Lauren Bell G5
1991 - 1992

THE

WINSTON

CANADIAN

DICTIONARY

FOR SCHOOLS

HOLT, RINEHART AND WINSTON OF CANADA, LIMITED
TORONTO

Copyright 1974 - 65 - 64 - 63 - 60, by

HOLT, RINEHART AND WINSTON OF CANADA, LIMITED

All rights reserved

Printed in Canada

ISBN 0-03-923504-1

CONTENTS

INTRODUCTORY MATTER

TO THE TEACHER

In the *Winston Canadian Dictionary for Schools* some 38,550 terms have been selected and defined. Most of these are used in a meaningful context in order to help explain them.

In the main listings, the short hyphen is used to show the syllabification, or division of the word into syllables. The pronunciation follows in parentheses. It, too, divides the word into syllables by means of the short hyphen, but omits the hyphen under the accents. Example: pop-u-lar-i-ty (pop'ū-lar'i-ti). The long hyphen is used to separate the parts of compound words. Examples: bat-tle–axe, jack–in–the–pul-pit.

The teacher should call the pupil's attention to such expressions as *Slang, Colloq., Archaic, Poetic,* so that he may early grasp something of the distinction between literary prose composition and daily speech. He should be shown that each has its own place and proper use.

Many compound terms, following the trend of the modern press of Canada, are written solid, rather than hyphenated. Examples: *eyetooth, radioactive, sagebrush, transcontinental, watermelon.*

As early as Grade 4, the teacher should introduce the pupil to the systematic phonetic respelling of words, even if it be but two or three per day. After he gains some mastery of accenting, precision in sounding vowels, and principles of syllabification, he should be encouraged to apply his knowledge in the articulation of the vowels and consonants by employing definite lip tension, especially in forming the long *a's, e's,* and *u's* of the accented syllables. By this means flabby, loose-lipped enunciation may be successfully combated. There is a close relationship between the use of the dictionary in the hands of an imaginative teacher and that clear, expressive utterance which is the delight of every listener.

The pronunciation key is a simple one, employing a minimum number of diacritical marks. It makes no use of the breve [˘], the modified breve [˘], or the modified macron [˘]. This simplification is based on the premise that if the pupil learns the correct accenting and the long vowels, the unaccented vowels should offer little difficulty. It will take him some time to realize that words pronounced in isolation (especially key words illustrating sound symbols) have by no means the same sound values as when spoken in connected oral speech, or when read aloud in a context. A Grade 4 pupil is not ready for this distinction; he will do well if he understands it by the time he reaches Grade 8.

The dictionary is complementary to the language programme. While it should frequently become a classroom text for practice in ascertaining the spelling, pronunciation, and meaning of words, its chief use must remain that of the reference book kept close at hand when one is reading, so that the fleeting impulse to look up a new word will not be inhibited, or evaporated, by the need to rise, walk two paces, and take the book from a shelf. Such appalling effort usually stifles the impulse as far as the young (and often older) reader is concerned.

KEY TO PRONUNCIATION

A. VOWELS

Symbol	Key Word
a	cat
ā	ape
ä	jar, car
å	ask, mast
â	care
e	ten
ē	eve
ė	writer
i	if, pity, begin, rely
ī	bite
o	top
ō	no
ô	dog, all, or
u	up
ū	mute
û	cur, her
oo	fool
oo	book, full

B. DIPHTHONGS

oi	oil
ou	out

C. (a) COMPOUND CONSONANT SOUNDS

ng	sing
sh	she
ch	chin
th	thin
th	this

hw	why
zh	azure
qu	kw, as in quit
x	(1) ks, as in ax
	(2) gz, as in exit
	(3) ksh or sh, as in anxious
	(4) zh, as in luxurious (-gzh)
	(5) z, as in xylophone (initial x)

(b) SINGLE CONSONANT SOUNDS

g	get
j	jet
y	yet

Fourteen consonants have their ordinary English values: b, d, f, h, k, l, m, n, p, r, t, v, w, z.

N.B.: c, q, and x do not appear as sound symbols since c has always the sound of k or s; qu is always kw, there being no q's unaccompanied by u's; and initial x is sounded as z, otherwise as ks, gz, ksh, sh, or zh.

D. FOREIGN SOUNDS

ö	Fr. feu, Ger. schön
ᐃo	Fr. coq, Ger. doch
ü	Fr. lune, Ger. für
kh	Sc. loch, Ger. ach
ṅ	Fr. enfant, nom
y'	Fr. Versailles (vâr'sày'')

USING THE PRONUNCIATION KEY

Key words illustrating the commoner sounds, especially of the vowels, are given at the bottom of each page. For pronunciation symbols other than these, the pronunciation key on p. iv and the illustrations of sound symbols on pp. v and vi of the introductory matter, should be consulted.

The characteristic sound of a word of more than one syllable is largely determined by its accenting. The primary or heavy stress is marked ['] and the secondary or light [']. Examples: avoirdupois (av'ĕr-dū-poiz'), civilization (siv'i-li-zā'shun), fortify (fôr'ti-fi').

The other important step towards mastery of pronunciation, is to note any long vowel(s) in a word. In the key, a long vowel is shown by a short line over it, called a macron [ˉ]. Examples: know (nō), duel (dū'el), unscrupulous (un-skrōō'pū-lus).

The pupil should practise daily the phonetic respelling of a few words as a prelude to the careful, correct pronunciation and clear enunciation that make listening to a speaker or reader a pleasure.

THE SYMBOLS ILLUSTRATED

a   as in cat, garret, canteen (short a).

ā   as in pale, age, prevail, weigh, steak, they, suede (long a).

ä   as in calm, father (broad or Italian a).

â   as in fare, parent, there, air, heir (usually in an unaccented syllable before r).

a̍   as in grass, staff, path, dance (the softened flat a).

e   as in edge, effort, set (short e).

ē   as in even, seize, people, quay, team, machine, weird (long e).

ĕ   as in later, beaver, beggar (slurred e before r).

i   as in (i) him, myth, ill (short i).

(ii) befall, become, rely, resume, (the long e sound when shortened in an unaccented syllable).

(iii) copy, honey, busy, fishy (final y).

(iv) savage, adage, garbage, preface, palace, prelate, climate (slurred a before a final consonant preceding silent e).

(v) ladies, hurries, parties (in words that change y to i and add es).

ī   as in mile, aisle, senile, ice (long i).

o   as in odd, God, prop, box, bottom, log, hot, doll (short o).

ō   as in hope, foam, beau, sew, road, oh, flow, doe (long o).

ô   as in horn, order, orb, talk, haul, broad, raw, fought, aught (intermediate o).

u   as in cup, honey, enough, hiccough (short u).

ū   as in cute, cure, unit, yew, you, few, feud, queue, beauty, adieu, cue, suit (long u).

û   as in burn, occur, fur, word, refer, learn, mirth, term, thirst, worm, myrtle, hurt (usually before an r in the same syllable).

ōō   as in boot, noon, mood, move, ooze, troupe, fruit, rule, canoe, true, soup, manoeuvre, rheumatism (the long oo sound).

oo   as in foot, put, pull, could, tearful, wolf, should, look, good, bull (the short oo sound).

oi   as in toil, foil, decoy, ahoy (diphthong).

ou   as in shout, brow, bough (diphthong).

g   as in get, gold, ghost (hard g).

THE SYMBOLS ILLUSTRATED

j as in *j*oy, a*g*e, *g*em, e*dg*e, cor*di*al (soft *g*).

s as in *s*ing, cea*s*e.

y as in *y*et, *y*ear, *y*ou, oni*o*n.

ng as in so*ng*, to*ng*ue, u*n*cle, fi*ng*er.

ch as in *ch*in, cat*ch*, ques*ti*on, righ*te*ous.

sh as in *sh*ow, *s*ure, ac*ti*on, ten*si*on, tena*ci*ous, o*c*ean, ma*ch*ine.

th as in *th*in, ba*th*, e*th*er (voiceless).

th as in *th*en, ba*the*, ei*th*er (voiced).

hw as in *wh*en, *wh*y, *wh*ere.

b, d, f, h, k, l, m, n, p, r, t, v, w, z (14 consonants) have their ordinary English values.

c, q, and **x** are not used as sound symbols. The *c* is equivalent to a *k* as in a*c*t, or an *s* as in *ce*de.

The letter *q* in English is found only in combination with *u*, that is, as *qu*, and is usually pronounced *kw*, as in *qu*ick, re*qu*est, *qu*ite. Sometimes it is sounded *k*, as in li*qu*or, uni*qu*e.

The letter **x** in sound is compound, being equivalent to

(1) *ks*, as in fi*x*, la*x*, e*x*cept

(2) *gz*, as in e*x*act, e*x*amine, e*x*ist

(3) *ksh* or *sh*, as in an*x*ious

(4) *zh*, as in lu*x*urious (-*gzh*)

(5) *z*, as in *x*ylem, *x*enon, an*x*iety (usually *x* as the first letter of a word).

Sounds in Foreign Languages

kh for the German or Scottish *ch*: a*ch* (akh); lo*ch* (lokh).

ṅ for the French nasal: e*n*fa*n*t (äṅ′fäṅ′); bie*n* (byâṅ).

âṅ for the French sound in voisi*n* (vwȧzâṅ′); si*m*ple (sâṅpl′).

ö for the German umlauted *o* of *oe*: sch*ö*n (shön), Go*e*the (gö′tĕ); also final *eu* or before *s*, *x*, *z*, *t* in French words: f*eu* (fö), j*eu* (zhö), dans*eu*se (dän′söz′).

Otherwise, French *eu* is like *û*: p*eu*r (pûr), dans*eu*r (dän′sûr′).

ü for the German umlauted *u*: f*ü*r (für), L*ü*beck (lü′bek), and for French *u*: l*u*ne (lün), d*u* (dü).

ŏ̥ for the short, open *o* of French c*o*q (kŏ̥k) and Germàn d*o*ch (dŏ̥kh), the *o* being pronounced more quickly than in English words like d*o*g, s*o*ft.

y′ French Vers*ailles* (vâr′sȧy″). The French *y′* is pronounced almost like ye, but does not make an extra syllable. Similarly, *r′*, *m′, l′* following a consonant are not sounded to make an extra syllable: si*m*ple (sâṅpl′).

In French, all full syllables are pronounced with nearly equal stress; but there is usually a rising inflection or slight stress on the last syllable, which has somewhat the effect of the English accent. In this book, French words are shown with a primary accent on the last syllable, representing this rising inflection or slight stress, and with secondary accents on all other full syllables.

SPELLING OF INFLECTED FORMS

A. Vagaries of English Spelling

1. *Doubling a Final Consonant*

One rule of spelling that governs over 2,000 common words, especially verb inflections, ought to be mastered by the student:

Whenever one-syllable words, and words of more than one syllable that are accented on the last syllable, *end in a single consonant preceded by a single vowel*, they double the final consonant before adding a suffix beginning with a vowel; otherwise, no doubling takes place. (For application of this rule, *qu* is considered to be two consonants, *kw*.) Examples: *abet, abettor; bag, baggage; big, bigger; equal, equalled; equip, equipped; occur, occurred; pin, pinned; plot, plotting; prefer, preferring; rebel, rebellious; tub, tubby.*

Examples of words that do not double the final consonant because they do not conform to the rule: *pain, pained; pine, pined; benefit, benefited; merit, meritorious; profit, profiting.*

An exception is *chagrin, chagrined.* The commonest exceptions concern words ending in *el* that do not conform to the rule. Examples: *apparelled, bevelled, cancelled, dialled, dishevelled, libelled, quarrelled, revelled, yodelled.* There is, however, a growing tendency to apply the rule fairly rigidly as is done in the U.S., with the result that sometimes the Canadian press spells these *appareled, beveled, canceled, dialed, disheveled, libeled, quarreled, reveled, yodeled,* though Canadian usage does not yet sanction so rigid an application of the rule as to permit such spellings as *kidnaped, marvelous, traveler,* and *worshiper.*

2. *Ei and ie Words*

Usually when the *ei* or *ie* combination is sounded like long *e* (ē), the "lice" rule applies, that is, *i* after *l* and *e* after *c.* Examples: *believe, relieve, conceive, deceive.*

3. *Dropping Final (Silent) E*

Final *e* is usually dropped before suffixes beginning with a vowel, but retained before those beginning with a consonant. Examples: *coming, famous, desirable, forcible, grievous, guidance, tonal, tonic; apelike, awesome, careless, dukedom, hateful, movement, shapely.*

Exceptions:

i) A few *-oe* endings: *canoeing, hoeing, shoeing, toeing.*

ii) A few that retain the *e* to prevent their being confused with words that look like them: *dyeing, singeing, tingeing.*

iii) Words ending in *-ce* and *-ge* that retain the *e* in order to make the *c* or *g* soft in sound: *advantageous, changeable, courageous, enforceable, manageable, noticeable, outrageous, peaceable, serviceable.*

iv) A few ending in *-ue: argument, duly, suing, truly, truism.*

v) Some verbs ending in *ie* change the *ie* to *y* when the suffix begins with a vowel: *tie, tying; vie, vying.*

vi) Some words may either drop or retain the final *e: acknowledgment, acknowledgement; judgment, judgement; milage, mileage; salable, saleable.*

4. *Words Ending in C*

When a suffix beginning with a vowel is added to words ending in *c,* a *k* is inserted to prevent a soft *s* sound: *picnicking, trafficked, mimicking, panicky, shellacked.*

Exceptions: Some one-syllable verbs ending in *c: arc, disc.*

5. *Final Y Preceded by a Consonant*

(a) Words ending in a *y* preceded by a consonant usually change *y* to *i* before a suffix, unless the suffix begins with *i: busy, busily, business; dry, driest, drily or dryly; icy, icier, icily, iciness; pity, pitiable, pitiful, pitiless; crying, drying, flying, trying.*

Exceptions: A word ending in *y* preceded by a consonant, especially if a one-syllable word, may

i) use either *y* or *i* for the comparative form of an adjective: *dryer, drier; spryer, sprier; shyer, shier;*

ii) retain *y* before *-ly* and *-ness:* *shyly, shyness; wryly, wryness; dryly, dryness; busyness;*

iii) use either *y* or *i* for the noun form: *flier; flyer;*

iv) arbitrarily retain the *y: lady-ship, fairylike, babyish, busy-ness; Spys, Storeys;*

v) use both adverbial forms: *dryly, drily; slyly, slily.*

vi) retain *y* in a possessive: *everybody's.*

(b) Words ending in *y* preceded by a consonant usually change *y* to *i* before adding *-es* (i) to form plurals of nouns: *allies, ladies;* (ii) to form the third person singular: *cries, defies, marries, tries.*

6. Final Y Preceded by a Vowel

These words simply add *s* (a) to form plurals of nouns: *boys, chimneys, keys, valleys;* (b) to form the third person singular: *allays, buys, obeys, says.*

They also simply add suffixes: *joy, joyful, joyous; key, keyed, keying; gluey, glueyness; gay, gayest;* but *gaily* or *gayly; gaiety* or *gayety.*

Exceptions: *day, daily; lay, laid; say, said; slay, slain.*

7. Words Ending in L

A number of words which end in an *l* that in U.S. practice is doubled before a suffix, leave the *l* undoubled in Canada and Great Britain: *enrol, enrolment; fulfil, fulfilment; install, instalment; thraldom; skilful; wilful.*

8. Sounding of a Retained Final Vowel

Words ending in a vowel retain the vowel sound before a suffix beginning with a vowel: *agree, agree-able; ski, skied; taxi, taxiing (taxying); weigh, weighing; bow, bowed; shampoo, shampooing; charivari, charivaried.*

If a verb ends in two vowels, the third person singular usually adds *s*, not *es: baas; boohoos; moos; hoodoos.*

If a word ends in two *ee*'s, the final *e* is dropped before a suffix beginning with *e: free, freed, freer, freest.*

B. Inflections: Their Spelling and Pronunciation

Plural of Nouns

1. Add *-s* (pronounced s) if the singular ends in the sound of *f, k, p, t,* or *th* as in *breath*—that is, any sound with which the sound of *s* readily combines; as, *puffs, rakes, tops, hopes, hats, births.* The sound of *th* in a few such words changes in the plural to that of *th* as in *breathe,* and the *s* is pronounced z (see 2 *b* below); as, *baths, mouths.*

2. Add *-s* (pronounced z) if the singular ends:

(*a*) In a vowel sound; as, *trees, laws.*

(*b*) In the sound of *b, d, g, ng, l, m, n, r, v,* or *th* as in *breathe*—that is, any voiced consonant sound with which the sound of *z* readily combines; as, *cabs, odes, bags, tongs, bells, plumes, tins, fires, Slavs, tithes.*

3. Add *-es* (pronounced ez) if the singular ends in a sibilant, or hissing sound, whether voiced or unvoiced—that is, in the sound of *s, sh, ch, z, zh,* or *j*—and has no final silent *-e;* as, *dresses, marshes, matches, topazes.*

4. Add *-s* if the singular ends in a sibilant sound and has a final silent *-e,* the final *e* combining with the *s* to form an additional syllable (pronounced ez); as, *laces, moustaches, avalanches, breezes, garages, edges.*

Plurals formed according to the rules stated above are considered regular, and are not given in the Dictionary unless required for some special reason.

The following classes of plurals are considered irregular, and are noted in this book:

5. Nouns ending in -*y* preceded by a consonant form the plural by changing the *y* to *i* and adding -*es* (the -*ies* being pronounced iz); as, *lady, ladies.* Nouns ending in -*y* preceded by a vowel add -*s* according to rule, but their plurals are usually given; as, *turkey, turkeys.*

6. Nouns ending in -*o* preceded by a vowel form the plural in -*os* (pronounced ōz); as, *cameos, folios;* nouns ending in -*o* preceded by a consonant usually form the plural in -*oes;* as, *echoes, heroes, mosquitoes, mottoes, Negroes, potatoes, tomatoes,* etc.; but musical terms ending in -*o* add -*s* only, whether a vowel or a consonant precedes the *o;* as, *sopranos, altos.*

7. A few nouns ending in the sound of *f* change the *f* to *v* and add -*es* (pronounced z); as, *loaf, loaves.*

8. A few plurals are formed in other ways than by the addition of -*s* or -*es.* Among these are *geese, mice, children, oxen, deer, sheep, dice;* foreign plurals, as *theses, alumni, alumnae, phemonena, cherubim;* and other scattered cases.

9. The plurals of symbols and abbreviations are usually formed by adding '*s:* a's, y's, +'s, —'s (pluses, minuses); 8's, 205's; if's, and's; but, pp. (*pl.* of *p.* for *page;* ll. (*pl.* of *l.* for *line*); MSS. (*pl.* of *MS.* for *manuscript*).

Examples: (1) *But* me no *but's.* (2) His *U's* were like *V's,* and his 2's and *Q's* looked like *Z's.*

10. The plurals of proper names are usually formed by adding *s* or *es,* as required: (1) There are three Marys and two Jameses in our class. (2) The Joneses were visiting the McColls.

Third Person Singular of Verbs

The third person singular indicative of all regular and most irregular verbs is formed according to rules 1–4 for the plural of nouns; as, *gets, hears, wishes, rises.*

Principal Parts of Verbs

1. Regular verbs add -*ed* to the infinitive to form the past tense and past participle, and -*ing* to form the present participle. The -*ing* is always pronounced as an additional syllable.

2. If the infinitive ends in -*d* or -*t* not silent, the -*ed* is pronounced ed or id; as, *ended, heated.*

3. If the infinitive ends in the sound of *b, g, ng, j, l, m, n, r, v, z, zh,* or *th* as in *breathe*—that is, any voiced consonant except *d*—or in a vowel sound, the -*ed* is pronounced d; as, *hurled, hurrahed;* but note rules 5 and 6 below.

4. If the infinitive ends in the sound of *f, k, p, s, sh, ch, th,* as in *breath*—that is, any unvoiced consonant except *t*—the -*ed* is pronounced t; as, *amassed, attacked, marched;* but note 5 and 6 below.

Principal parts derived according to the rules stated above are considered regular, and are not given in the Dictionary unless required for some special reason.

Principal parts formed according to the following rules are considered irregular, and are given in this book:

5. (*a*) Final -*e,* whether silent or not, is dropped before -*ed;* as, *agreed, judged.*

(*b*) Final silent -*e* preceded by a consonant is usually dropped before -*ing;* as, *racing, judging.* In words where final silent -*e* is preceded by a consonant and *l* or *r,* those letters unite with -*ing* to form a single syllable; as, *cou-pling* from *couple.*

(*c*) Final -*y* preceded by a consonant is changed to *i* before -*ed,* but is retained before -*ing;* as, *cried, crying; replied, replying.*

(*d*) Final silent -*e* preceded by *i* is dropped and the *i* is changed to *y* before -*ing;* as, *dying, lying.*

6. Verbs of one syllable, and verbs of more than one syllable if accented on the last syllable, ending in a single consonant preceded by a single vowel, double the final consonant before -ed and -ing; as, *plan, planned, planning; prefer, preferred, preferring.*

7. A considerable number of verbs have entirely irregular parts; as, *buy, bought, buying; bear,* past tense *bore,* past participle *borne* or *born,* present participle *bearing.* A few are defective, as *can* (no infinitive form), past tense *could.* Many verbs, once regular, have been contracted and now appear to be irregular; as, *put, set,* past tense and past participle *put, set; read* (pronounced red), *kept, slept,* past tense and past participle of *read, keep, sleep.*

Comparison of Adjectives and Adverbs

1. Adjectives of one syllable are regularly compared by adding -er and -est to the positive degree to form respectively the comparative and superlative; as, *old, older, oldest.*

2. Adjectives of more than two syllables are usually compared by using the words *more* and *most* with the positive; as, *beautiful, more beautiful, most beautiful.*

3. Adjectives of two syllables are compared by adding -er, -est (but see rule 5), if the resulting form is easily pronounced; as, *yellow, yellower, yellowest;* otherwise they are compared by the use of *more* and *most;* as, *spacious, more spacious, most spacious.* Usage varies according to individual taste; many adjectives can be compared in either way; as, *corrupt, corrupter* or *more corrupt,* etc.

4. Adverbs are usually compared by the use of *more* and *most,* though a few use -er and -est; as, *near, nearer, nearest; often, oftener, oftenest.* Some adverbs are not compared; as, *here, there, now, then.*

Comparatives and superlatives formed in accordance with the rules stated above are considered regular, and are not given in the Dictionary unless required for some special reason.

The following cases of comparison are considered irregular, and are noted in this book:

5. A final silent -e is dropped before the endings -er and -est; as, *fine, finer, finest; noble, nobler, noblest.*

6. Adjectives of one syllable, and adjectives of more than one syllable if accented on the last syllable, ending in a single consonant preceded by a single vowel, double the final consonant before -er and -est; as, *big, bigger, biggest.*

7. Adjectives ending in -y change the y to i before -er and -est; as, *happy, happier, happiest.*

8. A number of the commoner adjectives, and a few adverbs, are entirely irregular; as, *good, better, best; bad, worse, worst; ill* (the adverb), *worse, worst; far, farther, farthest.*

9. Many adverbs which may function also as prepositions have an adjective function when compared, forming the comparative in -er and the superlative by adding -most to the positive or comparative; as, *in, inner, inmost* or *innermost.* Some adjectives have only the superlative; as, *topmost, uttermost.*

ABBREVIATIONS USED IN THIS BOOK

A.D. .... anno Domini (Latin = in the year of our Lord); used in giving dates

adj. .... adjective

adv. .... adverb, adverbial

B.C. .... before Christ; used in giving dates

cap. .... capital

colloq. .... colloquial

comp. .... comparative

conj. .... conjunction

def. .... definition

esp. .... especially

etc. et cetera (Latin = and others)

fem. .... feminine

indef. .... indefinite

interj. .... interjection

masc. .... masculine

n. .... noun

neut. .... neuter

pl. .... plural

p.p. .... participle, past

p.pr. .... participle, present

prep. .... preposition

pron. .... pronoun, pronomial

p.t. .... past tense

sing. .... singular

superl. .... superlative

Syn. .... synonym(s)

U.S. .... United States

U.S.S.R. .... Union of Soviet Socialist Republics

v.i. .... verb, intransitive

v.t. .... verb, transitive

¹A, a (ā), *n.* [*pl.* A's, a's], **1,** the first letter of the alphabet; **2,** in *music*, the sixth note in the major scale of C:—**A,** *adj.* **1,** first in order or class; as, an *A* rating; **2,** having the form of an A; as, an *A* tent:—**A1** (ā′wun′), excellent; first-class.

²a (a; when stressed, ā), *adj.* or *indefinite article* one; any, as, *a* man was here; *a* man will protect his home: used instead of *an* before words beginning with a consonant or a consonant sound, or with a sounded *h*; as, *a* man, *a* unit, *a* youth, *a* holiday, *a* hotel.

a-back (a-bak′), *adv.* backward:—taken aback, surprised; disconcerted.

ab-a-cus (ab′a-kus), *n. pl.* abacuses (-kus-iz): abaci (-sī)], a frame with beads or balls sliding on wires, used for counting or calculating.

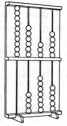
ABACUS

a-ban-don (a-ban′dun), *v.t.* **1,** to give up entirely; as, to *abandon* a house, a ship, or work; **2,** to yield (oneself) without restraint; as, he *abandoned* himself to grief:—*n.* reckless enthusiasm; as, he danced with *abandon.*—*n.* **a-ban′don-ment.**

a-ban-doned (a-ban′-dund), *adj.* **1,** deserted; as, an *abandoned* house; **2,** wicked; as, an *abandoned* wretch.

a-base (a-bās′), *v.t.* [abased, abas-ing], to humble; as, he *abased* himself.—*n.* **a-base′ment.**

a-bash (a-bash′), *v.t.* to embarrass; shame; disconcert; as, he was *abashed* at the rebuke.

a-bashed (a-basht′), *adj.* overcome with surprise or shame; confused; disconcerted.

a-bate (a-bāt′), *v.i.* [abat-ed, abat-ing], to decrease; subside; as, the flood has *abated:*—*v.t.* **1,** to put an end to; as, *abate* a nuisance; **2,** to reduce, as a debt.—*n.* **a-bate′ment.**

a-bat-toir (ab′a-twôr′), *n.* a building where animals are killed for market.

ab-bé (a′bā), *n.* in France, a title given to various persons, not necessarily priests, who wear religious garb.

ab-bess (ab′es), *n.* the head of a convent; the mother superior of an abbey.

ab-bey (ab′i), *n.* [*pl.* abbeys], **1,** one or more buildings where men or women live a religious life apart from the world, governed by an abbot or abbess; **2,** a church that was once part of a monastery; as, Westminster *Abbey.*

ab-bot (ab′ut), *n.* the head of a monastery; a father superior.

ab-bre-vi-ate (a-brē′vi-āt′), *v.t.* [abbrevi-at-ed, abbreviat-ing], to shorten; esp., to shorten (a word) by writing only a part, as *Apr.* for *April.*—*n.* **ab-bre′vi-a′tion.**

ab-dicate (ab′di-kāt′), *v.t.* [abdicat-ed, ab-dicat-ing], to give up, as kingly power; resign (a throne):—*v.t.* to give up sovereign power; as, the king *abdicated.*—*n.* **ab′di-ca′tion.**

ab-do-men (ab-dō′men; ab′dō-men), *n.* **1,** the large cavity of the body below the diaphragm, containing the digestive organs; **2,** in insects, the rear section of the body. —*adj.* **ab-dom′i-nal.**

ab-duct (ab-dukt′), *v.t.* to kidnap.—*n.* **ab-duc′tor.**—*n.* **ab-duc′tion.**

a-bed (a-bed′), *adv.* in bed.

ab-er-ra-tion (ab′ẽr-ā′shun), *n.* **1,** departure from what is right, true, proper, etc.; **2,** mental disorder; **3,** a deviation from the normal.

a-bet (a-bet′), *v.t.* [abet-ted, abet-ting], to encourage or aid, esp. in a crime; as, he aided and *abetted* the thief.—*n.* **a-bet′tor.**

a-bey-ance (a-bā′ans), *n.* a postponing of something; as, the project was left *in abeyance.*

ab-hor (ab-hôr′), *v.t.* [abhorred, abhor-ring], to shrink from with disgust; as, the humane man *abhors* cruelty,— *adj.* **ab-hor′rent.**—*n.* **ab-hor′rence.**

a-bide (a-bid′), *v.i.* [*p.t.* and *p.p.* abode (a-bōd′) or abid-ed, *p.pr.* abid-ing], **1,** to live; dwell; **2,** to endure; as, great love *abides;*—**abide by,** to remain faithful to; as, to *abide* by a promise:—*v.t.* to put up with; as, I cannot *abide* him.

a-bil-i-ty (a-bil′i-ti), *n.* [*pl.* abilities], power to do something; as, *ability* to work; also, skill; talent; as, a man of *ability.*

ab-ject (ab′jekt; ab-jekt′), *adj.* **1,** degraded; craven; as, an *abject* coward; **2,** contemptible; as, *abject* submission; hopeless; as, *abject* poverty.—*adv.* **ab′ject-ly.**

ab-jure (ab-jōōr′), *v.t.* [abjured, abjur-ing], to promise solemnly to give up; renounce, as one's religion.—*n.* **ab′ju-ra′tion.**

ab-la-tive (ab′la-tiv), *adj.* and *n.* a case form, esp. in Latin grammar, denoting *from, by, with, at, in,* etc.

a-blaze (a-blāz′), *adj.* **1,** on fire; as, the

cat, āge, fär, câre, ásk, ten, ēve, latẽr; (i) pity, rely, senate; īce; top, nō, all (ôl), ôr; up, mūte, cûr, cōōl, book; oil, out; th, thin; *th,* the.

1

hut was *ablaze;* **2,** aglow; full of colour, as autumn woods; **3,** ardent; eager.

a-ble (ā′bl), *adj.* **1,** having power, skill, or means; as, she is ill and not *able* to go: is he *able* to drive a car? they are not *able* to buy coal; **2,** skilful; unusually clever; as, an *able* lawyer. —*adv.* **a′bly.**

ab-lu-tion (a-blū′shun; -blōō), *n.* a washing or cleansing of the body or part of the body; as, he performs his *ablutions* religiously.

ab-ne-ga-tion (ab′ne-gā′shun), *n.* denial, esp. self-denial; a renouncing of self.

ab-nor-mal (ab-nôr′mal), *adj.* differing from what is usual or expected; out of the ordinary; above or below the average; as, *abnormal* weather.—*adv.* **ab-nor′mal-ly.**

a-board (a-bōrd′), *adv.* on or into a ship, train, etc.:—*prep.* on board of; in or into: as, to be, or go, *aboard* a ship.

a-bode (a-bōd′), *n.* a place of residence; home; as, this cottage is my *abode.*

a-bol-ish (a-bol′ish), *v.t.* to do away with; put an end to; as, to *abolish* slavery.

ab-o-li-tion (ab′o-lish′un), *n.* the destroying of, or doing away with, something; as, the *abolition* of slavery.—*n.* **ab′o-li′-tion-ist.**

a-bom-i-na-ble (a-bom′i-na-bl), *adj.* hateful; odious; as, he is a rude fellow with *abominable* manners.—*adv.* **a-bom′i-na-bly.**

a-bom-i-nate (a-bom′i-nāt′), *v.t.* [abominat-ed, abominat-ing], to detest; loathe.—*n.* **a-bom′i-na′tion.**

ab-o-rig-i-nes (ab′o-rij′i-nēz′), *n. pl.* the earliest known inhabitants of a country, as the Indians in North America, or Australian *aborigines.*

a-bor-tive (a-bôr′tiv), *adj.* **1,** fruitless; unsuccessful; as, an *abortive* attempt; **2,** imperfectly developed.

a-bound (a-bound′), *v.i.* **1,** to exist in great numbers or amount; as, deer *abound* in these hills; **2,** to be richly supplied; as, his speech *abounded* in wit.

a-bout (a-bout′), *adv.* **1,** around; on every side; near by; as, they stood *about;* **2,** in a reversed position; as to face *about;* **3,** in rotation; as, turn *about* is fair play; **4,** in a state of action; as, he is up and *about;* **5,** on the point of; as, I am *about* to shoot; **6,** approximately; nearly; as, *about* dead:—*prep.* **1,** concerning; relating to; as, a story *about* a bear; something wrong *about* the plan; **2,** on all sides of; near to; as,

trees *about* the lake; **3,** on the person of; as, I haven't a dollar *about* me.

a-bove (a-buv′), *adv.* **1,** in a higher place; overhead; as, directly *above;* **2,** in heaven; as, up *above;* **3,** before this; as, see page 6 *above:*—*prep.* **1,** over; higher than; **2,** superior to; as, to be *above* deceit; **3,** beyond; as, *above* reproach; **4,** in excess of; as, *above* a dollar;—*adj.* stated previously; as, the *above* objection.

a-bove-board (a-buv′bōrd′), *adv.* openly; without trickery; as, he acted *aboveboard:*—*adj.* honest; as, he was always *aboveboard* in his dealings.

ab-ra-sion (a-brā′zhun), *n.* **1,** the injury caused by rubbing or scraping; as a skin *abrasion:* **2,** a wearing or rubbing away.—*v.* **ab-rade′.**

a-breast (a-brest′), *adj.* and *adv.* side by side; as, the three boys walked *abreast;* not behind; as, *abreast* of the times.

a-bridge (a-brij′), *v.t.* [abridged, abridging], **1,** to shorten; condense, as a book; **2,** to deprive of (a right, privilege, liberty, etc.):—*n.* **a-bridg′-ment; a-bridge′ment.**

a-broad (a-brôd′), *adv.* **1,** far and wide; as, the news spread *abroad;* **2,** out of doors; as, to walk *abroad;* **3,** in, or to go to a foreign country.

ab-ro-gate (ab′ro-gāt′), *v.t.* [abrogated, abrogat-ing], to annul; abolish; repeal; as, to *abrogate* a law, rule, or custom.

ab-rupt (a-brupt′), *adj.* **1,** sudden; as, an *abrupt* turn; **2,** short or curt; as, an *abrupt* manner; **3,** steep, as a hill.

ab-scess (ab′ses), *n.* pus forming at a certain point, or focus, of infection.

ab-scond (ab-skond′), *v.i.* to flee secretly, esp. after some wrongdoing; as, he *absconded* with the stolen money.

ab-sence (ab′sens), *n.* **1,** a being away, or the period of being away; as, an *absence* of one week; **2,** lack; as, *absence* of heat.

ab-sent (ab′sent), *adj.* **1,** not present; missing; lacking; **2,** lost in thought; inattentive; as, an *absent* manner:—*v.t.* (ab-sent′), to withdraw (oneself).—*adv.* **ab′sent-ly.**

ab-sen-tee (ab′sen-tē′), *n.* one who is away from his work, school, duty, etc.—*adj.* away; as, *absentee* workman.

ab-sent—mind-ed (ab′sent-mīn′did), *adj.* lost in thought; hence, inattentive; forgetful.—*adv.* **ab′sent—mind′ed-ly.**

ab-so-lute (ab′so-lūt;-lōōt), *adj.* **1,** whole; complete; perfect; as, the *absolute* truth; **2,** having power or authority that is not restricted by laws or by a constitution; as, an *absolute* monarch; **3,** positive; certain; as, an *absolute* fact.—*adv.* **ab′so-lute-ly.**

ab-solve (ab-solv′), *v.t.* [absolved, absolving], **1,** to release or set free, as from a duty; **2,** to acquit; pronounce not guilty; as, a jury's verdict *absolved* him of guilt.—*n.* **ab′so-lu′tion** (ab′so-lū′shun).

ab-sorb (ab-sôrb′), *v.t.* **1,** to drink in; suck or swallow up; as, a sponge *absorbs* water; **2,** to interest deeply; take all of one's attention; as, baseball *absorbs* John now.—*adj.* **ab-sorb′ent.**—*n.* **ab-sorp′tion** (ab-sôrp′shun).

ab-sorb-ing (ab-sôrb′ing), *adj.* intensely interesting, as a story.

ab-stain (ab-stān′), *v.i.* to refrain; keep away; as, to *abstain* from the use of tobacco.—*n.* **ab-stain′er.**

ab-ste-mi-ous (ab-stē′mi-us), *adj.* sparing or moderate in eating or drinking; temperate; as, an *abstemious* diet.

ab-sti-nence (ab′sti-nens), *n.* a refraining from something; esp., the practice of denying oneself certain foods, drinks, etc.

ab-stract (ab′strakt), *n.* a summing-up of the main points, as of a book or an argument;—*adj.* (ab′strakt; ab-strakt′), **1,** considered apart from actual facts or a real situation; as *abstract* justice; **2,** withdrawn (in thought); as, he wore an *abstract* air; **3,** in *grammar*, describing a noun which expresses a quality or characteristic but does not name the person or thing that possesses it; thus "strength" is an *abstract* noun, but a word like "wrestler," which names a person, is a *concrete* noun:—*v.t.* (ab-strakt′), **1,** to take away or draw out, esp. secretly or dishonestly; **2,** to make a summary of (a book).—*n.* **ab-strac′tion.**

ab-stract-ed (ab-strak′tid), *adj.* absent-minded; lost in thought.

ab-struse (ab-strōōs′), *adj.* hard to understand; as, philosophy deals with *abstruse* problems; hidden; concealed.

ab-surd (ab-sûrd′), *adj.* contrary to reason or sense; ridiculous; silly.—*n.* **ab-surd′-i-ty.**—*adv.* **ab-surd′ly.**

a-bun-dance (a-bun′dans), *n.* overflowing quantity or amount; great plenty; as, an *abundance* of food.—*adj.* **a-bun′dant.**—*adv.* **a-bun′dant-ly.**

a-buse (a-būz′), *v.t.* [abused, abus-ing], **1,** to use improperly; misuse; as, to *abuse* a privilege; **2,** to maltreat; as, to *abuse* animals; **3,** to use violent language to; as, he *abused* his men; **4,** to strain; overtax; as, to *abuse* one's health:—*n.* (a-būs′), **1,** misuse, as of a privilege; **2,** cruel treatment, as of

animals; **3,** violent language; **4,** a straining or overtaxing, as of one's health; **5,** a corrupt or wrong practice; as, political *abuses.*—*adj.* **a-bu′sive** (a-bū′siv).—*adj.* **a-bu′sive-ly.**

a-but (a-but′), *v.i.* [abut-ted, abut-ting], to join end to end; end against; followed by *on, upon, against;* as, the house *abuts* on the hill.

a-byss (a-bis′), *n.* **1,** a deep chasm; **2,** anything bottomless or unbounded.—*adj.* **a-bys′mal** (a-biz′mal).

a-cad-e-my (a-kad′e-mi), *n.* [*pl.* academies], **1,** a private high school; **2,** a university; **3,** a school for special study; as, a military *academy.*—*adj.* **ac′a-dem′ic; ac′a-dem′i-cal.**

A-ca-di-a (a-kā′di-a), *n.* a former French colony, 1604–1713, in what is now Nova Scotia.—*adj.* **A-ca′di-an.**

ac-cede (ak-sēd′), *v.i.* [acced-ed, acceding], **1,** to agree or yield, as to a request; **2,** to succeed, as to a throne.

ac-cel-er-ate (ak-sel′ẽr-āt′), *v.t.* [acceler-at-ed, accelerat-ing], **1,** to cause to move, act, or change more quickly; as, to *accelerate* an engine; **2,** to cause to come sooner; as, death was *accelerated* by grief.—*n.* **ac-cel′er-a′tion.**

ac-cel-er-at-or (ak-sel′ẽr-āt′ẽr), *n.* **1,** a device, like the foot throttle of a motor car, for increasing the speed of a machine; **2,** anything that speeds up a process or chemical reaction.

ac-cent (ak′sent), *n.* **1,** emphasis; stress; esp., the stress laid upon a syllable of a word or upon a note of music; **2,** any of several characters, as [′, ′], used in writing and printing to show which syllable of a word is to be stressed; **3,** a special or peculiar method of pronouncing; as, to speak English with a foreign *accent:* **4,** tone of voice; as, she spoke in *accents* soft and low:—*v.t.* (ak-sent′; ak′sent), **1,** to utter with special stress, as a word; **2,** to mark with an *accent;* **3,** to emphasize; as, his remarks were *accented* by gestures.—*v.t.* **ac-cen′tu-ate′.**

ac-cept (ak-sept′), *v.t.* **1,** to take or receive, as a gift; consent to take, as an office; take with resignation, as one's fate; **2,** to agree to; as, I *accept* your terms; **3,** to recognize as true, as a creed; **4,** to admit (a person) to favour; as, the club *accepted* the stranger.—*adj.* **ac-cept′a-ble.**—*n.* **ac-cept′ance.**—*adv.* **ac-cept′a-bly.**

ac-cess (ak′ses), *n.* **1,** admittance or approach to a person or place; also, a way or means of approach; as, a drawbridge gave *access* to the castle; **2,** an attack; fit; as, an *access* of coughing; an *access* of rage.

all (ôl), ôr; up, mūte, cûr, cōōl, book; oil, out; th, thin; *th,* the.

ac-ces-si-ble (ak-ses′i-bl), *adj.* **1,** easy to reach; as, the book was easily *accessible* because the shelf was low; **2,** open to influence; as *accessible* to reason, pity, etc.; **3,** approachable; as, the mayor was *accessible* to every citizen.—*n.* **ac-ces′si-bil′i-ty.**

ac-ces-sion (ak-se′shun), *n.* the act of coming into an office, dignity, or estate; as, the *accession* of a king; or one's *accession* to wealth or property.

ac-ces-sor-y (ak-ses′or-i; ak′), *adj.* **1,** contributing to an effect; **2,** helping another in crime;—*n.* **1,** an article that adds to the use or appearance of something else; as, gloves and handbags are *accessories* of dress; **2,** a person who assists a criminal before or after a crime. Also, **ac-ces′sar-y.**

ac-ci-dent (ak′si-dent), *n.* **1,** an unexpected or unforeseen event, generally unfortunate; **2,** something done unintentionally; a mishap; **3,** chance; as, to lose or find something by *accident.*—*adj.* **ac′ci-den′tal.**—*adv.* **ac′ci-den′tal-ly.**

ac-claim (a-klām′), *v.t.* **1,** to applaud; **2,** to hail or proclaim by shouting; as, to *acclaim* a champion:—*n.* a shout of joy or praise.

ac-cla-ma-tion (ak′la-mā′shun), *n.* **1,** shout of approval, joy, etc. **2,** approbation in any form; **3,** an oral vote, or uncontested election, usually unanimous; as, elected by *acclamation.*

ac-cli-ma-tize (a-klī′ma-tīz′), *v.t.* [-tized (-tīzd), -tizing], to accustom to a new climate (or conditions); *v.i.* to become adapted (to); as shorthorns became *acclimatized* to our winters.

ac-cliv-i-ty (a-kliv′i-ti), *n.* a slope upwards.

ac-com-mo-date (a-kom′o-dāt′), *v.t.* [ac-commodat-ed, accommodat-ing], **1,** to supply lodgings, food, etc., as, this hotel can *accommodate* 100 guests; **2,** to oblige or help; as, he *accommodated* me by cashing a cheque; **3,** to fit or adapt; as, we *accommodated* ourselves to our new surroundings.

ac-com-mo-dat-ing (a-kom′o-dāt′-ing), *adj.* obliging; kind.

ac-com-mo-da-tion (a-kom′o-dā′-shun), *n.* **1,** .the act or process of adjusting or fitting something to something else; as, the *accommodation* of one's plans to those of others; the *accommodation* of the eye to distant objects; **2,** willingness to oblige; **3,** the thing furnished in order to oblige, as a loan of money; **4, accommodation,** lodgings; as, hotel *accommodation.*

ac-com-pa-ny (a-kum′pa-ni), *v.t.* [accompanied, accompany-ing], **1,** to go with; escort; as, a guide *accompanied* the party; **2,** to supplement or join (with); as, she *accompanied* her words with a glance; **3,** in *music,* to follow (a singer or player) on an instrument.—*n.* **ac-com′pa-ni-ment.**

ac-com-plice (a-kom′plis; -kum′), *n.* an associate or companion in crime; as, two robbers were caught, but an *accomplice* escaped.

ac-com-plish (a-kom′plish; -kum′), *v.t.* **1,** to complete; finish, as a task; **2,** to carry out; fulfil; as, she *accomplished* her purpose.

ac-com-plished (a-kom′plisht), *adj.* **1,** brought to fulfilment, as a plan; finished, as a piece of work; **2,** skilful; talented and well trained; as, an *accomplished* violinist.

ac-com-plish-ment (a-kom′plish-ment), *n.* **1,** fulfilment, as of a purpose; completion, as of a task; **2,** skill; an ability acquired through special training; as, acting was one of his many *accomplishments.*

ac-cord (a-kôrd′), *v.t.* to give; grant; as, to *accord* due praise;—*v.i.* to be in harmony; agree; as, your point of view *accords* with mine:—*n.* agreement; harmony; as, you and I are in *accord* on the way to solve the problem.—*n.* **ac-cord′ance;** as, I am acting *in accordance with* his wishes.

ac-cord-ing-ly (a-kôr′ding-li), *adv.* **1,** in agreement with what might be expected; suitably; as, you are now grown and must act *accordingly;* **2,** consequently; therefore.

ac-cor-di-on (a-kôr′di-un), *n.* a portable musical instrument, consisting of bellows, metal reeds, and a keyboard, played by alternately extending the ends of the instrument and pushing them together, thus forcing air through the reeds;—*adj.* folded and creased like the bellows of an accordion; as, *accordion* pleats.

ac-cost (a-kôst′), *v.t.* to speak to first; address; as, a beggar *accosted* me.

ac-count (a-kount′), *v.i.* **1,** to give a reckoning or make a report of money received and money spent; as, he *accounted* for all the money; **2,** to give an explanation or reason; as, I cannot *account* for his conduct;—*v.t.* to think of; consider as; as, although he failed, he was *accounted* a hero:—*n.* **1,** a record of business dealings involving money; a bill; as, an *account* with a store; **2,** any reckoning; as, he rendered an *account* of his expenses; **3,** a record or report, as of events; **4,** cause or explanation; as, give an *account* of your actions; **5,** importance; worth; as, of no *account,* **6, accounts,** financial records; bookkeeping records; as, his *accounts* are in order:—**turn to account,** to make use of.

ac-count-a-ble (a-koun'ta-bl), *adj.* **1,** bound to give an explanation of one's conduct; responsible; answerable; **2,** capable of being explained; as, his failure is *accountable* if you recall his lack of training.—*n.* **ac-count'a-bil'i-ty.**

ac-count-ant (a-koun'tant), *n.* one who is trained in keeping or adjusting accounts or financial records.—*n.* **ac-count'an-cy.**

ac-cred-it (a-kred'it), *v.t.* **1,** to authorize; furnish with credentials; as, an *accredited* delegate; **2,** to attribute; ascribe; as, the discovery is *accredited to* Copernicus; he is *accredited with* saying that; **3,** to take as valid; as, an *accredited* story.

ac-crue (a-krōō'), *v.i.* grow; increase; be added; as, interest *accrued* on the loan; prestige *accrued* from his social contacts.

ac-cu-mu-late (a-kū'mū-lāt'), *v.t.* and *v.i.* [accumulat-ed, accumulat-ing], to collect; gather; pile up; as, to *accumulate* a library; books *accumulate* on a table.—*n.* **ac-cu'mu-la'tion.**—*n.* **ac-cu'mu-la'tor** (wet battery).—*adj.* **ac-cu'mu-la'tive.**

ac-cu-ra-cy (ak'ū-ra-si), *n.* correctness; exactness; precision.

ac-cu-rate (ak'ū-rit), *adj.* free from error; as, an *accurate* list; precise; as, an *accurate* person.—*adv.* **ac'cu-rate-ly.**

ac-cursed (a-kûrst'; a-kûr'sid), *p. adj.* **1,** ill-fated; doomed; **2,** detestable; damnable.

ac-cuse (a-kūz'), *v.t.* [accused, accusing], to charge with guilt; blame; as, to *accuse* a person of theft.—*n.* **ac'cu-sa'tion.**—*n.* **ac-cus'er.**

ac-cus-tom (a-kus'tum), *v.t.* to make used to something; to familiarize; as, to *accustom* oneself to new conditions.

ace (ās), *n.* **1,** a card or die with a single spot; **2,** a fighter-pilot who has a large number of 'kills' credited to him; **3,** one who excels others in doing some particular thing; as, a football *ace.*

a-ce-tic (a-sē'tik; a-set'ik), *adj.* like vinegar. *Acetic acid,* the sour, pungent acid element in vinegar.

a-cet-y-lene (a-set'i-lēn'), *n.* a highly inflammable gas made from calcium carbide and water and used with oxygen for welding.

ache (āk), *n.* continuous pain, bodily or mental; as, tooth*ache;* heart*ache.*—*v.i.* [ached, ach-ing], **1,** to suffer from, or throb with, pain; as, my head *aches;* **2,** to have a strong desire; to long for.

a-chieve (a-chēv'), *v.t.* [achieved, achieving], **1,** to accomplish; as, he *achieved* his goal; **2,** to gain or get by effort; as, to *achieve* success.—*n.* **a-chieve'ment.**

acid (as'id), *adj.* sharp or biting to the taste, as vinegar; sour:—*n.* **1,** a sour substance, often liquid; **2,** in chemistry, that which combines with a base to form a salt.

a-cid-i-ty (a-sid'i-ti), *n.* **1,** sourness; **2,** the quality or state of being acid; as, vinegar has high *acidity.*

ac-knowl-edge (ak-nol'ij), *v.t.* [acknowledged, acknowledging], **1,** to admit as real or genuine; as, to *acknowledge* a fault or a signature; **2,** to respect; recognize; as, to *acknowledge* Dickens as a great novelist; **3,** to admit the receipt of; express thanks for; as, to *acknowledge* a letter or a gift.—*n.* **ac-knowl'edg-ment; ac-knowl'edge-ment.**

acme (ak'mi), *n.* the highest point; perfection; as, her dancing was the *acme* of grace.

ac-ne (ak'ni), *n.* a skin disease marked by eruption of pimples, due to a clogging of the oil glands.

ac-o-lyte (ak'ō-līt'), *n.* **1,** one who helps a priest at Mass: **2,** an altar-boy; **3,** an attendant.

a-corn (ā'kôrn; ā'kẽrn), *n.* the fruit of the oak, a nut with its base set in a woody cup.

a-cous-tic (a-kous'tik; a-kōōs'tik), *adj.* associated with the sense of hearing or with sound; as, the *acoustic* properties of a room.

ac-quaint (a̧-kwānt'), *v.t.* to make aware of something; familiarize; as, I *acquainted* him with the contents of this letter.

ac-quaint-ance (a-kwān'tans), *n.* **1,** knowledge of a person or a thing gained by contact or experience; as, an *acquaintance* with a book and with its author; **2,** a person whom one knows slightly.—*n.* **ac-quaint'ance-ship.**

ac-qui-esce (ak'wi-es'), *v.i.* [acquiesced, acquiesc-ing], to agree in silence; submit or assent without objection; as she *acquiesced* in her son's decision.—*adj.* **ac'-qui-es'cent.**—*n.* **ac'qui-es'cence.**

ac-quire (a-kwīr'), *v.t.* [acquired, acquiring], to gain or obtain, usually by one's own effort; as, she *acquired* speed in swimming; he *acquired* a name for honesty; he *acquired* a summer cottage. —*n.* **acquire'ment.**

ac-qui-si-tion (ak'wi-zish'un), *n.* **1,** the act of obtaining or gaining something; **2,** that which is gained, esp. a material possession.

all (ôl), ôr; up, mūte, cûr, cōōl, book; oil, out; th, thin; *th*, the.

ac-quis-i-tive (a-kwiz′i-tiv), *adj.* having a strong desire to get or gain property or money for oneself.

ac-quit (a-kwit′), *v.t.* [acquit-ted, acquit-ting], **1,** to free (a person) from an accusation or an obligation; to clear (of a charge); as, the court *acquitted* the prisoner; **2,** to discharge or carry out one's duty or obligations; as, the soldier *acquitted* himself nobly.— *n.* **ac-quit′tal.**

a-cre (ā′kėr), *n.* **1,** a measure of land area (43,560 square feet) about equivalent to the area of a lot 208 feet square; **2,** a piece of land; a field; **3,** **acres,** lands or a landed estate; as, ancestral *acres.*—*n.* **a′cre-age** (ā′kėr-ij).

ac-rid (ak′rid), *adj.* **1,** bitter; sharptasting; pungent, as smoke; **2,** illtempered; bitter; harsh and sharp; as, his *acrid* retort stung her.—*adv.* **ac′rid-ly.**

ac-ri-mo-ny (ak′ri-mo-ni), *n.* harshness or bitterness of speech or temper; as, he spoke with *acrimony.*

ac-ro-bat (ak′rō-bat′), *n.* one who performs skilled or daring gymnastic feats, such as tumbling, vaulting, etc.—*adj.* **ac′ro-bat′ic.**

A-crop-o-lis (a-krop′o-lis), *n.* the hill at Athens upon which the famed Parthenon stands.

a-cross (a-kros′), *prep.* **1,** from one side to the other of; as, she swam *across* the stream; **2,** on the other side of; as, she lives *across* the road:—*adv.* from one side to the other; as, to cut cloth straight *across*; to fly *across*.

a-cros-tic (a-kros′tik), *n.* verses (or sometimes lines of prose) of which the first or other, letters form a word, motto, etc.

act (akt), *n.* **1,** a deed; thing done; **2,** the process of doing; as, Mary is in the *act* of cleaning out her desk; **3,** a decree or law; as, an *act* of Parliament; **4,** one of the principal divisions of a play or an opera; a separately billed part of a vaudeville performance:—*v.t.* to perform or take the part of, as in a stage or screen play:—*v.i.* **1,** to do something; as, you must *act* quickly; **2,** to behave; as, she *acts* queerly; **3,** to take a part in a play; **4,** to produce an effect; as, the drug *acted* quickly.

act-ing (ak′ting), *adj.* performing the duties of another; as, the *acting* chairman:—*n.* **1,** the art of performing on the stage or screen; **2,** false or insincere behaviour; as, his enthusiasm was mere *acting*.

ac-tion (ak′shun), *n.* **1,** the doing of something; a deed; as, a kind *action*; **2,** the tendency to act; as, men of *action*; **3,** the effect of one body or substance upon another, as of sunlight on plants; **4,** a suit at law; **5,** the effective or acting part of a mechanism; as, the *action* of our piano needs repair; **6,** the progress of events, as in a play; **7,** a battle; **8, actions,** conscious acts; conduct; behaviour; as, we judge a man by his *actions*.

active (ak′tiv), *adj.* **1,** given or inclined to action; brisk; lively, as, an *active* body does not always house an *active* mind; **2,** in action or operation; as, an *active* volcano; **3,** in *grammar*, naming the voice of the verb which represents the subject as the doer of the action of the verb: opposite of passive.—*n.* **ac-tiv′i-ty.**—*v.t.* **ac′ti-vate′.**

ac-tor (ak′tėr), *n.* one who takes the part of a character in a play; a theatrical or motion-picture player.—*n. fem.* **ac′tress.**

ac-tu-al (ak′tū-al), *adj.* existing in fact; real: not imaginary.—*adv.* **ac′tu-al-ly.**

ac-tu-a-ry (ak′tū-er′i: ak′choo-ėr-i), *n.* an expert in computing insurance risks, premiums, etc.

ac-tu-ate (ak′tū-āt′), *v.t.* [actuat-ed, actuat-ing], to impel; move to action; as he was *actuated* by selfish motives; the carburettor was *actuated* by a throttle.

a-cu-men (a-kū′men), *n.* keenness; quickness of insight; as, he has business *acumen.*

a-cute (a-kūt′), *adj.* **1,** sharp-pointed: not blunt; **2,** mentally quick; as, an *acute* person; sensitive; keen; as, an *acute* sense of smell; *acute* insight; **3,** severe; as, *acute* pain; **4,** critical; as, the *acute* stage in a fever.—*adv.* **a-cute′ly.**—*n.* **a-cute′ness.**

ad-age (ad′ij), *n.* a pointed and wellknown saying; a proverb. "Waste not, want not," is an *adage.*

ad-a-mant (ad′a-mant; ad′a-mant′), *n.* a real or imaginary stone of great hardness; any substance of extreme hardness, such as the diamond:—*adj.* extremely hard; unyielding or inflexible; as, in this his will was *adamant.*—*adj.* **ad′a-man′tine** (tin; tēn; tīn).

a-dapt (a-dapt′), *v.t.* to make suitable; change so as to fit new conditions; as, I must *adapt* myself to the new house; his eyes *adapted* themselves to the dark. *adj.* **a-dapt′a-ble.** —*n.* **ad′ap-ta′tion.**

add (ad), *v.t.* to join or unite into a whole; esp. to sum up (a set of numbers); **2,** to bring (additional items); to put with others; as, to *add* books to a library; **3,** to go on to say.—*n.* **add′er.**

ad-dend (ad′end; a-dend′), *n.* a

number to be added to another number, called the *augend*.

ad-den-dum (a-den′dum), *n.* [*pl.* -da], something to be added; an appendix; a supplement.

adder (ad′er), *n.* 1, any of several harmless American snakes; 2, the poisonous viper of Europe.

ad-der's—tongue, *n.* the dogtooth violet.

ad-dict (a-dikt′), *v.t.* to devote or give (oneself) up to a habit, (sometimes a bad one); as, he *addicts* himself to music, alcohol, etc. —*n.* (ad′ikt), one who is given over to a habit; as, a drug *addict*.—*n.* **ad-dic′tion.**

ad-di-tion (a-dish′un), *n.* 1, the act, process, or result of summing up numbers, or of adding or joining something to something else; 2, a thing which is added or joined.—*adj.* **ad-di′-tion-al.**—*adv.* **ad-di′tion-al-ly.**

ad-dle (ad′l), *v.t.* and *v.i.* [ad-dled, ad-dling], 1, to make or become spoiled or rotten; as, *addled* eggs; 2, to make or become muddled; as, an *addled* mind:—*adj.* rotten, as an egg:— **addle**headed, **addle**pated, or **addle**-brained, weak-brained; muddled.

ad-dress (a-dres′), *v.t.* 1, to speak or write to; 2, to direct, as a letter; 3, to apply or devote (oneself) to a duty, task, etc.—*n.* 1, a speech delivered or written; 2, manners and bearing; 3, tact; cleverness; 4, (also, ad′res), the place to which one's mail is directed; the direction written on the letter or package.

ad-duce (a-dūs′), *v.t.* [adduced (-dūst′), adduc-ing], to bring forward (as proof or evidence); as, to *adduce* reasons.

ad-e-noids (ad′e-noidz), *n. pl.* a growth in the passage leading from the nose to the throat, often causing difficulty in breathing.

a-dept (a-dept′), *adj.* highly skilled:— *n.* (a-dept′; ad′ept), one who is fully proficient or skilled in an art; an expert; as, he is an *adept* at diving.

ad-e-quate (ad′e-kwit), *adj.* equal to requirement; enough to meet a certain need; as, his skill was *adequate* for the job.—*n.* **ad′e-qua-cy** (ad′e-kwa-si),— *adv.* **ad′e-quate-ly.**—*n.* **ad′e-quate-ness.**

ad-here (ad-hēr′), *v.i.* [adhered, adhering], 1, to stick fast as if glued; as, candy *adheres* to paper; 2, to be attached or devoted, as to a person, principle, or party; as, he *adhered* to his plans.—*n.* **ad-her′ence.**

ad-her-ent (ad-hēr′ent), *n.* a follower or supporter, as of a party, leader, cult, etc.—*adj. Grammar*, standing before (or attached to) a noun. In the phrase,

"a fond parent," *fond* is an *adherent* adjective.

ad-he-sion (ad-hē′zhun), *n.* 1, the state of sticking fast to something; 2, continued allegiance, as to a cause or party; 3, the sticking together, as in a wound, of tissues which normally are separated.

ad-he-sive (ad-hē′sive), *adj.* 1, holding fast; 2, sticky; made so as to stick; as *adhesive* tape:—*n.* a substance used to stick things together, as paste, sealing-wax, etc.—*n.* **ad-he′sive-ness.**

a-dieu (a-dū′; a′dyö′), *n.* [*pl.* adieus (a-dūz′), or adieux (a-dyö′)], a farewell:—*interj.* good-bye! farewell! (a French word).

ad-ja-cent (a-jā′sent), *adj.* 1, near; adjoining; as, *adjacent* fields; 2, in *geometry*, (two angles) with a common side between them.—*n.* **ad-ja′cen-cy.**

ad-jec-tive (aj′ik-tiv), *n.* a part of speech expressing quality or condition; a word used to limit or define a noun or pronoun, as, a *bad* law, a *wise* man; a *green* leaf.—*adj.* **ad′jec-ti′val** (aj′ik-tī′val).

ad-join (a-join′), *v.i.* to lie or be situated so as to touch, as two lots of land:—*v.t.* to lie next to; as, the field *adjoins* our yard.

ad-journ (a-jûrn′), *v.t.* to bring (a meeting) to a close; also, to put off to another time; as, to *adjourn* a debate: —*v.i.* to come to a close, or to cease business for a time; as, the court *adjourned*.—*n.* **ad-journ′ment.**

ad-judge (a-juj′), *v.t.* [adjudged adjudging], 1, to decide (a dispute) according to law; to declare or sentence by law; as, the defendant was *adjudged* insane; 2, to award or grant by law; as, the estate was *adjudged* to him.

ad-junct (aj′ungkt), *n.* something added to another thing, but not essentially part of it; as, a lean-to is an *adjunct* of a house; a subordinate, auxiliary, or dependent addition.

ad-jure (a-jōōr′), *v.t.* [adjured, adjuring], to charge or command solemnly, as if under oath or pain of penalty.

ad-just (a-just′), *v.t.* 1, to settle, as insurance claims, differences, disputes, etc.; 2, to put in proper order or position; regulate; as, to *adjust* eyeglasses, etc.—*adj.* **ad-just′a-ble.**—*n.* **ad-just′ment.**

ad-ju-tant (aj′oo-tant), *n.* 1, an assistant; esp., in the army, a regimental staff officer who assists the commanding officer; 2, a large Old World stork.

ad-lib (ad′lib′) *v.t.* and *v.i.* [-libbed (-libd), -lib-bing], 1, *Colloq.* to improvise or speak lines not in the script (on the stage, television, etc.) **2**, the full form is *ad libitum*, in *music* abbreviated to *ad lib'*: opposite of *obbligato*.

ad-min-is-ter (ad-min'is-tèr), *v.t.* **1**, to manage or conduct; as, to *administer* the affairs of state; **2**, to supply or give, as justice or relief; **3**, to cause to take; as, he *administered* the oath; **4**, in law, to settle; as, to *administer* an estate:—*v.i.* **1**, to manage affairs; **2**, in law, to settle an estate.

ad-min-is-tra-tion (ad-min'is-trā'- shun), *n.* **1**, the act of managing; management; as, his *administration* of the estate was honest; **2**, that part of a government which manages the affairs of a nation, state, city, etc.; the body of men who compose the government, or their term of office as, the policies of the *administration* were severely criticized. —*adj.* **ad-min'is-tra'tive.**—*n.* **ad-min'istra'tor.**

ad-mi-ra-ble (ad'mi-ra-bl), *adj.* worthy of wonder and approval; excellent; as, *admirable* behaviour.— *adv.* **ad'mi-ra-bly.**

ad-mir-al (ad'mi-ral), *n.* **1**, a naval officer of higher rank; a flag-officer, as rear-*admiral; Admiral* of the Fleet; **2**, any of a variety of vivid butterflies, as the *red admiral.*—*n.* **ad'mi-ral-ty.**

ad-mi-ra-tion (ad'mi-rā'shun), *n.* **1**, wonder mingled with approval and gratification or delight; as the listeners were filled with *admiration;* **2**, the object of these feelings; as, she was the *admiration* of her classmates.

ad-mire (ad-mīr'), *v.t.* [admired, ad-mir-ing], **1**, to regard with wonder, approval and delight; **2**, to esteem highly; as, Jane *admires* her teacher.— *n.* **ad-mir'er.**—*adv.* **ad-mir'ing-ly.**

ad-mis-si-ble (ad-mis'i-bl), *adj.* allowable; permissible; as, this form of argument is not *admissible.*—*adv.* **ad-mis'si-bly.**

ad-mis-sion (ad-mish'un), *n.* **1**, the power or permission to enter; as, *admission* is limited to certain days; **2**, the price paid for permission to enter; **3**, acknowledgment that something is true; as, he made full *admission* of his guilt.

ad-mit (ad-mit'), *v.t.* [admit-ted, admit-ting], **1**, to permit to enter; **2**, to allow as valid in argument; accept as true; as, I *admit* the justice of your viewpoint; **3**, to permit to have certain privileges; as, to *admit* to bail; **4**, to be capable of; allow; as, the words *admit* no other meaning.

ad-mit-tance (ad-mit'ans), *n.* the literal action of letting in, as distin-

guished from *admission*, which is the action of letting in together with granting the rights, privileges, society, etc., that belong to the place of admission.

ad-mix-ture (ad-miks'tŭr), *n.* mixing, or that which is added by mixing.

ad-mon-ish (ad-mon'ish), *v.t.* **1**, to reprove gently; as, she *admonished* the noisy child; **2**, to urge; exhort; as, the pastor *admonished* his flock to be patient.—*n.* **ad'mo-ni'tion** (ad'mo-nish'un).

a-do (a-dōō'), *n.* fuss; haste; trouble; as, much *ado* about nothing.

a-do-be (a-dō'bi), *n.* **1**, unburnt brick dried in the sun, used in southwestern U.S. and Mexico; **2**, a structure made of such brick.

ad-o-les-cent (ad'ō-les'ent), *adj.* growing up; passing from childhood to manhood or womanhood; youthful;— *n.* a person past childhood, but not yet fully grown.—*n.* **ad'o-les'cence.**

a-dopt (a-dopt'), *v.t.* **1**, to choose or take to be one's own; as, to *adopt* a child, or a plan; **2**, to approve and accept; as, the boys *adopted* his idea. —*n.* **a-dop'tion.**

a-dore (a-dōr'), *v.t.* [adored, ador-ing], **1**, to regard with warm admiration and affection; as, the mother *adores* her baby; **2**, to worship; as, to *adore* God. —*adj.* **a-dor'a-ble.**—*n.* **ad'o-ra'tion.**

a-dorn (a-dôrn'), *v.t.* to decorate; ornament; as, to *adorn* the room with flowers.—*n.* **a-dorn'ment.**

ad-ren-al-in (a-dren'a-lin), *n.* a hormone (exciting or stimulating substance) secreted by the kidney glands, and used to stop bleeding, raise blood pressure, etc.

a-drift (a-drift'), *adj.* and *adv.* floating at random; at the mercy of wind and tide; as, to cast a boat *adrift.*

a-droit (a-droit'), *adj.* clever; expert; skilful.—*adv.* **a-droit'ly.**—*n.* **a-droit'-ness.**

ad-u-la-tion (ad'ū-lā'shun), *n.* servile praise or flattery.—*adj.* **ad'u-la-tor-y.**

a-dult (a-dult'; ad'ult), *adj.* grown to full size:—*n.* a full-grown animal or person.

a-dul-ter-ate (a-dul'tèr-āt'), *v.t.* [adulter-at-ed, adulterat-ing], to make poorer or thinner by mixing in some other substance; as, to *adulterate* milk with water.—*n.* **a-dul'ter-a'tion.**

a-dul-ter-y (a-dul'tè-ri), *n.* sexual intercourse with a person other than one's spouse.—*n.* **a-dul'ter-er, a-dul'-ter-ess.**—*adj.* **a-dul'ter-ous.**

ad-vance (ad-vàns'), *v.i.* [advanced,

advanc-ing], **1,** to go forward; **2,** to rise in rank, price, etc. as, he *advanced* to the captaincy; the cost of food *advanced:*—*v.t.* **1,** to help forward; as, his money *advanced* the work; **2,** to promote; as, they *advanced* him to the principalship; **3,** to increase, as prices; **4,** to offer, as an opinion; **5,** to furnish (money) beforehand; as, he *advanced* me a dollar:—*n.* **1,** a moving forward; **2,** improvement; **3,** rise in rank or value; **4,** an approach, as to make someone's acquaintance, adjust a quarrel, etc.; as, John was the first to make *advances;* **5,** a loan.—*n.* **ad-vance′ment.**

ad-vanced (ad-vånst′), *adj.* far along in life or time, or far ahead of others in any course of action, outlook, or the like; as, a man of *advanced* ideas.

ad-van-tage (ad-vån′tij), *n.* **1,** superiority in position, skill, etc.; **2,** benefit from favourable circumstances; a useful or helpful result; as, the *advantages* of foreign travel.

ad-van-ta-geous (ad′van-tā′jus), *adj.* useful; favourable; profitable.

ad-vent (ad′vent), *n.* a coming; arrival; as, the *advent* of fall:—**Advent,** the period including the four Sundays before Christmas.

ad-ven-ti-tious (ad′ven-tish′us), *adj.* **1,** accidental; acquired; casual; added externally; not inherent; **2,** in *botany,* occurring in unusual places; as, *adventitious* leaves.

ad-ven-ture (ad-ven′tūr; -choor), *n.* **1,** a bold undertaking, involving risk and danger; as, the *adventures* of explorers; **2,** the encountering of new and exciting events; as, boys crave *adventure;* **3,** an unusual or exciting experience; as, one's first aeroplane ride is an *adventure:*—*v.t.* and *v.i.* [adventured, adventur-ing], to take a chance; venture.—*adj.* **ad-ven′ture-some.**—*n.* **ad-ven′tur-er.**

ad-ven-tur-ous (ad-ven′tūr-us; choor), *adj.* **1,** inclined to incur dangers; rash, as, an *adventurous* explorer; **2,** requiring courage; as, an *adventurous* journey.

ad-verb (ad′vûrb), *n.* a word used: **1,** to modify a verb, telling the time, place, or manner of the action; as, you came *early;* he came *here* yesterday; I read *slowly;* **2,** to modify an adjective or another adverb, indicating degree; as, *very* pretty; *too* quickly.—*adj.* **ad-ver′bi-al.**

ad-ver-sar-y (ad′vėr-sa-ri; -ser′), *n.* [*pl.* adversaries], an enemy; opponent; antagonist.

ad-verse (ad′vûrs; ad-vûrs′), *adj.* **1,** opposed; as, *adverse* winds; **2,** un-

favourable; as, *adverse* reports.—*adv.* **ad′verse-ly** or **ad-verse′ly.**

ad-ver-si-ty (ad-vûr′si-ti), *n.* [*pl.* —ties], misfortune; lack of prosperity.

ad-ver-tise (ad′vėr-tīz′; ad′vėr-tīz′), *v.t.* [advertised, advertis-ing], to turn the attention of others to; announce, esp. by printed matter, radio, or the like; as, to *advertise* a sale; publish:—*v.i.* to give public notice, as by circular, newspaper, radio, etc.:—**advertise for,** to ask for by public notice.—*n.* **ad′ver-tis′er.**

ad-ver-tise-ment (ad-vûr′tis-ment; -tiz-; or *U.S.* ad′vėr-tīz′ment), *n.* a printed notice or public announcement, esp. about something wanted or offered for sale.

ad-vice (ad-vīs′), *n.* an opinion offered as a guide to someone's action; recommendation; counsel; —**advices,** information from a distance; as, *advices* from Europe.

ad-vis-a-ble (ad-vīz′a-bl), *adj.* prudent; sensible; suitable; as, it is *advisable* to drive slowly.—*n.* **ad-vis′a-bil′i-ty.**

ad-vise (ad-vīz′), *v.t.* [advised, advising], **1,** to give advice to; as, he *advised* me to go; **2,** to notify; as, he *advised* me of my promotion:—*v.i.* to get advice; consult; as, he *advised* with me about his plans.—*n.* **ad-vis′er;** **ad-vi′sor.**

ad-vis-ed-ly (ad-vī′zid-li), *adv.* deliberately; after careful thought; as, he chose *advisedly* to delay payment.

ad-vi-so-ry (ad-vī′zo-ri), *adj.* having power to give advice; as, an *advisory* board.

ad-vo-cate (ad′vō-kāt′; -kit), *n.* **1,** one who pleads the cause of another, esp. in a court of law; **2,** one who is in favour of something; as, an *advocate* of peace:—*v.t.* (ad′vō-kāt′), [advocat-ed, advocat-ing], to urge; as, he *advocated* mercy.—*n.* **ad′vo-ca-cy** (ad′vō-ka-si).

adze or **adz** (adz), *n.* a cutting tool, somewhat like a short, heavy hoe, having a blade at right angles to the handle, and used in shaping and finishing timber.

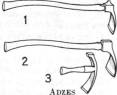

ADZES
1, ship-builder's adz; 2, carpenter's adz; 3, cooper's adz.

ae-on or **e-on** (ē′on; ē′un), *n.* a period of time too long to measure; an age.

aer-i-al (âr′i-al; ā-ē′ri-al), *adj.* **1,** living in the air, as do certain plants; also, produced in the air; as, *aerial* currents; **2,** high; lofty; as, *aerial* towers; **3,** not real or substantial; imaginary; as, *aerial* flights of fancy:— *n.* in radio systems, one or more wires suspended in the air to receive or radiate energy; an antenna.

aer-ie (ā′er-i; âr′i; ē′ri), *n.* the nest of a bird of prey, as an eagle. Also, **ey′rie.**

aer-o-bat-ics (ā′er-ō-bat′iks; âr′ō-bat′iks), *n.* [*pl.* used as *sing*], stunt flying.

aer-o-drome (ā′er-ō-drōm′; âr′ō-drōm′), *n.* an airport; airdrome.

aer-o-naut (ā′er-o-nôt′; âr′ō-nôt′), *n,* one who operates, or one who rides in, an airship or a balloon.

aer-o-nautics (ā′er-ō-nô′tiks; âr′ō-nô′tiks), *n.* [*pl.* used as *sing.*] the science of aviation, or of operating aircraft.— *adj.* **a′er-o-nau′tic; a′er-o-nau′ti-cal.**

aer-o-plane (ā′er-ō-plān′; âr′ō-plān′), *n.* an aircraft which is driven through the air by an engine and is kept aloft by the force of the air upon its winglike planes.

aes-thet-ic (es-thet′ik; ēs-thet′ik) or **es-thet-ic** (es-thet′ik), *adj.* **1,** having to do with the sense of beauty; **2,** sensitive to the beautiful in art or nature; having a cultivated, artistic taste.—*adj.* **aes-thet′-i-cal.**

ae-ther (ē′thèr), *n.* **1,** Same as **ether.**

a-far (a-fär′), *adv.* at, to, or from, a distance; as, he went *afar* seeking work.

af-fa-ble (af′a-bl), *adj.* courteous; friendly.—*n.* **af′fa-bil′i-ty.**— *adv.* **af′fa-bly.**

af-fair (a-fâr′), *n.* **1,** concern; proceeding; matter; as, luncheon is a simple *affair;* **2,** that which is done, or is to be done; as, a hard *affair* to manage; **3, affairs,** business of any kind; as, *affairs* of state.

¹af-fect (a-fekt′), *v.t.* to produce an effect upon; as, his tale *affected* me deeply.

²af-fect (a-fekt′), *v.t.* **1,** to pretend to do or to have; as, he *affected* a sympathy he did not feel; **2,** to show a liking for; as, he *affected* loud neckties.

af-fec-ta-tion (af′ek-tā′shun), *n.* the assuming of a manner merely to create an impression; also, an instance of this; as, *affectation* of wit, wealth, etc.

af-fect-ed (a-fek′tid), *adj.* not natural; assumed; as, *affected* manners.

af-fect-ing (a-fek′ting), *adj.* having power to excite the emotions; pathetic; as, the mother's grief was most *affecting.*

af-fec-tion (a-fek′shun), *n.* **1,** love; fondness; as, *affection* for animals; **2,** disease; as, an *affection* of the throat.

af-fec-tion-ate (a-fek′shun-it), *adj.* having or expressing love; kind; tender; as, she has an *affectionate* nature.

af-fi-ance (a-fī′ans), *v.t.* [affianced, affiancing], to betroth, or bind by promise of marriage; as, he is *affianced* to my sister.

af-fi-da-vit (af′i-dā′vit), *n.* a sworn statement in writing, esp. one made before a court or notary public.

af-fil-i-ate (a-fil′i-āt′), *v.t.* [affiliat-ed affiliat-ing], to join; as, to *affiliate* oneself with a certain set of people;— *v.i.* to become connected or associated; as, one company *affiliated* with the other.—*n.* **af-fil′i-a′tion.**

af-fin-i-ty (a-fin′i-ti), *n.* [*pl.* —ties], **1,** a close relationship; as, an *affinity* between two races of men, or between two languages; **2,** special attraction; as, the *affinity* of salt for water; **3,** a liking for a person; also, the person liked.

af-firm (a-fûrm′), *v.t.* and *v.i.* to declare solemnly, as to a court, but without taking oath; to declare vigorously and strongly; as, he *affirmed* his belief in my honesty.—*n.* **af′fir-ma′tion** (af′èr-mā′shun).

af-firm-a-tive (a-fûr′ma-tiv), *n.* the side in a debate which defends a proposition; as, the *affirmative* won:— *adj.* **1,** answering, or consisting of, "yes"; as, an *affirmative* answer; **2,** supporting a proposition; as, the *affirmative* side.—*adv.* **af-firm′a-tive-ly.**

af-fix (a-fiks′), *v.t.* to attach or add; as, I *affixed* my signature to the letter: —*n.* (af′iks), a part added to a word, as a prefix like *ad-* or *un-*, or a suffix like *-able* or *-ness.*

af-flict (a-flikt′), *v.t.* to distress with pain or great trouble; make miserable. —*n.* **af-flic′tion.**

af-flu-ent (af′loo-ent), *adj.* having abundance; wealthy; as, an *affluent* man; *affluent* times.—*n.* **af′flu-ence.**

af-ford (a-fōrd′), *v.t.* **1,** to supply; produce; yield; as, singing *affords* him pleasure; **2,** to bear the expense of; as, he can *afford* a car; **3,** to manage to give; spare; as, I can *afford* the time.

af-fray (a-frā′), *n.* a noisy quarrel; brawl.

af-fright (a-frīt′), *v.t.* to frighten; terrify; as, the noise *affrighted* the child.—*n.* fear.

af-front (a-frunt′), *v.t.* to insult intentionally; as, the boy *affronted* the teacher:—*n.* an insult; as, an *affront* to one's honour.

a-fire (a-fīr′), *adj.* and *adv.* on fire; as, a house *afire;* to set rubbish *afire.*

---

a-flame (a-flām′), *adj.* on fire; blazing; also, ardent; as, *aflame* with patriotism.

a-float (a-flōt′), *adj.* and *adv.* **1,** floating on water, as a vessel; on board ship, as the crew; **2,** awash; covered with water, as a deck; **3,** in circulation; commonly talked about; as, a rumour is *afloat.*

a-foot (a-foot′), *adj.* and *adv.* **1,** on foot; **2,** astir; as, a conspiracy was *afoot.*

a-fore-said (a-fōr′sed′), *adj.* mentioned before; as, the *aforesaid* person.

a-fore-thought (a-fōr′thôt′), *adj.* planned beforehand; as, malice *aforethought.*

a-fraid (a-frād′), *adj.* filled with fear; frightened; as, he was *afraid* of the dog.

a-fresh (a-fresh′), *adv.* again; anew; newly; over again; as, to start *afresh.*

Af-ri-ca (af′ri-ka), *n.* the second largest continent (11.5 million square miles), situated south of Europe.

aft (àft), *adj.* and *adv.* toward the stern of a ship; as, the *aft* cabin; to go *aft.*

aft-er (àf′tèr), *prep.* **1,** in succession to; as, B comes *after* A; **2,** later than; as, John arrived *after* Jim; **3,** in imitation of; in the manner of; as, a painting *after* Raphael; **4,** next below in rank or excellence; as, a captain comes *after* a major; **5,** in pursuit of; as, John ran *after* the dog; **6,** by the name of; as, he is named *after* his father; **7,** in spite of; as, *after* all your help, he failed:—*conj.* following the time when; as, *after* he has dinner, he may go.—*adv.* afterward; as, he arrived shortly *after:*—*adj.* **1,** later; as, in *after* days; **2,** in the rear; as, the *after* deck.

aft-er-math (àf′tèr-math′), *n.* result; (bad) consequences; as, the *aftermath* of the war.

aft-er-noon (àf′tèr-nōōn′), *n.* the time between noon and evening:—*adj.* occurring in the *afternoon* (af′tèr-nōōn′).

aft-er-thought (àf′tèr-thôt′), *n.* a second or later thought about something, esp. one that comes too late; as, the idea was an *afterthought.*

aft-er-wards (àf′tèr-wèrdz) or **aft-er-ward** (àf′tèr-wèrd), *adv.* at a later time.

a-gain (a-gen′; a-gān′), *adv.* **1,** a second time; once more; as, do it *again;* **2,** in return; as, give the book back *again;* **3,** further; on the other hand; as, then *again,* I need cash.

a-gainst (a-genst′; a-gānst′), *prep.* **1,** in contact with; near to; as, to lean *against* a tree; **2,** opposite to; facing; in the direction of; as, over *against* Jericho; **3,** in opposition to; as, a law *against* speeding.

a-gape (a-gāp′; a-gap′), *adj.* and *adv.* having the mouth wide open, as in wonder.

ag-ate (ag′it), *n.* **1,** a semi-precious stone, with colours in stripes and cloudy patches; **2,** a boy's marble made of agate, or striped like agate; **3,** a small size of type.

age (āj), *n.* **1,** a particular time or period in life; as, the *age* of six; the *age* of childhood; **2,** a period in history; as, the Elizabethan *age;* **3,** the latter part of life; as, the wisdom of *age;* **4,** *Colloq.* a long or weary time; as, it's an *age* since I saw you:—**of age,** 21 years old; as, he just came of *age:*—*v.i.* and *v.t.* [aged, ag-ing], to grow old, or cause to grow old.

ag-ed (ā′jid), *adj.* **1,** old; far on in years; as, an *aged* man; **2,** (ājd), of the age of; as, a child *aged* three.

a-gen-cy (ā′jen-si), *n.* [*pl.* agencies], **1,** the business or place of business of one who acts for another; as, a ticket *agency;* **2,** help; active influence; as, crops grow through the *agency* of rain.

a-gen-da (a-jen′da), *n. pl.* the items on a programme of business to be brought up for action.

a-gent (ā′jent), *n.* **1,** one who acts, esp. for another; as, an *agent* for a firm; **2,** an active power or cause; as, religion is an *agent* for good.

ag-gra-vate (ag′ra-vāt′), *v.t.* [aggravat-ed, aggravat-ing], **1,** to increase, as a burden; make worse; as, worry will only *aggravate* your illness; **2,** *Colloq.,* to annoy; irritate; as, his boasting *aggravates* me.—*adj.* **ag′gra-vat′ing.**—*n.* **ag′gra-va′tion.**

ag-gre-gate (ag′re-gāt′), *v.t.* [aggregat-ed, aggregat-ing], to collect or bring together; gather into one whole or mass; *n.* (ag′re-git), **1,** the entire number; total; **2,** a mass formed by the sticking together of similar particles —*adj.* taken as a whole; as, the *aggregate* amount.—*n.* **ag′gre-ga′tion.**

ag-gres-sion (a-gresh′un), *n.* an unprovoked attack or assault.—**ag-gres′sor.**

ag-gres-sive (a-gres′iv), *adj.* **1,** energetic; pushing; as, an *aggressive* salesman; **2,** first to attack or quarrel, esp. without a cause; as, an *aggressive* nation.—*adv.* **ag-gres′sive-ly.**—*n.* **ag-gres′sive-ness.**

ag-grieved (a-grēvd′), *adj.* having a grievance; having cause of grief or offence; as, he felt *aggrieved* at being left out.

a-ghast (a-gàst′), *adj.* struck with sudden surprise, horror, or terror; as, he stood *aghast* at the damage he had caused.

ag-ile (aj′il; aj′īl), *adj.* quick-moving; active; nimble; also, mentally quick; as, an *agile* mind.—*n.* **a-gil′i-ty** (a-jil′i-ti.)

ag-i-tate (aj′i-tāte′), *v.t.* [agitat-ed, agitat-ing], **1,** to stir violently; as, the storm *agitates* the sea; **2,** to excite; disturb; as, he was *agitated* about losing his job; **3,** to discuss publicly; argue for; as, to *agitate* the repeal of a law:—*v.i.* to stir up public interest; as, to *agitate* for shorter working hours.—*n.* **ag′i-ta′tion.**—*n.* **ag′i-ta′tor.**

a-glow (a-glō′), *adj.* bright; flushed; as, cheeks *aglow* with health.

ag-nos-tic (ag-nos′tik) *n.* one who holds that we cannot know whether there is a God or a future life.

a-go (a-go′), *adj.* and *adv.* past; in past time; as, an hour *ago;* long *ago.*

a-gog (a-gog′), *adj.* aroused; alive with interest; excited; eager, as we are *agog* with curiosity.

ag-o-nize (ag′o-nīz′), *v.i.* [agonized, agoniz-ing], to suffer extreme pain or grief:—*v.t.* to torment or torture.

ag-o-ny (ag′o-ni), *n.* [*pl.* agonies], **1,** intense suffering of body or mind; as, an earache is *agony;* she suffered *agonies* of remorse for her carelessness; **2,** the death struggle of a person, etc.

a-gree (a-grē′), *v.i.* [agreed, agree-ing], **1,** to consent; as, he *agreed* to the plan to go; **2,** to be in harmony; as, I *agree* with you:—**agree with, 1,** in *grammar,* to correspond with; as, the verb *agrees with* its subject in person and number; **2,** to suit physically; as, fruit *agrees* with me.

a-gree-a-ble (a-grē′a-bl), *adj.* **1,** ready or willing to agree; **2,** pleasant; as, an *agreeable* afternoon; having pleasing manners or personality; as, an *agreeable* companion.

a-gree-ment (a-grē′ment), *n.* **1,** harmony of opinions or feelings; **2,** in *grammar,* the correspondence of one word with another in gender, number, case or person; **3,** a compact; contract; as, the *agreement* for the sale was drawn up and signed.

ag-ri-cul-ture (ag′ri-kul′tūr), *n.* the cultivation of the soil; farming.—*adj.* **ag′ri-cul′tur-al.**—*n.* **ag′ri-cul′tur-ist.** *n.* **ag′ri-cul′tur-al-ist.**

a-ground (a-ground′), *adv.* and *adj.* stranded, as a ship on a shoal, reef, etc.

a-gue (ā′gū), *n.* **1,** a chill; a fit of shivering; **2,** a fever (with chills).

ah (ä, ô), *interj.* exclamation of pain, disgust, delight, surprise, etc.

a-ha (à-hä), *interj.* exclamation of triumph, mockery, irony, etc.

a-head (a-hed′), *adv.* in front; forward; onward.

a-hoy (a-hoi′), *interj.* a call used in hailing a vessel; as, ship *ahoy!*

aid (ād), *n.* help; assistance. Also *v.t.*

aide–de–camp (ād′–de–kamp′; ed′–de–kän′), *n.* [*pl.* aides–de–camp (ādz′–de–kamp′)], an officer who assists a general: often shortened to *aide.*

ail (āl), *v.t.* to trouble with pain or discomfort; as, what *ails* the child?— *v.i.* to feel pain; be ill; as, they are all *ailing.*

ai-ler-on (ā′lẽr-on), *n.* a hinged section on the rear edge of each wing of an airplane, used in banking or steadying the plane.

ail-ment (āl′ment), *n.* sickness; illness.

aim (ām), *v.t.* to point (a gun) before firing; hence, to direct; as, the remark was *aimed* at you:—*v.i.* **1,** to point a weapon at something; **2,** to direct one's efforts:—*n.* **1,** the pointing of a weapon; **2,** purpose.

aim-less (ām′lis), *adj.* without a definite intention or purpose; as, an *aimless* stroll.

air (âr), *n.* **1,** a mixture of gases, consisting chiefly of oxygen and nitrogen, which surrounds the earth; the atmosphere; **2,** a light breeze; **3,** an appearance or manner; as, an *air* of dignity; **4,** a tune or melody; as, she hummed an *air;* **5, airs,** affected manners:—*v.t.* **1,** to expose to the *air;* ventilate; **2,** to make a public display of; as, he is always *airing* his views.

air-borne (âr′bōrn′), *adj.* carried by or on air; as, *airborne* troops, *airborne* bacteria.

air cas-tle (kàs′l), an idle fancy; a daydream.

air–con-di-tion (âr′–kon-dish′un), *v.t.* to provide desirable temperature, humidity, and purity by circulating treated air within a structure.—*n.* **air-con-di′tion-ing.**

air-craft (âr′kråft′), *n.* [*pl.* aircraft], any type of machine for flying, as a balloon, glider, or airplane.

air-drome (âr′drōm′), *n.* Same as *aerodrome.*

Aire-dale (âr′dāl′), *n.* a large black-and-tan terrier with a rough coat.

air-i-ness (âr′i-nis), *n.* **1,** openness to the air; as, the *airiness* of an apartment; **2,** delicacy; lightness; **3,** sprightliness; jauntiness; as, an *airiness* of manner.

air lift, an airplane service ferrying supplies and personnel over inaccessible territory. Also **air′lift′.**

cat, āge, fär, câre, àsk; ten, ēve, latẽr; (i) pity, rely, senate; īce; top; nō.

air-line (âr'lïn'), *n.* **1,** a system of air transport; **2,** the route used by the air system.—*adj.* **air'line'**.

air-plane (âr'plān'), *n.* a motor-driven aircraft, kept aloft by the force of the air upon its winglike planes.

air-port (âr'pôrt'), *n.* a place with facilities for the departure, landing, loading, fuelling, or repairing of aircraft.

air-ship (âr'ship'), *n.* a motor-driven aircraft that is lighter than air; a dirigible.

air-strip (âr'strip'), *n.* a runway for the take-off and landing of airplanes.

air-tight (âr'tīt'), *adj.* **1,** so tight that no air can get in or out; **2,** without flaw; as, he has an *airtight* alibi.

air-y (âr'i), *adj.* [air-i-er, air-i-est], **1,** open to the air; breezy; **2,** of the air; as, *airy* spirits; **3,** delicate; light; as, *airy* chiffons; **4,** gay; lighthearted.—*adv.* **air'i-ly.**

aisle (īl), *n.* **1,** a passageway leading to the seats in a church, theatre, etc. **2,** in a store, a passageway for patrons.

a-jar (a-jär'), *adv.* and *adj.* slightly open.

A-ke-la (a-kā'la), *n.* the leader and instructor of a cub wolf-pack (Boy Scouts).

a-kimbo, (a-kim'bō), *adj.* and *adv.* with the hands supported on the hips and the elbows turned outward; as, he stood with arms *akimbo*.

a-kin (a-kin'), *adj.* **1,** related by blood; **2,** of the same kind; near in nature or character; as, the two schemes are closely *akin*.

al-a-bas-ter (al'a-bàs'tér), *n.* a kind of stone, usually white, of fine texture, often carved into vases or ornaments:—*adj.* made of alabaster; white like alabaster.

a-lack (a-lak'), *interj.* expressing regret, dismay, etc. (archaic).

a-lac-ri-ty (a-lak'ri-ti), *n.* eager readiness to do something; as, he accepted the invitation with *alacrity*.

a-larm (a-lärm'), *n.* **1,** a call to arms; hence, a warning of danger; as, he gave the *alarm;* **2,** the fear of danger; as, *alarm* seized the camp; **3,** a device to warn or awaken persons; as, a fire *alarm*:—*v.t.* to arouse to a sense of danger; startle; as, we were *alarmed* by the smell of smoke.

a-larm-ing (a-lär'ming), *adj.* causing a fear of danger; terrifying.—*adv.* **a-larm'ing-ly.**

a-larm-ist (a-lär'mist), *n.* one who exaggerates bad news or foretells calamities.

a-las (a-làs'), *interj.* an exclamation expressing sorrow, pity, or regret.

al-ba-tross (al'ba-trôs'), *n.* a very large web-footed sea bird, of southern waters, capable of remarkably long flights from land.

al-be-it (ôl-bē'it), *conj.* although; even though.

al-bum (al'bum), *n.* a book with blank pages, in which to keep a collection of photographs, stamps, autographs, etc.

al-bu-men (al-bū'men), *n.* **1,** the white of an egg; **2,** albumin.—*adj.* **al-bu'mi-nous.**

al-bu-min (al-bū'min), *n.* a protein found in its purest state in the white of an egg. It occurs in animal and vegetable tissues and fluids, and is used in sugar refining, etc.—*adj.* **al-bu'mi-nous.**

al-che-my (al'ke-mi), *n.* the art of changing baser metals to gold; hence, any mysterious change.

al-co-hol (al'kō-hol'), *n.* a colourless liquid, made by the fermentation of grapes, grain, etc. and forming the intoxicating substance in all fermented and distilled liquors.—*adj.* **al'co-hol'ic.**

al-cove (al'kōv), *n.* a recess in a room, as for a window-seat or bookcase; also, a very small room opening into a larger room.

al-der (ôl'dèr), *n.* any of several trees and shrubs related to the birches, often growing thickly in moist places. The bark is used in tanning and dyeing.

al-der-man (ôl'dèr-man), *n.* [*pl.* aldermen], in some cities of Canada and the U.S., a member of the city's governing body representing a ward or district.

ale (āl), *n.* a strong, fermented liquor like beer, made from malt and hops.

a-lert (a-lûrt'), *adj.* **1,** watchful; wide-awake; as, an *alert* watchdog; **2,** nimble; active; as, an *alert* child:—*n.* warning of an attack, as from the air —*v.t.* to warn of an attack:—**on the alert,** ready to act; on the lookout.—*adv.* **a-lert'ly.**—*n.* **a-lert'-ness.**

al-fal-fa (al-fal'fa), *n.* a kind of clover, having purple flowers and very deep roots. In Canada and the U.S. it is grown for hay, of which it may yield several cuttings a year.

al-gae (al'jē), *n. pl.* [*sing.* alga (al'ga)], a group of flowerless water plants, including the seaweeds.

al-ge-bra (al'je-bra), *n.* a branch of mathematics which represents quantities by the use of letters and other symbols, instead of by numbers, as in arithmetic.

a-li-as (ā'li-as), *n.* an assumed name;

as, the forger had two *aliases:*—*adv.* otherwise called; as, Max, *alias* Sam.

al-i-bi (al′i-bī′), *n.* [*pl.* alibis], **1,** the plea offered by a person accused of a crime, of having been elsewhere at the time the crime was committed; **2,** *Colloq.* an excuse.

al-ien (āl′yen; ā′li-en), *n.* a foreigner; a person who is not a citizen of the country in which he is living:—*adj.* **1,** foreign; as, *alien* peoples; **2,** strange; unnatural; as, language *alien* to persons of refinement.

al-ien-ate (āl′ye-nāte; ā′li-en-āt′), *v.t.* [alienat-ed, alienat-ing], to estrange (a person); cause (affection) to turn away; as, she was *alienated* from her brother; they *alienated* her affections from me.—*n.* **al′ien-a′tion** (āl′yen-ā′-shun;ā′li-en-ā′shun).—*adj.* **al′ien-a-ble.**

a-light (a-līt′), *adj.* **1,** kindled and burning, as a fire; **2,** lighted up; as, the child's face was *alight* with joy.

a-light (a-līt′), *v.i.* **1,** to come down, as from a horse or train; **2,** to descend and settle; land, as an aeroplane.

a-lign (a-līn′), *v.t.* and *v.i.* to put or get into line; as, to *align* troops; the men *aligned* quickly. Also, **a-line′.**

a-lign-ment or **a-line-ment** (a-līn′-ment), *n.* the act of arranging, or an arrangement, in a straight line; as, the *alignment* was good; the sergeant directed the *alignment*.

1 2 3 4 5 6

□□□□■□

ALIGNMENT
Blocks 1, 2, 3, 5, 6, are in alignment; block 4 is out of alignment.

a-like (a-līk′), *adj.* resembling one another; similar:—*adv.* in a similar manner.

al-i-men-ta-ry (al′i-men′ta-ri), *adj.* pertaining to food and nutrition.— **alimentary canal,** the digestive tract of the body, consisting of oesophagus (or gullet), stomach, and intestines, through which food passes.

a-line (a-līn′), *v.t.* and *v.i.* Same as **align.**

a-live (a-līv′), *adj.* **1,** having life; **2,** lively; animated; as, *alive* with excitement; **3,** attentive; sensitive; as, he is *alive* to his opportunities; **4,** full of living things; swarming; as, the stream is *alive* with fish.

al-ka-li (al′ka-lī′; al′ka-li), *n.* [*pl.* alkalis; -lies], a substance, as soda or potash, which neutralizes acids and combines with them to form salts; a base.—*adj.* **al′ka-line.**

all (ôl), *adj.* **1,** the whole of; every bit of; as, *all* the world; **2,** every one of; as, *all* men; **3,** as much as possible; as, with *all* speed; **4,** nothing but; as, *all* work and no play:—*n.* and *pron.* **1,** the

whole number or quantity; as, *all* of us, or *all* of the money we have; **2,** one's entire possessions; as, he lost, or gave, his *all.*—*adv.* **1,** wholly; as, *all* wrong; **2,** exhausted; as, *all* in.

Al-lah (al′a; ȧl-lä′), the name of the God of the Mohammedans; God.

al-lay (a-lā′), *v.t.* to quiet or calm; lessen; as, *allay* your fears.

al-lege (a-lej′), *v.t.* [alleged, alleg-ing], **1,** to offer as an argument, plea, or excuse; as, he *alleged* illness for his failure to come; **2,** to assert; as, he *alleges* his innocence.—*n.* **al′le-ga′tion.**

al-le-giance (a-lē′jens), *n.* **1,** the loyalty or obligation of a person to his sovereign or country; **2,** fidelity to a thing, cause, or person; as, we pledged *allegiance* to our new leader.

al-le-gor-y (al′e-gōr′i), *n.* [*pl.* allegories], a story, usually aiming to teach something, as the parables of the Bible or Bunyan's *Pilgrim's Progress,* in which the characters stand for ideas or qualities, such as truth, loyalty, or the like.—*adj.* **al′le-gor′i-cal**(al′e-gōr′i-kal) —*adv.* **al′le-gor′i-cal-ly.**

al-le-gro (äl-lā′grō), *adj.* and *adv.* in *music,* fast; lively.

al-le-lu-ia (al′e-lū′yȧ; -lōo′), *n.* a song of praise to God:—*interj.* praise ye the Lord.

al-ler-gic (a-lûr′jik), *adj.* sensitive to certain substances or conditions; as, he is *allergic* to feathers.

al-ler-gy (al′ẽr-ji), *n.* [pl. allergies], extreme sensitivity to certain things, as pollens, fruits, etc. Hives, asthma, and hay fever are common *allergies.*

al-le-vi-ate (a-lē′vi-āt′), *v.t.* [alleviat-ed, alleviat-ing], to lighten; lessen; make easier; as, a drug to *alleviate* pain.

¹al-ley (al′i), *n.* [*pl.* alleys], **1,** a narrow way or back street in a city; **2,** a long, narrow enclosure for games; as, a bowling-*alley.*

²al-ley (al′i), *n.*[*pl.* alleys], in marbles, a shooter, formerly made of alabaster.

al-ley-way (al′i-wā′), *n.* a narrow lane or passageway.

al-li-ance (a-lī′ans), *n.* **1,** a union between or among nations, groups, or persons; as an *alliance* by marriage; **2,** a group of persons, societies, or nations, united by treaty or agreement.

al-li-ga-tor (al′i-gā′tẽr), *n.* a large, lizard-like, carnivorous reptile related to the crocodiles, with a short, broad head and blunt snout. One kind, growing to about twelve feet, lives in the fresh waters of the southern U.S.

al-lit-er-a-tion (a-lit′ẽr-ā′shun), *n.* the repetition of initial sounds in a phrase; as, the *teeming trout twinkled* below.

al-lo-cate (al′ō-kāt′), *v.t.* [-cated, -cating], to assign; allot; set apart; as, they *allocated* funds for housing.

al-lot (a-lot′), *v.t.* [allot-ted, allot-ting], to distribute (amounts or shares); assign; as, to *allot* the work.—*n.* **al-lot′ment.**

al-low (a-lou′), *v.t.* **1,** to permit; as, smoking is not *allowed;* **2,** to concede; acknowledge, as a claim; **3,** to set apart; as, to *allow* ten per cent for breakage; **4,** to give; let someone have; as, he *allows* you too much money:—*v.i.* to make concession or provision; as, to *allow* for shrinking.

al-low-a-ble (a-lou′a-bl), *adj.* permissible; proper; acceptable.

al-low-ance (a-lou′ans), *n.* **1,** a quantity or sum allotted; as, a weekly *allowance;* **2,** an amount deducted or added; as, an *allowance* for cash.

al-loy (a-loi′; al′oi), *n.* **1,** any mixture of metals; as, steel is an *alloy* of iron and carbon; **2,** a baser metal used in mixture with a finer one; as, copper is often used as an *alloy* with gold; **3,** something that lowers or takes from the value or perfection of something; as, pleasure without *alloy:*—*v.t.* (a-loi′), **1,** to melt together (two or more metals); **2,** esp., to debase by mixture, as gold with copper; **3,** to lessen by mixing; as, hope *alloyed* with fear.

all right, *Colloq.* **1,** correct; satisfactory; **2,** yes; certainly.

all—round (ôl′round′), *adj.* **1,** able to do many things; as an *all-round* student; **2,** generally useful; as, an *all-round* tool.

all-spice (ôl′spīs′), *n.* **1,** the berry of the West Indian pimento tree; **2,** a spice made from it, combining the flavours of cinnamon, nutmeg, and cloves.

al-lude (a-lūd′), *v.i.* [allud-ed, alluding], to refer indirectly or in passing; as I *allude* to events familiar to you all.

al-lure (a-lūr′), *v.t.* [allured, allur-ing], to tempt by the offer of something desirable; entice; attract.—*adj.* **al-lur′ing.**

al-lu-sion (a-lū′zhun), *n.* **1,** a passing reference; as, do not make any *allusion* to his loss; **2,** a hint or reference, usually to something generally familiar, used by way of illustration; as, a literary *allusion*.

al-lu-vi-al (a-lū′vi-al), *adj.* composed of clay, mud, etc. deposited by running water; as, *alluvial* soil.

al-ly (a-lī′), *v.t.* [allied, ally-ing], to

unite or bind, as by marriage, treaty, league, confederacy, or friendship:—*n.* (a-lī′; al′ī), [*pl.* allies (a-liz′; al′īz)], a nation, family, or the like, so united to another, esp., a nation that helps another in war.

al-ma-nac (ôl′ma-nak′), *n.* a year-book, or calendar of days, weeks, and months, often giving information about the weather, the sun, moon, stars, tides, festivals, etc.

al-might-y (ôl-mīt′i), *adj.* having unlimited power; all powerful:—**the Almighty,** God.

al-mond (ä′mund; am′und), *n.* **1,** the nutlike fruit of a small tree somewhat like the peach; **2,** the tree itself.

al-most (ôl ′mōst; ôl-mōst′), *adv.* nearly.

alms (ämz), *n. sing.* and *pl.* money given to the poor; charity.

alms-house (ämz′ hous′), *n.* a free home for the poor, supported by public funds.

al-oe (al′ō), *n.* a plant with thick, spiny leaves found chiefly in South Africa:— **American aloe,** the century-plant.

a-loft (a-loft′; a-lôft′), *adv.* **1,** on high; far above the earth; **2,** esp., at the masthead, high above the deck of a ship.

a-lone (a-lōn′), *adj.* and *adv.* **1,** by oneself; apart; as, he usually walks *alone;* the house stands *alone;* **2,** only; as, he *alone* knows it; **3,** without the aid of another; as, he did that job *alone.*

a-long (a-long′), *prep.* by the length of; lengthwise of; as, *along* the shore:— *adv.* **1,** parallel; as, he ran *along* beside me; **2,** onward; as, step *along.*

a-long-side (a-long′sīd′), *adv.* by the side; side by side;—*prep.* by the side of; beside.

a-loof (a-loof′), *adj.* and *adv.* apart; as, he stood *aloof* from the crowd.—*n.* **a-loof′ness.**

a-loud (a-loud′), *adv.* loudly; as, to call *aloud* for help; also, with a normal voice; as, he read *aloud.*

alp (alp), *n.* a high mountain, or its peak.

al-pac-a (al-pak′a), *n.* **1,** a domesticated, sheeplike animal of the Andes, with fine long woolly hair; **2,** a thin cloth made from this hair, often mixed with silk or cotton.

al-pha-bet (al′fa-bet′), *n.* a set of letters used in writing a language; also, these letters arranged in a certain traditional order.—*adj.* **al′pha-bet′i-cal.**

al-pha-bet-ize (al′fa-be-tīz′), *v.t.* [betized, -betizing], to arrange, as a list of words, in alphabetical order.

al-read-y (ôl-red′i), *adv.* previously; before a particular time; beforehand; as, he has *already* left.

all (ôl), ôr; up, mūte, cûr, cōōl, bŏŏk; oil, out; th, thin; *th,* the.

al-so (ôl'sō), *adv.* in addition; besides; too.

al-tar (ôl'tėr), *n.* **1,** any raised place or structure on which, as formerly, incense was burned or sacrifices were offered by worshippers; **2,** in some Christian churches, the communion-table.

al-ter (ol'tėr), *v.t.* and *v.i.* to change; make or become different; as, she *altered* the dress; his manners *altered* for the better.—*adj.* **al'ter-a-ble.**—*n.* **al'ter-a'tion.**

al-ter-ca-tion (ôl'tėr-kā'shun; al'), *n.* a quarrel or dispute; wrangle; as, the baseball pitcher had an *altercation* with the umpire.

al-ter-nate (ôl-tûr'nit; al-; ôl'tėr-nit; al'-), *adj.* **1,** taking place by turns, first one and then the other; as, *alternate* chills and fever; **2,** every other (one) of a series; as, *alternate* months:—*n.* a substitute; as, an *alternate* took the sick man's place:—*v.t.* (ôl'tėr-nāt'; al') [alternat-ed, alternat-ing], to cause to occur by turns; interchange; as, he *alternated* his questions between the boys and the girls:—*v.i.* to take place by turns; as, day *alternates* with night.

al-ter-na-tion (ôl'tėr-nā'shun; al'), *n.* a following in succession, one after the other; as, the *alternation* of day and night.

ALTERNATION
White and black squares are arranged in alternation.

al-ter-na-tive (ôl-tûr'na-tiv; al-), *n.* **1,** a choice between two things or courses of action; as, she had the *alternative* of going to a concert or to a theatre; **2,** either of the two choices; as, she chose the second *alternative*, namely, the theatre:—*adj.* giving the choice of two things, only one of which may be taken, done, etc.—*adv.* **al-ter'na-tive-ly.**

al-though (ôl-thō'), *conj.* though; even if.

al-tim-e-ter (al-tim'e-tėr; al'ti-mē'tėr), *n.* an instrument for measuring altitude, as a barometer (on aircraft).

al-ti-tude (al'ti-tūd'), *n.* **1,** height; height above sea level; as, the *altitude* of a mountain; **2,** a high place or region.

al-to (al'tō), *n.* [*pl.* altos], **1,** the part sung by the lowest female voice; **2,** a person with such a voice, or the voice itself.—*adj.* **al'to.**

al-to-geth-er (ôl'too-geth'ėr), *adv.* **1,** completely; wholly; entirely; **2,** on the whole; in the main; as, *altogether*, the party was a success.

al-tru-ism (al'trōō-izm), *n.* unselfish regard for the interests of others.—*n.* **al'-tru-ist.**—*adj.* **al'tru-is'tic.**

al-um (al'um), *n.* a transparent, whitish mineral salt, used as a medicine, either externally to stop bleeding, or internally to cause vomiting; also in dyeing and in the purification of water.

a-lu-mi-num (a-lū'mi-num), *n.* a bluish-white, non-rusting metal, used where lightness and strength are needed. Also, **a'lu-min'i-um** (al'ū-min'i-um).

a-lum-nus (a-lum'nus), *n.* [*pl.* alumni (a-lum'nī; a-lum'nē)], a boy or man graduate of a school, college, or university, or the like.—*n. fem.* **a-lum'-na** [*pl.* **alumnae** (a-lum'nē; a-lum'nī)].

always (ôl'wāz; ôl'wiz), *adv.* at all times.

am (am), first person, *sing.*, present indicative, of *be.*

a-mal-ga-mate (a-mal'ga-māt'), *v.t.* [amalgamat-ed, amalgamat-ing], **1,** to alloy or mix (a metal) with mercury or with another metal; **2,** to mix to form a compound:—*v.i.* to mix or combine so as to become indistinguishable; unite; as, one race may *amalgamate* with another.—*n.* **a-mal'ga-ma'tion.**

a-mass (a-mas'), *v.t.* to collect into a heap; gather; accumulate; as, he *amassed* great wealth.

am-a-teur (am'a-tūr'; am'a-tûr'), *n.* **1,** one who engages in any art, study, or sport for pleasure, and not for money; as, a golf *amateur;* **2,** one whose work lacks professional finish:—*adj.* non-professional; as, *amateur* standing in athletics; *amateur* dramatics.—*adj.* **am'a-teur'ish.**

a-maze (a-māz'), *v.t.* [amazed, amazing], to overwhelm with astonishment; as, your news *amazes* me.—*n.* **a-maze'-ment.**—*adj.* **a-maz'ing.**—*adv.* **a-maz'-ing-ly.**

Am-a-zon (am'a-zon'; am'a-zun), *n.* one of a fabulous race of female warriors: —**amazon,** a tall, strong, masculine woman.—*adj.* **Am'a-zo'ni-an** (am'a-zō'ni-an).

am-bas-sa-dor (am-bas'a-dėr), *n.* **1,** a government agent of highest rank representing his country's interests at a foreign capital; **2,** any representative or agent charged with a special mission.

am-ber (am'bėr), *n.* **1,** a yellowish hard resin, or gum, capable of high polish, which is made into beads, cigar-holders, etc.; **2,** the reddish-yellow colour of amber:—*adj.* made of amber; also, amber-coloured.

am-big-u-ous (am-big'ū-us), *adj.* doubtful; having two or more possible meanings; as, *ambiguous* words; *ambiguous* actions.—*n.* **am'bi-gu'i-ty** (am'-bi-gū'i-ti).

---

cat, āge, fär, câre, ȧsk; ten, ēve, latėr; (i) pity, rely, senate; īce; top; nō.

am-bi-tion (am-bish′un), *n.* **1,** an eager desire to gain or do something; as, he has an *ambition* to be an explorer; **2,** the thing desired; as, he has attained his *ambition* to be a doctor.

am-bi-tious (am-bish′us), *adj.* **1,** full of ambition; determined to succeed; **2,** eager; aspiring; as, *ambitious* for knowledge; **3,** requiring great skill or effort for success; as, they planned an *ambitious* program.

am-ble (am′bl), *v.i.* [amb-led, ambling], **1,** to walk at an easy pace; meander; **2,** of horses, to pace, or go at a gait in which the animal lifts the two feet on the same side together:—*n.* **1,** the ambling gait of a horse; **2,** any easy gait.—*n.* **am′bler.**

am-bu-lance (am′bū-lans), *n.* an enclosed vehicle for carrying the sick and wounded.

am-bus-cade (am′bus-kād′), *n.* an ambush; a place where troops hide for sudden attack; also, troops so hidden: —*v.i.* [ambuscad-ed, ambuscad-ing], to lie in ambush;—*v.t.* to place (troops) in ambush.

am-bush (am′boosh), *n.* **1,** a concealed station from which to attack the enemy unexpectedly; **2,** troops so attacking: —*v.t.* to waylay; attack from ambush.

a-me-ba (a-mē′ba), *n.* Same as **amoeba.**

a-men (ā′men′; ä′men′), *interj.* verily; so be it: a word used at the end of a prayer, blessing, etc., to express solemn assent or approval.—*n.* **a′men′.**

a-me-na-ble (a-mē′na-bl; a-men′a-bl), *adj.* **1,** easy to lead; ready to accept advice; **2,** liable; as, *amenable* to the law.—*adv.* **a-me′na-bly.**

a-mend (a-mend′), *v.t.* **1,** to change for the better; improve; correct; as, he tried to *amend* his faults; **2,** to change formally; as, to *amend* a law.

a-mend-ment (a-mend′ment), *n.* **1,** a change for the better; as, an *amendment* in conduct; **2,** an alteration or change in a formal document, as in the constitution of a country.

a-mends (a-mendz′), *n. pl.* payment or reparation for loss or injury inflicted on someone else; as, he made *amends* for the results of his careless drinking.

a-men-i-ty (a-men′i-ti; a-mēn′i-ti), *n.* [*pl.* amenities], **1,** pleasantness; **2,** *pl.* civilities; as, please observe the social *amenities.*

A-mer-i-can (a-mer′i-kan), *adj.* relating to America or the U.S.—*n.* a native of America, esp. a citizen of U.S.

am-e-thyst (am′e-thist), *n.* a kind of purple or violet quartz, used as a gem.

a-mi-a-ble (ā′mi-a-bl), *adj.* friendly; kindly; as, an *amiable* disposition.— *adv.* **a′mi-a-bly.**—*n.* **a′mi-a-bil′i-ty.**

am-i-ca-ble (am′i-ka-bl), *adj.* friendly; peaceful; as, an *amicable* discussion.— *adv.* **am′i-ca-bly.**—*n.* **am′i-ca-bil′i-ty.**

a-mid (a-mid′), *prep.* in the middle of.

a-midst (a-midst′), *prep.* among.

a-miss (a-mis′), *adj.* wrong; faulty; as, nothing's *amiss:*—*adv.* wrongly; as, you take my words *amiss.*

am-i-ty (am′i-ti), *n.* [*pl.* amities], friendship; peaceful relations.

am-mo-ni-a (a-mō′ni-a; a-mōn′ya), *n.* **1,** a clear, sharp-smelling gas readily soluble in water, much used in fertilizers, in cleaning fluids, and in making ice; **2,** a solution of this gas in water, for household use.

am-mu-ni-tion (am′ū-nish′un), *n.* material, as powder and shot, used in charging cannon, firearms, etc.

am-ne-si-a (am-nē′zhi-a), *n.* loss of memory.

a-moeba (a-mē′ba), *n.* [*pl.* amoebae (a-mē′bē) or amoebas], a tiny water animal without definite shape, one of the simplest forms of life. Also, **a-me′ba.**

a-mok (a-mok′; a-muk′), *adv.* Same as *amuck.*

a-mong (a-mung′), *prep.* **1** in the group with; surrounded by; as, *among* friends; *among* all his wealth; **2,** by the united action of; as, *among* them all, they succeeded; **3,** in the time of; as, *among* the ancient Greeks; **4,** by distribution to; as, to divide the estate *among* the heirs.

a-mongst (a-mungst′), *prep.* among.

am-o-rous (am′o-rus), *adj.* inclined to love; having to do with love; as, an *amorous* nature; *amorous* letters.

a-mount (a-mount′), *v.i.* **1,** to be equal or equivalent; as, his answer *amounted* to a threat; **2,** to add up; as, it *amounts* to 100:—*n.* **1,** the total sum; as, the *amount* is 25 cents; **2,** a measure; quantity; as, an unusual *amount* of courage.

a-mour (a-mōōr′), *n.* a secret love-affair.

am-pere (am′pâr; am′pēr; am-pâr′; am-pēr′), *n.* a unit for measuring strength of electric current; viz., the amount sent by one volt through a resistance of one ohm.

am-phib-i-an (am-fib′i-an), *n.* **1,** a plant or animal that can live both on land and in water; as, frogs are *amphibians;* **2,** an aeroplane that can take off from, and alight upon, either land or water:—*adj.* able to live on land and in water; amphibious.

am-phib-i-ous (am-fib′i-us), *adj.* able to live both on land and in water.

am-phi-brach (am′fi-brak′), *n.* in verse, a foot of one accented syllable between two unaccented ones (◡′◡), as in the poems 'The Ride from Ghent to Aix' and 'Flow gently, Sweet Afton'.

am-phi-the-a-tre or **am-phi-the-a-ter** (am′fi-thē′a-tér), *n.* **1,** an oval or circular building with rows of seats rising in a slope around a central space, or arena; **2,** anything resembling an amphitheatre in shape or purpose.

am-ple (am′pl), *adj.* **1,** full; of large size, extent, or volume; **2,** abundant.

am-pli-fy (am′pli-fī′), *v.t.* [amplified, amplify-ing], to make larger, fuller or louder; as, she *amplified* her statement. —*n.* am′pli-fi-ca′tion.—*n.* am′pli-fi′er.

am-ply (am′pli), *adv.* fully; sufficiently.

am-pu-tate (am′pū-tāt′), *v.t.* [amputat-ed, amputat-ing], to cut off, as an arm or leg.—*n.* am′pu-ta′tion.

a-muck (a-muk′), *adv.* in a frenzy to kill; as, to run *amuck.* Also, **amok.**

am-u-let (am′ū-lit), *n.* something worn as a charm against evil or harm; a talisman.

a-muse (a-mūz′), *v.t.* [amused, amusing], **1,** to entertain; as, to *amuse* children with toys; **2,** to cause to smile or laugh; as, the antics of the clown *amused* her.—*adj.* **a-mus′ing.**—*adv.* **a-mus′ing-ly.**

a-muse-ment (a-mūz′ment), *n.* **1,** that which entertains; a pastime; **2,** pleasant entertainment, esp. if it is amusing.

an (an; *unstressed,* un), *indefinite sing. article* a; any; each: used instead of *a* before a vowel sound or silent *h*; as, *an* ell, *an* hour; but *a* hotel, *a* yoke, *a* union.

a-nach-ro-nism (a-nak′ro-nizm), *n.* an assigning of a person or an event to a period other (esp. earlier) than the correct one.

a-nae-mi-a or **a-ne-mi-a** (a-nē′mi-a), *n.* a diseased condition caused by loss of blood or by the lack of red cor-puscles in the blood.—*adj.* **a-nae′mic.**

an-aes-the-si-a or **an-es-the-si-a** (an-as-thē′zhi-a; an′es-thē′-zha; an′es-thē′-zi-a), *n.* a partial or complete loss of sensation, due to disease, inhaling of gas, hypnotism, etc.

an-aes-thet-ic or **an-es-thet-ic** (an′es-thet′ik), *adj.* causing loss of sensation:—*n.* a gas or drug which causes temporary loss of sensation, as ether or chloroform.

an-a-gram (an′a-gram′), *n.* a word or phrase obtained by changing the order

of the letters of another word or phrase, as "live" from "evil":—**anagrams,** a game in which the players strive to form the largest number of words from any given letters.

a-nal-o-gy (a-nal′o-ji), *n.* [*pl.* analo-gies], a partial agreement or likeness between two things somewhat different; as, the *analogy* between an eye and a camera.—*adj.* **a-nal′o-gous.**

an-a-lyse (an′a-līz′), *v.t.* [analysed, analysing], **1,** to separate into parts or elements; as, to *analyse* a chemical compound; **2,** to examine critically; as, to *analyse* evidence, motives, character, or the like. Also spelled **an′a-lyze.**—*n.* **an′a-lyst.**

a-nal-y-sis (a-nal′i-sis), *n.* [*pl.* analyses (a-nal′i-sēz′)], **1,** the separation of a thing into its parts to find out what it is made of; as, a chemical *analysis;* **2,** a critical examination of an idea, book, event, or the like.

an-a-lyt-ic (an′a-lit′ik) or **an-a-lyt-i-cal** (an′a-lit′i-kal), *adj.* separating things into their parts or elements, as for the purpose of study; as, an *analytic* mind.

an-a-paest, **an-a-pest** (an′a-pest′), *n.* a metrical foot of two short syllables followed by a long (◡◡′): 'And hĭs có/hŏrts wĕre gleám/ĭng ĭn púr/plĕ ănd góld.'

an-arch-ist (an′är-kist), *n.* **1,** one who regards all government as evil, and believes, as a political ideal, in living without any government; **2,** any person who stirs up violent revolt against established rule.

an-arch-y (an′är-ki), *n.* [*pl.* anarchies], the absence or lack of government; hence, a condition of general confusion and terror resulting from the overthrow or disregard of laws.

a-nath-e-ma (a-nath′i-ma), *n.* **1,** a solemn curse of the church, accom-panied by expulsion from the church; **2,** any curse; **3,** a thing or person greatly disliked.

a-nat-o-my (a-nat′o-mi), *n.* **1,** the science that treats of the structure of the parts of plants and animals, and the relation of these parts to one another; **2,** the cutting up of a plant or animal to study its structure; **3,** the structure of a plant or animal.—*adj.* **an′a-tom′ical; an′a-tom′ic.**

an-ces-tor (an′ses′tér), *n.* a person from whom one is descended.—*adj.* **an-ces′tral.**

an-ces-try (an′ses′tri), *n.* [*pl.* ances-tries], the line of one's descent traced back through parents, grandparents, etc.; also, one's ancestors.

an-chor (ang′kẽr), *n.* **1,** a heavy iron or steel implement that, being dropped, hooks into the ground and moors a ship in a particular place; **2,** any similar thing to hold fast a movable object:—*v.t.* to make or hold fast, as a ship:—*v.i.* to lie secure in harbour; as, the ship *anchored* in the bay.

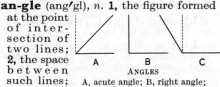

ANCHOR

A, ring; B, stock; C, shank; D, D, flukes; E, crown.

an-chor-age (ang′kor-ij), *n.* a place, or toll, for anchoring.

an-cho-vy (an-chō′vi; an′chō-vi), *n.* [*pl.* anchovies], a very small Mediterranean herring, used in sauces and as an appetizer.

an-cient (ān′shent), *adj.* **1,** of very great age; as, *ancient* rocks; **2,** pertaining to times long past; as, *ancient* history:—*n.* **1,** an aged person; **2,** one who lived in olden times:—**the ancients,** civilized peoples of times long past, as the Romans, Greeks, Egyptians, etc.—*adv.* **an′cient-ly.**

and (and), *co-ordinate conj.*, a connective that joins expressions (words, phrases, or clauses) of equal grammatical value; as, John *and* Mary are here; to have *and* to hold.

and-i-ron (and′ī′ẽrn), *n.* one of two metal supports or rests for holding logs in a fireplace.

an-ec-dote (an′ik-dōt′), *n.* a brief story intended to amuse or instruct, often told about a famous person.

a-ne-mi-a (a-nē′mi-a), *n.* Same as **anaemia.**—*adj.* **a-ne′mic** (a-nē′mik).

an-e-mom-e-ter (an′e-mom′e-tẽr), *n.* a gauge for measuring wind velocity.

a-nem-o-ne (a-nem′o-ni), *n.* **1,** a plant of the buttercup family; esp., the wind-flower, or wood anemone, the delicate white flower of which blooms in the woods in early spring; **2,** a seafish.

an-es-the-si-a (an′es-thē′zhi-a; an′es-thē′zha; an′es-thē′zi-a), *n.* Same as **anaesthesia.**

an-es-thet-ic (an′es-thet′ik), *adj.* and *n.* Same as **anaesthetic.**

a-new (a-nū′), *adv.* a second time; over again.

an-gel (ān′jel), *n.* **1,** a messenger of God; one of an order of spiritual beings pictured in human form, but with wings; **2,** an attendant spirit; **3,** a good, innocent, or lovely person; **4,** an English gold coin used in the 16th century.—*adj.* **an-gel′ic** (an-jel′ik).

an-ger (ang′gẽr), *n.* rage; a strong emotion aroused by a sense of injury or wrong:—*v.t.* to provoke to resentment; enrage.

an-gle (ang′gl), *n.* **1,** the figure formed at the point of intersection of two lines; **2,** the space between such lines; **3,** a corner; a sharp edge; **4,** a point of view; as, he sees it from all *angles*.

ANGLES

A, acute angle; B, right angle; C, obtuse angle.

an-gle (ang′gl), *v.i.* [an-gled, an-gling], **1,** to fish with hook and line; **2,** to use tricks in obtaining something; as, to *angle* for a compliment.

an-gler (ang′glẽr), *n.* **1,** a fisherman, esp., one who fishes for pleasure; **2,** a salt-water fish with a large, broad head, whose projections lure smaller fish within reach of the huge mouth.

an-gle-worm (ang′gl-wûrm′), *n.* an earthworm, used by anglers as bait.

An-gli-cize (ang′gli-sīz′), *v.t.* [Anglicized, Angliciz-ing], to make English in manners, customs, speech, etc.; as, we have *Anglicized* such a foreign word as *chauffeur*. Also written **an′gli-cise.**

an-gry (ang′gri), *adj.* **1,** feeling or showing wrath, rage, or resentment; as, an *angry* beast; an *angry* look; **2,** inflamed; red; as, an *angry* wound.—*adv.* **an′gri-ly.**

an-guish (ang′gwish), *n.* extreme suffering, esp. of mind; as, a mother's *anguish* over the death of her child.

an-gu-lar (ang′gū-lẽr), *adj.* **1,** having angles or points; sharp-cornered; as, *angular* figures; **2,** bony; ungainly; awkward; as, an *angular* youth.—*n.* **an′gu-lar′i-ty** (ang′gu-lar′iti).

an-i-mal (an′i-mal), *n.* **1,** a living being that can feel, and move about of its own will, as a man, dog, sparrow, fish, snake, fly, etc.; **2,** any mammal other than man, as a dog, monkey, etc:—*adj.* relating to animals; as, the *animal* kingdom; like or characteristic of an *animal*; as, *animal* spirits; sensual; bestial: opposite of *spiritual*.

an-i-mate (an′i-māt′), *v.t.* [animat-ed, animat-ing], to give life to; inspire with energy or activity; enliven; as, joy *animates* his face:—**animated, 1,** full of spirit and vigour; as, *animated* dialogue; **2,** taking on, through motion, the semblance of life; as, an *animated* cartoon:—*adj.* (an′i-mit), endowed with life; as, biology deals with *animate* beings.—*n.* **an′i-ma′tion.**

an-i-mos-i-ty (an′i-mos′i-ti), *n.* [*pl.* animosities], hostility; hatred; enmity.

an-ise (an′is), *n.* **1,** a plant cultivated for its spicy seeds, which are used both in medicine and in flavouring; **2,** the seed of this plant, often called *aniseed.*

an-kle (ang′kl), *n.* the joint connecting the foot with the leg.

an-klet (ang′klit), *n.* **1,** an ornamental ring or chain for the ankle; **2,** a sock that just covers the ankle.

an-nals (an′alz), *n. pl.* **1,** an account or history of events as they happen, written or issued year by year; as, the *Annals* of the Academy are published regularly; **2,** records; history; as, the *annals* of ancient Rome.

an-nex (a-neks′), *v.t.* to unite, as a smaller thing to a greater; as, to *annex* a province to a kingdom:—*n.* (a-neks′; an′eks), a building added to or adjoining another building.—*n.* **an′nex-a′tion.**

an-ni-hi-late (a-ni′i-lāt), *v.t.* [annihilat-ed, annihilat-ing], to blot or wipe out of existence; destroy; as, the people of Pompeii were *annihilated* by the eruption of Vesuvius.—*n.* **an-ni′hi-la′tion.**

an-ni-ver-sa-ry (an′i-vûr′sa-ri), *n.* [*pl.* anniversaries], the yearly return of the date of an event; as, we celebrate the *anniversary* of our birthdays.

an-no-tate (an′ō-tāt′), *v.t.* [annotat-ed, annotat-ing], to make notes upon, by way of comment or criticism; as, to *annotate* a book.—*n.* **an′no-ta′tion.**

an-nounce (a-nouns′), *v.t.* [announced, announc-ing], **1,** to proclaim; make known formally or publicly; publish; as, she *announced* her daughter's engagement; **2,** to state formally the presence or approach of; as, the butler *announced* the guests.

an-nounce-ment (a-nouns′ment), *n.* **1,** the act of announcing or declaring; **2,** the thing declared or made known; **3,** a public notice or advertisement.

an-nounc-er (a-noun′sèr), *n.* one who announces, esp. over radio or television.

an-noy (a-noi′), *v.t.* to vex or trouble; irritate; as, a dog growls when he is *annoyed.*—*adj.* **an-noy′ing.**

an-noy-ance (a-noi′ans), *n.* **1,** the act of causing vexation; as, he finds pleasure in the *annoyance* of his chums; **2,** the sense of being annoyed; vexation; as, my *annoyance* over the delay was great; **3,** the thing or act which vexes; as, his tardiness was an *annoyance.*

an-nu-al (an′ū-al), *adj.* **1,** occurring once a year; yearly; as, an *annual* banquet; **2,** taking a year to complete; as, the *annual* rotation of the seasons; **3,** done, reckoned, or published yearly; as, *annual* dues; an *annual* bulletin; **4,**

lasting but one year or season, as a plant:—*n.* **1,** a publication appearing once a year; **2,** a plant living only one year or season.—*adv.* **an′nu-al-ly.**

an-nu-i-ty (a-nū′i-ti), *n.* [*pl.* annuities], **1,** a sum of money paid, as by an insurance company, for a specified period in regular instalments; **2,** the right to receive such instalments; as, he invested his money in an *annuity.*

an-nul (a-nul′), *v.t.* [annulled, annulling], to abolish or do away with, as a law, decree, or compact; as, the marriage has been *annulled.*—*n.* **an-nul′ment.**

an-nu-lar (an′ū-lèr), *adj.* ring-shaped; as, an *annular* eclipse of the sun.

an-ode (an′ōd), *n.* the positive pole or electrode of a battery, vacuum tube, etc.

a-noint (a-noint′), *v.t.* **1,** to pour oil or other liquid upon; as, to *anoint* the body with olive oil; **2,** consecrate, as in a religious rite; as, a priest *anoints* a child in baptism.—*n.* **a-noint′-ment.**

a-nom-a-ly (a-nom′a-li), *n.* [*pl.* anomalies], irregularity; anything that varies from the common rule, or is abnormal or peculiar; as, a winter thunderstorm is an *anomaly.*—*adj.* **a-nom′a-lous.**

a-non (a-non′), *adv.* **1,** soon; in a little while; **2,** at another time; again.

a-non-y-mous (a-non′i-mus), *adj.* **1,** not known by name; as, an *anonymous* author; **2,** without the author's name; as, an *anonymous* poem.—*adv.* **a-non′-y-mous-ly.**—*n.* **an′o-nym′i-ty.**

an-oth-er (a-nuth′èr), *pron.* one more of the same kind; as, I have one hat, but need *another;* also, a different person or thing; as, in the dark I took him for *another:*—*adj.* **1,** additional; as, please give me *another* orange; **2,** different; as, he has become *another* man.

an-swer (àn′sèr), *n.* **1,** a response or reply, as to a letter; **2,** a reply to a charge; as, to say nothing in *answer* to an accusation; **3,** a solution, as of a mathematical problem:—*v.t.* **1,** to speak, write, or act in reply to; as, to *answer* the bell; to *answer* a letter; **2,** to reply to in defence; as, to *answer* a charge; **3,** to correspond to; as, he *answers* the description; **4,** to be sufficient for; as, this *answers* the purpose:—*v.i.* **1,** to speak, write, or act in reply; **2,** to be sufficient; as, this coat will *answer;* **3,** to be accountable; as, I cannot *answer* for this mixture.

an-swer-a-ble (àn′sèr-a-bl), *adj.* **1,** accountable; responsible; as, *answerable* to a person for one's conduct; **2,**

---

cat, āge, fär, câre, àsk; ten, ēve, latèr; (i) pity, rely, senate; īce; top; nō.

capable of being answered or disproved, as an argument.

ant (ant), *n.* a small insect, famed for its industry. Ants live in communities or colonies, in holes which they burrow in wood or in the ground.

an-tag-o-nism (an-tag′-o-nizm), *n.* dislike or opposition between two persons, forces, parties, etc.; hostility; hatred, as, their *antagonism* was of long standing.—*adj.* **an-tag′o-nis′tic.** —*adv.* **an-tag′o-nis′ti-cal-ly.**

an-tag-o-nist (an-tag′o-nist), *n.* one who fights or competes with another, as in sports or battle; an opponent; adversary.

an-tag-o-nize (an-tag′o-nīz′), *v.t.* [antagonized, antagoniz-ing], to make hostile; turn into an enemy; as, her rudeness *antagonizes* her associates.

ant-arc-tic (ant-ärk′tik), *adj.* **1,** opposite to the north polar, or arctic, regions; **2,** located in, or relating to, the south polar regions:—**Antarctic Circle,** an imaginary circle parallel to the equator and distant 23° 30′ from the South Pole.—**Antarctic Ocean,** the south polar ocean.

an-te (an′ti), *n. Poker,* the stake that each player puts into the pool before receiving cards or drawing new ones.— *v.t.* and *v.i.* to put in one's stake, as, to *ante in* or *ante up.*

ant-eat-er (ant′ēt′ėr), *n.* an animal which feeds upon ants. It has a long, sticky tongue, with which it licks up the ants.

an-te-ced-ent (an′ti-sē′dent), *n.* **1,** someone or something that goes before or precedes; **2,** in *grammar,* a noun, pronoun, etc., later referred to by a pronoun; as, in the sentence, "James played football until he hurt his leg," "James" is the *antecedent* of "he"; **2, antecedents,** the previous events or influences in a person's life; also, ancestry; as, his unfortunate *antecedents* account for his criminal traits:— *adj.* going before; preceding; as, the events *antecedent* to the meeting.

an-te-cham-ber (an′ti-chăm′bėr), *n.* a room leading into a principal room or apartment; a waiting-room.

an-te-date (an′ti-dāt′; an′ti-dāt′), *v.t.* [antedat-ed, antedat-ing], **1,** to occur at an earlier time than; as, sailing-ships *antedated* steamships; **2,** to mark with an earlier date than the correct one; as, to *antedate* a cheque.

an-te-lope (an′ti-lōp′), *n.* any of a large group of graceful Old World animals, including the gazelle, eland, and kudu. In western North America, the name is applied to the pronghorn, though it is not properly an antelope.

an-ten-na (an-ten′a), *n.* [*pl.* antennae (an-ten′ē)], **1,** one of the feelers which grows on the heads of insects, centipedes, lobsters, etc.; **2,** [*pl.* antennas], in radio and television a wire or set of wires for sending and receiving electromagnetic messages.

an-te-ri-or (an-tē′ri-ėr), *adj.* **1,** fore; toward the front; as, the *anterior* lobe of the brain; **2,** prior; coming earlier; as, the American Revolution was *anterior* to the French Revolution.

an-te-room (an′ti-room′), *n.* a room leading into another; an antechamber.

an-them (an′them), *n.* **1,** a song of praise or triumph; as, a national *anthem;* **2,** a piece of sacred music, often a Biblical passage set to music.

an-ther (an′thėr), *n.* in a flower, the part of the stamen which produces the pollen. (See illustration at flower.)

an-thol-o-gy (an-thol′o-ji), *n.* [*pl.* anthologies], a collection of choice poems or prose passages from a variety of authors.

an-thra-cite (an′thra-sīt′), *n.* a hard coal which burns with little smoke or flame.

an-thrax (an′thraks), *n.* an infectious and usually fatal disease of cattle and sheep, and sometimes of man.

an-thro-pol-o-gy (an′thrō-pol′o-ji), *n.* the science of man, his origins, institutions, myths, etc.

an-ti (an′ti; an′tī), *n.* [*pl.* antis], a person who is opposed to a policy, movement, law, etc.

an-ti-bi-ot-ic (an′ti-bī-ot′ik), *n.* a chemical substance extracted from living organisms, like molds and fungi, which is able to destroy other organisms, and is therefore useful in treatment of bacterial infection.

an-tic (an′tik), *n.* a comical trick or action; as, the *antics* of a puppy.

an-tic-i-pate (an-tis′i-pāt′), *v.t.* [anticipat-ed, anticipat-ing], **1,** to look forward to; expect; esp., to await with pleasure; as, to *anticipate* a party; **2,** to foresee (a command, need, wish, etc.) and do ahead of time what needs doing; as, they *anticipated* our hunger; **3,** to be before (another) in doing something; as, A *anticipated* B in the discovery.—*n.* **an-tic′i-pa′tion.**

an-ti-cli-max (an′ti-klī′maks), *n.* opposite of climax; descent from the sublime to the ridiculous, or from the important to the trivial and uninteresting; as, washing dishes after a party is an *anticlimax.*

an-ti-dote (an′ti-dōt′), *n.* **1,** a medicine which counteracts a poison; **2,** hence, a remedy; as, hard work served as an *antidote* to his troubles.

an-ti-freeze (an′ti-frēz′), *n.* a liquid, as alcohol or glycol, used in winter to prevent motor-car engines and radiators from freezing up.

an-tip-a-thy (an-tip′a-thi), *n.* [*pl.* antipathies], a strong, instinctive hatred or dislike.—*adj.* an′ti-pa-thet′ic.

an-tip-o-des (an-tip′o-dēz′), *n. pl.* places on exactly opposite sides of the earth; as, the North and the South Poles are *antipodes.*

an-ti-quar-i-an (an′ti-kwâr′i-an), *adj.* relating to ancient times or to the relics and ruins of past peoples; as, *antiquarian* studies:—*n.* an antiquary.

an-ti-quar-y (an′ti-kwėr-i), *n.* [*pl.* antiquaries], one who collects ancient relics, or who studies the customs, events, and records of past peoples.

an-ti-quat-ed (an′ti-kwāt′id), *adj.* old-fashioned; out of date; as, *antiquated* clothes; *antiquated* ideas.

an-tique (an-tēk′), *adj.* belonging to an age long past; ancient; as, an *antique* vase;—*n.* something of great age; a relic of a much earlier time than the present; as, this chair is an *antique.*

an-tiq-ui-ty (an-tik′wi-ti), *n.* [*pl.* antiquities], **1,** the early ages, esp. before the Middle Ages; as, the pyramids are a relic of *antiquity;* **2,** great age; as, the *antiquity* of ruins; **3,** antiquities, relics that throw light upon ancient times; as, Chinese *antiquities* in a museum.

an-ti-sep-tic (an′ti-sep′tik), *adj.* preventing the growth of germs, esp. those of disease or decay; as, salt in water makes an *antiseptic* gargle:—*n.* an *antiseptic* substance, as hydrogen peroxide or iodine.

an-ti-so-cial (an′ti-sō′shal), *adj.* opposed to the interests of society, or of people and citizens as a whole; as, robbery and murder are *antisocial* acts.

an-ti-the-sis (an-tith′e-sis), *n. pl.* antitheses (an-tith′e-sēz′)], **1,** the exact opposite; as, black is the *antithesis* of white; **2,** opposition; contrast; as, an *antithesis* of ideas; **3,** an expression that emphasizes contrast. "Give me liberty, or give me death," is an *antithesis.*

an-ti-tox-in (an′ti-tok′sin), *n.* a substance formed in the body of a person or animal suffering from a germ disease, such as diphtheria or scarlet fever, that helps the body to resist the effects of the germs. Antitoxins are used to prevent or cure disease. Some animal is given the disease in a mild form, and an antitoxin is thus produced in its blood. This antitoxin is then drawn off and introduced into the blood of a person, etc. to neutralize the poison of the disease germs.

ant-ler (ant′lėr), *n.* the horn, or a branch of the horn, of a deer.—*adj.* **ant′lered** (ant′lėrd).

an-to-nym (an′tō-nim), a word whose meaning is opposite to that of another word; as, "warm" is the *antonym* of "cool": opposite of *synonym.*

a-nus (ā′nus), *n.* in animals, the posterior opening of the digestive tract.

an-vil (an′vil), *n.* a block of iron on which metals are hammered and shaped.

anx-i-e-ty (ang-zī′e-ti), *n.* [*pl.* anxieties], **1,** mental uneasiness from fear of misfortune; as, their *anxiety* increased with the storm; **2,** eager desire tinged with fear; as, *anxiety* to make good.

anx-ious (angk′shus; ang′shus), *adj.* **1,** deeply concerned; greatly troubled or worried; as, *anxious* about one's health; **2,** desirous; as, *anxious* to please.—*adv.* anx′ious-ly.

an-y (en′i), *adj.* **1,** one of several, but no matter which; as, you may have *any* book here; **2,** some: used with a negative, or in a question; as, I haven't *any* time; **3,** every; as, I did what *any* man would do:—*pron.* some; as, give me some nails if you have *any:*—*adv.* to any extent; at all; in any degree; as, don't go *any* farther.

an-y-bod-y (en′i-bod′i; -bud′), *pron.* **1,** an ordinary person; any person of a group; as, *anybody* can do it if he tries; **2,** someone of importance; as, is he *anybody?*

an-y-how (en′i-hou′), *adv.* **1,** in any way; hence, carelessly; in haphazard way; as, she just does her work *anyhow;* **2,** at any rate; as, *anyhow,* you are here now.

an-y-one (en′i-wun′), *pron.* any person; anybody; as, *anyone* can do that.

an-y-thing (en′i-thing′), *pron.* a thing of any sort whatever; as, *anything* can happen.

an-y-way (en′i-wā′), *adv.* **1,** in any manner; as, do it *anyway* you like; **2,** nevertheless; as, I am tired, but I'm going *anyway.*

an-y-where (en′i-hwâr′), *adv.* in or at any place; as, put it *anywhere.*

an-y-wise (en′i-wīz′), *adv.* in any way or degree.

a-or-ta (ā-ôr′ta), *n.* [*pl.* aortas], the large artery which carries blood away from the heart to branch arteries that supply the entire body.

a-pace (a-pās′), *adv.* quickly; speedily; rapidly; as, the work grew *apace.*

---

cat, āge, fär, cåre, åsk; ten, ēve, latėr; (i) pity, rely, senate; īce; top; nō.

A-pach-e (a-pä′chä; a-pach′i), *n.* a fierce Athabascan Indian tribe of South-western U.S.

a-part (a-pärt′), *adv.* **1,** separately in time or place; as, to live *apart;* **2,** in, or into, pieces; as, it fell *apart;* he took the watch *apart:*—apart from, **1,** separated from; as, she lives *apart from* her parents; **2,** not considering; leaving out of account; as, *apart* from the plot, the book interested me.

a-part-heid (a-pärt′hīt′), *n.* racial separation, esp. as practised against the native Negroes and coloured peoples in South Africa.

a-part-ment (a-pärt′ment), *n.* a separate room, or suite of rooms, used to live in. Also **apartment house** and **apartment block.**

ap-a-thy (ap′a-thi), *n.* [*pl.* apathies], lack of feeling or interest; indifference; as, to arouse a person from *apathy.*— *adj.* **ap′a-thet′ic.**

ape (āp), *n.* **1,** a tailless monkey, like man in structure and organs, as the gorilla, chimpanzee, orang-outang; **2,** a silly mimic:—*v.t.* [aped, ap-ing], to imitate; as, the boy *apes* his elders.

ap-er-ture (ap′ẽr-tūr; -chẽr), *n.* an opening; gap; hole; as, an *aperture* in a wall.

a-pex (ā′peks), *n.* [*pl.* apices (ā′pi-sēz′; ap′i-sēz′) or apexes (ā′pek-sez)], the peak or summit of something, as of a mountain, triangle, etc.

a-phid (ā′fid; af′id), *n.* a small insect that sucks the sap of plants; also called *aphis.*

a-phis (ā′fis; af′is), *n.* [*pl.* aphides (āf′i-dēz′)], an aphid; a plant louse.

a-pi-ar-y (ā′pi-ẽr-i), *n.* [*pl.* apiaries], a place where bees are kept; also, a collection of beehives.

a-piece (a-pēs′), *adv.* for each one; as, the pencils cost five cents *apiece.*

a-pol-o-get-ic (a-pol′o-jet′ik) or **a-pol-o-get-i-cal** (jet′i-kal), *adj.* admitting or excusing a fault or failure; as, his *apologetic* attitude won him a new chance.

a-pol-o-gize (a-pol′o-jīz′), *v.i.* [apolo-gized, apologiz-ing], **1,** to make an excuse; **2,** to express regret for a fault, wrong, etc.

a-pol-o-gy (a-pol′o-ji), *n.* [*pl.* apolo-gies], **1,** an excuse or expression of regret for something one has said or done; as, he made an *apology* for being noisy; **2,** something spoken, written, or offered in defence; as, an *apology* for communism; **3,** a poor substitute; a makeshift; as, this drawing is only an *apology* for a map.

ap-o-plec-tic (ap′o-plek′tik), *adj.* **1,** afflicted or threatened with apoplexy; **2,** red of face; **3,** hot-tempered; easily angered.

ap-o-plex-y (ap′o-plek′si), *n.* the sudden loss of consciousness, or of the power to feel or move; a stroke. It is usually caused by the breaking of a blood-vessel in the brain.

a-port (a-pōrt′), *adv.* on or toward the left; as, rocks *aport;* to steer hard *aport.*

a-pos-ta-sy (a-pos′ta-si), *n.* [*pl.* apostasies], the giving up of what one has professed, believed, or followed; as, religious or political *apostasy.*—*n.* and *adj.* **a-pos′tate.**

a-pos-tle (a-pos′l), *n.* **1,** one of the twelve men chosen by Jesus to teach his gospel to the world (Luke 6:13); also, a disciple, like Paul, given the same work to do; **2,** a pioneer missionary; as, Livingstone was the *apostle* to Africa; **3,** a leader of any reform; as, an *apostle* of temperance.

ap-os-tol-ic (ap′os-tol′ik) or **ap-os-tol-i-cal** (-tol′i-kal), *adj.* **1,** relating to the twelve apostles of Christ, their times, doctrine, etc. **2,** coming from the Pope; papal; as, an *apostolic* blessing.

a-pos-tro-phe (a-pos′tro-fi), *n.* **1,** a breaking off in a speech to address a person, usually absent or dead, or an abstract idea or imaginary object; **2,** the sign used to show various things: **a,** a contraction, as *I'll* for *I will;* **b,** the omission of one or more letters from a word, as *can't* for *cannot;* '49 for 1849; **c,** the possessive case of nouns, as in *cat's* fur, *Ulysses'* shield; **d,** the plural of letters and figures, as *x's* and *v's, 6's* and *7's.*—*v.t.* **a-pos′tro-phize′.**

a-poth-e-car-y (a-poth′e-kẽr-i; -ker′), *n.* [*pl.* apothecaries], one who prepares and sells medicines and drugs; a pharmacist; druggist:—**apothecaries′ weight,** a system of weights used in dispensing drugs.

ap-pal or **ap-pall** (a-pôl′), *v.t.* [ap-palled, appal-ling], to frighten; shock; dismay; as, danger of war *appalled* us.

ap-pa-ra-tus (ap′a-rā′tus; ap′a-rat′-us), *n.* [*pl.* apparatuses or apparatus], **1,** an outfit of tools, utensils, or instruments for any kind of work; as, laboratory *apparatus;* **2,** the set of organs which performs some natural process; as, the digestive *apparatus.*

ap-par-el (a-par′el), *n.* clothing; dress; as, boys' *apparel:*—*v.t.* to clothe; fit out.

ap-par-ent (a-pâr′ent; a-par′ent), *adj.* **1,** open to view; easily seen; **2,** easily understood; evident; **3,** appearing or seeming, rather than true or real; as, his *apparent* remorse fooled us.—*adv.* **ap-par′ent-ly.**

ap-pa-ri-tion (ap′a-rish′un), *n.* something startling and unreal that suddenly appears; a ghost or spectre.

ap-peal (a-pēl′), *v.t.* to transfer or refer to a superior court or judge; as, to *appeal* a case:—*v.i.* **1,** to make an earnest request; as, he *appealed* for aid; **2,** to be of interest; make a favourable impression; as, good music *appeals* to me:—*n.* **1,** a call for aid or sympathy; **2,** interest; attraction; as, your proposal has no *appeal* for me; **3,** the transfer of a case from a lower to a higher court.—*adj.* **ap-peal′ing.**

ap-pear (a-pēr′), *v.i.* **1,** to come into sight; as, the moon *appeared;* **2,** to seem; as, he *appears* to be ill; **3,** to come before the public; as, the book *appeared* in June; this actor *appeared* in *Hamlet.*

ap-pear-ance (a-pēr′ans), *n.* **1,** the act of becoming visible; as, the *appearance* of the sun from behind a cloud; **2,** look; bearing; as, Charles Dickens had a dignified *appearance;* **3,** outward show; as, an *appearance* of humility; **4,** the act of coming before the public; as, an *appearance* in court.

ap-pease (a-pēz′), *v.t.* [appeased, appeasing], **1,** to quiet; pacify; as, to *appease* an angry person; **2,** to satisfy; as, to *appease* one's hunger or curiosity.

ap-pel-la-tion (ap′e-lā′shun), *n.* a name or title by which a person or thing is described or known; as, one *appellation* of England is "Albion."

ap-pend (a-pend′), *v.t.* **1,** to attach or affix, as a seal; **2,** to attach or add, as supplementary matter to a book.

ap-pend-age (a-pen′dij), *n.* something attached to a greater thing, and forming a part of it, as a leg to an animal's body, or a porch to a house.

ap-pen-dec-tomy (ap′en-dek′to-mi), *n.* [*pl.* appendectomies], removal of the vermiform appendix by surgery.

ap-pen-di-ci-tis (a-pen′di-sī′tis), *n.* an inflammation of the vermiform appendix.

ap-pen-dix (a-pen′diks), *n.* [*pl.* appendices (a-pen′di-sēz′) or appendixes (a-pen′dik-sez)], **1,** that which is added to give further information; as, the *appendix* to a book; **2,** a wormlike sac, three or four inches long, situated near the entrance to the large intestine, in the lower right-hand side of the abdomen; called in full *vermiform appendix.*

ap-per-tain (ap′ẽr-tān′), *v.i.* **1,** to belong by right, nature, or custom; as,

the lands *appertaining* to the abbey; the right to vote *appertains* to all citizens; **2,** to be related; pertain.

ap-pe-tite (ap′e-tīt′), *n.* **1,** a physical craving for food; **2,** a strong and active desire; as, an *appetite* for books; an *appetite* for fighting.

ap-pe-tiz-er (ap′e-tīz′ẽr), *n.* **1,** a food or drink served before a meal to stimulate the desire for food; **2,** anything that arouses interest in things to follow.

ap-pe-tiz-ing (ap′e-tīz′ing), *adj.* exciting or pleasing the appetite; as, an *appetizing* meal.

ap-plaud (a-plôd′), *v.t.* **1,** to express approval of, esp. by a clapping of the hands; **2,** to commend; as, I *applaud* your stand in the matter:—*v.i.* to clap the hands, or otherwise show approval.

ap-plause (a-plôz′), *n.* an expression of approval, as by hand-clapping.

ap-ple (ap′l), *n.* **1,** the round, fleshy fruit of a well-known tree, grown in temperate regions; **2,** the tree itself.

ap-pli-ance (a-pli′ans), *n.* an article or device for some special use or purpose, as an electric iron or a lawn-mower.

ap-pli-ca-ble (ap′li-ka-bl), *adj.* suitable; fit; capable of being used or applied; as, this excuse is not *applicable* to your case.—*n.* **ap′pli-ca-bil′i-ty.**

ap-pli-cant (ap′li-kant), *n.* one who applies for a position; a candidate; as, an *applicant* for a job.

ap-pli-ca-tion (ap′li-kā′shun), *n.* **1,** the act of putting on; as, the *application* of ice to a sprained ankle; **2,** the thing put on; as, cold *applications;* **3,** practical demonstration or use, as of a theory or law; **4,** close attention, as to work; **5,** a personal or written request, as for a job.

ap-ply (a-pli′), *v.t* [applied, apply-ing], **1,** to bring into contact with something; lay on; as, to *apply* a bandage; to *apply* a whip; **2,** to put into practice; as, to *apply* a rule; **3,** to devote to a particular purpose; as, *apply* yourself to study:—*v.i.* **1,** to ask; petition; as, *apply* early if you want a ticket; **2,** to have some connection; as, this does not *apply* to you.

ap-point (a-point′), *v.t.* **1,** to name for an office; as, to *appoint* a chairman; **2,** to set; fix; as, to *appoint* a day for a game.

ap-point-ee (a-poin′tē′), *n.* a person named to an office; as, political *appointees.*

ap-poin-tive (a-poin′tiv), *adj.* filled by appointment, not by election, as an office.

ap-point-ment (a-point′ment), *n.* **1,**

the act of naming or appointing to an office; **2,** the position or office so assigned; **3,** an engagement; mutual agreement to meet; **4,** appointments, furniture or equipment.

ap-por-tion (a-pōr′shun), *v.t.* to divide and distribute; allot; as, ample rations were *apportioned* to the sailors.—*n.* **ap-por′tion-ment.**

ap-po-site (ap′ō-zit), *adj.* relevant; pertinent; apt; as an *apposite* reply.

ap-po-si-tion (ap′ō-zish′un), *n.* **1,** the act of placing together; also, the condition of being in close contact; **2,** in *grammar*, the relation of a noun to another noun near which it is placed, as its equivalent, or as explanatory of it. In the expression, "Crusoe spoke to Friday, his servant," "servant" is in apposition to "Friday."

ap-pos-i-tive (a-poz′i-tiv), *adj.* in apposition; explanatory:—*n.* a word or phrase in apposition.—*adv.* **ap-pos′i-tive-ly.**

ap-praise (a-prāz′), *v.t.* [appraised, apprais-ing], to estimate or fix the price or value of; as, to *appraise* a man's worth; to *appraise* land for taxation.—*n.* **ap-prais′al.**—*n.* **ap-prais′er.**

ap-pre-ci-a-ble (a-prē′shi-a-bl); a-prē′sha-bl), *adj.* capable of being estimated; perceptible; as, an *appreciable* gain.—*adv.* **ap-pre′ci-a-bly.**

ap-pre-ci-ate (a-prē′shi-āt′), *v.t.* [appreciat-ed, appreciat-ing], **1,** to value justly; esteem; **2,** to have a cultivated understanding of; be sensitive to; as, to *appreciate* art:—*v.i.* to increase in price or value; as, real estate *appreciates* in boom times.—*n.* **ap-pre′ci-a′tion.**—*adj.* **ap-pre′ci-a′tive.**

ap-pre-hend (ap′ri-hend′), *v.t.* **1,** to lay hold of; seize; arrest; as, to *apprehend* a fugitive; **2,** to take mental hold of; as I *apprehend* his meaning; **3,** to anticipate with fear; as, to *apprehend* danger:—*v.i.* to catch the meaning.—*n.* **ap′pre-hen′sion.**

ap-pre-hen-sive (ap′ri-hen′siv), *adj.* afraid; fearful, as of trouble; worried, as for someone's safety.—*adv.* **ap′pre-hen′sive-ly.**—*n.* **ap′pre-hen′sive-ness.**

ap-pren-tice (a-pren′tis), *n.* **1,** a person who is learning a trade or craft by practical experience under a skilled worker; formerly, one bound by an agreement to work for a definite length of time in return for his training; **2,** a novice, or one slightly versed in anything:—*v.t.* [apprenticed, apprentic-ing], to put under a master for training in a trade.—*n.* **ap-pren′tice-ship.**

ap-prise (a-prīz′), *v.t.* [apprised, appris-ing], to give notice to; warn;

inform; as, I *apprised* him of danger.

ap-proach (a-prōch′), *v.i.* to draw near; as, a stranger is *approaching*:—*v.t.* to come near to (a thing, place, or condition); as, to *approach* a church; to *approach* perfection:—*n.* **1,** the act of drawing near; as, we noticed the *approach* of a car; **2,** the way by which one draws near; as, the *approaches* to the city were lined with trees; **3,** in *golf,* a shot which aims to place the ball on the green.—*adj.* **ap-proach′a-ble.**

ap-pro-ba-tion (ap′rō-bā′shun), *n.* the act of declaring good; commendation; approval; as, the audience clapped in *approbation.*

ap-pro-pri-ate (a-prō′pri-āt′), *v.t.* [appropriat-ed, appropriat-ing,] **1,** to take and use for one's own; as, I *appropriated* your pencil; **2,** to set apart for a particular purpose, often by legislative act; as, to *appropriate* money for roads:—*adj.* (a-prō′pri-it), fit; suitable; proper.—*adv.* **ap-pro′pri-ate-ly.**—*n.* **ap-pro′pri-ate-ness.**—*n.* **ap-pro′pri-a′tion.**

ap-prov-al (a-proov′al), *n.* favourable opinion; the thinking well of a person or his act; as, your idea has my *approval.*

ap-prove (a-proov′), *v.t.* [approved, approv-ing], to think or speak well of; commend; accept; as, to *approve* plans:—*v.i.* to express a favourable opinion; as, we *approve* of his friends.—*adv.* **ap-prov′ing-ly.**

ap-prox-i-mate (a-prok′si-mit), *adj.* almost equal; nearly correct; not exact but nearly so; as, an *approximate* price:—*v.t.* (a-prok′si-māt′), [approximat-ed, approximat-ing], to come close to; as, John's conduct *approximates* folly.—*adv.* **approx′i-mate-ly.**—*n.* **ap-prox′i-ma′tion.**

ap-pur-te-nance (a-pûr′te-nans), *n.* an accessory, adjunct, or appendage.

a-pri-cot (ā′pri-kot′, ap-), *n.* **1,** an orange-coloured fruit of the plum family, similar to the peach in texture of skin and flesh; **2,** the tree itself.

A-pril (ā′pril), *n.* the 4th month of the year (30 days).

a-pron (ā′prun), *n.* **1,** a garment, usually made of cloth, rubber, or leather, worn in front to protect one's clothes; **2,** such a garment worn as part of a costume; as, a bishop's *apron.*

ap-ro-pos (ap′rō-pō′), *adv.* with reference (to); as, *apropos* of that remark, I have this to say:—*adj.* appropriate; fitting; suitable; as, an *apropos* remark.

apt (apt), *adj.* **1,** suitable; appropriate; as, an *apt* reply; **2,** inclined; likely; as, he is *apt* to be careless; **3,** quick to learn; as, an *apt* student.—*adv.* **apt′ly.**

all (ôl), ôr; up, mūte, cûr, cōol, book; oil, out; th, thin; *th,* the.

ap-ti-tude (ap'ti-tūd'), *n.* **1,** talent; as, *aptitude* for painting; **2,** fitness; as, the *aptitude* of his remark; **3,** ability or quickness to learn.

aq-ua-ma-rine (ak'wa-ma-rēn'; ā'kwa-ma-rēn'), *n.* **1,** a transparent semiprecious stone, blue, green, or bluish green in colour; **2,** a pale blue-green colour:—*adj.* of this colour.

aq-ua-plane (ak'wa-plān'; ā'kwa-plān'), *n.* a board towed by a motor-boat, and ridden by a person standing on it:—*v.i.* [aquaplaned, aquaplaning], to ride an aquaplane.

a-quar-i-um (a-kwâr'i-um), *n.* [*pl.* aquariums or aquaria (a-kwâr'i-a)], **1,** a tank, bowl, or artificial pond in which living water plants and water animals are kept; **2,** a place devoted to the care and exhibition of large collections of water plants and animals.

A-quar-i-us (a-kwâr'i-us), *n.* **1,** a central constellation, the Water-Bearer; **2,** the 11th sign of the zodiac (♒), which the sun enters about January 21.

a-quat-ic (a-kwat'ik; a-kwot'ik; a-kwôt'ik), *adj.* **1,** in or on water; as, *aquatic* sports; **2,** growing in water:— *n.* an animal or plant that lives in water.

aq-ue-duct (ak'we-dukt), *n.* **1,** a pipe or artificial channel for conducting water from a distance; **2,** a bridgelike structure that supports such a conduit.

a-que-ous (ā'kwi-us; ak'wi-us), *adj.* **1,** of the nature of water; watery; **2,** produced by water; as, *aqueous* rocks.

aq-ui-line (ak'wi-līn'; ak'wi-lin), *adj.* curved like an eagle's beak; as, an *aquiline* nose.

ar-a-ble (ar'a-bl), *adj.* suitable for cultivation; tillable; as, *arable* land.

ar-bi-ter (är'bi-tėr), *n.* **1,** a person chosen or appointed to settle a dispute; an umpire; **2,** one who has full power to make decisions; as, one is the *arbiter* of one's own life.—*n.* **ar-bit'ra-ment.**

ar-bi-trar-y (är'bi-trėr-i; -treri), *adj.* **1,** ruled only by one's own wishes or ideas in making decisions; despotic; as, an *arbitrary* ruler; **2,** based on one's own opinions and wishes, and not on any rule or law; as, an *arbitrary* decision.—*adv.* **ar'bi-trar-i-ly.**

ar-bi-trate (är'bi-trāt'), *v.t.* [arbitrated, arbitrat-ing], **1,** to hear as a judge, and decide; as, the father *arbitrated* the family differences; **2,** to refer (a dispute) to others for settlement; as, we decided to *arbitrate* the issue:—*v.i.* to act as arbiter or judge.—*n.* **ar'bi-tra'tion.**—*n.* **ar'bi-tra'tor.**

ar-bo-re-al (är-bō'ri-al), *adj.* **1,** like trees; relating to trees; **2,** living in trees, as monkeys and squirrels.

ar-bour or **ar-bor** (är'bėr), *n.* **1,** a latticework bower of vines; as, a grape *arbour;* **2,** a shaded nook or walk.

ar-bu-tus (är-bū'tus), *n.* a trailing plant of eastern North America that bears very fragrant pink and white flowers very early in the spring; also called *trailing arbutus* and *Mayflower*: adopted in 1901 by an act of the legislature as Nova Scotia's floral emblem.

arc (ärk), *n.* **1,** part of a curved line; esp. a part of the circumference of a circle; **2,** in electricity, a short band of light, sometimes curved, formed when a powerful electric current passes across a space between two points, generally of carbon, in a broken circuit:—*v.i.* to form an arc.

ar-cade (är-kād'), *n.* **1,** a row of arches supported by pillars; **2,** an arched gallery or passageway, often between buildings, esp. one lined with shops.

¹arch (ärch), *n.* **1,** a structure of brick or masonry, the wedge-shaped parts of which follow a curved line, usually forming the top of a door, window, or gateway; **2,** an opening or passage covered by such a structure; an archway; **3,** anything arch-shaped; as, the *arch* of the foot:—*v.t.* **1,** to cover with a curved or arched structure; **2,** to bend or curve; as, the cat *arched* his back:—*v.i.* to form an arch-shaped bend or curve; as, *arching* trees.

²arch (ärch), *adj.* **1,** mischievous; roguish; as, an *arch* look; **2,** chief; of the first rank; as, an *arch* villain: often used as a prefix, as in *arch*bishop, *arch*duke.

ar-chae-ol-o-gy (är-ki-ol'o-ji), *n.* the scientific study of the human past from excavation of fossils, buildings, remains, etc.

ar-cha-ic (är-kā'ik), *adj.* old-fashioned; primitive; of words, no longer in common use; as, the word "methinks" is *archaic.*

arch-an-gel (ärk'ān'jel), *n.* a chief angel.

arch-bish-op (ärch'bish'up), *n.* a bishop of highest rank, with authority over a group of dioceses.—*n.* **arch'-bish'op-ric.**

arch-duke (ärch'dūk'), *n.* a prince of the imperial house of Austria.—*adj.* **arch'du'cal.**—*n.* **arch'duch'y.**

arch-er (är'chėr), *n.* a person skilled in using the bow and arrow.

arch-er-y (är'chė-ri), *n.* **1,** the use, or skill in the use, of bow and arrow; **2,** a company of archers.

ar-chi-pel-a-go (är'ki-pel'a-gō'), *n.* [*pl.* archipelagoes or archipelagos], a sea containing numerous islands; also, a group of islands.

ar-chi-tect (är'ki-tekt'), *n.* one who plans or designs houses, churches, bridges, etc., and superintends their construction.

ar-chi-tec-ture (är'ki-tek'tŭr; choor), *n.* 1, the science and art of building for both use and beauty; 2, the manner or style of building; as, the new church is an example of Gothic *architecture;* 3, construction; shape; workmanship; as, the *architecture* of this library has many defects.—*adj.* **ar'chi-tec'tur-al.**

ar-chive (är'kīv), *n.* a record preserved as evidence:—**archives,** the place in which public records or historical documents are kept; such records.

arch-ly (ärch'li), *adv.* in a coy manner; roguishly; playfully.

arch-ness (ärch'nis), *n.* coyness; roguishness; playfulness.

arch-way (ärch'wā'), *n.* an opening or entrance through an arch; also, a passage under an arch or curved roof.

arc-tic (ärk'tik), *adj.* located in, or relating to, the region of the North Pole; northern; frigid:—**Arctic Circle,** an imaginary circle parallel to the equator and distant 23° 30' from the North Pole:—*n.* in the U.S., a high, warmly lined, waterproof overshoe.— **Arctic Ocean,** the north-polar ocean.

ar-dent (ärd'ent), *adj.* blazing; hence, passionate; eager; as, an *ardent* desire.

ar-dour or **ar-dor** (är'dẽr), *n.* burning heat; hence, warmth of affection; eagerness.

ar-du-ous (är'dū-us; joo-), *adj.* 1, steep; hard to climb; 2, attended with great labour or exertion; difficult; as, an *arduous* task; 3, strenuous; as, *arduous* efforts.

¹are (âr; är), *n.* in the metric system, a measure of surface, esp. of land; 100 square meters (119.6 square yards).

²are (är), second person, singular and plural, present indicative, of *be.*

a-re-a (âr'i-a; ā'ri-a), *n.* [*pl.* areas], 1, any level, bounded surface; as, the *area* of a floor; the shaded *area* of a drawing; 2, extent of surface, esp. of the earth's surface; as, the *area* of Canada; 3, a region; as, a hilly *area;* 4, scope; range; as, his activities covered a wide *area;* 5, in geometry, the total surface of a plane or solid figure; as, the *area* of a square or of a cube.

a-re-na (a-rē'na), *n.* 1, the enclosed space of a Roman amphitheatre, in which fights between gladiators took place; 2, hence, any place of contest or rivalry; as, the *arena* of politics.

ar-gon (är'gon), *n.* a colourless, odourless, inert gaseous element found in the atmosphere.

Ar-go-nauts (är'go-nôts'), *n.* the legendary Greek heroes whom Jason led to find the Golden Fleece.

ar-go-sy (är'go-si), *n.* [*pl.* argosies], a large merchant vessel.

ar-gue (är'gū), *v.i.* [argued, argu-ing], 1, to give reasons for or against an opinion, measure, etc., try to prove or disprove something; as, to *argue* for a lower tariff; 2, to debate; dispute:— *v.t.* to persuade by force of words; as, he *argued* me into going along.

ar-gu-ment (är'gū-ment), *n.* 1, a reason for or against a thing; as, I know of no *argument* against it; 2, a discussion containing reasons for or against something; 3, the subject, as of a speech or essay; also, an outline or summary, as of a book.

ar-gu-men-ta-tive (är'gū-men'ta-tiv), *adj.* fond of arguing or discussing; hence, contentious; quarrelsome.

a-ri-a (âr'i-a; ä'ri-a), *n.* 1, an air or tune; 2, an elaborate solo part in an opera, oratorio, or the like.

ar-id (ar'id), *adj.* dry; parched; as, an *arid* desert.—*n.* **a-rid'i-ty** (a-rid'i-ti).

A-ri-es (â'ri-ēz'; âr'ēz), *n.* 1, a northern constellation, the Ram; 2, the first sign of the zodiac (♈), which the sun enters about March 21.

a-right (a-rīt'), *adv.* correctly; in a proper way or form.

a-rise (a-rīz'), *v.i.* [*p.t.* arose (a-rōz'), *p.p.* aris-en (a-riz'n), *p. pr.* aris-ing], 1, to stand up; change to a standing position from one of sitting, kneeling, or lying; get up after sleep; 2, to ascend; move upward; as, the sun *arose;* 3, to spring up; begin; as, then a dispute *arose.*

ar-is-toc-ra-cy (ar'is-tok'ra-si), *n.* [*pl.* aristocracies], 1, government by persons of the highest rank in a state; 2, a state with such a government; 3, the nobility; the few who, in rank, wealth, or intellect, are best fitted to rule.

ar-is-to-crat (a-ris'to-krat'; ar'is-), *n.* 1, a personage of high rank or noble birth, or one who has traits characteristic of such rank; 2, one who upholds aristocracy or favours government by the few.—*adj.* **ar'is-to-crat'ic.**

a-rith-me-tic (a-rith'me-tik), *n.* the science of numbers; the art of reckoning by the use of figures.—*adj.* **ar'ith-met'i-cal.**

ark (ärk), *n.* 1, a chest; 2, the oblong box containing the Covenant, or tables of the Law, in the Jewish Tabernacle

(Exodus 25); **3,** the ship in which Noah and his family remained during the Flood (Genesis 6).

¹arm (ärm), *n.* **1,** in man and monkey, one of the two upper limbs; esp., that part of the upper limb between shoulder and hand; **2,** the front or fore limb of any animal having a backbone; **3,** a part resembling, or corresponding to, an arm, as the side of a chair, an inlet of the sea, a branch of a tree, etc.

²arm (ärm), *n.* **1,** a weapon; as, the right to bear *arms;* **2,** a branch of the military service, as the infantry, navy, etc.:—*v.t.* to furnish with arms:—*v.i.* to fit oneself with arms; take up arms.

ar-ma-da (är-mä′da; är-mä′da), *n.* a fleet of armed vessels, aircraft, etc.

ar-ma-dil-lo (är′ma-dil′ō), *n.* [*pl.* armadillos], any of several South and Central American burrowing animals having the head and body protected by an armour of bony plates. Some kinds, when attacked, curl up into a ball.

ar-ma-ment (är′ma-ment), *n.* a nation's entire war equipment or military strength; also, equipment in guns and ammunition.

ar-ma-ture (är′ma-tūr; -chėr), *n.* in a dynamo, the rotary iron core with wire wound around it.

arm-chair (ärm′châr′; ärm′châr′), *n.* a chair with supports for the arms.

arm-ful (ärm′fool), *n.* [*pl.* armfuls], as much as one arm, or both, can hold.

arm-hole (ärm′hōl′), *n.* in a garment, an opening for the arm.

ar-mi-stice (är′mi-stis), *n.* a pause in war by agreement of both sides; a truce.

arm-let (ärm′lit), *n.* a decorative band worn around the upper arm.

ar-mor (är′mėr), **ar-mor-er** (är′mėr-ėr), *n.* Same as armour, armourer.

ar-mo-ri-al (är-mō′ri-al), *adj.* relating to armour or to coats of arms.

ar-mor-y (är′mė-ri), *n.* Same as armoury.

ar-mour (är′mėr), *n.* **1,** a covering, of metal, leather, etc., worn of old, to protect the body in battle or jousting; **2,** the steel plating of a warship; **3,** any protective covering, as the scales of a fish:—*v.t.* to furnish with a protective covering.—*adj.* ar′moured.

ar-mour-er (är′mėr-ėr), *n.* **1,** formerly, a maker of armour; now, a manufacturer of arms; **2,** on a battleship, the man in charge of cleaning and repairing arms.

ar-mour-y (är′mė-ri), *n.* [*pl.* armouries], **1,** a place where arms are stored; a large building in which soldiers

assemble, and which contains also drill halls, offices, etc.; **2,** a place where arms are manufactured.

arm-pit (ärm′pit′), *n.* the pit or hollow beneath the arm where it joins the shoulder.

arms (ärmz), *n.pl.* **1,** weapons of offence or defence; **2,** the military service; as, a call to *arms;* war as a profession; **3,** heraldic emblems or devices; as, the coat of *arms* of Canada.

ar-my (är′mi), *n.* [*pl.* armies], **1,** a large body of men trained and equipped for war; **2,** a great number or multitude; a host; as, an *army* of beetles; **3,** an organized body of persons engaged in furthering a common cause; as, an *army* of workmen:—**army—worm,** the larva of a kind of moth, so called because it spreads over a region like an army, stripping the land of grasses.

a-ro-ma (a-rō′ma), *n.* a pleasant, spicy odour.—*adj.* ar′o-mat′ic (ar′ō-mat′ik).

a-rose (a-rōz′), *v. p.t.* of arise.

a-round (a-round′), *adv.* **1,** in a circle; as, to go *around* on a merry-go-round; **2,** on every side; round about; as, to rush *around;* **3,** near at hand; as, no one is *around:*—*prep.* **1,** circling or encircling; as, to walk *around* a tree; a belt *around* a waist; **2,** on all sides of; as, the air *around* us.

a-rouse (a-rouz′), *v.t.* [aroused, arousing], **1,** to waken; as, she sleeps soundly but is easily *aroused;* **2,** to stir to life; excite to activity; as, his anger is not easily *aroused.*

ar-pent (är′pän′; är′pent), *n.* a French-Canadian land measure (.84 acre).

ar-raign (a-rān′), *v.t.* **1,** to summon (a prisoner) into court to answer a charge; accuse; **2,** to find fault with; call in question; as, I do not *arraign* his honesty.—*n.* ar-raign′ment.

ar-range (a-rānj′), *v.t.* [arranged, arrang-ing], **1,** to put into suitable order; as, to *arrange* flowers or books; **2,** to adjust or settle, as a dispute; bring about, as an interview or compromise:—*v.i.* to make preparations in advance; as, I have *arranged* for the use of the hall.—*n.* arrange′ment.

ar-rant (ar′ant), *adj.* notorious; out-and-out; utter; as, an *arrant* coward.

ar-ras (ar′as), *n.* tapestry; also, wall hangings of tapestry.

ar-ray (a-rā′), *n.* **1,** orderly or formal arrangement; as, troops in battle *array;* **2,** a fine or imposing collection or display; as, an *array* of silver; an *array* of talent; **3,** clothing, especially fine clothing; as, the crowds were in holiday *array:*—*v.t.* **1,** to place or dispose in order; to marshal; as, to *array* troops

---

cat, āge, fär, cåre, åsk; ten, ēve, latėr; (i) pity, rely, senate; īce; top; nō.

in battle formation; **2,** to deck or dress; as, the guests were beautifully *arrayed.*

ar-rears (a-rērz′), *n.pl.* that which should be done or paid, but is still undone or unpaid; as, *arrears* of work or rent:—**in arrears,** behindhand with what should have already been done or paid.—*n.* **ar-rear′age.**

ar-rest (a-rest′), *v.t.* **1,** to stop or check; as, to *arrest* a runaway horse; also, to attract and hold; as, bright colours *arrest* the eye; **2,** to seize and hold (a person) by legal authority; take prisoner:—*n.* **1,** the act of checking or stopping; as, the *arrest* of decay; **2,** the act of taking a person prisoner.

ar-riv-al (a-rīv′al), *n.* **1,** the act of coming to a place, or reaching a destination; as, her *arrival* was unexpected; **2,** a person arriving; as, a late *arrival.*

ar-rive (a-rīv′), *v.i.* [arrived, arriv-ing], **1,** to come to, or reach, a given place; **2,** to reach a result by a process of thought; as, to *arrive* at a conclusion.

ar-ro-gance (ar′ō-gans), *n.* a display of too great confidence in oneself, or one's abilities; extreme haughtiness; lordly contempt of others.—*adj.* **ar′ro-gant.**

ar-row (ar′ō), *n.* **1,** a slender, pointed shaft, often of wood, usually feathered and barbed, and made to be shot from a bow; **2,** a figure on maps, sign-boards, or the like, to indicate direction.

ar-row-head (ar′ō-hed′), *n.* the piercing end or tip of an arrow.

ar-se-nal (är′se-nal), *n.* a public building for storing, making, or repairing military equipment of all kinds.

ar-se-nic (är′se-nik; ärs′nik), *n.* a poisonous greyish-white chemical element:—*adj.* (är-sen′ik), containing arsenic.

ar-son (är′sn), *n.* the malicious or intentional act of setting fire to a building ,or other property.

¹**art** (ärt), *n.* **1,** skill acquired by study or practice; natural aptitude; knack; as, the *art* of sewing; **2,** the body of knowledge and experience related to a particular occupation or profession; as, the *art* of engineering; **3,** the study or creation of beautiful things; as in painting, drawing, sculpture, architecture, music, literature, and dancing: usually called *fine arts;* **4,** the work produced by painters, sculptors, musicians, etc.; **5,** arts, certain branches of learning such as literature, science, history, languages, etc.; **6,** craft; cunning; as, her *art* and wiles failed.

²**art** (ärt), *Poetic,* second person, *sing.* indicative, of *be;* as, "Art thou he?"

ar-ter-y (är′tė-ri), *n.* [*pl.* arteries], **1,**

one of the tubes which carry blood from the heart to all parts of the body; **2,** any great channel or main thoroughfare:—*adj.* **ar-te′ri-al** (är-tē′ri-al).

ar-te-sian well (är-tē′zhan; är-tē′zi-an) a well made by boring into the ground deep enough to reach water which, from internal pressure, will gush to the surface.

art-ful (ärt′fool), *adj.* **1,** skilful; clever; as, *artful* decoration; **2,** cunning; crafty; as, her *artful* ways displeased us.

ar-thri-tis (är-thrī′tis), *n.* inflammation of a joint (as in rheumatism).

ar-thro-pod (ar′thro-pod′), *n.* any spineless animal with jointed legs and segmented body, as crabs and lobsters, spiders, insects, centipedes and millipedes, etc.

ar-ti-choke (är′ti-chōk′), *n.* a tall plant the edible flower head of which is used as a vegetable; also, the vegetable.

ar-ti-cle (är′ti-kl), *n.* **1,** a thing belonging to a particular class of things; as, an *article* of clothing; **2,** a single section of a written document, as a clause of a contract, treaty, creed, or the like; **3,** a prose composition, complete in itself, in a newspaper, magazine, etc.; **4,** in grammar, any of the words *a, an,* or *the,* used before a noun:—*v.t.* [arti-cled, arti-cling], to bind by written agreement; as, he *articled* his son to a carpenter as an apprentice.

ar-tic-u-late (är-tik′ū-lāt′), *v.t.* [articulat-ed articulat-ing], **1,** to unite by means of joints; **2,** to utter in distinct syllables; as, do not mumble; *articulate* your words:—*v.i.* **1,** to utter distinct sounds; **2,** to be jointed:—*adj.* (är-tik′ū-lit), **1,** jointed; **2,** spoken with distinctness; **3,** able to speak, or to express oneself, clearly.—*adv.* **ar-tic′-u-late-ly.**—*n.* **ar-tic′u-la′tion.**

ar-ti-fice (är′ti-fis), *n.* **1,** skill in invention or design; **2,** a ruse or trick.

ar-tif-i-cer (är-tif′i-sėr), *n.* **1,** a skilled craftsman; **2,** an inventor.

ar-ti-fi-cial (är′ti-fish′al), *adj.* **1,** not natural; made by man in imitation of nature; as, *artificial* teeth; *artificial* ice; **2,** affected; insincere; as, an *artificial* smile:—*adv.* **ar′ti-fi′cial-ly.**—*n.* **ar′ti-fi′ci-al′i-ty.**

ar-til-ler-y (är-til′ė-ri), *n.* **1,** cannon, mounted guns, etc., together with their ammunition; **2,** that branch of an army which uses these arms.

ar-ti-san (är′ti-zan′; är′ti-zan), *n.* a man specially trained to work with his hands, as a bricklayer or carpenter.

art-ist (är′tist), *n.* **1,** a person who

practises an art, as painting, sculpture, music, literature, or the like; esp., a painter or sculptor; **2,** in any field, a person who shows creative power in his work; as, your cook is an *artist*.

ar-tis-tic (är-tis′tik), *adj.* **1,** pertaining to art or artists; **2,** designed and made with skill; **3,** readily responsive to beauty; as, an *artistic* nature.—*adv.* **ar-tis′ti-cal-ly.**

art-ist-ry (är′tis-tri), *n.* beauty of workmanship or effect; also, artistic skill.

art-less (ärt′lis), *adj.* **1,** lacking skill or art; clumsy; **2,** free from guile or deceit; natural.—*adv.* **art′less-ly.**

as (az), *adv.* **1,** equally; similarly; to the same extent; as, paper plates will do *as* well; he swam just *as* far yesterday; **2,** thus; for example: used in introducing an example or illustrative quotations:—*conj.* **1,** because; as, he sat down, *as* he was tired; **2,** while; when; as, they fled *as* we approached; **3,** in the way that; as, we did *as* we were told:—*prep.* in the rôle of; as, he entered the contest *as* an amateur:—*relative pron.* that; which: used after *such, same,* etc.; as, send me such books *as* you have ready.

as-bes-tos (as-bes′tos; az-) or **as-bes-tus** (az-bes′tus; as-), *n.* a fibrous, unburnable mineral substance, used in making fireproof materials.

as-cend (a-send′), *v.t.* and *v.i.* to climb or go up; also, to mount; as, to *ascend* the stairs; we watched the kite *ascend*.

as-cend-ant (a-sen′dant) or **as-cend-ent,** *adj.* **1,** rising; predominant; **2,** above the horizon.—*n.* **as-cend′an-cy; as-cend′en-cy.**

as-cen-sion (a-sen′shun), *n.* a moving upward; a rising.

as-cent (a-sent′), *n.* a rising; as, the *ascent* of an aeroplane; **2,** the act of climbing; as, the *ascent* of a mountain; **3,** an upward slope.

as-cer-tain (as′ėr-tān′), *v.t.* to find out definitely; discover; as, it is not so easy to *ascertain* truth.— *adj.* **as′cer-tain′a-ble.**—*n.* **as′cer-tain′ment.**

as-cet-ic (a-set′ik), *n.* one who renounces the comforts and pleasures of life and devotes himself to religious duties; also, one who practises self-denial:—*adj.* self-denying; as, the monks lived *ascetic* lives.—*n.* **as-cet′i-cism.**

as-cribe (a-skrīb′), *v.t.* [ascribed, ascrib-ing], **1,** to regard or speak of (something) as caused by something else; as, she *ascribed* her success to hard work; **2,** to regard or speak of (something) as belonging to someone;

as, the poem was *ascribed* to Burns; valour is *ascribed* to a hero.—*adj.* **as-crib′a-ble.**

a-sep-tic (a-sep′tik; ā-), *adj.* free from disease germs; surgically clean; as, *aseptic* bandages.—*n.* **a-sep′sis.**

¹ash (ash), *n.* a common timber and shade tree, or its tough, elastic wood.

²ash (ash), *n.* **1,** what remains of a substance that has been burned; as, wood *ash;* coal *ash;* **2,** the colour of wood ashes; a whitish or brownish grey.

a-shamed (a-shāmd′), *adj.* **1,** feeling shame or regret; as, he was *ashamed* of his rude act; **2,** fearful of reproach or scorn; as, *ashamed* to beg.

ash-en (ash′en), *adj.* of the colour of ashes; pale; as, in *ashen*-hued.

ash-es (ash′iz), *n. pl.* **1,** what remains of a thing after it is burned; as, wood *ashes* are good for a garden; **2,** that part of the body left after being reduced to dust, as by cremation.

a-shore (a-shōr′), *adv.* on shore; to the shore; as, a ship driven *ashore*.

ash-y (ash′i), *adj.* **1,** composed of ashes; as, an *ashy* soil; **2,** covered with ashes; as, an *ashy* floor; **3,** ash-coloured.

a-side (a-sīd′), *adv.* on or to one side; as, to pull a curtain *aside:*—*n.* a remark in a low tone, intended not to be overheard.

as-i-nine (as′i-nīn′), *adj.* like the ass; hence, stupid; silly; as, an *asinine* remark.

ask (ask), *v.t.* **1,** to seek an answer to; as, to *ask* a question; also, to put a question to; as, *ask* her how old she is; **2,** to beg or request; as, to *ask* a favour; **3,** to inquire about; as, to *ask* the way; **4,** to invite; as, I was *asked* to the party; **5,** to claim; demand; as, what price do you *ask?*—*v.i.* **1,** to make a request; as, to *ask* for money; **2,** to inquire; as, to *ask* for the chief.

a-skance (a-skans′), *adv.* with a side-long glance; hence, with suspicion or distrust; as, to look *askance* at a newcomer.

a-skew (a-skū′), *adv.* and *adj.* awry; out of order; off the true or straight; as, the picture is hanging *askew*.

a-slant (a-slant′), *adv.* and *adj.* in a sloping or slanting direction:—*prep.* in a slanting direction over; as, the rays of the sun fell *aslant* the barn.

a-sleep (a-slēp′), *adj.* and *adv.* **1,** sleeping; **2,** numb; as, my foot is *asleep*.

asp (asp), *n.* a small poisonous snake of Africa, Europe, and Arabia.

as-par-a-gus (a-spar′a-gus), *n.* the tender young stalks of a garden plant

---

cat, åge, fär, câre, åsk; ten, ēve, latėr; (i) pity, rely, senate; īce; top; nō.

of the lily family, used as a vegetable; also, the plant.

as-pect (as'pekt), *n.* **1,** appearance; look; as, the pirate's fierce *aspect;* **2,** a side or part facing a given direction; as, the southern *aspect* of the fort.

as-pen (as'pen; às'pen), *n.* a kind of poplar tree whose leaves tremble in the faintest breeze:—*adj.* relating to such a tree.

as-per-i-ty (as-per'i-ti), *n.* [*pl.* asperities], **1,** roughness of surface; unevenness; **2,** hence, harshness or sharpness of temper; as, he spoke with *asperity* of the trouble we had caused him.

as-perse (a-spûrs'), *v.t.* [aspersed, aspers-ing], to spread damaging or false reports about (a person or his character); to slander.—*n.* **as-per'sion.**

as-phalt (as'fôlt; as'falt), *n.* **1,** a dark-coloured, tarlike mineral substance; **2,** a preparation of this substance, used for paving, roofing, and cementing.

as-phyx-i-ate (as-fik'si-āt'), *v.t.* [asphyxiat-ed, asphyxiat-ing], to cause unconsciousness or death to by cutting off the supply of air; to suffocate.—*n.* **as-phyx'i-a'tion.**

as-pic (as'pik), *n.* a clear meat jelly, served cold, and used as a garnish, or to make a mould of meat, fish, or vegetables.

as-pi-ra-tion (as'pi-rā'shun), *n.* **1,** the act of breathing; a breath; **2,** the strong desire to attain a high or noble goal; ambition; as, an *aspiration* to become an artist; **3,** the pronunciation of the letter *h* as in "horse."

as-pire (a-spīr'), *v.i.* [aspired, aspiring], to have an earnest desire to attain something great or noble; as, he *aspired* to fame as an artist.—*n.* **as-pir'ant.**

as-pi-rin (as'pi-rin), *n.* a drug, usually in the form of white tablets, used as a remedy for rheumatism, headache, colds, etc.

ass (às; as), *n.* **1,** the donkey (with longer ears and shorter mane than the horse); **2,** a dull, stupid person.

as-sail (a-sāl'), *v.t.* to fall upon or attack violently; also, to attack with words; as, they *assailed* him with threats and jeers.—*adj.* **as-sail'a-ble.**

as-sail-ant (a-sāl'ant), *n.* a person who makes an attack or assault.

as-sas-sin (a-sas'in), *n.* a person who kills secretly or treacherously.

as-sas-si-nate (a-sas'i-nāt'), *v.t.* [assassinat-ed, assassinat-ing], to kill by secret or treacherous means.—*n.* **as-sas'si-na'tion.**

as-sault (a-sôlt'), *n.* a violent attack,

by physical force, or by force of words; as, an *assault* on the enemy's camp; an *assault* on the character of an opponent: —*v.t.* to attack violently, especially by armed force; assail.

as-say (a-sā'), *n.* **1,** the act or process of analyzing a metallic compound, ore, or alloy; esp., the testing of gold or silver coin or bullion to see if it is of standard purity; **2,** the substance tested:—*v.t.* **1,** to make a chemical analysis of; **2,** to attempt; as, to *assay* a hard task.—*adj.* **as-say'a-ble.**— *n.* **as-say'er.**

as-sem-ble (a-sem'bl), *v.t.* [assem-bled assem-bling], **1,** to gather together into one place or mass; collect; as, he *assembled* the committee; **2,** to fit together, as parts of machinery:—*v.i.* to meet or come together; convene; as, the Senate *assembles* today.—*n.* **as-sem'blage.**

as-sem-bly (a-sem'bli), *n.* [*pl.* assemblies], **1,** a collection or company of persons brought together in one place and for a common object; a meeting; congregation; **2,** a legislative body; **3,** the fitting together of parts to make a complete machine; as, the *assembly* of a motorcar.

as-sem-bly-man (a-sem'bli-man), *n.* [*pl.* assemblymen (-men)], a member of an assembly:—Assemblyman in certain States, a member of the lower body of the legislature.

as-sent (a-sent'), *v.i.* to agree; consent; express agreement; as, to *assent* to a request:—*n.* the act of agreeing; consent; as, do you *assent* to my plan?

as-sert (a-sûrt'), *v.t.* **1,** to state positively; declare with assurance; affirm; as, let me *assert* my belief; **2,** to insist upon; as, to *assert* one's rights; make (oneself) felt; as, he invariably *asserts* himself.

as-ser-tion (a-sûr'shun), *n.* **1,** the act of declaring positively; **2,** a positive declaration or statement.

as-ser-tive (a-sûr'tiv), *adj.* **1,** inclined to make very positive statements; overconfident; as, an *assertive* person is often disliked; **2,** declarative; as, this is an *assertive* sentence.—*n.* **as-ser'tive-ness.**

as-sess (a-ses'), *v.t.* **1,** to fix or determine the amount of; as, to *assess* the damages; **2,** to fix or set (a tax), as on property; **3,** to value officially for the purpose of taxation; as, the property was *assessed* at $500.—*adj.* **as-sess'a-ble.**—*n.* **as-sess'ment.**

as-ses-sor (a-ses'ėr), *n.* one appointed to estimate the value of property.

as-set (as'et), *n.* **1,** anything of value

that belongs to a business, a person, etc.; as, integrity is a business *asset;* bank deposits are an *asset;* **2, assets,** all the property of a person, firm, or estate which may be used to pay debts and obligations.

as-sid-u-ous (a-sid′ū-us; -sij′oo-), *adj.* persistent; persevering; hardworking; as, John was an *assiduous* worker for peace.—*n.* **as′si-du′i-ty** (as′i-dū′i-ti).

as-sign (a-sīn′), *v.t.* **1,** to allot, as seats; **2,** to appoint, as to a duty; **3,** to give out, as lessons; **4,** to settle definitely; as, to *assign* a time for a meeting; **5,** to transfer (property) to another.—*n.* **as-sign′ment.**

as-sim-i-late (a-sim′i-lāt′), *v.t.* [assimilat-ed, assimilat-ing], to absorb; make a part of oneself:—*v.i.* to be absorbed.

as-sim-i-la-tion (a-sim′i-lā′shun), *n.* **1,** a bringing into agreement; **2,** in physiology, the absorbing of digested food, and its change into bodily tissue.

as-sist (a-sist′), *v.t.* and *v.i.* to help; aid.

as-sist-ance (a-sis′tans), *n.* help; aid.

as-sist-ant (a-sis′tant), *adj.* **1,** helping; lending aid; **2,** acting under another person of higher authority; as, an *assistant* editor:—*n.* a helper.

as-size (a-sīz′) [*pl.* assizes (a-sīz′iz)] *n.* a court of justice, or a session, for the trial by jury of civil or criminal cases.

as-so-ci-ate (a-sō′shi-it; -āt′), *n.* **1,** a companion; **2,** someone joined with another in an undertaking; partner, as in business; **3,** a member of a society or institution:—*adj.* **1,** joined with someone in interest or purpose; **2,** sharing office or authority; as, an *associate* judge; **3,** admitted to some but not all rights or privileges; as, an *associate* member of a club:—*v.t.* (a-sō′shi-āt′) [associat-ed, associat-ing], to unite; combine; connect in thought; as, I *associate* green with grass:—*v.i.* to keep company; as, don't *associate* with evil persons.

as-so-ci-a-tion (a-sō′shi-ā′shun; a-sō′si-ā′shun), *n.* **1,** a joining together; **2,** fellowship; **3,** a body of persons organized for a common object; a corporation; **4,** a connection between related ideas.

as-so-nance (as′ō-nans), *n.* **1,** similarity of sound; **2,** a partial rhyme in which stressed words like *fate* and *take* have similar vowel, but unlike consonant, sounds.

as-sort (a-sôrt′), *v.t.* **1,** to separate into classes; sort; **2,** to agree; as, his actions *assort* well with his character.

as-sort-ed (a-sôr′tid), *adj.* of different kinds; various; as, *assorted* cakes.

as-sort-ment (a-sôrt′ment), *n.* **1,** a separating and arranging; **2,** a collection of articles of various kinds.

as-suage (a-swāj′), *v.t.* [assuaged, assuaging], to lessen; as, time *assuaged* her grief.

as-sume (a-sūm′), *v.t.* [assumed, assuming], **1,** to take upon oneself, especially without authority; as, to *assume* the leadership; **2,** to take for granted; as, to *assume* that something is true; **3,** to pretend; put on; as, he *assumed* an air of surprise; **4,** to undertake (an office or duty).—*n.* **as-sump′tion** (a-sump′shun).

as-sur-ance (a-shōōr′ans), *n.* **1,** a statement intended to give certainty or confidence; as, *assurances* of his safety came in every mail; **2,** certain proof; freedom from doubt; utmost certainty; as, *assurance* of success; **3,** self-reliance; self-confidence; as, frequent speaking in public gave him *assurance;* **4,** impudence; too much self-confidence; as, his *assurance* cost him his job; **5,** insurance.

as-sure (a-shōōr′), *v.t.* [assured, assuring], **1,** to make certain; as, practice *assures* skill; **2,** to declare confidently (to); promise; as, he *assured* us she would come; **3,** to insure against loss.

as-sur-ed-ly (a-shōōr′id-li), *adv.* certainly; without doubt.

as-ter (as′tėr), *n.* a leafy-stemmed plant related to the daisy, with white, pink, blue, or purple flower heads; also, its flower. Asters vary in size from small, star-shaped heads to large, many-flowered heads which often resemble chrysanthemums.

as-ter-isk (as′tėr-isk), *n.* the figure of a star [*], used in printing or writing as a reference mark, or to show an omission:—*v.t.* to mark with such a star.

a-stern (a-stûrn′), *adv.* **1,** at or toward the rear end of a ship; **2,** behind a ship.

as-ter-oid (as′tė-roid′), *n.* any of the small planets in orbit between Mars and Jupiter.

asth-ma (az′ma, as′ma), *n.* a disease attended by difficulty in breathing.—*adj.* **asth-mat′ic.**

a-stir (a-stûr′), *adj.* and *adv.* on the move; in activity; as, to be *astir* early.

as-ton-ish (a-ston′ish), *v.t.* to strike with sudden wonder; surprise; amaze. —*adj.* **as-ton′ish-ing.**—*n.* **as-ton′ish-ment.**

as-tound (a-stound′), *v.t.* to strike with amazement; shock.—*adj.* **as-tound′ing.**

a-strad-dle (a-strad'l), *adv.* with one leg on each side of something.

as-tra-khan or **as-tra-chan** (as'tra-kan'; as'tra-kan), *n.* 1, the skin of young lambs, with a curly wool like fur; 2, a cloth imitation of this.

as-tral (as'tral), *adj.* of, like, or from the stars; as, *astral* rays reach us from the constellation Orion.

a-stray (a-strā'), *adv.* out of the proper way or place; as, to go *astray:—adj.* wandering; confused.

a-stride (a-strīd'), *adv.* with one leg on each side:—*prep.* straddling.

as-trin-gent (a-strin'jent), *adj.* tending to pucker or wrinkle the skin, as alum:—*n.* a substance that contracts tissues.

as-trol-o-gy (a-strol'o-ji), *n.* the practice which claims to predict events by the position and mysterious influence on human affairs of the sun, moon, and planets.—*adj.* **as'tro-log'i-cal** (as'tro-loj'i-kal).—*n.* **as-trol'o-ger.**

as-tron-o-my (as-tron'o-mi), *n.* the science of the nature and movements of stars, planets, etc.—*n.* **as-tron'o-mer.** —*adj.* **as'tro-nom'i-cal.**

as-tro-phys-ics (as'trō-fiz'iks), *n.* the science that deals with the properties (physical, chemical, etc.) of heavenly bodies.—*adj.* **as'tro-phys'i-cal.**

as-tute (as-tūt'), *adj.* shrewd; cunning; crafty; subtle.—*n.* **as-tute'ness.**

a-sun-der (a-sun'dẽr), *adv.* apart; into parts; as, he tore the book *asunder.*

a-sy-lum (a-sī'lum), *n.* 1, a place of refuge or security; 2, an institution for the· care of the helpless or insane.

at (at), *prep.* 1, indicating nearness in place or time; as, to be *at* home *at* noon; 2, indicating such conditions as occupation, cause, price, etc.; as, *at* play; *at* ten cents; *at* will.

ate (āt), *p.t.* of *eat.*

a-the-ist (ā'thē-ist), *n.* one who disbelieves in, or denies, the existence of a God.—*n.* **a'the-ism.**—*adj.* **a'the-is'tic.**

a-thirst (a-thûrst'), *adj.* 1, thirsty; 2, having a keen desire; eager, as for fame.

ath-lete (ath'lēt), *n.* a person trained to contend in games of physical strength or endurance.—*adj.* **ath-let'ic** (ath-let'ik).

ath-let-ics (ath-let'iks), *n. pl.* sometimes used as *sing.* athletic sports.

a-thwart (a-thwôrt'), *adv.* from side to side; crosswise:—*prep.* 1, across the course or direction of; 2, from side to side of; as, beams set *athwart* the ship.

Atlantic Ocean, lies between the Americas and Europe-Africa; area, over 3¾ million square miles.

at-las (at'las), *n.* 1, a bound volume of maps or charts; 2, the vertebra of the neck which supports the skull.

at-mos-phere (at'mos-fēr'), *n.* 1, the air which surrounds the earth; 2, the air in any particular place; as, the damp *atmosphere* of a cellar; 3, a surrounding or pervading influence; as, an *atmosphere* of peace.—*adj.* **at'mos-pher'ic** (at'mos-fer'ik).

at-oll (a-tol'; at'ol), *n.* a circular coral reef surrounding a lake or lagoon.

at-om (at'um), *n.* 1, one of the smallest parts into which a substance may be divided; 2, a minute quantity or particle.

a-tom-ic (a-tom'ik), *adj.* relating to minute things or quantities:—**atomic bomb,** a highly destructive bomb, using the explosive energy stored in the smallest particles of matter:—**atomic theory,** the idea that elements consist of minute parts, having all the properties of the elements.

at-om-iz-er (at'o-mī'zẽr), *n.* a device for changing a liquid, esp. a medicine or perfume, into a fine spray.

a-tone (a-tōn'), *v.i.* [atoned, aton-ing], to do something to make up for some offence or wrong; as, Mary tried to *atone* for hurting Jane's feelings by giving her a doll.—*n.* **a-tone'ment.**

a-top (a-top'), *adv.* at or to the top:— *prep.* on top of.

a-tro-cious (a-trō'shus), *adj.* extremely wicked; outrageous.—*adv.* **a-tro'cious-ly.**

a-troc-i-ty (a-tros'i-ti), *n.* [*pl.* atrocities], 1, an outrageous or cruel deed; 2, *Colloq.*, something ugly or very faulty; as, that hat is an *atrocity.*

at-ro-phy (at'ro-fi), *v.i.* [atrophied (at'-ro-fid), atrophy-ing], to waste or wither away, from lack of food or from disuse:—*n.* a wasting of the body, or any part of it, due to lack of food or to disuse.

at-tach (a-tach'), *v.t.* 1, to fasten to or upon something; connect; as, to *attach* a cheque to a letter; 2, to assign, as to a military company; appoint; 3, to affix, as a signature; 4, to attribute; as to *attach* importance to something; 5, to bind by ties of affection or self-interest; 6, to take by law:—*v.i.* to be fixed; adhere.

at-ta-che (at'a-shā'; a-tash'ā), *n.* [*pl.* attachés], a member of a suite or staff; especially, a subordinate attached to the staff of a foreign minister or ambassador.

at-tach-ment (a-tach'ment), *n.* 1, the

act of fastening, or the thing fastened; **2,** affection; **3,** something extra that may be connected to something else; as, *attachments* for a vacuum cleaner; **4,** legal seizure of goods or persons.

at-tack (a-tak′), *v.t.* **1,** to set upon with physical force, or with words; assail; as, to *attack* with sword or pen; **2,** to begin to have a harmful effect upon; as, worms are *attacking* our trees; **3,** to begin work on; as, to *attack* a problem: *v.i.* to make an assault:—*n.* **1,** an assault; onset; **2,** a bitter criticism; **3,** the first step of an undertaking; **4,** a seizure, as of illness.

at-tain (a-tān′), *v.t.* **1,** to reach; arrive at; as, to *attain* the top of a hill; **2,** to achieve; gain; accomplish; as, *attain* one's goal:—*v.i.* to arrive.—*n.* **at-tain′ment.**—*adj.* **at-tain′a-ble.**

at-tempt (a-tempt′), *v.t.* **1,** to make an effort to do; try; as, to *attempt* a flight, or to fly; **2,** to try to take by force; as, to *attempt* a man's life:—*n.* trial; effort.

at-tend (a-tend′), *v.t.* **1,** to wait upon; care for; **2,** to escort; accompany; **3,** to be present at; as, to *attend* a church service:—*v.i.* **1,** to give heed to; as, *attend* to my warning; **2,** to be in waiting, as a bridesmaid at a wedding; **3,** to look after something; as, to *attend* to business.

at-tend-ance (a-ten′dans), *n.* **1,** the fact of being present, as at school; **2,** the state of looking after or waiting upon some person or thing; as, the nurse is in *attendance;* **3,** the number of persons present; also, the record of this number; as, to take the *attendance.*

at-tend-ant (a-ten′dant), *adj.* accompanying or immediately following; as, illness *attendant* on overeating:—*n.* **1,** one who serves or waits upon another; a servant or companion; as, he dismissed his *attendants;* **2,** one who is frequently present, as at church.

at-ten-tion (a-ten′shun), *n.* **1,** the fixing of one's thoughts closely on something; concentration; **2,** an act of courtesy, esp. on the part of a man in wooing a woman.

at-ten-tive (a-ten′tiv), *adj.* **1,** heedful; intent; as, an *attentive* student; **2,** polite; eager to offer courtesies.

at-ten-u-ate (a-ten′ū-āt), *v.t.* **1,** to make thin or slender; **2,** to weaken, lessen, or reduce (in force or intensity).

at-test (a-test′), *v.t.* **1,** to bear witness to; affirm the truth of, esp. by signing one's name or by oath; **2,** to give proof of; as, your work *attests* your ability.

at-tic (at′ik), *n.* the space immediately beneath the roof of a house; a garret.

at-tire (a-tīr′), *n.* clothes; finery:—*v.t.* [at-tired, attir-ing], to clothe; array.

at-ti-tude (at′i-tūd′), *n.* **1,** bodily position or pose; esp., position assumed to show feeling, purpose, mood, etc.; as, to take a threatening *attitude;* **2,** way of thinking or feeling; as, his *attitude* of indifference.

at-tor-ney (a-tûr′ni), *n.* [*pl.* attorneys], a lawyer; one legally appointed by another to act for him in any legal matter: also called *attorney-at-law.*

at-tor-ney–gen-er-al, *n.* [*pl.* attor-neys–general or attorney–generals], the chief law-officer of a state or nation.

at-tract (a-trakt′), *v.t.* **1,** to draw to oneself by personal charm, or the like; as, he *attracts* friends easily; **2,** to cause to approach; as, a magnet *attracts* steel; **3,** to draw forth; win; as, beauty *attracts* attention.

at-trac-tion (a-trak′shun), *n.* **1,** the power or act of drawing to or toward; **2,** the thing that attracts; as, beauty has an *attraction* for all.

at-trac-tive (a-trak′tiv), *adj.* having the power to attract; charming; alluring.

¹at-trib-ute (a-trib′ūt), *v.t.* [attribut-ed, attribut-ing], **1,** to consider (a quality) as belonging to a person or thing; as, we *attribute* grace to a dancer; **2,** to consider (a thing) as being caused by something else; as, I *attribute* Anne's popularity to her beauty.—*n.* **at′tri-bu′tion.**

²at-tri-bute (at′ri-būt′), *n.* **1,** a trait or characteristic, thought of as belonging to a person or thing; as, courtesy is an *attribute* of a gentleman; **2,** a symbol; as, the crown is an *attribute* of royalty.

at-trib-u-tive (a-trib′ū-tiv), *adj.* in *grammar,* an adjective which immediately precedes the noun which it modifies; as, "red," in the expression "red bricks," is an *attributive* (or adherent) adjective.

at-tri-tion (a-trish′un), *n.* a wearing away or down; as, our forces shrank in a war of *attrition.*

at-tune (a-tūn′), *v.t.* [attuned, attun-ing], **1,** to put in tune; **2,** to bring into harmony; as, his spirit was *attuned* to nature.

au-burn (ô′bẽrn), *adj.* reddish brown.

auc-tion (ôk′shun), *n.* a public sale of property to the highest bidder:—*v.t.* to sell to the highest bidder.

auc-tion-eer (ôk′shun-ēr′), *n.* a person who conducts an auction.

au-da-cious (ô-dā′shus), *adj.* **1,** bold; daring; **2,** too bold; insolent; impudent.

au-dac-i-ty (ô-das′i-ti), *n.* [*pl.* audaci-ties], **1,** rash boldness; **2,** impudence.

au-di-ble (ô′di-bl), *adj.* loud enough to

be heard.—*adv.* **au′di-bly.**—*n.* **au′di-bil′i-ty.**

au-di-ence (ô′di-ens), *n.* 1, a group of persons assembled to hear or to see, as at a lecture or a motion picture; 2, a formal interview with a person of authority.

au-di-o (ô′di-ō′), *adj.* 1, in television, the sound phase as distinct from the *video*, or picture, portion; 2, relating to apparatus using audible frequencies; as, *audio* amplifier.

au-di-o—vis-u-al aids, films, lantern slides, recordings, and materials other than textbooks used in classroom teaching.

au-dit (ô′dit), *n.* an official examination of claims or accounts:—*v.t.* to examine and adjust, as accounts or claims.

au-di-tion (ô-dish′un), *n.* 1, act or sense of hearing; 2, a test hearing given a singer, musician, actor, etc.—*v.t.* to give such a hearing.—*v.i.* to perform an audition.

au-di-tor (ô′di-tér), *n.* 1, a listener; 2, a person appointed to examine and verify accounts and claims.

au-di-tor-i-um (ô′di-tōr′i-um), [*pl.* auditoriums or auditoria], *n.* a building or room, designed for public gatherings; also, the part of a theatre, or the like, assigned to the audience.

au-di-tor-y (ô′di-tōr′i), *adj.* having to do with hearing or the organs of hearing; as, the *auditory* nerve.

au-gend (ô′jend; ô-jend′), *n.* a number to which another number, the *addend,* is to be added.

au-ger (ô′gér), *n.* a tool for boring holes.

aught (ôt), *n.* 1, any part; anything; as, for *aught* I know; 2, (usually *ought*), in arithmetic, a cipher; nothing.

aug-ment (ôg-ment′), *v.t.* to increase in size or extent; to make bigger; as, the general *augmented* his forces.—*n.* **aug′-men-ta′tion** (ôg′men-tā′shun).

au-gur (ô′gér), *n.* in Roman times, a religious official who foretold events by signs or omens, such as the flight of birds, thunder, etc.; a soothsayer; prophet:—*v.i.* to foretell events from signs:—*v.t.* to predict; give promise of; as, careful planning *augurs* success.

au-gu-ry (ô′gū-ri; ô′gér-i), *n.* [*pl.* auguries], 1, the art or practice of foretelling events by signs or omens; 2, an omen; a prediction.

au-gust (ô-gust′), *adj.* 1, majestic; having grandeur and dignity; 2, of high rank; noble.

Au-gust (ô′gust), *n.* the eighth month of the year (31 days).

auk (ôk), *n.* a kind of diving bird with small wings used as paddles, and a heavy body. It lives in the colder regions of the Northern Hemisphere.

aunt (ȧnt; änt), *n.* the sister of one's father or mother; also, an uncle's wife.

aunt-ie, aunt-y (ȧn′ti), *n.* familiar form of *aunt.*

au-ra (ô′ra), *n.* 1, an invisible emanation, as the aroma of flowers; 2, a distinctive atmosphere about a person or thing; as, an *aura* of culture.

au re-voir (ō′ re-vwär′), *French,* goodbye till I see you again.

au-ri-cle (ô′ri-kl), *n.* 1, the part of the ear outside the head; the outer ear; 2, either of the two upper chambers of the heart, which receive the blood from the veins and transmit it to the ventricles.

au-ror-a bor-e-a-lis (ô-rō′ra bō′ri-ā′lis; bō′ri-al′is), northern lights; a glow, or streamers of light, supposed to be of electrical origin, appearing in the northern sky at night, best seen in northern latitudes.

aus-pic-es (ôs′pi-siz), *n.pl.* 1, omens or signs, as those drawn from birds by the ancient Romans; 2, protection; patronage; as, a play given under the *auspices* of the club.

aus-pi-cious (ôs-pish′us), *adj.* 1, promising success or happiness; as *auspicious* circumstances; 2, successful; prosperous; as, an *auspicious* year.

aus-tere (ôs-tēr′), *adj.* 1, rigidly strict in manner of living or thinking; 2, severely simple; unadorned; as, an *austere* building.—*adv.* **aus-tere′ly.**—*n.* **aus-ter′i-ty.**

au-then-tic (ô-then′tik), *adj.* 1, genuine; original; as, an *authentic* painting by Raphael; 2, duly authorized; true; trustworthy; as, *authentic* information.—*n.* **au′then-tic′i-ty** (ô′-then-tis′i-ti).

au-then-ti-cate (ô-then′ti-kāt′), *v.t.* [authenticat-ed, authenticat-ing], to establish as real or genuine, as the authorship of a book, a signature, or the like.—*n.* **au-then′ti-ca′tion.**

au-thor (ô′thér), *n.* 1, one who composes or writes a book, articles, etc.; 2, a person who begins or originates anything. *Fem.* **au′thor-ess** (now rare).

au-thor-i-ta-tive (ô-thor′i-tā′tiv), *adj.* 1, having acknowledged authority, entitled to obedience or acceptance; 2, commanding in manner; imperative.

au-thor-i-ty (ô-thor′i-ti), *n.* [*pl.* authorities], 1, the right to act or command; as, a general's *authority;* 2, one whose knowledge or judgment on a subject is entitled to acceptance; an expert; as, Audubon is an *authority* on birds; also, a book, quotation, or the like, cited in justification of a statement or action; **3, authorities,** government officials.

au-thor-ize (ô′thẽr-īz′), *v.t.* [authorized, authoriz-ing], **1,** to give (a person) the right to act; as, he is *authorized* to act for us; **2,** to approve; allow; as, to *authorize* the purchase of supplies.—*n.* **au′thor-i-za′tion.**

au-to (ô′tō), *n.* [*pl.* autos], *Colloq.,* an automobile.

au-to-bi-og-ra-phy (ô′tō-bī-og′ra-fi; ô′-tō-bi-og′ra-fi), *n.* [*pl.* autobiographies], a life history of a person, written by himself.—*n.* **au′to-bi-og′ra-pher.**—*adj.* **au′to-bi′o-graph′ic** (ô′-tō-bī′o-graf′ik); **au′to-bi′o-graph′i-cal.**

au-toc-ra-cy (ô-tok′ra-si), *n.* [*pl.* autocracies], government by a person whose will is law; absolute monarchy.

au-to-crat (ô′tō-krat′), *n.* **1,** a ruler with unlimited power; **2,** a person who demands obedience to his will; as, Jack's father was an *autocrat* in his home.—*adj.* **au′to-crat′ic.**

au-to-graph (ô′tō-gráf), *n.* a person's own handwriting or signature:—*v.t.* to write one's signature in or on; as, to *autograph* a book or a photograph.

au-to-mat-ic (ô′tō-mat′ik), *adj.* **1,** designed to work without attention; as, an *automatic* oil burner; **2,** done unconsciously; as, breathing is *automatic:—n.* a firearm which continues to fire so long as the trigger is held and the ammunition lasts.—*adv.* **au′to-mat′i-cal-ly.**

au-to-ma-tion (ô′tō-mā′shun), *n.* the use of self-operating machines or electronic devices to control processes of production, inspection, calculation, sorting, etc.

au-tom-a-ton (ô-tom′a-ton′; -tun), *n.* [*pl.* automata], a person or apparatus that moves or acts in a mechanical way, like a robot.

au-to-mo-bile (ô′to-mō-bēl′; ô′to-mō′bēl), *n.* a vehicle carrying an engine by which it is propelled; a motor car:—*adj.* having to do with motor cars.—*n.* **au′to-mo-bil′ist** (ô′to-mō-bēl′ist; ô′to-mō′bil-ist).

au-to-mo-tive (ô′to-mō′tiv), *adj.* pertaining to self-propelled vehicles; as, the *automotive* industries.

au-ton-o-my (ô-ton′o-mi), *n.* [*pl.* -mies (-miz)], the power or right of self-government:—*adj.* **au-ton′o-mous.**

au-top-sy (ô′top-si; ô′tup-si), *n.* [*pl.* autopsies], the examination and dissection of a dead body to find the cause of death, extent of disease, injury, etc.

au-tumn (ô′tum), *n.* the season following summer, (in the Northern Hemisphere, about September 22 to December 21): also called *fall:—adj.* belonging to this season; as, *autumn* fruits.—*adj.* **au-tum′nal.**

aux-il-ia-ry (ôg-zil′ya-ri), *adj.* helping; assisting; as, *auxiliary* forces:—*n.* [*pl.* auxiliaries], **1,** a helper; an ally; aid of any kind; **2,** in *grammar,* a verb, such as *be, have, may,* which helps to form the moods and tenses of other verbs; as, in "they have come," "have" is the *auxiliary;* **3, auxiliaries,** foreign troops in the service of a nation at war.

a-vail (a-vāl′), *v.i.* to be of use or value:—*v.t.* to benefit; help; as, shouting did not *avail* us:—**avail oneself of,** to take advantage of; utilize:—*n.* use; means toward an end; as, crying was of no *avail.*

a-vail-a-ble (a-vāl′a-bl), *adj.* **1,** at hand; ready to be used; **2,** suitable for one's purpose.—*n.* **a-vail′a-bil′i-ty.**

av-a-lanche (av′a-lansh), *n.* **1,** a large mass of snow or earth sliding down a mountain; **2,** anything that overwhelms by speed and volume; as, an *avalanche* of words.

av-a-rice (av′a-ris), *n.* the passion for hoarding or acquiring wealth; greed.—*adj.* **av′a-ri′cious** (av′a-rish′us).

a-ve (ā′vē; ä′vā), *interj.* hail! farewell! a salutation, esp. to the Virgin.

a-venge (a-venj′), *v.t.* [avenged, avenging], **1,** to inflict just punishment in return for (a wrong or injury); as, to *avenge* an insult; **2,** to exact punishment on behalf of; as, to *avenge* a slain kinsman.—*n.* **a-veng′er.**

av-e-nue (av′e-nū′), *n.* **1,** a wide roadway or drive; **2,** a way of approach to a place or goal; as, an *avenue* to success.

a-ver (a-vûr′), *v.t.* [averred, aver-ring], to state positively; assert; as, the man averred that he had not slept.

av-er-age (av′ẽr-ij), *n.* **1,** something of a usual character, midway between extremes, as between too much and too little, very good and very bad, or the like; obtained by dividing the sum of several quantities by the number of quantities; as, the average of 5, 8, and 14 is 9:—*adj.* **1,** arrived at by dividing the sum of several quantities by their number; as, the *average* height of the boys; **2,** ordinary; usual:—*v.t.* [averaged, averag-ing], to find the average of (a series of numbers or the like):—*v.i.* to do, perform, or get as an average rate, sum, amount, or the like; as, the car *averaged* 20 miles an hour.

a-verse (a-vûrs′), *adj.* **1,** unwilling; reluctant; **2,** having a dislike; as, *averse* to hard work.—*n.* **a-ver′sion.**

a-vert (a-vûrt′), *v.t.* **1,** to turn aside, as one's eyes; **2,** to turn or ward off; **3,** to prevent; as, to *avert* a strike.

a-vi-ar-y (ā′vi-er′i), *n.* [*pl.* aviaries], a place for the keeping of birds.

a-vi-a-tion (ā′vi-ā′shun), *n.* the art or science of flying aeroplanes.

a-vi-a-tor (ā′vi-ā′tėr), *n.* the pilot of an airplane (whether male or female).

av-id (av′id), *adj.* extremely eager; as, *avid* of pleasure; greedy; as, *avid* for food.—*adv.* **av′id-ly.**—*n.* **a-vid′i-ty** (a-vid′i-ti).

av-o-ca-do (av′ō-kä′dō), *n.* a tropical pear-shaped American or West-Indian fruit; the alligator pear.

av-o-ca-tion (av′ō-kā′shun), *n.* an activity other than one's occupation; hobby; as, the lawyer's *avocation* is playing the violin.

av-o-cet or **av-o-set** (av′ō-set), *n.* a shore bird with webbed feet and up-curved bill.

a-void (a-void′), *v.t.* to keep away from; shun.—*n.* **a-void′ance:**—*adj.* **a-void′-a-ble.**

av-oir-du-pois (av′-ėr-dū-poiz′; av′-ėr-du-poiz′), *n.* **1,** the common system of measuring weight, in pounds of sixteen ounces each: used for weighing all articles except precious metals, gems, and drugs; **2,** *Colloq.*, weight; heaviness.

a-vouch (a-vouch′), *v.t.* to declare positively; maintain; confirm; as, the spectators *avouched* that the man was badly hurt; their evidence *avouched* the date of the accident.

a-vow (a-vou′), *v.t.* to declare openly; admit; as, to *avow* one's faults.—*n.* **a-vow′al.**—*adj.* **a-vowed′.**—*adv.* **a-vow′-ed-ly.**

a-wait (a-wāt′), *v.t.* **1,** to wait for; expect; as, to *await* news; **2,** to be ready for; as, I *await* your commands; **3,** to be in store for; as, happiness *awaits* you.

a-wake (a-wāk′), *v.t.* [*p.t.* and *p.p.* awoke (a-wōk′) or awaked (a-wākt′), *p.pr.* awak-ing], **1,** to rouse from sleep; **2,** to rouse from inactivity; stimulate; as, to *awake* interest:—*v.i.* **1,** to cease to sleep; **2,** to rouse oneself; become alert:—*adj.* **1,** not asleep; **2,** fully aware; on the alert; as, he was *awake* to his danger.

a-wak-en (a-wāk′en), *v.t.* and *v.i.* to rouse from sleep or as if from sleep; awake.—*n.* and *adj.* **a-wak′en-ing.**

a-ward (a-wôrd′), *v.t.* **1,** to give or

assign, as does a judge or an umpire, after careful consideration; **2,** to bestow, as a prize:—*n.* **1,** a careful and deliberate decision; **2,** that which is awarded.

a-ware (a-wâr′), *adj.* conscious; informed; as, he is well *aware* of his shortcomings.

a-wash (a-wosh′; a-wôsh′), *adj.* and *adv.* **1,** afloat; tossed about by water; **2,** washed over; covered with water.

a-way (a-wā′), *adv.* **1,** at or to a distance; off; aside; as, to be *away;* to look *away;* **2,** out of one's possession; as, to give *away;* **3,** continuously; as, to work *away;* **4,** out of existence; as, to die *away.*

awe (ô), *n.* wonder tinged with fear; reverence; as, to live in *awe* of nature: —*v.t.* [awed, aw-ing], to produce feelings of solemn respect or fear in; as, to be *awed* by mountains.

awe-some (ô′sum), *adj.* majestic and terrifying, as a volcano.—*n.* **awe′some-ness.**

aw-ful (ô′fool), *adj.* **1,** inspiring reverence or fear; **2,** appalling, as a calamity; **3,** *Colloq.,* extreme in any sense; very bad, great, ugly, etc.; as *awful* language; an *awful* dress; an *awful* thirst.—*n.* **aw′ful-ness.**—*adv.* **aw′ful-ly.**

a-while (a-hwīl′), *adv.* for a short time.

awk-ward (ôk′wėrd), *adj.* **1,** unskilful; bungling; clumsy; as, an *awkward* workman; **2,** ungraceful; ungainly in action or form; as, an *awkward* skater; **3,** ill at ease; embarrassed; as, he feels *awkward* in company; **4,** difficult to deal with; embarrassing; as, an *awkward* situation.—*adv.* **awk′ward-ly.** —*n.* **awk′ward-ness.**

awl (ôl), *n.* a pointed tool for making small holes, as in leather or wood.

awn (ôn), *n.* one of the sharp ends or bristles on a head of barley, oats, etc.

awn-ing (ôn′ing), *n.* a rooflike covering, as of canvas, stretched on a frame and used above or before any place as a shelter from rain or sun.

a-woke (a-wōk′), *p.t.* of *awake.*

a-wry (a-rī′), *adv.* and *adj.* **1,** turned or twisted to one side; out of the right line; crooked; **2,** wrong; amiss; as, the plan went *awry.*

axe or **ax** (aks), *n.* a hewing or chopping tool, consisting of an iron head with a steel cutting edge, fixed to a handle.

ax-il (ak′sil), *n.* the angle between a leaf or branch and the stem or trunk to which it it attached.

ax-i-om (ak′si-um), *n.* a self-evident truth; a statement accepted without proof. An axiom of geometry is,

all (ōl), ôr; up, mūte, cûr, cōōl, book; oil, out; th, thin; *th*, the.

"The shortest distance between two points is the straight line between them."—*adj.* **ax'i-o-mat'ic.**

ax-is (ak'sis), *n.* [*pl.* axes (ak'sēz)], a straight line, real or imaginary, about which a body turns, or may be supposed to turn; as, the earth's *axis.*

ax-le (ak'sl), *n.* the bar on which a wheel turns; also, the centre rod of a wheel which revolves along with it.

ax-le-tree (ak'sl-trē'), *n.* a bar between opposite wheels on a vehicle, on the ends of which the wheels turn.

ay (ī), *adv.* yes; even so:—*n.* [*pl.* ayes (īz)], a vote, or one who votes, in the affirmative.

aye (ā), *adv.* always; forever; on all occasions.

a-za-le-a (a-zā'li-a, a-zāl'ya), *n.* a shrub of the heath family, grown for its abundant and brilliant flowers.

az-ure (ā'zhūr; azh'ẽr), *adj.* sky blue:—*n.* 1, clear blue sky; 2, a sky-blue colour.

B

B, b (bē), *n.* [*pl.* B's, b's], 1, the second letter of the alphabet, following A; 2, the seventh tone in the major scale of C.

baa (bä), *v.i.* [baaed (bäd), baa-ing], to bleat or cry as a sheep or lamb:—*n.* the bleating of a sheep or lamb.

babble (bab'l), *v.i.* [bab-bled, bab-bling], 1, to talk indistinctly or imperfectly; 2, to talk childlishly or foolishly; 3, to chatter; also, to make a murmuring sound:—*v.t.* 1, to utter indistinctly or imperfectly; as, he *babbled* his words; 2, to blab (secrets):—*n.* 1, foolish talk; 2, a confused prattle or continuous murmuring:—*n.* **bab'bler.**

babe (bāb), *n.* a young child; baby.

ba-bel (bā'bel), *n.* a scene of noise and confusion; tumult.

ba-boon (ba-bōōn'), *n.* a kind of large, Old World monkey, usually with a short tail and a doglike face.

ba-by (bā'bi), *n.* [*pl.* babies], a child in arms; a young or small child.—*adj.* **ba'byish.**—*n.* **ba'by-hood:**—*n.* **ba'by-sit'ter.**

bac-cha-nal (bak'a-nal'), *n.* a drunken revel or reveller.

bach-e-lor (bach'e-lẽr), *n.* 1, a man who has never married; 2, one who has taken the first degree at a college or university; as, a *bachelor* of arts, etc.

ba-cil-lus (ba-sil'us), *n.* [*pl.* bacilli (-lī)], a rod-shaped bacterium; *pl.* loosely, any harmful bacteria.

back (bak), *n.* 1, in man and other animals having a backbone, the hinder or upper surface of the body from the neck to the end of the backbone; also, the corresponding part in other animals; 2, the opposite of the front; the hinder part; as, the kitchen is at the *back* of the house; 3, the side of anything away from, or out of sight of, the beholder; as, put the inkstand at the *back* of the desk; 4, the part of a book where the leaves are sewed in; 5, the part of a knife, sword, etc., opposite to the cutting edge; 6, the vertical part of a chair, bench, or the like, against which one can lean when sitting; as, the *back* of a sofa:—*v.t.* 1, to move backward or to the rear; as, to *back* a car; 2, to second or support; as, we *back* Jones for president; he *backed* up his proposal with a donation:—*v.i.* to go or move backward or to the rear:—*adj.* 1, lying or being behind as to time, situation, or direction; as, *back* numbers of a magazine; a *back* porch; 2, overdue; in arrears; as, *back* pay:—*adv.* 1, to or toward the rear; 2, to or toward a former place or state; as, to bring *back* a borrowed book; *back* to normal conditions; 3, to or toward time past; 4, in return; as, to pay *back.*

back-bench-er (bak'ben'chẽr), *n.* a member of Parliament who occupies a rear seat and seldom participates in debates.

back-bite (bak'bīt'), *v.t.* and *v.i.* to slander or speak evil of one absent.

back-bone (bak'bōn'), *n.* 1, the spine; 2, firmness; moral courage.

back-door (bak'dōr'), *adj.* underhand; unworthily secret; as, his *backdoor* methods revolted us. Also **back'stairs'.**

back-drop (bak'drop'), *n.* the rear curtain of a theatre's stage.

back-field (bak'fēld'), *n.* in *football,* the players behind the front line.

back-fire (bak'fīr'), *n.* 1, in a gasoline engine, an explosion of gas that occurs at the wrong time, or in the wrong part of the engine; 2, a fire started to check a prairie fire by burning a space in its path:—*v.i.* to bring opposite results to those expected; as, our plot *backfired.*

back-ground (bak'ground'), *n.* 1, the distant parts of any scene or landscape, or the corresponding part of a picture; **2**, a surface upon which patterns or designs are drawn, printed, etc.; **3**, a place out of sight; retirement; as, she modestly kept in the *background*.

back-hand (bak′hand′), *n*. **1**, backward-slanting handwriting; **2**, a backhanded stroke.

back-hand-ed (bak′han′did) or **backhand** (bak′hand′), *adj*. **1**, made with the back of the hand, or with the hand turned backward; as, a *backhanded* stroke; **2**, not straightforward; insincere; as, a *backhanded* warning.

back-ing (bak′ing), *n*. **1**, material used to strengthen (at the back); **2**, supporters; **3**, aid, support.

back-lash (bak′lash′), *n*. **1**, a play (in machinery) owing to worn or loose parts; **2**, a snarl in a reeled fishing-line.

back-log (bak′log′), *n*. a reserve, as of unfilled orders.

back-slide (bak′slīd′; bak′slīd′), *v.i.* [*p.t.* backslid (-slid′), *p.p.* backslid or backslid-den (-slid′n), *p.pr.* backsliding], to slip back, esp. to slip away from a religion, habit, etc.—*n.* **back′ slid′er.**

back-stop (bak′stop′), *n*. a screen or fence to stop balls from going too far.

back-ward (bak′wêrd), *adj*. **1**, directed to the rear; as, a *backward* look; **2**, retiring; bashful; **3**, behind in learning or progress; dull; as, a *backward* pupil; **4**, behindhand; late; as, a *backward* season.—*adv.* **back′ward; back′wards.** —*n.* **back′ward-ness.**

back-wa-ter (bak′wô′tẽr), *n*. **1**, dammed-up, or stagnant, water; hence, **2**, an isolated place; as, we live in a cultural *backwater*.

back-woods (bak′woodz′), *n.pl.* forests or partly cleared land on the outskirts of a new settlement.—*n.* **back′woods′man.**

ba-con (bā′kun), *n*. the salted and dried or smoked flesh of the hog, esp. that from the back and sides.

bac-te-ri-a (bak-tē′ri-a), *n.pl.* [*sing.* bacterium (bak-tē′ri-um)], a widely distributed group of tiny plants, invisible without a microscope, living on plant and animal tissues, dead or alive, and causing a great variety of processes and conditions affecting vegetable and animal life, as decay, fermentation, soil enrichment, and, in some cases, disease. —*adj.* **bac-te′ri-al.**

bac-te-ri-ol-o-gy (bak-tē′ri-ol′o-ji), *n*. the science that deals with bacteria:— *n.* **bac-te′ri-ol′o-gist.**

bad (bad), *adj.* [*comp.* worse, *superl.* worst], **1**, evil; morally wicked; vicious; as, *bad* company; **2**, of poor quality; defective; as, *bad* eggs; *bad* housing conditions; legally worthless, as a coin; **3**, severe; as, a *bad* cold; **4**, ill; in poor health:—*n.* that which is wrong, defective, corrupting, or the like.—*adv.* **bad′ly.**—*n.* **bad′ness.**

bade (bad), *p.t.* of *bid*.

badge (baj), *n*. a distinctive mark, sign, or token to denote the occupation or achievements of the person by whom it is worn; as, a policeman's *badge;* the Roman toga was the *badge* of manhood.

badg-er (baj′ẽr), *n*. a hairy, flesh-eating, burrowing animal, about two feet long:—*v.t.* to tease; worry; pester: from the former practice of baiting badgers for sport.

bad-lands (bad′landz′), *n*. barren lands where erosion has cut dry soil or soft rock into strange shapes; as, the Alberta *badlands*.

bad-min-ton (bad′min-ton), *n*. a tennis-like game in which feathered corks (shuttlecocks) are batted with light racquets to and fro across a net.

baf-fle (baf′l), *v.t.* [baf-fled, baf-fling], to check or interfere with (a person) by placing difficulties in his way; hence, to foil, or hamper (efforts or plans).

bag (bag), *n*. **1**, a sack; pouch; wallet; **2**, the amount contained in a sack; as, a *bag* of grain; **3**, all the game secured by a sportsman in a day:—*v.t.* [bagged, bagging], **1**, to enclose in a bag; **2**, to secure or capture; as, to *bag* game:— *v.i.* to bulge; hang down like a full bag.—*adj.* **bag′gy.**

bag-a-telle (bag′a-tel′), *n*. a trifle; as, a mere *bagatelle*.

bag-gage (bag′ij), *n*. **1**, the tents, clothing, utensils, etc., of an army; **2**, the trunks, packages, etc., which a traveller takes with him; luggage.

bag-pipe (bag′pīp′), *n*. a shrill Scottish musical instrument consisting of a leather bag from which air is forced by the player's arm into pipes.—*n.* **bag′-pip′er.**

¹bail (bāl), *v.t.* in law: **1**, to turn over (a defendant or prisoner) to persons who promise to be responsible for his appearance in court when summoned; as, the magistrate *bailed* the accused thief to Mr. Smith; **2**, to obtain the release of (a person) by promising to pay a certain sum if he does not appear in court or when wanted; as, Mr. Smith *bailed* his friend out of jail:—*n.* in law: **1**, temporary freedom given a defendant or prisoner, said to be out *on bail*, when security is given for his appearance when wanted; **2**, security so given.

²bail (bāl), *v.t.* **1**, to dip (water) out of a

boat; **2,** to empty (a boat) by this process:—*n.* the dipper used in bailing.

bail-iff (bāl'if), *n.* **1,** a sheriff's officer or constable; **2,** in England, an overseer on an estate.

bail out, *v.i.* leap, with a parachute, from a flying aircraft.

bairn (bârn), *n.* (Scottish), a child.

bait (bāt), *n.* any substance, esp. real or sham food, used to entice or allure fish or other animals with a view to catching them:—*v.t.* **1,** to prepare (a fishhook, trap, or snare) by placing bait so as to attract an animal; **2,** to torment or worry with dogs; as, bears were formerly *baited* for sport; to tease or annoy (a person).

baize (bāz), *n.* a coarse woollen fabric, often green in colour, used for table covers, etc.

bake (bāk), *v.t.* and *v.i.* [baked, bak-ing], **1,** to cook or be cooked in an oven; as, she is *baking* cakes; the cake is *baking;* **2,** to dry or harden by dry heat.—*n.* **bak'er.—*n.* bak'er-y.**

bak-ing—pow-der (bāk'ing–pou'dėr), *n.* a white powder used to bring about the quick rising of biscuits, cakes, etc.

bak-ing so-da, bicarbonate of soda.

bal-ance (bal'ans), *n.* **1,** an apparatus for weighing, consisting in its simplest form of a beam pivoted at its middle, with hooks, platforms, or pans suspended from the ends; **2,** the condition of a scale when the beam is about horizontal; hence, equality of any opposing forces; equilibrium or steadiness; **3,** general good sense; sanity; **4,** an equality between the two sides of an account; also, the excess shown on either side; **5,** in a watch, the wheel which regulates the rate of running:— *v.t.* [balanced, balanc-ing], **1,** to weigh on a balance; **2,** to weigh in the mind; hence, to compare or estimate; as, we *balanced* the good against the bad; **3,** to find out the difference between the debits and credits of (an account); **4,** to steady:—*v.i.* **1,** to be of the same weight, force or amount as something else; as, the advantages of the two plans *balance;* **2,** to keep one's balance.

bal-co-ny (bal'ko-ni), *n.* [*pl.* balconies], a platform or gallery built to jut out from a wall, and enclosed by a balustrade or railing. It may be either on the outside or the inside of a building.

bald (bôld), *adj.* **1,** bare of hair; **2,** without the natural or usual covering of hair, feathers, fur, or foliage, upon the head, top, or summit; **3,** of birds, having a white head; as, a *bald* eagle; **4,** unadorned; bare; as, a *bald* statement:—*adv.* **bald'ly.—*n.* bald'ness.**

bal-der-dash (bôl'dėr-dash'), *n.* nonsense; senseless talk or writing; jargon.

bal-dric (bôl'drik), *n.* an ornate belt, worn diagonally from shoulder to hip, to support a bugle, sword, etc.

bale (bāl), *n.* **1,** a large and closely pressed package of merchandise prepared for storage or transportation.— *v.t.* [baled, bal-ing], to make into bales; as, to *bale* cotton or hay.

bale-ful (bāl'fool), *adj.* full of deadly intent; destructive.—*adv.* **bale'ful-ly.**

balk (bôk), *v.i.* to stop short and refuse to go, as a stubborn horse:—*v.t.* to hinder or check; prevent (a person) from doing something:—*n.* **1,** a barrier; hindrance; **2,** in *baseball,* an incompleted pitch, entitling a runner to advance a base. Also spelled **baulk.—*adj.* balk'y; baulk'y.**

¹ball (bôl), *n.* **1,** a round or roundish body or mass; a sphere; esp., such a body, solid or inflated, used in playing a game; **2,** a bullet or other missile shot from firearms; **3,** a game played with a ball: **4,** in baseball, a pitched ball, not struck at, which does not pass over the plate between the levels of the batsman's shoulders and knees:—*v.t.* and *v.i.* to form into a ball.

²ball (bôl), *n.* a large, formal, social gathering for dancing.

bal-lad (bal'ad), *n.* **1,** a short narrative poem, suitable for reciting or singing; **2,** a simple song, often sentimental.

bal-last (bal'ast), *n.* **1,** heavy material carried to give steadiness or balance, as in a ship or a balloon; **2,** stones in the spaces between the ties of a railway track; **3,** that which gives strength to the character:—*v.t.* to steady with a weight; as, to *ballast* the bow of a canoe with a rock.

ball—bearing (bôl'–bâr'ing), *n.* a bearing in which a shaft turns smoothly upon balls of metal which turn with it.—*adj.* **ball'—bear'ing.**

ball—cock (bôl'–kok'), *n.* a self-regulating tap or valve, as in a flush-toilet. Also **ball valve.**

bal-let (bal'ā, ba-lā'), *n.* **1,** an elaborate and artistic dance; **2,** the company of persons who perform the dance.

bal-lis-tics (ba-lis'tiks), *n.pl.* the science of the motion of projectiles, as bullets, bombs, shells, etc. —ICBM, intercontinental *ballistic* missile.

bal-loon (ba-loon'), *n.* a large airtight bag of prepared silk or other material, which when filled with a gas that is lighter than air, such as hydrogen or helium, rises and floats in the air:—*v.i.* **1,** to go up in a balloon; **2,** to expand or swell out.—*n.* **bal-loon'ist.**

bal-lot (bal′ut), *n.* **1,** a ball, ticket, or paper used in voting; **2,** the system of secret voting by use of a printed form; **3,** the act of voting; as, the second *ballot;* also, the total number of votes cast:—*v.i.* to vote by ballot.

ball-room (bôl′rōōm′), *n.* a large room for dancing.

bal-ly-hoo (bal′i-hōō′; bal′i-hōō′), *n. Colloq.,* **1,** sensational advertising; propaganda; **2,** noisy uproar:—*v.t.* loud promotion of a cause or product.

balm (bäm), *n.* **1,** an oily, gummy substance coming from certain trees or shrubs, used for healing or soothing; balsam; **2,** anything that heals or soothes; as, praise was *balm* to his wounded vanity.

balm-y (bäm′i), *adj.* [balm-i-er, balm-i-est], soft; mild; soothing; also, spicy; fragrant.—*n.* **balm′i-ness.**

ba-lo-ney (ba-lō′ni), *interj. Slang,* nonsense; buncombe.

bal-sa (bôl′sa; bäl′sa), *n.* a light wood used for airplane models, rafts, etc.

bal-sam (bôl′sam), *n.* **1,** an oily, fragrant substance obtained from certain trees and used for medicine or in perfumery; balm; **2,** a kind of evergreen tree or shrub, yielding an oily, resinous substance; **3,** a flowering plant, with flowers like those of the Lady's slipper; **4,** Canada *balsam,* a fir.

bal-us-ter (bal′us-tėr), *n.* one of a set of small pillars that support the handrail of a parapet or balustrade.

bal-us-trade (bal′-us-trād′), *n.* a row of small pillars, or balusters, topped by a protective rail, as along the edge of a bridge, balcony, or staircase.

Balustrade

bam-boo (bam-bōō′), *n.* a tropical, treelike plant of the grass family, with hard, thick, jointed stems, used for poles, canes, etc.

bamboo-zle (bam-bōō′zl), *v.t.* [-zled, -zling], *Colloq.* to trick; cheat; mislead.

ban (ban), *n.* **1,** the formal forbidding of an act, as by law; as, a *ban* on lotteries; **2,** condemnation, as by public opinion; **3,** excommunication by the church:—*v.t.* [banned, ban-ning], **1,** to curse; call evil down upon; **2,** to prohibit; forbid; as, noise is *banned* in the library.

ban-al (bān′al; ba-nal′; ba′nal), *adj.* trite; hackneyed; commonplace.

ba-nan-a (ba-nan′a; ba-nä′na), a tropical treelike plant which grows 20 feet high and bears a long, hanging cluster of sweet fruit; also the fruit.

¹band (band), *n.* **1,** a thin, flat, flexible strip used for binding or supporting; a strip of trimming or lining, as on a hat or a sleeve; **2,** a stripe; as, a *band* of white around a pole:—*v.t.* to tie or mark with a band.

²band (band), *n.* **1,** a company united by a common purpose; as, a *band* of robbers or soldiers; **2,** a company of musicians, esp. one playing music suitable for outdoors:—*v.t.* and *v.i.* to unite; bring together into a company.

bandage (ban′dij), *n.* a strip of cloth used in dressing wounds, sprains, etc.:—*v.t.* [bandaged, bandaging], to dress, cover, or bind, as wounds, with a strip of any soft material.

ban-dann-a or **ban-dan-a** (ban-dan′-a), *n.* a large silk or cotton handkerchief, with figures on a coloured background.

band-box (band′boks′), *n.* a pasteboard box for holding hats, etc.

ban-deau (ban-dō′; ban′dō), *n.* a narrow headband; a ribbon for the hair.

ban-dit (ban′dit), *n.* [*pl.* bandits or banditti (ban-dit′i)], an outlaw; robber.

band-master (band′mås′tėr), *n.* a leader of a band.

ban-do-leer, ban-do-lier (ban′do-lēr′), *n.* a shoulder-belt with cartridge-loops.

band-wagon (band′wag′un), *n.* a wagon carrying a band (in a parade); to climb *on the band-wagon,* to be on the popular or winning side, as in an election.

ban-dy (ban′di), *v.t.* [bandied, bandy-ing], **1,** to knock to and fro, as a ball; **2,** to give and take; exchange; as, to *bandy* words.

ban-dy—leg-ged (ban′di–leg′id; -legd), *adj.* bowlegged.

bane (bān), *n.* **1,** originally, poison: still used in names of plants; as, wolf's-*bane;* **2,** a cause of ruin or destruction; curse; as, drink is the *bane* of his life.

bane-ful (bān′fool), *adj.* harmful; destructive; deadly.—*adv.* **bane′ful-ly.**

¹bang (bang), *v.t.* **1,** to beat noisily; thump; as, to *bang* an anvil or a piano; **2,** to shut or put down noisily; as, to *bang* a door; to *bang* down a book:—*v.i.* **1,** to strike a noisy blow; as, to *bang* upon a piano or a door; **2,** to make a loud or sudden noise; as, the gun *banged:—n.* **1,** a heavy, noisy blow; whack; as, I gave the pan a *bang;* **2,** a loud, sudden noise; an explosive sound:—*adv.* suddenly; with a noisy sound; as, *bang* went another tire.

²bang (bang), *v.t.* to cut (the hair over the forehead) straight across:—**bangs,** *n.pl.* or, sometimes, **bang,** *sing.* hair cut to a short fringe over the forehead.

ban-gle (bang′gl), *n.* **1,** an ornamental ring worn upon the wrists and ankles in India and Africa; **2,** one of several slender bracelets worn together.

ban-ian (ban′yan), *n.* an East Indian tree, the branches of which send roots down to the ground, so as to form new trunks. Also spelled **ban′yan.**

ban-ish (ban′ish), *v.t.* **1,** to drive out; condemn to exile; expel; as, to *banish* an alien from a country; **2,** to drive out of the mind; as, to *banish* care or fear.—*n.* **ban′ish-ment.**

ban-is-ter (ban′is-tėr), *n.* a baluster:— **banisters,** a balustrade of a staircase.

ban-jo (ban′jō), *n.* [*pl.* banjos], a stringed musical instrument somewhat like a guitar, having a long neck, and a body like a tambourine.—*n.* **ban′jo-ist.**

¹**bank** (bangk), *n.* **1,** a ridge of earth; **2,** a heap, mound, or large mass; as, a *bank* of clouds or snow; **3,** the land at the edge or margin of a stream; **4,** a shallow place in the sea or at the mouth of a river; a shoal; **5,** a slope:—*v.t.* **1,** to cover (a fire) with ashes or packed coal, to prevent rapid burning; **2,** to pile up; as, he *banked* leaves against the wall:—*v.i.* in aeronautics, to tip an aeroplane when going round a curve.

²**bank** (bangk), *n.* an institution which receives money from its depositors for safekeeping, lends money at interest, and assists in transactions requiring the transfer of money:—*v.t.* to place (money) in a bank:—*v.i.* **1,** to have an account with a bank; **2,** *Colloq.,* to rely; count; as, I *bank* on him to do his part.

bank-book (bangk′book′), *n.* a book recording a depositor's account at a bank; a pass-book.

bank-er (bangk′ėr), *n.* a person engaged in banking; **2,** a man or vessel employed in fishing on the Newfoundland Banks.

bank-ing (bangk′ing), *n.* the business of lending, issuing, or caring for money.

bank—note (bangk′—nōt), *n.* a piece of paper resembling government paper money, and used as money, but issued by a bank.

bank-rupt (bangk′rupt), *n.* a person who is legally declared to be unable to pay his debts, and whose property is divided among his creditors in proportion to their claims:—*adj.* unable to meet one's debts:—*v.t.* to make poor or insolvent.—*n.* **bank′rupt-cy.**

ban-ner (ban′ėr), *n.* a piece of cloth attached to a pole, and usually worked with some device or motto; an ensign; flag:—*adj.* unusually good; as, a *banner* year.

ban-nis-ter (ban′is-tėr) *n.* a banister.

ban-nock (ban′uk), *n.* a thick, flat, oatmeal cake baked on a griddle.

banns (banz), *n.pl.* notice, given in church, of a proposed marriage.

ban-quet (bang′kwit), *n.* an elaborate feast or large formal dinner:—*v.t.* and *v.i.* to feed elaborately; to feast.

ban-tam (ban′tam), *n.* **1,** a breed of small, but aggressive, fowl; **2,** a small pugnacious person; **3,** a small size or weight of boy eligible for a *bantam* team.

ban-tam—weight (ban′tam—wāt′), *n.* and *adj.* a boxer who weighs from 113 to 118 pounds.

ban-ter (ban′tėr), *n.* good-natured teasing:—*v.t.* tɔ make fun of; tease with good humour.—*adv.* **ban′ter-ing-ly.**

ban-yan (ban′yan), *n.* Same as **banian.**

bap-tize (bap-tīz′), *v.t.* [baptized, baptizing], **1,** to sprinkle with water, or immerse in water, as a religious ceremony, esp. in admitting to a Christian church; **2,** to purify; **3,** to christen; name; as, the boy was *baptized* John.—*n.* **bap′tism.**—*adj.* **bap-tis′mal** (bap-tiz′mal).

bar (bär), *n.* **1,** a rigid piece of wood, metal, or other solid matter, long in proportion to its thickness; **2,** a barrier; **3,** a bank of sand, gravel, or the like, under water, obstructing the passage of ships; **4,** the place in court where prisoners are stationed for trial or sentence; also, the court itself; **5,** those who are permitted to try cases in court; lawyers as a class; **6,** a counter over which liquor is sold as a beverage, or a room containing such a counter; **7,** a band or stripe; as, a *bar* of red in a border; **8,** one of the series of upright lines drawn through a staff of written music, dividing it into equal measures of time; also, the space between two such bars or lines; **9,** a meteorological unit of atmospheric pressure:—*prep.* but; except; as, *bar* none:—*v.t.* [barred, bar-ring], **1,** to fasten with a bar; as, to *bar* a door or a window; **2,** to hinder; obstruct; as, the police *barred* the way.

barb (bärb), *n.* the sharp point extending backward in an arrow, fishhook, etc.:—*v.t.* to furnish with barbs.—*adj.* **barbed.**

bar-bar-i-an (bär-bâr′i-an), *n.* **1,** in ancient history, a foreigner; one not a Greek or a Roman, and therefore regarded as uncivilized; **2,** a person of uncultivated taste:—*adj.* rude; uncivilized; savage.

bar-bar-ic (bär-bar′ik), *adj.* belonging to, or characteristic of, uncivilized people; as, *barbaric* cruelty; *barbaric* splendour.

bar-ba-rism (bär'ba-rizm), *n.* **1,** the state of being uncivilized; **2,** rudeness; ignorance of art and literature; **3,** a word or expression not in good use.

bar-bar-i-ty (bär-bar'i-ti), *n.* [*pl.* —ties], brutal or inhuman conduct.

bar-ba-rous (bär'ba-rus), *adj.* **1,** uncivilized; outlandish; rude; **2,** of language, crude; unpolished; **3,** cruel; inhuman.

bar-be-cue (bär'be-kū'), *n.* **1,** any meat broiled on a grill over an open fire; the grill and its frame; **2,** an out-of-doors feast where meat is so cooked and eaten:—*v.t.* so to prepare and serve meat, etc.

bar-ber (bär'bėr), *n.* one whose business is shaving, haircutting, and hairdressing.

bar-ber-ry (bär'bėr-i), *n.* [*pl.* barberries], a prickly shrub bearing berries which turn red in the fall; also, the berry.

bar-bi-tu-rate (bär-bit'ū-rāt'; bär'-bi-tū'rāt), *n.* one of a large group of drugs used to reduce tension, anxiety, etc.

bar-car-ole, -olle (bär'ka-rōl'), *n.* **1,** a boating song of Venetian gondoliers; **2,** any song in this style.

bard (bärd), *n.* in ancient times, a poet and singer who made and sang verses about heroes, etc.; hence, any poet.

bare (bâr), *adj.* **1,** not covered; as, a *bare* hillside; esp., not covered with clothing; as, *bare* arms; **2,** unadorned; simple; plainly or scantily furnished; as, *bare* lodgings; **3,** scanty; as, he earned a *bare* living:—*v.t.* [bared, baring], to uncover; expose.—*n.* **bare'ness.**

bare-back (bâr'bak'), *adj.* and *adv.* on a horse without a saddle.

bare-faced (bâr'fāst'), *adj.* unconcealed; bold; impudent; as, *barefaced* frauds.

bare-foot (bâr'foot'), *adj.* with bare feet.

bare-headed (bâr'hed'id), *adj.* with head bare.

bare-ly (bâr'li), *adv.* **1,** only just; hence, hardly; scarcely; as, he had *barely* enough time; **2,** scantily; poorly.

bar-gain (bär'gin), *n.* **1,** an agreement on the terms of a deal; as, they closed the *bargain* at $5 a load; **2,** something offered, bought, or sold, at a low price:—*v.i.* to make a bargain or trade; also, to discuss the terms of an agreement; haggle.

barge (bärj), *n.* **1,** a large, roomy, flat-bottomed vessel, used for carrying freight or passengers; **2,** a large boat of a warship, used by a flag-officer.—*n.* **barge'man.**

bar-i-tone (bar'i-tōn'), *n.* Same as **barytone.**

¹bark (bärk), *n.* the outer covering of trees and other woody plants:—*v.t.* to strip bark or skin from; as, to *bark* a tree; *bark* one's shin.

²bark, barque, bark-en-tine (bärk; bär'ken-tēn'), *n.* **1,** a three-masted sailing ship; **2,** *Poetic,* any small ship.

³bark (bärk), *n.* the sound made by a dog:—*v.i.* to utter a bark, as a dog.

bar-ker (bär'kėr), *n.* a person, often with megaphone or amplifier, who attracts customers at a sideshow, etc.

bar-ley (bär'li), *n.* **1,** a grain used as a food and in the manufacture of malt liquors; **2,** the plant yielding the grain.

barm (bärm), *n.* yeast formed on fermenting liquors.—*adj.* **barmy,** frothy; hence, silly (Colloq.).

barn (bärn), *n.* a farm building for housing livestock, keeping tools, and storing hay, grain, and other produce.

bar-na-cle (bär'na-kl), *n.* **1,** a small sea animal living in a white shell and fastening itself to rocks or the bottoms of ships; **2,** a hanger-on.

barn-storm (bärn'stôrm'), *v.i.* and *v.t.* **1,** to perform plays, give lectures, or stage exhibitions in small towns; as, the Maple Leafs went on a *barnstorming* tour of Japan.

barn-yard (bärn'yärd'), *n.* a yard adjoining a barn:—*adj.* fit for a barnyard; as, *barnyard* manners.

ba-rom-e-ter (ba-rom'e-tėr), *n.* an instrument for measuring the pressure of the air, used in showing height above sea level and in forecasting weather.—*adj.* **bar'o-met'ric** (bar'ō-met'rik) or **bar'-o-met'ri-cal.**

bar-on (bar'on), *n.* **1,** in English history, one who held an estate directly from the king; **2,** in Great Britain and other countries, a noble of the lowest rank within the nobility; also, the rank itself.—*n.fem.* **bar'on-ess.**—*adj.* **baro'ni-al.**

bar-on-et (bar'un-et), *n.* a rank of honour between baron and knight; also, a person holding this rank.—*n.* **bar'on-et-cy.**

bar-racks (bar'aks), *n.pl.* a large structure or a row of buildings for lodging soldiers or workmen.

bar-ra-cu-da (bar'a-kōō'da), *n.* a fierce, edible, pikelike fish of tropical seas.

¹bar-rage (ba-räzh'), *n.* **1,** a curtain of protective artillery or bombing fire under which an advance is made, or to prevent an enemy from advancing; **2,** an attack in words, blows, etc.

²bar-rage (bär′ij), *n.* a dam on a stream or river.

bar-rel (bar′el), *n.* 1, a round, bulging cask or vessel, greater in length than in width, usually of wood, with flat ends or heads; 2, the quantity which a full barrel contains; 3, a tubelike part; as, the *barrel* of a gun or of a fountain-pen:—*v.t.* [barrelled, barrel-ling], to put or pack in a barrel.

bar-ren (bar′en), *adj.* 1, unable to bear, or not bearing, children or young; also, not producing fruit; as, a *barren* plant; 2, not fertile; as, *barren* land; 3, without profit; empty; as, *barren* labour:—*n.* (usually *barrens*), a sandy, wooded track.

Barren Grounds or Lands, the bare windswept Canadian tundra northwest of Hudson Bay. It has a few Eskimos, trappers, etc.

bar-ri-cade (bar′i-kād′), *n.* a fortification made of such materials as are nearest to hand, and serving to obstruct an enemy or shield a besieged party:—*v.t.* [barricad-ed, barricad-ing], to obstruct or fortify with a barricade.

bar-ri-er (bar′i-ėr), *n.* 1, anything that prevents progress or approach; 2, a fence or wall to keep people out.

bar-ring (bär′ing), *prep.* except for; as, *barring* delay, I shall arrive Tuesday.

bar-ris-ter (bar′is-tėr), *n.* a lawyer who argues cases in superior courts; an attorney.

¹bar-row (bar′ō), *n.* a flat, oblong frame with projecting handles (a *hand-barrow*), or with a wheel at one end and shafts at the other (a *wheel-barrow*), for carrying or wheeling loads.

²bar-row (bar′ō), *n.* in early times, a mound of earth or stones raised over a grave.

bar-ten-der (bär′ten′dėr), *n.* one who serves liquor at a bar.

bar-ter (bär′tėr), *v.t.* to give in exchange for something; as, to *barter* oats for groceries:—*n.* the trade or exchange of one thing for another without the use of money.

bar-y-tone (bar′i-tōn′), *n.* a male voice between tenor and bass; also, a person who has a voice whose tones range between tenor and bass:—*adj.* having, or suited to, a barytone voice.

bas-al (bās′al), *adj.* having to do with a base or foundation; used as a base; also fundamental; basic.

ba-salt (ba-sôlt′; bas′ôlt), *n.* a dark, fine-grained, igneous rock of columnar structure.

bas-cule (bas′kūl), *n.* an apparatus on the principle of a seesaw or teeter-totter; as, a **bascule bridge**, a counterpoised drawbridge.

¹base (bās), *n.* 1, the part of a thing on which it rests; as, the *base* of a statue; 2, one of the principal or fundamental parts of which anything is made; as, the *base* of some soups is meat stock; 3, the line or point from which an operation starts, as in surveying or in a race; 4, in baseball and some other games, a station or goal; 5, a secure or fortified location used as a starting point for operations, for storage of supplies, etc.; as, a military or naval *base;* 6, in chemistry, a substance that combines with an acid to form a salt; an alkali:—*v.t.* [based, bas-ing], 1, to found; establish; as, he *bases* his hopes on news reports; his business is *based* on honesty; 2, to set on a base; as, to *base* a statue on concrete.

²base (bās), *adj.* 1, inferior in quality; of little value; as, *base* materials; 2, mixed with inferior metal; as, a *base* coin; 3, morally bad; mean; vile; as, *base* motives; 4, low or deep in sound; bass:—*adv.* **base′ly.**—*n.* **base′ness.**

base-ball (bās′bôl′),*n.* 1, a game, very popular in Canada and the U.S., played with a bat and ball by nine players on a side, on a field with four stations, or bases, arranged in the shape of a diamond; 2, the ball used in this game. Also, **base hit, base-line,** etc.

base-board (bās′bōrd′), *n.* a wide moulding running around the lower part of the wall, against the floor.

base-less (bās′lis), *adj.* without foundation; groundless; as, *baseless* fears.

base-ment (bās′ment), *n.* the lowest story of a building, usually below the level of the ground.

¹bas-es (bās′iz), *n.pl.* of base.

²bas-es (bā′sēz), *n.pl.* of basis.

bash (bash), *v.t.* [bashed, bashing], *Colloq.* to strike a smashing blow; as, to *bash in.*—*n.* a violent blow.

bash-ful (bash′fool), *adj.* shy; easily embarrassed; as, a *bashful* suitor.—*adv.* **bash′ful-ly.**—*n.* **bash′ful-ness.**

bas-ic (bās′ik), *adj.* fundamental; essential; as, *basic* reasons; a *basic* wage, fact, etc.

ba-sil-i-ca (ba-sil′i-ka), *n.* [*pl.* basilicas], 1, in ancient Rome, an oblong hall with columns along the two sides and a semicircular recess, or apse, at one end; 2, a church built on such a plan.

ba-sin (bā′sn), *n.* 1, a round, wide vessel for holding water or other liquid; 2, the quantity such a vessel will hold; 3, a hollow or enclosed place containing water, as a dock for ships; **4,** all the land drained by a river and its branches.

ba-sis (bā′sis), *n.* [*pl.* bases (bā′sēz)], **1,** a reason; cause; foundation; as, a a *basis* for doubt; **2,** a fundamental part or ingredient.

bask (bàsk), *v.i.* to lie in comfortable warmth, as in the sun or before a fire.

bas-ket (bàs′kit), *n.* **1,** a container made of woven rushes, reeds, etc.; **2,** the amount which such a container will hold.—*n.* **bas′ket-work′.**

bas-ket-ball (bàs′kit-bôl′), *n.* **1,** a game played by two teams of five players each, in which a ball about ten inches in diameter must be thrown into basketlike goals placed ten feet above the floor; **2,** the ball used in the game.

bas—re-lief (bä′—ri-lēf′; bä′—ri-lēf′), *n.* a form of sculpture in which the figures stand out very slightly from the background.

¹bass (bas), *n.* [*pl.* bass or basses], an edible fish of both fresh and salt water.

²bass (bās), *adj.* low-toned; deep; low in pitch; as, a *bass* note; a *bass* voice: —*n.* **1,** the lowest part in a musical composition; **2,** the lowest tones of a male voice or of an instrument; **3,** a bass-viol; **4,** a singer or an instrument with a bass part.

bas-si-net (bas′i-net′; bas′i-net), *n.* a wicker basket used as a baby's crib.

bas-soon (ba-sōōn′), *n.* a musical wind-instrument of deep tone, having a long, curved mouthpiece, and a wooden tube.

bass—vi-ol (bās–vī′al), *n.* a musical instrument similar in shape to the violin, the largest in size and lowest in tone of all the stringed instruments: also called *bass.*

bass-wood (bàs′wood′), *n.* a tree with broad leaves, yellowish flowers, and light, durable wood; the linden or lime.

bast (bàst), *n.* the fibrous inner bark of trees (linden, etc.) used for making mats and ropes.

bas-tard (bas′tèrd), *n.* a child born of unmarried parents.

¹baste (bāst), *v.t.* [bast-ed, bast-ing], to sew temporarily with long, loose stitches; as, Mary *basted* her dress before she stitched it on the machine.— *n.* **bast′ings.**

²baste (bāst), *v.t.* [bast-ed, bast-ing], to moisten (roasting meat), esp. with its own juice, to make it tender and juicy.

bas-tille or **bas-tile** (bas-tēl′), *n.* a prison:—**the Bastille,** an old prison in Paris, destroyed by the people in 1789.

bas-tion (bas′chun; bas′ti-un), *n.* a part projecting out from the main body of a fortification.

¹bat (bat), *n.* **1,** a heavy stick, esp. one used to strike the ball in cricket, baseball, etc.; **2,** a turn to hit; **3,** *Colloq.*, a hard blow; **4,** *Slang*, a spree; **5,** cotton batting or **batt:**—*v.t.* [bat-ted, bat-ting], to hit with a bat:—*v.i.* to use a bat in games; as, he *batted* once.— *n.* **bat′ter.**

²bat (bat), *n.* a small animal which flies by night and feeds on fruit and insects. It has a mouselike body and wings formed of skin stretched between the fore limbs, feet, and tail.

batch (bach), *n.* **1,** the quantity of bread baked at one time; **2,** a quantity of material to be used at one time; as, a *batch* of flour; **3,** a group or collection of similar things; as, a *batch* of letters.

bate (bāt), *v.t.* to lower; diminish; moderate; as, with *bated* breath.

ba-teau (bà-tō′), *n.* [*pl.* bateaux (-tōz′)], a light, flat-bottomed river-boat with tapering ends, used by French-Canadians.

bath (bàth), *n.* [*pl.* baths (bàthz)], **1,** a cleansing or washing of the entire body, esp. with water; **2,** the water, liquid, etc., used for bathing; **3,** a vessel holding water for bathing; as, a bird-*bath;* **4,** a building or room fitted up for bathing. Note also **bath′robe′, bath′room′, bath′tub′.**

bathe (bāth), *v.t.* [bathed, bath-ing], **1,** to wash by putting into water, etc.; **2,** to wet; wash; as, the ocean *bathes* the shore; **3,** to surround; envelop; as, a landscape *bathed* in moonlight: —*v.i.* to take a bath.—*n.* **bath′er.**

bat-man (bat′man), *n.* an army officer's orderly.

ba-ton (bà′ton′; bat′un), *n.* **1,** a staff used as a badge of office or symbol of authority; **2,** the stick used by a band or orchestra leader to beat time.

bat-tal-i-on (ba-tal′yun), *n.* two or more companies of foot soldiers.

bat-ten (bat′n), *n.* a thin strip of wood used to: **1,** fasten down canvas (on hatches); **2,** cover a crack; **3,** flatten the leech of a sail; **4,** carry lights for film work:—*v.t.* to fasten with such strips.

¹bat-ter (bat′ẽr), *v.t.* to strike with heavy, repeated blows; as, the sea *battered* the wall; the champion *battered* his opponent:—*v.i.* to strike repeatedly; as, he *battered* at the door:—*n.* a stiff liquid mixture, as of flour, eggs, etc., beaten together before being cooked.

²bat-ter (bat′ẽr), *n.* one who uses a bat, or is at bat. Also **bats′man.**

bat-ter-ing—ram (bat′ẽr-ing–ram′),

n. a large iron-headed beam, used in ancient days to beat down the walls of besieged places.

bat-ter-y (bat′ér-i), *n.*[*pl.* batteries], **1,** an unlawful attack on another; as, he was arrested for assault and *battery;* **2,** two or more cannons placed together for combined action, usually under a single command; as, a field-*battery;* also, the place where they are stationed; as, the forward *battery* on a battleship; **3,** an apparatus for producing or storing electric current; as, a storage-*battery;* **4,** in baseball, the combination of pitcher and catcher; **5,** a number of like things used as a unit; as, a *battery* of lights.

bat-tle (bat′l), *n.* a fight between opposing forces, esp. one between armies or fleets; also, any hard struggle; as, the game was a *battle:—v.i.* [battled, bat-tling], to fight; struggle. Note also **bat′tle-field′, bat′tle-ground′, bat′tle-ship′.**

bat-tle—axe or **bat-tle—ax** (bat′l-aks′), *n.* a broad-faced axe formerly used as a weapon in battle.

bat-tle-ment (bat′l-ment), *n.* a wall for defence, usually at the top of a building or tower with openings through which in ancient times defenders shot at the enemy.

bau-ble (bô′bl), *n.* a trifling piece of finery; anything showy or gay but without real value; as, the prizes given at the fair were mere *baubles.*

baulk (bôk), *n.* Same as **balk.**

baux-ite (bôk′sīt; bō′zīt), *n.* the principal ore of aluminum.

bawd-y (bôd′i), *adj.* lewd; obscene; as, *bawdy* songs or jokes.

bawl (bôl), *v.i.* to cry out loudly; howl; as, the child *bawled* more from temper than from pain:—*v.t.* to call loudly; shout.

¹bay (bā), *n.* an arm of the sea in a sheltered recess or curve in the shore.

²bay (bā), *n.* **1,** the laurel tree; also, a shrub or tree resembling the laurel; **2,** a garland or crown of laurel leaves, formerly given as a mark of honour to conquerors and successful poets.

³bay (bā), *n.* **1,** the deep-toned prolonged cry of a dog; **2,** the position of a person or animal compelled to turn and face an enemy or a danger when no escape is possible; as, a stag at *bay;* also, the position of the pursuers thus held off; as, the guard held five robbers at *bay:—v.i.* to bark with a deep sound; as, the hounds *bayed.*

⁴bay (bā), *adj.* reddish brown in colour: —*n.* a horse of a bay colour.

bayberry (bā′ber-i), *n.*[*pl.* bayberries], a low-growing shrub, common along the sea-coast, bearing round grey berries in clusters; also, the waxy berry. Candles are made from the berries, and the fragrant leaves are used to perfume bay rum.

bay-o-net (bā′o-nit), *n.* a daggerlike weapon attached to the muzzle of a rifle:—*v.t.* [bayonet-ed, bayonet-ing], to stab with a bayonet.

bay-ou (bī′ōō), *n.* [*pl.* bayous], a sluggish, marshy offshoot of a river or lake, as in the southern U.S.

bay rum, a fragrant toilet liquid, perfumed with the leaves of a species of bayberry found in Jamaica.

bay win-dow, the window or windows in a part of a room which extends outward from the line of the wall, built up from the ground level.

ba-zaar or **ba-zar** (ba-zär′), *n.* **1,** in Oriental countries, a market-place or street lined with shops; **2,** a hall or series of rooms with stalls for the sale of goods; **3,** a sale of fancy articles, as in aid of a charity.

ba-zoo-ka (ba-zōō′ka), *n.* a metal tube for launching electrically-fired, armour-piercing rockets.

BB shot (bē′bē′), *n.* a .18-inch size of shot used in air rifles or *BB* guns.

be (bē), *v.i.* [*present sing.* I am, you are, he is, *pl.* are; *p.t.* I was, you were, he was, *pl.* were; *p.p.* been; *p.pr.* be-ing], **1,** to exist; as, there *is* hope; **2,** to stay; remain; occupy a certain place; as, the lesson *is* on this page; **3,** to mean; signify; as, it *is* nothing to me; **4,** to coincide with; equal; as, it *is* I; the girl *is* my sister; **5,** to belong to the class or group of; as, the animal *is* a lion; **6,** as a helping verb used to form: **a,** the progressive form of other verbs; as, he *is* going; **b,** the passive voice; as, I *was* hit.

beach (bēch), *n.* the shore of a body of water which is washed by the waves, esp. the sandy or pebbly part:— *v.t.* and *v.i.* to haul up or land on a beach.

beach-comb-er (bēch′kŏm-ér),·*n.* **1,** a long ocean wave rolling in; **2,** one who lives by gathering wreckage, etc., on a shore, esp. in the South Seas.

beach-head (bēch′hed′), *n.* an area captured or secured by troops landing on a hostile shore.

bea-con (bē′kun), *n.* **1,** a fire or light used as a signal of warning or guidance, as for ships at sea or for aeroplanes on land; also the structure bearing this signal; **2,** anything which serves as a guide; as, faith was his *beacon.*

bead (bēd), *n.* **1,** a little ball of any material, such as wood, glass, or pearl, pierced through and intended to be strung with others to form an ornament; **2,** any small round body; a drop or bubble; as, a *bead* of dew; *beads* of perspiration; **3,** a small knob of metal at the end of a gunbarrel, used in taking aim:—*v.t.* to ornament with beads.— *adj.* **bead'y.**

bea-dle (bē'dl), *n.* a parish officer with minor duties.

bea-gle (bē'gl), *n.* a small, short-legged hound, used esp. in hunting hares.

beak (bēk), *n.* **1,** the bill of a bird; also, the long, sharp mouth of some insects and other animals; **2,** anything pointed or shaped like the bill of a bird, as the prow of ancient war vessels.—*adj.* **beaked** (bēkt; bēk'id).

beak-er (bēk'ēr), *n.* **1,** a large drinking cup or vessel with a wide mouth; **2,** an open-mouthed vessel with a projecting lip, used as a container in laboratories.

beam (bēm), *n.* **1,** a long heavy piece of wood or metal used in the framework of buildings; **2,** one of the principal horizontal supports of a ship; **3,** the widest part of a ship; **4,** the bar of a balance on which the scale pans are hung; **5,** the chief timber of a plow; **6,** a ray of light given out by the sun or any other luminous body; as, the *beam* from a lamp; **7,** a smile:—*v.i.* to gleam; shine; as, his face *beamed* with joy.

beam—ends (bēm'—endz'), *n. pl.* to be on one's beam-ends is to be at the end of one's money or resources, like a ship stranded on her side.

bean (bēn), *n.* **1,** the seed or the long pod of a pod-bearing plant used as food; also, the plant itself; as, a Lima or a string *bean;* **2,** any seed resembling a true bean; as, a coffee *bean.* Note also, *n.* **bean'pole'; bean'stalk'.**

bean-ie (bē'ni), *n.* a small brimless hat made of sections converging to the top. Beanie

¹bear (bâr), *n.* **1,** a large four-footed animal with long shaggy fur and a very short tail, as the cinnamon bear, grizzly bear, polar bear; **2,** a person with rough, uncouth, or surly manners; **3,** on the stock exchange, one who tries to lower prices for his own advantage: opposite of *bull:*—**Bear,** in astronomy, either of two groups of stars in the Northern Hemisphere, called *Great Bear,* containing the *Big Dipper,* and the *Little Bear,* containing the *Little Dipper.*

²bear (bâr), *v.t.* [*p.t.* bore (bōr), *p.p.* borne (bōrn) or born (bôrn), *born* is properly used only in the passive voice of sense 6 when *by* does not follow; as,

a son was *born* to him; he was *born* in 1800; a son *borne by* his first wife), *p.pr.* **bear-ing**], **1,** to support; hold up; as, the pillars *bore* all the weight; **2,** to carry; convey; as, this letter *bears* good news; **3,** to suffer or endure; stand; as, to *bear* pain or sorrow; **4,** to possess, wear, or use, as a weapon; **5,** to show; as, his past record *bears* proof of his guilt; **6,** to bring forth; as, she *bore* many children; **7,** to behave; as, he *bore* himself well:—*v.i.* **1,** to be capable of enduring trouble or pain; as, she *bears* up well under her grief; **2,** to be fruitful; as, this tree always *bears;* **3,** to press or weigh; as, he *bore* too hard on the tool and it broke; **4,** to refer; as, this *bears* on our talk.—*adj.* **bear'a-ble.**

beard (bērd), *n.* **1,** the hair on the chin and cheeks of a man; **2,** anything resembling a beard, esp. the hairs on the heads of certain grains, as barley:—*v.t.* to take by the beard; hence, to oppose face to face; defy.—*adj.* **beard'less.**— *adj.* **beard'ed.**

bear-er (bâr'ēr), *n.* **1,** one who or that which carries; **2,** one who presents a cheque or other order for the payment of money.

bear-ing (bâr'ing), *n.* **1,** the act of one who endures or bears; **2,** behaviour; as, the *bearing* of a gentleman; **3,** meaning; relation; as, this has no *bearing* on the subject; **4,** the act or power of producing; **5,** a part of a machine in which another part turns; as, ball-*bearings;* **6,** (usually *bearings*), direction; way; as, he lost his *bearings* in the fog.

bear-ish (bâr'ish), *adj.* rude: surly; as, *bearish* behaviour.—*n.* **bear'ish-ness.**

beast (bēst), *n.* **1,** a four-footed animal, as distinguished from a bird, insect, fish, or man; **2,** a brutal person.—*adj.* **beastly:**—*n.* **beast'li-ness.**

beat (bēt), *v.t.* [*p.t.* beat, *p.p.* beat-en (bēt'n), *p.pr.* beat-ing], **1,** to strike with many blows; **2,** in hunting, to range over in order to drive out game; as, to *beat* a thicket; **3,** to flap; as, the bird *beat* its wings; **4,** in cooking, to mix by stirring with a spoon or fork; **5,** in music, to measure (time) by strokes; **6,** to defeat; conquer; as, the first team *beat* the second:—*v.i.* **1,** to strike repeatedly; as, waves *beat* upon rocks; **2,** to throb; as, the heart *beats;* **3,** to sail against the wind by tacking; as, the ship *beat* to windward; **4,** *Colloq.,* to win in a contest; as, have you been to the game? who *beat?*—*n.* **1,** a stroke which is made again and again; as, the *beat* of marching feet; **2,** a round frequently traversed; as, a policeman's *beat;* **3,** in music, the rise

all (ôl), **ôr; up, mūte, cûr, cōōl,** book; **oil, out;** th, **thin;** *th,* **the.**

and fall of the stroke marking the divisions of time.—*n.* **beat′er.**

be-a-tif-ic (bē′a-tif′ik), *adj.* giving bliss or joy. **Beatific vision,** a view of the glories of heaven.

beau-ti-cian (bū-tish′un), *n.* one who does hairdressing, manicuring, and massaging in a beauty shop:—*v.t.* **beaut′i-fy.**

be-at-i-tude (bē-at′i-tūd′), *n.* supreme happiness:—**the Beatitudes,** nine statements made in the Sermon on the Mount (Matthew 5:3–12), blessing and declaring blessed, or supremely happy, those who possess certain virtues.

beau (bō), *n.* [*pl.* beaux (bōz; bō) or beaus (bōz)], **1,** a man who follows the latest fashion in dress; a dandy; **2,** an escort; a lover.

beau-te-ous (bū′tē-us), *adj.* beautiful.

beau-ti-ful (bū′ti-fool), *adj.* possessing qualities which delight the mind and senses; lovely.—*adv.* **beau′ti-ful-ly.**

beau-ty (bū′ti), *n.* [*pl.* beauties], **1,** that combination of qualities which pleases the eye or ear, or satisfies in a moral sense; **2,** a particular grace or charm; as, the *beauty* of the country; **3,** a beautiful thing or person, esp. a lovely or beautiful woman.—*v.t.* **beau′ti-fy.**

¹bea-ver (bē′ver), *n.* **1,** a small fur-bearing animal that lives both in water and on land, having a broad, flat, powerful tail, strong teeth formed for gnawing, and webbed hind feet: remarkable for the way in which it fells trees and dams streams; **2,** the fur of this animal; **3,** a gentleman's high hat, formerly made of beaver fur.

²bea-ver (bē′ver), *n.* on an ancient helmet, the movable part that served as protection for the lower part of the face.

be—bop (bē′-bop′), *n.* a jazz style of music marked by off-hand composing, clashing harmonies, lack of restraint, and weird effects.

be-calm (bi-käm′), *v.t.* to make calm or quiet:—**becalmed,** motionless because of a lack of wind, as a sailing vessel.

be-came (bi-kām′), *p.t.* of *become.*

be-cause (bi-kôz′), *conj.* for the reason that; since; as, we came in *because* it rained:—**because of,** on account of; as, I stayed late *because* of my work.

be-chance (bi-chàns′), *v.t.* and *v.i.* to happen; befall.

beck (bek), *n.* a nod or other silent signal given as a sign of command.

beck-on (bek′un), *v.i.* and *v.t.* to signal by a motion of the head or hand; also, to attract; call; as, pleasure *beckons.*

be-cloud (bi-kloud′), *v.t.* **1,** to darken; **2,** to confuse.

be-come (bi-kum′), *v.i.* [*p.t.* became (bi-kām′), *p.p.* become, *p.pr.* becoming], to come or grow to be; as, a boy *becomes* a man:—*v.t.* to suit; be suitable for; as, that hat *becomes* you.

be-com-ing (bi-kum′ing), *adj.* proper; suitable; appropriate; as, a *becoming* hat; a *becoming* pride.—*adv.* **be-com′-ing-ly.**

bed (bed), *n.* **1,** an article of furniture upon which one rests or sleeps; **2,** anything which serves as a bed or resting place; **3,** a portion of a garden; as, a *bed* of pansies; **4,** the base or bottom of anything; as, a *bed* of concrete; the *bed* of a river:—*v.t.* [bed-ded, bed-ding], **1,** to fix for the night; as, I *bedded* the horses; **2,** to plant; **3,** to set; fix; as, to *bed* a pole in concrete. Also, **bed′-cham′ber, bed′clothes′, bed′ding, bed′-pan′, bed′post′, bed′room′, bed′side′, bed′sore′, bed′spring′, bed′time′.**

bed-bug (bed′bug′), *n.* a biting, blood-sucking, flat-bodied insect, of vile odour, infesting furniture, esp. beds.

bed-lam (bed′lam), *n.* **1,** an insane asylum; **2,** any scene of uproar and confusion; as, the jail was a *bedlam* during the riot.

be-drag-gled (bi-drag′ld), *adj.* wet, soiled, and limp; as, a *bedraggled* dress.

bed-ridden (bed′rid′n), *adj.* confined to bed, as by age or illness.

bed-rock (bed′rok′), *n.* **1,** the solid rock underlying the looser upper crust of the earth; **2,** hence, the lowest state or bottom of a thing; as, my savings account has reached *bedrock.*

bed-spread (bed′spred′), *n.* a covering for a bed; a counterpane.

bed-stead (bed′sted′, bed′stid′), *n.* the wood or metal framework of a bed.

bee (bē), *n.* **1,** a winged insect with sucking and stinging organs; esp., the honeybee, which lives with many others in a hive, where it stores pollen and honey; **2,** a social meeting for work or amusement; as, a quilting-*bee;* a spelling-*bee.*

beech (bēch), *n.* a wide-spreading tree with smooth, ash-grey bark and deep-green leaves, yielding hard timber and edible triangular nuts.

beech-nut (bēch′nut′), *n.* the edible, triangular nut of the beech tree.

beef (bēf), *n.* **1,** the flesh of an ox, bull, or cow, used for food; **2,** [*pl.* beeves (bēvz) or beefs (bēfs)], a full-grown ox, bull, or cow, esp. when fattened for market:—*v.i. Slang,* to complain; grumble:—*n.* a complaint.

beef-eat-er (bēf′ēt′ėr), *n.* **1,** one who eats beef; **2,** a yeoman of the guard; esp. a guard of the Tower of London.

cat, āge, fär, câre, ȧsk; ten, ēve, latėr; (i) pity, rely, senate; īce; top; nō.

beef-steak (bēf′stāk′), *n.* a thin broad piece, or slice, of beef that can be broiled or fried.

beef-y (bēf′i), *adj.* [beef-i-er, beef-i-est], fat; brawny; fleshy:—*n.* **beef′i-ness.**

bee-hive (bē′hiv′), *n.* a box made to house a swarm of bees and store its honey.

bee-line (bē′lĭn′), *n.* 1, the straight course of a bee returning to the hive with honey or pollen; 2, the most direct way from one point to another; as, I made a *beeline* for home.

been (bin; bēn), *p.p.* of *be.*

beer (bēr), *n.* 1, an alcoholic liquor generally brewed from malted barley and flavoured with hops; 2, a non-alcoholic drink made from roots or plants, as root beer, ginger beer, etc.: —*adj.* **beer′y.**

bees-wax (bēz′waks′), *n.* a tough, yellowish-brown wax that bees make and use for honeycomb:—*v.t.* to rub or polish with beeswax.

beet (bēt), *n.* a plant cultivated for its root, which serves as a vegetable and as a source of sugar; also, the red or white root.

bee-tle (bē′tl), *n.* a kind of insect having four wings, the outer pair being hard and shiny and serving as a protection to the inner pair.

bee-tling (bē′tling), *adj.* jutting out; prominent; overhanging; as, bare and *beetling* cliffs; a *beetling* brow.

be-fall (bi-fôl′), *v.t.* [*p.t.* befell (bi-fel′), *p.p.* befall-en (bi-fôl′en), *p.pr.* befall-ing], to happen or occur to:—*v.i.* to come to pass; as, whatever *befalls.*

be-fit (bi-fit′), *v.t.* [befit-ted, befit-ting], to be worthy of; be suitable or appropriate for.—*adj.* **be-fit′ting.**

before (bi-fōr′), *prep.* 1, in front of; 2, preceding in space, time, or rank; as, the lawn *before* the house; *before* ten o'clock; a general comes *before* a colonel; 3, in the presence or sight of; as, the prisoner was brought *before* the judge:—*adv.* in front; previously; formerly; as, you never looked like that *before:*—*conj.* 1, previous to the time at which; as, I shall finish *before* I leave; 2, rather than; as, he would die *before* he would betray his country.

be-fore-hand (bi-fōr′hand′), *adv.* in advance; as, do it *beforehand.*

be-friend (bi-frend′), *v.t.* to act as a friend; aid.

be-fud-dle (bi-fud′l), *v.t.* to confuse, as with liquor.

beg (beg), *v.t.* [begged, beg-ging], 1, to entreat or ask for (food, money, etc.) as charity; 2, to beseech; implore; as,

I *beg* you to help me; 3, to ask as a favour; as, I *beg* you to hand me that book:—*v.i.* to ask, or to live by asking. alms; as, he *begs* from door to door.

be-gan (bi-gan′), *p.t.* of *begin.*

be-get (bi-get′), *v.t.* [*p.t.* begot (bi-got′) or, *Archaic,* begat (bi-gat′), *p.p.* begot or begot-ten (bi-got′n), *p.pr.* (begetting], 1, to become the father of; 2, to produce; cause; as, love *begets* love.

beg-gar (beg′ẽr), *n.* 1, one who asks for alms; 2, a very poor person; 3, a fellow: often used humorously; as, he's a cute little *beggar:*—*v.t.* to reduce to poverty.—*adj.* **beg′gar-ly.**

beg-gar's—lice (beg′ẽrz–lĭs′), *n.* a weed whose seeds catch on clothing; also, the seed. Also, **beg′gar—lice′.**

beg-gar-y (beg′ẽr-i), *n.* extreme poverty.

be-gin (bi-gin′), *v.i.* [*p.t.* began (bi-gan′), *p.p.* begun (bi-gun′), *p.pr.* beginning], 1, to come into existence; arise; commence; as, life *began* many million years ago; the stream *begins* up in the hills; the story *begins* on page 30; 2, to take the first step or do the first act; start; as, work *begins* to-morrow:—*v.t.* to commence.

be-gin-ner (bi-gin′ẽr), *n.* one who is just starting in; one who has had no training or experience; a novice.

be-gin-ning (bi-gin′ing), *n.* 1, origin; as, the *beginning* of the world; 2, source; as, the *beginning* of all evil; 3, the first part; as, the *beginning* of a book.

be-gone (bi-gôn′), *interj.* go away! get out!

be-go-ni-a (bi-gō′ni-a; bi-gōn′ya), *n.* a plant with ornamental leaves and red, pink, or white flowers, often grown in the house.

be-grimed (bi-grĭmd′), *adj.* deeply soiled.

be-grudge (bi-gruj′), *v.t.* [begrudged, begrudg-ing], 1, to envy (a person) the possession of (something); as, I *begrudge* him the honour; 2, to give reluctantly or unwillingly; as, I *begrudge* the money.—*adv.* **be-grudg′ing-ly.**

be-guile (bi-gīl′), *v.t.* [beguiled, beguiling], 1, to deceive; 2, to cause to pass pleasantly; as, to *beguile* many hours in reading; 3, to amuse; as, to *beguile* children with stories.

be-half (bi-hȧf; bi-häf′), *n.* used only in phrases: **—in behalf of,** in the defence or interest of; as, he spoke *in behalf of* the plan; **on behalf of,** in the place of; for; as, the agent acts *on behalf of* his employer.

be-have (bi-hāv′), *v.t.* and *v.i.* [behaved,

behav-ing], to conduct or carry (oneself); act; as, he *behaves* himself well; also, to conduct (oneself) properly; as, make him *behave*.

be-hav-iour (bi-hāv'yẽr), *n.* conduct; manners. In American usage, **be-hav'ior.**

be-head (bi-hed'), *v.t.* to cut off the head.

be-hest (bi-hest'), *n.* a command; order.

be-hind (bi-hīnd'), *prep.* **1,** at the back of; as, to hide *behind* the door; **2,** inferior to; as, he is *behind* the class in spelling; **3,** in support of; as, there is money *behind* the plan; **4,** remaining after; as, he left nothing but debts *behind* him:—*adv.* **1,** in the rear; as, to remain *behind;* **2,** backward; as, look *behind;* **3,** in arrears; as, he is *behind* in his dues.

be-hind-hand (bi-hīnd'hand'), *adj.* and *adv.* late; slow; behind, as in one's work.

be-hold (bi-hōld'), *v.t.* [*p.t.* beheld (bi-held'), *p.p.* beheld or, *Archaic,* beholden (bi-hōl'den), *p.pr.* behold-ing], to look at; gaze upon; see.—*n.* **be-hold'er.**

be-hoove (bi-hōōv'), *v.t.* [*p.t.* behooved (-hōōvd')], to be necessary; as, it *behooves* me to go. Also **be-hove'** (-hōv').

beige (bāzh), *n.* the light-tan colour of unbleached wool:—*adj.* of a light-tan colour.

be-ing (bē'ing), *n.* **1,** existence; life; as, to come into *being;* **2,** that which exists; esp., a person.

be-la-bour (bi-lā'bẽr), *v.t.* **1,** to beat; pummel; **2,** berate; as, he *belaboured* the mule with whip and voice.

be-lat-ed (bi-lāt'id), *adj.* delayed; as, a *belated* report; a *belated* arrival.

be-lay (bi-lā'), *v.t.* [belayed, belay-ing], *nautical,* to make fast, as a running rope, by winding around a pin, cleat, etc.:—**belaying—pin,** an adjustable pin to which ropes are made fast:—*interj.* stop!

belch (belch), *v.t.* and *v.i.* **1,** to discharge (gas) from the stomach through the mouth; **2,** to throw out with force; as, the volcano *belched* fire:—*n.* the act of belching.

bel-dam (bel'dam), *n.* an ugly old woman; hag; witch.

be-lea-guer (bi-lē'gẽr), *v.t.* to besiege; as, we *beleaguered* the fort.

bel-fry (bel'fri), *n.* [*pl.* belfries], a bell tower, or that part of a tower in which a bell is hung.

be-lie (bi-lī'), *v.t.* [belied, bely-ing], **1,** to give a false notion of; as, his appearance *belies* his feelings; **2,** to fail to come up to or to accord with; as, his acts *belie* his words.

be-lief (bi-lēf'), *n.* **1,** the acceptance of something as true or desirable; confidence; as, a *belief* in physical education; my *belief* in his innocence; **2,** creed; as, a religious *belief;* **3,** opinion; as, it is my *belief* that he is coming.

be-lieve (bi-lēv'), *v.t.* [believed, believing], **1,** to accept as true; as, I *believe* the evidence; **2,** to trust the word of; place confidence in; as, I *believe* him; **3,** to think; as, I *believe* that honesty pays:—*v.i.* to have faith, trust, or confidence; as, to *believe* in God; *believe* in our cause.—*adj.* **be-liev'ing.**—*adj.* **be-liev'a-ble.**—*n.* **be-liev'er.**

be-lit-tle (bi-lit'l), *v.t.* [belit-tled, belittling], **1,** to cause to appear small; as, he *belittled* the danger; **2,** to speak slightingly of; as, he *belittled* my work.

bell (bel), *n.* **1,** a hollow metal vessel, usually cup-shaped, which gives a ringing sound when struck with a clapper or hammer; **2,** anything shaped like a bell, as the flare at the mouth of a horn; **3,** on shipboard, the time is indicated by strokes on a bell, each stroke meaning a half hour after 12, 4, or 8 o'clock, so that 1 bell is 12:30, 4:30, or 8:30, 4 bells is 2, 6, or 10, etc.:—*v.t.* to put a bell on; as, to *bell* a cat or a sheep.

bell-boy (bel'boi'), *n.* a hotel, ship, or club employee who attends to the wants of guests. Also, *Slang,* **bell'hop'.**

bell—buoy (bel'–boi'), *n.* a buoy with a warning bell that is rung by the heaving of the sea.

belle (bel), *n.* a beautiful woman; a very popular young lady.

bel-li-cose (bel'i-kōs'), *adj.* quarrelsome; warlike.

bel-lig-er-ent (bi-lij'er-ent), *adj.* **1,** waging war; as, *belligerent* nations; **2,** quarrelsome; warlike; as, *belligerent* words; a *belligerent* person:—*n.* a nation or person at war; as, the *belligerents* took up arms.—*n.* **bel-lig'er-ence.**

bel-low (bel'ō), *v.i.* **1,** to roar like a bull; **2,** to make a similar noise; as, he *bellowed* with rage:—*v.t.* to utter with a loud, full voice; roar:—*n.* **1,** the roar of a bull or similar animal; **2,** a loud, deep cry or voice.

bel-lows (bel'ōz), *n.* [*pl.* bellows], **1,** instrument for producing a current of air, used for various purposes, such as blowing fires or filling the pipes of an organ; **2,** the creased casing that connects the front and back of a camera.

bel-ly (bel'i), *n.* [*pl.* bellies], **1,** the part of the body of man or animal between the chest and the thighs, containing the stomach, bowels, etc.; the abdomen; **2,** the front or lower surface of the body of man or an animal; **3,** the bulging

---

cat, āge, fär, câre, ásk; ten, ēve, latẽr; (i) pity, rely, senate; ice; top; nō.

part of any object; as, the *belly* of a flask:—*v.i.* [bellied, belly-ing], to swell and extend; bulge out, as sails in the wind:—*v.t.* to cause to swell out.

be-long (bi-lòng′), *v.i.* **1,** to be the duty, concern, or business; as, this work *belongs* to you; **2,** to be the property; as, the coat *belongs* to me; **3,** to be a part or member; as, the button *belongs* to my coat; he *belongs* to the Masons; **4,** to have a characteristic place or niche; as, the book *belongs* on this shelf.

be-lov-ed (bi-luv′id; bi-luvd′), *adj.* dearly loved.—*n.* one dearly loved.

be-low (bi-lō′), *prep.* **1,** farther down, or lower than, in place, rank, excellence, dignity, value, amount, price, or the like; **2,** undeserving or unworthy of; beneath; as, *below* your dignity:—*adv.* **1,** into or to a lower place; as, go *below*; **2,** on the earth; as, here below.

belt (belt), *n.* **1,** a strip of leather, cloth, etc., worn around the body as a support for a garment, or as an ornament or mark of rank; **2,** any broad band, strip, or series of things; as, a *belt* of forts; **3,** a region, with a given character, or where a certain kind of vegetation grows; as, the timber *belt;* **4,** an endless band connecting two wheels or pulleys, and passing motion from one to the other; as, a sewing-machine *belt:*—*v.t.* **1,** to encircle, as with a belt; **2,** to fasten on (a sword) with a belt; **3,** to flog soundly, as with a belt.

be-moan (bi-mōn′), *v.t.* to grieve for; bewail; as, to *bemoan* one's lot.

bench (bench), *n.* **1,** a long seat; **2,** a strong table on which mechanics do their work; as, a carpenter's *bench;* **3,** the seat where judges sit in court; hence, judges as a class; also, the court.

bend (bend), *v.t.* [bent (bent), bend-ing], **1,** to strain or make taut, as the string of a bow; **2,** to curve or make crooked; as, he *bent* the iron rod; **3,** to turn; deflect; as, the glass *bent* the rays of the sun; **4,** to direct to a certain point; as, we *bent* our energies to the task; **5,** to force to submit or yield; **6,** *nautical,* to fasten, as a sail to a spar:—*v.i.* **1,** to become curved or crooked; as, the board *bent* under his weight; **2,** to turn toward or away from; as, the road *bends* to the left; **3,** to bow or stoop; hence, to submit; as, I *bend* to fate:—*n.* **1,** a turn or curve; **2,** a knot by which one rope is fastened to another or to some object:—**the bends,** *Colloq.* cramps caused by a too-sudden change to normal air pressure from a high pressure, as in deep-sea diving.—*n.* **bender,** *Slang,* a spree.

be-neath (bi-nēth′; bi-nēth′), *prep.* **1,** under; as, *beneath* the sky; **2,** under the pressure of; as, to sink *beneath* troubles; **3,** lower than; as, *beneath* the rank of captain; **4,** undeserving of; as, the letter was *beneath* his notice; unworthy of; as, the work was *beneath* him:—*adv.* in a lower place; below.

ben-e-dict, ben-e-dick (ben′e-dikt; -dik), *n.* a newly married man, esp. one long a bachelor.

ben-e-dic-tion (ben′i-dik′shun), *n.* a blessing, esp. the short blessing pronounced at the end of a church service.

ben-e-fac-tor (ben′i-fak′tėr), *n.* one who has given help in the form of money or service.—*n.* **ben′e-fac′tion.**

be-nef-i-cence (bi-nef′i-sens), *n.* active kindness; a charitable gift; as, his *beneficence* relieved the poor.—*adj.* **be-nef′i-cent.**

ben-e-fi-cial (ben′i-fish′al), *adj.* useful; helpful; profitable; as, *beneficial* climate, advice, or experiences.

ben-e-fi-ci-ar-y (ben′i-fish′ėr-i; ben′i-fish′i-er′i), *n.* [*pl.* beneficiaries], one who receives anything as a gift or benefit; esp., the person named in a will or an insurance policy to receive the inheritance.

ben-e-fit (ben′i-fit), *n.* **1,** a help; advantage; as, the *benefits* of an education, or of sunshine; **2,** a play, concert, etc., the proceeds of which go to a particular person or cause:—*v.t.* [benefit-ed, benefit-ing], to do good to; help; as, the vacation *benefited* him:—*v.i.* to be helped; improve; as, he *benefited* from his rest.

Ben-e-lux (ben′i-luks), *n.* Belgium, Netherlands, and Luxembourg are the *Benelux* nations.

be-nev-o-lent (bi-nev′o-lent), *adj.* kindly; charitable; generous; as, a *benevolent* nature.—*n.* **be-nev′o-lence.**

be-night-ed (bi-nīt′id), *adj.* **1,** morally ignorant; as, a *benighted* heathen; **2,** overtaken by night.

be-nign (bi-nīn′), *adj.* **1,** of a kind or gentle disposition; **2,** favourable; healthful; as, a *benign* sea breeze; **3,** in medical usage, harmless.—*n.* **be-nig′ni-ty** (bi-nig′ni-ti).—*adj.* **be-nig′-nant** (bi-nig′nant).

bent (bent), *adj.* **1,** curved; crooked; **2,** strongly inclined; set; as, he is *bent* on going:—*n.* a natural interest or ability; as, Tom has a *bent* for painting.

be-numb (bi-num′), *v.t.* to stupefy; deprive of feeling; as, a foot *benumbed* by cold; a heart *benumbed* by grief.

ben-zene (ben′zēn; ben-zēn′), *n.* a highly inflammable, colourless liquid obtained from coal-tar, used as a motor fuel, in the manufacture of illuminating gas and of dyes, and in other processes.

ben-zine (ben′zēn; ben-zēn′), *n.* an inflammable liquid obtained from petroleum used in cleaning, dyeing, painting, etc., and as a motor fuel.

be-queath (bi-kwēth′), *v.t.* 1, to give or leave by will; 2, to hand down; as, the Greeks *bequeathed* to us a love of beauty.

be-quest (bi-kwest′), *n.* something given or left by will; a legacy; as, small *bequests* of money went to the servants.

be-rate (bi-rāt′), *v.t.* [berat-ed, berat-ing], to scold; rebuke severely.

be-reave (bi-rēv′), *v.t.* [bereaved (bi-rēvd′) or bereft (bi-reft′), bereav-ing], to deprive; leave desolate; as, *bereaved* of his children; fear *bereft* him of his wits.—*n.* **be-reave′ment.**

be-ret (be-rā′; be′rā), *n.* a flat, round, brimless cap of wool, felt, etc.

berg (bûrg), *n.* a large floating mass of ice; an iceberg.

ber-i-ber-i (ber′i-ber′i), *n.* an Oriental disease caused by a lack of vitamin B1 in the diet.

ber-ry (ber′i), *n.* [*pl.* berries], 1, any small pulpy fruit with many seeds, as the huckleberry; 2, the dry seed or kernel of certain plants; as, the coffee-berry:—*v.i.* [berried, berry-ing], to gather berries.

ber-serk (bûr′sûrk), *adj.* destructively frenzied; as, he went *berserk* and shot six persons.

berth (bûrth), *n.* 1, a bunk or bed for a passenger, as on a ship, train etc.; 2, a position or job; as, he has a good *berth* with the government; 3, *nautical,* a place where a ship ties up or lies at anchor.

ber-yl (ber′il), *n.* a hard, lustrous gem in striking colours, two of the best-known being emerald and aquamarine.

be-seech (bi-sēch′), *v.t.* [besought (be-sôt′), beseech-ing], 1, to entreat; implore; as, I *beseech* you to hear me; 2, to beg for; as, I *beseech* your favour.

be-seem (bi-sēm′), *v.t.* to be suitable or becoming to; befit; as, it hardly *beseems* you to bully your sister.

be-set (bi-set′), *v.t.* [beset, beset-ting], 1, to assail; harass; as, trouble *beset* him; his *besetting* sin; 2, to hem in; surround; as, a spy is *beset* by danger.

be-side (bi-sīd′), *prep.* 1, at or by the side of; near by; as, sit *beside* me; 2, in comparison with; as, my work is poor *beside* yours; 3, away from; as, *beside* the point:—**beside oneself,** out of one's senses.

be-sides (bi-sīdz′), *adv.* in addition; also; as well:—*prep.* over and above; in addition to.

be-siege (bi-sēj′), *v.t.* [besieged, besieg-ing], 1, to surround with armed forces; lay siege to; as, to *besiege* a city; 2, to pester or harass (a person) in any way, as with questions or requests.

be-smirch (bi-smûrch′), *v.i.* 1, to soil; 2, to dishonour; sully; as, slander can *besmirch* a man's good name.

be-sot-ted (bi-sot′id), *adj.* 1, muddled with drink; 2, infatuated; as, a *besotted* wretch.

be-sought (bi-sôt′), *p.t.* and *p.p.* of beseech.

be-speak (bi-spēk′), *v.t.* [*p.t.* bespoke (bi-spōk′), *p.p.* bespo-ken (bi-spō′ken), *p.pr.* bespeak-ing], 1, to ask for beforehand; order in advance; as, I *bespoke* two tickets; 2, to show or give evidence of; as, this *bespeaks* a kind heart.

best (best), *adj.* [*superl.* of *good*], 1, having the highest degree of goodness or excellence; as, he did the *best* work in class; 2, largest; as, the *best* part of a month:—*n.* 1, that which is finest; as, the *best* is none too good; 2, the highest degree of excellence; as, she was at her *best* in the school play:—*adv.* [*superl.* of ²*well*], 1, in the most successful way; 2, in the highest degree:—*v.t.* to get the better of; surpass.

be-stead (bi-sted′), *adj. Archaic,* placed; situated; as, he was sore *bestead* by enemies:—*v.t.* to help.

bes-tial (best′yal; bes′chal), *adj.* like the beasts; brutish; savage.—*n.* **bes′ti-al′i-ty** (bes′ti-al′i-ti; bes′chi-al′i-ti).

be-stir (bi-stûr′), *v.t.* [bestirred, bestir-ring], to rouse; exert.

be-stow (bi-stō′), *v.t.* to give or confer; as, to *bestow* a medal on a hero.

be-stride (bi-strīd′), *v.t.* [*p.t.* bestrode (bi-strōd′), *p.p.* bestrid-den (bi-strid′n), *p.pr.* bestrid-ing], to mount, sit, or ride with one leg on each side; straddle; as, to *bestride* a horse, fence, log, etc.

bet (bet), *v.t.* [bet or bet-ted, bet-ting], to stake, risk, or wager (money or the like) that something will or will not happen, or that a contest or situation will end in a certain way; as, I *bet* a dollar that it will rain today; I *bet* ten dollars on the home team:—*v.i.* to lay a wager; as, to *bet* on a horse:—*n.* 1, a wager; as, to make a *bet;* 2, the amount staked or wagered; 3, that on which a wager is laid; as, this horse is a safe bet.—*n.* **bet′ter; bet′tor.**

be-take (bi-tāk′), *v.t.* [*p.t.* betook (bi-took′), *p.p.* betak-en (bi-tāk′en), *p.pr.* betak-ing], to take (oneself); as, they *betook* themselves to a place of safety.

be-think (bi-thingk′), *v.t.* [bethought

(bi-thôt′), bethink-ing], to remember: used with *myself*, *himself*, or the like; as, I *bethought* myself of an errand.

be-tide (bi-tīd′), *v.t.* (betid-ed, betiding], to happen to; befall; as, who knows what will *betide* us:—*v.i.* to come to pass.

be-times (bi-tīmz′),*adv.* early; promptly.

be-to-ken (bi-tō′ken), *v.t.* to be a token or sign of; foreshadow; as, a red sunset is said to *betoken* hot weather.

be-tray (bi-trā′), *v.t.* **1,** to give into the hands of an enemy by treachery; as, Judas *betrayed* his Master; **2,** to be faithless to; as, to *betray* a trust; **3,** to disclose; reveal, as a secret; **4,** to disclose unintentionally; as, his manner *betrays* uneasiness.—*n.* **betray′er.**—*n.* **be-tray′al.**

be-troth (bi-trōth′; bi-trôth′), *v.t.* to promise to give (a daughter) in marriage:—**betrothed,** *n.* the person to whom one is engaged to be married.—*n.* **be-troth′al.**

bet-ter (bet′ẽr), *adj.* [*comp.* of *good*], **1,** having good qualities in a higher degree; as, your work is *better* than it was; these apples are *better* than those; **2,** preferable; as, it is *better* to walk than to wait for a car; **3,** improved in health; **4,** larger; greater; as, I waited the *better* part of an hour:—*adv.* [*comp.* of ²*well*], **1,** in a more excellent manner; as, you swim *better* than you did; **2,** more; as, you like swimming *better* now:—*v.t.* **1,** to improve; as, he has *bettered* his condition; **2,** to surpass, as a record:—*n.* **1,** that which is better or more desirable; as, to rise from the good to the *better;* **2,** advantage; as, to get the *better* of an opponent; **3,** **betters,** superiors, as in social standing, education, or the like; as, respect for one's *betters.*

bet-ter-ment (bet′ẽr-ment), *n.* a bettering; an improvement, as of land, a railway, a road, or the like.

be-tween (bi-twēn′), *prep.* **1,** in the space or time which separates one thing from another; as, *between* dark and daylight; **2,** from one to another of; as, a look passed *between* them; **3,** by the joint action of; as, *between* us we shall succeed; **4,** by comparison of; as, a choice *between* evils:—*adv.* in a place between other things.

be-twixt (bi-twikst′), *prep.* between; as, *betwixt* two perils:—**betwixt and between,** neither one thing nor the other.

bev-el (bev′el), *v.t.* [bevelled, bevelling], to give a sloping edge to; as, to *bevel* the edge of a table:—*v.i.* to slant or incline:—*n.* **1,** the slant or angle that one line or surface makes with another; **2,** an instrument used for drawing or measuring angles:—*adj.* slanting; as, a *bevelled* edge.

bev-er-age (bev′ẽr-ij), *n.* any kind of drink, as coffee, lemonade, wine, etc.

bev-y (bev′i), *n.* [*pl.* bevies], **1,** a company or group, esp. of girls or women; **2,** a flock of birds, esp. of quail or larks.

be-wail (bi-wāl′), *v.t.* to mourn or weep for; lament; as, he *bewailed* his loss.

be-ware (bi-wâr′), *v.i.* and *v.t.* be on one's guard (against); be wary (of).

be-wil-der (bi-wil′dẽr), *v.t.* to perplex; confuse; puzzle; as, this test paper *bewildered* us.—*n.* **be-wil′der-ment.**

be-witch (bi-wich′), *v.t.* **1,** to cast a spell over as by magic; as, the fairy *bewitched* the cow; **2,** hence, to fascinate; charm.

be-witch-ing (bi-wich′ing), *adj.* fascinating; charming.—*adv.* **be-witch′ing-ly.**

bey (bā), *n.* **1,** a governor of a Turkish province; **2,** title of ruler of Tunis.

be-yond (bi-yond′), *prep.* **1,** on the farther side of; as, *beyond* the hills; **2,** farther than; past; as, *beyond* the finish line; *beyond* five o'clock; **3,** out of the reach of; as, *beyond* medical aid; **4,** outside the experience of; too much for; as, algebra was *beyond* him:—*adv.* at a distance; yonder:—*n.* that which lies on the farther side:—**the Beyond,** life after death.

bi-an-nu-al (bī-an′ū-al), *adj.* occurring twice a year.—*adv.* **bi-an′nu-al-ly.**

bi-as (bī′as), *adj.* slanting; diagonal; as, a *bias* seam:—*n.* **1,** the diagonal direction of a cut, seam, or stitching made to slant across the threads of material; as, to cut a skirt on the *bias;* **2,** a leaning of the mind toward a particular thing, desire, or opinion; prejudice:—*v.t.* [biased or biassed, bias-ing or bias-sing], to give a particular direction to; influence; as, the newspapers *bias* our opinions.—*adj.* **bi′ased; bi′assed.**

bib (bib), *n.* an apronlike cloth tied under a child's chin to protect the clothes; also, the upper part of an apron.

Bi-ble (bī′bl), *n.* **1,** the sacred writings of the Old and New Testaments, whether in the original tongue or translated; **2,** a book of the sacred writings of any religion; as, the Koran is the Mohammedan *Bible.*—*adj.* **Bib′li-cal** (bib′li-kal).

bib-li-og-ra-phy (bib′li-og′ra-fi), *n.* a list of writings about a given subject or of a given author, publisher, etc.

all (ôl), ôr; up, mūte, cûr, cōōl, book; oil, out; th, thin; *th*, the.

bi-car-bon-ate (bī-kär′bon-āt′; -it), *n.* a salt of carbonic acid:—**bicarbonate of soda**, a white substance, in the form of powder or crystals, used as a leaven in cooking, and as a medicine.

bi-cen-ten-ni-al (bī′sen-ten′i-al), *adj.* occurring every 200 years:—*n.* a 200th anniversary or its celebration.

bi-ceps (bī′seps), *n.* [*pl.* bicepses (bī′sep-sez)], the large muscle on the front of the upper arm.

bi-cker (bik′ēr), *v.i.* to squabble; wrangle; as, these boys *bicker* over marbles:—*n.* an angry or petty dispute; a wrangle.

bi-cus-pid (bī-kus′pid), *adj.* with two points or cusps:—*n.* in man, one of eight teeth, placed in pairs, two on each side of each jaw, between the canines and the molars. (See illustration at *dentition*.)

bi-cy-cle (bī′sik-l), *n.* a light vehicle having a metal frame, two wheels, one behind the other, and a saddlelike seat for the rider, who propels the bicycle by means of pedals, and steers it by means of a handle-bar:—*v.i.* [bicy-cled, bicy-cling], to ride on a bicycle.—*n.* **bi′cy-cler.**—*n.* **bi′cy-clist.**

bid (bid), *v.t.* [*p.t.* bade (bad) or, in definition 3, bid, *p.p.* bid-den (bid′n) or, in definition 3, bid, *p.pr.* bid-ding], 1, to command; order; as, he *bade* me tell everything; 2, to offer by way of greeting; say; as, to *bid* someone welcome or good-bye; also, to invite; as, he *bade* me come again; 3, to propose a price for something, esp. at an auction; as, he *bid* ten dollars for the watch; 4, in *cards*, to state the number of tricks one expects to take:—*v.i.* to make an offer; offer a price:—*n.* 1, an offer of a price, as at an auction; also, the amount offered; as, a *bid* of five dollars; 2, the statement of a price, or the price itself, at which a person will do a piece of work; as, his *bid* on the new house was $15,000; 3, in *cards* (a) the number of tricks stated (b) a player's turn to bid:—*n.* **bid′der.**—*n.* **bid′ding.**—*adj.* **bid′da-ble.**

bid-der (bid′ēr), *n.* one who bids, esp. at an auction sale or a game of bridge.

bide (bīd), *v.t.* [*p.t.* bode (bōd) or bid-ed, *p.p.* bid-ed, *p.pr.* bid-ing], to wait for; as, you must *bide* your time.

bi-en-ni-al (bī-en′i-al), *adj.* 1, occurring once in two years; as, a *biennial* convention; 2, continuing or living for two years; as, *biennial* plants:—*n.* 1, a plant which produces roots and leaves in the first year, and flowers, fruit, and seed in the second, and then dies; 2, an event that occurs once in two years.

bier (bēr), *n.* the frame on which a corpse or coffin is placed or carried.

biff (bif), *v.t. Colloq.* to strike:—*n.* a sharp blow, as with a fist.

bi-fo-cal (bī-fō′kal), *adj.* having two focal points, as a lens:—*n.* a lens ground to form a combination of two lenses, one for near and the other for distant objects:—**bifocals,** eye-glasses with this type of lens.

big (big), *adj.* [big-ger, big-gest], 1, large, bulky; as, a *big* horse; a *big* load; 2, boastful; pompous; as, *big* talk; 3, important; serious; as, a *big* issue; a *big* mistake.

big-a-my (big′a-mi), *n.* the act of marrying a person while married to another.—*n.* **big′a-mist.**

big-horn (big′hôrn′), *n.* the wild sheep of the Rocky Mountains.

bight (bīt), *n.* a loop in a rope; a bay, or a curve in a shore-line.

big-ot (big′ut), *n.* a person who is unreasonably and obstinately attached to his beliefs and opinions on such subjects as religion, morals, etc.—*adj.* **big′ot-ed.**—*n.* **big′ot-ry.**

bike (bīk), *n. Colloq.* bicycle.

bi-lat-er-al (bī-lat′ēr-al), *adj.* having to do with two sides or two parties; as, a *bilateral* contract.

bil-ber-ry (bil′ber-i), *n.* a shrub of the heath family, with rose-coloured flowers and dark-blue berries.

bile (bīl), *n.* 1, the bitter, yellow or greenish fluid secreted by the liver to aid in the digestive processes; 2, ill humour; irritation.

bilge (bilj), *n.* 1, the bulging part of a cask; 2, the bottom of a ship up to the point where the sides become vertical:—**bilge-water,** water which gathers in the bottom of a ship, always very disagreeable in odour:—*v.i.* [bilged, bilg-ing], 1, to spring a leak by a break in the bilge; 2, to bulge:—*v.t.* to stave in the bottom of (a ship).

bi-lin-gual (bī-ling′gwal), *adj.* of, or using, two languages; as, Canada is a *bilingual* nation.

bil-ious (bil′yus), *adj.* 1, caused by a disorder of the liver; due to too much bile; as, a *bilious* headache; 2, bad-tempered; peevish.—*n.* **bil′ious-ness.**

bilk (bilk), *v.t.* to evade payment (of a debt); swindle; defraud.

¹**bill** (bil), *n.* 1, a draft of a proposed law presented to a legislature; 2, an account of money owed for goods sold, services given, or work done; as, a plumbing *bill;* 3, a piece of paper money; as, a ten-dollar *bill;* 4, a promissory note; 5, a printed advertisement; poster; 6, a paper giving a

list of items; as, the *bill* of the races; a *bill* of fare; **7,** in law, a written complaint or accusation:—*v.t.* **1,** to advertise by posters; enter on a programme; announce; as, the actor was *billed* to appear in person; **2,** to make a bill of; enter on a bill; make a list of; as, these purchases will be *billed* next month; **3,** to charge (a person); send a statement of indebtedness to; as, please *bill* me without delay; **4,** to ship by freight; as, *billed* to Toronto.

²bill (bil), *n.* **1,** the beak of a bird; **2,** a similar beak in other animals, as the jaw of a turtle:—*v.i.* to join bills; show affection; as, doves *bill* and coo.

bill-board (bil′bōrd′), *n.* a board for outdoor poster displays; **2,** a ledge on a ship's bow for an anchor to rest on.

bil-let (bil′et), *n.* **1,** a written order from a military officer directing the person to whom it is addressed to furnish a soldier with board and lodging; **2,** a place where a soldier is lodged; in the World War, a rest camp; **3,** a situation; appointment; as, he had a comfortable *billet* in Montreal:—*v.t.* [billet-ed, billet-ing], to quarter or lodge; as, the government *billeted* the soldiers in private homes.

bill-fold (bil′fōld′), *n.* a folding wallet for money, cards, etc.

bill-head (bil′hed′), *n.* a printed form, with a name and business address at the top, used for making out bills.

bil-liards (bil′yẽrdz), *n.* a game played with solid balls and a cue on an oblong, cloth-covered table which is bounded by a raised, cushioned ledge.

bil-lion (bil′yun), *n.* in Canada, U.S. and France, one thousand millions, written 1,000,000,000; in Britain and Germany, a million millions, written 1,000,000,000,000:—*adj.* **bil′lionth** (bil′yunth).—*n.* **bil′lion-aire′.**

bill-post-er (bil′pōs′tẽr), *n.* one who sticks posters on billboards.

bil-low (bil′ō), *n.* a great wave of the sea:—*v.i.* **1,** to rise and roll in large waves; **2,** to swell out; bulge; as, the ship's sails *billowed* in the breeze.—*adj.* **bil′low-y.**

bil-ly (bil′i), *n.* a club, esp. a policeman's.

billy—goat, *n. Colloq.* a male goat.

bi-month-ly (bī-munth′li), *adj.* and *adv.* occurring or appearing every two months; loosely (and less correctly) twice a month or semimonthly.

bin (bin), *n.* a box, crib, or enclosure, used for storage; as, a coal-*bin.*

bind (bīnd), *v.t.* [bound (bound), binding], **1,** to tie up, as with a cord or band; **2,** to hold together; confine; restrain; as, cement *binds* bricks; ice *binds* the river in winter; this shoe *binds* my foot; **3,** to hold in bonds of affection, loyalty, duty, or law; as, *bound* by friendship or by a promise; *bound* as an apprentice; **4,** to finish or protect with a band or border; as, to *bind* an edge of a garment; **5,** to bandage; **6,** to fasten together and into a cover; as, to *bind* a book:—*v.i.* **1,** to tie up something; **2,** to have the force of a duty or necessity; as, ties that *bind;* **3,** to stick together in a mass; to become hard or stiff; as, clay *binds* when heated.—*n.* **bind′ing.**

bind-er (bīn′dẽr), *n.* one who binds; as, a *bookbinder;* **2,** anything that binds, as tar on roads, or a stiff cover that holds loose sheets of paper; **3,** a machine that cuts and binds grain.

bind-er-y (bīn′dẽr-i), *n.* [*pl.* binderies], a place where books are bound.

bind-weed (bīnd′wēd′), *n.* a twining herb of the morning-glory family.

binge (binj), *n. Slang,* a spree.

bin-go (bing′gō), *n.* a game played by drawing numbered discs, etc., and covering corresponding numbers on cards.

bin-na-cle (bin′a-kl), *n.* a case or stand near the steering-wheel of a ship containing the ship's compass.

bin-oc-u-lar (bin-ok′ū-lẽr; bī-nok′ū-lẽr), *adj.* adapted to the use of both eyes at the same time; as, *binocular* glasses. Also, *n. pl.* **bin-oc′u-lars** (-lẽrz), field or opera glasses.

bi-nom-i-al (bī-nō′mi-al), *adj.* consisting of two terms, as $x - a$.

bi-og-ra-phy (bī-og′ra-fi; bi-og′ra-fi), *n.* [*pl.* biographies], **1,** a history of a person's life; **2,** the branch of literature dealing with the written history of person's lives.—*n.* **bi-og′ra-pher.**—*adj.* **bi′o-graph′ic** (bī′o-graf′ik); **bi′o-graph′i-cal.**

bi-ol-o-gy (bī-ol′o-ji), *n.* the science which includes both the study of plants (*botany*) and the study of animals (*zoology*).—*n.* **bi-ol′o-gist.**—*adj.* **bi′o-log′ic** (bī′o-loj′ik); **bi′o-log′i-cal.**

bi-ped (bī′ped), *n.* an animal with two feet. Men and birds are bipeds.

bi-plane (bī′plān′), *n.* an aeroplane with two main supporting surfaces, usually one above the other.

birch (bûrch), *n.* **1,** a kind of tree, valued for its close-grained wood, with smooth outer bark, which in some varieties may be removed in thin, papery sheets; **2,** the wood of this tree; **3,** a whip formed of birch twigs, used for flogging:—*adj.* made of birch:—*v.t.* to punish with a birch; whip.

bird (bûrd), *n.* **1,** any member of a class of warm-blooded, feathered, egg-laying animals, having wings that enable it to fly; **2,** any small game bird, as distinguished from a waterfowl; **3,** *Slang,* a fellow; chap; as, he is a queer *bird.*

bird-ie (bûr/di), *n.* **1,** a little bird; **2,** in *golf,* a score of one less than par on a hole.

bird's—eye (bûrdz/-ī/), *adj.* **1,** seen from above, as if by a flying bird; as, a *bird's-eye* view of the city; hence, general; sweeping; not detailed; as, a *bird's-eye* view of the labour problem; **2,** marked with spots resembling a bird's eye; as, *bird's-eye* maple.

birth (bûrth), *n.* **1,** the act of coming into life; **2,** origin; beginning; as, the *birth* of a republic; **3,** descent; lineage.

birth-day (bûrth/dā/), *n.* the day of one's birth.

birth-mark (bûrth/märk/), *n.* a mark or blemish on the skin from birth.

birth-right (bûrth/rīt/), *n.* **1,** any right, privilege, or possession to which a person is entitled by birth; **2,** the rights or inheritance of the oldest son.

bis-cuit (bis/kit), *n.* **1,** a flat cake of unraised bread, baked hard and dry; a cracker; **2,** in Canada, a small piece of dough, usually unsweetened, raised with baking-powder or baking soda, and baked.

bi-sect (bī-sekt/), *v.t.* to cut or divide into two equal parts.—*n.* **bi-sec/tion.** —*n.* **bi-sec/tor.**

bish-op (bish/up), *n.* **1,** a clergyman of high rank, the head of a diocese or church district; **2,** a piece used in playing chess.—*n.* **bish/op-ric.**

bi-son (bī/sn; bī/zn), *n.* **1,** a wild, shaggy-maned, oxlike animal of North America, popularly called *buffalo,* extinct except in protected herds; **2,** the European wild ox, now extinct except in protected herds in Lithuania: the bison appears as an emblem on the Manitoba coat of arms.

bisque (bisk), *n.* **1,** a thick, rich, cream soup made from meat, fish, or tomatoes; **2,** a kind of ice-cream containing finely chopped nuts or macaroons.

¹bit (bit), *n.* **1,** a tool for boring or drilling holes; **2,** the cutting part of a tool, as a blade in a carpenter's plane; **3,** the metal mouthpiece of a bridle; **4,** the part of a key that enters and works a lock.

²bit (bit), *n.* **1,** a small piece of anything; a little; as, a *bit* of bread; **2,** a little while; as, wait a *bit;* **3,** in the south-

western U.S., a money value of 12½ cents:—**not a bit,** not at all; none at all.

bitch (bich), *n.* the female of the dog, wolf, fox, etc.

bite (bīt), *v.t.* [*p.t.* bit (bit), *p.p.* bitten (bit/n) or bit, *p.pr.* bit-ing], **1,** to seize, grip or cut with the teeth; **2,** to sting; as, a spider *bit* him; **3,** to cut into; as, the saw *bites* the wood; **4,** to cause smarting pain to; as, vinegar *bites* my tongue; **5,** to eat into; as, acid *bites* metal:—**bite the dust,** to fall dead or dying, as in combat; be defeated:—*v.i.* **1,** to seize an object with the teeth; as, the dog *bites;* **2,** to sting or pierce; as, insects *bite;* **3,** to cut or take hold; as, the saw *bites* well; **4,** to smart; as, mustard *bites;* **5,** to take a bait; as, the fish are *biting;* **6,** to eat away; as, acid *bites;*—*n.* **1,** the act of seizing with teeth; **2,** a wound made by the teeth or by a sting; **3,** a mouthful; a slight meal; **4,** a smarting sensation.—*n.* **bit/er.**—*adj.* **bit/ing.**

bit-ter (bit/ėr), *adj.* **1,** sharp and unpleasant to the taste, as quinine; **2,** sharp; painful; as, *bitter* cold; grievous; as, *bitter* woe; **3,** severe; sarcastic; as, *bitter* words; **4,** relentless; as, a *bitter* enemy:—*n.* **1,** that which is hard or unpleasant; as, take the *bitter* with the sweet; **2,** bitters, liquor in which herbs or roots have been soaked. —*adv.* **bit/ter-ly.**—*n.* **bit/ter-ness.**— *adj.* **bit/ter-ish.**

bit-tern (bit/ėrn), *n.* a kind of marsh bird, related to the heron. It is noted for its peculiar booming cry.

bit-ter—sweet (bit/ėr-swēt/), *n.* **1,** a vine of the nightshade family; **2,** an American twining shrub showing in the fall scarlet seeds in open, orange pods: —*adj.* mingling bitter and sweet, or pain and pleasure.

bi-tu-mi-nous (bi-tū/mi-nus), *adj.* containing much volatile hydrocarbon and burning with a smoky flame, as *bituminous* (or soft) coal.

bi-valve (bī/valv/), *n.* a shellfish, such as the oyster or clam, with a shell consisting of two valves hinged at one side: —*adj.* having two valves.

biv-ou-ac (biv/oo-ak/; biv/wak), *n.* a temporary camp in the open air:—*v.i.* [bivouacked (biv/oo-akt; biv/wakt), bivouack-ing], to encamp, as for a night, in the open air.

bi-week-ly (bī/wēk/li), *adj.* occurring or appearing every two weeks:—*n.* [*pl.* bi-weeklies], a periodical issued once in two weeks:—*adv.* once every two weeks.

bi-year-ly (bī/yēr/li), *adj.* and *adv.* occurring twice a year.

bi-zarre (bi-zär/), *adj.* odd; grotesque; queer.

blab (blab), *v.t.* [blabbed, blab-bing], to tell thoughtlessly:—*v.i.* to tell tales; talk too much and unwisely:—*n.* one who lets out secrets, or tells tales.—*n.* and *v.* **blab′ber.**

black (blak), *adj.* 1, of the colour of coal; opposite of *white;* 2, almost without light; very dark; as, a *black* cellar; 3, dismal; as, a *black* sky; threatening; sullen; as, *black* looks; 4, without moral goodness; evil; as, *black* deeds; 5, indicating disgrace; as, he got a *black* mark for conduct; 6, dark-skinned, as a Negro; 7, grimy:—*n.* 1, the colour of coal; 2, a black colour or dye; 3, a Negro; a member of any dark-skinned race; 4, black clothes; mourning:—*v.t.* to blacken, as boots.—*n.* **black′ness.**

black-ball (blak′bôl′), *v.t.* to vote against, or reject, by use of a blackball.

black bass, either of two fresh-water game fishes of eastern North America, the *large-mouthed black bass* or the *small-mouthed black bass.*

black-ber-ry (blak′bĕr-i), *n.* [*pl.* black-berries], 1, a bramble bearing a small, dark, juicy fruit; 2, the fruit itself.

black-bird (blak′bûrd′), *n.* 1, an English thrush; 2, one of several North American birds related to the bobolink, including the red-winged blackbird and the purple grackle.

black-board (blak′bōrd′), *n.* a dark, smooth surface, often of slate, to be written or drawn upon with chalk, or coloured crayons.

black-en (blak′en), *v.i.* to grow black or dark:—*v.t.* 1, to make black; 2, to speak evil of; as, to *blacken* a person's character.

black—eyed (blak′–īd′), *adj.* having an eye with a black iris, or one discoloured as from a bruise.

black-face (blak′fās′), *n.* 1, an actor made up for a Negro rôle; 2, boldfaced type. Also *adj.*

black-guard (blag′ärd), *n.* a vicious and abusive scoundrel:—*adj.* low; abusive:—*v.t.* to revile.—*adv.* and *adj.* **black′guard-ly.**

black-head (blak′hed′), *n.* a small plug of fatty matter in a pore of the face.

black-ing (blak′ing), *n.* a black paste, cream, or liquid for polishing shoes, etc.

black-jack, (blak′jak′), a small, flexible club with a weighted head:—*v.t.* to hit with a blackjack.

black-leg (blak′leg′), *n.* 1, a deadly infection of sheep and cattle; also a fungous disease of cabbage, etc.; 2, a strikebreaker or scab.

black list, a list of persons, companies, etc., judged worthy of punishment, ex-clusion, or the like:—**black-list** (blak′-list′), *v.t.* to place the name of (a person or firm) on a black list.

black-mail (blak′māl′), *n.* 1, money got from a person by a threat to tell something bad about him; 2, an attempt to get money thus:—*v.t.* to get money by threats.—*n.* **black′mail′er.**

black-out (blak′out′), *n.* a temporary loss of consciousness; as, the pilot suffered a *blackout* in the steep dive; 2, the putting out of all lights, as in an air-raid; 3, censorship, as of news, etc.

black-smith (blak′smith′), *n.* a person who works in iron, by heating it in fire, and then hammering it into shape.

black-snake (blak′snāk′), *n.* 1, any of several dark, harmless snakes; 2, a heavy whip of cowhide.

black-thorn (blak′thôrn′), *n.* 1, the sloe; 2, a stick cut from its stem.

blad-der (blad′ĕr), *n.* 1, in man and other animals, a sac of elastic muscle in which fluid collects, esp. the fluid secreted by the kidneys; 2, any sac or bag containing fluid or gas.

blade (blād), *n.* 1, the cutting part of a knife or other instrument; 2, a long, slender leaf, as of grass; 3, the broad part of any leaf; 4, a broad, flat object or part; as, the shoulder-*blade;* 5, a sword or swordsman; 6, a dashing fellow.

blah (blä), *n.* and *interj. Slang,* nonsense!

blame (blām), *n.* 1, an expression of disapproval; censure; 2, responsibility for something that goes wrong or is done wrong; as, he bears the *blame:*—*v.t.* [blamed, blam-ing], 1, to find fault with; reproach; 2, to place responsibility for; as, she *blames* her errors on her sister:— **to blame,** at fault; as, she is *to blame.*—*adj.* **blam′a-ble.**—*adj.* **blame′less.**

blanch (blanch), *v.t.* 1, to whiten; 2, to scald quickly, so as to remove the skin; as, to *blanch* almonds:—*v.i.* to turn pale.

blanc-mange (bla-mänzh′), *n.* a jelly-like dessert composed of some starchy substance, such as cornstarch, combined with milk, sweetened and fla-voured.

bland (bland), *adj.* 1, soft-spoken; gentle; as, a *bland* manner; 2, mild; soothing; as, a *bland* diet.—*adv.* **bland′ly.**

blan-dish (blan′dish), *v.t.* to flatter; coax; wheedle.—*n.* **blan′dish-ment.**

blank (blangk), *n.* 1, any empty space; 2, a printed form with empty spaces to be filled in; as, an order-*blank;* 3, a void; as, his mind was a *blank:*—*adj.* 1, free from writing or print; 2, without variety or interest; as, a *blank* day; **3**, without expression; as, a *blank* look; **4**, unbroken; unmarked; as, *blank* silence; a *blank* wall.—*adv.* **blank′ly.**

blank verse, unrhymed 5-foot verse in iambic pentameter rhythm.

blan-ket (blang′kit), *n.* **1**, a soft piece of cloth, often of wool, used to cover a bed, a horse, a dog, etc.; **2**, any covering; as, a waterproof *blanket:* —*v.t.* to cover with, or as with, a blanket.

blare (blâr), *n.* a loud sound like that of a trumpet:—*v.i.* [blared, blar-ing], to give forth a loud, brazen sound like that of a trumpet:—*v.t.* to sound loudly.

blar-ney (blär′ni), *n.* wheedling flattery:—*v.t.* to win over by smooth talk: —**Blarney Stone**, a stone in the wall of Blarney Castle, in Ireland, near Cork, said to confer the gift of blarney upon those who kiss it.

bla-sé (blä′zā′), *adj.* bored; glutted, as with pleasure, etc.

blas-pheme (blas-fēm′), *v.t.* [blasphemed, blasphem-ing], to speak profanely or impiously of (God or sacred things):—*v.i.* to talk irreverently.—*n.* **blas-phem′er.**—*n.* **blas′phe-my.**—*adj.* **blas′phe-mous.**

blast (blàst), *n.* **1**, a strong gust of wind; **2**, a forcible stream of air or gas from an opening; as, a *blast* of heat from a furnace; **3**, a sudden sound, as from a wind-instrument; **4**, a sudden harmful influence upon plants or animals; a blight; **5**, an explosion, as of dynamite, used in blowing up rocks; also, the charge so used:—*v.t.* **1**, to cause to fade or wither; as, a late frost *blasted* the crops;ʹ **2**, to destroy; **3**, to break or shatter by an explosive.

blast-off (blast′-ôf′), *n.* the take-off of a rocket at the moment when its fuels explode and hurl it from its launching-pad. Also used as *v.*

bla-tant (blā′tant), *adj.* **1**, noisy; vociferous; **2**, vulgarly conspicuous; as, a *blatant* display of wealth.—*adv.* **bla′-tant-ly.**

bla-ther (blath′ẽr, blā-), *n.* foolish talk. —*v.t.* and *v.i.* to speak foolishly.

¹blaze (blāz), *n.* **1**, a fire; bright flame; **2**, intense direct light, as of the sun; **3**, brilliant display; splendour; **4**, a sudden outbreak; as, a *blaze* of fury:—*v.i.* [blazed, blaz-ing], **1**, to burst into flame; burn; **2**, to glow or shine like a flame; as, his eyes *blazed;* **3**, to be lighted up, as a house.

²blaze (blāz), *n.* **1**, a white spot on the face of an animal; **2**, a mark made on a tree by removing a piece of the bark:— *v.t.* [blazed, blaz-ing], **1**, to mark (a tree),

by chipping off bark; **2**, to indicate (a trail) by marking trees in this way.

blaz-er (blāz′ẽr), *n.* a brightly coloured or striped sports jacket.

bla-zon (blā′zn), *n.* a showy display.— *v.t.* to proclaim; as, he *blazoned* the news abroad.

bleach (blēch), *v.t.* to whiten by a chemical process or by exposing to the sun's rays:—*v.i.* to become white:—*n.* the process of whitening or bleaching; also, a chemical used in the process.

bleach-ers (blēch′ẽrz), *n.pl.* a roofless or temporary stand providing cheap seats at a game, such as baseball.

bleak (blēk), *adj.* **1**, exposed to wind and cold; desolate; unsheltered; as, a *bleak* house; **2**, piercing cold, as a wind; **3**, cheerless; as, a *bleak* day.— *n.* **bleak′ness.**

blear (blēr), *adj.* sore or dim from a watery discharge; as, *blear* eyes:—*v.t.* **1**, to make (the eyes) sore or watery; **2**, to dim or obscure (the sight).—*adj.* **blear′—eyed′.**—*adj.* **blear′y.**

bleat (blēt), *n.* the cry of a sheep, goat, or calf; also, any similar cry:—*v.i.* to utter any such cry.

bleed (blēd), *v.i.* [bled (bled), bleed-ing], **1**, to give forth or to lose blood; **2**, to lose sap or juice; as, the tree *bled* from trimming; **3**, to be filled with sympathy or pity; as, my heart *bleeds* for you:— *v.t.* **1**, to take blood or sap from; **2**, *Colloq.*, to extort money from.

blem-ish (blem′ish), *n.* any defect or flaw:—*v.t.* to injure; mar; disfigure.

blend (blend), *v.t.* [blend-ed or blent (blent), blend-ing], to mix together, as colours, liquids, teas, or the like, so as to secure a certain quality or flavour:— *v.i.* to mingle; as, oil and water do not *blend;* merge; harmonize:—*n.* **1**, a thorough mixture; **2**, a shading or merging, as of one colour or flavour into another.

bless (bles), *v.t.* [blessed or blest (blest), bless-ing], **1**, to make or declare holy; as, God *blessed* the seventh day; **2**, to call down the favour of God upon; as, the priest *blessed* the altar; **3**, to give happiness or protection to; as, *bless* thy people; **4**, to praise; extol; as, *bless* the Lord.—*adj.* **bless′ed.**—*n.* **bless′ed-ness.**

bless-ing (bles′ing), *n.* **1**, the favour of God; **2**, a prayer of thanks for such favour, as at a meal; a benediction; **3**, something which makes for happiness or well-being; as, good health is a *blessing.*

blew (blōō), *p.t.* of *blow.*

blight (blīt), *n.* **1**, any disease that causes plants to wither or decay; **2**,

---

insects, fungi, or the like, which cause such a disease; **3,** anything which brings about ruin or decay; as, the *blight* of poverty:—*v.t.* to cause to wither; destroy.

blimp (blimp), *n. Colloq.,* a small, motor-driven balloon.

blind (blīnd), *adj.* **1,** sightless; **2,** unable or unwilling to understand, judge, or realize; as, *blind* to one's own faults; **3,** heedless; unthinking; as, *blind* haste; **4,** without reason; as, *blind* instinct; **5,** hidden; as, a *blind* ditch; difficult to follow; as, a *blind* path; **6,** without an opening or outlet; as, a *blind* wall; a *blind* alley:—*n.* **1,** anything designed to obstruct vision, or light, as a window shade, a blinker on a bridle, or the like; **2,** something to mislead the eye or the understanding; a trick; **3,** a place or means of concealment, as in hunting:—*v.t.* **1,** to deprive of sight; also, to dazzle; as, the sunlight *blinded* him; **2,** to deprive of judgment; as, hate *blinded* him.—*adv.* **blind′ly.**—*n.* **blind′ness.**

blind-er (blīn′dėr), *n.* a blinker on a horse's bridle which prevents him from seeing objects beside or behind him.

blind-fold (blīnd′fōld′), *adj.* **1,** with the eyes covered and unable to see; **2,** without thinking clearly; hence, heedless; reckless; as, *blindfold* extravagance:—*v.t.* **1,** to cover the eyes of, as with a bandage.

blink (blingk), *v.i.* **1,** to wink quickly; **2,** to see through half-shut eyes; as, to *blink* at the sun; **3,** to twinkle; glimmer:—*v.t.* **1,** to wink (the eyes) rapidly; also, to turn (lights) off and on rapidly; **2,** to close the mind to:—*n.* **1,** a rapid winking; **2,** a glimmer, as of light.

blink-er (blingk′ėr), *n.* **1,** a leather flap placed one on each side of a horse's bridle to prevent him from seeing objects beside or behind him; **2,** a blinking light used as a warning signal, as at a crossing.

blip (blip), *n.* a glowing spot on a radar screen to mark the position of an airplane, submarine, etc

bliss (blis), *n.* great happiness; perfect joy.—*adj.* **bliss′ful.**—*adv.* **bliss′ful-ly.**

blister (blis′tėr), *n.* **1,** a small bladderlike swelling of the skin, containing watery fluid, resulting from a burn, friction, etc.; **2,** any similar swelling, as of the surface of a leaf, or of paint, an air bubble in glass, etc.:—*v.t.* to cause blisters to rise on:—*v.i.* to become covered with blisters

blithe (blīth), *adj.* gay; joyous; cheery; happy; as, a *blithe* spirit.—*adv.* **blithe′ly.**—*adj.* **blithe′some.**

blith-er-ing (blith′ėr-ing), *adj.* talking nonsense; as, a *blithering* idiot.

blitz (blits), *n.* a lightning attack, as by use of tanks, bombs, aircraft, etc.; any such attack, esp. by propaganda.—*v.t.* to attack swiftly and violently.

bliz-zard (bliz′ėrd), *n.* a furious windstorm accompanied by fine driving snow and extreme cold.

bloat (blōt), *v.t.* **1,** to cause to swell, as with water or air; **2,** hence, to inflate; make vain; as, *bloated* with pride.

blob (blob), *n.* a drop of a thick liquid; as, a *blob* of paint; a daub or splash of colour.—*v.t.* to splotch, as with blobs.

bloc (blok), *n.* a coalition of (political, racial, or other) groups for a common purpose.

block (blok), *n.* **1,** a solid piece of wood, stone, metal, or the like; **2,** a form for moulding or shaping articles, as hats; **3,** the solid piece of wood on which an executioner chops off the heads; **4,** a stand on which articles are put up for sale by an auctioneer; **5,** a grooved pulley in a frame: often called *pulley block;* **6,** a connected row of houses or shops; a large building divided into separate houses or shops; **7,** a part of a city bounded by four streets: also called *square;* also, the length of one side of such a square; **8,** a number or section of things taken as a unit; as, a *block* of theatre seats; **9,** an obstacle; hindrance; hence, standstill; as, a traffic *block:*—*v.t.* **1,** to secure or hold up, as by square wooden supports; **2,** to obstruct; hinder; as, do not *block* my way; **3,** to mould on a form; as, to *block* hats; **4,** to outline roughly; plan without details; **5,** in football or basketball, to check the progress of, or interfere with (an opponent or his play). —*n.* **block′age.**

block-ade (blok-ād′), *n.* the shutting up of a place, as a port, by ships or troops in order to prevent anything from coming in or going out, in hope to force surrender:—**blockade—runner,** a ship that evades the enemy's blockade:—*v.t.* [blockad-ed, blockad-ing], to surround (a place) with a blockade.

block-head (blok′hed′), *n.* a dunce; dolt.

block-house (blok′hous′), *n.* a fort, built of heavy timber, often made with a projecting upper storey, and with loopholes in the walls through which to shoot.

blond or **blonde** (blond), *adj.* having light hair and a fair skin; fair in colouring.—*n.masc.* **blond.**—*n.fem.* **blonde.**

blood (blud), *n.* **1,** in man and other animals, the red fluid which circulates through the body, supplying it with nourishment and oxygen, and carrying away waste matter; **2,** kinship; relationship; as, near in *blood;* **3,** descent; esp., noble or royal lineage; as, a prince of the *blood;* **4,** bloodshed; violence; as, deeds of *blood;* **5,** a man of fire and spirit; as, a young *blood;* **6,** temper; anger; as, my *blood* is up. Also, **blood'-bank', blood'bath', blood count, blood group or type, blood heat, blood'less, blood'let'ting, blood money, blood plasma, blood pressure.**

blood-cur-dling (blud'kûr'dling), *n.* frightening; terrifying.

blood-hound (blud'hound'), *n.* **1,** a powerful hound with long drooping ears, famous for its acute sense of smell, and used chiefly in tracking criminals; **2,** a person keen in pursuit; a detective.

blood-root (blŭd'rōot'), *n.* an early spring flower of Canada and U.S. with white petals, red root, and red sap.

blood-shed (blud'shed'), *n.* the shedding of blood, esp. of human beings.

blood-shot (blud'shot'), *adj.* red and inflamed; as, *bloodshot* eyes.

blood-thirs-ty (blud'thûrs'ti), *adj.* cruel; murderous.

blood—ves-sel (blud'–ves'l), *n.* a tube in which blood circulates in the body, as a vein.

blood-y (blud'i), *adj.* [blood-i-er, blood-i-est], **1,** stained or running with blood; as, a *bloody* field; **2,** bleeding; as, a *bloody* nose; **3,** marked by much bloodshed; as, a *bloody* fight:—*v.t.* [bloodied, bloody-ing], to stain with blood.—*n.* **blood'i-ness.**

bloom (blōom), *n.* **1,** a blossom or flower; **2,** the state of being in flower or having flowers; as, the tulips are in *bloom;* **3,** a state or period of health and beauty; prime; as, the *bloom* of youth; **4,** a delicate, waxy, or powdery coating on certain fruits or leaves; **5,** a rosy flush on the cheeks:—*v.i.* **1,** to produce blossoms; flower; **2,** to glow with youth and freshness; flourish.

bloom-er (blōom'ér), *n.* **1,** *Slang,* a bad mistake; **2,** *pl.* a short skirt and loose trousers gathered below the knee, used by women for gymnastics.

blos-som (blos'um), *n.* **1,** the flower of a plant; **2,** the state of being in bloom; as trees in *blossom:—v.i.* **1,** to put forth flowers; **2,** to flourish.

blot (blot), *n.* **1,** a spot or stain; **2,** a spot on the reputation; disgrace:—*v.t.* [blot-ted, blot-ting], **1,** to spot or stain, as with ink; **2,** to dishonour; stain with disgrace; **3,** to dry (ink) with absorbent paper; **4,** to cancel; as, to *blot* out an obligation; **5,** to destroy

utterly; as, Sodom was *blotted* out; **6,** to darken or hide; as, a cloud *blots* out the moon: *—v.i.* to become blotted.

blotch (bloch), *n.* **1,** a large irregular spot, as of ink; **2,** a disfiguring spot or blemish on the skin:—*v.t.* to mark or disfigure with spots.—*adj.* **blotch'y.**

blouse (blouz; blous), *n.* **1,** a loose outer garment, like a smock, originally worn by workmen; **2,** any similar garment, esp. a shirtwaist worn by women and children.

¹blow (blō), *v.t.* [*p.t.* blew (blōo), *p.p.* blown (blōn), *p.pr.* blow-ing], **1,** to cause to move or send forward by a current of air; as, the wind *blows* the paper about; **2,** to force air upon, with the mouth or otherwise; as, *blow* out the light; **3,** to make or shape by causing to swell with air; as, to *blow* bubbles; **4,** to cause to sound by forcing air or steam through, as a wind-instrument or a whistle; **5,** to clear by forcing air through, as a tube or a nostril; **6,** to shatter by explosives; also, to melt, by an electric overcharge, as a fuse; **7,** *Slang,* to spend freely, as money:—*v.i.* **1,** to move flowingly, as the wind; **2,** to send forth air; send up a spout of water, as whales do in breathing out; **3,** to give forth sound when air or steam is forced through; as, the whistle *blew;* **4,** to pant; breathe with quick gasps; **5,** to be moved or carried by the wind; as, the curtains are *blowing;* **6,** *Colloq.,* to brag:—*n.* a gale.

²blow (blō), *n.* **1,** a hard stroke with the hand or with a weapon; **2,** a calamity. Also, **blow'gun', blow'hole', blow'off', blow'pipe', blow'torch', blow'up'.**

blow-er (blō'ér), *n.* a device for producing an air current; as, a furnace *blower.*

blow-zy (blou'zi), *adj.* slovenly; dishevelled; as, *blowzy* hair.

blow-out (blō'out'), *n.* the bursting of something, as a tire, caused by too much pressure from within.

blub-ber (blub'ér), *v.i.* to weep noisily: *—v.t.* to utter sobbingly:—*n.* **1,** a noisy weeping; **2,** the fat of whales and some other animals; a source of oil.

bludg-eon (bluj'un), *n.* a short, heavy-headed stick used as a weapon:—*v.t.* to strike with, or as with, a club.—*n.* **bludg'eon-ing.**

blue (blōo; blū), *adj.* [blu-er, blu-est], **1,** of the colour of the clear sky; azure; **2,** gloomy; sad; dismal; as, the sad news made her *blue;* **3,** discoloured; as, my nose was *blue* with cold:—*n.* **1,** the colour between green and violet; **2,** a dye or powder that colours blue; **3,** **the blue,** the sky; the sea; **4, blues: a,** *Colloq.,* usually with *the,* melancholy; low spirits; **b,** a melancholy kind of folk-song, of Negro origin, widely adopted in popular music:—*v.t.* [blued, bluing, or blue-ing], **1,** to make or dye the colour of the clear sky, or any hue like it; **2,** to treat with bluing.—*n.* **blue′ness.**

blue-bell (blōō′bel′; blŭ′bel′), *n.* any of several plants, bearing blue, bell-shaped flowers, as the harebell.

blue-ber-ry (blōō′; blŭ′ber-i), *n.* [*pl.* blue-ber-ries], **1,** a shrub of the heath family, bearing round, blue, edible berries; **2,** the berry.

blue-bird (blōō′-; blŭ′bûrd′), *n.* a songbird of the thrush family. The male has a blue back.

blue-bot-tle (blōō′-; blŭ′bot′l), *n.* **1,** any of several species of loud-buzzing fly with steel-blue body; **2,** the cornflower or bachelor's button; **3,** the hyacinth.

blue-fish (blōō′-; blŭ′fish′), *n.* [*pl.* blue-fish or blue-fishes], a valuable food fish of the Atlantic Coast.

blue-grass (blōō′-; blŭ′gras′), *n.* a valuable pasture and lawn grass with slender, bluish-grey stems.

blue-ing (blōō′ing), *n.* Same as **bluing.**

blue jay, a bird of eastern North America, with bright blue plumage and handsome crest.

blue-nose, Blue-nose (blōō′-; blŭ′nōz′), *n.* a native of the Canadian maritime provinces, esp. Nova Scotia.

blue-print (blōō′print′), *n.* a photographic print, white on blue paper, used as a plan in building operations, etc. —*adj.* and *v.t.* **blue′print′.**

blu-et (blōō′et), *n.* a low-growing plant of the U.S., with small, bluish flowers, and tufted stems.

¹bluff (bluf), *n.* **1,** a high, steep bank, cliff, or headland; **2,** a grove or clump of trees in the prairie provinces:—*adj.* **1,** rising steeply or boldly, as a cliff; **2,** abrupt but hearty in manner.—*n.* **bluff′ness.**

²bluff (bluf), *v.t.* and *v.i.* **1,** to mislead or overawe (someone) by assuming a bold front or bold speech; **2,** to accomplish or attempt by pretence or bravado; as, to *bluff* a test:—*n.* **1,** a show of pretended confidence, knowledge, etc.; **2,** one who bluffs.—*n.* **bluff′er.**

blu-ing or **blue-ing** (blōō′ing), *n.* a bluish preparation used in laundering to make clothes white.

blu-ish (blōō′ish), *adj.* somewhat blue.

blun-der (blun′dèr), *n.* a stupid or careless mistake:—*v.i.* **1,** to make a mistake from stupidity, ignorance, or the like; **2,** to move clumsily, as in a dark room.—*n.* **blun′der-er.**

blun-der-buss (blun′dèr-bus), *n.* a short gun of former times with a flaring muzzle, for shooting at close range.

blunt (blunt), *adj.* **1,** having a thick or rounded edge or point; not sharp; as, *blunt* scissors; **2,** dull; not quick-witted; not sensitive; **3,** abrupt in speech or manner; plain-spoken:—*v.t.* **1,** to dull the edge or point of; as, to *blunt* a knife; **2,** to make less keen; as, fatigue *blunted* his wits.—*adv.* **blunt′ly.** —*n.* **blunt′ness.**

blur (blûr), *v.t.* [blurred, blur-ring], **1,** to make indistinct; as, fog *blurred* the road ahead; **2,** to dim (the senses or judgment); **3,** to stain; blemish; as, to *blur* a paper with blots:—*n.* **1,** a smudge, smear, as of ink; **2,** an indistinct or confused effect; as, the page was a *blur* to his tired eyes.

blurb (blûrb), *n. Colloq.* an announcement, esp. one of fulsome praise, as on a book jacket.

blurt (blûrt), *v.t.* to utter suddenly and impulsively; as, to *blurt* out a secret.

blush (blush), *v.i.* **1,** to become red in the face, as from shame or confusion; **2,** to feel shame; as, she *blushed* for his ignorance:—*n.* **1,** a reddening of the face from any emotion; **2,** a rosy tint; as, the *blush* of dawn.

blus-ter (blus′tèr), *v.i.* **1,** to blow gustily, as wind; to be rough and windy, as the weather; **2,** to talk in a noisy, threatening style:—*n.* **1,** the noise and violence of a storm, or of a high wind; **2,** noisy talk; empty threats.—*adj.* **blus′ter-y.**

bo-a (bō′a), *n.* **1,** a large, non-poisonous snake that crushes its prey by coiling around it; **2,** a long fur or feather neck-piece for women.

boar (bōr), *n.* a male pig; **2,** the wild hog.

board (bōrd), *n.* **1,** a thin, flat piece of sawn timber, longer than it is broad; **2,** a table for food, or spread with food; **3,** food; meals served, esp. at a fixed price; **4,** a group of persons with power to act or advise; as, a *Board* of Health; **5,** pasteboard, as for a book cover; **6,** a flat piece of wood or other material prepared for a definite use; as, a diving *board;* a chequer*board:*—**on board,** on a ship or other conveyance:—*v.t.* **1,** to cover with boards; **2,** to furnish with food, or food and lodging, in return for money; as, to *board* students; **3,** to cause to be lodged and fed, as a horse at a stable; **4,** to get on (a ship or train):—*v.i.* to get meals, or meals and lodging, regularly, at a fixed charge; as, I *board* at my aunt's.—*n.* **board′er.** Also, **board′inghouse′; board′walk′.**

boast (bōst), *v.i.* to brag; praise oneself or one's belongings or deeds in loud terms; to exult:—*v.t.* to possess as a thing to be proud of; as, he *boasted* a fine ranch:—*n.* 1, a proud, vainglorious speech; bragging; 2, a cause of pride or vanity; as, his garden was his *boast*. —*n.* **boast'er.**—*adj.* **boast'ful.**—*adv.* **boast'ful-ly.**

boat (bōt), *n.* 1, any kind of small open watercraft, named according to the power by which it moves; as, row*boat;* sail*boat;* motor*boat;* also, a ship; 2, a long, narrow dish; as, a gravy*boat:*—*v.i.* to ride in a small open vessel; row; sail.—*n.* **boat'ing.** Also, **boat'house'; boat'load'.**

boat-swain (bō'sn; bōt'swān'), *n.* an under officer of a ship in charge of the crew, and of the rigging and anchors.

bob (bob), *n.* 1, a jerking movement, as of the head; also, a curtsy; 2, a weight, as on a pendulum or a plumb-line; also, a cork or float on a fishing line; 3, a style of haircut, shoulder length or shorter, for women or children; 4, a bobsled:—*v.t.* [bobbed, bob-bing], 1, to move (the head) with short jerky motions; 2, to cut (a woman's or child's hair) to shoulder length or shorter:— *v.i.* 1, to move jerkily; also, to curtsy; 2, to fish with a float on the line.

bob-bin (bob'in), *n.* a spool or reel around which thread or yarn is wound.

bobby pin (bob'i pin'), *n.* a flat, wire hairpin with closed prongs.

bobby—soxer (bob'i–sok'sẽr), *n.* a teen-age girl who ardently follows the fashions, esp. in wearing bobby socks.

bob-cat (bob'kat'), *n.* a lynx; wildcat.

bob-o-link (bob'o-lingk), *n.* an American songbird: also called *ricebird* or *redbird.*

bob-sled (bob'sled'), *n.* a long sled made of two short sleds joined by a plank; also, either of the two short sleds. Also, **bob'sleigh'.**

bob-tail (bob'tāl'), *n.* 1, a short tail or a tail cut short; 2, hence, an animal with such a tail.—*adj.* **bob'tailed'.**

bob-white (bob'hwīt'), *n.* 1, a species of quail or partridge; 2, its cry.

bode (bōd), *v.t.* [bod-ed, bod-ing], to be a sign or omen of; betoken; as, his lack of perseverance *bodes* ill for his future.

bod-ice (bod'is), *n.* 1, the close-fitting waist of a woman's dress; 2, a wide belt or girdle, laced and tight-fitting.

bod-i-ly (bod'i-li), *adj.* having material form; belonging to the body; having to do with the body; as, *bodily* warmth:—*adv.* completely; in one body; as a whole; as, the class was sent out *bodily.*

bod-kin (bod'kin), *n.* a blunt, large-

eyed needle for drawing ribbon, tape, etc., through a hem or loop.

body (bod'i), *n.* [*pl.* bodies], 1, the physical form and substance of a person or an animal, living or dead; 2, the trunk or main portion of a person, animal, or plant; also, the greater part of anything; as, the *body* of a letter; 3, a person; as, she is a good *body;* 4, a group of persons or things; as, a legislative *body;* a *body* of facts; 5, a mass of matter; as, a heavenly *body;* 6, consistency; substance; as, this silk has very little *body.*

bod-y-guard (bod'i-gärd'), *n.* a guard, of one or more, to protect a person; as, the president's *bodyguard.*

bog (bog), *n.* wet, spongy ground composed of partially decayed vegetation; a quagmire; marsh:—*v.i.* and *v.t.* [bogged, bog-ging], to sink, or cause to sink, in wet ground; to mire.—*adj.* **bog'gy.**

bo-gan (bō'gan), *n.* a small bay, cove, or inlet (Canadian Atlantic provinces).

bo-gey (bō'gi), *n.* in *golf,* one stroke above par on a hole.

bog-gle (bog'l), *v.i.* 1, to shy away; as, the horse *boggled* at the jump; 2, to hesitate or demur:—*v.t.* to bungle.

bo-gus (bō'gus), *adj.* counterfeit; not genuine; sham; as, *bogus* money.

bo-gy (bō'gi), *n.* [*pl.* bogies], a bugbear; hobgoblin. Also spelled **bo'gey.**

¹**boil** (boil), *v.i.* 1, to bubble from the action of heat; throw off bubbles of vapour; 2, to be cooked in boiling water; 3, to be violently agitated; seethe, as if boiling; 4, to be excited, as by anger:—*v.t.* 1, to heat (a liquid) to the boiling-point, or temperature at which vapour rises in bubbles; 2, to cook in a boiling liquid:—*n.* a bubbling from the effect of heat; as, the water came to a *boil.*

²**boil** (boil), *n.* an inflamed, festering sore in the skin, caused by infection.

boil-er (boil'ẽr), *n.* 1, a strong metal vessel in which steam is produced, as for driving engines; 2, a tank for storing hot water; 3, a vessel in which things are boiled.

bois-ter-ous (bois'tẽr-us), *adj.* 1, stormy; rough; as, a *boisterous* sea; 2, noisily cheerful; as, *boisterous* laughter. —*adv.* **bois'ter-ous-ly.**—*n.* **bois'ter-ousness.**

bold (bōld), *adj.* 1, courageous; fearless; as, a *bold* knight; 2, steep; abrupt; as, a *bold* headland; 3, clear; wellmarked; as, *bold* strokes of a pen; 4, showing courage or daring in thought or expression; as, *bold* ideas; 5, audacious; as, a *bold* front.—*adv.* **bold'ly.**— *n.* **bold'ness.**

bold-face, *n.* in *printing,* a type with thick, heavy lines.—*adj.* **bold′faced′.**

bo-ler-o (bō-lâr′ō), *n.* **1,** a short, open, waist-length vest or jacket; **2,** a lively Spanish dance in 3/4 time.

bole (bōl), *n.* the trunk of a tree.

boll (bōl), *n.* the seed pod of a plant, as of cotton:—**boll weevil,** a greyish beetle about ¼-inch long, which lays its eggs on cotton bolls. The larvae cause serious damage to the cotton crop.

bol-lard (bol′ėrd), *n.* a metal post on a dock or a ship for holding a hawser fast.

bo-lo-gna (bo-lo′nyȧ; bo-lō′nȧ), *n.* a sausage of mixed veal, beef, and pork encased in a skin.

bo-lo-ney (bo-lō′ni), *n. Colloq.* **1,** bologna sausage; **2,** *interj.* piffle; bosh; nonsense (*slang*).

bolster (bōl′stėr), *n.* a long pillow; also, a cushioned pad or support:—*v.t.* to support.

bolt (bōlt), *n.* **1,** a short, heavy-headed arrow for a crossbow; a dart; **2,** hence, anything coming swiftly or suddenly; as, a *bolt* of lightning; **3,** a metal pin or rod for fastening together parts of machinery, furniture, etc., threaded to hold a nut; **4,** a sliding catch for a door or gate; that part of a lock which is shot or drawn back by the key; **5,** a roll of cloth, usually containing about 40 yards; **6,** a sudden dashing or darting away, as of a horse; **7,** in politics, to withdraw support from one's own party:—*v.t.* **1,** to fasten with a sliding catch, as a door; **2,** to fasten together with bolts, as metal plates; **3,** to swallow (food) very rapidly, or without chewing; **4,** in politics, to break away from (one's party):—*v.i.* to dash away suddenly:—*adv.* stiffly.

bomb (bom; bum), *n.* a hollow iron ball or shell filled with an explosive which may be exploded by a time fuse, or by the force with which it strikes:—*v.t.* to attack with bombs; drop bombs on; bombard.—*n.* **bomb′er.**

bom-bard (bom-bärd′; bum-bärd′), *v.t.* **1,** to attack with cannon; **2,** to assail persistently; as, they *bombarded* me for pennies.—*n.* **bom-bard′ment.**

bom-bas-tic (bom-bas′tik), *adj.* pompous; high-sounding.

bomb′er (bom′ėr), *n.* a heavy aeroplane, used in offensive warfare.

bomb-shell (bom′shel′), *n.* **1,** an explosive missile; **2,** a devastating effect; as, his death came as a *bombshell.*

bo-na fi-de (bō′na fī′dē), in good faith; genuine; without deceit.

bo-nan-za (bō-nan′za), *n. Colloq.* a lucky speculation.

bon-bon (bon′bon′), *n.* a sweetmeat; a piece of candy.

bond (bond), *n.* **1,** that which fastens or confines; **2, bonds,** fetters; chains; imprisonment; **3,** a force or an influence which unites; as, the *bond* of kinship; **4,** an agreement binding a person to pay a certain sum of money, if certain conditions are not fulfilled; **5,** a certificate issued and sold by a corporation or government, and promising to pay the purchaser a specified sum by a certain date, with interest, usually in instalments; **6,** a guarantee that owners of goods, liable to a tax and held in a warehouse pending disposal, will pay the tax when the goods are removed:—*v.t.* **1,** to place under the conditions of a bond; as, the firm *bonded* its employees; **2,** to put (goods) into a bonded warehouse; **3,** to mortgage (property).

bond-age (bon′dij), *n.* slavery; servitude.

bond-hold-er (bond′hōl′dėr), *n.* one who holds or owns a bond.

¹bonds-man (bondz′man), *n.* [*pl.* bondsmen (-men)], a person who pledges his credit and assets as guarantee that another will fulfil certain conditions by a given time.

²bonds-man (bondz′man), *n.* [*pl.* bonds-men (-men)], a male serf. Also, **bond′man.**—*n.* **bonds′wom′an; bond′-wom′an.**

bone (bōn), *n.* **1,** the hard, whitish material of which the skeleton of an animal is composed; **2,** one of the separate pieces of this skeleton; **3,** a substance similar to bone, as ivory, whalebone, etc.; **4,** a piece of bone with meat on it; as, a soup *bone:*—*v.t.* [boned, bon-ing], **1,** to remove the bones from; as, to *bone* a chicken; **2,** to make stiff with whalebone or the like, as a corset.

bon-fire (bon′fir′), *n.* an outdoor fire of refuse or rubbish.

bon-net (bon′it), *n.* **1,** a head covering worn by women and children; usually brimless, with ribbons or strings tied under the chin; **2,** in Scotland, a soft woollen cap worn by men.

bon-ny or **bon-nie** (bon′i), *adj.* [bon-ni-er, bon-ni-est], pretty; healthy-looking.

bon-spiel (bon′spēl′), *n.* a curling match (of clubs, towns, provinces, etc.).

bo-nus (bō′nus), *n* a sum paid over and above what is strictly due.

bon-y (bōn′i), *adj.* [bon-i-er, bon-i-est], **1,** made of bone; like bone; as, *bony* tissue; **2,** full of bones, as a shad; **3,** having prominent bones; as, a *bony* arm; **4,** thin; gaunt; emaciated.

boo (bōō), *interj.* a sound to express

scorn or disapproval, or to startle.—*v.t.*
and *v.i.* [booed (bōod), boo-ing], to
utter *boo.*

boo-by (bōo'bi), *n.* **1,** a stupid fellow;
dunce; nitwit; **2,** in *games,* the player
with poorest score; as, he won the
booby prize. Also, **boo'by—hatch'**,
boo'by—trap'.

boo-gie-woo-gie (bōo'gi-wōo'gi), *n.*
a primitive jazz style of blues played
(on the piano) with persistent bass
rhythms.

book (book), *n.* a collection of sheets of
paper or other writing material, fastened or bound together, and enclosed in
a cover; **2,** a volume containing a composition of some length or a number of
shorter ones; as, a text*book;* a *book* of
verse; **3,** a main division, section, or
part of a literary composition; as, a
book of the Bible; **4,** in bridge, a minimum of six tricks, after which the
counting of tricks won begins; **5,** in
horse racing, a list of horses entered and
the bets laid on them:—**the Book,** the
Bible:—*v.t.* **1,** to record or register; as,
to *book* an order; **2,** to engage beforehand; as, to *book* an orchestra.—*adj.*
book'ish.—*n.* **book'ish-ness.** Also,
**book'bind'er, book'case', book-ends,
bookjacket, book'let, book'lore', book'-
man, book'mark', bookseller, book'-
store'.**

bookkeep-ing (book'kēp'ing), *n.* the
work of recording business transactions
in an orderly manner; the keeping of
accounts.—*n.* **book'keep'er.**

book-worm (book'wûrm), *n.* **1,** an
insect larva that feeds on the paste or
leaves of books; **2,** a person very fond of
books and reading.

¹boom (bōom), *n.* **1,** a long pole or spar
attached to a ship's mast to extend the
bottom of a sail; **2,** a similar pole
attached to a derrick's mast to support
or guide the load; **3,** a chain or line of
connected floating timbers used on a
river to keep logs from drifting away.

²boom (bōom), *n.* a deep, rumbling
sound, as the roar of breakers:—*v.i.*
and *v.t.* to make, or utter with, such a
sound.

³boom (bōom), *n.* **1,** a sudden increase
of business activity or in prices; also,
rapid growth, as in population; **2,** a
vigorous endorsement for office; as, a
boom for president:—*v.i.* to grow or
rise rapidly; become suddenly prosperous; as, the town *boomed* when gold
was found:—*v.t.* to advertise (a town
or a product) widely and actively; to
advocate (a candidate) with vigour.

boom-er-ang (bōom'ĕr-ang), *n.* **1,** a
bent, flat piece of wood, used as a
weapon by Australian natives, which,

when thrown in a certain manner,
returns to the thrower; **2,** hence, anything that recoils to the disadvantage
of its author.

¹boon (bōon), *n.* a favour; gift; blessing.

²boon (bōon), *adj.* jovial; merry; as, a
boon companion.

boor (bōor), *n.* **1,** a peasant or rustic; **2,**
a clumsy, ill-mannered person; a lout:
—*adj.* **boor'ish.**—*n.* **boor'ish-ness.**

boost (bōost), *Colloq.,* *v.t.* **1,** to lift by
pushing from behind; hoist; as, *boost*
me over the fence; **2,** to raise; push up;
as, to *boost* wages; **3,** to support; promote; as, *boost* Smith for mayor:—*n.*
a push or shove that helps someone to
rise or advance.—*n.* **boost'er.**

boot (bōot), *n.* **1,** an outer covering for
the foot, usually of leather, coming
above the ankle; a high shoe; **2,** esp.,
in the U.S., such a covering, either of
leather or of rubber, and reaching either
the knee or the hip; **3,** a place for
baggage in a coach, etc.:—*v.t.* **1,** to put
boots on (someone); **2,** to kick.

boot-black (bōot'blak'), *n.* one whose
job is to shine shoes.

boot-ee (bōo-tē'), *n.* **1,** a woman's half-
boot; **2,** a baby's knitted shoe.

booth (bōoth; bōoth), *n.* **1,** a temporary
stall for the sale of goods for a puppet-
show, or the like; **2,** an enclosure to
ensure privacy; as, a telephone *booth.*

boot-leg-ger (bōot'leg'ĕr), *Slang, n.*
one who makes or sells something, esp.
alcoholic liquors, in violation of law.—
v.t., v.i., and *adj.* **boot'leg'.**—*n.* **boot'-
leg'ging.**

boot-less (bōot'lis), *adj.* useless; unavailing; as, the search was *bootless.*

boo-ty (bōo'ti), *n.* [*pl.* booties], **1,** food,
guns, and the like, taken from the
enemy in war; **2,** the plunder of thieves
and robbers; **3,** any rich prize or gain.

booze (bōoz), *n.* *Colloq.* drink; liquor:
—*v.i.* [boozed, booz-ing], to drink to
excess.

bo-peep (bō-pēp'), *n.* a child's game of
peek-a-boo.

bo-rac-ic (bō-ras'ik), *adj.* pertaining to
or produced from, boron; boric:—
boracic acid, a white powder used in
solution as an antiseptic; boric acid.

bor-ax (bō'raks), *n.* a white crystalline
compound of sodium, boron, and oxygen: used as a cleaning agent, antiseptic, water softener, or the like.

bor-der (bôr'dĕr), *n.* **1,** the edge of anything, as of a lake; **2,** a boundary or
frontier, as of a country; **3,** a narrow
strip along or around something; as, a

handkerchief with a lace *border:*—*v.t.*
1, to surround or line with a border; as,
to *border* a path with flowers; **2**, to
come in contact with; lie next to; as,
their land *borders* ours:—*v.i.* **1**, to touch;
as, the park *borders* on the lake front;
2, to come near to being; as, his ability
borders on genius. Also, **bor'der-land'**;
bor'der-line'.

¹bore (bōr), *v.t.* [bored, bor-ing], **1**, to
pierce or drill a hole in; as, to *bore* the
ground; **2**, to form (a hole) by piercing
or drilling; as, to *bore* a tunnel; **3**, to
force (a passage) with effort; as, he
bored his way through the crowd:—*v.i.*
1, to make a hole; pierce; as, they
bored all day; **2**, to be drilled by an
instrument; as, this wood *bores* easily:
—*n.* **1**, a hole made by piercing or
drilling; **2**, hence, the hollow of a gun
or tube; **3**, the inside diameter of a
drilled hole; calibre; **4**, a high tidal
wave or flow, esp. in a narrow channel
or estuary.—*n.* **bor'er**.

²bore (bōr), *v.t.* [bored, bor-ing], to
weary by tiresome repetition or by
dulness; as, her complaining *bores* me:
—*n.* a tiresome person or thing.—*n.*
bore'dom.

³bore (bōr), *p.t.* of *bear*.

bo-ric (bō'rik), *adj.* containing boron;
boracic:—**boric acid**, a white powder
used in solution as an eyewash and an
antiseptic; boracic acid.

born (bôrn), *p.p.* of *bear* when used (in
the passive) of *birth*.

bo-ron (bō'ron), *n.* a non-metallic
element always occurring in combination, as in borax, boric acid, or the like.

bor-ough (bur'ō), *n.* **1**, an incorporated
town; also, in England, a town represented in Parliament; **2**, one of the five
political divisions of New York City.

bor-row (bor'ō), *v.t.* **1**, to obtain (something) with the understanding that it is
to be returned; **2**, to copy; adopt; as,
English has *borrowed* many words from
Latin:—*v.i.* **1**, to obtain something on
the promise to return it; as, he *borrowed*
from his son; **2**, to copy or adopt
another's thought or words; as, Shakespeare *borrowed* from old chronicles.—*n.*
bor'row-er.

bosh (bosh), *interj. Colloq.* nonsense!

bos-om (boo͞'zum; boo͞z'um), *n.* **1**, the
breast of a human being; **2**, the part of
a garment which covers the breast; **3**,
the breast as the seat of affections,
passions, emotions, or desires; the
heart; as, my *bosom* swells with pride;
4, intimacy; privacy; as, in the *bosom*
of the family; **5**, anything thought of
as resembling the breast; as, the *bosom*
of the sea:—*adj.* intimate; as, a *bosom*
friend.

boss (bôs), *n.* **1**, a projection, as of a
rocky spur on a mountain or a stud on
a shield; **2**, *Colloq.* a superintendent,
foreman, manager, or employer; **3**, a
politician who controls a large number
of votes.—*v.t.* to manage.—*v.i.* to be
master.—*adj.* **boss'y**.

bot-a-ny (bot'a-ni), *n.* [*pl.* botanies],
the science which treats of plants, their
form, growth, classification, distribution, and importance to other forms of
life.—*n.* **bot'a-nist**.—*adj.* **bo-tan'i-cal**
(bo-tan'i-kal); **bo-tan'ic**.

botch (boch), *n.* bungled work:—*v.t.*
to spoil; bungle; do clumsily.—*adj.*
botch'y.

bot-fly (bot'flī'), *n.* a parasite whose
larvae infest horses, etc.

both (bōth), *adj.* the one and the other;
not one only, but two; as, *both* boys
were lost:—*pron.* the two; as, take
both:—*conj.* alike; including; as, *both*
men and women.

both-er (both'ẽr), *v.t. Colloq.* to annoy;
worry; give trouble to; as, I am busy,
don't *bother* me:—*v.i.* to take trouble; as,
don't *bother* about dinner:—*n. Colloq.* **1**,
a source of worry; **2**, one who gives
trouble.—*adj.* **both'er-some**.—*n.* **both'-
er-a'tion**.

bots (bots), *n.pl.* an infection in horses
from the parasitic larvae of the botfly.

bot-tle (bot'l), *n.* **1**, a hollow, narrow-
necked vessel without handles, usually
of glass; **2**, the contents of such a
vessel; as, I drank a *bottle* of milk:—
v.t. [bot-tled, bot-tling], **1**, to put into
a bottle; **2**, to shut in or hold back; as,
to *bottle* up one's feelings.

bot-tle-neck (bot'l-nek'), *n.* figuratively, a condition that checks progress;
as, labour shortage is a *bottleneck* in
industry.

bot-tom (bot'um), *n.* **1**, the lowest part
of anything, as of a hill; **2**, the part
underneath; the base, as of a barrel;
3, the basis; essential point; as, he got
to the *bottom* of the mystery; **4**, the
ground under any body of water; **5**,
low land bordering a river; **6**, the part
of a vessel below the water-line; hence,
a ship:—*adj.* lowest.—*adj.* **bot'tom-less**.

bou-doir (boo͞'dwär), *n.* a lady's private
sitting-room or dressing-room.

bough (bou), *n.* a limb or branch of a
tree.

bought (bôt), *p.t.* and *p.p.* of *buy*.

bouil-lon (boo͞'yôn'; bool'yun), *n.* a
clear soup made from beef, etc.

boul-der (bōl'dẽr), *n.* a large stone,
detached from its original bed, and
rounded by water, weather, or moving
ice. Also spelled **bowl'der**.

bou·le·vard (bōō′le-värd′; bool′e-värd), *n.* 1, a broad, parklike avenue; 2, a street reserved for pleasure cars.

bounce (bouns), *v.t.* [bounced, bouncing], to throw or toss (something) so that it will rebound; as, to *bounce* a ball:—*v.i.* 1, to rebound; as, this ball won't *bounce;* 2, to move suddenly and noisily; as, she *bounced* out of the room:—*n.* the rebound of an elastic body; a sudden bound or spring; as, she rose with a *bounce.*—*n.* **bounc′er.**

¹bound (bound), *v.i.* 1, to leap or spring lightly; as, to *bound* from rock to rock; 2, to rebound; bounce; as does a ball:—*n.* 1, a light, springing step or leap; a rebound; 2, the space covered by such a leap.

²bound (bound), *v.t.* 1, to form the boundary of; as, the Pacific Ocean *bounds* Canada on the west; 2, to name the countries or waters surrounding; as, to *bound* Canada:—*n.* 1, a boundary; limit; 2, **bounds**, extent of territory, as of a state; hence, range of action, thought, or the like; as, within the *bounds* of reason.

bound-a-ry (boun′da-ri), *n.* [*pl.* boundaries], that which marks the extent or limit of anything, as a line which bounds a territory on a map, a fence around a property, or the like; also, the limit itself; as, this river forms a *boundary* between the two states.

bound-en (boun′dn), *adj.* *Archaic*, binding; as, one's *bounden* duty.

bound-er (boun′dẽr), *n.* *Colloq.* a vulgar, ill-bred person; cad.

bound-less (bound′lis), *adj.* unlimited; vast; as, *boundless* prairies.

boun-te-ous (boun′tē-us), *adj.* 1, giving freely; generous; as, *bounteous* nature; 2, plentiful; as, a *bounteous* harvest.

boun-ti-ful (boun′ti-fool), *adj.* 1, liberal; generous; as, a *bountiful* giver; 2, plentiful; yielding abundantly; as, *bountiful* acres.

boun-ty (boun′ti), *n.* [*pl.* bounties], 1, generosity in giving; also, generous gifts; as, this hospital is supported by the *bounty* of one man; 2, a premium or reward, esp. one offered or given by a government; as, to give a *bounty* for the killing of a wolf.

bou-quet (bōō-kā′; bō′kā′), *n.* 1, a bunch of flowers; 2, aroma, as of wine; fragrance.

bour-geois (bōōr′zhwä; boor-zhwä′), *n.* a member of the middle class of society:—*adj.* belonging to the middle class or having its characteristics.

bour-geoi-sie (bōōr′zhwä-zē′), *n.* the middle classes of a nation or people.

bout (bout), *n.* a test of skill, strength, or endurance; a contest; as, a boxing *bout;* 2, a spell or turn at something; as, a *bout* of house-cleaning.

bou-ton-niere (bōō′to-nyâr′), *n.* a man's buttonhole flower or bouquet.

¹bow (bou), *v.t.* to bend (the head, body, or knee) to express greeting, thanks, or respect; as, to *bow* the head in prayer; 2, to express (greeting, thanks, or respect) by bending the head, body, or knee; as, be *bowed* his thanks; 3, to oppress; crush; as, sorrow has *bowed* him:—*v.i.* 1, to bend, as in greeting, thanks, or respect: 2, to yield; as, I *bow* to your wishes:—*n.* a bending of the head, body, or knee, in greeting, thanks, or respect.

²bow (bō), *n.* 1, anything curved, as a rainbow; 2, a weapon of elastic wood for shooting arrows; 3, a rod strung with tightly stretched horsehair, for playing instruments like the violin; 4, a knot with a loop or loops, as of ribbon:—**bow window**, a bay window:—*v.t.* to bend or curve like a bow:—*v.i.* to become bent or curved.—*n.* **bow′man; bow′knot′, bow′shot′, bow′-string′.**—*adj.* **bow′leg-ged** (-leg′id).

³bow (bou), *n.* the forward part of a ship, airship, or the like:—*adj.* situated at or near the bow; as, the *bow* oar.

bow-els (bou′elz), *n.pl.* 1, the intestines, esp. of man; 2, the innermost parts, as of the earth; 3, pity; compassion.

bow-er (bou′ẽr), *n.* 1, a shelter made of boughs or twining plants; an arbour; 2, a lady's private apartment. *adj.* **bow′er-y.**

bow-ie knife (bō′i; bōō′i), *n.* a single-edged hunting blade, about 15″ long.

¹bowl (bōl), *n.* 1, a kitchen dish or vessel in shape more or less spherical; 2, the contents of a bowl; as, she drank a *bowl* of milk; 3, the hollow part of anything, as of a spoon; 4, anything bowl-shaped, esp. an amphitheatre for athletics; as, the Varsity *bowl.*

²bowl (bōl), *n.* 1. a heavy ball of wood used in lawn or pin bowling; 2, **bowls**, in England, a game played with such balls; fivepins; ninepins; tenpins; 3, the act of rolling a bowl:—*v.i.* 1, to play at bowling; 2, to roll a bowl or ball; 3, to move rapidly and smoothly along; as, we *bowled* along the road in the carriage:—*v.t.* 1, to knock over; as, he *bowled* him off his feet; 2, in the game of cricket, to throw (the ball) with a stiff arm.—*n.* **bowl′er.**

bowl-der (bōl′dẽr), *n.* Same as **boulder.**

bowl-ing (bōl′ing), *n.* the game of

bowls, ninepins, tenpins, or fivepins; as, fivepin *bowling* is popular in Ontario.

bow-sprit (bō′sprit; bou′sprit), *n.* a large spar or boom projecting from the prow, or forward end, of a sailing-vessel.

bow-wow (bou′wou′), *n.* a dog's bark: —*v.i.* (bou-wou′), to bark.

¹box (boks), *n.* a slap on the face or a cuff on the ear:—*v.t.* to strike with the fist or hand:—*v.i.* to fight with fists, usually gloved as a sport, or for money.—*n.* **box′er.**—*n.* **box′ing.**

²box (boks), *n.* an evergreen tree or shrub, much used for borders and hedges.

³box (boks), *n.* **1,** a case or container, of wood, cardboard, steel, etc., usually with a lid; **2,** the contents or the quantity that such a container can hold; as, to use up a *box* of soap; **3,** a compartment in a theatre, courtroom, etc.; as, the jury *box;* **4,** a shed or stall used as shelter for a sentry; **5,** in baseball, the place where the pitcher or the batsman stands; **6,** the driver's seat on a coach or carriage; **7,** a trunk: —*v.t.* to enclose in a box; as, to *box* toys.

box elder, *n.* a fast-growing shade tree with compound leaves, in Canada usually called the Manitoba maple.

box-ing (bok′sing), *n.* the art of fighting with the fists, esp. using boxing gloves.

box-la (boks′-la′), *n.* in Canada, the game of lacrosse as played in an enclosure. See *lacrosse.*

boy (boi), *n.* **1,** a male child, up to the age of about fourteen; a lad; **2,** a male servant; as, an errand-*boy.*—*adj.* **boy′-ish.**—*n.* **boy′hood.**

boy-cott (boi′kot), *v.t.* **1,** to refuse, in agreement with others, to buy from, sell to, or have dealings with (a person, firm, nation, etc.); **2,** to refuse as a group to use or purchase (a thing):—*n.* an organized refusal to have any dealings with a person, firm, or nation, or to buy a product, in an effort to force someone to do something.

boy-sen-ber-ry (boi′zn-ber′i; boi′-sn-), *n.* a large, sweet fruit developed from crossing the raspberry, blackberry, and loganberry, relished as a dessert because of its fine flavour.

bra (brä), *n. Colloq.* brassière.

brace (brās), *n.* **1,** that which steadies a thing or supports it firmly, as a steel beam or timber in a building; also, a bandage or a steel support for a part of the body; **2,** a pair; as, a *brace* of pistols; **3,** a curved line as {or}, connecting two or more lines of print, staffs of music, etc.; **4,** a curved implement used to hold and turn boring tools; **5,**

braces, suspenders:—*v.t.* [braced, bracing], to steady; as, to *brace* a ladder; to *brace* one's courage:—*v.i.* to rouse oneself to efforts; as, we told him to *brace* up.

brace-let (brās′lit), *n.* an ornamental band or chain for the wrist or the arm.

brack-en (brak′n), *n.* a large coarse brake fern that grows luxuriantly in North American woods and clearings.

brack-et (brak′it), *n.* **1,** an L-shaped piece or framework of wood or metal projecting from a wall, as to support a shelf; **2,** one of a pair of marks, as [ ] or ( ), used to enclose a word, or to mark off a part of the text from the rest:—*v.t.* **1,** to enclose in brackets; as, to *bracket* a phrase; **2,** to mention or classify (two things) together; as, gossips *bracket* the two names.

brack-ish (brak′ish), *adj.* saltish; salty; as, *brackish* water.

bract (brakt), *n.* a small, modified or specialized leaf, or leaflike part (sometimes large and brilliantly coloured), at the base of a flower or on its stalk.

brad (brad), *n.* a small, thin nail.

brag (brag), *v.i.* [bragged, brag-ging], to boast:—*n.* boasting.—*n.* **brag′ger.**

brag-ga-do-ci-o (brag′a-dō′shi-ō), *n.* **1,** empty boasting; **2,** a braggart.

brag-gart (brag′ert), *n.* a person given to bragging; a boaster:—*adj.* boastful.

Brah-man (brä′man), *n.* [*pl.* Brahmans], a Hindu of the highest priestly caste. Also, **Brah′min.**

braid (brād), *n.* **1,** something plaited; as, a *braid* of hair; **2,** a flat band made of machine-plaited silk, cotton, or wool, used for binding or trimming:—*v.t.* **1,** to intertwine (three or more strands of hair, silk, or the like); plait; **2,** to trim with braid.

braille (brāl), *n.* a system of printing for the blind using raised dots to be read by touch.

brain (brān), *n.* **1,** the mass of nervous tissue filling the skull: the centre of thought and feeling; **2, brains,** intelligence; as, she has *brains:*—*v.t.* to dash out the brains of (a person or animal).— *adj.* **brain′less, brain′y.**

brain-wash (brān′wôsh′), *v.t.* to bring about a complete change in one's beliefs or convictions, esp. by suggestion, force, etc.

braise (brāz), *v.t.* [braised, brais-ing], to cook (meat) by browning first in fat, and then simmering in very little liquid in a covered vessel.

¹brake (brāk), *n.* a device for checking the motion of a locomotive, vehicle, or the like:—*v.t.* [braked, brak-ing], to slow down or stop by applying a brake.

²brake (brāk), *n.* a place overgrown with shrubs, bushes, etc.; a thicket.

brake'man (brāk'man), *n.* One who applies the brakes, or assists the conductor on a railway train.

bram-ble (bram'bl), *n.* **1,** any prickly bush or shrub; **2,** the blackberry, raspberry, etc.

bran (bran), *n.* the outer coat or husks of wheat, rye, etc., separated from flour by sifting.

branch (brånch), *n.* **1,** a shoot or limb, from the main trunk of a tree, shrub, or plant; **2,** any member or part of a body or system; a department or subdivision; as, the executive *branch* of the government; a *branch* of a family:—*adj.* **1,** turning off from the trunk or main body; as, the *branch* roads of a railway system; **2,** subordinate; as, a *branch* office:—*v.i.* to send out a branch, or branches; to divide into branches; as, the firm has *branched* out into many cities.

brand (brand), *n.* **1,** a charred or burning piece of wood; **2,** a mark burned with a hot iron upon animals, to indicate the owner, or upon things, often to indicate the producer; **3,** a trademark; hence, any particular kind or make of goods; as, they do not carry that *brand* of coffee; **4,** a mark of disgrace:—*v.t.* to mark with, or as with, a brand; as, the cattle were *branded;* these words were *branded* upon my mind.

bran-dish (bran'dish), *v.t.* to wave or shake menacingly; flourish; as, they threatened us by *brandishing* their swords and rifles.

brand—new (brand'-nū'), *adj.* quite new.

bran-dy (bran'di), *n.* [*pl.* brandies], an alcoholic liquor distilled from wine or other fermented fruit juice.

brant (brant), *n.* a small, dark, wild goose.

brash (brash), *adj.* **1,** brittle; **2,** *Colloq.,* impudent; saucy; rash.

bra-sier (brā'zhėr), *n.* **1,** one who works in brass; **2,** a pan for burning charcoal.

brass (bràs), *n.* **1,** an alloy made of copper and zinc; **2,** the deep-yellow colour of brass; **3,** *Slang,* impudence; as, he had the *brass* to say that; **4,** **brasses,** ornaments of brass; also, musical wind-instruments of brass.

bras-si-ère (bra-zēr'), *n.* an under-waist for supporting the breasts.

brat (brat), *n.* a child, esp. one who is

unruly or impudent; (used in contempt).

bra-va-do (bra-vä'dō; -vä'), *n.* [*pl.* bravadoes or bravados], pretence of courage or indifference; boastful defiance; as, timid people often assume an air of *bravado.*

brave (brāv), *adj.* [brav-er, brav-est], **1,** fearless; courageous; as, a *brave* deed; **2,** showy; as, a *brave* display of flags:— *n.* a North American Indian warrior:— **the brave,** all those who are brave:— *v.t.* [braved, brav-ing], to face or meet with courage; defy; as, he *braved* the storm.—*adv.* **brave'ly.**

brav-er-y (brāv'ėr-i), *n.* [*pl.* braveries], **1,** fearlessness; courage; **2,** splendid appearance; finery.

bra-vo (brä'vō; brä'vō), *interj.* [*pl.* bravos], well done! good!

braw (brô), *adj.* fine; excellent.

brawl (brôl), *n.* a noisy quarrel:—*v.i.* **1,** to quarrel or wrangle noisily; **2,** to make a loud noise, as rushing water.— *n.* **brawl'er.**

brawn (brôn), *n.* **1,** firm, strong muscles; muscular strength; as, a fighter's *brawn;* **2,** in England, potted meat.—*adj.* **brawn'y.**

bray (brā), *n.* the loud, harsh cry of the ass; also, any similar sound, as the blast of a trumpet:—*v.i.* to utter a loud, harsh sound or cry.

braze (brāz), *v.t.* to solder (with brass and zinc).

bra-zen (brā'zn), *adj.* **1,** made of brass; like brass; **2,** loud and harsh; as, a *brazen* voice; **3,** impudent; shameless; as, a *brazen* manner:—*v.t.* to face with impudence; as, to *brazen* out a situation.—*adv.* **bra'zen-ly.**

bra-zier (brā'zhėr), *n.* an open pan for holding burning charcoal or live coals.

breach (brēch), *n.* **1,** a gap or opening made by breaking through; as, a *breach* in a wall; **2,** the breaking of a law, contract, etc.; as, a *breach* of promise; **3,** a break in friendly relations; as, a *breach* between nations.

bread (bred), *n.* **1,** a food made from flour or meal, moistened, raised, kneaded, and baked; **2,** livelihood; as, he works for his *bread;*—*v.t.* to cover with bread-crumbs before cooking.—*n.* **bread'-board'**, **bread'stuff'.**

bread-fruit (bred'frōōt'), *n.* **1,** the large, round fruit of a tree native to the South Pacific islands, which, when roasted, somewhat resembles bread; **2,** the tree which bears this fruit.

breadth (bredth), *n.* **1,** the measure of a thing from side to side; width; hence, spaciousness; extent; **2,** a piece of fabric of a certain width; as, a *breadth* of carpet; **3,** freedom from narrowness; liberality; as, *breadth* of mind.

break (brāk), *v.t.* [*p.t.* broke (brōk), *p.p.* bro-ken (brō′ken), *p.pr.* breaking], **1,** to split or smash into pieces by a blow or strain; as, to *break* glasses; fracture, as a bone; **2,** to force (a path, hole, or the like) into or through something; **3,** to destroy the arrangement or completeness of; as, to *break* ranks; to *break* a dollar bill; **4,** to weaken the force of; as, the haystack *broke* my fall; **5,** to set aside, violate, or fail to obey; as, to *break* a promise or a law; also, to escape from; as, he *broke* jail; **6,** to tell cautiously; disclose; as, to *break* news; **7,** to tame, as a horse; **8,** to plough or dig up, as ground; **9,** to make bankrupt; as, he *broke* the bank at Monte Carlo; **10,** to discontinue; as, to *break* off relations; **11,** to exceed; as, to *break* a swimming record; **12,** to interrupt, as silence or an electric circuit:—*v.i.* **1,** to separate into pieces suddenly; burst; as, the plate *broke;* **2,** to change abruptly in gait, tone, etc.; as, the horse *broke* into a gallop; three times his voice *broke* during the questioning; **3,** to fail in health; weaken; **4,** to burst forth violently, as a storm or cry; **5,** to force a way; as, he *broke* into the safe; **6,** to begin to be; as, day *breaks;* **7,** to discontinue relations; as, the firms *broke* with each other; **8,** *Slang,* to occur or turn out in a given way; as, luck *broke* against him:—*n.* **1,** the act of breaking; as, the *break* of day; **2,** something produced by breaking; as, a *break* in a wire; an interruption; as, a *break* in a conversation; **3,** a sudden fall in prices; as, a *break* in the stock market; **4,** *Colloq.,* a blunder in speech or action; **5,** *Slang,* a turn of fortune; as, it was a lucky *break* for me.—*adj.* **break′-a-ble.**—*n.* **break′age.**—*n.* **break′-down′; break′through′; break′up′.**—*adj.* **break′neck′.**

break-er (brāk′ẽr), *n.* **1,** one who or that which smashes or breaks; **2,** a machine for crushing coal, rocks, etc.; **3,** a wave which dashes itself upon the shore in foam.

break-fast (brek′fast), *n.* the first meal of the day:—*v.i.* to eat breakfast.

break-wa-ter (brāk′wô′tẽr), *n.* a wall or dike built to break the force of the waves, as around a harbour.

breast (brest), *n.* **1,** the front part of the body between the neck and the abdomen; **2,** either one of the glands found on the chest of man and some other mammals, serving, in the female, for the secretion of milk; **3,** anything resembling the breast; as, the *breast* of a hill; **4,** the seat of the affections:—*v.t.* to face bravely.

breast-bone (brest′bōn′), *n.* the thin, flat, vertical bone in the front of the chest to which the seven upper pairs of ribs are attached.

breast-plate (brest′plāt′), *n.* in a suit of armour, the metal plate protecting the chest.

breast-work (brest′wûrk′), *n.* a hastily constructed wall built breast-high for defence.

breath (breth), *n.* **1,** the air drawn into and forced out of the lungs; **2,** a single act of drawing air into or forcing air out from the lungs; hence an instant; a pause; **3,** the power to breathe freely; as, to lose one's *breath;* hence, life; strength; **4,** a light breeze; as, a *breath* of air; **5,** a whisper; as, a *breath* of scandal; **6,** a film produced by the breath, as on a mirror.—*adj.* **breath′-tak′ing.**

breathe (brēth), *v.i.* [breathed, breathing], **1,** to use the lungs; be alive; as, the dying man still *breathes;* **2,** to rest from stress or action; pause; as, I can *breathe* again, now that the work is done; **3,** to blow softly, as wind:—*v.t.* **1,** to draw into and force out of the lungs; as, we *breathed* the fresh air; **2,** to exhale; give forth; as, he *breathed* a sigh of relief; the flower *breathes* perfume; **3,** to whisper softly; as, don't *breathe* a word of this.

breath-er (brēth′ẽr), *n.* a pause (for breath).

breath-less (breth′lis), *adj.* **1,** out of breath, as from exertion or emotion; as, *breathless* from running; *breathless* with fear; **2,** dead.—*adv.* **breath′less-ly.**

bred (bred), *p.t.* and *p.p.* of *breed.*

breech (brēch), *n.* **1,** the rear part of a firearm; **2,** the buttocks; rump.

breech-es (brich′iz), *n.pl.* **1,** short trousers, fastened below the knee; **2,** *Colloq.,* trousers.

breed (brēd), *v.t.* [bred (bred), breeding], **1,** to give birth to; **2,** to mate or raise, as animals or plants, for the purpose of maintaining or improving the stock; **3,** to train; rear; as, I was *bred* to be my father's successor; **4,** to nourish; as, swamps *breed* mosquitoes; poverty *breeds* misery:—*v.i.* **1,** to bear young; **2,** to be born; come into being; as, crime *breeds* in slums:—*n.* race; stock; strain; as, a good *breed* of cattle.—*n.* **breed′er.**

breed-ing (brēd′ing), *n.* **1,** the producing of young; **2,** the training or bringing up of young; esp., the results of training; good manners; as, a man of *breeding.*

breeks (brēks), *n. Colloq.* breeches.

breeze (brēz), *n.* a gentle wind.—*adj.* **breez'y.**

breeze-way (brēz'wā'), *n.* a covered passage (often closed in) between house and garage.

breth-ren (breth'ren), *n.pl.* brothers; fellow members of a church or fraternity.

breve (brēv), *n.* a mark [˘] often used above a vowel to show that it is short in sound; as, *flat* (flăt).

brev-i-ty (brev'i-ti), *n.* [*pl.* brevities], briefness; shortness.

brew (brōō), *v.t.* 1, to make, as beer, from malt and hops, by steeping, boiling, and fermenting; 2, to make by steeping, as tea, or by mixing, as punch; 3, to bring about; plot; as, to *brew* mischief:—*v.i.* 1, to make a liquor by fermentation or steeping; 2, to gather; grow in force; as, a storm *brews:*—*n.* a drink made by brewing.—*n.* **brew'er.**—*n.* **brew'er-y.**

¹bri-ar (brī'ẽr), *n.* Same as ¹**brier.**

²bri-ar (brī'ẽr), *n.* Same as ²**brier.**

bribe (brīb), *n.* a gift made or promised to a person to influence him to adopt a wrong course of action:—*v.t.* [bribed, brib-ing], to influence by a bribe.—*n.* **brib'er-y.**

bric—a—brac (brik'–a–brak'), *n.* small articles of artistic or sentimental value, displayed as ornaments; knickknacks.

brick (brik), *n.* 1, a material used in building or paving made from clay moulded into blocks, usually oblong, and baked in the sun or in kilns; also, one of these blocks; 2, anything shaped like such a block; as, a *brick* of ice-cream; 3, *Colloq.*, a good fellow; as, he's a *brick* to do it:—*v.t.* to lay bricks; wall in with bricks; as, to *brick* up a fireplace.—*n.* **brick'kiln'; brick'lay'er; brick'yard'.**

brick-bat (brik'bat'), *n.* 1, a piece of brick used as a missile; 2, an unkind remark.

brid-al (brīd'al), *n.* a wedding:—*adj.* pertaining to a bride or a wedding.

bride (brīd), *n.* a woman newly married, or about to be married.

bride-groom (brīd'grōōm'), *n.* a man newly married, or about to be married.

brides-maid (brīdz'mād'), *n.* a woman who attends a bride at her wedding.

bridge (brij), *n.* 1, a structure built to carry a road or path across a river, valley, or the like; 2, anything shaped like a bridge, as the upper part of the nose, the arch for the strings on a violin, or a mounting for artificial teeth;

3, an observation platform above the deck of a ship for the officer in charge or the pilot; 4, a movable passageway from a ship to the shore; 5, a modern card game developed from the game of whist:—*v.t.* [bridged, bridg-ing], 1, to build a bridge over; span; 2, to pass; get over; as, he helped me *bridge* the difficulty.—*n.* **bridge'work'** (of teeth).

bri-dle (brī'dl), *n.* 1, in a horse's harness, the headgear, with the bit and reins, by which the horse is governed; 2, a check; restraint; as, to put a *bridle* on the tongue:—*v.t.* [bri-dled, bri-dling], 1, to put a bit and reins on; 2, to control, as, the temper:—*v.i.* to throw back the head, as in anger or pride; as, she *bridled* at his words.

brief (brēf), *adj.* 1, short; not lengthy; as, a *brief* delay; 2, said in a few words; condensed; as, a *brief* description:—*n.* a summary; esp., a lawyer's outline of the argument of a case.—*adv.* **brief'ly.**

¹bri-er or **bri-ar** (brī'ẽr), *n.* 1, any thorny plant or shrub; 2, a thorn, as of a rose; 3, a patch of thorny bushes.

²bri-er or **bri-ar** (brī'ẽr), *n.* 1, the European white-heath; 2, a tobacco-pipe made from its root.

brig (brig), *n.* a two-masted square-rigged vessel.

bri-gade (bri-gād'), *n.* 1, in some armies a unit consisting of two regiments, under a brigadier-general; 2, an organized body of men acting under authority; as, a fire-*brigade.*

brig-a-dier (brig'a-dēr'), *n.* an officer in command of a brigade, ranking next below a major-general: more often called *brigadier-general.*

brig-and (brig'and), *n.* one of a gang of robbers; bandit.—*n.* **brig'and-age.**

brig-an-tine (brig'an-tēn', -tīn'), *n.* a two-masted square-rigged ship, unlike a brig in not having a square mainsail: it was often used as a pirate craft.

bright (brīt), *adj.* 1, giving much light; shining, as the sun; 2, vivid; as, *bright* green; 3, lively; cheerful; 4, clever; as, a *bright* idea; a *bright* child; 5, favourable; hopeful; as, a *bright* future. —*adv.* **bright'-ly.**—*n.* **bright'ness.**

bright-en (brīt'n), *v.i.* to grow clearer, lighter, or brighter; as, the day *brightens:*—*v.t.* to make light or bright; as, to *brighten* a room with flowers.

bril-liant (bril'yant), *adj.* 1, sparkling; glittering; as, the *brilliant* light of a chandelier; 2, very successful; distinguished; as, a *brilliant* reign; 3, distinguished by splendid mental ability; as, a *brilliant* scientist:—*n.* a diamond or other precious stone, cut to show its sparkling quality.—*n.* **bril′-liance; bril′lian-cy.**

bril-lian-tine (bril′yan-tēn′), *n.* a liquid used to give gloss to the hair.

brim (brim), *n.* **1,** the edge or brink, as of a lake; the rim, as of a cup; **2,** the projecting edge, as of a hat:—*v.i.* [brimmed, brimming], to be full to the very edge; as, her eyes *brimmed* with tears.—*adj.* **brim′less.**

brim-ful (brim′fool′; brim′fool′), *adj.* full to the edge; completely filled; as, a cup *brimful* of tea.

brim-stone (brim′stōn′), *n.* sulphur.

brin-dled (brin′dld), *adj.* streaked with gray, brown, or tawny markings; as, a *brindled* cow or dog. Also, **brin′ded.**

brine (brīn), *n.* **1,** water that is extremely salty; **2,** the ocean.—*adj.* **brin′y.**

bring (bring), *v.t.* [brought (brôt), bringing], **1,** to cause (a person or thing) to come along; as, *bring* your cousin home; also, to fetch; as, *bring* me a cake; **2,** to carry; as, the boat *brought* me to land; **3,** to draw; attract; as, this speaker always *brings* a crowd; **4,** to cause, or to result in; as, winter *brings* snow; sleep *brings* relief; **5,** to sell for (a price); as, diamonds *bring* a large sum; **6,** to recall; as, that *brings* up a story; **7,** to persuade; as, I cannot *bring* myself to go; **8,** in law, to begin; as, to *bring* suit.

brink (bringk), *n.* the edge or top, esp. of a steep place; as, the *brink* of a pit; hence, verge; as, on the *brink* of ruin.

bri-quette (bri-ket′), *n.* a pressed brick of coal dust (for fuel).

brisk (brisk), *adj.* **1,** active; lively; swift; nimble; as, a *brisk* walker; **2,** burning freely, as a fire; **3,** keen; enlivening, as a wind.—*adv.* **brisk′ly.**

bris-ket (bris′kit), *n.* the breast or lower chest of an animal used for food.

brist-le (bris′l), *n.* a short, stiff, coarse hair:—*v.i.* [bris-tled, bris-tling], **1,** to stand up in a stiff, prickly way, as an angry dog's hair; **2,** to be covered with bristly points; as, the battle front *bristles* with bayonets; **3,** to show signs of anger or defiance; as, the class *bristled* with revolt.—*adj.* **bris′tly.**

Brit-ain (brit′un), *n.* the island of England, Scotland, and Wales.

Brit-ish (brit′ish), *adj.* of, or relating to, Great Britain.

Brit-on (brit′un), *n.* a native or subject of Great Britain.

brit-tle (brit′l), *adj.* easily broken; apt to break, as ice, glass, or thin china.

broach (brōch), *n.* **1,** any pointed, spike-shaped tool, as a skewer for roasting meat; **2,** a tapered bit for boring holes, esp. in metal; a reamer:—*v.t.* **1,** to tap or pierce, as a keg of wine; **2,** to begin to talk about; as, to *broach* an unpleasant subject.

broad (brôd), *adj.* **1,** wide from side to side; **2,** spacious; vast; as, *broad* estates; **3,** liberal; as, *broad* views; **4,** open; clear; as, *broad* daylight; **5,** evident; plain; as, a *broad* hint; **6,** indelicate; as, a *broad* joke.—*adv.* **broad′ly.**

broad-axe or **broad-ax** (brôd′aks′), *n.* **1,** a broad-bladed axe for cutting timber; **2,** an ancient weapon with a wide blade.

broad-cast (brôd′kåst′), *v.t.* [broadcast or broadcast-ed, broadcast-ing], **1,** to scatter or throw by hand, as seed; **2,** to spread abroad, as news; **3,** to send out (messages or sound) by radio from a transmitting station:—*adv.* so as to scatter widely; as, to sow *broadcast*:—*n.* **1,** a scattering of seed far and wide; **2,** anything broadcast by radio, as a programme, speech, or game.—*n.* **broad′cast′er.**

broad-cloth (brôd′clôth′), *n.* **1,** a fine woollen cloth with a smooth surface, often used for suits; **2,** a fine grade of cotton or silk cloth, much used for shirts, dresses, etc.

broad-en (brôd′n), *v.i.* to grow wide or wider; as, the river *broadens* at this point:—*v.t.* to make wider or more liberal; as, education should *broaden* the mind.

broad-loom (brôd′lōōm′), *n.* seamless carpet 54″ to 8′, wide.

broad—mind-ed (brôd′–mīn′did),*adj.* liberal in opinions; tolerant.

broad-side (brôd′sīd′), *n.* **1,** the entire side of a ship above the water-line; also, the broad unbroken expanse of anything; **2,** all the cannon on one side of a warship; also, a discharge from all these at once; **3,** a sheet of paper printed on one side only, as a tract or advertisement; **4,** *Colloq.,* a printed or verbal attack on some person.

broad-sword (brôd′sōrd′), *n.* a sword with a broad blade.

bro-cade (brō-kād′), *n.* a silken fabric woven with gold and silver threads, or ornamented with raised designs of flowers, etc.:—*v.t.* [brocad-ed, brocading], to decorate or weave with a raised pattern.—*adj.* **bro-cad′ed.**

broc-co-li (brok′o-li), *n.* a vegetable of the mustard family, related to the cabbage and cauliflower.

bro-chure (brō-shyōōr′), *n.* a pamphlet or stitched booklet.

bro-gan (brō′gan), *n.* a man's heavy

oxford shoe, with decorative perforations.

¹**brogue** (brōg), *n.* a pronunciation characteristic of a dialect; esp., the Irish pronunciation of English.

²**brogue** (brōg), *n.* Same as *brogan.*

broil (broil), *v.t.* to cook directly over or under a hot fire:—*v.i.* to be exposed to great heat; as, we fairly *broiled* in the hot sun:—*n.* a broiled dish.

broil-er (broil′ėr), *n.* **1,** a utensil or device for cooking food directly over or under a fire; **2,** a young fowl suitable for broiling.

broke (brōk), *p.t.* of *break.*

bro-ken (brō′ken), *adj.* **1,** not entire; in pieces; shattered; as, a *broken* dish; **2,** fractured; as, a *broken* bone; **3,** cut into; as, ground *broken* by ploughing; **4,** uneven; as, *broken* country; **5,** incomplete; disorganized; as, a *broken* set; *broken* ranks; **6,** interrupted; as, *broken* sleep; **7,** violated; as, a *broken* vow; **8,** trained to obedience; as, a *broken* horse; **9,** enfeebled; weak; as, *broken* health; **10,** subdued; crushed; as, a *broken* spirit; **11,** imperfectly spoken; as, *broken* English.—*adv.* bro′-ken-ly.—*adj.* broken-down; broken-hearted.

bro-ker (brō′kėr), *n.* an agent for others in buying or selling anything, as real estate, stocks, bonds, or the like.

bro-ker-age (brō′kėr-ij), *n.* the business of a broker; also, his fee or commission.

bro-mine (brō′mēn; -mĭn; -min), *n.* an element of the chlorine–iodine group, used in dyes, photography, and medicine.

bron-chi (brong′kī), *n.pl.* [*sing.* bronchus (brong′kus)], the two main branches of the windpipe, or trachea.—*adj.* bron′chi-al.

bron-chi-tis (bron-kī′tis; brong-kī′-tis), *n.* an inflammation of the bronchi or their branches.

bron-co or **bron-cho** (brong′kō), *n.* [*pl.* broncos, bronchos], in western North America. a small, half-tamed horse.

bron-to-saur-us (bron′to-sô′rus), *n.* a prehistoric reptile (nearly 100′ long) of the dinosaur era.

bronze (bronz), *n.* **1,** an alloy or metallic mixture of eight or nine parts copper to one of tin; **2,** a work of art cast or wrought in this alloy; **3,** a yellowish or reddish brown, the colour of bronze:—*adj.* made of bronze; like bronze:—*v.t.* [bronzed, bronz-ing], to make of the colour of bronze; tan; as, the sun *bronzed* his face.

brooch (brōch), *n.* an ornamental pin or clasp, used for fastening the dress, esp. at the neck.

brood (brōod), *n.* **1,** all the young of birds hatched at one time; **2,** all the young of one mother; **3,** the eggs and larvae of bees when in the comb:—*v.i.* **1,** to sit on eggs, as a hen; **2,** to think about something long and moodily; as, to *brood* over losses:—*v.t.* to sit on and hatch (eggs).—*n.* brood′er.

¹**brook** (brook), *n.* a small, natural stream of water:—**brook trout,** a freshwater game fish of eastern North America, related to the salmon, and valued highly as food.

²**brook** (brook), *v.t.* to bear; put up with; as, I will *brook* no delay.

broom (brōom), *n.* **1,** a long-handled brush used for sweeping; **2,** a shrub of the pea family, with stiff, slender branches:—**broom corn,** a cornlike grass, eight to ten feet high, used in making brooms.—*n.* broom′stick′.

broth (brôth), *n.* thin soup made by boiling meat slowly in water.

broth-er (bruth′ėr), *n.* **1,** a male child of the same parents; **2,** a member of a fatherland or race; a fellow-man; **3,** one closely united to another or others by a common interest, such as a lodge, church, etc.

broth-er-hood (bruth′ėr-hood′), *n.* **1,** a group of men with similar interests and aims; a fraternity; as, the legal *brotherhood;* **2,** fellowship; kinship; as, the *brotherhood* of man.

broth-er—in—law (bruth′ėr-in-lô′), *n.* [*pl.* brothers-in-law], a brother of one's husband or wife, or husband of one's sister.

broth-er-ly (bruth′ėr-li), *adj.* like a brother; kind; friendly.—*n.* broth′er-li-ness.

brougham (brōom; brōo′um; brō′um), *n.* a closed automobile or carriage with the driver's seat outside.

brought (brôt), *p.t.* and *p.p.* of *bring.*

brow (brou), *n.* **1,** the forehead; **2,** the arch of hair over the eye; the eyebrow; **3,** the edge of a cliff; the top of a hill.

brow-beat (brou′bēt′), *v.t.* [*p.t.* browbeat (-bēt′), *p.p.* browbeat-en (-bēt′n), *p.pr.* browbeat-ing], to frighten by stern looks or words; bully.

brown (broun), *adj.* of a dusky colour between black and orange:—*n.* a dark colour between black and orange:—*v.i.* and *v.t.* to become or to make brown.

brown-ie (broun′i), *n.* **1,** a good-natured elf supposed to do certain useful household tasks by night, as sweeping, churning, etc.; **2,** a thin flat chocolate cake with nuts in it; **3,** **Brownie,** a girl scout 8 to 11 years of age.

browse (brouz), *n.* the tender shoots of shrubs and trees fit for the food of cattle, etc.:—*v.i.* [browsed, brows-ing], **1,** to nibble off twigs or grass; **2,** to read here and there in books; wander idly, as through an art gallery, etc.

bru-in (broo′in), *n.* the brown bear: so called in popular tales.

bruise (brooz), *n.* an injury to the flesh which discolours the skin:—*v.t.* [bruised, bruis-ing], to injure or hurt; as, to *bruise* one's leg; to *bruise* a friend's feelings:—*v.i.* to show the effects of bruises; as, I *bruise* easily.

bruit (broot), *v.i.* to report; rumour; as, it was *bruited* that he was ill.

bru-nette or **bru-net** (broo-net′), *adj.* having dark skin, hair, and eyes.— *n.masc.* **bru-net′.**—*n.fem.* **bru-nette′.**

brunt (brunt), *n.* the heaviest part of a shock or strain; as, to bear the *brunt.*

brush (brush), *n.* **1,** an implement made of bristles, feathers, or the like, fixed in a back or handle, used for cleaning, smoothing, applying paint, etc.; **2,** the tail of a fox; **3,** a slight battle; skirmish; **4,** the act of cleaning or smoothing with a brush; **5,** a thicket of small trees; **6,** branches cut from trees; brushwood; **7,** thin metallic plates or wires bound together, to conduct a current to or from an electric motor or dynamo:—*v.t.* **1,** to sweep, cleanse, or rub with a brush; **2,** to remove, as with a brush; as, to *brush* crumbs away; **3,** to touch lightly in passing; graze:— *v.i.* to pass quickly with a casual touch; as, he *brushed* by me.—*adj.* **brush′y.**

brush-wood (brush′wood′), *n.* **1,** a dense growth of bushes; thicket; **2,** cut branches, etc., suitable for a fire.

brusque (brusk; broosk), *adj.* abrupt; curt in manner or speech.—*adv.* **brusque′ly.**—*n.* **brusque′ness.**

Brus-sels sprouts, a food plant of the mustard family, with small, green, cabbagelike heads growing on a stalk.

bru-tal (broo′tal), *adj.* savage; cruel; inhuman.—*n.* **bru-tal′i-ty** (broo-tal′i-ti).

brute (broot), *adj.* **1,** without intelligence; not human; **2,** like a wild beast; cruel:—*n.* **1,** a beast; esp., a wild beast; **2,** a man without human kindliness.— *v.t.* **bru′tal-ize:**—*adj.* **brut′ish.**

bub-ble (bub′l), *n.* **1,** a small, globelike film filled with air or gas; **2,** a small body of air or gas rising in a liquid, as in soda-water, or held within a solid, as in ice or glass; **3,** anything unreal or fanciful; a delusion:—*v.i.* [bub-bled, bub-bling], **1,** to rise in bubbles; also,

to form bubbles, as soda-water; **2,** to make a gurgling sound, as a stream.— *adj.* **bub′bly.**

bu-bon-ic plague (bū-bon′ik), a contagious disease (often fatal), marked by inflamed swelling of glands in armpit or groin, chills and fever, and delirium: fleas from infected rats carry it.

buc-ca-neer (buk′a-nēr′), *n.* a pirate; a sea robber.

buck (buk), *n.* **1,** the male of an animal, as the deer or rabbit, of which the female is called *doe;* **2,** a sudden, vertical leap, as of an unruly horse; **3,** in football, a hard plunge into the opponents' line; **4,** *Slang,* a dollar:—*v.i.* to leap suddenly into the air with arched back as a horse does to throw off a rider:—*v.t.* **1,** to throw off by a sudden leap; **2,** in football, to charge into (the opposing line.)

buck-board (buk′bôrd′), *n.* a light wagon with the seat set on a long, flexible board fastened without springs to the axles.

buck-et (buk′it), *n.* **1,** a wooden pail for drawing water; **2,** any pail or holder in which something is collected or carried, as a dredge scoop; **3,** the amount a bucket holds; a bucketful.

¹buck-le (buk′l), *n.* **1,** a clasp for holding together the ends of a strap or the like; **2,** an ornament of similar shape for a dress, hat, etc.:—*v.t.* [buck-led, buck-ling], **1,** to fasten with a buckle; **2,** to apply (oneself) with energy:—*v.i.* **1,** to be held together by means of a buckle; **2,** to set to work with energy; as, to *buckle* down to studying.

²buck-le (buk′l), *v.i.* [buck-led, buckling], to bend or warp, as metal, from pressure or heat; crumple up:—*v.t.* to cause to buckle; crumple:—*n.* a bend, twist, or kink in a piece of metal.

buck-ler (buk′lẽr), *n.* a small, round shield, or similar protection.

buck-saw (buk′sô′), *n.* a saw set in a deep, H-shaped frame and used with both hands for sawing firewood.

buck-shot (buk′shot′), *n.* coarse lead shot, used for large game.

buck-skin (buk′skin′), *n.* a soft, pliable leather made from the skin of a deer or sheep:—*adj.* made of buckskin.

buck-toothed (buk′tootht′), *adj.* having projecting teeth.

buck-wheat (buk′hwēt′), *n.* a plant grown for its triangular seeds, which are ground into flour; also, the flour.

bud (bud), *n.* **1,** a growth, as a lump or point on a plant, that may develop into a branch, stem, leaf, or flower; **2,** a young girl in her first season in society: —*v.t.* [budded, bud-ding], to insert (a bud) into an opening cut in the bark of another plant; graft; as, to *bud* an apple on a quince stock:—*v.i.* to put forth new shoots; sprout.

bud-dy (bud′-i), *n. Colloq.* pal; comrade.

budge (buj), *v.i.* [budged, budg-ing], to move from one's place; stir:—*v.t.* to cause to move.

budg-et (buj′it), *n.* **1**, a quantity or store; as, a *budget* of news; **2**, a statement by a person, corporation, or government, of estimated income and expenses for a definite period; also, a plan for the best division of such income among the expenses:—*v.t.* to plan the spending of (one's income) by making a budget.

budg-ie (buj′i), *n. Colloq.* for **budg′er-i-gar′** (buj′ẽr-i-gär′), an Australian parakeet with blue, green, yellow, and brown markings.

buff (buf), *n.* **1**, a thick, soft, dull-yellow leather made from the skin of a buffalo, ox, or similar animal; **2**, a soldier's coat made from this skin; **3**, a pale or faded yellowish-orange colour; **4**, a wheel covered with buff, used for polishing:—*adj.* **1**, made of dull-yellow leather; **2**, of a faded yellowish-orange colour:—*v.t.* to polish with a buff.

buf-fa-lo (buf′a-lō′), *n.* [*pl.* buffaloes, buffalos, or buffalo], **1**, a kind of wild ox, as the Asiatic water buffalo, or the African Cape buffalo; **2**, in America, the bison:—**buffalo-bug,** a small beetle which in its larva stage is very destructive to wool, fur, and feathers: the buffalo appears as an emblem on the Manitoba coat of arms.

buf-fer (buf′ẽr), *n.* **1**, a device to keep two objects or forces from colliding, as a fender or bumper, or as a *buffer* state; **2**, a machine that buffs or polishes.

¹buf-fet (buf′it), *n.* **1**, a blow with the hand; **2**, any blow:—*v.t.* **1**, to strike with the hand or fist; knock about; **2**, to struggle against; as, to *buffet* the waves:—*v.i.* to fight; struggle.

²buf-fet (boo-fā′; buf′it), *n.* **1**, a cupboard or sideboard for a dining-room; **2**, (boo-fā′), a refreshment counter; also, a restaurant equipped with such counters:—**buffet luncheon** (boo-fā′), a light meal served to guests seated or standing about a room.

buf-foon (bu-foon′), *n.* one who amuses others by jokes, antics, etc.; a clown.—*n.* **buf-foon′er-y.**

bug (bug), *n.* **1**, one of a group of flattened insects, with or without wings, having a piercing or sucking mouth, as the squash bug; **2**, popularly any crawling insect; **3**, *Colloq.,* **1**, a disease germ; **2**, a defect (as in machine).

bug-a-boo (bug′a-boo′), *n.* [*pl.* bugaboos], an imaginary creature used to frighten children into obedience; hence, any fancied cause of fear.

bug-bear (bug′bâr′), *n.* **1**, a bugaboo or goblin; **2**, any object of dislike or dread.

bug-gy (bug′i), *n.* [*pl.* buggies], a light, one-seated carriage.

bu-gle (bū′gl), *n.* **1**, a hunting-horn; **2**, a trumpetlike brass wind instrument used for military calls:—*v.i.* and *v.t.* [bu-gled, bu-gling], to sound, or give forth (a sound) on, a bugle.—*n.* **bu′gler.**

build (bild), *v.t.* [built (bilt), build-ing]. **1**, to construct by putting materials or parts together according to some plan or practice; **2**, to base or found; as, he *built* his hopes on his invention; **3**, to establish gradually, as a business:—*v.i.* to construct a building:—*n.* style of construction; as, the *build* of an automobile; also, figure; form; as, a boy of sturdy *build.*—*n.* **build′er.**—*n.* **build′-up.**—*adj.* **built′-in′.**

build-ing (bil′ding), *n.* **1**, the art or business of erecting houses, churches, etc.; **2**, the act of constructing, raising, or establishing; **3**, a structure covering a piece of land, and designed for particular use, as a school, barn, etc.

bulb (bulb), *n.* **1**, the rounded part, usually under ground, of some plant, as the onion, the lily, and the narcissus, where the·plant food·is stored; **2**, a rounded end of a glass tube, as of a thermometer; **3**, a small glass globe containing an electric-light filament.—*adj.* **bulb′ous.**

bulge (bulj), *n.* **1**, a swelling outward, as from pressure; **2**, the part of a wall, ship, etc., designed to curve outward:—*v.i.* and *v.t.* [bulged, bulg-ing], to swell or bend outward.—*adj.* **bulg′y.**

bulk (bulk), *n.* **1**, mass; volume; esp., great size; **2**, the main mass; the greater part; as, the *bulk* of his property.—*adj.* **bulk′y.**

bulk-head (bulk′hed′), *n.* **1**, an upright partition in a ship, separating watertight compartments; **2**, a structure built to resist the pressure of water, air, or earth; esp., a sea wall.

bull (bool), *n.* **1**, the male of any animal of the ox family or of various other large animals, as the whale or elephant; **2**, a person who buys stocks, bonds, commodities, etc., because he thinks prices are going up and he can sell at a profit: opposite of *bear.*—*adj.* **bull′ish.**

bull-dog (bool′dôg′), *n.* a breed of short-haired, medium-sized dog with a heavy head and projecting lower jaw, remarkable for its courage and for its strong grip:—*adj.* having the qualities of a bulldog; courageous; tenacious.

bull-doze (bool′dōz′), *v.t.* [bulldozed, bulldoz-ing], to bully; compel by threats.

bull-doz-er (bool′dōz′ėr), *n.* **1,** a machine for grading and roadbuilding: a powerful tractor, pushing a heavy, broad-nosed scraper; **2,** a person who forces another by bluster or violence; also, anything used to threaten, as, esp., a pistol; **3,** a heavy, powerful machine for bending and shaping metal into shorter and thicker form.

bul-let (bool′it), *n.* a small metal ball, made to be fired from a firearm.

bul-le-tin (bool′e-tin), *n.* **1,** a brief official report on some matter of public interest; as, a doctor's *bulletin* on a famous patient's condition; **2,** a magazine published regularly, con-taining reports of a club or society:—*v.t.* to publish or announce in a brief authorized statement.

bull-fight (bool′fīt′), *n.* a spectacle in which a crowd is entertained by a fight between a man and a bull (esp. in Spain and Spanish America).

bull-finch (bool′finch′), *n.* **1,** a small, rosy-breasted European songbird with short, rounded beak.

bull-frog (bool′frog′), *n.* a large, heavy frog with a loud, bellowing croak.

bull-head (bool′hed′), *n.* any of various big-headed fishes, esp. the catfish.

bull-head-ed (bool′hed′id), *adj.* blindly stubborn or headstrong; as, he was too *bullheaded* to be reasoned with.

bul-lion (bool′yun), *n.* uncoined gold or silver in lumps, bars, or the like.

bull-ock (bool′uk), *n.* a castrated bull; a steer.

bull pen, *n.* **1,** a pen for bulls; **2,** at a jail, an enclosure where rioting prisoners are confined; **3,** an area by a baseball field where relief pitchers warm up.

bull's—eye (boolz′-ī′), *n.* **1,** a bulging lens used to bring together the rays of light from a lantern upon a small spot; also, a lantern having such a lens; **2,** a round piece of thick glass in a floor or deck to admit light; **3,** the centre point of a target, or a shot that hits it; hence, anything esp. successful; **4,** a hard, round candy which looks like a marble.

bul-ly (bool′i), *n.* [*pl.* bullies], a coward who tries to rule his weaker fellows by cruelty or threats:—*v.t.* [bullied, bully-ing], to rule with bluster and threats:— *v.i.* to be noisy and overbearing:—*adj. Colloq.*, excellent.

bul-rush (bool′rush′), *n.* a large plant

with slender stalks, growing in wet places. Also called *cattail.*

bul-wark (bool′wėrk), *n.* **1,** a barrier or wall built for defence; an earth-work; rampart; breakwater; **2,** the boarding round the sides of a ship, above the level of the deck; **3,** any means of protection.

bum (bum), *n. Colloq.,* **1,** a hobo; tramp; **2,** *Slang,* the buttocks:—*v.i.* to loaf.

bum-ble—bee (bum′bl-bē′), *n.* a large bee which makes a loud hum.

bum-bling (bum′bling), *adj.* blunder-ingly self-important.

bump (bump), *n.* **1,** a blow; collision; **2,** a swelling due to a knock or blow:— *v.t.* **1,** to bring violently together; as, to *bump* heads; **2,** to strike against; knock into:—*v.i.* to come together heavily.—*adj.* **bump′y.**

¹bump-er (bump′ėr), *n.* a device for absorbing shock from a collision, as on an automobile, engine, or the like.

²bump-er (bump′ėr), *n.* **1,** an over-flowing cup; esp., one used for a toast; **2,** *Colloq.,* anything unusually large:— *adj.* very large; as, a *bumper* crop.

bump-kin (bump′kin), *n.* an awkward clumsy fellow; lout; rustic.

bump-tious (bump′shus), *adj.* dis-agreeably pushing, forward, or con-ceited.

bun (bun), *n.* a sweetened, raised roll.

bunch (bunch), *n.* **1,** a cluster, as of grapes; a bouquet, as of flowers; **2,** a collection of things of the same kind fastened together; as, a *bunch* of keys: *v.i.* and *v.t.* **1,** to form into a cluster or bouquet; **2,** to gather into folds; **3,** to group together.

bun-combe (bung′kum), *n.* senti-ments that sound well but mean nothing; bunk.

bun-dle (bun′dl), *n.* **1,** a number of things bound together; a parcel; as, a *bundle* of rags; a *bundle* of books; **2,** a quantity of something in one mass; as, a *bundle* of carpet:—*v.t.* [bun-dled, bun-dling], **1,** to tie in a mass or roll; **2,** to send off in a hurry; as, they *bundled* him out of town:—*v.i.* to pack up and start in haste; as, they *bundled* off before daylight.

bung (bung), *n.* **1,** a stopper of wood or cork for the hole in the side of a cask or barrel; **2,** the bung hole:—*v.t.* to close (a bung hole) with a stopper.

bun-ga-low (bung′ga-lō′), *n.* a one-story house.

bung-hole (bung′hōl′), *n.* the small, round hole in the side of a cask.

all (ôl), ôr; up, mūte, cûr, cōōl, book; oil, out; th, thin; *th,* the.

bun-gle (bung'gl), v.i. and v.t. [bungled, bun-gling], to perform in a clumsy and unskilful manner:—n. a clumsy performance.—n. **bun'gler.**

bun-ion (bun'yun), n. an inflamed swelling on the foot, usually on the great toe.

¹bunk (bungk), n. a shelf or recess used for a bed, as in a ship, camp, or the like:—v.i. to sleep in a bunk or bed.

²bunk (bungk), n. Slang, humbug; buncombe.

bunk-er (bungk'ẽr), n. 1, a large bin, esp. for coal on shipboard; 2, on a golf links, a sand trap or rough hazard; hence, an obstacle of any kind.

bun-kum (bung'kum), n. buncombe; bunk.

bun-ny (bun'i), n. a pet name for a rabbit.

bunt (bunt), v.t. and v.i. 1, to butt or push, as with head or horns; 2, in baseball, to tap the ball a short distance within the infield by meeting it with a loosely held bat:—n. 1, a push, as with horns; 2, in baseball, a bunted ball.

¹bun-ting (bun'ting), n. a small, thick-billed bird akin to the finch.

²bun-ting (bun'ting) or **bun-tine** (bun'tin), n. a light fabric used for flags.

buoy (boi; boo'i), n. 1, a floating object to show the position of rocks or shoals, or of a channel; 2, a device to keep a person afloat; as, a life-buoy:—v.t. to support; as, to buoy up one's hopes.

buoy-ant (boi'ant; boo'yant), adj. 1, able to float in a fluid, as cork; 2, vivacious; light-hearted; gay.—n. **buoy'an-cy.**

bur or **burr** (bûr), n. 1, a prickly seedcase, or a plant bearing such; 2, a small, rough, or clinging object.

bur-den (bûr'dn), n. 1, something carried; a load; 2, something endured, as a trouble or sorrow; 3, the bearing of loads or packs; as, a beast of burden; 4, the cargo-carrying capacity of a vessel; tonnage; 5, a refrain or theme; as, the burden of a song:—v.t. 1, to load; 2, to put too much upon; oppress.—adj. **bur'den-some.**

bur-dock (bûr'dok'), n. a coarse weed with broad leaves and a prickly, clinging fruit.

bu-reau (bū'rō; bū-rō'), n. [pl. bureaux or bureaus (bū'rōz; bū-rōz')], 1, a low chest of drawers for clothing, usually with a mirror; 2, an office or department; as, an employment bureau; information bureau; 3, a government office or department; as, the Bureau of Standards.

bu-reauc-ra-cy (bū-rok'ra-si; bū-rō'kra-si), n. [pl. bureaucracies], 1, government by an organized system of bureaus or departments; 2, officials of such a government, spoken of as a whole.—n. **bu'reau-crat'** (bū'rō-krat').

burg (bûrg), n. Colloq. a town or city.—n. **burgh'er.**

bur-gess (bûr'jis), n. 1, a citizen or freeman of a borough; 2, a town executive.

bur-glar (bûr'glẽr), n. one who breaks into a building to steal.—n. **bur'gla-ry.**

bur-go-mas-ter (bûr'gō-mȧs'tẽr), n. in Holland, Flanders, or Germany, the chief magistrate or the mayor of a town.

bur-i-al (ber'i-al), n. the act or ceremony of placing a body in the grave.

burl (bûrl), n. a flattened or domelike outgrowth on a tree, often over 1' high and 2' across (like a wart): sliced thin to make burlwood veneer.

bur-lap (bûr'lap), n. a coarse fabric of jute or hemp, used for bags, curtains, etc.

bur-lesque (bûr-lesk'), n. 1, a ridiculous imitation; a parody; 2, a composition or play in which a trifling subject is treated with mock dignity, or a dignified subject with irreverence:—v.t. and v.i. [burlesqued, burlesquing], to ridicule by exaggeration:—adj. amusingly imitative.

bur-ly (bûr'li), adj. [bur-li-er, bur-li-est], strong and muscular.—n. **bur'li-ness.**

burn (bûrn), v.t. [burned (bûrnd) or burnt (bûrnt), burn-ing], 1, to destroy or damage by fire or heat; 2, to use or consume as fuel for heat or light; as, we burn coal; this lamp burns kerosene; 3, to affect or injure by heat, acid, or the like; as, the sun burned her skin; 4, to expose intentionally to the action of fire, as wood to make charcoal; 5, in surgery, to apply heat or acid to; cauterize:—v.i. 1, to be on fire; 2, to suffer from, or be injured by, too much heat; 3, to be inflamed with passion or desire; as, he burns to win fame; 4, to feel a sensation of heat; as, his ears burned; 5, to blaze; glow; be bright; as, the scene burned with colour:—n. an injury caused by fire; any damage caused by too much heat.—n. **burn'er.**

bur-nish (bûr'nish), v.t. to polish by rubbing, as metal:—n. polish; brightness.

burp (bûrp), v.i. Slang, to belch:—n. **burp'gun'**, a toy submachine gun.

burr (bûr), n. 1, a thin ridge or roughness left by a tool in cutting or shaping metal; 2, a small rotating drill used by dentists; 3, a prickly, clinging seedcase; a bur; 4, a rough, guttural pronunciation of *r:*—*v.i.* and *v.t.* to pronounce with a rough or guttural sound; as, to *burr* one's *r's.*

bur-ro (bur′ō; boor′ō), *n.* [*pl.* burros], in the southwestern U.S., a small donkey.

bur-row (bur′ō), *n.* **1,** a hole in the ground, such as is dug by an animal as a refuge or nest; **2,** hence, a secluded dwelling-place or place of retreat:—*v.i.* **1,** to dig a hole in the earth, as for shelter; **2,** to lodge in a burrow; **3,** to dig or search; as, he was *burrowing* in an old trunk:—*v.t.* to build by burrowing; as, to *burrow* a cave.

bur-sa-ry (bûr′sa-ri), *n.* a grant of money for support of a student.

bur-si-tis (bûr-sī′tis), *n.* in a joint, esp. the shoulder, inflammation of the small sac containing a lubricating fluid.

burst (bûrst), *v.i.* [burst, burst-ing], **1,** to explode; break open; fly to pieces; as, our steam-boiler *burst;* **2,** to break out into sudden action or expression of feeling; as, to *burst* into tears; **3,** to appear or disappear suddenly; as, a scene *burst* upon our view; **4,** to be full to overflowing; as, the bags are *bursting* with mail:—*n.* **1,** a violent or sudden breaking forth; as, a *burst* of applause; **2,** a broken place; as, a *burst* in a gas pipe; **3,** a rush; spurt; as, a *burst* of energy.

bur-y (ber′i), *v.t.* [buried, bury-ing], **1,** to place in a grave, tomb, or the like; **2,** to cover from sight; conceal, as treasure; **3,** to keep secret; as, to *bury* one's past; **4,** to engross; as, he *buried* himself in a book.

bus (bus) [*pl.* buses; also, *U.S.* busses], *n.* an omnibus; a large public vehicle.

bush (boosh), *n.* **1,** a shrub or low-growing plant which develops some wood in its stem; **2,** an uncleared forest region: used esp. of such land in Australia.—*n.* bush′man; bush′rang′-er; bush′land.

bushed (boosht), *adj.Colloq.* exhausted; fatigued.

bush-el (boosh′el), *n.* **1,** a unit of dry measure, containing four pecks, or 32 quarts; **2,** a container holding a bushel.

bush-ing (boosh′ing), *n.* a removable metal lining used as a bearing on a shaft or axle to reduce friction.

bush-mas-ter (boosh′más′tėr), *n.* a large, poisonous snake of tropical America.

bush pilot, an airplane pilot who flies above Canada's vast bushlands to frontier outposts.

bush-whacker (boosh′hwak′ėr), *n.* one used to travelling through dense bush afoot or by boat.

bush-y (boosh′i), *adj.* [bush-i-er, bush-i-est], **1,** growing thickly; as, *bushy* hair; **2,** overgrown with shrubs.

bus-i-ly (biz′i-li), *adv.* in a busy, active manner.

busi-ness (biz′nis), *n.* **1,** employment; regular occupation; **2,** duty; mission; as, I made it my *business* to see that the job was done; **3,** concern; as, it is no *business* of mine; **4,** affair; matter; as, the trial was an unpleasant *business;* **5,** a commercial enterprise; as, he started a hardware *business;* **6,** activity in trade; as, *business* was good last month:—*adj.* relating to commercial activities; as, a *business* deal.—*adj.* busi′ness-like′.—*n.* busi′ness-man′.

buss (bus), *v.t. Archaic,* to kiss.

bust (bust), *n.* **1,** the upper front of the body; the breast or bosom, esp. of a woman; **2,** a piece of sculpture representing the head and shoulders.

bus-tard (bus′tėrd), *n.* the largest European land bird (related to the crane and plover).

¹bus-tle (bus′l), *n.* noisy activity:—*v.i.* [bus-tled, bus-tling], to be noisily and fussily busy.

²bus-tle (bus′l), *n.* a pad, or a framework formerly worn under a women's skirt just below the back of the waist.

bus-y (biz′i), *adj.* [bus-i-er, bus-i-est], **1,** at work; active; not idle; **2,** produced by industry or activity; as, the *busy* hum of the factory; **3,** full of activity; as, a *busy* crossing; **4,** in use, as a telephone line:—*v.t.* [busied, busy-ing], to keep constantly occupied; as, *busied* with housework.

bus-y-bod-y (biz′i-bod′i), *n.* [*pl.* busy-bodies], a person who meddles in the affairs of others.

but (but), *adv.* only; as, speak but a word:—*prep.* except; as, I can bear all *but* that:—*conj.* **1,** still; yet; as, poor *but* honest; **2,** on the contrary; as, you go, *but* I stay; **3,** that; as, I do not doubt *but* it is true; **4,** that not; as, who knows *but* he will succeed?

butch-er (booch′ėr), *n.* **1,** a person who kills and dresses animals for food; **2,** a meat dealer; **3,** a cruel, bloody murderer:—*v.t.* **1,** to kill and dress (animals) for food; **2,** to murder by violence; **3,** to botch or mangle; ruin. —*n.* butch′er-y.

but-ler (but′lėr), *n.* a manservant, usually the chief servant in a household.

¹butt (but), *n.* **1,** the thicker, heavier, or lower part of anything, as of a whip or a gun; **2,** what is left after a part has been cut away or used up; **3,** any of several kinds of hinge or joint.

²butt (but), *v.t.* to strike with, or as with,

lowered head:—*v.i.* to bump; collide; as, he *butted* into the table:—*n.* a push or sudden thrust with the head.

³butt (but), *n.* that at which anything is aimed; a target, esp. for ridicule; as, to be the *butt* of jokes; *pl.* a rifle– or firing–range.

butte (būt), *n.* an isolated tablelike hill.

but-ter (but′ẽr), *n.* **1,** the fatty substance obtained from milk or cream by churning; **2,** any butterlike substance; as, peanut *butter;* peach *butter:*—*v.t.* to spread or season with butter.—*adj.* **but′ter-y.**

butter–and–eggs, *n.* the common toadflax with flowers in two shades of yellow.

but-ter-cup (but′ẽr-kup′), *n.* a common meadow plant with yellow, cup-shaped flowers; also, its flower.

but-ter-fly (but′ẽr-flī′), *n.* [*pl.* butterflies], **1,** a day-flying insect with a long sucking beak, two long knobbed feelers, and four wings, often bright-coloured; **2,** a gay idler:—**butterfly weed,** a milkweed with orange-coloured flowers.

but-ter-milk (but′ẽr-milk′), *n.* the liquid left when the butterfat of milk has been removed after churning.

but-ter-nut (but′ẽr-nut′), *n.* the American white walnut tree, or its edible nut.

but-ter-scotch (but′ẽr-skôch′), *n.* and *adj.* a taffy made of brown sugar and butter; as, a *butterscotch* sundae.

but-tock (but′uk), *n.* the part of the hip on which one sits; *pl.* the rump.

but-ton (but′n), *n.* **1,** a small disk or knob of bone, wood, glass, or the like, used for fastening or ornamenting a garment; **2,** anything like this, as the knob operating an electric switch:—*v.t.* and *v.i.* to fasten with buttons.

but-ton-hole (but′n-hōl′), *n.* a stitched slit for a button to pass through:—*v.t.* [buttonholed, buttonhol-ing], **1,** to furnish with buttonholes; **2,** to edge (cloth) with the stitching used in making buttonholes; **3,** to engage (a person) in conversation, often against his will.

but-ton-wood (but′n-wood′), *n.* the North American sycamore tree.

but-tress (but′ris), *n.* **1,** brickwork or masonry built against a wall or building to support it; **2,** any prop or support: —*v.t.* to support with, or as with, a buttress; strengthen; brace.

bux-om (buk′sum), *adj.* plump, healthy, and full of life.

buy (bī), *v.t.* [bought (bôt), buy-ing], **1,** to get by paying a price agreed on; **2,** to gain at a sacrifice; as, to *buy* peace by yielding; **3,** to be the means of getting; as, money cannot *buy* happiness; **4,** to bribe:—*v.i.* to make a purchase; as, I cannot *buy* without money.—*n.* **buy′er.**

buzz (buz), *n.* **1,** a continuous humming sound, as of bees; **2,** a confused or blended murmur, as of voices:—*v.i.* to make, or speak with, a low hum.

buz-zard (buz′ẽrd), *n.* **1,** any of several hawklike birds of prey of America and Europe; **2,** esp., in America, the turkey buzzard, a blackish vulture that feeds only on dead flesh.

by (bī), *prep.* **1,** beside or near to; as, a chair *by* the window; **2,** along; as, a road *by* the river; over; as, I came *by* the bridge; **3,** in, on, or at; as, *by* night; *by* land; **4,** past and beyond; as, to go *by* the spot; **5,** according to; from; as, known *by* his gait; to judge *by* appearances; **6,** not any later than; as, to finish *by* two o'clock; **7,** through the agency of; as, to send word *by* a boy; **8,** through the action of; as, a poem *by* Shelley; **9,** because of; as, to succeed *by* industry; **10,** to or in the amount of; as, taller *by* several inches; the game was won *by* one goal; **11,** with regard to; as, he dealt well *by* me; **12,** with the witness of; in the name of; as, to swear *by* the Book; **13,** in the measure of; as, sell tea *by* the pound; **14,** in the manner of; as, *by* accident; **15,** one point in the direction of; as, north *by* east:—*adv.* **1,** near; at hand; as, to stand *by;* **2,** aside; in reserve; as, put *by* some money; lay your armour *by;* **3,** past; as, he drove *by.*

by and by, after a while; before long.

by–and–by (bī′–and–bī′), *n.* the future.

bye-bye (bī′bī′), *n.* and *interj. Colloq.* good–bye.

by–election (bī′–e-lek′shun), *n.* an election between regular elections to fill one or more vacancies.

by-gone (bī′gôn′), *adj.* past; gone by:—*n.* a thing of the past.

by-law (bī′lô′), *n.* a rule or law made by a corporation, a city council, or the like, for the regulation of its affairs.

by–pass (bī′–pàs′), *n.* a detour; shunt; **2,** a road to enable motorists to avoid cities, etc.:—*v.t.* **1,** to detour; **2,** to outwit; **3,** to go over the head of (a superior, etc.).

by-path (bī′páth′), *n.* a side path.

by-play (bī′plā′), *n.* speech or action apart from the main situation, as on a stage.

by–prod-uct (bī′–prod′ukt), *n.* something of value produced in a manufacturing process, other than the principal product, as sawdust in a saw-mill; a secondary product.

byre (bīr), *n.* a cow stable; barn.

by-road (bī'rōd'), *n.* a side road.

by-stand-er (bī'stan'dėr), *n.* a person who looks on, but does not take part.

by-way (bī'wā'), *n.* a side path; a road little known or used.

by-word (bī'wûrd'), *n.* **1,** a proverb or saying; **2,** an object of scorn or ridicule; as, her vanity made her a *byword.*

C

C, c (sē), *n.* [*pl.* C's, c's], **1,** the third letter of the alphabet; **2,** the Roman numeral for 100; **3,** in music, the first tone in the major scale of C.

cab (kab), *n.* **1,** an automobile for hire to passengers; a taxicab; **2,** a public carriage drawn by one horse; **3,** on an engine, truck, steam shovel, crane, etc., the place for the operator.

ca-bal (ka-bal'), *n.* **1,** a secret scheme; **2,** a few people united in a secret plan.

cab-a-ret (kab'a-rā', kab'a-rā'), *n.* a restaurant where music, dancing, etc. are provided for the patrons.

cab-bage (kab'ij), *n.* a vegetable with dense leaves forming a round, hard head.

ca-ber (kā'bėr), *n.* a pole, used in a trial of strength, called 'tossing the *caber.*'

cab-in (kab'in), *n.* **1,** a small hut or cottage; **2,** on a ship or aeroplane, an enclosed place for passengers.

cab-i-net (kab'i-nit), *n.* **1,** a piece of furniture or a closet having shelves or drawers, in which a number of articles are kept or displayed; as, a curio-*cabinet;* a medicine-*cabinet;* a filing-*cabinet;* **2,** a group of persons chosen by the head of a government as advisers in managing a country's affairs.

ca-ble (kā'bl), *n.* **1,** a chain or strong rope of hemp or wire strands, variously used, as for supporting suspension-bridges, towing automobiles, mooring ships, etc.; **2,** an insulated bundle of electric wires; **3,** a message sent by submarine telegraph; as, a *cable* from London; **4,** a cable's length, about 100 fathoms or 600 feet:—*v.t.* and *v.i.* [ca-bled, ca-bling], to send by submarine telegraph; as, *cable* me your answer; he *cabled* today.

ca-ble-gram (kā'bl-gram'), *n.* a message sent by undersea cable.

ca-boose (ka-bōōs'), *n.* **1,** a kitchen on the deck of a ship; **2,** a small car in which trainmen rest, sleep, or eat, generally attached to the end of a freight train.

ca-ca-o (ka-kā'ō; ka-kä'ō), *n.* **1,** a small evergreen tree of tropical America **2,** the seeds of this tree, from which cocoa and chocolate are made.

cache (kåsh), *n.* a hidden store of food, supplies, etc., often left by explorers for a return, or later, trip.

cack-le (kak'l), *n.* **1,** the cry, or clucking, of a hen or goose just after it has laid an egg; **2,** chatter; noisy, idle talk; as, the *cackle* of the diners drowned the music:—*v.i.* [cack-led, cack-ling], **1,** to cry like a goose or a hen; **2,** to giggle; prattle; as, they *cackled* too much to get anything done.

ca-coph-o-ny (ka-kof'o-ni), *n.* harsh, unpleasant, or discordant sound; as, a *cacophony* arose when the new orchestra began to practice (opposite of *euphony*).

cac-tus (kak'tus), *n.* [*pl.* cacti (kak'tī) or cactuses], a leafless desert plant with sharp spines along a fleshy stem and branches. Some kinds bear very showy flowers.

cad (kad), *n.* an ill-bred, ungentlemanly man.

ca-dav-er-ous (ka-dav'ėr-us), *adj.* gaunt; ghastly; like a corpse.

cad-die (kad'i), *n.* [*pl.* caddies], a person who carries clubs for a golf-player:—*v.i.* [caddied, caddy-ing], to be a caddie.

cad-dy (kad'i), *n.*, [*pl.* caddies], a small box for holding tea; as, a tea-*caddy.*

ca-dence (kā'dens), *n.* **1,** the rise and fall of the voice in reading or speaking; **2,** rhythm, as in music; **3,** in music, chords at the end of part of a composition.

ca-det (ka-det'), *n.* **1,** a student in a naval or military academy; **2,** a younger brother or son; **3,** a schoolboy receiving military training.—*n.* **ca-det'-ship.**

ca-di (kä'di, kā'di), *n.* **1,** a Moslem judge; **2,** *Colloq.* a magistrate.

ca-du-ce-us (ka-dū'sē-us), *n.* Hermes' staff with two intertwined serpents, used as a symbol by the medical profession.

cae-su-ra (si-zhōōr'a), *n.* a break or

pause in a line of verse, usually about the middle; in scansion, marked ‖.

café (ka-fā′), *n.* a restaurant.

caf-e-te-ri-a (kaf′e-tē′ri-a), *n.* a restaurant where patrons serve themselves.

caf-fe-ine (kaf′i-in; kaf′ēn′; kaf′i-ēn′) or **caf-fe-in** *n.* the drug or stimulant in coffee and tea.

cage (kāj), *n.* **1,** a box or enclosure, usually of bars or wire, used to confine birds or animals; **2,** anything like a cage in form or effect; as, a *cage* for baseball practice; an elevator *cage:*— *v.t.* [caged, cag-ing], to confine; shut up in, or as if in, a cage.

cairn (kârn), *n.* a heap of stones set up as a landmark or memorial.

cais-son (kā′son), *n.* an airtight box in which men do underwater work, the bottom being open, and high air pressure used to keep the water out.

ca-jole (ka-jōl′), *v.t.* [cajoled, cajoling], to coax with flattery, etc.; wheedle; as, she *cajoled* the child into coming.—*n.* **ca-jol′er-y.**

cake (kāk), *n.* **1,** a small mass of dough, sweetened and baked; as, layer *cake;* **2,** a small portion of thin batter or of ground-up meat, fish, potatoes, etc., cooked on a griddle; **3,** any small compressed or flattened mass; as, a *cake* of soap or ice:—*v.i.* and *v.t.* [caked, cak-ing], to form or harden into a hard mass; as, the mud *caked.*

cal-a-bash (kal′a-bash′), *n.* **1,** a tropical American tree, or its hard-shelled, gourdlike fruit; **2,** a pipe, bowl, dipper, bottle, etc., made from the dried shell.

cal-a-mine (kal′a-mīn′, -min), *n.* a silicate of zinc used in lotions, as for a skin irritation like poison ivy.

ca-lam-i-ty (ka-lam′i-ti), *n.* [*pl.* calamities], **1,** an event that causes widespread destruction, as a hurricane or an earthquake; **2,** a great personal misfortune, as the death of a loved one, loss of sight, etc.—*adj.* **ca-lam′i-tous.**

cal-ci-mine (kal′si-mīn′; kal′si-min), *n.* a white or tinted wash for decorating walls or ceilings:—*v.t.* [calcimined, calcimin-ing], to cover with such a wash. Also spelled **kal′so-mine.**

cal-ci-um (kal′si-um), *n.* a soft, white metal, found only in combination with some other substance, as in lime, marble, chalk, or bone.

cal-cu-late (kal′kū-lāt′), *v.t.* [calculated, calculat-ing], **1,** to figure out by arithmetic; as, to *calculate* the cost of a house; **2,** to estimate in any way; as, to *calculate* the benefits of science; also, chiefly in *p.p.*, to intend; as, a programme *calculated* to help business:

—*v.i.* **1,** to make a computation or estimate; as, he *calculated* wrongly; **2,** *Colloq.*, to plan; as, he *calculated* on arriving before dark.—*n.* **cal′cu-la′tion.**

cal-cu-lus (kal′kū-lus), *n.* any of several branches of higher mathematics using algebraic symbols.

cal-dron (kôl′drun), *n.* a large kettle. Same as **cauldron.**

cal-en-dar (kal′en-der), *n.* **1,** a method of reckoning time, esp. as to the length and divisions of a year; **2,** a printed card, or sheets of paper, setting forth the days, weeks, and months of a year; **3,** a list of things to be done in order of time; as, a court *calendar;* the *calendar* for the day:—*v.t.* to register; list.

¹**calf** (kåf), *n.* [*pl.* calves (kåvz)], **1,** the young of the cow; **2,** the young of certain other large mammals, as of the whale, elephant, or moose; **3,** leather made of the skin of the calf.

²**calf** (kåf), *n.* [*pl.* calves (kåvz)], the fleshy hinder part of the human leg, between the knee and the ankle.

calf-skin (kåf′skin′), *n.* leather made from the skin of a calf, used esp. for shoes and bookbinding.

cal-i-bre or **cal-i-ber** (kal′i-ber), *n.* **1,** the inside diameter of the barrel of a pistol, gun, etc.; as, a pistol of .22 *calibre* has a bore 22 hundredths of an inch wide; **2,** mental capacity; degree of merit or importance; as, we play teams of our own *calibre.*

cal-i-co (kal′i-kō′), *n.* [*pl.* calicoes or calicos], a cheap cotton cloth, usually printed with figured or flowered patterns:—*adj.* made of calico.

ca-liph (kā′lif; ka′lif), *n.* the supreme ruler in a Moslem state; the successor to Mahomet. Also, **ka′liph, kha′lif.**

cal-is-then-ics (kal′is-then′iks), *n. pl.* Same as **callisthenics.**

calk (kôk), *v.t.* to drive hemp rope fibre into the seams of (a ship), to stop leaks; also, to seal (a house) by putting a similar substance in cracks, as around doors.—*n.*—**calk′ing.** The preferred spelling is **caulk.**

call (kôl), *v.t.* **1,** to utter in a loud voice; as, to *call* the roll; to announce, esp. with authority; as, the announcer *calls* the train; **2,** to summon or request to come; as, to be *called* home; **3,** to appeal to; as, he *called* God to witness; **4,** to bring up for action; as, to *call* a case in court; **5,** to arouse from sleep; **6,** to invite or summon to meet; as, to *call* delegates together; **7,** to issue a command for; as, to *call* a strike; **8,** to invite to a position; as, to *call* a minister; **9,** to direct; as, to *call* one's attention to something; **10,** to telephone to; as, he *called* me from Toronto; **11,** to demand payment of (a loan); **12,** to give a name to; **13,** to regard as being; as, I *call* him my friend; **14,** to estimate; as, I should *call* it six miles; **15,** in cards, to require (a player) to show his hand; **16,** in baseball, to designate (a pitched ball) as a strike or a ball; **17,** in *sports,* to order (a game) to begin or end; as, the game was *called* at two o'clock:—*v.i.* **1,** to cry out loudly; **2,** to make a brief visit; **3,** to communicate by telephone; as, he *called* from Toronto:—*n.* **1,** a loud shout, as for help; **2,** a summons; **3,** an invitation; as, a *call* to preach; **4,** need; occasion; as, he has no *call* to be offended; **5,** a short visit; **6,** the cry or note of an animal or bird:—*adj.* in business, payable on demand; as, a *call-*loan.

cal-la (kal′a), *n.* a house plant in which the flowers, clustered on a spike, are surrounded by a large, trumpet-shaped white or yellow sheath, or spathe: often called *calla lily.*

call-er (kôl′ėr), *n.* **1,** one who calls; esp., one who pays a brief visit; **2,** one who *calls off* or recites in a singsong the movements of a square dance.

call-ing (kôl′ing), *n.* **1,** a summons; **2,** a vocation or profession.

cal-li-o-pe (ka-lī′ō-pē′; popularly, kal′i-ōp′), *n.* a mechanical organ which produces tones by a set of whistles.

cal-li-pers (kal′i-pėrz), *n.pl.* a compass-like tool with two movable legs for measuring outside or inside diameters of pipes or distances between surfaces. Also, **cal′i-pers.**

cal-lis-then-ics (kal′is-then′iks), *n.pl.* **1,** setting-up or simple gymnastic exercises; **2,** used as *sing.,* the science of such exercises.—*adj.* **cal′lis-then′ic.**

cal-lous (kal′us), *adj.* **1,** hardened, as the skin forming a callus; **2,** unfeeling; insensitive; as, he was *callous* to criticism.—*adv.* **cal′lous-ly.**—*n.* **cal′-lous-ness.**

cal-low (kal′ō), *adj.* immature; raw; green; as, a *callow* youth.

cal-lus (kal′us), *n.* [*pl.* calluses or calli (kal′ī], **1,** a thick, hard place on the skin, as on the palm of the hand; **2,** new growth at the ends of fractured bones serving to knit them.

calm (käm), *adj.* peaceful; undisturbed; as, a *calm* scene:—*n.* stillness; peace and quiet; as, a *calm* after the storm:—*v.t.* to *calm* an excited child:—*v.i.* to become calm; as, to *calm* down after a fight.—*adj.* **calm′ly.**—*n.* **calm′ness.**

cal-o-rie or **cal-o-ry** (kal′o-ri), *n.* a unit of heat or energy: used also to measure the heat or energy derived from foods. One egg has 75 calories.

cal-u-met (kal′ū-met′), *n.* the ceremonial long-stemmed peace pipe of the North American Indian.

cal-um-ny (kal′um-ni), *n.* [*pl.* calumnies], a slanderous report; slander.—*v.t.* **ca-lum′ni-ate.**—*adj.* **ca-lum′ni-ous.**

Cal-va-ry (kal′va-ri), *n.* the place outside Jerusalem where Jesus was crucified.

calve (kàv), *v.i.* [calved, calv-ing], to bring forth young. Cows, whales, elephants, and does are said to *calve.*

ca-lyp-so (ka-lip′sō), *n.* and *adj.* a lively West-Indian Negro jazz marked by violent stresses, off-hand African rhythms and verse, and loose rhyming; as, a *calypso* singer or dancer.

cal-yx (kā′liks; ka′liks), *n.* [*pl.* calyces (kā′li-sēz′)], the outer sheath of a bud, composed of green sepals.

cam (kam), *n.* a device for changing circular to variable motion, often an oval or irregularly shaped wheel revolving with a shaft. Also, **cam′shaft′.**

CALYX (C)

cam-ber (kam′bėr), *n.* **1,** the setting of the front wheels of a motor vehicle closer together at the bottom than at the top; **2,** any slightly convex surface.

cam-bi-um (kam′bi-um), *n.* the layer of soft tissue between the sapwood and the bark of trees, which develops into the new wood and the new bark.

cam-bric (kām′brik), *n.* **1,** a fine, thin, white linen fabric; **2,** a cotton imitation of this in white or plain colours.

came (kām), *p.t.* of come.

cam-el (kam′el), *n.* a large four-footed, cud-chewing animal, of which there are two kinds, the Arabian camel or dromedary, with a single hump, and the Bactrian camel, with two humps: used as beasts of burden in the desert.

cam-e-o (kam′i-ō′), *n.* [*pl.* cameos], a gem, stone, or shell carved with a raised design.

cam-er-a (kam′ėr-a), *n.* an apparatus for taking photographs.

cam-i-sole (kam′i-sōl′), *n.* a woman's fancy underwaist.

cam-ou-flage (kam′oo-flázh), *n.* **1,** disguise; concealment; pretence; as, her calm manner is mere *camouflage;* **2,** the art or practice of disguising guns, ships, etc., to hide them from the enemy:—*v.t.* [camouflaged, camouflaging], to conceal by disguising.

camp (kamp), *n.* **1,** a collection of tents or other temporary dwellings; also, the ground on which these are set up: **2,** the people staying there; as, he belonged to a gipsy *camp;* **3,** a summer residence in the country; **4,** one side in war, religion, politics, or the like; as, the republican *camp:—v.i.* to pitch a camp; live in a camp.

cam-paign (kam-pān'), *n.* **1,** a series of military operations, conducted in a definite place, or with a single purpose; **2,** action organized to produce a certain result; as, a political *campaign:—v.i.* to take an active part in or go on a campaign.—*n.* **cam-paign'er.**

cam-phor (kam'fer), *n.* a whitish crystalline gum with pungent odour, obtained chiefly from the camphor tree of eastern Asia, and used in medicines, etc.

cam-pi-on (kam'pi-un), *n.* a plant of the pink family with red or white flowers and blue-green leaves, esp. the **bladder campion.**

cam-pus (kam'pus), *n.* in America, the grounds of a school or a college.

¹**can** (kan), *verb* [*p.t.* could (kood)], to be able to; have the power to; as, I *can* dance: distinguished from *may*, indicating permission, probability, etc.

²**can** (kan), *n.* **1,** a metal container for holding or preserving liquids, solids, or powders; as, a coffee *can;* **2,** the contents of a can; as, one *can* of peaches will be enough for lunch:—*v.t.* [canned, can-ning], **1,** to preserve in sealed cans, as fruits or vegetables; **2,** *Slang,* to stop; as, *can* that noise; also, to discharge; dismiss.

ca-nal (ka-nal'), *n.* **1,** a man-made water channel, used for either navigation or irrigation; **2,** any tubelike part of the body; as, the alimentary *canal.*

ca-nar-y (ka-nâr'i), *n.* [*pl.* canaries], **1,** a small, yellow songbird, originally from the Canary Islands; **2,** a light-yellow colour; **3,** a light wine from the Canary Islands:—*adj.* of a light-yellow colour.

ca-nas-ta (ka-nas'ta), *n.* a card game of the rummy family in which the aim is to meld sets of seven or more cards.

can-cel (kan'sel), *v.t.* [cancelled, cancel-ling], **1,** to cross out with a line or lines; mark so as to deprive of value; as, to *cancel* a stamp; **2,** to take back; withdraw; as, to *cancel* an order; **3,** to balance; offset; as, this item *cancels* that; **4,** in *arithmetic,* to strike out (a common factor) from the numerator and the denominator of a fraction.—*n.* **can'cel-la'tion.**

Can-cer (kan'ser), *n.* **1,** a northern constellation, the Crab; **2,** the 4th sign of the zodiac (♋), which the sun enters about June 22.

can-cer (kan'ser), *n.* **1,** a harmful, often deadly, tumour, or growth, that spreads and eats into the body; **2,** the diseased condition resulting from such a growth:—*adj.* **can'cer-ous. Tropic of Cancer,** the northern boundary of the torrid zone; **23° 27'** north latitude.

can-de-la-brum (kan'de-lā'brum; -lä'), *n.* a large ornamental branched candlestick.

can-did (kan'did), *adj.* **1,** outspoken; frank; as, a *candid* person; a *candid* opinion; **2,** unprejudiced; fair.

can-di-date (kan'di-dāt'), *n.* one who offers himself, or is proposed by others, as a contestant for an office, grade, etc. —*n.* **can'di-da-cy.**—*n.* **can'di-da'ture.**

can-dle (kan'dl), *n.* **1,** a slender stick of tallow or wax enclosing a wick, burned to furnish light; **2,** anything resembling a candle in form or purpose: —*v.t.* [can-dled, can-dling], to test or examine (eggs) by holding between the eye and a small light.

can-dle—pow-er (kan'dl-pou'ér), *n.* a unit of measure of light.

can-dle-stick (kan'dl-stik'), *n.* a device for holding a candle.

can-dour or **can-dor** (kan'dér), *n.* **1,** openness; frankness, as of speech; **2,** fairness; as, to judge with *candour.*

can-dy (kan'di), *n.* [*pl.* candies], something to eat made largely of sugar, usually cut or formed into small pieces: —*v.t.* [candied, candy-ing], to coat, cook, or preserve with sugar:—*v.i.* to turn into sugar; as, the syrup *candied:* —**candy bar,** a place in the foyer or rotunda of a theatre or hotel that sells candy; a confectionery counter.

cane (kān), *n.* **1,** the woody, jointed stem of certain palms or grasses, as the bamboo or rattan; **2,** sugar-cane; **3,** a walking-stick:—*v.t.* [caned, can-ing], **1,** to beat, as with a walking-stick; **2,** to furnish with parts made of cane; as, to *cane* chairs:—*adj.* made of cane, as a chair seat.

ca-nine (ka'nīn; kā'-; ka-nīn'), *adj.* **1,** pertaining to dogs; doglike; **2,** designating one of the four sharp-pointed teeth, found in most mammals, between the incisors and the bicuspids:—*n.* **1,** one of the canine teeth (see *dentition,* illustration); **2,** a dog.

can-is-ter (kan'is-tér), *n.* a box or small container, usually of metal, for holding tea, coffee, etc.

can-ker (kang'kér), *n.* **1,** anything which destroys by gradual eating or wearing away, as an ulcer in animals or rust in plants; **2,** a white sore in the mouth, caused by an upset stomach; **3,** a canker-worm.—*adj.* **can′ker-ous.**

can-ker—worm (kang′kẽr–wûrm′), a caterpillar esp. destructive to fruit-trees and shade trees.

can-nel (kan′el), *n.* a soft coal often burned in fireplaces for its bright flame and good heat.

can-ner-y (kan′ẽr-i), *n.* [*pl.* canneries], a factory where fruit, meat, fish, or vegetables are canned.—*n.* **can′ner.**

can-ni-bal (kan′i-bal), *n.* **1,** a human being who eats human flesh; **2,** any animal that eats its own kind:—*adj.* like a cannibal.—*n.* **can′ni-bal-ism.**—*adj.* **can′ni-bal-is′tic.**

can-non (kan′un), *n.* [*pl.* cannon or cannons], a large mounted gun.

can-non-ade (kan′un-ād′), *n.* a continuous discharge of artillery or cannon:—*v.t.* [cannonad-ed, cannonad-ing], to attack with artillery; to bombard.

can-not (kan′not), am, is, or are not able to; as, I *cannot* do this problem.

can-ny (kan′i), *adj.* [can-ni-er, can-ni-est], **1,** shrewd; cautious; as, a *canny* person; **2,** thrifty; frugal; **3,** quiet.—*adv.* **can′ni-ly.**

ca-noe (ka-nōō′), *n.* a light boat made of bark, canvas, or thin wood and moved by paddles:—*v.i.* [canoed (ka-nōōd′), canoeing], to paddle, or go in, a canoe.—*n.* **ca-noe′ing.**—*n.* **ca-noe′ist.**

ca-ñon (kan′yun), *n.* Same as **canyon.**

¹can-on (kan′un), *n.* **1,** an established standard or principle; **2,** a law of a church; **3,** the accepted books of the Bible; **4,** a list of saints.

²can-on (kan′un), *n.* a clergyman attached to a cathedral.

can-on-ize (kan′un-īz′), *v.t.* [canonized canoniz-ing], to declare (a deceased person) a saint; admit to the list of saints.—*n.* **can′on-i-za′tion.**

can-o-py (kan′o-pi), *n.* [*pl.* canopies], **1,** a covering fixed above a bed, hung over a throne, or held on poles over an important personage; **2,** any overhanging covering, as the arch of the sky:—*v.t.* [canopied, canopying], to cover with, or as with a canopy.

¹cant (kant), *n.* **1,** the words and phrases peculiar to a certain trade, profession, or group, as the slang used by thieves; **2,** the insincere use of religious or moral speech; hypocrisy; **3,** a whining manner of speech, esp. that used by beggars.

²cant (kant), *n.* **1,** a sloping position; a slant or tilt; as, the *cant* of a roof; **2,** a sudden, forceful thrust resulting in a change of course or position:—*v.t.* **1,** to

give a tilt or slant to; **2,** to push or pitch sideways; as, the wind *canted* the sailing-vessel:—*v.i.* to lean; lean to one side.

can-ta-loup (kan′ta-lōōp′; -lōp), *n.* a hollow, edible melon with a hard, rigid rind. Also, **can′ta-loupe.**

can-tan-ker-ous (kan-tang′kẽr-us), *adj. Colloq.* ill-tempered; quarrelsome; as, a *cantankerous* mood; a *cantankerous* person.—*n.* **can-tan′ker-ous-ness.**

can-ta-ta (kan-tä′ta), *n.* a choral composition, often sacred, with a story or play to be sung rather than acted.

can-teen (kan-tēn′), *n.* **1,** a shop in a military camp, for the sale of food, drink, tobacco, etc.; **2,** a metal bottle used for carrying water or other drink when on the march; **3,** a box containing mess utensils for active-service use.

can-ter (kan′tẽr), *n.* an easy gallop:—*v.i.* and *v.t.* to gallop, or cause (a horse) to gallop, without haste.

cant—hook (kant′–hook′), *n.* a wooden lever with a movable iron hook near the end: it is used for turning or handling (floating) logs.

can-ti-lev-er (kan′ti-lē′vẽr; -le′vẽr), *n.* and *adj.* a bridge with two steelwork arms projecting from piers and joined directly together or by a suspended centre span, as the Quebec bridge.

can-to (kan′tō), *n.* [*pl.* cantos], a part or section of a long poem.

can-ton (kan′ton′), *n.* one of the political divisions of a country, esp. Switzerland.

can-vas (kan′vas), *n.* **1,** a coarse, heavy cloth of hemp, cotton, or flax, used for tents, sails, etc., and as material on which to paint in oil; **2,** an oil-painting.

can-vas-back (kan′vas-bak′), *n.* a North American wild duck.

can-vass (kan′vas), *v.t.* **1,** to examine thoroughly; discuss in detail; as, we *canvassed* the subject from A to Z; **2,** to visit (a district, house, or person) in order to get votes or contributions, or make sales:—*v.i.* to seek orders, contributions, votes, etc.; as, to *canvass* for a charity:—*n.* **1,** a thorough examination or discussion; **2,** a solicitation of votes, orders, etc.—*n.* **can′vass-er.**

can-yon or **ca-ñon** (kan′yun), *n.* a deep gorge or valley made by a river or stream.

caou-tchouc (kou′chook; kōō′chook; kou-chook′), *n.* rubber; India-rubber.

cap (kap), *n.* **1,** a tight-fitting covering, esp. one with a peak and without a brim, for a person's head; **2,** anything resembling a cap in form or use; as, a *cap* on a bottle; a mushroom *cap;* a nurse's *cap;* a *cap* and gown; **3,** a small quantity of explosive, enclosed in paper, for toy pistols, or in metal, for setting off cartridges, artillery, shells, etc.; **4,** writing-paper of various large sizes; as, fools*cap;* legal *cap:—v.t.* [capped, cap-ping], **1,** to cover, as with a cap; as, to *cap* a bottle; **2,** to match or surpass; as, his story *caps* mine.

ca-pa-ble (kā′pa-bl), *adj.* **1,** having skill or ability; as, a *capable* servant, student, etc.; **2,** having the nature or spirit to do a given thing; as, he is quite *capable* of such a trick.—*n* **ca′pa-bil′i-ty.**

ca-pa-cious (ka-pā′shus), *adj.* roomy; able to hold much; as, a *capacious* trunk.

ca-pac-i-ty (ka-pas′i-ti), *n.* [*pl.* capacities], **1,** the power of receiving or holding; also, the amount that can be held; as, the *capacity* of a room, cup, etc.; **2,** mental ability; **3,** position; relationship; as, he served in the *capacity* of teacher.

1cape (kāp), *n.* a sleeveless outer garment worn loosely over the shoulders; also, a similar part of a garment, attached to a cloak or dress.

2cape (kāp), *n.* a point of land jutting out into the water; as, *Cape* Race.

1ca-per (kā′pėr), *n.* **1,** a playful leap or spring; **2,** a prank:—*v.i.* to skip or jump playfully; frolic.

2ca-per (kā′pėr), *n.* a kind of low, prickly shrub, grown in Europe:— **capers,** *pl.* buds of the caper, used to flavour salads and sauces.

cap-il-lar-y (kap′i-lėr-i), *n.* [*pl.* capillaries], a slender, hairlike tube; esp. a very minute blood vessel:—*adj.* **1,** hairlike; slender; **2,** relating to the minute blood-vessels of the body.—*n.* **cap′i-lar′i-ty.**

1cap-i-tal (kap′i-tal), *adj.* **1,** punishable by death; involving the death penalty; as, *capital* crime; *capital* punishment; **2,** in writing and printing, designating one of the large letters, as A, B, C, etc., used at the beginning of a sentence, line of verse, proper noun, etc.; **3,** first in importance; chief; as, the *capital* points in a discussion; **4,** first-rate; as, a *capital* plan:—*n.* **1,** the city or town which is the seat of a government in a country or state; **2,** a capital letter; **3,** accumulated wealth available for use in business; as, he has plenty of *capital* to finance the invention; **4,** any resources.—*adv.* **cap′i-tal-ly.**

2cap-i-tal (kap′i-tal), *n.* in architecture, the ornamental head or top of a column.

cap-i-tal-ism (kap′i-tal-izm), *n.* an economic system resting upon private ownership of wealth used in producing

goods.—*n.* **cap′i-tal-ist.**—*adj.* **cap′i-tal-is′tic.**

cap-i-tal-ize (kap′i-tal-īz′), *v.t.* [capitalized, capitaliz-ing], **1,** to furnish (a business) with capital; as, the firm was *capitalized* at $10,000; **2,** to make profitable use of; as, a guide *capitalizes* his wood lore; **3,** to print or write with capital letters; start (a word) with, or change (a small letter) to, a capital letter.—*n.* **cap′i-tal-i-za′tion.**

Cap-i-tol (kap′i-tl), *n.* **1,** the building at Washington in which Congress meets; **2,** *capitol,* the building in which a State legislature meets; a State-house.

ca-pit-u-late (ka-pit′ū-lāt′),*v.i.* [capitulat-ed, capitulat-ing], to surrender to an enemy on conditions agreed upon.

ca-pon (kā′pon), *n.* a castrated rooster fattened for eating.

ca-price (ka-prēs′), *n.* **1,** a sudden, unreasoning change of mind or conduct; whim; as, her refusal to go is mere *caprice;* **2,** the tendency to yield to whims.—*adj.* **ca-pri′cious** (ka-prish′us).

1Cap-ri-corn (kap′ri-kôrn′), *n.* **1,** a southern constellation, the Goat; **2,** the 10th sign of the zodiac (♑), which the sun enters about December 22.

2Cap-ri-corn (kap′ri-kôrn′), *n.* the tropic of Capricorn, or southern boundary of the torrid zone, 23° 27′ south latitude.

cap-size (kap-sīz′), *v.i.* and *v.t.* [capsized, capsiz-ing], to upset; turn over (a boat).

cap-stan (kap′stan), *n.* an upright drum or cylinder revolving upon a pivot. It may be turned by bars or levers in the top of the drum, or by steam. Around the centre of the drum a rope or cable is wound, by means of which heavy weights are raised. It is used esp. on ships.

cap-sule (kap′sūl), *n.* **1,** a small envelope of gelatin enclosing disagreeable medicine; **2,** a seedcase which bursts when ripe; **3,** a skinlike sac enclosing some part or organ of the body.—*adj.* **cap′su-lar.**

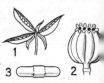

CAPSULES

1, of violet; 2, of poppy; 3, as used in medicine.

cap-tain (kap′tin), *n.* **1,** one in authority over others acting in a group; a leader; as, the *captain* of a football team; **2,** in the army, an officer ranking below a major and above a lieutenant and usually in command of a company; **3,** in the navy, an officer commanding a man-of-war; **4,** the master of a merchant ship:—*v.t.* to act as leader or captain of; to lead.

cap-tion (kap′shun), *n.* the heading of an article, chapter, section, etc.; as, the front page bore the *caption* 'War!'

cap-tious (kap′shus), *adj.* faultfinding; hard to please; as, his *captious* remarks irritated her.

cap-ti-vate (kap′ti-vāt′), *v.t.* [captivat-ed, captivat-ing], to attract; charm; fascinate.—*n.* **cap′ti-va′tion.**

cap-tive (kap′tiv), *n.* a prisoner, esp. one taken in war:—*adj.* taken or held prisoner; as, a *captive* army.—*n.* **cap-tiv′i-ty.**

cap-tor (kap′tẽr; kap′tôr), *n.* a person who captures a prisoner, or holds him captive.

cap-ture (kap′tūr; chẽr), *v.t.* [captured, captur-ing], to take or seize by force, skill, surprise, trickery, etc.; as, to *capture* a thief; to *capture* the attention:—*n.* **1**, the act of capturing; an arrest; **2**, the person or thing captured.

car (kär), *n.* **1**, a wheeled vehicle, as a railway car, trolley, automobile, etc.; **2**, the part of an airship or balloon in which freight, baggage, or passengers are carried; **3**, the cage of an elevator.

car-a-cul (kar′a-kul), *n.* Same as **karakul.**

ca-rafe (ka-raf′; -räf′), *n.* a glass water bottle or decanter.

car-a-mel (kar′a-mel), *n.* **1**, a kind of candy, of various flavours, generally in the shape of a cube; **2**, burnt sugar used for colouring and flavouring foods.

car-at or **kar-at** (kar′at), *n.* **1**, a unit of weight, one fifth of a gram, for precious stones; **2**, a 24th part: a measure of the purity of gold, pure gold being 24 carats; as, gold 22 *carats* fine contains 22 parts gold and 2 parts alloy.

car-a-van (kar′a-van′; kar′a-van′), *n.* **1**, a company of persons travelling together for safety, as across a desert or through dangerous country; **2**, a large covered wagon.

car-a-vel (kar′a-vel′) or **car-vel** (kär′vel), *n.* a small Spanish or Portuguese sailing-vessel, (such as was used by Columbus), of the 15th and 16th centuries. It had a high stern, three masts, and usually three or more three-cornered sails.

car-a-way (kar′a-wā′), *n.* a plant of the parsley family, whose seed is used to flavour small cakes, rye-bread, etc.

car-bine (kär′bīn), *n.* a short, light rifle used chiefly by cavalry.

car-bo-hy-drate (kär′-bō-hī′drāt), *n.* a compound of carbon, hydrogen, and oxygen, as sugar or starch.

car-bol-ic acid (kär-bol′ik), a poisonous acid, made from coal-tar, and used in solution as a disinfectant and antiseptic.

car-bon (kär′bon), *n.* **1**, a chemical element occurring pure in nature as the diamond and as graphite, and found in combination in all animal and vegetable substances, esp. fuels; **2**, either of two rods of hard carbon used in an arc-lamp. —*adj.* **car-bon′ic; car′bon-if′er-ous.**

car-bon-ate (kär′bon-āt′), *v.t.* to charge with carbonic-acid gas; hence, *carbonated* (or soda) water.

car-bo-run-dum (kär′bo-run′dum), *n.* a hard compound of carbon and silicon used for sharpening tools, etc.

car-bun-cle (kär′bung-kl), *n.* **1**, a painful inflamed swelling, more severe than a boil; **2**, a deep-red garnet.

car-bu-ret-tor or **car-bu-ret-or** (kär′bū-ret′ẽr), *n.* an apparatus used to mix air with gasoline in the form of a vapour or spray, as in the motor of an automobile.

car-cass or **car-case** (kär′kas), *n.* **1**, the dead body of an animal; **2**, contemptuously, the living or dead body of a human being.

¹card (kärd), *n.* a piece of pasteboard, usually small and rectangular; as, a post*card:* a calling-*card;* a playing-*card;* **2**, **cards,** any game or games played with playing-cards; card-playing.

²card (kärd), *n.* a toothed instrument for combing wool, flax, cotton, or the like, to prepare it for spinning:—*v.t.* to comb with a card, as wool.

card-board (kärd′bôrd), *n.* stiff pasteboard used for cards, posters, boxes, etc.

car-di-ac (kär′di-ak′), *adj.* pertaining to the heart; as, *cardiac* nerves or muscles.

car-di-gan (kär′di-gan), *n.* a knitted woollen jacket or waistcoat.

car-di-nal (kär′di-nal), *adj.* **1**, chief; of first importance; as, justice is one of the *cardinal* virtues; **2**, of a rich red colour:—*n.* **1**, a high official in the Roman Catholic Church, appointed by the Pope, and of his council; **2**, the red colour worn by cardinals; **3**, the cardinal bird:—**cardinal—bird,** an American songbird, the male of which has bright-red plumage and a pointed crest: also called *redbird;* **cardinal—flower,** a large, bright-red lobelia which blooms in late summer and early fall; **cardinal numbers,** the numbers *one, two, three,* etc., in distinction from the ordinal numbers, *first, second, third,* etc.; **cardinal points,** the main directions of the compass, north, east, south, and west.

car-di-o-gram (kär′di-o-gram′), *n.* a graph or tracing showing the action of the heart. Also, **car′di-o-graph′**.

care (kâr), *n.* **1,** a burdened state of mind caused by doubt, fear, or anxiety; **2,** the cause of such doubt, fear, or anxiety; as, the *cares* of state weighed heavily upon the King; **3,** heed; caution; pains; as, take *care* in crossing the street; work done with *care;* **4,** charge or oversight; as, under a nurse's *care:*—*v.i.* [cared, car-ing], **1,** to be anxious, concerned, or interested; as, she *cared* only for dancing; also, to feel affection; as, she *cared* a great deal for her sister; **2,** to provide oversight or protection; as, the nurse *cared* for the children while the mother was away; **3,** to desire; wish; as, I do not *care* to go.

ca-reen (ka-rēn′), *v.t.* to turn (a ship) over on one side, in order to clean or repair it:—*v.i.* to incline to one side; to lurch, as a ship in the wind.

ca-reer (ka-rēr′), *n.* **1,** a swift or sweeping course; full speed; as, a horse in full *career;* **2,** a course of action in the life of an individual, a nation, etc.; **3,** an occupation or calling; as, a scientific *career:*—*v.i.* to move rapidly, as a ship.

care-free (kâr′frē′), *adj.* happy; unworried.

car-fare (kär′fâr′), *n.* the sum paid for a ride on a bus or streetcar.

care-ful (kâr′fool), *adj.* **1,** done or made with care; as, a *careful* piece of work; **2,** attentive; concerned; as, the nurse is *careful* with his diet; **3,** watchful; cautious; as, *careful* with money.—*adv.* **care′-ful-ly.**—*n.* **care′ful-ness.**

care-less (kâr′lis), *adj.* **1,** not taking due care; inaccurate; as, a *careless* writer; *careless* work; **2,** unconcerned; heedless; as, *careless* of the outcome.—*adv.* **care′-less-ly.**—*n.* **care′less-ness.**

ca-ress (ka-res′), *n.* any act expressing affection, as a kiss or embrace:—*v.t.* to touch or stroke lovingly; fondle.

car-et (kar′et; kâr′et), *n.* a mark [ʌ] used in writing, or in correcting proof, to indicate where something is to be added.

care-tak-er (kâr′tāk′ẽr), *n.* one who takes care of places, persons, or things for someone else.

care-worn (kâr′wŏrn′), *adj.* showing marks of anxiety; wearied by care.

car-go (kär′gō), *n.* [*pl.* cargoes or cargos], the goods or merchandise carried by a ship.

car-i-bou (kar′i-bōō′), *n.* [*pl.* caribou], a North American reindeer: adopted as an official emblem by Newfoundland in 1928 to commemorate the loss of almost the entire Newfoundland Regiment at Beaumont Hamel, July 1, 1916.

car-i-ca-ture (kar′i-ka-tūr′; kar′i-ka-tūr′), *n.* a picture or description of a person or thing, in which the defects or peculiarities are so exaggerated as to appear ridiculous:—*v.t.* [caricatured, caricatur-ing], to make or give a caricature of; as, the cartoonist *caricatured* the actor.—*n.* **car′i-ca-tur′ist.**

ca-ri-es (kâr′i-ēz′; kâr′ēz), *n.* decay of the teeth, bones, or tissues.

car-il-lon (kar′i-lon′; ka-ril′yun), *n.* a set of fixed bells in a tower, usually operated from a keyboard.

car-mine (kär′min; -mīn), *n.* and *adj.* a deep purplish-red or crimson.

car-nage (kär′nij), *n.* great slaughter, esp. in battle.

car-nal (kär′nal), *adj.* **1,** fleshly or sensual; **2,** worldly; **3,** sexual; as, *carnal* lusts or appetites.

car-na-tion (kär-nā′shun), *n.* a cultivated pink with large red, pink, or white flowers.

car-ni-val (kär′ni-val), *n.* **1,** in Roman Catholic countries, the season just before Lent, devoted to merry-making; **2,** any revelry or feasting; **3,** an amusement enterprise, with side-shows, games, etc.

car-niv-o-rous (kär-niv′o-rus), *adj.* flesh-eating; as, dogs are *carnivorous*.

car-ol (kar′ul), *n.* a song of joy or praise; as, a Christmas *carol:*—*v.t.* and *v.i.* [carolled, carol-ling], to sing joyfully.

ca-rous-al (ka-rouz′al), *n.* a carouse.

ca-rouse (ka-rouz′), *n.* a drinking party:—*v.i.* [caroused, carous-ing], to take part in a drinking party.—*n.* **ca-rous′er.**

¹carp (kärp), *v.i.* to find fault; as, to *carp* at someone.—*adj.* **carp′ing.**

²carp (kärp), *n.* a freshwater fish that lives in ponds, sometimes to a great age.

car-pel (kär′pel), *n.* the part of a plant which bears seeds; one of the parts of a compound ovary.

car-pen-ter (kär′pen-tẽr), *n.* one who works in timber and builds or repairs the woodwork of houses, ships, etc.—*n.* **car′-pen-try.**

C

CARPELS (C)

car-pet (kär′pit), *n.* **1,** a thick woven or felted fabric used as a floor or stair covering; **2,** a soft covering upon which one may walk; as, a *carpet* of grass:—*v.t.* to cover with, or as with, a carpet.

car-riage (kar′ij), *n.* **1,** the act or business of carrying or transporting goods; also, the expense of carrying; **2,** a wheeled vehicle for carrying persons, esp. one drawn by horses; **3,** a wheeled support, as for a cannon; **4,** the moving part of a machine which carries another part, as in a typewriter; **5,** the manner of holding one's body; as, an erect *carriage.*

car-ri-er (kar′i-ér), *n.* **1,** a bearer, as of letters; **2,** a person or firm whose business is to transport goods or persons; **3,** a device in a machine for guiding something; as, a slide-*carrier* in a magic lantern; **4,** a person or thing that carries and transmits disease germs.

car-ri-on (kar′i-un), *n.* decaying flesh.

car-rot (kar′ut), *n.* a vegetable of the parsley family, with an edible, orange-yellow tapering root.—*adj.* **car′ rot-y.**

car-rou-sel or **car-ou-sel** (kar′oo-zel′), *n.* a merry-go-round.

car-ry (kar′i), *v.t.* [carried, carry-ing], **1,** to convey; transmit, as a cargo or a message; **2,** to support or sustain; as, the columns *carry* the weight of the building; **3,** to have upon one's person; as, to *carry* a scar; **4,** to hold (oneself); as, she *carries* herself well; also, to conduct (oneself); **5,** to win, as an election; **6,** to secure the passage of, as a bill in Parliament; **7,** to keep on hand for sale:—*v.i.* **1,** to bear or convey something; **2,** to have power to reach a distance, as a gun or a voice:—*n.* [*pl.* carries], **1,** the distance over which a gun will hurl a shot; **2,** in Canada and the northern U.S., the act of carrying between two bodies of water; also, the distance crossed: also called *portage;* **3,** in *golf,* the distance from the spot where a ball is struck to the point where it first lands.

car-ry—all (kar′i-ôl′), *n.* a large bag, basket, etc.

cart (kärt), *n.* **1,** a two-wheeled vehicle for carrying heavy goods; **2,** a light delivery wagon used by tradesmen; **3,** a light, two-wheeled carriage:—*v.t.* to carry in a cart.—*n.* **cart′age; cart′er.**

carte blanche (kärt′blänsh′), *n.* absolute freedom of action; as, anything you say; I give you *carte blanche.*

car-tel (kär-tel′; kär′tel), *n.* an international association of rival firms to regulate prices and production so as to create a monopoly.

car-ti-lage (kär′ti-lij), *n.* an elastic tissue composing most of the skeleton of young animals and children: it usually develops into bone; gristle.—*adj.* **car′-ti-lag′i-nous** (kär′ti-laj′i-nus).

car-ton (kär′t′n), *n.* a pasteboard or cardboard box.

car-toon (kär-tōōn′), *n.* a picture, esp. one in a newspaper or magazine, dealing with a public person or event in an exaggerated or satirical manner; as, the *cartoons* of the disaster aroused anger:—*v.t.* to draw a cartoon of:—*v.i.* to draw cartoons.—*n.* **car-toon′ist.**

car-tridge (kär′trij), *n.* **1,** a case of metal, cardboard, or other material containing powder and a bullet, as for a firearm, or one charge of powder, as of dynamite; **2,** a case shaped like a cartridge, used as a container; as, a *cartridge* of films for a camera.

carve (kärv), *v.t.* [carved, carv-ing], **1,** to produce by cutting; as, to *carve* a statue out of marble; **2,** to adorn by cutting; as, he *carved* a panel with floral designs; **3,** to cut, as meat; **4,** to make or get as if by cutting; as, he *carved* out a career for himself:—*v.i.* **1,** to work as a sculptor; **2,** to cut up meat.—*n.* **carv′er.**—*adj.* **carv′en.**

cas-cade (kas-kād′), *n.* **1,** a small waterfall or series of small falls; **2,** anything like this; as, a *cascade* of ruffles:—*v.t.* and *v.i.* to fall, or cause to fall as a cascade; as, to *cascade* electric circuits.

¹case (kās), *n.* **1,** any set of facts, conditions, or circumstances relating to a particular person or thing; as, the *case* of Mr. Jones; a *case* of robbery; **2,** an actual state of affairs; as, that was not the *case;* **3,** a certain form or instance of disease; also, the person having a given disease; a patient; as, there is a *case* of mumps in the house; **4,** a lawsuit; **5,** a person, family, or problem under the observation of a social-service organization; **6,** in *grammar,* the relation of a noun or pronoun to other words; as, the subject of a sentence is in the nominative *case;* **7,** *Colloq.* a peculiar person; as, he's a queer *case:*—**in case of,** in the event of; as, *in case of* fire, ring the alarm.

²case (kās), *n.* **1,** a covering or container; as, the *case* of a watch; a pillow-*case;* **2,** a container and its contents; as, a *case* of books; also, the amount of this content; as, to buy canned peas by the *case;* **3,** a glass box used for exhibiting goods; as, a show*case;* **4,** a frame or casing, as of a window; **5,** in printing, a tray for type, divided into *upper case,* which contains the capital letters, etc., and *lower case,* which contains small letters, etc.:—*v.t.* [cased, cas-ing], to protect with a case; encase.

ca-se-in (kā′si-in), *n.* a substance in milk which forms the main part of cheese.

case-ment (kās′ment), *n.* a window made to open on hinges like a door.

cash (kash), *n.* **1,** money; esp. ready

money; as, I have no *cash* in my pocket; **2**, money paid for an article at the time of purchase; as, sold for *cash*; **3**, in banking, strictly, coin, but also paper money, bank-notes, and commercial paper easily exchanged for coin:—*v.t.* to exchange for money in coin or bills; as, to *cash* a cheque.—*n.* **cash′book′**.

ca-shew (kash′ōō; ka-shōō′), *n.* a tropical American tree, or its kidney-shaped nut, which is used for food.

¹cash-ier (kash-ēr′), *n.* **1**, in a bank, an executive officer who has charge of paying and receiving money; **2**, a person in a store who pays out and receives cash.

²cash-ier (kash-ēr′), *v.t.* to dismiss in disgrace from a position of trust or from military service.

cash-mere (kash′mēr; kash′mēr′), *n.* **1**, a soft woollen fabric made from the wool of the goats of Kashmir, Tibet, etc.; **2**, a shawl made of this; **3**, a soft woollen imitation of real cashmere.

cas-ing (kās′ing), *n.* **1**, a covering, as for a pillow; **2**, a framework, as of a window.

ca-si-no (ka-sē′nō), *n.* [*pl.* casinos or casini (ka-sē′ni)], **1**, in Italy, a summer-house; **2**, a public room or building for dancing, gambling, etc.

cask (kȧsk), *n.* **1**, a barrel-shaped, wooden vessel for holding liquids; a keg; **2**, the amount contained in a cask; as, a *cask* of molasses was consumed in a month; **3**, the cask and its contents; as, a *cask* of wine was shipped.

cas-ket (kȧs′kit), *n.* **1**, a small chest or box, as for jewels; **2**, a coffin.

cas-sa-va (ka-sä′va), *n.* a tropical plant with a fleshy root that yields a starch from which tapioca is made: often called the *bitter cassava*.

cas-se-role (kas′e-rōl′), *n.* **1**, a covered glass or earthen dish in which food is baked and served; **2**, food cooked and served in a casserole.

cas-sock (kas′uk), *n.* a long, close-fitting gown worn by some clergymen.

cas-so-war-y (kas′ō-wer′i), *n.* [*pl.* cassowaries], a large, swift-running bird of Australia and Papua, resembling the ostrich, but smaller.

cast (kȧst), *v.t.* [*p.t.* and *p.p.* cast, *p.pr.* casting], **1**, to throw; hurl; as, to *cast* a fishing-line; to *cast* stones; **2**, to send or turn in a certain direction; as, to *cast* a glance; to *cast* a shadow; **3**, to put off; shed; as, a snake *casts* its skin; **4**, to deposit, as a vote; **5**, to assign, as the parts or actors in a play; **6**, to pour into a certain shape; as, to *cast* a bronze statue; **7**, to add; as, to *cast* up a column of figures:—*v.i.* **1**, to throw a

fishing-line; as, it was his turn to *cast*; **2**, to receive shape in a mould; **3**, in hunting, to search for game, or for a lost scent; hence, to search; as, he *casts* about for an idea:—*n.* **1**, the act or manner of throwing; the distance to which a thing can be thrown; **2**, a permanent turn, twist, or warp; as, a *cast* in the eye; **3**, calculation; the addition of columns of an account; **4**, the members of a company of actors to whom certain parts are assigned; **5**, something formed by moulding; as, a plaster *cast*; **6**, form; style; bent; as, a gloomy *cast* of countenance; **7**, a tinge or hue; as, a greyish *cast*; **8**, in hunting, the scattering of hounds in search of a lost scent:—*adj.* shaped in a mould while fluid.

cas-ta-nets (kas′ta-nets′; kas′ta-nets′), *n.pl.* a pair of spoon-shaped shells of hard wood or ivory, clicked with the fingers to beat time, esp. in Spanish dances and music.

cast-a-way (kȧst′a-wā′), *n.* **1**, a person cast adrift at sea, or a shipwrecked person cast ashore; **2**, a social or moral outcast:—*adj.* **1**, shipwrecked; **2**, thrown aside; rejected.

caste (kȧst), *n.* a distinct class of society, esp. as in India.

cast-er (kȧs′tèr), *n.* Same as **castor**.

cas-ti-gate (kas′ti-gāt′), *v.t.* **1**, to correct; chastise; **2**, criticize severely.

cast-ing (kȧst′ing), *n.* an object formed by pouring (molten metal) into a mold; hence, cast iron; cast steel.

cast i-ron, iron which has been melted and shaped by being run into moulds:—**cast-iron**, *adj.* **1**, made of cast iron; **2**, like iron; rigid; unyielding; as, a *cast-iron* will.

cas-tle (kȧs′l), *n.* **1**, a building or group of buildings fortified for defence; a fortress; **2**, any of these used now as a residence by a nobleman or wealthy person; **3**, anything resembling a castle; **4**, one of the pieces used in chess: also called *rook*.

cas-tor (kȧs′-tèr), *n.* **1**, a small vessel for salt, vinegar, or the like; a cruet; also, a stand for a number of such vessels; **2**, a small roller on a swivel, or a set of rollers in a frame, used under furniture, etc., to permit easy moving. Also spelled **cast′er**.

castor oil, a thick, yellowish oil from the castor bean, used as a physic.—*adj.* **cas′tor—oil′**.

cas-trate (kas′trāt), *v.t.* [castrat-ed, castrat-ing], to remove the male sex glands of (an animal); as, a steer is a *castrated* bull.

cas-u-al (kazh′ū-al; kaz′ū-al), *adj.* **1**,

happening by chance; accidental; as, a *casual* meeting; **2,** uncertain; occasional; as, *casual* profits; **3,** having an air of indifference; as, a *casual* manner.

cas-u-al-ty (kazh′ū-al-ti; kaz′ū-al-ti), *n.* [*pl.* casualties], **1,** a disaster; an accident; **2, casualties,** in the army and navy, losses in general, caused by death, wounds, illness, desertion, or discharge; **3,** anyone hurt or killed accidentally.

cat (kat), *n.* a small flesh-eating animal, often kept as a household pet; also, any closely related animal, as the lion or tiger.—*adj.* **cat′like′; cat′ty.**

cat-a-clysm (kat′a-klizm), *n.* **1,** a deluge; flood; **2,** a violent upheaval, as an earthquake or a great war.

cat-a-logue (kat′a-log′), *n.* a systematic list of names, places, books, etc., usually arranged alphabetically:—*v.t.* [catalogued, catalogu-ing], to make a list of; as, to *catalogue* a library. Also spelled **cat′a-log** [cataloged, catalog-ing].

ca-tal-pa (ka-tal′pa), *n.* a tree with large leaves, showy white flower-clusters, and winged seeds in long pods.

cat-a-lyst (kat′a-list), *n.* a substance or agent that causes or speeds up chemical (or other) action between two other substances without itself undergoing change.

cat-a-ma-ran (kat′a-ma-ran′), *n.* **1,** a raft or float of logs or pieces of wood lashed together, and propelled by sail, paddle, etc.; **2,** a craft with twin hulls.

cat-a-mount (kat′a-mount), *n.* a wildcat; in North America, esp. a lynx, or the cougar.

cat-a-pult (kat′a-pult), *n.* **1,** in ancient times, a military engine for hurling stones, arrows, or the like; **2,** in modern times, a similar device for launching an aeroplane from the deck of a ship; **3,** a slingshot:—*v.t.* to hurl (something) from a catapult:—*v.i.* to rush headlong; hurtle; as, the acrobat *catapulted* from a cannon into a net.

CATAPULT

cat-a-ract (kat′a-rakt′), *n.* **1,** a large waterfall; **2,** a furious rush of water; **3,** a disease of the eye which causes partial or total blindness.

ca-tarrh (ka-tär′), *n.* an inflammation of any mucous membrane, esp. of the air passages in the head and throat.

ca-tas-tro-phe (ka-tas′trō-fi), *n.* a sudden calamity or widespread disaster.

cat-bird (kat′bûrd′), *n.* an American songbird, slate-grey in colour, related to the mocking-bird. It utters a catlike mew when disturbed.

cat-boat (kat′bōt′), *n.* a small sailboat with one mast in the bow, and one large sail.

cat-call (kat′kôl′), *n.* a loud cry of disapproval, as from a theatre audience.

catch (kach), *v.t.* [caught (kôt), catching], **1,** to lay hold of; seize; as, the brambles *caught* her dress; tó *catch* a bird; to *catch* a ball; **2,** to reach or be in time for; as, to *catch* a train; **3,** to overtake; as, I will *catch* you; **4,** to attract; as, to *catch* the eye or the attention; **5,** to learn by hearing, as a tune; **6,** to understand; as, to *catch* a meaning; **7,** to become infected with, as a disease; **8,** to come upon suddenly; surprise; as, to *catch* a thief in the act; the storm *caught* him; **9,** to take (fire); **10,** please; charm; as, the music *caught* the public's fancy:—*v.i.* **1,** to grasp; snatch; as, to *catch* at an opportunity; to *catch* at straws; **2,** to be seized and held; as, my dress *caught* in the door; **3,** to take hold, as fire; **4,** to take and keep hold, as a bolt; **5,** to be stuck, as a window:—*n.* **1,** a fastening, as a hook, door-latch, etc.; **3,** a choking sensation in the throat; **3,** what is caught; as, a *catch* of fish; **4,** a trick or pitfall; as, a *catch* in a question; **5,** in ball games, the seizing of the ball before it touches the ground; **6,** a snatch of song; also, a round set to humorous words.—*n.* **catch′er.**—*adj.* **catch′y.**

catch-up (kach′up), *n.* a sauce made by boiling and spicing mushrooms, tomatoes, etc., used cold with meat. The preferred spelling is **ketch′up.**

catch-word (kach′wûrd′), *n.* **1,** a word or phrase repeated as a slogan, esp. by a political party; **2,** any word placed prominently to catch the eye; as in a dictionary; **3,** an actor's cue.

cat-e-chism (kat′e-kizm), *n.* **1,** a small book of questions and answers for instruction in the Christian religion; **2,** a method of teaching by questions and answers; **3,** a set of questions to be answered.

cat-e-chize (kat′e-kīz′), *v.t.* [catechized, catechiz-ing], **1,** to instruct by questions and answers, esp. in the Christian religion; **2,** to question closely. Also spelled **cat′e-chise′.**—*n.* **cat′e-chist.**

cat-e-gor-y (kat′e-go-ri), *n.* [*pl.* categories], a broad division or classification; as, there are three *categories* of matter: animal, vegetable, and mineral.

ca-ter (kā-tèr), *v.i.* **1,** to provide or supply food; as, to *cater* for a banquet; **2,** to supply what is desired; as, some writers *cater* to popular taste.—*n.* **ca′ter-er.**

cat-er-pil-lar (kat′ẽr-pil′ẽr), *n.* a wormlike larva, usually of a butterfly or moth.

cat-fish (kat′fish′), *n.* [*pl.* catfish or catfishes], a scaleless fish with long, whiskerlike feelers around the mouth, as the bullhead.

cat-gut (kat′gut′), *n.* a dried and twisted cord made from the intestines of animals, usually sheep, used chiefly for the strings of musical instruments, tennis-rackets, etc.

ca-thar-tic (ka-thär′tik), *adj.* cleansing the bowels; purgative; as, *cathartic* herbs:—*n.* a purgative medicine; a physic.

ca-the-dral (ka-thē′dral), *n.* **1**, the principal church of a church district under the special charge of the bishop; **2**, in careless use, any church of great size or importance.

cath-ode (kath′ōd), *n.* in *electrolysis,* the negative pole of a battery; a negatively charged electrode.

cath-o-lic (kath′o-lik), *adj.* **1**, universal; general; including all; as, he has a *catholic* taste in literature; **2**, liberal, as in thought or sympathies:—**Catholic, 1**, naming or having to do with the universal Christian church; **2**, naming or having to do with the Church of Rome:—*n.* a member of such a church.

cat-kin (kat′kin), *n.* a hanging, fingerlike flower-cluster, as of the willow or birch.

cat-nip (kat′nip), *n.* a common plant of the mint family, so called because cats like its pungent leaves.

cat-o'—nine—tails (kat′—o-nīn′–tālz′), *n.* **1**, a whip with nine lashes of knotted cord, formerly used for flogging; **2**, popularly, the cat's-tail, a marsh plant with long, furry spikes.

CATKIN OF A WILLOW

cat's—paw (kats′–pô′), *n.* **1**, a dupe; a person who is deceived and made use of by another; **2**, a light air that roughens calm water; **3**, a kind of hitch or knot.

cat-sup (kat′sup), *n.* Same as **ketchup**.

cat-tail (kat′tāl′), *n.* a tall marsh plant with long, narrow leaves and brownish spikes of flowers. Also, **cat's—tail**.

cat-tle (kat′l), *n.pl.* live-stock; esp. cows, etc., raised for profit.

Cau-ca-sian (kô-kā′zhan), *n.* Loosely, a member of *the white race,* esp. peoples of Nordic, Alpine, or Mediterranean stock:—*adj.* **1**, pertaining to the white race, or **2**, to the Caucasus area or mountains.

cau-cus (kô′kus), *n.* a meeting of political party leaders, to discuss party policies or to choose party candidates.

cau-dal (kô′dal), *adj.* like, or near, the tail; as, the *caudal* fin of a fish.

caught (kôt), *p.t.* and *p.p.* of *catch*.

caul-dron (kôl′drun), *n.* a large kettle or boiler.

cau-li-flower (ko′li-flou′ẽr), *n.* a variety of cabbage with a white, compact flowering head used as a vegetable.

caulk (kôk), *v.t.* to force hemp rope fibre into the seams of (a ship), to stop leaks.—*n.* **caulk′er**.—*n.* **caulk′ing**.

cause (kôz), *n.* **1**, a person who, or a thing which, makes something happen; as, the boy was the *cause* of the quarrel between them; **2**, a motive or reason; as, he had no *cause* for being angry; **3**, a subject, esp. one side of a question of wide interest, which is taken up by one or more persons and made into an issue, as in a political campaign; as, the temperance *cause*; **4**, in law, a ground for action; also, a lawsuit:—*v.t.* [caused, caus-ing], to bring about; effect.—*n.* **cau-sa′-tion** (kô-zā′shun).—*adj.* **caus′-al**.

cause-way (kôz′wā′), *n.* **1**, a raised path or road over wet ground, shallow water, or the like; **2**, a raised sidewalk.

caus-tic (kôs′tik), *adj.* **1**, having the power of gradually eating away or destroying by chemical action; as, *caustic* soda; **2**, sarcastic; biting; as, a *caustic* remark:—*n.* a substance which by chemical action burns or eats away animal tissues.—*adv.* **caus′ti-cal-ly**.

cau-ter-ize (kô′tẽr-īz′), *v.t.* [cauterized, cauteriz-ing], to burn or sear with a hot iron, or with some caustic agent; as, to *cauterize* a wound with carbolic acid.—*n.* **cau′ter-i-za′tion**.

cau-tion (kô′shun), *n.* **1**, an act, word or the like, that warns, as against danger; a warning; as, he heeded my *caution* against gambling; **2**, heedfulness; care in avoiding danger; as, handle chemicals with *caution*:—*v.t.* to warn of danger.

cau-tious (kô′shus), *adj.* taking care to avoid danger or trouble; heedful.—*adv.* **cau′tious-ly**.

cav-al-cade (kav′al-kād′), *n.* a procession of persons, usually on horseback.

cav-a-lier (kav′a-lẽr′), *n.* **1**, a horseman; often, an armed horseman; a knight; **2**, a gay adventurer; **3**, a lady's escort; a gallant:—*adj.* **1**, gay; frank and carefree; **2**, haughty; offhand or unceremonious; as, a *cavalier* refusal.

cav-al-ry (kav′al-ri), *n.* [*pl.* cavalries]

soldiers who fight on horseback; mounted troops.—*n.* **cav′al-ry-man.**

cave (kāv), *n.* a large hole in the earth, esp. a natural one:—**cave—man,** a man of the Stone Age; hence, humorously, any man who is rough or overbearing, esp. toward women:—*v.i.* [caved, caving], to fall in or down; as, the road *caved* in.

cav-ern (kav′ĕrn), *n.* a large, underground cave.—*adj.* **cav′ern-ous.**

cav-i-are, cav-i-ar (kav′i-är′; *n.* the pickled eggs, or spawn, of the sturgeon, salmon, etc., eaten as a relish or delicacy.

cav-il (kav′il), *v.i.* [cavilled, cavil-ling], to find fault or object on trivial grounds; as, Benny *cavilled* at the suggestion that he tip the waiter.

cav-i-ty (kav′i-ti), *n.* [*pl.* cavities], a hollow place; a hole or hollow.

ca-vort (ka-vôrt′), *v.i. Colloq.* to prance or caper about, as does a horse.

caw (kô), *n.* a cry like that of the crow: —*v.i.* to utter such a cry.

cay-enne (kī-en′; kā-en′), *n.* a hot, biting pepper made from the seeds or fruit of certain plants: also called *red pepper, cayenne pepper.*

cay-use (kī-ūs′), *n.* an Indian pony; a mustang.

cease (sēs), *v.i.* [ceased, ceas-ing], to come to an end; stop; as, at nightfall the singing of the birds *ceased*:—*v.t.* to discontinue; as, *cease* your quarrelling. —*adj.* **cease′less.**

ce-dar (sē′dĕr), *n.* **1,** an Old World evergreen tree of the pine family, with a very durable and fragrant wood; **2,** any one of several related North American trees, as the white cedar, red cedar, etc.; **3,** the wood of any of these trees: —*adj.* relating to cedar; made of cedar.

ce-dar-bird or **ce-dar wax-wing,** *n.* a bright, crested American bird with red patches on its wings.

cede (sēd), *v.t.* [ced-ed, ced-ing], **1,** to give up or surrender, as a tract of land; **2,** to grant (a point), as in an argument.

ceil-ing (sēl′ing), *n.* **1,** the inner overhead lining or covering of a room; **2,** an upper limit; as, a (price) *ceiling* on rents; **3,** the upper limit of visibility or height at which an airplane can fly under clouds, etc.

cel-e-brate (sel′e-brāt′), *v.t.* [celebrated, celebrat-ing], **1,** to perform publicly with suitable ceremonies, as a Mass; **2,** to make known with praise; honour; as, we *celebrate* the names of great men; **3,** to observe suitably, as with a holiday and ceremonies; as, to *celebrate* Christmas.—*n.* **cel′e-bra-′tion.**

cel-e-brat-ed (sel′e-brāt′id), *adj.* famous; illustrious.

ce-leb-ri-ty (se-leb′ri-ti), *n.* [*pl.* celebrities], **1,** fame; renown; **2,** a renowned or celebrated person; a public character.

ce-ler-i-ty (se-ler′i-ti), *n.* rapidity; speed.

cel-er-y (sel′ĕr-i), *n.* a garden plant, the stalks of which are bleached, during growth, and eaten as a vegetable; also, a stalk of this plant.

ce-les-tial (se-les′chal), *adj.* **1,** pertaining to the heavens; as, the stars are *celestial* bodies; **2,** heavenly; divine; as, *celestial* peace.

cel-i-bate (sel′i-bāt′; -bit), *n.* an unmarried person:—*adj.* single; unmarried; bound by vows not to marry. —*n.* **cel′i-ba-cy.**

cell (sel), *n.* **1,** a small, close room, as in a monastery or prison; **2,** a tiny mass of living matter, the unit of structure in both plants and animals; **3,** a small enclosed space, as in a honeycomb; **4,** in electricity, a vessel containing a fluid and two plates of different materials, or a similar apparatus, used to generate an electric current.—*adj.* **cel′lu-lar.**

cel-lar (sel′ĕr), *n.* a room or group of rooms, generally underground or under a building, most often used for storage.

cel-lo (chel′ō), *n.* [*pl.* cellos or celli (chel′ē)], the violoncello; a musical stringed instrument larger than the violin and deeper in tone. Also written ′cel′lo.—*n.* ′cel′list; cel′list.

cel-lo-phane (sel′o-fān′), *n.* a thin, transparent, waterproof material made from wood-pulp, and used as a wrapper for many articles.

cel-lu-loid (sel′ū-loid′), *n.* a compound of camphor and gun-cotton: a material often used to imitate amber or tortoise-shell, used in making combs, brushes, films, etc.

cel-lu-lose (sel′ū-lōs′), *n.* a substance related to starch, and forming the main part of plant tissue: used in making linen, paper, etc.

ce-ment (si-ment′), *n.* **1,** a substance usually made from clay and limestone and mixed with water to form a kind of mortar which soon hardens to the consistency of stone, used in building walls, laying floors, etc.; **2,** any similar substance which causes things to stick together, as glue or paste; **3,** the bony material which covers the root of a tooth; **4,** in dentistry, a material used for filling cavities:—*v.t.* **1,** to cause to stick together, as bricks; **2,** to cover or pave with cement.

cem-e-ter-y (sem′i-tĕr-i), *n.* [*pl.* cemeteries], a burial-ground; graveyard.

cen-o-taph (sen′ō-tȧf′), *n.* a monument or empty tomb erected in honour of a person buried elsewhere.

cen-ser (sen′sėr), *n.* a vessel with a perforated lid, in which incense is burned.

cen-sor (sen′sėr), *n.* **1,** in ancient Rome, one of the two magistrates who took the census and regulated morals; **2,** an official who examines books, plays, or the like, to prevent the publication or performance of anything immoral or offensive; **3,** an official who, in time of war, examines all printed matter, mail, telegrams, or the like, to suppress anything that might help the enemy; **4,** one who criticizes manners or morals:— *v.t.* to deal with as a censor.

cen-sure (sen′shyoor), *n.* blame; fault-finding; reproof:—*v.t.* [censured, censur-ing], to find fault with.—*adj.* **cen-sor′i-ous** (sen-sōr′i-us).

cen-sus (sen′sus), *n.* an official count of population: in ancient Rome, a registration of citizens and property for taxation purposes: in Canada, a count taken every ten years, including statistics as to sex, race, age, employment, etc.

cent (sent), *n.* **1,** the hundredth part of a dollar; **2,** a coin of this value.

cen-taur (sen′tôr), *n.* **1,** in mythology, a creature half man and half horse; **2,** a perfect horseman.

cen-te-na-ry (sen′ti-na-ri;), *n.* [*pl.* centenaries], a period of 100 years; also, a celebration of a 100th anniversary.—*n.* **cen′te-nar′i-an.**

cen-ten-ni-al (sen-ten′i-al), *adj.* relating to a period of 100 years:—*n.* the 100th anniversary of any event; also, the celebration of this anniversary.

CENTAUR

cen-ter (sen′tėr), *n.* Same as **centre.**

cen-ti-grade (sen′ti-grād′), *adj.* having 100 equal divisions called degrees:— **centigrade thermometer,** a thermometer on which the distance between the freezing-point of water, marked at 0°, and the boiling-point, marked at 100°, is divided into 100 equal degrees.

cen-ti-pede (sen′ti-pēd′), *n.* a small, wormlike animal with a pair of legs for each body segment.

cen-tral (sen′tral), *adj.* **1,** relating to the middle; situated in the middle; **2,** chief; leading; as, the *central* theme of a discussion:—*n.* a telephone exchange; also, a telephone operator at an exchange.—*adv.* **cen′tral-ly.**

cen-tral-ize (sen′tral-īz′), *v.t.* [centralized, centraliz-ing], to draw to one central point; to bring under one control; as, to *centralize* a government.—*n.* **cen′tral-i-za′tion.**

cen-tre (sen′tėr), *n.* **1,** that point of a circle or sphere which is equally distant from every point of the circumference; **2,** a point about which something turns, or about which things are collected or people gather; as, the *centre* of a wheel; a shopping *centre*; **3,** the principal point or object; as, she is the *centre* of attention:—*v.t.* [centred, cen-tring], **1,** to place (something) at the middle point; **2,** to gather to a point; concentrate, as the attention:—*v.i.* to gather at one point; converge toward a single point; as, his ambition *centred* on his son.

cen-tre-board (sen′tėr-bōrd′), *n.* on a sailboat, a movable fin keel that can be lowered to prevent leeward drifting, or raised for shallow water.

cen-trif-u-gal (sen-trif′ū-gal), *adj.* moving or tending to move away from a centre:— **centrifugal force,** a force which tends to make a rotating body fly away from its centre, as mud is thrown from a moving wheel.

cen-trip-e-tal (sen-trip′e-tal), *adj.* tending to move towards the centre; opposite of *centrifugal.*

cen-tu-ri-on (sen-tū′ri-un), *n.* in Roman history, an officer commanding a company of about 100 soldiers.

cen-tu-ry (sen′tū-ri; sen′choo-ri), *n.* [*pl.* centuries], **1,** a group of 100, esp. 100 years; **2,** each group of 100 years after some fixed date, as the birth of Christ; as, the years 1801 to 1900 inclusive belong to the 19th *century* A.D.; **3,** a score of 100 points; as, in cricket, to make a *century;* **4,** in Roman history, a group of citizens casting a single vote; also, a company of about 100 soldiers:— **century—plant,** the American aloe, a plant with long, fleshy spiny leaves and a treelike flower stalk, formerly supposed to bloom once every 100 years.

ce-ram-ics (se-ram′iks), *n.pl.* used as *sing.,* the art of moulding and baking clays in the form of pottery, tiles, etc.

ce-re-al (sē′ri-al), *n.* **1,** any grass that yields a grain or seed used for food, as rice, wheat, oats, etc.; **2,** any of these grains, in a natural state or as put on the market; **3,** a prepared food, esp. a breakfast food, made from any of these grains:—*adj.* pertaining to edible grains or the grasses which produce them.

cer-e-bral (ser′e-bral; se-rē′bral), *adj.* **1,** of, or relating to, the brain; as, *cerebral* excitement; **2,** intellectual; as, *cerebral* music.

cer-e-mo-ni-al (ser′e-mō′ni-al), *adj.* relating to rites or formalities; as, *ceremonial* garb:—*n.* **1,** a system of rites, etc.; as, the *ceremonial* of coronation; **2,** behaviour required by custom on a given social occasion; as, court *ceremonial.*—*adv.* **cer′e-mo′ni-al-ly.**

cer-e-mo-ny (ser′e-mo-ni), *n.* [*pl.* ceremonies], **1,** a formal rite or observance; as, the marriage *ceremony*; the inaugural *ceremony*; **2,** behaviour regulated by the laws of strict etiquette; formality.—*adj.* **cer′e-mo′ni-ous.**

ce-rise (se-rēz′; se-rēs′), *adj.* cherry red:—*n.* a bright, light-red colour.

cer-tain (sûr′tin), *adj.* **1,** beyond question; sure; as, it is *certain* that day follows night; **2,** destined; inevitable; as, death is the *certain* end for all; **3,** fixed; settled; as, it is *certain* that we leave tomorrow; **4,** confident; as, I am *certain* of your loyalty; **5,** particular; one or some; as, to travel by a *certain* road; *certain* senators disagreed.—*adv.* **cer′tain-ly.**

cer-tain-ty (sûr′tin-ti), *n.* [*pl.* certainties], **1,** the state of being sure; as, there is no *certainty* that we can leave today; **2,** something that is sure to happen; as, death is a *certainty.*

cer-tif-i-cate (ser-tif′i-kit), *n.* a formal, printed or written statement of a fact or privilege, signed by a public official or qualified person; as, a *certificate* of marriage; a medical *certificate*; a teacher's *certificate.*—*v.t.* (ser-tif′i-kāt′), [-cated, -cat-ing], **1,** to verify, or vouch for, in a written statement; as, to *certificate* a teacher; **2,** to issue a certificate.

cer-ti-fy (sûr′ti-fī), *v.t.* [certified, certifying], **1,** to confirm or verify by a signed statement; as, the doctor *certified* that John had been vaccinated; **2,** to guarantee; as, to *certify* a cheque. —*n.* **cer′ti-fi-ca′tion.**

cer-ti-tude (sûr′ti-tūd′), *n.* assurance; certainty.

cer-vi-cal (sûr′vi-kal), *adj.* pertaining to the neck; as, a *cervical* vertebra.

ces-sa-tion (se-sā′shun), *n.* a ceasing; a pause; stop; as, *cessation* of pain; *cessation* of hostilities.

ces-sion (sesh′un), *n.* a formal giving up to another; as, a *cession* of territory.

cess-pool (ses′pōōl′), *n.* **1,** a pit or well to receive drainage from sinks, toilets, etc. **2,** a filthy place; as, Sodom was a *cesspool* of iniquity.

chafe (chāf), *v.t.* [chafed, chaf-ing], **1,**

to rub with the hand, so as to restore warmth or sensation; as, to *chafe* numb hands; **2,** to wear away or make sore by rubbing; as, a frayed collar *chafes* the skin; **3,** to fret; irritate:—*v.i.* **1,** to rub; **2,** to be worn or made sore by rubbing; **3,** to be vexed; to fume; as, to *chafe* at the least delay.

chaf-er (chāf′ẽr), *n.* a species of large beetle, such as the June bug.

¹chaff (chȧf), *n.* **1,** the husks of grain, separated by threshing and winnowing; **2,** straw or hay cut fine for cattle; **3,** anything worthless.

²chaff (chȧf), *n.* good-natured teasing; banter:—*v.i.* and *v.t.* to tease.

chaf-ing dish (chāf′ing), *n.* a pan with lamp or electric element under it for cooking at table or keeping food hot.

cha-grin (sha-grin′; -grēn′), *n.* vexation due to disappointment, failure, or humiliation:—*v.t.* to vex; mortify; as, he was *chagrined* by the loss of his job.

chain (chān), *n.* **1,** a series of links or rings joined together; **2,** anything which binds or restrains; **3, chains,** imprisonment or bondage; **4,** a connected series or succession; as, a *chain* of events; **5,** a measure, used in surveying land, equal to 100 links or 66 feet:—*v.t.* **1,** to fasten with a chain; **2,** to fetter; restrain.

chair (châr), *n.* **1,** a movable single seat with a back; **2,** a position of honour or authority; **3,** the seat from which a professor delivers his lectures; hence, the office or position of a professor; as, the *chair* of English at a university; **4,** the presiding officer of an assembly; chairman; as, to address the *chair.*

chair-man (châr′man), *n.* [*pl.* chairmen (-men)], the presiding officer of an assembly or committee.—*n.* **chair′man-ship.**

chaise (shāz), *n.* a light carriage with a folding top. The most common type has two wheels, is drawn by one horse, and carries two persons: also called *shay*, regarded as the singular of *chaise.*

cha-let (shal′ā; sha-lā′), *n.* a Swiss-style wide-eaved cottage or resort, usually in hilly country for skiing, etc.

chal-ice (chal′is), *n.* **1,** a goblet; **2,** the cup used in celebrating the Eucharist, or Lord's Supper; **3,** the cup-shaped head of a flower, as of the tulip.

chalk (chôk), *n.* **1,** a soft, whitish limestone, composed chiefly of tiny seashells; **2,** a chalklike material used to make crayons; also, the crayon:—*v.t.* **1,** to rub or whiten with chalk; **2,** to mark or write with chalk.—*adj.* **chalk′y.**

chal-lenge (chal′inj), *n.* **1,** a summons or invitation to a duel or contest; a

all, (ôl), ôr; up, mūte, cûr, cōōl, book; oil, out; th, thin; *th,* the.

dare; **2,** a demand by a sentry that a passer-by show who he is; **3,** an objection made to a person's serving on a jury:—*v.t.* [challenged, challeng-ing], **1,** to summon to a duel or contest; **2,** to invite; as, to *challenge* investigation; **3,** to take exception to; dispute, as a statement; **4,** to claim as due; as, he *challenges* respect by his honesty; **5,** to demand identification from; as, the sentry *challenged* him; **6,** in law, to object to (a juror).—*n.* **chal′leng-er.**

cham-ber (chām′bėr), *n.* **1,** a room, esp. a bedroom; as, in my lady's *chamber*; **2, chambers,** a set of rooms used as a dwelling or business office; **3,** a hall where a legislative or other government body meets; **4,** the government body itself; as, in Canada the Senate is the upper *chamber* of Parliament; **5,** a group of persons organized for certain business purposes; as, the *Chamber* of Commerce; **6,** a hollow, enclosed space, as the part of a gun intended to hold the charge.

cham-ber-lain (chām′bėr-lin), *n.* the high court official who manages the household of a ruler or nobleman.

cha-me-le-on (ka-mē′li-un; ka-mēl′-yun), *n.* **1,** a lizard which has the power to change its colour to match its surroundings; **2,** a person of changeable disposition.

cham-ois (sha′mwä; in def. 2, sham′i), *n.* **1,** a small antelope found on high peaks in Europe and Asia; **2,** a soft, thin leather, originally made from the hide of the chamois, but now prepared from other skins, and used for gloves, polishing-cloths, etc.

champ (champ), *v.t.* and *v.i.* to bite or bite upon, noisily or impatiently; as, a horse *champs* the bit.

cham-pagne (sham-pān′), *n.* **1,** a light, sparkling, almost colourless wine made originally in the northeastern part of France; **2,** in careless use, any sparkling wine.

cham-paign (sham′pān), *n.* a flat, open country.

cham-pi-on (cham′pi-un), *n.* **1,** a successful competitor against all rivals; as, lightweight *champion* of Canada; **2,** a person who defends another or fights for a cause; as, a *champion* of free speech:—*adj.* above all rivals:—*v.t.* to defend or support.—*n.* **cham′pi-on-ship′.**

chance (chåns), *n.* **1,** the way things happen; fate; fortune; as, *chance* willed it; **2,** a possibility; probability; also, opportunity; as, a *chance* of a position; **3,** risk; as, to take a *chance*:—*adj.* accidental; unforeseen; as, a *chance* meeting:—*v.i.* [chanced, chanc-

ing], to happen; as, it *chanced* to rain:—*v.t. Colloq.*, to risk; as, I don't dare *chance* it.

chan-cel (chån′sel), *n.* in certain churches, the space surrounding the altar, reserved for the clergy and, sometimes, for the choir.

chan-cel-lor (chån′se-lėr), *n.* **1,** in some European countries, the chief minister of state; **2,** in many universities, the president:—**Chancellor,** 'in Great Britain: **1,** the highest judge of the realm, called *Lord Chancellor*; **2,** the minister of finance, called *Chancellor of the Exchequer.*—*n.* **chan′cel-lor-ship′.** —*n.* **chan′cel-ler-y.**

chan-cer-y (chån′sėr-i), *n.* **1,** the court of the Lord Chancellor; **2,** in the U.S., a court of equity.

chan-de-lier (shan′de-lēr′), *n.* a hanging lights fixture, with branches for electric light bulbs, candles, etc.

change (chānj), *v.t.* [changed, changing], **1,** to make different by substituting one thing for another; as, he *changed* his coat; he *changed* his job; **2,** to alter so as to make different in shape, size, colour, or the like; **3,** to exchange; as, to *change* rings with someone; **4,** to give an equivalent for; as, to *change* a dollar bill:—*v.i.* **1,** to vary; as, the weather *changes*; **2,** to be altered; as, her appearance has *changed* greatly; **3,** of the moon, to pass from one phase, or state, to another; as, the moon *changes* next week:—*n.* **1,** an alteration; a variation; as, a *change* of scenery; **2,** variety; as, she plays tennis almost every day, but likes golf as a *change*; **3,** small coins taken together; **4,** the difference, returned to a purchaser, between the price of a purchase and the amount paid.—*adj.* **change′a-ble; change′less.**

change-ling (chānj′ling), *n.* **1,** in *folklore,* an elf child left by fairies in exchange for a human infant; **2,** any child substituted for another.

chan-nel (chan′el), *n.* **1,** the bed of a stream; also, the deepest part of a bay, harbour, etc.; **2,** a strait separating two large bodies of land; as, the English *Channel*; **3,** a long groove or furrow; **4,** a course by which information, thought, or the like, travels; as, news comes through the *channel* of the press:—*v.t.* [channelled, channel-ling], to cut or wear (a groove or way); as, the brook *channelled* ,its way through the rock.

chant (chånt), *v.t.* **1,** to sing; **2,** to praise in song; **3,** to intone, or sing on one prolonged note; recite musically:— *v.i.* **1,** to make melody with the voice; **2,** to intone; sing slowly and solemnly: —*n.* **1,** a song; esp. a solemn, measured song; **2,** a special musical composition, chanted or intoned, used in church services.—*n.* **chant'er.**

chant-ey (shăn'ti; chăn'ti), *n.* a sailor's song sung in rhythm with his work; as, 'Blow the man down...'

chan-ti-cleer (chan'ti-klēr), *n.* a rooster.

cha-os (kā'os), *n.* **1,** the utter confusion formerly supposed to have existed before the universe; **2,** hence, utter disorder.—*adj.* **cha-ot'ic** (kā-ot'ik).

¹chap (chap), *v.t.* [chapped, chap-ping], to cause to crack or become rough; as, cold *chaps* the skin:—*v.i.* to crack or become rough; as, my hands *chap* quickly:—*n.* a crack, as in the skin.

²chap (chap), *n. Colloq.*, a boy or man.

cha-peau (shà'pō'), *n.* [*pl.* -peaux (-pōz')], *n.* a hat, esp. one that goes with an official costume.

chap-el (chap'el), *n.* **1,** a place of public worship, not so large or important as a church; **2,** a place of worship in a palace, school, etc.; **3,** in Great Britain, a church belonging to neither the Church of England nor the Roman Catholic Church.

chap-er-on (shap'ẽr-ōn'), *n.* an older woman who accompanies a young unmarried woman, or a group of young people, to the theatre, a dance, or other social function:—*v.t.* to act as chaperon to. Also, **chap'er-one.**

chap-lain (chap'lin), *n.* a clergyman who performs religious services in the army or navy, or in an institution, etc.

chap-let (chap'lit), *n.* **1,** a wreath or garland for the head; **2,** a string of beads, one third as long as a rosary, for counting prayers; also, the prayers; **3,** any string of beads.

chaps (chaps; shaps; chops), *n.* seatless leather breeches or overalls open at the back, worn by cowboys as a protection against cacti, thorns, etc. Short for **cha-pa-ra-jos** (chä'pä-rä'hōs).

chap-ter (chap'tẽr), *n.* **1,** a main division of a book; **2,** a local group which is part of a larger religious or fraternal order.

char (chär), *v.t.* [charred, char-ring], **1,** to burn partially; **2,** to reduce to charcoal.—*n.* a small red-bellied brook trout.

char-ac-ter (kar'ak-tẽr), *n.* **1,** a distinctive sign or mark; hence, the written or printed marks for letters and numbers; **2,** individuality; nature; the qualities that make a thing what it is, and different from other things; as, the *character* of mountain vegetation

differs from that of a valley; **3,** a person possessing distinctive qualities; as, a great historical *character*; **4,** mental or moral nature; as, a person of high *character*; **5,** reputation; **6,** a testimonial; **7,** a person in literature; as, a Dickens *character*.

char-ac-ter-is-tic (kar'ak-tẽr-is'tik), *adj.* showing the distinctive qualities or traits of a person or thing; typical; as, her *characteristic* kindness:—*n.* a distinguishing quality; as, the *characteristics* of a scholar.

char-ac-ter-ize (kar'ak-tẽr-īz'), *v.t.* [characterized, characteriz-ing], **1,** to describe as having specific qualities; as, the author *characterizes* his heroines as ugly, but interesting; **2,** to mark or distinguish; be characteristic of; as, obstinacy *characterizes* the donkey.—*n.* **char'ac-ter-i-za'tion.**

cha-rade (sha-rād'; sha-räd'), *n.* a game in which a word is to be guessed from the acting out of each syllable, as *persuaded* from the acting of *purr, sway, dead.*

char-coal (chär'kōl'), *n.* a very dark or black porous substance produced by charring wood in the absence of air: used as fuel, and in drawing pencils.

chard (chärd), *n.* **1,** a beet whose thick stalk and large leaves are used as food, the Swiss chard; **2,** the blanched leaves and stalk of the artichoke, used as food.

charge (chärj), *v.t.* [charged, charging], **1,** to load, as a gun with ammunition, or a battery with electricity; **2,** to command; instruct; as, the judge then *charged* the jury; **3,** to accuse; blame; as, he was *charged* with murder; **4,** to demand, as a price; **5,** to place (something) on record as not paid for; as, please *charge* this purchase to me; **6,** to rush upon or attack:—*v.i.* **1,** to demand or set a price or sum due; as, he *charges* reasonably for what he sells; **2,** to make an attack:—*n.* **1,** a quantity of material with which a firearm or other apparatus is loaded; as a *charge* of gunpowder; **2,** an office or trust; responsibility; **3,** a parish or congregation entrusted to the care of a minister; **4,** the price of an object; as, the *charge* is one dollar; **5,** an entry or account of what is owed; **6,** an accusation; as, a *charge* of theft; **7,** a violent onset or attack.—*adj.* **charge'a-ble.**

charg-er (chär'jẽr), *n.* **1,** a spirited warhorse; **2,** a large platter.

char-i-ot (char'i-ut), *n.* an ancient two-wheeled car used in war, state processions, and racing, drawn by two horses or, sometimes, by four.—*n.* **char'i-ot-eer'.**

char-i-ty (char'i-ti), *n.* [*pl.* charities],

1, generosity to the poor; **2,** a gift to the poor; **3,** brotherly love and good-will; **4,** leniency in judging others; **5,** an institution, founded by a gift, to help the needy.—*adj.* **char′i-ta-ble.** —*adv.* **char′i-ta-bly.**

cha-ri-va-ri (sha-riv′a-rē′; shi′va-rē′), *n.* a mock serenade (to newlyweds), by beating on pans, blowing horns, etc. Also, *Colloq.* **shiv′a-ree′.**

char-la-tan (shär′la-tan), *n.* a quack, esp. a pretender to medical skill; an impostor.

char-ley horse (chär′li), *n. Colloq.*, a stiffness in leg or arm muscles, as from strain suffered in football, etc.

charm (chärm), *n.* **1,** originally, a chanted verse supposed to have magic power; **2,** hence, anything which has magic power; **3,** something worn to bring good luck and avert ill luck; an amulet; **4,** a trinket worn on a watch fob; **5,** a quality of appearance or personality which attracts others; attractiveness:—*v.t.* **1,** to bewitch; put a spell on; **2,** hence, to affect as if by magic; as, to *charm* away pain; **3,** to fascinate.—*n.* **charm′er.**

charm-ing (chär′ming), *adj.* delight-ful; fascinating; pleasing.—*adv.* **charm′ing-ly.**

chart (chärt), *n.* **1,** a map, esp. a map of any part of a body of water, marking dangerous ledges, ocean currents, is-lands, etc., for the use of mariners; **2,** the map of a ship's course; **3,** a sheet of paper giving information in the form of tables, diagrams, or the like; as, a nurse's *chart*;—*v.t.* **1,** to map out; **2,** to put (information) in the form of a chart.

char-ter (chär′tẽr), *n.* **1,** an official paper bestowing certain rights and privileges; **2,** a written permit from the authorities of a society to establish a chapter, lodge, or branch:—*v.t.* **1,** to grant a charter or permit to; **2,** to hire; as, to *charter* a bus.

char-treuse (shär′tröz′), *n.* **1,** a pale yellowish-green colour; **2,** a sirupy alcoholic liqueur of this colour.

char-wom-an (chär′woom′an), *n.* a woman hired by the day who cleans and scrubs, as in office buildings, etc.

char-y (châr′i; chär′i), *adj.* **1,** cautious; careful; as, *chary* of fire; **2,** shy; as, *chary* of strangers; **3,** sparing; stingy; as, *chary* of praise.

chase (chās), *v.t.* [chased, chas-ing], **1,** to pursue with intent to capture or kill, as a fox; to hunt; **2,** to drive away; dispel; as, to *chase* crows; *chase* fears: —*n.* **1,** eager pursuit, esp. with the idea of capturing (a criminal) or killing (an animal); **2,** hunters (collectively).

chasm (kazm), *n.* a deep cleft or gap (in the earth); a vast empty space.

chas-sis (shas′ē; shas′is), *n.* [*pl.* chassis (shas′iz)], **1,** the frame, machinery, and wheels of an auto-mobile; **2,** the main frame of an aero-plane.

chaste (chāst), *adj.* **1,** virtuous; pure; **2,** simple and restrained in style or taste; unadorned.

chas-ten (chās′n), *v.t.* **1,** to punish for the purpose of making better; as, God *chastens* his people; **2,** to subdue; bring low; as, ridicule *chastens* a braggart.

chas-tise (chas-tīz′), *v.t.* [chastised, chastis-ing], to correct by punishment; as, to *chastise* a child.—*n.* **chas′tise-ment.**

chas-ti-ty (chas′ti-ti), *n.* **1,** moral purity; innocence; **2,** simplicity in design or style.

chat (chat), *v.i.* [chat-ted, chat-ting], to converse in an easy, familiar manner:— *n.* **1,** familiar, easy speech; an informal talk; **2,** a kind of songbird noted for its song.—*adj.* **chat′ty.**—*n.* **chat′ti-ness.**

cha-teau (shȧ-tō′), *n.* [*pl.* -teaux (-tōz′)], **1,** a feudal castle; **2,** a stately (French) manor or country seat.

chat-e-laine (shȧ′te-lān′), *n.* the lady or mistress of a chateau or fashionable household.

chat-tel (chat′l), *n.* personal property not including houses or land; a mov-able possession, such as furniture.

chat-ter (chat′ẽr), *v.i.* **1,** to utter sounds rapidly and indistinctly, as monkeys; **2,** to talk much and say little; **3,** to rattle, as parts of a machine in motion, or as teeth when one is shivering:—*n.* **1,** sounds like those of the magpie, monkey, etc.; **2,** idle, rapid talk; **3,** a rattling of the teeth, as from cold or fear.—*n.* **chat′ter-er.**

chat-ter-box (chat′ẽr-boks′), *n.Colloq.*, an incessant talker.

chauf-feur (shō′fẽr; shō-fûr′), *n.* one whose business is to drive an auto-mobile.

cheap (chēp), *adj.* **1,** low in price; inexpensive; **2,** low in quality; as, *cheap* goods are expensive in the long run; **3,** well worth the price; as, the car was *cheap* at $200; **4,** easily secured; hence, of little value; as, *cheap* popularity; **5,** connected with things of low price or value; as, a *cheap* street or store.—*adj.* **cheap′ly.**—*n.* **cheap′-ness.**

cheap-en (chēp′en), *v.t.* to lower in price or value:—*v.i.* to become cheap.

cheat (chēt), *n.* one who deceives or

swindles another:—*v.i.* to act dishonestly; as, to *cheat* at cards:—*v.t.* **1**, to deceive; deprive of something by trickery; **2**, to escape; as, to *cheat* the gallows.—*n.* **cheat′er.**

¹check (chek), *n.* **1**, restraint; control; as, to keep one's thoughts in *check*; also, a person or thing imposing restraint; **2**, a stop or interruption; as, a journey without *check*; **3**, a ticket or metal disk which shows that a person has the right to claim something; as, a hat-*check*; also, a ticket showing the amount of a bill; as, to pay the *check* in a restaurant; **4**, (preferably *cheque*), an order or draft on a bank for money; **5**, an examination into the accuracy of something; as, a *check* of a bank statement; **6**, a mark showing that something has been examined or verified:—*v.t.* **1**, to stop; as, to *check* the advance of the enemy; **2**, to examine for accuracy, or mark, as having been examined or verified; **3**, to deposit for safekeeping; as, to *check* a coat.

²check (chek), *n.* **1**, a pattern of squares of alternating colours, as on a chequerboard; **2**, any one of these squares; **3**, cloth showing this pattern:—*v.t.* to mark in checks.

check-er (chek′ẽr), *n.* Same as **chequer.**

check-mate (chek′māt′), *n.* **1**, in chess, the putting of an opponent's king in such a position that he cannot escape; **2**, hence, a complete obstruction or defeat:—*v.t.* [checkmat-ed, checkmat-ing], to obstruct or defeat utterly; as, to *checkmate* a plan.

check-off (chek′ôf′), *n.* an arrangement whereby an employer deducts union dues from wages, and turns them over to the union.

check-room (chek′rōōm′), *n.* a room where hats, coats, parcels, and baggage may be left temporarily.

check-up (chek′up′), *n.* an inspection; examination.

ched-dar (ched′ẽr), *n.* a standard Canadian and American cheese of smooth, firm texture.

cheek (chēk), *n.* **1**, the side of the face below the eye; **2**, *Slang*, saucy speech; effrontery; impudence.—*adj.* **cheek′y.** —*n.* **cheek′i-ness; cheek′bone′.**

cheep (chēp), *n.* a faint shrill note, as of a chick or bird; peep; chirp.—*v.t.* and *v.i.* to peep or chirp.

cheer (chēr), *n.* **1**, state of mind; esp. a state of gladness or joy; **2**, that which is furnished in the way of food or entertainment; **3**, a shout of joy, applause or encouragement:—*v.t.* **1**, to gladden; comfort; **2**, to greet, esp. with shouts of welcome; **3**, hence, to

applaud; encourage:—*v.i.* **1**, to become hopeful or glad; as, he soon *cheered* up; **2**, to applaud.

cheer-ful (chēr′fool), *adj.* **1**, in good spirits; gay; **2**, bringing cheer; as, a *cheerful* fire; **3**, willing; eager; as, a *cheerful* worker.—*adv.* **cheer′ful-ly.**—*n.* **cheer′ful-ness.**

cheer-i-o (chēr′i-ō′), *interj. Colloq.* **1**, good-bye; **2**, hello.

cheer-less (chēr′lis), *adj.* gloomy; forlorn; dismal; as, a damp, *cheerless* day.

cheer-y (chēr′i), *adj.* [cheer-i-er, cheer-i-est], **1**, cheerful; gay; as, a *cheery* voice; **2**, attractive; bright; as, a *cheery* room.—*n.* **cheer′i-ness.**—*adv.* **cheer′i-ly.**

cheese (chēz), *n.* a food made of the pressed curd of milk.—*adj.* **chees′y.**

cheese-cake (chēs′kāk′), *n.* a one-crust pie of curds, sugar, eggs, milk, etc. **2**, *Slang*, a display in newspaper photographs of the figure (esp. the legs) of a pretty girl.

cheese-cloth (chēz′clôth′), *n.* a thin loosely woven cotton cloth.

chee-tah (chē′ta), *n.* a Eurasian species of the cat family, leopard-like, long-legged, swift, black-spotted, able to be taught to hunt deer.

chef (shef), *n.* a head cook, as of a hotel or restaurant; hence, any male cook.

chem-i-cal (kem′i-kal), *adj.* **1**, pertaining to chemistry; as, a *chemical* experiment; **2**, produced by, or used in operations of, chemistry; as, a *chemical* compound:—*n.* a substance, such as alcohol, hydrogen, soda, or the like, produced by, or used in, a chemical process.—*adv.* **chem′i-cal-ly.**

che-mise (she-mēz′), *n.* a woman's sleeveless, knee-length undergarment.

chem-is-try (kem′is-tri), *n.* the science which treats of the nature of different kinds of substances, and of the laws which govern their combination and behaviour under various conditions.—*n.* **chem′ist.**

cheque (chek), *n.* an order or draft on a bank for money. Also spelled **check.**

cheq-uer (chek′ẽr), *n.* **1**, one of the squares of a pattern marked in squares of alternate colours; also, the pattern itself; **2**, one of the pieces used in playing chequers; **3**, **chequers**, a game played on a chequerboard by two persons each with twelve pieces:—*v.t.* to mark with small squares of alternate colours; also, to mark similarly; as, sunlight through the leaves *chequered* the ground.—*n.* **cheq′uer-board′.**

cheq-uered, check-ered (chek′ẽrd),

adj. **1,** varied; full of ups and downs; as, a *chequered* career; **2,** having a pattern of alternate squares or colours.

cher-ish (cher′ish), *v.t.* **1,** to protect; care for tenderly; **2,** to hold dear, as a memory; **3,** to cling to, as a hope.

che-root (she-rōōt′), *n.* a long, narrow (or tapering) cigar with both ends cut square.

cher-ry (cher′i), *n.* [*pl.* cherries], **1,** a tree related to the plum, bearing a small, smooth, fleshy fruit with a stone in the centre; also, the fruit or the wood of this tree; **2,** a bright red, like that of certain cherries:—*adj.* **1,** of the colour of ripe red cherries; **2,** made of cherry wood.

cher-ub (cher′ub), *n.* [*pl.* cherubs], **1,** a representation of a child, or the head of a child, with wings; **2,** a beautiful, innocent child; **3,** [*pl.* cherubim (cher′ū-bim; cher′oo-bim)], in the Bible, one of an order of angels.—*adj.* **che-ru′bic** (che-rōō′bik).

chess (ches), *n.* a game played by two persons, each with sixteen variously shaped pieces, or men, on a board of 64 squares.—*n.* **chess′board′; chess′man′.**

chest (chest), *n.* **1,** a strong case; a box with a lid; as, a seaman's *chest*; a tool *chest*; **2,** the quantity such a box contains; also, the box and the contents; as, a *chest* of tea; **3,** a place for keeping a fund of money; hence, the fund itself; as, a community *chest*, **4,** the breast or upper front part of the body enclosed by the ribs.

ches-ter-field (ches′tėr-fēld′), *n.* **1,** a large living-room sofa or divan with well-padded back and upright arms; **2,** a man's single-breasted topcoat, usually with concealed buttons and velvet collar.

chest-nut (ches′nut), *n.* **1,** a tree of the beech family, bearing nuts in a prickly bur; **2,** the nut or the timber of this tree; **3,** a reddish-brown colour; **4,** a horse of such colour; **5,** *Slang,* an old or stale joke:—*adj.* **1,** made of the wood of the chestnut; **2,** reddish brown.

chest-y (ches′ti), *adj. Colloq.,* boastful; conceited.

chev-a-lier (shev′a-lēr′), *n.* **1,** a knight; **2,** in France, a member of an order of merit, as The Legion of Honour.

chev-i-ot (shev′i-ut; chev′i-ut), *n.* **1,** a kind of rough woollen fabric; **2,** a similar fabric made of cotton.

chev-ron (shev′run), *n.* a badge of two or more stripes meeting at an angle, on the coat sleeve of a non-commissioned officer, policeman, etc., to show his rank.

chew (chōō), *v.t.* to crush and grind with the teeth:—*v.i.* to bite repeatedly with the teeth:—*n.* **1,** the act of chewing; **2,** that which can be chewed, as a quid of tobacco.

chic (shik; shēk), *n. Colloq.,* Parisian cleverness in dress; hence, smartness; style:—*adj.* stylish; as, a *chic* hat.

chi-can-er-y (shi-kān′ėr-i), *n.* **1,** trickery, esp. of a legal kind; **2,** sharp practice.

chick (chik), *n.* a young chicken or bird; **2,** a child; **3,** *Slang,* a young girl.

chick-a-dee (chik′a-dē′), *n.* a small, grey bird with a black cap.

chick-en (chik′en), *n.* **1,** the young of a fowl, esp. of the domestic fowl; **2,** a hen or rooster; **3,** the flesh of such fowl, prepared for the table; as, roast *chicken*.

chicken—pox (chik′en–poks′), *n.* a mild contagious disease of children, which is accompanied by a rash.

chic-le (chik′l), *n.* a juice of certain tropical American trees used in making chewing-gum.

chic-o-ry (chik′o-ri), *n.* **1,** a plant with blue flowers, the leaves of which are used as salad; **2,** the root of this plant which, when roasted, is used to adulterate coffee.

chick-weed (chik′wēd′), *n.* a common white-flowering weed, the seeds and young leaves of which are eaten by birds.

chide (chīd), *v.i.* and *v.t.* [*p.t.* chid (chid or chid-ed (chīd′ed), *p.p.* chid, chid-den (chid′n), or chid-ed, *p.pr.* chid-ing], to find fault (with); scold.

chief (chēf), *n.* a commander, leader, or principal person in an organization or group:—*adj.* principal; leading; most important; as, the *chief* news of the day.—*adv.* **chief′ly.**

chief-tain (chēf′tin), *n.* a leader or commander; esp. the military or civil head of a clan or tribe.

chif-fon (shi-fon′; shif′on), *n.* a soft thin, transparent fabric:—*adj.* very light and sheer in weight; as, *chiffon* hosiery.

chif-fo-nier (shif′o-nēr′), *n.* a high chest of drawers, sometimes with a mirror.

Chi-hua-hua (chi-wä′wä), *n.* one of the smallest of all dogs, a Mexican with large pointed ears.

chil-blain (chil′blān′), *n.* an itching sore or swelling on feet or hands from exposure to cold.

child (chīld), *n.* [*pl.* children (chil′dren)] **1,** a boy or a girl; **2,** a son or a daughter offspring; **3,** a baby; **4,** a descendant as, a *child* of Abraham; **5,** a product

---

cat, āge, fär, câre, ȧsk; ten, ēve, latėr; (i) pity, rely, senate; īce; too; nū

as of habit, environment, or temperament; as, a *child* of poverty.—*n.* **child'hood.**—*adj.* **child'less; child'like.**

child-ish (chĭl'dish), *adj.* 1, like, or suitable to, a child; 2, weak; foolish; as, a *childish* impulse in an adult.—*n.* **child'ish-ness.**

chill (chil), *n.* 1, coldness; 2, a sudden coldness of body with shivering; as, *chills* and fever; 3, a check upon enthusiasm; as, she put a *chill* on the party:—*adj.* 1, cool; as, a *chill* breeze; 2, unfriendly; not cordial; as, a *chill* welcome:—*v.t.* to make cold:—*v.i.* to become or feel cold.—*adj.* **chill'y.**—*n.* **chill'i-ness.**

chil-li or **chil-ly** (chil'i), *n.* a tropical plant, the pods of which, red when ripe, are dried and powdered to make cayenne pepper; also, the pods.

chime (chīm), *n.* 1, a set of bells musically attuned, as the bells in a clock tower; 2, (often *chimes*), the music of such bells:—*v.i.* [chimed, chim-ing], 1, to sound in harmony; as, hear the bells *chiming*; 2, to agree; as, your opinion *chimes* with mine:—*v.t.* to announce (the hour) by chimes.

chim-ney (chim'ni), *n.* [*pl.* chimneys], 1, the upright tube or flue, made of brick, stone, or the like, through which smoke and heated air may escape from a building; 2, the part of a flue above a roof; 3, a glass tube around the flame of a lamp.

chim-pan-zee (chim'pan-zē'; chim'-pan-zē'; chim'-pan'zi), *n.* a blackish-brown, anthropoid, or manlike ape of Africa, smaller than the gorilla.

chin (chin), *n.* the part of the face below the underlip; also, the rounded tip of the lower jaw: CHIMPANZEE ($\frac{1}{30}$) —*v.t.* [chinned, chin-ning], to pull (oneself) up, while hanging by the hands from a horizontal bar, until one's chin is on a level with the bar.

chi-na (chī'na), *n.* 1, porcelain or porcelain ware, brought originally from the Far East; 2, porcelain or earthenware dishes of any kind:—*adj.* made of porcelain.—*n.* **chi'na-ware'.**

chinch (chinch), *n.* 1, a stink bug that destroys grain and grass; 2, a bedbug.

chin-chil-la (chin-chil'a), *n.* 1, a small, South American, gnawing animal with a soft, fine, grey fur; 2, the fur of this animal; 3, a heavy woollen cloth.

¹chink (chingk), *n.* a narrow crack or opening; as, you can see through the *chink* in the wall:—*v.t.* 1, to make fissures or cracks in; 2, to fill the cracks of.

²chink (chingk), *n.* a sharp, ringing sound as of glass or metal struck lightly: —*v.t.* to cause to jingle:—*v.i.* to jingle.

chi-nook (shi-nook'; chi-nook'; chi-nook'), *n.* and *adj.* 1, a dry wind that blows at intervals down eastern Rocky Mountain slopes, esp. in Alberta and southward; 2, a warm moist southwest ocean wind that blows along the British Columbia coast and southward.

chintz (chints), *n.* a cotton cloth, printed in coloured patterns, often with a smooth, glossy finish.

chip (chip), *v.t.* [chipped, chip-ping], 1, to cut or break small bits or pieces from; 2, to shape by cutting away small bits; as, to *chip* an arrow from flint:—*v.i.* to break off in small bits; as, these cups *chip* easily:—*n.* 1, a small piece, as of stone or wood, cut or broken off; also, the gap left; as, a *chip* in the saucer; 2, a very small piece, as of a diamond; 3, a counter or disk used in games; as, a poker-*chip.*

chip-munk (chip'mungk), *n.* a small Canadian squirrel with striped markings on its back; in U.S. also called *ground squirrel.* Also spelled **chip'-muck.**

chip-per (chip'ẽr), *adj. Colloq.*, in good spirits; cheerful; as, I feel *chipper* today.

chip-ping spar-row, in Eastern North America, a small sparrow with red-brown crown.

chip shot, in *golf*, a short, lofting stroke used near the green.

chi-rop-o-dist (kī-rop'o-dist; ki-rop'-o-dist), *n.* one who treats ailments, esp. minor ailments, of the feet.—*n.* **chirop'o-dy.**

chi-ro-prac-tor (kī-rō-prak'tẽr), *n.* one who treats bodily diseases by manipulating the joints, esp. the joints of the spine.—*n.* and *adj.* **chi'ro-prac'tic.**

chirp (chûrp), *n.* a short, cheerful note, as that of a bird:—*v.i.* 1, to utter such a note; 2, to talk merrily:—*v.t.* to utter (a sound) resembling a chirp. Also, **chir'rup.**

chis-el (chiz'l), *n.* a steel-edged tool for cutting wood, stone, or metal:—*v.t.* and *v.i.* [chiseled, chisel-ing], 1, to cut or engrave with such a tool; 2, *Slang:* a, to cheat; b, to secure (something) by shrewd, often unfair, means.—*n.* **chis'el-ler, chis'e-ler.**

¹chit (chit), *n.* 1, a child; 2, a pert girl.

²chit (chit), *n.* 1, a letter, bill, note, etc. 2, a voucher for a small sum owed.

chit-chat (chit′chat′), *n.* **1**, small talk; **2**, gossip.

chiv-al-ry (shiv′al-ri), *n.* **1**, the system of knighthood in the Middle Ages; **2**, the characteristics of an ideal knight, as courage, courtesy, respect for women, and the like; **3**, a body of knights; hence a company of gallant gentlemen. —*adj.* **chiv′al-ric**.—*adj.* **chiv′al-rous**.

chive (chīv), *n.* a plant similar to the onion, used for seasoning.

chlo-ride of lime (klō′rīd, -rid), *n.* a white powder used in bleaching, and as a germ destroyer, esp. in drinking water.

chlo-rine (klō′rēn, klō′rin), *n.* a heavy, poisonous green-yellow gas of disagreeable odour used in bleaching, purifying water, and warfare.—*v.t.* **chlo′rin-ate′**. —*n.* **chlo′rin-a′tion**.

chlor-o-form (klōr′ō-fôrm′), *n.* a colourless liquid with sweetish odour, used in surgery to produce unconsciousness:—*v.t.* to make unconscious or to kill with chloroform.

chlor-o-phyll or **chlor-o-phyl** (klōr′-ō-fil), *n.* the green colouring matter of plants.

chock—full (chok′-fool′), *adj.* as full as possible; crammed.

choc-o-late (chok′o-lit), *n.* **1**, a food substance obtained by roasting and grinding cacao seeds; **2**, a small piece of candy made of, or coated with, this substance; **3**, a drink made from this food with milk and sugar:—*adj.* **1**, made of, or flavoured with, chocolate; **2**, of the dark-brown colour of chocolate.

choice (chois), *n.* **1**, selection; as, make your *choice*; also, power of selection; as, you have your *choice*; **2**, the thing or person chosen; as, the president is the *choice* of the society; **3**, the best or most desirable part or thing; as, this puppy is the *choice* of the litter; **4**, a number large enough to choose from; as, a *choice* of hats:—*adj.* [choic-er, choic-est], **1**, select; particularly fine; as, *choice* meats; **2**, selected with care; appropriate.

choir (kwīr), *n.* **1**, a group of trained singers, esp. in a church; **2**, the part of the church in which they sing.—*n.* **choir′boy′**; **choir′mas′ter**.

choke (chōk), *v.t.* [choked, chok-ing], **1**, to stop the breath of; stifle; as, this collar *chokes* me; **2**, to check the growth of by stifling, or as if by stifling; as, weeds *choked* the garden; to *choke* the fire; **3**, to cut down the air intake of the carburettor of (a motor) to enrich the mixture; as, to *choke* an engine; **4**, to block up; clog; as, rubbish *choked* the alley; **5**, to suppress (an emotion); as, to *choke* down anger:—*v.i.* to become

suffocated:—*n.* **1**, the act or sound of strangling; **2**, in an automobile, the carburettor valve which regulates the air intake.

choke-cher-ry (chōk′cher′i), *n.* a wild cherry tree of Canada and U.S. that grows along farm fences, roads, etc., and has a small fruit that dries and puckers the lips.

chok-er (chōk′ėr), *n. Colloq.*, a necklace, high collar, wide scarf, etc., worn close about neck or throat.

chol-er-a (kol′ėr-a), *n.* **1**, **cholera morbus** (môr′bus) or **summer cholera**, an acute, non-infectious inflammation of the digestive tract, occurring in hot summer months; **2**, **Asiatic cholera**, an infectious and often rapidly fatal disease.

chol-er-ic (kol′ėr-ik), *adj.* easily angered; quick-tempered; irascible.

choose (chōoz), *v.t.* [*p.t.* chose (chōz), *p.p.* cho-sen (chō′zn), *p.pr.* choos-ing], **1**, to pick; select from a number; as, he *chose* the reddest apple; **2**, to prefer; see fit; as, he *chose* to run:—*v.i.* to make a choice.

¹**chop** (chop), *v.t.* [chopped, chop-ping], **1**, to cut with repeated blows; as, to *chop* wood; **2**, to cut into very small pieces; as, to *chop* vegetables; **3**, to cut short, as words:—*v.i.* to make a quick stroke, as with an axe:—*n.* **1**, a small piece of meat containing a rib or section of bone; as, a lamb *chop*; **2**, a short, rough movement of the waves.— *n.* **chop′per**.

²**chop** (chop), *n.* **1**, a jaw; **2**, **chops**, the mouth or the fleshy parts about it.

¹**chop-py** (chop′i), *adj.* [chop-pi-er, chop-pi-est], full of short, rough waves; as, a *choppy* sea.

²**chop-py** (chop′i), *adj.* [chop-pi-er, chop-pi-est], changeable; as, a *choppy* wind.

chop-sticks (chop′stiks′), *n.pl.* two small sticks of wood, ivory, etc., used instead of a fork, esp. by the Chinese.

chor-al (kōr′al), *adj.* **1**, pertaining to a choir or chorus; as, *choral* singing; **2**, sung by a choir; as, a *choral* service.

¹**chord** (kôrd), *n.* **1**, a string of a musical instrument; **2**, in geometry, a straight line joining two points on the circumference of a circle; **3**, in the body, a chordlike structure; tendon.

²**chord** (kôrd), *n.* in music, a combination of three or more tones sounded together and in harmony.

CHORDS (AB, AC)

chore (chōr), *n.* **1,** a small job; **2, chores,** small or odd jobs; the daily humdrum work of a farm or household.

chor-is-ter (kôr'is-tėr; kor-), *n.* a singer in a choir, esp. a male choir.

chor-tle (chôr'tl), *v.i.* [chortled, chortling], to chuckle gleefully:—*n.* a low, deep, or inward, laugh.

chor-us (kōr'us, kôr-), *n.* **1,** a group of persons singing together or their song; also, any utterance by a number of persons at one time; as, a *chorus* of shouts; **2,** a piece of music arranged to be sung by a number of voices all together; **3,** a refrain at the end of each verse of a song:—*v.t.* and *v.i.* to sing or utter all together.

chose (chōz), *p.t.* of *choose*.

chow (chou) or **¹chow-chow** (chou'-chou'), *n.* a dog of a breed originating in China, having a muscular body, heavy coat, and short tail which curls over the back.

²chow-chow (chou'chou'), *n.* a relish.

chow-der (chou'dėr), *n.* a soup made by stewing fish, clams, or a vegetable, usually in milk, with bits of pork, onions, etc.

Christ (krīst), *n.* used as a title of Jesus, meaning the Messiah, whose coming was foretold by the Jewish prophets.

chris-ten (kris'n), *v.t.* **1,** to baptize; **2,** to name; as, to *christen* a ship; **3,** *Colloq.*, to use for the first time; as, to *christen* the new car.—*n.* **chris'ten-ing**.

Chris-tian (kris'chan; krist'yan), *n.* a believer in the religion of Christ; a member of the Christian Church:—*adj.* **1,** believing in, or practising, the religion of Christ; **2,** pertaining to Christ, his followers, or his teachings; **3,** showing Christlike qualities, as gentleness, forbearance, etc.:—**Christian name**, a person's first name.—*n.* **Chris'ti-an'i-ty**.

Christ-mas (kris'mas), *n.* the yearly festival (December 25) in honour of the birth of Christ.—*n.* **Christ'mas-tide'**.

chro-mat-ic (krō-mat'ik), *adj.* **1,** relating to colour; as, *chromatic* printing (in colours); **2,** in *music*, using or proceeding by half tones; as, a *chromatic* scale.

chrome (krōm), *n.* **1,** a bright colouring substance or pigment; as, *chrome* yellow, *chrome* green, *chrome* red; **2,** a shorter form of *chromium*.

chro-mi-um (krō'mi-um), *n.* a greyish-white, rust-resisting metallic element, much used in plating motor-car bumpers and trim, household wares, roller bearings, tools, dies, etc., and as an alloy.

chro-mo-some (krō'mo-sōm'), *n.* one of the rod-shaped, threadlike bodies that carry the genes which convey hereditary characteristics.

chron-ic (kron'ik), *adj.* **1,** continuing for a long time; as, he has a *chronic* cold; **2,** habitual; as, a *chronic* complainer.—*adv.* **chron'i-cal-ly**.

chron-i-cle (kron'i-kl), *n.* a record of events in the order of their happening: —*v.t.* [chroni-cled, chroni-cling], to enter, as in a record.—*n.* **chron'i-cler**.

chro-nol-o-gy (kro-nol'o-ji), *n.* [*pl.* chronologies], **1,** the science that deals with events and arranges their dates in proper order; **2,** a table of events given in the order of their occurrence; as, a *chronology* of the war.—*adj.* **chron'o-log'i-cal** (kron'o-loj'i-kal).

chro-nom-e-ter (kro-nom'e-tėr), *n.* a highly accurate timepiece such as those used on ships or aircraft for determining longitude.

chrys-a-lis (kris'a-lis), *n.* [*pl.* chrysalises], **1,** the inactive form through which an insect, esp. a moth or a butterfly, passes when it leaves the caterpillar stage and before it reaches its winged or perfect form; **2,** the case enclosing the insect during that stage; a cocoon.

CHRYSALIS OF A BUTTERFLY

chrys-an-the-mum (kris-an'the-mum; kriz-an'the-mum), *n.* **1,** a plant with showy flowers that blooms late in the fall; **2,** a flower of this plant.

chub (chub), *n.* a kind of fresh-water fish.

chub-by (chub'i), *adj.* [chub-bi-er, chub-bi-est], plump and round; as, a baby's *chubby* fists.—*n.* **chub'bi-ness**.

¹chuck (chuk), *v.t.* **1,** to tap or pat under the chin affectionately or playfully; **2,** to fling away; throw; toss; as, *chuck* me the ball:—*n.* a light tap; a pat under the chin.

²chuck (chuk), *n.* **1,** a clamp for holding a tool or piece of work in a lathe or drill press; **2,** a part of a side of beef or a carcass of lamb or mutton, including most of the neck, the shoulder, and about three ribs.

chuck-le (chuk'l), *n.* a quiet, suppressed laugh:—*v.i.* [chuck-led, chuck-ling], to laugh quietly to oneself.

chuck-wag-on (chuk'wag'un), *n.* *Colloq.*, in Western Canada and U.S., a kitchen on wheels to provide meals for cowboys, lumbermen, etc.;—the *chuck-wagon* race at the Calgary Stampede.

chum (chum), *n.* **1,** a roommate, as at school; **2,** an intimate friend:—*v.i.* [chummed, chum-ming], **1,** to occupy

all (ôl), ôr; up, mūte, cûr, cōōl, book; oil, out; th, thin; *th*, the.

the same room; **2,** to be very friendly.
—*adj.* **chum′my.**

chump (chump), *n.* **1,** a short, thick block of wood; **2,** *Slang,* a dolt, blockhead.

chunk (chungk), *n.* a short, thick piece. —*adj.* **chunk′y.**

church (chûrch), *n.* **1,** a building for public Christian worship; **2,** the entire body of Christians; **3,** (usually *Church*), a particular body or division of Christians; a denomination; as, the United *Church*; **4,** a regular service for Christian worship:—*adj.* having to do with a church; as, *church* music; *church* architecture.—*n.* **church′go′ing; church′man.**

church-ward-en (chûrch′wôr′dn), *n.* in the Anglican Church, an official who looks after church property, finances, etc.

church-yard (chûrch′yärd′), *n.* ground about a church, often used for burial.

churl (chûrl), *n.* **1,** formerly, a person of low birth; **2,** a surly, ill-bred person. —*adj.* **churl′ish.**—*adv.* **churl′ish-ly.**

churn (chûrn), *n.* a vessel in which milk or cream is made into butter:—*v.t.* **1,** to make (butter) by violently stirring cream; **2,** to stir by violent motion; as, the propeller *churned* the water:—*v.i.* **1,** to work a churn; **2,** foam; seethe; wash to and fro; as, the water *churns* around the rocks.

chute (shoot), *n.* **1,** a slanting trough for sliding things down; as, a coal-*chute*; **2,** a rapid in a stream; a shoot; **3,** a toboggan-slide:—*v.t.* [chut-ed, chuting], to send down a chute.

ci-ca-da (si-kā′da; si-kä′da), *n.* [*pl.* cicadas], a large insect with four transparent wings, noted for the long, shrill, chirping sound made by the male.

ci-der (sī′dėr), *n.* applejuice; also, cherry-juice: used as a drink or for making vinegar.

ci-gar (si-gär′), *n.* a roll of CICADA (⅖) tobacco leaf, used for smoking.

cig-a-rette (sig′a-ret′), *n.* a small roll made of finely cut tobacco wrapped in thin paper for smoking.

cinch (sinch), *n.* **1,** a saddle-girth firmly fastened in place by loops and knots; **2,** *Colloq.*, a sure grip or hold; **3,** *Slang,* a sure or easy thing:—*v.t.* **1,** to put a cinch upon; **2,** *Slang,* to get a sure hold on.

cin-cho-na (sin-kō′na), *n.* an evergreen tree of South America, the dried bark of which is a source of quinine.

cin-der (sin′dėr), *n.* **1,** a piece of partly burned coal or wood which has ceased to flame; **2, cinders,** ashes.

cin-e-ma (sin′i-ma), *n.* a motion-picture theatre or a photoplay. Short form of **cin′e-mat′o-graph.**

cin-e-ra-ma (sin′ė-ram′a) or **cin-e-ma-scope** (sin′e-ma-skōp′), *n.* a motion-picture system employing wide-angle lenses, two or more cameras, and wide curved screens.

cin-na-mon (sin′a-mun), *n.* **1,** an East Indian tree; also, its bark or the spice made from it; **2,** a red-brown colour.

ci-pher or **cy-pher** (sī′fėr), *n.* **1,** in mathematics, zero; naught [symbol 0]; **2,** hence, a person or thing without value or power; **3,** a secret manner of writing, or the key to it; a code:—*v.t.* and *v.i.* **1,** to work (arithmetical examples) with figures; calculate; **2,** to write in code.

cir-cle (sûr′kl), *n.* **1,** a plane surface bounded by a single curved line called its circumference, every part of which is equally distant from a point within it, called the centre; also, the curve bounding such a surface; **2,** any flat, round body; **3,** anything resembling a circle or part of a circle; as, the family *circle* in a theatre; **4,** a completed series; a system; cycle; round; as, the *circle* of the months; **5,** a number of persons grouped around a central interest or person; as, a *circle* of friends: —*v.i.* [cir-cled, cir-cling], to move in a circle; as, the aeroplane *circled* above: —*v.t.* **1,** to surround; as, a ring *circled* his finger; **2,** to revolve around; as, the earth *circles* the sun.—*n.* **cir′cler.**

cir-clet (sûr′klit), *n.* **1,** a small circle; **2,** a circular ornament for the head, arm, neck, or finger.

cir-cuit (sûr′kit), *n.* **1,** the boundary line around an area; also, the space enclosed; **2,** the distance around any space, whether circular or of other form; **3,** the act of going around anything; revolution; as, the *circuit* of the earth around the sun; **4,** the regular travelling from place to place of a judge or other person for the purpose of holding court or performing other specific duties; also, the territory or district over which he travels; **5,** the path of an electric current; **6,** a group of theatres under the same management:—**circuit—breaker,** *n.* an automatic device for interrupting an electric current, esp. when the current load becomes too heavy.

cir-cu-i-tous (sėr-kū′i-tus), *adj.* round about; indirect; as, to go by a *circuitous* route.—*adv.* **cir-cu′i-tous-ly.**

cir-cu-lar (sûr′kū-lėr), *adj.* **1,** of,

pertaining to, or like, a circle; as, a *circular* saw; **2,** moving in a circle; as, *circular* motion; **3,** published for distribution to.a group of persons; as, a *circular* letter:—*n.* a printed letter or notice for general distribution.—*adv.* **cir-cu-lar-ly.**—*v.t.* **cir-cu-lar-ize.**

cir-cu-late (sûr′kū-lāt′), *v.i.* [circulated, circulat-ing], **1,** to pass from place to place; as, he *circulated* among the guests; **2,** to move around in a course; as, in that heating system hot water *circulates* through the pipes; **3,** to be distributed, as a newspaper:—*v.t.* to send round; as, he *circulated* the report.—*n.* **cir′cu-la′tion.**

cir-cum-cise (sûr′kum-sīz′), *v.t.* [circumcised, circumcis-ing], to cut off part or all of the foreskin.—*n.* **cir′cum-ci′sion.**

cir-cum-fer-ence (sėr-kum′fer-ens], *n.* **1,** the line that bounds a circle or any curved plane figure; **2,** the distance around a circular body or area; circuit.

cir-cum-flex (sûr′kum-fleks′), *n.* an accent mark [^; ^; ~] to denote a rising–falling tone, as in the French word *rôle* or Spanish *cañon* (canyon).

cir-cum-nav-i-gate (sûr′kum-nav′i-gāt′), *v.t.* [circumnavigat-ed, circum-navigat-ing], to sail completely around (the earth, an island, etc.).—*n.* **cir′cum-nav′i-ga′tion.**

cir-cum-scribe (sûr′kum-skrīb′), *v.t.* [circumscribed, circumscrib-ing], **1,** to draw a line around; **2,** hence, to restrict; as, to *circumscribe* the powers of a king.

cir-cum-spect (sûr′kum-spekt′), *adj.* cautious; considering all sides of a problem before acting.—*n.* **cir′cum-spec′tion.**

cir-cum-stance (sûr′kum-stans′), *n.* **1,** an incident, occurrence, or fact relating to another fact, and throwing light on its meaning, importance, etc.; **2,** a detail; as, one *circumstance* was overlooked; **3,** pomp; ceremony; **4,** circumstances, **a,** the conditions under which an act occurs, such as time, place, or cause, etc.; as, the meeting occurred under peculiar *circumstances*; **b,** a condition or state of affairs; material welfare; as, he is living in poor *circumstances*.

cir-cum-stan-tial (sûr′kum-stan′-shal), *adj.* **1,** consisting of, or based on, particular incidents or apparent facts; not direct; as, *circumstantial* evidence; **2,** detailed; as, a *circumstantial* report.

cir-cum-vent (sûr′kum-vent′), *v.t.* to get the better of by crafty means; get around; outwit.—*n.* **cir′cum-ven′tion.**

cir-cus (sûr′kus), *n.* **1,** a large level space surrounded by seats, usually within a tent, for displaying acrobatic feats, animals, etc.; **2,** the performance in such a space: also, the company of performers; **3,** in ancient Rome, an oval space surrounded on three sides by tiers of seats, used for chariot races, games, etc.

cir-rho-sis (si-rō′sis), *n.* a disease in which the liver turns yellowish and becomes shrunken and deformed (often caused by drinking alcohol).

cir-rus (sir′us), *n.* and *adj.* a whitish, filmy, fleecy cloud-formation at high altitude.

cis-co (sis′kō), *n.* a Great Lakes species of whitefish, esp. that known as *lake herring*.

cis-tern (sis′tėrn), *n.* a tank or artificial reservoir, often underground, for storing water or other liquids.

cit-a-del (sit′a-del), *n.* **1,** a fortress, esp. one defending a city; **2,** any strongly fortified place; any refuge.

ci-ta-tion (sī-tā′shun), *n.* **1,** the quoting of a passage, as from a book; **2,** honourable mention, as for distinguished service.

cite (sīt), *v.t.* [cit-ed, cit-ing], **1,** to summon to appear in court; **2,** to quote; as, a minister *cites* as his text a passage from the Bible; **3,** to bring forward as proof; as, the lawyer *cited* the evidence; **4,** to give honourable mention to.—*n.* **ci-ta′tion.**

cit-i-zen (sit′i-zn), *n.* **1,** an inhabitant; a resident of a town or city; as, the *citizens* of Montreal; **2,** a member of a state or nation who enjoys political rights and privileges, and gives in return his allegiance to the government; **3,** a civilian as distinguished from a soldier, policeman, etc.

cit-i-zen-ship (sit′i-zn-ship′), *n.* the status of a person who owes allegiance to the government in return for his political rights and privileges.

cit-ric (sit′rik), *adj.* pertaining to, or derived from lemons, oranges, and other citrus fruits; as, *citric* acid.

cit-ron (sit′run), *n.* **1,** a small tree or shrub of oriental origin; **2,** its fruit, like the lemon, but larger and not so acid; **3,** the thick preserved rind of this fruit, used in cooking.

cit-ron-el-la (sit′run-el′a), *n.* a sharp-smelling oil used to keep away insects, esp. mosquitoes; also used for perfume, liniment, and soap.

cit-rus or **cit-rous** (sit′rus), *adj.* of or relating to a group of trees which includes the orange, lemon, lime, citron, etc.

cit-y (sit′i), *n*. [*pl*. cities], **1,** a large and important town; also, its inhabitants; **2,** in Canada and the U.S., a municipality having local self-government.

civ-ic (siv′ik), *adj*. of or relating to a city, a citizen, or citizenship; as, *civic* beauty; *civic* rights:—**civics,** *n.pl*. used as *sing*. the study of city government or of good citizenship.

civ-il (siv′il), *adj*. **1,** of, relating to, or characteristic of, a city, its government, or its citizens; as, *civil* duties; **2,** pertaining to civilians; not military or ecclesiastical; **3,** formally polite; often, barely polite.—*adv*. **civ′il-ly.**—*n*. **civil′i-ty.**

ci-vil-ian (si-vil′yan), *n*. one who is not a member of an armed service such as army, navy, airforce, marines.

civ-i-li-za-tion (siv′i-li-zā′shun; -lī-zā′shun), *n*. **1,** the act of making or becoming less savage or barbarous; as, the *civilization* of man has been a slow process; **2,** the state of being refined in manners; culture; refinement; a particular stage or type of this; as, Greek *civilization* is older than Roman; **3,** collectively, those countries which are in a high stage of development.

civ-i-lize (siv′i-līz′), *v.t*. [civilized, civiliz-ing], to reclaim from a savage state; instruct in the arts and refinements of life; enlighten.

clack (klak), *n*. **1,** a confused hubbub of voices; as, a *clack* of tongues; **2,** a sharp, abrupt sound; as, the *clack* of belting in a mill:—*v.t*. to gossip; blab (secrets).

clad (klad), *p.t*. and *p.p*. of *clothe*:— *p.adj*. dressed; clothed; as, he was *clad* in skins.

claim (klām), *v.t*. **1,** to demand or assert as one's own or one's due; as, to *claim* an inheritance; **2,** to call for; deserve; as, this matter *claims* our attention; **3,** *Colloq.*, maintain; as, I *claim* this to be true:—*n*. **1,** a demand for something as due; as, he put in a *claim* for damages; **2,** an assertion of a right to something; as, I have a *claim* to the property; **3,** the thing demanded; esp. a piece of land which a miner marks out.—*n*. **claim′ant.**

clam (klam), *n*. an edible shellfish with a hinged double shell, living partly or wholly buried in sand or mud:—*v.i*. [clammed, clam-ming], to dig for clams.

clam-bake (klam′bāk′), *n*. a picnic at which clams, along with other food, are baked on heated stones under a covering of seaweed.

clam-ber (klam′bèr), *v.t*. and *v.i*. to ascend or climb with difficulty; as, to *clamber* up a rocky slope.

clam-my (klam′i), *adj*. [clam-mi-er, clam-mi-est], damp, soft, and cold.

clam-our (klam′ẽr), *n*. a loud and continued outcry; a loud and persistent demand:—*v.i*. to make noisy demands; as, to *clamour* for food.—*adj*. **clam′or-ous.** Also spelled **clam′or.**

clamp (klamp), *n*. a device, as a brace, clasp, or band, usually of wood or metal, used to hold or press things together:—*v.t*. to fasten or bind with a clamp.

clan (klan), *n*. **1,** a tribe or association of families, esp. in the Scottish Highlands, united under one chieftain, claiming common ancestry, and having the same surname; **2,** a group of people closely united by some common interest or pursuit; a set; clique.—*adj*. **clan′-nish.**—*n*. **clans′man.**

clan-des-tine (klan-des′tin), *adj*. secret; private; underhand; as, a *clandestine* meeting.—*adv*. **clan-des′-tine-ly.**

clang (klang), *n*. a loud, ringing metallic sound; as, the *clang* of an anvil:—*v.i*. to give out such a sound; as, the bells *clanged*:—*v.t*. to cause to give out such a sound; as, he *clanged* the cymbals.

clan-gour (klang′gẽr; klang′ẽr), *n*. a ringing, clanking, metallic sound, as of chains, bells, etc.

clank (klangk), *n*. a sharp, harsh, brief, metallic sound:—*v.t*. and *v.i*. to rattle.

clap (klap), *v.t*. [clapped, clap-ping], **1,** to strike together with a quick, sharp noise; **2,** to applaud by striking the hands together noisily; **3,** to put, place, etc., quickly and suddenly; as, they *clapped* him into jail; **4,** to strike or slap suddenly; as, he *clapped* me on the back:—*v.i*. **1,** to show approval by striking the hands together; **2,** to come together with a quick, sharp noise; as, the door *clapped* shut:—*n*. **1,** a loud noise made by, or as by, a sudden collision; as, a *clap* of thunder; **2,** applause; **3,** a slap; as, a *clap* on the back.—*n*. **clap′per.**

clap-board (klap′bōrd′; klab′ẽrd), *n*. a long, narrow board, often thicker at one edge than at the other, used to cover the outside of wooden houses:— *v.t*. to cover or line with such boards; as, to *clapboard* a house.

clap-per (klap′ẽr), *n*. **1,** the tongue of a bell; **2,** one who claps hands; **3,** either of a pair of musical *bones*.

clap-trap (klap′trap′), *n*. empty, showy talk in order to gain applause; buncombe.

clar-et (klar′et), *n*. **1,** a red wine; **2,**

a deep, purplish-red colour:—*adj.* purplish red.

clar-i-fy (klar′i-fī′), *v.t.* [clarified, clarify-ing], 1, to make clear or pure; 2, to make intelligible or plain; as, to *clarify* a statement:—*v.i.* to become clear, pure, or transparent; as, the syrup *clarified* as it heated.—*n.* **clar′i-fi-ca′tion.**

clar-i-net (klar′i-net; klar′i-net′), *n.* a tube-shaped, musical wind-instrument. Also, **clar′i-o-net′.**

clar-i-on (klar′i-un), *n.* a small, high-pitched trumpet; also, its sound: —*adj.* clear and loud; as, a *clarion* call.

clar-i-ty (klar′i-ti), *n.* clearness; as, the *clarity* of his speech; *clarity* of the air.

CLARINETS
1, clarinet; 2, bass clarinet.

clash (klash), *v.i.* 1, to make a loud, harsh noise by striking together; as, the cymbals *clashed;* 2, to be in opposition; disagree; as, their interests *clashed:*—*v.t.* to strike violently together; as, they *clashed* the cymbals:—*n.* 1, the noise so produced; 2, opposition; conflict; as, a *clash* of ideas.

clasp (klȧsp), *n.* 1, a hook to hold anything close; a fastening device; 2, a grasp, as in shaking hands; a close embrace:—*v.t.* 1, to fasten together with, or as with, a clasp; 2, to enclose and hold with the arms; 3, to grasp, as hands in a handshake.

class (klȧs), *n.* 1, a number or body of persons with common characteristics, as social status, property, occupation, etc.; as, the middle *class;* 2, a body of students taught by the same teacher, or engaged in similar studies; as, a *class* in Latin; also, a group of students who are to graduate in the same year; 3, a division or grading on the basis of quality; as, first-*class* on a steamer; mail sent second-*class;* 4, in zoology, a group of animals; in botany, a group of plants:—*v.t.* to arrange according to a system; classify.

clas-sic (klas′ik), *n.* 1, any book or work of art that is, or may properly be regarded as, a standard; 2, esp., any Greek or Roman piece of literature or work of art; 3, any author whose productions are of such excellence that they are regarded as standards:—**the Classics,** the literature of ancient Greece and Rome:—*adj.* 1, pertaining to the highest class or rank in literature or art; 2, pertaining to, or like, the

Greek or Roman authors.—*n.* **clas′si-cism.**—*n.* **clas′si-cist.**—*adj.* **clas′si-cal.**

clas-si-fy (klas′i-fī′), *v.t.* [classified, classify-ing], to arrange in groups according to a system; as, to *classify* books by subject.—*n.* **clas′si-fi′er.**—*n.* **clas′si-fi-ca′tion.**

clat-ter (klat′ẽr), *v.i.* 1, to make a rattling sound; 2, to talk idly and noisily:—*v.t.* to cause to make a rattling sound; as, to *clatter* dishes:—*n.* 1, a rattling noise; 2, commotion; noisy talk.

clause (klôz), *n.* 1, a separate part of a written agreement or document; a distinct condition; as a *clause* in a treaty; 2, a division of a sentence containing a subject and predicate of its own. In the sentence, "I can go today, but I can't go tomorrow," there are two clauses connected by the conjunction "but."—*adj.* **claus′al.**

claus-tro-pho-bi-a (klos′trō-fō′bi-a), *n.* dread of enclosed or narrow places.

clav-i-cle (klav′i-kl), *n.* the collar bone.

claw (klô), *n.* 1, a sharp, hooked, horny nail on the foot of an animal or bird; 2, the whole foot equipped with these nails; as, the owl held a mouse in his *claw;* 3, the pincers of shellfish, such as crabs, lobsters, etc.; 4, anything sharp and hooked like a claw, as the curved end of some hammer-heads:—*v.t.* and *v.i.* to tear or scratch with, or as with, claws.

clay (klā), *n.* 1, an earthy material, easily moulded when moist, but hard when baked, used in making pottery, bricks, etc.; 2, the human body.—*adj.* **clay′ey.**

clay-more (klā′mōr′), *n.* a heavy two-edged sword, once used by Scottish Highlanders.

clean (klēn), *adj.* 1, free from dirt or filth; as, *clean* hands; 2, unmixed with foreign matter; as, *clean* seed, 3, pure; without moral or spiritual stain; as, he lives a *clean* life; 4, even; unobstructed; complete; as, a *clean* field; a *clean* sweep; 5, skilful; well done; as, a *clean* hit; 6, cleanly by habit; as, a *clean* housekeeper; 7, shapely; as, a car with *clean* lines:—*adv.* 1, so as to be clean; as, swept *clean;* 2, wholly; entirely; as, the apple was sound *clean* through:—*v.t.* 1, to remove dirt from; as, to *clean* house; 2, to remove undesirable parts of; as, to *clean* a fish by removing its head, scales, etc.—*n.* **clean′ness.**—*n.* **clean′er.**

¹clean-ly (klen′li), *adj.* [clean-li-er, clean-li-est], careful to keep clean; neat.—*n.* **clean′li-ness.**

²clean-ly (klēn′li), *adv.* in a clean manner.

cleanse (klenz), *v.t.* [cleansed, cleansing], to free from filth, guilt, sin, etc.— *n.* **cleans'er.**

clear (klēr), *adj.* **1,** bright; unclouded; as, a *clear* day; **2,** clean; pure; as, *clear* water; **3,** fresh; blooming; as, a *clear* skin; **4,** untroubled; as, a *clear* conscience; **5,** easily understood; plain; as, a *clear* explanation; **6,** audible; distinct; as, a *clear* voice; **7,** without further cost to be deducted; net; as, *clear* profit; **8,** unobstructed; as, a *clear* view; freed from obstruction; as, land *clear* of stumps:—*adv.* wholly, entirely; clean; as, I broke a piece *clear* off:—*v.t.* **1,** to make free from muddiness, cloudiness, smoke, stuffiness, etc.; **2,** to make plain; as, to *clear* up a puzzling situation; **3,** to free from obstruction; as, to *clear* the way; **4,** to remove; as, to *clear* away rubbish; **5,** to prove or declare to be innocent; as, to *clear* an accused person; **6,** to jump over or pass by without touching; as, the horse *cleared* the fence; **7,** to make beyond expenses; as, to *clear* ten dollars:—*v.i.* to become *clear.*—*adv.* **clear'ly.**—*n.* **clear'ness.**—*adj.* **clear—cut; clear'head'ed; clear—sighted.**

clear-ance (klēr'ans), *n.* **1,** removal of obstructions; **2,** a legal certificate issued by a custom-house permitting a vessel to leave port; **3,** the clear space between two passing objects, or between a vehicle and the top of an arch, bridge, etc.

clear-ing (klēr'ing), *n.* **1,** the act of removing obstructions; as, the *clearing* of land; **2,** a tract of land cleared of trees and bush.

cleat (klēt), *n.* **1,** a piece of wood or metal with branching arms, around which ropes are turned to prevent slipping; **2,** a strip of wood or metal fastened across a board, under a shelf, etc., to give support or strength, hold something in position, prevent slipping, or the like; as, the *cleats* on a gangplank, on football shoes, etc.

cleave (klēv), *v.t.* [*p.t.* cleft (kleft), cleaved (klēvd), clove (klōv), *p.p.* cleft, cleaved, clo-ven (klō'ven), *p.pr.* cleaving], to cut open; cut a way through; split; as, the axe *cleft* the log; the boat *cleaved* the water:—*v.i.* to split; divide; as, wood *cleaves* along the grain.—*n.* **cleav'age.**

cleav-er (klēv'er), *n.* a butcher's heavy hatchet or chopper for cutting meat or bone.

clef (klef), *n.* in *music,* a sign placed at the beginning of the staff to show the pitch of the notes on each line. The line on which the centre of the circle of the G clef falls is G; the line on which the dot of the F clef falls is F.

cleft (kleft), *n.* a crack; crevice; as, the water trickled from a *cleft* in the rock:—*adj.* partly divided.

clem-a-tis (klem'a-tis), *n.* a vine or bush of the buttercup family, with yellow, blue, purple, or white flowers.

CLEFS
Above, G clef; below, two forms of F clef.

clem-ent (klem'ent), *adj.* **1,** forgiving; gentle; kind; as, a *clement* judge; **2,** mild; as, *clement* weather.—*n.* **clem'-en-cy.**

clench (klench), *v.t.* **1,** to set closely together, as the teeth; close tightly, as the hands; **2,** to clinch or settle, as an argument; **3,** to grasp firmly; as, he *clenched* his sword:—*n.* a thing that grips or catches.—*n.* **clench'er.**

cler-gy (klûr'ji), *n.* [*pl.* clergies], the body of persons ordained for religious service, as ministers, priests, monks, etc.—*n.* **cler'gy-man.**

cler-ic (kler'ik), *n.* a clergyman.

cler-i-cal (kler'i-kal), *adj.* **1,** having to do with the clergy; as, *clerical* garb; **2,** pertaining to a clerk, writer, or copyist; as, *clerical* work.—*adv.* **cler'i-cal-ly.**

clerk (klärk; klûrk), *n.* **1,** a person, not of the clergy, with certain minor church duties; **2,** one who keeps records and does routine business; as, the town *clerk*; **3,** a general office assistant; typist; secretary; **4,** a salesman or saleswoman in a store:—*v.i.* to act as a clerk; as, he *clerks* in a law office.—*n.* **clerk'ship.**

clev-er (klev'ẽr), *adj.* **1,** skilful; **2,** mentally quick; talented.—*adv.* **clev'er-ly.**—*n.* **clev'er-ness.**

clev-is (klev'is), *n.* a U-shaped piece of iron with a pin through the two holes at the end, for attaching to a whippletree, drawbar, etc.

CLEVIS

clew or **clue** (klū; kloo), *n.* **1,** a ball of thread, yarn, etc.; esp., in mythology, a ball of thread by which one found one's way through a labyrinth; **2,** hence, (usually *clue*), a guide or key to a problem, plot, or mystery; **3,** a metal loop attached to the lower corner of a sail to hold the ropes that raise or lower the sail:—*v.t.* to draw (sails) up by the lower corners, as for furling.

cli-ché (klē'shā'), *n.* an expression worn, or made stale, by much use; as, *bright and early; sadder but wiser.*

click (klik), *n.* a slight, sharp sound like the turning of a key in a lock:—*v.i.* to make such a sound; as, hail *clicked* against the window.

cli-ent (klī′ent), *n.* one who consults or employs a lawyer, doctor, etc.; hence, a customer or patron.

cliff (klif), *n.* a high, steep face of rock; a precipice.

cli-mate (klī′mit), *n.* **1,** the weather conditions of a place, esp. as regards temperature, moisture, etc.; **2,** a region with certain conditions of weather, as of heat and cold, sunlight, etc.; as, a sunny *climate.*—*adj.* **cli-mat′ic** (klī-mat′ik).

cli-max (klī′maks), *n.* **1,** a series of ideas or expressions increasing in force; also, the last of such a series; **2,** hence, the highest point of interest, excitement, or development; as, the *climax* of a play.—*adj.* **cli-mac′tic.**

climb (klīm), *v.t.* **1,** to go up or down, esp. using both hands and feet; as, to *climb* a ladder; mount; ascend; as, the sun *climbs* the heavens; **2,** to ascend by twining; as, a vine *climbs* a trellis:—*v.i.* **1,** to go up and down something, using both hands and feet; as, to *climb* out of (or into) a tree; **2,** to rise by effort or achievement; as, to *climb* to the head of the class; *climb* to fame:—*n.* the act of climbing; as, a long, hard *climb;* also, a place to be ascended; as, there was a steep *climb* near the top.—*n.* **climb′er.**

clime (klīm), *n. Poetic,* place; region; climate.

clinch (klinch), *v.t.* **1,** to rivet; to fasten tightly; esp., to turn down the protruding point of (a nail); **2,** to confirm or settle, as a bargain or argument; **3,** to grasp tightly:—*v.i.* to grapple; seize one another, as in boxing:—*n.* **1,** the act of making a fastening on both sides of something; **2,** the fastening by which a tight hold is obtained; **3,** in the U.S., a struggle or scuffle at close grips, as in boxing; **4,** a kind of rope fastening.—*n.* **clinch′er.**

cling (kling), *v.i.* [clung (klung), cling-ing], **1,** to stick together or to something; as, snow *clings* to bushes; **2,** to adhere closely; stick; hold fast by embracing or entwining; hang on; as, a child *clings* to its mother's hand; ivy *clings* to a wall; **3,** hence, to be loyal; remain faithful.

clin-ic (klin′ik), *n.* **1,** in medicine and surgery, the treatment of patients before a class of students for the instruction of the class; **2,** an institution, or department of a hospital, devoted to the study, and often the free treatment, of disease or of problems of a particular type; as, an eye or a child-guidance *clinic.*—*adj.* **clin′i-cal.**

clink (klingk), *v.t.* to strike so as to make a slight, tinkling sound; as, they *clinked* glasses:—*v.i.* to make a tinkling noise; as, ice *clinks* in a glass:—*n.* a slight, tinkling noise; as, the *clink* of coins.

clink-er (kling′-kėr), *n.* the stony, fused mass of impurities left from burning coal, coke, etc., in a furnace, kiln, etc.

¹clip (klip), *v.t.* [clipped or clipt (klipt), clip-ping], to clasp or hold tightly; fasten; as, he *clipped* the papers together:—*n.* a clasp, as for holding papers; any device for gripping.—*n.* **clip′per.**

²clip (klip), *v.t.* [clipped or clipt (klipt), clip-ping], **1,** to cut or trim with shears or scissors, as hair, or the wool from sheep; **2,** to cut short, as final letters, syllables, etc., from words:—*n.* the act of cutting off with shears; **2,** the amount of wool obtained from a single shearing season.

clip-per (klip′ėr), *n.* **1,** one who or that which moves swiftly, as a horse or a ship; esp., a vessel, developed in New England, built with fine lines and rigged for fast sailing; **2,** a tool for clipping.

clique (klēk), *n.* a small exclusive, social group.—*adj.* **cli′quish** (klē′kish).

cloak (klōk), *n.* **1,** a loose outer garment, usually sleeveless; **2,** hence, that which covers or conceals; as, night is a *cloak* for crime:—*v.t.* to conceal; cover; disguise; as, to *cloak* grief with laughter.

cloak-room (klōk′rōōm′), *n.* a place where hats, coats, etc., may be left temporarily.

clob-ber (klob′ėr), *v.t. Slang,* to batter; maul; wound.

¹clock (klok), *n.* a mechanical device for keeping time, larger than a watch, with a moving pair of pointers, or hands, on a dial marked with the hours and minutes.—*adv.* and *adj.* **clock′wise′.**—*n.* **clock′work′.**

²clock (klok), *n.* a woven or embroidered ornament on the ankle of a sock or stocking.—*adj.* **clocked.**

clod (klod), *n.* **1,** a lump of earth, turf, or clay; **2,** a stupid fellow.—*adj.* **clod′dy.**

clod-hop-per (klod′hop′ėr), *n.* a clumsy fellow; boor; bumpkin; **2,** *pl.* heavy shoes as worn by a ploughman, etc.

clog (klog), *v.t.* [clogged, clog-ging], **1,** to hinder motion with a weight or burden; impede; **2,** hence, to hinder in any way; as, ignorance *clogs* progress; **3,** to obstruct; stop up; as, mud *clogs* a drain:—*v.i.* **1,** to be hindered; **2,** to stick together:—*n.* **1,** a load or weight; hence, any hindrance or restraint; **2,** a shoe with a wooden sole; **3,** a dance by one wearing such shoes.

clois-ter (klois′tẻr), *n.* **1,** a place of religious retirement; a monastery or convent; **2,** an arched way or covered walk along the outside walls of a monastery, college, etc., often surrounding an open court, or connecting buildings of a group: —*v.t.* to confine in, or as if in, a convent or monastery; seclude from the world. —*adj.* **clois′tered.**

CLOISTER

¹**close** (klōz), *v.t.* [closed, clos-ing], **1,** to shut, as a box, the mouth, a door, etc.; **2,** to fill; stop up; obstruct; as, to *close* an opening; **3,** to make an ending to; as, to *close* an argument:—*v.i.* **1,** to come together; as, the waters *closed* over him; **2,** to grapple or fight at close quarters; **3,** to come to an ending:—*n.* **1,** conclusion; **2,** in Great Britain, a court or quadrangle, esp. a school *close* (klōs) or playground.

²**close** (klōs), *adj.* **1,** shut; closed; **2,** contracted; narrow; shut in; as, *close* quarters; **3,** stifling; without ventilation; as, this room is *close;* **4,** stingy; **5,** near in space, time, etc.; **6,** accurate; careful; as, *close* thinking; **7,** firmly knit; compact; tight; as, *close* weaving; **8,** dear; familiar; as, a *close* friend; **9,** almost equal; as, a *close* race or contest; **10,** fitting tightly or snugly, as a turban to the head; **11,** accurate; precise; as, a *close* translation; **12,** confined; kept within bounds; as, a *close* prisoner:—*adv.* **1,** near in space or time; as, follow *close* after me; **2,** tightly; closely together; as, *close* knit; **3,** secretly; in hiding; as, keep *close.*—*adv.* **close′ly.**—*n.* **close′-ness.**

closed shop, an establishment that excludes nonunion labour.

close-fist-ed (klōs′fis′tid), *adj.* stingy.

close—hauled (klōs′–hôld′), *adj.* sailing as close into the wind as possible.

close—lipped, close—mouthed (-lipt; -mou*th*d; -mou*t*ht), *adj.* talking little.

clos-et (kloz′it), *n.* **1,** a small room for privacy or retirement; **2,** a small room for storing things, as cloths, dishes, etc.; a cupboard:—*adj.* private; secret:—*v.t.*

to shut up, as in a private room, esp. for secret conference.

close-up (klōs′up′), *n.* a picture, or inspection, at close range.

clo-sure (klō′zhoor), *n.* **1,** a shutting up; ending; as, the *closure* of a meeting **2,** in parliamentary law, a way of ending a debate and taking an immediate vote.

clot (klot), *v.i.* [clot-ted, clot-ting], to thicken into a soft, sticky, semi-solid mass; as, blood *clots:*—*v.t.* to form into lumps of thickened fluid; as, souring *clots* milk:—*n.* a lumpish mass of some thickened fluid, esp. blood.—*adj.* **clot′-ted.**

cloth (klôth), *n.* [*pl.* cloths (klô*th*z; klôths)], **1,** a woven fabric of wool, cotton, silk, linen, or the like; **2,** a piece of such fabric made for a certain use; as, a dish-*cloth;* a table-*cloth;* **3,** one's profession as shown by one's dress, esp. the profession of a clergyman:—**the cloth,** the clergy.

clothe (klō*th*), *v.t.* [clothed or clad (klad), cloth-ing], **1,** to dress; **2,** to cover with, or as with, a garment; as, flowers *clothed* the field; old age *clothes* a man with dignity.

clothes (klō*th*z; *Colloq.,* klōz), *n.pl.* **1,** garments; dress; **2,** bed-clothes. Note compounds, **clothes′brush′; clothes′-line′; clothes′peg′; clothes′pin′.**

clothes-horse (klō*th*z′hôrs′; klōz′-), *n.* a folding wooden frame with horizontal bars on which to dry or air clothes.

cloth-ier (klō*th*′yẻr), *n.* one who makes or deals in cloth or clothing.

cloth-ing (klō*th*′ing), *n.* clothes; dress; garments in general.

cloud (kloud), *n.* **1,** a visible mass of condensed water floating above the earth; **2,** a similar mass of smoke or dust; **3,** anything that threatens or darkens, as grief, disgrace, suspicion, etc.; **4,** anything that moves in or like a mass, as a large number of arrows, insects, horsemen, etc.:—*v.t.* **1,** to cover with a mist or cloud; **2,** hence, to make gloomy; as, grief *clouds* a face; **3,** to blacken; trouble; sully; as, a bad record *clouds* his reputation:—*v.i.* to grow cloudy; as, toward afternoon the sky *clouded* over.—*adj.* **cloud′less.**

cloud-burst (kloud′burst′), *n.* a violent, unusually heavy downpour of rain.

cloud-y (kloud′i), *adj.* [cloud-i-er, cloud-i-est], **1,** pertaining to a cloud or clouds; **2,** overcast; threatening rain; **3,** vague; obscure; **4,** not transparent; as, a *cloudy* liquid; **5,** gloomy.—*n.* **cloud′i-ness.**

clout (klout), *n.* **1,** *Archaic,* a patch; a rag; esp., a dish-cloth; **2,** in archery, the white canvas centre of a target; also, an arrow that hits the centre; **3,** *Colloq.,* a blow on the head with the hand:—*v.t.* **1,** to patch or mend coarsely; **2,** *Colloq.,* to strike; knock.

clove (klōv), *n.* **1,** the dried flower bud of a tropical evergreen tree of the myrtle family, used as spice; **2,** the tree.

clove hitch (klōv'hich'), *n.* a hitch for fastening a rope about a post; thus, two rounds of rope are passed about the post so that their ends come out in opposite directions between the crossed parts.

CLOVE HITCH

clo-ven (klō'vn), *p.p.* of *cleave;* as a *cloven,* or cleft, hoof.

clo-ver (klō'vẽr), *n.* a low-growing plant with three-parted leaves and sweet, round flower-heads of red, white, or purple, used for fodder.

clo-ver leaf (klō'vẽr-lēf'), *n.* a highway intersection allowing traffic to cross at different levels, and so called

CLOVER LEAF

because its shape resembles the outline of a four-leaf clover.

clown (kloun), *n.* **1,** a man of coarse manners; a boor; **2,** a jester, esp. in a play or circus:—*v.i.* to act the clown.—*adj.* **clown'ish.**

cloy (kloi), *v.t.* to surfeit or sate with food, esp. with rich or sweet food; also, to weary with pleasure.

club (klub), *n.* **1,** a heavy stick; **2,** one of a suit, called *clubs,* of playing-cards, marked with a black figure like a clover leaf; **3,** a number of persons united for a common purpose or mutual benefit; **4,** a building or room occupied by such persons; **5,** a stick used to hit the ball in certain games, esp. golf:—*v.t.* [clubbed, club-bing], **1,** to beat with a cudgel; **2,** to give to a common cause; as, the town *clubbed* its resources to help the flood victims:—*v.i.* to combine for a common purpose; as, to *club* together to buy a football.

club-foot (klub'foot'), *n.* a deformed or misshapen foot.—*adj.* **club'foot'ed.**

cluck (kluk), *n.* a hen's call to her chicks: *v.t.* to make a sound of suction in the side of the mouth; as, he *clucked* his disbelief.

clue or **clew** (klōo; klū), *n.* anything

that helps to solve a mystery or difficulty; as, a footprint was the only *clue* to the thief.

clump (klump), *n.* **1,** a cluster or group, as of trees; **2,** a mass; lump, as of earth; **3,** a sound like that of heavy treading:—*v.i.* to tread heavily; as, the labourers *clumped* along the road.

clum-sy (klum'zi), *adj.* [clum-si-er, clum-si-est], **1,** awkward; heavy; lacking in ease or grace; as, a *clumsy* person or action; **2,** ill-made; unwieldy; as, a *clumsy* tool.—*adv.* **clum'si-ly.**—*n.* **clum'si-ness.**

clung (klung), *p.t.* and *p.p.* of *cling.*

clus-ter (klus'tẽr), *n.* **1,** a number of things, such as fruits, of the same kind growing or collected together; a bunch; **2,** a group; as, a *cluster* of islands:—*v.i.* and *v.t.* to grow, or gather, in bunches.

clutch (kluch), *v.t.* to grasp, seize, or grip strongly; as, to *clutch* a dagger:—*v.i.* to snatch or reach out eagerly; as, he *clutched* at the rope:—*n.* **1,** a tight grasp; **2, clutches,** grasping claws or hands; as, a bird in the *clutches* of a hawk; **3,** a device for gripping or holding, as in a crane; also, a mechanical device which connects and disconnects the motor of a machine from certain other parts which do the work of the machine, as in an automobile; **4,** a nest of eggs; a brood of chicks.

clut-ter (klut'ẽr), *n.* disorder; litter:—*v.t.* to make untidy; disarrange.

coach (kōch), *n.* **1,** a large, closed, four-wheeled carriage; **2,** a tutor, esp. one who prepares others for an examination; also, a director of athletics, dramatics, etc.; **3,** a closed, two-door automobile; **4,** a railroad passenger car; **5,** a passenger airplane for a particular flight:—*v.t.* to teach; direct; as, to *coach* a team for a play.—*n.* **coach'er.**—*n.* **coach'man.**

co-ag-u-late (kō-ag'ū-lāt'), *v.t.* and *v.i.* [coagulat-ed, coagulat-ing], to clot or curdle; thicken; solidify; as, cooking *coagulates* the white of egg.—*n.* **co-ag'u-la'tion.**

coal (kōl), *n.* **1,** a black, hard, burnable mineral, formed under the earth by the decay of the vegetation of prehistoric times, and used as fuel; **2,** charcoal; **3,** a glowing or charred bit of wood, coal, etc.; an ember:—*v.t.* to furnish with coal, as a vessel:—*v.i.* to take in coal, as a ship.—*n.* **coal'er.**

co-a-lesce (kō'a-les'), *v.i.* [coalesced, coales-cing], to grow together; blend; as, the ends of the broken bone *coalesced.*

co-a-li-tion (kō'a-lish'un), *n.* and *adj.*

a temporary alliance of persons or parties; as, a *coalition* cabinet.

coal—oil (kōl'-oil'), *n.* kerosene.

coal—tar (kōl'-tär'), *n.* a thick, black, sticky substance obtained when gas is distilled from soft coal, yielding paraffin, dyes, etc.

coarse (kōrs), *adj.* [coars-er, coars-est], **1,** of poor or inferior quality or appearance; as, *coarse* cloth; **2,** large in texture or size; as, *coarse* sand; **3,** not refined; gross; as, *coarse* manners.—*adv.* **coarse'ly.**—*n.* **coarse'ness.**—*adj.* **coarse'-grained'.**

coars-en (kōr'sn), *v.t.* and *v.i.* to turn, or become, large, rough, common, etc.

coast (kōst), *n.* **1,** the land forming the margin or boundary of the sea; the seashore; also, the region adjoining the sea; **2,** a slide downhill over snow or ice on a sled, skis, or the like:—*v.i.* **1,** to sail along a shore, or from port to port; **2,** to ride along by the force of gravity, without power, as on a sled.—*adj.* **coast'al.**—*n.* **coast'line'.**

coast—guard (kōst'-gärd'), *n.* a coastal police force.

coast-wise (kōst'wīz'), *adj.* and *adv.* by way of, or along, the coast.

coat (kōt), *n.* **1,** a sleeved, outer garment covering the upper part of the body; **2,** any outside covering, as fur, skin, rind, etc.; also, any outer layer; as, a *coat* of paint:—*v.t.* to cover or spread over.—*n.* **coat-tail** (kōt'tāl').

coat of arms, 1, a group of emblems signifying rank or achievement, originally granted to a knight or person of distinction and adopted by his descendants; **2,** a shield or coat marked with such emblems.

coax (kōks), *v.t.* **1,** to wheedle; urge or influence with soft words or flattery; **2,** to handle with patience and skill; as, to *coax* a fire.—*adv.* **coax'ing-ly.**

co-ax-i-al cable (kō-ak'si-al), *n.* a cable with an outer insulated sheath composed of separately insulated wires overlying a similar inner core of insulated wires.

cob (kob), *n.* **1,** a corn-cob; **2,** a strong, short-legged horse.

co-balt (kō'bôlt; kō'bolt), *n.* **1,** a silver white metallic element; **2,** a deep-blue colouring matter made from it.

cob-ble (kob'l), *n.* a round stone, worn smooth by water, esp. one of a size used for street paving; a cobblestone:—*v.t.* [cob-bled, cob-bling], to pave with cobblestones.

cob-bler (kob'ler), *n.* **1,** one who mends boots and shoes; **2,** a clumsy workman; **3,** a cooling summer drink of iced wine and fruit juices; as, sherry *cobbler;* **4,** a deep-dish fruit pie with one crust.

cob-ble-stone (kob'l-stōne'), *n.* a rounded stone used for paving.

co-bra (kō'bra; ko'bra), *n.* a large, poisonous snake of Asia and Africa which, when irritated, swells its neck out like a hood.

cob-web (kob'web'), *n.* **1,** a spider's web or the material of which it is made; **2,** anything resembling the flimsy or entangling qualities of a cobweb.

co-caine or **co-cain** (kō-kān'; kō'kān), *n.* a powerful drug extracted from the leaves of a South American shrub called *coca,* used to dull pain and cause sleep.

coc-cyx (kok'siks), *n.* [*pl.* coccyges (kok-sī'jēz)], the last bone of the spinal column.

¹cock (kok), *n.* **1,** the male of the common domestic fowl; a rooster; **2,** any male bird; **3,** a weather-vane in the shape of a rooster; **4,** a leader; as, *cock* of the school; **5,** a turn-valve, tap, faucet, etc.; **6,** the hammer of a fire-arm, or its position when raised; as, a gun at full *cock.*

²cock (kok), *n.* a tilting or turning upward, as of a hat or an eye:—*v.t.* **1,** to turn up or set jauntily on one side; tilt defiantly, as a hat; **2,** to raise the hammer of (a gun), in readiness for firing.

cock-ade (kok-ād'), *n.* **1,** a rosette or knot of ribbon or leather worn on a hat to signify office or party; **2,** an ornament on a bridle.

cock-a-doodle-do (kok'a-dōō'dl-dōō'), *n.* the shrill crow of a rooster.

cock-a-too (kok'a-tōō'), *n.* a white or brilliantly coloured parrot, often with a crest, found chiefly in Australia.

cock-er-el (kok'ér-el), *n.* a rooster not over a year old.

cock-er span-iel (kok'ér span'yel), *n.* a spaniel, usually with long black, red, or cream-coloured hair, trained to hunt birds.

cock-horse (kok'hôrs'), *n.* a toy riding-horse.

cock-le (kok'l), *n.* **1,** an edible shellfish with two heart-shaped fluted shells; **2,** one of its shells; often called *cockleshell;* **3,** a frail or shallow boat; **4,** a species of weed found among grain; as, corn *cockle,* darnel, etc.

cock-ney (kok'ni), *n.* [*pl.* cockneys], a Londoner; esp., one born in the East End of London, and speaking a characteristic dialect:—*adj.* of or relating to cockneys.

cock-pit (kok′pit′), *n.* **1,** an enclosed space for cockfights; **2,** in small vessels, space aft lower than the deck; **3,** in a war vessel, the quarters of junior officers, used as a hospital during a battle; **4,** in some aeroplanes, the place where the pilots and passengers sit.

cock-roach (kok′rōch′), *n.* a black or brown, beetlelike insect found in kitchens and pantries.

cocks-comb (koks′kōm′), *n.* **1,** the comb or crest of a cock; **2,** a garden plant of the amaranth family with a crest-shaped red or yellow flower; **3,** (usually *coxcomb*), the red edge on a jester's cap; also, the cap; **4,** (usually *coxcomb*), a conceited fellow; a fop.

cock-sure (kok′shōōr′), *adj.* absolutely sure; positive.

cock-swain (kok′swān; kok′sn). Same as **cox′swain.**

cock-tail (kok′tāl′), *n.* **1,** an iced, mixed drink made of alcoholic liquors, bitters, fruit juices, etc.; **2,** an appetizer of shellfish, mixed fruits, or the like, served as a first course.

co-co (kō′kō), *n.* [*pl.* cocos], **1,** a palm which produces the coconut: also called *coconut-palm;* **2,** the fruit of this tree; a coconut.

co-coa (kō′kō), *n.* **1,** a powder made from the ground seeds of the cacao-tree; **2,** a drink made from it.

co-co-nut (kō′ko-nut′), *n.* **1,** the fruit of the coco-palm; **2,** loosely, the white meaty substance from it, prepared for use as food. Also spelled **co′coa-nut′.**

co-coon (ko-kōōn′), *n.* the silky case spun by the larvae of many insects, such as caterpillars and silk worms, as a protection while they are developing into butterflies, moths, or the like.

COCOON OF CECROPIA MOTH

cock-y (kok′i), *adj. Colloq.*, impudent; conceited; pert.

cod (kod), *n.* [*pl.* cod or cods], a large deep-sea food fish, averaging 10 to 20 pounds, found in the northern Atlantic.

cod-dle (kod′l), *v.t.* [cod-dled, cod-dling], **1,** to pet or pamper; treat tenderly; **2,** to stew gently; cook by allowing to stand in hot water.

code (kōd), *n.* **1,** a body of laws arranged in clear and regular order; as, the civil or penal *code;* **2,** a system of military or naval signals; **3,** any system of symbols used for messages, to secure their brevity or secrecy; **4,** a body of principles or standards governing the conduct of a society, class, or profession, under certain conditions; as, the social *code.—v.t.* **co′di-fy′:—***n.* **co′di-fi-ca′-tion.**

co-de-ine, co-de-in (kō′di-ēn); (ko′-dēn), *n.* a drug derived from opium, used to calm or soothe nerves or excitement, and to allay pain.

cod-fish (kod′fish′), *n.* the cod or its flesh, esp. when cured and salted, served as food.

cod-i-cil (kod′i-sil), *n.* a provision added to a will.

cod-ling (kod′ling), *n.* an unripe apple: **—codling—moth,** a small moth whose larvae damage apples, pears, etc.

co—ed (kō′—ed′), *n. Colloq.*, a female student, esp. at a college. Also, **co′ed′.**

co-ed-u-ca-tion (kō′ed-ū-kā′shun, *n.* the education of both boys and girls in the same school.—*adj.* **co′ed-u-ca′-tion-al.**

co-erce (kō-ûrs′), *v.t.* [coerced, coercing], to compel by force; as, he *coerced* the prisoner into submission.—*n.* **co-er′cion.**

co-ex-ist (kō′eg-zist′), *v.i.* to exist together at the same time.—*n.* **co′ex-ist′ence.**

cof-fee (kôf′i), *n.* **1,** a drink made from the seeds, roasted and ground, of a tropical shrub; **2,** the seeds: often called *coffee-beans;* **3,** the shrub or tree.

coffee break, a short rest from work for coffee, cake, etc.

cof-fer (kôf′ėr; kof′), *n.* **1,** a casket, chest or trunk in which to keep money or treasure; **2, coffers,** a treasury; funds.

cof-fin (kôf′in), *n.* the case or chest in which a dead person is buried.

cog (kog), *n.* one of a series of teeth on the rim of a wheel which gives or transmits motion by interlocking with the teeth on another wheel.

co-gent (kō′jent), *adj.* forceful; convincing; as, a *cogent* reason.—*adv.* **co′gent-ly.**

cog-i-tate (koj′i-tāt′), *v.i.* [cogitat-ed, cogitat-ing], to reflect; ponder; think: *—v.t.* to think over; plan.—*n.* **cog′i-ta′tion.**

cog-nate (kog′nāt), *adj.* having the same nature or origin; thus, in 'he dreamed a dream,' *dream* is an object *cognate* with the verb *dreamed;* the German and English are *cognate* peoples: —*n.* a related word, language, person, or thing.

cog-ni-zant (kog′ni-zant; kon′i-zant), *adj.* having knowledge; aware.—*n.* **cog′ni-zance.**

cog-wheel (kog′hwēl′), *n.* a wheel with teeth in its rim; a gearwheel: when small, called *pinion.*

co-hab-it (kō-hab′it), *v.i.* to live together as husband and wife; esp., to have sexual intercourse.

co-here (kō-hēr′), *v.i.* [cohered, cohering], to stick together in a mass, as mud; hold together, as cement and stone.

co-her-ent (kō-hēr′ent), *adj.* **1,** sticking together; **2,** logically connected, and developed; consistent.—*adv.* **co-her′-ent-ly.**—*n.* **co-her′ence; co-her′en-cy.**

co-he-sion (ko-hē′zhun), *n.* a sticking together; specifically, the force by which particles of the same material are held together; as, there is *cohesion* in clay, but not in gravel.—*adj.* **co-he′sive.**

co-hort (kō′hôrt), *n.* **1,** in ancient Rome a body of soldiers of 300 to 600 men, or the tenth part of a legion; **2,** any body of soldiers or band of persons.

coif-fure (kwä-fūr′), *n.* **1,** a headdress; **2,** the manner of arranging the hair.

coil (koil), *n.* **1,** anything wound in a circle or series of circles; a spiral; as, a *coil* of rope; **2,** a continuous spiral of pipe or wire for conducting hot water, electricity, or the like:—*v.t.* to wind into circles; as, to *coil* a rope:—*v.i.* to form coils.

coin (koin), *n.* **1,** a piece of metal legally stamped to be used as money; **2,** metal money:—*v.t.* **1,** to make (coins) by stamping pieces of metal; also, to change (metal) into coins; **2,** to invent (a word); as, he *coined* the word "cinemactor."

coin-age (koin′ij), *n.* **1,** the process of making pieces of money; **2,** the money made; **3,** the system of metal money used in a country; **4,** invention of new words and phrases.

co-in-cide (kō′in-sīd′), *v.i.* [coincided, coincid-ing], **1,** to occur at the same time; as, their rest periods *coincide;* **2,** to occupy the same space exactly; **3,** to agree; be alike; as, my idea *coincides* with yours.—*adj.* **co-in′ci-dent.**

co-in-ci-dence (kō-in′si-dens), *n.* **1,** the condition of happening at the same time or of occupying the same space; **2,** agreement; **3,** a remarkable happening together of events, apparently accidental and unconnected.

coke (kōk), *n.* **1,** coal from which some of the gases have been driven by intense heat: used for fuel; **2,** *Colloq.,* a variety of soft drink.

col-an-der (kul′an-dẽr; kol′an-dẽr), *n.* a strainer; a kitchen utensil pierced with holes, used for draining off liquids from vegetables, etc.

cold (kōld), *adj.* **1,** producing or feeling chilliness; of low temperature: opposite of *hot;* esp., less hot than the human body; as, a *cold* wind; *cold* food; **2,** indifferent; not moved; as, the news left him *cold;* **3,** unresponsive; unfriendly; as, a *cold* greeting; **4,** chilling; depressing; as, *cold* comfort; **5,** spiritless; dull; **6,** not fresh, as a scent in hunting:—*n.* **1,** lack of heat; as, to feel the *cold;* **2,** the sensation produced by lack of heat; **3,** in physics, a temperature below the freezing-point of water; as, five degrees of *cold;* **4,** cold weather; **5,** the shivering sensation caused by fear or despair; **6,** an inflammation of a mucous membrane, generally of the nose or throat.—*adv.* **cold′ly.**—*n.* **cold′-ness.** Also note compounds: *adj.* **cold—blood-ed** (kōld′—blud′id); **cold—heart-ed.**—*n.* **cold chisel; cold sore; cold war.**

cole—slaw (kōl′—slô′), *n.* a salad made of finely cut raw cabbage, served with a sauce or dressing.

co-le-us (kō′li-us), *n.* any of the mint family of plants grown for their showy, bright-coloured foliage.

col-ic (kol′ik), *n.* sharp pain in the abdomen or bowels.—*adj.* **col′ick-y.**

col-i-se-um (kol′i-sē′um), *n.* Same as *colosseum.*

col-lab-o-rate (ko-lab′o-rāt′), *v.i.* [-rated, -rat-ing], **1,** to work jointly, esp. on a literary, artistic, or scientific project; **2,** to work treacherously with an invader; as, he *collaborated* with the Nazis.—*n.* **col-lab′o-ra′tion.**

col-lapse (ko-laps′), *n.* **1,** a falling in or together, as of a roof or a balloon; **2,** a sudden and complete failure, as of a government; **3,** general breakdown; as, a nervous *collapse:*—*v.i.* [collapsed, collaps-ing], **1,** to fall in or shrink together; **2,** to fail completely and suddenly; **3,** to break down physically.—*adj.* **col-laps′i-ble.**

col-lar (kol′ẽr), *n.* **1,** the part of any garment which fits around the neck; also, an ornamental piece of lace, linen, silk, etc., worn around the neck; **2,** a leather or metal band for the neck of a dog or other animal; **3,** the part of a horse's harness which fits over the neck and shoulders and bears the strain of the load; **4,** in mechanics, a connecting ring or band:—*v.t.* **1,** to seize by the collar; **2,** to put a collar on.—*n.* **col′lar-bone′.**

col-lat-er-al (ko-lat′ẽr-al), *adj.* **1,** side by side; parallel; **2,** connected with something but of minor importance; **3,** pertaining to something, as stocks or bonds, offered as security, in addition to one's note, or other promise to pay; **4,** descended from the same stock, but not in a direct line: opposed to *lineal;* as, my sister is my *collateral* relative; my father is my *lineal* relative:—*n.* something given, as stocks or bonds, as a pledge for the repayment of a loan.— *adv.* **col-lat′er-al-ly.**

col-league (kol′ēg), *n.* an associate in office, or in a profession.

¹col-lect (ko-lekt′), *v.t.* **1,** to gather together; **2,** to secure payment of (money due, bills, taxes, etc.); **3,** to make a hobby of collecting (something); as, to *collect* stamps, rare books, or the like:—*v.i.* **1,** to accumulate; as, scum *collects* on stagnant water; **2,** to meet or assemble; as, a crowd *collects.*

²col-lect (kol′ekt), *n.* a brief prayer, part of a church's ritual suited to a particular occasion; as, a *collect* for peace.

col-lect-ed (ko-lek′tid), *adj.* calm; cool; undisturbed.—*adv.* **col-lect′ed-ly.**

col-lec-tion (ko-lek′shun), *n.* **1,** the process of gathering or assembling; as, the *collection* of outgoing mail; the *collection* of a crowd at a fire; **2,** any assemblage of persons or things; esp. a group of books, stamps, paintings, or the like, gathered for display or study; **3,** the taking in of money due; also, the amount received; **4,** a contribution asked for; as, they took up two *collections* at church.

col-lec-tive (ko-lek′tiv), *adj.* relating to, produced by, or affecting a number of individuals jointly, that is, a number of persons as if they were one body; as, the *collective* wisdom of the ages; *collective* action:—**collective noun,** a singular noun used to name a group or collection of individuals; as, "army" and "audience" are *collective nouns.*— *adv.* **col-lec′tive-ly:**—**collective bargaining,** the negotiating of terms between union and employer respecting wages, hours, fringe benefits, etc.

col-lec-tiv-ism (ko-lek′tiv-izm), *n.* the doctrine that the people should own and control the means of production and distribution; socialism.

col-lec-tor (ko-lek′tẽr), *n.* a person who collects; as, an art *collector;* a tax *collector.*

col-lege (kol′ij), *n.* **1,** an educational institution above the high school, which gives degrees to its students upon completion of certain courses of study; **2,** the buildings and grounds of such an institution; **3,** a school for special instruction; **4,** an association of men having a common profession; as, the *College* of Physicians.—*adj.* **col-le′gi-ate** (ko-lē′ji-it; -jit).

col-lide (ko-lid′), *v.i.* [collid-ed, collid-ing], to meet and strike together with force; crash; as, the two ships *collided;* also, to clash; conflict.

col-lie (kol′i), *n.* a large sheep-dog with a shaggy coat.

col-lier (kol′yẽr), *n.* **1,** a coal-miner; **2,** a ship for carrying coal.—*n.* **col′lier-y.**

col-li-sion (ko-lizh′un), *n.* the violent striking together of two bodies; a crash; also, a clash or conflict.

col-loid (kol′oid), *n.* a substance whose finely divided particles hang indefinitely suspended in a medium without crystallizing, as in glue, jelly, or gelatin.—*adj.* **col-loi′dal.**

col-lo-qui-al (ko-lō′kwi-al), *adj.* used in ordinary conversation, but not in formal or literary language; as, "movies" is a *colloquial* word.—*adv.* **col-lo′qui-al-ly.**—*n.* **col-lo′qui-al-ism.**

col-lo-quy (kol′o-kwi′), *n.* a somewhat formal conversation; conference; discussion; as, the students concerned held a *colloquy* at recess.

col-lu-sion (ko-lū′zhun), *n.* a secret agreement for an unlawful or evil purpose; as, *collusion* between witnesses in a lawsuit.

co-logne (ko-lōn′), *n.* a perfumed toilet water.

¹co-lon (kō′lun), *n.* a punctuation mark [:] used after the formal greeting with which a business letter begins, before a quotation of some length, and before a list, as of contents, illustrations, causes, etc.

²co-lon (kō′lun), *n.* the large intestine, which in a man is about six feet long.

colo-nel (kûr′nl), *n.* the commander of a regiment.—*n.* **colo′nel-cy.**

co-lo-ni-al (ko-lō′ni-al), *adj.* relating to a colony or colonies; esp., relating to the British colonies which have become part of the British Commonwealth.

col-o-nize (kol′o-niz′), *v.t.* [colonized, coloniz-ing], **1,** to migrate to and establish a colony in (a place); as, the French and English *colonized* Canada; **2,** to send colonists to; as, England *colonized* New Zealand.—*n.* **col′o-ni-za′tion.**—*n.* **col′o-nist.**

col-on-nade (kol′o-nād′), *n.* a row of columns, regularly spaced along the side or sides of a building.

col-o-ny (kol′o-ni), *n.* [*pl.* colonies], **1,** a body of people who leave their native country and settle in another land, but remain subject to the mother country; **2,** the country thus settled; **3,** a group of people allied by race, interests, or the like, living together; as, an artist *colony;* **4,** a group of plants or animals living together; as, a *colony* of honeybees.—*n.* **col′o-nist.**

col-o-phon (kol′o-fon′), *n.* a publisher's distinctive emblem placed on either the last page or the title page of a book.

col-or (kul′ẽr), *n.* an American spelling of *colour.*

col-o-ra-tu-ra (kul′ẽr-a-tū′ra; kō′lora-tōō′ra; kol-), *n.* **1,** brilliant trills, runs, etc., to show a singer's range and skill; **2,** a lyric soprano who sings in such a manner.

co-los-sal (ko-los′al), *adj.* huge; vast.

col-os-se-um (kol′o-sē′um), *n.* a large building used as a theatre, stadium, or place of public entertainment; as, the *Colosseum* at Rome or Toronto's Canadian National Exhibition. Also, **col′i-se′um.**

co-los-sus (ko-los′us), *n.* [*pl.* colossi (ko-los′ī) or colussuses (ko-los′us-iz)], **1,** a huge statue; **2,** any huge person or thing.

col-our or **col-or** (kul′ẽr), *n.* **1,** that quality of an object by which one can see whether it is red, blue, green, or the like; **2,** any hue, tint, or shade, sometimes including black and white; **3,** a paint or pigment; **4,** complexion:— **the colours,** the flag; as, a call to *the colours:*—*v.t.* **1,** to give a colour to; dye; **2,** to misrepresent; as, the witness *coloured* his story:—*v.i.* to blush.— *n.* **col′our-a′tion.**—*adj.* **col′our-less; colour—blind.**

col-our-cast (kul′ẽr-kast′), *n.* a telecast intended for colour production.

col-oured (kul′ẽrd), *adj.* **1,** having colour; not black or white; **2,** belonging to a dark-skinned race; esp. the Negro race.

col-our-ful (kul′ẽr-fōōl), *adj.* **1,** full of striking colour or colours; as, a *colourful* parade; **2,** exciting the fancy or imagination; as, *colourful* music.

colt (kōlt), *n.* a young horse, ass, zebra, etc.

col-ter (kōl′tẽr), *n.* Same as *coulter.*

col-um-bine (kol′um-bīn′), *n.* a plant of the buttercup family, having flowers with deeply spurred petals; also the flowers:—**Columbine,** the mistress of Harlequin in a pantomime.

col-umn (kol′um), *n.* **1,** an upright pillar supporting or adorning any part of a building or standing alone as a monument; **2,** anything that by its form, position, or use suggests a pillar; as, the spinal *column;* a *column* of mercury; **3,** a vertical division on a printed page; as, the *columns* of a

newspaper; **4,** a department in a newspaper, usually written by one person on one general subject; as, the society *column;* **5,** a body or file of soldiers or ships following one after the other.— *adj.* **co-lum′nar.**

col-um-nist (kol′um-nist), *n.* one who writes or edits a particular column in a newspaper.

co-ma (kō′ma), *n.* a state of prolonged unconsciousness and insensibility, produced by disease, injury, or poison.

comb (kōm), *n.* **1,** a toothed instrument of hard rubber, celluloid, metal, or the like, used to smooth, adjust, or hold in the hair; **2,** a toothed ornament for the hair; **3,** a toothed metal instrument used in grooming horses, separating and cleaning the fibres of flax or wool, etc.; **4,** the crest of a cock; **5,** the crest of a hill or wave:—*v.t.* **1,** to dress (the hair) with a comb; **2,** to cleanse (flax or wool) with a comb; **3,** to search through; as, they *combed* the city for the fugitive.

com-bat (kom′bat; kum′bat), *n.* a struggle; fight:—*v.i.* (kom′bat; kum′bat; kombat′), [combat-ed, combating; if accented on the last syllable, combat-ted, combat-ting], to struggle; as, good *combating* with evil:—*v.t.* to oppose; resist.—*adj.* **com′ba-tive.**

com-bat-ant (kom′ba-tant; kum′batant), *n.* a person who takes part in a fight or conflict:—*adj.* fighting.

¹**com-bine** (kom′bīn), *n.* a farm machine which harvests, threshes, and cleans grain in one continuous operation in the field.

²**com-bine** (kom-bīn′), *v.t.* [combined, combin-ing], to unite or join; as, to *combine* forces; to mix, as ingredients: —*v.i.* to unite; agree; as, two parties will *combine* to defeat a third:—*n.* (kom′bīn; kom-bīn′), *Colloq.,* a union; a joining of persons or parties in business or politics to effect a common purpose.—*n.* **com′bi-na′tion.**

com-bus-ti-ble (kom-bus′ti-bl), *adj.* **1,** capable of taking fire and burning; as, wood and coal are *combustible;* **2,** excitable; fierce; as, a *combustible* temper:—*n.* an inflammable substance, as *gasoline.*—*n.* **com-bus′ti-bil′i-ty.**

com-bus-tion (kom-bus′chun), *n.* the act or process of burning.

come (kum), *v.i.* [*p.t.* came (kām), *p.p.* come, *p.pr.* com-ing], **1,** to move toward; draw near; as, *come* here; spring is *coming;* also to arrive; **2,** to extend to a given point; as, the farm *comes* as far as the river; **3,** to amount to; as, the bill *comes* to $50; it all *comes* to the same thing; **4,** to become visible, audible, or the like; as, sounds *come* to the ear; **5,** to be descended; as, he *comes* from a humble family; **6,** to occur as a result; as, accidents *come* from carelessness; **7,** to happen; as, I don't know how we *came* to speak of it.

co-me-di-an (ko-mē′di-an), *n.* an actor who plays comic parts.—*n.fem.* **co-me′di-enne′** (ko-mē′di-en′).

com-e-dy (kom′e-di), *n.* [*pl.* comedies], an amusing play with a happy ending.

come-ly (kum′li), *adj.* [come-li-er, come-li-est], fair to look upon; of pleasing appearance; as, a *comely* girl. —*n.* **come′li-ness.**

com-et (kom′it), *n.* a heavenly body which moves about the sun. It often has a long, blazing train, or tail.

com-fort (kum′fèrt), *v.t.* to console or cheer (a person) in pain, grief, or trouble:—*n.* **1,** a person or thing that relieves distress or makes trouble easier to bear; as, a good friend is a *comfort;* **2,** enjoyment of freedom from mental or physical discomfort; **3,** contentment resulting from the satisfying of wants; also, the things that produce such a state; as, the *comforts* of home.

com-fort-a-ble (kum′fèrt-a-bl), *adj.* **1,** enjoying ease, contentment, or freedom from care; **2,** giving comfort; as, a *comfortable* chair:—*n.* a wadded or quilted bed-covering; a comforter.— *adv.* **com′fort-a-bly.**

com-fort-er (kum′fèrt-ėr), *n.* **1,** one who consoles or cheers; **2,** a long woollen scarf; **3,** a quilted bed-covering of cotton, wool, or feathers; a comfortable.

com-ic (kom′ik), *adj.* aiming to excite laughter; funny; as, a *comic* song. Also, **com′i-cal.**

com-ma (kom′a), *n.* a punctuation mark [,] used to indicate a slight separation of ideas or construction, as to set off a short quotation from the text, to separate words in a series, etc.

com-mand (ko-mand′), *v.t.* **1,** to give orders to, with authority; **2,** to have authority over; control; as, the captain *commands* his ship and crew; **3,** to overlook or dominate, as from a height; **4,** to be able to obtain; as, to *command* good prices; to *command* respect:—*v.i.* to act as leader; rule:—*n.* **1,** authority; the right to command or control; as, a captain is in *command* of a company; **2,** an order; as, he gave the *command* to fire; **3,** a district or a body of troops under a naval or military officer; **4,** mastery; as, the *command* of language; in *command* of one's temper.

com-man-dant (kom′an-dant′; kom′an-dänt′), *n.* the officer in command of a troop, a fort, a navy-yard, or the like.

com-man-deer (kom′an-dēr′), *v.t.* **1,** to compel (men) to military service; **2,** to take forcibly (food, clothing, horses, etc.) for military purposes; **3,** *Colloq.*, to seize for personal use.

com-mand-er (ko-man′dėr), *n.* **1,** a person in authority; **2,** a military leader or chief; **3,** a naval officer ranking next below a captain:—**commander— in—chief** [*pl.* commanders–in–chief], the person in supreme command of the army or the navy, or of both.

com-mand-ment (ko-mand′ment), *n.* an order; injunction; law; esp., any one of the Ten Commandments given by God to Moses on Mount Sinai (Exodus 20: 3–17).

com-mem-o-rate (ko-mem′o-rāt′), *v.t.* [commemorat-ed, commemorat-ing] to keep alive the memory of (a person, event, etc.), as by a celebration or a monument; as, the Peace Tower commemorates the Canadians killed in World War I.—*n.* **com-mem′o-ra′tion.**

com-mence (ko-mens′), *v.t.* and *v.i.* [commenced, commenc-ing], to begin.

com-mence-ment (ko-mens′ment), *n.* **1,** the beginning; origin; **2,** the occasion when degrees or diplomas are conferred at a school or a college; also, the graduation exercises.

com-mend (ko-mend′), *v.t.* **1,** to recommend as worthy of notice; as, I *commend* that play to your attention; **2,** to praise; as, to *commend* a child for promptness.—*n.* **com′men-da′tion.**

com-mend-a-ble (ko-men′da-bl), *adj.* praiseworthy.—*adv.* **com-mend′a-bly.**

com-men-su-rate (ko-men′sū-rit; -shoor), *adj.* corresponding in amount; proportionate; as, his skill is *commensurate* with his intelligence.

com-ment (kom′ent), *n.* **1,** a spoken or written remark; esp., a written note that explains, illustrates, or criticizes; **2,** talk; gossip; as, his unexpected departure caused *comment:*—*v.i.* (ko-ment′), to make observations or notes; as, to *comment* upon the news.

com-men-tar-y (kom′en-tėr-i; ter′-), *n.* [*pl.* commentaries], **1,** an explanation; **2,** a series of explanatory notes, as on passages in the Bible; also, a book of critical or explanatory notes.

com-men-ta-tor (kom′en-tā′tėr), *n.* one who writes or makes comments on a book or topic; as, a radio news-commentator.

com-merce (kom′ėrs), *n.* the buying

and selling of goods, esp. on a large scale; trade.—*adj.* and *n.* **com-mer'cial.**

com-mer-cial-ize (ko-mûr'shal-īz'), *v.t.* [commercialized, commercializ-ing], to reduce to a money-making or business basis; as, to *commercialize* football.—*n.* **com-mer'cial-ism; com-mer'cial-i-za'tion.**

com-mis-er-ate (ko-miz'ėr-āt'), *v.t.* [commiserat-ed, commiserat-ing], to feel or express pity for; sympathize with.—*n.* **com-mis'er-a'tion.**

com-mis-sar (kom'i-sär'), *n.* **1,** a deputy; esp., in the army, an officer charged with maintaining food supplies; **2,** in a republic of the U.S.S.R., the head of a government department.—*n.* **com'mis-sa'ri-at.**

com-mis-sar-y (kom'i-sėr-i), *n.* [*pl.* commissaries], **1,** one to whom some charge is committed by a superior; a deputy; **2,** in the army, an official in the department which has charge of provisions and supplies; **3,** a company store supplying food and equipment, as in a lumber-camp.

com-mis-sion (ko-mish'un), *n.* **1,** the doing or performing of some act: often implying wrongdoing; as, the *commission* of a crime; **2,** a matter entrusted to anyone to perform; as, he had a *commission* to buy land; **3,** the fee paid to an agent for doing business for another; as, the *commission* on the sale was $25; **4,** a group of persons appointed to perform certain duties; as, a *commission* to investigate housing; **5,** a document conferring military or naval rank or authority:—*v.t.* **1,** to empower; delegate; as, I *commission* you to paint the picture; **2,** in the army and navy, to confer rank or authority upon; **3,** to put into service, as a war-ship.—*n.* **com-mis'sion-er.**

com-mit (ko-mit'), *v.t.* [commit-ted, commit-ting], **1,** to give (someone) into another's care for safekeeping, care, custody, or the like; as, to *commit* an invalid to a hospital; to *commit* a man for trial; **2,** to entrust (something) for safekeeping, as by writing down or memorizing; as, to *commit* thoughts to paper or verses to memory; **3,** to do (something foolish or wrong); as, to *commit* a folly or a crime; **4,** to involve (oneself) in difficulties; as, he refused to *commit* himself by talking; also, to pledge; as, I am *committed* to the cause. —*n.* **com-mit'ment.**—*n.* **com-mit'al.**

com-mit-tee (ko-mit'i), *n.* a group of persons elected or appointed to deal with a certain phase of a business, or to act on, consider, or report on, one special matter; as, a *committee* for decorating the hall.

com-mo-di-ous (ko-mō'di-us), *adj.* roomy; spacious.—*adv.* **com-mo'di-ous-ly.**

com-mod-i-ty (ko-mod'i-ti), *n.* [*pl.* commodities], **1,** something useful; an article of commerce, such as wheat, copper, silk, hogs, or the like; **2,** commodities, goods; merchandise.

com-mo-dore (kom'o-dōr'), *n.* **1,** a naval commanding officer ranking above a captain and below a rear-admiral; **2,** a title of courtesy given to the president of a yacht club, the senior captain of a line of merchant ships, etc.

com-mon (kom'un), *adj.* **1,** belonging to, or shared by, more than one; general; as, death is the *common* lot; **2,** belonging, or relating, to a group or community; public; as, parks are *common* property; **3,** usual; frequent; as, a *common* saying; a *common* sight; **4,** of the ordinary kind; merely average in rank, ability, etc.; **5,** low; vulgar:— *n.* **1,** a tract of open public land; as, the village *common;* **2,** the average; as, a man above the *common.*

com-mon-ly (kom'un-li), *adv.* usually.

com-mon-place (kom'un-plās'), *n.* **1,** an ordinary topic of conversation; also, a remark oft repeated; **2,** an everyday object or event; one that is not uncommon; as, flying has become a *commonplace:*—*adj.* uninteresting; neither new nor striking.

common sense, common—sense, *n.* good sense; sound, practical judgment; normal intelligence.

com-mon-wealth (kom'un-welth'), *n.* the public; the whole body of people in a state; also, a state in which the people rule.

com-mo-tion (ko-mō'shun), *n.* **1,** violent physical disturbance; as, the *commotion* of the raging sea; **2,** stir and confusion; tumult; as, a *commotion* in the crowd.

com-mu-nal (kom'ū-nal; ko-mū'nal), *adj.* relating to the community; belonging to the people; as, *communal* land.

[1]**com-mune** (kom'ūn), *n.,* in some countries, the smallest political division hence, a local, self-governing community.

[2]**com-mune** (ko-mūn'), *v.i.* [commun-ed, commun-ing], **1,** to feel an intimate understanding or hold intimate intercourse; as, to *commune* with nature **2,** esp. in the U.S., to partake of Holy Communion.

com-mu-ni-cate (ko-mū-ni-kāt'), *v.t* [communicat-ed, communicat-ing], **1,** to impart; convey; as, to *communicate* happiness; to *communicate* a disease

2, to make known; tell, as news:—*v.i.* **1,** to partake of the Lord's Supper; **2,** to be connected; as, *communicating* rooms; **3,** to get into connection or touch, by letter, telephone, etc.; as, she *communicates* with us regularly. —*adj.* **com-mu′ni-ca′tive.**—*adj.* **com-mu′ni-ca-ble.**—*n.* **com-mu′ni-ca′tion.**

com-mun-ion (ko-mūn′yun), *n.* **1,** fellowship; esp., religious fellowship; an intimate exchange of spiritual thoughts and feelings; **2,** a group of persons having the same religious beliefs:—**Communion,** the sacrament of the Lord's Supper.

com-mu-ni-qué (ko-mū′ni-kā′), *n.* an official report to press or public, esp. in wartime.

com-mu-nist (kom′ū-nist), *n.* one who believes in communism, or the theory that the people should own in common the means of production, such as mines, factories, etc., and should share in both the work and the returns: —**Communist,** a member of a political party holding these views, esp. in the U.S.S.R.—*n.* **com′ mu-nism.**—*adj.* **com′mu-nis′tic.**

com-mu-ni-ty (ko-mū′ni-ti), *n.* [*pl.* communities], **1,** all the persons who live in one place, as the people of a town; hence, the public; **2.** a group of persons, bound by ties of religion or of common interest; as, a *community* of artists; **3,** likeness; similarity; as, *community* of interests.

com-mu-ta-tor (kom′ū-tā′tẽr), *n.* a device used in a generator or motor for changing the direction of an electric current, esp., alternating to direct; usually it is a revolving cylinder that collects the current from, or distributes it to, the brushes.

com-mute (ko-mūt′), *v.t.* [commut-ed, commut-ing], to exchange for something different; esp., to reduce the severity of; as, to *commute* a sentence of imprisonment from ten to five years: —*v.i.* to travel back and forth daily from a suburb to work in a city.—*n.* **com-mut′er.**—*n.* **com′ mu-ta′tion.**

com-pact (kom′pakt), *n.* an agreement.

²com-pact (kom-pakt′ ; kom′pakt), *adj.* **1,** closely or firmly united or packed together; solid; **2,** condensed; terse; as, a *compact* style:—*v.t.* to press or pack closely; make solid:—*n.* (kom′pakt), a small metal case, to be carried in the purse, which contains face powder.— *adv.* **com-pact′ly.**—*n.* **com-pact′ness.**

com-pan-ion (kom-pan′yun), *n.* **1,** a comrade or associate; sometimes, a person paid to live or travel with another;

2, one of a pair or set of objects designed to go together:—*v.t.* to accompany.—*n.* **com-pan′ion-ship.**

com-pan-ion-a-ble (kom-pan′yun-a-bl), *adj.* sociable; agreeable.

com-pan-ion—way (kom-pan′yun—wā′), *n.* on a ship, a stairway leading below from the deck.

com-pa-ny (kum′pa-ni), *n.* [*pl.* companies], **1,** companionship; society; as, I want *company* tonight; **2,** companions; associates; as, a man is known by the *company* he keeps; **3,** a guest or guests; **4,** a group of persons assembled; **5,** a business or commercial firm; **6,** a troupe of actors; **7,** a body of soldiers, esp. a section of infantry, normally commanded by a captain.

com-pa-ra-ble (kom′pa-ra-bl), *adj.* **1,** capable of being compared; as, the sound of cannon and of thunder are *comparable;* **2,** worthy or fit to be compared; as, Westminster Abbey is *comparable* to Notre Dame.—*adv.* **com′para-bly.**

com-par-a-tive (kom-par′a-tiv), *adj.* **1,** involving the use of comparison; as, the *comparative* study of animals; **2,** measured by comparison with something else; as, we live in *comparative* comfort; **3,** in *grammar,* naming that form of an adjective or adverb, as "longer" or "sooner," that expresses a higher degree of the quality indicated by the simple form:—*n.* the comparative degree; also, a comparative form; as, "better" is the *comparative* of "good." —*adv.* **com-par′a-tive-ly.**

com-pare (kom-pâr′), *v.t.* [compared, compar-ing], **1,** to liken; describe as similar; as, the poets *compare* death to sleep; **2,** to examine in order to discover likeness and unlikeness; as, to *compare* two specimens; **3,** in *grammar,* to give the positive, comparative, and superlative degrees of (an adjective or adverb):—*v.i.* to be worthy of comparison with something else; as, rayon *compares* favourably with silk:—*n.* comparison; as, beauty beyond *compare.*—*n.* **com-par′i-son.**

com-part-ment (kom-pärt′ment), *n.* a separate part or division, as of an enclosed space; a separate section; as, a watertight *compartment* in the hull of a ship; a *compartment* in a European passenger coach.

com-pass (kum′pas), *n.* **1,** the boundary of an area; as, within the *compass* of a city; **2,** an instrument for determining direction by means of a needle pointing to the magnetic north; **3,** the range of tones possible to a given voice or instrument; **4,** (usually *compasses*), an instrument for drawing and

all (ôl), **ôr;** **up, mūte, cûr, cōōl, book;· oil, out;** **th, thin;** *th,* **the.**

dividing circles, transferring measurements, etc., consisting of two small, upright rods joined together at the top by a hinge: also called *dividers:—v.t.* to bring about; achieve; as, he *compassed* his aims.

com-pas-sion (kom-pash′un), *n.* sorrow and pity for the sufferings of others.

com-pas-sion-ate (kom-pash′un-it), *adj.* merciful.—*adv.* **com-pas′sion-ate-ly.**

com-pat-i-ble (kom-pat′i-bl), *adj.* harmonious; consistent; mutually agreeable or suitable; as, this evidence is not *compatible with* your testimony.

com-pa-tri-ot (kom-pā′tri-ot; -pat′), *n.* a fellow-countryman.

com-pel (kom-pel′), *v.t.* [compelled, compel-ling], to oblige; force; as, a guilty conscience *compelled* him to confess.

com-pen-sate (kom′pen-sāt′), *v.t.* [compensat-ed, compensat-ing], to make a suitable return to; pay; as, to *compensate* you for your time:—*v.i.* to make up for something; supply an equivalent; as, nothing can *compensate* for loss of health.—*n.* **com′pen-sa′tion.**

com-pete (kom-pēt′), *v.i.* [compet-ed compet-ing], to enter into a contest or rivalry; contend; as, to *compete* for a prize.

com-pe-tence (kom′pe-tens), *n.* **1,** fitness; capability; ability; as, no one questions her *competence* to teach; **2,** a modest fortune; enough for comfort. Also, **com′pe-ten-cy.**

com-pe-tent (kom′pe-tent), *adj.* able; capable.—*adv.* **com′pe-tent-ly.**

com-pe-ti-tion (kom′pe-tish′un), *n.* **1,** the act of competing; rivalry; **2,** a contest; a trial of ability, as in sport; as, the *competition* in skiing drew a crowd; **3,** the effort of rival concerns to secure as much business as possible by making concessions as regards price, terms of payment, etc.—*adj.* **com-pet′i-tive** (kom-pet′i-tiv).—*n.* **com-pet′i-tor** (kom-pet′i-tėr).

com-pile (kom-pīl′), *v.t.* [compiled, compil-ing], to collect (data, facts, figures, literary extracts, or the like) from various sources and put into new form; as, to *compile* a table of contents or a book of verse.—*n.* **com-pil′er.**—*n.* **com′pi-la′tion.**

com-pla-cent (kom-plā′sent), *adj.* pleased with oneself; self-satisfied.—*adv.* **com-pla′cent-ly.**—*n.* **com-pla′cence.**

com-plain (kom-plān′), *v.i.* **1,** to give voice to grief, pain, resentment, or discontent; as, she *complained* of headache; **2,** to lament mournfully;

as, Job *complained* to the Lord; **3,** to find fault with; as, the teacher *complained* of John's tardiness; **4,** to make an accusation; as, the prisoner *complained* of injustice.—*n.* **com-plaint′.**—*adv.* **com-plain′ing-ly.**

com-plai-sant (kom-plā′zant; kom′-plā-zant′), *n.* polite; courteous; agreeable; obliging; as, the Parisians are *complaisant* in their reception of visitors.

com-ple-ment (kom′ple-ment), *n.* **1,** the full number or quantity, a complete set; as, the orchestra has its *complement* of instruments; **2,** that which makes an incomplete thing complete; **3,** one of two parts which together form a whole:—*v.t.* (kom′-ple-ment′), to finish out; make whole. —*adj.* **com′ple-men′ta-ry.**

com-plete (kom-plēt′), *adj.* **1,** lacking nothing; entire; perfect; full; as, a *complete* pack of cards; **2,** absolute; as, a *complete* surprise; **3,** finished; as, her work is now *complete:—v.t.* [completed, complet-ing], to make whole or perfect; finish.—*n.* **com-plete′ness.**—*n.* **com-ple′tion.**—*adv.* **com-plete′ly.**

com-plex (kom′pleks; kom-pleks′), *adj.* **1,** made of various parts; not simple; as, a *complex* business organization; **2,** involved; intricate; as, a *complex* situation:—*n.* (kom′pleks), a habitual emotional attitude toward a particular thing.—*n.* **com-plex′i-ty.**

com-plex-ion (kom-plek′shun), *n.* **1,** the colour, texture, and appearance of the skin, esp. of the face; **2,** general aspect or character; as, his story gave a different *complexion* to the case.—*adj.* **com-plex′-ioned.**

com-pli-ant (kom-plī′ant), *adj.* inclined to consent; yielding; obliging.— *adv.* **com-pli′ant-ly.**—*n.* **com-pli′ance.**

com-pli-cate (kom′pli-kāt′), *v.t.* [complicat-ed, complicat-ing], to make confused or hard to understand; to make difficult.—*adj.* **com′pli-cat′ed.**— *n.* **com′pli-ca′tion.**

com-plic-i-ty (kom-plis′i-ti), *n.* [*pl.* complicities], partnership in wrong-doing or crime.

com-pli-ment (kom′pli-ment), *n.* **1,** something pleasant said about a person or his work; **2, compliments,** formal greetings; as, the new ambassador paid his *compliments* to the Premier:— *v.t.* (kom′pli-ment′), to express approval of; praise.

com-pli-men-ta-ry (kom′pli-men′-ta-ri), *adj.* **1,** conveying approval or admiration; **2,** given free; as, *complimentary* tickets.

com-ply (kom-plī′), *v.i.* [complied, comply-ing], to assent; yield; agree; as, we *complied* with his wish to be alone.

---

c**a**t, **āge, fär, câre, åsk; ten, ēve, latėr; (i) pity, rely, senate; īce; top; nō.**

com-po-nent (kom-pō′nent), *n.* part; ingredient.—*adj.* helping to make up or constitute; as, bearings are a *component* part of a motor.

com-port (kom-pôrt′), *v.t.* to conduct or behave (oneself); as, he did not know how to *comport* himself at the party:— *v.i.* to agree; accord; harmonize; as, simplicity *comports* with beauty.—*n.* **com-port′ment.**

com-pose (kom-pōz′), *v.t.* [composed, compos-ing], **1,** to form by putting things together; as, bronze is *composed* of copper and tin; **2,** to construct or put together; as, to *compose* a sentence, sermon, piece of music, or picture; **3,** in a printing-office, to set (type); **4,** to settle or arrange (any matter) successfully; as, to *compose* a dispute; **5,** to calm; make tranquil; as, to *compose* one's mind.—*n.* **com-pos′er.**

com-pos-ite (kom′poz-it), *adj.* **1,** made up of various distinct parts; **2,** in botany, belonging to a group of plants whose flowers are made up of many small flowers, as the dandelion:— *n.* a compound.

com-po-si-tion (kom′pō-zish′un), *n.* **1,** the act of creating an artistic work; **2,** the work created, as a picture, a piece of music, a novel, or the like; **3,** a schoolroom exercise written for practice in the use of language; **4,** the setting up of type; **5,** a substance formed by mingling various materials; **6,** the make-up of anything; as, what is the *composition* of this substance?

com-pos-i-tor (kom-poz′i-tėr), *n.* one who sets type in a printing-office.

com-post (kom′pōst), *n.* a rotted mixture of dead leaves, manure, etc., for fertilizing soils.

com-po-sure (kom-pō′zhūr; -zhėr), *n.* calmness.

com-pound (kom-pound′), *v.t.* **1,** to mix or combine together, as two chemicals to make a medicine; **2,** to form by mixing, as a medicine:—*adj.* (kom′pound; kom-pound′), composed of two or more elements:—*n.* (kom′-pound), **1,** a combination of two or more elements or parts; **2,** in chemistry, a substance formed of two or more elements united in definite proportions; **3,** in *grammar*, a word composed of two or more elements, themselves usually words, as "housewife."

com-pre-hend (kom′pri-hend′), *v.t.* **1,** to understand; grasp the meaning of; **2,** to include; take in; as, Europe *comprehends* many nations.—*n.* **com′-pre-hen′sion.**—*adj.* **com′pre-hen′si-ble.**

com-pre-hen-sive (kom′pri-hen′siv), *adj.* **1,** including much; full; complete;

as, a *comprehensive* account of the war; **2,** able to understand readily; comprehending.

com-press (kom-pres′), *v.t.* to press together; condense:—*n.* (kom′pres), a pad applied hot or cold to some part of the body to reduce inflammation.—*adj.* **com-press′i-ble.**—*n.* **com-pres′sion.**

com-prise (kom-prīz′), *v.t.* [comprised, compris-ing], to consist of; include; as, the house *comprises* ten rooms.

com-pro-mise (kom′prō-mīz′), *n.* **1,** a method of settling a dispute whereby each side yields something; as, after hours of dispute they resorted to *compromise;* **2,** an agreement reached by mutual yielding; **3,** a line of action that follows a middle course; as, the plan adopted was a *compromise:*—*v.t.* [compromised, compromising], **1,** to settle by mutual yielding; **2,** to expose to suspicion; endanger; as, such actions will *compromise* your reputation:—*v.i.* to make a compromise.

comp-tom-e-ter (komp-tom′e-tėr), *n.* a high-speed machine for adding, subtracting, multiplying, and dividing.

comp-trol-ler (kon-trōl′ėr), *n.* a public officer who examines and certifies accounts; a controller.

com-pul-sion (kom-pul′shun), *n.* the act of compelling; force; also, the state of being compelled; constraint.

com-pul-so-ry (kom-pul′so-ri), *adj.* **1,** exercising force; as, *compulsory* laws; **2,** obligatory; enforced; required; as, vaccination is *compulsory.*—*adv.* **com-pul′so-ri-ly.**

com-punc-tion (kom-pungk′shun), *n.* a feeling (often slight or passing) of regret or uneasiness for wrongdoing; as, he felt *compunction* for the theft of the child's shoes.

com-pute (kom-pūt′), *v.t.* [comput-ed, comput-ing], to figure; number; reckon; calculate; as, he *computed* his expenses. —*n.* **com-put′er.**—*n.* **com′pu-ta′tion.**

com-rade (kum′rid; kom′rad), *n.* a friend; a companion.—*n.* **com′rade-ship.**

¹**con** (kon), *v.t.* [conned, con-ning], to study carefully; hence, to commit to memory.

²**con** (kon), *adv.* on the negative side; as, they argued the matter pro and *con.*

con-cave (kon′kāv; kon-kāv′), *adj.* curved inward, as the inside of a circle or ball: opposite of *convex.*—*n.* **con-cav′i-ty** (kon-kav′i-ti).

con-ceal (kon-sēl′), *v.t.* to hide; keep secret.—*n.* **con-ceal′ment.**

CONCAVE
The inside of the bowl is concave.

con-cede (kon-sēd'), *v.t.* [conced-ed, conced-ing], **1,** to admit to be true; yield; as, he *conceded* the point in the debate; **2,** to grant (a right, privilege, etc.); as, to *concede* an advance in wages.

con-ceit (kon-sēt'), *n.* **1,** a too flattering belief in one's own powers; vanity; **2,** a fanciful notion; a quaint thought.—*adj.* **con-ceit'ed.**

con-ceive (kon-sēv'), *v.t.* [conceived, conceiv-ing], **1,** to think of; imagine; **2,** to form (a purpose, design etc.) in the mind; devise; as, to *conceive* a plot; **3,** to become pregnant with (young):—*v.i.* **1,** to think; imagine; as, I cannot *conceive* of her doing that; **2,** to become pregnant.—*adj.* **con-ceiv'a-ble.**—*adv.* **con-ceiv'a-bly.**

con-cen-trate (kon'sen-trāt'), *v.t.* [concentrat-ed, concentrat-ing], **1,** to bring to a common centre; as, the general *concentrated* his troops in the city; **2,** to fix (the attention or energies) on one course or object; **3,** to increase in strength by reducing bulk; as, to *concentrate* soup by boiling away excess liquid:—*v.i.* **1,** to come together in one place; as, population *concentrates* in the cities; **2,** to fix the attention; as, to *concentrate* on a problem.—*n.* **con'cen-tra'tion.**

con-cen-tric (kon-sen'trik), *adj.* having a common centre; as, *concentric* circles.

con-cept (kon'sept), *n.* a mental impression of an object; a general notion.

CONCENTRIC
CIRCLES

con-cep-tion (kon-sep'shun), *n.* **1,** the act of forming a mental image or impression; **2,** an idea or notion; **3,** the fertilization of the egg and the beginning of a new life in the body of the mother.

con-cern (kon-sûrn'), *v.t.* **1,** to affect the welfare of; relate or belong to; interest or engage; as, that affair does not *concern* me; **2,** to make uneasy; as, don't let that *concern* you:—*n.* **1,** that which relates to one; affair; as, that is my *concern;* **2,** interest; anxiety; **3,** a business firm.

con-cern-ing (kon-sûr'ning), *prep.* relating to; regarding.

con-cert (kon-sûrt'), *v.t.* to plan together; settle by agreement:—*n.* (kon'sûrt), **1,** a musical entertainment; **2,** musical harmony; as, the boys like to sing in *concert;* **3,** agreement; co-operation; **4,** unison of voices; as, to recite in *concert.*

con-cer-to (kon-cher'tō; -châr), *n.*

symphonic music for one or more solo instruments, as a piano or organ, with accompaniments for a full orchestra, playing a composition with three movements.

con-cer-ti-na (kon'sėr-tē'na), *n.* a small musical instrument somewhat like an accordion.

con-ces-sion (kon-sesh'un), *n.* **1,** the act of granting or yielding something; **2,** an acknowledgement or admission; **3,** a grant of a privilege, or of land, for some special purpose; **4,** a government grant of land forming a division of a township; **5,** one of the roads (of a township) that run parallel, usually ⅞ to 1¼ miles apart; as, the fourth *concession* of Innisfil township.

conch (kongk; konch), *n.* a large spiral seashell.

con-cil-i-ate (kon-sil'i-āt'), *v.t.* [conciliat-ed, conciliat-ing], to gain the goodwill of (a person); win over from hostility; as, her many kind deeds finally *conciliated* her enemy.—*n.* **con-cil'i-a'tion.**—*n.* **con-cil'i-a-tor.**—*adj.* **con-cil'i-a-tor'y.**

con-cise (kon-sīs'), *adj.* terse; brief; expressing much in few words.—*adv.* **con-cise'ly.**—*n.* **con-cise'ness.**

con-clave (kon'clāv; kong'-), *n.* **1,** any private or secret meeting; **2,** the meeting-place, or meeting, of the cardinals to elect a pope.

con-clude (kon-klūd'; kon-klōōd'), *v.t.* [conclud-ed, conclud-ing], **1,** to bring to an end; as, to *conclude* a speech; **2,** to arrive at an opinion by reasoning; infer; as, it grew so late, I *concluded* you were not coming; **3,** to settle; bring about as a result; as, after hours of bickering, he *concluded* the agreement:—*v.i.* to come to an end. —*n.* **con-clu'sion.**—*adj.* **con-clu'sive.**

con-coct (kon-kokt'), *v.t.* **1,** to prepare, as food, by mixing various elements; **2,** to form; make up, as a plot.—*n.* **con-coc'tion.**

con-cord (kong'kôrd; kon'kôrd), *n.* agreement; peace; harmony.

con-course (kong'kōrs; kon'kōrs), *n.* **1,** a flowing together; as, a *concourse* of waters; **2,** an assembly or crowd; **3,** an open place where crowds gather or roads meet.

con-crete (kon'krēt; kon-krēt'), *adj.* **1,** actual; specific; capable of being seen, heard, tasted, etc.; not abstract; as, a table is a *concrete* object, but goodness is an abstract quality; **2,** consisting of the substance called *concrete:*—*n.* a hardened mixture of cement, sand, gravel, and water.—*adv.* **con'crete-ly.**

con-cu-bine (kong'kū-bīn'), *n.* [chiefly

Biblical), a woman who lives, or cohabits, with a man without being married to him; a common–law wife.

con-cur (kon-kûr′), *v.i.* [concurred, concur-ring], to agree or unite in action or opinion; as, all *concurred* in the decision.—*n.* **con-cur′rence.**—*adj.* **con-cur′rent.**

con-cus-sion (kon-kush′un), *n.* **1,** a shaking; shock; **2,** an injury, as to the brain or spine, from a blow or collision.

con-demn (kon-dem′), *v.t.* **1,** to blame; censure; declare to be wrong; **2,** to declare guilty; **3,** to declare to be forfeited or taken for public use; as, to *condemn* land; **4,** to pronounce unfit for use; as, to *condemn* a row of tenements.—*adj.* **con-dem′na-tor′y.**—*n.* **con′dem-na′tion.**

con-dense (kon-dens′), *v.t.* [condensed, condens-ing], **1,** to compress; make more close, compact, or dense; **2,** to reduce to fewer words; **3,** to change from a gas or vapour to a liquid, as steam to water; **4,** to increase in intensity, as an electric charge:—*v.i.* **1,** to become dense; **2,** to pass from gaseous or vaporous to liquid form.—*n.* **con′den-sa′tion.**—*n.* **con-dens′er.**

con-de-scend (kon′de-send′), *v.i.* to stoop or come down voluntarily to the level of one's inferiors; show courtesies, often with a superior air; as, the great man *condescended* to join us.—*n.* **con′de-scen′sion.**

con-di-ment (kon′di-ment), *n.* a spicy seasoning for food, as pepper or mustard.

con-di-tion (kon-dish′un), *n.* **1,** something that must exist if something else is to be or to take place; as, hard work is one of the *conditions* of success; **2,** state of being or of circumstances; as, the road is in bad *condition;* **3,** state of health; fitness for work, etc.; as, he is in good *condition;* **4,** rank; social position; as, a lady of high *condition;* **5,** in schools a failure that can be made up:—*v.t.* **1,** to render fit; as, to *condition* a boxer; **2,** to be a condition for; as, health *conditions* success.—*adj.* **con-di′tioned.**

con-di-tion-al (kon-dish′un-al), *adj.* **1,** depending upon certain provisions or conditions; **2,** in *grammar*, containing a provisional clause.—*adv.* **con-di′tion-al-ly.**

con-dole (kon-dōl′), *v.i.* [condoled, condol-ing], to express sympathy; as, we *condoled* with him over his loss.—*n.* **con-do′lence.**

con-done (kon-dōn′), *v.t.* [condoned, condon-ing], to forgive or overlook, as a fault or offence.—*n.* **con′do-na′tion.**

con-dor (kon′dor), *n.* a very large, South American vulture found in the Andes Mountains.

con-duce (kon-dūs′), *v.i.* [conduced, conduc-ing], to lead or tend toward a result; contribute.—*adj.* **con-du′cive.**

con-duct (kon-dukt′), *v.t.* **1,** to guide; **2,** to manage; direct, as an orchestra; **3,** to behave (oneself); **4,** to carry; as, the canal *conducts* water:—*v.i.* **1,** to direct; lead; **2,** to transmit electricity, heat, etc.:—*n.* (kon′dukt), **1,** personal behaviour or practice; **2,** management; guidance.—*n.* **con-duc′tion.**—*n.* **con′duc-tiv′i-ty.**

con-duc-tor (kon-duk′tẽr), *n.* **1,** a leader or guide; **2,** a manager; a director of a chorus or orchestra; **3,** an official who has charge of the passengers, collects fare, etc., on a bus, trolley-car, or railway train; **4,** a substance which transmits energy; as, metals are good *conductors* of heat and electricity.

con-duit (kon′dit; kun′dit; kon′doo-it), *n.* **1,** a canal or pipe for carrying water, etc.; **2,** an enclosed tube or passage for electric wires.

cone (kōn), *n.* **1,** a solid body which tapers uniformly to a point from a circular base; **2,** anything of similar shape; as, an ice-cream *cone;* **3,** the scaly, cone-shaped fruit of certain trees, as the pine, fir, etc.

con-fab-u-late (kon-fab′ū-lāt′), *v.i.* *Colloq.*, to chat or gossip.

con-fec-tion (kon-fek′shun), anything preserved in sugar; a sweetmeat; candy.

con-fec-tion-er-y (kon-fek′shun-er′i), *n.* [*pl.* confectioneries], **1,** candies, ice-cream, cakes, etc.; **2,** the business of a confectioner.—*n.* **con-fec′tion-er.**

con-fed-er-a-cy (kon-fed′er-a-si), *n.* [*pl.* confederacies], a group or league made up of persons, states, or nations united for mutual support of any kind; an alliance; as, a loose *confederacy* of Indian tribes:—**the Confederacy,** the Confederate States of America, a league of eleven southern States that seceded from the United States in 1860 and 1861.

con-fed-er-ate (kon-fed′ẽr-āt′), *v.t.* and *v.i.* [confederat-ed, confederat-ing], to unite in a league:—*adj.* (kon-fed′ẽr-it), united by a league or agreement:—**Confederate,** pertaining to the Confederacy:—*n.* (kon-fed′ẽr-it), **1,** a member of a league or union; **2,** an ally; accomplice:—**Confederate,** a person who sided with the Confederacy; a soldier of the Confederacy.—*n.* **con-fed′er-a′tion.**

con-fer (kon-fûr′), *v.t.* [conferred, conferring], to give or bestow; as, to *confer* a medal:—*v.i.* to consult with others; discuss; as, to *confer* with one's partner.—*n.* **con′fer-ence.**

con-fess (kon-fes′), *v.t.* **1,** to admit as true; esp., to acknowledge (a fault, crime, debt, etc.); **2,** to profess, as a religious belief; **3,** to hear a confession from: said of a priest:—*v.i.* **1,** to disclose the state of one's conscience to a priest; **2,** to make an acknowledgement or admission.

con-fes-sion (kon-fesh′un), *n.* **1,** the act of acknowledging or admitting; **2,** the act of making known one's sins to a priest; **3,** anything confessed.

con-fes-sor (kon-fes′ẽr), *n.* **1,** one who admits or acknowledges a wrong; **2,** a priest who hears confessions.

con-fet-ti (kon-fet′i), *n.* small discs of coloured paper used in celebrating at weddings, festivals, etc.

con-fi-dant (kon′fi-dant′; kon′fi-dant′), *n.* an intimate friend to whom private affairs are told.—*n.fem.* **con′fi-dante′.**

con-fide (kon-fīd′), *v.t.* [confid-ed, confid-ing], **1,** to put into another's trust or keeping; entrust; as, I will *confide* my daughter to your care; **2,** to tell in confidence; as, *confide* your secret to me:—*v.i.* **1,** to have confidence or trust; as, to *confide* in military force; **2,** *Colloq.*, to entrust secrets; as, you can *confide* in me.—*adj.* **con-fid′ing.**

con-fi-dence (kon′fi-dens), *n.* **1,** belief; trust; as, I have *confidence* in his ability; **2,** boldness; self-assurance; as, he spoke with *confidence;* **3,** trusting intimacy; as, to speak in *confidence;* also, a secret.—*adj.* **con′fi-dent.**—*adv.* **con′fi-dent-ly.**

con-fi-den-tial (kon′fi-den′shal), *adj.* **1,** private; secret; as, *confidential* information; also, intimate; as, he spoke in a *confidential* tone of voice; **2,** entrusted with secret matters; as, a *confidential* secretary.—*adv.* **con′fi-den‵tial-ly.**

con-fig-u-ra-tion (kon-fig′ū-ra′shun), *n.* outline; contour; pattern; as, the *configuration* of the constellation Orion.

con-fine (kon′fīn), *n.* a border, limit, or boundary; as, within the *confines* of a country:—*v.t.* (kon-fīn′), [confined, confin-ing], **1,** to restrict within limits; as, high dikes *confined* the sea; **2,** to keep within doors; imprison; as, illness *confined* him to his room.—*n.* **con-fine′ment.**

con-firm (kon-fûrm′), *v.t.* **1,** to establish more firmly; as, the book *confirms* my belief; **2,** to assure the truth of; verify; as, to *confirm* a report; **3,** to receive into church membership.—*n.* **con′fir-ma′tion.**

con-firmed (kon-fûrmd′), *adj.* settled, as in a habit; as, a *confirmed* invalid.

con-fis-cate (kon′fis-kāt; kon-fis′kāt), *v.t.* [confiscat-ed, confiscat-ing], to take over (private property) by public authority, or by any authority; as, the police *confiscated* the smuggled goods; the teacher *confiscated* the boy's marbles.—*n.* **con′fis-ca′tion.**

con-fla-gra-tion (kon′fla-grā′shun), *n.* a large and destructive fire.

con-flict (kon-flikt′), *v.i.* to clash; be in opposition; as, his story *conflicts* with mine:—*n.* (kon′flikt), **1,** a fight; struggle; battle; **2,** a clash between ideas, feelings, or the like; as, the *conflict* between duty and pleasure.

con-flu-ence (kon′floo-ens), *n.* **1,** a flowing together, esp., of two rivers; **2,** the place where rivers flow together; **3,** a throng; crowd.—*adj.* **con′flu-ent.**

con-form (kon-fôrm′), *v.t.* to make like or similar; as, I will *conform* my tastes to yours:—*v.i.* to act in agreement with a standard, pattern, etc.; as, to *conform* to rules or to the ways of the world.—*n.* **con-form′ist.**—*adj.* **con-form′a-ble.**

con-for-ma-tion (kon′fôr-mā′shun), *n.* form; structure; esp. the orderly arrangements of the parts of a thing.

con-form-i-ty (kon-fôr′mi-ti), *n.* [*pl.* conformities], **1,** a correspondence in form, manner, or character; agreement; as, *conformity* of tastes; **2,** action in agreement with a standard, pattern, etc.; as, *conformity* to fashion.

con-found (kon-found′; kon′found′), *v.t.* **1,** to perplex; bewilder; confuse; **2,** to mistake for another; mix up; as, he *confounds* Jim with his twin; **3,** to damn: used as a mild curse.

con-frère (kôn′frâr), *n.* an associate or colleague, as in a profession.

con-front (kon-frunt′), *v.t.* **1,** to bring face to face; as, to *confront* a prisoner with evidence; **2,** to face defiantly or with hostility; as, to *confront* an enemy.

con-fuse (kon-fūz′), *v.t.* [confused, confus-ing], **1,** to bewilder; perplex; embarrass; **2,** to mistake for another.—*adv.* **con-fus′ed-ly.**

con-fu-sion (kon-fū′zhun), *n.* **1,** perplexity; loss of self-possession; **2,** disorder; tumult.

con-fute (kon-fūt′), *v.t.* [confut-ed, confut-ing], **1,** to prove to be false or untrue; as, to *confute* a claim; **2,** to prove (a person) to be wrong.—*n.* **con′fu-ta′-tion** (kon′fū-tā′shun).

con-ga (kong′ga), *n.* a (Spanish-American) dance in which the dancers form a winding line and dance to a 4/4 ragtime rhythm.

con-geal (kon-jēl′), *v.t.* and *v.i.* to thicken by, or as if by, cold; as, fear *congealed* his blood.

con-gen-ial (kon-jēn′yal; kon-jē′ni-al), *adj.* 1, sympathetic; having the same tastes; as, *congenial* friends; 2, agreeable; naturally suited to one's nature; as, a *congenial* climate.—*adv.* con-gen′ial-ly.

con-gen-i-tal (kon-jen′i-tal), *adj.* existing at, or from, birth; as a *congenital* disease, deformity, etc.; thus, a *congenital* idiot.—*adv.* con-gen′i-tal-ly.

con-ger (kong′gẽr), *n.* and *adj.* a big, edible, salt-water eel, the *conger* eel.

con-gest (kon-jest′), *v.t.* 1, to cause (an organ or part of the body) to become too full of blood; 2, to make too crowded; as, parades *congest* traffic.—*n.* con-ges′tion.

con-glom-er-a-tion (kon-glom′er-ā′-shun), *n.* a compact mass or mixture of different things; as, a *conglomeration* of clay and pebbles, or of sense and nonsense. Also, con-glom′er-ate (rock).

con-grat-u-late (kon-grat′ū-lāt′), *v.t.* [congratulat-ed, congratulat-ing], to express sympathetic pleasure to (a person) on account of some happy event or honour.—*adj.* con-grat′u-la-tor′y.—*n.* con-grat′u-la′tion.

con-gre-gate (kong′gre-gāt′), *v.i.* and *v.t.* [congregat-ed, congregat-ing], to assemble; gather together; as, people *congregated* in the town hall.

con-gre-ga-tion (kong′gre-gā′shun), *n.* 1, a gathering or collection of persons or things; 2, a group of people meeting for religious worship or instruction.—*adj.* con′gre-ga′tion-al.

con-gress (kong′gres), *n.* 1, a meeting, as of delegates for discussion; 2, the chief law-making body of a republic; 3, CIO, Congress for (or of) Industrial Organization.—Congress, the national law-making body of the U.S., composed of the Senate and the House of Representatives.—*adj.* con-gres′sion-al.

con-gress—man (kong′gres–man), *n.* [*pl.* congress-men (-men)], a member of a congress, esp. of the House of Representatives.—*n.fem.* con′gress–wom′an.

con-gru-ent (kong′groo-ent), *adj.* agreeing; corresponding; as, *congruent* triangles, which coincide when placed one over the other.—*n.* con-gru′i-ty.

con-ic (kon′ik), or **con-i-cal** (kon′i-kal), *adj.* shaped like a cone.

co-ni-fer (kō′ni-fẽr; kon′i-fẽr), *n.* a cone-bearing tree, as the spruce or pine.—*adj.* co-nif′er-ous.

con-jec-ture (kon-jek′tūr), *n.* the act of forming an opinion without definite proof; a guess:—*v.t.* and *v.i.* [conjectured, conjectur-ing], to guess.—*adj.* con-jec′tur-al.

con-join (kon-join′), *v.t.* and *v.i.* to join or connect together; unite; as, his memory and wit *conjoined* charmed his audience.—*adj.* con-joint′.—*adv.* con-joint′ly.

con-ju-gal (kon′joo-gl), *adj.* of or relating to marriage; as, *conjugal* happiness.—*adv.* con′ju-gal-ly.—*n.* con′ju-gal′i-ty.

con-ju-gate (kon′joo-gāt′), *v.t.* [conjugated, conjugat-ing], in *grammar*, to give the various forms of (a verb) in order, as, "I am, you are, he is; we, you, they are."—*n.* con′ju-ga′tion.

con-junc-tion (kon-jungk′shun), *n.* 1, a joining together; union; 2, in *grammar*, a word, such as *and*, *if*, *but*, *as*, *or*, *though*, which is used to connect two words, phrases, clauses, or sentences.—*adj.* con-junc′tive.

con-junc-ti-vi-tis (kon-jungk′ti-vī′-tis), *n.* inflammation of the mucous membrane lining the inner surface of the eyelid, eyeball, etc.; pink-eye.

con-jure (kon′joor; kun′jẽr), *v.t.* [conjured, conjur-ing], 1, to cause to appear or disappear as if by magic; 2, (kon-joor′), to appeal to solemnly; implore; as, he *conjured* us to help:—to practice magical arts; also, to juggle.

con-jur-er or **con-jur-or** (kun′jẽr-ẽr), *n.* 1, a magician; 2, a juggler.

conk (kongk), *v.t. Slang*, to hit on the head. Conk out, to fail in operation, as the motor of a car or airplane.

con-nect (ko-nekt′), *v.t.* 1, to join; 2, to join by personal relationship; as, to *connect* by marriage; 3, to associate; as, I did not *connect* his name with his face:—*v.i.* to join; have a close relation.

con-nec-tion (ko-nek′shun), *n.* 1, the state of being joined; union; 2, relationship by blood or marriage; hence, a relative, esp. a distant one; 3, relationship by reason of a common interest or occupation; as, to make a good business *connection*; 4, the linking of words or ideas in speech or thought.—*adj.* and *n.* con-nec′tive.

con-nive (ko-nīv′), *v.i.* [connived, conniv-ing], to permit or help in secret what one should oppose or prevent; as, the jailer *connived* at his escape;—*n.* con-niv′ance.

con-nois-seur (kon′i-sūr′; -sûr′), *n.* one who is expert or competent in judging matters of art, taste, etc.

con-no-ta-tion (kon′ō-tā′shun), *n.* the suggested implied, or associated significance, feeling, or atmosphere of a

all (ôl), ôr; up, mūte, cûr, cōōl, book; oil, out; th, thin; *th*, the.

word, apart from its explicit meaning or denotation.—*v.t.* **con-note′**; thus, *house* connotes a refuge from the elements; *home*, a house plus warmth, love, toys, etc.

con-quer (kong′kẽr), *v.t.* **1,** to subdue by war; as, to *conquer* a country; **2,** to overcome by force of will, as a bad habit:—*v.i.* to be victorious.—*n.* **con′- quer-or.**

con-quest (kong′kwest), *n.* a winning, subduing, or conquering, esp. by war; as, the Norman *Conquest* of England; also, that which is conquered, subdued, or won.

con-science (kon′shens), *n.* a sense of the rightness or wrongness of one's own acts; as, he has a guilty *conscience.*

con-sci-en-tious (kon′shi-en′shus), *adj.* **1,** careful to follow one's sense of right; as, a *conscientious* girl; **2,** arising from one's feelings of right and wrong; as, *conscientious* objections.—*adv.* **con′- sci-en′ tious-ly.**—*n.* **con′sci-en′tious- ness.**

con-scious (kon′shus), *adj.* **1,** aware; as, *conscious* of a pain; **2,** mentally awake; having possession of one's senses; as, the patient is *conscious;* **3,** known to oneself; as, a *conscious* sin.— *adv.* **con′scious-ly.**

con-scious-ness (kon′shus-nis), *n.* **1,** awareness of one's own existence, or of what is happening; as, when asleep we lose *consciousness;* **2,** all that occurs in one's experience; one's sensations, thoughts, feelings, and actions; one's entire mental life.

con-script (kon-skript′), *v.t.* to force a (person) to serve in the army or navy: —*adj.* (kon′skript), forced into military or naval service; as, a *conscript* army: —*n.* (kon′skript), a person so forced.— *n.* **con-scrip′tion.**

con-se-crate (kon′se-krāt′), *v.t.* [consecrat-ed, consecrat-ing], to set apart for a holy purpose; regard as sacred; as, to *consecrate* one's life to God.—*n.* **con′ se-cra′tion.**

con-sec-u-tive (kon-sek′ū-tiv), *adj.* following without a break; as, Monday and Tuesday are *consecutive* days.

con-sen-sus (kon-sen′sus), *n.* general agreement in opinion, testimony, or feeling; as, the *consensus* of the committee.

con-sent (kon-sent′), *n.* agreement; approval; compliance; as, by common *consent:*—*v.i.* to comply; yield; agree.

con-se-quence (kon′se-kwens′), *n.* **1,** outcome; result; as, to suffer the *consequences* of an action; **2,** importance; as, a person of no *consequence.*

con-se-quent (kon′se-kwent′), *adj.*

following as a result; as, the disorder *consequent* to the fire.—*adv.* **con′sequent-ly.**—*adj.* **con′se-quen′tial.**

con-ser-va-tion (kon′sẽr-vā′shun), *n.* the prevention of waste or loss, esp. of natural resources, as forests or water-power, or of game-birds, wild flowers, etc.

con-serv-a-tive (kon-sûr′va-tiv), *adj.* inclined to prefer existing institutions to new ones:—*n.* a conservative person.

con-serv-a-tor-y (kon-sûr′va-tẽr-i), *n.* [*pl.* conservatories], **1,** a greenhouse, esp. a private one; **2,** a college for special study, as of music.

con-serve (kon-sûrv′), *v.t.* [conserved, conserv-ing], **1,** to keep from waste or destruction; as, to *conserve* game; **2,** to preserve with sugar:—*n.* (kon-sûrv′; kon′sûrv), preserved or candied fruit: —**conserves,** preserves.—*n.* **con′serva′tor.**

con-sid-er (kon-sid′ẽr), *v.t.* **1,** to think over with care; as, to *consider* an offer; **2,** to esteem; **3,** to regard as; believe; as I *consider* him rude:—*v.i.* to reflect; as, to take time to *consider.*

con-sid-er-a-ble (kon-sid′ẽr-a-bl), *adj.* worthy of notice; important; not small; as, a *considerable* sum of money.

con-sid-er-a-bly (kon-sid′ẽr-a-bli), *adv.* much; greatly.

con-sid-er-ate (kon-sid′ẽr-it), *adj.* thoughtful of others; kindly.

con-sid-er-a-tion (kon-sid′ẽr-ā′shun), *n.* **1,** careful thought; as, to take a thing into *consideration;* **2,** something taken, or worth taking, into account; a reason or motive; **3,** thoughtful regard for others; **4,** payment or compensation for something.

con-sid-er-ing (kon-sid′ẽr-ing), *prep.* taking into account; allowing for; as, crops are good, *considering* the drought.

con-sign (kon-sīn′), *v.t.* **1,** to deliver formally; hand over; as, to *consign* a man to jail; **2,** to ship, as merchandise. —*n.* **con-sign′ment.**—*n.* **con′sign-ee′.**

con-sist (kon-sist′), *v.i.* to be composed or made up; as, a day *consists* of 24 hours.

con-sist-en-cy (kon-sis′ten-si), *n.* [*pl.* consistencies], **1,** degree of firmness or thickness; as, this liquid has the *consistency* of syrup; **2,** harmony; agreement, as of one's deeds with one's statements.—*n.* **con-sist′ence.**

con-sist-ent (kon-sis′tent), *adj.* **1,** fitting in; in agreement; as, his story is *consistent* with facts; **2,** continuing without change, or with adherence to the same principles; as, a *consistent* Tory.—*adv.* **con-sist′ent-ly.**

¹con-sole (kon-sōl′), *v.t.* [consoled, consoling], to comfort in sorrow.—*n.* **con′-so-la′tion.**—*adj.* **con-sol′a-tor′y.**—*adj.* **con-sol′a-ble.**

²con-sole (kon′sōl), *n.* **1,** the part of a pipe-organ at which the organist sits, containing the keyboard, stops, and pedals; **2,** a radio cabinet or a table designed to stand against a wall.

con-sol-i-date (kon-sol′i-dāt′), *v.t.* and *v.i.* [consolidat-ed, consolidat-ing], to unite; combine; as, to *consolidate* two offices.—*n.* **con-sol′i-da′tion.**

con-sols (kon-solz′; kon′solz), *n.pl.* the British funded government securities.

con-som-mé (kon′so-mā′), *n.* a strong clear soup made by boiling meat, vegetables, etc., in water.

con-so-nant (kon′so-nant), *n.* **1,** a sound made by closing or narrowing the mouth or throat; **2,** a symbol of such a sound, as *b, c, d:*—*adj.* **1,** like a consonant; as, a *consonant* sound; **2,** harmonious; consistent; agreeing; as, an act *consonant* with one's beliefs.—*adj.* **con′so-nan′tal.**

con-sort (kon′sôrt), *n.* **1,** a husband or wife; **2,** a ship accompanying another: —*v.i.* (kon-sôrt′), to associate; keep company.

con-spic-u-ous (kon-spik′ū-us), *adj.* **1,** plainly visible; as, a *conspicuous* tower; hence, striking; attracting attention; as, a *conspicuous* costume; **2,** distinguished; notable; as, the play was a *conspicuous* success.—*adv.* **con-spic′u-ous-ly.**

con-spire (kon-spīr′), *v.i.* [conspired, conspir-ing], **1,** to plan secretly together to do something unlawful; plot; **2,** to work with other factors toward a given result; as, events *conspired* to injure him.—*n.* **con-spir′a-cy**(kon-spir′a-si).— *n.* **con-spir′a-tor.**

con-sta-ble (kon′sta-bl; kun′sta-bl), *n.* a police officer.

con-stab-u-lar-y (kon-stab′ū-lėr-i), *n.* [*pl.* constabularies], an armed force organized for police duty.

con-stant (kon′stant), *adj.* **1,** standing firm in one's beliefs or affections; steadfast; faithful; as, a *constant* friend; **2,** regular in a habit; unchanging; as, *constant* in attendance.—*n.* **con′stan-cy.**—*adv.* **con′stant-ly.**

con-stel-la-tion (kon′ste-lā′shun), *n.* any group of fixed stars with a special name, as the Big Dipper.

con-ster-na-tion (kon′stėr-nā′shun), *n.* terrified astonishment; dismay.

con-sti-pa-tion (kon′sti-pā′shun), *n.* a condition in which the bowels do not

move freely enough.—*adj.* **con′sti-pat′ed.**—*v.* **con′sti-pate′.**

con-stit-u-en-cy (kon-stit′ū-en-si), *n.* [*pl.* constituencies], a body of voters which elects a representative, as to Parliament.

con-stit-u-ent (kon-stit′ū-ent), *adj.* necessary in the make-up of something; as, a *constituent* part:—*n.* **1,** a necessary part; as, flour is a *constituent* of cake; **2,** a voter in a given district; as, the member addressed his *constituents.*

con-sti-tute (kon′sti-tūt′), *v.t.* [constituted, constitut-ing], **1,** to make up or form; compose; as, twelve things *constitute* a dozen; **2,** to appoint; elect; as, he *constituted* himself judge of the contest.

con-sti-tu-tion (kon′sti-tū′shun), *n.* **1,** the way in which a thing is made up; as, the *constitution* of the earth; **2,** bodily strength; vitality; **3,** the fundamental law on which a state or society is organized; as, the national *constitution.*

con-sti-tu-tion-al (kon′sti-tū′shun-al), *adj.* **1,** inherent in one's make-up; as, a *constitutional* liability to colds; **2,** relating to the fundamental law of a state or society; as, a *constitutional* amendment; also, in harmony with such law:—*n. Colloq.,* a walk taken for health's sake.

con-sti-tu-tion-al-i-ty (kon′sti-tū′-shun-al′i-ti), *n.* agreement with the constitution, or fundamental law; as, the *constitutionality* of an act of Parliament.

con-strain (kon-strān′), *v.t.* **1,** to hold in check; restrain; as, the presence of the captain *constrained* the crew; **2,** to urge strongly; compel; as, to *constrain* a child to eat.—*n.* **con-straint′.**

con-strict (kon-strikt′), *v.t.* to bind; tighten; contract; draw together or make narrow at a single place; as, the blood hardly moved in the *constricted* vein.—*n.* **con-stric′tion; con-stric′tor.** —*adj.* **con-stric′tive.**

con-struct (kon-strukt′), *v.t.* **1,** to fit together; arrange; build, as a house; **2,** to plan; compose; as, to *construct* a play.

con-struc-tion (kon-struk′shun), **1,** a putting together; the act or method of building; as, fireproof *construction;* also, the thing built; **2,** understanding; as, to put a wrong *construction* on a letter; **3,** in *grammar,* the way in which words are related to one another in a sentence.

con-struc-tive (kon-struk′tiv), *adj.* tending to build up rather than to destroy; creative; as, *constructive* ideas.

con-strue (kon′strōō; kon-strōō′), *v.t.*
[construed, constru-ing], **1,** to interpret;
explain; as, his act was *construed* as a
favour; **2,** in *grammar*, to apply the
rules of syntax to (a sentence).

con-sul (kon′sul), *n.* **1,** an official commissioned by a government to promote
his country's trade in a foreign city,
and to protect its citizens; **2,** one of the
two joint chief officials of the Roman
Republic.—*adj.* **con′su-lar.**—*n.* **con′su-
late.**

con-sult (kon-sult′), *v.t.* **1,** to ask
advice of; **2,** to have regard to; as, he
consulted my welfare:—*v.i.* to take
counsel together; confer.—*n.* **con′sul-
ta′tion.**—*n.* **con-sult′ant.**

con-sume (kon-sūm′), *v.t.* [consumed,
consum-ing], **1,** to destroy, as by fire;
2, to eat or drink up; use up; waste,
as time.

con-sum-er (kon-sūm′ẽr), *n.* a person
or thing that consumes anything; esp.
a person who buys goods to be used by
himself.

con-sum-mate (kon′su-māt′), *v.t.*
[consummat-ed, consummat-ing], to
complete; finish:—*adj.* (kon-sum′it),
perfect; carried to the highest degree;
as, a man of *consummate* skill.—*n.* **con′-
sum-ma′tion.**

con-sump-tion (kon-sump′shun), *n.*
1, a using up, as of food or other
materials; also, the amount used up;
2, tuberculosis of the lungs.

con-sump-tive (kon-sump′tiv), *adj.* **1,**
wasteful; **2,** ill with tuberculosis of the
lungs:—*n.* a person who has consumption.

con-tact (kon′takt), *n.* **1,** a touch;
touching; as, the *contact* of cold metal;
2, a meeting for conversation or consultation; also, acquaintance which
makes such a meeting possible; as, he
makes advantageous *contacts*:—*v.i.* to
touch together.—*v.t.* to get in touch
with (avoided by careful speakers and
writers).

contact lens, a thin glass or plastic
lens fitted to the eyeball, with its edges
under the eyelid.

con-ta-gious (kon-tā′jus), *adj.* **1,**
spreading easily from person to person;
as, a *contagious* disease; **2,** exciting a
similar action or feeling in others; as,
contagious laughter.—*n.* **con-ta′gion.**

con-tain (kon-tān′), *v.t.* **1,** to hold; as,
the box *contained* candy; the bucket
contained water; **2,** to include; as, the
book *contains* a good story; **3,** to be
equal to; as, a quart *contains* two pints;
4, to hold in check; as, to *contain* one's
anger; **5,** to be a multiple of; as, ten
contains five.

con-tain-er (kon-tān′ẽr), *n.* a receptacle in which goods are kept or shipped.

con-tam-i-nate (kon-tam′i-nāt′), *v.t.*
[contaminat-ed, contaminat-ing], to
pollute; make impure.—*n.* **con-tam′i-
na′tion.**

con-tem-plate (kon′tem-plāt′), *v.t.*
[contemplat-ed, contemplat-ing], **1,** to
look at or to think about with attention; meditate on; **2,** to intend; ˈpur-
pose; expect:—*v.i.* to meditate; reflect.
—*n.* **con′-tem-pla′tion.**—*adj.* **con′tem-
pla-tive.**

con-tem-po-rar-y (kon-tem′po-rẽr-i-i),
adj. existing or occurring at the same
time:—*n.* [*pl.* contemporaries], one who
lives at the same time as another; as,
Macdonald and Laurier were *contem-
poraries*.

con-tempt (kon-tempt′), *n.* **1,** scorn,
as of vile or mean acts; disdain; **2,** the
state of being despised; disgrace; **3,**
disregard of lawful orders; as, *contempt*
of court.—*adj.* **con-tempt′i-ble.**

con-temp-tu-ous (kon-temp′tū-us),
adj. disdainful; scornful; as, a *contemptuous* smile.—*adv.* **con-temp′tu-ous-ly.**

con-tend (kon-tend′), *v.i.* **1,** to strive
against opponents, as for a prize; **2,** to
dispute; debate.—*n.* **con-tend′er.**

¹con-tent (kon′tent; sometimes kon-
tent′), *n.* **1,** the subject matter or
thought, as of a magazine article; **2,**
(usually *contents*), all that is contained,
as in a vessel or book; also, the capacity, as of a measure.

²con-tent (kon-tent′), *adj.* **1,** satisfied
with one's lot; **2,** willing; as, I am
content to go:—*v.t.* to satisfy; as, he is
easily *contented*:—*n.* ease of mind.—*n.*
con-tent′ment.—*adj.* **con-tent′ed.**

con-ten-tion (kon-ten′shun), *n.* **1,** a
striving or struggling; dispute; quarrel; **2,** a point for which one argues; as,
my *contention* is that the price is too
high.

con-ten-tious (kon-ten′shus), *adj.* inclined to argue about trifles; quarrelsome.—*n.* **con-ten′tious-ness.**

con-test (kon-test′), *v.t.* to strive to
win or hold, as a battlefield; **2,** to dispute; call in question; as, to *contest* an
election:—*n.* (kon′test), a struggle for
victory, as a game, fight, lawsuit, etc.—
n. **con-test′ant.**

con-text (kon′tekst), *n.* the words just
before and after a particular word,
expression, or passage that determine
its exact meaning; as, please do not
quote me *out of context*.

con-tig-u-ous (kon-tig′ū-us), *adj.*
touching; adjoining; also, near; as, a
field *contiguous* to the village.—*adv.*
con-tig′u-ous-ly.—*n.* **con′ti-gu′i-ty.**

cat, āge, fär, câre, ȧsk; ten, ēve, latẽr; (i) pity, rely, senate; īce; top; nō.

con-tin-ence (kon′tin-ens), *n.* self-restraint; moderation; esp., abstinence from sexual intercourse.

con-ti-nent (kon′ti-nent), *n.* one of the large divisions of land on the earth; as, the *continent* of North America:—**the Continent,** the mainland of Europe as distinguished from the British Isles.—*adj.* temperate; not indulging the sexual appetites; esp., sexually chaste.

con-ti-nen-tal (kon′ti-nen′tal), *adj.* relating to a continent:—**Continental, 1,** relating to the mainland of Europe; **2,** in American history, having to do with the colonies at the time of the Revolution; as, the *Continental* Congress:—*n.* **1,** an American soldier during the Revolution; **2,** an inhabitant of the mainland of Europe:—**continental shelf,** the relatively shallow slope of a continent beneath the sea before the steep descent to the ocean floor begins.

con-tin-gen-cy (kon-tin′-jen-si), *n.* [*pl.* contingencies], possibility; also, an event which may or may not happen; as, ready for any *contingency.*

con-tin-gent (kon-tin′jent), *adj.* **1,** possible, but uncertain; also, accidental; **2,** depending on something else, or on chance; as, her coming is *contingent* on the weather:—*n.* any unit or group in a gathering of representative units; as, the Alberta *contingent* at the convention.

con-tin-u-al (kon-tin′ū-al), *adj.* **1,** occurring again and again; **2,** going on without a break; ceaseless.—*adv.* **con-tin′u-al-ly.**

con-tin-ue (kon-tin′ū), *v.t.* [continued, continuing], **1,** to keep on doing, without a break; as, he *continued* to sing; also, to persevere in; **2,** to take up again after a break, as a story; **3,** to keep in office; **4,** to postpone, as a law case:—*v.i.* **1,** to remain in a place or condition; stay; as, to *continue* sad; **2,** to last; persist.—*n.* **con-tin′u-ance.**—*n.* **con-tin′u-a′tion.**

con-ti-nu-i-ty (kon′ti-nū′i-ti), *n.* [*pl.* continuities], **1,** unbroken succession; connectedness; **2,** a motion-picture scenario; **3,** remarks by a radio announcer, connecting the items on a programme.

con-tin-u-ous (kon-tin′ū-us), *adj.* connected; unbroken.—*adv.* **con-tin′u-ous-ly.**

con-tort (kon-tôrt′), *v.t.* to bend or twist violently out of shape; distort.—*n.* **con-tor′tion.**—*n.* **con-tor′tion-ist.**

con-tour (kon′toor; kon-tōōr′), *n.* an outline, as of a body, or of a coast, mountain, or the like; also, an outline drawing:—**contour map,** a map with lines joining points of the same elevation above sea level (for example, fifty-foot differences in altitude).

con-tra-band (kon′tra-band′), *n.* **1,** anything forbidden to be brought into or out of a country, as in time of war; also, traffic in such goods; smuggling; **2,** smuggled goods:—*adj.* prohibited; forbidden.

con-tra-cep-tive (kon′tra-sep′tiv), *adj.* and *n.* a device or agent for the artificial prevention of conception.

con-tra-clock-wise (kon′tra-klok′-wīz′), *adj.* opposite to the direction in which the hands of a clock move.

con-tract (kon-trakt′), *v.t.* **1,** to draw closer together; condense; shorten and thicken, as a muscle; to wrinkle; as, to *contract* the brows; **2,** to enter into (a friendship); incur (a debt, disease, habit, etc.); **3,** (often kon′trakt), to enter upon by agreement, as an alliance or a marriage; **4,** in *grammar,* to shorten; as, to *contract* "over" to "o'er":—*v.i.* **1,** to shrink; **2,** (often kon′trakt), to make an agreement; as, to *contract* for the removal of snow:—*n.* (kon′trakt), **1,** a legal agreement; also, a written record of such an agreement; **2,** in cards, an undertaking to win a given number of tricks.—*n.* **con-trac′tion.**

contract bridge, a form of auction bridge in which the declarer counts points towards game only by taking all of the tricks he has bidden or contracted for.

con-trac-tor (kon-trak′tėr; kon′traktėr), *n.* **1,** one of the parties to a written agreement; **2,** one who undertakes to supply or construct something for a certain sum.

con-tra-dict (kon′tra-dikt′), *v.t.* **1,** to assert the opposite of (a statement); **2,** to deny the words of (a person).—*n.* **con′tra-dic′tion.**—*adj.* **con′tra-dic′to-ry.**

con-tral-to (kon-tral′tō), *n.* [*pl.* contraltos], **1,** the lowest female voice or part; **2,** a person with such a voice.

con-trap-tion (kon-trap′shun), *n.* *Colloq.,* a gadget; makeshift; device.

con-tra-ry (kon′trėr-i), *adj.* **1,** opposed; contradictory; conflicting; as, *contrary* opinions; **2,** opposite in direction; adverse; as, a *contrary* wind; **3,** (often kon-trâr′i), perverse; wayward:—*n.* [*pl.* contraries], the opposite; as, if he says one thing, I believe the *contrary.*—*adv.* **con′tra-ri-wise′** (conversely).

con-trast (kon-trȧst′), *v.t.* to place or state in such a way as to show differences; compare so as to show unlikeness:—*v.i.* to be very different, as shown by comparison; as, the white rose *contrasts* with her black dress:—*n.* (kon'tràst), **1**, striking difference; opposition; **2**, the thing or quality showing such difference.

con-tra-vene (kon'tra-vēn'), *v.t.* to go contrary to; disobey; infringe; as, do not *contravene* the traffic laws.—*n.* **con'tra-ven'tion.**

con-trib-ute (kon-trib'ūt), *v.t.* [contribut-ed, contribut-ing], to give, as to some fund or purpose, along with others; furnish as a share:—*v.i.* **1**, to help; assist; aid in the accomplishment of a purpose; as, every player *contributed* to the victory; **2**, to be of use; as, play *contributes* to health.—*n.* **con'tri-bu'tion.**—*n.* **con-trib'u-tor.**—*adj.* **con-trib'u-to'ry.**

con-trite (kon'trīt; kon-trīt'), *adj.* humble; repentant.—*n.* **con-tri'tion** (kon-trish'un).

con-trive (kon-trīv'), *v.t.* [contrived, contriv-ing], **1**, to devise cleverly; invent; plan; **2**, to achieve by clever management; as, to *contrive* an escape. —*n.* **con-triv'ance.**

con-trol (kon-trōl'), *n.* **1**, a check; restraint; **2**, effective authority; as, a teacher's *control* over a class; **3**, the apparatus regulating the operation of a machine:—*v.t.* [controlled, control-ling] **1**, to restrain; hold in check; as, to *control* one's anger; **2**, to govern.

con-trol-ler (kon-trōl'ẽr), *n.* a public official who examines accounts.

con-tro-ver-sy (kon'trō-vûr'si), *n.* [*pl.* controversies], a dispute; an argument.—*adj.* **con'tro-ver'sial.**

con-tro-vert (kon'trō-vûrt'; kon'trō-vûrt'), *v.t.* to dispute; contradict; oppose; as, he *controverts* your claim to the mine.—*adj.* **con'tro-vert'i-ble.**

con-tu-sion (kon-tū'zhun), *n.* a bruise.

co-nun-drum (ko-nun'drum), *n.* a riddle.

con-va-les-cent (kon'va-les'ent), *adj.* **1**, getting well; as, a *convalescent* patient; **2**, having to do with recovery from an illness; as, a *convalescent* home:—*n.* one who is getting well.—*n.* **con'va-les'cence.**—*v.i.* **con'va-lesce'.**

con-vec-tion (kon-vek'shun), *n.* the conveying of heat or electricity by the movement of heated or electrified gases or liquids.

con-vene (kon-vēn'), *v.i.* and *v.t.* [convened, conven-ing], to come or call together; assemble.—**con-ven'er.**

con-ven-ience (kon-vēn'yens), *n.* **1**, suitability; fitness of place or time; **2**, ease in use or action; a saving of trouble; advantage; as, the *convenience* of a car; **3**, a handy device; **4**,

conveniences, things that add to personal comfort, make work easier, or the like.—*adj.* **con-ven'ient.**—*adv.* **con-ven'ient-ly.**

con-vent (kon'vent), *n.* a society, usually of women, living together and devoted to a religious life; also, the building occupied by such a society; a nunnery.

con-ven-ti-cle (kon-ven'ti-kl), *n.* a meeting (or place) for (or of) religious worship, esp. a secret or nonconformist one.

con-ven-tion (kon-ven'shun), *n.* **1**, a formal meeting; an assembly of delegates; as, a political *convention;* **2**, a diplomatic agreement; **3**, a fixed custom or usage.

con-ven-tion-al (kon-ven'shun-al), *adj.* **1**, in harmony with established customs; customary; as, *conventional* evening clothes; **2**, regular; lacking in original thought.—*n.* **con-ven'tion-al'i-ty.**

con-verge (kon-vûrj'), *v.i.* [converged, converg-ing], to tend to come together, as crowds at a place of interest; to approach each other; as spokes of a wheel, or lines drawn toward a common point.—*adj.* **con-ver'gent.**—*n.* **con-ver'gence.**

CONVERGENT LINES
The two lines converge toward the point A.

con-ver-sant (kon'vẽr-sant), *adj.* familiar; as, to be *conversant* with music.

con-ver-sa-tion (kon'vẽr-sā'shun), *n.* informal or familiar talk of persons with one another.—*adj.* **con'ver-sa'tion-al.**

¹con-verse (kon-vûrs'), *v.i.* [conversed, convers-ing], to chat with a person:—*n.* (kon'vûrs), familiar talk; conversation.

²con-verse (kon'vûrs), *adj.* opposite:— *n.* the opposite of something else; as, "hot" is the *converse* of "cold."—*adv.* **con'verse-ly** (kon'vûrs-li; kon-vûrs'li).

con-vert (kon-vûrt'), *v.t.* **1**, to transform or change, as in form, substance, etc.; **2**, to bring (a person) to belief in a religion, course, opinion, etc.; **3**, to exchange for something else, as land for money:—*n.* (kon'vûrt), one who becomes a believer in something, as a religion or a political party; as, a *convert* to Christianity; **2**, in *football*, the kicking of a field goal after a touchdown to score an extra point.—*n.* **con-ver'sion.**

con-ver-ti-ble (kon-vûr'ti-bl), *adj.* capable of being changed or transformed.—*n.* a motorcar with a folding top.

cat, āge, fär, cáre, àsk; ten, ēve, latẽr; (i) pity, rely, senate; īce; top; nō.

convex 129 **coot**

con-vex (kon′veks; kon-veks′), *adj.* curved out like the outside of a circle or ball; bulging; as, a *convex* mirror: opposite of *concave.—n.* **con-vex′i-ty.** The outside of the bowl is convex.

con-vey (kon-vā′), *v.t.* **1,** to carry; transport; as, the train *conveyed* the children to the mountains; **2,** to transmit; be a means of carrying; as, pipes *convey* gas; **3,** to transfer (property) from one person to another. *—n.* **con-vey′er; con-vey′or.**

con-vey-ance (kon-vā′ans), *n.* **1,** the act of carrying from one place or person to another; **2,** anything used for carrying; esp., a vehicle; **3,** a written title or deed to property.

con-vict (kon-vikt′), *v.t.* to prove or find guilty of a crime or offence:—*n.* (kon′vikt), **1,** a person found guilty of a crime; **2,** a person serving a term in prison.

con-vic-tion (kon-vik′shun), *n.* **1,** the finding that someone is guilty of a crime or offence; also, the state of being found guilty; **2,** a firm or settled belief.

con-vince (kon-vins′), *v.t.* [convinced, convinc-ing], to cause (a person) to see or feel the truth of something.—*adj.* **con-vinc′ing.**—*adv.* **con-vinc′ing-ly.**

con-viv-i-al (kon-viv′i-al), *adj.* **1,** fond of feasting, drinking, merriment, etc.; **2,** gay; jovial.

con-voke (kon-vōk′), *v.t.* [convoked, convok-ing], to call together for a meeting; as, Parliament was *convoked* in June.—*n.* **con′vo-ca′tion.**

con-vo-lu-tion (kon′vō-lū′shun; -lōō′), *n.* a coiling, winding, or folding together, as the ridges on the surface of the brain.

con-vol-vu-lus (kon-vol′vū-lus), *n.* a genus of twining plants with trumpet-shaped flowers, like the *bindweed* and *morning-glory.*

con-voy (kon-voi′), *v.t.* to accompany on the way, so as to guide or protect; to escort; as, the cruiser *convoyed* our ship into port:—*n.* (kon′voi), **1,** a protecting force accompanying ships, goods persons, etc.; an escort; **2,** the goods, ships, persons, etc., so escorted.

con-vulse (kon-vuls′), *v.t.* [convulsed, convuls-ing], **1,** to agitate or disturb violently; shake; **2,** to affect with spasms, as of laughter or anger.—*n.* **con-vul′sion.**—*adj.* **con-vul′sive.**

co-ny, co-ney (kō′ni), *n.* a rabbit's fur, esp. when dyed to imitate Hudson seal.

coo (kōō), *n.* a murmuring sound like that of pigeons:—*v.i.* to utter such a sound.

cook (kook), *v.t.* **1,** to prepare (food) by applying heat, as in boiling, baking, frying, etc.; **2,** to invent falsely; as, to *cook* up an excuse:—*v.i.* to undergo cooking:—*n.* one who prepares food for the table.—*n.* **cook′er.**—*n.* **cook′er-y.**

cook-ie or **cook-y** (kook′i), *n.* [*pl.* cookies], a small, flat, sweet cake.

cool (kōōl), *adj.* **1,** slightly or moderately cold; **2,** not admitting or retaining heat; as, *cool* clothes; **3,** calm; self-possessed; as, he was the only *cool* one in the mob; **4,** lacking in cordiality; as, a *cool* response:—*v.t.* **1,** to make slightly cold; chill; **2,** to calm; quiet; as, his tears *cooled* my anger:—*v.i.* to become slightly cold:—*n.* a state or time of moderate cold; as, the *cool* of the evening.—*adj.* **cool′ish.**—*adj.* **cool′-head′ed.**—*adv.* **cool′ly.**

coo-lie (kōō′li), *n.* [*pl.* -lies (liz)], an unskilled native labourer of (or from) the Orient, esp. China or India.

coon (kōōn), *n.* a raccoon.

coop (kōōp), *n.* a cage or enclosure for fowls, rabbits, etc.; a pen:—*v.t.* to confine in a cage or pen.

coop-er (kōōp′ẽr), *n.* a maker or mender of barrels, casks, etc.—*n.* **coop′er-age.**

co—op-er-ate, co-öp-er-ate (kō–op′ẽr-āt′), *v.i.* [co-operat-ed, co-operat-ing], to act or work for a common end; work together; as, everyone *co-operated* in making the play a success.—*n.* **co—op′er-a′tion.**

co—op-er-a-tive, co-öp-er-a-tive (kō–op′ẽr-a-tiv; -ā′tiv), *adj.* **1,** working together for common ends; **2,** having to do with an organized group of people who work together for common ends and share their profits and losses; as, a *co-operative* shop for students.—*n.* **co—op, co-öp,** *Colloq.,* short form for **co—operative shop or store.**

co—opt, co-öpt (kō′-opt), *v.t.* to add or elect by combined action one or more persons to a committee, board, etc.

co—or-di-nate, co-ör-di-nate (kō–ôr′di-nāt′), *v.t.* [co-ordinat-ed, co-ordinat-ing], **1,** to place in the same order or class; to make equal in rank or importance; **2,** to put in harmony; adjust; as, to *co-ordinate* movements in swimming:—*v.i.* to harmonize:—*adj.* (kō-ôr′di-nit; nāt′), **1,** of the same rank or order, as the clauses of a compound sentence; **2,** pertaining to things of the same rank:—*n.* (kō-ôr′di-nit; nāt′), a person or thing of the same rank, order, or importance as another; an equal.—*n.* **co—or′di-na′-tion.**

coot (kōōt), *n.* **1,** a swimming and

all (ôl), ôr; up, mūte, cûr, cōōl, book; oil, out; th, thin; ɪh, the.

diving bird somewhat like a duck; **2,** a scoter.

coo-tie (kōō′ti), *n. Slang,* a louse.

cop (kop), *n. Slang,* a policeman (constable on *patrol*).—*v.t. Slang,* to steal; seize.

cope (kōp), *v.i.* [coped, cop-ing], to struggle successfully; as, he is able to *cope* with difficulties.

cop-ing (kōp′ing), *n.* the top layer of a wall, often of brick or stone, usually sloping so as to shed water.

COPING (C)

co-pi-lot (kō′pī′lot), *n.* an assistant pilot in an aircraft.

co-pi-ous (kō′pi-us), *adj.* plenteous; ample; abundant; as, a *copious* supply of pencils.—*adv.* **co′pious-ly.**

cop-per (kop′ẽr), *n.* **1,** a common reddish metal, easily worked, and an excellent conductor of heat and electricity; **2,** something made of this metal; **3,** a coin, usually made of copper but sometimes of bronze; a cent:—*adj.* of or like copper.—*adj.* **cop′per-y.**

cop-per-head (kop′ẽr-hed′), *n.* a poisonous snake, related to the rattlesnake, with brownish or reddish colouring, found in the eastern part of the U.S.

cop-pice (kop′is), *n.* a thicket of small trees or bushes; a copse.

copse (kops), *n.* a grove or thicket of small trees or bushes; a coppice.

cop-u-la (kop′ū-la), *n.* and *adj.* a verb (*to be, seem, taste,* etc.) which joins the subject of a sentence to the predicate; as, he *is* king; it *smells* sour (*copula* verbs).

cop-u-late (kop′ū-lāt′), *v.i.* to unite in sexual intercourse.—*n.* **cop′u-la′-tion.**

cop-y (kop′i), *n.* [*pl.* copies], **1,** an imitation; a reproduction; as, a *copy* of a portrait or of a will; **2,** an exercise written in imitation of a model; also, the model; **3,** something, as typewritten matter, to be set up in type; **4,** a single one of a number of reproductions, as of a book or magazine, etc.:—*v.t.* [copied, copy-ing], **1,** to make a likeness of; reproduce; as, to *copy* a report; **2,** to imitate.—*n.* **cop′y-ist.**

cop-y-right (kop′i-rīt′), *n.* the exclusive legal right of an artist or author, or his agent, to reproduce, publish, etc., a literary or artistic work for a certain time:—*adj.* protected by copyright:—*v.t.* to secure a copyright for; as, to *copyright* a book.

co-quet (kō-ket′), *v.i.* [coquet-ted coquet-ting], to flirt; trifle or dally with love, with danger, or the like.—*n.* **co′quet-ry.**

co-quette (kō-ket′), *n.* a woman who trifles with love; a flirt.—*adj.* **co-quet′tish.**—*adv.* **co-quet′tish-ly.**

cor-a-cle (kôr′a-kl), *n.* a short, broad basketlike (Welsh) boat.

cor-al (kor′al), *n.* **1,** a hard substance like limestone, varied and often brilliant in colour, built up of countless skeletons of certain animals which grow in shallow tropical seas, and often appearing at or above the surface as reefs or islands; **2,** one of the tiny animals that produce coral; **3,** the colour of orange red:—*adj.* **1,** made of coral; **2,** red in colour, as coral.

cor-bie, cor-by (kôr′bi), *n.* a raven or crow.

cord (kôrd), *n.* **1,** a string or small rope **2, cords,** any binding force; as, the *cords* of friendship; **3,** a measure of firewood, usually the amount in a pile eight feet by four feet by four feet, or 128 cubic feet; **4,** any ropelike structure, as a tendon or nerve:—*v.t.* **1,** to bind with string or rope; **2,** to stack (wood) in cords.—*n.* **cord′age; cord′ing; cord′wood′.**

cor-dial (kôr′jal; kôrd′yal), *adj.* **1,** tending to revive, as a medicine; **2,** hearty; sincere; as, a *cordial* manner —*n.* a medicine, food, or drink that revives or stimulates.—*n.* **cor-dial′i-ty.**

cor-dil-le-ra (kôr′dĕl-yâ′ra; kôr-dil′ẽr-a), *n.* a mountain chain, esp. the chief mountain axis of a continent; as the Rocky Mountains, etc.

cor-don (kôr′don), *n.* a line or circle of men, ships, etc., to guard a person or place; as, a *cordon* of police.

cor-du-roy (kôr′dū-roi′; kôr′dū-roi′) *n.* **1,** a stout ribbed or corded cotton cloth with a velvety surface; **2, corduroys,** trousers, or a suit, made of corduroy:—*adj.* **1,** of or like corduroy **2,** in Canada, made of logs laid crosswise, as a road.

core (kōr), *n.* **1,** the heart or innermost part of anything, esp. of certain fruits such as apples; **2,** the substance or essential point, as of an argument or speech; **3,** a bar of soft iron forming the centre of an electromagnet:—*v.t.* [cored, cor-ing], to remove the core from as an apple.—*n.* **cor′er.**

cor-gi (kôr′gi), *n.* a Welsh breed of dog resembling a dachshund, but with erect ears (two varieties: Cardigan and Pembroke).

co-re-op-sis (kō′ri-op′sis; ko′), *n.* a

garden plant cultivated for its bright, showy, yellow– or crimson–rayed flowers.

co-re-spond-ent (kō'ri-spon'dent), *n.* in a divorce suit, a defendant jointly charged with a husband or wife as guilty of adultery.

cork (kôrk), *n.* **1,** the light, elastic, outer layer of bark of a certain oak, used for floats, life-preservers, stoppers for bottles, etc.; **2,** a stopper for a bottle or cask; esp. one made of cork:—*v.t.* **1.** to stop with a cork, as a bottle; **2,** to restrain; as, to *cork* up one's anger:—*adj.* made of cork.

cork-screw (kôrk'skrōō'), *n.* a spiral wire or a screw, fastened to a handle, used for drawing corks from bottles:—*adj.* shaped like a corkscrew; as, a *corkscrew* path:—*v.i.* and *v.t. Colloq.*, to follow, or cause to follow, a winding course.

corm (kôrm), *n.* a short, fleshy or bulblike, underground stem as of the *crocus* or *gladiolus.*

cor-mo-rant (kôr'mo-rant), *n.* **1,** a large, greedy sea-bird that feeds on fish; **2,** a person who is greedy or covetous.

¹corn (kôrn), *n.* **1,** a grain or seed, esp. of a cereal plant; also, such a plant; **2,** any kind of cereal grain, as wheat, barley, etc.; in England, wheat; in Scotland and Ireland, oats; in North America, Indian corn, or maize.—*adj.* **corn'fed'.**—*n.* **corn'field'; corn'stalk'.**

²corn (kôrn), *n.* a horny thickening of the skin, esp. on the toe or foot.

corn–bor-er (kôrn'–bōr'ėr), *n.* a moth larva (from Europe in 1917) that feeds on plants, esp. the ear, cob, and stalk of corn.

corn-cob (kôrn'kob'), *n.* **1,** the woody centre of an ear of Indian corn, on which the grains are set; **2,** a tobacco-pipe made of a corncob.

cor-ne-a (kôr'ni-a), *n.* the front, transparent part of the outer coat of the eyeball, which covers the iris and pupil and admits light to the interior.

corned (kôrnd), *adj.* preserved in brine or salt; as, *corned* beef.

cor-ner (kôr'nėr), *n.* **1,** an angle; the point where two lines, sides, or edges meet; as, the *corners* of a desk; also, the area near this angle; as, a *corner* of the attic; **2,** the intersection of two or more streets; **3,** a nook; a secluded place; **4,** a remote point; as, the *corners* of the earth; **5,** an awkward situation; as, your question put me in a *corner;* **6,** a monopolizing of the supply of something in order to raise the price:

—*v.t.* **1,** to drive into a corner; **2,** to force into a situation having no escape; as, to *corner* a burglar:—*adj.* **1,** located at a corner; as, a *corner* store; **2,** usable in a corner; as, a *corner* cupboard.

cor-ner-stone (kôr'nėr-stōn'), *n.* **1,** a stone at an angle of a building, esp. one laid at the formal ceremony preceding erection; **2,** anything of fundamental importance; as, faith is a *cornerstone* of most religions.

cor-net (kôr'nit; kôr-net'), *n.* a brass wind-instrument somewhat similar to a trumpet.—*n.* **cor'net-ist; cor-net'-tist.**

cor-nice (kôr'nis), *n.* **1,** an ornamental moulding on a wall near the ceiling; **2,** a horizontal projecting piece forming the top of a wall or column.

CORNICE (C)

corn-starch (kôrn'-stärch'), *n.* a white, floury starch made from Indian corn, used in puddings and as a thickening for foods.

cor-nu-co-pi-a (kôr'nū-kō'pi-a), *n.* [*pl.* cornucopias], **1,** a horn full of fruit and flowers, symbolizing prosperity; **2,** hence, plenty; abundance; **3,** a cone-shaped paper holder for nuts and candy.

corn-y (kôr'ni), *adj. Slang,* stale; as, a *corny* joke.

co-rol-la (ko-rol'a), *n.* the inner envelope of a flower usually brightly coloured, and made up of the petals.

cor-ol-la-ry (ko-rol'a-ri; *U.S.* kôr'a-ler'i; kor'), *n.* **1,** an obvious inference or deduction; a result; **2,** in *geometry,* a proposition deduced from a proof already established.

COROLLA (C)

co-ro-na (ko-rō'na), *n.* **1,** the dazzling halo of burning gases surrounding the sun, seen only during an eclipse; **2,** a crown; garland.

cor-o-na-ry (kôr'o-nėr-i; -nėr'i), *adj.* relating to a crown or to the *coronary* artery of the heart.—*n. Colloq.*, a heart attack; as, he has had a *coronary* (thrombosis).

cor-o-na-tion (kor'o-nā'shun), *n.* the act or ceremony of crowning a king or queen.

cor-o-ner (kor'o-nėr), *n.* an officer whose chief duty is to find out the cause of any violent or mysterious death.

cor-o-net (kôr′o-net′; kor′o-nit), *n.* a small crown worn to show a high rank below that of a king, as of a duke or earl; **2,** an ornamental band or wreath worn around the head. CORONET

¹**cor-po-ral** (kôr′po-ral), *n.* the lowest non-commissioned officer in the army, next below a sergeant, and usually in command of a squad of eight men.

²**cor-po-ral** (kôr′po-ral), *adj.* having to do with the body; as, *corporal* punishment.

cor-po-ra-tion (kôr′po-rā′shun), *n.* a group of persons permitted by law to act as one person in carrying on a given kind of business, work, or the like.— *adj.* **cor′po-rate** (-rit).

cor-po-re-al (kor-pō′ri-al), *adj.* having a material body; tangible; physical; not mental or spiritual; as, man's *corporeal* frame.

corps (kōr), *n.* [*pl.* corps (kôrz)], **1,** a large unit of an army, containing two or more military divisions; **2,** a body of troops for special service; as, the signal *corps;* **3,** a body of persons associated in a common work; as, a *corps* of writers.

corpse (kôrps), *n.* a dead body, usually a human body.

cor-pu-lent (kôr′pū-lent), *adj.* fat; having a large, fleshy body.—*n.* **cor′pu-lence.**

cor-pus-cle (kôr′pus-l), *n.* **1,** a minute particle of matter; **2,** an electron; **3,** one of the small cells of the blood.

cor-ral (ko-ral′; ko-räl′), *n.* **1,** a pen or enclosure for horses, cattle, or the like; **2,** an enclosure or circle of wagons formed to protect an encampment:— *v.t.* (ko-ral′), [corralled, corral-ling], to drive into, or secure in, a pen or enclosure.

cor-rect (ko-rekt′), *v.t.* **1,** to set straight; make right; remove errors from; mark errors in (something written or printed) for removal; as, to *correct* compositions; **2,** to cure; as, to *correct* a bad habit; **3,** to reprove; as, the teacher *corrected* the student:—*adj.* **1,** exact; accurate; free from error; **2,** measuring up to a standard of morals, taste, manners, etc.; as, *correct* be-haviour.—*n.* **cor-rec′tion.**—*n.* and *adj.* **cor-rec′tive.**

cor-re-late (kôr′e-lāt′; kor), *v.t.* to connect by mutual relation; as, to *cor-relate* English and history in the school program.

cor-rel-a-tive (ko-rel′a-tiv), *adj.* de-pending upon or naturally related to something else; as, the size and weight of a stone are *correlative* qualities; in *grammar,* so related that one implies the other; as, *either* and *or* are *correla-tive* conjunctions.—*n.* one of two related terms; as *both, and; not only, but also; whether, or;* etc.—*n.* **cor′re-la′tion.**

cor-re-spond (kor′i-spond′), *v.i.* **1,** to be similar or equal in use, position, character, or amount; as, the U.S. Congress *corresponds* to the British Parliament; **2,** to agree; suit; match; harmonize; as, her actions do not *correspond* to our standards; **3,** to com-municate by letter.—*n.* **cor′re-spond′-ence.**—*n.* **cor′re-spond′ent.**

cor-ri-dor (kor′i-dôr; kor′i-dėr), *n.* a long passage into which rooms open.

cor-rob-o-rate (ko-rob′ō-rāt′), *v.t.* [corroborat-ed, corroborat-ing], to con-firm; make more certain; as, this evidence *corroborates* my opinion.—*n.* **cor-rob′o-ra′-tion.**—*adj.* **cor-rob′o-ra′-tive.**—*adj.* **cor-rob′o-ra-tor′y.**

cor-rode (ko-rōd′), *v.t.* and *v.i.* [corrod-ed, corrod-ing], to eat away or decay gradually, as by chemical action; dis-integrate; rust:—*n.* **cor′ro′sion.**—*adj* **cor-ro′sive.**

cor-ru-gate (kôr′oo-gāt′; kor′ū-gāt′) *v.t.* [corrugat-ed, corrugat-ing], to shape in wrinkles or alternate ridges and grooves, as *corrugated* iron or paper:— *v.i.* to contract into wrinkles or folds.— *adj.* **cor′ru-gat′ed.**

cor-rupt (ko-rupt′), *v.t.* **1,** to injure spoil; **2,** to make impure; debase; as, bad associations *corrupted* his morals **3,** to bribe; as, to *corrupt* a witness:— *adj.* spoiled; depraved; dishonest; as, *corrupt* practices; full of errors; as, he spoke corrupt English.—*adv.* **cor-rupt′-ly.**—*n.* **cor-rup′tion.**—*adj.* **cor-rup′tive** —*adj.* **cor-rupt′i-ble.**

cor-sage (kôr′sàzh′), *n.* **1,** a bouquet of flowers for a woman to wear; **2,** the bodice of a woman's dress.

cor-sair (kôr′sâr), *n.* **1,** formerly, a Turkish or Saracen privateer who attacked the ships and coasts of Christian nations; **2,** a corsair's ship **3,** a pirate.

corse-let, cors-let (kôrs′lit), *n.* **1,** formerly, armour for the body; breast plate; **2,** a woman's bra, girdle or corset and garters combined in one garment usually opening with a zipper at the side.

cor-set (kôr′sit), *n.* a woman's tight-fitting undergarment, worn to support the figure, or to modify its shape; stays

cor-tege (kôr-tezh′; -täzh′), *n.* a pro-cession; retinue; as a funeral *cortege*

cor-tex (kôr′teks), *n.* [*pl.* cortices

(kôr'ti-sēz)], **1,** a plant tissue lying below the epidermis, often storing starch; **2,** the outer layers of an organ, as of the brain.—*adj.* **cor'ti-cal.**

cor-ti-sone (kôr'ti-zōn'; -sōn'), *n.* a hormone obtained from ox bile or certain plants; used esp. for arthritis, etc.

cor-vette (kôr-vet'), *n.* a small, fast, naval-escort warship.

cos-met-ic (koz-met'ik), *n.* a preparation, as facial cream, powder, or the like, used to beautify the skin or hair: —*adj.* designed to beautify the complexion.

cos-mic (koz'mik), *adj.* **1,** relating to the universe and its laws; as, *cosmic* dust or *cosmic* rays; **2,** vast (as to time or space).

cos-mo-pol-i-tan (koz'mo-pol'i-tan), *n.* a person of wide information and sympathies:—*adj.* **1,** at home anywhere; having broad interests and sympathies; **2,** belonging to the world; not restricted to one nation or race; as, *cosmopolitan* ideals. Also, **cos-mop'o-lite'** (koz-mop'o-līt').

cos-mos (koz'mos), *n.* the universe conceived as a system of order and harmony (opposite of *chaos*).

cost (kôst), *v.t.* [*p.t.* and *p.p.* cost, *p.pr.* cost-ing], **1,** to be obtainable for (a certain price); as, the card *costs* five cents; **2,** to cause to spend or lose; as, carelessness *cost* him his job:—*v.i.* to involve or cause expenditure, loss, etc.; as, the accident *cost* dear:—*n.* **1,** a charge; expense; as, the *cost* of food; **2,** the price in terms of suffering, to work, etc.; as, at the *cost* of health; **3,** costs, the expenses of a lawsuit.

co—star (kō'—stär'), *v.t.* and *v.i.* to share prominently in a play, performance, etc.—Also used as *noun.*

cost-ly (kôst'li), *adj.* [cost-li-er, cost-li-est], involving great cost or expense, as of money or effort.—*n.* **cost'li-ness.**

cos-tume (kos'tūm; kos-tūm'), *n.* **1,** dress in general; style of dress; esp., the dress of a given time, period, class, etc.; **2,** historical dress; fancy dress:— *v.t.* (kos-tūm'), [costumed, costum-ing], to provide with appropriate dress; as, to *costume* an actor for a part.—*n.* **cos-tum'er.**

co-sy (kō'zi), *adj.* [co-si-er, co-si-est], warm and comfortable; snug;—*n.* [*pl.* cosies], **1,** a cover, padded, to keep a tea-pot warm; **2,** a corner seat. Also spelled **co'zy.**—*adv.* **co'si-ly.**

cot (kot), *n.* a small, light bed.

cote (kōt), *n.* a shelter, as for sheep; a coop, as for pigeons.

co-te-rie (kō'tê-ri; kō'tê-rē'), *n.* a set of intimate friends; a clique.

co-til-lion (kō-til'yun), *n.* a lively, intricate, 19th-century dance for eight or more persons.

cot-tage (kot'ij), *n.* a small dwelling; also, a house at a summer resort.—*n.* **cot'tag-er.**

cot-ter—pin (kot'êr—pin'), *n.* a split metal pin whose ends are bent after insertion through a hole or slot.

cot-ton (kot'n), *n.* **1,** a white, fibrous down enclosing the seeds of the cottonplant; **2,** the plant producing this; **3,** thread or cloth made of cotton:—*adj.* pertaining to cotton.—*adj.* **cot'ton-y.**

cotton batting, thin layers of fluffy absorbent cotton used for surgical dressings.

cot-ton—tail (kot'n—tāl'), *n.* a wild American rabbit.

cot-y-le-don (kot'i-lē'dun), a part of a seed containing food for the young root, stem, and first true leaves: often appearing above ground at germination as the seed-leaf, and later shrivelling up. —*adj.* **cot'y-le'don-ous.**

couch (kouch), *v.t.* **1,** to lay upon a bed or other resting-place; **2,** to put into words; express; as, to *couch* a letter in strong terms; **3,** to lower, as a lance or spear for attack:—*v.i.* **1,** to lie down, as on a bed; **2,** to cower; hide:—*n.* a bed; sofa; lounge.

couch grass, a variety of coarse grass that spreads rapidly by creeping rootstocks: also called *twitch grass* or *quick grass.*

cou-gar (kōō'gàr), *n.* a large, tawny American animal of the cat family: also called *puma, catamount, panther,* or *mountain-lion.* (See illustration under *puma.*)

cough (kôf), *v.i.* to force air from the lungs suddenly, with a sharp noise:— *v.t.* to expel from the lungs or air passages; as, he *coughed* up the bone:— *n.* **1,** the act or sound of coughing; **2,** an illness marked by a cough; as, to have a dry *cough.*

could (kood), *p.t.* of *can.*

cou-lee (kōō'li), *n.* in Western Canada and U.S., a deep, dry gulch with steeply sloping sides like those of a canyon.

coul-ter (kōl'têr), *n.* a blade on a plough to cut the turf ahead of the share.

coun-cil (koun'sil), *n.* **1,** a group of persons called together to discuss and settle problems, give advice, etc.; as, a *council* of teachers; **2,** a law-making or governing body, as of a city or town; **3,** the deliberation of such a body.—*n.* **coun'cil-lor; coun'ci-lor.**—*n.* **coun'cil-man.**

all (ôl), ôr; up, mūte, cûr, cōōl, book; oil, out; th, thin; *th,* the.

coun-sel (koun'sel), *n.* **1,** exchange of opinion; consultation; as, the general took *counsel* with his officers; **2,** instruction; advice; as, he was guided by his mother's *counsel;* **3,** prudence; foresight; **4,** an advocate or lawyer:—*v.t.* [counselled, counsel-ling], **1,** to give advice to; **2,** to recommend; as, I *counsel* patience.—*n.* **coun'sel-lor; coun'se-lor.**

¹count (kount), *v.t.* **1,** to tell off (units) in order to find their number; sum up; as, *count* your pennies; **2,** to give the numerals in regular order to a certain point; as, *count* ten before you answer; **3,** to consider; as, she *counts* herself generous; **4,** to include in an enumeration; as, he *counted* only the best:—*v.i.* **1,** to tell off articles or numbers in order; **2,** to rely; as, we *count* on her consent; **3,** to be of worth or value; as, this doesn't *count* much; **4,** to have effect; as, his support *counted* heavily in the victory:—*n.* **1,** the act of numbering; as, a *count* of the boys; **2,** the total ascertained.

²count (kount), *n.* a title of nobility in France, Spain, Italy, etc.: about the same as British *earl.*

count-down (kount'doun'), *n.* a counting downwards before the launching of a rocket (the counting ending . . . 3, 2, 1, zero) to measure the precise period preceding blast-off.

coun-te-nance (koun'te-nans), *n.* **1,** the face; **2,** the expression of the face showing feeling or character; as, an angry *countenance;* a noble *countenance;* **3,** approval; support; as, to lend *countenance* to a plan; **4,** composure; as, he kept *countenance* despite the insult:—*v.t.* [countenanced, countenanc-ing], to support; favour; as, he *countenanced* the affair.

¹coun-ter (koun'tėr), *n.* **1,** a person who keeps count; **2,** a small object used to keep score, as in a game; **3,** a sort of table, as in a store, at which goods are sold or money handled; **4,** a coinlike token.

²coun-ter (koun'tėr), *adj.* contrary; opposing; as, a *counter* opinion:—*n.* **1,** the opposite or contrary; **2,** in boxing, a blow to ward off a blow:—*v.i.* to make an opposite or contrary attack:—*v.t.* **1,** to combat; oppose:—*adv.* in a contrary way; against.

coun-ter-act (koun'tėr-akt'), *v.t.* to act in opposition to; neutralize; as, one medicine may *counteract* another.— *n.* **coun'ter-ac'tion.**

coun-ter-bal-ance (koun'tėr-bal'ans), *n.* a weight which balances another; hence, a power or influence that offsets another:—*v.t.* (koun'tėr-bal'ans),

[counterbalanced, counterbalanc-ing], to balance, as with an equal weight; make up for; as, his unusual mental powers *counterbalanced* his lameness.

coun-ter-feit (koun'tėr-fit), *v.t.* to copy or imitate exactly, as money, with intent to deceive or defraud:—*v.i.* to make imitations, esp. of money:—*adj.* made to resemble something genuine very closely, with intent to deceive; as, *counterfeit* money:—*n.* a copy made with intent to deceive; a forgery; as, this bill is a *counterfeit.*—*n.* **coun'ter-feit'er.**

coun-ter-mand (koun'tėr-mand'; koun'-tėr-mand'), *v.t.* **1,** to cancel (a purchase); **2,** to issue instructions reversing (an order, plan, or the like); as, the general *countermanded* the march: —*n.* (koun'tėr-mand'), a contrary order.

coun-ter-march (koun'tėr-märch'), *n.* **1,** a reversal; a marching back; returning; **2,** in drilling, a sharp turn, as if around a post, and a march back parallel and close to the line of advance: —*v.i.* (koun'tėr-märch'; koun'tėr-märch'), to march back; make a countermarch.

coun-ter-pane (koun'tėr-pān'), *n.* an outer covering for a bed; a bedspread.

coun-ter-part (koun'tėr-pärt'), *n.* a person or thing that corresponds closely to another; as, the right foot is a *counterpart* of the left; a duplicate; copy.

coun-ter-plot (koun'tėr-plot'), *n.* a plot in opposition.

coun-ter-sign (koun'tėr-sīn'; koun'-tėr-sīn'), *v.t.* to sign (a document) already signed by another:—*n.* (koun'tėr-sīn'), **1,** an additional signature to a document to make it of value; **2,** a word known to a special group, as a secret password.

count-ess (koun'tis), *n.* the wife or widow of a count or an earl; also, a lady who in her own right ranks with an earl or a count.

count-less (kount'lis), *adj.* innumerable; numberless.

coun-try (kun'tri), *n.* [*pl.* countries], **1,** a tract of land; region; as, level *country;* **2,** rural regions; as, we left the *country* for the city; **3,** one's native or adopted land; **4,** a territory that has a distinct existence as to name, language, government, and the like; as, Spain and other Mediterranean *countries;* **5,** the people of a nation as a whole; the public; as, the *country* voted for lower taxes:—*adj.* **1,** pertaining to the rural regions; as, *country* roads; **2,** unpolished; rustic; as, *country* ways.

coun-try-man (kun'tri-man), *n.* [*pl.*

country-men (-men)], **1,** a person who lives in the rural regions; **2,** a person who lives or was born in the same country as another.

coun-ty (koun'ti), *n.* [*pl.* counties], **1,** a definite political district of a country; **2,** in all States of the U.S. except Louisiana, the largest political subdivision; also, its people; as, the *county* voted the tax:—*adj.* pertaining to a county; as, *county* officials.

coup (kōō), *n.* a sudden, unexpected, and sometimes brilliantly successful move or stroke.

coup d'état (kōō'dā'tå'), *n.* an unexpected political change, usually the sudden overthrow of a government by force or an illegal measure.

cou-pé (kōō'pā'), *n.* **1,** a horse-drawn, fourwheeled closed carriage for two, with an outside driver's seat; **2,** a closed automobile with one seat.

cou-ple (kup'l), *n.* **1,** two persons or things of the same kind connected or thought of together; as, a *couple* of books; **2,** two persons of opposite sex, closely associated; as, a dancing *couple:*—*v.t.* [cou-pled, cou-pling], **1,** to join together, as railway cars; **2,** *Colloq.,* to unite in pairs; unite in wedlock:—*v.i.* to pair off; mate.

cou-plet (cup'lit), *n.* two successive lines of rhymed verse.

cou-pling (kup'ling), *n.* **1,** the act of joining or mating; **2,** a device for joining two parts of machinery or the like; as, a railroad *coupling.*

cou-pon (kōō'pon), *n.* **1,** a detachable slip or part of a ticket, certifying the holder's right to something, as to a theatre seat; **2,** a dated, detachable certificate which may be clipped from a bond and presented for collection of interest.

cour-age (kûr'ij), *n.* boldness; fearlessness.—*adj.* **cou-ra'geous.**

cour-eur de bois (kōō'rûr' de bwå'), *n.* a French or half-breed trapper, esp. of the early (or French) regime in Canada.

cour-i-er (koor'i-ẻr), *n.* **1,** a messenger, usually entrusted with important letters or documents to be delivered with great speed; **2,** a travelling attendant who arranges all the details of a journey, as tickets, hotel reservations, etc.

course (kōrs), *n.* **1,** the act of moving onward; progress in space; as, the *course* of the earth around the sun; progress in time; as, in the *course* of a week; **2,** ground to be passed over in a regular way; as, a golf-*course;* **3,** a path; direction taken; as, a ship's *course;* **4,** a channel through which

water flows; as, the *course* of a river; **5,** a succession; series; as, a *course* of lectures; **6,** method of procedure; as, a *course* of action; **7,** the part of a meal served at one time; **8,** in building, a layer of stone or bricks:—**of course,** naturally; as was to be expected:—*v.t.* [coursed, cours-ing], to pursue (game) with hounds:—*v.i.* to run; flow; as, tears *coursed* down her cheeks.

cours-er (kōr'sẻr), *n. Poetic,* a swift horse.

court (kōrt), *n.* **1,** an unroofed space wholly or partly surrounded by buildings or walls; **2,** a level space marked for playing games; **3,** a royal palace; also, the people in attendance at a palace; **4,** a prince or sovereign and his ministers considered as the ruling power; also, an official meeting of a sovereign and his councillors; **5,** a hall of justice; **6,** the judge or judges engaged in administering justice; also, the session at which they preside; **7,** flattering attentions paid to one in power; also, attention paid by a man to a woman in wooing her:—*v.t.* **1,** to pay attention to as a lover; woo; **2,** to seek favour of, by flattery and attention; **3,** to attempt to gain; seek.

cour-te-ous (kûr'ti-us; kōrt'yus), *adj.* polite. *adv.* **cour'te-ous-ly.**—*n.* **cour'-te-ous-ness.**

cour-te-sy (kûr'te-si; kōr'te-si), *n.* [*pl.* courtesies], **1,** politeness; **2,** an act of kindliness or respect; **3,** kindness or generosity; as, a programme presented through the *courtesy* of a large coal company; **4,** a bow, as made by women or girls; a curtsy.

court—house (kōrt'–hous'), *n.* a public building in which courts of law are held.

cour-ti-er (kōr'ti-ẻr; kōrt'yẻr), *n.* **1,** a person in attendance at a royal court; **2,** one who pays court to a superior.

court-ly (kōrt'li), *adj.* [court-li-er, court-li-est], polished; elegant; as, *courtly* manners.—*n.* **court'li-ness.**

court—mar-tial (kōrt'–mär'shal), *n.* [*pl.* courts-martial], a court made up of military or naval officers to try offences against military or naval law: also, a trial by such a court:—*v.t.* to try (a person) by such a court.

court-room (kōrt'rōōm'), *n.* a room where a court of law is held.

court-ship (kōrt'ship), *n.* attentions paid by a member of one sex to a member of the other sex, preparatory to marriage or mating.

court-yard (kōrt'yärd'), *n.* an enclosed space adjoining a house or castle.

cous-in (kuz'n), *n.* a son or daughter of one's uncle or aunt.

all (ôl), ôr; up, mūte, cûr, cōōl, book; oil, out; th, thin; *th,* the.

cove (kōv), *n.* **1,** a sheltered place or pass; esp., an inlet or creek on the coast; **2,** in *architecture*, a concave moulding.

cov-e-nant (kuv′e-nant), *n.* a compact or agreement:—*v.t.* and *v.i.* to promise by solemn agreement.

cov-er (kuv′ẽr), *v.t.* **1,** to put or lay something over (a person or thing); as, to *cover* a box; **2,** to lie over, so as to close or enclose; as, a lid *covers* the box; a shoe *covers* the foot; **3,** to hide; screen; as, clouds *cover* the mountain; to *cover* a mistake; **4,** to extend or pass over; as, the estate *covers* a wide area; we *covered* ninety miles today; **5,** to include; comprise; as, the book *covers* the subject; **6,** to hold within aim; as, to *cover* a man with a gun; **7,** in *journalism*, to report on a specific event.—*n.* **1,** that which is laid on something else; as, a *cover* for a bed; **2,** the binding of a book, or the outside page of a magazine; **3,** protection; as, to escape under *cover* of night; **4,** a thicket that may conceal game; **5,** the table equipment for the use of one person at a meal.

cov-er-alls (kuv′ẽr-ôlz′), *n.* a one-piece, external work garment worn by mechanics, etc.

cov-er-ing (kuv′ẽr-ing), *n.* **1,** that which covers; **2,** the act of putting on a cover.

cov-er-let (kuv′ẽr-lit), *n.* the outer cover of a bed; a bedspread.

cov-ert (kuv′ẽrt), *adj.* concealed, secret; veiled; as, a *covert* scheme, threat, or glance.

cov-et (kuv′it), *v.t.* to long for (something that belongs to another).—*adj.* cov′et-ous.

cov-ey (kuv′i), *n.* [*pl.* coveys], a brood or flock of game-birds, as quail.

¹cow (kou), *n.* [*pl.* cows (kouz), *Poetic* or *Archiac*, kine (kīn)], **1,** a full-grown female of the ox family, esp. of domestic cattle; **2,** a female of certain other large mammals, such as the moose, whale, etc.

²cow (kou), *v.t.* to make afraid.

cow-ard (kou′ẽrd), *n.* a person lacking in courage; a shamefully timid person. —*adj.* and *adv.* cow′ard-ly.

cow-ard-ice (kou′ẽr-dis), *n.* want of courage; shameful fear.

cow-bird (kou′bûrd′), *n.* a small, blackbird of North America, that follows cattle. It builds no nest, but lays its eggs in the nests of other birds.

cow-boy (kou′boi′), *n.* in the western part of Canada and of the U.S., a man who tends cattle, doing his work mostly on horseback.

cow-er (kou′ẽr), *v.i.* to crouch down, as from fear or shame.

cow-hide (kou′hīd′), *n.* **1,** the skin of a cow, esp. when tanned and dressed; **2,** a whip of rawhide or of braided leather:—*adj.* made of cowhide:—*v.t.* [cow-hid-ed, cow-hid-ing], to flog with a cowhide.

cowl (koul), *n.* a monk's hood, or hood and gown together.

cow-lick (kou′lik′), *n.* a tuft of hair on the forehead that will not lie flat.

cow-ling (kou′ling), *n.* the removable metal covering of an airplane engine.

cow-slip (kou′slip), *n.* **1,** in the U.S., the marsh marigold, a yellow-flowered swamp plant; **2,** in England, a wild primrose with fragrant flowers.

cox-comb (koks′kōm′), *n.* **1,** the red edge on a jester's cap; also, the cap; **2,** a vain fellow; fop; **3,** (usually *cocks-comb*), a garden plant with showy flowers.

cox-swain (kok′swān; kok′sn), *n.* one who steers or has charge of a boat, esp. a racing shell. Also cock′swain.

coy (koi), *adj.* **1,** bashful; shy; **2,** pretending to be shy; coquettish.

coy-ote (koi′ōt; k 1-ō′-ti), *n.* the prairie-wolf of western North America.

COYOTE ($\frac{1}{55}$)

co-zy (kō′zi), *adj.* [co-zi-er, co-zi-est], warm and comfortable; snug:—*n.* [*pl.* cozies], **1,** a cover, padded, to keep a teapot warm; **2,** a corner seat. Preferred spelling, co′sy.—*adv.* co′zi-ly.

¹crab (krab), *n.* any of various animals, most of which live in the sea, which have a broad, flattened body, ten walking legs, and the abdomen, or so-called tail, curled under the body:—*v.i.* [crabbed, crab-bing], to fish for or catch crabs.

²crab (krab), *n.* **1,** a tree bearing small, sour apples, often used in making jelly: usually called *crab-apple;* also, the fruit; **2,** a surly, ill-tempered person.— *adj.* crab′bed (kra′bid); crab′by.—*n.* crab grass (a coarse, creeping, weedy grass that infests lawns).—catch a crab, in *rowing*, to miss the water in making a stroke, or to fail to clear the water on a recovery stroke.

crack (krak), *v.i.* **1,** to make a sharp, snapping noise, as a whip; **2,** to be broken without dividing completely; as, the cup *cracked* in hot water; **3,** to break or become rasping, as a voice:— *v.t.* **1,** to cause to pop or snap; as, to *crack* a whip; **2,** to break without separating completely; break open; as, to *crack* nuts; **3,** to tell (a joke):—*n.* **1,** a sudden, sharp noise; as, a *crack* of thunder; **2,** an incomplete break; as, a *crack* in the ice; **3,** a broken note, as in a boy's voice when changing; **4,** *Colloq.*, a sharp blow; as, he gave the boy a *crack* on the head:—*adj. Colloq.*, first-rate; as, a *crack* hunter.—*adj.* **crack'-brained'**—*n.* **crack'down'** (*Slang*).

crack-er (krak'ẽr), *n.* **1,** a dry biscuit, often hard and crisp; **2,** in the south-eastern U.S., a poor white from the backwoods; **3,** a firecracker; **4,** a party favour which pops when pulled apart.

crack-le (krak'l), *v.i.* [crack-led, crack-ling], to make slight rustling or snapping noises, frequently repeated:—*n.* **1,** a slight, sharp, or snapping noise, esp. one that is often repeated; as, the *crackle* of a fire; **2,** the finely cracked glaze or surface of a kind of pottery, glass, or porcelain; also, ware having such a surface.—*adj.* **crack'ly.**

crack-pot (krak'pot'), *n. Colloq.*, an eccentric or crazy person.

crack-up (krak'up'), *n.* **1,** a crash, as of an airplane; **2,** *Colloq.*, a mental or physical breakdown. Also, *v.i.* to crack *up:* **1,** to crash; **2,** *Colloq.*, to break down.

cra-dle (krā'dl), *n.* **1,** a baby's crib or bed, often on rockers; **2,** birthplace; origin; as, the *cradle* of liberty; **3,** anything resembling a baby's cradle, as a supporting frame placed under a ship during construction, a trough on rockers used by miners in washing gold-bearing earth, etc.; **4,** a frame of wood, fastened to a scythe, used in harvesting; also, the scythe:—*v.t.* [cra-dled, cra-dling], **1,** to place or rock in a cradle; **2,** to shelter in infancy; as, the two brothers were *cradled* in luxury; **3,** to wash gold-bearing earth in a cradle; **4,** to reap with a cradle scythe.

craft (kràft), *n.* **1,** skill, esp. of the hand; **2,** deceit; cunning; **3,** a trade requiring artistic manual skill; also, those engaged in such a trade; **4,** [*pl.* craft], a ship or boat; also, an aeroplane or dirigible.

crafts-man (kràfts'man), *n.* [*pl.* crafts-men (-men)], a skilled workman.—*n.* **crafts'man-ship'.**

craft-y (kràf'ti), *adj.* [craft-i-er, craft-i-est], deceitful; wily; as, *crafty* schemes. —*adv.* **craft'i-ly.**—*n.* **craft'i-ness.**

crag (krag), *n.* a steep, rugged rock; also, a projecting point of a rock.—*adj.* **crag'gy.**

crake (krāk), *n.* a bird of the rail family, with long legs and short bill.

cram (kram), *v.t.* [crammed, cram-ming], **1,** to stuff; fill to overflowing, as with food; **2,** to pack or crowd in; **3,**

Colloq., to study intensively, as for an examination:—*v.i.* **1,** to eat greedily; **2,** *Colloq.*, to study hard for an examination.

¹cramp (kramp), *n.* **1,** an iron bar bent at the ends, used to hold together blocks of stone, timber, or the like; **2,** a piece of iron or steel, resembling a C, with a tightening screw, used for holding two things together: also called *clamp:*— *v.t.* **1,** to fasten or hold by a cramp; **2,** to hinder in action or growth; hamper; as, lack of knowledge *cramped* his progress.

²cramp (kramp), *n.* a sudden, sharp, painful contracting of the muscles, due to sudden chill, strain, or the like:—*v.t.* and *v.i.* to suffer, or cause to suffer, from cramp.

cran-ber-ry (kran'bẽr-i), *n.* [*pl.* cranberries], the small, tart, scarlet berry of a kind of bog plant; also, the plant.

crane (krān), *n.* **1,** a wading bird with very long legs, a long straight bill, and a long neck which it stretches to full length in flight; **2,** a machine for raising and moving heavy weights; **3,** a mechanical arm or support, as an iron arm for utensils in a fireplace:—*v.t.* and *v.i.* [craned, cran-ing], to stretch (the neck), in order to see better.

cra-ni-um (krā'ni-um), *n.* the skull, esp. the part enclosing the brain.—*adj.* **cra'ni-al.**

¹crank (krangk), *n.* an arm fastened at right angles to a shaft, and used for changing to-and-fro motion to circular motion, as in a grindstone, or the reverse, as in a windmill pump:—*v.t.* **1,** to work with a crank, as a motion-picture camera; **2,** to start (a motor) with a crank.

²crank (krangk), *n. Colloq.*, **1,** a person with a peculiar turn of mind; esp. one who pursues one idea exclusively; **2,** an irritable person.

crank-case (krank'kās'), *n.* the housing enclosing crankshaft, connecting rods, etc., of a motorcar.

crank-shaft (krank'shàft'), *n.* the shaft in a gasoline engine that transmits the piston movement to the propeller of a ship or airplane, or, through a clutch, to the wheels of a motorcar.

crank-y (krangk'i), *adj.* [crank-i-er, crank-i-est], **1,** ill-tempered; irritable; **2,** liable to upset, as a boat.—*adv.* **crank'i-ly.**—*n.* **crank'i-ness.**

cran-ny (kran'i), *n.* [*pl.* crannies], a crack or chink, as in a wall.

crape (krāp), *n.* a crinkly black silk fabric, used esp. as a sign of mourning.

¹crash (krash), *v.i.* **1,** to break to pieces

with a loud noise, esp. on falling; as, the vase *crashed* to the floor; **2**, to break one's way noisily through something; as, to *crash* through a jungle; **3**, to make a noise as of breakage on a vast scale; as, the thunder *crashed;* **4**, to collide, as two automobiles; also, to come into violent contact with the ground, as an aeroplane; **5**, to fail, as a business enterprise:—*v.t.* **1**, to break (something) to bits with noise and violence; smash; **2**, to land (an aeroplane) so as to damage it:—*n.* **1**, a smashing or shattering; **2**, a sudden loud sound, as of violent breakage; as, the *crash* of the orchestra; **3**, an aeroplane landing in which the craft is damaged; **4**, an automobile collision; **5**, the failure of a business; also, a general business and financial collapse; as, the *crash* of 1929.

²crash (krash), *n.* a coarse linen or cotton used for towelling, summer suits, etc.

crass (kras), *adj.* thick; coarse; gross; as, *crass* stupidity, ignorance, or carelessness.

crate (krāt), *n.* a wickerwork basket, or a case made of wooden slats, used for shipping goods:—*v.t.* [crat-ed, crat-ing], to pack in a crate, as apples.

cra-ter (krā′tẽr), *n.* **1**, the cup-shaped cavity forming the mouth of a volcano; **2**, a hole in the earth, caused by an explosion, as of an artillery shell.

cra-vat (kra-vat′), *n.* a necktie or neckcloth, usually worn by men.

crave (krāv), *v.t.* [craved, crav-ing], **1**, to beg earnestly for; as, I *crave* your help; **2**, to long for (food).—*n.* **crav′ing.**

cra-ven (krā′vn), *adj.* cowardly; base; as, a *craven* deserter:—*n.* an abject coward.

craw (krô), *n.* the crop of a bird or insect.

crawl (krôl), *v.i.* **1**, to move slowly by dragging the body along the ground; **2**, to go on hands and knees; **3**, to move very slowly; **4**, to be infested with creeping things; as, the ground *crawls* with ants; **5**, to feel as if live things were over one's body; as, to *crawl* with loathing:—*n.* **1**, the act of creeping, or of making one's way with difficulty; slow motion; **2**, a fast stroke in swimming.—*n.* **crawl′er.**

cray-fish (krā′fish′), *n.* [*pl.* crayfish or crayfishes], a shellfish related to, but much smaller than, the lobster, found in fresh water. Also called **craw′fish′.**

cray-on (krā′on), *n.* **1**, a stick or pencil, as of charcoal, chalk, or the like, for drawing or writing; **2**, a drawing

made with such material:—*v.t.* to draw with crayon.

craze (krāz), *n.* an intense but passing interest; infatuation; fad:—*v.t.* [crazed, craz-ing], to drive insane.—*adj.* **crazed.**

cra-zy (krā′zi), *adj.* [cra-zi-er, cra-zi-est], **1**, insane; mad; **2**, shaky; unsound, as a building; **3**, *Colloq.*, foolishly fond or eager; wildly enthusiastic; as, he is *crazy* about music.—*adv.* **cra′zi-ly.** —*n.* **cra′zi-ness.**

creak (krēk), *v.i.* to make a sharp, harsh, squeaking or grating sound:—*n.* a harsh, squeaking sound.—*adj.* **creak′y.**

cream (krēm), *n.* **1**, the rich, fat part of milk, which rises to the top; hence, the choicest part of anything; as, the *cream* of a story; **2**, a dessert or sweet made of cream, or like cream; as, ice-*cream;* butter *creams;* **3**, a light-yellow colour; **4**, a soft cosmetic; as, cold *cream:*—*v.t.* **1**, to skim the cream from (milk): **2**, to put cream into (tea or coffee); **3**, to bring to the consistency of thick cream; as, to *cream* butter, or butter and sugar; **4**, to cook with a dressing of cream or with a sauce of creamlike consistency.—*adv.* **cream′y.** *n.* **cream′er-y.**

crease (krēs), *n.* a mark or wrinkle left by a fold, as in paper:—*v.t.* [creased, creas-ing], to make a fold or wrinkle in; as, to *crease* a pair of trousers:—*v.i.* to fall into folds or wrinkles.—*adj.* **creas′y.**

cre-ate (krē-āt′), *v.t.* [creat-ed, creating], to cause to come into existence; make; originate; produce; also, to cause; occasion; as, to *create* a disturbance.

cre-a-tion (krē-ā′shun), *n.* **1**, the act of forming or originating; as, the *creation* of a new design; **2**, the thing made or originated; esp., the universe; also, the act by which it was created.—*adj.* **cre-a′tive.**

cre-a-tor (krē-ā′tẽr), *n.* one who makes or has the power to bring into existence: —**Creator**, the Supreme Being; God.

crea-ture (krē′tūr), *n.* **1**, any living being; an animal or a human being; **2**, a person who is the mere tool of another.

creche (krâsh), *n.* a public nursery for small children, esp. a day nursery.

cre-dence (krē′dens), *n.* **1**, belief; as, he gave *credence* to the rumour; **2**, credential; as, he had a letter of *credence* with him.

cre-den-tials (kre-den′shalz), *n.pl.* documents given to a person to be presented by him in proof of his identity, authority, record, or the like; letters of introduction; references.

cred-i-ble (kred′i-bl), *adj.* **1**, trustworthy; as, a *credible* witness; **2**, believable; as, a *credible* story.—*adv.* **cred′i-bly.**

cred-it (kred′it), *n.* **1,** belief; trust; confidence in the truth of a statement or the truthfulness of a person; as, do not place much *credit* in gossip; **2,** good name; reputation; as, a citizen of *credit* and renown; **3,** acknowledgment of worth; honour; as, he is given *credit* for trying; also, a source of honour; as, he is a *credit* to his family; **4,** the sum remaining at a customer's disposal or in his favour, as on the books of a bank; **5,** a record of satisfactory standing or achievement; as, college entrance *credits;* **6,** an extension of time allowed a customer to pay; as, goods bought on *credit;* **7,** financial standing or reputation; as, his *credit* is good for a charge account; **8,** in bookkeeping, the right-hand side of an account: opposite of *debit:*—*v.t.* **1,** to believe; trust; have confidence in; as, I *credit* her story; **2,** to give (a person) credit or honour; as, I *credit* you with good intentions; **3,** to enter a sum in favour of (a customer on his account); as, *credit* me with ten dollars.—*adj.* **cred′it-a-ble.**—*adv.* **cred′-it-a-bly.**

cred-i-tor (kred′i-tẽr), *n.* one to whom money is owed: opposite of *debtor.*

cre-do (krē′dō′), *n.* any creed or formal statement of belief.

cred-u-lous (kred′ū-lus), *adj.* ready to believe almost anything; easily deceived or imposed upon:—*n.* **cre-du′li-ty** (kre-dū′li-ti).—*adv.* **cred′u-lous-ly.**

creed (krēd), *n.* **1,** a brief, authoritative statement of religious belief; as, the Apostles' *creed;* **2,** a set of opinions or principles on any subject, such as politics, science, etc.; as, a business *creed.*

creek (krēk), *n.* **1,** a small stream; **2,** a long, narrow bay or inlet; also, a stream emptying into a bay or inlet.

creel (krēl), *n.* an angler's fish basket.

creep (krēp), *v.i.* [crept (krept), creeping], **1,** to move with the body near or touching the ground as does a cat stalking a bird, or a human being on hands and knees; **2,** to feel as if touching crawly things; as, my skin *creeps* when I see a snake; **3,** to grow along the ground, or over a surface, as a vine; **4,** to move cautiously or stealthily:—*n.* **creeps,** *Colloq.,* a prickly sensation in the skin or scalp; as, ghost stories give me the *creeps.*—*n.* **creep′er.**—*adj.* **creep′y.**

cre-mate (krē-māt′; krē′māt), *v.t.* [cremat-ed, cremat-ing], to burn to ashes, as a corpse.—*n.* **cre′ma-tor.**—*n.* **cre-ma′tion.**

cre-o-sote (krē′ō-sōt′), *n.* a heavy, oily liquid with a smoky smell, obtained from coal-tar or wood-tar: used as an antiseptic in medicine, and as a wood preservative.

crêpe or **crepe** (krāp), *n.* **1,** a soft fabric of silk, wool, cotton, or rayon, with a crinkled or wavy surface; **2,** (usually **crape**), a similar black silk fabric, used as a sign of mourning.

crept (krept), *p.t.* and *p.p.* of *creep.*

cre-scen-do (kre-shen′dō; -sen′), *n.* in *music,* an increasing or swelling of sound to its highest loudness or intensity.

cres-cent (kres′ent), *adj.* **1,** increasing; growing, as the new moon; **2,** shaped like the new moon: —*n.* **1,** the figure of the moon in its first or last quarter; **2,** anything shaped like the new moon; as, a jewelled *crescent.* CRESCENT

cress (kres), *n.* a green water plant of the mustard family with crisp, peppery leaves, used in salads and for garnishing.

crest (krest), *n.* **1,** a comb or tuft on the head of a bird; **2,** a tuft of feathers on a helmet, or the helmet itself; **3,** the top, as the ridge of a wave or the summit of a hill or ridge; **4,** the device or figure at top of a coat of arms; also, this device used by itself as a decoration or seal:—*v.t.* **1,** to serve as the crest of; as, woods *crest* the hills; **2,** to rise above; top.—*adj.* **crest′ed.**

crest-fall-en (krest′fôl′en), *adj.* dejected; disheartened; dispirited.

cre-ta-ceous (kri-tā′shus), *adj.* containing or like chalk.—*adj.* and *n.* **Cretaceous,** in *geology,* a period succeeding the age of dinosaurs and reptiles during which the remains of early mammals and flowering plants were fossilized in chalk beds.

cre-tin (krē′tin), *n.* a person arrested in physical and mental development owing to a lack of thyroid secretion.

cre-tonne (kri-ton′; krē′ton), *n.* a strong, unglazed cotton fabric, printed on one or both sides, and used for covering chairs, making draperies, etc.

cre-vasse (kre-vas′), *n.* a deep fissure or cleft in a glacier.

crev-ice (krev′is), *n.* a narrow split or crack; as, a *crevice* in a wall or rock.

crew (krōō), *n.* **1,** the group of men manning a ship or rowing a boat; **2,** a gang of men working together; as, a train *crew;* **3,** a company or throng; as, a *crew* of gipsies.

crib (krib), *n.* **1,** a manger for feeding stock; **2,** a bin with slatted walls, for storing unshelled corn; **3,** a child's bed with high, railed sides; **4,** a heavy framework, for strengthening a building that is being moved; **5,** *School Slang,* an unfair aid, as a key or translation, used by students; **6,** in *cribbage,* discarded cards used by the dealer in scoring.—*v.t.* [cribbed, crib-bing], **1,** to put (grain) into a crib; **2,** *Colloq.,* to steal and use as one's own; as, to *crib* a thought from Shakespeare:—*v.i.Colloq.,* to use a crib, as in a recitation or test.

crib-bage (krib′ij), *n.* a card game, usually for two, in which cards are discarded to form a *crib,* which adds to the dealer's score. The score is kept by moving pegs on a board with holes for them.

crib-bing (krib′ing), *n.* a framework of timber, as the lining of a mine, etc. Also, **crib′work′.**

crick (krik), *n.* a painful stiffness of the muscles of the neck or back.

¹crick-et (krik′it), *n.* a popular English game somewhat like baseball, but with eleven players on each side and two wickets instead of bases.—*n.* **crick′et-er.**

²crick-et (krik′it), *n.* a black, hopping insect. The male makes a chirping sound by rubbing his forewings together.

crime (krīm), *n.* **1,** an act which breaks the law and makes the offender liable to punishment; also, a sinful or wicked deed; **2,** wrongdoing; law-breaking.

crim-i-nal (krim′i-nal), *n.* one who is guilty of a grave offence against the law:—*adj.* having to do with crime; as, *criminal* acts; *criminal* law.—*adv.* **crim′i-nal-ly.**—*n.* **crim′i-nal′i-ty; crim′i-nol′o-gy.**

crimp (krimp), *v.t.* to fold or press into pleats; impart a wavy appearance to: —*n.* **1,** the act of waving, curling, or frilling; **2, crimps,** curled hair.—*adj.* **crimp′y.**

crim-son (krim′zn), *n.* a deep-red colour:—*adj.* deep-red:—*v.t.* to colour deep red; as, the sunset *crimsons* the lake:—*v.i.* to blush; become red.

cringe (krinj), *v.i.* [cringed, cring-ing], **1,** to wince with pain; shrink or cower in fear; **2,** to fawn; be basely humble in manner, as a beggar:—*n.* a servile bow.

crin-kle (kring′kl), *v.i.* [crin-kled, crin-kling], **1,** to wrinkle; twist; become rippled; as, paper *crinkles;* **2,** to rustle, as stiff silk:—*v.t.* to cause to wrinkle or ripple:—*n.* a wrinkle; a fold.—*adj.* **crin′kly.**

crin-o-line (krin′o-lin), *n.* **1,** a stiff cloth (formerly of horsehair and linen) used as a lining; **2,** a hoop skirt.

crip-ple (krip′l), *n.* one who is lame or

physically disabled:—*v.t.* [crip-pled, crip-pling], **1,** to disable; **2,** to weaken; as, the depression *crippled* business.

cri-sis (krī′sis), *n.* [*pl.* crises (krī′sēz)], **1,** a turning-point for better or worse in an illness; **2,** a turning-point in the progress of anything, as in history.

crisp (krisp), *adj.* **1,** hard but brittle; as, *crisp* toast; also, flaky; as, *crisp* pastry; **2,** brisk; decided; as, *crisp* speech; **3,** fresh and firm; as, *crisp* lettuce; **4,** fresh and bracing; as, *crisp* air; **5,** tightly curling; as, *crisp* hair:— *v.t.* and *v.i.* to make or become crisp.— *n.* **crisp′ness.**—*adj.* **cris′py.**—*adv.* **crisp′ly.**

criss-cross (kris′krôs′), *adj.* cross-wise, as in the game of *ticktacktoe.*—*n.* a cross used as a signature by one unable to write.

o	x
x
o	x

cri-te-ri-on (krī-tē′ri-un), *n.* [*pl.* criteria (krī-tē′ri-a)], a standard or rule by which to form a judgment; test: as, his words are no *criterion* of his thoughts.

crit-ic (krit′ik), *n.* **1,** a person skilled in judging art, literature, or the like; **2,** one who judges harshly.

crit-i-cal (krit′i-kal), *adj.* **1,** faultfinding; **2,** impartial and careful in forming judgments; **3,** decisive; important; as, a *critical* moment; **4,** involving risk; as, a *critical* operation.—*adv.* **crit′i-cal-ly.**

crit-i-cism (krit′i-sizm), *n.* **1,** the act or art of judging and defining the merits of a scientific or artistic work; **2,** a harsh judgment; faultfinding; **3,** the principles or method of judging works of art.—*v.t.* and *v.i.* **crit′i-cize.**

croak (krōk), *v.i.* **1,** to utter a low, harsh sound like that of a raven or frog; **2,** to grumble; forebode evil; **3,** *Slang,* to die: —*v.t.* to utter hoarsely or dismally:—*n.* a low, hoarse sound.—*n.* **croak′er.**

cro-chet (krō′shā), *v.t.* [crocheted (krō′-shād), crochet-ing (krō′shā-ing)], to make (a fabric or article) by looping a thread into other loops with a single hooked needle; as, to *crochet* a doily:— *v.i.* to make things in this manner; as, to *crochet* all day:—*n.* the kind of fabric thus made; as, a piece of *crochet.*

crock (krok), *n.* an earthenware pot or jar, esp. for kitchen use.

crock-er-y (krok′ẽr-i), *n.* earthenware, esp. kitchen dishes, bowls, etc.

croc-o-dile (krok′o-dīl′), *n.* tough-skinned, long-tailed, flesh-eating reptile, fourteen to twenty feet in length, with a long, narrow head and pointed snout, found in the fresh waters of Africa, Asia, Australia, and America.

cat, āge, fär, câre, ȧsk; ten, ēve, latẽr; (i) pity, rely, senāte; īce; top; nō.

cro-cus (krō′kus), *n.* one of the earliest spring-flowering bulbs, bearing purple, yellow, or white flowers. The **wild cro-cus** (*pulsatilla ludovic-iana*), also called pasque-flower, wind-flower (*anemone pat-ens*), and gosling plant (so named for its furry petals), was chosen in 1906 by the school children as Manitoba's official floral emblem. (Second: the prairie lily; third: the wild rose).

CROCUS (wild)

crone (krōn), *n.* a withered old woman; a hag.

cro-ny (krō′ni), *n.* [*pl.* cronies], a familiar friend; chum.

crook (krook), *n.* **1,** the bent or curved part of anything; **2,** a bent or hooked article or tool, as a shepherd's staff; **3,** *Colloq.*, a swindler:—*v.t.* to bend; as, to *crook* one's finger:—*v.i.* to curve; grow crooked.

crook-ed (krook′id), *adj.* **1,** bent; curved; not straight; as, a *crooked* path; **2,** not upright in conduct; dishonest.

croon (kroon), *v.i.* and *v.t.* to sing in a soft, plaintive, or sentimental manner:—*n.* the sound of such singing.—*n.* **croon′er.**

crop (krop), *n.* **1,** the amount, as of a grain or fruit, grown and gathered in one season; as, the corn *crop;* **2, crops,** plants grown for food, esp. grains and fruits; **3,** anything likened to a season's harvest; as, a *crop* of books; **4,** a pouch in a bird's gullet where food is prepared for digestion; **5,** a stout hunting-whip; **6,** hair cut close or short:—*v.t.* [cropped or, *Rare*, cropt (kropt), crop-ping], **1,** to mow; **2,** to bite off; as, the horse *cropped* the grass; **3,** to cut short, as hair, tail, ears, etc.:—*v.i.* **1,** to bite the tops off grass, or the like; **2,** to appear unexpectedly; as, an old friend *cropped* up yesterday.

crop—eared (krop′—ērd′), *adj.* having the ears cropped or clipped.

crop-per (krop′ėr), *n.* **1,** one who raises farm crops on shares; **2,** a disastrous failure; as, to come a *cropper.*

cro-quet (krō′ki), *n.* a lawn game in which wooden balls are driven by mallets from a starting-stake, through a series of wire wickets to a turning-stake and back.

cro-quette (krō-ket′), *n.* a ball of minced meat or fish, seasoned and fried.

cros-i-er (krō′zhi-ėr), *n.* a bishop's staff.

cross (krôs), *n.* **1,** an upright stake bearing a horizontal bar, or two stakes nailed together to form an X, an ancient Roman instrument of torture and death for slaves or foreign criminals; **2,** a sacred emblem, esp. of Christianity, as a symbol of the stake on which Jesus was crucified; **3,** any reproduction of this symbol, used as a shrine or monument; a crucifix; **4,** two intersecting straight lines, as the plus sign [+]; or as the sign of multiplication [×]; **5,** such a mark used as a signature by one who cannot write; **6,** a badge of distinction; as, he received the Victoria *Cross;* **7,** suffering or affliction to be borne; **8,** an intermixture of breeds or varieties of plants or animals; as, a mule is a *cross* between a horse and an ass:—*v.t.* **1,** to put or lay across; as, to *cross* timbers in building; **2,** to draw a mark across; as, to *cross* a *t;* **3,** to go to the opposite side of; as, to *cross* a bridge; **4,** to meet and pass; as, my letter *crossed* his on the way; **5,** to intersect; **6,** to make the sign of the cross upon (oneself); **7,** to cancel; as, I *crossed* out a word; **8,** to thwart; hinder; as, he is not in a mood to be *crossed;* **9,** to cause to interbreed, as plants or animals of different kinds:——*v.i.* **1,** to go, move, or lie from one side to the other; **2,** to meet and pass, going in opposite directions; **3,** to interbreed:—*adj.* **1,** intersecting; **2,** opposed; contrary; as, to work at *cross* purposes; **3,** ill-tempered; peevish:—**cross-cut saw,** any saw that cuts across the grain (opposite of *rip* saw, that cuts with the grain).

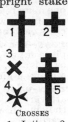
CROSSES
1, Latin; 2, Greek; 3, St. Andrew's; 4, Maltese; 5, papal.

cross-bow (krôs′bō′), *n.* a weapon of the Middle Ages, having a bow across a wooden stock which contained a groove for a stone or an arrow.

cross—ex-am-ine (krôs′—ig-zam′in), *v.t.* and *v.i.* to question closely, as a lawyer *cross-examines* a witness who has already been questioned at a trial. Also, **cross—ques′ tion.**

cross-grained (krôs′grānd′), *adj.* **1,** (of wood) having an irregular, transverse, or gnarled grain; **2,** (of persons) contrary; cantankerous.

cross-patch (krôs′pach′), *n.* a bad-tempered person.

cross-pol-li-nate (krôs′—pôl′i-nāt′), *v.t.* to transfer pollen from one flower to the stigma of another (by wind, insects, or artificially), in order to fertilize it.

cross-road (krôs′rōd′), *n.* **1,** a road

that crosses a main road, or runs from one main road to another; **2, crossroads,** the place where two or more roads cross each other.

cross—sec-tion (krôs′sek′shun), *n.* a piece cut off at right angles to its length or axis; as, the *cross–section* of a fruit, a stalk, a girder, etc.

cross-wise (krôs′wīz′), *adv.* **1,** across; athwart; **2,** in the shape of a cross; as, the church was built *crosswise;* **3,** contrarily.

crotch (kroch), *n.* **1,** a hook or fork; esp., a forked prop or support; **2,** the point of separation into two parts or branches; as, a *crotch* of a tree.

crotch-et-y (kroch′i-ti), *adj.* cantankerous; eccentric.

crouch (krouch) *v.i.* **1,** to stoop low, as if ready to spring; **2,** to cringe, as if in fear.

¹**croup** (krōōp), *n.* a child's disease, not infectious, marked by difficult breathing, choking, loss of voice, and a harsh, gasping cough.—*adj.* **croup′y.**

²**croup** (krōōp), *n.* a horse's rump.

¹**crow** (krō), *v.i.* [*p.t.* sometimes in sense 1, crew (krōō); otherwise regular], **1,** to make a shrill sound, like that of a barnyard cock; **2,** to boast in triumph; as, to *crow* over a victory; **3,** to utter a joyous cry:—*n.* the cry of a cock.

²**crow** (krō), *n.* **1,** a large, black bird, harsh-voiced, highly intelligent, and often destructive; **2,** any closely related bird, as a rook or raven; **3,** a crowbar.

crow-bar (krō′bär′), *n.* a long, straight iron bar, pointed or wedge-shaped at the working end, used as a lever.

crowd (kroud), *n.* **1,** a number of persons or things collected closely together; **2,** the masses, or common people; **3,** *Colloq.,* a certain set of people; clique:—*v.t.* **1,** to press (people or things) closely together; **2,** to fill too full; pack; stuff; **3,** to force (oneself or one's way) through; shove; push:— *v.i.* **1,** to assemble in large numbers; as, to *crowd* into a hall; **2,** to push; force oneself.

crown (kroun), *n.* **1,** a wreath, as of flowers, for the head; **2,** a headdress of gold and jewels, worn by kings or queens on ceremonial occasions; a diadem; **3,** the monarch himself, or his power; **4,** anything shaped like, or likened to, a crown; as, the *crown* of a hill, hat, or tooth; **5,** the top of the head; also, the head; **6,** completion; perfection; as, wisdom is the *crown* of age; **7,** in England, a coin worth five shillings; **8,** the heavy end of the shank of an anchor (see illustration

under *anchor*):—**crown prince,** the immediate heir to a throne; **crown princess,** a woman or girl who is next in succession to a throne; also, the wife of a crown prince:—*v.t.* **1,** to put a crown upon the head of; hence, to invest with regal power; reward; honour; **2,** to occupy the topmost part of; complete; as, a dome *crowns* a building; success *crowns* a career; **3,** in dentistry, to place an artificial top upon (a tooth); **4,** *Colloq.,* to hit on the head.—*n.* **crown′er.**

crow's—feet (krōz′–fēt′), *n.* small wrinkles that form at the corners of the eyes (of older persons).

crow's—nest (krōz′–nest′), *n.* a partly enclosed box or platform on the masthead of a ship, as shelter for the lookout man; any lookout.

cru-cial (krōō′shal), *adj.* important; decisive; as, a *crucial* test.—*adv.* **cru′cial-ly.**

cru-ci-ble (krōō′si-bl), *n.* an earthenware pot in which ores, metals, and the like, are melted.

cru-ci-fix (krōō′si-fiks), *n.* any image of Christ on the cross.

cru-ci-fix-ion (krōō′si-fik′shun), *n.* death upon a cross:—**Crucifixion,** the death of Christ on the cross; also a statue or picture representing this scene.—*v.t.* **cru′ci-fy′.**

crude (krōōd), *adj.* [crud-er, crud-est], **1,** in a raw state; unrefined; as, *crude* oil; **2,** uncultured; rude; as, *crude* manners; **3,** wanting in grace or taste; harsh in colour; as, a *crude* painting.— *adv.* **crude′ly.**

cru-el (krōō′el), *adj.* **1,** delighting in giving pain to others; merciless; hardhearted; **2,** painful; causing suffering, as a disease.—*adv.* **cru′el-ly.**—*n.* **cru′el-ty.**

cru-et (krōō′it), *n.* a small glass bottle, esp. for vinegar, oil, etc., for the dining table.

cruise (krōōz), *v.t.* [cruised, cruis-ing], to sail about with no special destination; as, pirates *cruised* the China Sea:—*v.i.* **1,** to sail about in search of enemy ships or to protect merchant ships in time of war; **2,** to travel by boat from port to port; **3,** to make a like trip over land:—*n.* a voyage from place to place.

cruis-er (krōōz′ẽr), *n.* a swift man-of-war with less armour than a battleship.

crul-ler (krul′ẽr), *n.* a ring-shaped or twisted cake, fried brown in deep fat: often called *doughnut.*

crumb (krum), *n.* **1,** the soft, inner part of bread; **2,** a fragment of bread, cake, etc.; **3,** a little bit; as, a *crumb* of cheer:—*v.t.* to break (bread) into little pieces.

crum-ble (krum'bl), *v.t.* [crum-bled, crum-bling], to break into crumbs or pieces:—*v.i.* **1,** to fall to pieces; **2,** to fall into decay or ruin.—*adj.* **crum'bly.**

crum-pet (krum'pit), *n.* a tea cake or thin muffin, usually toasted.

crum-ple (krum'pl), *v.t.* [crum-pled, crum-pling], to press into wrinkles; rumple:—*v.i.* to become wrinkled.

crunch (krunch), *v.t.* and *v.i.* **1,** to crush or grind noisily; as, feet *crunch* the ice; **2,** to chew noisily, as does a horse:—*n.* the act or sound of grinding or chewing noisily.

cru-sade (krōō-sād'), *n.* **1,** any one of seven military expeditions of European Christians, in the 11th, 12th, and 13th centuries, to recover the Holy Land from the Mohammedans; **2,** a vigorous movement for some cause, as against crime:—*v.i.* [crusad-ed, crusad-ing], to engage in a crusade.—*n.* **cru-sad'er.**

cruse (krōōs; krōōz), *n. Archaic,* a small vessel for holding oil, water, or the like.

crush (krush), *v.t.* **1,** to press between two bodies; break to pieces by pressure; **2,** to squeeze; press into a mass; as, to *crush* berries; **3,** to bruise so as to change the normal condition; as, to *crush* a leg; **4,** to break down; ruin; conquer:—*n.* **1,** violent pressure; **2,** a crowd; **3,** *Colloq.,* a crowded social gathering.—*n.* **crush'er.**

crust (krust), *n.* **1,** the hard outside covering on bread; also, a piece of this or of stale bread; **2,** any similar hard outside coating; as, a *crust* of ice over soft snow; **3,** the pastry casing of a pie; **4,** *Slang,* impudence:—*v.t.* and *v.i.* to cover, or become covered, with a crust.—*adj.* **crust'y.**—*adv.* **crust'i-ly.** —*n.* **crust'i-ness.**

crus-ta-cean (krus-tā'shan), *n.* any of a class of animals, most of which live in the water, having a crustlike shell, as crabs, lobsters, shrimps, etc.

crutch (kruch), *n.* **1,** a staff with a crosspiece to fit under the arm, used by lame or infirm persons; **2,** any forked prop or support.

crux (kruks), *n.* [*pl.* cruxes (-ez); cruces (krōō'sēz)], **1,** a puzzle; anything hard to explain; **2,** a basic or essential point; as, this is the *crux* of the problem.

cry (krī), *v.i.* [cried, cry-ing], **1,** to call aloud; complain loudly; wail; exclaim; **2,** to shed tears; weep; **3,** of an animal or bird, to call loudly:—*v.t.* **1,** to announce publicly; as, to *cry* the

hour of the night; **2,** to advertise or offer for sale; as, the pedlar *cries* his wares:—*n.* **1,** loud or passionate utterance; as, a *cry* of joy, fear, anger, pain, or the like; **2,** outcry; clamour; demand; **3,** the calling of goods for sale; as, the pedlar's *cry;* **4,** common report; rumour; **5,** the characteristic call of an animal; as, the *cry* of the wolf; **6,** a fit of weeping; **7,** a rallying call; as, a battle *cry.*

cry-ba-by (krī'bā'bi), *n.* one given to constant complaining.

cry-ing (krī'ing), *adj.* requiring action or redress; urgent; as, a *crying* evil.

crypt (kript), *n.* an underground vault, esp. one under a church.

cryp-tic (krip'tik), *adj.* not plain; secret, hidden, or ambiguous; as, *cryptic* remarks.

cryp-to-gam (krip'to-gam'), *n.* a plant that bears neither flower nor seed but propagates by spores, as the mosses, ferns, algae, etc.

cryp-to-gram or **cryp-to-graph** (krip'tō-gram'; -gràf'), *n.* a code or cypher; secret writing.

crys-tal (kris'tal), *n.* **1,** transparent quartz; **2,** a body with regular flat surfaces formed by some substances when they solidify; as, *crystals* of ice; **3,** a glass of superior clearness; **4,** the glass over a watch dial:—*adj.* of or like crystal; consisting of transparent glass; clear:—**crystal set,** a simple radio receiver using a crystal of galena, carborundum, etc., as a detector or rectifier.

crys-tal-line (kris'tal-īn'; kris'tal-in), *adj.* **1,** made of, or like, crystal; **2,** clear.

crys-tal-lize (kris'tal-īz'), *v.t.* [crystal-lized, crystalliz-ing], **1,** to cause to form grains or become crystalline; **2,** to give a fixed shape to; **3,** to coat with sugar crystals; as, to *crystallize* ginger: —*v.i.* **1,** to be converted into grains; become crystalline; **2,** to assume definite shape; as, his plans *crystallized* into deeds.—*n.* **crys'tal-li-za'tion.**

cub (kub), *n.* **1,** the young of the fox, bear, or the like; **2,** an inexperienced youth.

cub-by-hole (kub'i-hōl'), *n.* a small confined space.

cube (kūb), *n.* **1,** in geometry, a regular solid body with six equal square sides or faces; **2,** any body resembling this; as, candy *cubes;* **3,** the product obtained when a number is multiplied two times by itself; as, $5 \times 5 \times 5 = 125$, the *cube* of 5:—*v.t.* [cubed, cub-ing], **1,** to multiply (a number) twice by itself; raise to the third power; **2,** to form into cubelike shapes; as, to *cube* potatoes.—*adj.* **cu′bic.**—*adj.* **cu′bi-cal:** —**cube root,** a number or quantity that multiplied by itself to the third power (or two times) gives the number; thus, 2 is the *cube root* of 8.

cu-bi-cle (kū′bi-kl), *n.* a very small room, as a telephone booth or a bedroom.

cub-ism (kūb′izm), *n.* a modern school of painting and sculpture that uses geometric figures to suggest volume.

cu-bit (kū′bit), *n.* chiefly *Biblical,* a former measure of 18″ to 20″.

cuck-oo (kook′ōō′), *n.* an ash-grey European bird noted for laying its eggs in the nests of other birds, and leaving them to the care of the nest-owners; also, an American bird which rears its own young: both so named from their characteristic two-noted love call; **2,** the call of the cuckoo:— *adj.* **1,** relating to the cuckoo; **2,** *Slang,* silly; unbalanced.

cu-cum-ber (kū′kum-bėr), *n.* **1,** a creeping plant cultivated for its fruit, which is used as a salad or pickle; **2,** the fruit itself.

cud (kud), *n.* food which certain animals, called *ruminants,* bring back into the mouth from the first stomach to be chewed; as, cows, sheep, goats, and the like, chew the *cud.*

cud-dle (kud′l), *v.t.* [cud-dled, cud-dling], to embrace closely and lovingly; as, a mother *cuddles* a baby:—*v.i.* to lie close or snug; nestle.

cudg-el (kuj′el), *n.* a thick stick used as a weapon:—*v.t.* [cudgelled, cudgelling], to beat with a stick.

¹cue (kū), *n.* **1,** the tapering rod used to strike the ball in playing billiards, pool, and similar games; **2,** a pigtail; queue; **3,** a long line of people waiting. See **queue.**

²cue (kū), *n.* **1,** a hint; a suggestion as to what to do; **2,** the last words of a speech or scene in a play which indicate the time for another actor to enter or speak.

¹cuff (kuf), *n.* a blow, as with the open hand:—*v.t.* to strike with the open hand.

²cuff (kuf), *n.* a band worn about the wrist, as on a sleeve; also, a fold about the bottom of a trouser leg.

cui-sine (kwi-zēn′), *n.* the kitchen or cooking department of a hotel, home, etc.; the style or quality of cooking.

cu-li-nar-y (kū′li-nėr-i), *adj.* pertaining to the kitchen or to cooking.

cull (kul), *v.t.* to pick out; select; gather:—*n.* something sorted out from the rest of a group, as inferior or worthless; as, the *culls* of an orchard.

cul-mi-nate (kul′mi-nāt′), *v.i.* [culminat-ed, culminat-ing], to reach the highest point; come to a climax.—*n.* **cul′mi-na′tion.**

cul-pa-ble (kul′pa-bl), *adj.* guilty; criminal; blameworthy.—*adv.* **cul′pa-bly.**—*n.* **cul′pa-bil′i-ty.**

cul-prit (kul′prit), *n.* **1,** one formally accused of a crime; **2,** one guilty of a crime.

cult (kult), *n.* **1,** a particular system of worship; **2,** devotion to a person, idea, theory, or the like; as, the nudist *cult;* **3,** the group of people so devoted; also, the object of their devotion.

cul-ti-vate (kul′ti-vāt′), *v.t.* [cultivat-ed, cultivat-ing], **1,** to till, as the soil; raise by tillage, as crops; **2,** to improve by care, labour, or study; **3,** to devote oneself to; as, to *cultivate* literature; **4,** to seek the society of (a person or persons); **5,** to loosen the ground about (growing crops).—*n.* **cul′ti-va′-tion.**

cul-ti-va-tor (kul′ti-vā′tėr), *n.* **1,** one who tills; **2,** a farm implement for loosening earth about crops.

cul-ture (kul′tūr; chėr), *n.* **1,** care given to the growth and development of animals and plants; **2,** the breeding of germs for scientific study; also, the product of such breeding; **3,** improvement of mind or body by practice or training; as, voice *culture;* physical *culture;* **4,** the training of the mental or moral powers; refinement; **5,** the civilization of a race of people, including religion, arts, and social customs; as, Greek, Zulu, or Navajo *culture.*— *adj.* **cul′tur-al.**—*adj.* **cul′tured.**

cul-vert (kul′vėrt), *n.* a drain, sewer, conduit, etc., passing under a roadway.

cum-ber (kum′bėr), *v.t.* **1,** to burden; **2,** to perplex; as, he was *cumbered* with care.

cum-ber-some (kum′bėr-sum),′ *adj.* burdensome; clumsy.—*adv.* **cum′ber-some-ly.**

cu-mu-la-tive (kūm′ū-lā′tiv), *adj.* becoming larger by successive additions as, *cumulative* interest (on money invested).

cu-mu-lus (kūm′ū-lus), *adj.* said of clouds that pile up in rounded masses above a horizontal base; hence, **cu′mu-lo-cir′rus,** or small, light and filmy; **cu′mu-lo-nim′bus,** or thick, towering and black (pouring rain); **cu′mu-lo-strā′tus,** or swelling up from a horizontal base.

---

cat, āge, fär, cåre, åsk; ten, ēve, latėr; (i) pity, rely, senate; īce; top; nō.

cu-ne-i-form (kū-nē'i-fôrm), *n.* and *adj.* the wedge-shaped writing of ancient inscriptions found in Babylon, Persia, Assyria, etc.

Ox (Cuneiform word)

cun-ning (kun'ing), *adj.* 1, skilful; clever; done with skill or ingenuity; as, a *cunning* craftsman; a *cunning* escape; 2, crafty; sly; designing; 3, *Colloq.*, pretty; cute; as, a *cunning* child:—*n.* skill; ability; also, deceit; craftiness.—*adv.* **cun'ning-ly.**

cup (kup), *n.* 1, a small open vessel, usually with a handle, used for drinking or measuring; 2, something shaped like a cup; as, the *cup* of an acorn; 3, the amount a cup holds; as, a cupful; as, two *cups* of milk; 4, a cup-shaped prize of gold or silver; as, to win the yacht *cup*; 5, one's portion of happiness or misery; as, to drain the *cup* of sorrow; 6, **cups,** intoxication: usually in the expression *in his cups*:—*v.t.* [cupped, cup-ping], to form a cup with; as, to *cup* one's hands.

cup-board (kub'êrd), *n.* 1, a closet fitted with shelves for cups, plates, etc.; 2, any small closet.

cup-ful (kup'fool),*n.* two-fifths of a pint.

cu-pid-i-ty (kū-pid'i-ti), *n.* greed, esp. for money or wealth.

cu-po-la (kū'po-la), *n.* 1. a domelike roof; a dome; 2, any small domelike structure above the roof of a building.

cur (kûr), *n.* 1, a mongrel; a dog of mixed breed; 2, a surly, illbred person.

CUPOLA

cu-rate (kū'rit), *n.* an assistant to a priest or rector.

cu-ra-tor (kū-rā'tèr), *n.* one in charge of a museum, art gallery, or the like.

curb (kûrb), *v.t.* 1, to restrain; keep within bounds; 2, to furnish with a protecting rim, as of stone; as, to *curb* a street:—*n.* 1, that which checks, restrains, or subdues; as, he put a *curb* on his anger; 2, a chain or strap attached to a horse's bit and used as a check; 3, (also *kerb*), a protecting rim of stone bordering a sidewalk. Also,—*n.* **curb'stone**.

curd (kûrd), *n.* the thickened part of milk; as, cheese is formed of *curds*:—*v.t.* and *v.i.* to curdle.—*adj.* **curd'y.**

cur-dle (kûr'dl), *v.t.* [cur-dled, cur-dling], to thicken into curd:—*v.i.* to thicken; as, this milk has *curdled*.

cure (kūr), *n.* 1, the act of healing; as, the *cure* of a cold; 2, a method of treatment that cures; as, the milk *cure*;

the water *cure*; 3, a remedy; as, quinine is a *cure* for malaria:—*v.t.* [cured, cur-ing], 1, to heal; restore to health; 2, to remedy or remove (an evil of any kind); as, he *cured* his dread of the dark; 3, to preserve by salting, drying, etc.; as, to *cure* hams.—*adj.* **cur'a-ble; cur'a-tive.**

cur-few (kûr'fū), *n.* 1, in mediaeval Europe, the ringing of a bell at a fixed hour in the evening as a warning that fires and lights were to be put out; the law which required this; also, the bell itself; 2, hence, a bell rung at a certain hour in the evening, as a signal for children to leave the streets.

cu-ri-o (kū'ri-ō'), *n.* [*pl.* curios], a rare object of art; a curiosity.

cu-ri-ous (kū'ri-us), *adj.* 1, anxious to know; prying; as, *curious* eyes; a *curious* mind; 2, strange; full of mystery; as, a *curious* silence.—*n.* **cu'ri-os'i-ty.**

curl (kûrl), *n.* 1, a small ring of hair; a ringlet; 2, anything of similar shape; as, a *curl* of smoke; 3, the act of forming, or state of being formed into a curved or coiled shape; as, the *curl* of a wave; hair kept in *curl*:—*v.t.* to twist into ringlets or coils:—*v.i.* 1, to grow or move in spirals; as, smoke *curled* lazily from the chimney; 2, to play at curling.—*adj.* **curl'y.**

curl-er (kûr'lêr), *n.* 1, a person or thing that curls; 2, one who plays the game of *curling*.

cur-lew (kûr'lū), *n.* a long-legged shore-bird with a long, downward-curving bill.

curl-i-cue, curl-y-cue (kûr'li-kū'), *n.* a fancy flourish in handwriting.

curl-ing (kûr'ling), *n.* a game in which heavy, polished stones are slid on *ice* towards a *tee* about 38 yards away.

cur-rant (kur'ant), *n.* 1, a small seedless raisin; 2, a common garden shrub; also, its acid, red, black, or white berry, used for jellies and jams.

cur-ren-cy (kur'en-si), *n.* [*pl.* currencies], 1, a passing from person to person; circulation, as of bank-notes; 2, general acceptance; as, the *currency* of a scientific theory; 3, that which is generally used for money, as notes and coin; as, the *currency* of a nation.

cur-rent (kur'ent), *adj.* 1, widely circulated; passing from person to person; 2, now passing, as time; as, the *current* year; belonging to the present time; as, the *current* issue of a magazine; 3, generally accepted; common; as, *current* opinion:—*n.* 1, a flow or passing; a body of air or water flowing in a certain direction; esp., the swift part of a stream; **2,** the flow, or rate of flow, of electricity; **3,** general course or tendency; as, the *current* of the present time.—*adv.* **cur'rent-ly.**

cur-ric-u-lum (ku-rik'ū-lum), *n.* [*pl.* curriculums (ku-rik'ū-lumz) or curricula (ku-rik'ū-la)], a regular course of study in a university, school, or the like.—*adj.* **cur-ric'u-lar.**

¹cur-ry (kur'i), *n.* [*pl.* curries], **1,** a highly spiced East Indian sauce; **2,** a dish of meat, rice, or the like, cooked or seasoned with this sauce.

²curry (kur'i), *v.t.* **1,** to rub down and clean, as a horse:—**curry favour,** to try to gain favour, as by flattery, etc.

curse (kûrs), *n.* **1,** an oath; **2,** a prayer for injury to someone; **3,** that which brings or causes evil or trouble; also, the evil itself; as, crime is a *curse:—v.t.* [cursed or curst (kûrst), curs-ing], **1,** to wish, or bring, evil upon; blaspheme; swear at; **2,** to torment; to afflict; as, to be *cursed* with a bad temper:—*v.i.* to swear.—*adj.* **curs'ed.**

cur-so-ry (kûr'so-ri), *adj.* hasty; superficial; as, a *cursory* glance at a paper.

curt (kûrt), *adj.* **1,** short; **2,** abrupt; rude.

cur-tail (kûr-tāl'), *v.t.* to cut short; as, rain *curtailed* the exercises; reduce, as expenses.—*n.* **cur-tail'ment.**

cur-tain (kûr'tn; kûr'tin), *n.* **1,** a hanging covering or screen, usually of cloth, which can be drawn up or aside; as a window *curtain;* **2,** anything that serves to conceal; as, the fog was like a *curtain* over the city:—*v.t.* to furnish with draperies; enclose with a screen or the like.

curt-sy (kûrt'si), *n.* [*pl.* curtsies], a bow, made by bending the knees and lowering the body:—*v.i.* [curtsied, curtsy-ing], to make a curtsy. Also **curt'sey.**

cur-va-ture (kûr'va-tūr; chêr), *n.* a bending; curving; also, the amount of bending, as of a curved line or surface.

curve (kûrv), *n.* **1,** a bending without angles; also, that which is bent; **2,** in baseball, a ball so pitched as to turn from its expected course:—*v.t.* [curved, curv-ing], to cause to bend or turn from a straight line:—*v.i.* to bend; to turn.

cur-vet (kûr'vit), *n.* a horse's upward leap in which its hind legs are raised from the ground just before the forelegs come down again:—*v.i.* (kûr-vet'), to make such a leap; [curvetted (-id) or curveted, curvet-ting or curvet-ing].

cush-ion (koosh'un), *n.* **1,** a pillow or soft pad to sit, lie, or rest upon; **2,** anything resembling a cushion; as, a *cushion* of leaves:—*v.t.* **1,** to seat on, or

as on, a soft pad; **2,** to furnish with a soft pad.

cusp (kusp), *n.* **1,** the point or elevation where two curves meet and stop, as on the crown of a tooth or apex of a leaf; **2,** one of the points of the crescent moon.

cus-pid (kus'pid), *n.* a tooth with only one point for tearing food; a canine tooth.

cus-pi-dor (kus'pi-dôr'), *n.* a spittoon, or vessel into which one may spit.

cus-tard (kus'têrd), *n.* a mixture of eggs, milk, and sugar, baked or boiled.

cus-to-dy (kus'to-di),. *n.* **1,** guardianship; care; as, the *custody* of the jewels; **2,** restraint of liberty; imprisonment; as, the accused was taken into *custody.*—*n.* **cus-to'di-an.**

cus-tom (kus'tum), *n.* **1,** an established practice, habit, or usage; as, it is his *custom* to read in bed; the strange *customs* of the Indians; **2,** the regular buying of goods in one place; as, I give my *custom* to this store; **3, customs,** government taxes on imported or, less frequently, exported goods:—*adj.* **1,** made to order; as, *custom* hats; **2,** doing only work that is ordered; as, *custom* tailors.—*adj.* **cus'tom-ar'y.**—*adv.* **cus'tom-ar-i-ly.**—*adj.* **custom-built.**

cus-tom-er (kus'tum-êr), *n.* one who buys; esp., one who buys regularly at a certain store; a patron.

cut (kut), *v.t.* [*p.t.* and *p.p.* cut, *p.pr.* cut-ting], **1,** to slash with a sharp-edged tool; as, to *cut* one's finger; to hew; as, to *cut* down a tree; to pierce; as, the sleet *cut* his skin; **2,** to shape, as a garment, with a sharp instrument; as, she *cut* the sleeves for the dress; **3,** to shorten or reduce in length or extent; trim; as, to *cut* the hair; *cu* expenses; **4,** figuratively, to grieve or hurt; as, the remark *cut* him to the quick; to penetrate, as if with a sharp-edged tool; as, the wind *cut* him to the bone; **5,** to pretend not to recognize; **6,** to cross; to intersect; as, the two railroad lines *cut* one another; **7,** to dissolve or make less stiff; as, a strong soap will *cut* the grease in washing dishes; **8,** *Colloq.,* to absent oneself from (a lecture, class, or the like):—**to cut teeth,** to have new teeth appear through the gums:—*v.i.* **1,** to make a gash; as, the knife *cuts* well; also, to admit of being cut or divided; as, this meat *cuts* easily; **2,** to pass through or across by a direct route; as, to *cut* across is shorter:—*n.* **1,** the act of slashing or separating by a sharp instrument; also, a slash or wound made by a sharp instrument; **2,** a sharp stroke, as with a

whip; 3, a passage or channel made by digging; as, a *cut* for a railroad track; **4,** that which is severed or detached by a sharp instrument; a slice; as, a *cut* of cake; **5,** a straight, short passage; as, the path is a short *cut* to the house; **6,** the fashion of a garment; style; as, the *cut* of a coat; **7,** a reduction, as in price, expenses, or the like; **8,** absence, as from a lecture, class, or the like; **9,** the deliberate ignoring of an acquaintance; **10,** an engraved block of wood or metal from which a picture or the like is printed; also, the picture made from it:—*adj.* **1,** divided or separated; **2,** gashed, wounded; **3,** having the surface ornamented or fashioned, as a gem; **4,** reduced; as, dresses sold at *cut* prices: —**cut and dried, 1,** prearranged; **2,** boring; lifeless.

cute (kūt), *adj.* [cut-er, cut-est], *Colloq.*, **1,** clever; shrewd; **2,** attractive because of daintiness, etc.; as, a *cute* child.

cu-ti-cle (kū'ti-kl), *n.* **1,** the outer layer of skin; the epidermis; **2,** dead skin, as that around the base of a finger-nail.

cut-lass (kut'las), *n.* a short, heavy sword, with a wide, curved blade, used especially by sailors.

cut-ler (kut'lẽr), *n.* one who makes, sells, or repairs knives or other cutting tools.

cut-ler-y (kut'lẽr-i), *n.* **1,** edged or cutting tools collectively, as knives, scissors, etc.; esp., implements used in cutting or serving food; **2,** the business of a cutler.

cut-let (kut'lit), *n.* a slice of meat, generally of veal or mutton, cut from the ribs or leg of an animal, for frying or broiling; also, any preparation of fish, ground meat, or the like, shaped like a cutlet.

cut-off (kut'-ôf'), *n.* a device for shutting off a fluid, steam, etc., from an engine or mechanism, or the place where it is shut off; **2,** a road, passage, or channel that shortens the distance (across).

cut-out (kut'out'), *n.* **1,** a device to allow exhaust gases to bypass a motor-car's muffler; **2,** a design or shape prepared for cutting out of cardboard, etc.; **3,** a switch or electric circuit-breaker.

cut-ter (kut'ẽr), *n.* **1,** one who cuts out and shapes anything, as garments; **2,** that which cuts; **3,** a light sleigh for two persons; **4,** a small, single-masted sailing-vessel, or a boat used by ships of war; **5,** an armed boat used by the coast-guard; as, a revenue *cutter*.

cut-throat (kut'thrōt'), *n.* a murderous villain; an assassin:—*adj.* murderous.

cut-tle-fish (kut'l-fish'), *n.* a salt-water shellfish, which has ten arms or tentacles and which gives forth a cloud of black fluid when attacked.

cut-worm (kut'wûrm'), *n.* a destructive caterpillar which destroys the young shoots of cabbage, corn, or the like, by cutting part way through the stalk at or near the ground.

cy-an-ide (sī'an-īd'), *n.* potassium and sodium cyanide (deadly poisons), used in electroplating, case-hardening of steel, extracting gold from low-grade ores, and as a flux.

cy-cle (sī'kl), *n.* **1,** a period of time, or a round of events, that takes place regularly; **2,** a complete series; esp., a group of stories surrounding a famous event or hero; as, the Arthurian *cycle;* **3,** an age or long period of time; **4,** a bicycle, tricycle, or motorcycle:— *v.i.* [cy-cled, cy-cling], to ride a cycle; as, he *cycled* to town.—*adj.* **cy'clic.**—*n.* **cy'clist.**

cy-clom-e-ter (sī-klom'e-tẽr), *n.* a device for recording the revolutions of a wheel (as a bicycle), and hence the distance travelled.

cy-clone (sī'klōn), *n.* **1,** a violent storm in which the wind whirls inward toward a calm centre; **2,** loosely, any destructive storm.—*adj.* **cy-clon'ic** (si-klon'ik).

cy-clo-pae-di-a (sī'klō-pē'di-a), *n.* an encyclopaedia, or volume with wide range of summarized information.— *adj.* **cy'clo-pae'dic.** Also, **cy'clo-pe'di-a, cy'clo-pe'dic.**

cy-clo-tron (sī'klo-tron'; sik-), *n.* a device for increasing the speed of positive particles, esp. protons, etc., in order to bombard and split atoms; an atom-smasher.

cyl-in-der (sil'in-dẽr), *n.* **1,** a solid or hollow body, long and round, with its two ends equal and parallel; **2,** any body having the form of a cylinder, as the piston chamber of a gasoline or steam-engine, the barrel of a pump, a roller used in a printing-press, etc.—*adj.* **cy-lin'dri-cal; cy-lin'dric.**

CYLINDER

cym-bal (sim'bl), *n.* in *music,* either of two circular metal plates which when clashed together produce a ringing sound.

cyn-ic (sin'ik), *n.* one who doubts the goodness of human nature and believes that each person has only a desire to further his own interests; hence, a sarcastic, sneering person; a fault-finder:—*adj.* sarcastic; doubting.—*adj.* **cyn′i-cal.**—*adv.* **cyn′i-cal-ly.**—*n.* **cyn′i-cism.**

cy-no-sure (sī′nō-shoor′), *n.* an object of attraction and attention; as, the comet was the *cynosure* of every eye.

cy-pher (sī′fėr), *n.* Same as **cipher.**

cy-press (sī′pres), *n.* 1, a cone-bearing evergreen tree of the pine family; 2, the wood of a cypress tree:—*adj.* pertaining to, or made of, cypress.

cyst (sist), *n.* a sac, or pouch, in the body, containing diseased matter.

czar (zär) or **tsar** (tsär), *n.* 1, the title of the former emperors of Russia; 2, a dictator; as, the *czar* of an industry.—*n. fem.* **cza-ri′na; tsa-ri′na.**

D

D, d (dē), *n.* 1, the fourth letter of the alphabet, following C, or its sound; 2, in *music*, the second tone in the major scale of C; 3, the Roman numeral for 500.

dab (dab), *v.t.* [dabbed, dab-bing], to strike or touch lightly; smear in spots:—*n.* 1, a soft blow; 2, a quick, sharp stroke; 3, a small, soft lump; 4, a small portion.

dab-ble (dab′l), *v.t.* [dab-bled, dab-bling], to wet by dipping; spatter:—*v.i.* 1, to paddle in water, as with the hands; 2, to work at or do anything indifferently; as, to *dabble* in art.—*n.* **dab′bler.**

dachs-hund (däks′hoont′; daks′-hoond′; dash′-hund′; dash′-und), *n.* a hound, usually black or brown, with a long body and very short, crooked legs.

DACHSHUND ($\frac{1}{20}$)

da-cron (dā′kron), *n.* a strong, washable, moth-proof, wrinkle-resisting, synthetic cloth (a trade-mark).

dac-tyl (dak′til), *n.* in *verse*, a metrical foot (‾ ˘ ˘), consisting of a long syllable followed by two short ones; as Tĕnderlў/soōthĭnglў/. Homer's *Iliad*, Vergil's *Aenead*, and Longfellow's *Evangeline* are in *dactylic* hexameter.—*adj.* **dac-tyl′ic.**

dad, daddy (dad, da′di), *n. Colloq.* for father.

dad-dy—long-legs (dad′i–lông′legz′), a small-bodied spider-like animal with long, slender legs.

daf-fo-dil (daf′ō-dil), *n.* a plant, grown from a bulb, with long, narrow leaves and large yellow flowers.

daft (dȧft), *adj.* weak-minded; simple; foolish; crazy.

dag-ger (dag′ėr), *n.* 1, a short, sharp, pointed knife, used for stabbing; 2, in printing a mark [†] telling the reader to look elsewhere for more information.

dahl-ia (dāl′ya; däl′ya; dal′ya), *n.* 1, a garden plant that grows from a bulb to a height varying from three to nine feet, and bears in the early autumn large showy flowers of red, yellow, white, etc.; 2, the bulb or flower of this plant.

dai-ly (dā′li), *n.* [*pl.* dailies], a newspaper published every day:—*adj.* occurring, appearing, or done every day:—*adv.* on every day; day by day.

dain-ty (dān′ti), *n.* [*pl.* dainties], something choice or delicious; a choice bit of food:—*adj.* [dain-ti-er, dain-ti-est], 1, delicious; 2, pretty in a delicate way; 3, sensitive; having delicate tastes and feelings.—*adv.* **dain′ti-ly.**

dair-y (dâr′i), *n.* [*pl.* dairies], 1, a place where milk is kept and made into butter and cheese; 2, a farm, or part of a farm, which produces and sells milk, butter, and cheese; 3, a shop where milk, butter, and cheese are sold.—*n.* **dair′y-ing.**

da-is (dā′is; dās), *n.* [*pl.* daises (dā′is-ez; dās′ez)], a raised platform, as for a throne or seats of honour, in a large room or hall.

dai-sy (dā′zi), *n.* [*pl.* daisies], a flower of the aster family, with a brown or yellow centre surrounded by white, yellow, or pink petals; also, the plant itself. The *English daisy* is low-growing and has white or pink petals, while the common *ox-eye daisy*, in Canada, grows tall and has white petals.—*adj.* **dai′sied.**

dale (dāl), *n.* a valley; glen; as, they went up hill and down *dale*.

dal-ly (dal′i), *v.i.* [dallied, dally-ing], 1, to make sport; play; trifle, as with affections or an idea; 2, to waste time; loiter; as, he *dallied* over his work.—*n.* **dal′li-ance.**

Dal-ma-tian (dal-mā′shun), *n.* a breed of dog like a pointer, with black-and-white spots; a coach dog.

cat, āge, fär, câre, ȧsk; ten, ēve, latėr; (i) pity, rely, senate; īce; top; nō.

¹dam (dam), *n.* **1,** a bank or wall built so as to hold back a flow of water; **2,** water so held back:—*v.t.* [dammed, dam-ming], **1,** to provide with a dam; as, to *dam* a brook; **2,** to obstruct; restrain; confine.

²dam (dam), *n.* a mother: generally used of certain animals, as sheep.

dam-age (dam′ij), *n.* **1,** injury or harm; as, the flood did *damage* to the town; **2, damages,** money paid to one for injury or loss through the fault of another; as, the streetcar company paid him *damages:*—*v.t.* [damaged, damag-ing], to injure.—*adj.* **dam′age-able.**

dam-ask (dam′ask), *n.* **1,** a figured fabric of silk, linen, wool, or other material, used esp. for table-cloths: so named from the city of Damascus, where it was originally made; **2,** hard, elastic steel decorated with wavy lines, and formerly used for sword-blades; **3,** a deep-pink colour:—*adj.* **1,** pertaining to or coming from Damascus; **2,** made of damask; as, a *damask* table-cloth; **3,** of a deep-pink colour.

dame (dām), *n.* **1,** formerly, a lady of high rank; now, a lady member of an Order of the British Empire: also used as a title of respect, corresponding to *Sir;* **2,** a title used instead of Mistress or Madam; **3,** a matron; an elderly woman; **4,** *Slang,* a girl or woman.

damn (dam), *v.t.* [damned (damd), damning (dam′ing; often dam′ning, except in sense 3)], **1,** to condemn; **2,** to doom to eternal punishment; **3,** to curse; call down a curse upon; **4,** to judge as bad, faulty, or as a failure; as, the critics *damned* the book.—*adj.* **dam′na-ble.**—*n.* **dam-na′tion.**

damp (damp), *n.* **1,** moisture; fog; **2,** a poisonous gas sometimes found in coal-mines; **3,** depression of spirits:—*adj.* moist; a little wet; as, a *damp* cloth:—*v.t.* **1,** to moisten; **2,** to discourage; depress; **3,** to check; stifle.—*adv.* **damp′ly.**—*n.* **damp′ness.**

damp-en (damp′en), *v.t.* **1,** to make moist or wet; **2,** to depress or discourage.

damp-er (damp′ėr), *n.* **1,** something which depresses or discourages; as, to put a *damper* on fun; **2,** a movable plate to regulate a draught, as in a stove.

dam-sel (dam′zel), *n.* a maiden; girl.

dance (dáns), *v.i.* [danced, danc-ing], **1,** to move the body and feet rhythmically in time to music; **2,** to skip about lightly; as, the child *danced* in glee; sunbeams *dance* in the room:—*v.t.* **1,** to give a dancing motion to; as, to *dance*

the baby up and down; **2,** to perform; as, to *dance* a jig:—*n.* **1,** a rhythmical movement of the body and feet, usually to the accompaniment of music; **2,** a dancing party, less formal than a ball; **3,** one round of dancing at such a party; as, may I have this *dance*? **4,** a piece of music for dancing; as, the orchestra played a new *dance*.—*n.* **danc′er.**

dan-de-li-on (dan′di-lī′un), *n.* a common plant having yellow flowers and coarsely-toothed leaves; also, its flower.

dan-dle (dan′dl), *v.t.* [dan-dled, dan-dling], **1,** to dance (an infant) up and down, as on the knee; **2,** to fondle.

dan-druff (dan′druf), *n.* minute scales of dead skin that form on the scalp.

dan-dy (dan′di), *n.* [*pl.* dandies], **1,** a man who gives much attention to dress; **2,** *Colloq.,* something unusually fine:—*adj.* [dan-di-er, dan-di-est], *Colloq.,* excellent.

dan-ger (dān′jėr), *n.* **1,** peril; exposure to loss, injury, or death; risk; as, the *danger* of an explosion was very grave; **2,** something which may cause loss, injury, etc.

dan-ger-ous (dān′jėr-us), *adj.* **1,** unsafe; perilous; as, a *dangerous* road; **2,** likely to do harm; as, a *dangerous* criminal.

dan-gle (dang′gl), *v.i.* [dan-gled, dan-gling], **1,** to hang or swing loosely; **2,** to hang about anyone; as, flatterers *dangle* about a king:—*v.t.* to cause to swing loosely; as, he *dangled* the bag.

dank (dangk), *adj.* unpleasantly damp; moist; wet; as, *dank* seaweed.

dan-seuse (dän′söz′), *n.* a professional woman dancer; the leading woman in a ballet.

daph-ni-a (daf′ni-a), *n.* a genus of minute fresh-water crustaceans; a water-flea: used as a fish food in aquaria.

dap-per (dap′ėr), *adj.* **1,** small and active; **2,** trim and neat in appearance.

dap-ple (dap′l), *adj.* spotted; as, a *dapple*-grey horse:—*n.* a spotted animal, esp. a horse:—*v.t.* [dap-pled, dap-pling], to decorate with spots.—*adj.* **dap′pled.**

dare (dâr), *v.i.* [*p.t.* dared (dârd) or durst (dûrst), *p.p.* dared, *p.pr.* dar-ing], to have courage; be bold enough; venture; as, I do not *dare* to enter:—*v.t.* **1,** to have courage for; brave; as, to *dare* the perils of arctic travel; **2,** to challenge; as, he *dared* me to jump:—*n.* a challenge.

dare—dev-il (dâr′—dev′l), *adj.* bold; reckless:—*n.* a reckless, bold person.

dar-ing (dâr′ing), *n.* bravery; bold-ness:—*adj.* fearless; bold; venturous.

dark (därk), *adj.* **1,** having little or no light; **2,** of colours, nearer black than white; **3,** of a brunette complexion; **4,** gloomy; as, a *dark* mood; **5,** secret; mysterious; as, a *dark* saying; **6,** evil; as, a *dark* deed:—*n.* **1,** darkness; nightfall; **2,** secrecy; as, to work in the *dark;* **3,** ignorance; as, I am in the *dark* on the subject.—*adv.* **dark'ly.**—*n.* **dark'ness.**—*v.t.* and *v.i.* **dark'en.**

dark-room (därk'rōōm'), *n.* a room from which sunlight is excluded, for developing films, etc.

dark-some (därk'sum), *adj. Poetic,* dark; gloomy; hence, wicked; mysterious.

dark-y (där'ki), *n.* [*pl.* darkies], a Negro. Also spelled **dark'ey** [*pl.* darkeys].

dar-ling (där'ling), *n.* one dearly loved:—*adj.* tenderly loved; very dear.

darn (därn), *v.t.* to mend, as a hole in a fabric, by interweaving thread or yarn:—*n.* the place so mended.—*n.* **darn'ing.**

dar-nel (där'nel), *n.* a poisonous weed of grain fields, rye grass.

darn-ing—nee-dle (därn'ing-nē'dl), *n.* **1,** a long needle for darning; **2,** a dragon-fly.

dart (därt), *n.* **1,** a thin, pointed weapon, thrown by hand; **2,** a swift, sudden movement:—*v.t.* to throw out suddenly; as, to *dart* angry glances:—*v.i.* to move swiftly; as, the child *darted* here and there.

dash (dash), *v.t.* **1,** to throw violently or hastily; as, he *dashed* the vase to pieces; **2,** to push aside; **3,** to spatter; to splash; as, they *dashed* him with water; **4,** to ruin; destroy; as, you *dash* my hopes; **5,** to do hastily; as, to *dash* off a letter:—*v.i.* **1,** to rush with violence; as, he *dashed* madly away; **2,** to strike on a surface violently; as, rain *dashed* against the window:—*n.* **1,** a violent blow; **2,** a little bit; as, a *dash* of pepper; **3,** spirit; energy; as, with vim and *dash;* **4,** *Colloq.*, a vulgar display; as, to cut a *dash* with fine clothes; **5,** a mark [—] used in writing or printing to mark a pause or break; **6,** the striking of a liquid against a surface; **7,** a sudden rush; as, a *dash* for freedom; **8,** a short race; as, a hundred-yard *dash.*

dash-board (dash'bōrd'), *n.* in cars, airplanes, etc., a panel with gauges and instruments; **2,** a splashboard or screen on a boat, carriage, etc.

dash-er (dash'ẽr), *n.* **1,** one who or that which dashes; **2,** the part of an ice-cream freezer, etc., which stirs or churns a liquid; **3,** the plunger of a churn.

dash-ing (dash'ing), *adj.* **1,** spirited; bold; as, a *dashing* soldier; **2,** showy; gay.

das-tard (das'tẽrd), *n.* a base coward:—*adj.* mean; cowardly.—*adj.* **das'tard-ly.**

da-ta (dā'tȧ; dä'tȧ), *n.pl.* [*sing.* datum (dā'tum; dä'tum)], a collection of facts to be used as a basis for study; as, he has collected the *data* for his report.

¹date (dāt), *n.* **1,** the point of time at which something takes place or is done; as, the *date* of his death; **2,** the period or era to which anything belongs; as, art of an early *date;* **3,** *Colloq.* an engagement for a fixed time:—*v.t.* [dat-ed, dat-ing], **1,** to mark with a definite time; **2,** to find the definite time of:—*v.i.* to belong to a certain time; as, this house *dates* from the days of the 17th century.

²date (dāt), *n.* the edible fruit of the date-palm tree, oblong in shape and enclosing a single bed.

da-tive (dā'tiv), *n.* in *grammar,* the case of a noun, pronoun, or adjective that expresses the indirect object; as, he gave his *son* a toy; she got it for *me;* tell it to *George: son, me,* and *George* are datives.—*adj.* denoting an indirect object (usually a person or persons).

da-tum (dā'tum), *n. Sing.* of data.

daub (dôb), *v.t.* **1,** to cover or smear with mud, plaster, or the like; **2,** to paint coarsely or unskilfully:—*v.i.* **1,** to put on plaster, mud, or the like; **2,** to paint poor pictures:—*n.* **1,** a smear; smudge; **2,** a picture poorly painted.—*n.* **daub'er.**

daugh-ter (dô'tẽr), *n.* **1,** a female child; **2,** a female member of a race, church, etc.; as, a *daughter* of France.

daugh-ter—in—law (dô'tẽr–in–lô'), *n* [*pl.* daughters-in-law], a son's wife.

daunt (dônt; dänt), *v.t.* to frighten; dishearten; dismay.

daunt-less (dônt'lis; dänt'lis), *adj·* fearless; intrepid.

dau-phin (dô'fin), *n.* formerly, the title of the oldest son of the king of France.

dav-en-port (dav'en-pôrt'), *n.* a long upholstered sofa with back and arms; esp. one that can be converted, or changed, into a bed.

dav-its (dav'its), *n.* two cranes or r-shaped arms used in lowering and raising lifeboats from ships.

daw (dô), *n.* a bird of the crow family; a jackdaw.

daw-dle (dô′dl), *v.i.* [daw-dled, dawdling], to waste time; loiter; as, *dawdle* over work.—*n.* **daw′dler.**

dawn (dôn), *v.i.* **1,** to begin to grow light; as, when day *dawned*, the attack began; **2,** to become evident or plain; as, the solution of the problem finally *dawned* upon me; **3,** to begin to develop; as, with Pasteur, a new era *dawned* in medicine:—*n.* **1,** the first appearance of daylight; **2,** a beginning or unfolding; as, the *dawn* of history.

day (dā), *n.* **1,** the period of light between sunrise and sunset; daylight; **2,** a period of 24 consecutive hours; **3,** an age or period; as, the *day* of chivalry; *days* of old; **4,** the number of hours per day allowed or permitted for work; as, an eight-hour *day;* **5,** a particular 24-hour period connected with some observance; as, a birth*day;* Armistice *Day.*

day-book (dā′book′), *n.* a bookkeeping journal or diary in which transactions are entered as they occur; a book recording daily all sales, purchases, receipts, etc.

day-break (dā′brāk′), *n.* dawn.

day-dream (dā′drēm′), *n.* an idle fancy; a castle in the air:—*v.i.* to indulge in fanciful waking dreams.

day-light (dā′līt′), *n.* **1,** the light of day; **2,** the time between dawn and dusk; **3,** daybreak; as, he arose at *daylight:*—**daylight-saving time,** time that is reckoned one hour earlier than standard time and which thus gives an extra hour of daylight in the evening; as, when it is eight o'clock in the evening, standard time, it is nine o'clock *daylight-saving time.*

day-time (dā′tīm′), *n.* the period from dawn to sunset.

daze (dāz), *v.t.* [dazed, daz-ing], **1,** to confuse; stupefy; as, he was *dazed* by the blow; **2,** to dazzle; as, the display of jewellery *dazed* the spectators:—*n.* a state of confusion or bewilderment.— *adj.* **dazed.**

daz-zle (daz′l), *v.t.* [daz-zled, dazzling], **1,** to confuse with a glare of light; **2,** to bewilder or surprise with splendour; as, the richness of her house *dazzled* the guests:—*n.* glitter.— *adv.* **daz′zling-ly.**

dea-con (dē′kun), *n.* a subordinate church official who assists in certain ceremonies, in caring for the poor, etc. In the Roman Catholic and Protestant Episcopal churches, he is ordained, and ranks just below a priest; in other churches, he is a layman assisting the minister.—*n. fem.* **dea′con-ess** (dē′kon-is).

dead (ded), *adj.* **1,** having ceased to live; as, a *dead* man; *dead*wood; **2,** without life; inanimate; as, *dead* matter; **3,** inactive; showing no force, motion, liveliness, or the like; as, a *dead* electric wire; a *dead* tennis-ball; **4,** disused; as, a *dead* language; **5,** complete; utter; as, a *dead* loss:—*n.* **1,** one who has died; those who have died; as, the quick and the *dead;* **2,** the time of greatest inactivity or quietness; as, the *dead* of night:—*adv.* **1,** entirely; as, he is *dead* right; **2,** exactly; due; as, *dead* east.

dead-beat (ded′bēt′), *n.* in *physics,* a beat without a recoil.

dead—beat (ded′–bēt′), *adj. Colloq.,* exhausted.

dead beat (ded′bēt′), *n. Slang,* one who doesn't pay his bills; a sponger.

dead-en (ded′n), *v.t.* to deprive of force; lessen; as, medicine to *deaden* pain.

dead-fall (ded′fôl′), *n.* a trap made of a log or weight that falls on an animal to kill or disable it.

dead-head (ded′hed′), *n.* one who gets free tickets or passes for transportation, theatres, board, etc.

dead heat (ded′hēt′), *n.* a tie in a race.

dead letter, 1, a letter undelivered because of faulty address, usually sent to a *dead–letter* office; **2,** anything that has lost its force; as, this law is a *dead letter.*

dead-line (ded′līn′), *n.* the time-limit for doing something, such as paying a debt or completing copy to go to press.

dead-lock (ded′lok′), *n.* a standstill; the state of a contest when two opposing sides are so evenly balanced in strength or power that neither will give in and no progress can be made.— *adj.* **dead′locked.**

dead-ly (ded′li), *adj.* [dead-li-er, dead-li-est], **1,** causing death; fatal; as, Asiatic cholera is a *deadly* disease; **2,** relentless; as, a *deadly* enemy; **3,** resembling death; as, a *deadly* pallor:— *adv.* **1,** like death; as, *deadly* still; **2,** *Colloq.,* extremely; as, *deadly* dull.

dead—pan (ded′–pan′), *adj. Slang,* expressionless; as, the clown's *dead– pan* face was funny.

dead reckoning, in fog or cloudy weather, finding a ship's position by compass, speed, distance travelled, etc., rather than by using a sextant.

dead-wood (ded′wood′), *n.* anything useless, whether a person or an object.

deaf (def), *adj.* **1,** unable to hear; unable to hear clearly; **2,** unwilling to

listen; as, *deaf* to persuasion.—*n.* **deaf′ness.**

deaf-en (def′en), *v.t.* to make deaf; stun with noise.—*adj.* **deaf′en-ing.**

deaf—mute (def′—mūt′), *n.* a deaf-and-dumb person.

¹deal (dēl), *n.* **1.** a part; portion; an amount; as, a great *deal* of money; **2,** in card games, a distribution of cards to the players; also, a player's turn to distribute the cards; as, it's my *deal;* **3,** any distribution or redistribution; as, a new *deal;* **4,** a bargain or agreement; also, the result of such an agreement; as, to make a *deal;* to get a square *deal:*—*v.t.* [dealt (delt), dealing], **1,** to distribute (cards); **2,** to deliver; inflict; as, to *deal* a blow:—*v.i.* **1,** to buy and sell; trade; as, to *deal* in furs; **2,** to behave; as, he *dealt* honourably by his ward; **3,** to be concerned; as, the lesson *dealt* with fractions.—*n.* **deal′er.**

²deal (dēl), *n.* fir or pine wood cut into boards of a certain size; also, one of these boards:—*adj.* made of deal.

dean (dēn), *n.* **1,** the head of a group of clergy connected with a cathedral; **2,** the member of a college faculty who has charge of the students; **3,** the administrative officer of a college or university next below the president; **4,** the oldest member, in years of service, among men of similar calling; as, *dean* of the diplomatic corps.

dear (dēr), *adj.* **1,** highly esteemed; beloved; often, as in letters, merely a polite form of address; **2,** costly; also, charging high prices; as, that is a very *dear* shop; **3,** heart-felt; earnest; as, his *dearest* ambition:—*n.* a darling; loved one:—*adv.* at a high price:—*interj.* expressing surprise, pity, or the like.—*adv.* **dear′ly.**

dearth (dûrth), *n.* want; lack; scarcity; as, a *dearth* of coal during a strike.

death (deth), *n.* **1,** the end of life; also, the act of dying; **2,** total loss; end; as, the *death* of his hopes; **3,** that which causes death; as, his disgrace was the *death* of his father:—**Death,** the destroyer of life: usually represented as a skeleton with a scythe. Also, **death′-bed′; death′blow′; death′trap′.**

death-less (deth′lis), *adj.* never ending; never dying; as, *deathless* fame.

death-ly (deth′li), *adj.* [death-li-er, death-li-est], **1,** fatal; deadly; **2,** like death; as, a *deathly* stillness:—*adv.* to a degree like death; as, *deathly* pale.

de-bar (di-bär′), *v.t.* [debarred, debarring], to shut out; exclude; as, he was *debarred* from taking the test.

de-bark (di-bärk′), *v.i.* to go ashore from a vessel:—*v.t.* to remove from a vessel; as, to *debark* troops.—*n.* **de′bar-ka′tion.**

de-base (di-bās′), *v.t.* [debased, debasing], to lower in value, quality, purity, etc.; as, to *debase* the coinage.—*n.* **de-base′ment.**

de-bate (di-bāt′), *v.t.* [debat-ed, debating], to discuss by presenting arguments for and against; as, he *debated* whether or not to go:—*v.i.* to argue or discuss a point:—*n.* **1,** an argument; discussion; **2,** a formal presentation of arguments on both sides of a question by speakers before an audience.—*adj.* **de-bat′a-ble.**—*n.* **de-bat′er.**

de-bauch (di-bôch′), *v.t.* to corrupt or seduce (a person):—*n.* an orgy; excessive indulgence in sensual pleasures. —*n.* **de-bauch′er-y.**

de-ben-ture (di-ben′tūr; chẻr), *n.* **1** an interest-bearing bond, usually issued by a corporation (with or) without the security of a mortgage; **2,** a government voucher for money.

de-bil-i-tate (di-bil′i-tāt′), *v.t.* [debilitat-ed, debilitat-ing], to weaken; as, a bad cold *debilitates* one's health.

de-bil-i-ty (di-bil′i-ti), *n.* [*pl.* debilities], a weakness; lack of strength.

deb-it (deb′it), *n.* **1,** an entry in an account of something due; **2,** the left-hand, or debtor, side of an account: opposite of *credit:*—*v.t.* to charge (a sum due); enter a charge against (a person or an account).

deb-o-nair (deb′o-nâr′), *adj.* gay; courteous; elegant; winsome; as, a *debonair* youth.

de-bouch (di-bōōsh′), *v.i.* to emerge or issue; as, the troops *debouched* from a wood; from the valley the river *debouched* on the plain.

de-bris, dé-bris (deb′rē; de-brē′) or (dä′-brē; da-brē′; deb′rē), *n.* **1,** scattered fragments; rubbish; as, the yard was littered with paper and *debris;* **2,** piles of loose rock, as at the base of a mountain.

debt (det), *n.* **1,** that which one person owes to another; an amount owed; as, my *debts* total $100; for your kindness to my mother, I owe you a *debt* of gratitude; **2,** the state of owing money; esp. more than one can pay; as, to be in *debt;* **3,** *Archaic,* sin; as, "Forgive us our *debts.*"

debt-or (det′ẻr), *n.* a person who owes money; also, one who is under obligation to another: opposite of *creditor.*

de-bunk (di-bungk′), *v.t. Slang,* to strip of false claims, humbug, etc.; deflate; as, they *debunked* the popular hero.

---

cat, āge, fär, cảre, ȧsk; ten, ēve, latẻr; (i) pity, rely, senate; īce; top; nō,

de-but (dā-bū′; dā′bōō; de-bū′; dā′bū; deb′ū), *n.* **1,** the first formal appearance of a girl in society; **2,** a first appearance on the stage, in business, etc.

deb-u-tante (deb′ū-tänt′; dā′bōō-tänt′), *n.* a young woman who is making, or has recently made, her debut, or first appearance in society.

dec-ade (dek′ād), *n.* **1,** a group of ten; **2,** a period of ten consecutive years.

dec-a-dence (di-kā′dens; dek′a-dens), *n.* decay, as in morals, character, or quality.—*adj.* **dec′a-dent** (dek′a-dent; di-kā′dent).

de-cal (di-kal′), *n.* short for **de-cal-co-ma-ni-a** (di-kal′kō-mā′ni-a), the transfer of decorative designs or pictures from specially prepared paper to glass, wood, metal, or china.

Dec-a-logue (dek′a-log′), *n.* The Ten Commandments (Ex. 20).

de-camp (di-kamp′), *v.i.* to leave suddenly or secretly; run away; as, he *decamped* with my fishing-rod.

de-cant (di-kant′), *v.t.* to pour gently without disturbing the sediment, as wine from a bottle.

de-can-ter (di-kan′tėr), an ornamental glass bottle, with a stopper, used for wine or liquor.

de-cap-i-tate (di-kap′i-tāt′), *v.t.* [decapitat-ed, decapitat-ing], to cut off the head of; behead.

de-cath-lon (di-kath′lon), *n.* an athletic contest of ten separate events, in all of which all of the contestants take part.

de-cay (di-kā′), *v.i.* **1,** to decline from a condition of soundness or health; fail; as, business, beauty, or civilization may *decay;* **2,** to rot:—*n.* **1,** decline; gradual failure; **2,** rot; decomposition; as, I cut out the *decay* and ate the rest of the apple.

de-cease (di-sēs′), *v.i.* [deceased, deceas-ing], to die:—*n.* death.

de-ceased (di-sēst′), *adj.* dead; esp. recently dead:—**the deceased,** the dead person.

de-ceit (di-sēt′), *n.* **1,** the act or practice of misleading or cheating; as, he justified *deceit* as a means to an end; **2,** an instance of misleading; a trick.

de-ceit-ful (di-sēt′fool), *adj.* given to fraud and trickery; insincere; false.—*adv.* **de-ceit′ful-ly.**—*n.* **de-ceit′ful-ness.**

de-ceive (di-sēv′), *v.t.* [deceived, de-ceiv-ing], **1,** to cause (one) to believe what is untrue; as, do not *deceive* me, tell me the truth; **2,** to mislead; as, I was *deceived* by his looks.—*n.* **de-ceiv′er.**

De-cem-ber (di-sem′bėr), *n.* the 12th month of the year (31 days).

de-cen-cy (dē′sen-si), *n.* [*pl.* decencies], **1,** propriety in speech, actions, or dress; decorum; **2, decencies,** the requirements of a respectable or decent life, such as common courtesy, cleanliness, etc.

de-cent (dē′sent), *adj.* **1,** becoming; suitable; proper; as, *decent* behaviour; *decent* clothes; **2,** respectable; as, he comes from a *decent* home; **3,** passable; good enough; as, a *decent* living.—*adv.* **de′cent-ly.**

de-cep-tion (di-sep′shun), *n.* **1,** the act of tricking or cheating; as, *deception* aided his escape; **2,** a piece of trickery; fraud.—*adj.* **de-cep′tive.**

dec-i-bel (des′i-bel′), *n.* the unit used to measure volume of sound; thus, soft radio music is about 35 *decibels.*

de-cide (di-sīd′), *v.t.* [decid-ed, decid-ing], **1,** to settle; bring to a conclusion; as, he *decided* the matter without delay; **2,** to cause to make a decision; as, that trait *decides* me in his favour:—*v.i.* **1,** to make up one's mind; as, I have *decided* to leave early; **2,** to give a judgment or decision.

de-cid-ed (di-sīd′id), *adj.* **1,** definite; clear; as, *decided* opinions; **2,** determined; resolute; as, a very *decided* person.

de-cid-ed-ly (di-sīd′id-li), *adv.* definitely; certainly; as, she is *decidedly* pretty.

de-cid-u-ous (di-sid′ū-us), *adj.* **1,** losing foliage every year; not evergreen; as, the oak is a *deciduous* tree; **2,** shed, or falling, at certain seasons; as, *deciduous* leaves.

dec-i-mal (des′i-mal), *adj.* based upon the number ten; as, the *decimal* system:—**decimal fraction,** a fraction having as its denominator ten or some power of ten, usually written as a number preceded by a dot, called the *decimal point,* as .7 = 7/10, .07 = 7/100:—*n.* a decimal fraction.

dec-i-mate (des′i-māt′), *v.t.* to kill a large part of; as, we *decimated* the enemy; literally, to kill one in ten.

de-ci-pher (di-sī′fėr), *v.t.* to make out the meaning of; to translate (esp. something written in secret characters); as, to *decipher* a code message.

de-ci-sion (di-sizh′un), *n.* **1,** the act of reaching an opinion; also, the opinion or judgment reached; as, he is quick in making *decisions;* **2,** firmness; determination; as, he is a man of *decision.*

de-ci-sive (di-sī′siv), *adj.* **1,** final; conclusive; as, a *decisive* victory; **2,** prompt; positive; determined; as, *decisive* action.

¹deck (dek), *n.* **1,** a platform serving as

a floor in a ship; also, the space between floors; **2,** a pack of playing-cards:—*v.t.* to furnish (a ship) with a deck.

²deck (dek), *v.t.* to put finery or ornaments on; adorn; array; as, she *decked* herself out in her Sunday clothes.

de-claim (di-klām'), *v.i.* and *v.t.* **1,** to utter (words) in oratorical style; as, he does not speak naturally; he *declaims;* **2,** to recite in public.—*n.* **de-claim'er.**—*n.* **dec'la-ma'tion** (dek'la-mā'shun).

dec-la-ra-tion (dek'la-rā'shun), *n.* **1,** the act of announcing or proclaiming; as, the *declaration* of a holiday; **2,** that which is affirmed or proclaimed; also, the document embodying the proclamation; as, the *Declaration* of Independence.

de-clar-a-tive (di-klar'a-tiv), *adj.* making a statement or declaration; as, "The sun shone all day" is a *declarative* sentence.

de-clare (di-klâr'), *v.t.* [declared, declar-ing], **1,** to make known; tell openly or publicly; proclaim formally; as the Government *declared* a holiday; she *declared* that nothing would persuade her to go; **2,** to affirm solemnly before witnesses; as, the accused man *declared* his innocence; **3,** to make a complete statement of (dutiable goods, or the like); as, a traveller, returning to Canada, must *declare* his purchases:—*v.i.* to make a statement; take sides for or against something; as, the students *declared* for self-government. —*n.* **de-clar'er.**

de-clen-sion (di-klen'shun), *n.* **1,** in *grammar*, the changes in form of nouns or pronouns, and, in some languages, adjectives, to correspond to their use in the sentence; **2,** a sloping downward; descent; **3,** a falling away; deterioration.

de-cline (di-klīn'), *v.i.* [declined, declin-ing], **1,** to slope, bend, or lean downward; **2,** to sink toward the horizon, as the sun or a star; hence, to draw toward a close; as, day *declined;* **3,** to decay; fail; as, his vigour began to *decline;* **4,** to seek a lower level; as, prices have *declined;* **5,** to refuse; as, I *decline* to go:—*v.t.* **1,** to refuse; as, to *decline* an invitation; **2,** to give the declension of; as, to *decline* a noun:—*n.* **1,** a setting; lessening; decay; as, the *decline* of day, of prices, of fame; **2,** a wasting away with disease; as, she went into a *decline.*

de-cliv-i-ty (di-kliv'i-ti), *n.* [*pl.* de-clivities], a downward slope.

de-com-pose (dē'kom-pōz'), *v.t.* [de-composed, decompos-ing], **1** to separate (something) into parts; as, a prism *decomposes* sunlight; **2,** to rot:—*v.i.* to

decay.—*n.* **de'com-po-si'tion** (dē'kom-pō-zish'un).

de-com-press (dē'kom-pres'), *v.t.* to free from air pressure, as by means of an air lock (in a submarine, caisson, airplane, etc.)—*n.* **de'com-pres'sion.**

de-con-tam-i-nate (dē'kon-tam'i-nāt'), *v.t.* to free from a harmful substance, as poison gas, radioactivity, etc.

dé-cor (dā-kôr'), *n.* the decorative scheme of a room, stage setting, etc.

dec-o-rate (dek'o-rāt'), *v.t.* [decorat-ed, decorat-ing], **1,** to adorn; as, to *decorate* a stage; **2,** to confer a badge of honour upon; as, the general was *decorated* for bravery.—*n.* **dec'o-ra'tion.**—*adj.* **dec'o-ra'tive.**—*n.* **dec'o-ra'tor.**

de-cor-ous (di-kōr'us; dek'ō-rus), *adj.* seemly; fit; proper; as, *decorous* behaviour.

de-cor-um (di-kōr'um), *n.* propriety of dress, language, and conduct; seemliness; dignity; as, to act with *decorum.*

de-coy (di-koi'), *n.* **1,** a deceptive trick or snare; a lure; **2,** a real or imitation bird used to attract live birds within gunshot; **3,** a person used to lead another into a position of danger:—*v.t.* to draw into danger by a trick; entice.

de-crease (di-krēs'; dē'krēs), *v.i.* [de-creased, decreas-ing], to grow less; diminish in number, strength, or the like:—*v.t.* to cause to grow less:—*n.* (dē'krēs; dē-krēs'), a gradual lessening or falling off; also, the amount or degree of lessening.

de-cree (di-krē'), *n.* **1,** an ordinance; law; edict; **2,** in certain courts, the judgment or award of the court; as, a *decree* of divorce:—*v.t.* [decreed, decree-ing], to establish by law; as, to *decree* an amnesty:—*v.i.* to make a decision or law.

de-crep-it (di-krep'it), *adj.* broken down by age or use; as, a *decrepit* horse.—*n.* **de-crep'i-tude** (dē-krep'i-tūd).

de-cry (di-krī'), *v.t.* [decried, decry-ing], **1,** to condemn; censure; as, to *decry* modern dances; **2,** to make little of; as the ignorant may *decry* the value of education.

ded-i-cate (ded'i-kāt'), *v.t.* [dedicat-ed, dedicat-ing], **1,** to set apart by a solemn act or ceremony; as, to *dedicate* a church; **2,** to devote to some work or duty; as, to *dedicate* ourselves to peace; **3,** to address (a book) formally to a patron or friend.—*n.* **ded'i-ca'tion.**

de-duce (di-dūs'), *v.t.* [deduced, deduc-ing], to arrive at (a conclusion) by reasoning; infer; as, from your accurate work I *deduce* that you are an industrious student.—*adj.* **de-duc′i-ble.**

de-duct (di-dukt′), *v.t.* to take away; subtract; as, *deduct* a dollar from the bill.—*adj.* **de-duct′i-ble.**

de-duc-tion (di-duk′shun), *n.* 1, subtraction; also, that which is taken away; as, she expected a *deduction* from her pay; 2, the drawing of conclusions by reasoning from principles generally accepted as true; also, a conclusion thus reached.—*adj.* **de-duc′tive.**

deed (dēd), *n.* 1, that which is done; an act; 2, a brave action; exploit; as, *deeds* of prowess; 3, a legal document for the transfer of ownership of real estate:—*v.t.* to convey by deed; as, he *deeded* the land.

deem (dēm), *v.t.* to think; believe; judge; as, I *deem* it wise to call him back.

deep (dēp), *adj.* 1, extending far down from the surface; not shallow; as, a *deep* hole; also, extending well back; as a *deep* lot; 2, penetrating; thorough; as, *deep* insight; 3, difficult to understand; as, a *deep* subject; 4, absorbed; involved; as, *deep* in study; 5, low in pitch; as, a *deep* voice; 6, profound; heavy; as, a *deep* sleep; 7, dark; rich; as, a *deep* red; 8, heartfelt; as, *deep* sorrow:—**the deep,** the sea:—*adv.* far down; far on; in the heart of; as, dig *deep; deep* in the jungle.—*adv.* **deep′ly.** —*v.t.* and *v.i.* **deep′en.**

deep-freeze (dēp′frēz′), *n.* a refrigerator for storing perishable foods at temperatures down to zero Fahrenheit. —*v.t.* to store in a deepfreeze.

deer (dēr), *n.* [*pl.* deer], a swift, graceful, cud-chewing wild animal. The male deer has branching horns, or antlers, which are shed and renewed every year.

deer-fly (dēr′flī′), *n.* a blood-sucking fly with mottled wings; in northern Canadian woods it bites viciously, esp. in early summer.

deer-hound (dēr′hound′), *n.* a large, shaggy-haired hunting dog resembling a greyhound.

deer-skin (dēr′skin′), *n.* and *adj.* the hide of a deer, or leather made from it.

de-face (di-fās′), *v.t.* [defaced, defacing], to mar the appearance of; as, to *deface* a book with pencil marks.—*n.* **de-face**ꞁ**ment.**

de-fame (di-fām′) *v.t.* [defamed, defaming], to injure or destroy the good name of; speak evil of; slander.—*n.* **de-fam′er.**—*n.* **def′a-ma′tion** (def′a-māꞁshun).—*adj.* **de-fam′a-tor-y** (dē-fam′a-tẽr-i).

de-fault (di-fôlt′), *n.* 1, failure to do

something required by law; 2, failure to pay one's debts; 3, failure to start or to finish a game or contest:—*v.t.* and *v.i.* 1, to fail to fulfil a contract, esp. a financial contract); 2, to fail to start or to finish; hence, to lose (a contest) through such a failure.—*n.* **de-fault′er.**

de-feat (di-fēt′), *v.t.* 1, to overthrow or vanquish; as, to *defeat* an enemy; 2, to bring to naught; frustrate; as, to *defeat* a purpose:—*n.* 1, failure; as, the *defeat* of a plan or purpose; also, loss of a game or contest; 2, overthrow, as of an army.—*n.* **de-feat′ism; de-feat′ist.**

def-e-cate (def′e-kāt), *v.i.* to void or excrete faeces or waste matter from the bowels.

de-fect (di-fekt′; dē′fekt), *n.* 1, a mental or physical imperfection; 2, error; flaw; as, *defects* in writing.

de-fec-tion (di-fek′shun), *n.* the act of abandoning a friend, duty, allegiance, or the like; desertion.

de-fec-tive (di-fek′tiv), *adj.* 1, imperfect; incomplete; faulty; as, *defective* hearing; a *defective* radio-tube; 2, mentally deficient:—*n.* a person who is mentally lacking.

de-fence or **de-fense** (di-fens′), *n.* 1, resistance to attack; as, to fight in *defence* of one's country; 2, one who or that which protects; a protector; protection; as, a coat is a *defence* against a cold wind; 3, in law, the reply of the defendant to the charge against him.— *adj.* **de-fence′less.**

de-fend (di-fend′), *v.t.* 1, to protect from harm or violence; as, to *defend* a child from danger; 2, to maintain or uphold, as one's legal rights, by argument or evidence; to contest, as a suit. —*n.* **de-fend′er.**

de-fend-ant (di-fen′dant), *n.* a person ordered to answer a charge in a lawcourt.

de-fen-si-ble (di-fen′si-bl), *adj.* 1, capable of being protected, as a military position; 2, justifiable, as a point of view.

de-fen-sive (di-fen′siv), *adj.* 1, designed to guard or protect; as, *defensive* weapons; 2, carried on in self-defence; as, *defensive* warfare:—*n.* the position of one warding off attack; as, she is always on the *defensive.*—*adv.* **de-fen′-sive-ly.**

¹**de-fer** (di-fûr′), *v.t.* [deferred, deferring], to put off until later; delay; postpone; as, he *deferred* final action for a week.—*n.* **de-fer′ment.**

²**de-fer** (di-fûr′), *v.i.* [deferred, deferring], to yield; give in; bow (to); as, I *defer* to your judgment.

def-er-ence (def′ẽr-ens), *n*. **1,** a yielding to the opinions or wishes of another; **2,** respect; as, *deference* to the aged.— *adj.* **def′-er-en′tial** (def′ẽr-en′shal).

de-fi-ance (di-fī′ans), *n*. **1,** the act of challenging; a challenge; **2,** resistance; scornful opposition to authority.—*adj.* **de-fi′ant.**

de-fi-cient (di-fish′ent), *adj.* lacking; incomplete; defective.—*n.* **de-fi′cien-cy.**

def-i-cit (def′i-sit; dē′fi-sit), *n*. a shortage, as of money: opposite of *surplus*.

¹**de-file** (di-fīl′), *v.t.* [defiled, defil-ing], **1,** to make foul or impure; as, to *defile* a stream with refuse; **2,** to bring dishonour upon; as, to *defile* a person′s reputation.—*n.* **de-file′ment.**

²**de-file** (di-fīl′), *v.i.* [defiled, defil-ing], to march off in a line or in files:—*n.* (di-fīl′; dē′fīl), a long, narrow pass, as between mountains.

de-fine (di-fīn′), *v.t.* [defined, defin-ing], **1,** to state the exact meaning of; as, to *define* words; **2,** to fix the limits of; as, to *define* the extent of a tract of land; **3,** to prescribe authoritatively; as, the duties of the treasurer were *defined* in the by-laws.—*adj.* **de-fin′a-ble.**

def-i-nite (def′i-nit), *adj.* **1,** precise; exact; as, *definite* instructions; **2,** having fixed or distinct limits; as, a *definite* period of time:—**definite article,** the word *the:* so called because it limits the word it modifies.—*adv.* **def′i-nite-ly.**

def-i-ni-tion (def′i-nish′un), *n*. **1,** the act of explaining; **2,** an exact statement of the meaning of a word, term, or phrase.

de-fin-i-tive (di-fin′i-tiv), *adj.* final; conclusive; as, a *definitive* answer.

de-flate (di-flāt′), *v.t.* [deflat-ed, deflat-ing], **1,** to release air or gas from; as, to *deflate* a tire; **2,** to reduce (prices); also, to reduce the amount of (money in circulation); **3,** to expose a person′s pretensions; as, her rebuff *deflated* his ego.—*n.* **de-fla′tion.**

de-flect (di-flekt′), *v.t.* to cause to turn from a straight line; as, the wall *deflected* the bullet.—*n.* **deflec′tion.**—*n.* **de-flec′tor.**

de-form (di-fôrm′), *v.t.* **1,** to make ugly or unshapely; disfigure; **2,** to mar; deface.—*n.* **de-form′i-ty.**

de-fraud (di-frôd′), *v.t.* to cheat or deceive; deprive (one) of a possession, right, or the like, by trickery or deceit.

de-fray (di-frā′), *v.t.* to pay; settle; as, to *defray* the cost of a trip.—*n.* **de-fray′al.**

de-frost (di-frôst′), *v.t.* to remove frost from or cause to thaw.—*n.* **de-frost′er.**

deft (deft), *adj.* neat and skilful in action; nimble; as, piano-playing requires *deft* fingers.—*adv.* **deft′ly.**—*n.* **deft′ness.**

de-funct (di-fungkt′), *adj.* dead; extinct; **the defunct,** the dead person(s).

de-fy (di-fī′), *v.t.* [defied, defy-ing], **1,** to challenge or dare; as, to *defy* an enemy; **2,** to act in contempt of; as, a criminal *defies* the law; **3,** to resist successfully; as, the problem *defied* solution.

de-gen-er-ate (di-jen′ẽr-āt′), *v.i.* [de-generat-ed, degenerat-ing], to sink into a worse state; become inferior in goodness or quality:—*adj.* (di-jen′ẽr-it), below the former or typical standard; degraded; as, *degenerate* times; inferior to the true or former type; as, *degenerate* offspring:—*n.* (di-jen′ẽr-it), a degenerate person.—*n.* **de-gen′er-a-cy.**—*n.* **de-gen′er-a′tion.**

de-grade (di-grād′), *v.t.* [degrad-ed, degrad-ing], **1,** to reduce in grade or rank; deprive of honours, office, or dignity; as, to *degrade* a soldier; **2,** to lower morally; as, to tell lies *degrades* one:—*adj.* **de-grad′ed.**—*n.* **deg′ra-da′tion** (deg′ra-dā′shun).

de-gree (di-grē′), *n*. **1,** a step or grade in a series; **2,** rank in life; as, a person of low *degree;* **3,** a stage in progress; **4,** a title conferred by a college or university in recognition of work done or of special distinction; **5,** a relative amount, extent, quality; as,

DEGREES, def. 8

a good *degree* of skill; **6,** a unit for measuring temperature, as on a Fahrenheit or centigrade scale; **7,** a unit division on a mathematical or scientific instrument, as a compass; **8,** the 360th part of the circumference of a circle; **9,** in grammar, one of the three grades in the comparison of an adjective or adverb; as, "good," "better," "best" are the positive, comparative, and superlative *degrees* of "good"; **10,** in music, a line or a space on the staff for notes; also, a tone of a scale:—**by degrees,** gradually.

de-hy-drate (dē-hī′drāt), *v.t.* to remove water from; as, *dehydrated* (dē′hī-drā′tid) fruits or vegetables.

de—ice (dē′-is′), *v.t.* to remove ice from; as, to *de-ice* the wings of an airplane.

de-i-fy (dē′i-fī′), *v.t.* [defied, deify-ing], to worship as a god; to make into a god; as, the druids *deified* the oak tree.—*n.* **de′i-fi-ca′tion.**

deign (dān), *v.i.* to condescend; think

fit; as, he did not *deign* to heed our request:—*v.t.* to grant; condescend.

de-i-ty (dē'-i-ti), *n.* [*pl.* deities], **1,** a god or goddess; a being worshipped as divine; **2,** the character, nature, or attributes of God:—**the Deity,** God; Jehovah.

de-ject-ed (di-jek'tid), *adj.* cast down; sad; low-spirited.—*n.* **de-jec'tion.**

de-lay (di-lā'), *v.t.* to put off; postpone; hinder for a time; as, illness *delayed* my journey:—*v.i.* to act or proceed slowly: —*n.* a putting off; postponement; wait; as, a *delay* of two hours.

de-lec-ta-ble (di-lek'ta-bl), *adj.* pleasing; delightful.—*adv.* **de-lec'ta-bly.**— *n.* **de'lec-ta'tion.**

del-e-gate (del'e-git), *n.* one sent to represent, and act for, others; as, the *delegates* to a convention:—*v.t.* (del'e-gāt'), [delegated, delegat-ing], **1,** to send as an agent, with authority to act; as, I *delegate* you to deliver the message; **2,** to entrust, transfer, or commit; as, we *delegate* to Parliament the making of our laws.

del-e-ga-tion (del'e-gā'shun), *n.* **1,** the act of authorizing a person or persons to act for others; **2,** a body of persons chosen so to act; a body of representatives.

de-lete (di-lēt'), *v.t.* to remove; destroy; take out (something written or printed); as, *delete* this comma.—*n.* **de-le'tion.**

delf, delft (delf, delft), *n.* earthenware glazed in colours; china; pottery or dishes, delftware like that of Delft, Holland.

de-lib-er-ate (di-lib'ẽr-āt'), *v.t.* [deliberated, deliberat-ing], to reflect on; think upon; consider carefully; as, to *deliberate* a question:—*v.i.* to take counsel with oneself or others; as, to *deliberate* on a plan:—*adj.* (di-lib'ẽr-it), **1,** careful; slow; cautious; **2,** slow in determining or acting; **3,** intended; as, a *deliberate* insult.—*adv.* **de-lib'er-ate-ly.**—*n.* **de-lib'er-a'tion.**

del-i-ca-cy (del'i-ka-si), *n.* [*pl.* delicacies], **1,** a dainty; a rare or delightful food; **2,** fineness of form or texture; as, the *delicacy* of a spider web; **3,** fineness of touch; as in writing or painting; **4,** sensitiveness; as, *delicacy* of taste.

del-i-cate (del'i-kit), *adj.* **1,** pleasing to the taste; as, a *delicate* flavour; **2,** fine; dainty; exquisite in texture; as, *delicate* lace; **3,** of instruments, minutely accurate; as, a *delicate* scale; **4,** sensitive to injury or disease; as, a *delicate* child or plant; **5,** requiring skill or nicety; as, a *delicate* operation; **6,** soft or subdued, as a colour; **7,** capable

of making fine distinctions; as, a musician has a *delicate* ear; **8,** finely sensitive; as, a *delicate* touch.

del-i-ca-tes-sen (del'i-ka-tes'en), *n.pl.* **1,** prepared foods, as cooked meats, salads, and preserves; table delicacies; **2,** used as *singular*, a place where these are sold.

de-li-cious (di-lish'us), *adj.* highly pleasing, esp. to the taste.—*adv.* **de-li'-cious-ly.**—*n.* **de-li'cious-ness.**

de-light (di-līt'), *v.t.* to gratify or please greatly; charm; as, beauty *delights* the eye:—*v.i.* to take great pleasure or enjoyment; as, to *delight* in dancing:— *n.* **1,** an extreme degree of pleasure; high satisfaction; joy; **2,** that which causes pleasure.—*adj.* **de-light'ed.**— *adj.* **de-light'ful.**

de-lin-e-ate (di-lin'ē-āt'), *v.t.* [delineated, delineat-ing], **1,** to mark out with lines; sketch; draw; **2,** to describe minutely and accurately in words; as, an author *delineates* his characters.—*n.* **de-lin'e-a'tion.**

de-lin-quent (di-ling'kwent), *adj.* **1,** failing in duty; **2,** overdue; not paid, as, taxes:—*n.* **1,** one who neglects a duty; **2,** a lawbreaker; esp. a youthful offender.—*n.* **de-lin'quen-cy.**

de-lir-i-um (di-lir'i-um), *n.* **1,** a temporary mental disorder, often caused by fever, and marked by wandering speech; **2,** excitement; wild enthusiasm.—*adj.* **de-lir'i-ous.**

de-lir-i-um tre-mens (trē'menz), *n.* a fit marked by trembling, sweating, and terrifying visions, brought on by excessive drinking (of alcohol).

de-liv-er (di-liv'ẽr), *v.t.* **1,** to set free; save; **2,** to yield possession or control of, as a property; **3,** to give; transfer; as, to *deliver* a package; **4,** to send forth vigorously; as, to *deliver* a blow; **5,** to utter; as, to *deliver* a speech.—*n.* **de-liv'er-ance.**

de-liv-er-y (di-liv'ẽr-i), *n.* [*pl.* deliveries], **1,** the act of releasing; a setting free; **2,** a surrender; transfer; **3,** manner of speaking; as, a lecturer's *delivery;* **4,** a giving from one person to another; as, a mail *delivery;* **5,** the act or manner of pitching a ball; **6,** childbirth.

dell (del), *n.* a secluded valley; glen.

del-phin-i-um (del-fin'i-um), *n.* a garden plant with irregular flower spikes on tall stalks, esp. the blue larkspur.

del-ta (del'ta), *n.* **1,** the 4th letter of the Greek alphabet (Δ, δ); **2,** a fan-shaped alluvial deposit at the mouth of a river, as the *deltas* of the Nile; **3,** any triangular surface.

all (ôl), ôr; up, mūte, cûr, cōōl, book; oil, out; th, thin, *th,* the.

del-toid (del'toid), *n*. on the shoulder, a triangular muscle that raises the arm from the side.—*adj*. triangular.

de-lude (di-lūd'), *v.t*. [delud-ed, delud-ing], to mislead; deceive; as, to *delude* oneself with false hopes.—*n*. **de-lu'sion**. —*adj*. **de-lu'sive**.

del-uge (del'ūj), *n*. 1, a heavy downpour; 2, anything that overwhelms or floods; as a *deluge* of protests greeted the new rules:—**the Deluge**, the great flood of the time of Noah (Genesis 7):— *v.t*. [deluged, delug-ing], 1, to overflow; 2, to overwhelm; as, they *deluged* him with questions.

de luxe (di looks'; di luks'), of unusually fine quality; luxurious.

delve (delv), *v.i*. [delved, delv-ing], 1, to work with a spade; 2, to make earnest search for knowledge; as, to *delve* into a subject.

dem-a-gogue or **dem-a-gog** (dem'a-gog), *n*. a political agitator who gains and uses power by appealing to the ignorance or prejudice of the people.

de-mand (di-mand'), *v.t*. 1, to claim as due; exact; as, to *demand* an apology; 2, to question with authority; as, to *demand* one's name; 3, to require; have urgent need for; as, the letter *demands* an answer; 4, in law, to summon:—*n*. 1, the act of claiming as due; as, a *demand* for payment; 2, a desire to obtain; call; as, a great *demand* for books; 3, the state of being sought after.

de-mean (di-mēn'), *v.t*. to lower in dignity; degrade; as, he *demeaned* himself by taking the bribe.

de-mean-our (di-mēn'ėr), *n*. behaviour; bearing.

de-ment-ed (di-men'tid), *adj*. insane; mad; out of one's mind.

de-mer-it (di-mer'it), *n*. 1, something that deserves blame; a fault; 2, a mark for failure or misconduct.

de-mesne (di-mēn'; di-mān'), *n*. 1, the holding of land as one's own; 2, a landed estate attached to a manor house; 3, a region or domain.

dem-i-god (dem'i-god'), *n*. an inferior god; a hero.

de-mise (di-mīz'), *n*. death; thus, on his *demise* the crown went to his son.

dem-i-tasse (dem'i-tȧs'), *n*. a small cup (of black coffee).

de-mo-bi-lize (dē-mō'bi-līz'; -mo'), *v.t*. [demobilized, demobiliz-ing], to disband or dismiss, as troops; to change (an army or country) from a war to a peace footing.—*n*. **de-mo'bi-li-za'tion**.

de-moc-ra-cy (di-mok'ra-si), *n*. [*pl*. democracies], 1, government by the people; government in which the people hold supreme power and delegate it to elected representatives; also, a nation or state so governed; as, the United States is a *democracy;* 2, political or social equality as opposed to inherited rights and privileges.

dem-o-crat (dem'ō-krat), *n*. one who believes in and upholds the principles of popular government or social equality: —**Democrat**, in the U.S., a member of the Democratic party.

dem-o-crat-ic (dem'ō-krat'ik), *adj*. 1, pertaining to democracy, or government by the people; 2, ignoring differences of class; friendly; as, a *democratic* spirit makes one loved:— **Democratic party**, one of the great political groups in the U.S.: so named in 1828.—*adv*. **dem'o-crat'i-cal-ly**.

de-mol-ish (di-mol'ish), *v.t*. to pull down; destroy; as, they *demolished* the old house.

dem-o-li-tion (dem'ō-lish'un; dē'mō-lish'un), *n*. the act of tearing down; destruction.

de-mon (dē'mun), *n*. 1, an evil spirit; a devil; 2, a very cruel or fierce person. —*adj*. **de-mon'ic** (di-mon'ik).

de-mo-ni-ac (di-mō'ni-ak'), de-mo-ni-a-cal (dē'mo-nī'a-kl), *adj*. devilish; possessed by a demon.

dem-on-strate (dem'un-strāt'), *v.t*. [demonstrat-ed, demonstrat-ing], 1, to prove beyond a doubt; 2, to teach by examples; illustrate; 3, to show and explain publicly the good points of (an article or product).—*n*. **dem'on-stra'-tor**.—*adj*. **de-mon'stra-ble**.

dem-on-stra-tion (dem'un-strā'-shun), *n*. 1, the act of showing or proving; 2, a proof beyond any doubt; 3, an outward expression of feeling; as, a kiss is a *demonstration* of affection; 4, a public exhibition; as, a cooking *demonstration;* 5, a show of military force; 6, a show of public interest and sympathy, as by a street meeting or a parade.

de-mon-stra-tive (di-mon'stra-tiv), *adj*. 1, having the power of showing or proving; 2, in *grammar*, serving to point out; as, a *demonstrative* pronoun; 3, showing the feelings, esp. affection, openly and strongly:—*n*. a pronoun that serves to point out the object to which it refers, as *this, that, these, those*.

de-mor-al-ize (di-mor'al-īz), *v.t*. [demoralized, demoraliz-ing], 1, to corrupt; lower the morals of; as, bad company will *demoralize* anybody; 2, to weaken the courage, spirit, or energy of; throw into confusion; as, loss of their leader *demoralized* the army.—*n*. **de-mor'al-i-za'tion**.

de-mote (di-mōt′), *v.t.* to reduce to a lower grade or rank (in school or the army, etc.); opposite of *promote.*—*n.* **de-mo′tion.**

de-mur (di-mûr′), *v.i.* [demurred, demur-ring], **1,** to hesitate; **2,** to raise objections; as, he *demurred* at going so far:—*n.* **1,** an objection or exception; **2,** hesitation.

de-mure (di-mūr′), *adj.* [demur-er, demur-est], **1,** grave; sober; as, a *demure* child; **2,** affectedly modest, as in manner.—*adv.* **de-mure′ly.**

den (den), *n.* **1,** the lair of a wild beast; **2,** a cavern; cave; **3,** a cosy, private room; **4,** a haunt of criminals.

de-ni-al (di-nī′al), *n.* **1,** refusal to grant; as, *denial* of a request; **2,** contradiction; refusal to admit; as, the prisoner's *denial* of his guilt; **3,** refusal to acknowledge.

de-nim (den′im), *n.* a coarse twilled cotton used for overalls, hangings, floor coverings, etc.

den-i-zen (den′i-zn), *n.* **1,** a naturalized (but not native) citizen, plant, or animal; **2,** an inhabitant; as, gnats are *denizens* of the air.

de-nom-i-nate (di-nom′i-nāt′), *v.t.* to name or call; as, *Wm. I* was *denominated* the Conqueror.

de-nom-i-na-tion (di-nom′i-nā′-shun), *n.* **1,** a name; a descriptive title; **2,** a grouping of people or things under one name; as, botany and chemistry come under the *denomination* of science; **3,** a class or division; esp. a religious sect; as, the Methodist *denomination;* **4,** a name for a certain class or unit in a series; as, in Canada we have coins of many *denominations.*—*adj.* **de-nom′i-na′tion-al.**

de-nom-i-na-tor (di-nom′i-nā′tėr), *n.* in arithmetic, the part of a fraction below the line, showing into how many parts the number or units is to be divided; the divisor.

de-no-ta-tion (dē′nō-tā′shun), *n.* the literal or explicit meaning of a word as opposed to its *connotation;* thus, the denotation of cattle is *cows* or *livestock,* the connotation *dumb, driven beasts.*

de-note (di-nōt′), *v.t.* [denot-ed, denoting], **1,** to show; indicate; mark out plainly; as, the hands of a clock *denote* the hour; **2,** to be a sign of; mean or signify; as, the song of a robin *denotes* spring.

dé-noue-ment (dā′nōō′mäṅ′), *n.* the solving of the mystery or plot of a play, story, novel, etc.; the outcome or issue; as, the *dénouement* of *Macbeth* is Macduff's killing of Macbeth.

de-nounce (di-nouns′), *v.t.* [denounced,

denounc-ing], to accuse publicly; condemn; as, to *denounce* a cheat.

dense (dens), *adj.* **1,** thick; heavy; as, a *dense* fog; closely packed together; as, a *dense* crowd; **2,** stupid; dull; as, a *dense* person.—*n.* **dense′ness.**—*n.* **den′si-ty.**

dent (dent), *n.* a small hollow or depression:—*v.t.* to make a small hollow in:—*v.i.* to receive dents; as, tin *dents* easily.

den-tal (den′tal), *adj.* **1,** pertaining to the teeth or to dentistry; as, a *dental* clinic; **2,** pronounced by the aid of the teeth; as, *t* and *d* are *dental* letters:—*n.* a dental sound, as *t, d.*

den-ti-frice (den′ti-fris), *n.* a powder, liquid, or paste used for cleaning teeth.

den-tine (den′tēn; den′tin), or **den-tin** (den′tin), *n.* the hard, dense tissue which forms the main part of a tooth. (See illustration under *tooth.*)—*adj.* **den′ti-nal.**

den-tist (den′tist), *n.* one who treats teeth, as by filling or extracting them. —*n.* **den′tis-try.**

den-ti-tion (den-tish′un), *n.* **1,** the process or period of cutting teeth; **2,** the arrangement of the teeth.

den-ture (den′tūr; chėr), *n.* a set of teeth, esp. artificial ones.

de-nude (di-nūd′) *v.t.* [denud-ed, denud-ing], to make bare or naked; as, to *denude* a hillside of trees.

de-nun-ci-a-tion (di-nun′si-ā′shun; di-nun′shi-ā′-shun), *n.* a public accusation; also, condemnation of anything.

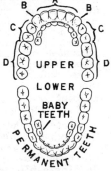

DENTITION
Arrangement of the teeth of a human being.
A, incisors; B,B, canines; C,C, bicuspids; D,D, molars.

de-ny (di-nī′), *v.t.* [denied, deny-ing], **1,** to refuse to believe or admit; contradict; as, I *deny* his statement; **2,** to withhold; refuse to grant; as, to *deny* help; **3,** to disown; as, to *deny* his son.

de-o-dor-ant (dē-ō′dėr-ant), *n.* a preparation that destroys odours.—*adj.* killing or disguising smells.—*v.t.* **de-o′dor-ize′.**

de-part (di-pärt′), *v.i.* **1,** to go away; leave; **2,** to vary; change; as, to *depart* from a habit; **3,** to start on a journey.—*n.* **de-par′ture.**

de-part-ment (di-pärt′ment), *n.* **1,** a distinct division or branch of a whole; **2,** a branch of business, study, or science; **3,** a division of government; as, the *Department* of Finance; **4,** in France, a division of local government: —**department store,** a store selling many kinds of goods, divided into departments, as for clothing, hardware, groceries, etc.—*adj.* **de′part-men′tal.**

de-pend (di-pend′), *v.i.* **1,** to rely for support; as, the old man *depends* on his son; **2,** to be determined by; rest; as, his answer *depends* on his mood; **3,** to trust or rely; as, I *depend* on your word.

de-pend-a-ble (di-pen′da-bl), *adj.* reliable; trustworthy; as, *dependable* news; a *dependable* servant.—*adv.* **de-pend′a-bly.**—*n.* **de-pend′a-bil′i-ty.**

de-pend-ence (di-pen′dens), *n.* **1,** the state of being influenced or determined by something; as, *dependence* of daylight on the sun; **2,** reliance; trust; **3,** that on which one relies; **4,** the state of needing aid; as, the *dependence* of a child on its parents.

de-pend-en-cy (di-pen′den-si), *n.* [*pl.* dependencies], **1,** the condition of relying on another; **2,** a country under the control of another country.

de-pend-ent (di-pen′dent), *adj.* **1,** hanging down; **2,** relying on someone or something else for support; **3,** conditioned by something; as, strength is *dependent* on health; **4,** in *grammar,* subordinate; as, a *dependent* clause:—*n.* (also *dependant*), one who relies on another for support.

de-pict (di-pikt′), *v.t.* to portray; describe vividly in words.—*n.* **de-pic′tion.**

de-plete (di-plēt′), *v.t.* [deplet-ed, depleting], to empty; reduce; exhaust; use up; as, illness *depleted* his strength. *n.* **de-ple′tion.**

de-plor-a-ble (di-plōr′a-bl), *adj.* **1,** sad; lamentable; grievous; as, a *deplorable* accident; **2,** shameful; regrettable; as, *deplorable* behaviour.— *adv.* **de-plor′a-bly.**

de-plore (di-plōr′), *v.t.* [deplored, deplor-ing], *v.t.* to lament; grieve for.

de-ploy (di-ploi′), *v.t.* to spread out on a wider front; as, to *deploy* troops.

de-pon-ent (di-pō′nent), *adj.* in *grammar,* a verb with a passive form but active meaning, as, the Latin verb *uti* (to use).—*n.* one who gives evidence under oath, esp. in writing.

de-pop-u-late (dē-pop′ū-lāt′), *v.t.* [depopulat-ed, depopulat-ing], to deprive of inhabitants; reduce the number of people in; as, an epidemic *depopulated* the country.—*n.* **de′pop-u-la′tion.**

de-port (di-pōrt′), *v.t.* **1,** to banish; exile; remove; as, we *deport* criminal

aliens; **2,** to behave (oneself); as, he *deported* himself with dignity.

de-por-ta-tion (dē′pōr-tā′shun), *n.* banishment; removal from the country.

de-port-ment (di-pōrt′ment), *n.* conduct; behaviour; manners.

de-pose (di-pōz′), *v.t.* [deposed, deposing], **1,** to remove from a throne or other high station; deprive of office; **2,** to bear witness; testify under oath. —*n.* **de-pos′al.**

de-pos-it (di-poz′it), *v.t.* **1,** to put or set down; place; **2,** to put into a bank, as money; entrust to another for safekeeping:—*n.* **1,** something committed to the care of another; **2,** a pledge; money given as a promise to pay more; as, a small *deposit* on a purchase; **3,** something laid down; esp. solid matter which settles at the bottom of a liquid; sediment.—*n.* **de-pos′i-tor.**

dep-o-si-tion (dep′o-zish′un; dē′pō-zish′un), *n.* **1,** a putting out of office; dethronement; as, the *deposition* of a king; **2,** a sediment; a laying down, as of sand or mud by a river; **3,** testimony under oath.

de-pot (dep′ō; dē′pō), *n.* **1,** a warehouse; **2,** a building for military supplies, food, or the like; **3,** in Canada, a railroad station.

de-prave (di-prāv′), *v.t.* [depraved, depraving], to make bad; to corrupt.— *adj.* **de-praved′.**—*n.* **de-prav′i-ty** (di-prav′i-ti).

dep-re-cate (dep′re-kāt′), *v.t.* [deprecat-ed, deprecat-ing], to express great disapproval of, or regret for; as, to *deprecate* gambling.—*adj.* **dep′re-ca-to′ry.**

de-pre-ci-ate (di-prē′shi-āt′), *v.t.* [depreciat-ed, depreciat-ing], **1,** to lower the value of; as, to *depreciate* the currency; **2,** to speak slightingly of; belittle; as, to *depreciate* another's work:—*v.i.* to fall in value; become of less worth; as, buildings *depreciate* if not kept in repair.—*n.* **de-pre′ci-a′tion.**

dep-re-da-tion (dep′ri-dā′shun), *n.* a laying waste; a plundering; robbery; as, the *depredations* of the invaders.

de-press (di-pres′), *v.t.* **1,** to press or thrust down; **2,** to sadden; to cast down; as, bad news *depresses* us; **3,** to lower; make less active, as trade.

de-pres-sion (di-presh′un), *n.* **1,** a sinking or falling in of a surface; as, a *depression* in the ground; **2,** low spirits; **3,** dullness of trade; also, the period of time in which business is dull.

de-prive (di-prīv′), *v.t.* [deprived, depriv-ing], **1,** to take away from; as, to *deprive* him of his house; **2,** to keep from having, using, enjoying.—*n.* **dep'-ri-va'tion** (dep'ri-vā'shun).

depth (depth), *n.* **1,** deepness; distance below the surface, or from the observer in any direction; as, the *depth* of a tank; the *depth* of the sky; **2,** profoundness; wisdom; as, the *depths* of learning; a man of *depth;* **3,** richness of tone or colour; **4,** the innermost part; as, the *depths* of a forest; the mid part; as, the *depth* of winter; **5,** that which is deep; as, the ocean *depths.*

dep-u-ta-tion (dep'ū-tā'shun), *n.* **1,** the act of appointing, or giving power to, an agent; **2,** a group of people appointed to act or speak for others; as, a *deputation* of citizens called on the mayor.

de-pute (di-pūt'), *v.t.* **1,** to appoint as an agent or deputy; **2,** to send with power to act; delegate; as, to *depute* authority.

dep-u-ty (dep'ū-ti), *n.* [*pl.* deputies], one appointed to act for another; an agent; as, a policeman is a *deputy* of the law.

de-rail (dē-rāl'), *v.t.* to cause (a train or trolley) to leave, or run off, the rails. *n.* **de-rail'ment.**

de-range (di-rānj'), *v.t.* [deranged, de-rang-ing], **1,** to disorder; confuse; disturb; **2,** to make insane.—*adj.* **de-ranged'.**—*n.* **de-range'ment.**

der-by (dûr'bi), *n.* [*pl.* derbies], **1,** a stiff felt hat, with a dome-shaped crown and a narrow, curved brim; a bowler; **2,** a race or contest, as of horses, motor-cars, airplanes, etc.; thus, a stork *derby.*

der-e-lict (der'e-likt), *adj.* **1,** abandoned; deserted; **2,** unfaithful; neglectful; as, to be *derelict* in one's duty:—*n.* **1,** anything left, forsaken, or cast away; esp. a waterlogged ship; **2,** a human wreck; a hopeless outcast. —*n.* **der'e-lic'tion.**

de-ride (di-rīd'), *v.t.* [derid-ed, derid-ing], to mock; laugh at; jeer.

de-ri-sion (di-rizh'un), *n.* ridicule; scorn; contempt.—*adj.* **de-ri'sive** (dē-rī'siv).

de-riv-a-tive (di-riv'a-tiv), *adj.* obtained from a source; as, *derivative* words:—*n.* something formed from something else; esp. a word formed from another.

de-rive (di-rīv'), *v.t.* [derived, deriv-ing], **1,** to get from a source; as, to *derive* pleasure from a game; **2,** to trace the origin of (a word); as, the word "garage" is *derived* from the French.— *n.* **der'i-va'tion.**

de-rog-a-tor-y (di-rog'a-tĕr-i), *adj.* tending to discredit; disparaging.

der-rick (der'ik), *n.* **1,** a machine equipped with ropes, gears, and pulleys, for lifting heavy weights; **2,** a scaffolding built above an oil-well, to which the drilling machinery is attached.

der-rin-ger (der'in-jẽr), *n.* a small, short-range pocket pistol.

der-vish (dûr'vish), *n.* a monk belonging to a Mohammedan religious order, whose members take vows to live a life of poverty and self-denial.

des-cant (di-skant'), *v.i.* to talk or comment at length; as, he *descanted* on the merits of his dog.—*n.* (des'kant).

de-scend (di-send'), *v.i.* **1,** to go or come down from a higher to a lower level; as, the rain *descended;* **2,** to fall upon in force; as, the soldiers *descended* upon the city; **3,** to pass by inheritance; as, the house *descended* from father to son; also, to come down from earlier times; as, the custom *descended* from the ancient Greeks; **4,** to come down or be derived, as from a source; as, this child *descended* from royalty:—*v.t.* to go down.

de-scend-ant (di-sen'dant), *n.* one who is descended from a given ancestor; offspring.

de-scent (di-sent'), *n.* **1,** change from a higher to a lower place; downward motion; **2,** a sudden hostile invasion or attack; **3,** ancestry; as, he is of English *descent;* **4,** a downward slope.

de-scribe (di-skrīb'), *v.t.* [described, describ-ing], **1,** to give an account of in words; as, he *described* the house; **2,** to draw the outline of; as, *describe* a circle.—*adj.* **de-scrib'a-ble.**

de-scrip-tion (di-skrip'shun), *n.* **1,** the act of giving an oral or written account of something; also, a picture in words; **2,** a class; sort; kind; as, his library contains books of every *description.*— *adj.* **de-scrip'tive.**

de-scry (di-skrī'), *v.t.* [descried, descry-ing], to discover with the eye, esp. in the distance or through obscurity; catch sight of; as, the shipwrecked sailors *descried* a sail on the horizon.

des-e-crate (des'i-krāt'), *v.t.* [desecrat-ed, desecrat-ing], to treat (something sacred) with contempt: opposite of *consecrate;* as, to *desecrate* the church by throwing stones through the windows. —*n.* **des'e-cra'tion.**

de-seg-re-ga-tion (dē'seg'ri-gā'shun), *n.* the process of abolishing racial segregation (separation) in schools, public resorts, buses, railways, etc., esp. in Southern U.S.—*v.t.* **de-seg're-gate.**

¹de-sert (di-zûrt'), *v.t.* **1,** to forsake; abandon; **2,** in military usage, to abandon without leave; as, to *desert* the army:—*v.i.* to run from duty; forsake a post.—*n.* **de-sert′er.**—*n.* **de-ser′-tion.**

²**de-sert** (di-zûrt′), *n.* often *deserts*, a deserved reward or punishment; as, he received his just *deserts.*

³**des-ert** (dez′ẽrt), *n.* a wilderness; a remote, lonely place; esp. a vast expanse of dry, sandy waste:—*adj.* pertaining to a wilderness; desolate.

de-serve (di-zûrv′), *v.t.* [deserved, deserv-ing], to earn by service; be worthy of; merit; as, he *deserved* his promotion:—*v.i.* to be worthy.—*adj.* **de-serv′ing.**—*adv.* **de-serv′ed-ly.**

des-ic-cate (des′i-kāt′), *v.t.* to dry up; free from moisture; as, *desiccated* eggs, beef, or fish.

de-sign (di-zīn′), *v.t.* **1,** to draw or plan out; also, to plan and draw in detail; as, to *design* a house or bridge; **2,** to mean; intend; as, a nod *designed* to warn:—*n.* **1,** an outline or sketch to serve as a pattern, as for a dress; **2,** purpose or intention; also, a plot; as, *designs* against the state; **3,** arrangement of details according to plan; as, a vase of fancy *design.*

des-ig-nate (dez′ig-nāt′; des′ig-nāt′), *v.t.* [designat-ed, designat-ing], **1,** to point out; indicate; show; as, to *designate* the boundaries of a country; **2,** to name; nominate; as, the teacher *designated* John and Mary to count the votes.—*n.* **des′ig-na′tion.**

de-sign-er (di-zīn′ẽr), *n.* one who makes plans, patterns, or original sketches.

de-sign-ing (di-zīn′ing), *adj.* scheming; artful; cunning; as, a *designing* person:—*n.* the art of making plans or sketches.

de-sir-a-ble (di-zīr′a-bl), *adj.* agreeable; pleasing; worth having; as, *desirable* companions.—*n.* **de-sir′a-bil′i-ty.**

de-sire (di-zīr′), *v.t.* [desired, desir-ing], **1,** to wish earnestly for; crave; **2,** to express a wish for; ask; as, I *desire* your help:—*n.* **1,** a longing for the possession of some object; an earnest wish; **2,** a request; **3,** the object longed for.—*adj.* **de-sir′ous.**

de-sist (di-zist′), *v.i.* to cease; stop; as, *desist* from evil.

desk (desk), *n.* a piece of furniture with a tablelike surface to support the paper or book of a writer or reader.

des-o-late (des′ō-lāt′), *v.t.* [desolat-ed, desolat-ing], **1,** to lay waste; make unfit for inhabitants; as, an earthquake *desolated* the city; **2,** to overwhelm with sorrow:—*adj.* (des′o-lit), **1,** deprived of inhabitants; abandoned; **2,**

in a condition of neglect or ruin; **3,** forlorn; miserable.—*adv.* **des′o-late-ly.** —*n.* **des′o-la′tion.**

de-spair (di-spâr′), *v.i.* to lose all hope or expectation:—*n.* **1,** loss of hope or confidence; hopelessness; **2,** that which causes loss of hope; as, she is the *despair* of her mother.—*adj.* **de-spair′ing.**

des-patch (dis-pach′), *v.t.* and *n.* Same as **dispatch.**

des-per-a-do (des′pẽr-ā′dō; des′pẽr-ä′dō), *n.* [*pl.* desperadoes or desperados], a bold and reckless criminal.

des-per-ate (des′pẽr-it), *adj.* **1,** without regard to danger; reckless; as, a *desperate* man; **2,** proceeding from despair; frantic; as, the swimmer made a *desperate* effort to reach shore; **3,** beyond hope or cure; as, a *desperate* illness.—*n.* **des′per-a′tion.**

des-pi-ca-ble (des′pi-ka-bl), *adj.* contemptible; mean; vile.—*adv.* **des′pi-ca-bly.**

de-spise (di-spīz′), *v.t.* [despised, despis-ing], to look down upon; scorn; disdain.

de-spite (di-spīt′), *prep.* notwithstanding; in spite of; as, the player continued in the game *despite* his injuries.

de-spoil (di-spoil′), *v.t.* to rob; deprive of belongings; as, to *despoil* a house of all its treasures.—*n.* **de-spoil′er.**

de-spond (di-spond′), *v.i.* to lose hope or courage; become depressed.

de-spond-en-cy (di-spon′den-si), *n.* absence of hope; mental depression.— *n.* **de-spond′ence.**—*adj.* **de-spond′ent.**

des-pot (des′pot), *n.* an absolute ruler; tyrant; as, Nero was a *despot.*—*adj.* **des-pot′ic.**

des-pot-ism (des′pot-izm), *n.* **1,** absolute government; **2,** any absolute control; tyranny; as, the *despotism* of dictators.

des-sert (di-zûrt′), *n.* a course of fruits, nuts, or sweets, such as pastry or pudding, served last at a meal.

des-ti-na-tion (des′ti-nā′shun), *n.* **1,** an end or object; goal; **2,** the stated end of a journey; as, Toronto is my *destination.*

des-tine (des′tin), *v.t.* [destined, destin-ing], **1,** to appoint to any purpose or end; as, he was *destined* for the ministry; **2,** to settle in advance; foreordain; as, his hopes were *destined* (des′tind) to be realized.

des-ti-ny (des′ti-ni), *n.* [*pl.* destinies], **1,** lot or fortune; fate; as, it was his *destiny* to die alone; **2,** the succession of events in life considered as something beyond the power or control of man; as, it is folly to whine against *destiny.*

cat, āge, fär, câre, ásk; ten, ēve, latẽr; (i) pity, rely, senate; īce; top; nō.

des-ti-tute (des'ti-tūt'), *adj.* 1, without means; penniless; 2, being wholly without something necessary or desirable; as, a man *destitute* of honour.—*n.* **des'ti-tu'tion.**

de-stroy (di-stroi'), *v.t.* 1, to pull down; overturn; lay waste; undo; 2, to kill; put an end to; 3, to render void; as, his acts *destroyed* his influence.

de-stroy-er (di-stroi'ẽr), *n.* 1, a person or thing that destroys; 2, a light, fast war vessel armed with guns, torpedoes, etc.

de-struct-i-ble (di-struk'ti-bl), *adj.* capable of being destroyed or ruined.

de-struc-tion (di-struk'shun), *n.* 1, the act of destroying; ruin; as, fire completed the *destruction* of the city; 2, a cause of ruin; as, gambling was his *destruction.*

de-struc-tive (di-struk'tiv), *adj.* 1, causing desolation; ruinous; hurtful; as, the boll-weevil is a *destructive* insect; 2, tearing down without building up; as, a *destructive* critic.—*adv.* **de-struc'-tive-ly.**

des-ul-tor-y (des'ul-tẽr-i), *adj.* passing from one thing to another without order or method; aimless; as, *desultory* reading.

de-tach (di-tach'), *v.t.* 1, to separate; disconnect; 2, to detail for a special duty; as, to *detach* men to guard a pass. *adj.* **de-tached', de-tach'a-ble.**

de-tach-ment (di-tach'ment), *n.* 1, the act of separating; as, the *detachment* of a key from a key-ring; 2, a body of troops or ships separated from the main body and sent on special service; 3, a standing apart or aloof; aloofness; isolation.

de-tail (di-tāl'), *v.t.* 1, to relate minutely; enumerate; as, she *detailed* to us all her troubles; 2, to tell off for a special duty; as, he *detailed* two men for guard duty:—*n.* (di-tāl'; dē'tāl), 1, a small part of a whole; a single item; as, the *details* of a scheme; such items considered together or taken one by one; as, a subject treated in great *detail;* to go into *detail;* 2, a particular or minute account; 3, a small body of troops assigned to special duty.

de-tain (di-tān'), *v.t.* 1, to hold back or delay; 2, to keep in custody.

de-tect (di-tekt'), *v.t.* to discover; find out; as, to *detect* a criminal; to *detect* an odour.—*n.* **de-tec'tion.**

de-tec-tive (di-tek'tiv), *n.* a person who investigates crimes and mysteries:—*adj.* fitted for, employed in, or connected with, finding out; as, a *detective* agency.

de-tec-tor (di-tek'tẽr), *n.* 1, one who

or that which finds out or discovers; 2, a device used in radio for making the presence of electric waves known.

de-ten-tion (di-ten'shun), *n.* 1, the act of keeping back or withholding; 2, confinement; restraint.

de-ter (di-tûr'), *v.t.* [deterred, deterring], to discourage or hinder, as by fear; restrain; dishearten; as, previous failures did not *deter* us from trying again.—*n.* **de-ter'ment.**

de-ter-gent (di-tẽr'jent), *n.* a cleansing substance or agent, as soap, water, disinfectant drugs, etc.

de-te-ri-o-rate (di-tē'ri-ō-rāt'), *v.t.* [deteriorat-ed, deteriorat-ing], to reduce the quality or value of; as, the rainy spell *deteriorated* the peach crop:—*v.i.* to grow worse; as, a boxer's skill *deteriorates* through idleness.—*n.* **de-te'ri-o-ra'tion.**

de-ter-mi-na-tion (di-tûr'mi-nā'-shun), *n.* 1, the act of deciding; 2, firmness; resolution; as, he spoke with *determination;* 3, measurement or calculation; as, the *determination* of iron in ore.

de-ter-mine (di-tûr'min), *v.i.* [determined, determin-ing], to reach a decision; as, he *determined* on quick action:—*v.t.* 1, to put an end to; 2, to settle; as, to *determine* a case in court; 3, to fix or decide upon beforehand; as, to *determine* the date for the game; 4, to find out for oneself; as, to *determine* the coldness of the wind; 5, to cause to come to a decision; as, this *determined* him to go at once; 6, to establish as a result, or give a definite direction to; as, an accident *determined* his career.—*adj.* **de-ter'mi-nate** (-nit).

de-ter-mined (di-tûr'mind), *adj.* resolute; decided; as, he was a *determined* sort of person.—*adv.* **de-ter'mined-ly** (di-tûr'mind-li; di-tûr'-min-id-li).

de-test (di-test'), *v.t.* to hate intensely; loathe; as, we *detest* people who cheat.—*adj.* **de-test'a-ble.**—*n.* **de'tes-ta'tion.**

de-throne (di-thrōn'), *v.t.* [dethroned, dethron-ing], to remove from a throne; deprive of authority or power; as, to *dethrone* a king.—*n.* **de-throne'ment.**

det-o-nate (det'o-nāt'; dē'), *v.t.* to explode; as, he *detonated* the charge of dynamite.—*n.* **det'o-na'tion; det'o-na'tor.**

de-tour (di-tōōr'; dē'tōōr), or **dé-tour** (dā-tōōr'), *n.* a roundabout way; a path or road that is used temporarily because of an obstruction in a main road.

de-tract (di-trakt'), *v.t.* and *v.i.* 1, to

take away; as, the dark colour *detracts* a great deal from the beauty of the hall; **2,** to malign; slander.—*n.* **de-trac′tion.**

de-train (dē-trān′), *v.i.* to get off a railway train; as, the troops *detrained.*

det-ri-ment (det′ri-ment), *n.* that which injures or reduces in value; injury; damage; loss; harm; as, you cannot do evil without *detriment* to your reputation.—*adj.* **det′ri-men′tal.**

de-tri-tus (di-trī′tus), *n.* fragments of rock worn away or broken down by action of weather, glaciers, etc.

deuce (dūs), *n.* **1,** a card or the side of a die marked with two spots; **2,** in *lawn tennis,* an even point score of forty points each, or an even game score of five or more games each.—*adj.* deu-cod (dū′sid; dŭst).—*adv.* **deu-ced′ly.**

de-val-u-ate (dē-val′ū-āt′), *v.t.* to reduce the legal value (of); as, France *devaluated* the franc. Also, **de-val′ue.**

dev-as-tate (dev′as-tāt′), *v.t.* [devastat-ed, devastat-ing], to lay waste; destroy; as, fire *devastated* the town.— *n.* **dev′as-ta′tion.**

de-vel-op (di-vel′up), *v.t.* **1,** to unfold gradually; make known in detail; as, he *developed* his plans for capturing the city; **2,** to make available for use; as, to *develop* a country's mineral wealth; **3,** to cause to grow; as, fresh air and exercise help to *develop* healthy bodies; **4,** to treat (a photographic plate, print, or film) with chemicals so as to bring out the picture:—*v.i.* to advance from one stage to another; as, boys *develop* into men.—*n.* **de-vel′op-ment.**

de-vel-op-er (di-vel′o-pér), *n.* in *photography,* a chemical solution used to develop a film, plate, etc.

de-vi-ate (dē′vi-āt′), *v.i.* [deviat-ed, deviat-ing], to turn aside or stray, as from a course, plan, or the like.—*n.* **de′vi-a′tion.**

de-vice (di-vīs′), *n.* **1,** a scheme; trick; **2,** an invention; apparatus; **3,** a fanciful design or pattern; a heraldic emblem; **3,** fancy or will; as, left to his own *devices.*

dev-il (dev′l), *n.* **1,** (usually *Devil*), the supreme spirit of evil; Satan; **2,** a false god or demon; also, a wicked person; **3,** an unfortunate person; as, the poor *devil* deserves pity; **4,** a daring or reckless person; **5,** a printer's helper:—*v.t.* [devilled, devilling], to tease; torment:—*v.i.* to do work for which one's employer gets credit.— *adj.* **dev′il-ish** (dev′l-ish).—*n.* **dev′il-ment; dev′il-ry; dev′il-try.**

dev-illed (dev′ld), *adj.* chopped and mixed with seasoning or relish; as, *devilled* crabs.

dev-il—fish (dev′l–fish′), *n.* **1,** any of various odd-shaped sea-fishes, as the angler or ray; **2,** a giant octopus.

de-vi-ous (dē′vi-us), *adj.* **1,** indirect; rambling; roundabout; as, *devious* paths; **2,** apart from the way of right and duty; as, *devious* methods.—*adv.* **de′vi-ous-ly.**

de-vise (di-vīz′), *v.t.* [devised, devis-ing], **1,** to think up or contrive; as, the prisoners *devised* a way to escape; **2,** to bequeath or give by will.

de-vis-er (di-vīz′ėr), *n.* one who contrives or invents.

de-vis-or (di-vīz′ėr), *n.* one who gives by will.

de-void (di-void′), *adj.* entirely without; lacking; as, *devoid* of sense.

de-volve (di-volv′), *v.i.* [devolved, devolv-ing], to be passed down or handed over; as, the duty *devolved* upon him.—*n.* **dev′o-lu′tion** (dē′vo-lū′shun).

de-vote (di-vōt′), *v.t.* [devot-ed, devot-ing], **1,** to dedicate or set apart; as, to *devote* the morning to meditation; **2,** to give up wholly; as, to *devote* oneself to study or music.—*adj.* **de-vot′ed.**

dev-o-tee (dev′ō-tē′), *n.* one entirely given up to a special interest; as, a *devotee* of the theatre; one zealous in religion; an enthusiast.

de-vo-tion (di-vō′shun), *n.* **1,** the act of devoting or the state of being devoted; **2,** strong affection; **3,** **devotions,** religious worship; prayer.— *adj.* and *n.* **de-vo′tion-al.**

de-vour (di-vour′), *v.t.* **1,** to swallow greedily or ravenously; as, the hungry man *devoured* the food; **2,** to destroy or lay waste; as, the fire *devoured* much timber; **3,** to take in eagerly with ears or eyes; as, to *devour* a new novel.

de-vout (di-vout′), *adj.* **1,** devoted to religious thoughts and exercises; **2,** expressing piety; as, a *devout* prayer; **3,** sincere; as, accept our *devout* wishes for success.—*adv.* **de-vout′ly.**—*n.* **de-vout′ness.**

dew (dū), *n.* **1,** moisture from the atmosphere condensed in small drops; **2,** anything refreshing like dew.—*adj.* **dew′y.**

dew-lap (dū′lap′), *n.* the loose fold of skin hanging from the neck of a cow, dog, etc.

dew-worm (dū′wûrm′), *n.* a variety of large earthworm found on lawns at night (used for fishing).

dex-ter-ous (dek′stėr-us) or **dex-trous** (deks′trus), *adj.* **1,** skilful with

cat, āge, fär, câre, àsk; ten, ēve, latėr; (i) pity, rely, senate; īce; top; nō.

the hands; as, a *dexterous* workman; **2,** quick mentally; adroit; clever; **3,** done with skill; as, *dexterous* tricks.—*n.* **dex-ter/i-ty** (deks-ter/i-ti).

di-a-be-tes (dī/a-bē/tis; -tēz), *n.* a disease marked by excessive urination, sugar in the urine, thirst and hunger.— *n.* and *adj.* **di/a-bet/ic** (-bet/; -bēt/).

di-a-bol-ic (dī/a-bol/ik) or **di-a-bol-i-cal** (dī/a-bol/i-kal), *adj.* devilish; outrageously wicked; cruel; as, he has a *diabolic* temper.

di-a-crit-i-cal (dī/a-krit/i-kal), *adj.* separating or distinguishing, as a mark or sign:—**diacritical marks,** the signs used to show the pronunciation of words, as ā, ė, ô, ü, etc.

di-a-dem (dī/a-dem), *n.* a crown; tiara.

di-ag-nose (dī/ag-nōz/; dī/ag-nōs/), *v.t.* [diagnosed, diagnos-ing], to determine the nature of something, as a disease, from the symptoms; as, the doctor *diagnosed* her illness as measles. *n.* **di/ag-no/sis.**

di-ag-o-nal (dī-ag/o-nal), *adj.* **1,** slanting; **2,** extending from one corner of a figure, as a square, to its opposite corner:—*n.* **1,** a straight line drawn or cut on a slant; **2,** a straight line drawn from one angle of a figure, as a square, to any other angle not adjacent; **3,** material with an oblique pattern.—*adv.* **di-ag/o-nal-ly.**

di-a-gram (dī/a-gram), *n.* **1,** a line drawing of something, made for purposes of explanation, and giving in outline the most important parts; a plan or chart, as of a building, machine, or the like; **2,** in *grammar*, an outline of a sentence showing its construction:— *v.t.* [diagrammed, diagramming], **1,** to illustrate by an outline or drawing; **2,** in *grammar*, to show the construction of (a sentence) by means of a diagram.— *adj.* **di/a-gram-mat/ic.**

di-al (dī/al), *n.* **1,** a flat surface on which a pointer casts a shadow in such a way as to show the time of day; **2,** the face of a watch, clock, or the like; **3,** any plate on which a pointer marks revolutions, direction, pressure, or the like; as, the *dial* on a gas-meter; **4,** in some telephones, a movable device by means of which connections may be made without giving the number to a central operator:—*v.t.* [dialled, dialling], **1,** to measure or indicate by a dial; as, they *dialled* the speed of the car; **2,** in telephoning, to call by operating a movable dial.

di-a-lect (dī/a-lekt), *n.* **1,** the special form of a language in a given region of the country; as, the Nova Scotia *dialect;* also, the customary speech of a

class; as, the Negro *dialect;* **2,** the special language of a trade or profession.—*adj.* **di/a-lec/tal.**

di-a-logue or **di-a-log** (dī/a-log), *n.* a conversation between two or more persons; also, the conversation in a novel or play.

dial tone, a low steady buzz or hum in a dial telephone to show that the line is open and a number may be dialled.

di-am-e-ter (dī-am/e-têr), *n.* **1,** a straight line through the centre of a circle, dividing it in half; **2,** the length of a straight line through the centre of an object; hence, thickness; as, the *diameter* of a tree.—*adj.* **di/a-met/ric** (dī/a-met/rik); **di/a-met/ri-cal.**—*adv.* **di/a-met/ri-cal-ly.**

di-a-mond (dī/a-mund), *n.* **1,** a brilliant, usually colourless, precious stone; crystallized carbon: the hardest known substance; **2,** a plane figure with four equal straight sides and two acute and two obtuse angles, called *diamonds,* of playing-cards, marked with a red figure like a diamond; **4,** in baseball, the space inside the lines connecting the bases; also, the entire playing-field:—*adj.* resembling, or made of, a diamond.

di-a-per (dī/a-pêr), *n.* **1,** cotton or linen cloth woven in geometric patterns; **2,** a breech cloth for an infant.

di-a-phragm (dī/a-fram), *n.* **1,** the muscular partition which divides the chest from the abdomen; **2,** a vibrating disk, as in a telephone; **3,** in a camera, optical instrument, or the like, a perforated device for regulating the admission of light.

di-ar-rhoe-a or **di-ar-rhe-a** (dī/a-rē/a), *n.* extreme looseness of the bowels.—*adj.* **di/ar-rhoe/al.**

DIAPHRAGM

A, abdominal cavity; C, thoracic cavity; D, diaphragm.

di-a-ry (dī/a-ri), *n.* [*pl.* diaries], **1,** a personal record of daily events; **2,** a book for daily memoranda.

di-a-ton-ic scale (dī/a-ton/ik), *n.* in *music,* a standard major or minor scale of eight tones to the octave with no chromatic (or semitone) intervals.

di-a-tribe (dī/a-trīb/), *n.* a bitter, abusive attack in words.

dib (dib), *n. Colloq.* a small marble used in playing a children's game in which the marble is propelled by thumb against an opponent's dib or marble.

dib-ble (dib/l), *n.* a pointed garden tool used to make holes for planting seeds, etc.

dice (dīs), *n.pl.* [*sing.* die (dī)], small cubes, marked on the sides with one to six spots, used in games of chance:—*v.i.* [diced, dicing], to play with dice: —*v.t.* **1,** to decorate with patterns resembling cubes or squares; to chequer; **2,** to cut into cubes or squares.—*n.* **dic′er.**

DICE

dick-er (dik′ẽr), *v.i.* to bargain or trade on a small scale; as, to *dicker* with a shopkeeper:—*n.* a small bargain or deal.

di-cot-y-le-don (dī-kot′i-lē′don), *n.* a plant with two seed leaves; in this largest class of some 172 orders are the shrubs, deciduous trees, legumes, etc.— *adj.* **di-cot′y-le′don-ous.**

dic-ta-phone (dik′ta-fōn′), *n.* a phonographic device used in offices for recording and reproducing dictation.

dic-tate (dik-tāt′), *v.t.* [dictat-ed, dictat-ing], **1,** to declare with authority; prescribe; **2,** to express orally for another to take down in writing; as, her employer *dictated* ten letters:—*v.i.* to speak with final authority:—*n.* (dik′tāt), **1,** a command; as, the king's *dictates;* **2,** a controlling principle; as, the *dictates* of conscience.—*n.* **dicta′tion.**

dic-ta-tor (dik-tā′tẽr; dik′tāt-ẽr), *n.* **1,** one who says something for another to write; **2,** one who rules with absolute powers of government; **3,** one exercising similar authority in any sphere; as, a *dictator* of styles.—*n.* **dic-ta′tor-ship.**

dic-ta-tor-i-al (dik′ta-tōr′i-al), *adj.* pertaining to one who gives positive commands; overbearing; imperious.

dic-tion (dik′shun), *n.* the manner of expressing ideas in words; choice of words.

dic-tion-ar-y (dik′shun-ẽr-i), *n.* [*pl.* dictionaries], a book explaining the words of a language arranged alphabetically; a lexicon; vocabulary.

dic-to-graph (dik′to-graf′), *n.* a telephonic device with sensitive transmitter used for secret listening to and recording of conversation in a nearby room.

did (did), *p.t.* of *do.*

di-dac-tic (di-dak′tik; dī-), *adj.* pertaining to, or of the nature of, teaching; conveying instruction; as, a *didactic* poem.—*adv.* **di-dac′ti-cal-ly.**—*n.* **di-dac′ti-cism.**

did-dle (did′l), *v.i.* and *v.t. Colloq.* **1,** to jiggle; **2,** swindle; **3,** trifle time away.

¹die (dī), *v.i.* [died, dy-ing], **1,** to cease to live; expire; **2,** to decay; wither: said of plants or flowers; **3,** to long

intensely; as, she is *dying* to hear your secret; **4,** figuratively, to fade; vanish; as, fame soon *dies.*

²die (dī), *n.* [*pl.* dies (dīz)], **1,** a metal form used in stamping coins, metals, or the like; **2,** tool used in cutting the threads of screws or bolts, or the like; **3,** a metal plate with holes for receiving a punch; also, a form of cutter, used in a press, for shaping leather, paper, sheet metal, or the like; **4,** [*pl.* dice (dīs)], a small cube used in gaming.

DIE, def, 2, for threading a pipe or bar, held in a frame or stock.

di-e-lec-tric (dī′e-lek′trik), *n.* any nonconducting or insulating material, as rubber, glass, etc.

die-sel (dē′zel), *n.* an internal–combustion engine in which crude oil is ignited by heat from air compression instead of by electric spark as in a gasoline engine.

¹di-et (dī′et), *n.* a formal assembly or congress; esp. the parliamentary assembly of some countries.

²di-et (dī′et), *n.* **1,** one's customary food; **2,** manner of living, with special reference to food; **3,** a prescribed course of food, intended as a health measure:—*v.t.* to regulate the eating and drinking of (a person); as, he *dieted* himself back to health:—*v.i.* to eat or drink according to prescribed rules:—*adj.* **di′e-tar-y.**

di-e-tet-ic (dī′e-tet′ik), *adj.* pertaining to diet:—**dietetics,** *n.pl.* used as *sing.,* that branch of hygiene relating to diet and its effects.—*adj.* **di′e-tet′i-cal.**

di-e-ti-tian or **di-e-ti-cian** (dī′e-tish′an), *n.* one trained to plan meals with a proper proportion of various food elements.

dif-fer (dif′ẽr), *v.i.* **1,** to be unlike; **2,** to disagree; dispute; quarrel.

dif-fer-ence (dif′ẽr-ens), *n.* **1,** the state of being unlike; unlikeness; **2,** controversy; quarrel; **3,** the amount by which numbers differ; remainder after subtraction; as, the *difference* between five and eight is three.

dif-fer-ent (dif′ẽr-ent), *adj.* unlike; distinct; not the same.—*adv.* **dif′fer-ent-ly.**

dif-fer-en-tial (dif′ẽr-en′shal), *adj.* **1,** showing a difference; **2,** distinguishing; **3,** making use of differences; as, a *differential* gear.—*n.* **1,** a difference; **2,** a differential gear; **3,** a difference in rates.

dif-fer-en-ti-ate (dif′ẽr-en′shi-āt′), *v.t.* [differentiat-ed, differentiat-ing], **1,** to observe or state an unlikeness between; as, to *differentiate* the various breeds of cattle; **2,** to mark (a person or thing) as unlike another; as, size *differentiates* the raven from the crow: —*v.i.* to acquire a distinctive character. —*n.* dif′fer-en′ti-a′tion.

dif-fi-cult (dif′i-kult), *adj.* **1,** not easy; hard to do, as a problem; **2,** not easily pleased or managed; as, a *difficult* child.

dif-fi-cul-ty (dif′i-kul-ti), *n.* [*pl.* difficulties], **1,** the state of being hard to do; as, the *difficulty* of the task; also, great effort; as, he reached home with *difficulty;* **2,** something hard to do; an obstacle; trouble; hard work; as, he had *difficulty* in starting the car; **3,** a scruple; objection; as, he made no *difficulty* about my going; **4,** **difficulties,** a trying situation; embarrassment; esp. want of money.

dif-fi-dent (dif′i-dent), *adj.* lacking self-reliance; shy; modest.—*n.* dif′fi-dence.

dif-frac-tion (di-frak′shun), *n.* **1,** the breaking of a ray of light into the colours of the spectrum or into dark and light bands; **2,** a similar breaking of wave motions, as of sound or electricity:—*v.t.* dif-fract′.

dif-fuse (di-fūz′), *v.t.* [diffused, diffus-ing], **1,** to send out; spread; as, the lamps *diffused* a pale light; **2,** in physics, to spread, as a gas or liquid, by mixing with another gas or liquid; as, to *diffuse* syrup in water:—*v.i.* to spread out in every direction:—*adj.* (di-fūs′), **1,** widely spread; scattered; **2,** wordy; as, a *diffuse* lecture.—*n.* dif-fu′sion.—*adv.* dif-fuse′ly.

dig (dig), *v.i.* [*p.t.* and *p.p.* dug (dug) or digged (digd), *p.pr.* dig-ging], **1,** to work with a spade, hands, claws, etc., in casting up earth; **2,** to make a way (under, through, in); as, they *dug* through the hill; **3,** *Colloq.,* to study hard:—*v.t.* **1,** to loosen or break up with a spade, hands, claws, or the like; **2,** to make, as a hole, by casting out earth; **3,** to bring up from underground; as, to *dig* potatoes; also, to bring to light; as, to *dig* up information; **4,** to thrust; poke; as, to *dig* spurs into a horse:—*n.* **1,** a poke or thrust; **2,** *Colloq.:* **a,** a cutting or spiteful remark; **b,** a plodding student.—*n.* dig′ger.

di-gest (di-jest′; dī-jest′), *v.t.* **1,** to change (food) in the stomach and intestines into a form which the body can use; **2,** to think over carefully until one understands or until the material becomes a part of one's knowledge; as, to *digest* a book; **3,** to arrange in condensed form and systematic order; classify; as, the laws of the state were *digested:*—*v.i.* to undergo change, as food in the stomach and intestines, for use in the body; as, fruits *digest* easily: —*n.* (dī′jest), **1,** an orderly and classified arrangement of materials, usually in condensed form; as, a *digest* of the laws of the state; **2,** a brief summary; as, he wrote a *digest* of the book.

di-gest-i-ble (di-jes′ti-bl; dī-jes′ti-bl), *adj.* capable of being changed in the stomach and intestines for use in the body.—*adv.* di-gest′i-bly.—*n.* di-gest′i-bil′i-ty.

di-ges-tion (di-jes′chun), *n.* the act or process of changing food by action of juices in the stomach and intestines for use in the body; also, the power of digesting; as, a weak *digestion.*

di-ges-tive (di-jes′tiv), *adj.* pertaining to, or promoting, absorption of food by the body.

dig-it (dij′it), *n.* **1,** a finger or toe; **2,** any one of the numerals from 1 to 9.

dig-i-ta-lis (dij′i-tā′lis), *n.* **1,** a drug used as a heart stimulant; **2,** a showy garden biennial, the foxglove.

dig-ni-fied (dig′ni-fīd′), *adj.* lofty in manner; noble; stately.

dig-ni-fy (dig′ni-fī), *v.t.* [dignified, dignify-ing], to exalt; confer honour upon; add distinction to; as, his presence *dignified* the meeting.

dig-ni-tar-y (dig′ni-tẽr-i), *n.* [*pl.* dignitaries], one who holds a position of rank or honour; esp. a high church official; as, a bishop is a *dignitary.*

dig-ni-ty (dig′ni-ti), *n.* [*pl.* dignities], **1,** nobleness; true worth; as, the *dignity* of labour; **2,** stateliness of manner or style; as, to walk with *dignity;* **3,** high rank or office; as, the *dignity* of a king; **4,** a person of high rank; as, the king will meet the other *dignities* of the state.

di-gress (dī-gres′; di-gres′), *v.i.* to turn aside; get away from the main subject or line of argument.—*n.* di-gres′sion.

dike (dīk), *n.* **1,** a ditch; **2,** a mound or bank of earth along a ditch; a causeway; **3,** a dam or bank thrown up as a protection against the sea or floods; as, the *dikes* of Holland:—*v.t.* [diked, dik-ing], **1,** to enclose or protect with a dike; **2,** to drain by means of ditching or dikes. Also spelled **dyke.**

di-lap-i-dat-ed (di-lap′i-dāt′ed), *adj.* in partial ruin; run-down; neglected; as, a *dilapidated* old house.—*n.* di-lap′i-da′tion.

di-late (dī-lāt′; di-lāt′), *v.t.* [dilat-ed, dilat-ing], **1,** to enlarge or widen; as, to *dilate* the eyes; **2,** to distend; as, to *dilate* the lungs with air:—*v.i.* **1,** to be extended or enlarged; **2,** to speak fully and copiously.—*n.* **di-lat′er.**—*n.* **di-la′tion.**—*n.* **dil′a-ta′tion.**

dil-a-tor-y (dil′a-tėr-i), *adj.* tending to cause delay; as, *dilatory* tactics; tardy; as, a *dilatory* reply.—*adv.* **dil′a-tor-i-ly.**

di-lem-ma (di-lem′a; dī-lem′a), *n.* a situation involving a choice between two or more evils; a difficult choice.

dil-et-tan-te (dil′e-tán′ti), *n.* one who dabbles in the fine arts, literature, or science as a pastime.

dil-i-gent (dil′i-jent), *adj.* industrious; careful.—*n.* **dil′i-gence.**

dill (dil), *n.* a plant whose spicy seeds are used in flavouring:—**dill pickle,** a large pickle seasoned with the seed of the dill.

dil-ly-dal-ly (dil′i-dal′i), *v.i.* [dilly-dallied, dillydallying], *Colloq.,* to loiter; trifle; waver.

di-lute (di-lūt′; dī-), *v.t.* [dilut-ed, dilut-ing], to weaken or thin by mixture with something, esp. by adding water:—*adj.* weakened; thinned; as, a *dilute* mixture.—*n.* **di-lu′tion.**

dim (dim), *adj.* **1,** faint; obscure; not bright; as, the *dim* light of evening; **2,** shedding little light; as, *dim* head-lights; **3,** hazy; ill-defined; as, a *dim* figure in the shadows; **4,** not understanding or seeing clearly; as, eyes *dim* with tears:—*v.t.* [dimmed, dim-ming], to make less bright or distinct; dull:—*v.i.* to become indistinct; fade.—*adv.* **dim′ly.**—*n.* **dim′ness.**

dime (dīm), *n.* a silver coin worth one tenth of a dollar, or ten cents.

di-men-sion (di-men′shun), *n.* **1,** measurement in any one direction, as length, breadth, height, or the like; **2, dimensions, a,** size in terms of these measurements; **b,** size; importance; scope; as, an undertaking of large *dimensions.*—*adj.* **di-men′sion-al.**

dim-e-ter (dim′e-tėr), *n.* in *verse,* a line of two feet or measures: as, In rai′n/ or shi′ne/ (iambic *dimeter*).

di-min-ish (di-min′ish), *v.t.* **1,** to make less in amount, size, number, or the like; as, the long winter *diminished* their supplies; **2,** to weaken; impair; as, the power of wealth was *diminished:*—*v.i.* to grow less in amount or importance; decrease.

di-min-u-en-do (di-min′ū-en′dō), *adj.* and *adv.* in *music,* decreasing or softening in volume of sound: opposite of *crescendo.*

dim-i-nu-tion (dim′i-nū′shun), *n.* a decreasing; a making or growing less; as, a *diminution* in foreign trade.

di-min-u-tive (di-min′ū-tiv), *adj.* **1,** small or little; as, a *diminutive* child; **2,** expressing smallness; as, "-kin" is a *diminutive* ending:—*n.* a word formed from another to express a smaller thing of the same kind; as, *lambkin,* a little *lamb.*

dim-i-ty (dim′i-ti), *n.* [*pl.* dimities], a cotton cloth with raised ornamental stripes or figures.

dim-out (dim′out), *n.* a partial blackout, in which street and other bright lights are dimmed but not necessarily concealed.

dim-ple (dim′pl), *n.* a small dent or hollow in the surface of anything, as in the cheek or chin:—*v.i.* [dim-pled, dim-pling], to form dimples:—*v.t.* to mark with dimples.

din (din), *n.* a continued and insistent noise:—*v.t.* [dinned, din-ning], to repeat over and over persistently; as, she *dinned* into him the lesson of honesty:—*v.i.* to make a noise; as, cries *dinning* in his ears.

di-nar (di-när′), *n.* a small silver coin, the monetary unit of Yugoslavia (worth about 19 cents).

dine (dīn), *v.i.* [dined, din-ing], to take dinner:—*v.t.* to give a dinner for; feed.

din-er (dīn′ėr), *n.* **1,** one who dines; **2,** a railroad car in which meals are served.

din-ette (dī′net′), *n.* an alcove used as a dining-room.

ding (ding), *v.i.* to sound like a bell.

ding-dong (ding′dong′), *n.* **1,** the sound of a bell; **2,** monotonous repetition.

din-ghy, din-gy, or **din-gey** (ding′gi), *n.* [*pl.* dinghies, dingies, dingeys], any of various kinds of small rowboats or sail-boats.

din-gle (ding′gl), *n.* a dell; a small deep, wooded valley.

din-gy (din′ji), *adj.* [din-gi-er, din-gi-est], grimy; faded; as, a *dingy* room.—*adv.* **din′gi-ly.**—*n.* **din′gi-ness.**

din-ner (din′ėr), *n.* **1,** the chief meal of the day; **2,** a formal party at which dinner is served.

din-ing—room (dīn′ing-rōom′), *n.* a room where meals are usually eaten.

dink-y (dingk′i), *adj. Colloq.,* small.

di-no-saur (dī′no-sôr′), *n.* any of a great variety of huge reptiles that lived millions of years ago.—*adj.* **di′no-sau′-ri-an.**

dint (dint), *n.* **1,** a blow; **2,** a mark left by a blow or pressure; a dent; **3,** force or power; as, the trunk was closed by *dint* of much effort:—*v.t.* to mark or dent.

di-o-cese (dī′ō-sēs; dī′ō-sis), *n.* the district in which a bishop has authority. —*adj.* **di-oc′e-san** (di-os′e-san; dī-os′e-zan).

di-ode (dī′ōd), *n.* a vacuum tube with a cold pole (anode) and a heated negative pole (cathode), used as a rectifier (a means of changing alternating to direct current).

di-ox-ide (dī-ok′sīd), *n.* an oxide with two atoms of oxygen to the molecule, as carbon *dioxide* (CO_2).

dip (dip), *v.t.* [dipped, dip-ping], **1,** to put quickly into liquid and take out again; immerse; as, to *dip* one's finger into water; or the like; as, to *dip* water from a brook; **3,** to baptize by putting under water; **4,** to lower and raise quickly, as a flag:—*v.i.* **1,** to immerse oneself; **2,** to enter slightly into anything; as, to *dip* into a book; **3,** to slope downward; as, the road *dips;* **4,** to sink; as, the sun *dipped* below the hills; **5,** to reach into to take something out; as, to *dip* into a barrel for flour:— *n.* **1,** the act of putting into water temporarily; a short plunge; as, a *dip* in the ocean; **2,** a downward slope; as, a *dip* in the road; **3,** a liquid preparation used in cleaning or colouring; **4,** a candle made by frequent dipping of a wick in fat or wax; **5,** in aviation, a quick descent followed by an ascent.

diph-the-ri-a (dif-thē′ri-a), *n.* an acute contagious disease of the throat.

diph-thong (dif′thông), *n.* the union of two vowel sounds to form a continuous sound, as in *oil, out, aisle.*

di-plo-ma (di-plō′ma), *n.* an official document conferring some honour or degree; esp. a paper showing the completion of a course of study in school or college.

di-plo-ma-cy (di-plō′ma-si), *n.* [*pl.* diplomacies], **1,** the art or practice of managing relations between states or nations; **2,** skill in conducting affairs; tact.

dip-lo-mat (dip′lō-mat′), *n.* **1,** one who conducts negotiations between nations; **2,** a tactful person.—*adj.* **dip′lo-mat′ic.**

dip-per (dip′ẽr), *n.* **1,** a vessel with a long handle for scooping up a liquid; **2,** a wrenlike bird skilled in diving: also called *waterouzel:—***Dipper,** either of two groups of seven stars in the northern heavens, arranged in the outline of a ladle. One is called the *Big Dipper*, the other the *Little Dipper.*

dire (dīr), *adj.* [dir-er, dir-est], **1,** dreadful; as, the *dire* news of an explosion;

2, extreme; as, in *dire* need.—*adv.* **dire′ly.**

di-rect (di-rekt′; dī-rekt′), *adj.* **1,** straight; as, a *direct* route; **2,** straightforward; sincere; as, a *direct* answer; **3,** immediate; not coming through someone else; as, he had *direct* knowledge; hence, personal; as, under his *direct* supervision; **4,** in an unbroken line of descent; as, a *direct* heir:—*v.t.* **1,** to address (a letter); also, to address with a definite aim; as, he *directed* his remarks to the students; **2,** to aim or point; as, to *direct* one's attention to peace; **3,** to show or guide; as, to *direct* him to the station; **4,** to conduct or manage; as, to *direct* a chorus; **5,** to order or instruct; as, to *direct* students:—*v.i.* to act as a guide.—*n.* **di-rect′ness.**—*n.* **di-rec′tive.**

di-rec-tion (di-rek′shun; dī-rek′shun), *n.* **1,** the act of controlling, managing, or guiding; management; **2,** instruction or command; as, he left *directions* for the servants; **3,** the address on a letter, or the like; **4,** a course or line of motion; as, he went in the opposite *direction:—***direction finder,** a rotating loop antenna used to find the direction of incoming radio waves.

di-rect-ly (di-rekt′li; dī-rekt′li), *adv.* **1,** in a direct line or manner; **2,** at once.

di-rec-tor (di-rek′tẽr; dī-rek′tẽr), *n.* a person who manages; a manager; esp. a member of the governing board of a company or society.—*n.fem.* **di-rec′tress.**—*n.* **di-rec′to-rate.**

di-rec-to-ry (di-rek′to-ri; dī-rek′to-ri), *n.* [*pl.* directories], an alphabetical list of names and addresses; as, a business *directory.*

dire-ful (dīr′fool), *adj.* dreadful; dire.

dirge (dûrj), *n.* a funeral hymn; a song of mourning.

dir-i-gi-ble (dir′i-ji-bl), *adj.* capable of being guided; as, a *dirigible* balloon:— *n.* a cigar-shaped balloon driven by motors.

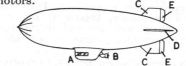

DIRIGIBLE
A, control car;   B, power car;   C, C, vertical fins; D, horizontal fin;   E, E, rudder.

dirk (dûrk), *n.* a kind of dagger.

dirt (dûrt), *n.* **1,** mud; filth; as, streets full of *dirt;* **2,** foulness in action, speech, or thought; scandal; **3,** loose earth or soil.

dirt-y (dûr′ti), *adj.* [dirt-i-er, dirt-i-est], **1,** soiled; as, a *dirty* dress; **2,** obscene; as, *dirty* language; **3,** base; low; as, a *dirty* scoundrel; **4,** not clear, as water or colour; **5,** disagreeable, as weather: —*v.t.* [dirtied, dirty-ing], to soil.—*n.* **dirt′i-ness.**

dis-a-bil-i-ty (dis′a-bil′i-ti), *n.* [*pl.* disabilities], **1,** the lack of power or ability to do something; **2,** that which deprives of power or ability, as old age or mental or physical illness.

dis-a-ble (dis-ā′bl), *v.t.* [disabled, disabling], to deprive of power or ability; cripple; incapacitate.—*adj.* **dis-a′bled.**

dis-a-buse (dis′a-būz′), *v.t.* [disabused, disabus-ing], to undeceive; set right.

dis-ad-van-tage (dis′ad-vàn′tij), *n.* **1,** unfavourable condition; obstacle; as, to work under *disadvantages;* **2,** loss or harm; as, a rumour to his *disadvantage.* —*adj.* **dis-ad′van-ta′geous.**

dis-af-fec-tion (dis′a-fek′shun), *n.* **1,** discontent; **2,** ill will; disloyalty; as, *disaffection* among troops.—*adj.* **dis′af-fect′ed.**

dis-a-gree (dis′a-grē′), *v.i.* [disagreed, disagree-ing], **1,** to differ in opinion; also, to quarrel; as, to *disagree* over money; **2,** to be unlike; as, this book *disagrees* with mine; **3,** to be unsuitable; as, the climate *disagrees* with him. —*n.* **dis′a-gree′ment.**

dis-a-gree-a-ble (dis′a-grē′a-bl), *adj.* unpleasant; distasteful; ill-tempered. —*adv.* **dis′a-gree′a-bly.**

dis-al-low (dis′a-lou′), *v.t.* to refuse to admit or allow (a claim or the like).

dis-ap-pear (dis′a-pēr′), *v.i.* to pass from sight or existence.—*n.* **dis′ap-pear′ance.**

dis-ap-point (dis′a-point′), *v.t.* **1,** to fail to fulfil the hope of; **2,** to balk.— *adj.* **dis′-ap-point′ed.**—*n.* **dis′ap-point′-ment.**

dis-ap-pro-ba-tion (dis′ap-rō-bā′-shun), *n.* disapproval; unfavourable opinion.

dis-ap-prove (dis′a-prōōv′), *v.t.* [disapproved, disapprov-ing], **1,** to regard with disfavour; condemn; blame; **2,** to refuse assent to:—*v.i.* to express an unfavourable judgment.—*n.* **dis′ap-prov′al.**

dis-arm (dis-ärm′), *v.t.* **1,** to deprive of weapons; **2,** to make harmless; as, his frank admission *disarmed* his foes:—*v.i.* to lay aside arms; reduce the size of armed forces; as, the country decided to *disarm.*

dis-ar-ma-ment (dis-är′ma-ment), *n.* **1,** the laying aside or depriving of weapons; **2,** the reduction of military, naval, and air forces.

dis-ar-range (dis′a-rānj′), *v.t.* [disarranged, disarrang-ing], to put out of

order; disturb the order of.—*n.* **dis′ar-range′ment.**

dis-ar-ray (dis′a-rā′), *v.t.* **1,** to unrobe; undress; **2,** to throw into disorder:— *n.* **1,** disordered dress; **2,** confusion; disorder.

dis-as-ter (di-zàs′tèr), *n.* a calamity; sudden misfortune; a serious accident. —*adj.* **dis-as′trous.**

dis-a-vow (dis′a-vou′), *v.t.* to refuse to acknowledge; disclaim.

dis-band (dis-band′), *v.t.* to break up and dismiss (an organized body of people); as, to *disband* the army after the armistice:—*v.i.* to disperse; as, the club *disbanded* after its meeting.—*n.* **dis-band′ment.**

dis-bar (dis-bär′), *v.t.* to expel a lawyer from the legal profession.

dis-be-lief (dis′bi-lēf′), *n.* lack of belief.

dis-be-lieve (dis′bi-lēv′), *v.t.* and *v.i.* [disbelieved, disbeliev-ing], to refuse to accept as true.—*n.* **dis′be-liev′er.**

dis-burse (dis-bûrs′), *v.t.* [disbursed, disburs-ing], to expend; pay out; as, a treasurer *disburses* money.—*n.* **dis-burs′er.**—*n.* **dis-burse′ment.**

disc (disk), *n.* Same as **disk.**

dis-card (dis-kärd′), *v.t.* **1,** to throw away as useless; **2,** in card-playing, to get rid of (a card or cards), as useless or extra:—*v.i.* to throw away a card or cards:—*n.* (also dis′kärd), **1,** the act of throwing away weak cards; also, the cards so thrown away; **2,** that which is cast aside as worthless.

dis-cern (di-zûrn′; di-sûrn′), *v.t.* **1,** to make out or perceive with the sense or mind; as, to *discern* a figure in the shadows; he *discerned* danger in the plan; **2,** to distinguish clearly; discriminate; as, to *discern* good from evil —*v.i.* to see, make, or understand distinctions; as, to *discern* between right and wrong.—*n.* **dis-cern′er.**

dis-cern-i-ble (di-zûr′ni-bl; di-sûr′ni-bl), *adj.* visible; as, the hills are barely *discernible* in the mist.

dis-cern-ing (di-zûr′ning; di-sûr′ning), *adj.* of keen insight or discriminating judgment; acute.—*adv.* **dis-cern′ing-ly.**

dis-cern-ment (di-zûrn′ment; di-sûrn′ment), *n.* the act or power of distinguishing or discriminating; keenness of insight.

dis-charge (dis-chärj′), *v.t.* [discharged, discharg-ing], **1,** to relieve of a load or burden; unload, as a ship; **2,** to remove, as a cargo from a ship or passengers from a train; **3,** to let fly, as an arrow; to shoot, as a gun; **4,** to set free; as, to *discharge* a prisoner; **5,** to dismiss, as servants; to end the services of; as, to *discharge* a jury, committee, or the.like; **6,** to give off; as, his wound *discharged* pus; **7,** to pay off, as a debt; **8,** to perform, as a duty:—*v.i.* to get rid of a load or burden; to empty; as, the lake *discharged* into a river:—*n.* **1,** an unloading or emitting; as, the *discharge* of a ship; **2,** that which is unloaded; **3,** a firing or shooting off, as of guns, arrows, dynamite; **4,** release from a burden, debt, accusation, confinement, responsibility; legal release, as of a prisoner; also, a certificate of release; as, a *discharge* from the army; **5,** dismissal; **6,** performance, as of a duty.

lis-ci-ple (di-sī′pl), *n.* a pupil or follower who accepts the teachings of a leader or master and who helps to spread them; esp. one of the followers of Jesus.

lis-ci-pli-nar-i-an (dis′i-pli-nâr′i-an), *n.* one who enforces strict rules and order.

lis-ci-pli-nar-y (dis′i-pli-nẽr-i), *adj.* pertaining to strict training; corrective.

lis-ci-pline (dis′i-plin), *n.* **1,** strict training of mind or character; **2,** obedience to rules and commands, as in a school, army, prison, or the like; as, a good teacher enforces *discipline;* **3,** punishment given by way of training or correction:—*v.t.* [disciplined, disciplin-ing], **1,** to train; drill; **2,** to punish.

lis-claim (dis-klām′), *v.t.* to disown; deny any connection with.—*n.* **dis-claim′er.**

lis-close (dis-klōz′), *v.t.* [disclosed, disclos-ing], **1,** to uncover; bring to light; as, the digging *disclosed* an old treasure; **2,** to make known; as, to *disclose* secrets.—*n.* **dis-clo′sure** (dis-klō′zhoor; dis-klō′zhẽr).

is-col-our (dis-kul′ẽr), *v.t.* to spoil or change the colour of; stain:—*v.i.* to change colour or fade.—*n.* **dis-col′our-a′tion.**

is-com-fit (dis-kum′fit), *v.t.* to defeat; to upset or throw into confusion; hence, to disconcert; embarrass.—*n.* **dis-com′fi-ture.**

is-com-fort (dis-kum′fẽrt), *n.* uneasiness; distress:—*v.t.* to make uneasy.

is-com-pose (dis′kom-pōz′), *v.t.* [discomposed, discompos-ing], to disturb the peace or calm of; disarrange.—*n.* **dis′-com-po′sure.**

is-con-cert (dis′kon-sûrt′), *v.t.* to disturb the calm or self-possession of; to disorder; as, sickness *disconcerted* his plans.

is-con-nect (dis′ko-nekt′), *v.t.* to

disunite; unfasten.—*n.* **dis′con-nec′-tion.**

dis-con-so-late (dis-kon′sō-lit), *adj.* without hope; forlorn; sad or unhappy.

dis-con-tent (dis′kon-tent′), *n.* dissatisfaction; restlessness:—*adj.* not satisfied:—*v.t.* to dissatisfy.—*adv.* **dis′-con-tent′ed.**

dis-con-tin-ue (dis′kon-tin′ū), *v.t.* [discontinued, discontinu-ing], to stop; cease doing; put an end to:—*v.i.* to cease; come to an end.—*n.* **dis′con-tin′u-ance.**

dis-cord (dis′kôrd), *n.* **1,** difference or lack of agreement; **2,** strife or conflict; **3,** a harsh noise; **4,** in music, lack of harmony.—*n.* **dis-cord′ance.**—*adj.* **dis-cord′ant.**

dis-count (dis-kount′; dis′kount), *v.t.* **1,** to deduct from an account, debt, or the like, for early payment; **2,** to get or advance money on, as a note not yet due, deducting interest for the period it still has to run; **3,** to make allowance for exaggeration in; as, they *discounted* his story of the accident; **4,** to reduce the importance of by considering beforehand; as, to *discount* the difficulties of the trip by careful planning:—*n.* (dis′-kount), **1,** a sum deducted from an account, bill, or the like, for early payment; as, ten per cent *discount* for cash; **2,** a deduction made for interest from the face value of a bill, note, or the like, when it is converted into cash or sold before it is due; **3,** the rate of interest so deducted.—*adj.* **dis′count-a-ble.**

dis-coun-te-nance (dis-koun′te-nans), *v.t.* to disapprove of.

dis-cour-age (dis-kur′ij), *v.t.* [discouraged, discourag-ing], **1,** to lessen the courage of; dishearten; **1,** to try to prevent or deter; as, laws *discourage* crime.—*n.* **dis-cour′age-ment.**

dis-course (dis′kōrs; dis-kōrs′), *n.* **1,** talk; conversation; **2,** a lecture, treatise, or sermon:—*v.i.* (dis-kōrs′), [discoursed, discours-ing], to talk; converse:—*v.t.* to send forth; utter; as, to *discourse* wisdom.

dis-cour-te-ous (dis-kûr′ti-us), *adj.* impolite; rude.—*n.* **dis-cour′te-sy.**

dis-cov-er (dis-kuv′ẽr), *v.t.* **1,** to find, find out, or learn for the first time; also, to catch sight of; **2,** *Archaic,* to reveal or make known.—*n.* **dis-cov′er-er.**

dis-cov-er-y (dis-kuv′ẽr-i), *n.* [*pl.* discoveries], **1,** a finding for the first time; **2,** the thing found out or discovered.

dis-cred-it (dis-kred′it), *v.t.* **1,** to refuse to believe; **2,** to destroy belief in or the reputation of; as, science *discredits* his theories:—*n.* **1,** loss of reputation; disgrace; **2,** doubt or disbelief; as, to bring old beliefs into *discredit.*

---

all (ôl), ôr; up, mūte, cûr, cōōl, book; oil, out; th, thin; *th*, the.

dis-cred-it-a-ble (dis-kred'it-a-bl), *adj.* disgraceful; unworthy.

dis-creet (dis-krēt'), *adj.* careful in speech and action; as, *discreet* behaviour.—*adv.* **dis-creet'ly.**—*n.* **dis-creet'-ness.**

dis-crep-an-cy (dis-krep'an-si), *n.* [*pl.* discrepancies], a difference; lack of agreement; as, the *discrepancy* between the two accounts.—*adj.* **dis-crep'ant.**

dis-crete (dis-krēt'; dis'krēt), *adj.* separate; detached; not continuous; as, photons of light and quanta of energy come in *discrete* units.

dis-cre-tion (dis-kresh'un), *n.* **1,** prudence; good judgment; **2,** freedom of choice or action; as, use your own *discretion.*

dis-crim-i-nate (dis-krim'i-nāt'), *v.t.* [discriminat-ed, discriminat-ing], to see or mark the difference between; distinguish; as, to *discriminate* good books from bad:—*v.i.* to make a distinction; as, to *discriminate* between good and evil.—*adv.* **dis-crim'i-nate-ly.**—*adj.* **dis-crim'i-na'tive.**

dis-crim-i-na-tion (dis-krim'i-nā'-shun), *n.* **1,** the act of distinguishing; **2,** the ability to make fine distinctions; discernment; **3,** a difference, often unfair, in the treatment of persons or things.

dis-cur-sive (dis-kûr'siv), *adj.* rambling from one topic to another; digressing; as, his *discursive* remarks bored us.

dis-cus (dis'kus), *n.* [*pl.* discuses (dis'kus-ez) or disci (dis'kī)], a heavy disk of metal or stone to be thrown in athletic contests.

dis-cuss (dis-kus'), *v.t.* to debate fully; talk over; consider.

dis-cus-sion (dis-kush'un), *n.* full and open consideration or argument; as, the assembly agreed after a two-hour *discussion;* also, talk; as, his absence caused much *discussion.*

dis-dain (dis-dān'), *v.t.* to scorn; look upon with contempt; as, he *disdained* our attempts to help:—*n.* contempt; scorn.—*adj.* **dis-dain'ful.**—*adv.* **dis-dain'ful-ly.**

dis-ease (di-zēz'), *n.* disorder of mind or body marked by definite symptoms; illness; sickness; any particular instance or kind of such disorder; as, heart-*disease.*

dis-em-bark (dis'em-bärk'), *v.t.* and *v.i.* to remove from, or go ashore from, a vessel; land; as, to *disembark* troops; to *disembark* at Quebec.—*n.* **dis-em'bar-ka'tion.**

dis-em-bod-ied (dis'im-bod'id), *adj.* free from a body, as a spirit, ghost, etc.

dis-en-chant (dis'en-chånt'), *v.t.* to set free from a charm, spell, or illusion. —*n.* **dis'en-chant'ment.**

dis-en-gage (dis'en-gāj'), *v.t.* [disengaged, disengag-ing], **1,** to set free; release; as, to *disengage* one from a promise; **2,** to extricate; free (oneself); as, he *disengaged* himself from his bonds: —**disengaged,** *adj.* at liberty; not in use.—*n.* **dis'en-gage'ment.**

dis-en-tan-gle (dis'en-tang'gl), *v.t.* [disentan-gled, disentan-gling], **1,** to free from confusion; as, to *disentangle* truth from error; **2,** to unravel; as, to *disentangle* a skein of yarn.—*n.* **dis'en-tan'gle-ment.**

dis-fa-vour (dis-fā'vėr), *n.* **1,** disapproval; as, to look with *disfavour* on a scheme; **2,** the condition of being regarded with disapproval or dislike; as, he was in *disfavour.*

dis-fig-ure (dis-fig'ūr), *v.t.* [disfigured, disfigur-ing], to mar or injure in shape, form, or beauty.—*n.* **dis-fig'ure-ment.** —*n.* **dis-fig'u-ra'tion.**

dis-fran-chise (dis-fran'chīz), *v.t.* to deprive of one's citizenship rights, voting, holding office, etc. Also, **dis'en-fran'chise.**

dis-gorge (dis-gôrj'), *v.t.* [disgorged, disgorg-ing], to discharge from, or as from, the throat with violence; to vomit; hence, also, to give up unwillingly; as, to *disgorge* plunder:—*v.i.* **1,** to discharge contents; **2,** to surrender unlawful gains.

dis-grace (dis-grās'), *n.* **1,** shame; dishonour; **2,** the cause of shame; as, the roads are a *disgrace* to the town:— *v.t.* [disgraced, disgrac-ing], to bring shame, reproach, or dishonour upon.— *adj.* **dis-grace'ful.**

dis-grun-tle (dis-grun'tl), *v.t.* to make discontented or displeased; as, he was *disgruntled* with the voters' decision.

dis-guise (dis-gīz'), *v.t.* [disguised, disguis-ing], **1,** to change in appearance so as to conceal the identity of (a person); as, they *disguised* him as a woman; **2,** to hide, conceal, or mask; as, to *disguise* one's intentions:—*n.* **1,** anything worn to conceal one's identity; **2,** anything, as a manner of speaking, assumed to deceive.

dis-gust (dis-gust'), *n.* strong distaste; loathing:—*v.t.* to offend by loathsome appearance, repulsive behaviour, or the like.

dish (dish), *n.* **1,** a vessel used for serving food; also, anything so shaped; **2,** any special food; as, ice-cream is a popular *dish:*—*v.t.* to put into a dish for serving.—*n.* **dish'cloth';** **dish'rag';** **dish'wat'er.**

dis-heart-en (dis-här'tn), *v.t.* to discourage; as, *disheartened* by failure.

di-shev-el (di-shev'el), *v.t.* [dishevelled, dishevel-ling], to throw into disorder; to tousle; as, the children *dishevelled* his hair.—*adj.* **di-shev'elled.**

dis-hon-est (dis-on'est), *adj.* 1, lacking in uprightness or fairness; as, lying is *dishonest;* 2, inclined to cheat or deceive; as, a *dishonest* person; 3, designed for unfair use; false; as, *dishonest* scales.—*n.* **dis-hon'es-ty.**

dis-hon-our (dis-on'ėr), *v.t.* 1, to disgrace; bring shame upon; 2, to refuse to pay (a bill or note):—*n.* disgrace; shame.

dis-hon-our-a-ble (dis-on'ėr-a-bl), *adj.* 1, shameful; 2, lacking in uprightness.

dis-il-lu-sion (dis'i-lū'zhun), *v.t.* to set free from a mistaken belief in the goodness or value of some person or thing.

dis-in-clined (dis'in-klīnd'), *adj.* unwilling.—*n.* **dis-in'cli-na'tion.**

dis-in-fect (dis'in-fekt'), *v.t.* to cleanse from infection; purify of disease germs; as, to *disinfect* a room.—*n.* **dis'in-fec'tion.**

dis-in-fect-ant (dis'in-fek'tant), *n.* a substance capable of destroying disease germs.

dis-in-gen-u-ous (dis'in-jen'ū-us), *adj.* not frank or candid; insincere; artfully simple; as, his excuse was *disingenuous.*

dis-in-her-it (dis'in-her'it), *v.t.* to cut off (a natural heir) from property.

dis-in-te-grate (dis-in'ti-grāt), *v.t.* [disintegrat-ed, disintegrat-ing], 1, to break into pieces; as, frost *disintegrates* rock; 2, to destroy the unity of; as, to *disintegrate* society:—*v.i.* to crumble to pieces; as, limestone *disintegrates* rapidly.—*n.* **dis-in'te-gra'tion.**

dis-in-ter-est-ed (dis-in'ter-es-tid; dis-in'tris-tid), *adj.* 1, not influenced by a personal or selfish motive; 2, not concerned; one's interests not affected.—*adv.* **dis-in'ter-est-ed-ly.**

dis-joint (dis-joint'), *v.t.* 1, to part at the joints; as, to *disjoint* a turkey; 2, to put out of joint; as, to *disjoint* one's shoulder:—**disjointed,** unconnected; incoherent; as, a *disjointed* speech.

disk or **disc** (disk), *n.* a flat, circular plate, or anything like it:—**disk harrow,** a harrow with sharp revolving disks for breaking up topsoil before sowing:—**disk jockey,** a radio announcer who provides recorded music punctuated with quips, commercials, etc.

dis-like (dis-līk'), *n.* a feeling of

distaste; aversion:—*v.t.* [disliked, dislik-ing], to regard with distaste; as, to *dislike* olives.

dis-lo-cate (dis'lō-kāt'), *v.t.* [dislocated, dislocat-ing], to displace; put out of place; esp. to put out of joint.—*n.* **dis'lo-ca'tion.**

dis-lodge (dis-loj'), *v.t.* [dislodged, dislodg-ing], to remove from a resting-place; drive from a hiding-place.

dis-loy-al (dis-loi'al), *adj.* false to duty, government, or friends; faithless.—*n.* **dis-loy'al-ty.**—*adv.* **dis-loy'al-ly.**

dis-mal (diz'mal), *adj.* 1, gloomy; depressing; as, *dismal* weather; 2, depressed; melancholy, as a mood.—*adv.* **dis'mal-ly.**

dis-man-tle (dis-man'tl), *v.t.* [dismantled, disman-tling], 1, to strip or deprive of furniture, equipment, or the like; 2, to take apart; as, to *dismantle* an engine.

dis-may (dis-mā'), *v.t.* 1, to terrify; 2, to dispirit; discourage:—*n.* 1, terrified amazement, as at a great danger or disaster; 2, discouragement, as at a hopeless task.

dis-mem-ber (dis-mem'bėr), *v.t.* to tear limb from limb; as, the ghouls *dismembered* the corpse.

dis-miss (dis-mis'), *v.t.* 1, to send away or permit to depart, as a class; 2, to discharge from office or employment, as a clerk; 3, to refuse to consider further; as, to *dismiss* a matter from one's mind.—*n.* **dis-miss'al.**

dis-mount (dis-mount'), *v.i.* to get down, as from a horse:—*v.t.* 1, to remove (a rider) by force from a horse; 2, to remove from a carriage, as a cannon; 3, to remove from a setting, as a jewel.

dis-o-be-di-ence (dis'o-bē'di-ens), *n.* neglect or refusal to obey a rule or command.

dis-o-be-di-ent (dis'o-bē'di-ent), *adj.* refusing or neglecting to obey; as, a *disobedient* boy.

dis-o-bey (dis'ō-bā'), *v.t.* and *v.i.* to refuse or fail to obey; as, to *disobey* parents.

dis-o-blige (dis'ō-blīj'), *v.t.* [disobliged, disoblig-ing], to refuse or neglect to accommodate; refuse a favour to.

dis-or-der (dis-ôr'dėr), *n.* 1, lack of system; confusion; a commotion; esp. a riot; 3, mental or physical disease:—*v.t.* 1, to throw into confusion; disarrange; 2, to derange in health of mind or body.—*adj.* **dis-or'dered.**—*adj.* **dis-or'der-ly.**

dis-or-gan-ize (dis-ôr'gan-īz), *v.t.* [disorganized, disorganiz-ing], to throw into confusion; as, their arrival *disorganized* the meeting.

dis-own (dis-ōn′), *v.t.* **1**, to reject; refuse to claim as one's own; as, to *disown* one's son; **2**, to renounce allegiance to; as, to *disown* one's flag.

dis-par-age (dis-par′ij), *v.t.* [disparaged, disparag-ing], to speak slightingly of; belittle; as, to *disparage* a rival.— *adv.* **dis-par′ag-ing-ly.**—*n.* **dis-par′age-ment.**

dis-par-i-ty (dis-par′i-ti), *n.* inequality; difference; as, the *disparity* in the ages of two boys.—*adj.* **dis′pa-rate** (-rit).

dis-pas-sion-ate (dis-pash′un-it), *adj.* free from passion; impartial; as, a *dispassionate* speech.—*adv.* **dis-pas′sion-ate-ly.**

dis-patch (dis-pach′), *v.t.* **1**, to send off promptly; as, to *dispatch* a messenger; **2**, to finish quickly; as, to *dispatch* a lunch; **3**, to put to death; kill:—*n.* **1**, promptness; as, he did the lesson with *dispatch;* **2**, a message; esp. an official communication; **3**, an item of news; as, a *dispatch* from Paris; **4**, a putting to death. Also spelled **des-patch′.**—*n.* **dis-patch′er.**

dis-pel (dis-pel′), *v.t.* [dispelled, dispelling], to drive apart; scatter; disperse; as, the wind *dispelled* the fog.

dis-pen-sa-ry (dis-pen′sa-ri), *n.* [*pl.* dispensaries], a place where medical advice and medicines are given free or very cheap.

dis-pen-sa-tion (dis′pen-sā′shun), *n.* **1**, distribution; **2**, divine management of the world; also, an instance of this; as, the flood was a *dispensation* of Providence; **3**, permission, esp. by a church official, to do something usually forbidden, or to omit something usually required.

dis-pense (dis-pens′), *v.t.* [dispensed, dispens-ing], **1**, to deal out in portions; **2**, to carry out; apply; as, to *dispense* justice:—**dispense with,** to do without.

dis-perse (dis-pûrs′), *v.t.* [dispersed, dispers-ing], **1**, to scatter; as, to *disperse* a crowd; **2**, to spread; as, to *disperse* funds; also, to cause to vanish; as, the sun *dispersed* the mist:—*v.i.* to break up and depart; as, the meeting *dispersed.*—*n.* **dis-pers′al.**—*n.* **dis-per′-sion.**

dis-pir-it-ed (dis-pir′i-tid), *adj.* disheartened; discouraged; depressed.

dis-place (dis-plās′), *v.t.* [displaced, displac-ing], **1**, to put out of place; **2**, to remove and replace with something else; as, to *displace* a cart with a truck; **3**, to take the place of; as, the automobile *displaced* the buggy; **4**, to remove from office.—*n.* **dis-place′ment.**

dis-play (dis-plā′), *v.t.* **1**, to spread out; unfold; as, the peacock *displayed* its feathers; **2**, to exhibit; show off:—*n.* **1**, an exhibit; as, a *display* of china; **2**, a parade or show; as, a fashion *display.*

dis-please (dis-plēz′), *v.t.* [displeased, displeas-ing], to offend; annoy; make angry; as, the results of the examination *displease* me.—*n.* **dis-pleas′ure** (dis-plezh′yoor; zhẽr).

dis-port (dis-pōrt′), *v.t.* to amuse (oneself); as, the picknickers *disported* themselves on the beach.

dis-pos-al (dis-pōz′al), *n.* **1**, arrangement; as, the *disposal* of goods in a store; **2**, a getting rid; as, the *disposal* of rubbish; **3**, control; command; as, to place money or other resources at one's *disposal.*

dis-pose (dis-pōz′), *v.t.* [disposed, dispos-ing], **1**, to arrange; distribute; **2**, to make willing; incline; as, weariness *disposed* him to yield.

dis-po-si-tion (dis′pō-zish′un), *n.* **1**, the act of placing or arranging; **2**, order; arrangement; as, the *disposition* of furniture in a room; **3**, the power of managing or distributing; as, to have the *disposition* of property; **4**, inclination; temper or habit of mind; as, a *disposition* to jealousy.

dis-pos-sess (dis′po-zes′), *v.t.* to oust; put out of possession; as, to *dispossess* a man of his home.—*n.* **dis′pos-ses′sion.**

dis-praise (dis-prāz′), *n.* and *v.* censure.

dis-pro-por-tion (dis′prō-pōr′shun), *n.* want of balance or symmetry; lack of proper relation in form, size, or the like.—*adj.* **dis′pro-por′tion-ate.**

dis-prove (dis-prōōv′), *v.t.* [disproved, disprov-ing], to show to be untrue or unreasonable; as, to *disprove* a statement.

dis-pute (dis-pūt′), *v.i.* [disput-ed, disput-ing], to debate; argue; quarrel —*v.t.* **1**, to contend for, by words or actions; as, the soldiers *disputed* every inch of the ground; **2**, to question the justice or fairness of; as, to *dispute* an election:—*n.* an argument; also, a quarrel.—*n.* **dis′pu-ta′tion.**—*adj.* and *n.* **dis′pu-tant** (dis′pū-tant).

dis-pu-ta-ble (dis′pū-ta-bl; dis-pūt′a-bl), *adj.* debatable; as, a *disputable* proposition or argument.

dis-qual-i-fy (dis-kwol′i-fī′; kwôl′-) *v.t.* [disqualified, disqualify-ing], **1**, to make unfit; disable; **2**, to deprive of a privilege; as, to *disqualify* a player.— *n.* **dis-qual′i-fi-ca′tion.**

dis-qui-et (dis-kwī′et), *v.t.* to make uneasy; worry; as, his look *disquieted* her:—*n.* uneasiness; anxiety.—*n.* **dis-qui′e-tude.**

dis-qui-si-tion (dis′kwi-zish′un), *n.* a formal discussion; dissertation.

dis-re-gard (dis′ri-gärd′), *v.t.* to fail to notice or give heed to; neglect; as, he *disregarded* instructions:—*n.* lack of attention.

dis-re-pair (dis′ri-pâr′), *n.* the state of needing repair, as of a building.

dis-rep-u-ta-ble (dis-rep′ū-ta-bl), *adj.* of bad reputation; not respectable.

dis-re-pute (dis′ri-pūt′), *n.* lack or loss of reputation; dishonour; ill repute.

dis-re-spect (dis′ri-spekt′), *n.* lack of courtesy or respect, esp. toward elders or superiors.—*adj.* **dis′re-spect′ful.**

dis-robe (dis-rōb′), *v.i.* and *v.t.* [disrobed, disrob-ing], to undress.

dis-rupt (dis-rupt′), *v.t.* to break apart; break up; as, to *disrupt* a government.—*n.* **dis-rup′tion.**

dis-sat-is-fac-tion (dis-sat′is-fak′-shun), *n.* discontent; lack of satisfaction.

dis-sat-is-fy (dis-sat′is-fī′), *v.t.* [dissatisfied, dissatisfy-ing], to cause discontent to, as by lack of something; to fail to satisfy; as, the house *dissatisfied* her.

dis-sect (di-sekt′), *v.t.* 1, to cut in pieces, in order to examine; as, to *dissect* a plant; 2, to examine; analyse; as, to *dissect* a person's motives.—*n.* **dis-sec′tion.**

dis-sem-ble (di-sem′bl), *v.t.* [dissembled, dissem-bling], to hide under a false appearance; as, to *dissemble* one's feelings:—*v.i.* to conceal the truth by some pretence; as, to *dissemble* in making excuses.

dis-sem-i-nate (di-sem′i-nāt′), *v.t.* [disseminat-ed, disseminat-ing], to scatter, as seed; diffuse; spread abroad, as news.—*n.* **dis-sem′i-na′tion.**

dis-sen-sion (di-sen′shun), *n.* angry disagreement; strife.

dis-sent (di-sent′), *v.i.* to disagree in opinion; as, to *dissent* from a judgment:—*n.* a disagreement in opinion.

dis-sent-er (di-sen′tėr), *n.* a person who differs from the prevailing opinion: —**Dissenter,** in Great Britain, a member of a Protestant sect which has broken away from the established church.

dis-ser-ta-tion (dis′ėr-tā′shun), *n.* a lengthy and formal discourse or treatise.

dis-sev-er (di-sev′ėr), *v.t.* to cut off; separate; disjoin.

dis-si-dent (dis′i-dent), *adj.* and *n.* disagreeing in opinion; as, the *dis-*

sident members formed a new club.—*n.* **dis′si-dence.**

dis-sim-i-lar (di-sim′i-lėr; dis-sim′i-lėr), *adj.* unlike; as, *dissimilar* tastes.— *n.* **dis-sim′i-lar′i-ty.**

dis-sim-u-late (di-sim′ū-lāt′), *v.i.* and *v.t.* [dissimulat-ed, dissimulat-ing], to dissemble; feign; pretend.—*n.* **dis-sim′u-la′tion.**

dis-si-pate (dis′i-pāt′), *v.t.* [dissipat-ed, dissipat-ing], 1, to scatter in different directions; as, the wind *dissipated* the smoke; 2, to waste foolishly; as, he *dissipated* his fortune: —*v.i.* 1, to disperse; vanish; 2, to engage in riotous amusement; esp. to drink to excess.—*n.* **dis′si-pa′tion.**

dis-si-pat-ed (dis′i-pāt′ed), *adj.* 1, scattered; dispersed; wasted; 2, intemperate.

dis-so-ci-ate (di-sō′shi-āt′), *v.t.* to sever relations; disunite; as, religion and politics became *dissociated.*

dis-so-lu-ble (dis′o-lū-bl; di-sol′ū-bl), *adj.* able to be dissolved (as, a substance or an assembly).

dis-so-lute (dis′ō-lūt′), *adj.* morally loose; given to vice or dissipation.

dis-so-lu-tion (dis′o-lū′shun), *n.* 1, the act of separating or breaking up; as, the *dissolution* of a partnership; 2, decay; ruin; death.

dis-solve (di-zolv′), *v.t.* [dissolved, dissolv-ing], 1, to cause to be absorbed by a liquid; as, to *dissolve* salt in water; 2, to break up; as, to *dissolve* an assembly; 3, to put an end to; as, to *dissolve* a partnership:—*v.i.* to be absorbed in a liquid.

dis-so-nant (dis′o-nant), *adj.* disagreeing (in sound); discordant; as, *dissonant* ditties.—*n.* **dis′so-nance.**

dis-suade (di-swād′), *v.t.* [dissuad-ed, dissuad-ing], to advise or counsel against; divert by persuasion from a purpose or action; as, they *dissuaded* him from going.—*n.* **dis-sua′sion.**

dis-syl-la-ble (dis-sil′a-bl), *n.* a two-syllable word, as *la′ter.*

dis-taff (dis′tåf), *n.* a stick on which the wool or flax used for spinning is wound:—**distaff side,** the female side (of a family).

dis-tance (dis′tans), *n.* 1, the extent of space between two objects or points; 2, a far-off place; as, hills are blue in the *distance;* 3, lack of familiarity; reserve; coldness; as, to keep one's *distance:*— *v.t.* [distanced, distanc-ing], to leave behind in a race; outstrip; as, to *distance* one's rivals.

dis-tant (dis′tant), *adj.* 1, far off in time, space, or relationship; as, a *distant* event; a *distant* cousin; **2,** reserved; not familiar; cold; as, he is *distant* with his employees.—*adv.* **dis′tant-ly.**

dis-taste (dis-tāst′), *n.* dislike; aversion; as, a *distaste* for buttermilk. —*adj.* **dis-taste′ful.**

dis-tem-per (dis-tem′pẽr), *n.* illness; esp. a disease of animals.

dis-tend (dis-tend′), *v.t.* to stretch out or expand; as, to *distend* the stomach: —*v.i.* to swell; enlarge, as a balloon.— *n.* **dis-ten′tion; dis-ten′sion.**

dis-til or **dis-till** (dis-til′), *v.i.* [distilled, distil-ling], to fall in drops; trickle forth:—*v.t.* **1,** to let fall in drops; **2,** to separate (a liquid) from a mixture by heating so as to form a vapour, which is carried off and condensed by cooling; **3,** to subject (a mixture) to this process. —*n.* **dis′til-la′tion.**—*n.* **dis-til′ler.**—*n.* **dis′till-ate** (-lit; -lāt′).

dis-til-ler-y (dis-til′ẽr-i), *n.* [*pl.* distilleries], a place where liquids, esp. alcoholic liquors, are distilled.

dis-tinct (dis-tingkt′), *adj.* **1,** separate; different; **2,** clear to the senses; as, a *distinct* sound or view; **3,** carefully thought out; lucid; as, a *distinct* statement.—*n.* **dis-tinct′ness.**—*adv.* **dis-tinct′ly.**

dis-tinc-tion (dis-tingk′shun), *n.* **1,** the act of noting clearly or marking off from others; **2,** a characteristic difference; as, the *distinction* between good and evil; **3,** special honour; eminence; superiority; as, to serve with *distinction.*

dis-tinc-tive (dis-tingk′tiv), *adj.* marking a difference; characteristic; as, a *distinctive* feature.—*adv.* **dis-tinc′tive-ly.**

dis-tin-guish (dis-ting′gwish), *v.t.* **1,** to mark off; as, speech *distinguishes* man from apes; **2,** to recognize by special features; as, to *distingusih* different makes of cars; **3,** to see clearly; **4,** to honour by a mark of preference:—*v.i.* to make a distinction; as, to *distinguish* between brown and tan.—*adj.* **dis-tin′guish-a-ble.**

dis-tin-guished (dis-ting′gwisht), *adj.* superior in ability, achievement, etc.

dis-tort (dis-tôrt′), *v.t.* **1,** to change from its natural shape; as, to *distort* the features; **2,** to change the meaning of; as, he *distorted* what I said.—*n.* **dis-tor′tion.**

dis-tract (dis-trakt′), *v.t.* **1,** to divert; bewilder; perplex; as, the many changes *distracted* him; **2,** to drive mad; derange.—*adj.* **dis-tract′ed.**—*adv.* **dis-tract′ed-ly.**

dis-trac-tion (dis-trak′shun), *n.* **1,** a

drawing away of the attention from an object; **2,** anything which diverts attention; **3,** bewilderment; mental confusion or distress; **4,** madness or frenzy.

dis-traught (dis-trôt′), *adj.* distracted; crazed (as with grief): the bereaved man was *distraught.*

dis-tress (dis-tres′), *v.t.* to inflict pain or grief upon; grieve:—*n.* **1,** physical or mental anguish; **2,** misfortune; danger; as, a ship in *distress.*

dis-trib-ute (dis-trib′ūt), *v.t.* [distribut-ed, distribut-ing], **1,** to deal or give out; allot; as, to *distribute* books; **2,** spread; scatter; as, to *distribute* fertilizer; **3,** to sort; classify.—*n.* **dis′tri-bu′tion.**—*n.* **dis-trib′u-tor.**

dis-trib-u-tive (dis-trib′ū-tiv), *adj.* apportioning.—*n.* in *grammar,* a word that makes the members of a group individual (hence *singular* when used in the subject of a sentence), as, *any, each, either, neither, every, everybody,* etc. *everyone is* to say *his* say.

dis-trict (dis′trikt), *n.* **1,** a section marked off within definite limits for administration; as, a school *district;* **2,** an indefinite region.

dis-trust (dis-trust′), *n.* want of confidence or reliance; suspicion:—*v.t.* to have no faith in; to doubt; suspect —*adj.* **dis-trust′ful.**

dis-turb (dis-tûrb′), *v.t.* **1,** to trouble; vex; **2,** to throw into confusion; agitate; **3,** to interfere with.— **dis-turb′ance.**

dis-u-nite (dis′ū-nīt′), *v.i.* and *v.t.* [disunit-ed, disunit-ing], to divide; separate.—*n.* **dis-un′ion.**

dis-use (dis-ūs′), *n.* the condition of not being in use; neglect.

ditch (dich), *n.* a trench cut in the earth:—*v.t.* **1,** to surround with ditch; **2,** to send into a ditch; as, to *ditch* a car.

dith-er (di*th*′ẽr), *n. Colloq.* trembling in a state of nervous excitement (to be *in a dither*).

dit-to (dit′ō), *n.* [*pl.* dittos], the same thing as has been said before:—*adv.* as before; likewise:—**ditto marks,** marks [″] used to avoid repetition.

dit-ty (dit′i), *n.* [*pl.* ditties], a little song; esp. one sung by country people

di-ur-nal (dī-ûr′nal), *adj.* **1,** relating to the day or lasting a day; as the *diurnal* revolution of the earth; occurring every day; daily; **3,** active during the daytime; as, *diurnal* insects.—*adv.* **di-ur′nal-ly.**

di-van (di-van′; dī′van), *n.* a long cushioned couch without back or ends; a sofa.

dive (dīv), *v.i.* [*p.t.* dived (dīvd) or, *Colloq.* dove (dōv), *p.p.* dived, *p.pr.* diving], **1,** to plunge head foremost, as into water; **2,** to go quickly and completely into a place or activity; as, to *dive* into a tunnel; he *dived* into his work:—*n.* **1,** a plunge head foremost, as into water; **2,** a low resort.

div-er (dīv′ẽr), *n.* **1,** a person who plunges into water; **2,** a person who makes a business of going under water, as for pearls; **3,** any bird of diving habit, as a loon.

di-verge (di-vûrj′; dī-), *v.i.* [diverged, diverg-ing], **1,** to spread out from a point; **2,** to differ, as from a standard. —*n.* **di-ver′gence.**—*adj.* **di-ver′gent.**

di-vers (dī′vẽrz), *adj.* various; several; as, *divers* points of view.

di-verse (di-vûrs′ dī′vûrs; dī-vûrs′), *adj.* different; unlike; dissimilar; varied.

di-ver-si-fy (di-vûr′si-fī; dī-vûr′si-fī), *v.t.* [diversified, diversify-ing], to make various; give variety to; as, hills *diversify* the view.—*n.* **di-ver′si-fi-ca′tion.**

d-iver-sion (di-vûr′shun; di-vûr′zhun; dī-vûr′shun; dī-vûr′zhun), *n.* **1,** a turning aside from a set course; as, the *diversion* of a river; **2,** a recreation.

di-ver-si-ty (di-vûr′si-ti; dī-vûr′si-ti), *n.* [*pl.* diversities], difference; variety; as, *diversity* of colour.

di-vert (di-vûrt′; dī-vûrt′), *v.t.* **1,** to turn from or to any direction or course; draw away; **2,** to entertain; amuse.

di-vest (di-vest′; dī-vest′), *v.t.* **1,** to strip; unclothe; **2,** to deprive, as of rights or office; despoil.

di-vide (di-vīd′), *v.t.* [divid-ed, dividing], **1,** to cut into two or more parts; **2,** to separate (a thing) from another or others; **3,** to cause to disagree; as, to *divide* friends; **4,** to share, as money; **5,** in *arithmetic*, to perform the operation of division on or with; as, to *divide* 30 by 6; to *divide* 6 into 30:—*v.i.* **1,** to be separated into parts; **2,** to perform the operation of division with two numbers: —*n.* a watershed.

div-i-dend (div′i-dend), *n.* **1,** a share of the profits of a company or business; **2,** in *arithmetic*, a number or quantity to be divided by another number or quantity.

di-vid-ers (di-vīd′ẽrz), *n.pl.* an instrument used in mechanical drawing, for dividing lines, checking distances, or the like.

div-i-na-tion (div′i-nā′shun), *n.* **1,** the act of foreseeing or foretelling; **2,** a forecast; guess.

¹di-vine (di-vīn′), *adj.* [diviner, divinest], **1,** relating to God; from God; **2,** godlike; holy; **3,** superhumanly excellent:—*n.* a person who knows theology; a priest; clergyman.—*adv.* **di-vine′ly.**

²di-vine (di-vīn′), *v.t.* [divined, divining], **1,** to foresee or foretell; **2,** to guess; perceive by reason or insight; as, he *divined* my purpose.—*n.* **di-vin′er.**

di-vin-i-ty (di-vin′i-ti), *n.* [*pl.* divinities], **1,** the state or quality of being godlike; Godhead; **2, the Divinity,** God; **3,** a god or deity; **4,** the study of theology.

di-vis-i-ble (di-viz′i-bl), *adj.* **1,** capable of being separated into parts; **2,** in *mathematics,* capable of division by a specified number without a remainder; as, 6 is *divisible* by 2.—*n.* **di-vis′i-bil′i-ty.**

di-vi-sion (di-vizh′un), *n.* **1,** a separation into parts; also, a portion or part; **2,** that which separates, as a partition; a dividing line; **3,** discord; difference in opinion; **4,** a department; as, the selling *division* of a firm; **5,** in the army, a unit complete in itself, comprising several thousand men under a major-general; **6,** in the navy, a section or unit of a fleet; **7,** the process of finding how many times one quantity contains, or is contained in, another.

di-vi-sor (di-vī′zẽr), *n.* in *arithmetic,* the number or quantity by which the dividend is to be divided.

di-vorce (di-vōrs′), *n.* **1,** a legal dissolving of a marriage; **2,** disunion of things formerly united:—*v.t.* [divorced, divorc-ing], **1,** to release from the marriage contract; **2,** to separate; as, to *divorce* church and state.

di-vor-cée (di-vōr′sē′; sā′), *n.* a divorced person (esp. a woman).—*n. masc.* **di-vor′cé′.** Customary usage, **di-vor′cee** (for both sexes).

div-ot (div′ot), *n.* in *golf,* a piece of turf cut out by a club in making a stroke.

di-vulge (di-vulj′), *v.t.* [divulged, divulg-ing], to make known, as a secret; tell.

diz-zy (diz′i), *adj.* [diz-zi-er, diz-zi-est], giddy; also, causing giddiness; as, a *dizzy* height.—*n.* **diz′zi-ness.**

¹do (dōō), *v.t.* [*p.t.* did (did), *p.p.* done (dun), *p.pr.* do-ing], **1,** to perform; execute; as, to do one's work; **2,** to render; pay; give; as, to *do* a favour; **3,** to produce, esp. by art; as, to *do* a painting; **4,** to arrange; as, to *do* one's hair; put in order; as, to *do* a room; also, to prepare, as lessons; **5,** to achieve (a given speed); as, the car *did* fifty miles an hour; **6,** *Colloq.* to cheat; as, he *did* me out of a job; **7,** *Colloq.* to visit as a tourist; as, to *do* England:— *v.i.* **1,** to try one's best to succeed; as, to *do* or die; **2,** to fare (well or ill); as, to *do* well in business; **3,** *Colloq.* to serve the purpose; as, this hat will *do:* —*auxiliary v.* used: **1,** in sentences so phrased as to be emphatic; as, *do* tell me; never *did* I see so large an apple; **2,** in interrogative and negative sentences; as, when *do* you get back? the parade *did* not come this way:— *substitute v.* used to replace a verb or verb construction in order to avoid repetition; as, he walks as his father *does.*—*adj.* **do-a-ble** (dōō′a-bl).—*n.* **do′er** (dōō′ėr).

²do (dō), *n.* in music, the first of the syllables commonly used in singing the scale.

dob-bin (dob′in), *n.* a family or farm horse; a gentle nag.

doc-ile (dō′sīl; dos′il), *adj.* easy to teach; easily managed; as, a *docile* child.—*n.* **do-cil′i-ty** (dō-sil′i-ti).

¹dock (dok), *n.* a long-rooted, coarse weed with red-veined leaves, and seeds in reddish husks.

²dock (dok), *n.* in a courtroom, the place reserved for the prisoner.

³dock (dok), *n.* **1,** an artificial basin or waterway for ships; **2,** a waterway between two piers; also, *Colloq.* a wharf:—*v.t.* to bring to a pier and moor, as a ship:—*v.i.* to arrive at a pier.

⁴dock (dok), *n.* the stump of an animal's tail:—*v.t.* **1,** to cut off; **2,** to make a deduction from (wages).

dock-age (dok′ij), *n.* **1,** a reduction or cutting down; **2,** a charge for the use of a dock or pier.

dock-et (dok′it), *n.* in *law*, a list of cases for trial.

dock-yard (dok′yärd′), *n.* a place where ships are built and repaired, and where ship's supplies are kept.

doc-tor (dok′tėr), *n.* **1,** a licensed physician or surgeon; **2,** a person who holds the highest degree conferred by a university:—*v.t.* *Colloq.* **1,** to treat medically; as, to *doctor* a cold; **2,** to tamper with.—*n.* **doc′tor-ate.**

doc-trine (dok′trin), *n.* that which is taught; the principles or beliefs of a church, sect, or party.—*adj.* **doc′tri-nal** (dok′tri-nal; dok-tri′nal).

doc-u-ment (dok′ū-ment), *n.* a record; an official paper that gives information or evidence, as a birth certificate.—*n.* and *adj.* **doc′u-men′ta-ry.**—*n.* **doc′u-men-ta′tion.**

dod-der (dod′ėr), *v.i.* to shake; tremble; totter, as from weakness or age.

dod-der-ing (dod′ėr-ing), *adj.* shaky as from old age; senile.

dodge (doj), *v.i.* [dodged, dodg-ing], **1,** to move aside quickly so as to escape something; **2,** to practise tricky devices —*v.t.* to escape from, by dodging; as, to *dodge* a car:—*n.* **1,** an act of evasion; **2,** a clever trick.

dodg-er (doj′ėr), *n.* **1,** one who dodges; **2,** a tricky fellow; **3,** a small handbill.

do-do (dō′dō), *n.* [*pl.* dodoes or dodos], a large bird, with short legs and wings too small for flight, related to the pigeons. It is now extinct.

doe (dō), *n.* the female of the deer; also, the female of the antelope, rabbit, or hare.

do-er (dōō′ėr), *n.* one who does or achieves things; as, he is a *doer,* not a dreamer.

doe-skin (dō′skin′), *n.* **1,** leather made from the skin of a female deer; **2,** woollen cloth made with a soft, smooth finish.

doff (dof), *v.t.* to take off, as one's clothes; raise (one's hat).

dog (dôg), *n.* **1,** a domesticated animal of which there are many breeds, some ancient, found the world over; **2,** a device for bracing, holding, etc.; as, fire-*dog;* also, a catch or ratchet; **3,** *Colloq.* any sort of fellow; as, a gay *dog;* a sly *dog:*—*v.t.* [dogged, dog-ging] to follow; track; trail.

dog-cart (dôg′kärt′), *n.* **1,** a light cart drawn by dogs; **2,** a horse-drawn, two-wheeled carriage with seats back to back.

doge (dōj), *n.* the chief magistrate in the old republics of Venice and Genoa.

dog—ear (dôg′-ēr′), *n.* and *v.* Same as *dog's—ear.*

dog-fish (dôg′fish′), *n.* any of various small, voracious sharks, often found in schools.

dog-ged (dôg′ed), *adj.* stubborn; persistent.

dog-ger-el (dôg′ėr-el), *n.* trivial, comic or inartistic verse.—*adj.* crude, poorly constructed (rhymes).

do-gie (dō′gi), *n.* Same as *dogy.*

dog-ma (dôg′ma), *n.* a principle, belief, or doctrine, accepted as authoritative, esp. one so accepted by the church.

dog-mat-ic (dôg-mat′ik) or **dog-mat-i-cal** (dôg-mat′i-kal), *adj.* **1,** pertaining to established doctrine or belief; **2,** making assertions in a positive manner without proof; arrogant; as, a *dogmatic* old man; **3,** asserted positively without proof; as, *dogmatic* opinions.—*adv.* **dog-mat′i-cal-ly.**

dog's—ear (dôgz′–ēr′) or **dog—ear** (dôg′–ēr′), *n.* the turned-down corner of a page in a book:—*v.t.* to disfigure (a book) in this way.—*adj.* **dog's′—eared′** or **dog′—eared′.**

dog's—leg (dôgz′–leg′), *n.* in *golf*, a bend in a fairway between tee and green.

dog's-tooth vi-o-let (dogz′tooth′), a plant of the lily family which has two mottled leaves and a single nodding yellow or white flower; also, the flower. Also written **dog′tooth′ vi′o-let.**

dog-trot (dôg′trot′) *n.* a slow, easy run.

dog-wood (dôg′wood′), *n.* any of a group of trees or shrubs with hard, close-grained wood, bearing in spring clusters of flowers, often surrounded by four pink or white petal-like parts.

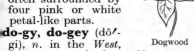

Dogwood

do-gy, do-gey (dō′-gi), *n.* in the *West*, a stray or motherless calf.

doi-ly (doi′li), *n.* [*pl.* doilies], a small mat of lace, linen, or the like.

dol-drums (dol′drumz), *n.pl.* 1, the state of being becalmed or at a standstill; as, a ship in the *doldrums;* 2, a windless region near the equator where ships are often becalmed; 3, hence, depression of mind.

do—it—your-self (doo′–it–ūr-self′), *n.* and *adj.* making, repairing, etc., done by oneself instead of hiring another.

dole (dōl), *n.* the dealing out of money, clothing, food, or the like, for charity; also, the gifts themselves:—*v.t.* doled, dol-ing], 1, to give as alms; 2, hence, to deal out sparingly or in small amounts.

dole-ful (dōl′fool), *adj.* sad; dismal; gloomy.—*adv.* **dole′ful-ly.**—*n.* **dole′ful-ness.**

doll (dol), *n.* 1, a puppet or toy baby; 2, a girl or woman with a pretty, childish face.

dol-lar (dol′èr), *n.* 1, a silver coin used in Canada and the U.S., equal to 100 cents; 2, a bank-note, treasury note, or the like, of the legal value of 100 cents; 3, any of various large silver coins of other countries; as, Mexican *dollar*.

doll-y (dol′i), *n.* 1, an appliance, as a low truck or frame, for moving heavy objects; 2, a tool for holding rivets; 3, a narrow-gauge yard-engine; 4, an agitator for washing clothes, ores, etc.

do-lour (dō′lèr). *n.* *Poetic*, grief; sorrow.—*adj.* **dol′or-ous.**

dol-phin (dol′fin), *n.* 1, a whalelike sea mammal, about six feet long, with a long snout; 2, an edible sea-fish remarkable for its rapid changes of colour when dying.

dolt (dōlt), *n.* a heavy, stupid fellow; a dunce; blockhead.—*adj.* **dolt′ish.**

do-main (dō-mān′), *n.* 1, an estate owned in one's own right; 2, a region under the rule of a king or government; dominion; realm; 3, a field of thought or action; as, the *domain* of science.

dome (dōm), *n.* 1, a large rounded roof on a circular base; as, the *dome* of St. Paul's Cathedral in London; 2, any domelike object:—*v.t.* to top with, or shape like, a dome.

do-mes-tic (dō-mes′tik), *adj.* 1, relating to one's home or household affairs; as, *domestic* cares; 2, staying at home; fond of home; 3, relating to, or made in, one's own country; not foreign; as, *domestic* trade; *domestic* products; 4, of animals, tame; living with man, as dogs; turned to the use of man, as cattle:—*n.* a household servant.

do-mes-ti-cate (dō-mes′ti-kāt′), *v.t.* [domesticat-ed, domesticat-ing], 1, to accustom (a person) to a home or home life; 2, to turn (an animal or plant) to the use of man; tame or cultivate; 3, to civilize; as, in some cases, savages die out before they can be *domesticated*.—*n.* **do-mes′ti-ca′tion.**

dom-i-cile (dom′i-sīl′), *n.* a place of abode; home:—*v.t.* [domiciled, domicil-ing], to establish in a fixed residence.

dom-i-nant (dom′i-nant), *adj.* controlling; ruling; also, most important; as, the *dominant* partner in a business. —*n.* **dom′i-nance.**

dom-i-nate (dom′i-nāt′), *v.t.* [dominat-ed, dominat-ing], 1, to govern or control; rule; as, the Romans once *dominated* Europe; 2, to occupy a commanding position; as, the mountain *dominates* the valley:—*v.i.* to exercise influence or control; as, the strong *dominate* over the weak.—*n.* **dom′i-na′tion.**

dom-i-neer (dom′i-nēr′), *v.i.* to exercise authority arrogantly or tyranically; be overbearing.—*adj.* **dom′i-neer′ing.**

dom-i-nie (dom′i-ni), *n.* 1, a schoolmaster; 2, (usually dō′mi-ni), a clergyman.

do-min-ion (dō-min′yun), *n.* 1, supreme authority or control; rule; 2, territory subject to a ruler or government; as, a king's *dominions;* 3, (usually *Dominion*), a self-governing territory within the British Commonwealth (as, the *Dominion* of Canada).

dom-i-no (dom'i-nō), *n.* [*pl.* dominoes or dominos], **1**, a loose cloak with a hood and mask, used as a masquerade costume; **2**, a flat, oblong, dotted piece of bone or wood used in playing a game:— **dominoes**, *n.pl.* used as *sing.* the game so played.

¹don (don), *v.t.* [donned, don-ning], to put on; as, to *don* one's coat.

²don (don), *n.* **1**, a Spanish lord or gentleman; **2**, a distinguished person; **3**, at English universities, a fellow, tutor, or head of a college:—**Don** (dôn), Sir; Mr.: a title used in Spain.—*n. fem.* **Do'ña** (dō'nyä).

do-nate (dō-nāt'; dō'nāt), *v.t.* [donat-ed, donat-ing], to give to charity; contribute.—*n.* **do-na'tion.**

done (dun), *p.p.* of *do.*

don-jon (don'jun; dun'jun), *n.* the tower of a mediaeval castle.

don-key (dong'ki), *n.* [*pl.* donkeys], **1**, an ass; **2**, a stupid or obstinate fellow:—**donkey—engine,** a small, movable steam-engine, used when not much power is required.

do-nor (dō'nẽr), *n.* a giver; one who makes a donation or contribution.

doo-dle (dōō'dl), *v.t., v.i.* idly or aimlessly to scribble or trace designs (as when talking on a telephone).

doom (dōōm), *n.* **1**, destiny which cannot be escaped; **2**, destructive fate; **3**, the Last Judgment; as, the crack of *doom;* **4**, judgment; sentence:—*v.t.* **1**, to condemn; sentence; as, to *doom* a man to death; **2**, to destine; as, *doomed* to disappointment.

door (dōr), *n.* **1**, a movable barrier, sliding or swinging on hinges, which opens and closes the entrance to a house, room, or the like; **2**, a means of entrance.

dope (dōp), *n. Slang:* **1**, narcotic drugs; **2**, information; inside information, as on a horse-race:—*v.t.* [doped, dop-ing], *Slang,* to treat with drugs.

dor-mant (dôr'mant), *adj.* sleeping; temporarily inactive; as, plants lie *dormant* in the winter; a *dormant* talent.—*n.* **dor'man-cy** (dôr'man-si).

dor-mer—win-dow (dôr'mẽr-win'-dō), *n.* a window built upright in a sloping roof; also, the structure that contains it.

dor-mi-tor-y (dôr'-mi-tẽr-i), *n.* [*pl.* dormitories], a sleeping-room containing several beds; also, a building containing a number of sleeping-rooms.

DORMER-WINDOW

dor-mouse (dôr'mous'), *n.* a smal hibernating, squirrel-like rodent of th Old World.

dor-sal (dôr'sal), *adj.* pertaining to, o on or near, the back; as, a *dorsa* muscle.

dor-y (dôr'i), *n.* [*pl.* dories], a dee flat-bottomed rowboat with a shar prow and flat, V-shaped stern, used b salt-water fishermen.

dos-a-dos (dō'za-dō'), *n.* **1**, any kin of seat where persons sit *back to back* **2**, (dō'sē-dō') a square-dance movemen in which dancers approach and pas *back to back.*

dose (dōs), *n.* a definite quantity (medicine to be taken at one time:—*v.* [dosed, dos-ing], to give medicine t(

dost (dust), *Biblical,* second person *sing.,* of *do.*

¹dot (dot), *n.* a very small spot (point, as over an *i* or *j;* a speck:—*v.* [dot-ted, dot-ting], to mark with dot!

²dot (dot), *n.* property which a bric brings to her husband; dowry.

dot-age (dōt'ij), *n.* **1**, the childishne of old age; **2**, foolish affection.

do-tard (dō'tẽrd), *n.* one whose mind weakened by age; a silly, foolis person.

dote (dōt), *v.i.* [dot-ed, dot-ing], **1**, to k feeble and foolish with age; **2**, to sho excessive love; as, to *dote* on a grand child.

dot-ty (dot'i), *adj.* feeble—mindec crazy. (*Colloq.*)

dou-ble (dub'l), *adj.* **1**, being in pair as, *double* doors; **2**, multiplied by tw twice as much or many; twice tl size, strength, value, etc.; as, a *doub* amount; **3**, combining two unlil qualities; as, his remark had a *doub* meaning; **4**, folded over, as cloth (paper; **5**, in botany, having more tha a single row of petals; as, a *doub* nasturtium:—*n.* **1**, twice as mucl twice the number or quantity; **2**, substitute or understudy; as, a actor's *double;* **3**, a duplicate; th which looks very much like somethir else; **4**, a sharp turn made whi running, as by a hunted animal, throw pursuers off the track; hence, (evasive trick:—*v.t.* [dou-bled, do bling], **1**, to make twice as mucl multiply by two; as, *double* five to g ten; **2**, to fold over; as, to *double* piece of paper; **3**, to pass around; as ship *doubles* a cape:—*v.i.* **1**, to increa to twice as much; as, his stock *doubl* in value; **2**, to turn and retrace tl same course; as, the fox *doubled* bacl **3**, to be a substitute or understudy; ;

he *doubles* for Mr. Smith:—*adv.* by twos; in a pair; as, to ride *double:*—
double—dealing, dishonest action; deceit.—*adv.* **dou´bly.**

dou-ble—cross (dub´l–krôs´), *v.t.* *Slang,* to betray.

dou-ble—head-er (dub´l–hed´ĕr), *n.* 1, a train with two engines in front; 2, in *baseball,* two games in succession on the one day (by the same two teams).

dou-blet (dub´let), *n.* 1, one of a pair; 2, a couple; 3, a close-fitting garment for the upper part of the body, worn by men in western Europe from the 15th to the 17th century.

DOUBLET

dou-bloon (dub-loon´), *n.* an old Spanish gold coin, worth about $8.00.

doubt (dout), *v.i.* to waver in opinion or belief; be uncertain or undecided:—*v.t.* to distrust; question; as, to *doubt* one's eyes:—*n.* 1, uncertainty of mind; unbelief; as, I have my *doubts;* 2, an unsettled question; an objection; as, to answer a *doubt;* 3, a state or condition of uncertainty; as, his life is in *doubt.*—*n.* **doubt´er.**—*adv.* **doubt´less.**

doubt-ful (dout´fool), *adj.* 1, questionable as to result; as, a *doubtful* venture; 2, questionable as to character; as, *doubtful* people; 3, undecided; doubting; as, he was *doubtful* of her ability. –*adv.* **doubt´ful-ly.**

douche (dōōsh), *n.* and *v.* cleansing or flushing out some cavity or organ of the body, etc.

dough (dō), *n.* a spongy paste of flour and other ingredients, esp. for bread.

dough-boy (dō´boi´), *n.* *Colloq.* in the U.S. army, an infantry soldier.

dough-nut (dō´nut´), *n.* a small cake of sweetened dough, fried in deep fat.

dough-ty (dou´ti), *adj.* [dough-ti-er, dough-ti-est], brave; strong and bold.

Dou-kho-bors (dōō´ko-bôrz´). Same as *Dukhobors.*

dour (dōōr), *adj.* stern, gloomy, or sour in manner; obstinate; as, a *dour* Scot.

douse, dowse (dous), *v.t.,* *v.i.* 1, to thrust into or pour a liquid over: he was *doused* in the pond; he was *dowsed* (or drenched) with water; 2, *Slang,* to put out (a light); as, *dowse* the glim.

dove (duv), *n.* a bird of the pigeon family, known by the cooing sounds it makes.

dove-tail (duv´tāl´), *n.* a tongue or a notch shaped like a dove's tail:—*v.t.* to fasten together by interlocking tongues and notches of this shape:—*v.i.* to fit closely and exactly.

DOVETAILS

dow-a-ger (dou´a-jĕr), *n.* 1, a widow who holds property or title from her husband; 2, *Colloq.* a dignified elderly woman.

dow-dy (dou´di), *n.* [*pl.* dowdies], a shabby, poorly dressed woman:—*adj.* [dow-di-er, dow-di-est], lacking style.

dow-el (dou´el), *n.* a pin to fasten two pieces of wood or metal together: also called *dowel* pin:—*v.t.* [dow-elled, dowel-ling], to fasten by such pins.

dow-er (dou´ĕr), *n.* 1, that part of a deceased husband's estate, usually a third, which the law gives to his widow to use during her life; 2, dowry; 3, one's natural talents or abilities:—*v.t.* to furnish with a dower or a dowry; endow.

DOWELS (D)

¹down (doun), *n.* 1, the first feathers of young birds; 2, the soft under-feathers of birds; 3, any velvety fuzz, as on a peach.

²down (doun), *n.* in England, a stretch of high, grassy land used for sheep grazing.

³down (doun), *adv.* 1, from a higher to a lower position or degree: opposite of *up;* 2, from an earlier to a later time; as, heirlooms are handed *down;* 3, at once, as if on the counter; as, to pay a dollar *down;* 4, to, or in, a lower state or condition, as of illness, defeat, or the like; as, to come *down* with a cold; to bring *down* one's price; 5, from a greater to a lesser quantity; as, to boil *down;* 6, seriously; as, to get *down* to work; 7, upon paper; as, take *down* what he says:—*adj.* 1, descending; as, a *down* elevator; 2, in a lowered position; as, the curtain is *down;* 3, in golf, behind one's opponent in holes or points; as, three *down;* 4, ill; inactive; as, he is *down* with the measles:—*prep.* from a higher to a lower point on; as, to row *down* the stream:—*v.t.* to bring or put down; as, *down* the enemy; *down* the drink:—*n.* a descent; figuratively, a reverse of fortune; as, to have ups and *downs.*

down-cast (doun´kàst´), *adj.* 1, directed downward; 2, sad; discouraged.

down-fall (doun´fôl´), *n.* 1, a falling downward; 2, a sudden fall from rank,

all (ôl), **ôr; up, mūte, cûr, cōōl, book; oil, out; th, thin;** *th,* **the.**

fortune, or reputation; disgrace; **3,** capture, as of a city.—*adj.* **down'fall'en.**

down-heart-ed (doun'här'tid), *adj.* downcast; sad.—*adv.* **down'—heart'ed-ly.**

down-pour (doun'pōr'), *n.* a heavy rain.

down-right (doun'rīt'), *adj.* **1,** complete; as, *downright* folly; **2,** going straight to the point; blunt; as, an honest and *downright* person:—*adv.* (doun'rīt'; doun'rit'), **1,** in plain terms; **2,** utterly; extremely.

down-stage (doun'stāj'), *adj.* and *adv.* towards the front of the stage.

down-stairs (doun'stârz'), *adv.* on or to a lower floor:—*adj.* (doun'stârz'), on a lower floor.

down-stream (doun'strēm'), *adj.* and *adv.* in the direction of the current.

down-town (doun'toun'), to or toward the centre of a city.

down-trod-den (doun'trod'n), *adj.* oppressed.

down-ward (doun'wẽrd), *adj.* moving from a higher to a lower level.

down-ward (doun'wẽrd) or **down-wards** (doun'wẽrdz), *adv.* **1,** from a higher to a lower level or condition; **2,** from an earlier time.

down-y (doun'i), *adj.* [down-i-er, down-i-est], **1,** made of, or covered with, soft feathers, hair, or wool; **2,** like down; soft.

dow-ry (dou'ri), *n.* [*pl.* dowries], **1,** the property a woman brings to her husband at marriage; **2,** an endowment or talent.

dowse (dous), *v.* Same as *douse.*

dox-ol-o-gy (doks-ol'o-ji), *n.* [*pl.* doxologies], a short hymn of praise to God.

doze (dōz), *v.i.* [dozed, doz-ing], to sleep lightly:—*n.* a light sleep.

doz-en (duz'n), *n.* [*pl.* dozen or dozens], twelve things of a kind, taken together.

drab (drab), *adj.* [drab-ber, drab-best], **1,** of a dull greyish brown; **2,** uninteresting.

drachm (dram), *n.* one eighth of an ounce in apothecaries' weight, or one sixteenth of an ounce in avoirdupois weight. Also, **dram.**

drach-ma (drak'ma), *n.* the monetary unit of Greece (since 1928); about 2000 to $1 (in value).

drae-ger-man (drā'gẽr-man), *n.* a Nova Scotian miner skilled in techniques of rescuing trapped miners.

draft or **draught** (drȧft), *n.* **1,** a line drawing or plan, as for an engine or building; **2,** a sketch or outline of some-

thing to be done; as, the first *draft* of a speech; **3,** a written order for the payment of money; also, a drawing of money from a bank or fund; **4,** a method of selecting men for compulsory military service; also, the men so selected; **5,** the pulling of a load by beasts; as, horses are often used for *draft;* **6,** a stream of air; as, a *draft* from an open door; **7,** a device for controlling the air stream in a stove, furnace, or the like; **8,** a taking away; drain; as, a *draft* on supplies; **9,** (usually *draught*), the depth of water to which a ship sinks, esp. when loaded; **10,** (usually *draught*), the hauling in of a net of fish; also, the quantity of fish caught in one haul; **11,** (usually *draught*), a single drink; as, a *draught* of water; also, the act of drawing (liquid) from a cask, barrel, or the like; as, beer on *draught:—adj.* **1,** (usually *draught*), used for pulling loads; as, *draught* animals; **2,** (usually *draught*), served or drawn from a keg; as, *draught* beer:—*v.t.* **1,** to sketch, write, or draw in outline; **2,** to select (men) for compulsory military service.

draf-tee (dråf-tē'), *n.* one conscripted for military service, etc.

drafts-man (dråfts'man), *n.* [*pl.* draftsmen (-men)], one who makes plans, mechanical drawings, etc.

draft-y (dråf'ti), *adj.* [draft-i-er, draft-i-est], exposed to currents of air.

drag (drag), *v.t.* [dragged, dragging], **1,** to draw along by force; haul; **2,** to search the bottom of (a river or lake) with a drag or grapnel:—*v.i.* **1,** to trail along the ground; as, her skirt *dragged;* **2,** to move or go slowly; hence, to be slow and uninteresting; as, the speech *dragged:—n.* **1,** a device for searching the bottom of a river or lake; **2,** a sledge for hauling loads; **3,** a harrow for breaking up soil; **4,** anything which holds back progress; **5,** a kind of coach; **6,** *Slang,* influence; pull.

drag-gle (drag'l), *v.t.* **1,** to wet or soil by dragging, as in mud; **2,** to lag behind.

drag-net (drag'net'), *n.* a net for drawing along the bottom of a river to catch fish, or along the ground to catch small game.

drag-on (drag'un), *n.* in mythology or folklore, a huge beast represented as a winged serpent, often many-headed, and breathing fire.

drag-on-fly (drag'on-flī'), *n.* [*pl.* dragon-flies], an insect with a long, slender body, large eyes, and four narrow, finely veined wings: often called *darning-needle.*

dra-goon (dra-gōōn'), *n.* a cavalry-man

or mounted soldier, heavily equipped:
—*v.t.* to oppress; force (someone) to do
something.

drain (drān), *v.t.* **1,** to draw off (a liquid)
gradually; as, to *drain* water from a
reservoir; **2,** to make empty; as, he
drained the cup:—*v.i.* to discharge
surface water; as, swamps *drain* into
ditches:—*n.* **1,** a channel or pipe for
useless water; **2,** a continuous demand.

drain-age (drān′ij), *n.* **1,** a flowing off
of water; **2,** a system of pipes or streams
for drawing off water; **3,** that which
flows away.

drake (drāk), *n.* a male duck.

dram (dram), *n.* **1,** a drachm; **2,** a small
drink, esp. of alcoholic liquor.

dra-ma (drä′ma; dram′a), *n.* **1,** a play;
a work, in prose or verse, intended for
acting on a stage; **2,** that branch of
literature concerned with plays; as, a
student of *drama;* **3,** any series of
human events leading to a climax.—
adj. **dra-mat′ic.**

dram-a-tize (dram′a-tīz′), *v.t.* [drama-
tized, dramatiz-ing], **1,** to adapt or re-
write for the stage; as, to *dramatize* a
novel; **2,** to portray anything vividly
or in a dramatic manner.—*n.* **dram′a-
tist.**—*n.* **dram′a-ti-za′tion.**

drank (drank), *p.t.* of *drink.*

drape (drāp), *v.t.* [draped, drap-ing], **1,**
to cover with cloth; **2,** to arrange
(cloth or hangings) in folds.

dra-per-y (drā′pėr-i), *n.* [*pl.* draperies],
fabrics used for garments or hangings,
esp. when hung loosely or in folds; also,
the hangings or draped robes.

dras-tic (dras′tik), *adj.* acting rapidly
and violently; severe; as, a *drastic*
remedy.—*adv.* **dras′ti-cal-ly.**

draught (dráft), *n.* **1,** a drink, as of
water; **2,** the depth of water required
to float a boat; **3,** a catch of fish:—*adj.*
drawn from a keg, as beer:—**draughts,**
the game of chequers. Spelled *draft* in
some uses. See **draft.**

draw (drô), *v.t.* [*p.t.* drew (drōō), *p.p.*
drawn (drôn), *p.pr.* draw-ing], **1,** to haul
or drag; **2,** to pull out; haul up, as a
fish-net; **3,** to come to (a conclusion) by
reasoning; **4,** to extend in length; as,
to *draw* out a performance; **5,** to extract
or bring out; as, to *draw* a cork; to
draw a sword; **6,** to represent on paper
with pen or pencil; **7,** to write in legal
form; as, to *draw* up a will; **8,** to
require in order to float; as, the boat
draws ten feet of water; **9,** to inhale;
as, to *draw* a long breath; **10,** to receive;
as, to *draw* one's pay; **11,** to obtain
(money) from a bank; **12,** to attract;
as, honey *draws* flies; **13,** to produce or

gain; as, money *draws* interest; **14,** to
select or obtain (a chance); as, to *draw*
lots; **15,** to influence (someone) to
reveal facts, talents, or the like; as, to
draw someone out; **16,** to get (something) from a source; as, to *draw* inspiration from a book:—*v.i.* **1,** to move;
as, to *draw* away; *draw* near; **2,** to
attract; as, a good show always *draws;*
3, to pull or haul something; to move
something by pulling; **4,** to make a
demand; as, to *draw* on a bank; **5,** to
practise the art of making designs or
pictures; **6,** to allow a current of air to
pass; as, the chimney *draws* well:—*n.*
1, the act or result of drawing; in
particular, a lottery; **2,** a contest left
undecided; a tie; **3,** the movable
section of a drawbridge.

draw-back (drô′bak′), *n.* a disadvantage; hindrance.

draw-bridge (drô′brij′), *n.* a bridge of
which the whole or a part may be lifted
up, let down, or drawn aside.

draw-er (drô′ėr; drôr), *n.* **1,** one who
draws; a draftsman; **2,** (drôr), a sliding
compartment in a bureau, table, or the
like; **3, drawers** (drôrz), an undergarment for the lower part of the body.

draw-ing (drô′ing), *n.* **1,** the act of
dragging, pulling, etc.; as, the *drawing*
of a load, or of a sword; **2,** a picture
made with a pen, pencil, chalk, or the
like; a sketch; **3,** the art of making
such a picture.

draw-ing—room (drô′ing–rōōm′), *n.*
a room for the reception of company.

drawl (drôl), *v.t.* and *v.i.* to speak in an
affected, lazy manner:—*n.* a slow, lazy
manner of speaking.

drawn (drôn), past participle of *draw:*—
adj. **1,** left undecided; as, a *drawn*
game; **2,** out of shape; twisted; as, a
face *drawn* with grief; **3,** melted; as,
drawn butter.

dray (drā), *n.* a stout low cart with
removable sides, used for heavy loads.

dread (dred), *v.t.* to look forward to
with shrinking or fear:—*n.* fear, esp. of
the future; **2,** fear mingled with awe:—
adj. **1,** terrifying; **2,** inspiring fear
mingled with awe; as, a *dread* lord.—
adj. **dread′ful.**—*adv.* **dread′ful-ly.**

dream (drēm), *n.* **1,** thoughts, feelings,
or pictures experienced or seen during
sleep; **2,** something imagined; as, a
dream of greatness:—*v.t.* [*p.t.* and *p.p.*
dreamed (drēmd) or dreamt (dremt),
p.pr. dreaming], **1,** to see, think, or feel
during sleep; **2,** to imagine or hope for:
—*v.i.* **1,** to have thoughts, see pictures,
etc., during sleep; **2,** to be lost in
thought.—*n.* **dream′er.**

dream-y (drēm′i), *adj.* [dream-i-er,

dream-i-est], **1**, like a dream; unreal; **2**, not awake to realities; **3**, soothing; as, *dreamy* music.—*adv.* **dream′i-ly.**—*n.* **dream′i-ness.**

drear-y (drēr′i), *adj.* [drear-i-er, drear-i-est], cheerless; gloomy; as a *dreary* day.—*adv.* **drear′i-ly.**—*n.* **drear′i-ness.**—*adj.* **drear.**

¹dredge (drej), *n.* **1**, a device for scooping up mud, as from the bottom of a river; **2**, a device for gathering oysters:—*v.t.* [dredged, dredg-ing], **1**, to deepen, as a river channel; **2**, to scoop with a dredge.—*n.* **dredg′er.**

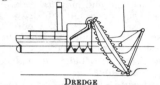

DREDGE

²dredge (drej), *n.* a box with perforated top, used to sprinkle flour, etc.:—*v.t.* [dredged, dredg-ing], to sprinkle with flour.

dregs (dregz), *n.pl.* **1**, the sediment of liquids; lees; **2**, hence, the worthless part of anything.

drench (drench), *v.t.* to wet thoroughly. —*n.* **1**, a drink, as a forced draught of medicine given to a horse, etc.; **2**, *Colloq.* a heavy rain.

dress (dres), *n.* **1**, clothes; wearing apparel; attire; **2**, a woman's or a child's gown; **3**, any outer garb or appearance; as, trees in autumn *dress:* —*v.t.* **1**, to clothe; as, to *dress* a baby; **2**, to deck out; as, to *dress* a window; **3**, to make ready for use; as, to *dress* meat; **4**, to treat or bind up, as a wound; **5**, to straighten (a line of soldiers) in military drill; **6**, to arrange (hair):— *v.i.* **1**, to put on clothes; **2**, in drilling, to form into a straight line; as, "Right, *dress!*"

dress-er (dres′ẽr), *n.* **1**, a chest of drawers with a mirror; **2**, a cupboard for dishes, glass, etc.; **3**, a bench used in dressing or preparing something for use; **4**, a surgeon's assistant who dresses wounds.

dress-ing (dres′ing), *n.* **1**, the act of putting on clothes, treating a wound, etc.; **2**, material for stiffening fabrics; **3**, sauce or stuffing; **4**, a bandage, compress, or the like, applied to a wound or sore:—**dressing—gown,** a loose robe worn while one is dressing or lounging.

dress-y (dres′i), *adj.* [dress-i-er, dress-i-est], **1**, given to showy dressing; **2**, *Colloq.* stylish; smart.

drew (drōō), *p.t.* of *draw.*

drib-ble (drib′l), *v.i.* [drib-bled, drib-bling], **1**, to fall in drops; **2**, to drool:— *v.t.* **1**, to let fall in drops; give out in small portions; **2**, in soccer and hockey, to give slight kicks or shoves to (the ball); **3**, in basketball, to bounce (the ball) rapidly along the floor; **4**, to drool:—*n.* a trickle of water.

drib-let (drib′lit), *n.* a small sum or portion; as, he paid his bill in *driblets.*

dri-er or **dry-er** (drī′ẽr), *n.* **1**, a person or thing that dries something; **2**, a substance added to paint or varnish to aid drying.

drift (drift), *n.* **1**, the direction in which anything is driven; tendency; meaning; as, the *drift* of a speech; **2**, that which is driven; as, a snow*drift;* **3**, in geology, loose rocks, earth, etc., carried by a glacier; **4**, the distance a ship is carried from its course by ocean or air currents or an aeroplane by air currents: —*v.t.* to drive along or heap up; as, the wind *drifts* dry leaves into piles:—*v.i.* **1**, to be carried along by a current or by circumstances; **2**, to gather or collect in heaps.—*n.* **drift′er.**

drift-wood (drift′wood′), *n.* floating wood cast ashore by water.

drill (dril), *n.* **1**, a tool for boring holes; **2**, a machine for sowing seeds in rows; also, a row so planted; **3**, military exercises; **4**, thorough training by frequent repetition:—*v.t.* **1**, to pierce with a drill; bore (holes); **2**, to train (soldiers) in military exercises; **3**, to instruct thoroughly; as, to *drill* pupils; **4**, to sow in rows.—*n.* **drill′er.**

drink (dringk), *v.i.* [*p.t.* drank (drangk), *p.p.* drunk or drunken (drungk′en), *p.pr.* drink-ing], **1**, to swallow a liquid; **2**, to take alcoholic liquors habitually: —*v.t.* **1**, to swallow (a liquid); **2**, to absorb; suck in; as, plants *drink* water; **3**, to receive through the senses; as, to *drink* in a scene:—*n.* **1**, any liquid to be swallowed; as, a cool *drink;* **2**, the quantity of liquid to be swallowed; as, a *drink* of water; **3**, strong or intoxicating liquor; as, he took to *drink.* —*adj.* **drink′a-ble.**—*n.* **drink′er.**

drip (drip), *v.i.* [dripped, drip-ping], **1**, to fall in drops; as, the oil *drips* ȯn the floor; **2**, to let fall drops; as, your umbrella *drips:*—*v.t.* to let fall in drops; as, the trees *drip* rain:—*n.* **1**, that which falls in drops; **2**, a projecting part so shaped as to throw off rain.

drip-o-la-tor (drip′o-lā′tẽr), *n.* a coffeepot in which boiling water from the top part drips slowly through fine holes on to fine-ground coffee in a second part, also perforated to allow the coffee to be caught in the lowest section.

drip-ping (drip′ing), *n.* the fatty juice from roasting meat.

drive (drīv), *v.t.* [*p.t.* drove (drōv), *p.p.* driv-en (driv'en), *p.pr.* driv-ing], **1,** to urge forward by force or threats; push forward forcibly; **2,** to control the motion of; steer, as an automobile; also, to carry in a driven vehicle; **3,** to carry on vigorously; to conclude; as, to *drive* a bargain; **4,** to put into a certain state; as, you *drive* me crazy; **5,** to overwork; as, he *drove* his employees to the limit:—*v.i.* **1,** to press, aim, or be moved, forward steadily or with violence; **2,** to travel in a carriage or motor-car; **3,** in *golf*, to strike the ball from a tee:—*n.* **1,** the act of sending forward; **2,** a road, usually one for pleasure vehicles; a driveway; **3,** a trip in a motor-car or carriage; **4,** a gathering together, or rounding up, as of cattle for branding, logs for floating, or the like; **5,** a campaign.

driv-el (driv'el), *n.* **1,** idle silly talk; as, to descend to *drivel;* **2,** saliva drooling from the mouth.—*v.t., v.i.* **1,** to talk nonsense; **2,** to drool (saliva).

drive–in (drīv'–in'), *adj.* built so that a patron can sit in his car while receiving service, as at a *drive-in* theatre, bank, restaurant, etc.

driv-er (drīv'er), *n.* **1,** one who or that which forces something into motion or directs persons or things in motion; **2,** in golf, a wooden club for driving the ball from a tee.

drive-way (drīv'wā'), *n.* a passageway for vehicles or animals.

driz-zle (driz'l), *v.i.* [driz-zled, drizzling], to rain slightly or mistily:—*n.* fine, misty rain.—*adj.* **driz'zly.**

droll (drōl), *adj.* queer; odd; amusing; as, a *droll* remark.—*n.* **droll'er-y.**

drom-e-dar-y (drom'i-dėr-i; drum'idėr-i), *n.* [*pl.* dromedaries], the Arabian, or one-humped, camel, noted for its speed.

drone (drōn), *v.i.* [droned, droning], to utter a monotonous sound; as, to *drone* through a lesson:—*v.t.* to read or speak in a monotonous tone:—*n.* **1,** a dull monotonous tone; as, the *drone* of bees; **2,** one of the pipes of a bagpipe; **3,** the male of a honey-bee, which produces no honey; **4,** a lazy fellow.

DROMEDARY ($\frac{1}{100}$)

drool (drōōl), *v.i.* **1,** to run at the mouth; drivel; **2,** to speak foolishly.

droop (drōōp), *v.i.* **1,** to sink or hang down, as from weariness; close, as eyelids; **2,** to fail or flag; as, his spirits

drooped:—*v.t.* to let hang down; as, to *droop* the head:—*n.* the act of drooping.—*adj.* **droop'y.**

drop (drop), *v.i.* [dropped, drop-ping], **1,** to fall in small rounded masses of liquid; **2,** to fall; sink to a lower position; as, the hat *dropped;* **3,** to fall behind or below, as in rank; **4,** to grow lower in sound or pitch; as, her voice *dropped* to a whisper; **5,** to cease or end; as, the matter *dropped;* **6,** to come or go naturally or casually; as, to *drop* in for tea:—*v.t.* **1,** to let fall in tiny masses; as, to *drop* medicine from a spoon; **2,** to let fall suddenly; as, I *dropped* the book; **3,** to lower, as one's eyes or voice; **4,** to fell with a blow or weapon; **5,** to have done with; as, to *drop* an argument:—*n.* **1,** a small rounded mass of liquid; as, a *drop* of water; **2,** anything like a small rounded mass of liquid; as, a chocolate-*drop;* **3,** any very small quantity; **4,** a sudden descent or fall; as, a *drop* in prices; **5,** the depth or distance of a descent or fall; as, a sheer *drop* of 50 feet; **6,** something arranged to be lowered or hung from above; as, a curtain *drop.*—*n.* **drop'per.**

drop–kick (drop'–kik'), *n.* in *football*, a kick given to a ball as it rises or bounces after being dropped to the ground (not a *placement* or *punt*). Also *v.t., v.i.,* as, he *drop–kicked* a field goal, from thirty yards out.

drop-let (drop'lit), *n.* a tiny drop.

drop-sy (drop'si), *n.* a disease marked by an excessive accumulation of water in any part of the body.

dross (drôs), *n.* **1,** the scum or refuse of melted metal; **2,** refuse; waste.

drought (drout) or **drouth** (drouth), *n.* continued absence of rain or moisture.

¹drove (drōv), *n.* **1,** a herd of animals driven in a body; **2,** a crowd of people, esp. when running along together.

²drove (drōv), *v.t., v.i., p.t.* of drive.

dro-ver (drō'vėr), *n.* **1,** one who drives cattle to market; **2,** a dealer in cattle.

drown (droun), *v.i.* to die from suffocation in water or other liquid:—*v.t.* **1,** to kill by plunging under water; **2,** to overpower; as, the noise *drowned* the music.

drowse (drouz), *v.i.* [drowsed, drowsing], to be heavy with sleep; doze:—*v.t.* to spend (time) dozing; as, to *drowse* an afternoon away:—*n.* a light sleep, or doze.

drow-sy (drou'zi), *adj.* [drow-si-er, drow-si-est], **1,** sleepy; as, a *drowsy* feeling; **2,** making one sleepy; as, a *drowsy* sound.—*adv.* **drow'si-ly.**—*n.* **drow'si-ness.**

drub (drub), *v.t.* [drubbed, drub-bing],

to thrash; beat or whip soundly; as, our team was *drubbed* to-day.—*n.* a thump; a blow, as with a club.

drudge (druj), *v.i.* [drudged, drudging], to work hard at disagreeable tasks; slave:—*n.* one employed in slavish work.—*n.* **drudg'er-y.**

drug (drug), *n.* 1, a medicine, or a substance used in making medicine; 2, a habit-forming substance, or narcotic, such as opium; 3, an article which sells slowly; as, a *drug* on the market:—*v.t.* [drugged, drug-ging], 1, to mix drugs with; as, to *drug* wine; 2, to render stupid or put to sleep with a drug; as, she *drugged* herself with headache powders.

drug-gist (drug'ist), *n.* a dealer in medicines and their ingredients.

drug-store (drug'stōr'), *n.* a shop where drugs and miscellaneous goods, such as candy, perfumes, and the like, are sold.

dru-id (drōō'id), *n.* a priest of a religious cult of ancient Britain and Gaul.—*adj.* **dru-id'ic; dru-id'i-cal.**

drum (drum), *n.* 1, a musical instrument consisting of a hollow cylinder with dried skin stretched across the ends, and beaten with sticks; 2, anything like a drum, as a cylinder for winding rope or wire, or a cylindrical container, as for oil; *v.i.* [drummed, drum-ming], 1, to beat or play a drum; 2, to beat rapidly upon something with the fingers:—*v.t.* 1, to cause to beat against something; as, to *drum* one's feet on the floor; 2, to beat (up) or summon; as, to *drum* up trade; 3, to repeat constantly; as, this idea has been *drummed* into me.

drum-mer (drum'ẽr), *n.* 1, one who plays a drum; 2, a travelling salesman.

drum-stick (drum'stik'), *n.* 1, a stick for beating a drum; 2, the lower joint of the leg of a dressed chicken, turkey, etc.

drunk (drungk), one form of the past participle of *drink:*—*adj.* intoxicated:—*n. Slang:* 1, a sot; 2, a spree.

drunk-ard (drungk'ẽrd), *n.* one who is habitually intoxicated; a sot.

drunk-en (drungk'en), one form of the past participle of *drink:*—*adj.* intoxicated; also, due to drink; as, a *drunken* stupor.—*adv.* **drunk'en-ly.**—*n.* **drunk'-en-ness.**

drupe (drōōp), *n.* a pulpy fruit inclosing a stone or pit, as the *peach, plum, cherry,* etc.

dry (drī), *adj.* [dri-er, dri-est], 1, without moisture or water; as, *dry* land; 2, empty of water; as, a *dry* well; also, *Colloq.* thirsty; 3, lacking in interest; as, a *dry* speech; 4, harsh; as, a *dry,*

hacking cough; 5, shrewd and sharp; as, *dry* wit; 6, naming a measure for grains, vegetables, etc.; 6, *Colloq.* forbidding the sale of intoxicants; as, *dry* cities; *dry* laws:—*v.t.* and *v.i.* [dried, dry-ing], to make or become dry:—*n.* [*pl.* drys], *Colloq.* a prohibitionist.—*n.* **dry'ness.**—*adv.* **dry'ly or dri'ly.**

dry-ad (drī'ad), *n.* in mythology, a nymph supposed to live in a tree.

dry—clean (drī'–klēn'), *v.t.* to clean garments, etc., with an agent other than water (as, gasoline or naphtha).

dry-dock (drī'dok'), *n.* a dock built so that the water can be pumped out after a ship has entered it, used for repairs, ship-building, etc.

dry-er (drī'ẽr), *n.* Same as **drier.**

dry goods, woven fabrics, such as cloth, lace, ribbon, or the like.

du-al (dū'al), *adj.* pertaining to two; composed of two; twofold; double; as, *dual* ownership.

du-al-ism (dū'al-izm), *n.* being of two parts, as in one human being (or universe) mind and matter, soul and body, good and evil, etc., the two parts or natures often being opposed or irreconcilable.

dub (dub), *v.t.* [dubbed, dub-bing], 1, to bestow knighthood upon, by tapping the shoulder with a sword; 2, to confer any title, name, or nickname upon; as, they *dubbed* her "Tommy"; 3, to do awkwardly; as, to *dub* a golf stroke:—*n. Slang,* an awkward player.

du-bi-ous (dū'bi-us), *adj.* 1, doubtful; as, a *dubious* venture; 2, questionable; as, a man of *dubious* reputation.

du-cal (dū'kal), *adj.* pertaining to a duke.

duc-at (duk'at), *n.* 1, a gold or silver coin formerly in use in many European countries; 2, *ducats,* money; cash.

du-ce (dōō'chā), *n.* Italian word for leader:—**Il Duce** (ēl), or **Duce,** the head of the Fascist government of Italy.

duch-ess (duch'es), *n.* 1, the wife or widow of a duke; 2, a woman with the rank or authority of a duke.

duch-y (duch'i), *n.* [*pl.* duchies], the territory or dominions of a duke.

¹**duck** (duk), *n.* 1, a flat-billed waterfowl with short legs and neck; 2, the female duck as distinguished from the male, or drake; 3, *Colloq.* a pet or favourite. —*adj. Slang,* **duck'y.**

²**duck** (duk), *v.t.* 1, to plunge (the head) for an instant under water; also, to throw (a person) into the water; 2, to bend down; as, to *duck* the head; 3, *Colloq.* to avoid, as by quickly bowing

the head; as, to *duck* a blow:—*v.i.* **1**, to take a quick dip into water; **2**, to move the head or body aside quickly; dodge:—*n.* **1**, a dip or quick plunge under water; **2**, a sudden lowering of the head.

³duck (duk), *n.* **1**, a linen or cotton fabric for sails and outer clothing; **2**, **ducks**, *Colloq.* sailors' trousers made of duck.

duck-bill (duk′bil′), *n.* the Australian platypus, a small aquatic, egg-laying mammal with webbed feet, beaver-like tail, and duck's bill.

duck-ling (duk′ling), *n.* a young duck.

duck-tailed (duk′tāld′), *adj.* shaped behind like a *duck's* tail; as, a *duck-tailed* haircut.

duck-weed (duk′wēd′), *n.* a genus of small free-floating aquatic plants (like a green scum), eaten by ducks.

duct (dukt), *n.* **1**, a canal, tube, or passage by which fluid is carried; **2**, a tube or vessel of the body, esp. one for carrying a secretion; **3**, a tube or pipe for cables, wires, or the like.—*adj.* **duct′less**.

duc-tile (duk′tīl), *adj.* **1**, capable of being drawn out into strands; as, copper is highly *ductile;* **2**, easily influenced or led.

dud (dud), *n.* a shell that fails to explode; hence, a futile person or device.

dude (dūd), *n.* a man who is over-refined in manner or dress; a dandy; fop.—*adj.* **dud′ish**.

dudg-eon (duj′un), *n.* resentment; sullen anger; indignation: he left in high *dudgeon.*

duds (dudz), *n. Colloq.* clothes; rags.

due (dū), *adj.* **1**, owed or owing; payable; as, the rent is *due* today; **2**, suitable; proper; as, *due* courtesy; **3**, scheduled or expected; as, *due* at noon; **4**, caused by; as, an accident *due* to carelessness:—*adv.* exactly; directly; as, *due* west:—*n.* **1**, that which rightfully belongs to someone; as, give him his *due;* **2**, **dues**, the money paid for membership in a club or society.

du-el (dū′el), *n.* a combat between two persons, usually planned beforehand and fought with deadly weapons before witnesses:—*v.i.* [duelled, duel-ling], to fight a duel.—*n.* **du′el-ling.**—*n.* **du′el-list.**

du-et (dū′et′), *n.* a musical composition for two performers.

duf-fel (duf′l), *n.* a camper's kit:—duffel bag, a large bag for carrying personal belongings, clothing, etc.

duf-fer (duf′ẽr), *n. Colloq.* a stupid, dull, or incompetent person.

dug (dug), *p.t.* and *p.p.* of *dig.*

dug-out (dug′out′), *n.* **1**, a trench or cave used as a shelter against bombs, gunfire, etc.; **2**, in *baseball,* an enclosure (one behind third base and one behind first) for the members of the two opposing teams; **3**, a canoe hollowed out from a log.

duke (dūk), *n.* **1**, in England and some other European countries, a member of the nobility next below a prince; **2**, the ruler of a duchy.—*n.* **duke′dom.**

Du-kho-bors (dōō′ko-bōrz′), *n. pl.* a sect driven by religious persecution from Russia to Canada in the 1890's; noted for frequently resorting to nudity in protest against certain Canadian laws. Also, **Doukhobors.**

dul-cet (dul′sit), *adj.* sweet, esp. to the ear; as, *dulcet* tones or notes.

dull (dul), *adj.* **1**, not sharp-edged; blunt; as, a *dull* knife; **2**, lacking keenness or liveliness; as, a *dull* fellow; **3**, slow of understanding or action; as, a *dull* pupil; **4**, not clear or vivid; as, a *dull* colour; a *dull* sound; **5**, pointless as a *dull* story:—*v.t.* and *v.i.* to make or become dull.—*adv.* **dul′ly.**—*n.* **dull′-ness; dul′ness.**

dul-lard (dul′ẽrd), *n.* a slow-witted person.

du-ly (dū′li), *adv.* in a fit and becoming manner; regularly; as, *duly* elected officers.

dumb (dum), *adj.* **1**, unable to speak; as, a deaf and *dumb* child; a *dumb* animal; **2**, *Colloq.* stupid; foolish.—*n.* **dumb′ness.**

dumb—bell (dum′-bel′), *n.* **1**, one of a pair of weights, each consisting of two balls of wood or metal joined by a short bar which serves as a grip, used for gymnastic exercise; **2**, *Slang,* an ignorant or stupid person.

dumb-found (dum′found′), *v.t.* to amaze; make dumb with surprise or fear.—*adj.* **dumb′found′ed.** Also, **dum∠found′.**

dumb—wait-er (dum′-wāt′ẽr), *n.* a small elevator for moving dishes or supplies from one floor to another.

dum-my (dum′i), *n.* [*pl.* dummies], **1**, one who is silent; also, a thick-witted person; **2**, a make-believe; hence, a form for showing clothing; **3**, in some card games, an exposed hand played by the partner; also, the player whose hand is exposed; **4**, a person who acts for another, when he seems to be acting for himself:—*adj.* sham; as, a *dummy* drawer.

dump (dump), *v.t.* to unload; as, they *dumped* sand from the barrel:—*n.* **1**, a place for rubbish; **2**, a heap of refuse.

dump-ling (dump′ling), *n.* **1**, a small

mass of dough boiled in soup or stew; 2, a shell of dough enclosing fruit or meat and either baked or boiled; as, an apple *dumpling*.

¹dun (dun), *n.* 1, an urgent request or demand for the payment of a debt; 2, one who demands payment of a debt repeatedly:—*v.t.* [dunned, dun-ning], to plague by frequent demands for payment.

²dun (dun), *adj.* of a dull brownish or grayish colour.

dunce (duns), *n.* a dull, ignorant person; esp. a backward student.

dune (dūn), *n.* a low hill of drifted sand piled up by the wind, esp. along the seashore.

dung (dung), *n.* waste material from animals; manure.

dun-geon (dun'-jun), *n.* a dark underground cell for prisoners.

dunk (dungk), *v.t.* to dip (dry food into soup, tea, etc., before eating it).

dun-nage (dun'ij), *n.* baggage or equipment, esp. of sailors, campers, etc.; duffel.

duo (dū'ō; dōō'ō), *n.* [*pl.* duos (-ōz); dui (dōō'i)], in *music*, a duet.

du-o-de-nal (dū'ō-dē'nl), *adj.* pertaining to that part of the small intestine just below the stomach, the *duodenum* (dū'ō-dē'num); as, *duodenal* ulcers.

du-o-de-num (dū'ō-dē'num), *n.* [*pl.* duodena (dū'o-dē'na)], the first part of the small intestine, just below the stomach.

dupe (dūp), *n.* one who is easily tricked, or believes everything he is told:—*v.t.* [duped, dup-ing], to deceive by trickery.

du-plex (dū'pleks), *adj.* double; as a *duplex* apartment or house. Also used as *noun*.

du-pli-cate (dū'pli-kāt'), *v.t.* [duplicated, duplicat-ing], to reproduce exactly; make a copy or copies of:—*adj.* (dū'pli-kit), 1, corresponding exactly with another; as, a *duplicate* key; 2, double; twofold:—*n.* (dū'pli-kit), 1, something exactly like another; a copy, as of a letter; 2, exact likeness between two things; as, documents in *duplicate*.—*n.* du'pli-ca'tion.

du-plic-i-ty (dū-pli'si-ti), *n.* deceitfulness; double-dealing.

du-ra-ble (dū'ra-bl), *adj.* permanent and lasting; resisting wear; as, *durable* cloth.—*adv.* du'ra-bly.—*n.* du'ra-bil'i-ty.

dur-ance (dū'rans), *n.* imprisonment; as, in *durance* vile.

du-ra-tion (dū-rā'shun), *n.* the time anything lasts; as, the *duration* of a war.

dur-ess (dū'res; dū-res'), *n.* 1, compulsion, as by threat or violence: he signed under *duress;* 2, imprisonment.

dur-ing (dūr'ing), *prep.* throughout the period of; in the time of.

durst (dûrst), *p.t.* of *dare*.

dusk (dusk), *adj.* dim; shadowy:—*n.* 1, the dim light at the beginning and end of daylight; 2, shadow; gloom.

dusk-y (dus'ki), *adj.* [dusk-i-er, dusk-i-est], somewhat dark; as, a *dusky* skin.

dust (dust), *n.* 1, fine, dry particles of earth or other matter; a cloud or film of such fine particles; 2, the earth or its surface; 3, the remains of a human body:—*v.i.* to remove dust from furniture, etc.:—*v.t.* 1, to brush away dust from; as, to *dust* the table; 2, to cover or sprinkle, as with powder.—*n.* dust'er. —*adj.* dust'y.—*n.* dust'i-ness.—*adj.* dust'less.

du-te-ous (dū'ti-us), *adj.* obedient; rendering service that is due; as, a *duteous* servant.—*adv.* du'te-ous-ly.

du-ti-ful (dū'ti-fool), *adj.* obedient and respectful to parents or superiors; as, a *dutiful* child.—*adv.* du'ti-ful-ly.

du-ty (dū'ti), *n.* [*pl.* duties], 1, the respectful behaviour due to parents or superiors; 2, action required in a certain office or position; as, the *duties* of a chairman; 3, that which one is morally bound to do; 4, a tax levied by the government.—*adj.* du'ti-a-ble.

dwarf (dwôrf), *n.* [*pl.* dwarfs (dwôrfs)], a person, animal, or plant much below average size:—*adj.* of smaller size or height than the average; as, a *dwarf* rose:—*v.t.* 1, to hinder from growing to natural size; as, the drought *dwarfed* the corn; 2, to cause to look small by comparison; as, the skyscraper *dwarfs* the church.—*adj.* dwarf'ish.

dwell (dwel), *v.i.* [dwelt (dwelt) or dwelled (dweld), dwell-ing], 1, to reside; live in a place; as, to *dwell* in England; 2, to linger; as, to *dwell* on a subject. —*n.* dwell'er.

dwell-ing (dwel'ing), *n.* a residence.

dwin-dle (dwin'dl), *v.i.* [dwin-dled, dwin-dling], to become gradually less; shrink.

dye (dī), *v.t.* [dyed, dye-ing], to stain or colour (fabric, fur, or the like):—*v.i.* to take colour in dyeing; as, this silk *dyes* well:—*n.* 1, colouring matter used in dyeing; a dye-stuff; 2, a colour produced by dyeing.

dyed—in—the—wool, *adj.* unchangeable; as, a *dyed-in-the-wool* Tory.

dye-stuff (dī'stuf'), *n.* any substance that yields a dye or stain; also, a dye.

dy-ing (dī'ing), present participle of ¹**die**:—*adj.* **1,** passing from life; as, a *dying* man; **2,** drawing to a close; as, the *dying* year; **3,** said or done at the time of death:—*n.* the act of passing from life.

dyke (dīk), *n.* Same as **dike.**

dy-nam-ic (dī-nam'ik; di-nam'ik), *adj.* **1,** relating to power or physical energy; **2,** forceful.—*adv.* **dy-nam'i-cal-ly.**

dy-na-mite (dī'na-mīt'), *n.* a highly explosive mixture, used for blasting:—*v.t.* [dynamit-ed, dynamit-ing], to destroy or blast by the explosion of dynamite.

dy-na-mo (dī'na-mō'), *n.* [*pl.* dynamos], a machine which converts mechanical energy, as that of a steam-engine or waterfall, into electric current.

dy-nas-ty (dīn'as-ti; dī'nas-ti), *n.* [*pl.* dynasties], a line or succession of sovereigns of the same family; as, the Tudor *dynasty.*—*adj.* **dy-nas'tic** (dī-nas'tik).—*n.* **dy'nast.**

dyne (dīn), *n.* in the *centimeter–gram–second* system, the force that, acting on a mass of one gram for one second, produces a velocity of one centimeter per second.

dys-en-ter-y (dis'en-tėr-i), *n.* a disease of the bowels, marked by severe inflammation and mucous, bloody discharges.

dys-pep-sia (dis-pep'si-a; dis-pep'-sha), *n.* poor digestion; indigestion.—*n.* **dys-pep'tic.**

dys-tro-phy (dis'trō-fi), *n.* a wasting disease that robs the muscles of power until the victim is helpless.

E

E, e (ē), *n.* [*pl.* E's, e's], **1,** the fifth letter of the alphabet, following D; **2,** in music, the third tone of the major scale of C.

each (ēch), *pron.* every one of a number considered separately; as, *each* of the girls brings her lunch:—*adj.* every (one) of two or more taken separately; as, they study *each* lesson carefully.

ea-ger (ē'gėr), *adj.* full of keen desire; impatiently anxious to do or have something; as, he was *eager* to learn.—*adv.* **ea'ger-ly.**

ea-gle (ē'gl), *n.* **1,** a bird of prey, akin to the hawks and kites, noted for its strength, size, and keen vision; **2,** the ten-dollar gold piece of the U.S.; **3,** in *golf*, a score of two strokes less than par on a hole.

ea-glet (ē'glit), *n.* a young eagle.

¹**ear** (ēr), *n.* **1,** the entire organ of hearing; also, the outer, visible part of that organ; **2,** the sense of hearing; unusual ability to hear delicate sounds; as, she has an *ear* for music; **3,** attention; heed; as, give *ear* to what I say; **4,** anything like an external ear in shape.—*adj.* **ear'split'ting.**—*n.* **ear'-wax'.**

²**ear** (ēr), *n.* the spike of a cereal plant, containing the grains; as, an *ear* of corn or wheat.

ear-ache (ēr'āk'), *n.* a pain in the ear.

ear-drum (ēr'drum'), *n.* the middle ear; esp. the thin membrane between the outer and the middle ear.

ear-ful (ēr'fool'), *n. Colloq.,* **1,** news; **2,** gossip; **3,** a scolding.

earl (ûrl), *n.* a British nobleman next below a marquis.—*n.* **earl'dom.**

ear-ly (ûr'li), *adj.* [ear-li-er, ear-li-est], **1,** near the beginning; as, *early* spring; **2,** before the usual time; in good time; as, an *early* riser:—*adv.* **1,** at or near the beginning; as, he arrived *early* in the week; **2,** before the usual time; in good time; as, he goes to bed *early.*—*n.* **ear'li-ness.**

ear-mark (ēr'mark'), *n.* a slit in the ear of a sheep or cow, used to identify it; hence, any distinguishing mark.

ear-muffs (ēr'mufs'), *n.* coverings for the ears in cold weather.

earn (ûrn), *v.t.* **1,** to gain or get as just pay for one's labour, service, etc.; as, he *earns* $50 a week; **2,** to deserve for one's labour, service, etc.; as, he *earned* a rest.

ear-nest (ûr'nist), *adj.* **1,** zealous; fervent; as, an *earnest* reformer; *earnest* requests; **2,** important; grave; as, life is *earnest.*

earn-ings (ûr'ningz), *n.pl.* money received for services; wages.

ear-ring (ēr'ring'), *n.* an ear ornament.

ear-shot (ēr'shot'), *n.* the distance within which the voice can be heard; the range of hearing; as, to walk beyond *earshot.*

earth (ûrth), *n.* **1,** the planet on which we live, which revolves about the sun; **2,** the solid materials which compose it;

all (ôl), ôr; up, mūte, cûr, cōōl, book; oil, out; th, thin; *th*, the.

dry land; **3**, ground; soil; as, rich *earth*.

earth-en (ûr′then), *adj.* made of earth or baked clay; as, an *earthen* floor or jar.

earth-en-ware (ûr′thn-wâr′), *n.* vessels, pottery, etc., of baked clay (of coarser kinds).

earth-ling (ûrth′ling), *n.* an earth dweller; a sordid mortal.

earth-ly (ûrth′li), *adj.* **1**, pertaining to this world or to the present life; material; as, *earthly* possessions; **2**, possible; as, he has no *earthly* reason to go.—*n.* **earth′li-ness**.

earth-quake (ûrth′kwāk′), *n.* a sudden shaking, often violent, of the earth's surface, usually caused by a splitting and sliding of the rock foundation.

earth-ward (ûrth′wẽrd), *adv.* toward the earth. Also, **earth′wards**.

earth-work (ûrth′wûrk′), *n.* an embankment made wholly or largely of earth.

earth-worm (ûrth′wûrm′), *n.* a burrowing worm that lives in the ground; an angle-worm.

earth-y (ûr′thi), *adj.* **1**, made of, or like, soil; as, *earthy* colours; **2**, material; worldly; as, *earthy* desires.—*n.* **earth′i-ness**.

ear-wig (ēr′wig′), *n.* **1**, an insect, formerly supposed to creep into the ear; **2**, a kind of centipede.

ease (ēz), *n.* **1**, freedom from pain, labour, worry, trouble, etc.; as, *ease* of body and mind; **2**, naturalness; as, *ease* of manner:—*v.t.* [eased, eas-ing], **1**, to free from pain, anxiety, stress, etc.; give relief to; as, medicine to *ease* pain; good news *eases* the mind; **2**, to loosen anything tight; as, to *ease* a band; also, to move gently; as, to *ease* a stretcher into an ambulance.

EARWIG (enlarged) def. 1.

ea-sel (ē′zl), *n.* a frame for supporting an artist's canvas, a blackboard, or the like.

eas-i-ly (ēz′i-li), *adv.* without difficulty; readily.

east (ēst), *n.* **1**, that part of the heavens where the sun is seen to rise; **2**, one of the four points of the compass: opposite of *west;* **3**, the part of the earth lying toward the sunrise:—**East**, **1**, the Orient; the countries of Asia; **2**, in Canada, the territory comprising the Atlantic Provinces (N.B., N.S., P.E.I. and Newfoundland):—*adj.* coming from the direction of the east; as, an *east*

wind; in the direction of the east; as, the *east* side of the street:—*adv.* in the direction of the east; as, facing *east*.

east-bound (ēst′bound′), *adj.* going eastward.

East-er (ēs′tẽr), *n.* a festival of the Christian church to commemorate the resurrection of Jesus Christ, observed on a Sunday between March 21 and April 26.

east-er-ly (ēs′tẽr-li), *adj.* **1**, eastward; as, an *easterly* direction; **2**, from the direction of the east; as, an *easterly* wind:—*adv.* in the direction of the east.

east-ern (ēs′tẽrn), *adj.* **1**, grown or produced in the east; as, *eastern* potatoes; **2**, situated in the east; as, an *eastern* city:—**Eastern**, pertaining to the Orient; Oriental; as, *Eastern* religions.—*n.* **east′ern-er**.—*adj.* **east′ern-most**.

¹**east-ward** (ēst′wẽrd), *adj.* to or toward the east; as, steer an *eastward* course.

²**east-ward** (ēst′wẽrd) or **east-wards** (ēst′wẽrdz), *adv.* to or toward the east; as, we journeyed *eastward*.—*adv.* **east′ward-ly**.

eas-y (ēz′i), *adj.* [eas-i-er, eas-i-est], **1**, free from troubles or worry; as, an *easy* life; **2**, comfortable; restful; **3**, not difficult; **4**, moderate; gentle; as, an easy pace; **5**, not exacting; as, an *easy* teacher.—*n.* **eas′i-ness**.

eat (ēt), *v.t.* [*p.t.* ate (āt) or eat (et), *p.p.* eat-en (ēt′n), *p.pr.* eat-ing], **1** to chew and swallow, as food; **2**, to destroy by eating; as, moths *eat* woollen blankets; **3**, to corrode; waste or wear away; as, the river *ate* away the banks:—*v.i.* **1**, to take food; as, we always *eat* here; **2**, to make a way (into), as by eating; as, acids *eat* into metal; expenses *eat* into one's money.—*n.* **eat′er**.

eat-a-ble (ēt′a-bl), *adj.* fit to eat.—*n.pl.* food.

eaves (ēvz), *n.pl.* the lower edges of a roof which project a little from the building.

eaves-drop (ēvz′drop′), *v.i.* [eaves-dropped, eavesdrop-ping], to listen secretly to the private conversation of others.—*n.* **eaves′-drop′ping**.—*n.* **eaves′drop′per**.

ebb (eb), *n.* **1**, the going out of the tide; **2**, a decline; low state; as, his courage was at its lowest *ebb*:—**ebb—tide**, the receding tide; also, the point or time of lowest tide: opposite of *flood-tide:*—*v.i.* **1**, to flow back or return; as, the tide *ebbs* to the sea; **2**, to decline; decay; as, his fortune *ebbs*.

eb-on-y (eb′un-i), *n.* [*pl.* ebonies], a hard, heavy, durable, black-coloured

wood; also, the tree furnishing it:—
adj. made of, or like, ebony; as, the
ebony keys on a piano.

e-bul-lient (i-bul′yent), *adj.* over-
enthusiastic; as, an *ebullient* youth.—*n.*
e-bul′lience.

ec-cen-tric (ek-sen′trik), *adj.* 1, out of
centre; not revolving about its centre;
2, not having the same centre; as,
circles which partly overlap are *eccentric;* 3, not in the line of a perfect circle,
as the earth's course around the sun;
4, peculiar in manner or character; as,
an *eccentric* person:—*n.* 1, a circle or
sphere not having the same centre as
another circle or sphere with which it
partly coincides; 2, one who or that
which is odd or peculiar.—*n.* **ec′cen-
tric′i-ty** (ek′sen-tris′i-ti).

ec-cle-si-as-tic (i-klē′zi-as′tik), *adj.*
pertaining to the church and its organization or government:—*n.* a person in
holy orders; a clergyman; priest.—
adj. **ec-cle′-si-as′ti-cal**.

ech-e-lon (esh′e-lon; āsh′), *n.* an
arrangement of troops, ships, airplanes,
etc., in a steplike formation; as, the
troops marched in *echelon*.

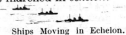

Ships Moving in Echelon.

ech-o (ek′ō), *n.* [*pl.* echoes], 1, the repetition of a sound caused by the throw-
ing back of sound waves; 2, any repetition or imitation:—*v.t.* [echoed,
echo-ing], to give back or repeat a
sound; as, the corridors *echoed* with
footsteps:—*v.t.* to repeat the sound of;
imitate.

e-cho-ic (e-kō′ik), *adj.* used of words
imitative in sound; as, *hiss, tinkle*, etc.

e-clair (ā-klâr′), *n.* a small, iced, oblong
pastry containing whipped cream or
custard.

e-clipse (i-klips′), *n.* 1, the total or
partial darkening of the light of the sun,
moon, or other heavenly body, caused
by its entering the shadow of another
body, or by having another body come
between it and the observer; 2, an
overshadowing; loss of brilliance or
glory:—*v.t.* [eclipsed, eclips-ing], 1, to
darken or conceal, as one body over-
shadows another; 2, to outshine; surpass; as, his success *eclipsed* his father's.

e-clip-tic (i-klip′tik), *n.* 1, the sun's
apparent annual orbit or path; 2, the
plane of the earth's orbit cutting the
sun's path and inclined 23° 27′ to the
celestial equator; 3, the orbit or path
of the earth as seen from the sun.

e-co-nom-ic (ē′ko-nom′ik; ek′o-
nom′ik), *adj.* relating to the production
and use of wealth; as, the *economic*

policy of a country:—**economics**, *n.pl.*
used as *sing.* the science dealing with
the production and use of wealth.—*n.*
e-con′o-mist (ē-kon′o-mist).

e-co-nom-i-cal (ē′ko-nom′i-kal; ek′o-
nom′i-kal), *adj.* prudent in the outlay
of money, use of goods, etc.; thrifty.—
adv. **e′co-nom′i-cal-ly**.

e-con-o-mize (ē-kon′o-mīz′), *v.t.*
[economized, economiz-ing], 1, to use
sparingly; 2, to use to the best advantage:—*v.t.* to be careful in spending
money; avoid extravagance; as, after
two months of unemployment, she
began to *economize*.

e-con-o-my (ē-kon′o-mi), *n.* [*pl.* econo-
mies], 1, freedom from waste in the use
of anything; thrift; 2, the regulation
and management of the resources of a
group.—*n.* **e-con′o-mist**.

ec-ru (ek′rōō; ā-krōō′; ā′krōō), *adj.*
pale brown; like unbleached linen in
colour:—*n.* the colour of unbleached
linen.

ec-sta-sy (ek′sta-si), *n.* [*pl.* ecstasies],
deep emotion; esp. rapturous joy.—
adj. **ec-stat′ic** (ek-stat′ik).

ec-u-men-i-cal (ek′ū-men′i-kal), *adj.*
world wide; universal; esp. of the
Christian church as a whole: an ecu-
menical council would represent the
entire Christian church.

ec-ze-ma (ek′zi-ma; ek′si-ma), *n.* a
skin-disease usually attended by the
formation of reddish scales and intense
itching.

ed-dy (ed′i), *n.* [*pl.* eddies], a current of
air, water, or the like, running opposite
to the main current, thus taking on a
circular motion; a small whirlpool:—
v.t. and *v.i.* [eddied, eddy-ing], to move
with a circular motion; whirl; as,
smoke *eddies* from a chimney.

edge (ej), *n.* 1, the thin, sharp, or cutting part of a knife or tool; 2, extreme
border; brink; margin; as, the *edge* of
a chair; the *edge* of a brook; 3, keenness; sharpness; as, her remarks had
an *edge*:—*v.t.* [edged, edg-ing], 1, to
make or put an edge upon; sharpen;
2, to furnish with a border; as, to *edge*
a handkerchief with lace; 3, to move
carefully, little by little; as, to *edge* a
car into traffic:—*v.i.* to move along
little by little; as, to *edge* along a cliff.
—*adj.* **edg′y**.

edge-ways (ej′wāz′) or **edge-wise**
(ej′-wīz′), *adv.* with the edge foremost;
edge first; also, sideways.

edg-ing (ej′ing), *n.* a narrow border, as
of lace, used as trimming.

ed-i-ble (ed′i-bl), *adj.* fit to be used for
food; as, the salmon is an *edible* fish.—
n. **ed′i-bil′i-ty**.

e-dict (ē′dikt), *n.* a public order issued by an official authority and having the force of a law; a decree.

ed-i-fice (ed′i-fis), *n.* a building, esp. one that is large and imposing.

ed-i-fy (ed′i-fī′), *v.t.* [edified, edify-ing], to benefit, esp. in religion or morals; as, good deeds *edify* us more than words.— *n.* **ed′i-fi-ca′tion.**

ed-it (ed′it), *v.t.* **1**, to revise and prepare (manuscript) for publication; **2**, to select, arrange, and compile for publication; as, to *edit* a collection of verse; **3**, to direct or be responsible for the work of preparing (a dictionary, encyclopaedia, or the like); **4**, to direct the policies of (a newspaper, magazine, or the like).

e-di-tion (i-dish′un), *n.* **1**, the published form of a literary work; **2**, the number of copies, all exactly alike, of a book, magazine, or newspaper, published at or near the same time.

ed-i-tor (ed′i-tėr), *n.* **1**, one who revises or prepares a literary work for publication; **2**, one who directs the policies of a newspaper, magazine, or the like.

ed-i-tor-i-al (ed′i-tōr′i-al), *adj.* connected with editors, or their work:—*n.* an article in a newspaper, magazine, etc., expressing the official opinions of the editors or publishers on some topic.

ed-u-cate (ed′ū-kāt′), *v.t.* [educat-ed, educat-ing], to develop and improve, esp. mentally, by teaching or training; instruct; as, to *educate* children.—*adj.* **ed′u-ca-ble; ed′u-ca′tive.**

ed-u-ca-tion (ed′ū-kā′shun), *n.* **1**, the training of the mental and moral powers, as by a system of study and discipline; also, the system itself; **2**, the knowledge and abilities gained by such training.—*adj.* **ed′u-ca′tion-al.**—*n.* **ed′u-ca′tion-al-ist.**—*n.* **ed′u-ca′tion-ist.**

e-duce (i-dūs), *v.t.* to draw out; elicit; as, to *educe* a boy's faults (in order to correct them) or his virtues (to develop them).—*adj.* **e-duc′i-ble.**

eel (ēl), *n.* a long, snakelike fish, smooth and slimy, used for food.

e'en (ēn), *adv.* a short form of ²*even*, meaning *exactly:*—*n.* a short form of ¹*even* or *evening.*

e'er (âr; ār), *adv.* a short form of *ever;* as, the sweetest song that *e'er* I heard.

ee-rie or **ee-ry** (ē′ri), *adj.* fearful; weird; as, an *eerie* shriek.—*adv.* **ee′ri-ly.**—*n.* **ee′ri-ness.**

ef-face (i-fās′), *v.t.* [effaced, effac-ing], **1**, to erase or blot out (writing); **2**, to wipe out or destroy, as if by erasing; as, time *effaces* sorrow.—*n.* **ef-face′-ment.**

ef-fect (i-fekt′), *v.t.* to accomplish; bring about; as, to *effect* a change in a plan:—*n.* **1**, result; consequence; **2**, impression; as, to do something for *effect;* **3**, **effects**, movable goods; personal property; as, household *effects.*

ef-fec-tive (i-fek′tiv), *adj.* **1**, having the power to produce a desired result; as, an *effective* censorship; **2**, impressive; striking; as, an *effective* picture; **3**, operative; enforced; as, after a law is passed, time may elapse before it becomes *effective.*—*adv.* **ef-fec′tive-ly.**

ef-fec-tu-al (i-fek′tū-al), *adj.* producing, or having the ability to produce, a desired result.—*adv.* **ef-fec′tu-al-ly.**

ef-fem-i-nate (i-fem′i-nit), *adj.* womanish; feeble; lacking in such manly qualities as endurance, strength, and courage.—*n.* **ef-fem′i-na-cy.**

ef-fer-vesce (ef′ėr-ves′), *v.i.* [effervesced, effervesc-ing], **1**, to bubble up; hiss; work, as does new wine; **2**, to be lively and gay.—*n.* **ef′fer-ves′cence.**—*adj.* **ef′fer-ves′cent.**

ef-fete (e-fēt′), *adj.* worn out; exhausted; spent; as, an *effete* government or civilization.

ef-fi-ca-cy (ef′i-ka-si), *n.* the power to produce desired results; as, the *efficacy* of a remedy.—*adj.* **ef′fi-ca′cious.**

ef-fi-cient (if-fish′ent), *adj.* capable; competent; able to get results; as, an *efficient* secretary.—*n.* **ef-fi′cien-cy.**

ef-fi-gy (ef′i-ji), *n.* [*pl.* effigies], a portrait, image, or other likeness of a person.

ef-flo-res-cence (ef′lo-res′ens), *n.* **1**, bloom or blossoming, as of flowers; **2**, coming to fullness, as of power, beauty, etc.—*adj.* **ef′flo-res′cent.**

ef-flu-ent (ef′loo-ent), *n.* that which flows out, as a stream from a lake, sewage from pipes, or lava from a volcano.

ef-flu-vium (e-floo′vi-um), *n.* a vapour or odour, esp. a disagreeable one, as from decaying matter.

ef-fort (ef′ėrt; ef′ôrt), *n.* the putting forth of exertion, physical or mental; as, it takes *effort* to lift a rock or work a problem; also, an attempt or endeavour; as, I shall make an *effort* to come.

ef-fron-ter-y (e-frun′tėr-i), *n.* [*pl.* effronteries], shameless impudence or audacity.

ef-ful-gence (i-ful′jens), *n.* brilliance, radiance or splendour, as of the sun.— *adj.* **ef-ful′gent.**

ef-fu-sion (i-fū′zhun), *n.* **1**, an act of pouring or gushing forth; as, an *effusion* of blood; **2**, an unrestrained outpouring of thought or feeling.—*adj.* **ef-fu′sive.**

eft (eft), *n.* a newt or small salamander.

egg (eg), *n.* an animal cell containing the germ of life, which may develop into a new individual; EFT ($\frac{1}{3}$) esp. the oval, rounded body produced by birds, insects, fish, and most reptiles, from which the young hatch out.—*n.* **egg'shell'**.

egg (eg), *v.t.* to urge or incite; as, they *egged* him on to try his luck.

egg-head (eg'hed'), *n.* *Slang,* an intellectual (term of contempt).

egg-nog (eg'nog'), *n.* a drink made of eggs beaten up with milk, sugar, spices, and wine or other liquor.

egg-plant (eg'plant'), *n.* a cultivated plant or its large, purplish, egg-shaped fruit, used for food.

eg-lan-tine (eg'lan-tīn'), *n.* a sweet-smelling wild rose with pink flowers and prickly stem; sweetbrier.

EGG-PLANT
Fruit and leaves.

e-go (ē'gō; e'gō), *n.* 1, the self; I; thus, his criticism bruised my *ego;* 2, *Colloq.* conceit; egotism.

e-go-ism (eg'ō-izm; ē'gō-izm), *n.* the belief that the aim of life is to perfect the self; hence, excessive interest in one's own concerns.—*n.* **e'go-ist.**—*adj.* **e'go-is'tic; e'go-is'ti-cal.**

e-go-tism (eg'o-tizm; ē'go-tizm), *n.* the habit of talking or writing too much about oneself; conceit.—*n.* **eg'o-tist.**—*adj.* **eg'o-tis'tic; eg'o-tis'ti-cal.**

e-gress (ē'gres), *n.* 1, a departure or going out; 2, a means of leaving; an exit.

e-gret (ē'grit; eg'rit), *n.* 1, a large wading bird of the heron family bearing, in the breeding season, long plumes drooping over the tail; 2, (usually *aigrette*), an egret's plume, often used as a head ornament.

eh (ā, e), *interj.* 1, an expression of surprise or doubt; 2, *Colloq.* an equivalent of "What did you say?"

EGRET ($\frac{1}{3}$), def. 1

ei-der (ī'dėr), *n.* a large salt-water duck of the northern regions, valued for its downy feathers: also called *eider-duck.*

ei-der-down (ī'dėr-down'), *n.* 1, the soft breast feathers of the eider-duck, used in pillows, coverlets, or the like; 2, a down-quilt.

eight (āt), *adj.* composed of one more than seven:—*n.* 1, the number consisting of seven plus one; 2, a sign representing eight units, as 8 or viii.

eight-een (ā'tēn), *adj.* composed of ten more than eight:—*n.* 1, the sum of seventeen and one; 2, a sign represensing eighteen units, as 18 or xviii.

eight-eenth (ā'tēnth'), *adj.* next after the 17th: the ordinal of *eighteen:*—*n.* one of the eighteen equal parts of anything.

eighth (ātth), *adj.* next after the seventh: the ordinal of *eight:*—*n.* one of the eight equal parts of anything.

eight-i-eth (ā'ti-eth), *adj.* next after the 79th: the ordinal of *eighty:*—*n.* one of the 80 equal parts of anything.

eight-y (ā'ti), *adj.* composed of one more than 79:—*n.* [*pl.* eighties], 1, the sum of 79 and one; 2, a sign representing 80 units, as 80 or lxxx.

eighty—one (ā'ti-wun'), *n.* and *adj.* the numbers *eighty—one* to *eighty—nine* are hyphenated.

ei-ther (ē'thėr; ī'thėr), *adj.* 1, one or the other of two; as, come *either* today or tomorrow; 2, each; as, along *either* bank:—*pron.* one of two; as, *either* of the two boys may go:—*conj.* in one of two cases: the correlative of *or;* as, *either* confess or die:—*adv.* also: used after a negative; as, he won't go, and she won't *either.*

e-jac-u-late (ē-jak'ū-lāt'), *v.t.* to utter suddenly or vehemently; exclaim; 2, to eject suddenly; discharge; emit.—*n.* **e-jac'u-la'tion.**

e-ject (ē-jekt'), *v.t.* to expel; dismiss (from office); evict or turn out; as, to *eject* a tenant.—*n.* **e-jec'tor.**—*n.* **e-jec'tion.**

eke (ēk), *v.t.* [eked, ek-ing], to piece out or add to, little by little; esp. to manage to make (a living) by some means or another; as, to *eke* out a living by writing.

el (el), *n.* a wing at right angles to a main building. Also, **ell.**

e-lab-o-rate (i-lab'o-rāt'), *v.t.* [elaborat-ed, elaborat-ing], to work out with great care and detail:—*adj.* (i-lab'o-rit), worked out in detail; highly finished; as, an *elaborate* stage-setting; complicated; as, an *elaborate* plan.—*adv.* **e-lab'o-rate-ly.**—*n.* **e-lab'o-ra'tion.**

e-land (ē'land), *n.* a large South

African antelope. Both the buck and the doe have twisted horns.

e-lapse (i-laps′), *v.i.* [elapsed, elapsing], to go by; pass, as hours, days, or years.

e-las-tic (i-las′tik), *adj.* 1, having the power of springing back to its original form after being stretched or pressed together, as rubber; 2, able to rebound from a state of depression; as, an *elastic* disposition; 3, flexible; easily changed; adaptable:—*n.* 1, a narrow woven strip or band made in part of india rubber; 2, a rubber band.—*n.* **e-las′tic′i-ty** (i-las′tis′i-ti; ē′las-tis′i-ti).

e-late (i-lāt′), *v.t.* [elat-ed, elat-ing], to make happy or proud; as, he was *elated* by the applause.—*adj.* **e-lat′ed.**—*n.* **e-la′tion.**

el-bow (el′bō), *n.* 1, the joint between the forearm and the upper arm; also, the outer part or curve of this joint; 2, a bend or angle like that of an elbow when the arm is bent; as, the *elbow* of a pipe:—*v.t.* to jostle or push (a person), as with the elbows:—*v.i.* to push one's way rudely.

¹**eld-er** (el′dèr), *adj.* [a *comp.* of *old*], older; superior in rank or station; senior; as, an *elder* brother; the *elder* statesmen:—*n.* 1, one who is older; 2, a leader or ruler of a tribe or family; 3, in certain Protestant churches, esp. the Presbyterian, a governing officer.

²**el-der** (el′dèr), *n.* a shrub with flattened clusters of white or pink flowers, and black, reddish, or purple berries.

el-der-ber-ry (el′dèr-ber′i), *n.* [*pl.* elderberries], the black, reddish, or purple fruit of the elder; also, the bush.

eld-er-ly (el′dèr-li), *adj.* somewhat old; beyond middle age.

eld-est (el′dest), *adj.* [a *superl.* of *old*], oldest; first-born; as, the *eldest* son inherits the throne.

e-lect (i-lekt′), *v.t.* 1, to choose; select; 2, to choose or select by vote; as, to *elect* a president:—*adj.* chosen for office but not yet in charge; as, the president *elect*.

e-lec-tion (i-lek′shun), *n.* the act of choosing or selecting; esp. the selection, by vote, of a person or persons for office.

e-lec-tive (i-lek′tiv), *adj.* 1, chosen by election, as an officer; filled by election, as an office; 2, open to choice; not compulsory; as, an *elective* course of study:—*n.* a course of study which a student may choose, as distinguished from one that is compulsory.

e-lec-tor (i-lek′tèr), *n.* 1, one lawfully qualified to vote; 2, in the U.S., a member of a body of men chosen every four years by the people of the individual States, to elect a president and vice-president.

e-lec-tric (i-lek′trik) or **e-lec-tri-cal** (i-lek′tri-kal), *adj.* 1, pertaining to or connected with electricity, its production, transmission, or use; as, an *electric* battery; *electric* wires; an *electric* iron; *electric* light; *electric* trains; 2, figuratively, as if charged with electricity; thrilling; exciting.

e-lec-tri-cian (ē′lek-trish′an; el′ek-trish′an), *n.* one who makes, repairs, or installs electrical appliances and equipment.

e-lec-tric-i-ty (ē′lek-tris′i-ti; el′ek-tris′i-ti), *n.* an invisible force in nature which causes the lightning's flash, the electric spark, and many other phenomena. When artificially produced by man, it is used as an important source of power, to produce heat, light, and motion.

e-lec-tri-fy (i-lek′tri-fī), *v.t.* [electrified, electrify-ing], 1, to charge with electricity; 2, to equip for the use of electric power, as a railway; 3, to thrill; startle; as, the acrobat's feat *electrified* the spectators.

e-lec-tro-cute (i-lek′tro-kūt), *v.t.* [electrocut-ed, electrocut-ing], 1, to put (a condemned criminal) to death by electricity; 2, to kill accidentally by an electric shock.—*n.* **e-lec′tro-cu′tion.**

e-lec-trode (i-lek′trōd), *n.* either pole of a battery, vacuum tube, electrolytic cell, etc.

e-lec-trol-y-sis (i-lek′trol′i-sis), *n.* the breaking down of a chemical compound in solution by passing an electric current through it.

e-lec-tro-lyte (i-lek′trō-līt′), *n.* a compound capable of being broken down by an electric current.—*adj.* **e-lec′tro-lyt′ic.**

e-lec-tro-mag-net (i-lek′trō-mag′nit), *n.* a piece of soft iron made into a magnet by passing an electric current through a coil of wire wrapped around it.—*adj.* **e-lec′tro-mag-net′ic.**

e-lec-tron (i-lek′tron), *n.* a very small, light, negatively charged particle, or component, of an atom: opposite of *proton*, a positively charged atom component.

e-lec-tron-ics (i-lek′tron′iks), *n.* the science that deals with electrons and their use in vacuum tubes for radio, television, radar, and equipment for purifying air, guiding missiles, computing, sorting, etc.

e-lec-tro-plate (i-lek′trō-plāt′), *v.t.* to cover with a thin coat of nickel, gold, chrome, etc., by means of electrolysis. —*n.* silver-plated articles.

e-lec-tro-scope (i-lek′trō-skōp′), *n.* an instrument for detecting small charges of electricity, and showing whether they are positive or negative.

e-lec-tro-ther-a-py (i-lek′trō-ther′a-pi), *n.* the use of electricity in treating disease.

el-e-gant (el′i-gant), *adj.* 1, marked by refinement, grace, and good taste, as dress or manners; 2, *Colloq.* excellent; very fine.—*adv.* **el′e-gant-ly.**—*n.* **el′e-gance.**

el-e-gy (el′i-ji), *n.* [*pl.* elegies], a poem lamenting the dead; a funeral poem.—*adj.* and *n.* **e-le-gi′ac** (el′e-jī′ak).

el-e-ment (el′i-ment), *n.* 1, in chemistry, a substance which cannot be broken down into simpler substances, such as gold, hydrogen, or oxygen; 2, a simple part of a larger whole; an ingredient; 3, a first or main principle of a subject which must be learned before the subject can be understood; 4, a condition or place particularly suited to a person or thing; as, she is in her *element* on the stage:—**the elements,** the forces of nature.—*adj.* **el′e-men′tal.**

el-e-men-ta-ry (el′i-men′ta-ri), *adj.* pertaining to first principles or beginnings; introductory; as, an *elementary* education.

el-e-phant (el′i-fant), *n.* the largest of living animals, native to India and Africa, with thick, wrinkled hide, a long, flexible snout, or trunk, and two long, curved ivory tusks.

el-e-vate (el′i-vāt′), *v.t.* [elevat-ed, elevat-ing], 1, to raise to a higher level; lift; as, to *elevate* a glass before drinking; 2, to raise in rank, as a lieutenant to a captaincy; 3, to raise or improve mentally or morally; as, study *elevates* the mind; 4, to make (the voice) louder or higher in pitch.—*adj.* **el′e-vat′ed.**

el-e-va-tion (el′i-vā′shun), *n.* 1, the act of raising or state of being raised; 2, a raised place; 3, height; often, height above sea level.

el-e-va-tor (el′i-vā′tėr), *n.* 1, a hoisting machine or lift; a cage that can be raised or lowered in a shaft, to carry people or goods from one level to another; 2, a continuous belt or chain conveyer with buckets for raising sand, earth, etc.; 3, a warehouse for the storage of grain.

e-lev-en (i-lev′en), *adj.* composed of one more than ten:—*n.* 1, the number consisting of ten plus one; 2, a sign representing eleven units, as 11 or xi; 3, a football or cricket team.

e-lev-enth (i-lev′enth), *adj.* next after the tenth: the ordinal of *eleven:*—*n.* one of the eleven equal parts of anything.

elf (elf), *n.* [*pl.* elves (elvz)], 1, in fairytales, a tiny goblin, dwarf, or fairy, sometimes mischievous, sometimes helpful, to man; 2, a small creature.—*adj.* **elf′in.**—*adj.* **elf′ish.**

e-lic-it (i-lis′it), *v.t.* to draw out; extract; as, to *elicit* a reply.

e-lide (i-līd′), *v.t.* to omit (as shown by an apostrophe) a letter, vowel, or syllable; as, *o′er, ′tis, destin′d.*—*n.* **e-li′sion** (-lizh′).

el-i-gi-ble (el′i-ji-bl), *adj.* fit to be chosen or elected; meeting given requirements; as, a disabled soldier is *eligible* for a pension.—*adv.* **el′i-gi-bly.** —*n.* **el′i-gi-bil′i-ty.**

e-lim-i-nate (i-lim′i-nāt′), *v.t.* [eliminat-ed, eliminat-ing], 1, to get rid of; expel; 2, to set aside; leave out of consideration.—*n.* **e-lim′i-na′tion.**

é-lite (ā-lēt′), *n.* the best or choicest members, as of a society or a profession.

e-lix-ir (i-lik′sėr), *n.* 1, a substance formerly believed capable of changing baser metals into gold; also, a liquid formerly believed capable of prolonging life; 2, hence, a remedy for all diseases or evils.

elk (elk), *n.* 1, the largest native deer of Europe and Asia, with spreading antlers; 2, in North America, the wapiti (see **wapiti**).

¹ell (el), *n.* an old measure of length, used chiefly for cloth, varying from 27 to 48 inches.

²ell (el), *n.* an addition to a house at right angles to the main structure.

el-lipse (i-lips′), *n.* a closed curve that differs from an oval in that it has symmetrical ends.—*adj.* **el-lip′tic; el-lip′ti-cal.**

el-lip-sis (i-lip′sis), *n.* [*pl.* ellipses (-sēz)], the omitting of a word or words that are understood; as, "*(he)* who steals my purse steals trash."

el-lip-ti-cal (i-lip′ti-kal), *adj.* 1, shaped like an ellipse; 2, shortened by the omission of a word or words needed for a complete construction, as an *elliptical* sentence (one in which even the subject and predicate may be omitted).

elm (elm), *n.* 1, a tall, graceful shade tree; 2, the hard, tough wood of this tree.

el-o-cu-tion (el′o-kū′shun), *n.* the art which teaches the proper use of voice and gesture in public speaking or reading.—*n.* **el'o-cu'tion-ist.**

e-lon-gate (ē'lông-gāt'; i-lông'gāt), *v.t.* and *v.i.* [elongat-ed, elongat-ing], to lengthen.—*n.* **e'lon-ga'tion.**

e-lope (i-lōp'), *v.i.* [eloped, elop-ing], to run away with a lover.—*n.* **e-lope'ment.**

el-o-quence (el'o-kwens), *n.* the art of speaking so as to move one's hearers; forceful and vivid use of language.—*adj.* **el'o-quent.**

else (els), *adv.* otherwise; besides; as, eat, *else* you will starve; where *else* shall I hunt?—*adj.* implying someone different or additional; as, somebody *else* has the book.

else-where (els'hwâr'), *adv.* in, at, or to, another place; somewhere else.

e-lu-ci-date (i-lū'si-dāt'), *v.t.* explain; make clear; as, please *elucidate* this verse of Browning's.

e-lude (i-lūd'), *v.t.* [elud-ed, elud-ing], to escape or evade through cleverness; as, to *elude* an enemy.

e-lu-sive (i-lū'siv), *adj.* tending to slip away or escape; as, an *elusive* criminal; also, hard to get hold of or to understand; as, an *elusive* fact.—*adv.* **e-lu'-sive-ly.**—*adj.* **e-lu'so-ry.**—*n.* **e-lu'sive-ness.**

em (em), *n.* in *printing*, a square of any size of type used as a unit of measure, esp. *em* pica, which is about ⅙ of an inch.

e-ma-ci-ate (i-mā'shi-āt'), *v.t.* [emaciat-ed, emaciat-ing], to cause to waste away; to make thin; as, he was *emaciated* by hunger and fatigue.—*adj.* **e-ma'ci-at'ed.**

em-a-nate (em'a-nāt'), *v.i.* [emanat-ed, emanat-ing], to flow out, issue, or proceed from a source, as light from the sun.—*n.* **em'a-na'tion.**

e-man-ci-pate (i-man'si-pāt'), *v.t.* [emancipat-ed, emancipat-ing], to set free from bondage or control; liberate. —*n.* **e-man'ci-pa'tion.**—*n.* **e-man'ci-pa'tor.**

e-mas-cu-late (i-mas'kū-lāt'), *v.t.* **1,** to castrate; hence, **2,** to weaken, esp. a book or play; as, this film has been *emasculated* by the censor.

em-balm (em-bäm'), *v.t.* **1,** to treat (a dead body) to preserve it from decay; **2,** to hold in memory.—*n.* **em-balm'er.**

em-bank-ment (em-bangk'ment), *n.* a structure of earth, stones, etc., built to prevent water from overflowing, to carry a roadway, or for some similar purpose.

▪ar-go (em-bär'gō), *n.* [*pl.* em- an order of government ▪ns of commerce to use its ▪lar order forbidding

transportation of certain freight:—*v.t.* to lay an embargo on.

em-bark (em-bärk'), *v.i.* **1,** to go on board a vessel; **2,** to engage in any affair; as, to *embark* in business.—*n.* **em'bar-ka'tion.**

em-bar-rass (em-bar'as), *v.t.* **1,** to disconcert; fluster; as, her manners *embarrassed* her mother; **2,** to worry; hinder; as, *embarrassed* by debt.—*n.* **em-bar'rass-ment.**

em-bas-sy (em'bas-si), *n.* [*pl.* embassies], **1,** the position of an ambassador also, his official residence; **2,** an ambassador and his assistants.

em-bed (em-bed'), *v.t.* [embed-ded, embed-ding], to lay in, or as in, a bed set firmly in surrounding matter; as to *embed* a thing in clay. Also, **im-bed'**

em-bel-lish (em-bel'ish), *v.t.* **1,** to beautify or ornament; as, to *embellish* a cloak with fur; **2,** to add fanciful details to (a story).—*n.* **em-bel'lish-ment.**

em-ber (em'bėr), *n.* a live coal or small piece of wood, smouldering in ashes.

em-bez-zle (em-bez'l), *v.t.* [embez-zled, embez-zling], to steal (funds entrusted to one's care); as, to *embezzle* a trust fund.—*n.* **em-bez'zler.**—*n.* **em-bez'zle-ment.**

em-bit-ter (em-bit'ėr), *v.t.* to make bitter or resentful; as, his scolding *embittered* her because it was unjust.

em-bla-zon (em-blā'zn), *v.t.* **1,** to decorate brightly; as, on the flag a maple leaf was *emblazoned;* **2,** to spread widely; praise; extol.

em-blem (em'blum), *n.* a symbol or representation of an idea; as, the olive-branch is an *emblem* of peace.—*adj.* **em'blem-at'ic; em'blem-at'i-cal.**

em-bod-y (em-bod'i), *v.t.* [embodied, embody-ing], **1,** to represent in bodily form; **2,** to express in a definite form; as, to *embody* thought in words; **3,** to collect into a united whole.—*n.* **em-bod'i-ment.**

em-bold-en (em-bōl'dn), *v.t.* make bolder; encourage; as, thus *emboldened,* I spoke out.

em-boss (em-bôs'), *v.t.* to ornament with raised work; also, to raise above a surface; as, the name was *embossed* on the card.

em-brace (em-brās'), *v.t.* [embraced, embrac-ing], **1,** to hold in the arms with affection; **2,** to adopt; turn to; as, the heathen *embraced* Christianity; **3,** to take up; enter on; as, to *embrace* a profession; **4,** to include; as, biology *embraces* botany and zoology:—*n.* the act of clasping in the arms; a hug.

em-bra-sure (em-brā′zhẻr), *n.* **1**, an opening in a wall or fort from which to fire guns; **2**, the space made by the slanting off of the wall at the sides of a door or window.

em-broi-der (em-broi′dẻr), *v.t.* **1**, to decorate or make beautiful with needle-work; **2**, to exaggerate, as a story:— *v.i.* to do decorative needlework; as, she *embroiders* beautifully.—*n.* **embroi′der-y.**

em-broil (em-broil′), *v.t.* to involve in strife; entangle; as, he became *embroiled* in the pipeline debate.

em-bry-o (em′bri-ō), *n.* [*pl.* embryos], **1**, the young of an animal in the earliest stages of its growth before birth or hatching; **2**, an undeveloped plant, contained in a seed; **3**, the first or undeveloped state of anything.—*adj.* **em′bry-on′ic** (em′bri-on′ik).

e-mend (ē-mend′), *v.t.* to alter or correct; as, to *emend* a text.—*n.* **e′men-da′tion.**

em-er-ald (em′ẻr-ald), *n.* **1**, a precious stone of a clear, deep-green colour; **2**, the colour of this stone.

e-merge (i-mûrj′), *v.i.* [emerged, emerg-ing], to rise up; come forth; appear.

e-mer-gen-cy (i-mûr′jen-si), *n.* [*pl.* emergencies], a sudden or unexpected happening or situation, demanding prompt action.

e-mer-i-tus (i-mer′i-tus), *adj.* retired from service with honorary title.

em-er-y (em′ẻr-i), *n.* a very hard, dark mineral substance used, when pow-dered, for grinding or polishing.

e-met-ic (i-met′ik), *adj.* causing vomit-ing:—*n.* a medicine that causes vomit-ing.

em-i-grant (em′i-grant), *n.* one who leaves his own country to settle in another:—*adj.* moving from one coun-try to settle in another; as, *emigrant* labourers.

em-i-grate (em′i-grāt′), *v.i.* [emigrat-ed, emigrat-ing], to leave one's own country to settle in another; as, many of Canada's early settlers *emigrated* from England.

é-mi-gré (ā′mē′grā′), *n.* an emigrant, esp. one who flees from political per-secution.

em-i-nence (em′i-nens), *n.* **1**, that which is high; an elevation; **2**, a high station or standing; as, to attain *eminence* as a lawyer.

em-i-nent (em′i-nent), *adj.* high in office, rank, or reputation; distin-guished; as, an *eminent* scholar.—*adv.* **em′i-nent-ly.**

e-mir (e-mēr′), *n.* **1**, an Arabian prince or chieftain; **2**, a title of certain Turkish officials; **3**, a title given to persons descended from Mohammed.

em-is-sar-y (em′i-sẻr-i), *n.* [*pl.* emis-saries], a person or agent sent on a mission, esp. of a secret nature.

e-mit (i-mit′), *v.t.* [emit-ted, emit-ting], to send forth; as, a stove *emits* heat.— *n.* **e-mis′sion.**

e-mol-u-ment (e-mol′ū-ment), *n.* pay for work; salary; fees; profit; as, the lawyer accepted a very small *emolument* for his services.

e-mo-tion (i-mō′shun), *n.* **1**, mental excitement; strong feeling; **2**, an in-tense feeling of love, hate, joy, awe, grief, etc.

e-mo-tion-al (i-mō′shun-al), *adj.* **1**, excitable; easily agitated; as, she has an *emotional* nature; **2**, tending to stir the feelings.—*adv.* **e-mo′tion-al-ly.**

em-pan-el (em-pan′el), *v.t.* Same as *impanel.*

em-pa-thy (em′pa-thi), *n.* the project-ing of oneself imaginatively into another's personality in order to under-stand him better.

em-per-or (em′pẻr-ẻr), *n.* the supreme ruler of an empire.

em-pha-sis (em′fa-sis), *n.* [*pl.* em-phases (em′fa-sēz)], **1**, a particular stress of the voice on a word or words in reading or speaking; **2**, importance; stress; as, to put too much *emphasis* on football.

em-pha-size (em′fa-sīz′), *v.t.* [empha-sized, emphasiz-ing], **1**, to pronounce clearly and positively; stress; as, he *emphasized* each word; **2**, to call atten-tion to; as, he *emphasized* the fine points of the picture.

em-phat-ic (em-fat′ik), *adj.* **1**, expres-sive; forceful; as, an *emphatic* gesture; **2**, positive; striking.—*adv.* **em-phat′i-cal-ly.**

em-pire (em′pīr), *n.* **1**, a group of nations united under one ruler; as, the Roman *Empire;* **2**, the country or territory ruled over by an emperor; as, the Japanese *Empire;* **3**, supreme power; imperial rule.

em-place-ment (em-plās′ment), *n.* assigning to a position or location.

em-ploy (em-ploi′), *v.t.* **1**, to make use of the services of; give occupation to; hire; as, he *employed* ten men; **2**, to make use of; as, he *employed* his know-ledge of Spanish in business:—*n.* the state of serving an employer for wages.

em-ploy-ee (em-ploi′ē; em′ploi-ē′), *n.* one who works for another for wages.

em-ploy-er (em-ploi′ẻr), *n.* a person who engages others in paid service.

em-ploy-ment (em-ploi′ment), *n.* 1, the state of being employed; 2, business; work.

em-pow-er (em-pou′ėr), *v.t.* to give authority to; make able.

em-press (em′pris), *n.* a woman ruler of an empire; the wife or widow of an emperor.

emp-ty (emp′ti), *adj.* [emp-ti-er, emp-ti-est], 1, containing nothing; as, an *empty* box; 2, vague; with no possibility of fulfilment; as, *empty* dreams; 3, having no force or sense; as, *empty* words; 4, vacant, as an unoccupied house:—*v.t.* [emptied, empty-ing], 1, to remove the contents from; make vacant; 2, to pour out; as, to *empty* the milk from a bottle:—*v.i.* 1, to become empty; 2, to discharge itself; as, the river *empties* into the ocean.—*n.* **emp′ti-ness.**

e-mu ē′mū), *n.* a large, three-toed Australian bird resembling the ostrich.

em-u-late (em′ū-lāt′), *v.t.* [emulat-ed, emulat-ing], to strive to equal or excel; imitate with the hope of equalling or excelling; as, to *emulate* great men.—*n.* **em′u-la′tion.**

e-mul-sion (i-mul′-shun), *n.* a liquid mixture in which a fatty substance is present in small globules which will not dissolve.—*v.t.* **e-mul′si-fy.**

en (en), *n.* 1, the letter *n* as pronounced; 2, a prefix (meaning in, into, on, etc.); as, *en*snare, *en*grave; a verbal intensive as in *en*danger; 3, in *printing*, half the width of an em.

e-na-ble (i-nā′bl), *v.t.* [ena-bled, ena-bling], to make able; as, the aeroplane *enables* us to travel faster than by train.

en-act (en-akt′), *v.t.* 1, to make into law; as, to *enact* a bill; 2, to act the part of; as, he *enacted* the hero.—*n.* **en-act′ment.**

e-nam-el (i-nam′el), *n.* 1, a hard, glassy substance used in coating the surface of metals, glass, or porcelain for ornamentation or protection; 2, any hard, glossy covering like enamel; 3, the hard, white outer coating of the teeth:—*v.t.* [enamelled, enamel-ling], 1, to cover or decorate with enamel; 2, to apply a glossy surface to.

en-am-our (en-am′ėr), *v.t.* to inspire with love; charm.

en-camp (en-kamp′), *v.t.* to settle in camp:—*v.i.* to make camp; as, let's *encamp* here.—*n.* **en-camp′ment.**

en-case (en-kās′), *v.t.* [encased, encasing], to enclose in a box; surround with anything. Also spelled **in-case′.**

en-chant (en-chȧnt′), *v.t.* 1, to charm by magic spells; 2, to fill with delight.

—*n.* **en-chant′er.**—*n.* **en-chant′ment.** —*n.* **en-chant′ress.**

en-cir-cle (en-sûr′kl), *v.t.* [encir-cled, encir-cling], 1, to surround; 2, to make a circle around; go around.—*n.* **encir′cle-ment.**

en-close (en-klōz′), *v.t.* enclosed, en-clos-ing], 1, to insert; as, he *enclosed* the cheque in a letter; 2, to surround with a barrier. Also, **in-close′.**—*n.* **en-clo′sure.**

en-co-mi-um (en-kō′mi-um), *n.* high praise; eulogy; as, he lavished *en-comiums* upon the artist.

en-com-pass (en-kum′pas), *v.t.* to surround; encircle; as, enemies *encom-passed* us.

en-core (äng-kōr′), *interj.* once more! again!—*n.* (äng′kōr), a repetition, as of a song, in response to a call by an audience:—*v.t.* (äng-kōr′; äng′kōr), [encored, encor-ing], to call for a repetition of (any part of a performance), by applause; also, to call upon (a person) for an encore.

en-coun-ter (en-koun′tėr), *v.t.* and *v.i.* 1, to meet in conflict; 2, to meet unexpectedly:—*n.* 1, a sudden or accidental meeting; 2, a conflict.

en-cour-age (en-kûr′ij), *v.t.* [encouraged, encourag-ing], 1, to help; 2, to inspire with courage or hope.—*n.* **encour′age-ment.**

en-croach (en-krōch′), *v.i.* 1, to intrude upon another's rights or property; trespass; 2, to go beyond normal limits.—*n.* **en-croach′ment.**

en-crust (en-krust′), *v.t.* 1, to cover with, or as with, a crust; to coat; as, barnacles *encrusted* the hull; 2, to overlay, as with mosaics. Also spelled **in-crust′.**

en-cum-ber (en-kum′bėr), *v.i.* 1, to impede or hinder; as, her long skirts *encumbered* her; 2, to burden, as with debt. Also, **in-cum′ber.**—*n.* **en-cum′-brance.**

en-cy-clo-pae-di-a or **en-cy-clo-pe-di-a** (en-sī′klo-pē′di-a), *n.* a work in one or more volumes, containing information on all branches of knowledge, with the articles arranged in alphabetical order. —*adj.* **en-cy′clo-pae′dic; en-cy′clo-pe′dic.**

end (end), *n.* 1, the extreme limit or terminal point of anything; as, the *end* of a railroad; 2, death; 3, that which is left over; as, odds and *ends;* 4, purpose; goal; as, work to some good *end;* 5, conclusion; as, bring the discussion to an *end;* 6, in football, a player stationed at the end of the line: —*v.t.* 1, to finish; 2, to destroy; put to death:—*v.i.* **1**, to come to an end; as, the road *ends* here; **2**, to result; as, the argument *ended* in a fight; **3**, to die.

en-dan-ger (en-dān′jẽr), *v.t.* to expose to danger; imperil; as, you *endanger* your health when you drink impure water.

en-dear (en-dēr′), *v.t.* to make beloved; make (a person) dear or precious to another; as, his thoughtfulness *endeared* him to us.—*adv.* **en-dear′ing-ly.**

en-dear-ment (en-dēr′ment), *n.* an act or utterance of affection; a caress.

en-deav-our (en-dev′ẽr), *v.i.* to strive; attempt; as, the team *endeavoured* to win the game:—*n.* an effort or attempt.

en-dem-ic (en-dem′ik), *adj.* peculiar to a nation, group, or locality; as, *endemic* plants or diseases; thus goitre is endemic in areas where iodine is lacking in the diet.

end-ing (en′ding), *n.* end; conclusion.

en-dive (en′div; en′dīv), *n.* a plant with curling leaves, used as a salad.

end-less (end′lis), *adj.* **1**, lasting for ever; without an end; **2**, having no ends; continuous; as, an *endless* chain.—*adv.* **end′-less-ly.**

en-do-crine (en′dō-krīn′; krin), *adj.* relating to such glands as the thyroid, adrenal, and pituitary, or their secretions which regulate bodily functions.

en-dorse (en-dôrs′), *v.t.* [endorsed, endors-ing], **1**, to approve; as, Parliament *endorsed* the plan; **2**, to write one's name on the back of, as a cheque. Also, **in-dorse′.**—*n.* **en-dorse′ment.**

en-dow (en-dou′), *v.t.* **1**, to bestow a permanent fund or source of income upon; as, to *endow* a college; **2**, to equip or furnish; as, Nature *endowed* man with reason.

en-dow-ment (en-dou′ment), *n.* **1**, property or a sum of money given to an institution, or devoted permanently to any cause; **2**, the act of making such a settlement; **3**, any talent that a person possesses by nature.

en-due (en-dū′), *v.t.* [endued, endu-ing], **1**, to clothe; **2**, to endow; **3**, furnish (a person) with qualities.

en-dure (en-dūr′), *v.t.* [endured, enduring], to bear up under; bear with patience:—*v.i.* **1**, to remain firm, as under suffering; **2**, to remain in existence; last.—*n.* **en-dur′ance.**—*adj.* **en-dur′a-ble.**

end-ways (end′wāz′), *adv.* **1**, on end; **2**, with the end forward; **3**, lengthwise.

end-wise (end′wīz′), *adv.* endways.

en-e-ma (en′i-ma; en-ē′ma), *n.* the injection of a fluid or gas into the rectum, esp. to produce bowel movement.

en-e-my (en′i-mi), *n.* [*pl.* enemies], **1**, one hostile to another; **2**, anything that harms another person or thing; as, laziness is an *enemy* of success.

en-er-get-ic (en′ẽr-jet′ik), *adj.* full of life; active; vigorous; as, she is an *energetic* worker.—*adv.* **en′er-get′i-cal-ly.**

en-er-gy (en′ẽr-ji), *n.* [*pl.* energies], capacities for work; power; force; vigour; as, he devoted all his *energy* to the task.

en-er-vate (en′ẽr-vāt′), *v.t.* [enervated, enervat-ing], to deprive of nerve, force, or vigour; weaken.—*n.* **en′er-va′tion.**

en-fee-ble (en-fē′bl), *v.t.* to weaken.—*n.* **en-fee′ble-ment.**

en-fold (en-fōld′), *v.t.* to wrap up; infold. Also spelled **in-fold′.**

en-force (en-fōrs′), *v.t.* [enforced. enforc-ing], **1**, to carry out; as, to *enforce* a law; **2**, to compel; impose; as, to *enforce* silence.—*adj.* **en-force′a-ble.**—*n.* **en-force′ment.**

en-fran-chise (en-fran′chīz), *v.t.* [enfranchised, enfranchis-ing], **1**, to admit to the right to vote; **2**, to free.—*n.* **en-fran′chise-ment** (en-fran′chiz-ment).

en-gage (en-gāj′), *v.t.* [engaged, engag-ing], **1**, to pledge or bind by oath or contract; **2**, to betroth; **3**, to win and hold; as, to *engage* the attention; **4**, in machinery, to come into gear with; **5**, to secure for aid or employment; as, to *engage* a workman; **6**, to encounter, as in battle; **7**, to occupy the time or attention of; as, to *engage* someone in conversation:—*v.i.* **1**, to promise, or assume an obligation; as, he *engaged* to pay his father's debts; **2**, to occupy oneself; as, to *engage* in business; **3**, to enter a conflict; **4**, in machinery, interlock.

en-gaged (en-gājd′), *adj.* **1**, busy or occupied; **2**, betrothed.

en-gage-ment (en-gāj′ment), *n.* **1**, betrothal; **2**, occupation; **3**, an appointment; obligation; **4**, in machinery, state of being in gear; **5**, a battle.

en-gag-ing (en-gāj′ing), *adj.* winning; pleasing; as, an *engaging* manner.

en-gen-der (en-jen′dẽr), *v.t.* to beget; cause; as, poverty often *engenders* crime.

en-gine (en′jin), *n.* **1**, a machine by which power is used to do work; **2**, an apparatus for converting some form of energy, as heat, into mechanical power; esp. a locomotive; **3**, a tool; an instrument.

en-gi-neer (en'ji-nēr'), *n*. **1,** one who designs and constructs machines, bridges, etc.; as, an electrical *engineer;* **2,** one who has charge of and drives an engine or locomotive; **3,** one of an army corps which constructs bridges, roads, etc.:—*v.t.* **1,** to plan or direct; as, he *engineered* the campaign; **2,** to plan and execute the construction of (a road, canal, etc.)

en-gi-neer-ing (en'ji-nēr'ing), *n.* the science and practice of designing and building machinery, roads, bridges, etc., and of developing natural resources, as waterpower, minerals, etc.

Eng-lish (ing'glish), *n.* **1,** the people of England; **2,** the language, chiefly spoken in the British Commonwealth and U.S.:—Also used as *adj.* —*n.* **Eng'lish-man; Eng'lish-wom'an.**

en-graft (en-gráft'), *v.t.* to graft; insert (a shoot) in a tree. Also, **en-graft'.**

en-grave (en-grāv'), *v.t.* [*p.t.* engraved, *p.p.* engraved or engrav-en, *p.pr.* en-grav-ing]. **1,** to cut or carve; as, to *engrave* words on a monument; **2,** to cut (letters, figures, designs, etc.) on stone, wood, or a metal plate, as for printing; **3,** to impress deeply; as, the words were *engraved* upon his mind.—*n.* **en-grav'er.**

en-grav-ing (en-grāv'ing), *n.* **1,** the process or art of cutting designs into metal, stone, or hardwood with a tool or with acid; **2,** a design so cut; **3,** a print made from an engraved plate.

en-gross (en-grōs'), *v.t.* to absorb; occupy wholly; as, the book *engrossed* her.

en-gulf (en-gulf'), *v.t.* to swallow up, as in a gulf; as, sorrow *engulfed* him.

en-hance (en-háns'), *v.t.* [enhanced, en-hanc-ing], to increase in attractiveness or value; add to; as, a good education will *enhance* your earning power.

e-nig-ma (i-nig'ma), *n.* a riddle; a re-mark, act, or person not easily under-stood.—*adj.* **en'ig-mat'ic** (en'ig-mat'-ik; ē'nig-mat'ik); **en'ig-mat'i-cal.**

en-jamb(e)-ment (än'zhänb'män'), *n.* in *versification,* the running on of a thought from one couplet or line into the next without a pause at the end of the line.

en-join (en-join'), *v.t.* **1,** to direct with authority; command; as, the teacher *enjoined* the students to silence; **2,** to prohibit or restrain by judicial order.

en-joy (en-joi'), *v.t.* **1,** to take delight in; as, we *enjoyed* the book; **2,** to have the use or possession of; as, I *enjoy* keen eyesight.—*adj.* **en-joy'a-ble.**—*n.* **en-joy'-ment.**

en-kin-dle (en-kin'dl), *v.t.* to stir up as a revolt; excite; arouse, as the passions.

en-large (en-lärj'), *v.t.* [enlarged, en larg-ing], to make larger; increase:— *v.i.* **1,** to become larger; **2,** to speak or write fully; as, he *enlarged* upon his theme.—*n.* **en-large'ment.**

en-light-en (en-līt'n), *v.t.* to furnish with increased knowledge; instruct.— *n.* **en-light'en-ment.**—*n.* **en-light'en-er**

en-list (en-list'), *v.t.* **1,** to enrol (a per son) for military service; **2,** to win ove for a cause; as, to *enlist* support for the Red Cross:—*v.i.* to enrol for militar service, or in any cause.—*n.* **en-list' ment.**

en-liv-en (en-līv'en), *v.t.* to make lively active, or gay; to put life into.

en-mi-ty (en'mi-ti), *n.* [*pl.* enmities] ill will; hatred; hostility.

en-no-ble (e-nō'bl; en-nō'bl), *v.t.* [en nobled, enno-bling], **1,** to dignify exalt; **2,** to raise to the nobility.

en-nui (än'nwē), *n.* boredom from lac of something to do; tedium.

e-nor-mi-ty (i-nôr'mi-ti), *n.* [*pl.* enor mities], **1,** the state of being outrageou or monstrous; as, the *enormity* of hi offence; **2,** a grave offence; **3,** hug size; vastness.

e-nor-mous (i-nôr'mus), *adj.* immense of great size or number.—*adv.* **e-nor' mous-ly.**—*n.* **e-nor'mous-ness.**

e-nough (i-nuf'), *adj.* sufficient:—*n.* sufficient amount:—*adv.* in a sufficien degree; sufficiently:—*interj.* stop!

en-plane (en-plān'), *v.i.* to board a airplane; as, he *enplaned* for Germany

en-quire (en-kwīr'), *v.t.* Same *inquire.*

en-rage (en-rāj'), *v.t.* [enraged, enrag ing], to make intensely angry; provok to fury.

en-rap-ture (en-rap'tūr), *v.t.* [enrap tured, enraptur-ing], to delight; charn enchant.

en-rich (en-rich'), *v.t.* **1,** to increase th wealth of; **2,** to make fertile, as soi **3,** to improve, as the mind; **4,** to ador —*n.* **en-rich'ment.**

en-rol or **en-roll** (en-rōl'), *v.t.* [er rolled, enrol-ling], to insert or write dow in a register; enlist; as, to *enrol* me for the army.—*n.* **en-rol'ment; er roll'ment.**

en route (än rōōt'), on the way; as, e *route* to Paris.

en-sconce (en-skons'), *v.t.* [ensconcec ensconc-ing], **1,** to settle comfortabl **2,** to establish in a secret place.

en-sem-ble (än-som′bl; än′som′bl; äṅ′-säṅbl′/), *n.* **1,** all the parts of anything considered as a whole; **2,** a costume of two or more pieces, worn together.

en-shrine (en-shrīn′), *v.t.* [enshrined, enshrin-ing], to place upon an altar or in a holy place; keep sacred.

en-shroud (en-shroud′), *v.t.* to cover completely; hide; as, fog *enshrouds* the city.

en-sign (en′sīn; en′sin), *n.* **1,** a flag, esp. a national standard; **2,** a badge of office, rank, etc.; **3,** (en′sin), in the U.S. navy, a commissioned officer of the lowest rank.

en-si-lage (en′si-lij), *n.* green fodder (usually corn) preserved in a silo.—*v.t.*

en-sile′ (en-sīl′; en′sil).

en-slave (en-slāv′), *v.t.* [enslaved, en-slav-ing], to bring into bondage; deprive of freedom.—*n.* **en-slave′ment.**

en-snare (en-snâr′), *v.t.* [ensnared, en-snar-ing], to trap; snare.

en-sue (en-sū′), *v.i.* [ensued, ensu-ing], to follow; result; come afterward; as, the ship ran aground, and panic *ensued.*

en-sure (en-shoor′), *v.t.* [ensured, en-sur-ing], to make sure; guarantee; as, it is difficult to *ensure* a happy outcome.

en-tail (en-tāl′), *v.t.* **1,** to leave (property), as money or land, to an heir or line of heirs, so that none of them can give or will it away; **2,** to necessitate; require; demand; as, success *entails* hard work.—*n.* **en-tail′ment.**

en-tan-gle (en-tang′gl), *v.t.* [entan-gled, entan-gling], **1,** to twist into a snarl; **2,** to ensnare; as, he was *entangled* in a plot; **3,** to perplex; bewilder.—*n.* **en-tan′gle-ment.**

en-ter (en′tẽr), *v.t.* **1,** to go or come into; as, he *entered* the house; **2,** to set down in writing; as, the clerk *entered* the account in the journal; **3,** to join; as, to *enter* a club; **4,** to go into or begin, as a business; **5,** to enrol as a competitor; as, he *entered* his horse in the race; **6,** to gain admission for; as, to *enter* a pupil in a school:—*v.i.* **1,** to go or come in; **2,** to take part; as, to *enter* into a discussion; **3,** to make a beginning, as into business; **4,** to come upon the stage, as an actor.—*n.* **en′trant.**

en-ter-prise (en′tẽr-prīz), *n.* **1,** an undertaking of importance or danger; as, a daring *enterprise;* **2,** readiness to undertake such projects.

en-ter-pris-ing (en′tẽr-prīz′ing), *adj.* energetic; active; progressive.

en-ter-tain (en′tẽr-tān′), *v.t.* **1,** to receive and treat hospitably; **2,** to amuse; as, she *entertained* the children

with stories; **3,** to harbour, as a grudge; **4,** to take into consideration; as, to *entertain* a proposal:—*v.i.* to receive guests.

en-ter-tain-ing (en′tẽr-tān′ing), *adj.* amusing; diverting; pleasing.

en-ter-tain-ment (en′tẽr-tān′ment), *n.* **1,** that which interests or amuses; **2,** provision for the wants of guests.

en-thral or **en-thrall** (en-thrôl′), *v.t.* [enthralled, enthral-ling], **1,** to enslave; **2,** to charm.—*n.* **en-thral′ment;** **en-thrall′-ment.**

en-throne (en-thrōn′), *v.t.* [enthroned, enthron-ing], to place on a seat of power; endow with royal power and authority.

en-thu-si-asm (en-thū′zi-azm), *n.* keen interest or feeling for something; as, the boys took up football with *enthusiasm.*

en-thu-si-ast (enthū′zi-ast), *n.* one who is filled with enthusiasm.

en-thu-si-as-tic (en-thū′zi-as′tik), *adj.* full of zeal.—*adv.* **en-thu′si-as′ti-cal-ly.**

en-tice (en-tīs′), *v.t.* [enticed, entic-ing], to allure; tempt; lead on by arousing hope or desire.

en-tire (en-tīr′), *adj.* **1,** with no part omitted; whole; unbroken; **2,** unqualified; as, my *entire* support.—*n.* **en-tire′ty.**

en-tire-ly (en-tīr′li), *adv.* **1,** wholly; **2,** solely; as, it is *entirely* his fault.

en-ti-tle (en-tī′tl), *v.t.* [enti-tled, enti-tling], **1,** to give a name to; **2,** to give a right to; as, this card *entitles* you to a seat.

en-ti-ty (en′ti-ti), *n.* being; essence; anything thought of as having real existence apart from its qualities and relations; thus, matter, space, time, and force are *entities.*

en-tomb (en-tōōm′), *v.t.* to place in a grave or tomb; bury.—*n.* **en-tomb′-ment.**

en-to-mol-o-gy (en′to-mol′o-ji), *n.* [*pl.* entomologies], that branch of zoology which treats of insects.—*adj.* **en′to-mo-log′i-cal.**—*n.* **en′to-mol′o-gist.**

en-tou-rage (äṅ′tōō′räzh′), *n.* **1,** surroundings; **2,** retinue; attendants; as, the queen's *entourage* accompanied her aboard the ship.

en-trails (en′trālz), *n.pl.* the internal parts of animals; intestines.

en-train (en-trān′), *v.i.* to board a train.

[1]**en-trance** (en′trans), *n.* **1,** the act of entering; **2,** a door, passage, etc., through which one goes into a place; **3,**

permission to enter; as, he gained *entrance* at once.

²en-trance (en-trȧns′), *v.t.* [entranced, entranc-ing], to throw into a trance; delight; enrapture.—*adv.* **en-tranc′ing-ly.**

en-trap (en-trap′), *v.t.* [entrapped, entrap-ping], to catch in a trap; entangle.

en-treat (en-trēt′), *v.t.* to ask earnestly; beg or beseech.—*n.* **en-treat′y.**

en-trée (än′trā; än′trā′), *n.* 1, entrance; privilege of entering; 2, a dish served between the chief courses of a meal.

en-trench (en-trench′) or **in-trench** (in-trench′), *v.t.* to surround or protect with trenches:—*v.i.* to trespass.—*n.* **en-trench′ ment; in-trench′ment.**

en-trust (en-trust′) or **in-trust** (in-trust′), *v.t.* 1, to give (something) in trust to someone; as, to *entrust* funds to a bank; 2, to confer a trust upon; as, to *entrust* a bank with funds.

en-try (en′tri), *n.* [*pl.* entries], 1, the act of entering; entrance; 2, a place through which one enters; 3, the act of writing an item in a list or record; also, the item.

en-twine (en-twīn′), *v.t.* [entwined, entwin-ing], to wind around; twist together.

e-nu-mer-ate (i-nū′mėr-āt), *v.t.* [enumerat-ed, enumerat-ing], to name one by one; count.—*n.* **e-nu′mer-a′tion.**—*n.* **e-nu′mer-a′tor.**

enun-ci-ate (i-nun′si-āt; i-nun′shi-āt), *v.t.* [enunciat-ed, enunciat-ing], 1, to declare; state; 2, to utter:—*v.i.* to pronounce; as, a public speaker should *enunciate* clearly.—*n.* **e-nun′ci-a′tion.**

en-ure (en-ūr′). *v.* Same as **inure.**

en-vel-op (en-vel′up), *v.t.* to cover; wrap up or in.—*n.* **en-vel′op-ment.**

en-ve-lope (en′ve-lōp′; on′ve-lōp′), *n.* 1, a paper wrapper for enclosing letters sent by post, messenger, etc.; 2, any covering.

en-vi-a-ble (en′vi-a-bl), *adj.* arousing a wish for possession; desirable; as, an *enviable* record.—*adv.* **en′vi-a-bly.**

en-vi-ous (en′vi-us), *adj.* feeling, or characterized by, a desire to possess something belonging to another.—*adv.* **en′vi-ous-ly.**

en-vi-ron (en-vī′run), *v.t.* to surround or enclose; hem in:—**environs,** *n.pl.* places near a town or city; suburbs; any surrounding region.

en-vi-ron-ment (en-vī′run-ment), *n.* the surroundings of one's life; outside conditions which influence growth or character.

en-vi-rons (en-vī′runz; en′), *n.* surroundings; suburbs; vicinity; as, the *environs* of Toronto.—*v.t.* **en-vi′ron** (en-vī′run), inclose; as, a ring of factories *environs* the city.

en-vis-age (en-viz′ij), *v.t.* 1, to face, confront; as, you must *envisage* the results; 2, see in the mind's eye; visualize; as, he *envisaged* a new house.

en-voy (en′voi), *n.* a government agent, next in rank to an ambassador; also, a person sent on a special mission.

en-vy (en′vi), *v.t.* [envied, envy-ing], 1, to wish for (what is another's); as, I *envy* his health; 2, to begrudge the excellence or prosperity of (another):—*n.* [*pl.* envies], 1, ill will or jealousy felt because of the excellence or good fortune of another; 2, a person or object exciting such feeling; as, she is the *envy* of her friends.

en-zyme (en′zīm), *n.* a complex organic substance that promotes chemical, or catalytic, changes in other substances; thus, pepsin is a digestive *enzyme.*

e-on (ē′on), *n.* Same as **aeon.**

ep-au-let or **ep-au-lette** (ep′o-let), *n.* a shoulder ornament on a military or naval uniform, usually signifying rank.

EPAULET

e-phem-er-al (i-fem′ėr-al), *adj.* existing only for a day, as a May fly; short-lived; transitory.

ep-ic (ep′ik), *adj.* 1, grand; noble, heroic; 2, narrative: said of a poem:—*n.* a long narrative poem of heroic deeds written in a lofty style.

ep-i-cure (ep′i-kūr′), *n.* a person devoted to pleasure; also, one fond of the delicacies of the table.—*adj.* **ep′i-cu-re′an.**

ep-i-dem-ic (ep′i-dem′ik), *adj.* attacking many at the same time; as, measles is an *epidemic* disease:—*n.* 1, a general attack of a disease throughout a locality; 2, a widespread occurrence of anything; as, an *epidemic* of cheap books.

ep-i-der-mis (ep′i-dûr′mis), *n.* 1, the outer layer of an animal's skin; 2, the outer coating of the leaf or bark of a plant.

ep-i-glot-tis (ep′i-glot′is), *n.* the leaf shaped lid of cartilage at the back of the mouth, which covers the upper part of the windpipe during swallowing.

ep-i-gram (ep′i-gram), *n.* a verse or short poem with a witty point; a wise thought given briefly, as "To err is human, to forgive, divine."—*adj.* **ep′i-gram-mat′ic.**

ep-i-lep-sy (ep'i-lep'si), *n.* a chronic nervous disease, often attended by convulsions and loss of consciousness.—*adj.* and *n.* **ep'i-lep'tic.**

ep-i-logue or **ep-i-log** (ep'i-log'), *n.* 1, a poem or speech at the end of a play; 2, an addition to a novel, play, etc., giving further comment or interpretation.

E-piph-a-ny (i-pif'a-ni), *n.* a Christian festival (January 6) celebrating the showing forth of Christ to the Gentiles in the persons of the three wise men.

e-pis-co-pal (i-pis'ko-pal), *adj.* 1, pertaining to bishops; as, *episcopal* robes; 2, governed by a bishop:—**Episcopal**, pertaining to the Protestant Episcopal Church.—*n.* **e-pis'co-pa-cy; E-pis'co-pa'li-an.**

ep-i-sode (ep'i-sōd), *n.* an incident within a series of events, connected with but not essential to the series; as, a comic *episode* in a tragic plot; an *episode* of the war.

e-pis-tle (i-pis'l), *n.* a formal letter; a written communication:—**Epistle**, any one of the letters written by the apostles, and recorded in the New Testament.

ep-i-taph (ep'i-tàf), *n.* an inscription or writing on a tomb.

ep-i-thet (ep'i-thet), *n.* an adjective expressing some characteristic quality, as "empty" in "empty fame"; also, a descriptive title, as "Fat" in "Charles the Fat."

e-pit-o-me (i-pit'o-mi), *n.* [*pl.* epitomes], a brief statement of the contents of a literary work; a summary; synopsis.—*v.t.* **e-pit'o-mize'.**

ep-och (ē'pok; ep'ok), *n.* 1, an event or a point of time which marks the beginning of a new period in history; 2, a period of unusual events.—*adj.* **ep'och-al** (ep'ok-al).

eq-ua-ble (ek'wa-bl; ē'kwa-bl), *adj.* 1, steady; free from change; as, an *equable* climate; 2, even and serene in temperament; tranquil.—*adv.* **eq'ua-bly.**

e-qual (ē'kwal), *adj.* 1, the same in number, size, or value; the same as; 2, of the same rank or degree; evenly balanced; 3, just; fair; as, an *equal* contest; 4, strong or brave enough; as, *equal* to a task:—*n.* a person or thing of the same rank or value as another:—*v.t.* [equalled, equal-ling], to have the same size, rank, value, etc., with; match in some way; as, to *equal* another in height.—*adv.* **e'qual-ly.**

e-qual-i-ty (ē-kwol'i-ti; ē-kwôl'i-ti), *n.* [*pl.* equalities], sameness in size, rank, value etc.

e-qual-ize (ē'kwal-īz), *v.t.* [equalized, equaliz-ing], to make the same in size, rank, value, etc.; make equal.—*n.* **e'qual-i-za'tion; e'qual-iz'er.**

e-qua-nim-i-ty (ē'kwa-nim'i-ti; ek'wa-nim'i-ti), *n.* evenness of temper or mind; calmness; serenity.

e-quate (ē-kwāt'), *v.t.* [equat-ed, equating], to make equal or treat as equal.

e-qua-tion (ē-kwā'zhun; ē-kwā'shun), *n.* in mathematics, a statement that two things are equal, as in "$2 + 2 = 4$".

e-qua-tor (i-kwā'tėr), *n.* 1, an imaginary line around the earth, equally distant from the North and South Poles; 2, a similar line dividing the sphere of the sky in two, called the *celestial equator.*

e-qua-tor-i-al (ē'kwa-tōr'i-al), *adj.* pertaining to, or situated near, the equator; as, *equatorial* islands; rice is an *equatorial* grain.

eq-uer-ry (ek'wėr-i), *n.* [*pl.* equerries], an officer in charge of the horses of a prince or nobleman.

e-ques-tri-an (i-kwes'tri-an), *adj.* 1, pertaining to horses or horsemanship; 2, mounted; also, showing a mounted figure; as, an *equestrian* statue:—*n.* a skilled horseman; also, a trick rider on horseback.—*n.fem.* **e-ques'tri-enne'** (i-kwes'tri-en').

e-qui-dis-tant (ē'kwi-dis'tant), *adj.* equally distant.

e-qui-lat-er-al (ē'kwi-lat'ėr-al), *adj.* having all sides equal.—*adv.* **e'qui-lat'er-al-ly.**

e-qui-lib-ri-um (ē'kwi-lib'ri-um), *n.* 1, the state of balance between opposing forces, actions, or weights; 2, even mental balance between opposing influences; hence, neutrality.

e-quine (ē'kwīn), *adj.* pertaining to a horse:—*n.* a horse.

e-qui-nox (ē'kwi-noks; ek'wi-noks), *n.* either of two times when the sun crosses the equator of the sky, making the days and nights of equal length, the *vernal equinox* occurring about March 21, and the *autumnal equinox* about September 22.—*adj.* **e'qŭi-noc'-tial** (ē'kwi-nok'shal).

e-quip (i-kwip'), *v.t.* [equipped, equipping], to fit out for any undertaking; as, to *equip* scouts with tents for camp. —*n.* **e-quip'ment.**

eq-ui-page (ek'wi-pij), *n.* 1, the arms and outfit of an army, vessel, traveller, etc.; 2, the carriage, , horses, and liveried servants of a person of rank.

eq-ui-se-tum (ek′wi-sē′tum), *n*. the horsetail, a widespread flowerless genus of plant found in Canada and U.S., having rough, jointed, hollow stems; the scouring rush.

eq-ui-ta-ble (ek′wi-ta-bl), *adj*. impartial; just; fair; honest; as, an *equitable* decision.—*adv.* **eq′ui-ta-bly.**

eq-ui-ty (ek′wi-ti), *n*. [*pl.* equities], **1,** justice; fair dealing; **2,** the value of a property beyond the total amount owed on it; as, I have now an equity of $7000 in my house and lot.

Horsetail, sterile (A) and fertile (B) sporophytes, showing leaves (a) and spore-producing cones of strobiles (b): C, enlarged view of strobile.

e-quiv-a-lent (i-kwiv′a-lent), *adj*. equal in value; the same in meaning or effect; as, cheating is *equivalent* to lying:—*n.* a thing of the same value, weight, power, effect, etc. —*n.* **e-quiv′a-lence.**

e-quiv-o-cal (i-kwiv′o kal), *adj*. of a doubtful or double meaning; uncertain; as, an *equivocal* reply.

e-quiv-o-cate (i-kwiv′o-kāt′), *v.i.* [equivocat-ed, equivocat-ing], to speak with double meaning; evade the truth by a statement which can be understood in more than one way; lie.—*n.* **e-quiv′o-ca′tion.**

e-ra (ē′ra), *n*. **1,** a period of time starting from a given point; as, the Christian *era;* **2,** a period of time with notable characteristics; as, the machine *era;* **3,** one of the five great divisions of geologic time.

e-rad-i-cate (i-rad′i-kāt′), *v.t.* [eradi-cat-ed, eradicat-ing], to destroy completely; get rid of; wipe out; as, to *eradicate* crime.—*n.* **e-rad′-i-ca′tion.**

e-rase (i-rās′), *v.t.* [erased, eras-ing], to rub or scrape out, esp. something written.—*n.* **e-ra′sure** (i-rā′zhẽr).

e-ras-er (i-rās′ẽr), *n*. a device for rubbing out written marks, often made of rubber.

ere (âr), *Poetic, conj.* **1,** before; as, "the joys that came *ere* I was old"; **2,** rather than; as, I will fight *ere* I will submit:—*prep.* before; as, *ere* daylight.

e-rect (i-rekt′), *v.t.* **1,** to construct; build, as a house; **2,** to raise upright, as a flagpole; **3,** to set up or establish; as, to *erect* a new government.—*adj.* **1,** upright; as, an *erect* posture; **2,** lifted up; as, to hold a banner *erect*.

e-rec-tion (i-rek′shun), *n*. **1,** the art of

raising a structure, such as a wall or building; also, the state of being constructed; **2,** the structure raised.

erg (ẽrg), *n*. in the metric system, the unit of work or energy; namely, the work expended in overcoming a resistance of one dyne acting through a distance of one centimetre.

er-mine (ûr′min), *n*. **1,** a weasel-like animal found in all northern countries, and valued for its fur, esp. the white winter coat with black tail tip; **2,** the fur itself; **3,** the dignity or office of a judge, the state robe of European judges being lined with ermine.

e-rode (i-rōd′), *v.t.* [erod-ed, erod-ing], to wear away; as, running water *erodes* rocks:—*v.i.* to wear away gradually, as do rocks.

e-ro-sion (i-rō′zhun), *n*. the act of wearing away; gradual destruction or eating away: used esp. of the action of water on rock or soil; as, forests hinder soil *erosion*.

e-rot-ic (i-rot′ik), *adj*. amorous; relating to sexual love; as, an *erotic* poem.—*n.* **e-rot′i-cism.**

err (ûr), *v.i.* **1,** to go astray morally; to sin; **2,** to be mistaken.

er-rand (er′and), *n*. **1,** a trip made to attend to some special business; **2,** the object for which the trip is made.

er-rant (er′ant), *adj*. **1,** roving; wandering in search of adventure; as, a knight-*errant;* **2,** mistaken; not standard; as, *errant* beliefs.—*n.* **er′ran-cy.**

er-ra-ta (e-rā′ta), *n.pl.* a list of a printer's or writer's errors with corrections.

er-rat-ic (e-rat′ik), *adj*. **1,** having no fixed course; wandering; **2,** irregular; eccentric; queer.—*adv.* **er-rat′i-cal-ly.**

er-ro-ne-ous (e-rō′ni-us), *adj*. incorrect; mistaken; wrong; as, an *erroneous* belief.—*adv.* **er-rō′ne-ous-ly.**

er-ror (er′ẽr), *n*. **1,** false belief; as, superstition leads to *error;* **2,** a mistake; an inaccuracy; as, an *error* in a sum; **3,** a sin; as, to repent of an *error*.

erst-while (ûrst′hwīl′; ûrst′hwīl′), *adv. Archaic,* formerly; long ago.

er-u-dite (er′oo-dīt; er′ū-dīt), *adj*. learned; scholarly.—*adv.* **er′u-dite′ly.**

er-u-di-tion (er′oo-dish′un; er′ū-dish′un), *n*. knowledge obtained by study; book learning; scholarship.

e-rupt (i-rupt′), *v.i.* to burst forth, as a volcano:—*v.t.* to hurl out; as, a volcano *erupts* lava.

e-rup-tion (i-rup′shun), *n*. **1,** a bursting out or forth, as of a volcano, war, or disease; **2,** that which bursts forth, as water from a geyser; **3,** a rash on the skin.—*adj.* **e-rup/tive.**

er-y-sip-e-las (er/i-sip/i-las), *n.* an acute bacterial infection of the skin or mucous membrane, marked by fever, intense local redness, swelling and severe itching and burning; St. Anthony's fire.

es-ca-la-tor (es/ka-lā/ter), *n.* a moving stairway.

es-ca-pade (es/ka-pād/; es/ka-pād/), *n.* a breaking loose from restraint; a foolish or reckless adventure.

e-scape (i-skāp/), *v.t.* [escaped, escaping], **1,** to flee from; avoid; as, to *escape* a task; **2,** to be unaffected by; as, he *escaped* the disease; **3,** to issue from unawares; as, a sigh *escaped* him; **4,** to elude the notice, memory, or understanding of; as, his name *escapes* me; **5,** to get away from; be saved from; as, to *escape* danger:—*v.i.* **1,** to get out of danger; avoid harm or capture; **2,** to break loose from confinement; as, to *escape* from prison; **3,** to flow out; as, gas *escapes* from a pipe; **4,** to slip away; as, to *escape* from memory:—*n.* **1,** a successful flight, as from prison, **2,** deliverance from harm or danger; as, a narrow *escape;* **3,** an outlet for water, steam, etc.; **4,** leakage; outflow.

es-cap-ism (es-kāp/izm), *n.* the effort, often unconscious, to escape harsh reality, responsibility, or routine by means of entertainment, fantasy, alcohol, etc., or even by reading, art, etc., pursued for this reason.

es-carp-ment (es-kärp/ment), *n.* a long cliff; steep slope; sharp ridge; as, the Niagara *escarpment.*

es-chew (es-chōō/; es-chū/), *v.t.* to shun; abstain from; avoid; as, to *eschew* bad company; *eschew* strong drink.

es-cort (es/kôrt), *n.* **1,** a body of men, ships, aeroplanes, automobiles, etc., accompanying a person, another ship, aeroplane, etc., or goods, for protection or honour; **2,** a person accompanying another as a guard or guide, or to show honour; esp. a gentleman accompanying a lady in public:—*v.t.* (es-kôrt/), to accompany as escort.

es-crow (es/krō; es-krō/), *n.* an agreement, such as a bond or deed, placed in the care of a third party, not to be delivered (or in effect) until certain conditions are met.

es-cutch-eon (es-kuch/un), *n.* the surface, usually shield-shaped, on which a coat of arms is displayed.

Es-ki-mo (es/ki-mō/), *n.* [*pl.* -mos, -mo], one of a race living above the

Arctic Circle,—short, muscular, with broad, flat, light-brown faces.—**Eskimo dog,** a powerful, half-tamed dog, with long gray hair, used by the Eskimos for drawing sleds.

e-soph-a-gus (i-sof/a-gus), *n.* the gullet, or tube through which food and drink pass from the throat to the stomach. The preferred spelling is **oe-soph/a-gus.**

es-pe-cial (es-pesh/al), *adj.* **1,** particular; chief; special; **2,** exceptional of its kind; as, an *especial* friend.—*adv.* **es-pe/cial-ly.**

es-pi-o-nage (es/pi-o-nij; es/pi-ō-näzh/; es-pī/o-nij), *n.* **1,** the secret watching of another; spying; **2,** employment of secret agents or spies; esp, systematic spying on an enemy in time of war.

es-pla-nade (es/pla-nād/), *n.* a public walk or roadway, often along a waterfront: a promenade.

es-pouse (es-pouz/), *v.t.* [espoused, espous-ing], **1,** to give in marriage; **2,** to wed; **3,** to become a follower of; as, to *espouse* a cause.—*n.* **es-pous/al.**

es-prit de corps (es-prē/de kôr/), *n.* group spirit, marked by strong morale, enthusiasm, devotion, and resolve to maintain the group's honour: esp. used of an organization, as a school, team, etc.

es-py (es-pī/), *v.t.* [espied, espy-ing], **1,** to see at a distance; catch sight of; as, to *espy* a ship on the horizon; **2,** to discover or detect (something hard to find).

es-quire (es-kwir/), *n.* **1,** originally, the armour-bearer or attendant of a knight; **2,** a member of the English gentry ranking below a knight:—**Esquire,** a title of courtesy, written after a man's name.

es-say (es/ā), *n.* **1,** a literary composition on some special subject, usually of moderate length and expressing the personal views of the author; **2,** (often e-sā/), an attempt; experiment:—*v.t.* (e-sā/), to try.—*n.* **es/say-ist.**

es-sence (es/ens), *n.* **1,** the extract of a substance dissolved in alcohol; as, *essence* of peppermint; **2,** a perfume; **3,** that which is the real character of a thing; as, the *essence* of politeness is kindness.

es-sen-tial (e-sen/shal), *adj.* **1,** pertaining to the real character of a thing; as, the *essential* element of a situation; **2,** necessary; indispensable; as, water is *essential* to life:—*n.* that which is a necessary element; as, the three R's are the *essentials* of education.—*adv.* **es-sen/tial-ly.**

all (ôl), ôr; up, mūte, cûr, cōōl, book; oil, out; th, thin; *th,* the.

es-tab-lish (es-tab'lish), *v.t.* **1,** to fix firmly; settle; as, he has *established* a reputation for efficiency; **2,** to prove legally; to prove beyond doubt; as, to *establish* a claim; **3,** to found, as an institution.—*n.* **es-tab'lish-ment.**

es-tate (es-tāt'), *n.* **1,** condition of life; rank, position, or quality; a man of low *estate;* **2,** an order or class of people, politically or socially distinct, as nobles or clergy; **3,** property in land or buildings; esp., large possessions; **4,** in *law,* property in general.

es-teem (es-tēm'), *v.t.* **1,** to value highly; prize; **2,** to think; consider; as, to *esteem* it a privilege:—*n.* a favourable opinion; respect; regard.

es-ter (es'tėr), *n.* a compound formed by the chemical reaction between an acid and an alcohol; a fragrant salt used in flavouring extracts, fruit essences, perfumes, etc.

es-thet-ic (es-thet'ik), *adj.* Same as aesthetic.

es-ti-ma-ble (es'ti-ma-bl), *adj.* **1,** worthy of respect or honour; deserving esteem; **2,** that may be estimated; calculable; as, *estimable* damages.— *adv.* **es'ti-ma-bly.**

es-ti-mate (es'ti-māt'), *v.t.* [estimat-ed, estimat-ing], **1,** to form an opinion of; as, to *estimate* a man's character; **2,** to reckon approximately; calculate (the amount, cost, or value); as, to *estimate* the cost of a job:—*n.* (es'ti-mit), **1,** a valuation of qualities; opinion; **2,** a judgment, esp. of the amount, cost, or value of anything.—*n.* **es'ti-ma'tion.**

es-ti-vate, æs-ti-vate (es'ti-vāt'), *v.i.* [estivat-ed, estivat-ing], to spend the summer in a dormant condition, as certain snails: opposite of *hibernate.*— *n.* **es'ti-va'tion, æs'ti-va'tion,** *Bot.* the arrangement of floral parts in a bud.

es-trange (es'trānj'), *v.t.* [estranged, estrang-ing], to turn from affection to indifference or dislike; to *estrange* friends by neglect.—*n.* **es-trange'ment.**

es-tu-ar-y (es'tū-ėr-i), *n.*[*pl.* estuaries], the wide mouth of a tidal river.

et cet-er-a (et set'ėr-a), and others of the same kind; abbreviated to *etc.*

etch (ech), *v.t.* to engrave with a special needle a design on metal, glass, etc., through a wax coating that protects the rest of the plate from acids that eat out the lines:—*v.i.* to practise the art of etching.—*n.* **etch'er.**

etch-ing (ech'ing), *n.* **1,** a picture or design printed from an etched plate; also, the plate itself; **2,** the art or process of making etched plates.

e-ter-nal (i-tûr'nal), *adj.* **1,** without

beginning or end; everlasting; **2,** never ceasing; as, *eternal* chatter:—the Eternal, God.—*adv.* **e-ter'nal-ly.**

e-ter-ni-ty (i-tûr'ni-ti), *n.* [*pl.* eterni-ties], **1,** time without beginning or end; time everlasting; **2,** indefinite time; time that seems endless; as, to wait an *eternity;* **3,** life after death.

eth-ane (eth'ān), *n.* a methane gas used as a refrigerant.

e-ther (ē'thėr), *n.* **1,** the upper, purer air; clear sky; **2,** a liquid anaesthetic, the vapour of which, when inhaled, produces unconsciousness and deadens pain; **3,** in *physics,* a substance formerly believed by many to fill all space, and to carry rays of light.

e-the-re-al (i-thē'ri-al), *adj.* **1,** light; exquisite; airy; delicate: *ethereal* music; **2,** heavenly; not earthly.

eth-i-cal (eth'i-kal), *adj.* **1,** pertaining to questions of right and wrong; **2,** morally right or good; as, *ethical* behaviour.—*adv.* **eth'i-cal-ly.**

eth-ics (eth'iks), *n.pl.* **1,** used as *sing.,* the science of morals; **2,** used as *pl.,* moral principles or practice; as, every profession has its own *ethics.*

eth-nic (eth'nik), *adj.* of, or relating to, races or peoples as distinguished by speech, customs, characteristics, etc.; as, *ethnic* religions.

eth-nol-o-gy (eth-nol'o-ji), *n.* the science that treats of races, their cultures, differences, etc.—*n.* **eth-nol'o-gist.**—*adj.* **eth'no-log'i-cal.**

eth-yl (eth'il), *n.* **1,** the base of alcohol, ether, and other hydrocarbons; **2,** any of several motor fuels containing an antiknock lead compound.

et-i-quette (et'i-ket'; et/i-ket'), *n.* rules of conduct observed in polite society or in official intercourse; the forms of polite behaviour demanded by good breeding.

e-tude (ā'tūd'), *n.* a study; in *music,* an exercise affording practice on a special point of technique, but often performed for its artistic value.

et-y-mol-o-gy (et/i-mol'o-ji), *n.* [*pl.* etymologies], a statement of the origin of a word and the history of its changing forms and meanings; also, the science treating of the origin and history of words.—*n.* **et/y-mol'o-gist.**—*adj.* **et/y-mo-log'i-cal.**

eu-ca-lyp-tus (ū'ka-lip'tus), *n.* [*pl.* eucalypti (ū'ka-lip'tī) or eucalyptuses], any of various trees of the myrtle family, including the gum tree of Australia, many species of which furnish timber, aromatic gum, and an oil valuable as a medicine.

Eu-cha-rist (ū'ka-rist), *n.* **1,** in many

Christian churches, the Holy Communion, or the sacrament of the Lord's Supper; **2**, the consecrated bread and wine used in that sacrament.

eu-chre (ū′kėr), *n.* a card game for two to four persons played with 24 cards, all cards below the nines (except the aces) being removed.—*v.t.* **1**, to defeat an opponent's bid by taking three of the five tricks; **2**, *Colloq.* to outwit; get the better of.

Eu-clid (ū′klid), *n.* a work on geometry written about 300 B.C. by Euclid of Alexandria.—*adj.* **Eu-clid′e-an.**

eu-gen-ics (ū-jen′iks), *n. pl.* used as *sing.*, the science of improving the human race by careful selection of parents.

eu-lo-gy (ū′lo-ji), *n.* [*pl.* eulogies], high praise, either written or spoken, of the life or character of a person, esp. of a dead person.—*v.t.* **eu′lo-gize** (ū′lo-jīz).

eu-nuch (ū′nuk), *n.* a man who has been castrated.

eu-phe-mism (ū′fe-mizm), *n.* the use of a pleasing expression for a harsh or blunt one; as, *pass away* for *die* or *fib* for *lie.*—*adj.* **eu′phe-mis′tic.**

eu-pho-ny (ū′fo-ni), *n.* pleasantness of sound; as, the *euphony* of his accents charmed his audience.—*adj.* **eu-phon′ic.**

eu-re-ka (ū-rē′ka), *interj.* Greek, "I have found (it)"; an expression of triumph at success.

eu-tha-na-si-a (ū′tha-nā′zhi-a; -zi-a), *n.* **1**, painless death; **2**, mercy killing (by sedatives), esp. for incurable sufferers.

e-vac-u-ate (i-vak′ū-āt), *v.t.* [evacuated, evacuat-ing], **1**, to empty; **2**, to abandon possession of; as, to *evacuate* a town; also, to withdraw (persons) from a place.—*n.* **e-vac′u-a′tion.**

e-vade (i-vād′), *v.t.* [evad-ed, evad-ing], **1**, to escape from by some trick; as, to *evade* pursuers or the law; **2**, to baffle or foil; as, a face which *evades* description.

e-val-u-ate (i-val′yoo-āt′), *v.t.* to determine the worth of; appraise; as, this service cannot be *evaluated* in dollars.—*n.* **e-val′u-a′tion.**

e-van-gel-i-cal (ē′van-jel′i-kal; ev′an-jel′i-kal), *adj.* **1**, pertaining to, or agreeing with the teachings of, the four Gospels; **2**, holding certain doctrines, as that of redemption through faith, believed by many Protestants to represent the true teaching of the Gospels. Also, **e-van-gel′ic.**

e-van-ge-list (i-van′je-list), *n.* **1**, one of the four writers of the Gospels; **2**, one who spreads the gospel; esp. a travelling preacher.—*adj.* **e-van′ge-lis′tic.**—*n.* **e-van′gel.**

e-vap-o-rate (i-vap′o-rāt), *v.i.* [evaporat-ed, evaporat-ing], **1**, to change from solid or liquid into vapour, as water into steam; **2**, to pass away without effect; as, his zeal soon *evaporated:*—*v.t.* **1**, to change into vapour; as, heat *evaporates* water; **2**, to dry or concentrate, by removing moisture; as, to *evaporate* fruit or milk.—*n.* **e-vap′o-ra′tor.**—*n.* **e-vap′o-ra′tion.**

e-va-sion (i-vā′zhun), *n.* **1**, an artful avoidance; as, the *evasion* of a question; **2**, an artful escape; **3**, an excuse.—*adj.* **e-va′sive.**—*adv.* **e-va′sive-ly.**

eve (ēv), *n.* **1**, the evening before a church festival or saint's day; as, Christmas *eve;* **2**, the period immediately before some important event; as, on the *eve* of departure; **3**, *Poetic*, evening.

¹**e-ven** (ē′ven), *n. Poetic*, evening.

²**e-ven** (ē′ven), *adj.* **1**, level; smooth; as, an *even* surface; **2**, equal in quantity, size, number; **3**, on the same line; parallel; as, water *even* with the top of a bucket; **4**, divisible by two without a remainder; as, six is an *even* number; **5**, impartial; fair; as, *even* justice; **6**, satisfied as to an account or grudge; as, to get *even* with a person; **7**, calm; unruffled; as, an *even* temper; **8**, whole; exact; as, an *even* mile:—*v.t.* **1**, to level; make smooth; as, to *even* a lawn; **2**, to make equal; as, to *even* up a score:—*adv.* **1**, exactly; just; as, *even* so; **2**, precisely; just; as, *even* as I spoke; **3**, quite; so much as; as, I never *even* spoke; **4**, used to emphasize or imply comparison; as, clear *even* to a child.—*adv.* **e′ven-ly.**—*n.* **e′ven-ness.**

eve-ning (ēv′ning), *n.* the close of day and beginning of night:—*adj.* pertaining to the latter part of the day; as, the *evening* meal.

e-vent (i-vent′), *n.* **1**, an occurrence; incident; happening; **2**, the fact of something happening; as, in *event* of war; **3**, the result or outcome of an action; as, in any *event;* **4**, a single item in a programme of sports.

e-vent-ful (i-vent′fool), *adj.* full of incidents or happenings; momentous; important.—*adv.* **e-vent′ful-ly.**

e-ven-tu-al (i-ven′tū-al), *adj.* **1**, depending on a future or possible event; as, *eventual* succession to a throne; **2**, final; as, an *eventual* reward.—*adv.* **e-ven′tu-al-ly.**

ev-er (ev′ėr), *adv.* **1**, at any time; as, if I *ever* go; **2**, forever; always; as, the poor are *ever* with us; **3**, in any degree; used to strengthen an expression; as, study as hard as *ever* you can:—**ever so,** very; as, *ever so* much better.

ev-er-glade (ev′ẽr-glād′), *n.* a low, swampy tract of land.

ev-er-green (ev′ẽr-grēn′), *n.* a tree or plant which remains green throughout the year, as the pine, cedar, holly, etc.:—*adj.* always green or fresh.

ev-er-last-ing (ev′ẽr-lås′ting), *adj.* **1,** endless; eternal; as, the *everlasting* hills; **2,** never ceasing; lasting too long; as, an *everlasting* noise:—*n.* **1,** any of various plants whose flowers keep their form and colour when dried; **2,** eternity:—**the Everlasting,** God.—*adv.* **ev′er-last′ing-ly.**

ev-er-more (ev′ẽr-mōr′), *adv.* eternally; always; forever.

ev-er-y (ev′ri; ev′ẽr-i), *adj.* **1,** all, taken one at a time; each; as, *every* man will do his duty; **2,** all possible; as, *every* kindness.

ev-er-y-bod-y (ev′ri-bod′i; ev′ẽr-i-bod′i), *pron.* every person; everyone.

ev-er-y-day (ev′ri-dā′; ev′ẽr-i-dā′), *adj.* happening on each day; usual; commonplace; as, *everyday* matters.

ev-er-y-one (ev′ri-wun; ev′ẽr-i-wun′), *pron.* every person; everybody.

ev-er-y-thing (ev′ri-thing′; ev′ẽr-i-thing′), *pron.* all things; all that relates to a given matter; as, to tell *everything* about it.

ev-er-y-where (ev′ri-hwâr′; ev′ẽr-i-hwâr′), *adv.* in all places or parts; as, they looked *everywhere.*

e-vict (ē-vikt′), *v.t.* to put out by force; expel, esp. by legal force; as, to *evict* a tenant.—*n.* **e-vic′tion.**

ev-i-dence (ev′i-dens), *n.* facts from which to judge; proof; testimony; as, *evidence* of guilt:—*v.t.* [evidenced, evidenc-ing], to prove; make evident or plain; indicate.

ev-i-dent (ev′i-dent), *adj.* clear to the eyes and mind; obvious; as, his dislike was *evident.*—*adv.* **ev′i-dent-ly.**

e-vil (ē′vl; ē′vil), *adj.* **1,** bad; wicked; sinful; as, *evil* acts; **2,** hurtful; disastrous; **3,** of ill repute; as, an *evil* name:—**evil eye,** the power to cause harm by a glance: a popular superstition:—*n.* **1,** disaster; injury; anything that destroys happiness or well-being; **2,** sin; wrongdoing: opposite of *good.*—*adv.* **e′vil-ly.**—*adj.* **e′vil—min′-ded.**

e-vil-do-er (ē′vl-dōō′ẽr), *n.* a wicked person.—*n.* **e′vil—do′ing.**

e-vince (i-vins′), *v.t.* [evinced, evinc-ing], to show; make evident; as, the soldiers *evinced* bravery.—*adj.* **e-vin′ci-ble.**

e-voke (i-vōk′), *v.t.* [evoked, evok-ing], to call forth; as, to *evoke* an answer.

ev-o-lu-tion (ev′o-lū′shun), *n.* **1,** development; growth; as, the *evolution* of a moth from a caterpillar; **2,** the theory that all present forms of plant and animal life have developed gradually through the ages from lower and simpler forms; also, the long process of this development; **3,** an ordered move or manœuvre of troops or ships changing position; **4,** a movement that is one of a series of movements; as, an *evolution* in a dance.—*adj.* **ev′o-lu′tion-ar′y.**

e-volve (ē-volv′), *v.t.* [evolved, evolving], to develop; unfold; expand; as, he *evolved* a new method of doing the work:—*v.i.* to become developed; as, from the invention of the radio a new industry *evolved.*

ewe (ū), *n.* a female sheep.

ex-ac-er-bate (eg-zas′ẽr-bāt′), *v.t.* **1,** to make sharper or more intense (anger, disease, etc.); as, this event *exacerbated* the ill-feeling between them; **2,** irritate; annoy.—*n.* **ex-ac′er-ba′tion.**

ex-act (eg-zakt′), *adj.* **1,** correct; precise; **2,** methodical; thorough; particular:—*v.t.* **1,** to require or insist upon; as, to *exact* attention; **2,** to compel payment of; demand; as, he *exacted* money from his debtors.—*n.* **ex-act′ness.**—*n.* **ex-act′i-tude′.**

ex-act-ing (eg-zak′ting), *adj.* making unreasonable demands; severe; difficult; as, an *exacting* task.

ex-ac-tion (eg-zak′shun), *n.* **1,** the act of firmly demanding; **2,** something demanded, esp. more than what is due; an illegal or excessive demand.

ex-act-ly (eg-zakt′li), *adv.* **1,** correctly; in an accurate manner; **2,** quite so; just as you say.

ex-ag-ger-ate (eg-zaj′ẽr-āt′), *v.t.* [exaggerat-ed, exaggerat-ing], to enlarge beyond truth or reason; overstate.—*n.* **ex-ag′ger-a′tion.**

ex-alt (eg-zôlt′), *v.t.* **1,** to raise in rank, position, or dignity; **2,** to delight; elate; **3,** to glorify; extol; as, *exalt* His holy name.—*n.* **ex′al-ta′tion** (eg-zôl-tā′shun).

ex-am-i-na-tion (eg-zam′i-nā′shun), *n.* **1,** an investigation; a careful inquiry or inspection; as, an *examination* of the accounts; **2,** a test of knowledge, fitness, or ability; esp. a written test; **3,** in law, a questioning, as of a witness.

ex-am-ine (eg-zam′in), *v.t.* [examined, examin-ing], **1,** to inspect closely; investigate carefully; **2,** in law, to question, as a witness; **3,** to find out

cat, āge, fär, câre, åsk; ten, ēve, latẽr; (i) pity, rely, senate; īce; top; nō.

example 209 **exclamation**

the knowledge, qualifications, etc. of, (a person) by a spoken or written test; as, he *examined* the class in history.—*n.* **ex-am'in-er.**

ex-am-ple (eg-zam'pl), *n.* 1, a person, thing, or act fit to be copied; 2, something that illustrates a rule; as, an *example* in subtraction; 3, a sample; specimen, as of workmanship; 4, a warning; as, let his punishment be an *example* to you.

ex-as-per-ate (eg-zas'pėr-āt'), *v.t.* [exasperat-ed, exasperat-ing], to irritate greatly; enrage; as, delay *exasperates* him.—*n.* **ex-as'per-a'tion.**

ex-ca-vate (eks'ka-vāt'), *v.t.* [excavated, excavat-ing], 1, to dig or hollow out; scoop or cut into; as, to *excavate* a hill; 2, to bring to light by digging; as, to *excavate* ruins.—*n.* **ex'ca-va'tion.** —*n.* **ex'ca-va'tor.**

ex-ceed (ek-sēd'), *v.t.* 1, to go beyond the limit of; overdo; as, he *exceeded* his authority; 2, to excel; surpass.

ex-ceed-ing-ly (ek-sēd'ing-li), *adv.* very; to a remarkable degree.

ex-cel (ek-sel'), *v.t.* [excelled, excelling], to possess good qualities in a great degree; as, this tea *excels* in flavour:—*v.t.* to be superior to; outdo in comparison; as, John *excels* Mary in arithmetic.

ex-cel-lence (ek'se-lens), *n.* superior merit; worth; special virtue.

ex-cel-len-cy (ek'se-len-si), *n.* [*pl.* excellencies], superior merit:—**Excellency**, a title of honour of various high officials.

ex-cel-lent (ek'se-lent), *adj.* of unusually high quality; very good of its kind.

ex-cel-si-or (ek-sel'si-ėr), *n.* a packing material made of long, fine, wood shavings.

ex-cept (ek-sept'), *v.t.* to leave out of account; omit:—*prep.* not including; outside of; as, he knows little *except* music.

ex-cept-ing (ek-sep'ting), *prep.* not including; except.

ex-cep-tion (ek-sep'shun), *n.* 1, an omission; exclusion; 2, that which is not included; as, he is an *exception* to the rule; 3, objection; offence taken; as, to take *exception* to what was said.

ex-cep-tion-a-ble (ek-sep'shun-a-bl), *adj.* 1, open to blame; objectionable; as, his conduct is *exceptionable*; 2, liable to omission.—*adv.* **ex-cep'tion-a-bly.**

ex-cep-tion-al (ek-sep'shun-al), *adj.* unusual; uncommon; extraordinary; as, music of *exceptional* beauty.

ex-cerpt (ek'sûrpt; ek-sûrpt'), *n.* a passage or selection (from a book); as, mimeograph this *excerpt* from Milton's prose.—*v.t.* (ek-sûrpt'), to pick out a passage; extract.

ex-cess (ek-ses'), *n.* 1, abundance; more than enough; 2, the amount by which one thing is more than another; 3, intemperance; 4, an added charge, as for fare on fast trains:—*adj.* over and above what is ordinary; extra; as, *excess* profits.

ex-ces-sive (ek-ses'iv), *adj.* extreme; unreasonable; immoderate.—*adv.* **ex-ces'sive-ly.**—*n.* **ex-ces'sive-ness.**

ex-change (eks-chānj'), *v.t.* [exchanged, exchang-ing], to give in return for something; barter; trade:—*n.* 1, the giving of one thing for another; barter; 2; giving and receiving; as, an *exchange* of ideas; 3, the giving up of one thing for another; as, the *exchange* of country life for city life; 4, a place for settling special business accounts or where persons, as brokers, meet to carry on particular business transactions; 5, a central office; as, a telephone *exchange*.—*adj.* **ex-change'a-ble.**

ex-cheq-uer (eks-chek'ėr; eks'chek-ėr), *n.* 1, a treasury, esp. of a government; 2, cash or funds.

¹**ex-cise** (ek-sīz'; ek'sīz), *n.* a tax levied on articles or commodities within the country where they are manufactured, sold, or used.—*adj.* **ex-cis'a-ble.**

²**ex-cise** (ek-sīz'), *v.t.* 1, to cut out, as a tumour; 2, to delete, as a word, passage, etc., in an article or book.—*n.* **ex-ci'sion.**

ex-cit-a-ble (ek-sīt'a-bl), *adj.* easily roused or stirred up.—*n.* **ex-cit'a-bil'i-ty.**

ex-cite (ek-sīt'), *v.t.* [excit-ed, exciting], 1, to set in motion; stir up; as, to *excite* anger; 2, to encourage; impel; incite; as, to *excite* men to revolt; 3, to arouse mentally or emotionally; move; perturb; as, news of the accident *excited* him.—*n.* **ex-cit'er.**—*n.* **ex'ci-ta'tion.**

ex-cite-ment (ek-sīt'ment), *n.* 1, the condition of being stirred up; commotion; 2, the act of stirring up; stimulation.

ex-claim (eks-klām'), *v.i.* to speak or cry out suddenly or passionately; as with surprise, anger, pleasure, etc.

ex-cla-ma-tion (eks'kla-mā'shun), *n.* 1, a sudden crying out; 2, an expression of surprise, pain, etc.:—**exclamation point**, a mark (!) in writing or printing to denote emotion, surprise, etc.—*adj.* **ex-clam'a-tor-y** (eks-klam'a-tėr-i).

ex-clude (eks-klōōd'), *v.t.* [exclud-ed, exclud-ing], to shut out; keep from entrance or admission; debar; as, they *excluded* him from the club.—*n.* **ex-clu'sion.**

ex-clu-sive (eks-klōō'siv), *adj.* 1, shutting out; 2, including everything but what is mentioned; as, twenty members *exclusive* of officers; 3, open to a chosen or privileged number; as, an *exclusive* club; 4, sole; as, an *exclusive* agency for a certain machine; 5, entire; complete; as, *exclusive* devotion to work.—*adv.* **ex-clu'sive-ly.**

ex-com-mu-ni-cate (eks'ko-mū'ni-kāt'), *v.t.* [excommunicat-ed, excommunicat-ing], 1, to punish by cutting off from the membership and communion of the church; 2, to expel from membership in any association or club.—*n.* **ex'com-mu'ni-ca'tion.**

ex-co-ri-ate (eks-kō'ri-āt'), *v.t.* 1, to strip the skin off; flay; 2, to blame severely; censure; denounce; as, the judge *excoriated* the press for the libel.

ex-cre-ment (eks'kri-ment), *n.* waste matter discharged from the body.

ex-cres-cence (eks-kres'ens), *n.* 1, an abnormal outgrowth, as a wart or bunion; 2, a normal one, as a hair or toenail.

ex-cre-tion (eks-krē'shun), *n.* the act of throwing off waste matter from the body; also, the waste matter thrown off.

ex-cru-ci-at-ing (eks-krōō'shi-āt'ing), *adj.* torturing; extremely painful.

ex-cul-pate (eks'kul-pāt'; ik-skul'-pāt), *v.t.* to free from blame; as, I *exculpate* you, whatever your crime.—*n.* **ex'cul-pa'tion.**

ex-cur-sion (eks-kûr'shun; eks-kûr'-zhun), *n.* 1, a pleasure trip, often one made by a number of people; also, the persons on such a trip; 2, a short or rapid tour.—*n.* **ex-cur'sion-ist.**

ex-cuse (eks-kūz'), *v.t.* [excused, excus-ing], 1, to pardon; as, to *excuse* one for being late; 2, to free from blame, obligation, or duty; as, the teacher *excused* her from the test; 3, to make an apology or explanation for; as, illness *excuses* his absence; 4, to justify; as, only ignorance *excuses* bad grammar: —*n.* (eks-kūs'), 1, a plea offered to justify some fault or neglect of duty; an apology; 2, a reason; as, an *excuse* for absence.—*adj.* **ex-cus'a-ble.**

ex-e-crate (eks'si-krāt'), *v.t.* [execrat-ed, execrat-ing], 1, to curse; 2, to detest; abhor; abominate:—*v.i.* to curse. —*adj.* **ex'e-cra-ble.**—*n.* **ex'e-cra'tion.**

ex-e-cute (eks'si-kūt'), *v.t.* [execut-ed,

execut-ing], 1, to carry into effect; complete; as, to *execute* a plan; 2, to make legal by signing or sealing; as, to *execute* a lease; 3, to put to death under sentence of the law; 4, to perform, as a musical selection; to make according to a design; as, to *execute* a memorial in marble.

ex-e-cu-tion (ek'si-kū'shun), *n.* 1, performance; the carrying of anything into effect; 2, workmanship; as, a portrait of perfect *execution*; 3, the making of a legal paper binding; 4, punishment by death.

ex-e-cu-tion-er (ek'si-kū'shun-ẽr), *n.* one who puts to death condemned criminals.

ex-ec-u-tive (eg-zek'ū-tiv; ek-sek'ū-tiv), *adj.* 1, pertaining to, or skilful in, the carrying out of plans; as, he has *executive* ability; 2, referring to that branch of government that administers the laws; as, the *executive* power is distinct from the legislative power:—*n.* 1, any person charged with putting laws or plans into effect; 2, the administrative branch of a government.

ex-e-cu-tor (ek'si-kū'tẽr), *n.* 1, one who carries something into effect; 2, (eg-zek'ū-tẽr; ek-sek'ū-tẽr), a person appointed in a will to see that its terms are carried out.—*n.fem.* **ex-e'cu-trix** (eg-zek' or ek-sek'ū-triks).

ex-em-pla-ry (eg-zem'pla-ri), *adj.* serving as a copy or model; praiseworthy; as, the boy's conduct was *exemplary.*

ex-em-pli-fy (eg-zem'pli-fī'), *v.t.* [exemplified, exemplify-ing], to show by example; illustrate; as, a story to *exemplify* honesty.—*n.* **ex-em'pli-fi-ca'tion.**

ex-em-pli gra-ti-a (eg-zem'plī grā'-shi-a), *Latin*, for example: abbreviated to *e.g.*

ex-empt (eg-zempt'), *v.t.* to free from an obligation or duty; excuse; release; as, to *exempt* a man from military service:—*adj.* free from a duty, restriction, or other limitation, to which others are subject; as, goods *exempt* from import duties.—*n.* **ex-emp'tion.**

ex-er-cise (ek'sẽr-sīz'), *v.t.* [exercised, exercis-ing], 1, to train by use; practise; 2, to employ actively, as the muscles or the mind; 3, to make anxious; as, the girl's absence *exercised* her mother:—*v.i.* to undergo training —*n.* 1, physical or mental activity for the sake of development; 2, a lesson or example for practice; 3, **exercises,** a ceremony; formal programme; as, graduation *exercises;* 4, performance as, in the *exercise* of duty.

ex-ert (eg-zûrt'), *v.t.* to put forth; bring to bear: to *exert* influence, will power, etc. —*n.* **ex-er'tion.**

ex-e-unt (ek'si-unt), *Latin,* a stage direction showing that two or more persons go off-stage (used in plays).

ex-hale (eks-hāl'; eg-zāl'), *v.t.* [exhaled, exhal-ing], to breathe out; give off; as, we *exhale* air in breathing; swamps *exhale* mist:—*v.i.* to rise in vapour.—*n.* **ex'ha-la'-tion.**

ex-haust (eg-zôst'), *v.t.* **1,** to empty by letting out all the contents; drain; **2,** to weaken; wear out; use up, as strength or a supply of money; **3,** to discuss or treat thoroughly; as, to *exhaust* a topic:—*n.* **1,** the drawing off or escape of used fuel, as steam, gas, etc., from an engine; **2,** the steam, gas, etc., that escapes; **3,** an instrument or device for drawing off or letting escape, as bad air from a room, or used fuel from an engine.—*adj.* **ex-haust'ed.**—*adj.* **ex-haust'less; ex-haust'i-ble.**

ex-haus-tion (eg-zôs'chun), *n.* **1,** the act of draining or the state of being drained; **2,** utter fatigue.

ex-haus-tive (eg-zôs'tiv), *adj.* complete; thorough: *exhaustive* research, study, etc.—*adv.* **ex-haus'tive-ly.**

ex-hib-it (eg-zib'it), *v.t.* **1,** to show: he *exhibited* impatience; **2,** to show publicly; present formally or officially: to *exhibit* an artist's work:—*n.* **1,** an object or collection of objects offered for public view: an *exhibit* of paintings; **2,** in *law,* an article, paper, etc., marked to be used as evidence.—*n.* **ex-hib'-i-tor.**—*n.* **ex'-hi-bi'tion** (ek'si-bi'shun).—*n.* **ex'hi-bi'tion-ist.**

ex-hil-a-rate (eg-zil'a-rāt'), *v.t.* [exhilarat-ed, exhilarat-ing], to make joyous; gladden; enliven.—*adj.* **ex-hil'a-rat'ing.**—*n.* **ex-hil'a-ra'tion.**

ex-hort (eg-zôrt'), *v.t., v.i.* to urge by appeal or argument, esp. to good deeds; advise; warn.—*n.* **ex'hor-ta'tion.**

ex-hume (eks-hūm'), *v.t.* to dig out of the earth; as, the judge ordered the corpse *exhumed.*

ex-i-gence (ek'si-jens), *n.* [*pl.* exigencies], **1,** a situation that needs immediate attention; **2,** pressing necessity; urgency. Also, **ex'i-gen-cy.**

ex-ile (ek'sīl), *v.t.* [exiled, exil-ing], to banish from home or country:—*n.* **1,** banishment, either forced or voluntary; as, to live in *exile;* **2,** a person banished from or living out of his own country.

ex-ist (eg-zist'), *v.i.* **1,** to have actual being; live; be; **2,** to be found; occur: salt *exists* in solution.

ex-ist-ence (eg-zis'tens), *n.* **1,** the state of being: new truths come into *exist-*ence; **2,** life: food is necessary for *existence;* **3,** manner of life: a happy *existence;* **4,** reality: he believes in the *existence* of devils.—*adj.* **ex-ist'ent;ex'is-ten'tial** (shal).

ex-it (eg'zit; ek'sit), *n.* **1,** the act of going out; **2,** a way out, as a door; **3,** the departure of an actor from the stage:—*v.i.* *sing.* goes off stage; as, *exit* Hamlet:—**exeunt** (ek'si-unt; eg'zi-unt), *pl.* go off stage.

ex-o-don-tist (ek'sō-don'tist), *n.* a dentist who specializes in pulling teeth.

ex-o-dus (ek'so-dus), *n.* a going out; departure.

ex of-fi-ci-o (eks o-fish'i-ō), because of right of office and without other authority; as, the Governor-General of Canada is *ex officio* commander-in-chief of the army.

ex-on-er-ate (eg-zon'ẽr-āt'), *v.t.* [exonerat-ed, exonerat-ing], to free from blame; as, the jury *exonerated* the accused man.—*n.* **ex-on'er-a'tion.**

ex-or-bi-tant (eg-zôr'bi-tant), *adj.* going beyond due limits; excessive; as, an *exorbitant* price.—*n.* **ex-or'bi-tance.**

ex-or-cize **ex-or-cise** (ek'sôr-sīz'), *v.t.* [exorcized, exorciz-ing], to expel (an evil spirit), as by religious or magic ceremonies; to deliver or free from evil spirits.—*n* **ex'or-cism.**

ex-ot-ic (eg-zot'ik; ek-sot'ik), *adj.* **1,** foreign, imported from another country or world; as, *exotic* plants, words, fashions, etc.; **2,** *Colloq.* fascinating or beautiful, because strange or foreign.

ex-pand (eks-pand'), *v.t.* **1,** to spread or stretch out; **2,** to dilate; swell; as, to *expand* the chest; **3,** to give more details of; enlarge upon; as, *expand* your topic into an essay:—*v.i.* to increase in size.

ex-panse (eks-pans'), *n.* wide extent; unbroken stretch or area: an *expanse* of ocean or sky.—*n.* **ex-pan'sion.**

ex-pan-sive (eks-pan'siv), *adj.* **1,** capable of being spread or stretched out; **2,** widely extended; large; **3,** free and unrestrained in the expression of feeling; effusive; as, an *expansive* manner.—*adv.* **ex-pan'sive-ly.**

ex-pa-ti-ate (eks-pā'shi-āt'), *v.i.* to talk at length; as, he *expatiated* upon the virtues of his dog; elaborate.

ex-pect (eks-pekt'), *v.t.* **1,** to look forward to as likely to happen: I *expect* him to arrive soon; **2,** *Colloq.* to suppose: I *expect* it is all for the best.

ex-pect-ant (eks-pek'tant), *adj.* looking forward confidently; expecting. —*adv.* adds **ly.**—*n.* **ex-pect'an-cy.**

ex-pec-ta-tion (eks'pek-tā'shun), *n.* 1, a looking forward to something; anticipation; as, in *expectation* of a good dinner; 2, (usually *expectations*), the prospect of future benefit, esp. of advancement or wealth; as, his *expectations* are good.

ex-pec-to-rate (eks-pek'to-rāt'), *v.t.* and *v.i.* to spit.

ex-pe-di-en-cy (eks-pē'di-en-si), *n.* [*pl.* expediencies], 1, suitableness; fitness for a purpose; 2, the doing of something, regardless of fairness or justice, in order to gain a certain end; as, *expediency* made him refuse. Also, **ex-pe'di-ence.**

ex-pe-di-ent (eks-pē'di-ent), *adj.* 1, fit for a special purpose; 2, helpful toward self-interest; as, an *expedient* friendship:—*n.* 1, that which acts as a means to an end; 2, a device.—*adv.* **ex-pe'di-ent-ly.**

ex-pe-dite (eks'pi-dīt'), *v.t.* [expedited, expedit-ing], 1, to hasten; help forward; quicken; 2, to carry out quickly; as, to *expedite* work.—*adj.* **ex'pe-di'tious.**

ex-pe-di-tion (eks'pi-dish'un), *n.* 1, haste; dispatch; promptness; as, he did his work with *expedition;* 2, a journey or voyage for some particular purpose; as, an exploring *expedition;* 3, the body of persons engaged in such an enterprise.—*adj.* **ex'pe-di'tion-ar-y.**

ex-pel (eks-pel'), *v.t.* [expelled, expelling], 1, to drive away; force out; as, to *expel* an enemy from a region; 2, to turn out; send away; as, to *expel* someone from a club, school, or the like.

ex-pend (eks-pend'), *v.t.* to pay out; spend; as, to *expend* strength, time, or money.—*adj.* **ex-pend'a-ble.**

ex-pend-i-ture (eks-pen'di-tūr), *n.* 1, a spending, as of money, time, labour, etc.; 2, that which is spent.

ex-pense (eks-pens'), *n.* 1, money, labour, time, etc., laid out or spent; cost; as, the *expenses* of a college education; he worked long hours at the *expense* of his health; 2, a source or cause of spending; as, war is a great *expense.*

ex-pen-sive (eks-pen'siv), *adj.* costly; high-priced.—*adv.* **ex-pen'sive-ly.**

ex-pe-ri-ence (eks-pē'ri-ens), *n.* 1, knowledge or skill gained by direct action, observation, enjoyment, or suffering; 2, the actual observation or living through anything, as a series of events, or of feeling anything through sensation; 3, anything lived through, enjoyed, or felt; as, war *experiences:—v.t.* [experienced, experienc-ing], to feel; live through; as, to *experience* hardship.

ex-pe-ri-enced (eks-pē'ri-enst), *adj.* having experience; made expert by experience.

ex-per-i-ment (eks-per'i-ment), *n.* a trial or test to discover something previously unknown, or to confirm or disprove something; as, the *experiment* showed he was right:—*v.i.* (eks-per'i-ment), to make tests to find out something; as, Edison *experimented* for years trying to perfect electric lighting. —*n.* **ex-per'i-ment-er.**—*adj.* **ex-per'i-men'tal.**

ex-pert (eks-pûrt'; eks'pûrt), *adj.* skilful; clever; dextrous:—*n.* (eks'-pûrt), one who is skilled or thoroughly informed in any particular subject; a specialist; as, a financial *expert.*—*adv.* **ex-pert'ly.**

ex-pi-ate (eks'pi-āt'), *v.t.* [expiat-ed, expiat-ing], to atone or make amends for; as, he *expiated* his theft by restoring the plunder.—*n.* **ex'pi-a'tion.**

ex-pire (ek-spīr'), *v.t.* [expired, expiring], to breathe out from the lungs:— *v.i.* 1, to die; 2, to come to an end; as, his term *expired.*—*n.* **ex'pi-ra'tion** (eks'pi-rā'shun).—*n.* **ex-pi'ry.**

ex-plain (eks-plān'), *v.t.* 1, to make plain or clear; tell the meaning of; as, to *explain* a problem; 2, to account for; as, to *explain* one's conduct.—*n.* **ex'pla-na'tion.**

ex-plan-a-tor-y (eks-plan'a-tėr-i), *adj.* serving to make clear.

ex-ple-tive (eks'ple-tiv), *n.* in *grammar* a word, such as *it* or *there*, used to fill in for the real subject; as, *it* is foolish to worry; *there* is nothing left.—*interj.* used for emphasis like an oath or exclamation; as, his salty *expletives* startled her.

ex-pli-ca-ble (eks'pli-ka-bl), *adj.* capable of being explained.

ex-plic-it (eks-plis'it) *adj.* plain; definite; expressed clearly and in detail; as, *explicit* instructions.—*adv.* **ex-plic'it-ly.**

ex-plode (eks-plōd'), *v.i.* [explod-ed, explod-ing], 1, to burst with sudden noise and violence; as, the bomb *exploded;* 2, to break forth suddenly into laughter, anger, etc.:—*v.t.* 1, to cause to burst suddenly with a loud noise; as, to *explode* dynamite; 2, to refute or disprove; as, Copernicus *exploded* the theory that the earth was the centre of the solar system.

ex-ploit (eks-ploit'), *v.t.* 1, to make use of for one's own profit; put to use selfishly; as, to *exploit* one's friends; 2, to make use of; work; develop; as, to *exploit* natural resources:—*n.* (eks'ploit; eks-ploit'), a remarkable deed or heroic act.—*n.* **ex-ploit′er.**—*n.* **ex′ploi-ta′tion.**

ex-plore (eks-plōr′), *v.t.* [explored, explor-ing], **1,** to search or examine thoroughly; as, to *explore* a wound; **2,** to travel in or over (a region) to discover its geographical characteristics as, to *explore* unknown islands.—*n.* **ex′plo-ra′tion.**—*n.* **ex-plor′er.**—*adj.* **explor′a-to-ry.**

ex-plo-sion (eks-plō′zhun), *n.* **1,** a sudden and violent bursting with a loud noise; as, the *explosion* of a bomb; **2,** a sudden and violent outburst, as of anger.

ex-plo-sive (eks-plō′siv), *adj.* pertaining to explosion; likely to explode; as, dynamite is an *explosive* substance: —*n.* any substance, liquid, solid, or gaseous, which will explode or cause an explosion, as gunpowder, TNT, etc.— *adv.* **ex-plo′sive-ly.**

ex-po-nent (eks-pō′nent), *n.* **1,** one who explains or interprets; as, an *exponent* of democracy; **2,** a person or thing that represents a principle or theory; as, Disraeli was the *exponent* of imperialism.

ex-port (eks-pōrt′; eks′pōrt), *v.t.* to send or carry out (goods) to another country for sale; as, to *export* cattle:— *n.* (eks′pōrt), **1,** (usually *exports*), goods sold and sent to a foreign country; also, their amount or value; **2,** the act or business of sending goods to a foreign country to be sold; as, the *export* of wheat is an important industry in Canada.—*n.* **ex′por-ta′tion.** —*adj.* **ex-port′a-ble.**—*n.* **ex-port′er.**

ex-pose (eks-pōz′), *v.t.* [exposed, exposing], **1,** to lay open to view; uncover; make known; as, to *expose* a secret, an opinion, or a villain; **2,** to leave without shelter or defence; as, to *expose* a child to the cold; **3,** to lay open or put in the way of; as, to *expose* a plant to the sun; *expose* a friend to blame; **4,** in *photography*, to subject (a film) to the action of light.

ex-po-sé (eks′pō′zā′), *n.* the public disclosure of the details of a scandal, crime, etc.

ex-po-si-tion (eks′pō-zish′un), *n.* an explanation or interpretation (as distinct from narration, description, or argument); a piece of writing that explains or interprets; **2,** an exhibition on a large scale.—*adj.* **ex-pos′i-to-ry.**

ex-pos-tu-late (eks-pos′tū-lāt), *v.i.* [expostulat-ed, expostulat-ing], to plead earnestly, as with a friend about his faults; remonstrate.—*n.* **ex-pos′tu-la′-tion.**

ex-po-sure (eks-pō′zhėr), *n.* **1,** a revealing or making known; as, the *exposure* of a crime; **2,** the state of being open or subject to attack, contamination, etc.; as, *exposure* to disease; **3,** position; outlook; as, a house with a southern *exposure;* **4,** in *photography*, an exposing to light.

ex-pound (eks-pound′), *v.t.* to set forth, explain, or interpret.—*n.* **ex-pound′er.**

ex-press (eks-pres′), *adj.* **1,** plainly stated; special; definite; as, an *express* answer or wish; **2,** having to do with quick or direct transportation; as, an *express* train; **3,** pertaining to the business of transporting goods rapidly; as, an *express* company:—*adv.* by express; quickly; as, send the package *express:*—*n.* **1,** a fast railway train stopping only at principal stations; **2,** a system of transportation for mails, goods of small bulk, or the like; also, goods so forwarded:—*v.t.* **1,** to make known, esp. by language; utter; as, he *expressed* the idea clearly; **2,** to show; reveal; as, to *express* relief, joy, etc.; **3,** to represent; as, the symbol of the arrow *expresses* direction; **4,** to send by express.—*adj.* **ex-press′i-ble.**

ex-pres-sion (eks-presh′un), *n.* **1,** the act of expressing or revealing, esp. in words; manner of speech, change in tone of voice, etc., revealing thought and feeling; as, to speak with *expression;* **2,** a look on the face that betrays feeling; as, a joyous *expression;* **3,** a saying; as, "Never say die" is an old *expression.*

ex-pres-sive (eks-pres′iv), *adj.* full of meaning; serving to point out or express; as, a look *expressive* of sorrow.—*adv.* **ex-pres′sive-ly.**—*n.* **ex-pres′sive-ness.**

ex-press-ly (eks-pres′li), *adv.* **1,** particularly; specially; **2,** in direct terms; plainly; as, told *expressly* to go home.

ex-pro-pri-ate (eks-prō′pri-āt), *v.t.* to take property from an owner, esp. for public use; as, the province *expropriated* his land for a new highway. —*n.* **ex-pro′pri-a′tion.**

ex-pul-sion (eks-pul′shun), *n.* **1,** a forcing out or away; **2,** banishment; as, the *expulsion* of an enemy.—*adj.* **ex-pul′sive.**

ex-pur-gate (eks′pėr-gāt′), *v.t.* to remove obscene or objectionable passages; as, we read an *expurgated* edition of *Hamlet.*—*n.* **ex′pur-ga′tion.**

ex-qui-site (eks′kwi-zit), *adj.* **1,** delicately beautiful; as, *exquisite* lace; *exquisite* workmanship; **2,** intensely or sensitively felt; as, *exquisite* joy.—*adv.* **ex′qui-site-ly.**

all (ôl), ôr; up, mūte, cûr, cōōl, book; · oil, out; th, thin; *th*, the.

ex-tant (ek-stant′; eks′tant), *adj.* in existence; not destroyed or lost; as, old prints or writings that are still *extant*.

ex-tem-po-ra-ne-ous (eks-tem′po-rā′ni-us), *adj.* made without preparation or study; extemporary.—*adv.* **ex-tem′po-ra′ne-ous-ly.**

ex-tem-po-rar-y (eks-tem′po-rėr-i), *adj.* 1, without notes or previous study; as, an *extemporary* speech; 2, made on the spur of the moment.—*adv.* **ex-tem′po-rar-i-ly.**

ex-tem-po-re (eks-tem′po-ri), *adj.* and *adv.* without preparation; as, to recite *extempore*.

ex-tem-po-rize (ex-tem′po-rīz′), *v.i.* to sing, play an instrument, speak, etc., improvising music or words as one proceeds.—*n.* **ex-tem′po-ri-za′tion.**

ex-tend (eks-tend′), *v.t.* 1, to lengthen, as a railroad; prolong, as a visit; 2, to enlarge; increase, as power, influence, etc.; 3, to straighten out, as the arm; 4, to offer, as friendship:—*v.i.* to reach, in time or distance; as, Canada *extends* from the U.S. to the Arctic Circle.

ex-ten-sion (eks-ten′shun), *n.* 1, the act of reaching or stretching out; 2, the state of being lengthened; enlargement; 3, an addition; as, an *extension* to a house.

ex-ten-sive (eks-ten′siv), *adj.* wide; comprehensive; far-reaching; as, *extensive* business interests; an *extensive* view.—*adv.* **ex-ten′sive-ly.**

ex-ten-sor (eks-ten′sor), *n.* a muscle that straightens out some part of the body, as an arm or leg; opposite of *flexor*.

ex-tent (eks-tent′), *n.* the space or degree to which a thing is extended; size; length; limit; as, the *extent* of his lands.

ex-ten-u-ate (eks-ten′ū-āt′), *v.t.* [extenuat-ed, extenuat-ing], to offer excuses for; lessen the blame for; as, he sought to *extenuate* his fault.—*n.* **ex-ten′u-a′tion.**

ex-te-ri-or (eks-tē′ri-ėr), *adj.* 1, outward; external; as, the *exterior* covering of a box; 2, coming, or acting, from without; as, *exterior* aid:—*n.* the outer surface or the outside of anything.

ex-ter-mi-nate (eks-tûr′mi-nāt′), *v.t.* [exterminat-ed, exterminat-ing], to destroy utterly; root out; as, to *exterminate* moths.—*n.* **ex-ter′mi-na′tion.** —*n.* **ex-ter′mi-na′tor.**

ex-ter-nal (eks-tûr′nal), *adj.* 1, outside; exterior; as, an *external* force; 2, foreign; as, the *external* debt of a

country; 3, visible; as, *external* proof; 4, superficial; as, *external* culture:—*n.* 1, an outward part; 2, (often *externals*), outward form or ceremony; as, the *externals* of religion.—*adv.* **ex-ter′nal-ly.**

ex-tinct (eks-tingkt′), *adj.* 1, no longer burning; gone out, as a fire; inactive, as a volcano; 2, destroyed, as life or hope; 3, no longer living or surviving; as, buffaloes are almost *extinct*.

ex-tinc-tion (eks-tingk′shun), *n.* annihilation; death.

ex-tin-guish (eks-ting′gwish), *v.t.* 1, to put out, as a light; 2, to destroy; as, to *extinguish* hope.—*n.* **ex-tin′guish-er.**

ex-tir-pate (eks′tėr-pāt′), *v.t.* to root out or destroy totally, as weeds, ideas, heresies, etc.; as, we used 24D to *extirpate* the weeds on our lawn.—*n.* **ex′tir-pa′tion.**

ex-tol (eks-tol′; eks-tōl′), *v.t.* [extolled, extol-ling], to praise highly; as, to *extol* the name of God.

ex-tort (eks-tôrt′), *v.t.* to obtain by force or threats; as, to *extort* money.

ex-tor-tion (eks-tôr′shun), *n.* 1, the act of obtaining by force or threat; 2, unjust exaction, as of excessive interest on loans; 3, that which has been exacted unlawfully.—*adj.* **ex-tor′tion-ate.**—*adv.* **ex-tor′tion-ate-ly.**—*n.* **ex-tor′tion-er.**

ex-tra (eks′tra), *adj.* 1, more than usual; 2, unusually good; as, *extra* meats:—*n.* 1, something additional; 2, a newspaper edition issued between regular editions:—*adv.* exceptionally; as, *extra* fine silk.

ex-tract (eks-trakt′), *v.t.* 1, to obtain from a substance by some process; as, to *extract* perfume from flowers; 2, to pull out, as a tooth; 3, to get by effort; as, to *extract* money from a miser; 4, to select, as a passage from a book; 5, in *mathematics*, to calculate, as the root of a number:—*n.* (eks′trakt), 1, that which has been extracted, or taken out; as, *extract* of beef; 2, a passage from a book, speech, etc.

ex-trac-tion (eks-trak′shun), *n.* 1, the act of extracting; 2, origin; descent; as, a person of English *extraction*.

ex-tra-cur-ric-u-lar (eks′tra-ku-rik′ū-lėr), *adj.* outside the regular course of studies; as, athletics, debating, and dramatics are *extracurricular* activities.

ex-tra-dite (eks′tra-dīt′), *v.t.* to give up a prisoner or fugitive to the jurisdiction of another country; as, the murderer was *extradited* from the U.S.—*n.* **ex′tra-di′tion.**

ex-tra-ne-ous (ek-strā′ni-us), *adj.*

coming from without; not belonging or essential to a thing; external; foreign; as, no *extraneous* influences molded the islanders' culture.

ex-tra-or-di-nar-y(eks-trôr'di-nėr-i; eks'tra-ôr'di-nėr-i), *adj.* **1**, unusual; **2**, remarkable; rare; **3**, special; as, an envoy *extraordinary*.—*adv.* **ex-tra-or'di-nar-i-ly**.

ex-trav-a-gant (eks-trav'a-gant), *adj.* **1**, exceeding reasonable limits; **2**, wasteful; needlessly lavish in spending; **3**, very high, as prices.—*adv.* **ex-trav'a-gant-ly**.—*n.* **ex-trav'a-gance**.

ex-trav-a-gan-za (eks-strav'a-gan'za), *n.* a drama or musical, as a comic opera, marked by fantastic plot, irregular form, farce, etc.; a spectacular.

ex-treme (eks-trēm'), *adj.* **1**, of the highest degree; as, *extreme* old age; *extreme* danger; **2**, outermost; farthest away; as, the *extreme* ends of the world; **3**, most severe or strict; as, *extreme* measures; **4**, excessive; immoderate; as, *extreme* fashions; **5**, advanced; radical; as, *extreme* ideas:—*n.* **1**, the extremity; the very end; **2**, the utmost degree of anything; **3**, excess; as, to go to *extremes*.—*adv.* **ex-treme'ly**.—*n.* **ex-trem'ist**.

ex-trem-i-ty (eks-trem'i-ti), *n.* [*pl.* extremities], **1**, the farthest point, or end; as, the western *extremity* of the bridge; **2**, an arm, hand, leg, or foot; **3**, the utmost degree; as, an *extremity* of pain; **4**, extreme need or distress; as, people were reduced to *extremity* by the drought.

ex-tri-cate (eks'tri-kāt'), *v.t.* [extricated, extricat-ing], to free or set loose; as, to *extricate* an animal from a trap; also, to free from difficulties; as, to *extricate* oneself from debt.

ex-trin-sic (eks-trin'sik), *adj.* not inherent in; external; opposite of *intrinsic;* as, *extrinsic* values, causes, advantages, etc.

ex-tro-vert (eks'trō-vûrt'), *n.* one who is more interested in his environment and other persons than in himself; an active, practical person concerned with the objective world about him: opposite of *introvert*.

ex-trude (eks-trōōd'), *v.t.* force out; expel; as, heated metals and plastics are extruded through dies or minute holes to form tubing or fibres:—*v.i.* to stick out; project.—*n.* **ex-tru'sion**.

ex-u-ber-ance (eg-zū'bėr-ans), *n.* an overflowing; abundance, as of high spirits.—*adj.* **ex-u'ber-ant**.

ex-ude (eks-ūd'; eg-zūd'), *v.t.* [exuded, exud-ing], to discharge gradually through the pores, as by sweating; give out (moisture):—*v.i.* to ooze out.—*n.* **ex'u-da'tion**.

ex-ult (eg-zult'), *v.i.* to rejoice exceedingly; as, to *exult* in victory.—*adj.* **ex-ult'** ant.—*n.* **ex'ul-ta'tion**.—*adv.* **ex-ult'ing-ly**.

ey-as (ī'as), *n.* a young hawk; a nestling; an unfledged bird.

eye (ī), *n.* **1**, the organ of sight; **2**, sight; power to see or appreciate; as, an *eye* for beauty; **3**, a look; gaze; **4**, close observation; as, to keep an *eye* on someone; **5**, estimation; judgment; as, in the *eyes* of the world; **6**, that which resembles an eye; as, the *eye* of a needle:—*v.t.* [eyed, ey-ing or eye-ing], to look at; watch closely.

eye-ball (ī'bôl'), *n.* all of the eye within the lids and socket.

eye-brow (ī'brou'), *n.* the ridge above either eye; also, the hair on this ridge.

eye-glass (ī'glås'), *n.* **1**, a lens for the eye, to improve faulty sight; **2**, the lens of a telescope or microscope; **3**, **eye-glasses**, a pair of lenses for the eyes.

eye-lash (ī'lash'), *n.* the fringe of hair that grows on the edge of the eyelid; also, one of the hairs of this fringe.

eye-let (ī'let), *n.* **1**, a small hole to receive a lace or cord; **2**, a ring of metal to strengthen such a hole.

eye-lid (ī'lid'), *n.* the movable upper or lower cover of skin which closes and protects the eye.

eye-piece (ī'pēs'), *n.* in a telescope or other optical instrument, the lens or system of lenses nearest the eye of the user.

eye-sight (ī'sīt'), *n.* **1**, the ability to see; **2**, range of vision; as, within *eyesight*.

eye-sore (ī'sōr'), *n.* anything offensive to look at; as, the broken window was an *eyesore*.

eye-tooth (ī'tōōth'), *n.* [*pl.* eyeteeth (-tēth')], one of the two canine teeth in the upper jaw, the third tooth from the front on either side.

eye-wash (ī'wosh'), *n.* **1**, a lotion for the eyes; **2**, *Slang*, flattery (intended to deceive); nonsense.

eye-wit-ness (ī'wit'nes), *n.* one who has seen something happen; one who can testify to what he has actually seen; as, an *eyewitness* of the crime.

ey-rie (âr'i; ēr'i; ī'ri), *n.* the nest or brood of a bird of prey, as an eagle or a hawk; an aerie. Also spelled **a'er-ie; ey'ry**.

F

F, f (ef), *n.* [*pl.* F's, f's], **1,** the sixth letter of the alphabet, following E; **2,** the fourth note in the major scale of C.

fa (fä), *n.* in *music,* the name of the fourth note in the scale.

fa-ble (fā′bl), *n.* **1,** a story, esp. one with a moral, in which, usually, animals talk and act like human beings; **2,** an untrue statement; a lie; also, a fabulous thing.—*n.* **fab′u-list.**

fab-ric (fab′rik), *n.* **1,** woven or knitted cloth; **2,** texture or workmanship; as, cloth of fine *fabric;* **3,** structure; as, the social *fabric.*

fab-ri-cate (fab′ri-kāt′), *v.t.* [fabricated, fabricat-ing], **1,** to invent; as, to *fabricate* a tale; **2,** to manufacture; construct; as, to *fabricate* boxes; to *fabricate* a bridge.—*n.* **fab′ri-ca′tion.**

fab-u-lous (fab′ū-lus), *adj.* **1,** occurring in fable; legendary; as, Ulysses is a *fabulous* hero; **2,** hard to believe; incredible; hence, enormous; amazing; as, *fabulous* wealth.—*adv.* **fab′u-lous-ly.**

fa-cade (fa-säd′), *n.* the chief front of a building, or any of its principal faces.

face (fās), *n.* **1,** the front part of the head; **2,** expression or look; as, a happy *face;* also, a grimace; as, don't make a *face* at Ann; **3,** impudence; as, she had the *face* to go, uninvited; **4,** the principal side, as of a building, clock, card, etc.; **5,** reputation; as, to save his *face;* **6,** personal presence; sight; as, to say it to his *face:*—*v.t.* [faced, fac-ing], **1,** to turn toward; as, she *faced* them; be situated opposite; as, my room *faced* the south; **2,** to confront; as, he *faced* danger; **3,** to cover, or partly cover, with something in front; as, to *face* a fireplace with brick; also, to cover (some part of a garment) with another layer of material; as, to *face* a hem:—*v.i.* to turn the face; stand or front in any given direction; as, the windows of the living-room *face* south.

face—off (fās′-ôf′), *n.* in *hockey,* the referee's starting of play by dropping the puck between the sticks of two opposing players:—*v.i.* to begin play in such a way; as, they *faced-off* at the Leafs' blue line.

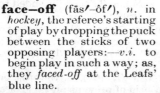

FACETS
Gem cut with facets: top view and side view.

fac-et (fas′et), *n.* **1,** one of the small, polished surfaces of a gem that has been cut. **2.** an aspect; as of a topic, personality, etc.

fa-ce-tious (fa-sē′shus), *adj.* humourous; harmlessly teasing; as, a *facetious* remark.—*adv.* **fa-ce′tious-ly.**

fa-cial (fā′shal), *adj.* pertaining to the face; as, *facial* expression:—*n. Colloq.,* a facial massage.

fac-ile (fas′il), *adj.* **1,** easily done; **2,** quick in doing; fluent; expert; as, a *facile* writer; **3,** gentle; mild.

fa-cil-i-tate (fa-sil′i-tāt′), *v.t.* [facilitat-ed, facilitat-ing], to make easier; as, an electric washer *facilitates* laundering.

fa-cil-i-ty (fa-sil′i-ti), *n.* [*pl.* facilities], **1,** ease; freedom from difficulty; also, skill; as, he writes with *facility;* **2, facilities,** the device or means by which anything may be more easily done; as, kitchen *facilities.*

fac-ing (fās′ing), *n.* **1,** a covering in front as for ornament; as, the stone *facing* of a house; **2,** material applied near the edge of a garment for ornament or protection; as, a grey dress with red sleeve *facings.*

fac-sim-i-le (fak-sim′i-lē), *n.* an exact reproduction or duplicate.

fact (fakt), *n.* **1,** a statement of something that has been done or is strictly true; as, give me the *facts;* **2,** the quality of being real or actual; as, a question of *fact* rather than of fancy; **3,** that which actually happens or is known to be true; as, the *fact* that fire burns.—*adj.* **fac′tu-al.**

fac-tion (fak′shun), *n.* a group of persons who attempt, often by destructive means, to bring about changes, as in government or in the existing state of affairs; a clique.—*adj.* **fac′tion-al.**—*adj.* **fac′tious.**

fac-tor (fak′tèr), *n.* **1,** any one of the causes of a given result; as, opportunity is one of the great *factors* in success; **2,** in *arithmetic,* any of the numbers which, when multiplied together, form a given product; as, two and three are the *factors* of six; **3,** in *commerce,* an agent:—*v.t.* to find the factors of (a number).

fac-to-ri-al (fak-tō′ri-al), *n.* in *mathematics,* the product of all the integers from any given number down to unity (one); as, *factorial* four is 4 × 3 × 2 × 1, or 24.

fac-to-ry (fak′to-ri), *n.* [*pl.* factories], **1,** a place where goods are manufactured; **2,** an establishment where factors, or agents, carry on business in a foreign country.

fac-ul-ty (fak′ul-ti), *n.* [*pl.* faculties], **1,** the ability to act or do; usually, a special ability; a talent; as, he had a *faculty* for painting; **2,** a physical or mental power; as, the *faculty* of hearing; **3,** the teaching staff in an educational institution.

fad (fad), *n.* a passing fancy or fashion; as, large hats were the *fad* that year.

fade (fād), *v.i.* [fad-ed, fad-ing], **1,** to grow pale or faint; as, colours *fade* in the sun; the music *faded* in the distance; **2,** to wither:—*v.t.* to cause to lose colour; as, the sun *faded* the curtains.

fae-ces or **fe-ces** (fē′sēz), *n.pl.* waste matter expelled from the bowels or intestines; excrement.

fag (fag), *v.i.* to become dead tired; as, I am *fagged out.*—*n. Slang,* a cigarette; as, he was smoking a *fag* (end).

fag-got or **fag-ot** (fag′ut), *n.* a bundle of sticks bound together.

Fahr-en-heit (far′en-hīt′; fär′en-hīt′) *adj.* naming, or pertaining to, the scale on the thermometer introduced by G. D. Fahrenheit:—*n.* the Fahrenheit scale, on which 32° represents the freezing-point, and 212° the boiling-point, of water.

fail (fāl), *v.i.* **1,** not to succeed; as, to *fail* to learn; **2,** to fall short of what is expected or desired; be insufficient; as, the crop *failed;* to *fail* in one's duty; **3,** to lose strength; **4,** to become bankrupt; as, his business *failed:*—*v.t.* **1,** to forsake; give no help to; as, friends *failed* me; **2,** to give a mark of failure to (a pupil):—**without fail,** certainly; surely.

fail-ing (fāl′ing), *n.* a defect; fault.

fail-ure (fāl′ūr), *n.* **1,** lack of success; as, *failure* in a test; **2,** a falling short of something expected or desired; as, *failure* of crops; *failure* to be on time; **3,** bankruptcy; **4,** an unsuccessful person or thing.

fain (fān), *adv.* willingly; as, *fain* would I do it:—*adj.* glad; willing; as, she was *fain* to keep silence.

faint (fānt), *v.i.* to lose consciousness:—*n.* the act or state of fainting:—*adj.* **1,** weak; about to faint; as, to feel *faint;* **2,** timid; as, a *faint* heart; **3,** dim; indistinct; as, a *faint* sound or colour; **4,** feeble; inadequate; as, a *faint* attempt.—*n.* **faint′ness.**—*adv.* **faint′ly.**

fair (fâr), *adj.* **1,** pleasing to the sight; as, a *fair* city; **2,** light in complexion; blond; as, *fair* skin; **3,** without blemish; clean; as, a *fair* name; **4,** not cloudy;

clear; as, today will be *fair;* **5,** honest; just; as, *fair* play; **6,** moderately good; as, a *fair* score; **7,** open to lawful pursuit; as, *fair* game:—*adv.* in a fair manner; as, to play *fair.*—*adv.* **fair′ly.**—*n.* **fair′ness.**

²fair (fâr), *n.* **1,** a gathering at a fixed time and place, for the sale or exhibition of farm products, etc.; **2,** a sale of useful and fancy goods, as for charity.

fair-way (fâr′wā′), *n.* in *golf,* the grassy lane between tee and putting-green.

fair-y (fâr′i), *n.* [*pl.* fairies], an imaginary being of graceful and tiny human form, supposed to interfere in the affairs of mankind for good or for evil:—*adj.* having to do with, or like, fairies.

fair-y-land (fâr′i-land′), *n.* the home of the fairies; hence, an enchanting place.

fait ac-com-pli (fà′tä′kôn′plē′), *n.* an accomplished fact; a thing done (hence opposition is useless).

faith (fāth), *n.* **1,** belief in God; **2,** belief in something without proof; as, he had *faith* that his son was safe; **3,** confidence or trust in another person; as, we had *faith* in the captain; **4,** a promise; as, he broke *faith* with us; **5,** a system of religious belief; as, the Christian *faith.*

faith-ful (fāth′fool), *adj.* **1,** loyal; as, a *faithful* friend; **2,** trustworthy; as, a *faithful* servant; **3,** accurate; as, a *faithful* copy.—*adv.* **faith′ful-ly.**—*n.* **faith′ful-ness.**

faith-less (fāth′les), *adj.* **1,** without faith; **2,** untrustworthy; disloyal.—*adv.* **faith′-less-ly.**—*n.* **faith′less-ness.**

fake (fāk), *v.t. Colloq.* **1,** to pretend; as, he *faked* illness; in *football,* he *faked* a pass; **2,** to tamper with (in order to deceive); as, a *faked* label; to counterfeit.—*n. Colloq.* a deception; as, this so-called Rembrandt is a *fake.*—*adj. Colloq.* sham; not genuine.—*n. (Colloq.)* **fa′ker.**

fa-kir (fà-kēr′), *n.* a Moslem monk or mendicant; **2,** loosely, a Hindu mystic or ascetic.

fal-con (fô′kun; fôl′kun), *n.* any one of several small, swift hawks, esp. one trained for hunting.—*n.* **fal′con-ry** (fô′kn-ri).

fall (fôl), *v.i.* [*p.t.* fell (fel), *p.p.* fall-en (fôl′ en), *p.pr.* fall-ing], **1,** to drop from a higher to a lower place; as, the rain *fell;* **2,** to hang down; as, a cloak *falls* in folds; **3,** to be overthrown; as, a city *falls;* **4,** to die; as, to *fall* in battle; **5,** to lose moral dignity or character; as, to *fall* from grace; **6,** to decrease; diminish in value or degree; as, prices *fall;* the thermometer *falls;* **7,** to slope, as land; **8,** to come by chance or by inheritance; as, this part *falls* to me; **9,** to pass gradually into some state of mind or body; as, to *fall* asleep; **10,** to reach or strike; as, moonlight *fell* on the water; **11,** to occur; as, Christmas *fell* on Sunday that year:—*n.* **1,** the act of falling; **2,** something which has fallen; as, a heavy *fall* of rain; **3,** autumn; **4,** ruin or downfall; as, the *fall* of a city; **5,** decrease in price, value, etc.; **6,** **falls,** a cascade.

fal-la-cy (fal′a-si), *n.* [*pl.* fallacies], **1,** a mistaken idea; as, it is a *fallacy* that the good die young; **2,** unsound reasoning.—*adj.* **fal-la′cious** (fa-lā′shus).

fall-en (fôl′en), *adj.* **1,** ruined; as, a *fallen* empire; **2,** dropped, as leaves, acorns, etc.; **3,** degraded; as, a *fallen* woman; **4,** dead; as, *fallen* soldiers.

fal-li-ble (fal′i-bl), *adj.* liable to err; as, all men are *fallible.*

fall—out (fôl′-out′), *n.* the descent of radioactive particles after a nuclear explosion, esp. of particles of strontium 90 or caesium 132.

fal-low (fal′ō), *n.* **1,** land which is ploughed, but left unseeded for a season; **2,** the ploughing of land without sowing it for a season, in order to increase its fertility:—*adj.* **1,** ploughed, but not seeded; as, a *fallow* field:—*v.t.* to make or keep fallow.

false (fôls), *adj.* [fals-er, fals-est], **1,** untrue; wrong; as, a *false* idea; **2,** disloyal; **3,** dishonest; lying; as, a *false* witness; **4,** artificial; as, *false* hair; *false* teeth.—*adv.* **false′ly.**—*n.* **false′-ness.**

false-hood (fôls′hood), *n.* a lie.

fal-set-to (fôl-set′ō), *n.* [*pl.* falsettos], a voice, esp. a man's voice, pitched unnaturally high; also, one who sings with such a voice:—*adj.* pertaining to a falsetto.

fals-ies (fôl′sēz), *n.pl. Colloq.* a padded brassiere to make the breasts look fuller.

fal-si-fy (fôl′si-fī), *v.t.* [falsified, falsifying], **1,** to make false; alter, so as to deceive; as, to *falsify* records; **2,** to prove to be false; disprove.—*n.* **fal′si-fi-ca′tion.**

fal-si-ty (fôl′si-ti), *n.* [*pl.* falsities], **1,** the quality of being untrue; **2,** that which is untrue; an error; falsehood.

fal-ter (fôl′tẽr), *v.i.* **1,** to hesitate; waver; as, he started, then *faltered;* **2,** to move unsteadily; **3,** to speak hesitatingly; stammer:—*v.t.* to utter with hesitation; as, he *faltered* a few words.

fame (fām), *n.* reputation; renown.—*adj.* **famed.**

fa-mil-iar (fa-mil′yẽr), *adj.* **1,** well acquainted; intimate; as, *familiar* friends; **2,** well known; as, *familiar* scenes; **3,** taking liberties; bold; **4,** informal; as, a *familiar* greeting.—*n.* **fa-mil′i-ar′i-ty.**

fa-mil-iar-ize (fa-mil′yẽr-īz), *v.t.* [familiarized, familiariz-ing], **1,** to make (a person) feel well acquainted or at ease with something; as, to *familiarize* oneself with new surroundings; **2,** to make well known.

fam-i-ly (fam′i-li), *n.* [*pl.* families], **1,** a group of closely related people, as parents and their children; **2,** the children alone of such a group; **3,** a household; a group of persons under one roof; **4,** a body of persons descended from a common ancestor; tribe; clan; **5,** distinguished lineage; as, they are people of good *family;* **6,** a group of things with some common characteristics; as, a mineral *family;* **7,** in *biology,* a classification of plants or animals, larger than a genus, but smaller than an order; as, the cat *family.*

fam-ine (fam′in), *n.* **1,** extreme scarcity of food; starvation; **2,** shortage of some special thing; as, a wheat *famine.*

fam-ish (fam′ish), *v.t.* to destroy with hunger:—*v.i.* to suffer from extreme hunger.

fa-mous (fā′mus), *adj.* renowned; celebrated; as; a *famous* scientist.

fan (fan), *n.* **1,** any device used to start currents of air; **2,** a small hand device, often one which unfolds into a semicircular shape, used to stir up the air; **3,** anything like a fan in shape; **4,** an enthusiast; as, a football *fan:*—*v.t.* [fanned, fan-ning], **1,** to winnow, or separate, as chaff from grain; **2,** to drive a current of air upon; cool the face of; kindle (a fire); **3,** hence, to rouse, as rage; **4,** *Slang,* in baseball, to strike out (a batter).

fa-nat-ic (fa-nat′ik), *n.* one who holds extravagant and unreasonable views, esp. of religion; one who is carried away by his beliefs:—*adj.* **fa-nat′i-cal.**—*adv.* **fa-nat′i-cal-ly.**—*n.* **fa-nat′i-cism.**

fan-ci-er (fan′si-ẽr), *n.* one who has a special interest in something; as, a cat *fancier;* a bird-*fancier.*

fan-ci-ful (fan′si-fool), *adj.* **1** led by imagination; **2,** unreal; as, a *fanciful* story; **3,** curiously designed.—*adv.* **fan′ci-ful-ly.**—*n.* **fan′ci-ful-ness.**

fan-cy (fan′si), *v.t.* [fancied, fancy-ing], **1,** to suppose; as, I *fancy* he will come; **2,** to imagine; as, he *fancies* himself to be king; **3,** to take a liking to:—*adj.* [fan-ci-er, fan-ci-est], **1,** ornamental; not plain; as, *fancy* dress; **2,** extravagant; as, *fancy* prices; **3,** superior to the average; as, *fancy* groceries:—*n.* [*pl.* fancies], **1,** imagination; **2,** an idea; a notion or whim; **3,** a liking.

fancy—free (fan′si–frē′), *adj.* **1,** not in love; **2,** carefree.

fan-dan-go (fan-dang′gō), *n.* a lively Spanish dance (or tune) in 3/4 time.

fang (fang), *n.* a long, sharp tooth, as of a dog, wolf, or poisonous snake.

fan-light (fan′līt′), *n.* a fan-shaped window above a door; a transom.

fan-tan (fan′tan′), *n.* a Chinese gambling game.

fan-ta-si-a (fan-tä′zi-a; zhi-a; zē′a), *n.* in *music*, **1,** a medley of well-known tunes; **2,** a composition of no fixed form that follows the composer's fancy.

fan-tas-tic (fan-tas′tik) or **fan-tas-ti-cal** (-tas′ti-kal), *adj.* **1,** imaginary; unreal; as, *fantastic* fears; **2,** odd; grotesque; as, shadows assume *fantastic* shapes.—*adv.* **fan-tas′ti-cal-ly.**

fan-ta-sy (fan′ta-si; fan′ta-zi), *n.* [*pl.* fantasies], **1,** imagination; **2,** a product of the imagination. Also, **phan′ta-sy.**

far (fär), *adj.* [far-ther, far-thest], **1,** distant in time or space; as, the *far* past; a *far* land; **2,** more distant of two; as, the *far* side; **3,** reaching to great distances; as, a *far* journey:—*adv.* **1,** to or at a great, or definite, distance in time or space; as, to go *far;* to go only so *far;* **2,** by a great deal; very much; as, he is *far* wiser than I am.

far-ad (far′ad), *n.* a unit that measures the electrical capacity of a condenser.

far-a-day (far′a-dā′), *n.* a unit that measures the quantity of electricity (used esp. in electrolysis).

far-a-way (fär′a-wā′), *adj.* **1,** distant; remote; **2,** dreamy; as, a *far-away* look.

farce (färs), *n.* **1,** a play full of exaggerated situations intended to be very funny; **2,** a ridiculous sham; as, the election was a mere *farce.*—*adj.* **far′ci-cal.**

fare (fâr), *v.i.* [fared, far-ing], **1,** to experience either good or bad fortune; as, to *fare* well or ill; **2,** to journey; travel; **3,** to be fed; as, I *fared* well at lunch:—*n.* **1,** the sum paid for a journey; **2,** a person paying this sum; **3,** food.

fare-well (fâr′wel′), *interj.* good-bye! —*adj.* final; parting; as, a *farewell* tour:—*n.* (fâr′wel′), **1,** a wish of welfare at parting; a good-bye; **2,** a departure; as, a sad *farewell.*

far-fetched (fär′fetcht′), *adj.* forced; strained; as, a *farfetched* simile.

fa-ri-na (fa-rē′na), *n.* **1,** flour or meal from cereal grains, beans, potatoes, etc.; **2,** starch, esp. from potatoes.

farm (färm), *n.* a single holding of tillable land with the buildings belonging to it:—*v.t.* and *v.i.* to cultivate (land).—*n.* **farm′ing.**—*n.* **farm′er.**—*n.* **farm′house′.**—*n.* **farm′yard′.**

far-o (fâr′ō), *n.* a card game in which the dealer bets against all the other players.

far—reach-ing (fär′–rēch′ing), *adj.* having a wide influence or effect.

far-row (far′ō), *n.* **1,** a litter of pigs; **2,** *v.i.* and *v.t.* to give birth (to pigs).

far-see-ing (fär′sē′ing), *adj.* having foresight; farsighted.

far-sighted (fär′sīt′id), *adj.* **1,** able to see distant objects more clearly than near ones; **2,** having good judgment; prudent.—*n.* **far′sight′ed-ness.**

far-ther (fär′thėr), *adj.* (*comp.* of *far*], **1,** more distant; as, the *farther* side; **2,** additional; further; as, to take no *farther* notice:—*adv.* **1,** to or at a greater distance; as, to go *farther;* **2,** moreover.—*adj.* **far′ther-most′.**

far-thest (fär′thest), *adj.* [*superl.* of *far*], most distant:—*adv.* to or at the greatest distance.

far-thing (fär′thing), *n.* a British coin worth one fourth of a British penny.

far-thin-gale (fär′thing-gāl′), *n.* a hoop skirt or frame for holding the skirt out (worn in the 16th and 17th centuries).

fas-ci-nate (fas′i-nāt′), *v.t.* [fascinated, fascinat-ing], **1,** to bewitch or hold motionless by some strange power; as, snakes are said to *fascinate* small birds; **2,** hence, to enchant; charm irresistibly. —*adv.* **fas′ci-nat′ing-ly.**—*n.* **fas′ci-na′-tion.**

fas-cism (fash′izm), *n.* a centralized, one-party governmental system, suppressing unions and rival parties, and marked by aggressive nationalism, racism, and hostility to socialism: Italy and Germany were fascist states before World War II.—*n.* and *adj.* **fas′cist** (sh). Also, **Fas′cism; Fas′cist.**

fash-ion (fash′un), *n.* **1,** the shape or form of anything; **2,** manner or way of doing something; as, he eats in a queer *fashion;* **3,** the prevailing style or custom at any time, esp. in dress; as, high shoes are no longer the *fashion:*— *v.t.* to mould, shape, or form; as, to *fashion* a model out of clay.—*adj.* **fash′ion-a-ble.**—*adv.* **fash′ion-a-bly.**

¹fast (fàst), *adj.* **1,** securely fixed; attached; as, frozen *fast* in the snow; **2,** faithful; steadfast; as, *fast* friends; **3,** deep; sound; as, a *fast* sleeper; **4,** not fading; as, *fast* colours; **5,** rapid; swift; as, a *fast* runner; also, allowing quick motion; as, a *fast* track; **6,** ahead of the standard time; as, my watch is *fast;* **7,** wild; too gay; as, *fast* society:—*adv.* **1,** fixedly; firmly; **2,** rapidly; **3,** wildly; too gaily; **4,** deeply; as, *fast* asleep.

²fast (fȧst), *v.i.* to take little or no food: —*n.* the act or period of fasting.

fas-ten (fȧs′n), *v.t.* **1,** to fix securely, as a door; cause to hold together, as a dress; to attach to something else; as, to *fasten* a shelf to a wall; **2,** to keep fixed steadily, as the attention; **3,** to attach, as blame:—*v.i.* to take hold; become attached.—*n.* **fas′ten-er.**

fas-ten-ing (fȧs′n-ing), *n.* something that fastens; a lock, chain, clasp, etc.

fas-tid-i-ous (fas-tid′i-us), *adj.* hard to please; daintily particular.—*adv.* **fas-tid′ i-ous-ly.**—*n.* **fas-tid′i-ous-ness.**

fast-ness (fȧst′nes), *n.* **1,** swiftness; **2,** a stronghold; as, a mountain *fastness.*

fat (fat), *adj.* [fat-ter, fat-test], **1,** plump; fleshy; **2,** greasy; rich; as, *fat* gravy; **3,** well-filled or -stocked; as, a *fat* wallet; **4,** profitable; as, a *fat* job; **5,** fertile; as, a *fat* soil:—*n.* **1,** an oily, yellow or white substance found in animal and vegetable tissues; **2,** the best or richest part of anything:—*v.t.* [fat-ted, fat-ting], to make fat.

fa-tal (fā′t′l), *adj.* **1,** causing death; as, a *fatal* accident; **2,** causing great harm; as, a *fatal* error.—*adv.* **fa′tal-ly.** —*n.* **fa′tal-ist.**—*adj.* **fa′tal-is′tic.**—*n.* **fa′tal-ism.**

fa-tal-i-ty (fā-tal′i-ti), *n.* [*pl.* fatalities], **1,** a condition of being doomed by fate; as, a *fatality* attends everything he tries to do; **2,** a fatal influence; deadly quality; as, the *fatality* of cancer; **3,** a calamity; also, death in a disaster; as, there were only two *fatalities* in the fire.

fate (fāt), *n.* **1,** a power beyond man's control that is believed to determine events; **2,** that which is decided by fate; one's lot or destiny.—*adj.* **fat′ed.**

fate-ful (fāt′fool), *adj.* **1,** important; significant; as, tomorrow is the *fateful* day; **2,** prophetic; as, a *fateful* tolling of the bell; **3,** deadly; as, a *fateful* blow; **4,** controlled by fate.—*adv.* **fate′ful-ly.**

fat-head (fat′hed′), *n. Colloq.* a stupid person.

fa-ther (fä′thėr), *n.* **1,** a male parent; **2,** an ancestor; **3,** one who stands in the relation of a father; **4,** an originator or founder; **5,** a clergyman, esp. a Roman Catholic priest:—**Father,** God: —*v.t.* **1,** to beget or adopt (a child); **2,** to assume authorship of or accept responsibility for; as, to *father* a plan.

—*n.* **fa′ther-hood.**—*adj.* **fa′ther-less.** —*adj.* **fa′ther-ly.**

fa-ther—in—law (fä′thėr—in—lô′), *n.* [*pl.* fathers-in-law], the father of one's husband or of one's wife.

fa-ther-land (fä′thėr-land′), *n.* one's native country.

Fa-ther's Day, the third Sunday in June, set aside to honour fathers.

fath-om (fath′um), *n.* a measure of length equal to six feet:—*v.t.* **1,** to find the depth of (water); **2,** to reach an understanding of; as, I was able to *fathom* his meaning.

fath-om-less (fath′um-lis), *adj.* **1,** so deep that the bottom cannot be reached; **2,** not possible to understand; as, a *fathomless* mystery.

fa-tigue (fa-tēg′), *n.* weariness resulting from labour; bodily or mental exhaustion:—*v.t.* and *v.i.* [fatigued, fatiguing], to weary; tire or become wearied.

fat-ten (fat′n), *v.t.* and *v.i.* to make or become fat.

fat-ty (fat′i), *adj.* [fat-ti-er, fat-ti-est], **1,** containing fat; **2,** greasy; oily.

fat-u-ous (fat′ū-us), *adj.* silly; as, a *fatuous* remark.—*n.* **fa-tu′i-ty.**

fau-cet (fô′set), *n.* a device for controlling the flow of liquid from a pipe or other container; a tap.

faugh (fô), *interj.* an exclamation of disgust or contempt.

fault (fôlt), *n.* **1,** a weakness in character; **2,** a slight offence; **3,** blame or responsibility for something; as, it was not his *fault;* **4,** a break in layers of rock that were previously continuous:—**find fault,** to complain; as, he was forever *finding fault.*—*adj.* **fault′less.**—*n.* **fault′fin′der.**

fault-y (fôl′ti), *adj.* [fault-i-er, fault-i-est], imperfect; defective.—*n.* **fault′i-ness.**

faun (fôn), *n.* in *mythology,* a woodland deity, half-human, with pointed ears, small horns and, sometimes, a goat's tail and hind legs.

fau-na (fô′na), *n.* the animals belonging to a special region or period; as, the *fauna* of the African jungle.

faux pas (fō′pä′), *n.* a false step, as a breach of good breeding or morals; a tactless deed or word.

fa-vor (fā′vėr), *n.* an American spelling of *favour.*

fa-vour or **fa-vor** (fā′vėr), *n.* **1,** an act of kindness; as, do me a *favour;* **2,** approval; as, he looked on with *favour;* **3,** partiality; special consideration; as, he asked no *favour;* **4,** a small gift or token:—*v.t.* **1,** to regard with good will; approve; **2,** to show partiality to; **3,** to make possible or easy; as, fair weather *favours* our plan; **4**, to oblige; as, *favour* me with your attention; **5**, to look like (a person); as, she *favours* her mother.

fa-vour-a-ble (fā′vėr-a-bl), *adj.* **1**, expressing approval; as, a *favourable* account; **2**, advantageous; as, *favourable* weather; **3**, giving assent; helpful. —*adv.* **fa′vour-a-bly.**

fa-vour-ite (fā′vėr-it), *n.* **1**, one who or that which is particularly liked; **2**, a contestant thought to have the best chance of winning:—*adj.* preferred; best-liked; as, a *favourite* book.—*n.* **fa′vour-it-ism.**

¹fawn (fôn), *n.* a deer less than one year old:—*adj.* of a light yellowish brown; as, she bought a *fawn* coat.

²fawn (fôn), *v.i.* **1**, to show pleasure or affection by wagging the tail, whining, etc., as a dog does; **2**, to seek favour by flattery and cringing behaviour.

fay (fā), *n.* an elf; a fairy.

faze (fāz), *v.t. Slang,* to disconcert; disturb; as, it didn't *faze* him.

fe-al-ty (fē′al-ti), *n.* in the feudal period, the pledge of a vassal to be faithful to his lord; hence, loyalty; a pledge of allegiance.

fear (fēr), *n.* **1**, a feeling of alarm or dread of possible evil or danger; **2**, reverence; as, the *fear* of God:—*v.t.* **1**, to regard with dread; be afraid of; **2**, to revere:—*v.i.* to be afraid.

fear-ful (fēr′fool), *adj.* **1**, causing fear or awe; terrible; as, a *fearful* sight; **2**, full of alarm; timid; lacking courage. —*adv.* **fear′ful-ly.**

fear-less (fēr′lis), *adj.* without fear; not afraid; courageous.—*adv.* **fear′less-ly.**—*n.* **fear′less-ness.**

fea-si-ble (fē′zi-bl), *adj.* capable of being done; possible; as, a *feasible* scheme.—*n.* **fea′si-bil′i-ty.**

feast (fēst), *n.* **1**, a lavish meal; **2**, a festival in memory of an event; esp. a religious festival; **3**, anything pleasing to the taste or mind:—*v.t.* **1**, to make a rich meal for; **2**, to delight; as, to feast the eyes on beauty:—*v.i.* to partake of a feast.

feat (fēt), *n.* an act or deed displaying great courage, strength, skill, etc.; as, flying the Atlantic is a remarkable *feat.*

feath-er (feth′ėr), *n.* one of the light outgrowths from the skin of a bird:— *v.t.* **1**, to cover or line with feathers; **2**, to turn the blade of (an oar) horizontally as it leaves the water:—*v.i.* **1**, to become covered with feathers; **2**, to feather one's oars while rowing.

feath-er-bed-ding (feth′ėr-bed′ing),

n. the forcing of an employer by a union to pay unnecessary employees.

feath-er-brain (feth′ėr-brān′), *n.* a giddy, silly, or weak-minded person.

feath-er-weight (feth′ėr-wāt′), *n.* the weight of a boxer between 118 and 126 pounds.

feath-er-y (feth′ėr-i), *adj.* like a feather in shape, lightness, or softness; as, a *feathery* fern.—*n.* **feath′er-i-ness.**

fea-ture (fē′tūr), *n.* **1**, something noticeable about a thing; as, the architectural *features* of a church; **2**, the chief attraction on a programme; as, her dance was the *feature;* **3**, any part of the face, as the eyes, chin, etc.; **4**, **features**, the whole face:—*v.t.* [featured, featur-ing], **1**, to portray the features of; outline; **2**, to make prominent; as, to *feature* an actor.

fe-brile (fē′brīl; feb′ril), *adj.* feverish; as, *febrile* symptoms.

Feb-ru-a-ry (feb′roo-ėr-i), *n.* the second month of the year.

fe-ces (fē′sēz), *n.* **1**, animal excrement; **2**, dregs; sediment. Also spelled **faeces.**

fec-und (fē′kund; fek′und), *adj.* fruitful; prolific; as, a *fecund* mind (one rich in ideas).—*v.t.* **fe′cun-date′.**—*n.* **fe-cun′di-ty.**

fed-er-al (fed′ėr-al), *adj.* relating to a nation formed by the union of several smaller states; as, a *federal* republic.

Fed-er-al (fed′ėr-al), *adj.* **1.** relating to the government of federated states; as, *federal* taxes; **2**, favouring the North in the War between the States; as, a *Federal* soldier:—*n.* a person on the side of the Union in the War between the States.

fed-er-ate (fed′ėr-āt′), *v.t.* and *v.i.* [federat-ed, federat-ing], to combine (states or societies) into a union.—*n.* **fed′er-a′tion.**

fe-do-ra (fi-dō′ra), *n.* a soft felt hat with the crown creased lengthwise and brim curved a little.

fee (fē), *n.* **1**, payment for a service or a privilege; as, a lawyer's *fee;* a licence *fee;* **2**, under the feudal system, land held from an overlord; also, the terms under which such land was held; a fief; as, to hold land in *fee:*—*v.t.* [feed, fee-ing], to give a tip or fee to.

fee-ble (fē′bl), *adj.* [fee-bler, fee-blest], **1**, without strength; **2**, lacking in vigour; faint; as, a *feeble* effort.—*n.* **fee′ble-ness.**—*adj.* **fee′bly.**

fee-ble—mind-ed (fē′bl-mīn′did), *adj.* having very little power to think or to learn.—*n.* **fee′ble—mind′ed-ness.**

feed (fēd), *v.t.* [fed (fed), feed-ing], **1**, to

supply with food; as, to *feed* a beggar; **2,** to put food into the mouth of; as, to *feed* a baby; **3,** to give as food; as, to *feed* meat to a dog; **4,** to nourish; as, soil *feeds* plants; **5,** to supply (a fire) with fuel:—*v.i.* to take food; as, the pup *fed* eagerly:—*n.* food for animals; fodder.—*adj.* and *n.* **feed′er.**

feed-back (fēd′bak′), *n.* in a vacuum tube, the feeding back of some of the energy of the plate circuit to the grid circuit.

feel (fēl), *v.t.* [felt (felt), feel-ing], **1,** to examine by touch; as, to *feel* a person's pulse; **2,** to be aware of (something) by touch; as, I *felt* rain; **3,** to have a sense of; as, to *feel* pity; **4,** to be moved or disturbed by; as, to *feel* a slight; **5,** to be sure of, without proof; as, I *feel* it to be so:—*v.i.* **1,** to search by touch; grope; as, to *feel* for a match; **2,** to be aware of being in some definite condition of mind or body; as, to *feel* faint; **3,** to have sympathy; as, to *feel* deeply for someone; **4,** to seem to the touch; as, the air *feels* damp:—*n.* a quality perceived by touch; as, the silky *feel* of velvet.

feel-er (fēl′ẽr), *n.* **1,** an organ of touch, as, one of a cat's whiskers; **2,** a remark made to draw out the opinions of others; as, to throw out a *feeler*.

feel-ing (fēl′ing), *n.* **1,** the sense, usually called *touch*, by which a person tells hot from cold, rough from smooth, etc.; **2,** any sensation of the skin, or of the body in general; as, a *feeling* of pain, cold, hunger, etc.; **3,** an emotion of hope, hate, love, or the like; **4,** emotional excitement; as, *feeling* over the game ran high; **5,** opinion; as, it is my *feeling* that you ought to go; **6,** **feelings,** sensitive nature; as, to hurt her *feelings*.

feet (fēt), *n.pl.* of *foot*.

feign (fān), *v.t.* and *v.i.* to pretend; as, to *feign* illness.—*n.* **feign′er.**

feint (fānt), *n.* a pretence; esp. a pretence of attack at one point while really attacking at another:—*v.i.* to make a sham thrust; as, to *feint* with the left hand and strike with the right.

feld-spar (feld′spär′), *n.* an aluminum silicate with potassium, sodium, or calcium, usually white or pink; found in common rocks such as granite, gneiss, etc.

fe-lic-i-tate (fe-lis′i-tāt′), *v.t.* [felici-tat-ed, felicitat-ing], to congratulate; wish happiness to.—*n.* **fe-lic′i-ta′tion.**

fe-lic-i-ty (fe-lis′i-ti), *n.* [*pl.* felicities], **1,** great happiness; also, a source of happiness; **2,** a pleasing way of speaking or writing; also a well-chosen expression.—*adj.* **fe-lic′i-tous.**

fe-line (fē′līn), *adj.* **1,** of, or relating to a cat or the cat family; **2,** stealthy sly; treacherous; as, a *feline* step in the darkness.

¹fell (fel), *p.t.* of *fall*.

²fell (fel), *n.* skin; pelt; hide; as, a *fell* of hair.

³fell (fel), *n.* in Britain, **1,** a barren or rocky hill; **2,** a moor; heath; down.

⁴fell (fel), *v.t.* **1,** to cause to fall; cut down, as a tree; knock down, as by a blow; **2,** to fold over and sew down flat, as a seam:—*n.* a seam made by fell-ing.

FELLED SEAM

1, stitch the pieces of material, A, B, as at *a*; 2, fold B over A; 3, fold B down upon A and stitch through B and A at *c*.

⁵fell (fel), *adj.* cruel; savage; terrible; deadly.

fel-low (fel′ō), *n.* **1,** a companion; as, a *fellow* in misery; **2,** one of a pair; a mate; match; as, the *fellow* of this shoe; **3,** *Colloq.* a man or boy; anybody; as, a *fellow* has to eat; also, a girl's beau; **4,** an honoured member, as of certain learned societies; also, a student supported by an endowment:—*adj.* associated with others; as, *fellow* members.

fel-low-ship (fel′ō-ship′), *n.* **1,** membership in a group, as a church; also, the group itself; as, to admit to *fellowship;* **2,** friendly association; companionship; as, I enjoy his *fellowship;* **3,** a position endowed to enable the holder to continue study, free of expense for board, tuition, etc., as in a university.

¹fel-on (fel′un), *n.* a person who is guilty of a serious crime.

²fel-on (fel′un), *n.* a painful inflammation on a finger or toe, usually near the nail.

fel-o-ny (fel′o-ni), *n.* [*pl.* felonies], a serious crime, as murder or robbery.—*adj.* **fe-lo′ni-us** (fe-lō′ni-us).

felt (felt), *n.* a fabric made of wool, hair, and fur, matted or forced together by pressure:—*adj.* made of felt; as, a *felt* hat:—*v.t.* to mat into a mass; as, to *felt* wool together; also, to cover with felt.—*n.* **felt′ing.**

fe-male (fē′māl), *adj.* having to do with or belonging to the sex that bears young:—*n.* a person or an animal of this sex.

fem-i-nine (fem′i-nin), *adj.* **1,** relating to women; like women; as, *feminine* fashions or ways; **2,** in *grammar*, of the gender to which names of females belong; as, "doe" is a *feminine* noun.—*n.* **fem′i-nin′i-ty.**

fem-i-nism (fem'i-nizm), *n.* the belief that women are mentally as highly endowed as men, and should be given social, economic, and political equality.—*n.* **fem'i-nist.**

fe-mur (fē'mẽr), *n.* [*pl.* femurs (-mẽrz), femora (fem'o-ra)], the thighbone, longest and largest bone in the body (from hip to knee).

fen (fen), *n.* low, marshy land.

fence (fens), *n.* 1, a barrier or boundary of stone, wood, or other material; 2, a receiver of stolen goods:—*v.t.* [fenced, fencing], to enclose with a fence; as, to *fence* a field:—*v.i.* to practise the use of swords or foils.—*n.* **fenc'er.**

fenc-ing (fen'-sing), *n.* 1, the art of using a foil or sword; 2, materials used for making a fence; 3, the fences on a plot of land.

FENCING, def. 1

fend (fend), *v.t.* to ward off, as a blow:—*v.i.* to provide; as, I must *fend* for myself.

fend-er (fen'dẽr), *n.* 1, a device on the front of a locomotive or a streetcar to prevent or lessen injuries from collisions; 2, a metal guard in front of a fireplace; 3, a guard over an automobile or bicycle wheel.

fen-nel (fen'el), *n.* a fragrant plant of the carrot family. Its seeds are used in cooking and in medicine.

fer-ment (fûr'ment), *n.* 1, a substance, as yeast, that causes chemical change with effervescence; 2, a state of excitement; unrest; as, the town is in a *ferment:*—*v.i.* (fẽr-ment'), 1, to be in a state of fermentation, as milk when it turns sour, or cider when it bubbles; 2, to become stirred up or excited:—*v.t.* 1, to cause fermentation in; 2, to excite or stir up.

fer-men-ta-tion (fûr'men-tā'shun), *n.* 1, a change, such as is caused by yeast, producing gas bubbles, alcohol, or acid, as in the souring of milk, the working of cider, etc.; 2, excitement; unrest.

fern (fûrn), *n.* any one of many flowerless plants with broad feathery, leaflike fronds.—*n.* **fern'er-y.**—*adj.* **fern'y.**

fe-ro-cious (fe-rō'shus), *adj.* savage; fierce; as, a *ferocious* tiger.—*n.* **fe-roc'i-ty.** (fe-ros'i-ti).

fer-ret (fer'it), *n.* a weasel-like animal used to hunt rats and rabbits:—*v.t.* 1, to hunt (rats, etc.) with ferrets; 2, to search perseveringly for; as, to *ferret* out a secret.—*v.i.* to hunt with ferrets; search.—*n.* **fer'ret-er.**

fer-ric (fer'ik) and **fer-rous** (fer'us),

adj. relating to, or containing, iron; as, *ferric* oxide (Fe_2O_3) and *ferrous* sulphate ($FeSO_4$).

fer-rule (fer'ool; fer'il), *n.* a metal ring or cap placed around the end of a stick, tool handle, or the like, to strengthen it.

fer-ry (fer'i), *n.* [*pl.* ferries], 1, a boat used to carry passengers or vehicles across a river, lake, or the like; 2, a place where such a boat lands:—*v.t.* [ferried, ferry-ing], to take across a body of water on a ferry; as, to *ferry* a car across a lake; also, to cross by ferry; as, to *ferry* the lake:—*v.i.* to go by ferry.

fer-tile (fûr'tl; fûr'tīl), *adj.* 1, producing abundantly; fruitful; as, *fertile* land; 2, capable of producing seed; as, a *fertile* flower; 3, capable of developing; as, a *fertile* seed or egg.—*n.* **fer-til'i-ty.**

fer-ti-lize (fûr'ti-līz'), *v.t.* [fertilized, fertiliz-ing], to make productive; esp. to supply with plant food; as, to *fertilize* soil.—*n.* **fer'ti-li-za'tion.**—*n.* **fer'ti-liz'er.**

fer-ule (fer'ool; fer'il), *n.* a stick or ruler used to punish children:—*v.t.* [feruled, ferul-ing], to punish with a ferule.

fer-vent (fûr'vent), *adj.* warmly felt; intense; earnest; as, a *fervent* prayer.—*adv.* **fer'vent-ly.**—*n.* **fer'ven-cy.**

fer-vid (fûr'vid), *adj.* fiery in feeling; earnest; as, a *fervid* speech.—*adv.* **fer'vid-ly.**—*n.* **fer'vid-ness.**

fer-vour (fûr'vẽr), *n.* glowing warmth of feeling; zeal; as, patriotic *fervour.*

fes-cue (fes'kū), *n.* a small, hardy meadow grass used for pasture and lawns.

fes-tal (fes't'l), *adj.* relating to a feast or holiday; joyful; as, her birthday was a *festal* occasion.

fes-ter (fes'tẽr), *v.i.* 1, to become filled with pus; as, his wound *festered;* 2, to linger painfully; cause a sore feeling; rankle; as, the insult *festered* in his mind:—*n.* a pus-forming sore.

fes-ti-val (fes'ti-val), *n.* a time of rejoicing and feasting, usually in honour of some great event; a special public celebration; as, a Thanksgiving *festival.*

fes-tive (fes'tiv), *adj.* 1, suitable to a feast or holiday; 2, gay; as, a *festive* room.—*n.* **fes-tiv'i-ty.**

fes-toon (fes-toon'), *n.* a decorative chain of flowers, or the like, hung in curves; also, a carved likeness of such a chain:—*v.t.* to decorate with festoons, or decorative chains of flowers, etc.; as, the church was *festooned* with ivy.

all (ôl), ôr; up, mūte, cûr, cōol, book; oil, out; th, thin; *th*, the.

fetch (fech), *v.t.* **1,** to go after and bring; as, *fetch* me a pen; **2,** to sell for; as, the land *fetched* a high price.

fetching (fech'ing), *adj. Colloq.* charming; attractive; as, a *fetching* costume.

fête (fāt), *n.* a festival; an entertainment; esp. an elaborate outdoor entertainment:—*v.t.* [fêt-ed, fêt-ing], to entertain as the guest of honour. Also, **fete.**

fet-id (fet'id; fē'tid), *adj.* stinking; as, a *fetid* breath; *fetid* air.

fe-tish (fē'tish; fet'), *n.* an object of blind or unreasoning devotion; as, she makes a *fetish* of dress.

fet-lock (fet'lok'), *n.* the tufted projection (or hair) on the back of a horse's leg just above the hoof.

fet-ter (fet'ér), *n.* **1,** a chain to bind the feet; **2,** a restraint; hindrance; as, the *fetters* of ignorance:—*v.t.* to put in chains; also, to hinder; restrain.

fet-tle (fet'l), *n.* condition; state; as, the speaker was in fine *fettle.*

fe-tus (fē'tus), *n.* the child in the uterus from the third month of pregnancy till birth (before then called the *embryo*). Also spelled **foe'tus.**—*adj.* **fe'tal** or **foe'tal.**

feud (fūd), *n.* a quarrel, generally of long standing, between clans or families.

feu-dal (fū'd'l), *adj.* relating to the method of holding land in the Middle Ages:—**feudal system,** the form of political organization common in Europe in the Middle Ages, based on the relationship between lord and vassal, the vassal holding land from his lord in return for military and other service.— *n.* **feu'dal-ism.**

fe-ver (fē'vér), *n.* **1,** a diseased condition marked by weakness, quick pulse, and high body temperature; also, a disease causing such symptoms; **2,** great excitement; as, a *fever* of anxiety.— *adj.* **fe'ver-ish.**—*adj.* **fe'vered.**

few (fū), *adj.* and *pron.* small in number; not many; as, his words were *few.*—*n.* **few'ness.**

fez (fez), *n.* [*pl.* fezzes], a red felt, tasselled cap, formerly worn by Turkish men.

fi (fē), *n.* in *music,* a tone between fa and sol of the diatonic scale.

fi-an-cé (fē'än-sā'; fi-än'sā; *French,* fyän'sā'), *n.* a man engaged to be married.—*n.fem.* **fi'an-cée'** (fē'än-sā'; fi-än'sā; *French,* fyän'sā').

fi-as-co (fi-ås'kō), *n.* an ignominious failure, as an actor's or opera singer's failure to please an audience.

fi-at (fī'at), *n.* a decree; command; as, a king's *fiat.*

fib (fib), *n.* a petty lie:—*v.i.* [fibbed, fib bing], to tell fibs.—*n.* **fib'ber.**

fi-ber-glas (fī'bér-glas'), *n.* finel spun glass filaments made into a wooll yarn and woven into textiles for build ing insulation, protecting boat hulls, etc

fi-bre or **fi-ber** (fī'bér), *n.* **1,** one c many slender, threadlike parts formin certain plant and animal substances as, flax *fibres;* nerve *fibres;* also, substance made up of such parts; ! raw material which can be separate into threads and spun or woven; a cotton *fibre;* **3,** quality or characte as, a man of tough *fibre.*—*adj.* **fi'broi**

fi-brous (fī'brus), *adj.* **1,** threadlik 2, made of threadlike stuff; as, *fibrou* bark.

fib-u-la (fib'yoo-la), *n.* the oute smaller bone of the leg below the kne the larger, inner one is the *tibia.*

fick-le (fik'l), *adj.* uncertain; chang able; as, *fickle* weather.—*n.* **fick'l** ness.

fic-tion (fik'shun), *n.* **1,** novels, sho stories, etc., telling of imaginary even and characters; **2,** anything imagine or invented as contrasted with thin which are real or true; as, that story his wealth is a *fiction.*—*adj.* **fic'tion-a**

fic-ti-tious (fik-tish'us), *adj.* imagine not real; as, a *fictitious* character.

fid-dle (fid'l), *n. Colloq.* a violin:—*v* [fid-dled, fid-dling], **1,** to play the violi **2,** to trifle; as, to *fiddle* at writing:—*v Colloq.* to play (a tune) on a violin; a he can *fiddle* the latest songs.

fid-dle—fad-dle (fid'l—fad'l), *n.* ar *interj. Colloq.* nonsense; fuss:—*v.i.* fuss.

fid-dler (fid'lér), *n.* **1,** a violinist; **2,** kind of burrowing crab having one cla much larger than the other: also call *fiddler crab.*

fidel-i-ty (fi-del'i-ti; fī-del'i-ti), *n.* [*p* fidelities], faithfulness to a perso cause, or trust; loyalty; trustwort! ness.

fidg-et (fij'et), *v.i.* to be restless a uneasy; as, the boys *fidgeted* during t long play:—*v.t.* to make uneasy; wor as, the heat *fidgets* me:—*n.* **1,** a restle person; as, the child is a *fidget* in churc **2, fidgets,** a state of restlessness; as, have the *fidgets.*—*adj.* **fidg'et-y.**

fie (fī), *interj.* for shame! (used humc ously to indicate a pretence of bei shocked).

field (fēld), *n.* **1,** a piece of farm la cleared for cultivation, pasture, et often enclosed by a fence or hedge; a plot of ground set aside for a spec use; as, a football *field;* **3,** a regi

cat, āge, fär, câre, ȧsk; ten, ēve, latėr; (i) pity, rely, senate; īce; top; i yielding some natural product; as, oil-*fields;* **4,** the scene of military operations; a battlefield; also, a battle; **5,** in sports, all those who engage or compete in a contest or sport; as, in the fox-hunt he led the *field;* **6,** in baseball, cricket, or the like, the side not batting; **7,** the background against which a thing is seen; as, stars in a blue *field;* **8,** an open space; as, a *field* of snow; **9,** a range or sphere of activity; as, the *field* of art:—*v.t.* and *v.i.* in cricket or baseball, to catch or stop and return (a ball) from the field.—*n.* **field′er.**

ield mar-shal, in Europe, a military officer next below the commander-in-chief.

ield-piece (fēld′pēs′), *n.* a cannon mounted on wheels.

iend (fēnd), *n.* **1,** an evil spirit; a devil; also, an unnaturally wicked or cruel person; **2,** *Colloq.* a person much given to a habit; as, a drug *fiend;* a speed *fiend.*—*adj.* **fiend′ish.**—*adv.* **fiend′ish-ly.**

ierce (fērs), *adj.* [fierc-er, fierc-est], **1,** furiously violent and intense; as, a *fierce* fighter; **2,** cruel; savage.—*adv.* **fierce′ly.**—*n.* **fierce′ness.**

i-er-y (fī′ẽr-i; fī′ri), *adj.* [fier-i-er, fier-i-est], **1,** hot and lively in feeling; as, a *fiery* speech; **2,** having a reddish glow; as, a *fiery* sun.

ies-ta (fyäs′tä; fi-es′ta), *n.* a religious festival; holiday; saint's day.

ife (fīf), *n.* a shrill-toned musical instrument of the flute class:—*v.t.* and *v.i.* [fifed, fif-ing], to play (a tune) on a fife. —*n.* **fif′er.**

if-teen (fif′tēn′), *adj.* composed of ten more than five:—*n.* **1,** the sum of fourteen and one; **2,** a sign representing fifteen units, as 15 or xv.—*adj.* **fif′-teenth′.**

ifth (fifth), *adj.* next after the fourth: the ordinal of *five:*—*n.* **1,** one of the five equal parts of anything; **2,** in music, an interval of three steps and a half step, as from C to G in the scale of C major.—*adv.* **fifth′ly.**

if-ti-eth (fif′ti-eth), *adj.* next after the 49th: the ordinal of *fifty:*—*n.* one of the 50 equal parts of anything.

if-ty (fif′ti), *adj.* composed of ten more than 40:—*n.* [*pl.* fifties], **1,** the sum of 49 and one; **2,** a sign representing 50 units, as 50 or l.

if-ty—one (fif′ti-wun′), *adj.* the numbers fifty-one to fifty-nine are hyphenated.

fig (fig), *n.* **1,** a small, sweet, pear-shaped fruit, grown in warm countries; also, the tree which bears it; **2,** *Colloq.* the least amount; as, I don't care a *fig.*

fight (fīt), *v.i.* [fought (fôt), fight-ing], **1,** to strive in battle or in single combat; as, to die *fighting;* **2,** to strive against difficulties or opponents; as, to *fight* for a goal:—*v.t.* **1,** to strive against; make war upon; as, to *fight* an enemy; crime, disease, etc.; **2,** to engage in (a conflict); as, to *fight* a duel:—*n.* **1,** a battle; conflict with firearms, ships, armies, etc.; also, a physical conflict between persons; a brawl; **2,** any strife or struggle; as, the *fight* for lower taxes; **3,** willingness or eagerness to struggle; as, John is full of *fight.*—*n.* **fight′er.**

fig-ment (fig′ment), *n.* something imagined; fiction; as, your ghost is a mere *figment.*

fig-ur-a-tive (fig′ūr-a-tiv; fig′yẽr-a-tiv), *adj.* expressing an idea or meaning in an unusual way, esp. by the use of language which tends to call up a picture; as, "armed to the teeth" is a *figurative* way of saying "completely armed."—*adv.* **fig′ur-a-tive-ly.**

fig-ure (fig′ūr; fig′yẽr), *n.* **1,** a shape; outline; appearance; as, a *figure* in the fog; a girlish *figure;* **2,** a person as he appears to others; as, the old beggar was a pitiful *figure;* **3,** a likeness of something; as, a *figure* on a coin; **4,** an illustrative drawing; **5,** a design or pattern, as in fabrics; also, a movement of a dance; **6,** a symbol of a number, as 1, 2, etc.; **7,** price; as, sold at a high *figure;* **8, figures,** numbers; arithmetic:—**figure of speech,** the saying of something in a fanciful manner in order to make it more striking or forceful:—*v.t.* [figured, figur-ing], **1,** to calculate; as, to *figure* up the cost; also, to think; as, to *figure* out a way; **2,** to imagine; as, he *figures* himself a hero:—*v.i.* **1,** to be prominent; as, to *figure* in the news; **2,** *Colloq.* to use arithmetic; as, he likes to *figure.*

fig-ure-head (fig′ūr-hed′; yẽr), *n.* **1,** a carved image at the prow of a ship; **2,** a person who is important in name only; as, the king was a mere *figure-head.*

fig-u-rine (fig′ū-ren′; yẽr), *n.* a small ornamental statuette, esp. of molded and painted terra cotta or metalwork.

fil-a-ment (fil′a-ment), *n.* **1,** a fine wire or thread; **2,** in a flower, the stalk of a stamen (see *flower,* illustration).

fil-bert (fil′bẽrt), *n.* the nut of the hazel.

filch (filch), *v.t.* to take by stealth; to steal.

¹file (fīl), *n.* **1,** a folder or a case, for keeping papers in order; also, papers arranged in order, as letters; **2,** a row of persons or things, one behind another:—*v.t.* [filed, fil-ing], to put (papers) away in order:—*v.i.* to march in line, one person following behind another.

²**file** (fīl), *n.* a steel tool with a rough face for smoothing or wearing away surfaces, as wood or metal:—*v.t.* [filed, fil-ing], to smooth or cut with a file.—*n.* **fil′ing.**

fi-let mi-gnon (fē′le′mē′nyŏn′), *n.* a round cut of beef garnished with pork or bacon.

fil-i-al (fil′i-al; fil′yal), *adj.* due to a parent from a child; as, *filial* respect.

fil-i-bus-ter (fil′i-bus′tėr), *n.* a long speech made merely to consume time in a legislature, esp. to prevent a bill from coming to a vote; use of dilatory tactics to thwart the will of a majority:—*v.i.* to use such tactics.—*n.* **fil′i-bus′ter-er.**

fil-i-gree (fil′i-grē′), *n.* ornamental lacelike work in gold or silver wire; also, any delicate tracery, as of frost:—*adj.* made of or like such work.

fill (fil), *v.t.* to make full; as, to *fill* a glass; **2,** to close or stop up the pores or cavities of; as, to *fill* teeth; **3,** to satisfy, as with food; **4,** to take up all the space in; as, the crowd *filled* the room; **5,** to supply what is required by; as, to *fill* an order; **6,** to perform the duties of; as, he *fills* the office well:—*v.i.* **1,** to become full; as, her eyes *filled* with tears; **2,** to become full of wind, as sails:—*n.* **1,** enough to satisfy; as, I ate my *fill;* **2,** anything put in to fill up a space; as, a *fill* of sand.—*n.* **fill′er.**

fil-let (fil′et), *n.* **1,** a narrow band, esp. one worn around the forehead; **2,** a flat moulding separating other mouldings; **3,** (often fil′ā; fil′i), in cooking, a boneless piece of meat or fish: also spelled *filet:*—*v.t.* to bind or ornament with a narrow band.

fil-ly (fil′i), *n.* [*pl.* fillies], a young mare; a female foal or colt.

film (film), *n.* **1,** a thin layer, or coating, as of oil on water; **2,** a roll of celluloid for taking photographs; **3,** a motion picture:—*v.t.* **1,** to cover with a thin coating; **2,** to make a motion picture of.

fil-ter (fil′tėr), *n.* any material, as sand or cloth, used to strain out solid matter from liquids; also, an apparatus so used:—*v.t.* and *v.i.* to pass (a liquid) through a filter.—*n.* **fil-tra′tion** (fil-trā′shun).—*adj.* **fil′ter-a-ble** or **fil′tra-ble** (as, a *filterable* virus).—*v.* and *n.* **fil′trate.**

filth (filth), *n.* **1,** loathsome dirt; **2,** dirty language or thought.—*n.* **filth′i-ness.**—*adj.* **filth′y.**

fin (fin), *n.* one of the fanlike parts of fish, which helps to move and steer i through the water; also, anything lik a fin; as, an aeroplane *fin.*

fi-na-gle (fi-nā′gl), *v.t. Colloq.* **1,** to ge by guile or underhand means; as, h *finagled* passes to the game; **2,** reneg (at cards).—*n.* **fi-na′gler.**

fi-nal (fī′nal), *adj.* **1,** coming at the end last; as, the *final* page; **2,** putting a end to doubt; as, a *final* decision:— **finals,** *n.pl.* **1,** the last event or game i a series; **2,** the last examinations of th term.—*n.* **fi-nal′i-ty** (fī-nal′i-ti).— **fī′nal-ist.**—*v.t.* **fi′nal-ize′** (*U.S. Colloq.*

fi-na-le (fi-nä′li; fi-nä′lā), *n.* **1,** th final movement of a symphony or othe musical composition; **2,** the closin scene of an opera or play.

fi-nal-ly (fī′nal-i), *adv.* **1,** lastly; **2,** ε last; as, they *finally* came; **3,** once f all; as, to settle a matter *finally.*

fi-nance (fi-nans′; fī-nans′; fī′nans *n.* **1,** the science of the management money; **2, finances,** income; funds; a the family *finances* are low:—*v.t.* [nanced, financ-ing], to provide the mo ey for; as, the bank *financed* the factor —*adj.* **fi-nan′cial.**—*adv.* **fi-nan′cial-l**

fin-an-ci-er (fi-nan′si-ėr; fin′an-sėr fī′nan-sėr′), *n.* a person skilled in mon matters.

fin-back (fin′bak′), *n.* a whalebo whale with a prominent dorsal fin, es the rorqual of the North Atlantic coa of America: length 60′ to 80′.

finch (finch), *n.* any of various sma songbirds, as the bunting, canar sparrow, linnet, grosbeak, etc.

find (fīnd), *v.t.* [found (found), find-in **1,** to discover by chance or acciden as, to *find* a dime; **2,** to learn by obse vation or experiment; as, to *find* t way a thing works; **3,** to reach; get t as, the arrow *found* its mark; **4,** determine and declare; as, the ju *found* him guilty; **5,** to succeed getting; as, to *find* favour:—*n.* a val able discovery; as, the postage stam on the old letters were a *find.*

find-er (fīn′dėr), *n.* an extra lens on camera, used to locate the object in t field of vision and to show on a ve small scale the picture to be taken.

find-ings (fīnd′ingz), *n.pl.* **1,** materi (other than leather) used in makin shoes; **2,** thread, buttons, binding etc., provided by a dressmaker:—*sin* in *law,* the verdict of a jury or cou

¹**fine** (fīn), *n.* money paid as a penal for breaking a law:—*v.t.* [fined, fin-in to punish by imposing a fine.

²**fine** (fīn), *adj.* [fin-er, fin-est], **1,** superior quality; as, *fine* silk; fi

music; **2,** slender; not coarse; as, a *fine* needle; *fine* sand; **3,** delicate; refined; as, a man of *fine* feelings; **4,** excellent in character; as, a *fine* boy; **5,** pleasant; bright; as, a *fine* day:— **fine arts,** arts whose chief concern is with the creation of beauty, as music and painting.—*adv.* **fine/ly**—*n.* **fine/ness.**

fin-er-y (fīn/ėr-i), *n.* [*pl.* fineries], showy clothing or ornaments.

fi-nesse (fi-nes/), *n.* **1,** adroitness; delicate skill; artifice; as, he handled the diplomatic mission with *finesse;* **2,** at *cards,* to try, as second or third player, to take a trick with a lower card, in the hope that a higher one is held by the right-hand opponent; as, he *finessed* the queen.

fin-ger (fing/gėr), *n.* **1,** one of the five separate divisions of the hand; esp. any one of four not including the thumb; **2,** any one of many mechanical devices used like a finger; **3,** a division of a glove into which a finger is put:—*v.t.* **1,** to touch; as, to *finger* objects on a counter; **2,** to play (an instrument) with the fingers.

in-ger-ling (fing/gėr-ling), *n.* a young fish no longer than a man's finger; as, to stock a stream with trout *fingerlings.*

in-i-cal (fin/i-kl) or fin-ick-ing (fin/i-king) or fin-ick-y (fin/i-ki), *adj.* affectedly fussy; precise in trifles; fastidious; as, he was *finicky* about his food.

i-nis (fī/nis), *n.* the end.

in-ish (fin/ish), *v.t.* **1,** to bring to an end; complete; conclude; as, to *finish* a piece of work; **2,** to fix the surface of in some way; as, to *finish* wood, cloth, etc.; **3,** *Colloq.* to dispose of; render powerless; kill:—**finished,** done very carefully; excellent; as, a *finished* performance:—*v.i.* to come to an end; stop; as, the book *finished* abruptly:—*n.* **1,** the completion; end; as, the *finish* of a race; **2,** surface or texture; as, tweed cloth has a rough *finish;* wood with a smooth *finish.*—*n.* **fin/ish-er.**

i-nite (fī/nīt), *adj.* having limits.

in-nan had-die (fin/an had/i) or **fin-nan had-dock** (had/uk), a smoked haddock, a kind of food fish.

iord or **fjord** (fyôrd), *n.* a long, narrow inlet, or arm of the sea, between high banks, as on the coast of Norway.

ir (fûr), *n.* a cone-bearing, evergreen tree valued for its resin and timber; also, the timber.

.re (fīr), *n.* **1,** the visible heat or light produced by burning; a spark or flame; **2,** wood, coal, or other fuel burning; as, a hot *fire* in the stove; **3,** a destructive burning; as, a forest *fire;* **4,** a discharge of firearms; as, the soldiers

heard the *fire* of cannon; **5,** strong feeling; spirit; as, the speech lacked *fire;* **6,** brilliancy or light; as, the *fire* of a diamond:—*v.t.* [fired, fir-ing], **1,** to set on fire; as, to *fire* a haystack; **2,** to animate; excite; as, ambition *fires* his genius; **3,** to cause to explode; as, to *fire* a gun; **4,** to apply intense heat to; as, to *fire* pottery; **5,** *Colloq.* to dismiss; discharge; as, the boss *fired* his secretary:—*v.i.* **1,** to become ignited; take fire; **2,** to discharge artillery; as, they *fired* at the enemy.—*adj.* **fire/less.**

fire-arm (fīr/ärm/), *n.* a small weapon, as a rifle, revolver, etc., from which a shot is discharged by an explosive.

fire-brand (fīr/brand/), *n.* **1,** a piece of burning wood; **2,** one who kindles strife; esp. one who inflames the emotions of a crowd.

fire-crack-er (fīr/krak/ėr), *n.* a small roll of paper filled with gunpowder and set off by a fuse.

fire-damp (fīr/damp/), *n.* a gas, esp. methane, that forms in coal mines, and explodes when ignited.

fire—en-gine (fīr/—en/jin), *n.* an apparatus for forcing liquid on a fire to put it out.

fire—es-cape (fīr/—es-kāp/), *n.* a ladder or staircase that provides an escape from a burning building.

fire—ex-tin-guish-er (fīr/—eks-ting/-guish-ėr), *n.* an apparatus, usually a portable tank containing chemicals, for immediate use in putting out a fire.

fire-fly (fīr/flī/), *n.* [*pl.* fireflies], a small beetle which gives forth light.

fire-light (fīr/līt/), *n.* light from a fire; as, shadows dance in the *firelight.*

fire-lock (fīr/lok/), *n.* an old form of gun fired by a spark from flint and steel.

fire-man (fīr/man), *n.* [*pl.* fireman (-men)], **1,** one trained to put out fires; **2,** one who tends fires; a stoker.

fire-place (fīr/plās/), *n.* an opening in a chimney, where a fire may be built; a hearth.

fire-plug (fīr/plug/), *n.* a street hydrant where a fire hose may be attached to a water main.

fire-proof (fīr/proof/), *adj.* made of material that resists fire; as, *fireproof* buildings:—*v.t.* to make proof against burning.

fire-side (fīr/sīd/), *n.* **1,** the place near the fire; **2,** the hearth; home:—*adj.* pertaining to the home; as, *fireside* comfort.

fire-wood (fīr/wood/), *n.* wood for fuel.

fire-works (fīr/wûrks/), *n.pl.* devices, as firecrackers, rockets, etc., used in celebrations to make noise or a display of light.

¹firm (fûrm), *adj.* compact; solid; as, *firm* muscles; **2,** not easily moved; stable; as, a *firm* foundation; **3,** steady and vigorous; as, a *firm* step; **4,** steadfast; loyal; as, a *firm* belief; **5,** resolute; positive; as, he is *firm* of purpose:—*v.t.* to compact; fix firmly.—*adv.* **firm′ly.** —*n.* **firm′ness.**

²firm (fûrm), *n.* **1,** a partnership of two or more persons for doing business; **2,** the name under which a partnership operates.

fir-ma-ment (fûr′ma-ment), *n.* the sky.

first (fûrst), *adj.* **1,** earliest in time or order; as, the *first* page; **2,** foremost in importance, time, excellence, etc.; as, he was *first* in his class: also used as the ordinal of *one:*—*adv.* **1,** before everyone else, as in order, place, rank, etc.; **2,** sooner; rather; as, I would die *first:*—*n.* **1,** the beginning; **2,** any person or thing that is first; as, we were the *first* to go.

first aid, temporary treatment given the sick or injured while awaiting regular medical treatment.—*adj.* **first′— aid′.**

first—born (fûrst′–bôrn′), *adj.* earliest produced or born; eldest:—*n.* the eldest.

first—class (fûrst′–klás′), *adj.* of the highest rank or quality:—*adv.* with the best accommodations; as, to travel *first-class.*

first—hand (fûrst′–hand′), *adj.* obtained directly from the source; as, *first-hand* facts:—*adv.* directly.

first-ly (fûrst′li), *adv. Colloq.* used sometimes with *secondly, thirdly,* etc., but *first* is more correct.

first—rate (fûrst′–rāt′), *adj.* **1,** of the highest excellence; very good; as, a *first-rate* writer; **2,** *Colloq.* very well; as, I feel *first-rate:*—*adv. Colloq.* excellently.

firth (fûrth), *n.* an arm of the sea.

fis-cal (fis′kal), *adj.* relating to financial matters; financial.

fish (fish), *n.* [*pl.* fish or fishes], **1,** an animal, usually with a scaly body and limbs modified into fins, living in water, and breathing through gills instead of lungs; **2,** the flesh of fish used for food:—*v.i.* **1,** to catch, or try to catch, fish; **2,** to search for anything hidden, buried, etc.; as, he *fished* in his pocket for a match; **3,** to seek to gain something by indirect means; as, he *fished* for information by sly questions:—*v.t.* **1,** to catch or try to catch (fish); **2,** to try to catch fish in; as, to *fish* a stream.—*n.* **fish′er.**—*n.* **fish′er-man.**

fish-er-y (fish′ẽr-i), *n.* [*pl.* fisheries], **1** the business of catching fish; **2,** a fishing ground.

fish-hook (fish′hook′), *n.* a hook which when fastened to a line and baited, i used for catching fish.

fish-y (fish′i), *adj.* [fish-i-er, fish-i-est] **1,** like fish or abounding in fish; **2** *Colloq.* unlikely; as, the story sound *fishy* to me.

fis-sion (fish′un), *n.* a splitting int parts; in *biology,* reproduction by cel division, as of bacteria; in *physics,* th splitting of an atomic nucleus, as b bombardment of uranium or plutoniur with neutrons.

fis-sure (fish′yoor; yẽr), *n.* a narrov opening; a crack; a cleft; as, a *fissur* in the earth:—*v.t.* or *v.i.* [fissured fissur-ing], to break or split.

fist (fist), *n.* the hand when closed o clenched; as, he struck with his *fist:*— *adj.* **fist′ic** (as, a *fistic* encounter).—*n* **fist′i-cuffs.**—*n.* **fist′ful.**

fis-tu-la (fis′tyoo-la; choo), *n.* a ulcerous narrow passage leading to a abscess, cavity, or organ (caused b injury or disease).

¹fit (fit), *n.* **1,** a sudden, violent attac of disease, as of epilepsy or indigestior **2,** a sudden outburst, as of laughter c energy.

²fit (fit), *adj.* [fit-ter, fit-test], **1,** suitabl proper; as, a dress *fit* for a queen; **2** ready; prepared; as, the team is *fit* fc work; **3,** in good condition; as, I fe *fit* again:—*v.t.* [fit-ted, fit-ting], **1,** t make suitable; adapt; as, I will *fit* m time to yours; **2,** to furnish with wha is right in size, shape, etc.; as, can yo *fit* me in shoes? **3,** to equip; prepare as, to *fit* a boy for college; **4,** to b properly adjusted to; be suitable fo as, this dress *fits* me:—*v.i.* to be adapte to one; as, his gloves *fit* well:—*n.* th adaptation of one thing to another; a this coat is an excellent *fit.*—*adv.* **fit′l** —*n.* **fit′ness.**—*n.* **fit′ter.**

fit-ful (fit′fool), *adj.* changeable; capr cious; also, irregular; restless; as, *fi ful* sleep.—*adv.* **fit′ful-ly.**

fit-ting (fit′ing), *adj.* suitable; prope as, you come at a *fitting* moment:— **fittings,** *n.pl.* the equipment or neces sary fixtures of a house, car, shop, et

five (fiv), *adj.* composed of one mor than four:—*n.* **1,** the number cor sisting of four plus one; **2,** a sig representing five units, as 5 or v.

fix (fiks), *v.t.* **1,** to make fast or firm; a they *fixed* a stake in the ground; **2,** t determine; as, they *fixed* the time fo the concert; **3,** to place definitely on person, as blame, responsibility, etc **4,** to make fast or permanent, as

colour, a photographic negative, etc.;
5, to direct or hold steadily, as the eyes; **6,** *Colloq.* to repair; as, the plumber *fixed* the leak; also, to arrange; as, to *fix* one's hair:—*v.i.* to become fixed:—*n. Colloq.* an awkward situation; as, I'm in a *fix.*—*n.* **fix-a/tion.**—*n.* **fix/i-ty.**

fixed (fikst), *adj.* firmly established; set; as, a *fixed* purpose:—**fixed star,** a star whose position with relation to other stars always seems the same: distinguished from a *planet.*—*adv.* **fix/ed-ly.**

fix-ture (fiks/tŭr), *n.* **1,** something permanently attached to an office, house, or the like; as, an electric-light *fixture;* plumbing *fixtures;* **2,** a person permanently placed; as, he's a *fixture* in our town.

fizz or **fiz** (fiz), *n.* **1,** a hissing sound; **2,** an effervescent or bubbling liquid, as soda-water:—*v.i.* [fizzed, fizz-ing], to make a hissing noise.

fiz-zle (fiz/l), *v.i.* [fiz-zled, fiz-zling], **1,** to make a hissing noise; **2,** *Colloq.* to fail miserably:—*n.* **1,** a hissing or spluttering; **2,** *Colloq.* a failure; as, he made a *fizzle* of his part in the play.

fjord (fyôrd), *n.* Same as **fiord.**

flab-ber-gast (flab/ẽr-gast), *v.t., Colloq.* astound; amaze; esp. by startling news.

flab-by (flab/i), *adj.* [flab-bi-er, flab-bi-est], **1,** yielding to the touch; limp; not firm; as, *flabby* cheeks; **2,** feeble; weak; as, a *flabby* will.—*n.* **flab/bi-ness.**

flac-cid (flak/sid), *adj.* flabby; soft; limp; as, *flaccid* muscles.

flag (flag), *n.* a piece of cloth bearing some design or symbol and often attached by one edge to a staff or stick, and intended to be spread or held aloft, as a national banner, signal, decoration, etc.:—*v.t.* [flagged, flagging], **1,** to signal with, or as with, a flag; as, to *flag* a train; **2,** to place a flag upon; also, to deck with flags.—*n.* **flag/pole/.**

flag (flag), *v.i.* [flagged, flag-ging], to droop; lag; lose strength; as, his courage *flagged.*

flag (flag), *n.* a plant with long, narrow leaves and showy, brightly coloured flowers; the iris: the fleur-de-lis or wild flag (yellow: *Iris pseudacorus;* blue: *Iris germanica;* the common North American blue flag: *Iris versicolor*) appears on the coat of arms of Quebec province.

Wild flag

⁴flag (flag), *n.* a large, flat slab of stone for pavements; a flagstone:—*v.t.* [flagged, flag-ging], to pave with flags.

flag-on (flag/un), *n.* a vessel for holding liquors, with a spout, a handle, and often a lid; as, a wine *flagon.*

fla-grant (flā/grant), *adj.* openly wicked; outrageous; notorious; as, a *flagrant* crime.—*n.* **fla/gran-cy.**

flag-ship (flag/ship/), *n.* a ship that flies the flag of the commander of a fleet.

flag-staff (flag/stȧf/), *n.* [*pl.* flag-staffs], a pole on which a flag is flown.

flag-stone (flag/stōn/), *n.* a large, flat stone used esp. for paving walks.

flail (flāl), *n.* an instrument consisting of a handle with a short stick hung loosely at one end, used for threshing grain by hand:—*v.t.* **1,** to thresh (with a flail); **2,** whip; flog.

flair (flâr), *n.* aptitude; bent; instinct; knack; as, a *flair* for writing.

flak (flak), *n.* antiaircraft fire.

flake (flāk), *n.* a small, thin chip or fragment of anything; as, a *flake* of soap:—*v.i.* [flaked, flak-ing], to break off into flakes; peel or scale off.—*adj.* **flak/y.**

flam-boy-ant (flam-boi/ant), *adj.* **1,** flaming; as, *flamboyant* colours; **2,** flowery, as *flamboyant* language or style; **3,** ornate, as *flamboyant* architecture.

flame (flām), *n.* **1,** a burning gas or vapour, often tonguelike in shape; **2,** a burning emotion or feeling; as, a *flame* of rage; **3,** *Colloq.* a sweetheart; as, she's an old *flame* of mine:—*v.i.* [flamed, flam-ing], to burn with a flame; burst into flame; as, the beacon *flamed* in the night:—*v.t.* **1,** to subject to the action of flame; **2,** to send (a signal) by fire.

fla-min-go (fla-ming/gō), *n.* [*pl.* flamingos or flamingoes], a long-legged, tropical wading bird, with rosy-white to bright-red plumage.

flamma-ble (flam/a-bl), *adj.* easily set on fire; inflammable; (preferred to this latter term by underwriters as less ambiguous).

flange (flanj), *n.* a raised or projecting rim on a wheel to keep it in place upon a track, or on a pipe to give a place for attaching it to a wall, floor, or the like.

flank (flangk), *n.* **1,** the fleshy part of an animal, between the ribs and hip; **2,** the side of anything, as of an army, building, etc.; as, the enemy attacked our right *flank:*—*v.t.* **1,** to stand at the side of; border; as, large trees *flanked* the road; **2,** to attack, go around, or guard the side of (an army).

flan-nel (flan'el), *n.* **1,** a soft, loosely woven cloth, usually made of wool; **2, flannels,** garments made of this material.

flan-nel-ette (flan'el-et'), *n.* a soft cotton cloth with a nap on one side.

flap (flap), *n.* **1,** anything broad and flat, hanging loose, and attached on one side only; as, the *flap* of an envelope; **2,** the motion of anything broad and flat swinging loosely and striking against something else; also, the sound thus made; **3,** a blow or slap; as, a *flap* of a beaver's tail:—*v.t.* [flapped, flap-ping], **1,** to strike with, or as with, a flap; **2,** to move to and fro; as, the bird *flaps* its wings:—*v.i.* to sway about loosely, often with a beating noise; as, the shades *flapped* against the windows.—*n.* **flap'per.**

flap-jack (flap'jak'), *n.* a cake of thin batter baked on a griddle; a pancake.

flare (flâr), *n.* **1,** a large, unsteady, glaring light; **2,** a fire or blaze serving as a signal; **3,** a sudden bursting forth; as, a *flare* of trumpets; **4,** a spreading outward; as, the vase has a *flare* at the top:—*v.i.* [flared, flar-ing], **1,** to burn with a broad, unsteady flame; **2,** to spread outward; as, a skirt that *flares* at the bottom.

flash (flash), *n.* **1,** a sudden burst of light; as, a *flash* of lightning; **2,** a sudden outburst, as of merriment, wit, or genius; **3,** a momentary light displayed as a signal; **4,** cheap display or show; **5,** an instant; as, he saw it in a *flash*:—*v.t.* **1,** to send forth swiftly or suddenly; as, to *flash* a light; to *flash* a look; **2,** to send out in flashes; as, to *flash* a signal:—*v.i.* **1,** to shine for a moment with a sudden light; as, beacons *flash* at night; **2,** to appear suddenly; pass at great speed; as, the train *flashed* by.—*n.* **flash'er.**

flash-back (flash'bak'), *n.* the interruption of a film, novel, etc., to present an earlier scene or episode.

flash-ing (flash'ing), *n.* sheet metal, etc., used to waterproof angles, joints, or edges of roofs and chimneys.

flash-light (flash'lit'), *n.* **1,** a small, portable electric light; **2,** a sudden brilliant light for taking photographs; also, the photograph so taken; **3,** a light that comes and goes in flashes, as a signal.

flash-y (flash'i), *adj.*] flash-i-er, flash-i-est], **1,** brilliant for a moment; **2,** gaudy; showy, but cheap-looking; as, *flashy* clothes.—*adv.* **flash'i-ly.**—*n.* **flash'i-ness.**

flask (flåsk), *n.* **1,** a narrow-necked bottle, made of glass, metal, or leather, for holding liquids, powder, etc.; **2,**

a metallic bottle with flat sides; as, pocket *flask.*

¹flat (flat), *adj.* [flat-ter, flat-test], **1,** having a level, horizontal surfac as, *flat* country; **2,** stretched out full length; as, to lie *flat* on the groun **3,** having a smooth and even surfac or nearly so, whether horizontal (not; as, the *flat* face of a cliff; broad and smooth, but not very thic **5,** dull or uninteresting; as, a *fl* sermon; tasteless or stale; as, *flat* foc or wine; not clear or sharp; as, *flat* sound; **6,** unqualified; downrigh as, a *flat* refusal; **7,** based on a fixe unit; uniform; as, a *flat* rate for gas; deflated; as, a *flat* tire; **9,** henc *Colloq.* low-spirited; without energ; also, without funds; **10,** dull; n glossy; as, a *flat* paint or finish; **11,** music: **a,** below the true pitch; as, *flat* note; **b,** lowered by a half step; a B *flat:*—*adv.* **1,** in a flat manner; a he sprawled *flat* on the ground; positively; directly; as, he came o *flat* against the candidate; **3,** exactl said of numbers; as, he ran 100 yar in ten seconds *flat;* **4,** in music, belo the true pitch; as, she sang slight *flat:*—*n.* **1,** a level surface or plai esp. low-lying country; as, the riv *flats;* **2,** the smooth, wide part of thing; as, the *flat* of a sword; **3,** deflated tire; **4,** in music, a sign [indicating a lowering of pitch by a ha step; also, the note so lowered:—*v.i.* and *v.i.* [flat-ted, flat-ting], **1,** to mal or become flat; **2,** to lower or becon lower in pitch.—*adv.* **flat'ly.**—*n.* **flat ness.**

²flat (flat), *n.* a set of rooms on o floor, usually planned for a sing family and forming complete livi quarters.

flat-fish (flat'fish'), *n.* a fish with broad, flat body, and both eyes on o side, as the flounder.

flat-foot-ed (flat'–foot'id), *adj.* having flat feet; **2,** firm; uncompr mising; **3,** unprepared; taken surprise; as, I caught him *flat-foote*

flat-iron (flat'i'ern), *n.* a heavy ir with a flat, smooth bottom and handle on top, used when heated f pressing or smoothing cloth.

flat-ten (flat'n), *v.t.* **1,** to make level smooth; **2,** to beat down; as, the ra *flattened* the corn; hence, to sadden depress; **3,** to make dull or tasteless:—*v.i.* **1,** to become even or level; **2,** become stale; as, ginger ale *flatte* when it stands.

flat-ter (flat'ẽr), *v.t.* **1,** to please, seek to please, with praise which usually insincere; as, he got the job l *flattering* the boss; **2,** to portray too favourably; as, the snapshot *flatters* him:—*v.i.* to give false praise.—*n.* **flat′ter-er.**—*adj.* **flat′ter-ing.**

flat-ter-y (flat′ẽr-i), *n.* [*pl.* flatteries], insincere, false, or undue praise.

flat-top (flat′top′), *n. Colloq.* an aircraft carrier.

flat-u-lent (flat′yoo-lent), *adj.* **1,** having or producing gas in the stomach or intestines; **2,** pompous or pretentious (in language); as, a *flatulent* style.

flat-ware (flat′wâr′), *n.* knives, plates, etc., as distinguished from bowls and cups (or *hollow* ware).

flat-worm (flat′wûrm′), *n.* any flat, unsegmented, parasitic worm, as the tapeworm.

flaunt (flônt; flänt), *v.t.* to show off; display impudently; as, the girl *flaunted* her new clothes:—*v.i.* **1,** to wave showily; as, flags *flaunting* in the wind; **2,** to make a showy appearance.—*adv.* **flaunt′ing-ly.**

fla-vour (flā′vẽr), *n.* **1,** that quality which affects the sense of taste; as, a spicy *flavour* in a cake; **2,** that quality which affects the sense of smell; as, the *flavour* of a perfume; **3,** a substance that gives a particular taste to food or drink; **4,** a particular or characterizing quality; as, his stories have a *flavour* of the sea:—*v.t.* to give flavour to.

fla-vour-ing (flā′vẽr-ing), *n.* an extract or substance used to give a particular taste.

flaw (flô), *n.* a blemish; a weak spot; defect; crack; as, a *flaw* in the glass.— *adj.* **flaw′less.**—*adv.* **flaw′less-ly.**

flax (flaks), *n.* a slender blue-flowered plant whose stem yields the fibres from which linen is spun, and from whose seeds linseed oil is made.

flax-en (flak′sn), *adj.* **1,** made of, or resembling, flax; **2,** of a pale-yellow colour; as, *flaxen* curls.

flax-seed (flaks′sēd′; flak′sēd′), *n.* the seed of the flax, much used in medicine and in the making of linseed oil.

flay (flā), *v.t.* **1,** to strip the skin from; skin; **2,** to scold; criticize or reprove severely or harshly.

flea (flē), *n.* a small jumping insect that sucks the blood of man and some other animals.

fleck (flek), *n.* a streak or spot; as, the bird had *flecks* of white on its breast:— *v.t.* to streak or spot; as, clouds *flecked* the sky.

fled (fled), *p.t.* and *p.p.* of *flee.*

fledge (flej), *v.i.* [fledged, fledg-ing], to acquire the feathers necessary for

flight; as, some birds are quicker than others to *fledge* and fly:—*v.t.* to furnish with feathers for flying; as, the young birds are not yet *fledged;* to *fledge* an arrow.—*n.* **fledg′ling** or **fledge′ling.**

flee (flē), *v.t.* [fled (fled), flee-ing], to run away from; avoid; shun; as, to *flee* evil:—*v.i.* **1,** to run away, as from danger or evil; as, they *fled* from their burning homes;. **2,** to vanish; disappear swiftly.

fleece (flēs), *n.* **1,** the woolly coat of a sheep; also, all the wool shorn from a sheep at one time; **2,** anything like the coat of a sheep:—*v.t.* [fleeced, fleec-ing], **1,** to shear (a sheep) of its wool; **2,** to rob; strip; as, the thieves *fleeced* him of all his money.—*adj.* **fleec′y.**

¹**fleet** (flēt), *adj.* swift; nimble; as, *fleet* as a deer:—*v.i., Poetic,* to pass or fly quickly; as, the hours *fleeted* by.— *adv.* **fleet′ly.**—*n.* **fleet′ness.**

²**fleet** (flēt), *n.* a number of warships under one command; hence, a number of vessels or vehicles moving together or under a single ownership; as, a *fleet* of taxicabs.

fleet-ing (flēt′ing), *adj.* passing quickly as, a *fleeting* glance.—*adv.* **fleet′ing-ly.**

flesh (flesh), *n.* **1,** the soft muscular tissues beneath the skin of a human or animal body; **2,** the body of animals used as food: more often called *meat;* **3,** the soft pulp of fruit; **4,** the human body; **5,** kindred, stock, or race; as, his own *flesh* and blood.—*adj.* **flesh′y.**— *n.* **flesh′i-ness.**

flesh-ly (flesh′li), *adj.* pertaining to the body; worldly.—*n.* **flesh′li-ness.**

fleur—de-lis (flûr′–dẽ-lē′; flûr′–dẽ-lēs′), *n.* [*pl.* fleurs-de-lis (flûr′–dẽ-lēz′)], **1,** the iris; **2,** the emblem of the former royal family of France; **3,** the wild flag (yellow: *Iris pseudacorus;* blue: *Iris germanica;* the common North American blue flag: *Iris versicolor*) appears on the coat of arms of Quebec province.

FLEUR-DE-LIS, def. 2

flew (floo), *p.t.* of *fly.*

flews (flooz), *n.* the hanging side-flaps of the upper lip of some dogs, as the bloodhound.

flex (fleks), *v.t.* to bend; as, he *flexed* his biceps.

flex-i-ble (flek′si-bl), *adj.* **1,** easily bent without breaking; **2,** yielding to persuasion; hence, easily managed or led; tractable; **3,** adaptable; as, a *flexible* form of government.—*adv.* **flex′i-bly.**—*n.* **flex′i-bil′i-ty.**

flex-or (flek′sẽr), *n.* a muscle that bends an arm, leg, etc.

flick (flĭk), *n.* **1,** a light, quick stroke, as of a whip; **2,** a streak or speck; as, a *flick* of dust:—*v.t.* to whip or strike gently with a quick jerk, as with a whip; as, to *flick* the dust off one's coat.

¹flick-er (flĭk'ẽr), *v.i.* **1,** to waver, shine, or burn unsteadily, as a flame; **2,** to flutter; vibrate; quiver:—*n.* an unsteady light or movement.—*adj.* and *n.* flick'er-ing.—*adv.* flick'er-ing-ly.

²flick-er (flĭk'ẽr), *n.* the golden-winged woodpecker of North America.

flied (flīd), *v.i.* in *baseball*, a past form of *fly;* as, he *flied* out to left field.

fli-er (flī'ẽr), *n.* Same as **flyer**.

flight (flīt), *n.* **1,** the act, process, manner, or power of flying; **2,** a passage, or the distance travelled, through the air; as, the *flight* of an aeroplane; hence, a swift passage; as, the *flight* of time; **3,** a hasty departure; as, the enemy took *flight;* **4,** a number of things or creatures, as birds, insects, arrows, or the like, passing through the air together; **5,** a soaring out beyond ordinary bounds; as, a *flight* of the imagination; **6,** a series of steps.

flight-y (flīt'ĭ), *adj.* [flight-i-er, flight-i-est], **1,** given to wild flights, as of fancy, humour, etc.; fickle; unsteady; **2,** mildly crazy.—*n.* flight'i-ness.

flim-flam (flĭm'flam'), *v.t. Colloq.* to trick; deceive.

flim-sy (flĭm'zĭ), *adj.* [flim-si-er, flim-si-est], **1,** thin; weak; without strength; as, a *flimsy* box; **2,** without reason; as, a *flimsy* argument.—*adv.* flim'si-ly.—*n.* flim'si-ness.

flinch (flĭnch), *v.i.* to draw back from pain, danger, an unpleasant duty, or the like.

fling (flĭng), *v.t.* [flung (flŭng), fling-ing], **1,** to throw or cast from, or as if from, the hand; as, to *fling* stones into a lake; **2,** to put away violently; as, he was *flung* into prison; **3,** to jerk suddenly; as, he *flung* back his head; **4,** to send out; as, the lantern *flung* out a dim light; **5,** to throw aside or cast off; as, to *fling* caution to the winds:—*v.i.* to rush out or about impatiently; as, to *fling* out of the room:—*n.* **1,** a cast or throw; **2,** a sneer or gibe; as, a *fling* at politicians; **3,** a period, usually brief, of unrestrained pleasure; as, he has had his *fling;* **4,** a lively dance; as, the Highland *fling*.

flint (flint), *n.* a hard kind of quartz or rock which strikes sparks from steel.—*adj.* flint'y.

flint-lock (flint'lok'), *n.* an old form of gun, or the lock of such a gun, in which the charge was set off by a spark from a flint struck on steel.

flint-y (flint'ĭ), *adj.* [flint-i-er, flint-i-est], composed of, or like, flint; hard; unyielding; as, a *flinty* heart.—*n.* flint'i-ness.

flip (flĭp), *v.t.* [flipped, flip-ping], **1,** to flick with the fingers; tap gently; as, to *flip* the ash from a cigar; **2,** to toss so as to turn over; as, to *flip* a coin: —*v.i.* to move jerkily; flap; as, the fish *flipped* in the boat:—*n.* a short, quick tap or flick:—*adj. Colloq.* pert; flippant.

flip-pant (flĭp'ant), *adj.* disrespectfully pert; saucy; as, a *flippant* child or a *flippant* answer.—*adv.* flip'pant-ly.—*n.* flip'pant-ness. flip'pan-cy.

flip-per (flĭp'ẽr), *n.* a broad, flat limb or fin adapted for swimming, as those of seals.

flirt (flûrt), *v.t.* **1,** to toss to and fro jerkily; as, the bird *flirts* its tail; **2,** to throw with a jerk; as, they *flirted* water at each other:—*v.i.* **1,** to move jerkily; dart; also, to shift constantly from one thing to another; trifle; **2,** to make love frivolously; play at love; **3,** to play, toy, or dally; as, to *flirt* with an idea:—*n.* **1,** one who plays at making love; **2,** a sudden jerk or toss; as, the *flirt* of a fan.—*n.* flir-ta'tion.

flit (flĭt), *v.i.* [flit-ted, flit-ting], **1,** to move lightly from place to place; **2,** to pass or dart along; as, the birds *flit* by.

flitch (flĭch), *n.* the side of a hog salted and cured; as, a *flitch* of bacon.

fliv-ver (flĭv'ẽr), *n. Slang,* a small, cheap motor-car, airplane, etc.

float (flōt), *v.i.* to be buoyed or held up on the surface of a liquid or within a volume of gas; as, a boat *floats;* a balloon *floats:*—*v.t.* **1,** to cause to rest or move gently on the surface of a liquid; as, the tide will *float* the boat again; to *float* a cargo down the river; also, to cause to be suspended or move in a volume of gas; as, to *float* balloons. **2,** to start or set going, as a company, scheme, or rumour:—*n.* **1,** anything that floats, as a raft, an anchored landing-place, a life-preserver, a cork on a fishing-line, a hollow metal ball in a tank or cistern, or the like; **2,** a low platform on wheels to carry an exhibit in a parade, or the exhibit so carried; also, a low under-slung platform or wheels for carrying heavy loads.—*n.* float'er.—*n.* flo-ta'tion.

flock (flok), *n.* **1,** a number of animals or birds of one kind keeping together; as, a *flock* of wild ducks; **2,** a large number of persons together; as, they came in great *flocks;* **3,** a group of people in charge of some person; as, the minister preached to his *flock:*—*v.i.* to come together or move in crowds; as, people *flocked* to hear her.

floe (flō), *n.* a large mass of drifting ice.

flog (flog), *v.t.* [flogged, flog-ging], to whip; beat or strike with a rod.

flood (flud), *n.* 1, a great flow of water; esp. a body of water overflowing its banks; 2, an abundant supply or outpouring of anything; as, a *flood* of light; a *flood* of music:—*v.t.* to cover or fill with water; as, to *flood* a valley; to supply; fill to excess; as, to *flood* a stage with light.

flood-gate (flud'gāt'), *n.* a sluice or gate to regulate the flow of water.

flood-light (flud'līt'), *n.* an artificial light of high intensity, used to illuminate playing fields, exteriors of buildings, etc.

floor (flōr), *n.* 1, the bottom surface of a room or hall; as, there is a pine *floor* in the kitchen; 2, any bottom surface like a floor; as, the *floor* of the ocean; 3, all the rooms on one level in a building; a storey; 4, the main part of an assembly-hall where members sit and speak; hence, the right to speak in an assembly; as, he has the *floor:*—*v.t.* 1, to cover with a floor; 2, to strike down; as, the boxer *floored* his opponent; 3, to put to silence; as, that argument *floored* him.

flop (flop), *v.t.* [flopped, flop-ping], to drop, or let fall heavily; as, to *flop* a suitcase on the floor:—*v.i.* 1, to strike about; as, the fish *flops* in the boat; flap, as the brim of a hat; 2, to throw oneself heavily; as, to *flop* down on a chair; 3, *Colloq.* to change over suddenly, as from one political party to another; 4, *Slang,* to fail:—*n.* 1, *Colloq.* the act or sound of flopping; 2, *Slang,* a failure.—*adj. Colloq.* **flop'py.**

flop-house (flop'hous'), *n. Slang,* a cheap hotel, often just for men.

flor-a (flōr'a), *n.* the plants of a particular region or period of time.

flor-al (flōr'al), *adj.* of or resembling flowers; as, a *floral* decoration.

flo-res-cent (flō-res'ent), *adj.* blossoming.—*n.* **flo-res'cence.**

flo-ri-cul-ture (flō'ri-kul'tyoor; chėr), *n.* flower cultivation.

flor-id (flor'id), *adj.* 1, bright in colour; flushed; as, a *florid* complexion; 2, flowery; richly decorated; showy; as, a *florid* style.

flor-in (flor'in; flor'), *n.* 1, an English silver coin worth two shillings; 2, any of several European gold or silver coins.

flor-ist (flor'ist; flôr'ist), *n.* one whose business is raising or selling flowers.

floss (flôs), *n.* 1, strands of silk used in embroidering, crocheting, or the like; 2, the downy, silky substance in certain pods, as of milkweed:—**floss silk,** an untwisted soft silk fabric used in embroidery; when waxed used as dental *floss* for cleaning between teeth.

flo-til-la (flō-til'a), *n.* 1, a fleet of small vessels; 2, a small fleet.

flot-sam (flot'sam), *n.* pieces of shipwreck or lost cargo found floating.

¹flounce (flouns), *n.* a gathered piece of cloth sewed by its upper border to the skirt of a dress; a deep ruffle:—*v.t.* [flounced, flounc-ing], to trim with deep ruffles.

²flounce (flouns), *n.* a jerk or sudden movement, often showing impatience; as, a *flounce* of the head:—*v.i.* [flounced, flounc-ing], to move suddenly and jerkily; as, to *flounce* out of a room.

¹floun-der (floun'dėr), *v.i.* 1, to plunge around; struggle awkwardly; as, to *flounder* through a swamp; 2, to make mistakes; blunder; as, to *flounder* through a speech.

²floun-der (floun'dėr), *n.* a food fish with a flat body and both eyes on the same side.

flour (flour), *n.* 1, the fine meal of ground wheat or other grain; 2, any fine, soft powder:—*v.t.* 1, to grind into flour; 2, to sprinkle flour upon.—*adj.* **flour'y.**

flour-ish (flûr'ish), *v.i.* 1, to grow; prosper; thrive; be vigorous; as, palm trees *flourish* in the tropics; 2, to make showy movements, as with a sword; 3, to make ornamental strokes with a pen:—*v.t.* 1, to swing about or brandish; as, to *flourish* a sword; 2, to ornament (letters) in writing:—*n.* 1, a showy waving; as, a *flourish* of a flag or a weapon; 2, a decoration in handwriting; 3, a showy musical passage played by trumpets, bugles, etc.

flout (flout), *v.t.* to insult; mock; disdain; as, to *flout* a kindness:—*n.* a scoffing remark or action.—*adv.* **flout'ing-ly.**

flow (flō), *v.i.* 1, to move or run along as a fluid; as, water *flows;* blood *flows* in the body; 2, to abound; be plentiful; as, wine *flows* at a feast; 3, to pour out easily and plentifully; as, words *flow;* 4, to come from; proceed; as, energy *flows* from health; 5, to hang loose; as, her long hair *flows;* 6, to rise, as the tide:—*n.* 1, a flowing; as, the *flow* of a river; 2, the amount of fluid passing through an opening or by a certain point in a given time; 3, any easy, continuous movement or procedure; as, a *flow* of speech, music, or thought; 4, the coming in of the tide.

flow-er (flou'ėr), *n.* 1, that part of a

seed-bearing plant or tree from which the seed develops; a blossom; **2,** a plant grown for its blossoms; **3,** the

FLOWER, partly cut away to show its parts.

best part; as, the *flower* of a nation's youth:—*v.i.* to blossom; as, fruit-trees *flower* in the spring.

flow-er-et (flou′ẽr-et), *n.* a little flower.

flow-er-y (flou′ẽr-i), *adj.* **1,** abounding in, or like, flowers; **2,** full of showy words and phrases; as, *flowery* language.

flown (flōn), *p.p.* of *fly*.

flu (flōō), *n. Colloq.* influenza, a contagious disease, marked by inflamed air passages, muscular pains, headache, digestive disturbances, and exhaustion.

fluc-tu-ate (fluk′tū-āt′), *v.i.* [fluctuated, fluctuat-ing], **1,** to rise and fall like waves; **2,** to keep changing or wavering as prices or temperature; as, the price of meat *fluctuates* daily.—*n.* **fluc′tu-a′tion.**

flue (flōō), *n.* **1,** a pipe or passage for smoke, air, etc., as in a chimney; **2,** the opening in an organ-pipe.

flu-ent (flōō′ent), *adj.* **1,** proceeding smoothly; flowing; **2,** ready or easy in the use of words, esp. in speaking.—*n.* **flu′en-cy.**

fluff (fluf), *n.* light down or fur nap:— *v.t.* **1,** to puff up into a light mass; as, to *fluff* the hair; to *fluff* a pillow; **2,** on stage, radio, television, etc., to make an error in speaking one's lines; as, the mayor *fluffed* the difficult phrase.—*adj.* **fluff′y.**—*n.* **fluff′i-ness.**

flu-id (flōō′id), *adj.* capable of flowing; liquid or gaseous:—**fluid drachm** or **dram,** a measure equal to one eighth of a fluid ounce; about a teaspoonful:— **fluid ounce,** a liquid measure of $\frac{1}{16}$ of a pint:—*n.* a substance which is capable of flowing, as a liquid or a gas.

[1]fluke (flōōk), *n.* **1,** the flattened, pointed end of an arm of an anchor; **2,** one of the broad lobes on the tail of a whale; **3,** the broad head of a harpoon, arrow, or lance.

[2]fluke (flōōk), *n.* a stroke of good or bad luck, esp. in a game.

flume (flōōm), *n.* **1,** an artificial channel for carrying water; **2,** a gap or gorge through which a stream or river flows.

flung (flung), *p.t.* and *p.p.* of *fling*.

flunk (flungk), *v.t. Colloq.* to fail; as, he *flunked* the English test; his teacher *flunked* him in Latin.

flunk-y or **flunk-ey** (flung′ki), *n.* a liveried servant, as a footman; a toady.

flu-or-i-date (flōō′ẽr-i-dāt′), *v.t.* to treat with fluorine.—*n.* **flu′o-ri-da′tion.**

flu-or-ide (flōō′ẽr-īd′; -id), *n.* a fluorine compound, as sodium *fluoride*, NaF.

flu-or-ine (flōō′ẽr-ēn′; -in), *n.* a pungent, green-yellow, corrosive gas (a member of the chlorine-bromine family).

flu-o-res-cent (flōō′ẽr-es′ent), *adj.* luminous when exposed to radiation:— **fluorescent lighting,** the light from a tubular electric lamp, the inside of which is coated with a phosphoric mixture that emits light when acted on by a stream of electrons from the cathode.—*n.* **flu′o-res′cence.**

flu-o-ro-scope (flōōr′e-skōp′), *n.* an instrument used by doctors for examining internal body structures by observing their shadows cast on a fluorescent screen when X-rays are passed through the structures.

flur-ry (flûr′i), *v.t.* [flurried, flurry-ing] to excite; confuse; bewilder; as, to be *flurried* by a question:—*n.* [*pl.* flurries], **1,** a sudden commotion or excitement; as, we were in a *flurry* at the news; **2,** a sudden gust of wind, rain, or snow.

[1]flush (flush), *v.t.* **1,** to redden; cause to blush; **2,** to excite; fill with elation as, to be *flushed* with victory; **3,** to wash or cleanse by a strong flow of water:—*v.i.* to blush; glow:—*n.* **1,** a blush; glow; **2,** a sudden rush, as of water; **3,** a thrill, as of excitement, elation, or pleasure:—*adj.* **1,** abundantly supplied, as with money; **2,** even; level; as, nail the board *flush* with the other; **3,** vigorous; spirited; full of life.

[2]flush (flush), *v.t.* to startle into flight, as birds.

flus-ter (flus′tẽr), *v.t.* to confuse, excite; agitate:—*n.* agitation or confusion.

flute (flōōt), *n.* **1,** a musical wind-instrument, a wooden pipe with finger stops and a hole across which the player blows; **2,** a long, rounded decorative groove, as in a column:—*v.i.* [flut-ed, flut-ing], to play on a flute:— *v.t.* to form grooves or folds in; as, to *flute* a ruffle.—*adj.* **flut′ed.**—*n.* **flut′ist.**

flut-ing (flōōt′ing), *n.* **1,** a set of grooves cut lengthwise in a column; **2,**

cat, āge, fär, câre, ásk; ten, ēve, latẽr; (i) pity, rely, senate; ice; top; nō.

a series of folds in a collar, ruffle, or the like.

flut-ter (flut′ẽr), *v.t.* to flap quickly without flying; as, the bird *flutters* his wings:—*v.i.* **1,** to move quickly and irregularly; as, curtains *flutter* in the wind; **2,** to be confused; flit about aimlessly; as, to *flutter* about at odd jobs:—*n.* **1,** a quick, irregular motion; vibration; as, the *flutter* of wings; **2,** a stir; excitement:—**flutter kick,** a short, rapid, up-and-down movement of the legs while using the crawl or the back-stroke in swimming.

flux (fluks), *n.* **1,** any flow or discharge of matter; **2,** continuous flowing; constant change; as, in a state of *flux;* **3,** a substance used to promote fusing in metals:—*v.t.* to fuse or melt; make fluid.

fly (flī), *v.i.* [*p.t.* flew (flōō), *p.p.* flown (flōn), *p.pr.* fly-ing], **1,** to move through the air with wings, or as with wings; as, birds *fly;* we *flew* in an aeroplane; **2,** to float in the air; as, the flag *flies;* **3,** to move or go swiftly; as, he *flies* to her aid: **4,** to run away; flee:—*v.t.* to cause to fly or float; as, to *fly* an aeroplane:—*n.* [*pl.* flies (flīz)], **1,** any of a large number of insects with a single pair of wings; esp. the common house-fly; **2,** a fishhook fitted with feathers to resemble an insect; **3,** in *baseball,* a ball batted so as to rise high in the air; **4,** a strip of material on a garment to cover or contain fastenings; **5,** a piece of canvas stretched over something to form an extra roof.

fly-blown (flī′blōn′), *adj.* full of flies' eggs; hence, tainted; as, *flyblown* meat.

fly-catch-er (flī′kach′ẽr), *n.* **1,** a small bird which feeds on insects, capturing them while flying; **2,** a plant which traps insects, as the pitcher-plant.

fly-er (flī′ẽr), *n.* **1,** one who or that which flies, as, a bird or an aviator; **2,** anything that moves very rapidly, as an express train; **3,** *Colloq.* a daring venture; as, he took a *flyer* in stocks. Also spelled **fli′er.**

fly-ing (flī′ing), *adj.* **1,** moving through the air, as on wings; **2,** capable of gliding through the air; as, a *flying* squirrel; **3,** floating or moving freely, as a flag; **4,** moving rapidly; as, a *flying* horse; **5,** fleeting; brief; as, a *flying* visit:—**flying buttress,** an arched brace against the wall of a building to resist the outward thrust of the roof, as in the mediaeval cathedrals.

fly-weight (flī′wāt′), *n.* a boxer of 112 pounds or less.

fly-wheel (flī′hwēl′), *n.* a heavy wheel

used to stabilize the speed of a machine, esp. to carry a piston over dead centre.

foal (fōl), *n.* the young of the horse or similar animal; a colt:—*v.i.* to give birth to a foal.

foam (fōm), *n.* the white substance formed on a liquid by shaking or fermentation; froth:—*v.i.* to form or produce foam; as, the dog *foamed* at the mouth.—*adj.* **foam′y.**

fob (fob), *n.* **1,** a small pocket for a watch; **2,** a short watch-chain or ribbon; also, a small ornament at the end of it.

fo-cal (fō′k′l), *adj.* relating to a focus; placed at a central point.

fo-cus (fō′kus), *n.* [*pl.* foci (fō′sī) or focuses (fō′kus-ez)], **1,** the point at which rays of heat, light, sound, etc., meet after being bent or turned from the straight lines in which they radiate; **2,** an adjustment of eyes, glasses, camera lenses, etc., to produce clear sight or images; **3,** a central point; centre of interest:—*v.t.* [focused, focus-ing], **1,** to adjust the focus of (eyes, a telescope, camera, etc.) **2,** to bring into focus; **3,** to centre; concentrate; as, he *focused* his attention on history.

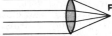

Focus, def. 1
Parallel rays of light brought to a focus (F) by a convex lens.

fod-der (fod′ẽr), *n.* coarse food, such as dried corn-stalks, for cattle.

foe (fō), *n.* **1,** an enemy; **2,** anything injurious; as, ill health is a *foe* to happiness.

foe-man (fō′man), *n.* *Poetic,* foe; enemy.

foe-tus (fē′tus), *n.* Same as *fetus.*

fog (fog), *n.* **1,** a cloud of water vapour near the surface of the sea or land; **2,** any haziness, as on a photographic plate; **3,** bewilderment; as, my thoughts are in a *fog:*—*v.i.* [fogged, fog-ging], to become clouded, as with a fog:—*v.t.* to cover as with a fog; cloud.—*adj.* **fog′gy.**

fog-bound (fog′bound′), *adj.* held up by heavy fog (said of a ship, airplane, etc.).

fog-horn (fog′hôrn′), *n.* a siren or horn for warning ships in a fog.

fo-gy or **fo-gey** (fō′gi), *n.* [*pl.* fogies], a person of old-fashioned or dull habits and ideas.

foi-ble (foi′bl), *n.* a weak point; a failing or weakness of character; as, humorists write about the *foibles* of mankind.

¹foil (foil), *n.* **1,** a thin, flexible sheet

of metal; as, tin-*foil;* gold-*foil;* **2,** a thin coat of metal placed on the back of a mirror to reflect light; also, such a coat placed under stones in jewellery to set off their brightness; **3,** anything that sets off another thing to advantage by contrast; as, her poor clothes are a *foil* to her beauty.

²foil (foil), *n.* a long, thin sword with a blunt point, used in fencing.

³foil (foil), *v.t.* to baffle; defeat; as, every attempt was *foiled* by the enemy.

foist (foist), *v.t.* to palm off; pass (something false or counterfeit) as genuine; as, to *foist* a false gem on a buyer.

¹fold (fōld), *v.t.* **1,** to double; bend over; as, to *fold* a letter; **2,** to clasp, as the hands; to bend close to the body; as, to *fold* one's arms; a bird *folds* its wings; **3,** to envelop; as, peaks *folded* in clouds:—*v.i.* to become closed by bending or doubling; as, the aeroplane's wings *folded* up:—*n.* a part doubled over another; also, a hollow or crease made by folding.

²fold (fōld), *n.* **1,** a pen for sheep; **2,** a flock of sheep; **3,** a body of religious believers:—*v.t.* to shut up (sheep) in a pen.

fold-er (fōl′dėr), *n.* **1,** a small folded circular, map, or the like; **2,** a cover for holding loose papers.

fo-li-age (fō′li-ij), *n.* leaves; all the leaves of a plant.

fo-li-o (fō′li-ō; fōl′yō), *n.* [*pl.* folios], **1,** a sheet of paper folded once; **2,** a book of the largest size, made of sheets of paper folded only once, with two leaves or four pages to each sheet; **3,** the size of a book so ·made; **4,** a folder for carrying music, loose papers, etc.; **5,** in *printing,* the number of a page:—*adj.* consisting of sheets of paper folded once; having the form or size of a folio; as, a *folio* edition:—*v.t.* to number the pages of (a book or manuscript).

fo-li-ate (fō′li-it; -āt′), *adj.* **1,** covered with leaves; **2,** leaflike:—*v.t.* to beat into foil or divide into thin layers.

folk (fōk), *n.* **1,** a race or nation; **2,** **folks** or **folk,** *pl.,* people collectively, esp. common people; as, town *folk;* some *folks* like to travel; **3,** **folks,** *Colloq.* one's own kindred; as, my *folks* are away:—*adj.* originating with the people; as, a *folk*-tale.

folk-lore (fōk′lōr′), *n.* the beliefs, legends, customs, etc., of a people.

fol-li-cle (fol′i-kl), *n.* a small sac or gland for secretion or excretion; as, when the hair *follicles* dry up, baldness results.

fol-low (fol′ō), *v.t.* **1,** to go or come after; as, we *followed* the guide; **2,** to come after in time or rank; as, he *followed* his father in office; **3,** to go along; as, to *follow* a road; **4,** to strive after; aim at; as, to *follow* fame; **5,** to copy; imitate; as, your idea *follows* his; **6,** to accept as guide; obey; as, to *follow* advice; **7,** to practise as a profession; as, he *followed* medicine; **8,** to pay attention to; to understand; as, to *follow* a lecture; **9,** to result from; as, illness *follows* neglect of health:—*v.i.* **1,** to go or come after another; as, go ahead, and we will *follow;* **2,** to result from; as, it *follows* from your remark that you intend to leave.—*n.* **fol′low-er.**

fol-low-ing (fol′ō-ing), *adj.* coming after; next; as, the *following* year; read the *following* page:—*n.* **1,** a body of followers or supporters; as, a political leader with a very large *following;* **2,** those about to be mentioned; as, the *following* were there.

fol-ly (fol′i), *n.* [*pl.* follies], **1,** lack of sense; want of understanding; foolishness; **2,** a foolish act or idea.

fo-ment (fō-ment′), *v.t.* **1,** to bathe with warm liquids; **2,** to foster; excite; stir up; as, to *foment* a riot.—*n.* **fo′men-ta′tion.**

fond (fond), *adj.* **1,** affectionate; loving; **2,** interested in; as, *fond* of music; **3,** cherished; as, my *fond* hope.—*adv.* **fond′ly.**

fon-dle (fon′dl), *v.t.* [fon-dled, fon-dling], to caress; pet; as, to stroke and *fondle* a cat.

¹font (font), *n.* **1,** a vessel to hold holy water or water for baptizing; **2,** a fountain or spring.

²font (font), *n.* in *printing,* a complete assortment of one size and style of type.

food (fōod), *n.* **1,** nourishment taken into the body to keep it alive and make it grow; also, any nourishing substance; **2,** solid nourishment in contrast to liquid.

food-stuff (fōod′stuf′), *n.* anything used as food, as meats, cereals, and fruits.

fool (fōol), *n.* **1,** a person of little sense or intelligence; **2,** in former times, a jester or clown; **3,** a dupe; a victim of a joke; as, to make a *fool* of him:—*v.t.* to deceive or trifle:—*v.i.* to trifle; play the fool.—*adj.* and *n.* **fool′ing.**—*n.* **fool′er-y.**—*n.* **fool′har′dy;** **fool′har′di-ness.**—*adj.* **fool′proof′.**

fools-cap (fōolz′kap′), *n.* writing paper about 17″ × 14″ (originally watermarked with a jester's cap and bells).

fool's gold (fo͞olz′gōld′), *n.* iron pyrites (looks like gold).

fool-ish (fo͞ol′ish), *adj.* 1, without reason or judgment; 2, silly; ridiculous.—*adv.* **fool′ish-ly.**—*n.* **fool′ish-ness.**

foot (foot), *n.* [*pl.* feet (fēt)], 1, that part of the leg on which man and other animals walk or stand; 2, the lowest part; base; as, the *foot* of a tree or a hill; 3, the lowest part in rank; as, the *foot* of the class; 4, the part of a boot or stocking which receives the foot; 5, that part of anything where the feet lie; as, the *foot* of a bed; 6, a measure of length, equal to twelve inches; 7, unmounted soldiers; infantry; 8, in *poetry*, a group of syllables containing one accented syllable and one or more unaccented syllables; as, the line "Peter,/Peter,/pumpkin/eater" has four metrical *feet*:—*v.t.* 1, to add a foot to (a stocking or sock); 2, to add up (a column of figures) and place the total at the bottom; 3, *Colloq.* to pay; as, to *foot* the bill.—*adj.* **foot′-stool′; foot′wear′; foot′work′.**

foot-ball (foot′bôl′), *n.* 1, a game in which an inflated leather ball must be carried or kicked across the opposing team's goal-line; 2, the ball used in this game.

foot-fall (foot′fôl′), *n.* a footstep; the sound of the tread of the foot.

foot—fault (foot′–fôlt′), *n.* in *tennis*, failure to keep both feet behind the white baseline in serving; hence, loss of the point.

foot-hill (foot′hil′), *n.* a low, outlying hill near the base of a mountain range.

foot-hold (foot′hōld′), *n.* a secure place to set foot; firm footing.

foot-ing (foot′ing), *n.* 1, firm placing of the feet; foothold; as, to lose one's *footing;* 2, a place to stand or walk; as, there was no *footing* along the cliff; 3, relationship; basis; as, a friendly *footing;* 4, the adding up, or the sum total, of a column of figures.

foot-lights (foot′līts′), *n.pl.* a row of lights along the front of the floor of the stage of a theatre.

foot-loose (foot′lo͞os′), *adj.* free (to go anywhere).

foot-man (foot′man), *n.* [*pl.* footmen (-men)], a male servant, usually in uniform, who attends a carriage, waits on table, etc.

foot-note (foot′nōt′), *n.* a note of explanation at the bottom of a page in a book.

foot-pad (foot′pad′), *n.* a highwayman who goes on foot.

foot-path (foot′path′), *n.* a path for the use of persons who are walking.

foot-print (foot′print′). *n.* the mark made by a foot, as in mud, snow, or the like.

foot-step (foot′step′), *n.* 1, an act of stepping; a step; 2, the sound of a step; 3, the mark of a foot, as in earth; footprint; track.

foo-zle (fo͞o′zl), *v.t. Colloq.* to bungle; as, he *foozled* the short putt.

fop (fop), *n.* a man who is fond of fine dress; a dandy.—*n.* **fop′per-y.**—*adj.* **fop′pish.**

for (fôr), *prep.* 1, in place of; as, Jones ran base *for* Brown; 2, as being; as, I took him *for* an honest man; 3, in return for, in a trade; as, two pencils *for* five cents; 4, because of; as, he could not walk *for* weakness; 5, because of a hindrance or lack of; as, I'd go but *for* my lessons; pressed *for* time; 6, on account of; in the interest of; as, do it *for* your mother; fear *for* his safety; 7, in favour, support, or defence of; as, to vote *for* White; 8, in spite of; as, *for* all his money, he has no influence; 9, to the amount of; as, a bill *for* five dollars; 10, as regards; as, so much *for* that point; a love *for* poetry; 11, in comparison or contrast with; as, wise *for* his years; one success *for* every ten failures; 12, with the hope, intention, or expectation, of reaching, getting, doing, etc.; as, he left *for* Europe; to try *for* a prize; 13, with a view to; for the purpose of; as, to go *for* a walk; 14, suited to; as, a salve *for* burns; the man *for* the job; 15, about; as, I don't care *for* cards; 16, for the use of; as, books *for* the class:—*conj.* because; since; seeing that; as, get up, *for* day is here.

for-age (fôr′ij), *n.* 1, food for horses and cattle; 2, a search for food or provisions for an army:—*v.i.* [foraged, forag-ing], to go in search of provisions: —*v.t.* to strip of provisions; ravage, as a land in wartime.—*n.* **for′ag-er.**

for-as-much as (fôr′az-much′az), *conj.* since; because.

for-ay (fôr′ā), *n.* in warfare, a raid:— *v.t. and v.i.* to plunder or ravage.

¹for-bear (fôr′bâr), *n.* an ancestor. Also spelled **fore′bear.**

²for-bear (fôr-bâr′), *v.t.* [*p.t.* forbore (fôr-bōr′), *p.p.* forborne (fôr-bōrn′), *p.pr.* forbear-ing], to refrain; keep from; as, he *forbore* to ask questions:— *v.i.* to restrain oneself; be patient.—*n.* **for-bear′ance.**

for-bid (fôr-bid′), *v.t.* [*p.t.* forbade or forbad (fôr-bad′). *p.p.* forbid-den (fôr-bid′n), or, *Archaic*, forbid, *p.pr.* forbidding], 1, to prohibit; not to allow; 2, to command (a person) not to do.

for-bid-ding (fôr-bid′ing), *adj.* stern; discouraging; as, a *forbidding* manner.

force (fōrs), *n.* **1,** energy; power; vigour; strength; violence; as, the *force* of a blow; **2,** power to convince or persuade; as, the *force* of an argument; **3,** real meaning, as of a word; **4,** (often *forces*), military or naval strength; armed men; warships or aircraft; **5,** hence, any trained or organized body of persons; as, the police *force;* the night *force* of a hospital; **6,** any powerful person or thing; as, a *force* for social reform; **7,** mental or moral strength; as, *force* of character; **8,** great numbers; as, the people ran out in *force;* **9,** violence to persons or property; **10,** in *physics,* anything which causes or changes motion in a body; as, the *force* of gravity, electricity, heat, etc.:—**force-pump,** a pump that forces water through valves under pressure:—*v.t.* [forced, forc-ing], **1,** to compel; as, to *force* her to talk; **2,** to push; get by strength; as, to *force* one's way; **3,** to produce by unnatural or special effort; as, to *force* a smile; **4,** to break open; as, to *force* a lock; **5,** to press or impose; as, to *force* a gift on someone; **6,** to hasten the growth of (a plant) artificially.

force-ful (fōrs′fool), *adj.* having vigour; strong; powerful; as, a *forceful* speech. —*adv.* **force′ful-ly.**—*n.* **force′ful-ness.**

for-ceps (fôr′seps), *n. sing.* and *pl.* pincers, pliers, or tongs, esp. those used by dentists, doctors, watchmakers, etc.

for-ci-ble (fôr′si-bl), *adj.* **1,** vivid; convincing; powerful; as, *forcible* speech; **2,** accomplished by violence; as, a *forcible* entry.—*adv.* **for′ci-bly.**

ford (fōrd), *n.* a shallow part of a stream, which can be crossed on foot:— *v.t.* and *v.i.* to pass through (water, a stream, etc.), on foot.

fore (fōr), *n.* the front part:—*adj.* and *adv.* at or near the front:—*interj.* used as a warning on a golf-course.

fore—and—aft (fōr′-and-àft′), *adj.* lengthwise of a ship; as, *fore-and-aft* sails.

fore-arm (fōr′ärm′), *n.* the arm between the wrist and the elbow.

fore-bear (fōr′bâr), *n.* an ancestor. Another spelling of **for′bear.**

fore-bode (fōr-bōd′), *v.t.* [forebod-ed, forebod-ing], **1,** to have a feeling or suspicion of (coming misfortune); fore-see (evil); **2,** to be a sign or warning of; as, conditions *forebode* war.

fore-bod-ing (fōr-bōd′ing), *n.* a feeling that misfortune is coming.

fore-cast (fōr′kàst), *n.* a foretelling,

as of the weather:—*v.t.* (fōr-kàst′; fōr′kàst′), [forecast or forecast-ed, forecast-ing], to plan or calculate beforehand; to predict.

fore-cas-tle (fōk′sl; fōr′kàs-l), *n.* the part of a vessel forward of the foremast.

fore-close (fōr-klōz′), *v.t.* [foreclosed, foreclos-ing], to terminate (a mortgage) by obtaining the legal right to the property mortgaged.—*n.* **fore-clo′sure.**

fore-fa-ther (fōr′fä′thĕr), *n.* an ancestor.

fore-fin-ger (fōr′fing′gĕr), *n.* the first or index finger, next to the thumb.

fore-foot (fōr′foot′), *n.* [*pl.* forefeet (-fēt′)], a front foot of a four-legged animal.

fore-gath-er (fōr-gath′ĕr). Same as *forgather.*

fore-go (fōr-gō′), *v.t.* Same as **forgo.**

fore-go-ing (fōr-gō′ing), *adj.* coming ahead of something else; preceding.

fore-gone (fōr-gôn′; fōr′gôn), *adj.* settled in advance; as, a *foregone* conclusion.

fore-ground (fōr′ground′), *n.* that part of a picture or scene nearest the observer.

fore-hand (fōr′hand′), *adj.* in *tennis,* made, as a stroke, with the arm at the side, not extended across the body.

fore-hand-ed (fōr′han′did), *adj.* **1,** ahead of time; **2,** looking to the future; prudent; as, be *forehanded* and save your pennies.

fore-head (for′id; fōr′hed′), *n.* the part of the face above the eyes; the brow.

for-eign (fôr′in), *adj.* **1,** belonging to another nation or country; as, a *foreign* language; **2,** not native; as, of *foreign* birth; **3,** not belonging or suitable; as, remarks *foreign* to the topic.—*n.* **for′eign-er.**

fore-knowl-edge (fōr-nol′ij), *n.* the knowing of a thing before it happens or exists; as, God's *foreknowledge* of what we will do.

fore-leg (fōr′leg′), *n.* either front leg, as of a horse, dog, etc.

fore-lock (fōr′lok′), *n.* a lock of hair growing on the front part of the head.

fore-man (fōr′man), *n.* [*pl.* foremen (-men)], **1,** the man in charge of a group of workmen; **2,** the chairman and spokesman of a jury.—*n. fem.* **fore′-wom′an.**

fore-mast (fōr′mast; fōr′màst′), *n.* the mast nearest the bow of a ship.

fore-most (fōr′mōst), *adj.* first; most important; chief.

fore-noon (fōr'noōn'), _n._ the time between sunrise and midday.

fo-ren-sic (fo-ren'sik), _adj._ relating to public debate or law courts; as, _forensic_ eloquence.

fore-paw (fōr'pô'), _n._ a front foot of any animal that has claws.

fore-run-ner (fōr-run'ẽr), _n._ **1,** a messenger sent in advance; **2,** anything which precedes or foreshadows another.

fore-sail (fōr'sāl; fōr'sl; fō'sl), _n._ **1,** the largest and lowest sail on the foremast of a square-rigged vessel; **2,** the big fore-and-aft sail on the foremast of a schooner.

fore-see (fōr-sē'), _v.t._ [_p.t._ foresaw (fōr-sô'), _p.p._ foreseen (fōr-sēn'), _p.pr._ foresee-ing], to know or see beforehand.

fore-shad-ow (fōr-shad'ō), _v.t._ to point to as coming; predict.

fore-short-en (fōr-shôr'tn), _v.t._ in drawing or painting, to shorten (lines or objects) so that they will appear to be at the true distance from the observer, as compared with other lines or objects.

fore-sight (fōr'sīt'), _n._ **1,** knowing or seeing beforehand; **2,** thought for the future; prudence.

fore-skin (fōr'skin'), _n._ the fold of skin covering the end of the penis (usually removed by circumcision).

for-est (fōr'est), _n._ a growth of trees covering a large tract of land; wild woodland:—_adj._ of or relating to woodland; as, _forest_ animals:—_v.t._ to cover with trees or woods.

fore-stall (fōr-stôl'), _v.t._ to hinder or prevent, by action taken in advance.

fore-stay (fōr'stā'), _n._ a rope from the foremast head forwards to the side of a ship, to support the foremast.

for-est-ry (fôr'est-ri), _n._ the science of caring for forests.—_n._ **for'est-er.**

fore-taste (fōr-tāst'), _v.t._ [foretast-ed, foretast-ing], to taste beforehand:—_n._ (fōr'tāst'), anticipation.

fore-tell (fōr-tel'), _v.t._ and _v.i._ [foretold (fōr-tōld'), foretell-ing], to tell beforehand; predict; prophesy.

fore-thought (fōr'thôt'), _n._ **1,** the planning of something beforehand; **2,** heedfulness for the future.

for-ev-er (fôr-ev'ẽr), _adv._ **1,** at all times; as, she was _forever_ nagging him; **2,** through eternity; perpetually.

fore-warn (fōr-wôrn'), _v.t._ to caution in advance.—_n._ **fore-warn'ing.**

fore-wom-an (fōr'woom'an), _n._ **1,** a woman in charge of factory workers or a workshop; **2,** a woman who presides over a jury.

fore-word (fōr'wûrd), _n._ a preface; introductory note or remarks.

for-feit (fôr'fit), _n._ something lost because of a crime or fault; hence, a fine or penalty; **2, forfeits,** a game in which one must perform a silly task to regain some article given:—_v.t._ to lose by neglect or fault; as, to _forfeit_ a game by coming late:—_adj._ lost by neglect or crime.—_n._ **for'fei-ture.**

for-gath-er (fôr-ga_th_'ẽr), _v.i._ to assemble; meet, esp. by chance.

¹forge (fōrj), _v.i._ [forged, forg-ing], to go on steadily; as, to _forge_ ahead.

²forge (fōrj), _v.t._ [forged, forg-ing], **1,** to shape (metal) by hammering while it is soft with heat; **2,** to shape; form; invent; **3,** to make a false imitation of; esp. to counterfeit (a signature):—_n._ **1,** an open fire for heating metal in preparation for hammering or shaping; **2,** a shop for heating and working metal.—_n._ **forg'er.**

for-ger-y (fōr'jẽr-i), _n._ [_pl._ forgeries], **1,** the act of copying or imitating something, esp. a signature, with intent to deceive; **2,** a false signature; **3,** anything counterfeit.

for-get (fôr-get'), _v.t._ [_p.t._ forgot (fôr-got'), _p.p._ forgot-ten (fôr-got'n) or forgot, _p.pr._ forget-ting], **1,** to fail to remember or recall; **2,** to cease to think of; as, he has _forgotten_ me; **3,** to omit to take or do; as, I have _forgotten_ my tonic; **4,** to neglect; disregard; as, to _forget_ a debt:—_v.i._ to fail to remember.—_adj._ **for-get'ful.**—_n._ **for-get'fulness.**

for-get—me—not (fôr-get'—mē—not'), _n._ a plant with tiny, yellow-eyed blue or white flowers and hairy, rough leaves.

for-give (fôr-giv'), _v.t._ [_p.t._ forgave (fôr-gāv'), _p.p._ forgiv-en (fôr-giv'en), _p.pr._ forgiv-ing], **1,** to cease to resent; to pardon; as, to _forgive_ an unkindness; _forgive_ him for doing it; **2,** to refrain from exacting, as a debt.—_adj._ **for-giv'ing.**—_adv._ **for-giv'ing-ly.**—_n._ **for-give'ness.**—_adj._ **for-giv'a-ble.**

for-go (fôr-gō'), _v.t._ [_p.t._ forwent (fôr-went'), _p.p._ forgone (fôr-gôn'), _p.pr._ forgo-ing], to give up; deny oneself. Also, **fore-go'.**

fork (fôrk), _n._ **1,** a farm tool with two or more prongs and a handle, used for digging, picking up, carrying, etc.; as, a pitch_fork_; **2,** a small, pronged implement for dining-room or kitchen use; **3,** anything branching like a fork; as, a _fork_ in a road or a tree:—_v.t._ **1,** to make in the shape of a fork; **2,** to raise, throw, or dig with a fork; as, to _fork_ hay:—_v.i._ to branch; as, the road _forks_ here.

for-lorn (fôr-lôrn′), *adj.* forsaken; miserable; pitiful; as, a *forlorn* beggar.

form (fôrm), *n.* 1, the outward appearance or shape of anything; 2, a body, esp. the human body; 3, special arrangement or method of composition; as, poetic *form;* sonata *form;* 4, established practice or ritual; as, *forms* of worship; 5, a definite manner of doing something; etiquette; as, the *form* for an introduction; 6, a standard of conduct; as, tattling is bad *form;* 7, athletic fitness; as, he's in good *form* to-day; 8, a mould or pattern; as, a *form* for jelly; 9, a typewritten or printed blank with spaces left to be filled in; also, a typewritten or printed letter to be sent out in great numbers; 10, in printing, type locked in a frame ready for printing; 11, a kind; variety; as, a tree is a *form* of plant life; 12, a long bench without a back; 13, a class in a school; as, in the fifth *form;* 14, in *grammar*, the composition of a word in reference to spelling, pronunciation, inflection, etc.; as, "narcissus" has two plural *forms*, "narcissuses" and "narcissi":—*v.t.* 1, to give shape to; make; as, to *form* a figure out of clay; 2, to mould by influence; train; as, education helps to *form* the mind; 3, to go to make up; as, music *formed* the greater part of the programme; 4, to develop; as, to *form* a habit; 5, to construct (a word) by grammatical rules; as, to *form* the plural of a noun by adding *s*:—*v.i.* to take shape; as, lumps *formed* in the pudding.—*adj.* **form′less; form′a-tive.**

for-mal (fôr′mal), *adj.* 1, according to established rules or conventions; as, a *formal* ceremony; 2, having outward show but lacking reality; as, a *formal* friendship.—*adv.* **for′mal-ly.**

form-al-de-hyde (fôr-mal′de-hīd′), *n.* a pungent gas, used in solution as a preservative, antiseptic, and disinfectant.

for-mal-i-ty (fôr-mal′i-ti), *n.* [*pl.* formalities], 1, rigid observance of forms or established rules; 2, a regular order of procedure; as, legal *formalities*.

for-mat (fôr′mat), *n.* the whole style and size of a book, magazine, etc., including the paper, type, and binding.

for-ma-tion (fôr-mā′shun), *n.* 1, moulding or shaping; as, *formation* of character; 2, that which is shaped; structure; as, rock *formations;* also, shape; form; as, the *formation* of the brain; 3, arrangement of a body of troops; as, marching *formation*.

for-mer (fôr′mèr), *adj.* preceding in time or order; as, *former* days; of the two speakers I prefer the *former*.

for-mer-ly (fôr′mèr-li), *adv.* in past time; as, he *formerly* lived in France.

for-mic (fôr′mik), *adj.* 1, pertaining to a pungent, corrosive acid distilled from glycerine and oxalic acid (formerly from red ants); 2, of ants.

for-mi-da-ble (fôr′mi-da-bl), *adj.* fearinspiring; hard to deal with or overcome; as, a *formidable* army.—*adv.* **for′mi-da-bly.**

for-mu-la (fôr′mū-la), *n.* [*pl.* formulas or formulae (fôr′mū-lē′)], 1, a set rule for doing something; 2, the specified way of performing a ceremony or of expressing a faith or doctrine; 3, a prescription, as for drugs;. a recipe

for-mu-late (fôr′mū-lāt′), *v.t.* [formulat-ed, formulat-ing], to put into a definite form; state in definite terms as, to *formulate* a law.—*n.* **for′mu-la′tion.**

for-ni-ca-tion (fôr′ni-kā′shun), *n.* il licit sexual intercourse, esp. adultery.—*v.i.* **for′ni-cate′.**

for-sake (fôr-sāk′), *v.t.* [*p.t.* forsook (fôr-sook′), *p.p.* forsak-en (fôr-sāk′en) *p.pr.* forsak-ing], to give up; abandon as, his friends will not *forsake* him.

for-swear (fôr-swâr′), *v.i.* [forswore (fôr-swôr′), *p.p.* forsworn (fôr-swôrn′) *p.pr.* forswear-ing], to take an oath falsely:—*v.t.* 1, to deny on oath; 2, to renounce earnestly; 3, to perjure (oneself).

for-syth-i-a (fôr-sith′i-a; fôr-sī′thi-a) *n.* an ornamental shrub of the olive family bearing bright yellow flowers in early spring before the leaves appear

fort (fôrt), *n.* a strongly fortified place esp. a structure built for defence.

forte (fôrt), *n.* one's strong point special talent; as, his *forte* is music.—*adj.* (fôr′tā), in *music*, loudly.

forth (fôrth), *adv.* 1, onward in time place, or order; forward; as, from thi day *forth;* 2, out; outward; as, th sun sends *forth* light.

forth-com-ing (fōrth′kum′ing), *ad* ready or about to appear; approach ing; as, our *forthcoming* trip; a *fortl coming* answer.

forth-right (fōrth′rīt′), *adv.* straigh forward; at once.—*adj.* direct; decisive as, a *forthright* answer.

forth-with (fōrth′with′; fōrth′with′) *adv.* immediately; directly.

for-ti-eth (fôr′ti-eth), *adj.* next afte the 39th: the ordinal of *forty:*—*n.* on of the 40 equal parts of anything.

for-ti-fi-ca-tion (fôr′ti-fi-kā′shun), *n.* 1, the act of building or strengthenin military defences; 2, a military worl erected for defence; a fort.

for-ti-fy (fôr'ti-fī'), *v.t.* [fortified, forti-fy-ing], **1,** to strengthen by forts, walls, etc.; as, to *fortify* a town; **2,** to make strong; as, to *fortify* one's courage.

for-tis-si-mo (fôr-tis'i-mō'), *adj.* in *music*, very loud.—*adv.* very loudly (stronger than *forte*).

for-ti-tude (fôr'ti-tūd'), *n.* strength of endurance or courage in pain or trouble.

fort-night (fôrt'nīt; fôrt'nit), *n.* a period of two weeks.—*adv.* **fort'-night-ly.**

or-tress (fôr'tres), *n.* a fortified place; a stronghold.

for-tu-i-tous (fôr-tū'i-tus), *adj.* accidental; happening by chance; as, to many the evolution of life is not *fortuitous.*

for-tu-nate (fôr'tū-nit), *adj.* **1,** bringing good fortune; as, a *fortunate* play; **2,** lucky; successful; as, a *fortunate* person.—*adv.* **for'tu-nate-ly.**

or-tune (fôr'tūn), *n.* **1,** the good or ill that happens to a person; chance; luck; as, the good *fortune* to find friends; **2,** wealth; riches; **3,** future fate; as, tell my *fortune.*

or-ty (fôr'ti), *adj.* composed of one more than 39:—*n.* [*pl.* forties], **1,** the number consisting of 39 plus one; **2,** a sign representing forty units, as 40 or xl.

or-ty—one (fôr'ti—wun'), *n.* and *adj.* the numbers *forty-one* to *forty-nine* are hyphenated.

or-um (fōr'um), *n.* [*pl.* forums or fora (fōr'a)], **1,** the public meeting-place in ancient Rome where the law courts, public offices, etc., were situated; **2,** a place of gathering for public discussion.

for-ward (fôr'werd) or **for-wards** (fôr'werdz), *adv.* toward the front; on or onward; as, to march *forward:—interj.* on!

for-ward (fôr'werd), *adj.* **1,** situated near the front; as, the *forward* ranks; **2,** early; ahead of time; as, *forward* crops; **3,** onward; as, a *forward* movement; **4,** ready; prompt; also, too confident; bold; as, a *forward* manner:—*v.t.* **1,** to help on; advance; as, to *forward* a cause; **2,** to send on; as, to *forward* mail.—*n.* in *football,* a forward pass.—*n.* **for'ward-ness.**

os-sil (fos'il), *n.* **1,** a petrified animal or plant; a trace or remnant of a prehistoric animal or plant, imbedded or preserved in the earth, in rocks, or in caves; **2,** an oldfashioned person:—*adj.* **1,** petrified; like a fossil; **2,** out of date.

os-ter (fos'tèr), *v.t.* **1,** to nourish;

rear up; as, to *foster* a child; **2,** to support; cherish; as, to *foster* ideas:—*adj.* giving, receiving, or sharing nurture or care, though not related by blood; as, a *foster*-mother; *foster*-brother.

fought (fôt), *p.t.* and *p.p.* of *fight.*

foul (foul), *adj.* **1,** offensive; disgusting; as, a *foul* taste; **2,** dirty; soiled; as, *foul* linen; **3,** vulgar; obscene; as, *foul* language; **4,** morally offensive; odious; as, a *foul* deed; **5,** unfair; as, *foul* play; **6,** stormy; as, *foul* weather; **7,** clogged; as, a *foul* chimney; **8,** entangled; as, a *foul* rope; **9,** in collision; as, the ship ran *foul* of the rock:—*n.* **1,** in many games, as football, a play or act that is against the rules; **2,** in baseball, a batted ball which first strikes the ground outside of the lines marking out the playing-field:—*v.t.* **1,** to make impure; as, to *foul* the air; **2,** to dishonour; as, to *foul* one's name; **3,** to collide with or entangle; as, to *foul* a cable:—*v.i.* **1,** to become dirty; **2,** to come into collision, as two boats; to become entangled; **3,** in baseball, to hit a foul ball.—*adv.* **foul'ly.**—*n.* **foul'-ness.**

found (found), *v.t.* to lay the basis of; to originate; establish; as, to *found* a city or an institution.—*n.* **found'er.**

foun-da-tion (foun-dā'shun), *n.* **1,** the act of establishing; as, the *foundation* of a school; **2,** the ground work of a structure; as, a stone *foundation;* basis; as, the rumour has no *foundation;* **3,** an endowment or gift of money to support an institution; **4,** an endowed institution or charity.

foun-der (foun'dėr), *v.i.* **1,** to fill and sink, as a ship; **2,** to go lame, as a horse; **3,** to fall down; collapse, as a building:—*v.t.* **1,** to cause (a ship) to fill with water and sink; **2,** to make (a horse) break down.

found-ling (found'ling), *n.* a child found after being deserted by its unknown parents.

foun-dry (foun'dri), *n.* [*pl.* foundries], **1,** the place where metal casting is carried on; as, an iron *foundry;* **2,** the act or process of casting metals.

fount (fount), *n.* a spring of water; a source.

foun-tain (foun'tin), *n.* **1,** a natural spring of water; **2,** a spring or source; as, a *fountain* of truth; **3,** an artificial jet or spout of water; also, the apparatus for producing it; **4,** a reservoir, as for ink in a pen, or oil in a lamp.—*n.* **foun-tain-head** (foun'tin-hed').

four (fōr), *adj.* consisting of one more than three:—*n.* **1,** the sum consisting of three plus one; **2,** a sign representing four units, as 4 or iv.

four-flush-er (fōr′flush′ėr), *n. Slang,* one who fails to implement his pretensions; a bluffer.

four—in—hand (fōr′–in–hand′), *n.* **1,** a team of four horses under one driver, or a coach drawn by it; **2,** a long necktie tied in a slipknot:—*adj.* pertaining to such a coach or necktie.

four-score (fōr′skōr′), *adj.* four times twenty; 80; as, *fourscore* years.

four-some (fōr′sum), *n.* in certain games, such as golf, a match in which four players, two on a side, take part.

four-square (fōr′sqwâr′), *adj.* upright; honest.—*adv.* in a square form.

four-teen (fōr′tēn′), *adj.* consisting of one more than thirteen:—*n.* **1,** the number consisting of thirteen plus one; **2,** a sign representing fourteen units, as 14 or xiv.

four-teenth (fōr′tēnth′), *adj.* next after the 13th: the ordinal of *fourteen:* —*n.* one of the fourteen equal parts of anything.

fourth (fōrth), *adj.* next after the third: the ordinal of *four:*—*n.* one of four equal parts of anything; a quarter.— *adv.* **fourth′ly.**

fowl (foul), *n.* [*pl.* fowl or fowls], **1,** a bird; esp. the common rooster or hen; **2,** the flesh of the domestic fowl used as food:—*v.i.* to hunt wild birds.

fowl-er (foul′ėr), *n.* one who catches or kills wild birds for sport or food.

fox (foks), *n.* **1,** a wild animal of the dog family, with pointed ears and a bushy tail, noted for its cunning; **2,** the fur of this animal; **3,** a sly person.—*adj.* **fox′y.**

fox-glove (foks′gluv′), *n.* a plant having showy, upright spikes of bell-shaped flowers. Its leaves are used in medicine.

fox-hole (foks′hōl′), *n.* a small hole dug by one or two soldiers for a protection against gunfire.

fox-hound (foks′hound′), *n.* a hound trained to hunt foxes.

fox—ter-ri-er (foks′–ter′i-ėr), *n.* a small, active, alert dog of the terrier family. There are two kinds, the smooth-haired fox-terrier and the wire-haired fox-terrier.

fox-trot (foks′trot′), *n.* a dance in 2/4 or 4/4 time, performed by couples in a variety of short, quick steps; a two-step.—*v.i.* to dance a foxtrot.

fox-y (foks′i), *adj.* cunning; crafty; sly.

foy-er (fwä′yā′; foi′ėr), *n.* the lobby or entrance hall of a hotel, theatre, etc.

fra-cas (frȧ′kä′; frā′kas), *n.* a loud quarrel; brawl; uproar.

frac-tion (frak′shun), *n.* **1,** a fragment; a part; **2,** in *mathematics,* a part or an indicated number of equal parts of a whole; as, in the *fraction* ⅞ the whole has been divided into eight equal parts of which seven are indicated.— *adj.* **frac′tion-al.**—*adv.* **frac′tion-al-ly.**

frac-tious (frak′shus), *adj.* unruly; cross; as, a *fractious* child.—*adv.* **frac′tious-ly.**

frac-ture (frak′tūr), *n.* **1,** the act of breaking; **2,** a break, esp. of a bone:— *v.t.* and *v.i.* [fractured, fractur-ing], to break or crack.

frag-ile (fraj′il; fraj′īl), *adj.* easily broken; delicate; as, a *fragile* dish.—*n.* **fra-gil′i-ty.**

frag-ment (frag′ment), *n.* a part broken off from a whole; a portion, piece, or incomplete part; as, a *fragment* of the story.—*adj.* **frag′men-tar′y.**—*n.* **frag′men-ta′tion.**

fra-grant (frā′grant), *adj.* sweet-smelling; having a pleasing odour; as, a *fragrant* spice.—*adv.* **fra′grant-ly.**—*n.* **fra′grance.**

frail (frāl), *adj.* **1,** fragile or easily broken; as, a *frail* stem; **2,** physically weak; as, a *frail* child; **3,** morally weak.—*adv.* **frail′ly.**

frail-ty (frāl′ti), *n.* [*pl.* frailties], **1,** weakness; as, *frailty* of character; **2,** a failing or sin due to moral weakness.

frame (frām), *v.t.* [framed, fram-ing], **1,** to put together; build; as, to *frame* a house; **2,** to invent; plan; as, to *frame* a conspiracy; express; as, to *frame* an answer; **3,** to surround or enclose with a stiff rim; as, to *frame* a picture; **4,** *Slang,* to falsify evidence to make a person look guilty:—*n.* **1,** anything built or made of parts fitted together; as, the *frame* of a ship; **2,** bodily structure; as, the slender *frame* of a girl; **3,** a structure of wood, metal, or the like, for holding, enclosing, or supporting something; as, a *frame* of a door; an embroidery *frame;* **4,** established order; system; as, the *frame* of society; **5,** in *bowling,* any of the ten divisions of a game; in *pool,* the triangular form in which the balls are racked to begin a game.—*n.* **fram′er.**

frame-work (frām′wûrk′), *n.* that which supports; a skeleton; as, the *framework* of a house or of the body.

franc (frangk), *n.* the French monetary unit (worth about ⅕ of a cent in 1959) also a unit of Switzerland, Belgium, and Italy.

fran-chise (fran′chĭz), *n.* **1,** citizenship; the right to vote; **2,** a specia privilege granted by a government to a person or company; as, a *franchise* to run a bus line.

an-gi-ble (frăn′ji-bl), *adj.* breakable; brittle; as glass or delftware.

rank (frăngk), *adj.* candid; outspoken; as, a *frank* opinion.—*adv.* **rank′ly.**

rank (frăngk), *n.* a signature or mark that exempts mail matter from payment of postage:—*v.t.* to send postfree.

ank-furt-er (frăngk′fẽr-tẽr), *n.* a highly seasoned beef and pork sausage.

ank-in-cense (frăngk′in-sens′), *n.* a fragrant resin from balsam trees, burned as incense.

an-tic (frăn′tĭk), *adj.* wild; frenzied; as, *frantic* cries.—*adv.* **fran′ti-cal-ly.**

a-ter-nal (fra-tûr′nal), *adj.* 1, pertaining to, or like, a brother or brothers; as, *fraternal* love; 2, naming or pertaining to a group or society of men who bind themselves together like brothers; as, a *fraternal* order.—*adv.* **ra-ter′nal-ly.**

a-ter-ni-ty (fra-tûr′ni-ti), *n.* [*pl.* raternities], 1, brotherly relationship; 2, a body of men joined by a common interest, esp. such an organization in high schools and colleges:—*v.i.* **frat′er-ize′.**

at-ri-cide (frăt′ri-sīd′), *n.* the killing of a brother or sister; 2, one who does so.

aud (frôd), *n.* 1, deceitfulness; trickery; 2, a trick; 3, *Colloq.* one who cheats.

aud-u-lent (frôd′ū-lent), *adj.* 1, guilty of trickery; deceitful; dishonest; 2, characterized by, or obtained by, unfair methods; as, *fraudulent* measures; *fraudulent* gains.—*adv.* **raud′u-lent-ly.**—*n.* **fraud′u-lence; raud′u-len-cy.**

aught (frôt), *adj.* laden; filled; as, the voyage was *fraught* with danger.

ray (frā), *n.* a riot; a fight; as, in the midst of the *fray.*

ray (frā), *v.t.* and *v.i.* to rub; wear into shreds; as, a sleeve *frayed* at the edge.

az-zle (frăz′l), *v.t.* and *v.i.* [fraz-zled, raz-zling], 1, to fray or ravel, as cloth; hence, to tire or wear out:—*n.* 1, a ragged end; 2, the state of being exhausted.

eak (frēk), *n.* 1, a capricious change of mind; whim; 2, an abnormal person, animal, or plant.—*adj.* **freak′ish.**

eck-le (frek′l), *n.* a brownish spot on the skin:—*v.t.* and *v.i.* [freck-led, eck-ling], to mark, or become marked, with freckles.

free (frē), *adj.* [fre-er, fre-est], 1, having full personal and political liberty; as, a *free* people; 2, loose; not attached; as, the *free* end of a rope; 3, independent; as, a *free* church; 4, at liberty; released; not caught or shut up; as, a *free* person or animal; 5, not following rigid rules of form; as, *free* verse; 6, not following the original exactly; as, a *free* translation; 7, frank; also, informal; as, a *free* and easy manner; 8, lavish; generous; as, *free* with praise; abundant; as, a *free* flow of blood; 9, clear of obstructions; open; as, a *free* field; a *free* course; 10, rid of or exempt from; as, *free* from disease or punishment; 11, unhampered; not influenced by others; as, a *free* choice; 12, given without cost; as, a *free* ticket; open to all; as, a *free* fight; 13, impudent; as, a *free* tongue:—*v.t.* [freed, free-ing], 1, to let go; set at liberty; as, to *free* an animal from a trap; 2, to rid of; clear; as, to *free* someone of a charge of murder:—*adv.* without charge; as, to get in *free.*—*adv.* **free′ly.**—*adj.* **free′-born′.**

free-board (frē′bōrd′), *n.* the part of a boat or ship between waterline and gunwale.

free-boot-er (frē′bōōt′ẽr), *n.* one who roves in search of plunder, as the Elizabethan *freebooters* (Drake, Raleigh, etc.); a pirate; buccaneer.

free-dom (frē′dum), *n.* 1, personal and political liberty; independence; as, a slave is given his *freedom;* the colonies won their *freedom;* 2, free use; as, to be given the *freedom* of a clubhouse; 3, exemption from; lack of; as, *freedom* from disease; *freedom* from taxes; 4, state of being clear or unmixed; as, *freedom* from impurities; 5, ease; as, to move with *freedom;* 6, frankness; as, *freedom* in expressing his feelings; 7, undue familiarity; as, he assumes too much *freedom* with his superiors.

free-hand (frē′hănd′), *adj.* done or drawn by hand without the aid of ruler, compasses, etc.; as, a *freehand* sketch.

free-hold (frē′hōld′), *n.* the holding for life of land, etc., with the right to pass it on to one's heirs; 2, land so held.

free lance *n.* a writer, actor, etc., who is not bound by contract to one employer, but sells his services where he wishes.—*adj.* **free′—lance′.**

free-man (frē′man), *n.* [*pl.* freemen (-men)], one who is not a slave.

free-stone (frē′stōn′), *n.* 1, a stone, as limestone or sandstone, that cuts easily with outsplitting; 2, a peach, plum, etc., whose pit does not cling to the fruit when ripe.

free-think-er (frē′think′ėr), *n.* one who forms his opinions independently of authority, esp. in religious matters; an agnostic.

free verse, poetry marked by lack of rhyming, and by irregular metre and length of line.

freeze (frēz), *v.t.* [*p.t.* froze (frōz), *p.p.* fro-zen (frō′zn), *p.pr.* freez-ing], **1,** to harden with cold; as, to *freeze* ice-cream; **2,** to chill, damage, or kill with cold; as, to *freeze* plants:—*v.i.* **1,** to be changed into or covered with ice; as, the lake *freezes;* **2,** to be killed by cold or frost; as, the plants *froze* last night; **3,** to be very cold; **4,** to be chilled with fear or horror; **5,** to stick or adhere because of cold; as, their hands *froze* to the oars.—*n.* freez′er.

freight (frāt), *n.* **1,** the goods with which a vessel or car is loaded; cargo; **2,** a method of transporting bulky goods, esp. by train; also, a train that carries bulky goods; **3,** the sum paid for hauling goods:—*v.t.* **1,** to load with goods for hauling; **2,** to send (goods) by freight.

freight-er (frāt′ėr), *n.* **1,** one who loads a ship or car; also, one who sends goods by freight; **2,** a vessel for carrying cargoes.

French horn, a musical wind-instrument of the brass group, consisting of a long coiled tube ending in a flaring bell.

fren-zied (fren′zid), *adj.* maddened; frantic; as, *frenzied* efforts to swim.

fren-zy (fren′zi), *n.* [*pl.* frenzies], **1,** violent mental derangement; delirium; **2,** wild excitement or enthusiasm.

fre-quen-cy (frē′kwen-si), *n.* [*pl.* frequencies], **1,** the repeated happening of anything at short intervals; as, the *frequency* of storms; **2,** the number of happenings in a given time; rate of occurrence; **3,** the cycles per second of an alternating current.

fre-quent (frē′kwent), *adj.* **1,** occurring often; as, *frequent* delays; **2,** habitual; as, a *frequent* visitor:—*v.t.* (frē-kwent′), to go to often or habitually; as, to *frequent* the theatre.—*adv.* fre′quent-ly.

fres-co (fres′kō), *n.* [*pl.* frescos or frescoes], **1,** the method or art of painting on plaster before it has dried; **2,** a painting made in this manner:—*v.t.* [frescoed, fresco-ing], to decorate or paint in fresco.

fresh (fresh), *adj.* **1,** new; not known or used before; as, a *fresh* sheet of paper; **2,** additional; different; as, to make a *fresh* start; **3,** recent; just made or arrived; as, a *fresh* report; **4,** newly gathered or produced; as, *fresh* grapes; not faded; as, *fresh* flowers; **5,**

pure and cool; refreshing; as, *fresh* a **6,** not preserved by salting or picklin as, *fresh* ham; **7,** not salt; as, *fre* water; **8,** not stale; not spoiled; ɛ *fresh* fish; **9,** not tired; vigorous; ɛ to feel *fresh* after a nap; **10,** n experienced; as, a *fresh* recruit; **1** *Slang,* bold; impudent; as, don't g *fresh.*—*adv.* fresh′ly.

fresh-en (fresh′en), *v.t.* **1,** refres revive; as, I *freshened* myself after hard day's work; **2,** to render le salt:—*v.i.* to become brisk; as, t wind *freshens.*

fresh-et (fresh′et), *n.* a flood caused melting snow or heavy rain.

fresh-man (fresh′man), *n.* [*pl.* fres men (fresh′men)], a college or hig school student in his first year.

¹**fret** (fret), *v.t.* [fret-ted, fret-ting], **1,** chafe; wear or rub away; as, wat *frets* a channel in a rock; **2,** to worr irritate:—*v.i.* to be irritated; as, s *frets* over little things:—*n.* **1,** a wo spot; **2,** vexation; irritation.

²**fret** (fret), *n.* a small ridge or bar wood, metal, ivory, etc., on the neck certain stringed instruments, as t mandolin, to regulate fingering.

fret-ful (fret′fool), *adj.* peevish; irr able; as, a *fretful* child.—*adv.* fret′ful-l —*n.* fret′ful-ness.

fret—saw (fret′–sô′), *n.* a saw wi thin, fine-toothed blade for cuttī thin boards, metal, etc., into patterr

fret-work (fret′wûrk′), *n.* a kind carved, raised, or open ornament work.

fri-a-ble (frī′a-bl), *adj.* crumbli readily (to powder), as *friable* rock.

fri-ar (frī′ėr), *n.* a brother, or memb of any of certain religious orders; monk.

fric-as-see (frik′a-sē), *n.* a dish chicken, rabbit, or other meat cut in small pieces and stewed in gravy sauce.

fri-ca-tive (frik′a-tiv), *n.* and *adj.* sound produced by forcing the brea through a narrow opening, used ɛ of the letters or sounds (fricatives) *f*, *v*, *th*, *z*.

fric-tion (frik′shun), *n.* **1,** the rubbi of one thing against another; **2,** machinery; the resistance one thi encounters when moving agair another; **3,** conflict; difference opinion.—*adj.* fric′tion-al.

Fri-day (frī′di; dā), *n.* the sixth day the week.

fried (frīd), *p.t.* and *p.p.* of *fry.*

friend (frend), *n.* **1,** a person bound another by affection, esteem, a intimacy; **2**, a sympathizer; helper; a supporter of a cause; **3**, an ally.—*adj.* **friend'less**.

friend-ly (frend'li), *adj.* [friend-li-er, friend-li-est], **1**, like a friend; kind; **2**, not hostile; as, a *friendly* tribe; **3**, played for mere sport; as, a *friendly* contest; **4**, favourable; as, a *friendly* breeze.—*n.* **friend'li-ness**.

friend-ship (frend'ship), *n.* the relationship or attachment between people arising from mutual affection and admiration.

fri-er (fri'ẽr), *n.* Same as *fryer*.

frieze (frēz), *n.* an ornamental or sculptured band around a wall.

frig-ate (frig'it), *n.* **1**, originally, a light, swift vessel propelled both by oars and sails; **2**, a fast three-masted, square-rigged war-vessel of the 18th and early 19th centuries.

fright (frīt), *n.* **1**, violent fear; terror; alarm; **2**. *Colloq.* anything ugly or ridiculous in appearance.

fright-en (frīt'n), *v.t.* to terrify; alarm; startle.—*adj.* **fright'ened**.

fright-ful (frīt'fool), *adj.* **1**, terrible; dreadful; frightening; as, a *frightful* accident; **2**, *Colloq.* grotesque; ugly; as, a *frightful* dress.—*adv.* **fright'ful-ly**.

frig-id (frij'id), *adj.* **1**, very cold; freezing; as, *frigid* weather; **2**, unfriendly; stiff; formal; as, a *frigid* welcome.—*adv.* **frig'id-ly**.—*n.* **fri-gid'i-ty** (fri-jid'i-ti).

frill (fril), *n.* **1**, an ornamental edging made of a strip of material gathered on one edge; a ruffle; **2**, *Colloq.* an affectation of manner, speech, or dress.

fringe (frinj), *n.* **1**, a ravelled, frayed edge on a fabric; also, a separate ornamental border of hanging cords, tassels, etc.; **2**, any border or edging like a fringe.

fringed gentian. Same as **gen'tian**.

frip-per-y (frip'ẽr-i), *n.* [*pl.* fripperies], tawdry finery; cheap gewgaws.

frisk (frisk), *v.i.* to skip or dance in frolic or playfulness.—*adj.* **frisk'y**.—*adv.* **frisk'i-ly**.

frit-ter (frit'ẽr), *n.* a fried cake made of batter, often containing meat or fruit.

frit-ter (frit'ẽr), *n.* a fragment:—*v.t.* to cut or break into small pieces; hence, to waste; as, to *fritter* away one's time.

friv-o-lous (friv'o-lus), *adj.* **1**, of little importance; trivial; as, *frivolous* pastimes; **2**, not serious; giddy; as, *frivolous* people.—*n.* **fri-vol'i-ty** (fri-vol'i-ti).

friz-zle (friz'l), *v.t.* **1**, to curl (the hair): **2**, to fry with a sputter (bacon). Also, **frizz**.—*adj.* **friz'zly**; **friz'zy**.

fro (frō), *adv.* away from; backward or back: used only in the phrase *to and fro*.

frock (frok), *n.* **1**, a loose upper garment worn by children and women; a dress; **2**, a monk's habit; **3**, a coarse outer garment worn by workmen.

frog (frog), *n.* **1**, a small, tailless amphibian with smooth skin, webbed feet, and remarkable swimming and leaping ability; **2**, soreness in the throat.

frol-ic (frol'ik), *n.* **1**, a scene of merry-making or gaiety; **2**, a wild prank:— *v.i.* [frolicked, frolick-ing], to make merry.—*adj.* **frol'ic-some**.

from (from), *prep.* **1**, indicating a starting-point in space, time, or a series; as, a letter *from* home; ten feet *from* a post; *from* morning to night; *from* childhood on; *from* 10 to 20; **2**, indicating a place, person, or thing left behind; as, turn your steps *from* folly; **3**, indicating removal; as, take candy *from* a box; pick berries *from* a bush; steal candy *from* a baby; **4**, indicating separation or freedom; as, excused *from* school; free *from* disease; **5**, indicating some condition changed for another; as, to go *from* bad to worse; **6**, indicating origin or source; as, translated *from* the French; weak *from* hunger; **7**, indicating a model or copy; as, drawn *from* life.

frond (frond), *n.* the leaf of a fern, palm, or seaweed.—*adj.* **frond'ed**.

front (frunt), *n.* **1**, the foremost part of anything; **2**, the forehead; **3**, land that faces the sea, a river, stream, etc.; as, the beach *front;* the river *front;* **4**, in warfare, the scene of the actual fighting:—*adj.* situated at the foremost part; as, a *front* wall:—*v.t.* **1**, to stand, or be situated, opposite to; as, your house *fronts* mine; **2**, to confront; meet; as, to *front* danger; to *front* an enemy:—*v.i.* to have the front turned in a certain direction; as, his house *fronts* north.

front-age (frunt'ij), *n.* the boundary line (of a lot or building) fronting a street or road; the exposure.

fron-tal (frun'tal; fron'tal), *adj.* having to do with the front or forehead; as, a *frontal* artery:—*n.* the bone of the forehead.

fron-tier (frun-tẽr'; fron'tẽr), *n.* **1**, the boundary of a country; **2**, the most remote settled part of a country, adjoining wild territory:—*adj.* pertaining to, or situated near, the

boundary of a country; as, a *frontier* custom; a *frontier* town.

fron-tis-piece (frun'tis-pēs'), *n.* 1, a picture facing the front page or title-page of a book; 2, a facade or front of a building.

frost (frôst), *n.* 1, minute frozen particles of dew or vapour; hoarfrost; 2, a temperature low enough to cause freezing of water; freezing weather; 3, *Slang.* a failure:—*v.t.* 1, to cover with frost, or with something like frost; 2, to injure by frost; 3, to cover (a cake) with icing.—*adj.* **frost'y.**—*n.* **frost'i-ness.**

frost-ing (frôs'ting), *n.* 1, a preparation of sugar mixed with a liquid, used in covering or icing cakes or pastry; 2, a dull finish, as for metal or glass.

froth (frôth), *n.* 1, a mass of small bubbles formed on the surface of a liquid, as by shaking or fermentation; foam; 2, shallow knowledge:—*v.t.* to become covered with foam; as, the mad dog *frothed* at the mouth.—*adj.* **froth'y.**—*n.* **froth'i-ness.**

fro-ward (frō'wėrd; frō'ėrd), *adj.* wilful; disobedient; wayward; contrary.

frown (froun), *n.* a wrinkling of the brow showing displeasure; a scowl; a stern look:—*v.i.* 1, to contract the brows in anger, deep thought, uncertainty, etc.; 2, to show disapproval; as, to *frown* upon gambling:—*v.t.* to rebuke or suppress by frowning; as, to *frown* a person down.

frow-zy or **frou-zy** (frou'zi), *adj.* slovenly; unkempt; dirty; as, a *frowzy* room or person.

fro-zen (frō'zn), *p.p.* of *freeze:*— **frozen assets,** property that for the present cannot be converted to cash for face value, as a *frozen* loan.

fru-gal (froo'gl), *adj.* 1, thrifty; economical; not wasteful; 2, sparingly used or supplied; simple; as, a *frugal* meal.—*adv.* **fru'gal-ly.**—*n.* **fru-gal'i-ty.**

fruit (froot), *n.* 1, in general, a seed and all its enveloping parts; 2, usually, a particular fruit, as the apple, peach, pear, etc. generally eaten raw, or cooked with sugar and water and used as a dessert; 3, any product, result, or profit; as, the *fruit* of labour:—*v.i.* to produce fruit:—**fruited,** *adj.* laden with fruit.—*adj.* **fruit'y.**

fruit-ful (froot'fool), *adj.* yielding fruit; fertile; as, a *fruitful* tree; *fruitful* soil; profitable; productive; as, a *fruitful* venture; a *fruitful* year.— *n.* **fruit'ful-ness.**

fru-i-tion (froo-ish'un), *n.* 1, the bearing of fruit; 2, realization or

attainment; as, the *fruition* of his cherished hopes.

fruit-less (froot'lis), *adj.* 1, not bearing fruit; 2, without result; useless; as, a *fruitless* effort.

frump (frump), *n.* a dowdy (or sometimes cross) woman.—*adj.* **frump'y; frump'ish.**

frus-trate (frus'trāt), *v.t.* [frustrated, frustrat-ing], to defeat or disappoint; thwart or oppose; bring to nothing; as, to *frustrate* a plan.—*n.* **frus-tra'tion.**

frus-tum (frus'tum), *n.* the part of a cone or pyramid left when the top is cut off parallel to the base.

fry (frī), *v.t.* [fried, fry-ing], to cook with fat or oil in a pan or on a griddle:—**small fry,** *Colloq.*, 1, children; 2, unimportant people.—*n.* **fry'er** or **fri'er.**

fuch-si-a (fū'shi-a; fū'-sha), *n.* a plant of the evening primrose family with drooping pink, red, or purple flowers.

fud-dled (fud'ld), *adj.* confused or muddled, as with alcoholic liquor; befuddled. —*v.t.* **fud'dle.**

fud-dy—dud-dy (fud'i—dud'i), *n. Slang*, a fussy or old-fashioned person.

FRUSTUM of a cone.

fudge (fuj), *n.* a candy made of a stiff sugary mixture flavoured with maple chocolate, etc.:—*interj.* nonsense.

fu-el (fū'el), *n.* 1, material that can be burned to supply heat, as coal, wood, oil, etc.; 2, anything that keeps an emotion active; as, the news adds *fuel* to his anger:—*v.t.* [fuelled, fuel-ling], to furnish with fuel; as, they *fuelled* the vessel for a long trip.

fu-gi-tive (fū'ji-tiv), *adj.* 1, fleeting; not lasting very long; as, a *fugitive* idea; 2, fleeing from danger, pursuit, or duty; as, a *fugitive* slave:—*n.* one who flees; a runaway or deserter.

fugue (fūg), *n.* in *music*, a composition in which a number of parts, voices, or instruments successively repeat the theme to a climactic end.

ful-crum (ful'krum), *n.* [*pl.* fulcrum or fulcra (ful'kra)], the support, often wedge-shaped, on which a lever turns when it lifts something.

ful-fil (fool-fil'), *v.t.* [fulfilled, fulfil-ling], 1, to complete or accomplish; 2, to do; carry out (that which is

FULCRUM A, lever; B, fulcrum; C, weight

promised, foretold, ordered, or expected); **3,** to satisfy, as a wish.—*n.* **ful-fil'ment.**

full (fool), *adj.* **1,** filled; having no empty space; as, a *full* pail; **2,** well supplied; as, a *full* cellar; **3,** rounded out; plump; as, a *full* figure; **4,** complete; filling the normal allowance, quota, or the like; as, a *full* hour; a *full* orchestra; *full* speed; **5,** having excess material arranged in folds; as, a *full* skirt; **6,** clear; distinct; as, a *full* tone; **7,** *Colloq.* intoxicated:—*n.* the highest state, or extent; as, enjoy it to the *full:—v.t.* to give fulness to; as, to *full* a skirt:—*adv.* completely; quite: often with a hyphen; as, a *full*-blown rose.—*n.* **full'ness; ful'ness.**

full-back (fool'bak'), *n.* in *football,* one of the players farthest behind the line of scrimmage.

full—fledged (fool'–flejd'), *adj.* fully developed; as, a *full-fledged* lawyer.

full-y (fool'i), *adv.* completely; abundantly; as, *fully* equipped for a journey.

ful-mi-nate (ful'mi-nāt'), *v.t.* **1,** to explode; detonate; **2,** to denounce; as, he *fulminated* against the new law.—*n.* **ful'mi-na'tion.**

ful-some (fool'sum; ful'sum), *adj.* offensive to good taste; excessive; immoderate; as, *fulsome* flattery.—*adv.* **ful'some-ly.**

fum-ble (fum'bl), *v.i.* [fum-bled, fumbling], to grope or feel about in search; as, he *fumbled* in his pocket for a match:—*v.t.* to handle or manage awkwardly, or drop; as, to *fumble* the ball in a game.—*n.* **fum'bler.**

fume (fūm), *n.* smoke, vapour, or gas, esp. if offensive; as, the air was thick with tobacco *fumes:—v.i.* [fumed, fuming], **1,** to send forth smoke; **2,** to complain angrily; as, he *fumed* over his losses.

fu-mi-gate (fū'mi-gāt'), *v.t.* [fumigated, fumigat-ing], **1,** to disinfect or purify with fumes; esp. to free of disease germs, insects, etc., with fumes; as, to *fumigate* a sickroom; **2,** to perfume.—*n.* **fu'mi-ga'tion.**—*n.* **fu'mi-ga'tor.**

fun (fun), *n.* pleasure; mirth; sport; amusement; play.

func-tion (fungk'shun), *n.* **1,** the special work or use of anything; as, the *function* of the heart is to pump blood; the *function* of a judge is to interpret the law; **2,** a formal social or official ceremony; as, the inauguration was the most important *function* of the year:—*v.i.* to perform the duty for which a person or thing is intended.—*adj.* **func'tion-al.**

fund (fund), *n.* **1,** a permanent supply of something; a stock; as, a *fund* of information; **2,** money set apart for carrying out some object; as she has a *fund* saved for vacation; **3,** a stock in reserve; **4, funds,** securities; money.

fun-da-ment (fun'da-ment), *n.* the buttocks; **2,** the anus.

fun-da-men-tal (fun'da-men'tal; -men'tl), *adj.* serving as a foundation or basis; essential; as, a *fundamental* reason:—*n.* a rule or principle that serves as the groundwork of a system; as, a *fundamental* of arithmetic.—*adv.* **fun'da-men'tal-ly.**

fun-da-men-tal-ist (fun'da-men'tal-ist), *n.* one who believes in a literal interpretation of the Bible (esp. its miracles, virgin birth, etc.) as an essential to Christian faith.—*n.* **fun'da-men'tal-ism.**

fu-ner-al (fū'nėr-al), *n.* the ceremony of burying a dead human body, or the services that take place at such a time:—*adj.* pertaining to, or for, a funeral.—*adj.* **fu-ne're-al** (fū-nē'ri-al).

fun-gi-cide (fun'ji-sīd'), *n.* any substance that kills bacteria, moulds, mildews, etc. (usually a spray or dust).

fun-gus (fung'gus), *n.* [pl. fungi (fung'gī; fun'jī) or funguses (fung'gus-ez)], one of the plants without green colour, including bacteria, moulds, mushrooms, mildews, lichens, rusts, smuts, toadstools, etc., which feed upon other plants or decaying animal matter:—*adj.* pertaining to, or growing like, a fungus; as, a *fungus* growth.

funk (fungk), *n.* *Colloq.* panic; fright; as, to be in a blue *funk.*—*v.i.* to flinch or cower from fear; shrink from.

fun-nel (fun'el), *n.* **1,** a wide-mouthed vessel shaped like a cone with a tube or hole at the bottom, used for pouring liquids into a small opening; **2,** the smokestack of a steamship or steam-engine.

fun-ny (fun'i), *adj.* [fun-ni-er, fun-ni-est], **1,** comical; droll; causing laughter; **2,** *Colloq.* strange; odd; queer.

fur (fûr), *n.* **1,** the thick, soft hair of certain animals; **2,** the dressed skin of fur-bearing animals; also, (often *furs*), clothing made from these skins; **3,** any light, fuzzy covering, as a coating on the tongue:—*adj.* lined or trimmed with fur, or made of fur:—*v.t.* [furred, fur-ring], to cover, line, or trim with fur.—*adj.* **furred.**

fur-be-low (fûr'bi-lō'), *n.* flounce, ruffle, etc. (on women's clothing).

fur-bish (fûr'bish), *v.t.* to polish; burnish; as, he *furbished* his medals.

fu-ri-ous (fū′ri-us), *adj.* **1,** very angry; mad; **2,** violent, as a storm.—*adv.* **fu′ri-ous-ly.**

furl (fûrl), *v.t.* to roll up and fasten to a mast, pole, or the like, as a sail or flag.

fur-long (fûr′lông), *n.* one eighth of a mile; 40 rods; 220 yards.

fur-lough (fûr′lō), *n.* leave of absence; as, the soldier came home on *furlough:*—*v.t.* to give leave of absence to.

fur-nace (fûr′nis), *n.* an apparatus in which fuel is burned to make heat for various purposes, as to melt ores, heat a house, bake pottery, etc.

fur-nish (fûr′nish), *v.t.* **1,** to fit out or fit up with what is needed; as, to *furnish* a house; **2,** to provide; give; as, he *furnished* the money for the trip.

fur-nish-ings (fûr′nish-ingz), *n.pl.* **1,** the necessary fittings of a house; **2,** apparatus or fixtures of any kind.

fur-ni-ture (fûr′ni-tūr; -chẽr), *n.* the necessary fittings of a house, a ship, or a trade; outfit; esp. the movable articles of a house, as beds, chairs, utensils, etc.

fu-ror (fū′rôr), *n.* **1,** rage; **2,** a great outburst of excitement or enthusiasm. Also spelled **fu-ro′re** (fū-rôr′i).

fur-ri-er (fur′i-ẽr), *n.* one who prepares or sells furs.

fur-row (fur′ō), *n.* **1,** a trench made in the ground by a plough; **2,** a groove; a wrinkle:—*v.t.* **1,** to plough; **2,** to make grooves or wrinkles in.

fur-ry (fûr′i), *adj.* **1,** covered with fur; as, a *furry* animal; **2,** like fur or made of fur.

fur-ther (fûr′thẽr), *adj.* **1,** more distant; as, the *further* field; **2,** additional; as, he needs *further* help:—*adv.* **1,** to a greater distance or degree; as, to go *further;* **2,** moreover; also; as, she remarked *further* that you were late:—*v.t.* to promote; help forward; as, he *furthered* my plans.

fur-ther-ance (fûr′thẽr-ans), *n.* advancement; aid.

fur-ther-more (fûr′thẽr-mōr′), *adv.* besides; in addition; also.

fur-ther-most (fûr′thẽr-mōst), *adj.* most distant or remote; as, the *furthermost* point inland.

fur-thest (fûr′thest), *adj.* and *adv.* most distant in time or space; as, the *furthest* island of the group.

fur-tive (fûr′tiv), *adj.* sly; secret; stealthy; as, *furtive* glances or actions. —*adv.* **fur′tive-ly.**—*n.* **fur′tive-ness.**

fu-ry (fū′ri), *n.* [*pl.* furies], **1,** violent anger; rage; **2,** great violence; fierceness; as, the *fury* of the storm; **3,** a violently angry person.

furze (fûrz), *n.* **1,** in Europe a low spiny shrub with yellow flowers (also known as *gorse* or *whin*).

¹fuse (fūz), *v.t.* [fused, fus-ing], **1,** to melt, esp. by heat, as metals; make liquid; **2,** to join or blend by melting:—*v.i.* **1,** to become melted, as by heat; **2** to blend, as if melted.—*adj.* **fu′si-ble.**

²fuse (fūz), *n.* **1,** a small tube or casing filled with a material easily set on fire or a cord saturated with such material along which fire will run: used for exploding gunpowder, dynamite, etc. **2,** a piece of metal put in an electric circuit, which melts and breaks the circuit when the current gets too strong for safety:—*v.t.* [fused, fus-ing] to attach a fuse to.

fu-see (fū-zē′), *n.* **1,** a coloured railroad flare; **2,** a friction match that will burn in the wind.

fu-se-lage (fū′ze-lij; fū′ze-läzh′), *n.* the body of an aeroplane, to which the wings and the tail are fastened, and which contains the controls, space for the pilot, passengers, cargo, etc.

fu-sil-eer (fū′zi-lēr′), *n.* formerly, soldier armed with a flintlock; *pl.* name of a number of British regiments.

fu-sil-lade (fū′zi-lād′), *n.* a rapid discharge of many firearms; an outpouring; as, a *fusillade* of questions.

fu-sion (fū′zhun), *n.* **1,** the act of melting, or state of being melted together; as, the *fusion* of metals; **2,** union or blending together; as, *fusion* of ideas:—**fusion bomb,** a hydrogen bomb.

fuss (fus), *n.* **1,** unnecessary or disturbing activity, esp. in small matters; confusion; stir; **2,** a complaint:—*v.i.* **1,** to worry; **2,** to be busy over trifles:—*v.t. Colloq.* to annoy or embarrass.—*adj.* **fuss′y.**

fu-tile (fū′til; fū′til), *adj.* **1,** without result; useless; as, *futile* shouting; **2,** of no importance; worthless.—*adv.* **fu′tile-ly.**—*n.* **fu-til′i-ty** (fū-til′i-ti).

fu-ture (fū′tūr; chẽr), *adj.* yet to happen or come; as, a *future* event:—*n.* **1,** time yet to come; **2,** the future tense:—**future tense,** in *grammar,* tense of a verb indicating action in time yet to come; as, I *shall go* tomorrow; **future perfect,** in *grammar,* a tense of the verb indicating action taking place before a future time; as, when you arrive, I *shall have finished* the task.

fu-tu-ri-ty (fū-tū′ri-ti), *n.* [*pl.* futurities], **1,** time to come; **2,** a future event.

fuzz (fuz), *n.* tiny particles of down, wool, etc.:—*v.i.* to come off in small fluffy bits.—*adj.* **fuzz′y.**—*n.* **fuzz′i-ness.**

cat, āge, fär, câre, ásk; ten, ēve, latẽr; (i) pity, rely, senate; īce; top; n

G

G, g (jē), *n.* [*pl.* G's, g's], **1,** the seventh letter of the alphabet, following F; **2,** in music, the fifth tone in the major scale of C.

gab (gab), *v.i. Colloq.* to talk much or idly.—*n.* idle talk; chatter; as, a gift of the *gab.*—*n.* **gab'ber.**

gab-ar-dine (gab'ẽr-dēn'; gab'ẽr-dēn'), *n.* **1,** a kind of woollen or cotton cloth like serge; **2,** a gaberdine.

gab-ble (gab'l), *v.i.* to make rapid, inarticulate sounds; as, the *gabbling* of geese.

gab-er-dine or **gab-ar-dine** (gab'ẽr-dēn'; gab'ẽr-dēn'), *n.* a long, loose gown or coat; esp. a loose gown worn by the Jews in the Middle Ages.

ga-ble (gā'bl), *n.* **1,** the triangular part of a wall of a building between opposite slopes of a sloping roof; **2,** any similar construction, as over a window.

gad (gad), *v.i.* [gad-ded, gad-ding], to go about without purpose; to ramble; as, to *gad* about all day.—*n.* **gad'der.**

gad (gad), *n.* a goad, spike, or switch, as for driving an animal, or loosening ore in a mine.

gad-a-bout (gad'a-bout'), *n. Colloq.* one who moves about aimlessly for gossip, or out of curiosity.

gad-fly (gad'flī'), *n.* [*pl.* gad-flies], any of various flies which sting cattle, horses, etc.

gadg-et (gaj'et), *n.* a device; contrivance.

Gael-ic (gāl'ik), *n.* (and *adj.*) the language or people of the Scottish Highlands, Ireland, and the Isle of Man.

gaff (gaf), *n.* **1,** a large hook with a handle, used for getting large fish out of the water; **2,** a spar branching from the mast of a sailing-vessel, to which is attached the top of a fore-and-aft sail; **3,** *Slang,* a trial; ordeal; as, to stand the *gaff*:—*v.t.* to seize (a fish) with a gaff.

gag (gag), *n.* **1,** something put in the mouth to hinder speech, or to keep the mouth open; **2,** *Slang,* a practical joke; **3,** in a play, words added by an actor, or any remark, trick, or act inserted to get a laugh:—*v.t.* [gagged, gag-ging], **1,** to stop up the mouth; **2,** to silence by force or law:—*v.i.* to strain, as in vomiting.

gage (gāj), *n.* **1,** a promise; pledge; **2,** a pledge to appear and fight, as in support of a claim: indicated by the throwing down of a glove; **3,** a challenge to fight; a glove, cap, or the like, thrown down as a challenge:—*v.t.* [gaged, gag-ing], to bet; wager.

gage (gāj), *n.* Same as **gauge.**

gai-e-ty (gā'e-ti), *n.* [*pl.* gaieties], **1,** merriment; glee; jollity; **2,** brilliancy, as of dress. Also spelled **gay'e-ty.**

gai-ly or **gay-ly** (gā'li), *adv.* **1,** merrily; happily; **2,** showily; as, to dress *gaily.*

gain (gān), *n.* **1,** advantage; profit; as, to be greedy for *gain;* **2,** increase; as, a *gain* in weight:—*v.t.* **1,** to obtain, as profit or advantage; earn; **2,** to win; as, he *gained* his point; **3,** to obtain through an increase; as, to *gain* ten pounds in weight:—*v.i.* **1,** to improve; increase; as, to *gain* in knowledge; **2,** to advance; as, to *gain* on the runner ahead.—*n.* **gain'er.**—*adj.* **gain'ful.**

gain-say (gān'sā'), *v.t.* [gainsaid (gān'-sād'; gān'sed'), gainsay-ing], to contradict; deny.

gait (gāt), *n.* a manner of walking or running; as, the old man's shuffling *gait.*

gai-ter (gā'tẽr), *n.* **1,** a covering of cloth or leather for the lower leg or ankle, fitting over the top of the boot; **2,** in the U.S., a shoe with elastic strips at the sides; also, a kind of overshoe with a cloth top.

ga-la (gā'la; gä'la), *n.* a festival; a celebration:—*adj.* festive; as, *gala* attire:—**gala day,** a day of pleasure; a holiday.

gal-ax-y (gal'ak-si), *n.* [*pl.* galaxies (-siz)], **1,** a system of stars or suns many light-years apart; an island universe; **2,** an assemblage of famous persons:—**the Galaxy,** the Milky Way, or island universe to which our sun belongs: to the eye it appears as a luminous band across the sky.—*adj.* **ga-lac'tic.**

gale (gāl), *n.* **1,** a strong wind, less violent than a hurricane; **2,** an outburst.

ga-le-na (ga-lē'na), *n.* the chief ore of lead, lead sulphide, occurring in cube-shaped crystals: used as a detector or rectifier in the earliest wireless receivers.

gall (gôl), *n.* **1,** the bile, a bitter fluid separated out of the blood by the liver and stored in the gall-bladder; **2,** the gall-bladder; **3,** anything bitter or distasteful; **4,** spite; hate; **5,** *Slang,* insolence.

gall (gôl), *n.* a swelling or growth on the bark or leaves of numerous plants, esp. oaks, caused by, and growing around, the larva of certain insects, esp. the gallfly.

all (ôl) ôr; up, mūte, cûr, cōōl, book; oil, out; th, thin; *th,* the.

³gall (gôl), *v.t.* **1**, to chafe, or fret by friction, as a horse's collar; **2**, to vex; irritate; annoy.—*n.* a skin sore caused by chafing; a place rubbed bare; flaw. *adj.* **gall′ing.**

gal-lant (gal′ant), *adj.* **1**, brave; high-spirited; chivalrous; as, a *gallant* knight; **2**, of noble or stately appearance; **3**, (ga-lant′; gal′ant), showing elaborate courtesy and respect to women:—*n.* (gal′ant; ga-lant′), **1**, a man of fashion; **2**, a beau; a man elaborately polite to women.—*n.* **gal′lant-ry.**

gall—blad-der, (gôl′—blad′ẽr), *n.* a pear-shaped sac which receives and stores bile.

gal-le-on (gal′i-un), *n.* a large sailing-vessel with a high stern and three or four decks, usually armed, used esp. by the Spaniards from the 15th to the 17th century.

gal-ler-y (gal′-ẽr-i), *n.* [*pl.* galleries], **1**, a long, narrow hall, often with windows on one side only; **2**, a platform projecting from the side and end walls of a theatre, church, assembly-room, etc., containing seats; a balcony; **3**, the occupants of such seats; **4**, a building or room for exhibiting works of art or the like; **5**, an underground passage for communication, as in a mine or an underground fort.—*adj.* **gal′ler-ied.**

gal-ley (gal′i), *n.* [*pl.* galleys], **1**, a low, flat, one-decked, sea-going vessel, propelled by sails and oars, used in ancient and mediaeval times; **2**, a large, open rowboat; **3**, the cooking quarters of a ship; **4**, in printing, an oblong tray to hold set-up type; also, a printer's proof, often called *galley proof*, made from such type on a long sheet of paper.

gall-fly (gôl′fli′), *n.* [*pl.* gallflies], an insect that deposits its eggs on plants, causing a swelling of the plant tissue, called a *gall.*

gal-li-vant (gal′i-vant′) or **gal-a-vant,** *v.i.* to play the beau or gallant; to gad about in search of passing pleasure.

gal-lon (gal′un), *n.* a unit of liquid measure; the imperial gallon of Great Britain being equal to 277.42 cubic inches, the standard gallon; in the U.S., to four quarts or 231 cubic inches.

gal-lop (gal′up), *n.* **1**, the fastest gait of a horse, in which he takes all four feet off the ground in the same stride; **2**, a ride at this gait:—*v.i.* **1**, to run with leaps, like a horse; **2**, to ride a horse at a gallop; **3**, to hasten; as, to *gallop* through one's work:—*v.t.* to cause to move at a gallop; as, to *gallop* a horse.

gal-lows (gal′ōz; gal′us), *n.* [*pl.* gallowses], a structure consisting of

two uprights with a crossbar on the top, used for hanging criminals.

gall-stone (gôl′stōn′), *n.* a crystalline fatty alcohol (sometimes a calcium salt) that forms in the gall bladder liver, or bile duct.

gal-lus-es (gal′us-ez), *n. pl. Colloq* braces; suspenders.

ga-lore (ga-lōr′), *adj.* very many abundant: used after the noun i modifies; as, pretty girls *galore*:—*adv* in great plenty.

ga-losh (ga-losh′), *n.* any protective overshoe; esp. a high rubber overshoe also called *arctic.* Also spelled **go-losh′**

gal-va-nize (gal′va-nīz′), *v.t.* [gal vanized, galvaniz-ing], **1**, to coat wit metal, as iron with zinc, by means o electricity; **2**, to excite or shock, as i by electricity; as, to *galvanize* a person into action:—**galvanized iron** iron, often in thin sheets, coated by an electric process with zinc to keep it from rusting.—*adj.* **gal-van′ic.**

gal-va-nom-e-ter (gal′va-nom′e-tẽr *n.* an instrument that uses a magneti needle or a coil in a magnetic field t detect and measure slight electri currents.

gambit (gam′bit), *n.* **1**, in *chess,* a opening move that sacrifices a paw or piece in hope of an advantag hence, **2**, an opening move in a dis cussion, battle of wits, etc.

gam-ble (gam′bl), *v.i.* [gam-bled, gam bling], **1**, to play for money or a prize **2**, to risk money on a possible happen ing; **3**, to run any great risk for th sake of uncertain gain:—*v.t.* to squar der by playing for stakes; as, h *gambled* away his savings:—*n.* **1**, an game or act involving the risking c stakes; **2**, an act accompanied b uncertainty or by any special risk; ε mountain climbing is quite a *gamble.*— *n.* **gam′bler.**

gam-bol (gam′bul), *n.* a dancing c skipping about for joy or sport; froli —*v.i.* [gambolled, gambol-ling], t skip and dance about in play.

game (gām), *n.* **1**, sport or amusemen fun; frolic; also, jest; as, to mak *game* of a poor man; **2**, a contes carried on according to rules, succes depending upon superiority in strengt skill, luck, etc.; as, the *game* of basebal football, etc.; **3**, a single unit or divisic of play; as, four *games* in the first s at tennis; **4**, a scheme, or pla sometimes not praiseworthy; as, I'v spoiled your little *game*; the *game* is u **5**, wild animals, birds, or fish pursue by a hunter or fisherman; also, the flesh used for food:—*v.i.* [gamed, gan ing], to play for a stake or prize:—*ad*

1, pertaining to animals or birds hunted or taken for sport; **2,** *Colloq.* ready; spirited; plucky; as, he was a *game* lad.—*adv.* **game/ly.**

game-keep-er (gām/kēp/ėr), *n.* one in charge of wild animals or birds that are to be protected or preserved for hunting.

game-ster (gām/stėr), *n.* one who habitually bets or plays for stakes; a gambler.

gam-in (gam/in), *n.* a neglected street child; an outcast boy or girl.

gam-ma (gam/a), *n.* the third letter of the Greek alphabet (Γ, γ = English G, g): —**gamma rays,** penetrating short-wave radiations, similar to X-rays, emitted by radium, uranium, etc., and used in treating cancer: the γ-rays from nuclear blasts are deadly.

gam-ut (gam/ut), *n.* **1,** the great scale or whole series of recognized musical notes; **2,** the major scale; **3,** hence, the entire range of anything; as, to run the *gamut* from joy to despair.

gam-y (gām/i), *adj.* [gam-i-er, gam-i-est], **1,** abounding in game; **2,** plucky; ready; spirited; **3,** having the flavour of game.

gan-der (gan/dėr), *n.* **1,** a male goose; **2,** a simpleton.

gang (gang), *n.* **1,** a number of persons banded together for a particular purpose; as, a *gang* of thieves; **2,** a group of workmen under one foreman; **3,** an outfit or set of tools or machines arranged for use together; as, a *gang* of snowploughs.

gan-gling (gang/gling), *adj.* spindly; awkwardly tall; lanky; as, a *gangling* youth.

gan-gli-on (gang/gli-un), *n.* [*pl.* ganglia or ganglions], **1,** a mass of nerve cells (as in the brain or spinal cord) serving as a nerve centre; **2,** any centre of energy, force, or activity; as, a telephone exchange is a vital *ganglion* of modern life.

gan-grene (gang/grēn/), dying or decomposing tissue, owing to interruption of blood circulation.—*adj.* **gan/gre-nous.**

gang-plank (gang/plangk/), *n.* a movable platform or bridge by which to enter or leave a ship; gangway.

gang-ster (gang/stėr), *n.* a member of a lawless gang; a criminal.

gang-way (gang/wā/), *n.* **1,** a movable platform or bridge between a wharf and a ship; **2,** a passageway; aisle.

gan-net (gan/et), *n.* a large, fish-eating bird of the North Atlantic which breeds in colonies on cliffs and rocky islands.

¹**gant-let** (gônt/let; gȧnt/let), *n.* **1,** a former military punishment in which an offender, stripped to the waist, ran between two files of men who struck him with clubs or other weapons as he passed; **2,** a similar torture practised by Indians upon captives; **3,** figuratively, a series of tests or trials; as, he ran the *gantlet* of public opinion.

²**gant-let** (gänt/let; gȧnt/let), *n.* Same as **gauntlet.**

gan-try (gan/tri), *n.* **1,** a large, bridge-like frame structure carrying a travelling crane; **2,** a bridge over several railroad tracks carrying signals; **3,** a small overhead crane used in machine shops, mills, etc.; **4,** a frame for supporting barrels.

gaol (jāl), *n.* a place of confinement; a jail.—*n.* **gaol/er.**

gap (gap), *n.* **1,** an opening; passage; **2,** a pass in a mountain ridge; **3,** an unfilled interval; as, a *gap* in the conversation.

gape (gāp; gap; gȧp), *v.i.* [gaped, gap-ing], **1,** to open the mouth wide; as from drowsiness, wonder, etc.; yawn; **2,** to stare with open mouth, as in amazement:—*n.* **1,** the act of opening the mouth and staring; **2,** a yawn; **3,** an opening; gap; **4,** the opening between the jaws of birds or of fishes.

gar (gär), *n.* an elongated fish with long narrow jaws. Also called **garfish, gar pike,** and **needlefish.**

ga-rage (gar/äzh; ga-räzh/; gar/ij), *n.* a building in which automobiles are sheltered or repaired.

garb (gärb), *n.* dress; clothing, esp. of a distinctive kind; as, the *garb* of a priest:—*v.t.* to clothe.

gar-bage (gär/bij), *n.* waste matter from a kitchen, market, store, etc.

gar-ble (gär/bl), *v.t.* to corrupt; mutilate (a story, text, etc.) so as to mislead; as, a *garbled* account.

gar-den (gär/dn), *n.* a piece of ground set aside for growing flowers, fruit, vegetables, etc.; also, a place set aside for the display of plant and animal life to the public; as, the zoological *gardens:*—*v.i.* to labour in or cultivate a garden.

gar-den-er (gär/dn-ėr; gärd/nėr), *n.* one who gardens; also, one hired to care for a garden.

gar-de-ni-a (gär-dē/ni-a), *n.* **1,** any of a group of shrubs and trees cultivated for their fragrant yellow or white flowers; **2,** the flower of any of these.

gar-fish (gär/fish/), *n.* Same as **gar.**

gar-gan-tu-an (gär-gan/tū-an), *adj.*

unbelievàbly huge; enormous; as, a *gargantuan* appetite.

gar-gle (gär′gl), *n.* a medicinal or antiseptic liquid for washing the throat or mouth:—*v.t.* [gar-gled, gargling], to wash or disinfect (the throat) with a medicinal liquid kept moving in it by slowly expelling the breath:—*v.i.* to use a gargle.

gar-goyle (gär′goil), *n.* a grotesque waterspout or ornament in the form of an animal or human head projecting from a gutter or corner of a building; as, the *gargoyles* of Westminister Abbey.

gar-ish (gâr′ish), *adj.* gaudy; showy (without taste); cheaply flashy; as, *garish* dress, buildings, writings, etc.

gar-land (gär′land), *n.* a wreath, as of flowers, branches, or leaves, worn on the head:—*v.t.* to deck or adorn with a wreath.

gar-lic (gär′lik), *n.* a plant of the lily family, with a strong, biting taste and an unpleasant odour; also, the bulb of this plant, used in cooking.

gar-ment (gär′ment), *n.* any article of clothing, as a dress, hat, or the like.

gar-ner (gär′nėr), *n.* a storehouse for grain; a granary:—*v.t.* to gather for safekeeping; store, as in a granary; gather up; as, to *garner* grain.

gar-net (gär′net), *n.* 1, a semi-precious stone, used as a gem, usually deep red; 2, a deep-red colour.

gar-nish (gär′nish), *n.* 1, an ornament or decoration; 2, something laid about food in a dish as a decoration:—*v.t.* 1, to adorn; 2, to decorate (food); as, to *garnish* potatoes with parsley.—*n.* **gar′ni-ture.**

gar-ni-shee (gär′ni-shē′), *v.t.* to seize by legal process a debtor's property, as to *garnishee* wages.

gar pike (gär′ pīk′), *n.* Same as *gar.*

gar-ret (gar′et), *n.* the uppermost part of a house, beneath the roof; an attic.

gar-ri-son (gar′i-sun), *n.* 1, a body of troops stationed in a fort; 2, the place where such soldiers are stationed:—*v.t.* 1, to furnish (a place) with troops; as, to *garrison* a town; 2, to defend by means of a fort or forts manned by soldiers; as, they built a fort to *garrison* the pass.

gar-rote (ga-rot′; rōt′), *v.t.* to disable or kill by strangling; throttle.

gar-ru-lous (gar′ū-lus), *adj.* very talkative, esp. about unimportant things. —*adv.* **gar′ru-lous-ly.** —*n.* **gar-ru′li-ty.**

gar-ter (gär′tėr), *n.* a band or strap by which a stocking is held up:—*v.t.* to bind or fasten with a garter.

garter—snake (gär′tėr-snāk′), *n.* a small harmless snake with yellow stripes along the back, common in North America.

gas (gas), *n.* 1, any airlike fluid, without shape or volume, tending to expand indefinitely; 2, any combustible gaseous mixture used to give light and heat; 3, any similar fluid used as an anaesthetic; esp. a mixture of nitrous oxide and oxygen: often called *laughing gas*; 4, any fumes or vapour which make breathing difficult or impossible; as, *gases* used in warfare; 5, *Colloq.* gasoline; petrol:—*v.t.* [gassed, gas-sing], to poison by a gas.—*adj.* **gas′e-ous** (gä′si-us; ga′si-us).—*n.* **gas′light′.**

gash (gash), *n.* a deep or gaping cut or wound:—*v.t.* to cut deeply; as, he *gashed* his hand with a sharp knife.

gas-ket (gas′kit), *n.* 1, a band of metal, rubber, hemp, fibre paper, etc., to pack pistons and make joints leakproof; 2, a cord used to tie a furled sail to a yard.

gas-o-line or **gas-o-lene** (gas′o-lēn′; gas′o-lēn′), *n.* an inflammable liquid commonly obtained by distilling petroleum and used esp. for fuel and cleansing.

gasp (gàsp), *n.* a quick painful effort to catch the breath; as, his breath came in *gasps*:—*v.i.* to catch the breath with the mouth open; as, he was *gasping* for air:—*v.t.* to emit with quick, painful breaths; as, he *gasped* forth his words in terror.

gas-tric (gas′trik), *adj.* pertaining to the stomach; as, *gastric* fluid; *gastric* fever:—**gastric juice,** a thin, digestive liquid, secreted by glands in the lining of the stomach.—**gas-tri′tis** (gas-trī′tis) *n.* inflammation of the lining of the stomach.

gas-tro-nom-ic (gas′tro-nom′ik), *adj.* pertaining to good eating; as, a *gastronomic* treat for dinner.

gat (gat), *n. Slang,* pistol; revolver.

gate (gāt), *n.* 1, an opening in a wall, fence, or the like, to allow entrance or passage; 2, a barrier, frame, or door which opens or closes such an entrance; 3, a valve or door to stop or permit a flow, as of water, in a pipe, canal, etc.; 4, the number of people paying to see an athletic contest; also, the amount of money taken in at the entrance-gate.

gate-leg (gāt′leg′), *n.* and *adj.* a type of table with gatelike legs that can be folded to let the leaves drop.

gate-way (gāt′wā′), *n.* 1, an opening in a wall or fence for entrance and exit; 2, the frame or structure around a gate.

gath-er (gath′ẽr), *v.t.* **1,** to collect; bring together; as, to *gather* information; **2,** to pick and collect; as, to *gather* flowers; **3,** to summon; as, to *gather* one's strength; **4,** to amass gradually; as, to *gather* a fortune; **5,** to pucker; draw together; as, to *gather* a skirt to a blouse; **6,** to conclude; infer; as, they *gathered* that she was leaving:—*v.i.* **1,** to collect; come together; as, people *gathered* on all sides; **2,** to generate pus, as an abscess; **3,** to increase; as, the storm *gathers*:—*n.* one of the folds in cloth, drawn together by a thread.

gauche (gōsh), *adj.* **1,** awkward; clumsy; boorish; as, a *gauche* bearing or reply. —*n.* **gau′che-rie** (gōsh′e-ri).

gaud-y (gôd′i), *adj.* [gaud-i-er, gaud-i-est], showy; vulgarly gay; as, *gaudy* imitation jewelry.—*adv.* **gaud′i-ly.**—*n.* **gaud′i-ness.**

gauge (gāj), *n.* **1,** any of various standards of measurement; **2,** a means of estimating or judging; a test; **3,** the distance between railway rails, standard gauge being 4 feet 8½ inches; **4,** any measuring or recording instrument, as one for measuring rainfall, wind velocity, steam pressure, diameter of a wire, etc.; **5,** a carpenter's tool for marking a line parallel with the edge of a board:—*v.t.* [gauged, gaug-ing], **1,** to measure exactly; **2,** to ascertain the contents or capacity of; **3,** to make standard or uniform; **4,** to estimate; as, to *gauge* one's strength. Also, **gage.**

gaunt (gônt; gänt), *adj.* **1,** haggard and lean, as from hunger or suffering; **2,** barren and grim; desolate; as, a *gaunt* hillside.—*adv.* **gaunt′ly.**—*n.* **gaunt′ness.**

gaunt-let (gônt′let; gänt′let) or **gant-let** (gänt′let; gànt′let), *n.* **1,** in the Middle Ages, a mailed glove to protect the hand and wrist from wounds; **2,** a heavy glove with a long cuff; **3,** that part of such a glove which covers the wrist; **4,** a former punishment or torture in which a person ran between two files of men who struck him as he passed:—**throw down the gauntlet,** to give a challenge.

gauze (gôz), *n.* a thin, light, transparent fabric of silk, cotton, etc.—*adj.* **gauz′y.**

gave (gāv), *v.t.*, *p.t.* of **give.**

gav-el (gav′el), *n.* a small mallet used by a chairman or auctioneer to signal for order or attention.

ga-votte (ga-vot′), *n.* a lively French dance in 4/4 time, or the music for it.

gawk (gôk), *v.i. Colloq.* to stare stupidly: —*n.* a booby.

gawk-y (gôk′i), *adj.* [gawk-i-er, gawk-i-est], awkward; clumsy.—*adv.* **gawk′i-ly.**

gay (gā), *adj.* **1,** lively; merry; full of glee; cheerful; sportive; **2,** showy; bright-coloured; as, a *gay* red; **3,** addicted to pleasure; as, he leads a *gay* life.

gay-e-ty (gā′e-ti), *n.* Same as **gaiety.**

gay-ly (gā′li), *adv.* Same as **gaily.**

gaze (gāz), *v.i.* [gazed, gaz-ing], to look earnestly or steadily; as, he *gazed* straight ahead:—*n.* a fixed, earnest look.

ga-zelle (ga-zel′), *n.* a small, swift antelope of Africa and Asia, with large black eyes.

ga-zette (ga-zet′), *n.* **1,** a newspaper; **2,** an official government journal which prints lists of promotions, appointments, etc.:—*v.t.* [gazet-ted, gazet-ting], publish in a gazette.

gaz-et-teer (gaz′-e-tēr′), *n.* a dictionary of geographical names.

gear (gēr), *n.* **1,** equipment; as, hunting and fishing *gear*; **2,** a harness for draft animals; **3,** a unit of machinery which performs a certain function, such as transmitting power or changing timing; as, first, second, third, or reverse *gears* on an automobile change the speed and power of the motor; **4,** a condition in which the parts of a machine are adjusted to each other in order to act; as, a car cannot go unless it is in *gear*:—**gear wheel,** a wheel with teeth, which fit into the cogs of another wheel: also written *gearwheel*:—*v.t.* **1,** to put into gear; **2,** to provide with a gear or gears:—*v.i.* to be in, or come into, gear.

gear-ing (gēr′ing), *n.* the parts of a machine by which motion is transmitted from one section to another.

gear-shift (gēr′shift′), *n.* a mechanism for engaging and disengaging gears.

geck-o (gek′ō), *n.* a species of small, insect-eating lizards with weak limbs, large heads, and suction pads on their feet.

gee (jē), *interj.* a command to oxen and other animals to turn toward the right.

geese (gēs), *n. pl.* of **goose.**

Gei-ger count-er (gī′gẽr), an instrument used to detect and measure radioactivity.

gei-sha (gā′sha), *n.* a Japanese dancing-girl.

gel-a-tin (jel′a-tin) or **gel-a-tine** (jel′a-tin; jel′a-tēn′), *n.* a transparent, tasteless substance extracted from the bones, hoofs, and other parts of animals by prolonged boiling; animal jelly.—*adj.* **ge-lat′i-nous.**

gel-ding (gel′ding), *n.* a castrated horse.

gel-id (jel′id), *adj.* frozen; icy; as *gelid* arctic blasts; the *gelid* tundra.

gem (jem), *n.* **1,** a precious stone; **2,** any rare object; as, a *gem* of a picture; **3,** a kind of muffin:—*v.t.* [gemmed, gem-ming], to adorn with, or as with, precious stones.

Gem-i-ni (jem′i-ni), *n.* **1,** a northern constellation, the Twins, containing two bright stars, Castor and Pollux; it is in the Milky Way, opposite Orion and Taurus; **2,** the third sign of the zodiac.

gen-darme (zhän′därm′), *n.* in France, a member of an armed, uniformed police, trained as troopers or soldiers.

gen-der (jen′dėr), *n.* in English *grammar,* any one of the three divisions (masculine, feminine, neuter) into which nouns and pronouns are put, according to whether the objects named are regarded as male, female, or without sex.

gene (jēn), *n.* an element of a reproductive cell by which hereditary characteristics (colour of hair, shape of leaf, etc.) are determined and transmitted; each individual resulting from a union of two such cells receives a set of genes from each of its parents.

gen-e-al-o-gy (jen′e-al′o-ji; jē′), *n.* **1,** a recorded history of the descent of a person or his family from one or more ancestors; **2,** lineage; pedigree.

gen-er-a (jen′er-a), *n. pl.* of *genus.*

gen-er-al (jen′er-al), *n.* a military officer ranking higher than a colonel and usually placed in command of an army or one of the chief divisions of an army:—*adj.* **1,** pertaining to or affecting one and all; universal; as, food is the *general* need of man; a *general* epidemic; **2,** indefinite; not specific or detailed; as, a *general* outline; **3,** prevailing; usual; as, a *general* custom; **4,** whole; not local or divided; as, a *general* vote; the *general* public; **5,** not specializing in any one thing; as, a *general* store; **6,** indicating superiority of rank; as, postmaster *general.*

gen-er-al-is-si-mo (jen′ėr-al-is′i-mō′), *n.* [Italian], a commander-in-chief, esp. of combined armies in the field.

gen-er-al-i-ty (jen′ėr-al′i-ti), *n.* [*pl.* generalities], **1,** the greatest part; majority; as, the *generality* of mankind; **2,** a general statement, or one that is true as a rule but may have exceptions.

gen-er-al-ize (jen′ėr-al-īz′), *v.t.* [generalized, generaliz-ing], to derive general principles from:—*v.i.* to draw general conclusions or notions from particular instances.—*n.* **gen′er-al-i-za′tion.**

gen-er-al-ly (jen′ėr-al-i), *adv.* **1,** commonly; as a rule; as, we *generally* go to the shore; **2,** in a broad sense; as, *generally* speaking, children go to school; **3,** extensively, but not universally; as, this condition exists *generally.*

gen-er-ate (jen′ėr-āt′), *v.t.* [generat-ed, generat-ing], **1,** to bring into existence, as plants, animals, etc.; **2,** to produce, as steam in a boiler.

gen-er-a-tion (jen′ėr-ā′shun), *n.* **1,** the act or process of producing by natural or artifical means; **2,** a single step in a line of succession; as, a mother and son represent two *generations*; **3,** people born in the same period; as, the people of our *generation*; **4,** the average period of time between generations, considered as 33 years.

gen-er-a-tor (jen′ėr-ā′tėr), *n.* one who or that which causes or produces; esp. an apparatus by which steam, electricity, or gas is produced.

gen-er-os-i-ty (jen′ėr-os′i-ti), *n.* [*pl.* generosities], the quality of being liberal; greatness of heart; as, he showed *generosity* in his dealings with his enemies.

gen-er-ous (jen′ėr-us), *adj.* **1,** characterized by liberality; **2,** unselfish; honorable; **3,** rich; abundant; noble; as, a *generous* harvest.—*adv.* **gen′er-ous-ly.**

gen-e-sis (jen′i-sis), *n.* a coming to birth; **2,** origin; creation, esp. of the world and human life, as told in the Book of *Genesis.*

ge-net-ics (ji-net′iks), *n.pl.* used as *sing.,* the science of heredity, esp. that accounting for variations traceable to the interaction of genes and environment.—*adj.* **ge-net′ic.**—*n.* **ge-net′i-cist.**

gen-ial (jēn′yal; jē′ni-al), *adj.* **1,** favorable to comfort and growth; as, a *genial* climate; **2,** kindly; sympathetic; cordial; as, a *genial* disposition.—*adv.* **gen′ial-ly.**—*n.* **ge′ni-al′i-ty.**

ge-nie (jē′ni), *n.* Same as jinni.

gen-i-tals (jen′i-talz), *n.pl.* the reproductive organs, esp. the external sex organs of the male.

gen-i-tive (jen′i-tive), *adj.* in Latin, Greek, etc., the case denoting possession, separation, origin, etc.; loosely, the *possessive* case in English.

gen-ius (jēn′yus; jē′ni-us), *n.* [*pl.* geniuses], **1,** [*pl.* genii (jē′ni-ī′)], **a,** in *Roman religion,* a guardian spirit; hence, the controlling spirit of a place or person; **b,** in *Mohammedan and Arabian lore,* a nature spirit; a jinni; **2,** remarkable ability or natural fitness for a special pursuit; as, a *genius* for music; **3,** exceptional creative, intellectual, or artistic power; also, the one possessing it; **4,** a person who has a powerful influence over another.

gent (jent), *n. Slang,* gentleman.

gen-teel (jen-tēl′), *adj.* polite; wellbred: now used only humorously or sarcastically.—*adv.* **gen-teel′ly.**

gen-tian (jen′shan), *n.* any of certain plants, prized for their deep-blue flowers; esp. the tall European gentian and the U.S. fringed gentian.

Gen-tile (jen′tīl), *n.* **1,** one who is not Jewish; **2,** a pagan; heathen; a Christian.—*adj.* non-Jewish. Also, **gen′-tile.**

gen-til-i-ty (jen-til′i-ti), *n.* [*pl.* gentilities], gentle birth; refinement; good manners; as, he has no claim to *gentility.*

gen-tle (jen′tl), *adj.* [gen-tler, gen-tlest], **1,** mild; not severe in manner; kind; **2,** light; not rough; as, a *gentle* touch; **3,** friendly; docile; as, a *gentle* dog; **4,** gradual; as, a *gentle* slope; **5,** well-born:—*v.t.* [gen-tled, gen-tling], to train; make docile; as, to *gentle* a pony. —*adv.* **gen′tly.**

gen-tle-man (jen′tl-man), *n.* [*pl.* gentlemen (-men)], **1,** a well-bred and honourable man; **2,** a man; as, show the *gentleman* in; **3,** formerly, a man entitled to bear arms, but not included in the nobility.—*adj.* **gen′tle-man-ly.**

gen-tle-wom-an (jen′tl-woom′an), *n.* a woman of good birth or breeding; a lady.

gen-try (jen′tri), *n.* **1,** people of education and breeding; **2,** in England, those ranking next below the nobility; **3,** people of a particular class: usually contemptuous.

gen-u-flec-tion or **gen-u-flex-ion** (jen′ū-flek′shun), *n.* the bending of the knee (in worship).

gen-u-ine (jen′ū-in), *adj.* **1,** real; not imitation; as, a *genuine* pearl; **2,** sincere; as, *genuine* affection.—*adv.* **gen′u-ine-ly.**

ge-nus (jē′nus), *n.* [*pl.* genera (jen′ėr-a)], a group of plants or animals which have certain fundamental likenesses, yet differ in minor characteristics; as, the lion, tiger, and lynx are different species of the same *genus.* —*adj.* **ge-ner′ic** (je-ner′ik).

ge-o-det-ic (jē′o-det′ik), *adj.* relating to the science of measuring the size and shape of the earth; as, a *geodetic* survey.

ge-og-ra-phy (ji-og′ra-fi), *n.* [*pl.* geog-raphies], **1,** the science that deals with the surface of the earth, its divisions into continents, its climates, plants, animals, inhabitants, and their distribution, industries, etc.; **2,** the natural features of a certain area; as, the *geography* of France.—*n.* **ge-og′ra-pher.**—*adj.* **ge′o-graph′ic** (jē′o-graf′ik); **ge′o-graph′i-cal.**

ge-ol-o-gy (ji-ol′o-ji), *n.* [*pl.* geologies], the science of the structure of the earth and the history of its successive physical changes, esp. as recorded in the rocks. —*adj.* **ge′o-log′ic; ge′o-log′i-cal.**—*n.* **ge-ol′o-gist.**

ge-om-e-try (ji-om′e-tri), *n.* [*pl.* geometries], that branch of mathematics which treats of the properties and measurements of lines, angles, surfaces, and solids.—*adj.* **ge′o-met′ric; ge′o-met′ri-cal.**

ge-o-phys-i-cal (jē′o-fiz′ i-kal), *adj.* pertaining to phenomena of the earth's physics such as tides, magnetism, meteorology, cosmic rays, the Van Allen radiation belts, etc.:—the International Geophysical Year, an 18-month period (1957–58) devoted to a major study of earth phenomena by world scientists.

ge-ra-ni-um (ji-rā′ni-um), *n.* **1,** a plant, the *wild geranium,* with blue or rose-coloured flowers; **2,** a cultivated plant with red, white, or pink flowers.

ger-fal-con (jûr′fô′kn; fôl′kn), *n.* a large falcon found in the Arctic regions of America, Europe, and Asia.

ger-i-at-rics (jer′i-at′riks), *n.* the branch of medicine dealing with old age and its diseases.

germ (jûrm), *n.* **1,** that from which anything springs; origin; as, the *germ* of life, war, etc.; **2,** the undeveloped beginning of an animal or plant; a sprout; seed; **3,** a microbe, esp. one that may cause disease.

ger-mane (jėr-mān′; jûr′mān), *adj.* closely pertinent; relevant; as, your remark is (not) *germane* to the argument.

ger-mi-cide (jûr′mi-sīd′), *n.* a substance used to destroy germs, as carbolic acid or iodine.

ger-mi-nate (jûr′mi-nāt′), *v.t.* [germinat-ed, germinat-ing], to sprout or bud; begin to develop:—*v.t.* to cause to develop; as, to *germinate* seeds.—*n.* **ger′mi-na′tion.**

ger-ry-man-der (jer′i-man′dėr; ger′), *v.t.* to divide, or change the boundaries of, a voting district so as to give a political party an unfair advantage; to manipulate; misrepresent. Also used as *noun.*

ger-und (jer'und), *n.* a verbal noun; as, *seeing* is *believing.—adj.* **ge-run'di-al.**

ge-sta-po (ge-stä'pō), *n.* a high-handed secret police, as in Germany under the Nazi regime.

ges-ta-tion (jes-tā'shun), *n.* the carrying of young in the womb; pregnancy.

ges-tic-u-late (jes-tik'ū-lāt'), *v.i.* [gesticulat-ed, gesticulat-ing], to make expressive motions, esp. while speaking; as, an orator *gesticulates* to emphasize a point.—*n.* **ges-tic'u-la'tion.**

ges-ture (jes'tūr), *n.* **1,** a movement of the face, body, or limbs, to express an idea or emotions; **2,** something said or done as a courtesy or for effect; as, her visit was a kindly *gesture;*—*v.i.* [gestured, gestur-ing], to make expressive motions.

get (get), *v.t.* [*p.t.* got (got), *p.p.* got or got-ten (got'n), *p.pr.* get-ting], **1,** to acquire; win; realize; as, to *get* a new hat; *get* first prize; *get* three wishes; **2,** to obtain by calculating; as, to *get* 40 by adding 20 and 20; **3,** to understand; as, to *get* an idea; **4,** to contract; catch; as, to *get* the measles; **5,** to receive as one's lot; as, to *get* the worst of it; to *get* ten years' imprisonment; **6,** to learn; as, to *get* a lesson; **7,** to obtain by effort or some process; as, to *get* coal from a mine; *get* power from a waterfall; also, to prepare; as, to *get* dinner; **8,** to succeed in bringing about; bring into some state; as, to *get* the grass cut; *get* him talking; **9,** *Colloq.* to overcome; also, to catch or kill; as, he *got* his man:—*v.i.* **1,** to arrive; as, to *get* home by five; **2,** to bring oneself into a certain state; as, to *get* ready; *get* well; **3,** to become; as, to *get* hungry or tired.

get-a-way (get'a-wā'), *n.* **1,** *Colloq.* the start (of a race); **2,** *Slang,* escape, as from pursuers, etc.

gew-gaw (gū'gô), *n.* a showy trifle.

gey-ser (gī'zėr), *n.* a hot spring which frequently throws forth jets of hot water, steam, and mud.

ghast-ly (gȧst'li), *adj.* **1,** deathlike; pale; **2,** horrible; as, a *ghastly* crime.

gher-kin (gûr'kin), *n.* a small young cucumber used for pickling.

ghet-to (get'ō), *n.* [*pl.* ghettos], formerly, the only part of a city where Jews might live; now, the Jewish quarter.

ghost (gōst), *n.* **1,** the spirit of a dead person, thought of as living in an unseen world, or as returning to earth in bodily form to haunt the living; **2,** a shadowy resemblance; as, the *ghost* of a smile.—*adj.* **ghost'ly.**

ghost writer, one who writes speeches,

articles, etc., for another, who takes credit for them.

ghoul (gōōl), *n.* **1,** a grave-robber; **2,** one who enjoys doing loathsome acts. —*adj.* **ghoul'ish.**

G.I. (jē'ī'), *n. Colloq. U.S. army,* government issue; hence, an enlisted man.— *adj.* relating to an armed service; as, *G.I.* shoes, haircut, etc.

gi-ant (jī'ant), *n.* **1,** in *mythology* and *folklore,* a person of human form but of supernatural size and power; **2,** an unusually large person, animal, or plant; **3,** a person of unusual physical or mental strength or courage:—*adj.* huge; unusually powerful; monstrous. —*n.fem.* **gi'ant-ess.**

gib-ber (jib'ėr; gib'ėr), *v.i.* and *v.t.* **1,** to chatter rapidly and meaninglessly; as, monkeys *gibber;* **2,** to talk foolishly.

gib-ber-ish (gib'ėr-ish; jib'ėr-ish), *n.* **1,** rapid, disconnected talk; **2,** nonsense; as, his arguments were *gibberish.*

gib-bet (jib'et), *n.* a kind of gallows; an upright post with an arm projecting from the top from which the bodies of executed criminals used to be hung and left as a warning:—*v.t.* **1,** to execute by hanging; **2,** to hang (the body of an executed person) on a gibbet as a warning; **3,** hence, to expose to public ridicule or scorn.

gib-bon (gib'un), *n.* a small long-armed ape of southeastern Asia.

gib-bous (gib'us), *adj.* bulging; swelling; as, the *gibbous* moon.

gibe (jīb), *n.* a taunt or scoff; sneering or sarcastic expression:—*v.t.* [gibed, gib-ing], to sneer at; taunt; as, they *gibed* him for his mistakes:—*v.i.* to sneer; scoff; as, they *gibed* at his singing. Also spelled **jibe.**

GIBBOUS MOON

gib-lets (jib'litz), *n.* the internal organs of poultry, as heart, liver, gizzard, etc., used as food.

gid-dy (gid'i), *adj.* [gid-di-er, gid-di-est], **1,** light-headed; dizzy; **2,** causing dizziness or staggering; as, a *giddy* height; **3,** frivolous; fickle; as, a giddy young girl.—*adv.* **gid'di-ly.**—*n.* **gid'di-ness.**

gift (gift), *n.* **1,** something given; a present; **2,** the power to give or bestow; as, the position is in his *gift;* **3,** natural talent or ability; as, a *gift* for oratory.

gift-ed (gif'ted), *adj.* talented; endowed with unusual natural ability.

gig (gig), *n.* **1,** a light, two-wheeled, open

carriage drawn by one horse; **2,** a ship's light boat, for the captain's use.

gi-gan-tic (jī-gan′tik), *adj.* huge; immense; of extraordinary size.

gig-gle (gig′l), *n.* a nervous, silly laugh: —*v.i.* [gig-gled, gig-gling], to laugh in a nervous, tittering manner.—*adj.* **gig′gly.**

gi-go-lo (zhig′o-lō′), *n.* a professional male dancing partner.

Gi-la mon-ster (hē′la), *n.* a poisonous, black-and-orange lizard of southwestern U.S. deserts (about 20″ long).

¹gild (gild), *v.t.* [gild-ed or gilt (gīlt), gild-ing], **1,** to coat or cover with a thin layer of gold, or something resembling gold; **2,** to make (something) seem more attractive than it really is; gloss over; as, to *gild* a lie.—*n.* **gild′ing.**

²gild (gild), *n.* Same as **guild.**

¹gill (gil), *n.* an organ for breathing air under water, as in fish and amphibians.

²gill (jil), *n.* a unit of liquid measure equal to one fourth of a pint.

gilly-flow-er (jil′i-flou′ẽr), *n.* a yellow-flowered, clove-scented perennial, as the European wallflower and common stock.

gilt (gilt), *adj.* covered with, or of the colour of, gold; as, *gilt* chairs:—*n.* a thin layer of gold or something resembling it put on a surface; as, a picture-frame covered with *gilt.*

gim-bals (jim′b′lz; gim′), *n.* a device used at sea to keep a suspended object (compass, lantern, etc.) horizontal; it consists of a pair of rings pivoted so as to swing freely within each other.

gim-let (gim′let), *n.* a small tool for boring holes.

gim-mick (gim′ik), *n. Slang,* **1,** a device by which a magician works a trick; **2,** any tricky device or contrivance used to obtain an end.

¹gin (jin), *n.* an alcoholic liquor made from grain mash and flavoured with juniper berries, etc.

²gin (jin), *n.* **1,** a trap or snare; **2,** a machine for clearing cotton fibres of seeds; a cotton gin:—*v.t.* [ginned, ginning], to clear (cotton) of seeds with a cotton gin.

gin-ger (jin′jẽr), *n.* **1,** a tropical plant cultivated for its spicy, sharp-tasting root; **2,** the dried, usually scraped, roots of such a plant used as a sweetmeat when candied; **3,** the powder obtained by grinding such dried roots, used as a spice or medicine; **4,** *Colloq.* courage; vim; spirit:—**ginger ale,** a non-alcoholic drink flavoured with ginger.

gin-ger-bread (jin′jẽr-bred′), *n.* **1,** a dark-coloured cake sweetened with molasses and flavoured with ginger, sometimes cut into fanciful shapes and gilded or frosted; **2,** hence, cheap, flimsy ornamentation, esp. on a house: —*adj.* gaudy; over-ornamented.

gin-ger-ly (jin′jẽr-li), *adv.* with extreme care; timidly:—*adj.* cautious; careful.

gin-ger-snap (jin′jẽr-snap′), *n.* a thin, crisp molasses cooky flavoured with ginger.

ging-ham (ging′am), *n.* a cotton dress cloth, usually in stripes, plaids, or checks, woven of dyed yarn.

gin-gi-vi-tis (jin′ji-vī′tis), *n.* inflammation of the gums.

ging-ko (ging′kō; jing′kō), *n.* [*pl.* gingkoes], a cone-bearing tree with fan-shaped leaves, native to Japan and China. Also written **gink′go** (gingk′gō).

gip (jip), *v.* Same as *gyp.*

gip-sy (jip′si), *n.* [*pl.* gipsies], **1,** one of a wandering, dark-skinned race of Eastern, probably Hindu, origin; **2,** the language of the gipsies: also called *Romany:*—**gipsy—moth,** a European moth. Also spelled **gyp′sy.**

gi-raffe (ji-ràf′), *n.* a cud-chewing animal of Africa, remarkable for its long legs and neck. It has a spotted skin, and feeds on the leaves and twigs of trees.

gird (gûrd), *v.t.* [gird-ed or girt (gûrt), gird-ing], **1,** to encircle or bind with a cord, belt, or the like; **2,** to encircle; **3,** to make ready; as, to *gird* oneself for combat.

gird-er (gûr′dẽr), *v.* a main beam of wood, iron, or steel, used to support the weight of a structure; as, the steel *girders* of a bridge.

gir-dle (gûr′dl), *n.* something which surrounds, encircles, or confines, as a sash or belt:—*v.t.* [gir-dled, gir-dling], **1,** to bind or surround with, or as with, a belt; **2,** to enclose; **3,** to cut the bark of (a tree or branch) clear around.

girl (gûrl), *n.* **1,** a female child; a young unmarried woman; **2,** a female servant; **3,** *Colloq.* a sweetheart.—*adj.* **girl′ish.**— *n.* **girl′hood.**

girth (gûrth), *n.* **1,** a band around an animal to hold a saddle, blanket, etc., in place; **2,** the measure around anything; as, a man's *girth.*

gist (jist), *n.* the main point of a matter; as, the *gist* of a story or speech.

give (giv), *v.t.* [*p.t.* gave (gāv), *p.p.* giv-en (giv′en), *p.pr.* giv-ing], **1,** to hand over as a present; as, I *gave* him a hat; **2,** to pay in exchange for something received; as, to *give* a dollar for a doll; he *gave* money for candy; **3,** to bestow freely; devote; as, he *gave* his life for his country; **4,** to administer, as medicine or gas; **5,** to deliver, as a message; as, *give* her my love; **6,** to read, recite, or utter; as, to *give* a speech; **7,** to furnish; as, fire *gives* heat; **8,** to furnish as entertainment; as, to *give* a dance; **9,** to put forth; as, *give* a jump or a shout; **10,** to impart; be the source of; as, to *give* some one a cold; the play *gave* pleasure; **11,** to allot; assign; as, to *give* a child a name; **12,** to grant; as, to *give* permission; **13,** to entrust; as, I *give* it into your charge; **14,** to pledge; as, to *give* one's word; **15,** to present for action or consideration; as, to *give* a reason; **16,** to perform; present; as, to *give* a play:—*v.i.* **1,** to present gifts; to contribute; bestow charity; as, he *gave* freely to the hospital; **2,** to yield, as to force, pressure, motion, etc.; as, the marshy ground *gave* under my feet; **3,** to afford a view or passage; as, the window *gives* on a court:—*n.* a yielding to pressure; elasticity; as, the *give* of new rubber.

giv-en (giv'en), *adj.* **1,** inclined; disposed; as, *given* to lying; **2,** stated; as, to meet at a *given* time:—**given name,** the Christian name given to a child by his parents or guardian.

giz-zard (giz'ėrd), *n.* the second stomach of birds, with thick, muscular walls for crushing and grinding food, often by means of pebbles previously swallowed.

gla-cier (gla'si-ėr; glā'shėr), *n.* a mass or river of ice, formed in high, cold regions, which moves slowly down through a valley until it melts, or else, on sea coasts, breaks off into icebergs. —*adj.* **gla'cial.**

glad (glad), *adj.* [glad-der, glad-dest], **1,** joyous; cheerful; **2,** pleased; as, I am *glad* that you came; **3,** causing joy; as, *glad* news; **4,** bright; beautiful; as, a *glad* sky:—*adv.* **glad'ly.**—*v.t.* and *v.i.* **glad'den.**

glade (glād), *n.* an open space in a forest.

glad-i-a-tor (glad'i-ā'tėr), *n.* in ancient Rome, a man trained or hired to fight for the amusement of the public.

glad-i-o-lus (glad'i-ō'lus; gla-dī'ō-lus), *n.* [*pl.* gladioluses or gladioli (glad'i-ō'lī; gla-dī'ō-lī)], a plant of the iris family, with sword-shaped leaves and spikes of coloured, showy flowers.

glam-our or **glam-or** (glam'ėr), *n.* **1,** magical charm; enchantment; as, the *glamour* of the moonlight; **2,** false or alluring charm of a person, place or thing.

The *-our* spelling is preferred for the noun, and the *-or* spelling for the words derived from it.—*adj.* **glam'or-ous.**

glance (glȧns), *n.* **1,** a swift, side-wise look; **2,** a hasty look; as, a *glance* into a room; a *glance* at a paper:—*v.i.* [glanced, glanc-ing], **1,** to view with a quick movement of the eye; **2,** to strike at a slant and fly off; as, the stone *glanced* off his armour.

gland (gland), *n.* an organ which secretes a special substance or substances to be used in, or discharged from, the body; as, the salivary *glands.*—*adj.* **glan'du-lar.**

glan-ders (glan'dėrz), *n.pl.* a contagious disease of horses, marked by swelling in the glands of the lower jaw and discharge of mucous from the nose.

glare (glâr), *n.* **1,** a brilliant light; dazzling brightness; as, the *glare* of the sun; **2,** a fierce, piercing look:—*v.i.* [glared, glar-ing], **1,** to shine with a dazzling light; as, the light *glared* through the windows; **2,** to look with fierce, piercing eyes; as, she *glared* at me when I spoke:—*v.t.* to express with a fierce look; as, he *glared* his hate.

glar-ing (glâr'ing), *adj.* **1,** dazzlingly bright; as, a *glaring* light; **2,** fierce; angry; as, a *glaring* eye; **3,** evident; extremely conspicuous; as, a *glaring* error.

glass (glȧs), *n.* **1,** a hard, brittle substance, usually transparent or translucent, made from sand mixed with soda, potash, and other chemicals, and shaped at high heat by pressing or blowing; **2,** an article made of this substance, as a mirror, a table-tumbler, telescope, etc.; **3,** the amount of anything contained in a drinking-tumbler; as, a *glass* of milk; **4, glasses,** spectacles; eye-glasses:—*adj.* made of such a substance; as, *glass* flowers:—*v.t.* to put into a jar, for preservation; as, to *glass* fruits.—*n.* **glass'ful.**—*n.* **glass'-mak-ing.**—*n.* **glass'ware'.**

glass-y (glȧs'i), *adj.* [glass-i-er, glass-i-est], **1,** like glass in being smooth, transparent, etc.; **2,** staring without expression: said of the eye or look.—*adv.* **glass'i-ly.**

glau-co-ma (glô-kō'ma), *n.* an eye disease marked by tension and hardness of the eyeball, leading to loss of sight.

glaze (glāz), *v.t.* [glazed, glaz-ing], **1,** to furnish or fit with glass; **2,** to cover or overlay with a thin coating of glass, or a substance resembling glass; hence, to make smooth and glossy; as, to *glaze* pottery or paper; **3,** in cooking, to coat with crystallized sugar; as, *glazea* fruit; **4,** to make (the eye) staring or glassy; as, death *glazed* his eyes:—*v.i.* to become staring or glassy; as, his eyes *glazed:*—*n.* 1, a substance used for glazing; 2, a glossy or glazed surface; as, a *glaze* of ice.—*n.* **gla′zier** (glā′zhẻr).

gleam (glēm), *n.* 1, a brief flash of light; a beam; 2, something resembling a flash of light; as, a *gleam* of hope:—*v.i.* to send out rays of light; as, candles *gleamed* in the windows.

glean (glēn), *v.t.* 1, to gather (grain, or other produce) which the reapers have left; 2, to collect bit by bit; as, facts *gleaned* from many books:—*v.i.* to gather grain left by reapers.—*n.* **glean′er.**

glee (glē), *n.* 1, gaiety; mirth; entertainment; 2, a song, without musical accompaniment, for three or more voices, singing different parts in harmony:—**glee club,** a club organized to sing songs in harmony.—*adj.* **glee′ful.** —*adv.* **glee′ful-ly.**

glen (glen), *n.* a narrow secluded valley.

glib (glib), *adj.* [glib-ber, glib-best], speaking or spoken with readiness and ease, but often with little sincerity or thought; as, a *glib* talker; a *glib* statement.—*adv.* **glib′ly.**

glide (glīd), *v.i.* [glid-ed, glid-ing], to flow, or move along smoothly or noiselessly; as, the boat *glided* through the water:—*n.* the act of moving along smoothly or noiselessly; also, a smooth, sliding step or motion, as in dancing.

glid-er (glīd′ẻr), *n.* 1, one who or that which moves along smoothly; 2, a form of aircraft similar to an aeroplane but without any engine.

glim (glim), *n.* *Slang,* light; candle.

glim-mer (glim′ẻr), *n.* 1, a faint, unsteady light; 2, a glimpse or hint; as, a *glimmer* of hope:—*v.i.* to flicker; shine faintly and waveringly; as, lights *glimmer* afar.

glimpse (glimps), *n.* 1, a hurried view; as, they caught a *glimpse* of her as she passed; 2, a hint; a notion; as, a *glimpse* of what is to come:—*v.t.* [glimpsed, glimps-ing], to catch a hurried view of; as, they *glimpsed* the garden as they hurried by.

glint (glint), *n.* a faint gleam; a flash:— *v.i.* to sparkle or flash; reflect light; as, the armour *glinted* in the sunlight.

glis-ten (glis′n), *v.i.* to sparkle; shine; gleam; as, her eyes *glistened* with tears:—*n.* glitter; sparkle.

glit-ter (glit′ẻr), *v.i.* 1, to sparkle or flash, as diamonds; 2, to be showy, as jewels:—*n.* brilliancy; sparkle; as, the *glitter* of gold.—*adj.* **glit′ter-y.**

gloam-ing (glōm′ing), *n.* twilight; dusk.

gloat (glōt), *v.i.* to feast the eyes or mind in triumph, greed, or spite; as, a thief *gloats* on stolen jewels; to *gloat* over an enemy's failure.

globe (glōb), *n.* 1, an object which is round like a ball; a ball; a sphere; 2, a sphere showing a map of the earth (*terrestrial globe*); a similar sphere showing the arrangement of the heavenly bodies (*celestial globe*):—**the globe,** the earth.—*adj.* **glob′u-lar** (glob′ū-lẻr).— *adj.* **glob′al.**

glob-ule (glob′ūl), *n.* a tiny globe-shaped particle; as, a *globule* of fat.

gloom (glōōm), *n.* 1, partial darkness; 2, unhappiness; low spirits; sadness:— *v.i.* 1, to be or become cloudy or partially dark; 2, to frown or look sullen; be sad or unhappy.—*adj.* **gloom′y.**—*adv.* **gloom′i-ly.**—*n.* **gloom′i-ness.**

glor-i-fy (glōr′i-fī), *v.t.* [glorified, glorify-ing], 1, to confer honour and splendour upon; as, to *glorify* a hero; 2, to, worship; adore; as, to *glorify* God; 3, to give beauty and charm to; as, kindliness *glorifies* a homely face.—*n.* **glor′i-fi-ca′tion.**

glor-i-ous (glōr′i-us), *adj.* 1, praiseworthy; noble; as, a *glorious* victory; 2, of splendid beauty; magnificent; as, a *glorious* scene; 3, *Colloq.* delightful; as, *glorious* fun.—*adv.* **glor′i-ous-ly.**

glor-y (glōr′i), *n.* [*pl.* glories], 1, distinction, fame, or honour, given to someone or something by others; 2, splendour; radiant beauty; as, the *glory* of the sunset; 3, a reason for pride; as, the Colosseum was the *glory* of ancient Rome; 4, highest state of magnificence or prosperity; as, Greece in her *glory*; 5, praise given in worship; as, *glory* be to God; 6, in art, a halo: —*v.i.* [gloried, glory-ing], to rejoice or exult; as, to *glory* in one's power.

gloss (glôs), *n.* 1, a smooth, glistening lustre; as, the *gloss* of satin; 2, an insincere or false appearance; 3, a glossary:—*v.t.* 1, to make smooth and lustrous; 2, to give a fair appearance to; cover up or lessen by excuses; as, to *gloss* over a mistake.—*adj.* **gloss′y.**— *n.* **gloss′i-ness.**

glos-sa-ry (glos′a-ri), *n.* [*pl.* glossaries], 1, a collection of notes explaining obsolete, technical, or other unusual words in a book or text, or as used by some author; 2, a dictionary of a dialect.

glot-tis (glot′is), *n.* the small opening between the vocal cords in the larynx.

glove (gluv), *n.* 1, a covering for the hand, of leather, wool, silk, or the like, with a separate division for each finger; **2,** a padded covering to protect the hand in certain sports, as boxing, baseball, etc,

glow (glō), *v.i.* **1,** to give off heat and light without flame; as, embers *glow* after a fire dies down; **2,** to be red; show brilliant colour; as, the sun *glows* in the west; **3,** to be warm or flushed, as from exercise; **4,** to burn with the fervour of emotion or excitement:—*n.* **1,** intense or shining heat; **2,** redness, or brightness of colour; **3,** passion; ardour; **4,** warmth of body.

glow-er (glou′ẽr), *v.i.* to stare threateningly or angrily; scowl; as, the angry man *glowered* at the boy.

glow-worm (glō′wûrm′), *n.* any of various insects and their larvae which glow or flicker in the dark.

glu-cose (glōō′kōs), *n.* **1,** a form of sugar in honey and most fruits; **2,** in Canada, a syrup made from cornstarch, and used to sweeten food: also called *corn-syrup*.

glue (glōō), *n.* **1,** a substance, made by boiling fish or the skins, hoofs, etc., of animals, and used, when heated or boiled with water, for sticking things together; **2,** any substance that is like glue:—*v.t.* [glued, glu-ing], to join with glue.—*adj.* **glue′y.**

glum (glum), *adj.* [glum-mer, glummest], gloomy; moody; sullen; as, a *glum* expression.—*adv.* **glum′ly.**

glut (glut), *n.* too large a supply; as, a *glut* of wheat on the market:—*v.t.* [glut-ted, glut-ting], **1,** to more than satisfy; as, he *glutted* his appetite with rich food; **2,** to over-supply; as, to *glut* the market.

glu-ten (glōō′ten), *n.* a nutritious and sticky substance, found in the flour of certain grains, esp. wheat.—*adj.* **glu′ti-nous.**

glut-ton (glut′n), *n.* **1,** one who eats too much; a greedy person; **2,** a small flesh-eating and fur-bearing animal of the northern regions; the wolverine.—*adj.* **glut′ton-ous.**—*n.* **glut′ton-y.**

glyc-er-ine (glis′ẽr-in; glis′ẽr-ēn′) or **glyc-er-in** (glis′ẽr-in), *n.* a sweetish colourless, sticky liquid obtained from oils, fat, etc., used in medicines, explosives, etc.

gly-col (glī′kol), *n.* an organic compound (of the nature of alcohol or glycerine) used as an antifreeze in automobiles.

gnarled (närld), *adj.* full of knots; distorted; twisted; as, an old, *gnarled* oak.

gnash (nash), *v.t.* and *v.i.* to strike or grind the teeth together, as in anger or in pain.

gnat (nat), *n.* a small, two-winged insect, which stings or bites.

gnaw (nô), *v.t.* [*p.t.* gnawed (nôd), *p.p.* gnawed or gnawn (nôn), *p.pr.* gnaw-ing], **1,** to bite off, or eat away, little by little; to corrode; **2,** hence, to torment; as, *gnawed* by remorse:—*v.i.* **1,** to bite repeatedly; as, to *gnaw* at a crust; **2,** to torment.

gneiss (nīs), *n.* a granite-like rock of banded appearance, consisting of alternate layers of feldspar, quartz, mica, and hornblende.

gnome (nōm), *n.* a dwarf, supposed to live in the earth to guard the earth's treasures.

gno-mon (nō′mon), *n.* **1,** anything that points out the time of day by its shadow, as the arm of a sundial, or a pillar; **2,** that part of a parallelogram left after a similar paralello-gram has been cut from the corner.

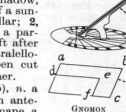
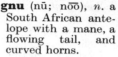

gnu (nū; nōō), *n.* a South African antelope with a mane, a flowing tail, and curved horns.

GNOMON
1, on a sundial, 2, on a parallelogram (figure *abcdef*).

go (gō), *v.i.* [*p.t.* went (went), *p.p.* gone (gôn), *p.pr.* go-ing], **1,** to pass from place to place; travel; proceed; as, to *go* from Montreal to Toronto; *go* ahead; gossip *goes* through a town; a telegram *goes* by wire; **2,** to move away; depart; start; as, the train *goes* at five; the train has *gone;* **3,** to follow or be guided; as, to *go* by rule; she *goes* with the fashion; **4,** to be (in a certain condition); as, to *go* dirty; *go* in daily dread; *go* prepared; **5,** to be in working order; as, a clock or an engine *goes;* **6,** to make a particular motion; as, *go* like this; **7,** to make a particular sound; as, guns *go* bang; the cat *goes* "miaow"; **8,** to have a certain wording or tune; as, the song *goes* like this; **9,** to result; as, the election *went* Conservative; **10.** to adopt certain views or a course of action; as, Russia *went* Communist; to *go* to war; **11,** to lead; as, the road *goes* to town; **12,** to pass by; elapse; as, an hour *goes* quickly; **13,** to be known; as, she *goes* by the name of Sue; **14,** to be sold; as, a house *goes* at auction; the ring *went* for a dollar; **15,** to be missing; as, my ring is *gone;* **16,** to disappear; be abolished or lost; as, crime must *go;* his health is *gone;* **17,** to be spent; as, my money *went* for food; **18,** to die; as, all men *go* at last; **19,** to fail; give way; collapse; as, his mind *went;* the scaffolding *went;* **20,** to attend; as, he *goes* to McGill; **21,** to become; as, to *go* crazy; *go* blind; **22,** to fit; belong; harmonize; as, this shoe *goes* on this foot; that book *goes* on that shelf; brown *goes* well with green; **23,** to be contained; as, three *goes* into nine:—going to, about to; intending to; as, I was just *going* to leave:—*v.t. Colloq.* **1,** to bet; wager; as, I'll *go* you one better; **2,** to endure; tolerate; as, I can't *go* her chatter:—*n. Colloq.* **1,** energy; enthusiasm; as there is *go* in him yet; **2,** an agreement; as, it's a *go;* **3,** success; as, the business is a *go.*

goad (gōd), *n.* **1,** a sharp, pointed stick to urge on cattle; **2,** anything which urges one to action:—*v.t.* to drive with a goad; as, to *goad* cattle; hence, to urge to action by irritating means; to drive; as, his taunts *goaded* me to try.

goal (gōl), *n.* **1,** a point marking the end of a race or journey; **2,** an aim; purpose; as, a *goal* in life; **3,** the place into, over, or through which the players in football, hockey, etc., must put the ball in order to score; also, the score thus made.—*n.* **goal'keep'er;** *Colloq.* **goal'ie.**

goat (gōt), *n.* **1,** a small, very active, cud-chewing animal, with horns and a beard, much valued for its milk, flesh, and hair; **2,** *Colloq.* one who gets or takes the blame for another's deed; a scapegoat; one who is a butt for ridicule or jokes.—*n.* and *adj.* **goat'-skin'.**

goat-ee (gō'tē'), *n.* a pointed beard (on chin or lower lip).

¹gob (gob), *n. Colloq.* a slimy lump or mass; as, a *gob* of paint.

²gob (gob), *n. Slang,* a sailor in the U.S. navy.

¹gob-ble (gob'l), *v.t.* [gob-bled, gob-bling], **1,** to swallow hastily or greedily; as, he *gobbled* his food; **2,** *Slang,* to seize greedily; as, to *gobble* the front seats.

²gob-ble (gob'l), *n.* the cry of a male turkey:—*v.i.* [gob-bled, gob-bling], to utter this cry.

gob-bler (gob'lēr), *n.* a male turkey.

go—be-tween (gō'–bi-twēn'), *n.* one who goes from one person to another to make peace, do business, or settle difficulties.

gob-let (gob'let), *n.* a drinking-glass with a stem and a base, but without a handle.

gob-lin (gob'lin), *n.* an evil, mischievous, ugly spirit; gnome.

go-cart (gō'kärt'), *n.* **1,** a baby carriage with small front wheels, and a back that can be raised or lowered; **2,** a light cart.

god (god), *n.* **1,** a being thought of as having greater than human powers and traits; *esp.* one to whom worship is due; **2,** anything believed to have divine powers, as an image, animal, phase of nature; **3,** a thing or person that is an object of supreme interest or devotion; as, money is his *god;* his teacher is his *god:*—**God,** the Supreme Being; the Lord: also called *Creator; the Almighty; Jehovah.*—*n.* **god'hood.** —*n.fem.* **god'dess.**

god-child (god'chīld') *n.* a child for whose religious training a godparent or godparents promise to assume responsibility at the baptism of the child; a goddaughter or godson.

god-dess (god'is), *n.* **1,** a female deity; hence, **2,** a woman of unusual charm, beauty, or goodness.

god-fa-ther (god'fä'thėr), *n.* a man who promises, at the baptism of a child, to be responsible for its religious training.

God-head (god'hed'), *n.* **1,** divinity; **2,** God. Also, **god'head'.**

god-less (god'lis), *adj.* having no god; not believing in God; hence, wicked.

god-like (god'līk'), *adj.* like, or suitable for, a god.

god-ly (god'li), *adj.* pious; obedient to the commands of God; as, the minister is a *godly* man.—*n.* **god'li-ness.**

god-mother (god'muth'ėr), *n.* a woman who promises, at the baptism of a child, to be responsible for its religious training.

god-par-ent (god'pâr'ent), *n.* a man or woman who promises, at a child's baptism, to be responsible for its religious training.

god-send (god'send'), *n.* unexpected aid or good fortune which comes as if sent by God.

God-speed (god'spēd'), *n.* success: a wish for good luck, as to one going on a journey.

gog-gle (gog'l), *v.i.* [gog-gled, gog-gling], to roll the eyes; stare:—*adj.* staring; prominent; rolling; as, *goggle* eyes:—*n.* **1,** a strained or affected rolling of the eyes; **2,** goggles, eyeglasses worn to protect the eyes from dust, sun, etc.

go-ing (gō'ing), *n.* **1,** departure; as, her *going* was unexpected; **2,** the state of the ground or roads, as for travelling, racing, etc.; as, the *going* is good:—*adj.* working; successful; as, a *going* concern.

goi-tre or **goi-ter** (goi′tèr), *n.* an enlargement of the thyroid gland (often seen as a swelling on the front of the neck), caused by lack of iodine in the diet.

gold (gōld), *n.* **1,** a precious metal, widely used for coinage and jewellery, which is heavy and easily bent, and, when pure, of a bright yellow colour; **2,** money; wealth; **3,** the colour of gold; **4,** precious or pure quality; as, she is *gold* all through.

gold-en (gōl′den), *adj.* **1,** made of, or like, gold; **2,** shining; bright like gold; **3,** excellent; as, a *golden* opportunity.

gold-en-eye (gōl′den-ī′), *n.* a diving wild duck with white breast, dark-green back and bright-yellow eyes.

gold-en-rod (gōl′den-rod′), *n.* a summer- or fall-blooming plant with wandlike stems and spike-shaped clusters of small, yellow flowers.

gold-eye (gōld′ī′), *n.* a silvery, herring-like game fish of cold-water lakes, as the Winnipeg *goldeye* (noted for its delectable flavour).

gold-finch (gōld′finch′), *n.* **1,** a brightly coloured European songbird; **2,** an American songbird with a yellow body, and black crown, wings, and tail.

gold-fish (gōld′fish′), *n.* a small, yellow or orange-coloured fresh-water fish native to China. It is related to the carp and is often kept in ponds, bowls, or aquariums.

gold-smith (gōld′smith′), *n.* one who makes gold utensils and ornaments, or who deals in gold plate.

golf (golf), *n.* a game played with a small, hard ball and long-handled clubs, on a course, or tract of land, called *links*, the object being to drive the ball into a series of holes with the fewest possible strokes:—*v.i.* to play the game of golf.

go-losh (go-losh′), *n.* Same as *galosh.*

gon-do-la (gon′dō-la), *n.* **1,** a long, narrow, flat-bottomed boat, with high, pointed ends, moved, usually, by one oar, and used on the canals of Venice; **2,** in the U.S., an open freight-car with a flat bottom and low sides; **3,** a long car slung under a dirigible balloon. —*n.* **gon′do-lier′.**

gone (gôn), *p.p.* of go.

gong (gông), *n.* a saucer-shaped, metal bell which resounds when struck; as, a dinner-*gong;* a fire-*gong.*

good (good), *adj.* [*comp.* bet-ter, *superl.* best], **1,** adapted to the end in view; suited to its purpose; as, fish are *good*

to eat; a *good* saddle-horse; **2,** efficient; as, a *good* doctor; a *good* driver; **3,** satisfactory in quality; as, *good* silk; **4,** giving pleasure; as, a *good* time; **5,** not less than; complete; as, a *good* mile; **6,** real; genuine; as, *good* money; **7,** considerable; as, a *good* distance; a *good* number; **8,** well-behaved; as, a *good* child; a *good* dog; **9,** morally excellent; virtuous; as, a *good* man; **10,** kind; benevolent; as, God is *good;* **11,** right; proper; as, a *good* rule to live by; **12,** favourable; advantageous; as *good* news; **13,** of high or respectable birth; as, to come of a *good* family; **14,** able to endure or perform; as, a coat *good* for two years; **15,** valid; sound; as, a *good* excuse; **16,** thorough; as, a *good* scolding; **17,** financially sound; trustworthy; as, *good* for a debt:—*n.* **1,** whatever is excellent, right, desirable, or sound: opposite of *evil;* as, let *good* prevail; **2,** profit; advantage; welfare; as, I tell you for your own *good;* **3,** use; as, what *good* is it?—*interj.* an exclamation of approval.—*adj.* **good′look′ing; good′hu′moured.**

good—bye or **good—by** (good′–bī′), *n.* a farewell; as, a fond *good-bye:*—*interj.* farewell! a contraction of "God be with you." (Also spelled **goodbye, goodby.**)

good—for—noth-ing (good′fèr–nuth′-ing), *n.* a useless or worthless person. Also used as *adj.*

good-ly (good′li), *adj.* [good-li-er, good-li-est], **1,** handsome; **2,** of pleasing quality or character; **3,** of considerable size.

good-ness (good′nis), *n.* the state or quality of being good; virtue; kindness; excellence:—*interj.* an exclamation of surprise.

good-will (good′wil′), *n.* **1,** kindly feeling; benevolence; **2,** good intention; well-wishing; as, you have my *goodwill;* **3,** the value to a business of an established trade. Also, **good will.**

goof (goof), *n. Slang,* a silly, stupid, or gullible person:—*v.i. Slang,* to fail, blunder, etc.—*adj.* **goof′y.**

goon (goon), *n. Slang,* **1,** a person hired by racketeers, unionists, etc., to terrorize by slugging, bombing, etc.; a thug hired as a strikebreaker; **2,** an awkward, stupid person.

goose (goos), *n.* [*pl.* geese (gēs)], **1,** a web-footed, flat-billed water-bird, larger than a duck but smaller and more awkward than a swan; **2,** a female goose: in contrast to *gander;* **3,** the flesh of the goose, used as food; **4,** a silly person.

goose-ber-ry (goos′bèr-i; gooz′bèr-i),

n. [*pl.* gooseberries], **1,** a sour, hairy berry, used in pies and jams; **2,** the bush that bears this berry.

goose-flesh (gōos'-flesh), *n.* a temporary roughness of the skin, resembling that of a plucked goose, caused by cold or fear: also called *goose-skin.*

goose-step (gōos'step'), *n.* the German stiff-legged parade step:—*v.i. Colloq.* to march thus (often used figuratively).

go-pher (gō'fer), *n.* **1,** a ground squirrel of the prairies of North America; **2,** a ratlike, burrowing animal with large cheek pouches; **3,** a burrowing land-tortoise of the southern U.S.

¹gore (gōr), *n.* blood; esp. thick or clotted blood.—*adj.* **gor'y.**

²gore (gōr), *n.* **1,** a three-cornered or triangular piece of cloth sewed into a dress, sail, etc., to vary its width; **2,** one of the triangular or wedge-shaped pieces needed to make a dome-shaped object, as an umbrella, balloon, etc.:—*v.t.* [gored, goring], to piece with gores or a gore.

³gore (gōr), *v.t.* [gored, gor-ing], to pierce with, or as with, a horn; as, the bull *gored* him.

Gor-gon (gôr'gon), *n.* in *Greek mythology,* one of three snaky-haired sisters so horrible that the beholder was turned to stone; one (Medusa) was slain by Perseus. Also **gor'gon,** an ugly or repulsive woman.

gorge (gôrj), *n.* **1,** the throat; **2,** that which is swallowed; **3,** a mass of anything which chokes up a channel; as, a *gorge* of ice in a river; **4,** a narrow passage, as between mountains; a ravine:—*v.t.* [gorged, gorging], **1,** to swallow greedily; to stuff; **2,** to stop up:—*v.i.* to eat greedily.

gor-geous (gôr'jus), *adj.* rich in colour; magnificent; showy.—*adv.* **gor'geous-ly.**

go-ril-la (go-ril'a), *n.* an African manlike ape, the largest ape known.

gor-mand (gôr'mand), *n.* Same as **gourmand.**

gor-mand-ize (gôr'man-dīz'), *v.i.* to eat gluttonously.

gorse (gôrs), *n.* a low, spiny European shrub; furze; whin.

gos-hawk (gos'hôk'), *n.* any of several powerful, short-winged hawks.

gos-ling (goz'ling), *n.* a young goose.

gos-pel (gos'pel), *n.* **1,** good news or tidings; esp. the teachings of Jesus and the apostles; **2,** anything believed as absolutely true; as, I take his word for *gospel;* **3,** any principle which guides actions and in which its supporters earnestly believe:—**Gospel, 1,**

the history of the life and teachings of Jesus Christ, contained in the first four books of the New Testament; **2,** any one of these books.

gos-sa-mer (gos'a-mer), *n.* **1,** a light film of spider's web or cobweb; **2,** any very thin, filmy fabric:—*adj.* thin; delicate; gauzy; as, a *gossamer* scarf.

gos-sip (gos'ip), *n.* **1,** familiar or idle talk; talebearing; **2,** one who makes a habit of talking about other people and their affairs:—*v.i.* to chat; tell idle tales about others; tattle.—*adj.* **gos'sip-y.**

gos-soon (go-sōon'), *n.* (Irish), a boy.

got (got), *p.t.* and alternative *p.p.* of *get.*

Gothic (goth'ik), *adj.* characteristic of a style of architecture with pointed arches and steep roofs:—*n.* a style of architecture.

gouge (gouj), *n.* **1,** a curved, hollow chisel for scooping out grooves or holes; **2,** a groove or hole, made with, or as with, a gouge:—*v.t.* [gouged, goug-ing], to scoop out with, or as with, a gouge.—*n.* **goug'er.**

gou-lash (gōo'lash; gōo'läsh), *n.* a highly seasoned stew of pieces of beef or veal, and vegetables.

gourd (gōord; gōrd), *n.* **1,** any of a number of fleshy, many-seeded fruits with hard shells, related to the melon, pumpkin, etc.; also, the vine bearing this fruit; **2,** the dried shell of such fruits, used for cups, dippers, etc.; **3,** a bottle, cup, or the like, made from a gourd shell.

gour-mand (gōor'mand), *n.* **1,** a glutton; **2,** a judge of fine foods; epicure; gourmet.

gour-met (gōor'mā'), *n.* a judge of fine foods and drinks; an epicure.

gout (gout), *n.* **1,** a disease marked by painful inflammation of the joints, esp. of the big toe; **2,** a splash or drop, as of rain or blood.—*adj.* **gout'y.**—*n.* **gout'i-ness.**

gov-ern (guv'ern), *v.t.* **1,** to control, manage, or direct; as, to *govern* a nation or household; **2,** to decide; determine; influence; as, the financial report *governed* their decision; **3,** to require to be in a particular grammatical mood, case, etc.; as, a transitive verb *governs* a noun in the objective case:—*v.i.* to rule.

gov-ern-ess (guv'er-nis), *n.* a woman employed to take care of, and often to teach, children in their own home.

gov-ern-ment (guv'ern-ment), *n.* **1,** control or management; as, the *government* of a nation; school *government;* **2,** the system of governing; method of ruling; as, a democratic

government; **3,** a person or persons who govern; **4,** a territory or country governed.—*adj.* **gov′ern-men′tal.**

gov-er-nor (guv′ĕr-nẽr), *n.* **1,** one who governs; as, the Board of *Governors* of a hospital; esp. the head of a British colony, or of a state in the U.S.; **2,** a device attached to an engine, etc. to regulate its speed.

gov-er-nor—gen-er-al (guv′ĕr-nẽr-jen′ĕr-al), *n.* [*pl.* governor-generals or governors-general], a viceroy's or sovereign's deputy, as in Canada, where each province has a lieutenant-governor or deputy governor.

gown (goun), *n.* **1,** a woman's dress; esp. an elaborate dress; as, an evening *gown;* **2,** a long, loose robe worn by judges, priests, etc.; **3,** any loose robe or dress; as, a night*gown:*—*v.t.* to clothe with a gown.

grab (grab), *v.t.* and *v.i.* [grabbed, grabbing], to seize suddenly; snatch; as, the thief *grabbed* the purse:—*n.* a sudden snatch at something; as, to make a *grab* at a life-preserver.

grace (grās), *n.* **1,** attractiveness; charm; esp. beauty and ease of motion or manner; as, the *grace* of a dancer; **2,** favour; goodwill; as, in the teacher's good *graces;* **3,** hence, kindness; mercy; **4,** favour shown by granting a delay; as, three days' *grace* to pay a note already due; **5,** any charming quality, natural or affected; as, to be full of pleasant *graces;* **6,** a sense of right and wrong; as, he had the *grace* to apologize; **7,** a prayer of thanks before or after a meal; **8,** God's mercy or his divine favour:—*v.t.* **1,** [graced, gracing], to adorn; decorate; **2,** to honour; favour; as, the queen's presence *graced* the banquet.—*adj.* **grace′ful.** —*adv.* **grace′ful-ly.**

grace-less (grās′lis), *adj.* **1,** unlovely; awkward; **2,** bad; wicked; as, a *graceless* prisoner.—*adv.* **grace′less-ly.**

gra-cious (grā′shus), *adj.* **1,** kindly; courteous; also, merciful; as, the *gracious* king pardoned him; **2,** attractive and kind in manner and character. —*adv.* **gra′cious-ly.**

grack-le (grak′l), *n.* **1,** a variety of blackbird, esp. the purple or bronze *grackle;* **2,** one of the European starling family.

gra-da-tion (gra-dā′shun), *n.* **1,** a gradual change from one thing to another; as, *gradation* in colour from blue to purple; **2,** the act of arranging into a series in order of size, rank, colour, etc.; the series so formed; a step in such a series; **3, gradations,** steps; stages; degrees.

grade (grād), *n.* **1,** a step or degree in rank, quality, order, etc.; **2,** position in a scale; as, a general holds the highest *grade* in the army; **3,** a class of persons or things of the same degree, rank, etc.; as, meat of a good *grade;* **4,** a division of the school course, consisting of a year of work; as, the elementary school has eight *grades;* also, the pupils in such a division; **5,** the mark or rating given to a pupil for school work; **6,** the rate at which a road, railroad, etc., slopes or inclines; also, the slope of a road, railroad, etc., as, the train goes slowly on a downward *grade:*—*v.t.* [graded, grading], **1,** to sort out according to size, quality, rank, or value; as, to *grade* milk or fruits; to arrange into classes; as, to *grade* children according to age; **2,** to level, or to ease the slope of, as a road; **3,** to assign a mark to; as, to *grade* test papers.—*n.* **grad′er.**

gra-di-ent (grā′di-ent), *n.* **1,** slope (or degree of slope), as of a road, ramp, etc.; **2,** in *physics,* the rate of change (as of pressure, temperature, electrical potential, etc.); **3,** a curve or graph showing such a rate of change.—*adj.* rising or descending by steps or degrees.

grad-u-al (grad′ū-al), *adj.* proceeding, or moving slowly, by degrees; not sudden; as, a *gradual* slope.—*adv.* **grad′u-al-ly.**

grad-u-ate (grad′ū-āt′), *v.t.* [graduated, graduat-ing], **1,** to confer a degree or diploma upon; as, a university *graduates* students; **2,** to mark in grades or degrees; as, to *graduate* a measuring-glass:—*v.i.* **1,** to receive a diploma or degree; as, he *graduated* from high school; **2,** to change gradually from one degree to another; as, the brightness of the light *graduates* in the electric sign:—*adj.* (grad′ū-it), **1,** having received a degree; as, a *graduate* student; **2,** designed for one who has received a degree; as, a *graduate* course:—*n.* (grad′-ū-it), one who has received a diploma or degree.—*n.* **grad′u-a′tion.**

graft (gráft), *v.t.* **1,** to insert (a shoot) from one plant into another plant, on which it continues to grow; **2,** to transplant (living tissue) from one part of the body to another; as, to *graft* skin; **3,** *Colloq.* to get by unfair or dishonest means; as, to *graft* money

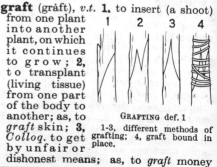

GRAFTING def. 1

1-3, different methods of grafting; 4, graft bound in place.

or votes:—*n.* **1,** the act of grafting; also, a shoot or piece of tissue used in grafting; **2,** in the U.S., the getting of money or positions by dishonest means —*n.* **graft'er.**

gra-ham (grā'am), *adj.* made of wholewheat flour, as *graham* wafers.

Grail (grāl), *n.* the cup used by Jesus at the Last Supper, called the *Holy Grail*, famous in literature.

grain (grān), *n.* **1,** the seedlike fruit of any cereal grass, such as oats, rice, wheat, etc.; also, the plant itself; **2,** any very small, hard particle; as, a *grain* of sand or sugar; **3,** any tiny bit; as, a *grain* of salt for seasoning; a *grain* of hope; **4,** a very small unit of weight, obtained from the weight of a grain of wheat; **5,** the arrangement of fibres or the texture of wood, stone, or the like; **6,** the nature or instincts of a person; as, dishonesty goes against my *grain:*—*v.t.* to paint in imitation of the grain of wood.

gramme or **gram** (gram), *n.* a unit or measure of weight and mass in the metric system, equal to 15.432 grains.

gram-mar (gram'ẽr), *n.* **1,** the science which deals with the forms of words and their relation to each other; **2,** the use of words according to this science; **3,** a book on this science:—**grammar—school, 1,** in the U.S., the grades between the primary grades and those of the high school; **2,** in England, a school where Latin, Greek, and other subjects are taught, to prepare a student for college.—*adj.* **gram-mat'i-cal** (gra-mat'i-kal).—*n.* **gram-mar'i-an** (gra-mâr'i-an).

gram-o-phone (gram'o-fōn'), *n.* one of the earliest machines producing speech or music from a record; phonograph.

gran-a-ry (gran'a-ri), *n.* [*pl.* granaries] a storehouse for grain.

grand (grand), **1,** main; principal; as, the *grand* entrance to a theatre; **2,** magnificent; splendid; as, a *grand* ball; **3,** showing high social standing and wealth; as, a *grand* lady; **4,** dignified; noble; as, the *grand* manner **5,** imposing; stately; as, a *grand* mountain; **6,** higher in rank than others of the same class; as, a *grand* duke; **7,** great in size, value, or consequence; as, a *grand* prize; *grand* climax; **8,** including everything; as, a *grand* total; **9,** *Colloq.* very good; as, a *grand* time.

Grand Banks, a shoal 300 miles long (40,000 sq. mi. in area), southeast of Newfoundland, famous for fishing.

Grand Canyon, a gorge of the

Colorado River, 217 miles long, 2,000 to 6,000 ft. deep.

grand-child (grand'chīld'), *n.* [*pl.* grand-children (grand'chil'dren)], the child of one's son or daughter.

grand-daugh-ter (grand'dô'tẽr), *n.* a daughter of one's son or daughter.

grand duke, 1, in certain countries of Europe, as Luxemburg, a sovereign duke, who is next below a king in rank; **2,** formerly, in Russia, a son of a czar. —**grand duch'ess.**

gran-dee (gran-dē'), *n.* a man of high rank, esp. a Spanish or Portuguese nobleman.

gran-deur (gran'dūr), *n.* **1,** great power, rank, or fame; **2,** sublime beauty; as, the *grandeur* of the Alps; **3,** social splendour.

grand-fa-ther (grand'fä'thẽr), *n.* the father of one's father or mother; also, any forefather.—*adj.* **grand'fa'ther-ly.**

gran-dil-o-quence (gran-dil'o-kwens), *n.* the use of pompous, high-flown, or bombastic words or expressions.—*adj.* **gran-dil'o-quent.**

gran-di-ose (gran'di-ōs'), *adj.* **1,** imposing; impressive; **2,** pompous; showy; as, *grandiose* schemes.

grand ju-ry, a group of jurors chosen to examine into accusations against people, and decide whether or not to send them for trial to a regular court.

grand-ma (grand'mä'; gran'mä'; gram' mä'), *n.* a grandmother. Also, **grand'-mam-ma'.**

grand-moth-er (grand'muth'ẽr), *n.* the mother of one's father or mother.

grand-pa (grand'pä'; gran'pä'; gram'-pä'), *n.* a grandfather. Also, **grand'papa'.**

grand-par-ent (grand'pâr'ent), *n.* either parent of one's father or mother.

grand-sire (grand'sīr'), *n. Archaic:* **1,** a grandfather or forefather; **2,** an aged man.

grand slam, in *bridge,* the (bidding and) taking of all 13 tricks.

grand-son (grand'sun'), *n.* a son of one's son or daughter.

grand-stand, the principal seatingplace for the spectators at a race-course, athletic field, etc.

grange (grānj), *n.* **1,** a farm, esp. with all its buildings; **2,** in the U.S., one of the lodges of a secret national association of farmers.

gran-ite (gran'it), *n.* a hard, durable rock, pink, whitish, or grey in colour, used for buildings, monuments, etc.

gran-ny knot (gran'i), *n.* a knot like a reef or square knot, but with the ends crossed the wrong way.

grant (grant), *v.t.* **1,** to give or confer, esp. in response to a prayer or request; as, to *grant* permission; *grant* pardon; **2,** to agree to; admit as true; as, to *grant* a point in an argument:—*n.* **1,** the act of granting; also, the thing granted; as, to receive land as a *grant* from a government; **2,** in law, a transfer of property.

gran-u-late (gran'ū-lāt'), *v.t.* [granulat-ed, granulat-ing], **1,** to form into small grains; as, to *granulate* metal; **2,** to roughen the surface of:—*v.i.* to form into small grains; as, syrup *granulates*:—**granulated** sugar, sugar which has been whitened and made into small, separate grains.—*adj.* **gran'-u-lar.**

gran-ule (gran'ūl), *n.* a small grain.

grape (grāp), *n.* **1,** an edible, juicy berry, growing in clusters on a vine and used for making wine and raisins; **2,** the grapevine.

grape-fruit (grāp'frōōt'), *n.* a large, round, yellow fruit, related to the orange.

grape-vine (grāp'vīn'), *n.* a vine which bears grapes.

graph (grăf), *n.* a diagram showing by means of dots and lines the relationship between any two quantities or things; as, a *graph* of the temperature, hour by hour.

graph-ic (graf'ik) or **graph-i-cal** (graf'i-kal), *adj.* **1,** pertaining to the art of writing, drawing, engraving, etc.; **2,** illustrated by graphs, diagrams, etc.; **3,** vividly written or told.

graph-ite (graf'īt), *n.* a kind of soft black carbon used in lead pencils.

grap-nel (grap'nel), *n.* **1,** a grappling iron, often with six hooks or claws; **2,** a small anchor with three or more flukes: used on boats, balloons, etc.

grap-ple (grap'l), *v.t.* [grap-pled, grap-pling], to lay fast hold of:—*v.i.* to struggle in, or as in, a fight; as, to *grapple* in wrestling; to *grapple* with a problem:—*n.* **1,** a close fight; a close hold, as in wrestling; **2,** a mechanical device for seizing anything: often called a *grappling-iron.*—*n.* **grap'pler.**

grasp (gràsp), *v.t.* **1,** to seize; catch at; hold by clasping; as, *grasp* the rope; **2,** to take hold of mentally; understand; as, to *grasp* the situation:—*v.i.* to try to seize; as, to *grasp* at power:—*n.* **1,** the grip of the hand; **2,** power of seizing; **3,** mental hold; comprehension; control; possession.

grasp-ing (gràs'ping), *adj.* greedy.

grass (gràs), *n.* **1,** green herbage, on which grazing animals feed; esp. plants having jointed stems and narrow leaves; **2,** land for grazing; any grass-covered ground.—*adj.* **grass'y.**

grass-hop-per (gràs'hop'ēr), *n.* any one of numerous slender, leaping, plant-eating insects, sometimes winged, which do great damage to crops.

grass widow, a woman divorced, or otherwise separated, from her husband.

¹grate (grāt), *v.t.* [grat-ed, grat-ing], **1,** to reduce to small particles by rubbing on a rough surface; as, to *grate* cheese; **2,** to rub so as to produce a rasping sound; as, to *grate* metal on stone:—*v.i.* **1,** to produce a harsh noise by rubbing; **2,** to cause annoyance; as, her voice *grates* on me.

²grate (grāt), *n.* **1,** an iron frame of parallel or crossed bars; as, a *grate* on a prison window; **2,** a framework of iron bars to hold burning fuel:—*v.t.* [grat-ed, grat-ing], to furnish with iron bars; as, to *grate* a window.—*n.* **grat'er.**

grate-ful (grāt'fool), *adj.* **1,** thankful; appreciative; **2,** pleasant; soothing.—*adv.* **grate'ful-ly.**—*n.* **grate'ful-ness.**

grat-i-fi-ca-tion (grat'i-fi-kā'shun), *n.* **1,** satisfaction; **2,** that which pleases; **3,** reward or recompense.

grat-i-fy (grat'i-fī), *v.t.* [gratified, gratify-ing], to please; indulge; humour; as, to *gratify* a taste for music.

¹grat-ing (grāt'ing), *adj.* harsh; irritating.

²grat-ing (grāt'ing), *n.* a framework of crossed or parallel bars, used to cover an opening without shutting out light and air.

gra-tis (grā'tis), *adv.* without charge; free.

grat-i-tude (grat'i-tūd'), *n.* thankfulness.

gra-tu-i-tous (gra-tū'i-tus), *adj.* **1,** freely given; as, *gratuitous* information; **2,** without cause; as, a *gratuitous* insult.

gra-tu-i-ty (gra-tū'i-ti), *n.* **1,** a return for a service or favour, as a tip; **2,** a financial gift or bounty at retirement, as a pensioner's or soldier's *gratuity.*

¹grave (grāv), *v.t.* [*p.t.* graved, *p.p.* grav-en (grāv'en) or graved, *p.pr.* grav-ing], **1,** to shape by cutting with a chisel; also, to cut, as letters, on a hard surface; **2,** to impress deeply, as on the mind:—*n.* **1,** a hole dug in the earth as a place of burial; any place of burial; **2,** death; destruction.—*n.* **grav'er.**

²grave (grāv), *adj.* [grav-er, grav-est], **1,** needing serious thought; as, a *grave* problem; **2,** solemn; serious; as, a *grave* face; **3,** not gay; dull; sombre; **4,** low in pitch, as in music.—*adv.* **grave'ly.**

rave accent (gráv), **1,** a mark [`ˋ`] over a vowel to show that it is pronounced, as in *belovèd;* **2,** in *French* (a) to distinguish words spelt alike, as *là* and *la;* (b) to suggest open *e* as in *père.*

rav-el (grav'el), *n.* material consisting of pieces of rock and pebbles coarser than sand:—*v.t.* [gravelled, gravel-ling], to cover with gravel; as, to *gravel* a road.

rav-en (grāv'en), *adj.* sculptured; carved:—**graven image,** an idol.

rave-stone (grāv'stōn'), *n.* a stone placed to mark a grave; a tombstone.

rav-ing (grā'ving), *n.* and *adj.* **1,** carving; **2,** scraping a ship's hull in a *graving* dock or dry-dock.

rav-i-ta-tion (grav'i-tā'shun), *n.* **1,** the force which draws all bodies in the universe toward one another; **2,** the force which draws all objects on the earth toward its centre; **3,** a natural movement toward a centre of attraction or influence:—*v.i.* **grav'i-tate'.**—*adj.* **grav'i-ta'tion-al.**

rav-i-ty (grav'i-ti), *n.* [*pl.* gravities], **1,** seriousness; solemnity; as, the *gravity* of those attending a funeral; dignity, as of a judge; **2,** importance; serious significance; as, the *gravity* of war; **3,** the force which draws all objects on the earth toward its centre; also, gravitation of any kind.

ra-vure (grà-vūr'; grā'vūr), *n.* **1,** engraving by the use of plates from photographs (short for *photogravure* or *rotogravure);* **2,** the print made in this way.

ra-vy (grā'vi), *n.* [*pl.* gravies], the fatty juice which comes out of meat in cooking; also, this juice made into a food dressing.

ray (grā), *n.* Same as **grey.**

ray-ling (grā'ling), *n.* a fresh-water game fish of the trout family, but with a larger dorsal fin of bright colour, found from U.S. to the Arctic, esp. in northwestern Canada.

graze (grāz), *v.t.* [grazed, graz-ing], **1,** to feed growing grass to; to pasture; as, to *graze* cattle; **2,** to eat grass from:—*v.i.* to eat grass.—*n.* **graz'er.**

graze (grāz), *v.t.* and *v.i.* [grazed, graz-ng], to touch, rub, or scrape lightly; to scratch, or become scratched, by rubbing:—*n.* a slight rub.

rease (grēs), *n.* **1,** melted animal fat; **2,** any thick oily substance:—*v.t.* (grēs; grēz), [greased, greas-ing], **1,** to smear with fat; **2,** to oil; to lubricate; as, 'to *grease* a car.—*adj.* **greas'y** (grēz'i; grē'si).—*n.* **greas'i-ness.**

reat (grāt), *adj.* **1,** large in size; big;

vast; opposite of *small* or *little;* as, *great* plains stretch to the west; **2,** large in number; as, a *great* herd of cattle; **3,** prolonged; as, a *great* while; a *great* wait; **4,** extreme; as, *great* ignorance; *great* danger; **5,** plentiful; elaborate; as, a *great* feast; in *great* detail; **6,** of remarkable genius, skill, or character; noble; distinguished; as, a *great* artist; **7,** important; as, *great* things depend on his decision; **8,** considerable in size or intensity; as, a *great* storm; *great* pain; **9,** more than usual; as, take *great* precautions; **10,** more remote in relationship by one generation; as, a *great*-grandfather, a *great*-grandson; **11,** *Colloq.* having unusual skill or knowledge; as, he's *great* at swimming; **12,** *Colloq.* favourite; as, a *great* joke of his; **13,** *Colloq.* intimate; as, *great* friends; **14,** *Slang,* excellent; as, that's *great!*—**Great War,** the war of 1914–18, which involved nearly all the important nations of the world: also called *World War I.*—*adv.* **great'ly.**—*n.* **great'ness.**

great—aunt (grāt'-ànt'), *n.* a father's or mother's aunt.

Great Bear, the seven bright stars forming the Great Dipper, or Ursa Major.

great-coat (grāt'kōt'), *n. Military,* a heavy overcoat.

great—grand-child (grāt'-grand'-child'), *n.* [*pl.* great-grandchildren (-chil'dren)], a child of one's grandson or granddaughter.

great—grand-fa-ther (grāt'-grand'-fä'thèr), *n.* the father of one's grandfather or grandmother.

great—grand-moth-er (grāt'-grand'muth'èr), *n.* the mother of one's grandfather or grandmother.

grebe (grēb), *n.* a diving bird with a short body, partly webbed feet, and almost no tail, related to the loon.

greed (grēd), *n.* intense and selfish hunger or desire; as, *greed* for wealth.—*adj.* **greed'y.**—*adv.* **greed'i-ly.**—*n.* **greed'i-ness.**

green (grēn), *n.* **1,** the colour of growing grass or plants; a colour between blue and yellow; **2,** a grass plot or common; **3,** in *golf,* the closely cut turf around a hole; **4, greens: a,** green leaves or branches cut for decorations; as, Christmas *greens;* **b,** spinach or similar vegetables, used for food:—*adj.* **1,** having the colour of, or covered with, growing grass or plants; **2,** fresh; full of life; **3,** having a sickly colour; **4,** unripe; as, *green* fruit; **5,** not salted; as, *green* hams; **6,** not dried; as, *green* wood; **7,** untrained; inexperienced.

green-back (grēn'bak'), *n.* a piece of

U.S. paper money, so called because its back is printed in green ink.

green-horn (grēn′hôrn), *n.* an inexperienced person; a simpleton.

green-house (grēn′hous′), *n.* a house made of glass, for growing flowers and plants.

greening (grēn′ing), *n.* any of several apples which have green skins when ripe.

green-ish (grēn′ish), *adj.* somewhat green.

green-sward (grēn′swôrd′), *n,* smooth turf which is well covered with grass.

Greenwich Time (grin′ij; ich), the mean solar time of the first meridian at Greenwich, England: used as the basis of standard time everywhere in the world.

green-wood (grēn′wood′), *n.* a forest in full leaf.

greet (grēt), *v.t.* **1,** to address courteously; welcome; **2,** to receive or meet, as with a demonstration; as, to *greet* the mayor with a parade; **3,** to appear before; as, a view of the sea *greets* us.

greet-ing (grēt′ing), *n.* an expression of goodwill, written or spoken; a welcome.

gre-ga-ri-ous (gri-gâr′i-us), *adj.* **1,** of *animals,* living in flocks or herds; **2,** of *persons,* fond of company; sociable: some wolves are *gregarious* hunters, for they prowl in packs.

grem-lin (grem′lin), *n.* an imaginary, small, invisible mischievous being, humorously supposed to interfere with a process or mechanism, esp. an airplane.

gre-nade (gre-nād′), *n.* **1,** a bomb containing poison gas, explosives; **2,** a flask containing chemicals which scatter when the container is thrown and broken: used for putting out fires.

gren-a-dier (gren′à-dēr′), *n.* a footsoldier who throws grenades; also, a member of the British infantry regiment called *Grenadier Guards.*

grew (grōō), *p.t.* of *grow.*

grey (grā), *n.* any colour that is formed by mixing black with white:—*adj.* **1,** of the colour grey; hence, dull; as, a *grey* day; **2,** dismal; cheerless; **3,** old; mature:—*v.t.* and *v.i.* to make or become grey.—*adj.* **grey′ish; gray′-ish.** Also, **gray.**

grey-hound (grā′hound′), *n.* a graceful, slender dog with long legs, keen sight, and great speed, used for hunting and racing.

grid (grid), *n.* **1,** a grating of parallel bars; **2,** a gridiron for broiling meat,

fish, etc.; **3,** in *electricity,* (a) a perforated lead plate in a storage battery (b) in a vacuum tube an electrode o wire mesh for controlling the flow o electrons:—*grid circuit,* the part of th circuit that includes the grid an cathode:—*grid condenser,* a condense in series with the grid circuit.

grid-dle (grid′l), *n.* an iron, aluminium or soapstone plate used to cool griddle-cakes.

grid-dle—cake (grid′l–kāk′), *n.* a thin cake, usually made of wheat or buck wheat flour batter, and cooked on both sides on a griddle.

grid-i-ron (grid′ī′ĕrn), *n.* **1,** an iror utensil with parallel bars, used fo broiling meat or fish; **2,** anythin resembling a gridiron, or marked wit parallel lines, as a football-field.

grief (grēf), *n.* **1,** deep sorrow as result of trouble, a death, or the like also, the cause of sorrow; **2,** failure disaster; as, his plans came to *grief* —*adj.* **grief′—strick′en.**

griev-ance (grēv′ans), *n.* a real o fancied wrong or hardship; also, cause of complaint; as, taxatio without representation was the *griev ance* of the Colonies.

grieve (grēv), *v.t.* [grieved, griev-ing] to cause grief to; afflict mentally as, his death *grieved* his friends:—*v.* to be in sorrow; as, to *grieve* for friend.

griev-ous (grēv′us), *adj.* **1,** causin physical or mental suffering; severe as, *grievous* wounds; *grievous* wrongs **2,** showing grief; as, a *grievous* ex pression.

grif-fin (grif′in), *n.* a fabled monste with body and legs of a lion and wing and beak of an eagle.

grill (gril), *n.* **1,** a gridiron for broilin food; **2,** a dish of meat or fish cooke on a gridiron; **3,** a grillroom:—*v.* **1,** to broil (meat, fish, etc.) on a grid iron; **2,** hence, to torment, esp. wit merciless questioning; as, police *gri* a criminal.

grilse (grils), *n.* a young salmon on it first return from the sea to fresh wate

grim (grim), *adj.* [grim-mer, grim mest], **1,** stern; forbidding; threaten ing; as, a *grim* expression; **2,** fierce cruel; merciless; as, a *grim* story a *grim* smile.

gri-mace (gri-mās′), *n.* a twisting c the face to show disgust or disapprova or to provoke laughter; also, a unconscious twisting of the face in pair —*v.i.* [grimaced, grimac-ing], to mak faces.

grime (grīm), *n.* dirt rubbed or groun

into the skin or other surface:—*v.t.*
[grimed, grim-ing], to soil; make
dirty.—*adj.* **grim′y.**—*n.* **grim′i-ness.**

grin (grin), *v.i.* [grinned, grin-ning], to
show the teeth in smiling or as the
result of pain:—*v.t.* to express by
smiling; as, he *grinned* his delight:—*n.*
a broad smile.

grind (grīnd), *v.t.* [ground (ground),
grind-ing], **1,** to make into powder or
small bits by crushing; as, to *grind*
wheat; also, to make by a crushing
process; as, to *grind* flour; **2,** to
sharpen by wearing down to a fine edge;
as, to *grind* a knife; **3,** to rub together;
grate; as, to *grind* the teeth; **4,** to
oppress; harass; as, to *grind* a
people down; **5,** to operate by turning
a crank; as, to *grind* an organ:—*v.i.*
to study hard:—*n. Colloq.* hard or
tedious work; also, a student who
studies hard.—*n.* **grind′er.**

grind-stone (grīnd′stōn′), *n.* a flat
round stone which turns on an axle,
used to sharpen tools.

grin-go (gring′gō), *n.* [*pl.* -gos], a
Spanish-American term (of contempt)
for a foreigner, esp. an Anglo-Saxon.

grip (grip), *n.* **1,** a tight grasp; a firm
hold; as, take a *grip* on the rope; **2,**
holding power; as, a dog with a strong
grip; **3,** a handle; **4,** a particular way
of clasping hands, as among members
of a secret society; **5,** a mechanical
device for holding something; **6,** mental
or physical mastery; as, a good *grip*
on the situation; **7,** *Colloq.* a valise;
8, grippe:—*v.t.* [gripped, grip-ping],
to grasp firmly; seize:—*v.i.* to take a
fast hold.

gripe (grīp), *v.t.* [griped, grip-ing], **1,** to
seize; grip; **2,** to cause pain in the
bowels of; **3,** to distress; oppress; as,
remorse *gripes* the mind:—*n.* **1,** a firm
hold or grip; also, control; **2,** distress;
oppression; as, the *gripe* of sorrow;
3, *gripes,* pain in the intestines.

grippe (grip), *n.* a severe cold accompanied by fever and bodily aches;
influenza.

grip-ping (grip′ing), *adj.* absorbing;
intense; as, a *gripping* drama.

gris-ly (griz′li), *adj.* [gris-li-er, gris-li-
est], horrible; ghastly; gruesome;
grim.

grist (grist), *n.* grain to be ground;
also, grain that has been ground.

gris-tle (gris′l), *n.* a transparent,
tough, elastic substance found in
animal tissue; cartilage.—*adj.* **gris′tly.**

grit (grit), *n.* **1,** tiny hard particles, as
of sand; **2,** strength of character;
courage; endurance:—*v.i.* [grit-ted, grit-

ting], to make a grating sound:—*v.t.*
to grind; grate; as, to *grit* the teeth.
—*adj.* **grit′ty.**

Grit (grit), *n. Colloq.* in politics, a
(dyed-in-the-wool) Liberal.

grits (grits), *n.* grain, such as wheat or
oats, hulled and coarsely ground:
used as a breakfast food.

griz-zled (griz′ld), *adj.* streaked with
grey; grey-haired; as, a *grizzled*
veteran.

griz-zly (griz′li), *n.* [*pl.* grizzlies], a big
fierce bear of the western mountains of
North America: also called *grizzly
bear:*—*adj.* [griz-zli-er, griz-zli-est],
somewhat grey; grizzled.

groan (grōn), *n.* a low, deep sound of
pain or sorrow; a moan:—*v.i.* **1,** to
utter a deep sound of pain or sorrow;
2, to creak, as a rusty hinge; **3,** to be
overburdened or oppressed:—*v.t.* to
express by groans; as, the audience
groaned its disappointment.

groat (grōt), *n.* a trifling sum, as, not
worth a *groat.*

gro-cer (grō′sėr), *n.* one who sells
articles of food, such as tea, sugar,
butter, etc.

gro-cer-y (grō′sėr-i), *n.* [*pl.* groceries],
1, a grocer's shop; **2,** **groceries,** food
supplies, such as tea, sugar, coffee, etc.

grog (grog), *n.* an unsweetened mixture
of rum or whisky with water; hence,
any intoxicating liquor.

grog-gy (grog′i), *adj.* [grog-gi-er, grog-
gi-est], **1,** tipsy; drunk; **2,** dazed;
staggering; as, *groggy* with sleep.—*n.*
grog′gi-ness.

groin (groin), *n.* **1,** the curved hollow
where the thigh joins the body; **2,** the
curved ridge made by the intersection
of two arches:—*v.t.* to build or form
with such ridges; as, to *groin* a roof.

grom-met (grom′it), *n.* a metal
eyelet or ring, used on the edge of a
sail, top of a mailbag, etc.

groom (grōōm) *n.* **1,** a man or boy who
has charge of horses; **2,** a bridegroom;
3, one of several officers of a royal
household:—*v.t.* **1,** to feed, curry, and
brush (a horse); **2,** to make neat.

groove (grōōv), *n.* **1,** a channel or
furrow, esp. one cut by a tool or worn
by flowing water; a rut; **2,** an unchanging way of living or working;
routine; habit:—*v.t.* [grooved, groov-
ing], to make a groove in; as, to *groove*
a panel.

grope (grōp), *v.i.* [groped, grop-ing],
to feel one's way with the hands, as in
the dark:—*v.t.* to search out, as in
the dark; as, to *grope* one's way through
a forest.

---

all (ôl), ôr; up, mūte, cûr, cōōl, book; oil, out; th, thin; *th*, the.

gros-beak (grōs'bēk'), *n.* any one of a number of songbirds, related to the finches, as the rose-breasted grosbeak or the cardinal grosbeak.

gross (grōs), *adj.* **1,** thick; heavy; **2,** indelicate; coarse; vulgar; as, *gross* remarks; **3,** flagrant; glaring; as, *gross* errors; **4,** heavy; fat; **5,** very great; shameful; as, *gross* injustice; **6,** whole; total; as, *gross* income: distinguished from *net:*—*n.* **1,** twelve dozen; **2,** the entire amount.—*adv.* **gross'ly.**—*n.* **gross'ness.**

gro-tesque (grō-tesk'), *adj.* distorted; odd; fantastic; as, a *grotesque* mask; *grotesque* antics:—*n.* a painting or carving which combines human and animal forms in a fantastic way.

grotto (grot'ō), *n.* [*pl.* grottoes or grottos], **1,** a picturesque cavern in the earth; **2,** an artificial cave, used as a retreat.

grouch (grouch), *v.i. Colloq.* to grumble; sulk; be morose or ill-tempered.—*n.* one who acts in such a way.—*adj.* **grouch'y.**

ground (ground), *n.* **1,** the surface of the earth; the soil; **2,** a topic; subject; as, to be familiar with the *ground* covered in a talk; **3,** land put to special use; as, a play*ground;* **4,** distance or extent on a surface; as, to gain *ground* in football; **5,** cause; reason; as, a *ground* for argument; **6,** in *painting,* a neutral background or undecorated part; **7,** the bottom of a body of water; as, the boat touched *ground:*—**grounds,** **1,** lawns and gardens about a house; **2,** dregs; sediment; as, coffee or tea *grounds:*—*v.t.* **1,** to establish; as, to *ground* a government on proper principles; **2,** to bring to rest by touching the earth or bottom; as, to *ground* an aeroplane or a boat; **3,** to teach the first principles to; as, to *ground* a class in Latin; **4,** in *electricity,* to connect with the earth, as a wire conductor:—*v.i.* to run upon land; as, the vessel *grounded:*—*adj.* on or near the ground; as, the *ground* floor.

ground crew, the personnel in charge of maintaining and repairing aircraft (chiefly technicians).

ground-er (groun'dẽr), *n.* in *baseball,* etc., a ball that does not rise into the air when batted, but bounces or rolls on the ground.

ground-hog (ground'hog') *n.* the woodchuck, a burrowing animal of the rat family.

ground-less (ground'lis), *adj.* without foundation or cause; as, *groundless* fear.

ground-work (ground'wûrk'), *n.* basis; foundation; fundamentals.

group (grōōp), *n.* a number of people or objects considered as a whole; also, a cluster; as, a *group* of houses:—*v.t.* to combine into a group; as, to *group* the boys by themselves:—*v.i.* to gather in a group; as, the men *grouped* around the fire.

grouse (grous), *n.* [*pl.* grouse], any of several game-birds having, usually, a mottled reddish-brown plumage, as the partridge, or ruffed grouse, and the prairie-chicken: in 1945 the prairie hen was declared a provincial emblem of Saskatchewan.

grove (grōv), *n.* a small wood; also, a group of cultivated fruit-trees.

grov-el (grov'l; gruv'l), *v.i.* [grov-elled, grovel-ling], **1,** to lie face downward in fear or in seeking favour; to crawl; as, to *grovel* before a king; **2,** to humble oneself basely.—*n.* **grov'el-ler.**

grow (grō), *v.t.* [*p.t.* grew (grōō), *p.p.* grown (grōn), *p.pr.* grow-ing], to produce by cultivation, as vegetables:—*v.i.* **1,** to become bigger by natural development; as, puppies *grow* rapidly; **2,** to arise or spring up naturally; as, moss *grows* in damp places; **3,** to increase; as, to *grow* in understanding; **4,** to become gradually; as, to *grow* stronger; **5,** to become attached, or become one; as, the broken bone *grew* together.—*n.* **grow'er.**

growl (groul), *n.* **1,** a deep, throaty and threatening sound, as made by a dog; **2,** an angry, muttered complaint —*v.i.* **1,** to snarl like a dog; **2,** to find fault in a surly tone; grumble:—*v.t.* to say in an angry muttering tone; as, he *growled* his answer.

grown-up (grōn'up'), *n.* an adult.— *adj.* **grown'—up'.**

growth (grōth), *n.* **1,** the progressive increase of animal or vegetable bodies; as, the *growth* of a plant; **2,** increase; as, *growth* in skill; **3,** that which is produced; result; as, a season's *growth* of corn; **4,** a tumour; cancer; etc.

grub (grub), *v.t.* [grubbed, grub-bing] to dig up; root out of the ground, as stumps:—*v.i.* **1,** to dig in the earth; **2,** to drudge or toil; do menial labour:— *n.* **1,** the wormlike larva of some insects; **2,** *Slang,* food.—*adj.* **grub'by.**

grub-stake (grub'stāk'), *n.* money, supplies, etc., advanced to a prospector in return for a share in any profit from his discoveries.

grudge (gruj), *n.* secret ill will; as, to hold a *grudge:*—*v.t.* [grudged, grudg-ing], to envy; as, he *grudges* me my good luck; also, to begrudge; as, he *grudges* every cent he spends.—*adv.* **grudg'ing-ly.**

gru-el (grōō'el), *n.* a thin porridge made by boiling meal or flour in water or milk.

gru-el-ling (grōō'el-ing), *adj.* a severe, trying, or exhausting experience; as, the tire was submitted to a *gruelling* road-test.—*v.t. Colloq.* **gru'el,** to question relentlessly; exhaust.

grue-some (grōō'sum), *adj.* revolting and horrifying, repulsive; as, the decaying corpse was a *gruesome* sight.

gruff (gruf), *adj.* rough; surly; harsh; as, a *gruff* reply; hoarse; as, a *gruff* voice.—*adv.* **gruff'ly.**—*n.* **gruff'ness.**

grum-ble (grum'bl), *v.i.* [grum-bled, grum-bling], to murmur discontentedly; growl; find fault:—*v.t.* to mutter; as, he *grumbled* a reply:—*n.* a surly speech or reply; growl.—*n.* **grum'bler.**

grump-y (grump'i), *adj.* [grump-i-er, grump-i-est], surly; dissatisfied; as, a *grumpy* old man.—*adv.* **grump'i-ly.**—*n.* **grump'i-ness.**

grunt (grunt), *n.* **1,** the gruff sound made by a hog; also, any similar sound; **2,** a fish that makes a grunting noise when caught:—*v.t.* to utter with a gruff sound; as, to *grunt* assent:—*v.i.* to make a grunting noise.

gry-phon (grif'in), *n.* Same as *griffin.*

gua-no (gwä'nō), *n.* the manure of sea-birds, esp. from islands off the coast of Peru, used widely as fertilizer.

guar-an-tee (gar'an-tē'), *n.* **1,** anything that makes something else sure or certain; as, a *guarantee* of quality; **2,** a statement that something is as represented; as, a *guarantee* goes with this fountain-pen; **3,** in law: **a,** a promise made by one person that another will fulfil an agreement to a third; **b,** one who becomes surety for the performance of another's promises; **c,** property pledged as security for the performance of promises:—*v.t.* [guaranteed, guarantee-ing], **1,** to make sure; as, to *guarantee* success; **2,** in *law*, to be legally responsible for.—*n.* **guar'an-tor** (gar'an-tôr; gar'an-tôr').—*n.* **guar'an-ty** (gar'en-ti).

guard (gärd), *v.t.* **1,** to protect; preserve by caution; defend; **2,** to watch over; as, to *guard* a prisoner:—*v.i.* to watch; be cautious; as, to *guard* against disease:—*n.* **1,** defence against injury or attack; **2,** a state or duty of watchfulness or attention; as, be on *guard;* **3,** a position of defence, as in fencing; **4,** a device for protection; as, a mud*guard;* **5,** a man or body of men employed for control, as in a prison; **6,** in *football,* either of two players in the line, one on each side of the centre.

guard-ed (gär'did), *adj.* **1,** defended; protected; as, a heavily *guarded* fort;

2, careful; cautious; as, a *guarded* answer.—*adv.* **guard'ed-ly.**—*n.* **guard'-ed-ness.**

guard-i-an (gär'di-an), *n.* **1,** one who legally has the care of a person or his property; a warden; as, a *guardian* of a child; **2,** one who or that which protects anything.

guards-man (gärdz'man), *n.* [*pl.* guardsmen (-men)], **1,** a man employed for defence or watching; **2,** an officer or soldier of any military body termed *Guards.*

gu-ber-na-to-ri-al (gū'ber-na-tō'ri-al), *adj. chiefly U.S.* pertaining to a governor or his office.

guer-don (gûr'dun), *n.* a reward, esp. for courage or high deeds.

gue-ril-la or **guer-ril-la** (ge-ril'a), *n.* one who carries on irregular warfare; esp. one of an independent band engaged in harassing an enemy in wartime. Also used as *adj.*

guess (ges), *n.* a hasty conclusion; an opinion formed without knowledge:—*v.t.* **1,** to form an opinion of without certain knowledge; **2,** to surmise; estimate; as, to *guess* the height of someone; **3,** to solve correctly by surmising; as, to *guess* a riddle; **4,** to think; suppose:—*v.i.* to form a chance judgment.

guest (gest), *n.* **1,** one who is entertained at the house or table of another; a visitor; **2,** a patron of a hotel or a restaurant.

guff (guf), *n. Slang,* foolish talk; nonsense.

guf-faw (gu-fô'), *n.* a coarse or loud burst of laughter:—*v.i.* to laugh noisily.

guid-ance (gīd'ans), *n.* direction; leadership; influence.

guide (gīd), *n.* **1,** one who or that which directs; **2,** a person hired to conduct travellers in a strange place; **3,** that by which one finds his way; a guide-book; guide-post:—*v.t.* [guid-ed, guiding], **1,** to lead; conduct; pilot; **2,** to direct; instruct.

guide-book (gīd'book'), *n.* a book of information for travellers.

guide-post (gīd'pōst'), *n.* a post or marker to direct travellers at forks in a road or at crossroads.

guild or **gild** (gild), *n.* **1,** an association for mutual protection and aid of people in a common trade; **2,** a society for a useful or charitable purpose.

guile (gīl), *n.* deceit; cunning; trickery; as, he's full of *guile.*—*adv.* **guile'ful-ly.**

guile-less (gīl'les), *adj.* innocent; frank; as, a *guileless* child.—*adv.* **guile'less-ly.**

guil-le-mot (gil'e-mot), *n.* a narrow-billed Arctic diving bird of the auk family.

guil-lo-tine (gil'ō-tēn'), *n.* a machine for cutting off a person's head by means of a knife which descends between two posts:—*v.t.* (gil'ō-tēn'), [guillotined, guillotin-ing], to behead with the guillotine.

guilt (gilt), *n.* 1, the fact of having done a wrong, esp. an act punishable by law; as, his *guilt* was proved by his own confession; 2, wrongdoing; sin; as, he led a life of *guilt* and shame.—*adj.* guilt'less.

guilt-y (gil'ti), *adj.* [guilt-i-er, guilt-i-est], 1, responsible for a crime; having committed a wrong; as, he was judged *guilty* by the jury; 2, showing guilt; not innocent; as, a *guilty* look.—*adv.* guilt'i-ly.

guin-ea (gin'i), *n.* a gold coin, formerly current in England, worth 21 shillings; now, the amount of 21 shillings.

guin-ea—fowl (gin'i–foul'), *n.* a noisy, domesticated fowl, originally from Guinea. Its plumage is bluish grey dotted with white spots: also called *guinea* and *guinea-hen*.

guin-ea—pig (gin'i–pig'), *n.* a small, short-tailed rodent, usually white, black, or tan, originally from South America.

guise (gīz), *n.* 1, manner or external appearance; likeness; as, the *guise* of a beggar; 2, hence, cloak or pretence; as, to cheat under the *guise* of friend-ship.

gui-tar (gi-tär'), *n.* a long-necked musical instrument with a hollow, wooden body and six strings, played with the fingers.

gulch (gulch), *n.* in the western U.S., a narrow, deep valley or ravine; gorge.

gulf (gulf), *n.* 1, an arm of the sea extending into the land, larger than a bay; 2, a deep hollow in the earth; an abyss; 3, wide separation; as, the *gulf* between a king and a beggar.

gull (gul), a large, graceful, web-footed sea-bird, usually white with grey or black markings, known all over the world, valuable as a harbour scavenger.

gul-let (gul'it), *n.* the tube by which food travels from the mouth to the stomach; the throat.

gul-li-ble (gul'i-bl), *adj.* easily fooled. *n.* gul'li-bil'i-ty.

gul-ly (gul'i), *n.* [pl. gullies], a channel worn by water; a narrow ravine:—*v.t.* [gullied, gully-ing], to wear channels in.

gulp (gulp), *v.t.* 1, to swallow hastily or greedily; 2, to check; keep back; as, to *gulp* down angry words or tears:—*n.* a big swallow; a mouthful; a choke

¹gum (gum), *n.* the flesh around the teeth of human beings and animals.

²gum (gum), *n.* 1, a sticky substance that comes out of certain trees and shrubs and hardens on the surface; as *gum* arabic; spruce *gum;* 2, any natural gum prepared for some indus trial use, as in drugs or chewing gum 3, a gum-tree; 4, gums, overshoes:— *v.t.* [gummed, gum-ming], to smear o fasten with mucilage:—*v.i.* to becom stiff or sticky; to exude gum, as doe a tree.—*adj.* gum'my.—*n.* gum'mi ness.

gum-bo (gum'bō), *n.* 1, a prairie sil or mud, as in Southern Saskatchewan that becomes sticky when wet; 2, soup thickened with okra pods.

gum-boil (gum'boil'), *n.* a smal abscess on the gums.

gum-drop (gum'drop'), *n.* a cand made of flavoured gelatin, cast i moulds, and covered with sugar cry stals.

gum-shoe (gum'shoo'), *n.* 1, a rubbe shoe; *pl.* sneakers; 2, *Colloq.* a detec tive:—*v.i.* *Colloq.* to move abou stealthily; sneak.

gump-tion (gump'shun), *n.* *Colloc* energy; initiative; spirit; as, h hasn't *gumption* enough to speak u for himself.

gum—tree (gum'–trē), *n.* in the U.S. a gum-yielding tree, as the sweet gun

gum-wood (gum'wood'), *n.* wood fron a Western U.S. gum tree, or fron Australian eucalyptus.

gun (gun), *n.* 1, a weapon for discharg ing a missile through a tube by th force of an explosive, as a cannor rifle, pistol, or revolver; 2, any simila implement; 3, a discharge of canno given as an honour:—*v.i.* [gunned, gun ning], to shoot or hunt with a gun.— gun'fire'; gun'play'; gun'run'ne gun'shot'.

gun-boat (gun'bōt'), *n.* a small, arme patrol ship.

gun-cot-ton (gun'kot'n), *n.* a powerf explosive made by treating cotton wit nitric and sulphuric acids.

gun-man (gun'man), *n.* [pl. gunme (-men)], an armed robber or murdere

gun—met-al (gun'–met'l), *n.* 1, variety of bronze, formerly used i making cannon, etc., but now sup planted by steel; 2, the colour of th bronze, dark grey with a blue or purp tinge. Also used as *adj.*

gun-ner (gun'ėr), *n.* 1, one who work a gun; 2, one who hunts with a gu 3, in the navy, a warrant-officer i charge of the ship's ordnance or military supplies.—*n.* **gun'ner-y.**

gun-ny (gun'i), *n.* a strong, coarse fabric made from jute or hemp, used for bags, esp. *gunny* sacks.

gun-pow-der (gun'pou'dér), *n.* an explosive powder made of sulphur, saltpetre, and charcoal, used in blasting and in guns.

gun-wale or **gun-nel** (gun'el), *n.* the upper edge of the side of a boat.

gup-py (gup'i), *n.* a tiny, live-bearing, fresh-water fish, kept in aquaria at about 70°F.; the males have brilliant colouring: found in Trinidad, Barbados, and Venezuela.

gur-gle (gûr'gl), *n.* a broken, bubbling sound, as of a liquid when poured from a bottle:—*v.i.* [gur-gled, gur-gling], to make a low bubbling sound.

gush (gush), *n.* **1,** a sudden and free flow of liquid, as of blood from a wound, or of water from a spring; **2,** a violent outbreak, as of anger; **3,** *Colloq.* silly, sentimental talk or display of affection:—*v.i.* **1,** to flow out suddenly with force; flow abundantly; as, oil *gushed* from the well; **2,** *Colloq.* to display affection and enthusiasm in a silly, showy manner.—*adj.* **gush'y.**

gush-er (gush'ér), *n.* **1,** one who gushes; esp. one who makes a show of sentiment; **2,** an oil- or gas-well with a large natural flow.

gus-set (gus'it), *n.* **1,** a small triangular piece sewn into a garment, glove, etc., to make it stronger or roomier; **2,** a triangular metal plate used to strengthen angles and joints.

gust (gust), *n.* **1,** a sudden rush of wind; **2,** a violent outburst, as of laughter.—*adj.* **gust'y.**—*adv.* **gust'i-ly.**—*adj.* **gust'-ing.**

gus-ta-to-ry (gus'ta-to-ri), *adj.* relating to the sense of taste; as the *gustatory* nerve, buds, etc.

gus-to (gus'tō), *n.* zest; relish; enjoyment; as, to eat or drink with great *gusto.*

gut (gut), *n.* **1,** the intestinal canal; **2,** catgut, as used for violin strings; **3,** a narrow channel; also, a gully:—*v.t.* [gut-ted, gut-ting], **1,** to extract the entrails from; **2,** to plunder, or empty; destroy the inside of; as, fire *gutted* the building.

gut-ta—per-cha (gut'a–pûr'cha), *n.* a greyish or yellowish substance similar to rubber, made of the juice of a tree of the Malay Archipelago; also, the tree itself.

gut-ter (gut'ér), *n.* **1,** a trough under the eaves of a building to carry off rain-water; **2,** a slope at the roadside

to carry off surface water; **3,** any shallow trench:—*v.t.* to cut into, or make furrows in:—*v.i.* to become channelled, as the rim of a burning candle.

gut-ter-snipe (gut'ér-snīp'), *n. Slang,* a street urchin or arab; gamin.

gut-tur-al (gut'ér-al), *adj.* **1,** having to do with the throat; **2,** formed in the throat; harsh; as, a *guttural* sound:—*n.* a sound formed or modified in the throat, as *g* in *go* or *goose.*—*adv.* **gut'tur-al-ly.**

¹guy (gī), *n.* a rope, chain, wire, or the like, used to secure or keep something steady; as, the *guy* of a tent pole:—*v.t.* to fasten or steady with a guy.

²guy (gī), *n.* **1,** a person of queer looks or dress; **2,** *Slang,* a fellow:—*v.t. Colloq.* to ridicule; as, his friends *guyed* him good-naturedly.

guz-zle (guz'l), *v.t.* and *v.i.* [guz-zled, guz-zling], to eat or drink greedily and to excess; as, to *guzzle* beer:—*n.* **guz'zler.**

gym (jim), *n. Colloq.* a gymnasium.

gym-na-si-um (jim-nā'zi-um), *n.* [*pl.* gymnasiums (jim-nā'zi-umz) or gymnasia (jim-nā'zi-a)], a room or building for athletic practice.

gym-nast (jim'nast), *n.* one who is expert in physical exercises; esp. one skilled in the use of gymnasium apparatus.

gym-nas-tics (jim-nas'tiks), *n.pl.* physical exercises for developing the body.

gyn-e-col-o-gist (jin'i-kol'o-jist; jī'; gī'), *n.* a medical specialist who deals with the functions and diseases peculiar to women.—*n.* **gyn'e-col'o-gy.**

gyp (jip), *v.t. Slang,* to swindle; cheat.

gyp-sum (jip'sum), *n.* a common mineral, calcium sulphate ($CaSO_4$.-$2H_2O$), used for making plaster of Paris and for soil dressings or fertilizer.

gyp-sy (jip'si), *n.* [*pl.* gypsies], **1,** one of an ancient wandering, dark-skinned, dark-eyed race of Eastern, probably Hindu, origin; **2,** the language of the gypsies: also called *Romany;* **3,** a person who looks or acts like a gypsy: —**gypsy—moth,** a European moth, the caterpillars of which are very destructive to fruit-trees. The preferred spelling is **gip'sy.**

gy-rate (jī'rāt; jī-rāt'), *v.i.* to whirl; revolve; spiral; as, a *gyrating* toe-dancer.—*n.* **gy-ra'tion.**

gyr-fal-con (jûr'fô'kn), *n.* Same as *gerfalcon.*

gy-ro-scope (jī'rō-skōp; gī'rō-skōp), *n.* an apparatus consisting of a wheel mounted in a ring so as to move freely in one or more directions. It is used to

illustrate the laws of rotation, and to stabilize aeroplanes, ships, etc.—*adj.*
gy-ro-scop-ic (jĭ′rō-skop′ik; gĭ′rō-skop′ik).

gy-ro-sta-tics (jĭ′rō-sta′tiks), *n.* th science that deals with rotating bodie

gyves (jīvz), *n.* leg irons, shackles, c fetters.

H

H, h (āch), *n.* [*pl.* H's, h's], the eighth letter of the alphabet, following G.

ha-be-as cor-pus (hā′bi-us kôr′pus), in *law*, a writ requiring a prisoner to be brought before a judge or court to determine the justice of his detention.

hab-er-dash-er (hab′ėr-dash′ėr), *n.* a dealer in men's furnishings, as hats, neckties, etc.—*n.* **hab′er-dash′er-y.**

hab-it (hab′it), *n.* **1,** an action so often repeated as to become a fixed characteristic; as, it is his *habit* to rise at six; the *habit* of neatness; **2,** usual physical or mental condition; as, a cheerful *habit* of mind; **3,** a woman's riding-costume; **4,** the distinctive dress worn by members of a religious order; as, a nun's *habit:*—*v.t.* to dress; clothe.

hab-it-a-ble (hab′it-a-bl), *adj.* fit to be lived in; as, repairs have made the house *habitable.*

hab-it-ant (hab′i-tant), *n.* **1,** a dweller; permanent resident; **2,** (a′bē′tän′), in Canada (esp. Quebec) or Louisiana, a farmer of French descent.

hab-i-tat (hab′i-tat′), *n.* **1,** the natural abode of an animal or plant; **2,** a dwelling-place; habitation.

hab i-ta-tion (hab′i-tā′shun), *n.* **1,** an abode or dwelling-place; **2,** the act of inhabiting or dwelling in; as, the house is ready for *habitation.*

ha-bit-u-al (ha-bit′ū-al), *adj.* **1,** formed or acquired by custom; usual; as, *habitual* promptness; **2,** given over to a regular practice, or habit; as, a *habitual* coffee drinker.—*adv.* **ha-bit′u-al-ly.**

ha-bit-u-ate (ha-bit′ū-āt′), *v.t.* [-ated, -ating], to accustom; familiarize; as, *habituated* to hardship.

ha-cien-da (ä-syän′dä; has′i-en′da), *n.* in Spanish America, a landed estate, as a ranch or plantation; an establishment for farming, mining, or stock-raising.

¹hack (hak), *v.t.* to cut unevenly or irregularly:—*v.i.* **1,** to make rough cuts; **2,** to give short dry coughs:—*n.* **1,** a cutting or notching tool, as a mattock; **2,** a cut or gash; **3,** a short dry cough.

²hack (hak), *n.* **1,** a horse that may be hired for work; also, a saddle- or

carriage-horse; **2,** a carriage which ma be hired; **3,** one who hires out h services for pay, esp. in literary worl a drudge.

hack-a-more (hak′a-mōr′), *n.* in th West, a rawhide halter used in breakin horses, or a rope loop passed around horse's neck and through his mout

hack-le (hak′l), *n.* **1,** any of the feathe on a bird's neck (esp. a rooster's), the bristles on a dog's neck, that ri to indicate rage or anger; **2,** a fishin fly made from a rooster's hackles.

hack-ney (hak′ni), *n.* [*pl.* hackneys], a horse used chiefly for riding driving; **2,** a coach or hack kept f hire:—*adj.* let out for hire as, *hackney*-coach.

hack-neyed (hak′nid), *adj.* common place; trite; as, a *hackneyed* phrase.

hack-saw (hak′sô′), *n.* a fine-toothe saw for cutting metal.

had (had), *p.t.* and *p.p.* of *have.*

had-dock (had′uk), *n.* a North Atlant food fish of the cod family.

Ha-des (hā′dēz), *n.* in the *Bible* and Greek *mythology*, the place or abode departed spirits.

hae-mo-glo-bin (hē′mō-glō′bi hem-), *n.* the red oxygen-carryir matter of the red corpuscles. Als **hemoglobin.**

hae-mo-phil-i-a (hēm′ō-fil′i-a; hem *n.* a tendency to excessive bleedir from the smallest cut: it occurs males, but is transmitted by female

haem-or-rhage (hem′o-rij), *n.* blee ing from the lungs, arteries, veins, etc esp. a great or continuous flow of bloo

haft (håft), *n.* a handle, as of a cuttir tool, dagger, or knife.

hag (hag), *n.* **1,** a witch; **2,** an ugly o woman.

hag-gard (hag′ėrd), *adj.* worn an anxious in appearance; as, *haggard* fro worry.

hag-gis (hag′is), *n.* a dish (esp. Scotland) made of the heart, liver, etc of a sheep or calf, highly seasone minced with onions and oatmeal, ar boiled in a sheep's stomach.

hag-gle (hag'l), *v.i.* [hag-gled, hag-gling], to argue or wrangle; as, the woman *haggled* over the price of the butter.

¹hail (hāl), *n.* 1, small, icy particles that fall from the sky, generally in winter, but sometimes during a thunderstorm; 2, anything falling abundantly and with great force; as, a *hail* of shrapnel: —*v.i.* to come down in the form of hail: —*v.t.* to shower; pour down; as, they *hailed* blows upon me.

²hail (hāl), *n.* a salutation; greeting:— *v.t.* to greet; salute; accost; as, he *hailed* me as I was entering the store.

hail-stone (hāl'stōn'), *n.* a single particle of hail or frozen rain.

hair (hâr), *n.* 1, the mass of threadlike growths, forming the coat or fur of an animal; the natural growth on a person's head; any one of these threadlike growths; 2, a hairlike fibre growing on the stems and leaves of plants; 3, a very small distance, degree, or quantity; as, the bullet missed him by a *hair*.—*adj.* **hair'y.**—*n.* **hair'i-ness.**— *adj.* **hair'less.**—Compounds: **hair'-brush'; hair'cut'; hair'do'; hair'-dres'ser; hair'breadth', hair's'breadth',** or **hair's'—breadth'.**—*adj.* **hair'split'-ting.**

hair-pin (hâr'pin'), *n.* a two-pronged pin, as of wire or celluloid, for holding the hair in place.

hair-spring (hâr'spring'), *n.* the delicate hairlike spring which regulates the balance-wheel in a watch.

hake (hāk), *n.* any fish of the cod family, esp. the white *hake*, preserved as boneless cod.

hal-berd (hal'bèrd) or **hal-bert** (hal'-bèrt), *n.* a weapon of the Middle Ages that was a combination spear and battle-axe.

¹hale (hāl), *adj.* sound in body; robust; as, a *hale* old man.

²hale (hāl), *v.t.* [haled, hal-ing], to drag by violence; as, they *haled* him into court.

half (hâf), *n.* [*pl.* halves (hâvz)], one of two equal parts:—*adj.* forming a half; as, a *half* pound:—*adv.* 1, to the extent of a half; 2, partially.

half-back (hâf'bak'), *n.* in *football*, a player behind the forward line.

half—breed (hâf'—brēd'), *n.* one whose parents are of different races.

half—broth-er (hâf—bruth'èr), *n.* a brother related through one parent only.

half—heart-ed (hâf'—här'ted), *adj.* uninterested; not enthusiastic; as, a *half-hearted* response to a suggestion.— *adv.* **half'—heart'ed-ly.**—*n.* **half'—heart'ed-ness.**

half life, in *nuclear physics*, the time required for half of the atoms of a radioactive element to disintegrate: thus, plutonium 238 has a *half life* of some 50 years.

half—mast (hâf—mâst'), *n.* a point near the middle of a mast or staff. A flag flies at half-mast in token of mourning or as a signal of distress.

half—nelson (nel'sun), *n.* in *wrestling*, a hold consisting of thrusting an arm from behind under an opponent's arm and placing the hand on the nape of his neck.

half-pen-ny (hā'pen-i; hāp'ni), *n.* [*pl.* halfpence (hā'pens), or halfpennies (hā'-pen-iz; hāp'niz)], an English bronze coin, worth half an English penny.

half—sis-ter (hâf'—sis'tèr), *n.* a sister related through one parent only.

half—track (hâf'—trak'), *n.* a motor vehicle whose rear drive-wheels operate on caterpillar treads, as in some army trucks.

half—way (hâf'wā'), *adj.* 1, situated mid-way between two points; as, a *halfway* house; 2, midway between two states or conditions; as, twilight, the *halfway* state between night and day; 3, partial; not extreme; as, *halfway* measures:—*adv.* 1, midway; at half the distance; as, they met *halfway* between the two towns; 2, partially; as, he *halfway* consented.

half—wit-ted (hâf'—wit'ed), *adj.* mentally lacking; feeble-minded.—*n.* **half'-wit'.**—*adv.* **half'—wit'ted-ly.**

hal-i-but (hal'i-but; hol'i-but), *n.* the largest of the flatfish, prized as food.

hal-i-to-sis (hal'i-tō'sis), *n.* offensive, or bad, breath.

hall (hôl), *n.* 1, the main living-room of a castle; 2, a large building or room for entertainments; as, a dance *hall;* 3, a public building; as, City *Hall;* 4, a university building used for residence, instruction, etc.; 5, a passageway in a house or other building; also, the passage or room through which one enters a building; 6, in England, the residence of a landed proprietor; a manor-house.

hal-le-lu-jah or **hal-le-lu-iah** (hal'e-lōō'ya), *n.* an exclamation or song of praise to God:—*interj.* praise be to God! The preferred spelling is **al'le-lu'ia.**

hal-liard (hal'yèrd), *n.* Same as **halyard.**

hall-mark (hôl'märk'), *n.* a mark or stamp of high quality, as on gold or silver articles assayed by the Goldsmiths' Company, London, Eng.

hal-lo or **hal-loa** (ha-lō′), *interj.* Same as hollo.

hal-loo (ha-lōō′), *n.* [*pl.* halloos], and *interj.* a shout to attract attraction or to call dogs:—*v.i.* and *v.t.* to cry out (to).

hal-low (hal′ō), *v.t.* **1,** to make sacred; mark or set apart as holy; as, this ground has been *hallowed* by the brave men who died here; **2,** to honour as holy; reverence; as, *hallowed* be the name of the Lord.

Hal-low-e'en or **Hal-low-een** (hal′ō-ēn′), *n.* the evening of October 31st (which precedes All-Saints' Day or Allhallows) celebrated with fun, masquerading, etc. Also, **Allhallows Eve.**

hal-lu-ci-na-tion (ha-lū′si-nā′shun), *n.* **1,** the seeing or hearing of a thing or sound, seemingly (but not) real, as in some mental disorders; **2,** the object supposed seen or heard.

hall-way (hôl′ wā′), *n.* a corridor, or entrance hall.

ha-lo (hā′lō), *n.* [*pl.* halos or haloes], **1,** a circle of light around a shining body, such as the sun or moon; **2,** in pictures, a bright ring drawn or painted around the head of a holy person or saint; **3,** the splendour or glory with which one endows a person or an object highly prized:—*v.t.* to surround with a halo.

hal-o-gen (hal′ō-jen), *n.* an element (chlorine, bromine, iodine, or fluorine) that forms a salt by uniting with a metal: example, *sodium chloride.*

¹halt (hôlt), *adj.* crippled or lame:—*v.i.* **1,** to limp; **2,** hence, to proceed slowly and hesitatingly; as, his lecture began smoothly, but later *halted* painfully.

²halt (hôlt), *n.* a stop or pause on a march or journey:—*v.i.* to come to a stop for a longer or shorter period:— *v.t.* to bring to a stop.

hal-ter (hôl′tèr), *n.* **1,** a rope or strap for leading or fastening a horse or other animal; **2,** a rope for hanging criminals; **3,** a woman's or girl's sports waist, tied behind neck and back, leaving arms and back bare.

halt-ing (hôl′ting), *adj.* **1,** lame; limping; **2,** hesitating; faltering; as, *halting* speech.

halve (hàv), *v.t.* [halved, halv-ing], **1,** to divide into two equal parts, as an apple; to share equally; **2,** to lessen by half; as, the teacher *halved* the assignment.

hal-yard (hal′yèrd), *n.* on a ship, a rope or tackle for hoisting and lowering a sail, yard, or flag. Also, **hal′liard.**

¹ham (ham), *n.* the thigh of an animal

prepared for food; esp. the thigh of a hog, salted and sometimes dried in smoke; also, the meat so prepared.

²ham (ham), *n.* [From *am*, Cockney form of *amateur*], a licensed amateur radio operator.

ham-bur-ger, (ham′bûr-gèr) *n.* **1,** a patty of cooked Hamburg (finely ground beef); **2,** a sandwich in the form of a round bun, made with such a patty.

hames (hāmz), *n.pl.* two curved pieces of wood or metal on a horse's collar to which traces are fastened.

ham-let (ham′let), *n.* a small village.

ham-mer (ham′èr), *n.* **1,** an instrument with a handle and an iron head used for driving nails, beating metals etc.; **2,** anything resembling this tool in its action or shape; as, the *hammer* of a gun-lock:—*v.t.* **1,** to pound or beat with a hammer or a similar instrument **2,** to drive into place by pounding **3,** to produce by hard work; as, to *hammer* out a plan:—*v.i.* **1,** to strike heavy blows; **2,** to make a noise like that of a hammer blow; **3,** to work hard.

ham-mer-head (ham′èr-hed′), *n* a voracious species of shark with extensions from the head that give i a double-headed hammer appearance.

ham-mer—lock (ham′èr–lok′), *n.* in *wrestling*, a hold in which one twists an opponent's arm and bends it behind his back.

ham-mock (ham′uk), *n.* a swinging bed or couch, usually of network o canvas, suspended by cords at the ends

¹ham-per (ham′pèr), *n.* a large basket usually wickerwork with a cover, used to carry or hold clothes, food, etc.

²ham-per (ham′pèr), *v.t.* to obstruct hinder; as, the snow *hampered* th traffic.

ham-ster (ham′stèr), *n.* a stout bodied, ratlike, burrowing rodent of th Old World, with large cheek pouche for carrying grain: it is raised as a pet the *golden hamster* is also used like a guinea pig for medical research.

ham-string (ham′string), *v.t.* **1,** t cripple by cutting tendons at the back o the knee or of the hock of a quadrupe (as, a horse); **2,** (figuratively) to disable

hand (hand), *n.* **1,** that portion of th human arm extending downward from the wrist, made up of the palm, fou fingers, and a thumb, and fitted fo grasping objects; also, a like part o an ape, an opossum, or certain othe animals that grasp; **2,** an index o pointer on a dial; as, the *hands* of clock; **3,** a measure of four inches used chiefly in measuring the heigh

---

cat, āge, fär, câre, àsk; ten, ēve, latèr; (i) pity, rely, senate; ice; top; nō

of horses; **4,** deftness or skill; as, try your *hand* at this game; **5,** direction to the left or right; as, on the right *hand* of the passage; **6,** penmanship; **7,** an employee who labours with his hands; **8,** a player in a game of cards; also, the cards held by a player; a single round in a game of cards; **9,** possession; control; as, the matter is in your *hands;* **10,** assistance; as, lend a *hand;* **11,** a pledge, esp. of betrothal; **12,** source; as, knowledge at first*hand;* **13,** one who is skilled at a particular thing:—*v.t.* **1,** to pass or transfer by hand; as, *hand* me the book; **2,** to pass (down) from time past; as, these dishes were *handed* down to me from my grandmother; **3,** to lead or assist with the hand; as, he *handed* her into the car:—*adj.* pertaining to the hand; used or carried by the hand. *adj.* **hand′ed.**

hand-bag (hand′bag′), *n.* **1,** a satchel **2,** a small bag to hold a purse, powder, etc.

hand-ball (hand′bôl′), *n.* a game played in a walled court, or against a single wall, in which the players bat the ball against a wall with their hands.

hand-bar-row (hand′bar′ō), *n.* a barrow, without a wheel, carried by four handles.

hand-bill (hand′bil′), *n.* a printed advertisement distributed by hand.

hand-book (hand′book′), *n.* a small guidebook: a manual.

hand-breadth (hand′bredth′), *n.* a measure of about 2¼ to 4 inches, the width of a hand. Also, **hand′s′— breadth′.**

hand-cuff (hand′kuf′), *n.* one of a pair of metal, braceletlike devices, locked around a prisoner's wrist to prevent his escape:—*v.t.* to restrain with handcuffs.

hand-ful (hand′fool), *n.* [*pl.* handfuls], the amount a hand can hold; hence, a small quantity or number.

hand-i-cap (han′di-kap), *n.* **1,** a disadvantage imposed on a superior contestant, or an advantage granted to an inferior contestant, in order to equalize chances of winning; also, a race, contest, or game in which such a condition exists; **2,** a hindrance:— *v.t.* [handicapped, handicap-ping], **1,** to be a disadvantage to; **2,** to impose a handicap upon.—*n.* **hand′i-cap′per.**

hand-i-craft (han′di-kráft), *n.* a trade or craft requiring a skilled hand; manual skill.—*n.* **hand′i-crafts′man.**

hand-i-ly (han′di-li), *adv.* expertly; deftly; as, he won *handily.*

hand-i-work (han′di-wûrk′), *n.* **1,** work done by hand; **2,** anything done by personal effort.

hand-ker-chief (hang′kėr-chif; chēf), *n.* a square piece of cloth for wiping the face, nose, etc.; also, one worn around the neck.

han-dle (han′dl), *n.* that part of a tool, vessel, etc., grasped by the hand:—*v.t.* [han-dled, han-dling], **1,** to hold, touch, or move with the hand; **2,** to manage; control; as, he *handled* the aeroplane with skill; **3,** to deal with or treat in a given way; as, he *handles* complaints tactfully; **4,** to buy and sell; deal in; as, a broker *handles* stocks and bonds.

hand-made (hand′mād′), *adj.* made by hand.

hand-maid (hand′mād′), *n.* a female servant or personal attendant.

hand-some (han′sum), *adj.* [hand-som-er, handsom-est], **1,** pleasing to look upon; good-looking; **2,** ample; generous; as, a very *handsome* gift.— *adv.* **hand′some-ly.**—*n.* **hand′some-ness.**

hand-spike (hand′spīk′), *n.* a bar used as a lever for lifting heavy weights.

hand-spring (hand′spring′), *n.* a feat in which one places one or both hands on the ground and turns the body in the air so as to land on the feet.

hand-writ-ing (hand′rīt′ing), *n.* **1,** a person's style of penmanship; **2,** writing done by hand.

hand-y (han′di), *adj.* [hand-i-er, hand-i-est], **1,** skilful with the hands; **2,** convenient; as, a *handy* footstool near the chair.—*n.* **hand′i-ness.**

hang (hang), *v.t.* [*p.t.* and *p.p.* hung (hung) or, in def. 3, hanged (hangd), *p.pr.* hanging], **1,** to attach to something above; suspend; as, to *hang* curtains; **2,** to fasten (something) so that it can swing to and fro; as, to *hang* a door; **3,** to suspend by the neck until dead; as, the murderer was *hanged;* **4,** to cause to droop; as, he *hung* his head; **5,** to decorate; as, she *hung* the wall with pictures:—*v.i.* **1,** to dangle; be suspended; **2,** to hover threateningly; as, ill fortune *hangs* over him; **3,** to rest; depend; as, my decision *hangs* on your answer; **4,** to die by hanging; **5,** to hold for support; as, *hang* on to me:—*n.* **1,** the manner in which a thing hangs; as, the *hang* of a coat; **2,** *Colloq.:* **a,** the manner of doing or using; knack; **b,** general idea; as, the *hang* of a story.—*n.* **hang′er.**

hang-ar (hang′ėr; hang′gär), *n.* a shed for housing aeroplanes and other aircraft.

hang-dog (hang'dôg'), *adj.* ashamed; cowering; as, a *hang-dog* expression.

hanger—on (hang'ėr—on'), *n.* [*pl.* hangers–on (-ėrz–on')], **1,** one who, though not wanted, attaches himself to another person, group, etc.; **2,** a dependent; follower; favour-seeker.

hang-ing (hang'ing), *n.* **1,** the act of suspending; **2,** execution by suspending a person by the neck until dead; **3,** hangings, drapery for walls, windows, etc.

hang-man (hang'man), *n.* [*pl.* hangmen (-men)], a public officer whose duty it is to execute convicted criminals.

hang-nail (hang'nāl'), *n.* a small piece of loose skin around a fingernail.

hang-ov-er (hang'ō'vėr), *n.* **1,** *Colloq.* a survival from the past, as a custom; **2,** *Slang,* nausea, headache, etc., resulting from much drinking of alcoholic liquor.

hank (hangk), *n.* a coil or skein, as of woollen or cotton yarn.

han-ker (hang'kėr), *v.i.* to yearn or crave; as, to *hanker* after pleasure.

Han-sard (han'sėrd), *n.* the official printed reports of the proceedings of Parliaments of the British Commonwealth at London, Ottawa, etc.

han-som (han'sum), *n.* a two-wheeled, covered cab, with an outside seat for the driver at the back: also called *hansom cab.*

hap (hap), *v.i.* [happed, hap-ping], to happen; befall:—*n.* chance; lot; fortune.

hap-haz-ard (hap'haz'ėrd), *adj.* accidental; as, a *haphazard* remark:—*adv.* by chance:—*n.* an accident.

hap-less (hap'lis), *adj.* unlucky; unfortunate.—*adv.* **hap'less-ly.**

hap-ly (hap'li), *adv.* perhaps; perchance.

hap-pen (hap'en), *v.i.* **1,** to occur; as, how did it *happen?* **2,** to chance; as, I *happened* to be there; **3,** to come by chance; as, we *happened* on a house in the woods.

hap-pen-ing (hap'en-ing), *n.* an occurrence.

hap-py (hap'i), *adj.* [hap-pi-er, hap-pi-est], **1,** enjoying or expressing pleasure; as, a *happy* girl with a *happy* smile; **2,** fortunate; lucky; as, a *happy* turn of events; **3,** apt; suitable; as, a *happy* remark.—*adv.* **hap'pi-ly.**—*n.* **hap'pi-ness.**

hap-py—go—lucky (hap'i–gō–luk'i), *adj.* **1,** gay; light-hearted; **2,** trusting to luck.

ha-ra ki-ri (hä'ra ki'ri), *n.* the ritual of Japanese suicide by disembowelling, formerly practised by the samurai or ruling class.

ha-rangue (ha-rang'), *n.* a public speech; usually, a loud, ranting address:—*v.i.* and *v.t.* [harangued, harangu-ing] to address in a loud, ranting speech.

har-ass (har'as; ha-ras'), *v.t.* **1,** to annoy or vex; as, she was *harassed* by daily complaints; **2,** to plunder; lay waste; pillage.—*n.* **har'ass-ment.**

har-bin-ger (här'bin-jėr), *n.* a herald; forerunner; as, the cock, *harbinger* of day.

har-bour (här'bėr), *n.* **1,** a partly sheltered portion of a sea, lake, etc. which serves as a port or haven for ships; **2,** any place of refuge or safety:—*v.t.* **1,** to give lodging to; shelter; **2,** to cherish; indulge; as, to *harbour* resentment:—*v.i.* to find or take shelter. In American usage, **har'bor.**

hard (härd), *adj.* **1,** solid; firm; not easily pierced or broken; as, *hard* bone; **2,** difficult; as, a *hard* task; **3,** difficult to bear; as, *hard* times; **4,** hardy; strong; as, *hard* as steel; **5,** done with exertion or energy; as, *hard* labour; **6,** industrious; as, a *hard* worker; **7,** harsh; unsympathetic; as, a *hard* master; **8,** severe in action or effect; as, a *hard* winter; **9,** containing a high per cent of alcohol; as, *hard* cider; **10,** violent; as, a hard rain; **11,** pronounced with the sound of *g* in "go" or *c* in "come," not soft like the *g* in "gin" or *c* in "cent":—*adv.* **1,** vigorously; as, work *hard;* **2,** firmly; securely; as, bound *hard* and fast; **3,** with a struggle; as, friendship dies *hard;* **4,** close; near; as, *hard* by; **5,** severely; as, the loss bore *hard* on me.

hard—boiled (härd'–boild'), *adj. Colloq.* callous; unyielding to appeal; argument, sentiment, etc.; as, a *hard-boiled* person.

hard-en (här'dn), *v.t.* **1,** to make firm, solid, or unyielding; as, to *harden* steel; *harden* one's will; **2,** to toughen; make hardy; as, to *harden* the body:—*v.i.* to become firm, solid, harsh, unyielding, hardy, etc.—*n.* **hard'en-er.** —*adj.* **hard'ened.**

hard—head-ed (härd'–hed'ed), *adj.* **1,** having shrewd judgment; practical; **2,** obstinate; stubborn.

hard—heart-ed (härd'–här'ted), *adj.* unfeeling; cruel.—*n.* **hard'—heart'edness.**

har-di-hood (här'di-hood), *n.* robustness; hence, boldness; audacity; impudence.

har-di-ly (här'di-li), *adv.* boldly.

hard-ly (härd'li), *adv.* **1,** with difficulty; **2,** scarcely; as, he has *hard* recovered; **3,** severely; as, to deal *hardly* with someone.

hard-ness (härd'nis), *n.* the quality or state of being solid, unyielding, etc.; as, *hardness* of rock; *hardness* of heart.

hard-pan (härd'pan'), *n.* a hard, cementlike soil layer difficult to dig through.

hard-ship (härd'ship), *n.* that which is hard to bear, as toil, privation, etc.

hard-tack (härd'tak'), *n.* a large, unsalted biscuit, used in the army and navy.

hard-top (härd'top'), *n.* a motor-car with rigid metal top and without centre posts between windows.

hard-ware (härd'wâr'), *n.* articles manufactured from metal, as cutlery, kitchen utensils, tools, etc.

hard-wood (härd'wood'), *n.* a heavy, close-grained wood, such as oak, maple, or mahogany:—*adj.* made of hardwood; as, *hardwood* floors.

har-dy (här'di), *adj.* [har-di-er, har-di-est], **1,** robust; capable of bearing hardship; **2,** bold; resolute; **3,** able to survive winter weather: used of plants. —*n.* **har'di-ness.**

hare (hâr), *n.* a timid, swift-footed animal, like a rabbit, with a divided upper lip, long ears, and a short fluffy tail.

hare-bell (hâr'bel'), *n.* a slender plant with blue, bell-shaped flowers; also, the flower: also called *bluebell.*

hare-brained (hâr'brānd'), *adj.* heedless; rash; as, a *hare-brained* fool.

hare-lip (hâr'lip'), *n.* a lip, usually the upper, that from birth is divided or cleft like that of a hare.

ha-rem (hâr'em; hā'rem), *n.* **1,** the part of a Mohammedan house where the women live; **2,** a Mohammedan's wives and female relatives living in this part of the house. Also, **ha-reem'.**

ha-ri ki-ri (hä'ri ki'ri), *n.* Same as hara kiri. Erroneously *hari-kari.*

hark (härk), *v.i.* to listen: often used as an exclamation; as, *Hark!* the hounds!

hark-en (här'ken), *v.i.* Same as **hearken.**

har-le-quin (här'le-kwin; -kin), *n.* a buffoon or clown, usually masked, wearing spangled tights of many colours, and carrying a wooden sword or magic wand.

har-lot (här'lot), *n.* a woman of bad character; a prostitute.

harm (härm), *n.* **1,** injury; damage; **2,** moral evil or wrongdoing:—*v.t.* to hurt or damage.

harm-ful (härm'fool), *adj.* hurtful; injurious; as, *harmful* drugs.—*adv.* **harm'ful-ly.**

harm-less (härm'lis), *adj.* having no power to damage or hurt; as, a *harmless* snake; also, producing no ill effect; as, a *harmless* drug.—*adv.* **harm'less-ly.**

har-mon-ic (här-mon'ik), *adj.* **1,** relating to the science dealing with musical sounds; **2,** agreeing in sound; concordant:—*n.* **1,** a tone, higher than the main tone, and heard along with it; an overtone; **2, harmonics,** *n.pl.* used as *sing.* the science dealing with musical sounds.

har-mon-i-ca (här-mon'i-ka), *n.* a small musical wind-instrument, provided with metal reeds, which is played by the mouth; a mouth-organ.

har-mo-ni-ous (här-mō'ni-us), *adj.* **1,** combining so as to form a pleasing and agreeable whole; as, *harmonious* voices; **2,** agreeing in action and feeling; peaceable; friendly; as, *harmonious* neighbors.—*adv.* **har-mo'ni-ous-ly.**

har-mo-ni-um (här-mō'ni-um), *n.* a small organ whose notes are made by forcing air through reeds.

har-mo-nize (här'mo-nīz'), *v.t.* [harmo-nized, harmoniz-ing], **1,** to arrange in musical harmony; **2,** to bring into agreement; as, to *harmonize* colours; **3,** to cause to agree; reconcile; as, to *harmonize* conflicting opinions:— *v.i.* **1,** to play or sing in harmony; **2,** to go suitably or pleasingly together; as, these colours *harmonize.*

har-mo-ny (här'mo-ni), *n.* [*pl.* harmonies], **1,** the combination of parts so as to form an agreeable or connected whole; as, the *harmony* of motion in dancing; **2,** agreement in feeling, opinions, etc.; as, *harmony* in the Senate; **3,** the arrangement of similar passages, as in the Bible, so as to show their points of agreement or disagreement; as, a *harmony* of the four Gospels; **4,** in music, the combination of musical notes so as to form chords, or the science treating of this; also, the composition of a piece of music with reference to its chords.

har-ness (här'nes), *n.* the fittings used to attach a horse or other animal to a wagon, plough, etc.:—*v.t.* **1,** to put a harness upon; **2,** to make (something) produce power, by installing machinery; as, to *harness* a waterfall.

harp (härp), *n.* a stringed musical instrument of triangular shape, played with the fingers:—*v.i.* **1,** to play on a harp; **2,** to dwell unduly on some particular subject.—*n.* **harp'er.**—*n.* **harp'ist.**

har-poon (här-pōōn'), *n.* a long spear

with a rope attached, used to strike and kill whales or large fish:—**harpoon—gun** a gun used for throwing a harpoon:— *v.t.* to strike or kill with a harpoon; as, the sailor *harpooned* the whale.—*n.* **har-poon′er.**

harp-si-chord (härp′si-kôrd), *n.* an instrument with wire strings and a keyboard, similar to the grand piano in form and arrangement, in general use before the piano.

har-py (här′pi), *n.* **1,** in *Greek mythology,* a ravenous monster with a woman's head and a bird's body; **2,** a greedy, grasping person.

har-ri-dan (har′i-dan), *n.* a disreputable, shrewish woman; a vicious old hag.

har-row (har′ō), *n.* a farming implement with sharp iron or wooden teeth, or sharp steel disks, for breaking up clods or covering sown seeds with earth: —*v.t.* **1,** to drive a harrow over; as, to *harrow* ploughed land; **2,** to distress deeply; as, his feelings were *harrowed* by his friend's misery.

har-ry (har′i), *v.t.* [harried, harry-ing], **1,** to plunder; lay waste; as, the invaders *harried* the country; **2,** to annoy or vex.

harsh (härsh), *adj.* **1,** wounding the feelings; cruel; severe; as, the *harsh* father; a *harsh* command; **2,** rough or irritating to the hearing, or touch; as, a *harsh* voice; a *harsh* piece of cloth; also, disagreeable; rigorous; as, a *harsh* climate.

hart (härt), *n.* a male of the red deer over five years of age; a stag.

har-te-beest or **hart-beest** (härt′-bēst′; härt′ti-bēst′), *n.* a large swift South African antelope with doubly curved horns (now nearly extinct).

har-um—scar-um (hâr′um–skâr′um), *adj. Colloq.* reckless; irresponsible; wild; rash.—*n.* such a person.

har-vest (här′vist), *n.* **1,** a crop, as of grain or fruit, ready for gathering or already gathered; **2,** the gathering in of such a crop; **3,** the season, usually late summer or early fall, for gathering in a crop; **4,** result; reward; as, his good marks are the *harvest* of hard work:— *v.t.* to gather in (a crop); as, to *harvest* wheat.—*n.* **har′vest-er.**

has (haz), 3rd person sing. pres. of *have.*

has—been (haz′–bin′), *n. Colloq.* a person or thing once effective, useful, etc., but no longer so.

hash (hash), *v.t.* **1,** to chop into small pieces, as meat; **2,** to botch; bungle:— *n.* **1,** a mixture of meat and vegetables, chopped into small pieces and cooked;

also, the dish so prepared; **2,** a mixture or jumble; **3,** a botch.

hash-ish (hash′ēsh; hash′ish), *n.* a preparation of Indian hemp, smoked or chewed for its intoxicating or narcotic effect.

hasp (hȧsp), *n.* a hinged metal clasp for a door or a box, which folds over a staple and is fastened with a pin or padlock.

has-sock (has′uk), *n.* **1,** a heavy, stuffed cushion, used to kneel or sit upon; a footstool; **2,** a tuft of coarse grass.

haste (hāst), *n.* **1,** quickness of movement; hurry; speed; **2,** undue, rash, or excessive speed:—*v.t.* and *v.i.* [hast-ed, hast-ing], to hurry.

has-ten (hās′n), *v.t.* to cause (a person) to hurry; to urge (work) forward:—*v.i.* to move with speed; hurry; as, *hasten* home.

hast-y (hās′ti), *adj.* [hast-i-er, hast-i-est], **1,** speedy; hurried; as, a *hasty* departure; **2,** careless; superficial; as, *hasty* work; **3,** quick-tempered; impetuous.—*adv.* **hast′i-ly.**—*n.* **hast′i-ness.**

hat (hat), *n.* a covering for the head, usually with a crown and brim. Compounds: hat′band′; hat′box′; hat′pin′; hat′rack′.

¹hatch (hach), *n.* **1,** an opening in a deck, roof, floor, etc., often with a removable cover or trapdoor; a hatchway; **2,** a cover for a hatch.

²hatch (hach), *v.t.* **1,** to produce young from; as, to *hatch* eggs; **2,** to produce (young) from eggs; as, to *hatch* chickens; **3,** to plot or plan; as, to *hatch* a rebellion:—*v.i.* **1,** to yield young; as, the eggs *hatched* in three weeks; **2,** to come forth from the egg, as a young chick:—*n.* the brood of young produced at one time.—*n.* **hatch′er-y.**

hatch-et (hach′et), *n.* a small axe with a hammer-head and short handle.

hatch-way (hach′wā′), *n.* an opening, as in the deck of a vessel, for passage below; a hatch.

hate (hāt), *v.t.* [hat-ed, hat-ing], **1,** to dislike thoroughly; detest; **2,** to be averse to; dislike; as, I *hate* sewing:— *n.* extreme abhorrence or dislike; hatred.—*n.* **hat′er.**

hate-ful (hāt′fool), *adj.* deserving or causing hatred; abominable; as, murder is a *hateful* thing; also, displaying hatred; as, a *hateful* glance.—*adv.* **hate′ful-ly.**—*n.* **hate′ful-ness.**

ha-tred (hā′tred), *n.* intense dislike; enmity.

---

cat, āge, fär, câre, ȧsk; ten, ēve, later; (i) pity, rely, senate; īce; top; nō.

haugh-ty (hô′ti), *adj.* [haugh-ti-er, haugh-ti-est], proud; disdainful; as, a *haughty* empress; a *haughty* gesture.— *adv.* **haugh′ti-ly.**—*n.* **haugh′ti-ness.**

haul (hôl), *v.t.* **1,** to pull or draw forcibly; to drag; **2,** to move or transport by pulling; as, to *haul* a load:—*v.i.* **1,** to change the course of a ship; as, the sailors *hauled* into the wind; **2,** to change direction; as, the wind *hauls* to the west:—*n.* **1,** a strong pull; **2,** a single pulling in of a net; also, the quantity of fish caught at one time; **3,** booty; loot; as, the thief made a good *haul;* **4,** the distance over which anything is drawn; as, a *haul* of 30 miles.— **haul′age.**—*n.* **haul′er.**

haunch (hônch; hänch), *n.* **1,** the hip and buttocks of a man or other animal; the hind part; **2,** of meats, the leg and loin taken together; esp. a joint of venison or mutton.

haunt (hônt; hänt), *n.* **1,** a place of frequent meeting or resort; as, the *haunt* of outlaws; **2,** (hänt; hant), *Colloq.* in the U.S., a ghost:—*v.t.* **1,** to visit frequently or habitually; **2,** to trouble persistently; as, dreams *haunt* me.

hau-teur (ō′tör′; hō-tûr′), *n.* haughtiness; arrogance; disdainful pride.

have (hav), *v.t.* [*present sing.* I have, you have, he has (haz), *pl.* have, *p.t.* and *p.p.* had (had), *p.pr.* hav-ing], **1,** to hold; possess; own; as, to *have* money; **2,** to be compelled; as, I *have* to sell it; **3,** to hold or harbour in one's mind; as, to *have* a grudge; **4,** in a general way, to engage in, experience, suffer, enjoy, or the like; as, to *have* a good time or an argument; to *have* a headache; **5,** to bear (a child); **6,** to cause to do or to be done; as, *have* Tom go; *have* this bill paid; **7,** to allow; permit; as, I will not *have* disobedience; **8,** to obtain; get; as, he *has* his way; **9,** to state as a fact; as, the papers *have* it that war is declared; **10,** to beat; get the better of; as, he *had* me in that argument; **11,** to show; use; as, to *have* mercy; **12,** as a helping verb, used to form the present perfect, past perfect, and future perfect tenses of verbs, indicating action occurring before the present, past, or future; as, I *have* gone; I *had* gone; I *shall have* gone.

ha-ven (hā′ven), *n.* **1,** a sheltered anchorage for ships; **2,** any harbour or shelter.

hav-er-sack (hav′ėr-sak′), *n.* a strong canvas bag or pack for carrying provisions or rations, esp. on a march or hike.

hav-oc (hav′uk), *n.* devastation; ruin.

haw (hô), *interj.* a word meaning *left*, used in driving teams without reins: opposite of *gee:*—*v.t.* and *v.i.* to turn toward the left.

¹hawk (hôk), *n.* any of several strong, swift-flying birds of prey, as falcons, buzzards, kites, etc.:—*v.i.* to hunt wild birds or game with the help of hawks.— *adj.* and *n.* **hawk′ing.**

²hawk (hôk), *v.t.* to peddle; cry out (wares) for sale as one goes from place to place.—*n.* **hawk′er.**

haw-ser (hô′zėr; hô′sėr), *n.* a rope or cable used to tow or moor a vessel.

haw-thorn (hô′thôrn), *n.* any of several thorny trees or shrubs, with white or pink fragrant flowers and small red berries. Also, the flower.

hay (hā), *n.* various grasses, clover, etc., cut and dried for fodder:—*v.i.* to make hay.

hay-cock (hā′kok′), *n.* a small cone-shaped pile of hay in a field.

hay fe-ver, a disease affecting the nose, eyes, and throat, caused by the pollen of certain plants.

hay-mak-er (hā′māk′ėr), *n.* **1,** one who handles hay, by spreading it, etc.; **2,** *boxing slang,* a wild swinging blow.

hay-mow (hā′mou′), *n.* **1,** a mass of hay laid up in a barn; **2,** the part of a barn in which the hay is stored.

hay-rick (hā′rik′), *n.* a large pile of hay stacked in the open air; a haystack.

hay-stack (hā′stak′), *n.* a stack or pile of hay in the open air; a hayrick.

hay-wire (hā′wīr′), *n.* wire for baling hay, esp. when tangled after removal from bales; hence, *adv.* and *adj. Slang,* **1,** out of order; wrong; **2,** crazy; as, he went *haywire.*

haz-ard (haz′ėrd), *n.* **1,** an old gambling game at dice; **2,** chance; risk; danger; **3,** in *golf,* an obstacle, such as rough ground, a stream, or a sand-pit:—*v.t.* **1,** to subject to risk, or take the risk of; as, to *hazard* one's fortune; to *hazard* a loss; **2,** to offer; venture; as, to *hazard* a guess.—*adj.* **haz′ard-ous.**

¹haze (hāz), *n.* **1,** a slight fog, mist, or smoke in the atmosphere; **2,** mental vagueness or confusion.—*adj.* **ha′zy.**— *n.* **ha′zi-ness.**

²haze (hāz), *v.t.* [hazed, haz-ing], to play practical jokes upon, as in school or college initiations; bully.—*n.* **haz′er.**

ha-zel (hā′zl), *n.* **1,** any of various shrubs or small trees bearing a small, rounded, edible nut; **2,** the nut borne by this tree; a filbert; **3,** a light, reddish-brown colour:—*adj.* light reddish brown.—*n.* **ha′zel-nut′.**

H-bomb (āch′bom′), *n.* Abbreviation for **hydrogen bomb.**

he (hē), *masc. pron.* of the third person [*nominative*, he, *possessive*, his (hiz), *objective*, him (him)], **1**, one particular man or boy; as, where is Charles? *he's* absent; **2**, anyone; as, *he* who runs may read:—*n.* [*pl.* he's or hes (hēz)], a man or boy.

head (hed), *n.* **1**, the uppermost part of the body in man, or, in most animals, the foremost part, containing the mouth, eyes, nose, ears, and brain; **2**, the top or upper end of anything, as of a flagpole, cane, stairs, page, etc.; also the side of a coin showing a head; **3**, anything resembling a head; *esp.* the top part of a plant, or a round compact bloom; as, a *head* of lettuce; a *head* of clover; **4**, imagination; intelligence; as, a story out of one's *head;* he talks over my *head;* a good *head* for figures; **5**, mental calm or control; as, to keep one's *head;* **6**, the front or foremost part of anything, as of a parade or an army; also, the bow of a ship; **7**, the position of command or leadership; as, to be at the *head* of a firm; also, a leader or chief; **8**, a separate topic; a class or subject; as, optics comes under the *head* of science; **9**, a head's length; as, the horse won by a *head;* **10**, a person; as, to charge so much a *head;* also, [*pl.* head], a single one; an individual; as, 50 *head* of sheep; **11**, crisis; as, the situation came to a *head;* **12**, source; beginning; as, the *head* of a river; **13**, force; pressure; as, a *head* of steam; **14**, a cape or promontory, as of land:—*adj.* **1**, principal; chief; as, a *head* clerk; **2**, coming toward one; as, a *head* wind; **3**, placed at the front or top:—*v.t.* **1**, to lead; direct; as, to *head* an expedition; **2**, to take the first place in; as, Tom *heads* his class; **3**, to get in front of; as, to *head* off a horse; prevent; as, to *head* off a quarrel:—*v.i.* **1**, to move in a given direction; as, to *head* south; **2**, to form a head, as a plant or flower; hence, to come to a climax.—*adj.* **head′less.**

head-ache (hed′āk′), *n.* a continuous pain in the head.

head-cheese (hed′chēz′), *n.* jellied meat made *esp.* from the head and feet of pigs, cut up, boiled, and pressed.

head-dress (hed′dres′), *n.* **1**, a covering, often ornamental, for the head; **2**, a manner of wearing the hair.

head-first, **1**, headlong; **2**, in rash, thoughtless haste.—**head′fore′most′.**

head-ing (hed′ing), *n.* **1**, the title of a chapter, page, etc.; **2**, the subject or topic discussed; **3**, a gallery in a mine.

head-land (hed′land), *n.* a cape or promontory.

head-light (hed′līt′), *n.* a bright light on the front of a locomotive, automobile, etc.

head-line (hed′līn′), *n.* a heading, often in large type, at the top of a newspaper column or at the beginning of an article.

head-lock (hed′lok′), *n.* a hold in which a wrestler locks his arm around his opponent's head.

head-long (hed′lông), *adv.* **1**, head foremost; **2**, rashly:—*adj.* **1**, rash; violent; thoughtless; as, a *headlong* decision; **2**, plunging head first.

head-man (hed′man′), *n.* [*pl.* headmen (-men′)], a leader; the chief man of a tribe.

head mas-ter ,the principal teacher or the principal of a school.

head—on (hed′—on′), *adj.* with fronts facing: used *esp.* of collisions.

head-quar-ters (hed′kwôr′tẽrz), *n.* [*pl.* headquarters], **1**, the residence or office of a commanding officer from which orders are issued; **2**, any centre of activity or authority.

head-ship (hed′ship), *n.* the position of head, chief, or leader.

head-stone (hed′stōn′), *n.* **1**, a stone set at the head of a grave; **2**, a cornerstone.

head-y (hed′i), *adj.* [-ier, -iest], **1**, wilful; rash; impetuous; as, a *heady* youth; a *heady* horse; **2**, intoxicating as, *heady* wine.—*n.* **head′i-ness.**

head-strong (hed′strông), *adj.* ungovernable; self-willed.

head wa-ters, the source and upper waters of a stream.

head-way (hed′wā′), *n.* **1**, forward motion, as of a ship; progress; **2**, a clear space permitting passage under an arch, bridge, etc.

heal (hēl), *v.t.* to restore to health cure:—*v.i.* to become well or sound.—*n.* **heal′er.**

health (helth), *n.* **1**, freedom from pain or disease; vigour of body or mind; **2**, a toast to a person's health and happiness.

health-ful (helth′fool), *adj.* promoting bodily welfare; giving health; as *healthful* exercise; a *healthful* climate —*adv.* **health′ful-ly.**—*n.* **health′ful ness.**

health-y (hel′thi), *adj.* [health-i-er health-i-est], **1**, in a sound or whole some condition; as, a *healthy* child; **2** showing health; as, a *healthy* look.— *adv.* **health′i-ly.**—*n.* **health′i-ness.**

heap (hēp), *n.* **1**, a number of thing piled up together; **2**, a large quantity —*v.t.* **1**, to make a pile of; **2**, to bestow generously; as, to *heap* gifts upon; **3,** to fill to overflowing; as, to *heap* a plate with food.

hear (hēr), *v.t.* [heard (hûrd), hear-ing], **1,** to perceive by the ear; **2,** to attend or listen to; give heed to; **3,** to become informed of; as, to *hear* news; **4,** to grant (a favour or a prayer):—*v.i.* **1,** to have the sense of hearing; **2,** to be told; as, I *heard* of his death; **3,** to listen.—*n.* **hear′er.**

hear-ing (hēr′ing), *n.* **1,** the sense by which sound is perceived; **2,** the distance over which a sound may be heard; as, to be within *hearing;* **3,** a chance to be heard; attention; as, to get a *hearing.*

heark-en or **hark-en** (här′ken), *v.i.* to listen; pay attention.

hear-say (hēr′sā′), *n.* rumour; gossip.

hearse (hûrs), *n.* a vehicle for carrying dead bodies to the grave.

heart (härt), *n.* **1,** a hollow, muscular organ which pumps the blood through the body; **2,** hence, an essential part; as, the *heart* of a book; also, the central or inmost part; as, the *heart* of a tree; **3,** tenderness; sympathy; as, one's *heart* goes out to a child; also courage; as, I haven't the *heart* to tell her; **4,** a conventional figure representing a heart; **5,** one of a suit, called *hearts,* of playing-cards, marked with a red figure like a heart; **6,** memory; as, to learn by *heart;* **7,** liking; approval; as, after one's own *heart;* **8, hearts,** a card game. Compounds: **heart′ache′; heart′beat′; heart′break′; heart′bro′ken; heart′-rend′ing; heart′sick′; heart′string′.**

HUMAN HEART
Partly laid open to show: 1, right auricle; 2, left auricle; 3, right ventricle; 4, left ventricle; 5, aorta; 6, pulmonary artery.

heart-burn (härt′bûrn), *n.* **1,** a burning sensation in the stomach region, caused by high acidity, indigestion, etc.; **2,** jealousy; discontent; envy. Also, **heart′burn′ing.**

heart-en (här′tn), *v.t.* to give courage to; to cheer or inspire.

heart-felt (härt′felt′), *adj.* earnest; sincere; with true emotion.

hearth (härth), *n.* **1,** the floor or base of a fireplace, usually of brick or stone; **2,** the family circle; home.

hearth-stone (härth′stōn′), *n.* **1,** a flat stone forming a hearth; **2,** the fireside.

heart-less (härt′lis), *adj.* **1,** without feeling or affection; **2,** cruel; merciless. —*adv.* **heart′less-ly.**—*n.* **heart′less-ness.**

heart-wood (härt′wood′), *n.* the hard inner wood of a tree trunk.

heart-y (här′ti), *adj.* [heart-i-er, heart-i-est], **1,** sincere; cordial; as, a *hearty* welcome; **2,** vigorous; strong; as, a *hearty* handclasp; **3,** abundant and nourishing; as, a *hearty* meal.—*adv.* **heart′i-ly.**—*n.* **heart′i-ness.**

heat (hēt), *n.* **1,** a form of energy due to the motion of invisible particles of matter and capable of passing from one body to another; **2,** hotness; warmth; high temperature; as, the *heat* of summer; also, the sensation caused by heat; **3,** intensity of feeling; rage; zeal; as, the *heat* of a quarrel; **4,** one race in an event which is made up of two or more races:—*v.t.* **1,** to make hot; **2,** to excite or arouse:—*v.i.* to become hot; as, an engine *heats* up.—*n.* **heat′er.**—*adv.* **heat′ed-ly** (hēt′id-li).

heath (hēth), *n.* **1,** a tract of waste or level land, covered with heather or other coarse vegetation, esp. in Great Britain; **2,** an evergreen shrub; heather.

hea-then (hē′then), *n.* [*pl.* heathens or, collectively, heathen], a person who is not of the Jewish, Christian, or Mohammedan faith; a pagan; idolater: —*adj.* pertaining to the heathen; as, a *heathen* land.

heath-er (heth′ėr), *n.* a small evergreen shrub with lavender flowers, that blooms profusely in late summer: also called *heath.*—*adj.* **heath′er-y.**

heave (hēv), *v.t.* [*p.t.* and *p.p.* heaved (hēvd) or hove (hōv), heav-ing], **1,** to hoist or lift up with effort; **2,** to utter (a sob or sigh); **3,** to throw; hurl:—*v.i.* **1,** to be lifted up; swell up; **2,** to rise and fall alternately; as, the sea *heaves;* **3,** to struggle; strain; **4,** to haul; move; as, the ship *hove* in sight: —*n.* **1,** an effort to move or pull something; a lift; **2,** the act of throwing; **3,** a swell or rising; as, a *heave* of the breast.

heav-en (hev′en), *n.* **1,** the abode of God and the blessed; **2,** a state or condition of bliss; supreme happiness; **3, the heavens,** the firmament; sky.— *adj.* and *adv.* **heav′en-ward.**—*adv.* **heav′en-wards.**

heav-en-ly (hev′en-li), *adj.* **1,** pertaining to the sky; as, a *heavenly* body; **2,** pertaining to the abode of God; divine; as, *heavenly* joy; **3,** beyond compare; as, *heavenly* beauty.—*n.* **heav′en-li-ness.**

heaves (hēvz), *n.pl.* used as *sing.* an asthmatic disease of horses, marked by wheezing, heaving of the flanks, and persistent coughing; broken wind.

heav-y (hev′i), *adj.* [heav-i-er, heav-i-est], **1,** weighty; ponderous; as, a *heavy* load; **2**, large in extent, or effect; as, a *heavy* rain; **3**, oppressive; grievous; as, a *heavy* punishment; also, rough or hard to travel over; as, a *heavy* road; **4**, grave; serious; as, *heavy* reading; **5**, dejected; sad; as, a *heavy* heart; **6**, dull; stupid; as, a *heavy* mind; **7**, powerful; loud; as, a *heavy* voice; **8**, thick; coarse; as, *heavy* linen; **9**, loaded; as, a tree *heavy* with apples; **10**, dense, as storm-clouds.—*adv.* **heav′i-ly.**—*n.* **heav′i-ness.**

heavy hydrogen, a hydrogen isotope of twice the mass of ordinary hydrogen.

heavy water, water in which the ordinary hydrogen atom is replaced by that of heavy hydrogen.

heav-y-weight (hev′i-wāt′), *n.* a boxer of 175 lbs. or over.

heck-le (hek′l), *v.t.* [heck-led, heck-ling], to question sharply, so as to annoy or confuse; as, to *heckle* a speaker.—*n.* **heck′ler.**

hec-tic (hek′tik), *adj.* **1**, feverish; flushed and hot; **2**, *Colloq.* exciting; wild; as, a *hectic* life.

hec-to— (hek′tō–), a *prefix* in the *metric system* signifying 100, as in **hec′tare** (100 ares or 2.471 acres), **hec′to-gramme′** or **hec′to-gram′** (100 grams or 3.527 oz.), **hec′to-li′ter** (100 litres or about 2–3/4 bu.), **hec′to-me′tre** (100 metres or 328.089 feet).

hec-tor (hek′tẽr), *v.t.* and *v.i.* to bully; threaten; bluster.

hedge (hej), *n.* **1**, a fence of bushes, shrubs, or low trees; **2**, a barrier:—*v.t.* [hedged, hedg-ing], **1**, to enclose with a border of bushes or shrubs; **2**, to obstruct; hem in; surround; as, an army *hedges* in the enemy:—*v.i.* **1**, to bet on both sides in order to protect oneself against heavy loss; **2**, to speak evasively; avoid frank speech, esp. in answer to questions.

hedge-hog (hej′hog′), *n.* **1**, a spiny, insect-eating animal, with the power of rolling itself into a ball for defence; **2**, the North American porcupine.

hedge-row (hej′rō′), *n.* a hedge or fence of small trees or shrubs.

heed (hēd), *v.t.* to notice; pay attention to; regard:—*n.* careful attention; as, give *heed.*—*adj.* **heed′ful.**—*adv.* **heed′-ful-ly.**—*n.* **heed′ful-ness.**

heed-less (hēd′lis), *adj.* careless; inattentive; neglectful.—*adv.* **heed′less-ly.**—*n.* **heed′less-ness.**

hee-haw (hē′hô′), *n.* [Imitative], **1**, rude laughter; a guffaw; **2**, the braying of an ass:—*v.i.* to laugh a loud or silly laugh.

¹**heel** (hēl), *v.i.* to lean to one side; to list: said of a ship:—*v.t.* to cause (a ship) to list.

²**heel** (hēl), *n.* **1**, the back part of the foot; **2**, the corresponding part of a boot, shoe, or stocking; **3**, anything resembling a heel in position or shape; as, the *heel* of a scythe or a golf-club:—*v.t.* to furnish with a heel; as, to *heel* boots.—*n.* **heel′ing.**

heft (heft), *n. Colloq.* weight; heaviness; bulk:—*v.t. Colloq.* to try the weight of; as, he *hefted* the sack of sand:—*v.i.* to weigh.—*adj.* **heft′y.**

he-gi-ra or **he-ji-ra** (hej′i-ra; hi-jī′ra), *n.* **1**, Mohammed's flight from Mecca to Medina, A.D. 622, that marks the beginning of the Moslem era; **2**, any flight to safety.

heif-er (hef′ẽr), *n.* a young cow that has not yet calved.

heigh (hā; hī), *interj.* calling attention or expressing surprise, a question, jubilation, etc.

heigh—ho (hā′–hō′; hī′–hō′), *interj.* an exclamation of (a) weariness, mild surprise, melancholy, etc., (b) joy gaiety, etc.

height (hīt), *n.* **1**, distance from the base to the top; of man, stature; as, he is six feet in *height;* **2**, altitude; the distance anything rises above the earth or above sea level; **3**, a mountain or hill; **4**, the highest point; top summit; hence, the utmost degree; as the *height* of madness.

height-en (hīt′n), *v.t.* **1**, to raise; make higher; **2**, to intensify, as a colour increase; aggravate; as, to *heighten* anger:—*v.i.* to rise in height; increase.

hei-nous (hā′nus), *adj.* hateful; extremely wicked; as, a *heinous* crime.—*adv.* **hei′nous-ly.**—*n.* **hei′nous-ness.**

heir (âr), *n.* **1**, one who receives or has the right to receive an estate, title, etc. on the death of the owner; **2**, one who inherits anything, as property or mental qualities; as, he fell *heir* to his father's temper.

heir-ess (âr′is), *n.* a woman or girl who inherits, or is heir to, title or property

heir-loom (âr′lōōm′), *n.* a piece of personal property handed down in a family for generations.

held (held), *p.t.* and *p.p.* of *hold.*

hel-i-cop-ter (hel′i-kop′tẽr), *n.* a flying machine lifted and propelled by large horizontal propellers turned by motor power.

he-li-o-graph (hē′li-ō-gràf′), *n.* an apparatus using a mirror for signalling by reflecting flashes of sunlight:—*v.* and *v.i.* to signal by such a device

he-li-o-trope (hē′li-ō-trōp′), *n.* **1,** a cultivated plant bearing purplish, sweet-scented flowers; **2,** a purplish colour.

he-li-um (hē′li-um), *n.* a rare gas, very light and not inflammable, used for inflating balloons.

hell (hel), *n.* **1,** the place of punishment for the wicked after death; **2,** any place or condition of extreme misery or evil; **3,** the dwelling-place of the dead.—*adj.* **hell′ish.**—*n.* **hell′ish-ness.**

hell-bend-er (hel′ben′dẻr), *n.* **1,** an edible (but rarely eaten) salamander, about 18″ long, found esp. in Lake Erie and the Ohio Valley; **2,** *Slang*, a drunken spree (or person).

Hel-len-ic (he-len′ik; -lē′nik), *adj.* relating to Greece, esp. its social and cultural aspects; as, *Hellenic* sculpture.

hel-lo (he-lō′), *interj.* an exclamation of informal greeting, surprise, etc.:—*n.* a salutation; greeting.

helm (helm), *n.* **1,** the steering apparatus of a ship, esp. the tiller or the wheel; **2,** hence, any post of command or control; as, at the *helm* of the nation.

hel-met (hel′met), *n.* a covering, as of metal or leather, worn to protect the head.

helms-man (helmz′man), *n.*[*pl.* helmsmen (-men)], the person who steers a ship or boat; a pilot.

hel-ot (hel′ot), *n.* a member of the lowest class of serf in ancient Sparta; a slave.

help (help), *v.t.* **1,** to give assistance to; support; **2,** to avoid; prevent; as, I cannot *help* his going; **3,** to distribute food to; serve; **4,** to remedy; as, nothing *helps* my headache:—*v.i.* to lend aid; be useful:—*n.* **1,** aid; support; **2,** remedy; relief; **3,** that which forwards or promotes; **4,** a hired servant or servants; as, she never has trouble with her *help*.—*n.* **help′er.**

help-ful (help′fool), *adj.* giving aid; beneficial; useful.—*n.* **help′ful-ness.**

help-ing (hel′ping), *n.* a portion of food served at table.

help-less (help′lis), *adj.* unable to take care of oneself; feeble; dependent.—*adv.* **help′less-ly.**—*n.* **help′less-ness.**

help-mate (help′māt′) or **help-meet** (help′mēt′), *n.* a helper, esp. a wife.

hel-ter—skel-ter (hel′tẻr–skel′tẻr), *adj.* and *adv.* in hurried confusion; pell-mell:—*n.* disorder; hasty confusion.

hem (hem), *n.* the edge of material turned under and sewed down to prevent fraying:—*v.t.* [hemmed, hem-

ming], **1,** to fold under and sew down the edge of (a cloth or garment); **2,** to shut in; surround; as, the enemy *hemmed* us in.

hem-a-tite (hem′a-tīt′; hēm′), *n.* an important ore of iron, Fe_2O_3 (iron oxide).

hem-i-sphere (hem′i-sfēr), *n.* a half sphere; esp. a half of the earth. The equator divides the earth into the Northern and the Southern Hemispheres. A meridian divides the earth into the Eastern Hemisphere, including Europe, Asia, Africa, and Australia, and the Western Hemisphere, including North America and South America.

hem-lock (hem′lok), *n.* **1,** any of several evergreen trees of the pine family; also, the lumber from such a tree; **2,** any of several poisonous plants of the parsley family.

he-mo-glo-bin (hē′mō-glō′bin), *n.* Same as **haemoglobin.**

he-mo-phil-i-a (hēm′ō-fil′i-a), *n.* Same as **haemophilia.**

hem-or-rhage (hem′o-rij), *n.* bleeding esp. a great or continuous flow of blood. The preferred spelling is **haem′or-rhage.**

hem-or-rhoids (hem′o-roidz), *n.pl.* painful swelling and bleeding of the veins about the anus; piles.

hemp (hemp), *n.* a herb of Asia, the fibre of which is used for ropes and various kinds of coarse linen. The leaves and flowers are the source of the drug hashish.—*adj.* **hemp′en.**

hem-stitch (hem′stich′), *n.* an ornamental stitch used in hemming, in which crosswise threads are pulled out and lengthwise threads fastened into small bundles; also, needle-work so finished:—*v.t.* to finish with hemstitch.

hen (hen), *n.* the female of the domestic fowl; also, the female of other birds.

hence (hens), *adv.* **1,** from this place, source, or time; as, a week *hence;* **2,** for this reason:—*interj.* begone!

hence-forth (hens′fôrth′; hens′fôrth′) or **hence-for-ward** (hens′fôr′wẻrd), *adv.* from this time on.

hench-man (hench′man), *n.*[*pl.* henchmen (-men)], a trusted follower; a political supporter.

hen-na (hen′a), *n.* a reddish-brown dye made from the leaves of the henna, a tropical Asian shrub with fragrant white or rose leaves.

hen-pecked (hen′pekt′), *adj.* governed or domineered over by one's wife.

hen-ry (hen′ri), *n.* [*pl.* henrys]; the unit for measuring induced currents, that is, the inducing of one volt by a current varying at the rate of one ampere per second.

he-pat-i-ca (he-pat′i-ka), *n.* any of several spring-blooming plants of the buttercup family, with hairy stems, heart-shaped leaves, and pink, lavender, or white flowers.

hep-a-ti-tis (hep′a-tī′tis), *n.* inflammation of the liver.

hep-cat (hep′kat′), *n. Slang,* an enthusiast in jazz or swing music.

hep-ta-gon (hep′ta-gon′), *n.* in *geometry,* a plane figure having seven sides and seven angles.

hep-tam-e-ter (hep-tam′e-tẽr), *n.* a line or verse with seven metrical feet. Also used as *adj.*   HEPTAGON

her (hûr), *adj.* a possessive form of *she,* belonging to her; as, *her* book:—*pron.* the objective from of *she;* as, I see *her.*

her-ald (her′ald), *n.* **1,** an official who made state proclamations, carried important messages, and assisted at public ceremonies; **2,** a messenger; forerunner:—*v.t.* to introduce; proclaim.

her-ald-ry (her′ald-ri), *n.* [*pl.* heraldries], **1,** the science that treats of coats of arms and of pedigrees; **2,** a coat of arms; also, pomp and splendour. —*adj.* **he-ral′dic.**

herb (ûrb; hûrb), *n.* a plant with a soft, juicy stem, which, after flowering, either dies completely, or withers to the ground; esp. one used for medicine, food, flavour, etc.—*adj.* **herb′al.**—*n.* **herb′al-ist.**

her-ba-ceous (hûr-bā′shus), *adj.* of the nature of an herb; also, planted with herbs.

herb-age (ûr′bij; hûr′bij), *n.* grass or herbs; pasturage.

her-biv-o-rous (hûr-biv′u-rus), *adj.* feeding on plants, as do horses and dairy cattle.

her-cu-le-an (hûr-kū′li-an; hûr′kū-lē′an), *adj.* **1,** of great strength or power (like Hercules); **2,** difficult; as, a *herculean* task.

herd (hûrd), *n.* **1,** a group of animals, esp. cattle, feeding or travelling together; **2,** a large crowd of people; **3,** the common people as a mass; mob:—*v.i.* **1,** to flock together, as beasts; **2,** to associate:—*v.t.* to form (cattle) into a herd.

herds-man (hûrdz′man), *n.* [*pl.* herdsmen (-men)], one who owns or tends cattle.

here (hēr), *adv.* **1,** in this place; as, I live *here;* in answer to a roll-call, present; **2,** in this direction; hither; as, look *here;* **3,** at this point or moment; as, *here* he paused; **4,** in this world; as, *here* below.

here-a-bout (hēr′a-bout′) or **here-a-bouts** (hēr′a-bouts′), *adv.* in this locality.

here-aft-er (hēr-áf′tẽr), *adv.* after this; henceforth; also, in the life to come:— *n.* the future; also, the life to come.

here-by (hēr-bī′), *adv.* by means of this.

he-red-i-tar-y (he-red′i-tẽr-i), *adj.* **1,** descending from a person to his heir; as, a *hereditary* estate; **2,** holding rank or position by inheritance; as, a *hereditary* ruler; **3,** passed on from parent to child; as, *hereditary* diseases.

he-red-i-ty (he-red′i-ti), *n.* [*pl.* heredities], **1,** the passing on from parent to child of physical or mental traits; **2,** hereditary traits.

here-in (hēr-in′), *adv.* in this.

here-of (hēr-ov′), *adv.* of this; about this; as, we will speak further *hereof.*

here-on (hēr-on′), *adv.* on this; hereupon.

her-e-sy (her′e-si), *n.* [*pl.* heresies], an opinion or doctrine contrary to those commonly accepted on such subjects as religion, politics, or art.

her-e-tic (her′e-tik), *n.* one who holds an opinion contrary to accepted views. —*adj.* **he-ret′i-cal** (he-ret′i-kal).

here-to-fore (hēr′too-fōr′), *adv.* previously; formerly; until now.

here-un-to (hēr′un-tōō′), *adv.* to this; up to the present.

here-up-on (hēr′u-pon′), *adv.* on this; hereon; at this point.

here-with (hēr-wi*th*′; hēr-with′), *adv.* with this; at this point.

her-it-age (her′i-tij), *n.* that which is handed down to an heir; inheritance; also, the lot or condition into which one is born.

her-maph-ro-dite (hûr-maf′ro-dīt′), *n.* a plant or animal having both male and female sexual organs.

her-met-i-cal-ly (hûr-met′i-kal-i), *adv.* made airtight; as, a *hermetically* sealed container.

her-mit (hûr′mit), *n.* one who withdraws from society and lives alone; a recluse.

her-mit-age (hûr′mi-tij), *n.* the home of a recluse or hermit.

her-ni-a (hûr′ni-a), *n.* [*pl.* hernias (hûr′ni-az)], the pushing of part of the intestine through a break in the inner wall of the abdomen; a rupture.

he-ro (hē′rō), *n.* [*pl.* heroes], **1,** a man famed for courage or deeds of prowess; **2,** the chief character in a play, novel, etc.—*n.fem.* **her′o-ine** (her′ō-in).

he-ro-ic (hē-rō′ik) or **he-ro-i-cal** (hē-rō′i-kal), *adj.* **1,** having the qualities of a hero; courageous; as, a *heroic* warrior; **2,** worthy of a hero; bold; brave; as, *heroic* deeds; **3,** having to do with heroes and their deeds; as, *heroic* poetry; the *heroic* age described in Homer's "Iliad."—*adv.* **he-ro′i-cal-ly.**

her-o-in (her′ō-in; hēr), *n.* a white, crystalline narcotic powder derived from morphine.

her-o-ism (her′ō-izm), *n.* heroic conduct; high and noble courage.

her-on (her′un), *n.* a wading bird with long legs, neck, and bill, living in marshes, and feeding on fish, frogs, and insects.

her-pes (hûr′pēz), *n.* an acute skin inflammation in which clusters of blisters keep spreading, as in cold sores or shingles.

her-ring (her′ing), *n.* [*pl.* herring or herrings], a food fish found in North Atlantic waters.

her-ring—bone (her′ing-bōn′), *adj.* composed of rows of short parallel lines slanting in opposite directions from a central rib, like the spine of a herring.

hers (hûrz), a possessive form of *she*, used alone: **1,** as *adj.*, in the predicate, belonging to her; as, whose is that hat? it is *hers;* **2,** as *pron.*, a person or thing that belongs to her; as, which hat have you? I have *hers.*

her-self (hûr-self′), *pron.* **1,** a reflexive form of *her;* as, she cut *herself;* **2,** an emphatic form of *she;* as, she did it *herself;* **3,** her normal or true self; as, she is now *herself* again.

hes-i-tant (hez′i-tant), *adj.* undecided; wavering; hesitating.—*n.* **hes′i-tan-cy.**

hes-i-tate (hez′i-tāt′), *v.i.* [hesitat-ed, hesitat-ing], **1,** to be uncertain; undecided; as, he *hesitates* about going; also, to be unwilling; as, I *hesitate* to take the risk; **2,** to pause for a moment.

hes-i-ta-tion (hez′i-tā′shun), *n.* **1,** uncertainty; doubt; indecision; **2,** a faltering in speech; stammering.

het-er-o-ge-ne-ous (het′ẽr-ō-jē′ni-us), *adj.* dissimilar; consisting of parts of different kinds: opposite of *homogeneous;* as, the *heterogeneous* population of the U.S.

hew (hū), *v.t.* [*p.t.* hewed, *p.p.* hewn (hūn) or hewed, *p.pr.* hew-ing], **1,** to cut or chop, as with an axe; as, to *hew* wood; **2,** to cut down (trees); **3,** to cut into shape; as, to *hew* out a beam:—*v.i.* to strike blows, as with an axe.—*n.* **hew′er.**

hex (heks), *n. Colloq.* spell; enchant-

ment; jinx; as, to put a *hex* on one:—*v.t.* to jinx; bewitch.

hex-a-gon (hek′sa-gon′), *n.* a plane figure with six angles and six sides.—*adj.* **hex-ag′o-nal** (heks-ag′o-nal).

hex-am-e-ter (hek-sam′e-tẽr), *n.* a line or verse with six metrical feet, as in Longfellow's *Evangeline*, Vergil's *Aenead*, or Homer's *Iliad*. HEXAGON

hey-day (hā′dā′), *n.* the time of greatest strength, vigour, bloom, etc.; as, the *heyday* of youth; the *heyday* of chivalry.

hi (hī), *interj.* an exclamation of greeting.

hi-a-tus (hī-ā′tus), *n.* **1,** a break or gap, as where something is missing; thus, a *hiatus* in a manuscript; **2,** a slight pause between two vowels sounded separately, as co-operate.

hi-ber-nate (hī′bẽr-nāt′), *v.i.* [hibernat-ed, hibernat-ing], to pass the winter in a state like sleep, as does the bear; to winter; also, to be inactive.—*n.* **hi′ber-na′tion.**

hi-bis-cus (hī-bis′kus; hi-), *n.* a genus of plants of the mallow family, as the rose of Sharon, a shrub having large showy flowers.

hic-cup (hik′up), *n.* a short, convulsive gasp:—*v.i.* [hiccuped, hiccup-ing], to have hiccups. Also spelled **hic′cough** (hik′up).

hick (hik), *n. Slang*, a farmer; rustic; hayseed (term of contempt).

hick-o-ry (hik′o-ri), *n.* [*pl.* hickories], a North American nut-bearing tree of the walnut family; also, the nut or the tough wood of this tree.

¹hide (hīd), *n.* **1,** the skin, raw or dressed, of an animal; **2,** the human skin:—*v.t.* [hid-ed, hid-ing], *Colloq.* to whip.

²hide (hīd), *v.t.* [*p.t.* hid (hid), *p.p.* hidden (hid′n) or hid, *p.pr.* hid-ing], to conceal; keep secret or unknown; as, to *hide* a letter or a piece of news; also, to turn away; as, to *hide* one's face:—*v.i.* to conceal oneself or to be concealed.

hide-bound (hīd′bound′), *adj.* **1,** having the skin or bark tight (said of cattle or trees); **2,** bigoted; narrow-minded.

hid-e-ous (hid′i-us), *adj.* frightful to look upon; horrible to think of.—*adv.* **hid′e-ous-ly.**—*n.* **hid′e-ous-ness.**

hie (hī), *v.i.* [hied, hy-ing or hie-ing], to make haste.

hi-er-arch-y (hī′ẽr-är′ki), *n.* a system of persons or things in graded ranks, order, etc., as the zoological *hierarchy* of *phylum, class, order, family,* and *species;* **2,** a government of clergy by graded ranks.

hi-er-o-glyph-ic (hī/ĕr-ō-glif/ik), *n*. 1, a picture used as one of the characters in the writing of the ancient Egyptians, Mexicans, etc.; 2, **hieroglyphics**, the picture-writing of the ancient Egyptians; hence, any writing hard HIEROGLYPHICS to read:—*adj*. 1, pertaining to hieroglyphics; 2, symbolic; 3, illegible.

hi-fi (hī/fī/), *n*. Short for *high fidelity*, esp. in sound reproduction.

hig-gle-dy—pig-gle-dy (hig/l-di-pig/l-di), *adv*. in disorder:—*adj*. jumbled together; topsy-turvy:—*n*. confusion; disarray.

high (hī), *adj*. 1, far above the ground or sea level; as, a *high* plateau; also, tall; as, a *high* tree; a tower 30 feet *high*; 2, noble; lofty; as, *high* aims; 3, chief; important; as, *high* government officials; 4, elated; lively; as, *high* spirits; 5, intense or extreme; as, *high* speed; *high* favour; a *high* colour; 6, strong, violent, or tempestuous; as, *high* winds; angry; as, *high* words; 7, at the full; as, *high* tide; 8, expensive; as, food is *high;* not low; as, prices are *high;* 9, shrill or sharp; as, a *high* tone:—*adv*. 1, to a great altitude or degree; 2, extravagantly; as, to live *high;* 3, proudly; as, to hold one's head *high;* 4, in a shrill or loud pitch.

high-ball (hī/bôl/), *n*. 1, a railroad signal meaning 'go ahead'; 2, an alcoholic drink diluted with soda water, ginger ale, etc., and served with ice in a tall glass.

high-brow (hī/brou/), *n*. *Slang*, a person highly educated or intellectual, or affecting to be so:—*adj*. *Slang*, intellectual; cultured.

high-fa-lu-tin or **high-fa-lu-ting** (hī/fa-lōo/tin; ting), *adj*. *Colloq*. pretentious; pompous.

high—hand-ed (hī/–han/did),*adj*.arbitrary; overbearing.

high-hole (hī/hōl/) or **high-holder** (-hōl/dĕr),—*n*. the flicker.

high-land (hī/land), *n*. high or mountainous land.

high-ly (hī/li), *adv*. in a high degree; as, *highly* coloured; favourable; as, to speak *highly* of someone; also, at a high price or rate; as, *highly* paid.

high—mind-ed (hī/–mīn/did), *adj*. honourable; having a lofty or noble character.

high-ness (hī/nes), *n*. the state or condition of being high; height:—**Highness**,

a title of honour applied to persons of royal rank; as, His Royal *Highness*.

high-road, a chief or much-travelled road or highway.

high-way (hī/wā/), *n*. 1, a main road; highroad; 2, any public road.

high-way-man (hī/wā/man), *n*. one who robs on a public road by holding up his victims.

hi-jack-er or **high-jack-er** (hī/jak/-ĕr), *n*. *Colloq*. one who steals goods in transit, esp. by holdup of trucks carrying bootleg or smuggled liquor.—*v.t.* **hi/jack/**.

hike (hīk), *Colloq. v.i.* [hiked, hik-ing], to tramp or walk:—*n*. a long walk or march.

hi-lar-i-ty (hi-lar/i-ti; hī-lâr/i-ti), *n*. [*pl.* hilarities], noisy merriment; jollity. —*adj*. **hi-lar/i-ous** (hi-lâr/i-us; hī-lâr/i-us).

hill (hil), *n*. 1, a natural elevation lower than a mountain; 2, a small mound or heap; as, an ant-*hill*:—*v.t.* to form into a mound; surround with a mound of earth; as, to *hill* potatoes.—*adj*. **hill/y**. —*n*. **hill/i-ness**.

hill-bil-ly (hil/bil/i), *n*. and *adj*. *U.S. Colloq*. a person, often illiterate or uncouth, from the mountains or backwoods of Southern U.S.; *hillbilly* music.

hill-ock (hil/uk), *n*. a small hill.

hill-side (hil/sīd/), *n*. the side of a hill

hilt (hilt), *n*. a handle of a sword or dagger.

him (him), *pron*. the objective case of *he;* as, they found *him*.

him-self (him-self/), *pron*. 1, a reflexive form of *him;* as, he hurt *himself;* 2 an emphatic form of *he;* as, he *himself* went; 3, his normal or true self; as, he came to *himself*.

¹**hind** (hīnd), *adj*. [*comp*. hind-er, *superl* hind-most or hind-er-most], at the rear as, the *hind* wheels of a wagon.

²**hind** (hīnd), *n*. the female of the red deer, esp. in and after the third year opposite of *stag*.

¹**hind-er** (hīn/dĕr), *adj*. [*comp*. of *hind*] rear; back.

²**hind-er** (hin/dĕr), *v.t.* to keep back slow up; as, the snow *hindered* ou progress.

hind-most (hīnd/mōst) or **hind-er-most** (hīnd/ĕr-mōst), *adj*. [*superl*. o *hind*], farthest back.

hind quar-ter, the back part of half carcass, as of beef, lamb, or veal.

hin-drance (hin/drans), *n*. the act o hindering; also, an obstruction.

hind-sight (hīnd/sīt/), *n*. seeing, afte

an event, what should have been done: opposite of *foresight*.

hinge (hinj), *n.* a jointed device or mechanism by means of which a movable part, as a door or lid, is made to turn or swing:—*v.t.* [hinged, hinging], to furnish or attach with a hinge: *v.i.* to turn or depend, as on a hinge; as, my answer *hinges* on the decision you make.

hint (hint), *v.t.* to suggest slightly; refer to indirectly:—*v.i.* to make an indirect suggestion:—*n.* an indirect or veiled suggestion.

hin-ter-land (hin′tẽr-land′), *n.* an inland region; **2,** remote or undeveloped part of a country.

hip (hip), *n.* the widening fleshy part of the body on either side below the waist, formed by the sides of the pelvis and the upper part of the thigh; the haunch.

hip-po-drome (hip′o-drōm′), *n.* a building or arena for circuses, games, theatricals, etc.

hip-po-pot-a-mus (hip′o-pot′a-mus), *n.* [*pl.* hippopotamuses or hippopotami (hip′o-pot′-a-mī)], a huge land and water animal, common near rivers in Africa, with big head and mouth, thick hide, and short legs.

HIPPOPOTAMUS ($\frac{1}{125}$)

hire (hīr), *v.t.* [hired, hir-ing], **1,** to engage the service of, for a price; employ (a servant) for wages; **2,** to secure the temporary use of, for a price; to rent; as, to *hire* a horse for a day; **3,** to grant the temporary use of, for a price; as, to *hire* out a horse:—*n.* **1,** the act of hiring; **2,** the wages paid for personal service; **3,** the price paid for the use of anything.

hire-ling (hīr′ling), *n.* one who serves for wages, esp. one whose interest is centred in the wages rather than in the work:—*adj.* mercenary; working for pay.

hir-sute (hûr′sūt; hẽr-sōōt′), *adj.* rough with hair or bristles; as, a *hirsute* skin or face.

his (hiz), the possessive form of *he,* used: **1,** as *adj.,* belonging to him; as, this is *his* hat; this hat is *his;* **2,** as *pron.,* a person or thing that belongs to him; as, I have my hat, and he has *his.*

hiss (his), *n.* **1,** the sharp sound made in the pronunciation of the letter *s;* also, this sound uttered as an exclamation of disapproval or contempt; **2,** a similar sound; as, the *hiss* of water on a hot stove; the *hiss* of a snake:—*v.i.* to make a hiss; as,. they *hissed* during his speech:—*v.t.* **1,** to express contempt for by hissing; as, the audience *hissed* the actors; **2,** to utter with a hiss; as, to *hiss* one's words.—*n.* **hiss′ing.**

hist (hist), *interj.* hush! hark! as, *hist!* what was that sound?

his-tor-ic (his-tor′ik), *adj.* belonging to, connected with, or famous in history; as, a *historic* spot.

his-tor-i-cal (his-tor′i-kal), *adj.* **1,** of or pertaining to history; as, *historical* studies; **2,** based on history; as, a *historical* play; **3,** true to history; not legendary; as, a *historical* event.—*adv.* **his-tor′i-cal-ly.**

his-to-ry (his′to-ri), *n.* [*pl.* histories], **1,** a written narrative of past facts and events affecting one or more peoples, countries, institutions, sciences, etc., usually with comments and explanations; **2,** the branch of learning that studies, records, and explains past facts and events; **3,** past facts or events referring to a particular person, nation, etc.; as, this house has a strange *history.*—*n.* **his-tor′i-an.**

his-tri-on-ic (his′tri-on′ik), *adj.* pertaining to the stage or acting; as, she has *histrionic* ability.—*n.* **his′tri-on′ics.**

hit (hit), *v.t.* hit, [hit-ting], **1,** to strike or give a blow to; as, to *hit* an opponent; **2,** to bring hard against something; as, to *hit* one's head on a post; **3,** to deliver; as, to *hit* a hard blow; **4,** to touch or reach; as, to *hit* the ceiling; **5,** to wound the feeling of; as, he was hard *hit* by failure:—*v.i.* **1,** to strike or deliver a blow; as, *hit* hard; **2,** to clash or collide; as, the two cars *hit* head-on; **3,** to come or light (upon); as, to *hit* upon the answer; **4,** *Colloq.* of gasoline engines, to fire or explode; as, the motor *hits* on all four cylinders:—*n.* **1,** a stroke or blow; **2,** a success; as, the song was a *hit;* **3,** in baseball, a ball so hit as to enable the batter to reach first base successfully.—*n.* **hit′ter.**

hitch (hich), *v.t.* **1,** to fasten or tie; as, the pony was *hitched* to the post; **2,** to pull up with a jerk; as, *hitch* up your skirt:—*v.i.* **1,** to become fastened or entangled; **2,** to move jerkily; hobble: —*n.* **1,** a sudden pull or jerk; as, a *hitch* of the reins; **2,** a sudden stop; an obstacle; as, there was no *hitch* in the arrangements; **3,** a kind of noose or knot, used esp. on shipboard for temporary fastening.

hitch-hike (hich′hīk′), *v.i.* to travel by thumbing rides from motorists.

hith-er (hith′ẽr), *adv.* to or toward this place; here:—*adj.* nearer to the speaker.

hith-er-to (hith'ẽr-tōō'), *adv.* to this time; till now.

hith-er-ward (hith'ẽr-wẽrd) or **hith-er-wards** (hith'ẽr-wẽrdz), *adv.* to this place; in this direction.

hive (hīv), *n.* 1, a box or house for bees; 2, a swarm of bees in a hive; 3, a very busy place; also, a swarming multitude:—*v.i.* [hived, hiv-ing], to enter a hive, as bees; also, to live together in swarms; as, people *hive* in a city:—*v.t.* 1, to put (bees) into a hive; 2, to store, as, honey.

hives (hīvz), *n.pl.* a disease marked by the appearance of a rash accompanied by intense itching.

ho (hō), *interj.* 1, an expression of delight, surprise, etc., or, when repeated, mockery; 2, stop! also, **whoa.**

hoar (hōr), *adj.* 1, white; as, *hoar*frost; 2, grey with age; as, *hoar* locks.

hoard (hōrd), *n.* a secret store or treasure; a collection of things kept in reserve:—*v.i.* to lay up money or goods: *v.t.* to lay up or store secretly; as, to *hoard* gold.—*n.* **hoard'er.**—*n.* **hoard'ing.**

hoar-frost (hōr'frost'), *n.* white frost; tiny ice particles from the moisture in the night air.

hoar-hound (hōr'hound'), *n.* Same as **hore'hound'.**

hoarse (hōrs), *adj.* [hoars-er, hoars-est], 1, harsh or rough in sound; as, a *hoarse* voice; 2, having a rough voice or making a rough rasping sound; as, a *hoarse* foghorn.—*adv.* **hoarse'ly.**—*n.* **hoarse'ness.**

hoar-y (hōr'i), *adj.* [hoar-i-er, hoar-i-est], 1, white or grey with age; as, *hoary* hair; 2, old; venerable.

hoax (hōks), *n.* a mischievous trick or practical joke; also, a fraud:—*v.t.* to trick.

hob (hob), *n.* 1, the projecting ledge of a fireplace for keeping a kettle warm; 2, mischief (as by elf or goblin); hence, to *play hob with.*

hob-ble (hob'l), *v.i.* [hob-bled, hob-bling], to walk with a limp or go unevenly:—*v.t.* 1, to make lame; 2, to hamper, as a horse, by tying its legs:— *n.* 1, a limping walk; 2, a rope or fetter for hobbling horses.

hob-by (hob'i), *n.* [*pl.* hobbies], a favourite interest aside from one's business.

hob-by-horse (hob'i-hôrs'), *n.* 1, a stick with a horse's head, on which children pretend to ride; 2, a wooden rocking-horse; 3, a wooden horse on a merry-go-round.

hob-gob-lin (hob'gob'lin), *n.* 1, a mischievous elf; 2, an evil sprite of frightful appearance; a bogy.

hob-nail (hob'nāl), *n.* a short, thick large-headed nail for protecting the soles of heavy boots, and to prevent slipping.

hob-nob (hob'nob'), *v.i.* [hob-nobbed, hob-nob-bing], to drink or talk together be on intimate terms; as, the old cronies *hobnobbed* all winter.

ho-bo (hō'bō), *n.* [*pl.* hobos or hoboes], an idle, shiftless vagrant; a tramp.

¹hock (hok), *n.* the joint, as of a horse's hind leg, corresponding to the human ankle.

²hock (hok), *v.t. Slang,* to pawn.

hock-ey (hok'i), *n.* 1, a game originating in Canada played on ice skates in a rink by teams of 6 men to a side (goalie, 2 defencemen, 3 forwards) with sticks having blades for controlling and shooting a rubber puck; 2, **field hockey**, a similar game played with a ball in a field.

ho-cus—po-cus (hō'kus-pō'kus), *n.* 1 meaningless words used as a formula by a magician or conjurer; 2, sleight of hand; 3, trickery; deception.

hod (hod), *n.* 1, a wooden trough for carrying mortar or bricks; 2, a coal scuttle.

hodge-podge (hoj'poj'), *n.* a stew of meat and vegetables; hence, any mixture or jumble.

hoe (hō), *n.* a flat-bladed, long-handled garden tool for loosening soil, removing weeds, etc.:—*v.t.* [hoed (hōd), hoe-ing] 1, to till or loosen with a hoe; 2, to clean of weeds; as, he *hoed* his garden every week:—*v.i.* to work with a hoe.

hoe-down (hō'doun'), *n.* a lively rollicking dance, as a square dance.

hog (hog), *n.* 1, a full-grown domestic swine; also, any of various similar animals, as the wart-hog; 2, *Colloq.* a grasping or greedy person; also, a coarse, dirty person:—*v.t.* [hogged hog-ging], *Slang,* to take more than a fair share of. Compounds: hog'barn' hog'house'; hog'pen'.

hogs-head (hogz'hed'), *n.* 1, a liquid measure equal to 52½ imperial gallons 2, a large cask holding up to 140 gallons.

hog-wash (hog'wôsh'), *n. Colloq.* 1 swill fed to hogs; 2, empty phrases worthless matter.

hoi pol-loi (hoi' po-loi'), *n. Greek* the common people; the masses: used patronizingly or contemptuously (Often wrongly for "upper classes."

hoist (hoist), *v.t.* to raise aloft; as, to *hoist* a flag; to raise by means of a pulley or other tackle:—*n.* 1, an apparatus for hoisting; a tackle; an elevator; **2,** *Colloq.* a push; a lift.

ɪo-kum (hō′kum), *n. Slang,* humbug; nonsense; bunk.

hold (hōld), *n.* the interior of a ship below deck.

hold (hōld), *v.t.* [*p.t.* held (held), *p.p.* held or, *Arcahic,* hold-en (hōl′dn), *p.pr.* holding], **1,** to have in one's hand or grasp; as, to *hold* a book; also, to keep in place; support; as, a shelf *holds* books; **2,** to keep possession of; defend; as, the defenders *held* the fortress; **3,** to contain; as, this bottle *holds* a quart; **4,** to restrain or check; as, *hold* your tongue; to detain; as, to *hold* a train; **5,** to believe or accept; as, to *hold* an opinion; to think; consider; as, the court *held* that the defendant was guilty; **6,** to keep in a particular state; as, to *hold* one's head erect; to *hold* someone in esteem; **7,** to maintain or carry on; as, to *hold* an argument; **8,** to conduct; as, the club *held* a meeting; also, to preside at; as, the judge *holds* court; **9,** to keep or observe (a festival); **10,** to occupy; have title to; as, to *hold* political office: —*v.i.* **1,** to keep a grasp on something; as, the anchor *holds;* **2,** to remain faithful; as, to *hold* to a purpose; **3,** to remain unbroken or unchanged; as, our ranks *held;* my offer still *holds* good; **4,** to keep going; as, to *hold* to one's course:—*n.* **1,** the act of holding; grasp; **2,** something that may be grasped for support; **3,** influence or control; as, the supernatural has a strong *hold* on him; **4,** in *music,* a character placed over [↑] or under [↓] a note or rest to show that it is to be prolonged; a pause.—*n.* hold′er. Compounds: hold′out′; hold′o′ver; hold′-up′.—*n.* holding company, a company organized to hold stocks or bonds of other companies, which it usually controls, in order to derive income from them.

ɪole (hōl), *n.* **1,** an opening in or through something; as, a *hole* in the roof; **2,** a cavity in something solid; as, a *hole* in a tooth; **3,** an abrupt hollow in the ground, as a pit or a cave; also, a deep place in a stream; as, a swimming-*hole;* **4,** the burrow of an animal; hence, a den, or hiding-place; **5,** *Colloq.* a difficulty; **6,** in *golf:* a, a cup, or hollow, in the putting-green into which the ball is to be played; b, the part of a course from a tee to such a cup:—*v.t.* [holed, hol-ing], **1,** to drive or put into a hole; **2,** to make holes in; as, to *hole* a board for pegs:—*v.i.* **1,** to go into a hole; **2,** to make a hole; as, to *hole* through a wall; **3,** in *golf,* to put a ball in the hole.—*adj.* hole′y.

hol-i-day (hol′i-dā′), *n.* **1,** a day of gaiety and joy, as in celebration of some event; **2,** a day of freedom from labour:—*adj.* festive; gay; as, in holiday dress.

ho-li-ness (hō′li-nis), *n.* the state or equality of being free from sin; saintliness:—**His Holiness,** a title of the Pope.

hol-land (hol′and), *n.* fine unbleached linen or cotton used for window shades, garments, upholstery, etc.

hol-ler (hol′ėr), *v.i.* and *v.t. Colloq.* to shout; yell; as, he *hollered* for help.

hol-lo (ho-lō′; hol′ō), *interj.* What ho! Stop! Also, hal-lo′; hal-loa′.

hol-low (hol′ō), *n.* **1,** a cavity; as, the *hollow* of a tree; **2,** space between hills; a valley:—*v.t.* to scoop out; as, he *hollowed* out the sand:—*adj.* **1,** having an empty space within; as, a *hollow* shell; **2,** sunken; haggard; as, a *hollow* face; **3,** unreal; insincere; as, *hollow* words of sympathy; **4,** deep or dull; as, a *hollow* roar:—*adv. Colloq.* completely; as, they beat us all *hollow.*—*adv.* hol′low-ly.—*n.* hol′low-ness.

hol-ly (hol′i), *n.* [*pl.* hollies], a shrub or tree, the glossy leaves and red berries of which are much used as decorations at Christmas-time.

hol-ly-hock (hol′i-hok), *n.* a tall plant, much cultivated in gardens, that has large flowers of various colours.

hol-o-caust (hol′o-kôst′), *n.* a great destruction of lives or property, esp. by fire.

hol-ster (hōl′stėr), *n.* a leather pistol-case, carried at the belt or fixed to a saddle.

ho-lus—bo-lus (hō′lus-bō′lus), *adv. Colloq.* all at once; all together; as, he swallowed the story *holus-bolus.*

ho-ly (hō′li), *adj.* [ho-li-er, ho-li-est], **1,** dedicated to the service of God; as, *holy* ground; **2,** perfect; divine; as, the *Holy* Spirit; **3,** devoted to God; given over to piety; as, the *holy* saints: —*n.* [*pl.* holies], a sacred thing; anything that is holy.

hom-age (hom′ij), *n.* **1,** reverence; respect; **2,** in feudal times, the ceremony in which a vassal promised loyalty and service to his lord in return for protection.

hom-bre (ôm′brä; om′bri), *n.* [*Spanish,* man], *Slang,* fellow.

Hom-burg (hom′burg; hom′boorkh), *n.* a man's soft felt hat with partially rolled brim, worn with the crown dented lengthwise.

home (hōm), *n.* **1,** one's fixed residence

or dwelling-place; hence, the unit of society formed by a family living together; **2,** one's native land; **3,** an institution or asylum for the care or relief of some class of persons; as, an orphans' *home;* **4,** in various games, a goal:—*adv.* **1,** to or at home; **2,** to the heart or core; as, the blow struck *home:* —*v.i.* [homed, hom-ing], to return home as pigeons; also, to have a home; dwell.—*adj.* **home′less.** Compounds: **home′land′; home′like′; home′made′ home′sick′; home′work′.**

home-ly (hōm′li), *adj.* [home-li-er, home-li-est], **1,** homelike; plain; simple; as, *homely* fare; **2,** plain-featured; **3,** unpolished; unpretending; as, *homely* manners.

ho-mer (hō′mẽr), *n. Colloq.* in *baseball,* a home run.

home-spun (hōm′spun′), *n.* **1,** cloth made of yarn spun at home; **2,** a loosely woven, woollen fabric:—*adj.* **1,** made at home; **2,** plain and homely.

home-stead (hōm′sted), *n.* a family home with the adjoining lands and buildings.—*n.* **home′stead′er.**

home-ward (hōm′wẽrd), *adj.* and *adv.* toward home or one's native land; as, *homeward* bound.—*adv.* **home′wards.**

hom-i-cide (hom′i-sīd′), *n.* **1,** the killing of a human being by another; **2,** one who kills another.—*adj.* **hom′i-cid′al.**

hom-i-ly (hom′i-li), *n.* **1,** a sermon; **2,** a tedious, moralizing lecture.

hom-i-ny (hom′i-ni), *n.* hulled Indian corn, or maize, coarsely ground or broken, used as a cereal and as a vegetable.

ho-moe-o-path-ic (hō′mi-ō-path′ik; hom′i-ō-path′ik), *adj.* naming or employing a method of treating disease in which drugs are given that will produce in healthy persons effects like those of the disease. Also spelled **ho′me-o-path′ic.**

ho-mo-ge-ne-ous (hō′mō-jē′nē-us; hom′ō-jē′nē-us), *adj.* uniform; of the same kind or nature; made up of similar parts: opposite of *heterogeneous;* as, the *homogeneous* population of Japan.

ho-mo-gen-ize (ho-moj′en-īz′; hō′), *v.t.* to make more uniform in texture by breaking down and blending the particles, esp. to break up the fat and casein globules of milk to make it more digestible.

hom-o-nym (hom′o-nim), *n.* any of two or more words, the same in sound but different in meaning and often in

spelling, as pair, pare, pear, and to, too, two.

ho-mo-sex-u-al (hō′mō-sek′shoo-al), *n.* and *adj.* one who feels sexually attracted to a person of the same sex.— *n.* **ho′mo-sex′u-al′i-ty.**

hone (hōn), *n.* a fine-grained stone for sharpening razors and keen-edged tools —*v.t.* [honed, hon-ing], to sharpen on such a stone.

hon-est (on′est), *adj.* **1,** upright; just; as, an *honest* man; truthful; sincere as, an *honest* opinion; **2,** genuine without fraud; as, *honest* weight; **3,** frank; expressing sincerity; as, an *honest* countenance.—*adv.* **hon′est-ly** —*n.* **hon′es-ty.**

hon-ey (hun′i), *n.* **1,** a sweet, sticky substance, produced by bees from the nectar which they collect from flowers **2,** sweetness; **3,** darling; sweetheart

hon-ey-bee (hun′i-bē′), *n.* a be which gathers nectar from flowers t make honey. Man keeps honeybees i hives for the sake of their wax an honey.

hon-ey-comb (hun′i-kōm′), *n.* **1,** wax structure of six-sided cells mad by bees to hold their honey and thei eggs; **2,** any similar structure:—*v.t.* an *v.i.* to fill, or become filled, with hole passages, or cells; as, miners ha *honeycombed* the ground beneath th town.

hon-ey-dew (hun′i-dū′), *n.* **1,** a swee liquid that exudes from some plants i hot weather; **2,** a pale-green musl melon of sweet flavour and whit flesh, the **honeydew melon.**

hon-eyed (hun′id), *adj.* **1,** covered o filled with honey; **2,** sweet; coaxin as, *honeyed* words. Also, **hon′ied.**

hon-ey-moon (hun′i-mōōn′), *n.* holiday spent together by a new married couple; a wedding trip:—*v.* to spend a honeymoon.

hon-ey-suck-le (hun′i-suk′l), *n.* climbing plant with fragrant white, re or yellow tube-shaped flowers.

honk (hongk), *n.* **1,** the call of a wil goose; **2,** any sound resembling thi as, the *honk* of an automobile horn:- *v.i.* to make such a sound:—*v.t.* t sound or blow (a horn).

hon-o-ra-ri-um (on′o-râ′ri-um), *n.* a payment recognizing profession services for which propriety forbids set price; **2,** a fee for the services of professional person.

hon-or-ar-y (on′ẽr-a-ri), *adj.* **1,** give as a mark of honour, esteem, meri etc.; as, an *honorary* title or degree; holding a position or office as honour without its responsibilities, pay, etc.; as, *honorary* president.

hon-our or **hon-or** (on′ĕr), *n.* **1,** respectful regard; high esteem; as, to show *honour* to one's parents; an outward mark of high esteem; as, military *honours;* **2,** glory; fame; as, Hector fought for the *honour* of Troy; **3,** distinction; as, the *honour* of being president; also, a cause of glory; a credit; as, he is an *honour* to the town; **4,** uprightness; integrity; as, a man of *honour;* **5,** **honours,** distinguished standing in school or college; as, he was graduated with *honours:*—**Honour,** a title of respect; as, his *Honour,* the mayor:— *v.t.* **1,** to treat with respect or deference; revere; as, "*Honour* thy father and thy mother"; **2,** to bestow marks of esteem upon; as, he was *honoured* with the title of captain; **3,** to accept and pay when due; as, the bank will *honour* my cheque. In U.S., often spelled **hon′or.**

hon-our-a-ble or **hon-or-a-ble** (on′ĕr-a-bl), *adj.* **1,** noble; illustrious; as, *honourable* deeds; **2,** upright; honest; as, an *honourable* man; an *honourable* purpose; **3,** in accord with honour; as, an *honourable* discharge; **4,** accompanied with honour or marks of respect; as, *honourable* burial:— **Honourable,** a title of distinction of certain officials.—*adv.* **hon′ our-a-bly.**

hood (hood), *n.* **1,** a soft wrapper or covering for the head, sometimes attached to a cloak; **2,** something resembling such a head-covering in shape or use, as a folding cover for a carriage, automobile engine, etc.; **3,** an ornamental fold hanging down the back of a gown worn by a graduate of a college or university, denoting, by its colour, the wearer's degree:—*v.t.* to cover, or furnish with, or as with, a hood.—*adj.* **hood′ed.**

hood-lum (hood′lum), *n. Colloq.* a rowdy; street rough; ruffian. Sometimes abbreviated to *hood* (*slang*).

hoo-doo (hoo′doo′), *n. Colloq.* a person or thing that causes bad luck:—*v.t.* [-dooed (dood), -dooing], to bring bad luck; bewitch.

hood-wink (hood′wingk), *v.t.* **1,** to deceive; mislead; **2,** to blindfold.

hoof (hoof), *n.* [*pl.* hoofs (hoofs) or, rarely, hooves (hoovz)], the horny substance covering the toes of some animals, as horses; also, the whole foot. —*adj.* **hoofed.** Also used as *v.* (*Slang*).

hook (hook), *n.* **1,** a curved piece of metal, bone, etc., to hold or catch something; as, a crochet-*hook;* a fish*hook;* **2,** a curved instrument, as a sickle, for looping or cutting; **3,** a sharp bend or curve, as in a river; **4,** *Nautical* (*Colloq.*), an anchor; **5,** in *music,* a line or stroke at the end of the stem of a note to show that it is an eighth, sixteenth, etc.; **6,** in *baseball,* a curve; **7,** in *boxing,* a swinging blow; **8,** in *golf,* a stroke that is curved or pulled sharply to the left by a right-handed player, or to the right by a left-handed player.—**by hook or by crook,** by fair means or foul:—*v.t.* to catch with, or as with, a hook; as, to *hook* a fish; hence, to steal; also, to fasten with a hook or hooks; as, *hook* the gate:—*v.i.* **1,** to bend or curve sharply; as, this road *hooks* to the left; **2,** to be fastened by a hook; as, this skirt *hooks* on the side.

hook-ah (hook′a), *n.* an Oriental smoking pipe with a long flexible tube for drawing the smoke through water contained in a vase.

hooked (hookt; hook′id), *adj.* **1,** curved like a hook; as, a *hooked* nose; **2,** made with a hook; as, a *hooked* rug; **3,** furnished with hooks; as, a *hooked* dress; **4,** *Slang,* trapped.

hook-up (hook′up′), *n.* **1,** the connecting with wires, as of apparatus for radio or television reception or transmission; **2,** a chain of radio or television stations linked for a broadcast; as, a continent-wide *hookup.*

hook-worm (hook′wûrm′), *n.* a worm, most common in warm climates, that sometimes enters the intestines of man and certain animals, as through infected drinking-water or food, and causes a disease marked by progressive weakness and emaciation.

hook-y (hook′i), *n. School slang,* used only in the expression *to play hooky,* or truant.

hoo-li-gan (hoo′li-gan), *n. Slang,* a hoodlum; a young ruffian, esp. a member of a street gang.—*n.* **hoo′li-gan-ism.**

hoop (hoop), *n.* **1,** a circular metal or wooden band to hold together narrow, curving strips forming the sides of a cask, tub, etc.; **2,** a large circle of metal or wood rolled along the ground by children; **3,** **hoops,** a circular framework of wire, whalebone, etc., formerly used to expand a woman's skirt; a hoop skirt; **4,** in *croquet,* a metal arch or wicket:—*v.t.* to bind with a hoop; encircle.

hoop skirt, a skirt expanded by means of a circular framework of wire, whalebone, etc.

hoot (hoot), *n.* **1,** the cry of an owl; as, a long *hoot* sounded through the woods; **2,** a sound like this cry; **3,** a shout of contempt:—*v.t.* to jeer with contemptuous shouts; as, to *hoot* an actor: *v.i.* **1,** to utter a sharp cry, as an owl; **2,** to utter shouts of derision or contempt; as, the audience *hooted* and jeered at the speaker.

¹hop (hop), *n.* **1,** a vine with small, greenish, cone-shaped flowers; **2, hops,** the dried, ripened cones of this plant, used to give a bitter flavour to beer, ale, etc.:—*v.t.* [hopped, hop-ping], to flavour with hops:—*v.i.* to pick hops.

²hop (hop), *v.t.* [hopped, hop-ping], to jump over; as, to *hop* a fence:—*v.i.* **1,** to move by short jumps, using one leg only; **2,** to jump with both or all feet at once, as do frogs:—*n.* **1,** a short, brisk jump, esp. on one leg; **2,** *Colloq.* an informal dance.

hope (hōp), *n.* **1,** desire accompanied by expectation; anticipation; confidence; as, an invalid's *hope* of speedy recovery; **2,** the thing desired; as, success in business was his constant *hope;* **3,** a cause or source of hope; as, he was the *hope* of his parents:—*v.t.* [hoped, hop-ing], to desire; expect; as, he *hopes* his efforts will be successful:—*v.i.* to cherish a desire; as, we *hope* for better times.

hope-ful (hōp'fool), *adj.* **1,** full of confident expectations; as, he is *hopeful* that he will be able to go; **2,** promising success; as, *hopeful* news.— *adv.* **hope'ful-ly.**—*n.* **hope'ful-ness.**

hope-less (hōp'lis), *adj.* **1,** without expectation of good; despairing; as, *hopeless* grief; **2,** without promise of good; as, a *hopeless* situation.—*adv.* **hope'less-ly.**—*n.* **hope'less-ness.**

hop-per (hop'ẽr), *n.* **1,** one who or that which hops; **2,** any of various leaping insects; as, the grass*hopper;* **3,** a wooden funnel through which grain passes into a mill, or any device like this.

hop-scotch (hop'skoch'), *n.* a child's game, in which the players hop or skip from one space to another of a design on the ground.

horde (hōrd), *n.* **1,** a wandering tribe or clan; as, a gipsy *horde;* **2,** a vast multitude, as of insects.

hore-hound (hōr'hound'), *n.* **1,** an Old World herb having a bitter juice good for colds and coughs; **2,** a hard brittle candy flavoured with this juice. Also, **hoar'hound'.**

HOP-SCOTCH

ho-ri-zon (ho-rī'zn), *n.* **1,** the line where the sky and earth, or the sky and sea, appear to meet; **2,** the range or limit of one's mental experience or interest.

hor-i-zon-tal (hor'i-zon'tal), *adj.* parallel to, or in the direction of, the line where earth meets sky; level: opposite of *vertical.*—*adv.* **hor'i-zon'-tal-ly.**

hor-mone (hôr'mōn), *n.* a secretion of organs or glands, such as the adrenal and pituitary, that excites or increases a vital process in remoter cells when carried to them by body fluids.

horn (hôrn), *n.* **1,** a hard, usually pointed, outgrowth on the head of certain animals, esp. cattle, goats, deer, etc.; **2,** the material of which animals' horns are composed, or a similar material; **3,** anything made of or resembling the horns of an animal, as one of the ends of the moon when in crescent form; **4,** a musical wind-instrument, as a French horn or an English horn.

horn-bill (hôrn'bil'), *n.* any of the large tropical birds with enormous horny bills and partly united toes.

horn-blende (hôrn'blend'), *n.* a dark silicate of calcium and magnesium found in granite and other igneous rocks.

hor-net (hôr'nit), *n.* a large wasp which inflicts a severe sting.

horn-pipe (hôrn'pīp'), *n.* **1,** a lively dance, esp. popular with sailors; **2,** music for this dance; **3,** a musical wind-instrument, once much used in Wales.

horn-y (hôr'ni), *adj.* [horn-i-er, horn-i-est], **1,** hard like horn; **2,** made of horn; **3,** having horns.

hor-o-scope (hor'o-skōp'), *n.* **1,** the conjunction, or relative position, of the planets and stars at one's birth; **2,** the foretelling of the events of one's life from such position (not regarded as scientific); **3,** the diagram showing the 12 signs of the zodiac (used by astrologers).

hor-ren-dous (ho-ren'dus), *adj.* frightful; exciting terror.

hor-ri-ble (hor'i-bl), *adj.* **1,** terrible; dreadful; as, a *horrible* train wreck; **2,** *Colloq.* severe; extreme; as, a *horrible* headache.—*adv.* **hor'ri-bly.**

hor-rid (hor'id), *adj.* terrible; hideous; as, a *horrid* monster.

hor-ri-fy (hor'i-fī'), *v.t.* [horrified, horrify-ing], to fill or strike with great fear or dread.

hor-ror (hor'ẽr), *n.* **1,** excessive fear; extreme dread; as, they were filled with *horror* at the thought of war; **2,** great

cat, āge, fär, câre, àsk; ten, ēve, latẽr; (i) pity, rely, senate; īce; top· nō.

disgust or aversion; as, she has a *horror* of dirt; **3,** that which causes dread.

hors d'oeuvres (ôr'dûvr'), *French,* an appetizer, as olives or radish, served at the beginning of a meal.

horse (hôrs), *n.* **1,** a large, solid-hoofed, four-footed animal, used for drawing burdens or riding; **2,** mounted soldiers; cavalry; **3,** a framework for the support of anything; as, a clothes-*horse;* **4,** in *gymnastics,* a padded and raised wooden block used for vaulting: —**dark horse, 1,** in horse-racing, a horse whose chances of success have been overlooked; *esp.* an unexpected winner; **2,** in *politics,* an unforeseen competitor:—*v.t.* [horsed, hors-ing], to mount on, or furnish with, a horse.

horse-back (hôrs'bak'), *n.* the back of a horse:—*adv.* on horseback.

horse—chest-nut (hôrs'—ches'nut), *n.* a tree with large clusters of white or pink blossoms and brown seeds growing in burs; also, the seed of this tree.

horse-fly (hôrs'flī'), *n.* [*pl.* horse-flies], a large, two-winged fly that stings animals.

horse-hair (hôrs'hâr'), *n.* **1,** the hair of the mane or tail of a horse; **2,** cloth made from this hair.

horse-hide (hôrs'hīd'), *n.* the skin of a horse or the leather made from it.

horse-man (hôrs'man), *n.* [*pl.* horse-men (-men)], **1,** a rider on horseback; **2,** a person who is clever at managing horses.—*n. fem.* **horse'wom'an.**—*n.* **horse'man-ship.**

horse opera, *Slang,* a play about cowboys, rustlers, etc.

horse-play (hôrs'plā'), *n.* rough fun.

horse-power (hôrs'pou'ėr), *n.* a unit of power; the amount of power required to raise 30,000 pounds one foot in one minute.

horse-rad-ish (hôrs'rad'ish), *n.* **1,** a plant of the mustard family, the root of which is ground and used as a relish with meats, fish, etc.; **2,** the relish made from this root.

horse-shoe (hôrs'shoo'), *n.* **1,** a U-shaped metal shoe to protect the hoof of a horse; **2,** anything shaped like a horseshoe.

horse-tail (hôrs'tāl'), *n.* the scouring rush or equisetum, a widely growing flowerless plant with hollow, jointed stems.

horse-whip (hôrs'whip'), *n.* a leather whip for managing horses:—*v.t.* [horse-whipped, horse-whip-ping], to flog.

hor-sy (hôr'si), *adj. Colloq.* fond of horses, racing, fox-hunting, etc., or

affecting the ways of those who are; as, *horsy* talk.

hor-ti-cul-ture (hôr'ti-kul'tūr), *n.* the art or science of growing vegetables, fruits, and flowers.—*adj.* **hor'ti-cul'tur-al.**—*n.* **hor'ti-cul'tur-ist.**

ho-san-na (hō'zan-a), *n.* and *interj.* an exclamation of praise to God.

hose (hōz), *n.* [*pl.* hose], **1,** a covering for the leg; a stocking; **2,** a tight-fitting covering for the legs and waist, formerly worn by men; **3,** [*pl.* sometimes hoses], flexible tubing for carrying liquids; as, a *hose* for sprinkling the lawn:—*v.t.* [hosed, hos-ing], to water or drench with a hose.

ho-sier-y (hō'zhėr-i), *n.* stockings.

hos-pi-ta-ble (hos'pi-ta-bl), *adj.* disposed to welcome guests with generosity and kindness; as, a *hospitable* hostess. —*adv.* **hos'pi-ta-bly.**

hos-pi-tal (hos'pi-tal), *n.* a place for treatment and care of the sick and injured.—*v.t.* **hos'pi-tal-ize'.**—*n.* **hos'-pi-tal-i-za'tion.**

hos-pi-tal-i-ty (hos'pi-tal'i-ti), *n.* [*pl.* hospitalities], the entertaining of guests with kindness and liberality.

¹host (hōst), *n.* a large army; a great number; a throng.

²host (hōst), *n.* **1,** one who entertains others; one who provides food and lodging for pay, as the landlord of an inn; **2,** an animal or plant organism that gives nourishment to a parasite.

Host (hōst), *n.* the consecrated bread or wafer of the Mass.

hos-tage (hos'tij), *n.* **1,** a person who remains in the hands of another as a guarantee that certain conditions will be fulfilled; as, prisoners of war are sometimes held as *hostages;* **2,** any pledge or guarantee.

hos-tel (hos't'l), *n.* an inn or hotel.

host-ess (hōs'tes), *n.* **1,** a woman who receives and entertains guests; **2,** the mistress of an inn; also, an attendant in a restaurant who welcomes guests, conducts them to a table, etc.

hos-tile (hos'til; hos'til), *adj.* **1,** belonging to an enemy; as, a *hostile* fleet; **2,** unfriendly; as, *hostile* criticism.—*n.* **hos-til'i-ty.**

hos-tler (os'lėr; hos'lėr), *n.* one who takes care of horses; a groom; an ostler.

hot (hot), *adj.* [hot-ter, hot-test], **1,** of high temperature: opposite of *cold;* as, a *hot* stove; *hot* soup; **2,** fiery; passionate; as, a *hot* temper; **3,** having a sharp or biting taste, as spices; **4,**

fresh; strong; as, a *hot* scent.—*adv.*
hot′ly.—*n.* **hot′ness.**

hot-bed (hot′bed′), *n.* **1,** a bed of earth
heated by decaying manure for forcing
plants; **2,** any place or condition
promoting rapid growth; as, a *hotbed*
of intrigue, vice, treason, etc.

hot—blood-ed (hot′blud′id), *adj.* excitable; impetuous.

hotch-potch (hoch′poch′), *n.* a hodge-
podge.

hot—dog (hot′–dog′), *n.* *Colloq.* a
heated wiener, usually in a split roll.

ho-tel (hō-tel′), *n.* an establishment
where food and lodging are provided for
pay.

hot-head (hot′hed′), *n.* a rash, fiery-
tempered person.—*adj.* **hot′—head′ed.**

hot-house (hot′hous′), *n.* a glass-
roofed house, heated for growing or
forcing flowers or vegetables.

hou-dah (hou′da), *n.* Same as **howdah.**

hound (hound), *n.* any of several
breeds of hunting-dog, with large,
drooping ears and very keen scent:—
v.t. **1,** to chase with hounds; **2,** to
pursue; nag; as, his debtors *hounded*
him.

hour (our), *n.* **1,** the 24th part of a day;
60 minutes; **2,** the time of day; as,
clocks tell the *hours;* **3,** a particular or
stated time; as, school *hours;* **4,** a unit
of distance reckoned by the time taken
to travel it; as, three *hours* distant.—
adj. and *adv.* **hour′ly.**

hour-glass (our′glás′), *n.* a device
consisting of two glass bulbs,
one above the other, con-
nected by a narrow neck,
used for measuring time.
It takes an hour for the sand,
mercury, or water with which
the uppermost bulb is filled
to pass through the narrow   HOUR-
neck to the lower bulb.   GLASS

house (hous), *n.* **1,** a building for people
to live in; **2,** a building for some
particular purpose; as, a work*house;*
court*house;* also, a shelter for animals;
as, a dog*house;* **3,** family or race; as,
the royal *house* of England; **4,** one of
the divisions of a law-making or church-
governing body; as, the *House* of
Bishops; also, the place where each
body meets; as, the *Houses* of Parliament; **5,** a theatre or its audience; **6,** a
business firm or place of business:—*v.t.*
(houz), [housed, hous-ing], **1,** to shelter
or lodge; **2,** to store (goods); **3,** to
secure; put into a safe place; as, to
house a yacht:—*v.i.* to take shelter.—*n.*
house′ful.

house-bro-ken (hous′brō′ken), *adj.*
trained to live in a house (that is, to
urinate, etc., in the proper place), as a
cat, dog, etc.

house-fly (hous′flī′), *n.* [*pl.* house
flies], the common domestic fly.

house-hold (hous′hōld′), *n.* a group of
persons living together; a family:—
adj. pertaining to a family or home
domestic; as, *household* duties.

house-keep-ing (hous′kēp′ing), *n.* the
management of domestic affairs:—*adj.*
pertaining to the management of a
household; domestic.—*n.* **house′keep**-
er.

house-maid (hous′mād′), *n.* a gir
hired to do housework; a female
servant.

house-warm-ing (hous′wôr′ming), *n.*
a party celebrating a family's moving
into a new home.

house-wife (hous′wīf′), *n.* **1,** [*pl.*
housewives (-wīvz′)], the mistress of a
home; one who manages domestic
affairs; **2,** (huz′if), [*pl.* housewive
(huz′ivz)], a small case for sewing
materials.

house-work (hous′wûrk′), *n.* the work
of housekeeping, as cooking, cleaning
etc.

hous-ing (houz′ing), *n.* **1,** the act of
giving shelter; **2,** that which give
shelter; **3,** hence, provision of home
for people; as, *housing* is a problem of a
large city; **4,** in *mechanics*, a frame of
support; as, the *housing* of gears in the
rear axle of a motor vehicle.

hove (hōv), *p.t.* and *p.p.* of *heav*
(nautical).

hov-el (hov′el; huv′el), *n.* a wretched
little cottage; a hut.

hov-er (hov′ĕr; huv′ĕr), *v.i.* **1,** to
flutter over or about; as, pigeon
hovered over the square; **2,** to wait nea
at hand; move to and fro near a place
as, the fleet *hovers* in the bay; **3,** to
waver; hesitate.

how (hou), *adv.* **1,** in what manner or
way; as, *how* did you do it? **2,** to what
degree or extent; as, *how* far did you
go? **3,** at what price; as, *how* much did
you pay for it? **4,** in what condition
as, *how* are you? **5,** with what reason or
meaning; as, *how* is it that you are late

how-be-it (hou-bē′it), *conj.* *Archaic*
nevertheless; be this as it may.

how-dah or **hou-dah** (hou′da), *n.* a
canopied seat for riding on an elephan
or camel.

how-ev-er (hou-ev′ĕr), *adv.* in what
ever manner or degree; as, every gift

however small, is a help to the cause:— *conj.* nevertheless; as, I cannot, *however,* agree.

how-itz-er (hou′it-sėr), *n.* a short cannon that fires a shell at a high angle.

howl (houl), *n.* 1, the long, wailing cry of a dog or a wolf; 2, a cry of pain or distress; 3, a loud shout of ridicule; as, *howls* and jeers from the audience:—*v.i.* 1, to utter a loud, wailing cry, like a dog or wolf; 2, to utter a prolonged cry of pain or distress; lament; 3, to roar like the wind:—*v.t.* to utter in a wailing tone:—**howl down,** to silence or deride by howling.

how-ler (hou′lėr), *n.* 1, one who howls; 2, a species of tropical monkey; 3, *Colloq.* a glaring blunder; as, a schoolboy *howler.*

how-so-ev-er (hou′sō-ev′ėr), *adv.* in whatever manner or degree; however.

hoy (hoi), *interj.* an exclamation to attract attention.

hoy-den (hoi′dn), *n.* a rude, boisterous girl; a tomboy.

hub (hub), *n.* 1, the central part of a wheel; 2, anything that resembles the centre of a wheel in position or importance.

hub-bub (hub′ub), *n.* uproar; tumult; as, the class was in a *hubbub* when the teacher returned.

huck-le-ber-ry (huk′l-ber′i), *n.* [*pl.* huckleberries], the blue-black, berry-like, edible fruit of a low-growing shrub; also, the shrub.

huck-ster (huk′stėr), *n.* 1, a pedlar or hawker; esp. one who deals in fruit and vegetables; 2, a mean, tricky fellow.

hud-dle (hud′l), *v.t.* and *v.i.* [hud-dled, hud-dling], to crowd or press together in disorder:—*n.* 1, confusion; crowd; 2, in *football,* the gathering together of the players of a team for the giving of signals, instructions, etc.

hue (hū), *n.* colour; tint; as, wild flowers of every *hue.*

huff (huf), *n.* a fit of ill humour; sudden offence taken:—*v.t.* and *v.i.* to bully or offend; to take offence.—*adj.* **huff′y.**

hug (hug), *n.* a close embrace:—*v.t.* [hugged, hug-ging], 1, to embrace closely; 2, to hold fast to; cling to; as, to *hug* a belief; 3, to keep close to; as, to *hug* the shore.

huge (hūj), *adj.* [hug-er, hug-est], 1, of great bulk; vast; very large; as, a *huge* mountain; 2, great; as, the party was a *huge* success.—*adv.* **huge′ly.**

hu-la—hu-la (hōō′la–hōō′la), *n.* a native Hawaiian women's dance, pantomimic and suggestive. Also, **hu′la.**

hulk (hulk), *n.* 1, the body of a wrecked or unseaworthy ship; 2, an old, clumsy vessel; also, any clumsy object or person.

hulk-ing (hul′king), *adj.* clumsy; bulky; as, a *hulking* fellow.

¹hull (hul), *n.* the outer covering of certain fruits, vegetables, and grains:— *v.t.* to shell (peas), husk (corn), etc.

²hull (hul), *n.* the body or frame of a ship or airship.

hul-la-ba-loo (hul′a-ba-lōō′), *n.* [Imitative], uproar; confusion; hubbub; noisy disturbance.

hul-lo (hu-lō′), *n.* and *interj.* 1, a call to attract attention; 2, hello:—*v.i.* and *v.t.* to call out; shout aloud.

hum (hum), *v.i.* [hummed, hum-ming], 1, to make a sound without opening the lips, suggesting the sound of a prolonged *m;* 2, to make a buzzing noise, as a bee in flight; to drone; 3, to sing with lips closed; 4, *Colloq.* to be in energetic motion or action; as, to make things *hum:*—*v.t.* to sing with the lips closed; as, to *hum* a song:—*n.* 1, the noise made by bees and other insects in flying; a low sound like the letter *m;* 2, a distant sound as of machinery in motion, aeroplanes in flight, etc.

hu-man (hū′man), *adj.* pertaining to, or characteristic of, man or mankind; as, *human* progress; *human* kindness: —*n.* a human being.

hu-mane (hū-mān′), *adj.* having or exhibiting the feelings proper to man; benevolent; kind; as, *humane* laws.— *adv.* **hu-mane′ly.**—*n.* **hu-mane′ness.**

hu-man-ism (hū′man-izm), *n.* 1, liberal education, esp. in the Greek and Roman classics; 2, a conception of religion that regards man as the highest entity so far attained.—*n.* **hu′man-ist.**

hu-man-i-tar-i-an (hū-man′i-târ′i-an), *n.* a charitably inclined person; one who is devoted to the welfare of human beings:—*adj.* charitable; devoted to the welfare of people.—*n.* **hu-man′i-tar′i-an-ism.**

hu-man-i-ty (hū-man′i-ti), *n.* [*pl.* humanities], 1, mankind; 2, the nature which distinguishes man from other creatures; 3, charity toward others; kindness.

hu-man-ize (hū′man-īz′), *v.t.* and *v.i.* [-ized, -izing], to make kind, considerate, etc.; to civilize:—*v.i.* to become human.

hu-man-kind (hū′man-kīnd′), *n.* mankind collectively; human beings.

hu-man-ly (hū'man-li), *adv.* **1,** in a human or kind manner; as, to speak *humanly;* **2,** within human power or knowledge; as, we will do whatever is *humanly* possible.

hum-ble (hum'bl), *adj.* [hum-bler, hum-blest], **1,** not proud; as, a *humble* attitude; **2,** obscure; unassuming; as, they lived in a *humble* cottage:—*v.t.* [hum-bled, hum-bling], to subdue; humiliate; as, the loss of his job *humbled* him.—*n.* **hum'ble-ness.**

hum-bug (hum'bug'), *n.* **1,** a fraud or sham; **2,** an impostor or deceiver; **3,** a kind of peppermint candy:—*v.t.* [hum-bugged, humbug-ging], to swindle.

hum-drum (hum'drum'), *adj.* dull; monotonous; as, a *humdrum* life:—*n.* **1,** monotony; **2,** a stupid person; a bore.

hu-mer-us (hu'mėr-us), *n.* the bone of the upper arm from shoulder to elbow.

hu-mid (hū'mid), *adj.* damp; moist; as, a *humid* climate.—*n.* **hu-mid'i-ty.**

hu-mid-i-fy (hū-mid'i-fī'), *v.t.* [-fied, -fying], to moisten or make humid:—*n.* hu-mid'i-fi'er.

hu-mi-dor (hū'mi-dôr'), *n.* a case for tobacco or cigars that is kept humid, as by moistened sponges.

hu-mil-i-ate (hū-mil'i-āt'), *v.t.* [hu-miliat-ed, humiliat-ing], to humble; put to shame; as, his behaviour *humiliated* me.

hu-mil-i-a-tion (hū-mil'i-ā'shun), *n.* the act of putting to shame or the state of being put to shame; mortification.

hu-mil-i-ty (hū-mil'i-ti), *n.* [*pl.* humilities], meekness; modesty.

hum-ming-bird (hum'ing-bûrd'), *n.* a small American bird noted for its bright colours. Its wings, during flight, move so rapidly as to make a hum-ming noise.

hum-mock (hum'uk), *n.* a knoll; a low rounded hill.

hu-mor (hū'mėr; ū'mėr), an American spelling of **humour.**

hu-mour (hū'mėr; ū'mėr), *n.* **1,** a state of mind; mood; as, he is in a bad *humour;* **2,** the capacity to see or appreciate things that are funny; as, a sense of *humour;* **3,** the quality of being funny or amusing; as, the *humour* of a story:—*v.t.* to yield to the mood of; to indulge.—*n.* **hu'mor-ist.**—*adj.* **hu'-mor-ous.**

hump (hump), *n.* a bulging lump, as that on the back of a camel:—*v.t.* to make into such a shape; bend or curve, as the back.

hump-back (hump'bak'), *n.* **1,** one with a deformed or crooked back; **2,** a crooked back.—*adj.* **hump'backed';** **humped; hump'y.**

humpf (humf), *interj.* a snort or grunt expressing doubt, disgust, disbelief, contempt, etc.

hu-mus (hū'mus), *n.* the black or dark substance in soils formed by the decay of vegetable or animal matter.

hunch (hunch), *n.* **1,** a hump; a rounded lump; **2,** *Colloq.* a strong feeling that something will happen, or happen in a certain way:—*v.t.* to round (the back).

hunch-back (hunch'bak'), *n.* **1,** a person with a crooked back; **2,** a crooked back.—*adj.* **hunch'—backed'.**

hun-dred (hun'dred), *adj.* composed of ten times ten:—*n.* **1,** the number consisting of ten times ten; **2,** a sign representing this number, as 100 or C.—*adj.* and *n.* **hun'dredth.**

hun-dred-fold (hun'dred-fōld'), *adj.* *adv.,* and *n.* a hundred times as much or as great.

hun-dred-weight (hun'dred-wāt'), *n.* in North America, 100 pounds avoirdu pois; in England, 112 pounds avoirdu pois.

hun-ger (hung'gėr), *n.* **1,** a craving or need for food; **2,** any strong desire; as a *hunger* for excitement:—*v.i.* **1,** to fee a desire or longing for food; **2,** to long eagerly for something; as, the bo *hungered* for an education.—*adj.* **hun' gry.**—*adv.* **hun'gri-ly.**

hunk (hungk), *n.* *Colloq.* a lump large piece; chunk, as of bread or meat

hun-kers (hungk'ėrz), *n. pl.* th haunches or hams; as, he squatted o his *hunkers.*

hunt (hunt), *v.t.* **1,** to pursue, or try t catch or kill (game or wild animals); **2** to search through for something; as, t *hunt* the library for a book; **3,** to follo closely; hound; as, they *hunted* th fugitive over the countryside; **4,** t search after; as, to *hunt* gold:—*v.i.* **1** to follow the chase; **2,** to seek; as, t *hunt* for gold:—*n.* **1,** the pursuing o game or wild animals; **2,** an associatio of huntsmen; **3,** a search.—*n.* **hunt'ing**

hunt-er (hunt'ėr), *n.* **1,** one wh pursues game; a huntsman; **2,** a hors or hound trained for use in hunting; **3** one who searches or looks for some thing.—*n. fem.* **hunt'ress.**

hunts-man (hunts'man), *n.* [*pl.* hunts men (-men)], **1,** one who pursues game **2,** one who manages a hunt or chase

hunts-man's—cup (hunts′manz– kup′), *n.* the pitcher plant or Indian dipper (*Sarracenia purpurea*), with large cuplike or pitcher-shaped leaves and purple or greenish flowers: adopted in 1954 as Newfoundland's official floral emblem.

Huntsman's-cup

hur-dle (hûr′dl), *n.* **1,** a frame or framework of interwoven twigs, branches, or the like, used in making fences; **2,** a fence or barrier to be·leaped in steeple-chasing or racing; **3,** hurdles, a race in which such hurdles must be leaped; **4,** any barrier or obstacle; **5,** in England, a rude frame on which criminals were formerly dragged to execution:—*v.t.* [hur-dled, hur-dling], **1,** to leap over an obstacle while running; **2,** to surmount or overcome; as, to *hurdle* a difficulty.—*n.* hur′dler.

hur-dy—gur-dy (hûr′di–gûr′di), *n.*[*pl.* hurdy-gurdies], a musical instrument played by turning a crank, and pulled through the streets on wheels.

hurl (hûrl), *v.t.* **1,** to throw with violence; fling forcibly; as, he *hurled* the javelin; **2,** to cast down; overthrow; as, they *hurled* the despot from power; **3,** to utter with vehemence; as, to *hurl* threats:—*v.i. Slang,* in *baseball,* to pitch:—*n.* a cast; a violent throw.—*n.* hurl′er.

hurl-y—burl-y (hûr′li–bûr′li), *n.* tumult; confusion.

hur-rah (hoo-rä′; hu-rä′; hoo-rô′; hu-rô′), *interj.* expressing joy, triumph, applause, etc.:—*n.* a triumphant shout; a cheer:—*v.i.* to utter such a shout; to cheer.

hur-ray (hoo-rā′; hu-rā′), *interj.* hurrah!

hur-ri-cane (hûr′i-kān; -kan), *n.* a violent wind storm accompanied by rain, thunder, and lightning, esp. common in tropical regions.

hur-ried (hûr′id), *adj.* showing haste; hasty; as, a *hurried* meal.

hur-ry (hûr′i), *v.t.* [hurried, hurry-ing], to impel to greater speed; hasten:—*v.i.* to act or move with haste; as, the woman *hurried* through the station:— *n.* haste; urgency.

hurt (hûrt), *v.t.* [hurt, hurt-ing], **1,** to injure or inflict pain upon; wound; as, the blow *hurt* his arm; **2,** to grieve; offend; as, your indifference *hurts* me; **3,** to injure; impair or damage; as, don't *hurt* the book:—*n.* **1,** a wound or other injury causing physical pain; also, pain caused by such an injury; **2,** an

injury or loss causing mental pain; as, a *hurt* to one's pride; **3,** harm or damage of any kind.

hurt-ful (hûrt′fool), *adj.* injurious; harmful.

hur-tle (hûr′tl), *v.i.* [-tled, -tling], **1,** to move violently or noisily; as, rocks *hurtled* through the air; **2,** to collide with a crash, clatter, or shock.

hus-band (huz′band), *n.* a married man:—*v.t.* to manage, direct, or use with economy; as, to *husband* one's income.

hus-band-man (huz′band-man), *n.* [*pl.* husbandmen (-men)], a tiller of the soil; farmer.

hus-band-ry (huz′band-ri), *n.* **1,** agriculture; farming; **2,** economical management.

hush (hush), *interj.* be still! silence!—*v.t.* **1,** to make silent; to calm; **2,** to conceal; as, to *hush* scandal:—*v.i.* to become or keep quiet:—*n.* silence; as, in the *hush* of the night.

hush-a-by (hush′a-bī′), *interj.* an expression used in hushing infants.

husk (husk), *n.* **1,** the dry outer covering of certain fruits or seeds, as that of an ear of corn; **2,** any rough worthless outside covering:—*v.t.* to remove the husk from.—*n.* husk′er.

¹**husk-y** (hus′ki), *adj.* [husk-i-er, husk-i-est], **1,** consisting of, or like, husks; **2,** dry and hoarse; as, a *husky* voice.— *adv.* husk′i-ly.—*n.* husk′i-ness.

²**hus-ky** (hus′ki), *Colloq.* in the U.S., *adj.* [hus-ki-er, hus-ki-est], well-developed; powerful:—*n.* [*pl.* huskies], a stalwart, well-developed man.

Hus-ky (hus′ki), *n.* [*pl.* Huskies], **1,** an Eskimo; **2,** an Eskimo dog.

hus-sar (hoo-zär′), *n.* in European armies, a soldier belonging to the light cavalry.

hus-sy (huz′i), *n.* **1,** a pert or saucy girl; wench; **2,** a woman, esp. of low morals (used in contempt).

hus-tings (hus′tingz), *n. pl.* a platform used for electioneering speeches.

hus-tle (hus′l), *v.t.* [hus-tled, hus-tling], **1,** to push or crowd roughly; jostle; **2,** *Colloq.* to cause to be done quickly; as, to *hustle* work:—*v.i.* **1,** to jostle; crowd; **2,** *Colloq.* to exhibit energy and alacrity; hurry:—*n.* **1,** a pushing or jostling; **2,** *Colloq.* activity; vigour.—*n.* hus′tler.

hut (hut), *n.* a small, roughly built shelter; a hovel or shanty.

hutch (huch), *n.* **1,** a bin, box, or chest in which things may be stored; as, a grain-*hutch;* **2,** a coop or pen for animals; as, a rabbit-*hutch.*

hy-a-cinth (hī′a-sinth), *n.* a plant of

the lily family with spikes of bell-shaped, and very fragrant, white, pink, yellow, blue, or purple flowers.

hy-brid (hī′brid), *n*. **1**, an animal or plant produced from the crossing of two distinct varieties or species; as, some roses are *hybrids;* **2**, anything formed of parts of unlike origin; esp. a compound word, as *cablegram*, the elements of which are derived from different languages:—*adj*. **1**, produced from two kinds or classes; as, the mule is a *hybrid* animal; **2**, composed of mixed elements; as, a *hybrid* word.—*v.t.* **hy′brid-ize**.

hy-dran-ge-a (hi-drān′ji-a), *n.* a shrub with large, round clusters of showy white, blue, or pink flowers.

hy-drant (hī′drant), *n.* a pipe with a valve and spout through which water may be drawn from a water-main.

hy-drate (hī′drāt), *n.* a compound formed by the chemical union of water with another substance; as plaster of Paris (2CaSO₄·H₂O) or copper sulphate (CaSO₄·5H₂O).

hy-drau-lic (hī-drô′lik), *adj*. **1**, pertaining to water in motion; **2**, operated by water-power; as, a *hydraulic* elevator; **3**, accomplished by water-power; as, *hydraulic* mining; **4**, hardening under water; as, *hydraulic* cement.

hy-dride or **hy-drid** (hī′drīd; hī′drid), *n.* a compound of hydrogen with another element.

hy-dro-e-lec-tric (hī′drō-e-lek′trik), *adj.* pertaining to electric energy generated by water-power or steam.— *n.* **hy′dro-e-lec′tric′i-ty**.

hy-dro-gen (hī′drō-jen), *n.* a colourless, tasteless, odourless gas, which burns easily, and is the lightest substance known. It combines with oxygen to form water.

hydrogen bomb, a nuclear-fusion bomb, in which atoms of a heavy hydrogen isotope are fused into helium under intense heat and pressure. It is much more powerful than an atom, or fission, bomb.

hy-drol-y-sis (hī-drol′i-sis), *n.* the breaking down of organic compounds by interaction with water.

hy-drom-e-ter (hī-drom′e-tėr), *n.* a float for measuring the specific gravity of liquids.

hy-dro-pho-bi-a (hī′drō-fō′bi-a), *n.* an infectious disease, esp. of dogs, etc., marked by convulsions and dread of water; rabies.

hy-dro-plane (hī′drō-plān′), *n.* **1**, a motorboat with a sloping bottom, the bow of which rises partly out of water

when driven at high speed; **2**, an aeroplane so constructed that it can take off from, or alight on, a body of water; a seaplane.

hy-dro-pon-ics (hī′drō-pon′iks), *n*. *pl.* used as *sing.*, the science of growing plants without soil by using a solution with the proper plant foods; soilless gardening.

hy-drous (hī′drus), *adj*. **1**, containing water in combination; **2**, containing hydrogen.

hy-drox-ide (hī-drok′sīd), *n.* a compound containing the chemical unit [OH].

hy-e-na (hī-ē′na), *n.* a night-prowling, flesh-eating animal, somewhat resembling a wolf or large dog, native to Africa and Asia.

hy-giene (hī′jēn; hī′ji-ēn), *n.* the science which treats of the preservation of health.—*n.* **hy′gi-en-ist** (hī′ji-en-ist)

hy-gi-en-ic (hī′ji-en′ik), *adj*. **1**, pertaining to health or to the science of health; **2**, not injurious to health; sanitary.

hy-grom-e-ter (hī-grom′e-tėr), *n.* an instrument for measuring atmospheric moisture.

hymn (him), *n.* **1**, a sacred song expressing praise or adoration of God; **2**, any song of praise, thanksgiving, etc.

hym-nal (him′nal; him′nl), *n.* a collection of sacred songs; a book of hymns.

hy-per- (hī′pėr), *prefix* (*Greek*), **1**, over beyond; **2**, excessive; as, *hyperacidity;* opposite of *hypo-* (having a deficiency)

hy-per-bo-la (hī-pûr′bo-la), *n.* a curve formed by a conic section cut by a plane that makes a greater angle with the base than the side of the cone makes.

hy-per-bo-le (hī-pûr′bo-lē′), *n.* extravagant exaggeration; as, 'his arms dangled *a mile* out of his sleeves.'

HYPERBOLA

hy-per-sen-si-tive (hī′pėr-sen′si-tiv) *adj.* over-sensitive.

hy-phen (hī′fen), *n.* a punctuation mark [-] used to join compound words, as in *self-denial*, or to divide a word into syllables, as in *hy-phen-ate:*—*v.t.* to join (words) with, or separate (syllables) by, such a mark; hyphenate.

hy-phen-ate (hī′fen-āt′), *v.t.* [hyphen-at-ed, hyphenat-ing], to insert a hyphen between (two words) or between the syllables of (a word); to hyphen.

hyp-no-tism (hip′no-tizm), *n.* the act

or method of producing a state resembling sleep, in which the mind readily responds to suggestions, esp. from the person who caused the state.—*n.* **hyp′no-tist.**—*v.t.* **hyp′no-tize′** (hip′-no-tīz′).—*adj.* **hyp-not′ic** (hip-not′ik)

hy-po (hī′pō), *n.* short for **hyposulphite** (hī′pō-sul′fīt), a photographic fixing agent.

hy-po-chon-dri-a (hī′pō-kon′dri-a; hip′), *n.* morbid anxiety about fancied illnesses; severe melancholy.—*n.* **hy′po-chon′dri-ac.**

hy-poc-ri-sy (hi-pok′ri-si), *n.* [*pl.* hypocrisies], a pretending to be what one is not; the putting on of an appearance of virtue which one does not possess.

hyp-o-crite (hip′ō-krit), *n.* one who puts on an appearance of virtue which he does not possess.—*adj.* **hyp′o-crit′i-cal.**

hy-po-der-mic (hī′pō-dûr′mik; hip), *adj.* pertaining to the tissues under the skin; as, a *hypodermic* injection by hypodermic needle.

hy-pot-e-nuse (hī-pot′i-nūz′; hi-pot′-i-nūz′), *n.* in *geometry*, the side of a right-angled triangle which is opposite the right angle.

hy-poth-e-sis (hī-poth′e-sis; hi-poth′e-sis), *n.* [*pl.* hypotheses (hī-poth′e-sēz; hi-poth′e-sēz)], something which may or may not prove to be true for the sake of argument.

HYPOT-ENUSE (H)

hys-te-ri-a (his-tē′ri-a), *n.* a persistent nervous condition, marked chiefly by uncontrolled emotional excitement and outbursts of senseless weeping and laughter.

hys-ter-ic (his-ter′ik) or **hys-ter-i-cal** (his-ter′i-kal), *adj.* **1,** pertaining to, or affected by, hysteria; **2,** violently emotional; uncontrolled; as, *hysterical* laughter.—*adv.* **hys-ter′i-cal-ly.**

hys-ter-ics (his-ter′iks), *n. pl.* used as *sing.* a fit of nervous and uncontrollable laughing and crying; any hysterical outburst.

I

¹I, i (ī), *n.* [*pl.* I's, i's], **1,** the ninth letter of the alphabet, following H; **2,** as a Roman numeral, 1.

²I (ī), *pron.* of the first person, [*nominative* I, *possessive* my, mine, *objective* me], the pronoun by which the speaker or writer denotes himself.

i-amb (ī′amb) or **i-am-bus** (ī-am′-bus), *n.* in *verse metre*, a foot of two syllables, the first short or unaccented, the second long or accented; as, "Ĭn sooth/Ĭ know/nŏt why/Ĭ am/sō sad" (*iambic* pentameter).—*adj.* and *n.* **i-am′bic.**

i-bex (ī′beks), *n.* [*pl.* ibices (ī′bi-sēz) or ibexes (ī′bek-siz)], a wild goat with large, backward-curving horns.

i-bis (ī′bis), *n.* [*pl.* ibises or ibis], a large, wading bird of the heron family, with a long, slender, curving beak, found in warm climates:—**sacred ibis,** an ibis found along the Nile, regarded as sacred by the ancient Egyptians.

ice (īs), *n.* **1,** frozen water; **2,** any substance resembling ice; as, menthol *ice;* **3,** a frozen dessert, made with fruit juices instead of cream; as, raspberry *ice;* **4,** cake frosting; icing:—*v.t.*[iced, icing], **1,** to freeze; **2,** to supply with ice; **3,** to cool by ice as beverages or fruit; **4,** to cover, as cake, with

frosting:—*adj.* **1,** of ice; as, *ice* cubes; **2,** having to do with ice; as, *ice* hockey; an iceboat, 1. Compounds: **ice′box′; ice′break′er; ice′cap′; ice′—cold′: ice′—floe′; ice′—free′; ice′house′.**

ice—age (īs′-āj′), *n.* the glacial epoch, or time when ice covered much of the world.

ice-berg (īs′bûrg′), *n.* a large mass of ice broken off from a glacier, and floating in the sea, often extending to a great height above the water.

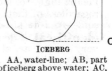

ICEBERG
AA, water-line; AB, part of iceberg above water; AC, part of iceberg below water, about nine times the size of AB.

ice-boat (īs′-bōt′), *n.* **1,** a heavily-built steamboat with a very strong bow, used to break a channel in frozen rivers, lakes, or harbours: also called *ice-breaker;* **2,** a boat or frame mounted on runners and propelled by sails over ice

ice—cream (īs′-krēm′), *n.* flavoured cream, etc., sweetened and frozen.

ich-neu-mon fly (ik-nū′mon), a member of a large group of wasplike, but stingless, insects whose larvae live on caterpillars and other larvae.

all (ôl), ôr: up, mūte, cûr, cōōl, book; oil, out; th, thin; *th,* the.

i-ci-cle (ī′sik-l), *n.* a hanging piece of ice, tapering downward to a point, formed by the freezing of dripping water.

ic-ing (īs′ing), *n.* a coating or frosting for cakes, made of sugar, flavouring, etc.

i-con (ī′kon), *n.* [*pl.* icons or icones (ī′ko-nēz′)], an image; likeness; **2,** in the *Greek Church,* a sacred image or picture, as of the Virgin Mary or a saint. Also, **i′kon.**

i-con-o-clast (ī-kon′ō-klast), *n.* **1,** a breaker of images; hence, **2,** one who attacks cherished beliefs or institutions.

ic-y (īs′i), *adj.* [ic-i-er, ic-i-est], **1,** pertaining to, like, or covered with, ice; as, *icy* pavements; cold; frosty; as, an *icy* gale; **2,** chilling in manner; indifferent; as, an *icy* welcome.—*adv.* **ic′i-ly.**—*n.* **i′ci-ness.**

i-de-a (ī-dē′a), *n.* **1,** a mental picture of a thing; as, his *idea* of an elephant; **2,** an ideal; also, a plan; as, John has the *idea* of becoming an actor; **3,** the purpose or meaning of anything; as, the *idea* is to get votes; **4,** a supposition; fancy; as, I have an *idea* she will come.

i-de-al (ī-dē′al), *adj.* **1,** existing in imagination or fancy only; not real or practical; **2,** equal to one's highest wish; perfect; as, *ideal* weather:—*n.* any perfect person or thing, or one regarded as worthy of imitation.—*adv.* **i-de′al-ly.**

i-de-al-ism (ī-dē′al-izm), *n.* **1,** the tendency to see things as they should be instead of as they are; **2,** the effort to live according to a standard of perfection; **3,** in *art* and *literature,* the effort to depict beauty and perfection rather than fact: opposite of *realism.*—*n.* **i-de′al-ist.**—*adj.* **i-dē′al-is′tic.**

i-de-al-ize (ī-dē′al-īz′), *v.t.* [idealized, idealiz-ing], to look upon as perfect, regardless of fact; as, she *idealizes* her son.—*n.* **i-de′al-i-za′tion.**

i-den-ti-cal (ī-den′ti-kal), *adj.* **1,** the very same; as, the *identical* spot; **2,** exactly alike; as, no two faces are *identical.*—*adv.* **i-den′ti-cal-ly.**

i-den-ti-fy (ī-den′ti-fī′), *v.t.* [identified, identify-ing], **1,** to make, consider, or treat as the same; as, we *identify* sportsmanship with good character; **2,** to prove to be the same or prove as one's own; as, I *identified* my umbrella; **3,** to recognize or classify, as a plant or a person.—*n.* **i-den′ti-fi-ca′tion.**

i-den-ti-ty (ī-den′ti-ti), *n.* [*pl.* identities], **1,** sameness or likeness; as, the *identity* of this pen with the one I lost; **2,** the fact of being as represented; as,

to establish one's *identity.*—*adj.* **i-dent′-i-fi′a-ble.**

i-de-ol-o-gy (ī′di-ol′o-ji; id′), *n.* **1,** the theory that ideas originate from sensation; **2,** the ideas, prejudices, beliefs, etc., that determine one's view of life.

id est (id est), *Latin,* that is: usually abbreviated to *i.e.*

id-i-om (id′i-um), *n.* **1,** the language of a people; also, the dialect of a group or section; as, the New England *idiom;* **2,** the peculiar form or character of a language; **3,** an expression which, as a whole, has a meaning different from the meanings of the individual words joined together, as "to be hard put to it" means "to have difficulty"; **4,** a method of expression characteristic of an individual; as, Shakespeare's *idiom.* —*adj.* **id′i-o-mat′ic.**

id-i-o-syn-cra-sy (id′i-ō-sing′kra-si), *n.* a peculiarity of one's disposition; a mannerism.

id-i-ot (id′i-ut), *n.* **1,** a person lacking in mind from birth; **2,** a fool; a dunce.

id-i-ot-ic (id′i-ot′ik), *adj.* **1,** pertaining to, or like, an idiot; **2,** senseless; foolish.—*n.* **id′i-o-cy.**

i-dle (ī′dl), *adj.* [i-dler, i-dlest], **1,** unused; as, the house stands *idle;* **2,** useless; futile; of no importance; as, an *idle* tale; **3,** not working; lazy; as, *idle* servants:—*v.i.* [i-dled, i-dling], **1,** to waste or lose time; do nothing; **2,** to run slowly in neutral gear, as an automobile engine:—*v.t.* to waste (time) as, to *idle* time away gossiping.—*n.* **i′dle-ness.**—*n.* **i′dler.**—*adv.* **i′dly.**

i-dol (ī′d'l), *n.* **1,** an image of a god used as an object of worship; **2,** a person or thing greatly loved or adored.

i-dol-a-try (ī-dol′a-tri), *n.* [*pl.* idolatries], **1,** the worship of idols; **2,** extreme admiration for any person or thing.—*n.* **i-dol′a-ter.**—*adj.* **i-dol′a-trous.**

i-dol-ize (ī′d'l-īz′), *v.t.* [idolized, idolizing], **1,** to worship (an image regarded as a god, or as divine); to make an idol of; **2,** to love or admire to excess; as, small boys *idolize* great football stars.

i-dyll or **i-dyl** (ī′dil), *n.* **1,** a short poem describing a scene or event in country life; a similar prose description; **2,** an episode suitable for such a piece.

i-dyl-lic (ī-dil′ik), *adj.* **1,** pertaining to, or of the nature of, the idyll; **2,** charming and simple.

if (if), *conj.* **1,** on the condition that; as, *if* I let you have the book, you must read it; supposing that; as, *if* I go to Quebec, what is the best train to take? 2, whether; as, he asked *if* he might go; 3, although; as, even *if* the answer is correct, the work is not neatly done; 4, whenever; as, *if* I have a question, I will come to you:—*n.* a supposition or condition.

ig-loo or **ig-lu** (ig′lōō), *n.* an Eskimo hut, dome-shaped, usually made of blocks of snow or ice.

ig-ne-ous (ig′ni-us), *n.* and *adj.* produced by heat, as an *igneous* rock (like granite).

ig-nite (ig-nīt′), *v.t.* [ignit-ed, igniting], to set on fire; as, to *ignite* coal:—*v.i.* to catch fire; as, the paper *ignited* from sparks.

ig-ni-tion (ig-nish′un), *n.* 1, the act of setting on fire; kindling; 2, the state of being ignited; 3, the means of producing fire; 4, the device for, or the process of, igniting the fuel mixture in gasoline engines.

ig-no-ble (ig-nō′bl), *adj.* 1, of low birth; as, an *ignoble* family; 2, of mean character or quality; degraded; vile; as, an *ignoble* act.—*adv.* **ig-no′bly.**

ig-no-min-i-ous (ig′nō-min′i-us), *adj.* disgraceful; humiliating; shameful; as, an *ignominious* punishment.—*n.* **ig′no-min-y.**

ig-no-ra-mus (ig′nō-rā′mus), *n.* an ignorant person.

ig-no-rance (ig′no-rans), *n.* lack of knowledge.

ig-no-rant (ig′no-rant), *adj.* 1, lacking knowledge; uninformed; 2, unaware; as, he was *ignorant* of the fact; 3, betraying, or caused by, lack of knowledge; as, an *ignorant* reply.—*adv.* **ig′no-rant-ly.**

ig-nore (ig-nōr′), *v.t.* [ignored, ignoring], to disregard intentionally; as, to *ignore* a request; to overlook; as, to *ignore* rudeness.

i-kon (ī′kon), *n.* Same as **i′con.**

ilk (ilk), *n.* family; breed; kind; as, thieves and others of that *ilk.*

ill (il), *adj.* [*comp.* worse, *superl.* worst], 1, sick; not well; as, the child is *ill;* 2, disagreeable; hostile; as, *ill* humour; *ill* will; 3, harmful; as, an *ill* turn:—*n.* 1, evil: the opposite of *good;* 2, something unfavourable or injurious; as, to work *ill* to one's neighbour; 3, misfortune:—*adv.* 1, badly; as, to fare *ill;* 2, unkindly; as, to treat someone *ill.* Compounds: **ill′—fa′ted;** **ill′—man′nered;** **ill′—o′mened;** **ill′—us′age.**

ill—bred (il′—bred′), *adj.* badly reared; impolite; rude.

il-le-gal (il-lē′gal), *adj.* against the law;

unlawful; as, it is *illegal* to drive a car without a licence.—*n.* **il′le-gal′i-ty** (il′li-gal′i-ti).—*adv.* **il-le′gal-ly.**

il-leg-i-ble (il-lej′i-bl), *adj.* not readable; difficult to read; as, an *illegible* manuscript; an *illegible* date on a coin. —*adv.* **il-leg′i-bly.**—*n.* **il-leg′i-bil′i-ty.**

il-le-git-i-mate (il′li-jit′i-mit), *adj.* 1, born out of wedlock; 2, unlawful; illegal; as, an *illegitimate* business.

ill—hu-moured (il′—hū′mẽrd), *adj.* cross; disagreeable; in a bad humour.

il-lic-it (il-lis′it; i-lis′it), *adj.* not allowed; illegal; as, *illicit* trade in drugs.

il-lim-it-a-ble (il-lim′it-a-bl), *adj.* immeasurable; vast; as, *illimitable* space.

il-lit-er-ate (il-lit′ẽr-it), *adj.* 1, unlearned; ignorant of letters or books; esp. unable to read or write; 2, showing lack of learning; as, an *illiterate* letter: —*n.* one unable to read or write.—*n.* **il-lit′er-a-cy.**

ill-ness (il′nes), *n.* the state of being ill; also, a disease or malady.

il-log-i-cal (i-loj′i-kal), *adj.* contrary to sound reason.

il-lu-mi-nate (i-lū′mi-nāt′), *v.t.* [illuminat-ed, illuminat-ing], 1, to give light to; as, one large lamp *illuminated* the room; 2, to decorate with lights, as in token of rejoicing; 3, to make clear, as a difficult point; 4, to ornament (an initial letter on the borders of a page) with designs in colours, as in ancient manuscripts.—*n.* **il-lu′mi-na′tion.**

il-lu-mine (i-lū′min), *v.t.* [illumined, illumin-ing], to light up; brighten; as, the moon *illumines* the night; a smile *illumined* her face.

il-lu-sion (i-lū′zhun), *n.* 1, an unreal or misleading appearance; as, that

ILLUSION
The two horizontal lines appear farther apart at the centre than at the ends of the drawing.

cloud gives the *illusion* of a castle; 2, a false idea; a delusion.—*adj.* **il-lu′sive, il-lu′so-ry.**

il-lus-trate (il′us-trāt′; i-lus′trāt), *v.t.* [illustrat-ed, illustrat-ing], 1, to make clear; as, to *illustrate* the definition of a word by a phrase in which the word is used; 2, to make plain by means of pictures or diagrams; also, to ornament with pictures.—*adj.* **il′lus-trat′ed.**— *adj.* **il-lus′tra-tive** (i-lus′tra-tiv; il′us-trā′tiv).—*n.* **il′lus-tra′tor.**

il-lus-tra-tion (il′us-trā′shun), *n.* 1, the process of making plain, or explaining, by the use of examples; 2, the art of ornamenting with pictures; **3,** that which makes clear, as a comparison or an example; **4,** that which decorates a text, as a picture.

il-lus-tri-ous (i-lus′tri-us), *adj.* famous; distinguished.—*adv.* **il-lus′tri-ous-ly.**

ill will, unfriendliness.

im- (im), *prefix* (1) meaning *not,* as in **im-plau′si-ble; im-pol′i-tic;** or (2) often used instead of *em,* as in **im-bod′y; im-plant′.**

im-age (im′ij), *n.* **1,** a statue, bust, or similar representation of a person or thing; as, an *image* of the Virgin Mary; **2,** a close likeness; as, he is the *image* of his brother; **3,** a mental picture; an idea; **4,** a reflection in a mirror or something seen through a camera lens, magnifying glass, or the like:—*v.t.* [imaged, imag-ing], **1,** to form a likeness or picture of (something); portray; **2,** to represent to oneself; imagine; **3,** to picture vividly in words.

im-age-ry (im′ij-ri; im′ij-ėr-i), *n.* [*pl.* imageries], mental pictures, esp. as conveyed in words; also, language which causes the mind to form pictures.

im-ag-i-na-ble (i-maj′i-na-bl), *adj.* capable of being pictured by the mind; conceivable.

im-ag-i-nar-y (i-maj′i-nėr-i), *adj.* existing only in the mind; unreal.

im-ag-i-na-tion (i-maj′i-nā′shun), *n.* **1,** the picture-forming power of the mind; the ability to form mental pictures of things not actually present; **2,** a product of this power; a mental picture or idea; a fancy.—*adj.* **im-ag′i-na′tive** (i-maj′i-na-tiv; i-maj′i-nā′tiv).

im-ag-ine (i-maj′in), *v.t.* and *v.i.* [imagined, imagin-ing], **1,** to form an idea or mental picture of (something); **2,** to suppose; fancy.

im-be-cile (im′bi-sil; im′bi-sīl; im′bi-sēl′), *adj.* **1,** feeble-minded; idiotic; **2,** marked by stupidity; inane; as, an *imbecile* remark:—*n.* one of weak mind. —*n.* **im′be-cil′i-ty.**

im-bed (im-bed′), *v.t.* Same as **embed.**

im-bibe (im-bīb′), *v.t.* [imbibed, imbib-ing], **1,** to drink; **2,** to receive or absorb into the mind; as, to *imbibe* knowledge.

im-bue (im-bū′), *v.t.* [imbued, imbu-ing], **1,** to cause to absorb; tinge deeply; dye; as, the setting sun *imbues* the lake with rose; **2,** to impress deeply; inspire; as, a soldier *imbued* with patriotism.

im-i-tate (im′i-tāt′), *v.t.* [imitat-ed,

imitat-ing], **1,** to make a likeness of; **2,** to follow as a model or pattern; mimic; **3,** to look like; resemble; as, paper doilies are made to *imitate* lace ones.—*adj.* **im′i-ta′tive** (im′i-tā-tiv; im′i-tā′tiv).—*n.* **im′i-ta′tor.**

im-i-ta-tion (im′i-tā′shun), *n.* **1,** the act of copying or following a model; as, *imitation* is the sincerest form of flattery; **2,** a copy:—*adj.* made to resemble something superior; as, *imitation* lace.

im-mac-u-late (i-mak′ū-lit), *adj.* **1,** absolutely clean; as, *immaculate* hands; **2,** without fault; stainless; pure:— *adv.* **im-mac′u-late-ly.**

im-ma-nent (im′a-nent), *adj.* indwelling; inherent: as, God is *immanent* in the universe.

im-ma-te-ri-al (im′ma-tē′ri-al), *adj.* **1,** not consisting of matter; without physical form; as, ghosts are *immaterial;* **2,** unimportant; as, *immaterial* details.

im-ma-ture (im′a-tūr′), *adj.* **1,** not ripe; not fully grown or developed; **2,** not finished or perfected; crude.—*adv.* **im′ma-ture′ly.**—*n.* **im′ma-tu′ri-ty.**

im-meas-ur-a-ble (i-mezh′ōōr-a-bl), *adj.* incapable of being measured; as, the *immeasurable* heavens; *immeasurable* joy.

im-me-di-ate (i-mē′di-it), *adj.* **1,** closely related; as, one's *immediate* family; **2,** next; as, the *immediate* succession to the throne; **3,** direct; as, *immediate* cause; **4,** present; as, the *immediate* question; **5,** instant, urgent; as, *immediate* needs; **6,** *Colloq.* near at hand; as, the *immediate* neighbourhood; **7,** happening or coming at once; as, an *immediate* answer.

im-me-di-ate-ly (i-mē′di-it-li), *adv.* **1,** at once; **2,** closely; directly.

im-me-mor-i-al (im′me-mōr′i-al), *adj.* extending beyond the reach of memory or written record; as, life has existed on this earth from time *immemorial.*

im-mense (i-mens′), *adj.* vast; enormous.—*adv.* **im-mense′ly.**—*n.* **im-men′si-ty.**

im-merse (i-mûrs′), *v.t.* [immersed, immers-ing], **1,** to plunge into some liquid; dip; as, to *immerse* clothes in water; **2,** to baptize by plunging (a person) entirely under water; **3,** to absorb the attention of; as, he was *immersed* in a book.—*adj.* **im-mersed**. —*n.* **im-mer′sion.**

im-mi-grant (im′i-grant), *n.* a foreigner who enters a country to settle there permanently.

im-mi-grate (im′i-grāt′), *v.i.* [immigrat-ed, immigrat-ing], to enter a foreign country intending to settle there permanently.—*n.* **im′mi-gra′tion.**

im-mi-nent (im′i-nent), *adj.* threatening; about to occur: said esp. of misfortune or danger; as, *imminent* death.—*n.* **im′mi-nence.**

im-mo-bile (i-mō′bil; bīl; bēl), *adj.* motionless.—*n.* **im′mo-bil′i-ty.**

im-mod-er-ate (im-mod′ẽr-it), *adj.* extreme; excessive; as, the *immoderate* use of slang.—*adv.* **im-mod′er-ate-ly.**

im-mod-est (i-mod′est), *adj.* **1,** not decent or proper; as, *immodest* behaviour; **2,** forward; brazen; as, *immodest* boasting.—*n.* **im-mod′es-ty.**

im-mor-al (i-môr′al), *adj.* **1,** contrary to what is considered right; as, *immoral* conduct; **2,** wicked; evil; unscrupulous; as, an *immoral* age.—*n.* **im′mo-ral′i-ty.**

im-mor-tal (i-môr′tal), *adj.* never dying; living or lasting forever; as, the Greeks considered their gods *immortal;* an *immortal* poem:—*n.* **1,** one who never dies; **2,** one whose fame is undying:—**the immortals,** in *mythology,* the gods.—*adv.* **im-mor′tal-ly.**—*n.* **im-mor-tal′i-ty.**—*v.t.* **im-mor′tal-ize.**

im-mov-a-ble (i-mōōv′a-bl), *adj.* **1,** incapable of being moved; firmly fixed; as, *immovable* rocks; **2,** firm; unchanging.

im-mune (i-mūn′), *adj.* **1,** safe; free; as, *immune* from punishment; **2,** protected from a particular disease; as, vaccination makes one *immune* to smallpox.—*n.* **im-mu′ni-ty.**—*v.t.* **im′-mun-ize′**—*n.* **im′mu-ni-za′tion.**

im-mure (i-mūr′), *v.t.* [immured, immur-ing], to confine within walls; shut up in, or as, in prison.

im-mu-ta-ble (i-mū′ta-bl), *adj.* unchangeable; unalterable.—*n.* **im-mu′-ta-bil′i-ty.**

imp (imp), *n.* **1,** a little demon; offspring of the devil; **2,** an annoying child.

im-pact (im′pakt), *n.* a collision; a forcible coming together of two objects; as, the *impact* of billiard balls.—*adj.* **im-pact′ed** (as, an *impacted* tooth).

im-pair (im-pâr′), *v.t.* to make worse; lessen the quantity, excellence, value, or strength of; weaken; harm; as, reading in a dim light *impairs* the eyesight.—*n.* **im-pair′ment.**

im-pale (im-pāl′), *v.t.* [impaled, impaling], **1,** to pierce through with anything sharp; **2,** to kill by thrusting through and fixing with a sharp stake.

im-pal-pa-ble (im-pal′pa-bl), *adj.* that cannot be felt or known by sense of touch; intangible; as, the *impalpable* air: said of gases, shadows, etc.

im-pan-el (im-pan′el), *v.t.* **1,** to enter on a list, or panel, for jury duty; **2,** to choose (a jury) from the list and swear in (as jurors for a trial).

im-part (im-pärt′), *v.t.* **1,** to bestow a share or portion of; give; as, flowers *impart* beauty to a room; **2,** to tell; disclose; as, to *impart* a secret.

im-par-tial (im-pär′shal), *adj.* not favouring one more than another; fair; just; as, a judge must be absolutely *impartial* in his decisions.—*n.* **im′par-ti-al′i-ty.**

im-pass-a-ble (im-pàs′a-bl), *adj.* not capable of being traversed or travelled; as, an *impassable* swamp; an *impassable* road.

im-passe (àṅ′pàs′), *French,* **1,** a blind alley; hence, **2,** a position from which there is no escape; a deadlock; as, to reach an *impasse* in negotiations.

im-pas-si-ble (im-pas′i-bl), *adj.* insensible to pain; apathetic.

im-pas-sioned (im-pash′und), *adj.* showing strong emotion; as, an *impassioned* orator; an *impassioned* appeal for aid.

im-pas-sive (im-pas′iv), *adj.* feeling no emotion; showing no feeling; unmoved; calm; as, *impassive* faces.

im-pa-tience (im-pā′shens), *n.* **1,** rebelliousness against delay, restraint, or the like; restless eagerness; as, she was all *impatience* to be gone; **2,** inability to tolerate or endure; intolerance; as, *impatience* of lying; **3,** irritability; lack of control.—*adj.* **im-pa′tient.**

im-peach (im-pēch′), *v.t.* **1,** to charge (a person in public office), before a court, with misconduct in office; as, to *impeach* a judge; **2,** to question or challenge (a person's honor, motives, etc.).—*adj.* **im-peach′a-ble.**—*n.* **im-peach′ment.**

im-pec-ca-ble (im-pek′a-bl), *adj.* faultless; flawless; as, his manners are *impeccable.*

im-pe-cu-ni-ous (im′pi-kū′ni-us), *adj.* lacking money; poor.

im-ped-ance (im-pēd′ans), *n.* the apparent resistance of a circuit to the flow of an alternating current.

im-pede (im-pēd′), *v.t.* [imped-ed, imped-ing], to obstruct or hinder; retard; as, snow and ice *impeded* our progress.

im-ped-i-ment (im-ped′i-ment), *n.* **1,** that which hinders or obstructs; an obstacle; **2,** a defect in speech, as a stammer.

im-pel (im-pel′), *v.t.* [impelled, impelling], to drive forward; force; compel; as, fear and remorse *impelled* him to confess.

im-pend (im-pend′), *v.i.* **1,** to overhang; as, the sword *impending* over Damocles' head; **2,** to be at hand; threaten; as, death *impends.*

im-pen-e-tra-ble (im-pen′i-tra-bl), *adj.* **1,** not capable of being entered; allowing no entrance or passage; as, *impenetrable* forests; an *impenetrable* wall; **2,** not capable of being understood; as, an *impenetrable* plot; **3,** closed to reason, sympathy, etc.

im-pen-i-tent (im-pen′i-tent), *adj.* not sorry or repentant for one's sin:—*n.* a hardened sinner.—*n.* **im-pen′i-tence.**

im-per-a-tive (im-per′a-tiv), *adj.* **1,** in *grammar*, expressing command or exhortation; as, the *imperative* mood; **2,** commanding; peremptory; authoritative; as, an *imperative* gesture of dismissal; **3,** necessary; urgent; as, it is *imperative* to leave at once:—*n.* in *grammar*, the mood expressing command; also, the form of a verb used in this mood.

im-per-cep-ti-ble (im′pėr-sep′ti-bl), *adj.* **1,** so small, slow, or gradual, as hardly to be seen or felt; as, the *imperceptible* growth of a plant from day to day; **2,** too slight to be grasped by the mind; subtle; as, *imperceptible* shades of meaning.—*adv.* **im′per-cep′ti-bly.**

im-per-fect (im-pûr′fekt), *adj.* lacking perfection; faulty; incomplete:—**imperfect tense,** a tense of a verb which indicates action in the past going on but not completed; as, he *was walking:* —*n.* the imperfect tense, or a verb in that tense.—*adv.* **im-per′fect-ly.**—*n.* **im′per-fec′tion.**

im-pe-ri-al (im-pē′ri-al), *adj.* **1,** pertaining to an empire or an emperor; as, *imperial* policies; *imperial* majesty; **2,** splendid; magnificent:—*n.* a small, pointed beard.—*adv.* **im-pe′ri-al-ly.**

im-pe-ri-al-ism (im-pē′ri-al-izm), *n.* **1,** the power or government of an emperor; **2,** the policy of any nation which aims at the acquisition of new territory and, usually, closer union of the territory already possessed.—*adj.* **im-pe′ri-al-is′tic.**—*n.* **im-pe′ri-al-ist.**

im-per-il (im-per′il), *v.t.* [imperilled, imperil-ling], to put in danger; endanger; as, to *imperil* one's life to save a child.

im-pe-ri-ous (im-pē′ri-us), *adj.* overbearing; urgent.—*adv.* **im-pe′ri-ous-ly.**

im-per-ish-a-ble (im-per′ish-a-bl), *adj.* enduring permanently; immortal; as, he won *imperishable* fame.

im-per-me-a-ble (im-pûr′mi-a-bl), *adj.* not permitting passage, esp. of fluids; impervious; as, the skin is *impermeable* to water; *impermeable* rock.

im-per-son-al (im-pûr′sun-al), *adj.* **1,** not relating to any particular person or thing; as, an *impersonal* discussion; **2,** not existing as a person; as, fate and luck are *impersonal* forces:—**impersonal verb,** a verb which usually has *it* for a subject, used only in the third person singular, as it *seems,* it *follows.*—*adv.* **im-per′son-al-ly.**

im-per-son-ate (im-pûr′sun-āt′), *v.t.* [impersonat-ed, impersonat-ing], **1,** to play the part of, esp. on the stage; **2,** to typify; represent; as, Jack Canuck *impersonates* Canada.—*n.* **im-per′son-a′tion.**—*n.* **im-per′son-a′tor.**

im-per-ti-nent (im-pûr′ti-nent), *adj.* insolent; rude.—*n.* **im-per′ti-nence.**

im-per-turb-a-ble (im′pėr-tûr′ba-bl), *adj.* calm; serene; not easily excited; as, *imperturbable* composure.

im-per-vi-ous (im-pûr′vi-us), *adj.* not permitting entrance or passage; as, slickers are *impervious* to rain; *impervious* to insult.

im-pe-ti-go (im′pi-tī′gō), *n.* a skin disease characterized by pus spots which later become crusted.—*adj.* **im′pe-tig′i-nous.**

im-pet-u-ous (im-pet′ū-us), *adj.* **1,** rushing with force and violence; as, an *impetuous* wind; **2,** acting with sudden energy; passionate; impulsive; as, an *impetuous* child.—*n.* **im-pet′u-os′i-ty.**

im-pe-tus (im′pi-tus), *n.* **1,** the force or momentum by which a moving body tends to overcome resistance and go on moving; **2,** a moving force; stimulus; incentive; as, the desire for fame is an *impetus* to action.

im-pi-e-ty (im-pī′e-ti), *n.* [*pl.* impieties], **1,** lack of religious reverence; **2,** an act of irreverence or wickedness.—*adj.* **im′pi-ous.**—*adv.* **im′pi-ous-ly.**

im-pinge (im-pinj′), *v.i.* to strike (*on, upon, against*); as, rays of light *impinge* on the eye.

im-pish (imp′ish), *adj.* mischievous.

im-pla-ca-ble (im-plā′ka-bl; im-plak′a-bl), *adj.* not able to be pacified or appeased; relentless; as, *implacable* hatred.—*adv.* **im-pla′ca-bly.**

im-ple-ment (im′pli-ment), *n.* an instrument, tool, or utensil; as, garden *implements:*—*v.t.* to make possible, or to put into effect; as, to *implement* a plan.

im-pli-cate (im′pli-kāt′), *v.t.* [implicat-ed, implicat-ing], to involve deeply; as, the accusation *implicated* a dozen men.

im-pli-ca-tion (im′pli-kā′shun), *n.* 1, close connection; entanglement; 2, something not expressed but suggested; a hint; as, *implications* of theft.

im-plic-it (im-plis′it), *adj.* 1, understood, though not expressed; implied; as, an *implicit* threat; 2, trusting in the word or authority of another without question; complete; as, *implicit* faith; *implicit* obedience.—*adv.* **im-plic′it-ly.**

im-plore (im-plōr′), *v.t.* [implored, implor-ing], to entreat earnestly and humbly; as, to *implore* God for mercy; pray for; beg; as, to *implore* aid.—*adv.* **im-plor′ing-ly.**

im-ply (im-plī′), *v.t.* [implied, implying], 1, to mean something not directly expressed; suggest; as, silence *implies* consent; 2, to involve as a result; as, wealth *implies* responsibility.

im-po-lite (im′pō-līt′), *adj.* discourteous; rude.—*adv.* **im′po-lite′ly.**

im-pon-der-a-ble (im-pon′dẽr-a-bl), *adj.* without weight:—*n.* usually *pl.*, problems, situations, etc., difficult to assess; as, the *imponderables* of war.

¹**im-port** (im-pōrt′; im′pōrt), *v.t.* to bring in from a foreign country, esp. for commercial purposes:—*n.* (im′pōrt), an article brought from a foreign country; esp. merchandise intended for sale: usually *imports.*—*n.* **im-port′er.**

²**im-port** (im-pōrt′), *v.t.* to signify or express:—*v.i.* to have consequence; be of moment:—*n.* (im′pōrt), 1, meaning; as, the *import* of a sentence; 2, importance; as, a decision of great *import.*

im-por-tant (im-pôr′tant), *adj.* 1, of much consequence; significant; momentous; as, an *important* election; 2, having an air of importance; pompous.—*adv.* **im-por′tant-ly.**—*n.* **im-por′tance.**

im-por-ta-tion (im′pōr-tā′shun), *n.* the act or practice of bringing merchandise into a country from abroad; also, the merchandise so imported.

im-por-tune (im′pôr-tūn′; im-pôr′-tūn), *v.t.* [importuned, importun-ing], to ask repeatedly; beg persistently.—*n.* **im′por-tu′ni-ty.**—*adj.* **im-por′tu-nate.**

im-pose (im-pōz′), *v.t.* [imposed, impos-ing], 1, to lay (a burden, punishment, etc.) upon persons or property; as, to *impose* taxes; 2, to force (oneself); obtrude; as, to *impose* one's company

on others:—*v.i.* to take advantage; presume; as, do not *impose* upon his kindness.

im-pos-ing (im-pōz′ing), *adj.* stately; impressive.

im-po-si-tion (im′pō-zish′un), *n.* 1, the act of imposing a burden; 2, the tax, punishment, etc., imposed; also, an excessive burden imposed; 3, a trick; fraud.

im-pos-si-ble (im-pos′i-bl), *adj.* 1, not capable of occurring or existing; 2, not convenient or easy; as, it is *impossible* to call a meeting for tomorrow; 3, *Colloq.* utterly objectionable; intolerable.—*n.* **im-pos′si-bil′i-ty.**

im-post (im′pōst), *n.* a tax, esp. a duty levied by a government on imports into a country.

im-pos-tor (im-pos′tẽr), *n.* one who attempts to deceive others by adopting a false name or character; a swindler.

im-po-tent (im′po-tent), *adj.* 1, lacking physical, mental, or moral power; weak; 2, lacking sexual power (said of males).—*n.* **im′po-tence.**

im-pound (im-pound′), *v.t.* 1, to shut in a pen; as, to *impound* stray dogs; 2, to seize and hold; as, the police *impounded* his car.

im-pov-er-ish (im-pov′ẽr-ish), *v.t.* 1, to make poor; as, his gambling *impoverished* him; 2, to use up the strength or fertility of; as, to *impoverish* land.—*n.* **im-pov′er-ish-ment.**

im-prac-ti-ca-ble (im-prak′ti-ka-bl), *adj.* that cannot be worked or used; as, an *impracticable* plan; an *impracticable* device.

im-prac-ti-cal (im-prak′ti-kal), *adj.* not inclined to pay attention to what is useful or profitable; not practical.

im-pre-ca-tion (im′pri-kā′shun), *n.* the calling down of evil upon someone; a curse.

im-preg-na-ble (im-preg′na-bl), *adj.* 1, not to be captured by force; unconquerable; as, an *impregnable* fort; 2, not to be overcome by temptation; as, a man of *impregnable* honesty.

im-preg-nate (im-preg′nāt), *v.t.* [impregnat-ed, impregnat-ing], 1, to make pregnant; fertilize; 2, to cause to be filled or saturated with; as, to *impregnate* wood with creosote.—*n.* **im′preg-na′tion.**

im-pre-sa-ri-o (im′pre-sär′i-ō), *n.* the organizer, manager, or conductor of an opera or concert company.

im-press (im-pres′), *v.t.* 1, to mark by applying pressure; stamp; as, the king *impressed* the wax with the royal seal; **2,** to affect or influence deeply; as, the speech *impressed* me; **3,** to imprint or fix deeply on the mind; as, *impress* the fear of the law upon him:— *n.* (im′pres), **1,** a mark produced by pressure, as by a stamp; **2,** a distinguishing mark.

im-pres-sion (im-presh′un), *n.* **1,** the act of marking or stamping; also, the mark made; as, the *impression* of a seal on wax; **2,** the effect produced on the mind or emotions by something outside them; as, his first ascent in an aeroplane made a profound *impression* upon him; **3,** a vague notion, remembrance, or belief; as, my *impression* is that I have seen you before.—*adj.* **im-pres′-sion-a-ble.**

im-pres-sive (im-pres′iv), *adj.* able to influence the mind or feelings; as, an *impressive* ceremony.—*adv.* **im-pres′-sive-ly.**

im-print (im-print′), *v.t.* **1,** to mark by pressure; impress; **2,** to stamp or print, as letters, postmarks, etc., on paper; **3,** to impress (an idea) deeply on the mind:—*n.* (im′print), **1,** an impression or mark left by something; as, the *imprint* of a foot; **2,** the printer's or publisher's name, and the place and date of publication, printed on the title-page or at the end of a book.

im-pris-on (im-priz′n), *v.t.* to put in jail or prison.—*n.* **im-pris′on-ment.**

im-prob-a-ble (im-prob′a-bl), *adj.* unlikely to happen, exist, or be true; as, an *improbable* result; an *improbable* story.—*adv.* **im-prob′a-bly.**—*n.* **im-prob′a-bil′i-ty.**

im-promp-tu (im-promp′tū), *adv.* and *adj.* without preparation; off-hand; as, to speak *impromptu;* an *impromptu* picnic:— *n.* something, as a musical composition, that is made, done, or performed without preparation.

im-prop-er (im-prop′ẽr), *adj.* **1,** not suited to the purpose; **2,** not according to good manners; indecent; as, *improper* conduct; **3,** incorrect; as, *improper* usage of words.—*adv.* **im-prop′er-ly.**

im-pro-pri-e-ty (im′prō-prī′e-ti), *n.* [*pl.* improprieties], **1,** the fact or quality of being improper; **2,** something, as in language or conduct, that is incorrect or indecent.

im-prove (im-prōōv′), *v.t.* [improved, improv-ing], **1,** to make better; as, to *improve* the mind; **2,** to use to advantage; as, to *improve* an opportunity:— *v.i.* to grow better. as in health.—*n.* **im-prove′ment.**

im-prov-i-dent (im-prov′i-dent), *adj.* lacking foresight; not providing for the future: opposite of *thrifty.*

im-pro-vise (im′prō-vīz′; im′prō-vīz′) *v.t.* [improvised, improvis-ing], **1,** to compose without plan; make up on the spur of the moment, as verses or music; **2,** to contrive; as, we *improvised* a bed out of pine branches.—*n.* **im′pro-vi-sa′tion.**

im-pru-dent (im-prōō′dent), *adj.* lacking caution; heedless and rash; as, it is *imprudent* to go sailing in a storm.—*adv.* **im-pru′dent-ly.**—*n.* **im-pru′dence.**

im-pu-dent (im′pū-dent), *adj.* insolent; rude; disrespectful; as, an *impudent* reply.—*n.* **im′pu-dence.**

im-pugn (im-pūn′), *v.t.* to attack by argument; question; as, I do not *impugn* your veracity.

im-pulse (im′puls), *n.* **1,** a driving forward; the motion so produced, or the force producing it; **2,** a sudden, unthinking desire or inclination to act in a particular way; as, to give a beggar money under an *impulse* of pity; **3,** tendency to act without thinking; as, many people are guided by *impulse* rather than by reason.—*adj.* **im-pul′-sive.**—*adv.* **im-pul′sive-ly.**—*n.* **im-pul′-sive-ness.**

im-pu-ni-ty (im-pū′ni-ti), *n.* freedom from punishment, injury, or loss; as, you cannot break the law with *impunity.*

im-pure (im-pūr′), *adj.* **1,** not clean; unwholesome; as, *impure* milk; **2,** mixed with foreign or inferior substance as, *impure* gold; **3,** bad; corrupt in thought, word, or deed.—*adv.* **im-pure′ly.**—*n.* **im-pu′ri-ty.**

im-pute (im-pūt′), *v.t.* [imput-ed, imput-ing], to set to the account of; attribute or ascribe; as, to *impute* a theft to poverty.—*n.* **im′pu-ta′tion** (im′pū-tā′shun).

in (in), *prep.* **1,** within the bounds or limits of; as, lost *in* the woods; hurt *in* the hand; **2,** being surrounded by (circumstances, interests, etc.); as, *in* business; *in* trouble; **3,** within (a state, condition, occupation, etc.); as, *in* chains; *in* pain; **4,** within (a period of time); during; as, *in* winter; **5,** after; as, return *in* two days; **6,** at the time of; as, *in* the beginning; **7,** in the person or case of; as, you have a friend *in* me; **8,** in the range of; as, *in* mathematics; in the capacity of; as, it isn't *in* him to do that; **9,** made of; as, a statue *in* bronze; **10,** dressed in; as, a woman *in* black; **11,** expressed in; as, a letter *in* French; **12,** as a means of; as, *in* explanation:—*adv.* **1,** toward

the inside; as, he went *in;* **2,** inside a place; at home; as, my mother is *in:*—*adj.* **1,** incoming; as, the *in*-line of traffic; **2,** in power; as, the *in*-party; **3,** *Colloq.* the richer by; as, he was *in* five dollars; **4,** *Slang,* in a certain relation; as, he's *in* bad with the officials:—**ins,** *n.pl.* those in office or power:—**ins and outs,** all the details; as, to know the *ins and outs* of a business.

in-a-bil-i-ty (in/a-bil/i-ti), *n.* the condition of being unable; lack of power.

in-ac-ces-si-ble (in/ak-ses/i-bl), *adj.* not easy to get to or into; not obtainable or approachable; as, *inaccessible* heights.—*n.* in/ac-ces/si-bil/i-ty.

in-ac-cu-rate (in-ak/ū-rit), *adj.* incorrect; not exact; as, *inaccurate* figures made by *inaccurate* people.—*n.* in-ac/cu-ra-cy.

in-ac-tive (in-ak/tiv), *adj.* unable to move or act; not active; sluggish; idle; as, an *inactive* volcano.—*n.* in-ac/tion.—*n.* in/ac-tiv/i-ty.

in-ad-e-quate (in-ad/i-kwit), *adj.* not equal to some demand; not sufficient; as, *inadequate* resources.—*adv.* in-ad/e-quate-ly.—*n.* in-ad/e-qua-cy (in-ad/e-kwa-si).

in-ad-mis-si-ble (in/ad-mis/i-bl), *adj.* not to be granted, allowed, or conceded (as true).

in-ad-vert-ent (in/ad-vûr/tent), *adj.* due to heedlessness; unintentional; thoughtless; as, an *inadvertent* slight.—*n.* in/ad-vert/ence.

in-ad-vis-a-ble (in/ad-vīz/a-bl), *adj.* not to be recommended; unwise.

in-al-ien-a-ble (in-āl/yen-a-bl), *adj.* that cannot be transferred or taken away; as, *inalienable* rights.

in-ane (in-ān/), *adj.* empty; senseless; silly; as, an *inane* remark or smile.—*n.* in-an/i-ty.

in-an-i-mate (in-an/i-mit), *adj.* **1,** without animal life; as, *inanimate* rocks; **2,** deprived of life; as, an *inanimate* human body; **3,** dull; spiritless; as, *inanimate* conversation.—*adv.* in-an/i-mate-ly.

in-ap-pli-ca-ble (in-ap/li-ka-bl), *adj.* not fit, suitable, or relevant.

in-ap-pro-pri-ate (in/a-prō/pri-it), *adj.* not suitable, fit, or proper; as, *inappropriate* dress or speech.—*adv.* in/ap-pro/pri-ate-ly.—*n.* in/ap-pro/pri-ate-ness.

in-ar-tic-u-late (in/är-tik/ū-lit), *adj.* **1,** not expressed in words; as, *inarticulate* rage; **2,** incapable of speech; dumb; as, *inarticulate* animals; surprise made him *inarticulate;* **3,** not

jointed; as, a jelly-fish has an *inarticulate* body.

in-ar-tis-tic (in/är-tis/tik), *adj.* **1,** not in accord with the principles of art; as, *inartistic* designs; **2,** lacking in appreciation of art; as, an *inartistic* nature; **3,** not graceful; not skilful; as, *inartistic* movements.—*adv.* in/ar-tis/ti-cal-ly.

in-as-much (in/az-much/), *adv.* in so far; because; as, *inasmuch* as you wish to, you may go. Also written **in as much.**

in-at-ten-tion (in/a-ten/shun), *n.* failure to fix one's mind on a matter; heedlessness; as, he failed because of *inattention.*—*adj.* in/at-ten/tive.—*adv.* in/at-ten/tive-ly.

in-au-di-ble (in-ô/di-bl), *adj.* incapable of being heard; as, an *inaudible* remark.—*adv.* in-au/di-bly.

in-au-gu-ral (in-ô/gū-ral), *adj.* pertaining to the dedication of a public building, the formal installation of a person in an office, etc.:—*n.* a speech made on such an occasion.

in-au-gu-rate (in-ô/gū-rāt/), *v.t.* [inaugurat-ed, inaugurat-ing], **1,** to admit or swear into office with special ceremony; as, to *inaugurate* a president; **2,** to make a formal beginning of; as, to *inaugurate* a custom; **3,** to celebrate the first public use of; as, to *inaugurate* a court-house.—*n.* in-au/gu-ra/tion.

in-aus-pi-cious (in/ôs-pish/us), *adj.* unlucky; unfavourable; as, an *inauspicious* beginning.—*adv.* in/aus-pi/cious-ly.

in-born (in/bôrn/), *adj.* present at birth; innate; natural; as, an *inborn* sense of courtesy.

in-breed-ing (in/brēd/ing), *n.* **1,** mating of animals or persons closely related; **2,** the self-fertilizing of plants.—*adj.* in/bred/.

in-cal-cu-la-ble (in-kal/kū-la-bl), *adj.* **1,** beyond estimate; hence, very great; as, he did *incalculable* harm; **2,** not dependable; as, a person of *incalculable* moods.

in-can-des-cent (in/kan-des/ent), *adj.* glowing with white heat; hence, brilliant; shining:—**incandescent lamp,** a kind of lamp in which a filament gives off light as a result of intense heat.—*n.* in/can-des/cence.

in-can-ta-tion (in/kan-tā/shun), *n.* **1,** the use of charms or spells, sung or spoken, as a part of a magic ritual; **2,** the words used.

in-ca-pa-ble (in-kā/pa-bl),

INCANDESCENT LAMP

adj. **1,** not having power or ability; as, *incapable* of walking; **2,** not open or susceptible to; as, *incapable* of improvement.—*n.* in′ca-pa-bil′i-ty.

in-ca-pac-i-tate (in′ka-pas′i-tāt′), *v.t.* [incapacitat-ed, incapacitat-ing], to make powerless or unfit; as, old age *incapacitates* one for hard labour.—*n.* in′ca-pac′i-ty.

in-car-cer-ate (in-kär′sėr-āt′), *v.t.* [incarcerat-ed, incarcerat-ing], to shut up in a prison; imprison; confine.

in-car-na-tion (in′kär-nā′shun), *n.* **1,** the taking on of material form; embodiment in human flesh; **2,** esp. in the Christian religion, the taking upon himself of human flesh by the Son of God in the person of Jesus; **3,** a person thought of as representing a principle, ideal, etc.; as, he is the *incarnation* of honesty.—*adj.* in-car′nate.

in-case (in-kās′), *v.t.* [incased, incasing], to enclose in a box or solid covering; surround with anything; as, the mediaeval knights *incased* themselves in armour. The preferred spelling is **en-case′.**

in-cau-tious (in-kô′shus), *adj.* heedless; careless; unwary; indifferent.

in-cen-di-ar-y (in-sen′di-er′i), *adj.* **1,** pertaining to the malicious setting on fire of property; **2,** tending to stir up passion, strife, or violence; as, an *incendiary* article:—*n* [*pl.* incendiaries], **1,** one who maliciously sets fire to property; **2,** one who excites quarrels; **3,** *Military,* a bomb which sets fire to its target: short for *incendiary bomb* (World War II).

¹in-cense (in-sens′), *v.t.* [incensed, incens-ing], to make angry; enrage; as, the lie *incensed* her.

²in-cense (in′sens), *n.* **1,** any material which gives off perfume when burned; **2,** the smoke or odour of such material when burned, esp. in religious rites; **3,** any pleasant odour or perfume; as, the *incense* of flowers.

in-cen-tive (in-sen′tiv), *adj.* arousing to action; encouraging:—*n.* motive; as, hope of gain is an *incentive* to work.

in-cep-tion (in-sep′shun), *n.* beginning; initiation; first stage; as, *inception* of a new project.

in-ces-sant (in-ses′ant), *adj.* unceasing; constant; repeated; as, the *incessant* dropping of water.—*adv.* in-ces′sant-ly.

in-cest (in′sest), *n.* sexual intercourse between persons related within the degrees wherein marriage is forbidden by law.—*adj.* in-ces′tu-ous.

inch (inch), *n.* **1,** a unit of length equal to one twelfth of a foot; **2,** a small

distance or degree; as, he came within an *inch* of being struck by the automobile:—*v.i.* to move slowly; as, to *inch* along.

in-ci-dence (in′si-dens), *n.* the range or extent of occurrence or effect; as, the *incidence* of poliomyelitis that year.

in-ci-dent (in′si-dent), *adj.* apt to happen; naturally belonging; as, the dangers *incident* to a career as an aviator:—*n.* an episode; an event of small importance in relation to a larger event or experience.

in-ci-den-tal (in′si-den′tal), *adj.* occurring in connection with something else more important; as, a play with *incidental* music; *incidental* worries:—**incidentals,** *n. pl.* relatively unimportant items, esp. minor expenses.—*adv.* in′ci-den′tal-ly.

in-cin-er-a-tor (in-sin′ėr-ā′tėr), *n.* a furnace for burning waste matter or cremating dead bodies.

in-cip-i-ent (in-sip′i-ent), *adj.* beginning to be or appear; as, *incipient* tuberculosis.

in-ci-sion (in-sizh′un), *n.* **1,** the act of cutting into something; **2,** a cut made with a sharp instrument; as, a surgical *incision.*

in-ci-sor (in-sī′zėr), *n.* a cutting tooth; in man, one of the four front teeth in either jaw. (See illustration under *dentition.*)

in-cite (in-sīt′), *v.t.* [incit-ed, incit-ing], to rouse; stir up; as, hunger *incited* the mob to riot.—*n.* in-cite′ment.

in-ci-vil-i-ty (in′si-vil′i-ti), *n.* impoliteness; lack of courtesy.

in-clem-ent (in-klem′ent), *adj.* harsh; severe; as, *inclement* weather, climate.

in-cli-na-tion (in′kli-nā′shun), *n.* **1,** the act of bending or leaning towards something; esp. a bending of the head or body in reverence, recognition, etc.; a bow; **2,** a turning aside from a given direction or position; a slanting position; slope; as, the *inclination* of the Tower of Pisa; also, the amount of slant; **3,** a tendency of the mind; a liking; preference; as, an *inclination* for music.

in-cline (in-klīn′), *v.t.* [inclined, inclining], **1,** to cause to lean; slant; as, to *incline* a board; **2,** to bow; as, to *incline* the head in prayer; **3,** to give a tendency to; turn; dispose; as, this statement *inclines* me to believe:—*v.i.* **1,** to turn from a given direction; slant; lean; **2,** to bow; **3,** to have a tendency or preference:—*n.* (in-klīn′; in′klīn), a slant; a sloping surface; as, we travelled up a steep *incline.*

in-close (in-klōz′), v.t. Same as **enclose.**

in-clude (in-klūd′; klōōd′), v.t. [included, includ-ing], to enclose within limits; contain as part of the whole; as, biology *includes* both botany and zoology.—*n.* **in-clu′sion.**

in-clu-sive (in-klū′siv; klōō′), adj. 1, containing a great deal; as, an *inclusive* survey; 2, taking in the two extremes or limits mentioned; as, study lessons from one to five *inclusive.*—*adv.* **in-clu′sive-ly.**

in-cog-ni-to (in-kog′ni-tō′), adj. having one's true identity concealed or disguised; going under an assumed name; as, the prince travelled *incognito.*

in-co-her-ent (in′kō-hēr′ent), adj. 1, consisting of parts that do not cling together; 2, without logical connection; rambling; as, an *incoherent* sentence.—*n.* **in′co-her′ence.**

in-com-bus-ti-ble (in′kom-bus′ti-bl) adj. unburnable; fireproof; as, asbestos is *incombustible.*

in-come (in′kum), *n.* the receipts, usually money, derived from labour, business, property, or capital; wages or salary.

in-com-ing (in′kum′ing), adj. 1, coming in; as, the *incoming* tide; 2, beginning; coming into office; as, the *incoming* mayor:—*n.* the act of coming in; arrival.

in-com-pa-ra-ble (in-kom′pa-ra-bl), adj. not to be compared; unequalled; as, *incomparable* beauty.—*adv.* **in-com′pa-ra-bly.**

in-com-pat-i-ble (in′kom-pat′i-bl), adj. 1, incapable of existing together in harmony; 2, inconsistent; as, desires *incompatible* with one's income.—*adv.* **in′com-pat′i-bly.**—*n.* **in′com-pat′i-bil′i-ty.**

in-com-pe-tent (in-kom′pi-tent), adj. 1, unfit; without ability; as, an *incompetent* servant; 2, not legally qualified.—*adv.* **in-com′pe-tent-ly.**—*n.* **in-com′pe-tence.**

in-com-plete (in′kom-plēt′), adj. not fully finished or developed; as, an *incomplete* design; not having all its parts; imperfect; as, an *incomplete* set.

in-com-pre-hen-si-ble (in′kom-pri-hen′si-bl), adj. not to be understood or grasped by the mind; as, *incomprehensible* points of view.—*adv.* **in′com-pre-hen′si-bly.**

in-con-ceiv-a-ble (in′kon-sēv′a-bl), adj. incapable of being grasped by the mind or imagined; unbelievable; as, *inconceivable* cruelty.—*n.* **in′con-ceiv′a-bil′i-ty.**

in-con-gru-ous (in-kong′groo-us), adj. unsuitable; inappropriate; as, his solemn voice was *incongruous* with the gaiety of the poem he was reciting.—*n.* **in′con-gru′i-ty.**

in-con-se-quen-tial (in-kon′si-kwen′shal), adj. unimportant; trivial; irrelevant.

in-con-sid-er-ate (in′kon-sid′ėr-it), adj. not heeding the wishes, thoughts, or feelings of others; thoughtless; as, an *inconsiderate* son; an *inconsiderate* remark.—*adv.* **in′con-sid′er-ate-ly.**

in-con-sist-en-cy (in′kon-sis′ten-si), *n.* [*pl.* inconsistencies], 1, lack of agreement; as, the *inconsistency* of two stories; 2, a contradiction; as, testimony full of *inconsistencies.*

in-con-sist-ent (in′kon-sis′tent), adj. 1, not in keeping (with); as, stealing is *inconsistent* with honesty; 2, self-contradictory; not logical; as, a person *inconsistent* in argument.

in-con-so-la-ble (in′kon-sōl′a-bl), adj. not to be comforted; as, *inconsolable* grief.

in-con-spic-u-ous (in′kon-spik′ū-us), adj. not noticeable; not prominent or striking; as, *inconspicuous* colours.

in-con-stant (in-kon′stant), adj. subject to change; fickle; as, *inconstant* lovers.—*n.* **in-con′stan-cy.**

in-con-tro-ver-ti-ble (in-kon′tro-vûr′ti-bl), adj. indisputable; undeniable; as, this is the *incontrovertible* truth.

in-con-ven-ience (in′kon-vēn′yens), *n.* 1, discomfort; trouble; as, an interruption in electrical service causes a great deal of *inconvenience;* 2, that which causes trouble; a hindrance; annoyance; as, the late arrival of the train was an *inconvenience* to me:—*v.t.* to put to trouble; annoy; as, we might *inconvenience* our hosts if we stayed overnight.—*adj.* **in′con-ven′ient.**

in-cor-po-rate (in-kôr′po-rāt′), v.t. [incorporat-ed, incorporat-ing], 1, to combine into one body; unite; esp. to establish as a corporation, or group of people entitled by law to conduct a business as if they were one person; as, to *incorporate* a town or a club; 2, to embody; include; put; as, to *incorporate* an idea into a story; 3, to blend; mix, as one substance with another:—*v.i.* to unite with something else to form a single body:—*adj.* (in-kôr′po-rit), 1, closely united; united in one body; 2, formed into, or united with others in, a body of persons authorized by law to conduct a business as one individual.—*n.* **in-cor′po-ra′tion.**

in-cor-rect (in'ko-rekt'), *adj.* 1, not according to model or rule; faulty; as, an *incorrect* copy; 2, not according to fact; inaccurate; as, *incorrect* information; 3, not in accordance with what is right or proper; improper; as, *incorrect* behaviour; *incorrect* dress.—*adv.* in'-cor-rect'ly.

in-cor-ri-gi-ble (in-kor'i-ji-bl), *adj.* not capable of being corrected or set right; too accustomed to a bad habit to be reformed; as, an *incorrigible* drinker or gambler.—*adv.* in-cor'ri-gi-bly.—*n.* in-cor'ri-gi-bil'i-ty.

in-cor-rupt-i-ble (in'ko-rup'ti-ble), *adj.* 1, not liable to decay; 2, not open to bribery; as, a man of *incorruptible* integrity.

in-crease (in-krēs'), *v.t.* and *v.i.* [increased, increas-ing], to make or become greater; enlarge; as, the number of students *increases* year by year:—*n.* (in'krēs), 1, grown in size, number, intensity, etc.; as, an *increase* in business; an *increase* in popularity; 2, that which is added to the original number, stock, capital, etc.; as, an *increase* of ten students.

in-cred-i-ble (in-kred'i-bl), *adj.* hard to believe; unimaginable; as, *incredible* tales; *incredible* wealth.—*adv.* in-cred'-i-bly.

in-cred-u-lous (in-kred'ū-lus), *adj.* 1, indicating lack of belief; as, an *incredulous* smile; 2, unbelieving; doubting; sceptical; as, even after the evidence was set before her, she was still *incredulous*.—*adv.* in-cred'u-lous-ly.—*n.* in'cre-du'li-ty.

in-cre-ment (in'kre-ment; ing'), *n.* an increase or addition, esp. one of several additions, as an annual *increment* in salary; gain, growth, or profit.

in-crim-i-nate (in-krim'i-nāt'), *v.t.* [incriminat-ed, incriminat-ing], to charge with, or involve in, a crime; as, his words *incriminated* him.—*n.* in-crim'i-na'tion.

in-crust (in-krust'), *v.t.* 1, to cover with, or as with, a crust; to coat; as, barnacles *incrust* the hulls of ships; 2, to overlay with a decorative covering, as with mosaics. The preferred spelling is **en-crust'**.—*n.* in'crus-ta'tion.

in-cu-bate (in'kū-bāt'; ing'kū-bāt'), *v.t.* [incubat-ed, incubat-ing], 1, to sit upon (eggs) in order to hatch them; brood; 2, to keep (eggs) under proper conditions, esp. of warmth, for hatching them:—*v.i.* 1, to sit on eggs; brood; 2, to develop or hatch.—*n.* in'cu-ba'tion.

in-cu-ba-tor (in'kū-bā'tėr; ing'kū-bā'tėr), *n.* 1, an apparatus for hatching eggs by artificial warmth; 2, an apparatus to help the growth of exceptionally small new-born or prematurely born babies.

in-cul-cate (in'kul-kāt'; in-kul'kāt), *v.t.* [inculcat-ed, inculcat-ing], to impress upon the mind urgently; as, the mother tried to *inculcate* honesty on her children.—*n.* in'cul-ca'tion.

in-cum-bent (in-kum'bent), *adj.* 1, lying or leaning with its weight on something else; 2, pressing upon as a duty; as, it is *incumbent* upon every good citizen to vote:—*n.* the holder of an office, esp. a church office.—*n.* in-cum'ben-cy.

in-cum-ber (in-kum'bėr), *v.t.* Same as **encumber**.—*n.* in-cum'brance.

in-cur (in-kûr'), *v.t.* [incurred, incurring], to meet with, fall into, or bring down upon oneself; as, to *incur* hatred, punishment, etc.

in-cur-a-ble (in-kūr'a-bl), *adj.* incapable of being healed; beyond the skill of medicine; as, an *incurable* disease:—*n.* a person diseased or crippled beyond remedy.—*adv.* in-cur'a-bly.—*n.* in-cur'a-bil'i-ty.

in-cur-sion (in-kûr'shun), *n.* raid; inroad; invasion; as, an *incursion* into enemy territory; an *incursion* of the sea.

in-curve (in-kûrv'), *v.t.* and *v.i.* to curve inward:—*n.* (in'kûrv'), in *base-ball*, a pitched ball that curves towards the batter.

in-debt-ed (in-det'id), *adj.* 1, owing money; 2, under obligation; owing gratitude; as, I am *indebted* to you for your kindness.—*n.* in-debt'ed-ness.

in-de-cent (in-dē'sent), *adj.* 1, unfit to be heard or seen; as, *indecent* language or pictures; 2, unbecoming; in bad taste; as, he spoke and left in *indecent* haste.—*adv.* in-de'cent-ly.—*n.* in-de'cen-cy.

in-de-ci-pher-a-ble (in'di-sī'fėr-a-bl), *adj.* that cannot be read; illegible; as, the note was *indecipherable*.

in-de-ci-sive (in'di-sī'siv), *adj.* 1, not settling a matter; as, *indecisive* evidence; 2, not positive; uncertain; irresolute; as, an *indecisive* manner of speech.—*adv.* in'de-ci'sive-ly.—*n.* in'-de-ci'sion.

in-de-co-rous (in'di-kō'rus; in-dek'-or-us), *adj.* improper; violating the rules of good breeding; as, *indecorous* conduct.

in-deed (in-dēd'), *adv.* in fact; in truth; as, I was *indeed* surprised.

in-de-fat-i-ga-ble (in'de-fat'i-ga-bl).

adj. tireless; as, *indefatigable* exertion, —*adv.* in**/**de**/**fat**/**i-ga-bly.

in-de-fen-sib-le (in**/**di-fen**/**si-bl), *adj.* without defence; esp. not capable of being held, maintained, or justified; as, an *indefensible* argument.—*n.* in**/**de-fen**/**si-bil**/**i-ty.

in-de-fin-a-ble (in**/**di-fīn**/**a-bl), *adj.* that cannot be exactly described or explained.

in-def-i-nite (in-def**/**i-nit), *adj.* **1,** not exact; vague; uncertain; as, his answers were *indefinite;* **2,** having no fixed limit, amount, or number:— **indefinite article,** either of the words *a* or *an.*—*adv.* in-def**/**i-nite-ly.

in-del-i-ble (in-del**/**i-bl), *adj.* incapable of being erased; as, *indelible* ink; also, incapable of being forgotten; as, an *indelible* impression.—*adv.* in-del**/**i-bly.

in-del-i-cate (in-del**/**i-kit), *adj.* lacking refinement; offensive to modesty or propriety; coarse; as, *indelicate* remarks.

in-dem-ni-fy (in-dem**/**ni-fī**/**), *v.t.* [indemnified, indemnify-ing], to repay or compensate a person for loss, expense, or damage.—*n.* in-dem**/**ni-fi-ca**/**tion.

in-dem-ni-ty (in-dem**/**ni-ti), *n.* [*pl.* indemnities], **1,** insurance against loss, damage, or punishment; **2,** repayment for loss or injury.

in-dent (in-dent**/**), *v.t.* **1,** to give a zigzag outline to; notch; as, many small bays *indent* the coast; **2,** in writing or printing, to begin (a line) with a blank space; **3,** to make a depression in; dent; stamp; as, to *indent* the sand with footsteps.—*n.* in**/**den-ta**/**tion.

in-den-tion (in-den**/**shun), *n.* Same as in**/**den-ta**/**tion.

in-den-ture (in-den**/**tūr), *n.* **1,** a dent; depression; indentation; **2,** a written agreement or contract, esp. one binding a servant or an apprentice to a master: —*v.t.* [indentured, indentur-ing], to bind by a written agreement, as an apprentice.

in-de-pend-ence (in**/**di-pen**/**dens), *n.* **1,** freedom from support, control, or government by others; **2,** an income or money sufficient for one's needs.

in-de-pend-ent (in**/**di-pen**/**dent), *adj.* **1,** not relying on, supported by, or governed by, others; as, the American colonies declared themselves *independent* of England; **2,** having enough money to live on; as, his family is *independent;* **3,** not easily influenced; not biased; as, an *independent* thinker;

4, disinclined, through pride, to accept help:—*n.* one who in politics, art, etc., acts or thinks for himself.

in-de-scrib-a-ble (in**/**di-skrīb**/**a-ble), *adj.* **1,** not sufficiently definite to be described; indefinite; vague; as, an *indescribable* pain; **2,** too great, beautiful, terrible, etc., to be described; beyond description; as, jewels of *indescribable* beauty.—*adv.* in**/**de-scrib**/**a-bly.

in-de-struct-i-ble (in**/**di-struk**/**ti-bl), *adj.* not capable of being broken up, ruined, or destroyed; durable; lasting. —*adv.* in**/**de-struct**/**i-bly.—*n.* in**/**de-struct**/**i-bil**/**i-ty.

in-de-ter-mi-nate (in**/**di-tûr**/**mi-nit), *adj.* not settled or fixed; indefinite; vague; as, an *indeterminate* sentence for a crime.

in-dex (in**/**deks), *n.* [*pl.* indexes (in**/**dek-sez) or indices (in**/**di-sēz**/**), **1,** that which points out or indicates; a sign; as, busy factories are an *index* of prosperity; **2,** the finger next to the thumb; **3,** a pointer, as the hand on a dial; **4,** a table of the contents of a book, arranged alphabetically and telling on what page each subject is treated; **5,** in *printing,* a mark [☞] used to call attention to:—*v.t.* **1,** to provide (a book) with an alphabetical table of references; **2,** to indicate.

In-di-an club (in**/**di-an), a bottle-shaped club swung by hand for exercise.

Indian dipper, Same as hunts**/**man's-cup**/**.

Indian Ocean, a large ocean south of Asia between Africa and Australia: area, about 28½ million square miles.

India paper, a strong, opaque paper used for thin-paper editions of books.

india—rubber, *n.* Same as *rubber* (definition 3).

in-di-cate (in**/**di-kāt**/**), *v.t.* [indicat-ed, indicat-ing], **1,** to point out; show; mark; as, signposts *indicate* the road; **2,** to suggest; also, to state briefly.—*n.* in**/**di-ca**/**tion.—*n.* in**/**di-ca**/**tor.

in-dic-a-tive (in-dik**/**a-tiv), *adj.* **1,** pointing out; suggesting; as, cold hands are *indicative* of poor circulation; **2,** in *grammar,* designating, or having to do with, that mood of the verb used to state a fact or ask a direct question: —*n.* the indicative mood.—*adv.* in-dic**/**a-tive-ly.

in-dict (in-dīt**/**), *v.t.* to accuse; charge with a crime after finding evidence enough to warrant a trial; as, he was *indicted* for theft.—*n.* in-dict**/**ment.— *adj.* in-dict**/**a-ble (in-dīt**/**a-bl).

in-dif-fer-ent (in-dif′fẽr-ent), *adj*. **1,** not caring or concerned about something; feeling no interest; as, a poor ruler is *indifferent* to the wishes of his people; **2,** neither good nor bad; mediocre; as, *indifferent* work; **3,** having no preference; taking neither side, as in an argument; as, he maintained an *indifferent* attitude.—*n*. **in-dif′fer-ence.**

in-di-gence (in′di-jens), *n*. poverty; need.

in-dig-e-nous (in-dij′i-nus), *adj*. born or produced in a particular place or country; native; as, tobacco is *indigenous* to America.—*adv*. **in-dig′e-nous-ly.**

in-di-gent (in′di-jent), *adj*. very poor; needy; as, an *indigent* widow.

in-di-gest-i-ble (in′di-jes′ti-bl; in′dī-jes′ti-bl), *adj*. hard or impossible to digest.

in-di-ges-tion (in′di-jes′chun), *n*. difficulty in digesting food; the discomfort caused by such difficulty; dyspepsia.

in-dig-nant (in-dig′nant), *adj*. feeling anger and scorn because of unfair treatment.—*n*. **in′dig-na′tion.**

in-dig-ni-ty (in-dig′ni-ti), *n*. [*pl*. indignities], an act or saying which injures the dignity of someone else; an insult.

in-di-go (in′di-gō′), *n*. [*pl*. indigos or indigoes], **1,** a manufactured blue dye, formerly obtained from the indigo plant; **2,** a deep-violet blue: also called *indigo blue*.

in-di-rect (in′di-rekt′; in′dī-rekt′), *adj*. **1,** not straight; not in a direct line; as, an *indirect* road; **2,** roundabout; as, *indirect* taxation; **3,** not straightforward; as, an *indirect* reply.—*adv*. **in′di-rect′ly.**

in-dis-cern-i-ble (in′di-zûr′ni-bl), *adj*. that cannot be seen.

in-dis-creet (in′dis-krēt′), *adj*. not cautious or careful; unwise; imprudent; as, an *indiscreet* remark.—*adv*. **in′dis-creet′ly.**

in-dis-cre-tion (in′dis-kresh′un), *n*. **1,** rashness; lack of caution; **2,** an indiscreet or imprudent act.

in-dis-crim-i-nate (in′dis-krim′i-nit), *adj*. not distinguishing differences between one person or thing and another or others; not choosing or chosen carefully; as, an *indiscriminate* reader; *indiscriminate* reading.—*adv*. **in′dis-crim′i-nate-ly.**

in-dis-pen-sa-ble (in′dis-pen′sa-bl), *adj*. not to be done without; absolutely necessary; as, food is *indispensable* to life.

in-dis-posed (in′dis-pōzd′), *adj*. **1,** ill; unwell; **2,** unwilling; averse.

in-dis-po-si-tion (in′dis-po-zish′un), *n*. **1,** an illness, esp. one that is not serious; **2,** aversion; unwillingness.

in-dis-pu-ta-ble (in-dis′pū-ta-bl), *adj*. unquestionable; clearly evident: prefix *in*- means *not*.

in-dis-so-lu-ble (in-dis′o-lū-bl; in′di-sol′ū-bl), *adj*. **1,** that cannot be broken up or destroyed; **2,** forever binding, as a contract, agreement, etc.

in-dis-tinct (in′dis-tingkt′), *adj*. not distinct or clear; as, an *indistinct* sound.—*adv*. **in′dis-tinct′ly.**

in-dis-tin-guish-a-ble (in′dis-ting′-gwish-a-bl), *adj*. not separable; blurred.

in-di-vid-u-al (in′di-vid′ū-al), *adj*. **1,** of or belonging to a single person or thing; as, *individual* lockers; **2,** one's own; as, an *individual* style of speaking:—*n*. a single or separate person, animal or thing.—*adv*. **in′di-vid′u-al-ly.**

in-di-vid-u-al-i-ty (in′di-vid′ū-al′i-ti), *n*. [*pl*. individualities], **1,** the quality or state of existing separately, or apart from other persons or things; separate existence; **2,** the sum of all the characteristics that mark one person or thing as different and separate from another; personality; **3,** an individual person or thing.—*adj*. **in′di-vid′u-al-is′tic.**

in-di-vis-i-ble (in′di-viz′i-bl), *adj*. not capable of being divided into parts.—*n*. **in′di-vis′i-bil′i-ty.**

in-doc-tri-nate (in-dok′tri-nāt′), *v.t.* [-nated, -nating], to teach, impress deeply with a doctrine, principle, idea etc.—*n*. **in-doc′tri-na′tion.**

in-do-lent (in′do-lent), *adj*. fond of ease; avoiding labour; lazy.—*n*. **in′dolence.**

in-dom-i-ta-ble (in-dom′i-ta-bl), *adj* unconquerable; stubborn; unyielding as, an *indomitable* will.—*adv*. **in-dom′i-ta-bly.**

in-door (in′dōr′), *adj*. pertaining to the inside of a building; living, belonging or done, within doors; as, *indoor* sports.

in-doors (in′dōrz′; in′dōrz′), *adv*. in or into the house; as, to play *indoors*.

in-dorse (in-dôrs′), *v.t.* Same a *endorse*.

in-dorse-ment (in-dôrs′ment), *n* Same as *endorsement*.

in-du-bi-ta-ble (in-dū′bi-ta-bl), *adj*

sure beyond doubt or question.—*adv.* **in-du'bi-ta-bly.**

n-duce (in-dūs'), *v.t.* [induced, inducing], **1,** to persuade; influence; prevail upon; as, money will *induce* him to go; **2,** to bring on; effect; cause; as, illness *induced* by overwork; **3,** to arrive at (a conclusion or principle) from the observation or study of particular cases.—*n.* **in-duce'ment.**

n-duc-tance (in-duk'tans), *n.* in *electricity*, the capacity of a circuit for magnetic induction.

n-duc-tion (in-duk'shun), *n.* **1,** the introduction of a person into office; **2** in *electricity*, the act or process by which a conductor becomes electrified when near, but not in contact with, a body that is charged; **3,** the process of reasoning by which a general conclusion is reached from a study of particular facts.—*adj.* **in-duc'tive.**—*v.t.* **in-duct'.**

n-dulge (in-dulj'), *v.t.* [indulged, indulg-ing], **1,** to give way to; humour; as, the nurse *indulged* the sick child; **2,** to yield to; as, to *indulge* a love of sweets:—*v.i.* to gratify one's desires, usually without restraint; as, to *indulge* in candy.

n-dul-gent (in-dul'jent), *adj.* yielding to the humour or wishes of another; as an *indulgent* parent; also, too forbearing; too lenient.—*n.* **in-dul'gence.**

n-dus-tri-ous (in-dus'tri-us), *adj.* diligent; hard-working; as, an *industrious* wife.—*adv.* **in-dus'tri-ous-ly.**

n-dus-try (in'dus-tri), *n.* [*pl.* industries], **1,** steady application to a task; diligence; **2,** all forms of business and manufacture; **3,** in a more limited sense, the occupations that produce goods, as distinguished from finance and commerce; **4,** a particular branch of work or trade; as, the cotton *industry.*—*adj.* **in-dus'tri-al.**—*n.* **in-dus'tri-al-ist.**—*v.t.* **in-dus'tri-al-ize'.**—*n.* **in-dus'-tri-al-i-za'tion.**

n-dwell (in'dwel'), *v.t.* and *v.i.* to abide or exist in, as a spirit or principle.

n-e-bri-ate (in-ē'bri-āt'), *v.t.* [-ated, -ating], to make drunk; intoxicate (mentally or emotionally).—*n.* (-it), an habitual drunkard.—*adj.* drunken.—*n.* **in-e'bri-a'tion.**

n-ed-i-ble (in-ed'i-bl), *adj.* not fit to be eaten.—*n.* **in-ed'i-bil'i-ty.**

n-ef-fa-ble (in-ef'a-bl), *adj.* incapable of being expressed in words; beyond description; as, *ineffable* joy.—*adv.* **in-ef'fa-bly.**

n-ef-fec-tive (in'e-fek'tiv), *adj.* not producing, or unable to produce, the desired result; ineffectual; as, his urgent plea was *ineffective.*—*adv.* **in'ef-fec'tive-ly.**

in-ef-fec-tu-al (in'e-fek'tū-al), *adj.* without result; weak; unsuccessful; as, all his efforts were *ineffectual.*

in-ef-fi-cient (in'e-fish'ent), *adj.* **1,** not producing, or not capable of producing, the desired effect; as, *inefficient* labour; **2,** incapable; lacking in skill or in willingness to work well: as, an *inefficient* workman.—*n.* **in'ef-fi'cien-cy.**

in-el-e-gant (in-el'e-gant), *adj.* lacking in beauty, refinement, good taste, etc.

in-el-i-gi-ble (in-el'i-ji-bl), *adj.* **1,** unfit; unsuitable; as, a lame man is *ineligible* for the army; **2,** not qualified legally for an office or position; as, his age makes him *ineligible* for Parliament.—*adv.* **in-el'i-gi-bly.**—*n.* **in-el'i-gi-bil'-i-ty.**

in-ept (in-ept'), *adj.* **1,** unsuitable; unfit; **2,** absurd; foolish; as, an *inept* remark; **3,** clumsy; inefficient.—*n.* **in-ep'ti-tude'.**

in-e-qual-i-ty (in'i-kwol'i-ti; in'i-kwôl'i-ti), *n.* [*pl.* inequalities], **1,** the quality of being unequal; difference of rank, station, size, number, etc.; **2,** unevenness, as in surface; changeableness in the condition of a person or thing; as, *inequalities* of temper, the weather, etc.

in-eq-ui-ta-ble (in-ek'wi-ta-bl), *adj.* unfair; unjust.

in-ert (in-ûrt'), *adj.* **1,** without power to move; lifeless; as, an *inert* mass of rock; **2,** slow; sluggish; **3,** having no active chemical powers; as, an *inert* drug.

in-er-tia (in-ûr'sha; in-ûr'shi-a), *n.* **1,** the tendency not to move, change, or exert oneself; **2,** in *physics*, that property of matter which causes a body at rest to stay motionless, or a body in motion to continue moving in the same direction, unless acted upon by some outside force.

in-es-cap-a-ble (in'es-kā'pa-bl), *adj.* that cannot be escaped; as, an *inescapable* conclusion.

in-es-ti-ma-ble (in-es'ti-ma-bl), *adj.* beyond measure or price; as, the work of our public schools is of *inestimable* value.

in-ev-i-ta-ble (in-ev'i-ta-bl), *adj.* not to be escaped or shunned; unavoidable; as, *inevitable* death.—*adv.* **in-ev'i-ta-bly.**

in-ex-act (in'eg-zakt'), *adj.* not exact or accurate; incorrect.—*adv.* **in'ex-act'ly.**

in-ex-cus-a-ble (in′eks-kūz′a-bl), *adj.* not to be excused or justified; as, *inexcusable* rudeness.—*adv.* in′ex-cus′a-bly.

in-ex-haust-i-ble (in′eg-zôs′ti-bl), *adj.* **1,** incapable of being used up; unfailing; as, *inexhaustible* resources; **2,** of tireless power, vigour, or strength; unwearied.

in-ex-o-ra-ble (in-ek′so-ra-bl), *adj.* not to be moved by prayers; unyielding; unrelenting; as, an *inexorable* enemy.

in-ex-pe-di-ent (in′eks-pē′di-ent), *adj.* not advisable; not suitable or wise; as, it would be *inexpedient* to increase taxes now.—*n.* in′ex-pe′di-en-cy.

in-ex-pen-sive (in′eks-pen′siv), *adj.* cheap; costing little.

in-ex-pe-ri-ence (in′eks-pē′ri-ens), *n.* want of experience; lack of firsthand knowledge.—*adj.* in′ex-pe′ri-enced.

in-ex-pli-ca-ble (in-eks′pli-ka-bl), *adj.* not capable of being explained or understood; as, an *inexplicable* mystery —*adv.* in-ex′pli-ca-bly.—*n.* in-ex′pli-ca-bil′i-ty.

in-ex-press-i-ble (in′eks-pres′i-bl), *adj.* not capable of being put into words; unutterable.—*adv.* in′ex-press′i-bly.

in-ex-tin-guish-a-ble (in′eks-ting′-gwish-a-bl), *adj.* that cannot be put out, as a fire; unquenchable.

in-ex-tri-ca-ble (in-eks′tri-ka-bl), *adj.* incapable of being untied or disentangled; hopelessly confused; incapable of being solved; as, an *inextricable* difficulty.

in-fal-li-ble (in-fal′i-bl), *adj.* **1,** incapable of failing; unerring; not capable of making a mistake; as, God is *infallible;* **2,** absolutely trustworthy; unfailing; as, an *infallible* remedy; an *infallible* friend.—*adv.* in-fal′li-bly.—*n.* in-fal′li-bil′i-ty.

in-fa-mous (in′fa-mus), *adj.* **1,** having a bad reputation; notorious; as, an *infamous* traitor; **2,** villainous; as, an *infamous* plot to kill the king.—*adv.* in′fa-mous-ly.

in-fa-my (in′fa-mi), *n.* [*pl.* infamies], **1,** public disgrace; dishonour; **2,** baseness; vileness; also, a disgraceful act.

in-fan-cy (in′fan-si), *n.* **1,** babyhood and early childhood; **2,** the first stage of anything; as, the *infancy* of a nation.

in-fant (in′fant), *n.* **1,** a baby; a young child; **2,** in *law,* a person who has not attained the age of 21:—*adj.* pertaining to, or intended for, babies or young children; as, *infant* diet; also, pertaining to the earliest stages of anything;

very young; undeveloped; as, an *infan* industry.

in-fan-ti-cide (in-fan′ti-sīd′), *n.* the murder, or murderer, of an infant.

in-fan-tile (in′fan-tīl′), *adj.* **1,** childish as *infantile* behaviour; **2,** relating t infants; as *infantile* diseases:—**infantil paralysis,** a spinal disease marked by inflammation of nerve cells, ofte resulting in permanent deformity.

in-fan-try (in′fan-tri), *n.* soldiers wh are armed, equipped, and trained fo service on foot; foot-soldiers.—*n.* in′ fan-try-man.

in-fat-u-at-ed (in-fat′ū-āt′ed), *adj* showing foolish fondness; so inspire with an extravagant passion for some thing as to be wanting in soun judgment about it.—*n.* in-fat′u-a′tion

in-fect (in-fekt′), *v.t.* **1,** to affect (ε person or persons) with disease by spreading germs; as, nurses are no inoculated against typhoid fever, s that they cannot be *infected* with th disease; **2,** to taint or poison (a wound instrument, drinking-water, etc.) wit germs; **3,** to affect or influence with ä mood, feeling, or idea; as, Jane' giggles *infected* her playmates.

in-fec-tion (in-fek′shun), *n.* **1,** th communication of disease germs; **2,** ε disease communicated by germs in an manner.

in-fec-tious (in-fek′shus), *adj.* **1,** cap able of spreading by means of germ as, mumps and typhoid fever ar *infectious* diseases; **2,** readily com municated or spread; as, *infectiou* gaiety.—*adv.* in-fec′tious-ly.

in-fer (in-fûr′), *v.t.* [inferred, infer-ring] **1,** to arrive at (a conclusion) b reasoning; as, they *inferred* from th student's improved health that gym nasium work was a benefit; **2,** (*loosel* and *incorrectly*) to indicate; imply suggest; your haste *infers* eagernes —*n.* in′fer-ence (in′fer-ens).

in-fe-ri-or (in-fē′ri-ėr), *adj.* **1,** lower i place, rank, or value; secondary; as an *inferior* court; an *inferior* officer; **2** second-rate; poor; as, *inferior* work manship:—*n.* one who ranks belov another.—*n.* in-fe′ri-or′i-ty.

in-fer-nal (in-fûr′nal), *adj.* **1,** belong ing to, or resembling, hell; hellish; **2** fiendish; outrageous.—*adv.* in-fer′nal ly.

in-fer-no (infûr′nō), *n.* [*pl.* -nos (nōz)] **1,** hell; **2,** a place or scene of flames o great heat; as, the blazing buildin became an *inferno.*

in-fest (in-fest′), *v.t.* to overrun; swarr in or over; trouble or annoy constantl or in numbers; as, moths *infested* the woollen material; pirates *infested* the coast.

in-fi-del (in′fi-del), *n.* one who does not believe in a certain religion; an unbeliever, as, among Mohammedans, one who is not a Mohammedan, and among Christians, one who is not a Christian:—*adj.* 1, unbelieving; heathen; 2, pertaining to, or like, infidels; as, *infidel* contempt for the faith.

in-fi-del-i-ty (in′fi-del′i-ti; in′fī-del′i-ti), *n.* [*pl.* infidelities], 1, disbelief in religion, esp. in the Christian religion; 2, the breaking of a trust; disloyalty; unfaithfulness.

in-field (in′fēld′), *n.* in baseball: 1, the space enclosed within the base lines; the diamond as distinguished from the *outfield*; 2, the infield players as, a whole.—*n.* **in′field′er.**

in-fil-trate (in-fil′trāt), *v.t.* to pass through (gaps, openings, etc.): as our scouts *infiltrated* the enemy lines.—*n.* **in′fil-tra′tion.**

in-fi-nite (in′fi-nit), *adj.* 1, without limit in greatness, power, knowledge, etc.; as, *infinite* wisdom; 2, unlimited; endless; as, space is *infinite:*—*n.* that which has no limit:—**the Infinite,** God; the Supreme Being.—*adv.* **in′fi-nite-ly.** —*n.* **in-fin′i-tude** (as, an *infinitude* of stars).

in-fin-i-tes-i-mal (in′fin-i-tes′i-mal), *adj.* too small to be measured; microscopic.—*adv.* **in′fin-i-tes′i-mal-ly.**

in-fin-i-tive (in-fin′i-tiv), *n.* in *grammar*, a part of the verb which expresses the general meaning of the verb without any inflection for person or number, usually having the same form as the stem of the present tense: often though not always used with *to;* as, he longs *to go;* this is a good road on which *to travel;* help me *finish* the job:—*adj.* pertaining to, or formed with, the infinitive; as, an *infinitive* phrase.

in-fin-i-ty (in-fin′i-ti), *n.* [*pl.* infinities], 1, the state of being infinite or beyond measure in time, space, number, etc.; boundlessness; 2, space or time considered as boundless; 3, an infinite quantity or number.

in-firm (in-fûrm′), *adj.* 1, not well or sound physically; weak; 2, weak of mind, will, or character; irresolute; wavering; as, a man *infirm* of purpose. —*n.* **in-fir′mi-ty.**

in-fir-ma-ry (in-fûr′ma-ri), *n.* [*pl.* infirmaries], a room or building in which the sick or injured are cared for, esp. in a school or institution.

in-flame (in-flām′), *v.t.* [inflamed, inflaming], 1, to set on fire; 2, to excite; arouse; as, the speaker *inflamed* the crowd's anger; 3, to put into a state of redness, swelling, and pain; as, weeping *inflames* the eyes.

in-flam-ma-ble (in-flam′a-bl), *adj.* 1, easily set on fire; as, kerosene is *inflammable;* 2, easily excited; as, an *inflammable* temper.

in-flam-ma-tion (in-fla-mā′shun), *n.* 1, the act of inflaming; 2, an unnatural condition of any part of the body, marked by redness, heat, swelling, and pain.

in-flam-ma-tor-y (in-flam′a-tér-i), *adj.* 1, tending to excite anger or rebellion; 2, causing, or showing, inflammation.

in-flate (in-flāt′), *v.t.* [inflat-ed, inflating], 1, to swell out with air or gas, as a balloon or a tire; 2, to puff up; to elate; as, *inflated* with pride; 3, to raise beyond reason, as prices.—*n.* **in-fla′tion.**

in-flect (in-flekt′), *v.t.* 1, to change the pitch or tone of (the voice); 2, to vary the form of (a word) so as to show grammatical changes in person, number, case, etc., as *he, his, him, they, their* or *theirs, them.*—*n.* **in-flec′tion.**

in-flex-i-ble (in-flek′si-bl), *adj.* 1, not able to be bent; rigid; as, an *inflexible* rod of iron; 2, not to be moved by entreaty; unyielding; as, he has an *inflexible* will.—*adv.* **in-flex′i-bly.**—*n.* **in-flex′i-bil′i-ty.**

in-flict (in-flikt′), *v.t.* 1, to cause by or as if by, striking; as, to *inflict* a wound; 2, to impose (a punishment or penalty) on someone.—*n.* **in-flic′tion.**

in-flo-res-cence (in′flo-res′ens), *n.* a flowering or blossoming.

in-flu-ence (in′floo-ens), *n.* 1, a power tending to produce results by indirect or invisible means; the power of personality; moral power; as, the *influence* of a good example; 2, power arising from wealth or station; as, political *influence;* 3, one who, or that which, exerts a power:—*v.t.* [influenced, influenc-ing], 1, to have power over, physically or mentally; 2, to affect; as, weather *influences* crops.

in-flu-en-tial (in′floo-en′shal), *adj.* having or exerting power; as, an *influential* citizen.—*adv.* **in′flu-en′tial-ly.**

in-flu-en-za (in′floo-en′za), *n.* a severe infectious disease, frequently occurring in epidemic form, characterized by inflammation of the air passages, severe muscular pains, and headache: popularly called *flu*.

in-flux (in′fluks), *n.* an inflow; a pouring in; as, an *influx* of money into a bank.

in-fold (in-fōld′), *v.t.* to wrap; envelop; embrace. The preferred spelling is **en-fold′**.

in-form (in-fôrm′), *v.t.* to supply with knowledge; notify; tell:—*v.i.* to give information, esp. in accusation; as, the neighbours *informed* against him.— *adj.* **in-form′a-tive.**—*n.* **in-form′ant.**— *n.* **in-form′er.**

in-for-mal (in-fôr′mal), *adj.* not according to custom or rule; without ceremony; as, an *informal* dance; an *informal* talk.—*adv.* **in-for′mal-ly.**—*n.* **in′for-mal′i-ty.**

in-for-ma-tion (in′fôr-mā′shun), *n.* knowledge given or acquired; esp. knowledge of facts; also, news.

in-frac-tion (in-frak′shun), *n.* the act of breaking; esp. the act of breaking a law or rule.

in-fra-red (in′fra-red′), *adj.* relating to the penetrating, hot invisible rays that lie beyond the visible red end of the spectrum: the rays are longer than those of the spectrum colours, but shorter than radio waves.

in-fre-quent (in-frē′kwent), *adj.* seldom occurring; as, *infrequent* visits; *infrequent* rains.—*adv.* **in-fre′quent-ly.** —*n.* **in-fre′quence; in-fre′quen-cy.**

in-fringe (in-frinj′), *v.t.* [infringed, infring-ing], to disregard or break, as a law:—*v.i.* to trespass; as, to *infringe* upon another person's liberty.—*n.* **in-fringe′ment.**

in-fu-ri-ate (in-fū′ri-āt′), *v.t.* [infuriated, infuriat-ing], to enrage; madden; as, anything of a red colour is said to *infuriate* a bull.—*n.* **in-fu′ri-a′tion.**

in-fuse (in-fūz′), *v.t.* [infused, infusing], **1,** to introduce, as by pouring; **2,** to instil; inspire; as, to *infuse* a spirit of goodwill into a class; **3,** to steep in liquid; as, to *infuse* tea in boiling water.—*n.* **in-fu′sion.**

in-gen-ious (in-jēn′yus), *adj.* **1,** creative; gifted; clever; as, an *ingenious* mind; **2,** skilfully made or contrived; as, an *ingenious* device.—*n.* **in′ge-nu′i-ty.**

in-gen-u-ous (in-jen′ū-us), *adj.* frank; innocent; sincere; as, an *ingenuous* child.

in-gle or **in-gle-nook** (ing′gl-nook′), *n.* a chimney-corner.

in-glor-i-ous (in-glōr′i-us), *adj.* **1,**

without fame; humble; **2,** disgraceful; shameful; as, an *inglorious* defeat.

in-got (ing′got), *n.* a mass of cast metal, such as gold, silver, or steel.

in-graft (in-gràft′), *v.t.* Same as **engraft.**

in-grained (in′grānd′; in′grānd′), *adj.* deep-rooted; fixed; as, an *ingrained* habit or vice.

in-grate (in′grāt), *n.* one who is ungrateful; a thankless person.

in-gra-ti-ate (in-grā′shi-āt′), *v.t.* [-ated, -ating], to work oneself into another's favour or good graces: as, he *ingratiated* himself into her affections.

in-grat-i-tude (in-grat′i-tūd′), *n.* lack of thankfulness; ungratefulness.

in-gre-di-ent (in-grē′di-ent), *n.* a part of a compound or mixture; as, sugar is the principal *ingredient* of candy.

in-gress (in′gres), *n.* entrance; access.

in-grown (in′grōn′), *adj.* **1,** grown into the flesh; as, an *ingrown* toenail; **2,** native; inborn. Also, **in′grow′ing.**

in-gulf (in-gulf′), *v.t.* Same as **engulf.**

in-hab-it (in-hab′it), *v.t.* to dwell in; live in; occupy; as, man *inhabits* the earth; tigers *inhabit* the jungle.—*adj.* **in-hab′it-a-ble.**—*n.* **in-hab′it-ant.**

in-hale (in-hāl′), *v.t.* [inhaled, inhaling], to draw into the lungs; to breathe in, as air, ether, etc.—*n.* **in′ha-la′tion.**

in-har-mo-ni-ous (in′här-mō′ni-us), *adj.* **1,** unmusical; as, *inharmonious* sounds; **2,** conflicting; clashing; as *inharmonious* colours.—*adv.* **in′har-mo′ni-ous-ly.**

in-her-ent (in-hēr′ent), *adj.* existing in something as a permanent or essential part; inborn; as, love of beauty is *inherent* in poets.—*adv.* **in-her′ent-ly;** —*v.i.* **in-here′** (in).

in-her-it (in-her′it), *v.t.* **1,** to come into possession of (property, as land or money) by right of succession or by will; as, he *inherited* his father's house; **2,** to derive (mental or physical qualities) from one's ancestors; receive by birth; as, to *inherit* intelligence or a strong constitution; **3,** to be heir to.— *n.* **in-her′i-tor.**

in-her-it-ance (in-her′i-tans), *n.* **1,** the act of inheriting, or coming into property; **2,** property inherited; also, a trait or quality handed down from parent to offspring.

in-hib-it (in-hib′it), *v.t.* to restrain; hold in check; as, to *inhibit* a selfish impulse.—*n.* **in′hi-bi′tion** (in′hi-bish′-un).

in-hos-pi-ta-ble (in-hos′pi-ta-bl), *adj.*
1, not disposed to welcome strangers or
guests; as, an *inhospitable* household;
2, barren; cheerless; as, an *inhospitable*
shore.

in-hu-man (in-hū′man), *adj.* cruel;
brutal; unfeeling.—*n.* in′hu-man′i-ty.

in-im-i-cal (in-im′i-kal), *adj.* 1, unfavourable; adverse; as, this drug is
inimical to health; 2, unfriendly;
hostile; as, an *inimical* attitude.

in-im-i-ta-ble (in-im′i-ta-bl), *adj.*,
matchless; impossible to imitate; as
an *inimitable* style.—*adv.* in-im′i-ta-
bly.

in-iq-ui-ty (i-nik′wi-ti), *n.* [*pl.* iniqui-
ties], 1, wickedness; unrighteousness;
2, a wicked act or crime; a sin.—*adj.*
in-iq′ui-tous.

in-i-tial (i-nish′al), *adj.* 1, placed at the
beginning; first; as, the *initial* letter of
a word; 2, marking, or pertaining to,
the beginning; as, the *initial* chapter in
a book; the *initial* step in an undertaking:— *n.* 1, a letter at the beginning
of a word, paragraph, etc.; 2, initials,
the first letter of each part of a person's
name; as, *A. S.* are the *initials* of
Adam Smith:—*v.t.* to mark with one's
initial or initials.—*adv.* in-i′tial-ly.

in-i-ti-ate (i-nish′i-āt′), *v.t.* [initiat-ed,
initiat-ing], 1, to instruct in the first
principles of anything; as, to *initiate* a
student into the study of French; 2, to
begin; as, to *initiate* a new fashion; 3,
to introduce into a club, secret society,
tribe, etc., by special rites and ceremonies:—*n.* (i-nish′i-it), one who has
been, or is about to be, initiated.—*n.*
in-i′ti-a′tion.

in-i-ti-a-tive (i-nish′i-a-tiv), *n.* 1, an
introductory or first step; as, to take
the *initiative* in a deal; 2, a natural
ability to take the lead; also, an ability
to foresee what needs doing and to do
it; as, people with *initiative* advance
rapidly; 3, the right, also the method,
by which citizens may introduce new
laws.

in-ject (in-jekt′), *v.t.* 1, to drive or force
into: introduce, as a liquid; 2, to
throw in; interject; as, to *inject*
humour into a story.—*n.* in-jec′tion.

in-ju-di-cious (in′jōō-dish′us), *adj.*
unwise; lacking in judgment; as, an
injudicious governess; not carefully
thought out; as, *injudicious* advice; an
injudicious remark.—*adv.* in′ju-di′-
cious-ly.

in-junc-tion (in-jungk′shun), *n.* 1, a
command; an order; 2, a writ to

command or forbid certain proceedings;
as, to issue an *injunction* against a
strike.

in-jure (in′joor), *v.t.* [injured, injur-
ing], to harm; damage, physically or
morally.—*adj.* in-ju′ri-ous.—*adv.* in-
ju′ri-ous-ly.

in-ju-ry (in′joor-i), *n.* [*pl.* injuries], any
hurt or harm; damage to one's person,
property, rights, etc.

in-jus-tice (in-jus′tis), *n.* the quality of
being unfair; lack of justice; also, an
injury; a wrong.

ink (ingk), *n.* a coloured fluid used for
writing or drawing with a pen; also, a
sticky paste used for printing:—*v.t.* to
mark or smear with ink.

ink-ling (ingk′ling), *n.* a faint idea or
suspicion; as, an *inkling* of the truth.

ink-stand (ingk′stand′), *n.* a small
container for ink, pens, etc.; sometimes,
a container for ink only; an ink-well.

ink-well (ingk′-wel′), *n.* a cup for ink,
fitted into a desk or an inkstand.

ink-y (ingk′i), *adj.* [ink-i-er, ink-i-est],
like ink; spotted with ink; black; as,
an *inky* blotter; *inky* darkness.

in-laid (in-lād′; in′lād′), *adj.* 1, set
into a surface for ornament; as, ivory
inlaid in ebony; 2, ornamented with
inlay.

in-land (in′land), *adj.* 1, pertaining to,
or situated in, the interior of a country;
away from the sea; as, an *inland* town;
2, carried on within a country; as,
inland commerce:—*adv.* (in′land′; in′-
land), toward the interior:—*n.* (in′-
land; in′land′), the interior of a
country.

in-lay (in-lā′), *v.t.* [inlaid (in-lād′),
inlaying], to ornament (a surface) by
setting in pieces of ivory, wood, metal,
etc.; also, to set (pieces of ivory, wood,
etc.) into a surface:—*n.* (in′lā), materials
for inlaying; also, a pattern or design
formed by inlaying.

in-let (in′let), *n.* a small bay or creek
along a coast; an arm of the sea.

in-mate (in′māt), *n.* a member of a
family or other group of persons living
under one roof; now, usually, a person
confined in an institution; as, an
inmate of a prison, a poorhouse, etc.

in-most (in′mōst), *adj.* most inward;
deepest; as, the *inmost* wish of my
heart is to be a great pianist.

inn (in), *n.* a house for the lodging and
entertainment of travellers; a tavern.
—*n.* inn′keep′er.

---

all (ôl), ôr; up, mūte, cûr, cōōl, book; oil, out; th, thin; *th*, the.

in-nate (in′nāt; i-nāt′), *adj.* inborn; natural; as, *innate* courtesy; *innate* intelligence.—*adv.* **in′nate-ly.**

in-ner (in′ẽr), *adj.* **1,** internal; interior; inside; as, an *inner* lining; **2,** pertaining to the mind or soul; as, the *inner* nature of man.

in-ner-most (in′ẽr-mōst), *adj.* farthest in from the outside; inmost.

in-ning (in′ing), *n.* **1,** in baseball. cricket, etc., one of the divisions of the game during which one side is at bat or each side in turn is at bat once; **2,** **innings,** the period when a person or party is in power.

in-no-cent (in′ō-sent), *adj.* **1,** free from guilt or wrongdoing; blameless; **2,** pure in heart and life; **3,** foolishly ignorant; **4,** without evil effect or meaning; as, an *innocent* joke; **5,** lacking; as, *innocent* of humour or brains:—*n.* **1,** one who is free from, or unacquainted with sin; **2,** a simpleton. —*adv.* **in′no-cent-ly.**—*n.* **in′no-cence.**

in-noc-u-ous (i-nok′ū-us), *adj.* harmless; as, an *innocuous* dose.

in-no-va-tion (in′ō-vā′shun), *n.* **1,** the introduction of something new; **2,** a new custom, device, style, etc.

in-nu-en-do (in′ū-en′dō), *n.* [*pl.* -does (dōz)], an indirect remark, reference, etc., that implies something derogatory; insinuation.

in-nu-mer-a-ble (i-nū′mẽr-a-bl; in-nū′mẽr-a-bl), *adj.* without number; countless; as, *innumerable* stars.

in-oc-u-late (in-ok′ū-lāt′), *v.t.* [inocu-lat-ed, inoculat-ing], **1,** to produce a mild case of disease in (a person or animal) by the insertion of germs into body tissues in order to prevent future attacks; as, to *inoculate* against typhoid; **2,** to fill or infect the mind of (a person, community, etc.) with a feeling, opinion, or habit.—*n.* **in-oc′u-la′tion.**

in-of-fen-sive (in′o-fen′siv), *adj.* **1,** harmless; **2,** not disagreeable or disgusting.

in-op-er-a-tive (in-op′ẽr-a-tiv), *adj.* not working; not in operation; in-effective.

in-op-por-tune (in-op′or-tūn′), *adj.* happening at the wrong time; unsuit-able; as, an *inopportune* remark; the *inopportune* moment.—*adv.* **in-op′por-tune′ly.**

in-or-di-nate (in-ôr′di-nit), *adj.* too much; excessive; as, it took him an *inordinate* amount of time; *inordinate* vanity.

in-or-gan-ic (in′ôr-gan′ik), *adj.* with-out a living body; not belonging to the animal or vegetable kingdom; not par of, nor produced by, a plant or anima Rocks and metals are inorganic sub stances; wood, bone, and blood ar organic substances.

in-put (in′poot′), *n.* what is put in, esp electricity supplied to a machine.

in-quest (in′kwest), *n.* an officia inquiry, with the aid of a jury, esp into the cause of a sudden death.

in-quire (in-kwīr′), *v.t.* [inquired, in quir-ing], to seek after by questions as, to *inquire* the way to the station:— *v.i.* **1,** to ask; seek information; as *inquire* at the office; **2,** to mak examination or search; as, to *inquir* into a murder; to *inquire* about some thing; **3,** to ask concerning the where abouts or welfare of someone; as, t *inquire* for or about a person.

in-quir-y (in-kwīr′i; in′kwi-ri), *n.* [*p* inquiries], **1,** the act of seeking informa tion, knowledge, etc.; research; **2,** a investigation; **3,** a question.

in-qui-si-tion (in′kwi-zish′un), *n.* in quiry; examination; esp. an officia inquiry before a jury; also, th findings of the jury:—**Inquisition,** the Roman Catholic Church, a cour which was esp. active in the 15th an 16th centuries in seeking out an punishing heretics, but is now chief concerned with heretical literature.—*n* **in-quis′i-tor.**

in-quis-i-tive (in-kwiz′i-tiv), *ad* given to asking questions; curious; as a gossip is *inquisitive* about he neighbours.

in-road (in′rōd′), *n.* **1,** an invasio esp. if sudden; entry by force; as, a *inroad* into enemy territory; **2,** a advance which destroys or decrease the thing attacked; as, the sea make *inroads* upon the land; overwor makes *inroads* on endurance.

in-sane (in-sān′), *adj.* **1,** mentall disordered or ill; mad; crazy; **2,** ver unreasonable or foolish; as, an *insan* desire to dance in church; **3,** intende for the mentally disordered; as, a *insane* asylum.—*adv.* **in-sane′ly.**—*n* **in-san′i-ty.**

in-san-i-tary (in-san′i-ta-ri), *adj.* un healthful; as, *insanitary* plumbing.

in-sa-ti-a-ble (in-sā′shi-a-bl; in-sā′ sha-bl), *adj.* immoderate; not to b satisfied; greedy; as, an *insatiabl* appetite.

in-scribe (in-skrīb′), *v.t.* [inscribe inscrib-ing], **1,** to write or engrav (letters or words) on parchment, bras etc.; as, to *inscribe* a date on a ring;

surgical *instruments;* **3,** a mechanical device for producing musical sounds; as, a horn is a wind-*instrument;* **4,** in *law,* a formal writing; a document.

in-stru-men-tal (in′stroo-men′tal), *adj.* **1,** helping to bring about; as, he was *instrumental* in settling the quarrel; **2,** performed on, or composed for, a musical instrument or instruments.—*n.* in′stru-men-tal′i-ty.

in-sub-or-di-nate (in′su-bôr′di-nit), *adj.* rebelling against authority; disobedient; mutinous.—*n.* in′sub-or′di-na′tion.

in-sub-stan-tial (in′sub-stan′shal), *adj.* **1,** imaginary; unreal; as, this *insubstantial* pageant; **2,** not solid; flimsy.

in-suf-fer-a-ble (in-suf′ẽr-a-bl), *adj.* unbearable; as, *insufferable* pride.

in-suf-fi-cient (in′su-fish′ent), *adj.* not enough, as of quality, amount, power, etc.; as, *insufficient* light for reading.—*adv.* in′suf-fi′cient-ly.—*n.* in′suf-fi′cien-cy.

in-su-lar (in′sū-lẽr), *adj.* **1,** relating to an island or to the inhabitants of an island, their customs, etc.; **2,** hence, narrow-minded; prejudiced.—*n.* in′su-lar′i-ty.

in-su-late (in′sū-lāt′; in′su-lāt′), *v.t.* [insulat-ed, insulat-ing], to separate; set apart; esp. to separate by, or enclose in, a material that will not conduct electricity, heat, etc.; as, to *insulate* an electric wire or an oven.—*n.* in′su-la′tion.

in-su-la-tor (in′sū-lā′tẽr; in′su-lā′-tẽr), *n.* a material or body that does not carry electricity, heat, or sound; a nonconductor.

in-su-lin (in′sū-lin), *n.* an extract from the pancreas of animals, used in treating diabetes: it reduces the sugar content of the blood and urine.

in-sult (in′sult), *n.* **1,** an affront or indignity; **2,** a gross abuse in word or action:—*v.t.* (in-sult′), to treat with intentional rudeness or abuse.

in-su-per-a-ble (in-sū′pẽr-a-bl), *adj.* not to be surmounted or overcome; as, *insuperable* difficulties.—*adv.* in-su′per-a-bly.

in-sup-port-a-ble (in′su-pōr′ta-bl), *adj.* unendurable.

in-sur-ance (in-shoor′ans), *n.* **1,** a system of protection against financial loss resulting from fire, accident, death, etc.; **2,** a contract whereby one party, usually a company, guarantees to repay the other party for such loss, in

return for the yearly payment of a smaller sum, called a *premium;* **3,** the premium; **4,** the amount of payment thus guaranteed.

in-sure (in-shoor′), *v.t.* [insured, insuring], **1,** to protect (a person), by a special contract, against financial loss resulting from fire, accident, theft, etc., in return for payments of a premium; as, to *insure* a farmer against the burning of his barn; **2,** to make such a contract about (property); as, the farmer *insures* his barn; **3,** to make such a contract about (one's life), providing for payment of a fixed sum to a specified person in case of one's death, or to oneself at a specified age; as, he has *insured* his life for $5,000:—*v.i.* to protect oneself by insurance.

in-sur-gent (in-sûr′jent), *adj.* rising against authority:—*n.* a rebel.—*n.* in-sur′gence; in-sur′gen-cy.

in-sur-mount-a-ble (in′sẽr-moun′-ta-bl), *adj.* unconquerable; as, *insurmountable* obstacles.

in-sur-rec-tion (in′su-rek′shun), *n.* active or open rebellion against authority, esp. against a government.

in-tact (in-takt′), *adj.* entire; uninjured; untouched; as, the house was *intact* after the earthquake.

in-take (in′tāk′), *n.* **1,** a thing taken in. as money in a store; also, a taking in, as of breath; **2,** the place where a fluid enters a pipe, channel, etc.

in-tan-gi-ble (in-tan′ji-bl), *adj.* **1,** not touchable; as, ghosts are *intangible;* **2,** hence, vague; not easily expressed or defined; as, an *intangible* idea. *adv.* in-tan′gi-bly.—*n.* in-tan′gi-bil′i-ty.

in-te-ger (in′ti-jẽr), *n.* a whole number, as 1, 2, 3, etc.

in-te-gral (in′ti-gral), *adj.* **1,** making a whole; complete; **2,** necessary as a part; as, sincerity is an *integral* part of friendship:—*n.* a whole made up of parts.

in-te-grate (in′ti-grāt′), *v.t.* **1,** to bring (the parts) together into a whole; unify; **2,** to remove barriers (social, educational, legal, etc.) that separate racial groups.—*n.* in′te-gra′tion.

in-teg-ri-ty (in-teg′ri-ti), *n.* **1,** uprightness; virtue; honesty; as, the *integrity* of a person; **2,** soundness; as, the *integrity* of an argument; **3,** unbroken condition; completeness; as, the *integrity* of an army.

in-tel-lect (in′te-lekt′), *n.* **1,** the powers of the mind that know and reason: distinguished from *feeling* and *will;* the mind; **2,** mental power; ability to reason; **3,** a person of high intelligence.

in-tel-lec-tu-al (in′te-lek′tū-al), *adj.* **1,** pertaining to the intellect or mind; as, *intellectual* interests; **2,** possessing a high degree of intellect or understanding; as, an *intellectual* person; **3,** demanding keen thinking; as, *intellectual* subjects:—*n.* a person of superior mind; as, Emerson was an *intellectual.* —*n.* in′tel-lec′tu-al/i-ty.

in-tel-li-gence (in-tel′i-jens), *n.* **1,** ability to learn and to use what one has learned to the best advantage; understanding; **2,** information or news, particularly secret information, as that secured for the government in wartime. —**intelligence quotient,** a number (derived from tests) that indicates one's level of intelligence; thus, a 10-year-old with a mental age of 12 would have an I.Q. of 120.

in-tel-li-gent (in-tel′i-jent), *adj.* **1,** able to learn and to use what one has learned; possessing understanding; **2,** showing understanding; as, an *intelligent* answer.

in-tel-li-gent-si-a (in-tel′i-jent′si-a; -gent′), *n.* the educated classes; intellectuals.

in-tel-li-gi-ble (in-tel′i-ji-bl), *adj.* capable of being understood; clear; as, an *intelligible* explanation.—*n.* in-tel′li-gi-bil′i-ty.—*adv.* in-tel′li-gi-bly.

in-tem-per-ate (in-tem′pėr-it), *adj.* **1,** severe; not mild; as, an *intemperate* climate; **2,** lacking in moderation or self-control; violent; as, *intemperate* conduct; **3,** given to excess, esp. in the use of alcoholic liquors.—*n.* in-tem′per-ance.

in-tend (in-tend′), *v.t.* **1,** to plan; mean; as, we *intend* to stay; **2,** to design or destine (a person or thing) for some purpose; as, his son is *intended* for the legal profession.

in-ten-dant (in-ten′dant), *n.* **1,** a manager or superintendent; **2,** formerly, in French colonies, an official in charge of a district.

in-tense (in-tens′), *adj.* **1,** extreme; excessive; as, *intense* cold; **2,** violent; eager; earnest; as, *intense* love.—*adv.* in-tense′ly.

in-ten-si-fy (in-ten′si-fī′), *v.t.* [intensi-fied, intensify-ing], to make greater in degree; as, to *intensify* pain.—*n.* in-ten′si-fi-ca′tion.

in-ten-si-ty (in-ten′si-ti), *n.* [*pl.* intensities], **1,** the state or quality of being extreme; violence; as, the

intensity of anger or joy; **2,** strength or degree; as, *intensity* of light.

in-ten-sive (in-ten′siv), *adj.* **1,** concentrated; thorough; as, an *intensive* study of literature; *intensive* thought; **2,** in *grammar,* giving emphasis or force; as, in the sentence, "He did it himself," the word "himself" is *intensive.*—*adv.* in-ten′sive-ly.

in-tent (in-tent′), *adj.* concentrated closely occupied; as, he was *intent* on his work:—*n.* purpose; aim; as, study with *intent* to learn.—*adv.* in-tent′ly

in-ten-tion (in-ten′shun), *n.* that which is intended or planned; purpose aim; as, to act with good *intention.*

in-ten-tion-al (in-ten′shun-al), *adj.* done on purpose; as, an *intentional* wrong.

in-ter (in-tûr′), *v.t.* [interred, inter ring], to bury.—*n.* in-ter′ment.

in-ter— (in′tėr–), *prefix,* **1,** among between; as, in′ter-con′ti-nen′tal; in′ter-de-nom′i-na′tion-al; in′ter-plan′e-tar′y; **2,** together; mutually; as in′ter-ac′tion; in′ter-fuse′; in′ter lock′; in′ter-weave′.

in-ter-cede (in′tėr-sēd′), *v.i.* [interced ed, interced-ing], to act as peacemaker mediate; also, to plead for another; as I *interceded* for him with his father

in-ter-cept (in′tėr-sept′), *v.t.* **1,** t seize or catch on the way; stop; as, th spy *intercepted* the message; **2,** t obstruct; cut off, as a view; **3,** t interfere with the course of; stop; a to *intercept* a forward pass.—*n.* in′ter cep′tion.—*n.* in′ter-cept′er or in′ter cept′or.

in-ter-ces-sion (in′tėr-sesh′un), *n.* an attempt to restore friendshi between persons who are unfriendly **2,** the act of pleading for someone else a prayer.—*n.* in′ter-ces′sor.

in-ter-change (in′tėr-chānj′), *v.t.* [terchanged, interchang-ing], **1,** to ex change the position of, by putting on thing or person in the place of another **2,** to vary; alternate; as, to *inter change* study with play:—*n.* (in′tė chānj′), **1,** the exchange of two thing one for the other; as, an *interchange* calling-cards; **2,** alternate successio as of the seasons.—*adj.* in′ter-change a-ble.—*adv.* in′ter-change′a-bly.

in-ter-col-le-gi-ate (in′tėr-ko-lē′ji-it jit), *adj.* **1,** carried on, as game between colleges; **2,** existing, as league among colleges or universities.

in-ter-com (in′tėr-kom′), *n. Slang* short for in′ter-com-mu′ni-ca′tio system, as of an airplane or army tan

---

cat, āge, fär, cåre, åsk; ten, ēve, latėr; (i) pity, rely, senate; īce; top; n

in-ter-course (in'tẻr-kōrs), *n.* connection, correspondence, or communication between individuals, nations, etc.

in-ter-dict (in'tẻr-dikt'), *v.t.* 1, to prohibit or forbid; 2, to cut off from the spiritual services of a church:—*n.* (in'tẻr-dikt), a formal prohibition, esp. of church privileges.—*n.* **in'ter-dic'-tion.**

in-ter-est (in'tẻr-est), *n.* 1, a feeling of concern or curiosity about something; also, that which arouses it; as, suspense gives *interest* to a story; 2, that which is of advantage; benefit; as, he acts for the public *interest;* 3, a share or part ownership; as, he has an *interest* in the business; 4, a sum paid by the borrower for the use of borrowed money; as, 2% *interest* on a loan; 5, personal influence over the actions of others; as, he used his *interest* with the president; 6, **interests,** the persons occupied in some field of business or industry, taken all together; as, the coal *interests:*—*v.t.* 1, to engage the attention of; arouse to curiosity, sympathy, etc., as, the play *interested* him; 2, to cause to take an interest or a share in.

in-ter-est-ing (in'tẻr-es-ting), *adj.* attracting, provoking, or holding attention, curiosity, or emotion.

in-ter-fere (in'tẻr-fẽr'), *v.i.* [interfered, interfer-ing], 1, to meddle; 2, to clash; be opposed; as, their views *interfered;* 3, in *football*, to block an opposing player.—*n.* **in'ter-fer'ence.**

in-ter-im (in'tẻr-im), *n.* the time or period between happenings; the meantime:—*adj.* belonging to, or occurring or done in, an intervening period; temporary; as, an *interim* report.

in-te-ri-or (in-tē'ri-ẻr), *adj.* 1, inner; internal; 2, far from the coast or frontier:—*n.* 1, the inside, as of a building; 2, the inland; 3, the home affairs of a nation; as, the Department of the *Interior.*

in-ter-ject (in'tẻr-jekt'), *v.t.* to put or throw in; insert; as, to *interject* a question.

in-ter-jec-tion (in'tẻr-jek'shun), *n.* 1, the act of throwing in or interjecting; also, that which is thrown in; an exclamation; 2, in *grammar*, a word used as an exclamation, having no grammatical connection with the rest of the sentence; as, "Ah!" and "Oh!" are *interjections.*

in-ter-lace (in'tẻr-lās'), *v.t.* and *v.i.* [interlaced, interlac-ing], to join by weaving or lacing together; to intermingle.

in-ter-lard (in'tẻr-lärd'), *v.t.* to diversify; intermingle; as, to *interlard* a talk with jokes, oaths, etc.

in-ter-line (in'tẻr-līn'), *v.t.* [interlined, interlin-ing], 1, to fit (a garment) with an extra lining beneath the usual one; 2, to insert words between the lines of (a book, etc.).

in-ter-lock (in'tẻr-lok'), *v.t.* and *v.i.* to lock or clasp together.

in-ter-loc-u-tor (in'tẻr-lok'ū-tẻr), *n.* a questioner, esp. the middle man in a minstrel show who questions the end men.

in-ter-lop-er (in'tẻr-lōp'ẻr), *n.* an outsider who interferes; an intruder.

in-ter-lude (in'tẻr-lūd), *n.* 1, a short entertainment given between the acts of a play; 2, a short passage of music played between the stanzas of a hymn, parts of a church service, acts of an opera, etc.; 3, any period of time coming between; as, an *interlude* of play in a day of work.

in-ter-mar-riage (in'tẻr-mar'ij; in'-tẻr-mar'ij), *n.* marriage between different families, tribes, races, etc.—*v.i.* **in'ter-mar'ry.**

in-ter-me-di-ate (in'tẻr-mē'di-it), *adj.* existing or lying in the middle; coming between:—*n.* 1, that which lies between; 2, a go-between.—*adv.* **in'ter-me'di-ate-ly.**

in-ter-ment (in-tûr'ment), *n.* burial.

in-ter-mez-zo (in'ter-met'sō; -med'), *n.* [*pl.* -mezzi (-tzē)], *n.* 1, dramatic or musical entertainment between acts in a play, opera, etc.; 2, music connecting parts of a larger musical composition.

in-ter-mi-na-ble (in-tûr'mi-na-bl), *adj.* endless; exceptionally long; as, an *interminable* speech.—*adv.* **in-ter'-mi-na-bly.**

in-ter-min-gle (in'tẻr-ming'gl), *v.t.* and *v.i.* [intermin-gled, intermin-gling], to mix together.

in-ter-mis-sion (in'tẻr-mish'un), *n.* 1, a short or temporary break; an interruption; a pause; 2, an interval of time between two parts, as acts of a play:—*v.t.* **in'ter-mit'.**

in-ter-mit-tent (in'tẻr-mit'ent), *adj.* ceasing for short periods and starting again; coming and going; as, *intermittent* rain.—*adv.* **in'ter-mit'tent-ly.**

in-tern (in'tûrn; in-tûrn'), *n.* 1, a resident doctor on a hospital staff, usually a recent medical graduate; 2, an inmate:—*v.i.* (in-tûrn'), to perform an intern's duties. Also, **interne.**—*v.t.* 1, to hold or detain, as (enemy) aliens in time of war; 2, to detain ships or persons in port.—*n.* **in-tern'ment.**

in-ter-nal (in-tûr'nal), *adj.* **1,** belonging to the inside; inner: opposite of *external;* as, the *internal* parts of an engine; **2,** inherent; coming from within the thing itself; as, *internal* evidence; **3,** having to do with affairs within a country; domestic; as, *internal* products.—*adv.* **in-ter'nal-ly:—internal combustion engine,** an engine used in motor vehicles, airplanes, boats, etc., in which the power is produced by the exploding of a fuel-and-air mixture in cylinders.

in-ter-na-tion-al (in'tĕr-nash'un-al), *adj.* relating to, or carried on between, two or more nations or their people; as, *international* trade.—*adv.* **in'ter-na'-tion-al-ly.**

in-ter-pose (in'tĕr-pōz'), *v.t.* [interposed, interpos-ing], **1,** to place or set between; **2,** to thrust in; put forth, in order to interfere; **3,** to introduce (a remark) into a conversation:—*v.i.* **1,** to come between parties in a quarrel; mediate; **2,** to interrupt; **3,** to be between.

in-ter-pret (in-tûr'pret), *v.t.* **1,** to explain the meaning of; as, to *interpret* a foreign word or a difficult passage; **2,** to bring out the meaning of, as a poem, a work of art, etc.; as, to *interpret* the rôle of Hamlet; **3,** to take one's own meaning from (words, actions, etc.); as, to *interpret* a friend's motives.—*n.* **in-ter'pre-ta'tion.**—*n.* **in-ter'pret-er.**

in-ter-ro-gate (in-ter'o-gāt'), *v.t.* [interrogat-ed, interrogat-ing], to question; examine by asking questions; as, to *interrogate* a witness.—*adj.* **in'ter-rog'-a-tor'y.**

in-ter-ro-ga-tion (in-ter'o-gā'shun), *n.* **1,** the act of asking questions; **2,** a question; inquiry:—**interrogation—point** or **—mark,** a mark [?] indicating a direct question; a question mark.

in-ter-rog-a-tive (in'te-rog'a-tiv), *adj.* indicating, or containing a question; as, an *interrogative* glance; an *interrogative* sentence:—*n.* in *grammar,* a word which asks a question, as *why, where, who,* etc.

in-ter-rupt (in'te-rupt'), *v.t.* **1,** to stop or hinder by breaking in upon; as, to *interrupt* a speech; to *interrupt* a speaker; **2,** to obstruct; as, a wall *interrupts* a view; **3,** to break the continuity of; as, only the clock's tick *interrupts* the silence.—*n.* **in'ter-rup'-tion.**

in-ter-sect (in'tĕr-sekt'), *v.t.* to cut across; as, one line *intersects* another:—*v.i.* to cross each other.—*n.* **in'ter-sec'tion.**

in-ter-sperse (in'tĕr-spûrs'), *v.* [interspersed, interspers-ing], **1,** insert here and there; as, to *intersper* comments in the reading of a play; to scatter about; place here and the among other things; as, to *intersper* shrubbery with flowers.

in-ter-state (in'tĕr-stāt), *adj.* b tween states; as, *interstate* railways.

in-ter-stel-lar (in'tĕr-stel'ĕr), *ad* between or among the stars; *interstellar* space.

in-ter-twine (in'tĕr-twīn'), *v.t.* and *v* [intertwined, interwin-ing], to twis wind or coil together.

in-ter-val (in'tĕr-val), *n.* **1,** the time space between events, periods, et as, the *interval* between two illnesses; a space between objects; as, *interval* of ten feet between tents; **3,** *music,* the difference in pitch betwe two tones.

in-ter-vene (in'tĕr-vēn'), *v.i.* [inte vened, interven-ing], **1,** to come betwe (things or events); as, a minu *intervened* between his remarks; **2,** step in; interfere, as a force to influen action; as, friends *intervened* when t two men quarrelled; **3,** to be betwee as, a fence *intervened* between t yards.—*n.* **in'ter-ven'tion.**

in-ter-view (in'tĕr-vū'), *v.t.* question, esp. in order to obta information for the press:—*n.* **1,** personal conference or meeting; **2,** *journalism,* the act of talking with, being questioned by, a reporter; al the published account of such conversation.—*n.* **in'ter-view'er.**

in-tes-tate (in-tes'tāt), *adj.* leaving will; as, he died *intestate.*

in-tes-tine (in-tes'tin), *n.* a tu extending from the stomach to the rectum, which helps to digest and absorb food and to eliminate waste matter: composed of the *large* and the *small intes-tine;* the bowels.— *adj.* **in-tes'ti-nal.**

in-ti-mate (in'ti-mit), *adj.* **1,** close in friendship; familiar; as, *intimate* friends; **2,** resulting from close study; as, an *intimate* knowledge of art; **3,** having to do with the inner nature of anything; innermost; as, a person's *intim*

INTESTINES
S.I., small intesti
L.I., large intesti
Appendix; R, rect

feelings:—*n.* a close friend:—*v.t.* (in′ti-māt′), [intimat-ed, intimat-ing], to suggest; hint; make known indirectly; as, he *intimated* his disapproval of the plan.—*adv.* in′ti-mate-ly.—*n.* in′ti-ma-cy.

in-ti-ma-tion (in′ti-mā′shun), *n.* 1, an indirect hint; 2, an announcement.

in-tim-i-date (in-tim′i-dāt′), *v.t.* [intimidat-ed, intimidat-ing], to frighten; overawe, esp. by threats.—*n.* in-tim′i-da′tion.

in-ti-tle (in-tī′tl), *v.t.* Same as entitle.

in-to (in′tōō; in′too), *prep.* 1, to the inside of (a place. matter, occupation, state, etc.); as, come *into* the room; look *into* the affair; go *into* business; get *into* trouble; 2, to the condition of; as, the rain later turned *into* snow.

in-tol-er-a-ble (in-tol′ẽr-a-bl), *adj.* unbearable; not to be endured; as, *intolerable* heat; an *intolerable* insult.—*adv.* in-tol′er-a-bly.

in-tol-er-ant (in-tol′ẽr-ant), *adj.* 1, scorning difference of opinion, belief, or behaviour in others, esp. in religion and morals; 2, unable to bear or endure; as, *intolerant* of pain.—*n.* in-tol′er-ance.

in-tone (in-tōn′), *v.t.* and *v.i.* to recite in a musical monotone; chant; as, the priest *intoned* the liturgy.—*n.* in′to-na′tion.

in-tox-i-cate (in-tok′si-kāt′), *v.t.* [intoxicat-ed, intoxicat-ing], 1, to make drunk, as by alcoholic liquors; 2, to excite exceedingly; to elate; as, happiness *intoxicated* him.—*n.* in-tox′i-ca′tion.—*n.* in-tox′i-cant.

in-trac-ta-ble (in-trak′ta-bl), *adj.* unmanageable; not easily controlled; as, an *intractable* horse; an *intractable* temper.

in-tra-mu-ral (in′tra-mū′ral), *adj.* entirely within the limits of a city, college, etc.; as, *intramural* sports.

in-tran-si-gent (in-tran′si-jent), *adj.* refusing to come to an understanding, agreement, etc.; uncompromising, as in politics, U.N. debates, etc.

in-tran-si-tive (in-tran′si-tiv), *adj.* in *grammar*, not taking a direct object because none is needed to complete the action or the meaning: said of verbs; as, he *sits;* he *laughed.*—*adv.* in-tran′si-tive-ly.

in-treat (in-trēt′), *v.t.* Same as entreat.

in-trench (in-trench′), *v.t.* Same as entrench.

in-trench-ment (in-trench′ment), *n.* Same as entrenchment.

in-trep-id (in-trep′id), *adj.* bold; fearless; brave.—*n.* in′tre-pid′i-ty.

in-tri-cate (in′tri-kit), *adj.* entangled; complicated; involved; as, an *intricate* plot; an *intricate* carving.—*n.* in′tri-ca-cy.

in-trigue (in-trēg′), *v.i.* [intrigued, intriguing], 1, to carry on a secret plot; 2, to engage in a secret love affair:—*v.t.* 1, to arouse curiosity in; hence, to interest keenly; as, your plan *intrigues* me; 2, to plot; perplex:—*n.* (in-trēg′; in′trēg), 1, a plot; 2, a secret love affair.

in-trin-sic (in-trin′sik), *adj.* relating to the inner nature; true; as, a man's *intrinsic* worth.—*adv.* in-trin′si-cal-ly.

in-tro-duce (in′trō-dūs′), *v.t.* [introduced, introduc-ing], 1, to bring in; usher in; as, he *introduced* me into the room; 2, to bring into use or notice; as, to *introduce* a new fad; Newton *introduced* the theory of gravity; 3, to make known, as one person to another; 4, to put into; insert; as, to *introduce* lime into the soil; 5, to make known or bring to notice; as, to *introduce* the poetry of Keats to a class; 6, to present in a formal manner; as, to *introduce* a bill into Parliament; 7, to open; begin; as, a phrase may *introduce* a sentence.—*n.* in′tro-duc′-tion.—*adj.* in′tro-duc′to-ry.

in-tro-spec-tion (in′trō-spek′shun), *n.* the act of observing or examining one's own mental processes.—*adj.* in′-tro-spec′tive.

in-tro-vert (in′trō-vûrt′), *n.* one who is concerned with his own thoughts rather than external events or objects:—*v.t.* to turn inward (one's attention, etc.):—*n.* in′tro-ver′sion.

in-trude (in-trōōd′), *v.i.* [intrud-ed, intrud-ing], to enter without invitation or welcome:—*v.t.* to thrust or force in; as, to *intrude* remarks.—*n.* in-trud′er. —*n.* in-tru′sion.—*adj.* in-tru′sive.

in-trust (in-trust′), *v.t.* Same as entrust.

in-tu-i-tion (in′tū-ish′un), *n.* knowledge that comes to one instinctively or without conscious thought or study; sudden insight; as, his *intuition* warned of danger.—*adj.* in-tu′i-tive.—*adv.* in-tu′i-tive-ly.

in-un-date (in′un-dāt′), *v.t.* [inundat-ed, inundat-ing], 1, to fill to overflowing; flood; 2, hence, to spread over.—*n.* in′un-da′tion.

in-ure (in-ūr′), *v.t.* [inured, inur-ing], to accustom; toughen; as, to *inure* oneself to cold baths:—*v.i.* (often *enure*, chiefly in legal sense), to come into use; take effect; as, the fund *inured* to his benefit.

in-vade (ın-vād′), *v.t.* [invad-ed, invading], **1,** to enter in a hostile manner; as, the Romans *invaded* Gaul; worry *invades* the mind; **2,** to infringe upon; to violate; as, to *invade* the rights of a people.—*n.* **in-vad′er.**

¹in-val-id (in-val′id), *adj.* of no force, authority, or value; as, an *invalid* reason.

²in-val-id (in′va-lid; -lēd′), *n.* one who is weak or sick; also, a disabled soldier or sailor:—*adj.* **1,** sick; enfeebled by ill health; **2,** for a sick person; as, an *invalid* chair:—*v.t.* (also, in-va-lēd′), **1,** to make sick or weak; **2,** to send away as sick; as, *invalided* home.

in-val-u-a-ble (in-val′ū-a-bl), *adj.* priceless; exceedingly valuable.

in-var-i-a-ble (in-vâr′i-a-bl), *adj.* constant; unchanging.—*adv.* **in-var′i-a-bly.**

in-va-sion (in-vā′zhun), *n.* **1,** the act of entering in a hostile manner; **2,** an attack of anything injurious, as a disease.

in-vec-tive (in-vek′tiv), *n.* a violent, bitter attack in words; abusive language.

in-veigh (in-vā′), *v.i.* to attack violently in words; rail; as, he *inveighed against* democracy.

in-vei-gle (in-vē′gl), *v.t.* to trick or entice one into doing something; beguile; as, he *inveigled* me into a game of poker.

in-vent (in-vent′), *v.t.* **1,** to create as a result of original study; originate; produce for the first time; as, to *invent* a machine; **2,** to make up; as, to *invent* a strange story.—*n.* **in-ven′tion.** —*adj.* **in-ven′tive.**—*n.* **in-ven′tor.**

in-ven-tor-y (in′ven-tėr-i), *n.* [*pl.* inventories], a catalogue or detailed list of goods, furniture, books, etc.:—*v.t.* [inventoried, inventory-ing], to make an inventory of; to include in a list; catalogue.

in-verse (in-vûrs′; in′vûrs), *adj.* directly opposite; reversed; as in *inverse* order or ratio.—*n.* the direct opposite; as, subtraction is the *inverse* of addition:—*v.t.* to invert; reverse.— *adv.* **in-verse′ly.**

in-vert (in-vûrt′), *v.t.* **1,** to turn upside down, inside out, or in an opposite direction; **2,** to reverse, as in meaning or order; as, to *invert* AB by making BA.—*adj.* **in-vert′ed.**—*n.* **in-ver′sion.**

in-ver-te-brate (in-vûr′ti-brāt′), *n.* an animal without backbone or spinal

column:—*adj.* having no backbone; hence, weak-willed.

in-vest (in-vest′), *v.t.* **1,** to lay out (money) for income or profit; as, he *invested* money in stocks; **2,** to clothe with an office, dignity, etc.; as, to *invest* a judge with the authority of his position:—*v.i.* to put money out for profit.—*n.* **in-vest′ment.**—*n.* **in-ves′tor** —*n.* **in-ves′ti-ture** (sense 2).

in-ves-ti-gate (in-ves′ti-gāt′), *v.t.* and *v.i.* [investigat-ed, investigat-ing], to examine systematically; to make careful inquiry (about); as, to *investigate* the cause of a disaster.—*n.* **in-ves′ti-ga′tor.**—*n.* **in-ves′ti-ga′tion.**

in-vet-er-ate (in-vet′ėr-it), *adj.* **1,** of long standing; deep-rooted; as, *inveterate* hatred; **2,** habitual; as, an *inveterate* liar.

in-vid-i-ous (in-vid′i-us), *adj.* likely to provoke ill will or envy; unfairly partial.

in-vig-o-rate (in-vig′o-rāt′), *v.t.* [invigorat-ed, invigorat-ing], to give vitality to; strengthen; as, sea air *invigorates* the weak.

in-vin-ci-ble (in-vin′si-bl), *adj.* not to be overcome or subdued; unconquerable; as, an *invincible* will.—*adv.* **in-vin′ci-bly.**—*n.* **in-vin′ci-bil′i-ty.**

in-vi-o-la-ble (in-vī′ō-la-bl), *adj.* sacred; not to be violated; as *inviolable* territory; **2,** not to be broken; as, an *inviolable* promise; *inviolable* laws.

in-vi-o-late (in-vī′o-lit; -lāt′), *adj.* kept sacred or unbroken, as a promise, oath, etc.

in-vis-i-ble (in-viz′i-bl), *adj.* not capable of being seen; out of sight; as, clouds make the stars *invisible*.—*adv.* **in-vis′i-bly.**—*n.* **in-vis′i-bil′i-ty.**

in-vi-ta-tion (in′vi-tā′shun), *n.* a request to a person to come to some place or to do something; also, the written or spoken form of such a request.

in-vite (in-vīt′), *v.t.* [invit-ed, inviting], **1,** to ask (a person) to come somewhere or to do something; as, *invite* him for a walk; **2,** to request; as, to *invite* an opinion; **3,** to tempt; as, the music *invites* us to dance.

in-vit-ing (in-vīt′ing), *adj.* tempting; alluring; as, an *inviting* meal.

in-vo-ca-tion (in′vō-kā′shun), *n.* **1,** a prayer; a supplication, esp. to a divine being; **2,** the act of conjuring up devils, or the magic words for doing so.

in-voice (in′vois), *n.* **1,** a written list of

goods sent to a purchaser, with their prices, quantity, and charges; **2,** the goods listed:—*v.t.* [invoiced, invoicing], to make an invoice of; to include in an invoice.

in-voke (in-vōk′), *v.t.* [invoked, invoking], **1,** to address in prayer or supplication; as, to *invoke* the Lord; **2,** to ask for earnestly; as, to *invoke* a blessing; **3,** to conjure up; as, to *invoke* evil spirits.

in-vol-un-tar-y (in-vol′un-tẽr-i), *adj.* **1,** not under the control of the will; as, the beating of the heart is an *involuntary* activity; **2,** against one's will; compulsory; **3,** unintentional; as, an *involuntary* sigh.—*adv.* **in-vol′un-ta-ri-ly.**

in-volve (in-volv′), *v.t.* [involved, involv-ing], **1,** to entangle; complicate; as, he *involved* his friends in debt; **2,** to make difficult; complicate; as, these new facts certainly *involve* the mystery; **3,** to include as a necessity; require; as, a career *involves* hard work; **4,** to engage completely; as, study *involves* all my time.—*n.* **in-volve′ment.**

in-vul-ner-a-ble (in-vul′nẽr-a-bl),*adj.* **1,** incapable of being injured; **2,** incapable of being answered or refuted; as, an *invulnerable* argument.—*n.* **in-vul′ner-a-bil′i-ty.**

¹in-ward (in′wẽrd), *adj.* **1,** situated within; internal; as, *inward* organs; **2,** of the inner self; as, *inward* happiness; **3,** toward the inside or centre; as, an *inward* curve.

²in-ward (in′wẽrd) or **in-wards** (in′-wẽrdz), *adv.* **1,** toward the inside or centre; as, to bend *inward;* **2,** into or toward the mind; as, turn the thoughts *inward.*

in-ward-ly (in′wẽrd-li), *adv.* internally; esp. in the mind or feelings; secretly; as, to grieve *inwardly.*

in-wrap (in-rap′), *v.t.* Same as **enwrap.**

i-o-dide (ī′ō-dīd′), *n.* a compound of iodine and another element or a radical.

i-o-dine (ī′ō-dīn′; ī′ō-din; ī′ō-dēn′) or **i-o-din** (ī′ō-din), *n.* a black-grey crystalline element found in mineral springs, sea-weed, etc. A solution of these crystals in alcohol is much used as an antiseptic.

i-o-dize (ī′ō-dīz′), *v.t.* to treat with iodine or an iodide (a wound, photographic plate, etc.); as, *iodized* salt.

i-on (ī′on), *n.* one of the particles bearing electrical charges which trans-

mit electric current through other gases.

i-on-ize (ī′o-nīz′), *v.t.* and *v.i.* to into ions.—*n.* **i′on-i-za′tion.**

i-o-ta (ī-ō′ta), *n.* a very small quant jot; as, there is not an *iota* of truth in the rumour.

ir- (ir), *prefix,* signifying *not,* as in ir′re-claim′a-ble; ir′re-deem′a-ble; ir′-re-duc′i-ble; ir′re-fut′a-ble or ir-ref′u-ta-ble; ir′re-me′di-a-ble; ir′re-vers′i-ble.

i-ras-ci-ble (i-ras′i-bl; ī-), *adj.* easily angered; as, an *irascible* old man.

i-rate (ī-rāt′; ī′rāt), *adj.* angry, enraged.

ire (īr), *n.* anger; wrath.—*adj.* **ire′ful.**

ir-i-des-cent (ir′i-des′ent),*adj.* having changing, shimmering, rainbowlike colours, as an opal.—*n.* **ir′i-des′cence.**

i-rid-i-um (ī-rid′i-um; i-), *n.* a hard, silvery metallic element used to harden platinum alloys, pen points, etc.

i-ris (ī′ris), *n.* [*pl.* irises], **1,** the rainbow; also, a rainbowlike shimmer; **2,** the coloured portion of the eye around the pupil; **3,** a plant with large, showy flowers and sword-shaped leaves: often called *flag.*

irk (ûrk), *v.t.* to weary; bore; annoy; as, it *irked* me to wait.

irk-some (ûrk′sum), *adj.* tedious; wearisome; dull; as, an *irksome* lesson.

i-ron (ī′ẽrn), *n.* **1,** a silver-white metal which can be melted and worked into tools and implements: the most common of all the metals, used over almost all the world in three commercial forms, *wrought iron, cast iron,* and *steel;* **2,** any tool or weapon made of iron, esp. a flat-iron, pistol, branding-iron, or harpoon; **3,** firmness; rigidity; strength; as, a man of *iron;* **4,** in *golf,* any of several clubs with an iron head; **5, irons,** chains or fetters:—*adj.* **1,** pertaining to, or made of, iron; as, an *iron* bar; **2,** resembling iron in hardness, strength, etc.; as, an *iron* will:—*v.t.* **1,** to smooth with an iron; as, to *iron* clothes; **2,** to fetter.—*n.* **i′ron-er** (ī′ẽr-nẽr):—**iron lung,** a chamber enclosing all but the head, used to force normal lung action in infantile paralysis, gas poisoning, etc. Compounds: **i′ron-clad′; i′ron-ware′; i′ron-wood′.**

i-ron-i-cal (ī-ron′i-kal) or **i-ron-ic** (ī-ron′ik),*adj.* **1,** expressing the opposite of what is meant; disguisedly sarcastic; as, an *ironical* remark; **2,** describing a circumstance the reverse of what was, or might be, expected; as, an *ironical* turn of fate made him the rival of his best friend.

ro-ny (ī′ro-ni), *n.* [*pl.* ironies], **1,** hidden sarcasm; the expression of the opposite of what is really meant; as, ridicule disguised as praise is *irony;* **2,** any situation or event the opposite of what would normally be expected; as, the *irony* of it was that he was killed by his own invention.

ir-ra-tion-al (ir-rash′un-al), *adj.* **1,** lacking reasoning powers, as beasts; **2,** without reason; as, an *irrational* fear.

ir-rec-on-cil-a-ble (ir-rek′on-sīl′a-bl; ir-rek′on-sīl′a-bl), *adj.* **1,** not adjustable, as a quarrel; unchangeably hostile, as two persons who have quarrelled; **2,** not in agreement; as, his actions are *irreconcilable* with his promises.—*adv.* **ir-rec′on-cil′a-bly.**

ir-reg-u-lar (ir-reg′ū-lẽr), *adj.* **1,** not straight or symmetrical; not uniform in shape, order, etc.; as, *irregular* lines and figures; **2,** not according to rule or established method; as, an *irregular* proceeding; **3,** in *grammar*, not following the regular rule for conjugation or inflection; as, "go" is an *irregular* verb. —*adv.* **ir-reg′u-lar-ly.**—*n.* **ir-reg′u-lar′-i-ty.**

ir-rel-e-vant (ir-rel′i-vant), *adj.* not bearing upon the case; unrelated to the matter discussed; as, *irrelevant* evidence or arguments.—*adv.* **ir-rel′e-vant-ly.**—*n.* **ir-rel′e-vance; ir-rel′e-van-cy.**

ir-re-li-gious (ir′ri-lij′us), *adj.* lacking religion or respect for religion; profane; as, *irreligious* conduct.—*adv.* **ir′re-li′gious-ly.**

ir-rep-a-ra-ble (i-rep′a-ra-bl), *adj.* not capable of being repaired, restored, or remedied; as, his losses are *irreparable.*

ir-re-press-i-ble (ir′ri-pres′i-bl), *adj.* incapable of being checked or controlled; as, *irrepressible* laughter.

ir-re-proach-a-ble (ir′ri-prōch′a-bl), *adj.* blameless; faultless; as, *irreproachable* conduct.

ir-re-sist-i-ble (ir′ri-zis′ti-bl), *adj.* too strong or desirable to be resisted; overpowering; as, an *irresistible* temptation.—*adv.* **ir′re-sist′i-bly.**

ir-res-o-lute (i-rez′o-lūt′), *adj.* undecided; wavering; as, a man *irresolute* in his decisions.—*n.* **ir-res′o-lu′tion.**

ir-re-spec-tive (ir′ri-spek′tiv), *adj.* regardless; as, all men must die, *irrespective* of rank.—*adv.* **ir′re-spec′-tive-ly.**

ir-re-spon-si-ble (ir′ri-spon′si-bl), *adj.* **1,** not to be held accountable; as, an *irresponsible* child; **2,** not trustworthy; as, *irresponsible* servants.—

adv. **ir′re-spon′si-bly.**—*n.* **ir′re-spon′si-bil′i-ty.**

ir-re-triev-a-ble (ir′ri-trēv′a-bl), *adj.* not recoverable; not to be regained; as an *irretrievable* loss.—*adv.* **ir′re-triev′a-bly.**

ir-rev-er-ent (i-rev′ẽr-ent), *adj.* disrespectful; showing a lack of respect or veneration, esp. for things held sacred. —*n.* **ir-rev′er-ence.**

ir-rev-o-ca-ble (i-rev′o-ka-bl), *adj.* incapable of being recalled or undone; as, an *irrevocable* act.

ir-ri-gate (ir′i-gāt′), *v.t.* [irrigat-ed irrigat-ing], **1,** to supply with water, as land under cultivation, by means of ditches, channels, etc.; **2,** to wash out, as a wound, with a flow of liquid, in order to clean or disinfect it.—*n.* **ir′ri-ga′tion.**

ir-ri-ta-ble (ir′i-ta-bl), *adj.* easily annoyed or angered; cranky; also very sensitive.—*adv.* **ir′ri-ta-bly.**—*n.* **ir′ri-ta-bil′i-ty.**

ir-ri-tate (ir′i-tāt′), *v.t.* [irritat-ed irritat-ing], **1,** to annoy or make angry as, his manner *irritates* me; **2,** to make sore; inflame; as, smoke *irritates* the eyes.—*n.* **ir′ri-ta′tion.**

ir-rup-tion (i-rup′shun), *n.* a bursting or rushing in; sudden invasion; as, an *irruption* of the enemy.

is (iz), 3rd person, sing., present indicative of *be.*

i-sin-glass (ī′zing-glas′), *n.* **1,** a white semi-transparent substance or gelatin prepared from the air bladders of the sturgeon, cod, etc., used as an adhesive for stiffening silks, linens, etc.; **2** *Colloq.* a mineral that readily separates into thin, semi-transparent sheets mica.

Is-lam (is′lam; iz), *n.* the Moslem religion, people, or territory; Mohammedan belief in one God, Allah.

is-land (ī′land), *n.* **1,** a tract of land surrounded by water; **2,** anything detached and isolated like an island; as floating *islands* of ice.—*n.* **is′land-er.**

island universe, a galaxy of stars such as the Milky Way.

isle (īl), *n.* a small island; usually *Poetic*, except in proper names.

is-let (ī′let), *n.* a small island.

i-so-bar (ī′sō-bär′), *n.* a line on a map connecting places of equal barometric pressure.

i-so-late (ī′sō-lāt′; is′ō-lāt′), *v.t.* [isolat-ed, isolat-ing], to place alone and away from others; as, the doctor *isolates* contagious cases.

i-so-la-tion (ī′sō-lā′shun; is′ō-lā′ shun), *n.* a setting apart, or the state of being placed apart or in solitude; loneliness.—*n.* i′**so-la′tion-ist.**

i-sos-ce-les (ī-sos′e-lēz′), *adj.* having two equal sides; as, an *isosceles* triangle.

i-so-therm (ī′sō-thûrm′), *n.* a line on a map connecting points on the earth's surface having the same temperature. —*adj.* i′**so-ther′mal.**

ISOSCELES TRIANGLES

i-so-tope (ī′sō-tōp′), *n.* one of two or more forms of an element having the same place in the periodic table and having almost identical properties, but differing in atomic weight; as, uranium 235 and uranium 238 are *isotopes.*

is-sue (ish′ōō), *n.* **1,** the act of passing or flowing out; as, an *issue* of water, as from a tap; **2,** an outlet; also, the point of outlet, as the mouth of a river; **3,** that which is sent forth or produced; as, an *issue* of bank-notes; **4,** an edition of a book, newspaper, etc., esp. the entire number put out at one time; **5,** offspring; progeny; as, to die without *issue;* **6,** the final result; outcome; as, the *issue* of an election; **7,** a point of contention between two parties; as, political *issues:*—*v.t.* [issued, issu-ing], **1,** to send out; discharge; as, a crater *issues* smoke; **2,** to publish; send out officially; as, to *issue* a decree; **3,** to put into circulation; as, to *issue* currency:—*v.i.* **1,** to come or pass forth; as, blood *issues* from a cut; **2,** to arise, as from a source; as, a river *issues* from a lake; **3,** to end; as, the struggle *issued* in peace.—*n.* **is′su-ance.**

isth-mus (is′mus), *n.* [*pl.* isthmuses], a neck of land connecting two larger bodies of land; as, the *isthmus* of Panama.

it (it), *neut. pron.* of third person [*nominative* it, *possessive* its (its), *objective* it], the thing in question; as, where is my book? *It* is on the table: also used impersonally; as, *it* is

raining:—*n.* in children's games, the player whom the other players oppose.

I-tal-i-an (i-tal′yan), *adj.* pertaining to Italy, its people, or its language. Also used as *n.*

i-tal-i-cize (i-tal′i-sīz′), *v.t.* [italicized, italiciz-ing], to print (words) in a slender, sloping style of type called *italics.*

itch (ich), *n.* **1,** a contagious skin disease causing great irritation; **2,** a sensation of irritation in the skin; **3,** a constant and craving desire; as, an *itch* to paint:—*v.i.* **1,** to have a feeling in the skin causing a desire to scratch; **2,** to have a longing; crave; as, he *itched* to run away to sea.—*adj.* **itch′y;**—*n.* **itch′i-ness.**

i-tem (ī′tem), *n.* **1,** a separate article, entry, or particular; a sum entered in an account; **2,** a newspaper paragraph.

i-tem-ize (ī′tem-īz′), *v.t.* [itemized, itemiz-ing], to state by separate entries; give particulars of; as, to *itemize* a bill.

i-tin-er-ant (ī-tin′ẽr-ant; i-), *adj.* passing from place to place; as, an *itinerant* preacher:—*n.* one who travels from place to place.

i-tin-er-ar-y (ī-tin′ẽr-ẽr-i; i-tin′ẽr-ẽr-i), *n.* [*pl.* itineraries], **1,** a traveller's guide-book; also, a plan for a journey; **2,** a route actually taken; also, a record of a journey.

its (its), *adj.* the possessive form of the personal pronoun *it:* of or belonging to it; as, the tree has lost *its* leaves.

it-self (it-self′), *pron.* the intensive or reflexive form of *it;* as, he loved the work *itself;* the cat washes *itself.*

i-vo-ry (ī′vo-ri), *n.* [*pl.* ivories], **1,** the hard, white substance which forms the tusks of the elephant, walrus, etc.; **2,** the colour of ivory; **3,** a substance resembling ivory; **4,** an article, as a carving, made of ivory:—*adj.* made of, or like, ivory.

i-vy (ī′vi), *n.* [*pl.* ivies], any of several clinging vines with shiny, green, ornamental leaves, as English ivy, Boston ivy.—*adj.* i′**vied.**

J

J, j (jā), *n.* [*pl.* J's, j's], the tenth letter of the alphabet, following I.

jab (jab), *v.t.* and *v.i.* [jabbed, jab-bing], to stab with something pointed:—*n.* a sharp thrust; as, a *jab* of a needle.

jab-ber (jab′ẽr), *v.i.* and *v.t.* to talk rapidly and indistinctly; chatter:—*n.* chatter; unintelligible talk.

jack (jak), *n.* **1,** a young man, esp. of the labouring class; often written *Jack;* **2,**

hence, any one of several mechanical devices which may be considered to do the work of a labourer or assistant, as a bootjack, a roasting-jack for turning meat on a spit, or a portable device for lifting a great weight; **3**, the male of any of several animals, esp. the ass; **4**, in *cards*, any one of the four knaves; **5**, in *bowling*, a small bowl used as a mark; **6**, a small flag used on a ship, as a signal or a sign of nationality; **7**, a jackstone; **8**, **jacks**, the game of jackstones:—*v.t.* **1**, to raise or hoist by means of a jack, lever, block, or other mechanical device; **2**, *Colloq.* to spur on; as, to *jack* up the lazy boy.

jack-al (jak′ôl), *n*. **1**, a doglike, flesh-eating animal of the Old World which lives on small animals and carrion; **2**, one who does base work for another: from the false idea that the jackal hunts prey for the lion.

jack-a-napes (jak′a-nāps′), *n*. a conceited or impertinent fellow.

jack-ass (jak′ås′), *n*. **1**, the male ass; donkey; **2**, a conceited fool; blockhead.

jack-daw (jak′dô′), *n*. a European bird of the crow family, which can be taught to make sounds imitating human speech.

jack-et (jak′it), *n*. **1**, a short coat; **2**, a covering for protection, insulation, etc.; as, a water-*jacket* for cooling an engine.

jack—in—the—box, a toy consisting of a box from which a grotesque figure springs out when the lid is released.

jack—in—the—pul-pit (jak′—in—*thu*-pool′pit), *n*. a plant that grows in damp woods and bears inconspicuous yellow flowers on a fleshy stalk covered by a leaflike hood or spathe.

jack-knife (jak′nīf′), *n*. [*pl.* jack-knives (jak′—nīvz′)], **1**, a pocket-knife larger and stronger than a penknife; **2**, a dive used in fancy diving.

jack-o′—lan-tern (jak′—o-lan′tẽrn), *n*. **1**, a pumpkin hollowed out and cut to resemble a human face, and used as a lantern at Hallow-e′en; **2**, a will-o′-the-wisp.

jack-pot (jak′pot′), *n*. **1**, in *poker*, a pot that keeps increasing until a player can open with a pair of jacks or better; **2**, any high or cumulative stakes, as in bingo, slot machines or enterprise involving risk; as, he hit the *jackpot*.

jack—rab-bit (jak′—rab′it), *n*. a hare of western North America, having very long ears and long hind legs.

jacks (jaks), *n*. a common Canadian term for jackstones.

jack-stones (jak′stōnz′), *n.pl.* a set of pebbles or small metal pieces which are picked up in various ways in a children′s game; also, the game so played.

jack-straws (jak′strôz′), *n.pl.* **1**, a game in which the players try in turn to lift light pieces of wood or metal out of a pile without moving other strips; **2**, the pieces used.

jade (jād), *n*. **1**, a hard, semi-precious stone, green, white, or blue, often carved; **2**, a worn-out or worthless horse; **3**, a woman (derogatory use).

jag (jag), *n*. a sharp projecting point; a notch:—*v.t.* [jagged (jagd), jag-ging], to cut or tear unevenly.—*adj.* **jag′ged** (jag′ed).

jag-uar (jag′wär), *n*. a fierce, catlike, flesh-eating animal of tropical America, spotted like the leopard, but heavier and more powerful.

jail (jāl), *n*. a prison; esp. a lock-up for persons guilty of small offences, or for persons awaiting trial:—*v.t.* to imprison.—*n.* **jail′er**.

ja-lop-y (ja-lop′i), *n*. a ramshackle automobile or airplane.

jal-ou-sie (zhal′oo-zē′; jal′oo-sē′), *n*. *French*, a window or door made of overlapping glass slats, louvres, etc., to keep out rain but admit air.

¹jam (jam), *v.t.* [jammed, jam-ming], **1**, to squeeze or press in tightly; crowd; push; as, to *jam* things into a box; block; as, to *jam* traffic; **2**, to crush or bruise; as, to *jam* one's finger in a heavy door; **3**, to render (a machine or some movable part of it) unworkable by wedging:—*v.i.* **1**, to become tightly packed; as, the logs *jammed;* **2**, to become unworkable by the wedging of some part; stick; as, the engine *jammed:*—**jam session**, a meeting of musicians to enjoy the spontaneous performing of jazz or swing music (without scores).

²jam (jam), *n*. a thick preserve, made by boiling fruit with sugar.

jamb (jam), *n*. one of the side pieces of a door, window, fireplace, or other opening.

jam-bo-ree (jam′bo-rē′), *n*. **1**, a noisy revel or merrymaking; **2**, a boy-scout rally, esp. international or interregional.

jan-gle (jang′gl), *v.i.* and *v.t.* [jan-gled, jan-gling], **1**, to sound harshly or out of tune, as bells; **2**, to speak or utter in a loud, wrangling manner:—*n.* **1**, a discordant sound; **2**, a wrangling.

jan-i-tor (jan′i-tẽr), *n*. **1**, a doorkeeper; **2**, the caretaker of a public building.—*n.fem.* **jan′i-tress**.

Jan-u-ar-y (jan′ū-a-ri), *n.* the first month of the year.

Ja-nus (jā′nus), *n.* the Roman god of the gateway, having two faces, one looking in front and one behind: hence *January.*

ja-pan (ja-pan′), *n.* a hard, brilliant lacquer, varnish, coating, etc.:—*n.* objects ornamented with such lacquer: —*v.t.* to coat with a hard, black gloss; **2,** to lacquer with japan.

Jap-a-nese bee-tle (jap′a-nēz′; jap′a-nēs′), a small bronze-green beetle, very destructive to vegetation.

¹jar (jär), *v.i.* [jarred, jar-ring], **1,** to give out a harsh sound; be discordant; **2,** to shake; vibrate, as doors and windows in an earthquake; **3,** to strike with harsh effect; as, his laugh *jars* on my nerves:—*v.t.* **1,** to make discordant; **2,** to cause to shake; as, the blast *jarred* the house:—*n.* **1,** a harsh sound; discord; **2,** a sudden shake or quivering **3,** a conflict of opinion.

²jar (jär), *n.* **1,** a broad-mouthed vessel of earthenware or glass; **2,** a jar and its contents; as, I bought a *jar* of jelly; also, the amount a jar holds; as, we ate a *jar* of cookies.

jar-di-niere (zhär′di-nyâr′; jär′di-nēr′), *n.* an ornamental container for potted plants.

jar-gon (jär′gun; jär′gon), *n.* **1,** confused talk that cannot be understood; **2,** a mixture of two or more languages; **3,** the technical or special vocabulary of a profession, trade, etc.; cant; as, chemical *jargon;* thieves' *jargon.*

jas-mine or **jas-min** (jas′min; jaz′-min), *n.* a shrub of the olive family with shiny leaves and fragrant red, white, or yellow flowers; also a perfume made from the flowers: also called *jessamine.*

Ja-son (jā′son), *n.* in *Greek Mythology,* the man who, with Medea's help, stole the Golden Fleece, after leading his Argonauts to Colchis.

jas-per (jas′pèr), *n.* **1,** an opaque, cloudy stone, usually red, brown, or yellow; **2,** in the Bible, a stone, probably green, used in the breastplate of the high priest.

ja-to (jā′tō), *n.* in *flying,* jet-assisted take-off.

jaun-dice (jôn′dis; jän′dis), *n.* **1,** a disease characterized by yellowness of the eyeballs, skin, etc., caused by too much bile in the system; **2,** hence, a mental condition such as jealousy, which distorts the judgment:—*v.t.* [jaundiced, jaundic-ing], **1,** to affect with jaundice; **2,** to affect with envy or prejudice.

jaunt (jônt; jänt), *n.* a short excursion or ramble.

jaun-ty (jôn′ti; jän′ti), *adj.* [jaun-ti-er, jaun-ti-est], airy; gay; carefree; as, a hat at a *jaunty* angle.—*adv.* **jaun′ti-ly.** —*n.* **jaun′ti-ness.**

jave-lin (jav′lin; jav′e-lin), *n.* a short, light spear to be thrown by hand.

jaw (jô), *n.* **1,** either of the two bony structures which frame the mouth and in which the teeth are set: also called *jawbone;* **2,** the lower part of the face; **3,** anything that resembles an animal's jaw in form or power of gripping; as, the *jaws* of a vise; **4,** mouth or entrance; as, the *jaws* of a chasm.

jay (jā), *n.* any of several noisy birds of the crow family, of Europe and North America, having bright-coloured plumage, and sometimes a crest; esp. in Canada and the U.S., the blue jay.

jay-walker (jā′wôk′ėr), *n. Colloq.* one who crosses a street contrary to traffic regulations:—*v.i.* **jay′walk′.**

jazz (jaz), *n.* **1,** a kind of American music of Negro, and probably African origin, supposedly named for Jasbo Brown, a Mississippi Negro, used as dance music because of its syncopated rhythms; **2,** a dance to this music:— *v.t. Slang,* **1,** to play (music) so as to make it resemble jazz; **2,** to make lively; as, to *jazz* up a party:—*v.i. Slang,* to act in a gay, lively manner.— *adj.* **jazz′zy.**

jeal-ous (jel′us), *adj.* **1,** characterized by suspicious fear or envy; as, to be *jealous* of another's wealth; **2,** unwilling to have, or afraid of having, a rival in love; as, a *jealous* suitor; **3,** demanding exclusive worship and love: said of God; **4,** anxiously careful or watchful; as, *jealous* of a good name.— *n.* **jeal′ous-y.**

jean (jēn), *n.* **1,** a twilled cotton cloth; **2, jeans,** a garment of this cloth, as overalls.

jeep (jēp), *n.* a small automobile truck, usually for four persons, used during Allied armies during World War II.

jeer (jēr), *v.t.* to sneer at; ridicule; as, the crowd *jeered* the losing team:—*v.i.* to speak in a sneering or sarcastic manner:—*n.* a sneer; coarse ridicule.

Je-ho-vah (ji-hō′va), *n.* [Hebrew, *Yahweh*], God; the Lord; the Almighty.

jell (jel), *v.i.* and *v.t. Colloq.* **1,** to become jelly; **2,** to crystallize or take definite form; as, our plans have not yet *jelled.*

jel-ly (jel′i), *n.* [*pl.* jellies], **1,** the juice

of fruit, meat, etc., which becomes semi-solid and semi-transparent after boiling and cooling; **2,** any similar substance:—*v.i.* [jellied, jelly-ing], to become jelly:—*v.t.* to cause to become jelly.

jel-ly-bean (jel′i-bēn′), *n.* a small gelatinous bean-shaped candy.

jel-ly-fish (jel′i-fish′), *n.* any of several swimming sea animals, with boneless, disk-shaped bodies, somewhat transparent, some of which have long tentacles with stinging hairs: often called *sea-nettle*.

jen-ny (jen′i), *n.* [*pl.* jennies], **1,** a machine for spinning; **2,** a female: used before the names of animals; as, the *jenny* ass.

jeop-ard-y (jep′ẽr-di), *n.* risk; danger; as, the escape of the criminal put the safety of the community in *jeopardy.*—*v.t.* jeop′ard-ize.

jerk (jûrk), *v.t.* **1,** to give a quick pull, twist, or push to; as, he *jerked* off his coat; to *jerk* a fish out of water; **2,** to throw with a sudden, quick movement:—*v.i.* to move with a sudden convulsive movement:—*n.* a sudden, quick pull, twist, push, or throw; as, a *jerk* of the head:—**jerked beef,** beef sliced into strips and dried in the sun or over a fire.

jer-kin (jûr′kin), *n.* a short, close-fitting, sleeveless coat, often made of leather, formerly worn by men.

jerk-wa-ter (jûrk′wô′tẽr), *adj. Colloq.* small; unimportant; as, a *jerkwater* town (one on a branch railroad line).

jerk-y (jûr′ki), *adj.* [jerk-i-er, jerk-i-est], full of jerks; moving with sudden starts and stops; as, a *jerky* walk; not smooth; as, a *jerky* style of writing.—*adv.* jerk′i-ly.

jer-ry—built (jer′i–bilt′), *adj.* flimsy; built of cheap or inferior material: said of houses.

jer-sey (jûr′zi), *n.* a close-fitting pull-on of wool, cotton, rayon, etc. (often knitted).

jess (jes), *n.* a strap fastened to a falcon's leg and attached to a leash.

jes-sa-mine (jes′a-min), *n.* Same as jasmine.

jest (jest), *n.* **1,** a joke; fun; as, many a true word is spoken in *jest;* **2,** the person or thing laughed at or jeered:—*v.i.* to joke; as, I was only *jesting.*

jest-er (jes′tẽr), *n.* **1,** one who makes jokes; **2,** in mediaeval times, a court fool.

Jes-u-it (jez′ū-it), *n.* a member of the Society of Jesus, a Roman Catholic order founded by Ignatius Loyola in

1534; **2,** a crafty person; schemer: hostile term used by anti-Jesuits.

Je-sus (jē′zuz), in the Bible, the Son of Mary, founder of Christianity: also called *Jesus of Nazareth, Jesus Christ,* or *Christ.*

¹jet (jet), *v.t.* and *v.i.* [jet-ted, jet-ting], to shoot or spout out:—*n.* **1,** a stream of liquid or gas issuing from an opening; as, the whale spouts a *jet* of water; **2,** a spout or nozzle for the issuing of a fluid or gas; as, a gas *jet;* **3,** a jet-propelled airplane:—**jet propulsion,** the propelling of airplanes, boats, bombs, etc., by use of heated gases emitted under pressure through a vent or orifice; hence, **jet′plane.**

²jet (jet), *n.* **1,** a hard, black mineral, akin to coal, which is polished and used in making ornaments and buttons; **2,** the colour of jet, a deep, glossy black.—*adj.* **1,** made of, or like, jet; **2,** very black.—*adj.* **jet′—black′.**

jet-sam (jet′sam), *n.* goods thrown overboard to ease a ship in danger of sinking: esp. such goods when washed ashore.

jet-ti-son (jet′i-son), *v.t.* **1,** to throw cargo overboard, esp. to lighten a ship or airplane in distress; **2,** to throw away anything useless or a burden.

jet-ty (jet′i), *n.* [*pl.* jetties], **1,** a structure extending into the water, used as a pier, breakwater, or wall to direct currents; **2,** a landing pier.

jew-el (jōō′el; jū′el), *n.* **1,** a gem or precious stone; **2,** a valuable ornament or trinket set with gems; **3,** a piece of precious stone used as a bearing in the works of a watch; **4,** a person or thing of great value or dearness:—*v.t.,* [jewelled, jewel-ling], to adorn with, or supply with jewels, as a dress or watch.—*n.* **jew′el-er.**

jew-el-ler-y (jōō′el-ẽr-i; jū′el-ẽr-i), *n.* precious stones set in rings, brooches, etc.; also, personal ornaments of gold and silver. Also, **jew′el-ry** (jōō′el-ri).

jew-el-weed (jōō′el-wēd′), *n.* a genus of related plants with spotted orange or yellow flowers having three sepals and a spur.

Jew's—harp or **Jews′—harp** (jōōz′-härp′; jūz′-härp′), *n.* a small musical instrument, with a thin, flexible metal tongue which, when placed between the teeth and struck by the finger, gives forth tones.

JEW'S-HARP

jib (jib), *n.* **1,** a three-cornered sail extending from the foremast to the bowsprit, or to the jibboom, of a vessel; **2,** the projecting arm or beam of a crane or lifting machine:—**flying jib,** a smaller, three-cornered sail set outside the jib to an extension of the jibboom called *flying jibboom.*

jib-boom (jib′bōōm′), *n.* a spar which serves to lengthen the bowsprit of a vessel: a jib is attached to it.

jibe (jīb), *n.* Same as **gibe.**

jibe (jīb), *v.i.* [jibed, jib-ing], *Colloq.* to agree; hang together.

jibe (jīb), *v.i.* to shift suddenly from one side to the other, as when a sail or boom snaps across in a following wind.

jif-fy (jif′i), *n.* [jiffies], *Colloq.* an instant; a moment; as, to do it in a *jiffy.*

jig (jig), *n.* **1,** a quick, lively dance; also, music for such a dance; **2,** a particular kind of fishhook:—*v.i.* [jigged, jig-ging], **1,** to dance a jig; **2,** to fish with a jig.

jigger (jig′ẽr), *n.* a small flea: also spelled **chig′ger.**

jig-ger (jig′ẽr), *n.* **1,** in *mechanics,* a device with a jerky up-and-down motion, as a railway handcar; **2,** in *mining,* a kind of sieve; **3,** in *nautical usage,* a small tackle, sail, or mast near the stern; **4,** in *radio,* an oscillation transformer; **5,** *Colloq.,* any gadget or device.

jig-gle (jig′l), *v.t.* [-gled, -gling], to move with quick, short jerks:—*n.* a light rapidly repeated jerky motion.

jig-saw (jig′sô′), *n.* a narrow saw, moving vertically in a frame, used to cut curved or irregular patterns, as in scroll work:—**jigsaw puzzle,** a picture puzzle made up of pieces cut by a jigsaw.

jilt (jilt), *n.* a person who discards an accepted suitor:—*v.t.* to discard or desert (a lover).

jim-my (jim′i), *n.* [*pl.* jimmies], a short crowbar used by burglars:—*v.t.* to pry open; as, to *jimmy* a safe, window, etc.

jim-son—weed (jim′sn–wēd′), *n.* a coarse, poisonous weed of the nightshade family, with white or violet trumpet-shaped flowers and rank-smelling leaves.

jin-gle (jing′gl), *n.* **1,** a sharp, tinkling sound, as of bells or coins clinking; **2,** a pleasing or catchy succession of rhymes, often with little sense:—*v.i.* [jin-gled, jin-gling], **1,** to give a tinkling sound; as, the keys *jingled* in his pocket; **2,** to sound with a pleasing or

catchy succession of rhymes:—*v.t.* to cause to jingle; as, to *jingle* coins.

jin-go (jing′gō), *n.* a supporter of an aggressive policy in foreign affairs; a blustering patriot.—*n.* **jin′go-ism.**

jinks (jingks), *n.pl. Colloq.* lively or boisterous pranks; frolics; as, **high jinks.**

jin-nee or **jin-ni** (ji-nē′), *n.* [*pl.* jinn], in Mohammedan and Arabian folklore, a spirit made of fire, able to appear in both human and animal forms, and having a supernatural influence over mankind for good and evil: also called *genie* or *genius.*

jin-rik-isha (jin-rik′shä; jin-rik′shô), *n.* a small two-wheeled, man-drawn Japanese carriage. Also spelled **jin-rick′sha.**

jinx (jingks), *n. Slang,* a hoodoo:—*v.t.* to bring bad luck (to).

jit-ney (jit′ni), *n. Slang,* a five-cent piece; **2,** *Colloq.* a car or bus that carries one for a small fare (originally a nickel).

jit-ter-bug (jit′tẽr-bug′), *n.* one who, either alone or with a partner, dances rhythmically to swing music, using improvised acrobatic movements:—*v.i.* to dance in such a manner.

jit-ters (jit′ẽrz), *n.pl. Slang,* extreme nervousness; as, he has the *jitters.*— *adj.* **jit′ter-y.**

jiu-jit-su or **jiu-jut-su** (jōō-jit′sōō; jōō-jut′sōō), *n.* Same as **ju-jut′su.**

jive (jīv), *n. Slang,* **1,** swing music; **2,** the special vocabulary of swing enthusiasts.

job (job), *n.* **1,** a piece of work; as, a little *job* of sewing; **2,** anything one has to do; a responsibility; a duty; as, that's your *job,* not mine; **3,** any scheme for making money or securing private advantage at the expense of duty; **4,** *Colloq.* work; a position; as, out of a *job:*—*adj.* done by the piece; as, *job* work; handled in the gross, or as a total; as, a *job* lot:—*v.i.* [jobbed, job-bing], **1,** to do an occasional piece of work for wages; **2,** to work for one's own gain in a position of trust:—*v.t.* **1,** to buy up (goods) for resale in smaller quantities; **2,** to do, or cause to be done by the lot or piece.

job-ber (job′ẽr), *n.* **1,** one who buys in quantity, from a wholesaler or importer, and sells to a retailer; **2,** one who deals in odd or job lots; **3,** a pieceworker.

jock-ey (jok′i), *n.* [*pl.* jockeys], **1,** a professional horseman hired to ride in a race; **2,** *Slang,* one who drives anything:—*v.t.* **1,** to ride (a horse) as a jockey; **2,** to bargain for position or advantage.

jock-strap (jok′strap′), _n._ an athletic supporter for the genitals, worn by men participating in sports.

jo-cose (jo-kōs′), _adj._ full of jokes; humorous; playful.—_n._ **jo-cos′i-ty.**

joc-u-lar (jok′ū-lėr), _adj._ **1,** given to joking; as, a _jocular_ person; **2,** humorous; comic; as, a _jocular_ reply. —_adv._ **joc′u-lar-ly.**—_n._ **joc′u-lar′i-ty** (jok′ū-lar′i-ti).

joc-und (jok′und; jō′kund), _adj._ jovial; merry; as, a _jocund_ laugh.

jodh-purs (jod′pėrz), _n.pl._ a type of riding breeches worn over the boot.

jog (jog), _v.t._ [jogged, jog-ging], **1,** to push or shake slightly; nudge; **2,** to arouse; as, to _jog_ the memory:—_v.i._ to travel along at a slow trot, as an old horse:—_n._ **1,** a slight push or shake; **2,** a slow trot; **3,** a notch; an irregularity; as, a _jog_ in the road.

jog-gle (jog′l), _v.t._ [jog-gled, jog-gling], to jerk slightly; nudge:—_v.i._ to totter: —_n._ a sudden shake; jolt.

john-ny-cake (jon′i-kāk′), _n._ a flat cake of corn meal mixed with milk or water, eggs, etc., and baked.

join (join), _v.t._ **1,** to unite; connect; put or bring together; as, to _join_ a hose to a faucet; _join_ hands;· **2,** to unite in marriage; **3,** to become a member of; as, to _join_ a club; **4,** to engage in, with others; as, to _join_ battle; **5,** to be next to; as, his yard _joins_ ours:—_v.i._ **1,** to be in contact; **2,** to become associated or united; as, two roads _join_ at this point: —_n._ a joint; a joining.

join-er (join′ėr), _n._ **1,** one who or that which joins; **2,** a skilled workman who finishes the inside woodwork for houses.

joint (joint), _n._ **1,** the place where two or more things join; esp. the point where two bones of the body are joined; **2,** the part between two joinings; as, a _joint_ in a grass stem; **3,** a large piece of meat cut for roasting; **4,** _Slang,_ a low or disreputable resort:—_adj._ **1,** united; combined; as, _joint_ efforts; **2,** used, held, or owned by two or more; as, _joint_ property:—_v.t._ **1,** to connect by joints; **2,** to cut into pieces at the joints.—_adv._ **joint′ly.**

joist (joist), _n._ a piece of timber to which the boards of a floor or ceiling are fastened for support.

joke (jōk), _n._ **1,** something said or done to cause mirth; a jest; **2,** a laughing-stock; as, he was the _joke_ of the town: —_v.i._ [joked, jok-ing], to jest.

jok-er (jō′kėr), _n._ **1,** one who tells humorous stories or plays pranks; **2,** an extra card used in certain card games as the highest trump; **3,** a clause in a legislative bill, a written agreement, etc., which is inconspicuous, but which actually changes the entire meaning of the document.

jol-ly (jol′i), _adj._ [jol-li-er, jol-li-est], **1,** full of mirth; gay; as, a _jolly_ time; **2,** causing or expressing mirth or gaiety; as, a _jolly_ laugh:—_v.t._ [jollied, jolly-ing] _Colloq._ to flatter; make good-humored fun of.—_n._ **jol′li-ty.**—_n._ **jol′li-fi-ca′-tion** (_Colloq._).

Jol-ly Rog-er (roj′ėr), _n._ the emblem of piracy, a black flag with white skull and crossbones.

jolt (jōlt), _v.t._ to shake by sudden jerks: —_v.i._ to have a jerky motion; as, the carriage _jolted_ down the hill:—_n._ a sudden jerk; as, the train stopped with a _jolt._

jon-quil (jong′kwil; jon′kwil), _n._ a plant of the narcissus family, with yellow or white fragrant flowers and sword-shaped leaves; also, the flower.

josh (josh), _v.t._ and _v.i. Colloq._ to tease; banter; chaff; ridicule good-naturedly; as, he took the _joshing_ in good part.

jos-tle (jos′l), _v.t._ [jos-tled, jos-tling], to push against; elbow; as, we _jostled_ one another in the subway.

jot (jot), _v.t._ [jot-ted, jot-ting], to make a brief note of; as, to _jot_ down an address:—_n._ a very small particle or quantity; as, not a _jot_ of intelligence.

joule (joul; jool), _n._ in _electricity,_ the unit of work or energy, namely, the work done, or heat generated, in maintaining for one second a current of one ampere against a resistance of one ohm; ten million ergs.

jounce (jouns), _v.t._ and _v.i._ [jounced, jounc-ing], to shake up and down; jolt:—_n._ a jolt.

jour-nal (jûr′nal), _n._ **1,** a daily record of news or events; **2,** a daily newspaper or other periodical; **3,** a diary;· **4,** a book in which business transactions are entered daily; **5,** a ship's logbook; **6,** a record of the daily proceedings of a legislative body; **7,** that portion of an axle or of a rotating shaft that rests on bearings.

jour-nal-ism (jûr′nal-izm), _n._ the occupation of publishing, editing, or writing for a newspaper or periodical.— _adj._ **jour′nal-is′tic.**—_n._ **jour′nal-ist.**

jour-ney (jûr′ni), _n._ [_pl._ journeys], **1,** a trip from one place to another; as, a _journey_ from France to Spain; **2,** the amount of time consumed or space covered in travel:—*v.i.* to travel, esp. by land.

jour-ney-man (jûr'ni-man), *n.* a craftsman or mechanic who has served his apprenticeship, or learned a trade and works for another, esp. by the day.

joust (joōst; just), *n.* a combat with lances between two mounted knights, usually as part of a tournament:—*v.i.* to engage in such a combat.

jo-vi-al (jō'vi-al), *adj.* jolly; merry; gay; as, a *jovial* comrade.—*adv.* **jo'vi-al-ly.**—*n.* **jo'vi-al'i-ty.**

jowl (joul; jōl), *n.* 1, the jaw; esp. the under jaw; 2, the cheek.

joy (joi), *n.* 1, a feeling of happiness; gladness; as, the holidays bring *joy;* 2, that which causes gladness; as, "a thing of beauty is a *joy* forever":—*v.i.* to rejoice.—*adj.* **joy'less.**—*n.* and *v.* **joy'—ride'.**

joy-ful (joi'fool), *adj.* full of, or causing gladness; as, *joyful* days; *joyful* news. —*adv.* **joy'ful-ly.**—*n.* **joy'ful-ness.**

joy-ous (joi'us), *adj.* having or causing happiness; glad; as, a *joyous* occasion. —*adv.* **joy'ous-ly.**—*n.* **joy'ous-ness.**

ju-bi-lant (joō'bi-lant), *adj.* showing great joy; exultant; as, *jubilant* over winning a game.—*adv.* **ju'bi-lant-ly.**

ju-bi-la-tion (joō'bi-lā'shun), *n.* triumphant exultation; rejoicing.

ju-bi-lee (joō'bi-lē'), *n.* 1, the anniversary, generally the 50th, but sometimes the 25th, of any event; 2, any occasion of rejoicing; also, a state of rejoicing; 3, a year of special indulgence which was formerly granted by the Pope every 25th year, but may now be granted at any time.

judge (juj), *n.* 1, the official who presides in a court of law and hears and tries cases; 2, a person appointed to decide in a trial of skill, speed, etc., between two or more persons; 3, one who has enough knowledge or experience to decide on the quality or value of anything; as, a *judge* of gems:—*v.t.* [judged, judg-ing], 1, to hear and pass sentence on (a person or a matter), as in a court of law; 2, to estimate; criticize; as, we *judged* him unfairly; 3, to think or suppose; as, I *judged* this to be true:—*v.i.* 1, to form an opinion after careful consideration; as, to *judge* in a debate; 2, to hear and determine a case and pass sentence; 3, to think; consider.

judg-ment (juj'ment), *n.* 1, the act of passing sentence; also, the decision of a court; 2, the mental process by which we are able to see differences and likenesses, and by which we are able to weigh values; 3, good sense; discernment; as, a man of *judgment;* 4, estimate; opinion; as, in my *judgment* he is sane; 5, any calamity attributed to the anger of God. Also spelled **judge'ment.**

ju-di-ca-ture (joō'di-ka-tūr; -chėr), *n.* 1, a court of justice; judges collectively; 2, the power to do justice by legal trial and judgment; 3, the territory and matter over which the authority of a court extends.

ju-di-cial (joō-dish'al), *adj.* 1, pertaining to a judge, to a court of law, or to the administration of justice; as, *judicial* power; 2, proceeding from, or inflicted by, a court of justice; as, a *judicial* decision; 3, considering all aspects of a situation before deciding; impartial.

ju-di-ci-ar-y (joō-dish'i-a-ri), *n.* [*pl.* judiciaries], the system of courts of justice in a country; also, the judges collectively:—*adj.* pertaining to judges, courts of justice, or the procedure of a court.

ju-di-cious (joō-dish'us), *adj.* showing good judgment; wise; as, a *judicious* act.

ju-do (joō'dō), *n.* jujutsu.

jug (jug), *n.* 1, a narrow-necked vessel, usually with a handle, for holding liquids; also, a pitcher; 2, the vessel and its contents; as, a *jug* of wine; also, the amount of liquid the vessel can hold.

jug-gle (jug'l), *v.t.* [jug-gled, jug-gling], 1, to perform tricks with; as, to *juggle* balls; 2, hence, to misrepresent; as, to *juggle* facts:—*v.i.* 1, to perform entertaining tricks; 2, to play tricks so as to deceive.—*n.* **jug'gler.**—*n.* **jug'gler-y.**

jug-u-lar (jug'ū-lėr), *adj.* pertaining to neck or throat.—*n.* the **jugular vein,** one of two large veins on either side of the throat that return the blood from the head to the heart.

juice (joōs), *n.* the liquid part of fruits, meats, etc.—*adj.* **juic'y.**—*n.* **juic'i-ness.**

ju-jube (joō'joōb), *n.* a lozenge flavoured with the fruit of the tropical jujube tree or shrub.

ju-jut-su (joō-jut'soō), *n.* the Japanese art of wrestling, which turns an opponent's own strength and weight against him. Also, **ju-jit'su; jiu-jut'su; jiu-jit'su.**

juke box (joōk), *n. Colloq.* an electric

all (ôl), **ôr; up, mūte, cûr, cool, book; oil, out; th, thin;** *th,* **the.**

phonograph in a restaurant, etc., that operates when a coin is deposited in it.

ju-lep (jōō′lip), *n.* **1,** a drink made of brandy or whisky sweetened and flavoured; as, mint *julep;* **2,** a mixture of sugar and water in which medicine is given.

ju-lienne (zhü′lyen′; jōō′li-en′), *n.* and *adj.* French, a clear meat soup with chopped vegetables, esp. carrots (cut in thin strips).

Ju-ly (jōō-li′), *n.* the 7th month of the year.

jum-ble (jum′bl), *n.* **1,** a confused mass or mixture; disorder; **2,** a thin round cake:—*v.t.* [jum-bled, jum-bling], to mix in a confused mass; throw together messily.

jum-bo (jum′bō), *n. Colloq.* a large clumsy animal, person, or thing.—*adj.* very large; as, *jumbo* olives.

jump (jump), *n.* **1,** a spring or bound; hence, a sudden rise; as, a *jump* in temperature; **2,** the space covered by a leap or bound; **3,** something to be leaped or hurdled; as, the third *jump* was easy; **4,** a sudden movement or start:—*v.i.* **1,** to leap or spring; **2,** to start suddenly; as, she *jumped* when she saw the mouse; **3,** to rise suddenly; as, prices *jumped* as the supply gave out:—*v.t.* **1,** to cause to leap; as, to *jump* a horse over a brook; **2,** to leap on or over; **3,** to jump upon or aboard; as, to *jump* a passing freight train; **4,** to seize in the owner's absence; as, to *jump* a mining claim.

¹jump-er (jump′ėr), *n.* a person or thing that jumps.

²jump-er (jump′ėr), *n.* **1,** a loose outer jacket worn by workmen; **2,** a woman's outer blouse reaching to the hips.

jum-py (jum′pi), *adj.* nervous; on edge.—*n.* **jump′i-ness.**

jun-co (jung′kō), *n.* [*pl.* juncos], an American finch about the size of the English sparrow; a snowbird.

junc-tion (jungk′shun), *n.* **1,** the act of joining or state of being joined; **2,** a point of union; esp. a station where two or more railroad lines meet or cross.

junc-ture (jungk′tūr), *n.* **1,** the point at which two things join; joint; junction; **2,** a union of events, esp. a crisis.

June (jōōn), *n.* the 6th month of the year.

June bug, a large brown beetle that emerges from the ground about June 1st: its white larva, curled and plump, is about 1½″ long.

jun-gle (jung′gl), *n.* any tract of land overrun with dense, tangled vegetation, usually tropical.

jun-ior (jōōn′yėr), *adj.* **1,** younger: used of a son named for his father; as, John Smith, *Junior;* **2,** of lower standing; as, the *junior* partner in a firm; **3,** naming or relating to the next to the last year of a college or high-school course:—*n.* **1,** a younger person; **2,** one of lower standing; **3,** in high schools and colleges, a student in the next to last year.

ju-ni-per (jōō′ni-pėr), *n.* any of several evergreen trees or shrubs of the pine family, with blue, berrylike fruits, as the common juniper and red cedar.

¹junk (jungk), *n.* a jumble of useless articles, paper, broken glass, etc.; trash:—*v.t.* to cast off as worthless or unusable; also, to destroy or make unusable.

²junk (jungk), *n.* a kind of flat-bottomed Chinese vessel with a high stern.

jun-ket (jung′kit), *n.* **1,** milk that has been curdled, sweetened, and flavoured; **2,** a feast; a picnic; **3,** an excursion at public expense:—*v.i.* to feast or picnic.

jun-ta (jun′ta), *n.* in Spain and Spanish America, an assembly for making or administering laws: less correctly **jun′to.**

Ju-pi-ter (jōō′pi-tėr), *n.* **1,** the ancient Roman supreme god (same as the Greek *Zeus*); **2,** the largest planet fifth from the sun, takes 11.86 years to revolve around it, is 483,000,000 miles from it (diameter 87,000 miles).

ju-rid-i-cal (jōō-rid′i-kal), *adj.* pertaining to law, legal proceedings, or the office of a judge.

ju-ris-dic-tion (jōōr′is-dik′shun), *n.* **1,** the right to apply legal authority; as the *jurisdiction* of a court or state; **2,** authority of a sovereign power; **3,** the district over which any authority extends.

ju-ris-pru-dence (jōō′ris-prōō′dens), *n.* **1,** the science of law; **2,** a system of laws; a department of law.

ju-rist (jōōr′ist), *n.* one skilled in the science of law.

ju-ror (jōōr′ėr), *n.* a member of a jury.

¹ju-ry (jōōr′i), *n.* [*pl.* juries], **1,** a body of persons, usually twelve in number selected and sworn to inquire into, or to try, matters of fact submitted to them in a court of law; **2,** a committee of experts selected to pass judgment on something, award prizes, etc.

'ju-ry (jōō′ri), *adj. Nautical*, for temporary use in an emergency; as, a *jury* mast.

ju-ry-man (jōō′ri-man), *n.* a juror.

just (just), *adj.* 1, fair; impartial; as, the judge gave a *just* decision; 2, based on reasonable grounds; as, a *just* accusation; 3, exact; as, *just* weight; 4, legally right; as, a *just* case; 5, according to divine or human laws; upright; as, a *just* life:—*adv.* 1, exactly; as, *just* how many? 2, but now; a moment ago; as, he was *just* here; 3, only; barely; as, *just* a little; 4, *Colloq.* simply; quite; as, *just* beautiful.

jus-tice (jus′tis), *n.* 1, the principle or practice of dealing uprightly with others; 2, absolute fairness; as, the *justice* of a decision; 3, legal administration; as, a court of *justice;* 4, a judge.

jus-ti-ci-ar-y (jus-tish′i-a-ri), *n.* a judge of a superior court.

jus-ti-fy (jus′ti-fī′), *v.t.* [justified, justifying], 1, to show or prove to be right; warrant; as, the result *justified* the expense; 2, to clear; free from blame: —*v.i.* to show lawful grounds for an act. —*adj.* **jus′ti-fi′a-ble.**—*n.* **jus′ti-fi-ca′-tion** (jus′ti-fi-kā′shun).

jut (jut), *v.i.* [jut-ted, jut-ting], to project; stick out; as, a peninsula *juts* into the sea:—*n.* a projection.

jute (jōōt), *n.* the fibre of an East Indian plant, used for ropes, bags, etc.; also, the plant itself.

ju-ve-nile (jōō′vi-nīl; jōō′vi-nil), *adj.* 1, childlike; youthful; 2, like or for young people; as, *juvenile* literature:— *n.* 1, a child under sixteen; 2, a book for children; 3, an actor in youthful roles.

jux-ta-po-si-tion(juks′ta-pō-zhis′un), *n.* a placing side by side or close together:—*v.t.* **jux′ta-pose′.**

K

K, k (kā), *n.* [*pl.* K's, k's], the 11th letter of the alphabet, following J.

kale or **kail** (kāl), *n.* a plant belonging to the same family as the cabbage, with crisp, curly leaves. It is used as a vegetable.

ka-lei-do-scope (ka-lī′dō-skōp′), *n.* 1, an instrument containing small, loose bits of coloured glass and an arrangement of mirrors, in which the bits of glass are reflected in a variety of beautiful patterns when their position is changed by rotation of the instrument; 2, anything which shows a succession of changing aspects.—*adj.* **ka-lei′do-scop′ic** (ka-lī′do-skop′ik).

ka-lif or **kha-lif** (kā′lif), *n.* Same as **caliph.**

kal-so-mine (kal′sō-mīn′), *n.* Same as **calcimine.**

kan-ga-roo (kang′ga-rōō′), *n.* [*pl.* kangaroos], an animal of Australia, which has short forelegs, powerful hind legs with which it leaps, and a strong tail, used as a support in standing or leaping. The female has an external pouch in which it carries its young: —**kangaroo court,** an irregular or unauthorized court, as in a frontier area, among prison inmates, etc.

ka-o-lin (kā′ō-lin), *n.* a pure white clay used in making porcelain.

ka-pok (kā′pok; kȧ′), *n.* the mass of silky fibres within the seed pods of a certain tropical tree, called *kapok tree:* used as stuffing for mattresses and cushions.

kar-a-kul or **car-a-cul** (kar′a-kōōl), *n.* 1, a kind of Asiatic broad-tailed sheep; 2, the curly black coat of the new-born lambs of this sheep, highly valued as a fur.

kar-at (kar′at), *n.* Same as **carat.**

ka-ty-did (kā′ti-did′), *n.* a large, green insect similar to a grasshopper, so named because of the sound it makes.

kau-ri (kou′ri), *n.* a tall New Zealand pine yielding long timbers and a resin gum valuable for varnish.

kay-ak (kī′ak), *n.* an Eskimo canoe, made of sealskin stretched over a light frame about sixteen feet in length, and seating one person.

ka-zoo (kȧ-zōō′), *n.* a toy musical instrument consisting of a tube containing a thin membrane of paper, catgut, etc., that vibrates to make a buzzing or humming when one blows into the tube.

kedge (kej), *n.* a light anchor:—*v.t.* to pull or warp a ship along by a rope attached to an anchor.

keel (kēl), *n.* 1, the lowest timber or steel plate in the framework of a vessel, extending lengthwise along the

all (ôl), ôr; up, mūte, cûr, cōōl, book; oil, out; th, thin; *th*, the.

bottom, and often projecting below the planking; **2,** anything resembling a ship's keel:—*v.t.* and *v.i.* to turn up the keel (of); turn over.

keen (kēn), *adj.* **1,** sharp; cutting; as, a *keen* blade; **2,** piercing; bitter; as, a *keen* wind; *keen* sarcasm; **3,** acute or sharp; as, *keen* eyesight; alert; quick; as, a *keen* mind; **4,** eager; ardent; as, a *keen* sportsman.

keep (kēp), *v.t.* [kept (kept), keep-ing], **1,** to watch; defend; as, to *keep* goal; **2,** to take care of; as, to *keep* dogs; to provide with lodging or food; as, to *keep* boarders; **3,** to manage; as, to *keep* a shop; *keep* house; **4,** to have and retain in use, ownership, or possession; as, whatever you find you may *keep;* **5,** to observe; fulfil; as, to *keep* a holiday or a promise; **6,** to guard; as, to *keep* a secret; **7,** to detain; as, to *keep* a boy after school; **8,** to have on hand or in stock, as for sale; as, to *keep* shoes; **9,** to maintain; as, to *keep* one's health; to *keep* silence; preserve; as, to *keep* food; **10,** to maintain (a record of events, transactions, etc.); as, to *keep* books; to *keep* accounts:—*v.i.* **1,** to remain or continue; as, to *keep* cheerful; to *keep* on with one's work; **2,** to continue sweet, fresh, or unspoiled; as, food will not *keep* at this time of year:—*n.* **1,** means of subsistence; maintenance; board and lodging; as, he worked for his *keep;* **2,** the stronghold of a castle.—*n.* **keep'er.**

keep-ing (kēp'ing), *n.* **1,** maintenance; support; as, the *keeping* of bees or a dog; observance; as, the *keeping* of customs; **2,** custody; charge; as, the book was given into his *keeping;* **3,** harmony; agreement; as, a speech in *keeping* with the occasion.

keep-sake (kēp'sāk'), *n.* something kept in memory of the giver; a memento.

keg (keg), *n.* a small, strong barrel, with a capacity of five to ten gallons.

kelp (kelp), *n.* any of several large, brown seaweeds: a source of alkali, iodine, and other commercial products.

ken (ken), *n.* view; reach of sight or knowledge; comprehension; as, beyond one's *ken*:—*v.t.* [kenned, ken-ning], *Scottish*, to know.

ken-nel (ken'el; ken'l), *n.* **1,** a doghouse; **2, kennels,** a place where dogs are bred and raised:—*v.t.* [kennelled, kennel-ling], to confine in a kennel; as, to *kennel* a dog:—*v.i.* to live or rest in a kennel.

ker-chief (kûr'chif), *n.* **1,** a square of cloth worn by women on the head or around the neck; **2,** a handkerchief.

ker-nel (kûr'nl), *n.* **1,** a seed; a grain of wheat, corn, or other cereal; **2,** the softer, inner portion of a nut, fruit, stone, etc., sometimes used for food; **3,** the central or important part of anything; gist; as, the *kernel* of a plan or theory.

ker-o-sene (ker'o-sēn'; ker'o-sēn'), *n.* a thin, colourless oil, made from petroleum, and used in lamps and stoves.

ketch (kech), *n.* a small sailing-vessel with a large mainmast, and a smaller mizzenmast just forward of the rudder-post.

ketch-up (ketch'up), *n.* a sauce made of tomatoes, mushrooms, etc. Also, **catch'up.**

ket-tle (ket'l), *n.* a metal vessel for heating liquids; esp. a teakettle having a handle and a spout.

ket-tle-drum (ket'l-drum'), *n.* a drum consisting of a large hollow bowl of copper or brass, with parchment stretched over the opening.

¹key (kē), *n.* **1,** a metal instrument for moving the bolt of a lock; **2,** anything resembling this instrument in use or form; as, the *key* of a clock; a fraternity *key;* **3,** that which allows or hinders entrance or control; as, Gibraltar is the *key* to the Mediterranean; **4,** that by means of which a difficulty is removed or something difficult to understand is explained; as, the *key* to a translation; a *key* to a code or cipher; **5,** in certain musical instruments, as the piano, and in typewriters and similar devices, any of a series of levers by means of which the instrument is played or operated; **6,** the general pitch of tone of the voice; as, men usually speak in a lower *key* than women; also, tone of thought or expression; as, a poem in minor *key;* **7,** an arrangement or series of musical tones bearing a fixed relation to a given note, called the keynote; as, the *key* of G major:—*v.t.* **1,** to regulate the pitch of; as, to *key* a violin; **2,** to stimulate; make tense; as, the thought of the game *keyed* him up to a state of great excitement.

²key (kē), *n.* a low, small reef or island; as, the Florida *keys.*

key-board (kē'bôrd'), *n.* **1,** the row of keys on a piano, organ, etc., by means of which the instrument is played; **2,**

KEY
1, bow; 2, stem; 3, collar; 4, pin; 5, bit.

the bank of keys on a typewriter, or any similar machine, by means of which the instrument is operated.

key-hole (kē′hōl′), *n.* a small opening, as in a door or lock, for inserting a key.

key-note (kē′nōt′), *n.* 1, in *music*, the first note of a scale; the note on which a scale or system of tones is based; 2, the main idea or principle; as, the *keynote* of a plan.

key-stone (kē′stōn′), *n.* 1, the wedge-shaped stone at the topmost point of an arch, which holds the whole structure in place; 2, something essential, on which other connected things depend.

kha-ki (kä′ki), *n.* 1, a dull, yellowish-brown or olive-drab colour; 2, a wool or cotton cloth of this colour, much used for uniforms; also, a uniform of this material:—*adj* of a dull, yellowish-brown colour.

kha-lif (kā′lif; kal), *n.* Same as **caliph.**

khan (kän), *n.* 1, a title of respect in Iran, Afghanistan, India, etc.; 2, an inn, esp. one where caravans stop for the night.

khe-dive (ke-dēv′), *n.* the title of Turkish viceroys in Egypt, 1867–1914.

kib-itz-er (kib′it-sėr), *n. Colloq.* one who looks on at a card game, and gives unasked advice; hence, 2, a meddler:—*v.i.* **kib-itz** (kib′its).

ki-bosh (kī′bosh), *n. Slang,* nonsense: —to **put the kibosh on,** to veto or squelch.

kick (kik), *v.t.* to thrust at, or strike, with the foot:—*v.i.* 1, to strike out with the foot; 2, to spring back, as a gun after it has been fired; 3, *Slang,* to grumble; rebel; as, he *kicked* against staying indoors:—*n.* 1, a blow with the foot; 2, a backward spring, as of a gun; 3, *Slang:* **a,** an objection or protest; **b,** thrill; excitement; as, to get a *kick* out of skiing.

kick-back (kik′bak′), *n. Colloq.* a giving back of part of a sum received as a commission, fee, etc., often as a result of a previous understanding, coercion, etc.

kick-off (kik′ôf′), *n.* in *football,* the opening of play by the kicking of the ball.

kid (kid), *n.* 1, a young goat; also, its flesh; 2, leather made from the skin of a kid, used esp. for shoes and gloves; 3, *Colloq.* a child:—*adj.* made of leather called kid; as, *kid* gloves:—*v.i.* [kid-ded kid-ding], *Slang,* to joke teasingly with someone:—*v.t. Slang,* to tease.

kid-die or **kid-dy** (kid′i), *n.* [*pl.* -dies], *Colloq.* child.

kid-nap (kid′nap), *v.t.* [kidnapped, kidnap-ping], to steal or carry off (a person) by force or fraud; as, to *kidnap* a child.—*n.* **kid′nap′per.**

kid-ney (kid′ni), *n.* [*pl.* kidneys], 1, one of two bean-shaped glands situated in the back, near the spinal column, which separate waste matter from the blood, and pass it off in liquid form through the bladder; 2, this organ in certain animals, used for food; 3, sort or kind; disposition; as, a man of his *kidney*:— **kidney bean,** a reddish-brown, kidney-shaped bean.

kill (kil), *v.t.* 1, to deprive of life; as, the frost *killed* the flowers; the farmer *killed* the cow; 2, to destroy; as, to *kill* one's hopes; 3, to use up; as, to *kill* time; 4, to reject; discard; as, to *kill* a legislative bill:—*v.i.* to destroy life; as, it is a crime to *kill*:—*n.* 1, in hunting, the act of killing; 2, the animal or animals killed.—*n.* **kill′er.**

kill-deer (kil′dēr′), *n.* a North American bird, greyish-brown and white in colour, with a much repeated, penetrating cry; a plover.

kiln (kil; kiln), *n.* a furnace or oven for burning, drying, or hardening something, as lime, brick, tiles, etc

kil-o-cy-cle (kil′ō-sī′kl), *n.* in *electricity* 1,000 cycles per second, a unit used esp. in radio to give the frequency of an alternating current or oscillation; as CJBC, 860 *kilocycles.*

kil-o-gramme or **kil-o-gram** (kil′ō-gram), *n.* a unit of weight equal to 1,000 grammes, or 2.2046 pounds avoirdupois.

kil-o-me-tre or **kil-o-me-ter** (kil′-ō-mē′tèr), *n.* a measure of distance equal to 1,000 meters, or 3280.89 feet. —*adj.* **kil′o-met′ric** (kil′ō-met′rik); **kil′o-met′ri-cal.**

kil-o-watt (kil′ō-wot′; kil′ō-wôt′), *n.* a unit of electrical power equal to 1,000 watts:—**kilowatt hour,** the energy expended, or work done, in one hour by one kilowatt (about 1⅓ horsepower).

kilt (kilt), *n.* a short pleated skirt, usually of tartan cloth, worn by men of the Scottish Highlands; also, any similar garment:—*v.t.* 1, to form into pleats; 2, in Scotland, to tuck up (the skirts).

kil-ter (kil′tèr), *n. Colloq.* order; condition.

ki-mo-no (ki-mō′nō; ki-mō′na), *n.* [*pl.* kimonos], 1, a loose outer robe, tied by a sash, worn by the Japanese; 2, a similar garment sometimes worn as a dressing-gown by women of other nations.

kin (kin), *n*. **1,** a person's family or relatives; kinsfolk; kindred; as, my *kin* live in England; **2,** family relationship:—*adj*. of the same ancestry; related; as, John is *kin* to me.

¹kind (kīnd), *adj*. sympathetic; inclined to be considerate of others; as, a *kind* master; also, showing such sympathy or consideration; as, a *kind* deed.

²kind (kīnd), *n*. **1,** a natural group, class, or division; as, the cat *kind;* **2,** variety; sort; as, all *kinds* of food; **3,** nature; character; style; as, prose and poetry differ in *kind*.

kin-der-gar-ten (kin′der-gär′tn), *n*. a school for children too young to go to regular school, in which they are taught by the use of games, toys, songs, etc.

kin-dle (kin′dl), *v.t*. [kin-dled, kin-dling], **1,** to set fire to; as, the spark *kindled* the wood; **2,** to arouse or excite; stir; as, the speech *kindled* his anger; **3,** to make bright or shining; as, enthusiasm *kindled* her face:—*v.i*. **1,** to catch fire; as, the wood *kindled* rapidly; **2,** to become excited or aroused; **3,** to become bright or glowing; as, his eyes *kindled* with joy.

kin-dling (kin′dling), *n*. material, easily lighted, for starting a fire, such as light, dry wood.

kind-ly (kīnd′li), *adj*. [kind-li-er, kind-li-est], sympathetic; gracious; kind:—*adv*. **1,** in a kind or friendly manner; **2,** naturally; as, willows take *kindly* to damp ground.—*n*. kind′li-ness.

kind-ness (kīnd′nis), *n*. **1,** the state or quality of being ready to do good to others; **2,** a helpful or gracious act; as, she has done us many *kindnesses*.

kin-dred (kin′dred), *adj*. **1,** of like nature or character; as, football and soccer are *kindred* sports; also, congenial; as, *kindred* spirits; **2,** related by birth or marriage:—*n*. **1,** relationship by birth or marriage; kinship; **2,** one's relatives.

kine (kīn), *n*. *Archaic*, cows; cattle.

kin-e-scope (kin′e-skōp′; kīn), *n*. in *television*, a receiving tube with a screen on which pictures or images are reproduced; picture tube: a trademark.

ki-net-ic (ki-net′ik; kī-), *adj*. pertaining to, or resulting from, motion.—**kinetic energy,** the energy possessed by a moving body due to its motion, and equal to one-half the product of its mass and the square of its velocity: opposite of *potential* energy.—**kinetics,** the branch of dynamics treating of changes in motion as produced by unbalanced forces: opposite of *statics*.

king (king), *n*. **1,** a male sovereign or ruler; **2,** one who has power or importance that can be compared with that of a ruler or sovereign; as, a *king* of painters; a cotton *king;* **3,** the principal piece in the game of chess; **4,** in *cards*, a card which bears the picture of a king; **5,** in *chequers*, a piece which has crossed the board to the opponent's last row.—*adj*. king′ly.—*n*. king′li-ness; king′ship.

king-bird (king′–bûrd′), *n*. an American flycatcher.

king-dom (king′dum), *n*. **1,** a country ruled by a king or queen, or the territory comprising such a country; **2,** a realm or sphere in which one has control; as, the *kingdom* of the mind; his home is his *kingdom;* **3,** one of the classes into which natural objects are divided; as, the animal, mineral, and vegetable *kingdoms*.

king-fish-er (king′fish′er), *n*. any of a family of bright-coloured, long-billed birds that feed on fish and insects.

king-pin (king′pin′), *n*. **1,** a main or large bolt, esp. one passing through an axle and acting as a pivot; **2,** *Colloq*. the chief person in an enterprise, company, etc.; **3,** in *bowling*, the pin at the apex or centre.

king—size (king′–size′), *adj*. *Colloq*. larger than usual. Also, king′–sized′.

kink (kingk), *n*. **1,** a twist, curl, or loop in rope, wire, thread, hair, etc., **2,** a notion or odd whim; a twist in one's mind or disposition:—*v.i*. to form twists or curls:—*v.t*. to cause to kink.—*adj*. kink′y.

kins-folk (kinz′fōk′), *n*. relatives; kin.

kin-ship (kin′ship), *n*. relationship by birth or by marriage; also, similarity in qualities or character; as, there is close *kinship* in their ideas.

kins-man (kinz′man), *n*. [*pl*. kinsmen (-men)], a male relative; a man related by birth or marriage.—*n.fem*. kins′-wom′an.

kip-per (kip′er), *v.t*. to cure by cleaning, salting, and drying or smoking.—*n*. **1,** a salmon or herring so cured; **2,** a male salmon or sea trout during or after spawning season, when it is unfit to eat.

kirk (kûrk), *n*. *Scottish*, church.

kis-met (kiz′met; kis), *n*. *Arabic*, fate; destiny.

kiss (kis), *n*. **1,** a touching with the lips in a caress or greeting; **2,** a slight touch; **3,** a kind of candy:—*v.t*. **1,** to touch with the lips as a sign of affection;

greeting, etc., **2,** to touch slightly; as, a soft breeze *kissed* the flowers:—*v.i.* **1,** to touch or salute a person with the lips; **2,** to touch gently.

kit (kit), *n.* an outfit of tools, articles of travel, etc., as a plumber's *kit;* a salesman's *kit;* also, the box or bag holding such an outfit.

kitch-en (kich'en), *n.* a room in which cooking is done.

kitch-en-ette (kich'e-net'), *n.* a small, compactly arranged kitchen.

kite (kīt), *n.* **1,** a light frame of wood, covered with paper or other thin material, to be flown in the air while held by a string; **2,** a bird of the hawk family, small or medium in size, with long, narrow wings.

kith (kith), *n.* friends; neighbours: used in the expression *kith and kin.*

kit-ten (kit'n), *n.* a young cat.

¹kit-ty (kit'i), *n.* **1,** a pool, as in a poker game, contributed by players for a special purpose; **2,** in some card games, an extra hand (or part of one) dealt to the table.

²kit-ty (kit'i), *n. Colloq.* a pet term for kitten.

klep-to-ma-ni-a (klep'tō-mā'ni-a), *n.* an abnormal, often irresistible, impulse to steal.—*n.* **klep'to-ma'ni-ac.**

knack (nak), *n.* cleverness in performance; ability to do something skilfully; as, she could never acquire the *knack* of tatting.

knap-sack (nap'sak'), *n.* a leather or canvas bag, worn strapped across the shoulders, for carrying toilet articles or clothes.

knave (nāv), *n.* **1,** a dishonest or deceitful person; a rascal; **2,** a playing-card with the figure of a soldier upon it; a jack.—*n.* **knav'er-y.**—*adj.* **knav'ish.**

knead (nēd), *v.t.* **1,** to mix and work into a mass, usually with the hands; as, to *knead* dough; **2,** to work over or treat with the hands or fingers; to massage.

knee (nē), *n.* **1,** in man, the joint between the thigh and the lower leg; **2,** the part of a garment covering this joint; as, the *knee* of your trousers is torn; **3,** anything resembling the human knee, esp. when bent, as a sharp angle in an iron pipe.

knee-cap (nē'kap'), *n.* a flattened, triangular, movable bone on the front part of the knee.

kneel (nēl), *v.i.* [knelt (nelt) or kneeled, kneel-ing], **1,** to bend the knee; as, he *knelt* to pick up his hat; **2,** to rest on bent knees; as, to *kneel* in prayer.

knell (nel), *n.* **1,** the sound of a bell, esp. when tolled for a death or at a funeral; **2,** hence; a sign of the ending or extinction of something; as, "The curfew tolls the *knell* of parting day":— *v.i.* to toll dolefully.

knick-er-bock-ers (nik'ér-bok'érz), *n.pl.* short, wide breeches gathered at the knee.

knick-ers (nik'érz), *n.pl.* knickerbockers.

knick-knack (nik'nak'), *n.* a trifle; toy; small ornament.

knife (nīf), *n.* [*pl.* knives (nīvz)], **1,** a cutting instrument with a sharp-edged blade or blades, set in a handle; **2,** a sharp-edged blade in a machine:—*v.t.* [knifed, knif-ing], to stab or cut with a knife.

knight (nīt), *n.* **1,** in the Middle Ages, a mounted warrior who served a king or lord; esp. one of noble birth who, after serving as page and squire, and pledging himself to chivalrous conduct, was admitted by solemn ceremonies to a high military rank; **2,** in modern times in Great Britain, a man ranking next below a baronet, who has the title *Sir;* **3,** a member of any of certain orders or societies; **4,** in *chess,* a piece bearing the figure of a horse's head:— *v.t.* to raise (a man) to the rank of knight.

knight—er-rant (nīt'-ér'ant), *n.* [*pl.* knights-errant], in the Middle Ages, a knight who went in search of adventure.

knight-hood (nīt'hood), *n.* **1,** the character, rank, or dignity of a knight; **2,** knights as a class or body.

knight-ly (nīt'li), *adj.* [knight-li-er, knight-li-est], **1,** chivalrous; brave, gentle, and courteous; **2,** consisting of knights.

knit (nit), *v.t.* [knit-ted or knit, knit-ting], **1,** to form (a fabric, garment, etc.) by hand or by machine, by looping or weaving a single thread or yarn on needles; as, to *knit* a sweater; **2,** to unite closely; lock together; as, he *knitted* his fingers; **3,** to draw together by a tie of some kind; as, common interests *knit* them to each other; **4,** to draw (the brow) into wrinkles:—*v.i.* **1,** to weave thread or yarn in loops by the use of needles; **2,** to become closely jointed or united; as, the broken bone *knitted* well.

knob (nob), *n.* **1,** the rounded handle of a door, an umbrella, etc.; **2,** a round swelling, mass, or lump; **3,** a rounded hill.—*adj.* **knob'by.**

knock (nok), *v.i.* **1,** to strike with a blow;

esp. to rap on a door; **2,** to collide; bump; **3,** of machinery parts, to jar or pound noisily; **4,** *Slang,* to make unfavourable comments:—*v.t.* **1,** to strike or beat; give a blow to; **2,** to strike (something) against something else; as, to *knock* one's head against a wall; **3,** *Slang,* to criticize unfavourably —*n.* a sharp, quick blow; rap; **2,** a noise like that of a knock.—*n.* **knock′er.** Compounds: **knock′down′**; **knock′-kneed′**; **knock′out′.**

knoll (nōl), *n.* a rounded hillock; mound.

knot (not), *n.* **1,** an interweaving or tying together of the parts of one or more threads, cords, ropes, etc., so that they will not slip or come apart; also, the tie so formed; **2,** something resembling a knot, as a lump or knob in a piece of wood or in a tree; **3,** a difficulty; hard problem; **4,** a group or cluster of people; **5,** a nautical mile (6,080 ft.), the unit used in stating the speed of a moving ship:—*v.t.* [knot-ted, knot-ting], **1,** to tie in a knot; **2,** to unite closely:—*v.i.* to form knots.— *adj.* **knot′ty.**

knot-grass (not′gras′), *n.* a widespread trailing weed with jointed or knotted stems, growing esp. in crevices of sidewalks, etc.; also called **knot′-weed′.**

knot-hole (not′hōl′), *n.* a hole in a tree or in lumber caused by the rotting or falling out of a knot.

knout (nout; nōot), *n.* a whip of twisted leather thongs, formerly used for flogging criminals.

know (nō), *v.t.* [*p.t.* knew (nū), *p.p.* known (nōn), *p.pr.* know-ing], **1,** to perceive with the mind; understand clearly; as, he *knows* what he is doing; **2,** to recognize; as, he *knew* the beggar; **3,** to be familiar with; as, to *know* Spanish; **4,** to have information about; as, I *know* his reasons; **5,** to have in the memory; as, I *know* the names of all the bones; **6,** to be skilled in; as, he *knows* the art of swimming; **7,** to be certain; as, I *know* it is true:— *v.i.* to be informed; have certain knowledge.—*adj.* **know′a-ble.**

know—how (nō′-hou′), *n. Colloq.* the special ability, or technical skill (usually from experience), enabling one to execute an operation efficiently.

know-ing (nō′ing), *adj.* **1,** having knowledge; intelligent; **2,** shrewd; showing special knowledge; as, a *knowing* look.

know-ing-ly (nō′ing-li), *adv.* **1,** in a

knowing or shrewd way; **2,** intentionally.

knowl-edge (nol′ij), *n.* **1,** that which has been acquired by study or observation; learning; **2,** understanding of a subject; as, a *knowledge* of history; **3,** skill; familiarity from experience; as, a *knowledge* of boating; **4,** extent of one's information; as, not to my *knowledge.*

knuck-le (nuk′l), *n.* **1,** the lump formed where the ends of two bones meet in a joint, esp. the joint of a finger; **2,** in cookery, the knee-joint of a calf or pig:—*v.i.* [knuck-led, knuckling], **1,** in *marbles,* to place the knuckles on the ground in shooting; **2,** to yield or submit; as, make him *knuckle* under; **3,** *Colloq.* to apply oneself earnestly:—**knuckle ball,** in *baseball,* a slow ball thrown with the thumb and little finger gripping the sides of the ball, the first joints of the other fingers tucked under and pressed against the top of the ball:—**knuckle-dusters,** brass knuckles worn for rough fighting.

knurl (nûrl), *n.* a ridge, or series of ridges, as on a nut, coin, etc., to aid in gripping it.—*adj.* **knurled.**

ko-a-la (kō-ä′la), *n.* a tailless, pouch-bearing animal of Australia with ash-gray, woolly fur: it is about 2′ long and resembles a small bear.

ko-dak (kō′dak), *n.* a portable camera using a continuous roll of sensitized film on which successive negatives are made: incorrectly applied to *any* hand camera; trade name.

kohl-rab-i (kōl′rä′bi), *n.* [*pl.* kohlrabies], a cabbage with an enlarged, edible, turniplike stem.

koo-doo (kōō′dōō), *n.* Same as **kudu.**

ko-peck (kō′pek), *n.* a small Russian copper coin worth 1/100 of a rouble (about a half cent).

ko-sher (kō′shẽr), *adj.* clean and fit to eat according to Jewish law; as, *kosher* meat.

Ko-ran (kō′ran; rän), *n.* the sacred book of the Moslems, who believe it to be Allah's (God's) revelations to Mohammed.

kow-tow (kou-tou′), or **ko-tow** (kō-tou′), *n.* the Chinese custom of kneeling and touching the ground with the forehead as a token of respect or worship:—*v.i.* to perform such an act; hence, to be obsequious.

kraal (kräl), *n.* **1,** a South African native village enclosed by a stockade; **2,** a sheepfold or cattle pen.

cat, āge, fär, cãre, ȧsk; ten, ēve, latẽr; (i) pity, rely, senate; īce; top; nō.

kraft (kråft), *n.* a strong wrapping paper, usually of brown colour, made from sulphate pulp.

krem-lin (krem'lin), *n.* a Russian citadel or fortress:—**the Kremlin**, in Moscow, the place of government of the Soviet Union (USSR).

kryp-ton (krip'ton), *n.* a rare inert gaseous element of the atmosphere (about one volume per million).

ku-du (kōō'dōō), *n.* a large gray-brown African antelope with white markings: the male has long corkscrewlike horns. Also, **koodoo.**

L

L, l (el), *n.* [*pl.* L's, l's], **1,** the 12th letter of the alphabet, following K; **2,** the Roman numeral for fifty.

la (lä), *n.* in music, the name of the sixth note of the scale.

la-bel (lā'bl), *n.* **1,** a small slip of paper, cloth, metal, etc., attached to anything, indicating its maker, contents, size, owner, destination, etc.; a tag; as, a *label* on a garment; **2,** a short phrase or catch-word applied to persons or theories:—*v.t.* [labelled, label-ling], **1,** to mark with a label, as a medicine bottle; **2,** to classify; apply a descriptive word to; as, they *labelled* him a radical.

la-bi-al (lā'bi-al), *adj.* and *n.* formed by the lips, as *labial* consonants *b, p,* and rounded vowels *ō, ōō.*

la-bor (lā'bẽr), U.S. spelling of *labour.*

lab-o-ra-tor-y (lab'o-ra-tōr'i; la-bōr'a-tẽr-i), *n.* [*pl.* laboratories], a place where scientific experiments and research are carried on, or where drugs, chemicals, etc., are made, or tested for purity or strength.

-bor-i-ous (la-bōr'i-us), *adj.* **1,** difficult; requiring toil; **2,** hard-working.

a-bour or **la-bor** (lā'bẽr), *n.* **1.** physical or mental toil; work; **2,** a difficult task; **3,** hired workers who do physical, rather than mental, work, esp. when considered as a class; as, laws benefiting *labour:*—*v.i.* **1,** to use muscular strength; toil; **2,** to be hard pressed; as, to *labour* under a difficulty; to move slowly and heavily; as, a wagon *labours* up a hill; **3,** to strive; take pains; as, he *laboured* to understand the problem; **4,** to pitch and roll heavily, as a ship in a storm.—*n.* **la'bour-er.**

a-boured (lā'bẽrd), *adj.* produced with toil or care; not fluent; as, a *laboured* speech.

a-bur-num (la-bûr'num), *n.* a genus of tree or shrub of the pea family; it

has 3-part leaves and clusters of pea-shaped, yellow flowers.

lab-y-rinth (lab'i-rinth), *n.* **1,** a maze or confusing network of passages winding into and about one another, so that it is almost impossible to find one's way through it; **2,** hence, a confusing or puzzling state of affairs.—*adj.* **lab'y-rin'thine.**

lac (lak), *n.* a dark-red resinous substance left by the lac insect on trees in India, used in making shellac, lacquer, varnish, sealing wax, etc.

lace (lās), *n.* **1,** an ornamental fabric of fine threads, as of linen, cotton, or silk, woven in a delicate open design; **2,** a cord or string, passed through eyelets or other holes to fasten together parts of a garment, shoe, or the like:—*v.t.* [laced, lac-ing], **1,** to fasten with a lace; as, *lace* your shoes; **2,** to adorn or trim with lace; **3,** to weave or twine together; **4,** to lash; beat:—*v.i.* to be fastened with a lace; as, a blouse *laces* at the neck.—**lac'y.**

lac-er-ate (las'ẽr-āt'), *v.t.* [lacerat-ed, lacerat-ing], **1,** to tear or mangle; as, the claws of the tiger *lacerated* his arm; **2,** to distress, as the feelings.—*n.* **lac'er-a'tion.**

lac-ing (lās'ing), *n.* **1,** the act of fastening with a lace; **2,** a cord, string, braid, etc., passed through eyelets to fasten something or serve as a trimming; **3,** *Colloq.* a sound thrashing.

lack (lak), *v.t.* to be without; not to have; as, his remarks *lack* common sense; I *lack* the money:—*v.i.* to have need; be short; as, he *lacks* in wisdom: —*n.* want; as, *lack* of fresh air.

lack-a-dai-si-cal (lak'a-dā'zi-kal), *adj.* lazily indifferent; listless.

lack-ey (lak'i), *n.* [*pl.* lackeys] a male attendant of low rank; a footman.

lack-lus-tre (lak'lus'tẽr), *adj.* dull; lacking brightness; as, *lacklustre* eyes.

la-con-ic (la-kon'ik), *adj.* using few

words; concise; pithy; terse; as, a *laconic* reply.

lac-quer or **lack-er** (lak′ẽr), *n.* **1**, a varnish made of shellac dissolved in alcohol, and used to protect brass, silver, etc., from tarnish and as a finish for automobiles; **2**, any of various varnishes made from resin, esp. one made from the sap of certain Oriental trees, and used for polishing wood and other surfaces; **3**, Chinese or Japanese woodwork finished with a hard, polished varnish and often inlaid with gold, ivory, etc.:—*v.t.* to paint with lacquer.

la-crosse (là-krôs′), *n.* a field game played by two teams of twelve players each, in which the object is to send a small ball into the opponent's goal by means of sticks or rackets, called *crosses*.

lac-te-al (lak′ti-al), *adj.* of, or relating to, milk; as, the *lacteal* fluid; *lacteal* ducts.

lac-tose (lak′tōs), *n.* a white, sweetish powder made from evaporated whey and used in infant foods: also called *milk sugar* and *sugar of milk*.

lad (lad), *n.* a boy or youth; stripling.

lad-der (lad′ẽr), *n.* **1**, a device for scaling or climbing, consisting usually of two long uprights of wood, connected by cross-pieces, called *rungs*, forming steps; **2**, hence, any means by which one mounts or ascends; as, the *ladder* of ambition.

lade (lād), *v.t.* [*p.t.* lad-ed, *p.p.* lad-en (lād′n) or lad-ed, *p.pr.* lad-ing], **1**, to load (goods); put a cargo aboard (a ship); **2**, to lift out or in with a scoop; bail; as, to *lade* water out of a vat.

lad-en (lād′n), one form of the past participle of *lade:—adj.* **1**, loaded; burdened; as, *laden* with packages; **2**, oppressed or burdened in spirit; as, *laden* with sorrow.

lad-ing (lād′ing), *n.* **1**, the act of loading or of bailing; **2**, freight.

la-dle (lā′dl), *n.* a deep spoon or dipper, with a long handle, for dipping out liquids:—*v.t.* [la-dled, la-dling], to dip out with a ladle.

la-dy (lā′di), *n.* [*pl.* ladies], **1**, originally, a woman of authority over a house or an estate, of the same rank as a lord; **2**, a well-bred woman; a woman of good family or of high social position; a gentlewoman:—*n.* **la′dy-ship** (usually with *her, your,* etc.).

la-dy-bird (lā′di-bûrd′), *n.* a small, round-backed beetle, usually reddish brown with black spots: also called *ladybug.*

la-dy-like (lā′di-līk′), *adj.* befitting a gentlewoman; well-bred; as, *ladylike* behaviour.

La-dy's slip-per or **la-dy slip-per**, any of a group of orchids with a slipper-shaped flower: it is a popular floral emblem in Prince Edward Island.

LADY'S SLIPPER

¹lag (lag), *v.i.* [lagged, lag-ging], to move slowly; fail to keep pace; fall behind; as, to *lag* behind other runners in a race; to *lag* in one's studies:—*n.* a falling behind in movement or progress; as, a *lag* in the speed of a race or in the progress of work.

²lag (lag), *v.t.* to cover, as a steam boiler, to prevent loss of heat.

lag-gard (lag′ẽrd), *n.* one who acts slowly; a backward person; as, he is a *laggard* in his studies:—*adj.* backward; slow.

la-ger (lä′gẽr), a light malt beer, aged for several months after brewing.

la-goon (la-gōōn′), *n.* **1**, a shallow lake or channel, usually near the sea, and connected with it; **2**, the shallow water inside an atoll, or ring-shaped coral island.

laid (lād), *v.t.*, *p.t.* and *p.p.* of *lay.*

lain (lān), *v.i.*, *p.p.* of *lie.*

lair (lâr), *n.* the den of a wild animal.

laird (lârd), *n.* in Scotland, the owner of a landed estate.

la-i-ty (lā′i-ti), *n.* [*pl.* laities], **1**, laymen, as distinguished from the clergy; **2**, those outside any particular profession.

lake (lāk), *n.* a large body of water entirely surrounded by land.

la-ma (lä′ma), *n.* a Buddhist priest or monk of Tibet, Mongolia, or western China: the chief is called *Dalai Lama.* —*n.* **la′ma-ser′y.**

lamb (lam), *n.* **1**, the young of sheep; **2**, the flesh of young sheep, used as food; **3**, one who is gentle or innocent: —*v.i.* to bring forth lambs.

lam-baste (lam-bāst′), *v.t. Slang,* to beat severely; thrash.

lamb-kin (lam′kin), *n.* **1**, a little lamb; **2**, a tenderly cherished child.

lame (lām), *adj.* [lam-er, lam-est], **1**, crippled or disabled, esp. in a leg or foot; also, sore; painful; as, a *lame* shoulder; **2**, not sound or effective; as, a *lame* excuse:—*v.t.* [lamed, lam-ing], to cripple.

la-ment (la-ment′), *v.i.* and *v.t.* to mourn; bewail:—*n.* an expression of sorrow.

lam-en-ta-ble (lam′en-ta-bl), *adj.* 1, regrettable; deplorable; unfortunate; as, a *lamentable* mistake; 2, mournful. —*adv.* **lam′en-ta-bly.**

lam-en-ta-tion (lam′en-tā′shun), *n.* an expression of grief; a lament.

lam-i-nat-ed (lam′in-ā′tid), *adj.* in the form of thin sheets or layers, as plywood:—*v.t.* **lam′i-nate′.**

lamp (lamp), *n.* 1, in olden days, a vessel in which oil or other inflammable liquid was burned by means of a wick to produce light; 2, in modern times, any vessel or device for producing light by gas, electricity, etc. Compounds: **lamp′light′; lamp′post′.**

lam-poon (lam-poon′), *v.t.* to ridicule, satirize, or abuse (in prose or verse). —*n.* a bitter satire in writing.

lam-prey (lam′pri), *n.* an eellike fish with large circular mouth, pouchlike gills, and horny teeth that aid it to suck its victim's blood (by rasping a hole in the flesh).

lance (làns), *n.* 1, a weapon consisting of a long shaft of wood with a sharp steel head; also, a soldier equipped with a lance; 2, any sharp-pointed instrument resembling a lance; esp. one used in spearing fish:—*v.t.* [lanced, lanc-ing], 1, to pierce with a lance; 2, to cut open, as a boil, with a lancet, or surgeon's knife.

lanc-er (làn′sèr), *n.* 1, a person who uses a lance; 2, a cavalry soldier armed with a lance; 3, **lancers,** a square dance for four or more couples; also, the musical accompaniment.

lan-cet (làn′set), *n.* a small, pointed, two-edged surgical knife.

land (land), *n.* 1, the solid part of the surface of the globe; 2, a division of the earth's surface marked off by natural, political, or other boundaries; a country; district; also, the people of a country; a nation; 3, soil; ground; as, fertile *land*:—*v.t.* 1, to set on shore; as, to *land* passengers from a ship; 2, to capture and bring to shore; as, to *land* a fish; 3, *Colloq.* to win; as, to *land* a prize; 4, to bring to a destination; as, the train *landed* him in Toronto on time:—*v.i.* 1, to come or go ashore; disembark, as a passenger; 2, to arrive at a destination; 3, to come to the end of a course; get into a situation; as, he *landed* in jail; 4, to alight; come to

earth, as an aeroplane. Compounds: **land′hold′er; land′own′er.**

lan-dau (lan′dô; lan′dou), *n.* a four-wheeled enclosed carriage with a top in two parts, so that it may be used closed, half open, or fully open.

land-ed (lan′did), *adj.* 1, owning land; as, a *landed* proprietor; 2, consisting of land; as, a *landed* estate.

land-fall (land′fôl′), *n.* the first sighting of land after a voyage; the land so sighted.

land-ing (lan′ding), *n.* 1, the act of going or putting ashore or of alighting on earth from the sky; 2, a place or platform, as a wharf, where passengers may embark or disembark, and goods may be loaded or unloaded; 3, a platform, as at the end of a flight of steps.

land-la-dy (land′lā′di), *n.* [*pl.* land-ladies], 1, a woman who rents her house or land to others; 2, the mistress of a boarding-house or inn; also, the wife of a landlord.

land-locked (land′lokt′), *adj.* 1, nearly surrounded by land; as, a *landlocked* bay; 2, confined to waters shut off from the sea by some barrier; as, *landlocked* fish.

land-lord (land′lôrd′), *n.* 1, one who rents his buildings or land to others; 2, the keeper of a hotel or inn.

land-lub-ber (land′lub′èr), *n.* one who is awkward or inexperienced on ship-board.

land-mark (land′märk′), *n.* 1, an object that marks the boundary of a tract of land; 2, a familiar or easily seen object that serves as a guide for a traveller or a navigator; 3, any event which marks or is associated with a stage or turning-point in history; as, the discovery of fire is a *landmark* in the history of mankind.

land-scape (land′skāp′), *n.* 1, a stretch of land or of land and water seen as one view; 2, a picture of a scene from nature.

land-slide (land′slid′), *n.* 1, the slipping of a mass of earth, stones, etc., down a steep slope; 2, the material that slips down; 3, a decisive, overwhelming victory in an election. Also, in senses 1 and 2, **land′slip′** (land′slip′).

land-ward (land′wèrd), *adj.* facing or moving toward the shore:—*adv.* toward the shore.—*adv.* **land′wards.**

lane (lān), *n.* 1, a narrow path or by-way between hedges, walls, etc.; 2, an unpaved or little used road, or a narrow street; any narrow way or track; 3, one of the ocean courses fixed as routes for vessels.

lang-syne (lang'sīn'; zīn'), *adv. Scottish*, long since; long ago.

lan-guage (lang'gwij), *n*. 1, the power or ability to express ideas in words; human speech; 2, the means of such expression, as letters, sounds, words, etc., current among members of a single people; as, the German *language;* also, the means of expression, as words, phrases, etc., peculiar to special fields of knowledge; as, technical *language;* 3, any style of verbal expression; as, simple *language;* 4, any means of expressing ideas; as, the *language* of pictures; the *language* of flowers.

lan-guid (lang'gwid), *adj*. weak, as from exhaustion; dull; listless.

lan-guish (lang'gwish), *v.i.* 1, to lose strength or animation; become languid; also, to pine away, as with longing; 2, to appeal for sympathy by pretending feebleness or fatigue.

lan-guor (lang'gẽr), *n*. 1, lack of energy; listlessness; 2, dreaminess; a soft, tender mood; 3, heaviness; oppressiveness; as, the *languor* of a humid day.—*adj.* **lan'gour-ous.**

lank (langk), *adj*. 1, lean; thin; as, a tall, *lank* figure; 2, straight and limp, as hair that will not curl.—*adj.* **lank'y.** —*n.* **lank'i-ness.**

lan-o-lin (lan'ō-lin'), *n*. a fatty substance obtained from sheep's wool: it is purified and used in ointments, cosmetics, etc.

lan-tern (lan'tẽrn), *n*. 1, a transparent case enclosing a light and protecting it from wind, rain, etc.; 2, the room at the top of a lighthouse where the light is kept.

lan-yard (lan'yẽrd), *n*. 1, a cord used by sailors, as for securing shrouds, stays, etc.; 2, a cord once used to fire cannon.

¹lap (lap), *n*. 1, the loose part of a garment which may be doubled or folded over; the skirt of a coat or the overlapping part of a gown; 2, that part of the clothing that rests upon the thighs and knees of a person in a sitting position; also, the part of the body thus covered; as, sit in my *lap;* 3, a place for supporting, sheltering, or rearing; as, the *lap* of luxury; 4, that part of an object, as a shingle, that extends over another; also, the distance or amount of such extension; as, a *lap* of two inches; 5, the length of a course or track which has to be passed over more than once in a race:—*v.t.* [lapped, lap-ping], 1, to lay or fold over,

as cloth; also, to wrap; 2, to place over something else so as partly to cover it; as, to *lap* one shingle over another; 3, to enfold; surround; as, *lapped* in luxury:—*v.i.* to lie partly over something; as, the boards *lap;* also, to be folded; as, the cuff *laps* back.

²lap (lap), *v.t.* [lapped, lap-ping], 1, to lick up with the tongue, as liquid; 2, to splash gently against; as, the waves *lap* the shore:—*v.i.* 1, to take up liquid with the tongue; 2, to make a lapping or rippling sound:—*n*. the act or sound of lapping.

la-pel (la-pel'), *n*. the part of a garment which is folded back; esp. the fold at each side of a coat front, forming a continuation of the collar.

lapse (laps), *v.i.* [lapsed, laps-ing], 1, to glide or slip slowly away; as, to *lapse* into unconsciousness; his attention *lapsed*, 2, to slip or depart from a normal standard; fall into error; as, to *lapse* from good behaviour; 3, to cease or to pass to another, as insurance, an estate, etc., because of the holder's failure to fulfil certain conditions:—*n*. 1, a gliding or passing away slowly; as, the *lapse* of time; 2, a slight mistake; a slip, as of memory, tongue, or pen; 3, the loss of a claim, right, etc., through failure to use or renew it; 4, a passing into a lower rank or condition; as, a *lapse* into poverty; a *lapse* into drunkenness.—*adj.* **lapsed.**

lap-wing (lap'wing'), *n*. a crested plover of the Old World with an iridescent green and violet back and white breast. It is well known for its flapping flight and shrill cry.

lar-board (lär'bōrd; lär'bẽrd), *n*. the left side of a ship as one faces the bow: now called *port:—adj.* naming, or pertaining to, the left, or port, side of a ship.

lar-ce-ny (lär'se-ni), *n*. [*pl.* larcenies], the unlawful taking away of another's property; theft.—*adj.* **lar'ce-nous.**

larch (lärch), *n*. any of a group of graceful trees of the pine family, with small cones and short needlelike leaves which drop in the fall; also, the wood of these trees, which is unusually durable.

lard (lärd), *n*. a white, greasy substance made from the fat of swine:—*v.t.* 1, to smear with fat; 2, to insert strips of bacon into (meat) before roasting.

lard-er (lär'dẽr), *n*. the place where household provisions are kept; a pantry; also, the stock or supply of food.

large (lärj), *adj.* [larg-er, larg-est], **1,** big; great in size; bulky; wide; extensive; as, a *large* estate; **2,** wide in scope; broad in understanding and sympathy; as, a *large* mind:—**at large, 1,** free; unconfined; as, the convict is *at large;* **2,** chosen to represent a whole section instead of one of its districts; as, a delegate *at large.*—*adv.* **large′ly.**— *n.* **large′ness.**

lar-gess or **lar-gesse** (lär′jes), *n.* liberal giving, as of a great person on a festive occasion.

lar-i-at (lar′i-at), *n.* **1,** a rope with a sliding noose, used for catching horses or cattle; a lasso; **2,** a rope for picketing horses.

¹lark (lärk), *n.* **1,** any of various small European song-birds, as the skylark; **2,** any of many birds similar to larks but of different families, as the meadow lark.

²lark (lärk), *n.* a frolic; spree; an amusing adventure:—*v.i. Colloq.* to frolic.

lark-spur (lärk′spûr), *n.* a tall plant cultivated for its showy spikes of pink, blue, or white flowers; also, the flowers.

lar-rup (lar′up), *v.t. Colloq.* beat; thrash; flog; as, he *larruped* the mule.

lar-va (lär′va), *n.* [*pl.* larvae (lär′vē)], the early, often wormlike, form of insects in the stage between the egg and the pupa; also, the early form of any animal which changes in form as it develops; hence, an animal in this form, as a tadpole.—*adj.* **lar′val.**

lar-yn-gi-tis (lar′in-jī′tis), *n.* inflammation of the upper end of the windpipe.

lar-ynx (lar′ingks), *n.* [*pl.* larynges (la-rin′jēz) or larynxes], an enlargement of the upper end of the windpipe, containing the vocal cords.

las-civ-i-ous (la-siv′i-us), *adj.* lustful; tending to excite sensual passion; as, a *lascivious* picture.

¹lash (lash), *v.t.* **1,** to strike or beat violently with a whip; flog; also, to beat upon; as, the waves *lashed* the shore; **2,** to rebuke or scold severely; **3,** to switch backward and forward like a lash; as, the puma *lashed* his tail; **4,** to stir up or arouse; as, the orator *lashed* the crowd to fury:—*v.i.* **1,** to apply the whip; also, to rebuke severely; **2,** to rush, pour, or beat, as wind or rain:—*n.* **1,** the flexible part, or thong, of a whip; **2,** a stroke with a whip or anything used like a whip; as, a *lash* of sarcasm; **3,** one of the little hairs on the edge of the eyelid.

²lash (lash), *v.t.* to tie or bind with a rope.

lash-ing (lash′ing), *n.* **1,** a whipping; **2,** a sharp scolding; **3,** the act or process of binding; **4,** a cord, rope, etc., used for binding.

lass (las; làs), *n.* **1,** a girl or young woman; usually, a country girl; **2,** a sweetheart.

las-si-tude (las′i-tūd′), *n.* bodily or mental weariness; lack of energy.

las-so (las′ō), *n.* [*pl.* lassos or lassoes], a rope, usually of hide, with a slip-knot, used for catching wild horses and cattle; a lariat:—*v.t.* to catch with a noosed rope.

¹last (làst), *n.* a foot-shaped model in wood or metal on which shoes are made.

²last (làst), *adj.* one form of the superlative of *late:* **1,** coming after all others in time, place, order, etc.; as, the *last* man to go; **2,** next before the present; as, *last* week; **3,** authoritative; conclusive; as, his writings are regarded as the *last* word in literary criticism; **4,** least likely; least fitted; as, he is the *last* person for the position:—*adv.* **1,** after all others; **2,** on the time or occasion next preceding the present; **3,** at the end; finally:—*n.* the end:—**at last,** finally; at the end of a long period of time.—*adv.* **last′ly.**

³last (làst), *v.i.* **1,** to continue; as, the play *lasted* three hours; **2,** to be enough for a given time; hold out; as, this coffee will *last* a week; **3,** to wear well; endure.

latch (lach), *n.* a fastening device for a door or gate, made of a small bar and catch:—*v.t.* and *v.i.* to fasten with a catch.

late (lāt), *adj.* [*comp.* lat-er or lat-ter (lat′ẽr), *superl.* lat-est or last (làst)], **1,** coming after the usual time; tardy; as, a *late* spring; **2,** far on toward the end; as, a *late* hour of the day; **3,** of recent date; as, a *late* occurrence; **4,** formerly in office; as, the *late* lieutenant-governor; **5,** deceased; as, the *late* Mr. Smith:—*adv.* **1,** after the usual or appointed time; as, to arrive *late;* **2,** far into the day, night, etc.; as, to work early and *late:*—**of late,** recently; as, I have not seen you *of late.*—*n.* **late′ness.**

la-teen sail (la-tēn′), a three-cornered sail attached to a yard crossed obliquely on a low mast.

late-ly (lāt′li), *adv.* not long ago; recently; as, she has not been here *lately.*

la-tent (lā′tent), *adj.* concealed; not

visible; present, but not active; as, *latent* disease germs; *latent* discontent.

lat-er-al (lat′ėr-al), *adj.* pertaining to, at, or coming from, the side.—*adv.* **lat′er-al-ly.**

la-tex (lā′teks), *n.* a milky juice secreted by plants such as the rubber tree, milkweed, poppy, etc.: the basis of rubber.

lath (làth), *n.* [*pl.* laths (làthz; làths)], one of the thin, narrow strips of wood nailed to the framework of a house to support the plaster:—*v.t.* to cover with such strips.—*n.* **lath′ing.**

lathe (lāth), *n.* a machine which holds and turns articles of wood, metal, etc., while they are being shaped and polished.

lath-er (lath′ėr), *n.* **1,** froth made from soap and water; **2,** the foamy sweat of a horse:—*v.t.* to cover with froth or foam, as in shaving:—*v.i.* to form foam or suds.

lat-i-tude (lat′i-tūd′), *n.* **1,** the distance north or south of the equator measured in degrees; **2,** breadth; range; as, his remarks cover a wide *latitude* of subjects; **3,** degree of freedom from rules; as, he was given great *latitude* in arranging the meeting; **4,** a region or locality; as, a warm *latitude*.

la-trine (la-trēn′), *n.* a privy, esp. in a camp, factory, etc.: often equipped also as a washroom.

lat-ter (lat′ėr), *adj.* one form of the comparative of *late:* **1,** the second of two things already mentioned; **2,** more recent; later; as; the *latter* half of the century.

lat-tice (lat′is), *n.* crossed or interlaced open work of metal or wood; hence, any door, window, gate, etc., made of such work:—*v.t.* [latticed, lattic-ing], **1,** to cross or interlace (strips) as in a lattice; **2,** to furnish with a lattice.—*n.* **lat′tice—work′.**

laud (lôd), *v.t.* to praise; glorify:—*n.* a hymn extolling God; a song of praise. —*adj.* **laud′a-ble.**—*adj.* **laud′a-tor′y.**

lau-da-num (lô′da-num; lod′n-um), *n.* tincture of opium: a poisonous narcotic drug.

laugh (làf), *v.i.* to express mirth, enjoyment, or derision by a series of chuckling sounds:—*v.t.* **1,** to express or utter with laughter; as, he *laughed* his pleasure; **2,** to move or affect by merriment or ridicule; as, we *laughed* her out of her pout:—*n.* the act of laughing or its sound:—**laugh up one's sleeve,** to laugh to oneself.—*adj.*

laugh′a-ble.—*n.* **laugh′er.**—*adv.* **laugh′ing-ly.**—**laughing gas,** a colourless gas, nitrous oxide (N_2O): used as an anaesthetic in dentistry, it often produces exhilaration and laughter.

laugh-ing—stock (làf′ing-stok′), *n.* a person who makes himself ridiculous.

laugh-ter (làf′tėr), *n.* the act or sound of laughing.

¹launch (lônch; länch), *v.t.* **1,** to move or cause to slide into the water, as a vessel; **2,** to start off, as a business; **3,** to hurl; throw:—*v.i.* **1,** to put to sea; **2,** to plunge or start swiftly and with vigour; as, he *launched* into a torrent of abuse; **3,** to enter on a new career.

²launch (lônch; länch), *n.* **1,** the largest boat of a battleship; **2,** a large, open pleasure-boat, usually motor-driven.

laun-der (lôn′dėr; län′dėr), *v.t.* to wash and iron (clothes).—*n.* **laun′dress.**

laun-dry (lôn′dri; län′dri), *n.* [*pl.* laundries], **1,** a commercial establishment, or a room in a home, where clothes are washed and ironed; **2,** articles sent to be washed.

lau-re-ate (lô′rē-it; lô′rē-āt′), *adj.* decked or crowned with laurel; hence, worthy of honour:—**poet laureate,** the official court poet of Great Britain:—*n.* a poet laureate.—*n.* **lau′re-ate-ship′.**

lau-rel (lô′rel; lor′el), *n.* **1,** an evergreen shrub of southern Europe, used by the ancient Greeks and Romans as a symbol of fame and distinction: also called *bay* or *bay laurel;* **2,** any of several shrubs resembling the true laurel, esp. the flowering mountain laurel; **3,** a crown or wreath of bay given as a prize or honour; **4,** laurels, fame; honour.

la-va (là′va), *n.* melted rock such as erupts from a volcano.

lav-a-tor-y (lav′a-tôr′i), *n.* [*pl.* lavatories], **1,** a room for washing the hands and face; **2,** a basin fixed on a stand, usually with running water, for washing; **3,** often used as a euphemism for *toilet*.

lave (lāv), *v.i.* [laved, lav-ing], to bathe; wash oneself:—*v.t.* **1,** to wash bathe; **2,** to flow or wash gently against; as, the calm sea *laves* the beach.

lav-en-der (lav′en-dėr), *n.* **1,** a plant with lilac-coloured flowers and narrow woolly leaves, cultivated for its perfume and used, when dried, to sweeten and scent clothes, linens, etc.; **2,** the pale-lilac colour of its flowers.

lav-ish (lav′ish), *adj.* **1,** very liberal, almost too generous; **2,** excessive; as *lavish* praise:—*v.t.* to spend or bestow liberally; squander; waste.—*adv.* **lav′ish-ly**.—*n.* **lav′ish-ness.**

law (lô), *n.* **1,** a rule of action, established by authority or custom, for a nation or a group of people; also, a body of such rules or customs; as, maritime *law;* social *law;* **2,** an act or enactment of a leglislative, or law-making, body; **3,** the legal profession: **4,** in sport, games, etc., the generally accepted rules of procedure; as, the *laws* of football; **5,** trial in the courts; as, take it to *law;·* **6,** in *science*, a statement of what, under given conditions, invariably happens, or of relations between things in nature; as, the *law* of gravitation; **7,** in the Bible, the set of rules and commands given by Moses. Compounds: **law′—a- bid′ing; law′book′; law′break′er; law′mak′ing.**

law-ful (lô′fool), *adj.* **1,** according to law; right, not wrong; as, *lawful* acts; **2,** recognized by law; rightful; as, *lawful* ownership.—*adv.* **law′ful-ly.**—*n.* **law′ful-ness.**

law-less (lô′lis), *adj.* **1,** without laws; **2,** not obedient to, or controlled by, authority; unruly.—*adv.* **law′less-ly.**— *n.* **law′less-ness.**

¹lawn (lôn), *n.* a thin, fine cotton or linen fabric used for dresses, blouses, etc.

²lawn (lôn), *n.* a plot of grass kept closely mowed.—*n.* **lawn′—mow′er.**

law-suit (lô′sūt), *n.* a case in a law court to settle a claim or enforce a right.

law-yer (lô′yėr), *n.* one who knows and practises law; an attorney.

lax (laks), *adj.* **1,** loose; not firm, tense, or rigid; **2,** careless; inexact; not strict; as, *lax* principles.—*adv.* **lax′ly.** —*n.* **lax′i-ty.**

lax-a-tive (lak′sa-tiv), *adj.* loosening; causing the bowels to move:—*n.* a medicine which causes the bowels to move.

¹lay (lā), *n.* **1,** a short lyric or poem intended to be sung; **2,** any poem or song.

²lay (lā), *adj.* **1,** having to do with persons outside the clergy; as, *lay* opinion; **2,** relating to those outside any particular profession; as, the *lay* mind cannot understand all the fine points of law.

³lay (lā), *v.t.* [laid (lād), lay-ing], **1,** to cause to lie; place or put; as, to *lay* a card on the table; **2,** to bring or beat down; as, the blow *laid* him low; **3,** to produce and deposit (an egg); **4,** to bet; **5,** to impose, as a tax, burden, duty,

etc.; **6,** to spread over a surface; as, to *lay* rugs; **7,** to keep down or quiet; suppress; make disappear; as, rain *lays* dust; to *lay* doubt; *lay* a ghost; **8,** to reduce to a certain condition; as, to *lay* waste a city; **9,** to set, in time or place; as, the scene was *laid* in ancient Rome; **10,** to place; impute; as, to *lay* blame for a crime on someone; **11,** to construct, as a floor, foundation, etc.; **12,** to present for consideration; as, to *lay* facts before a committee:— *v.i.* **1,** to produce eggs; **2,** to bet; **3,** on shipboard, to take up a position (as specified); as, to *lay* aft:—*n.* the manner or direction in which something lies; as, the *lay* of the land.

lay-er (lā′ėr), *n.* **1,** one that lays; as, a brick*layer;* **2,** one thickness; a stratum, row, coating, etc.; as, a *layer* of earth; a *layer* of paint.

lay-ette (lā-et′), *n.* a complete outfit of bedding, clothes, etc., for a newborn child.

lay-man (lā′man), *n.* [*pl.* laymen (-men)], **1,** a person not of the clergy; **2,** a person not belonging to a particular profession.

lay-off (lā′ôf′), *n.* the temporary discharge of an employee.

lay-out (lā′out′), *n.* **1,** plan; arrange- ment; as, the make-up of a book, page, advertisement, etc.; **2,** an outfit or supply of tools, equipment, etc., as a burglar's *layout*.

laze (lāz), *v.i. Colloq.* to lie, act, or enjoy (oneself) lazily; loaf; idle.

la-zy (lā′zi), *adj.* [la-zi-er, la-zi-est], disinclined to work; indolent; idle.— **la′zi-ly.**—*n.* **la′zi-ness.**

lea (lē), *n.* a grassy meadow; a stretch of pasture land.

¹lead (led), *n.* **1,** a soft, heavy, bluish- grey metallic element; **2,** a weight attached to a rope for sounding depths at sea; **3,** a thin strip of metal for separating lines of type in printing; **4,** a stick of graphite or black carbon in a pencil; **5, leads,** strips of lead used for framing window-panes, stained glass, etc.:—*adj.* consisting wholly or partly of lead:—*v.t.* **1,** to cover, fit, or join with lead; **2,** in *printing*, to spread (lines of type) by the insertion of thin metal strips.

²lead (lēd), *v.t.* [led (led), lead-ing], **1,** to conduct by the hand; as, to *lead* a child through a crowd; **2,** to conduct or guide by going on in advance; **3,** to guide or conduct by advice or counsel; **4,** to be first among; as, to *lead* one's class; **5,** to influence; as, hunger *led* him to steal; **6,** to direct; as, to *lead* the singing; **7,** to pass; spend; as, to *lead* a happy life; **8,** to play (a card) as the opening play of a trick:—*v.i.* **1,** to take the first place; **2,** to act as a guide, director, or manager; **3,** to take a course; extend in a direction: **lead to,** to bring about; pave the way to; as, waste often *leads to* poverty:—*n.* **1,** guidance; example; **2,** first place or position; as, in the *lead;* also, the distance by which one competitor is in advance of another; **3,** in card games, the right to play first; also, the play thus made; **4,** something that may act as a guide; a tip or hint; **5,** the principal actor in a play; also, his part.

lead-en (led′n), *adj.* **1,** made of lead; of the colour or weight of lead; **2,** dull; spiritless; as, a *leaden* step.

lead-er (lēd′ẽr), *n.* **1,** one who guides, directs, or conducts; as, an orchestra *leader;* **2,** one who occupies, or is fitted to occupy, the first or chief place; as, a *leader* among men; **3,** the piece of catgut at the end of a fishing-line to which the hooks are attached.—*n.* **lead′er-ship.**

leaf (lēf), *n.* [*pl.* leaves (lēvz)], **1,** one of the thin, flat parts of a plant, usually green, variously shaped, and borne on a stem or growing from the roots; also, a petal; as, a rose-*leaf;* **2,** foliage in general; as, a tree in *leaf;* **3,** a sheet of metal beaten thin; as, gold-*leaf;* **4,** any of various thin, flat parts, esp. a single page of a book, a part of the top of a folding table, etc.:—*v.i.* to put forth foliage:—*v.t.* to turn the pages of (a book).—*n.* **leaf′age.**—*adj.* **leaf′y.**—*n.* **leaf′i-ness.**

leaf hopper, one of various leaping insects that suck juices from plants.

leaf-let (lēf′let), *n.* **1,** a single division of a compound leaf; **2,** a printed sheet or circular; pamphlet.

¹league (lēg), *n.* **1,** an agreement entered into by two or more persons or nations for their common good; also, the union so formed; **2,** an organization of groups of persons with a common interest; as, a baseball *league:*—*v.t.* and *v.i.* [leagued, lea-guing], to combine for mutual interests; as, *leagued* together for protection.

²league (lēg), *n.* a varying measure of distance, equal to about three miles.

leak (lēk), *n.* a hole, crack, or other opening, which accidentally lets anything, esp. a fluid, in or out; also, the escaping of gas or fluid; leakage:—*v.i.* **1,** to go in or out through a leak; as, air *leaks* in through a crack; **2,** to lose

contents through a hole or a crack; as, a bucket *leaks;* **3,** to become gradually known; as, the news *leaked* out.—*n.* **leak′age.**—*adj.* **leak′y.**

¹lean (lēn), *v.i.* [leaned (lēnd), sometimes leant (lent), lean-ing], **1,** to slant from an upright position; as, the *leaning* Tower of Pisa; **2,** to rest on something for support; as, to *lean* on a crutch; **3,** to rely; as, she *leans* on her mother in all things; **4,** to tend or be inclined to; as, I *lean* toward his opinion:—*v.t.* to place in a slanting position; as, he *leaned* the gun against a tree.

²lean (lēn), *adj.* **1,** thin; as, a *lean* person; lacking in fat; as, *lean* meat; **2,** not productive; as, *lean* years:—*n.* meat without fat.—*n.* **lean′ness.**

lean-to (lēn′-tōō′), *n.* a building that rests against another building and has a roof sloping one way only; also, a crude shelter built against a tree, rock, etc.

leap (lēp), *v.t.* [leaped (lēpt) or leapt (lept), leap-ing], **1,** to pass over by a bound or jump; as, to *leap* a ditch; **2,** to cause to jump or spring; as, to *leap* a horse over a hedge:—*v.i.* **1,** to jump or spring off the ground, or from a high place; **2,** to bound or move suddenly; as, my heart *leaps* up:—*n.* **1,** the act of passing over with a bound; also, a jump; spring; **2,** the space covered in jumping.

leap-frog (lēp′frog′), *n.* a game in which each player in turn runs, places his hands on the bent back of another, and leaps over him.

learn (lûrn), *v.t.* [learned (lûrnd) or learnt (lûrnt), learn-ing], **1,** to acquire knowledge of, or skill in; as, to *learn* French; **2,** to gain information of; as, I regret to *learn* the sad news; **3,** to memorize; as, to *learn* a poem:—*v.i.* to gain or receive knowledge or skill; as, she knows no algebra as yet, but *learns* quickly.—*n.* **learn′er.**

learn-ed (lûr′nid), *adj.* having much knowledge; scholarly; as, a *learned* professor.—*adv.* **learn′ed-ly.**

learn-ing (lûr′ning), *n.* **1,** the act or process of acquiring knowledge; **2,** knowledge or skill gained by study.

lease (lēs), *n.* **1,** a written contract for the renting of land or buildings for a specified time; **2,** property so rented; also, the time for which property is so rented:—*v.t.* [leased, leas-ing], **1,** to grant possession of, for a specified time, by a contract or lease; as, the owner *leases* a house to a tenant; **2,** to take possession of by lease.

lease-hold (lēs'hōld'), *n.* the holding of land by lease or contract for a specified rate and fixed payments.—*n.* **lease'hold'er.**

leash (lēsh), *n.* a thong of leather, or a long cord or chain, for holding a hawk or dog:—*v.t.* to fasten or hold with a leash.

least (lēst), *adj.* [*superl.* of *little*], smallest in degree, size, importance, etc.:—*adv.* in the lowest or smallest degree:—*n.* the smallest amount; as, to say the *least.*

leath-er (leth'ẽr), *n.* the skin of an animal, tanned and prepared for use; also, anything made of the skin so prepared.

leath-er-ette (leth'ẽr-et'), *n.* an imitation or substitute leather, as paper or cloth.

leath-ern (leth'ẽrn), *adj.* made of leather.

leath-er-y (leth'ẽr-i), *adj.* like leather.

¹leave (lēv), *v.t.* [left (left), leav-ing], **1,** to fail to take; allow to remain behind; as, I *left* my purse at home; **2,** to have remaining at death; as, they say she *left* three children; **3,** to allow to remain or continue in the same place or condition; as, the appeal *left* him indifferent; **4,** to depart or withdraw from; as, to *leave* a job; *leave* home; **5,** to deliver; as, the postman *leaves* letters; **6,** to cease from; stop; as, *leave* your quarrelling; **7,** to give by will; as, she *left* the money to charity; **8,** to refer (a matter) for decision; as, I *leave* the choice to you:—*v.i.* to go away;, depart.

²leave (lēv), *n.* **1,** a permission granted; **2,** departure; formal farewell.

³leave (lēv), *vi.* [leaved, leav-ing], to put forth leaves; come out in leaf.

leav-en (lev'en), *n.* **1,** a ferment mixed with a substance to render it light, as yeast in dough; **2,** an influence which cheers or lightens; as, humour is the *leaven* of life:—*v.t.* **1,** to make light by fermentation; to cause to ferment; as, yeast *leavens* dough; **2,** to mix with some modifying element; as, he *leavens* correction with a little praise.

leav-ings (lēv'ingz), *n.pl.* what is left over; discarded remains.

lech-e-ry (lech'ẽr-i), *n.* gross sensuality; lewdness.—*adj.* **lech'er-ous;** as, a *lecherous* man; *lecherous* plays.

lec-tern (lek'tẽrn), *n.* a reading desk, esp. that from which a lesson is read in a church.

lec-ture (lek'tūr), *n.* **1,** a formal talk or address on any subject; **2,** a lengthy reproof; scolding:—*v.i.* [lectured, lecturing], to deliver a formal talk:—*v.t.* to rebuke.—*n.* **lec'tur-er.**

led (led), *p.t.* and *p.p.* of *lead.*

ledge (lej), *n.* **1,** a shelf or shelflike projection from an upright surface; as, a window *ledge*, or a *ledge* of rock; **2,** a ridge of rock, esp. one under water, not far from shore.

ledg-er (lej'ẽr), *n.* the principal account-book of a business house, in which the final summaries of debits and credits are recorded.

lee (lē), *n.* **1,** the direction opposite to that from which the wind blows; **2,** the side of anything which is protected from the wind; **3,** shelter; as, in the *lee* of the rock:—*adj.* **1,** pertaining to the part which is protected from the wind; as, the *lee* side of a ship; **2,** in the direction toward which the wind blows; as, a *lee* tide.

leech (lēch), *n.* **1,** any of various blood-sucking worms, usually water-dwelling, formerly much used in medicine as a means of withdrawing blood from patients; **2,** one who gets all he can out of another; **3,** the free or after edge of a sail: opposite of *luff:*—*v.t.* to bleed with leeches.

leek (lēk), *n.* an onionlike plant used as food or flavouring.

leer (lēr), *n.* a sly, sidelong look of malice or evil desire:—*v.i.* to look slyly or evilly.

leer-y or **lear-y** (lē'ri), *adj.* *Colloq.* **1,** suspicious; afraid; wary; **2,** wide-awake; knowing.

lees (lēz), *n.pl.* the sediment at the bottom of a vessel containing liquor; dregs.

lee-ward (lē'wẽrd; lū'ẽrd), *adj.* pertaining to the lee; away from the wind:—*adv.* toward the lee or sheltered side:—*n.* the lee side.

lee-way (lē'wā'), *n.* **1,** the sideward drift of a vessel caused by the wind; **2,** *Colloq.* extra room or time for action; margin; as, he has ten minutes' *leeway* to catch the boat.

left (left), *adj.* **1,** naming, or relating to, that side of the human body which is toward the north when one faces east: opposite of *right;* **2,** placed or located on the left side; as, the *left* eye:—*n.* **1,** the direction or region which lies on the left side; as, look to the *left;* **2,** in *politics*, the liberal or radical party: so called because in some parliaments this party is often seated on the left:—*adv.* to the left.

left—hand (left′–hand′), *adj.* relating to, or situated on, the left side.

left—hand-ed (left′–han′did), *adj.* **1,** using the left hand with greater strength or skill than the right; **2,** done with, or adapted to, the left hand; **3,** awkward.

left-ist (left′ist), *n.* one who is a member of, or sympathetic to, a socialistic or radical party. Also used as *adj.*

leg (leg), *n.* **1,** one of the limbs which support the body and by which men and animals walk; sometimes, in man, the lower limb from knee to ankle; **2,** anything resembling a leg; as, a chair *leg;* **3,** the part of a garment covering the leg; **4,** the course covered by a vessel on one tack; **5,** in *mathematics,* one of two sides of a triangle, the third being the base; **6,** in *cards,* the first game toward a rubber.—*adj.* **leg′gy; leg′less.**

leg-a-cy (leg′a-si), *n.* [*pl.* legacies], **1,** a gift by will; **2,** anything that has come down from one's predecessors.

le-gal (lē′g'l), *adj.* **1,** pertaining to law; **2,** permitted or authorized by law; as, Sunday baseball is *legal* in some places. —*n.* **le-gal′i-ty.**—*adj.* **le′gal-ly.** **legal tender,** money or currency lawfully proper for paying debts; thus, over $10 in dimes is not *legal tender* for discharge of a debt.

le-gal-ize (lē′gal-īz′), *v.t.* [-ized, i-zing], to make lawful; as, to *legalize* the sale of drugs.—*n.* **le′gal-i-za′tion.**

leg-ate (leg′it), *n.* **1,** an ambassador, delegate, or envoy; **2,** in the Roman Catholic Church, a representative of the Pope.

leg-a-tee (leg′a-tē′), *n. Law:* a person to whom money or other property is left by will.

le-ga-tion (li-gā′shun), *n.* **1,** an ambassador or envoy and his associates; **2,** the official residence of a diplomatic representative in a foreign country.

le-ga-to (li-gä′tō; lā-gä′tō), *adj.* and *adv.* in *music,* in a smooth, flowing manner without breaks between notes: opposite of *staccato.*

leg-end (lej′end; lē′jend), *n.* **1,** a story handed down from the past; esp. a story which centers about a historic person or event, but which cannot be proved to be true; **2,** the words of a title or inscription, as on a coin or under an illustration in a book.—*adj.* **leg′end-ar′y.**

leg-er-de-main (lej′ẽr-de-mān′), *n.* **1,** sleight of hand; jugglery; hence, **2,** any deceit or trickery.

leg-ging (leg′ing), *n.* either of a pair of long gaiters worn to protect the legs from cold or wet.

leg-horn (leg′hôrn; lig-ôrn′; leg′ẽrn), *n.* **1,** a braid made of fine Italian straw; **2,** a hat made of such straw.

leg-i-ble (lej′i-bl), *adj.* capable of being read; clear; distinct.—*n.* **leg′i-bil′i-ty.**—*adv.* **leg′i-bly.**

le-gion (lē′jun), *n.* **1,** a division of the ancient Roman army, of 3,000 to 6,000 foot-soldiers; **2,** an army; **3,** a vast number.

le-gion-ar-y (lē′jun-ẽr-i), *adj.* **1,** belonging to, or consisting of, legions; **2,** too great to be numbered:—*n.* [*pl.* legionaries], a soldier of a legion.

le-gion-naire (lē′jun-âr′), *n.* and *adj.* a member of, or pertaining to, a legion; a legionary.

leg-is-late (lej′is-lāt′), *v.i.* [legislat-ed, legislat-ing], to make or enact a law or laws; as, to *legislate* against gambling. —*adj.* **leg′is-la′tive.**—*n.* **leg′is-la′tor.**

leg-is-la-tion (lej′is-lā′shun), *n.* **1,** the act of making a law or laws; **2,** laws made or enacted.

leg-is-la-ture (lej′is-lā′tūr), *n.* the law-making body of a state or nation.

le-git-i-mate (li-jit′i-mit), *adj.* **1,** lawful; rightful; as, the *legitimate* heir to a throne; **2,** born lawfully, of wedded parents; **3,** according to accepted rules; as, a *legitimate* pass in football; **4,** reasonable; just; as, illness is a *legitimate* reason for absence:—*v.t.* (li-jit′i-māt′), [legitimat-ed, legitimat-ing], to permit or recognize by law.—*n.* **le-git′i-ma-cy.**

leg-ume (leg′ūm; li-gūm′), *n.* **1,** a type of podlike fruit, as the pea and the bean; **2,** a plant bearing such fruit; **3, legumes,** the seed of such fruit used as food.—*adj.* **le-gu′mi-nous.**

lei-sure (lē′zhẽr; lezh′ẽr), *n.* spare time:—*adj.* free; unoccupied by work; as, *leisure* hours.—*adj.* and *adv.* **lei′sure-ly.**

lem-ming (lem′ing), *n.* a short-tailed, mouselike rodent with furry feet, found in the Arctic.

lem-on (lem′un), *n.* **1,** a small tropical fruit with pale-yellow skin and very acid juice; **2,** the tree, related to the orange, which bears this fruit; **3,** a pale-yellow colour:—*adj.* flavoured or coloured like a lemon; as, *lemon*-pie; *lemon* taffeta.

lem-on-ade (lem′un-ād′), *n.* a drink of sweetened water flavoured with lemon juice.

---

cat, āge, fär, câre, àsk; ten, ēve, latẽr; (i) pity, rely, senate; ice; top; nō

le-mur (lē'mẽr; lem'ẽr), *n.* any of various small sharp-nosed, tree-dwelling woolly mammals, which are related to monkeys, found chiefly in Madagascar.

lend (lend), *v.t.* [lent (lent), lend-ing], 1, to turn over to someone to use for a time; 2, to give (aid); provide; as, distance *lends* enchantment; 3, to devote or accommodate; as, to *lend* oneself to a scheme:—*v.i.* to make a loan or loans.—*n.* lend'er.

length (length), *n.* 1, the measure of anything from end to end; as, the *length* of a boat; 2, extent in space, degree, or time; as, the *length* of a journey or a vacation; 3, a specified distance, as from head to tail of a horse; as, to win by a *length;* 4, a single piece, as of a series of objects that may be connected; as, a *length* of pipe; 5, the quantity of a vowel measured by the time it takes to utter it; as, the *length* of *e* in "he" is greater than that of *e* in "bet":—at length, 1, in full detail; as, read the letter *at length;* 2, at last; finally.

length-en (leng'then), *v.t.* to make long or longer; as, to *lengthen* a skirt:—*v.i.* to grow longer; as, the days *lengthen* in spring.

length-wise (length'wīz'), *adj.* and *adv.* in the direction from end to end; as, a *lengthwise* measurement; we sleep *lengthwise* in bed. Also, *adv.* length'-ways.

length-y (leng'thi), *adj.* [length-i-er, length-i-est], long; drawn out; tedious. *adv.* length'i-ly.—*n.* length'i-ness.

le-ni-ent (lē'ni-ent; lēn'yent), *adj.* not severe; mild; merciful; as, a *lenient* judge.—*adv.* le'ni-ent-ly.—*n.* le'ni-en-cy. Also, le'ni-ence; len'i-ty.

lens (lenz), *n.* 1, a piece of glass or other transparent substance, with one or both of its surfaces curved, used in cameras, eye-glasses, telescopes, etc., producing a change in the direction of rays of light, as a result of which, in some lenses, the rays that pass through make an image on a screen or a camera film; 2, a lenslike part of the eye, which focuses light on the retina.

Lent (lent), *n.* the 40 week-days before Easter Sunday, observed in some Christian churches with fasting and penitence.—*adj.* Lent'en.

len-til (len'til), *n.* a pod-bearing plant, of which the small seeds are cooked as a vegetable or ground into meal, and the stalks used for fodder.

len-to (len'tō), *adj.* in *music,* slow.—*adv.* slowly.

Le-o (lē'ō), *n.* 1, a northern constellation, the Lion; 2, the 5th sign of the zodiac (♌), which the sun enters about July 22.

leop-ard (lep'ẽrd), *n.* a large carnivorous cat of southern Asia and Africa, with a black-spotted tawny coat: also called *panther.*

le-o-tard (lē'ō-tärd), *n.* a sleeveless, close-fitting, one-piece garment worn by aerial gymnasts, ballet dancers, etc.

lep-er (lep'ẽr), *n.* a person who is afflicted with leprosy

lep-re-chaun (lep're-kôn'; -khôn'), *n.* in *Irish folklore,* a sprite or fairy, usually in the form of a little old man.

lep-ro-sy (lep'ro-si), *n.* [*pl.* leprosies], a loathsome, infectious skin disease marked by external ulcers and a scaling off of dead tissue.—*adj.* lep'-rous.

le-sion (lē'zhun), *n. Medical,* a hurt; injury, esp. to the working or structure of an organ; as, a brain *lesion.*

less (les), *adj.* [*comp.* of *little*], 1, not so much; not so large; 2, inferior:—*prep.* minus; as, ten *less* seven:—*adv.* in a lower degree; as, *less* famous:—*n.* a smaller quantity; as, to eat *less.*

les-see (les-ē'), *n.* one to whom a lease is granted; tenant.

less-en (les'n), *v.t.* to make smaller or fewer; reduce; as, to *lessen* the length of a rope; *lessen* working hours:—*v.i.* to become less.

less-er (les'ẽr), *adj.* [a *comp.* of *little*], smaller; inferior; less; as, the *lesser* evil.

les-son (les'n), *n.* 1, that which is assigned to a pupil to learn; 2, the instruction given at one time; 3, any person, thing, etc., by which one learns; as, his fate is a *lesson* to me; 4, in Christian church services, a reading from the Bible.

les-sor (les'ôr; les-ôr'), *n.* one who gives a lease or rents property to another.

lest (lest), *conj.* for fear that; as, in dread *lest* the thief come; so that not: as, hurry *lest* you be too late.

¹let (let), *n.* 1, *Archaic,* an obstacle; hindrance; 2, in *tennis,* a served ball which touches the net in going over.

²let (let), *v.t.* [let, let-ting], 1, to permit; allow; as, *let* me try again; 2, to rent; lease; 3, to allow (something) to escape; as, to *let* air out of a tire:—*v.i.* to be hired or leased; as, the house *lets* for $50 a month.

le-thal (lē′thal), *adj.* **1,** deadly; fatal; as, a *lethal* dose; a *lethal* chamber; **2,** pertaining to death.

leth-ar-gy (leth′ẽr-ji), *n.* [*pl.* lethargies], **1,** unnatural drowsiness; **2,** lack of interest; listlessness.—*adj.* **le-thar′-gic** (li-thär′jik).

let-ter (let′ẽr), *n.* **1,** a mark or character used to represent a sound; an alphabetical symbol; **2,** a written or printed communication; epistle; as, a *letter* of introduction; a *letter* of thanks; **3,** the exact or word-for-word meaning; as, the *letter* of the law; **4, letters,** knowledge; learning; literature; as, men of *letters:*—*v.t.* to mark with letters.

let-ter-head (let′ẽr-hed′), *n.* **1,** a printed form at the top of a sheet of writing-paper, usually containing the name and address of the sender; **2,** a sheet of paper so printed.

let-tuce (let′us; let′is), *n.* a garden plant with tender, crisp leaves which are used as a salad or garnish.

let-up (let′up′), *n.* pause; cessation; as, it rained without *letup*, (*Colloq.*).

leu-co-cyte (lū′kō-sīt′), *n.* the white blood corpuscle, useful in destroying harmful bacteria.

leu-ke-mi-a (lū-kē′mi-a), *n.* a disease, usually fatal, in which there is uncontrolled multiplying of the white blood cells. Also, **leu-kae′mi-a.**

¹lev-ee (lev′i; le-vē′), *n.* **1,** a morning reception, esp. by a person of high rank; **2,** any assemblage of guests.

²lev-ee (le-vē′; lev′i), *n.* **1,** a wall or embankment built along a river to keep it from flooding adjoining land; **2,** a pier.

lev-el (lev′el; lev′l), *n.* **1,** an unbroken horizontal surface or line; **2,** equality of height; as, this house is on a *level* with that; **3,** a standard elevation; as, sea *level;* **4,** an instrument used to find or test a horizontal line:—*adj.* **1,** having a flat, horizontal surface; as, *level* ground; **2,** equal to something else in height or importance; **3,** steady; judicious; well-balanced; as, a *level* head:—*v.t.* [levelled, level-ling], **1,** to make smooth or flat in a horizontal plane; as, to *level* a road; **2,** to bring to the same plane, height, or condition as something else; specifically, to bring to the level of the ground; raze; **3,** to point; aim, as a gun.—*n.* **lev′el-ler.**—*adj.* **lev′el—head′-ed.**

le-ver (lē′vẽr; lev′ẽr), *n.* **1,** a bar used to move a heavy object by prying; a crowbar; **2,** in *mechanics*, a rigid bar,

fixed at one point, the fulcrum, around which it moves as on an axis, used to transmit or modify power.

le-ver-age (lē′vẽr-ij; lev′ẽr-ij), *n.* **1,** the action of a lever; **2,** the mechanical power gained by using a lever.

le-vi-a-than (li-vī′a-than), *n.* **1,** in the Bible, a sea animal of enormous size; **2,** anything huge, as a whale or a large ship.

lev-i-ta-tion (lev′i-tā′shun), *n. Spiritualism,* the process or illusion of raising and suspending a heavy body in air without physical support.

lev-i-ty (lev′i-ti), *n.* [*pl.* levities], lack of seriousness; unseemly frivolity.

lev-y (lev′i), *n.* [*pl.* levies], **1,** the act of collecting men or raising money under compulsion; **2,** the number or amount collected:—*v.t.* [levied, levy-ing], raise or collect by force or order, as an army or a tax:—*v.i.* to raise money by seizing property; as, to *levy* on an estate for a debt.

lex-i-con (lek′si-kon), *n.* a dictionary, esp. of an ancient language, as Greek or Latin.

li-a-bil-i-ty (lī′a-bil′i-ti), *n.* [*pl.* liabilities], **1,** the state of being held responsible for a loss, debt, etc.; **2,** the state of being subject to something or apt to do something; tendency; as, *liability* to disease or to error; **3, liabilities,** debts; the obligations which must be paid out of assets.

li-a-ble (lī′a-bl), *adj.* **1,** answerable; responsible; as, a person is *liable* for his debts; **2,** exposed to some damage, danger, misfortune, penalty, etc.; as, a lazy student is *liable* to fail.

li-ai-son (li-ā′zn; lē′a-zŏn′; lye-zŏn′), *n.* **1,** a connecting link; bond; union; as, a *liaison* between church and state, or between departments of the army, government, etc.; **2,** in *phonetics*, the carrying over of a final consonant to sound as the first letter of the next word, esp. one beginning with a vowel as, a *nold* crow (an old crow).

li-a-na (li-ä′na), *n.* any tropical vine such as climbs high, twining around tree-trunks, etc.

li-ar (lī′ẽr), *n.* one who tells lies.

li-ba-tion (lī-bā′shun), *n.* the act of pouring out wine or other liquid in honour of a god; **2,** the liquid so poured out.

li-bel (lī′bel; lī′bl), *n.* a malicious written or printed statement tending to defame, or to injure the reputation of another; also, the publishing of such statement:—*v.t.* [libelled, libel-ling], to publish a malicious, injurious statement against; defame.—*n.* li′bel-ler.—*adj.* li′bel-lous.

lib-er-al (lib′ẽr-al), *adj.* 1, generous; 2, abundant; plentiful; as, a *liberal* supply; 3, free from narrowness in ideas; broadminded; 4, in *politics*, in favour of social and governmental change and progress:—*n.* 1, any freethinking person; a progressive; 2, **Liberal**, a member of a liberal political party.—*n.* lib′er-al′i-ty.

lib-er-ate (lib′ẽr-āt′), *v.t.* [liberat-ed, liberat-ing], to set free from restraint or bondage; as, to *liberate* slaves.—*n.* lib′er-a′tor.—*n.* lib′er-a′tion.

lib-er-tine (lib′ẽr-tēn′; -tin; -tīn′), *n.* one who gives free play to his evil impulses, appetites, and desires; a rake:—*adj.* loose in morals; dissolute.

lib-er-ty (lib′ẽr-ti), *n.* [*pl.* liberties], 1, freedom from control or bondage; 2, freedom to do as one pleases; 3, an overstepping of the rules of propriety; undue freedom; as, to take *liberties* with a person; 4, leisure; freedom from business.

Li-bra (lī′bra), *n.* 1, a southern constellation, the Balance; 2, the 7th sign of the zodiac (♎), which the sun enters about September 23.

li-brar-y (lī′bẽr-i), *n.* [*pl.* libraries], 1, a collection of books; 2, a room or building where books are kept.—*n.* li-brar′i-an (lī-brâr′i-an).

li-bret-to (li-bret′ō), *n.* the text of an opera or other long musical composition.

lice (līs), *n. pl.* of *louse*.

li-cence (lī′sens), *n.* 1, legal authorization or permission to do something; also, the document which gives such permission; as, a fishing *licence;* 2, unrestrained liberty; abuse of freedom. Also spelled **li′cense**.

li-cense (lī′sens), *v.t.* [licensed, licensing], to authorize, or grant permission to, by law. Also spelled **li′cence**.

li-cen-tious (lī-sen′shus), *adj.* lewd; unrestrained; dissolute.—*adv.* li-cen′-tious-ly.—*n.* li-cen′tious-ness.

li-chen (lī′ken), *n.* a flowerless, leafless plant growing flat on rocks, tree trunks, etc.

lick (lik), *v.t.* 1, to pass the tongue over; as, to *lick* a lollipop; 2, to play or pass over lightly, as do flames; 3, *Colloq.* to whip; also, to conquer or defeat:—*n.* 1, the act of passing the tongue over something; 2, a small amount; as, a

lick of flour; 3, a deposit of natural salt, to which animals go for salt.

lic-o-rice (lik′ō-ris), *n.* liquorice; the dried root of a plant of the pea family, or an extract made from it, which is used in medicines and candy; also, the plant.

lid (lid), *n.* 1, a movable cover for an opening, as of a box; a top; 2, the cover of the eye; eyelid.

¹lie (lī), *n.* 1, an untrue statement; falsehood; 2, anything that misleads or is intended to mislead:—*v.i.* [lied (līd), ly-ing], 1, to speak a falsehood; 2, to make false representations; as, figures never *lie*.

²lie (lī), *v.i.* [*p.t.* lay (lā), *p.p.* lain (lān), *p.pr.* ly-ing], 1, to assume, or rest in, a reclining position; 2, to be in a flat or horizontal position; as, the tree *lay* in the road; 3, to be situated; as, the town *lies* yonder; also, to extend; as, there *lies* the path; 4, to be; exist; as, the trouble *lies* in the engine; also, to remain; as, the factory *lay* idle all summer.

lief (lēf), *adv.* willingly; as, I should as *lief* go as stay.

liege (lēj), *adj.* 1, having the right to devotion and service; as, faithful to his *liege* lord; 2, bound to give service and devotion, as to a feudal lord; 3, hence, loyal; faithful:—*n.* 1, one bound to give service and devotion; a vassal; 2, a sovereign; lord and master.

lien (lē′en; lēn), *n.* 1, a legal claim upon property until a debt owing on it is paid; as, a *lien* on an automobile; 2, security for payment.

lieu (lū), *n. French,* place; stead; as, he used Scotch tape *in lieu* of string.

lieu-ten-ant (lef-ten′ant), *n.* 1, one who acts for a superior: used also with names of ranks to indicate the next lower rank; as, *lieutenant*-governor; 2, in the army, a commissioned officer next below a captain; 3, in the navy, a commissioned officer ranking next below a lieutenant-commander.—*n.* **lieu-ten′-an-cy**.

life (līf), *n.* [*pl.* lives (līvz)], 1, the particular quality which distinguishes an animal or a plant from rocks, earth, water, etc.; 2, the state of being alive; existence; as, a living person; as, a *life* was saved by the operation; also, living beings collectively; as, human *life;* animal *life;* 4, the period between birth and death; as, all the years of a man's *life;* 5, a biography; as, a *life* of Tennyson; 6, animation; vivacity; as, to be full of *life;* **7,** a manner of living; as, a *life* of hardship. Compounds: **life'blood'; life'less; life'like'; life'-long'; life'time'; life'work'.**

life-boat (līf'bōt'), *n.* a strong boat for use in rescuing persons at sea.

life-guard (līf'gärd'), *n.* an expert swimmer at public bathing-beaches or pools, detailed to look after the safety of bathers.

lift (lift), *v.t.* **1,** to raise to a higher point; take up; pull up; as, to *lift* a heavy weight; **2,** to exalt; **3,** *Colloq.* to steal:—*v.i.* to rise or have the appearance of rising; as, the fog *lifts:—n.* **1,** the act of rising to a higher point; also, a rise; increase; as, a *lift* in prices; **2,** aid; assistance; hence, a free ride along one's way; **3,** an elevator; a hoist; **4,** a rope from the mast to the end of a yard below, supporting the yard.—*n.* **lift'er.**

lig-a-ment (lig'a-ment), *n.* a band of tough, fibrous tissue which connects the ends of bones or holds an organ of the body in place.

lig-a-ture (lig'a-tūr'; -choōr'), *n.* **1,** a tying or binding together; **2,** a narrow bandage; **3,** in *music,* a slur; in *printing,* two or more letters forming a single character, as *fl* or *œ*; in *surgery,* a thread or wire to tie blood vessels to stop bleeding.

¹light (līt), *n.* **1,** the condition of illumination upon which sight depends; as, I need more *light;* **2,** anything which gives light, as the sun, a candle, etc.; **3,** also, the brightness or radiance given off by these; **4,** something like light that leads to mental clearness and understanding; as, to throw *light* on a problem; **5,** the state of being visible, esp. in public; as, his sins were brought to *light;* **6,** brightness; shining quality; as, the *light* in her eyes; **7,** a famous or model person; as, he is a shining *light:—adj.* **1,** clear; bright; not dark; **2,** pale in colour:—*v.t.* [light-ed or lit (lit), light-ing], **1,** to kindle, as a fire; also, to set on fire; **2,** to cause to shine and give forth brightness; as, *light* the lamp; **3,** to give brightness to; as, the lamp *lights* up the room; **4,** to furnish with, or guide by, a light; as, to *light* someone on his way:—*v.i.* to become bright; as, her face *lit* up when we praised her.

²light (līt), *adj.* **1,** not heavy; of little weight; as, a *light* package; **2,** not burdensome; easy to endure, understand, or do; as, a *light* loss; *light* reading; *light* tasks; **3,** delicate; dainty; also, graceful; nimble; as, a

light step; **4,** cheerful; gay; as, a *light* heart; **5,** frivolous; fickle; **6,** small in amount; as, a *light* snowfall; **7,** of food, easily digested; **8,** of wines, containing little alcohol; **9,** not heavily equipped; as, *light* infantry:—*v.i.* [lit (lit) or light-ed, light-ing], to descend and rest; come down; settle; alight; as, the bird *lit* on the lawn.—*adv.* **light'ly.**

¹light-en (līt'n), *v.t.* to make clear or bright; illumine:—*v.i.* **1,** to become bright; **2,** to shine with flashes of lightning.

²light-en (līt'n), *v.t.* **1,** to reduce in weight, as a load; **2,** to make less burdensome; as, her sympathy *lightened* my trouble.

light-er (līt'ẽr), *n.* **1,** anything that ignites to produce a light or flame; as, a cigarette *lighter;* **2,** a large boat or barge used to load and unload ships not docked but lying at anchor.

light—foot-ed (līt'—foot'id), *adj.* nimble.

light—head-ed (līt'—hed'id), *adj.* **1,** dizzy; also, delirious, as from fever; **2,** thoughtless; heedless.

light—heart-ed (līt'—här'tid), *adj.* free from care; gay; happy; cheerful; as, *light-hearted* laughter.—*adv.* **light'—heart'ed-ly.**—*n.* **light'—heart'ed-ness.**

light-house (līt'hous'), *n.* a tower or other structure with a brilliant light at the top to guide ships at night.

light—mind-ed (līt'—mīn'did), *adj.* frivolous; silly.

light-ning (līt'ning), *n.* a flash of light caused by electricity as it travels between clouds or from clouds to the earth.

light-ning—bug (līt'ning–bug), *n.* a firefly.

light-ning—rod (līt'ning–rod'), *n.* a metal rod, fastened on a building and connected with the earth below, to protect the building from lightning.

light-ship (līt'ship'), *n.* a vessel carrying a warning light and moored at sea in a dangerous place to warn other ships or to mark a channel.

light—year (līt'—yẽr'), *n.* the distance that light travels in a year (about 6×10^{12} miles), a unit of stellar distance.

lig-ne-ous (lig'ni-us), *adj.* composed of, or like, wood; as, *ligneous* plants.

lig-nite (lig'nīt), *n.* a woody, brownish-black coal, softer than bituminous but harder than peat; brown coal.

lik-a-ble or **like-a-ble** (līk'a-bl), *adj.*

attractive; so pleasant as to gain the liking and friendship of people.

¹like (līk), *adj.* [*comp.* lik-er, *superl.* lik-est, now chiefly poetical], **1,** similar; exactly or nearly the same; as, my hat is *like* hers; **2,** in a mood for; as, I feel *like* reading; **3,** characteristic of; as, it was *like* him to be kind; **4,** giving indications of; as, it looks *like* rain:—*prep.* in the manner of; as, act *like* a man:—*n.* the equal of a person or thing; as, I have never seen its *like*.

²like (līk), *v.t.* [liked, lik-ing], to have a taste for; enjoy; find agreeable:—*v.i.* to choose; prefer; as, we'll go, if you *like*:—**likes,** *n.pl.* the things one enjoys.

like-li-hood (līk′li-hood), *n.* probability.

like-ly (līk′li), *adj.* [like-li-er, like-li-est], **1,** probable; believable; as, a *likely* tale; **2,** suitable; promising; as, a *likely* place for lunch; a *likely* fellow; **3,** expected; as, it is *likely* to snow today.

lik-en (līk′en), *v.t.* to compare; as, I will *liken* him unto a wise man.

like-ness (līk′nis), *n.* **1,** resemblance; similarity; as, the *likeness* between the two brothers was amazing; **2,** a portrait; **3,** shape; external appearance guise; as, an enemy in the *likeness* of a friend.

like-wise (līk′wīz′), *adv.* **1,** in a similar manner; as, watch him and do *likewise;* **2,** also; furthermore.

li-lac (lī′lak), *n.* **1,** a shrub with clusters of white or pale-violet flowers; **2,** the flower of this shrub; **3,** the pale-violet colour of the flowers.

lilt (lilt), *n.* **1,** a light or lively tune; a merry song; **2,** rhythmic movement, as, the *lilt* of verse:—*v.t.* to sing in a gay, rhythmic way:—*v.i.* to sing gaily; as, to *lilt* and play.

lil-y (lil′i), *n.* [*pl.* lilies], a plant with bell-shaped flowers and a bulblike root:—*adj.* pure; pale.

lil-y of the val-ley, a low-growing plant with stalks of fragrant, bell-shaped flowers; also, the flowers.

lil-y pad, one of the floating leaves of the water lily.

Li-ma bean (lī′ma), a flat-podded bean; also, its seed, fresh or dried, used as food.

limb (lim), *n.* **1,** a leg or arm of man or some other animal; also a bird's wing; **2,** a main branch of a tree.

lim-ber (lim′bèr), *adj.* **1,** flexible; **2,** supple; lithe:—*v.t.* and *v.i.* to make or become flexible or supple.—*n.* **lim′ber-ness.**

lim-bo (lim′bō), *n.* a place of confinement or oblivion; as, a *limbo* of lost reputations: originally conceived to be a place between heaven and hell.

¹lime (līm), *n.* a white, earth-like substance obtained by the action of heat upon limestone, marble, bones, sea-shells, etc., and used in making cement, mortar, and the like:—*v.t.* [limed, lim-ing], to treat (land) with lime in order to sweeten it.—*adj.* **lim′y.**

²lime (līm), *n.* a tree bearing a small, juicy, lemonlike fruit; also, its small, sour fruit; the linden or basswood.

lime-ade (līm′ād′), *n.* a drink made of lime juice, water, and sugar.

lime-light (līm′līt′), *n.* **1,** the brilliant light, formerly thrown upon the central figure or group on a stage, so called because it was produced by playing a hot flame upon lime: also called *calcium light;* **2,** glare of publicity.

lim-er-ick (lim′ėr-ik), *n.* a nonsense poem of five anapaestic lines, of which 1, 2, and 5 have three feet, and 3 and 4 two feet: rhyme scheme, *aabba:* the last line is the "punch" line.

lime-stone (līm′stōn′), *n.* a rock used as building stone, for road construction, etc.

lim-it (lim′it), *n.* **1,** a border or boundary; that which confines, ends, or checks; **2,** a point not to be passed; end; as, to reach the *limit* of one's endurance:—*v.t.* to restrict; as, his share of the profits is *limited* to 25 per cent.—*n.* **lim′i-ta′tion.**—*adj.* **lim′it-less.**

limn (lim), *v.t.* [limned (limd), lim-ning (lim′ing)], to paint or draw; to depict; as, to *limn* a picture.

lim-ou-sine (lim′oo-zēn′), *n.* a large automobile, often with a passenger compartment separated from the driver's seat.

¹limp (limp), *n.* a lame, halting motion in walking:—*v.i.* to walk lamely.

²limp (limp), *adj.* not stiff or firm.—*adv.* **limp′ly.**—*n.* **limp′ness.**

lim-pet (lim′pit), *n.* a variety of shellfish with broad cone-shaped shell, and thick fleshy foot with which it clings tightly to rocks: used often as a food.

lim-pid (lim′pid), *adj.* transparent; sparklingly clear; as, a *limpid* pool.

linch-pin (linch′pin′), *n.* an axle pin used to keep a wheel on.

lin-den (lin′den), *n.* a large tree with heart-shaped leaves and small clusters of cream-coloured flowers; the basswood: also called *lime*.

all (ôl), ôr; up, mūte, cûr, cōōl, book; oil, out; th, thin; *th,* the.

¹line (līn), *n*. **1,** a mark having length, but very little width, made with pen, pencil, etc.; **2,** a wrinkle, as in the skin; a crease; **3,** a strong, slender string, cord, etc.; as, a clothes-*line;* also, a wire of a telephone or telegraph system; **4,** a boundary; as, they crossed the *line* into Canada; also, a limit; **5,** a plan or method; course of action or thought; as, a *line* of reasoning; **6,** a succession of persons or objects that form a line or row; as, a long waiting *line;* a *line* of tents; **7,** a profession; branch of business; as, the restaurant *line;* **8,** a row of printed or written letters or words; **9,** family; descent; as, a *line* of kings; **10,** vehicles, cars, trains, ships, etc., making up a system of transportation; also, direction; route; as, a *line* of travel; **11,** outline; shape; as, the *line* of the face; **12, lines,** the words of a part in a play; as, the actors were not sure of their *lines:—v.t.* [lined, lining], **1,** to draw lines upon; **2,** to form or make a line along; as, roses *line* the path; to *line* a street with trees; **3,** to arrange in a line, as soldiers:—*v.i.* to form a row.

²line (līn), *v.t.* [lined, lin-ing], to provide with an inside covering; as, to *line* curtains; to *line* a coat.—*n.* **lin′er.**

lin-e-age (lin′i-ij), *n*. ancestry; also, all the descendants of one ancestor.

lin-e-al (lin′i-al), *adj.* **1,** pertaining to direct descent from an ancestor; as, *lineal* heirs; **2,** linear.—*adv.* **lin′e-al-ly.**

lin-e-a-ment (lin′i-a-ment), *n*. [often *lineaments*] a feature; the features; profile.

lin-e-ar (lin′i-ėr), *adj.* **1,** pertaining to, or composed of, lines; **2,** having, or pertaining to, length only; as, *linear* measure.

line-man (līn′man), *n*. **1,** a man who repairs and maintains a telephone or telegraph line; **2,** in *surveying*, the one who carries tape, line, or chain; **3,** one who inspects rails on a railroad; **4,** in *football*, a player on a forward line.

lin-en (lin′en), *n*. **1,** thread spun from flax; **2,** the material made of this thread; **3,** articles made of this material, as napkins, towels, sheets, shirts, collars, etc.:—*adj.* made of linen.

¹lin-er (lī′nėr), *n*. a large swift ship or aeroplane belonging to a regular system of transport.

²lin-er (līn′ėr), *n*. **1,** one who makes, fits or provides linings; **2,** in *baseball*, a hard-hit ball that travels horizontally.

lines-man (līnz′man), *n*. [*pl.* linesmen (-men)], **1,** one who puts up or repairs telephone or telegraph lines; **2,** in *football*, an official who records the distance gained or lost in each play; **3,** in *tennis*, an official who decides whether the ball lands inside or outside the boundary-lines of the court.

¹ling (ling), *n*. **1,** a large Atlantic fish, resembling the cod; **2,** other such varieties as the *burbot* and *hake.*

²ling (ling), *n*. the common heather of the United Kingdom.

lin-ger (ling′gėr), *v.i.* to delay; loiter.

ling-e-rie (lȧṅ′zhė-rē′; popularly, län′-zhė-rē′), *n*. women's undergarments.

lin-go (ling′gō), *n*. [*pl.* lingoes], dialect; often, humorously, any queer speech; jargon; as, baseball *lingo.*

lin-gual (ling′gwal), *adj.* pertaining to, or shaped like, the tongue.—*n.* in *phonetics*, a letter or sound formed by the tongue, as *l, r, th,* etc.

lin-guist (ling′gwist), *n*. one skilled in languages.—*adj.* **lin-guis′tic.**—*n.* **lin-guis′tics.**

lin-i-ment (lin′i-ment), *n*. a healing or stimulating liquid rubbed on the skin.

lin-ing (līn′ing), *n*. an inside covering; also, material of which such a covering is made.

link (lingk), *n*. **1,** a single loop or division of a chain; **2,** anything that serves to connect the parts of a series:—*v.t.* and *v.i.* to connect, or be connected, by a link.—*n.* **link′age.**—**linking verb** or **link verb,** one requiring a predicate adjective, noun, or pronoun to complete it, as *to be, appear, seem, taste,* etc.; as, I *feel* ill.

links (lingks), *n.pl.* a golf-course.

lin-net (lin′it), *n*. a small songbird of the finch family, common in Europe.

li-no-le-um (li-nō′li-um), *n*. a floor covering made of a hardened mixture of ground cork and linseed oil on a backing of burlap or canvas.

lin-o-type (līn′o-tīp′), *n*. a typesetting machine, with keyboard, that casts solid lines of type.

lin-seed (lin′sēd′), *n*. the seed of flax.

linseed oil, a pale-yellow oil pressed from flax-seed, used in paint, linoleum, etc.

lint (lint), *n*. **1,** the soft down obtained by scraping linen, used for dressing wounds; **2,** ravellings from textiles.

lin-tel (lin′t'l), *n*. the horizontal piece of wood, stone, etc., over the top of a door-frame or a window-frame to support the structure above it.

li-on (lī′un), *n*. **1,** a powerful, flesh-eating mammal of the cat family, found in Africa and southern Asia; **2,** a celebrated person who is much sought after by society.—*n.fem.* **li′on-ess.**— *v.t.* **li′on-ize′.**

lip (lip), *n.* **1,** one of the two fleshy borders of the mouth; **2,** an edge of anything hollow; as, the *lip* of a cup:— *adj.* spoken but not felt; insincere; as, *lip* service.

lip-stick (lip′stik′), *n.* a stick of rouge or colouring for the lips.

liq-ue-fy (lik′wi-fī′), *v.i.* and *v.t.* [liquefied, liquefy-ing], to become, or to change into, a liquid.

li-queur (li-kūr′; lē′kûr′), an alcoholic drink, sweetened and flavoured, as creme de menthe, chartreuse, etc.

liq-uid (lik′wid), *adj.* **1,** not solid; freely flowing; **2,** pure or clear in sound; as, *liquid* tones of voice; **3,** smooth; flowing, as the consonants *l* and *r;* **4,** in *finance,* easily and quickly salable for cash; as, *liquid* assets:—*n.* **1,** a liquid substance; **2,** any of the consonant sounds *l, r,* and, sometimes, *m, n,* and *ng.*—*n.* **li-quid′i-ty.**

liq-ui-date (lik′wi-dāt′), *v.t.* [liquidat-ed, liquidat-ing], **1,** to pay off or settle, as a debt; **2,** to wind up or settle the affairs of (a business, estate, etc.) by turning the assets into cash, paying the debts in full or in whatever proportion may be possible, and dividing up what is left among the owners; **3,** to get rid of, as by killing:—*v.i.* to wind up a business.—*n.* **liq′ui-da′tion.**

liq-uor (lik′ẽr), *n.* any liquid sub-stance; esp. an alcoholic drink.

li-quo-rice (lik′o-ris), *n.* the dried root of a plant of the pea family, or an extract made from it; also, the plant.

li-ra (lē′rä), *n.* [*pl.* lire (lē′rā) or liras] an Italian silver coin worth about eight cents.

lisle (līl), *n.* a fine, hard-twisted cotton thread, or a fabric knitted from it.

lisp (lisp), *v.i.* to pronounce *s* and *z* incorrectly, giving them the sound of *th:*—*v.t.* to utter imperfectly:—*n.* the incorrect pronunciation of *s* and *z* as *th.*

¹list (list), *n.* **1,** a series of names, items, etc.; a catalogue, roll, or register; **2,** an edge or selvage of cloth:—*v.t.* to catalogue, register, or enrol.

²list (list), *v.i.* to tilt toward one side, as a ship:—*n.* a leaning to one side, as of a ship.

lis-ten (lis′n), *v.i.* **1,** to attend closely, so as to hear; harken; **2,** to heed; obey.

list-less (list′lis), *adj.* lacking energy or interest; spiritless.—*adv.* **list′less-ly.** —*n.* **list′less-ness.**

lists (lists), *n.pl.* in days of old, the barriers of a field where tournaments were held; hence, now, any place of contest.

lit (lit), *p.t.* and *p.p.* of *light.*

lit-a-ny (lit′a-ni), *n.* [*pl.* litanies], a certain form of prayer; esp. in a church service, a responsive prayer in which the clergyman repeats a series of petitions to which the congregation makes responses.

li-ter (lē′tẽr), *n.* Same as litre.

lit-er-a-cy (lit′ẽr-a-si), *n.* the ability to read and write.—*adj.* **lit′er-ate.**

lit-er-al (lit′ẽr-al), *adj.* **1,** following the given words; exact; as, a *literal* translation; **2,** precise; not exaggera-ted; as, the *literal* truth; **3,** matter-of-fact.—*adv.* **lit′er-al-ly.**—*n.* **lit′er-al-ness.**

lit-er-ar-y (lit′ẽr-ẽr-i), *adj.* relating to literature or to men of letters.

lit-er-a-ture (lit′ẽr-a-tūr′; chōōr′), *n.* **1,** the written or printed productions of a country or period; esp. such poetry or prose as is notable for beauty of matter, style, etc.; **2,** the occupation of authors; **3,** the body of writings on a given subject; as, the *literature* of music; advertising *literature.*

lith-arge (lith′ärj), *n.* lead monoxide, PbO, a yellow or red substance used in making glass, pottery, varnish, drying oils, rubber, and cement.

lithe (līth), *adj.* [lith-er (līth′ẽr), lith-est (līth′est)], bending easily; supple.

li-thog-ra-phy (li-thog′ra-fi), *n.* in *offset printing,* the design or page is reproduced by photography on a thin metal plate curved to fit the printing-press cylinder, and transferred to, or offset on, paper by means of a rubber blanket that runs over another cylinder. This process is also called *lithoprint* and *planograph:*—*v.t.* and *n.* **lith′o-graph′;** **li-thog′ra-pher.**—*adj.* **lith′o-graph′ic.**

lit-i-gant (lit′i-gant), *n.* either party in a lawsuit:—*adj.* engaged in a lawsuit.

lit-i-ga-tion (lit′i-gā′shun), *n.* the act or process of carrying on a lawsuit; also, a lawsuit.—*v.t.* and *v.i.* **lit′i-gate′.**

lit-mus (lit′mus), *n.* a violet-blue colouring matter obtained from lichens: it is turned red by an acid, and restored to blue by an alkali.—**litmus paper,** a paper saturated with litmus, and used for testing acid and alkali solutions.

li-tre or **li-ter** (lē′tẽr), *n.* a metric unit

all (ôl), **ôr;** **up, mūte, cûr, cōōl, book;** **oil, out;** **th, thin;** *th,* **the.**

of capacity equal to 0.88 quarts liquid measure.

lit-ter (lit′ẽr), *n.* **1,** a couch with a canopy, borne on men's shoulders by means of long shafts; **2,** a cot or stretcher for carrying a sick or wounded person; **3,** straw, hay, etc., used as bedding for animals; **4,** odds and ends scattered about; **5,** young born at one time to pigs, dogs, etc.; as, a *litter* of puppies:—*v.t.* **1,** to supply, as with straw, for bedding; **2,** to make (a place) untidy by scattering odds and ends about:—*v.i.* to bring forth young.

lit-tle (lit′l), *adj.* [*comp.* less, lesser, or *Colloq.* lit-tler, *superl.* least or, *Colloq.* lit-tlest], **1,** small in size or quantity; **2,** small in dignity or importance; **3,** brief in time; as, a *little* while; **4,** petty; mean: as, a *little* mind:—*adv.* in small degree; not much:—*n.* a small quantity.—*n.* **lit′tle-ness.**

lit-ur-gy (lit′ẽr-ji), *n.* **1,** the prescribed ritual for public worship in Christian churches; **2,** the *Mass* of Roman Catholic and *Divine Liturgy* of Eastern Orthodox Churches.

liv-a-ble (liv′a-bl), *adj.* **1,** fit or agreeable to live in or with; **2,** endurable; as, such a life is hardly *livable.*

¹live (liv), *v.i.* [lived, liv-ing], **1,** to exist, or have life; **2,** to reside or dwell; as, to *live* in the woods; **3,** to continue to have life; as, to *live* to be old; **4,** to pass life in a particular manner; as, to *live* happily; **5,** to win a livelihood; as, to *live* by hard work; **6,** to be nourished; as, to *live* on meat:—*v.t.* to pass or spend; as, to *live* a happy life.

²live (līv), *adj.* **1,** having life; alive; **2,** burning, as a hot coal; also, charged with electricity; as, a *live* wire; **3,** full of enthusiasm; wide awake; as, a *live* club; also, of present interest; as, a *live* subject.

live-li-hood (līv′li-hood), *n.* a means of existence; regular support.

live-li-ness (līv′li-nis), *n.* gaiety; vigour.

live-long (liv′lông′), *adj.* whole; entire; as, the children played the *livelong* day.

live-ly (līv′li), *adj.* [live-li-er, live-li-est], **1,** animated; brisk; spirited; as, a *lively* dance; **2,** alert; keen; as, a *lively* concern in affairs; **3,** vivid; bright; as, a *lively* red; **4,** vigorous; as, a *lively* manner; **5,** bounding back easily and quickly, as a ball.

liv-en (līv′en), *v.t.* and *v.i. Colloq.* to make or become cheerful or lively.

liv-er (liv′ẽr), *n.* a large glandular organ in the upper part of the abdomen,

which produces bile and causes important changes in certain substances in the blood.

liv-er-wort (liv′ẽr-wûrt′), *n.* in *botany*, a class of mosslike plants with a thallus, or flat leaflike structure, and rudimentary roots.

liv-er-y (liv′ẽr-i), *n.* [*pl.* liveries], **1,** a particular costume worn by servants or by any other special group of persons; **2,** a stable where horses are boarded or hired out: also called *livery stable.*—*n.* **liv′er-y-man.**—*adj.* **liv′er-ied.**

live-stock (līv′stok′), *n.* domestic animals, as horses, cattle, sheep, or hogs, raised for profit or for farm purposes.

liv-id (liv′id), *adj.* **1,** black and blue; discoloured, as by a bruise; **2,** ashy pale; as, *livid* with anger.

liv-ing (liv′ing), *adj.* **1,** having life; alive; as, *living* beings; **2,** now existent; now in use; as, French is a *living* language; **3,** vigorous; active; as, a *living* hope; a *living* faith; **4,** exact; very; as, he is the *living* image of his father:—**the living,** all who are alive:— *n.* **1,** state of existence; **2,** mode of life; as, plain *living;* **3,** livelihood; as, to earn a *living;* **4,** in England, a church appointment.—*n.* **liv′ing—room′.**

liz-ard (liz′ẽrd), *n.* a long, slender reptile, with four legs and a tapering tail.

lla-ma (lä′ma), *n.* a South American animal somewhat like the camel, but much smaller and without a hump. It is used as a beast of burden in the Andes.

lla-no (lä′nō; Spanish, lyä′nō), *n.* [*pl.* -nos], a broad grassy plain, esp. in South America and Texas.

lo (lō), *interj.* behold! see! look!

load (lōd), *v.t.* **1,** to put into or upon (a wagon, ship, animal, etc.) as much as can be carried; **2,** to put (the cargo) into or upon a vehicle, ship, etc.; **3,** to burden; weigh down; as, to *load* a man with work; my heart is *loaded* with sorrow; **4,** to supply lavishly; as, to *load* a man with gifts; **5,** to put a cartridge into; as, to *load* a gun:—*v.i.* **1,** to put a cartridge into a gun; **2,** to put on, or take on, a cargo:—*n.* **1,** the mass of weight usually carried at one time; cargo; as, this truck carries a *load* of ten tons; **2,** a burden; as, a *load* of care; **3,** the powder, bullet, etc., with which a gun is charged; **4,** the amount of electricity drawn from a given source.—*n.* **load′er.**

load-star or **lode-star** (lōd'stär'), *n.* the North Star.

load-stone or **lode-stone** (lōd'stōn'), *n.* **1,** a kind of iron ore that is magnetic and attracts iron; **2,** anything that has great powers of attraction.

¹loaf (lōf), *n.* [*pl.* loaves (lōvz)], **1,** a shaped mass of bread or cake; **2,** a dish of food made in the shape of a loaf of bread; as, meat *loaf*.

²loaf (lōf), *v.i.* and *v.t.* to pass (time) in idleness; idle.

loaf-er (lō'fẽr), *n. Slang,* one who does not work; a lounger or idler; **2,** *Colloq.* a moccasinlike sports shoe.

loam (lōm), *n.* a fertile soil of clay mixed with sand and decayed vegetable matter.—*adj.* **loam'y.**

loan (lōn), *n.* **1,** something that is borrowed or lent; esp. a sum of money borrowed to be returned with or without interest; **2,** the act of lending; as, the *loan* of a coat:—*v.t.* and *v.i.* in the U.S., to lend.

loath or **loth** (lōth), *adj.* unwilling; reluctant; as, I was *loath* to go.

loathe (lōth), *v.t.* [loathed, loath-ing], to regard with extreme dislike or disgust; detest; as, I *loathed* the sight of food when I was seasick.—*n.* **loath'ing.**

loath-some (lōth'sum), *adj.* causing disgust; detestable; as, a *loathsome* disease.

lob (lob), *n.* in *cricket,* a slow underhand ball in bowling; in *tennis,* a stroke that sends the ball high so as to pass over an opponent's head. Also used as *v.*

lob-by (lob'i), *n.* [*pl.* lobbies], **1,** a hall or waiting room; **2,** persons who try to influence the votes of members of a law-making body:—*v.i.* [lobbied, lobbying], to try by personal influence to get the votes of members of a legislature for a particular measure.—*n.* **lob'by-ist.**

lobe (lōb), *n.* any rounded projection or part; as, the *lobe* of the ear.

lo-be-li-a (lō-bē'li-a; lō-bel'ya), *n.* a plant with red, blue, or white flowers.

lob-ster (lob'stẽr), *n.* a large shellfish with five pairs of legs, the first developed into powerful pinchers.

lo-cal (lō'k'l), *adj.* **1,** relating to a particular place or places; as, *local* customs; **2,** limited to a certain part of the body; as, a *local* sprain; **3,** of a train, making all stops; **4,** serving a limited district; as, a *local* gas company:—*n.* a train which stops at all stations on a given route.—*adv.* **lo'cal-ly.**—*v.t.* **lo'cal-ize'** (as, to *localize* an

infectious disease).—*n.* **lo'cal-i-za'tion.** (-i-).

lo-cale (lō'kal'; käl'), *n.* a place or locality, esp. with reference to some event or circumstance connected with it.

lo-cal-i-ty (lō-kal'i-ti), *n.* [*pl.* localities], a general region, place, or district; neighbourhood.

lo-cate (lō-kāt'; lō'kāt), *v.t.* [locat-ed, locat-ing], **1,** to settle in a particular spot; as, the firm *located* its office in Toronto; **2,** to mark out and determine the position of; as, to *locate* a gold mine; **3,** to find the position of; as, to *locate* the enemy:—*v.i. Colloq.* to settle in a place.—*n.* **lo-ca'tion.**

loch (lokh), *n. Scottish,* a lake; also, a bay or arm of the sea.

¹lock (lok), *n.* **1,** a curl or tress of hair; **2,** a tuft of wool, silk, etc.

²lock (lok), *n.* **1,** a device for fastening a door, trunk, safe, etc., so that it can be opened only by a special key or a combination of turns of a knob; **2,** an enclosure between two gates in a canal or stream, used in raising or lowering boats from one water level to another; **3,** the mechanism used to fire a gun:—*v.t.* **1,** to fasten or secure with, or as with, a lock; as to *lock* a safe; **2,** to make secure; to confine; to shut in, out, or up; as, to *lock* up a criminal; **3,** to make fast or rigid by the linking of parts; as, to *lock* the wheels of a truck:—*v.i.* to become locked; as, the door *locks* automatically.—*n.* **lock'nut'.**

lock-er (lok'ẽr), *n.* a drawer or compartment secured by a lock; esp. a cupboard for individual use.

lock-et (lok'it), *n.* a small, ornamental, hinged case, usually of gold or silver, made to hold a portrait or other small token, and to be worn on a necklace or chain.

lock-jaw (lok'jô), *n.* a form of the disease tetanus, in which the jaws become firmly locked together.

lock-out (lok'out'), *n.* the refusal of an employer to let his employees come to work unless they agree to his terms.

lock-smith (lok'smith'), *n.* a maker or repairer of locks.

lock-up (lok'up'), *n.* jail.

lo-co-mo-tion (lō'ko-mō'shun), *n.* the act of moving, or ability to move, from place to place.

lo-co-mo-tive (lō'ko-mō'tiv), *adj.* relating to a machine that moves about under its own power:—*n.* a steam or electric engine for drawing railway cars.

lo-co-weed (lō'kō-wēd'), *n.* a poisonous plant of the western U.S., which produces a nervous disease in the horses, cattle, and sheep which eat it.

loc-us (lō'kus), *n.* [*pl.* loci (-sī)], **1,** in *geometry*, a line or curve traced by a moving point; **2,** a place; locality.

lo-cust (lō'kust), *n.* **1,** a grasshopper; esp. one of a certain kind, destructive to vegetation, which migrates in great swarms; **2,** a cicada or seventeen-year locust; **3,** a large North American tree, esp. the common locust, or false acacia, having rough bark and yellow-white flowers; also, its wood; **4,** any of several other trees, as the honey locust.

lo-cu-tion (lō-kū'shun), *n.* a peculiar phrase; idiom; a particular style of speech; as, he used an odd *locution.*

lode (lōd), *n.* **1,** any deposit of metallic ore containing gold, silver, etc., found in a vein or crack in a rock; **2,** a vein filled with ore.

lode-stone (lōd'stōn'), *n.* Same as **load-stone.**

lodge (loj), *v.t.* [lodged, lodg-ing], **1,** to furnish with a temporary dwelling; **2,** to deposit for safety; **3,** to settle, or bring to rest, in some spot; as, the stone was *lodged* on a ledge; **4,** to place formally before the proper authorities; as, to *lodge* a complaint:—*v.i.* **1,** to be deposited or come to rest; **2,** to be a lodger:—*n.* **1,** a small house; cottage; **2,** the den of a wild animal or group of animals; **3,** a place where members of a local branch of a society meet; also, the members themselves.

lodg-er (loj'ẽr), *n.* one who lives in a rented room or apartment in another's house.

lodg-ing (loj'ing), *n.* **1,** a place to sleep; as, *lodging* for the night; **2,** **lodgings,** a room or rooms rented as living quarters.

loft (lôft), *n.* **1,** a room directly beneath a roof; an attic; **2,** a floor or gallery above the main floor; as, a *loft* for hay in a barn; an organ-*loft* in a church; **3,** an upper floor in a warehouse or business building.

loft-y (lôf'ti), *adj.* [loft-i-er, loft-i-est], **1,** very high; as, a *lofty* spire; **2,** dignified; proud; as, a *lofty* manner; **3,** elevated in thought or language; as, *lofty* sentiments.—*adv.* **loft'i-ly.**—*n.* **loft'i-ness.**

log (log), *n.* **1,** a bulky piece of felled timber, usually in its natural or unhewn state; **2,** a heavy, stupid person; **3,** a device consisting of a wooden float on a line and reel, used for measuring the rate of progress of a ship; **4,** a book in which the record of a ship's daily

progress and other items of interest are entered; also called *logbook:*—*v.t.* [logged, log-ging], **1,** to fell and cut into logs, as a tree; **2,** to fell and remove the timber on (a tract of woodland); **3,** to enter in the logbook of a ship:—*v.i.* to cut or transport logs.—*n.* **log'ger.**

lo-gan-ber-ry (lō'gan-bẽr-i), *n.* [*pl.* loganberries], **1,** a plant obtained by crossing the raspberry with the blackberry; **2,** the fruit of this plant.

log-a-rithm (log'a-rith'm; -ri*th*'m), *n.* the exponent, or index, of the power to which a given number must be raised in order to give a required number; as, the *logarithm* of 100 to the base 10 is 2, or of 1000, 3; the *logarithm* of 8 to the base 2 is 3: logarithmic tables are usually computed to the base of 10.

log-book (log'book'), *n.* a ship's diary, or journal, recording its progress, position, daily occurrences, etc.: also called *log.*

loge (lōzh), *n.* a box or compartment, esp. in a theatre or opera house.

log-ger-head (log'ẽr-hed'), *n.* a blockhead.—**to be at loggerheads,** to dispute or quarrel.

log-ic (loj'ik), *n.* **1,** the science or art of reasoning; **2,** correct reasoning.—*n.* **lo-gi'cian** (lō-jish'an).

log-i-cal (loj'i-kal), *adj.* **1,** relating to reasoning; **2,** according to the rules of correct reasoning; as, a *logical* conclusion; reasonable; as, a *logical* explanation; **3,** skilled in reasoning; as, a *logical* thinker.

lo-gis-tics (lō-jis'tiks), *n.* the branch of military science dealing with the moving, quartering, and provisioning of armies.

lo-gy (lō'gi), *adj. Colloq.* dull or sluggish, as from overeating.

loin (loin), *n.* **1,** that part of the body of an animal or man, on either side of the spine, between the lowest rib and the hip-bone; **2,** a special cut of meat from this part of an animal.

loi-ter (loi'tẽr), *v.i.* to linger; saunter; as, don't *loiter* on your way home from school:—*v.t.* to spend idly; as, he *loitered* his time away.—*n.* **loi'ter-er.**

loll (lol), *v.i.* **1,** to lounge at ease; as, to *loll* in a chair; **2,** to hang out loosely; as, the dog's tongue *lolls* out:—*v.t.* to permit (the tongue) to hang out.

lol-li-pop (lol'i-pop), *n.* a lump of hard candy on a stick.

lone (lōn), *adj.* **1,** solitary; as, a *lone* star in the sky; **2,** unfrequented; as, a *lone* road.

lone-ly (lōn'li), *adj.* [lone-li-er, lone-li-est], **1,** solitary; without companions; as, a *lonely* traveller; **2,** not often visited; as, a *lonely* valley; **3,** depressed because alone; lonesome.—*n.* **lone'li-ness.**

lone-some (lōn'sum), *adj.* [lonesom-er, lonesom-est], **1,** lonely; depressed because alone; as, to feel *lonesome;* **2,** desolate; not often visited; as, a *lonesome* place.

¹long (lông), *adj.* **1,** not short; covering great distance from end to end; as, a *long* road; **2,** extended in time; not brief; as, a *long* wait; **3,** far-reaching; as, a *long* memory; **4,** extended (to a specified measure) in space or time; as, a yard *long;* an hour *long;* **5,** of a vowel: **a,** sounded like its name: as, the *long a* in "hate," the *long e* in "eve," the *long u* in "use," etc.; **b,** taking more time to pronounce than the corresponding short sound, as the vowel in "palm" compared with the corresponding short vowel in "what": —*adv.* **1,** to a great length or extent; as, something *long* drawn out; **2,** at a distant point in time; as, *long* before the war; **3,** for a long time; as, to wait *long.* Compounds: **long'boat'; long'-bow'; long'—drawn'; long'hand'; long'head'ed; long'horn'; long'—lived'; long'—range'; long'—suf'fering.**

²long (lông), *v.i.* to desire something eagerly; yearn; as, I *long* to go.

lon-gev-i-ty (lon-jev'i-ti), *n.* great length of life.

long-house (lông'hous'), *n.* the council house or communal dwelling of the Iroquois and of other North American Indian tribes.

long-ing (lông'ing), *n.* an earnest desire; wish; as, a *longing* for wealth.

lon-gi-tude (lon'ji-tūd'), *n.* distance east or west on the earth's surface, measured in degrees, from the meridian of Greenwich, England.

lon-gi-tu-di-nal (lon'ji-tū'di-nal), *adj.* **1,** relating to longitude or to length; **2,** running lengthwise; as, *longitudinal* veins on the wings of an insect.

long-shore-man (lông'shôr'man), *n.* one who works about wharves, as in loading ships.

long—wind-ed (lông'—win'did), *adj.* tedious; long drawn out; tiresome.

look (look), *v.i.* **1,** to direct the eyes upon something; as, to *look* at a picture; **2,** to front or face; as, my windows *look* out on a garden; **3,** to appear; as, she *looks*

happy; **4,** to pay attention; take care; as, *look* before you leap:—*v.t.* **1,** to show by an expression of the face; as, he *looked* his contempt; **2,** to regard or survey with the eyes; as, he *looked* the boy up and down:—*n.* **1,** the act of looking; glance; as, I took a *look* at the picture; **2,** (often *looks*), appearance; **3,** expression of face.

look-er—on (look'ėr-on'), *n.* [*pl.* lookers-on], a bystander; a passive observer.

look-ing—glass (look'ing-glås'), *n.* a mirror.

look-out (look'out'), *n.* **1,** the act of watching for someone to come or something to happen; **2,** a place for watching; **3,** a person engaged in watching.

¹loom (loom), *n.* a frame or machine for weaving cloth.

²loom (loom), *v.i.* to come into view in an indistinct and enlarged form; as, the buildings *loomed* dark above the deserted street.

¹loon (loon), *n.* a fish-eating, diving bird, noted for its shrill cry.

²loon (loon), *n.* a boorish, ignorant person.

loon-y (loon'i), *adj. Slang,* crazy; silly.

loop (loop), *n.* **1,** a folding or doubling of string, rope, etc., forming a ring or eye through which a cord may be run; a noose; **2,** a ring-shaped formation in a line, stream, road, etc.; **3,** a manoeuvre in which an aeroplane makes a circular turn in the air:—*v.t.* to form into, furnish with, or fasten with, loops:—*v.i.* to make a loop.

loop-hole (loop'hōl'), *n.* **1,** a narrow opening in a wall for shooting through, as in a fort; **2,** a means of escape.

loose (loos), *adj.* [loos-er, loos-est], **1,** not held fast; as, a *loose* button; unbound; as, *loose* papers; **2,** free from bonds or fetters, as an escaped criminal; **3,** not tightly fitted; not snug; as, a *loose* garment; **4,** wanting in accuracy or system; as, *loose* logic; **5,** vague; unfounded; as, *loose* ideas; **6,** not close or compact in substance or texture; as, *loose* soil; **7,** lax in principles; unstable morally:—*adv.* in such a manner as not to bind:—*v.t.* [loosed, loos-ing], **1,** to set free; **2,** to relax (one's hold); **3,** to untie; unbind; **4,** to release, as an arrow.—*adv.* **loose'ly.**—*n.* **loose'ness.**

loos-en (loos'n), *v.t.* **1,** to make loose; as, to *loosen* a screw; **2,** to allow to become less rigid; as, to *loosen* discipline:—*v.i.* to become less tight, compact, or firm.

all (ôl), ôr; up, mūte, cûr, cōōl, book; oil, out; th, thin; *th*, the.

loot (lo͞ot), *v.t.* and *v.i.* to rob or plunder; steal:—*n.* booty thus taken.

lop (lop), *v.t.* [lopped, lop-ping], **1,** to cut off, as branches from a tree; **2,** to cut twigs, branches, etc., from; trim.

lope (lōp), *n.* an easy, swinging gait, as of a horse:—*v.i.* [loped, lop-ing], to move with an easy, swinging gait.

lop-sid-ed (lop′sīd′id), *adj.* larger or heavier on one side than on the other; hence, unevenly balanced.

lo-qua-cious (lō-kwā′shus), *adj.* talkative; garrulous.—*n.* **lo-quac′i-ty** (lō-kwas′i-ti).

lord (lôrd), *n.* **1,** a ruler or governor; master; one who has supreme power; **2,** in feudal times, a person from whom a vassal held land and to whom he owed service; **3,** in Great Britain, a nobleman; **4, Lords,** the upper house of the British Parliament:—**the Lord,** God; also, Jesus Christ:—*v.i.* to rule with absolute power.

lord-ly (lôrd′li), *adj.* [lord-li-er, lord-li-est], **1,** suited to, or like, one of high rank; noble; **2,** proud; haughty.

lord-ship (lôrd′ship), *n.* **1,** the territory under the control of a lord; **2,** authority; control; **3,** in England, the rank of a lord:—**Lordship,** in England, a title or term of address to judges and noblemen.

Lord's Sup-per, 1, the last supper partaken of by Jesus with his disciples the night before his crucifixion; **2,** the sacrament of the Holy Communion or Eucharist.

lore (lōr), *n.* knowledge; esp. the body of traditions and facts about a particular subject; as, folk*lore*; bird *lore*.

lor-gnette (lôr′nyet′), *n.* **1,** a pair of eyeglasses fixed to a handle; **2,** a long-handled opera glass.

lorn (lôrn), *adj.* forsaken; desolate; lone.

lor-ry (lor′i), *n.* [*pl.* -ries], **1,** a long, low-wheeled wagon without sides; **2,** a large low autotruck for heavy supplies.

lose (lo͞oz), *v.t.* [lost (lôst), los-ing], **1,** to cease to have, or to be deprived of, as by death, separation, accident, negligence, etc.; as, to *lose* a son; to *lose* a finger; to *lose* money; **2,** to fail to keep or sustain; as, to *lose* one's health, to *lose* interest in one's work; **3,** to wander from; as, to *lose* one's way; **4,** to waste; let go by; as, to *lose* time; to *lose* an opportunity; **5,** to fail to keep in sight or follow mentally; as, to *lose* track of something; **6,** to fail to win; as, to *lose* a battle; **7,** to cause (a

person) the loss of (a thing); as, illness *lost* him his job; **8,** to obscure; submerge; as, the stream *lost* itself in the marsh; **9,** to ruin; destroy; as, the ship was *lost* at sea:—*v.i.* **1,** to experience loss; **2,** to fail of success.—*n.* **los′er.**

loss (lôs), *n.* **1,** the state or fact of being lost or destroyed; as, the *loss* of a ship; also, that which is lost, or its value: opposite of *profit*; as, heavy *losses*; **2,** failure to keep a thing; as, *loss* of wealth; **3,** failure to win or obtain; as, the *loss* of a contract; **4,** waste; as, *loss* of gasoline; **5, losses,** the number of soldiers killed, wounded, or captured in battle.

lost (lôst), *adj.* **1,** missing; as, a *lost* child; **2,** not won; as, a *lost* race; **3,** ruined; destroyed; as, a *lost* soul; **4,** preoccupied; as, *lost* in thought; **5,** wasted; as, *lost* efforts; **6,** no longer visible; as, *lost* in the distance; **7,** insensible; as, *lost* to honour.

lot (lot), *n.* **1,** a method of deciding questions by drawing numbers, or by throwing blocks, dice, etc.; as, to choose by *lot*; also, the object used; **2,** what falls to a person in such a decision; share; also, fortune; one's fate; as, it is not my *lot* to become famous; **3,** a portion or parcel; esp. a plot of land; **4,** a number of objects in a group; as, the store has received a new *lot* of dresses; **5,** *Colloq.* a great deal.

loth (lōth), *adj.* Same as **loath.**

lo-tion (lō′shun), *n.* a liquid preparation for cleansing the skin, healing a wound, etc.

lot-ter-y (lot′ẽr-i), *n.* [*pl.* lotteries], a scheme for distributing prizes by lot to persons holding tickets corresponding to numbers drawn at random.

lot-to (lot′ō), *n.* a game resembling bingo, played with discs, and cards marked in squares.

lo-tus (lō′tus), *n.* **1,** a plant of the water-lily family found in Egypt, or one that is held sacred in India; **2,** in Greek legend, a fruit supposed to cause forgetfulness of care; **3,** a plant of the pea family, with red, pink, or white flowers. Also, **lo′tos.**

loud (loud), *adj.* **1,** not low; as, *loud* music; noisy; as, *loud* streets; **2,** striking; emphatic; as, *loud* protests; **3,** *Colloq.* showy in dress or manner; also, unpleasantly vivid; as, *loud* colours:—*adv.* not in a quiet manner.—*adv.* **loud′ly.**—*n.* **loud′ness.**

loud—speak-er (loud′–spēk′ẽr), *n.* a device on a radio for magnifying sound.

lounge (lounj), *v.i.* [lounged, lounging], to move, act, or recline in a lazy manner:—*n.* 1, a couch or sofa; 2, a comfortable and informal parlour in a hotel, club, etc.—*n.* loung′er.

lour (lour) or **low-er** (lou′ẽr), *v.i.* 1, to appear dark, gloomy, or threatening; as, the sky *loured;* 2, to look sullen; scowl:—*n.* a frown.—*adj.* lour′ing.

louse (lous), *n.* [*pl.* lice (līs)], 1, a small, flat, wingless insect living and feeding on the bodies of animals or men; 2, a similar insect which lives on plants.—*adj.* lous′y (louz′i).

lout (lout), *n.* an awkward fellow; a clown.—*adj.* lout′ish.

lou-vre or **lou-ver** (lōō′vẽr), *n.* any one of a series of slits or openings for light and air, as in gable, automobile, etc.—**louvre boards,** sloping slats to keep rain out but let air and light in.

lov-a-ble (luv′a-bl), *adj.* worthy of love; endearing.—*n.* lov′a-ble-ness.

love (luv), *n.* 1, warm and tender attachment; as, mother *love;* also, passionate devotion; 2, strong liking; as, *love* for music; 3, a sweetheart; 4, in *tennis,* no score:—*v.t.* [loved, lov-ing], 1, to have a feeling of deep affection for; as, I *love* my sisters; 2, to delight in; as, to *love* dancing.—*adj.* love′less; love′sick′.

love-bird (luv′bûrd′), *n.* a species of small African or South American parrot that shows great affection for its mate.

love-lorn (luv′lôrn′), *adj.* pining from love. Also used as *n.*

love-ly (luv′li), *adj.* [love-li-er, love-li-est], 1, beautiful; charming; 2, *Colloq.* delightful; as, *lovely* music.—*n.* love′liness.

lov-er (luv′ẽr), *n.* 1, one who has a deep affection for another of the opposite sex; 2, one who has a great liking for anything.

lov-ing (luv′ing), *adj.* affectionate; devoted; as, a *loving* friend.—*adv.* lov′ing-ly.

lov-ing—kind-ness (luv′ing–kind′nis), *n.* affectionate sympathy; mercy; tenderness.

¹low (lō), *adj.* 1, not high; as, a *low* mound; 2, below the normal level; as, *low* waters; 3, deep in pitch; not loud; as, a *low* voice; 4, near the horizon; as, the sun is *low;* 5, lacking bodily or mental strength; 6, depressed; as, *low*

spirits; 7, relatively small in amount, value, etc.; as, *low* prices; 8, humble; as, a *low* station in life; 9, unfavourable; as, a *low* opinion; 10, vulgar; as, *low* company; 11, slow; as, at *low* speed:—*adv.* 1, not high; as, to fly *low;* 2, at a deep pitch; 3, softly; 4, at a small price; ′5, in humbleness, poverty, or disgrace.—*adj.* low′ly; low′born′; low′brow′ (*Slang*).

²low (lō), *n.* the moo or soft call of cattle:—*v.i.* to moo.

low-boy (lō′boi′), *n.* a chest of drawers, table high, mounted on short legs.

¹low-er (lō′ẽr), *v.t.* 1, to let or bring down; let fall; as, to *lower* a curtain; 2, to reduce in price or value; as, to *lower* the rent; 3, to reduce the height of; as, to *lower* the crown of a hat; 4, to weaken; as, illness *lowers* one's resistance; 5, to humble; as, to *lower* the pride:—*v.i.* to sink; decrease; become less, as in price or value.

²low-er (lō′ẽr), *adj.* [*comp.* of ¹*low*], below in position, rank, or the like; as, a *lower* drawer; *lower* station.

³low-er (lou′ẽr), *v.i.* Same as **lour.**

lower case, in *printing,* the small letters, or letters not capitals (the latter being *upper case*).

low-er-most (lō′ẽr-mōst′), *adj.* lowest: opposite of *uppermost.*

low-land (lō′land), *adj.* pertaining to low, flat country:—*n.* low, level country.

low-li-ness (lō′li-nis), *n.* humbleness.

low-ly (lō′li), *adj.* [low-li-er, low-li-est], humble; modest:—*adv.* modestly; humbly.

loy-al (loi′al), *adj.* 1, faithful, esp. to one's ruler or country; 2, true to friend, promise, or duty; 3, showing faithfulness.—*n.* loy′al-ty.

loy-al-ist (loi′al-ist), *n.* one who supports the authority of his ruler or country, esp. in time of revolt.

loz-enge (loz′enj; inj), *n.* anything diamond-shaped, as a cough drop or candy, pane of glass, shield, etc.

lub-ber (lub′ẽr), *n.* an awkward clumsy fellow; 2, a raw sailor.

lu-bri-cant (lū′bri-kant), *n.* a substance, as oil or grease, for oiling machine parts.

lu-bri-cate (lū′bri-kāt′), *v.t.* [lubricated, lubricat-ing], 1, to make smooth or slippery; 2, to apply oil to in order to reduce friction, as in gears.—*n.* lu′bri-ca′tion.

lu-cent (lū′sent), *adj.* 1, shining; as,

pines half *lucent* in the dawn; **2,** transparent.

lu-cid (lū′sid), *adj.* **1,** clear; readily understood; as, a *lucid* explanation; **2,** characterized by mental soundness or clarity; as, she has *lucid* moments; **3,** clear; transparent; as, *lucid* water.—*n.* **lu-cid′i-ty.**

lu-ci-fer (lū′si-fẽr), *n.* a friction match. —**Lucifer**, Satan.

lu-cite (lū′sīt), *n.* a clear synthetic plastic resin used for reflectors, store fronts, airplane windshields, etc. (trade name).

luck (luk), *n.* **1,** chance; fortune, whether good or bad; **2,** good fortune.

luck-less (luk′lis), *adj.* unfortunate.

luck-y (luk′i), *adj.* [luck-i-er, luck-i-est], **1,** having good fortune; as, a *lucky* mortal; **2,** turning out well; as, a *lucky* venture; a *lucky* day.—*n.* **luck′i-ness.**—*adv.* **luck′i-ly.**

lu-cra-tive (lū′kra-tiv), *adj.* profitable; money-making; as, a *lucrative* business.

lu-cre (lū′kẽr; lōō′kẽr), *n.* money; profits.

lu-di-crous (lū′di-krus), *adj.* ridiculous.

luff (luf), *v.i.* **1,** to sail close into the wind (usually with sails shaking); as, to *luff* past a buoy.—*n.* the forward edge, or weather leech, of a fore-and-aft sail.

lug (lug), *v.t.* [lugged, lug-ging], to pull, draw, or carry, with effort; as, there goes Mary, *lugging* a suitcase.—*n.* a projecting piece to support or carry something, as a tractor with *lugs;* (*Colloq.*) the ear.

lug-gage (lug′ij), *n.* baggage.

lug-ger (lug′ẽr), *n.* a vessel with one or more lugsails.

lug-sail (lug′sāl′), *n.* a four-sided sail held out by a yard, which is slung obliquely to the mast.

lu-gu-bri-ous (lū-gū′bri-us), *adj.* sad; mournful; as, a *lugubrious* air, tone(s), etc.

luke-warm (lōōk′wôrm′; lūk′), *adj.* **1,** moderately warm; **2,** indifferent; not enthusiastic.

lull (lul), *v.t.* and *v.i.* to make or become quiet:—*n.* a lessening of noise or violence; temporary calm; as, a *lull* in a storm.

lull-a-by (lul′a-bī′), *n.* [*pl.* lullabies], a song to lull small children to sleep.

lum-ba-go (lum-bā′gō), *n.* rheumatic pain in the muscles of the lower back.

lum-bar (lum′bär), *n.* and *adj.* the regions of the lower back, or loins; as, a *lumbar* nerve or vertebra.

¹lum-ber (lum′bẽr), *n.* **1,** timber that has been sawn into boards, planks, etc.; **2,** rubbish; articles of no value:—*v.i.* to cut and prepare timber for market:—*v.t.* to clutter; as, please don't *lumber* up this room.—*n.* **lum′ber-ing; lum′-ber-jack′; lum′ber-man; lum′ber-yard′.**

²lum-ber (lum′bẽr), *v.i.* to roll heavily along; as, the lorry *lumbered* up the hill.

lu-mi-nar-y (lū′mi-nẽr-i), *n.* [*pl.* luminaries], **1,** a light-giving body, such as the sun or moon; **2,** a person who is a shining light, or leader, in his field.

lu-mi-nous (lū′mi-nus), *adj.* **1,** giving light; bright; as, *luminous* stars; **2,** easily understood; as, a *luminous* remark.—*n.* **lu′mi-nos′i-ty.**

lump (lump), *n.* **1,** a small, shapeless mass; as, a *lump* of clay; **2,** a swelling —*v.t.* to unite in one body or amount as, to *lump* expenses:—*v.i.* to form into a mass.

lump-ish (lump′ish), *adj.* heavy; dull

lump-y (lump′i), *adj.* [lump-i-er, lump i-est], **1,** full of lumps; as, *lumpy* bread **2,** like a lump; lumpish.

lu-na-cy (lū′na-si), *n.* [*pl.* lunacies] insanity; also, extreme foolishness.

lu-nar (lū′nẽr), *adj.* relating to the moon.

lu-na-tic (lū′na-tik), *adj.* **1,** foolish utterly absurd; as, *lunatic* notions; **2,** relating to the insane; as, a *lunati* asylum:—*n.* an insane person.

lunch (lunch), *n.* a light meal, usually eaten between breakfast and dinner luncheon:—*v.i.* to eat a lunch.—*n* **lunch′room′.**

lunch-eon (lun′chun), *n.* a light mea between breakfast and dinner; lunch often, a lunch to which guests ar invited.

lu-nette (lū-net′), *n.* a crescent-shape space, often containing a mural, staine glass, etc., above a door or window, o placed in a dome or ceiling.

lung (lung), *n.* either of the two organ of breathing in man and other air breathing animals.

lunge (lunj), *n.* **1,** a sudden thrust o pass with a fencing foil or a sword; **2,** sudden leap:—*v.i.* [lunged, lung-ing], to make a sudden thrust; **2,** to plung forward.

¹lu-pine (lū′pin), *n.* **1,** a garden plan

of the pea family with blue, purple, yellow, or white flowers; **2,** the flower of this plant.

²lu-pine (lū'pīn), *adj.* wolflike; savage.

¹lurch (lûrch), *n.* a sudden roll to one side; as, the *lurch* of a ship; a swaying, staggering motion:—*v.i.* to stagger; as, the drunken man *lurched* down the street.

²lurch (lûrch), *n.* a difficult, embarrassing situation: used only in *to leave in the lurch.*

lure (lūr), *n.* **1,** anything that attracts by promising profit or pleasure; **2,** a decoy; artificial bait; **3,** attraction; as, the *lure* of adventure:—*v.t.* [lured, lur-ing], to tempt with promise of profit or pleasure.

lu-rid (lū'rid), *adj.* **1,** ghastly; pale; **2,** shining with a red glow; as, a *lurid* sky; **3,** shockingly vivid; as, a *lurid* tale.

lurk (lûrk), *v.i.* **1,** to stay secretly in or about a place; as, the thief *lurked* in the shrubbery until the police had gone; **2,** to move about stealthily; **3,** to exist in secret; as, resentment *lurked* in his heart.

lus-cious (lush'us), *adj.* **1,** sweet and delicious; as, a *luscious* peach; **2,** pleasing to smell, hear, see, or feel.

lush (lush), *adj.* rich in growth or vegetation; as, *lush* meadows.

lust (lust), *n.* **1,** a strong, urgent desire to possess; as, a *lust* for gold; **2,** sinful, impure desire:—*v.i.* **1,** to have a very strong desire; as, he *lusted* for power; **2,** to be filled with impure desire.—*adj.* lust'ful.

lust-i-ly (lus'ti-li), *adv.* heartily; with vigour or energy.

lus-tre or **lus-ter** (lus'tėr), *n.* **1,** the quality of shining by reflected light; gloss; **2,** brightness; **3,** splendour; renown; **4,** a kind of pottery with a gleaming, metallic finish.

lus-trous (lus'trus), *adj.* gleaming; brilliant; as, *lustrous* eyes.

lust-y (lus'ti), *adj.* [lust-i-er, lust-i-est], vigorous; healthy.

lute (lūt), *n.* a stringed musical instrument with a body like that of a mandolin.

lux-a-tion (luk-sā'shun), *n.* dislocation (of a joint):—*v.t.* lux'ate.

luxe (lüks), *n. French,* (of) fine quality or elegance; as, a *de luxe* automobile.

lux-u-ri-ant (lug-zhoor'i-ant; luks-ū'ri-ant), *adj.* **1,** abundant and vigorous in growth; **2,** profuse or elaborate.—*n.* lux-u'ri-ance.

lux-u-ri-ate (lug-zhoor'i-āt'; luks-ū'ri-āt'), *v.i.* [luxuriat-ed, luxuriating], **1,** to grow abundantly; **2,** to revel without restraint.

lux-u-ri-ous (lug-zhoor'i-us; luks-ū'ri-us), *adj.* **1,** having a strong taste for costly pleasures or ease; **2,** lavishly furnished and comfortable; as, a *luxurious* hotel.

lux-u-ry (luk'shoo-ri; lug'zhoo-ri), *n.* [*pl.* luxuries], **1,** indulgence in costly pleasure or ease; **2,** something costly or difficult to get; **3,** anything beyond the merest necessity.

lye (lī), *n.* an alkali obtained from wood ashes, used in cleaning, making soap, etc.

ly-ing (lī'ing), *n.* the act of telling lies; untruthfulness:—*adj.* untruthful.

lymph (limf), *n.* a transparent, colourless fluid in animal bodies, carried in vessels called *lymphatics.*

lym-phat-ic (lim-fat'ik), *adj.* relating to, or carrying, lymph:—*n.* a tiny vessel which carries lymph.

lynch (linch), *v.t.* to hang or put to death, without legal trial.

lynx (lingks), *n.* a large, fierce wildcat with short tail, tufted ears, and valuable fur.

lyre (līr), *n.* a harplike musical instrument used by the ancients to accompany singing.

lyr-ic (lir'ik), *adj.* suggesting song; like, or relating to, a song-like poem:—*n.* **1,** a short, musical poem expressing personal feelings; **2,** in music: **a,** a short, melodious song; **b,** in a musical play, the words of a song. Also, *adj.* lyr'i-cal.

LYRE

ly-sol (lī'sôl), *n.* a disinfectant and germicide made of soap dissolved in a coal-tar oil (a trade name).

M

M, m (em), *n.* [*pl.* M's, m's], **1,** the 13th letter of the alphabet, following L; **2,** the Roman numeral for 1,000.

ma (ma), *n. Colloq.* mamma; mother.

mac-ad-am (mak-ad'am), *n.* **1,** a roadway or pavement of crushed stone, usually with oil or tar for binding; **2,** crushed stone for such a road:—*v.t.* **mac-ad′am-ize.**

mac-a-ro-ni (mak′a-rō′ni), *n.* [*pl.* macaronies or macaronis], **1,** a food made of a flour paste dried in long, thin tubes; **2,** a dandy.

mac-a-roon (mak′a-rōōn′), *n.* a small cake made of white of egg, crushed almonds, and sugar.

ma-caw (ma-kô′), *n.* a large, gaily coloured tropical American parrot with a strong, hooked bill, a long tail, and a harsh voice.

¹**mace** (mās), *n.* **1,** a large and heavy club, often spiked, formerly used as a war club; **2,** a staff carried by or before an official as a symbol of power; **3,** the bearer of such a staff.

²**mace** (mās), *n.* a fragrant spice ground from the dried outer covering of the nutmeg.

ma-che-te (mä-chä′tä; ma-shet′), *n.* a large heavy knife, sometimes several feet in length, used in Cuba and South MACHETE America as a weapon and for cutting sugar-cane.

mach-i-na-tion (mak′i-nā′shun), *n.* a plotting or scheming to do evil; as, the *machinations* of an enemy.

ma-chine (ma-shēn′), *n.* **1,** any contrivance or apparatus designed to produce or utilize power or energy; also, a mechanism which lightens human labour; as, a sewing-*machine;* **2,** a vehicle, esp. an automobile; **3,** one who acts without intelligence or with unfailing regularity; **4,** an organization which controls the policies of a political party.—*n.* **ma-chin′ist.**

ma-chin-er-y (ma-shēn′ėr-i), *n.* **1,** machines collectively; as, the *machinery* in a factory; also, the parts of a machine; as, the *machinery* of a clock; **2,** any means by which something is kept in action or a desired result is gained; as, the *machinery* of law enforcement.

mack-er-el (mak′ėr-el), *n.* [*pl.* mackerel], a food fish, from twelve to eighteen inches in length, found in schools in the North Atlantic:— **mackerel sky,** a sky covered with small white flecks of cloud.

mack-i-naw (mak′i-nô′), *n.* **1,** a short, double-breasted coat of thick plaid, woollen material; **2,** a blanket of such material in bright colours, used by Indians, lumbermen, etc., of northern U.S. and Canada.

mack-in-tosh (mak′in-tosh), *n.* a waterproof overcoat.

mac-ro— (mak′rō–), a Greek *prefix* signifying *large* or *great,* as in *macro*cosm, *macro*physics, *macro*scopic opposite of *micro*–.

ma-cron (mā′kron; ma), *n.* a mark [¯] over a vowel to show that it is pronounced long, as the *a* in *fate* (fāt).

mad (mad), *adj.* [mad-der, mad-dest], **1,** mentally disordered; insane; **2,** rashly foolish; as, he is *mad* to try to swim across the lake; **3,** carried away by strong feeling; excited; as, *mad* with delight; *mad* about antiques; **4,** rabid as, a *mad* dog: **5,** wild; as, a *mad* rush; **6,** *Colloq.* angry.—*adv.* **mad′ly**

mad-am (mad′am), *n.* [*pl.* mesdames (mā/dàm/)], a complimentary title or form of courteous address to a lady.

mad-ame (mà/dàm′; mad′am), *n.* [*pl.* mesdames (mā/dàm′)], the French title of address to a married woman.

mad-cap (mad′kap′), *n.* a wild thoughtless, impulsive person:—*adj.* given to wild follies; reckless.

mad-den (mad′n), *v.t.* and *v.i.* to make or become, crazed or furious.

made (mād), *p.t.* and *p.p.* of *make.*

ma-de-moi-selle (màd′mwä′zel′ mad′à-ma-zel′; *Colloq.* màm/zel′), *n.* [*pl.* mesdemoiselles (mād′mwä/zel/)] Miss: a French title of address to an unmarried woman.

mad-man (mad′man), *n.* [*pl.* madmen (-men)], a lunatic; an insane person

mad-ness (mad′nis), *n.* **1,** insanity; **2** great foolishness; as, it was *madness* to walk so far; **3,** great anger; rage.

Ma-don-na (ma-don′a), *n.* [Italian my lady], a picture or statue of the Virgin Mary.

mad-ri-gal (mad′ri-gl), *n.* **1,** a short love poem; **2,** a musical setting for such a poem, written for three to eight or more voices, without any instrumental accompaniment.

mael-strom (māl′strom), *n.* **1,** a large violent whirlpool; **2,** any widespread destructive influence; as, the *maelstrom* of war: **the Maelstrom,** a dangerous whirlpool off the northwest coast of Norway.

ma-es-tro (mīs′trō; mä-es′trō), *n.* a master of an art, esp. a great musical composer, conductor, or teacher.

mag-a-zine (mag′a-zēn′), *n.* **1,** (often mag′a-zēn′), a publication, containing articles, stories, poems, etc., and issued at regular times; **2,** a place for storing military supplies; as, a powder-*magazine;* **3,** a warehouse; **4,** a chamber in a gun containing a supply of cartridges.

ma-gen-ta (ma-jen′ta), *n.* a red dye made from coal-tar; also, its peculiar shade of purplish red.

mag-got (mag′ut), *n.* **1,** the wormlike larva of an insect, esp. the house-fly, often found in decaying flesh, food, etc.; a grub; **2,** a caprice; notion; whim.—*adj.* **mag′got-y.**

Ma-gi (mā′jī), *n.pl.* [sing. Magus (mā′gus)], the wise men who came from the East to see the child Jesus.

mag-ic (maj′ik), *n.* **1,** the art, or pretended art, of compelling supernatural forces, as demons or spirits, to do one's bidding in the natural world: a part of all primitive religions; sorcery; witchcraft; **2,** any unexplainable, bewitching power; as, the *magic* of music; **3,** sleight-of-hand:—*adj.* pertaining to, produced by, or having magic; as, a *magic* touch.—*adj.* **mag′i-cal.**

ma-gi-cian (ma-jish′an), *n.* one skilled in magic; a wizard; sorcerer.

mag-is-trate (maj′is-trāt), *n.* **1,** a government official; **2,** a justice of the peace.—*n.* **mag′is-tra-cy** (maj′is-tra-si).—*adj.* **mag′is-te′ri-al.**

mag-ma (mag′ma), *n.* in *geology,* the molten, fluid matter deep in the earth from which igneous rock is formed: when ejected from volcanoes it is called *lava.*

mag-nan-i-mous (mag-nan′i-mus), *adj.* great of mind; above pettiness; generous; noble.—*n.* **mag′na-nim′i-ty.**

mag-nate (mag′nāt), *n.* a person of rank or importance; esp. a man of power in an industry; as, an oil *magnate.*

mag-ne-sia (mag-nē′sha; mag-nē′zha), *n.* a white, tasteless, earthy powder, used as a medicine.

mag-ne-si-um (mag-nē′zhi-um; shi-), *n.* a light, silver-white metallic element used in alloys for airplane construction; used also in flash bulbs as it burns with a hot, white light.

mag-net (mag′nit), *n.* **1,** loadstone, a variety of iron ore which has the property of attracting iron; **2,** a bar of iron or steel to which the power of attracting iron or steel has been artificially given; **3,** a person or thing that attracts. MAGNET

mag-net-ic (mag-net′ik), *adj.* **1,** relating to a magnet, or its power of attraction; **2,** relating to the earth's magnetism; **3,** having the power to attract; winning; as, a *magnetic* smile:—**magnetic needle,** a light needle of magnetized steel, which, when suspended in a compass, points in the direction of the earth's magnetism, which is approximately north and south:—**magnetic field,** the space around a magnet or an electric current occupied by magnetic lines of force:—**magnetic pole, 1,** either pole of a magnet where the lines of force converge; **2,** the **North Magnetic Pole,** just northwest of Hudson Bay: it is not fixed, but extends over an elliptical zone about 50 miles long: it is moving from Prince of Wales Island and should reach Bathurst Island in the 1970's.

BAR MAGNET
Showing lines of force in the magnetic field.

mag-net-ism (mag′ne-tizm), *n.* **1,** the property of a substance, naturally possessed by some substances, as loadstone, and artificially given to others, as iron or steel, of attracting certain substances according to fixed, physical laws; **2,** the science of magnetism; **3,** personal charm.—*v.t.* **mag′net-ize′.**

mag-ne-to (mag-nē′tō), [*n. pl.* magnetos], a small dynamo, with permanent magnets, for generating electric current.

mag-nif-i-cent (mag-nif′i-sent), *adj.* **1,** grand in appearance; splendid; as, a *magnificent* display of jewels; **2,** sublime; noble; as, a *magnificent* idea.—*adv.* **mag-nif′i-cent-ly.**—*n.* **mag-nif′i-cence.**

mag-ni-fy (mag′ni-fī), *v.t.* [magnified, magnify-ing], **1,** to cause to appear larger in size; as, a microscope *magnifies* objects seen through it; **2,** to exaggerate; as, he *magnifies* the danger.

mag-nil-o-quent (mag-nil′o-kwent), *adj.* pompous in style or speech; boastful.

mag-ni-tude (mag′ni-tūd′), *n.* **1,** greatness of size; as, the *magnitude* of a mountain; **2,** importance; as, the *magnitude* of Columbus's discovery was not recognized.

mag-no-li-a (mag-nō′li-a; mag-nōl′-ya), *n.* an ornamental tree, with shiny, dark-green leaves, large white or pink flowers, and cone-shaped fruit. It grows in Asia and North America.

mag-pie (mag′pī′), *n.* **1,** a black-and-white bird of the crow family, noted for its incessant chatter; **2,** hence, one who talks continuously; a chatterer.

ma-ha-ra-jah (mä′ha-rä′ja), *n.* in India, the title of a sovereign native prince. Also, **ma′ha-ra′ja.**—*n. fem.* **ma′ha-ra′ni; ma′ha-ra′nee.**

ma-hog-a-ny (ma-hog′a-ni), *n.* [*pl.* mahoganies], the hard, usually reddish-brown wood of a tropical American tree, used for fine furniture; also, the tree.

Ma-hom-et (ma-hom′it), *n.* Same as **Mohammed.**

ma-hout (ma-hout′), *n.* in the East Indies, an elephant driver or keeper.

maid (mād), *n.* **1,** a girl or unmarried woman; **2,** a female servant.

maid-en (mād′n), *n.* a girl or unmarried woman; a maid:—*adj.* **1,** not married; as, a *maiden* lady; **2,** pure; unsoiled; **3,** earliest or first; as, a *maiden* voyage; **4,** unused; untried; as, a *maiden* sword.—*adj.* and *adv.* **maid′en-ly.**

maid-en-hair (mād′n-hâr′), *n.* **1,** a delicate fern found in damp and shady woods; **2,** the gingko.

¹mail (māl), *n.* **1,** body armour of steel rings, net, or scales; hence, plate or other armour; **2,** the shell-like protective coat of some animals, as the turtle.

²mail (māl), *n.* **1,** the letters, newspapers, packages, etc., delivered by post; **2,** the government system for carrying letters, packages, etc.; **3,** something that carries the mail, as an aeroplane or boat:—*v.t.* to post, or send by post; as, to *mail* a letter.

maim (mām), *v.t.* to deprive of the use; of any necessary part of the body; cripple.

main (mān), *adj.* **1,** chief; principal; as, the *main* street; the *main* reason; **2,** sheer; as, by *main* strength:—*n.* **1,** any wide expanse; esp. the sea; as, to sail the *main;* **2,** strength: now used only in the phrase *with might and main;* **3,** a principal conduit or pipe; as, a water-*main.*

main-land (mān′land′; mān′land), *n.* a continent; a broad stretch of land as contrasted with the islands off its coast.

main-ly (mān′li), *adv.* principally; chiefly; for the most part.

main-mast (mān′mast; mān′màst′), *n.* the chief mast of a ship; in vessels of more than two masts, the second mast from the bow.

main-sail (mān′sāl′; mān′sl), *n.* **1,** in a square-rigged vessel, the lowest and largest sail on the mainmast; **2,** in a fore-and-aft rigged vessel, the big sail on the mainmast.

main-spring (mān′spring′), *n.* **1,** the principal spring, or driving spring, in a mechanism, such as a trigger or watch; **2,** a chief motive or reason.

main-stay (mān′stā′), *n.* **1,** any of the large, strong ropes supporting the mainmast of a ship; **2,** the chief support; as, the *mainstay* of a cause.

main-tain (mān-tān′), *v.t.* **1,** to support or bear the expense of; as, many Canadian provinces *maintain* a university; **2,** to sustain; keep unimpaired; as, to *maintain* a reputation; **3,** to continue; keep up; as, to *maintain* a war; **4,** to affirm and defend by argument, as a claim; **5,** to retain possession of; hold to, as a belief.

main-te-nance (mān′ti-nans), *n.* **1,** the act of sustaining or defending; support; **2,** means of support; food and other necessities.

maize (māz), *n.* Indian corn; field corn; also, its grain.

ma-jes-tic (ma-jes′tik) or **ma-jes-ti-cal** (ma-jes′ti-kal), *adj.* having great dignity of person or appearance; stately.

maj-es-ty (maj′es-ti), *n.* [*pl.* majesties], sovereign power or dignity; royal stateliness:—**Majesty,** the title of a sovereign ruler; as, His *Majesty,* the King.

ma-jor (mā′jẽr), *adj.* greater in number, extent, dignity, or quality; as, he worked the *major* part of a day:—**major scale,** in music, the most commonly used scale, consisting of eight tones arranged at intervals of a step or a half step:—*n.* **1,** a military officer next in rank above a captain; **2,** the course of study in which a student specializes:—*v.i.* to specialize in a certain subject; as, he *majored* in history.

ma-jor-i-ty (ma-jor′i-ti), *n.* [*pl.* majorities], **1,** the greater of two numbers looked upon as parts of a whole; also, the difference between this greater number and the smaller; as, in the class election she won by 24 to 18, a *majority* of six; **2,** the full legal age of 21 years.

make (māk), *v.t.* [made (mād), mak-ing], **1,** to build; create; fashion; as, to *make* a dress; **2,** to prepare for use; as, to *make* a garden or a bed; **3,** to get; win; as, to *make* friends; **4,** to profit or gain; clear; as, to *make* five dollars; also, to score; as, we *made* ten points in the game; **5,** to arrive at; draw near or into sight of; as, the ship *made* Halifax; **6,** to cause to be or become; as, the club *made* him president; you *make* me happy; **7,** to cause; compel; as, to *make* a child behave; **8,** to perform; as, to *make* a gesture; **9,** to carry on, as war; **10,** to amount to; as, two and two *make* four; **11,** in electricity, to complete or close (a circuit):—*v.i.* **1,** to move; as, he *made* toward the goal; **2,** to prepare; as, to *make* ready for a journey; **3,** to act in a certain manner; as, to *make* merry:—*n.* **1,** character; style; build; **2,** brand; act or method of manufacture; as, this car is of a well-known *make;* **3,** the completion of an electric circuit.

make—be-lieve (māk'–bi-lēv'), *n.* pretence; pretending, as in the play of children:—*adj.* pretended; false.

mak-er (māk'ėr), *n.* a composer, producer, or creator: — **Maker,** the Creator.

make-shift (māk'shift'), *n.* a thing which can be used for the time being until something better is obtained:— *adj.* temporary; as, a box may be used as a *makeshift* table.

make—up (māk'–up'), *n.* **1,** the way the parts of anything are put together; as, the make-up of a team; **2,** the dress, grease-paint, powder, etc., used by an actor for the part he is to play; **3,** the personality or character of a person.

mal- (mal-), *prefix,* meaning *bad, ill, evil,* as in *mal*administration, *mal*adjusted, *mal*formation, *mal*nutrition, *mal*odorous, *mal*practice, *mal*treat.

mal-a-droit (mal'a-droit'), *adj.* lacking skill; awkward; bungling.

mal-a-dy (mal'a-di), *n.* [*pl.* maladies], a mental or physical disease or ailment.

ma-la-mute or **ma-le-mute** (ma'la-mūt'), *n.* a powerful breed of dog or husky native to arctic regions like Yukon, Alaska, etc.: it has a thick black-and-white or gray furry coat.

ma-lar-i-a (ma-lâr'i-a), *n.* a disease caused by a parasite left in the blood by the bite of certain mosquitoes, and characterized by chills and fever.—*adj.* **ma-lar'i-al.**

mal-con-tent (mal'kon-tent'), *adj.* discontented, esp. with established authority:—*n.* one who is discontented with the established order of things.

male (māl), *adj.* **1,** pertaining to the sex that begets young; **2,** consisting of men or boys; masculine; as, a *male* choir:—

n. a human being, animal, or plant of this sex.

mal-e-dic-tion (mal'e-dik'shun), *n.* **1,** a curse; **2,** slander.

mal-e-fac-tor (mal'i-fak'tėr), *n.* a wrongdoer; a criminal.—*n.* **mal'e-fac'tion.**

mal-e-mute (ma'le-mūt'), *n.* Same as malamute.

ma-lev-o-lent (ma-lev'o-lent), *adj.* wishing evil or injury to others; spiteful.—*adv.* **ma-lev'o-lent-ly.**—*n.* **ma-lev'o-lence.**

mal-ice (mal'is), *n.* evil desire to injure others; ill will.

ma-li-cious (ma-lish'us), *adj.* **1,** bearing ill will; filled with hatred or spite; **2,** arising from ill will; as, a *malicious* act.

ma-lign (ma-līn'), *v.t.* to speak of spitefully; slander; as, to *malign* an innocent person:—*adj.* **1,** possessed of an evil disposition; malicious; **2,** tending to injure; as, *malign* influences.—*n.* **ma-lign'er.**

ma-lig-nant (ma-lig'nant), *adj.* **1,** feeling or showing ill will; doing evil; malicious; **2,** in medical usage, tending to produce death; as, a *malignant* tumour.—*n.* **ma-lig'ni-ty.**—*n.* **ma-lig'-nan-cy.**

ma-lin-ger (ma-ling'gėr), *v.i.* to feign or pretend illness to escape a duty; shirk.—*n.* **ma-lin'ger-er.**

mall (môl), *n.* **1,** a public walk shaded by trees; **2,** a mallet or maul.

mal-lard (mal'ėrd), *n.* a large wild duck, esp. the male, which is marked by a greenish-black head.

mal-le-a-ble (mal'i-a-bl), *adj.* capable of being hammered or rolled out without being broken; as, gold and silver are *malleable* metals.

mal-let (mal'it), *n.* **1,** a short-handled hammer with a wooden head, used to drive a wedge or chisel; **2,** a wooden stick, hammerlike at one end, used for driving the balls in croquet or polo.

mal-low (mal'ō), *n.* a plant with showy, five-petalled flowers of pink, purple, white, or yellow colour.

malt (môlt), *n.* barley or other grain which has been sprouted in water and then dried for use in brewing:—*v.t.* to make into, or with, malt:—*adj.* made with malt; as, beer and ale are *malt* liquors.

Mal-tese (môl-tēz'), *adj.* of, or relating to, Malta; as, *Maltese* cat (with slate-gray fur); *Maltese* cross (with four equal, wide-notched ends).

malt-ose (môl′tōs), *n.* a white sugary substance, like glucose; grape sugar.

mam-bo (mam′bō), *n.* a ballroom dance of Cuban-Negro origin in 4/4 syncopated time, the 2nd and 4th beats being heavily accented. Also used as *v.*

mam-ma or **ma-ma** (mä′mä), *n.* mother.

mam-mal (mam′al), *n.* a member of that group of animals which feed their young by means of milk glands, or mammae. Most of the common, four-footed, furry or hairy animals, as well as elephants, human beings, bats, and whales, are mammals.

mam-ma-ry (mam′a-ri), *adj.* pertaining to the breasts, or mammae.

mam-mon (mam′un), *n.* wealth; worldly gain:—**Mammon,** greed; the god of greed.

mam-moth (mam′uth), *n.* an enormous prehistoric elephant: —*adj.* gigantic; huge; as, the pageant was a *mammoth* production.

SKELETON OF MAMMOTH ($\frac{1}{160}$)

m a m - m y (mam′i), *n.* [*pl.* mammies], **1,** mother: a childish name; **2,** in the U.S., a Negro servant or nurse entrusted with the care of children.

man (man), *n.* [*pl.* men (men)], **1,** a human being; also, the human race; mankind; **2,** an adult male of the human race; an adult male person; **3,** a male servant; valet; **4,** one possessed of manly qualities in a high degree; **5,** one of the pieces in chess, chequers, etc.; also, a player in a game, whether male or female; **6,** a husband; as, *man* and wife:—*v.t.* [manned, man-ning], **1,** to furnish with men; as, to *man* a ship; **2,** to brace or nerve (oneself); as, he *manned* himself for the unpleasant task.

man-a-cle (man′a-kl), *n.* a handcuff; fetter:—*v.t.* [mana-cled, mana-cling], to place handcuffs upon; put into chains.

man-age (man′ij), *v.t.* [managed, man-aging], **1,** to carry on; conduct; as, to *manage* a store; **2,** to govern; make obedient, as a child; **3,** to bring about by clever means; contrive; as, he *managed* an escape.—*adj.* **man′age-a-ble.**

man-age-ment (man′ij-ment), *n.* **1,** the act of directing or controlling; as, skilful *management* saves money; **2,** skill in controlling or directing; **3,** those in charge of a business or enterprise; as, the *management* chooses the store decorations.

man-ag-er (man′ij-ėr), *n.* **1,** one who directs or conducts anything; as, the *manager* of a store; **2,** a person who conducts business or household affairs with skill and economy.—*adj.* **man′a-ge′ri-al.**

man-a-kin (man′a-kin), *n.* Same as **man′i-kin.**

man-da-rin (man′da-rin), *n.* **1,** in China, a high official belonging to any one of nine grades, distinguished by a kind of button worn on the cap; **2,** a kind of small orange, with easily detachable rind and sweet pulp.

man-date (man′dāt; man′dit), *n.* **1,** a command; an official order; **2,** formerly a charge from the League of Nations to a member nation authorizing it to govern conquered territory; also, an area so governed; **3,** political instructions from voters to their representatives in a legislature.—*adj.* **man′da-tor-y** (man′da-tėr-i).

man-di-ble (man′di-bl), *n.* **1,** a jawbone, usually the lower; **2,** in birds, the upper or lower part of the beak; **3,** in insects or shellfish, one of the biting jaws.

man-do-lin (man′do-lin′), *n.* a musical instrument with a pear-shaped soundbox and metal strings arranged in pairs. Also, **man-do-line′** (man-do-lēn′).

man-drake (man′drāk), *n.* **1,** a plant of the nightshade family with a very large, forked root and a white or purple flower; **2,** in the U.S., the May-apple, a low-growing plant of the barberry family.

man-drel or **man-dril** (man′dril), *n.* **1,** a tight-fitting, cone-shaped (or cylindrical) piece of metal for holding something while it is being machined or turned, as in a lathe; **2,** a similar core used in forging, wire-winding, etc.

man-drill (man′dril), *n.* the blue-nosed baboon of West Africa: one of the largest and most ferocious of the baboons.

mane (mān), *n.* the long hair on or about the neck of certain animals, as the horse and the lion.

ma-neu-ver (ma-nōō′vėr; ma-nū′vėr), *n.* Same as **manœuvre.**

man-ful (man′fool), *adj.* courageous; bravely determined.—*adv.* **man′ful-ly.**

man-ga-nese (mang′ga-nēz′), *n.* a hard, brittle, gray-white metallic element used in hardening steel, alloys, etc.

mange (mānj), *n.* a contagious skin-disease of domestic animals and sometimes man, caused by parasites.—*adj.* **man'gy.**

man-gel (mang'gl) or **man-gold** (mang'gold), *n.* a coarse variety of beet grown as food for cattle (now largely replaced in Canada by fodder corn).

man-ger (mān'jėr), *n.* a feeding-trough for horses or cattle.

¹**man-gle** (mang'gl), *n.* a machine for ironing cloth, esp. damp linen, between hot rollers:—*v.t.* [man-gled, man-gling], to iron in a mangle, as tablecloths, sheets, etc.

²**man-gle** (mang'gl), *v.t.* [man-gled, man-gling], **1,** to cut to pieces; maim; mutilate by cutting or hacking; **2,** to spoil in the making or doing.—*n.* **man'gler.**

man-go (mang'gō), *n.* [*pl.* mangoes or mangos], **1,** a tropical tree bearing a pear-shaped, juicy, yellow-red, edible fruit; **2,** the fruit.

man-grove (mang'grōv), *n.* a genus of tropical shore tree or shrub that spreads densely in swampy ground by sending down prop roots.

manhole (man'hōl'), *n.* an opening by which workmen enter a tank or sewer.

man-hood (man'hood), *n.* **1,** the state of being a man; **2,** men collectively; as, the *manhood* of a nation; **3,** the qualities belonging to a man; courage; bravery.

ma-ni-a (mā'ni-a; mān'ya), *n.* **1,** insanity marked by excitement and violence; **2,** excessive enthusiasm; a craze; as, a *mania* for collecting stamps.

ma-ni-ac (mā'ni-ak), *adj.* affected with insanity; raving; as, a *maniac* fury:— *n.* a madman.—*adj.* **ma-ni'a-cal** (ma-nī'a-kal).

ma-nic (man'ik), *adj.* Medical, of (or having) madness; as, he is a *manic* depressive (one who alternates between fits of mania and depression).

man-i-cure (man'i-kūr'), *n.* **1,** the care of the hands and fingernails; **2,** one whose business is caring for people's hands and fingernails:—*v.t.* [manicured, manicur-ing], to care for (hands and fingernails).—*n.* **man'i-cur'ist.**

man-i-fest (man'i-fest), *adj.* clear; apparent to the sight or understanding; as, the truth of that statement is *manifest*:—*v.t.* **1,** to make clear; show; as, to *manifest* anger; **2,** to show the list of (a ship's cargo):—*n.* the list of a

cargo to be shown to the custom-house officials.

man-i-fes-ta-tion (man'i-fes-tā'shun), *n.* a revelation, display, or proof of the existence or nature of something; as, the *manifestation* of political feeling.

man-i-fes-to (man'i-fes'tō), *n.* [*pl.* -toes (tōz)], a public proclamation or declaration of political measures, intentions, principles, etc.; as, a dictator's *manifesto.*

man-i-fold (man'i-fōld), *adj.* **1,** various in kind or quality; numerous; as, *manifold* favours; **2,** comprehensive; as, *manifold* wisdom:—*v.t.* to make many copies of by means of a duplicating machine:—*n.* **1,** a copy made by a duplicating machine; **2,** a pipe with two or more outlets along its length, used for connecting one pipe with others.—*adv.* **man'i-fold'ly.**

man-i-kin (man'i-kin), *n.* a dwarf; little man; **2,** a model of the human body (often of detachable parts for study); **3,** an artist's or dressmaker's model (usually, *mannequin*) or a person who models clothes.

ma-nil-a or **ma-nil-la** (ma-nil'a), a hemplike fibre used for ropes, textiles, paper, etc.; as, *manila* hemp; *manila* paper. Also, **Ma-nil'a, Ma-nil'la.**

man-i-oc (man'i-ok'), *n.* a tropical plant, the cassava, whose edible roots yield starch used in making bread and tapioca.

ma-nip-u-late (ma-nip'ū-lāt'), *v.t.* [manipulat-ed, manipulat-ing], **1,** to operate or work skilfully as tools, by means of the hands; **2,** to treat or influence artfully; control the action of, by skilful management; **3,** to falsify, as books in bookkeeping.—*n.* **ma-nip'u-la'tion.**

man-i-tou (man'i-tōō'), **man-i-to** (-tō'), or **man-i-tu** (tōō'), *n.* *Algonquin,* **1,** among certain North American Indians, a good or evil spirit regarded with awe and reverence; **2,** a being, fetish, or charm of supposed supernatural power.

man-kind (man'kīnd'), *n.* **1,** the human race; **2,** (man'kīnd'), men, as distinguished from women.

man-ly (man'li), *adj.* [man-li-er, man-li-est], having the qualities befitting a man; courageous; noble; dignified; resolute.—*n.* **man'li-ness.**

man-na (man'a), *n.* **1,** in the Old Testament, the food miraculously supplied to the Israelites during their 40 years wandering in the wilderness; **2,** hence, anything much needed which is unexpectedly supplied.

man-ne-quin (man′i-kin), *n.* Same as **man′i-kin.**

man-ner (man′ẽr), *n.* **1,** method or way of acting; as, to speak in a rapid *manner;* **2,** sort; kind; species; as, what *manner* of man is he? all *manner* of fish in the bay; **3,** personal, habitual behaviour; as, his *manner* is kind; **4,** style in literature or art; as, a painting in the Chinese *manner;* **5,** habit; custom, as of a race or nation; **6, manners; a,** social behaviour; as, to have good or bad *manners;* **b,** rules of social conduct; as, the *manners* of today.—*adv.* **man′ner-ly.**

man-ner-ism (man′ẽr-izm), *n.* an odd or peculiar action, gesture, style of speech, etc., esp. if affected or habitual.

ma-nœu-vre (ma-nōō′vẽr; ma-nū′vẽr) *n.* **1,** a planned and supervised movement, or change of position, of troops or ships; an evolution; in war, a strategic change of position by troops or ships; **2,** a skilful plan of action; as, a clever *manœuvre:*—*v.i.* [manœu-vred (ma-nōō′vẽrd), manœu-vring], **1,** to perform certain movements: said of troops or war vessels; **2,** to manage with skill; as, the driver had to *manœuvre* to put the car into the garage:—*v.t.* **1,** to cause to make certain movements, as troops; **2,** to handle skilfully. Also spelled **ma-neu′ver.**

man—of—war (man′—ov-wôr′), *n.* [*pl.* men-of-war (men′—ov-wôr′)], **a,** large armed vessel belonging to a navy.

man-or (man′ẽr), *n.* in England, originally, a piece of land held by a nobleman, part of which he occupied, the rest being occupied and farmed by serfs; now, a landed estate held by a lord, part of which he rents to tenants. —*adj.* **ma-nor′i-al.**

manse (mans), *n.* **1,** the residence of a Presbyterian minister, esp. in Scotland; **2,** loosely, any parsonage.

man-sion (man′shun), *n.* a large residence.

man-slaugh-ter (man′slô′tẽr), *n.* the killing of a human being by another or others, unlawfully but without intention.

man-ta ray (man′ta), *n.* a large tropical ray (fish) with wide expanded fins at each side, and slender whiplike tail.

man-tel (man′tl), *n.* **1,** a structure of wood, marble, brick, etc., around and above a fireplace; **2,** the shelf above a fireplace: also called *mantelpiece.*

man-til-la (man-til′a), *n.* **1,** a woman's

cloak or hood; **2,** a veil worn over the head by Spanish women.

man-tis (man′tis), *n.* any of several insects with long, grotesque bodies and rolling eyes, which prey on other insects and are noted for taking a position with the front legs folded as if praying: popularly called *praying mantis.*

MANTIS (⅓)

man-tle (man′tl), *n.* **1,** a loose cloak or cape; also, any enveloping covering; as, a tree in a *mantle* of bloom; **2,** a conelike network of material that will not burn, which fits like a cap over a flame and gives light by glowing at high temperature:—*v.t.* [man-tled, man-tling], to cover with, or as with, a cloak; to disguise:—*v.i.* to become covered; as, her face *mantled* with blushes.

man-u-al (man′ū-al), *adj.* pertaining to, or done by, the hands; as, *manual* skill; *manual* work:—*n.* **1,** a small book for easy reference; a handbook; **2,** a systematic exercise in the handling of a weapon; as, the *manual* of arms in the army.—*adv.* **man′u-al-ly.**

man-u-fac-to-ry (man′ū-fak′to-ri), *n.* [*pl.* manufactories], a place where goods are manufactured.

man-u-fac-ture (man′ū-fak′tūr), *v.t.* [manufactured, manufactur-ing], **1,** to make, as shoes, paper, etc., by hand or machinery, from raw materials; **2,** to make over into a more useful form; as to *manufacture* yarn from wool:—*n.* **1,** the making, usually on a large scale, of articles by hand, machinery, or a combination of processes; **2,** anything made from raw material by these processes; also, such articles collectively; **3,** hence, production in general.—*n.* **man′u-fac′tur-er.**

ma-nure (ma-nūr′), *n.* any fertilizing substance, esp. waste from stables, used for enriching the soil:—*v.t.* [manured, manur-ing], to enrich, as a field or garden, with fertilizing substances.

man-u-script (man′ū-skript′), *adj.* written by hand:—*n.* **1,** a book or paper written by hand; esp. an author's copy of his work in hand writing or in typewriting; **2,** writing as opposed to printing.

Manx (mangks), *adj.* relating to the Isle of Man; as, *Manx* cat; *Manx* dialect (Gaelic).

man-y (men′i), *adj.* [*comp.* more, *superl.* most], consisting of a great number:—*n.* a great number.

map 377 **marital**

map (map), *n.* **1,** a representation, on a flat surface, of the earth or some portion of it, showing the relative size and position of the parts or places represented; **2,** a chart of the heavens: —*v.t.* [mapped, map-ping], **1,** to picture or lay down in a chart; describe clearly; **2,** to plan in detail; as, to *map* out a journey.

ma-ple (mā′pl), *n.* **1,** any of a large group of trees of the North Temperate Zone with deeply indented leaves and two-winged fruits, valued for their wood and for the sap of certain varieties which is used in making a kind of sugar and syrup; **2,** the wood of any of these trees, esp. of the sugar-maple.

mar (mär), *v.t.* [marred, mar-ring], **1,** to disfigure; damage; as, to *mar* a painting; **2,** to injure; ruin; as, to *mar* one's record.

ma-ra-ca (ma-ra′ka), *n.* *Portuguese*, a percussion instrument consisting of a dried gourd with loose pebbles in it.

mar-a-schi-no (mar′a-skē′nō), *n.* a cordial or liqueur made by fermenting a small, black cherry, the marasca: *maraschino* cherries are flavoured in a syrup of this cordial.

mar-a-thon (mar′a-thon′), *n.* **1,** a foot-race of 26 miles, 385 yards; **2,** any contest requiring prolonged endurance.

ma-raud (ma-rôd′), *v.t.* to plunder:— *v.i.* to rove in search of plunder; as, wild beasts *maraud* at night.—*n.* **ma-raud′er.**

mar-ble (mär′bl), *n.* **1,** a hard limestone, white or of various colours, capable of taking a fine polish, used for building and sculpture; **2,** anything like such stone in hardness, smoothness, or coldness; **3,** a sculptured piece of such stone; **4,** a small clay or glass ball used as a child's plaything; **5, marbles:** **a,** the game played with these balls; **b,** a collection of sculpture in marble:— *adj.* **1,** made of, or like, marble; **2,** cold; hard; unfeeling:—*v.t.* [mar-bled, mar-bling], to stain or vein like marble.

mar-cel (mär-sel′), *n.* a deep, regular wave put in the hair by means of a special curling iron:—*v.t.* [marcelled, marcel-ling], to wave (the hair) with this iron.

march (märch), *n.* **1,** a regular, measured step or walk, esp. of soldiers; **2,** the distance passed over in marching from one place to another; as, a *march* of ten miles; **3,** steady onward movement; as, the *march* of years; **4,** a musical composition to be played as troops march:—*v.t.* **1,** to cause to move

at a march; **2,** to cause to go by force; as, to *march* a child to bed:—*v.i.* to move with regular steps, or in military form.—*n.* **march′er.**

March (märch), *n.* the 3rd month of the year (31 days).

mar-chion-ess (mär′shun-es′), *n.* the wife or widow of a marquis; a woman of the rank of a marquis.

mare (mâr), *n.* the female of the horse, donkey, zebra, etc.

mar-ga-rine (mär′ja-rēn′; mär′ga-rēn′), *n.* oleomargarine; a butter substitute made from animal or vegetable fats.

mar-gin (mär′jin), *n.* **1,** a border; an edge; as, the *margin* of a pool; **2,** the unprinted edge of a page; **3,** an amount in reserve, as of money or time; as, he allowed a *margin* of ten dollars for the trip.—*adj.* **mar′gin-al.**

mar-gue-rite (mär′ge-rēt′), *n.* the ox-eye daisy.

mar-i-gold (mar′i-gōld), *n.* **1,** any of a group of strong-scented garden plants of the aster family, with showy orange, yellow, or variegated flowers; **2,** any of numerous other yellow-flowered plants, as the marsh marigold; **3,** the flower of any of these.

ma-ri-jua-na or **ma-ri-hua-na** (mä′ri-hwä′na), *n.* a narcotic obtained from the dried leaves and flowers of the Indian hemp plant and smoked in cigarettes.

ma-rim-ba (ma-rim′ba), *n.* a musical instrument consisting of graduated lengths of hardwood, each with a sounding-box, which are played upon with wooden mallets.

ma-rine (ma-rēn′), *adj.* **1,** pertaining to, living in, or formed by, the sea; as, *marine* plants; *marine* deposits; **2,** naval; relating to commerce at sea; as, *marine* law; **3,** having to do with soldiers who serve on warships; as, the *marine* corps:—*n.* **1,** a soldier who serves on a warship; **2,** the navy of a nation; also, the executive department dealing with naval affairs; **3,** the collective mercantile and naval shipping of a country; as, the merchant *marine;* **4,** a picture of a sea-scene.

mar-i-ner (mar′i-nėr), *n.* a sailor or seaman; one of a ship's crew.

mar-i-o-nette (mar′i-o-net′), *n.* a doll moved by strings or by the hand, as in a puppet-show; a puppet.

mar-i-tal (mar′i-t'l), *adj.* relating to marriage or the married state; as, *marital* rights (those accruing to a husband by virtue of marriage).

mar-i-time (mar′i-tīm′), *adj.* **1**, pertaining to, or bordering upon, the sea; as, a *maritime* province; **2**, esp. relating to sea trade or navigation:— **the Maritimes**, N.S., N.B., P.E.I. (Newfoundland is the *Atlantic* province).

¹mark (märk), *n.* **1**, the target at which one aims, as in shooting; an aim or goal; **2**, a visible imprint, as a line, scratch, written word, etc.; as, an ink *mark;* **3**, a sign by which anything is known; a brand, label, trade mark, etc.; **4**, a trait; distinguishing feature; as, a *mark* of intelligence; **5**, high position; distinction; as, a man of *mark;* **6**, a figure or letter indicating a student's grade; **7**, a boundary or limit; a set standard; as, to fall below the *mark;* **8**, a line, object, etc., serving to indicate position; **9**, a symbol, often a cross, made by one who cannot sign his name:—*v.t.* **1**, to furnish with an identifying sign; **2**, to characterize or indicate, as by a sign; as, faith and courage *mark* the leader; **3**, to single out or select, as by a sign; as, they *marked* him for promotion; **4**, to notice; observe; as, I *marked* that incident; **5**, to rank or grade, as examination papers; **6**, to set apart by or as if by a boundary; as, to *mark* out a tennis-court:—*v.i.* to notice; consider; observe critically:—*n.* mark′er.

²mark (märk), *n.* **1**, the gold monetary unit of the former German Empire, worth almost 24 cents; **2**, the monetary unit of Germany: officially called *reichmark*.

marked (märkt), *adj.* **1**, ranked or graded; as, *marked* papers; **2**, having a distinguishing mark or marks upon it; as, a *marked* bill; **3**, noticeable; conspicuous; clearly defined; as, *marked* ability in music.—*adv.* mark′-ed-ly (märk′kid-li).

mar-ket (mär′ket), *n.* **1**, a place for the sale or purchase of goods, esp. of meat, fresh vegetables, etc.; **2**, a region or country where something can be sold; as, Canada is a *market* for Java coffee; **3**, the state of trade as shown by rate or price; as, a dull *market;* **4**, demand; as, there is a big *market* for radios:—*v.i.* to deal in a public place where provisions are exposed for sale; buy or sell goods or provisions:—*v.t.* to offer for sale, or to sell, in a public place.—*adj.* mar′ket-a-ble.

marks-man (märks′man), *n.* [*pl.* marks-men (-men)], one skilled in shooting.—*n.* marks′man-ship′.

marl (marl), *n.* clay or sand containing much lime, used as a fertilizer and in making bricks and cement.

mar-line (mär′lin) or **mar-lin**, *n.* and *adj. Nautical,* loosely-twisted, two-strand cord used to bind ends of ropes. —mar′line-spike′ (used in splicing ropes).

mar-ma-lade (mär′ma-lād′), *n.* a thick preserve made of oranges or other fruits boiled with sugar.

mar-mo-set (mär′mō-zet), *n.* a small South or Central American monkey.

mar-mot (mär′mut), *n.* a small, coarse-furred, stout-bodied animal with a short bushy tail, akin to the rat and squirrel; a woodchuck.

¹ma-roon (ma-rōōn′), *n.* **1**, one of a class of Negroes, originally fugitive slaves, living in the wilder parts of the West Indies and Dutch Guiana; **2**, one who is left alone or abandoned on a lonely coast:—*v.t.* to abandon on a lonely coast.

²ma-roon (ma-rōōn′), *n.* a dark brown-red colour:—*adj.* of the colour of maroon.

mar-quee (mär-kē′), *n.* **1**, a large field tent; **2**, a canopy from curb to door of a theatre, hotel, etc.

mar-quis (mär′kwis) or **mar-quess** (mär′kwis), *n.* a nobleman ranking below a duke and above an earl or count.

mar-quise (mär-kēz′), *n.* the wife or widow of a marquis; a marchioness.

mar-qui-sette (mär′ki-zet′; mär′kwi-zet′), *n.* a kind of sheer cotton cloth used for dresses, curtains, etc.; also, a thin silk cloth.

mar-riage (mar′ij), *n.* **1**, the act of legally uniting a man and woman in wedlock; the wedding ceremony; **2**, the state of being wedded; the relation existing between husband and wife.—*adj.* mar′riage-a-ble.

mar-row (mar′ō), *n.* **1**, the fatty tissue filling the cavities of bones; **2**, hence, the real meaning or significance of anything; as, the *marrow* of a speech.

mar-ry (mar′i), *v.t.* [married, marry-ing], **1**, to unite as husband and wife; as, the minister *married* Tom and Mary; **2**, to take in marriage; wed; as, Tom *married* Mary; **3**, to dispose of in wedlock; as, to *marry* off a daughter:— *v.i.* to enter into the state of wedlock; become married.

Mars (märz), *n.* **1**, the Roman god of war (Greek, *Ares*); **2**, the planet next outside the earth (4th from the sun), with a year of 687 days, diameter 4,230 miles, orbit about 142 million miles from the sun.—*adj.* and *n.*

Mar'tian.

Mar-seil-laise (mär'se-läz'; mär'se-yâz'), *n.* the rousing national anthem of France (since 1792).

marsh (märsh), *n.* a swampy tract of land.—*adj.* **marsh'y.**

mar-shal (mär'shal), *n.* 1, an official of high rank who superintends and regulates ceremonies; 2, in some foreign armies, an officer of highest rank: also called *fieldmarshal;* 3, an officer who has certain police duties; sometimes, the head of a fire or police department:—*v.t.* [marshalled, marshalling], 1, to arrange or dispose in order, as facts or military forces; 2, to lead; guide.

¹**marsh-mal-low** (märsh'mal'ō), *n.* a confection made from corn syrup, starch and gelatin, beaten to a creamy consistency and coated with powdered sugar.

²**marsh mal-low,** a coarse plant of the mallow family with large, five-petalled, white or rose-coloured flowers, growing in salt-marshes.

marsh mar-i-gold, a plant of the buttercup family with rounded leaves and bright-yellow flowers, growing in swamps and wet meadows.

mar-su-pial (mär-sū'pi-al), *adj.* an order of mammal, like the kangaroo, opossum, etc., that carries its young in an abdominal pouch containing the teats.

mart (märt), *n.* a market.

mar-ten (mär't'n), *n.* 1, a small animal' of the weasel family; 2, the valuable fur of this animal.

mar-tial (mär'shal), *adj.* 1, of, like, or suited to, war; 2, military; as, *martial* music.—*adv.* **mar'tial-ly.**

mar-tin (mär'tin), *n.* 1, in Europe, a bird of the swallow family which builds a mud nest on the walls of buildings; 2, in America, an insect-eating bird of the swallow family, nesting in colonies, and having blue-black plumage and a forked tail.

mar-ti-net (mär'ti-net'), *n.* a rigid disciplinarian; a stickler for form: derogatory use.

mar-ti-ni (mär-tē'ni), *n.* a cocktail of gin and dry vermouth.

mar-tyr (mär'tėr), *n.* 1, one who dies rather than forsake or betray a faith, cause, or principle; 2, one who suffers keenly or sacrifices much, esp. for a

cause or principle:—*v.t.* 1, to put to death for loyalty to some belief, esp. Christianity; 2, to persecute; torture.

mar-tyr-dom (mär'tėr-dum), *n.* death or suffering for the sake of a faith or cause; as, the *martyrdom* of Joan of Arc.

mar-vel (mär'v'l), *n.* something extraordinary and astonishing; a wonder:—*v.i.* [marvelled, marvel-ling], to be struck with wonder; as, to *marvel* at a person's courage.

mar-vel-lous (mär'vel-us), *adj.* causing wonder; scarcely to be believed as, a *marvellous* sight.—*adv.* **mar'vel-lous-ly.**

Marx-ist (märk'sist), *n.* a believer in, or follower of, the communistic theory of Marx and Engels that a classless society (the proletariat) will eventually replace a capitalistic one.—*n.* **Marx'ism.**

mas-car-a (mas-kar'a), *n.* a cosmetic for colouring the eyelashes and eyebrows.

mas-cot (mas'kot; mas'kut), *n.* a person or thing that is supposed to bring good luck; as, the team's *mascot* is a bulldog.

mas-cu-line (mas'kū-lin), *adj.* 1, pertaining to, having the qualities of, or suitable for, a man; manly; powerful; virile; 2, mannish: said of a woman; 3, in *grammar,* designating the gender of words which name male persons or animals.—*n.* **mas'cu-lin'i-ty.**

mash (mash), *n.* 1, a soft or pulpy mass; 2, a warm mixture of bran and water for horses and other animals; 3, bruised malt or meal soaked in hot water for making brews:—*v.t.* 1, to mix, as malt, with hot water, in brewing; 2, to change into a soft, pulpy state by crushing; as, to *mash* turnips.—*n.* **mash'er.**

mask (màsk), *n.* 1, a full or partial cover for the face to disguise or protect it; as, a dancer's *mask;* a baseball *mask;* also, a caricatured false face; 2, a disguise or pretence; as, to hide sorrow under a *mask* of laughter; 3, a likeness of a human face made of clay, wax, or a similar material; 4, (usually *masque*), a masquerade; 5, in classical drama, a huge figure of a head worn by actors to identify the character played; 6, (usually *masque*), an old form of drama characterized by masks, music, and pantomime:—**gas-mask,** a covering for the head and face, attached to a breathing device, to protect against poisonous gases that are found in mines and are used in warfare:—*v.t.* to cover with, or as with, a mask:—*v.i.* to put on a mask; be disguised.—*n.* **mask'er.**

mas-ka-longe (mas'ka-lunj'; lonj), *n.* a large game fish of the pike family, found in lakes and rivers of central North America: valuable for food. Also, **mas'kal-longe'**; **mas'ka-nonge'**; **mas'ki-nonge'**; **mus'kel-lunge'**; **mus'-kal-lunge'**.

ma-son (mā'sn), *n.* a builder in stone or, loosely, in brick; hence, a brick-layer.

ma-son-ry (mā'sn-ri), *n.* [*pl.* masonries], **1,** the art or occupation of a builder in stone; **2,** a structure made of stone.

masque (mask), *n.* **1,** a masquerade; **2,** an old form of drama, characterized by music, dancing, dialogue, and spectacular pageantry, performed by bands of amateur actors in court and castle, popular in the 16th and 17th centuries. Also spelled **mask.**

mas-quer-ade (mas'kėr-ād'), *n.* **1,** a ball or festive gathering where masks are worn; **2,** an acting or living under false pretences; as, his show of honour is a *masquerade;* **3,** a disguise:—*v.i.* [masquerad-ed, masquerad-ing], **1,** to take part in a ball where the guests are disguised; **2,** to take the part or character of another for amusement or deceit; as, to *masquerade* as the heir to a fortune.—*n.* **mas'quer-ad'er.**

mass (mas), *n.* **1,** a quantity of matter or collection of things united into one body; **2,** a large quantity or number; as, a *mass* of corrections; **3,** bulk; size; **4,** the main part:—**the masses,** the common people:—*v.t.* to collect into a lump or body; arrange in close relation; as, to *mass* shrubbery:—*v.i.* to make or gather into a lump or group.

Mass (mas), *n.* in certain churches, the celebration of the Holy Communion.

mas-sa-cre (mas'a-kėr), *n.* the killing of many people or animals with violence and cruelty; wholesale slaughter or murder:—*v.t.* [massa-cred (mas'a-kėrd), massa-cring (mas'a-kėr-ing; mas'a-kring)], to slaughter in great numbers.

mas-sage (ma-säzh'), *n.* a method of treating the body, for health purposes, by rubbing and kneading with the hands:—*v.t.* [massaged, massag-ing], to rub and knead with the hands.

mas-sa-sau-ga (mas'a-sô'ga), *n.* a small rattlesnake, found chiefly in a belt 25 miles wide along Lake Erie, Lake Huron, and Georgian Bay: Ontario's only poisonous snake.

mas-seur (ma'sûr'), *n.* a man who massages.—*n. fem.* **mas'seuse'** (söz').

mas-sive (mas'iv), *adj.* **1,** weighty; huge; bulky; **2,** hence, imposing; impressive.

mast (mast), *n.* **1,** a long, round spar or pole of iron or timber set upright on the keel and through the decks of a vessel, to support the sails and rigging; **2,** any upright pole, as the main post of a derrick.

mas-ter (mås'tėr), *n.* **1,** a man who rules or commands; a director; employer; owner; **2,** the head of a household, college, school, etc.; **3,** an expert; hence, a skilled workman; **4,** a winner in a contest; **5,** a great artist; also, a painting by a great artist; as, a gallery of old *masters;* **6,** the commander of a merchant vessel:—**Master 1,** a person holding an advanced university degree; as, a *Master* of Arts; **2,** a title used before the names of young boys; **3,** a legal title:—*adj.* chief; skilled; as, a *master*-mason:—*v.t.* to subdue or overcome; as, to *master* a task.

mas-ter-ful (mås'tėr-fool), *adj.* **1,** commanding; powerful; as, a *masterful* speaker; **2,** domineering.—*adv.* **mas'-ter-ful-ly.**

mas-ter-ly (mås'tėr-li), *adj.* characteristic of a chief or expert; as, he played with a *masterly* touch:—*adv.* like, or with the skill of, an expert.

mas-ter-piece (mås'tėr-pēs'), *n.* **1,** a thing which surpasses in excellence everything else done by the maker; as Cervantes's "Don Quixote" is his *masterpiece;* **2,** anything made with extraordinary skill.

mas-ter-y (mås'tėr-i), *n.* [*pl.* masteries], **1,** dominion; rule, as of a country; **2,** superiority or triumph, as in a contest; **3,** skill in, or full knowledge of, a subject.

mast-head (mast' hed'), *n.* **1,** the top of a mast, esp. the top of a lower mast used for a lookout; **2,** in all issues of newspapers, magazines, etc., a printed listing of owners, publishers, editors, subscription rates, dates of publication, etc.

mas-tic (mas'tik), *n. and adj.* **1,** a brown resin used in varnish, chewing gum, etc.; **2,** a quick-drying cement used in fastening wall tiles, etc.

mas-ti-cate (mas'ti-kāt'), *v.t.* [masticated, masticat-ing], to grind (food) with the teeth; chew.—*n.* **mas'ti-ca'tion.**

mas-tiff (mås'tif), *n.* one of a breed of

dogs that were originally used as hunting-dogs. The mastiff is extremely large and has a deep powerful chest.

mas-to-don (mas'to-don), *n.* a huge, elephantlike animal, that no longer exists on the earth.

mas-toid (mas'toid), *adj.* nipple-shaped; as, the *mastoid* bone, a projection of the temporal (or temple) bone behind the ear.

mas-tur-ba-tion (mas'tėr-bā'shun),*n.* sexual stimulation without intercourse.

¹mat (mat), *n.* **1**, a flat piece of coarse, woven fabric, made of straw, grass, rags, etc.; **2**, such a fabric placed before a door for wiping the feet; **3**, anything thickly grown or tangled, as hair, weeds, or wool; **4**, a piece of cloth, lace, asbestos, etc., placed under dishes or used as an ornament:—*v.t.* [mat-ted, mat-ting], to mass, knot, or twist together:—*v.i.* to become closely tangled.

²mat (mat), *adj.* dull, lustreless, but uniform: said of surfaces and colours:—*n.* **1**, a border of paper, cardboard, silk, etc., used to set off or protect a picture; **2**, a dull finish on a gilded or painted surface.

mat-a-dor (mat'a-dōr'; -dôr'), *n.* the man appointed to kill the bull with a sword-thrust at the end of a bullfight.

¹match (mach), *n.* **1**, anything which agrees with, or is exactly like, another thing; **2**, an equal; one able to cope with another; **3**, a game or contest; as, a hockey *match;* **4**, a marriage; also, a marriageable person:—*v.t.* **1**, to marry; esp. to marry advantageously; **2**, to compete with successfully; equal; as, their team *matched* ours:—*v.i.* to agree with, or be like, each other.

²match (mach), *n.* **1**, a slender piece of wood tipped with material that is easily set afire by friction, now almost universally used for starting fires; **2**, a wick which burns at a certain speed, used for firing cannon and guns.

match-less (mach'lis), *adj.* not capable of being equalled; peerless.

mate (māt), *n.* **1**, a companion or associate; as, a play*mate;* **2**, a partner in marriage; one of a pair of animals or birds for breeding; as, the lion's *mate;* **3**, one of a pair; as, the *mate* to a shoe; **4**, a merchant ship's officer ranking below the captain:—*v.t.* and *v.i.* [mat-ed, mat-ing], **1**, to match; **2**, to marry; of animals, to pair.

ma-te-ri-al (ma-tē'ri-al), *adj.* **1**, consisting of matter or substance; not spiritual; **2**, pertaining to bodily wants; as, the *material* needs of the poor; **3**, important; noticeable; as, a *material* improvement:—*n.* the substance of which anything is made.

ma-te-ri-al-ism (ma-tē'ri-al-izm), *n.* the doctrine that all reality (including thought, will, feeling) can be explained only in terms of matter.—*n.* **ma-te'ri-al-ist**.—*adj.* **ma-te'ri-al-is'tic**.

ma-te-ri-al-ize (ma-tē'ri-al-īz'), *v.t.* [materialized, materializ-ing], **1**, to give substance, reality, or form to; **2**, to express (an idea) through outward objects; as, to *materialize* an idea in a statue:—*v.i.* **1**, to become a fact; **2**, to assume actual form.

ma-te-ri-al-ly (ma-tē'ri-al-i), *adv.* **1**, with respect to body or substance; **2**, actually; considerably; as, his gift helps *materially*.

ma-ter-nal (ma-tûr'nal), *adj.* pertaining to motherhood or to one's mother; as, *maternal* love.—*adv.* **ma-ter'nal-ly**.

ma-ter-ni-ty (ma-tûr'ni-ti), *n.* [*pl.* maternities], the state of being a mother; motherhood.

math-e-mat-i-cal (math'i-mat'i-kal) *adj.* **1**, pertaining to, or performed by, mathematics; **2**, exact; precise; accurate; as, they measured the distance with *mathematical* precision.—*adv.* **math'e-mat'i-cal-ly**.

math-e-ma-ti-cian (math'i-ma-tish'an), *n.* one skilled in mathematics.

math-e-mat-ics (math'i-mat'iks), *n. pl.* used as *sing.* the science which deals with quantities, expressed in numbers or other symbols, and the relations between them.

mat-in (mat'in), *adj.* pertaining to morning:—**Matins**, *n.pl.* **1**, in the Roman Catholic Church, a service at midnight or at daybreak; **2**, in the Church of England, the morning service.—*adj.* **mat'in-al**.

mat-i-nee (mat'i-nā'; mat'i-nā'), *n.* a play, musicale, reception, etc., taking place in the afternoon.

mat-ri-cide (mat'ri-sīd'; mā), *n.* the murder of a mother by her son or daughter.

ma-tric-u-late (ma-trik'ū-lāt'), *v.t.* to enrol or register a student (or candidate for a degree) in a college or university:—*v.i.* to gain admission, or right of admission, to such an institution.—*n.* **ma-tric'u-la'tion; ma-tric'u-lant**.

mat-ri-mo-ny (mat'ri-mo-ni), *n.* marriage.—*adj.* **mat'ri-mo'ni-al** (-mō').

ma-trix (mā'triks), *n.* **1**, any die or

mold for casting or shaping (an object); **2,** the rock in which a fossil, gem, etc. is embedded; **3,** a papier-mâché or plaster impression of type used in electrotypy or stereotypy (printing from page plates cast in type metal).

ma-tron (mā´trun), *n.* **1,** a married woman or widow; esp. one who has borne children; **2,** a woman who superintends the housekeeping in a hospital or other institution; also, a woman whose duty it is to maintain order among women or children in a prison, dormitory, etc.

ma-tron-ly (mā´trun-li), *adj.* like or pertaining to a matron; dignified; sedate; as, a *matronly* manner.

mat-ted (mat´id), *adj.* **1,** covered with a mat or mats; **2,** closely tangled together; as, *matted* hair.

mat-ter (mat´ẽr), *n.* **1,** substance, as opposed to mind, spirit, etc.; **2,** the substance of which physical things are made; **3,** an instance of, or occasion for, something; as, a *matter* of habit; a laughing *matter;* **4,** the content of a book or speech; as, subject *matter;* **5,** anything sent by mail; as, second-class *matter;* **6,** importance; as, no *matter;* **7,** affair; business; hence, a thing; as, this *matter* needs prompt attention; **8,** amount; space; as, a *matter* of ten days or miles; **9,** pus; **10,** material set up in type; also, material printed from type:—*v.i.* **1,** to be of importance; as, health *matters;* **2,** to form pus; fester.

mat-ter—of—fact (mat´ẽr-ov-fakt´), *adj.* literal; practical; not imaginative.

mat-ting (mat´ing), *n.* a coarse fabric of straw, hemp, grass, etc., used for covering floors.

mat-tock (mat´uk), *n.* a tool which has a steel head with one end flat and the other pointed like a pick, used for digging, grubbing, etc.

mat-tress (mat´ris), *n.* a flat case or bag made of strong material, stuffed with hair, straw, cotton, etc., for use as a bed, or as a soft pad for a bed.

ma-ture (ma-tūr´), *v.i.* [matured, maturing], **1,** to become ripe; develop fully **2,** to fall due, as a note:—*v.t.* to bring to full growth or completion:—*adj.* [matur-er, matur-est], **1,** ripe; full-grown, as fruit; **2,** perfected; ready for use, as a plan; **3,** due, as a note.—*n.* **ma-tu´ri-ty.**

maud-lin (môd´lin), *adj.* **1,** easily moved to tears; weakly sentimental; as, *maudlin* sympathy; **2,** fuddled; drunkenly silly.

maul or **mall** (môl), *n.* a large, heavy

hammer:—*v.t.* to beat or bruise; treat in a rough manner.

maun-der (môn´dẽr; män), *v.i.* to drivel; talk foolishly, incoherently, or aimlessly.

mau-so-le-um (mô´sō-lē´um), *n.* a stately, magnificent tomb.

mauve (mōv), *n.* a soft lilac, violet, or purple colour.

mav-er-ick (mav´ẽr-ik), *n.* **1,** an unbranded animal, esp. a lost calf running at large; **2,** *Colloq.* one who bolts his group or party and becomes an independent.

ma-vis (mā´vis), *n.* the European song thrush.

maw (mô), *n.* **1,** the stomach of an animal; **2,** in birds, the craw or crop.

mawk-ish (môk´ish), *adj.* foolishly sentimental; as, a *mawkish* lover.

max-im (mak´sim), *n.* a general truth or rule expressed briefly; as, "Waste not, want not" is a useful *maxim*.

max-i-mum (mak´si-mum), *n.* [pl. maxima (mak´si-ma) or maximums] the greatest possible number, quantity or degree: opposite of *minimum:—adj.* greatest in quantity or highest in degree.

may (mā), *auxiliary v.* [p.t. might (mīt)], **1,** to be allowed or to be free to as, you *may* look; **2,** to be likely, but not certain; as, it *may* rain; **3,** would: that: expressing the earnest desire, o wish, of the speaker; as, *may* th report prove untrue.

May (mā), *n.* the 5th month (31 days)

may-be (mā´bē; mā´bi), *adv.* perhaps possibly.

may-hem (mā´hem), *n.* the crime o wilfully injuring a person by causin mutilation or loss, as of a limb o organ: a form of *maim*.

may-on-naise (mā´o-nāz´), *n.* a thick rich sauce or seasoned dressing made o raw egg-yolks, vegetable oil, an vinegar, beaten together until thick.

may-or (mā´ẽr; mâr), *n.* the chie official of a city or borough.—*r* **may´or-al-ty.**

maze (māz), *n.* **1,** a confusing networl of passages; a labyrinth; **2,** con fusion of mind; bewilderment.—*ad* **ma´zy.**

ma-zur-ka (ma-zûr´ka; -zōōr´), *n.* lively Polish dance, or music for it.

me (mē), *pron.* the objective case of ₁ the pronoun of the first person.

mead (mēd), *n.* **1,** *Poetic,* a meadow; ₃

formerly (a) a fermented drink (b) a soft drink.

mead-ow (med′ō), *n.* a field used for pasture; also, a field in which hay is grown.

meadow lark, a North American songbird of the oriole family, with a yellow breast marked with a black crescent.

mea-gre (mē′gėr), *adj.* 1, lacking in flesh; lean; 2, poor; scanty; as, a *meagre* meal.— *adv.* **mea′gre-ly.**—*n.* **mea′gre-ness.**

¹meal (mēl), *n.* coarsely ground grain; esp. ground Indian corn, or maize.

²meal (mēl), *n.* a repast; a time or occasion of taking food; also, the food eaten.

meal-y (mēl′i), *adj.* [meal-i-er, meal-i-est], 1, like meal; dry and soft; as, *mealy* soil; 2, covered with meal; floury; 3, pale.

meal-y—mouthed (mē′li–mou*th*d′; mouth*t*′), *adj.* afraid to speak out plainly or bluntly; using soft words.

¹mean (mēn), *v.t.* [meant (ment), meaning], 1, to intend; as, he *means* to go; he *means* mischief; 2, to express a certain thought; signify; as, charity *means* love; 3, to refer to; designate; as, I *mean* you; 4, to design or intend for a purpose; as, a pitcher is *meant* for holding and pouring a liquid.

²mean (mēn), *adj.* 1, humble; common; as, of *mean* birth; 2, inferior; ordinary; as, a *mean* grade of coal; 3, poor; shabby; as, a *mean* house; 4, lacking in generosity; stingy; as, a *mean* man; 5, lacking in honour; base; as, a *mean* motive; 6, *Colloq.* unkind.—*n.* **mean′-ness.**—*adv.* **mean′ly.**

³mean (mēn), *adj.* 1, occupying the middle position between two extremes; as, a *mean* height; a *mean* course; 2, average:—*n.* 1, a condition, quality, course of action, etc., which is midway between two extremes; as, grey is the *mean* between black and white; 2, hence, moderation; 3, **means; a,** that by which something is done or accomplished; as, a boat was the *means* of rescue; **b,** wealth; as, a man of *means.*

me-an-der (mi-an′dėr), *v.i.* 1, to follow a winding course, as a river; 2, to wander aimlessly.

mean-ing (mēn′ing), *adj.* expressive; full of significance; as, a *meaning* glance:—*n.* 1, object; intention; as, the *meaning* of her visit; 2, that which is meant; as, the *meaning* of a word.—*adv.* **mean′ing-ly.**—*adj.* **mean′ing-ful.**

mean-ing-less (mēn′ing-lis), *adj.* without meaning or sense; not significant.

mean-time (mēn′tīm′), *adv.* 1, in the time between two occasions; 2, at the same time:—*n.* the time between two occasions.

mean-while (mēn′hwīl′), *adv.* meantime:—*n.* the intervening time.

mea-sles (mē′zlz), *n.pl.* used as *sing.* a contagious disease, common esp. among children, marked by fever and itching small red spots on the skin.

meas-ure (mezh′ėr), *n.* 1, the size, quantity, or capacity of a thing, as found by a rule or standard; 2, a unit of measurement, as a pint, inch, etc.; also, an instrument for measuring, as a yardstick; 3, a system of measurement; as, dry *measure;* 4, an amount; degree; as, a small *measure* of pity; 5, a reasonable limit; as, the normal *measure* of life is 70 years; 6, a course of action; as, preventive *measure;* 7, an act of legislation; 8, rhythm, as in poetry; 9, in *music,* the time of a piece; also, the group of notes between two bars on a staff:—*v.t.* [measured, measuring], 1, to find out the extent, size, or volume of, by comparison with a fixed or known standard; 2, to give out; allot; as, to *measure* out rations; 3, mark off (size, rate, etc.); as, a speedometer *measures* the rate of speed:—*v.i.* 1, to find dimensions, volume, etc.; 2, to extend or be of a given length; as, the room *measures* 21 feet.—*adj.* **meas′ur-a-ble.**

meas-ured (mezh′ėrd), *adj.* 1, regulated or determined by some standard; 2, uniform; regular; also, rhythmical; 3, carefully considered; as, *measured* words.

meas-ure-ment (mezh′ėr-ment), *n.* 1, the act of finding size, quantity, amount, etc., by a standard; 2, the size or quantity found; 3, a system of units of measure.

meas-ur-ing worm, the caterpillar larva of any geometrid moth, that moves by bringing the rear end of the body forward (to form a loop) and then advancing at the front end. Also called *inch worm* and *looper.*

meat (mēt), *n.* 1, animal flesh used as food; 2, food in general; 3, the food parts within a shell, rind, etc.; as, the *meat* of a nut.—*adj.* **meat′y.**

me-chan-ic (mi-kan′ik), *n.* a skilled workman, esp. one who understands the construction and use of machinery and tools:—*adj.* relating to manual labour; esp. relating to machinery and tools.

me-chan-i-cal (mi-kan′i-kal), *adj.* **1,** relating to, or made by, machinery; **2,** done without thought, as if from force of habit; as, *mechanical* movements; **3,** run by machinery;. as, a *mechanical* piano.

me-chan-ics (mi-kan′iks), *n.pl.* used as *sing.* **1,** the science of machinery; **2,** the science which treats of the action of forces on bodies.—*adj.* **mech′a-nis′tic**: —*v.t.* **mech′a-nize′.**

mech-a-nism (mek′a-nizm), *n.* **1,** the structure or arrangement of the working parts of a machine of any kind; **2,** a mechanical device; **3,** any system of interworking parts; as, the *mechanism* of government.

med-al (med′l), *n.* a coinlike piece of metal marked with a design or with words to commemorate some event, deed, etc., or to serve as a reward or decoration for merit.—*n.* **med′al-ist** or **med′al-list.**

me-dal-lion (mi-dal′yun), *n.* **1,** a large medal; **2,** a design or decorative panel, often oval or circular, used in lace, carpets, textiles, portraits, carvings, etc.

med-dle (med′l), *v.i.* [med-dled, meddling], to interfere with what does not concern one; as, he loses his friends, because he *meddles* in their affairs.—*n.* **med′dler.**

med-dle-some (med′l-sum), *adj.* apt to interfere in the affairs of others.

me-di-ae-val or **me-di-e-val** (med′i-ē′val; mē′di-ē′val), *adj.* relating to, or characteristic of, the Middle Ages, a period extending approximately from A. D. 500 to A. D. 1400.

me-di-an (mē′di-an), *adj.* in the middle:—*n.* a point or number in a series having the same numbers of points or numbers before as after it; as, in the series 4, 5, 8, 16, 22, the *median* is 8.

me-di-ate (mē′di-āt′), *v.i.* [mediat-ed, mediat-ing], to act as a peacemaker between those who are openly disagreeing:—*v.t.* to bring about by acting as an agent between enemies; as, to *mediate* a peace:—*adj.* (mē′di-it), not direct; acting by or through some intervening person or thing.—*n.* **me′di-a′tion.**

me-di-a-tor (mē′di-ā′tėr), *n.* one who intervenes to effect agreement or compromise; intercessor.

med-i-cal (med′i-kal), *adj.* relating to medicine, or the treatment of disease; as, *medical* training.—*adv.* **med′i-cal-ly.** —*n.* **med′i-ca′tion.**

me-dic-i-nal (mi-dis′i-nal), *adj.* having the power to cure or relieve disease.— *adv.* **me-dic′i-nal-ly.**

med-i-cine (med′sin; med′i-sin; med′-i-sn), *n.* **1,** the science which deals with the prevention, treatment, and cure of disease; **2,** any drug or remedy for the treatment and cure of disease.

me-di-e-val (med′i-ē′val; mē′di-e′-val), *adj.* Same as **mediaeval.**

me-di-o-cre (mē′di-ō′kėr; mē′di-ō′-kėr), *adj.* of medium quality; commonplace.—*n.* **me′di-oc′ri-ty** (mē′di-ok′ri-ti).

med-i-tate (med′i-tāt′), *v.i.* [meditat-ed, meditat-ing], to think deeply; reflect; as, to *meditate* upon revenge:— *v.t.* to consider; plan; as, to *meditate* a change.—*n.* **med′i-ta′tion.**—*adj.* **med′-i-ta′tive.**

me-di-um (mē′di-um), *n.* [*pl.* media (mē′di-a) or mediums], **1,** that which comes between or in the middle; **2,** means; that by which or through which something is done; as, the newspaper is an advertising *medium;* **3,** the space or substance in which bodies exist or move; as, water is the *medium* in which we swim; also, a substance through which something acts or is carried; as, the air is a *medium* for sound; **4,** a person who claims to receive messages from the spirit world:—*adj.* middle; moderate; as, cloth of *medium* weight.

med-ley (med′li), *n.* [*pl.* medleys], **1,** a mixture or confused mass; **2,** in *music,* a composition made up of passages selected from different songs or pieces.

me-dul-la (mi-dul′a), *n.* **1,** in *botany,* the spongy centre of a stem; pith; **2,** in *zoology,* (a) the marrow of bones (b) the **medulla ob′lon-ga′ta,** a broadening of the spinal cord where it enters the skull to become a brain centre controlling breathing, blood circulation, etc.

med-ul-la-ry ray (mi-dul′a-ri; med′), in *botany,* a vertical band or plate of tissue radiating between the pith and the bark.

meed (mēd), *n.* reward; that which is given in consideration of merit or worth.

meek (mēk), *adj.* **1,** mild of temper; patient; gentle; **2,** easily imposed upon; spiritless.—*adv.* **meek′ly.**—*n.* **meek′ness.**

meer-schaum (mēr′shum), *n.* a fine white clay (a silicate of magnesium) used for tobacco pipes.

[1]meet (mēt), *v.t.* [met (met), meet-ing].

1, to come upon; come face to face with; as, he *met* her down town; 2, to be at the place of arrival of; as, I *met* the boat at the dock; 3, to connect with; join; as, this path *meets* the main road; 4, to oppose in a battle, contest, duel, etc.; 5, to be introduced to; 6, to experience; as, he *met* strange adventures; 7, to be perceived by; to catch the attention of; as, to *meet* the eye; 8, to equal; satisfy; as, will you *meet* my demands?—*v.i.* 1, to collect in one place; assemble; 2, to come together:—*n.* a gathering or assemblage for some definite purpose; as, a track *meet*.

²meet (mēt), *adj.* fitting; proper; as, it is *meet* that we should observe the law.

meet-ing (mēt′ing), *n.* 1, a coming together of persons; 2, an assembly; a gathering for a special purpose, esp. for a religious service; 3, a place where two or more things come together; union; a junction, as of roads.

meet-ing—house (mēt′ing–hous′), *n.* a building for public worship, esp. one used by Quakers.

meg-a— (meg′a–), *prefix,* 1, great; very large, as in *mega*phone; 2, a million times (or of), as in *mega*cycle; *mega*ton (explosive force of a million tons of TNT).

meg-a-lo- (meg′a-lō–), *prefix,* great, very large, as in *megalo*mania (mania for greatness).

meg-a-phone (meg′a-fōn′), *n.* a large horn or speaking-trumpet used to increase the sound of the voice or to carry it a long distance.

mel-an-chol-y (mel′an-kol′i), *n.* [*pl.* melancholies], a gloomy state of mind or mood; depression of spirits:—*adj.* dejected; downcast; sad.—*adj.* **mel′-an-chol′ic.**

me-lee (mâ′lā′; mā′), *n.* 1, a confused conflict between opposing fighters; hence, 2, a lively debate.

mel-lif-lu-ous (me-lif′lo͞o-us), *adj.* flowing sweetly and smoothly; as, *mellifluous* poetry, song, etc. Also, **mel-lif′lu-ent.**

mel-low (mel′ō), *adj.* 1, soft, juicy, and sweet, because of ripeness; as, a *mellow* peach; 2, of a delicate, rich flavour; well matured; as, *mellow* wine; 3, soft; rich, as soil; 4, pure; rich, as a colour or sound; 5, softened by age or maturity:—*v.t.* and *v.i.* to make or become ripe, gentle, or sweet; as, sorrow *mellowed* her nature.

me-lo-de-on (mi-lō′di-on), *n.* a small

reed organ with bellows operated by pedals.

mel-o-dra-ma (mel′ō-drä′ma; mel′ō-drä′ma; mel′ō-dram′a), *n.* 1, a highly exciting, romantic play, with a happy ending; 2, hence, sensational language or behaviour.—*adj.* **mel′o-dra-mat′ic.**

mel-o-dy (mel′o-di), *n.* [*pl.* melodies], 1, an agreeable arrangement of sounds; 2, a song or tune; as, the *melody* was simple; 3, the principal part in a song; the air; as, the sopranos carry the *melody*.—*adj.* **me-lod′ic** (mi-lod′ik).—*adj.* **me-lo′di-ous** (mi-lō′di-us).

mel-on (mel′un), *n.* 1, a trailing plant of the gourd family; also, its edible fruit; a musk melon; 2, a watermelon.

melt (melt), *v.i.* [*p.t.* melt-ed, *p.p.* melt-ed or, *Archaic,* mol-ten (mōl′ten), *p.pr.* melting], 1, to be changed from a solid to a liquid state, often by heat; as, ice *melts;* 2, to dissolve; as, sugar *melts* in the mouth; 3, to waste away; grow gradually less; as, his anger *melts* under kindness; 4, to disappear; vanish; as, the fog *melts* away; 5, to become gentle or tender; as, my heart *melts;* 6, to blend as colours,:—*v.t.* 1, to change from a solid to a liquid state; as, heat *melts* butter; 2, to make gentle.

mem-ber (mem′bėr), *n.* 1, one who belongs to a group or society; as, a class *member;* 2, a part of the body, esp. a leg or arm; hence, one part of any whole.

mem-ber-ship (mem′bėr-ship), *n.* 1, the state of being a member; 2, all the persons belonging to an organization.

mem-brane (mem′brān), *n.* a thin, soft sheet of tissue which serves as a cover, connection, or lining in an animal or vegetable body.—*adj.* **mem′-bra-nous.**

me-men-to (mi-men′tō), *n.* [*pl.* mementoes or mementos], that which serves as a reminder; a souvenir; token.

mem-o (mem′ō), *n. Colloq.* Short for *memorandum.*

mem-oir (mem′wär; mem′wôr), *n.* 1, a memorandum; 2, a record or account of events written from the author's personal knowledge or experience; 3, a biography; a biographical sketch or notice.

mem-o-ra-ble (mem′o-ra-bl), *adj.* worthy of being remembered; notable; as, a *memorable* battle.—*adv.* **mem′o-ra-bly.**

mem-o-ran-dum (mem′o-ran′dum), *n.* [*pl.* memoranda (mem′o-ran′da) or memorandums], **1,** a note to help one to remember; **2,** a brief, informal note or report.

me-mor-i-al (mi-mōr'i-al), *adj.* in memory of a person or an event; as, a *memorial* address:—*n.* **1,** a thing serving to keep alive the memory of a place, person, etc.; as a soldier's *memorial;* **2,** a record or account of something; **3,** a written statement of facts addressed to a person or persons in authority, usually accompanied by a request or protest.

mem-o-rize (mem'o-rīz'), *v.t.* [memorized, memoriz-ing], to commit to memory; to learn by heart; as, to *memorize* poetry.

mem-o-ry (mem'o-ri), *n.* [*pl.* memories], **1,** the ability or power to remember things; **2,** a particular period or experience remembered; as, a trip to the circus is one of my earliest *memories;* **3,** the length of time within which past happenings are remembered; as, it happened within grandmother's *memory;* **4,** reputation after death; as, his *memory* is honoured.

men-ace (men'is), *n.* a danger or evil that threatens; as, the *menace* of flood:—*v.t.* [menaced, menac-ing], to threaten; as, war *menaced* the world.—*adv.* **men'ac-ing-ly.**

me-nag-er-ie (mi-naj'ĕr-i; mi-nazh'-ĕr-i), *n.* **1,** a place where wild animals are kept; **2,** a collection of wild animals, kept in cages, for exhibition.

mend (mend), *v.t.* **1,** to repair (that which is broken or worn); as, to *mend* a torn sleeve; **2,** to make better; correct; reform; as, the prisoner *mended* his ways:—*v.i.* to grow better or stronger; improve; as, the man who had been ill *mended* rapidly:—*n.* **1,** the act of growing better; as, he is on the *mend* after his illness; **2,** a repaired part of something.

men-da-cious (men-dā'shus), *adj.* lying; false; as, a *mendacious* rascal; a *mendacious* account.—*n.* **men-dac'i-ty** (-das').

men-di-cant (men'di-kant), *n.* a beggar:—*adj.* practising begging; as, a *mendicant* rascal.

me-ni-al (mē'ni-al; mēn'yal), *n.* a domestic servant, esp. one who does lowly or degrading work:—*adj.* relating to, or suitable for, a servant; lowly; humble; as, a *menial* task.—*adv.* **me'ni-al-ly.**

men-in-gi-tis (men'in-jī'tis), *n.* an inflammation of the membranes of the brain and spinal cord.

men-stru-a-tion (men'strōō-ā'shun), the menses or monthly discharge of blood from the uterus (womb):—*v.i.* **men'stru-ate'.**—*adj.* **men'stru-al.**

men-su-ra-tion (men'shoo-rā'shun), *n.* **1,** the act or process of measuring; **2,** in *mathematics*, the branch of applied geometry dealing with the finding of lengths, areas, and volumes.

men-tal (men'tal), *adj.* relating to the mind; intellectual; as, *mental* exercise; done by the mind; as,. to make a *mental* note of something.—*adv.* **men'-tal-ly.**—*n.* **men-tal'i-ty.**

men-thol (men'thol; men'thōl), *n.* a solid, white substance with a mintlike odour, obtained from oil of peppermint and used in medicine, toilet preparations, etc.—*adj.* **men'tho-lat'ed.**

men-tion (men'shun), *n.* a brief notice; a light or chance remark; as, he made *mention* of the fact:—*v.t.* to speak briefly of; name; refer to; as, he did not *mention* you.

men-tor (men'tor), *n.* a wise and faithful adviser, friend, or teacher.

men-u (men'ū; mā'nū; *French,* mė-nü'), *n.* a bill of fare; a list of the dishes served at a meal; also, the dishes served.

mer-can-tile (mûr'kan-tīl'; mûr'kan-til), *adj.* having to do with, or engaged in trade; relating to merchants.

Mer-ca-tor's pro-jec-tion (mėr-kā'-tėrz), *n.* the use of lines on flat maps to show latitude and longitude: the distortion in the polar areas results from trying to show a global surface as a rectangle.

mer-ce-nar-y (mûr'si-nėr-i), *n.* [*pl.* mercenaries], a hired soldier:—*adj.* **1,** acting only for pay or reward; eager for money; **2,** prompted by greed; as, a *mercenary* crime.

mer-chan-dise (mûr'chan-dīz'), *n.* goods or articles that are bought and sold.

mer-chant (mûr'chant), *n.* **1,** one who buys and sells goods for profit; esp. one who carries on trade on a large scale; **2,** a shopkeeper:—*adj.* relating to, or employed in, trade; as, *merchant* ships.

mer-chant-man (mûr'chant-man), *n.* [*pl.* merchantmen (-men)], a trading ship.

mer-ci-ful (mûr'si-fool), *adj.* full of mercy; tender-hearted.—*adv.* **mer'ci-ful-ly.**

mer-ci-less (mûr'si-lis), *adj.* without pity; unfeeling; cruel.—*adv.* **mer'ci-less-ly.**

cat, āge, fär, câre, ásk; ten, ēve, latėr; (i) pity, rely, senate; īce; top; nō

mer-cu-ry (mûr′kū-ri), *n.* a heavy, liquid, silver-white metal, used in thermometers, medicines, etc.; quicksilver.—*adj.* **mer-cu′ri-al** (changeable). **mer-cy** (mûr′si), *n.* [*pl.* mercies], **1,** willingness to forgive an offender, or to treat him with kindness; pity; **2,** willingness to help suffering; **3,** an act of kindness:—**at the mercy of,** in the power of; as, the man was *at the mercy of* his captors.

mere (mēr), *adj.* [*superl.* mer-est], nothing but; no more than; simple; as, this error is a *mere* trifle; he is a *mere* child.

mere-ly (mēr′li), *adv.* simply; purely; only; as, not unkind, *merely* thoughtless.

mer-gan-ser (mėr-gan′sėr), *n.* a kind of fish-eating duck, often crested, with a slender, hooked, somewhat toothed bill.

merge (mûrj), *v.t.* [merged, merg-ing], to cause (something) to be absorbed into something else:—*v.i.* to be absorbed; lose separate character or identity; as, the two small banks *merged* with a larger one.

merg-er (mûr′jėr), *n.* the legal combination of two estates, or of two or more business corporations, into one.

me-rid-i-an (mi-rid′i-an), *adj.* **1,** relating to the highest point reached by a heavenly body, as the sun, in its daily course; **2,** relating to, or characteristic of, the point of greatest success or splendour (of a person, state, etc.):—*n.* **1,** the highest point reached by a heavenly body; **2,** the highest point, as of success, wealth, fame, etc.; **3,** an imaginary circle around the earth, passing through the North and South Poles and any given place; also, a line on a map representing a meridian.

me-ringue (mė-rang′), *n.* a mixture of beaten white of egg and sugar, used as an icing or made into small cakes.

me-ri-no (mi-rē′nō), *n.* and *adj.* [*pl.* -nos (-nōz)], **1,** a superior breed of sheep, originally from Spain (the male having heavy twisted horns), with long slim legs and fine, closely set, soft, silky wool; **2,** the wool itself, one of the best, widely used for hosiery, sweaters, underwear, etc.; **3,** a cloth like fine French cashmere, twilled on both sides, used as a women's dress-fabric.

mer-it (mer′it), *n.* **1,** due reward or punishment; usually, reward; **2,** the condition of deserving, or not deserving; as, we are treated according to our merits; **3,** excellence; worth; that which deserves praise; as, the *merit* of honesty; **4,** the right or wrong of anything; as, to judge a case on its *merits*:—*v.t.* to deserve.

mer-i-tor-i-ous (mer′i-tōr′i-us), *adj.* deserving of reward or praise; as, *meritorious* conduct.—*adv.* **mer′i-tor′i-ous-ly.**

mer-maid (mûr′mād′), *n.* a sea-nymph with the body of a woman and the tail of a fish.—*n.masc.* **mer′man′.**

mer-ry (mer′i), *adj.* [mer-ri-er, mer-ri-est], full of mirth and fun; gay; jolly; pleasant.—*adv.* **mer′ri-ly.**—*n.* **mer′ri-ment.**

mer-ry—go—round (mer′i-gō—round′.), *n.* **1,** a large, revolving, circular platform fitted with wooden animals or seats, on which persons ride; a carrousel; **2,** a whirl of gaiety; as, a *merry-go-round* of parties.

mes-dames (mā′dàm′), *n.* [*French*], *pl.* of madam and madame.

mesh (mesh), *n.* **1,** one of the openings between the threads of a net or of a wire screen; **2,** hence, any network, or something that entangles; as, the *meshes* of the spider's web; **3,** in machinery, the uniting, or engaging, of the teeth of two gear-wheels so that power can be passed along from one to the other:—*v.t.* to catch or entangle in, or as in, a net:—*v.i.* **1,** to become entangled; **2,** in machinery, to unite with one another: said of gear-teeth.

mes-mer-ism (mez′mėr-izm), *n.* the producing of a hypnotic sleep or trance in which the subject's behaviour and sensations are easily influenced by suggestion:—*v.t.* **mes′mer-ize′.**

mess (mes), *n.* **1,** a number of persons who take their meals together, esp. soldiers or sailors; also, the meal itself; **2,** enough for one meal; as, a *mess* of fish; **3,** a state of dirt or confusion; a muddle; a botch:—*v.t.* **1,** to provide food for; **2,** *Colloq.* to muddle; as, he *messed* the job; **3,** to soil:—*v.i.* **1,** to eat together, as sailors; **2,** to potter; trifle.

mes-sage (mes′ij), *n.* a word, notice, etc., written, spoken, or otherwise delivered, from one person to another.

mes-sen-ger (mes′en-jėr), *n.* **1,** one who carries a message; also, one who does errands; **2,** a herald or bringer of news.

Mes-si-ah (me-sī′a), *n.* Christ.

Messrs. (mes′ėrz), *n.pl.* [*French*, messieurs], the plural of *Mr.*

mess-y (mes′i), *adj.* [mess-i-er, mess-i-est], disorderly; soiled; botched; as, a *messy* job.—*adv.* **mess′i-ly.**—*n.* **mess′i-ness.**

met (met), *p.t.* and *p.p.* of *meet.*

me-tab-o-lism (me-tab′o-lizm), *n.* the process of building up food matter into living cells, or protoplasm, which in turn, is broken down into simpler substances, or waste matter, thereby releasing energy for vital processes.

met-al (met′l), *n.* **1,** any of a number of solid, heavy, lustrous substances, as gold, tin, copper, etc., that conduct electricity and that can be drawn into fine threads, hammered into thin plates, and melted by heat; also, a mixture of some of these substances, as brass; **2,** the material, as broken stone, used for making a road or as ballast for a railway track; **3,** spirit; temper; as, a woman of fine *metal.*—*adj.* **me-tal′lic** (mi-tal′ik).

met-al-lur-gy (met′al-ûr′ji), *n.* the art and science of refining metals from ores, making alloys, and treating them to give them desired properties.—*n.* **met′al-lur′gist.**

met-a-mor-pho-sis (met′a-môr′fo-sis; met′a-môr-fō′sis), *n.* [*pl.* metamorphoses (met′a-môr′fo-sēz′; -mor-fō′sēz)], change of form, shape, or

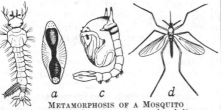

a *c* *d*
b
METAMORPHOSIS OF A MOSQUITO
a, egg; b, larva; c, pupa; d, adult.

structure; transformation; esp. a striking change in the form and habits of an animal as it grows and develops from the egg to the adult stage; as, the *metamorphosis* of a caterpillar into a moth.—*v.t.* **met′a-mor′phose.**—*adj.* **met′a-mor′phic.**

met-a-phor (met′a-fẽr; met′a-fôr′), *n.* a figure of speech in which a name, action, or term ordinarily applied to a certain object is applied to another in order to suggest a likeness between them: distinguished from *simile* by not having *like* or *as* to introduce it. In "His voice *cut* through the silence," 'cut' is a *metaphor.*—*adj.* **met′a-phor′i-cal** (met′a-for′i-kal).

met-a-physics (met′a-fiz′iks), *n.* the branch of philosophy that deals with the nature, character, and causes of being and knowing, the existence of God, etc.

mete (mēt), *v.t.* [met-ed, met-ing], **1,** to measure; **2,** to give out by measure; apportion; as, to *mete* out rewards.

me-te-or (mē′ti-ẽr), *n.* a mass of matter coming from outer space that glows and burns as it enters and passes through the earth's atmosphere.—*adj.* **me′te-or′ic** (mē′ti-or′ik).

me-te-or-ite (mē′ti-ẽr-īt′), *n.* a body of stone or metal which has fallen upon the earth from outer space.

me-te-or-ol-ogy (mē′ti-ôr-ol′o-ji), *n.* the science that treats of atmosphere, esp. its changes in temperature, moisture, etc.: applied to weather forecasting.—*adj.* **me′te-or-o-log′i-cal.**—*n.* **me′te-or-ol′o-gist.**

¹me-ter (mē′tẽr), *n.* Same as **¹metre, ²metre.**

²me-ter (mē′tẽr), *n.* an instrument for measuring and recording the passage of liquids, gases, or electric current; as, a water *meter.*

meth-ane (meth′ān), *n.* a light, colourless, odourless, highly inflammable gas (a compound of hydrogen and carbon): its chief forms are natural gas, marsh gas, and the fire damp of coal mines.

me-thinks (mi-thingks′), *v.impersonal* [*p.t.* methought (mi-thôt′)], *Archaic* or *Poetic,* it appears or seems to me.

meth-od (meth′ud), *n.* **1,** an established order or regular way of doing something; as, a *method* of teaching; **2,** an orderly arrangement of ideas, subjects, etc.

me-thod-i-cal (mi-thod′i-kal), *adj.* **1,** arranged in order; as, a *methodical* outline; **2,** devoted to order; systematic; as, a *methodical* person.—*adv.* **me-thod′i-cal-ly.**

me-tic-u-lous (me-tik′ū-lus), *adj.* unduly careful of details; as, his enunciation was *meticulous.*

me-ton-y-my (me-ton′i-mi), *n.* a figure of speech in which not the literal word but one associated with it, is used; as, he is addicted to the *bottle;* the *kettle* boils.

¹me-tre (mē′tẽr), *n.* **1,** the arrangement of a line of poetry into measured groups of words or syllables, called feet, which gives to the line a regular beat; **2,** in *music,* rhythm or time.

²me-tre (mē′tẽr), *n.* the standard unit of length in the metric system, equal to 39.37 inches.

met-ric (met´rik), *adj.* having to do with some kind of measurement, esp. the metric system:—**metric system,** a decimal system of weights and measures using the *metre* (39.37 inches) as the unit of length and the *gramme* (equal to about a cubic centimetre of water) as the unit of weight.

met-ri-cal (met´ri-k´l), *adj.* 1, relating to, like, or composed in, metre or rhythm; as, a *metrical* translation; a *metrical* effect; 2, relating to measurement; metric.—*adv.* **met´ri-cal-ly.**

met-ro-nome (met´ro-nōm´), *n.* an instrument which beats time, used esp. in practising music.

METRONOME

me-trop-o-lis (mi-trop´o-lis), *n.* the chief city or capital of a country, state, or region; also, a principal centre of population and civilization.

met-ro-pol-i-tan (met´ro-pol´i-tan), *adj.* relating to or belonging to a large city; as, *metropolitan* police:—*n.* 1, a resident of a large city; 2, an archbishop.

met-tle (met´l), *n.* spirit; courage; as, to try one's *mettle.*—*adj.* **met´tled.**

met-tle-some (met´l-sum), *adj.* high-spirited; fiery; as, a *mettlesome* horse.

¹mew (mū), *n.* a gull; esp. the common European gull.

²mew (mū), *n.* the cry of a cat:—*v.i.* to utter a sound or cry resembling the cry of a cat.

mez-za-nine (mez´a-nēn´; mez´a-nin), *n.* in a building, an extra floor between two others, usually the first and second, often in the form of a gallery.

mez-zo—so-pra-no (met´zō-sō-prà´-nō; med´zō), *n.* [*pl.* -nos (-nōz); -ni (nē)], a voice between soprano and alto, or one with such a voice.

mi (mē), *n.* in music, the name of the third note of the scale.

mi-as-ma (mī-az´ma), *n.* [*pl.* -mata (-ma-ta)], *n.* poisonous germs, etc., in the atmosphere.

mi-ca (mī´ka), *n.* a mineral easily separated into thin, transparent plates which are used in lanterns, stove doors, etc.: often incorrectly called *isinglass.*

mice (mīs), *n.pl.* of *mouse.*

mi-cro— (mī´krō-), *prefix* meaning *very small,* as in *micro*biology, *micro*-

cosm, *micro*film, *micro*graph, *micro*organism, etc.

mi-crobe (mī´krōb), *n.* a living animal or plant so tiny as to be seen only under the microscope; a germ; esp. a germ carrying disease.

mi-crom-e-ter (mī-krom´e-tèr), *n.* an instrument for measuring minute distances (often with a telescope or microscope).

mi-cro-phone (mī´krō-fōn´), *n.* an instrument which strengthens or passes along sound waves by means of electricity; as, a radio *microphone.*

mi-cro-scope (mī´krō-skōp´), *n.* an optical instrument with a lens for making very tiny objects appear larger.

mi-cro-scop-ic (mī´krō-skop´ik), *adj.* 1, seen or discovered by means of, or relating to, a microscope; 2, having the power of a microscope; as, a *microscopic* eye; 3, very small; invisible without a microscope; as, a *microscopic* insect or plant.

mid (mid), *adj.* [*superl.* midmost], middle; as, *mid*way, or *mid*-ocean.

mid-day (mid´dā´), *n.* the middle hours of the day; noon:—*adj.* at noon; as, the *midday* meal.

mid-dle (mid´l), *n.* a point or part halfway between two given points, ends, or sides; centre; as, the *middle* of a river:—*adj.* 1, halfway between two given points; as, the *middle* point of a line; 2, intermediate; in-between; as, *middle* age.—*adj.* **mid´dling.**

mid-dle—aged (mid´l-ājd´), *adj.* neither young nor old: said of a person between the ages of about 40 and 60 years.

Middle Ages, the period from about A.D. 500–1400.

mid-dle-man (mid´l-man´; mid´l-man), *n.* [*pl.* middlemen (-men´; -men)], one who acts as a go-between; esp. one who buys goods from the producer to sell to the retail merchant.

mid-dy (mid´i), *n.* [*pl.* middies], *Colloq.* a midshipman, or naval cadet:—**middy blouse,** a loose sailor blouse, worn esp. by children.

midge (mij), *n.* 1, a very small fly or gnat; 2, a dwarf; midget.

midg-et (mij´et), *n.* 1, a dwarf; a little person; 2, a small fly or gnat.

mid-land (mid´land), *adj.* inland; in the central part of a country; as, a *midland* farming district:—*n.* the interior of a country.

mid-most (mid´mōst), *adj.* in the very middle; hence, innermost.

mid-night (mid'nīt'), n. the middle of the night; twelve o'clock at night.

mid-rib (mid'rib'), n. in *botany*, the vein along the centre of a leaf.

mid-riff (mid'rif), n. the part of the body between chest and abdomen; diaphragm:—adj. pertaining to a garment that exposes this part.

mid-ship-man (mid'ship'man), n. [pl. midshipmen (-men)], in the British Navy, a person holding a rank between that of cadet and of sublieutenant; in the U.S. Navy, one who ranks next below an ensign.

midst (midst), n. the middle; the central place; as, in the *midst* of danger:—prep. amidst; as, *midst* the excitement.

mid-sum-mer (mid'sum'ẽr), n. the middle of summer; also, the period about June 21, the longest day of summer:—adj. (mid'sum'ẽr), in or like the middle of the summer; as, *midsummer* heat.

mid-way (mid'wā'), adj. and adv. halfway; as, *midway* to town:—n. the amusement section of an exposition or fair.

mid-wife (mid'wīf'), n. a woman who assists women in childbirth.

mid-win-ter (mid'win'tẽr), n. the middle of winter; also, the period about December 21, the shortest day of winter:—adj. (mid'win'tẽr), in or like the middle of winter.

mien (mēn), n. outward appearance; air; look; manner; as, a dignified *mien*.

miff (mif), v.t. and v.i. *Colloq.* to offend or be offended; put out of humour; vex.—n. a huff.

might (mīt), n. force or power of body or mind; as, fight with all your *might*.

might-y (mīt'i), adj. [might-i-er, might-i-est], 1, powerful; strong; 2, of unusual size, amount, etc.; as, a *mighty* wave:—adv. *Colloq.* very or exceedingly; as, *mighty* glad.—adv. **might'i-ly.**—n. **might'i-ness.**

mi-gnon-ette (min'yun-et'), n. a fragrant garden plant with small, greenish-white flowers.

mi-graine (mē'grān; mi-grān'; mī'grān), n. a headache, usually affecting one side of the head only, often accompanied by nausea.

mi-grate (mī-grāt'), v.i. [migrat-ed, migrat-ing], 1, to move from one country or locality to another for permanent residence; 2, to travel periodically from one climate or feeding

ground to another at certain times o the year, as do many birds.—n

mi-gra-tion (mī-grā'shun).—adj. mi gra-tor-y.—n. and adj. **mi'grant.**

mi-ka-do (mi-kä'dō), n. a popular titl for the Emperor of Japan.

mike (mīk), n. *Colloq.* Short for **mi'cro phone.**

mil-age (mīl'ij), n. Same as *mileage*

milch (milch), adj. yielding milk; as, milch cow.

mild (mīld), adj. 1, gentle; kind; calm as, a *mild* answer; 2, moderate i quality or degree; not sharp, sour, o bitter; as, *mild* cheese; not severe; as *mild* weather.

mil-dew (mil'dū), n. 1, any of severa kinds of tiny fungi, found on plants o decaying substances; 2, a disease o plants produced by these fungi; 3 spots of mould caused by their growtl on cloth, leather, paper, etc., usuall when exposed to dampness:—v.t. t affect with mildew:—v.i. to be affectec with mildew; as, leather *mildews* when it remains damp.

mile (mīl), n. a measure of lengtl containing 5,280 feet.

mile-age (mīl'ij), n. 1, an allowance fo travelling expenses, at so much pe mile; 2, total distance in miles, as o travel; as, the *mileage* of a trip; 3, th use that one gets from something expressed in miles; as, to get gooc *mileage* from tires.

mile-post (mīl'pōst'), n. a signpos stating the distance in miles to a certain point.

mile-stone (mīl'stōn'), n. a stone serving as a milepost; hence, any even in history, a person's life, etc., whicl marks a definite stage.

mil-i-tant (mil'i-tant), adj. 1, at war also, warlike; as, a *militant* nation; 2 combative or aggressive in promoting a cause; as, a *militant* clergyman:—n one who fights; also, one who use aggressive methods in aid of a cause.

mil-i-ta-rism (mil'i-ta-rizm), n. 1, a disposition to uphold a nation's powe by means of a strong army and navy; 2 a warlike policy; the policy of readines to fight on slight grounds; 3, rule o government by military interests.—n **mil'i-ta-rist.**—adj. **mil'i-ta-ris'tic** (mil i-ta-ris'tik).

mil-i-tar-y (mil'i-tẽr-i), adj. 1, relating to soldiers, arms, or war; as, *military* force; 2, performed or supported by soldiers; as, *military* rule:—n. the army; troops.

mil-i-tate (mil′i-tāt′), v.i. to have force or weight; tell; as, his record *militated against* him.

mi-li-tia (mi-lish′a), n. a body of citizens enrolled and trained for the defence of a state or nation as a regular military force, but not called into active service except in an emergency.

milk (milk), n. **1,** a white fluid produced by female mammals and used by their young as food; **2,** this fluid taken by man from certain animals, esp. the cow, and used as food; **3,** the white juice of certain plants, as of the milkweed; **4,** any whitish fluid resembling milk; as, the *milk* of the coconut:—v.t. to draw milk from; as, to *milk* a cow.—n. milk′man′; milk′shake′; milk′sop′ (a sissy).

milk-weed (milk′wēd′), n. any of various wild plants which exude a milklike fluid when bruised.

milk-y (mil′ki), adj. [milk-i-er, milk-i-est], **1,** containing milk, or like milk; as, *milky* water; **2,** yielding milklike juice, as do certain plants.

Milk-y Way, the Galaxy or island universe to which our sun belongs: it appears as a broad, faintly luminous band of countless stars.

¹mill (mil), n. the thousandth part of a dollar; one tenth of a cent.

²mill (mil), n. **1,** a building equipped with machinery to grind grain; as, a flour *mill;* **2,** any machine for grinding solid substances, as coffee, pepper, etc., for finishing or transforming raw materials, or for extracting juice or sap; as, a cider *mill;* **3,** a manufacturing plant; as, a steel *mill;* a paper *mill;* **4,** any unpleasant or exhausting experience; as, to go through the *mill:*—v.t. **1,** to grind (grain), cut or saw (timber), roll or press (steel); crush (ore), etc., in a mill; **2,** to make a raised border around the edges of (a coin); **3,** to make frothy, as chocolate, by churning or whipping:—v.i. **1,** to move in circles; as, the cattle *milled* about the pen; **2,** to move confusedly, as a crowd.

mil-len-ni-um (mi-len′i-um), n. [pl. -iums or -lennia], **1,** a period of 1,000 years; **2,** the thousand years that Christ will reign on earth (Rev. 20:1-5); **3,** any period of joy, peace, and righteousness.

mill-er (mil′ẽr), n. **1,** one who owns or works a flour mill; **2,** any moth whose wings look as if powdered with flour.

mil-let (mil′it), n. **1,** a grain-bearing grass, widely used in Europe and Asia as food for man and birds, and, in the U.S., cut for hay; **2,** the seed of this grass.

mil-li- (mil′i-), prefix, signifying a thousandth part, as in **mil′li-am′pere** ($\frac{1}{1000}$) ampere, **mil′li-gram′** ($\frac{1}{1000}$) gram, **mil′li-me′tre** ($\frac{1}{1000}$) metre, **mil′li-li′tre** ($\frac{1}{1000}$) litre.

mil-li-ner (mil′i-nẽr), n. a person, usually a woman, who deals in, makes, or trims women's hats, headdresses, etc.—n. mil′li-ner-y (mil′i-nẽr-i).

mil-lion (mil′yun), n. **1,** one thousand thousand: written 1,000,000; **2,** an indefinitely large number.—n. and adj. mil′lionth.

mil-lion-aire (mil′yun-âr′), n. **1,** one who has a million, or more, dollars, etc.; **2,** a very rich person.

mil-li-pede or **mil-le-pede** (mil′i-pēd′), n. any of the many-footed invertebrates (spineless creatures) with 25 to 100 body segments, each having two pairs of legs, esp. the common wood louse.

millrace (mil′rās′), n. a channel through which water flows with a swift current to a mill wheel; also, the current driving the wheel.

mill-stone (mil′stōn′), n. **1,** one of two flat, circular stones used for grinding grain in a mill; **2,** something that crushes; a heavy burden.

mim-e-o-graph (mim′i-ō-gráf′), n. a machine for duplicating letters, drawings, etc., by means of a stencil:—v.t. to make copies in this way: a trade-mark.

mim-ic (mim′ik), n. one who imitates, esp. to make fun of the person or thing imitated:—v.t. [mimicked, mimicking], to imitate closely; esp. to ridicule (a person) by imitating his manners, characteristics, etc.:—adj. **1,** imitative; **2,** mock; pretending to be real; as, *mimic* warfare.—n. mim′ic-ry.

min-a-ret (min′a-ret′; min′a-ret), n. a tall, slender tower connected with a Mohammedan mosque, or place of worship, encircled by several balconies from which the call to prayer is made by a public crier.

mince (mins), v.t. [minced, minc-ing], **1,** to cut or chop into very small pieces; **2,** to tell in part or by degrees, lessen the harshness of; as, to *mince* matters; **3,** to utter with assumed elegance or daintiness; as, she *minces* her words:—v.i. **1,** to talk with assumed elegance; **2,** to walk primly or with assumed daintiness.

all ·(ôl), ôr; up, mūte, cûr, cōōl, book; oil, out; th, thin; *th*, the.

mince-meat (mins′mēt′), *n.* a mixture of raisins, suet, lemon peel, etc., and usually meat, chopped fine and used as a filling for pies.

mind (mīnd), *n.* **1,** memory; recollection; as, to call to *mind;* **2,** one's thoughts, opinions, etc.; as, to speak one's *mind;* **3,** the part of a person that is aware, knows, thinks, feels, wills, etc.; consciousness: opposite of *matter;* **4,** the understanding or intellect; as, he has a good *mind:*—*v.t.* **1,** to pay attention to; as, *mind* your step; **2,** to be troubled by; object to; as, to *mind* the heat; **3,** to obey; as, *mind* your parents; **4,** to watch; take care of; as, to *mind* the baby:—*v.i.* **1,** to be troubled; feel annoyance; as, never *mind* if you can't do it; **2,** to be careful; as, *mind* you put on your overcoat.

mind-ed (mīn′did), *adj.* **1,** disposed or inclined; intending; as, *minded* to swim; **2,** having a mind of a certain kind or with a certain interest; as, pure-*minded;* mathematically *minded.*

mind-ful (mīnd′fool), *adj.* taking thought or heed; heedful; attentive; as, *mindful* of one's duty.—*adv.* **mind′-ful-ly.**

mind-less (mīnd′lis), *adj.* **1,** forgetful; disregarding; as, *mindless* of danger; **2,** without mind; stupid.

¹**mine** (mīn), *n.* **1,** in mining, an excavation from which minerals, precious stones, etc., are dug; also, a deposit of ore or coal; **2,** hence, an inexhaustible supply of anything, or a source of great wealth; **3,** an underground passage or cavity under an enemy's fortification in which a high explosive is set off; also, a case containing high explosive, moored where it will destroy enemy ships:—*v.t.* [mined, min-ing], **1,** to get by digging underground; as, to *mine* coal; **2,** to dig into, as for ore or metals; **3,** to destroy slowly or secretly; undermine; **4,** to place explosives under (an enemy's trenches); moor submerged explosives in (a harbour, river, ocean lane, etc.):—*v.i.* **1,** to carry on the work of digging for metals, coal, etc.; **2,** to lay explosives, as under an enemy's trenches or in a harbour.—*n.* **min′er.**

²**mine** (mīn), a possessive form of the personal pronoun *I:* **1,** as *adj.,* belonging to me: **a,** in the predicate; as, whose is that hat? it is *mine;* **b,** *Archaic* or *Poetic,* used for *my* before a vowel or *h;* as, *mine* eyes; *mine* host; **2,** as *pron.,* a person or thing that belongs to

me; as, which hat has he? he has *mine;* your hat is red, *mine* is blue.

min-er-al (min′ẽr-al), *n.* **1,** any substance not animal or vegetable in origin, ordinarily solid, except in the case of mercury and water; **2,** ore; a substance obtained by mining:—*adj.* pertaining to, containing, or mixed with, minerals, or a mineral; as, *mineral* ore; *mineral* water.

min-er-al-o-gy (min′ẽr-al′o-ji), *n.* the science of minerals.—*n.* **min′er-al′o-gist.**

min-gle (ming′gl), *v.t.* [min-gled, min-gling], **1,** to combine by mixing; blend; **2,** to associate:—*v.i.* **1,** to mix or blend; **2,** to enter into close relation; mix; as, to *mingle* with the crowd.

min-i-a-ture (min′i-a-tũr; min′ya-tũr), *n.* **1,** a very small painting, esp. a portrait, usually on ivory or vellum; **2,** a small model of any object:—*adj.* on a very small scale; as, a *miniature* railway.

min-i-fy (min′i-fī′), *v.t.* [-fied, -fying], to make less; as, he tried to *minify* the fault: opposite of *magnify.*

min-im (min′im), *n.* **1,** in *liquid measure,* 1/60 drachm or about one drop; **2,** in *music,* a half note.—*adj.* smallest; most minute.—*adj.* **min′i-mal** (as *minimal* areas, distances, energy, etc.).

min-i-mize (min′i-mīz′), *v.t.* [mini-mized, minimiz-ing], to reduce to the smallest degree, part, or proportion; make little of; as, to *minimize* one's illness.

min-i-mum (min′i-mum), *n.* [*pl.* minima (min′i-ma) or minimums], **1,** the least quantity possible or allowable: opposite of *maximum;* **2,** the lowest point reached or recorded, as of temperature:—*adj.* lowest; least possible or allowable; as, the *minimum* mark for passing.

min-ing (mīn′ing), *adj.* **1,** relating to the excavating of metals, ores, precious stones, etc.; **2,** relating to the laying of explosives:—*n.* the act of working mines for ores or minerals, or of laying explosive mines.

min-ion (min′yun), *n.* **1,** a fawning servant or agent who obeys without question; **2,** a favourite; a pet; **3,** in *printing,* a size of type.

min-is-ter (min′is-tẽr), *n.* **1,** one entrusted by the head of a government with the direction of a department; as, *Minister* of Labour; **2,** a diplomatic agent sent to a foreign country to represent his own government; **3,** a

cat, āge, fär, câre, ȧsk; ten, ēve, latẽr; (i) pity, rely, senate; īce; top; nō.

clergyman or pastor of a church, esp. of a Protestant church:—*v.i.* **1,** to serve or act as pastor; **2,** to give aid by doing helpful things; as, to *minister* to the poor.—*adj.* **min′is-te′ri-al.**—*n.* **min′is-tra′tion.**

min-is-try (min′is-tri), *n.* [*pl.* ministries], **1,** service; **2,** the service of one who preaches a religion; **3,** the office or duties of an officer of state; also, a department of government under the direction of a minister; as, the *Ministry* of Foreign Affairs; **4,** the clergy; **5,** the officers of state, as a group; **6,** the term of service of an officer of state or of a clergyman.

mink (mingk), *n.* **1,** an animal somewhat like the weasel, living part of the time in water; **2,** its valuable brown fur.

min-now (min′ō), *n.* **1,** a tiny freshwater fish of the carp family; **2,** loosely, any of several very small fish

mi-nor (mī′nėr), *n.* **1,** a person of either sex under full legal age, which is usually 21 years; **2,** in U.S. colleges, a subject next in importance to a student's major subject:—*adj.* **1,** unimportant; as, a *minor* injury; **2,** in *music,* less by half a step than the major interval; hence, designating a scale, chord, etc., in which such intervals occur.

mi-nor-i-ty (mi-nor′i-ti; mī-nor′i-ti), *n.* [*pl.* minorities], **1,** the smaller of two parts of a group; **2,** the state of being under age.

Min-o-taur (min′o-tôr′), *n.* in *Greek Mythology,* a monster with a bull's head and man's body, that inhabited the labyrinth of King Minos of Crete: it was slain by Theseus.

min-ster (min′stėr), *n.* **1,** the church of a monastery; **2,** in England, a cathedral.

min-strel (min′strel), *n.* **1,** in the Middle Ages, a poet, singer, and musician; **2,** now, one of a group of performers with blacked faces, who sing Negro songs, tell jokes, etc.—*n.* **min′strel-sy.**

¹mint (mint), *n.* any of a large family of spicy-leaved plants, as the peppermint.

²mint (mint), *n.* **1,** a place where money is coined under government authority and supervision; **2,** an abundant supply; a vast amount; as, he has a *mint* of money; **3,** hence, any source of invention or supply:—*v.t.* **1,** to coin or stamp (money); **2,** to make into money; as, to *mint* silver.

min-u-end (min′ū-end′), *n.* the number from which another is to be subtracted, as 6 in 6 − 3: opposite of *subtrahend.*

min-u-et (min′ū-et′; min′ū-et), *n.* **1,** a graceful and stately dance in triple measure; **2,** the music for such a dance; also, music having a similar style and rhythm.

mi-nus (mī′nus), *adj.* **1,** indicating subtraction; as, the *minus* sign; **2,** indicating a negative quantity; as, a *minus* three:—*n.* the sign [−] indicating subtraction:—*prep.* **1,** less; as, five *minus* two; **2,** deprived of; as, he came out of the wreck *minus* a leg.

¹min-ute (min′it), *n.* **1,** the 60th part of an hour or of a degree of an arc; **2,** a short time; a moment; **3,** an official note; a memorandum; **4, minutes,** the official record made of the proceedings of a meeting.

²mi-nute (mī-nūt′; mi-nūt′), *adj.* **1,** tiny; as, a *minute* particle; **2,** precise; detailed; as, a *minute* description.—*adv.* **mi-nute′ly.**

min-ute-man (min′it-man′), *n.* [*pl.* minutemen (-men′)], in the American Revolution, a citizen ready to arm at a minute's notice.

min-u-ti-a (mi-nū′shi-a), *n.* [*pl.* -tiae (-shi-ē′)], a small, precise, or trivial detail: usually *pl.*

minx (mingks), *n.* a bold or saucy girl.

mir-a-cle (mir′a-kl), *n.* an act or happening in the material or physical world which seems to depart from the laws of nature or to go beyond what is known of these laws; a wonder; a marvel.—*adj.* **mi-rac′u-lous.**

mi-rage (mi-räzh′), *n.* the image, usually upside down and often distorted, of some object actually beyond the range of sight, reflected in the sky over deserts, oceans, and plains. Mirages are common in hot countries, esp. in sandy deserts, where a traveller often imagines he sees a body of water where no water exists.

mire (mīr), *n.* deep mud; wet earth; slush; dirt:—*v.t.* [mired, mir-ing], **1,** to soil; **2,** to cause to be stuck in the mud; as, to *mire* the wheels of a cart:—*v.i.* to sink in mud.—*adj.* **mir′y.**

mirk (mûrk), *n.* Same as *murk.*—*adj.* **mirk′y.**

mir-ror (mir′ėr), *n.* **1,** a looking-glass; any surface that reflects images, as water or polished metal; **2,** that which gives a true likeness; **3,** hence, a model; a pattern:—*v.t.* to reflect; as, a lake *mirrors* a tree.

mirth (mûrth), *n.* noisy gaiety; social merriment; jollity.—*adj.* **mirth′ful.**

all (ôl), **ôr;** **up, mūte, cûr, cōol, book;** **oil, out;** **th, thin;** *th,* **the.**

mis- (mis-), a *prefix* signifying *wrong* or *wrongly,* as in *mis*belief, *mis*count, *mis*cue, *mis*deal, *mis*direct, *mis*quote, *mis*read, *mis*rule, *mis*trial, etc.

mis-an-thrope (mis'an-thrōp'), *n.* one who hates or distrusts mankind.— *adj.* **mis'an-throp'ic.**—*n.* **mis-an'thro-py.**

mis-ap-pre-hend (mis'ap-ri-hend'), *v.t.* to fail to understand.—*n.* **mis'ap-pre-hen'sion.**

mis-ap-pro-pri-ate (mis'a-prō'pri-āt'), *v.t.* (misappropriat-ed, misappropriat-ing], to apply to a wrong use or purpose; esp. to use (another's money) as one's own.—*n.* **mis'ap-pro'pri-a'tion.**

mis-be-have (mis'bi-hāv'), *v.i.* [misbehaved, misbehav-ing], to act in a wrong or improper fashion.—*n.* **mis'behav'iour.**

mis-cal-cu-late (mis-kal'kū-lāt'), *v.t.* [miscalculat-ed, miscalculat-ing], to make a mistake in; misjudge; as, to *miscalculate* a distance.—*n.* **mis'calcu-la'tion.**

mis-call (mis-kôl'), *v.t.* to name wrongly.

mis-car-riage (mis-kar'ij), *n.* **1,** failure; mismanagement; **2,** a premature birth.

mis-car-ry (mis-kar'i), *v.i.* [miscarried miscarry-ing], to go astray or go wrong; as, my plans *miscarried.*

mis-cel-la-ne-ous (mis'e-lā'ni-us), *adj.* **1,** consisting of several kinds mixed together; **2,** many-sided; consisting of various qualities.—*adv.* **mis'cel-la'ne-ous-ly.**

mis-cel-la-ny (mis'e-lā'ni), *n.* [*pl.* miscellanies], **1,** a collection of various things of different kinds; **2,** a book containing a variety of literary compositions.

mis-chance (mis-chàns'), *n.* bad luck.

mis-chief (mis'chif), *n.* **1,** harm; injury; damage; misfortune; as, to do someone *mischief;* **2,** discord; as, to make *mischief* between friends; **3,** vexatious behaviour; also, a tendency to cause annoyance; as, there was more *mischief* than evil in him; **4,** one who acts in an annoying manner; as, that child is a *mischief.*

mis-chie-vous (mis'chi-vus), *adj.* producing injury or damage; full of pranks; annoying.—*adv.* **mis'chie-vous-ly.**

mis-con-cep-tion (mis'kon-sep'shun, *n.* a false opinion; wrong understanding.

mis-con-duct (mis-kon'dukt), *n.* im-

proper or wrong behaviour:—*v.t.* (mis'-kon-dukt'), to manage or handle badly; as, to *misconduct* a business.

mis-con-struc-tion (mis'kon-struk'-shun), *n.* misunderstanding; the giving of a wrong meaning to something; as, the *misconstruction* of a word or an act.

mis-con-strue (mis-kon'-strōō); mis'-kon-strōō'), *v.t.* [misconstrued, misconstru-ing], to get the wrong meaning from; as, you *misconstrue* my words.

mis-cre-ant (mis'kri-ant), *n.* a villain; wrongdoer:—*adj.* villainous.

mis-deed (mis-dēd'), *n.* a wrong act; a crime.

mis-de-mean-our (mis'di-mēn'ẽr), *n.* a wrongdoing; esp. in law, an offence less serious than a felony. Also, **mis'de-mean'or.**

mis-di-rect (mis'di-rekt'; mis'dī-rekt'), *v.t.* **1,** to give false or incorrect instructions to; **2,** to place a wrong address on, as a letter; **3,** to apply wrongly, as one's talents.

mis-do-ing (mis-dōō'ing), *n.* wrongdoing.

mi-ser (mī'zẽr), *n.* one who accumulates money for its own sake; a greedy, stingy person.—*adj.* **mi'ser-ly.**—*n.* **mi'ser-li-ness.**

mis-er-a-ble (miz'ẽr-a-bl), *adj.* **1,** very unhappy; wretched; **2,** worthless; poor in quality; as, *miserable* food; **3,** causing discomfort; as, *miserable* weather.—*adv.* **mis'er-a-bly.**

mis-er-y (miz'ẽr-i), *n.* [*pl.* miseries], extreme pain, distress, or misfortune; great unhappiness; wretchedness.

mis-fit (mis'fit'), *n.* **1,** anything which does not fit; **2,** a person in a position for which he is unfitted (mis'fit).

mis-for-tune (mis-fôr'tūn), *n.* bad luck.

mis-giv-ing (mis-giv'ing), *n.* doubt or uncertainty; anxiety.

mis-guide (mis-gīd'), *v.t.* [misguid-ed, misguid-ing], to mislead; to influence to wrong conduct or thought.

mis-hap (mis'hap; mis-hap'), *n.* ill fortune; an unlucky accident.

mis-in-form (mis'in-fôrm'), *v.i.* and *v.t.* to give incorrect or false information (to).

mis-in-ter-pret (mis'in-tùr'pret), *v.t.* **1,** to misunderstand; **2,** to give a wrong explanation of.—*n.* **mis'in-ter'pre-ta'tion.**

mis-judge (mis-juj'), *v.t.* [misjudged, misjudg-ing], to form a wrong or unjust opinion of:—*v.i.* to be mistaken in opinion.

mis-lay (mis-lā/), *v.t.* [mislaid (mis-lād/), mislay-ing], to lose temporarily; put in the wrong place unintentionally.

mis-lead (mis-lēd/), *v.t.* [misled (mis-led/), mislead-ing], 1, to deceive; give a wrong idea to; 2, to lead astray.

mis-man-age (mis-man/ij), *v.t.* and *v.i.* [mismanaged, mismanag-ing], to manage badly.—*n.* **mis-man/age-ment.**

mis-no-mer (mis-nō/mẽr), *n.* a wrong naming, or name, of a person or thing, esp. in a legal document.

mi-sog-y-nist (mi-soj/i-nist; mī-), *n.* one who hates women.—*n.* **mi-sog/y-ny.**

mis-place (mis/plās/), *v.t.* [misplaced, misplac-ing], 1, to put in a wrong place; 2, to bestow on an undeserving object; as, he *misplaced* his trust.—*n.* **mis-place/ment.**

mis-play (mis-plā/), *n.* a wrong or improper play, as in baseball.

mis-print (mis/print/), *v.t.* to print incorrectly:—*n.* a mistake in type.

mis-pro-nounce (mis/prō-nouns/), *v.t.* and *v.i.* [mispronounced, mispronounc-ing], to speak with a wrong sound or accent.—*n.* **mis/pro-nun/ci-a/tion** (mis/prō-nun/si-ā/shun; -shi-ā/-shun).

mis-rep-re-sent (mis/rep-ri-zent/), *v.t.* and *v.i.* to report incorrectly, wilfully or carelessly.—*n.* **mis/rep-re-sen-ta/tion.**

¹**miss** (mis), *v.t.* 1, to fail to hit; as, to *miss* the mark; 2, to feel the need or absence of; as, he *misses* his mother; 3, to escape by good luck; as, he just *missed* the snowstorm; 4, to fail to meet or catch; as, to *miss* a train; 5, to let go by; fail to grasp, attend, etc.; as, to *miss* a chance; *miss* church; 6, to fail to hear, notice, or understand; as, he *missed* that point:—*v.i.* 1, to fail to make a hit; 2, to fail to secure, attain, do, etc.; as, to *miss* in spelling:—*n.* a failure to hit, reach, see, obtain, etc.

²**miss** (mis), *n.* [*pl.* misses (mis/ēz/), a young girl:—**Miss,** a title used before the name of a girl or an unmarried woman.

mis-sal (mis/al), *n.* in the *Roman Catholic Church,* a book containing the order of service for the Mass; hence, 2, any book of devotions.

mis-shap-en (mis-shāp/en), *adj.* deformed; out of shape.

mis-sile (mis/il), *n.* an object, as a spear, shot, etc., thrown or hurled as a weapon.

miss-ing (mis/ing), *adj.* lost; absent.

mis-sion (mish/un), *n.* 1, the act of sending, or state of being sent, with specific powers, to do a special service; 2, a business or duty on which one is sent; any errand; 3, one's life-work; a calling, esp. to preach and spread a religion; 4, an organization or a centre for doing religious and charitable work; 5, a body of people sent on some special work; 6, in military action, a task given to an individual, or to a whole unit; 7, in air warfare, a flight assignment for one aeroplane or a whole group of aeroplanes; 8, **missions,** missionary work.

mis-sion-ar-y (mish/un-ẽr-i), *n.* [*pl.* missionaries], a person who is sent to spread the knowledge of a religion and convert people to it, esp. in foreign lands:—*adj.* pertaining to missions or to missionaries; as, *missionary* service.

mis-sive (mis/iv), *n.* a letter.

mis-spell (mis-spel/), *v.t.* [mis-spelled or mis-spelt, mis-spel-ling], to spell incorrectly.

mis-spent (mis/spent/), *adj.* spent foolishly or for the wrong purposes; wasted.

mis-state (mis/stāt/), *v.t.* [mis-stat-ed, mis-stat-ing], to state falsely or incorrectly; misrepresent.—*n.* **mis/-state/ment.**

mis-step (mis/step/), *n.* a wrong step; hence a wrong act.

mist (mist), *n.* 1, visible water vapour in the atmosphere, at or near the earth's surface; fog; haze; 2, anything that dims the sight or the mind:—*v.i.* to rain in very fine drops.—*adj.* **mist/y.** —*n.* **mist/i-ness.**

mis-take (mis-tāk/), *v.t.* [*p.t.* mistook (mis-took/), *p.p.* mistak-en (mis-tāk/-en), *p.pr.* mistak-ing], 1, to misunderstand; as, to *mistake* a meaning or a motive; 2, to put wrongly in place of another person or thing; as, he *mistook* her for her sister:—*v.i.* to err in judgment or opinion; be wrong:—*n.* an error; fault; misunderstanding.—*adj.* **mis-tak/a-ble.**

mis-tak-en (mis-tāk/en), *adj.* 1, wrong; as, a *mistaken* idea; 2, wrong in judgment; as, he is *mistaken;* 3, misunderstood; as, a *mistaken* meaning. —*adv.* **mis-tak/en-ly.**

mis-ter (mis/tẽr), *n.* a title of address to a man: written *Mr.* before a man's name.

mis-tle-toe (mis/l-tō; miz/l-tō), *n.* an evergreen parasitic plant with white waxen berries, which grows and feeds on apple trees, oak trees, etc.

mis-treat (mis'trēt'), *v.t.* to treat wrongly; abuse.

mis-tress (mis'tris), *n.* **1,** a woman at the head of a family, school, etc.; also, a woman with authority or power; as, she is *mistress* of her own business; **2,** a woman skilled in anything; as, a *mistress* of needlework; **3,** a woman courted and beloved; a sweetheart; **4,** a female paramour.

mis-trust (mis-trust'), *n.* lack of confidence:—*v.t.* to doubt; suspect.

mis-un-der-stand (mis'un-dėr-stand'), *v.t.* and *v.i.* [misunderstood (mis'un-dėr-stood'), misunderstanding], to take (a person, remark, etc.) in a wrong sense; mistake the meaning of (words or actions).

mis-un-der-stand-ing (mis'un-dėr-stan'ding), *n.* **1,** disagreement; a quarrel; as, a *misunderstanding* between friends; **2,** a mistake as to meaning or motive.

mis-use (mis'ūs'), *n.* **1,** wrong use; **2,** abuse:—*v.t.* (mis'ūz'), [misused, misusing], to use wrongly; ill-treat; as, to *misuse* a horse.

¹mite (mīt), *n.* any of various tiny animals of the spider family, which live as parasites on animals, insects, plants, and stored goods, such as cheese.

²mite (mīt), *n.* **1,** a small coin used in ancient Palestine; as, the widow's *mite* (Mark 12:42); hence, any small contribution; **2,** *Colloq.* a very small object or quantity; a small child.

mit-i-gate (mit'i-gāt'), *v.t.* [mitigated; mitigat-ing], to make less severe or painful; soften; as, time *mitigates* grief.

mi-tre or **mi-ter** (mī'tėr), *n.* **1,** a kind of crown or tall cap with two peaks, worn by archbishops, bishops, and sometimes by abbots at special ceremonies, as a symbol of office; **2,** a slanting joint, as at corners in mouldings, edgings, etc.: also called *mitre joint*:—*v.t.* **1,** to place a bishop's crown upon; hence, to raise to the office of a bishop; **2,** to join on a slanting line at a corner.

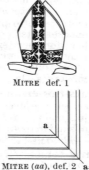

MITRE def. 1

MITRE (*aa*), def. 2

mitt (mit), *n.* **1,** a kind of glove, often of lace or net, without fingers or with half fingers; **2,** a glove with a thick protective pad over the palm, used in baseball.

mit-ten (mit'n), *n.* a glove for winter wear, covering the four fingers together and the thumb separately.

mix (miks), *v.t.* [*p.t.* and *p.p.* mixed or mixt (mikst), *p.pr.* mix-ing], **1,** to unite or blend into one mass or compound; **2,** to make by putting ingredients together; as, to *mix* a cake; **3,** to confuse; as, to *mix* facts:—*v.i.* **1,** to become united in a compound; as, oil will not *mix* with water; **2,** to mingle; associate; take part; as, to *mix* with the crowd; to *mix* well.—*n.* mix'er.

mixed (mikst), *adj.* **1,** composed of different kinds; as, *mixed* sweets or cakes; **2,** for persons of both sexes; as, a *mixed* school; **3,** not restricted by class or condition; as, a *mixed* crowd; **4,** confused; mentally muddled; as, to be *mixed* up.

mixed num-ber, a whole number and a fraction, as 4½ or 3.1416.

mix-ture (miks'tūr), *n.* **1,** the state of being blended or mingled; **2,** a compound or mass formed of two or more things.

miz-zen (miz'n), *n.* **1,** a fore-and-aft sail set on the mizzen-mast; **2,** the lowest square sail on the mizzen-mast of a full-rigged ship; **3,** a mizzen-mast.

miz-zen—mast (miz'n-mȧst'; miz'n-mast), *n.* **1,** the mast nearest the stern in a two-masted or three-masted vessel; **2,** the third mast from the bow in a vessel with four or more masts.

moan (mōn), *v.i.* to utter a low sound from, or as from, pain or sorrow:—*v.t.* to utter in a low wail:—*n.* a low, drawn-out sound of sorrow or pain; any similar sound; as, the *moan* of the wind.

moat (mōt), *n.* a deep ditch around a fortress or castle, usually containing water.

mob (mob), *n.* **1,** the common people; **2,** a rude, disorderly crowd:—*v.t.* [mobbed, mob-bing], to attack in a disorderly crowd.

mo-bile (mō'bīl; mō'bil), *adj.* **1,** easily moved; as, *mobile* troops; **2,** flowing freely, as some liquids; **3,** easily changing in expression; as, a *mobile* face.—*n.* mo-bil'i-ty.

mo-bi-lize (mō'bi-līz'; mob'), *v.t.* [mobilized, mobiliz-ing], to call and prepare for active service; as, to *mobilize* an army or a navy.—*n.* mo'bi-li-za'tion.

moc-ca-sin (mok'a-sin), *n.* **1,** a deerskin or other soft leather sandal worn by the North American Indians; **2,** any of several poisonous, mottled snakes of the southern U.S., esp. the water moccasin; **3,** a kind of wild orchid.

mock (mok), *v.t.* **1,** to ridicule; mimic in sport or contempt; make fun of; deride; **2,** to defy or scorn; as, to *mock* the law; **3,** to deceive; tantalize; as, the mirage in the desert *mocked* the travellers:—*n.* **1,** ridicule; **2,** a jeer or gibe; **3,** an object of ridicule:—*adj* false; not real; as, a *mock* battle.

mock-er-y (mok'ėr-i), *n.* [*pl.* mockeries], **1,** the act of making fun of a person or thing; **2,** ridicule; **3,** a poor or disrespectful imitation; **4,** an empty sham.

mock-ing-bird (mok'ing-bûrd'), *n.* a thrush of the southern U.S., about the size of a robin, noted for imitating the calls of other birds.

mock—or-ange (mok'—or'inj), an ornamental flowering shrub; syringa.

mock-up (mok'up'), *n.* a full-sized model in plywood, cardboard, etc., built accurately to scale, of a machine, weapon, airplane, etc., for instructional and test purposes.

mod-al (mōd'al), *adj.* pertaining to a manner, form, or mode: in *grammar*, **1,** of a verb; as *modal* auxiliaries (*may, might, must, can, would, should*); **2,** *modal* adverbs (*never, perhaps, certainly,* etc.) which indicate the speaker's point of view, or degrees of certainty; **3,** *mood* in verbs (assertion, doubt, command).

mode (mōd), *n.* **1,** way, method, or manner of doing something; as, a *mode* of speech; **2,** usual custom; fashion; style; as, hooped skirts are no longer the *mode;* **3,** in *grammar,* a certain form of a verb indicating whether or not the verb states a fact, a command, a condition, etc.; as, the indicative, imperative, or subjunctive *modes:* often called *mood.*

mod-el (mod'el), *n.* **1,** a pattern of something to be made, copied, or imitated; a standard copy; **2,** a small-sized, exact, and detailed representation of something to be made; as, an engine or ship *model;* a clay or wax *model* for a statue; **3,** a person who poses for a painter or sculptor; **4,** a woman who tries on costumes so that customers may see their effect; **5,** a person or thing to be imitated; as, let Laurier be your *model:*—*v.t.* [modelled, model-ling], to form or mould; as, to *model* a head in clay:—*v.i.* **1,** to shape objects out of clay; make designs; **2,** to pose, as for an artist, or to try on costumes for customers:—*adj.* **1,** serving

as a pattern; **2,** worthy of being imitated.

mod-er-ate (mod'ėr-āt'), *v.t.* [moderat-ed, moderat-ing], **1,** to keep within bounds; make less violent, intense, or extreme; as, to *moderate* rage, heat, etc.; **2,** to preside over, as a meeting:—*v.i.* to become less violent or intense; as, the storm gradually *moderated:*—*adj.* (mod'ėr-it), **1,** not extreme; calm; mild; **2,** limited; mediocre; medium. —*n.* mod'er-a'tion.

mod-er-a-tor (mod'ėr-ā'tėr), *n.* one who or that which regulates or restrains; **2,** in the (Presbyterian) Church, a presiding official, as of a session, presbytery, synod, or General Assembly; **3,** the presiding officer of a town council, debating team, TV panel, etc.

mod-ern (mod'ėrn), *adj.* **1,** having to do with the present time; recent; as, *modern* inventions; **2,** relating to, or originating in, the centuries after about 1500 A.D.:—*n.* a person of recent and present times; also, one up-to-date in his views or manners.—*n.* mod'ern-ism; mo-der'ni-ty.—*adj.* mod'ern-is'tic.

mod-ern-ize (mod'ėr-nīz'), *v.t.* [modernized, moderniz-ing], to make like, or adapt to, present usage, taste, or speech.

mod-est (mod'est), *adj.* **1,** not boastful or vain of one's own worth; **2,** retiring; not showy; as, the *modest* violet; **3,** not excessive or extreme; as, a *modest* ambition; **4,** pure; chaste.—*adv.* mod'-est-ly.

mod-es-ty (mod'es-ti), *n.* **1,** regard for what is proper in behaviour or manner; **2,** reserve concerning one's own powers; lack of conceit; **3,** freedom from what is extreme; moderation; as, *modesty* in dress.

mod-i-cum (mod'i-kum), *n.* a small amount; as, a *modicum* of common sense.

mod-i-fy (mod'i-fī'), *v.t.* [modified, modify-ing], **1,** to change slightly; as, to *modify* an idea; **2,** to limit; reduce; **3,** in *grammar,* to qualify; as, adjectives *modify* nouns.—*n.* mod'i-fi-ca'-tion.—*n.* mod'i-fi'er.

mod-ish (mōd'ish), *adj.* fashionable.

mod-u-late (mod'ū-lāt'), *v.t.* [modulat-ed, modulat-ing], **1,** to vary the tone of; as, to *modulate* the voice; **2,** to tone down:—*v.i.* in *music,* to pass from one key to a related key.—*n.* mod'u-la'tion.

mo-hair (mō'hâr'), *n.* **1,** a woven

material made from the hair of the Angora goat; **2,** an imitation of such a material.

Mo-ham-med-an (mō-ham'ed-an), *n.* and *adj.* a follower of Mohammed (A.D. 570–632) or of Islam, the religion founded by him. Also, **Ma-hom'et-an; Ma-hom'ed-an.**

moil (moil), *v.i.* to toil; drudge:—*n.* **1,** drudgery; **2,** confusion; turmoil.

moist (moist), *adj.* **1,** slightly wet; damp; **2,** tearful; as, *moist* eyes.

mois-ten (mois'n), *v.t.* and *v.i.* to make, or become, damp or slightly wet.

mois-ture (mois'tūr), *n.* **1,** a moderate degree of dampness; **2,** water, or other liquid, in small quantity in the air as vapour, or condensed on a surface.

mo-lar (mō'lēr), *n.* a double tooth, or grinder (see illustration under *dentition*): —*adj.* used for grinding.

mo-las-ses (mō-las'iz), *n.* [*pl.* molasses], a dark-coloured syrup, obtained as a by-product in the making of sugar; treacle.

mold (mōld), *n.* Same as ¹**mould,** ²**mould,** ³**mould.**

¹**mole** (mōl), *n.* a dark-coloured spot or growth on the skin.

²**mole** (mōl), *n.* a tiny, burrowing, worm-eating animal with soft, blackish-brown fur, imperfectly developed eyes, and broad forefeet with which it digs underground tunnels.

mol-e-cule (mol'i-kūl'; mō'li-kūl'), *n.* **1,** the smallest quantity of any substance which can exist separately and still retain the characteristics of the substance; a group of atoms bound together by chemical forces and acting as a physical unit; **2,** loosely, any tiny particle.—*adj.* **mo-lec'u-lar** (mō-lek'ū-lēr).

mole-hill (mōl'hil'), *n.* **1,** a little mound made by the burrowing of a mole; **2,** a small, trivial hindrance or difficulty.

mole-skin (mōl'skin'), *n.* **1,** the soft, fragile, gray fur of the mole; **2,** a strong twilled fabric used in sportsmen's and labourers' trousers; as, when football ended that year, he hung up his *moleskins* for good.

mo-lest (mō-lest'), *v.t.* to interfere with; disturb; pester.—*n.* **mo'les-ta'tion** (mol').

mol-li-fy (mol'i-fī'), *v.t.* [mollified, mollify-ing], to calm; soften; make less severe.

mol-lusc (mol'usk), *n.* any of numerous soft-bodied, hard-shelled animals,

loosely called *shellfish,* as oysters, clams, etc.

mol-ly-cod-dle (mol'i-kod'l), *v.t.* to pamper; as, she *mollycoddled* her son: *n.* one so pampered; a milksop.

molt (mōlt), *v.i.* Same as **moult.**

mol-ten (mōl'tn), *adj.* melted by heat, as, *molten* iron, lava, etc.

mo-lyb-de-num (mo-lib'di-num), *n.* a hard, silvery white, metallic element used in alloys, sparkplug points, etc.

mom (mom), *n. Colloq.* mother.

mo-ment (mō'ment), *n.* **1,** a portion of time; an instant; **2,** the present time; as, the man of the *moment;* **3,** importance; as, news of great *moment.*

mo-men-tar-y (mō'men-tēr-i), *adj.* lasting only for, or done in, an instant; as, a *momentary* rage.—*adj.* **mo'men-tar-i-ly.**

mo-men-tous (mō-men'tus), *adj.* very important; of great consequence; as, a *momentous* decision.

mo-men-tum (mō-men'tum), *n.* **1,** in *mechanics,* the force of motion in a moving body as measured by the product of its weight and speed; **2,** popularly, impetus gained by motion.

mon-ad (mon'ad; mō'nad), *n.* in *chemistry,* an element, radical or atom with a combining power equal to that of one atom of hydrogen.

mon-arch (mon'ērk), *n.* **1,** a supreme ruler or sovereign, as a king, queen, emperor, etc.; also, the hereditary ruler of a constitutional monarchy; **2,** the chief of its class or kind; as, the lion is *monarch* of all beasts.—*adj.* **mo-nar'chal** (mo-när'kal); **mo-nar'-chi-al** (mo-när'ki-al).—*adj.* **mo-nar'-chi-cal** (-ki-kal).

mon-arch-ist (mon'ēr-kist), *n.* one who believes in, or supports, a government whose power is possessed by a king, emperor, etc.—*n.* **mon'arch-ism.**

mon-arch-y (mon'ēr-ki), *n.* [*pl.* monarchies], **1,** a state ruled by a monarch whose power is supreme: called *absolute monarchy;* **2,** a state whose constitution limits the monarch's powers: called a *limited* or *constitutional monarchy;* **3,** a kingdom; an empire.

mon-as-ter-y (mon'as-tēr-i), *n.* [*pl.* monasteries], a house of seclusion occupied by persons, esp. monks, bound by vows to a religious life.—*adj.* **mon'as-te'ri-al.**

mo-nas-tic (mo-nas'tik) or **mo-nas'ti-cal** (mo-nas'ti-kal), *adj.* pertaining to religious houses called *monasteries,* or to monks and their manner of life; as, *monastic* discipline.—*n.* **mo-nas'ti-cism.**

Mon-day (mun′di; -dā), *n.* the second day of the week, following Sunday.

mon-e-tar-y (mon′i-tėr-i; mun′i-tėr-i), *adj.* 1, of or relating to money; as, a *monetary* gift; 2, pertaining to coinage or currency; as, the dollar is the *monetary* unit of Canada.

mon-ey (mun′i), *n.* [*pl.* moneys], 1, coin; gold, silver, etc. coined by a government and used as a means of exchange; 2, bank-notes, cheques, drafts, etc., used as a means of exchange; 3, wealth; 4, **monies**, sums of money.

Mon-gol-ism (mong′go-lizm), *n.* mental deficiency from birth, marked by wide, flattened skull and narrow slanting eyes; congenital idiocy.—*adj.* **Mon-go′li-an; Mon′go-loid.**

mon-goose (mong′gōōs), *n.* [*pl.* mongooses], a small, ferretlike animal of India, dingy brown in colour, noted for its ability to kill poisonous snakes.

mon-grel (mung′grel; mong′grel), *adj.* 1, of a mixed breed or kind; 2, of mixed origin: used esp. of a language or a word:—*n.* an animal of mixed breed or kind.

mon-i-tor (mon′i-tėr), *n.* 1, one who warns or advises; 2, in a school, a pupil appointed to oversee the younger ones; 3, an iron-clad warship, having low sides and one or more mounted with guns; 4, a large lizard of Africa, Asia, and Australia, reputed to give warning of crocodiles.

monk (mungk), *n.* one of a body of men who have taken religious vows and are living in a monastery apart from the world.—*adj.* **monk′ish.**

mon-key (mung′ki), *n.* [*pl.* monkeys], in the broadest sense, any one of the highest order of animals below man; in a narrower sense, one of the smaller, long-tailed forms differing from the larger, nearly tailless forms, called *apes:*—*v.i.* to play the fool; also, to meddle:—*v.t.* to ape; imitate.

monkey—wrench (mung′ki—rench′), a wrench with an adjustable jaw, useful for turning a nut, bolt, etc.

monks-hood (mungks′hood′), *n.* a plant of the crowfoot family with long spikes of blue hooded flowers and extremely poisonous roots: also called *aconite* and *wolfsbane.*

mon-o-chrome (mon′ō-krōm′), *n.* a picture in one colour or in different shades of one colour.

mon-o-cle (mon′o-kl), *n.* an eye-glass for one eye.

mon-o-cot-y-le-don (mon′ō-kot′i-lē′dun), *n.* a seed plant having a single seed leaf, or cotyledon, in the embryo. —*adj.* **mon′o-cot′y-lē′don-ous.**

mo-nog-a-my (mo-nog′a-mi), *n.* marriage to but one person at a time (as opposed to *bigamy* and *polygamy*).

mon-o-gram (mon′ō-gram′), *n.* a decorative character formed of two or more letters, often a person's initials, combined or interwoven.

mon-o-graph (mon′ō-gråf′), *n.* a short treatise on one particular subject, esp. a vocation; as, a *monograph* on chemical engineering.

mon-o-lith (mon′ō-lith), *n.* a single large stone, used in architecture or sculpture, as a statue, pillar, etc.

mon-o-lith-ic (mon′ō-lith′ik), *adj.* 1, massively solid; 2, *figuratively,* solid, single and uniform; as a *monolithic* culture or party.

mon-o-logue or **mon-o-log** (mon′ō-log′), *n.* 1, a long speech by one person, either in conversation or in a play; 2, a dramatic scene in which only one person speaks.

mon-o-ma-ni-a (mon′ō-mā′ni-a), *n.* a madness or craze in regard to a single subject or idea.—*n. and adj.* **mon′o-ma′ni-ac.**

mon-o-plane (mon′ō-plān′), *n.* an aeroplane with but one main supporting surface, consisting of a wing on each side of the body.

mo-nop-o-ly (mo-nop′o-li), *n.* [*pl.* monopolies], 1, the exclusive control and possession of anything, esp. of some commercial product, as sugar or rubber, or of some public service, as that of providing a community with gas or electricity or water; 2, the commodity or service so controlled; 3, a company that has such control; 4, a grant, or charter, of monopoly.—*v.t.* **mo-nop′o-lize.**

mon-o-rail (mon′ō-rāl′), *n.* a single rail on which cars run suspended.

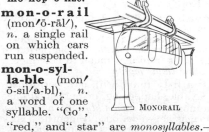

MONORAIL

mon-o-syl-la-ble (mon′ō-sil′a-bl), *n.* a word of one syllable. "Go", "red," and" star" are *monosyllables.*—*adj.* **mon′o-syl-lab′ic.**

mon-o-the-ism (mon′ō-thē′izm), *n.* the belief in one God only.—*adj.* **mon′-o-the-is′tic.**

mon-o-tone (mon′ŏ-tōn′), *n.* **1,** utterance of one syllable after another without change of pitch or key; **2,** sameness of style or colour, as in writing or painting.

mo-not-o-nous (mo-not′o-nus), *adj.* constantly the same; lacking variety; tiresome; as, a *monotonous* voice; a *monotonous* round of work.—*n.* **mo-not′o-ny.**

mon-o-type (mon′ŏ-tīp′), *n.* in *printing*, equipment with typewriter keyboard and a separate casting unit, as distinct from *linotype* (which combines both).

mon-ox-ide (mon-ok′sīd), *n.* an oxide with but one oxygen atom to the molecule; as, he died from carbon *monoxide* (CO) poisoning.

mon-sieur (mė-syö′; msyö), *n. French,* [*pl.* messieurs (mā′syö′)], *Sir* or *Mr.*; *pl. Messrs.*

mon-soon (mon-soon′), *n.* **1,** a wind of the Indian Ocean and southern Asia that blows from the northeast in winter and from the southwest in summer; **2,** the rainy season of the southwest monsoon.

mon-ster (mon′stėr), *n.* **1,** a misshapen animal or plant; as, a five-legged calf is a *monster;* **2,** an imaginary animal of grotesque form, such as a dragon, or the Minotaur; **3,** something very huge, deformed, or hideous; **4,** a person remarkable for wickedness or ugliness:—*adj.* huge.

mon-strous (mon′strus), *adj.* **1,** out of the common course of nature; abnormal; **2,** enormous; huge; as, a *monstrous* elephant; **3,** horrible; causing disgust; as, a *monstrous* crime.—*adv.* **mon′strous-ly.**—*n.* **mon-stros′i-ty.**

mon-tage (mŏṅ′tàzh′), *n.* in *motion pictures*, the cutting and arranging of film for a picture so that it tells a consecutive story or produces a desired effect.

month (munth), *n.* **1,** one of the twelve parts into which the year is divided, each containing about four weeks: called *calendar month;* **2,** the period of 28 days from new moon to new moon: called *lunar month.*

month-ly (munth′li), *adj.* performed, payable, happening, or published once a month; as, a *monthly* bill; a *monthly* magazine:—*adv.* once a month; every month; as, she pays her bills *monthly:*—*n.* [*pl.* monthlies], a magazine published each month.

mon-u-ment (mon′ū-ment), *n.* **1,** anything that keeps alive the memory of a person or event, as a pillar, a statue, etc.; **2,** a conspicuous and lasting example; an achievement worthy to be remembered; as, a *monument* of science.—*adj.* **mon′u-men tal.**

¹mood (mōōd), *n.* in *grammar,* one of the forms that the verb can take to show the manner in which the action or state, expressed by the verb, is to be understood, whether as a fact, wish, command, etc.

²mood (mōōd), *n.* a state of mind; humour; as, children in a merry *mood.*

mood-y (mōōd′i), *adj.* [mood-i-er, mood-i-est], **1,** subject to changes in the state of mind or temper; **2,** often ill-humoured or depressed; sullen.—*adv.* **mood′i-ly.**

moon (mōōn), *n.* **1,** the heavenly body that revolves around the earth once a month; **2,** any heavenly body that revolves about a planet; **3,** a month; as, "the *moon* of roses"; **4,** anything shaped like the moon, whether in its full or crescent phase:—*v.i.* to wander or look about listlessly.

moon-beam (mōōn′bēm′), *n.* a ray of light from the moon.

moon-light (mōōn′līt′), *n.* the light given by the moon:—*adj.* **1,** lighted by the moon; **2,** occurring by moonlight; as, a *moonlight* sail:—*v.i. Colloq.* to hold or do two jobs at once (one by night as well as one by day).

moon-stone (mōōn′stōn′), *n.* a semi-precious stone, lustrous and translucent.

moon-struck (mōōn′struk′), *adj.* lunatic; ill; dazed or crazed.

¹moor (mōōr), *n.* a tract of open, barren land, esp. one covered with heather.

²moor (mōōr), *v.t.* to secure (a vessel) in a particular place by a cable or anchor. —*n.* **moor′age.**—*n.pl.* **moor′ings.**

moor-land (mōōr′land′), *n.* barren land covered with heather.

moose (mōōs), *n.* the largest member of the deer family, related to the European elk, found in the forests of Canada and the northern U.S. It often attains a weight of 1,000 pounds or more.

moot (mōōt), *v.t.* to propose for discussion; also, to argue, debate, or discuss (a question):—*adj.* open to discussion; as, a *moot* question.

mop (mop), *n.* **1,** a bundle of cloth, rags, etc., fastened to the end of a long handle and used for washing floors, cleaning walls, etc.; **2,** a thick head of hair like a mop:—*v.t.* [mopped, mopping], **1,** to clean with a mop; as, to *mop* a floor; also, to remove with a mop; as, to *mop* up dust; **2,** to wipe; as, to *mop* the brow.

mope (mōp), *n.* one who is dull or out of spirits:—*v.i.* [moped, mop-ing], to be listless or low-spirited.

mop-pet (mop'it), *n.* **1,** a young girl; **2,** a rag doll: hence, a baby; dear child; darling; **3,** a lap dog.

mo-raine (mo-rān'), *n.* a ridge or heap of rocks or gravel gathered by a glacier and deposited at its edge (*lateral moraine*) or base (*terminal moraine*).

mor-al (mor'al), *n.* **1,** the lesson taught by a fable, story, or event; **2,** **morals,** standards of conduct; also, conduct; behaviour:—*adj.* **1,** referring to right and wrong; ethical; as, *moral* standards; a *moral* sense; **2,** virtuous; good; as, a *moral* way of living; a *moral* people; **3,** able to distinguish between right and wrong; as, man is a *moral* being.

mo-rale (mō-rȧl'; mō-räl'), *n.* the mental state which enables men to sustain courage, zest, hope, etc., in the face of danger or discouragement; as, defeat did not rob the team of its *morale.*

mo-ral-i-ty (mō-ral'i-ti), *n.* [*pl.* moralities], **1,** morals; standards of conduct; **2,** virtuousness; upright behaviour.

mor-al-ize (mor'al-īz'), *v.t.* [moralized, moraliz-ing], to make moral, or improve the morals of; as, to *moralize* the heathen:—*v.i.* to talk at length about right and wrong, duty, goodness, truth, etc.—*n.* **mor'al-ist.**

mor-al-ly (mor'al-i), *adv.* **1,** according to standards of right and wrong; as, though declared innocent by law, he is *morally* guilty.

mo-rass (mō-ras'), *n.* a swamp; tract of soft, wet ground; bog.

mor-a-to-ri-um (mor'a-tō'ri-um), *n.* **1,** in *law,* an enactment to allow a debtor or bank to delay payment of money due; **2,** the period that such an act is in force.

mo-ray (mō'rā; mō-rā'), *n.* a voracious, bright-coloured, marine eel with sharp, knife-like teeth: found in all warm seas.

mor-bid (môr'bid), *adj.* **1,** relating to disease; as, a *morbid* condition; **2,** sickly; hence, gloomy; unwholesome; as, a *morbid* imagination.—*adv.* **mor'-bid-ly.**

more (mōr), *adj.* [*comp.* of *many* and *much*], **1,** greater in number, quantity, extent, etc.; as, we know *more* people than you; you have *more* energy and *more* time than I; **2,** additional; as, one *more* word:—*adv.* **1,** to a greater degree; **2,** again; as, we shall see her once *more;* **3,** used often to form the comparative of adjectives and adverbs; as, *more* hopeful; *more* hopefully:—*pron.* **1,** a greater quantity, number, etc.; **2,** something further or additional.

mor-el (mor-el'), *n.* an edible mushroom of spongelike tissues.

more-o-ver (mōr-ō'vėr), *adv.* besides; in addition.

morgue (môrg), *n.* a building where bodies of persons found dead are placed for identification.

mor-i-bund (môr'i-bund'), *adj.* in a dying condition; as, fascism is by no means *moribund* today.

morn (môrn), *n.* *Poetic,* morning; dawn.

morn-ing (môr'ning), *n.* the early part of the day, not later than noon:—*adj.* pertaining to the morning; early.

morn-ing—glor-y (môr'ning-glōr'i), *n.* [*pl.* morning-glories], a twining plant with heart-shaped leaves and red, blue, or white funnel-shaped flowers.

mo-roc-co (mo-rok'ō), *n.* [*pl.* moroccos], a fine variety of leather made from goatskin, tanned with sumac, and used for bookbinding.

mor-on (mōr'on), *n.* a person whose mental ability or intelligence is below normal.—*adj.* **mo-ron'ic.**

mo-rose (mō-rōs'), *adj.* sullen; gloomy.

mor-phine (môr'fēn; môr'fin), *n.* a drug made from opium and used in medicine to deaden pain or to produce sleep.

mor-phol-o-gy (môr-fol'o-ji), *n.* the science of the form and structure of plants and animals, as against *physiology,* the science of functions and life processes.

mor-row (mor'ō), *n.* **1,** the next day after any given day; tomorrow; **2,** *Archaic,* morning; as, good *morrow.*

Morse code, a telegraphic system of dots and dashes, transmitted by sounds, flashes, etc.; there are two codes, the American telegraphic and the Continental (which differ in 11 letters of the 26).

mor-sel (mor's'l). *n.* a small piece; a little bit; a titbit.

mor-tal (môr'tal), *n.* a being subject to death; a human being:—*adj.* **1,** subject to death; as, *mortal* man; **2,** causing death; fatal; as, a *mortal* wound; causing spiritual death; deadly; as, *mortal* sin; **3,** involving death; as, *mortal* combat; **4,** filled with desire to kill; as, a *mortal* enemy; **5,** extreme; as, *mortal* fear; **6,** accompanying death; as, *mortal* agony; **7,** belonging to human beings; as, *mortal* fame.

mor-tal-i-ty (môr-tal′i-ti), *n.* [*pl.* mortalities], **1,** the condition of being subject to death; **2,** death; destruction; as, the *mortality* from war or disease; **3,** the number of deaths in a given period in a given area; death-rate.

mor-tal-ly (môr′tal-i), *adv.* **1,** in such a manner as to cause death; as, *mortally* wounded; **2,** deeply; bitterly; as, *mortally* grieved.

mor-tar (môr′tẽr), *n.* **1,** a bowl-like vessel in which substances are pounded or ground with a pestle; **2,** a short cannon used for shells at a high angle; **3,** a building cement made of lime, sand, and water.

MORTAR AND PESTLE

mor-tar-board (môr′- tẽr-bôrd′), *n.* **1,** a square board with a handle on the under side, for holding mortar; **2,** an academic cap, with a flat, projecting top.

mort-gage (môr′gij), *n.* a legal paper given by one person, usually a borrower, to another, usually a lender, which signs over certain property of the former, as security in case the debt is not paid:—*v.t.* [mortgaged, mortgaging], to make over (property) as security to one to whom a debt is owed.

mort-ga-gee (môr′ga-jē′), *n.* a person who holds a mortgage (security for a loan) on another's property.

mort-ga-gor (môr′ga-jôr′), *n.* one who gives a mortgage in order to borrow money.

mor-ti-cian (môr-tish′an), *n.* an undertaker.

mor-ti-fy (môr′ti-fī′), *v.t.* [mortified, mortify-ing], **1,** to subdue by self-denial; as, to *mortify* the appetites; **2,** to embarrass; put to shame; as, his rudeness *mortified* me:—*v.i.* to be affected with gangrene, as a foot or hand.—*n.* mor′ti-fi-ca′tion.

mor-tise (môr′tis), *n.* a hollowed-out space in a piece of wood into which a corresponding projection (the tenon) is inserted to form a joint.

mor-tu-a-ry (môr′tū-a-ri), *n.* and *adj.* **1,** a morgue; **2,** a burial place.

mo-sa-ic (mō-zā′ik), *n.* a design made of small pieces of coloured glass, stone, etc., inlaid in some other material; also, a piece of work so made:—*adj.* made of or like mosaic; as, *mosaic* jewellery.

mosque (mosk), *n.* a Moslem temple.

mos-qui-to (mus-kē′tō), *n.* [*pl.* mosquitoes], a two-winged insect, the female of which punctures the skin of man and animals, feeding on the blood it sucks out.

moss (môs), *n.* a spore-bearing, small-leaved plant, which grows like a thick mat on damp ground, trees, rocks, etc.: —**Iceland moss,** a kind of lichen.—*adj.* moss′y.

most (mōst), *adj.* [*superl.* of *many* and *much*]. greatest in number, quantity, degree, etc.; as, this house has the *most* rooms:—*pron.* the greatest number, part, quantity, or value; as, give him the *most:*—*adv.* **1,** in the greatest degree; as, I like plums *most;* **2,** used often to form the superlative of adjectives and adverbs; as, *most* hopeful; *most* hopefully.

most-ly (mōst′li), *adv.* mainly; usually.

mote (mōt), *n.* a tiny particle of dust.

mo-tel (mō-tel′), *n.* a hotel primarily for motorists.

moth (môth), *n.* [*pl.* moths (mo*th*z; mô*th*s)], **1,** any. of numerous, four-winged, night-flying insects, related to the butterfly, having antennae, and feelers, which are not knobbed; **2,** an insect of this kind whose larva feeds on wool, fur, etc.: also called *clothes moth.*

moth-er (mu*th*′ẽr), *n.* **1,** a female parent; **2,** origin or source; as, oppression is the *mother* of revolt; **3,** a title given to the head of a religious house for women:—*adj.* native; as, one's *mother* tongue:—*v.t.* to act as a mother to.—*adj.* moth′er-ly.

moth-er-hood (mu*th*′ẽr-hood), *n.* **1,** the state of being a mother; **2,** all the mothers of a country or region.

moth-er—in—law (mu*th*′ẽr-in-lô′), *n.* [*pl.* mothers-in-law], the mother of one's husband or of one's wife.

moth-er of pearl, the hard, rainbow-tinted lining of certain shells, including that of the pearl-oyster. It is used for buttons, ornaments, etc.

Moth-er's Day, the second Sunday in May, observed in honour of mothers.

mo-tif (mō-tēf′), *n.* the subject or main idea of a work of art or literature; in *music,* a theme which may be repeated many times with variations; also, a unit of design.

mo-tion (mō'shun), *n.* **1,** the act or process of moving from one place or position to another; action, as opposed to rest; as, the ceaseless *motion* of the waves; **2,** a gesture; as, a beckoning *motion;* **3,** a formal proposal made in a meeting; as, a *motion* to adjourn:—*v.i.* to express one's meaning in a gesture instead of words:—*v.t.* to guide or invite by a gesture; as, he *motioned* me in.—*adj.* **mo'tion-less.**

mo-tion pic-ture, a series of pictures of persons and things in action, taken by a special camera in such a way that when thrown on a screen in rapid succession they form a continuous picture in which the action is reproduced: also called *moving picture* and *cinema.*

mo-tive (mō'tiv), *n.* **1,** that which causes a person to act as he does under certain circumstances; the inner reason for any act; as, hunger might be the *motive* for stealing; **2,** in art, literature, and music, the main idea or theme; motif:—*adj.* causing motion; as, *motive* power.—*v.t.* **mo'ti-vate.**—*n.* **mo'ti-va'-tion.**

mot-ley (mot'li), *adj.* **1,** consisting of different colours; **2,** wearing particoloured clothing; as, a *motley* fool; **3,** composed of various kinds; as, a *motley* crowd:—*n.* a garment of various colours, formerly worn by jesters.

mo-tor (mō'tēr), *n.* **1,** an engine that produces action or mechanical power; as, an electric *motor;* **2,** an automobile: —*adj.* **1,** having to do with motors or with motor-driven vehicles; as, *motor* traffic; **2,** imparting action; as, *motor* nerves:—*v.i.* and *v.t.* to travel or transport by automobile.

mo-tor-boat, a boat that is driven by a motor.

mo-tor-cade (mō'tēr-kād'), *n.* a procession of automobiles.

mo-tor-car (mō'tēr-kär'), *n.* an automobile.

mo-tor-cy-cle, a bicycle run by a motor of one or more cylinders.—*n.* **mo'tor-cy'clist.**

mo-tor-drome (mō'tēr-drōm'), *n.* a track for racing or testing motor vehicles.

mo-tor-ist (mō'tēr-ist), *n.* one who usually travels by automobile.

mo-tor-man (mō'tēr-man), *n.* [*pl.* motor-men (-men)], one who operates a motor, esp. on an electric tram or train.

mot-tle (mot'l), *v.t.* [mot-tled, mot-tling], to mark with spots of various colours.

mot-to (mot'ō), *n.* [*pl.* mottoes], **1,** a short sentence, a phrase, or a single word, suggesting some guiding principle **2,** a quotation used as a chapter heading, a slogan, or an inscription.

¹mould (mōld), *n.* fine, soft soil rich in decayed matter.

²mould (mōld), *n.* **1,** a hollow form into which anything is poured to be shaped, as melted metals, jelly, puddings, etc.; **2,** the shape in which a thing is cast; form; **3,** kind; character; as, a man of honest *mould;* **4,** bodily shape or form:—*v.t.* **1,** to fashion in, or as in, a form; as, to *mould* a candle; to *mould* butter; **2,** to shape into a mass of the desired consistency; knead, as dough.

³mould (mōld), *n.* a fuzzy surface growth, composed of fungi, which develops chiefly on decaying animal or vegetable matter under warm, moist conditions, spreading by means of tiny spores and forming dense, feltlike mats:—*v.i.* to become covered with mould.—*adj.* **mould'y.**

mould-er (mōl'dēr), *v.i.* to crumble to dust by natural decay.

mould-ing (mōl'ding), *n.* **1,** anything made in or by a mould or form; **2,** an ornamental strip, usually of wood, used on a wall, cornice, picture-frame, etc.

moult (mōlt), *v.i.* to cast off and renew the hair, feathers, etc.:—*v.t.* to shed, as the skin, hair, horns, etc.:—*n.* the shedding of hair, feathers, etc., or the season when such shedding takes place.

mound (mound), *n.* an artificial bank of earth or stone; also, a small hill.

¹mount (mount), *n.* a high hill; mountain.

²mount (mount), *v.t.* **1,** to climb, ascend, or get up on; as, to *mount* a platform or a horse; **2,** to set up for use; as, to *mount* cannon; also, to be equipped with; as, the fort *mounts* 30 guns; **3,** to set up or arrange for exhibition or preservation; as, to *mount* photographs or insects; **4,** to put on, or furnish with, a horse:—*v.i.* **1,** to rise or increase; as, his debts *mounted* steadily; **2,** to get up on a horse, platform, etc.:—*n.* **1,** a saddle-horse; **2,** that on which something, as a photograph or drawing, may be fixed or mounted.

moun-tain (moun'tin; moun'ten), *n.* **1,** a natural elevation of rock or earth rising high above the level of the surrounding country; a towering hill; **2,** anything huge.—*adj.* **moun'tain-ous.**

mountain ash, a hardy tree or tall

shrub bearing clusters of brilliant red berries.

moun-tain-eer (moun'ti-nēr'), n. 1, a mountain dweller; 2, a mountain climber.

mountain goat, a pure-white goatlike animal of the north-western U.S. and Canada.

mountain lion, the cougar or American panther.

moun-te-bank (moun'ti-bangk), n. 1, one who sells quack medicines, esp. from a public platform; 2, a person who tricks or deceives people.

moun-tie or **moun-ty** (moun'ti), n. Colloq. a member of the Royal Canadian Mounted Police.

mount-ing (moun'ting), n. 1, the act of rising, climbing, etc.; 2, a support, fixture, or setting; as, the mounting of a jewel; the mounting of a gun.

mourn (môrn), v.i. and v.t. to grieve (for); sorrow (over); lament.—n. mourn'er.

mourn-ful (môrn'fool), adj. sad; doleful.

mourn-ing (môr'ning), n. 1, the act of grieving; 2, an outward expression of sorrow, as the wearing of black clothes; 3, the clothes themselves.

mourn-ing cloak, in America and Europe, a butterfly having purplish-brown wings with a wide yellow border.

mouse (mous), n. [pl. mice (mīs)], a small rodent related to, but smaller than, the rat, with soft fur and a long tail:—v.i. (mouz), [moused, mous-ing], 1, to watch for or catch mice; 2, to prowl and pry.—n. mous'er (mouz'ẽr). —adj. mous'y.

mousse (mōōs), n. a frozen dessert made of whipped cream sweetened and flavoured.

mous-tache (mus-tàsh'; mus'tash), n. the hair growing on a man's upper lip.

mouth (mouth), n. [pl. mouths (mouthz)], 1, the opening through which an animal takes food into the body; the space containing the teeth and tongue; 2, this opening, as the channel of voice or speech; 3, an opening or outlet; as, the mouth of a jug, tunnel, or river; 4, a face; grimace; as, to make a mouth:—mouth—organ, a small musical wind-instrument, held horizontally against the lips and played by blowing or sucking air through it; a harmonica:—v.t. (mouth), 1, to utter with a swelling or pompous voice; 2, to take in the mouth; as, a

dog mouths a bone:—v.i. 1, to make faces; grimace; 2, to declaim.

mouth-ful (mouth'fool), n. [pl. mouthfuls], 1, as much as is usually put into the mouth at one time; 2, a small amount.

mouth-piece (mouth'pēs'), n. 1, that part of a wind-instrument which is held in or against the player's mouth and through which he blows the air to produce the tone; 2, one who speaks for others; as, he was the mouthpiece of the Conservatives.

mou-ton (mōō'ton'), n. a water-proofed sheep fur, dyed esp. to resemble beaver.

mov-a-ble (mōōv'a-bl), adj. 1, capable of being carried from one place to another; 2, changing from one date to another; as, a movable holiday:— movables, goods or furniture that can be carried from place to place.

move (mōōv), v.t. [moved, mov-ing], 1, to change from one place or position to another; as, to move a table; 2, to set in motion; as, the breeze moves the grass; 3, to cause to act; to impel; as, no plea could move him to consent; 4, to arouse the feelings of; as, to move an audience to tears; 5, to put (a formal motion) before a meeting; as, I move we adjourn; 6, to cause (the bowels) to act:—v.i. 1, to change place or position; also, to advance; as, time moves on; 2, to change one's residence; 3, to take action; 4, to live; pass one's life or time; as, to move in society; 5, to apply (for); as, to move for a new trial; 6, to act: said of the bowels:—n. 1, a changing of place or position; as, a move in chequers; 2, a step in carrying out a plan; 3, a change of residence.— n. mov'er.

move-ment (mōōv'ment), n. 1, the act of changing place; any change of position; 2, a joint effort directed toward a desired end; as, the temperance movement; 3, the delicate mechanism of a watch or clock; 4, a main division of a long musical composition; 5, an emptying of the bowels.

mov-ie (mōōv'i), n. Colloq. a motion picture or a motion-picture theatre: often pl.

mov-ing (mōōv'ing), adj. 1, changing place or position; 2, causing motion or action; 3, stirring the emotions.

mov-ing pic-ture, a series of pictures, thrown on a screen, showing persons or things in motion; a motion picture.

¹**mow** (mō), v.t. [p.t. mowed (mōd), p.p. mowed or mown (mōn), p.pr. mow-ing],

1, to cut down with a scythe or a machine; as, to *mow* hay; **2,** to cut grass, grain, etc., from; as, to *mow* a lawn; **3,** to kill (living beings) as if mowing down grain; as, the guns *mowed* down the enemy:—*v.i.* to cut grass, grain, etc.—*n.* **mow′er.**

²mow (mou), *n.* **1,** a heap of hay, grain, etc., stored in a barn; **2,** the compartment in a barn for hay or grain:—*v.t.* to stow in a mow.

Mr. (mis′tėr), *abbreviation,* [*pl.* Messrs. (mes′rz)], Mister, a title used before a man's name:—**Mrs.** (mis′iz), Mistress, a title used before the name of a married woman.

much (much), *adj.* [*comp.* more, *superl.* most], great in quantity, extent, or degree:—*adv.* **1,** to a great degree or extent; greatly; as, *much* obliged; **2,** nearly; as, *much* of a size:—*indefinite pron.* a great quantity.

mu-ci-lage (mū′si-lij), *n.* a fluid, gummy substance used to stick things together.

muck (muk), *n.* **1,** moist manure; **2,** a mixture of rich earth and decayed matter, esp. when used as a fertilizer; **3,** anything filthy or dirty.—*adj.* **muck′y.**

mu-cous (mū′kus), *adj.* pertaining to, like, or producing, mucus:—**mucous membrane,** the moist lining of the nose, throat, and other passages of the body that open to the outside.

mu-cus (mū′kus), *n.* the slimy substance secreted by the mucous membrane.

mud (mud), *n.* soft, wet earth; mire.

mud-der (mud′ėr), *n.* in *horseracing,* a horse that does well on a muddy track.

mud-dle (mud′l), *n.* a state of confusion or disorder; a mess; also, mental confusion:—*v.t.* [mud-dled, mud-dling], **1,** to confuse or stupefy; to make slightly drunk; **2,** to make a mess of; bungle; as, to *muddle* accounts:—*v.i.* to act ineffectively and at haphazard; as, to *muddle* along.

mud-dy (mud′i), *adj.* [mud-di-er, mud-di-est], **1,** thick with mud; **2,** cloudy; not clear; as, *muddy* coffee; a *muddy* skin; **3,** confused; as, *muddy* ideas:—*v.t.* [muddied, muddy-ing], to make dirty.

mud-guard (mud′gärd′), *n.* a casing over a cycle or vehicle wheel to catch or deflect mud.

mud–hen, any of various rail-like birds, as the rail, coot, gallinule, etc.; a marsh hen.

mud pup-py, a large North American aquatic salamander with bushy red gills (esp. the *hellbender*).

mu-ez-zin (mū-ez′in), *n.* a Moslem crier, from a minaret or mosque, who calls the Faithful to prayer five times daily.

¹muff (muf), *n.* a warm, soft cover into the ends of which the hands may be thrust for protection against cold.

²muff (muf), *n.* in games such as baseball, a clumsy miss, or failure to keep hold of a ball:—*v.t.* and *v.i.* to handle clumsily; fail to hold (a ball); bungle.

muf-fin (muf′in), *n.* a small, usually unsweetened cake, served hot with butter.

muf-fle (muf′l), *v.t.* [muf-fled, muf-fling], **1,** to cover up so as to deaden the sound of; as, to *muffle* a bell; **2,** to wrap up closely and warmly.

muf-fler (muf′lėr), *n.* **1,** a scarf for the throat; **2,** a device for deadening noise; as, the *muffler* of an automobile.

mug (mug), *n.* an earthen, glass, or metal cup with a handle; also, a mugful; as, bring a *mug* of ale.

mug-gy (mug′i), *adj.* [mug-gi-er, mug-gi-est], warm, damp, and close; as, a *muggy* day.

muf-ti (muf′ti), *n.* **1,** civilian dress when worn by one who usually wears a uniform, esp. a military one; **2,** in Turkey and India, an interpreter of the Koran and the law: **Grand Muf′ti.**

muk-luk (muk′luk), *n.* a sealskin boot worn by Eskimos, trappers, flyers, etc., in arctic regions.

mu-lat-to (mū-lat′ō), *n.* [*pl.* mulattoes], the child of a Negro and a white person.

mul-ber-ry (mul′bėr-i), *n.* [*pl.* mulberries], a tree with broad leaves and a sweet, edible, berrylike fruit. The white mulberry is grown for its leaves, on which silk-worms feed.

mulch (mulch), *n.* a layer of leaves, straw, paper, etc., used to protect the roots of trees and plants:—*v.t.* to cover or protect with mulch.

mule (mūl), *n.* **1,** an animal bred from a donkey and a mare; **2,** *Colloq.* a stubborn person; **3,** a kind of spinning-machine.—*adj.* **mul′ish.**—*n.* **mul′ish-ness.**—*n.* **mu′le-teer′.**

mull (mul), *v.i. Colloq.* to cogitate; ponder; as, all day he *mulled over* the proposition.

mul-lein (mul′in) or **mul-len** (mul′-en), *n.* a plant having coarse, fuzzy leaves and yellow flowers in tall spikes.

mul-let (mul′it), *n.* **1,** a food fish with a

cylindrical body, such as the *gray mullet* and *red mullet;* **2,** *Colloq.* the sucker.

mul-li-gan (mul′i-gan), *n. Slang,* a stew of meat, vegetables, etc.

mul-lion (mul′yun), *n.* and *v.* an upright bar dividing the lights of a window, wainscot panels, etc.; as, a *mullioned* window.

mul-ti- (mul′ti-), *prefix* meaning *many,* as in **mul′ti-form′;** **mul′ti-mil′lion-aire′.**

mul-ti-fa-ri-ous (mul′ti-fâ′ri-us), *adj.* many and diverse; as, *multifarious* duties.

mul-ti-ple (mul′ti-pl), *n.* a number or quantity which contains another number or quantity an exact number of times; as, 12 is a *multiple* of 6; also, the result of the multiplication of one number by another:—*adj.* **1,** having many parts; **2,** repeated many times.

mul-ti-pli-cand (mul′ti-pli-kand′), *n.* a number to be multiplied by another—

mul-ti-pli-ca-tion (mul′ti-pli-kā′ shun), *n.* **1,** the act or process of increasing in number; as, a *multiplication* of details; **2,** in *arithmetic,* the operation, shown by the sign ×, by which a number (the *multiplicand*) is taken a given number of times (the number of times being indicated by the *multiplier*), to form a result called the *product;* as, 5 (the *multiplicand*) × 2 (the *multiplier*) = 10 (the *product*).

mul-ti-pli-er (mul′ti-plī′ẽr), *n.* the number which tells how many times another number is to be taken or multiplied.

mul-ti-ply (mul′ti-plī′), *v.t.* [multiplied, multiply-ing], **1,** to cause to increase in number or quantity; **2,** to repeat or take (a number or quantity) a given number of times; as, to *multiply* 4 by 3 means to take 4 three times, getting a result of 12:—*v.i.* to increase in number or extent; as, sorrows *multiply* as one grows old.—*n.* mul′ti-plic′i-ty.

mul-ti-tude (mul′ti-tūd′), *n.* **1,** a great number; crowd; **2,** people in general; as, the *multitude* came to hear him.— *adj.* mul′ti-tu′di-nous.

¹mum (mum), *adj.* silent:—*interj.* be silent!

²mum (mum), *n. Colloq. abbreviation* for (1) chrysanthemum (2) mother.

mum-ble (mum′bl), *v.t.* and *v.i.* [mum-bled, mum-bling], **1,** to mutter, or speak indistinctly; **2,** to chew (food) lightly with partly closed lips or without closing the teeth:—*n.* a muttering.

mum-bo jum-bo (mum′bō jum′bō) *n.* **1,** gibberish; meaningless ritual; **2** an idol; fetish.

mum-mer (mum′ẽr), *n.* one wh takes part in masked revels; an actor

mum-mer-y (mum′ẽr-i), *n.* [*pl.* mum mer-ies], **1,** masquerading; **2,** cere monies or performances regarded a silly or insincere.

mum-my (mum′i), *n.* [*pl.* mummies] the body of a human being or anima embalmed in the ancient Egyptia manner.

mumps (mumps), *n.pl.* used as *sing.* contagious disease marked by inflam mation and swelling of the glands whicl secrete saliva.

munch (munch), *v.t.* and *v.i.* to chev with a crunching noise, as does a horse

mun-dane (mun′dān), *adj.* relating t the world; worldly: *mundane* desire

mu-nic-i-pal (mū-nis′i-pal), *adj.* per taining to a city or town, or to its loca self-government; as, *municipal* build ings.

mu-nic-i-pal-i-ty (mū-nis′i-pal′i-ti) *n.* [*pl.* municipalities], a town, city, o borough with local self-government.

mu-nif-i-cence (mū-nif′i-sens), *n* generosity; liberality.—*adj.* mu-nif′i cent.

mu-ni-tion (mū-nish′un), *n.* ammuni tion and war material.

mu-ral (mū′ral), *adj.* pertaining to wall; on a wall:—*n.* a painting on wall.

mur-der (mûr′dẽr), *n.* the unlawfu intentional killing of a human being esp. **capital murder,** slaying wit deliberate intent.—*v.t.* **1,** to kill (person) deliberately; **2,** to spoil; as, t *murder* a song.—*adj.* mur′der-ous.—*n* mur′der-er; mur′der-ess.

mu-ri-at-ic acid (mū′ri-at′ik), *n* commercial hydrochloric acid, on part hydrogen by volume to one c chlorine dissolved in water.

murk (mûrk), *n.* darkness.—*ad* murk′y.

murk-y (mûr′ki), *adj.* [murk-i-e murk-i-est], dark; gloomy; as, murky night.

mur-mur (mûr′mẽr), *n.* **1,** a lov indistinct sound, as of voices or of running stream; **2,** a grumbling com plaint in a low, muttering tone; grumble:—*v.i.* **1,** to make a sound lik the hum of bees; speak in a low voice **2,** to grumble:—*v.t.* to utter com plainingly or in a low voice.

mus-cle (mus′l), *n.* **1,** an organ o

fibre-like tissue, which contracts and expands, thus producing movement in an animal body; also, the tissue of such an organ; **2**, *Colloq.* bodily strength; physical power.—*adj.* **mus′cu-lar.**

muse (mūz), *v.i.* [mused, mus-ing], to meditate in silence; think deeply; dream.

mu-se-um (mū-zē′um), *n.* a building in which objects of interest, esp. of scientific, artistic, or literary interest, are kept and displayed.

¹mush (mush), *n.* **1**, a porridge of corn meal boiled in water; hasty pudding; **2**, any soft, thick mixture like mush.— *adj.* **mush′y.**

²mush (mush), *interj.* in northwest Canada and Alaska, a shout ordering sled dogs to move along:—*v.i.* to travel, esp. with dog team, on foot over snow. —*n.* such a march on foot.

mush-room (mush′rōōm), *n.* **1**, a fast-growing fungus, usually shaped like an umbrella, some kinds of which are poisonous and some good for food; **2**, anything like this fungus in quickness of growth:—*adj.* **1**, made from mushrooms; **2**, like mushrooms in quickness of growth:— *v.i.* to spread rapidly.

mu-sic (mū′zik), *n.* **1**, the art of making pleasing or harmonious combinations of tones; **2**, harmony; melody **3**, a musical composition; also, the written or printed score of a musical composition; **4**, any succession of melodious sounds.

mu-si-cal (mū′zi-k'l), *adj.* **1**, relating to music; **2**, full of music; melodious; as, a *musical* voice; **3**, skilled in music: **musical comedy**, a light, amusing play, with songs, choruses, etc.—*adv.* **mu′si-cal-ly.**

mu-si-cale (mū′zi-kàl′), *n.* a social musical entertainment, usually private.

mu-si-cian (mū-zish′an), *n.* one who is skilled in some field of music.

musk (musk), *n.* **1**, a substance with a strong odour, obtained from the male musk deer, and used in perfumes; **2**, the odour of musk.—*adj.* **musk′y.**

mus-keg (mus′keg), *n.* a bog or marsh formed in a depression or hollow of the land surface by accumulation of water, moss, and thick layers of decaying vegetation. It is found esp. in the Pre-Cambrian Shield of Canada: in Chippewa, *grassy bog:* in French, *savane.*

mus-kel-lunge (mus′ke-lunj′), *n.* a large game fish of the pike family, found in lakes and rivers of central North America: valuable for food.

Also, **mus′kal-lunge′**; **mas′kal-longe′**; **mas′ki-nonge′.**

mus-ket (mus′kit), *n.* a riflelike gun formerly carried by foot-soldiers.

mus-ket-eer (mus′ke-tēr′), *n.* a foot-soldier armed with a musket.

mus-ket-ry (mus′kit-ri), *n.* **1**, the art of firing small arms; also, the fire of small arms; **2**, muskets collectively.

musk-mel-on, *n.* the cantaloup; the juicy, sweet, edible fruit of a trailing plant of the gourd family; also, the plant.

musk-rat (musk′rat′), *n.* a ratlike water animal of North America, with valuable, dark-brown fur and webbed hind feet; also, the fur.

mus-lin (muz′lin), *n.* **1**, a fine, soft cotton cloth, plain or figured, used for women's dresses, etc.; **2**, a heavier, plain cloth, used for sheets, underwear, etc.:—*adj.* made of muslin.

muss (mus), *n. Colloq.* confusion; disorder:—*v.t. Colloq.* to disarrange, as clothing; also, to soil.—*adj. Colloq.* **mus′sy.**

mus-sel (mus′l), *n.* any of several shellfish found in fresh and salt water, some of which are fit for food.

MUSSEL ($\frac{1}{8}$)

must (must), *auxiliary v.* [*p.t.* must], **1**, to be obliged or compelled; as, he *must* go; **2**, to be logically necessary; as, this *must* be what he means.

mus-tache (moos-tásh′; mus′tash), *n.* Same as **moustache.**

mus-tang (mus′tang), *n.* the small, hardy, half-wild horse of the Western plains.

mus-tard (mus′tėrd), *n.* **1**, a plant with yellow flowers and long, slender seed pods; **2**, the seed of this plant, esp. when ground into a fine, yellow powder which is used as a seasoning.

mus-ter (mus′tėr), *n.* **1**, a gathering; esp. an assembly of troops; **2**, the number of troops thus assembled:—*v.t.* **1**, to assemble, esp. troops for inspection, for actual warfare, etc.; **2**, to collect and show; as, to *muster* one's courage.

mus-ty (mus′ti), *adj.* [mus-ti-er, mus-ti-est], **1**, spoiled by dampness; mouldy; as, *musty* books; **2**, spoiled by age; stale.—*n.* **mus′ti-ness.**

mu-ta-ble (mū′ta-bl), *adj.* changeable. —*n.* **mu′ta-bil′i-ty.**

mu-ta-tion (mū-tā′shun), *n.* change; variation, esp. one which appears suddenly in a species and is inheritable; as, *gene mutations* (effected by X-ray), or *bud mutations,* as in the producing of the nectarine from the peach, or the navel (seedless) from the seeded orange.

mute (mūt), *n.* **1,** one who cannot speak or who remains silent; **2,** a contrivance to deaden or soften the sound of a musical instrument:—*adj.* **1,** silent; speechless; as, the child stood *mute;* **2,** unable to speak; dumb:—*v.t.* [mut-ed, mut-ing], to muffle the tone of.

mu-ti-late (mū′ti-lāt′), *v.t.* [mutilated, mutilat-ing], to cut off or remove a necessary part of.—*n.* **mu′ti-la′tion.**

mu-ti-neer (mū′ti-nēr′), *n.* one who is guilty of rebellion against authority.

mu-ti-ny (mū′ti-ni), *n.* [*pl.* mutinies], rebellion against authority; esp. rebellion of soldiers or sailors against their officers:—*v.i.* [mutinied, mutiny-ing], to rise against authority.—*adj.* **mu′ti-nous.**

mutt (mut), *n.* *Slang,* **1,** a stupid person; **2,** a mongrel dog.

mut-ter (mut′ẽr), *n.* a murmur:—*v.i.* **1,** to speak indistinctly in a low voice; **2,** to make a low, rumbling noise, as does thunder:—*v.t.* to utter indistinctly.

mut-ton (mut′n), *n.* the flesh of a sheep used as food.

mu-tu-al (mū′tū-al), *adj.* interchanged; given and received; as, *mutual* admiration.

muz-zle (muz′l), *n.* **1,** the projecting jaws and nose of an animal; snout; **2,** a guard or cover for the mouth of an animal to prevent its biting; **3,** the mouth of a gun:—*v.t.* [muz-zled, muzzling], **1,** to enclose the mouth of, to prevent biting; **2,** to restrain from free expression of opinion; as, to *muzzle* the newspapers.

my (mī), *adj.* a possessive form of *I:* belonging or relating to me; as, it is *my* hat.

my-e-li-tis (mī′e-lī′tis), *n.* inflammation of the spinal cord or of bone marrow, as in polio*myelitis.*

my-o-pi-a (mī-ō′pi-a), *n.* **1,** near-sightedness; **2,** shortsightedness.—*adj.* **my-op′ic** (-op).

myr-i-ad (mir′i-ad), *n.* a very large number:—*adj.* innumerable; as, *myriad* stars.

myrrh (mûr), *n.* a gummy substance obtained from a shrub of Arabia and East Africa, used in medicine, perfumes, etc.

myr-tle (mûr′tl), *n.* **1,** an evergreen shrub with glossy leaves and white or pink flowers followed by black berries; **2,** a creeping vine with dark-green leaves and blue flowers: also called *periwinkle.*

my-self (mī-self′), *pron.* [*pl.* ourselves (our-selvz′)], **1,** an emphatic form of *I;* **2,** a reflexive form of *me;* as, I hurt *myself;* **3,** my natural self; as, I am not *myself* today.

mys-ter-y (mis′tẽr-i), *n.* [*pl.* mysteries], **1,** something secret, hidden, or unexplained; as, the cause of the murder is a *mystery;* **2,** that which is beyond human understanding; as, the *mystery* of the creation of life; **3,** in the Middle Ages, a play based on incidents from the Bible.—*adj.* **mys-te′ri-ous** (mis-tē′ri-us).

mys-tic (mis′tik), *n.* one who believes that he can have direct spiritual communication with God:—*adj.* **1,** having a hidden meaning; mysterious; **2,** magical.—*adj.* **mys′ti-cal.**—*n.* **mys′ti-cism.**

mys-ti-fy (mis′ti-fī′), *v.t.* [mystified, mystify-ing], to bewilder; puzzle; as his acts *mystify* me.—*n.* **mys′ti-fi-ca′tion.**

myth (mith), *n.* **1,** a traditional story often founded on some fact of nature, or an event in the early history of a people, and embodying some religious belief of that people; **2,** any imaginary person, thing, or event.—*adj.* **myth′i-cal.**

my-thol-o-gy (mi-thol′o-ji), *n.* [*pl.* mythologies], **1,** a body of myths in which are recorded a people's beliefs concerning their origin, gods, heroes, etc.; **2,** the study of these beliefs.—*n* **my-thol′o-gist.**—*adj.* **myth′o-log′i-cal** (mith′o-loj′i-kal).

N

N, n (en), *n.* [*pl.* N′s, n′s], the 14th letter of the alphabet, following M.

nab (nab), *v.t.* [nabbed, nab-bing], to catch or seize unexpectedly; grab; arrest; as, the police *nabbed* the thief.

na-bob (nā′bob), *n.* **1,** a native ruler in India; **2,** a very rich man.

na-dir (nā′dẽr; dēr), *n.* **1,** the point o

the heavens directly opposite to the zenith, that is, the point of the celestial sphere directly under the observer; **2,** the lowest point (of anything); as, he had reached the *nadir* of his fortunes.

¹nag (nag), *n.* a small horse; hence, any horse, esp. one that is worn out.

²nag (nag), *v.i.* [nagged, nag-ging], to scold or find fault continually, often about little things; as, she *nagged* at him to stop smoking:—*v.t.* to torment with tiresome insistence; as, the boys *nag* their mother for sweets.—*adj.* **nag′ging.**—*adv.* **nag′ging-ly.**

na-iad (nā′yad; nī′ad), *n.* in *mythology*, a water-nymph.

nail (nāl), *n.* **1,** the thin, horny growth at the end of a finger or a toe; **2,** a slender, short bar or rod of metal, with a head at one end, used chiefly for driving into woodwork to hold two pieces together:—*v.t.* **1,** to fasten with a nail; as, to *nail* a lid down; **2,** to clinch or make certain; as, I *nailed* my argument by showing the figures; **3,** to answer or disprove; as, he *nailed* the lie.

na-ïve or **na-ive** (nä-ēv′), *adj.* artless; unaffected; as, a *naive* girl.—*n.* **na-ïve-te′** (nȧ′ēv′tā′).

na-ked (nā′kid), *adj.* **1,** entirely undressed; nude; as, *naked* swimmers; **2,** bare; without its usual covering; as, a *naked* hillside; a *naked* sword; **3,** plain; without addition; as, the *naked* truth: —**with the naked eye,** without the aid of a telescope or similar glass.

nam-by—pam-by (nam′bi–pam′bi), *adj.* weakly sentimental in writing or talk; affectedly nice.—*n.* such a person.

name (nām), *n.* **1,** the term or title by which a person or thing is called or known; **2,** character; reputation; fame; as, he has made a *name* for himself in literature:—*v.t.* [named, nam-ing], **1,** to give a name to; **2,** to appoint for a special purpose; specify; as, to *name* the day; **3,** to mention or specify; as, I asked him to *name* his reasons.—*adj.* **name′less.**

name-ly (nām′li), *adv.* that is to say; to state more particularly; as, three tools are needed, *namely,* saw, hammer, and plane.

name-sake (nām′sāk′), *n.* one who is named for another, or has the same name as another.

nan-ny—goat (na′ni–gōt′), *n. Colloq.* a she-goat.

¹nap (nap), *n.* a short sleep; a doze:— *v.i.* [napped, nap-ping], to take a nap, or short sleep; doze; hence, to be inattentive or off one's guard.

²nap (nap), *n.* short hairs or fuzz on the surface of some fabrics; the pile.

nape (nāp), *n.* in man or animals, the back of the neck.

naph-tha (naf′tha), *n.* a clear, inflammable liquid obtained from petroleum, coal-tar, etc., somewhat like gasoline.

nap-kin (nap′kin), *n.* **1,** a small square piece of cloth or paper held across the lap at table for protecting the clothing or for wiping the fingers or lips; **2,** a diaper.

nap-py (nap′i), *n.* a small, shallow, flat-bottomed dish, used for serving food.

nar-cis-sus (när-sis′us), *n.* [*pl.* narcissi (när-sis′ī) or narcissuses (när-sis′us-ez)] a spring-flowering plant, that grows from a bulb. The jonquil and the daffodil are kinds of narcissus.

nar-cot-ic (när-kot′ik), *n.* a drug which produces drowsiness or sleep, and which lessens pain by making the nerves dull:—*adj.* having the power to produce drowsiness, sleep, or insensibility to pain.

nar-rate (na-rāt′), *v.t.* [narrat-ed, narrat-ing], to tell (a story); give an account of (events or happenings); relate; as, he *narrated* his adventures. —*n.* **nar-ra′tion.**—*n.* **nar-ra′tor** (-tẽr).

nar-ra-tive (nar′a-tiv), *n.* a story or tale, or an account of real or imaginary happenings:—*adj.* having to do with story-telling; of the nature of a story; as, a *narrative* poem.

nar-row (nar′ō), *adj.* **1,** not wide; of little breadth or width; as, a *narrow* lane; **2,** small; as, to move within a *narrow* range; **3,** lacking wide knowledge or breadth of view; having little imagination; as, a *narrow* mind:—*v.t.* to make smaller in width or extent; hence, to limit or restrict:—*v.i.* to become less wide.—*n.* **nar′row-ness.**— *adv.* **nar′row-ly.**

nar-thex (när′theks), *n.* a church vestibule leading to the nave.

nar-whale, nar-whal, or **nar-wal** (när′hwȧl; wȧl), *n.* a whalelike arctic mammal, 15–20 feet long, (the male having a long twisted tusk projecting forward from the upper jaw), valued for its oil and ivory; sea unicorn.

na-sal (nā′zal), *adj.* having to do with the nose; esp. pronounced through the nose; as, *m, n,* and *ng* represent *nasal* sounds:—*n.* a nasal sound, or a letter used to represent it.—*adv.* **na′sal-ly.**— *v.t.* **na′sal-ize** (zal).

nas-cent (nas′ent), *adj.* **1,** beginning to develop or come into being; as, a *nascent* culture, city, etc.; a *nascent* larva; **2,** in *chemistry,* uncombined: said of an element at the instant of its being set free from a compound, when it has unusual energy and combining power: a *nascent* condition.

na-stur-tium (na-stûr′shum), *n.* a garden plant having brilliantly coloured, fragrant flowers with spurs.

nas-ty (nás′ti), *adj.* [nas-ti-er, nas-ti-est], **1,** dirty; filthy; **2,** disgusting to taste or smell; as, *nasty* medicine; **3,** obscene; indecent; **4,** troublesome; as, a *nasty* cut; **5,** *Colloq.:* **a,** ill-natured; mean; **b,** unpleasant; as, a *nasty* day. —*n.* **nas′ti-ness.**

na-tal (nā′tal), *adj.* pertaining to one's birth:—**natal day,** birthday.

na-tion (nā′shun), *n.* **1,** the people of one country, as Great Britain, living under one government; **2,** a race of people having the same religion and customs, but not always living in the same country or speaking the same language; as, the Jewish *nation.*—*adj.* **na′tion-al** (nash′un-al).—*adv.* **na′tion-al-ly.**

na-tion-al-ism (nash′un-al-izm), *n.* **1,** patriotic devotion; a sense of national unity; **2,** demand for national independence.—*n.* **na′tion-al-ist.**—*adj.* **na′-tion-al-is′tic.**

na-tion-al-i-ty (nash′un-al′i-ti), *n.* [*pl.* nationalities], one's connection with a particular nation by birth or citizenship, or one's political status because of this connection; as, he showed his French *nationality.*

na-tion-al-ize (nash′un-al-īz′), *v.t.* [nationalized, nationaliz-ing], **1,** to put under the control of the government, as mines or railways; **2,** to make or change into a nation; as, Garibaldi *nationalized* Italy; **3,** to admit to citizenship in a country; as, to *nationalize* an immigrant.—*n.* **na′tion-al-i-za′tion.**—*n.* **na′tion-al-iz′er.**

na-tive (nā′tiv), *adj.* **1,** pertaining to one's birth or to the place of one's birth; as, one's *native* land or language; **2,** born or produced in, or belonging to, a country; as, *native* plants; **3,** produced by nature; not artificial; as, *native* copper; **4,** inborn; not acquired; as, *native* charm:—*n.* one who is born in a given country or place.

na-tiv-i-ty (nā-tiv′i-ti), *n.* [*pl.* nativities], **1,** birth; **2,** the time, place, and manner of birth:—**the Nativity,** the birth of Christ.

NATO, North Atlantic Treaty Organization, a pact for collective defence (1948) by Gt. Britain, France, U.S.A., Canada, the Benelux nations, Norway, Denmark, Ireland, Italy, and Portugal: Greece and Turkey joined in 1952, Western Germany in 1954.

nat-ty (nat′i), *adj.* [nat-ti-er, nat-ti-est], tidy; neat; smart; trim.—*adv.* **nat′ti-ly.**

nat-u-ral (nat′ū-ral), *adj.* **1,** pertaining to one's nature; innate; inborn; as, *natural* gifts; **2,** occurring in the ordinary course of things; as, a *natural* result; **3,** true to life; as, a *natural* likeness; **4,** pertaining to the world and the things in it; as, *natural* science; **5,** in *music,* written without sharps or flats; as, the *natural* scale of C:—**natural history,** the study of plants, minerals, and natural objects in general; esp. the study of animals with relation to their life, habits, etc.:—*n.* in *music,* a sign [♮] placed on a line or space of the staff, to remove the effect of a preceding sharp or flat.

nat-u-ral-ism (nat′ū-ral-izm), *n.* **1,** in *art* and *literature,* the presenting of nature and life realistically without idealizing them; **2,** in *philosophy,* the doctrine that everything can be traced to natural causes; **3,** in *theology,* the doctrine that true religion may be learned from observing nature and does not depend on supernatural experiences.

nat-u-ral-ist (nat′ū-ral-ist), *n.* one who makes a special study of natural objects, as plants, minerals, and, esp. animals.

nat-u-ral-ize (nat′ū-ral-īz′), *v.t.* [nat-uralized, naturaliz-ing], **1,** to admit (an alien) to citizenship; **2,** hence, to accept or adopt, as a foreign word or custom; to introduce and make grow as, a foreign plant.—*n.* **nat′u-ral-i-za′tion.**

nat-u-ral-ly (nat′ū-ral-i), *adv.* **1,** in a natural way or manner; as, to act *naturally;* **2,** by nature; as, she was *naturally* clever at music; **3,** as might be expected; as, *naturally,* I was pleased when I won.

na-ture (nā′tūr), *n.* **1,** real character, the qualities that naturally belong to a person or thing; as, she is affectionate by *nature;* **2,** kind or sort; as, things of this *nature;* **3,** the outdoor world; as the beauties of *nature;* **4,** the physical universe as a whole, including what it is and what happens in it; as, the laws of *nature.*

naught (nôt), *n.* **1,** nothing; **2,** a cipher or zero; the character [0] used to represent an arithmetical value of nothing.

naugh-ty (nô′ti), *adj.* [naugh-ti-er, naugh-ti-est], bad; wayward; mischievous; disobedient.—*adv.* **naugh′ti-ly.**—*n.* **naugh′ti-ness.**

nau-se-a (nô′shi-a; nô′si-a; nô′zi-a), *n.* 1, sickness of the stomach, with a desire to vomit, as in seasickness; 2, loathing; disgust.—*adj.* **nau′seous.**—*v.t.* **nau′se-ate.**

nau-ti-cal (nô′ti-kal), *adj.* pertaining to ships, sailors, or navigation; maritime:—**nautical mile**, 6,080 feet (in American usage, 6,080.2 feet).—*adv.* **nau′ti-cal-ly.**

nau-ti-lus (nô′ti-lus), *n.* [*pl.* nautiluses or nautili (nô′ti-lī)], any of several molluscs with a spiral shell, found esp. in the South Pacific and Indian oceans.

Nav-a-ho or **Nav-a-jo** (nav′a-hō′), *n.* [*pl.* -hos or -hoes (-hōz)], a North American Indian tribe of Arizona and New Mexico.

na-val (nā′val), *adj.* pertaining to war vessels or a navy.

nave (nāv), *n.* the central part of the main body of certain churches from the choir to the main entrances, between the aisles.

na-vel (nā′vel), *n.* the depression or mark in the centre of the abdomen.

nav-i-ga-ble (nav′i-ga-bl), *adj.* 1, capable of being travelled over by a boat or aeroplane; as, a *navigable* stream; 2, capable of being steered; as, a *navigable* balloon; an easily *navigable* boat.—*n.* **nav′i-ga-bil′i-ty.**—*n.* **nav′i-ga-ble-ness.**

nav-i-gate (nav′i-gāt′), *v.i.* [navigated, navigat-ing], 1, to travel by water or air; 2, to sail or direct a ship or an aeroplane:—*v.t.* 1, to travel by water in any type of ship, or by air in any aeroplane; 2, to steer or manage a ship or an aeroplane.—*n.* **nav′i-ga′tion.**—*n.* **nav′i-ga′tor.**

nav-vy (nav′i), *n.* an unskilled labourer, esp. on railroads, canals, drains, etc.

na-vy (nā′vi), *n.* [*pl.* navies], 1, the warships of a nation; 2, the sea war force of a nation, including ships, shipyards, shops, officers, men, etc.; 3, a fleet, as of merchant ships:—**navy blue**, a dark blue.

nay (nā), *adv.* 1, no; 2, not only so, but: introducing a more emphatic statement; as, I suspect, *nay* I know, that he has gone:—*n.* 1, a refusal or denial; 2, a negative vote or reply; also, a negative voter.

Na-zi (nä′tsi), *n.* [*pl.* Nazis], a member of the National Socialist German Workers party, founded by Adolf Hitler.—*n.* **Na′zism; Na′zi-ism.**

neap (nēp), *adj.* and *n.* a name for the tides just after the moon's first and third quarters, in which they attain the least height.

Ne-a-pol-i-tan (nē′a-pol′i-tan), *adj.* of Naples.—**Neapolitan ice cream**, a brick in layers of different flavours, as vanilla, strawberry, and chocolate.

near (nēr), *adj.* 1, not far distant in time, place, or degree; close; 2, intimate; dear; as, a *near* friend; 3, with a narrow margin; bare; as, a *near* escape; 4, closely akin; as, a *near* relative; 5, direct or quick; as, to go by the *near* way; 6, mean or stingy; 7, on the left-hand side of a vehicle, animal, or team:—*adv.* 1, not distant in time, place, or degree; as, Easter is *near;* 2, almost; approximately; as, *near* dead with cold; 3, closely; as, as *near* as I can tell:—*prep.* close to or by; as, he sat *near* the stream:—*v.i.* and *v.t.* to come close (to); approach.—*n.* **near′ness.**

near-by (nēr′bī′), *adj.* not far off; close:—*adv.* (preferably *near by*), near; at hand.

near-ly (nēr′li), *adv.* 1, almost; all but; as, *nearly* frozen; 2, closely; as, *nearly* related.

near-sight-ed (nēr′sīt′id), *adj.* able to see objects with distinctness only when they are quite close to the eyes.—*n.* **near′sight′ed-ness.**—*adv.* **near′sight′-ed-ly.**

neat (nēt), *adj.* 1, tidy; trim; 2, simple and elegant; well made; as, a *neat* costume; 3, brief; cleverly phrased; as, a *neat* reply; 4, skilful; deft; as, a *neat* job of carpentering.—*adv.* **neat′ly.** —*n.* **neat′ness.**

neb (neb), *n.* 1, a beak, as of a bird; bill; 2, a snout; 3, the pointed end of a thing.

neb-u-la (neb′ū-la), *n.* [*pl.* -lae (-lē)], 1, any luminous, cloudlike mass of gaseous matter or misty star clusters far out in space; as, the Great *Nebula* in Andromeda; 2, an opaque spot on the cornea of the eye; 3, cloudiness in the urine; 4, an oily preparation for use in an atomizer.—*adj.* **neb′u-lar; neb′u-lous.**

nec-es-sar-y (nes′e-sèr′i), *adj.* 1, existing or happening naturally; true according to natural laws; as, a *necessary* conclusion; 2, not to be done without; essential; as, food is *necessary* to life; 3, unavoidable; inevitable; as, the *necessary* result of an act:— **necessaries**, *n. pl.* things which cannot be done without.—*adv.* **nec′es-sar′i-ly.**

ne-ces-si-tate (ni-ses´i-tāt´), *v.t.* [necessitat-ed, necessitat-ing], to make unavoidable; as, illness *necessitated* his removal.

ne-ces-si-ty (ni-ses´i-ti), *n.* [*pl.* necessities], **1,** great need of aid or help; as, send for me in case of *necessity;* **2,** something greatly needed; as, sunshine is a *necessity* for health; **3,** extreme poverty; **4,** that which compels one to act in a certain way; as, he felt the *necessity* of leaving immediately; **5, necessities,** the things needed for a decent living.

neck (nek), *n.* **1,** that part of the body connecting the head with the shoulders; **2,** the part of a garment which fits closely around the neck; the collar; **3,** a long, extended part of an object, esp. if near one end; as, the *neck* of a bottle.

neck-lace (nek´lis), *n.* a decorative chain, as of gold, or a string of beads, jewels, etc., worn around the neck.

neck-tie (nek´tī´), *n.* a narrow scarf or band worn around the neck and tied in front.

neck-wear (nek´wâr´), *n.* articles such as ties, collars, etc., worn around the neck.

nec-ro- (nek´rō-), a *prefix* meaning *dead, death,* or *corpse,* as in **nec-rop´o-lis** (cemetery); **nec-ro´sis** (decay of body or bone tissue).

nec-ro-man-cy (nek´rō-man´si), *n.* black magic.

nec-tar (nek´tėr), *n.* **1,** in *mythology,* the wine of the gods; **2,** any delicious beverage; **3,** a sweet fluid in plants, esp. in the flowers, used by bees in making honey.

nec-tar-ine (nek´ta-rēn´; nek´ta-rēn´), *n.* and *adj.* a kind of peach with a smooth, thin skin and firm pulp.

née (nā), *adj.* *French,* born: often placed before the maiden name of a married woman; as, Mrs. Jones, née May Smith.

need (nēd), *n.* **1,** lack of anything desired or useful; as, he felt the *need* of sleep; **2,** necessity; time of trouble; as, a friend in *need* is a friend indeed; **3,** urgent want; poverty:—*v.t.* to be in want of; require; have use for:—*v.i.* **1,** to be necessary; as, it *needs* to be done; **2,** to be under obligation; as, he *need* not go.—*adj.* **need´y.**

need-ful (nēd´fool), *adj.* **1,** necessary; required; **2,** needy.—*adv.* **need´ful-ly.**

nee-dle (nē´dl), *n.* **1,** a small, sharp-pointed steel instrument furnished with an eye to hold thread; **2,** a thin,

straight rod used in knitting or, when hooked at the end, for crocheting; **3,** anything sharply pointed like a needle, as the leaf of a pine or fir tree; **4,** the **magnetic needle,** a slender piece of magnetized steel in a compass.

need-less (nēd´lis), *adj.* unnecessary; useless; not needed.—*adv.* **need´less-ly.**

nee-dle-work (nē´dl-wûrk´), *n.* hand sewing; embroidery done by hand.

needs (nēdz), *adv.* necessarily; as, he *needs* must come.

ne'er—do—well (nâr´-dōō-wel´), *n.* one who does nothing worth-while.

ne-fa-ri-ous (ni-fâr´i-us), *adj.* extremely wicked; villainous; as, *nefarious* practices, schemes, etc.

ne-ga-tion (ni-gā´shun), *n.* **1,** denial; as, he shook his head in *negation;* **2,** the opposite or absence of something real or positive; as, death is the *negation* of life.

neg-a-tive (neg´a-tiv), *adj.* **1,** expressing or implying refusal or denial; as, he gave me a *negative* answer; **2,** lacking positive qualities; not forceful or influential; as, a *negative* sort of person; **3,** naming the kind of electricity made in silk by rubbing it on glass: the opposite of *positive;* **4,** in *mathematics,* naming a quantity to be subtracted; minus:—*n.* **1,** a refusal or denial; **2,** the side of a question which denies what the opposite side upholds; as, to support the *negative* in a debate; **3,** in *mathematics,* a quantity less than zero; also, its symbol; **4,** in *photography,* a picture made on a plate or film by exposure in a camera, in which light objects appear dark and dark objects light, and from which is printed the picture ordinarily shown as a finished photograph, called a *positive;* **5,** a word expressing denial, as the words *no, not, neither:—v.t.* [negatived, negativ-ing], **1,** to deny the truth of; contradict; **2,** to refuse assent to; veto; **3,** to counteract; neutralize.

neg-lect (neg-lekt´), *n.* **1,** failure to do that which should be done; as, her garden showed *neglect;* **2,** habitual lack of attention; disregard; as, his friends resented his *neglect;* **3,** carelessness:—*v.t.* **1,** to fail (to act or to do something), by carelessness or design; **2,** to slight; pay little attention to; as, to *neglect* a warning; **3,** to leave uncared for; as, the boy *neglects* his dog.

neg-lect-ful (neg-lekt´fool), *adj.* careless; disregardful.—*adv.* **neg-lect´-ful-ly.**

neg-li-gee (neg´li-zhā´; neg´li-zhā´), *n.*

1, a loose lounging robe worn by women; **2,** easy and informal dress in general.

neg-li-gent (neg′li-jent), *adj.* **1,** careless; heedless; inattentive; **2,** neglectful.—*adv.* **neg′li-gent-ly.**—*n.* **neg′ligence.**

neg-li-gi-ble (neg′li-ji-bl), *adj.* that may be disregarded because small, trifling, or unimportant.

ne-go-ti-a-ble (ni-gō′shi-a-bl), *adj.* that may be transferred to another, as a cheque or promissory note (usually by endorsement).

ne-go-ti-ate (ni-gō′shi-āt′), *v.t.* [negotiat-ed, negotiat-ing], **1,** to put through, obtain, or arrange for; as, to *negotiate* a sale, loan, treaty, peace; **2,** to sell, convert into cash, or transfer to another for a consideration; as, to *negotiate* business papers representing money value or credit, such as bonds, stocks, cheques, etc.; **3,** to deal with successfully; as, I knew the horse could *negotiate* the fence:—*v.i.* to treat with others in political or business affairs.— *n.* **ne-go′ti-a′tor.**—*n.* **ne-go′ti-a′tion.**

Ne-gro (nē′grō), *n.* [*pl.* Negroes], a person belonging to the African race:— **negro,** a black man, esp. one who has some Negro blood.—*adj.* **Ne′gro; ne′gro** —*n. fem.* **Ne′gress.**—*adj.* and *n.* **Ne′-groid; ne′groid.**

neigh (nā), *n.* the cry of a horse; a whinny:—*v.i.* to utter the cry of a horse.

neigh-bour or **neigh-bor** (nā′bėr), *n.* **1,** one who lives near another; **2,** a person or thing that is near another; **3,** a fellow being; as, love thy *neighbour* as thyself.

neigh-bour-hood (nā′bėr-hood′), *n.* **1,** the region near by; vicinity; as, it is in the *neighbourhood* of the river; **2,** all the people living near one another, or within a certain range; as, the *neighbourhood* welcomed the strangers.

neigh-bour-ing (nā′bėr-ing), *adj.* living or being near; adjoining.

neigh-bour-ly (nā′bėr-li), *adj.* friendly kindly.—*n.* **neigh′bour-li-ness.**

nei-ther (nē′thėr; nī′thėr), *pron.* not the one nor the other; as, I want *neither* of the books:—*adj.* not either; as, *neither* book will do:—*conj.* **1,** not either; not (one or the other): often with *nor;* as, *neither* the book *nor* the paper; **2,** nor; nor yet; and . . . not; as, I know not; *neither* can I guess.

nem-a-tode (nem′a-tōd′), *n.* and *adj.* a class or phylum of long, smooth, threadlike worms, as the hookworm, pinworm, vinegar eel, roundworm, etc., often parasitic.

nem-bu-tal (nem′bū-tôl′), *n.* a barbiturate, used as a sedative or to produce insensitivity to pain, calm the nerves, etc.: a trade-mark.

nem-e-sis (nem′i-sis), *n.* retributive justice whereby the punishment fits the crime; as, a fear of divine *nemesis.* Also, **Nemesis,** (the goddess of retribution).

ne-o- (nē′ō-), *prefix* meaning *new:* example, *neo*plasm (new growth, as in a tumour).

ne-o-lith-ic (nē′ō-lith′ik), *adj.* pertaining to the late stone age (New Stone Age), marked by use of polished stone implements, beginnings of agriculture, and domesticated animals (the *Neolithic* Age).

ne-on (nē′on), *n.* and *adj.* an inert gaseous element of which traces occur in the atmosphere (15 parts in a million):—**neon lamp,** a (vacuum) tube filled with neon, that ionizes and glows when an electric current is passed through it.

ne-o-phyte (nē′ō-fīt′), *n.* **1,** a beginner; novice, esp. a newly ordained priest or one just entering a convent; **2,** a convert.

neph-ew (nev′ū; nef′ū), *n.* the son of one's brother or sister; also, in careless use, the son of a brother-in-law or a sister-in-law.

ne-phri-tis (ni-frī′tis), *n.* inflammation of the kidneys, or Bright's disease.

Nep-tune (nep′tūn), *n.* **1,** in *Roman mythology,* the god of the sea (Greek *Poseidon*); **2,** the 8th planet from the sun (diameter 33,000 miles; takes about 165 years to complete its orbit of about 2.8 billion miles).

nerve (nûrv), *n.* **1,** one of the cordlike fibres which connect the brain and spinal cord with all parts of the body; **2,** boldness; coolness in danger; courage; as, a high dive takes *nerve:*—*v.t.* [nerved, nerv-ing], to arouse courage or strength in; as, he *nerved* himself for the battle.

nerve-less (nûrv′lis), *adj.* **1,** without nerves; **2,** hence, lacking vigour; paralysed; as, the pen fell from her *nerveless* grasp.—*adv.* **nerve′less-ly.**

nerv-ous (nûr′vus), *adj.* **1,** pertaining to, or made of, nerves; as, the *nervous* system; **2,** having weak nerves; hence, easily excited; timid; as, she is *nervous* in the dark; **3,** forceful; vigorous; as, he is full of *nervous* energy; **4,** restless or uneasy; as, *nervous* from suspense.— *adv.* **nerv′ous-ly.**—*n.* **nerv′ous-ness.**

all (ôl), ôr; up, mūte, cûr, cōol, book; oil, out; th, thin; *th*, the.

nest (nest), *n.* **1,** the bed or place made or chosen by a bird for the hatching of its eggs and rearing of its young; **2,** a hatching-place for insects, turtles, etc.; as, a hornet's *nest;* **3,** a cozy retreat or residence; **4,** a number of boxes, bowls, tables, etc., one fitting inside another:—*v.i.* to build and occupy a nest:—*v.t.* to place in, or as if in, a nest.

nes-tle (nes′l), *v.i.* [nes-tled, nes-tling], to lie close and snug; as, a child *nestles* in its mother's arms:—*v.t.* to cherish or cuddle.

nest-ling (nest′ling; nes′ling), *n.* a young bird recently hatched and not yet able to fly:—*adj.* recently hatched.

¹net (net), *n.* **1,** a fabric made of twine knotted into meshes, used for catching birds, fish, etc.; **2,** any fine open-work fabric, very often of silk, used for bridal veils, laces, etc.; **3,** that which entraps; an entanglement; as, the criminal cannot escape the *net* of justice; a snare:—*adj.* of or like net or netting; as, a *net* dress:—*v.t.* [net-ted, net-ting], **1,** to make into a net or network; **2,** to catch in a net; hence, to entrap by clever stratagem; snare; **3,** to cover or protect with a net:—*v.i.* **1,** to make nets or network; **2,** to use nets in fishing, hunting game, etc.; as, the fishers *netted* while I watched.

²net (net), *adj.* remaining after the deduction of all necessary expenses; as, *net* gain; also, excluding all waste, refuse, etc.; as, *net* weight:—*v.t.* [net-ted, net-ting], to earn as clear profit; as, the deal *netted* $2,000.

neth-er (neth′ẽr), *adj.* **1,** situated below, lying beneath; as, *nether* garments; **2,** pertaining to the regions below the heavens or the earth; as, Pluto ruled the *nether* world.

net-ting (net′ing), *n.* **1,** the act or method of making nets; **2,** a fabric made of meshes; as, fish *netting;* **3,** a fabric of crossed wires, as for fences; **4,** network.

net-tle (net′l), *n.* any of a group of coarse plants having prickles or sting-ing hairs:—*v.t.* [net-tled, net-tling], **1,** to sting, as with nettles; **2,** hence, to provoke; irritate; vex; as, his remark *nettled* me.

net-work (net′wûrk′), *n.* **1,** an open-work fabric made by interlaced threads; **2,** any system of lines that cross like those in a net; as, a *network* of roads, vines, wires, etc.; a radio or TV *network.*

neur- or **neu′ro-** (nūr-; nūr′ō-), *prefix,* pertaining to the nerves, as in **neu′ras-the′ni-a** (nervous exhaustion); **neu-**

rol′o-gy (study of nerves); **neu′ro-path′** (a specialist on nerves, or a patient abnormally given to nerve disease).

neu-ral-gi-a (nū-ral′ji-a), *n.* acute intermittent pain (in the face or head) along the course of, and over, a nerve.

neu-ri-tis (nū-rī′tis), *n.* inflammation of a nerve or nerves.

neu-ro-sis (nū-rō′sis), *n.* [*pl.* -ses (-sēz)], any mental disorder in which anxiety, fixed ideas, and complaints not traceable to a physical cause, dominate the mind: less serious than *psychosis,* in which there is a break-down of personality and loss of touch with the real world.—*adj.* **neu-rot′ic.**

neu-ter (nū′tẽr), *adj.* **1,** in *grammar,* neither masculine nor feminine; as, "book" is a *neuter* noun; **2,** in *biology:* **a,** having no sex, as certain plants; **b,** without fully developed sex organs; as, the worker bees are *neuter:*—*n.* a neuter word or organism.

neu-tral (nū′tral), *adj.* **1,** not affected by a special or personal interest; indifferent; as, my feelings on the matter were altogether *neutral;* **2,** not taking sides in a quarrel, war, etc.; as, a *neutral* nation; also, belonging to a neutral nation; as, *neutral* ships; **3,** neither good nor bad; with no decided characteristics; **4,** neither acid nor alkaline; **5,** having little or no colour; as, grey is *neutral:*—*n.* one who does not take sides in a dispute or conflict.—*adv.* **neu′tral-ly.**—*n.* **neu-tral′i-ty.**

neu-tral-ize (nū′tral-īz′), *v.t.* [neu-tralized, neutraliz-ing], **1,** to render inactive; make of no effect; counter-act; as, to *neutralize* the effects of a poison; **2,** to make neutral; as, to *neutralize* small nations.—*n.* **neu′tral-i-za′tion.**

neu-tron (nū′tron), *n.* a minute constituent of an atomic nucleus, about the mass of a proton, but without either positive or negative charge.

nev-er (nev′ẽr), *adv.* **1,** not ever; not at any time; **2,** in no degree; under no condition: used for emphasis; as, *never* fear.

nev-er-more (nev′ẽr-mōr′), *adv.* not ever again; at no future time.

nev-er-the-less (nev′ẽr-thẽ-les′), *adv.* and *conj.* notwithstanding; in spite of that; yet; however; still.

new (nū), *adj.* **1,** made for the first time; not existing before; as, a *new* dress; a *new* house; **2,** lately made, produced, invented, or discovered; as, a *new* type of engine; **3,** beginning afresh; recurring anew; as, a *new* year; a *new* start in life; **4,** freshly made or grown; as, *new* cheese; *new* peas; **5,** not yet used or worn; as, a *new* broom; a *new* suit; **6,** changed in character, health, etc.; as, I feel like a *new* man; **7,** different from that previously existing, known, or used; as, a *new* language; a *new* race of settlers:—*adv.* newly; recently; as, a field of *new*-mown hay.—*adv.* **new'ly.**—*n.* **new'ness.**—*adj.* **new'born'.** Compounds: **news'let'ter; news'man'; news'print'; news'room'; news'-stand'; news'worth'y.**

new-com-er (nū'kum'ẽr), *n.* one who has lately arrived.

new-el (nū'ẽl), *n.* **1,** in a winding staircase, the central upright pillar around which the steps turn; **2,** the post at the foot of a stairway.

new-fan-gled (nū'fang'gld; nū'-fang'gld), *adj.* **1,** novel; of a new kind; as, *newfangled* ideas or notions; **2,** inclined to new theories, fashions, etc.

new-ly-wed (nū'li-wed'), *adj.* and *n.* recently married.

news (nūz), *n.* recent or fresh information; as, we have no *news* of the accident; hence, recent events reported in the newspapers.

news-boy (nūz'boi'), *n.* a boy who delivers or sells newspapers.

news-cast (nūz'kàst'), *n.* and *v.* a radio or TV broadcast of news reports.

news-pa-per (nūz'pā'pẽr), *n.* a daily or weekly paper containing recent news, advertisements, pictures, etc.

news-reel (nūz'rēl'), *n.* a reel of motion pictures of current events.

newt (nūt), *n.* any of several small, harmless animals resembling lizards, found in water or damp places.

new-ton (nū'tn), *n.* in the MKS system, the absolute unit of force (10^5 dynes).

next (nekst), *adj.* immediately following in order; nearest in time, place, degree, or rank; as, the *next* day; the *next* street; the *next* quality; *next* in order:—*adv.* immediately succeeding; in the nearest time, place, or order; as, you go *next*:—*prep.* nearest to; as, you sit *next* the end.

nib (nib), *n.* **1,** the point of anything, esp. of a pen; **2,** a bird's bill or beak:—his nibs, *Colloq.* a person of authority, esp. a self-important one.

nib-ble (nib'l), *v.t.* and *v.i.* [nib-bled, nib-bling], to bite a little at a time; eat in little bites; as, to *nibble* lettuce; the

mouse *nibbled* at the cheese:—*n.* a small bite.

nice (nīs), *adj.* [nic-er, nic-est], **1,** particular; dainty; as, *nice* in one's dress; **2,** requiring care and accuracy; exact; as, a *nice* experiment; *nice* proportions; **3,** able to find or feel small differences; as, a *nice* ear for music; **4,** requiring the best; too particular; as, he is too *nice* about his food; **5,** *Colloq.* pleasing; agreeable; good; kind; as, she is a *nice* person to meet; **6,** *Colloq.* well-behaved; as, they are *nice* children; **7,** *Colloq.* pleasant; agreeable; as, to have a *nice* time.

ni-ce-ty (nī'se-ti), *n.* [*pl.* niceties], **1,** a dainty, elegant, or delicate thing; as, the *niceties* of life; **2,** a very small difference, point, or detail; as, to learn the *niceties* of drawing; **3,** accuracy; careful attention to details; as, to describe the scene with great *nicety;* **4,** the point at which a thing is just right; as, baked to a *nicety.*

niche (nich), *n.* **1,** a recess or hollow in a wall, as for a statue; **2,** a condition or position esp. suitable to a person or thing; as, she found a *niche* in business.

nick (nik), *n.* **1,** a notch; slit; **2,** a broken place in any edge or surface; as, a *nick* in the table; **3,** the exact or critical point (of time); as, he arrived in the *nick* of time:—*v.t.* **1,** to cut notches in; **2,** to hit upon exactly; strike at the right place or proper moment.

nick-el (nik'l), *n.* **1,** a hard, silver-white, metallic element; **2,** in Canada and the U.S., a coin of the value of five cents, made of nickel and copper.

nick-name (nik'nām'), *n.* a familiar form of a given name, as "Bill" for "William," or a wholly new name given in derision, sport, or familiarity:—*v.t.* [nicknamed, nicknam-ing], to give a nickname to; call by a familiar name; as, they *nicknamed* him "Red."

nic-o-tine (nik'ō-tēn'; nik'ō-tin), *n.* a pungent, colourless poison contained in tobacco.

niece (nēs), *n.* the daughter of one's brother or sister; also, the daughter of a brother-in-law or sister-in-law.

nif-ty (nif'ti), *n. Slang,* smart; attractive; stylish.

nig-gard-ly (nig'ẽrd-li), *adj.* **1,** stingy; miserly; as, a *niggardly* person; **2,** scanty, as a meal:—*adv.* stingily; miserly; scantily; meanly.—*n.* **nig'-gard-li-ness.**—*n.* and *adj.* **nig'gard.**

nig-gle (nig'l), *v.i.* to putter; work

fussily; **2,** to trifle:—*v.t.* to work out with too elaborate care; **2,** to deceive. —*adj.* **nig′gling.**

nigh (nī), *adj.* **1,** near in time or place; as, the hour of his triumph is *nigh;* **2,** closely related by blood or friendship: —*adv.* **1,** near in time or place; **2,** almost; as, he was *nigh* starved:—*prep.* near to; not far from; as, the well was *nigh* the house.

night (nīt), *n.* **1,** the time from sunset to sunrise; **2,** the close of the day; **3,** the darkness of night.

night-fall (nīt′fôl′), *n.* the coming of darkness at evening.

night-gown (nīt′goun′), *n.* a loose garment worn in bed. Also, **night′-dress′** and (*Colloq.*) **night′y.**

night-hawk (nīt′hôk′), *n.* **1,** any of a group of American birds, not properly hawks, which fly at night; **2,** a person who stays up late at night.

night-in-gale (nīt′in-gāl′; nīt′ing-gāl′), *n.* **1,** any of several small Old World thrushes noted for the melodious song of the male, heard oftenest at night; **2,** a person who sings beautifully.

night jar (nīt′jär′), *n.* any of various nocturnal insect-eating birds, as the American nighthawks.

night-ly (nīt′li), *adj.* **1,** happening, coming, or occurring at night; as, the army made *nightly* marches; **2,** occurring every night; as, he does *nightly* exercises:—*adv.* night by night; every night; at or by night.

night-mare (nīt′mâr′), *n.* **1,** a terrifying dream accompanied by a feeling of helplessness; **2,** hence, any frightful experience or haunting fear.

night-shade (nīt′shād′), *n.* any of a group of plants including the potato plant, the bittersweet, and the egg-plant; esp. any of several poisonous or medicinal species, as the common night-shade.

night-shirt (nīt′shûrt′), *n.* a man's or boy's garment to be worn in bed.

nil (nil), *n.* **1,** nothing; as, in that game his score was absolutely *nil;* **2,** a thing of no account whatever.

nim-ble (nim′bl), *adj.* **1,** quick and active; alert; as, a *nimble* mind; **2,** lively; brisk; swift; as, *nimble* feet.— *adv.* **nim′bly.**

nim-bus (nim′bus), *n.* **1,** a rain cloud, heavy and gray (nimbo-stratus); **2,** any kind of cloud enveloping a person or thing; **3,** a halo or circle about the heads of divinities, saints, sovereigns, etc., on medals and pictures.

nin-com-poop (nin′kom-pōōp′; kum-), *n. Colloq.* a silly or stupid person; fool.

nine (nīn), *adj.* composed of one more than eight:—*n.* **1,** the number consisting of eight plus one; **2,** a sign representing nine units, as 9 or ix.

nine-pins (nīn′pinz′), *n.pl.* used as *sing.* a game which consists in bowling a ball at nine wooden pins set up at one end of a bowling alley.

nine-teen (nīn′tēn′), *adj.* composed of ten more than nine:—*n.* **1,** the sum of eighteen and one; **2,** a sign representing nineteen units, as 19 or xix.

nine-teenth (nīn′tēnth′), *adj.* next after the 18th: the ordinal of *nineteen:* —*n.* one of nineteen equal parts.

nine-ti-eth (nīn′ti-eth′), *adj.* next after the 89th: the ordinal of *ninety:*—*n.* one of the 90 equal parts of anything.

nine-ty (nīn′ti), *adj.* composed of one more than 89:—*n.* [*pl.* nineties], **1,** the number consisting of 89 plus one; **2,** a sign representing 90 units, as 90 or xc.

nine-ty—one (nīn′ti-wun′), *n.* and *adj.* the numbers *ninety-one* to *ninety-nine* are hyphenated.

nin-ny (nin′i), *n.* [*pl.* -nies (iz)], *n.* a foolish person; simpleton; dunce.

ninth (nīnth), *adj.* next after the eighth: the ordinal of *nine:*—*n.* one of the nine equal parts of anything.

nip (nip), *v.t.* [nipped, nip-ping], **1,** to pinch; to cut off the end of; clip; **2,** to blight; blast; destroy, as by frost.

nip-per (nip′ėr), *n.* **1,** one who or that which pinches or cuts off; **2,** the large claw of a crab or lobster; **3,** a horse's front tooth; **4, nippers** any of various tools with jaws, such as forceps, pliers, tongs, etc.

nip-ple (nip′l), *n.* **1,** that part of a breast through which a baby or young animal draws milk; **2,** the mouthpiece of a nursing bottle.

Nip-pon-ese (nip′o-nēz′), *n.* and *adj.* Japanese.

nit (nit), *n.* **1,** the egg of a parasitic insect, as a flea or louse; **2,** the young insect; **3,** a very small speck.

nit-chie (nich′i), *n.* a North American Indian (a term occasionally used in the three prairie provinces of Canada); as, the young *nitchies* are learning English.

ni-ter or **ni-tre** (nī′tėr), *n.* a white crystalline salt, potassium nitrate, used in making gunpowder: also called *saltpeter.*

cat, āge, fär, câre, ȧsk; ten, ēve, latėr; (i) pity, rely, senate; īce; top; nō.

ni-trate (nī'trāt), *n.* **1**, a salt of nitric acid; **2**, potassium or sodium nitrate, extensively used as a fertilizer.

ni-tric ac-id (nī'trik as'id), a very powerful acid which eats into and destroys flesh, wood, metal, etc., and is used in making explosives, dyestuffs, etc.

ni-tro- (nī'trō-), *prefix* indicating **1**, a compound of nitrogen or its acids, as *nitro*bacteria, *nitro*cellulose, *nitro*glycerin(e), *nitro*hydrochloric acid (aqua regia), **2**, the presence of the [NO_2] radical, as in *nitro*benzene, *nitro*paraffin.

ni-tro-gen (nī'trō-jen), *n.* a colourless, odourless, tasteless gas, which forms four-fifths of the volume of the air.—*adj.* **ni-trog'e-nous** (nī-troj'i-nus).

ni-trous (nī'trus), *adj.* **1**, containing nitre or saltpetre; **2**, having less oxygen than compounds designated by *nitric:* —**nitrous oxide** (N_2O), a colourless gas of sweetish odour and taste, used as an anaesthetic, esp. by dentists: called *laughing gas.*

nit-wit (nit'wit'), *n.* a simpleton; stupid person.

nix (niks), *n.* **1**, a water elf:—*n. fem.* **nix'ie; 2**, *interj. Slang*, stop! I disagree, refuse, etc.:—*adv.* no; not at all.

no (nō), *n.* [*pl.* noes (nōz)], **1**, a denial; a refusal by saying "no"; as, my *no* was received in silence; **2**, a negative vote; as, my *no* lost him the election; **3**, **noes**, the voters in the negative:—*adv.* **1**, nay; not so; as, *No*, I cannot go: opposite of *yes;* **2**, not any; not at all; as, he is *no* better; **3**, not; as, whether or *no:*—*adj.* not any.

no-bil-i-ty (nō-bil'i-ti), *n.* [*pl.* nobilities], **1**, the quality of being lofty in character, mind, or rank; **2**, the rank of persons of noble birth:—**the nobility**, the body of nobles or persons of title in a country.

no-ble (nō'bl), *adj.* [no-bler, no-blest], **1**, lofty in character or mind; as, a *noble* woman; **2**, high in rank; of ancient lineage or descent; as, of *noble* birth; **3**, stately in appearance; grand; as, *noble* architecture:—*n.* a peer or person of high rank and title.—*adv.* **no'bly.**

no-ble-man (nō'bl-man), *n.* [*pl.* noblemen (-men)], a man of rank or title.—*n. fem.* **no'ble-wom'an.**

no-bod-y (nō'bod-i; nō'bud-i), *pron.* no one:—*n.* [*pl.* nobodies], a person of no importance or influence.

nock (nok), *n.* **1**, a notch or groove at an arrow's end to receive the bowstring; **2**, a groove for the bowstring at either end of the bow.

noc-tur-nal (nok-tûr'nal), *adj.* **1**, done or occurring at night; as, a *nocturnal* visit; **2**, active at night; as, the bat is a *nocturnal* animal.—*adv.* **noc-tur'nal-ly.**

noc-turne or **noc-turn** (nok'tûrn), *n.* **1**, a quiet, dreamy song without words (usually for piano); **2**, a painting of a night scene.

nod (nod), *n.* **1**, a quick bending of the head, used as a sign of greeting, assent, approval, etc.; **2**, a bending of the head as a sign of supreme authority; as, the ruler's *nod:*—*v.t.* [nod-ded, nodding], **1**, to say by means of a nod; as, he *nodded* his farewells; **2**, to incline or bend with a quick movement; as, to *nod* one's head:—*v.i.* **1**, to swing or sway quickly; as, flowers *nod* in the breeze; **2**, to bend the head in token of assent or as a salute; **3**, to be drowsy; bend the head forward sleepily.

node (nōd), *n.* **1**, a knot; knob; swelling; **2**, a hard swelling on a tendon or bone; **3**, the point on the stem of a plant from which a leaf springs.—*adj.* **nod'al.**

nod-ule (nod'ūl), *n.* a little knot, or irregular, rounded lump; as, he inoculated the alfalfa with *nodule*-bearing bacteria.—*adj.* **nod'u-lar.**

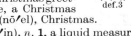

NODES (N,N), def.3

no-el (nō-el'), *n.* **1**, a shout of joy, as of Christmas greeting; **2**, hence, a Christmas carol:—**Noel** (nō'el), Christmas.

nog-gin (nog'in), *n.* **1**, a liquid measure of one gill, **2**, *Colloq.* the head.

noise (noiz), *n.* sound, esp. when confused or disagreeable:—*v.t.* [noised, nois-ing], to spread by rumour; as, the report was *noised* abroad.—*adv.* **nois'i-ly.**—*adj.* **nois'y.**—*n.* **nois'i-ness.**

noise-less (noiz'lis), *adj.* **1**, silent; still; **2**, making little sound; as, a *noiseless* engine.—*adv.* **noise'less-ly.**

noi-some (noi'sum), *adj.* **1**, injurious to health; harmful; as, *noisome* gases; **2**, offensive; disgusting; as, *noisome* odours.—*adv.* **noi'some-ly.**—*n.* **noi'-some-ness.**

no-mad (nō'mad), *n.* a member of a roving tribe of people, as the Arabs or gipsies, who have no fixed home but wander about in search of game, pasture, etc.:—*adj.* wandering; roving.—*adj.* **no-mad'ic.**

nom de plume (nom'de plōōm'), *n.* a pen-name; pseudonym; as, he wrote to the *Star* under a *nom de plume.*

no-men-cla-ture (nō'men-klā'tūr; chĕr), *n.* the system of names used for things, as in an art or science; thus, the *nomenclature* of botany, chemistry, etc.

nom-i-nal (nom'i-nal), *adj.* **1,** existing in name only; not real or actual; as, though the king was the *nominal* ruler, his son governed the country; **2,** so small as to be hardly worth mentioning; as, we paid only the *nominal* sum of ten dollars for the car.—*adv.* **nom'i-nal-ly.**

nom-i-nate (nom'i-nāt'), *v.t.* [nominat-ed, nominat-ing], to propose or name for an office; as, to *nominate* a man for election.—*n.* **nom'i-na'tor.**—*n.* **nom'i-na'tion.**

nom-i-na-tive (nom'i-na-tiv), *adj.* naming the case of the subject of a verb; as, in the sentence "I am ready," "I" is in the *nominative* case:—*n.* **1,** the case of the subject of a verb; the nominative case; **2,** a word in this case.

nom-i-nee (nom'i-nē'), *n.* one who is named or proposed for an office or duty; as, the *nominee* for president.

non-a-ge-na-ri-an (non'a-ji-nâr'i-an; -nā'ri-an), *n.* and *adj.* one between 90 and 100 years old.

non-cha-lance (non'sha-làns), *n.* lack of interest; easy unconcern; jauntiness; as, he pretended *nonchalance* to cover his embarrassment.—*adj.* **non'-cha-lant.**

non-com-mis-sioned (non'ko-mish'-und), *adj.* not having a certificate to engage in a service:—**noncommissioned officer** an enlisted man who has risen to the rank of sergeant or corporal.

non-com-mit-tal (non'ko-mit'al), *adj.* not revealing one's opinion or purpose; as, his answer was wholly *noncommittal.*

non-con-duc-tor (non'kon-duk'tẽr), *n.* any substance, such as rubber, through which heat, light, electricity, etc., will not pass readily; an insulator.

non-con-form-ist (non'kon-fôr'mist) *n.* one who does not conform to, or agree with, established beliefs, esp. church beliefs.—*n.* **non'con-form'i-ty.**

non-de-script (non'di-skript), *adj.* not easily described; odd; of no particular character; as, she wore a *nondescript* garment:—*n.* a nondescript thing or person.

none (nun), *pron.* **1,** not any; as, I will have *none* of it; **2,** not one; no one or ones: used as *sing.* or *pl.;* as, we needed a ball, but *none* was to be had; *none* of them were there:—*adv.* not at all; not in the least; as, he felt *none* the better for his trip.

non-en-ti-ty (non-en'ti-ti), *n.* [*pl.* -ties (-tiz)], **1,** a person of no influence

or individuality; as, he is a *nonentity;* **2,** an imaginary thing; **3,** the state of not existing.

non-par-ti-san (non-pär'ti-zn), *adj.* not strongly in favour of, or influenced by, a cause or a party; as, a *nonpartisan* meeting.

non-plus (non'plus), *v.t.* [nonplussed (non'plust), nonplus-sing], to throw into complete perplexity; bring to a standstill; as, I was *nonplussed* as to how to settle the quarrel:—*n.* inability to decide or proceed; as to be at a *nonplus.*

non-re-stric-tive (non'ri-strik'tiv), *adj.* in *grammar,* not limited: used of a parenthetical (descriptive) expression amplifying, but not necessary to, the sense of a sentence; as, the boy, *who was tall and strong,* won his match; distinguished from *restrictive;* as, he *who hesitates* is lost.

non-sense (non'sens), *n.* **1,** a thing without sense; language without meaning; absurdity; **2,** things of little worth; trifles; as, why spend money for such *nonsense?*—*interj.* absurd.—*adj.* **non-sen'si-cal.**

non-stop (non'stop'), *adj.* and *adv.* without a stop; as, a *nonstop* flight to fly *nonstop* from New York to Paris —*n.* a nonstop flight or trip.

noo-dle (nōō'dl), *n.* **1,** a narrow strip of dried dough, resembling macaroni and used chiefly in soups; **2,** a simpleton; **3** *Slang,* the head.

nook (nook), *n.* **1,** a cosy, out-of-the-way place; **2,** a corner in a room; **3,** a sheltered recess out of doors.

noon (nōōn), *n.* the middle of the day:—*adj.* pertaining to midday.

noon-day (nōōn'dā'), *n.* midday; noon —*adj.* pertaining to midday.

no one (nō'wun'), *pron.* nobody; no person.

noon-tide (nōōn'tīd'), *n.* noon.

noose (nōōs), *n.* **1,** a loop, made with a slipknot, as in a lasso, which binds the closer the more tightly it is drawn; **2** any snare:—*v.t.* [noosed, noos-ing], to catch or capture in a noose.

nor (nôr), *conj.* and not: a negative connecting word used after the negatives *neither* and *not,* to continue or complete their meaning; as, he has neither money *nor* friends; she is neither tall *nor* short; not a word *nor* a sign betrayed him.

norm (nôrm), *n.* a standard; model pattern; esp. the median or average achievement in a large group.

ıor-mal (nôr′mal), *adj.* according to rule; regular; natural; serving as a standard or model:—**normal school,** a school for the training of teachers:—*n.* the usual or ordinary condition, quantity, etc.; as, the rain raised the river two feet above *normal.*—*adv.* **nor′mal-ly.**—*n.* **nor-mal′i-ty.**—*n.* **nor′mal-cy.**

Norse (nôrs), *n.* and *adj.* of *Scandinavia*, the language or people.—*n.* **Norse′man.**

ıorth (nôrth), *n.* **1,** one of the four points of the compass; the point opposite to the south, or to the left of a person facing the sunrise; **2,** a section of country lying north of another; as, the *north* of Europe:—*adj.* having to do with, situated in, or coming from, the north; as, a *north* wind:—*adv.* to the north; as, walk *north* one block.— **North,** *n.* in the U.S., that district lying generally north of the Ohio River and the southern boundary of Pennsylvania; **North Pole,** the northern end of the earth's axis; **North Star,** the star which is very nearly over the North Pole; Polaris.—*n.* **north′land.**

orth-east (nôrth′ēst′), *n.* **1,** the point of the compass halfway between north and east; **2,** country lying in the direction of that point:—*adj.* having to do with the northeast, or in or from the northeast; as, a *northeast* wind:—*adv.* toward the northeast.—*adj.* and *adv.* **north′east′ward.**—*adv.* **north′east′-ward-ly.**

orth-east-er (nôrth′ēs′tėr), *n.* a violent wind or storm from the north-east.

orth-east-er-ly (nôrth′ēs′tėr-li), *adj.* and *adv.* from or toward the northeast.

orth-east-ern (nôrth′ēs′tėrn), *adj.* of, from, or situated in, the northeast.

orth-er-ly (nôr′thėr-li), *adj.* pertaining to the north, or situated in or coming from the north:—*adv.* toward the north.

orth-ern (nôr′thėrn), *adj.* in, from, or toward, the north; as, a *northern* course.—*adj. superl.* **north′ern-most.**

orth-ern-er (nôr′thėr-nėr), *n.* a person living in, or coming from, the north:—**Northerner,** a person living in, or coming from, the part of the U.S. north of the southern boundary-line of Pennsylvania.

orthern lights, the aurora borealis, or streams of light seen in the sky at night, best observed in northern latitudes.

orth—north-east (nôrth′–nôrth′ēst′) *ı.* 22° 30′ east of due north.

orth—north-west (nôrth′–nôrth′-vest′), *n.* 22° 30′ west of due north.

north-ward (nôrth′wėrd), *adj.* and *adv.* to or toward the north; leading to the north. Also, *adv.* **north′wards.**—*adj.* and *adv.* **north′ward-ly.**

north-west (nôrth′west′), *n.* **1,** the point of the compass halfway between north and west; **2,** country lying in the direction of that point:—*adj.* having to do with the northwest, or in or from the northwest:—*adv.* toward the northwest.—*adj.* and *adv.* **north′west′ward.**

north-west-er (nôrth′wes′tėr), *n.* a strong wind or storm from the northwest.

north-west-er-ly (nôrth-wes′tėr-li), *adj.* and *adv.* from or toward the northwest.

north-west-ern (nôrth′wes′tėrn), *adj.* of, from, or situated in, the northwest.

nose (nōz), *n.* **1,** in man and other animals, that part of the face or head containing the nostrils and nerves of smell; **2,** the sense of smell; as, the deer has a keen *nose;* **3,** anything like a nose, as a spout:—*v.t.* [nosed, nos-ing], **1,** to smell or scent; **2,** to rub or push with the nose or front; as, horses *nose* each other; the boat *nosed* its way through the ice:—*v.i.* **1,** to smell or scent; **2,** to pry into another person's affairs. Compounds: **nose′bleed′; nose′piece′; nose′cone.**

nose-gay (nōz′gā)′, *n.* a bouquet or bunch of flowers.

nos-ing (nōz′ing), *n.* the part of the tread of a step projecting beyond the riser.

nos-tal-gi-a (nos-tal′ji-a), *n.* homesickness.—*adj.* **nos-tal′gic.**

nos-tril (nos′tril), *n.* one of the two external openings in the nose.

nos-trum (nos′trum), *n.* a medicine recommended as a cure-all; as, an old nurse's *nostrums;* a patent or quack medicine; hence, **3,** a pet remedy for a social evil; as, political *nostrums.*

nos-y or **nos-ey** (nōz′i), *adj. Colloq.* inquisitive; prying.

not (not), *adv.* a word that expresses denial, prohibition, or refusal; as, he will *not* go.

no-ta be-ne (nō′ta bē′ni), *Latin,* note well: usually N. B.

no-ta-ble (nō′ta-bl), *adj.* **1,** worthy of attention; memorable for any reason; as, a *notable* event; a *notable* play; **2,** distinguished; as, a *notable* speaker was the guest of honour:—*n.* a person or thing of distinction.—*n.* **no′ta-ble-ness.**

no-ta-bly (nō′ta-bli), *adv.* in a remarkable manner; strikingly; as, he was a *notably* clever cartoonist.

no-ta-ry (nō′ta-ri), *n.* [*pl.* notaries], an official permitted by law to witness or certify contracts etc., or to record the fact that a certain person swears something is true, etc.: also called *notary public* [*pl.* notaries public].

no-ta-tion (nō-tā′shun), *n.* **1,** the act or practice of recording by marks or symbols; also, a note; as, he made a *notation* on an envelope; **2,** a system of signs or symbols used in place of language, for brevity or clearness; esp. the system of numbers, letters, and signs used in arithmetic and algebra, and the signs used in writing or printing music.

notch (noch), *n.* **1,** a small nick or V-shaped cut in the edge of something; **2,** a narrow pass through mountains:— *v.t.* **1,** to nick or cut into small hollows; **2,** to keep count of by nicks.

note (nōt), *n.* **1,** a brief memorandum to assist the memory; **2,** a brief explanation or comment; as, the *notes* make the book clearer; **3,** a short, informal letter; as, drop me a *note* about your plans; **4,** a formal letter from one government to another; **5,** characteristic quality; as, a *note* of gaiety in the voice; **6,** reputation; fame; distinction; as, a family of *note;* **7,** notice; attention; as, a matter worthy of *note;* **8,** a cry, song, or call, as of a

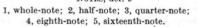

NOTES, def. 9
1, whole-note; 2, half-note; 3, quarter-note; 4, eighth-note; 5, sixteenth-note.

bird; **9,** in *music,* a written sign or character representing the pitch and relative length of a tone; also, a single tone itself, as made by a musical instrument or the voice; **10,** a legal paper acknowledging a debt, and promising payment; as, a promissory *note;* a bank-*note:*—*v.t.* [not-ed, not-ing], **1,** to make a memorandum of; as, he *noted* the date in his memorandum book; **2,** to make mention of; **3,** to observe; notice; as, he *noted* her beauty; **4,** to set down in musical notation.

note-book (nōt′book′), *n.* a book in which memoranda are made; esp. a student's book for notes, assignments, etc.

not-ed (nōt′id), *adj.* well-known; celebrated; as, a *noted* musician.

note-wor-thy (nōt′wûr′thi), *adj.* wor-

thy of notice; remarkable.—*adv* **note′wor′thi-ly.**—*n.* **note′wor′thi-ness**

noth-ing (nuth′ing), *pron.* not any thing; as, she has *nothing* to hope for —*n.* **1,** a thing of no value, use, or importance; **2,** a nobody:—*adv.* in no degree; not at all; as the copy is *nothing* like the original.—*n.* **noth′ing-ness.**

no-tice (nō′tis), *n.* **1,** a taking heed attention; observation; as, to take *notice* of events; **2,** information warning; as, he received *notice* to vacate the building; **3,** a printed announcement or sign; as, a *notice* of a death; **4,** a brief printed article or paragraph on a book, play, picture etc.:—*v.t.* [noticed, notic-ing], **1,** to see or observe; regard; **2,** to make remarks upon; speak of; **3,** to pay polite attention to; as, she didn't even *notice* me.

no-tice-a-ble (nō′tis-a-bl), *adj.* **1** capable of being observed or noticed as, a *noticeable* lack of interest; **2** conspicuous; likely to attract attention **3,** worthy of attention; notable; as his last play was a *noticeable* one.—*adv* **no′tice-a-bly.**

no-ti-fy (nō′ti-fī′), *v.t.* [notified, notify ing], **1,** to give warning or information to; **2,** to make known; declare publish.—*n.* **no′ti-fi′er.**—*n.* **no′ti-fi ca′tion.**

not-ion (nō′shun), *n.* **1,** a general idea as, I have no *notion* what he means; **2** a theory or belief; as, that is th common *notion;* **3,** inclination; fancy; as, to have a *notion* to do some thing; **4, notions,** in Canada and th U.S., small useful articles, such as pin thread, etc.

no-to-ri-e-ty (nō′to-rī′e-ti), *n.* [*pl* notorieties], the state of being wel known, esp. in an undesirable or ba way.

no-tor-i-ous (nō-tōr′i-us), *adj.* com monly known; noted; famous usually in a bad sense; as, a *notoriou* criminal.—*adv.* **no-tor′i-ous-ly.**—*n.* **no tor′i-ous-ness.**

not-with-stand-ing (not′with-stan′ ding), *prep.* in spite of; as, *notwith standing* the rain, he went to the party —*adv.* nevertheless; still; howeve all the same; as, his mother forbac his going, but he went *notwithstanding*

nought (nôt), *n.* **1,** a person or thing o no importance; **2,** in *arithmetic,* zer [0]; a cipher; a naught.

noun (noun), *n.* in *grammar,* a wor used to name a person or thing.

nour-ish (nur′ish), *v.t.* **1,** to feed (a plant or animal) with the material necessary to keep it alive and make it grow; **2,** to foster; encourage; as, a doctor *nourishes* hope in his patients:— *v.i.* to be nutritious; as, good food *nourishes.*—*n.* **nour′ish-ment.**

no-va (nō′va), *n.* [*pl.* -vae (vē); -vas (vaz)], a star that suddenly flashes out with unusual brilliancy and then gradually grows fainter.

¹nov-el (nov′el), *adj.* **1,** modern; unknown formerly; of recent origin; as, not many years ago airplanes were *novel* things; **2,** hence, new or unusual.

²nov-el (nov′el), *n.* a story, with a plot, long enough to fill one or more volumes, presenting characters and actions as they might occur in real life.

nov-el-ette (nov′el-et′), *n.* a short novel.

nov-el-ist (nov′el-ist), *n.* a writer of novels.

nov-el-ty (nov′el-ti), *n.* [*pl.* novelties], **1,** unusualness; newness; as, the new game was fun at first, but the *novelty* soon wore off; **2,** something new; a change or innovation; as, travel by airplane is still a *novelty;* **3,** **novelties,** attractive manufactured articles, usually of small value, offered for sale.

No-vem-ber (nō-vem′bėr), *n.* the 11th month (30 days).

nov-ice (nov′is), *n.* **1,** a beginner; an inexperienced person; **2,** a monk or nun who has entered a religious house, but has not yet taken the vows.

no-vi-ti-ate (nō-vish′i-it; -āt′), *n.* **1,** a period of probation or apprenticeship; **2,** a novice or beginner, or the state of being one; **3,** in a monastery, the quarters set apart for novices.

no-vo-ca-ine or **no-vo-ca-in** (nō′vo-kā′in; usually, nō′vo-kān′), *n.* a local anaesthetic, an alkaloid in solution, used by dentists, surgeons, etc.: a trade-mark.

now (nou), *adv.* **1,** at the present time; as, the danger is *now* over; **2,** a short time ago; quite recently; as, he left just *now;* **3,** immediately; at once; as, I am going *now;* **4,** under the present circumstances; as, *now* what can we do? **5,** used without any idea of time; as, oh, come *now,* don't do that; *now* you know better than that:—*conj.* since; now that; as, I need not stay, *now* you are here:—*n.* the present moment.—*adv.* **now′a-days.**

no-way (nō′wā′) or **no-ways** (nō′-wāz′), *adv.* not at all; as, he was *noway* to blame.

no-where (nō′hwâr′), *adv.* not in, at, or to, any place.

no-wise (nō′wīz′), *adv.* not at all; noway.

nox-ious (nok′shus), *adj.* harmful; injurious; deadly; as, *noxious* gases.— *adv.* **nox′ious-ly.**—*n.* **nox′ious-ness.**

noz-zle (noz′l), *n.* a projecting mouth-piece or spout, as on a hose, through which liquid can be discharged.

nth (enth), *adj.* the last in a series of infinitely increasing or decreasing amounts, values, etc.; hence, the *nth* degree, a very great one.

nu-ance (nü′äns′; nū′äns), *n. French,* a delicate shade, tone, colour, meaning, feeling, or expression; as, a *nuance* of green ivory.

nub (nub), *n.* **1,** knob; lump; knot; **2,** *Colloq.* the gist or point (of a story).

nu-cle-us (nū′kli-us), *n.* [*pl.* nuclei (nū′klē-ī) or nucleuses (nū′kli-us-ez)], **1,** a kernel; a central part or thing about which other matter collects; anything that serves as the centre of growth or development; as, John's few books became the *nucleus* of the town library; **2,** in *biology,* the central part of a seed or animal cell, necessary to growth and development.—*adj.* **nu′cle-ar.**

nude (nūd), *adj.* bare; naked.

nudge (nuj), *v.t.* [nudged, nudg-ing], to touch or push gently, as with the elbow: —*n.* a gentle touch or poke, as with the elbow.

nu-dism (nū′dizm), *n.* the cult or practice of going naked for healthful recreation, esp. by groups of persons.— *n.* **nu′dist.**—*n.* **nu′di-ty.**

nug-get (nug′it), *n.* a lump of native gold or other precious metal.

nui-sance (nū′sans), *n.* anything that offends or annoys.

null (nul), *adj.* of no force or value; not binding.—*n.* **nul′li-ty.**

nul-li-fy (nul′i-fī′), *v.t.* [nullified, nullifying], **1,** to deprive of effect or legal force; as, to *nullify* a decision or a law; **2,** to make of no value; destroy.—*n.* **nul′li-fi′er.**—*n.* **nul′li-fi-ca′tion.**

numb (num), *adj.* deprived of feeling or motion:—*v.t.* to deprive of sensation; benumb; as by cold.—*adv.* **numb′ly.**

num-ber (num′bėr), *n.* **1,** a total of units, persons, or things taken together; sum; as, to find out the *number* of persons present; **2,** the figure or mark that stands for this total; as, the *number* 20; **3,** a certain numeral by which one person or thing is identified from others; as, the convict's *number* was 665; **4,** a considerable collection; as, a *number* of people were present; **5,** one of a series; as, the October *number* of a magazine; **6,** in *grammar*, the characteristic of a word form whereby it refers either to one or to more than one; as, "man" is in the singular *number*, "men" is in the plural *number:*— **number one,** oneself:—*v.t.* **1,** to count; as, to *number* the persons in the crowd; **2,** to put a number on; **3,** to amount to; as, the class *numbers* 25; **4,** to include; as, we *number* her among our friends; **5,** to limit the number of; as, her days are *numbered*.

num-ber-less (num'bėr-lis), *adj.* **1,** having no number; **2,** very many; countless.

nu-mer-al (nū'mėr-al), *n.* a word, sign, or figure expressing a number; as, the Arabic *numerals* are 1, 2, 3, etc., the Roman *numerals* are I, II, III, etc.

nu-mer-a-tor (nū'mėr-ā'tėr), *n.* in fractions, the number above the line. In "⅞ of a bushel," the numerator, 7 indicates that seven of the eight equal parts of a bushel are to be taken.

nu-mer-i-cal (nū-mer'i-kal), *adj.* having to do with, or expressed in, numbers; as, *numerical* equations.— *adv.* **nu-mer'i-cal-ly.**

nu-mer-ous (nū'mėr-us), *adj.* consisting of a great number; many.—*adv.* **nu'mer-ous-ly.**—*n.* **nu'mer-ous-ness.**

nu-mis-mat-ics (nū'miz-mat'iks: mis-), *n. pl.* used as *sing.*, the collecting of coins, medals, etc., their science or study.—*adj.* **nu'mis-mat'ic.**

num-skull or **numb-skull** (num'-skul'), *n. Colloq.* a dolt; blockhead; dunce.

nun (nun), *n.* a woman living under certain vows in a convent and devoted to a religious life. Some nuns do charitable work, nursing, teaching, etc.

nun-ci-o (nun'shi-ō'), *n. [pl.* -os (ōz)], a permanent papal ambassador at a foreign capital.

nun-ner-y (nun'ėr-i), *n. [pl.* nunneries], a convent, or place where nuns live.

nup-tial (nup'shal), *adj.* pertaining to marriage; as, the *nuptial* day:— **nuptials,** *n.pl.* a wedding; marriage.

nurse (nûrs), *n.* **1,** one who cares for a young child or children; **2,** one who takes care of the sick or infirm:—*v.t.* [nursed, nurs-ing], **1,** to feed (an infant) at the breast; **2,** to take care of (a child, or young children); also, to caress or treat fondly; as, the little girl was *nursing* her doll; **3,** to care for or wait upon in sickness; **4,** to encourage; cherish; tend; make grow;

as, to *nurse* an industry, a grudge, a fire, a plant, etc.:—*v.i.* **1,** to suck milk from a mother; **2,** to care for the sick or infirm.—*n.* **nurse'maid'.**

nurs-er-y (nûr'sėr-i), *n. [pl.* nurseries], **1,** a room where young children sleep or play; **2,** a place or garden for raising young trees and plants.

nurs-er-y-man (nûr'sėr-i-man), *n. [pl.* nurserymen (-men)], a man who raises and sells plants.

nurs-ling (nûrs'ling), *n.* an infant; a child or thing needing tender care.

nur-ture (nûr'tūr), *n.* **1,** food; nourishment; **2,** feeding; promotion of growth; education; training:—*v.t.* [nurtured, nurtur-ing], **1,** to bring up; educate; **2,** to nourish; feed.

nut (nut), *n.* **1,** the dry fruit of certain trees, as the walnut, pecan, etc., consisting of a kernel, or seed, enclosed in a hard, woody or leathery shell; **2,** the kernel itself; **3,** a small metal block with a threaded hole, used to screw on a bolt to make it fast; **4,** *Slang:* **a,** the head: **b,** an insane or queer person.— *adj.* **nut'ty.**

nut-crack-er (nut'krak'ėr), *n.* **1,** an instrument for cracking nuts; **2,** a European bird of the crow family, feeding on nuts, seeds, and insects.

nut-hatch (nut'hach'), *n.* a small sharp-beaked, short-tailed bird that goes upside down up and down trees, eating nuts, beetles, etc.: found from Yukon to Quebec and south to Mexico; chief varieties are the *white-breasted,* the *red-breasted,* the *brownheaded,* and the *pygmy.*

nut-meg (nut'meg), *n.* the hard, nut-like kernel of the seed of an East Indian tree, which is grated and used as spice.

nu-tri-ent (nū'tri-ent), *n.* anything, as food, that nourishes and promotes growth:—*adj.* promoting growth; nourishing; as, milk is a *nutrient* fluid.

nu-tri-ment (nū'tri-ment), *n.* that which provides nourishment; food.

nu-tri-tion (nū-trish'un), *n.* **1,** food; **2,** the process by which an animal or plant uses food to promote growth.— *adj.* **nu-tri'tion-al.**

nu-tri-tious (nū-trish'us), *adj.* promoting growth; nourishing.—*adv.* **nu-tri'tious-ly.**—*n.* **nu-tri'tious-ness.**

nu-tri-tive (nū'tri-tiv), *adj.* **1,** nourishing; **2,** having to do with the process of growth in the body.

nuz-zle (nuz'l), *v.t.* [-zled, -zling], **1,** to rub or poke with the nose, muzzle, etc.; as, the pony *nuzzled* the boy's shoulder; **2,** to root up with the nose; as, the pig *nuzzled* for acorns:—*v.i.* to snuggle; nestle; as, ten whalers *nuzzled* the sand-bank.

ιy-lon (ni´lon), *n.* a strong, elastic, synthetic fabric made from coal, air, and water, used for hosiery, brush bristles, etc.; *pl.* women's stockings.

ιymph (nimf), *n.* 1, in *mythology*, a lesser goddess of nature, living in the mountains, woods, streams, etc.; 2, in *zoology*, a pupa or chrysalis; also, an immature insect stage like an un-developed adult form, seen in bugs, grasshoppers, etc.

nym-pho-ma-ni-ac (nim´fō-mā´ni-ak), *n.* a woman with excessive or uncontrollable sexual desire.—*n.* **nym´-pho-ma´ni-a.**

O

O, o (ō), *n.* [*pl.* O's, o's], 1, the 15th letter of the alphabet; 2, as a numeral, zero; 3, anything shaped like the letter O.

ɔ' (ō; o), *prep.* a contraction of *of;* as, ten o'clock; also, *Colloq.* a contraction of *on;* as, knocked o' the head.

ɔaf (ōf), *n.* 1, a deformed or idiotic child; a changeling; 2, an awkward or foolish person; an idiot.

ɔak (ōk), *n.* 1, any of several large European and American trees bearing a one-celled fruit, the acorn, in a woody cup, and yielding a strong, tough wood used as timber; 2, the wood of this tree; 3, a plant that is like an oak in some respect:—*adj.* made of oak.—*adj.* **oak´en.**

ɔa-kum (ō´kum), *n.* loose hemp fibre obtained by untwisting old ropes, used esp. for stopping leaks in boats.

ɔar (ōr), *n.* 1, a light pole with a broad, flat or spoon-shaped blade at one end, used for rowing or steering a boat; 2, one who rows a boat; an oarsman:—*v.t.* to row.

ɔar-lock (ōr´lok´), *n.* a U-shaped metal device, a notch, or a pin, on the side of a boat, in which a rower rests the oar in rowing or sculling; a rowlock.

ɔars-man (ōrz´man), *n.* [*pl.* oarsmen (-men)], one who rows.

ɔ-a-sis (ō-ā´sis; ō´a-sis), *n.* [*pl.* oases (ō-ā´sēz; ō´a-sēz´)], a fertile place in a desert.

ɔat (ōt), *n.* (usually *oats*), a cereal plant or its seed, used as food, esp. for horses. —*adj.* **oat´en.**

ɔath (ōth), *n.* [*pl.* oaths (ōthz)], 1, a solemn declaration that one speaks the truth, with an appeal to God as witness; 2, a profane use of the name of God or of any sacred thing.

ɔat-meal (ōt´mēl´), *n.* 1, meal made from oats; 2, porridge or pudding made from this meal or from rolled oats.

ob- (ob-), a *prefix* meaning *opposite* or *inverse*, as in *obverse; to* or *toward*, as in *object; in the way of*, as in *ob*vious; *completely*, as in *ob*solete: in this sense often called an *intensive*. Note that in Latin compounds the *b* may change as in *oc*cur, *of*fer, *op*press, etc.

ob-bli-ga-to (ob´li-gä´tō), *adj.* in *music* required; indispensable (as applied esp. to accompaniment): opposite of *ad libitum* (at pleasure).

ob-du-rate (ob´dū-rit; ob-dū´rit), *adj.* 1, not to be moved by appeals to the feelings; hard-hearted; 2, unrepentant; 3, stubborn; unyielding; firm.—*n.* **ob´du-ra-cy** (ob´dū-ra-si; ob-dū´ra-si).

o-be-di-ence (ō-bē´di-ens), *n.* the act of yielding to control by others; sub-mission to authority.—*adj.* **o-be´di-ent.**

o-bei-sance (ō-bā´sans; ō-bē´), *n.* a movement or bending of the body that shows obedience or respect; a bow.

ob-e-lisk (ob´e-lisk), *n.* 1, a four-sided, tapering stone pillar shaped at the top like a pyramid; 2, in books, a mark of reference [†].

o-bese (ō-bēs´), *adj.* very fat.—*n.* **o-bese´ness.**—*n.* **o-bes´i-ty** (ō-bes´i-ti).

o-bey (ō-bā´), *v.t.* 1, to submit to the rule or authority of (a law or a person); to follow or mind; as, to *obey* the commandments; to *obey* one's parents; 2, to respond to the guidance or control of; as, a horse *obeys* the rein:—*v.i.* to yield; do as bidden.

o-bit (ō´bit; ob´it), *n.* an obituary notice.

o-bit-u-ar-y (ō-bit´ū-ėr-i), *n.* [*pl.* obitu-aries], a printed notice of the death of a person, esp. one with a brief account of his life:—*adj.* pertaining to a person's death; as, an *obituary* notice.

¹ob-ject (ob-jekt´), *v.i.* 1, to offer opposition; as, he *objected* to my idea; 2, to feel or express disapproval:—*v.t.* to urge as a reason against a plan,

all (ôl), ôr; up, mūte, cûr, cōōl, book; oil, out; th, thin; *th*, the.

proposal, etc.; as, when asked to speak, he *objected* his lack of preparation.

²ob-ject (ob′jekt), *n.* **1,** that which can be seen or touched; **2,** a person or thing arousing some action or feeling; as, an *object* of charity; **3,** an aim; as, my *object* in school is to learn; **4,** in *grammar,* a word or clause governed by a verb: called *direct object* when immediately affected by the action of the verb, and *indirect object* when less directly affected as, in the sentence "he gave the boy money for a hat," "money" is the *direct object,* and "boy" the *indirect object,* of the verb "gave"; also, a word governed by a preposition; as, "hat" is the *object* of the preposition "for."

ob-jec-tion (ob-jek′shun), *n.* **1,** a feeling or expression of opposition or disapproval; **2,** a reason against anything.

ob-jec-tion-a-ble (ob-jek′shun-a-bl), *adj.* **1,** liable or open to opposition; **2,** arousing disapproval; undesirable; unpleasant.—*adv.* **ob-jec′tion-a-bly.**

ob-jec-tive (ob-jek′tiv), *n.* **1,** the end or goal toward which any action is directed; an aim; **2,** that which exists outside the mind; an outward fact; reality; **3,** in *grammar,* the objective case; also, a word in the objective case; **4,** the lens of a microscope or telescope nearest to the object observed:—*adj.* **1,** serving as an end or goal of action or feeling; as, the *objective* point of military operations; **2,** having to do with an outward fact, or that which exists outside the mind, rather than with thoughts or feelings: opposite of *subjective;* **3,** in *grammar,* naming the case of the object of a verb or a preposition.—*adv.* **ob-jec′tive-ly.**—*n.* **ob′jec-tiv′i-ty.**

ob-la-tion (ob-lā′shun), *n.* **1,** the act of making an offering or sacrifice to God or to the gods: used esp. in reference to the bread and wine of the Communion; **2,** anything presented as a religious offering or sacrifice; a religious gift.

ob-li-ga-tion (ob′li-gā′shun), *n.* **1,** the binding power of a vow, promise, contract, or sense of duty; **2,** any duty imposed by law, by social relations, or by goodwill; as, the *obligations* of good citizenship; **3,** the state of being bound to perform some duty or to do something burdensome; as, under *obligation* to pay a debt; **4,** a written deed or bond by which one binds oneself to do a thing; a contract; a promise.—*adj.* **ob-li-ga-to-ry** (ob′li-ga-tẽr-i; o-blig′a-tẽr-i).—*v.t.* **ob′li-gate′.**

ob-li-ga-to (ob′li-gä′tō), *n.* incorrect form of **ob′bli-ga′to.**

o-blige (ō-blīj′), *v.t.* [obliged, oblig-ing], **1,** to compel by force, moral, legal, or physical; as, the policeman *obliged* his young prisoner to walk in front; **2,** to place under obligation; as, I was *obliged* to him for his help; **3,** to render a favour to; as, he *obliged* the audience with an encore.

o-blig-ing (ō-blīj′ing), *adj.* willing to do favours; courteous; kindly; as, an *obliging* neighbour.—*adv.* **o-blig′ing-ly.**

ob-lique (ob-lēk′), *adj.* neither horizontal nor vertical; slanting.—*adv.* **ob-lique′ly.**—*n.* **ob-liq′ui-ty** (ob-lik′-wi-ti).

ob-lit-er-ate (ob-lit′ẽr-āt′), *v.t.* [obliterat-ed, obliterat-ing], to erase or blot out; destroy all traces of; as, to *obliterate* a mark; time *obliterates* sorrow.—*n.* **ob-lit′er-a′tion.**

ob-liv-i-on (ob-liv′i-un), *n.* **1,** the state of being forgotten; **2,** forgetfulness of the past.—*adj.* **ob-liv′i-ous.**

ob-long (ob′lông), *adj.* longer than broad: said usually of a figure that is rectangular or nearly so; as, an *oblong* box:—*n.* a rectangle or figure longer than it is broad.

ob-lo-quy (ob′lo-kwi), *n.* **1,** disgrace, esp. from public blame or censure; as, Mr. Harding suffered the *obloquy* of the Teapot Dome scandal; **2,** defamation.

ob-nox-ious (ob-nok′shus), *adj.* hateful; offensive; odious.—*adv.* **ob-nox′-ious-ly.**

o-boe (ō′boi; ō′bō), *n.* a high-pitched musical instrument of the woodwind

OBOE

group with a penetrating tone.—*n.* **o′bo-ist.**

ob-scene (ob-sēn′), *adj.* offensive to modesty; impure in language or action; indecent.—*adv.* **ob-scene′ly.**—*n.* **ob-scen′i-ty** (ob-sen′i-ti).

ob-scure (ob-skūr′), *adj.* **1,** not clear or distinct; as, an *obscure* view; **2,** shadowy; dim; dark; as, an *obscure* room; **3,** not easily understood; as, an *obscure* meaning; **4,** illegible; as, faint and *obscure* writing; **5,** remote; unknown; as, he lived in an *obscure* little village; **6,** humble; inconspicuous; as, he occupied an *obscure* position:—*v.t.* [obscured, obscur-ing], **1,** to darken; hide from view; **2,** to disguise; render less intelligible.—*n.* **ob-scu′ri-ty.**—*n.* **ob′scu-ra′tion.**

ob-se-quies (ob′si-kwiz), *n.pl.* funeral rites or ceremonies.

ob-se-qui-ous (ob-sē′kwi-us), *adj.* servile; fawning, usually in order to gain a selfish end.—*adv.* **ob-se′qui-ous-ly.**

ob-serv-ance (ob-zûr′vans), *n.* 1, the act of keeping, or of paying attention to, laws or customs; as, the *observance* of the Sabbath; 2, an act, as a ceremony, performed in token of worship or respect.

ob-serv-ant (ob-zûr′vant), *adj.* 1, quick to notice; attentive; 2, watchful; mindful of duties or authority.

ob-ser-va-tion (ob′zėr-vā′shun), *n.* 1, the act, power, or habit of seeing and noting; thorough, careful notice; 2, that which is noticed or learned; 3, a remark, judgment, or conclusion based on something noticed; 4, the fact of being seen; as, he tried to avoid *observation;* 5, the accurate examination of natural objects or events for the purpose of recording their cause, effect, etc.; as, *observation* of an eclipse.

ob-serv-a-tor-y (ob-zûr′va-tėr-i), *n.* [*pl.* observatories], 1, a building fitted up with a telescope and other instruments for studying the heavens; 2, a tower or other high place built to give an extensive view.

ob-serve (ob-zûrv′), *v.t.* [observed, observ-ing], 1, to take notice of; 2, to watch closely; study; 3, to keep or celebrate; commemorate; 4, to remark; 5, to comply with; as, to *observe* the social conventions:—*v.i.* 1, to take notice; 2, to comment.—*n.* **ob-serv′er.** —*adj.* **ob-serv′a-ble.**

ob-sess (ob-ses′), *v.t.* to rule the mind of; preoccupy; as, the idea *obsessed* him.—*n.* **ob-ses′sion.**

ob-so-lete (ob′so-lēt′), *adj.* gone out of use; as, *obsolete* firearms; no longer practised or accepted; as, an *obsolete* custom.—*adj.* **ob′so-les′cent.**—*n.* **ob′-so-les′cence.**

ob-sta-cle (ob′sta-kl), *n.* that which hinders or stands in the way; an obstruction; impediment; hindrance.

ob-stet-rics (ob-stet′riks), *n. pl.* used as *sing. Medical,* the science or art of the care and treatment of women before, during, and after childbirth; midwifery.—*n.* **ob′ste-tri′cian.**—*adj.* **ob-stet′ri-cal.**

ob-sti-nate (ob′sti-nit), *adj.* 1, not yielding to argument, persuasion, or entreaty; headstrong; firm in opinion or purpose; 2, not yielding to treatment as a disease.—*adv.* **ob′sti-nate-ly.**—*n.* **ob′sti-na-cy.**

ob-strep-er-ous (ob-strep′ėr-us), *adj.* noisy; unruly; turbulent; as, an *obstreperous* child.

ob-struct (ob-strukt′), *v.t.* 1, to block up or close so as to prevent passage; 2, to prevent or retard the progress of; as, to *obstruct* work; 3, to be in the way of; cut off from sight; as, to *obstruct* the view.—*n.* **ob-struc′tion.**—*n.* **ob-struc′-tion-ist.**—*adj.* **ob-struc′tive** (as, *obstructive* tactics).

ob-tain (ob-tān′), *v.t.* to get possession of; gain; as, to *obtain* knowledge:—*v.i.* to be established in practice or use; prevail or be in fashion; as, that custom still *obtains* here.—*adj.* **ob-tain′a-ble.**

ob-trude (ob-trōōd′), *v.t.* [obtrud-ed, obtrud-ing], to thrust forward boldly: —*v.i.* to force oneself upon others; intrude.

ob-tru-sive (ob-trōō′siv), *adj.* unduly inclined to push forward; intrusive.

ob-tuse (ob-tūs′), *adj.* 1, not pointed or acute; blunt; 2, of angles, greater than a right angle; 3, dull or stupid; as, an *obtuse* person.—*adv.* **ob-tuse′ly.**

OBTUSE ANGLE

ob-verse (ob′vûrs), *n.* 1, the front surface, esp. of a coin or medal, with the main design on it: opposite of *reverse;* 2, a corollary, different aspect, or counterpart of a fact or truth; as the science of medicine and its *obverse,* witchcraft.

ob-vi-ate (ob′vi-āt), *v.t.* [obviat-ed, obviat-ing], to remove, or clear away, beforehand, as difficulties or objections.

ob-vi-ous (ob′vi-us), *adj.* easily understood or seen; evident; plain; as, the effect is *obvious.*—*adv.* **ob′vi-ous-ly.**

oc-a-ri-na (ok′a-rēn′a), *n.* a small musical instrument, with finger-holes and mouthpiece, that gives a soft, pleasing sound: it is usually made of terra cotta: sometimes, from its shape, called *sweet potato.*

oc-ca-sion (o-kā′zhun), *n.* 1, a particular event or celebration; as, the king's visit was an *occasion;* 2, occurrence; as, on the *occasion* of her last visit; 3, something that leads to unexpected results; an incidental cause as, his carelessness was the *occasion* of the whole trouble; 4, need; reason; as, having *occasion* to buy food; no *occasion* for anger; 5, a favourable chance or opportunity; as, he seized the *occasion* to speak:—*v.t.* to cause; give rise to; as, the law *occasioned* widespread revolt.

oc-ca-sion-al (o-kā′zhun-al), *adj.* **1,** happening now and then, but not regularly; as, *occasional* visits; **2,** meant for, or suitable to, a special event; as, an *occasional* poem.—*adv.* **oc-ca′sion-al-ly.**

oc-ci-dent (ok′si-dent), *n.* the west: opposite of *orient,* or the east:— **Occident,** the countries west of Asia; western Europe and the Western Hemisphere: opposite of *Orient.*—*adj.* and *n.* **oc′ci-den′tal; Oc′ci-den′tal** (ok′si-den′tal).

oc-clu-sion (o-klū′zhun; -klōō), *n.* in *dentistry,* the shutting or fitting together of the cusps of the upper and lower teeth (in biting); **2,** in *chemistry,* absorption; as the *occlusion* of hydrogen by palladium; **3,** *medical,* closure, as of the pores:—*v.t.* **oc-clude′.**

oc-cult (o-kult′), *adj.* concealed; secret; mysterious: usually said of magic alchemy, astrology, etc. (*occult* sciences, rites, etc.):—*v.t.* and *v.i.* to hide, as a moon's or planet's passing in front of a star and blotting it out.—*adj.* **oc-cult′-ing,** respecting lighthouses, buoys, etc., said of a light that is cut off from view for a few seconds at regular intervals.

oc-cu-pant (ok′ū-pant), *n.* one who dwells in, has possession of, or uses a house, property, etc.—*n.* **oc′cu-pan-cy.**

oc-cu-pa-tion (ok′ū-pā′shun), *n.* **1,** the act of holding in possession, or occupying; also, the time during which a property or position is held; **2,** regular business, employment, or calling.

oc-cu-py (ok′ū-pī′), *v.t.* [occupied, occupy-ing], **1,** to take possession of; dwell in; as, to *occupy* a room; **2,** to fill or cover the time or space of; as, household duties *occupy* her day; **3,** to employ; busy; as, to *occupy* oneself with work; **4,** to hold; fill; as, to *occupy* the office of mayor.

oc-cur (o-kûr′), *v.i.* [occurred, occurring], **1,** to happen or take place; as, the mistake must not *occur* again; **2,** to be found; exist; as, such plants *occur* in Africa; **3,** to come to mind; as, did it *occur* to you to go?—*n.* **oc-cur′rence.**

o-cean (ō′shan), *n.* **1,** the vast body of salt water covering three fourths of the globe; also, any one of its chief divisions; as, the Atlantic *Ocean;* **2,** a vast expanse or amount; as, an *ocean* of tears.—*adj.* **o′ce-an′ic.**

o-cean-og-ra-phy (o′shan-og′ra-fi), *n.* geography dealing with the ocean.—*n.* **o′ce-a-nog′ra-pher** (-shi).

o-ce-lot (ō′se-lot; os′e-lot), *n.* a leopard-like cat, yellowish grey with elongated fawn-coloured spots edged in black, found in Central and South America.

o-chre or **o-cher** (ō′kėr), *n.* **1,** a fine clay (an ore of iron) pale yellow, orange, and red, used as paint pigments; **2,** a colour, esp. dark yellow.

o′-clock (o-klok′), *adv.* contraction for *of the clock,* according to the clock.

oc-ta-gon (ok′ta-gon′, ok′ta-gun), *n.* a plane figure of eight sides and eight angles.—*adj.* **oc-tag′o-nal** (ok-tag′o-nal).

oc-tam-e-ter (ok-tam′e-tėr), *adj.* having eight metrical feet.—*n.* a verse of eight feet, as in 'March: an Ode' (Swinburne).

oc-tane (ok′tān), *n.* a hydrocarbon, C_8H_{18}, obtained in the refining of petroleum: valuable for its high volatility:—**octane rating,** a number used in grading the antiknock quality of a gasoline.

oc-tang-u-lar (ok-tang′gu-lėr), *adj.* having eight angles.

oc-tave (ok′tiv; ok′tāv), *n.* in *music:* **1,** an interval of eight steps, as from C in the scale to the C next above or below; **2,** the series of tones comprised in such an interval; **3,** the harmonic combination of two tones at such an interval; **4,** the eighth note in the ordinary musical scale:—in *poetry,* the first eight lines, or octet, of an Italian sonnet.—*adj.* consisting of eight.

oc-tet or **oc-tette** (ok-tet′), *n.* **1,** in *music* (a) a composition with eight parts for voices or instruments (b) the eight performers of such a composition; **2,** in *poetry,* the first eight lines of an Italian sonnet.

Oc-to-ber (ok-tō′ber), *n.* the **10th** month of the year (31 days).

oc-to-ge-na-ri-an (ok′tō-ji-nâ′ri-an; -nā), *n.* one who is 80 years old, or between 80 and 90.

oc-to-pus (ok′tō-pus), *n.* [*pl.* octopuses (ok′tō-pus-ez) or octopi (ok′tō-pī′)], **1,** a sea mollusc related to the cuttlefish, having eight arms provided with suckers with which it holds on to its prey; **2,** any organization with a harmful, far-reaching hold on the public.

oc-u-lar (ok′ū-lėr), *adj.* **1,** pertaining to the eye or to eyesight; **2,** depending on, or seen by, the eye; as, *ocular* evidence.

oc-u-list (ok′ū-list), *n.* one who is skilled in the treatment of eye diseases: distinguished from *optician* and *optometrist.*

odd (od), *adj.* **1,** not paired or matched

with another; as, an *odd* glove; **2,** not exactly divisible by two; as, seven is an *odd* number; **3,** left over after equal division; extra; as, you may have the *odd* one; **4,** additional; as, fifty and some *odd* miles; also, plus a few more; as, thirty *odd;* **5,** unusual; as, an *odd* occurrence; **6,** eccentric; as, an *odd* person; **7,** occasional; as, *odd* jobs; **8,** not occupied; as, *odd* moments.—*adv.* **odd′ly.**—*n.* **odd′ness.**—*n.* **odd′i-ty.**

odds (odz), *n.pl.* **1,** inequality; **2,** advantage; superiority of one as compared with another; as, the *odds* are in her favour; **3,** probability; as, the *odds* are that he will succeed; **4,** in betting, an advantage in the amount wagered to compensate for a smaller chance of winning; as, *odds* of ten to one.

ode (ōd), *n.* a lyric poem expressing noble sentiments in a dignified style.

o-di-ous (ō′di-us), *adj.* deserving of, or causing, hatred; offensive; as, his conduct was *odious.*—*adv.* **o′di-ous-ly.** —*n.* **o′di-um.**

o-dour or **o-dor** (ō′dẽr), *n.* **1,** a scent; smell, whether pleasant or offensive; **2,** repute; as, in bad *odour.*—*adj.* **o′dor-ous.**—*adj.* **o′dour-less;** **o′dor-if′er-ous.**

o′er (ōr), *prep.* and *adv. Poetic,* over.

oe-soph-a-gus (i-sof′a-gus), *n.* the gullet, or tube through which food and drink pass from the throat to the stomach.

of (ov), *prep.* **1,** from; as, to cure *of* a fever; born *of* a line of kings; north *of* the city; **2,** forced by; as, he did it *of* necessity; **3,** about; concerning; as, talk *of* success; news *of* victory; **4,** in; as, quick *of* speech; **5,** belonging to, related to, or connected with; as, the palace *of* the king; **6,** containing; having; consisting of; as, a glass *of* milk; a man *of* brains; a line *of* trees; made from; as, a house *of* stone; **7,** named: esp. of political divisions; as, the province of Quebec; **8,** *Colloq.* on; as she died *of* a Monday; **9,** *Archaic,* by; as, admired *of* men:—**of late,** lately.

off (ôf), *adv.* **1,** away from a place; to run *off;* to stand *off* to sea; from, so as not to be on; as, take *off* your coat, gloves, hat; also, on one's way; as, he is *off* to town; **2,** into the condition of; as, to drop *off* to sleep; **3,** so as to stop the flow of; as, to turn *off* the gas; **4,** so as to end or be rid of; as, to break *off* a friendship; to shake *off* a feeling; **5,** in full; as, to pay *off* a mortgage; **6,** away from work; as, he has a day *off;* **7,** less; as, ten per cent *off* for cash:—

adj. **1,** on the right-hand side of a vehicle, animal, or team; **2,** removed; not on; as, he stood with his hat *off;* **3,** not in use; disconnected; as, the gas is *off;* the radio was *off* all day; **4,** given up; cancelled; as, all arrangements are *off;* **5,** wrong; mistaken; he is *off* in his estimate; **6,** out of order; not functioning properly; as, his heart is *off;* **7,** unlucky; as, it is an *off* day for him; **8,** not up to the usual standard; as, his playing was *off* today; **9,** provided for; situated; as, he is well *off;* **10,** not very probable; as, an *off* chance:—*prep.* **1,** away from; as, take your hands *off* the table; removed from; as, the cover is *off* my book; **2,** distant from; as, a mile *off* shore; **3,** temporarily relieved of; as, he is *off* duty; **4,** less than; as ten per cent *off* the regular price:—*interj.* begone!

of-fal (ôf′al), *n.* **1,** worthless scraps; refuse; **2,** waste parts of a butchered animal.

off—col-our (ôf′-kul′ẽr),*adj.* **1,** varying from standard colour, as a gem; **2,** improper; as, an *off-colour* story.

of-fence or **of-fense** (o-fens′), *n.* **1,** a sin; crime; **2,** the act of offering an injury; **3,** the state of being offended; **4,** an attack or assault.—*adj.* **of-fence′-less.**

of-fend (o-fend′), *v.t.* to displease or make angry; vex or annoy:—*v.i.* **1,** to transgress; sin; as, to *offend* against the law; **2,** to do anything displeasing. —*n.* **of-fend′er.**

of-fen-sive (o-fen′siv), *adj.* **1,** insulting; as, *offensive* actions; **2,** disagreeable; as, an *offensive* odour; **3,** used in attack; as, *offensive* weapons:—*n.* an aggressive method or attitude.—*adv.* **of-fen′sive-ly.**

of-fer (ôf′ẽr), *n.* **1,** a proposal; **2,** a price bid; **3,** an attempt or endeavour; as, to make an *offer* of resistance:—*v.t.* **1,** to present for acceptance or refusal; as, to *offer* money; **2,** to proffer; as, to *offer* help or advice; **3,** to propose; as, to *offer* a plan; **4,** to present in worship or sacrifice; as, to *offer* a prayer; **5,** to attempt to make or give; as, to *offer* resistance:—*v.i.* to present itself; appear; arise; as, a favourable opportunity soon *offered.*

of-fer-ing (ôf′ẽr-ing), *n.* **1,** the act of making a proffer or proposal; **2,** that which is offered or given; a gift.

of-fer-to-ry (ôf′ẽr-tō-ri), *n.* **1,** the act of offering, or the thing offered; **2,** the offering of money at a religious service; **3,** a vocal or organ selection rendered at such a time.

---

all (ôl), **ôr;** **up, mūte, cûr, cōōl, book;** **oil, out;** th, **thin;** *th,* **the.**

off-hand (ôf′hand′), *adj.* **1,** done without preparation; as, an *offhand* speech; **2,** informal:—*adv.* (ôf′hand′), usually *off hand*, without preparation.

of-fice (ôf′is), *n.* **1,** a position of trust or authority; as, the *office* of president; **2,** a function; as, the *office* of the ears is to hear; **3,** a religious ceremony or rite; **4,** a duty or service; as, an *office* of kindness; **5,** a place for the transaction of business; as, a doctor's *office;* an express *office.*

of-fi-cer (ôf′i-sėr), *n.* **1,** a person empowered to perform a public duty, as a policeman; **2,** one elected to manage the affairs of an organization; **3,** in the Army or Navy, one appointed, esp. by commission, to a position of rank and authority:—*v.t.* **1,** to furnish with leaders; **2,** to command.

of-fi-cial (o-fish′al), *n.* one who holds an office:—*adj.* **1,** pertaining to an office; as, *official* duties; **2,** derived from the proper authority; authorized; as, an *official* ruling.—*n.* **of-fi′cial-dom.**

of-fi-ci-ate (o-fish′i-āt′), *v.i.* [officiated, officiat-ing], **1,** to perform the duties of a divine service; **2,** to perform the duties of an office, etc.

of-fi-cious (o-fish′us), *adj.* too bold in offering services; meddling.—*adv.* **of-fi′cious-ly.**—*n.* **of-fi′cious-ness.**

off-ing (ôf′ing), *n.* the open sea, visible from shore but beyond anchoring-ground; hence, distance; future; as, a job in the *offing.*

off-scour-ing (ôf′skour′ing), *n.* filth; dregs; rubbish; refuse; usually *pl.*, as the *offscourings* of the slums.

off-set (ôf′set′; of′set′), *v.t.* [offset, offset-ting], to make up for; compensate; balance; as, her bad manners are *offset* by her beauty:—*n.* (ôf′set′), **1,** that which proceeds or develops from something else; an offshoot; **2,** one thing which makes up for another; a compensation.—**offset printing,** a process by which an inked impression is made on a rubber-covered roller and then transferred to paper.

off-shoot (ôf′shōōt′), *n.* **1,** a lateral branch from a main stem; **2,** anything that springs from a main stock; as, the offshoot of a noble house (descendant).

off-shore (of′shōr′), *adj.* **1,** moving toward the sea; **2,** located out from the shore:—*adv.* (ôf′shōr′), (usually *off shore*), away from, or at some distance from, the shore.

off-side (ôf′sīd′), *n.* in *football* and *hockey,* being ahead of a certain line of play and hence ineligible to receive the ball or puck: otherwise the play (or player) is *offside.*

off-spring (of′spring′), *n.* [*pl.* off-spring], a child or children; a descendant or descendants of a plant or animal.

off—stage (ôf′-stāj′), *n.* back-stage (in the wings).—*adj.* in the off-stage; as, an *off-stage* whisper. Also used as *adv.*

off—white (ôf′-hwīt′), *adj.* having a touch of gray in the white.

oft (oft), *adv. Poetic,* often.

of-ten (ôf′en), *adv.* frequently.

of-ten-times (ôf′en-tīmz′), *adv.* often.

oft-times (ôft′tīmz′), *adv. Poetic,* often.

o-gle (ō′gl), *v.t.* [o-gled, o-gling], to eye with familiar or amorous glances:—*n.* an amorous or too familiar look.—*n.* **o′gler.**

o-gre (ō′gėr), *n.* in fairy tales, a man-eating monster or giant; hence, a cruel, ugly person.

oh (ō), *interj.* **1,** an exclamation of wonder, surprise, sorrow, shame, pain, etc.; **2,** (preferably *O*), a word used in earnest address, as in prayer.

ohm (ōm), *n.* the unit of electrical resistance; namely, the resistance of a circuit in which one volt produces a current of one ampere.

o-ho (ō-hō′), *interj.* an exclamation of surprise, exultation, etc.

oil (oil), *n.* **1,** a greasy or fatty substance, of animal, vegetable, or mineral origin, and used variously as a lubricant, fuel, medicine, food, etc.; **2,** in art: **a,** a pigment mixed with oil: called *oil-colour* or *oil-paint;* **b,** a picture painted with this material:—*v.t.* **1,** to lubricate with oil; **2,** to anoint.—*n.* **oil′er.**—*adj.* **oil′y.**

oil-cloth (oil′klôth′), *n.* a coarse cloth coated with oil or oil-paint, used for covering floors, shelves, tables, etc.

oil-skin (oil′skin′), *n.* **1,** a cloth treated with oil and made waterproof; **2,** **oilskins,** waterproof clothing made of such cloth.

oil-stone (oil′stōn′), *n.* a fine-grained whetstone, moistened with oil, used to sharpen edged tools; a hone.

oint-ment (oint′ment), *n.* a medicinal preparation, usually made of a fat, applied to the skin to heal or beautify.

O.K., OK, or **o-kay** (ō′kā′), *adj., adv., n.,* and *interj. Colloq.* all right; correct: —*v.t.* to endorse or acknowledge; as, the engineer and conductor O.K.'d the despatcher's orders.

o-kra (ō′kra; ok′ra), *n.* a West Indian

plant, cultivated for the seed pods which are used as vegetables and in soups.

old (ōld), *adj.* [old-er or eld-er, old-est or eld-est], **1,** having existed or lived many years; aged; as, an *old* oak; an *old* man; **2,** having an appearance of age; as, an *old* face; **3,** having reached a certain age; as, twenty-one years *old;* **4,** decayed by time; as, an *old* ruin; **5,** ancient; out of date; as, *old* customs; *old* coins; **6,** long used; not new; as, *old* shoes; **7,** long practised; as, *old* habits; **8,** belonging to the past; as, one's *old* home; **9,** *Colloq.* familiar and dear; as, *Old* England; **10,** long experienced; as, he is an *old* hand at that work:—*n.* former times; as, in days of *old*.

old-en (ōl'den), *adj.* ancient; bygone; as, in *olden* times.

old—fash-ioned (ōld'–fash'und), *adj.* **1,** having or adhering to old ideas or customs; as, an *old-fashioned* person; **2,** out of style.

old—world (ōld'–wûrld'), *adj.* **1,** of or relating to ancient times; **2,** (usually *Old World*), relating to the Eastern Hemisphere.

o-le-an-der (ō'li-an'dẽr), *n.* a sub-tropical, poisonous, evergreen shrub of the dogbane family: it grows 20 feet high and has fragrant rose and white flowers.

o-le-o-mar-ga-rine (ō'li-ō-mär'jẽr-ēn'; -mär'ga-rin; -mär'ga-rēn'), *n.* a fatty substance extracted from animal or vegetable fats and used in place of butter: also called *mar'gar-ine*.

ol-fac-to-ry (ol-fak'to-ri), *adj.* pertaining to smelling; as, an *olfactory* nerve.

ol-i-gar-chy (ol'i-gär'ki), *n.* [*pl.* -chies (kiz)], *n.* **1,** a rule by a few (often vested in a clique, junto, or dominant class); **2,** the state so governed.—*n.* ol'i-garch'.

ol-ive (ol'iv), *n.* **1,** an Old World evergreen cultivated for its oily fruit; **2,** the wood of this tree; also, its fruit, brownish black when ripe; **3,** a dull yellowish-green colour, as of an unripe olive:—*adj.* of a dull yellowish-green or yellowish-brown colour.

O-lym-pic games, or **O-lym-pics** (ō-lim'pik), **1,** in ancient Greece, a festival of athletic contests, music, poetry, drama, etc., celebrated every four years in honour of Zeus; in modern times, various international athletic contests held every four years in a chosen city (since 1896): they include track and field, swimming, pole-vaulting, shot-put, etc.—*n.* **O-lym'pi-ad** (the four-year interval between celebrations).

o-me-ga (ō-mē'ga; ō'mi-ga; ō-meg'a), *n.* **1,** the last letter of the Greek alphabet equivalent of English long ō; hence, **2,** the last; the end; as, "I am *Alpha* and *Omega*, the beginning and the end."

om-e-let (om'e-let; om'let), *n.* a dish consisting of eggs and milk, often with other ingredients, beaten together and browned in a pan. Also spelled **om'e-lette**.

o-men (ō'men), *n.* a prophetic sign of some future event; augury.

om-i-nous (om'i-nus), *adj.* foreboding evil; threatening.—*adv.* **om'i-nous-ly**.

o-mis-sion (ō-mish'un), *n.* **1,** the act of omitting; state of being left out; **2,** something left out or neglected.

o-mit (ō-mit'), *v.t.* [omit-ted, omit-ting] to leave out; fail to include; also, to neglect; leave undone.

om-ni-bus (om'ni-bus'; om'ni-bus), *n.* a large four-wheeled public vehicle for passenger traffic over a fixed route; bus:—*adj.* including or providing for many different objects or cases; as, an *omnibus* bill was introduced into Parliament.

om-nip-o-tent (om-nip'o-tent), *adj.* all-powerful:—**the Omnipotent**, God.—*n.* **om-nip'o-tence**.

om-ni-pres-ent (om'ni-prez'ent), *adj.* present everywhere at the same time.—*n.* **om'ni-pres'ence**.

om-ni-sci-ent (on-nish'i-ent; om-nis'), *adj.* knowing all; infinitely wise.—*n.* **om-nis'ci-ence**.

om-niv-o-rous (om-niv'o-rus), *adj.* **1,** eating both animal and vegetable food, as the bears, crows, etc.; **2,** figuratively, taking in everything with the mind; as, an *omnivorous* reader.

on (on), *prep.* **1,** upon; supported by; as, to sit *on* a chair; **2,** in contact with the upper surface of; as, we live *on* the earth; **3,** covering; as, shoes *on* one's feet; **4,** along or by; situated by the edge of; as, Paris is *on* the Seine; **5,** in the state of; as, *on* fire; *on* sale; also, with a view to; as, to go *on* business; to go *on* a trip; **6,** toward; as, have pity *on* the needy; **7,** forming part of; as, *on* the committee; **8,** following; as, they are *on* his trail; **9,** in the direction of; as, the door opens *on* a lawn; from above in the direction of; as, the sun shone *on* the porch; **10,** about; concerning; as, an address *on* peace; with reference to; as, to unite *on* a plan; **11,** at the time of; as, *on* June first; **12,** against or hanging from; as, a picture *on* the wall; **13,** upon the event of; as, she saw him *on* his arrival; **14,** by means of; as, to play *on* a violin; **15,** as witness; by the strength of; as, *on* my honour; **16,** after; in addition to; as, he made error *on* error:—*adv.* **1,** forward; as, to go *on;* without interruption; longer; as, to talk *on* and *on;* at or toward something; as, to look *on;* **2,** in such a way as to cover, support, etc.; as, put *on* your coat; **3,** into action or use; as, to turn *on* the gas; **4,** in progress; as, the fight is *on.*

once (wuns), *adv.* **1,** at one time; formerly; as, *once* upon a time; this was *once* my home; **2,** one time only; as, read it over *once;* **3,** at any time; ever; as, if *once* they lose heart, their cause will be lost:—*n.* one time:—**at once, 1,** together; as, all talk *at once;* **2,** immediately; as, do it *at once.*

on-com-ing (on′kum′ing), *adj.* advancing; approaching.

one (wun), *adj.* **1,** a; a single; single; as, *one* person at a time; no *one* man can do that; **2,** a person named; as, I sold it to *one* Jones; a certain; as, *one* day long ago; some; we'll go there one day very soon; **3,** united; as, they answered with *one* voice; to be forever *one;* **4,** the same; as, don't put all your eggs in *one* basket; they were all going in *one* direction; **5,** only; as, the *one* thing to do:—*n.* [*pl.* ones (wunz)], **1,** the first number in counting by units; also, its symbol, as **1,** I, or i; hence, any person or thing designated by the number; as, who has number *one?* **2,** a person or thing; as, never a *one;* pick me out some good *ones;* if this *one* is right, the other is wrong; what a *one* he is to get into trouble:—*pron.* **1,** a single person or thing; as, *one* of them was lost; may I take *one* now? they saw *one* another often; *one* by *one; one* is wise, another foolish; **2,** any person or thing; as, *one* must eat to live; *one* can hardly sleep because of the noise.—*n.* **one′ness.**

on-er-ous (on′ėr-us), *adj.* burdensome; weighty; as, an *onerous* duty.

one-self (wun-self′), *pron.* **1,** a reflexive form of *one;* **2,** an emphatic form of *one;* **3,** one's true self.

on-ion (un′yun), *n.* **1,** a plant of the lily family, having a strong-smelling bulb used as food; **2,** the bulb of the plant.

on-ion-skin (un′yun-skin′), *n.* a thin, tough, translucent glazed paper.

on-look-er (on′look′ėr), *n.* a spectator; a casual observer.

on-ly (ōn′li), *adj.* **1,** sole; single; as, the *only* man there; an *only* daughter; **2,** best; most suitable; as, he is the *only* man to choose:—*adv.* no more than; merely:—*conj.* except for the fact that; but.

on-o-mat-o-poe-ia (on′ō-mat′o-pē′ya), *n.* **1,** the forming of a word by imitating the sound associated with the thing or action named, as *buzz, mumble, hiss, splash, trickle, cuckoo;* imitative harmony; **2,** the use of such words in poetry, etc.—*adj.* **on′o-mat-o-poe′ic** (-pē′ik).

on-rush (on′rush′), *n.* a violent onset; assault; headlong dash forward; as, an *onrush* of air, troops, etc.

on-set (on′set′), *n.* **1,** an assault; attack; **2,** a first step or stage; beginning.

on-side (ōn′sīd′), *adj.* and *adv.* in *football* and *hockey,* a person who, according to the rules, is in the proper position for play.

on-slaught (on′slôt′), *n.* a furious attack.

on-to (on′tōō), *prep. Colloq.* on.

o-nus (ō′nus), *n.* a burden; duty; obligation; responsibility; as, the *onus* of proof is on you.

on-ward (on′wėrd), *adj.* advancing; as, the *onward* march of troops:—*adv.* forward; as, to move *onward.* Also *adv.* **on′wards.**

on-yx (on′iks; ō′niks), *n.* a kind of quartz in layers of various colours, such as brown, black, red, and white.

oo- (ō′o-), a *prefix* meaning *egg* or *ovum,* as in o-ōl′o-gy (study of eggs) and o′ō-spore (the fertilized egg of bacteria, fungi, algae, and lichens).

oo-mi-ak (ōō′mi-ak), *n.* Same as **umiak.**

ooze (ōōz), *n.* a gentle flow, as of a stream through sedges or sweat from pores:—*v.i.* [oozed, ooz-ing], **1,** to flow gently; as, the water *oozed* through a crack in the wall; **2,** to leak out gradually; as, so the news *oozed* out:—*v.t.* to give off slowly; as, the sponge *oozed* moisture.—*adj.* **ooz′y.**

o-pal (ō′pal), *n.* a stone having constantly changing and delicate colours —*adj.* **o′pal-es′cent** (ō′pal-es′ent).—*n.* **o′pal-es′cence.**

o-paque (ō-pāk′), *adj.* **1,** not allowing light to pass through; as, *opaque* window-shades; **2,** having no lustre; dull; not shining; as, an *opaque* surface —*n.* **o-paci-ty** (pas′).

o-pen (ō′pen), *adj.* **1,** not shut; unclosed; as, an *open* door; **2,** unsealed or unstopped, as a letter or a bottle; **3,** uncovered or exposed; not enclosed; as, an *open* boat; **4,** not obstructed; as, a river *open* to navigation; **5,** clear of trees; as, *open* country; away from shore or land; as, the *open* sea; **6,** unfilled; unoccupied; as, the position is still *open*; **7,** undecided; as, an *open* question; **8,** mild; free from ice and snow; as, an *open* winter; **9,** unfolded or spread out; as, an *open* newspaper; **10,** not hidden; in plain view; as, *open* lawlessness; unreserved; as, an *open* criticism; **11,** public; free to all; as, an *open* meeting; **12,** ready to hear or to receive suggestion; as, an *open* mind; **13,** generous; as, to give with an *open* hand; **14,** frank; sincere; as, an *open* countenance:—*v.t.* **1,** to unclose or unlock, as a window or door; **2,** to spread out, as a fan; **3,** to break the seal of or untie, as an envelope or package; **4,** to remove obstructions from; as, to *open* a road; **5,** to begin; as, to *open* the discussion; **6,** to start, as a business; as, to *open* a store; **7,** to unburden; as, to *open* one's mind to a friend; **8,** to offer for settlement, use, etc.; as, to *open* undeveloped land:—*v.i.* **1,** to unclose itself; as, the door *opened*; **2,** to commence; as, the service *opened* with a hymn; **3,** to lead; as, the door *opens* into the hall; **4,** to unfold; as, the bud slowly *opened* in the sun; **5,** to become more clearly visible; as, the view *opened* before our eyes:—*n.* any wide, clear space; outdoors; as, we lived in the *open* all summer.

o-pen-ing (ōp′ning; ō′pen-ing), *n.* **1,** the act of making, or the fact of becoming, open; **2,** a hole; gap; passage; as, an *opening* in a fence; **3,** a space in a woods with few trees and little undergrowth; **4,** the first steps; a beginning; as, the *opening* of a trial; **5,** an opportunity or a chance; also, a vacant position; as, John applied for the *opening* in the bank:—*adj.* first in order; as, the *opening* song in assembly.

o-pen-ly (ō′pen-li), *adv.* without secrecy; as, he was *openly* envious of his chum.

o-pen-ness (ō′pen-nis), *n.* **1,** a being open; **2,** lack of secrecy; frankness; sincerity; as, *openness* of manner.

op-er-a (op′ẽr-a), *n.* a drama set to music and produced with scenery and costumes.

op-er-ate (op′ẽr-āt′), *v.i.* [operat-ed, operat-ing], **1,** to work; act; as, the engine *operates* smoothly; **2,** to produce or have a certain effect; as, many drugs *operate* harmfully on the body; **3,** to perform a surgical operation on the human body:—*v.t.* **1,** to cause to work; as, to *operate* a machine; **2,** to manage; work; as, to *operate* a coal mine.

op-er-at-ic (op′ẽr-at′ik), *adj.* of, suitable for, or like, opera; as, *operatic* music.

op-er-a-tion (op′ẽr-ā′shun), *n.* **1,** the act, method, result, etc., of operating; **2,** regular action; as, the machine is in *operation*; **3,** action; a working; as, by *operation* of the law of gravitation, objects fall to earth; **4,** a surgical treatment upon the living body to remove diseased parts, correct deformity, etc.; **5,** a series of movements of an army or fleet; as, naval *operations*.

op-er-a-tive (op′ẽr-a-tiv; op′ẽr-ā′tiv), *adj.* **1,** having the power of acting; **2,** having effect; also, in operation; as, an *operative* law; **3,** concerned with work, either with the hands or with machinery; as, an *operative* art; **4,** having to do with surgical operations; as, *operative* surgery:—*n.* (usually op′-ẽr-a-tiv), an artisan or workman; as, *operatives* in a factory.

op-er-a-tor (op′ẽr-ā′tẽr), *n.* **1,** one who or that which works or acts; **2,** one who is employed in a telephone exchange to make connections between lines; **3,** one who runs a machine, as in a factory.

op-er-et-ta (op′ẽr-et′a), *n.* a short, humorous, musical play.

o-pi-ate (ō′pi-it; ō′pi-āt′), *n.* **1,** a medicine containing, or made from, opium, that causes sleep; **2,** anything that soothes:—*adj.* soothing; quieting; as, an *opiate* drink.

o-pin-ion (ō-pin′yun), *n.* **1,** belief; what one thinks about any subject; as, that is my *opinion*; **2,** estimation; as, I have a good *opinion* of him; **3,** the formal statement of an expert; as, a doctor's *opinion.*—*adj.* **o-pin′ion-at′ed.**

o-pi-um (ō′pi-um), *n.* a powerful drug, which is used to cause sleep and dull pain. It is obtained from the juices of a certain kind of poppy.

o-pos-sum (o-pos′um), *n.* a small American animal with dark-greyish fur, which lives in trees and, if captured or in danger, pretends to be dead.

op-po-nent (o-pō′nent), *n.* one who works against, or takes the opposite side from, another, in a debate, race,

all (ôl), ôr; up, mūte, cûr, cōōl, book; oil, out; th, thin; *th*, the.

game, etc.; a rival:—*adj.* acting against each other; as, *opponent* forces in a tug of war.

op-por-tune (op′ẽr-tūn′; op′ẽr-tūn′), *adj.* well-timed; convenient; suitable; as, this is an *opportune* time to start the campaign.—*adv.* **op′por-tune-ly.**—*n.* **op′por-tun′ist.**

op-por-tu-ni-ty (op′ẽr-tū′ni-ti), *n.* [*pl.* opportunities], convenient time or occasion; a good chance; as, I have not had the *opportunity* to ask him.

op-pose (o-pōz′), *v.t.* [opposed, opposing], **1,** to stand in the way of; resist; to object to; as, to *oppose* a candidate's election; **2,** to set up in opposition or in contrast.

op-po-site (op′o-zit), *adj.* **1,** placed or standing in front of; facing; as, the *opposite* side of the street; the houses were *opposite* to each other; **2,** contrary; as, in the *opposite* way; **3,** antagonistic; much different; as, *opposite* opinions:—*n.* one who or that which is contrary or in marked contrast; as, "slow" is the *opposite* of "fast."— *adv.* **op′po-site-ly.**

op-po-si-tion (op′o-zish′un), *n.* **1,** the act of placing one thing opposite or over against another; also, the state of being so placed; **2,** resistance; as, *opposition* to authority; **3,** one who or that which is opposite or contrary to another; esp. a political party not in power.

op-press (o-pres′), *v.t.* **1,** to crush by hardships or severity; treat with cruelty; as, the cruel ruler *oppressed* his subjects; **2,** to weigh heavily upon; burden; as, sorrow *oppressed* him.—*n.* **op-pres′sor.**—*n.* **op-press′ion.**

op-pres-sive (o-pres′iv), *adj.* **1,** unreasonably burdensome; as, *oppressive* laws; **2,** unjustly severe; tyrannical; as, an *oppressive* ruler; **3,** overpowering; as, the *oppressive* air of a closed room.

op-pro-bri-ous (o-prō′bri-us), *adj.* **1,** expressing disrespect, contempt, or abuse; as, *opprobrious* language; **2,** notoriously vile; disgraceful; as, *opprobrious* conduct.—*adv.* **op-pro′bri-ous-ly.**—*n.* **op-pro′bri-um.**

op-pugn (o-pūn′), *v.t.* **1,** to be contrary to; **2,** to call in question:—*v.i.* to dispute; argue; contend.

op-tic (op′tik), *adj.* pertaining to the eye or to vision.

op-ti-cal (op′ti-kal), *adj.* **1,** pertaining to the science of light and vision; **2,** pertaining to the eyesight; **3,** constructed to aid the vision; as, *optical* instruments.

op-ti-cian (op-tish′an), *n.* one who makes or sells eye-glasses, lenses, etc.

op-tics (op′tiks), *n.pl.* used as *sing.* the science of light and its properties; the laws of vision and of making lenses as for microscopes, telescopes, etc.

op-ti-mism (op′ti-mizm), *n.* **1,** the belief that everything in life happens for the best; **2,** the inclination to look on the best side of things: opposite of *pessimism.*—*n.* **op′ti-mist.**—*adj.* **op′ti-mis′tic.**

op-ti-mum (op′ti-mum), *adj.* and *n.* best; most favourable; as, *optimum* conditions for growth.

op-tion (op′shun), *n.* **1,** the right or power of choosing; as, you have the *option* of taking it or leaving it; **2,** the act of choosing; choice; **3,** that which can be or is chosen; **4,** a right, usually purchased, to buy or sell something at a specified price within a specified time. —*adj.* **op′tion-al.**—*adv.* **op′tion-al-ly.**

op-tom-e-trist (op-tom′i-trist), *n.* one who examines and tests the eyes for the purpose of fitting glasses to correct any visual defect.—*n.* **op-tom′e-try.**

op-u-lence (op′ū-lens), *n.* great riches.

op-u-lent (op′ū-lent), *adj.* wealthy; rich.

o-pus (ō′pus), *n.* in *music,* a work or composition; as, *opus* 47 of Beethoven (the Kreutzer sonata).

or (ôr), *conj.* **1,** a connecting word introducing the second of two (or the last of several) possibilities; as, this book *or* that; go *or* stay, as you please; any city, town, *or* village: often used after *either* or *whether* to complete the sense; as, we'll go either tomorrow *or* Sunday; it is all the same whether you go *or* stay; **2,** that is; in other words; as, draw a triangle, *or* a figure with three sides and three angles; **3,** otherwise; as, hurry, *or* you will be late.

or-a-cle (or′a-kl), *n.* **1,** among the ancients, the reply of a god, through an inspired priest, to a question or petition; **2,** the place where a god was consulted; **3,** the person through whom the god spoke; **4,** a prophet or person of great wisdom.—*adj.* **o-rac′u-lar** (o-rak′ū-lẽr).

or-al (ōr′al), *adj.* **1,** spoken; not written; as, an *oral* quiz; **2,** of or pertaining to the mouth; as, the *oral* cavity; **3,** using the lips in instructing the deaf; as, *oral* teaching.—*adv.* **or′al-ly.**

or-ange (or′inj; ôr′enj), *n.* **1,** an evergreen tree with fragrant flowers and a deep golden-coloured or reddish-yellow juicy fruit; **2,** the fruit itself; **3,** the golden or reddish-yellow colour of such fruit:—*adj.* **1,** pertaining to such fruit; as, an *orange* grove; **2,** of a deep golden or reddish-yellow colour.

or-ange-ade (or'inj-ād'; ôr'enj-ād'), *n.* a drink of orange juice, sugar, and water.

o-rang—ou-tang (ō-rang'–oo-tang') or **o-rang—u-tan** (ō-rang'–ōō-tan'; ôr'ang-ōō'tan), *n.*: a large, reddish-brown manlike ape of Borneo and Sumatra.

o-ra-tion (ō-rā'shun), *n.* a formal and dignified public speech, esp. one delivered on a particular occasion; as, a funeral *oration*.

or-a-tor (or'a-tẽr), *n.* a public speaker, esp. one of skill and power.—*n.* or'a-tor-y.—*adj.* or'a-tor'i-cal.

or-a-tor-i-o (or'a-tōr'i-ō), *n.* [*pl.* oratorios], in *music,* a dramatic poem on a sacred theme, sung with orchestral accompaniment, without action, scenery, or costume.

orb (ôrb), *n.* a globe or sphere; esp. one of the heavenly bodies, as the moon.

orbed (ôrbd), *adj.* **1,** round; **2,** encircled; as, *orbed* with light; **3,** having eyes.

or-bit (ôr'bit), *n.* **1,** the bony cavity which contains the eye; **2,** the course followed by one heavenly body around another, as the path of the earth around the sun.—*adj.* or'bit-al.

or-chard (ôr'chẽrd), *n.* a place where fruit-trees are grown; also, the trees themselves.

or-ches-tra (ôr'kes-tra), *n.* **1,** a band of performers on musical instruments, esp. stringed instruments; **2,** the collection of instruments on which they play; **3,** in a theatre or opera-house, the place occupied by the musicians; also, the front part or all of the main floor of a theatre.—*adj.* or-ches'tral.

or-ches-trate (ôr'kes-trāt'), *v.t.* and *v.i.* [-trated, -trating], to compose or arrange (music) for an orchestra.—*n.* or'ches-tra'tion.

or-chid (ôr'kid), *n.* **1,** any one of a large family of plants bearing blossoms with two petals similar, and a third (the lip) usually enlarged and often queerly shaped; **2,** the blossom of any of these plants.

or-dain (ôr-dān'), *v.t.* **1,** to set apart for, or admit to, the Christian ministry or the priesthood by a special ceremony or rite; **2,** to give orders for; decree; regulate by law.—*n.* or'di-na'tion.

or-deal (ôr'di-al; ôr'dēl), *n.* **1,** an ancient method of trial by fire, combat, etc., to determine the guilt or innocence of an accused person, the person being judged guilty if harmed; **2,** hence, a severe trial or experience; as, the *ordeal* of taking three examinations in one day.

order (ôr'dẽr), *n.* **1,** sequence; succession; as, alphabetical *order;* also, regular arrangement; as, the house is in *order;* **2,** a fixed method of acting; established custom; as, the *order* of church worship; **3,** public observance of law; as, *order* in the streets; **4,** working condition; as, the engine was out of *order;* **5,** rule; command; as, by *order* of the governor; **6,** a direction to buy, sell, or supply goods; as, an *order* for books; also, the goods bought or sold; **7,** a written direction to pay money; as, a money *order;* **8,** a rank, degree, or class in the social scale; as, the *order* of nobility; **9,** a group of persons united in a society; as, a Masonic *order;* a monastic society; as, the Franciscan *order;* **10,** the rank or degree of a priest or clergyman; as, the *order* of deacon, priest, bishop, etc.; **11,** a badge indicative of an honour or membership in a society; as, he wore all his *orders;* **12,** in *botany* and *zoology,* a group larger than the family and smaller than the class; as, the amaryllis and the iris belong to the same *order* but to different families; **13,** in *architecture,* the form of a column and the capital just above it; as, the Doric, Ionic, and Corinthian *orders* of Greek architecture:—*v.t.* **1,** to command; as, to *order* someone to appear before court; **2,** to regulate or manage; direct; **3,** to give an order for; as, to *order* coal.

or-der-ly (ôr'dẽr-li), *adj.* **1,** tidy; as, an *orderly* room; also, having regard for order and system; as, an *orderly* person; **2,** well conducted or managed; as, an *orderly* meeting; **3,** methodical; as, done in an *orderly* manner; **4** peaceable; as, an *orderly* crowd:—*n.* [*pl.* orderlies], **1,** a soldier who attends an officer to carry out his orders; **2,** a man who acts as attendant in a hospital.—*n.* or'der-li-ness.

or-di-nal (ôr'di-nal), *n.* or **or-di-nal num-ber** (num'bẽr), one of the numbers *first, second, third,* etc., showing order or position in a series: distinguished from *cardinal number,* as *one, two, three,* etc.

or-di-nance (ôr'di-nans), *n.* an authoritative rule, law, or decree; as, a city *ordinance* against the sale of unbottled milk.

all (ôl), ôr; up, mūte, cûr, cōōl, book; oil, out; th, thin; *th,* the.

or·di·nar·i·ly (ôr′di-na-ri-li), *adv.* usually; commonly.

or·di·nar·y (ôr′di-nẻr-i), *adj.* **1,** usual; customary; as, he followed his *ordinary* routine; **2,** commonplace; not distinguished; as, an *ordinary* dress; an *ordinary* pupil.

ord·nance (ôrd′nans), *n.* **1,** the heavy guns used in warfare; **2,** military supplies.

or·di·nate (ôr′di-nit), *n.* in *plane geometry*, one of two lines used in fixing a point on a graph.

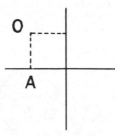

Ordinate

ore (ōr), *n.* a metal-bearing mineral or rock, esp. one containing sufficient metal to be commercially valuable.

or·gan (ôr′gan), *n.* **1,** a part of a plant or animal fitted for a special use; as, the ear is the *organ* of hearing; **2,** a medium of public communication, as a newspaper; **3,** an agency by which something is done; as, the court is an *organ* of justice; **4,** a large, musical wind-instrument with one or many sets of pipes, sounded by air blown from bellows, and played by one or more keyboards.—*n.* **or′gan·ist.**

or·gan·die or **or·gan·dy** (ôr′gan-di), *n.* a fine, thin, stiff muslin, used for dresses, curtains, trimmings, etc.

or·gan·ic (ôr-gan′ik), *adj.* **1,** of, relating to, or affecting, some organ of the body; as, an *organic* disease; **2,** relating to, or derived from, something that lives or has lived; as, fossils are remains of *organic* bodies; **3,** belonging to, or inherent in, the organization or constitution of something; fundamental; as, an *organic* fault; **4,** having a systematic arrangement of parts; as, an *organic* whole.

or·gan·ism (ôr′gan-izm), *n.* **1,** a living being composed of parts performing special duties, but dependent upon each other; **2,** anything like such a body in having many parts; as, the social *organism*.

or·gan·i·za·tion (ôr′gan-i-zā′shun;

-i-zā′shun), *n.* **1,** the act of grouping and arranging related parts into one whole, or the condition of being so organized; as, the *organization* of a campaign; the *organization* of a club; **2,** a body made up of parts dependent upon one another but each functioning separately; also, the way in which the separate parts of a living being are united in a whole; as, the *organization* of the human body; **3,** a body of persons united for some end or work.

or·gan·ize (ôr′gan-īz′), *v.t.* [organized; organiz-ing], to cause to unite and work together in orderly fashion; as, to organize forces for a campaign; to arrange in good order; as, to *organize* one's facts:—*v.i.* to become organized —*n.* **or′gan·iz′er.**

or·gasm (ôr′gazm), *n.* violent excitement, esp. the crisis or climax of the sexual act.

or·gy (ôr′ji), *n.* [*pl.* orgies], **1,** among the ancient Greeks and Romans, a secret celebration in honour of the gods, esp. the god of wine, accompanied by wild singing, dancing, etc.; **2,** a drunken revel.—*adj.* **or′gi·as′ti** (ji-); as, *orgiastic* rites.

or·i·ent (ôr′i-ent), *n.* the east: opposite of *occident*, or west:—**Orient,** countries of Asia or the Far East, and the countries bordering the eastern Mediterranean, or the Near East: opposite of *Occident*:—*adj.* **1,** rising; dawning **2,** bright; clear, as pearls; **3,** *Poetic* eastern:—*v.t.* (ôr′i-ent′), **1,** to place so as to face the east; **2,** to place (a person or oneself) in right relation to unfamiliar conditions.—*adj.* and *n* **or′i·en′tal; Or′i·en′tal.**—*n.* **o′ri·en·ta′tion.**

or·i·fice (ôr′i-fis), *n.* a mouth o opening.

or·i·gin (ôr′i-jin), *n.* **1,** a source beginning; as, theories about the *origin* of man; **2,** hence, parentage ancestry.

o·rig·i·nal (o-rij′i-nal), *adj.* **1,** of o relating to the beginning; first in existence or order; primary; as, th *original* edition of a book; **2,** not copied as, an *original* painting; not translated as, he read the story in the *origina* French; **3,** new; as, an *original* idea **4,** able to create or invent somethin new; as, an *original* writer:—*n.* **1,** tha from which anything is copied; as the *original* of that picture is in th museum; **2,** the literary text, or the language of such a text, from which translation is made; **3,** an unusua person.—*adv.* **o·rig′i·nal·ly.**

o·rig·i·nal·i·ty (o-rij′i-nal′i-ti), *n.* [*pl*

originalities], **1,** the ability to create or make something new; as, the *originality* of an inventor; **2,** the quality of being new or novel; as, the *originality* of a story.

o-rig-i-nate (o-rij'i-nāt'), *v.t.* [originat-ed, originat-ing], to bring into existence; invent; create; as, to *originate* a style of dancing:—*v.i.* to begin to exist; start; as, the fire *originated* in the chemical room.—*n.* o-rig'i-na'tion.—*n.* o-rig'i-na'tor.

or-i-ole (ōr'i-ōl'), *n.* **1,** any of various black-and-yellow songbirds of the Old World, akin to the crow, which build hanging nests; **2,** any of various American songbirds which build hanging nests, as the orange-and-black Baltimore oriole and the black-and-chestnut orchard oriole; esp. the Baltimore oriole.

O-ri-on (ō-rī'un), *n.* a constellation of seven stars near the celestial equator: noted for its belt of three bright stars.

or-na-ment (ôr'na-ment), *n.* **1,** anything that adorns; decoration; as, Christmas tree *ornaments;* **2,** a thing or person that adds beauty, honour, or grace to the surroundings:—*v.t.* (ôr'na-ment), to adorn; bedeck; as, to *ornament* a hall with holly.—*adj.* or'na-men'tal.—*n.* or'na-men-ta' tion.

or-nate (ôr-nāt'), *adj.* elaborately decorated or adorned.

or-ner-y (ôr'nėr-i), *adj.* chiefly, *U.S. dialect,* ugly or mean in disposition; hard to manage.

or-ni-thol-o-gy (ôr'ni-thol'o-ji), *n.* the branch of zoology that deals with birds.—*n.* or'ni-thol'o-gist.—*adj.* or'-ni-tho-log'i-cal.

or-phan (ôr'fan), *n.* a child who has lost one or, more commonly, both parents by death:—*adj.* being without parents:—*v.t.* to deprive of a parent or parents.

or-phan-age (ôr'fan-ij), *n.* an institution or home for the care of orphans.

or-tho- (ôr'thō), a *prefix* meaning *straight,* (*up*)*right, correct,* as in **or-thog'-ra-phy** (correct spelling), or **or'tho-pae'-dic** (relating to correction of deformities, etc., in bones, esp. of children).

or-tho-don-tist (ôr'tho-don'tist), *n.* a dentist who specializes in straightening teeth.

or-tho-dox (ôr'thō-doks), *adj.* **1,** holding what is regarded as the correct or sound opinion, esp. in regard to religion; **2,** approved; accepted; also, conventional; as, *orthodox* behaviour.—*n.* or'tho-dox'y.

or-thol-o-gy (ôr-thol'-o-ji), *n.* the art of using words correctly.—*adj.* or'tho-log'i-cal.—*n.* or'tho-lo'gian.

os-cil-late (os'i-lāt'), *v.i.* **1,** to swing to and fro, as a clock's pendulum; vibrate; **2,** to waver, as in purpose or opinion; fluctuate; vacillate; **3,** to alternate or vary, as an electric current; thus, a vacuum tube *oscillates.*—*n.* os'cil-la'tion; os'cil-la'tor.

os-cu-late (os'kū-lāt'), *v.t.* and *v.i.* to kiss or touch closely together; **2,** in *biology,* to have (characteristics) in common; **3,** in *geometry,* an *osculating circle* has three or more points in common with a curve at the point of contact.—*n.* os'cu-la'tion.—*adj.* os'cu-la-to-ry.

os-mo-sis (os-mō'sis; oz-), *n.* the tendency of liquids to pass through a porous membrane or partition that separates them: living cells depend on osmosis for most of their activity.—*adj.* os-mot'ic (mot').

os-prey (os'pri), *n.* a large fish-eating hawk.

os-si-fy (os'i-fī'), *v.t.* and *v.i.* [-fied, -fying], to change, or become changed, into bone, or hard like bone.—*n.* os'si-fi-ca'tion.

os-ten-si-ble (os-ten'-si-bl), *adj.* professed; apparent; as, an *ostensible* reason.—*adv.* os-ten'si-bly.

os-ten-ta-tion (os'-ten-ta'shun), *n.* unnecessary show; ambitious or vain display.—*adj.* os'ten-ta'tious.

os-te-o- (os'ti-ō'-), *n.* a *prefix* meaning *bone,* as in **os'te-o-my'e-li'tis** (inflammation of bone marrow).

os-te-op-a-thy (os'ti-op'a-thi), *n.* a system of medicine which, while recognizing the value of ordinary medical and surgical treatment, holds that disease is chiefly due to displacements of parts of the body, esp. of the vertebrae of the spinal column, and in healing lays stress on working the displaced parts into place with the hands.—*n.* os'te-o-path'.—*adj.* os'te - o-path'ic.

ost-ler (os'lėr), *n. obsolete,* **1,** a groom or stableman; **2,** an innkeeper.

os-tra-cize (os'tra-siz'), *v.t.* [-cized, -cizing], **1,** in *ancient Greece,* to banish by popular vote (using shells or ostrakons); **2,** to exclude from social fellowship, privileges, etc.; as, his club *ostracized* him because of his wife's drunkenness.

os-trich (os'trich), *n.* a swift-running African bird which cannot fly. It is the

all (ôl), ôr; up, mūte, cûr, cōōl, book; oil, out; th, thin; *th,* the.

largest bird known, and is highly valued for its feathers.

oth-er (uth′ẽr), *adj.* **1,** not the same; different; as, I have *other* matters to attend to; **2,** additional; more; as, I have *other* sisters; **3,** opposite; as, the *other* side of the street; **4,** alternating; second; as, every *other* line:—*adv.* otherwise; as, she could not do *other* than help him:—*pron.* and *n.* **1,** the second person or thing of two; as, one or the *other* of you must do it; some boys stayed, *others* left; they fought each *other;* **2,** a different person or thing; as, do good to *others;* have you any *other?* there will be many *others* here; the few *others* I have.

oth-er-wise (uth′ẽr-wīz′), *adv.* **1,** in a different way; differently; as, you evidently think *otherwise;* **2,** in different conditions or respects; as, I know him professionally, but not *otherwise:*—*conj.* else; as, it was told me in confidence, *otherwise* I would tell you:—*adj.* different; as, the facts were *otherwise.*

ot-ter (ot′ẽr), *n.* **1,** a fish-eating animal which lives in and near the water and is valued for its fur; **2,** the fur of this animal.

ot-to-man (ot′ō-man), *n.* a cushioned footstool.—**Ottoman,** pertaining to the Turks or Turkey, as the *Ottoman* Empire (a dynasty about 1300 A.D.).

ouch (ouch), *interj.* an exclamation expressing sudden pain.

¹ought (ôt), *v.i.* [no other form], **1,** to be or feel bound, obliged, or under obligation; as, we *ought* to finish our work; we *ought* to have paid the men; **2,** to be expected; as, this top *ought* to fit the jar; you *ought* to have been able to go; **3,** to be forced by necessity; as, we *ought* to go at once if he is to get his train; **4,** to need; as, this dress *ought* to have a collar.

²ought (ôt), *n.* **1,** anything; any part; **2,** carelessly, in arithmetic, nought.

oui-ja (wē′ja), *n.* and *adj.* a small board, often heart-shaped, resting on a larger one marked with letters of the alphabet: with the fingers of two (or more) persons resting lightly on it, it is used to spell out messages, answers to questions, etc., as at spiritualistic séances.

ounce (ouns), *n.* **1,** a weight of 1/16 of a pound avoirdupois; **2,** a weight of 1/12 of a pound in either troy or apothecaries' weight; **3,** a small amount; as, "an *ounce* of prevention is worth a pound of cure."

our (our), *adj.* a possessive form of the personal pronoun *we:* **1,** belonging to

us; as, *our* house; **2,** of or relating to us; as, *our* children; in *our* midst.

ours (ourz), a possessive form of the personal pronoun *we*, used alone: **1,** as *adj.* in the predicate, belonging to us; as, whose is that car? it is *ours;* **2,** as *pron.*, a person or thing that belongs to us; as, their car is black, *ours* is blue.

our-self (our-self′), *pron.* I myself: used only in formal speech or writing; as, the king said, "*ourself* will pardon him."

our-selves (our-selvz′), *pron.* **1,** a reflexive form of *us;* as, we fooled *ourselves* instead; **2,** an emphatic form of *we.*

ou-sel (ōō′zl), *n.* Same as **ou′zel.**

oust (oust), *v.t.* to drive, push, or turn out; as, to *oust* a person from a position.—*n.* **oust′er.**

out (out), *adv.* **1,** outdoors; not within doors; as, stay *out* in the fresh air; not in; not at home; as, she is *out* today; not within the limits; as, he is *out* of town; at liberty; as, *out* on bail; **2,** abroad; away from home; forth; as, to go *out* to India; to send a chair *out* to be fixed; **3,** not in a state or condition; as, *out* of practice; my elbow is *out* of joint; not in power or office; as, the leaders are *out;* **4,** forth from concealment; as, the sun came *out;* he brought *out* an old bag; in or into full bloom; as, the flowers are *out;* into the open; as, the story came *out;* **5,** to or at a conclusion or end; as, the fire burned *out;* to figure *out* a problem; March went *out* like a lion; **6,** from one's possession or use to another's; as, he lends *out* money; the father parcelled *out* the land to his sons; **7,** in error; as, your figures are *out;* **8,** minus; as, he is *out* five dollars; **9,** so as to clear of obstruction; as, to sweep *out* a room; **10,** on strike; as, the workers are *out;* **11,** loudly; without restraint; as, to speak *out;* **12,** in baseball: **a,** not at bat, as a team; fielding; **b,** deprived of the right to continue at bat or to continue a run around the bases for a score:—**outs,** *n.pl.* those not in office or power, or, in games, the side not having its inning:—*v.i.* to become known; as, the truth will *out:*—Compounds: *n.* **out′build′ing; out′flow′** (also *v.*); **out′pour′** (also *v.*):—*v.* **out-flank′; out-foot′; out-guess′; out′-ma-noeu′vre; out-num′ber; out-play′; out-point′.**—*adj.* **out-dat′ed; out′-spread′.**

out—and—out (out′–and–out′), *adj.* complete; thorough; utter; great; as, an *out-and-out* injustice; an *out-and-out* scoundrel.

out-bid (out-bid′), *v.t.* [outbid, out-bidding], to offer to pay more for something than (another person); as, he *outbid* all other bidders at the auction.

out-board (out′bōrd′) **motor**, a portable gasoline engine with a propeller and tiller, clamped on to the stern of a boat.

out-bound (out′bound′), *adj.* outward bound; leaving a port, railway terminal, etc.; as, a ship *outbound* for Europe.

out-break (out′brāk′), *n.* **1,** a sudden bursting forth; an epidemic; as, an *outbreak* of scarlet fever; **2,** a revolt; riot.

out-burst (out′bûrst′), *n.* a breaking forth; outbreak; as, an *outburst* of anger.

out-cast (out′kast′), *n.* one who is driven from home, friends, or country; an exile:—*adj.* friendless; homeless; hence, also, forlorn; wretched.

out-class (out-klȧs′), *v.t.* to surpass or excel in quality, skill, etc.

out-come (out′kum′), *n.* the result or consequence of an act.

out-crop (out′krop′), *n.* and *v.i.* in *geology,* a vein or stratum of rock or mineral, that emerges to the surface.

out-cry (out′krī′), *n.* [*pl.* outcries], a loud cry; clamour; uproar; confused noise.

out-curve (out′cûrv′), *n.* in *baseball,* a pitched ball that curves away from a (right-handed) batter.

out-dis-tance (out-dis′tans), *v.t.* [outdistanced, outdistanc-ing], to outstrip; surpass, esp. in a race.

out-do (out-dōō′), *v.t.* [*p.t.* outdid (-did′), *p.p.* outdone (-dun′), *p.pr.* outdo-ing], to surpass; excel.

out-door (out′dōr′), *adj.* not inside the walls of a building; done, used, or played in the open air.

out-doors (out′dōrz′), *n.* the world outside of the walls of buildings:—*adv.* outside of a building; in the open air.

out-er (out′ėr), *adj.* on the outside; farther out; as, *outer* garments; *outer* fortifications.

out-er-most (out′ėr-mōst′), *adj.* farthest outside; farthest from the centre or inside; as, the *outermost* layer of birch bark.

out-field (out′fēld′), *n.* **1,** in *baseball,* the part of the field outside or beyond the diamond; **2,** the players who play in the outfield; **3,** in *cricket,* the field remote from pitch, or the ground between wickets.—*n.* **out′field′er.**

out-fit (out′fit), *n.* all the articles required for a special purpose; equipment; as, a camping *outfit*; a baseball *outfit*:—*v.t.* (out′fit′), [outfit-ted, outfit-ting], to furnish with an outfit.—*n.* **out′fit′ter.**

out-gen-er-al (out-jen′ėr-al), *v.t.* to excel in military skill; hence, to outwit.

out-go (out′gō′), *n.* [*pl.* outgoes], that which goes out or is paid out; outlay; as, the *outgo* was greater than the income.

out-go-ing (out′gō′ing), *adj.* leaving; departing; as, *outgoing* baggage; also, going out of office; as, the *outgoing* president:—*n.* **1,** departure; **2,** expense.

out-grow (out-grō′), *v.t.* [*p.t.* outgrew (-grōō′), *p.p.* outgrown (-grōn′), *p.pr.* outgrow-ing], **1,** to excel in growing; as, weeds *outgrow* crops; **2,** to grow away from; as, to *outgrow* a habit; **3,** to become too big for; as, to *outgrow* clothes.

out-growth (out′grōth′), *n.* anything that grows out of anything else; a result.

out-house (out′hous′), *n.* a building belonging to, but apart from, a main house, as a barn, stable, etc.

out-ing (out′ing), *n.* a short excursion or pleasure trip; esp., a party or a walk in the open air.

out-land-ish (out-lan′dish), *adj.* strange; unfamiliar; odd; as, *outlandish* dress.

out-last (out-last′), *v.t.* to last longer than; outlive; as, these shoes will *outlast* the others.

out-law (out′lô′), *n.* **1,** one who is deprived of the benefits and protection of the law; **2,** one who flees from the law; a lawless wanderer:—*v.t.* **1,** to deprive of legal benefits and protection; as, to *outlaw* a criminal; **2,** to remove from legal control; to put beyond the power of the law to enforce or collect; as, to *outlaw* a debt.

out-lay (out′lā′), *n.* that which is spent, either money or effort, in an undertaking; cost; expenditure; as, an *outlay* of several thousand dollars.

out-let (out′let), *n.* **1,** a means of escape; as, games are an *outlet* for a child's energy; **2,** a passage or way out; as, the *outlet* of a lake.

out-line (out′līn′), *n.* **1,** a line showing the outer limits of an object; **2,** a drawing, or manner of drawing, showing shapes or contours, without light and shade; **3,** a draft or sketch of a story, speech, etc.—*v.t.* [outlined, out-lin-ing], **1,** to draw the outline of; **2,** to state the plan of.

out-look (out'look'), *n.* **1,** a view seen from a point of vantage, as from a window; **2,** the place from which such a view is obtained; lookout; **3,** the present state or future prospect of things; as, a favourable *outlook;* **4,** point of view; attitude; as, a happy *outlook* on life.

out-ly-ing (out'lī'ing), *adj.* far from the centre or main body; remote; as, the *outlying* districts of the city.

out-mod-ed (out-mōd'id), *adj.* out of fashion; no longer accepted; as, *outmoded* theories, doctrines, etc.

out—of—date (out'—ov—dāt'),·*adj.* no longer in fashion; as, *out-of-date* styles in dress.

out—of—door (out'—ov—dōr') or **out—of—doors** (–dōrz'), *adj.* outside a building; outdoor.—*n.* and *adv.* **out'—of–doors'.**

out—of—the—way (out'—ov—*the*—wā'), *adj.* **1,** hard to reach or find; remote; hidden; as, an *out-of-the-way* village; **2,** hence, strange; unusual; as, *out-of-the-way* events.

out-pa-tient (out'pā'shent), *n.* a patient who receives treatment at a hospital, but is not an inmate.

out-post (out'pōst'), *n.* **1,** a soldier, or troops, stationed at a distance from the main army to guard from surprise attack; **2,** the place so occupied.

out-put (out'poot'), *n.* the amount put out or produced, as from a mine, mill, etc.; the yield.

out-rage (out'rāj), *n.* gross insult or wrong; a cruel or violent act:—*v.t.* [out-raged, out-rag-ing], **1,** to inflict shame or wrong upon; to injure violently or grievously; **2,** to be contrary to; as, his drunkenness *outraged* all decency. *adj.* **out-ra'geous.**

out-ride (out-rīd'), *v.t.* [*p.t.* outrode (-rōd'), *p.p.* outrid-den (-rid'n), *p.pr.* outrid-ing], to ride better or faster than; outstrip in riding; as, the scout *outrode* his pursuers.

out-rig-ger (out'rig'er), *n.* **1,** the brace holding an oarlock out from the side of a racing shell (to give better leverage); **2,** a native canoe with a timber rigged out from the side to prevent tipping.

out-right (out'rīt'; out'rīt'), *adv.* **1,** not by instalments; all at once; as, to buy *outright;* **2,** at once; immediately; as, killed *outright;* **3,** straightforwardly: —*adj.* (out'rīt'; out'rīt'), downright;

straightforward; out-and-out; as, an *outright* denial.

out-run (out-run'), *v.t.* [*p.t.* outran (-ran'), *p.p.* outrun, *p.pr.* outrun-ning], **1,** to run faster than; get ahead of by running; **2,** hence, to pass beyond; as, his ambition *outran* his ability.

out-set (out'set'), *n.* a start; the beginning, as of a business or journey.

out-shine (out-shīn'), *v.t.* [*p.t.* and *p.p.* outshone (-shon';), *p.pr.* outshining], **1,** to shine more brightly than; surpass in brightness; **2,** hence, to excel; as, John *outshines* the rest in arithmetic.

out-side (out'sīd'), *n.* **1,** the part of anything that is on the surface or that is seen; **2,** the farthest limit; as, I shall return in a week at the *outside:*—*adj.* **1,** of or on the surface; exterior external; **2,** of or from one who does not belong to a group; as, *outside* help **3,** apart from one's regular duties; as *outside* interests:—*adv.* **1,** on or to the outer side; as, painted green *outside* **2,** outdoors; as, to go *outside:*—*prep* (out'sīd'; out'sīd'), beyond the limits of; on the outer side of.

out-sid-er (out'sīd'er), *n.* one no belonging to a given group, set, etc

out-skirts (out'skûrts'), *n.pl.* edge o edges; outlying part or parts; as, sh lives on the *outskirts* of the town.

out-spo-ken (out'spō'ken), *adj.* free o bold of speech; frank; as, he was *out spoken* in his criticism.—*adv.* **out' spo'ken-ly.**

out-stand-ing (out-stan'ding), *adj.* **1** prominent, as a person; **2,** unpaid, a debts.

out-strip (out-strip'), *v.t.* [out stripped outstrip-ping], **1,** to outrun, as in a race **2,** to excel; surpass.

out-ward (out'werd), *adj.* **1,** of or o the outside; external; as, *outwar* appearance; **2,** away from the shore as, the *outward* course of a ship; **3** visible; apparent; as, *outward* show:— *adv.* **1,** from the inside; toward th outside; as, to move *outward;* to fac *outward;* **2,** away from a place; a the ship was *outward* bound.

out-ward-ly (out'werd-li), *adv.* o the surface; in appearance; as, sh remained *outwardly* calm.

out-wards (out'werdz), *adv.* towar the outside; outward.

out-weigh (out'wā'), *v.t.* to excee in value, importance, etc.; as, th plan's merits *outweighed* its defect

out-wit (out-wit'), *v.t.* [outwit-ted outwit-ting], to get the better of b superior skill or cunning; as, to *outwit* an enemy.

out-work (out′wûrk′), *n.* a defence or protection built beyond the main body of a fort:—*v.t.* (out-wûrk′), to work faster or better than; outdo.

out-worn (out′wôrn′), *adj.* 1, worn out; as, *outworn* shoes; 2, out-of-date; as, an *outworn* point of view.

ou-zel (ōō′zl), *n.* the water ouzel or dipper (Alaska and western Alberta to New Mexico: also of Europe).

o-val (ō′vl), *adj.* shaped like an egg:—*n.* anything eggshaped; an ellipselike curve with one end broader than the other.

o-va-ry (ō′va-ri), *n.* [*pl.* ovaries], 1, in a female animal, the organ in which the ova, or egg cells, are formed; 2, the part of a plant in which the seeds are formed (see illustration under *flower*).

o-va-tion (o-vā′shun), *n.* enthusiastic applause; a hearty public tribute; as, the flyers received a tremendous *ovation.*

ov-en (uv′en), *n.* an enclosed chamber for baking, heating, or drying, esp. one inside a stove or range.

ov-en-bird (uv′en-bûrd′), *n.* a common American songbird which builds an ovenlike nest on the ground.

o-ver (ō′vêr), *prep.* 1, above in position, authority, dignity, excellence, etc. as, the sky is *over* our heads; a captain is *over* a lieutenant; a governor rules *over* the state; 2, across; from one side to another; as, to jump *over* a ditch; 3, on the surface of; upon; as, to wear a cape *over* the shoulders; to wander *over* the plains; 4, more than; as, he spent *over* ten dollars; 5, during; throughout; as, to stay *over* the weekend; 6, along; as, to drive *over* a new road; 7, on account of; as, to weep *over* defeat:—*adv.* 1, from beginning to end; as, to talk the matter *over;* 2, from one to another; as, to make *over* property; from one side to the other; as, to cross *over* to France; to go *over* to the enemy; 3, in addition; remaining; as, all that is left *over;* 4, so as to bring the under side up; as, to turn a coin *over;* so as to be upright no longer; as, to topple *over;* 5, from end to end; throughout; as, a landscape dotted *over* with trees; 6, again; once again; as, to do a thing *over;* 7, down from the edge, top, or brim; as, the water is running *over;* 8, at an end; as, all is *over;* 9, *Colloq.*, successfully; with the effect planned; as, the play went *over* the first night. Compounds:—*n.* **o′ver-**

a-bun′dance; o′ver-dose′; o′ver-drive′; o′ver-lay′; o′ver-lord′; o′ver-pass′; o′ver-plus′; o′ver-skirt′; o′-ver-trick′.—*adj.* o′ver-age′; o′ver-all′; o′ver-blown′; o′ver-con′fi-dent; o′ver-much′; o′ver-nice′; o′ver-ripe′; o′ver-strung′; o′ver-weight′.—*v.* o′-ver-bur′den; o′ver-dress′; o′ver-eat′; o′ver-in-dulge′; o′ver-lay′; o′ver-lie′; o′ver-pay′; o′ver-ride′; o′ver-shoot′; o′ver-step′; o′ver-stay′; o′-ver-tax′; o′ver-train′; o′ver-trump′; o′ver-val′ue.—*adv.*and*adj.* o′ver-seas′; o′ver-land′.—*n.*, *adj.*, and *adv.* o′ver-time′.

o-ver-alls (ō′vêr-ôlz′), *n.pl.* loose-fitting trousers supported by shoulder-straps, worn over, or in place of, other garments.

o-ver-awe (ō′vêr-ô′), *v.t.* [overawed, overaw-ing], to hold in check through fear, respect; hold spellbound; as, the man's manner *overawed* us.

o-ver-bal-ance (ō′vêr-bal′ans), *v.t.* [overbalanced, overbalanc-ing], 1, to be greater than, in weight or influence; 2, to upset the balance of.

o-ver-bear (ō′vêr-bâr′), *v.t.* [*p.t.* overbore (-bōr′), *p.p.* overborne (-bōrn′), *p.pr.* overbear-ing], 1, to bear down, as by greater physical weight or force; overthrow; 2, to overcome; triumph over.

o-ver-bear-ing (ō′vêr-bâr′ing), *adj.* haughty; domineering; as, his attitude is so *overbearing* that even his friends rebel.

o-ver-board (ō′vêr-bōrd′), *adv.* over the side of a ship or boat, into the water.

o-ver-cast (ō′vêr-kàst′), *v.t.* [overcast, overcast-ing], 1, to cover over; cloud; darken; as, the sky is *overcast;* 2, (ō′-vêr-kàst′), to take long, loose stitches over the edges of (a seam) to prevent ravelling.

o-ver-charge (ō′vêr-chärj′), *v.t.* [overcharged, overcharg-ing], 1, to load too heavily, as a gun; 2, to ask too high a price from:—*n.* (ō′vêr-chärj′), 1, too heavy a load, as of electricity; 2, too high a price.

o-ver-coat (ō′vêr-kōt′), *n.* a heavy, out-of-door coat worn in cold weather; esp. such a coat for a man or a boy.

o-ver-come (ō′vêr-kum′), *v.t.* [*p.t.* overcame (-kām′), *p.p.* overcome, *p.pr.* overcom-ing], 1, to become master of; as, to *overcome* fear; 2, to overpower; as, terror *overcame* him.

o-ver-do (ō′vêr-dōō′), *v.t.* [*p.t.* overdid (-did′), *p.p.* overdone (-dun′), *p.pr.*

overdo-ing], **1,** to carry too far; exaggerate; **2,** to weary by overwork; **3,** to cook too long:—*v.i.* to work too hard; do too much.

o-ver-draft (ō′vẽr-draft′), *n.* a cheque or draft drawn in excess of one's bank account or credit balance.

o-ver-draw (ō′vẽr-drô′), *v.t.* [*p.t.* overdrew (-drōō′), *p.p.* overdrawn (-drôn′), *p.pr.* overdraw-ing], **1,** to exaggerate; as, John's story of the robbery was greatly *overdrawn;* **2,** to draw against (a bank account) by writing a cheque for a sum greater than the amount on deposit.

o-ver-due (ō′vẽr-dū′), *adj.* **1,** unpaid at the time for payment; as, an *overdue* account; **2,** not on hand at the scheduled time; as, the train is *overdue.*

o-ver-es-ti-mate (ō′vẽr-es′ti-māt′), *v.t.* [overestimat-ed, overestimat-ing], to set too high a value on; as, he *overestimates* his own ability:—*n.* (ō′vẽr-es′ti-mit), too high a valuation, or estimate.

o-ver-flow (ō′vẽr-flō′), *n.* **1,** the spreading of water or other liquid beyond its proper limits; **2,** the excess water or liquid; also, an outlet for excess liquid; **3,** excess; superabundance; as, an *overflow* of enthusiasm:—*v.t.* and *v.i.* (ō′vẽr-flō′), to flood; overrun; spread all over.

o-ver-grow (ō′vẽr-grō′), *v.t.* [*p.t.* overgrew (-grōō′), *p.p.* overgrown (-grōn′), *p.pr.* overgrow-ing], **1,** to cover; grow over; as, the path is *overgrown* with weeds; **2,** to outgrow:—*v.i.* to grow too large or too fast.

o-ver-hand (ō′vẽr-hand′), *adj.* **1,** down from above; as, an *overhand* blow; **2,** grasping with the hand over the object, and with the palm downward; as, an *overhand* grip; **3,** in baseball, cricket, etc., thrown or bowled with the arm swung above the shoulder:—*n.* the simplest kind of knot:—*adv.* (ō′vẽr-hand′), with the palm of the hand down; as, to haul in a fishline *overhand.*

o-ver-hang (ō′vẽr-hang′), *v.t.* [overhung (-hung′), overhang-ing], to jut over; project above:—*v.i.* to project over and beyond something; as, the ledge *overhangs* several feet:—*n.* (ō′vẽr-hang′), a part as of a building or mountain, that projects.

o-ver-haul (ō′vẽr-hôl′), *v.t.* **1,** to examine thoroughly in order to make repairs; **2,** to overtake; catch up with.

o-ver-head (ō′vẽr-hed′), *adv.* above one's head; as, stars shine *overhead:*—*adj.* (ō′vẽr-hed′), **1,** situated or operating above one's head; as, *overhead*

ventilation; **2,** referring to the cost or expenses of a business which are directly chargeable not to any particular department, but to the running of the business as a whole:—*n.* (ō′vẽr-hed′), overhead expenses; as, rent, light, and heat are items in our *overhead.*

o-ver-hear (ō′vẽr-hēr′), *v.t.* [overheard (-hûrd′), overhear-ing], to hear (a remark, conversation) which one is not intended to hear.

o-ver-joyed (ō′vẽr-joid′), *adj.* made very glad; as, he was *overjoyed* at the news.

o-ver-lap (ō′vẽr-lap′), *v.t.* [overlapped, overlap-ping], **1,** to lie so as partly to cover; as, each shingle *overlaps* the one below; also, to lay so as to cover the edge of something; **2,** to coincide partly with; as, the treasurer's duties *overlap* those of the secretary:—*v.i.* **1,** to lie so that part of one thing covers part of another; **2,** to coincide in part:—*n.* (ō′vẽr-lap′), **1,** the extension, or amount of extension, of one thing over the edge of another; **2,** that which partly covers, or laps over, something.

o-ver-lay (ō′vẽr-lā′), *v.t.* [overlaid (-lād′), overlay-ing], to spread or cover (a surface) with something:—*n.* (ō′vẽr-lā′), that which is laid on as a covering.

o-ver-load (ō′vẽr-lōd′), *v.t.* to load, or burden, too heavily.—*n.* **o′ver-load′.**

o-ver-look (ō′vẽr-look′), *v.t.* **1,** to look down on from above; **2,** to keep an eye on; superintend; **3,** to fail to see; miss; as, I *overlooked* part of the problem; **4,** to disregard deliberately; pass over without noticing; ignore.

o-ver-night (ō′vẽr-nīt′), *adv.* in or during the night; as, it happened *overnight:*—*adj.* (ō′vẽr-nīt′), **1,** lasting through a night; as, an *overnight* trip by train; **2,** for a night, or short visit; as, an *overnight* bag; *overnight* guests.

o-ver-power (ō′vẽr-pou′ẽr), *v.t.* **1,** to crush by superior force; **2,** to affect greatly; as, he was *overpowered* by grief and sorrow.—*adj.* **o′ver-pow′er-ing.**

o-ver-rate (ō′vẽr-rāt′), *v.t.* [overrat-ed, overrat-ing], to set too high a value upon; as, to *overrate* one's ability.

over-reach (ō′vẽr-rēch′), *v.t.* **1,** to defeat (oneself) by reaching too far or attempting too much; **2,** to get the better of (another) by trickery.

o-ver-rule (ō′vẽr-rōōl′), *v.t.* [overruled, overrul-ing], **1,** to set aside; nullify; as, the judge *overruled* a previous decision; **2,** to decide against; disallow; as, the chairman *overruled* my objections.

o-ver-run (ō′vẽr-run′), *v.t.* [*p.t.* overran (-ran′), *p.p.* overrun, *p.pr.* overrunning], **1,** to grow or spread over in great quantity or numbers; as, weeds had *overrun* the garden; the enemy *overran* the country; **2,** to run beyond; as, to *overrun* first base.

o-ver-see (ō′vẽr-sē′), *v.t.* [*p.t.* oversaw (-sô′), *p.p.* overseen (-sēn′), *p.pr.* oversee-ing], to keep watch over; superintend.—*n.* **o′ver-se′er.**

o-ver-shad-ow (ō′vẽr-shad′ō), *v.t.* **1,** to darken, or obscure, with, or as with, a shadow; **2,** to cause (something) to lose importance or significance; as, his early success was *overshadowed* by his later failures.

o-ver-shoe (ō′vẽr-sho͞o′), *n.* a waterproof shoe, generally of rubber, worn over another shoe, for protection against wet.

o-ver-sight (ō′vẽr-sīt′), *n.* **1,** failure to see or think of something; a slip or mistake resulting from such failure; **2,** supervision; as, he has general *oversight* of the boys at recess time.

o-ver-spread (ō′vẽr-spred′), *v.t.* [overspread, overspread-ing], to cover the surface of; spread over; as, a mossy carpet *overspread* the ground.

o-ver-state (ō′vẽr-stāt′), *v.t.* [overstated, overstat-ing], to state or express too strongly; exaggerate.—*n.* **o′ver-state′-ment.**

o-ver-step (ō′vẽr-step′), *v.t.* [overstepped, overstep-ping], to go beyond; exceed; as, he *overstepped* his authority.

o-vert (ō′vẽrt), *adj.* publicly or openly performed; not secret or hidden; as, the bombing of the city was an *overt* act of war.—*adv.* **o′vert-ly.**

o-ver-take (ō′vẽr-tāk′), *v.t.* [*p.t.* overtook (-took′), *p.p.* overtak-en (-tāk′en), *p.pr.* overtak-ing], **1,** to catch or come up with; **2,** to come upon suddenly; take by surprise; as, the storm *overtook* us.

o-ver-tax (ō′vẽr-taks′), *v.t.* **1,** to tax too heavily; **2,** to lay too great a burden upon; as, to *overtax* one's strength.

o-ver-throw (ō′vẽr-thrō′), *v.t.* [*p.t.* overthrew (-thro͞o′), *p.p.* overthrown (-thrōn′), *p.pr.* overthrow-ing], **1,** to cause to fall or to fail; as, to *overthrow* a government; **2,** to overturn; upset; as, to *overthrow* a chair:—*n.* (ō′vẽr-thrō′), ruin; defeat, as of an army.

o-ver-tone (ō′vẽr-tōn′), *n.* in *music*, **1,** a harmonic or partial tone; **2,** a higher or secondary tone attending the

production of a basic one:—*v.t.* (ō′vẽr-tōn′), in *photography*, to give too much tone (to).

o-ver-ture (ō′vẽr-tūr), *n.* **1,** a preliminary offer or proposal; as, an *overture* of peace; **2,** music composed and played as the prelude to an opera, oratorio, etc.

o-ver-turn (ō′vẽr-tûrn′), *v.t.* **1,** to cause to upset or turn over; as, to *overturn* a footstool; **2,** to overthrow; bring to ruin:—*v.i.* to upset:—*n.* (ō′vẽr-tûrn′), an upsetting; as, the *overturn* of a political party.

o-ver-ween-ing (ō′vẽr-wēn′ing), *adj.* conceited; arrogant; also, excessive; exaggerated; as, *overweening* pride.

o-ver-whelm (ō′vẽr-hwelm′), *v.t.* **1,** to submerge; flood; as, he was *overwhelmed* with applause; **2,** to crush utterly; as, to *overwhelm* a person by harsh criticism.—*adj.* **o′ver-whelm′ing.**

o-ver-work (ō′vẽr-wûrk′), *v.t.* to place too much work upon:—*v.i.* to work beyond one's strength—*n.* (ō′vẽr-wûrk′) work beyond one's capacity; too much work.

o-ver-wrought (ō′vẽr-rôt′), *adj.* **1,** excited; unstrung; **2,** too elaborately adorned.

o-vi- (ō′vi-), a *prefix* meaning *egg* or *ovum*, as in **o′vi-duct′** (a tube by which eggs pass from the ovary to the uterus or egg sac), **o-vip′a-rous** (producing eggs that are expelled from the body, as of birds, some reptiles, and fishes), **o-vif′er-ous** (bearing eggs), **o′vi-form′** (egg-shaped), and **o′vi-pos′i-tor** (a special egg-laying organ, as in crickets and grasshoppers).

o-vule (ō′vūl), *n.* **1,** in *plants*, an undeveloped seed; **2,** in *female animals*, a little or undeveloped egg, or germ cell.

o-vum (ō′vum), *n.* [*pl.* ova (ō′va)], the female germ cell or seed.

owe (ō), *v.t.* [owed, ow-ing], **1,** to be under obligation to pay; as, to *owe* ten dollars; **2,** to be indebted for; as, I *owe* my success to you:—*v.i.* to be in debt.

ow-ing (ō′ing), *adj.* due as a debt:— **owing to,** because of.

owl (oul), *n.* any one of a group of night-flying birds of prey, which have large heads and eyes, short hooked bills and sharp claws, and a peculiar call or hoot. —*adj.* **owl′ish.**

owl-et (oul′et), *n.* a young owl; also a small owl.

own (ōn), *adj.* **1,** belonging to the individual person or thing; as, your *own* house; the sun's *own* light; **2,** of the same parents; as, my *own* sister:—*v.t.* **1,** to be the possessor of; as, this book is mine; I *own* it; **2,** to acknowledge; as, to *own* a fault; **3,** to grant; as, I *own* the truth of your argument.

own-er (ōn′ẽr), *n.* one who owns or possesses; a proprietor.—*n.* **own′er-ship.**

ox (oks), *n.* [*pl.* ox'n (ok′s'n)], **1,** a steer, or castrated male of the family of domestic cattle, that has been trained to do hauling and farm work; **2,** any of several animals related to domestic cattle, as the wild ox and the musk-ox.

ox-al-ic ac-id (ok-sal′ik), a violently poisonous, colourless, transparent, crystalline acid used in dyeing, bleaching iron stains, and making ink.

ox-a-lis (ok′sa-lis), *n.* any of a group of plants with small white or pink flowers, and leaves divided into three parts.

ox-blood (oks′blud′), *n.* a deep red colour.

ox-bow (oks′bō′), *n.* **1,** a U-shaped or S-shaped bend in a river; **2,** the land enclosed by it.

ox-eye dais-y (oks′ī′), the common white daisy.

Ox-ford or **ox-ford** (oks′fẽrd), *n.* a low shoe, laced or tied over the instep.

ox-ide (ok′sīd; ok′sid), *n.* a compound of oxygen with another element.

ox-i-dize (ok′si-dīz′), *v.t.* and *v.i.*

[oxidized, oxidiz-ing], to combine with oxygen.—*n.* **ox′i-diz′er.**—*n.* **ox′i-da′-tion.**

ox-tail (oks′tāl′), *n.* and *adj.* the ox's tail, used in *oxtail* soup.

[1]ox-y- (ok′si-), a *prefix* meaning *containing oxygen,* as in **ox′y-a-cet′y-lene′** or **ox′y-cal′ci-um.**

[2]ox-y- (ok′si-), a *prefix* meaning *sharp, acute, pointed,* or *acid,* as in *oxygen* or *oxy*moron.

ox-y-gen (ok′si-jen), *n.* a gas without odour, colour, or taste, forming about 1/5 of the total volume of the atmosphere: essential to life: part of many substances, such as water, acids, etc.

ox-y-gen-ate (ok′si-jen-āt′), *v.t.* to mix or enrich with oxygen. Also, **ox′y-gen-ize′.**—*n.* **ox′y-gen-a′tion.**

ox-y-mo-ron (ok′si-mō′ron), *n. Greek,* sharp-dull, a figure of speech combining opposite' or contradictory ideas, as *cruel kindness, bitter sweet, make haste slowly, falsely true:* used to give point to an epigram, etc.

oys-ter (ois′tẽr), *n.* a shellfish, valued as food, having a rough, hinged shell, and living in shallow water of sea coasts.

o-zone (ō′zōn; ō-zōn′), *n.* a bluish gas, O_3, with odour of weak chlorine, formed by the discharge of electricity through air or by other means: it is present after a thunderstorm: a powerful oxidizing agent, used in bleaching, sterilizing water, etc.

P

P, p (pē), *n.* [*pl.* P's, p's], the 16th letter of the alphabet, following O.

pace (pās), *n.* **1,** a step; the space covered by a step in walking; **2,** gait, or manner of moving; **3,** a certain gait of a horse; **4,** rate of speed; as, to keep the *pace:*—*v.t.* [paced, pac-ing], **1,** to measure by steps; as, to *pace* off 50 yards; **2,** to walk over with even steps; as, the guard *paces* his round; **3,** in racing, to set the *pace* for:—*v.i.* **1,** to walk with long, even steps; **2,** to go at a *pace,* as a horse.—*n.* **pac′er.**

pach-y-derm (pak′i-dûrm′), *n.* **1,** any thick-skinned, hoofed quadruped, as the elephant or rhinoceros; **2,** *humorously,* a person lacking sensitivity.

pa-cif-ic (pa-sif′ik), *adj.* **1,** peacemaking; as, *pacific* words; **2,** peaceful;

tranquil; as, *pacific* waters.—*adv.* **pa-cif′i-cal-ly.**—**Pacific Ocean,** the largest ocean (about 65 million square miles), lying between Australia-Asia and the Americas.

pac-i-fi-er (pas′i-fī′ẽr), *n.* a rubber nipple, teething ring, etc., for babies to bite or suck.

pac-i-fist (pas′i-fist), *n.* one who opposes war as wrong, and who believes in, and works for, peace among nations.—*n.* **pac′i-fism.**

pac-i-fy (pas′i-fī′), *v.t.* [pacified, pacify-ing], to calm; soothe; appease; as, to *pacify* an angry man.—*n.* **pac′i-fi-ca′tion.**

pack (pak), *n.* **1,** a bundle tied up for carrying, esp. on the back of a man or animal; **2,** a full set of things; as, a *pack* of cards; **3,** a number of animals

cat, āge, fär, câre, ásk; ten, ēve, latẽr; (i) pity, rely, senate; īce; top; nō.

of the same kind living or hunting together; as, a *pack* of hounds; **4**, a large area of floating cakes of ice driven close together:—*v.t.* **1**, to stow away, arrange compactly, or press into a bundle; as, to *pack* clothes for a trip; **2**, to fill (a receptacle or space) entirely; as, to *pack* a trunk with clothes; **3**, to crowd together; as, to *pack* people into a room; **4**, to press into a hard mass; as, to *pack* earth; **5**, to fill in (a joint or crack) to prevent leaking; **6**, to send away; as, to *pack* him off in a hurry; **7**, to arrange unfairly to suit one's own ends; as, to *pack* a jury:—*v.i.* **1**, to press or crowd together into a hard mass; as, ice *packs* together; **2**, to stow things for safety or for carrying; **3**, to admit of being stowed; as, these articles *pack* well; **4**, to depart or move in haste; as, she sent him *packing.*—*n.* pack′er. —*n.* pack′—horse′; pack′sack′; pack′-sad′dle.

pack-age (pak′ij), *n.* a bundle or bale of goods; a parcel; packet.

pack-et (pak′it), *n.* **1**, a small bundle or parcel; package; **2**, a vessel sailing between two or more ports at regular periods, carrying passengers, mail, and merchandise.

pack-ing (pak′ing), *n.* **1**, the act of packing; **2**, material, as straw or paper, used to protect goods packed for carrying.

pact (pakt), *n.* an agreement or contract.

pad (pad), *v.i.* [pad-ded, pad-ding], to walk slowly and wearily; also, to walk noiselessly, as a cat does.

pad (pad), *n.* **1**, a soft cushion used to fill a hollow space, lessen pressure or friction, protect from blows, etc.; **2**, the cushionlike part of the foot of some animals, as the dog and cat; **3**, a writing- or drawing-tablet; **4**, the floating leaf of certain water plants, as the water-lily; **5**, a cushioned, inked block used for inking a rubber stamp: —*v.t.* [pad-ded, pad-ding], **1**, to stuff with pads; line, as a coat; **2**, to expand with unnecessary material; as, to *pad* a newspaper story.

pad-ding (pad′ing), *n.* **1**, material used to pad; stuffing; **2**, material of no value used to fill up space.

pad-dle (pad′l), *n.* **1**, a short oar with a broad blade at one or both ends, used to propel a canoe; **2**, a short, broad-bladed instrument used for stirring, mixing, etc.; **3**, one of the wide boards of a water-wheel or a paddle-wheel:— *v.i.* and *v.t.* [pad-dled, pad-dling], to propel (a canoe) with a paddle.

²**pad-dle** (pad′l), *v.i.* [pad-dled, pad-dling], to wade; to dabble with the hands in water.

pad-dock (pad′uk), *n.* an enclosure near a stable or racetrack where horses are exercised.

pad-dy (pad′i), *n.* growing rice; rice in the husk; a rice field (loosely).

pad-lock (pad′lok′), *n.* a removable lock, which hangs by a curved bar, hinged at one end and snapped shut at the other:—*v.t.* to fasten with such a lock.

pad-re (pàd′ri), *n,* **1**, *Military,* a chaplain; **2**, a priest or monk, esp. in Europe and Latin America.

pae-an (pē′an), *n.* a loud and joyous song of praise or triumph; as, a *paean* of victory.

pa-gan (pā′gan), *n.* **1**, a heathen; one who is not Christian, Jewish, or Mohammedan; **2**, a person having no religious beliefs:—*adj.* heathen.—*n.* pa′gan-ism.

¹**page** (pāj), *n.* **1**, in the days of chivalry, a boy, usually of high birth, attending on a person of distinction as the first stage in the process of his training toward knighthood; **2**, an errand boy in a law-making body; also, a uniformed serving boy, as in a hotel: —*v.t.* [paged, pag-ing], **1**, to attend as a page; **2**, to call for or summon (a person), as by page in a hotel.

²**page** (pāj), *n.* one side of a leaf, as of a book; also, what is written or printed on it:—*v.t.* [paged, pag-ing], to arrange or number in pages.

pag-eant (paj′ant; pā′jant), *n.* a brilliant, stately display or procession in celebration of an event or in honour of a person.—*n.* pag′eant-ry.

pa-go-da (pa-gō′da), *n.* in the Far East a sacred tower or temple of many stories, usually built in the form of a pyramid, and richly painted and ornamented.

PAGODA

paid (pād), *p.t.* and *p.p.* of pay.

pail (pāl), *n.* an open vessel of wood or metal with a handle, for carrying liquids; a bucket; also, the amount a pail will hold.—*n.* pail′ful.

pain (pān), *n.* **1**, originally, penalty: now rare, except in such phrases as *on* *pain of death;* **2,** suffering of body; an ache; as, a *pain* in the stomach; **3,** distress of mind; sorrow; **4, pains,** diligent effort; as, he took great *pains* with his work:—*v.t.* **1,** to cause bodily suffering to; **2,** to make uneasy; grieve; as, Mary's impoliteness *pained* her mother.

pain-ful (pān′fool), *adj.* **1,** full of pain; causing pain; **2,** difficult, as a task.

pains-tak-ing (pānz′tāk′ing), *adj.* taking great pains; careful; as, a *painstaking* worker.—*adv.* **pains′tak′-ing-ly.**

paint (pānt), *v.t.* **1,** to picture in colours; as, to *paint* a portrait; **2,** to describe vividly; as, to *paint* a scene in words; **3,** to coat or cover with colour; as, to *paint* a house; **4,** to coat, as with paint; as, the doctor *painted* my throat with iodine:—*v.i.* to practise the art of making pictures with colour:—*n.* **1,** a colouring substance composed of pigment mixed with oil or water; **2,** cosmetic rouge.—*n.* **paint′er.**

paint-ing (pān′ting), *n.* **1,** the act, art, or work of a painter; **2,** a picture in colours.

pair (pâr), *n.* **1,** two things of a kind, similar in form, intended to be used together, or corresponding to each other in some way; as, a *pair* of oars; a *pair* of shoes; **2,** a single thing composed of two like parts; as, a *pair* of scissors; **3,** two members of different parties in a legislative body who agree that neither will vote on a given motion:—*v.t.* to join in couples; mate:—*v.i.* **1,** to come together in couples; as, to *pair* off in a dance; **2,** to match; form a pair.

pa-ja-mas (pa-jàm′az), *n.* Same as **py-ja′mas.**

pal (pal), *n. Colloq.* an intimate friend; chum; comrade.

pal-ace (pal′as; pal′is), *n.* **1,** the official residence of a king or other ruler; **2,** a magnificent house.

pal-a-din (pal′a-din), *n.* a knightly or heroic champion.

pal-ate (pal′at; pal′it), *n.* **1,** the roof of the mouth, consisting of the *hard palate,* or the bony front part of the roof of the mouth, and the *soft palate,* or the fleshy back part of the roof of the mouth; **2,** the sense of taste; as, a delicate *palate.*—*adj.* **pal′a-tal.**

pa-la-tial (pa-lā′shal), *adj.* pertaining to, or resembling, a palace; magnificent.

pa-la-ver (pa-lav′ėr), *n.* **1,** chatter; talk, esp. cajoling or idle talk; **2,**

in Africa, a conference with tribesmen:—*v.i.* to chatter; flatter:—*v.t.* to wheedle; talk deceitfully.

¹pale (pāl), *adj.* [pal-er, pal-est], **1,** wanting in colour; as, a face *pale* from illness; **2,** dim; not bright; as, *pale* blue:—*v.i.* [paled, pal-ing], to turn white, or lose colour:—*v.t.* to make dim or pale.—*n.* **pale′ness.**

²pale (pāl), *n.* **1,** a pointed stake or fence picket; **2,** a place enclosed by such a fence; hence, a district with clearly marked bounds; **3,** limits or bounds:—*v.t.* [paled, pal-ing], to enclose or fence with pales.

pale-face (pāl′fās′), *n.* an American Indian name for the white man.

pa-le-o- or **pa-lae-o-** (pā′li-ō; pal), *Greek prefix meaning very old* or *ancient,* as in **pa-le-on-tol-o-gy** (pā′li-on-tol′o-ji),—*n.* the branch of geology treating of fossil remains of plants and animals.

pa-le-o-lith-ic or **pa-lae-o-lith-ic** (pā′li-ō-lith′ik; pal′),—*adj.* relating to the Old Stone Age or earliest period of human development (when crude stone tools were used).

Pa-le-o-zo-ic or **pa-lae-o-zo-ic** (pā′li-ō-zō′ik; pal′), *adj.* relating to a geological era (55 to 215 million years ago) of rocks with fossils of developing fish and sea plants, the first amphibians, land plants and reptiles: coal and oil were produced then.

pal-ette or **pal-let** (pal′it), *n.* **1,** a thin wood, porcelain, or plastic plate with a hole for the thumb, used by artists for mixing and holding colours; **2,** the colours used.

pal-frey (pôl′fri), *n.* [*pl.* palfreys], a saddlehorse, esp. a small one for a lady.

pal-ing (pāl′ing), *n.* **1,** a fence made of narrow, upright boards called pales, usually pointed at the top; **2,** a pale; also, wood for making pales.

pal-i-sade (pal′i-sād′), *n.* **1,** a fence or fortification made of strong, pointed stakes, or pales, set close together and driven into the ground, **2, palisades,** a long line of cliffs, usually along a river: —*v.t.* [palisad-ed, palisad-ing], to enclose with stakes.

¹pall (pôl), *n.* **1,** a heavy, velvet covering for a coffin, hearse, or tomb; also, the coffin itself; **2,** any heavy, dark covering; as, a *pall* of smoke.

²pall (pôl), *v.i.* to become distasteful or wearisome; lose power to interest; as too much joking *palls* on him.

pall-bear-er (pôl′bâr′ėr), *n.* one of

the persons who carry or attend the coffin at a funeral.

pal-let (pal′it), *n.* a small, rough bed.

pal-li-ate (pal′i-āt′), *v.t.* [palliat-ed, palliat-ing], **1,** to excuse or cause to appear less wrong; as, to *palliate* a fault; **2,** to ease without curing; as, to *palliate* a disease.—*n.* and *adj.* **pal′li-a-tive.**—*n.* **pal′li-a′tion.**

pal-lid (pal′id), *adj.* pale; lacking in colour; as, a *pallid* face.—*n.* **pal′-lid-ness.**

pal-lor (pal′ẽr), *n.* lack of colour, as in the face; paleness.

¹palm (päm), *n.* **1,** the inner surface of the human hand, between the fingers and the wrist; **2,** a measure of length varying from three to four inches:—*v.t.* **1,** to conceal in, or about, the hand, as in a sleight-of-hand trick; **2,** hence to pass by fraud; as, to *palm* off worthless stock on investors.

²palm (päm), *n.* **1,** a tropical tree with a crown of large fanshaped leaves generally radiating from the summit of a slender trunk from which no large branches grow; **2,** a leaf of the tree, formerly used as an emblem of victory; hence victory; honor.

palm-er (päm′ẽr), *n.* a pilgrim to the Holy Land who brought back a palm branch as a token or sign of his pilgrimage.

pal-met-to (pal-met′ō), *n.* [*pl.* -tos, -toes (-ōz)], any of several palm trees with fan-shaped leaves (West Indies and Southern U.S.); the cabbage palm.

palm-is-try (päm′is-tri; palm′), *n.* the practice of reading character or foretelling the future from the lines and marks on the palm of the hand.—*n.* **palm′ist.**

palm-y (päm′i), *adj.* [palm-i-er, palm-i-est]; **1,** abounding in palm trees; **2,** flourishing; prosperous; as, *palmy* days.

pal-o-mi-no (pal-o-mē′nō), *n.* a creamy or golden-coloured saddle horse with white tail and mane, bred chiefly in southwestern U.S.

pal-pa-ble (pal′pa-bl), *adj.* **1,** capable of being touched or felt; **2,** easily seen; plain; as, a *palpable* error.—*adv.* **pal′pa-bly.**

pal-pi-tate (pal′pi-tāt′), *v.i.* to beat or throb rapidly, as the heart; to flutter. —*n.* **pal′pi-ta′tion.**

pal-sy (pôl′zi), *n.* [*pl.* palsies], paralysis; loss of sensation, or of power to move or to control motion, in any part of the body:—*v.t.* [palsied, palsy-ing], to paralyze.—*adj.* **pal′sied.**

pal-ter (pôl′tẽr), *v.i.* to use deceit or trickery; to trifle, esp. in speech.

pal-try (pôl′tri), *adj.* [pal-tri-er, pal-tri-est], worthless; contemptible; small; as, a *paltry* gift.—*n.* **pal′tri-ness.**

pam-pas (pam′paz), *n.pl.* the vast treeless plains of South America, esp. Argentina.

pam-per (pam′pẽr), *v.t.* to humor; gratify; indulge (a person) in every wish.

pam-phlet (pam′flet), *n.* a small unbound book, usually with a paper cover.

pan- (pan-), a Greek *prefix* meaning *all,* as in *pan-American* (relating to both North and South America, or to all Americans), **pan′chro-mat′ic** (sensitive to any colour, as a *panchromatic* film), and **pan′the-ism** (the doctrine that God exists, not as a person, but as manifest in all forms of matter, including man and every natural object).

pan (pan), *n.* **1,** a broad, shallow metal or earthenware dish for cooking and other household uses; **2,** any similar vessel, as either of the dishes for holding things weighed on scales, or the shallow receptacle for washing out gold from dirt or gravel; **3,** in old-fashioned guns, the hollow part of the lock that held gunpowder for firing the gun; **4,** a bed or layer of solid soil or gravel: usually called *hardpan:*—*v.t.* [panned, pan-ning], **1,** in mining, to wash (gravel or dirt) in a pan to separate out the gold; **2,** to cook in a pan; as, to *pan* oysters; **3,** *Slang,* to ridicule without mercy.

pan-a-ce-a (pan′a-sē′a), *n.* a remedy or medicine for all ills: a cure-all.

pan-cake (pan′kāk′), *n.* a thin cake made of batter fried in a pan or on a griddle.

pan-cre-as (pan′kri-as; pang′kri-as), *n.* a large, fleshy gland near the stomach, producing a fluid, called *pancreatic juice,* that helps digestion. The pancreas of animals, when cooked for food, is called *sweetbread.*—*adj.* **pan′cre-at′ic.**

pan-da (pan′da), *n.* **1,** the lesser panda of the Himalayas is a raccoonlike, rusty-coloured animal; **2,** the giant panda of Asia is bearlike, with white-and-black markings.

pan-de-mo-ni-um (pan′di-mō′ni-um) *n.* **1,** a place of lawless disorder; **2,** wild uproar; utter confusion.

pan-der (pan′dẽr), *v.i.* to cater to the

baser passions; as, lewd pictures *pander* to men's lusts.

pane (pān), *n.* a square or oblong piece of glass in a window or door.

pan-e-gyr-ic (pan'i-jir'ik), *n.* praise formally written or spoken in honor of a person or event; any high praise.

pan-el (pan'el), *n.* **1**, a division or section of a wall, ceiling, or door, raised above, or sunk below, the surrounding parts; **2**, a thin board on which a picture is painted; also, the picture itself; **3**, a list of persons summoned to serve as jurors; also, an entire jury; **4**, an ornamental strip placed lengthwise on a dress or skirt; **5**, a group of speakers organized specially for discussing, judging, etc.:—*v.t.* [paneled, panel-ing], to form, fit, or decorate with panels.—*n.* **pan'el-ist** or **pan'el-list**.—*n.* **pan'el-ing**.

pang (pang), *n.* **1**, a violent, sudden pain; as, *pangs* of hunger; **2**, a sudden, bitter emotion; as, *pangs* of remorse.

pan-han-dler (pan'han'dler), *n.* *Colloq.* beggar:—*v.i.* **pan'han'dle** (to beg, esp. on the streets).

pan-ic (pan'ik), *n.* **1**, sudden, extreme fright, often groundless, or inspired by a trifling cause; **2**, general alarm and distrust in financial circles; as, the closing of several banks caused a *panic.*—*adj.* **pan'ick-y**.

pan-i-cle (pan'i-kl), *n.* *Botany*, an irregularly branched flower cluster.

pan-nier (pan'yėr; pan'i-ėr), *n.* **1**, a bread basket; **2**, one of two wicker baskets suspended across the back of an animal for carrying market produce; also, a single basket for carrying on a person's back; **3**, a framework of whalebone, steel wire, etc., formerly used to enlarge a woman's skirts at the hips.

pan-o-ply (pan'o-pli), *n.* [*pl.* panoplies] **1**, a complete suit of armor; **2**, any complete covering; also, a splendid array.—*adj.* **pan'o-plied**.

pan-o-ra-ma (pan'o-rä'ma; pan'o-ram'a), *n.* **1**, a picture giving a view in every direction, seen from a central standpoint; **2**, a picture seen part at a time as it is unrolled or unfolded and made to pass before the spectator; **3**, a complete view of a region; **4**, a scene that moves constantly before one, as from the window of a moving train; **5**, a general view of a subject.—*adj.* **pan'-o-ram'ic**.

pan-sy (pan'zi), *n.* [*pl.* pansies], a common garden plant of the violet family, with blossoms of rich color and velvety texture; also, its flower.

pant (pant), *v.i.* **1**, to breathe rapidly; gasp; as, the walk uphill made him *pant;* **2**, to desire earnestly:—*v.t.* to utter with a gasp:—*n.* a short, rapid breath; also, the puff of an engine.

pan-ta-loon (pan'ta-lōōn'), *n.* **1**, a clown or foolish character in pantomime; **2**, **pantaloons**, trousers.

pan-ther (pan'thėr), *n.* **1**, a large American wildcat: also called *cougar;* **2**, the leopard; **3**, less frequently, the jaguar.

pan-ties (pan'tiz), *n.* *pl.* short underpants, with closed crotch, worn by children and women.

pan-to-mime (pan'to-mīm'), *n.* **1**, a series of actions, chiefly gestures and facial expressions, that express meaning without words; **2**, a musical play usually based on a fairy-tale; **3**, in the U.S., a play without any talking.—*adj.* **pan'to-mim'ic**.

pan-try (pan'tri), *n*, [*pl.* pantries], a room or closet for storing food, dishes, etc.

pants (pants), *n.pl.* **1**, *Colloq.*, trousers; **2**, drawers.

pan-zer (pän'tsėr; zėr), *n.* *German,* armoured; as, a *panzer* division.

pap (pap), *n.* **1**, soft food for infants; **2**, pulp of fruits.

pa-pa (pȧ-pä'), *n.* a child's name for *father.*

pa-pa-cy (pā'pȧ-si), *n.* [*pl.* papacies], the office, dignity, or term of authority of the Pope:—**Papacy**, the government of the Roman Catholic Church.

pa-pal (pā'pal), *adj.* of or pertaining to the Pope, or to the Roman Catholic Church:—**papal cross**, a cross with three cross-bars.

pa-per (pā'pėr), *n.* **1**, a material made of finely divided fibres from rags, wood-pulp, etc., commonly in the form of a thin, smooth, flexible sheet, used for writing, printing, etc.; **2**, a piece or sheet of this material; **3**, a packet wrapped in this material; as, a *paper* of needles; **4**, a newspaper or journal; **5**, an essay or special article; as, a *paper* read before a club; **6**, a legal document; **7**, banknotes or bills of exchange: called *commercial paper:*—*adj.* **1**, having to do with paper; as, a *paper*-cutter; **2**, made of paper; as, *paper* dolls; **3**, having no reality; existing only on paper; as, *paper* profits:—**paper money**, notes issued by a government, a bank, etc., and used as currency:—*v.t.* to cover or line with paper.—*adj.* **pa'per-y**.

pa-pier—mâché (på/pyā/—mä/shā/; pā/pėr-ma-shā/), *n.* paper pulp, mixed with glue, rosin, oil, casein, etc., and moulded into various shapes.

pa-poose (pa-pōōs/), *n.* a baby of North American Indian parents.

pap-pus (pap/us), *n.* [*pl.* pappi (-pī)], *Botany,* the downy tuft of chaff or bristles on the fruit of Compositae plants, as dandelion, thistle, etc.

pap-ri-ka (pa-prē/ka; pap/ri-ka), *n.* mildly pungent, red spice made from the dried ripe fruit of certain peppers.

pa-py-rus (pa-pī/rus), *n.* [*pl.* papyri (pa-pī/rī)], **1,** a kind of Egyptian reed from which the ancients made paper; **2,** the paper made from the pith of this plant; **3,** a manuscript or writing on papyrus.

par (pär), *n.* **1,** full or normal value; as, the stock is below *par;* **2,** equality; equal footing; as, the man is not on a *par* with his associates; **3,** normal conditions; as, to feel below *par;* **4,** in *golf,* the standard number of strokes for a given course or hole.

¹par-a- (par/a-), *Greek prefix* meaning **1,** beside; beyond; aside from; as in *parallel;* **2,** *Medical,* secondary; abnormal; like; as in *paratyphoid.*

²par-a- (par/a-), *Latin prefix* meaning protecting, as in *parapet, parachute.*

par-a-ble (par/a-bl), *n.* a made-up story, usually about something that might naturally occur, from which a moral may be drawn.

pa-rab-o-la (pa-rab/o-la), *n.* in *geometry,* the curve formed when a cone is cut by a plane parallel to one of its sides; the curve described by a projectile.—*adj.* **par/a-bol/ic.**

par-a-chute (par/a-shōōt/), *n.* a folding apparatus, umbrella-shaped when open, used in descending from a balloon or airplane high in the air.

pa-rade (pa-rād/), *n.* **1,** show; pompous display; as, a *parade* of wealth; **2,** a military display, or review of troops; **3,** a place of assembly for exercising and inspecting troops; **4,** any march or procession; as, a circus *parade;* **5,** a promenade or public place for walking:—*v.t.* [parad-ed, parad-ing], **1,** to assemble and form (troops, etc.) in military order, as for review; **2,** to march over or through; as, to *parade* the city; **3,** to make a display of:—*v.i.* **1,** to walk about so as to exhibit or show oneself; **2,** to take part in a formal march.

par-a-dise (par/a-dīs/), *n.* **1,** the place in which the souls of the righteous abide after death; heaven; **2,** a state of bliss.

par-a-dox (par/a-doks), *n.* **1,** something which seems absurd or unbelievable, yet may be true; **2,** a statement that appears contradictory; as, the child is father of the man.—*adj.* **par/a-dox/i-cal.**

par-af-fin (par/a-fin) or **par-af-fine** (par/-a-fin; par/a-fēn/), *n.* a tasteless, waxy substance obtained from wood, coal, etc., and used to make candles, seal jars, etc.

par-a-gon (par/a-gon/, par/a-gun), *n.* a model of excellence or perfection.

par-a-graph (par/a-gråf/), *n.* **1,** a small section of a piece of writing, dealing with one topic; a short passage; **2,** a reference mark [¶] indicating the beginning of a paragraph; **3,** an item in a newspaper, magazine, etc.:—*v.t.* **1,** to arrange in paragraphs; **2,** to write a brief passage about.

par-a-keet (par/a-kēt/), *n.* any of several small, slender parrots with long, tapering tails: noted for their chattering and their gay plumage. Also, **par/ra-keet/, par/ro-ket/,** or **par/ro-quet/.**

par-al-lel (par/a-lel/), *adj.* **1,** equally distant from each other at all points; as, *parallel* lines; **2,** having the same course; as, *parallel* roads; **3,** similar; corresponding; as, *parallel* circumstances:—*n.* **1,** a line or plane equally distant at all points from another line or plane; **2,** one of the imaginary lines drawn on the surface of the earth, or one of the lines drawn on a map or globe, parallel to the equator, which mark degrees of latitude; **3,** a person or thing closely resembling another; **4,** a presentation of resemblance; as, to draw a *parallel* between two careers:—*v.t.* [paralleled, parallel-ing], **1,** to compare; **2,** to be parallel with; **3,** to correspond to.—*n.* **par/al-lel-ism.**

PARALLEL LINES

par-al-lel-o-gram (par/a-lel/o-gram), *n.* a four-sided plane figure whose opposite sides are equal and parallel.

par-a-lyse (par/a-līz/), *v.t.* [paralysed, paralys-ing], **1,** to affect with paralysis; **2,** to unnerve; render useless or ineffective.

PARALLELO-GRAMS

pa-ral-y-sis (pa-ral/i-sis), *n.* [*pl.* paralyses (pa-ral/i-sēz/)], **1,** loss of feeling or of power to move in one or more parts of the body; palsy; **2,** a state of complete inactivity from lack of power to move.—*adj.* **par′a-lyt′ic.**

par-a-mount (par′a-mount′), *adj.* above all others; supreme; as, of *paramount* importance.

par-a-mour (par′a-moor′), *n.* an illicit lover, esp. a married person.

par-a-noi-a (par′a-noi′a), *n.* a mental disorder marked by delusions, esp. of persecution or grandeur.—*n.* **par′a-noi′ac.**

par-a-pet (par′a-pet′), *n.* **1,** a low wall at the edge of a roof, platform, balcony, bridge, etc.; **2,** in fortification, a wall of earth or stone to protect troops from enemy fire.

par-a-pher-na-li-a (par′a-fer-nā′li-a), *n. pl.* **1,** personal belongings; as, trappings, finery, regalia, etc.; **2,** equipment; apparatus: as, the *paraphernalia* of a circus.

par-a-phrase (par′a-frāz′), *n.* and *v.* rewording of the sense or meaning of a passage, text, etc., in terms clearer or simpler, ampler or more precise.

par-a-pleg-ic (par′a-plej′ik; -plēj′ik), *n.* and *adj.* one whose entire lower half of the body is paralysed.—*n.* **par′a-ple′gi-a** (-plē′).

par-a-site (par′a-sīt′), *n.* **1,** one who lives at another's expense, usually by flattery; a toady; **2,** an animal or plant which lives on or within another, called the host, at the latter's expense. —*adj.* **par′a-sit′ic** (par′a-sit′ik); **par′-a-sit′i-cal.**

par-a-sol (par′a-sôl′), *n.* a small, light umbrella used as a sunshade.

par-a-troops (par′a-troops′), *n.* troops trained and equipped to drop by parachute for battle action behind enemy lines.—*n.* **par′a-troop′er.**

par a-vion (par′ à-vyôn′), *French,* by airmail.

par-boil (pär′boil′), *v.t.* to cook partially by boiling.

par-cel (pär′sl), *n.* **1,** a bundle or package; **2,** a separate part; as, a *parcel* of land:—*v.t.* [parcelled, parcel-ling], **1,** to divide into parts; distribute; as, to *parcel* out candy; **2,** to do up in a package.

parcel post, a government system of carrying packages by mail at postal rates.

parch (pärch), *v.t.* **1,** to roast slightly; dry by heating; as, to *parch* corn; **2,** to dry up:—*v.i.* to become dry and hot.

par-che-si (pär-chē′zi), *n.* Same as *pachisi.*

parch-ment (pärch′ment), *n.* **1,** the skin of a sheep, goat, etc., dressed and prepared for writing purposes; **2,** a deed or document on such a skin.

par-don (pär′dn), *v.t.* **1,** to free from punishment; forgive; as, to *pardon* a criminal: **2,** to overlook; excuse:—*n.* **1,** forgiveness; **2,** polite indulgence; as, I beg your *pardon;* **3,** an official act setting one free from penalty.—*adj.* **par′don-a-ble.**

pare (pâr), *v.t.* [pared, par-ing], **1,** to cut or shave off the outside or ends of; peel; as, to *pare* an apple; **2,** to lessen; reduce; as, to *pare* expenses.

par-ent (pâr′ent), *n.* **1,** a father or mother; hence, the source of any living thing, as a plant; **2,** cause; origin.— *adj.* **pa-ren′tal.**

par-ent-age (pâr′en-tij), *n.* **1,** fatherhood or motherhood; **2,** birth or descent; as, of noble *parentage.*—*n.* **par′ent-hood′.**

pa-ren-the-sis (pa-ren′thi-sis), *n.* [*pl.* parentheses (pa-ren′thi-sēz′)], **1,** an explanatory word, phrase, or clause put into a sentence which is grammatically complete without it: indicated by the marks ( ); **2,** either or both of the marks ( ).—*adj.* **par′en-thet′ic; par′-en-thet′i-cal.**

par-e-sis (par′i-sis; pa-rē′sis), *n.* partial paralysis, affecting motion but not sensation.

par ex-cel-lence (pär′ ek′se′läns′; pär ek′se-lans′), *French,* excellent in the greatest degree; beyond comparison; as, Shakespeare is a poet *par excellence.*

pa-ri-ah (pâr′i-a; pa-rī′a), *n.* a social outcast (as of a low Hindu caste in India).

pa-ri—mu-tu-el (par′i—mū′tū-el; chōō), *n.* **1,** a form of betting (on horse races) in which those who bet on the winners divide the stakes, less a percentage for management and taxes; **2,** the race or bet itself; **3,** the machine used to record the bet.

par-ing (pâr′ing), *n.* **1,** the act of cutting from a surface; **2,** the part cut off.

par-ish (par′ish), *n.* **1,** originally, a church district under the particular charge of one priest, clergyman, or minister; **2,** in England, a civil district, or part of a county, looking after its own education, charities, etc.; **3,** a congregation; also, the locality covered by its activities; **4,** in Louisiana, a state division, the same as a county in other states:—*adj.* pertaining to, or maintained by, a church, congregation, or district; as, a *parish* school.

pa-rish-ion-er (pa-rish'un-ėr), *n.* **1,** one who belongs to a certain parish; **2,** a member of a congregation.

par-i-ty (par'i-ti), *n.* **1,** equality, as in character status, amount, etc., **2,** in *finance*, equality in the value of the the currency or products of two countries.

park (pärk), *n.* **1,** a tract of ground set apart as a public place for recreation; **2,** a large extent of woods and fields attached to a country-house; **3,** a train of artillery; an artillery encampment: —*v.t.* **1,** to enclose, as in a park; **2,** to collect and station in order; as, to *park* artillery; **3,** to place and leave for a time:—*v.i.* to place and leave a vehicle temporarily.

par-ka (pär'ka), *n.* a fur jacket, fleece-lined coat, or heavy woollen shirt, with hood attached for protecting the head from the cold: worn in Yukon, Alaska, etc.

park-way (pärk'wā'), a broad (motor) roadway, often divided by, or bordered with, trees, shrubs, grass, etc.

par-lance (pär'lans), *n.* way of speaking; idiom; language; as legal, military, or newspaper *parlance*.

par-lay (pär'lā; li), *v.t.* and *v.i.* *U.S.* **1,** to bet one's original wager plus its winnings on another race, contest, etc.; **2,** to exploit any asset successfully; as, to *parlay* to fame one's voice, beauty, skill, etc.

par-ley (pär'li), *n.* [*pl.* parleys], a conference, esp. one with an enemy: —*v.i.* to hold a conference, esp. with an enemy, with a view to peace.

par-lia-ment (pär'li-ment), *n.* a general council; a meeting of the people or their representatives to consider matters of common interest:—**Parliament, 1,** the supreme law-making body of Great Britain, consisting of the House of Lords and the House of Commons; **2,** a similar assembly in certain other countries.—*adj.* **par'lia-men'ta-ry:—Parliament Hill,** the eminence overlooking the Ottawa River, etc., on which Canada's parliament buildings stand at Ottawa, Ontario.

par-lour (pär'lėr), *n.* **1,** a room for conversation and the reception of visitors, in a private dwelling, inn, or club; **2,** in England, a family sitting-room; **3,** in the U.S., a shop furnished with some pretensions to elegance; as, a beauty *parlour*:—**parlour car,** a railroad car with individual chairs and sofas, providing more comfortable travel than the usual coach. In American usage, **par'lor.**

pa-ro-chi-al (pa-rō'ki-al), *adj.* **1,** of or pertaining to a parish, or church district; as, a *parochial* school; **2,** narrow; local.

par-o-dy (par'o-di), *n.* [*pl.* parodies], **1,** a humorous imitation of a serious writing; **2,** a burlesque of a musical composition; **3,** hence, a burlesque imitation of anything:—*v.t.* [parodied, parody-ing], to write a humorous imitation of.

pa-role (pa-rōl'), *n.* **1,** word of honour; esp., a promise given by a prisoner of war that in return for partial freedom or privileges he will not try to escape, will not take up arms within a given time, etc.; **2,** the freeing of a prisoner before his time is up, on certain conditions; also, the duration of the conditions:—*v.t.* [paroled, paroling], to release (a prisoner) on his word of honour to observe certain conditions.

par-ox-ysm (par'ok-sizm), *n.* **1,** a spasm, or fit of acute pain, recurring at intervals; **2,** a sudden and violent outburst of emotion; a fit of any kind; as, a *paroxysm* of rage.—*adj.* **par'ox-ys'mal.**

par-ra-keet (par'a-kēt'), *n.* Same as **par'a-keet'.** Also, **par'ro-ket';** **par'-ro-quet'.**

par-ri-cide (par'i-sīd'), *n.* the murder, or murderer, of a close relative, esp. a parent.

par-rot (par'ut), *n.* a tropical bird with a hooked bill and brilliant feathers: it can be taught to repeat words.

par-ry (par'i), *v.t.* [parried, parrying], **1,** to ward off, as a blow; **2,** to evade; as, to *parry* a question:—*v.i.* to ward off or turn something aside; as, to *parry* with the sword:—*n.* [*pl.* parries], a warding off, as of a blow.

parse (pärs; pärz), *v.t.* [parsed, parsing], in *grammar* **1,** to analyse or describe (a sentence) by stating the parts of speech and their relation to one another; **2,** to state the part of speech of a word and its value in a sentence.

par-si-mo-ni-ous (pär'si-mō'ni-us), *adj.* close; stingy; miserly.—*n.* **par'-si-mo-ny.**

pars-ley (pärs'li), *n.* a garden plant, whose leaves are used as a garnish and for flavouring.

pars-nip (pärs'nip), *n.* a plant with an edible carrotlike root.

all (ôl), ôr; up, mūte, cûr, cōōl, book; oil, out; th, thin; *th*, the.

par-son (pär′sn), *n.* **1,** a clergyman in charge of a parish; **2,** *Colloq.* any minister or preacher.

par-son-age (pär′sn-ij), *n.* the residence of a minister in charge of a parish: esp., a house owned by a church or parish and set aside for the use of the minister.

part (pärt), *n.* **1,** something less than the whole; as, *part* of a pear; a piece, section, or division; an individual portion; **2,** a share in action, duty, or responsibility; as, to do one's *part;* **3,** an essential member or organ; as, *part* of the body; automobile *parts;* **4,** a side in a quarrel; as, they took his *part;* **5,** a character assigned to an actor in a play; also, the words spoken by that character; as, he took the *part* of Hamlet; **6,** a division of the hair of the head by a straight line; **7,** in *music,* one of the melodies in a harmony; as, a bass *part;* **8,** one of a given number of equal quantities into which a number, quantity, or object may be divided; as, three is the third *part* of nine; **9, parts, a,** a region or section; as, to live in these *parts;* visit foreign *parts;* **b,** ability or talent; as, a man of *parts:*— *v.t.* **1,** to divide into two or more pieces or sections; **2,** to disunite; force to go apart; **3,** to separate; as, to *part* the fighters:—*v.i.* **1,** to divide into two or more parts; break; as, the rope *parted;* **2,** to separate; as, to *part* from a friend.—*adj.* **part′ed.**

par-take (pär-tāk′), *v.i.* [*p.t.* partook (pär-took′), *p.p.* partak-en (pär-tāk′en), *p.pr.* partak-ing], **1,** to have or receive a share in common with others; as, men *partake* of the ability to talk; **2,** to take a portion; as, to *partake* of food.—*n.* **par-tak′er.**

Par-the-non (pär′thi-non′), *n.* the temple of Athena, "the Virgin", on the Acropolis at Athens.

par-tial (pär′shal), *adj.* **1,** inclined to favour one side or party; **2,** having a liking for; as, she is *partial* to candy; **3,** not entire; incomplete.—*adv.* **par′-tial-ly.**—*n.* **par′ti-al′i-ty** (pär′shi-al′-i-ti; pär-shal′i-ti).

par-tic-i-pate (pär-tis′i-pāt′), *v.i.* [partici-pat-ed, participat-ing], to share with others; to take part; as, everyone *participated* in the fun.—*n.* **par-tic′-i-pa′tor.**—*n.* **par-tic′i-pa′tion.**—*n.* and *adj.* **par-tic′i-pant.**

par-ti-ci-ple (pär′ti-si-pl), *n.* a part of a verb used as both verb and adjective; as, in "running, the man caught the train," the *participle* "running" shows action as a verb, and describes the

noun "man" as an adjective.—*adj.* **par′ti-cip′i-al.**

par-ti-cle (pär′ti-kl), *n.* **1,** a very small piece; a bit; **2,** the smallest possible amount of anything; as, not a *particle* of courage; **3,** in *grammar,* a short, subordinate part of speech, as a conjunction, article, preposition or interjection.

par-ti-col-oured (pär′ti-kul′érd), *adj.* having varied colours.

par-tic-u-lar (pär-tik′ū-lér), *adj.* **1,** distinct from others; as, a *particular* kind of paint; **2,** special; as, of *particular* importance; **3,** exact; nice; as, *particular* in dress; **4,** detailed; precise; as, a *particular* report:—*n.* a detail; as, the *particulars* of the story.—*n.* **par-tic′u-lar′i-ty.**—*v.t.* and *v.i.* **par-tic′u-lar-ize′.**

par-tic-u-lar-ly (pär-tik′ū-lér-li), *adv.* **1,** in detail; in a particular manner; as, *particularly* accurate; **2,** especially; as, he *particularly* wanted to go.

par-ti-san or **par-ti-zan** (pär′ti-zn), *n.* a devoted, sometimes prejudiced, follower, esp. of a political cause or faction:—*adj.* pertaining to, or strongly in favour of, a person, cause, or faction, esp. a political party or faction.

par-ti-san-ship or **par-ti-zan-ship** (pär′ti-zan-ship′), *n.* loyalty; esp., unreasonable loyalty to a person or cause.

par-ti-tion (pär-tish′un), *n.* **1,** the act of dividing or state of being divided; **2,** a separation; a dividing wall, as in a building; **3,** a section or division:—*v.t.* **1,** to divide into shares or parts; **2,** to divide by walls.

part-ly (pärt′li), *adv.* in part; not wholly.

part-ner (pärt′nér), *n.* **1,** one who is associated with another or others for mutual benefit or united action; as, a business *partner;* **2,** one who shares something with another; as, *partners* in misery; **3,** in games, one who plays with another on a side against opponents; **4,** one who dances with another; **5,** a husband or wife.

part-ner-ship (pärt′nér-ship), *n.* **1,** joint interest or ownership; **2,** the union of two or more persons in the same business.

par-tridge (pär′trij), *n.* **1,** any of various Old World game-birds allied to the quails and pheasants; **2,** in America, any of a number of similar game-birds, as the bob-white, quail, and ruffed grouse.

par-tridge—berry (pär'trij-ber'i), n. [pl. partridge-berries], an American trailing evergreen plant, bearing a bright-red berry; also, the berry.

par-ty (pär'ti), n. [pl. parties], 1, a number of persons united for a particular purpose; group; faction; as, a political party; 2, one who has an interest in an affair, as one of the two sides in a lawsuit; 3, a social gathering; as, a dinner-party.

pass (pås) v.i. [p.t. passed (påst), p.p. passed or past, p.pr. pass-ing], 1, to go from one place or condition to another; move along; as, the parade passes down the street; 2, to move from one to another; circulate freely, as money; 3, to elapse or go by; as, the night passed; 4, to make or force one's way; as, to pass through a crowd; 5, to go unnoticed; as, his action passed without rebuke; 6, to be approved, as a bill or law; 7, to go through a test with success; 8, to decide on the quality of something; as, to pass on someone's work; 9, in cards, to let one's turn go by without playing or bidding; 10, to be known or accepted: as, to pass for a lawyer; 11, to end; as, old customs pass and new ones take their place; 12, to happen; occur; as, see what passed:—v.t. 1, to go by, through, beyond, etc.; as, to pass the house; 2, to cause or allow to go; hand; as, to pass the butter; also to give to some-one; cause to circulate; as, to pass bad money; 3, to spend time; as, to pass the day; 4, to exceed; as, it passes belief; 5, to give as a judgment; as, to pass sentence; 6, to utter or pronounce; as, to pass an opinion; 7, to give legal status to (a bill or law); 8, to go through (a test) successfully; 9, to examine and approve: as, to pass a candidate:—n. 1, a narrow passage, as in the mountains; 2, a permit allowing free admission or passage; as, a railway pass; 3, critical condition; as, matters have come to a sad pass; 4, in fencing, a thrust; 5, in an examination, a standard that satisfies examiners without securing honours.—n. **pass'er.**—adj. **pass'a-ble.**—adv. **pass'a-bly** (moderately).

pas-sage (pas'ij), n. 1, course or progress; as, the passage of time; 2, a journey; esp., a voyage; 3, a way by which one passes; a hall or corridor; 4, the right to go; as, a free passage; 5, legal enactment; as, the passage of a law; 6, a single portion of a book, speech, etc.; 7, a conflict; as, a passage at arms.—n. **pas'sage-way'.**

pass-book (pås'book'), n. a bank-

book; 2, a customer's book in which a dealer enters items bought on credit.

pas-sé (på'sā'), adj. French, out-of-date; superseded; as, that style is passé.

pas-sen-ger (pas'en-jėr), n. one who travels usually at a stated fare, by a public conveyance, as a boat, train, omnibus, etc.

pass-er-by (pås'ėr-bī'), n. [pl. passers-by], one who goes past.

pas-sion (pash'un), n. 1, any intense feeling or emotion, as joy, fear, love, etc.; 2, an outburst of rage; 3, love; intense desire; enthusiasm; as, a passion for music; 4, the object of love, interest, etc.; as, poetry's my passion; 5, passions, the emotions.—adj. **pas'-sion-ate.**

pas-sive (pas'iv), adj. 1, suffering without resisting; submitting; 2, not acting but acted upon; 3, in grammar, indicating that form of the transitive verb which carries the idea that the subject is acted upon: opposite of active; as, in the sentence, "the boy was thrown from the horse," the subject "boy" receives the action expressed in the passive form "was thrown."—adv. **pas'sive-ly**—n. **pas-siv'i-ty** (pa-siv'i-ti).—n. **pas'siv-ism.**

pass-key (pås'kē'), n. 1, a private key; 2, a master key that opens a group of locks.

pass-port (pås'pōrt), n. 1, an official paper from one's own government giving one permission to travel in a foreign country; 2, anything that opens the way to success.

pass-word (pås'wûrd'), n. a secret word known only to those on guard and to those allowed to pass the guard; a watchword.

past (påst), adj. 1, having formerly been; gone by; as, the past generation; 2, just gone by; last; as, the past hour; 3, thoroughly experienced; as, a past master:—n. 1, time gone by; as, memories of the past; 2, previous life or history; as, we know nothing of his past; 3, in grammar, the past tense:—adv. by; beyond; as, he just walked past:—prep. beyond in time, age, or condition; as, he is past 21; she is past cure:—past tense, in grammar, a tense of the verb indicating time gone by; as, he went; past perfect, a tense of the verb indicating action that took place before a time in the past; as, when we arrived, he had gone.

paste (påst), n. 1, a sticky mixture, often of flour and water, used for making things stick together; **2,** dough prepared for piecrust, etc.; **3,** a preparation, as of fish, nuts, or other foods, finely ground to a creamy consistency; as, anchovy or almond *paste;* also, a jellylike confection; as, Turkish *paste;* **4,** a hard, glassy mixture used for making artificial gems:—*v.t.* [past-ed, past-ing], to cover or fasten with a sticky mixture.—*adj.* **past'y.**

paste-board (pāst'bōrd'), *n.* stiff material made by pressing paper pulp or pasting together sheets of paper.

pas-tel (pas-tel'),*n.* a soft, pale shade of any colour; **2,** a crayon of ground colouring matter mixed with gum, or the ground pigment paste itself; **3,** a drawing made with such crayons, or the art of drawing with them; **4,** a light, short prose study.—*adj.* done in subdued tints; as, the interior was in *pastel* shades.

pas-tern (pas'tẽrn), *n.* the part of a horse's foot between the fetlock and hoof.

pas-teur-ize (pas'tūr-iz', pas'tẽr-iz'), *v.t.* [pasteurized, pasteuriz-ing], to heat a liquid, as milk, to a temperature high enough to destroy harmful germs without destroying the nourishing value of the liquid.—*n.* **pas'teur-i-za'tion.**

pas-time (pas'tīm'), *n.* diversion; sport; amusement; any activity that fills time agreeably.

pas-tor (pás'tẽr), *n.* a minister in charge of a church and congregation.

pas-to-ral (pás'to-ral), *adj.* **1,** pertaining to the duties of a minister; as, *pastoral* calls; **2,** pertaining to shepherds or the shepherd's life; as, *pastoral* poetry:—*n.* a poem, play, etc., depicting country life.

pas-try (pās'tri), *n.* [*pl.* pastries], desserts, as pies, tarts, etc., made with a rich crust enclosing, usually, fruit or meat.

pas-tur-age (pás'tūr-ij), *n.* land used for grazing cattle or other animals.

pas-ture (pás'tūr), *n.* land or grass on which cattle feed:—*v.t.* [pastured, pasturing], to supply with grass or pasture:—*v.i.* to graze.

past-y (pās'ti, pas'ti; *n.* [*pl.* pasties], a pie, usually of highly seasoned meat covered with a crust.

¹pat (pat), *n.* **1,** a light, quick blow with the hand or fingers; **2,** a small shaped lump, as of butter; **3,** a light sound or tap:—*v.t.* [pat-ted, pat-ting], to strike gently with a flat surface, esp. with the hand or fingers; stroke gently.

²pat (pat), *adj.* [pat-ter, pat-test], **1,**

suitable; as, a *pat* answer; **2,** resolute; as, to stand *pat:—adv.* aptly; readily.

patch (pach), *n.* **1,** a piece of material, as cloth or metal, put on to cover a hole or to strengthen a worn place; **2,** a small piece; **3,** a spot or blotch of colour; as, the cat had a *patch* of white on its side:—*v.t.* **1,** to cover or strengthen by putting on a patch; **2,** to mend clumsily; **3,** to piece together with pieces of material; as, to *patch* a quilt; **4,** to settle; mend; as, to *patch* up a quarrel.—*n.* **patch'work'.**—*adj.* **patch'y.**

pate (pāt), *n.* the head; crown of the head.

paté (pȧ'tā'), *n. French,* a meat paste, used in sandwiches, pies, etc.

pa-tel-la (pa-tel'a), *n.* the knee-cap.

pa-tent (pā'tent; pat'ent), *adj.* **1,** open for anyone to view or to read: said esp. of an official paper which confers a privilege; as, letters *patent;* medicines; **3,** (usually pā'tent), evident; plain; as, his honesty was *patent:—n.* **1,** a privilege granted by the government that gives to an inventor the sole right of making, using, or selling his invention for a definite number of years; **2,** the thing so protected; as, he owned several *patents:—v.t.* to grant or secure the sole right to.—*adj.* **pat'ent-a-ble.**—*adv.* **pa'tent-ly** (pā'tent-li).—*n.* **pat'ent-ee'** (a person granted a patent).

pa-ter-nal (pa-tûr'nal), *adj.* **1,** pertaining to a father; as, *paternal* advice; **2,** inherited from a father; as, *paternal* lands; **3,** related through the father; as, a *paternal* uncle.—*n.* **pa-ter'ni-ty** (fatherhood).—*n.* **pa-ter'nal-ism.**

path (páth), *n.* [*pl.* paths (páthz), **1,** a road; foot-path; **2,** a track; **3,** a course of conduct or action.—*adj.* **path'less.**

pa-thet-ic (pa-thet'ik), *adj.* arousing sympathy and pity; pitiful; as, a *pathetic* cripple.—*adv.* **pa-thet'ical-ly.** —**pathetic fallacy,** in *literature,* the portraying of nature as having human feeling; as, the *angry* sea; the sky *weeps.*

path-o- (path'ō-), *Greek prefix* meaning *suffering* or *feeling,* as in **pa-thol'o-gy** (the science of the cause, nature, and course of diseases).

pa-thos (pā'thos), *n.* that quality which excites sympathy and pity.

path-way (páth'wā'), *n.* **1,** a narrow footpath; **2,** any course or road.

pa-tient (pā'shent), *adj.* **1,** enduring pain, hardship, etc., without complaint; **2,** tolerant; tender; forgiving; **3,**

untiring in labour; persevering; as, a *patient* worke r; **4**, waiting with calmness:—*n.* one under the care of a doctor —*n.* **pa'tienc e.**

pa-ti-o (pá'ti-ō'; pä'tyō), *n.* [*pl.* patios], an open courtyard within a house or other building.

pa-tois (pat'wä; pà'twä'), *n.* [*pl.* patois], a local or provincial dialect that differs from the accepted standard; as, the Dutch *patois* of South Africa.

pa-tri-arch (pā'tri-ärk), *n.* **1**, a founder or head of a family or tribe; esp. one of the early ancestors of the Jews; **2**, an aged and venerable man; **3**, in the Greek Church a bishop of the highest rank.—*adj.* **pa'tri-ar'chal** (pā'tri-är'-kal).

pa-tri-cian (pa-trish'an), *n.* **1**, a member of the ancient Roman aristocracy: contrasted with *plebeian;* **2**, a person of noble birth:—*adj.* **1**, pertaining to the ancient Roman aristocracy; **2**, noble; aristocratic.

pat-ri-cide (pat'ri-sīd'), *n.* **1**, one who murders his father; **2**, such a murder.

pat-ri-mo-ny (pat'ri-mo-ni), *n.* [*pl.* patrimonies], **1**, property inherited from a father or other ancestor; **2**, property settled upon a religious institution for its support.—*adj.* **pat'ri-mo'ni-al.**

pa-tri-ot (pā'tri-it; pat'ri-ot), *n.* one who loves his government or country. —*adj.* **pa'tri-ot'ic** (pā'tri-ot'ik; pat'ri-ot'ik).

pa-tri-ot-ism (pā'tri-ot-izm; pat'), *n.* love of one's country.

pa-trol (pa-trōl'), *n.* **1**, a guard; policeman; **2**, the act of going the rounds of a district in order to protect it; **3**, a body of soldiers on guard or reconnoitring duty; **4**, a division of eight scouts in a troop of boy scouts:— *v.t.* [patrolled, patrol-ling], **1**, to go or walk round in order to protect; as, a policeman *patrols* his beat; **2**, to act as a guard to (a camp, sea coast, etc.).

pa-trol-man (pa-trōl'man), *n.* [*pl.* patrolmen (-men)], a policeman or watchman whose duty it is to patrol a certain beat or district.

pa-tron (pā'trun), **1**, a guardian or protector; **2**, an upholder or supporter; as, a *patron* of music or painting; **3**, in business, a regular customer; **4**, a man who lends his support to a social or charitable event:—*adj.* aiding, or acting as guardian; as, *patron* saints.—*n.fem.* **pa'tron-ess** (pā'trun-es; pat').

pa-tron-age (pā'trun-ij; pat'), *n.* **1**,

special favour or encouragement; guardianship or protection; **2**, the act of buying goods regularly at one store, of stopping regularly at one hotel, etc.; **3**, politically, the power to control nominations, or to give jobs, favours, etc.

pa-tron-ize (pā'trun-īz', pat') *v.t.* [patronized, patroniz-ing], **1**, to act as guardian or benefactor toward; support or protect; favour; **2**, to treat with condescension; **3**, *Colloq.* to deal with regularly as a customer; as, to *patronize* a store.—*n.* **pa'tron-iz'er.**— *adj.* **pa'tron-iz'ing.**

¹**pat-ter** (pat'ėr), *v.i.* **1**, to mumble or mutter something over and over rapidly, esp. a prayer; **2**, to talk glibly:—*v.t.* to mumble indistinctly:— *n.* **1**, rapid, cheap, fluent talk; **2**, thieves' jargon.

²**pat-ter** (pat'ėr), *n.* a quick succession of light sounds:—*v.i.* **1**, to run with quick, short steps; **2**, to strike with a quick succession of light taps.

pat-tern (pat'ėrn), *n.* **1**, a model, sample, or specimen; **2**, anything cut out or formed into a shape to be copied; as, a *pattern* for a dress; **3**, an example to follow, esp. a good example; **4**, a design or figure; as, the *pattern* in a carpet:—*v.t.* **1**, to make in imitation of; copy; as to *pattern* a dress after a model. **2**, to decorate, as with a design:—*v.i;* to follow a pattern or example.

pat-ty (pat'i), *n.* [*pl.* patties], a small, cupshaped shell of pastry, holding meat, oysters, etc.

pau-ci-ty (pô'-si-ti), *n.* small number (of); fewness; scarcity; as, *paucity* or workers, supplies, evidence, etc.

paunch (pônch; pänch), *n.* the abdomen; the belly and its contents.

pau-per (pô'pėr), *n.* a very poor person, esp. one who is supported by the public or by charity.—*n.* **pau'per-ism.**—*v.t.* **pau'per-ize.**

pause (pôz), *n.* **1**, a temporary stop or rest; interruption; as, a *pause* in the day's work; **2**, an intermission or break in speaking or reading, **3**, a break in writing indicated by a punctuation mark; **4**, a mark in music over or under a note or rest to show that it is to be prolonged: also called *hold:—v.i.* [paused, paus-ing], to make a short stop; wait; as, to *pause* for breath.

pave (pāv), *v.t.* [paved, pav-ing], **1**, to cover with stones, bricks, etc.; as, to *pave* a street; **2**, to make smooth or easy.—*n.* **pav'er.**

all (ôl), ôr; up, mūte, cûr, cōōl, book; oil, out; th, thin; *th*, the.

pave-ment (pāv′ment), *n.* **1**, a roadway or floor covered or laid with stone, brick, tile, etc.; **2**, a sidewalk; **3**, any material, as of stones, concrete, etc. used in covering a road, pathway, or floor.

pa-vil-ion (pa-vil′yun), *n.* **1**, a light, ornamental building, as in a garden; **2**, a large tent with a peaked roof; **3**, a temporary open building for shelter, entertainment, etc.

pav-ing (pāv′ing), *n.* **1**, the surfacing of a road or sidewalk; **2**, material for covering roads, walks, etc.; also, the surface itself; as, stone or brick *paving.*

paw (pô), *n.* **1**, the foot of an animal that has claws, as a cat, dog, tiger, etc.; **2**, *Colloq.* a hand:—*v.t.* **1**, to scrape or beat with the feet; as, the horse *pawed* the ground; **2**, *Colloq.* to handle roughly; **3**, to strike wildly with the hands; as, to *paw* the air:—*v.i.* **1**, to scrape or touch something with the forefoot; **2**, *Colloq.* to handle a thing awkwardly; grope clumsily.

pawl (pôl), *n.* a short bar or catch on a machine, made to fall into notches in another part, as a wheel, in order to prevent it from turning backward.

¹pawn (pôn), *n.* **1**, something given or deposited as a pledge for the payment of a debt or return of a loan; **2**, the state of being so pledged; as, my watch is in *pawn:*—*v.t.* to give as security for a loan; as, to *pawn* a ring.

²pawn (pôn), *n.* **1**, in *chess*, a piece of lowest value; **2**, a person deliberately used or sacrificed by another.

pawn-bro-ker (pôn′brō′kėr), *n.* a person whose business it is to lend money on goods left with him.

pawn-shop (pôn′shop′), *n.* a shop run by a pawnbroker.

pay (pā), *v.t.* [paid (pād), or, in sense **5**, payed (pād), pay-ing], **1**, to give money to, in return for work done or goods received; as, to *pay* workmen; **2**, to discharge, as a debt, by giving over the money required; **3**, to be profitable to; as, it will *pay* you to do what I say; **4**, to give without any sense of obligation; as, to *pay* a compliment; **5**, to allow to run out; to pass out through the hands; as, we *payed* out all the slack in the rope:—*v.i.* **1**, to make recompense; discharge a debt; as, he always *pays* promptly; **2**, to make suitable return for effort; be worth while; as, the business *pays* well; it *pays* to be honest:—*n.* money given for work done; wages; salary.—*n.* **pay′er.**

pay-a-ble (pā′a-bl), *adj.* due, as a bill.

pay-ee (pā-ē′), *n.* the one to whom money is paid, or payable.

pay-ment (pā′ment), *n.* **1**, the act of giving money for wages, a debt, etc.; **2**, that which is given to discharge a debt, etc.

pay-o-la (pā-ō′la), *n.* money or gifts given to corrupt integrity of choice, esp. to a disc jockey to favour certain records on a hit parade, to a television performer to take part in a rigged show, or to one so placed as to choose between products, contracts, sponsors, etc.

pea (pē), *n.* [*pl.* pease or peas (pēz)], **1**, a pod-bearing plant of the same family as the bean, widely grown as a vegetable; **2**, its round, green seed, which is used for food; **3**, a related plant; as, the sweet *pea.*

peace (pēs), *n.* **1**, a state of rest or calm; quiet; esp. freedom from war or disorder; **2**, friendly relations between persons; **3**, a treaty or agreement to end a war.—*n.* **peace′mak′er.**

peace-a-ble (pēs′a-bl), *adj.* **1**, not quarrelsome; **2**, calm; quiet.

peace-ful (pēs′fool), *adj.* **1**, free from war or commotion; **2**, mild; calm; undisturbed; quiet; as, a *peaceful* evening.—*adv.* **peace′ful-ly.**

peach (pēch), *n.* **1**, a sweet, juicy fruit, with white or yellow flesh, a downy pink-tinted skin, and a large, rough stone containing one large seed; **2**, the tree bearing this fruit; **3**, a soft yellowish-pink colour.

pea-cock (pē′kok′), *n.* the male bird of the peafowl, noted for its long, handsome tail feathers, marked with iridescent, eyelike spots.—*n. fem.* **pea′hen′.**

pea-jacket (pē′jak′it), *n.* a short, heavy, woollen overcoat, worn esp. by sailors.

peak (pēk), *n.* **1**, the sharp-pointed top of a mountain or hill; **2**, a mountain standing alone; **3**, a pointed end of anything; as, the *peak* of a roof; **4**, the most intense or highest point; as, the *peak* of happiness; **5**, the visor of a cap; **6**, the narrow part of a vessel's bow or stern.

¹peaked (pēkt), *adj.* pointed; as, a *peaked* roof; also, projecting; as, a *peaked* cap.

²peak-ed (pēk′id), *adj. Colloq.* sharp-featured; thin; wan; sickly; as, a *peaked* face.

peal (pēl), *n.* **1**, a loud sound or succession of sounds, as of thunder, bells etc.; **2**, a set of bells, or a musical phrase rung on them:—*v.i.* to give

forth loud sounds, as a bell or organ:—
v.t. to cause to sound loudly; as, to
peal a bell.

pea-nut (pē'nut'), *n.* a yellow-flowered
plant of the pea family, whose pods
ripen under the ground; also, its
nutlike fruit.

pear (pâr), *n.* 1, a sweet, juicy, oblong-
shaped fruit related to the apple; 2, the
tree which bears this fruit.

pearl (pûrl), *n.* 1, a small, smooth,
lustrous gem formed as a growth inside
the shells of oysters or other shellfish;
2, something resembling a pearl in
shape, size, colour, or value; 3, a pale,
greyish-white colour; 4, in printing,
a small size of type: (5 point):—
mother of pearl, the tinted lining of the
shell of various shellfish.—*adj.* **pearl'y.**

peas-ant (pez'ant), *n.* in Europe, one
who tills the soil; a farmer or farm
labourer:—*adj.* rustic; as, *peasant*
manners.

peas-ant-ry (pez'ant-ri), *n.* those who
till the soil; peasants; farmers.

peat (pēt), *n.* a substance formed of
partly decayed vegetable matter in
swamps and marshy places, and much
used, as in Ireland, for fuel.—*adj.*
peat'y.

pea-vey or **pea-vy** (pē'vi), *n. U.S.* a
lumberman's cant-hook (used in log-
ging).

peb-ble (peb'l), *n.* a small stone; a
stone worn smooth by water.—*adj.*
peb'bly.

pe-can (pi-kan'; pi-kän'), *n.* 1, a kind
of hickory tree of southern U.S.; 2, its
oblong, smooth, thin-shelled nut.

pec-ca-dil-lo (pek'a-dil'ō), *n.* [*pl.*
-dillos or -dilloes (ōz)], a trifling fault;
as, the boy's *peccadillos.*

pec-ca-ry (pek'a-ri), *n.* [*pl.* peccaries],
a night-roving, hoglike wild animal
found in America from Texas to
Paraguay.

¹peck (pek), *n.* 1, in dry measure, one
quarter of a bushel; eight quarts;
also, a vessel for measuring out a peck;
2, a lot; a great deal; as, a *peck* of
trouble.

²peck (pek), *v.t.* 1, to strike with the
beak; as, the bird *pecked* my hand; 2,
to strike with a pointed instrument, as
a pick; 3, to pick up with the beak; as,
the hen *pecks* corn; 4, *Colloq.* to eat
sparingly; as, she *pecks* her food:—*v.i.*
1, to make strokes with the beak or a
sharp instrument; 2, to pick up food
with the beak:—*n.* 1, a quick, sharp
stroke, as with the beak; 2, a mark

made by a blow with a pointed
instrument.

pec-tin (pek'tin), *n.* a white, water-
soluble substance found in ripe fruit,
etc., used as a jellying agent in vegetable juices.

pec-to-ral (pek'to-ral), *adj.* of or
placed on the chest; as, a *pectoral*
muscle.

pe-cul-iar (pi-kūl'yẻr), *adj.* 1, one's
own; individual; belonging to a
particular person or place; as, a tree
peculiar to New England; 2, strange;
queer; as, her actions are *peculiar.*—*n.*
pe-cu'li-ar'i-ty.

pe-cu-ni-ar-y (pi-kū'ni-er-i), *adj.* of or
concerned with money; financial; as,
pecuniary losses.

ped- (ped-), **pe-do-** (pē'dō-), or **pedi-**
(ped'i-), *prefix* meaning (1) *foot* (2)
child; as in **ped'a-go'gy** (teaching),
ped'i-cure (footcare), and **pe-dom'e-
ter** (an instrument that measures the
distance walked).

ped-a-gogue (ped'a-gog), *n.* a school
teacher; often, a dull schoolmaster.—
adj. **ped'a-gog'i-cal** (ped'a-goj'i-kal).

ped-al (ped'l), *adj.* concerning or
operated by a foot:—*n.* the treadle, or
foot-operated lever, of a machine, organ,
piano, or harp; —*v.t.* and *v.i.* [pedalled,
pedal-ling], to move or operate by
working a pedal or pedals.

ped-al push-ers, knee-length trousers
for women or girls (worn originally for
cycling).

ped-ant (ped'ant), *n.* one who makes
a show of his learning.—*adj.* **pe-dan'tic.**

ped-dle (ped'l), *v.i.* [ped-dled, ped-
dling], to travel about selling small
wares:—*v.t.* 1, to sell from house to
house; hawk; 2, hence, to deal out
little by little.—*n.* **ped'dler.**

ped-es-tal (ped'es-t'l), *n.* 1, the base of
a column; also, the support of a statue,
lamp, etc; 2, any base or foundation; 3, a
position of high regard or admiration;
as, he put his friend on a *pedestal.*

pe-des-tri-an (pi-des'tri-an), *n.* one
who travels on foot; a walker:—*adj.*
1, walking; on foot; 2, hence, slow-
moving; dull; uninspired; as, *pedes-
trian* argument or writing.

pe-di-a-tri-cian (pē'di-a-trish'an), *n.*
a specialist in the care of infants and
the treatment of children's diseases.

ped-i-cel (ped'i-s'l), *n.* a slender flower
stem branching from a peduncle.

pe-dic-u-lo-sis (pi-dik'ū-lō'sis), *n.*
the state of being infested with lice.—
adj. **pe-dic'u-lous.**

ped-i-gree (ped′i-grē′), *n.* **1**, a record or list of ancestors; **2**, lineage; ancestry; as, a man of noble *pedigree*.

ped-lar (ped′lẽr), *n.* one who travels around selling small articles; a hawker.

pe-dro (pē′drō), *n.* a variety of the card game seven-up in which the five of trumps counts five.

pe-dun-cle (pi-dung′kl), *n.* the main stem of a flower or cluster of flowers.

peek (pēk), *v.i.* to look slyly through half-closed eyes; to look through a crevice or crack; peep:—*n.* a peep; a sly glance.

PEDUNCLE (A) AND PEDICEL (B)

peel (pēl), *v.t.* **1**, to strip off an outer covering from; as, to *peel* an orange; **2**, to strip off; as, to *peel* bark from a tree:—*v.i.* to come off; as, bark *peels*:—*n.* skin or rind.

¹**peep** (pēp), *v.i.* **1**, to chirp; cry, as young birds; **2**, to speak in a weak, high voice:—*n.* **1**, chirp; squeak; **2**, a baby chick.

²**peep** (pēp), *v.i.* **1**, to look through a crack or from a hiding place; look slyly; **2**, to begin to appear; as, the moon *peeped* from behind a cloud:—*n.* **1**, a quick, sly look; **2**, a glimpse; as, I took a *peep* at the first chapter; **3**, first appearance, as of the sun.—*n.* peep′er.

¹**peer** (pēr), *n.* **1**, a person of the same rank; an equal or associate; as, a jury of his *peers;* **2**, a member of the British nobility; a nobleman.—*n. fem.* peer′ess.

²**peer** (pēr), *v.i.* **1**, to look closely or out of curiosity; as, they all *peered* at me; **2**, to peep out; come into sight; as, the sun *peered* from behind the cloud.

peer-age (pēr′ij), *n.* **1**, the rank or dignity of a nobleman; **2**, the whole body of noblemen; **3**, a record or list of peers.

peer-less (pēr′lis), *adj.* without equal; matchless; as, a *peerless* voice.

peeve (pēv), *v.t.* and *v.i. Colloq.* to become or make bad-tempered.—*n. Colloq.* the person or thing disliked, or that annoys; as, his pet *peeve.*—*adj. Colloq.* peeved (pēvd).

pee-vish (pē′vish), *adj.* childishly fretful; hard to please; as, a *peevish* disposition.

pee-wee (pē′wē′), *n. Colloq.* an unusually small person or thing.

peg (peg), *n.* **1**, a pointed wooden or metal pin used as a fastening; as, a shoe *peg;* a tent-*peg;* **2**, a piece of wood serving as a nail; as, to hang one's coat on a *peg;* **3**, a step or degree; as, he took her down a *peg;*—*v.t.* [pegged, peg-ging], **1**, to fasten with pegs; as, to *peg* furniture; **2**, to mark by driving in small stakes of wood; as, to *peg* out a mining claim:—*v.i.* to work steadily; as, to *peg* away at one's lessons.

Pe-kin-ese (pē′kin-ēz′; pē′kin-ēs′)

Pe-king-ese (pē′king-ēz′; pē′king-ēs′), *n.* a small, pug-nosed, long-haired dog, originally from China.

pe-koe (pē′kō), *n.* a choice black tea of Ceylon and India, from a smaller leaf than that used for orange pekoe: it is superior since the leaf is picked young with the down still on it.

pelf (pelf), *n.* **1**, stolen property; **2**, money; wealth; riches.

pel-i-can (pel′i-kan), *n.* a large, web-footed water-bird, which has a large pouch attached to the lower jaw of its huge bill.

pe-lisse (pe-lēs′), *n.* a woman's long cloak, esp. one lined with fur.

pel-lag-ra (pe-lag′ra; -lā′), *n.* a skin disease, caused by faulty diet, and marked by nervous disorders, often leading to insanity.

pel-let (pel′it), *n.* **1**, a little ball, as of food or medicine; **2**, a missile; bullet.

pell—mell or **pell-mell** (pel′–mel′), *adv.* **1**, in a disorderly manner; **2**, headlong; in a great hurry; as, to rush out *pellmell.*

¹**pelt** (pelt), *n.* a raw hide; the untanned skin of an animal.

²**pelt** (pelt), *v.t.* **1**, to strike with a number of missiles; as, to *pelt* pebbles at the windows:—*v.i.* **1**, to strike repeated blows with something thrown; **2**, to beat down heavily, as rain or hail:—*n.* **1**, a blow from something thrown; **2**, a rapid speed:—**full pelt,** (at) full speed; as, to ride *full pelt.*

pel-vis (pel′vis), *n.* [*pl.* pelves (pel′-vēz)], in man's anatomy, the basin-shaped structure of bones which supports the spinal column and to which the lower limbs are attached; in animals, a similar structure where the backbone and hipbones meet.—*adj.* pel′vic.

pem-mi-can (pem′i-kan), *n.* **1**, a North American Indian food made of dried lean meat pounded into a paste with fat and pressed into cakes; **2**, a concentrate of dried beef, raisins, suet, and sugar, used by explorers.

¹**pen** (pen), *n.* a small enclosure, esp. one for confining animals; a coop:—*v.t.* [penned (pend) or pent (pent), penning], to shut up in, or as if in, a pen or enclosure.

²**pen** (pen), *n.* an instrument for writing with ink, originally a quill; now, ordinarily, a split point of metal to be fitted into a holder; also, the holder and the point together:—*v.t.* [penned, penning], to write; compose and put upon paper, as a letter.

pe-nal (pē'nal), 1, *adj.* having to do with punishment or with punished persons; as, *penal* laws; *penal* labour; a *penal* colony; 2, meriting punishment; as, a *penal* offence.

pe-nal-ize (pē'nal-īz'), *v.t.* [penalized, penaliz-ing], to inflict a penalty upon; as, the referee *penalized* our football team.

pen-al-ty (pen'al-ti), *n.* [*pl.* penalties] 1, legal punishment for breaking the law; as, the *penalty* for murder is death; 2, a fine; forfeit; 3, a punishment or handicap imposed for the breaking of a rule.

pen-ance (pen'ans), *n.* 1, an act of devotion, often prescribed, to show sorrow or repentance for a sin; 2, hardship or suffering as a result of a mistake or wrongdoing.

pence (pens), *n. pl.* of *penny*.

pen-cil (pen'sil), *n.* a stick of black lead, coloured chalk, etc., generally encased in wood, and used for writing, drawing, etc.:—*v.t.* [pencilled, pencilling], to write or sketch with a pencil.— *adj.* **pen'cilled.**

pend-ant (pen'dant), *n.* something hanging; esp., a hanging ornament.

pen-dent (pen'dent), *adj.* 1, hanging; swinging; as, a *pendent* bough; 2, overhanging; jutting over, as, a *pendent* rock; 3, undetermined; in suspense.

pend-ing (pen'ding), *adj.* not yet finished or decided; as, a *pending* trial: —*prep.* 1, during; as, *pending* the negotiations for peace, an armistice was declared; 2, until; as, *pending* his arrival, we did nothing.

pen-du-lous (pen'dū-lus), *adj.* hanging down; swaying; as, *pendulous* branches, fruits, etc.

pen-du-lum (pen'dū-lum), *n.* a body suspended from a fixed point so that it is free to swing to and fro; as, the *pendulum* of a clock.

pen-e-trate (pen'i-trāt'), *v.t.* [penetrat- ed, penetrat-ing], 1, to enter into; pierce; 2, to soak through; spread itself through; as, the dampness *penetrated* his clothes; 3, to understand; as, to *penetrate* a secret:—*v.i.* 1, to pierce something; 2, to affect the feelings or mind deeply.—*adj.* **pen'e-trat'ing.**

pen-e-tra-tion (pen'i-trā'shun), *n.* 1, the act of entering or piercing; 2, mental acuteness or keenness; sagacity.

pen-guin (peng'gwin; pen'gwin), *n.* a large antarctic sea-bird which cannot fly but uses its winglike appendages as paddles in swimming.

pen-i-cil-lin (pen'i-sil'in), *n.* a sub- stance produced by a common mould (usually of bread) which checks the growth of several disease-producing germs; not poisonous, but useful in the treatment of such infections as pneu- monia.

pen-in-su-la (pen-in'sū-la), *n.* a piece of land almost surrounded by water.— *adj.* **pen-in'su-lar.**

pe-nis (pē'nis), *n.* the male organ of sexual intercourse.

pen-i-tence (pen'i-tens), *n.* sorrow for sin or wrongdoing; repentance.—*adj.* and *n.* **pen'i-tent.**—*adj.* **pen'i-ten'tial.**

pen-i-ten-tia-ry (pen'i-ten'sha-ri), *adj.* 1, pertaining to penance; 2, per- taining to prisons or reformatories; 3, making a person liable to imprison- ment; as, a *penitentiary* offence:—*n.* [*pl.* penitentiaries], a prison in which convicts are confined.

pen-knife (pen'nīf'), *n.* [*pl.* penknives (pen'nīvz')], a small pocket-knife.

pen-man-ship (pen'man-ship), *n.* art or style of handwriting; as, good *penmanship*.

pen-nant (pen'ant), *n.* 1, a long, narrow naval flag or streamer; 2, a small, triangular flag; 3, a flag given to a champion team in a sport; 4, hence, championship.

pen-ni-less (pen'i-lis), *adj.* without a penny; very poor; destitute.

pen-non (pen'un), *n.* 1, a flag or streamer, swallow-tailed or triangular, borne on a lance; 2, any flag or banner.

pen-ny (pen'i), *n.* [*pl.* pennies, meaning a number of coins; pence (pens), meaning, generally, an amount valued in pennies], 1, in England, a coin, formerly copper, now bronze, equal to one twelfth of a shilling, or about two cents of Canadian or U.S. money; 2, in Canada and the U.S., one cent.

all (ôl), ôr; up, mūte, cûr, cōōl, book; oil, out; th, thin; *th*, the.

pen-ny-weight (pen′i-wāt′), *n.* a troy weight equal to 24 grains, or ²⁄₂₀ of an ounce troy.

pe-nol-o-gy (pi-nòl′o-ji), *n.* the science of (a) reforming and rehabilitating criminals (b) managing prisons.

pen-sion (pen′shun), *n.* **1,** a certain sum paid regularly by a government, employer, or corporation to a person retired after a long period of service; **2,** an allowance paid by governments to provide for certain needy classes; as, old-age *pensions;* **3,** (in French, pän′-syôn′; in German, pän-syōn′), in Europe, a boarding-house or boarding-school:—*v.t.* to grant a regular allowance of money to.

pen-sion-er (pen′shun-ėr), *n.* a person who receives a pension.

pen-sive (pen′siv), *adj.* **1,** engaged in, or given to, serious thought; musing; as, a *pensive* mood; a *pensive* nature; **2,** expressing serious thought; as, a *pensive* poem.

pent (pent), *adj.* shut or penned up. —*adj.* **pent′-up′** (as, *pent-up* emotions).

pen-ta-gon (pen′ta-gon; *n.* in *geometry* a figure with five sides and five angles.—*adj.* **pen-tag′-o-nal** (pen-tag′o-nal).

pen-tam-e-ter (pen-tam′-e-tėr), *n.* a verse or line of PENTAGON five metrical feet; as, 'My̆ stron|gėr guílt|defeats|my̆ strong|intent' (*iambic pentameter*).

pen-tath-lon (pen-tath′lon), *n.* an athletic contest of five events, esp. the broad jump, 200-metre dash, 1500-metre run, javelin throw, and discus throw of the Olympic Games.

pent-house (pent′hous′), *n.* **1,** a house or apartment built on a roof; **2,** a shed or roof sloping from a wall or building; **3,** a sloping covering like an awning, canopy, etc.

pe-nult (pē′nult; pi-nult′), *n.* the second-last syllable of a word.

pen-um-bra (pi-num′bra), *n.* the partial, as distinct from the total, shadow, esp. that which surrounds the total shadow of the moon, or of the earth, during an eclipse.

pen-u-ry (pen′ū-ri), *n.* want of the necessities of life; extreme poverty. *adj.* **pe-nu′ri-ous.**

pe-on (pē′on), *n.* in Spanish America and in the southern U.S., a labourer, esp. one forced to work to pay a debt.

pe-o-ny (pē′o-ni), *n.* [*pl.* peonies], a garden plant that springs up in a cluster of red shoots; also, one of its large, usually double, red, pink, or white flowers.

peo-ple (pē′pl), *n.* **1,** a body of persons united into a community, race, tribe, nation, etc.; inhabitants; as, the American *people;* **2,** men, women, and children; as, only ten *people* were present; **3,** the persons of a particular place or group; as, country *people,* **4,** the lower classes; the masses; as, the *people* revolted against the nobles; **5,** relatives; as, my own *people;*—*v.t.* [peo-pled, peo-pling], to fill with inhabitants; as, to *people* a country.

pep (pep), *n. Slang,* liveliness; energy; vim;—*v.t.* to stimulate; invigorate; used with *up.*—*adj.* **pep′py.**

pep-per (pep′ėr), *n.* **1,** a hot seasoning made of the ground berries of an East Indian plant; also, the plant which bears these berries; **2,** a plant whose red berries make a similar hot seasoning; **3,** a garden plant, whose hollow red or green fruit is used as a vegetable:—*v.t.* **1,** to season with pepper; **2,** to sprinkle or strew thickly; also, to shower or pelt with small missiles.

pep-per-mint (pep′ėr-mint), *n.* **1,** a strong-smelling plant of the mint family; **2,** an oil prepared from it; **3,** a candy flavoured with this oil.

pep-per-y (pep′ėr-i), *adj.* **1,** containing pepper; **2,** hot-tempered; fiery; spirited.

pep-sin (pep′sin), *n.* **1,** a ferment formed in the gastric juice of animals as a natural aid to digestion; **2,** a preparation from this substance used in medicine.

pep-tic (pep′tik), *adj.* **1,** digestible, or aiding digestion; caused by pepsin, as *peptic* ulcers.

per- (pûr-), *prefix,* meaning *thoroughly* or *completely,* as in **per-fer′vid** (ardent) and **per-vert′** (corrupt).

per (pėr), *prep.* **1,** through; by means of; by; as, *per* bearer; **2,** for or in each; as, two dollars *per* man; 1000 revolutions *per* second.

per-ad-ven-ture (pûr′ad-ven′tūr), *adv. Archaic* perhaps; as, *peradventure* he will come:—*n.* doubt; question.

per-am-bu-late (pėr-am′bū-lāt′), *v.t.* to walk through:—*v.i.* to stroll about. —*n.* **per-am′bu-la′tor** (a baby-carriage) —*n.* **per-am′bu-la′tion.**

per an-num (an′um), *Latin,* by the year; yearly; as, 5% *per annum.*

per-cale (pėr-kāl′), *n.* a closely woven cotton fabric with a linen finish and often, a printed pattern.

per-ceive (pėr-sēv'), v.t. [perceived, perceiv-ing], **1,** to become aware of through the senses; see, hear, feel, taste, or smell; **2,** to understand; comprehend.

per cent or **per-cent** (pėr-sent'), in or to every hundred; as, six *per cent* of a dollar is six cents; five *per cent* of 200 is ten.

per-cent-age (pėr-sen'tij), *n.* a certain part or number in each hundred; loosely, any part or proportion of a whole.

per-cep-ti-ble (pėr-sep'ti-bl), *adj.* capable of being known through the senses.—*adv.* **per-cep'ti-bly.**—*n.* **per-cep'ti-bil'i-ty.**

per-cep-tion (pėr-sep'shun), *n.* **1,** power or ability to become aware of something through the senses; **2,** a mental impression; also, understanding—*adj.* **per-cep'tive.**

¹perch (pûrch), *n.* **1,** a spiny-finned fresh-water fish of which the yellow perch is the commonest variety; **2,** any of various spiny-finned, salt-water fishes, as the sea perch or cunner, and the white perch.

²perch (pûrch), *n.* **1,** a rod or pole on which birds sit or roost; **2,** any high seat; **3,** a measure of length equal to 5½ yards; a rod; also, a surface measure equal to 30¼ square yards; a square rod:—*v.i.* to sit on a high seat; roost.

per-chance (pėr-chàns'), *adv. Archaic,* perhaps; maybe.

per-cip-i-ent (pėr-sip'i-ent), *adj.* seeing or perceiving keenly or readily.—*n.* **per-cip'i-ence.**

per-co-late (pûr'kō-lāt'), v.i. [percolat-ed, percolat-ing], to pass, as a liquid, through very small spaces; to filter; as, water *percolates* through sand:—*v.t.* **1,** to cause to pass through very small spaces; to filter; **2,** to pass boiling water through, in order to extract a flavour; as, to *percolate* coffee.

per-co-la-tor (pûr'kō-lā'tėr), *n.* anything that filters; esp. a coffee-pot in which boiling water filters through ground coffee.

per-cus-sion (pėr-kush'un), *n.* **1,** a violent crashing together of two bodies; **2,** the striking of sound waves against the eardrum.

per-di-tion (pėr-dish'un), *n.* **1,** ruin; esp., loss of all happiness after death; **2,** hell; the place of lasting torment.

per-emp-to-ry (per'emp-tėr-i, pėr-emp'to-ri; *adj.* positive; final; allow-ing no discussion; as, a *peremptory* command.—*adv.* **per-emp'to-ri-ly.**

per-en-ni-al (pėr-en'i-al),*adj.* **1,** lasting throughout the year, as, *perennial* summer; **2,** living more than one year; living on from year to year; as, *perennial* flowers; **3,** enduring; as, *perennial* youth:—*n.* a plant that lives more than one year.

per-fect (pûr'fekt), *adj.* **1,** complete; finished; whole; **2,** without defect or blemish; as, a *perfect* apple; a *perfect* diamond; **3,** lacking nothing; exact; as, a *perfect* likeness; **4,** of the highest type of excellence; as, a *perfect* answer; **5,** very skilled or accomplished; as, a *perfect* defence; **6,** *Colloq.* utter; entire; as, a *perfect* stranger:—**perfect tense,** in *grammar,* any of three tenses of the verb, called more specifically *present perfect, past perfect,* and *future perfect,* which indicate action that has taken place before the time of the present, the past, or the future; as, I *have seen,* I *had seen,* I *shall have seen;* esp. the present perfect:—*n.* in *grammar,* the present perfect tense:—*v.t.* (pėr-fekt'; pûr'fekt), **1,** to complete or finish; as, to *perfect* an invention; **2,** to bring to final excellence; as, to *perfect* one's speaking ability.

per-fec-tion (pėr-fek'shun), *n.* **1,** completion; as, the *perfection* of the plan was left to the captain; **2,** completeness; as, to bring a plan to *perfection;* **3,** that which is faultless; also, highest excellence or skill; as, the *perfection* of the boy's playing amazed the musician.—*n.* **per-fec'tion-ist.**

per-fect-ly (pûr'fekt-li), *adv.* in a per-fect manner; exactly; completely.

per-fid-i-ous (pėr-fid'i-us), *adj.* treach-erous; faithless; disloyal; as, a *perfidious* friend.—*adv.* **per-fid'i-ous-ly.**—*n.* **per'fi-dy.**

per-fo-rate (pûr'fo-rāt'), v.t. [perforat-ed, perforat-ing], to pierce; make a hole or a series of holes in; as, to *perforate* cheques for purposes of cancellation.—*n.* **per'fo-ra'-tion.**

per-force (pėr-fōrs'), *adv.* of necessity.

per-form (pėr-fôrm'), v.t. **1,** to do; carry out; execute; as, to *perform* a task; **2,** to discharge; fulfil; as, to *perform* a duty; **3,** to represent; render; portray; as, to *perform* a part in a play:—*v.i.* **1,** to act a part; as, to *perform* on the stage; **2,** to exhibit skill in public; as, to *perform* on the piano.—*n.* **per-form'er.**

per-form-ance (pėr-fôr'mans), *n.* **1,**

the carrying out of something; completion; as, the *performance* of a duty; **2,** a thing done; deed; feat; **3,** a public exhibition, esp. on the stage.

per-fume (pėr-fūm′), *v.t.* [perfumed, perfum-ing], to fill with a pleasant odour; scent:—*n.* [pûr′fūm; pėr-fūm′] **1,** a pleasing scent; a fragrance; **2,** a fluid mixture esp. prepared to give out a pleasing odour.—*n.* **per-fum′er.**

per-fum-er-y (pėr-fūm′ėr-i), *n.* [*pl.* perfumeries], **1,** a perfume or perfumes in general; **2,** the place where perfumes are made or sold.

per-func-to-ry (pėr-fungk′to-ri), *adj.* done half-heartedly, carelessly, or as if to get rid of a duty; as, a *perfunctory* inspection.—*adv.* **per-func′to-ri-ly.**

per-haps (pėr-haps′), *adv.* possibly; maybe; it may be.

per-i- (per′i-), *Greek prefix* meaning (1) around, as in **per′i-pa-tet′ic** (walking around or about); **pe-riph′er-y** (perimeter or outside), (2) *near*, as in **per′i-gree′** (the point in the moon's orbit where it is nearest the earth); **per′i-he′li-on** (the point in a planet's or comet's orbit where it is nearest the sun).

per-i-anth (per′i-anth′), *n.* the sepals and petals of a flower considered together.

per-il (per′il), *n.* exposure to injury; danger; risk:—*v.t.* [perilled, peril-ling], to expose to danger or risk.—*adj.* **per′il-ous.**

per-im-e-ter (pe-rim′e-tėr), *n.* the outer boundary or circumference of an area; as, the *perimeter* of a field.

pe-ri-od (pē′ri-ud), *n.* **1,** a definite portion of time, the beginning and end of which are fixed; **2,** any space of time as, a *period* of rainy weather; also, a number of years looked on as an era; as, the World War *period;* **3,** a full pause at the end of a complete sentence; **4,** a dot [.] used as a mark of punctuation at the end of a complete declarative sentence, or after an abbreviation; **5,** a complete sentence, esp. a complex one.

pe-ri-od-ic (pē′ri-od′ik), *adj.* **1,** pertaining to a definite period of time; **2,** occurring at intervals; as, *periodic* fever; **3,** designating a kind of sentence so framed that the thought is not complete until the end.

pe-ri-od-i-cal (pē′ri-od′i-kal), *adj.* **1,** ·pertaining to a definite period of time; **2,** occurring at intervals; **3,** published at regular intervals:—*n.* a periodical magazine.—*adv.* **pe′ri-od′i-cal-ly.**

per-i-scope (per′i-skōp′), *n.* an upright tube with lenses and mirrors so arranged that a person below a certain level, as below ground or sea level, can view objects on or above that level.

per-ish (per′ish), *v.i.* **1,** to lose life; decay or die; **2,** to be destroyed or come to nothing as, empires *perish.*

per-ish-a-ble (per′ish-a-bl), *adj.* liable to decay; easily spoiled; as, *perishable* food.

per-i-to-ne-um (per′i-to-nē′um), *n.* [*pl.* peritonea (per′i-tō-nē′a)], the thin membrane which lines the abdomen and covers the organs in it.—*adj.* **per′i-to-ne′al.**

per-i-to-ni-tis (per′i-tō-nī′tis), *n.* acute inflammation of the peritoneum, or lining membrane of the abdomen.

per-i-win-kle (per′i-wing′kl), *n.* a creeping evergreen plant, esp. the common myrtle, which has shiny leaves, and blue or white flowers.

per-jure (pûr′jėr), *v.t.* [perjured, perjuring], to make (oneself) guilty of swearing falsely, or breaking a vow; as, to *perjure* oneself.—*n.* **per′jur-er.**

per-ju-ry (pûr′jėr-i), *n.* [*pl.* perjuries], **1,** the wilful breaking of an oath or solemn promise; **2,** wilful giving, under oath, of false testimony, usually in a court of law.

perk (pûrk), *v.t.* **1,** to lift quickly; as the little bird *perked* up its head; **2,** to make (oneself) trim or neat:—*v.i.* **1** to hold up the head saucily; **2,** to become brisk or jaunty.

perk-y (pûr′ki), *adj.* [perk-i-er, perk-i est], pert; lively; jaunty.

per-ma-nent (pûr′ma-nent), *adj.* lasting; durable; continuing in the same state; as, *permanent* improvements to real estate.—*adv.* **per′ma-nent-ly.**—*n.* **per′ma-nence.**

per-man-ga-nate (pėr-mang′ga-nāt′) *n.* a dark purple crystalline salt, *potas sium permanganate*, used in bleaching and as an antiseptic.

per-me-ate (pûr′mē-āt′), *v.t.* [permeated, permeat-ing], **1,** to pass through the pores or crevices of; as, water *per meates* sand; **2,** spread itself through pervade; as, gas *permeates* a room.—*n.* **per′me-a′tion.**—*adj.* **per′me-a-ble.**

per-mis-si-ble (pėr-mis′i-bl), *adj.* tolerable; allowable; as, *permissible* conduct.

per-mis-sion (pėr-mish′un), *n.* **1,** the act of allowing; **2,** consent; leave as, he asked *permission* to go early

per-mit (pėr-mit′), *v.t.* [permit-ted

permit-ting], **1,** to allow by not trying to prevent; tolerate; as, swimming is *permitted* in the creek; **2,** to give consent to; as, to *permit* a marriage:—*v.i.* to give consent; allow; as, if the weather *permits,* I shall go:—*n.* (pûr′-mit), a written licence to do something, as to drive an automobile.

per-mu-ta-tion (pûr′mū-tā′shun), *n.* any of the ways of arranging a number of objects, letters, etc.; thus, the possible *permutations* of *a, b, c,* are *abc, acb, bac, bca, cab, cba.*

per-ni-cious (pėr-nish′us), *adj.* highly injurious; destructive; as, a *pernicious* habit.

per-nick-et-y (pėr-nik′et-i), *adj. Colloq.* fussy; overprecise; finical; as, the actor was *pernickety* about his makeup.

per-o-ra-tion (per′o-rā′shun), *n.* the summing up or conclusion of a speech, often emphatic, eloquent, etc.

per-ox-ide (pėr-ok′sīd), *n.* a compound which contains a large proportion of oxygen; as, *peroxide* of hydrogen. Also spelled **per-ox′id.**

per-pen-dic-u-lar (pûr′pen-dik′ū-lėr) *adj.* **1,** at right angles to a given line or surface; **2,** perfectly upright; also, steep; as, a *perpendicular* hill:—*n.* **1,** a line or plane at right angles with another; **2,** a vertical line or direction.—*adv.* **per′pendic′-u-lar-ly.**

A

C —— D

B

PERPENDICU-
LAR
AB is perpendicular to CD.

per-pe-trate (pûr′pi-trāt), *v.t.* [perpetrat-ed, perpetrat-ing], to do; perform: usually in a bad sense; as, to *perpetrate* a crime.—*n.* **per′pe-tra′tion.** —*n.* **per′pe-tra′tor.**

per-pe-tu-al (pėr-pet′ū-al), *adj.* never ceasing; continuous; endless; everlasting.—*adv.* **per-pet′u-al-ly.**

per-pet-u-ate (pėr-pet′ū-āt), *v.t.* [perpetuat-ed, perpetuat-ing], to make everlasting; to continue indefinitely. —*n.* **per-pet′-u-a′tion.**—*n.* **per-pet′u-a′tor.**—*n.* **per′pe-tu′i-ty** (pûr′pi-tū′i-ti).

per-plex (pėr-pleks′), *v.t.* to fill with uncertainty or doubt; to puzzle; distract.—*adj.* **per-plexed′.**—*n.* **per-plex′i-ty.**

per-qui-site (pûr′kwi-zit), *n.* a gain or profit attaching to an office, above the usual wage or salary, as a tip or gratuity.

per-se-cute (pûr′si-kūt), *v.t.* [persecut-ed, persecut-ing], **1,** to keep on inflicting injury upon; to oppress,

esp. for religious reasons; **2,** to harass or treat cruelly; annoy; vex:—*n.* **per′se-cu′tor.**

per-se-cu-tion (pûr′si-kū′shun), *n.* **1,** the continued infliction of unjust pain or punishment; as, religious *persecution;* **2,** the state of being unjustly treated; repeated injury of any kind.

per-se-ver-ance (pûr′si-vēr′ans), *n.* refusal to give up; continued effort, esp. under a handicap; persistence.

per-se-vere (pûr′si-vēr′), *v.i.* [persevered, persever-ing], to persist steadfastly in a purpose or undertaking.— *adj.* **per′se-ver′ing.**—*adv.* **per′se-ver′-ing-ly.**

per-si-flage (pûr′si-flȧzh′), *n.* light, frivolous talk; banter.

per-sim-mon (pėr-sim′un), *n.* **1,** a pulpy, orange-red fruit that is good to eat only when thoroughly ripened by frost; **2,** the tree bearing this fruit.

per-sist (pėr-sist′; pėr-zist′), *v.i.* **1,** to continue steadily or obstinately in saying or doing something; **2,** to continue to last or endure; as, his cold *persists.*

per-sist-ence (pėr-sis′tens; pėr-zis′-tens), *n.* **1,** continuous effort, esp. in spite of obstacles or opposition; **2,** lasting quality; as, the *persistence* of an illness. Also, **per-sist′en-cy.**

per-sist-ent (pėr-sis′tent; pėr-zis′-tent), *adj.* **1,** persisting; persevering; as a *persistent* worker; **2,** continuing for a long time; enduring; lasting; as, a *persistent* rain.—*adv.* **per-sist′ent-ly.**

per-son (pûr′sn), *n.* **1,** a human being as distinguished from a thing or an animal; an individual; **2,** the body of a human being; bodily appearance; **3,** in *grammar,* one of the three classes of personal pronouns, the *first person* referring to the person speaking, the *second person* to the person spoken to, the *third person* to the person or thing spoken of; also, any of the corresponding distinctions in verbs.—**per′-son-a-ble.**

per-son-age (pûr′sun-ij), *n.* **1,** a person; esp. a man or woman of distinction; **2,** a character in a play, novel, etc.

per-son-al (pûr′sun-al), *adj.* **1,** relating to, or peculiar to, a person and his private affairs; **2,** pertaining to the outward appearance or looks; as, *personal* beauty; **3,** given, performed, etc., in person, or by oneself; as, a *personal* greeting; **4,** relating to a certain person; as *personal* remarks; **5,** movable; as, *personal* property; **6,** in *grammar,* expressing person; as, *personal* endings in verbs; "I," "you," "he," "she," "it," etc., are *personal* pronouns.

per-son-al-i-ty (pûr'su-nal'i-ti), *n.* [*pl.* personalities], **1,** the quality or fact of being a person and not a thing; **2,** that which makes one human being different from another; individuality; **3,** outstanding qualities of character; also, a person who has such qualities; **4,** an offensive remark made about a person.

per-son-al-ly (pûr'sun-al-i), *adv.* **1,** in person; as, to attend to business *personally;* **2,** as a person; as, *personally,* he is charming; **3,** as far as I am concerned; as, *personally,* I should prefer to stay home.

per-son-i-fi-ca-tion (pêr-son'i-fi-kā'shun), *n.* **1,** a figure of speech by which things, qualities, or abstract ideas have a personal nature given to them; as, "the cruel waves" is a *personification* of "waves"; "Giant Despair" is a *personification* of the quality "despair"; Peter Pan is a *personification* of the abstract idea of "childhood"; **2,** a striking example of some quality; as, she is the *personification* of neatness.

per-son-i-fy (pêr-son'i-fi'), *v.t.* [personified, personify-ing], **1,** to regard or represent (a thing, quality, or idea) as a person; **2,** to be a striking example of; as, Caesar *personifies* power.

per-son-nel (pûr'so-nel'), *n.* all the people employed in any business, public service, factory, office, etc.

per-spec-tive (pêr-spek'tiv), *n.* **1,** the art of drawing an object on a flat surface in such a way as to give one the impression he is looking at the object itself; **2,** a view that includes things in the distance as well as things near by; hence, the ability to see things in their right relation to each other; as, a true *perspective* of historical events; **3,** the right relationship of things to each other; as, to look at the causes of the World War in *perspective*.

per-spi-ca-cious (pûr'spi-kā'shus), *adj.* mentally keen; penetrating; discerning.—*n.* **per'spi-cac'i-ty.**

per-spi-cu-i-ty (pûr'spi-kū'i-ti), *n.* clearness, as of thought or expression.—*adj.* **per-spic'u-ous.**

per-spi-ra-tion (pûr'spi-rā'shun), *n.* the act of secreting sweat; also, the sweat secreted.

per-spire (pêr-spīr'), *v.t.* and *v.i.* [perspired, perspir-ing], to sweat.

per-suade (pêr-swād'), *v.t.* [persuad-ed, persuad-ing], to win over to a point of

view; to convince by argument, advice, entreaty, etc.; as, he *persuaded* his mother to let him go.

per-sua-sion (pêr-swā'zhun), *n.* **1,** the act of persuading; the power to persuade, or the state of being persuaded by argument or entreaty; **2,** a conviction; belief, generally religious; as, of the Baptist *persuasion*.

per-sua-sive (pêr-swā'siv), *adj.* having power to convince or influence; as, a *persuasive* argument.—*adv.* **per-sua'sive-ly.**

pert (pûrt), saucy; bold; as, a *pert* answer.—*adv.* **pert'ly.**

per-tain (pêr-tān'), *v.i.* to belong; also, to relate or refer to something; as, the —telegram *pertains* to business.

per-ti-na-cious (pûr'ti-nā'shus), *adj.* obstinate; holding stubbornly to a purpose, belief, or course of action.—*n.* **per'ti-nac'i-ty.**

per-ti-nent (pûr'ti-nent), *adj.* fitting or appropriate; to the point; as, a *pertinent* remark.—*adv.* **per'ti-nent-ly.** —*n.* **per'ti-nence;**—*n.* **per'ti-nen-cy.**

per-turb (pêr-tûrb'), *v.t.* to agitate; disturb greatly, esp. in mind.—*n.* **per' tur-ba'tion** (pûr'têr-bā'shun).

pe-ruse (pi-rōōz'), *v.t.* [perused, perus-ing], to read; esp. to read with care and attention.—*n.* **pe-rus'al.**

per-vade (pêr-vād'), *v.t.* [pervad-ed, pervad-ing], to pass or spread through every part of; as, a perfume *pervades* the air.—*adj.* **per-va'sive.**

per-verse (pêr-vûrs'), *adj.* **1,** wilfully wrong; set against doing right; **2,** obstinate or stubborn, usually in a wrong action; **3,** hence, petulant; ill-tempered; as, a *perverse* child.—*adv* **per-verse'ly.**—*n.* **per-verse'ness.**

per-ver-sion (pêr-vûr'shun; pêr-vûr'zhun), *n.* **1,** a turning from the true or proper use, purpose, or meaning; **2,** a wrong form of something, as of the spelling of a word.

per-ver-si-ty (pêr-vûr'si-ti), *n.* [*pl.* perversities], **1,** wilful refusal to do right; **2,** stubbornness; contrariness.

per-vert (pêr-vûrt'), *v.t.* **1,** to turn from the true end or proper purpose; misuse; **2,** to give a wrong meaning to purposely; as, to *pervert* what someone has said:—*n.* (pûr'vûrt), one who has turned from right to wrong.—*adj.* **per-vert'ed.**

pes-ky (pes'ki), *adj. Colloq.* troublesome; annoying; as, *pesky* weather.

pe-so (pā'sō), *n.* [*pl.* -sos (-sōz; sōs)], *n.* the dollar of several Latin American countries, as of Mexico (worth about 8 cents: 1960).

pes-si-mism (pes'i-mizm), *n.* 1, the belief that there is more evil in the world than good; 2, a habit of looking on the dark side of life: opposite of *optimism.—n.* **pes'si-mist.—***adj.* **pes'si-mis'tic.**

pest (pest), *n.* 1, a widespread, fatal, contagious disease, as smallpox; a plague or pestilence; 2, anything or anyone very mischievous or annoying.

pes-ter (pes'tèr), *v.t.* to vex; . bother, esp. with petty irritations; as, he *pestered* his sister with questions.—*adj.* **pes-tif'er-ous.**

pes-ti-lence (pes'ti-lens), *n.* a widespread, infectious, fatal disease.—*adj.* **pes'ti-len'tial.**

pes-ti-lent (pes'ti-lent), *adj.* 1, poisonous; deadly; 2, bad for health, morals, or society; 3, making mischief; vexatious.

pes-tle (pes'l; pes'tl), *n.* a tool for pounding substances to a powder, used chiefly by druggists:—*v.t.* and *v.i.* [pes-tled, pestling], to pound with a pestle.

MORTAR AND PESTLE

¹pet (pet), *n.* 1, a tame animal, kept, treated kindly, and played with; 2, a person treated with special affection; a favourite:—*adj.* favourite; accustomed to fondling and indulgence:—*v.t.* [pet-ted, pet-ting], to fondle and indulge.

²pet (pet), *n.* a sudden fit of peevishness or ill humour.

pet-al (pet'al), *n.* one of the parts, usually bright-coloured, of the flower of a plant.—*adj.* **pet'alled** or **pet'aled.**

pet-i-ole (pet'i-ōl'), *n.* the stem or stalk of a leaf.

pet-it (pet'i), *adj.* in *law*, minor; as, a *petit* jury.

pe-tite (pe-tēt'), *adj.* small and trim in figure; as, Joan is *petite*.

pe-ti-tion (pe-tish'un), *n.* 1, an earnest request or prayer; 2, a formal request from an inferior to a superior; 3, a document containing a request supported by many signatures; as, a *petition* to the King:—*v.t.* 1, to present a formal request to; 2, to solicit or ask for earnestly.—*n.* **pe-ti'tion-er.**

Pe-trar-chan sonnet (pi-trär'kan), the Italian sonnet, with 8 lines or an octet rhymed *abba*, *abba*, and 6 lines or a sestet, rhymed variously (often *cde*, *cde*): the theme is stated in the octet and amplified in the sestet.

pet-rel (pet'rel), *n.* a sea-bird which flies far from the land.

pet-ri-fy (pet'ri-fī'), *v.t.* [petrified, petrify-ing], 1, to change into stone; 2, to make motionless with amazement or fear; as, the approach of danger *petrified* him:—*v.i.* to become stone or of a stony hardness.—*n.* **pet'ri-fac'-tion** (-fak'shun).

pet-ro- (pet'rō-), *prefix* meaning *rock*, as in **pe-trog'ra-phy** (the study of rocks) and **pet'ro-la'tum** (a basis for ointments).

pet-rol (pet'rol; pet'rul), *n.* gasoline.

pe-tro-le-um (pi-trō'li-um), *n.* a dark, yellowish-brown liquid that is obtained from the earth by means of wells, and is the source of gasoline, kerosene, etc.

pet-ti-coat (pet'i-kōt'), *n.* a loose underskirt worn by women and girls.

pet-ti-fog-ging (pet'i-fog'ing), *adj.* mean; dishonest in petty matters; as, a *pettifogging* lawyer, transaction, etc.

pet-tish (pet'ish), *adj.* cross; petulant.

pet-ty (pet'i), *adj.* [pet-ti-er, pet-ti-est], 1, trifling; unimportant; as, a *petty* quarrel; 2, small-minded; occupied with trivial things; as, *petty* people.—*n.* **pet'ti-ness.**

pet-u-lant (pet'ū-lant), *adj.* fretful; cross; impatient; pettish; as, a *petulant* answer.—*adv.* **pet'u-lant-ly.** —*n.* **pet'u-lance.**

pe-tu-ni-a (pi-tū'ni-a), *n.* a common garden plant with funnel-shaped flowers, usually white, pink, or purple.

pew (pū), *n.* one of the long, fixed benches in a church.

pe-wee (pē'wē), *n.* 1, a small American fly-catcher, so named from its note: also called *wood-pewee;* 2, the phoebe.

pew-ter (pū'tèr), *n.* 1, a lustrous metal, silvery grey in colour, made of tin and lead, or of tin and some other metal, as copper; 2, dishes or utensils made of this metal:—*adj.* made of pewter; as, a *pewter* tray.

phae-ton (fā'tn), *n.* 1, a light, open four-wheeled carriage; 2, an open automobile with a top that folds back.

phag-o-cyte (fag'o-sīt'), *n.* a white blood corpuscle that absorbs and destroys disease germs.

phal-anx (fal'angks; fā'langks), *n.* 1, among the ancient Greeks, a company of heavy-armed soldiers drawn up in a close rank; 2, hence, any compact body of persons united for some purpose; 3, [*pl.* phalanges (fa-lan'jēz)], a bone of the fingers or toes.

all (ôl), ôr; up, mūte, cûr, cōol, book; oil, out; th, thin; *th*, the.

phan-tasm (fan'tazm), *n.* **1,** an imaginary vision, as of a ghost or spectre; **2,** a supposed appearance of an absent person.

phan-ta-sy (fan'ta-si; fan'ta-zi), *n.* Same as **fantasy.**

phan-tom (fan'tum), *n.* an apparition; spirit; ghost; phantasm:—*adj.* having no substance but said to have been seen; as, a *phantom* ship.

phar-ma-cy (fär'ma-si), *n.* [*pl.* pharmacies], **1,** the art of preparing medicines; **2,** an apothecary's shop; a drugstore.—*adj.* **phar'ma-ceu'ti-cal** (as a *pharmaceutical* chemist).—*n.* **phar'-ma-col'o-gy** (study of drugs).—*n.* **phar'-ma-co-poe'ia** (a list, or stock, of drugs).—*n.* **phar'ma-cist.**

phar-ynx (far'ingks), *n.* [*pl.* pharynges (fa-rin'jēz) or pharynxes (far'ingk-sez)] the part of the alimentary canal between the cavity of the mouth and the oesophagus.—*adj.* **pha-ryn'ge-al** (fa-rin'ji-al; far'in-jē'al).—*n.* **phar'yn-gi'tis** (far'in-jī'tis); sore throat.

phase (fāz), *n.* **1,** in *astronomy*, a particular appearance presented by the moon or a planet, as full moon, new moon, etc.; **2,** one stage or period in the development of a thing; **3,** one side of a subject; as, a *phase* of history.

pheas-ant (fez'ant), *n.* **1,** a large, Old World game-bird with brilliant feathers; **2,** any of various birds that look like the pheasant, as the ruffed grouse.

phe-no-bar-bi-tal (fē'nō-bär'bi-tôl'), *n.* a sleep-inducing drug and sedative.

phe-nol (fē'nôl), *n.* an acid (carbolic) derived from benzene, and used as an antiseptic or a disinfectant.

phe-nom-e-non (fi-nom'i-non; fi-nom'i-nun), *n.* [*pl.* phenomena (fi-nom'-i-na)], **1,** any natural fact or event that can be seen; **2,** something uncommon, as snow in summer.—*adj.* **phe-nom'e-nal.**

phew (fū), *interj.* an exclamation of disgust, discomfort, etc.

phi-al (fī'al), *n.* a small glass bottle.

phil-an-throp-ic (fil'an-throp'ik) or **phil-an-throp-i-cal** (-throp'i-kal), *adj.* loving mankind; benevolent.

phi-lan-thro-pist (fi-lan'thro-pist), *n.* one who loves and seeks to benefit mankind, esp. one who uses his wealth for this.—*n.* **phi-lan'thro-py.**

phi-lat-e-ly (fi-lat'e-li), *n.* the collecting and study of postage stamps.—*n.* **phi-lat'e-list.**

phil-har-mon-ic (fil'här-mon'ik), *adj.* fond of music, as, a *philharmonic* concert, orchestra, society, etc.

phi-lip-pic (fi-lip'ik), *n.* a bitter verbal attack; as, Churchill's *philippic* against Hitler.

philo (fil'ō-), *prefix* meaning *loving* or *liking*, as in **phi-lan'der-er** (a man of many flirtations) and **phi-lol'o-gy** (the love, or study, of literature).

phi-los-o-pher (fi-los'o-fẻr), *n.* **1,** a student of philosophy; **2,** one who keeps calm and courageous in misfortune.

phi-los-o-phy (fi-los'o-fi), *n.* [*pl.* philosophies], **1,** the study of the principles that cause, control, or explain facts and events; **2,** the calmness of temper characteristic of a philosopher; resignation; **3,** a particular system of beliefs or views, as regarding God, existence, etc.—*adj.* **phil'o-soph'i-cal** (fil'o-sof'i-kal); **phil'o-soph'ic.**

phle-bi-tis (fli-bī'tis), *n.* inflammation of a vein.

phlegm (flem), *n.* a thick mucus, or sputum, from throat or lungs, as during a cold; **2,** apathy, sluggishness; **3,** self-possession; coolness.

phleg-matic (fleg-mat'ik) or **phleg-mat-i-cal** (fleg-mat'-i-kal), *adj.* sluggish; not easily excited; cool; as, a *phlegmatic* person.—*adv.* **phleg-mat'i-cal-ly.**

phlo-ëm (flō'em), *n.* in *botany*, the bast or softer cell tissue that carries food, as distinct from the xylem or woody tissue that gives stiffness (to the stems of higher plants).

phlox (floks), *n.* a plant that bears showy clusters of white, reddish, or purplish flowers.

pho-bi-a (fō'bi-a), *n.* a morbid fear or dread of a particular situation or thing.

phoe-be (fē'bi), *n.* any of several small American fly-catching birds, esp. a species with dark-brown upper parts and white or yellowish-white under parts, and a plaintive note: also called *pewee.*

phoe-nix (fē'niks), a mythical bird, symbol of immortality, said to live 500 or 600 years in the Arabian desert, burn itself to ashes on a funeral pyre, and rise to a new life of youth and beauty.

¹phone (fōn), *n.* any simple speech sound, as a vowel or consonant.—*adj.* **pho-net'ic.**—*n.* **pho-net'ics** (the science of producing sounds and using symbols to denote them).—*adj.* **phon'ic.**—*n.* **phon'ics** (the use of phonetics in teaching beginners to read).

²phone (fōn), *n. Colloq.*, a telephone:—*v.t.* and *v.i.* [phoned, phon-ing], *Colloq.* to telephone.

---

cat, āge, fär, câre, ȧsk; ten, ēve, latėr; (i) pity, rely, senate; īce; top; nō

pho-no- (fō′nō-), a *prefix* meaning *sound*, as in **pho′no-gram′** (a sound recorder) and **pho-nol′o-gy** (the science of sounds).

pho-no-graph (fō′nō-gràf′), *n.* an instrument to record and reproduce accurately speech, music, or other sounds.—*adj.* **pho′no-graph′ic.**

pho-ny (fō′ni), *adj. Slang,* sham; fake; bogus; as, *phony* money.

phos-gene (fos′jēn), *n.* a colourless poison gas with odour of musty hay, used in making dyes and in warfare.

phos-phate (fos′fāt), *n.* **1,** a salt of phosphoric acid; as *calcium phosphate,* used as a fertilizer, in medicine, etc.; **2,** a soda water drink and fruit syrup flavoured with a little phosphoric acid (H_3PO_4).

phos-pho-res-cence (fos′fo-res′ens), *n.* the giving of light without heat by certain bodies, such as phosphorus and decaying wood, and by some insects and sea animals.—*adj.* **phos′pho-res′cent.**

phos-pho-rus (fos′fo-rus), *n.* a yellowish-white, waxy, poisonous substance that has an unpleasant odour and easily bursts into flame: formerly used in making matches.—*adj.* **phos′-pho-rous** (fos′fo-rus; fos-for′us).—*adj.* **phos-phor′ic.**

pho-to (fō′tō), *n. Colloq.* a photograph.

pho-to-en-gra-ving (fō′tō-en-grā′-ving), *n.* **1,** a process by which photographs are reproduced in relief on metal plates for printing; **2,** a picture so printed.

pho-to-gen-ic (fō′tō-jen′ik), *adj.* **1,** photographing well (used esp. of a person artistically a good subject); **2,** phosphorescent.

pho-to-graph (fō′tō-gràf), *n.* a picture produced by exposing to the light a plate or film made sensitive to light by being coated with certain chemicals:—*v.t.* to take a picture of, by exposing a sensitized plate or film to the action of light.—*n.* **pho-tog′ra-pher** (fō-tog′ra-fèr —*adj.* **pho′to-graph′ic.**

pho-tog-ra-phy (fō-tog′ra-fi), *n.* the art or process of making pictures by the action of light on a material, as paper, glass, or celluloid, that has been coated with a film of chemicals to make it sensitive to light.

pho-to-gra-vure (fō′tō-gra-vūr′), *n.* the reproducing of a photographic negative by cutting into the surface of a metal plate, which transfers inked impressions to paper.

pho-ton (fō′ton), *n.* in *physics,* the smallest unit of light energy, called a quantum; a corpuscle of light.

pho-to-play (fō′tō-plā′), *n.* a motion-picture play.

pho-to-stat (fō′tō-stat′), *n.* **1,** a copy of a document, map, page, etc. made by photographing it directly as a positive on prepared, or sensitized paper; **2,** the process itself (a trade-name).

pho-to-syn-the-sis (fō′tō-sin′the-sis), *n.* in living plants, the forming of carbon-hydrogen compounds from water and carbon dioxide by the action of sunlight on the green colouring matter (chlorophyll).

phrase (frāz), *n.* **1,** in *grammar,* a group of related words not containing a subject and a predicate; as, "to the city" is a *phrase;* **2,** any brief, pithy expression containing a single idea; **3,** a characteristic style or manner of talking; as, speaking in the simple *phrase* of the day:—*v.t.* [phrased, phras-ing], to put into words, esp. into suitable words; as, he *phrased* his apology carefully.—*adj.* **phras′al.**

phra-se-ol-o-gy (frā′zi-ol′o-ji), *n.* [*pl.* phraseologies], selection and arrangement of words; manner of expression; as, legal *phraseology* contains many repetitions.

phre-nol-o-gy (fre-nol′o-ji), *n.* the study of the shape of the skull as an index of mental faculties.

phy-lum (fī′lum), *n.* in *biology,* a basic or primary division of the animal or vegetable kingdom, as the vertebrates, molluscs, crustaceans, etc.

phys-ic (fiz′ik), *n.* **1,** *Archaic,* the science of medicine, or the art of healing; **2,** medicine in general; **3,** specifically, a medicine for cleansing the bowels; a cathartic:—*v.t.* [physicked, physick-ing], to treat with medicine, esp. a cathartic.

phys-i-cal (fiz′i-k'l), *adj.* **1,** relating to natural science, or to the natural features and changes in the universe; as, *physical* geography; **2,** pertaining to the world around us, or to the material rather than to the mental or spiritual; as, the *physical* world; **3,** pertaining to the science of physics; as, *physical* changes in matter; **4,** pertaining to the body; as *physical* weakness.

phy-si-cian (fi-zish′an), *n.* one skilled in the art of healing and legally qualified to treat disease; a doctor of medicine.

phys-ics (fiz′iks), *n. pl.* used as *sing.* the science which deals with matter and its ability to perform work, including the study of mechanics, heat, light, sound, electricity, etc.

phys-i-og-no-my (fiz′i-og′no-mi), (fiz′i-on′o-mi); *n.* [*pl.* physiognomies], 1, the face; esp. the peculiar form or expression of the face; 2, outward appearance, as of a landscape.

phys-i-og-ra-phy (fiz′i-og′ra-fi), *n.* physical geography; the study of the earth's natural features, as climate, surface, etc.

phys-i-ol-o-gy (fiz′i-ol′o-ji), *n.* [*pl.* physiologies], that branch of biology which deals with the functions of the organs, tissues, cells, etc., in living plants, animals, and human beings.— *adj.* **phys-i-o-log′i-cal.**

phys-i-o-ther-a-py (fiz′i-ō-ther′a-pi) *n.* healing by the use of massage, exercise, light, heat, etc.

phy-sique (fi-zēk′), *n.* the structure and appearance of the body; as, the football player has a powerful *physique.*

¹pi (pī) *n.* in *mathematics*, the Greek letter π, designating the ratio of the circumference of a circle to its diameter, viz.: 22/7 (about 3.1416).

²pi (pī), *n.* 1, a jumble of printing type; hence, any mixture.

pi-a-nis-si-mo (pē′a-nis′i-mō′; pyä-nēs′si-mō′), *adv.* in *music*, very softly.

pi-an-ist (pi-an′ist; pē′a-nist), *n.* a person who plays the piano.

pi-an-o (pi-an′ō; pi-ä′nō), *n.* [*pl.* pianos], a large, modern musical instrument, enclosed in a case, and played from a keyboard. The keyboard, when struck, operates hammers which strike steel wires giving forth musical tones. Pianos are called *grand* (*concert grand*, *baby grand*), *upright*, and *square*, according to the shape of the case. Also, **pi-an′o-forte′.**

pi-az-za (pi-az′a; pi-ad′za), *n.* 1, in Italy, a large, open square surrounded by buildings or columns; 2, in America a porch, usually roofed.

pi-broch (pē′brokh; brok), *n.* wild, warlike music on Scottish bagpipes: sometimes dirgelike.

pi-ca (pī′ka), *n.* a printer's unit of measurement equivalent to ⅙ inch.

pic-a-dor (pik′a-dōr′), *n.* a horseman who opens a bullfight by pricking the bull with a lance.

pic-a-yune (pik′i-yūn′), *adj.* and *n.* anything small or trifling; as, his quibbling was *picayune.*

pic-co-lo (pik′o-lō′), *n.* [*pl.* piccolos],

a small, flute-shaped instrument with very shrill tones an octave higher than the tones of the ordinary flute.

PICCOLO

pick (pik), *n.* 1, a heavy tool for breaking earth or rock; a pickaxe; 2, a pointed instrument used for piercing or pecking; as, an ice-*pick;* 3, the amount of a crop gathered at one time; a picking; 4, choice; as, take your *pick;* 5, the best of anything; as, the *pick* of the lot:—*v.t.* 1, to strike or break open with a sharp instrument, or with the beak; pierce or peck; as, to *pick* a hole; 2, to open by a sharp instrument; as, to *pick* a lock or safe; 3, to lift or raise; as, to *pick* up something fallen; 4, to pluck or gather; as, to *pick* berries; 5, to choose or select; as, to *pick* the best one; 6, hence, to bring about by choice or intention; as, to *pick* a quarrel; 7, to rob; as, to *pick* a pocket; 8, to separate with the fingers; as, to *pick* rags; 9, to clean or clear of something; as, to *pick* a chicken; 10, to pluck the strings of (a musical instrument); as, to *pick* a banjo:—*v.i.* 1, to eat slowly and daintily; 2, to pilfer; as, to *pick* and steal; 3, *Colloq.* to find fault; nag.—*n.* **pick′er.**

pick-a-back (pik′a-bak′), *adv.* on the shoulders or back; as, he carried the boy *pickaback:—pickaback plane,* an airplane carried aloft at take-off on a larger plane, and then released to fly by itself.

pick-a-nin-ny (pik′a-nin′i), *n.* [*pl.* pickaninnies], a coloured baby or child.

pick-axe or **pick-ax** (pik′aks′), *n.* a hand tool for digging, with a wooden handle and a curved or straight iron head pointed at one end or at both ends.

pick-er-el (pik′ér-el), *n.* a kind of freshwater fish of the pike family, used for food; sometimes, the pike.

pick-et (pik′it), *n.* 1, an upright pointed stake, used in making fences for tethering a horse, etc.; 2, in warfare a military guard stationed at a given place to prevent surprise by an enemy; 3, one or more persons appointed by a labour union to watch at a factory, shop, etc., during a strike, to persuade, or otherwise influence, nonunion men not to work there; 4, hence, any person or persons appointed by an organization to watch at a given place for any purpose:—*v.t.* 1, to fence with pointed stakes; as, to *picket* a farm 2, to fasten to a stake; as, to *picket* a horse; **3,** to watch or guard; as, to *picket* a certain position; **4,** to place on guard; as, to *picket* men for duty:—*v.i.* to serve as a picket.

ick-le (pik′l), *n.* **1,** brine, or a mixture of salt and water, used for preserving meat, fish, etc.; also, vinegar, with or without spices, for preserving vegetables, fruit, meat, etc.; **2,** something preserved in pickle; esp. a pickled cucumber; **3,** an embarrassment; difficulty:—*v.t.* [pick-led, pick-ling], to preserve in brine or vinegar.

ick-pock-et (pik′pok′it), *n.* a thief who steals purses or the contents of pockets.

ick-up (pik′up′), *n.* **1,** a small (open) delivery truck; **2,** reception of sound or light, as by radio or television; **3,** *Colloq.* a stimulant (beverage); **4,** the pivot arm with the needle of an electric phonograph.

ic-nic (pik′nik), *n.* a short trip by a pleasure party carrying its own food for an outdoor meal:—*v.i.* [picnicked, picnick-ing], to go on, or hold, an outdoor pleasure party.—*n.* **pic′nick-er.**

ic-to-graph (pik′tō-gràf′), *n.* a picture expressing an idea, as in the picture-writing of primitive peoples; hieroglyph.

ic-tor-i-al (pik-tōr′i-al), *adj.* **1,** pertaining to, shown by, or containing, pictures; as, a *pictorial* magazine; **2,** suggesting a picture or clear mental image; as, *pictorial* description.—*adv.* **ic-tor′i-al-ly.**

ic-ture (pik′tūr; chėr), *n.* **1,** a painting, drawing, or photograph, of a person, object, scene, etc.; **2,** a likeness or image; as, she is the *picture* of her mother; representation; as, he was the *picture* of despair; **3,** a vivid portrayal in words; as, the speaker drew a *picture* of future prosperity; **4,** a mental image; as, my mind carried a *picture* of the beautiful scene; **5, pictures,** *Colloq.* motion pictures:—*v.t.* [pictured, pictur-ing], **1,** to present in a painting, drawing, etc.; as, the artist *pictured* a country scene; **2,** to describe vividly in words; **3,** to form a mental image of; imagine; as, I *pictured* myself in his place.

ic-tur-esque (pik′tūr-esk′), *adj.* **1,** giving a vivid impression, as a picture does; as, a *picturesque* description of one's travels; **2,** suitable to be drawn or painted as an interesting or striking picture; as, *picturesque* mountain scenery.—*adv.* **pic′tur-esque′ly.**—*n.* **ic′tur-esque′ness.**

¹pie (pī), *n.* a prepared dish consisting of meat, fruit, etc., baked between two layers of pastry or on one lower crust.

²pie (pī), *n.* the magpie, a black-and-white member of the crow family.

pie-bald (pī′bôld′), *adj.* having patches of different colours, esp. black and white; as, a *piebald* horse.

piece (pēs), *n.* **1,** a part of anything; a fragment; as, a *piece* of bread; a plot or division; unit; as, a *piece* of land; **2,** a fixed quantity or size in which goods or various articles are made up for sale; as, muslin comes at twelve yards to the *piece;* **3,** a separate instance, example, or performance; as, a bad *piece* of business; **4,** a single object of a group; as, each *piece* in the set; **5,** a single, distinct, literary or artistic composition; as, a *piece* of music; **6,** the amount of work done as a distinct job; as, the work is paid for by the *piece;* **7,** a coin; as, a five-cent *piece;* **8,** a gun; as, a field-*piece;* fowling-*piece;* **9,** one of the counters or men with which chess, draughts, or similar games are played:—*v.t.* [pieced, piecing], **1,** to enlarge or mend by adding material; as, to *piece* a skirt; **2,** to make by joining sections together; as, to *piece* a quilt.

piece-meal (pēs′mēl′), *adv.* in portions or parts; by degrees; gradually; as, the work was done *piecemeal.*

pied (pīd), *adj.* having two or more colours in blotches; piebald; as, a *pied* coat; also, wearing a many-coloured coat; as, "The *Pied* Piper of Hamelin."

pier (pēr), *n.* **1,** a support for an arch, bridge, etc., **2,** a projecting part of a wall, such as a buttress; **3,** a wharf or dock built out over the water, as for a landing-place, pleasure resort, etc.

pierce (pērs), *v.t.* [pierced, pierc-ing], **1,** to puncture or run through; stab; as, the knife *pierced* her hand; **2,** to make a hole in; as, she *pierced* her ears for earrings; **3,** to affect deeply; as, to *pierce* the heart with sorrow; **4,** to force a way through; as, they *pierced* the enemy lines; **5,** to see through or solve, as a mystery:—*v.i.* to enter; penetrate; as, the sun *pierced* through the clouds.

pi-e-ty (pī′e-ti), *n.* [*pl.* pieties], **1,** devotion to religion; **2,** reverence for God; **3,** honour and duty to parents.

pif-fle (pif′l), *n.* and *interj. Colloq.* nonsense; bosh; trifling talk.

pig (pig), *n.* **1,** a hoofed, two-toed animal raised for its meat; a hog, esp.

a young one; **2,** *Colloq.* a greedy or selfish person; **3,** an oblong mass of metal, esp. of iron or lead, formed by being run into moulds when melted:— *v.i.* [pigged, pig-ging], **1,** to give birth to pigs; **2,** to live like pigs.—*n.* **pig′ger-y; pig′pen′; pig′sty′.**

pi-geon (pij′un), *n.* a bird, often domesticated, with stocky body, short legs, long wings, and handsome plumage.

pi-geon-hole (pij′un-hōl′), *n.* **1,** a hole in which pigeons nest; **2,** a small, open, boxlike space in a desk, case, etc., for documents or letters:—*v.t.* [pigeon-holed, pigeonhol-ing], **1,** to place (letters, documents, etc.) in such a boxlike space; to file; **2,** to lay aside and forget; shelve; as, the committee *pigeon-holed* the proposal.

pi-geon—toed (pij′un–tōd′), *adj.* with the toes turned in.

pig-gish (pig′ish), *adj.* like a pig; stubborn, greedy, or dirty.—*adv.* **pig′-gish-ly.**—*n.* **pig′gish-ness.**

pig-gy-back (pig′i-bak′), *adj.* and *adv.* pickaback.

pig-head-ed (pig′hed′id), *adj.* obstinate or stubborn.

pig iron, crude iron, as it comes from the blast-furnace cast into moulds, or pigs.

pig-ment (pig′ment), *n.* **1,** any substance used to give colouring; esp. dry colouring matter which, when mixed with the proper fluid, forms paint; **2,** the colouring matter in persons, animals, or plants.—*n.* **pig′men-ta′tion.**

pig-my (pig′mi), *n.* Same as **pygmy.**

pig-skin (pig′skin′), *n.* **1,** the hide of a pig or the leather made from it; **2,** *Colloq.:* **a,** a football; **b,** a saddle.

pig-tail (pig′tāl′), *n.* **1,** hair twisted into a braid, usually hanging down from the back of the head; **2,** a long twist of tobacco.

pig-weed (pig′wēd′), *n.* a coarse garden weed of the goosefoot family, esp. the *white-* and *red-*root pigweeds, with tassellike reddish heads.

¹pike (pīk), *n.* a weapon formerly carried by foot-soldiers, consisting of a long wooden shaft with a spearhead at one end.

²pike (pīk), *n.*. a large, greedy fresh-water fish with a pointed head, found esp. in the great lakes in North America.

³pike (pīk), *n.* **1,** a road on which a charge is made for driving; a turnpike; **2,** any main road.

pik-er (pīk′ėr), *n. Slang,* **1,** an over cautious gambler; **2,** *Slang,* one who does things in a cheap or small way; a quitter; shirker.

¹pile (pīl), *n.* **1,** a mass or heap; as, a pile of sand; **2,** a heap of wood for burning a body; a pyre; **3,** *Colloq.* a great quantity; a lot; **4,** *Slang,* a fortune:—*v.t.* [piled, pil-ing], **1,** to place or throw in a heap; arrange; as, to pile bricks; **2,** to accumulate; amass as, he *piled* up a big fortune; **3,** to fill load; as, to *pile* a car full of people:— *v.i.* **1,** to form a mass or heap; accumulate; as, the snow *piled* up around the door; **2,** to press forward in a mass crowd.

²pile (pīl), *n.* **1,** a timber driven into the ground, as for a wharf, foundation for a building, etc.; also, metal or concrete columns similarly used; **2,** a pointed stake or post:—**pile—driver,** a machine for driving piles into the ground:—*v.t.* [piled, pil-ing], to drive piles into

³pile (pīl), *n.* **1,** nap of cloth; esp., the furry or velvety surface of velvet, plush, carpet, etc.; **2,** short, soft hair; down

pi-le-at-ed (pī′li-āt′id), *adj.* **1,** crested; as, the *pileated* woodpecker; **2,** capped, as a mushroom.

piles (pīlz), *n.* hemorrhoids, or painful swelling or bleeding of veins under the skin of the anus.

pil-fer (pil′fėr), *v.t.* and *v.i.* to steal in small amounts.—*n.* **pil′fer-er.**

pil-grim (pil′grim), *n.* **1,** one who travels from a distance to visit some sacred place; **2,** a traveller:—**Pilgrims** the Puritan settlers of the first colony in Massachusetts in 1620: also called *Pilgrim Fathers.*

pil-grim-age (pil′gri-mij), *n.* a long journey, esp. to some sacred place.

pill (pil), *n.* **1,** medicine prepared in the form of a small ball; **2,** something disagreeable that must be accepted; as defeat was a bitter *pill.*

pil-lage (pil′ij), *n.* **1,** the act of plundering, or robbing openly, esp. in war; **2,** booty; spoil:—*v.t.* and *v.i.* [pillaged pillaging], to plunder, or rob openly despoil; sack.—*n.* **pil′lag-er.**

pil-lar (pil′ėr), *n.* **1,** a column to support a structure or to serve as a monument; **2,** any support or mainstay; as a *pillar* of society.—*adj.* **pil′lared.**

pil-lion (pil′yun), *n.* and *adv.* a pad cushion, etc., behind a saddle, esp., for woman rider; as, she rode *pillion* (on horse or motorcycle).

pil-lo-ry (pil'o-ri), *n.* [*pl.* pillories], an old instrument used to punish offenders publicly, consisting of a wooden frame supported by an upright post, and having holes through which the head and hands of a person were passed and secured:—*v.t.* [pilloried, pillory-ing], 1, to punish (an offender) by putting into a pillory; 2, to expose to public disgrace or ridicule.

PILLORY

pil-low (pil'ō), *n.* a case filled with feathers, down, etc., to support the head of a person lying down:—*v.t.* to place on a pillow.

pi-lot (pī'lut), *n.* 1, one who steers a ship; one licensed to conduct a ship in or out of a port or in waters where sailing is difficult or dangerous; 2, one who flies any kind of aircraft; 3, a guide of any sort; as, the Prime Minister is the *pilot* of our national affairs; 4, the cow-catcher of a locomotive: —pilot—biscuit, hard tack:—*v.t.* 1, to direct the course of (a vessel, airship, etc.); 2, to guide or escort through difficulties.—*adj.* 1, serving as a guide, or as a test unit; as, a *pilot* plant, dye, parachute, etc.; 2, serving to start a larger device; as, a *pilot* lamp, light, etc.

pi-men-to (pi-men'tō), *n.* [*pl.* pi-mentos], 1, allspice, an unripe fruit, dried and used as a flavouring; also, the tree bearing it; 2, a variety of sweet pepper; pimiento.

pi-mien-to (pi-myen'tō), *n.* [*pl.* pimientos], a variety of sweet pepper, used as a vegetable, stuffing for olives, etc.: often called *pimento*.

pim-per-nel (pim'pėr-nl), *n.* a plant of the primrose family, with scarlet, white, or blue flowers that close in bad or rainy weather.

pim-ple (pim'pl), *n.* a small, inflamed swelling of the skin, often containing pus.—*adj.* **pim'pled.**—*adj.* **pim'ply.**

pin (pin), *n.* 1, a short piece of wire with a sharp point at one end and a round head at the other, used for fastening things together; 2, a piece of wood, metal, etc., having a similar use or appearance; as, a clothes*pin*, a hair*pin*, a hat*pin*, etc.; 3, an ornament, badge, or jewel fitted with a pin and a clasp; as, a fraternity *pin*; 4, a bolt or peg; 5, a wooden roller; as, a rolling-*pin*; 6, a wooden peg, shaped like a bottle, which is a target in bowling:— *v.t.* [pinned, pin-ning], 1, to fasten with,

or as with, a pin; as, to *pin* a pattern on cloth; 2, to hold fast in one position; as, the steering-wheel *pinned* him in the wrecked car; 3, to hold or keep (a person) to an obligation, course of action, etc.; as, to *pin* him down to his promise. Also, **pin'cush'ion; pin'-feath'er; pin'point'; pin'wheel'.**

pin-a-fore (pin'a-fōr'), a loose sleeve-less apron or covering to protect the clothing of a child or young girl.

pin-ball (pin'bôl'), *n.* and *adj.* a game played on a sloping board, the aim being to cause a ball, driven by a spring, to fall into the highest-num-bered hole(s): there are several kinds of *pinball* machines.

pin-cers (pin'sėrz), *n. pl.* sometimes used as *sing.* 1, an instrument with two handles and jaws working on a pivot, used for gripping things; nip-pers; 2, the claws of lobsters, crabs, etc.

pinch (pinch), *v.t.* 1, to squeeze or nip between the thumb and a finger, or between two hard edges; as, to *pinch* a finger in a door; 2, to press on so as to hurt; as, the shoe *pinches* my toe; 3, to oppress or distress; as, to be *pinched* by poverty; 4, to make thin or worn; as, to be *pinched* with hunger; 5, *Slang;* **a,** to arrest; **b,** to steal:—*v.i.* 1, to press hard; as, my shoe *pinches;* 2, to be mean or miserly:—*n.* 1, a squeeze or nip, as with the fingers and thumb; 2, painful pressure; as, the *pinch* of poverty; 3, a sudden difficulty or necessity; emergency; as, anything will do in a *pinch;* 4, as much as can be held between the thumb and a finger; as, a *pinch* of salt.

¹pine (pīn), *n.* 1, a kind of cone-bearing tree having clusters of evergreen needlelike leaves; 2, the timber of the tree; 3, a pineapple.—*adj.* **pin'y** or **pin'ey.**

²pine (pīn), *v.i.* [pined, pin-ing], 1, to grow thin and weak from distress, anxiety, etc. 2, to long intensely; as, to *pine* for friends.

pine-ap-ple (pīn'ap'l), *n.* 1, a tropical plant with spiny leaves, bearing a large fruit somewhat resembling a pine cone; 2, the edible, juicy fruit of this plant.

ping (ping), *n.* a slight ringing sound, as from a bullet's flight through the air, or from the bullet's striking something.

ping—pong (ping'-pong'), *n.* table-tennis.

¹pin-ion (pin'yun), *n.* 1, the last group of bones of a bird's wings; 2, a wing; 3, a feather:—*v.t.* 1, to bind the wings of, or to clip off the pinion of; as, to *pinion* a bird; **2,** to bind or confine; as, to *pinion* a person's arms to his sides.

²**pin-ion** (pin´yun), *n.* a wheel, the cogs of which come into gear with those of a larger toothed wheel or rack, so that motion is imparted from one to the other; also, in a pair of gears, the smaller gear.

¹**pink** (pingk), *v.t.* **1,** to cut the edges of (cloth, leather, paper, etc.) in points or scallops, esp. with *pinking* shears; **2,** to prick or pierce, as with a sword.

²**pink** (pingk), *n.* **1,** a very pale red; **2,** a garden plant with sharp-pointed leaves and red, pink, or white flowers, which are either fringed or ruffled and have a sweet, spicy fragrance; also, the flower; **3,** the highest degree; the peak; as, in the *pink* of perfection;—*adj.* of a very pale-red colour.—*adj.* **pink´ish.**

pink-eye (pink´ī´), *n.* inflammation of the membrane lining the inner surface of the eyelid; conjunctivitis.

pin-nace (pin´as; pin´is), *n.* **1,** a small, light, schooner-rigged vessel with oars; **2,** a man-of-war's eight-oared boat.

pin-na-cle (pin´a-kl), *n.* **1,** a small tower or turret above the rest of a building; **2,** a high point like a spire; as, a pinnacle of rock; **3,** the highest point; as, few men reach the *pinnacle* of fame.

pin-nate (pin´āt), *adj.* in *botany*, having a featherlike arrangement of leaves along a stem, as in the sumac, ash, locust, etc.

pi-noc-le or **pi-noch-le** (pē´ nuk´l), a game of cards the object of which is the making of certain card combinations of differing point values.

pint (pīnt), *n.* a measure of capacity equal to half a quart.

pin-tail (pin´tāl´), *n.* a species of long-necked duck with pointed tail.

pin-to (pin´tō), *n.* [*pl.* -tos], in Western U.S. and Canada, a mottled or piebald horse or pony.

pi-o-neer (pī´o-nēr´), *n.* one who goes before to prepare the way for others, esp. an original settler in a frontier country:—*v.i.* to prepare a way:—*v.t.* to open up (new country) or take the lead in (new causes).

pi-ous (pī´us), *adj.* **1,** showing reverence for God; religious; devout; as, *pious* nuns; **2,** done under pretence of religion; as, *pious* deception.—*adv.* **pi´ous-ly.**

pip (pip), *n.* **1,** a small seed, as of an apple, orange, etc.; **2,** *Colloq.* a star on

the shoulder of an army officer's uniform, to show his rank; **3,** *Humorous,* a minor ailment; as, it gives me the *pip;* **4,** a disease of poultry or birds, marked by a thick mucus in mouth and throat; **5,** any of the spots on dice, dominoes, playing cards, etc.

pipe (pīp), *n.* **1,** any long, hollow tube; as, a water-*pipe;* **2,** a tube of clay, wood, etc., with a bowl for smoking tobacco, blowing bubbles, etc.; **3,** a high-pitched voice; as, the *pipe* of a child; **4,** the note or call of a bird or insect; **5,** a musical wind-instrument consisting of a hollow tube, as a flute; **6,** one of the graduated tubes in which the notes of some organs, called *pipe-organs*, are produced; **7,** **pipes,** the bagpipe:—*v.t.* [piped, pip-ing], **1,** to play on a musical pipe; as, to *pipe* a tune; **2,** to utter in a high key; as, to *pipe* a song; **3,** to furnish with pipes; as, to *pipe* a house for water; **4,** to carry through a pipe or tube; as, to *pipe* water into a city:—*v.i.* **1,** to play on a pipe; **2,** to speak shrilly.—*adj.* **pipe´ful.**—*n.* **pipe´-line´.**

pip-er (pīp´ẽr), *n.* one who plays on a pipe; esp., one who plays on a bagpipe.

pip-ing (pīp´ing), *n.* **1,** the music of a pipe; also, a shrill sound; as, the *piping* of birds; **2,** a system of tubes for drainage, gas, etc.; **3,** a narrow fold of material used in trimming dresses. —*adv.* hissing; sizzling; as, *piping* hot.—*adj.* tranquil; as *piping* times of peace.

pip-it (pip´it), *n.* a small bird, similar to the lark, which sings as it flies.

pip-pin (pip´in), *n.* any one of several varieties of apple.

pip-squeak (pip´skwēk´), *n.* a high-velocity shell (1916).

pi-quant (pē´kant), *adj.* **1,** agreeably sharp to the taste; as, a *piquant* sauce; **2,** arousing interest or curiosity; having a lively charm; as, *piquant* remarks; a *piquant* face.—*n.* **pi´quan-cy.**

pique (pēk), *n.* slight anger or resentment, esp. as a result of wounded pride; as, she left the party in a fit of *pique:*—*v.t.* [piqued (pēkt), pi-quing (pē´king), **1,** to wound the pride of; irritate; displease; **2,** to pride or value (oneself); as, she *piqued* herself on her ability; **3,** to stir or arouse; as, to *pique* the curiosity.

pi-que (pi-kā´), *n.* a ribbed silk or cotton cloth.

pi-ra-cy (pī´ra-si), *n.* [*pl.* piracies], **1,** robbery upon the high seas; **2,** the using, without permission of another's literary work, invention, etc. for profit.

i-ra-gua (pi-rä′gwa), *n.* **1,** in the Carribean, a canoe, made by hollowing out a log; **2,** a two-masted barge.

ir-ah-na (pi-rän′ya), *n.* a small voracious South American fish, dangerous, even to man.

i-rate (pī′rit), *n.* **1,** a robber on the high seas; **2,** hence, anyone using lawless methods in gaining something; esp. one who uses another's literary work for profit without permission, or claims it as his own product; **3,** a ship engaged in robbery on the high seas:— *v.t.* and *v.i.* [pirat-ed, pirat-ing], **1,** to rob at sea; **2,** to take and publish without permission or payment.—*adj.* **pi-rat′ic** (pī-rat′ik); **pi-rat′i-cal.**

ir-ou-ette (pir′ōō-et′), *n.* a whirl or turn made on the toes (by a person or a horse):—*v.i.* [-etted, -et-ting], to turn or spin in one spot.

is-ces (pis′ēz), *n.* **1,** an equatorial constellation, the Fishes (south of Andromeda); **2,** the 12th sign of the zodiac (♓), which the sun enters about February 21.

is-ta-chi-o (pis-tä′shi-ō; pis-tā′ shi-ō), *n.* [*pl.* pistachios], **1,** a small tree of Asia and southern Europe, or its nut, the kernel of which is used for flavouring; **2,** the flavouring; **3,** the greenish colour of the kernel.

is-til (pis′til; pis′tl), *n.* in *botany*, the seed-bearing organ in the centre of a flower.

is-tol (pis′tl), *n.* a small, short gun intended for use with one hand. Pistols are now usually of two types, the revolver and the automatic.

is-ton (pis′tun), *n.* a closely fitting disk or cylinder designed to slide to and fro within a larger tube or cylinder.

PISTIL

Section of a flower showing pistil (P) and stamens (S, S).

pit (pit), *n.* **1,** a hole or cavity in the earth; **2,** the shaft of a mine, or the mine itself; **3,** a deep gulf; abyss; **4,** a hole used for trapping wild animals; **5,** a small scar, such as that left by smallpox; **6,** a depression in some part of the body; as, the arm-*pits;* **7,** in England, the cheaper downstairs seats in a theatre; **8,** an enclosed place set aside for dog-fighting, cockfighting, etc.; **9,** that part of the floor of an exchange where a special business is carried on; as, a grain *pit:*—**the pit,** hell or Hades:—*v.t.* [pit-ted, pit-ting],

1, to mark with small pits; as, smallpox had *pitted* his face; **2,** to match or set to fight against another; as, to *pit* one's strength against a foe; **3,** to place in a pit.

²pit (pit), *n.* the kernel or stone of certain fruits, as the peach, cherry, date, etc.:—*v.t.* [pit-ted, pit-ting], to remove the pits of.

pit-a-pat (pit′a-pat′), *adv.* with quick beat; flutteringly; as, my heart went *pitapat.*—*n.* a succession of light, quick beats, taps, etc.

¹pitch (pich), *n.* **1,** a thick, sticky, black substance, soft when heated, left over after distillation of coal-tar or turpentine: much used in roofing and filling seams in ships; commonly called *tar;* **2,** the sticky resin of certain trees:—*v.t.* to cover or smear with pitch or tar.

²pitch (pich), *v.t.* **1,** to fix in or on the ground; set up; as, to *pitch* a tent; **2,** throw or fling; as, to *pitch* hay; to *pitch* quoits; **3,** in *music*, to determine the key of; start, as a tune, by sounding the keynote:—*v.i.* **1,** to fall headlong; as, to *pitch* forward; **2,** to fix the choice; decide; as, they finally *pitched* on the right candidate; **3,** to rise alternately forward and aft as a ship in heavy seas; to toss; **4,** in *baseball,* to throw the ball to the batter; act as pitcher:—*n.* **1,** a plunging forward or down; as, a headlong *pitch* from a ladder; **2,** the act or manner of throwing or tossing; as, a good *pitch* in baseball; **3,** a tossing motion, as of a ship in a storm; **4,** degree or rate; as, the highest *pitch* of excitement; **5,** the tone of a voice; **6,** slope; as, the *pitch* of a roof; **7,** the distance between two successive threads of a screw; **8,** in *music,* the highness or lowness of a sound or a tone; **9,** in *cricket,* the part of the field between the wickets.

pitch-blende (pich′blend′), *n.* a shiny ore occurring in black masses: chief source of uranium and radium: found esp. in Canada.

¹pitch-er (pich′ẽr), *n.* **1,** one who throws or hurls; **2,** in *baseball,* the player who throws the ball to the batter.

²pitch-er (pich′ẽr), *n.* a container, usually with an open spout and a handle, used to hold or pour liquids:— **pitcher plant.** Same as **hunts′man's— cup′.**

pitch-fork (pich′fôrk′), *n.* a fork with a long handle for tossing hay, straw, etc.:—*v.t.* to toss, as hay or straw, with, or as with, a pitchfork.

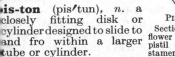

pit-e-ous (pit′i-us), *adj.* exciting sorrow or sympathy; mournful.—*adv.* **pit′e-ous-ly.**

pit-fall (pit′fôl′), *n.* **1,** a hole lightly covered, so that animals may fall into it; a trap; **2,** any hidden source of danger or temptation.

pith (pith), *n.* **1,** the soft, spongy substance in the centre of the stem of some plants; **2,** any similar soft tissue, as the marrow in a bone; **3,** energy or force; vigour; **4,** gist; substance; as, the *pith* of his speech.—*adj.* **pith′less.**

pith-y (pith′i), *adj.* [pith-i-er, pith-i-est], **1,** like or full of the soft, spongy substance called pith; **2,** forcible; full of meaning; as, Benjamin Franklin is noted for his *pithy* sayings.—*adv.* **pith′i-ly.**

pit-i-a-ble (pit′i-a-bl), *adj.* **1,** deserving sympathy; as, he was in a *pitiable* condition; **2,** poor; mean; as, *pitiable* makeshifts.—*adv.* **pit′i-a-bly.**

pit-i-ful (pit′i-fool), *adj.* **1,** miserable; sad; as, a *pitiful* sight; **2,** small; meagre; as, a *pitiful* amount; **3,** contemptible; as, a *pitiful* ambition.—*adv.* **pit′i-ful-ly.**

pit-i-less (pit′i-lis), *adj.* without sympathy or mercy.—*adv.* **pit′i-less-ly.**

pit-tance (pit′ans), *n.* a small allowance, esp. of money; as, my income is a mere *pittance*; a dole.

pit-ter—pat-ter (pit′ėr–pat′ėr), *n.* and *adv.* a rapid succession of light beats or taps; as, the *pitter-patter* of raindrops.

pi-tu-i-tar-y (pi-tū′i-ta-ri), *adj.* and *n.* a small two-lobed gland at the base of the brain; hormones secreted by one lobe are said to control the growth or size of the body, and by the other the blood pressure.

pit-y (pit′i), *n.* [*pl.* pities], **1,** a feeling of sorrow for the suffering of others; mercy; **2,** a reason for regret or grief; as, it is a *pity* he was not promoted with his classmates:—*v.t.* [pitied, pity-ing], to sympathize with; feel sorry for.

piv-ot (piv′ut), *n.* **1,** a fixed pin or short shaft on which some object, as a ball or wheel, turns; **2,** that on which something important depends:—*v.t.* to place on, or supply with, a pivot:—*v.i.* to turn on a pivot.

pix-y or **pix-ie** (pik′si), *n.* [*pl.* pixies], in old folk-tales, a fairy; an elf.

piz-za (pēt′sa), *n. Italian*, a kind of pie, baked in an oven at 750° Fahrenheit, made of tomato pulp and strips of cheese, meat, anchovies, etc., highly flavoured.

plac-ard (plak′ärd), *n.* a printed bill or notice posted in a public place, as an advertisement; a poster:—*v.t.* (plak′ärd; pla-kärd′), **1,** to advertise by a bill posted publicly; **2,** to post a bill on notice on.

place (plās), *n.* **1,** originally, an open space, as a public square, in a town or city; sometimes, a part of a street also, a city or town; **2,** a particular location; **3,** rank; social position; esp high rank; **4,** a position; job; **5,** in a race, a position among the winning competitors; **6,** in *arithmetic*, the position occupied by a figure in relation to the other figures of a series; **7,** a building devoted to a special purpose as, a *place* of worship; **8,** the location of a given body; as, it is out of *place*; **9,** duty; as, it is your *place* to do it, **10,** position in order; as, in the first *place;* **11,** a particular spot in a surface as, a sore *place* on my arm:—*v.t.* [placed, placing], **1,** to put in a particular spot or position; **2,** to put in office or authority; **3,** to identify by connecting with some place, circumstance, etc.; as, we *placed* him as a former neighbour; **4,** to put; as, I *place* trust in him.

pla-ce-bo (pla-sē′bō), *n.* [*pl.*—bos or -boes (-bōz)], a medicine or pill given to please or humour a patient (chiefly for its psychological effect).

place-ment kick (plās′ment), *n.* a placing of the ball on the ground in order to kick a field goal: it is neither a convert after a touchdown nor a drop kick. Also called *place* kick.

plac-er (plas′ėr) **mining**, the mining of placers (plas′ėrz) or deposits of sand or gravel containing ore, as of gold, by washing (as in the Yukon goldrush o 1898).

plac-id (plas′id), *adj.* calm; peaceful —*adv.* **plac′id-ly.**—*n.* **pla-cid′i-ty.**

plack-et (plak′it), *n.* a finished opening or slit in the upper part of a skirt or petticoat, to make it easy to put on

pla-gi-a-rism (plā′ji-a-rizm; plā′ja-rizm), *n.* stealing the ideas, plots, or writings of another, and passing them off as one's own.—*n.* **pla′gi-a-rist.**

plague (plāg), *n.* **1,** a deadly, epidemic disease; **2,** anything very troublesome or causing misery; **3,** *Colloq.* a nuisance —*v.t.* [plagued, pla-guing], **1,** to afflict with disease, evil or disaster; **2,** to trouble or annoy greatly.—*adj.* **pla′guy** (plā′gi).

plaid (plad), *n.* **1,** a barred or chequered woollen cloth; **2,** a garment made of a large rectangle of such material, worn

---

cat, āge, fär, câre, ȧsk; ten, ēve, latėr; (i) pity, rely, senate; ice; top; nō

by the Highlanders of Scotland; **3,** any material with such a pattern; also, the pattern:—*adj.* having a barred or chequered pattern; as, a *plaid* dress.

plain (plān), *adj.* **1,** level; flat; even; **2,** clear; evident; as, in *plain* sight; **3,** easily understood; as, your meaning is *plain;* **4,** unlearned; unpolished; simple in manners; as, a *plain,* blunt man; **5,** frank; sincere; as, a *plain* speech; **6,** not luxurious; as, *plain* living; **7,** without ornament; as, *plain* furniture; **8,** all of one colour; as, a dress of *plain* material; **9,** without beauty; homely; as, a *plain* face:—*adv.* clearly:—*n.* **1,** a wide stretch of level land; a flat expanse; **2, plains,** great tracts of level country without trees.—*adv.* **plain'ly.**

plain–spo–ken (plān'–spō'ken), *adj.* candid; frank in speech.

plaint (plānt), *n.* **1,** *Poetic,* a mournful song; lamentation; **2,** a complaint.

plain-tiff (plān'tif), *n.* one who brings suit in a court of law.

plain-tive (plān'tiv), *adj.* expressing sorrow; mournful; sad; as, a *plaintive* song.

plait (plat; plēt), *n.* **1,** a flattened fold made by doubling cloth over upon itself; a pleat, as in a skirt; **2,** (plat), a braid, as of hair:—*v.t.* **1,** to double over in folds; pleat; **2,** to braid or interweave.

plan (plan), *n.* **1,** a drawing, diagram, or map showing the outline or design of anything; as, an architect's *plan* of a building; **2,** the arrangement of parts according to a fixed design; **3,** a way of doing something; **4,** a scheme or project:—*v.t.* [planned, plan-ning], **1,** to make a sketch or design of; outline; **2,** to arrange beforehand:—*v.i.* make a plan.

¹plane (plān), *n.* a carpenter's tool for smoothing wood:—*v.t.* [planed, planing], to make smooth with such a tool, as a board:—*v.i.* to work with a plane.

²plane (plān), *adj.* flat; level; even; as, a *plane* surface:—*n.* **1,** a flat or even surface; **2,** a grade or level; as, a high *plane* of living; **3,** one of the flat supporting surfaces of the wings of an aeroplane; **4,** an aeroplane.

³plane (plān), *n.* any of several large trees with broad, spreading leaves and light-brown, flaky bark, including the American sycamore, or buttonwood: also called *plane-tree.*

plan-et (plan'it), *n.* in *astronomy,* any heavenly body revolving round the sun and shining by reflected light.

plan-e-tar-i-um (plan'i-târ'i-um), *n.*

[*pl.* planetaria (plan'i-târ'i-a)], a mode of the planetary system, showing the planets, their motions round the sun, their relative sizes, etc.

plan-e-tar-y (plan'e-tér-i), *adj.* **1,** pertaining to a planet or to the planets; **2,** like a planet.

plane—tree (plān'–trē'), *n.* Same as **³plane.**

plan-gent (plan'jent), *adj.* beating with a loud sound, as of waves: the *plangent* sea.

plank (plangk), *n.* **1,** a long, broad piece of sawn timber thicker than a board; **2,** an item in the platform of a political party:—*v.t.* **1,** to cover with thick boards; **2,** *Colloq.* to lay down, as on a plank; hence, to pay; as, to *plank* down money; **3,** to cook on a board; as, to *plank* shad.—*n.* **plank'ing.**

plank-ton (plangk'tun), *n.* the floating or drifting microscopic plant and animal life of seas and lakes used by fish as food.

plant (plant), *n.* **1,** a member of the vegetable kingdom, usually with roots in the soil from which it draws part of its food in the form of minerals and water, and with stems, branches, leaves and flowers above the ground, as a bush herb, or tree; **2,** a sprout or young shoot ready for transplanting; **3,** the tools, machinery, fixtures, and sometimes buildings, of any trade or business; as, a manufacturing *plant;* **4,** the equipment of an institution, as a college or hospital:—*v.t.* **1,** to put into the ground for growth; as, to *plant* seed; **2,** to provide or prepare with seeds, roots, etc.; as, to *plant* a garden; **3,** to fix firmly; place; **4,** to establish, as a colony; **5,** to implant or introduce, as an idea.

plan-tain (plan'tān), *n.* a common garden or roadside weed with a rosette of broad leaves, and a stalk bearing many seeds.

plan-ta-tion (plan-tā'shun), *n.* **1,** a place where anything is sown, set out, or cultivated; as, a *plantation* of trees; **2,** in southern countries, esp. in America a large estate where cotton, sugar-cane, etc., are cultivated; **3,** a colony.

plant-er (plan'tér), *n.* **1,** the owner or cultivator of a plantation; **2,** a person who sows or plants; **3,** a planting machine.

plaque (plàk), *n.* a thin, flat plate of metal, porcelain, ivory, etc., used esp. as a wall ornament.

plas-ma (plaz'ma), *n.* the colourless watery part of the blood in which the corpuscles float; also, the liquid part of milk, in which the fat globules are suspended.

plas-ter (plås′tẽr), *n.* **1,** a mixture of lime, sand, and water, which hardens on drying, used for coating walls and partitions of buildings; **2,** a substance with medicinal qualities, which is spread upon cloth and applied to some part of the body as a remedy; as, a mustard *plaster*:—*v.t.* **1,** to cover with plaster; as, to *plaster* the walls; **2,** to treat with a plaster. **Plaster of Paris,** a white powder of calcium sulphate or gypsum, used, when mixed with water, for finishing walls, making moulds, casts, statues, etc.

plas-tic (plas′tik), *adj.* **1,** capable of being formed or moulded; as, clay is *plastic;* hence, quick to receive impressions; as, a *plastic* mind; **2,** giving form to matter; as, *plastic* art; **3,** of, pertaining to, or characteristic of, moulding or modelling.—*n.* any of various non-metallic synthetic compounds, as bakelite, lucite, vinylite (trade-names): used instead of glass, wood, metal, etc. **plas-tic′i-ty** (plas-tis′i-ti).

plas-tics (plas′tiks), *n. sing.* an article fabricated by chemical synthesis, which imitates and resembles natural articles, as substitute for glass, wood, leather, cloth, etc.—*adj.,* as a *plastics* part.

plate (plāt), *n.* **1,** a thin, flat piece of metal or glass, rigid, and of uniform thickness; as, armour *plate;* **2,** a shallow, usually circular, dish from which food is eaten; **3,** as much food as such a plate will hold; a plateful; also, food served to one person at a meal; **4,** a piece of metal on which something is engraved; as, a door *plate;* **5,** a print made from an engraved metal surface; also, the surface; **6,** in *photography,* a thin sheet of glass treated with chemicals to make it sensitive to light, on which a picture is taken; **7,** household articles of gold or silver; **8,** a thin piece of rubber, metal, etc., fitted to the mouth, and holding artificial teeth; also, a device for straightening irregular teeth; **9,** in *baseball,* the home base; **10,** a cut of beef from the lower part of the side; **11,** in *architecture,* a horizontal timber upon which the lower ends of the rafters are set; **12,** the mould of a page or section of type:—*v.t.* [plat-ed, plat-ing], **1,** to coat with metal; **2,** to cover with sheets of metal.

pla-teau (pla-tō′), *n.* [*pl.* plateaux (-tō′) or plateaus], an elevated tract of flat land; tableland.

plat-en (plat′n), *n.* **1,** in a printing press, the flat part that brings the paper against the type; **2,** in a typewriter, the roller against which the type strikes.

plat-form (plat′fôrm′), *n.* **1,** a structure raised above the level of the ground or of the main floor, as a stage for public speakers, or along the tracks at a railway station; **2,** a statement of principles and policies, as of a political party.

plat-i-num (plat′i-num), *n.* a heavy, silver-white, precious metal much used for chemical utensils and for jewelry.

plat-i-tude (plat′i-tūd′), *n.* a commonplace or dull remark, esp. when used as though fresh or profound.

pla-toon (pla-tōōn′), *n.* **1,** a small unit of soldiers, usually three squads of twelve men each; **2,** any similar group, as a *platoon* of police, football players, etc.

pla-ty (plā′ti), *n.* an aquarium fish, *Platypoecilus maculatus,* (native to Mexico), varying from light gray with tail crescent, to red, yellow, or black; females 3″, male 2″, long; (male, scarlet and black): require water 70–85°F.: used in genetic research. Also called **blue-moon fish.**

plat-ter (plat′ẽr), *n.* a large, flat dish for serving meat, poultry, etc.

plat-y-pus (plat′i-pus), *n.* [*pl.* -puses, -pi (pī)], a small egg-laying Australian mammal with ducklike bill; the duckbill.

plau-dit (plô′dit), *n.* applause, esp. by clapping: enthusiastic praise or approval; as, he won the *plaudits* of his audience.

plau-si-ble (plô′zi-bl), *adj.* **1,** seeming to be true; having the appearance of truth; as, a *plausible* excuse; **2,** persuasive; as, a *plausible* speaker.—*n.* **plau′si-bil′i-ty.**—*adv.* **plau′si-bly.**

play (plā), *v.i.* **1,** to move lightly or capriciously; flutter, as leaves in the wind; **2,** to sport or frolic; **3,** to take part in a game; also, to gamble; **4,** to perform on a musical instrument; **5,** to act on the stage; **6,** to dally; trifle: —*v.t.* **1,** to take part in; as, to *play* chequers; also, to compete with, in a game; as, our team *played* the high-school team; **2,** to put into action in a game or contest, as by laying a card on the table; **3,** to imitate in sport; as, to *play* school; **4,** to perform; as, to *play* a comedy; also, to perform music on; as, to *play* the violin; **5,** to act in the character of; as, to *play* Othello; *play* the fool; **6,** to set in action; as, to *play* a trick; **7,** to operate continuously; as, to *play* a hose on the grass:—*n.* **1,** brisk, sometimes irregular, motion; as, the *play* of light and shade; **2,** freedom or room to act; as, to give one's arm full *play* in throwing a ball; **3,** action or use; as, all their resources were brought into *play;* **4,** exercise, esp. in a contest of strength or skill; as, the *play* of a duellist's sword; **5,** a game or sport; **6,** recreation; **7,** gambling; as, to lose money at *play;* **8,** any single action in a game; also, one's turn to move a piece, lay down a card, etc.; as, it is your *play;* **9,** fun; jest; as, she did it in *play* **10,** conduct; as, fair *play;* **11,** a drama intended for the stage; also, its performance.—*n.* **play′er.**—*adj.* **play′a-ble** —*n.* **play′boy′; play′-off′; play′go′er; play′room′.**

play-fel-low (plā′fel′ō), *n.* a playmate.

play-ful (plā′fool), *adj.* full of play; lively; as, a *playful* kitten.

play-ground (plā′ground′), *n.* a plot of ground set aside for children's play.

play-house (plā′hous′), *n.* **1,** a theatre; **2,** a house for children's play.

play-mate (plā′māt′), *n.* one who takes part in games with another; a playfellow.

play-thing (plā′thing′), *n.* a toy.

play-wright (plā′rīt′), *n.* a writer of plays; a dramatist.

pla-za (plä′za), *n.* an open square or market place surrounded by buildings.

plea (plē), *n.* **1,** an excuse or apology; **2,** an entreaty; **3,** the defendant's answer to the charges in a lawsuit.

plead (plēd), *v.i.* [*p.t.* and *p.p.* plead-ed or, *Colloq.* plead (pled), *p.pr.* plead-ing], **1,** to argue or reason in support of a cause against another; **2,** to argue before a court of law; as, to *plead* for an acquittal; **3,** to beg earnestly; pray; as, to *plead* for mercy:—*v.t.* **1,** to defend by arguments; as, to *plead* a case; **2,** to answer, as to a charge; as, to *plead* not guilty; **3,** to offer as an excuse; as, to *plead* poverty.—*n.* **plead′er.**

pleas-ant (plez′ant), *adj.* **1,** pleasing; delightful; agreeable; as, a *pleasant* smell; **2,** characterized by charming manners or behaviour; cheerful; as, a *pleasant* fellow.

pleas-ant-ry (plez′ant-ri), *n.* [*pl.* pleasantries], **1,** merriment; lively talk; gaiety; **2,** a laughable speech; a joke.

please (plēz), *v.t.* [pleased, pleas-ing], **1,** to gratify; give enjoyment to; **2,** to be the will of; suit; as, *please* God, we may return safely:—*v.i.* **1,** to give

satisfaction or enjoyment; as, we strive to *please;* **2,** to like or choose; as, to do as you *please.*

pleas-ur-a-ble (plezh′ẽr-a-bl), *adj.* delightful; gratifying; as, a *pleasurable* occasion.—*adv.* **pleas′ur-a-bly.**

pleas-ure (plezh′ẽr), *n.* **1,** a feeling of delight or satisfaction; enjoyment; **2,** a source of delight; a joy; **3,** choice; wish; as, I await your *pleasure.*

pleat (plēt), *n.* a fold, as of cloth doubled over upon itself:—*v.t.* to fold in pleats. Also spelled **plait.**

ple-be-ian (pli-bē′an; pli-bē′yan), *adj.* **1,** originally, pertaining to the plebs, or common people, of ancient Rome; **2,** hence, vulgar or common; as, *plebeian* tastes:—*n.* **1,** one of the common people of ancient Rome; opposite of *patrician;* **2,** any person of common breeding.

pleb-i-scite (pleb′i-sīt′; -sit), *n.* a direct vote of all the people; as, the liquor law was submitted to a *plebiscite.*

plec-trum (plek′trum) or **plec-tron,** *n.* a small, thin piece of ivory, metal, etc., used to pluck the strings of a guitar, mandolin, etc.

pledge (plej), *n.* **1,** anything given or considered as a security or guarantee; a pawn; **2,** the state of being given as security; as, goods held in *pledge;* **3,** a drinking of a health as an expression of goodwill; also, a person so pledged; **4,** an agreement or promise to do or not to do something; **5,** a token or sign of goodwill; as, a *pledge* of friendship:—*v.t.* [pledgėd, pledg-ing], **1,** to give as security or guarantee; as, to *pledge* one's honour; to put in pawn; as he *pledged* his watch; **2,** to bind by a promise; as, to *pledge* oneself to secrecy; **3,** to drink to the health of.

ple-na-ry (plē′na-ri; plen′), *adj.* full; complete; absolute; as, *plenary* powers or authority.

plen-i-po-ten-ti-a-ry (plen′i-pō-ten′-shi-a-ri; -ten′sha-ri), *n.* and *adj.* an ambassador or diplomatic agent (esp. to a foreign court) with full authority to act.

plen-te-ous (plen′ti-us), *adj.* abundant; amply sufficient; plentiful.— *adv.* **plen′ te-ous-ly.**—*n.* **plen′te-ous-ness.**

plen-ti-ful (plen′ti-fool), *adj.* **1,** yielding abundance; as, a *plentiful* harvest; **2,** existing in great quantity.—*adv.* **plen′ti-ful-ly**—*n.* **plen′ti-ful-ness.**

plen-ty (plen′ti), *n.* [*pl.* plenties], abundance; a full supply; more than enough.

pleu-ri-sy (ploŏr'i-si), *n.* [*pl.* pleurisies] inflammation of the membrane lining the chest and covering the lungs.—*adj.* **pleu'ral.**

pli-a-ble (plī'a-bl), *adj.* **1,** easily bent; flexible; **2,** easily influenced; docile.— *adv.* **pli'a-bly.**—*n.* **pli'a-bil'i-ty.**

pli-ant (plī'ant), *adj.* **1,** easily bent; pliable; as, a *pliant* twig; **2,** easily influenced.—*adv.* **pli'ant-ly.**—*n.* **pli'an-cy.**

pli-ers (plī'ẽrz), *n.pl.* used as *sing.* small pincers for bending wire, handling small objects, etc.

¹plight (plīt), *n.* a state or condition, usually unfavourable or dangerous; a predicament; as, they found us in a sorry *plight.*

²plight (plīt), *n.* a pledge or solemn promise:—*v.t.* **1,** to pledge, as one's faith; **2,** to betroth.

Plim-soll (plim's'l) **mark,** a line on the hull of a British merchant ship to show the depth to which it may be loaded.

plod (plod), *v.i.* [plod-ded, plod-ding], **1,** to walk slowly and heavily; trudge; **2,** to drudge or toil steadily and with perseverance:—*v.t.* to walk over heavily and slowly.—*n.* **plod'der.**

plop (plop), *n.* the sound made by a smooth object's dropping into water without splashing:—*v.i.* [plopped, plopping], to fall with a plop. Also used as *adv.* and *interj.*

plot (plot), *n.* **1,** a small area of ground; **2,** a plan of a piece of land, an estate, etc.; a diagram; chart; map; **3,** a scheme or plan; esp., a secret conspiracy; **4,** the plan of a play, novel, etc.:—*v.t.* [plot-ted, plot-ting], **1,** to lay plans for; scheme; as, to *plot* a crime; **2,** to make a plan or map of; **3,** to locate or show on a map or chart:—*v.i.* to scheme; as, to *plot* against an enemy.—*n.* **plot'ter.**

plough (plou), *n.* **1,** a farming implement for cutting and turning up the soil in preparation for planting; **2,** any implement that works in a similar way by cutting, shoving, furrowing, etc.; as, a snow*plough*:—*v.t.* to turn up with such an implement; till; as, to *plough* a field:—*v.i.* **1,** to break or turn up soil with, or as with, a *plough;* **2,** to move onward by cutting or pushing a way; as, the ship *ploughed* on; we *ploughed* through the mud.

plough-man (plou'man), *n.* [*pl.* ploughmen (-men)], one who operates a plough; hence, a farmer. Also, **plow'-man.**

plough-share (plou'shâr'), *n.* the strong, pointed blade of the plough, which cuts the soil.

plov-er (pluv'ẽr; plō'vẽr), *n.* a shorebird somewhat resembling the sandpiper, with a short bill, long, pointed wings, and short tail.

plow (plou), *n.* Same as **plough.**

ploy (ploi), *n.* **1,** a calculated move to gain an end; a trick; **2,** a pastime; sport.

pluck (pluk), *v.t.* **1,** to pull off, out, or up as, to *pluck* weeds; **2,** to pick or gather; harvest; as, to *pluck* grapes; **3,** to pull or twitch; as, to *pluck* the strings of a banjo; **4,** to strip completely of feathers as, to *pluck* a goose:—**pluck up,** to summon; as, *pluck up* your courage:— *v.i.* to give a sudden pull; tug:—*n.* **1,** spirit; courage; as, a man of *pluck;* **2,** a pull; snatch; tug.

pluck-y (pluk'i), *adj.* [pluck-i-er, pluck-i-est], brave; courageous.—*adv.* **pluck'i-ly.**

plug (plug), *n.* **1,** a piece of wood, rubber metal, etc., used to fill or stop a hole; **2,** a device to make an electrical connection; **3** a cake of pressed tobacco; **4,** a point in a water system where a hose may be attached; a fire-hydrant: —*v.t.* [plugged, plug-ging], to stop or make tight with a piece of wood, cork, etc.; as, to *plug* a leak; **2,** to advertise, as a song, book, etc., by reference to it on radio, television, etc.—*v.i. Colloq.* to work hard; plod:—**plug in,** to make an electrical connection by inserting a plug into a socket.

plum (plum), *n.* **1,** a tree somewhat like the peach and cherry; also, its red, green, purple, or yellow, smoothskinned fruit; **2,** something like this fruit in sweetness or shape; as, a sugar*plum;* **3,** a raisin when used in cooking; **4,** a dark-purple colour; **5,** a choice or best part; a desirable job or appointment.

plum-age (ploōm'ij), *n.* **1,** a bird's feathers; **2,** bright and ornamental costume.

plumb (plum), *n.* **1,** a small weight fastened to a cord, used by builders to test the accuracy of vertical work: also called *plumb-bob;* **2,** a similar weight used to find the depth of water; a plummet; **3,** the perpendicular or vertical:—*adj.* vertical; upright:—*adv.* **1,** vertically; **2,** *Slang,* completely; entirely; as, *plumb* crazy:—*v.t.* **1,** to test with a plumb-line; **2,** to straighten make vertical; as, to *plumb* up a wall; **3,** to sound (the depth of water) by a plummet; hence, to get to the bottom of; solve.

plum-ba-go (plum-bā'gō), *n.* **1,** graphite used in lead pencils, lubricants.

electrical apparatus, rubber-manufacturing, etc.; **2,** lead (the metal).

plumb-er (plum´ẻr), *n.* a workman who supplies, repairs, or installs bathroom fixtures, water-pipes, gas-pipes, etc.

plumb-ing (plum´ing), *n.* **1,** the occupation of putting in or repairing the piping and other fittings for the water or gas supply or sewage disposal of a building; **2,** the pipes and fittings so installed.

plumb—line (plum´-līn´), *n.* **1,** a cord attached to a plumb; **2,** a vertical line.

plume (ploom), *n.* **1,** a long and beautiful feather or tuft of feathers; **2,** a feather worn as an ornament:— *v.t.* [plumed, plum-ing], **1,** to clean and adjust; as, a bird *plumes* its feathers; **2,** to adorn with feathers or with fine clothes; **3,** to feel proud of (oneself); as, to *plume* oneself on one's skill.

plum-met (plum´it), *n.* a weight attached to a plumb-line:—*v.i.* to plunge; drop or fall straight down; as, the rocket *plummeted* to earth.

plump (plump), *adj.* well-filled or rounded out; as, a *plump* figure:—*v.i.* **1,** to grow round or full; **2,** to vote for but one on a ballot from which two or more are to be elected: to plump *for:—* *v.t.* to cause to fill out or become round.

plun-der (plun´dẻr), *n.* the act of robbing or taking by force; also, that which is taken; booty:—*v.t.* to rob by open force, esp. in war.—*n.* **plun´der-er.**

plunge (plunj), *v.t.* [plunged, plung-ing] **1,** to thrust suddenly into a liquid, or into any substance that can be penetrated; **2,** hence, to place suddenly in an unexpected condition; as, to *plunge* a friend into difficulty:—*v.i.* **1,** to dive, fall, or rush, as into water; **2,** to enter suddenly; as, to *plunge* into danger:— *n.* a sudden dive or leap; a headlong rush.—*n.* **plung´er.**

plunk (plungk), *v.t.* and *v.i.* to pluck or twang (the strings of a banjo, etc.); **2,** *Colloq.* to throw down; as, he *plunked* down a silver dollar.—*n. Colloq.* a hard blow; **2,** a plunking or twanging sound.

plu-per-fect (ploo´´pûr´fekt; ploo´-pûr´fekt), *adj.* in *grammar*, the tense that shows an action as complete before a given past time; past perfect; as, he *had gone* when I *arrived; had gone* is the pluperfect (completed action) in relation to *arrived.*

plu-ral (ploor´al), *adj.* **1,** consisting of more than one; **2,** in *grammar*, relating to the form of a word that names more than one; as, "girls" is a *plural* noun: —*n.* in *grammar*, that form of a word that names more than one; as, *churches* is the plural of *church, men* of *man, oxen* of *ox, sons-in-law* of *son-in-law.*

plu-ral-i-ty (ploo-ral´i-ti), *n.* [*pl.* pluralities], **1,** the state of consisting of more than one; **2,** the larger number; the majority; **3,** in *politics*, the excess of votes cast for one candidate over an other over those for any other candidate.

plus (plus), *adj.* **1,** extra; as, *plus* value; **2,** and more; as, 100 *plus;* **3,** indicating addition; as, the *plus* sign; **4,** indicating a positive quantity; as, a *plus* three:—*n.* **1,** an extra quantity; an addition; **2,** the plus sign [+]:—*prep.* with the addition of; and; as, 4 *plus* 2 makes 6.

plush (plush), *n.* thick, soft cloth with a pile or nap longer than that of velvet.— *adj. Slang,* luxurious.

plu-to-crat (ploo´tō-krat´), *n.* a member of a group that governs, or influences a government, by virtue of its wealth; a rich person.—*n.* **plu-toc´-ra-cy.**

plu-ton-ic (ploo-ton´ik), *adj.* formed by action of intense heat; igneous; as, *plutonic* rock.

plu-to-ni-um (ploo-tō´ni-um), *n.* a radioactive element with an isotope produced by bombarding uranium 238 with neutrons: it is fissionable, and is used in A-bombs.

¹ply (plī), *v.t.* [plied, ply-ing], **1,** to work at steadily; as, to *ply* a trade; **2,** to use diligently or earnestly; as, to *ply* an oar; **3,** to urge; offer something persistently to; as, to *ply* one with food:— *v.i.* to run regularly on a fixed course between two parts or places, as does a boat.

²ply (plī), *n.* [*pl.* plies], a thickness or layer, as in a carpet; a turn or twist.

ply-wood (plī´wood´), *n.* a building material made of two or more layers, or plies, of wood glued together.

pneu-mat-ic (nū-mat´ik), *adj.* **1,** pertaining to air; **2,** inflated with air; as, a *pneumatic* tire; **3,** made to work by air pressure or vacuum; as, a *pneumatic* drill.

pneu-mo-ni-a (nū-mō´ni-a), *n.* inflammation of the tissues of the lungs.

¹poach (pōch), *v.t.* to cook (eggs) by breaking (them) into boiling water.

²poach (pōch), *v.t.* and *v.i.* to hunt or fish, without permission, on another's property.—*n.* **poach´er.**

pock (pok), *n.* **1,** a small swelling (like

a blister or pimple), as in smallpox; **2,** the scar left by such a swelling; as, *pock*marked by chickenpox.

pocket (pok′it), *n.* **1,** a small pouch or bag attached to a garment, for carrying small articles; **2,** a small netted bag in a billiard-table for catching the balls; **3,** in a mine, a cavity or place where a deposit of ore is found; as a gold *pocket*; **4,** in aeroplane travel, a region marked by a sudden variation in the density of the air, which causes the plane to drop suddenly:—*v.t.* **1,** to put into a pocket; **2,** to take unlawfully, as profits; **3,** to receive (an insult) without showing any feeling:—*adj.* small-sized; as, a *pocket* Bible.—*n.* **pock′et-ful′.**

pock-et-book (pok′it-book′), *n.* a small case or folder for carrying money, papers, etc., in the pocket.

pock-et-knife (pok′it-nīf′), *n.* [*pl.* pocket-knives (-nīvz′)], a small knife with blades that close into the handle.

pock-mark (pok′märk′), *n.* a scar or small hole, as one left by smallpox.

pod (pod), *n.* a seed-vessel, esp. of the pea, bean, etc.

po-di-um (pō′di-um), *n.* a small raised platform for an orchestra leader; **2,** in *botany*, a support, as a stalk.

po-em (pō′im), *n.* a composition in verse; a piece of poetry.

po-e-sy (pō′i-si; pō′i-zi), *n.* [*pl.* poesies], the art of writing poetry; also, poetry.

po-et (pō′it), *n.* one who writes verses; esp. one who writes such verse or poetry as is characterized by beauty of thought and language.—*n.fem.* **po′et-ess.**

po-et-ic (pō-et′ik) or **po-et-i-cal** (pō-et′i-kal), *adj.* **1,** connected with, or characteristic of, poetry or poets; as, *poetic* language; **2,** written in verse; as, Milton's *poetical* works.—*adv.* **po-et′i-cal-ly.**

po-et-ry (pō′it-ri), *n.* **1,** the art of expressing beautiful or elevated thought or feeling in verse; **2,** a poem or poems.

po-go (pō′gō) **stick,** a strong stilt with a metal spring, enabling one to move forward in a series of short jumps.

poign-ant (poin′ant; poin′yant), *adj.* **1,** acute; as, *poignant* thirst; **2,** piercing; keenly felt; as, *poignant* regrets; **3,** keen; as, *poignant* wit.—*n.* **poign′an-cy.**

poin-set-ti-a (poin-set′-i-a), *n.* a plant on which tiny greenish flowers are surrounded by large, showy, bright-red, petal-like leaves.

point (point), *n.* **1,** the sharp or tapering end of a thing; as, the *point* of a pin; a pencil *point;* a *point* of land; **2,** a particular or separate part; detail; as the *points* of an argument; a trait; as *points* of character; also, the most important feature of a speech, story action, etc.; as, you missed the *point* **3,** purpose; as, she gained her *point* **4,** a particular spot or position; as a certain *point* on a road; also, a definite degree or stage; as, the boiling *point;* a turning-*point;* **5,** the unit of scoring in certain games; **6,** a dot printed or written; period; decimal point; **7,** one of the 32 equal divisions of the compass or one of the points marking them; **8,** a physical feature in an animal, esp. one by which excellence is judged:—*adj.* made with the needle as, *point* lace:—*v.t.* **1,** to sharpen; as to *point* a pencil; **2,** to give liveliness or force to; show the purpose of as, to *point* a moral; **3,** to show the direction of; as, to *point* the way; **4,** to direct or aim; as, to *point* a gun; **5,** to separate with a decimal point; as to *point* off figures; **6,** to fill the joint of (masonry) with mortar and smooth with a trowel; **7,** to show the presence of (game) by standing in a certain position, as some hunting dogs do **8,** to indicate; direct attention to as, to *point* out errors:—*v.i.* **1,** to call attention by extending the finger **2,** to face; tend (to or toward) be directed; **3,** to indicate the presence of game by standing in a certain position, as do some dogs.

point—blank (point′–blangk′), *adj* aimed straight at the mark; hence direct; blunt; as, a *point-blank* question:—*adv.* (point′–blangk′), directly.

point-ed (poin′tid), *adj.* **1,** sharpened having a sharp end, as a needle; **2** direct; telling; as, *pointed* repartee also, having a personal application as, a *pointed* allusion.

point-er (poin′tèr), *n,* **1,** a thing that points or shows position; **2,** a breed of large hunting dog with short hair and long ears, trained to point, that is, to stop and show the place where game is hidden; **3,** *Colloq.,* a timely hint suggestion; tip.

poise (poiz), *n.* **1,** equilibrium; balance **2,** the manner of carrying the head and body; **3,** mental balance; self-possession; as, she kept her *poise* under trying conditions:—*v.t.* and *v.i.* [poised pois-ing], to balance.

poi-son (poi′zn), *n.* **1,** a substance which causes injury or death to living body by chemical action when taken in or absorbed; **2,** an influence that damages the character:—*v.t.* **1,** to injure or kill by some deadly substance; **2,** to put a deadly substance into or upon; as, to *poison* food; **3,** to corrupt. —*adj.* **poi'-son-ous.**

poi-son—i-vy, (poi'zn–ī'vi), *n.* a common vine with leaves formed of three leaflets, the mere touch of which brings out, on many persons, a painful, itching rash.

poke (pōk), *v.t.* [poked, pok-ing,] **1,** to thrust or push against, esp. with a pointed object; prod; as, to *poke* the fire; **2,** to thrust (in or out); as, to *poke* one's head out of the door:—*v.i.* **1,** to thrust or push; as, to *poke* at the fire; **2,** to move lazily; dawdle:—*n.* **1,** a thrust or push; **2,** a projecting brim on the front of a woman's bonnet; **3,** a bonnet with a projecting rim: also called *poke bonnet;* **4,** *archaic,* pouch, wallet.

¹pok-er (pōk'ẽr), *n,* a rod of metal used for stirring fires.

²pok-er (pōk'ẽr), *n.* a card game in which two or more players bet on the value of their hands.

poke-weed (pōk'wēd') or **poke** (pōk) *n.* a common American plant with white flowers, purple berries, and poisonous root.

pok-y or **poke-y** (pōk'i), *adj.* [pok-i-er, pok-i-est], **1,** slow; dull; **2,** small; shabby.

po-lar (pō'lẽr), *adj.* pertaining to, or situated near, either pole of the earth; **2,** pertaining to either pole of a magnet.

Po-la-ris (pō-lâr'is; -lā'), *n.* the polestar, or North Star.

po-lar-ize (pō'lar-īz'), *v.t.* **1,** in *magnetism* and *electricity,* to give opposite magnetic properties to the poles of a bar, coil, battery, etc.; **2,** in *optics,* the process of affecting light or radiant heat so that the paths of the vibrations become straight lines, circles or ellipses. —*n.* **po-lar'i-ty; po'lar-i-za'tion.**

¹pole (pōl), *n,* **1,** either of the two ends of the axis of a sphere; esp., either of the two ends of the earth's axis, called the *North Pole* and the *South Pole;* **2,** either of the two terminals or ends of a magnet, electric battery, etc.

²pole (pōl), *n.* **1,** a long piece of wood or metal; as, a fishing-*pole;* also, an upright timber, such as a mast; as, a telegraph-*pole;* **2,** a rod, or linear measure, equal to 16½ feet, or 5½ yards: —*v.t.* [poled, poling], to push with a

pole; as, to *pole* a boat:—*v.i.* to propel a boat with a pole.

pole-cat (pōl'kat'), *n.* **1,** a small, flesh-eating European animal of the weasel family, which throws out a strong, offensive odour, and is valued for its dark-brown fur; **2,** a skunk.

pol-der (pōl'dẽr), *n.* an area of low land, as in Holland, reclaimed from the sea by use of dikes, etc.

pole-star (pōl'–stär'), *n.* **1,** the North Star, or Polaris, a guide to navigators and explorers; **2,** hence, a guiding light; guide.

po-lice (pō-lēs'), *n.* **1,** that part of a government which enforces the laws, investigates crimes, makes arrests, and keeps order; **2,** the men in this department:—*v.t.* [policed, polic-ing], **1,** to watch, protect, and keep in order by means of policemen; **2,** in the U.S. Army, to clean up (quarters or a camp): —*adj.* connected with the police; as, *police* protection:

—police dog, the German shepherd dog, or any of a variety of wolflike dogs trained to aid police.

po-lice-man (pō-lēs'man), *n.* [*pl.* police men (-men)], a member of a police force.—*n.* **po-lice'wom'an.**

¹pol-i-cy (pol'i-si), *n.* [*pl.* policies], **1,** wise management of public affairs; **2,** a course of conduct; as, it is good *policy* not to meddle; esp. a line of conduct of a government, business corporation, etc.; as, an immigration *policy.*

²pol-i-cy (pol'i-si), *n.* [*pl.* policies], a document containing a contract of insurance between an insurance company and the person or persons insured.

pol-i-o-my-e-li-tis (pol'i-ō-mī'i-lī'tis; pol'), *n.* an inflammation and wasting of the grey matter of the spinal cord: **acute anterior poliomyelitis,** an infectious form of the disease which esp. attacks children, causing a paralysis, sometimes permanent, of muscles of the arms and legs: also called *infantile paralysis,* or *polio.*

pol-ish (pol'ish), *v.t.* **1,** to make smooth or glossy by rubbing; as, to *polish* brass; **2,** to make polite or cultured:— *v.i.* to become smooth or glossy:— *n.* **1,** the act of polishing; **2,** a smooth glossy surface; **3,** a mixture for making a surface smooth and glossy; as, shoe *polish;* **4,** elegance of manners.— *n.* **pol'ish-er.**

Po-lit-bu-ro or **Po-lit-bu-reau** (po-lit'bū'rō), *n.* the inner executive committee of the Communist Party of the U.S.S.R. that examines questions before referring them to the government; it also acts independently.

po-lite (po-līt′), *adj.* [polit-er, polit-est], 1, well-bred; refined; as, *polite* society; 2, courteous; as, a *polite* child.

pol-i-tic (pol′i-tik), *adj.* 1, prudent; shrewd; as, a *politic* adviser; 2, useful; advisable; as, a *politic* decision.

po-lit-i-cal (po-lit′i-kal), *adj.* associated with the science of government, or the management of public affairs.

pol-i-ti-cian (pol′i-tish′an), *n.* a person who works for a political party.

pol-i-tics (pol′i-tiks), *n.pl.* used as *sing.* 1, the science or art of government; political science; 2, one's political opinions; the party to which one belongs.

pol-ka (pōl′ka), *n.* 1, a lively dance of Bohemian origin, performed by two persons; 2, music suitable for such a dance.

—polka dot, one of the small round dots used to form regular patterns on textile fabrics; as, a *polka dot* tie.

poll (pōl), *n.* 1, the head, esp. the part of it on which hair grows; 2, a count of persons, or the resulting number; hence, a list of persons, as of those entitled to vote at an election; 3, an election; 4, the number of votes recorded at an election; 5, (usually *polls*), the place where votes are cast; 6, a tax on each person: also called *poll-tax:—v.t.* 1, to lop, clip, or shear; as, to *poll* trees or sheep; also, to cut the horns of (cattle); 2, to enrol, as for voting; 3, to examine or record the votes of; as, to *poll* a jury; 4, to receive votes from; as, he *polled* a large majority; 5, to cast or drop into a ballot-box; as, to *poll* one's vote.

pol-len (pol′en), *n.* the fine powder produced by the anthers of a flower, which, when carried to the pistil, usually of another flower, fertilizes the seeds.

pol-li-nate (pol′i-nāt′), *v.t.* —pollinated, pollinat-ing], to carry and drop pollen upon the pistil of (a flower) for fertilization, as bees do.—*n.* pol′lina′tion.

pol-li-wog (pol′i-wog′), *n.* a tadpole, or immature frog.

pol-lute (po-lūt′), *v.t.* [pollut-ed, polluting], 1, to make unclean; as, to *pollute* water with filth; 2, to destroy the purity of; corrupt.—*n.* pol-lu′tion.

po-lo (pō′lō), *n.* a game similar to field hockey, in which the players are mounted on ponies and equipped with long-handled mallets:—**water-polo**, a ball game played in the water by swimmers.—*n.* po′lo-ist.

po-lo-ni-um (po-lō′ni-um), *n.* a radioactive element first obtained by the Curies from pitchblende: it gives off alpha rays and is identical with radium F (atomic number, 84).

pol-troon (pol-trōōn′), *n.* a mean-spirited, lazy coward.

pol-y- (pol′i-), *Greek prefix* meaning *many*, as in **pol′y-mor′phic** (having various forms), **pol′y-nu′cle-ar** (having many nuclei), **pol′y-the′ism** (belief in many gods).

po-lyg-a-my (po-lig′-a-mi), *n.* the practice or state of having more than one wife or more than one husband at the same time.—*adj.* po-lyg′a-mous (po-lig′a-mus).

pol-y-glot (pol′i-glot′), *adj.* containing, or made up of, several languages; as, a *polyglot* Bible or dictionary.

pol-y-gon (pol′i-gon; pol′i-gun), *n.* in geometry, a closed plane figure of straight sides.

POLYGONS

pol-yp (pol′ip), *n.* a small salt-water animal, as the coral, with a tubelike body, one end of which forms a mouth surrounded by tentacles, the other end being attached to shells, rocks, etc.

pol-y-syl-la-ble (pol′i-sil′a-bl), *n.* a word of many syllables.

po-made (pō-mād′; mäd′), *n.* perfumed hair ointment.

pome (pōm), *n.* any fleshy fruit, as apple, pear, etc.

pome-gran-ate (pom′gran′it; pom-gran′it; pum-gran′it; pum′gran′it), *n.* 1, a tropical Asiatic tree yielding a fruit with a thick rind and a very seedy, crimson pulp, of pleasant, acid taste; 2, the fruit of this tree.

Pom-er-a-ni-an (pom′er-ā′ni-an), *n.* a small dog with long, thick, black or white, silky hair, bushy, curled-up tail, and pointed muzzle.

pom-mel (pum′el), *n.* 1, the knob on a sword-hilt; 2, the ridge on the front of a saddle:—*v.t.* [pommelled, pommelling], to beat, esp. with the fists. Also spelled pum′mel.

pomp (pomp), *n.* display; magnificence.

pom-pa-dour (pom′pa-door; pom′pa-dôr;), *n.* a style of wearing the hair brushed back from the forehead without a part, and often over a roll.

pom-pom (pom'pom), *n.* an automatic, rapid-fire, anti-aircraft gun.

pom-pon (pom'pon), *n.* **1,** an ornamental tuft or ball of silk, feathers, etc., for women's or children's hats; **2,** a chrysanthemum with small, round flowers.

pom-pous (pom'pus), *adj.* self-important; pretentious; as, a *pompous* orator.—*n.* pom-pos'i-ty

pond (pond), *n.* a small body of still water.

pon-der (pon'dėr), *v.t.* to consider carefully; think about:—*v.i.* to reflect.

pon-der-ous (pon'dėr-us), *adj.* **1,** very heavy; **2,** laboured; dull; as, a *ponderous* style of writing.

pone (pōn), *n,* in the U.S., bread made of corn meal, with or without milk or eggs: also called *corn pone.*

pon-gee (pon-jē'; pun-jē'), *n.* a soft, thin, unbleached silk from China; also, any similar dyed silk fabric.

pon-iard (pon'yėrd), *n.* a dagger.

pon-tiff (pon'tif), *n.* a bishop; esp., the Pope.—*adj.* pon-tif'i-cal.

pon-toon (pon-tōōn'), *n.* **1,** a small, low, flat-bottomed boat; **2,** a flat-boat, a raft, a hollow metal cylinder, etc., used to support a floating bridge, called a *pontoon-bridge;* **3,** a boatlike attachment on the bottom of an aeroplane, to enable it to land on water.

po-ny (pō'ni), *n.* [*pl.* ponies], **1,** a horse of any one of certain small breeds; as, a Shetland *pony;* **2,** in the U.S., a literal translation into English of some foreign text, used by students in preparing lessons; a trot.

pooch (pōōch), *n. Slang,* a dog.

poo-dle ((pōō'dl), *n.* one of a breed of intelligent, black or white, curly-haired dogs.

pooh (pōō), *interj.* an exclamation of scorn or contempt; pshaw! nonsense!

pooh—pooh (pōō'–pōō'), *v.t.* to make light of.

¹pool (pōōl), *n.* **1,** a small body of still water; a pond; **2,** also, a small body of any standing liquid.

²pool (pōōl), *n.* **1,** a game played on a special table, with balls which are shot with a cue into the pockets at the edge of the table; **2,** in betting games, the total amount of the player's bets; the money at stake; **3,** a combination of persons, rival business corporations, etc., united for some special purpose, intended to result in profit to all involved; also, the resources combined in furtherance of this end:—*v.t.* to put

into a common fund for a joint undertaking or in order to share the profits.

poop (pōōp), *n.* the raised deck in the stern of a vessel; also, the stern itself.

poor (pōōr), *adj.* **1,** having little or no means; lacking riches; **2,** lacking in good qualities such as strength, beauty, or dignity; **3,** inferior in skill or execution; as, a *poor* piece of work; **4,** wretched; feeble; also, spiritless; **5,** of no great value; as, in my *poor* opinion; **6,** not fertile; as, *poor* soil; scanty; as, a *poor* harvest.—*adv.* poor'ly.

poor-house (poor'hous'), *n.* a place where paupers live at public expense; an alms-house.

pop (pop), *n.* **1,** a short, sharp, quick sound; **2,** a shot from a small firearm; **3,** a bubbling non-intoxicating drink; as, soda-*pop:*—*v.t.* [popped, pop-ping], **1,** to cause to burst open by heat; as, to *pop* corn; **2,** to fire (a gun); **3,** to push or thrust suddenly; as, she *popped* her head through the door:—*v.i.* **1,** to make a short, sharp, quick sound; **2,** to move quickly; dart; as, to *pop* in or out; **3,** come suddenly into view; to burst open with a sound:—*adv.* suddenly.

pop-corn (pop'kôrn'), *n,* **1,** a kind of Indian corn with small, hard grains which, when exposed to heat, burst open with a sharp noise, or pop, and become white and puffy; **2,** the white, puffed kernels.

Pope (pōp), *n.* the Bishop of Rome and head of the Roman Catholic Church:— pope, a church dignitary with great power.

pop-gun (pop'gun'), *n.* a child's toy gun that shoots a pellet (such as a cork) with a loud pop (by air compression).

pop-in-jay (pop'in-jā'), *n.* a vain, talkative person, esp. a fop or dude.

pop-lar (pop'lėr), *n.* a fast-growing slender tree with shiny, heart-shaped leaves, rough bark, and soft wood; also, the wood.

pop-lin (pop'lin), *n* a finely ribbed fabric, usually of silk or silk and worsted. It is used for dresses, curtains, etc.

pop-o-ver (pop'ō'vėr), *n,* a hot bread made of a batter of eggs, milk, and flour, thoroughly beaten. When baked, it becomes a hollow shell.

pop-per (pop'ėr), *n.* a utensil, as a wire net, for popping corn.

pop-py (pop'i), *n.* [*pl.* poppies], any of a number of plants with showy red,

all (ôl), ôr; up, mūte, cûr, cōol, book; oil, out; th, thin; *th,* the.

yellow, or white flowers; also, the flower of a poppy plant.

pop-py-cock (pop'i-kok'), *n.* and *interj. Colloq.* nonsense; bosh.

pop-u-lace (pop'ū-lis), *n.* the common people; the masses.

pop-u-lar (pop'ū-lėr), *adj.* **1,** having to do with the common people; as, *popular* taste; a *popular* form of government; **2,** suitable for the majority; as, *popular* music; **3,** held in favour by many people; as, a *popular* writer; **4,** within the means of the average purchaser; as, *popular* prices. —*adv.* **pop'u-lar-ly:**—*v.t.* **pop'u-lar-ize.**

pop-u-lar-i-ty (pop'ū-lar'i-ti), *n.* the state of. being liked and admired by many people.

pop-u-late (pop'ū-lāt'), *v.t.* [populated, populat-ing], **1,** to furnish with inhabitants; as, to *populate* a country; **2,** to inhabit.

pop-u-la-tion (pop'ū-lā'shun), *n.* **1,** the total number of people of a country, state, town, etc. **2,** the people themselves; also, any one group of the people; as, the adult *population;* **3,** the process of furnishing with inhabitants.

pop-u-lous (pop'ū-lus), *adj.* containing many inhabitants.—*n.* **pop'u-lous-ness.**

por-ce-lain (pôr'se-lin; pôrs'lin), *n.* and *adj.* **1,** a fine, white, glazed earthenware, unusually hard, and so thin that light can be seen through it; **2,** dishes or ornaments of such ware.

porch (pōrch), *n.* **1,** a partly-enclosed approach to a doorway, extending out from the main wall of a building and having a separate roof; **2,** a veranda; piazza.

por-cu-pine (pôr'kū-pīn'), *n.* an animal akin to the rat and beaver, with spines or sharp quills in its hairy coat which protect it from its enemies.

¹pore (pōr), *n.* a tiny hole or opening, esp. one of many in the skin through which perspiration is discharged.

²pore (pōr), *v.i.* [pored, poring], to study with close attention; ponder; as, to *pore* over lessons.

pork (pōrk), *n.* the flesh of pigs or hogs, used for food.

pork-er (pōr'kėr), *n.* a pig or hog fattened for food.

por-nog-ra-phy (pôr-nog'ra-fi), *n.* writings or pictures intended to arouse sexual desire.—*adj.* **porn'no-graph'ic.**

por-ous (pōr'us), *adj.* full of tiny holes through which a fluid may pass or be absorbed.—*n.* **po-ros'i-ty** (po-ros'i-ti).

por-poise (pôr'pus), *n.* **1,** a sea animal, five to eight feet long, related to the whales, and like the whale, a mammal; **2,** a dolphin.

por-ridge (por'ij), *n.* a food made by boiling a cereal or a vegetable slowly in water or milk until it thickens; as, oat-meal *porridge.*

¹port (pōrt), *n.* **1,** a place where vessels arrive and depart; harbour; as, the *port* of New York; **2,** a harbour town.

²port (pōrt), *n.* **1,** a round opening or window in the side of a ship, through which air and light may enter. or out of which cannon may be discharged; a loophole in a wall, fort, etc. Also called *porthole;* **2,** an outlet, as for steam or water.

³port (pōrt), *n.* the left side of a ship as one faces the bow: formerly called *larboard:* opposite of *starboard:*—*adj.* on the left side of a ship; as, a *port* cabin:—*v.t.* to turn to the port, or left, side of a ship; as, to *port* the helm.

⁴port (pōrt), *n.* a strong, sweet wine, usually dark red in colour.

port-a-ble (pōr'ta-bl), *adj.* capable of being easily carried; as, a *portable* typewriter.

por-tage (pōr'tij; pōr-täzh'), *n.* **1,** the carrying of boats, goods, etc., overland from one navigable lake or river to another; also, the overland route taken; **2,** any cargo to be carried, or the cost of such carriage.

por-tal (pōr't'l), *n.* a gateway; entrance.

port-cul-lis (pōrt-kul'is), *n.* a strong grating hung over the gateway of a fortress or castle, capable of being let down to close the gate and aid in defence.

por-tend (pôr-tend'), *v.t.* to give warning in advance of something that is to happen; as, clouds *portend* a storm.

por-tent (pōr'tent; pôr'tent), *n.* an omen or sign, esp. of calamity to come.

por-ten-tous (pôr-ten'tus), *adj,* **1,** foreshadowing evil; threatening; as, a *portentous* dream; **2,** remarkable; extraordinary.

¹por-ter (pōr'tėr), *n.* a doorkeeper.

²por-ter (pōr'tėr), *n.* **1,** one who carries luggage, as at railway stations and hotels; **2,** an attendant in a sleeping-car or parlour car; **3,** a dark-brown, bitter beer.

por-ter-house (pōr'tėr-hous') **steak,** a choice cut of beef from between the tenderloin and the sirloin.

cat, āge, fär, câre, àsk; ten, ēve, latėr; (i) pity, rely, senate; īce; top; nō.

port-fo-li-o (pōrt-fō′li-ō; pōrt-fōl′yō), *n.* [*pl.* portfolios], **1,** a case for carrying loose papers, drawings, etc.; a brief-case; **2,** the office of a minister of the government; as, the *portfolio* of war.

port-hole (pōrt′hōl′), *n.* **1,** a round opening, or window, in the side of a ship; **2,** an opening in the wall of a fort, blockhouse, etc., through which to shoot.

por-ti-co (pōr′ti-kō′), *n.* [*pl.* porticos or porticoes], a colonnade or walk covered by a roof supported on columns; esp. a porch with columns at the front of a building.

por-tiere (pōr′tyâr′; pōr′ti-âr′), *n.* a curtain or drapery hanging at a doorway.

por-tion (pōr′shun), *n.* **1,** a piece or part of anything; as, a *portion* of pie; **2,** hence, a share, or a part given; a part of an estate left to an heir; also, a dowry:—*v.t.* **1,** to divide into shares; **2,** to give a share to.

port-ly (pōrt′li), *adj.* [port-li-er, port-li-est], **1,** corpulent; stout; as, a *portly* chef; **2,** stately and dignified; as, a man of *portly* mien.—*n.* **port′li-ness.**

por-trait (pōr′trāt; pôr′trit), *n.* a picture of a person; a likeness.—*n.* **por′trai-ture.**

por-tray (pōr-trā′) *v.t.* **1,** to make a likeness of; **2,** to describe; **3,** to play the part of; as, to *portray* Hamlet.—*n.* **por-tray′al.**

por-tu-la-ca (pōr′tū-lā′ka; pōr′tū-lak′a), *n.* a garden plant with leaves like fleshy needles, and flowers of various colours.

¹pose (pōz), *v.i.* [posed, pos-ing], **1,** to assume and keep an attitude; as, the model *posed* for an hour; **2,** to pretend to be what one is not; as, he *posed* as an expert:—*v.t.* **1,** to place in a suitable attitude; as, to *pose* a person for a portrait; **2,** to put or set forth; as, he *posed* a question:—*n.* **1,** attitude or position; **2,** a mental attitude assumed for the sake of effect.

²pose (pōz), *v.t.* [posed, pos-ing], to perplex.

pos-er (pō′zėr), *n.* **1,** one who poses; an affected person; **2,** a perplexing or baffling problem.

po-si-tion (po-zish′un), *n.* **1,** the place where a thing is set or placed; situation; as, the *position* of a house; **2,** the manner in which anything is placed or arranged; as, an awkward sleeping *position;* **3,** social standing or rank; **4,** employment; job; **5,** mental attitude toward any subject; as, a conservative *position;* **6,** correct or proper place; as, take your *positions.*

pos-i-tive (poz′i-tiv), *adj.* **1,** clearly stated; as, a *positive* assertion; uttered with authority; as, *positive* instructions; **2,** leaving no doubt; as, proof *positive;* **3,** of real, practical value; as, self-reliance is a *positive* virtue; **4,** confident; sure; as, people were once *positive* that the sun moved round the earth; **5,** in *grammar,* naming the simplest form of an adjective or adverb; as, "easy" is a *positive* form, "easier" is comparative; **6,** in *arithmetic,* a quantity larger than zero; a plus quantity; **7,** naming the kind of electricity formed on a glass rod when it is rubbed with silk: opposed to the electricity on the silk, which is called *negative;* **8,** in *photography,* matching the original in the distribution of light and shade: opposite of *negative;* **9,** *Colloq.,* utter; absolute; as, a *positive* beauty:—*n.* **1,** in *grammar,* the simplest degree of comparison; also, an adjective or adverb in that degree; **2,** a photographic plate, film, or slide, reproducing the light and shade of the original: opposite of *negative,* in which the light and shade of the original are reversed.—*adv.* **pos′i-tive-ly.**

pos-i-tron (poz′i-tron), *n.* in an atom, a particle of positive electricity having a mass and charge equal to that of the electron.

pos-se (pos′i), *n.* a number of men summoned by a sheriff to assist in carrying out the law.

pos-sess (po-zes′), *v.t.* **1,** to own; have; as, to *possess* great wealth; to *possess* one's soul in patience; **3,** to occupy; seize; as, to *possess* a city during war:—**possessed,** *adj.* as if in the power of evil spirits; crazy.

pos-ses-sion (po-zesh′un), *n,* **1,** control; occupancy; as, *possession* of a town by an enemy; **2,** the thing owned; as, a small *possession;* **3, possessions,** property.

pos-ses-sive (po-zes′iv), *adj.* **1,** showing ownership, or a desire to own; as, a *possessive* manner; **2,** in *grammar,* naming the case used to express ownership, origin, etc., as "Mary's" in the expression "Mary's book":—*n.* the possessive case; also, a word in that case.

pos-ses-sor (po-zes′ėr), *n.* one who owns or holds something.

pos-si-bil-i-ty (pos′i-bil′i-ti), *n.* [*pl.* possibilities], **1,** anything that may happen; as, snow is a *possibility* today; **2,** the chance that a thing may happen; as, the *possibility* of failure.

pos-si-ble (pos′i-bl), *adj.* **1,** capable of existing or coming into being; capable of happening; as, the *possible* result of an act; **2,** available; worth considering; as, a *possible* candidate.—*adv.* **pos′si-bly.**

pos-sum (pos′um), *n. Colloq.,* in Canada and the U.S., an opossum.

¹post (pōst), *n.* an upright piece of timber, metal, etc., used esp. as a support for something:—*v.t.* **1,** to fasten, as a notice, to a wall; **2,** to make known by means of notices fastened to a wall; **3,** to place (a person's name) on such a notice; **4,** to put notices upon (a place) forbidding entrance or warning against use; as, to *post* a hunting-preserve or an unsafe bridge; to *post* a trout stream.

²post (pōst), *n.* **1,** formerly, one of a number of riders, placed at fixed stations along a road, each of whom in turn carried the mail forward to the next station; a postman; also, formerly one of the stations where relays of horses were kept for such riders; **2,** a system of carrying and delivering letters; the mail:—*v.i.* to travel with speed:—*v.t.* **1,** to send by mail; esp., to drop, as a letter, into a letter-box; **2,** in bookkeeping, to transfer (an entry or item) from journal to ledger; **3,** *Colloq.,* to inform fully:—*adv.* speedily.—*n.* **post′box′; post′free′.**

³post (pōst), *n.* **1,** a place where a person or thing is stationed; **2,** a position of trust; **3,** a trading settlement; **4,** a military station; also, the soldiers occupying it:—*v.t.* to station.

post- (pōst-), *prefix* meaning *after,* as in **post′gla′cial, post′grad′u-ate, post meridiem** (p.m. or afternoon), **post′ na′tal** (after birth), **post′ nup′tial** (after marriage), **post′ pran′di-al** (after-dinner).

post-age (pōs′tij), *n.* the cost of sending letters by mail:—**postage stamp,** a government stamp to be pasted on mail as a sign that postage has been paid.

post-al (pōs′tal), *adj.* of or pertaining to the post-office or mail service; as, *postal* rates:—**postal card, 1,** a card for mailing, with a postage stamp officially printed on it; **2,** a postcard.

post-card (pōst′kärd′), *n.* a private card for mailing, to which a stamp must be attached. Also written **post card.**

post-date (pōst′dāt′), *v.t.* [-dated, -dating], to date with a date later than the current date; as, a *postdated* cheque or invoice.

post-er (pōs′tėr), *n.* a placard or bill put up in a public place, as on a wall, to advertise or announce something.

pos-te-ri-or (pos-tē′ri-ėr) *adj.* **1,** later; **2,** rear; hinder:—*n.* often in *pl.,* the rump; buttocks.

pos-ter-i-ty (pos-ter′i-ti), *n.* **1,** a person's descendants, considered as a group; **2,** future generations.

pos-tern (pōs′tėrn; post′ėrn), *n.* **1,** formerly, a back door or gate; private entrance; **2,** in a fort, an underground passage, closed by a door, leading inward from the trench:—*adj.* behind; private; rear.

post-haste (pōst′hāst′), *adv.* quickly.

post-hu-mous (pos′tū-mus), *adj.* **1,** born after the death of the father; as, a *posthumous* child; **2,** published after the death of an author; as, a *posthumous* book; **3,** arising or occurring after one's death; as, *posthumous* fame.—*adv.* **post′hu-mous-ly.**

pos-til-ion or **pos-til-lion** (pōs-til′-yun; pos-til′yun), *n.* a person who rides the left-hand horse of a carriage team to guide the team.

post-man (pōst′man), *n.* [*pl.* postmen (-men)], a letter-carrier.

post-mark (pōst′märk′), *n.* a mark stamped upon mail to show the place and date of mailing:—*v.t.* to stamp thus.

post-mas-ter (pōst′más′tėr), *n.* **1,** the superintendent of a post-office; **2,** formerly, one who furnished horses for travelling.

post-mis-tress (pōst′mis′tris), *n.* a woman superintendent of a post-office.

post—mor-tem (pōst′—môr′tem), *adj.* happening after the death of the person involved; as, the *post-mortem* examination of a body:—*n.* an examination made of a body after death, esp. to find the cause of death.

post—of-fice (pōst′—ôf′is), *n.* **1,** the department of a government which handles the mail; **2,** any local office of this department.

post-paid (pōst′pād′), *adj.* having the postage paid in advance.

post-pone (pōst-pōn′), *v.t.* [postponed, postpon-ing], to put off to another time.—*n.* **post-pone′ment.**

post-script (pōst′skript), *n.* a written addition to a book, article, etc.; esp., a paragraph added to a letter after the writer's signature.

pos-ture (pos/tūr), *n.* personal bearing or carriage:—*v.t.* [postured, postur-ing], to place in a particular attitude:—*v.i.* to take a certain position, esp. an artificial or affected pose.

post-war (pōst/wôr/), *adj.* after any war, as contrasted with *prewar*.

po-sy (pō/zi), *n.* [*pl.* posies], **1,** a flower or a bunch of flowers; **2,** a motto or verse sent with a bouquet or inscribed in a ring.

pot (pot), *n.* **1,** a metal or earthenware vessel used for cooking; **2,** the quantity such a vessel will hold; **3,** such a vessel with its contents; **4,** a vessel of earthenware for holding growing plants; **5,** *Slang:* **a,** a sum of money made up as a bet by contributions from a group, to go to one of them; **b,** a large sum of money:—*v.t.* [pot-ted, pot-ting], **1,** to preserve in a pot, as meat; **2,** to transplant into a pot; **3,** to shoot (a bird or animal) for food.—*adj.* **pot/bel/lied.**—*n.* **pot/hold/er.**

pot-ash (pot/ash/), *n.* a salt of potassium; esp., impure potassium carbonate, a white salt obtained from wood ashes, and used in making soap and glass.

po-tas-si-um (po-tas/i-um), *n.* a soft, very light, bluish-white metal, found only in union with other substances. It is used in making fertilizers, glass, etc.

po-ta-to (po-tā/tō), *n.* [*pl.* potatoes], **1,** a plant related to the tomato, grown for its starchy, edible tubers: also called *white potato* and *Irish potato;* **2,** one of these tubers used as food; **3,** the sweet potato:—**potato bug,** a beetle with yellow and black stripes, which destroys the leaves of the potato and related plants.

po-tent (pō/tent), *adj.* **1,** powerful; mighty; as, a *potent* drug; **2,** having great authority or influence; as, a *potent* prince.—*n.* **po/ten-cy.**

po-ten-tate (pō/ten-tāt/), *n.* a ruler who has great power or authority; a monarch; sovereign; prince.

po-ten-tial (pō-ten/shal), *adj.* **1,** capable of existing, but not yet in existence; possible, but not actual; as, Canada has great *potential* wealth; **2,** in *grammar*, expressing power or possibility, as the word "can" in the sentence "I can come":—*n.* the amount of electrical force in an electrical conductor, usually measured in volts.—*n.* **po-ten/ti-al/i-ty.**

po-ten-ti-om-e-ter (pō-ten/shi-om/e-

tẻr), *n.* an instrument for measuring the differences in the charge or potential of electric circuits.

pot-hole (pot/hōl/), *n.* **1,** a cylindrical hole left in a river's rocky bed from the action of whirling gravel or boulders, as at Rockwood, Ontario; **2,** a hole left in a road by action of frost, erosion, etc.

po-tion (pō/shun), *n.* a drink, esp. of liquid medicine.

pot-latch (pot/lach/), *n. Chinook,* a winter festival, esp. among the Indians of Canada's Pacific Coast, at which lavish gifts were exchanged chiefly for fame or prestige: now forbidden by the Canadian Government.

pot-luck (pot/luk/), *n.* and *adj.* whatever a family is having for a meal; a potluck dinner; as, will you take *potluck* with us today?

pot—pie (pot/—pī/), *n.* **1,** a meat pie; **2,** a meat stew with dumplings.

pot-pour-ri (pō/poo-rē/; pot-poor/i), *n.* any mixture or medley as of spices, songs, writings, edibles, perfumes, etc.

pot-tage (pot/ij), *n.* a stew or thick soup of meat and vegetables, or of both.

¹pot-ter (pot/ẻr), *n.* a maker of vessels of earthenware, stoneware, etc.

²pot-ter (pot/ẻr) or **put-ter** (put/ẻr), *v.i.* to work lazily, or with little purpose; as, to *potter* around at gardening.

potter's field, a plot of ground set aside for the burial of criminals, of unidentified persons, and of persons who have neither friends nor money.

pot-ter-y (pot/ẻr-i), *n.* [*pl.* potteries], **1,** pots, dishes, vases, etc., moulded from moistened clay and hardened in ovens or kilns; **2,** a place where such ware is manufactured; **3,** the art of making it.

pouch (pouch), *n.* **1,** a bag or·sack of any sort; as, a tobacco-*pouch;* **2,** in certain animals, any baglike part, as that in which the kangaroo carries its young:—*v.t.* **1,** to put (something) into a small bag; as, to *pouch* money; **2,** to give a pouchlike form to (part of a dress, etc.):—*v.i.* to form a pouchlike cavity.

poul-tice (pōl/tis), *n.* a moist mixture of bread, herbs, etc., usually heated, spread on a cloth, and applied to a sore or inflamed spot:—*v.t.* [poulticed, poultic-ing], to apply such a mixture to (a sore place).

poul-try (pōl/tri), *n,* domestic fowls, as chickens, turkeys, etc.

all (ôl), ôr; up, mūte, cûr, cōōl, book; oil, out; th, thin; *th*, the.

pounce (pouns), *n.* a sudden swooping attack:—*v.i.* [pounced, pounc-ing], to spring suddenly or unexpectedly; as, the terrier *pounced* on the rat.

¹pound (pound), *n.* **1,** a measure of avoirdupois weight, equal to sixteen ounces; also, a measure of troy weight, equal to twelve ounces; **2,** the standard of money in Great Britain, called the *pound sterling*, equivalent to about $2.80 (1960).

²pound (pound), *n.* **1,** a place for confining or keeping stray animals; as, a dog *pound;* **2,** a shelter for livestock; **3,** an enclosure for trapping wild animals; **4,** an area or space where fish are caught or kept:—*v.t.* to confine, as in a pound.

³pound (pound), *v.t.* **1,** to beat; strike forcibly; **2,** to reduce to powder; **3,** to make solid by blows; tamp, as loose earth; **4,** to walk with heavy steps:— *v.i.* to deal blows; beat heavily or steadily, as waves against the seashore: —*n.* **1,** a blow; **2,** the sound of a blow.

pour (pōr), *v.t.* **1,** to cause to flow in a stream; **2,** to send forth freely; utter freely:—*v.i.* to flow down freely:—*n.* a heavy rain.

pout (pout), *v.i.* to push out the lips, as in sullenness, contempt, or displeasure; look sulky:—*v.t.* to push (the lips) out; pucker:—*n.* **1,** a sullen puckering of the lips; **2,** pouts, a fit of sullenness.

pout-er (pout′ėr), *n.* a kind of pigeon which puffs out its crop.

pov-er-ty (pov′ėr-ti), *n.* **1,** the state of being poor; necessity; want; **2,** any lack of excellence in quality; scarcity; as, a *poverty* of ideas.

pow (pou), *interj.* an exclamation, imitative of a bullet's ping, used by boys as in gunplay.

pow-der (pou′dėr), *n.* **1,** any dry substance in fine particles; a fine dust; **2,** an explosive in powder form; as, blasting-*powder;* **3,** a fine, dustlike cosmetic for use on the skin; **4,** a medicine in powder form; also, a dose of this; as, a sleeping-*powder:*—*v.t.* **1,** to reduce to powder; pulverize; **2,** to dust with powder; to decorate, as with powder; as, a box *powdered* with gilt stars; **3,** to sprinkle for flavouring; as, to *powder* cake with sugar:—*v.i.* **1,** to use powder; as, she *powders* lightly; **2,** to be reduced to powder; as, sugar *powders* easily.—*adj.* **pow′-der-y.**

pow-er (pou′ėr), *n.* **1,** ability to act or to do something; as, the *power* to fly;

the *power* to think; **2,** strength; vigour; as, the *power* of a blow; **3,** rule; influence; as, to have *power* over a group; also, official right to rule; authority; as, the *power* to levy taxes; **4,** a person or thing of great influence; as, he is a *power* in the city; **5,** an influential nation; as, Spain was once a great *power;* **6,** any form of force or energy to do work; as, mechanical or electrical *power;* **7,** the magnifying capacity of a lens; **8,** the result of multiplying a number by itself a given number of times; as, 27 is the third *power* of three, that is $3 \times 3 \times 3 = 27$. —*adj.* **pow′er-less.**

pow-er-ful (pou′ėr-fool), *adj.* having great power, influence, or strength; as, a *powerful* man, engine, telescope, odour, etc.

pow-wow (pou′wou′), *n,* **1,** a public feast or dance, esp. one intended to secure religious or magical aid in a hunt, war, etc., as among the North American Indians; **2,** the working of magic, as in the cure of disease; **3,** a worker of magic; medicine-man; **4,** *Colloq.,* in the U.S., a meeting; esp., a noisy meeting, often a political one:— *v.i.* (pou′wou′; pou′wou′), to hold such a meeting.

pox (poks), *n.* any disease marked by skin eruptions; syphilis.

prac-ti-ca-ble (prak′ti-ka-bl), *adj.* capable of being done, practised, or used; as, fire prevention is *practicable;* a *practicable* idea.—*adv.* **prac′ti-ca-bly.** —*n.* **prac′ti-ca-bil′i-ty.**

prac-ti-cal (prak′ti-kal), *adj.* **1,** relating to, or obtained through, experience or use; as, *practical* wisdom; **2,** capable of being put to use; useful; as, a *practical* suggestion; **3,** inclined to useful action rather than thought; as, a *practical* disposition; **4,** skilled, but without complete training; as, a *practical* nurse.—*n.* **prac′ti-cal′i-ty.**

prac-ti-cal-ly (prak′ti-kal-i), *adv.* **1,** really; as, his painting is *practically* worthless; **2,** through actual experience or practice; as, he is *practically* familiar with all types of radio; **3,** virtually; in fact, though not in name; as, he is *practically* the president.

prac-tice (prak′tis), *n.* **1,** custom; habit; **2,** the putting of knowledge to actual use; as, the *practice* of good manners; **3,** the exercise of any profession; as, the *practice* of medicine; **4,** regular exercise as a means of learning; as, *practice* in writing.

prac-tise (prak'tis), *v.t.* [practised, practis-ing], **1,** to do in reality; as, *practise* what you preach; **2,** to do frequently or as a rule; as, to *practise* plain eating; **3,** to work at, as a profession; as, to *practise* law; **4,** to perform in order to learn; as, to *practise* baseball:—*v.i.* **1,** to do something as a habit; **2,** to follow a profession; **3,** to do something often in order to learn. Also spelled **prac'tice.**

prac-ti-tion-er (prak-tish'un-ẽr), *n.* a person who is engaged in any profession, esp. medicine or law.

prag-mat-ic (prag-mat'ik), *adj.* concerned with practical values or consequences, also with the testing of an idea by experience; as, a *pragmatic* method.—*n.* **prag'ma-tism; prag'ma-tist.**

prai-rie (prâr'i), *n.* a large, treeless tract of level or rolling grassland, esp. in Western Canada.

prairie—chicken or **sharp—tailed grouse,** a large, brown-and-white, henlike grouse with short rounded tail: in 1945 it was declared a provincial emblem of Saskatchewan.

prairie—dog (prâr'i-dôg'), *n.* a small animal resembling a woodchuck: so called because it barks. It lives in large, underground colonies in western Canada.

prai-rie lil-y or **orange-red lily** (*Lilium philadelphicum* L.var.*Andinum*) was adopted.in 1941 as Saskatchewan's official floral emblem: it has orange flowers with purplish-black spots.

prairie—wolf (prâr'i-woolf'), *n.* a small wolf of western North America; a coyote.

praise (prāz), *n.* **1,** approval; applause; **2,** glorification of God:—*v.t.* [praised, prais-ing], **1,** to speak well of; approve; **2,** to glorify or extol (God).—*adj.* **praise'wor'thy.**

pram (pram), *n. Colloq.* a perambulator.

prance (prȧns), *v.i.* [pranced, prancing], **1,** to move by springing or bounding from the hind legs, as a high-spirited horse; **2,** to ride a prancing horse; **3,** to swagger; strut; **4,** *Colloq.,* to dance; caper:—*v.t.* to cause (an animal) to prance:—*n.* a prancing or swaggering.—*n.* **pranc'er.**

prank (prangk), *n.* a mischievous trick.

prate (prāt), *v.i.* [prat-ed, prat-ing], to talk idly:—*v.t.* to prattle; talk idly.

prattle (prat'l), *v.t.* and *v.i.* [prat-tled, prat-tling], to babble like a child; chatter:—*n.* childish talk.—*n.* **prat'tler.**

prawn (prôn), *n.* an edible, shrimplike shellfish with reddish-brown spots.

pray (prā), *v.i.* **1,** to make request or confession, or offer praise,'esp. to God; **2,** to make a petition to a human being or authority:—*v.t.* **1,** to make request of; as, to *pray* the court for relief; **2,** to make request for; as, we *pray* Thy forgiveness; **3,** to bring about by praying.

prayer (prâr), *n.* earnest entreaty, esp. that offered to God with thanks and praise.

prayer-ful (prâr'fool), *adj.* given to devout appeal to God.—*adv.* **prayer'-ful-ly.**

praying mantis, *n.* Same as *mantis.*

pre- (prē-), *prefix* meaning *before* (in time, place, rank, etc.) or *beforehand,* as in **pre'ar-range', pre'con-ceived', pre'de-cease'** (die before), **pre'con-cert'ed** (arranged beforehand), **pre-cur'sor** (forerunner), **pre'dis-posed', pre'-ex-ist', pre-fab'ri-cate** (*Colloq.* **pre'-fab**), **pre-fig'ure** (foreshadow), **pre-heat', pre-judge', pre-med'i-cal, pre-na'tal** (before birth), **pre'or-dain', pre'-school', pre'—shrunk', pre'view', pre'-vo-ca'tion-al.**

preach (prēch), *v.i.* and *v.t.* **1,** to talk or teach publicly on a religious subject, esp. from a text of Scripture; as, to *preach* eloquently; to *preach* Christ; **2,** to advise on moral, religious, or social subjects; as, his teacher *preached* to him.—*n.* **preach'er.**

pre-am-ble (prē'am'bl, pri-am'bl), *n.* **1,** an introduction to a speech or writing; **2,** an introduction to a statute or law, giving the reason for passing the law; as, the *preamble* to the Constitution.

pre-car-i-ous (pri-kâr'i-us), *adj.* depending on circumstances; uncertain; hence, dangerous; risky.—*adv.* **pre-car'i-ous-ly.**

pre-cau-tion (pri-kô'shun), *n.* care taken beforehand to prevent harm, loss, etc.—*adj.* **pre-cau'tion-ar'y.**

pre-cede (prē-sēd'), *v.t.* and *v.i.* [pre-ced-ed, preced-ing], to go before in time,·place, rank, or importance.

pre-ced-ence (pres'i-dens; pri-sēd'-ens), *n.* **1,** the act of going before another or others in time, order, rank, etc.; **2,** superiority in rank; specifically, the right of going before others in ceremonies and social formalities. Also, **pre-ced'en-cy.**

prec-e-dent (pres'i-dent), *n.* something said or done in the past, that serves as a model for the future:—*adj.* (pri-sēd'ent), going before.

pre-cept (prē'sept), *n.* a rule of conduct or action to be used as a guide.—*n.* **pre-cep'tor** (pri-sep'tẽr).

pre-ces-sion (pri-sesh'un), *n.* a going before or forward:—**precession of the equinoxes**, the earlier occurrence of the equinoxes each year owing to the westward motion of the equinoctial points on the ecliptic (the sun's apparent path), caused by the slow and regular shifting of the earth's axis in space (forming a completed cone of motion once every 26,000 years). Precession is the result of the sun's and moon's action on the mass of matter about the earth's equator.

pre-cinct (prē'singkt), *n.* **1,** a boundary; also, the region within it; **2,** a small district marked off, as for voting or police purposes; **3, precincts,** the surrounding regions.

pre-cious (presh'us), *adj.* **1,** of great price or value; as, *precious* metals; **2,** very dear; as, my *precious* child, highly esteemed; as, a *precious* privilege; **3,** *Colloq.* thorough; extreme; as, a *precious* nuisance.

prec-i-pice (pres'i-pis), *n.* the steep, nearly vertical face of a cliff or rock.

pre-cip-i-tate (pri-sip'i-tāt'), *v.t.* [precipitat-ed, precipitat-ing], **1,** to throw headlong; **2,** to hurry on rashly; bring to a crisis; as, his act *precipitated* the disaster; **3,** to cause to change from vapour to liquid or solid, and fall, as rain or snow; **4,** in *chemistry*, to cause to separate in solid form from a solution, as salt crystals from brine:—*n.* (pri-sip'i-tāt', pri-sip'i-tit), any solid substance which separates from a solution:—*adj.* (pri-sip'i-tit), **1,** rash; hasty; as, a *precipitate* departure; **2,** falling or rushing headlong, as a waterfall.—*n.* **pre-cip'i-ta'tion.**

pre-cip-i-tous (pri-sip'i-tus), *adj.* very steep, as a cliff.

pré-cis (prā'sē), *n.* a concise or shortened statement; a summary of the main points in a piece of writing, usually in ¼ to ⅓ the number of words of the original.

pre-cise (pri-sīs'), *adj.* **1,** exact; careful; as, a *precise* speaker; *precise* measurements; **2,** keeping closely to rule; prim.—*adv.* **pre-cise'ly.**—*n.* **pre-ci'sion** (pri-sizh'un).

pre-clude (pri-klōōd'; klūd'), *v.t.* [preclud-ed, preclud-ing], to shut out; prevent.

pre-co-cious (pri-kō'shus), *adj.* showing unusual mental development for one's age; as, a *precocious* child.

—*adv.* **pre-co'cious-ly.**—*n.* **pre-coc'i-ty** (-kos').

pred-a-tor-y (pred'a-tẽr-i), *adj.* living by plunder, or by preying on others; as, a *predatory* tribe or beast. Also, **pre-da'cious.**—*n.* **pred'a-tor** (tẽr).

pred-e-ces-sor (prē'di-ses'ẽr; pred'i-ses'-ẽr; pred'i-ses'ẽr), *n.* a person who has gone before another, as in the same office, position, etc.: opposite of *successor.*

pre-des-ti-na-tion (pri-des'ti-na'shun), *n.* the doctrine that from eternity God has determined whatever is to be, esp. with regard to the salvation or damnation of souls:—*v.t.* **pre-des'ti-nate'.**—*adj.* **pre-des'tined** (tind).

pre-dic-a-ment (pri-dik'a-ment), *n.* an unpleasant or dangerous situation.

pred-i-cate (pred'i-kāt'), *v.t.* [predicat-ed, predicat-ing], to declare (something) to be true or characteristic of something else; as, to *predicate* wetness of water:—*n.* (pred'i-kit), in *grammar*, the part of a sentence which makes a statement about the subject; as, in the sentence, "Tom caught the ball," the expression "caught the ball" is the *predicate*:—*adj.* (pred'i-kit), belonging in the predicate; as, in the sentence, "This is my hat," the word "hat" is a *predicate* noun.—*n.* **pred'i-ca'tion.**

pre-dict (pri-dikt'), *v.t.* and *v.i.* to tell or make known beforehand; foretell.—*n.* **pre-dic'tion.**

pre-di-lec-tion (prē'di-lek'shun), *n.* a preconceived liking; a preference.

pre-dis-pose (prē'dis-pōz'), *v.t.* [predisposed, predispos-ing], **1,** to incline beforehand; as, good humour in strangers *predisposes* us to like them; **2,** to make liable or subject, as to a disease; as, to be *predisposed* to tuberculosis.—*n.* **pre'dis-po-si'tion.**

pre-dom-i-nant (pri-dom'i-nant), *adj.* superior in numbers, strength, influence etc.—*n.* **pre-dom'i-nance.**

pre-dom-i-nate (pri-dom'i-nāt'), *v.i.* [predominat-ed, predominat-ing], to be superior in power or influence; prevail.

pre—em-i-nent (pri—em'i-nent), *adj.* highly superior to others; distinguished from others who are eminent.—*n.* **pre—em'i-nence.** Also, **preëminent.**

preen (prēn), *v.t.* **1,** to cleanse and smooth (the feathers) with the beak; **2,** to dress or groom (oneself) with care.

pref-ace (pref'is), *n.* an introduction, as to a book, preceding the body of the work:—*v.t.* [prefaced, prefac-ing], **1,** to introduce (a book, speech, etc.) by some act or statement; **2,** to serve as an introduction to; as, the program was *prefaced* by a talk.—*adj.* **pref′a-tor-y** (pref′a-tĕr-i).

pre-fer (pri-fûr′), *v.t.* [preferred, preferring], **1,** to like (something) more than something else; as, to *prefer* candy to cake; **2,** to offer for consideration; as, to *prefer* a claim.

pref-er-a-ble (pref′ĕr-a-bl), *adj.* more desirable; as, death is *preferable* to slavery.

pref-er-a-bly(pref′ĕr-a-bli),*adv.* rather than something else; by choice; as, come soon, *preferably* in the morning.

pref-er-ence (pref′ĕr-ens), *n.* **1,** choice of one thing rather than another; **2,** that which is favoured or chosen.—*adj.* **pref′er-en′tial.**

pre-fer-ment (pri-fûr′ment), *n.* promotion to higher rank or office; as, political *preferment;* also, a high post of honour or profit, esp. in the church.

pre-fix (prē′fiks), *n.* a syllable, or syllables, placed at the beginning of a word to modify its meaning, as *sub-* in the word "subway," and *super-* in the word "superfine":—*v.t.* (prē-fiks′), to place before, or at the beginning of, anything; as, he *prefixed* "Doctor" to his name.

preg-nant (preg′nant), *adj.* **1,** about to have young; carrying unborn young; **2,** fruitful; fertile; **3,** full of meaning; important; as, a *pregnant* thought.—*n.* **preg′nan-cy.**

pre-hen-sile (prē-hen′sīl), *adj.* adapted for seizing or grasping, as a monkey's tail, or *prehensile* fingers or toes.

pre-his-toric (prē′his-tôr′ik) or **pre-his-tor-i-cal** (prē′his-tôr′i-kal), *adj.* relating to the time before there were written records.

prej-u-dice (prej′ū-dis), *n.* **1,** an opinion, often unfavourable, formed without a fair examination of the facts; bias; **2,** injury or harm resulting from hasty or unfair judgment:—*v.t.* [prejudiced, prejudic-ing], to cause to form an opinion, usually unfavorable, before examination of the facts; as, your story *prejudiced* me against him.

pre-j-u-di-cial (prej′ū-dish′al), *adj.* injurious; damaging; as, his bad record was *prejudicial* to him.—*adv.* **prej′u-di′cial-ly.**

prel-ate (prel′it), *n.* a clergyman of high rank, as a bishop or archbishop.

pre-lim-i-nar-y (pri-lim′i-nĕr-i), *adj.* introductory; preparatory:—*n.*[*pl.* preliminaries], an introductory act or step.

prel-ude (prel′ūd; prē′lūd), *n.* **1,** a preface; something preceding and preparing for something of greater importance; as, a lie may be the *prelude* to a quarrel; **2,** a piece of music played at the opening of church services, or as an introduction to a musical composition:—*v.t.* and *v.i.* [prelud-ed, prelud-ing], to precede; preface; introduce.

pre-ma-ture (prem′a-tūr′; prē′ma-tūr′; prē′ma-tūr′, *adj.* coming before the usual or proper time; untimely.

pre-med-i-tate (prē-med′i-tāt′), *v.t.* and *v.i.* [premeditat-ed, premeditating], to think over carefully or plan beforehand.—*n.* **pre′med-i-ta′tion.**

pre-mi-er (prē′mi-ĕr; prem′yĕr), *adj.* **1,** foremost; chief; **2,** earliest in time: —*n.* (prē′mi-ĕr; prē-mēr′; prem′yir), the chief officer of a state; a prime minister.

pre-miere (prė-myâr′), **1,** the first performance of a play; a 'first night'; **2,** the leading lady (in a play).

prem-ise (prem′is), *n.* **1,** a statement accepted as true, from which a conclusion is to be drawn; esp. in *logic,* one of the first two statements of a form of argument called a syllogism; as, major *premise,* men must eat to live; minor *premise,* John is a man; conclusion, John must eat to live; **2, premises: a,** facts previously stated, as in a legal document; **b,** the property, such as lands, houses, etc., which is the subject of a legal document; **c,** hence, a house or building with its grounds.

pre-mi-um (prē′mi-um), *n.* **1,** a reward or prize for excelling, as in a competition; **2,** a sum agreed upon as the price to be paid for a contract of insurance; **3,** an amount exceeding the par value of something; as, the stock sold at a *premium;* **4,** that which is given in return for a loan of money, over and above the interest; as, he paid a *premium* of $5 for a loan of $100.

pre-mo-ni-tion (prē′mo-nish′un), *n.* **1,** a warning in advance; as, a *premonition* of a flood; **2,** a foreboding; a feeling that something is about to happen.—*adj.* **pre-mon′i-tor-y** (pri-mon′i-tĕr-i).

pre-oc-cu-pied (prē-ok′ū-pīd′), *adj.* **1,** lost in thought; absorbed; **2,** already occupied or in use.—*n.* **pre-oc′cu-pa′-tion.**

pre-oc-cu-py (prē-ok′ū-pī′), *v.t.* [preoccupied, preoccupy-ing], to fill the mind of; hold the attention of.

prep-a-ra-tion (prep'a-rā'shun), *n.* **1,** the act of making fit or ready for use; as, the *preparation* of dinner took an hour; **2,** a state of readiness; **3,** that which makes fit or ready; as, *preparations* for war; **4,** a substance, as a medicine or a salve, made up or compounded for a special use.—*adj.* **pre-par'a-tor'y** (pri-par'a-tèr-i).

pre-pare (pri-pâr'), *v.t.* [prepared, prepar-ing], **1,** to fit for some purpose or make ready for use; as, to *prepare* a house for occupancy; to *prepare* food; **2,** to make (a person) mentally ready or fit for something; as, we *prepared* him for bad news; **3,** to provide or fit out; as, to *prepare* an expedition:—*v.i.* to make things or oneself ready; as, to *prepare* for cold weather; to *prepare* for bad news.—*n.* **pre-par'ed-ness.**

pre-pay (prē'pā'), *v.t.* [prepaid, prepay-ing], to pay, or pay for, in advance.—*n.* **pre-pay'ment.**

pre-pon-der-ance (pri-pon'dèr-ans), *n.* superiority in power, influence, number, or amount; as, there was a *preponderance* of women in the audience.

prep-o-si-tion (prep'o-zish'un), *n.* in *grammar*, a part of speech, as *to*, *from*, *by*, etc., used with a noun or pronoun in the objective case, to show the relation between the noun or pronoun and some other word or words in the sentence; as, in "a bag for the mail," the word "for" is a *preposition* showing a relation between "bag" and "mail." *adj.* **prep'o-si'tion-al.**

pre-pos-sess-ing (prē'po-zes'ing), *adj.* tending to win favour, love, affection, confidence, etc.; attractive.

pre-pos-ter-ous (pri-pos'tèr-us), *adj.* contrary to common sense; absurd.

pre-req-ui-site (prē-rek'wi-zit), *n.* that which is required before something else can follow; as, reading is a *prerequisite* of all other studies:—*adj.* required before something else can follow.

pre-rog-a-tive (pri-rog'a-tiv), *n.* a right or privilege belonging to a person, class, or body of persons, by virtue of rank or position; as, the *prerogatives* of a sovereign, of a citizen, etc.

¹pres-age (pres'ij), *n.* **1,** a sign or omen foretelling what is going to happen; **2,** a feeling of what is going to happen; a foreboding.

²pre-sage (pri-sāj'), *v.t.* [presaged, presag-ing], **1,** to give a warning or sign of; **2,** to foretell.

pres-by-ter (prez'bi-tèr; pres'), *n.* a minister, priest, or elder in a Christian church.—*n.* **pres'by-ter-y.**

pre-scribe (pri-skrīb'), *v.t.* [prescribed, prescrib-ing], **1,** to advise the use of (a medicine or treatment); **2,** to set down as a rule of action:—*v.i.* **1,** to write or give medical directions; **2,** to give laws, rules, or directions.—*n.* **pre-scrip'tion.**

presence (prez'ens), *n.* **1,** the state of being in a certain place; **2,** nearness; immediate neighbourhood; as, in the *presence* of danger; **3,** one's appearance or bearing; as, a girl of pleasing *presence*:—**presence of mind,** quickness of thought or action in an emergency.

¹pres-ent (prez'ent), *adj.* **1,** being at hand or in sight at a given place; as, all people here *present;* **2,** existing now; as, my *present* situation:—*n.* **1,** the time now here; as, I do not know at *present;* **2,** the present tense:—**present tense,** a tense of the verb which indicates an action now going on; as, he *runs;* **present perfect,** in *grammar*, a tense of the verb indicating: **1,** action begun in the past and continuing to the present; as, I *have waited* an hour; **2,** an action the results of which are still going on; as, he *has stolen* my dog; **3,** an action just completed; as, I *have done* the deed.

²pre-sent (pri-zent'), *v.t.* **1,** to introduce (one person) to another; as, let me *present* Mrs. Brown to you; **2,** to bring (oneself) into the presence of someone; as, he *presented* himself before the judge; **3,** to bring to the view or attention of the public; as, to *present* a play; **4,** to submit; hand in; as, to *present* a bill; **5,** to give as a gift; as, we *presented* a book to him; also, to give a gift to; as, we *presented* him with a book; **6,** to display; offer to view; as, he *presented* a sad appearance.—*n.* **pres'en-ta'tion** (prez'en-tā'shun; prē'-zen-tā'shun).

³pres-ent (prez'ent), *n.* a gift; anything given or presented; as, a birthday *present*.

pre-sent-a-ble (pri-zen'ta-bl), *adj.* **1,** suitable to be offered, given, or introduced; **2,** suitable in appearance; fit to be seen.

pre-sen-ti-ment (pri-zen'ti-ment), *n.* a feeling that some particular thing is going to happen; a foreboding.

pres-ent-ly (prez'ent-li), *adv.* soon; before long; as, I shall be there *presently*.

pre-serv-a-tive (pri-zûr'va-tiv), *n.* a substance which tends to prevent decay or injury:—*adj.* acting as a preservative.

cat, āge, fär, câre, ásk; ten, ēve, latèr; (i) pity, rely, senate; īce; top; nō.

pre-serve (pri-zûrv′), *v.t.* [preserved, preserv-ing], **1,** to keep from injury; save; **2,** to keep (fruit or vegetables) from spoiling by canning, pickling, cooking with sugar, etc.; **3,** to keep up; maintain; as, to *preserve* peace:—*n.* **1,** (usually *preserves*), fruit or vegetables preserved with sugar; **2,** a place set apart for keeping game, fish, etc., for sport.—*n.* **pre-serv′er.**—*n.* **pres′er-va′-tion** (prez′ẽr-vā′shun).

pre-side (pri-zīd′), *v.i.* [presid-ed, presid-ing], **1,** to direct or control; as, to *preside* over a home; **2,** to act as chairman of a meeting; as, Mr. Jones *presided.*

pres-iden-cy (prez′i-den-si), *n.* [*pl.* presidencies], the office, or term of office, of a president.

pres-i-dent (prez′i-dent), *n.* **1,** the chief officer of a company, college, club, etc.; **2,** (often *President*), the highest executive officer of a modern republic. —*adj.* **pres′i-den′tial** (prez′i-den′shal).

pre-sid-i-um (pri-sid′i-um), *n.* in the U.S.S.R., a permanent administrative committee of the government.

press (pres), *v.t.* **1,** to bear down upon; **2,** to compress; squeeze; as, to *press* fruit to extract juice; also, to squeeze out; as, to *press* juice from a fruit; **3,** to thrust or push; as, to *press* a crowd back; **4,** to embrace; hug; as, she *pressed* the baby to her; **5,** to urge; entreat; as, we *pressed* him to stay; **6,** to hasten or urge; as, heavy anxiety *pressed* him on; **7,** to thrust upon others; impose; as, she *pressed* gifts upon them; **8,** to smooth or shape by pressure; as, to *press* clothes; **9,** to place in an urgent situation; as, to be *pressed* for time:—*v.i.* **1,** to bear down heavily; **2,** to hasten; strive eagerly; as, we *pressed* to the gate; **3,** to urge or impel to action; as, time *presses*:—*n.* **1,** the act of pushing forward; **2,** a dense crowd; **3,** a machine which presses or stamps anything; as, a printing-*press;* **4,** newspaper and magazine literature, or those who write and publish it; as, the power of the *press;* a statement issued by the *press;* **5,** urgent demand; as, the *press* of business; **6,** an upright cupboard, as for clothes.—*n.* **press′er.** Also, **press′-man; press′room′; press′work′.**

press-board (pres′bōrd′), *n.* **1,** a board of stiff, heavy, highly sized paper (or wood), used in presses for finishing paper, books, knit underwear, etc.; **2,** a heavy glazed paper used to cover the platen or cylinder of a printing press.

pres-sure (presh′ẽr), *n.* **1,** a bearing down upon; as, the *pressure* of a roller on a lawn; **2,** weight on the mind; distress; as, the *pressure* of worry; **3,** burden; oppression; as, the *pressure* of high expenses; **4,** weight of influence or authority; as, parental *pressure* changed his mind; **5,** urgent demand on one's time or energies; as, the *pressure* of work; **6,** in *physics*, force exerted on a body so as to tend to change its shape or lessen its volume. —*v.t.* **pres-sur-ize** (presh′ẽr-īz′), to maintain normal air pressure, esp. in an airplane at high altitudes or when descending.

pres-tige (pres-tēzh′; pres′tij), *n.* reputation or influence resulting from past achievement or associations.

pres-to (pres′tō), *adj.* in *music,* fast tempo.—*adv.* at once.—*interj.* an exclamation to alert (an audience); as, "presto, change!" (used by jugglers in doing their feats).

pre-sum-a-ble (pri-zūm′a-bl), *adj.* probable; to be expected; as, the *presumable* results of an act.—*adv.* **pre-sum′a-bly.**

pre-sume (pri-zūm′), *v.t.* [presumed, presum-ing], **1,** to take for granted; suppose; **2,** to venture; dare (to do something); as, to *presume* to offer advice:—*v.i.* to take liberties; act with unwarranted boldness.

pre-sump-tion (pri-zump′shun), *n.* **1,** boldness; arrogance; **2,** acceptance and belief of something not fully proved; as, the argument is based on *presumption;* **3,** that which is taken for granted.

pre-sump-tu-ous (pri-zump′tū-us), *adj.* bold or overconfident.

pre-sup-pose (prē′su-pōz′), *v.t.* [presupposed, presuppos-ing], to take for granted in advance.

pre-tence (pri-tens′; prē′tens), *n.* **1,** make-believe; a putting on of a false appearance in order to hide what is real; deception; as, she made a *pretence* of friendship; **2,** a false show; display; as, a man without *pretence;* **3,** a claim; as, she had no *pretence* to beauty.

pre-tend (pri-tend′), *v.t.* **1,** to make believe; as, he *pretends* to be a prince; **2,** to make a false show of; as, to *pretend* friendship:—*v.i.* **1,** to put forward a claim, true or false; as, to *pretend* to a title; **2,** to play at make-believe.—*n.* **pre-tend′er.**

pre-ten-sion (pri-ten′shun), *n.* **1,** a claim made, whether true or false; **2,** outward show; display;

pre-ten-tious (pri-ten′shus), *adj.* **1,** making claims to importance, worth, etc.; as, a *pretentious* book; **2,** made or done for show or display; as, a *pretentious* house.

pre-ter- (prē′tẽr-), *prefix* meaning *beyond* or *more than*, as in **pre′ter-hu′man** or **pre′ter-nat′u-ral.**

pre-text (prē′tekst), *n.* a pretence or excuse; a false motive put forward to conceal the real one.

pret-ty (prit′i), *adj.* [pret-ti-er, pret-ti-est], **1,** pleasing to look at; attractive; **2,** nice; fine; as, a *pretty* wit: often used slightingly; as, a *pretty* mess: —*adv.* fairly; moderately; as *pretty* well. —*adv.* **pret′ti-ly.**—*n.* **pret′-ti-ness.**

pret-zel (pret′s′l), *n.* a hard biscuit, made in a twisted form and glazed and salted on the outside.

pre-vail (pri-vāl′), *v.i.* **1,** to be victorious; triumph; as, right will *prevail;* **2,** to be or become widespread; be in general use; as, the English language *prevails* in America; **3,** to persuade; as, she finally *prevailed* on him to go.—*adj.* **pre-vail′ing.**—*n.* **prev′a-lence.**—*adj.* **prev′a-lent.**—*adv.* **prev′a-lent-ly.**

pre-var-i-cate (pri-var′i-kāt′), *v.i.* [prevaricat-ed, prevaricat-ing], to stray from the truth; lie.—*n.* **pre-var′i-ca′tor.**—*n.* **pre-var′i-ca′tion.**

pre-vent (pri-vent′), *v.t.* to stop or keep from happening, doing, etc.; hinder.—*n.* **pre-ven′tion.**—*adj.* **pre-vent′a-ble** or **pre-vent′i-ble.**

pre-ven-tive (pri-ven′tiv), *adj.* serving to hinder:—*n.* that which hinders; esp. something that wards off disease.

pre-vious (prē′vi-us), *adj.* earlier; preceding; as, he spoke of you in a *previous* letter.—*adv.* **pre′vi-ous-ly.**

pre-war (prē-wôr′), *adj.* before any war, as contrasted with *postwar.*

prex-y (prek′si), *n. Slang.* **1,** a higher official, esp. in an organized sport (baseball, hockey, etc.); **2,** a U.S. college president.

prey (prā), *n.* **1,** any animal hunted or killed by another animal for food; **2,** hence, a person who is a victim of another person or of anything which is hostile or evil:—**bird, or beast, of prey,** a bird or beast that devours other animals:—*v.i.* **1,** to plunder for the sake of booty; **2,** to seize and devour an animal as food; **3,** to exert a destructive influence; as, his guilt *preyed* upon his mind.

price (prīs), *n.* **1,** worth; value; as,

pearls of great *price;* **2,** something, usually money, given or asked in exchange for a thing; cost; **3,** reward; as, to set a *price* on a criminal's head; **4,** the cost at which something is obtained; as, the *price* of victory was the loss of a thousand lives:—*v.t.* [priced, pric-ing], **1,** to set a price on; **2,** *Colloq.,* to inquire the price of; as, to *price* goods in various stores.

price-less (prīs′lis), *adj.* too valuable to be bought at any price; invaluable.

prick (prik), *n.* **1,** a dot or mark made by a pointed instrument; also, the instrument; **2,** a sharp, stinging pain; hence, remorse:—*v.t.* **1,** to pierce with something pointed; **2,** to mark out by puncturing; **3,** to pain or sting, as with remorse; **4,** to erect or raise; as, a dog *pricks* up its ears; **5,** to spur; urge; as, to *prick* a horse on:—*v.i.* to feel a sharp, stinging pain.

prick-le (prik′l), *n.* **1,** a sharp point; esp. a small, slender projection growing from the surface of a plant; **2,** a slight stinging sensation:—*v.t.* [prick-led, prick-ling], **1,** to give a stinging sensation to (the skin); **2,** to cover with small dots:—*v.i.* to tingle.—*adj.* **prick′-ly.**—*n.* **prick′li-ness.**

pride (prīd), *n.* **1,** a high opinion of one's own qualities; conceit; **2,** haughtiness; disdain; **3,** dignity; self-respect:—*v.t.* [prid-ed, prid-ing], to be proud of; as, he *prides* himself on his speech.

priest (prēst), *n.* one with authority to perform religious rites and services.— *adj.* **priest′ly.**

priest-ess (prēs′tes), *n.* a woman priest, esp. in pagan times.

priest-hood (prēst′hood), *n.* **1,** the whole body of priests; **2,** the office or duties of a priest.

prig (prig), *n.* a conceited person who is over-particular about speech, conduct, etc.—*adj.* **prig′gish.**

prim (prim), *adj.* [prim-mer, prim-mest], extremely neat or precise.—*adv.* **prim′ly.**

pri-ma don-na (prē′ma don′a), [*pl.* prima donnas], the principal female singer in an opera or concert.

pri-mal (prī′mal), *adj.* **1,** first; original; **2,** primary; chief.

pri-ma-ri-ly (prī′ma-ri-li), *adv.* **1,** at first; originally; **2,** principally.

pri-ma-ry (prī′mar-i), *adj.* **1,** first in time; original; as, the *primary* meaning of a word; **2,** naming the first three grades of elementary school; **3,** basic; fundamental; as, the *primary* colours; **4,**

chief; principal; as, a *primary* purpose; **5,** pertaining to the large flight feathers of a bird's wing:—*n.* [*pl.* primaries], **1,** that which is first in rank, place, or importance; **2,** in the U.S., a district meeting of the voters of a party to name candidates for a coming election; **3,** (also *primary election*), a preliminary election in which parties nominate their respective candidates; **4,** one of the large flight feathers in a bird's wing; **5,** one of the primary colours.

pri-mate (prī'mit), *n.* **1,** an honorary title given to the archbishop, or, sometimes, to the bishop, who holds first place in a district or districts; **2,** a member of the highest order [the *Primates* (prī-mā'tēz)] of mammals, which includes man, monkeys, apes, etc.

¹prime (prīm), *adj.* **1,** first in time; original; **2,** chief; principal; as, a matter of *prime* importance; **3,** first in excellence or value; as, a *prime* grade of beef:—*n.* **1,** the early stage or beginning, as of a day, year, etc.; **2,** the spring of life; youth; also, the period of the greatest health, beauty, etc.; as, a man in the *prime* of life; **3,** the best one of a group or the best part of anything.—*n.* **prim'a-cy** (prī').

²prime (prīm), *v.t.* [primed, prim-ing], **1,** to prepare (a gun) for firing; also, to prepare (a pump) to lift water, by pouring water into it; **2,** to cover with the first coat of paint or plaster; **3,** to instruct (a person) beforehand as to what must be said; as, the lawyer *primed* the witness before he put him on the stand.—*n.* **prim'ing.**

pri-mer (prim'ẽr), *n.* **1,** a small book from which children receive their first lessons in reading; **2,** a textbook containing the first principles of any subject.

pri-me-val or **pri-mae-val** (prī-mē'-val), *adj.* pertaining to the earliest age or time; primitive; original.—*adv.* **pri-me'val-ly.**

prim-i-tive (prim'i-tiv), *adj.* **1,** belonging to the earliest ages; first; as, *primitive* man lived by hunting and fishing; **2,** characterized by the style of early times; hence, simple or crude; as, the savages used *primitive* weapons.

pri-mor-di-al (prī-môr'di-al), *adj.* **1,** existing from the beginning; original; as, *primordial* matter; **2,** in *biology* (a) earliest formed in the course of growth, as leaves, fruit, etc. (b) in a rudimentary or developing stage, as tissues, germ cells, etc.

primp (primp), *v.t.* and *v.i. Colloq·* to dress for show (with exaggerated care).

prim-rose (prim'rōz'), *n.* a plant bearing flowers which are usually pale yellow and which blossom in the early spring; also, the flower:—*adj.* pale yellow.

prince (prins), *n.* **1,** a ruler or sovereign, esp. of a small state; **2,** the son of a ruler; **3,** a male member of a royal family or of a high order of nobility; **4,** a distinguished member of a class of men; as, a merchant *prince.*—*adj.* **prince'ly.**

prin-cess (prin'ses'), *n.* **1,** the daughter or granddaughter of a sovereign; **2,** the wife of a prince; **3,** a female member of a royal family.

prin-ci-pal (prin'si-pal), *adj.* highest in rank, value, or importance; main; foremost; chief; as, the *principal* reason for his failure was his lack of confidence:—*n.* **1,** a leader; the chief person in authority; **2,** the head of a school; **3,** a sum of money drawing interest; **4,** a person or group of persons for whom an agent acts.—*adv.* **prin'ci-pal-ly.**

prin-ci-pal-i-ty (prin'si-pal'i-ti), *n.* [*pl.* -ities], the territory of a prince or the country from which he obtains his title.

prin-ci-ple (prin'si-pl), *n.* **1,** a truth or law on which other truths, laws, etc., are based; as, *principles* of government; **2,** a settled rule of action; as, *principles* of conduct; **3,** honesty; uprightness; as, a man of *principle;* **4,** a natural law; esp. one which is utilized in the construction and operation of a machine; as, an automobile engine works on the *principle* of the expanding power of gases.

prink (pringk), *v.t.* and *v.i.* to dress up in a showy fashion.

print (print), *n.* **1,** a mark or character made by pressure; as, a foot*print;* **2,** a stamp or die for making an impression; also, that which has received the impression; **3.** letters produced from type; as, the child's book was in large *print;* **4,** the state of being in published form; as, the story has just got into *print;* **5,** anything produced by type or from an engraved plate, as a newspaper, engraving, etc.; **6,** cloth decorated with a printed design:—*v.t.* **1,** to make an impression on; as, their feet *print* the sand; **2,** to fix or stamp in or on something; as, to *print* footsteps in the sand; **3,** to reproduce from type, engraved plates etc., as books, pictures, newspapers, etc.; **4,** to make in letters, like those of type; as, a child *prints* a letter; **5,** in *photography*, to produce (a picture) from a negative:—*v.i.* to make letters like those used in type; as, the child *prints* well.

print-er (prin'tẽr), *n.* one whose trade is the setting of type or the making of impressions from type.

print-ing (print'ing), *n.* the setting of reading matter in type, or the making of printed books, magazines, etc.

pri-or (prī'ẽr), *adj.* going before in time, order, or importance; previous: —*n.* the head of a monastery; also, in an abbey, the religious officer next below an abbot.—*n. fem.* **pri'or-ess.**

pri-or-i-ty (prī-or'i-ti), *n.* the state of being first in rank, time, or place.

prism (prizm), *n.* **1,** a solid object with ends that are parallel and exactly the same in size and shape, and sides that are parallelograms; **2,** such a solid, usually three-sided, made of glass or a similar substance, which breaks up a ray of sunlight into the colours of the rainbow.—*adj.* **pris-mat'ic** (priz-mat'ik).

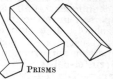
PRISMS

pris-on (priz'n), *n.* a place of confinement or detention for criminals; a gaol.

pris-on-er (priz'n-ẽr; priz'nẽr), *n.* anyone held against his will, as a person under arrest, in jail, or captured in war.

pris-sy (pris'i), *adj. Colloq.* affectedly prim or precise.

pris-tine (pris'tēn; -tin; tīn), *adj.* original; former; as, its *pristine* purity.

prith-ee (prith'ē),*interj. Archaic,*please.

pri-va-cy (prī'va-si), *n.* [*pl.* privacies], **1,** the state of being away from public view; seclusion; retirement; **2,** secrecy; as, to plot a scheme in *privacy.*

pri-vate (prī'vit), *adj.* **1,** concerning or belonging to oneself alone; personal; not public; as, one's *private* affairs; **2,** away from public view or knowledge; secret; as, he obtained *private* information; **3,** not holding a public position; as, a *private* citizen:—*n.* a common soldier.—*adv.* **pri'vate-ly.**

pri-va-teer (prī'va-tẽr'), *n.* **1,** an armed ship, privately owned, but permitted by the government to attack the enemy's ships; **2,** the commander or one of the crew of such a ship:—*v.i.* to sail in, or as, a privateer.

pri-va-tion (prī-vā'shun), *n.* need; hardship; want of the usual comforts of life.

priv-a-tive (priv'a-tiv), *n.* in *grammar,* a prefix (or suffix) that changes a positive term to a negative. Some common *privatives: a-* or *ab, e-* or *ex-, in* or *un-, non-;* as in *ab*normal, *e*gress, *ex*ile, *in*apt, *un*able, *non*acid.

priv-et (priv'it), *n.* a shrub with dark green leaves and small white flowers, much used for hedges.

priv-i-lege (priv'i-lij), *n.* a special favour or right granted to a person or body of persons:—*v.t.* [privileged, privileg-ing], to give some particular right to; as, employees are *privileged* to buy at a discount.

priv-y (priv'i), *adj.* **1,** for private, not public use; personal; as, the *privy* purse; **2,** secretly informed; as, to be *privy* to a plot:—**Privy Council,** a body of advisers appointed by the crown: —*n.* [*pl.* privies], an out-of-door toilet. —*adv.* **priv'i-ly.**

prize (prīz), *n.* **1,** a reward offered or won in a contest; **2,** anything of value; **3,** that which is taken from an enemy in war; esp., a captured vessel:—*adj.* **1,** given a prize; as a *prize* painting; **2,** worthy to be given a prize; as, a *prize* pupil; **3,** given as a prize; as, he won the *prize* box of candy:—*v.t.* [prized, priz-ing], to value or esteem highly; as, to *prize* a gift.

¹pro (prō), *adv.* on the affirmative side; as, they argued *pro* and con.

²pro (prō), *n. Colloq.*, a professional.

prob-a-bil-i-ty (prob'a-bil'i-ti), *n.* [*pl.* probabilities]; **1,** the quality or state of being likely; **2,** something likely to happen; **3,** chance; as, the *probabilities* at present are against war.

prob-a-ble (prob'a-bl), *adj.* **1,** likely; expected; **2,** giving grounds for belief; having the appearance of truth; as, a *probable* explanation.—*adv.* **prob'a-bly.**

pro-bate (prō'bāt), *v.t.* to prove the validity of a will.—*adj.* having jurisdiction over wills; as, a *probate* court: —*n.* legal proof of a will, or a copy of a will with the certificate of its legal proof.

pro-ba-tion (prō-bā'shun), *n.* **1,** a trial or test of a person's character, ability, etc.; also, the period of trial; **2,** a system of permitting young offenders against the law to go free, though under police supervision.—*adj.* **pro-ba′tion-al.**—*adj.* **pro-ba′tion-ar-y.** —*n.* **pro-ba′tion-er.**

probe (prōb), *n.* **1,** a slender surgical instrument for examining a wound, cavity, etc.; **2,** a searching inquiry:— *v.t.* [probed, prob-ing], **1,** to examine with a probe; **2,** to inquire into closely.

prob-i-ty (prō′bi-ti), *n.* integrity, uprightness; honesty; as, a man of *probity.*

prob-lem (prob′lem), *n.* **1,** a question hard to understand; a matter hard to solve or settle; **2,** in *mathematics,* something that is to be worked out or solved.—*adj.* **prob′lem-at′i-cal.**

pro-bos-cis (prō-bos′is), *n.* [*pl.* pro-boscides (-i-dēz′)], **1,** the trunk of an elephant; **2,** the long snout of certain other animals, as the tapir; **3,** the elongated mouth parts of certain insects.

pro-ce-dure (prō-sē′dūr), *n.* **1,** a course of action; a proceeding; as, his *procedure* in the matter was very fair; **2,** a system of proceeding; manner of conducting a business transaction, a lawsuit, etc.; **3,** the established manner of conducting a meeting.

pro-ceed (prō-sēd′), *v.i.* **1,** to go on or forward; advance; continue acting, speaking, etc.; as, to *proceed* on a journey; *proceed* with your speech; **2,** to issue; result; as, the tides *proceed* from the attraction of the sun and moon; **3,** to carry on a series of actions in a systematic manner.

pro-ceed-ing (prō-sēd′ing), *n.* **1,** a transaction, as in business; **2,** a course of conduct; **3, proceedings,** the record of the business accomplished at a meeting of a society, board of directors, etc.

pro-ceeds (prō′sēdz), *n.pl.* results from a transaction; esp., the amount of money realized from a sale.

pro-cess (prō′ses; pros′es), *n.* **1,** progress; course; as, the house is in *process* of construction; **2,** a continuous action or series of actions which lead to the accomplishment of a result; as, getting an education is a long *process;* **3,** in industry, esp. manufacturing, a method of operation or treatment which brings about a certain result; as, the Bessemer *process* of making steel; **4,** an official written summons to appear in court; **5,** an outgrowth or projecting part, esp. on a bone:—*v.t.* to subject to a special treatment or process; as, to *process* leather.

pro-ces-sion (prō-sesh′un), *n.* **1,** the act of going on or forward; **2,** a formal parade; as, a religious *procession.*

pro-ces-sion-al (prō-sesh′un-al), *adj.* pertaining to a procession:—*n.* **1,** a hymn sung at the beginning of a church service; **2,** organ music suitable for a procession.

pro-claim (prō-klām′), *v.t.* to make known publicly; declare; publish abroad.

proc-la-ma-tion (prok′la-mā′shun), *n.* **1,** the act of announcing publicly; **2,** that which is announced; a formal announcement.

pro-cliv-i-ty (prō-kliv′i-ti), *n.* a natural inclination; tendency; used esp. in a bad sense, as a *proclivity* to vice.

pro-cras-ti-nate (prō-kras′ti-nāt′), *v.i.* [procrastinat-ed, procrastinat-ing], to delay; put off action from day to day.—*n.* **pro-cras′ti-na′tion.**

pro-cre-ate (prō′kri-āt′), *v.t.* and *v.i.* to produce offspring; beget; as, couples marry and *procreate.*

pro-cure (prō-kūr′), *v.t.* [procured, procur-ing], **1,** to get; obtain; **2,** to cause or bring about; as, she *procured* his arrest.—*n.* **pro-cure′ment; pro-cur′er.**

prod (prod), *n.* **1,** a pointed implement for pricking, as a goad or pointed stick; **2,** a prick; hence, a poke or dig:—*v.t.* [prod-ded, prod-ding], **1,** to punch or poke with a pointed instrument; **2,** hence, to urge.

prod-i-gal (prod′i-g'l), *adj.* reckless with money; lavish; wasteful:—*n.* a spendthrift.—*n.* **prod′i-gal′i-ty.**

pro-di-gious (prō-dij′us), *adj.* **1,** unusually great in size, quantity, etc.; enormous; **2,** marvellous; amazing.

prod-i-gy (prod′i-ji), *n.* [*pl.* prodigies], **1,** anything both unusual and unnatural; as, comets were once thought of as *prodigies;* **2,** anything causing wonder; a marvel; as, a *prodigy* of learning; **3,** a person, esp. a child, unusually gifted or precocious.

¹pro-duce (prō-dūs′), *v.t.* [produced, produc-ing], **1,** to exhibit or bring to view; as, he *produced* the papers from the safe; **2,** to yield or bring forth; as, trees *produce* fruit; **3,** to manufacture; **4,** to lead to; as, wealth *produces* comfort; **5,** to present upon the stage, as a play.—*n.* **pro-duc′er.**

²prod-uce (prod′ūs), *n.* that which is brought forth or yielded; esp. the products of farm and garden.

all (ôl), ôr; up, mūte, cûr, cōōl, book; oil, out; th, thin; *th,* the.

prod-uct (prod'ukt), *n.* **1,** that which is yielded by nature, or made by labour, thought, manufacture, etc.; as, farm or factory *products;* poetry is a *product* of the imagination; **2,** in *arithmetic,* the result obtained by multiplying two or more numbers together; as, the *product* of 1, 3, and 5, is 15.

pro-duc-tion (prō-duk'shun), *n.* **1,** that which is yielded by nature or made by labour, thought, etc.; **2,** a performance on the stage; **3,** the act of producing.

pro-duc-tive (prō-duk'tiv), *adj.* **1,** having the power to create something; creative; **2,** creating in abundance; fertile; as, *productive* soil; **3,** causing to exist; as, *productive* labour.—*n.* pro'duc-tiv'i-ty.

pro-fane (prō-fān'), *adj.* **1,** not sacred or holy; hence, having to do with this world only; as, *profane* history; **2,** showing disrespect or irreverence toward God or sacred things; as, *profane* language:—*v.t.* [profaned, profan-ing], **1,** to treat (something sacred) with irreverence, contempt, or abuse; **2,** to put to an improper use.—*n.* prof'a-na'tion (prof'a-nā'shun).

pro-fan-i-ty (prō-fan'i-ti),*n.* [*pl.* profanities], irreverent conduct or speech.

pro-fess (prō-fes'), *v.t.* **1,** to make a public statement of (one's belief, intentions, etc.); as, to *profess* allegiance to the flag; **2,** to pretend; claim; as, to *profess* friendship; he *professed* to have expert knowledge.—*adv.* pro-fess'ed-ly.

pro-fes-sion (prō-fesh'un), *n.* **1,** the act of declaring; declaration; as, a *profession* of friendship; **2,** a calling or vocation, esp. one that requires special education; as, the *professions* of medicine and law; **3,** all the persons engaged in any one calling of this kind.

pro-fes-sion-al (prō-fesh'un-al), *adj.* **1,** pertaining to, or associated with, a profession; as, *professional* duties; **2,** pertaining to sport engaged in for profit or pay, or to the act or practice of engaging in a sport for pay; as, a *professional* boxer; *professional* golf: —*n.* one who engages in a sport or other pleasurable pursuit for gain: opposite of *amateur.*

pro-fes-sor (prō-fes'ẽr), *n.* **1,** a teacher of the highest rank in a college or university; **2,** loosely, a teacher; **3,** one who makes an open declaration of his opinions, esp. concerning religion. —*adj.* prof'es-sor'i-al (prof'e-sōr'i-al; prō'fe-sōr'i-al).

prof-fer (prof'ẽr), *v.t.* to offer for acceptance; as, to *proffer* help:—*n.* an offer.

pro-fi-cient (prō-fish'ent), *adj.* thoroughly skilled; expert; as, *proficient* in drawing:—*n.* an expert.—*n.* pro-fi'cien-cy.

pro-file (prō'fil; prō'fēl), *n.* **1,** outline or contour; as, the *profile* of a mountain **2,** a side-view of a human face, or a drawing, photograph, etc., made from it.

prof-it (prof'it), *n.* **1,** gain in money; the amount by which income exceeds expenses in a given time: opposite of *loss;* **2,** **profits,** the gain, as from the operation of a business, after all expenses, charges, etc., have been met; **3,** benefit or advantage:—*v.i.* and *v.t.* to benefit; as, to *profit* from a transaction; the transaction *profited* him. —*adj.* prof'it-a-ble.—*adv.* prof'it-a-bly.

prof-it-eer (prof'i-tēr'), *n.* one who makes undue or unjust profits, as during a period of scarcity:—*v.i.* to make, or try to make, undue profits.— *n.* prof'it-eer'ing.

prof-li-gate (prof'li-gāt'), *adj.* **1,** given up to vice; dissolute; **2,** recklessly extravagant:—*n.* a vicious or immoral person.—*n.* prof'li-ga-cy.

pro-found (prō-found'), *adj.* **1,** deep, as to space; as, the *profound* depths of ocean; **2,** deep, as to mental state; thorough; as, *profound* thought; *profound* learning; **3,** deep, as to feeling; intense; as, *profound* sorrow; **4,** bowing low; hence, humble; lowly; **5,** coming from the depths; as, a *profound* sigh.—*adv.* pro-found'ly.

pro-fun-di-ty (prō-fun'di-ti), *n.* [*pl.* profundities], **1,** deepness; depth; **2,** depth of thought, knowledge, feeling, etc.; **3,** that which is deep in any sense.

pro-fuse (prō-fūs'), *adj.* **1,** pouring forth freely; giving or given with great generosity; as, *profuse* kindness; **2,** produced or shown in great abundance; as, *profuse* foliage.—*adv.* pro-fuse'ly. *n.* pro-fu'sion (-fū'zhun).

pro-gen-i-tor (prō-jen'i-tẽr), *n.* an ancestor; forefather.

prog-e-ny (proj'e-ni), *n.* offspring; children; descendants or a descendant.

prog-no-sis (prog-nō'sis), *n.* a forecast, esp. by a doctor about the probable course of a disease.

prog-nos-ti-cate (prog-nos'ti-kāt'), *v.t.* to predict or foretell (from present signs); prophesy.—*n.* prog-nos'ti-ca'tion.

pro-gramme or **pro-gram** (prō'-gram), *n.* **1,** a brief outline giving in order the features that make up a public entertainment, ceremony, etc.; as, a concert *programme;* **2,** the features that make up such an entertainment; **3,** a clearly defined plan of action in any undertaking.

pro-gress (prō'gres; prog'res), *n.* **1,** a moving forward; as, the *progress* of a boat; hence, advancement or improvement; as, the patient made slow *progress* to recovery; **2,** growth or development; as, the *progress* of a campaign.

pro-gress (prō-gres'), *v.i.* **1,** to move forward; as, time *progresses;* **2,** to grow; improve; develop; as, science *progresses.*

pro-gres-sion (prō-gresh'un), *n.* the act or method of advancing.

pro-gres-sive (prō-gres'iv), *adj.* **1,** moving forward step by step; as, *progressive* improvement; **2,** ready to accept new ideas or to introduce changes for the sake of improvement; as, a *progressive* schoolteacher; **3,** in *grammar,* designating a form (of a verb) that expresses an action as going on; as, I *am thinking* (present progressive); in December he *was working* (past progressive or imperfect):—*n.* one who believes in, and works for, changes and reforms, esp. in political matters.—*adv.* **pro-gres'sive-ly.**

pro-hib-it (prō-hib'it), *v.t.* **1,** to forbid by law; as, to *prohibit* the sale of liquor; **2,** to hinder; prevent.—*adj.* **pro-hib'i-to-ry.**

pro-hi-bi-tion (prō'i-bish'un; prō'-hi-bish'un), *n.* **1,** the act of forbidding; esp. the forbidding by law of the manufacture and sale of intoxicating drinks; **2,** a law or injunction forbidding something.—*n.* **pro'hi-bi'tion-ist.**

pro-hib-i-tive (prō-hib'i-tiv), *adj.* tending to forbid, prevent, or hinder; as, *prohibitive* prices keep us from buying.

pro-ject (prō-jekt'), *v.t.* **1,** to throw or shoot forward; **2,** to cause (a beam of light, a shadow, etc.) to fall on a surface; as, to *project* a picture on a screen; **3,** to plan (something to be done, a course of action, etc.):—*v.i.* to jut out; extend forward; as, a bay window *projects.*—*n.* **pro-jec'tion.**—*n.* **pro-jec'tor.**—*n.* **pro-jec'tion-ist.**

project (prō'jekt; proj'ekt), *n.* **1,** a design; scheme; plan; **2,** in school, a problem or lesson intended to make

pupils rely on their own effort and natural ability.

pro-jec-tile (prō-jek'til; prō-jek'til), *n.* something thrown or shot forward; esp. a ball, shell, torpedo, etc., intended to be shot from a cannon.

pro-le-tar-i-at (prō'le-târ'i-it), *n.* **1,** in the Marxist sense, the industrial working class; **2,** the labouring class; earners of day wages.—*adj.* **pro'le-ta'-ri-an.**

pro-lif-ic (prō-lif'ik), *adj.* **1,** producing young or fruit abundantly; fertile; as, a *prolific* vine; **2,** producing ideas or results abundantly; as, a *prolific* writer.

pro-lix-i-ty (prō-lik'si-ti), *n.* wordiness; long-windedness;—*adj.* **pro'lix** or **pro-lix'.**

pro-logue or **pro-log** (prō'log), *n.* **1,** an introduction or preface to a poem, drama, etc.; esp. verses spoken or sung by an actor before the performance of a play or an opera; **2,** the actor by whom these verses are delivered.

pro-long (prō-lông'), *v.t.* to lengthen in time or space; draw out; extend; as, to *prolong* a conversation; to *prolong* a line.—*n.* **pro'lon-ga'tion.**

prom-e-nade (prom'i-näd'; i-nād'), *n.* **1,** a walk for pleasure or exercise; **2,** a place for walking; **3,** a ball or dance:—*v.i.* [promenad-ed, promenad-ing], to walk for pleasure.—*Colloq.* **prom.**

prom-i-nent (prom'i-nent), *adj.* **1,** standing or jutting out; projecting; **2,** conspicuous; noticeable; as, a *prominent* shop window; **3,** distinguished; as, a *prominent* diplomat.—*n.* **prom'i-nence.**

pro-mis-cu-ous (prō-mis'kū-us), *adj.* **1,** made up of a mixture, grouped without order; as, a *promiscuous* assembly; **2,** not confined to one person (used esp. of sexual intercourse); not discriminating; as, *promiscuous* hospitality. **3,** casual; accidental; unplanned.—*n.* **prom'is-cu'i-ty** (prom').

prom-ise (prom'is), *n.* **1,** a pledge that one will or will not do something; **2,** a cause or ground for hope or expectation; as, a *promise* of fair weather:—*v.i.* [promised, promis-ing], **1,** to pledge or engage to do or not to do something; **2,** to give reason for hope or expectation; as, the garden *promises* well:—*v.t.* **1,** to pledge or engage (to do or not to do); as, he *promised* to go; **2,** to agree to give to, or get for, someone; as, he *promised* her a position; **3,** to give reason to expect (something); as, the day *promised* rain.—*n.* **prom′is-er.**

prom-is-sor-y (prom′i-sêr-i), *adj.* containing an agreement to do or not to do something:—**promissory note,** a written agreement to pay a certain sum of money on demand or at a fixed date.

prom-on-tor-y (prom′un-têr-i), *n.* [*pl.* promontories], a high point of land extending into a body of water.

pro-mote (prō-mōt′), *v.t.* [promot-ed, promot-ing], **1,** to raise to a higher rank or class; as, the teacher *promoted* Mary to the sixth form; **2,** to set on foot or organize (a business venture); **3,** to help the growth or development of; as, to *promote* interest in outdoor sports.—*n.* **pro-mot′er.**—*n.* **pro-mo′-tion.**

prompt (prompt), *adj.* **1,** ready and quick to act; as, *prompt* to forgive; **2,** done or given without delay; as, *prompt* service; **3,** on time; not tardy; as, you must learn to be *prompt:*—*v.t.* **1,** to rouse to action; incite; **2,** to suggest; inspire; as, generosity *prompted* the gift; **3,** to remind or help (a speaker at a loss for words).—*n.* **prompt′er.**

prom-ul-gate (prom′ul-gāt′; prō-mul′gāt), *v.t.* [promulgat-ed, promulgat-ing], to make known formally and officially; proclaim; as, to *promulgate* a law.

prone (prōn), *adj.* **1,** naturally disposed or inclined; as, she is *prone* to forget; **2,** lying face downward.

prong (prông), *n.* one of the pointed ends of a fork; also, any sharp point or sharp-pointed instrument.

prong-horn (prông′hôrn′), *n.* a cud-chewing animal resembling an antelope, found on the western plains of North America.

pro-noun (prō′noun), *n.* a word which refers to, or is used in the place of, a noun or name, as, "this," "which," "he," "who," etc.—*adj.* **pro-nom′i-nal.**

pro-nounce (prō-nouns′), *v.t.* [pro-nounced, pronounc-ing], **1,** to utter the sounds of; as, to *pronounce* a name; **2,** to declare; as, they *pronounced* him a failure; **3,** to speak or utter with formal solemnity; as, to *pronounce* a benediction:—*v.i.* **1,** to utter words, esp. with care and precision; enunciate; **2,** to speak with confidence or authority.—*adj.* **pro-nounce′a-ble.**—*n.* **pro-nounce′-ment.**

pro-nounced (prō-nounst′), *adj.* strongly marked; decided; as, a *pronounced* change in the weather.

pron-to (pron′tō), *adj.* and *adv. Slang,* quick(ly); prompt(ly).

pro-nun-ci-a-tion(prō-nun′si-ā′shun; shi-ā′shun), *n.* the act or manner of uttering the sounds which form words.

proof (proof), *n.* **1,** the means by which something is shown to be true or correct; **2,** convincing evidence; as, *proof* of guilt; **3,** a test or trial; as, "the *proof* of the pudding is in the eating"; **4,** in *photography,* a trial print from a negative; **5,** in *printing,* an impression taken from type for correction:—*adj.* **1,** used in proving or testing; **2,** of a standard strength or purity; as, *proof* whisky; **3,** capable of resisting; as, *proof* against infection.

proof-read (proof′rēd′), *v.t.* and *v.i.* to read in order to correct errors, etc.; as, the boy had failed to *proofread* his essay.

prop (prop), *v.t.* [propped, prop-ping], **1,** to support by placing something under or against; as, to *prop* up a book; **2,** to sustain; support; as, to *prop* up a friend's courage:—*n.* a support or stay.

prop-a-gan-da (prop′a-gan′da), *n.* **1,** any organization or scheme for spreading special opinions or beliefs; **2,** the opinions or beliefs thus spread.—*n.* **prop′a-gan′dist.**

prop-a-gate (prop′a-gāt′), *v.t.* [propa-gated, propagat-ing], **1,** to cause to increase or multiply by natural reproduction; as, to *propagate* plants; **2,** to spread from person to person; as, to *propagate* news.—*n.* **prop′a-ga′tor.** —*n.* **prop′a-ga′tion.**

pro-pane (prō′pān), *n.* a methane gas, C_3H_8, obtained from petroleum, used for heating, etc.

pro-pel (prō-pel′), *v.t.* [propelled, pro-pel-ling], to push or urge forward; drive onward; as, to *propel* ships by steam.

pro-pel-lant (prō-pel′ant), *n.* an explosive charge that propels, esp. fuel plus an oxidizing agent used in rocket engines; a propelling agent.—*adj.* and *n.* **pro-pel′lent.**

pro-pel-ler (prō-pel′ẽr), *n.* one who or that which drives forward; esp. a device, usually a revolving shaft with blades, for causing an aeroplane or a ship to move forward.

pro-pen-si-ty (prō-pen′si-ti), *n.* [*pl.* propensities], natural inclination or tendency; as, a *propensity* to exaggerate.

prop-er (prop′ẽr), *adj.* **1,** suitable; fitting; appropriate; as, *proper* clothes for wet weather; **2,** belonging naturally to some person or thing; characteristic; as, trees *proper* to a region; **3,** according to accepted usage; correct; conventional; respectable; as, *proper* table manners; **4,** in a narrow or restricted sense; as, the spider is not an insect *proper.—adv.* **prop′er-ly.**

prop-er-ty (prop′ẽr-ti), *n.* [*pl.* properties], **1,** any quality or attribute that belongs to a thing, or one that esp. marks it; as, sourness is a *property* of vinegar; **2,** ownership; as, the duties and rights of *property;* **3,** the thing owned; possessions, namely, real estate, movable goods, etc.; **4, properties,** all the stage furnishings and articles required by actors in performing a play, except stage scenery and the costumes of the actors.

proph-e-cy (prof′i-si), *n.* [*pl.* -cies], a foretelling or prediction of future events, esp. one made under divine influence.

proph-e-sy (prof′i-sī′), *v.t.* [prophesied, prophesy-ing], to foretell, esp. under divine influence.

proph-et (prof′it), *n.* **1,** in the Bible, one inspired by God to teach His will to men and to announce future events; **2,** one who foretells the future.—*n. fem.* **proph′et-ess.**

pro-phet-ic (prō-fet′ik), *adj.* **1,** pertaining to the foretelling of future events or to one who foretells; as, the *prophetic* gift; **2,** containing a prophecy; as, a *prophetic* vision.

pro-phy-lax-is (prō′fi-lak′sis; prof′i-), *n.* the preventing of diseases, esp. through study of their behavior, causes, etc.—*adj.* **pro′phy-lac′tic.**

pro-pin-qui-ty (prō-ping′kwi-ti), *n.* nearness in time, place, or blood relationship; as, a factor in many marriages is *propinquity.*

pro-pi-ti-ate (prō-pish′i-āt′), *v.t.* [propitiat-ed, propitiat-ing], to win over (one who is offended or angry); conciliate.—*n.* **propi′ti-a′tion.**—*adj.* **pro-pi′ti-a-tor-y.**

pro-pi-tious (prō-pish′us), *adj.* **1,** favourably inclined; gracious; **2,** favourable; suitable, as *propitious* weather.

pro-po-nent (prō-pō′nent), *n.* an advocate or supporter; as, he is a *proponent* of state ownership, and state medicine.

pro-por-tion (prō-pōr′shun), *n.* **1,** the relation between the size, amount, or degree of one thing and the size, amount, or degree of another; ratio; as, the *proportion* of week-days to Sundays is six to one; **2,** proper or just

share; as, what is my *proportion* of the profits? **3,** in *mathematics,* a statement of equality between two ratios; as, 4 : 8 = 6 : 12 is a *proportion;* **4, proportions,** dimensions; size; as, the *proportions* of a rug:—*v.t.* to cause (one thing) to be in suitable relation to another; as, to *proportion* one's expenses to one's income; also, to give suitable dimensions to.—*adj.* and *n.* **pro-por′tion-al.**—*adj.* **pro-por′tion-ate.**

pro-pose (prō-pōz′), *v.t.* [proposed, propos-ing], **1,** to put forward for consideration; suggest; as, he *proposed* that I should go; I *proposed* a later date; **2,** to suggest the name of, for an office; nominate:—*v.i.* **1,** to make an offer of marriage; **2,** to form a plan; make known a plan; hence, to intend; purpose; as, I *propose* to stay at home.—*n.* **pro-pos′al.**

prop-o-si-tion (prop′o-zish′un), *n.* **1,** that which is offered for consideration; a proposal; **2,** the formal statement of a topic to be discussed; **3,** in *mathematics,* the statement of a theorem or problem for solution.

pro-pound (prō-pound′), *v.t.* to offer for discussion or debate; to set forth, as a question, problem, etc.

pro-pri-e-tar-y (prō-prī′e-ta-ri), *adj.* **1,** pertaining to an owner; **2,** holding property; **3,** held under patent, etc.; as, a *proprietary* medicine.

pro-pri-e-tor (prō-prī′e-tẽr), *n.* one who has a legal title to property; an owner; as, the *proprietor* of a farm.—*n. fem.* **pro-pri′e-tress.**—*n.* **pro-pri′e-tor-ship′.**

pro-pri-e-ty (prō-prī′e-ti), *n.* [*pl.* proprieties], **1,** fitness or suitability; also, correctness of manners or conduct; **2, proprieties,** the manners expected in polite society.

pro-pul-sion (prō-pul′shun), *n.* the act of propelling, or the state of being propelled.

pro ra-ta (prō rā′ta), in proportion; as, the loss was shared *pro rata.*

pro-rogue (prō-rōg′), *v.t.* and *v.i.* to end the meetings of a legislative assembly; as the Parliament at Ottawa *prorogued* on July 15.—*n.* **pro′ro-ga′-tion.**

pro-sa-ic (prō-zā′ik), *adj.* commonplace; unimaginative; dull.

pro-scribe (prō-skrīb′), *v.t.* [proscrib-ed, proscrib-ing], **1,** to put (a person) outside the protection of the law; outlaw; banish; **2,** to condemn; prohibit; as, free speech is still *proscribed* there. —*n.* **pro-scrip′tion.**

prose (prōz), *n.* ordinary spoken or written language without the metre, rhyme, rhythm, etc., of poetry: distinguished from *verse:—v.i.* [prosed, prosing], to write or speak tediously and at length:—*adj.* pertaining to composition that is not verse.—*adj.* **pros'y**.

pros-e-cute (pros'i-kūt'), *v.t.* [prosecut-ed, prosecut-ing], **1,** to follow up or pursue (an undertaking) in order to complete it; as, to *prosecute* an investigation; **2,** to bring legal proceedings against (someone):—*v.i.* **1,** to conduct the case against a person accused of crime; **2,** to carry on a lawsuit.—*n.* **pros'e-cu'tor.**—*n.* **pros'e-cu'tion.**—*n. fem.* **pro-sec'u-trix.**

pros-e-lyt-ize (pros'i-līt-īz'; -lit), *v.t.* and *v.i.* to win converts (to a religion or belief); as, this sect *proselytizes* vigorously.—*n.* **pros'e-lyte** (a convert).

pros-o-dy (pros'o-di), *n.* the art of versification, including metre, accent, rhythm, rhyming, etc.

pros-pect (pros'pekt), *n.* **1,** a scene spread out before the sight; view; outlook; as, a *prospect* of green, rolling prairie; **2,** a looking forward or, esp. that which one looks forward to, or expects; expectation; as, a *prospect* of fair weather; **3,** a possible customer or client:—*v.t.* and *v.i.* (pros-pekt'; pros'-pekt), to search or explore, esp. for gold, oil, etc.

pro-spec-tive (pro-spek'tiv), *adj.* **1,** concerned with the future; **2,** expected; hoped for; as, *prospective* profits.

pro-spec-tor (pro-spek'tėr; pros'pektėr), *n.* one who explores a region, searching for oil, gold, etc. of the earth.

pro-spec-tus (pro-spek'tus), *n.* a printed outline of a forthcoming book or a new enterprise (to win financial support for it).

pros-per (pros'pėr), *v.i.* to thrive; make progress; flourish.—*n.* **pros-per'i-ty.**—*adj.* **pros'per-ous.**

pros-ti-tute (pros'ti-tūt'), *v.t.* to devote to a low or unworthy purpose; as, to *prostitute* one's talents;—*n.* one (esp. a woman) who enters into sex relations for pay.—*n.* **pros'ti-tu'tion.**

pros-trate (pros'trāt), *adj.* **1,** lying face down on the ground; bending to the ground; in token of defeat, humility, or worship; as, the vanquished foe, *prostrate* before the victor; **2,** flung down to the ground as, the *prostrate* pillars of a ruined temple; **3,** overcome, as with emotion; also, drained of vitality; lifeless; as, a *prostrate* industry:—*v.t.* (pros-strāt'), [prostrat-ed, prostrat-ing]

1, to humble (oneself) by lying face down on the ground; as, to *prostrate* oneself before God; **2,** to exhaust; as, she is *prostrated* with fatigue.—*n.* **pros-tra'tion.**

pro-tag-o-nist (prō-tag'o-nist), *n.* the leading character in a play (as *Shylock* in Shakespeare's M. of V.).

pro-tect (prō-tekt'), *v.t.* to shield from harm; guard; shelter; as, a lightning-rod *protects* a building against fire from lightning.—*adj.* **pro-tec'tive.**—*n.* **pro-tec'tor.**

pro-tec-tion (prō-tek'shun), *n.* **1,** the act of keeping in safety; **2,** the state of being kept in safety; **3,** that which keeps safe; defence; security; as, an overcoat is a *protection* against a cold wind; **4,** the placing of duties on imported goods for the encouragement of home industry, a policy opposed to that of free trade.—*n.* **pro-tec'tion-ist** (one opposed to free trade).

pro-tec-tor-ate (prō-tek'tėr-it), *n.* **1,** government by a person appointed to rule in place of a king; **2,** the relation of a great nation to a weak one which it defends and partly controls; also, the period during which this control is maintained; **3,** the nation so defended and controlled.

pro-té-gé (prō'te-zhā; prô'tā/zhā'), *n.* one who is under the guardianship or care of another.—*n.fem.* **pro'té-gée.**

pro-te-in (prō'tē-in; prō'tēn), *n.* a substance containing nitrogen, found as a vital element in all living organisms, animal and vegetable. Protein is an essential part of any diet, and is contained in meat, butter, cheese, eggs, nuts, pease, beans, etc.

pro-test (prō-test'), *v.i.* to make a formal declaration of disapproval or dissent:—*v.t.* **1,** to affirm or assert; as, the defendant *protested* that he was telling the absolute truth; **2,** to object to; dissent from; as, to appeal to a higher court is to *protest* the judgment of the lower; **3,** to make a formal statement of refusal to honour or pay; as, to *protest* a cheque:—*n.* (prō'test). **1,** a formal declaration of opinion against something; **2,** a formal notification that a note, cheque, etc., will not be honoured or paid.

Prot-es-tant (prot'es-tant), *adj.* naming, or pertaining to, any of the branches of the Christian church which separated from the Roman Catholic Church in the 16th century:—*n.* a member of a Protestant church.—*n.* **Prot'es-tant-ism.**

cat, āge, fär, câre, ȧsk; ten, ēve, latėr; (i) pity, rely, senate; īce; top; nō

prot-es-ta-tion (prot'es-tā'shun), *n.* 1, a solemn declaration; as, *protestations* of friendship; 2, a formal objection or protest; as, a *protestation* against war or against unjust taxes.

pro-tho-rax (prō-thōr'aks), *n.* the front part of an insect's thorax bearing the first pair of legs.

pro-to-col (prō'tō-kol'), *n.* the proper courtesies in ceremonies of state, esp. the etiquette governing official visits between heads of states and their ministers.

pro-ton (prō'ton), *n.* one of the basic constituents, or particles, of an atom's nucleus: it carries, or consists of, a charge of positive electricity: the proton of the hydrogen atom has a mass 1840 times that of its electron.

pro-to-plasm (prō'tō-plazm), *n.* the essential living substance of both animal and plant cells. It is usually a colourless, jellylike substance, in which tiny grains of solid matter are suspended.—*adj.* **pro'to-plas'mic.** (plaz').

pro-to-type (prō'tō-tīp'), *n.* an original; model; pattern; as, Shakespeare has no *prototype* in British dramatic poetry.

pro-to-zo-a (prō'tō-zō'a), *n.* a phylum, or division, of animals, such as the *amoeba*, chiefly microscopic and aquatic, consisting of a single cell and reproducing by fission (splitting and dividing).—*n.* and *adj.* **pro'to-zo'an.**

pro-tract (prō-trakt'), *v.t.* 1, to draw out; prolong, as a meeting; 2, to draw to scale.—*n.* **pro-trac'tion.**—*adj.* **pro-tract'ed.**

pro-trac-tor (prō-trak'tėr), *n.* an instrument for measuring angles.

PROTRACTOR

pro-tu-ber-ant (prō-tū'bėr-ant), *adj.* swelling out beyond the surrounding surface; bulging; as, a *protuberant* nose.—*n.* **pro-tu'ber-ance.**

pro-trude (prō-trōōd'), *v.t.* and *v.i.* [protrud-ed, protrud-ing], to stick out; project; as, to *protrude* the tongue; pencils *protrude* from his pocket—*n.* **pro-tru'sion.**

proud (proud), *adj.* 1, having or exhibiting too great self-esteem; overbearing; haughty; as, a *proud* lady with her *proud* airs; 2, having worthy self-respect; as, too *proud* to beg; 3, having a feeling of glad satisfaction;

gratified; as, *proud* of his boy's success; 4, noble; magnificent; as, a *proud* old castle.—*adv.* **proud'ly.**

prove (prōōv), *v.t.* [*p.t.* proved (prōōvd), *p.p.* proved or prov-en (prōōv'-en), *p.pr.* prov-ing], 1, to test by an experiment; as, to *prove* the purity of copper; 2, to demonstrate by reasoning or evidence; as, to *prove* a theorem in geometry; 3, to cause to be accepted as genuine; as, to *prove* a will:—*v.i.* to turn out to be; be found to be; as, the new coat *proved* warm.

prov-en-der (prov'en-dėr), *n.* dry feed for livestock, as hay, oats, or corn.

prov-erb (prov'ûrb), *n.* 1, a short, homely saying, expressing a truth in few words; an adage, as "a stitch in time saves nine"; 2, a byword.

pro-ver-bi-al (pro-vûr'bi-al), *adj.* 1, contained in, or resembling, proverbs; as, *proverbial* wisdom; 2, widely spoken of or known; as, her kindness is *proverbial.*—*adv.* **pro-ver'bi-al-ly.**

pro-vide (prō-vīd'), *v.t.* [provid-ed, provid-ing], 1, to supply or furnish (a thing) for use; as, to *provide* food and lodging; also, to outfit or equip (a person); as, to *provide* a child with books; 2, to set forth as a condition; stipulate; as, her will *provided* that a new hospital be built:—*v.i.* to make preparations in advance; as, to *provide* against cold weather.

pro-vid-ed (prō-vīd'id), *conj.* on condition that; if; as, I'll go, *provided* you go.

prov-i-dence (prov'i-dens), *n.* 1, prudence; foresight; also, prudent management; thrift; 2, an instance of divine care; as, her recovery was God's special *providence:*—**Providence,** God; as, to trust in *Providence.*

prov-i-dent (prov'i-dent), *adj.* 1, mindful of the future; prudent; 2, economical; thrifty.—*adv.* **prov'i-dent-ly.**

prov-i-den-tial (prov'i-den'shal), *adj.* 1, of or by divine foresight; as, a *providential* recovery from illness; 2, fortunate.—*adv.* **prov'i-den'tial-ly.**

prov-ince (prov'ins), *n.* 1, a division of an empire or country; as, Alberta is a *province* of Canada; 2, a country governed by a distant authority; 3, limits or range; a proper sphere of action; as, this task is outside your *province;* 4, **provinces,** regions remote from a capital or a very large city; as, a company left London for the *provinces.*

pro-vin-cial (prō-vin'shal), *adj.* 1, of

or belonging to a division of an empire or country; as, *provincial* government; **2,** countrified; crude; **3,** restricted to the ideas and customs of one special region; hence, narrow; limited:—*n.* **1,** an inhabitant of a province; **2,** an uncultivated person.—*n.* **pro-vin′cial-ism.**

pro-vi-sion (prō-vizh′un), *n.* **1,** preparation; care beforehand; as, *provision* must be made for a long journey; **2,** (often *provisions*), a supply or stock of food; as, *provisions* for the winter; **3,** a condition; proviso; stipulation; as, a *provision* in a contract:—*v.t.* to supply with food, esp.—*adj.* **pro-vi′sion-al** (temporary).—*n.* **pro-vi′sion-er.**

pro-vi-so (prō-vī′zō), *n.* [*pl.* provisoes or provisos], a conditional clause or stipulation, as in a deed or will.

prov-o-ca-tion (prov′o-kā′shun), *n.* **1,** that which excites to anger or resentment; as, he fairly rages on the slightest *provocation;* **2,** the act of provoking; as, the *provocation* of a quarrel.—*adj.* **pro-voc′a-tive** (pro-vok′a-tiv).

pro-voke (prō-vōk′), *v.t.* [provoked, provok-ing], **1,** to excite; stir up; as, to *provoke* a laugh; **3,** to irritate; rouse; incite; as, to *provoke* another to anger.—*adj.* **pro-vok′ing.**

prov-ost (prov′ust), *n.* **1,** a chief official or superintendent, esp. of a college; **2,** *Military* (prō′vō), a guard of soldiers to help civil authorities keep order near an army post or camp.

prow (prou), *n.* the forward end or part, as the nose of an aeroplane or bow of a ship.

prow-ess (prou′es), *n.* **1,** daring; bravery; valour; **2,** very great skill or ability; as, he was noted for his *prowess* as a wrestler.

prowl (proul), *v.i.* to move about stealthily; as, wolves *prowl* for food:—*v.t.* to roam over, as woods or fields, in search of prey:—*n.* a roving for prey or plunder; as, beasts on the *prowl.*—*n.* **prowl′er.**

prox-im-i-ty (proks-im′i-ti), *n.* nearness; closeness; as, *proximity* to danger.

prox-y (prok′si), *n.* [*pl.* proxies], **1,** authority to act for another; hence, the document giving the authority; as, to vote by *proxy;* **2,** a person who is given authority to act for another.

prude (prōōd), *n.* a person who is extremely or affectedly proper in dress, speech, or behaviour.—*adj.* **prud′ish.** —*n.* **prud′er-y.**

pru-dent (prōō′dent), *adj.* **1,** mindful

of the future; using judgment an foresight; cautious; as, a *pruder* housewife; **2,** showing forethought as, a *prudent* act.—*n.* **pru′dence.**—*ad* **pru-den′tial.**

¹prune (prōōn), *v.t.* [pruned, prun-ing] **1,** to cut unnecessary twigs or branche from (a vine, bush, or tree); trim **2,** to cut out or clear away the useles parts of; as, the author *pruned* hi novel:—*v.i.* to remove useless branche or parts.—*n.* **prun′er.**

²prune (prōōn), *n.* a kind of plum, es one that has been dried or is capable o being dried without fermentation.

pru-ri-ent (prōō′ri-ent), *adj.* lustfu lewd; as, *prurient* longings.—*n.* **pru′ri** **ence.**

prus-sic acid (prus′ik), a colourles poisonous, gaseous acid, HCN (*hydro cyanic acid*), soluble in water: it has a odour of bitter almonds: used as an in secticide, and in mining and metallurgy

¹pry (prī), *v.i.* [pried, pry-ing], to loo or peer closely and inquisitively as, some people *pry* into other people affairs.—*adj.* **pry′ing.**

²pry (prī), *v.t.* [pried, pry-ing], **1,** to rais or open with a lever; **2,** to budge o move with difficulty; as, you can't *pr* Sally away from the piano:—*n.* a lever

psalm (säm), *n.* a sacred song or poem —*n.* **psalm′ist.**

pseu-do or **pseu-do-** (sū′dō), *adj.* an *prefix,* false; sham; pretended; as i *pseudo*aquatic (found in moist regions and *pseudo*-volcano (one that emit smoke or flame, but no lava).

pseu-do-nym (sū′do-nim), *n.* a fic titious or false name taken by a writer a pen-name; as, Mark Twain was th *pseudonym* of Samuel L. Clemens.

pshaw (shô), *interj.* an exclamation o contempt, impatience, disgust, etc.

psy-che (sī′ki), *n.* the human sou mind, or spirit; as, the failure left hin with a bruised *psyche.*

psy-chi-a-try (sī-kī′a-tri), *n.* the study and treatment of mental disorders —*n.* **psy-chi′a-trist.**

psy-chic (sī′kik), *n.* a person sensitiv to forces which cannot be explained by any known laws; a medium:—*adj.* **1** concerning the soul or mind; spiritual **2,** lying outside the realm of knowr physical processes; as, *psychic* forces **3,** sensitive to forces of this kind; as a *psychic* person.—*adj.* **psy′chi-cal.**

psy-cho- (sī′kō-), *prefix* meaning *menta*

cat, āge, fär, câre, àsk; ten, ēve, latér; (i) pity, rely, senate; īce; top; nō or *mind* (processes), as in **psy'cho-a-nal'y-sis**: this is the treating of neuroses, etc., on the theory that many desires, repressed by the conscious mind and persisting in the unconscious to the harm of one's mental life and conduct, can be directed into better channels through an analysis of the patient's emotional history. —*v.t.* **psy'cho-an'a-lyze'.**

psy-chol-o-gy (sī-kol'o-ji), *n.* [*pl.* psychologies], the science that studies the mind, particularly the human mind, and its activities.—*adj.* **psy'cho-log'i-cal** (sī'ko-loj'i-kal),—*n.* **psy-chol'o-gist.**

psy-cho-path (sī'kō-path'), *n.* a mentally deranged person.

psy-cho-sis (sī'kō'sis), *n.* [*pl.* psychoses (-sēz)], severe mental disorder that (a) lacks any apparent physical cause, (b) is accompanied by some organic damage, as in alcoholism, brain tumours, etc.: a *psychosis* is a mental, a *neurosis* a nervous, disorder (primarily).—*adj.* **psy-chot'ic.**

psy-cho-ther-a-py (sī'kō-ther'a-pi), *n.* the use of such aids as suggestion, hypnosis, and psychoanalysis to cure mental and nervous disorders.

ptar-mi-gan (tär'mi-gan), *n.* a northern grouse whose grey or black plumage turns white in winter.

pter-o-dac-tyl (ter'ō-dak'til) or **pter-o-saur** (ter'ō-sôr'), *n.* a flying reptile of the dinosaur era: it had wings (about 18' across) between the hind leg and the very long fourth digit of the forelimb.

pto-maine (tō-mān') or **pto-main** (tō'mān), *n.* a substance, usually poisonous, found in decaying organic matter.

pu-ber-ty (pū'bèr-ti), *n.* the earliest age at which one can beget or bear children: the age of puberty is about 12 for girls, 14 for boys.

pub-lic (pub'lik), *adj.* **1,** pertaining to the people as a whole; as, the *public* welfare; **2,** common to all; open to general use; as, a *public* park; a *public* library or school; **3,** generally known; not secret; as, the facts were made *public;* **4,** serving the people; as, a *public* utility:—*n.* **1,** the people in general or as a whole; **2,** a special section or group of the people; as, the voting *public.*—*adv.* **pub'lic-ly.**

pub-li-can (pub'li-kan), *n.* **1,** in Great Britain, one who keeps an inn or public house; **2,** in ancient Rome or in the Bible, a collector of taxes and public revenues.

pub-li-ca-tion (pub'li-kā'shun), *n.* **1,** the act or business of printing and placing on sale; as, the *publication* of books; **2,** a book, magazine, etc.; **3,** a making known to the public; as, this information is not for *publication.*

pub-lic-i-ty (pub-lis'i-ti), *n.* **1,** the state of being open to common knowledge; notoriety; public notice; as, unfavourable *publicity;* a *publicity* seeker; **2,** news that advertises; as, theatrical *publicity.*—*v.t.* **pub'li-cize'.** —*n.* **pub'li-cist.**

pub-lish (pub'lish), *v.t.* **1,** to make generally known; as, to *publish* one's intentions; also, to proclaim, as an edict; **2,** to print and offer for sale, as a book, magazine, etc.—*n.* **pub'lish-er.**

puck (puk), *n.* in *hockey*, a hard rubber disk pushed or driven along the ice with a stick.

puck-er (puk'èr), *v.t.* to draw up into small folds; wrinkle; as, in perplexity he *puckered* up his brow:—*v.i.* to become drawn up into folds; as, the cloth *puckered* badly after being wet: —*n.* a small fold or wrinkle.

pud-ding (pood'ing), *n.* **1,** a kind of soft food, often a dessert, made of flour, milk, eggs, etc.; **2,** a kind of sausage; as, blood-*pudding.*

pud-dle (pud'l), *n.* **1,** a small pool of dirty water; ` 2,` a mixture of clay and water used as a watertight covering or filling:—*v.t.* [pud-dled, pud-dling], **1,** to make muddy; **2,** to work water into (clay) so as to make a mixture through which water cannot pass; **3,** to stir (molten pig-iron) so as to produce wrought-iron.—*n.* **pud'dler.**

pudg-y (puj'i), *adj.* [pudg-i-er, pudg-i-est], short and fat; as, a *pudgy* hand. —*n.* **pudg'i-ness.**

pueb-lo (pweb'lō), *n.* [*pl.* pueblos], **1,** a building made of sun-dried brick by the Indians of New Mexico, Arizona, etc., often several stories high, housing the entire village or tribe; **2,** in the U.S. and Spanish America, an Indian or Spanish village.

pu-er-ile (pū'èr-īl'; -il), *adj.* **1,** pertaining to childhood; **2,** immature; foolish; as, a *puerile* remark; a *puerile* display of temper.

puff (puf), *n.* **1,** a short, quick blast, as of wind, steam, gas, breath, etc.; also, the accompanying sound or vapour; as, one may both hear and see the *puffs* of a locomotive; **2,** a soft pad; as, a powder-*puff;* **3,** a light pastry shell filled with whipped cream, custard, etc.; as, a cream-*puff;* **4,** in dressmaking, a piece of material gathered on two sides so as to stand out in the centre; **5,** exaggerated praise; as, the critic gave the new play quite a *puff;* **6,** a loose mass or roll of hair:—*v.i.* **1,** to send out air, smoke, breath, etc., in puffs; **2,** to breathe quickly and hard, as a runner; **3,** to swell with air; **4,** to swell with importance:—*v.t.* **1,** to emit or blow out, with whiffs or little blasts; **2,** to cause to swell, as with wind, or, figuratively, with importance; as, to *puff* out the cheeks; **3,** to praise in too high terms; as, to *puff* a book; **4,** to arrange in puffs, as the hair, dress material, etc.

puff-ball (puf'bôl'), *n.* a ball-shaped fungus, somewhat similar to a mushroom, which, when dried and broken open, sends out a dustlike puff of spores.

puf-fin (puf'in), *n.* a North Atlantic sea-bird, about a foot long, black above and white below, with short neck and bright-coloured, grooved beak.

puff-y (puf'i), *adj.* [puff-i-er, puff-i-est], **1,** swollen; bloated; as, infection made his hand *puffy;* **2,** breathing hard; puffing; as, a *puffy* old man; **3,** blowing in little gusts; as, a *puffy* wind.

pug (pug), *n.* a small stocky dog with short, broad nose, wrinkled face, and tightly curled tail: also called *pug-dog.*

pugh (pū; pōō), *interj.* an exclamation of disgust, contempt, etc.

pu-gil-ist (pū'ji-list), *n.* a prize-fighter; a boxer.—*adj.* **pu'gil-is'tic.**—*n.* **pu'-gil-ism.**

pug-na-cious (pug-nā'shus), *adj.* desiring to fight; quarrelsome.

pu-is-sant (pū'i-sant), *adj.* *Poetic,* powerful (esp. against opposition).—*n.* **pu'is-sance.**

puke (pūk), *v.i.* and *v.t. Vulgar,* to vomit.

pul-chri-tude (pul'kri-tūd'), *n.* beauty (esp. in women).

pull (pool), *v.t.* **1,** to draw out or toward one by exerting force; as, to *pull* a nail; *pull* a tooth; **2,** to draw in any direction; drag; haul; **3,** to pluck up by the roots; as, to *pull* weeds; **4,** to rend or tear; as, to *pull* a dress to pieces; **5,** to work by stretching; as, to *pull* candy:—*v.i.* to draw forcibly; tug:—*n.* **1,** the act of pulling; a tug; as, he gave

my sleeve a *pull;* **2,** a hard climb; as, a long *pull* up the mountain; **3,** a handle or cord by which something is pulled; **4,** *Slang,* influence.

pul-let (pool'it), *n.* a young hen.

pul-ley (pool'i), *n.* [*pl.* pulleys], a tackle which consists of a wood or metal frame for a wheel with a grooved rim, into which fits a rope. A pulley is used for hauling, lifting, and pulling or for changing the direction of a pull

Pull-man (pool'man), *n.* a railway car with sleeping-berths; also, a car with comfortable individual chairs. Also, **Pull'man car.**

pul-mo-nar-y (pul'mo-nėr-i), *adj.* pertaining to the lungs; as, tuberculosis is a *pulmonary* disease.

pulp (pulp), *n.* **1,** the soft fleshy part of fruit, plant stems, etc.; **2,** the inner fleshy part of a tooth; **3,** any soft, wet mass; as, wood-*pulp.*—*adj.* **pulp'y.**

pul-pit (pool'pit), *n.* **1,** a raised platform or desk in a church, from which the sermon is delivered; **2,** the preaching profession.

pulp-wood (pulp'wood'), *n.* soft wood, as spruce, etc., used in making paper.

pul-sate (pul'sāt; pul-sāt'), *v.i.* [pul-sat-ed, pulsat-ing], **1,** to throb; beat as the heart; **2,** to quiver; vibrate with life or feeling; as, a *pulsating* voice —*n.* **pul-sa'tion.**

pulse (puls), *n.* **1,** the throbbing or beating in an artery as the blood is pumped through; **2,** a stroke or beat occurring at regular intervals:—*v.i.* [pulsed, puls-ing], to beat or throb, as an artery.

pul-ver-ize (pul'vėr-īz'), *v.t.* [pulverized, pulveriz-ing], to crush, grind or beat into powder or dust; as, to *pulverize* sugar:—*v.i.* to become dust as, even rocks *pulverize* in time.

pu-ma (pū'ma), *n.* a large tawny American wildcat; the mountain lion, or cougar.

PUMA (1/45)

pum-ice (pum'-is), *n.* a hard light porous volcanic rock, used for cleaning polishing: also called *pumice-stone.*

pum-mel (pum'el), *n.* Same as **pommel.**

¹pump (pump), *n.* a machine for raising or moving liquids or compressing gases by means of pressure suction:—*v.t.* **1**, to raise or draw, as water, by means of a pump; **2**, to remove water or gases from; as, to *pump* a boat dry; **3**, to draw out by artful questions; as, to *pump* a secret, or a friend; **4**, to force, as does a pump; as, the heart *pumps* blood to all parts of the body:—*v.i.* **1**, to work a pump; as, to *pump* faster; **2**, to work like a pump; as, your heart *pumps* too fast.—*n.* **pump′er.**

²**pump** (pump) *n.* a low light-weight shoe, esp. one without a lace, strap or other fastening.

pump-kin (pump′kin; *Colloq.*, pung′-kin), *n.* a vine or plant that bears large yellow or orange fruit, like squashes; also, the fruit, used esp. for pies and as feed for animals.

pun (pun), *n.* a form of jesting expression in which one word is used with two meanings, or two different words pronounced nearly alike are used close together, as in "*stand* by what you say or you will *stand* the penalty" and "he went and *told* the sexton and the sexton *tolled* the bell":—*v.i.* [punned, pun-ning], to make or utter a pun; as, he is always *punning*.

¹**punch** (punch), *n.* **1**, a tool for making dents or holes; **2**, a machine tool for stamping and forming sheetmetal articles; **3**, a blow or thrust, esp. with the closed fist:—*v.t.* **1**, to strike with the fist; **2**, to drive along; as, to *punch* cattle; **3**, to press the key or keys of (a machine); as, to *punch* a typewriter; **4**, to make (a hole) in; **5**, to cut or mark with a tool:—*v.i.* **1**, to hit with the fist; as, to *punch* hard; **2**, to make a hole; as, this tool *punches* cleanly.

²**punch** (punch), *n.* a drink made of rum, whisky, or other liquor, with water, lemon juice, sugar, etc.; also, a drink made from fruit juices, sweetened and flavoured.

punch-eon (pun′chun), *n.* a large cask for liquor.

punc-til-i-ous (pungk-til′i-us), *adj.* nice or precise in conduct; as, *punc-*tilious etiquette.—*n.* **punctil′i-o.**

punc-tu-al (pungk′tū-al), *adj.* prompt; arriving or appearing at the proper time.—*adv.* **punc′tu-al-ly.**—*n.* **punc′tu-al′i-ty.**

punc-tu-ate (pungk′tū-āt′), *v.t.* [punc-tuat-ed, punctuat-ing], **1**, to mark or set off the parts of, with a period, comma, semicolon, etc.; as, to *punc-*tuate a paragraph; **2**, to emphasize; as, he *punctuated* his remarks with

gestures; **3**, to interrupt at intervals, or now and then; as, cheers *punctuated* the speaker's words.

punc-tu-a-tion (pungk′tū-ā′shun), *n.* in writing or printing, the marking, or setting off, of words, phrases, sentences, etc., by the use of certain special marks:—**punctuation marks,** the comma [,], semicolon [;], period[.], interrogation mark [?], exclamation mark [!], dash [—], parentheses [()], brackets [], double quotation marks ["..."], and single quotation marks ['...'].

punc-ture (pungk′tūr), *n.* a hole or wound made by something pointed; as, a *puncture* in a tube; also, deflation, as of a balloon:—*v.t.* [punctured, punc-tur-ing], **1**, to make a hole in, or pierce, as with a pointed instrument; prick; **2**, to deflate; destroy; as, a sharp reproof may *puncture* pride.

pun-dit (pun′dit), *n.* a learned man; scholar (esp. a Hindu); **2**, *Humorously,* an authority, expert or teacher.

pun-gent (pun′jent), *adj.* **1**, stinging; pricking; biting; as, a *pungent* acid; **2**, piercing; keen; as, *pungent* wit; **3**, sarcastic; caustic; as, *pungent* satire. —*adv.* **pun′gent-ly.**—*n.* **pun′gen-cy.**

pun-ish (pun′ish), *v.t.* **1**, to cause (a person) to pay the penalty for a crime or fault; as, to *punish* a child; **2**, to inflict the penalty for (something); as, to *punish* disobedience.—*n.* **pun′ish-ment.**—*adj.* **pu′ni-tive;** **pun′ish-a-ble.**

punk (pungk), *n.* **1**, partly decayed wood; tinder; **2**, a substance (made of decayed vegetable matter) used to light fireworks.

¹**punt** (punt), *n.* a flat-bottomed boat.

²**punt** (punt) *v.t.* and *v.i.* to drop a football from the hands and kick it *before* it strikes the ground: in a drop-kick the ball is kicked *after* it rebounds from the ground. Also used as *n.*

pu-ny (pū′ni), *adj.* [pu-ni-er, pu-ni-est], **1**, undersized; weak; as, a *puny* baby; **2**, hence, feeble; half-hearted; as, a *puny* effort.

pup (pup), *n.* **1**, a young dog; a puppy; **2**, the young of several other mammals, as of the seal.

pu-pa (pū′pa), *n.* [*pl.* pupae (pū′pē) or pupas], the stage in the life of an insect when it is in a cocoon or case. The pupa is the stage between the caterpillar and the butterfly.—*adj.* **pu′pal.**—*v.i.* **pu′pate** (to become a pupa, chrysalis, or cocoon).

¹**pu-pil** (pū′pl; pū′pil), *n.* a young

person under the care and instruction of a teacher.

²**pu-pil** (pū′pl; pū′pil), *n.* the dark centre in the iris of the eye, through which rays of light pass to the retina.

pup-pet (pup′it), *n.* **1**, a small doll or figure, esp. one moved by wires from behind a screen in a mock drama, called a *puppet-show;* a marionette; **2**, one who, though properly his own master, is under the control of another; as, the king was the *puppet* of his ministers:—*adj.* controlled (by another) as, a *puppet* state.

pup-py (pup′i), *n.* [*pl.* puppies], **1**, a young dog; **2**, a conceited, silly young man.

pur (pûr), *v.* and *n.* Same as **purr.**

pur-chase (pûr′chis), *v.t.* [purchased, purchas-ing], to get by paying money; buy:—*n.* **1**, the act or process of buying; as, the *purchase* and sale of goods or land; **2**, the thing bought; as, he examined his *purchase;* **3**, a firm hold or grasp to help one to move something or to keep oneself from slipping; as, to take a *purchase* on a rock with a crowbar.—*n.* **pur′chas-er.**

pure (pūr), *adj.* [pur-er, pur-est], **1**, free from any foreign matter that might lower its quality; clear; clean; **2**, free from sin; chaste; innocent; **3**, sheer; mere; nothing but; as, *pure* foolishness.—*n.* **pure′ness.**—*n.* **pur′ist.**

pu-ree (pū-rā′; pü′rā′), *n.* a thick soup, made of meat, beans, etc., boiled and strained through a sieve.

pure-ly (pūr′li), *adv.* entirely; merely; as, I have a *purely* unselfish interest in it.

pur-ga-tive (pûr′ga-tiv), *adj.* having the power of cleansing:—*n.* a medicine for the purpose of cleansing the system of waste and impurities; a cathartic or physic.—*n.* **pur-ga′tion.**

pur-ga-to-ry (pûr′ga-to-ri), *n.* **1**, in Roman Catholic theology, a place or state in which those who die in the grace of God are cleansed by suffering; **2**, any place of torment or misery.

purge (pûrj), *v.t.* [purged, purg-ing], **1**, to cleanse or free from impurities; **2**, to clear of guilt; free from sin; as, to *purge* one's mind of evil thoughts; **3**, to cleanse (the bowels) by the action of a cathartic medicine:—*n.* **1**, the act or process of cleansing or freeing from impurities; **2**, a purgative.

pu-ri-fy (pū′ri-fī′), *v.t.* [purified, purifying], **1**, to make clean; to free from impurities; **2**, to make ceremonially

clean, as by baptism.—*n.* **pu′ri-fi-ca′tion.**

pu-ri-tan (pū′ri-tan), *n.* one who is very strict in his religious life or in his attitude toward worldly pleasures; often, one who is bigoted and narrow-minded.—*adj.* **pu′ri-tan′i-cal.**

pu-ri-ty (pū′ri-ti), *n.* **1**, freedom from impurities; as, *purity* of spring water; **2**, virtue; innocence; freedom from evil; as, *purity* of thought; **3**, accuracy; refined elegance; as, *purity* of style.

¹**purl** (pûrl), *v.t.* and *v.i.* **1**, to edge with a chain of loops, as in knitting; **2**, to invert stitches for a ribbed effect.

²**purl** (pûrl), *v.i.* to flow with a gentle murmur, as a stream; to swirl, as an eddy.

pur-loin (pûr-loin′), *v.t.* and *v.i.* to steal; pilfer; filch; as, he *purloined* the key of the car.

pur-ple (pûr′pl), *n.* **1**, a colour resulting from a mixture of red and blue; formerly, a deep crimson; **2**, a robe of this colour formerly worn by royalty; **3**, hence, royal power or dignity; also, great wealth or high rank; as, born to the *purple:*—*adj.* of the colour of blended blue and red.—*adj.* **pur′plish.**

pur-port (pûr′pōrt), *n.* meaning; sense; substance; as, the *purport* of his reply was that he would do what we wished: —*v.t.* (pûr-pōrt′; pûr′pōrt), to profess; as, the book *purported* to be a real account of the author's experiences in the jungle.

pur-pose (pûr′pus), *n.* **1**, settled intention; design; aim; as, his *purpose* in consenting was merely to help his friends; **2**, end; result; as, he saved his money, but to little *purpose,* because his children spent it foolishly:—*v.t.* [purposed, purpos-ing], to intend; resolve; as, I *purpose* to go on with my studies.—*adj.* **pur′pose-ful.**

pur-pose-ly (pûr′pus-li), *adv.* intentionally; deliberately; on purpose; as, he hit me *purposely.*

purr or **pur** (pûr), *n.* a low murmuring sound, as made by a cat when it is comfortable or contented:—*v.i.* [purred, purr-ing], to utter such a sound.

purse (pûrs), *n.* **1**, a small bag or pouch for money; **2**, a sum of money collected for a purpose; as, they made up a *purse* for the widow; also, a sum of money offered as a prize; **3**, money; treasury; as, the public *purse:*—*v.t.* [pursed, purs-ing], to pucker or wrinkle as, to *purse* the lips.

purs-er (pûr′sèr), *n.* on shipboard, the officer who has charge of the accounts.

purs-lane (pûrs'lān), *n.* a low-spreading, fleshy plant, esp. the portulaca.

pur-sue (per-sū'), *v.t.* [pursued, pursuing], **1,** to follow with the aim of overtaking; chase; as, to *pursue* a thief; **2,** to seek; engage in; as, to *pursue* pleasure; **3,** to go on with; continue; as, to *pursue* an inquiry; **4,** to follow; engage in (studies, a profession, etc.). —*n.* **pur-su'er.**—*n.* **pur-su'ance** (in *pursuance of*).—*adj.* **pur-su'ant** (to).

pur-suit (per-sūt'), *n.* **1,** the act of following or seeking; chase; as, the *pursuit* of game; **2,** occupation; employment; as, scientific or mercantile *pursuits*.

pur-vey (pûr-vā'), *v.t.* to provide; supply, as provisions for an army:—*v.i.* to make a business of supplying provisions or food to others.—*n.* **pur-vey'or.**

pus (pus), *n.* the yellowish-white substance produced by inflammation in sores, abscesses, etc.; matter.—*adj.* **pus'sy.**

push (poosh), *v.t.* **1,** to press against with force, for the purpose of moving; **2,** to urge forward or extend by effort; as, to *push* one's interests; **3,** to dun urgently; press; urge; as, to *push* a debtor:—*v.i.* **1,** to make a steady forward effort; as, the army *pushed* on; **2,** to press hard in order to move:—*n.* **1,** a thrust; force applied; a shove; **2,** *Colloq.* enterprise; energy; as, I admire his *push*.—*n.* **push'er.**

pu-sil-lan-i-mous (pū'si-lan'i-mus), *adj.* cowardly; mean-spirited; opposite of *magnanimous*.

puss (poos), *n.* a cat; pussy.

puss-y (poos'i), *n.* [*pl.* pussies], a cat.

puss-y—wil-low (poos'i–wil'ō), *n.* a dwarf willow which bears furry buds along its branches.

pus-tule (pus'tūl), *n.* a small, inflamed swelling on the skin, as a pimple or blister full of pus.

put (poot), *v.t.* [put, put-ting], **1,** to move so as to place (something) in some position; to place; set; as, *put* on your hat; **2,** hence, to cause to be in a certain condition; as, to *put* things in order; *put* one's parents to shame; **3,** to state; propose; as, to *put* a question; **4,** to assign; set a value on (a thing); as, *put* a price on the desk; **5,** to express; as, to *put* a thought into words; **6,** to apply; set; as, he *put* himself to the task; **7,** to throw or hurl with an upward and forward motion of the arm; as, to *put* a shot; **8,** to force

or urge; as, to *put* a horse through its paces:—*v.i.* to go; proceed; as, to *put* out to sea.

pu-tre-fy (pū'tri-fī'), *v.t.* [putrefied, putrefy-ing], to rot; corrupt:—*v.i.* to decay or become rotten.—*n.* **pu'tre-fac'tion.**—*n.* **pu-tres'cence.**—*adj.* **pu-tres'cent.**

pu-trid (pū'trid), *adj.* **1,** corrupt; rotten; **2,** foul.—*n.* **pu'trid-ness.**—*n;* **pu-trid'i-ty.**

putt (put), *n.* in *golf*, a short, careful stroke to play the ball into a hole:—*v.t.* and *v.i.* to drive (a golf ball) into a hole. Also, **put.**

put-tee (put'i), *n.* **1,** a strip of cloth wrapped spirally from ankle to knee, esp. by soldiers, sportsmen, etc.; **2,** a stiff, heavy leather legging.

[1]put-ter (put'er), *n.* in *golf*, a short club used for playing the ball into a hole.

[2]put-ter (put'er), *v.i.* Same as [2]potter.

put-ty (put'i), *n.* a cement of whiting and linseed oil used for filling cracks, holding panes in window-sashes, etc.: —*v.t.* [puttied, putty-ing], to fill, as a crack or a hole, with such cement.

puz-zle (puz'l), *n.* **1,** something that perplexes, confuses, or bewilders; **2,** a toy or problem made to tax one's skill or ingenuity; **3,** a problem; riddle:— *v.i.* [puz-zled, puz-zling], to be perplexed; as, to *puzzle* over a mystery: —*v.t.* **1,** to perplex; entangle; **2,** to solve by clever thinking; as, to *puzzle* out a riddle.—*n.* **puz'zler.**

pyg-my (pig'mi), *n.* [*pl.* pygmies], a very small person or thing; dwarf:— *adj.* dwarflike; very small. Also, **pig'my.**

py-ja-mas (pi-jä'maz), *n.* a sleeping-suit consisting of jacket and trousers.

py-lon (pī'lon), *n.* a slender tower or shaft flanking a gateway or marking a course for air flights: the Canadian war memorial on Vimy Ridge has two beautiful *pylons* rising from its base.

py-or-rhe-a or **py-or-rhoe-a** (pī'o-rē'a), *n.* discharge of pus, esp. from the gums, often with loosening, or loss, of teeth.

pyr-a-mid (pir'a-mid), *n.* **1,** in *geom-etry*, a solid body standing on a triangular, square, or polygonal base, with triangular sides which meet in a point at the apex or top; **2,** anything having the shape of a pyramid:—**The**

PYRAMIDS
1, Triangular; 2, square; 3, pentagonal.

pyramids, a group of Egyptian monuments built by the early kings to serve as their tombs:—*v.t.* and *v.i.* to build in the form of a pyramid; to pile up. —*adj.* **py-ram′i-dal** (pi-ram′i-dal).

pyre (pīr), *n.* a pile of wood for burning a corpse; a funeral pile.

py-rite (pī′rīt), *n.* iron disulfide (FeS₂), a bright, brass-yellow mineral used in

making sulphuric acid: called *iron pyrites* (pī-rī′tēz) or fool's gold.

py-ro- (pī′rō-), a *prefix* meaning *fire* or *heat,* as in **py′ro-ma′ni-ac** (one with a mania for setting fires) and **py′ro-tech′nics** (display of fireworks).

py-thon (pī′thun; pī′thon), *n.* a large, non-poisonous Old World serpent which crushes its prey.

Q

Q, q (kū), *n.* [*pl.* Q's, q's], the 17th letter of the alphabet, following P.

¹quack (kwak), *n.* the cry of a duck, or a harsh sound like it:—*v.i.* to utter a quack.

²quack (kwak), *n.* **1,** an ignorant person who claims to have skill in medicine; **2,** hence, one who pretends to have knowledge which he does not really possess:—*adj.* making false claims; not genuine.—*n.* **quack′er-y.**

quack grass, couch grass.

quad-ran-gle (kwod′ran′gl; kwôd′-; kwod-rang′gl; kwôd-), *n.* **1,** in *geometry,* a plane figure with four angles and four sides; **2,** a four-sided court, surrounded by buildings, esp. on a college campus.—*adj.* **quad-ran′gu-lar.**

quad-rant (kwod′rant; kwôd′-), *n.* **1,** one fourth of the circumference of a circle, an arc of 90 degrees; **2,** the area bounded by such an arc and the lines from its ends to the centre of the circle; **3,** an instrument used in surveying, astronomy, etc., to measure altitude.

QUADRANT def. 1

quad-ri-lat-er-al (kwod′ri-lat′ẽr-al; kwôd′-), *n.* a plane figure bounded by four straight lines, as a parallelogram: —*adj.* having four sides.

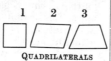

1   2   3

QUADRILATERALS

1, square; 2, rhomboid; 3, trapezoid.

qua-drille (kwo-dril′), *n.* an old-fashioned square dance for four or more couples, or music arranged for it.

quad-ru-ped (kwod′-roo-ped; kwôd′-) *n.* a four-footed animal:—*adj.* having four feet; as, a horse is a *quadruped* animal.

quad-ru-ple (kwod′roo-pl; kwôd′-; kwod-rōō′pl; kwôd-), *adj.* fourfold; composed of, or including, four parts: —*n.* (kwod′roo-pl; kwôd′-), a sum or

quantity four times as great as another: —*v.t.* (kwod-rōō′pl; kwôd-; kwod′-roo-pl; kwôd′-), [quadru-pled, quadrupling], to multiply by four:—*v.t.* to increase fourfold:—*n., v.,* and *adj.* **quad-ru′pli-cate′.**

quad-ru-plet (kwod′roo-plet; kwôd′-) *n.* **1,** a combination of four of one kind; **2,** one of four children born at one birth.

quad-ru-plex (kwod′roo-pleks′), *n.* and *adj.* fourfold; anything that is fourfold, as a telegraph system that can handle four messages at the same time, or a building with four suites of apartments.—*adj.* **quad-ru′pli-cate′** (*mathematics,* raised to the fourth power).

quaff (kwȧf), *v.t.* to drink in deep draughts:—*v.i.* to drink deeply.

quag (kwag), *n.* soft, miry ground.— *adj.* **quag′gy.**

quag-mire (kwag′mīr′), *n.* **1,** wet, boggy ground that yields under the feet; **2,** a perplexing situation, as of sinking into a morass of troubles.

¹quail (kwāl), *n.* [*pl.* quail or quails], any of several small game-birds, as the European quail and the bob-white: often called *partridge.*

²quail (kwāl), *v.i.* to shrink from pain or danger; lose heart; cower.

quaint (kwānt), *adj.* pleasingly odd in appearance or manner; esp. attractive because of an old-fashioned daintiness or prettiness.—*n.* **quaint′ness.**

quake (kwāk), *v.i.* [quaked, quak-ing], **1,** to shake from internal shock or convulsion; as, the earth *quakes;* **2,** to tremble or shake with fear, cold, etc.; quiver:—*n.* a shaking or trembling; esp. an earthquake.

qual-i-fi-ca-tion (kwol′i-fi-kā′shun; kwôl′-), *n.* **1,** the act of making, or the state of being, fit or qualified; **2,** that which makes a person or thing fit for a special task, position, etc.; fitness; **3,**

that which limits; a restriction; as, he told the story with the *qualification* that it be kept secret for a week.

qual-i-fied (kwol'i-fīd'; kwôl'-), *adj.* **1,** fitted; adapted; as, she is well *qualified* for the task; **2,** limited; as, *qualified* praise.

qual-i-fy (kwol'i-fī'; kwôl'-), *v.t.* [qualified, qualify-ing], **1,** to make fit for any office, occupation, sport, etc.; as, his work *qualified* him to compete for the prize; **2,** to alter slightly; change; limit; as, to *qualify* a statement; **3,** to moderate; lessen; soften; as, to *qualify* a rebuke; **4,** to give legal authorization to; as, the state has *qualified* him to practise medicine; **5,** in *grammar*, to limit the meaning of (a word); as, adverbs *qualify* verbs, adjectives, or other adverbs:—*v.i.* to be or become competent or fit for any office or employment; as, he *qualified* for the college crew.—*n.* **qual'i-fi'er.**

qual-i-ty (kwol'i-ti; kwôl'-), *n.* [*pl.* qualities], **1,** that which distinguishes one person or thing from others, as colour, weight, skill, etc.; **2,** the essential nature of a person or thing; a characteristic; as, elasticity is a *quality* of rubber; **3,** degree of excellence; as, a fine *quality* of wool; **4,** worth.—*adj.* **qual'i-ta'tive** (as, a *qualitative* analysis).

qualm (kwäm; kwôm), *n.* **1,** a feeling of illness or faintness that lasts only a moment; **2,** hence, a sudden fear; **3,** uneasiness of conscience.—*adj.* **qualm'-ish.**

quan-da-ry (kwon'da-ri; kwon-dâr'i), *n.* [*pl.* quandaries], a state of hesitation or doubt; uncertainty.

quan-ti-ty (kwon'ti-ti; kwôn'-), *n.* [*pl.* quantities], **1,** amount; bulk; as, this bag contains one bushel in *quantity;* **2,** any uncertain, usually considerable, amount; as, to buy ice in *quantity;* **3,** the relative time occupied in uttering a sound or syllable; **4,** in *mathematics*, anything that can be increased, divided, or measured.—*adj.* **quan'ti-ta'tive** (as, a *quantitative* analysis).

quan-tum (kwän'tum), *n.* [*pl.* quanta], in *physics*, the quantum theory holds that the energy of the electrons is discharged in specific, or discrete, amounts (or quanta).

quar-an-tine (kwor'an-tēn'; kwôr'-), *n.* **1,** the time during which an incoming vessel may not dock, while its passengers are inspected for contagious diseases; hence, the means taken to enforce this inspection; also, the place where the ships are held; **2,** any enforced restriction placed on a person, thing, or place because of contagious disease:—*v.t.* (kwor'an-tēn'; kwôr'-; kwor'an-tēn'; kwôr'-), [quarantined, quarantin-ing], to keep (a person or thing) away from others.

quar-rel (kwor'el; kwôr'-), *n.* **1,** an angry dispute; a petty fight; **2,** a cause for dispute; as, he has no *quarrel* with us; **3,** a disagreement or falling out; a breach of friendship:—*v.t.* [quarrelled, quarrel-ling], **1,** to dispute violently; fight; **2,** to disagree; fall out; **3,** to find fault; as, to *quarrel* with a decision.—*adj.* **quar'rel-some.**

¹quar-ry (kwor'i; kwôr'i), *n.* [*pl.* quarries], an open excavation or hole from which stone is obtained by cutting or blasting:—*v.t.* [quarried, quarry-ing], to dig or take from, or as from, an excavation or hole.

²quar-ry (kwor'i; kwôr'i), *n.* [*pl.* quarries], an animal that is hunted, caught, or killed, as in a chase; game.

quart (kwôrt), *n.* **1.** a measure of capacity; two pints, or one fourth of a gallon, or, in dry measure, one eighth of a peck; **2,** a vessel containing a quart, or its contents.

quar-ter (kwôr'tẽr), *n.* **1,** one of the four equal parts into which a thing may be, or is, divided; **2,** three months or a fourth of one year; **3,** one half of a semester at school or college; **4,** a fourth of a dollar, or 25 cents; also, a silver coin of this value; **5,** one of the four cardinal points of the compass; hence, any part or division of the earth; as, men came from all *quarters;* **6,** a particular place or district; as, the French *quarter* in Montreal; **7,** one of the four limbs of an animal with the parts near it; as, a *quarter* of beef; **8,** a measure for grain, consisting of eight bushels; **9,** the aspect or phase of the moon when halfway between new and full; **10,** life granted to a captive or enemy; mercy; as, to give no *quarter;* **11,** the after part of a ship's side; **12,** **quarters,** lodging; as, bachelor *quarters:* —*adj.* consisting of, or equal to, a fourth part of something; as, a *quarter*-hour:—*v.t.* **1,** to divide into fourths, or quarters; **2,** to furnish with food and lodging; as, to *quarter* soldiers in a town.

quar-ter-back (kwôr'tẽr-bak'), *n.* in *football*, a player just behind the line of scrimmage, who calls the signals and conducts the field strategy in the huddles.

quar-ter—deck (kwôr'tẽr–dek'), *n.* that part of the upper deck of a ship between the stern and mizzen-mast, used as a promenade for officers.

quar-ter-ly (kwôt´tẽr-li), *n.* [*pl.* quarterlies], a publication issued once every three months:—*adj.* 1, consisting of, or containing, a fourth part; 2, coming, or falling due, once every three months:—*adv.* once in each quarter.

quar-ter-mas-ter (kwôr´tẽr-màs´tẽr) *n.* 1, in the army, an officer whose duty it is to provide lodgings, food, clothing, and other supplies for soldiers; 2, in the navy, a petty officer who attends to the steering, signals, soundings, etc., of ships.

quar-tet or **quar-tette** (kwôr-tet´), *n.* 1, a musical composition for four voices or instruments; 2, the four performers of such a composition; 3, anything made up of four.

quartz (kwôrts), *n.* a very common, hard mineral, found in brilliant crystals or in masses. Many semi-precious stones, such as agates, amethysts, onyx, and jasper are forms of quartz.

quash (kwosh), *v.t.* 1, to crush, as a rebellion; 2, to stop, as a lawsuit; to set aside (by a judge), as an indictment (owing to an irregularity).

qua-si (kwā´sī), *prefix* meaning *as it were; as if;* virtually; seemingly; pseudo; as, *quasi*-historical.

quat-rain (kwät´rān), *n.* a stanza of four lines, usually rhyming *abab, abba,* or *abcb.*

qua-ver (kwā´vr), *n.* 1, a shaking or trembling, as of the voice; 2, a trill in singing or playing; 3, in *music*, an eighth-note:—*v.i.* to quiver; vibrate:—*v.t.* to utter or sing with trills.

quay (kē), *n.* a permanent wharf, often of masonry, where ships may load or unload.

quea-sy (kwē´zi), *adj.* [quea-si-er, quea-si-est], nauseated; easily upset; as, a *queasy* stomach; hence, squeamish; over-scrupulous; as, a *queasy* conscience.—*n.* **quea´si-ness.**

queen (kwēn), *n.* 1, a woman who rules a country in her own right; 2, the wife of a king; 3, a woman who is a leader in a certain sphere; as, a social *queen;* 4, the perfect female of bees, ants, etc., usually the only female in the group able to lay eggs; 5, a playing card bearing a conventional drawing of a queen; 6, in *chess*, the piece ranking next to the king; 7, the best or chief of her kind; as, the *queen* of beauty.—*adj.* **queen´ly.**—*n.* **queen´li-ness.**

queer (kwēr), *adj.* 1, differing from the

ordinary or normal; droll; strange; 2, giddy; faint; sick; as, a *queer* feeling; 3, *Colloq.*: **a,** mentally unsound; **b,** open to question:—*v.t.* 1, to spoil; upset; to interfere with; as, to *queer* one's chances for a job; 2, to place in an embarrassing situation; as, he *queered* himself at the party.—*n.* **queer´ness.**

quell (kwel), *v.t.* to suppress or subdue; put an end to; as, to *quell* a riot.

quench (kwench), *v.t.* 1, to put out; extinguish; as, to *quench* a fire; hence, to suppress; stifle; as, to *quench* a desire for revenge; 2, to relieve; slake; as, to *quench* thirst.—*adj.* **quench´a-ble; quench´less.**

quer-u-lous (kwer´ū-lus; kwer´oo-lus) *adj.* 1, complaining; fretful; as, a *querulous* old man; 2, whining; as, a *querulous* voice.

que-ry (kwē´ri), *n.* [*pl.* queries], 1, a question; an inquiry; 2, a question mark [?]:—*v.t.* [queried, query-ing], 1, to inquire into; ask, 2, to express a doubt in regard to; as, to *query* his loyalty:—*v.i.* to ask questions.

quest (kwest), *n.* 1, a search; as, an animal in *quest* of food; 2, in mediaeval romance, an expedition for a particular object; as, the *quest* for the Holy Grail: —*v.i.* to make search; to seek.

ques-tion (kwes´chun), *n.* 1, the act of asking or inquiring; 2, that which is asked; 3, the subject under discussion or to be decided upon; as, the *question* before the meeting; 4, dispute, doubt, or objection; as, beyond *question*, these are the facts:—**question mark,** an interrogation point; a mark [?] of punctuation in writing or printing put at the end of a question:—*v.t.* 1, to ask; examine by queries; 2, to consider doubtful; 3, to challenge; take exception to; as, I *question* that statement: —*v.i.* to make inquiries.—*n.* **ques´tion-er.**

ques-tion-a-ble (kwes´chun-a-bl), *adj.* 1, open to question or doubt; 2, arousing suspicion; as, a *questionable* character.

ques-tion-naire (kes´chun-âr´; kwes´), *n.* a list of questions submitted to a number of persons, whose replies serve as the basis of a report on a subject.

queue (kū), *n.* 1, a braid of hair hanging down the back; a pigtail; 2, a line of people, automobiles, etc., awaiting their turn to proceed. Also, spelled **cue.**

quib-ble (kwib´l), *n.* a skilful evasion of the point in question by advancing a trifling argument or by using words with a double meaning:—*v.i.* [quib-bled, quib-bling], to avoid the truth by a skilful but trifling objection.—*n.* **quib'-bler.**

quick (kwik), *adj.* **1,** rapid; swift; as, *quick* in action; **2,** nimble; as, *quick* on one's feet; **3,** prompt to respond to impressions; alert; as, a *quick* mind; **4,** accurate; unhesitating; ready; as, a *quick* eye; *quick* wit; **4,** easily excited; hasty; as, a *quick* temper; **6,** sensitive; as, a *quick* ear:—*adv.* with haste; rapidly:—*n.* **1,** living beings; **2,** the living flesh; as, to cut the nails down to the *quick;* hence, the seat of the feelings and emotions; as, she was hurt to the *quick.—adv.* **quick'ly.**

quick-en (kwik'en), *v.i.* **1,** to come to life; become alive; **2,** to act or move more rapidly:—*v.t.* **1,** to increase the speed of; hasten; as, to *quicken* one's steps; **2,** to bring to life; **3,** to make keen; arouse; kindle.—*n.* **quick'en-er.**

quick-lime (kwik'līm'), *n.* the white oxide of calcium obtained by subjecting limestone to intense heat: changed by action of water into slaked lime, used in cement, mortar, etc.; unslaked lime.

quick-sand (kwik'sand'), *n.* a bed of wet, loose sand that allows any heavy object that comes upon it to sink.

quick-step (kwik'step'), *n.* a march in quick, or lively, time.

quid (kwid), *n.* a piece of tobacco, etc., held in the mouth and chewed.

qui-es-cent (kwī-es'ent), *adj.* calm; still; tranquil.—*n.* **qui-es'cence.**

qui-et (kwī'et), *adj.* **1,** without sound; silent; as, a *quiet* night; **2,** not moving; still; as, *quiet* hands; **3,** tranquil; peaceful; secluded; as, a *quiet* country-side; **4,** peaceable; gentle; as, a *quiet* disposition; **5,** informal; as, a *quiet* wedding; **6,** not showy; as, *quiet* colours:—*v.t.* to make peaceful; as, to *quiet* a child:—*v.i.* to become still or calm; as, the sea has *quieted:*—*n.* **1,** freedom from motion, noise, or disturbance; **2,** gentleness or composure of manner; **3,** peace; rest.—*n.* **qui'e-tude.**—*v.t.* and *v.i.* **qui'et-en.**

qui-e-tus (kwī-ē'tus), *n.* **1,** death; as, to make one's *quietus;* **2,** anything that kills, ends, or finishes; as, to give the *quietus* to a rumour.

quill (kwil), *n.* **1,** a large, strong feather; also, the hollow shaft of a feather; **2,** a pen made from a feather; **3,** a long, sharp spine, as of a porcupine.

quilt (kwilt), *n.* a bed-cover made by stitching together two layers of fabric, usually in an ornamental pattern, with a layer of cotton or wool between; also, any warm bed-cover:—*v.t.* to stitch and interline (layers of cloth) in the manner of a quilt:—*v.i.* to do quilting. —*n.* **quilt'ing.**

quince (kwins), *n.* **1,** a tree related to the apple; **2,** the hard yellowish fruit of this tree, used for preserves and jellies.

qui-nine (kwi-nēn'; kwī'nīn), *n.* a bitter drug obtained from the bark of the cinchona tree and used esp. in treating malaria.

quin-quen-ni-al (kwin-kwen'i-al), *adj.* and *n.* occurring every five years, or lasting five years.

quin-que-reme (kwin'kwi-rēm'), *n.* in classical times, a galley with five banks of oars.

quin-sy (kwin'zi), *n.* inflammation of the tonsils and throat, with swelling and pus formation.

quin-tes-sence (kwin-tes'ens), *n.* the concentrated essence, or most perfect embodiment, of anything; as, a becoming humility is the *quintessence* of wisdom.

quin-tet or **quin-tette** (kwin-tet'), *n.* a group of five persons or things, or a musical composition for five voices or instruments.

quin-tu-plet (kwin'tū-plet), *n.* **1,** a combination of five of one kind; **2,** one of five children born at one birth.

quip (kwip), *n.* **1,** a clever or sarcastic remark; **2,** an evasion of a point by clever use of words; a quibble; **3,** something odd.

quire (kwīr), *n.* a pack of 24 uniform sheets of paper.

quirk (kwûrk), *n.* **1,** a sudden twist or turn, as of a pen in writing; **2,** a quick turn of fancy; a quip; **3,** a clever evasion of the truth in speaking.

quirt (kwûrt), *n.* a short-handled riding-whip with a lash of braided rawhide.

quis-ling (kwiz'ling), *n.* one who, from within, aids an enemy power to invade one's country; a traitor.

quit (kwit), *v.t.* [quit-ted or quit, quit-ting], **1,** to pay off (a debt); **2,** to stop; give up; as, to *quit* work; **3,** to go away from; as, to *quit* a neighbourhood:— *v.i.* to stop doing something; as, to *quit* at noon: —*adj.* free; as, we're *quit* of that fellow.

quite (kwīt), *adv.* **1,** totally; completely; as, *quite* mistaken; **2,** *Colloq.*, to a considerable extent; rather; as, *quite* cold.

quits (kwits), *adj.* even or equal (with someone), as upon the repayment of a favour or an injury; as, now we're *quits*.

quit-tance (kwit′ns), *n.* **1,** a receipt; **2,** release from a debt or obligation; **3,** recompense; repayment.

quit-ter (kwit′ėr), *n.* one who gives up; esp., a shirk or a coward.

¹quiv-er (kwiv′ėr), *n.* a light case for carrying arrows.

²quiv-er (kwiv′ėr), *n.* a trembling or shivering:—*v.i.* to shake, as from excitement.

quix-ot-ic (kwiks-ot′ik), *adj.* absurdly chivalrous, romantic, or idealistic.

quiz (kwiz), *n.* [*pl.* quizzes], **1,** an absurd or puzzling question; **2,** an informal examination of a pupil or class; a test:—*v.t.* [quizzed, quiz-zing], to examine informally.

quiz-zi-cal (kwiz′i-kal), *adj.* comical; humorously serious; as, a *quizzical* look.

quoit (kwoit, koit), *n.* **1,** a flat iron ring about six inches across; **2,** **quoits,** a game in which players pitch such rings at a peg.

quor-um (kwôr′um), *n.* the number of members of an assembly that the rules require to be present in order that business may legally be transacted.

quo-ta (kwō′ta), *n.* the part of a total that any individual or group is to contribute or receive; a share; as, each class paid its *quota* toward the school picnic.

quot-a-ble (kwōt′a-bl), *adj.* suitable for quoting from, as an author or a poem.

quo-ta-tion (kwō-tā′shun), *n.* **1,** the repeating of another's words; **2,** the words repeated; **3,** a passage from a book, poem, etc.; **4,** the current market-price of something, or a statement of this; as, a *quotation* on wheat: —**quotation mark,** a mark of punctuation placed at the beginning ["] and end ["] of a word or passage to show that it is quoted. A quotation within a quotation is usually enclosed in single quotation marks [']; as, "the boy said, 'I am going home.' "

quote (kwōt), *v.t.* [quot-ed, quot-ing], **1,** to repeat (another's words, either written or spoken); as, I *quoted* your poem; **2,** to repeat a passage from; refer to as an authority; as, to *quote* Ruskin; **3,** to give the present price of:—*v.i.* to repeat the words of another; as, he *quoted* accurately:—*n.* **1,** in *printing,* a quotation-mark; **2,** *Colloq.* a quotation.

quoth (kwōth), *v.t. Archaic,* said; spoke; as, "I met a fool," *quoth* he.

quo-tient (kwō′shent), *n.* the result obtained when one number is divided by another; as, if 10 is divided by 5, the *quotient* is 2.

R

R, r (är), *n.* [*pl.* R's, r's], the 18th letter of the alphabet, following Q:—**the three R's,** reading, 'riting, and 'rithmetic.

rab-bet (rab′it), *n.* **1,** a groove or slot cut out of the edge or face of a board, etc., so that another piece may be fitted into it to form a joint; **2,** a joint so made:—*v.t.* and *v.i.* to cut such a groove in.

rab-bi (rab′ī), *n.* [*pl.* rabbis or rabbies (rab′īz)], in the Jewish religion, a teacher and interpreter of the law and ritual.—*adj.* **rab-bin′i-cal.**

rab-bit (rab′it), *n.* a small, short-tailed animal of the hare family. Its fur is used to make imitations of expensive furs.

rab-ble (rab′l), *n.* a noisy crowd or mob:—**the rabble,** the common people, esp. those of the lowest class.

rab-id (rab′id), *adj.* **1,** furious; raging; **2,** extremely unreasonable; excessively zealous; as, a *rabid* reformer; **2,** infected with rabies; as, a *rabid* dog.

ra-bi-es (rā′bi-ēz; rā′bēz), *n.* an infectious and often fatal disease of the dog and other animals, esp. flesh-eating animals; hydrophobia: often transmitted to man by the bite of an infected animal.

¹race (rās), *n.* **1,** a swift current of water, or the channel for such a current; as, a mill *race;* **2,** course of life; career; as, my *race* is run; **3,** a competitive contest of speed, as in

cat, āge, fär, cåre, åsk; ten, ēve, latėr; (i) pity, rely, senate; īce; top; nō.

running or swimming; also, any contest or rivalry; as, a political *race:* —*v.i.* [raced, rac-ing], **1,** to run swiftly; as, to *race* a motor; **2,** to try to beat in a speed contest; as, I'll *race* you to the corner.

²race (rās), *n.* **1,** the descendants of a common ancestor; a family; **2,** a people or group of peoples united by a common language, religion, or culture; as, the English *race;* **3,** a division of mankind, made up of tribes descended from a common stock; as, the Negro *race;* **4,** a class of persons with common interests and traits; as, the *race* of poets.—*adj.* **ra'cial** (rā'shal).

ra-ceme (ra-sēm'; rā-), *n.* a flower cluster in which blooms grow single-stemmed at almost regular distances on a stalk, as in the lily of the valley.

rac-er (rās'ẽr), *n.* **1,** a person who engages in a speed contest; also, anything that can go at great speed, as an unusually swift horse; **2,** a swift snake, esp. the American black snake.

rac-ism (rās'izm), *n.* fear or dislike of a race other than one's own, or the doctrine that some races are inferior to others:—*n.* **rac'ist.**

¹rack (rak), *n.* **1,** a framework on or in which articles are arranged, held, or displayed; as, a meat-*rack;* a towel-*rack;* **2,** a frame of bars above a manger for holding fodder; **3,** a framework fitted to a wagon for hauling hay; **4,** a bar with teeth on one side that engage the teeth of a gear.

²rack (rak), *n.* **1,** in former times, an instrument for torturing the body by stretching and straining the limbs; **2,** intense physical or mental anguish; —*v.t.* **1,** to stretch, as on the rack; **2,** to subject to great pain or anguish: as, remorse *racked* him; **3,** to strain; exert to the utmost; as, to *rack* one's brain for a word.

³rack (rak), *n.* wreck; ruin: used only in the expression *rack and ruin.* See **wrack.**

¹rack-et (rak'it), *n.* **1,** a clattering noise; din; noisy talk or play; **2,** a dishonest trick or scheme; esp., an organized activity of the criminal underwórld, such as the extortion of money from merchants by threats of violence:—*v.i.* to make a loud and confused noise.

²rack-et or **rac-quet** (rak'it), *n.* a network bat used in tennis, badminton, etc.

rack-et-eer (rak'e-tēr'), *n.* a person

who, acting for himself, or as a member of a gang, extorts money by threats.

ra-con-teur (ra'kŏn'tûr'), *n.* one skilled or clever at telling stories.

ra-coon or **rac-coon** (ra-kōon'), *n.* **1,** a greyish-brown, tree-dwelling animal of North America, with a bushy, ringed tail: often called *coon;* **2,** its fur.

rac-y (rās'i), *adj.* **1,** retaining traces of origin; full-flavoured; as, *racy* fruit; **2,** lively; spirited; as, a *racy* style; **3,** *Colloq.* close to being improper; daring: as a *racy* story.

ra-dar (rā'där), *n.* a device which sends out radio waves of ultra high frequency, and locates a distant object, such as a ship, by the radio waves reflected from the object.

ra-di-al (rā'di-al), *adj.* arranged like the spokes of a wheel.—*adv.* **ra'di-al-ly.**

ra-di-an (rā'di-an), *n.* an arc of a circle equal in length to the radius; also the angle at the centre measured by such an arc (about 57.3°).

ra-di-ant (rā'di-ant), *adj.* **1,** sending out rays of light or heat; as, the *radiant* sun; shining; brilliant; as, *radiant* beauty; **2,** beaming with joy, delight, etc.; as, a *radiant* face; **3,** coming out in rays from some source; as, the *radiant* energy of the sun:—**radiant energy,** energy issuing from any source, as electromagnetic waves, sound, heat, light, X-rays, gamma rays etc.:—**radiant heating,** heating as by electric coils, steam, or hot-water pipes, etc., installed in floors or walls:—*adv.* **ra'di-ant-ly.** —*n.* **ra'di-ance.**

ra-di-ate (rā'di-āt'), *v.t.* [radiat-ed, radiat-ing], **1,** to send out in rays; as, a lamp *radiates* light; **2,** to spread abroad; as, to *radiate* happiness:—*v.i.* **1,** to send forth beams; shine; glow; **2,** to come out in rays, as heat from a fire; **3,** to come out from a centre; as, the spokes of a wheel *radiate* from the hub.—*n.* **ra'di-a'tion.**

ra-di-a-tor (rā'di-ā'tẽr), *n.* **1,** a set of pipes heated by hot water or steam, for heating a room; **2,** an appliance used to cool a motor.

rad-i-cal (rad'i-k'l), *adj.* **1,** having to do with a root or origin; deep-seated; fundamental; as, a *radical* cure; **2,** advocating extreme change; as, a *radical* speech:—*n.* **1,** (often Radical), a person who wishes to root out old customs and institutions, rather than to reform them; esp. in politics, an extremist; **2,** a root; a fundamental part or principle; **3,** a word or root from which other words are formed; **4**, in *chemistry*, a group of atoms (part of a molecule in a compound) that act as a single atom; as, the radical [OH]: also, *radicle*; **5**, in *mathematics*, a quantity considered as the root of another quantity: shown by use of the radical sign [√]; the sign itself.

ra-di-o (rā′di-ō), *n.* [*pl.* radios], **1**, any message, music, etc., transmitted or received by means of electromagnetic waves without the use of wires between sender and receiver; also, this system of sending and receiving messages; **2**, equipment for transmitting messages in this way; esp an instrument for receiving such messages:—*adj.* having to do with radio; as, *radio* supplies; a *radio* program:—**radio frequency**, vibrations too high to be heard by the human ear: over 10,000 cycles per second.

ra-di-o-ac-tive (rā′di-ō-ak′tiv), *adj.* giving off radiant energy in the form of particles or rays (alpha, gamma, etc.) by the breakdown of atomic nuclei of radium, thorium, uranium, etc.

ra-di-o-graph (rā′di-ō-gràf′), *n.* a picture made by invisible rays, as X-rays; a radiogram:—*v.t.* to produce a picture by X-rays, radium rays, etc. —*n.* **ra′di-og′ra-phy; ra′di-og′ra-pher.**

ra-di-o-i-so-tope (rā′di-ō-ī′so-tōp′), *n.* a radioactive isotope, artifically produced from a chemical element normally inert: used in biological research, medical therapy, etc.

ra-di-ol-o-gy (rā′di-ol′o-ji), *n.* the science of radiant energy and its uses, esp. in treating disease by X-rays.

ra-di-o-ther-a-py (rā′di-ō-ther′a-pi), *n.* the use of radioactivity to treat disease, as by X-rays, radium rays, etc.

rad-ish (rad′ish), *n.* a garden plant of the mustard family, with a pungent root; also, the root, which is eaten raw.

ra-di-um (rā′di-um), *n.* a rare white metal found in various minerals. Its atoms break down into lead and other metals, giving off rays which are used in treating cancer, etc.

ra-di-us (rā′di-us), *n.* [*pl.* radii (rā′di-ī) or radiuses], **1**, a straight line from the centre of a circle to its circumference, or from the centre of a sphere to its surface; **2**, an area about a point, bounded by a circle with a given radius; as, within a *radius* of a mile from the post office.

raf-fi-a (raf′i-a), *n.* **1**, the fibre of a Madagascar palm, used in weaving hats, baskets, etc.; **2**, the palm itself.

raf-fle (raf′l), *n.* a lottery in which each person pays a part of the value of something for a chance of winning it: —*v.t.* [raffled, raffling], to dispose of by selling chances on; as, to *raffle off* a car.

raft (ràft), *n.* a floating framework of logs or boards:—*v.t.* to convey on such a float.

raft-er (ràf′tèr), *n.* a sloping beam that helps support the roof of a house.

rag (rag), *n.* **1**, a worn or torn piece of cloth; a shred; **2**, **rags**, tattered or worn-out clothes; as, the children were dressed only in *rags*:—*v.t.* [ragged (ragd), rag-ging], **1**, *Colloq.*, to play (music) with a catchy shifting of the beat; play in ragtime; **2**, *Slang*, to tease; also, to scold.

rag-a-muf-fin (rag′a-muf′in), *n.* a ragged, dirty child, esp. a boy.

rage (rāj), *n.* **1**, uncontrolled anger; **2**, violence; fury; **3**, *Colloq.*, anything for the moment popular or fashionable; as, coloured shoes are the *rage* this spring:—*v.i.* [raged, rag-ing], **1**, to be furious with anger; **2**, to act or speak violently; **3**, to have furious force as, the tornado *raged* through the town.

rag-ged (rag′id), *adj.* **1**, having holes or tears resulting from wear; torn; as, a *ragged* coat; **2**, clothed in tatters; as, a *ragged* fellow; **3**, rough; jagged; as, a *ragged* stone.

ra-gout (ra-gōō′), *n.* a stew of meat and vegetables highly seasoned.

rag-time (rag′tīm′), a dance music in fast, syncopated rhythm: of Negro origin, it was a forerunner of jazz.

rag-weed (rag′wēd′), *n.* a coarse weed with small, yellowish-green flowers. Its pollen often causes hay fever: in Britain called **rag′wort′** (-wûrt′).

rah (rä), *interj.* Short for *hurrah.*

raid (rād), *n.* **1**, a hostile invasion; a sudden attack; as, an air *raid*; **2**, a forced entrance by police, to make arrests or seize stolen goods:—*v.t.* **raid.**

¹rail (rāl), *n.* **1**, a bar of wood or metal placed level between two posts, as in a fence; **2**, a wooden or iron barrier to keep persons from falling; as, a hand*rail;* **3**, one of the two metal bars forming a track for trolley cars or trains; **4**, a railroad; as, to travel by *rail:*—*v.t.* to enclose with bars; as, to *rail* in an exhibit.

rail (rāl), *n*. a wading bird resembling a small crane.

rail (rāl), *v.i.* to use bitter, scornful, or reproachful language; as, to *rail* at a beggar; to *rail* against fate.—*n*. and *adj*. **rail′ing**.

ail-ing (rāl′ing), *n*. **1,** material for rails; **2,** a fence or barrier made of rails and held up by posts.

ail-ler-y (rāl′ēr-i; ral′ēr-i), *n*. [*pl*. railleries], good-natured ridicule or banter.

ail-road (rāl′rōd′), *n*. **1,** a permanent track formed of two parallel rails, on which trains move; **2,** a railroad system, including land, equipment, etc.:—*v.t. Colloq.*, to put through rapidly; as, to *railroad* a bill through a legislature.

ail-way (rāl′wā′), *n*. **1,** a railroad; **2,** any track with rails for wheels to run on.

ai-ment (rā′ment), *n*. clothing; attire.

ain (rān), *n*. **1,** water falling in drops condensed from moisture in the air; **2,** the fall of such drops; as, a heavy *ain;* **3,** a shower of anything; as, a *rain* of bullets:—*v.i.* to fall in drops, or ike rain:—*v.t.* to pour down like rain; as, to *rain* blows on someone.—*adj*. **ain′less**.—*adj*. **rain′y**. Also, **rain′coat′; ain′drop′; rain′proof′; rain′storm′.**

ain-bow (rān′bō′), *n*. an arc or bow, containing the colours of the spectrum, formed in the sky opposite the sun by he reflection of the sun's rays from drops of falling rain, spray, or mist:—**ainbow trout**, *Salmo gairdner*, has osy side bands, with brown spots on ail: native to Pacific Coast, but found videly over the world; a superior ame and food fish; breeds best in treams flowing into the sea. Canadian ine record, 37 lb. 40½″ (1947).

ain-fall (rān′fôl′), *n*. **1,** a shower; **2,** the amount of rain that falls during a definite period on any given area.

aise (rāz), *v.t.* [raised, rais-ing], **1,** to set upright; lift up; **2,** to stir up (game); o rouse from sleep; also, to restore the dead) to life; **3,** to erect; construct; as, to *raise* a building; **4,** to ause to come into existence; as, to *aise* a smile; to *raise* trouble; **5,** to row; breed (crops, cattle, etc.); **6,** o procure; collect; muster; as, to *aise* money, armies, etc.; **7,** to bring up for consideration (a question, laim, etc.); **8,** to cause to increase in egree, amount, intensity, etc.; as, to *aise* prices, the voice, one's courage; , to terminate; put an end to (a

blockade); **10,** to cause (bread) to rise; **11,** to make higher in rank or power; as, to *raise* a prince to the throne; **12,** to rear; bring up (children): —*n. Colloq.*, an increase, as in salary.

rai-sin (rā′zn), *n*. a variety of sweet grape, often sold in dried form.

raj (raj), *n. India*, rule; supreme power; as, the British *raj*.

ra-jah or **ra-ja** (rä′ja), *n*. a Hindu king or prince.

¹rake (rāk), *n*. a farm or garden tool with teeth at one end of a long handle, used for loosening or smoothing soil, or for gathering loose matter, such as dead leaves, hay, etc.:—*v.t.* [raked, rak-ing], **1,** to gather, smooth, or loosen with a rake; as, to *rake* the lawn; **2,** to gather by diligent effort; as, to *rake* up evidence; to *rake* a few dollars together; **3,** to search carefully; as, to *rake* the library for a special book; **4,** in military language, to fire along the length of; as, to *rake* the deck of a ship:—*v.i.* **1,** to work with a rake; **2,** to make a close search.

²rake (rāk), *n*. a slant or tilt; as, the *rake* of a hat; also, a slant from the perpendicular, as of a ship's mast or funnel:—*v.i. and v.t.* [raked, rak-ing], to slant, or cause to slant, as a mast.—*adj*. **rak′ish**.

³rake (rāk), *n*. a man of loose morals.

rake—off (rāk′-ôf′), *n. Slang*, a commission, share, or rebate, often illegitimate, esp. from a public enterprise.

ral-ly (ral′i), *v.t.* [rallied, rally-ing], **1,** to bring together (troops in flight) and restore (them) to order; **2,** to call together for any purpose:—*v.i.* **1,** to return to order; **2,** to come together for action; be aroused to vigorous action; as, *rally* round the flag; **3,** to recover strength; as, to *rally* from fever; **4,** in *tennis*, to send the ball rapidly back and forth over the net: —*n.* [*pl*. rallies], **1,** a restoring or recovery of order and discipline, as among defeated troops; **2,** a quick sharp rise after a dip; as, a *rally* in prices; **3,** a mass meeting; **4,** in *tennis*, the repeated return of the ball in play until one player misses.

ram (ram), *n*. **1,** a male sheep; **2,** in *war*, a heavy pole for battering a wall; a battering-ram:—*v.t.* [rammed, ramming], **1,** to strike or butt against; **2,** to pack with sharp blows; as, to *ram* earth into a hole; also, to pack hastily; cram.

ram-ble (ram′bl), *v.i.* [ram-bled, rambling], **1,** to wander or rove aimlessly about; to stroll for pleasure; **2,** to talk or write at length and aimlessly; **3,** to grow or spread at random, as vines:—*n.* a leisurely, aimless stroll.—*n.* **ram′bler.**

ram-bling (ram′bling), *adj.* **1,** wandering at will; **2,** built on no single plan; growing or spreading at random; as, a *rambling* garden; **3,** loose and unorganized; as, a *rambling* tale.

ram-bunc-tious (ram-bungk′shus), *adj. U.S. Slang,* wild or unruly of behaviour.

ram-i-fi-ca-tion (ram′i-fi-kā′shun), *n.* **1,** the act, manner, or arrangement of branching; **2,** a small branch or offshoot; as, a *ramification* of a tree or a nerve; **3,** a dividing or separating into branches; **4,** a division of anything complex:—*v.t.* and *v.i.* **ram′i-fy′** (to divide into parts or branches; to grow by such division).

ramp (ramp), *n.* a sloping roadway by which persons or vehicles may go from one level to another.

ram-page (ram-pāj′; ram′pāj), *n.* a fit of excitement or rage:—*v.i.* (rampāj′; ram′pāj), [rampaged, rampag-ing], to dash about in a wild rage:—*adj.* **ram-pa′geous.**

ramp-ant (ram′pant), *adj.* **1,** showing a fierce, high spirit; violent; as, the *rampant* foe; **2,** bold and unchecked; as, *rampant* crime; also, growing rankly, as weeds; **3,** reared on the hind legs, with one foreleg raised above the other, as a lion on a coat of arms.

ram-part (ram′pärt; ram′pėrt), *n.* **1,** an embankment or earthen wall, built around a fort for better defence; **2,** any protection against danger.

ram-rod (ram′rod′), *n.* a rod used for ramming down the charge of a gun which loads through the muzzle.

ram-shack-le (ram′shak-l), *adj. Colloq.* loose; tumble-down; rickety; as, a *ramshackle* cottage.

ran (ran), *p.t.* of *run*.

ranch (ranch), *n.* **1,** in western Canada and U.S., a farm for the raising of cattle, horses, or sheep in large herds; **2,** a large farm for a special crop; as, a fruit *ranch:*—*v.i.* to manage, or work on, a ranch.—*n.* **ranch′er.**—*n.* **ranch′man.**

ran-cid (ran′sid), *adj.* not fresh; having the rank, tainted smell or taste of spoiled fat.—*n.* **ran′cid-ness.**

ran-cour (rang′kėr), *n.* deep spite or malice; a bitter, cherished grudge. In U.S.A., **ran′cor.**—*adj.* **ran′cor-ous.**

ran-dom (ran′dum), *adj.* done without aim or purpose; guided by chance; as, a *random* guess:—**at random,** without definite direction or aim; as, books picked *at random*.

ra-nee or **ra-ni** (rä′nē), *n.fem.* the wife of a rajah (India).

rang (rang), *p.t.* of *ring*.

range (rānj), *v.t.* [ranged, rang-ing], **1,** to set in a row or in regular order; as to *range* cups on a shelf; also, to classify; as, to *range* books by subjects; **2,** to put (oneself) in a certain position with reference to others; as, he *ranged* himself with the rebels; **3,** to wander over; as, cattle *range* the plains:—*v.i.* **1,** to wander; roam; as, he lets his fancy *range;* **2,** to vary within certain limits; as, these apes *range* in height from five to six feet; **3,** to be found or to occur, over a certain area; as the magnolia *ranges* northward to Ohio:—*n.* **1,** a line or row; series; chain, as of hills or mountains; **2,** direct line; as, in *range* with my window; **3,** the limits of space or time included or covered; scope; extent; as, the whole *range* of history; **4,** the limits within which something varies; as, her voice has a *range* of two octaves; **5,** a tract of land over which cattle graze; **6,** the distance to which a gun, cannon, etc., can shoot; as, *range* of one mile; also, the distance of the target from the gun; **7,** a place for target practice; as, a rifle-*range*; **8,** the area over which a plant or animal may be found; as, the *range* of the violet; **9,** a large cooking-stove.

ran-gy (rān′ji), *adj.* [rangier, rangiest], **1,** long in limb, lean and muscular, as animals or persons; **2,** adapted to ranging or wandering far and wide; **3,** *Australia,* mountainous.

¹**rank** (rangk), *n.* **1,** a row or line of persons or objects; also, an orderly arrangement, esp. a line of soldiers side by side; **2,** high station or position; as, a man of *rank;* **3,** a grade or social or official position; as, the *rank* of duke; the *rank* of admiral; **4,** degree of worth or eminence; as, a poet of the first *rank;* **5, ranks: a,** the army as a whole; **b,** the body of privates, as distinguished from the officers; as, the captain was reduced to the *ranks* for disobedience:—**rank and file,** the whole body of common soldiers; hence, the common people:—*v.t.* **1,** to place in rows; draw up (soldiers) in line; **2,** to include in a certain class, order, or division; as to *rank* students by their marks; **3,** to

be of higher rank than (another); outrank; as, a major *ranks* a captain:—*v.i.* to hold a certain grade or position; as, she *ranks* high in her classes.

²rank (rangk), *adj.* **1,** plentiful and coarse in growth; as, *rank* grass; **2,** producing too freely; as, *rank* soil; **3,** coarse; strong in taste or smell; as, *rank* fat; **4,** gross; inexcusable; extreme; as, *rank* carelessness.

ran-kle (rang′kl), *v.i.* [ran-kled, ran-kling], **1,** to fester or cause to fester; **2,** to cause mental pain or irritation; as, the insult *rankled.*

ran-sack (ran′sak), *v.t.* **1,** to make a thorough search of; as, I *ransacked* my desk in vain; **2,** to pillage; to plunder; as, the enemy *ransacked* the town.

ran-som (ran′sum), *n.* **1,** the returning of a captive or seized property upon payment of a price; as, they negotiated the *ransom* of the prisoners from the pirates; **2,** the sum so paid or demanded:—*v.t.* **1,** to free from prison, slavery, or punishment, by a payment; **2,** to set free on receipt of a payment.

²ant (rant), *n.* noisy, empty speech:—*v.i.* to speak loudly and at length; to rave on.—*n.* rant′er.—*adj.* rant′ing.

²ap (rap), *v.i.* [rapped, rap-ping], to strike a quick, sharp blow; to knock:—*v.t.* **1,** to strike sharply; **2,** to utter sharply as, to *rap* out a command.

ra-pa-cious (ra-pā′shus), *adj.* **1,** given to robbery; seizing by violence; as, *rapacious* highwaymen; **2,** greedy; grasping; as, a *rapacious* money-lender.—*n.* ra-pac′i-ty (ra-pas′i-ti).

²ape (rāp), *v.t.* [raped, rap-ing], to take by force; to assault or ravish (a woman).—*n.* a taking or carrying off by force.—*n.* rap′ist.

²ape (rāp), *n.* a plant of the mustard family, used as food for sheep and hogs. From its seeds an oil is obtained.

ap-id (rap′id), *adj.* very quick or swift; as, to run at a *rapid* rate; a *rapid* runner:—**rapids,** *n.pl.* a place in a river where the water rushes swiftly because of a steep slope in the river-bed.—*n.* ra-pid′i-ty.

a-pi-er (rā′pi-ėr), *n.* a straight, slender, light, two-edged sword, used for thrusting.

ap-ine (rap′in; rap′in), *n.* the act of plundering or of carrying off property ruthlessly or by force; destruction.

ap-port (ra′pôr′; ra-pōrt′), *n. French,* a sympathetic relationship; harmony; as, he was *en rapport* with his audience: used of speakers, singers, actors, etc.

rapt (rapt), *adj.* **1,** carried away with delight; enraptured; **2,** absorbed; engrossed; as, he gave *rapt* attention to his book.

rap-ture (rap′tūr), *n.* the state of being transported or carried away with great joy; extreme delight or pleasure.—*adj.* rap′tur-ous.—*adv.* rap′tur-ous-ly.

¹rare (râr), *adj.* [rar-er, rar-est], **1,** thin; not dense; as, a *rare* atmosphere; **2,** scarce; not frequent; as, on one of his *rare* visits to the country; **3,** unusual; precious; as, *rare* old lace.—*n.* rar′i-ty (rar′i-ti; râr′i-ti):—*v.t.* rar′e-fy′.—*adv.* rare′ly.

²rare (râr), *adj.* [rar-er, rar-est], not cooked through; underdone; as, *rare* beef.

rare-bit (râr′bit), *n. Welsh rabbit,* a dish made of melted cheese cooked with milk, ale, beer, etc., seasoned, and spread on toast or crackers: incorrectly called Welsh *rarebit.*

ras-cal (ras′k'l), *n.* a scoundrel; rogue.—*adj.* and *adv.* ras′cal-ly.—*n.* ras-cal′i-ty.

¹rash (rash), *n.* an eruption of the skin, showing red spots, as in scarlet fever.

²rash (rash), *adj.* **1,** hasty in thought or act; reckless; as, he was *rash* to drive that car; **2,** done, made, or given through lack of caution; as, a *rash* promise.

rash-er (rash′ėr), *n.* a thin slice of bacon (or ham), to be fried, etc.

rasp (rasp), *v.t.* **1,** to rub or scrape with, or as with, a file or other rough instrument; **2,** to irritate; as, her voice *rasps* my nerves:—*v.i.* **1,** to scrape or grate roughly; **2,** to make a harsh, grating noise:—*n.* **1,** a rough file with a toothed rather than a ridged surface; **2,** the act of rasping or scraping; also, a harsh, grating noise; as, the *rasp* of rusty hinges.

rasp-ber-ry (raz′bėr-i), *n.* [*pl.* raspberries], the red, black, yellow, or white seedy, edible fruit of a prickly shrub or vine; also, the shrub or vine.

rat (rat), *n.* a gnawing animal that looks like a mouse but is larger:—*v.i.* [rat-ted, rat-ting], to hunt or catch rats.—*n.* rat′ter.

rat-chet (rach′it), *n.* **1,** a hinged tongue, or pawl, which drops into the notches of a toothed wheel and prevents it from turning backward; **2,** the toothed wheel; **3,** a mechanism or device consisting of the toothed wheel and the tongue: also called *ratchet-wheel.*

rate (rāt), *n.* **1,** the amount or number of one thing measured in units of another; as, a *rate* of 50 miles an hour; **2,** a fixed charge for a certain amount of material, piece of work, length of time, etc.; as, the *rate* of wages is $45 a week; **3,** a relative standard in respect to manner, style, etc.; as, to drive at a fast *rate;* to spend at an extravagant *rate;* also, class; quality; as, first-*rate* food:—**at any rate,** in any case:—*v.t.* [rat-ed, rat-ing], **1,** to settle or fix the value, rank, or degree of; **2,** to consider; regard; as, we *rate* him among the best authors:—*v.i.* to be estimated or ranked; as, he *rated* very high in his class.

rate-pay-er (rāt′pā′ẽr), *n.* one who pays rates, or local taxes.

rath-er (rȧth′ẽr), *adv.* **1,** more gladly; sooner; as, I should rather read than write; **2,** on the contrary; instead; as, ask *rather* those who really know; **3,** more accurately; as, a pale purple, or *rather,* a deep lavender; **4,** somewhat; to a certain extent; as, I *rather* like it that way.

rat-i-fy (rat′i-fī′), *v.t.* [ratified, ratify-ing], to approve; endorse; make valid by signing; as, Parliament *ratified* the treaty.—*n.* **rat′i-fi-er.**—*n.* **rat′i-fi-ca′tion.**

rat-ing (rāt′ing), *n.* **1,** the act of classifying according to relative value; **2,** rank; class; as, a high scholastic *rating.*

ra-tio (rā′shi-ō; rā′shō), *n.* [*pl.* ratios], the relation in number, degree, or quantity, existing between two things; proportion; as, our school has average students and brilliant students in the *ratio* of 10 to 1.

ra-tion (rā′shun; rash′un), *n.* **1,** a definite quantity of food or supplies allowed daily to a soldier or sailor in the service; **2,** any fixed or stated share; as, a daily *ration* of sugar:—*v.t.* to furnish (soldiers) with a fixed allowance of food, supplies, etc.; also, to distribute (food, supplies, etc.) on a limited basis.

ra-tion-al (rash′un-al), *adj.* **1,** having the power to reason, or think con-nectedly; as, man is a *rational* being; **2,** based on, or in accordance with, reason; intelligent; not foolish; as, *rational* thought or conduct.—*n.* **ra′-tion-al′i-ty;**—*v.t.* **ra′tion-al-ize′.**—*n.* **ra′tion-al-ist.**

rat-lin or **rat-line** (rat′lin), *n.* **1,** one of a series of small cross ropes forming a ladder in a ship's shrouds; **2,** light, tarred rope used for this.

rat-tan (ra-tan′), *n.* **1,** a climbing palm with long, smooth, reedlike stems; **2,** the stems of such a palm, used particularly in making wicker furniture; **3,** a walking-stick or cane of rattan.

rat-tle (rat′l), *v.i.* [rat-tled, rat-tling], **1,** to produce short, sharp noises in quick succession; clatter; as, a door *rattles* in the wind; **2,** to talk in a noisy rapid manner; prattle; as, she *rattled* on for an hour; **3,** to move with a clatter; as, the wagon *rattled* along the road:—*v.t.* **1,** to cause to make a succession of rapid, sharp noises; as, the wind *rattles* the shutters; **2,** to utter in a rapid, noisy way; as, he *rattled* off his speech; **3,** *Colloq.,* to confuse or daze; as, this unexpected news *rattled* him:—*n.* **1,** a series of short, sharp, clattering sounds follow-ing one another quickly; as, the *rattle* of hail against the windows; **2,** any-thing for making a rattling sound, as a child's toy.

rat-tler (rat′lẽr), *n.* **1,** anything that makes a rattling noise; **2,** a rattlesnake.

rattle-snake (rat′l-snāk′), *n.* a poison-ous snake with hard bony rings or scales on the tail which make a rattling sound.

rau-cous (rô′kus), *adj.* hoarse; rough; as, a *raucous* voice.

rav-age (rav′ij), *v.t.* [ravaged, ravag-ing], to lay waste; pillage; plunder; *v.i.* to work havoc: as, the enemy *ravaged* the country: —*n.* destruction by violence; ruin; waste; as, the *ravages* of the storm.

rave (rāv), *v.i.* [raved, rav-ing], **1,** to act or talk madly; **2,** to speak enthusi-astically; as, he *raved* about her singing; **3,** to rage, as a high wind.—*adj.* **rav′ing.**

rav-el (rav′el), *v.t.* [ravelled, ravel-ling], to draw out the threads of (a woven or knitted fabric):—*v.i.* to become un-woven or unknit; as, a stocking *ravels* out:—*n.* a pulled-out thread; ravelled material.

rav-el-ling (rav′el-ing), *n.* a thread drawn from woven or knitted material; something that has ravelled.

ra-ven (rā′ven), *n.* a large bird of the crow family, noted for its glossy-black colour:—*adj.* like a raven; jet black and shining.

rav-en-ous (rav′-en-us), *adj.* mad for food; starving; as, *ravenous* beasts of prey; also, extremely sharp; greedy; as, a *ravenous* appetite.—*adv.* **rav′en-ous-ly.**—*n.* **rav′en-ous-ness.**

ra-vine (ra-vēn′), *n.* a long, deep

hollow, worn by the action of a stream or torrent; a mountain gorge; gully.

ra-vi-o-li (rav/i-ō/li), *n.* small squares of dough enclosing highly seasoned chopped meat and spinach cooked and served in soup or a savoury sauce.

rav-ish (rav/ish), *v.t.* **1,** to seize and remove by force; rape; **2,** to affect overpoweringly, as with delight, rapture, grief, etc.; as, they were *ravished* by the divine music.—*n.* **rav/ish-er.** —*n.* **rav/ish-ment.**

rav-ish-ing (rav/ish-ing), *adj.* very charming; entrancing; as, a *ravishing* voice.

raw (rô), *adj.* **1,** uncooked; as, a *raw* potato; **2,** without the covering of the skin; as, a *raw* spot on the hand; **3,** in its natural form or state; unprepared; as, *raw* silk; **4,** crude; inexperienced; unpractised; as, *raw* judgment; *raw* troops; **5,** cold and damp; as, *raw* weather.—*n.* **raw/ness.**

raw-boned (rô/bōnd/), *adj.* having little flesh; gaunt; lean.

raw-hide (rô/hīd/), *n.* **1,** untanned skin or hide, as of cattle; **2,** a whip made of a roll or braid of tanned leather.

ray (rā), *n.* **1,** a single line of light appearing to stream from a bright centre or source; as, a *ray* of sunlight; also, light or illumination; as, they studied by the *ray* of the lamp; **2,** a glimmer; trace; as, a *ray* of hope; **3,** one of a number of thin lines spreading from a common centre like the spokes of a wheel; **4,** a beam of energy, electricity, etc.; as, an X-*ray;* **5,** something that resembles a ray, as one of the yellow, petal like flowers around the dark disk of a black-eyed Susan, one of the radiating arms of a starfish, etc.:—*v.t.* to send forth (light):—*v.i.* to shine forth; radiate.—*adj.* **ray/less.**

ray (rā), *n.* a fish with a broad, flat body and a thin tail. The skate and the torpedo are rays.

ray-on (rā/on), *n.* a shiny, silklike fabric made from wood fibre spun into thread.

raze (rāz), *v.t.* [razed, razing], to level to the ground; tear down, as a building.

RAY (1/16)

ra-zor (rā/zẽr), *n.* a sharp-edged instrument used in shaving.

ra-zor-back (rā/zẽr-bak/), *n.* and

adj. **1,** in southern U.S., a semiwild hog with ridgelike back and long legs; **2,** the red whale with dorsal fin: also called *finback* and *rorqual.*

razz (raz), *v.t.* and *v.i. Slang,* to ridicule, tease, heckle, or disconcert.

re- (rē-). Latin *prefix* denoting: **1,** in return, mutual (*repay*); against (*resist*); back, backward (*recall*); off, away, down (*refuge*, *relax*); repeated action (*reduplicate*); an intensive (*redolent*); or a negative (*resign*); **2,** again, renew (*reread*); or back to a previous or better state (*reform*, *recondition*).

re (rā; rē), *n.* in *music,* the name of the second note of the scale.

reach (rēch), *v.t.* **1,** to stretch out; as, the children *reached* out their hands for pennies; **2,** to touch or grasp; as, they could not *reach* the railing; **3,** to pass or deliver to another; to hand; as, please *reach* me my coat; **4,** to arrive at or come to; attain; as, to *reach* a goal; **5,** to extend as far as; penetrate to; as, this road *reaches* the lake:—*v.i.* **1,** to extend the hand so as to touch or seize something; **2,** to endeavour to obtain something; as, to *reach* for fame; **3,** to extend in time, space, amount, etc.; as, the cost *reaches* into thousands; **4,** to cover a distance as does the eye:—*n.* **1,** the act or power of stretching out the arm in order to touch or grasp something; also, the distance one can stretch; as, he has a long *reach;* **2,** the distance within which one can touch, observe, etc.; as, he lives within *reach* of town; **3,** an unbroken stretch, as of water.

re-act (ri-akt/), *v.i.* **1,** to rebound; act as a boomerang; as, John's cruelty to his friend *reacted* on John and made him suffer; **2,** to respond to an influence or stimulus; as, the patient *reacted* favourably to the doctor's treatment; **3,** in *chemistry,* to undergo change; as, some substances are inert, that is, slow to *react.*—*n.* **re-ac/tion.**

re-ac-tion-ar-y (ri-ak/shun-ẽr-i), *n.* [*pl.* reactionaries], **1,** a person who favours a return to former conditions; **2,** one who seeks to block social or political progress:—*adj.* pertaining to, or favouring, a return to a former state of affairs; as, a *reactionary* political party.

re-ac-tor (ri-ak/tẽr), *n.* **1,** anything that reacts; **2,** a condenser used to modify the current of an alternating-current circuit; **3,** an apparatus in which a controlled chain reaction of atomic fission may be maintained for

all (ôl), ôr; up, mūte, cûr, cōōl, book; oil, out; th, thin; *th,* the.

the production of fissionable material, radioactive isotopes, or power; an atomic pile. Also called **nuclear reactor.**

read (rēd), *v.t.* [read (red), read-ing], **1,** to look at and understand the meaning of (something written or printed); to peruse; as, to *read* a book; **2,** to utter aloud (something written or printed); as, he *reads* his sermons; **3,** to discover, by observation, the meaning of certain lines or marks on; as, to *read* palms; to *read* a thermometer; **4,** to make a study of; as, to *read* law; **5,** to interpret (dreams or riddles); also, to foretell (the future); **6,** to show; indicate; as, the meter *reads* 35 miles:—*v.i.* **1,** to peruse written or printed matter; **2,** to learn from written or printed matter; as, to *read* about politics; **3,** to utter aloud written or printed words; as, he often *reads* to us; **4,** to have a special form; as, the passage *reads* thus.—*n.* **read′er.**

read-ing (rēd′ing), *n.* **1,** the act of one who reads; perusal of written or printed matter; **2,** utterance aloud of the words of books, letters,; **3,** a public recital; as, to give a *reading* from Kipling; **4,** a form of a particular passage in a book; as, various *readings* of a passage may be found in different editions of Sheakespeare; **5,** written or printed matter to be perused; as, "Ivanhoe" is good *reading;* **6,** the manner of interpreting something written; as, an actor's *reading* of his lines; **7,** that which is shown by an instrument; as, the *reading* of our gas-meter is taken monthly.

re-ad-just (rē′a-just′), *v.t.* to set in order again; set to rights once more.

read-y (red′i), *adj.* [read-i-er, read-i-est], **1,** in condition for immediate action; as, I am *ready* to go; prepared for instant use; as, your dress is *ready;* **2,** quick; prompt; as, *ready* payment; **3,** mentally fit or prepared; willing; as, *ready* to obey; **4,** on the point of; about to; as, that tree is *ready* to fall; **5,** awaiting use; available; as, *ready* cash.—*adv.* **read′i-ly.**—*n.* **read′i-ness.**

read-y—made (red′i—mād′), *adj.* **1,** not made to individual order; made in standard forms; as, *ready-made* clothing; **2,** prepared beforehand; as, a *ready-made* speech.

re-al (rē′al), *adj.* **1,** not imaginary; actually existing as a thing, or occurring as a fact; as, *real* events; a *real* illness; **2,** genuine; not imitation; as, *real* silk; **3,** in *law,* pertaining to land or buildings; as, *real* property.

re-al-ism (rē′al-izm), *n.* the theory that art and literature should present life and nature as they really are, ever when sordid or disgusting.—*n.* **re′al-ist**

re-al-is-tic (rē′al-is′tik), *adj.* presenting people and scenes as they actually are; true to life; as, a *realistic* novel

re-al-i-ty (ri-al′i-ti), *n.* [*pl.* realities] **1,** the state or quality of being real or actual; as, we believe in the *reality* of what we see; **2,** that which exists or i actual; a fact; as, the *reality* prove less horrible than his fear.

re-al-ize (rē′al-īz′), *v.t.* [realized, realiz ing], **1,** to bring into actual existence hence, to accomplish; as, he *realize* his plan to go abroad; **2,** to see clearly understand; as, he *realized* his error **3,** to obtain as profit; as, he *realize* $50 from the sale:—*v.i.* to tur property into money; as, to *realize* o a building.—*n.* **re′al-i-za′tion.**

re-al-ly (rē′al-i), *adv.* actually; as matter of fact.

realm (relm), *n.* **1,** a kingdom; a empire; **2,** hence, any region or state as, the *realm* of dreams.

re-al-tor (rē′al-tẽr; -tôr′), *n.* a dea in real estate.

re-al-ty (rē′al-ti), *n.* real estate; lande property.

¹ream (rēm), *n.* twenty quires, about 480 sheets of paper.

²ream (rēm), *v.t.* to enlarge or tap (a hole), esp. in metal.

ream-er (rēm′ẽr), *n.* **1,** one who or th which reams; esp., a tool with sha edges for enlarging or tapering hole **2,** a device for squeezing fruit, co sisting of a dish with a ridged, cor shaped centre.

reap (rēp), *v.t.* **1,** to cut down with scythe, sickle, or machine; gather i as, to *reap* grain; **2,** to cut a crop fro as, to *reap* a field; **3,** to receive reward; as, to *reap* the benefit of ha study:—*v.i.* to cut and gather gra —*n.* **reap′er.**

re-ap-pear (rē′a-pēr′), *v.i.* to co into view again.

¹rear (rēr), *n,* **1,** the back or back pa as, the door at the *rear* of the roo **2,** that part of a fleet or an arr behind the rest:—*adj.* pertaining or situated at, the back part; as, *re* stairs.

rear admiral, in the navy, a fl officer next below a vice-admiral.

²rear (rēr), *v.t.* **1,** to raise or lift up;

---

cat, āge, fär, cåre, ásk; ten, ēve, latẽr; (i) pity, rely, senate; ice; top;

a snake *rears* its head; **2,** to construct; erect; as, to *rear* a palace; **3,** to bring up and educate; as, to *rear* children; **4,** to breed; grow; as, to *rear* horses: —*v.i.* to rise up on the hind legs, as a horse.

re-ar-range (rē'a-rānj'), *v.t.* [rearranged, rearrang-ing], to put back in order or place; to change the position of.

rea-son (rē'zn), *n.* **1,** an explanation given for a belief, act, etc.; as, she gave no *reason* for leaving; **2,** the grounds for an opinion or the motive of an act; as, there were *reasons* for his belief; **3,** the power to understand or think; as, the sick man lost his *reason;* **4,** sanity; common sense; as, to bring a child to *reason:*—*v.i.* **1,** to exercise the power of thinking; to draw logical conclusions; **2,** to argue; as, you cannot *reason* with a stubborn person:—*v.t.* **1,** to persuade by argument; as, to *reason* a child out of his fears; **2,** to prove or explain by means of the intellect; as, to *reason* out a solution.—*n.* **rea'son-er.**

rea-son-a-ble (rē'zn-a-bl), *adj.* **1,** having the power to think clearly and to reach sound conclusions; as, a *reasonable* being; **2,** governed by reason; just; as, a *reasonable* employer; **3,** moderate or fair; as, a *reasonable* charge; **4,** sound or sensible; as, a *reasonable* decision.—*adv.* **rea'son-a-bly.**

rea-son-ing (rē'zn-ing), *n.* **1,** the process of reaching conclusions by careful and connected thinking; **2,** a line of argument; a presentation of reasons; as, the pupils understood the teacher's *reasoning.*

re-as-sure (rē'a-shoor'), *v.t.* [reassured, reassur-ing], to give back courage to; give new confidence to.—*n.* **re'as-sur'ance.**

re-bate (rē'bāt; ri-bāt'), *n.* money paid back; discount; as, John got a *rebate* of two dollars on the books he bought. Also used as *v.t.*

re-bel (ri-bel'), *v.i.* [rebelled, rebelling], **1,** to take up arms against the law or government; **2,** to resist any authority.

reb-el (reb'l), *n.* **1,** one who takes up arms against his government or resists its laws; **2,** one who resists any authority:—*adj.* opposing or resisting authority.

re-bel-lion (ri-bel'yun), *n.* **1,** the act of taking up arms, or the state of being in revolt, against the government; **2,**

defiance of any authority.—*adj.* **re-bel'lious.**

re-bound (ri-bound'), *v.i.* to spring or fly back from that which has been struck; as, the ball *rebounded* from the wall:—*n.* (rē'bound'; ri-bound'), the act of springing back or rebounding.

re-buff (ri-buf'), *n.* a sudden check; repulse; defeat:—*v.t.* to refuse or repel sharply; snub (someone).

re-build (rē'bild'), *v.t.* [rebuilt (rē'-bilt'), rebuild-ing], to construct again.

re-buke (ri-būk'), *n.* a sharp reproof; scolding:—*v.t.* [rebuked, rebuk-ing], to censure sharply; as, to *rebuke* a child.

re-but-tal (ri-but'al), *n.* the answering, refuting, or contradicting of the arguments of one's opponent in a debate: —*v.t.* **re-but'.**

re-cal-ci-trant (ri-kal'si-trant), *adj.* and *n.* refusing to comply, submit, obey, etc.; stubbornly defiant; as, this boy is *recalcitrant.*

re-call (ri-kôl'), *v.t.* **1,** to order or summon back; as, to *recall* an ambassador; **2,** to remember; recollect; as, to *recall* a name; **3,** to withdraw; annul; as, to *recall* a decision:—*n.* **1,** the act of summoning or calling back; **2,** the power by which an unsatisfactory public official may be put out of office by vote of the people.

re-cant (ri-kant'), *v.t.* to withdraw publicly (something previously believed or said):—*v.i.* to renounce formally an opinion previously held.

re-ca-pit-u-late (rē'ka-pit'ū-lāt'), *v.t.* recapitulat-ed, recapitulat-ing], to sum up the chief points of; as, after listening to the speakers, he *recapitulated* their main arguments:—*v.i.* to repeat briefly what has been said at length.—*n.* **re'ca-pit'u-la'tion.**

re-cap-ture (rē'kap'tūr), *n.* the act of seizing or taking again; as, the *recapture* of a town:—*v.t.* [recaptured, recaptur-ing], to seize or take again; also, to recollect.

re-cast (rē'kàst'), *v.t.* [recast, recasting], **1,** to plan or lay out anew; as, I must *recast* the first chapter; **2,** to mould or cast again; as, to *recast* a medal.

re-cede (ri-sēd'), *v.i.* [reced-ed, receding], **1,** to fall back; retire; as, the tide *recedes;* **2,** to withdraw, as from a claim or proposal; **3,** to slope or incline backward; as, his forehead *recedes.*

re-ceipt (ri-sēt'), *n.* **1,** the act of getting, or state of having received, something given, sent, etc.; as, the *receipt* of a letter; in *receipt* of news; **2,** a written acknowledgment of anything, usually money or goods; as, he signed a *receipt* for the package; **3,** esp. in cookery, a direction for making something by mixing certain ingredients; a recipe; **4,** (usually *receipts*), that which is taken in, as distinguished from what is paid out:—*v.t.* to sign (a paper) in acknowledgment of payment or of something received; as, to *receipt* a bill.

re-ceiv-a-ble (ri-sēv′a-bl), *adj.* due; payable; as accounts *receivable.*

re-ceive (ri-sēv′), *v.t.* [received, receiving], **1,** to get (a gift, message, payment, etc.) from another; as, I *received* your letter; **2,** to be informed of; as, to *receive* news; **3,** to admit to one's company; greet; entertain; as, to *receive* guests; **4,** to serve as a holder for; as, a box to *receive* books; **5,** to get; experience; as, to *receive* a shock; to *receive* a sword thrust:—*v.i.* **1,** to entertain; welcome guests; as, she *receives* on Wednesdays; **2,** to change or convert electric waves into sounds that one can hear, as does a radio.

re-ceiv-er (ri-sēv′ėr), *n.* **1,** one who or that which takes or holds; **2,** a receptacle; as, a trash *receiver;* **3,** the part of a telephone which receives the electric waves and turns them into sound; **4,** a person appointed by a court to hold and manage the property of a bankrupt person or firm:—*n.* **re-ceiv′er-ship′.**

re-cent (rē′sent), *adj.* **1,** pertaining to time not long past; as, a *recent* occurrence; **2,** new; modern; fresh; as, a *recent* book.

re-cep-ta-cle (ri-sep′ta-kl), *n.* **1,** anything, such as a cup, barrel, or vault used to hold other things; **2,** in a plant, the part of the stalk to which the parts of the flower are attached.

RECEPTACLE
Diagram of a flower showing: P, pistil; St, stamen; Pe, petal; S, sepal; R, receptacle.

re-cep-tion (ri-sep′-shun), *n.* **1,** the act of receiving, or the state of being received; as, the *reception* of news; **2,** the act or manner of welcoming; as, a cool *reception;* **3,** a formal entertainment; as, a *reception* was held in honour of the Mayor and his wife:—*adj.* **re-cep′tive.** —*n.* **re-cep′tion-ist.**—*n.* **re-cep′tor** (a sensory nerve-ending for reception of stimuli).

re-cess (ri-ses′; rē′ses), *n.* **1,** a receding part or space that breaks the line of a wall; an alcove or niche; **2,** a natural hollow or indentation in a coast line, a mountain range, etc.; **3,** a brief time during which work ceases; an intermission; as, the school *recess:—v.t.* (ri-ses′), to put back; set into a recess: —*v.i. Colloq.* to take a recess or intermission.

re-ces-sion (ri-sesh′un), *n.* **1,** in *economics,* a temporary decline in business, esp. in a recovery period following a depression; **2,** the withdrawal of the clergy and choir at the end of a service; **3,** a giving back, as to a former owner.

re-ces-sion-al (ri-sesh′un-al), *n.* **1,** a hymn sung, or music played, at the close of a church service as the clergy and choir leave the chancel; **2,** music played when a service, performance, etc., is over and the audience is leaving: —*adj.* pertaining to withdrawal or retirement.

re-ces-sive (ri-ses′iv), *adj.* **1,** receding; tending to recede, or go back; **2,** in *biology,* relating to a character, or characteristic, that does not appear in the immediate, but may be transmitted to later, offspring: opposite of *dominant* character.

rec-i-pe (res′i-pē′), *n.* **1,** a set of directions for mixing or preparing anything, as in cookery; as, a good *recipe* for cake; **2,** general directions for accomplishing a result; as, there is no *recipe* for success.

re-cip-i-ent (ri-sip′i-ent), *n.* one who receives; as, a *recipient* of high honours:—*adj.* receiving or ready to receive.

re-cip-ro-cal (ri-sip′ro-kl), *adj.* **1,** mutual; done, given, or offered by each to the other; as, *reciprocal* benefits; **2,** corresponding; equivalent; as, to ask for *reciprocal* privileges; **3,** in *grammar,* showing mutual action or relation: used of certain pronouns; as, in the sentence "John and Jim spoke to each other," "each" and "other" are *reciprocal* pronouns, showing that John spoke to Jim and Jim spoke to John. —*n.* **1,** that which is given or done by each to the other; an equivalent; **2,** in *mathematics,* the quotient obtained by dividing the number 1 by another number; as, the *reciprocal* of 3 is ⅓.— *adv.* **re-cip′ro-cal-ly.**

re-cip-ro-cate (ri-sip′ro-kāt′), *v.t.* [reciprocat-ed, reciprocat-ing], **1,** to give and take in exchange; as, they *reciprocate* each other's affection; **2,** to give something in return for; as, to *recipro-cate* a favour; **3,** in *mechanics,* to cause to move to and fro:—*v.i.* **1,** in *mechanics,* to move to and fro; **2,** to interchange; make an exchange with one another; **3,** to pay back; make a return; as, she *reciprocated* with a gift.—*n.* **rec′i-proc″i-ty** (res′i-pros′i-ti).

re-cit-al (ri-sīt′al), *n.* **1,** a telling of the details of an event; narration; as, a *recital* of one's adventures; also, the thing told; a story; **2,** an entertainment, usually consisting of music, instrumental or vocal.

rec-i-ta-tion (res′i-tā′shun), *n.* **1,** a public delivery of prose or poetry from memory; **2,** the selection of prose or poetry so delivered; as, the pupils liked John's *recitation* in assembly; **3,** the reciting by pupils in a classroom of a lesson prepared in advance; as, a *recitation* in history.

re-cite (ri-sīt′), *v.t.* [recit-ed, recit-ing], **1,** to repeat aloud from memory; declaim; as, to *recite* a poem; **2,** to tell in detail; relate; as, to *recite* the story of a trip; **3,** to repeat (a lesson) to a teacher:—*v.i.* to repeat something from memory.

reck (rek), *v.t.* and *v.i. Archaic,* to care for; heed; as, he *recks* not of danger.

reck-less (rek′lis), *adj.* heedless of consequences or danger; rash; careless; as, a *reckless* driver; *reckless* spending.

reck-on (rek′un), *v.t.* **1,** to count or number; compute; as, to *reckon* the cost; **2,** to look upon as being; consider; as, we *reckon* him a friend; **3,** *Colloq.* to think; suppose; as, I *reckon* it will rain:—*v.i.* **1,** to depend or rely; as, he *reckoned* on our votes; **2,** to make calculations.

reck-on-er (rek′un-ėr), *n.* one who, or something that, reckons, esp. a book of mathematical, or other, tables (often called a *ready reckoner*).

reck-on-ing (rek′un-ing), *n.* **1,** calculation, computation, or the result of it; **2,** a settling of accounts, as between debtor and creditor; **3,** a bill at a hotel, etc.; **4,** in *navigation,* the determining of a ship's position; as, **dead reckoning,** the use of log and compass instead of sextant, owing to cloudiness, fog, etc.; **5,** a calculated guess.

re-claim (ri-klām′), *v.t.* **1,** to demand or obtain the return of; as, to *reclaim* a book; **2,** to reform; as, to *reclaim* a drunkard; **3,** to bring under cultivation; as, to *reclaim* swampy land.—*n.* **rec′la-ma″tion.**

re-cline (ri-klīn′), *v.i.* [reclined, reclining], to lie down for rest or repose:—*v.t.* to cause to lean or lie back; as, he *reclined* his tired body on the cot.

re-cluse (ri-klōōs′; rek′lōōs), *n.* one who lives alone; a hermit.

rec-og-nize (rek′og-nīz′), *v.t.* [recognized, recogniz-ing], **1,** to know the identity of; recall as having known before; as, to *recognize* a voice; **2,** to admit acquaintance with; salute; as, she *recognized* her old friend with a smile; **3,** to take formal notice of; acknowledge; as, America *recognized* Cuba; **4,** to appreciate; as, to *recognize* true worth; **5,** to concede as true; admit; as, I *recognize* that you are right; **6,** in a meeting, to acknowledge (someone) as the person entitled to be heard at the time.—*n.* **rec′og-ni″tion.**

re-coil (ri-koil′), *v.i.* **1,** to start back or shrink, as in horror, fear, etc.; as, they *recoiled* at the sight of the mangled body; **2,** to spring back; kick, as a gun; **3,** to retreat or fall back; as, the enemy *recoiled;* **4,** to come back to the starting-point; as, evil *recoils* on the doer:—*n.* **1,** a shrinking back; **2,** a rebound; **3,** the springing back or kick of a gun or spring; also, the distance it moves.

rec-ol-lect (rek′o-lekt′), *v.t.* to call back to the mind; remember.

rec-ol-lec-tion (rek′o-lek′shun), *n.* **1,** the act of remembering; also, the power of remembering; as, age impairs the *recollection;* **2,** a person's memory or the time over which it extends; as, the coldest winter in my *recollection;* **3,** something remembered; as, boyhood *recollections.*

rec-om-mend (rek′o-mend′), *v.t.* **1,** to give in charge or trust, as to God; **2,** to offer to the favour, attention, or use of another; speak in favour of; as, to *recommend* a servant; **3,** to advise; suggest; as, I *recommend* a change of diet; **4,** to make attractive or deserving; as, her gentleness *recommends* her.

rec-om-men-da-tion (rek′o-men-dā′-shun), *n.* **1,** the act of offering to favourable notice; **2,** something that procures or deserves favourable attention; as, a neat appearance is a good *recommendation;* **3,** something recommended or advised; as, the committee's *recommendation* is to wait.

rec-om-pense (rek′om-pens′), *v.t.* [recompensed, recompens-ing], **1,** to give an equivalent to (a person); reward; repay; as, she *recompensed* him for his devotion; **2,** to make amends for; atone for; as, to *recompense* a loss:—*n.*

something given by way of reward or amends.

rec-on-cile (rek′on-sīl′), *v.t.* [reconciled, reconcil-ing], 1, to restore peace between; as, to *reconcile* brothers who have quarrelled; 2, to adjust; settle; as, to *reconcile* differences; 3, to make content or submissive; as, to *reconcile* a person to his fate; 4, to make consistent; as, it is hard to *reconcile* her words with her actions.

rec-on-cil-i-a-tion (rek′on-sil′i-ā′-shun), *n.* 1, a renewing of friendship after disagreement; 2, a settlement or adjustment of differences; compromise.

rec-on-dite (rek′on-dīt′; re-kon′dīt), *adj.* 1, too difficult for the ordinary mind to understand; obscure; 2, dealing in profound or abstruse things; as, *recondite* studies; 3, little known (used of writers or sources).

re-con-nais-sance (ri-kon′i-sans), *n.* 1, the making of a preliminary survey, as for military or scientific purposes; 2, a party of men sent on such a survey.

rec-on-noi-tre (rek′o-noi′tėr; rē′ko-noi′tėr), *v.t.* and *v.i.* [reconnoitred (-tėrd), reconnoi-tring], to explore and investigate, esp. for military or scientific purposes. Also spelled **rec′on-noi′ter**.

re-con-sid-er (rē′kon-sid′ėr), *v.t.* 1, to think over 'or ponder again; as, to *reconsider* a proposal; 2, in a legislative body, to bring up (a bill or motion) for renewed deliberation.—*n.* **re′con-sid′er-a′tion**.

re-con-struct (rē′kon-strukt′), *v.t.* to rebuild; remodel.—*n.* **re′con-struc′-tion**.

¹**re-cord** (ri-kôrd′), *v.t.* 1, to write out or set down in some permanent form; as, to *record* events; to *record* a voice by means of a phonograph; 2, to register; as, to *record* a deed; 3, to mark or indicate; as, the clock *records* time.

²**rec-ord** (rek′ôrd; rek′ėrd), *n.* 1, the act of writing down or recording facts or events for the purpose of history or evidence; also, what is written or recorded; as, a family *record;* 2, an official report, written or printed, of public acts; as, a legislative *record;* a court *record;* 3, the body of facts, known and preserved, giving the history of a person or thing; as, the prisoner's *record;* 4, the cylinder, disk, or paper roll for reproducing sounds in phonographs, mechanical pianos, etc.; 5, in *sports*, the best performance so far officially recognized; as, the track team

broke two *records:*—*adj.* best, greatest, or most remarkable of its kind up to a given time; as, *record* heat.

re-cord-er (ri-kôr′dėr), *n.* 1, a person whose business it is to keep an official record; as, a *recorder* of wills; 2, in some cities, a judge or a magistrate; 3, any of various devices that register mechanically; 4, a soft-toned flute, played in vertical position.

re-count (ri-kount′), *v.t.* to tell or repeat in full the particulars of; recite: —*n.* (rē′kount), a second counting, as of votes.

re-coup (ri-kōōp′), *v.t.* 1, to make up for; indemnify; compensate; as to *recoup* one's losses; 2, pay back; reimburse (for damage, loss, etc.).

re-course (ri-kōrs′; rē′kōrs), *n.* 1, an appeal for aid or protection; 2, the person to whom one appeals, or the thing to which one turns.

re-cov-er (ri-kuv′ėr), *v.t.* 1, to get back or regain; as, to *recover* one's health; to *recover* lost property; 2, to obtain by judgment in a court of law; as, to *recover* damages; 3, to make up for or make good the loss or waste of; as, to *recover* lost time; 4, to find again; as to *recover* a scent:—*v.i.* 1, to regain health, strength, or any former state 2, to win a lawsuit.—*adj.* **re-cov′er-a-ble**.—*n.* **re-cov′er-y**.

rec-re-ant (rek′ri-ant), *n.* 1, a faithless person; a traitor; 2, a coward:—*adj* 1, cowardly; 2, unfaithful to one's duty or to a cause; false; as, a *recrean* knight.

rec-re-ate (rek′ri-āt′), *v.t.* and *v.i.* t revive or refresh, as after toil or exer tion; amuse; divert; 2, (rē′kri-āt′), t create anew.

rec-re-a-tion (rek′ri-ā′shun), *n.* re freshment of mind or body after toil play.

re-crim-i-na-tion (ri-krim′i-nā′ shun), *n.* an accusing in return, o counter accusation; as *recrimination* i a defence of weak minds:—*v.i.* re **crim′i-nate′**.

re-cru-des-cence (rē′krōō-des′ens), a breaking out afresh; as, a *recrudes cence* of smallpox:—*v.i.* **re′cru-desce′**

re-cruit (ri-krōōt′), *n.* 1, a man newl enlisted in an army or a navy; 2, on who has just joined any cause:—*v.t.* 1 to gather together; to add to, or suppl with, fresh members; as, to *recruit* a army, a party, an association; also, t enlist (soldiers, sailors, etc.); 2, t build up; restore; as, to *recruit* one strength:—*v.i.* 1, to obtain fres supplies of men or members; **2**, to recover health and strength.

rec-tan-gle (rek′tang′gl), *n.* a four-sided figure with four right angles.— *adj.* **rec-tan′gu-lar.**

rec-ti-fi-er (rek′ti-fī′ẻr), *n.* a device, as a commutator or a vacuum tube, that (1) changes alternating into direct current, or (2) changes high frequencies into audible ones (as a galena crystal, or a vacuum tube in a radio).

rec-ti-fy (rek′ti-fī′), *v.t.* [rectified, rectify-ing], **1**, to correct; as, to *rectify* an error; to remedy; as, to *rectify* abuses; **2**, to refine or purify (liquids) by distillation; **3**, in *electricity*, to change (an electric current) from alternating to direct;—*adj.* **rec′ti-fi′a-ble.**—*n.* **rec′ti-fi-ca′tion.**

rec-ti-lin-e-ar (rek′ti-lin′i-ẻr), *adj.* **1**, moving in straight lines; **2**, bounded or formed by straight lines; **3**, in *optics*, corrected (as a lens) so as not to distort straight lines.

rec-ti-tude (rek′ti-tūd′), *n.* rightness of intention and action; honesty; uprightness.

rec-tor (rek-tẻr), *n.* **1**, in the Protestant Episcopal Church, a clergyman in charge of a parish; **2**, in the Roman Catholic Church, the head of a religious house for men; also, a parish priest; **3**, the head of a university, college, or school.—*n.* **rec′to-ry.**

rec-tum (rek′tum), *n.* the lower end of the large intestine.

re-cum-bent (ri-kum′bent), *adj.* lying down; reclining; as, a *recumbent* figure.

re-cu-per-ate (ri-kū′pẻr-āt′), *v.t.* [recuperat-ed, recuperat-ing], to regain (one's health):—*v.i.* to recover from illness, losses, etc.; as, it took her months to *recuperate*. *n.* **re-cu′per-a′-tion.**

re-cur (ri-kûr′), *v.i.* [recurred, recur-ring], **1**, to go back, as in memory or in speech; as, he *recurred* to his former opinion; **2**, to come back or return; as, a thought *recurs* to the mind; **3**, to come again, or at intervals, as malaria. —*n.* **re-cur′rence.**—*adj.* **re-cur′rent.**

red (red), *n.* **1**, the colour of blood, that part of the visible spectrum having the longest wave-length; **2**, any colouring matter that produces this colour; **3**, (often *Red*), a communist or revolutionary socialist; also, loosely, any radical:—*adj.* [red-der, red-dest], **1**, of the colour of blood; **2**, pertaining to or favouring revolution; as, a *red* agitator.

red admiral, a butterfly with white spots near the tips of the forewings and bright-orange bands edging the hind wings and across the forewings.

red-breast (red′brest′), *n.* the robin.

red-cap (red′cap′), *n.* a railway-station porter.

Red Chamber, the Senate Chamber of Canada's Parliament, as distinguished from the Green Chamber or House of Commons: its rugs, curtains, and furnishings are in red (traditional colour of the House of Lords at Westminister).

red-den (red′n), *v.t.* to make red:—*v.i.* to become red; blush; flush.

red-dish (red′ish), *adj.* somewhat red; tinged with red.

re-deem (ri-dēm′), *v.t.* **1**, to buy back; **2**, to rescue or free from bondage or claim by paying a ransom or price; **3**, to ransom or free from sin and its consequences; **4**, to make good; perform; as, to *redeem* a promise; **5**, to make up for; as, to *redeem* a fault; **6**, to pay off (a promissory note); also, to pay off (bank-notes) in coin; **7**, to recover (mortgaged property) by paying a price. *n.* **re-demp′tion.**—*adj.* **re-deem′a-ble.**

re-deem-er (ri-dēm′ẻr), *n.* one who saves or redeems:—**the Redeemer,** Jesus Christ.

red—hand-ed (red′–han′did), *adj.* with bloodstained hands; hence, in the very act; as, caught *red-handed* (in a crime); violent.

red—let-ter (red′–let′ẻr), *adj.* memorable; lucky; as, a *red-letter* day.

red-ness (red′nis), *n.* the state or quality of being red.

red-o-lent (red′ō-lent), *adj.* **1**, sweet-smelling; as, *redolent* of new-mown hay; **2**, suggestive (of).—*n.* **red′o-lence.**

re-doubt-a-ble (ri-dout′a-bl), *adj.* formidable; commanding respect; as, a *redoubtable* opponent: often used ironically.

re-dound (ri-dound′), *v.i.* **1**, to result (in) or contribute (to); as, this will *redound* to your credit; **2**, to recoil (upon): said of glory, disgrace, etc.

red pep-per, cayenne pepper. See **cayenne.**

re-dress (ri-dres′), *v.t.* **1**, to right (a wrong); **2**, to correct or do away with (abuses):—*n.* (ri-dres′; rē′dres), **1**, the act of setting right; as, *redress* of grievances; **2**, compensation for a wrong or loss; as, to seek *redress* in the courts.

red-root (red'rōōt'), *n.* a coarse weed about 3' high, with small green flowers crowded into dense bristly spikes and enclosed in stiff awl-shaped bracts: it is widespread in America, Europe, Asia, Australia, etc., and common in Canada except Newfoundland. Also called *rough pigweed* and *green amaranth.*

red-skin (red'skin'), *n.* a North American Indian.

red-start (red'stärt'), *n.* **1,** a small European bird of the thrush family; **2,** a North American warbler.

red-top (red'top'), *n.* in eastern Canada and U.S., a hay and pasture grass (*Agrostis* genus) having a reddish panicle with one-flowered spikelets. Also called *bent grass.*

re-duce (ri-dūs'), *v.t.* [reduced, reducing], **1,** to make less in value, size, etc.; lessen; lower; as, to *reduce* a debt; **2,** to bring from a higher to a lower rank or position; degrade; as, to *reduce* an officer to the ranks; **3,** to subdue; conquer; as, to *reduce* a hostile tribe; **4,** to bring into order; as, to *reduce* spelling to rules; **5,** to bring to a specified condition; as, she *reduced* her family to despair; **6,** to change into some other physical state; as, to *reduce* sugar to syrup; **7,** in *arithmetic,* to change from one form to another without changing the value, as gallons to pints; **8,** in *chemistry,* to remove non-metallic elements from; as, to *reduce* iron ore; **9,** in *surgery,* to restore (a displaced part) to its right position; also, to set; as, to *reduce* a fracture.—*adj.* **re-duc'i-ble.**

re-duc-tion (ri-duk'shun), *n.* **1,** the act of cutting down or reducing; also, the state of being reduced; **2,** the amount by which something is reduced; as, a *reduction* of ten pounds in weight; **3,** a duplicate on a smaller scale; as, the *reduction* of a map.

re-dun-dant (ri-dun'dant), *adj.* exceeding what is needed; superfluous in writing or speaking; too full or too wordy.—*n.* **re-dun'dance.**

re-du-pli-cate (ri-dū'pli-kāt'), *v.t.* to double; repeat; multiply.—*n.* **re-du'pli-ca'tion.**

red-wing (red'wing'), *n.* **1,** a small European thrush with an orange-red patch on the underside of the wing; **2,** the American red-winged blackbird.

red-wood (red'wood'), *n.* **1,** a very large California evergreen tree; **2,** the big tree, or giant sequoia. Both trees are sequoias.

reed (rēd), *n.* **1,** any of certain tall, coarse grasses that grow in wet places; also, one of their jointed hollow stems; **2,** a musical pipe made of the hollow stem of a plant; **3,** a thin, elastic tongue attached to the mouthpiece of certain musical instruments, as the clarinet; **4,** *Poetic,* an arrow.—*adj.* **reed'y.**

reed-bird (rēd'bûrd'), *n.* the bobolink.

¹reef (rēf), *n.* that part of a sail which can be drawn in and secured by small ropes in shortening sail:—*v.t.* to reduce (a sail) by drawing in or folding up part of it.

²reef (rēf), *n.* a sandbar or a shelf of rock at or just below the surface of the water.

reef-er (rēf'ẽr), *n.* a short, close-fitting, double-breasted jacket of thick cloth (esp. worn by sailors).

reef knot, a double knot in which the free ends come out parallel to the standing parts; a square knot.

reek (rēk), *n.* vapour, steam, or smoke; also, a disagreeable odour:—*v.i.* to send out vapour or unpleasant fumes.—*adj.* **reek'y.**

¹reel (rēl), *n.* **1,** any of various devices with a revolving frame for winding yarn, wire, rope, etc. **2,** a spool or bobbin for holding thread; **3,** in motion pictures, a strip of film, usually either 1,000 or 2,000 feet long, held by one spool:—*v.t.* **1,** to wind on a frame or bobbin; **2,** to draw in by winding a line on a reel; as, to *reel* in a trout; **3,** to tell rapidly and easily; as, to *reel* off a long story.

²reel (rēl), *v.i.* **1,** to stagger or sway from side to side in walking; **2,** to turn round and round; feel dizzy; as, his head *reeled;* **3,** to give way; waver; as, the whole line *reeled:*—*n.* the act of staggering or swaying.

³reel (rēl), *n.* **1,** a lively country or folk dance; **2,** the music for such dance.

re—e-lect (rē'–i-lekt'), *v.t.* to elect (a person) to another term.—*n.* **re'–e-lec'tion.**

¹reeve (rēv), *v.t.* to pass the end of a rope through a hole, block, or ring, as in a pulley block.

²reeve (rēv), *n.* an elected officer who presides over a village or township council.

re-fec-tion (ri-fek'shun), *n.* a light meal; refreshment(s).

re-fec-to-ry (ri-fek′to-ri), *n.* [*pl.* refectories], a dining-hall, esp. in a monastery, convent, or school.

re-fer (ri-fûr′), *v.t.* [referred, refer-ring], **1,** to submit to another person or authority for information or decision; as, they *referred* the question to experts; **2,** to direct or send somewhere for information or help; as, to *refer* students to the encyclopaedia: **3,** to explain as due to a certain cause; as, I *refer* his actions to ignorance: —*v.i.* **1,** to make mention of something; allude; as, he *referred* frequently to progress; **2,** to turn to something; apply; as, he *referred* frequently to his notes; **3,** to point or call attention; as, that sign *refers* to a footnote; **4,** to direct one person to another for information or recommendation; as, he had permission to *refer* to Mr. Jones.—*adj.* **ref′er-a-ble.**

ref-er-ee (ref′ėr-ē′), *n.* one to whom a matter in dispute is handed over for decision and settlement; an umpire: —*v.t.* and *v.i.* to umpire.

ref-er-ence (ref′ėr-ens), *n.* **1,** the act of submitting a matter for settlement, or of applying for information; **2,** a source of information which may be consulted; as, a dictionary is a book of *reference;* **3,** a passing allusion; as, he made no *reference* to politics; **4,** a passage or note in a book, article, etc., directing attention to some other book or passage; also, the book or passage to which attention is directed; **5,** a person to whom inquiries may be addressed regarding another person; **6,** a written statement about a person's character or ability; **7,** regard; respect; as. with *reference* to your request.

ref-er-en-dum (ref′ėr-en′dum), *n.* [*pl.* referendums (ref′ėr-en′dumz) or referenda (ref′ėr-en′da)], **1,** the submitting of a legislative act to the vote of the people for approval or rejection; **2,** the right of the people to vote upon a legislative act; **3,** a direct popular vote on a proposed measure.

re-fine (ri-fīn′), *v.t.* [refined, refin-ing], **1,** to make pure; clear from dross or worthless matter; as, to *refine* sugar; **2,** to free from coarseness, rudeness, etc.; improve; as, to *refine* one's manners.

re-fined (ri-fīnd′), *adj.* **1,** freed from impurities; as, *refined* ore; **2,** well-bred; polished; as, *refined* speech.

re-fine-ment (ri-fīn′ment), *n.* **1,** a freeing from impurities; **2,** freedom from what is coarse or lacking in good taste; culture.

re-fin-er-y (ri-fīn′ėr-i), *n.* [*pl.* refineries] a place where anything is refined or made pure; as, a sugar *refinery.*

re-flect (ri-flekt′), *v.t.* **1,** to throw or give back (rays of light, heat, or sound); **2,** to give back or show an image of, as does a mirror; **3,** to give back as a result; as, his act *reflects* honour upon him:—*v.i.* **1,** to consider carefully; think; **2,** to cast reproach, blame, etc.; as, his faulty grammar *reflects* upon his early schooling.—*n.* **re-flec′tor.**

re-flec-tion (ri-flek′shun), *n.* **1,** the act of throwing back; as, the *reflection* of light; **2,** that which is reflected, as an image; also, an effect or influence; as, the *reflection* of early associations on the character; **3,** careful consideration or thinking; as, this question requires prolonged *reflection;* **4,** criticism; reproach; as, a *reflection* on one's honesty; **5,** a remark, thought, or opinion; as, that was a profound *reflection;* **6,** in *anatomy* and *zoology,* the bending, turning, or folding of a part back on itself.—*adj.* **re-flec′tive.**

re-flex (rē′fleks), *adj.* **1,** thrown back; recoiling; as, *reflex* consequences; **2,** in *physiology,* showing automatic response to some outside stimulus; as, *reflex* action:—*n.* **1,** an image or reflection; as, public opinion is often a *reflex* of the newspapers; **2,** in *physiology,* an involuntary movement of some part of the body in response to a stimulus.

re-flex-ive (ri-flek′siv), *adj.* in *grammar,* indicating an action which the subject performs upon himself; as, "cut" in the sentence "he cut himself" is a *reflexive* verb:—**reflexive pronoun,** a pronoun which, though used as the object of a verb, is invariably identical with the subject, as "himself" in the sentence "he hurt himself accidentally." —*adv.* **re-flex′ive-ly.**

re-flux (rē′fluks′), *n.* a flowing back; ebbing; as of the tide: the flux and *reflux* of fortune.

re-for-est-a-tion (rē′fôr-is-tā′shun; for-), *n.* the replanting (of deforested land) with trees.—*v.t.* **re-for′est** (-for).

re-form (ri-fôrm′), *v.t.* to improve or make better by changing the form, removing the faults, or correcting or ending abuses; as, to *reform* the calendar, a thief, the courts:—*v.i.* to abandon evil ways:—*n.* a change for the better; a removal of some evil or abuse; as, *reforms* in the school system; also, improvement in character:—*adj.*

pertaining to reform; as, a *reform* movement.—*n.* **re-form′er.**

ref-or-ma-tion (ref′or-mā′shun), *n.* the act of changing for the better; improvement, esp. in social, political, or religious affairs:—**Reformation,** the great religious movement begun by Martin Luther in the 16th century which resulted in the establishment of Protestantism.

re-form-a-tor-y (ri-fôr′ma-ter-i), *n.* [*pl.* reformatories], an institution or school for correcting the habits and conduct, esp. of young offenders:—*adj.* tending to correct; as, *reformatory* schools.

re-fract (ri-frakt′), *v.t.* to bend from a straight line; as, to *refract* rays or waves of light, heat, or sound (in passing through media or layers of different density).—*n.* **re-frac′tion.**

re-frac-to-ry (ri-frak′ter-i), *adj.* **1,** disobedient; hard to manage; as, a *refractory* boy; **2,** resisting heat; hard to work or fuse, as ore or metals; **3,** not yielding to treatment, as a disease or wound.

¹re-frain (ri-frān′), *n.* a phrase or verse repeated at intervals in a poem or song.

²re-frain (ri-frān′), *v.i.* to hold oneself back; restrain oneself; as, to *refrain* from comment.

re-fresh (ri-fresh′), *v.t.* **1,** to make fresh again; revive; as, to *refresh* flowers; **2,** to restore after fatigue; as, rest *refreshes* the body; **3,** to quicken; as, to *refresh* the mind.

re-fresh-ment (ri-fresh′ment), *n.* **1,** the act of reviving, or state of being revived; restoration of strength, liveliness, etc.; **2,** that which restores or revives, esp. food, drink, or rest; **3, refreshments,** food and drink served to guests.

re-frig-er-ant (ri-frij′ẽr-ant), *n.* a substance (as ice, solid carbon dioxide, or liquid air) that reduces the temperature below freezing:—*adj.* cooling; reducing fever or heat.

re-frig-er-ate (ri-frij′ẽr-āt′), *v.t. and v.i.* [refrigerat-ed, refrigerat-ing], to cool or become cool.—*n.* **re-frig′er-a′tion.**

re-frig-er-a-tor (ri-frij′ẽr-ā′tẽr), *n.* a receptacle or a room where food and other perishable things are kept cool by ice, cold air, or other means.

ref-uge (ref′ūj), *n.* **1,** a place of safety from trouble or danger; a shelter or secure retreat; as, to seek *refuge* from the storm; **2,** one who or that which protects or defends from danger or misfortune; as, he is my *refuge.*

ref-u-gee (ref′ū-jē′), *n.* one who flees for safety, esp. from political or religious persecution, to a foreign land.

re-ful-gent (ri-ful′jent), *adj.* shining; splendid; radiant; as, a *refulgent* smile.—*n.* **re-ful′gence.**

re-fund (ri-fund′), *v.t. and v.i.* to give back or pay back (money); as, the game was cancelled and the money for the tickets *refunded:*—*n.* (ri-fund′; rē′fund), the money paid back.

re-fus-al (ri-fūz′al), *n.* **1,** the act of rejecting or denying; **2,** the right to refuse or take something which others are given an opportunity to take it; as, to have the *refusal* of an office.

¹re-fuse (ri-fūz′), *v.t.* [refused, refusing], **1,** to decline to take; be unwilling to accept; **2,** to decline to do or grant; deny; as, to *refuse* aid:—*v.i.* to decline to take an offer; decline to do something.

²ref-use (ref′ūs), *n.* waste material; trash; rubbish:—*adj.* worthless.

re-fute (ri-fūt′), *v.t.* [refut-ed, refuting], to prove to be false or wrong; to overthrow by argument or proof —*adj.* **ref′u-ta-ble** (ref′ū-ta-bl; ri-fūt′a-bl).—*n.* **ref′u-ta′tion** (ref′ū-tā′shun).

re-gain (ri-gān′), *v.t.* **1,** to get back; recover; as, to *regain* a fortune; **2,** to reach again; as, to *regain* shelter.

re-gal (rē′gal), *adj.* royal; fit for a king; hence, resplendent; magnificent.

re-gale (ri-gāl′), *v.t.* [regaled, regaling], to entertain in regal manner; feast; delight; as, he *regaled* us with anecdotes.

re-ga-li-a (ri-gāl′ya; -li-a), *n.* **1,** the decorations or insignia of an order or office, as the Shriners; **2,** the rights, privileges, or emblems of a king.

re-gard (ri-gärd′), *v.t.* **1,** to observe closely; look upon attentively; as, she *regarded* him with a frown; **2,** to consider; as, I *regard* her as an enemy; **3,** to heed; respect; as, *regard* my words; she does not *regard* her mother′s wishes; **4,** to relate to; concern; as, the matter *regards* your happiness; **5,** to esteem; admire; as, I *regard* him highly:—*n.* **1,** a look or gaze; close attention or notice; **2,** care; consideration; as, *regard* for others; **3,** respect; affection; as, I hold him in high *regard;* **4, regards,** good wishes; as, my best *regards* to your mother.

re-gard-ing (ri-gär′ding), *prep.* about; in respect to.

re-gard-less (ri-gärd′lis), *adj.* careless; negligent; heedless; as, *regardless* of danger.

re-gat-ta (ri-gat′a), *n.* a boat race, or series of boat races.

re-gen-cy (rē′jen-si), *n.* [*pl.* regencies], 1, the office of a temporary ruler; 2, a person or body of persons governing for another; 3, the office, powers, or government of such a person or body; 4, the period during which someone rules for another.

re-gen-er-ate (ri-jen′ėr-āt′), *v.t.* [regenerat-ed, regenerat-ing], 1, to renew spiritually; 2, to make a change for the better in; reform; as, the economic system needs to be *regenerated;* 3, to produce anew; as, the body *regenerates* tissue; also, to fill with new life or power:—*adj.* (ri-jen′ėr-it), 1, having new life; 2, spiritually reborn; as, a *regenerate* soul.—*n.* **re-gen′er-a′tion.**

re-gent (rē′jent), *n.* 1, a person appointed to govern while the rightful ruler is unable to do so, or until he is able to take the throne; 2, in certain universities, a member of the governing board:—*adj.* ruling in place of another; as, prince *regent.*

reg-i-cide (rej′i-sīd′), *n.* the murder, or murderer, of a king.

re-gime (rā-zhēm′), *n.* 1, a system of government, social or political; 2, a systematized method of living; as, a daily *regime.*

reg-i-men (rej′i-men), *n.* 1, a regulated course of diet, exercise, sleep, etc., prescribed for some special purpose; 2, orderly government; control.

reg-i-ment (rej′i-ment), *n.* an organized body of soldiers under the command of a colonel:—*v.t.* to systematize; subject to discipline.—*n.* **reg′i-men-ta′-tion.** *adj.* **reg′i-ment′al.**

re-gion (rē′jun), *n.* 1, an indefinitely large section of land; a district; as, the Rocky Mountain *region;* 2, one of the divisions or portions into which the earth, the sea, or the air may be thought of as divided; as, the inner *regions* of the earth; the upper *regions* of the atmosphere; 3, a division or part of the body.—*adj.* **re′gion-al.**

reg-is-ter (rej′is-tėr), *n.* 1, an official written record; as, a *register* of births and deaths; also, a book for keeping such a record; 2, a person who keeps a record; as, a *register* of deeds; 3, a device that records; as, a cash *register;* 4, a device for regulating the entrance

of heated air to a room; 5, the compass or range of a voice or an instrument:—*v.t.* 1, to enter in a list or formal record; enrol; as, to *register* securities; to *register* students; 2, to mark or read; as, the thermostat *registers* 60 degrees; 3, to indicate by facial expression; as, to *register* surprise:—*v.i.* to write one's name in a list or record; as, to *register* at a hotel.—*n.* **reg′is-try; reg′is-trar′.**

re-gret (ri-gret′), *v.t.* [regret-ted, regret-ting], 1, to look back upon, or recall, with remorse or distress; as, to *regret* one's mistakes; 2, to feel sorry about or grieve over; as, he *regretted* leaving:—*n.* 1, sorrow for the loss or want of something; as, *regret* for vanished wealth; 2, distress of mind over some past event with the wish that it had been otherwise; as, *regret* for harsh words; 3, sadness; disappointment; as, I hear with *regret* that you will not come; 4, **regrets,** a polite expression of refusal in answer to an invitation.

re-gret-ful (ri-gret′fool), *adj.* remembering with distress; expressing regret. —*adv.* **re-gret′ful-ly.**—*n.* **re-gret′fulness.**

re-gret-ta-ble (ri-gret′a-bl), *adj.* arousing regret; deplorable; as, a *regrettable* accident.—*adv.* **re-gret′ta-bly.**

reg-u-lar (reg′ū-lėr), *adj.* 1, according to some established rule, order, or custom; occurring on a fixed date; as, a *regular* holiday; without a break; as, in *regular* succession; fully qualified; as, a *regular* student; orthodox; as, a *regular* Republican; orderly or methodical; as, *regular* habits; unvarying, steady, or uniform; as, a *regular* pulse; 2, following a certain design; symmetrical; as, *regular* features; 3, belonging to a religious order; bound by religious rule; as, *regular* clergy; 4, permanent; as, the *regular* army; 5, in *grammar*, following the usual rules of declension, comparison, or conjugation; 6, *Colloq.*, thorough; as, she is a *regular* bookworm:—*n.* 1, a soldier belonging to a standing army; 2, a member of the clergy who belongs to a religious order.—*adv.* **reg′u-lar-ly.** —*n.* **reg′u-lar′i-ty.**

reg-u-late (reg′ū-lāt′), *v.t.* [regulat-ed, regulat-ing], 1, to govern according to rule, method, or established custom; as, to *regulate* one's conduct; 2, to put or keep in proper order; as, to *regulate* a household; 3, to adjust to some desired or standard condition ; as, *regulate* a thermostat.—*n.* **reg′u-la′tor.**

reg·u·la·tion (reg′ū-lā′shun), *n.* **1,** the act of adjusting; as, the *regulation* of temperatures; also, the state of being adjusted; **2,** a rule or law; as, hospital *regulations:*—*adj.* conforming to a regular style, method, or rule; as, a *regulation* uniform.

re·gur·gi·tate (rē-gûr′ji-tāt′), *v.t.* to pour or throw back; surge or rush back, esp. from the stomach; as cows *regurgitate* the food which forms their cuds; the housefly *regurgitates*, or vomits, its stomach contents before each new meal.

re·ha·bil·i·tate (rē′ha-bil′i-tāt′), *v.t.* **1,** to restore (a former state, rank, privilege, etc.); re-instate; **2,** to re-establish (in social position); clear the character or reputation; **3,** to put on a firm basis, as the currency of a country.—*n.* **re′ha-bil′i-ta′tion.**

re·hearse (ri-hûrs′), *v.t.* [rehearsed, rehears-ing], **1,** to narrate; tell the story of; as, she *rehearsed* the most interesting events of her career; **2,** to practice in preparation for a public performance; as, to *rehearse* a play or a piano solo.—*n.* **rehears′al.**

reichs·mark (rikhs′märk′), *n.* the monetary unit of Germany, established in 1924, worth about 23 cents.

reign (rān), *n.* **1,** supreme rule; royal power; **2,** the time during which a ruler holds sway:—*v.i.* **1,** to exercise royal authority; rule; **2,** to hold sway; prevail; as, terror *reigned* in the village.

re·im·burse (rē′im-bûrs′), *v.t.* [reimbursed, reimburs-ing], to repay (a person); as, to *reimburse* a man for the loss of his time.—*n.* **re′im-burse′ment.**

rein (rān), *n.* **1,** either of two leather straps fastened to rings in the ends of the bit of a horse or other animal as a means of guiding and controlling it; **2,** (often *reins*), any means of restraint or control; as, the *reins* of government: —**give rein to,** allow to be unchecked or uncontrolled; as, to *give rein to* grief: —*v.t.* **1,** to hold in, direct, or stop, by means of reins; as, to *rein* a horse; **2,** to restrain; control; as, to *rein* one's anger.

re·in·car·na·tion (rē′in-kär-nā′shun,) *n.* **1,** the belief that the soul reappears after death in another and different bodily form, a doctrine held esp. by certain oriental religions; **2,** the re-birth of the soul in a new body:—*v.t.* **re′in-car′nate.**

rein·deer (rān′dēr′), *n.* [pl. rein-deer], a large deer with branched antlers,

found in northern countries and used as a draught animal. Its flesh and hide are used for food and clothing.

re·in·force (rē′in-fōrs′), *v.t.* [rein-forced, reinforc-ing], to give new strength to; support; strengthen; as, to *reinforce* the foundations of a building.—*n.* **re′in-force′ment.**

re·in·state (rē′in-stāt′), *v.t.* [reinstat-ed, reinstat-ing], to restore to a former position; as, to *reinstate* a suspended pupil.

re·it·er·ate (re-it′ẽr-āt′), *v.t.* [reiterat-ed, reiterat-ing], to do or say again and again; as, to *reiterate* a denial.—*n.* **re-it′er-a′tion.**

re·ject (ri-jekt′), *v.t.* **1,** to throw away as worthless; discard; as, to *reject* all imperfect specimens; **2,** to refuse to take; decline; as, to *reject* an offer of assistance; **3,** to refuse to grant, believe, or agree to; as, to *reject* a suggestion.—*n.* **re-jec′tion.**

re·joice (ri-jois′), *v.i.* [rejoiced, rejoic-ing], to feel or express joy or gladness; as, I *rejoice* in your happiness:—*v.t.* to make joyful; gladden; as, the sight of her gifts *rejoiced* Mary greatly.—*n.* **re-joic′ing.**

re·join (rē′join′), *v.t.* to join again; return to after separation:—*v.i.* (ri-join′), to make answer to a reply; retort.

re·join·der (ri-join′dẽr), *n.* a reply; retort.

re·ju·ve·nate (ri-jōō′ve-nāt′), *v.t.* **1,** to make young again; restore youth, vigour, etc.; to renew; refresh.—*n.* **re-ju′ve-na′tion.**

re·lapse (ri-laps′), *v.i.* [relapsed, relaps-ing], to fall back into a former bad state or habit; as, he *relapsed* into unpunctuality; also, to fall back into illness after a state of partial recovery: —*n.* a slipping back; a setback.

re·late (ri-lāt′), *v.t.* [relat-ed, relat-ing], **1,** to tell (a story); recite; narrate; **2,** to show a connection between; as, to *relate* poverty and crime:—*v.i.* to refer or allude (to); have to do (with;) as, the letter *relates* to his success.—*adj.* **re-lat′ed.**

re·la·tion (ri-lā′shun), *n.* **1,** the act of narrating or telling; also, the thing narrated or told; **2,** a connection between two or more things; as, the *relation* of lack of nourishment to disease; **3,** reference; regard; as, in *relation* to the matter of which you spoke; **4,** connection by birth or marriage; also, a relative; **5, relations,**

dealings; affairs; as, foreign *relations;* business *relations.—n.* re-la'tion-ship.

rel-a-tive (rel'a-tiv), *n.* **1,** that which refers to, or is thought of in its connection with, something else; **2,** a person connected with another by blood or marriage; **3,** in *grammar,* a word, such as the pronouns *who, which, that,* which refers to an antecedent: *—adj.* **1,** having or expressing connection with, or reference to, something; as, their conversation was *relative* to business; **2,** comparative; as, the *relative* speed of field-hockey and ice-hockey; **3,** having meaning only in connection with something else; as, "more" and "less" are *relative* terms; **4,** in *grammar,* referring to an antecedent; as, a *relative* pronoun.—*adv.* rel'a-tive-ly.—*n.* rel'a-tiv'i-ty.

re-lax (ri-laks'), *v.t.* **1,** to slacken; make less tight or firm; as, to *relax* one's hold; **2,** to make less strict, harsh, or severe; as, to *relax* rules of conduct; **3,** to relieve from strain; ease; as, seeing a good comedy *relaxes* one's mind:—*v.i.* **1,** to become less tight, firm, or severe; **2,** to cease from effort; lessen tension; rest; as, to *relax* after the day's labour.—*n.* re'lax-a'tion.

re-lay (ri-lā'; rē'lā), *n.* a new or additional supply of men, horses, etc., held ready to replace or relieve others: —relay—race, a race in which a number of contestants replace one another, each covering a definite part of the course:—*v.t.* (ri-lā'), to send as if by successive messengers; as, to *relay* a message across the border.

re-lease (ri-lēs'), *v.t.* [released, releasing], **1,** to set free; as, the man was *released* from prison; **2,** to free from obligation or penalty; as, to *release* a person from a promise; **3,** to deliver from pain, care, etc.; **4,** to permit the showing or sale of; as, to *release* a book:—*n.* **1,** the act of setting free; the state of being set free; **2,** deliverance from pain, anxiety, distress, etc.; **3,** a freeing from an obligation or a penalty; as, *release* from debt; **4,** a device for holding or freeing part of a machine; as, a *release* on an automobile clutch; **5,** a placing on the market or before the public; as, the *release* of a film.

rel-e-gate (rel'e-gāt'), *v.t.* [-gated, -gating], **1,** to send or put away; exile; **2,** to remove, often to a less desirable place; as, to *relegate* furniture to the attic.

re-lent (ri-lent'), *v.i.* to become less harsh, severe, or cruel; to become more merciful; as, the tyrant *relented.—adj.* re-lent'less.

rel-e-vant (rel'e-vant), *adj.* bearing on the matter in hand; pertinent; as, *relevant* testimony (at a trial).—*n.* rel'e-van-cy.

re-li-a-ble (ri-lī'a-bl), *adj.* trustworthy fit to be depended upon; as, *reliable* servants; *reliable* news.—*n.* re-li'a-bil'i-ty.—*adv.* re-li'a-bly.

re-li-ant (ri-lī'ant), *adj.* having confidence; depending, as upon a person or thing.—*n.* re-li'ance.

rel-ic (rel'ik), *n.* **1,** that which remains; a survival; a trace or memorial, as of a custom, period, people, etc.; as, arrowheads are *relics* of primitive peoples; **2,** anything held in religious reverence as having belonged to a martyr or saint.

re-lief (ri-lēf'), *n.* **1,** the release in whole or in part from pain, grief, want, etc.; hence, comfort; ease; **2,** that which aids or relieves; as, exercise is a *relief* from overstudy; **3,** release from a task or duty; as, the *relief* of a sentinel by another; **4,** charitable help given to the poor; also, help given in time of danger or difficulty; **5,** fresh supplies of men, animals, food, etc.; esp. fresh troops, coming to take the place of those tired out in action; **6,** the raising of a sculptured design from a flat surface; as, the figures carved in *relief* on an altar; hence, sharpness of outline, due to contrast; as, a tower in bold *relief* against the sky.

re-lieve (ri-lēv'), *v.t.* [relieved, relieving], **1,** to remove; reduce in severity; lessen; as, to *relieve* pain; **2,** to free from suffering, distress, etc.; to help; as, to *relieve* a famine-stricken people; **3,** to release from a post; take the place of; as, he *relieved* the guard at midnight; **4,** to set off; bring out by contrast; as, a white collar *relieves* a black dress.

re-li-gion (ri-lij'un), *n.* **1,** belief in a divine or superhuman power, esp. in a personal God, to whom obedience and honour are due; **2,** the outward acts and practices of life that grow out of the worship of such a god; **3,** any system of faith and worship; as, the Christian *religion.—adj.* re-li'gious.

re-lin-quish (ri-ling'kwish), *v.t.* to give up; leave; surrender; as, to *relinquish* a claim.—*n.* re-lin'quish-ment.

rel-ish (rel'ish), *n.* **1,** a taste or preference; as, a *relish* for adventure; also, enjoyment; as, he ate his meal with *relish;* **2,** the quality that makes a thing pleasurable; as, novelty gave *relish* to the journey; **3,** a sauce, ketchup, etc., that adds flavour to food and stimulates the appetite:—*v.t.* **1,** to enjoy; take pleasure in; as, to *relish* gossip; **2,** to eat with pleasure or zest; as, he *relishes* his dinner.

re-luc-tant (ri-luk′tant), *adj.* **1,** unwilling; disinclined; as, *reluctant* to admit defeat; **2,** marked by unwillingness; as, a *reluctant* acceptance.—*n.* **re-luc′tance.**

re-ly (ri-lī′), *v.i.* [relied, rely-ing], to trust; have confidence; depend; as, you can *rely* on John.

re-main (ri-mān′), *v.i.* **1,** to stay behind when others go; as, only he *remained* in the room; **2,** to be left after a part has been used, taken away, lost, or destroyed; as, the walls of the house *remain;* **3,** to be left for further consideration or action; as, that *remains* to be seen; **4,** to continue in the same state; as, he *remains* a bachelor.

re-main-der (ri-mān′dėr), *n.* **1,** the portion left after anything is taken away; the rest; as, the *remainder* of one's life; **2,** in *arithmetic,* the quantity left after subtraction; as, 9 − 3 leaves a *remainder* of 6; also, the part, less than the divisor, left over after division.

re-mains (ri-mānz′), *n.pl.* **1,** the part or parts left; as, the *remains* of a meal; **2,** ruins; relics, esp. of antiquity; as, the extensive *remains* of ancient Rome; **3,** a dead body; corpse.

re-mand (ri-mand′), *v.t.* to call, order, or send back; as, to *remand* an officer to his post; to *remand* a prisoner (to jail until more evidence can be collected).

re-mark (ri-märk′), *v.t.* **1,** to take note of; observe; as, we *remarked* his worried look; **2,** to utter briefly and casually; mention; as, he *remarked* that he would be in Toronto today:—*v.i.* to comment upon something:—*n.* **1,** observation; notice; comment; as, her dress made her an object of *remark;* **2,** a brief or casual comment or statement; as, we laughed at his *remarks.*

re-mark-a-ble (ri-mär′ka-bl), *adj.* worthy of observation or comment; extraordinary; as, *remarkable* wit.— *adv.* **re-mark′a-bly.**

rem-e-dy (rem′i-di), *n.* [*pl.* remedies], **1,** anything designed to cure or relieve illness; a helpful medicine; **2,** that which removes or corrects an evil; a

relief:—*v.t.* [remedied, remedy-ing], **1,** to cure, or cause to improve, with medicine; as, to *remedy* a cough; **2,** to repair; make right; correct (an evil). —*adj.* **re-me′di-al** (-mē′); **rem-e′di-a-ble.**

re-mem-ber (ri-mem′bėr), *v.t.* **1,** to retain in the mind; recall; as, I don't *remember* how to play chequers; **2,** to keep in mind carefully; know by heart; as, to *remember* a poem; **3,** to carry greetings from; as, *remember* me to her; **4,** to give a present to; tip; as, *remember* the porter:—*v.i.* to possess or use the faculty of memory; as, he doesn't *remember* from one day to the next.

re-mem-brance (ri-mem′brans), *n.* **1,** the act or power of recalling to, or keeping in, the mind; recollecting; **2,** the state of being held in, or recalled to, mind; memory; as, in *remembrance* of someone; **3,** the length of time over which one's memories extend; as, a remarkable event in my *remembrance;* **4,** that which is remembered; also, a memento or keepsake; **5,** **remembrances,** greetings showing regard.

re-mind (ri-mīnd′), *v.t.* to bring to the mind of; cause to recollect.—*n.* **re-mind′er.**—*adj.* **re-mind′ful.**

rem-i-nis-cence (rem′i-nis′ens), *n.* the recollection of past experiences; remembrance; also, a particular event or experience which is remembered and told:—*v.t.* and *v.i. Colloq.* **rem′i-nisce′** [-nisced, -niscing].

rem-i-nis-cent (rem′i-nis′ent), *adj.* **1,** bringing memories of the past; as, a *reminiscent* scene; **2,** given to recalling the past; dwelling on the past; as, a *reminiscent* letter; **3,** suggestive; as, a poem *reminiscent* of Burns.

re-miss (ri-mis′), *adj.* careless in matters of duty, business, etc.; neglectful; lax; as, he is apt to be *remiss* in keeping his engagements.—*n.* **re-miss′-ness.**

re-mis-sion (ri-mish′un), *n.* **1,** the act of cancelling, as a fine or debt; also, forgiveness, as of sins or other offences; **2,** temporary lessening; as, a *remission* of pain.

re-mit (ri-mit′), *v.t.* [remit-ted, remitting], **1,** to forgive or pardon; as, to *remit* sins; **2,** to send (money) in payment of debts or bills due; **3,** to refrain from demanding or insisting upon; as, to *remit* a fine; **4,** to make less severe; relax; as, to *remit* one's watchfulness: —*v.i.* **1,** to abate; lessen in force; slacken; **2,** to send money, as in payment of goods.—*n.* **re-mit′ter.**

re-mit-tance (ri-mit′ans), *n.* **1,** the sending of money, esp. to someone at a distant place; **2,** the sum so sent:— **remittance man,** a person living in a foreign country largely on money sent from home.

rem-nant (rem′nant), *n.* that which is left over; remainder; esp. a short length of fabric, the last of a piece, offered at a low price.

re-mon-strate (ri-mon′strāt), *v.i.* [remonstrat-ed, remonstrat-ing], to urge or put forward strong reasons against some act or course; as, to *remonstrate* against low wages.—*n.* **re-mon′strance.**

re-morse (ri-môrs′), *n.* anguish of mind caused by sense of guilt; bitter reproach of oneself; repentance.—*adj.* **re-morse′-ful.**—*n.* **re-morse′ful-ness.**

re-morse-less (ri-môrs′lis), *adj.* cruel; merciless; pitiless.—*n.* **re-morse′ less-ness.**

re-mote (ri-mōt′), *adj.* [remot-er, re-mot-est], **1,** far off in time; as, *remote* centuries; **2,** distant in place; as, *remote* lands; **3,** far removed; not closely related; as, his remarks were *remote* from the subject; a *remote* cousin; **4,** slight; not plainly seen; as, a *remote* likeness; a *remote* possibility.

re-move (ri-mōōv′), *v.t.* [removed, re-mov-ing], **1,** to take from its place; transfer from one place to another; as, to *remove* toys from a counter; **2,** to put an end to; push out of the way; as, to *remove* a hindrance; **3,** to dismiss; displace; as, to *remove* a man from office:—*v.i.* to go from one place to another; change residence:—*n.* a step or interval; as, unemployment is but one *remove* from poverty.—*n.* **re-mov′er.**—*adj.* **re-mov′a-ble.**—*n.* **re-mov′al.**

re-mu-ner-ate (ri-mū′nėr-āt′), *v.t.* [remunerat-ed, remunerat-ing], to pay (someone) in return for service, time spent, etc.—*n.* **re-mu′ner-a′tion.**—*adj.* **re-mu′ner-a-tive.**

ren-ais-sance (ri-nā′sans; ren′e-säns′), *n.* a revival of interest and effort in any line of endeavour, esp. in art or literature:—**Renaissance,** the period of a great revival of learning and classical art in Europe during the 15th and 16th centuries, marking the transition from mediaeval to modern civilization. Also spelled **re-nas′cence; Re-nas′cence** (ri-nas′ens).

rend (rend), *v.t.* [rent (rent), rend-ing], **1,** to tear apart with violence; split; as, the wind *rends* the sail; **2,** to take away by force or violence.

ren-der (ren′dėr), *v.t.* **1,** to give in return; pay back; as, to *render* blow for blow; **2,** to pay, as something owed; as, to *render* homage; **3,** to present for payment; as, to *render* an account; **4,** to utter as final; as, to *render* a decision; **5,** to yield; as, to *render* one's life; **6,** to furnish; give; as, to *render* aid; **7,** to cause to be; make; as, to *render* a house fit for habitation; **8,** to translate; as, to *render* French into English; **9,** to express or interpret, as music; **10,** to extract and purify (lard) by melting. —*n.* **ren-di′tion** (-dish′).

ren-dez-vous (rän′dā-vōō′; ren′de-vōō′), *n.* [*pl.* rendezvous (rän′dā-vōōz′; ren′de-vōōz′)], **1,** an appointed place of meeting; **2,** a meeting by appointment; as, John had a *rendezvous* with his chums:—*v.i.* and *v.t.* to meet or bring together at a certain place.

ren-e-gade (ren′i-gād′), *n.* one who denies or gives up his faith; a deserter.

re-nege (ri-neg′; -nēg′; popularly, -nig′), *v.i.* **1,** at *cards,* to fail to follow suit when required to do so; revoke; **2,** *Colloq.* to go back on a promise or an agreement.

re-new (ri-nū′), *v.t.* **1,** to cause to become new once more; bring back the youth and strength of; revive; as, spring *renews* the earth; **2,** to take up again; resume; as, Mary *renewed* her piano lessons; **3,** to grant or obtain an extension of; as, to *renew* a magazine subscription; **4,** to replace; as, to *renew* furniture.—*n.* **re-new′al.**

ren-net (ren′it), *n.* **1,** a mass of curdled milk (from the stomach of an unweaned calf) used in curdling milk for cheese; **2,** the inner membrane lining the fourth stomach of a calf (or other ruminant), or a preparation made from it used in curdling milk, making junkets, etc.

re-nounce (ri-nouns′), *v.t.* [renounced, renounc-ing], **1,** to disown; cast off; as, to *renounce* an heir; **2,** to abandon; surrender; as, to *renounce* a claim.

ren-o-vate (ren′ō-vāt′), *v.t.* [renovat-ed, renovat-ing], to make as good as new; restore to a former or better condition of freshness; as, to *renovate* a house.—*n.* **ren′o-va′tion.**

re-nown (ri-noun′), *n.* fame; celebrity; as, a man of great *renown.*—*adj.* **re-nowned′.**

¹rent (rent), *p.t.* and *p.p.* of *rend:*—*n.* a tear; a hole or slit made by tearing, as in cloth.

²rent (rent), *n.* a fixed amount payable

at a stated time or times for the use of property:—*v.t.* **1,** to lease; hire; hold or use without ownership, in consideration of stated, regular payments; as, to *rent* a house from the owner; **2,** to give possession of, in return for rent; lease; as, to *rent* a house to a tenant: —*v.i.* to be leased or to let; as, the house *rents* for $900 a year.—*n.* **rent′er.**

rent-al (ren′tal), *n.* the amount of money paid or received as rent.

re-nun-ci-a-tion (ri-nun′si-ā′shun; re-nun′shi-ā′shun), *n.* the act of disowning, casting off, or giving up.

re-or-gan-ize (rē′ôr′gan-īz′), *v.t.* and *v.i.* [reorganized, reorganiz-ing], to arrange or organize anew; change to a more satisfactory form or system; as, to *reorganize* a club.—*n.* **re′or-gan-i-za′tion.**

rep (rep) *n.* a silk, wool, or silk-and-wool fabric with a finely corded surface.

re-pair (ri-pâr′), *v.t.* **1,** to put in good condition again after decay, injury, etc.; mend; renovate; as, to *repair* a roof; **2,** to remedy; set right; as, to *repair* a mistake:—*n.* **1,** the act of restoring to a sound condition, or the state of being thus restored; **2,** (usually *repairs*), the results of such restoration; as, he made the needed *repairs* on the barn; **3,** general condition in regard to soundness, need of repair, etc.; as, the house is in good *repair.*—*adj.* **rep′a-ra-ble.**

rep-a-ra-tion (rep′a-rā′shun) *n.* **1,** the act of remedying a mistake, a wrong, an injury, etc.; as, he made *reparation* for his neglect; **2,** that which is done by way of amends; **3, reparations,** money paid in compensation, as for war damages.

rep-ar-tee (rep′är-tē′), *n.* a quick-witted, clever reply; also, a conversation full of such replies; as, she is expert at *repartee.*

re-past (ri-pàst′), *n.* a meal; food.

re-pa-tri-ate (rē-pā′tri-āt′), *v.t.* to restore a person to his own country, esp. a prisoner-of-war, refugee, etc.

re-pay (ri-pā′), *v.t.* [repaid (ri-pād′), repay-ing], **1,** to pay back, as money; **2,** to pay back money to; as, to *repay* a creditor; **3,** to make a return to; as, to *repay* one for kindness.—*n.* **re-pay′-ment.**

re-peal (ri-pēl′), *v.t.* to cancel; take back; revoke; as, to *repeal* an amendment:—*n.* a cancelling; an abolition; as, the *repeal* of a law.—*adj.* **re-peal′a-ble.**

re-peat (ri-pēt′), *v.t.* **1,** to do or speak a

second time; as, to *repeat* a command; **2,** to say over from memory; recite; as, to *repeat* the alphabet; **3,** to say after another; tell; as, to *repeat* gossip: —*v.i.* to say or do anything over again: —*n.* **1,** the act of doing or saying over again; also, something done or said again; repetition; **2,** in *music,* a sign [:] or [:] placed at the beginning and end, or only at the end of a part to be played twice.—*n.* **re-peat′er.**—*adv.* **re-peat′ed-ly.**

re-pel (ri-pel′), *v.t.* [repelled, repel-ling], **1,** to force back; check the advance of; as, to *repel* invaders; **2,** to reject; refuse to consider; as, to *repel* an offer; **3,** to cause disgust in; as, the idea *repels* me.—*adj.* **re-pel′lent.**

re-pent (ri-pent′), *v.i.* **1,** to feel regret or sorrow on account of something done or left undone; **2,** to change one's way because of regret for sin:—*v.t.* to feel regret or sorrow for; as, to *repent* hasty words.—*n.* **re-pent′ance.**—*adj* **re-pent′ant.**

re-per-cus-sion (rē′pẽr-kush′un), *n* **1,** reaction; as, the launching of the first sputnik had world-wide *repercussions;* **2,** a forcing or throwing back of one thing by another, as waves from a sea-wall; **3,** reflection; echo; reverberation (as of sound); **4,** in *music* reiteration of a tone or chord; in a *fugue,* the reappearance of the main subject and answer after an episode.

rep-er-toire (rep′ẽr-twär′), *n.* a list of plays, operas, songs, etc., that a performer or company has ready to render often called **rep′er-to-ry,** which may also be a collection, or a place where the collection is stored.

rep-e-ti-tion (rep′i-tish′un), *n.* the act of doing or saying something more than once; a repeating; also, that which is repeated; as, this work is a *repetition* of what you did yesterday.—*adj.* **rep′e-ti′tious.**—*adj.* **re-pet′i-tive.**

re-pine (ri-pīn′), *v.i.* [repined, repining], to fret; complain; feel discontent

re-place (ri-plās′), *v.t.* [replaced, replac-ing], **1,** to put back in place; as, to *replace* a dish on a shelf; **2,** to fill the place of; as, a new house *replaces* the old one; **3,** to supply an equivalent in place of; as, to *replace* a broken doll —*n.* **re-place′ment.**

re-plen-ish (ri-plen′ish), *v.t.* to fill up again; stock in abundance; as, to *replenish* food supplies.

re-plete (ri-plēt′), *adj.* completely filled, esp. with food.—*n.* **re-ple′tion.**

rep-li-ca (rep′li-ka), *n.* **1,** a copy of

picture or statue; esp. a copy made by the original artist or sculptor; 2, any exact copy or duplicate.

re-ply (ri-pli'), n. [pl. replies], 1, something spoken, written, or done by way of an answer; a response; as, he sent in his reply to the advertisement; 2, the act of answering:—v.i. [replied, reply-ing], to say or write something in answer; as, to reply to a request.

re-port (ri-pôrt'), v.t. 1, to give an oral or written account of; as, to report the results of an investigation; 2, to make a charge or accusation against; as, to report an offender:—v.i. 1, to make, prepare, or present, a written or oral statement; 2, to present oneself at a given place; as, to report for work:—n. 1, an official or authorized presentation of facts; as, a government report; the report of a case at law; a school report; 2, something widely talked of; rumour; hearsay; hence, fame; reputation; as, a man of good report; 3, a loud and sudden noise; the sound of an explosion as, the report of a pistol.

re-port-er (ri-pōr'tér), n. one who reports; esp. a person who collects news for a newspaper.—adj. rep'or-to'ri-al.

1re-pose (ri-pōz'), v.t. [reposed, reposing], to lay or place; as, to repose one's faith in God.

2re-pose (ri-pōz'), v.t. [reposed, reposing], to place in a position of rest; lay down to rest; as, to repose oneself on a bed:—v.i. to lie at rest; hence, to sleep: n. 1, rest; sleep; 2, quietness of manner.

re-pos-i-tor-y (ri-poz'i-to-ri), n. 1, a place for storing and safekeeping, as a bank, warehouse, etc.; 2, a place of sale or exhibition; museum; as, the Canadian tundra is a repository of untapped mineral wealth; 4, a burial vault; 5, a person in whom one confides.

rep-re-hend (rep'ri-hend'), v.t. 1, to blame, censure, or sharply reprove; as, the judge reprehended the delinquent parent.

rep-re-hen-si-ble (rep'ri-hen'si-bl), adj. blamable; deserving reproof or rebuke.

rep-re-sent (rep'ri-zent'), v.t. 1, to show a likeness of; portray; as, this statue represents General Byng; 2, to make (oneself) out to be; describe (oneself); as, she represents herself as belonging to the nobility; 3, to act for or speak in place of; as, he represents his father in the business; 4, to take

or act the part of; as, he represented a clown in the play; 5, to stand for; as, letters represent sound.

rep-re-sen-ta-tion (rep'ri-zen-tā'-shun), n. 1, the act of standing for, or representing; also, the state of being represented, esp. in a legislative body; as, each of the ten provinces is given representation in the Senate; 2, a picture, statue, etc., that portrays something; an image; as, a representation of a saint; 3, a statement of fact; also, an argument in behalf of someone or something; 4, a sign or symbol.

rep-re-sent-a-tive (rep'ri-zen'ta-tiv), n. 1, one who or that which stands as a type, or shows the marked features of a group; as, he was a splendid representative of the American Indian; 2, one who has power or authority to act for another or others; 3, a member of a legislative body, elected by the people: —**Representative**, in the U.S., a member of the lower house in Congress, or in a State legislature:—adj. 1, serving to represent; portraying; 2, acting, or having power to act, for another or others, esp. in government; also, founded on representation by delegates; as, representative government; 3, characteristic of; typical; as, they made a representative selection of the author's work.

re-press (ri-pres'), v.t. 1, to keep under control; check; as, to repress a wish; 2, to crush; subdue; as, to repress a rebellion.—n. **re-pres'sion.**—adj. **re-pres'sive.**

re-prieve (ri-prēv'), n. 1, a temporary delay in carrying out the sentence of a judge; 2, a temporary relief from pain or escape from danger:—v.t. [reprieved, repriev-ing], 1, to grant a delay in the execution of; as, to reprieve a condemned prisoner; 2, to free for a time from pain or danger.

rep-ri-mand(rep'ri-mand'),n. a severe reproof or rebuke:—v.t. (rep'ri-mand', rep'ri-mand'), to rebuke severely for a fault; esp. to reprove officially.

re-pris-al (ri-prīz'al), n. 1, in war, injury or loss inflicted upon an enemy in return for an injury or loss suffered; 2, any repayment of injury with injury.

re-proach (ri-prōch'), n. 1, the act of scolding or rebuking; censure; as, a reproach for tardiness; 2, the cause or object of blame, scorn, or shame; as, the tenement district is a reproach to the town:—v.t. 1, to charge with something wrong or disgraceful; rebuke or blame; as, he reproached the clerk for carelessness; **2,** to bring shame or dishonour upon; disgrace.

re-proach-ful (ri-prōch′fool), *adj.* expressing rebuke or censure; as, a *reproachful* look.

rep-ro-bate (rep′rō-bāt′), *n.* a sinful or wicked person; a scoundrel:—*v.t.* [reprobat-ed, reprobat-ing], to disapprove of strongly; condemn:—*adj.* given up to sin; wicked.

re-pro-duce (rē′prō-dūs′), *v.t.* [reproduced, reproduc-ing], **1,** to bring about or show again; repeat; as, to *reproduce* a play, a sound, or a gesture; **2,** to bear, yield, or bring forth (offspring); **3,** to copy; make an image of; as, to *reproduce* a person's features in marble.—*n.* re′pro-duc′tion.

re-pro-duc-tive (rē′prō-duk′tiv), *adj.* pertaining to, or employed in, the process of bringing forth; as, the *reproductive* organs.

re-prove (ri-prōōv′), *v.t.* [reproved, reprov-ing], to blame; rebuke; as, to *reprove* a naughty child.—*n.* **re-proof′.**

rep-tile (rep′til), *n.* **1,** any of a class of cold-blooded, air-breathing, scaly animals, usually egg-laying, as snakes, lizards, alligators, and turtles; **2,** a mean, debased person.—*adj.* **rep-til′i-an.**

re-pub-lic (ri-pub′lik), *n.* a state or country in which the supreme power is held by the voting public, which elects its own representatives and executive officers, who are responsible directly to the people; also, the form of government of such a state or country.—*adj.* and *n.* **re-pub′li-can.**

Re-pub-li-can (ri-pub′li-kan), *adj.* naming, or relating to, the Republican party:—**Republican party,** one of the two major political parties in the U.S., established in 1854:—**Republican,** *n.* a member of the Republican party.

re-pu-di-ate (ri-pū′di-āt′), *v.t.* [repudiated, repudiat-ing], **1,** to refuse to recognize; disown; as, to *repudiate* an old friend; **2,** to decline to acknowledge or pay; as, to *repudiate* a debt; **3,** to reject; refuse to honour; as, to *repudiate* authority; to *repudiate* a statement.—*n.* **re-pu′di-a′tion.**

re-pug-nance (ri-pug′nans), *n.* extreme dislike; disgust.

re-pug-nant (ri-pug′nant), *adj.* **1,** highly distasteful or disagreeable; as, a *repugnant task*; **2,** contrary; opposed; as a course *repugnant* to one's principles.

re-pulse (ri-puls′), *v.t.* [repulsed, repuls-ing], **1,** to drive back; beat off; as,

to *repulse* an attack; **2,** to drive away by coldness, lack of sympathy, etc.:—*n.* **1,** the act of forcefully driving back; also, a defeat or setback; as, the army met with a *repulse;* **2,** a decided refusal; rejection; as, his request met with another *repulse.*—*n.* **re-pul′sion.**

re-pul-sive (ri-pul′siv), *adj.* disgusting; loathsome; as, a *repulsive* sight.

rep-u-ta-ble (rep′ū-ta-bl), *adj.* having a good reputation; decent; respectable. —*adv.* **rep′u-ta-bly.**

rep-u-ta-tion (rep′ū-tā′shun), *n.* **1,** good name or standing; honour; as, the artist has achieved world *reputation;* **2,** the general opinion held of a person, whether good or bad; as, he has a *reputation* for meanness.

re-pute (ri-pūt′), *v.t* [reput-ed, reputing], to regard or consider; as, he is *reputed* to be rich:—*n.* the estimation, good or bad, in which a person, place, or thing is held; also, fame; as, a man of *repute.*—*adv.* **re-put′ed-ly.**

re-quest (ri-kwest′), *n.* **1,** the act of asking for something; as, a *request* for information; **2,** that which is asked for; as, to grant a *request;* **3,** the condition of being in demand; as, he is in great *request* as a public speaker:—*v.t.* **1,** to ask for; express a wish for; as, to *request* a favour; **2,** to ask (someone) to do something; as, she *requested* him to make haste.

re-qui-em (rek′wi-em; rē′kwi-em), *n.* a solemn musical service, hymn, Mass, etc., for the dead.

re-quire (ri-kwīr′), *v.t.* [required, requir-ing], **1,** to demand or insist upon; as, to *require* promptness at school; **2,** to have need of; call for; as, this will *require* haste.—*n.* **re-quire′ment.**

req-ui-site (rek′wi-zit), *n.* anything that cannot be done without; a necessity; as, honesty is a *requisite* of fine character:—*adj.* so needful that it cannot be done without; necessary; as, a *requisite* amount of food.

req-ui-si-tion (rek′wi-zish′un), *n.* **1,** a written demand or claim made by right or authority; as, a *requisition* for office supplies; **2,** the condition of being demanded or put to use; as, his new bicycle was in constant *requisition* for family errands:—*v.t.* **1,** to demand; claim by authority; as, to *requisition* supplies; **2,** to make a demand upon, as for supplies; esp., to require (a country invaded in war) to deliver horses, food, or other military supplies.

re-quite (ri-kwīt′), *v.t.* [requit-ed, requit-ing], **1,** to repay (someone) for something; compensate; as, to *requite* a person for a kindness; **2,** to repay (something) with something else; as, to *requite* kindness with ingratitude. —*n.* **re-quit′al.**

re-scind (ri-sind′), *v.t.* to annul; repeal; cancel; as, to *rescind* a law.

res-cue (res′kū), *n.* deliverance from danger, imprisonment, or violence; as, the police aided in the *rescue* of the kidnapped boy:—*v.t.* [rescued, rescuing], to set free from danger, evil, violence, or imprisonment; save; as, the firemen *rescued* the entire family. —*n.* **res′cu-er.**

re-search (ri-sûrch′; rē′sûrch), *n.* careful study or investigation in an effort to find new information in history, science, literature, etc., by experiment or by a thorough examination of sources; as, much time, money, and effort are being devoted to cancer *research.*

re-sem-ble (ri-zem′bl), *v.t.* [resembled, resem-bling], to be similar to in appearance or character; as, the brothers *resemble* each other.—*n.* **re-sem′blance.**

re-sent (ri-zent′), *v.t.* to be angry because of; be indignant at; as, to *resent* criticism.—*adj.* **re-sent′ful.**

re-sent-ment (ri-zent′ment), *n.* strong anger or displeasure, often accompanied by a feeling of ill will, because of a real or fancied wrong, insult, etc.

res-er-va-tion (rez′ẽr-vā′shun), *n.* **1,** the act of holding back or hiding; **2,** a limiting condition; as, they gave their consent with *reservations;* **3,** accommodations arranged for in advance, as on a sleeping-car, on a steamship, in a hotel, etc.; **4,** a tract of public land set aside for some special use; as, an Indian *reservation.*

re-serve (ri-zûrv′), *v.t.* [reserved, re-serv-ing], **1,** to hold back for later use; as, to *reserve* the best till last; arrange for in advance; as, to *reserve* a room; **2,** to keep as one's own; keep control of; as, he *reserves* all rights in this book: —*n.* **1,** the act of setting aside, keeping back, or excepting; restriction; qualification; as, to accept a report without *reserve;* **2,** that which is kept in store for future use or for a particular purpose; extra supply; as, a large *reserve* of ammunition; **3,** a tract of land set apart for a special purpose; as, a game-*reserve;* **4,** restraint in speech and manner; **5,** funds kept on hand by a bank as a basis for credits;

6, reserves, a body of troops withheld from action and kept in readiness as reinforcements.

re-served (ri-zûrvd′), *adj.* **1,** keeping one's thoughts and feelings to oneself; also, undemonstrative; as, a *reserved* manner; **2,** set aside; arranged for, or capable of being arranged for, in advance; as, *reserved* seats.

res-er-voir (rez′ẽr-vwär′; rez′ẽr-vwôr′), *n.* **1,** a place where anything, esp. water, is collected and stored for current and future use; **2,** a part of an apparatus or instrument in which a liquid is held; **3,** a reserve; a storehouse; as, natural resources are a *reservoir* of wealth.

re-side (ri-zīd′), *v.i.* [resid-ed, residing], **1,** to dwell for a length of time; live; as they *reside* in the country; **2,** to exist as a fixed or essential quality, characteristic, right, etc.; as, the power to issue currency *resides* in the national governmet.—*n.* and *adj.* **res′i-dent.**

res-i-dence (rez′i-dens), *n.* **1,** the place where one lives; a settled or permanent home; **2,** the act or fact of living in a place for a period of time; also, the period during which one lives in a place; as, during his *residence* abroad.—*adj.* **res′i-den′tial.**

res-i-due (rez′i-dū′), *n.* **1,** that which remains after a part has been removed by filtration, burning, etc.; as, ash is the *residue* of coal; **2,** that part of an estate remaining after payment of all debts, charges, and particular bequests. —*adj.* **re-sid′u-al** (-zid′); **re-sid′u-ar-y** (as, a *residuary* bequest).

re-sign (ri-zīn′), *v.t.* **1,** to give up; surrender; as, to *resign* an office, to *resign* hope; **2,** to submit calmly; reconcile; as, she *resigned* herself to staying at home:—*v.i.* to withdraw from a position or office.

res-ig-na-tion (rez′ig-nā′shun), *n.* **1,** the act of giving up or yielding; a withdrawal; also, the official or written notice of such withdrawal; as, he handed in his *resignation;* **2,** patient submission; a bowing to misfortune; as, she accepted the loss with *resignation.*

re-signed (ri-zīnd′), *adj.* showing resignation; uncomplaining; submissive.

re-sil-i-ent (re-zil′i-ent), *adj.* springing back to a former position or shape; elastic; **2,** able to recover quickly (after being depressed, etc.); buoyant; as, a *resilient* temperament.—*n.* **re-sil′i-ence.**

res-in (rez′in), *n.* a hardened or dried brownish or yellowish substance obtained from certain trees, such as the pine and the fir, and used in making varnish, medicine, etc. The resin obtained from pine is often called *rosin.*—*adj.* res′in-ous.

re-sist (ri-zist′), *v.t.* 1, to stop or repel; to succeed in standing against, warding off, etc.; as, the armour *resisted* all weapons; 2, to strive against; oppose:—*v.i.* to offer opposition; refuse to obey or agree.

re-sist-ance (ri-zis′tans), *n.* 1, the act of opposing: *resistance* to arrest; an underground *resistance;* 2, power to ward off disease: his body lacked *resistance;* 3, a retarding force: air *resistance* to an airplane; 4, the opposition of a substance to an electric current: measured in ohms.—*adj.* re-sist′ant; re-sist′less.

re-sis-tor (ri-zis′tẽr), *n.* in an electric circuit, a device providing resistance for protection or control.

res-o-lute (rez′o-lūt′), *adj.* having a fixed purpose; determined; firm; as, a *resolute* will.—*adv.* res′o-lute-ly.

res-o-lu-tion (rez′o-lū′shun), *n.* 1, fixed determination; purpose, or firmness of purpose; as, a man of *resolution;* 2, that which is determined; as, we seldom keep our new-year's *resolutions;* 3, a formal proposal or statement voted on in a legislative assembly or public meeting; 4, the act of reducing a chemical compound to a simpler form or to component parts.

re-solve (ri-zolv′), *v.t.* [resolved, resolving], 1, to determine by vote; decide; as, they *resolved* that no additional funds should now be paid out; 2, to explain; clear up; as, he *resolved* all doubts by confessing everything; 3, to reduce by breaking up; transform; as, the argument *resolves* itself into three heads:—*v.i.* 1, to come to a determination; decide firmly; as, he *resolved* to do better; 2, to change to some simpler form or state; 3, to pass or adopt a resolution:—*n.* 1, fixed purpose; determination; 2, that which has been determined on; a resolution. —*adj.* re-solv′a-ble.

res-o-nant (rez′o-nant), *adj.* 1, echoing back; resounding; able to return, reinforce, or prolong sound; as, *resonant* walls; 2, round, full, and vibrant in sound.—*n.* res′o-nance; res′o-na′tor.

re-sort (ri-zôrt′), *v.i.* 1, to go often, habitually, or in numbers; betake one-

self; 2, to go or turn to for help, relief, or the gaining of an end: to *resort* to law:—*n.* 1, the act of turning to: a *resort* to arms; 2, the person or thing applied to for aid; recourse; a refuge: a last *resort;* 3, a place much visited: a summer *resort.*

re-sound (ri-zound′), *v.i.* 1, to sound loudly; as, his voice *resounded* far; 2, to be full of sound; echo; as, the woods *resound* with song; 3, *Poetic,* to be famous; as, his name *resounded* far and wide.

re-source (ri-sōrs′; rē′sōrs), *n.* 1, knowledge of what to do in an emergency or difficulty; as, a man of *resource;* 2, that to which one turns in a difficulty or emergency; as, flight was his only *resource;* 3, **resources,** a stock or reserve upon which one can draw when necessary; wealth in money, property, raw materials, etc.; as, a country's natural *resources.*

re-source-ful (ri-sōrs′fool), *adj.* 1, abounding in resources or riches; as, a *resourceful* country; 2, capable of meeting unusual demands or sudden needs; as, a *resourceful* housekeeper can make ends meet when funds are low.

re-spect (ri-spekt′), *n.* 1, regard for worth; honour and esteem; as, the world's *respect* for a great man; regard; as, *respect* for property; consideration; as, *respect* for old age; 2, **respects,** expression of good will or regard; as, to pay one's *respects;* 3, a special point or particular; as, in certain *respects* the book is good; 4, relation, reference, or regard; as, with *respect* to your question:—*v.t.* 1, to honour or esteem; as, the world *respects* a good man; also, to obey; as, *respect* the law; 2, to feel esteem for; defer to; heed: to *respect* a parent's advice; 3, to relate to; concern; 4, to avoid intruding upon: *respect* his privacy.—*n.* re-spect′er.

re-spect-a-ble (ri-spek′ta-bl), *adj.* 1, worthy of regard or esteem; as, an honest and *respectable* merchant; 2, of moderate excellence or size; passably good; as, a *respectable* income; 3, presentable; as, a *respectable* suit of clothes.—*adv.* re-spect′a-bly.—*n.* re-spect′a-bil′i-ty.

re-spect-ful (ri-spekt′fool), *adj.* showing, or marked by, proper regard, esteem, or courtesy; polite.—*adv.* res-pect′ful-ly.

re-spec-tive (ri-spek′tiv), *adj.* belonging to each of several persons or things;

particular; as, the boys took their *respective* positions in line.

re-spec-tive-ly (ri-spek'tiv-li), *adv.* as relating to each; in the order named; as, the red, blue, and green ties are for James, George, and William, *respectively*.

res-pi-ra-tion (res'pi-rā'shun), *n.* the act or process of breathing; as, artificial means are used to produce *respiration* in persons rescued from the sea.—*adj.* **re-spir'a-tor-y** (ri-spīr'a-tẽr-i; res'pi-ra-tẽr-i).—*n.* **res'pi-ra'tor.**

re-spire (ri-spīr), *v.t.* and *v.i.* [respired, respir-ing], to breathe; inhale and exhale.

res-pite (res'pit), *n.* **1,** a putting off; postponement, esp. in the carrying out of a sentence; as, the murderer was granted a *respite;* **2,** a brief period of rest; as, a *respite* from labour:—*v.t.* [respit-ed, respit-ing], to grant a respite to.

re-splend-ent (ri-splen'dent), *adj.* shining brilliantly; intensely bright; as, the heavens were *resplendent* with stars.—*n.* **re-splen'dence.**

re-spond (ri-spond'), *v.i.* **1,** to return an answer; make a reply; as, to *respond* to a question; **2,** to act, or show some feeling, in answer or sympathy; as, to *respond* to a friend's need; **3,** to react; as, to *respond* quickly to medicine.—*n.* **re-sponse'.**—*n.* and *adj.* **re-spond'ent.**

re-spon-si-bil-i-ty (ri-spon'si-bil'i-ti), *n.* [*pl.* responsibilities], **1,** the state or.fact of being answerable or accountable; as, I will assume no *responsibility* for debts contracted by you; **2,** that for which one is answerable or accountable; a duty or charge; as, this work is your *responsibility;* **3,** ability to meet obligations; as, a bank checks a man's *responsibility* before granting him a loan.

re-spon-si-ble (ri-spon'si-bl), *adj.* **1,** involving trust, duty, or obligation; as, he is capable of holding a *responsible* position; **2,** answerable; accountable; as, a guardian is *responsible* to the law; I will not be *responsible* for his debts; **3,** able to answer for one's conduct; trustworthy; as, only a *responsible* person can hold this position.—*adv.* **re-spon'si-bly.**

re-spon-sive (ri-spon'siv), *adj.* **1,** containing responses; as, *responsive* reading in a church service; **3,** easily moved; sympathetic; as, a *responsive* audience.

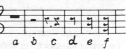

¹rest (rest), *n.* **1,** freedom from motion; as, a machine at rest; freedom from work or activity; as, a day of *rest;* freedom from disturbance of mind or spirit;

MUSICAL RESTS
a, whole; *b*, half; *c*, quarter (two forms); *d*, eighth; *e*, sixteenth; *f*, thirty-second.

peace of mind; as, a *rest* from worry; **2,** sleep; as, a good night's *rest;* **3,** a place of quiet or repose; a shelter or lodging-place; as, a sailors' *rest;* **4,** that on which anything leans for support; as, a back *rest;* **5,** in *music* and in *reading aloud,* a pause or a sign indicating such a pause:—*v.i.* **1,** to stop moving or acting; pause; relax; as, to *rest* from work; **2,** to take repose; sleep; as, I *rested* well all night; **3,** hence, to lie dead; as, the unknown soldier *rests* in his tomb; **4,** to be supported; as, the house *rests* upon its foundation; to lean; as, her hand *rested* upon the arm of the chair; to be fixed; as, his eyes *rested* on the book; **5,** to rely; depend; as, the success of this campaign *rests* on you; to be based or founded; as, the case *rested* on the evidence of one man; **6,** to remain for action or accomplishment; as, the matter *rests* with you:—*v.t.* **1,** to place at rest or in repose; as, *rest* yourself after a hard day's work; **2,** to lean; as, he *rested* his arm on the table; **3,** to base or ground; as, we *rest* our hopes in him.

²rest (rest), *n.* that which remains or is left; as, the *rest* of the book; the others; those who remain; as, the *rest* of the party:—*v.i.* to be and to continue to be; stay; as, we *rest* satisfied.

res-tau-rant (res'to-ränt'), *n.* a public place which serves meals or refreshments.

rest-ful (rest'fool), *adj.* **1,** giving repose; as, *restful* sleep; **2,** tranquil; peaceful; as, a *restful* hour.

res-ti-tu-tion (res'ti-tū'shun), *n.* **1,** the act of giving back to the rightful owner that which has been taken away or lost; **2,** the act of making good any loss, injury, or damage.

res-tive (res'tiv), *adj.* **1,** actively resisting control; unruly; as, a *restive* horse; **2,** rebellious; as, a people *restive* under slavery; **3,** restless; uneasy; as, the children grew *restive* in church.

rest-less (rest'lis), *adj.* **1,** always active or in motion; as, a *restless* child; *restless* waves; **2,** eager for change; as, a *restless* spirit; **3,** affording no repose; uneasy; as, a *restless* night. —*adv.* rest′less-ly.—*n.* rest′less-ness.

re-stor-a-tive (ri-stōr′a-tiv), *adj.* having the power to bring back to a former condition or place; as, a *restorative* medicine:—*n.* something which has power to restore; esp., a medicine used to bring back health or to restore consciousness.

re-store (ri-stōr′), *v.t.* [restored, restor-ing], **1,** to bring back to a former or original condition; as, to *restore* health; to *restore* a painting; *restore* a person to office; **2,** to bring back to the owner; as, to *restore* a lost pet.—*n.* res′to-ra′tion.—*n.* and *adj.* re-stor′a-tive.

re-strain (ri-strān′), *v.t.* to check; hold back; as, I could not *restrain* my desire to laugh.

re-straint (ri-strānt′), *n.* **1,** the act of holding back or hindering from action of any kind; **2,** the state of being held back or hindered; **3,** that which limits or hinders; **4,** reserve; as, to speak with *restraint.*

re-strict (ri-strikt′), *v.t.* to keep within bounds; to confine or limit; as, to *restrict* a patient to a certain diet.—*n.* re-stric′tion.

re-stric-tive (ri-strik′tiv), *adj.* **1,** limiting; restraining; as, *restrictive* trade laws; **2,** in *grammar,* limiting and necessary to identify the antecedent; as, men *who work hard* succeed: opposite of *nonrestrictive* (non-identifying); as, idlers, *who seldom work hard,* rarely succeed.

re-sult (ri-zult′), *n.* **1,** consequence; outcome; as, the *result* of hard work; **2,** in *arithmetic,* the answer to a problem or example:—*v.i.* **1,** to follow as a consequence or effect; as, benefits will *result* from this law; **2,** to end; lead to something as an outcome; as, the quarrel *resulted* in a fight.—*adj.* and *n.* re-sult′ant.

re-sume (ri-zūm′), *v.t.* [resumed, resum-ing], **1,** to take up again after interruption; begin again; as, to *resume* work; **2,** to take or occupy again after leaving; as, he *resumed* his seat. —*n.* re-sump′tion.

ré-su-mé (rā′zü′mā′; rā′zū-mā′), *n.* *French,* a summary; a condensed analysis or outline, as of a book.

re-sur-gence (ri-sûr′jens), *n.* a rising again (into life); as, *resurgence* of hope. —*adj.* re-sur′gent.

res-ur-rect (rez′u-rekt′), *v.t.* **1,** to raise from the dead; **2,** to bring again to notice or use; as, to *resurrect* an old style.—*n.* res′ur-rec′tion.

re-sus-ci-tate (ri-sus′i-tāt′), *v.t.* [resuscitat-ed, resuscitat-ing], to bring back to life from apparent death; as, artificial respiration to *resuscitate* a drowning person.—*n.* re-sus′ci-ta′tion. —*n.* re-sus′ci-ta′tor.

ret (ret) *v.t.* to soak, as flax, hemp, etc., to loosen the fibres.

re-tail (rē′tāl), *n.* the sale of goods in small quantities: opposite of *wholesale:* —*adj.* pertaining to, or engaged in, the sale of goods in small quantities; as, *retail* price; *retail* store; *retail* merchant:—*v.t.* (ri-tāl′; rē′tāl), **1,** to sell in small quantities; **2,** to tell in detail; pass on to others; as, to *retail* gossip:—*v.i.* to sell at retail price; as, this cloth *retails* for two dollars a yard. —*n.* re′tail-er (ri-tāl′ẽr; rē′tāl-ẽr).

re-tain (ri-tān′), *v.t.* **1,** to hold or keep in possession, practice, control, use, etc.; as, the Scot *retained* his accent; **2,** to engage by payment of a fee beforehand; as, to *retain* a lawyer; **3,** to keep in mind; as, he *retains* faces well:—**retained object,** in *grammar,* an object in a passive construction that would be a direct or an indirect object in the corresponding active construction: thus, "I gave John a book" in the passive becomes "John was given a *book* (retained *direct* object) by me", or "A *book* was given *John* (retained *indirect* object) by me". —*n.* re-tain′ment.

re-tain-er (ri-tān-ẽr), *n.* **1,** one kept in the service of a person of high rank or position; as, a lord's *retainers;* **2,** a person or thing that keeps possession; **3,** an advance fee paid to a barrister, adviser, etc.

re-tal-i-ate (ri-tal′i-āt′), *v.i.* [retaliat-ed, retaliat-ing], to give like for like, esp. evil for evil; as, to *retaliate* upon a man for an insult:—*v.t.* to repay (an injury or wrong) with something of the same kind.—*n.* re-tal′i-a′tion.—*adj.* re-tal′i-a-tor-y.

re-tard (ri-tärd′), *v.t.* to cause to move less quickly; to hinder; delay; as, the heavy snow *retarded* traffic.—*n.* re′tar-da′tion.

retch (rech), *v.i.* to try to vomit: strain, as in vomiting.

re-ten-tion (ri-ten′shun), *n.* **1,** the act of keeping in one's power or possession; **2,** the state of being kept in possession; **3,** the act or power of keeping things in mind; memory.—*adj.* **re-ten′tive.** —*n.* **re′ten-tiv′i-ty.**

ret-i-cent (ret′i-sent), *adj.* disposed to be silent; reserved in speech.—*n.* **ret′i-cence.**

re-tic-u-late (ri-tik′ū-lit), *adj.* 1, marked or veined like network, as leaves; 2, formed of fibres woven like network.

ret-i-na (ret′i-na), *n.* the inner sensitive coating of the eyeball containing the ends of the nerves of sight. Upon the retina are focused the images of objects.

ret-i-nue (ret′i-nū′), *n.* the body of persons who attend a prince or person of distinction ; a train of attendants.

re-tire (ri-tīr′), *v.i.* [retired, retir-ing], 1, to go to a place of privacy; as, to *retire* to a monastery; 2, to withdraw; retreat; as, to *retire* from a field of battle; 3, to withdraw from business, or active life; 4, to go to bed:—*v.t.* 1, to withdraw; as, to *retire* forces; 2, to withdraw (currency) from circulation, or (securities) from the market; 3, to cause to give up active service; as, to *retire* an employee with a pension.—*n.* **re-tire′ment.**

re-tired (ri-tīrd′), *adj.* 1, apart or withdrawn from society; secluded; as, a *retired* life; 2, having given up business or active life; as, a *retired* physician.

re-tir-ing (ri-tīr′ing), *adj.* modest; shy.

¹re-tort (ri-tôrt′), *n.* a quick, witty, or angry reply; as, her insulting remark brought a quick *retort:*—*v.t.* and *v.i.* to answer sharply, wittily, or angrily.

²re-tort (ri-tôrt′), *n.* a (glass) vessel with a long tube, in which substances are distilled or decomposed by heat.

re-touch (rē′tuch′), *v.t.* to touch up; improve by going over; as, to *retouch* a painting.

re-trace (ri-trās′), *v.t.* [retraced, re-trac-ing], to go over again; as, to *retrace* one's steps.

re-tract (ri-trakt′), *v.t.* and *v.i.* 1, to draw back or in; as, the cat can *retract* its claws; muscles *retract;* 2, to take back (something said or written).—*n.* **re-trac′tion.**

re-tread (rē-tred′), *v.t.* 1, to put a new tread on a worn tire by recapping or cutting new treads in the smooth rubber; regroove; 2, to tread again. —*n.* (rē′tred′), a recapped tire.

re-treat (ri-trēt′), *n.* 1, the act of with-drawing or retiring; esp. the retiring of troops before an enemy; also, the signal for retiring; 2, a place of safety

or shelter; as, the birds' forest *retreat:* —*v.i.* to withdraw; retire.

re-trench (ri-trench′), *v.t.* 1, to reduce; as, to *retrench* unnecessary expenses; 2, to take away; as, to *retrench* privileges:—*v.i.* to cut down expenses. —*n.* **re-trench′ment.**

ret-ri-bu-tion (ret′ri-bū′shun), *n.* re-ward or punishment suitable to a good or bad action; esp. loss or suffering considered as just punishment for sins. —*adj.* **re-trib′u-tive.**

re-trieve (ri-trēv′), *v.t.* [retrieved, re-triev-ing], 1, to recover; regain; as, to *retrieve* a lost book; 2, to restore; revive; as, to *retrieve* one's good name; 3, to repair the harm done by; as, to *retrieve* a misfortune; 4, in *hunting,* to fetch (wounded or killed game):—*v.i.* to find and bring in dead or wounded game; as, the hunter trained his dog to *retrieve.*

re-triev-er (ri-trēv′ėr), *n.* a dog trained to find and bring in game after it has been killed or wounded by the hunter.

ret-ro-ac-tive (ret′rō-ak′tiv), *adj.* ex-tending in scope or effect to matters that have occurred in the past; as, a *retroactive* law.

ret-ro-grade (ret′rō-grād′), *adj.*, 1, moving in reverse direction; as, a *retrograde* planet, satellite, etc.; 2, backwards; as, neo-fascism is a *retro-grade* movement.

ret-ro-spect (ret′rō-spekt′; rē′trō-), *n.* a looking back on things past; a review of the past; as, life is pleasant in *retrospect.*—*n.* **ret′ro-spec′tion.**—*adj.* **ret′ro-spec′tive.**

re-turn (ri-tûrn′), *v.i.* 1, to come or go back to a place, person, or condition; as, to *return* to one's home; 2, to begin or appear again; as, spring *returns;* 3, to come or go back in thought or con-sideration; as, to *return* to the subject; 4, to reply; make answer:—*v.t.* 1, to bring, send, carry, or put back; restore; as, to *return* a borrowed book; 2, to say in reply; as, to *return* an answer; also, to repay; as, to *return* a visit; 3, to yield; as, the fields *returned* a good crop; 4, to give back (an official report); as, to *return* the results of an election; 5, in various games, to strike or play (the ball) back:—*n.* 1, a coming or going back; as, a *return* from a vacation; 2, a restoring or giving back; as, a *return* of lost keys; 3, that which is restored or given back; 4, profit or yield; as, a good *return* on an invest-ment; 5, **returns,** results; as, election *returns;* also, proceeds; as, the *returns*

all (ol), ôr; up, mūte, cûr, cōōl, book; oil, out; th, thin; *th,* the.

from the sale:—*adj.* pertaining to a return; as, a *return* journey; a *return* engagement.—*adj.* **re-turn′a-ble.**

re-un-ion (rē-ūn′yun), *n.* **1,** the act of coming or bringing together again; **2,** a gathering of persons who were once closely associated but who have been separated; as, a class *reunion.*

re-u-nite (rē′ū-nīt′), *v.t.* [reunit-ed, reunit-ing], **1,** to bring together again; **2,** to reconcile:—*v.i.* to become joined again.

re-vamp (rē-vamp′), *v.t.* **1,** to renew the vamp, or upper (of a shoe); **2,** hence, to patch, reconstruct, or renovate.

re-veal (ri-vēl′), *v.t.* **1,** to make known; disclose; as, a chance word *revealed* his secret ambition; **2,** to display; unveil; expose to view; as, the curtain rose to *reveal* a forest scene.

re-veil-le (ri-val′i; rev′i-li), *n.* a morning signal, as of bugle, drum, etc., to call enlisted men to the day's duties.

rev-el (rev′el), *v.i.* [revelled, revel-ling], **1,** to make merry; be wildly gay; **2,** to take great delight; as, to *revel* in music: —*n.* a gay or noisy festivity; merry-making.—*n.* **rev′el-ler.**—*n.* **rev′el-ry.**

rev-e-la-tion (rev′e-lā′shun), *n.* **1,** the telling or making known of something secret or private; **2,** that which is made known.

re-venge (ri-venj′), *v.t.* [revenged, re-veng-ing], **1,** to inflict pain or injury in return for; as, to *revenge* an insult; **2,** to avenge a wrong done to; as, to *revenge* oneself:—*n.* **1,** the returning of injury for injury; **2,** the desire to return evil for evil; as, his heart was still filled with *revenge;* **3,** a chance to obtain satisfaction; as, to give a loser at cards his *revenge.*—*adj.* **re-venge′ful.**

rev-e-nue (rev′e-nū′), *n.* **1,** the sum that is yielded by an investment of any kind; income; **2,** the general income of a government from taxes, customs, and other sources.

re-ver-ber-ate (ri-vûr′bēr-āt′), *v.i.* [reverberat-ed, reverberat-ing], to re-sound; reëcho; as, thunder *reverberates* in the mountains:—*v.t.* to cause (sound) to echo; also, to reflect (heat or light). —*n.* **re-ver′ber-a′tion.**

re-vere (ri-vēr′); *v.t.* [revered, rever-ing], to regard with respectful and affectionate awe; to honour; venerate.

rev-er-end (rev′ēr-end), *adj.* worthy of reverence or deep respect:—**Reverend,** a title of respect given to clergymen.

rev-er-ent (rev′ēr-ent), *adj.* feeling

or expressing respect and affection mingled with awe or fear; deeply respectful.—*adj.* **rev′er-en′tial.**—*n.* and *v.t.* **rev′er-ence.**—*adv.* **rev′er-ent-ly.**

rev-er-ie (rev′ēr-i), *n.* deep musing; dreaminess; the state of being lost in thought or dreams. Also spelled **rev′er-y.**

re-verse (ri-vûrs′), *adj.* **1,** turned backward; opposite; as, the *reverse* order of subject and verb in an interrogative sentence; **2,** causing an opposite motion; as, the *reverse* gear in a motorcar:—*n.* **1,** the direct contrary or opposite, generally a backward, motion; as, a car in *reverse;* **3,** the back or less important side, as of a coin; **4,** a change for the worse; as, business *reverses;* also, a check or defeat; as, the enemy met with a *reverse:*—*v.t.* [reversed, revers-ing], **1,** to turn back; **2,** to cause to move in an opposite direction; **3,** to exchange; transpose; as, to *reverse* positions; **4,** to set aside or annul; as, to *reverse* a judgment:—*v.i.* to move in an opposite direction.—*adj.* **re-vers′i-ble.**—*n.* **re-ver′sal.**—*adv.* **re-verse′ly; re-vers′i-bly.**

re-vert (ri-vûrt′), *v.i.* **1,** to go back to an idea, purpose, etc.; **2,** to return to the original owner or his heirs; **3,** in *biology,* to return to an earlier type.—*n.* **re-ver′sion** (ri-vûr′shun; ri-vûr′zhun). —*adj.* **re-vert′i-ble.**

rev-er-y (rev′ēr-i), *n.* Same as **reverie.**

re-view (ri-vū′), *n.* **1,** a going over anything again to consider or examine it; **2,** an examination by a higher court of a decision of a lower court; **3,** a lesson studied or recited again; **4,** a general survey; as, a *review* of the news; **5,** a criticism, esp of a new publication or a work of art; **6,** a magazine or newspaper featuring criticisms of new books, timely essays, etc.; **7,** a military inspection:—*v.t.* **1,** to study or examine again; as, to *review* a legal decision; **2,** to go over in order to make corrections; revise; examine critically; also, to write a critical notice of; as, to *review* a concert; **3,** to look back on; as, to *review* one's life; **4,** to inspect (troops): —*v.i.* to write criticisms of books, works of art, etc.—*n.* **re-view′er.**

re-vile (ri-vīl′), *v.t.* [reviled, revil-ing], to address with abusive language; heap abuse upon; as, to *revile* an enemy.

re-vise (ri-vīz′) *v.t.* [revised, revis-ing], **1,** to go over and examine in order to correct; also, to change and correct; as, to *revise* a manuscript; **2,** to reconsider; amend; as, to *revise* one's judgment.—*n.* **re-vi′sion** (ri-vizh′un).

re-viv-al (ri-vīv′al), *n.* **1,** a bringing back, or the state of being brought back, to life, consciousness, or energy; as, the *revival* of flagging spirits; a *revival* of trade; **2,** a bringing or coming back to public attention and use; as, the *revival* of an old fashion; also, a new performance of an old play or opera; **3,** a religious awakening or reawakening of a community; also, the series of meetings held with this purpose in view.—*n.* **re-viv′al-ist.**

re-vive (ri-vīv′), *v.i.* [revived, reviv- -ing], **1,** to come back to life; **2,** to return to consciousness, as after a faint; **3,** to return to vigour or activity; as, learning *revived* in the 15th century:— *v.t.* **1,** to restore to life; **2,** to give new vigour to; as, efforts to *revive* interest in handicrafts; **3,** to bring back from a state of neglect; as, to *revive* folk- songs; **4,** to recall (memories).

rev-o-ca-ble (rev′ō-ka-bl), *adj.* capable of being repealed, reversed, or with- drawn.

re-voke (ri-vōk′), *v.t.* [revoked, revok- ing], to cancel; repeal; annul; as, to *revoke* a law or a license:—*v.i.* in card- playing, to fail to follow suit when one could and should:—*n.* in card-playing, a failure to follow suit when one could and should.—*n.* **rev′o-ca′tion.**

re-volt (ri-vōlt′; ri-volt′), *n.* an up- rising against authority; rebellion:— *v.i.* **1,** to rebel; **2,** to turn from some- thing in disgust or loathing; as, the civilized mind *revolts* against canni- balism:—*v.t.* to disgust.

rev-o-lu-tion (rev′o-lū′shun; -lōō′), *n.* **1,** the turning of a body, esp. a heavenly body, around a central point or axis; rotation; **2,** the course or motion of such a body around another body in a fixed orbit; as, the *revolution* of the earth around the sun; also, the time it takes to complete such a revolu- tion; **3,** any far-reaching change in habits of thought, methods of labour, manner of life, etc.; as, one century has seen a *revolution* in transportation from sail to steamships, and from horse- power to railroads, automobiles, and aircraft; **4,** a sudden change in the government of a country; the over- throw of one form of government and the setting up of another.

rev-o-lu-tion-ar-y (rev′o-lū′shun- ĕr-i), *adj.* associated with a sudden and complete change in thought, method, government, etc.:—*n.* [*pl.* revolution- aries], a believer in sudden and com- plete change.

rev-o-lu-tion-ist (rev′o-lū′shun-ist), *n.* one who advocates sudden and com- plete change, esp. in government.

rev-o-lu-tion-ize (rev′o-lū′shun-īz′), *v.t.* [revolutionized, revolutioniz-ing], to cause an entire change in the govern- ment, affairs, or character of; as, electricity *revolutionized* all kinds of industry.

re-volve (ri-volv′), *v.i.* [revolved, re- volv-ing], **1,** to turn around on an axis; rotate; as, the earth *revolves* once in 24 hours; wheels *revolve;* **2,** to move in a curved path around a centre, as the moon around the earth; **3,** to occur regularly; come round again and again; as, the seasons *revolve:*—*v.t.* **1,** to turn over and over in the mind, as an idea or plan; **2,** to cause to turn.—*adj.* **re-volv′ing.**

re-volv-er (ri-vol′vẽr), *n.* something that turns round or revolves; specifical- ly, a pistol with several bullet-chambers in a cylinder that revolves, bringing a fresh cartridge into position, so that several shots may be fired without reloading.

re-vue (ri-vū′), *n.* a musical show reviewing, satirizing, or parodying current fashions, events, plays, etc.

re-vul-sion (ri-vul′shun), *n.* a sudden and violent change, esp. of feeling; a sharp recoil; as, a *revulsion* of feeling from a popular favourite.

re-ward (ri-wôrd′), *n.* **1,** something given in return; as, this prize is a *reward* for diligence; **2,** money offered for service or for the return of some- thing lost:—*v.t.* to make a return to (somebody) or for (something): as, to *reward* a soldier; to *reward* his courage.

re-write (rē-rīt′), *v.t.* and *v.i.* [*p.t.* re- wrote (rē-rōt′), *p.p.* rewrit-ten (rē′- rit′n), *p.pr.* rewrit-ing], to write in different words; write (something) again.

rey-nard (rā′nãrd; ren′ẽrd), *n.* a fox. Also, **Rey′nard.**

rhap-so-dy (rap′so-di), *n.* [*pl.* rhapso- dies], **1,** a piece of literature, highly emotional in tone; **2,** an utterance of extravagant feeling; as, on Christmas morning there were *rhapsodies* of delight; **3,** in *music,* an instrumental composition, emotional in tone and irregular in form.

rhe-o-stat (rē′ō-stat′), *n.* an instru- ment for regulating the strength of an electric current by varying the resis- tance in the circuit.

rhe-sus (rē′sus), *n.* and *adj.* a small,

short-tailed, brownish-yellow monkey of India: used in medical and space research, esp. in testing the Salk vaccine for poliomyelitis and the effect of space travel on living beings.

rhet-o-ric (ret′o-rik), *n.* 1, the art of correct and forceful language, written or spoken; 2, the use of words to make a fine show.—*adj.* **rhe-tor′i-cal.**

rheu-ma-tism (rōō′ma-tizm), *n.* a disease causing stiffness and pain in the muscles and joints.—*adj.* and *n.* **rheu-mat′ic.**

rhine-stone (rīn′stōn′), *n.* a colourless paste gem made in imitation of a diamond.

rhi-noc-er-os (rī-nos′ėr-us), *n.* a massive thick-skinned, three-toed, herb-eating animal of tropical Asia and Africa, having either one or two horn-like projections on the snout.

rhi-zome (rī′zōm), *n.* any rootlike stem that sends out roots from its lower surface and leafy shoots from its upper surface, as in the mandrake.

rho-do-den-dron (rō′dō-den′dron), *n.* a shrub with shiny, usually evergreen, leaves and large clusters of variously coloured flowers.

rhom-boid (rom′boid), *n.* a four-sided plane figure with equal opposite sides and two acute and two obtuse angles.

RHOMBUS (1) and RHOMBOID (2)

rhom-bus (rom′bus) or **rhomb** (rom), *n.* an equilateral, four-sided figure having oblique angles. If one pair of sides is greater than the other, the figure is called a **rhom′boid** (rom′boid).

rhu-barb (rōō′bärb), *n.* 1, a plant with large green leaves and long, fleshy, reddish stems or stalks; 2, the stalks of this plant used as food; 3, a medicine made from the roots of a certain kind of rhubarb.

rhyme (rīm), *n.* 1, the identity in sound of the final sounds or syllables of two or more words; as, the words "bewail" and "nightingale," and "willow" and "billow," form *rhymes;* 2, words with identical final sounds; as, "flame" and "name" are *rhymes;* 3, verse or poetry that consists of lines ending in a rhyme or a series of rhymes:—*v.i.* [rhymed, rhyming], 1, to end in identical sounds; as, "bone" and "stone" *rhyme;* also, to end in words that end in identical sounds; as, the lines "Tell me where is

fancy bred" and "Or in the heart or in the head" *rhyme;* 2, to compose verses:—*v.t.* to make (lines of poetry) rhyme. Also spelled **rime.**—*n.* **rhym′er.**

rhyme-ster (rīm′stėr), *n.* a person who writes ordinary or poor verse.

rhythm (ri*th*m; rithm), *n.* 1, in prose and poetry, the harmonious rise and fall of the sounds of language, produced by patterns, more or less regularly repeated, of stressed and unstressed syllables; 2, in *music*, the ebb and flow of sound in measured intervals of time set off by beats; 3, in any action, the regular repetition of movement or sound; as, the *rhythm* of the pulse; the *rhythm* of the oarsmen.—*adj.* **rhyth′mi-cal; rhyth′mic.**

rib (rib), *n.* 1, in man and other animals, one of the set of long, flat, curved bones joined in pairs to the spine, which encircle and protect the cavity of the chest; 2, anything like a rib, as a ridge in fabrics or knitted work, a rod in an umbrella frame, one of the curved pieces of timber that shape and strengthen the side of a ship, etc.; 3, the main vein of a leaf:—*v.t.* [ribbed, rib-bing], to enclose or strengthen with, or as with, ribs; as, to *rib* an umbrella.

ri-bald (rib′ald), *adj.* 1, indecent; low; as a *ribald* song; 2, noisy and profane; as, *ribald* mirth.

rib-bon (rib′un), *n.* 1, a woven strip of fabric used for trimming, tying back the hair, etc.; 2, a fabric strip; as, a typewriter *ribbon;* 3, a shred; as, torn to *ribbons*.

ri-bo-fla-vin (rī′bō-flā′vin), *n.* a factor of the vitamin B complex found in milk, fresh meat, eggs, fresh vegetables, yeast, etc.: it is necessary for growth. Also called *vitamin B_2, vitamin G,* and *lactoflavin.*

rice (rīs), *n.* 1, a grass, valuable for its seed, grown in wet soil in a warm climate; 2, the seed or grain itself, the chief article of food in China, India, and Japan.

rice-bird (rīs′bûrd′), *n.* the bobolink so called in the southern U.S. because in the autumn it feeds on rice.

rich (rich), *adj.* 1, having much money or many possessions; wealthy; 2, expensive; valuable; as, *rich* clothing 3, great in amount; abundant; as, *rich* crops; 4, fertile; as, *rich* soil; productive; as, a *rich* mine; 5, heavily spiced or seasoned; made with large quantities of butter, eggs, sugar, etc.; as, a *rich* pudding; 6, having depth and vividness; as, a *rich* colour; 7, mellow and full in sound; as, a *rich* voice; **6,** highly humorous or entertaining; as, a *rich* situation:—**the rich,** those who have wealth.—*n.* **rich′ness.**

rick (rik), *n.* a stack, as of hay or grain: —*v.t.* to stack.

rick-ets (rik′its), *n.* a disease of children caused by insufficient or improper nourishment, and marked by softness and curving of the bones.

rick-et-y (rik′it-i), *adj.* **1,** shaky; likely to collapse; as, a *rickety* chair; **2,** infirm; tottering; **3,** affected with rickets, a child's disease marked by softness and curving of the bones.

ric-o-chet (rik′o-shā′; -shet′), *n.* a skipping or rebounding of anything, as of a missile over the ground or of a stone over the surface of the water:— *v.i.* [-cheted (-shād′) or -chetted (-shet′id), -cheting (-shā′ing)], to so skip or rebound and glance off, as a cannon-ball.

rid (rid), *v.t.* [rid-ded or rid, rid-ding], to free, as of a burden; clear; as, to *rid* oneself of an unpleasant task; *rid* a room of flies.—*n.* **rid′dance.**

rid-dle (rid′l), *n.* **1,** a question or problem so worded that one is puzzled to find the answer; **2,** a person or thing that is difficult to understand; a mystery:—*v.t.* [riddled, rid-dling], to explain; solve; as, *riddle* me this:—*v.i.* to speak with doubtful meaning.

ride (rīd), *v.i.* [*p.t.* rode (rōd), *p.p.* ridden (rid′n), *p.pr.* rid-ing], **1,** to be carried on the back of a horse or other animal; **2,** to be borne on or in a vehicle of any kind; **3,** of a vessel, to lie at anchor; **4,** to serve as a means of travel; as, this horse *rides* well:—*v.t.* **1,** to sit upon and manage; as, to *ride* a horse; **2,** to be carried on; as, to *ride* the waves; **3,** to take part in, as a race; **4,** to cause to ride; as, he *rode* the baby on his back; **5,** to oppress; as, the foreman *rode* his men:—*n.* a journey on horseback, in a vehicle, on a bicycle, etc.; as, a horseback *ride;* a *ride* in a train or motorcar.

ridge (rij), *n.* **1,** a range of hills or mountains; **2,** the projecting backbone of an animal; **3,** the angle formed by the meeting of two sloping sides; as, the *ridge* of a roof; **4,** any raised strip or line; as, the *ridges* in ploughed ground:—*v.t.* and *v.i.* [ridged, ridg-ing], to mark, or become marked, with raised lines, or ridges.

ridge-pole (rij′pōl′), *n.* **1,** the horizontal timber along the ridge of a sloping roof, to which the rafters are nailed; **2,** the horizontal pole at the top of a tent.

rid-i-cule (rid′i-kūl′), *n.* words, looks, or acts intended to make fun of someone, or to make something seem absurd: —*v.t.* [ridiculed, ridicul-ing], to make fun of.

ri-dic-u-lous (ri-dik′ū-lus), *adj.* deserving or exciting ridicule or laughter.

rid-ing (rīd′ing), *n.* an electoral district or constituency arbitrarily divided off for administrative and voting purposes: Metropolitan Toronto comprises several such ridings.

rife (rīf), *adj.* **1,** common; widespread; as, gossip is *rife* in the town; **2,** abounding; as, the town is *rife* with gossip.

rif-fle (rif′l), *v.t.* and *v.i.* to shuffle cards by dividing the deck in two, raising the corners or edges slightly, and allowing them to fall alternately together.—*n.* **1,** a method of shuffling cards, or of leafing rapidly through a book; **2,** a ripple, as on water; **3,** in a mining sluice, the lining of wooden slats, etc., arranged with grooves or openings between them for catching and holding particles of gold; **4,** any such slat, groove, or opening.

riff-raff (rif′raf′), *n.* **1,** the scum of society; **2,** trash; scraps.

¹ri-fle (rī′fl), *v.t.* [ri-fled, ri-fling], **1,** to ransack and rob; as, the safe was *rifled;* **2,** to make off with; steal.

²ri-fle (rī′fl), *n.* a firearm with the barrel spirally grooved inside to secure greater accuracy in firing:—*v.t.* [ri-fled, ri-fling], to groove (a gun barrel) spirally.—*n.* **ri′fle-man.**

rift (rift), *n.* **1,** an opening made by splitting; a cleft, as a crevice in a rock; **2,** any opening or separation; as, a *rift* in friendship; a *rift* in a fog:—*v.t.* and *v.i.* to split; burst open.

rig (rig), *v.t.* [rigged, rig-ging], **1,** to furnish (a ship) with spars, ropes, sails, etc.; **2,** to make; equip; as, to *rig* up a fishing-pole; **3,** to dress; as, she *rigged* herself out in an old costume; **4,** *Colloq.* to manipulate fraudulently; as, to *rig* the market, a TV quiz, prices, etc.:—*n.* **1,** a special arrangement of sails, masts, etc., on a ship; as, a square *rig;* **2,** *Colloq.* an odd style of dress; outfit; as, a cowboy's *rig;* **3,** *Colloq.* a cart or carriage with horse(s).

rig-ging (rig′ing), *n.* **1,** the ropes, chains, etc., by which the masts and spars of a vessel are supported, and the sails trimmed or set; **2,** any gear or tackle.—*n.* **rig′ger.**

---

all (ôl), ôr; up, mūte, cûr, cōōl, book; oil, out; th, thin; *th*, the.

right (rīt), *adj.* **1,** straight; as, a *right* line; **2,** just; honourable; as, it is *right* to fulfil one's obligations; **3,** fit; suitable; as, the *right* man for the job; **4,** correct; not mistaken; as, his opinion is usually *right;* **5,** in good condition; well; healthy; as, to be all *right;* **6,** meant to be placed or worn so as to be seen; as, the *right* side of a rug; the *right* side of a blouse; **7,** naming the side of the body on which are the arm and hand which most people naturally use for writing, carrying, etc.: opposite of *left:*—*adv.* **1,** in a direct line; as, he went *right* to the place; **2,** justly; honourably; truthfully; as, to act *right;* **3,** suitably; properly; as, nothing has been done *right;* **4,** exactly; as, *right* now; **5,** in the direction of the right side; as, then you should turn *right;* **6,** very; as, *right* honourable:—*n.* **1,** that which is proper, just, honourable: opposite of *wrong;* as, to fight for the *right;* **2,** the right-hand side; **3,** something to which one has a moral or legal claim; as, to defend one's *rights;* **4,** in *politics,* the conservative party: opposite of *left:* —*v.t.* **1,** to restore to proper condition; correct; as, to *right* an injustice; **2,** to make straight or upright; as, to *right* a chair:—*v.i.* to go back to a natural, generally an upright, position.

right an-gle, an angle of 90 degrees formed by two straight lines perpendicular to each other.

A
|
|
C —————— D
B

RIGHT ANGLES (ABC and ABD)

right-eous (rī′chus), *adj.* **1,** just; upright; honourable; as, a *right-eous* sovereign; **2,** justifiable; as, *righteous* indignation.—*adv.* **right′eous-ly.**—*n.* **right′eous-ness.**

right-ful (rīt′fool), *adj.* **1,** having a just claim according to law; as, the *rightful* heir; **2,** just; fair; as, a *rightful* claim; **3,** held by just claim; as, a *rightful* inheritance.—*n.* **right′ful-ness.**

right—hand (rīt′-hand′), *adj.* **1,** pertaining to, or situated on, the right; **2,** chiefly relied upon; as, my *right-hand* man; **3,** intended for the right hand, as a glove.

right—hand-ed (rīt′-han′did), *adj.* **1,** able to use the right hand more skilfully than the left; **2,** done or used with the right hand; **3,** turning in the same direction as the hands of a clock seen from the front; as, a *right-handed* screw.

right-ist (rīt′ist), *n.* and *adj.* in *politics,* one who is conservative or reactionary.

right-ly (rīt′li), *adv.* **1,** honestly; uprightly; as, duty *rightly* performed; **2,** properly; suitably; as, he is *rightly* called our benefactor; **3,** correctly; in accordance with fact; as, you are *rightly* informed.

right tri-an-gle, a triangle with one right angle.

rig-id (rij′id), *adj.* **1,** stiff; immovable; as, the *rigid* bone of the upper jaw; **2,** strict; severe; as, *rigid* discipline.—*n.* **ri-gid′ i-ty** (ri-jid′i-ti).

RIGHT TRIANGLE

rig-ma-role (rig′ma-rōl′), *n.* foolish, disconnected talk; nonsense: —*adj.* incoherent; frivolous.

ri-gor mor-tis (rī′gẽr; rī′gẽr môr′-tis), *n.* the stiffening of the body soon after death.

rig-our (rig′ẽr), *n.* **1,** strictness; severity; as, to enforce a law with *rigour;* **2,** severity of climate; hardship; as, the *rigours* of Arctic life.—*adj.* **rig′or-ous.**

rill (ril), *n.* a very small stream; rivulet.

rim (rim), *n.* a border, edge, or margin, esp. when round or raised; as, spectacle *rims:*—*v.t.* [rimmed, rim-ming], **1,** to furnish with a border or edge; **2,** to serve as a border around; as, silver *rims* the cup.

¹**rime** (rīm), *n.* Same as **rhyme.**—*n.* **rim′er.**

²**rime** (rīm), *n.* a rough, white, or icy covering deposited on trees, shrubs, etc., as *white frost* or *hoarfrost:* it is formed from fog- or vapour-laden air. —*adj.* **rim′y.**

rime-ster (rīm′stẽr), *n.* Same as **rhyme′ster.**

rind (rīnd), *n.* the outer skin or coat of a thing; as, the *rind* of a lemon; the *rind* of cheese; also, the bark of a tree.

¹**ring** (ring), *n.* **1,** any circular band or hoop; esp., a small ornamental hoop, as of gold or platinum, often set with gems, worn as an ornament or distinctive mark; as, an engagement *ring;* a class *ring;* **2,** an ornament for the ear; as, an ear*ring;* **3,** anything circular in shape; as, a key-*ring;* a *ring* of smoke; any circular arrangement; as, a *ring* of dancers; **4,** an arena or space used for contests or displays; as, a circus with three *rings;* **5,** a group of persons working together secretly, often towards some unlawful end:—*v.t.* [ringed, ring-ing], **1,** to put a ring around; encircle; hem in; **2,** to

fit or decorate with a ring or rings; **3**, to put a ring through; as, to *ring* the nose of a bull; **4**, in certain games (**ringtoss**), to throw a loop over (a peg).

²ring (ring), *v.i.* [*p.t.* rang (rang), *p.p.* rung (rung), *p.pr.* ring-ing], **1**, to sound musically or resound, as a bell when struck; **2**, to cause a bell to sound; as, to *ring* for breakfast; **3**, to sound loudly and clearly; as, his voice *rang* out; **4**, to give the impression of a quality; as, his excuse *rings* false; **5**, to be filled with a buzzing sound; as, my ears *ring;* **6**, to resound; echo; as, the woods *ring* with song; **7**, to be known far and wide; be famous; as, his deeds *ring* through the country:—*v.t.* **1**, to cause (particularly a bell or other metal object) to give forth a resonant sound; **2**, to announce or proclaim by a bell; as, to *ring* the hours; **3**, to summon, control, or otherwise affect by a bell signal; as, to *ring* up a friend on the telephone; *ring* up the curtain:—*n.* **1**, the sound made by a blow on metal; as, the *ring* of a hammer on iron; also, any similar sound; as, the musical *ring* of glass; **2**, a summons by, or as by, a bell; as, the *ring* of an alarm; **3**, a characteristic quality of spoken or written words; as, his words have the *ring* of sincerity; **4**, any echoing or repeated sound; as, the *ring* of applause.—*n.* **ring′er.**

ring-lead-er (ring′lēd′ėr), *n.* the leader of a number of persons banded together, usually for some unlawful act.

ring-let (ring′lit), *n.* **1**, a small ring; **2**, a curl, or lock, of hair.

ring-worm (ring′wûrm′), *n.* a contagious skin-disease marked by circular patches.

rink (ringk), *n.* **1**, an expanse of ice marked off for skating; **2**, an artificial sheet of ice in a building, for skating, or a floor for roller skating; also, the building.

rinse (rins), *v.t.* [rinsed, rins-ing], **1**, to put through clear water to remove all traces of soap; as, to *rinse* clothes; **2**, to wash lightly; as, to *rinse* the mouth:—*n.* a light wash, esp. to remove soap.

ri-ot (rī′ut), *n.* **1**, disorderly or uproarious behaviour; revelry; **2**, a disturbance of the public peace by a number of persons who are ready for violence; as, a bread *riot;* **3**, unrestrained display or growth; as, a *riot* of colour; a *riot* of weeds:—*v.i.* **1**, to

raise an uproar; engage in a public disturbance; **2**, to eat and drink without restraint; revel.—*n.* **ri′ot-er.** —*adj.* **ri′ot-ous.**—*adv.* **ri′ot-ous-ly.**

rip (rip) *v.t.* [ripped, rip-ping], **1**, to tear or cut with violence; as, she *ripped* open the package; he *ripped* off the bandage from his arm; **2**, to undo the seam of, by cutting or pulling out the stitches; as, please *rip* both sleeves; **3**, to saw (wood) along, or with, the grain:—*v.i.* to become torn apart:—*n.* a rent made by the breaking of stitches; also, a tear.

ripe (rīp), *adj.* [rip-er, rip-est], **1**, grown to maturity; ready for harvest; **2**, just right for use; mellow; as, *ripe* ale; **3**, advanced to a high degree; mature; as, *ripe* wisdom; **4**, ready; prepared; as, *ripe* for action.—*v.t.* and *v.i.* **rip′en.**

rip-ple (rip′l), *n.* **1**, a tiny wave on the surface of water; **2**, any slight, curling wave; as, *ripples* of hair; **3**, the sound made by gentle waves of water, or a sound like it; as, a *ripple* of mirth:—*v.t.* [rip-pled, rip-pling], to make small curling waves upon or in; as the wind ripples the water;—*v.i.* **1**, to become ruffled or waved on the surface; **2**, to sound like running water; as, the laughter of children *rippled* below us.

rip-saw (rip′sô′), *n.* a coarse-toothed saw with teeth raking forward, for cutting wood with the grain.

rip-tide (rip′tīd′), *n.* a sea or body of water roughened by the meeting of opposing tides or currents: also called a *rip.*

rise (rīz), *v.i.* [*p.t.* rose (rōz), *p.p.* ris-en (riz′n), *p.pr.* ris-ing], **1**, to go from a lower position to a higher; mount; ascend; as, a bird or lift *rises;* **2**, to extend upward; reach or attain; as, the building *rises* to a height of 80 feet; also, to slope upward; as, *rising* ground; **3**, to get up from kneeling sitting, or lying down; stand up; **4**, to appear above the horizon, as the sun; **5**, to come into view or existence; as, hills *rose* on my right; also, to have an origin; as, this river *rises* in the north; **6**, to swell up, as bread-dough in fermentation; **7**, to increase in value, force, intensity, etc,; as, milk is expected to *rise* in price; his fears *rose;* **8**, to thrive; prosper; also, to be promoted in rank; as, to *rise* in the world; **9**, to revolt; rebel; as, to *rise* against authority; **10**, to prove equal to something; as, to *rise* to one's opportunities; **11,** to live again; as, to *rise* from the dead:—*n.* **1,** the act of going up; ascent; **2,** the distance anything rises or ascends; as, the *rise* of a step; **3,** a small hill; **4,** appearance above the horizon; **5,** origin; source; as, the *rise* of a river; **6,** increase in value, amount, etc.; as, a steady *rise* of prices; **7,** an increase in salary or wages; **8,** advance in power or rank; **9,** rebellion.

ris-er (rīz′ẽr), *n.* **1,** one who rises, esp. with reference to the hour of rising; as, we are all late *risers;* **2,** the upright part of a step or stair.

ris-i-ble (riz′i-bl), *adj.* **1,** having the power to laugh; as, man is the only *risible* animal; **2,** laughable; ridiculous; as *risible* jokes; **3,** used in laughing; as, *risible* muscles.—*n.* **ris′i-bil′i-ty** (*pl.* sensitiveness to the ridiculous).

risk (risk), *n.* possibility of loss or injury; peril:—*v.t.* **1,** to expose to danger; as, to *risk* life and limb; **2,** to hazard; as, to *risk* a battle.—*adj.* **risk′y.**

ris-qué (rēs′kā′), *adj.* daringly close to being improper or indelicate; as, a *risque* story.

rite (rīt), *n.* the prescribed form for conducting a solemn ceremony; also, the ceremony; as, funeral *rites.*

rit-u-al (rit′ū-al), *adj.* pertaining to formal, solemn ceremonies; as, *ritual* observances:—*n.* **1,** a set form for conducting a solemn, esp. a religious, ceremony; **2,** a book of such forms; **3,** a set of ceremonies used in any church or order.—*n.* **rit′u-al-ism.**—*n.* **rit′u-a-list.**—*adj.* **rit′u-a-lis′tic.**

ri-val (rī′val), *n.* one who strives to equal or surpass another in some way; a competitor; as, *rivals* in tennis:—*v.t.* [rivalled, rival-ling], to try to equal or surpass; compete with; also, to be the equal of or match for; as, New York *rivals* London in banking:—*adj.* competing; as, *rival* businesses.—*n.* **ri′val-ry.**

rive (rīv), *v.t.* to split; cleave; as, lightning *rived* the oak.

riv-er (riv′ẽr), *n.* a large stream of water flowing in a definite channel into another stream, or into a lake or sea. —*n.* **river horse,** a hippopotamus.

riv-et (riv′it), *n.* a metal bolt with a head on one end, used to fasten together two or more pieces of wood, metal, etc., by passing it through holes and hammering down the plain end to form another head:—*v.t.* **1,** to

secure with, or as with, such a bolt; as, to *rivet* parts of a ship; **2,** to make firm or secure; as, to *rivet* a friendship; **3,** to fix (the eyes, mind, etc.) attentively.—*n.* **riv′et-er.**

riv-u-let (riv′ū-lit), *n.* a little stream.

roach (rōch), *n.* a household insect pest; a cockroach.

road (rōd), *n.* **1,** a public way for travel; highway; **2,** a way or means by which anything is reached; as, the *road* to happiness; **3,** a place near the shore where ships may ride at anchor; a roadstead.—*n.* **road′bed′; road′block′; road′house′; road′side′; road′way′.**

road-stead (rōd′sted), *n.* an anchorage for ships offshore, less sheltered than a harbour.

road-ster (rōd′stẽr), *n.* **1,** an open automobile, usually for two passengers; **2,** a horse used for light driving.

roam (rōm), *v.i.* to wander about aimlessly; ramble:—*v.t.* to wander over; as, to *roam* the countryside.

roan (rōn), *adj.* reddish brown, black, or chestnut, thickly sprinkled with grey or white; as, a *roan* horse:—*n.* **1,** a roan colour; **2,** a horse of roan colour.

roar (rōr), *n.* **1,** the deep, full cry of a large animal; as, the *roar* of a tiger; **2,** any loud, confused noise; as, the *roar* of traffic; **3,** loudly expressed mirth; as, a *roar* of laughter:—*v.i.* **1,** to cry with a loud, full, deep sound; as, a bull *roars;* **2,** to cry loudly, as in pain, distress, or anger; **3,** to laugh loudly; **4,** to make a loud, confused noise, as wind, waves, passing vehicles, etc.:—*v.t.* to utter boisterously; cry aloud; as, he *roared* his defiance.

roast (rōst), *v.t.* **1,** to cook before a fire or in a closed oven; **2,** to dry and parch under the action of heat; as, to *roast* groundnuts:—*v.i.* to be cooked by heat, as before a fire or in an oven: —*n.* a piece of meat cooked, or suitable to be cooked, before a fire or in an oven; as, a *roast* of veal:—*adj.* roasted.—*n.* **roast′er.**

rob (rob), *v.t.* [robbed, rob-bing], **1,** to take something forcibly away from; as, to *rob* a man; to steal from; as, to *rob* a bank; **2,** to deprive (a person) of something unjustly; as, to *rob* people of their rights:—*v.i.* to commit a theft. —*n.* **rob′ber.**—*n.* **rob′ber-y.**

robe (rōb), *n.* **1,** a long, loose outer garment, esp. one indicating rank or honour; **2, robes,** state or ceremonial costume; as, *robes* of office; **3,** a wrap or covering:—*v.t.* and *v.i.* [robed, robing], to dress in, or put on, a robe.

rob-in (rob′in), *n.* **1,** a small European bird of the thrush family; the robin redbreast; **2,** an American thrush somewhat like the English robin, but larger.

ro-bot (rō′bot), *n.* **1,** a manlike machine that does manual and routine work for human beings; an automaton; **2,** one who acts or works mechanically; a brutal, insensitive (but efficient) person.—*n.* **ro′bot-ry.**

ro-bust (rō-bust′), *adj.* strong; vigorous; sturdy; as, *robust* health.

roc (rok), *n.* an enormous bird of Arabian mythology.

¹rock (rok), *n.* **1,** a large mass of stone or of stony matter; also, stony fragments; **2,** mineral matter; a bed or mass of one mineral; **3,** that which resembles such a mass in firmness; a firm support; **4,** anything that may bring a person or thing to ruin; as, the business was wrecked on the *rock* of extravagance.—*adj.* **rock′y.**

²rock (rok), *v.t.* **1,** to move to and fro, or backward and forward; as, to *rock* a cradle, etc.; also, to move or swing (a baby) in a cradle; **2,** to lull to sleep; **3,** to cause to vibrate or shake; as, the explosion *rocked* the building:—*v.i.* **1,** to move backward and forward; as, to *rock* in a rocking-chair; **2,** to sway or reel:—*n.* a rocking movement.—*n.* **rock′er.**

rock-er-y (rok′ėr-i), *n.* a rock garden.

rock-et (rok′it), *n.* a tubelike vehicle, missile, or firework, powered by a gaseous, liquid, or solid propellant (kerosene, liquid oxygen, liquid hydrogen, hydrogen peroxide, etc.): the future points to multi-stage rockets of enormous thrust from atomic energy:—*v.i.* to dart swiftly ahead.—*n.* **rock′-et-ry.**

rock-weed (rok′wēd′), *n.* coarse seaweed (esp. *Fucus* and *Sargassum*) growing on tide-washed rocks.

rock wool, a fibrous insulation made by forcing a jet of steam through molten rock or slag; mineral wool.

ro-co-co (ro-kō′kō), *adj.* and *n.* old-fashioned; tastelessly florid; over-elaborate; as, *rococo* architecture (of 17th and 18th centuries).

rod (rod), *n.* **1,** a straight, slender stick of wood or metal; **2,** a fishing-pole; **3,** a switch or whip; hence, correction or discipline; as, to spare the *rod;* **4,** *U.S. Slang,* a revolver; **5,** a measure of length containing 5½ yards or 16½ feet.

rode (rōd), *p.t.* of ride.

ro-dent (rō′dent), *n.* any one of various gnawing animals, such as rats, mice, squirrels, and beavers:—*adj.* gnawing.

ro-de-o (rō′di-ō′; rō-dā′ō), *n.* **1,** a roundup or driving together of cattle to be branded; **2,** an exhibition of cowboys' skill in cattle roping, horsemanship, etc.

¹roe (rō), *n.* the eggs of a fish.

²roe (rō), *n.* **1,** a hind or doe; **2,** the small graceful roe deer of Eurasia.

roe-buck (rō′buk′), *n.* a male roe deer.

Roent-gen ray (rönt′jen; rönt′gen; rent′gen). Same as **Röntgen ray.**

rogue (rōg), *n.* **1,** a dishonest person; cheat; **2,** a mischievous person; as, a playful little *rogue.*—*adj.* **ro′guish.**

roil (roil), *v.t.,* **1,** to make (water, etc.) muddy by stirring (sediment or dregs); **2,** to vex; disturb.

roist-er (rois′tėr), *v.i.* to swagger; act in a noisy or blustering way.—*n.* **roist′er-er.**

role or **rôle** (rōl), *n.* **1,** a part or character taken by an actor in a play; **2,** any assumed part; as, she played the *role* of mother to the child.

roll (rōl), *v.t.* **1,** to cause to move onward by turning over and over; as, to *roll* a ball; **2,** to move or push along on casters or wheels; as, to *roll* a wheel-chair; **3,** to wrap upon itself or on some other object; as, to *roll* a rug; **4,** to wrap up; as, to *roll* oneself in a blanket; **5,** to cause to sway sidewise, as a ship; **6,** to utter or express with a deep, vibrating sound; as, the organ *rolls* forth its music; **7,** to level with a heavy revolving cylinder; as, to *roll* a lawn; **8,** to pronounce with a prolonged trilling sound; as, to *roll* one's r's:—*v.i.* **1,** to move onward by turning over and over; as, a ball *rolls;* **2,** to run on wheels; as, the wagon *rolls* along; **3,** to rock, as does a ship; **4,** to sweep along, as do waves; **5,** to give forth a long, deep, rumbling sound; as, the thunder *rolls;* **6,** to form, when being wound, the *shape* of a ball or cylinder; as, the cloth *rolls* easily; **7,** to rise and fall in gentle slopes, as land; **8,** to flatten under some kind of roller; as, dough *rolls* easily; **9,** *Colloq.,* to pile up; as, debts *roll* up quickly:—*n.* **1,** the act of turning over and over, or of tossing from side to side; **2,** the state of being rolled; **3,** that which revolves; a roller; as, a towel *roll;* **4,** anything wrapped upon itself in the form, or nearly the form, of a cylinder; as, a *roll* of oilcloth; **5,** a list of persons, generally official in character; as, a class *roll;* **6,** a kind of biscuit or bread, rolled or rounded; **7,** a continued, deep sound, as of a beaten drum, thunder, etc.; **8,** a swell or unevenness on a surface, as of a rough sea.

roll-a-way (rōl′a-wā′), *adj.* having casters for easy moving and storing; as, a *rollaway* bed.

roll-er (rōl′ẽr), *n.* **1,** anything that turns round and round, or over and over; **2,** a heavy cylinder used for grinding, smoothing, etc.; as, a hand *roller;* **3,** a small wheel on which something moves along, as on a roller skate; **4,** a long, huge wave; **5,** one of the cylinders on a clothes-wringer; **6,** a rod on which to roll up a curtain; **7,** a kind of pigeon which turns somersaults in the air; **8,** a canary with a trilling song.—*n.* **roller coaster** (an amusement railway); **roll′er—skates′; rolling stock** (railway vehicles).

rol-lick-ing (rol′ik-ing), *adj.* very jovial or gay; as, *rollicking* fun.

roll-ing (rōl′ing), *adj.* **1,** moving along by turning over and over; as, a *rolling* ball; **2,** moving on, or as on, wheels; as, a *rolling* chair; **3,** rising and falling in gentle slopes; as, *rolling* country; **4,** rumbling; as, *rolling* thunder:—*n.* **1,** the act of a person or thing that rolls; also, a person who works with a rolling tool; **2,** a deep sound.

rolling mill, 1, a mill in which metal is rolled into plates, bars, rails, etc.; **2,** a machine for so doing.

ro-ly—po-ly (rō′li-pō′li), *adj.* short and fat; dumpy; as, a *roly-poly* little girl.—*n.* such a person or thing.

ro-mance (rō-mans′; rō′mans), *n,* **1,** a long prose or poetical tale of adventure, chivalry, etc., as Malory's "Morte d'Arthur"; **2,** a novel or prose narrative full of imagination and adventure, as "Ivanhoe"; **3,** a series of acts or happenings that are strange and fanciful; **4,** a disposition to delight in what is fanciful; **5,** a falsehood:—*v.i.* [romanced, romanc-ing], **1,** to invent fanciful stories; **2,** to indulge in dreamy imaginings.—*n.* **ro-manc′er.**

Ro-man-esque (rō′man-esk′), *adj.* and *n.* a style of architecture marked by use of the round or semicircular arch, massive walls, etc.: found esp. in Italian churches of the 11th and 12th centuries.

ro-man-tic (rō-man′tik), *adj.* **1,** pertaining to, or like, what is imaginary, sentimental, or idealistic; fanciful; impractical; as, *romantic* ideas; **2,** pertaining to, or suggesting, what is strange or heroic; as, *romantic* literature; **3,** of a disposition to ignore what is real and delight in what is fanciful; as, a *romantic* girl; **4,** strangely wild and picturesque; as, *romantic* scenery; **5,** pertaining to a style of literature, art, or music, which places more value on imagination than on things as they are.

ro-man-ti-cism (rō-man′ti-sizm), *n.* **1,** the quality of being imaginative, sentimental, or extravagantly ideal; **2,** a movement in Europe at the end of the 18th century to restore imagination and feeling to literature, art, and music.—*n.* **ro-man′ti-cist.**

romp (romp), *n.* **1,** one who plays boisterously; a tomboy; **2,** rough, noisy, boisterous play:—*v.i.* to play in a rough manner.

romp-ers (romp′ẽrz), *n.pl.* an outer garment consisting of a waist with bloomers attached, worn by small children at play.

ron-deau (ron′dō; ron-dō′), *n.* a lyric poem of 3 stanzas with 5, 3, and 5 lines, respectively: the title, which forms the opening part of line 1, is repeated after lines 8 and 12, respectively: only two rhymes are used (aabba, aab, aabba): example, Col. John McCrae's "In Flanders Fields" (actually 15 lines).

Rönt-gen ray (rönt′jen; rönt′gen; rent′ gen). Same as **X-ray.**

rood (rōōd), *n.* **1,** a cross with the figure of Christ upon it; a crucifix, esp. over an altar; **2,** a measure equal to one fourth of an acre, or 40 square rods.

roof (rōōf), *n.* **1,** the top covering of a building; **2,** any similar top covering, as of a car or a cave:—*v.t.* to cover with a roof.—*n.* **roof′er.**

¹rook (rook), *n.* **1,** a European bird with glossy black plumage, similar to the crow; **2,** a cheat, esp. at dice or cards:—*v.t.* and *v.i.* to cheat; defraud.—*n.* **rook′er-y.**

²rook (rook), *n.* a piece used in chess: also called *castle.*

rook-ie (rook′i), *n. Colloq.* a first-year player in a league of professional sport (hockey, football, baseball, etc.).

room (rōōm; room), *n.* **1,** a space separated by partitions from the rest of the structure in which it is located; as, a living-*room;* **2,** space; as, there is *room* in this closet for their coats; **3,** opportunity; as, *room* for development:—*v.i.* to occupy a room or rooms:—*v.t.* to accommodate with a room or lodgings.—*n.* **room′ful.**

room-er (room/er; room/er), *n.* a lodger; one who rents a room.

room-ette (room-et/), *n.* a small, private room with folding bed and toilet facilities in a railroad sleeping car.

room-y (room/i), *adj.* [room-i-er, room-i-est], having plenty of room; spacious; as, a *roomy* garage.—*n.* **room/i-ness.**

roost (roost), *n.* **1,** the pole, perch, etc., upon which a bird rests at night; **2,** a number of fowls resting together; **3,** a temporary resting-place:—*v.i.* to sit or sleep upon a perch or pole.

roost-er (roos/ter), *n.* the domestic cock; a male fowl.

¹root (root), *n.* **1,** that part of a plant, usually growing downward into the soil, which holds the plant in place, and absorbs and stores food; **2,** in popular usage, any underground part of a plant; esp. a large part suitable for food, as a beet, turnip, etc.; **3,** anything like a root in position, use, etc.; as, the *root* of a tooth; **4,** a cause or source; as, laziness is the *root* of his poverty; **5,** in *arithmetic*, a number which, used as a factor a given number of times, produces a given number; as, since 2 × 2 × 2 = 8, 2 is the third *root* of 8; **6,** the basic part of a word, apart from prefixes, suffixes, etc.; as, "roll" is the *root* of "roller" and "enrol":—*v.t.* **1,** to plant and fix in the earth; **2,** to implant deeply; as, his dislike was *rooted* in fear; **3,** to tear or dig up by the roots; to destroy; as, to *root* out vice:—*v.i.* **1,** to take root; as, the bulbs began to *root* in February; **2,** to become firmly or permanently established; **3,** *Slang,* to support a team or a contestant by cheering, applauding, etc.: to root *for.*—*n.* **root/let** (a little root).

²root (root), *v.t.* **1,** to dig with the snout, as swine; **2,** to get by searching or hunting; as, to *root* out a secret:—*v.i.* **1,** to turn up the earth with the snout; **2,** to rummage.

root-stock (root/stok/), *n.* **1,** a creeping, underground, rootlike stem producing roots below and leaves above, as the ferns, horsetails, and club mosses: also called *rhizome;* **2,** the primary cause of anything.

rope (rop), *n.* **1,** a thick, stout cord made of several strands of hemp, cotton, etc., twined together; **2,** a collection of things braided or twined together in a line or string; as, a *rope* of pearls; **3,** a stringy thread formed in a liquid:—*v.t.* [roped, roping], **1,** to fasten, or tie with a rope; **2,** to mark or enclose by means of a rope; as, to *rope* off a field; **3,** to lasso; as, to *rope* a steer:—*v.i.* to form stringy threads, as syrup does.—*adj.* **rop/y.**

ro-quet (ro-ka/), *v.t.* and *v.i.* [-queted (-kad), -queting (-ka/ing)], in *croquet* to strike (another player's ball) with one's own ball:—*n.* the act of so striking.

ro-sa-ceous (ro-za/shus), *adj.* like a rose, esp. in having a 5-petalled corolla.

ro-sa-ry (ro/za-ri), *n.* [*pl.* rosaries], **1,** a string of beads for counting a series of prayers to be said one after the other in a certain order; also, the series of prayers thus recited; **2,** a rose bed or rose garden; a place where roses grow.

rose (roz), *n.* **1,** a thorny shrub, erect or climbing, bearing showy, fragrant flowers; also, the flower; **2,** the most typical colour of a rose; deep pink; **3,** a certain shape in which diamonds are cut.—*adv.* **ros/i-ly.**—*n.* **ros/i-ness.** —*adj.* **ros/e-ate/.**

rose-mary (roz/mer-i), *n.* [*pl.* rosemaries], a fragrant evergreen shrub. The leaves are used as a seasoning and in making perfume. It is also a symbol of remembrance and constancy.

Ro-set-ta stone (ro-zet/a), a tablet found in 1799 near Rosetta, Egypt, with parallel inscriptions in Greek, Egyptian hieroglyphics, and demotic or simplified Egyptian script: it proved the key to decipher ancient Egyptian writing.

ro-sette (ro-zet/), *n.* an ornament, as a knot or bunch of ribbon, made into the shape of a rose.

rose-wood (roz/wood/), *n.* a valuable hard, dark-red wood, usually fragrant, yielded by various tropical trees and used for fine furniture; also, any of the trees from which such wood is obtained.

ro-sin (roz/in), *n.* the resin, or solid substance, that remains after distilling crude turpentine:—*v.t.* to rub with rosin; as, to *rosin* the bow of a violin.

ros-ter (ros/ter), *n.* **1,** an enrolment or list of names; **2,** a schedule or programme; as, the *roster* of the day's events.

ros-trum (ros/trum), *n.* [*pl.* rostra (ros/tra) or rostrums], a pulpit, platform, or stage for public speaking.

ros-y (roz/i), *adj.* [ros-i-er, ros-i-est], **1,** like a rose; red; blooming; blushing; **2,** favourable; hopeful; as, *rosy* prospects.

all (ôl), ôr; up, mūte, cûr, cōōl, book; oil, out; th, thin; *th*, the.

rot (rot), *v.i.* [rot-ted, rot-ting], to decay; as, the fruit was *rotting* in the orchard:—*n.* **1**, process of decay; **2**, the state of being decayed; **3**, decayed matter; **4**, a disease of certain animals, esp. sheep; as, foot-*rot;* also, a disease or decay of plant tissues; as, dry-*rot.*

ro-ta-ry (rō′ta-ri), *adj.* **1**, turning or rotating; **2**, having parts that turn around; as, a *rotary* engine.

ro-tate (rō-tāt′; rō′tāt), *v.t.* [rotat-ed, rotat-ing], **1**, to cause to turn on, or as on, an axis; as, to *rotate* a wheel; **2**, to alternate or change about; as, to *rotate* crops:—*v.i.* **1**, to turn around on its own centre of axis; revolve; **2**, to take turns at anything; as, the members of the club *rotated* in office. —*n.* **ro-ta′tion.**—*adj.* **ro′ta-tor-y.**—*n.* **ro-ta′tor.**

rote (rōt), *n.* the repeating of words over and over to learn them, without paying much attention to their meaning; as, to learn rules by *rote.*

rot-i-fer (rō′ti-fėr), *n.* any of a group of complex, microscopic water animals, having cilia or hairlike processes that (in motion) resemble rotating wheels.

ro-to-gra-vure (rō′tō-gra-vūr′; -grā′-vūr), *n.* a photographic process for rapid printing of illustrations from plates etched on copper cylinders; a picture so printed.

ro-tor (rō′tėr), *n.* a part that revolves in a stationary part, esp. in an electrical machine.

rot-ten (rot′n), *adj.* **1**, decayed; as, *rotten* food; **2**, likely to break; not firm; as, a *rotten* plank; **3**, corrupt; dishonest.—*adv.* **rot′ten-ly.**—*n.* **rot′-ten-ness.**

ro-tund (rō-tund′), *adj.* **1**, plump; rounded out; as, a *rotund* little man; **2**, full-toned; as, a *rotund* voice.

ro-tun-da (rō-tun′da), *n.* **1**, a round hall or room, esp. one with a dome; **2**, popularly, the lobby or foyer of a hotel, theatre, etc.

rou-ble or **ru-ble** (rōō′bl), *n.* a silver coin, the monetary unit of the U.S.S.R. since 1947 (worth about 19 cents); 100 kopecks.

rou-é (rōō′ā′), *n.* an evil, dissipated man; a rake.

rouge (rōōzh), *n.* a red powder or paste used for colouring the cheeks and lips: *v.t.* and *v.i.* [rouged, roug-ing], to colour with rouge; redden.

rough (ruf), *adj.* **1**, having an uneven surface; not smooth; as, a *rough* road; *rough* cloth; **2**, not polished; unfinished;

as, *rough* diamonds; *rough* sketches; **3**, harsh; violent; as, *rough* treatment; *rough* sports; also, stormy; as, *rough* weather; **4**, not refined; rude in character; as, *rough* people:—*n.* **1**, a low, coarse fellow; a rowdy; **2**, a crude or unfinished condition; as, diamonds in the *rough;* **3**, in *golf*, the long grass bordering a fairway:—*v.t.* **1**, to make rough; ruffle; as, the bird *roughed* its feathers; **2**, to shape or sketch roughly; as, to *rough* in an outline:—**rough it,** to do without conveniences, as on a camping trip.—*adv.* **rough′ly.**—*n.* **rough′ness.**—*adj.* and *adv.* **rough′shod′;** as, to ride *roughshod* (domineer) *over:*—*v.t.* **rough′hew′.**

rough-age (ruf′ij), *n.* coarse food, as bran, vegetable fibre, etc., used in the diet to stimulate bowel movement.

rough-cast (ruf′càst′), *n.* and *v.t.* a coarse plaster for the outside of buildings; as, to *roughcast* a wall.

rough-en (ruf′n), *v.t.* to destroy the smoothness of; as, the wind *roughens* one's skin:—*v.i.* to become uneven or coarse on the surface.

rou-lette (rōō-let′), *n.* **1**, a game of chance played with a revolving disc marked off in red and black sections; **2**, small, consecutive punctures, as between some postage stamps to facilitate their separation.

round (round), *adj.* **1**, like, or nearly like, a circle or sphere in shape; as, a *round* plate; an apple is *round;* **2** having a curved surface; as, a *round* cheek; **3**, semicircular; as, opposed to pointed; as, a *round* arch; also, moving in a circle; as, a *round* dance; **4**, full or whole; as, a *round* dozen; **5**, going from and returning to, the same place; as a *round* trip; **6**, full in sound; not jarring; as, the *round* tones of a voice; **7**, outspoken; frank; as, a *round* scolding; **8**, brisk; as, a good *round* pace:—**in round numbers**, expressed approximately, as in even tens, dozens, etc.:—*n.* **1**, a circle or sphere; also, a curved part; **2**, a fixed course or route; a beat; routine; as, the day's *round* of duties; **3**, a series of events or acts; as, a *round* of gaiety; **4**, one of a series of regular periods, esp. in a game or contest; as, the *rounds* in a fight; **5**, a rung of a ladder; **6**, a cut of beef between the rump and the leg; **7**, a simultaneous volley of shots, each soldier firing once; also, the ammunition needed for such a volley, or enough for a single shot; **8**, a song sung by several persons or groups starting one after the other at intervals:—*v.t.* **1**, t give a curved or rounded form to; **2**, to travel or pass around; as, they *rounded* the cape; **3**, to bring to complete perfection or finish; as, to *round* out a plan; **4**, to drive in, or gather together; as, to *round* up cattle:—*v.i.* **1**, to become curved, spherical, or circular in form; **2**, to grow full, complete, or perfect; develop: —*adv.* **1**, in the neighbourhood; near by; as, they waited *round* for orders; **2**, in a circle or group; as, to gather *round;* **3**, in a circular motion; as, the earth goes *round;* **4**, from one side or party to another; as, he came *round* to our belief; **5**, in a complete circuit from person to person, or point to point; as, food to go *round;* **6**, by outside measure; as, a hole two inches *round;* **7**, so as to face in the opposite direction; as, to turn *round:*—*prep.* **1**, about; on every side of; as, a wall *round* a town; **2**, taking a curved or bent course to the other side of; as, walk *round* the corner.—*n.* **round′ness.** —*adv.* **round′ly.**

round-a-bout (round′a-bout′), *adj.* indirect; not straightforward; as, *roundabout* methods:—*n.* **1**, a merry-go-round; **2**, a short jacket, as for boys or sailors.

roun-de-lay (roun′de-lā′), *n.* **1**, a simple tune; **2**, a song in which a simple melody is often repeated; **3**, a dance in a circle.

roundup (round′up′), *n.* **1**, the herding together and corralling of cattle; **2**, the men and horses that herd them; **3**, any similar drive or roundup; as, a *roundup* of voters.

round-worm (round′wûrm′), *n.* a round unsegmented worm, as the pinworm, hookworm, etc.; a parasite in the intestine of man and other animals; a nematode.

roup (rōōp) *n.* a dangerous, infectious disease of poultry.—*adj.* **roup′y.**

rouse (rouz), *v.t.* [roused, rous-ing], **1**, to awaken; also, to stir to thought or action; **2**, to bring into existence; as, to *rouse* indignation:—*v.i.* **1**, to awake from sleep; **2**, to show signs of activity; as, the crowd *roused* at the sound of a shot.

roust-a-bout (roust′a-bout′), *n.* one who does odd jobs at a waterfront, ranch, circus, etc.

rout (rout), *n.* **1**, a total defeat and flight, as of an army; **2**, disorder resulting from such a defeat; **3**, a noisy crowd; mob:—*v.t.* to defeat and put to flight.

²**rout** (rout), *v.t.* **1**, to root up, as with the snout; **2**, to dig out, as with a gouging tool; **3**, *Colloq.*, to drag by force; as, to *rout* someone out of bed.

route (rōōt; rout), *n.* a way or road travelled; course; journey:—*v.t.* [rout-ed, rout-ing], to send or ship forward, as freight or express, by a certain road or railway.

rou-tine (rōō-tēn′), *n.* a customary course of action in business, pleasure, or duty.

rove (rōv), *v.t.* and *v.i.* [roved, rov-ing], to wander aimlessly (over); to ramble; as, buffaloes *roved* over the land.—*n.* **rov′er.**

¹**row** (rō), *n.* **1**, a series of persons or things in a line; **2**, a line of houses side by side on a street; also, the street.

²**row** (rō), *v.i.* **1**, to move a boat by means of oars; as, John has learned to *row;* **2**, to be moved by means of oars; as, the boat *rows* easily:—*v.t.* **1**, to propel by means of oars; **2**, to carry in a boat; as, he *rowed* her across:—*n.* the act of moving a boat by oars; also, a trip taken in a rowboat.

³**row** (rou), *n. Colloq.*, a noisy quarrel; brawl; fight:—*v.i. Colloq.*, to quarrel.

row-boat (rō′bōt′), *n.* a boat propelled by means of oars.

row-dy (rou′di), *n.* [*pl.* rowdies], a rough fellow; ruffian:—*adj.* [row-di-er, row-di-est], disorderly; rough.—*n.* **row′di-ness; row′dy-ism.**

row-lock (rō′lok; rul′uk), *n.* a notch, a pair of wooden pins, or a piece of metal with a U-shaped top, in which the oar rests in a rowboat: also called *oarlock.*

roy-al (roi′al), *adj.* **1**, pertaining to, or belonging to, a king; kingly; as, the *royal* household; **2**, pertaining to, or connected with a kingdom; as, the *royal* navy; **3**, suited to or like a king; regal; as, *royal* dignity:—*n.* a small sail above the top-gallant sail and under the skysail.—*n.* **roy′a-list.**

roy-al-ly (roi′al-i), *adv.* in a grand manner.

roy-al-ty (roi′al-ti), *n.* [*pl.* royalties], **1**, the station, dignity, etc., of a king; **2**, the king himself; also, any person of sovereign rank; as, *royalty* was present at the theatre; **3**, kingly nature or quality; **4**, a tax paid to the crown; **5**, a share of the profits paid to the owner for the use of a property; **6**, a percentage paid to an inventor or author for the use of a patent or copyright; as, *royalties* from the sale of a book.

rub (rub), *v.t.* [rubbed, rub-bing], **1,** to cause (a surface) to undergo friction and pressure; as, to *rub* one's face with a towel; **2,** to touch with a scraping or brushing movement; as, the wheel *rubbed* my dress; **3,** to cause to move over something with pressure; as, to *rub* the eraser over the paper; **4,** to cleanse or scour by rubbing; as, she *rubbed* the silver with a cloth; **5,** to erase; as, to *rub* out a mark; **6,** to cause to penetrate; spread; as, to *rub* wax on a floor:—*v.i.* **1,** to move along a surface with pressure; scrape; as, two things *rub* together; **2,** to get along with difficulty; as, to *rub* along somehow:—*n.* **1,** the use of friction and pressure upon a surface; a rubbing; as, give the table a good *rub;* **2,** that which makes progress difficult; a hindrance; as, what's the *rub?*—*n.* **rub′down′.**

¹**rub-ber** (rub′ẽr),*n.***1,** one who polishes, erases, massages, or rubs in any way; **2,** anything used for erasing, polishing, as, a *rubber* on a pencil; **3,** the prepared, solidified sap from various tropical trees, used for waterproofing, insulating, etc.; caoutchouc: also called *india-rubber;* **4,** an article made of this, as an overshoe or an elastic band:—*adj.* made of, like, or pertaining to, rubber. —*adj.* **rub′ber-y.**

²**rub-ber** (rub′ẽr), *n.* specifically, in the game of bridge, the winning of two games out of three; also, the games played until one side has won two; sometimes, the third, decisive game played after each side has won one; hence, generally, any game that breaks a tie.

rub-bish (rub′ish), *n.* anything value-less; trash.

rub-ble (rub′l), *n.* rough, broken stone, brick, etc., or masonry built from it.

ru-by (rōō′bi), *n.* [*pl.* rubies], **1,** a precious stone, varying in colour from carmine to crimson; **2,** the colour of the stone.

ruck (ruk), *n.* the general run of common persons or things; as, a horse left *in the ruck* (the horses undistinguished behind the leaders).

ruck-sack (ruk′sak′), *n.* a knapsack for hikers, etc.

ruck-us (ruk′us), *n. Colloq.* row; noisy disturbance; uproar.

ruc-tion (ruk′shun), *n. Slang,* commotion; free-for-all; row. Usually *pl.*

rud-der (rud′ẽr), *n.* **1,** a broad, flat piece of wood or metal, hinged vertically to the stern of a vessel and used for steering; **2,** a similar part in an aeroplane.—*adj.* **rud′der-less.**

rud-dy (rud′i), *adj.* [rud-di-er, rud-di-est], **1,** red or reddish; as, a warm, *ruddy* glow; **2,** having the colour of good health; as, a *ruddy* complexion. —*n.* **rud′di-ness.**

rude (rōōd), *adj.* [rud-er, rud-est], **1,** primitive; uncivilized; as, a *rude* people; **2,** impolite; disrespectful; as, *rude* behaviour; **3,** crude; unskilful; as, a *rude* carving; **4,** rough; severe; as, a *rude* awakening.

ru-di-ment (rōō′di-ment), *n.* **1,** one of the first principles of an art, science, etc.; as, the *rudiments* of algebra; **2,** in *biology,* a part or organ partially developed; as, the *rudiments* of antlers. —*adj.* **ru′di-men′ta-ry.**

rue (rōō), *v.t.* [rued, ru-ing], to be sorry for; wish undone; as, he shall *rue* his wicked deeds:—*n.* remorse; regret.— *adj.* **rue′ful.**

¹**ruff** (ruf), *n.* **1,** a large pleated or fluted collar, worn in the 16th and 17th centuries; **2,** anything like such a collar, as a prominent growth of feathers round the neck of a bird.—*adj.* **ruffed.**

²**ruff** (ruf), *v.t.* to trump (an opponent's card) when one has no card of the suit led:—*v.i.* to play a trump.

ruffed grouse, a partridge ranging from Alaska to Nova Scotia and south to Georgia and California; a superior game bird, it is conspicuous with black band near tip of tail, and crest on head.

ruf-fi-an (ruf′i-an; ruf′yan), *n.* a brutal, lawless fellow; one given to cruel deeds:—*adj.* brutal; cruel; violent; as, *ruffian* rage.

ruf-fle (ruf′l), *n.* a pleated or gathered strip of material used as a trimming: —*v.t.* [ruf-fled, ruf-fling], **1,** to draw into folds or plaits; **2,** to furnish or adorn with plaited or gathered strips; **3,** to cause to stand up or out; as, a bird *ruffles* its feathers; **4,** to disturb slightly or make ripples upon; as, the wind *ruffled* the pond; **5,** to disarrange; disorder (the hair); **6,** to annoy or vex: —*v.i.* **1,** to form small folds; **2,** to become vexed or annoyed.

rug (rug), *n.* **1,** a heavy floor-covering, usually made in one piece and often of a size to cover only part of the floor; **2,** a skin or a piece of heavy cloth used as a robe or blanket.

rug-by (rug′bi), *n.* a kind of football first played at Rugby, Warwickshire, the forerunner of modern Canadian and U.S. football.

rug-ged (rug′id), *adj.* **1,** having an uneven surface; rough; as, *rugged* country; also, steep and rocky; as, a *rugged* cliff; **2,** crude; plain; as, a *rugged* peasant; **3,** hard; austere; harsh; as, a *rugged* character; **4,** healthy; strong.—*n.* rug′ged-ness.

ru-in (rōo′in), *n.* **1,** overthrow; destruction; downfall; as, political *ruin;* also, a cause of destruction; **2, ruins,** the remains of a building destroyed or fallen into decay; as, the *ruins* of an old castle; **3,** the state of decay or desolation:—*v.t.* to pull down, overthrow, or destroy; as, the scandal *ruined* his career.—*n.* ru′in-a′tion.

ru-in-ous (rōo′i-nus), *adj.* **1,** bringing or causing ruin; destructive; as, a *ruinous* war; **2,** dilapidated; as, a barn in a *ruinous* state.—*adv.* ru′in-ous-ly.

rule (rōol), *n.* **1,** a standard or principle of conduct; as, the golden *rule;* school *rules;* an established usage or law, as in arithmetic or grammar; **2,** government; authority; as, a country under foreign *rule;* **3,** usual course of action; as, he works late as a *rule;* **4,** that which may be generally expected; as, scholarship is the *rule* in a university; **5,** a straight-edged strip of wood or metal, marked off in inches, used in drawing lines or measuring:—*v.t.* [ruled, rul-ing], **1,** to govern; as, to *rule* a country; **2,** to guide, influence, or control; as, he was *ruled* by hatred; **3,** to establish by a decision, as does a court; **4,** to mark with lines by the use of a ruler:—*v.i.* **1,** in *law,* to decide a point; **2,** to exercise superior authority; as, he *ruled* over the country for ten years.

rul-er (rōol′ẽr), *n.* **1,** one who governs; as, a wise *ruler;* **2,** a strip of wood, metal, etc., used in drawing lines or in measuring.

rul-ing (rōol′ing), *adj.* chief; predominant:—*n.* **1,** a decision laid down by a judge or court; **2,** the act of making lines; also, ruled lines.

¹rum (rum), *n.* **1,** a strong, alcoholic liquor made from molasses or the juice of the sugar-cane; **2,** any intoxicating drink.

²rum (rum), *adj. Slang,* **1,** queer; odd; as, a *rum* customer; **2,** rowdyish; dangerous.—*adj.* rum′my.

rum-ba (rum′ba), *n.* **1,** a dance of Cuban-Negro origin, marked by rhythmic movements of the lower part of the body; **2,** the music for it. Also, rhum′ba.

rum-ble (rum′bl), *n.* **1,** a low, heavy, rolling sound; as, the *rumble* of city traffic; **2,** a seat for servants at the back of a carriage; **3,** in an automobile, a folding outside seat at the back: also called *rumble-seat:*—*v.i.* and *v.t.* rum-bled, rum-bling], to make, or cause to make, rumbling sounds.

ru-mi-nant (rōo′mi-nant), *n.* and *adj.* any hoofed, four-footed animal that chews a cud, esp. the cow, bison, goat, deer, camel, giraffe, and llama.

ru-mi-nate (rōo′mi-nāt′), *v.i.* [ruminat-ed, ruminat-ing], **1,** to chew the cud; **2,** to meditate or muse; reflect; as, to *ruminate* on the future.—*n.* ru′mi-na′tion.

rum-mage (rum′ij), *n.* a thorough search made by turning things over in a disorderly way:—*v.t.* [rummaged, rummag-ing], to search thoroughly by turning over the contents of; ransack: —*v.i.* to make a thorough but disorderly search; as, to *rummage* in a closet.

rum-my (rum′i), *n.* a card game in which the aim is to match cards into sets of the same denomination or sequences of the same suit.

ru-mour (rōo′mẽr), *n.* **1,** talk; hearsay; **2,** a current story that has not been verified; as, a *rumour* of strikes:—*v.t.* to spread by report. In U.S. usage, ru′mor.

rump (rump), *n.* the hind part of an animal; the buttocks; also, a cut of beef from this part.

rum-ple (rum′pl), *n.* a wrinkle or crease:—*v.t.* and *v.i.* [rum-pled, rumpling], to wrinkle; muss; as, to *rumple* cloth.

rum-pus (rum′pus), *n.* and *adj. Colloq.,* a disturbance; brawl; shindy: —**rumpus room,** a (basement or attic) recreation room.

run (run), *v.i.* [*p.t.* ran (ran), *p.p.* run, *p.pr.* run-ning], **1,** to go on the feet at a speed faster than a walk; depart suddenly; **2,** to hurry; rush; as, he ran through his work too fast; **3,** to travel; proceed; as the express *runs* 60 miles an hour; **4,** to make regular trips; as, a bus *runs* between Toronto and Hamilton; **5,** to move in a stream; flow, as a river; **6,** to act; be in action; operate; as, the engine will not *run;* **7,** to extend; be placed; as, a path *runs* round the house; **8,** to become unfastened; ravel; as, a thread *runs* in a stocking; **9,** to engage in a contest; be a competitor; as, to *run* for office; **10,** to climb; creep; trail; as, the vine *runs* along the wall; **11,** to be written or related; as, so the story *runs;* 12, to spread or dissolve; as, dye *runs;* 13, to discharge a fluid; ooze; as, the nose *runs;* a sore *runs:*—*v.t.* 1, *Colloq.*, to cause to move or operate; as, to *run* an engine; to *run* a theatre; 2, to thrust; stick; as, to *run* a pin into one's finger; 3, to drive or dash forcibly; as, to *run* one's head against a wall; 4, to do by running; as, to *run* errands; 5, to go through (some danger) successfully; as, to *run* a blockade; 6, to expose oneself to; as, to *run* a risk; 7, to permit to mount up, as debts; 8, to sew with small, even stitches; as, to *run* a seam:—*n.* 1, the act or power of going at a pace swifter than a walk; 2, a trip or journey; progress; as, the boat made its usual *run;* 3, the act of flowing or that which flows; as, a *run* of maple sap; 4, a course or succession; repetition; as, a *run* of ill luck; 5, the average kind; as, the *run* of workers; 6, a place passed over frequently by animals; also, an enclosed place for animals; 7, a herd of animals or school of fish moving together; 8, a period of operation; as, the play had a year's *run;* 9, sudden and pressing demand; as, a *run* on a bank; 10, in baseball, cricket, etc., the unit of scoring, made by running once over a specified course; 11, a brook; 12, *Colloq.*, free use or enjoyment; as, the *run* of a friend's house—*adj.* and *n*.**run′—down′; run′—in′; run′—off′.**

run-a-bout (run′a-bout′), *n.* 1, a light, motorcar or carriage; 2, a light motorboat; 3, one who gads about.

run-a-way (run′a-wā′), *n.* 1, one who escapes; a fugitive; 2, the act of running away; also, a horse of which the driver has lost control:—*adj.* 1, escaping from control; as, a *runaway* engine; 2, brought about by eloping, or running away; as, a *runaway* wedding.

¹rung (rung), *n.* a crosspiece or round, esp. of a ladder or a chair.

rung (rung), *p.p.* of *ring.*

run-nel (run′el), *n.* a small stream; brook. Also, **run′let.**

run-ner (run′ėr), *n.* 1, one who runs, as a racer, a messenger, etc.; 2, one of the long, narrow pieces on which a sleigh, skate, or sled moves; 3, a long strip of linen or carpet; 4, a vertical rip in a stocking; 5, a slender, trailing branch that takes root at the end or at the joints; also, a plant that spreads in this way.—*n.* **run′ner(s)—up′.**

runt (runt), *n.* 1, any undersized

animal; especially, the smallest and weakest of a litter; 2, a person of stunted growth.

run-way (run′wā), *n.* 1, a beaten way or path along which animals pass; 2, a track, as for the take-off of aeroplanes; 3, a fenced place; as, a *runway* for dogs.

ru-pee (rōō-pē′), *n.* a silver coin, the monetary unit of India, worth about 20 cents (in Pakistan, about 30 cents).

rup-ture (rup′tūr), *n.* 1, a bursting or breaking apart; 2, the state of being broken or violently burst apart; 3, a breach or an interruption of friendly relations; 4, a hernia:—*v.t.* [ruptured, ruptur-ing], 1, to burst violently apart; 2, to cause a hernia to; 3, to bring about a breach of (friendship): —*v.i.* to suffer a breach or break.

ru-ral (rōō′ral), *adj.* pertaining to, or like, the country or country life.

ruse (rōōz), *n.* a trick; fraud or deceit.

¹rush (rush), *n.* any of certain plants growing in wet ground, having long hollow stems, which are used for caning chairs.

²rush (rush), *v.i.* 1, to move with great speed; press forward with violent haste; 2, to act with extraordinary haste or eagerness; as, to *rush* through one's work:—*v.t.* 1, to cause to move or act with great speed; hurry; as, to *rush* an order; 2, to make an attack upon and occupy; as, to *rush* a fortification:—*n.* 1, a driving forward with eagerness and haste; 2, a sudden migration; as, a gold-*rush;* 3, *Colloq.*, extraordinary activity; as, the Christmas *rush:*—*adj.* requiring haste; as, a *rush* job.

rusk (rusk), *n.* 1, a sweet, raised bread rebaked in the oven until browned and crisp; 2, a light, soft, sweetened biscuit.

rus-set (rus′it), *n.* 1, a reddish-brown colour; 2, cloth, esp. homespun, of such colour; 3, a kind of winter apple:—*adj.* reddish brown in colour.

rust (rusṭ), *n.* 1, the reddish matter formed on iron and steel and some other metals through exposure to air; red oxide of iron; 2, anything like rust, as mildew on wheat, corn, etc.:—*v.i.* 1, to form rust; 2, to grow worthless because of idleness:—*v.t.* to cause to rust.—*adj.* **rust′y.**—*n.* **rust′i-ness.**—*adj.* **rust′less; rust′proof′.**

rus-tic (rus′tik), *n.* a person reared in the country, esp. one who is unpolished: —*adj.* 1, relating to the country; 2, simple; artless; 3, awkward; crude. —*n.* **rus-tic′i-ty.**—*v.i.* **rus′ti-cate′.**

rus-tle (rus′l), *n.* a soft, crackling sound, such as that made by leaves: —*v.i.* [rus-tled, rus-tling], to make a soft, crackling sound, as taffeta when moved:—*v.t.* **1,** to cause to make such a sound; **2,** to steal (cattle).—*n.* **rus′tler.**

rut (rut), *n.* **1,** a hollow track or groove made by a wheel; **2,** a fixed habit:—*v.t.* [rut-ted, rut-ting], to cut into hollows; make wheel tracks in.—*adj.* **rut′ty.**

ru-ta-ba-ga (rōō′ta-bā′ga), *n. Swedish,* the yellow turnip: used now of any table turnip washed, waxed, and ready for market.

ruth-less (rōōth′lis), *adj.* cruel; without mercy; savage; as, a *ruthless* fighter.—*adv.* **ruth′less-ly.**—*n.* **ruth** (pity).

rye (rī), *n.* a hardy cereal plant closely related to wheat; also, its seed, used in making bread and whisky.

S

S, s (es), *n.* [*pl.* S's, s's], **1,** the 19th letter of the alphabet; **2,** anything having the shape of an S.

Sab-bath (sab′ath), *n.* **1,** the seventh day of the week, observed by the Jews and certain others as a day of rest, commencing at sunset on Friday and ending at sunset on Saturday; **2,** the Christian Sunday, or the first day of the week, observed as a day of rest and worship.

sab-bat-i-cal (sa-bat′i-kl), *adj.* relating to (a) the Sabbath; as, *Sabbatical* peace (b) a period of absence for study, travel, rest, etc.; as, a *sabbatical* leave or year (sometimes every seventh for teachers in colleges, etc.).

sa-ble (sā′bl), *n.* **1,** a small, flesh-eating animal valued for its handsome, dark fur; **2,** the fur of this animal:—*adj.* **1,** made of the fur of the sable; as, a *sable* coat; **2,** very dark; black; as, *sable* night.

sa-ble-fish (sā′bl-fish′), *n.* a large, edible, mackerellike fish common off the southern B.C. coast and northward.

sa-bo-tage (sab′o-tàzh′; -tij), *n.* malicious or wanton destruction, esp. of an employer's property during a strike, or of a country's resources or equipment in wartime.—*n.* **sab′o-teur′** (-tûr).

sa-bre or **sa-ber** (sā′bėr), *n.* a cavalry sword with a curved blade—*v.t.* to cut down with a sabre.

sa-bre—toothed ti-ger, a fierce tigerlike mammal, with long, curved, upper canine teeth: it lived from one to forty million years ago.

sac (sak), *n.* a baglike part of a plant or an animal, often containing a fluid.

sac-cha-rin (sak′a-rin), *n.* a crystalline substance about 400 times sweeter than sugar, used as a cheap sugar substitute by diabetics, and in the manufacture of candy, jam, etc.—*adj.* **sac′cha-rine** (-rin; -rīn′).

sac-er-do-tal (sas′ėr-dō′tal), *adj.* pertaining to a priest; priestly; as, *sacerdotal* robes.

sa-chem (sā′chem), *n.* a hereditary chief of the highest rank, as of the Iroquois, Algonquins, etc.

sa-chet (sa′shā; sa-shā′), *n.* a small bag or cushion filled with a perfume in the form of powder; also, the powder.

¹sack (sak), *n.* **1,** a bag; esp. a large coarse bag open at one end, for holding grain, potatoes, etc.; **2,** a sackful; as a *sack* of sugar; **3,** (often *sacque*), a loose jacket worn by women and children; **4,** *Slang,* dismissal; as, to get the *sack:* —*v.t.* to put into a bag.—*n.* **sack′ful.**

²sack (sak), *n.* the plundering by soldiers of a town taken in war; as, the *sack* of Rome by the Vandals:—*v.t.* **1,** to plunder or pillage; ravage; **2,** to rob; ransack.

sack-cloth (sak′klôth′), *n.* **1,** a coarse material of which sacks are made; **2,** a coarse, rough cloth worn in ancient times as a token of mourning or repentance.

sack-ing (sak′ing), *n.* a coarse flax, hemp, or jute cloth used for sacks, bags, etc.

sac-ra-ment (sak′ra-ment), *n.* **1,** a religious act or ceremony regarded as an outward, visible sign of inward, spiritual grace, as baptism and the Eucharist, or Lord's Supper; **2,** (also *Sacrament*), the consecrated elements of the Eucharist.—*adj.* **sac′ra-ment′al.**

sa-cred (sā′krid), *adj.* **1,** set apart for religious uses; consecrated; holy; as, a *sacred* edifice; **2,** pertaining to religion; as, *sacred* literature; **3,** to be treated with reverence; not to be violated; as, a *sacred* trust.

sac-ri-fice (sak′ri-fīs′), *n.* **1,** the act of presenting an offering to God or to a god; **2,** that which is offered; anything offered or consecrated to God; **3,** the giving up of something in order to gain something else; as, the *sacrifice* of leisure time for money; also, self-sacrifice; **4,** a price below cost; as, the house sold at a *sacrifice*:—*v.t.* [sak′ri-fīs′], [sacrificed, sacrific-ing], **1,** to offer to God or to a god; **2,** to give up for the sake of some other person or object; as, to *sacrifice* health for riches; **3,** to sell at a loss:—*v.i.* to offer up a sacrifice.—*adj.* **sac′ri-fi′cial** (sak′ri-fish′al): **—sacrifice bunt,** in *baseball*, the bunting of the ball by the batter in such a way that, though he is put out, a base-runner advances:—**sacrifice fly,** when there are fewer than two outs, a long fly that enables a runner to score from third base.

sac-ri-le-gious (sak′ri-lē′jus; sak′ri-lij′us), *adj.* treating sacred things irreverently; profane.—*n.* **sac′ri-lege.**

sac-ro-sanct (sak′rō-sangkt′), *adj.* very holy, sacred, or inviolable: said of persons, obligations, laws, things, etc. (often ironically).

sad (sad), *adj.* [sad-der, sad-dest], **1,** full of grief; mournful; doleful; **2,** causing mournfulness; as, a *sad* event.—*v.t.* and *v.i.* **sad′den.**

sad-dle (sad′l), *n.* **1,** a padded leather seat for a rider on horseback; also, the seat of a bicycle; **2,** the part of a horse's harness which rests on the horse's back; **3,** anything shaped like a saddle, as a cut of meat consisting of the two loins; **4,** a ridge between two hills or summits:—*v.t.* [sad-dled, sad-dling], **1,** to equip with a seat for a rider; **2,** to burden or embarrass; as, to be *saddled* with debt.—*n.* **sad′dler.**

sa-dism (sād′izm; sad′), *n.* a form of sex perversion marked by love of cruelty; any abnormal tendency to inflict pain.—*n.* **sa′dist.**—*adj.* **sa-dis′tic.**

saf-a-ri (sa-fär′i; suf′a-rē′), *n.* an expedition or journey, esp. for hunting (as in eastern Africa); a caravan.

¹**safe** (sāf), *adj.* [saf-er, saf-est], **1,** free from danger or harm; as, *safe* and sound; **2,** out of danger; secure; as, the soldier was *safe* from pursuit; **3,** incapable of doing injury or harm; securely kept, as a prisoner; **4,** reliable; trustworthy; involving no risk of loss; as, a *safe* investment.—*adv.* **safe′ly.**

²**safe** (sāf), *n.* a steel chest, usually fire-proof or burglar-proof, specially designed for safeguarding money and other valuables.

safe—con-duct (sāf′–kon′dukt), *—n.* a guard, or document, to guarantee safe passage (in wartime).

safe-guard (sāf′gärd′), *n.* a person or thing that guards or protects; a means of security; defence; as, traffic lights are a *safeguard* for both pedestrians and motorists:—*v.t.* to protect or defend.

safe-keep-ing (sāf′kēp′ing), *n.* care; protection.

safe-ty (sāf′ti), *n.* freedom from danger, injury, or damage; security:—*adj.* protecting against accident or injury; as, *safety* devices.—*n.* **safe′ty—pin′.**

saf-fron (saf′run), *n.* **1,** a purple-flowered, fall-blooming species of crocus; **2,** the yellow colour obtained from the dried stigmas of this plant, used as a dye and in medicine; **3,** a deep-yellow colour:—*adj.* deep yellow.

sag (sag), *v.i.* [sagged, sag-ging], **1,** to sink or droop in the middle, from weight or pressure; as, the wire *sags*; **2,** to lean to one side; become lopsided; as, the door *sags*; **3,** to lose firmness; weaken; as, his spirits *sagged*:—*n.* the fact or the extent of sinking or drooping under weight or pressure; as, the *sag* of a door.

sa-ga (sä′ga), *n.* a story of heroic achievement or marvellous adventure, as in heroic Scandinavian legends.

sa-ga-cious (sa-gā′shus), *adj.* having good judgment; shrewd; as, a *sagacious* ruler.—*n.* **sa-gac′i-ty** (sa-gas′-i-ti).

sag-a-more (sag′a-mōr′), *n.* a hereditary North American Indian chief of secondary rank (below *sachem*); a sachem.

¹**sage** (sāj), *adj.* [sag-er, sag-est], wise; shrewd:—*n.* an extremely wise man.

²**sage** (sāj), *n.* **1,** a plant of the mint family, whose spicy, dull-green leaves are used for flavouring meats, soups, etc.; **2,** the American sagebrush.

sage-brush (sāj′brush′), *n.* a low shrub of the plains of the western U.S.

Sag-it-ta-ri-us (saj′i-târ′i-us), *n.* **1,** the 9th sign of the zodiac (♐); **2,** a constellation, the Archer (a centaur drawing his bow).

sa-go (sā′gō), *n.* [*pl.* sagos], **1,** a powdered starch used in puddings, soups, etc., obtained from the pith of certain East Indian palms; **2,** a palm tree from which sago is made. Also, *sago palm.*

sa-hib (sä′ib), *n.* in India, a title

formerly used by natives to Europeans, signifying lord, master, or sir.

said (sed), *p.t.* and *p.p.* of *say*.

sail (sāl), *n*. 1, a sheet of canvas or cloth which is rigged to the masts and spars of a vessel and extended to catch the wind; 2, all the sails of a ship; as, under full *sail*; 3, (*pl.* sail), any ship; as, a squadron of 50 *sail*; 4, an excursion in a sailboat; as, we went for a *sail*; 5, anything resembling a sail, as the arms of a windmill:—*v.i.* 1, to be driven or propelled by the force of the wind upon spread canvas; 2, hence, to go by water; as, we *sailed* to Liverpool; 3, to begin a voyage; as, the ship *sailed* at noon; 4, to glide smoothly; as, the eagle *sailed* through the air:—*v.t.* 1, to pass over in a ship; as, to *sail* the seas; 2, to navigate or steer (a ship). *n.* **sail′boat′**.

sail-fish (sāl′fish′), *n*. a large game fish with a large sail-like dorsal fin. As in the swordfish, its upper jaw lengthens out into a swordlike projection.

sail-or (sāl′ẽr), *n*. 1, a member of the crew of a vessel; a seaman; 2, a straw hat with a flat brim and crown.

saint (sānt), *n*. 1, a person of exceptionally upright or holy life; 2, one of the blessed in heaven; 3, in the Roman Catholic Church, an exceptionally godly person, who, after death, is declared holy by the church:—*v.t.* to canonize; declare officially to be a saint.—*adj.* **saint′ly**.—*n.* **saint′hood**; **saint′li-ness**.

saint-ed (sān′tid), *adj*. 1, pious; also, sacred; holy; 2, canonized.

sake (sāk), *n*. 1, purpose; cause; as, for the *sake* of argument; 2, one's own welfare or the welfare of others; as, for my own *sake;* for my country's *sake*.

sa-laam (sa-läm′), *n*. and *v.i.* an Oriental greeting or salutation: a low bow with right palm on forehead.

sal-a-ble (sāl′a-bl), *adj*. capable of being sold; easily sold; as, a *salable* commodity. Also spelled **sale′a-ble**. —*n.* **sal′a-bil′i-ty**.

sa-la-cious (sa-lā′shus), *n*. lewd; tending to provoke lust; as, *salacious* fiction, pictures, etc.

sal-ad (sal′ad), *n*. a cold dish, as of lettuce with vegetables, fruit, meat, fish, etc., mixed with, or covered by, dressing.

sal-a-man-der (sal′a-man′dẽr), *n*. 1, a small, lizardlike but scaleless, animal living in water or damp places: formerly fabled to live unharmed in fire; 2, hence, one who can bear intense heat.

sa-la-mi (sa-lä′mi), *n*. a salted, garlic-flavoured sausage, dried or smoked so as to keep indefinitely in a dry atmosphere.

sal-a-ry (sal′a-ri), *n*. [*pl.* salaries], a regular, periodic payment for services; as, teachers receive a monthly *salary*. —*adj.* **sal′a-ried**.

sale (sāl), *n*. 1, the act of selling; the exchange of a commodity or goods for an agreed price; as, to arrange for the *sale* of a house; 2, a disposal of goods at a reduced price, by auction or in some other special way; as, the store is holding its annual *sale;* 3, a chance to dispose of goods; a demand for goods; as, there is a great *sale* for toys at Christmas.

sale-a-ble (sāl′a-bl), *adj*. Same as **salable**.

sales-man (sālz′man), *n*. [*pl.* salesmen (-men)], a man whose business it is to sell goods.—*n.fem.* **sales′wom′an**.— **sales′man-ship′**.

sa-li-ent (sā′li-ent), *adj*. 1, outstanding; conspicuous; noticeable; as, a *salient* angle (of a defended position). —*n.* projecting line of battle, trenches, etc.

sa-line (sā′līn), *adj*. 1, consisting of, or containing, salt or a salt; as, a *saline* solution; 2, pertaining to salt; salty; as, a *saline* taste.—*n.* **sa-lin′i-ty**.

sa-li-va (sa-lī′va), *n*. the watery fluid secreted by the salivary glands and discharged into the mouth; spit.—*adj.* **sal′i-var-y** (sal′i-vẽr-i).

sal-low (sal′ō), *adj*. of a pale, sickly yellow colour; as, the *sallow* complexion of a confined invalid.—*n.* **sal′low-ness**.

sal-ly (sal′i), *n*. [*pl.* sallies], 1, a sudden rushing forth of troops from a fortified place to attack the enemy; 2, a sudden outburst of wit or fancy; as, his *sally* made the crowd laugh:—*v.i.* [sallied, sally-ing], 1, to rush out, as troops from a besieged town; 2, to set out, as on a pleasure trip.

salm-on (sam′un), *n*. [*pl.* salmon], 1, a silver-scaled, salt-water or fresh-water fish, prized as a game and food fish; 2, the orange-pink colour of cooked salmon flesh:—*adj.* of an orange-pink colour:—**salmon trout**, 1, any of various large salmonlike fishes of North American lakes and rivers; 2, the smaller European sea trout.

sa-lon (sa-lon′; så′lōn′), *n*. [*pl.* salons (så′lon′; så′lônz′)], 1, a large reception-room; 2, a group of distinguished persons who meet from time to time for discussions or social intercourse; **3,** an art gallery; also, the paintings or sculpture exhibited there.

sa-loon (sa-lōōn′), *n.* **1,** a large room or apartment in a hotel or on a steamship, often elaborately decorated and used for exhibitions, receptions, etc; as, a dining-*saloon;* **2,** in the U.S., a tavern or barroom where liquors are sold.

salt (sôlt), *n.* a white, crystalline substance found in sea water, mineral springs, etc., and used universally for seasoning foods and preserving meats; **2,** anything which, like salt, gives flavour or character; savour; **3,** in *chemistry,* a compound, generally crystalline, formed by the union of an acid with a base; **4, salts,** in *medicine,* a substance resembling salt, used as a cathartic; **5,** *Colloq.,* a sailor:—*adj.* **1,** flavoured or seasoned with salt; **2,** preserved with salt; **3,** growing in salt water; as, *salt* weed:—*v.t.* **1,** to preserve with salt; as, to *salt* meat; **2,** to sprinkle or season with salt; **3,** to furnish with salt; as, to *salt* cattle. —*adj.* **salt′y.**—*n.* **salt′i-ness.**

salt-cel-lar (sôlt′sel′ẽr), *n.* a dish or shaker used on the table to hold salt.

salt-pe-tre (sôlt′pē′tẽr), *n.* a white, crystalline compound used in making gunpowder and matches, and in preserving foods.

sa-lu-bri-ous (sa-lū′bri-us), *adj.* healthful; wholesome; as, a *salubrious* climate.

sal-u-tar-y (sal′ū-tẽr-i), *adj.* **1,** producing health; as, *salutary* exercises; **2,** promoting good; as, *salutary* reforms.

sal-u-ta-tion (sal′ū-tā′shun), *n.* the act or manner of addressing or greeting another; also, the words or the gestures used.

sa-lute (sa-lūt′), *n.* **1,** a greeting; **2,** a gesture, bow, etc., expressing welcome, respect, etc.; **3,** in the army and navy, a gesture or position prescribed for respectful recognition of a superior officer, consisting of raising the fingers to the cap; also, the discharge of cannon, the lowering and raising again of a flag, etc., as a mark of honour:—*v.t.* [salut-ed, salut-ing], **1,** to address with words or gestures of greeting; **2,** in the army and navy, to honour or receive with an official salute or with a formal demonstration, as a discharge of guns, the lowering of a flag, etc.; as, the private *saluted* the captain; the fleet *saluted* the King with a discharge of 21 guns:—*v.i.* to make a gesture of respect.

sal-vage (sal′vij), *n.* **1,** the act of saving

a ship or goods from the sea, from a wreck, from a fire, etc.; **2,** the ship or the goods so saved; **3,** payment given to those who help to save property under such circumstances:—*v.t.* [salvaged, salvaging], to save (a ship or goods) from destruction.

sal-va-tion (sal-vā′shun), *n.* **1,** the act of saving; rescue; **2,** the setting free of the soul from sin and from eternal punishment; **3,** that which saves or rescues; as, a raft was their *salvation* from the sea.

¹**salve** (såv), *n.* **1,** an ointment or greasy mixture, used for the relief and healing of wounds and sores on the skin; **2,** anything that calms, soothes, or pacifies; as, the compliment *salved* his wounded pride.

²**salve** (salv), *v.t.* [salved, salv-ing], to salvage (a ship or its cargo).

sal-ver (sal′vẽr), *n.* a tray, as for refreshments, visiting cards, letters, etc.

sal-vi-a (sal′vi-a), *n.* a plant of the mint family grown for its showy, scarlet flowers.

sal-vo (sal′vō), *n.* a simultaneous discharge of artillery, etc., often as a salute; **2,** a burst of cheers; as, a *salvo* of applause.

sam-ba (sam′ba), *n.* a Brazilian dance of African origin, distinguished by a dip with knee-bending and springing up in time to the music.

same (sām), *adj.* **1,** being one; identical; as, he goes to the *same* school as his sister; **2,** similar in kind or quality; as, suits of the *same* cloth; **3,** equal; as, the *same* distance; **4,** just mentioned; as, these *same* words:—*pron.* the identical person or thing; as, give me more of the *same.*—*n.* **same′ness.**

sam-o-var (sam′o-vär′), *n.* a (Russian) tea-urn with a heating tube through the centre.

sam-pan (sam′pan), *n.* a flat-bottomed Chinese river or harbour skiff, with roofing of mats, and propelled by a single scull over the stern.

sam-ple (sam′pl), *n.* a specimen; model; pattern; also, a part of something, by which the whole is judged; as, she showed us a *sample* of the silk:—*v.t.* [sam-pled, sam-pling], to test by trying a small piece; as, to *sample* candy.

san-a-tor-i-um (san′a-tōr′i-um), *n.* [*pl.* sanatoria (san′a-tōr′i-a) or sanatoriums], **1,** a health resort; **2,** an institution for the care of invalids; a sanitarium.

sanc-ti-fy (sangk′ti-fī′), *v.t.* [sanctified, sanctify-ing], **1,** to make holy; set apart for some sacred use; as, "God blessed the seventh day and *sanctified* it"; **2,** to purify (human beings) from sin.—*n.* **sanc′ti-fi-ca′tion.**

sanc-ti-mo-ni-ous (sangk′ti-mō′ni-us), *adj.* making a show of piety or holiness; as, a *sanctimonious* humbug.

sanc-tion (sangk′shun), *n.* formal approval or consent by those in authority:—**sanctions,** a legal term given to coercive measures imposed for securing obedience to law, as by a group of nations' withholding loans, freezing assets abroad, imposing a blockade, etc.:—*v.t.* to approve; authorize; as, their parents *sanctioned* the marriage.

sanc-ti-ty (sangk′ti-ti), *n.* [*pl.* sanctities], **1,** holiness; purity; **2,** sacredness; solemnity; as, the *sanctity* of a cathedral; **3, sanctities,** sacred objects, duties, etc.

sanc-tu-ar-y (sangk′tū-ėr-i), *n.* [*pl.* sanctuaries], **1,** a consecrated place; a church or temple; **2,** the part of a Christian church nearest the altar; **3,** a place of shelter and protection; as, a *sanctuary* for wildfowl; **4,** hence, security; shelter; as, to seek *sanctuary* from the world.

sand (sand), *n.* **1,** dry soil composed of fine particles of crushed or worn rock, found chiefly along the shores of large bodies of water or in deserts; **2, sands,** moments; time: from the custom of measuring time by sand in an hourglass; as, the *sands* of life run fast:—*v.t.* to sprinkle, mix, or rub with sand; as, to *sand* floors.

san-dal (san′dl), *n.* **1,** a kind of low shoe, worn by the ancient Greeks and Romans, consisting of a sole without uppers fastened by straps over the instep or ankle; **2,** in modern times, a similar shoe for children; also, a woman's openwork street shoe or evening slipper; **3,** a low overshoe.

san-dal-wood (san′dl-wood′), *n.* **1,** a tree that grows in the Malay Archipelago and India; **2,** the close-grained fragrant wood of this tree, used for fine carving, and valued for the perfume which it yields: three varieties grow in Canada.

san-der (san′dėr), *n.* an apparatus for sanding or sandpapering.

sand-man (sand′man′), *n.* in nursery language, a personification of sleep or drowsiness.

sand-pa-per (sand′pā′pėr), *n.* a heavy paper with a coating of sand on one side, used for smoothing and polishing:—*v.t.* to smooth or polish with sandpaper.

sand-piper (sand′pīp′ėr), *n.* a small wading bird which feeds along sandy or muddy shores.

sand-stone (sand′stōn′), *n.* a rock composed chiefly of quartz sand hardened into a solid mass by a natural cement.

sand-wich (sand′wich; san′wij), *n.* two or more slices of fresh or toasted bread with meat, cheese, or other filling between them:—*v.t.* to place (a person or thing) between two others.

sand-y (san′di), *adj.* [sand-i-er, sand-i-est], **1,** entirely or chiefly composed of sand; as, *sandy* soil; **2,** of a yellowish-red colour; as, *sandy* hair.—*n.* **sand′i-ness.**

sane (sān), *adj.* [san-er, san-est], **1,** mentally sound or healthy; **2,** coming from a sound mind; sensible; as, a *sane* suggestion.

sang (sang), *p.t.* of *sing.*

san-guine (sang′gwin), *adj.* **1,** of the colour of blood; ruddy; as, a *sanguine* complexion; **2,** hopeful; confident; as, *sanguine* of victory.—*adj.* **san′gui-na-ry.**

san-i-tar-i-um (san′i-târ′i-um), *n.* [*pl.* sanitariums or sanitaria (san′-i-târ′i-a)], a place for the care of invalids or the treatment of certain diseases; also, a sanitorium; health resort.

san-i-tar-y (san′i-tėr-i), *adj.* **1,** relating to health; as, *sanitary* laws; **2,** preserving health; hygienic; as, *sanitary* conditions.

san-i-ta-tion (san′i-tā′shun), *n.* the science and practice of bringing about conditions that protect health; hygiene.

san-i-ty (san′i-ti), *n.* soundness of mind.

sank (sank), *p.t.* of *sink.*

San-ta Claus (san′ta klôz), in *nursery lore,* a chubby, white-bearded old man who brings children gifts on Christmas Eve in a sleigh drawn by eight reindeer.

¹sap (sap), *n.* the watery juice of a tree or plant. From the sap of certain trees come products useful to man, as rubber, sugar, etc.—*adj.* **sap′less.**

²sap (sap), *v.t.* [sapped, sap-ping], **1,** to wear away by digging beneath; undermine; as, the flood waters *sapped* the foundations of the house; **2,** to weaken; wear away; as, continual defeats *sapped* his courage.

sa-pi-ent (sā′pi-ent), *adj.* wise: often ironical.—*n.* **sa′pi-ence.**

sap-ling (sap′ling), *n.* **1,** a flexible young tree; **2,** hence, a youth.

sap-phire (saf′ir), *n.* a precious stone, hard and transparent, and of a deep-blue colour; **2,** the deep-blue colour of this gem.

sap-ro-phyte (sap′rō-fit′), *n.* any vegetable organism that lives on dead organic matter, as some fungi, bacteria, etc.

sap-suck-er (sap′suk′ėr), *n.* a small American woodpecker which feeds partly on the sap of trees.

sap-wood (sap′wood′), *n.* the soft living wood between the bark and the inner wood of most trees.

sar-casm (sär′kazm), *n.* a bitter, cutting remark; also, ironical language expressing scorn or contempt.—*adj.* **sar-cas′tic.**—*adv.* **sar-cas′ti-cal-ly.**

sar-coph-a-gus (sär-kof′a-gus), *n.* [*pl.* -gi (-jī); -guses], a stone coffin, esp. for a distinguished person, as that of King Tutankhamen of Egypt, (unearthed in 1922).

sard (särd), *n.* a gem varying from pale yellow to red orange.

sar-dine (sär-dēn′; sär′dēn), *n.* a small fish of the herring family, preserved in oil for use as food.

sar-don-ic (sär-don′ik), *adj.* sneering; mocking; bitterly ironic or derisive; as, a *sardonic* grin.

sar-do-nyx (sär′do-niks), *n.* a kind of onyx with bands of sard.

sar-gas-so (sär-gas′ō), *n.* a mass of floating brown seaweeds and gulfweeds: —**Sargasso** Sea, a tract of North Atlantic Ocean between the Azores, Canaries, and Cape Verde Islands, where masses of sargasso are found.

sa-rong (sa-rông′), *n.* the chief garment of both sexes in Malay and the East Indies: it is a long strip of cloth, worn tucked around the waist like a skirt.

sar-sa-pa-ril-la (sär′sa-pa-ril′a), *n.* **1,** a tropical American plant, the root of which is used as medicine or for flavouring; **2,** a cooling drink of soda-water flavoured with its extract.

sar-to-ri-al (sär-tō′ri-al), *adj.* relating to a tailor or his work; as, *sartorial* splendour or elegance.

¹**sash** (sash), *n.* [*pl.* sashes], an ornamental band, ribbon, etc., worn around the waist or over the shoulder.

²**sash** (sash), *n.* [*pl.* sashes or sash], a window-frame, or a similar part of a door, made to hold one or more panes.

sas-ka-toon (sas′ka-tōōn′), *n.* a shrub, *Amelanchier Canadensis,* 3′ to 14′ high, of which 13 species grow in Canada: the fruit is a purple berry, sweet and juicy, of which large quantities are harvested and preserved in Western Canada. Also called *serviceberry, juneberry,* and *shadbush.*

sas-sa-fras (sas′a-fras), *n.* **1,** a tree of the laurel family, whose root, wood, and flowers have a spicy smell and a pungent taste; **2,** its root bark is used in medicine and for flavouring.

sat (sat), *p.t.* and *p.p.* of *sit.*

Sa-tan (sā′tn), *n.* the Devil.

sa-tan-ic (sa-tan′ik), *adj.* pertaining to, or like, Satan; devilish; wicked; as, *satanic* wickedness.

satch-el (sach′el), *n.* a small bag, usually of fabric or of leather, in which to carry small personal belongings, papers, etc.

sate (sāt), *v.t.* [sat-ed, sat-ing], **1,** to satisfy fully (an appetite or desire); **2,** to disgust or weary with an excess of something; as, he was *sated* with flattery.

sa-teen (sa-tēn′), *n.* a cotton fabric with a glossy, satinlike finish.

sat-el-lite (sat′e-līt′), *n.* **1,** a heavenly body revolving round a larger one; as, the moon is a *satellite* of the earth; **2,** a persistent attendant or follower of a great person; **3,** a state economically or politically dependent on a more powerful one.

sa-ti-ate (sā′shi-āt′), *v.t.* [satiat-ed, satiat-ing], to gratify to excess; as, to *satiate* one's appetite.—*n.* **sa-ti′e-ty** (sa-tī′e-ti).

sat-in (sat′in), *n.* a closely woven, glossy silk:—*adj.* made of, or like, this silk.

sat-ire (sat′ir), *n.* a poem, essay, story, etc., exposing and ridiculing evil or folly; **2,** biting sarcasm or ridicule. —*adj.***sa-tir′ic**(sa-tir′ik); **sa-tir′i-cal.**

sat-is-fac-tion (sat′is-fak′shun), *n.* **1,** the act of supplying a need or desire; also, the act of paying off, compensating, contenting, etc.; **2,** the condition of having one's wishes filled, or of being gratified, paid off, contented, etc.; contentment; **3,** that which satisfies or gratifies; as, your visit will be a great *satisfaction.*

sat-is-fac-to-ry (sat′is-fak′to-ri), *adj.* sufficient; adequate; producing satisfaction.—*adv.* **sat′is-fac′to-ri-ly.**

sat-is-fy (sat′is-fī′), *v.t.* [satisfied,

cat, āge, fär, câre, ásk; ten, ēve, latėr; (i) pity, rely, senate; īce; top; nō.

satisfy-ing], **1,** to content; fill the wishes of; as, they were *satisfied* with the new house; also. to gratify to the full; as, to *satisfy* one's hunger; **2,** to free from doubt; convince; as, the explanation *satisfied* the child; **3,** to pay off; as, to *satisfy* a creditor:— *v.i.* to give gratification; as, riches do not always *satisfy.*

sat-u-rate (sat′ū-rāt′), *v.t.* [saturat-ed, saturat-ing], to cause to become soaked; to fill to the limit of capacity for absorbing; as, to *saturate* the ground with water.—*n.* **sat′u-ra′tion.**

Sat-ur-day (sat′ẽr-di; -dā′), *n.* the 7th and last day of the week.

Sat-urn (sat′ẽrn), *n.* the sixth planet from the sun and second largest: it is remarkable for its three thin, concentric rings.

sat-ur-nine (sat′ẽr-nīn′), *adj.* gloomy; sluggish; taciturn; as, a *saturnine* countenance, temper, person, etc.

sat-yr (sat′ẽr; sā′tẽr), *n.* in *mythology,* a forest god, represented with long, pointed ears, short horns, and the tail of a horse or goat, who indulged in riotous merriment and wantonness.

sauce (sôs), *n.* **1,** a dressing or seasoning for food; also, any highly seasoned mixture of ingredients, used as a relish; as, chilli *sauce;* **2,** stewed fruit; as, apple*sauce;* **3,** *Colloq.,* insolence; pertness:—*v.t.* [sauced, sauc-ing], **1,** to put seasoning into; add flavour to; **2,** *Colloq.,* to treat with pertness or sauciness.

sauce-pan (sôs′pan′), *n.* a small metal pan, with a handle, used in cooking.

sau-cer (sô′sẽr), *n.* a shallow dish, esp. one to hold a cup.

sau-cy (sô′si), *adj.* [sau-ci-er, sau-ci-est], pert; impudent; also, roguish; as, a *saucy* smile.—*adv.* **sau′ci-ly.**—*n.* **sau′ci-ness.**

sauer-kraut (sour′krout′), *n.* finely sliced cabbage, fermented in a brine made of its own juice.

sau-ger (sô′gẽr), *n.* a small perch or sand pike (*Stizostedion Canadense*): Canada's annual crop is over 13 million pounds, chiefly from the Great Lakes.

sault (sōō), *n.* a rapid or waterfall, as at *Sault* Ste. Marie.

saun-ter (sôn′tẽr; sän′tẽr), *v.i.* to wander idly; stroll; as, to *saunter* along the beach:—*n.* **1.** a leisurely manner of walking; **2,** an idle walk or ramble.

sau-ri-an (sô′ri-an), *n.* and *adj.* a reptile of the order *Sauria,* esp. croco-dile, alligator, lizard, etc., and any extinct lizardlike monster of the dinosaur period.

sau-sage (so′sij), *n.* meat, usually pork, ground fine and highly seasoned. It is often stuffed into a thin, tubelike casing.

sav-age (sav′ij), *adj.* **1,** relating to the forest or wilderness; wild; as, *savage* country; **3,** cruel; fierce; as, *savage* beasts; **3,** uncivilized; barbaric; as, *savage* tribes:—*n.* **1,** an uncivilized person; a barbarian; **2,** a fierce, brutal person.—*adv.* **sav′age-ly.**

sav-age-ry (sav′ij-ri), *n.* [*pl.* savageries], **1,** the condition of being wild or uncivilized; **2,** brutal roughness or cruelty.

sa-van-na or **sa-van-nah** (sa-van′a), *n.* a grassy, open plain, esp. in tropical America; a prairie.

sa-vant (sa-vänt′), *n.* a man of learning esp. one famed for scientific research.

¹save (sāv), *v.t.* [saved, sav-ing], **1,** to bring out of danger; deliver; rescue; as, the soldier *saved* his comrade's life; also, to preserve from damage, decay, etc.; as, rubbers *save* shoes; **2,** to spare; avoid; as, to *save* trouble; prevent the waste of; as, to *save* time; **3,** to refrain from spending; hoard; as, to *save* money; **4,** to free from the power and result of sin; as, to *save* souls:—*v.i.* **1,** to refrain from spending or wasting money or supplies; **2,** to lay by money a little at a time.—*n.* **sav′er.**

²save (sāv), *prep.* except; not including; as, he attended every game *save* one.

sav-ing (sāv′ing), *adj.* **1,** preserving from sin or destruction; as *saving* faith; **2,** redeeming; compensating; as, a *saving* sense of humour; **3,** economical; not wasteful; as, a very *saving* individual:—*n.* **1,** economy; as, the habit of *saving;* **2,** rescue; **3,** **savings,** money saved:—*prep.* except.

sav-iour or **sav-ior** (sāv′yẽr), *n.* one who rescues or saves:—**Saviour,** Jesus Christ, the Redeemer.

sa-vor-y (sā′vẽr-i), *n.* a fragrant herb of the mint family, used in cooking.

sa-vour or **sa-vor** (sā′vẽr), *n.* flavour; taste; as, a spicy *savour:*—*v.t.* **1,** to flavour; as, to *savour* a soup; **2,** to taste or smell with delight:—*v.i.* to partake of a quality or characteristic; as, this book *savours* of personal prejudice.—*adj.* **sa′vour-less.**

sa-vour-y (sā′vẽr-i), *adj.* with appetizing taste or smell; as, a *savoury* stew:—*n.* a light, highly seasoned dish served, usually, at the end of a dinner.

¹saw (sô), *n.* a cutting tool with a thin toothed blade, worked mechanically or by hand; also, a cutting machine having one or more such blades:—*v.t.* [*p.t.* sawed (sôd), *p.p.* sawn (sôn) or sawed, *p.pr.* saw-ing], **1,** to cut with a saw; as, to *saw* wood; **2,** to form or fashion with such a tool; as, he *sawed* the board so that it fitted into place; **3,** to make motions as if sawing; as, the excited speaker *sawed* the air: —*v.i.* **1,** to be cut with a saw; as, the wood *saws* easily; **2,** to use a saw; also to make motions as if using a saw; **3,** to cut.

²saw (sô), *n.* a proverb; an adage.

saw-dust (sô′dust′), *n.* the fine particles or chips that fly when wood is sawn.

saw-fish (sô′fish′), *n.* a giant ray, with long flat snout bearing toothlike spines on each edge.

saw-fly (sô′flī′), *n.* an insect family (*Tenthredinidae*), of which the female has a pair of sawlike organs for cutting slits in plants to hold her eggs.

saw-horse (sô′hôrs′), *n.* a rack or frame to hold sticks of wood while they are being sawn by hand.

saw-mill (sô′mil′), *n.* a mill where logs are sawn into lumber by machines; also, a sawing machine.

sax-horn (saks′hôrn′), *n.* a brass, wind instrument fitted with valves, as the tuba, cornet, etc.

sax-o-phone (sak′so-fōn′), *n.* a musical instrument consisting of a metal tube with keys and a reed mouthpiece.

say (sā), *v.t.* [said (sed), say-ing], **1,** to utter in words; tell; **2,** to declare; state as a decision; assert; as, I *say* he shall go; **3,** to estimate; assume; as, *say* he has ten houses, how long will he keep them? **4,** to recite; repeat; as, to *say* a poem:—*n.* **1,** something that one has said or intends to say; as, to have one's *say;* **2,** one's turn or right to express an opinion; as, it's your *say* next; also, the right to decide; as, the teacher has the whole *say.*

say-ing (sā′ing), *n.* that which is often said; a proverb or maxim.

scab (skab), *n.* **1,** a crust formed over a wound or sore; **2,** a disease of animals, esp. sheep, characterized by spots that resemble scabs; also, a similar disease of plants; **3,** a nonunion worker, esp. one who takes a striker's job.—*adj.* **scab′by.**

scab-bard (skab′ẽrd), *n.* the case in which the blade of a sword, bayonet, etc. is sheathed.

sca-bi-es (skā′bi-ēz′), *n.* the itch; a contagious skin disease of human beings and animals, due to a parasite, the itch mite.

scad (skad), *n.* a mackerellike fish, sometimes found in large numbers off the west coast of Vancouver Island and the Queen Charlotte Islands.—*pl. Slang,* a very large quantity or number; as, *scads* of money.

scaf-fold (skaf′uld), *n.* **1,** a temporary timber structure serving as a support for workmen while building, painting, etc.; **2,** an elevated platform on which the execution of criminals takes place by hanging, beheading, etc.

scaf-fold-ing (skaf′ul-ding), *n.* **1,** a scaffold or series of scaffolds; **2,** the materials used in erecting scaffolds.

scal-a-wag, scal-la-wag (skal′a-wag′), or **scal-ly-wag** (skal′i-wag′), *n. Colloq.,* a disreputable fellow; good-for-nothing; one who will not work; a scamp; rascal.

scald (skôld), *v.t.* **1,** to burn or injure, as does hot liquid; also, to burn with steam; **2,** hence, to pain as if by burning; as, hot tears *scalded* her face; **3,** to bring near to the boiling-point; as, to *scald* milk; **4,** to rinse or dip in boiling water; as, to *scald* dishes; to *scald* tomatoes:—*n.* a burn or injury from hot liquid or steam.

¹scale (skāl), *n.* **1,** one of the pans or dishes of a balance; **2,** (usually *scales*), the balance itself; **3,** any instrument or machine for weighing:—*v.t.* [scaled, scal-ing], to weigh by means of scales.

²scale (skāl), *n.* **1,** one of the thin, bony or horny plates forming the outer covering of many fishes, lizards, snakes, etc.; **2,** any thin plate resembling a scale; **3,** one of the small flaky pieces of dead skin which fall off in certain diseases:—*v.t.* [scaled, scal-ing], to strip (a fish) of scales:—*v.i.* **1,** to form or drop scales; separate and come off in thin layers; **2,** to become rough and hard; become crusted.—*adj.* **scal′y.** —*n.* **scal′i-ness.**

³scale (skāl), *n.* **1,** a measure consisting of a series of marks, laid down at definite, regular distances along a line; as, the *scale* on a tape-measure; **2,** a basis for a system of numbering; as, the decimal *scale;* **3,** a series of numbers, similar objects, etc., which progress from a low to a high point or degree; as, the *scale* of marks in the arithmetic test ranged from 47 to 98; **4,** the relation between the actual size of an object and the size of the object as it appears in a drawing, painting, etc.; as, a drawing of a house on the *scale* of five feet to one inch; **5,** any standard for judging or estimating; **6,** in *music,* a series of tones in a regular order, whether ascending or descending; also, a succession of tones beginning on a certain keynote; as, the *scale* of F:—*v.t.* [scaled, scal-ing], **1,** to climb up; as, to *scale* a wall; **2,** to reduce in accordance with a settled ratio or scale; as, to *scale* down expenses; **3,** to make (a drawing, etc.) in accordance with a definite scale.

scal-lion (skal′yun), *n.* an onionlike plant; a leek.

scal-lop (skol′up; skal′up) or **scol-lop** (skol′up), *n.* **1,** a salt-water shellfish with two fan-shaped, usually ribbed, shells, that are hinged together; **2,** the muscle by which the shell is closed, valued for food; **3,** one of a series of curves that form an ornamental edge, as on lace, linens, etc.:—*v.t.* **1,** to cut the edge or border of, in a series of curves; **2,** to mix with crumbs, butter, etc., and bake; as, to *scallop* tomatoes.

scalp (skalp), *n.* the skin on the top of head, normally covered with hair:—*v.t.* to torture or kill by cutting off the skin and hair of the head; as, the Indians *scalped* the prisoners.

scal-pel (skal′p′l). *n.* a surgeon's small light, straight knife with very sharp blade for operations and dissections.

scal-per (skal′pėr), *n.* one who buys stocks, tickets for games, etc., and peddles them (sometimes illegally) at a profit:—*v.t.* and *v.i.* **scalp** (*Colloq.*)

scamp (skamp), *n.* a rascal; a worthless fellow:—*v.t.* to do (work) negligently.

scam-per (skam′pėr), *v.i.* to run or skip; as, the frightened rabbit *scampered* to cover:—*n.* a hasty flight.

scan (skan), *v.t.* [scanned, scan-ning], **1,** to look at the details or scrutinize; as, Columbus *scanned* the horizon for land; **2,** to read or mark (a line of poetry) to show the number and kind of metrical feet used.

scan-dal (skan′dal), *n.* **1,** a cause of reproach; also, shame; disgrace; as, the tenement district was a *scandal* to the city; **2,** careless or malicious gossip injurious to another's reputation; backbiting.

scan-dal-ize (skan′dal-īz′), *v.t.* [scandal-ized, scandaliz-ing], to offend or shock by an opinion, action, etc.

scan-dal-ous (skan′dal-us), *adj.* **1,** tending to harm the good name or reputation of someone; as, *scandalous* rumours; **2,** shocking; wicked; as, *scandalous* neglect.

scan-sion (skan′shun), *n.* in *poetry,* the dividing of verses into metrical feet and marking the beats or accents [′] or [-].

scant (skant), *adj.* **1,** having only a small amount; short; as, *scant* of material; **2,** barely enough; as, a *scant* supply of food; also, a little less than; as, it weighs a *scant* pound:—*v.t.* to stint; limit the supply of.

scant-ling (skant′ling), *n.* a small upright timber, 2″ by 4″, used in the frame of a building, or, collectively, timber in this form; a stud.

scant-y (skan′ti), *adj.* [scant-i-er, scant-i-est], barely sufficient; scarcely enough; as, *scanty* supplies.

scape-goat (skāp′gōt′), *n.* **1,** in an ancient Jewish custom, a goat selected by lot, on whose head the high priest laid the sins of the people, after which it was driven into the wilderness; **2,** hence, one who bears the blame for others.

scape-grace (skāp′grās′), *n.* an unreliable, unprincipled person, esp. a mischievous, troublesome child.

scar (skär), *n.* **1,** the mark left after a wound or burn heals; **2,** any mark like a scar; as, knife *scars* on the table; **3,** a lasting effect caused by grief, trouble, etc.:—*v.t.* [scarred, scarring], to mark with, or as with, a scar:—*v.i.* to form a scar.

scar-ab (skar′ab), *n.* **1,** a kind of beetle; esp., a beetle held sacred by the ancient Egyptians as a symbol of immortality; **2,** a gem or seal cut in the form of this beetle.

scarce (skârs), *adj.* [scarc-er, scarc-est], **1,** not common; rarely seen; as, real diamonds are *scarce;* **2,** not plentiful; not equal to the demand; as, peaches are *scarce* this year.—*n.* **scarce′-ness.**—*n.* **scar′ci-ty.**

scarce-ly (skârs′li), *adv.* **1,** surely not; hardly; as, you can *scarcely* run as fast as that; **2,** almost not; barely; as, I *scarcely* saw him before he left.

scare (skâr), *v.t.* [scared, scar-ing], to strike with sudden terror; frighten: *n.* a sudden fright or panic.—*adj.* **scar′y.**

scare-crow (skâr′krō′), *n.* **1,** a figure, usually a crude representation of a man, dressed in ragged clothes, set up to frighten birds and animals away from crops; **2,** anything which frightens without real cause; **3,** a person dressed in rags.

scarf (skärf), *n.* [*pl.* scarfs or scarves (skärvz)], **1,** a neckerchief or necktie; **2,** a strip of lace, silk, wool, etc., worn loosely, for ornament or warmth, about the neck, head, or shoulders; **3,** a cover, often long and narrow, used on a bureau, piano, etc.

scarf-skin (skärf'skin'), *n.* the outermost layer of skin; cuticle; epidermis.

scar-let (skär'lit), *n.* a bright-red colour tinged with orange:—*adj.* of a scarlet colour.—**scarlet runner,** a climbing bean plant of tropical America with bright-red flowers and red-and-black seeds.—**scarlet tanager,** a treetop songbird related to the finch family, with scarlet body and black wings and tail: breeds from Saskatchewan to Nova Scotia and to Southern U.S., and winters in Central and South America.

scar-let fe-ver (fē'vėr), a highly contagious disease, characterized by a severe sore throat, high fever, and scarlet rash.

scat (skat), *interj. Colloq.* Begone!

scath-ing (skāth'ing), *adj.* severe; bitter; as, *scathing* remarks.—*adv.* **scath'ing-ly.**

scat-ter (skat'ėr), *v.t.* **1,** to throw here and there; strew; as, to *scatter* clothes about a room; *scatter* seed; **2,** to drive apart; disperse; as, the soldiers *scattered* the mob:—*v.i.* to separate and go in different directions; as, the covey of quail *scattered*.

scaup (skôp), *n.* an Arctic game duck related to the canvasback and redhead: two varieties, the *greater scaup* and the *lesser scaup* breed in the Canadian tundra in great numbers: distinguishable by a white area around the base of the bill or on the face.

scav-en-ger (skav'en-jėr), *n.* **1,** a man employed to keep the streets clean by carrying off all filth, refuse, etc.; **2,** any animal, bird, etc., that eats refuse.

sce-na-ri-o (si-när'i-ō; si-nä'ri-ō), *n.* [*pl.* scenarios], the complete, detailed story of the plot of a photoplay, including the cast of characters and acting directions.

scene (sēn), *n.* **1,** one of the parts into which an act of a play is divided; **2,** the painted background, hangings, etc., used on the stage to picture the place where the action is going on; **3,** the time, place, or circumstances in which

the action of a play, story, etc., takes place; as, the *scene* of the play is a farm; **4,** a particular episode or happening of a story, play, etc.; as, the storm *scene* in "David Copperfield"; **5,** a display of feeling or emotion; as, to make a *scene;* **6,** a landscape; view.

scen-er-y (sēn'ėr-i), *n.* **1,** painted hangings, screens, etc., used on a stage; the background; **2,** a landscape.

sce-nic (sē'nik; sen'ik), *adj.* **1,** pertaining to the stage; **2,** pertaining to a landscape; also, offering beautiful views of nature.

scent (sent), *n.* **1,** odour; fragrance; **2,** the sense of smell; as, hounds have a keen *scent;* **3,** an odour left lingering about a place by a person or animal; as, the dogs caught the wolf by following his *scent;* **4,** hence, the trail or track, as of a criminal; **5,** a perfume:—*v.t.* **1,** to smell; **2,** hence, to get a hint of; as, to *scent* trouble; **3,** to perfume; as, handkerchiefs *scented* with lavender.—*adj.* **scent'less.**

scep-tic (skep'tik), *n.* **1,** a person of doubting mind; **2,** one who doubts the truth of any fact or theory, and questions the possibility of human knowledge of anything; **3,** one who doubts the truth of a religious belief, as Christianity.—*adj.* **scep'ti-cal.**—*adv.* **scep'ti-cal-ly.**—*n.* **scep'ti-cism.**

scep-tre or **scep-ter** (sep'tėr), *n.* a ruler's staff; an emblem of authority or power.

sched-ule (shed'ūl; sked'ūl), *n.* **1,** a slip of paper containing a list or inventory; as, a *schedule* of household goods; **2,** a list of things to be done in a certain order of time; as, according to the *schedule,* the job will take a month; also, a timetable:—*v.t.* [scheduled, schedul-ing], **1,** to make a list or schedule of; as, to *schedule* one's possessions; **2,** to include in a list or schedule; as, I'll *schedule* your speech for tomorrow.

scheel-ite (shēl'īt), *n.* the chief ore of tungsten: it is a by-product of gold refining, esp. in Salmo, B.C.

scheme (skēm), *n.* **1,** a carefully arranged and systematic plan; a system; as, a *scheme* for old-age pensions; **2,** an underhand plan; plot; as, a *scheme* to rob a house; **3,** an arrangement or system in which everything is related or in harmony; as, the colour *scheme* of a costume:—*v.t.* [schemed, schem-ing], to design or plan; plot:—*v.i.* to form a plot or plan.—*adj.* **sche-mat'ic.**

scher-zo (sker'tsō), *n.* a sprightly movement or passage, esp. as the 2nd or 3rd division of a sonata or a symphony.

schism (sizm), *n.* 1, a split or division; esp., a split in the Christian church; 2, the offence of causing such a split or division; 3, a group that has separated from the main body of the church.

schist (shist), *n.* any crystalline rock that splits readily into sheets or layers. —*adj.* **schist'ose.**

schiz-o-phre-ni-a (skiz'ō-frē'ni-a), *n.* a psychosis or form of insanity marked by delusions, hallucinations, withdrawal, and (often) impaired intelligence.

schnau-zer (shnou'zėr; tsėr), *n.* a small, active terrier with small ears, heavy eyebrows, moustache, beard, and wiry coat.

chol-ar (skol'ėr), *n.* 1, one who attends a school or learns from a teacher; 2, one who has acquired thorough and expert knowledge in one or more fields of learning.—*adj.* **schol'-ar-ly.**

chol-ar-ship (skol'ėr-ship'), *n.* 1, the knowledge and attainments of a learned man; learning; erudition; 2, money given to a student to enable him to follow or continue a course of study.

cho-las-tic (sko-las'tik), *adj.* relating to learned men, students, schools, education, academic life, etc.

school (skōōl), *n.* 1, a place where instruction is given; a schoolhouse; as, the new *school* was opened yesterday; 2, a regular meeting or session at which instruction is given and received; as, there will be no *school* tomorrow afternoon; 2, the whole body of pupils in any educational institution; as, the *school* is happy over the victory; 4, the followers or imitators of a teacher or leader; as, the Platonic *school* of philosophy; 5, a division of a university devoted to one branch of learning; as, a *school* of dentistry:—*v.t.* to train or instruct in, or as in, a school.

school (skōōl), *n.* a great number of fish feeding or swimming together; a shoal:—*v.i.* to swim together in great numbers.

chool-book (skōōl'book'), *n.* a book used in schools; a textbook.

chool-boy (skōōl'boi'), *n.* a boy who attends school.—*n.fem.* **school'girl'.**

chool-house (skōōl'hous'), *n.* a building where school is held.

school-ing (skōō'ling), *n.* instruction in school; education.

school-master (skōōl'màs'tėr), *n.* a man who teaches in, or is the head of, a school.

school-mate (skōōl'māt'), *n.* a companion or associate at school; schoolfellow.

school-room (skōōl'rōōm'), *n.* a room in which pupils are taught.

school-teach-er (skōōl'tē'chėr), *n.* one who teaches in a school.

schoon-er (skōō'nėr), *n.* 1, a vessel with two or more masts, rigged fore-and-aft; 2, a covered wagon, formerly used by pioneers on the western prairies; a prairie schooner.

schot-tische or **schot-tish** (sho-tēsh'; shot'ish), *n.* a 19th-century dance, or its music, in 2/4 time: like a polka, but slower.

schwa (shwä), *n.* an inverted *e* [ə], used in some dictionaries as a diacritical (or pronunciation) mark to indicate a slurred vowel sound in an unaccented syllable; as, *a* in *ago* or *e* in *agent.*

sci-at-i-ca (sī-at'i-ka), *n.* a neuralgic pain of the sciatic nerve in the region of the hip or thigh.

sci-ence (sī'ens), *n.* 1, knowledge, or the pursuit of knowledge, of things as they are, and of why they act as they do; also, the classification and systematic arrangement of such knowledge, and the formulation, where possible, of general laws, or truths, deduced from it; 2, a special branch of such knowledge; as, the *science* of botany; the *science* of economics.

sci-ence fic-tion, stories about possible future scientific developments, often of travel through space or time.

sci-en-tif-ic (sī'en-tif'ik), *adj.* 1, relating to, or used in, a science; as, *scientific* instruments; 2, in accordance with the methods of science; applying the laws of science; as, *scientific* mining.—*adv.* **sci'en-tif'i-cal-ly.**

sci-en-tist (sī'en-tist), *n.* a person who is learned in science; also, one whose profession is scientific research.

scim-i-tar or **scim-i-ter** (sim'i-tėr), *n.* an Oriental sword with a curved blade.

scin-til-la (sin-til'a), *n.* a particle; iota: used figuratively (with a negative); as, there is not a *scintilla* of truth in the rumour.

scin-til-late (sin'ti-lāt'), *v.i.* 1, to give

off sparks, fire, or firelike particles; **2,** to twinkle, as stars; **3,** figuratively, to flash, as wit.—*n.* **scin′til-la′tion.**

sci-on (sī′un), *n.* **1,** the sprout or shoot of a plant, cut off and used for planting or grafting; **2,** a descendant; heir, esp. of a noble family.

scis-sors (siz′ẽrz), *n.pl.* an instrument, smaller than shears, with two sharp blades which open and close on a pivot, and cut when they meet.

scle-ro-sis (skli-rō′sis), *n.* [*pl.* -oses (-sēz)], **1,** the hardening of a part of the body, esp. of the nervous system, due to overgrowth of fibrous connective tissue; **2,** the hardening of a plant's cell wall, as by the formation of wood.

scoff (skôf), *n.* an expression of scorn or contempt; also, an object of scorn or contempt; a laughingstock:—*v.i.* to show scorn or contempt by mocking language; to jeer; as, do not *scoff* at the mistakes of others:—*v.t.* to mock or jeer at.—*n.* **scoff′er.**

scold (skōld), *v.i.* to chide sharply or rudely:—*v.t.* to find fault with; rebuke severely; as, the teacher *scolded* him for being late:—*n.* one who habitually finds fault; esp., a rude, quarrelsome woman.—*n.* **scold′ing.**

scol-lop (skol′up), *n.* Same as **scallop.**

sconce (skons), *n.* an ornamental bracket, fastened to a wall, holding one or more candlesticks.

scone (skōn), *n.* **1,** a rich, baking-powder tea biscuit, with currants; **2,** a batter cake of barley, oatmeal, or wheat (baked on a griddle).

scoop (skoop), *n.* **1,** a large long-handled ladle for skimming or dipping out liquids; **2,** a shovel for snow, coal, etc.; also, a small utensil, shaped like a shovel, for dipping out flour, sugar, etc., from a bin or bag; **3,** the act of dipping out or making a hollow; **4,** any gesture or motion like that made with a scoop; as, with a *scoop* of his hand, he splashed water into my face; **5,** the hollow left from scooping; **6,** the quantity dipped out in one scoop; as, two *scoops* will be enough; **7,** the scoop-like bucket of a dredging machine, water wheel, etc.; **8,** *Colloq.,* the securing and publishing of a piece of news before a rival (or rivals); also, the article printed:—*v.t.* **1,** to take out or up with a scoop; **2,** to make hollow.

¹scoot (skoot), *v.i. Colloq.,* **1,** to walk or run hastily; dart; scurry off; **2,** to skim along, as a bird.

²scoot (skoot), *n.* a small, speedy craft,

driven by an aircraft motor, used for winter travel in Georgian Bay in combined conditions of slob ice, snow, and open water at 40 to 50 miles per hour: it resembles the airboat of the U.S. Everglades.

scoot-er (skoot′ẽr), *n.* a child's toy vehicle, hung low on two wheels.

scope (skōp), *n.* **1,** extent of understanding; range of mental activity; as, a book beyond the *scope* of high-school pupils; **2,** the field covered; range of subjects embraced; as, a book limited in *scope;* **3,** room or outlet for action; as, he craved ample *scope* for his abilities.

scorch (skôrch), *v.t.* **1,** to burn the surface of; as, to *scorch* linen; **2,** to parch; wither; as, a hot sun *scorches* grass.—*n.* **scorch′er.**

score (skōr), *n.* **1,** a line, groove, or mark that has been drawn, cut, or scratched on a surface; **2,** a debt; bill; also, a grudge; as, to pay off old *scores;* **3,** reason; ground; as, he was freed on the *score* of insufficient evidence; **4,** the number of points, runs, etc., made in a game or contest; as, the *score* was five to one; **5,** [*pl.* score], twenty; as, three *score* and ten; **6,** in *music,* a copy of a composition showing all the parts for all the instruments or voices; **7,** **scores,** a great many; as, *scores* of people were there:—*v.t.* [scored, scoring], **1,** to notch or mark with lines, scratches, etc., as wood or paper; **2,** to make a record of; **3,** to win (a run, a point, etc.); hence, to achieve (a hit, success, etc.); **4,** to grade (test papers); also, to remove by marking out; as, to *score* out a line; **5,** to blame; find fault with:—*v.i.* **1,** to keep the tally in a game; **2,** to win points in a game.

scorn (skôrn), *n.* **1,** extreme contempt; haughty disdain and indignation; **2,** an object of contempt; as, the *scorn* of the neighbourhood:—*v.t.* **1,** to hold in extreme disdain; reject with contempt; as, to *scorn* underhand methods; **2,** *Archaic,* to taunt; scoff at; as, to *scorn* a liar.—*adj.* **scorn′ful.**

Scor-pi-o (skôr′pi-ō′), *n.* **1,** a southern constellation, the Scorpion; its brightest star is Antares; **2,** the 8th sign of the zodiac (♏), which the sun enters about October 24.

scor-pi-on (skôr′pi-un), *n.* an animal of the same class as the spider, two to eight inches in length. Each of the front legs is equipped with a pair of pincers, and the tip of the tail has a poisonous sting.

cat, āge, fär, câre, ȧsk; ten, ēve, latẽr; (i) pity, rely, senate; īce; top; nō

scotch (skoch), *v.t.* to wound without killing; as, to *scotch* a snake.

sco-ter (skō'tēr), *n.* a diving duck of two species, the *American* and the *white-winged*, that breed from the Arctic Circle to the St. Lawrence and Newfoundland: a better game than food bird: drakes are black, ducks brown. Also called *coot.*

scot—free (skot'–frē'), *adj.* safe; unpunished; as, the prisoner went *scot-free.*

scoun-drel (skoun'drel), *n.* a low, worthless rascal.—*adj.* **scoun'drel-ly.**

¹scour (skour), *v.t.* 1, to rub hard with some rough material, in order to make clean and shiny; as, we *scoured* the pots and pans; 2, to wash or clear of dirt, grease, etc., by rubbing with soap and water, flushing, etc.; as, to *scour* a rug; to *scour* a pipe:—*n.* the act of scouring; as, she gave the floor a good *scour.*—*n.* **scour'er.**

²scour (skour), *v.t.* to go through thoroughly, as on a search; as, the police *scoured* the city for the criminal.

scourge (skûrj), *n.* a whip used to inflict pain or punishment; 2, a means of inflicting punishment; hence, harsh punishment; 3, one who or that which afflicts or destroys; as, the *scourge* of pestilence:—*v.t.* [scourged, scourg-ing], 1, to whip severely; 2, to grieve or torment greatly; harass; as, the plague *scourged* the land.

scour-ing rush, the common horsetail or equisetum, formerly used to scour wood, metals, etc.

¹scout (skout), *n.* 1, a person sent out to obtain and bring back information; esp., a soldier sent out to obtain information about the enemy; 2, the act of gathering such information; 3, a member of the Boy Scouts or the Girl Guides:—*v.i.* 1, to act as a scout; to go about for purposes of securing information; esp., to ascertain the movements, position, strength, etc., of an enemy; 2, to perform the duties of a boy scout or a girl scout.—*n.* **scout'mas'ter.**

²scout (skout), *v.i.* to mock; scoff; gibe; —*v.t.* to reject with disdain; as, she *scouted* all objections to her plan.

scow (skou), *n.* a large flat-bottomed boat with square ends, (used to carry garbage and other refuse to be dumped).

scowl (skoul), *v.i.* to wrinkle the brows in displeasure, anger, or the like:—*n.* an angry wrinkling of the brow.

scrab-ble (skrab'l) *v.i.* and *v.t.* 1, to scrawl or scribble (hastily); 2, scramble (on hands and knees); scrape, scratch, or paw with the hands.—*n.* a game played by forming words with letters of the alphabet on small blocks: the rarer consonants, like *j* or *z*, carry higher scoring values.

scrag-gly (skrag'li), *adj.* 1, unkempt, as a beard; 2, jagged, irregular, or splintered, as rocks.

scrag-gy (skrag'i), *adj.* 1, lean, thin, or bony; 2, scraggly.

scram (skram), *interj. Slang,* begone!

scram-ble (skram'bl), *v.i.* [scram-bled, scram-bling], 1, to clamber or move along on the hands and feet; as, to *scramble* over sand dunes; 2, to struggle eagerly or roughly for something; as, the children *scrambled* for the candy: —*v.t.* 1, to toss together at random; 2, to prepare (eggs) by cooking the mixed yolks and whites:—*n.* 1, a disorderly struggle; 2, a climb.

¹scrap (skrap), *n.* 1, a small piece, cut or broken off; 2, worn out, discarded, or broken machinery, or used and discarded metal of any kind; junk metal; 3, **scraps,** odds and ends; esp., small pieces of food left over from a meal: —*adj.* in the form of fragments or pieces; as, *scrap*-metal:—*v.t.* [scrapped, scrap-ping], to break up; discard, as broken machinery.

²scrap (skrap), *v.i. Slang,* to fight; quarrel; also, to box:—*n. Slang,* a scuffle; a fight with blows or words. —*n.* **scrap'per.**—*adj.* **scrap'py.**

scrap-book (skrap'book'), *n.* a blank book for pasting in clippings, pictures, etc.

scrape (skrāp), *v.t.* [scraped, scrap-ing], 1, to drag harshly or gratingly; as, to *scrape* a chair along the floor; 2, to remove by rubbing with something sharp or rough; as, to *scrape* paint from a door; also, to remove paint, paper, etc., from: as, to *scrape* furniture; *scrape* walls; 3, to gather or accumulate in small amounts, with effort; as, to *scrape* together a small sum:—*v.i.* to manage by being extremely economical; as, to pinch and *scrape:*—*n.* 1, the act, noise, or effect of harsh rubbing or grating; 2, a difficult or awkward situation; as, if he had obeyed his mother, he would not be in this *scrape.*—*n.* **scrap'er.**

scrap-ple (skrap'l), *n.* a food made by boiling together seasoned, chopped meat, usually pork, and corn-meal or flour. It is served in fried slices.

all (ôl), ôr; up, mūte, cûr, cōōl, book; oil, out; th, thin; *th*, the.

scratch (skrach), *v.t.* **1,** to mark or tear the surface of, with something rough or pointed; as, to *scratch* a table with a pin; **2,** to cancel or erase; as, *scratch* this item out; **3,** to scrape or rub lightly with the finger-nails, etc.; as, he *scratched* his cheek; **4,** to strike on an uneven surface; as, to *scratch* matches:—*v.i.* **1,** to make a grating noise; as, the chalk *scratches;* **2,** to cause irritation or pain by rubbing; as, the collar *scratches:*—*n.* **1,** a mark or tear made by something pointed or rough; **2,** a slight wound or cut, as that made by a pin; **3,** a grating sound, as of chalk on a slate; **4,** the starting line in a race; also, the beginning; as, we will start this work from *scratch.*—*n.* **scratch′er.**

scrawl (skrôl), *v.t.* and *v.i.* to write or draw hastily, or in badly formed characters:—*n.* careless handwriting; a scribble.

scraw-ny (skrô′ni), *adj.* [scraw-ni-er, scraw-ni-est], lean; skinny.

scream (skrēm), *n.* a sharp, shrill cry, as of fear or pain:—*v.i.* to utter such a cry:—*v.t.* to utter in a loud, piercing voice; as, to *scream* a warning.

scree (skrē), *n.* loose rock, débris, or pebbles at the base of a cliff, or on a mountain slope, glacier, etc.

screech (skrēch), *n.* a harsh, shrill cry, as of fright or pain:—*v.i.* to utter a harsh, shrill cry:—*v.t.* to cry out in a shrill voice.

screech owl, a small owl with erect ear tufts and an eerie, wailing screech instead of a hoot: there are 15 species in Canada, U.S., and Mexico: often called *barn owl* and *little horned owl.*

screen (skrēn), *n.* **1,** a light, covered framework, partition, or curtain, that protects or conceals; as, the nurse put a *screen* around his bed; **2,** anything in the nature of a protective curtain; as, a smoke-*screen;* the villain was concealed behind a *screen* of shubbery; **3,** a frame covered with wire or cotton fabric to exclude insects; as, a window *screen;* **4,** a coarse sieve for separating coal, gravel, etc., into different sizes; **5,** a surface on which images are projected by a motion-picture machine; **6,** hence, motion pictures:—*v.t.* **1,** to shut off from danger, observation, etc.; shelter or conceal; protect; **2,** to sift through a coarse sieve; **3,** to project (a picture) upon a screen with a motion-picture machine.

screw (skrōō), *n.* **1,** a slender, nail-like, round bar of metal, with a spiral groove, or thread, for holding together pieces of wood, metal, etc.; **2,** anything resembling such a device; **3,** a contrivance to propel steamships, motorboats, etc.: also called *screw propeller;* **4,** a turn of a screw; as, give it another *screw:*—*v.t.* **1,** to tighten or fasten with, or as with, a screw; **2,** to twist or distort; as, to *screw* up one's face; **3,** to force (something) from someone as if by the use of screws; as, to *screw* information out of a prisoner:—*v.i.* to turn with a motion like a screw.—*n.* **screw′nail′.**

screw-dri-ver (skrōō′drī′vér), a tool with a blunt blade, the tip of which fits into a slot in the head of a screw, and is used for turning the screw. Also written **screw driv′er.**

screw-y (skrōō′i), *adj. Slang,* **1,** unpractical; as, a *screwy* proposal; **2,** misleading; **3,** unbalanced; eccentric; irrational (of a person).

scrib-ble (skrib′l), *v.t.* [scrib-bled, scrib-bling], **1,** to write hastily and carelessly; **2,** to cover (paper, books, etc.) with careless or meaningless scrawls:—*v.i.* to scrawl: —*n.* hasty, careless writing.

scrib-bler (skrib′lér), *n.* **1,** one who scribbles; **2,** a tablet, or writing-pad.

scribe (skrīb), *n.* **1,** a skilled penman; esp., in former times, one who copied manuscripts, or acted as an official or public secretary; **2,** among the Jews, in ancient times, a teacher and lawgiver; **3,** humorously, an author.

scrim (skrim), *n.* a thin, loosely woven but strong, fabric of cotton or linen, used esp. in making curtains.

scrim-mage (skrim′ij), *n.* **1,** a general quarrel or fight; a tussle; **2,** in *football,* play following the snapping back of the ball when both teams are lined up.

scrimp (skrimp), *v.i.* to be sparing, frugal, or niggardly:—*v.t.* **1,** to skimp; allow too little of; as, to *scrimp* a garment; **2,** to stint; restrict to a scant allowance.

scrimp-y (skrimp′i), *adj.* [scrimp-i-er, scrimp-i-est], *Colloq.,* scanty.

script (skript), *n.* **1,** ordinary handwriting; written characters; also, style of writing; **2,** type that is an imitation of writing; **3,** in *motion pictures,* a written summary of the action, the cast of characters, etc.

Scrip-ture (skrip′tūr), *n.* the Bible: chiefly in *pl.* with *the:*—**scripture,** any sacred writing; as, the Buddhist *scriptures.*

scrof-u-la (skrof′ū-la), *n.* a disease marked by swelling and abscesses of the lymphatic glands, esp. in the neck, and defective nutrition of the bodily tissues.—*adj.* **scrof'u-lous.**

scroll (skrōl), *n.* **1,** a manuscript of paper or parchment in the form of a roll; **2,** a spiral, ornamental design in carving or printing; **3,** an ornamental flourish to a signature.

scro-tum (skrō'tum), *n.* in male mammals, the pouch of skin enclosing the testicles.

scrounge (skrounj), *v.t.* and *v.i.* *Slang,* to hunt about for and take without permission; pilfer.

¹scrub (skrub), *v.t.* [scrubbed, scrubbing], **1,** to wash by hard rubbing; as, to *scrub* clothes; **2,** to rub hard with a wet cloth or brush; as, to *scrub* floors, woodwork, hands, etc.:—*v.i.* to do cleaning and scouring; as, she *scrubs* for a living:—*n.* the act or process of cleaning by hard rubbing.

²scrub (skrub), *n.* **1,** a shrub, tree, bush, etc., stunted or inferior in growth; also, a growth of thicket of such stunted trees; as, pine *scrub;* **2,** anything, as a person, plant, or animal, that is inferior in size, quality, or breed; also, a member of a second or inferior team; as, the varsity played the *scrubs:*—*adj.* **1,** mean or small; also, below normal size; stunted; **2,** consisting of, or pertaining to, players who are not members of a regular team; as, a *scrub*-game.—*adj.* **scrub'by.**

scruff (skruf), *n.* the back of the neck; the loose skin at the back of the neck.

scrump-tious (skrump'shus), *adj.* *Slang,* delightful; enjoyable; first-rate; as, we had a *scrumptious* time.

scrunch (skrunch), *v.t.* to crunch, chew, or crush noisily:—*v.i.* to grind violently; squeeze:—*n.* the act or sound of crunching.

scru-ple (skrōō'pl), *n.* **1,** an apothecaries' weight of twenty grains or one third of a dram; **2,** a very small quantity; **3,** a feeling of doubt, uneasiness, or uncertainty arising from one's conscience; as, he had *scruples* about disregarding his mother's advice: —*v.i.* [scru-pled, scru-pling], to hesitate on grounds of conscience; as, he *scrupled* to leave his work so long.

scru-pu-lous (skrōō'pū-lus), *adj.* **1,** conscientious; attentive to details; as, a *scrupulous* student; **2,** unswerving; strict; as, *scrupulous* honesty.

scru-ti-nize (skrōō'ti-nīz'), *v.t.* and *v.i.* [scrutinized, scrutiniz-ing], to inspect closely; examine carefully.—*n.* **scru'ti-ny.**

scud (skud), *v.i.* [scud-ded, scud-ding], to run or move swiftly; of a ship, to run before a gale with little or no sail spread:—*n.* **1,** the act of scudding; **2,** foam or spray driven by the wind.

scuff (skuf), *v.t.* **1,** to wear a rough place on the surface of; as, to *scuff* new shoes; **2,** to shuffle or drag (the feet): —*v.i.* **1,** to become rough on the surface; as, soft leather *scuffs* easily; **2,** to drag the feet in a slovenly manner:—*n.* a rough or worn spot.

scuf-fle (skuf'l), *v.i.* [scuf-fled, scuffling], **1,** to fight or struggle in a confused, disorderly manner; **2,** to drag the feet in a slovenly fashion; scuff: —*n.* a close grappling; a confused or disorderly struggle or fight.

scull (skul), *n.* **1,** one of a pair of short, light oars; **2,** an oar used at the stern of a boat and worked from side to side to propel the boat forward; **3,** a boat, usually for racing, propelled by short oars:—*v.i.* and *v.t.* to propel or move (a boat) with an oar used at the stern. —*n.* **scull'er.**

scul-ler-y (skul'ėr-i), *n.* a back kitchen for washing and storing pots, pans, etc.

scul-lion (skul'yun), *n.* a servant who cleans cooking-utensils, scrubs floors, and does menial kitchen service.

scul-pin (skul'pin), *n.* a scaleless fish with a big head armed with spines, from 15 pounds (the *great sculpin*) to tiny 1″ forms: 40 species are found off the Pacific coast. Also called *grunt-fish.*

sculp-tor (skulp'tėr), *n.* one who practices the art of carving, cutting, or modelling figures or designs in wood, stone, etc.—*n.fem.* **sculp'tress.**

sculp-ture (skulp'tūr), *n.* **1,** the art of fashioning figures or other objects in stone, metal, wood, or clay; **2,** a piece of such work:—*v.t.* [sculptured, sculptur-ing], to carve, chisel, model, cast, in stone, wood, clay, or metal.

scum (skum), *n.* **1,** a layer of impurities which forms on the surface of a liquid; **2,** anything worthless or vile; hence, low, worthless people.—*adj.* **scum'my.**

scup-per (skup'ėr), *n.* a hole, tube, or gutter in the side of a ship to carry off water from the deck.

scurf (skûrf), *n.* **1,** small, dry scales shed by the skin, as dandruff; **2,** any flaky or scaly coating.

scur-ri-lous (skûr'i-lus), *adj.* grossly or obscenely vulgar or abusive; as, a *scurrilous* attack, speaker, journal, etc. —*n.* **scur-ril'i-ty.**

all (ôl), ôr; up, mūte, cûr, cōōl, book; oil, out; th, thin; *th*, the.

scur-ry (skur′i), *v.i.* (scurried, scurrying], to hasten or move rapidly along:—*n.* [*pl.* scurries], a scampering.

scur-vy (skûr′vi), *n.* a disease caused by lack of fresh vegetable food, and marked by great weakness, thinness of the body, bleeding gums, etc.:—*adj.* [scur-vi-er, scur-vi-est], contemptible; mean; as, a *scurvy* trick.

¹**scut-tle** (skut′l), *v.i.* [scut-tled, scut-tling], to hasten or hurry away:—*n.* a hurried flight.

²**scut-tle** (skut′l), *n.* a small opening with a lid, as in the roof of a house, or in the deck, bottom, or side of a ship; also, the lid covering such an opening:—*v.t.* [scut-tled, scut-tling], to sink (a ship) by cutting holes in the bottom or sides.

³**scut-tle** (skut′l), *n.* a deep metal vessel or hod for holding a small quantity of coal.

scythe (sī*th*), *n.* a cutting instrument for mowing grain, grass, etc., by hand.

sea (sē), *n.* **1,** a body of salt water, smaller than an ocean; as, the Aegean *Sea;* **2,** an inland body of water; as, the *Sea* of Galilee; **3,** the ocean as a whole; **4,** a billow or large wave; the swell of the ocean or other body of water in a storm; as, the high *sea* kept on after the storm; **5,** a large quantity; anything like the sea in vastness; as a *sea* of troubles; a *sea* of faces.

sea-board (sē′bōrd′), *n.* the land bordering the sea or ocean; the seacoast or seashore:—*adj.* near or on the seacoast.

sea-coast, the coast, or land bordering upon the sea or ocean; seashore.

sea-far-er (sē′fâr′ėr), *n.* a person who travels by sea or follows the life of a sailor.—*adj.* **sea′far′ing.**

sea-go-ing (sē′gō′ing), *adj.* **1,** seafaring; **2,** suitable or fitted for use on the open sea; as, a *seagoing* yacht.

sea—horse (sē′-hôrs′), *n.* **1,** in *mythology,* a fabulous creature, half horse and half fish; **2,** a small fish with a head resembling that of a horse.

¹**seal** (sēl), *n.* **1,** any of various flesh-eating sea animals, found chiefly in polar regions, and hunted for their hide and oil, and, in some species, for their valuable fur; **2,** the dressed fur of this animal; sealskin; **3,** a leather made from the skin of the seal:—*v.i.* to hunt seals. —*n.* seal′er.

SEA-HORSE (⅓) def. 2.

²**seal** (sēl), *n.* **1,** a stamp or die engraved with a device, image, etc., used for making an impression in wax or some similar substance; **2,** wax or a similar substance fixed upon a letter or document and stamped with an emblem or design as proof of genuineness; **3,** anything that closes another thing securely in order to prevent its being opened or tampered with; hence, anything that secures; a pledge; as, a *seal* of silence on his lips; **4,** a decorative stamp used in sealing a letter or package; as, a Christmas *seal:*—*v.t.* **1,** to fasten with a device so that it cannot be tampered with; as, to *seal* a letter; **2,** to set or affix a seal to; as, to *seal* a deed; **3,** to ratify or confirm; as, the bargain was *sealed;* **4,** to keep secure or secret; as, to *seal* documents for later examination; **5,** to settle (a person's fate) once and for all; **6,** to enclose; confine; as, a fly *sealed* in amber; **7,** to close tightly, as a pipe, a jar of fruit, etc.; also, to fill up the cracks of.—*n.* seal′er.

seal brown, a rich, dark-brown colour like that of the fur of the seal after it is dyed.

sea lev-el, the level of the sea halfway between high and low tide: used as the standard in measuring the height of land; as, 300 feet above *sea level.*

sea li-on, any of several large seals of the Pacific Ocean.

seal-skin (sēl′skin′), *n.* the skin of a fur seal or a garment made of it.

seam (sēm), *n.* **1,** the line formed by sewing together two edges of material; **2,** a visible line of junction or union, as between two boards; **3,** a scar; also, a wrinkle; **4,** a layer or bed of mineral or rock; as, a *seam* of copper ore:—*v.t.* **1,** to join or sew together, as the parts of a garment; **2,** to scar; line; as, the wind had *seamed* his face with wrinkles.—*adj.* seam′less.

sea-man (sē′man), *n.* [*pl.* seamen (-men)], a sailor; mariner.—*n.* sea′manship.—*adj.* sea′man-ly.

seam-stress (sēm′stres), *n.* a woman who does sewing for a living; a needlewoman.

seam-y (sēm′i), *adj.* [seam-i-er, seam-i-est], **1,** showing or having seams, esp. roughly finished seams; **2,** hence, rough; harsh and unpleasant; as, the *seamy* side of life.

se-ance (sā′äns; sä′äns′), *n.* a session or meeting, as of a society; esp. a meeting of spiritualists to receive spirit messages.

cat, āge, fär, câre, ȧsk; ten, ēve, latėr; (i) pity, rely, senate; īce; top; nō.

sea otter, a marine mammal of the Canadian Pacific coast: its beauty and pelt value led to its becoming almost extinct: since 1911 a treaty protects it, and in the 1950's it began to reappear.

sea-plane (sē'plān'), *n.* an aeroplane so constructed that it can alight or travel upon the surface of water.

sea-port (sē'pōrt'), *n.* a town, harbour, or port that can be reached by seagoing vessels.

sear (sēr), *v.t.* **1,** to cause to dry up or wither; scorch; as, the summer sun *sears* the fields; **2,** to burn to dryness and hardness on the surface; cauterize; as, to *sear* a wound; **3,** to render callous or unfeeling, as the conscience:—*adj.* (also *sere*), withered; dried; as leaves.

search (sûrch), *v.t.* **1,** to seek; as, to *search* out the truth; **2,** to look for something by examining carefully the contents of (a place or object), the clothing of (a person), etc.; as, to *search* a room; to *search* a prisoner for weapons; **3,** to probe; try or test; as, to *search* one's heart:—*n.* **1,** the act of seeking or looking for something; **2,** a careful investigation; examination.

search-ing (sûr'ching), *adj.* penetrating; thorough; keen; as, a *searching* glance.—*adv.* **search'ing-ly.**

search-light (sûrch'līt'), *n.* a powerful electric light that can throw a beam of light in any direction; also, the beam.

search—war-rant (sûrch'-wor'ant), *n.* a written order giving a police-officer authority to search a house.

sea-scape (sē'skāp'), *n.* a view, or picture, of the sea.

sea-shore (sē'shōr'), *n.* the land bordering the sea; seacoast.

sea-sick (sē'sik'), *adj.* suffering from nausea caused by the pitching and rolling of a boat.—*n.* **sea'sick'ness.**

sea-side (sē'sīd'), *n.* the shore along the sea; the seashore.

sea-son (sē'zn), *n,* **1,** one of the four periods into which the year is divided, as spring, summer, autumn, and winter; **2,** any particular time; as, the holiday *season;* **3,** a suitable, convenient, or legal time; as, the shooting *season:*—*v.t.* **1,** to bring to the best state for use; as, to *season* timber; **2,** to make palatable, as with salt or spices; also, to make more delightful; as, he *seasoned* his lecture with humour:—*v.i.* to become fit for use; as, timber *seasons* well in the open air.

sea-son-a-ble (sē'zn-a-bl), *adj.* **1,** occurring or coming in good or proper time; as, *seasonable* advice; **2,** in keeping with the time of year; as, *seasonable* weather.

sea-son-al (sē'zn-al), *adj.* relating to or influenced by certain periods of the year; as, *seasonal* rates; *seasonal* diseases; *seasonal* trades; *seasonal* labour.—*adv.* **sea'son-al-ly.**

sea-son-ing (sē'zn-ing), *n.* that which is added to give relish to food, as salt, pepper, spices, etc.

seat (sēt), *n.* **1,** an object on which one sits; a bench, chair, or stool; **2,** that part of a chair, stool, or bench, on which one sits; **3,** that part of the body on which one sits; also, the part of a garment covering it; as, the *seat* of one's trousers; **4,** the place where anything flourishes; location; site; as, the brain is the *seat* of the intellect; a university is a *seat* of learning; **5,** a capital town or city; as, a county *seat;* **6,** the right to sit; specifically, membership; as, a *seat* on the stock exchange; **7,** room or space for a spectator; as, *seats* for a football game:—*v.t.* **1,** to place on a chair or bench; cause to sit down; **2,** to furnish with places to sit; as, this hall *seats* 800 persons; **3,** to repair the bottom of; as, to *seat* a chair.

SEATO (sē'tō), Southeast Asia Treaty Organization.

sea urchin, a sea animal less than 2″ through, with flattened globular body of lime plates covered by spines ¾″ long: it has 5 double rows of sucker-bearing tube feet: found on continental shelves: eggs used for food, esp. in Europe.

sea-ward (sē'wẽrd), *adj.* going toward, or situated in the direction of, the sea: —*adv.* toward the sea.—*adv.* **sea'-wards.**

sea-way (sē'wā'), *n.* **1,** a route by sea; **2,** a ship's forward motion; **3,** an inland passage for ocean-going ships, as the St. Lawrence Seaway.

sea-weed (sē'wēd'), *n.* any plant growing in the sea, as kelp.

sea-wor-thy (sē'wûr'thi), *adj.* fit for a voyage on the open sea; as, a *seaworthy* boat.—*n.* **sea'wor'thi-ness.**

se-cant (sē'kant), *n.* **1,** a straight line that cuts a curve in two points; **2,** a ratio in trigonometry.

se-cede (si-sēd'), *v.i.* [seced-ed, seceding], to withdraw formally from fellowship, union, or association; esp., to withdraw from a political or religious body.—*n.* **se-ces'sion** (si-sesh'un).

se-clude (si-klōōd'), *v.t.* [seclud-ed,

seclud-ing], to withdraw or keep apart from others; to place in solitude.—*n.* **se-clu′sion.**

sec-ond (sek′und), *adj.* **1,** immediately following the first; next to the first in order of place or time; **2,** next to the first in value, excellence, merit, dignity, or importance; as, a *second* lieutenant; **3,** being of the same kind as another that has gone before; another; as, a *second* Laurier; additional; as, a *second* helping; **4,** in *music*, rendering a part next to the highest in pitch and importance; as, a *second* violin:—*n.* **1,** one who or that which is next to the first in place, rank, excellence, or power; **2,** one who attends another, as in a duel or boxing match; **3,** a unit of time; the 60th part of a minute; **4,** hence, *Colloq.*, a short space of time; as, wait just a *second;* **5,** an article of merchandise of a grade inferior to the best; as, these *seconds* are very cheap:—*v.t.* **1,** to act as an assistant or supporter of; assist; **2,** in parliamentary practice, to support a motion, resolution, or nomination proposed by another.—*adj.* and *n.* **sec′ond-ar-y.**

sec-ond-hand (sek′und-hand′), *adj.* **1,** not new; as, *secondhand* furniture; **2,** dealing in goods that are not new; as, a *secondhand* shop; **3,** heard or learned indirectly; as, *secondhand* news.

sec-ond-ly (sek′und-li), *adv.* in the next place; in the second place.

se-cre-cy (sē′kre-si), *n.* [*pl.* secrecies], **1,** the state or quality of being secret or hidden; concealment; as, done in *secrecy;* **2,** the habit of keeping information to oneself.

se-cret (sē′krit), *adj.* **1,** concealed; private; as, *secret* information; **2,** withdrawn from public view or knowledge; as, a *secret* treaty; also, operating in secrecy; as, a *secret* society; **3,** permitting concealment; secluded; as, a *secret* chamber; **4,** mysterious; unknown; as, the *secret* operations of nature:—**secret service,** government detective service:—*n.* **1,** that which is purposely concealed or left untold; **2,** something not widely known; as, the *secrets* of science; **3,** a hidden reason or cause; as, unselfishness is the *secret* of his happiness; **4,** secrecy; as, prepared in *secret*.—*adv.* **se′cret-ly.**

sec-re-tar-y (sek′re-tėr-i; sek′ri-ter′i), *n.* [*pl.* secretaries], **1,** one who does writing for another; esp., one who attends to records, letters, etc., for an individual or an organization; **2,** an official of a company or society in charge of records and correspondence; **3,** a state executive who superintends the business of a government department; as, the *Secretary* of State; **4,** a writing-desk.—*adj.* **sec′re-tar′i-al** (sek′ri-târ′i-al).

se-crete (si-krēt′), *v.t.* [secret-ed, secreting], **1,** to hide or conceal; **2,** to separate from the blood and make into a new substance; produce; as, the liver *secretes* bile.—*n.* **se-cre′tion.**

se-cre-tive (si-krē′tiv), *adj.* inclined to keep things to oneself; not frank or open; reticent.—*adv.* **se-cre′tive-ly.**

sect (sekt), *n.* a number of persons who, following a teacher or leader, hold certain opinions in common, esp. certain religious opinions.—*n.* and *adj.* **sec-tar′i-an.**

sec-tion (sek′shun), *n.* **1,** the act of cutting; separation by cutting; **2,** a part or portion cut off; **3,** a representation of an object cut in two crosswise or lengthwise; as, the cross-*section* of a tomato; **4,** a division or subdivision of a chapter, often marked with the character [§]; **5,** a distinct part of a country, people, community, etc.; as, the business *section* of the city; **6,** in a sleeping-car, a compartment including an upper and a lower berth:—*v.t.* to divide or cut into sections.

sec-tion-al (sek′shun-al), *adj.* **1,** relating to a section or district; local; as, *sectional* strife; **2,** consisting of parts; as, a *sectional* bookcase.

sec-tor (sek′tėr), *n.* the area enclosed by two radii and the arc of a circle, ellipse, or other curve cut by them.

sec-u-lar (sek′ū-lėr), *adj.* **1,** relating to things of the world or to things not sacred; worldly; as, *secular* art; of the state as opposed to the church; as, *secular* courts; **2,** not bound by monastic communities; as, a parish priest belongs to the *secular* clergy —*v.t.* **sec′u-lar-ize′**.—*n.* **sec′u-lar-i-za′tion.**

SECTOR of a circle

se-cure (si-kūr′), *adj.* **1,** free from fear, care, or worry; **2,** safe; free from danger; as, *secure* against attack; in safekeeping; as, the prisoners are *secure;* affording safety; as, a *secure* retreat; firm or steady; as, a *secure* foundation; **3,** confident; as, *secure* of welcome; certain; assured; as, the victory is *secure:*—*v.t.* [secured, securing], **1,** to make safe; protect; **2,** to guarantee repayment of; as, he gave a mortgage to *secure* the loan; also, to protect oneself against the loss of; as, he took a mortgage to *secure* the loan; **3,** to make fast; latch or lock; as, to *secure* a door; also to place in custody; as, to *secure* a prisoner; **4,** to gain possession of; as, to *secure* wealth.—*adv.* **se-cure′ly.**—*adj.* **se-cur′a-ble.**

se-cu-ri-ty (si-kū′ri-ti), *n.* [*pl.* securities], **1,** the state or quality of being safe or protected; certainty; **2,** a means of safety or protection; as, insurance offers *security;* **3,** something given as a guarantee of performance or payment; as, he offered stock as *security* for the loan; **4,** one who becomes responsible for another; a surety; **5, securities,** bonds or stock that may be bought and sold.

se-dan (si-dān′), *n.* **1,** a portable covered chair or vehicle accommodating one passenger, usually slung between two poles and carried by two men: also called *sedan-chair;* **2,** a closed automobile for four or more persons.

se-date (si-dāt′), *adj.* calm; composed; serious; as, a *sedate* young lady.

sed-a-tive (sed′a-tiv), *n.* and *adj.* a remedy that calms or soothes by lessening excitement, irritation, etc. —*n.* **se-da′tion.**

sed-en-ta-ry (sed′en-ta-ri), *adj.* **1,** requiring a sitting posture; as, typing is a *sedentary* occupation; **2,** caused by sitting; as, a *sedentary* ailment.

sedge (sej), *n.* any of many grasslike herbs or plants growing in marshes —*adj.* **sedg′y.**

sed-i-ment (sed′i-ment), *n.* **1,** the solid substance which settles at the bottom of a liquid; dregs; **2,** sand, gravel, mud, etc., deposited, as by water—*adj.* **sed′i-men′ta-ry.**—*n.* **sed′i-men-ta′tion.**

se-di-tion (si-dish′un), *n.* agitation against a government, just short of insurrection or treason; the stirring up of discontent, rebellion, or resistance against lawful authority.—*adj.* **se-di′-tious.**

se-duce (si-dūs′), *v.t.* [seduced, seducing], to lead away from the paths of right, duty, or virtue, by flattery, promises, etc.; lead astray; tempt to do wrong.—*n.* **se-duc′er.**—*n.* **se-duc′tion.** —*adj.* **se-duc′tive.**

sed-u-lous (sed′ū-lus), *adj.* steadily industrious; diligent in application and attention; as, a *sedulous* worker, *sedulous* flattery.—*adv.* **sed′u-lous-ly.**

see (sē), *v.t.* [*p.t.* saw (sô), *p.p.* seen (sēn), *p.pr.* see-ing], **1,** to perceive with the eyes; behold; **2,** to discern mentally;

understand; as, to *see* a meaning; **3,** to accompany or escort; as, he *saw* the visitor to the door; **4,** to find out or learn by observation or experience; as, he wished to *see* what the result would be; **5,** to have personal experience of; as, he *saw* service in the war; **6,** to make sure; as, *see* that you address him properly; **7,** to visit, call on, or talk with; as, we went to *see* her; **8,** to admit to one's presence; receive; as, she refused to *see* us:—*v.i.* **1,** to possess or use the power of sight; **2,** to understand or discern; **3,** to consider; reflect; as, will you do it? I will *see;* **4,** to take care; attend; as, *see* to the dinner; **5,** to look: used only in the imperative; as, *See!* here he comes!

²**see** (sē), *n.* the official local seat of a bishop; the diocese of a bishop; the office or authority of a bishop:—**Holy See,** the seat of the papacy; the papal court or authority.

seed (sēd), *n.* [*pl.* seed or seeds], **1,** that part of a flowering plant that holds the germ of life, capable of developing into another plant; **2,** any small, seedlike fruit; as, dandelion or grass *seed;* **3,** a source or origin; as, *seeds* of discord; **4,** offspring; descendants; as, the *seed* of Jacob:—**to go to seed, 1,** to develop seed; **2,** *Colloq.*, to become shabby; to lose vitality or vigour:—*v.i.* **1,** to sow seed; **2,** to mature or produce seed; also, to shed seed:—*v.t.* **1,** to sow with seed, as a lawn; **2,** to remove the seeds from. —*n.* **seed′er.**—*adj.* **seed′less.**

seed-case (sēd′kās′), *n.* a dry hollow fruit containing seeds, as the pod of a pea.

seed-ling (sēd′ling), *n.* **1,** a plant grown from a seed; **2,** a young plant or tree.

seed-y (sēd′i), *adj.* [seed-i-er, seed-i-est], **1,** full of seed; having run to seed; **2,** *Colloq.*, shabby; threadbare.

seek (sēk), *v.t.* [sought (sôt), seeking], **1,** to go in search of; **2,** to aim at; as, to *seek* wealth; **3,** to ask or appeal for; as, to *seek* aid; **4,** to resort to; as, he *sought* the theatre for recreation; **5,** to attempt or try; as, he *sought* to undo the harm he had done:—*v.i.* to make search; inquire; make efforts to find someone or something.

seem (sēm), *v.i.* **1,** to appear; look; have the semblance of; as, the sky *seems* clear; **2,** to appear to exist; as, there *seems* little difference of opinion; **3,** to appear to one's own mind or imagination; as, I *seemed* to be floating in space.

all (ôl), **ôr;** up, mūte, cûr, cōol, book; **oil, out;** th, thin; *th*, the.

seem-ly (sēm′li), *adj.* [seem-li-er, seem-li-est], fit or becoming; decent; proper; as, *seemly* behaviour.—*n.* **seem′li-ness.**

seep (sēp), *v.i.* to leak out slowly; ooze.

seep-age (sēp′ij), *n.* **1,** a slow leaking through; **2,** the liquid that leaks through.

se-er (sē′ėr), *n.* **1,** one who sees; **2,** (sēr), one who claims to foresee the future; a prophet.

seer-suck-er (sēr′suk′ėr), *n.* a thin linen or cotton fabric, usually striped and of a crinkly or puckered weave.

see-saw (sē′sô′), *n.* **1,** a game in which children, sitting or standing on opposite ends of a balanced plank, move alternately up and down; also, the plank; **2,** any movement to and fro or up and down:—*v.i.* to move up and down or to and fro.

seethe (sēth), *v.i.* [*p.t.* seethed, *p.p.* seethed or, rarely, sod-den (sod′n), *p.pr.* seething], **1,** to boil; as, a *seething* pot; to move in violent agitation; as, a *seething* whirlpool; **2,** to be violently agitated; as, the crowd *seethed* with excitement.

seg-ment (seg′ment), *n.* **1,** any of the parts into which an object naturally separates or divides; a section; as, a *segment* of an orange; **2,** in *geometry*, a part cut off from a figure by one or more lines; esp., the part of a circle included between an arc and its chord.—*n.* **seg′men-ta′tion.**

SEGMENT (S) of a circle.

seg-re-gate (seg′ri-gāt′), *v.t.* **1,** to separate from others; cut off; set apart; isolate; **2,** in *science*, to put into a new or separate class.—*n.* **seg′re-ga′-tion.**

seign-ior (sēn′yėr) or **seigneur** (sân′-yûr′), *n.* in French Canada, the holder of a **seign′ior-y** (sēn′yėr-i) or **seign′-eur-y** (sân′yû-ri), a landed estate, held (until 1854) by feudal tenure (esp. along the St. Lawrence River).

seine (sān; sēn), *n.* a large fishing-net equipped with sinkers and floats:—*v.t.* [seined, sein-ing], to catch (fish) with such a net:—*v.i.* to fish with a seine.

seis-mo-graph (sīs′mō-grȧf′; sīz′), *n.* an instrument that automatically records the time, intensity, and direction of earthquakes.

seis-mol-o-gy (sīs-mol′o-ji), *n.* the science of earthquakes, their causes, etc.

seize (sēz), *v.t.* [seized, seiz-ing], **1,** to take possession of forcibly or suddenly; as, soldiers *seized* the fort; **2,** to grasp; snatch; take hold of; as, *seize* him by the arm; **3,** to take into legal custody on a warrant; as, the officers *seized* the kidnappers; **4,** to grasp mentally; understand:—**seize** (*up*), to become stuck owing to excessive heat, etc.; as, his motor *seized up* from lack of oil.

sei-zure (sē′zhŭr; zhėr), *n.* **1,** the act of taking forcible possession; **2,** a sudden attack, as of a disease; a fit.

sel-dom (sel′dum), *adv.* rarely; not often.

se-lect (si-lekt′), *adj.* **1,** carefully chosen or picked out; **2,** hence, of great excellence; choicest or best; as, a volume of *select* poems; **3,** exclusive; made up of chosen persons; as, a *select* club:—*v.t.* to pick out from among a number; choose.—*n.* **se-lec′tor.**—*adj.* **se-lec′tive.**—*n.* **se′lec-tiv′i-ty.**

se-lec-tion (si-lek′shun), *n.* **1,** the act of choosing; choice; as, the *selection* of one from so many is difficult; **2,** the thing or things chosen; as, the Scott novel is my *selection;* **3,** a part of a book, a piece of music, etc.; as, he read a *selection* from Shakespeare.

se-le-ni-um (si-lē′ni-um), *n.* a rare element of the sulphur group (by-product of copper refining), used in photoelectric devices, as talking films.

¹self (self), *n.* [*pl.* selves (selvz)], **1,** the entire person or character of an individual; that which makes one person quite different from others; personality; **2,** a phase or side of a person's character which may show itself under certain conditions or at specific times; as, her nobler *self;* **3,** personal or private interest; as, *self* was always present in his thoughts:—*adj.* same or very: now used only in the compound *selfsame;* as, I bought some of the *self*same material.

²self- (self-), *prefix* meaning *of, by, in,* or *to oneself* or *itself,* as in *self*-restraint, *self*-appointed, *self*-centred, *self*-ad-dressed, etc.

self—com-mand (self′–ko-mand′), *n.* control of one's actions and emotions; self-possession.

self—con-fi-dence (self′–kon′fi-dens), *n.* belief in one's own ability; sometimes, too great a belief in oneself; conceit.—*adj.* **self′—con′fi-dent.**

self—con-scious (self′–kon′shus), *adj.* too keenly aware of one's own actions, manner, feelings, etc.; embarrassed in the presence of others; ill at ease.

---

cat, āge, fär, câre, ȧsk; ten, ēve, latėr; (i) pity, rely, senȧte; īce; top; nō

self—con-trol (self'-kon-trōl'), *n.* control of one's desires, acts, and emotions.

self—de-fence (self'-di-fens'), *n.* the act of protecting one's person, property, or name against attack.

self—de-ni-al (self'-di-nī'al), *n.* refusal to consider one's own wishes or needs; self-sacrifice.—*adj.* **self'—de-ny'ing.**

self—es-teem (self'-es-tēm'), *n.* **1,** proper respect for oneself; self-respect; **2,** too high an opinion of oneself; conceit.

self—gov-ern-ment (self'-guv'ėrn-ment), *n.* **1,** government of a nation by the united action of its people, as in a republic; **2,** a similar form of government in a state, town, school, etc.; **3,** of persons, self-control.—*adj.* **self'—gov'ern-ing.**

self—im-por-tant(self'-im-pôr'tant), *adj.* having an exaggerated idea of oneself; pompous.—*n.* **self'—im-por'-tance.**

self—in-ter-est (self'-in'tėr-est; –in'-trist), *n.* concern for one's own welfare, regardless of the rights of others; selfishness.

self-ish (sel'fish), *adj.* **1,** putting one's own wishes and advantages before the wishes and advantages of others; **2,** prompted or marked by undue regard for oneself; as, a *selfish* act.—*adv.* **self'ish-ly.**—*n.* **self'ish-ness.**

self—made (self'-mād'), *adj.* having risen by one's own efforts from poverty and obscurity to wealth and power.

self—pos-sessed (self'-po-zest'), *adj.* having, or seeming to have, composure and calmness; poised.—*n.* **self'—pos-ses'sion.**

self—pres-er-va-tion (self'-prez'ėr-vā'shun), *n.* the keeping of oneself from harm or danger; esp., the instinct to protect oneself when danger threatens.

self—re-li-ance (self'-ri-lī'ans), *n.* confidence in, and dependence on, one's own ability, efforts, or judgment. —*adj.* **self'—re-li'ant.**

self—re-spect (self'-ri-spekt'), *n.* proper regard or respect for oneself; self-esteem.—*adj.* **self'—re-spec'ting.**

self—re-straint (self'-ri-strānt'), *n.* self-control; self-command.

self—sac-ri-fice (self'-sak'ri-fīs'; –sak'ri-fiz'), *n.* the sacrifice of one's personal interests or of one's life, whether from affection for another person, or devotion to a duty or cause. —*adj.* **self'—sac'ri-fic'ing.**

self—same (self'sām'), *adj.* identical.

self—seek-ing (self'-sēk'ing), *n.* the act or practice of looking out for one's own interests:—*adj.* selfish.

self—suf-fi-cient (self'-su-fish'ent), *adj.* **1,** needing no help from others; **2,** having undue confidence in oneself; self-confident.—*n.* **self'—suf-fi'cien-cy.**

self—sup-port-ing (self'-su-por'-ting), *adj.* **1,** earning one's own living; **2,** paying for itself without outside help; as, a *self-supporting* institution.

self—willed (self'-wild'), *adj.* bent on having one's own way; stubborn; wilful.

sell (sel), *v.t.* [sold (sōld), sell-ing], **1,** to give in return for a price, esp., money; as, this store *sells* shoes; also, to act as a salesman of; as, he *sells* insurance; **2,** to betray for a reward; as, to *sell* one's country:—*v.i.* **1,** to dispose of for a price; **2,** to find a market; as, eggs *sell* at a lower price in summer than in winter.—*n.* **sell'er.**

sel-vage or **sel-vedge** (sel'vij), *n.* the edge of cloth so woven as to prevent ravelling.

se-man-tics (si-man'tiks), *n.pl.* used as *sing.* the science of the meaning and sense development of words, together with the effect of language symbols upon the intellectual, emotional, and physiological life of the individual: the Canadian Institute of General Semantics was founded in Montreal in 1956. —*adj.* **se-man'tic.**

sem-a-phore (sem'a-fōr'), *n.* **1,** an apparatus for signalling, by day or night, by means of mechanical arms, lanterns, flags, etc.; **2,** in the army, a system of signaling in which the operator uses a flag in each hand, the letters of the alphabet being represented by various positions of the arms in relation to the body and to each other.

sem-blance (sem'blans), *n.* **1,** image; representation; as, a crucifix is the *semblance* of Christ crucified; **2,** outward appearance; hence, pretence; as, a *semblance* of truth.

se-men (sē'men), *n.* [*pl.* semina], the whitish fertilizing fluid of the male reproductive organs.—*adj.* **sem'i-nal.**

se-mes-ter (si-mes'tėr), *n.* a six-months period, esp. one of the two terms of a college or university year.

sem-i (sem'i-), a *prefix* meaning *half*, *partly* or *imperfectly*, or *twice* (in a specified period), as in *semi*circle, *semi*conscious, and *semi*weekly, respectively.

sem-i—an-nu-al (sem/i–an/ū-al), *adj.* occurring, published, due, etc., each half year, or twice a year; as, *semiannual* interest payments.—*adv.* **sem/i-an/nu-al-ly.**

sem-i-breve (sem/i-brēv/), *n.* in *music,* a whole note.

sem-i-cir-cle (sem/i-sûr/kl), *n.* half of a circle.—*adj.* **sem/i-cir/cu-lar.**

sem-i-co-lon (sem/i-kō/lun), *n.* a mark of punctuation [;], indicating a separation in the parts of a sentence greater than that marked by a comma.

sem-i-month-ly (sem/i-munth/ly), *adj.* occurring or done every half month, or twice a month:—*n.* [*pl.* semimonthlies], anything published or produced twice a month:—*adv.* at intervals of half a month.

sem-i-nar (sem/i-när/), *n.* a group of students as at a university, doing advanced work, esp. original research, under an instructor.

sem-i-nar-y (sem/i-nèr/i), *n.* [*pl.* seminaries], **1,** a private school or academy, usually one which prepares pupils for college; **2,** a school or college which prepares students for the priesthood or the ministry.

sem-i-pre-cious (sem/i-presh/us), *adj.* not among the most valuable; used of gems, such as the opal and amethyst, to distinguish them from *precious* gems, such as the diamond and ruby.

Sem-it-ic (se-mit/ik), *adj.* pertaining to the **Sem/ites,** a speech family comprising esp. the Hebrews, Arabs, Assyrians, and Aramaeans.

sem-i-tone (sem/i-tōn/), *n.* in *music,* a tone at an interval of half a step from a given tone: also called *half step* and *the interval.*

sem-i-trail-er (sem/i-trāl/ėr), *n.* a large trailer (with four or more wheels) attached to a tractor cab for hauling heavy loads.

sem-i-week-ly (sem/i-wēk/li), *adj.* occurring, published, or produced twice a week:—*n.* [*pl.* semiweeklies], anything published or produced twice a week:—*adv.* at intervals of half a week.

sen-ate (sen/it), *n.* **1,** in ancient Rome, the supreme legislative and administrative body; **2,** in modern times, an assembly or council of citizens with governmental powers; a legislative body:—**Senate,** the upper and smaller branch of the legislature, in such countries as the U.S., France, Canada, and Australia.

sen-a-tor (sen/a-tėr), *n.* a member of the senate, or upper house of a legislature.

sen-a-tor-i-al (sen/a-tōr/i-al), *adj.* **1,** referring to, or befitting, a senator or a senate; as, *senatorial* dignity; **2,** entitled to elect a senator; as, a *senatorial* district.

send (send), *v.t.* [sent (sent), send-ing], **1,** to cause to go, often to some special destination; as, to *send* a messenger; to *send* a child to school; **2,** to cause to be carried; as, to *send* a letter, greetings, or news; **3,** to cause to come or happen; bestow; as, fate *sent* much happiness to him; **4,** to throw or drive, as a ball:—*v.i.* to send word of some kind; as, he *sent* for me; I *sent* to warn him.—*n.* **send/er.**

se-nile (sē/nīl; -nil), *adj.* showing weaknesses of old age; as, *senile* babblings.—*n.* **se-nil/i-ty** (dotage).

sen-ior (sēn/yėr), *adj.* **1,** superior in dignity, rank, or office; older in standing; as, the *senior* member of the firm; **2,** older in years: generally used after a person's name, often in abbreviated form, *Sr.,* to distinguish the older of two persons having the same name; as, John Moore, *Sr.;* **3,** connected with the last year of a high-school or college course:—*n.* **1,** one who is older than others, or superior in dignity, rank, or office; **2,** a student in the final year of his high-school or college course.—*n.* **sen-ior/i-ty** (sēn-yor/i-ti).

sen-sa-tion (sen-sā/shun), *n.* **1,** a bodily feeling, usually produced by an external object or condition; as, a *sensation* of warmth; also, a mental feeling or emotion; as, a *sensation* of fear; **2,** a state of general excitement or interest; as, the new pianist produced a great *sensation;* also, the cause of the excitement.

sen-sa-tion-al (sen-sā/shun-al), *adj.* **1,** pertaining to bodily sensation; **2,** extraordinary; as, a *sensational* escape; **3,** exciting; thrilling; as, a *sensational* novel.

sense (sens), *n.* **1,** any one of the special faculties of the body by which impressions are received from the outside world; as, the *senses* of sight, smell, hearing, taste, touch, etc.; **2,** bodily feeling; sensation; as, a *sense* of pleasure or pain, heat or cold; **3,** understanding; judgment; as, he is a man of *sense;* a *sense* of the fitness of things; **4,** lively appreciation; as, a *sense* of humour:—*v.t.* [sensed, sensing], **1,** to perceive; be aware of; as, to *sense* hostility; **2,** *Colloq.*, to understand; as, I *sense* your meaning.

sense-less (sens'lis), *adj.* **1,** without feeling; unconscious, as a person in a faint; **2,** stupid; meaningless; as, a *senseless* argument.—*n.* **sense'less-ness.**

sen-si-bil-i-ty (sen'si-bil'i-ti), *n.* [*pl.* sensibilities], **1,** the capacity to feel; as, the *sensibility* of the skin; **2,** sensitiveness; capacity for emotion, in contrast to intellect; esp., acute feelings of delight, sorrow, appreciation, etc., in response to impressions; as, the *sensibility* of an artist.

sen-si-ble (sen'si-bl), *adj.* **1,** capable of affecting the senses; noticeable; as, a *sensible* rise in temperature; **2,** capable of being grasped by the mind; as, a *sensible* difference; **3,** conscious; aware; as, I am *sensible* of your kindness to me; **4,** having good common sense; reasonable.—*adv.* **sen'si-bly.**

sen-si-tive (sen'si-tiv), *adj.* **1,** quick to receive impressions from external objects or conditions; as, a *sensitive* skin; **2,** responding to or recording slight shades or changes of sound, light, etc.; as, a *sensitive* photographic film; **3,** easily moved; impressionable; also, easily offended; touchy.—*n.* **sen'si-tiv'i-ty.**—*v.t.* **sen'si-tize'.**

sen-so-ry (sen'so-ri), *adj.* **1,** pertaining to the senses or to sensation; as, *sensory* impressions; **2,** conveying messages from the organs of sense, as the eyes, ears, etc., to the brain; as, *sensory* nerves.

sen-su-al (sen'shoo-al; sen'sū-al), *adj.* **1,** associated with the pleasures of the body; not mental or spiritual; as, a *sensual* life; **2,** indulging in the pleasures of the body.—*n.* **sen'su-al'i-ty; sen'su-al-ism; sen'su-al-ist.**

sen-su-ous (sen'shoo-us; sen'sū-us), *adj.* **1,** appealing to the senses; as, *sensuous* music; **2,** sensitive to the beauty of colour, tone, texture, etc.—*adv.* **sen'su-ous-ly.**

sen-tence (sen'tens), *n.* **1,** in *grammar*, a series of words usually containing a subject and a predicate and expressing a complete thought; **2,** in *law*, judgment pronounced by a court; also, a penalty imposed:—*v.t.* (sentenced, sentenc-ing], to pronounce judgment or impose a penalty upon; as, the judge *sentenced* the thief to two months' imprisonment.

sen-ten-tious (sen-ten'shus), *adj.* **1,** full of proverbs or terse, pithy sayings; hence, moralizing; as, a *sententious* style; **2,** using a terse or moralizing style; as, a *sententious* orator.

sen-ti-ent (sen'shi-ent; sen'shent), *adj.* **1,** able to feel or perceive; conscious: opposite of *inanimate*; **2,** experiencing sensation.—*n.* **sen'ti-ence.**

sen-ti-ment (sen'ti-ment), *n.* **1,** an opinion or attitude of mind based on, or strongly influenced by, feeling or emotion; as, a person of strong patriotic *sentiment*; **2,** a feeling or emotion, as of pity or affection; **3,** a thought or opinion as distinct from the words in which it is expressed; as, I like the *sentiment* but not the language.

sen-ti-men-tal (sen'ti-men'tal), *adj.* **1,** easily moved to pity, sympathy, etc.; also, given to indulging one's emotions freely, or too freely; as, a *sentimental* girl; **2,** appealing to the emotions; as, *sentimental* poetry.—*n.* **sen'ti-men-tal'-i-ty.**—*n.* **sen'ti-men'tal-ism; sen'ti-men'tal-ist.**

sen-ti-nel (sen'ti-nl), *n.* a person who watches or guards; esp., a soldier on guard at a camp or fort; a sentry.

sen-try (sen'tri), *n.* [*pl.* sentries], a person stationed as a sentinel or guard.

se-pal (sē'pal; sep'al), *n.* one of the leaflike sections of the calyx, outside the coloured petals of a flower.

sep-a-rate (sep'a-rāt'), *v.t.* [separat-ed, separat-ing], **1,** to part or divide; disunite; set apart; as, please *separate* the pens from the pencils; **2,** to come

SEPALS (S.S)

in between; keep apart; as, a hedge *separates* the two gardens:—*v.i.* to part; withdraw from each other or from one another; scatter; as, rain began to fall, and the crowd *separated* in a hurry:—*adj.* (sep'a-rit; sep'rit), **1,** divided; no longer united; as, they have turned the second floor into two *separate* apartments; **2,** distinct; single; as, each *separate* item on a bill.—*n.* **sep'a-ra'tion.**—*n.* **sep'a-ra'tor.**—*adj.* **sep'a-ra-ble.**—*adv.* **sep'a-rate-ly.**

se-pi-a (sē'pi-a), *n.* **1,** a dark-brown pigment made from an inky fluid ejected by the European cuttle-fish; **2,** this cuttlefish; also, the inky fluid; **3,** a dark-brown colour.

Sep-tem-ber (sep-tem'bér), *n.* the ninth month of the year (30 days).

sep-tic (sep'tik); *adj.* and *n.* infected by germs; as, *septic* poisoning; putrefying.

sep-tu-a-ge-na-ri-an (sep′tū-a-ji-nā′ri-an), *n.* one who is 70, or between 70 and 80, years old.

se-pul-chral (se-pul′kral), *adj.* 1, pertaining to a tomb or to the burial of the dead; 2, gloomy or funereal; as, a *sepulchral* mansion; 3, deep and solemn; as, a *sepulchral* voice.

sep-ul-chre (sep′ul-kėr), *n.* a grave or tomb; a place of burial:—*v.t.* to bury; entomb. Also spelled **sep′ul-cher.**

sep-ul-ture (sep′ėl-chėr), *n.* burial.

se-quel (sē′kwel), *n.* 1, a succeeding part; continuation; as, the *sequel* of his fiery speech was a riot.

se-quence (sē′kwens), *n.* 1, the act of following; the coming of one thing after another; as, the *sequence* of cause and effect; 2, the order in which things occur or are arranged; as, the *sequence* of words in a sentence; 3, a series; as, a *sequence* of plays; 4, an event that follows another.

se-ques-tered (si-kwes′tėrd), *adj.* secluded; retired; quiet.

se-ques-trate (si-kwes′trāt), *v.t.* to seize by court order as security for a debt, claim, etc.; 2, to confiscate (esp. by a government).—*n.* **se′ques-tra′tion.**

se-quin (sē′kwin), *n.* a small spangle or shiny metal disc used to ornament dresses, etc.

se-quoi-a (si-kwoi′a), *n.* either of two evergreen trees of California, called *big tree* and *redwood* respectively, which grow to immense size.

ser-aph (ser′af), *n.* [*pl.* seraphim (ser′a-fim) or seraphs], an angel of the highest order of angels.—*adj.* **se-raph′ic.**

sere (sēr), *adj. Poetic,* dry; withered; as, a *sere* leaf.

ser-e-nade (ser′e-nād′), *n.* 1, music sung or played at night, often by a lover under his lady's window; 2, a piece of music suitable to such an occasion:—*v.t.* and *v.i.* [serenad-ed, serenad-ing], to sing or play a serenade in honour of (a person).

se-rene (se-rēn′), *adj.* 1, clear and calm; as, a *serene* summer day; 2, placid; composed.—*adv.* **se-rene′ly.**—*n.* **se-ren′i-ty** (si-ren′i-ti).

serf (sûrf), *n.* 1, originally, a slave; 2, in the Middle Ages, a tiller of the soil who belonged to the land he tilled, and stayed with the land whenever it was sold.—*n.* **serf′dom.**

serge (sûrj), *n.* a woollen material, woven with fine diagonal ridges, used for dresses, suits, and coats.

ser-geant (sär′jent), *n.* 1, a sergeant-at-arms; 2, a police-officer of minor rank; 3, a noncommissioned officer of the army or the marines, ranking next above a corporal. Also, **ser′jeant.**

sergeant—at—arms (sär′jent—at—ärmz′), *n.* [*pl.* sergeants-at-arms], an officer of a judicial, legislative, or deliberative body, who is responsible for keeping order at meetings.

ser-geant—ma-jor, the highest rank of noncommissioned officer; a warrant-officer.

se-ri-al (sē′ri-al), *adj.* consisting of parts or units which follow one another; esp., published in successive parts or numbers; as, a *serial* story:—*n.* a story, photoplay, etc., appearing in successive instalments.—*adv.* **se′ri-al-ly.**

se-ries (sē′riz), *n.* [*pl.* series], a number of similar things or events following one another in regular order or succession; as, a short *series* of lectures:—**series circuit,** an electric circuit in which the cells, conductors, or units are connected positive pole to negative pole so that the current passes through each in succession: opposite of *parallel circuit.*—**series wound,** in a motor or dynamo, the connecting of the armature and field magnet coil in series with the outer circuit: opposite of *shunt* wound.

ser-if (ser′if), *n.* in *printing,* one of the fine cross strokes at top or bottom that finish a letter.

se-ri-ous (sē′ri-us), *adj.* 1, responsible; earnest; as, a *serious* student; 2, not trifling; not comic; as, a *serious* play; 3, demanding thought and attention; as, *serious* reading; 4, disastrous; as, *serious* consequences.—*adv.* **se′ri-ous-ly.**

ser-mon (sûr′mun), *n.* 1, a formal talk or lecture based on a moral or religious subject, often based on Scripture and usually delivered by a priest or a minister; 2, any serious talk or address.

ser-pent (sûr′pent), *n.* 1, a snake, esp. a large one; 2, a sly, deceitful person.

ser-pen-tine (sûr′pen-tīn′; sûr′pen-tēn′), *adj.* 1, snakelike; winding in coils or curves; as, the *serpentine* course of a stream; 2, sly and crafty; as, *serpentine* wisdom:—*n.* (sûr′pen-tēn′), a kind of dull-green, sometimes mottled, rock which takes a high polish.

ser-rat-ed (ser′ā-tid), *adj.* having sawlike notches, as of leaves, knives, etc.; also, **ser′rate;** as, a *serrate* leaf of hydrangea.

ser-ried (ser′id), *adj.* close; as, *serried* ranks of soldiers.

se-rum (sē′rum), *n.* [*pl.* sera (sē′ra) or serums], **1,** the yellowish, clear, watery fluid which remains after blood has coagulated; **2,** such a fluid, taken from the blood of an animal which has been inoculated with a given disease, and used to fight the disease in human beings.

ser-vant (sûr′vant), *n.* a person who works for wages; esp., one who performs domestic duties in return for board, lodging, and wages.

serve (sûrv), *v.t.* [served, serv-ing], **1,** to attend or wait upon; work for; **2,** to obey and honour; as, to *serve* God; **3,** to put on the table and distribute, as food; also, to wait upon (persons) at table or in a shop; **4,** to be of use to; as, the car *served* him very well all summer; the coat *served* her for a pillow; **5,** to defend; take the part of; as, to *serve* one's country; also, to promote; make a contribution to; as, to *serve* science; **6,** to treat; deal with; act toward; as, he *served* me shamefully; **7,** to supply (customers) at regular or stated times; as, the milkman *serves* us with milk every morning; **8,** to deliver, as a legal writ or summons; **9,** to undergo; as, to *serve* a prison sentence; **10,** in games, such as tennis, to put (the ball) into play:—*v.i.* **1,** to be employed by another; be a servant, slave, or employee; **2,** to discharge the duties of an office or employment; as, to *serve* in the army or navy; to *serve* on a committee; **3,** to be sufficient; act as substitute; answer the purpose; as, rain will not *serve* as an excuse for absence; **4,** in games, such as tennis, to put (the ball) into play by sending it to an opponent as the first stroke:—*n.* in games, as tennis, the act of serving (the ball); also, the ball as served or the turn for serving; as, whose *serve* is it?—*n.* **serv′er.**

serv-ice (sûr′vis), *n.* **1,** the state or position of a servant; as, she was in *service* for ten years before her marriage; **2,** duty or function performed or required; as, have you need of our *services?* also, the manner of performing work; as, poor hotel *service;* **3,** a set of implements for special use; as, a silver tea-*service;* also, any formal religious ceremony; as, the funeral *service;* **5,** professional or official functions or duties; as, a lawyer's *services;* military *service;* **6,** employment; as, civil *service;* **7,** benefit; advantage; as, an education is often of great *service;* **8,** in games, such as tennis, that stroke of the ball which

puts it into play:—*v.t.* [serviced, servicing], to put into, or maintain in, condition; put back into good shape; as, to *service* a radio set.

serv-ice-a-ble (sûr′vis-a-bl), *adj.* **1,** useful; helpful; as, colonies may in many ways be *serviceable* to the parent country; **2,** having good wearing qualities; durable.

ser-vi-ette (sûr′vi-et′), *n.* a table napkin.

ser-vile (sûr′vīl; sûr′vil), *adj.* **1,** pertaining to a slave; as, of *servile* origin; **2,** characteristic of a slave; as, *servile* fear; **3,** cringing; slavishly humble; as, a *servile* flatterer.—*n.* **ser-vil′i-ty** (sûr-vil′i-ti).

ser-vi-tor (sûr′vi-tėr), *n.* a servant.

ser-vi-tude (sûr′vi-tūd′), *n.* **1,** slavery; bondage; **2,** service or labour enforced as a punishment; as, penal *servitude.*

ses-a-me (ses′a-mi), *n.* an East Indian herb whose seeds yield an oil and are used as food:—**open sesame,** any magical charm, password, etc., that removes barriers: from "Ali Baba and the Forty Thieves".

ses-sion (sesh′un), *n.* **1,** a meeting of a school, court, legislative body, etc.; **2,** a series of such meetings; **3,** the time occupied by a single meeting or by a series of meetings; as, a two-hour *session;* a two-month *session.*—*adj.* **ses′sion-al.**

ses-tet or **ses-tette** (ses-tet′), *n.* **1,** the last six lines of a sonnet (Italian); **2,** a musical composition for six voices or instruments.

set (set), *v.t.* [set, set-ting], **1,** to place or fix in a certain position; as, they *set* the basket on the floor; **2,** to put (a hen) upon a nest of eggs, or (eggs) under a hen; **3,** to put in order; make ready for use; as, to *set* a table; *set* a trap; **4,** to regulate (a clock); **5,** to cause to become stiff, as jelly; to make permanent or fast, as colours; **6,** to prepare (a broken bone) to knit; **7,** to fix (a price); **8,** to adapt, as words to music; **9,** to put into a special condition; as, to *set* a house on fire; **10,** to arrange (type) in words; **11,** to fix or determine; as, to *set* one's mind on, to, or against something:—*v.i.* **1,** to sink below the horizon, as the sun; **2,** to become firm, as jelly, or rigid, as cement; **3,** to apply oneself; as, to *set* to work; **4,** to flow or tend; as, the current *sets* to the north; **5,** to start; as, to *set* out on a journey; **6,** to fit; as, this coat *sets* well; **7,** to sit; hatch eggs; as, a *setting* hen:—*adj.* **1,** fixed or established; as, a *set* wage; **2,** immovable; obstinate; as, *set* in his ways; **3,** regular; formal; as, a *set* speech: —*n.* **1,** a number of things of the same kind, to be used in conjunction; as, a *set* of golf-clubs; a *set* of surgical instruments; also, apparatus; as, a radio receiving-*set;* **2,** a congenial group of persons; clique; as, the younger *set;* **3,** a series of games which counts as a unit, as in tennis; **4,** a setting, either on a stage or in a photoplay; **5,** posture; as, the *set* of the head; **6,** fit; as, the *set* of a coat or a skirt.

set-back (set′bak′), *n.* a check to progress or advancement; a reverse.

set-screw (set′skrōō′), *n.* a screw to regulate tension on a spring, etc., or to prevent movement, as of a ring around a shaft.

set-tee (se-tē′), *n.* a long seat or short sofa with arms and a back.

set-ter (set′ėr), *n.* **1,** one who or that which sets; as, a type*setter;* **2,** a longhaired hunting-dog trained to stand rigid and point on scenting game.

set-ting (set′ing), *n.* **1,** that in which something is fastened, as the mounting of a jewel; **2,** the scenery and stage properties for a play or a scene in a play; the background of a story; **3,** music composed for a written text; **4,** the eggs placed under a hen for hatching.

¹set-tle (set′l), *v.t.* [set-tled, set-tling], **1,** to place in a fixed state or position; as, *settle* yourself in this hammock; also, to establish in business or in a home; as, they were finally *settled* in the new house; **2,** to make calm; free from unrest; as, you must *settle* your nerves; **3,** to agree on; as, to *settle* a price; adjust, as a quarrel; pay, as a bill; **4,** to free of dregs by causing them to sink; as, to *settle* coffee; **5,** to make firm or solid; as, to *settle* a roadway; **6,** to colonize; as, the French and English *settled* Canada; **7,** to dispose of; as, to *settle* an estate; bestow legally; as, to *settle* an annuity on someone; put into shape, as one's affairs:—*v.i.* **1,** to become fixed; assume a lasting form; **2,** to come to rest, as a bird; establish a residence, as a colonist; **3,** to become established in business or in a way of life; as to *settle* down; **4,** to sink to the bottom of a liquid, as dregs; be cleared of dregs, as coffee; **5,** to become firm or solid, as a roadbed; find a permanent level, as the foundations of a building; **6,** to determine; as, to *settle* on a course

of conduct; **7,** to pay a bill.—*n.* **set′tler.**

²set-tle (set′l), *n.* a long, wooden bench with arms, a straight, high back, and, often, an enclosed boxlike base.

set-tle-ment (set′l-ment), *n.* **1,** the act of settling or establishing; also, the state of being fixed or established, as in a business or profession; **2,** the payment of an account; adjustment of a dispute; **3,** a legal gift; as, a marriage *settlement;* **4,** the process of colonizing; also, a colony, esp. one in a state of development; **5,** a small town or village; **6,** in a poor and crowded section of a large city, an institution providing instruction, entertainment, etc., for the people of the neighbourhood.

sev-en (sev′en), *adj.* composed of one more than six:—*n.* **1,** the sum of one and six; **2,** a sign representing seven units, as 7 or vii.—*adj.* and *adv.*

sev′en-fold′ (seven times as much or as many).

sev-en-teen (sev′en-tēn′), *adj.* composed of ten more than seven:—*n.* **1,** the sum of sixteen and one; **2,** a sign representing seventeen units, as 17 or xvii.

sev-en-teenth (sev′en-tēnth′), *adj.* next after the 16th: the ordinal of *seventeen:*—*n.* one of the seventeen equal parts of anything.

sev-enth (sev′enth), *adj.* next after the sixth: the ordinal of *seven:*—*n.* one of the seven equal parts of anything.

sev-en-ti-eth (sev′en-ti-eth), *adj.* next after the 69th: the ordinal of *seventy* —*n.* one of the 70 equal parts of anything.

sev-en-ty (sev′en-ti), *adj.* composed of one more than 69:—*n.* [*pl.* seventies] **1,** the number consisting of 69 plus one **2,** a sign representing 70 units, as 70 or lxx.

sev-en-ty—one (sev′en-ti-wun′), *n* and *adj.* the numbers seventy-one to seventy-nine are hyphenated.

sev-er (sev′ėr), *v.t.* **1,** to divide or separate with violence; cut; as, they *severed* the cords that bound him; **2** to put apart (two or more persons or things); divide:—*v.i.* to part; be torn apart.—*n.* **sev′er-ance.**

sev-er-al (sev′ėr-al), *adj.* **1,** distinct separate; as, they went their *several* ways; **2,** more than two but not many some; as, *several* members of the club arrived late.—*adv.* **sev′er-al-ly.**

se-vere (si-vēr′), *adj.* [sever-er, sever est], **1,** strict; stern; as, *severe* method of discipline; **2,** austere; grave in manner; **3,** extremely plain; as, a gown of a *severe* style; **4,** extreme; sharp; violent; as, *severe* anguish; **5,** hard to bear or undergo; trying; as, a *severe* test.—*adv.* **se-vere′ly.**—*n.* **se-ver′i-ty** (si-ver′i-ti).

sew (sō), *v.i.* [*p.t.* sewed (sōd), *p.p.* sewn (sōn) or sewed (sōd), *p.pr.* sew-ing] **1,** to work with needle and thread; **2,** to do dressmaking for a living:—*v.t.* **1,** to put together, as a dress, etc., by means of stitches; **2,** to join or fasten to something with stitches, as a ruffle on a skirt; **3,** to close or mend by sewing; as, to *sew* up a tear.

sew-age (sū′ij), *n.* foul liquids or waste matter carried off by sewers.

sew-er (sū′ėr), *n.* an underground pipe to carry off water, waste, etc.; a public drain.

sew-er-age (sū′ėr-ij; sōō), *n.* **1,** a drainage system (of pipes or sewers) to carry off the refuse matter of a town or city; **2,** sewage.

sex (seks), *n.* **1,** the physical characteristics that make a human being, animal, or plant, distinctively male or female; **2,** one of the two divisions of animals or plants, called male and female. —*adj.* **sexed.**—*adj.* **sex′y** (*Slang*). —*adv.* **sex′u-al-ly.**

sex-a-ge-nar-i-an (sek′se-je-nâr′i-an), *n.* one who is 60 years old, or between 60 and 70.

sex-tant (seks′tant), *n.* an instrument used by mariners esp. for observing the altitude of the sun in order to determine latitude and longitude at sea.

sex-tet or **sex-tette** (seks-tet′), *n.* a musical composition for six performers, or the six performers; **2,** any group of six.

sex-ton (seks′tun), *n.* an under-official or janitor of a church, whose duty it is to take care of the church building and property, attend to burials, etc.

shab-by (shab′i), *adj.* [shab-bi-er, shab-bi-est], **1,** threadbare or worn; as, *shabby* clothes; **2,** poorly dressed; seedy; **3,** petty or unworthy; mean; as, that was a *shabby* trick.—*adv.* **shab′bi-ly.**—*n.* **shab′bi-ness.**

shack (shak), *n.* **1,** a roughly built cabin or shanty, as of logs, etc.; **2,** a shabby old house; hut.

shack-le (shak′l), *n.* **1,** (usually *shackles*), anything that confines the arms or legs so as to prevent free action, as a strap or chain; a fetter; handcuff; **2,** hence, anything which restrains or prevents free action; **3,** any of various fastenings, as a link for coupling cars:—*v.t.* [shack-led, shack-ling], **1,** to embarrass or hinder; **3,** to join or fasten with a shackle.

shad (shad), *n.* [*p.* shad], a large fish of the herring family, highly valued as food, found along the Atlantic coast.

shad-bush (shad′boosh′), *n.* a white-flowering, tall shrub or small tree, bearing purple, edible, berrylike fruit. Also called *saskatoon* and *serviceberry.*

shade (shād), *n.* **1,** partial darkness caused by cutting off rays of light; **2,** a spot not exposed to the sun; a shady place; hence, a secluded retreat; **3,** something which cuts off or softens the rays of light; esp., a screen or curtain fitting close to a windowpane and adjustable so as to regulate the amount of light admitted; **4,** a special degree or variety of a colour; as, this *shade* of blue is difficult to match; often, a dark colour; as, tints and *shades;* **5,** a slight degree or amount; a trace; as, there was a *shade* of doubt in his voice; **6,** a shadow; a ghost or phantom; an unreal thing; **7, shades,** the shadows that gather as light fails; darkness; dimness; as, the *shades* of night:—*v.t.* [shad-ed, shad-ing], **1,** to screen from light or heat; **2,** to darken or make dim; **3,** to mark or paint with varying degrees of light or colour:—*v.i.* to merge or change by slight degrees; as, the sunset *shaded* from a flame colour to pale yellow.

shad-ow (shad′ō), *n.* **1,** comparative darkness, or shade, caused by cutting off the direct rays coming from the sun or other source of light; **2,** a dark figure or image projected by a body or person cutting off the direct light from a given source; as, his figure cast a *shadow* on the wall; **3,** that which follows inseparably; a constant companion; as, Jane is Mary's *shadow;* **4,** a reflection, as in water; hence, an imaginary likeness; **5,** the darker portion of a picture; **6,** protection; as, under the *shadow* of the Almighty; **7,** a weakened counterpart; a mere semblance; as, after her illness, she was only a *shadow* of her former self; **8,** a ghost; phantom; wraith; **9,** an unsubstantial or unreal thing; **10,** slightest trace; as, without a *shadow* of excuse:—*v.t.* **1,** to darken; cloud; **2,** to indicate indirectly or in outline; **3,** to keep under observation; as, the detective *shadowed* his man.—*adj.* **shad′ow-y.**

shad-o-w-box-ing (shad'ō-bok'sing), *n*. as training or exercise, to spar with an imaginary opponent.

shad-y (shād'i, *adj*). [shad-i-er, shad-i-est], **1**, giving shade or shelter; as, a *shady* tree; **2**, sheltered from the glare of light or heat; as, a *shady* path; **3**, *Colloq.*, questionable; of doubtful honesty; as, *shady* business deals.—*n*. **shad'i-ness.**

shaft (shàft), *n*. **1**, the long stem or handle of an arrow or similar missile; also, an arrow; spear; dart; **2**, any long, slender part resembling the stem of an arrow, as the stalk of a plant or the handle of a golf-club; **3**, the long, narrow, vertical or slanted entrance to a mine; **4**, the pole of a wagon or carriage; **5**, in an engine or a machine, a bar to hold or to help move wheels or other rotating parts; **6**, an open well-like space through which air and light reach the windows of a building, as a tenement or factory; also, the vertical well in which an elevator runs; **7**, the body of a column between the base and the top.

¹shag (shag), *n*. **1**, a coarse nap on cloth (or such cloth); **2**, a coarse-cut tobacco:—*v.t. Slang*, in *baseball*, to chase and catch (balls) in batting practice; as, to *shag* flies.

²shag (shag), *n*. a small crested cormorant, common on the Atlantic coast: *Shag* Harbour, N.S., was named for it (about 1785).

shag-bark (shag'bärk'), *n*. a nut-bearing tree with ragged bark; a hickory.

shag-gy (shag'i), *adj*. [shag-gi-er, shag-gi-est], **1**, rough-haired; as, a *shaggy* dog; **2**, unkempt; tangled.—*n*. **shag'gi-ness.**

shah (shä), *n*. *Persian*, the title of Iran's ruler.

¹shake (shāk), *v.t.* [*p.t.* shook (shook), *p.p.* shak-en (shāk'en), *p.pr.* shak-ing], **1**, to move with a quick back and forth motion; as, a terrier *shakes* a rat; **2**, to cause to tremble; as, chills *shook* his body; **3**, to cause (a person) to waver or doubt; also, to weaken; impair; as, to *shake* a person's faith; **4**, to throw off or dispel; as, to *shake* off sleepiness; **5**, to loosen; unfasten; as, to *shake* out a sail:—*v.i.* to tremble; quake:—*n*. the act of moving or causing to move with a quick short motion.

²shake (shāk), *n*. a thick B.C. red cedar shingle used for both roofing and

siding: some shakes are made by hand with a steel froe (a cleaving tool with handle at right angles to the blade).

shake-down (shak'doun'), *n*. **1**, a makeshift bed; **2**, *Slang*, extortion of money, as by blackmail.

shak-er (shāk'ēr), *n*. **1**, one who shakes; **2**, that from which something is shaken; as, a salt-*shaker*.

Shake-spear-e-an son-net (shāk-spēr'i-an), a sonnet composed of 3 groups of 4 lines each (quatrains), the rhyme scheme being *abab, cdcd, efef,* and a final couplet, rhymed *gg*.

shake-up (shāk'up'), *n*. a drastic reorganization, as of personnel or policy.

shak-y (shāk'i), *adj*. [shak-i-er, shak-i-est], **1**, ready to fall to pieces; unsound; as, a *shaky* table; **2**, feeble; tottering.

shale (shāl), *n*. a rock of clayey origin, easily split into sheets, and somewhat resembling slate.

shall (shal), *auxiliary v.* [*p.t.* should (shood)], used in the first person to express simple futurity, and in the second and third persons to express command, determination, promise, etc.; as, I *shall* be in town tomorrow; "Curfew *shall* not ring tonight."

shal-lop (shal'up), *n*. a dinghy; a small open boat with oars or sail (or both).

shal-low (shal'ō), *adj*. **1**, not deep; as, a *shallow* stream; **2**, having no mental depth; superficial; as, a *shallow* mind: —*n*. a place where the water is not deep; a shoal.

sham (sham), *n*. **1**, one who or that which deceives; a trick, fraud, or pretence; **2**, an ornamental cover for a pillow or bolster:—*adj*. **1**, feigned; false; as, a *sham* attack by the fleet; **2**, unreal; pretentious; as, *sham* finery:—*v.t.* [shammed, sham-ming], to make a pretence of, in order to deceive; feign; as, to *sham* death:—*v.i.* to pretend.

sham-ble (sham'bl), *v.i.* [sham-bled, sham-bling], to walk awkwardly and uncertainly, as if with weak knees; shuffle:—*n*. a shuffling gait.—*adj*. **sham'bling.**

sham-bles (sham'blz), *n.pl.* used as *sing.*, any scene of bloodshed, destruction, or disorder; as, the boys left the house a *shambles*.

shame (shām), *n*. **1**, a painful feeling caused by the knowledge that one has been guilty of something wrong, immodest, or dishonourable; also, that which causes a feeling of shame; **2**, disgrace; dishonour; **3,** a restraining sense of modesty or decency:—*v.t.* [shamed, sham-ing], **1,** to cause to blush with shame or guilt; **2,** to disgrace; as, to *shame* one's family; **3,** to make (a person) do a thing through a sense of decency; as, his friends *shamed* John into apologizing.—*adj.* **shame′less; shame′faced′.**

shame-ful (shām′fool), *adj.* causing disgrace; disgraceful; as, *shameful* conduct.

sham-poo (sham-pōō′), *v.t.* to cleanse (the head and hair) with soap and water, or other cleansing preparation:—*n.* **1,** the act of washing the hair; **2,** a preparation used in washing the hair.

sham-rock (sham′rok), *n.* a kind of three-leaved plant of the clover family. It is the national emblem of Ireland.

shang-hai (shang′hī), *v.t.* [-haied (hīd), -hai-ing], to drug and ship aboard as a sailor; to kidnap.

shank (shangk), *n.* **1,** the leg; esp., in man, the leg from the knee to the ankle; the shin; also, a corresponding part in animals; **2,** in dressed beef, a cut from the upper part of the foreleg; **3,** the portion of a tool, implement, etc., between the cutting or working part and the handle, as the stem of a key, bit, or drill, or the central part of an anchor; **4,** in a shoe, the part of the sole under the instep.

shan-ty (shan′ti), *n.* [*pl.* shanties], a rude shack or cabin.

shape (shāp), *n.* **1,** the form or figure of a person or thing; outline; as, the *shape* of a boat; **2,** that which has form or figure, whether real or imaginary; a person or thing indistinctly seen; hence, a ghost; **3,** a pattern for guiding a cutter; a mould; **4,** concrete or definite form; as, to whip an idea into *shape;* **5,** *Colloq.,* condition or state of being; as, his affairs were in bad *shape:*—*v.t.* [shaped, shap-ing], **1,** to make into a certain form; fashion; as, eyebrows *shaped* in a long curve; **2,** to adapt to a particular end; regulate; adjust; as, to *shape* plans:—*v.i.* to take form; develop; give signs of future form or fate.—*adj.* **shape′less.** —*n.* **shap′er.**

shape-ly (shāp′li), *adj.* [shape-li-er, shape-li-est], well-formed.—*n.* **shape′li-ness.**

shard (shärd), *n.* **1,** a broken piece, esp. of pottery; **2,** any hard, thin covering, as the shell or wing cover of a beetle.

share (shâr), *n.* **1,** a certain portion or part that falls to an individual; as, he has had more than his *share* of trouble; **2,** an equitable part given or belonging to one of a number of persons claiming or owning something jointly; as, he received his *share* of the estate; **3,** one's proportional contribution of any kind to a joint undertaking; as, he gave his *share* of time and money to the club; **4,** one of the equal portions into which a company's capital stock is divided, each represented by a certificate entitling the holder to a proportionate part of the earnings:—*v.t.* [shared, shar-ing], **1,** to give away a part of; divide and distribute; as, to *share* one's wealth; **2,** to possess in common; partake of, experience, enjoy, or suffer, with others; as, to *share* the common lot:—*v.i.* to take part; as, to *share* in the fun.

share—crop-per (shâr′–krop′ẽr), *n.* one who works another's farm in return for a share of the crop.

share-hold-er (shâr′hōl′dẽr), *n.* a stockholder; one who owns one or more of the transferable shares of the capital stock of a company or corporation.

shark (shärk), *n.* **1,** a large, carnivorous, sharp-toothed fish, found mostly in warm seas; **2,** a swindler or cheat; **3,** *Slang,* a person unusually talented in some special line; as, a *shark* at mathematics.

sharp (shärp), *adj.* **1,** having a very thin, fine edge; as, a *sharp* knife; **2,** ending in a fine point; as, a *sharp* needle; **3,** well-defined; distinct; as, *sharp* features; **4,** angular; abrupt; as, a *sharp* bend in the road; **5,** quick; keen; alert; as, a *sharp* eye; also, clever; shrewd; intelligent; **6,** close in dealing; hence, dishonest; unscrupulous; as, a *sharp* dealer; **7,** severe; intense; as, a *sharp* pain; **8,** piercing; shrill; penetrating; as, a *sharp* voice; **9,** acid; sour; tart; as, a *sharp* taste; **10,** frosty; cutting; as, *sharp* cold; **11,** quick; hasty; as, a *sharp* temper; **12,** sarcastic; bitter; as, a *sharp* tongue; **13,** fierce; violent; as, a *sharp* contest; **14,** in *music:* **a,** above the true pitch; as, a *sharp* note; **b,** raised by a half step; as, C *sharp:*—*adv.* **1,** in *music,* above the true pitch; **2,** *Colloq.,* promptly; precisely; as, six o'clock *sharp;* **3,** in a sharp manner; alertly; as, look *sharp:*—*n.* in music, a tone or note raised a half step in pitch; also, the sign [#] showing that a note is to be so raised:—*v.t.* and *v.i.* in *music,* to make (a note) higher in pitch by a half step; also, to sing or play above the correct pitch.

sharp-en (shär′p'n), *v.t.* to make keen or keener; give point or keenness to; as, to *sharpen* a tool:—*v.i.* to become sharp.

sharp-er (shär′pėr), *n.* one who drives a close bargain; hence, a cheat; swindler.

sharp-shoot-er (shärp′sho͞ot′ėr), *n.* an expert marksman, esp. with a rifle.

shat-ter (shat′ėr), *v.t.* 1, to break violently into many pieces; smash; as, to *shatter* a vase; 2, to derange or disorder; as, the accident *shattered* his nerves; 3, to defeat; ruin; as, *shattered* hopes:—*v.i.* to fly into pieces; break. —*adj.* shat′ter-proof′.

shave (shāv), *v.t.* [*p.t.* shaved (shāvd), *p.p.* shaved or shav-en (shāv′en), *p.pr.* shav-ing], 1, to cut off or remove with a razor or similar sharp-edged instrument; free (the face, chin, etc.) of hair; 2, to cut in very thin slices; as, to *shave* citron; 3, to come very close to; graze:—*v.i.* to use the razor to remove hair:—*n.* 1, the act or operation of removing hair with a razor; 2, any of various woodworking instruments for paring or smoothing the surface of wood; 3, *Colloq.*, a very small time or distance; also, a narrow escape; as, a close *shave*.

shav-er (shāv′ėr), *n.* 1, one who, or that which, shaves; 2, *Colloq.*, a boy; lad; as, he is a little *shaver*.

shav-ing (shāv′ing), *n.* a thin slice pared off with a knife or plane, as from a plank or board.

shawl (shôl), *n.* a scarf made of a square or oblong piece of cloth, used chiefly by women as a loose outer covering for the shoulders.

shay (shā), *n. Colloq.*, a chaise; a light carriage; as, the one-horse *shay*.

she (shē), *fem.pron.* of the third person personal pronoun [*nominative* she, *possessive* her (hûr) or hers (hûrz), *objective* her], 1, one particular woman or girl, previously mentioned; as, where is Ann? *she* is here; 2, any female animal, or thing personified as female: —*n.* a woman; any female.

sheaf (shēf), *n.* [*pl.* sheaves (shēvz)], 1, a quantity of cut grain, laid lengthwise and bound together; 2, any bundle of things tied together, as arrows, papers, etc.

shear (shēr), *v.t.* [*p.t.* sheared (shērd), *p.p.* shorn (shôrn) or sheared, *p.pr.* shear-ing], 1, to cut off or clip (hair, wool, etc.), esp. with large scissors or shears; 2, to cut or clip wool or hair

from; as, to *shear* sheep:—*n.* 1, a machine for cutting or clipping metal; 2, **shears: a,** any of various large cutting instruments, working much like scissors, by the crossing of cutting blades or edges; **b,** large scissors.—*n.* shear′er.

sheath (shēth), *n.* [*pl.* sheaths (shēthz)], 1, a close-fitting cover or case for a sword or knife; a scabbard; 2, any covering enclosing a part or organ, as the wing case of an insect.

sheathe (shēth), *v.t.* [sheathed, sheathing], 1, to put into, furnish, or cover with, a case; as, to *sheathe* a sword; 2, to encase or protect with a covering; as, to *sheathe* a roof with tin.

sheath-ing (shēth′ing), *n.* that which covers, or protects; esp., the protective boarding on the outside of a frame house.

sheave (shēv), *n.* [*pl.* sheaves], a pulley or grooved wheel in a block (used with a rope for raising weights).

sheaves (shēvs), *n.pl.* of the nouns *sheaf* and *sheave.*

¹shed (shed), *v.t.* [shed, shed-ding], 1, to pour out; drop; spill; as, to *shed* tears; 2, to cause to flow; as, to *shed* blood; 3, to pour forth; spread about; as, the sun *sheds* light; 4, to cause to flow off; as, oilskins *shed* water; 5, to cast away; let fall; as, birds *shed* their feathers:—*v.i.* to cast off or let fall hair, feathers, etc.

²shed (shed), *n.* a small building, often with the front or sides open, used for sheltering animals, or for storing supplies, farm implements, etc.

sheen (shēn), *n.* lustre; radiance.

sheep (shēp), *n.* [*pl.* sheep], 1, a timid, cud-chewing animal, related to the goat, valued for its wool, skin, and flesh; 2, a timid, defenceless person; 3, leather made of sheepskin and used in bookbinding.

sheep-fold (shēp′fōld′), *n.* an enclosure for sheep.

sheep-ish (shēp′ish), *adj.* awkwardly bashful; somewhat silly; as, a *sheepish* look.

sheep-skin (shēp′skin′), *n.* 1, the dressed skin of a sheep, preserved with the wool on, and used for garments; 2, leather or parchment made from the skin of sheep; 3, a document written on parchment; hence, *Colloq.*, a graduation diploma.

¹sheer (shēr), *adj.* 1, pure; utter; absolute; as, *sheer* folly; 2, very thin, fine, or transparent: said of fabrics; **3**, straight up and down; perpendicular; steep; as, a *sheer* precipice:—*adv.* **1**, steeply; straight up and down; **2**, quite; completely.

²sheer (shēr), *v.i.* to turn from the course; swerve; as, the ship *sheered* to the north.

sheet (shēt), *n.* **1**, a large, broad, thin piece of any substance, as of cloth, glass or metal; **2**, a broad piece of linen or cotton, used as bedding; **3**, a single piece of paper; **4**, a newspaper; **5**, a broad expanse or surface; as, a *sheet* of ice; **6**, a rope attached to the lower corner of a sail to hold and regulate it.—*n.* **sheet′ing.**

sheet—an-chor (shēt′–ang′kėr), *n.* a larger anchor used only in an emergency; **2**, figuratively; a final reliance, resource, or refuge.

sheet bend, a knot used to fasten a rope to a bight (loop) or eye of another rope, esp. where the two ropes are of different thicknesses.

sheik (shēk; shāk), *n.* the head of an Arab family, tribe, or clan. Also, **sheikh.**

shek-el (shek′el), *n.* an ancient Hebrew unit of weight and money; a coin.

shel-drake (shel′drāk′), *n.* a fish-eating wild duck of the Old World: it resembles the goose.

shelf (shelf), *n.* [*pl.* shelves (shelvz)], **1**, a flat board, usually long and narrow, fastened to a wall or set into a bookcase or cupboard; **2**, something resembling a shelf in appearance or position, as a sandbank or a reef; **3**, a flat projecting ledge of rock.

shell (shel), *n.* **1**, a hard outside case or covering, as on a fruit, egg, nut, or seed, or on certain animals, as a crab or oyster; also, a husk, as on corn; **2**, the covering of a tortoise or a manufactured material resembling it, used in making combs, spectacle frames, etc.; **3**, a framework or skeleton, as of a building; **4**, a very light, long, narrow racing boat; **5**, a metal or paper case holding ammunition for a rifle, pistol, etc.; **6**, [*pl.* shell], a metal projectile filled with explosive, for use in a cannon or mortar:—*v.t.* **1**, to take from the shell, pod, etc., as peas from the pod; **2**, to separate from the cob, as corn; **3**, to bombard; as, to *shell* an enemy fort.

shel-lac (she-lak′; shel′ak), *n.* a sticky, resinous substance used in

making sealing-wax, varnish, etc.; also, a solution of dry shellac, esp. in alcohol, used as a varnish:—*v.t.* [shellacked, shellack-ing], to coat or treat with this substance. **2**, *Slang*, to beat; defeat; as, our team was *shellacked.*

shell-fish (shel′fish′), *n.* a water animal having a shell, as a clam, lobster, etc.

shel-ter (shel′tėr), *n.* **1**, anything that protects, covers, or shields; a refuge, esp., from the weather; a house or cabin; **2**, the state of being protected, covered, or shielded; safety:—*v.t.* to protect; defend:—*v.i.* to take refuge; as, during the storm we *sheltered* in the cave.

¹shelve (shelv), *v.t.* [shelved, shelv-ing], **1**, to place on a shelf; **2**, to dismiss from service; as, to *shelve* an officer; **3**, to postpone indefinitely; as, to *shelve* a petition; **4**, to furnish with shelves, as a closet.—*n.* **shelv′ing.**

²shelve (shelv), *v.i.* [shelved, shelv-ing], to slope; as, the bottom *shelves* from the shore.

she-nan-i-gans (shi-nan′i-ganz), *n. pl. Colloq.*, trickery; as, none of your *shenanigans.*

shep-herd (shep′ėrd), *n.* **1**, one who tends sheep; **2**, one who guides the religious life of others; a pastor; minister:—*v.t.* to tend or guard, as sheep; also, to protect; lead.—*n.fem.* **shep′herd-ess.**

sher-bet (shûr′bet), *n.* **1**, a cooling drink of sweetened fruit juices; **2**, a water-ice, usually with a fruit flavour.

sher-iff (sher′if), *n.* the chief law-enforcing officer of a county.

sher-ry (sher′i), *n.* [*pl.* sherries], a white wine made in Jerez, Spain; also, a similar stronger, darker wine.

shew (shō), *v.t.* an archaic form of *show.*

shied (shīd), *p.t.* and *p.p.* of *shy.*

shield (shēld), *n.* **1**, a broad piece of metal or wood, or a frame covered with leather or a similar material, carried on the arm to protect the body in fighting; **2**, hence, any person or thing that serves to ward off attack or injury: —*v.t.* to protect with, or as with, a shield; defend.

shift (shift), *v.t.* **1**, to transfer; as, to *shift* the blame; **2**, to exchange; substitute; as, to *shift* places in a boat:—*v.i.* **1**, to change position; as, sand-dunes *shift;* also, to veer; as, the wind *shifted* to the north; **2**, to make one's way; as, to *shift* for oneself:—*n.* **1,** a turning away from one thing to another; change; substitution; as, a *shift* of public enthusiasm toward a new leader; **2,** an expedient; as, to make one's way by *shifts;* hence, a trick; **3,** the system of working groups in relays; any one of these groups; as, an early *shift;* also, the working time of each group; as, an eight-hour *shift;* **4,** in *football,* a change in position of the line just before the ball is snapped.

shift-less (shift′lis), *adj.* lazy; thriftless; taking no thought for the future.

shift-y (shif′ti), *adj.* [shift-i-er, shift-i-est], **1,** able to turn circumstances to advantage; **2,** hence, not to be trusted.

shil-ling (shil′ing), *n.* a British silver coin: value of twelve pence, or 14¢.

shil-ly—shal-ly (shil′i–shal′i), *v.i.* to hesitate; trifle; be irresolute; as, don't *shilly-shally.*

shim (shim), *n.* a thin piece of wood, metal, etc., often tapered, as for levelling a railroad tie, taking up wear in a bearing, filling space, etc.

shim-mer (shim′ėr), *v.i.* to shine waveringly; gleam and glitter, as moonlight on the water:—*n.* **1,** a tremulous gleam; flicker; **2,** gloss; sheen, as, of satin.

shim-my (shim′i), *n.* **1,** vibration; a shaking; as, a *shimmy* in a steeringwheel; **2,** *Colloq.* a foxtrot done with a shaking motion:—*v.i.* to shake; quiver; vibrate; **2,** *Colloq.* to dance the shimmy.

shin (shin), *n.* the front part of the leg between the ankle and knee; shank: —*v.i.* [shinned, shin-ning], to climb a tree, pole, etc., by gripping it alternately with the arms and legs.

shin-dig (shin′dig), *n. Slang.* **1,** a dance; **2,** a party or social affair.

shine (shin), *v.i.* [shone (shon; shōn), shin-ing], **1,** to emit or give forth rays of light, as the sun or moon; also, to reflect light; gleam; sparkle; as, the lake *shone* in the sunlight; **2,** to be brilliant; excel in some particular line; as, he *shines* in English:—*v.t.* [*p.t.* and *p.p.* shined (shind)], *Colloq.,* to cause to glisten; polish; as, to *shine* an automobile:—*n.* **1,** lustre; sheen; **2,** bright weather; sunshine; as, rain and *shine;* **3,** *Colloq.,* a polish; as, my shoes need a *shine.*—*adj.* **shin′y.**

shin-er (shīn′ėr), *n.* **1,** one of many varieties of small silvery fishes. **2,** *Slang,* a black eye (as from a bruise, etc.).

¹shin-gle (shin′gl), *n.* **1,** one of the thin, oblong pieces of wood, slate, etc., used in overlapping rows for roofing and siding; **2,** *Colloq.,* a signboard, as on a doctor's office:—*v.t.* [shin-gled, shin-gling], **1,** to cover, as a roof, with shingles; **2,** to cut (the hair) progressively shorter toward the nape of the neck, so as to reveal the outline of the back of the head.

²shin-gle (shin′gl), *n.* **1,** water-worn pebbles, such as lie in loose sheets or beds on a seashore; **2,** a beach.

³shingles (shing′glz), *n.pl.* a painful skin eruption in the form of blisters that cluster along the course of a nerve, or spread about the body like a belt.

¹shin-ny (shin′i), *v.i. Colloq.* to climb, using the shins: chiefly used with *up;* as, to *shinny up* a tree.

²shin-ny (shin′i), *n.* a kind of informal hockey, or the stick used in playing it.

ship (ship), *n.* **1,** any large seagoing vessel; **2,** a large sailing-vessel with three, four, or five square-rigged masts; **3,** an airship or aeroplane:—*v.t.* [shipped, ship-ping], **1,** to load on a vessel; as, to *ship* cargo; **2,** to carry or transport by water; **3,** to send through any regular channel of transportation, as by rail; **4,** to fix in its proper place or position on a ship, as a mast or a rudder; **5,** to hire for service on a ship; as, to *ship* sailors:—**ship a sea,** to have a wave break over the decks:—*v.i.* **1,** to engage oneself for service on a vessel, as a sailor; **2,** to embark on a ship; as, to *ship* for Spain.—*n.* **ship′per.**

ship-ment (ship′ment), *n.* **1,** the act of having goods transported; **2,** the goods transported.

ship-ping (ship′ing), *n.* **1,** the act or business of one who ships goods; **2,** all the ships in a port or harbour; all the ships belonging to a country; tonnage.

ship-shape (ship′shāp′), *adj.* in good order; neatly arranged:—*adv.* neatly; orderly.

shire (shīr; as an ending, -shėr; -shir), *n.* in England, a district or county.

shirk (shûrk), *v.t.* **1,** purposely to neglect, shun, or evade a duty or obligation:—*v.i.* to avoid work; neglect a duty or obligation.—*n.* **shirk′er.**

shirr (shûr), *n.* a puckering of a cloth or fabric by means of parallel gathers: —*v.t.* in *sewing,* to draw up (cloth) by gathering on parallel running stitches; in *cookery,* to cook (eggs) in a buttered dish or casserole.—*adj.* **shirred.**

shirt (shûrt), *n.* **1,** a man's sleeved blouse, usually worn under a coat or vest; **2,** a close-fitting undergarment for the upper part of the body.—*n.* shirt'ing.

shirt-waist (shûrt'wāst'), *n.* a woman's sleeved blouse, made long enough to be tucked under a skirt.

shiv-a-ree (shiv'a-rē'), *n.* Same as *charivari* (a mock serenade to newly-weds, with kettles, pans, horns, etc.).

¹shiv-er (shiv'ẽr), *v.i.* to tremble, as from cold or fright; to quiver; shake: —*n.* a trembling from cold, fear, etc. —*adj.* shiv'er-y.

²shiv-er (shiv'ẽr), *v.i.* and *v.t.* to break, or cause to break, into small pieces; shatter:—*n.* a small fragment splintered off by a fall or blow; a sliver.

¹shoal (shōl), *n.* a large number; as, a *shoal* of fish.

²shoal (shōl), *adj.* of little depth; shallow; as, *shoal* water:—*n.* **1,** a shallow place in any body of water; a shallow; **2,** a sandbank or bar which shows only at low tide; **3,** hence, a hidden or unexpected danger:—*v.i.* to grow shallow.

shoat (shōt), *n.* a young weaned pig.

¹shock (shok), *n.* **1,** a forcible blow; impact; violent jar; as, the *shock* of a collision; **2,** an unexpected and violent jarring of the feelings; as, a *shock* of grief; **3,** the effect of the passage of an electric current through the body; as, he got a *shock* when he touched the live wire; **4,** a condition of extreme physical exhaustion caused by the pain of severe wounds or blows, loss of blood, etc.:—*v.t.* to strike with surprise, horror, disgust, etc.; as, the crime *shocked* the country.—*adj.* shock'ing.

²shock (shok), *n.* a stack of sheaves of grain set upright together in a field: —*v.t.* to collect and stack (sheaves of grain).

³shock (shok), *n.* a bushy mass, as of hair.

shod (shod), *p.t.* and *p.p.* of *shoe.*

shod-dy (shod'i), *n.* **1,** refuse fibre from carding or weaving wool; **2,** inferior material (esp. from reclaimed wool); **3,** showy pretension; sham:—*adj.* inferior; not genuine; sham; as, *shoddy* cloth; a *shoddy* aristocracy.

shoe (shōō), *n.* **1,** an outer covering for the human foot, made of leather, suede, satin, etc.; **2,** a U-shaped metal bar nailed on the hoof of a horse, donkey, etc.; **3,** something resembling a shoe in form or use, as the strip of steel fastened on the runners of a sleigh, or the lining inside the brake-drum of a wheel:—*v.t.* [shod (shod), shoe-ing], **1,** to furnish with a shoe or shoes; as, the blacksmith *shod* the horse; **2,** to protect, strengthen, or ornament, by adding a tip, rim, etc., of harder material; as, to *shoe* a wooden pole with an iron point.

shoe-mak-er (shōō'māk'ẽr), *n.* a person whose business it is to make or mend shoes.—*n.* shoe'mak'ing.

shone (shon; shōn), *p.t.* and *p.p.* of *shine.*

shoo (shōō), *interj.* and *v.t.* begone! be off! used esp. in scaring away fowls.

shook (shook), *p.t.* of *shake.*

shoot (shōōt), *v.t.* [shot (shot), shoot-ing], **1,** to let fly, send out, or discharge with sudden force; as, to *shoot* an arrow; **2,** to strike, kill, or wound with a missile discharged from a gun; **3,** to fire or discharge (a missile, weapon); **4,** to streak with different colours; as, the setting sun *shot* the sky with crimson; **5,** to move (a bolt) into or out of a fastening; **6,** to push forward; stick out; as, the snake *shot* out its tongue; **7,** to throw; as, to *shoot* dice; **8,** to flip or propel by a sharp, quick movement of the thumb or fingers; as, to *shoot* marbles; **9,** to pass or rush rapidly through or over; as, to *shoot* the rapids in a canoe; **10,** in *motion pictures,* to photograph (a scene):—*v.i.* **1,** to protrude or project; jut; as, the peninsula *shoots* out into the sea; **2,** to rush or flash along swiftly; as, the meteor *shot* through the sky; **3,** to bud; sprout; **4,** to dart with a stabbing sensation; as, a sharp pain *shot* up her arm; **5,** to discharge a missile from a gun; cause a gun, bow, etc., to let fly a missile; **6,** to grow rapidly; grow taller; **7,** to stream forth; spurt:—*n.* **1,** a young branch or growth; **2,** a shooting-match; a hunt.

shop (shop), *n.* **1,** a room or building where goods are sold at retail; a store; **2,** a place where mechanics carry on their trade; as, an automobile repair *shop;* **3,** (usually *shops*), a factory; **4,** one's own business as a subject of conversation; as, to talk *shop:*—*v.i.* [shopped, shop-ping], to visit stores to look over or purchase goods.—*n.* and *adj.* shop'ping.—*adj.* shop'worn'. —*n.* shop'per; shop'keep'er.

shop-lift-er (shop'lif'tẽr), *n.* a person who steals goods from a shop while pretending to buy or inspect.—*n.* shop'lift'ing.

¹shore (shōr), *n.* the land bordering on a body of water, as on the sea, a lake, etc.—*adj.* and *adv.* **shore′ward.**

²shore (shōr), *n.* a prop or support, esp. a timber used to prop up a ship in dock, a wall, etc.: used usually with *up.*—*n.* **shor′ing.**

shorn (shōrn), *p.p.* of *shear.* Also, **sheared.**

short (shôrt), *adj.* **1,** brief in time; as, a *short* vacation; **2,** not long; of little length; as, a *short* piece of string; a *short* walk; **3,** below the average height; not tall; as, a *short* man; **4,** scant; deficient; as, a *short* supply of food; also, insufficiently provided with; as, to be *short* of cash; **5,** curt; abrupt; uncivil; as, a *short* answer; **6,** rich; flaky, as pastry; **7,** of vowels: **a,** taking less time than the corresponding long sound, as the vowels in "fed" and "foot" compared with those in "fare" and "food"; **b,** sounded like *a* in "hat," *e* in "met," *i* in "sit," *o* in "hot," *u* in "but":—**short ton,** a weight of 2,000 pounds: called *ton* in Canada and the U.S.:—**shorts,** *n.pl.* short, loose trousers:—*adv.* **1,** abruptly; suddenly; **2,** less than what is desired or regular; as, to fall *short* of the mark.

short-age (shôr′tij), *n.* the amount by which anything is short; a deficit; as, his accounts last year showed a *shortage.*

short-cake (shôrt′kāk′), *n.* a cake resembling biscuit in texture, or a sweetened sponge-cake, split and served with fruit between the layers; as, strawberry *shortcake.*

short-com-ing (shôrt′kum′ing; shôrt/kum′ing), *n.* a failing; fault.

short-en (shôr′tn), *v.t.* **1,** to make short or shorter in time, extent, or measure; lessen; as, the new road will *shorten* our trip to town; **2,** to make crisp or short, as pastry, by using butter, lard, etc.: —*v.i.* to grow or become shorter or briefer.

short-en-ing (shôr′tn-ing), *n.* that which makes pastry crisp, as lard, butter, etc.

short-hand (shôrt′hand′), *n.* a system of rapid writing in which characters, symbols, or abbreviations are used for letters, words, phrases, etc.; stenography.

short-horn (shôrt′hôrn′), *n.* a large heavy (red, white, and roan) breed of cattle with short, curved horns: used for beef and milk.

short-ly (shôrt′li), *adv.* **1,** soon; **2,** in a few words; concisely; **3,** curtly; abruptly.

short—sight-ed (shôrt′—sīt′id), *adj.* **1,** seeing clearly at short distances only; unable to see far; **2,** due to, or marked by, lack of foresight; imprudent; as, a *short-sighted* business venture.

short-stop (shôrt′stop′), *n.* in *baseball,* the infielder who plays between second and third base.

shot (shot), *n.* **1,** the discharge of a firearm; **2,** a bullet, shell, cannon-ball, etc.; also, anything let fly or discharged with force; **3,** [*pl.* shot], a small ball or pellet of lead, or a number of such pellets combined in one charge, and used in a shotgun for killing birds and small animals; **4,** the distance which is or can be covered by a missile; hence, range; as, the soldiers were within gun*shot;* **5,** in certain games, a stroke; throw; **6,** hence, an attempt; a try; **7,** a marksman; as, he is a good *shot;* **8,** in *sports,* a heavy ball-shaped weight to be thrown in competition for distance; **9,** in *motion pictures,* the film record of a scene; also, the process of photographing a single scene.

shot-gun (shot′gun′), *n.* a gun with a smooth bore, for firing at short range.

shot-put (shot′poot′), *n.* a sports contest that consists in heaving a heavy metal ball with an overhand thrust.

should (shood), *auxiliary v.* past tense of *shall,* used: **1,** in quoting a thought or expression in which *shall* was originally used; as, "I *shall* stay until six" becomes "I said that I *should* stay until six"; "he *shall* not leave" becomes "I said that he *should* not leave"; **2,** to express doubt, uncertainty, condition, etc.; as, if it *should* rain, don't try to go; I *should* like to see the play, if it is a good one; **3,** to express obligation that ought to be or ought to have been fulfilled; as, he *should* telephone this afternoon; he *should* have telephoned yesterday.

shoul-der (shōl′dèr), *n.* **1,** either of the two projecting parts of the human body between the neck and the place where the arm joins the trunk; **2,** in animals, the forequarter; also, a cut of meat consisting of the upper joint of the foreleg and adjacent parts of the animal; **3,** the part of a garment that covers the shoulder; **4,** anything resembling a shoulder; as, the *shoulder* of a vase; **5,** the graded edge of a road:—*v.t.* **1,** to take upon the shoulder; as, to *shoulder* a pack; **2,** hence, to assume the responsibility of; as, to *shoulder* an obligation; **3,** to push with the shoulders; hence, to make (one's way) by pushing with the shoulders; as, he *shouldered* his way through the crowd.

shout (shout), *n.* a loud and sudden cry, as of joy, command, encouragement, etc.:—*v.i.* to make an outcry; as, he *shouted* with joy:—*v.t.* to utter with a loud voice; as, he *shouted* out his orders.

shove (shuv), *n.* a forcible push:—*v.t.* [shoved, shov-ing], **1,** to push (something) along; as, to *shove* a book across the table; **2,** to jostle; crowd; as, she *shoved* me rudely:—*v.i.* to crowd against others.

shov-el (shuv′l), *n.* **1,** a tool consisting of a broad, flat scoop with a handle, for lifting and throwing coal, grain, etc., or for digging; **2,** anything which resembles a shovel in shape or use; **3,** the amount that a shovel holds; as, a *shovel* of ashes:—*v.t.* [shovelled, shovel-ling], **1,** to take up and throw with such a tool; **2,** to gather up with, or as with, a shovel; as, to *shovel* one's food; **3,** to dig, clear, or clean out with this tool; as, to *shovel* a path through snow.—*n.* shov′el-ler; shov′el-ful.

show (shō), *v.t.* [*p.t.* showed (shōd), *p.p.* shown (shōn) or showed, *p.pr.* showing], **1,** to present to view; exhibit; as, *show* your stamps to me; to *show* anger; **2,** to make known; disclose; as, a fortune-teller claims to *show* the future; **3,** to make clear or explain (something); as, let me *show* just what I mean; hence, to teach; as, *show* me how to skate; **4,** to prove; demonstrate; as, I shall *show* that he is wrong; **5,** to indicate; point out; as, this *shows* who did it; **6,** to direct; as, to *show* a person to his seat; **7,** bestow or manifest; as, to *show* mercy:—*v.i.* to be visible or noticeable; as, pity *showed* in his face; the stain still *shows:—n.* **1,** the act of exhibiting or displaying; **2,** an exhibition or display; as, a dog *show;* **3,** an imposing or proud display; as, a *show* of wealth; **4,** a deceitful appearance or pretence; as, a *show* of enthusiasm; **5,** *Colloq.,* a theatrical performance. Also, show′case′; show′-man-ship′; show′piece; show′room′.

show-down (shō′doun′), *n.* **1,** in the game of poker, a laying of cards, face up, on the table; **2,** hence, a full disclosure of facts or plans; as, to force a *showdown.*

show-er (shou′ẽr), *n.* **1,** a brief fall of rain, sleet, or hail; **2,** something resembling a shower; a brief outburst; as, a *shower* of stones; a *shower* of abuse; **3,** a party at which gifts are given to a future bride; **4,** a shower-bath:—*v.t.* **1,** to cause a liquid to fall upon; as, he *showered* me with water; **2,** to bestow liberally upon a person; as, honours were *showered* on the hero: —*v.i.* **1,** to rain for a short time; **2,** to fall in a shower.—*adj.* show′er-y.

show-ing (shō′ing), *n.* a display or exhibition; as, a *showing* of fall clothes; also, the impression made by a person's appearance or actions, or by a presentation of facts; as, a poor financial *showing.*

show-y (shō′i), *adj.* [show-i-er, show-i-est], attracting attention; gaudy; as, a *showy* dress; a *showy* garden.—*adv.* show′i-ly.—*n.* show′i-ness.

shrap-nel (shrap′nel), *n.* bullets of iron in a shell timed to explode and scatter its contents over a desired area or point; also the shells so charged.

shred (shred), *n.* a long, narrow strip torn or cut off; a scrap or fragment; as, to tear a handkerchief to *shreds:* —*v.t.* [*p.t.* and *p.p.* shred-ded or shred, *p.pr.* shred-ding], to tear or cut into strips; as, to *shred* cabbage.

shrew (shrōō), *n.* **1,** a scolding, quarrelsome woman; **2,** a mouselike animal with a long snout, which feeds chiefly on insects and worms.

shrewd (shrōōd), *adj.* sharp-witted; clever in practical affairs; keen; as, a *shrewd* buyer.

shrew-ish (shrōō′ish), *adj.* scolding; sharp-tongued; as, a *shrewish* wife.

shriek (shrēk), *v.t.* and *v.i.* to cry out sharply; scream; as, "Fire!" he *shrieked;* he *shrieked* for help:—*n.* a piercing scream; a shrill outcry.

shrift (shrift), *n.* a brief respite (as for confession of sins):—**to give short shrift to,** to make short work of; dismiss quickly.

shrike (shrīk), *n.* any of various birds which feed chiefly on insects but which sometimes kill smaller birds, mice, etc.

shrill (shril), *adj.* sharp and piercing in tone; as, a *shrill* cry:—*v.i.* and *v.t.* to speak in a piercing, sharp tone.—*adv.* shril′ly.

shrimp (shrimp), *n.* **1,** a small shellfish used for food; **2,** *Colloq.* a puny person; one of little account.

shrine (shrīn), *n.* **1,** a case or box in which sacred relics are kept; **2,** the tomb of a saint; **3,** any consecrated place or object, as a chapel or the statue of a saint; also, a place considered sacred because of its history; as, Keats's tomb is a *shrine* for lovers of poetry:—*v.t.* [shrined, shrin-ing], to cherish as sacred; put in a sacred place; enshrine.

shrink (shringk), *v.i.* [*p.t.* shrank (shrangk) or shrunk (shrungk), *p.p.* shrunk or esp. as *adj.*, shrunk-en (shrungk'en), *p.pr.* shrink-ing], **1,** to contract; become smaller or shorter; as, the blanket *shrank* when it was washed; **2,** to draw back; recoil; as, to *shrink* from punishment or an unpleasant sight:—*v.t.* to cause to contract or grow smaller; as, to *shrink* flannel by washing—*n.* **shrink'age.** —*adj.* **shrink'a-ble.**

shriv-el (shriv'l), *v.t.* and *v.i.* [shrivelled, shrivel-ling], to wrinkle, wither, or dry up; as, the heat *shrivelled* the leaves of the plant; some plants *shrivel* quickly.

shroud (shroud), *n.* **1,** a dress or covering for the dead; anything that envelops and conceals; as, a *shroud* of mystery; **3, shrouds,** a set of ropes, usually two to five, connected by rope rungs, or ratlins, which support and steady the masts of a vessel: —*v.t.* **1,** to clothe (a corpse) in a shroud; **2,** to hide or conceal with a covering; veil; as, the hills were *shrouded* in gray mist.

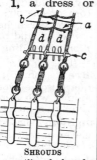

SHROUDS
a, ratlins; *b,* shrouds; *c,* rail for belaying pins, *d, d.*

Shrove Tuesday, the day before Ash Wednesday, a day of penitence and confession immediately preceding Lent. Also, **Shrove Sunday,** the 50th day before Easter.

shrub (shrub), *n.* a woody plant not so tall as a tree; a bush. It usually has many separate stems starting near the ground.—*adj.* **shrub'by.**

shrub-ber-y (shrub'er-i), *n.* [*pl.* shrub-beries], **1,** a group or collection of shrubs; **2,** ground planted with shrubs.

shrug (shrug), *v.t.* and *v.i.* [shrugged, shrug-ging], to draw up or hunch (the shoulders) in doubt, surprise, contempt, etc.:—*n.* a drawing up or hunching of the shoulders; as, his answer was a *shrug.*

shrunk or **shrunk-en** (shrunk'en), *p.p.* of *shrink.*

shuck (shuk), *n.* a husk or pod; the

outer covering of a nut; a shell:—*v.t.* to shell, as peanuts; husk, as corn.

shud-der (shud'er), *v.i.* to tremble or shake, as with fear or cold; to quake; shiver:—*n.* a sudden trembling, as from fear, aversion, cold, or excitement.

shuf-fle (shuf'l), *v.t.* [shuf-fled, shuf-fling], **1,** to shift from place to place or from person to person; as, we *shuffled* the money from hand to hand; **2,** to rearrange or mix up the order of (cards in a pack); **3,** to jumble together in a disorderly heap; as, to *shuffle* papers into a desk; **4,** to drag or trail (the feet) in walking or dancing; **5,** to slip off carelessly; as, to *shuffle* off a burden: —*v.i.* **1,** to shift things from one position to another; **2,** to rearrange the cards in a pack; **3,** to drag the feet in a slow, lagging manner; scuffle; as, he *shuffled* along in his big slippers; also, to dance with a sliding or scraping motion of the feet; **4,** to do something in a careless, clumsy manner; as, to *shuffle* through one's work:—*n.* **1,** the act of shifting, rearranging, etc.; esp., the rearranging of cards in a pack; **2,** a lazy, dragging gait or movement; also, a dance characterized by a scraping or sliding motion of the feet.—*n.* **shuf'fler.**

shuf-fle-board (shuf'l-bōrd'), *n.* a game in which disks are pushed with a cue along a flat surface toward numbered squares.

shun (shun), *v.t.* [shunned, shun-ning], to avoid; keep clear of; as, to *shun* evil.

shunt (shunt), *v.t.* and *v.i.* **1,** to turn to one side; switch, as a car or train; **2,** to put off on someone else, as a task or duty; **3,** to change; shift; as an opinion or course:—*adj.* **shunt-wound,** said of a dynamo or motor in which a winding is so arranged as to divide the armature current and lead a portion of it around a field magnet: opposite of **series-wound.**

shush (shush), *interj.* and *v.t.* to tell (someone) to hush or be quiet.

shut (shut), *v.t.* [shut, shut-ting], **1,** to close, so as to prevent entrance or exit; as, to *shut* a gate; **2,** to bar or deny entrance to; as, the country *shut* its ports to trade; **3,** to prevent the entrance of; as, to *shut* out certain imports; **4,** to confine; imprison; as, to *shut* a child in his room; **5,** to keep from functioning by turning a screw, dial, etc.; as, to *shut* off the radio; **6,** to bring together the parts of; as, to *shut* an umbrella, a knife, or a book: —*v.i.* **1,** to become closed; as, the door *shut* with a bang; **2,** to cease working; as, the factory *shut* down for six weeks.—*n.* **shut/down/.**

shut-out (shut/out/), *n.* **1,** a lockout (of employees); **2,** in a game, the preventing of an opposing team from scoring.

shut-ter (shut/ẽr), *n.* **1,** a movable metal or wood cover or screen for a window; **2,** in *photography,* a device for regulating the exposure of a sensitive plate to light.

shut-tle (shut/l), *n.* **1,** in *weaving,* an instrument used to carry the thread of the weft, or woof, back and forth through the warp; **2,** in a sewing-machine, the sliding holder which encloses the bobbin and carries the lower thread to meet the upper thread in order to form a single stitch; **3,** any similar device, as one used in tatting; **4,** a train making short trips back and forth between two points: also called *shuttle-train:*—*v.t.* and *v.i.* [shut-tled, shut-tling], to move backwards and forwards like a shuttle.

¹shy (shī), *adj.* [shy-er or shi-er, shy-est or shi-est], **1,** easily scared away; timid, as a fawn; **2,** reserved; bashful; as, a *shy* girl; **3,** *Slang,* short; lacking; as, this pack is one card *shy:*—*v.i.* [shied, shy-ing], to start suddenly aside, as from fear; as, a horse that *shies.*—*adv.* **shy/ly.**—*n.* **shy/ness.**

²shy (shī), *v.t.* [shied, shy-ing], to throw with a jerk; fling; as, the boy *shied* a stone at the kitten:—*n.* [*pl.* shies], **1,** a fling; throw; **2,** *Colloq.,* a try; a trial.

shy-ster (shī/stẽr), *n. Colloq.* one who carries on a business in a mean or tricky manner, esp. a rascally lawyer.

si (sē), *n.* in music, the seventh note of the scale: now often called *ti.*

sib-i-lant (sib/i-lant), *n.* and *adj.* a hissing sound, esp. of a letter of the alphabet: the sibilants are *s, sh, z,* and *zh* (or any symbol representing one of these sounds).

sick (sik), *adj.* **1,** in ill health; indisposed; **2,** affected with nausea; inclined to vomit; **3,** tired (of); as, *sick* of flattery; **4,** longing (for); as, *sick* for recognition; **5,** used by, or set apart for the use of, a person who is ill; as, a *sick*-bed; a *sick* benefit:—**the sick,** those who are ill.—*n.* **sick/ness.**

sick bay, a ship's hospital and drug dispensary.

sick-en (sik/en), *v.i.* **1,** to become ill; as, to *sicken* and die; **2,** to become tired of; as, to *sicken* of vain effort:—*v.t.* **1,** to make ill; as, the tainted meat *sickened* me; **2,** to disgust; as, she is *sickened* by vulgarity.

sick-le (sik/l), *n.* a hand tool consisting of a curved steel blade fitted into a short handle, used to cut grass, etc.

sick-ly (sik/li), *adj.* [sick-li-er, sick-li-est], **1,** habitually ailing; weak; as, a *sickly* baby; **2,** caused by, or characteristic of, illness; as, a *sickly* look; **3,** unfavourable to health; as, the *sickly* tropics; **4,** weak; faint; as, a *sickly* grin.—*n.* **sick/li-ness.**

side (sīd), *n.* **1,** one of the edges or lines that bound a surface; esp., in a rectangle, one of the longer lines as distinguished from the ends; **2,** one of the surfaces of a solid object; as, one of the six *sides* of a box; also, either of the surfaces of an object that has no appreciable thickness; as, the shiny *side* of a piece of silk; **3,** the particular surfaces of a structure which are not the top, bottom, front, or back; as, the *sides* of a house; **4,** a position to the right or to the left of the centre; as, he kicked the ball to the right *side* of the field; **5,** either lengthwise half of a person or an animal; as, a *side* of beef; **6,** a party or group upholding one view or aspect of a cause; **7,** line of descent through the father or mother; as, a cousin on my mother's *side:*—*adj.* **1,** pertaining to a side or sides; **2,** directed from or toward one side; as, a *side*-step; **3,** placed or situated on one side; as, a *side*-door; **4,** minor; incidental; as, a *side* issue:—*v.i.* [sid-ed, sid-ing], to take the part of one against another; as, he invariably *sided* with them in the argument.

side-board (sīd/bōrd/), *n.* a piece of dining-room furniture with drawers and compartments for holding flat silverware, dishes, linens, etc.

side-burns (sīd/bûrnz/), *n.* short whiskers worn only on the cheeks, esp. near the ears (the chin being shaven).

side-long (sīd/lông/), *adv.* sideways:—*adj.* directed to one side; as, a *sidelong* glance.

sid-er-ite (sid/ẽr-īt/), *n.* an important ore of iron: large deposits are mined at the Helen mine, Algoma District, Ontario.

side-slip (sīd/slip/), *v.i.* and *v.t.* and *n.* in *flying,* to slip or glide sideways and downward by banking steeply on a turn: opposite of *skid*.

side-track (sīd'trak'), *v.t.* 1, to transfer (a car or train) from the main track to a siding; 2, *Colloq.*, to put off for consideration at some future time; set aside; as, to *sidetrack* a legislative bill:—*v.i.* to run a train upon a siding:—*n.* a siding.

side-walk (sīd'wôk'), *n.* a path or pavement beside a road or street for foot travel.

side-ways (sīd'wāz'), *adv.* 1, toward the side; as, to glance *sideways;* 2, from the side; as, to see a thing *sideways;* 3, with the side foremost; as, to turn *sideways:—adj.* directed or turned to one side; as, a *sideways* look.

side-wise (sīd'wīz'), *adv.* and *adj.* sideways.

sid-ing (sīd'ing), *n.* 1, a short railroad track by the side of the main track, to which cars may be switched; a side-track; 2, boarding, plywood, metal, or composition used for covering the sides of a building.

si-dle (sī'dl), [si-dled, si-dling], to move sideways; edge along, as if from shyness or fear; as, the boy *sidled* up to us.

siege (sēj), *n.* 1, the surrounding of a fortified place by an army or fleet to compel its surrender; 2, a persistent attempt to gain possession of something; as, he laid *siege* to her heart.

si-en-na (si-en'a), *n.* 1, a yellowish-brown pigment containing iron and manganese; 2, a reddish-brown pigment, *burnt sienna*, made from burning the former; 3, the colour of either of these.

si-er-ra (si-er'a), *n.* a mountain chain or range rising in irregular peaks.

si-es-ta (si-es'ta), *n.* a sleep or rest taken during the hottest part of the day, as in Spain and Mexico; any midday or after-dinner rest or nap.

sieve (siv), *n.* a utensil with meshes usually of wire, for separating the finer from the coarser parts of a substance; as, a flour-*sieve*.

sift (sift), *v.t.* 1, to separate, as the finer part from the coarser, with a sieve; 2, to put through a sieve; also, to sprinkle with a sieve; as, the cook *sifted* flour over the meat; 3, to examine critically; as, the jury *sifted* the facts in the case.—*n.* **sift'er.**

sigh (sī), *n.* 1, a deep, audible breath expressing fatigue, sorrow, etc.; as, to heave a *sigh;* 2, a similar sound; as, the *sigh* of the wind:—*v.i.* 1, to breathe a sigh; as, to *sigh* with regret; 2, to long; grieve; as, the old lady *sighs* for the past; 3, to make a sound like sighing; as, trees murmur and *sigh:* —*v.t.* to express by sighs; as, she *sighed* her relief.

sight (sīt), *n.* 1, the power of seeing; vision; as, eye-glasses help to correct defects in *sight;* 2, the act of seeing; as, she was thrilled by her first *sight* of mountains; 3, that which is seen; a view or spectacle; as, the sunset was a *sight* to remember; also, something ludicrous or grotesque; a fright; as, my hair is a *sight* on a windy day; 4, the limit or range within which a person can see, or an object can be seen; as, in *sight;* out of *sight;* 5, manner of looking at or considering something; opinion; as, in his *sight,* she did well; 6, inspection; as, this report is intended for the *sight* of the committee only; 7, any of several devices, as on a gun, optical instrument, etc., to help in guiding the eye or aim; 8, careful aim or observation taken by means of such a device; as, take *sight* before firing:—**at sight, on sight,** as soon as seen; upon presentation to sight:—*v.t.* 1, to see with the eye; as, to *sight* an object through the telescope; 3, to direct by means of an aiming device; as, to *sight* a gun:—*v.i.* 1, to aim a gun by means of a sight; 2, to look carefully in a certain direction. —*adj.* **sight'less.**

sign (sīn), *n.* 1, a symbol, emblem, or character typifying or representing an idea; as, the *sign* of the cross; 2, that by which anything is made known; a mark; token; proof; as, his gift was a *sign* of his love; also, indication; evidence; as, there was no *sign* of anyone stirring in the house at that hour; 3, an omen; as, the breaking of a mirror is said to be a *sign* of bad luck; 4, a gesture or motion used instead of words to express some thought, command, or wish; as, the teacher gave the *sign* to rise; 5, a lettered board or plate displaying the name of a business, giving information, etc.; as, a shoemaker's *sign;* a *sign* to keep off the grass; 6, one of the twelve equal divisions of the zodiac or its symbol; 7, in *arithmetic*, a symbol for adding, subtracting, multiplying, or dividing, as $+$, $-$, $\times$, or $\div$: —*v.t.* 1, to write one's name at the end of; as, to *sign* a letter; 2, to transfer (a right to property) by putting one's signature to a document; as, the old man *signed* away all his property; **3,** to hire by getting the signature of; as, to *sign* a person for a particular job:—*v.i.* **1,** to write one's signature; as, I am ready to *sign;* **2,** to signal; motion; as, he *signed* for them to approach.—*n.* sign'er.—*n.* sign'board'.—*n.* sign'post'.

sig-nal (sig'nal), *n.* **1,** a sign agreed upon for sending information, giving notice of danger, etc.; as, a train *signal;* **2,** that which brings about action; as, the blowing of the fire whistle was the *signal* for panic:—*adj.* memorable; extraordinary; remarkable; as, a *signal* success:—*v.t.* [signalled, signal-ling], to communicate with by means of flags, lights, etc.; make signs to; as, the scoutmaster *signalled* the boys to return to camp:—*v.i.* to make signs.—*n.* sig'nal-ler or sig'nal-er.

sig-nal-ly (sig'nal-i), *adv.* in an extraordinary or striking manner.

sig-na-to-ry (sig'na-tōr'i), *n.* and *adj.* one bound jointly with others, esp. a state or power, by a signed agreement.

sig-na-ture (sig'na-tūr), *n.* **1,** the name of a person in his own handwriting; autograph; **2,** in *music,* the signs at the beginning of a staff indicating key and time.

sig-net (sig'nit), *n.* **1,** a seal; esp., in England, one of the private seals of the monarch; **2,** an imprint made by, or as by, a seal.

sig-nif-i-cance (sig-nif'i-kans), *n.* **1,** meaning; as, the full *significance* of his remark escaped me; **2,** importance; as, he must realize this is a matter of some *significance;* **3,** expressiveness; as, he gave the boy a look of deep *significance.*

sig-nif-i-cant (sig-nif'i-kant), *adj.* **1,** full of meaning; expressive; as, Caesar has come to be a *significant* name; also, suggestive; having some concealed or special meaning; as, a *significant* silence; **2,** important; conspicuous; as, *significant* progress.

sig-ni-fy (sig'ni-fī'), *v.t.* [signified, signify-ing], **1,** to show by a sign, mark or token; make known; declare; as, to *signify* one's consent; **2,** to denote; mean; as, that gesture *signifies* refusal:—*v.i.* to be of importance; to matter or count.—*n.* sig'ni-fi-ca'tion.

si-lence (sī'lens), *n.* **1,** the state of being still or mute; as, he listened in *silence;* **2,** entire absence of sound or noise; general stillness; as, there was *silence*

in the courtroom; **3,** absence of mention; as, to pass over a subject in *silence:*—*v.t.* [silenced, silenc-ing], **1,** to cause to be still; as, to *silence* the dogs; **2,** to quiet; put to rest; as, to *silence* opposition; **3,** to force (guns) to cease firing.—*n.* si'lenc-er.

si-lent (sī'lent), *adj.* **1,** saying nothing; mute; also, not given to frequent or copious words; as, a *silent* man; **2,** quiet; still; free from noise; as, a *silent* place; **3,** not expressed; not spoken; as, a *silent* command; **4,** having a share, not publicly acknowledged, in a business; as, a *silent* partner; **5,** written, but not pronounced: said of a letter; as, the "b" in "doubt" is *silent.*—*adv.* si'lent-ly.

sil-hou-ette (sil'oo-et'), *n.* an outline drawing, esp. a profile portrait, filled in with solid colour, usually black; **2,** the figure cast by a shadow, as on a wall or screen:—*v.t.* [silhouet-ted, silhouet-ting], to cause to appear in outline or silhouette; as, his form was *silhouetted* against the wall.

sil-i-ca (sil'i-ka), *n.* a hard, white or colourless mineral, silicon dioxide (SiO_2), found in many forms, as quartz, sand, opal, onyx, etc., used in making glass, flux for pottery manufacture, etc.

sil-i-cate (sil'i-kāt'; kit), *n.* a salt or ester derived from silica, used in making glass.

sil-i-con (sil'i-kon'), *n.* a nonmetallic element, ranking next to oxygen in abundance, found in a combined state in minerals and rocks making up $\frac{1}{4}$ of the earth's crust: used in steelmaking, etc.

sil-i-cone (sil'i-kōn), *n.* any compound made by replacing carbon with silicon in an organic substance: the chief silicones are oils, greases, resins, plastics, polishes, and synthetic rubber.

sil-i-co-sis (sil'i-kō'sis), *n.* a lung disease caused by inhaling silica dust, esp. in quarrying or cutting quartz or other rock.

silk (silk), *n.* **1,** a fine, soft, lustrous fabric made from threads spun by silkworm larvae to form their cocoons; **2,** the thread as produced by the larvae; **3,** any similar thread, as that spun by certain spiders; **4,** anything like silk, as the down of the milkweed pod:—*adj.* made of silk.—*adj.* silk'en.—*adj.* silk'y.—*n.* silk'i-ness.

silk-worm (silk'wûrm'), *n.* the larva of a certain kind of moth. The silkworm makes a strong silk fibre in spinning its cocoon.

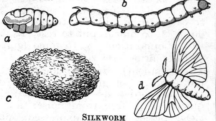

SILKWORM
a, pupa; *b*, larva (caterpillar); *c*, silk cocoon enclosing pupa; *d*, adult female moth.

sill (sil), *n.* **1,** a horizontal piece forming the foundation, or part of the foundation, of a structure; **2,** a threshold; as, a door-*sill;* **3,** the bottom piece in a window-frame.

sil-ly (sil'i), *adj.* [sil-li-er, sil-li-est], **1,** weak-minded; **2,** stupid; absurd; as, a *silly* answer.—*n.* **sil'li-ness.**

si-lo (sī'lō), *n.* [*pl.* silos], a pit or tower for storing and preserving green fodder.

silt (silt), *n.* mud or fine earth suspended in, or deposited by, water:—*v.t.* and *v.i.*, **1,** to choke, fill, or block with such deposit: usually with *up;* as, the channel is *silted up;* **2,** to ooze through crevices, as water carrying a fine sediment.

sil-van (sil'van), *adj.* **1,** pertaining to woods, forests or trees; rustic; as, a *silvan* deity; **2,** wooded; as, a *silvan* scene. Also, **syl'van.**

sil-ver (sil'vėr), *n.* **1,** a soft, shining, white metal, used for table implements, dishes, jewellery, etc.; **2,** anything made of this metal, as silverware or money; **3,** anything that has the lustre or colour of silver; as, cloth of *silver:*—*adj.* **1,** made of silver; as, a *silver* cup; **2,** having a soft, silvery lustre; as, *silver* dew; **3,** soft and clear, as the tones of a silver bell; hence, eloquent; as, a *silver* tongue; **4,** relating to silver; as, *silver* legislation; a *silver* mill:—*v.t.* **1,** to cover or coat with silver, or with something resembling it; **2,** to give a silverlike polish to; make the colour of silver:—*v.i.* to turn silvery white or grey; as, her hair *silvered* at a very early age.—*adj.* **sil'ver-y.**

sil-ver-fish (sil'vėr-fish'), *n.* a wingless insect with silvery scales, long feelers, and bristly tail: it likes dampness, and lives on the starches and sugars of wallpaper, books, etc.

sil-vi-cul-ture (sil'vi-kul'tūr; chėr), *n.* forestry.

sim-i-an (sim'i-an), *adj.* pertaining to, or like, an ape or monkey.—*n.* an ape or monkey, as the gorilla and chimpanzee.

sim-i-lar (sim'i-lėr), *adj.* **1,** having a general likeness; like, but not exactly the same; as, pink and rose are *similar* colours; **2,** in *geometry*, shaped alike, but not of the same size, position, etc.; as, *similar* triangles.—*n.* **sim'i-lar'i-ty.** —*adv.* **sim'i-lar-ly.**

sim-i-le (sim'i-lē), *n.* a figure of speech in which two different things having some likeness are compared by the use of *like* or *as:* as, the ice is *like* glass; the night is black *as* ink.

sim-mer (sim'er), *v.t.* **1,** to boil gently; **2,** to cook in liquid at or just below the boiling-point:—*v.i.* **1,** to cook at or just below the boiling-point; as, let the stew *simmer;* **2,** to make a gentle, low, murmuring sound, as a liquid about to boil; **3,** to be in a state of suppressed emotion; to be on the verge of breaking out; as, the savage tribes were *simmering* with revolt:—*n.* **1,** a heated state at or near the boiling-point; as, to cook meat at a *simmer;* **2,** a state of suppressed emotion or excitement.

sim-per (sim'pėr), *v.i.* to smile in an affected, silly, or self-conscious manner; smirk:—*n.* an affected smile; a smirk.

sim-ple (sim'pl), *adj.* [sim-pler, sim-plest], **1,** not mixed or compounded; as, a *simple* fraction; not divided into parts; as, a *simple* leaf; **2,** not involved or elaborate; easy to solve or understand; as, *simple* words; a *simple* problem; **3,** plain; as, *simple* food; unadorned; as, *simple* clothes; **4,** mere; unqualified; as, a *simple* fact; **5,** sincere; straightforward; as, a *simple,* unaffected manner; **6,** humble; of low rank or degree; as, *simple* folk; **7,** weak in intellect; foolish.—*n.* **sim'ple-ness.**

sim-ple-ton (sim'pl-tun), *n.* one who is foolish or weak-minded.

sim-plic-i-ty (sim-plis'i-ti), *n.* [*pl.* simplicities], **1,** the state or quality of being clear, plain, or unaffected; as, *simplicity* of language; *simplicity* of dress; **2,** lack of cunning; sincerity; **3,** lack of common sense, or of average ability to judge.

sim-pli-fy (sim'pli-fī'), *v.t.* [simplified, simplify-ing], to make easier; make plainer to the understanding.—*n.* **sim'-pli-fi-ca'tion.**

sim-ply (sim'pli), *adv.* **1,** plainly; clearly; as, to write *simply;* **2,** without elaborate show; as, to dress *simply;* **3,** only; merely; as, it is *simply* a question of money; **4,** absolutely; as, you *simply* must go.

sim-u-late (sim′ū-lāt′), *v.t.* to feign or counterfeit; as, to *simulate* insanity. —*n.* sim′u-la′tion.

sim-ul-ta-ne-ous (sim′ul-tā′ni-us; sī′), *adj.* happening, done, or existing at the same time; as, *simultaneous* explosions.—*adv.* sim′ul-ta′ne-ous-ly.

sin (sin), *n.* **1,** the breaking or violation of God's laws; also, any instance of such violation, as dishonesty; **2,** any serious offence:—*v.i.* [sinned, sin-ning], **1,** to transgress, offend, or neglect the law of God in any way; **2,** to commit evil deeds.—*adj.* sin′ful.—*n.* sin′fulness.

since (sins), *adv.* **1,** from a certain past time until now; as, he left six years ago and has not been seen *since;* **2,** at some time after a certain past event and before now; as, he was then treasurer, but has *since* been elected president; **3,** before this; ago; as, not long *since:*—*prep.* from the time of; during the time after; ever after; as, *since* his departure, I have never seen him:—*conj.* **1,** from and after a time when; as, I have not seen him *since* that happened; **2,** seeing that; because; as, *since* that is the case, I shall go.

sin-cere (sin-sēr′), *adj.* [sincer-er, sin-cer-est], honest; frank; as, a *sincere* man; genuine; as, a *sincere* friend; also, honestly felt or intended; as, *sincere* wishes for your success.—*adv.* sin-cere′ly.—*n.* sin-cer′i-ty (sin-ser′-i-ti).

sine (sīn), *n.* the ratio of the side opposite an acute angle of a right-angled triangle to the hypotenuse.

si-ne-cure (sī′ni-kūr′; sin′), *n.* a position requiring little or no work, yet well paid.

sin-ew (sin′ū), *n.* **1,** a tendon or tough piece of tissue joining muscle to bone; **2,** strength; power; energy; **3,** anything supplying strength; the mainstay of anything; as, money, the *sinews* of war.—*adj.* sin′ew-y.—*adj.* sin′ew-less.

sing (sing), *v.i.* [*p.t.* sang (sang), *p.p.* sung (sung), *p.pr.* sing-ing], **1,** to make musical sounds with the voice; **2,** to make a shrill or humming noise; as, a flying arrow *sings;* **3,** to make pleasant, melodious sounds; as, the brook *sings* merrily; **4,** to celebrate some event in verse; as, Vergil *sang* of the deeds of Aeneas; **5,** to ring with a constant humming or buzzing sound; as, my

ears are *singing:*—*v.t.* **1,** to utter with musical tones of the voice; as, to *sing* a song; to chant; as, to *sing* Mass; **2,** to celebrate in poetry; **3,** to lull by singing; as, to *sing* a child to sleep.—*n.* sing′er.

singe (sinj), *v.t.* [singed, singe-ing], **1,** to burn slightly or on the surface; scorch; **2,** to pass over a flame to remove the feathers or down; as, to *singe* a plucked chicken before cooking it:—*n.* a slight burn.

sin-gle (sing′gl), *adj.* **1,** consisting of one only; as, a *single* page; **2,** not married; as, they employ *single* girls only; **3,** performed by one person; having only one on each side; as, *single* combat; **4,** for the use of one person only; as, a *single* room; **5,** straightforward; sincere; as, a man of *single* purpose; **6,** in *botany,* having only one row of petals; as, a *single* tulip: —*v.t.* [sin-gled, sin-gling], to select (one person or thing) from others; as, they *singled* him out for honourable mention:—*v.i.* to make a base hit:—*n.* **1,** in baseball, a base hit; **2,** in *golf,* a game between two players; in *tennis,* (usually *singles*), a game with only one person on each side.

sin-gle—hand-ed (sing′gl—han′did), *adj.* done without aid or assistance.

sin-gle-ness (sing′gl-nis), *n.* **1,** the state of being separate or alone; the state of being unmarried; **2,** freedom from selfish ends; sincerity; as, *singleness* of purpose.

sin-gle-ton (sing′gl-tun), *n.* a single thing, as distinguished from several, esp. the only card of a suit in a hand (of playing cards).

sing-gle-tree (sing′gl-trē′), *n.* Same as whip′ple-tree′.

sin-gly (sing′gli), *adv.* **1,** individually; one by one; as, we took up each matter *singly;* **2,** without others; alone; single-handed.

sing-song (sing′song′), *n.* and *adj.* a monotonous or unvaried tone or rhythm.

sin-gu-lar (sing′gū-lėr), *adj.* **1,** in *grammar,* relating to the form of a word naming one person or thing; as, the word "girl" is a *singular* noun; **2,** extraordinary; exceptional; as, *singular* strength; **3,** peculiar; strange; as, *singular* habits:—*n.* in *grammar,* that form of a word naming one person or thing; as, "man" is the *singular* of "men."—*n.* sin′gu-lar′i-ty.

sin-is-ter (sin′is-tėr), *adj.* **1,** ill-omened; threatening; evil; as, a *sinister* look; **2,** base; dishonest; as, *sinister* intentions; **3,** left: applied in heraldry to the side of a shield on the left of the person bearing it.

sink (singk), *v.i.* [*p.t.* sank (sangk) or sunk (sungk), *p.p.* sunk, *p.pr.* sink-ing], **1,** to become wholly or partly submerged, as in water; **2,** to descend gradually; as, the sun *sinks;* to slope downward; as, land *sinks* to the sea; **3,** to decline gradually, as in strength; also, to degenerate, as in morals; **4,** to become hollow: often said of the cheeks; **5,** to enter deeply; as, a thought *sinks* into the mind:—*v.t.* **1,** to cause to go to the bottom; as, to *sink* a boat in a river; **2,** to make by digging downward; as, to *sink* a well; also, to place in an excavation thus made; as, to *sink* a pipe; **3,** to invest or spend unprofitably; as, to *sink* money in worthless stocks:—*n.* **1,** a kind of basin, as in a kitchen, with a drain to carry off dirty or excessive water; **2,** any slight hollow of land, esp. one that has little or no water outlet; **3,** a place of vice and corruption.—*n.* **sink′er.**

sin-ner (sin′ėr), *n.* one who breaks the law of God or man; an offender.

sin-u-ous (sin′ū-us), *adj.* **1,** winding or curving in and out; twisting; **2,** devious; morally crooked; as, he won honour by no *sinuous* path.

si-nus (sī′nus), *n.* a natural cavity or hollow in bone, esp. an air cavity in a bone of the skull.

sip (sip), *v.t.* [sipped, sip-ping], to drink by taking a small portion at a time; as, she *sips* her chocolate:—*v.i.* to drink a liquid in sips:—*n.* a small taste or mouthful.

si-phon (sī′fun), *n.* **1,** a pipe or tube bent like an in- verted U, with one leg longer than the other, used for drawing off liquids from a higher to a lower level; **2,** a bottle for soda- water, fitted with a siphon, through which the water is forced by pressure of gas in the bottle: —*v.t.* to draw off by such a tube.

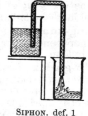

Siphon. def. 1

sir (sûr), *n.* a term of respect in addressing a man, esp. an elder or a superior.

sire (sīr), *n.* **1,** (*Sire*), a title of respect used in addressing a sovereign or king;

2, a father; the head of a family; **3,** among animals, the male parent:—*v.t.* [sired, siring], to be or become the father of: used esp. of animals.

si-ren (sī′ren), *n.* **1,** (often *Siren*), in Greek mythology, one of the sea nymphs who captivated sailors by their sweet singing; **2,** an alluring or captivating woman; **3,** a device for producing a shrill sound; as, a *siren* on an ambulance:—*adj.* **1,** pertaining to, or like, a siren; **2,** bewitching; alluring.

sir-loin (sûr′loin′), *n.* a choice cut of beef, taken from the upper part of the loin.

sir-up (sir′up), *n.* Same as **syrup.**

si-sal (sis′l; sī′sl), *n.* the fibre of the leaf of the agave or the aloe of Yucatan, used for making rope. Also, **sisal hemp.**

sis-sy (sis′i), *n.* *Colloq.* an effeminate boy or man.

sis-ter (sis′tėr), *n.* **1,** a woman or girl who has the same father and mother as another person; also, a woman or girl who is a very good friend; as, she's been a *sister* to me; **2,** a woman of the same religious society, order, or community as others; a nun.—*adj.* **sis′-ter-ly.**

sis-ter-hood (sis′tėr-hood′), *n.* **1,** the relationship between sisters; **2,** a number of women united by a common interest, as a religious society.

sis-ter—in—law (sis′tėr-in-lô′), *n.* [*pl.* sisters-in-law], **1,** a husband's or wife's sister; **2,** a brother's wife.

sit (sit), *v.i.* [sat (sat), sit-ting], **1,** to rest with the weight of the body on the lower part of the trunk; occupy a seat; as, to *sit* on a bench; to *sit* on the porch; **2,** to perch; as, the birds *sit* in the tree; **3,** to have place or position; be situated; as, the box *sits* on the floor; **4,** to fit; suit; as, the dress *sits* well; **5,** to press or weigh, as sorrow on the mind; **6,** to occupy a seat officially; be a member of a council or assembly; as, to *sit* in Parliament; **7,** to meet or hold a session, as a court; **8,** to cover eggs to be hatched, as does a fowl; **9,** to pose; as, to *sit* for a portrait:— *v.t.* **1,** to have, or keep, a seat upon; as, to *sit* a horse; **2,** to seat (oneself).—*n.* **sit′ter.**

site (sīt), *n.* **1,** position or place; as, the *site* of a battle; **2,** a plot of land suitable for a building.

sit-ting (sit′ing), *adj.* **1,** resting on the haunches; seated; as, a *sitting* figure; **2,** pertaining to, or used for sitting; as, a *sitting*-room:—*n.* **1**, the position or act of one who sits; **2**, a session or meeting; **3**, the time during which one sits; as, a long *sitting;* **4**, a set of eggs for hatching.

sit-u-at-ed (sit/ū-āt/id), *adj.* having a position; located; placed.

sit-u-a-tion (sit/ū-ā/shun), *n.* **1**, position; location; as, the *situation* of a hospital; **2**, a combination of circumstances; as, a ludicrous *situation;* **3**, a position of employment; as, a *situation* as nurse.

six (siks), *adj.* composed of one more than five:—*n.* **1**, the number consisting of five plus one; **2**, a sign representing six units, as 6 or vi.

six-er (siks/ẽr), *n.* *Boy Scouts,* the leader of one of the sixes, or groups of six, which form a wolf-cub pack.

six-pence (siks/pens), *n.* a small British silver coin, of the value of six English pence, or about seven cents.

six-teen (siks/tēn/), *adj.* composed of ten more than six:—*n.* **1**, the sum of fifteen plus one; **2**, a sign representing sixteen units, as 16 or xvi.

six-teenth (siks/tēnth/), *adj.* next after the 15th: the ordinal of *sixteen:*—*n.* one of the sixteen equal parts of anything.

sixth (siksth), *adj.* next after the fifth: the ordinal of *six:*—*n.* one of the six equal parts of anything.

six-ti-eth (siks/ti-eth), *adj.* next after the 59th: the ordinal of *sixty:*—*n.* one of the 60 equal parts of anything.

six-ty (siks/ti), *adj.* composed of one more than 59:—*n.* [*pl.* sixties], **1**, the number consisting of 59 plus one; **2**, a sign representing 60 units, as 60 or lx.

six-ty—one (siks/ti-wun/), *n.* and *adj.* the numbers sixty-one to sixty-nine are hyphenated.

siz-a-ble (sīz/à-bl), *adj.* of considerable bulk; quite large; as, a *sizable* income.—*adv.* **siz/a-bly.**

size (sīz), *n.* any of various thin, sticky washes, used by painters, paper-makers, etc., for glazing the surface of various materials:—*v.t.* [sized, siz-ing], to prepare, stiffen, or cover with thin glue. —*n.* **siz/ing.**

¹**size** (sīz), *n.* **1**, dimensions; bigness; as, to measure the *size* of a room; a building of great *size;* **2**, a measure showing how large something is; as, a medium *size;* a *size* four shoe:—*v.t.* [sized, siz-ing], **1**, to arrange in order of bulk, height, volume, or extent;

2, *Colloq.*, to form a conclusion about; as, to *size* up a situation.

siz-zle (siz/l), *v.i.* [siz-zled, siz-zling], to make a hissing sound, as in frying: —*n.* a hissing sound.

¹**skate** (skāt), *n.* a broad, flat-bodied fish with a very narrow tail.

²**skate** (skāt), *n.* **1**, a frame, with a metal runner attached, shaped to fit a shoe and used for gliding rapidly over ice; **2**, a device consisting of small wheels attached to a frame which clamps to the sole of the shoe; a roller skate:—*v.i.* [skat-ed, skat-ing], to move or glide along on skates. —*n.* **skat/er.**

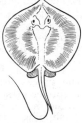

SKATE (⅒₈)

ske-dad-dle (ski-dad/l), *v.i. Colloq.* to run away in haste; scamper.

skeet (skēt), *n.* a kind of trap-shooting popular since 1925: the shooter, from eight different angles, shoots in succession 25 clay targets (thrown from two traps forty yards apart).

skein (skān), *n.* a quantity of thread, yarn, etc., coiled together.

skel-e-ton (skel/i-tun), *n.* **1**, the bony framework of man and other animals; **2**, the supporting framework of anything, as of a building.—*adj.* **skel/e-tal.**

skep-tic (skep/tik), *n.* **1**, a sceptic; a person of doubting mind; **2**, one who doubts the truth of any fact or theory, and questions the possibility of human knowledge of anything; **3**, one who doubts the truth of a religious belief, as Christianity. Usually spelled **scep/-tic.**—*adj.* **skep/ti-cal.**—*adv.* **skep/ti-cal-ly.**—*n.* **skep/ti-cism.**

sketch (skech), *n.* **1**, a simple, quickly made drawing; as, a crayon *sketch;* **2**, an outline; a rough draft or preliminary study; as, a *sketch* for a story; **3**, a short, simple piece of literature or music; also, a short, simple, dramatic performance:—*v.t.* to make an outline or sketch of; as, to *sketch* plans; to *sketch* a flower:—*v.i.* to make a sketch. —*n.* **sketch/er.**

sketch-y (skech/i), *adj.* [sketch-i-er, sketch-i-est], of the nature of a sketch; given in outline only; incomplete; as, a *sketchy* description.—*adv.* **sketch/i-ly.**

skew-er (skū/ẽr), *n.* a pin of wood or metal for holding meat in shape while cooking:—*v.t.* to fasten with, or as with, a skewer.

ski (skē; shē), *n.* [*pl.* ski or skis (skēz; shēz)], one of a pair of long, narrow pieces of wood, to be fastened one on each foot for sliding or travelling over snow:—*v.i.* [skied (skēd; shēd), skiing], to slide on skis.—*n.* **ski′er.**

skid (skid), *n.* 1, a device used on the wheel of a vehicle to check its motion; 2, one of a pair or set of logs, rails, etc., used to form a track down which heavy objects roll or slide; 3, a piece of timber on which a boat rests during the process of building or repair; 4, a runner attached under an aeroplane to aid in landing; 5, the act of sliding or slipping sideways; as, a *skid* on the ice:—*v.t.* [skid-ded, skid-ding], 1, to cause to move on skids; 2, to protect or check with a drag or skid:—*v.i.* to slip sideways on the road: said of an automobile.

skiff (skif), *n.* a small, light boat that can be rowed.

skil-ful (skil′fool), *adj.* 1, having expert training; clever; as, a *skilful* worker; 2, showing expertness; as, *skilful* work. —*adv.* **skil′ful-ly.**

skill (skil), *n.* knowledge of any art or science, with ability to use it; dexterity; as, *skill* in surgery.

skilled (skild), *adj.* 1, expert; as, *skilled* in painting; 2, having or requiring special training; as, *skilled* labour.

skil-let (skil′it), *n.* 1, a shallow, metal vessel with a handle, used for frying; a frying-pan; 2, a long-handled sauce-pan.

skim (skim), *v.t.* [skimmed, skim-ming], 1, to remove floating substances from the top of; as, to *skim* milk; 2, to take from the surface of a liquid, with a ladle or spoon; as, to *skim* cream from milk; 3, to touch the surface of, lightly; as, the boat *skims* the water; 4, to read hurriedly:—*v.i.* 1, to pass lightly over a surface; also, to glide, as through the air; 2, to read without thoroughness; as, to *skim* through a book:—**skim milk,** milk left after removal of cream.—*n.* **skim′mer.**

skimp (skimp), *Colloq.: v.t.* 1, to do badly or carelessly; to slight; 2, to be sparing with; as, to *skimp* material in making a dress:—*v.i.* to save; be miserly.—*adj.* **skimp′y.**

skin (skin), *n.* 1, in man and other animals, the outer covering of the body; 2, the pelt of an animal after it is removed from the body; as, a fur coat

made of valuable *skins;* 3, rind; as, an orange *skin;* 4, a vessel made of an animal's skin, used to hold liquids; 5, anything like a skin, as the outside covering of an airship:—*v.t.* [skinned, skin-ning], 1, to strip the skin from; as, to *skin* a rabbit; 2, *Slang,* to get the better of; cheat:—*v.i.* to become covered over with skin, as a wound. —*n.* **skin′ner.**

skin-flint (skin′flint′), *n.* a miser; a niggardly or avaricious person.

skin-ny (skin′i), *adj.* [skin-ni-er, skin-ni-est], 1, like skin in appearance or texture; 2, lean; without much flesh.

skip (skip), *v.t.* [skipped, skip-ping], 1 to jump lightly over; as, to *skip* rope 2, to pass over or omit; as, he *skipped* three pages in reading; she was bright enough to *skip* a grade in school:—*v.i.* 1, to leap or bound lightly; move with light trips and hops; 2, to pass along rapidly; hurry along, omitting portions, as in reading:—*n.* 1, a light leap 2, an omission; a passing over.

skip-per (skip′er), *n.* the master of a small trading or fishing vessel; the master or captain of any ship.

skirl (skirl), *n.* a shrill, piercing sound esp. that of the bagpipe:—*v.i.* to play the bagpipes.

skir-mish (skûr′mish), *n.* 1, a brisk fight between small parties of soldiers during a war; 2, any slight struggle or encounter:—*v.i.* to engage in a skirmish

skirt (skûrt), *n.* 1, the lower and loose part of a coat, dress, or other garment 2, an outer garment for women and girls, covering the body below the waist 3, an edge or border; 4, **skirts,** the outskirts or suburbs; 5, on a saddle one of the side flaps:—*v.t.* to border run or pass along the edge of; as, we *skirted* the town.

skit (skit), *n.* 1, a short comic sketch or play, as a revue; 2, a short satire or humorous piece of writing.

skit-tish (skit′ish), *adj.* 1, shy, excitable; nervous; easily frightened; as a *skittish* horse; 2, lively; high spirited; as, a *skittish* fancy; 3, un certain; fickle.

skit-tles (skit′lz), *n.* a game like nine pins; figuratively, amusement; as, life is not all beer and *skittles.*

skul-dug-ger-y (skul-dug′er-i), *n.* Colloq. mean trickery; dishonesty; crafti ness: often humorous.

skulk (skulk), *v.i.* to hide or get out of the way in a sneaking or underhand manner:—*n.* an idle, good-for-nothing fellow.—*n.* **skulk′er.**

skull (skul), *n.* **1,** in man and other animals, the skeleton or framework of the head; **2,** the head, as the seat of intelligence.

skunk (skungk), *n.* **1,** a small American mammal, usually black with white markings, which gives forth a liquid of very offensive odour when frightened or attacked; **2,** its skin valued as fur; **3,** *Colloq.*, a contemptible person.

skunk cab-bage, a plant with thick fleshy roots, large wide leaves, and disagreeable odour: common from N.S. to Ontario, and in northern U.S. Also called **skunk′weed′.**

sky (skī), *n.* [*pl.* skies], **1,** the heavens or upper atmosphere; the region of the clouds and winds; **2,** heaven.—*adj.* and *adv.* **sky′ward.**

sky-lark (skī′lärk′), *n.* a small Old World lark, noted for its song.

sky-light (skī′līt′), *n.* a window in a roof or in the ceiling of a room.

sky-line (skī′līn′), *n.* **1,** the line where land and sky, or water and sky, seem to meet; the horizon; **2,** the outline of mountains, trees, buildings, etc., against the sky.

sky-rock-et (skī′rok′it), *v.i. Colloq.* to rise rapidly, as prices, etc.

sky-scrap-er (skī′skrāp′ẽr), *n.* a building many storeys high.

sky-way (skī′wā′), *n.* **1,** an airlane or air-travel route; **2,** an elevated highway, as over a railroad, harbour, or waterway; as, the Hamilton *skyway.*

slab (slab), *n.* a thick piece of anything, as of marble, wood, or stone; also, a thick slice, as of bread or cheese.

slack (slak), *adj.* **1,** slow; lacking in vigour or energy; as, a *slack pace;* **2,** sluggish, as a backwater; **3,** relaxed; not tight; as, a *slack* wire; **4,** lazy; careless; as, a *slack* housekeeper; **5,** inactive; slow; as, business is *slack:* —*n.* **1,** that part of a wire, rope, etc., which is not stretched taut; **2,** a dull period, as in business; **3, slacks,** wide, loosely fitting trousers:—*v.t.* **1,** to loosen or slacken (a rope); **2,** to slake (lime):—*v.i.* to be or become sluggish or slack.

slack-en (slak′en), *v.i.* **1,** to become less firm, tense, or rigid; **2,** to let up; become slower; as, the coal business *slackens* in warm weather:—*v.t.* **1,** to make slower; relax; as, to *slacken* speed or efforts; **2,** to loosen; as, do not *slacken* the rope.

slack-er (slak′ẽr), *n.* a person who shirks his work or his duty.

slag (slag), *n.* **1,** the dross or dregs of melted metal; **2,** lava from a volcano.

slain (slān), *p.p.* of **slay.**

slake (slāk), *v.t.* [slaked, slak-ing], **1,** to quench; relieve; appease; as, to *slake* one's thirst; **2,** to combine chemically with water; as, to *slake* lime:—*v.i.* to be chemically mixed with water.

sla-lom (slä′lōm), *n.* a downhill skiing race over a zigzag course marked out by flags, posts, etc.

slam (slam), *v.t.* [slammed, slam-ming], **1,** to shut violently and noisily; **2,** to put, or throw, with force and loud noise; as, to *slam* down a book:—*v.i.* to bang; as, the door *slams:*—*n.* **1,** a blow; a bang; **2,** the act of shutting noisily: in *bridge,* the winning of all 13 tricks is a **grand slam,** or, when one trick short of this, a **little slam.**

slan-der (slan′dẽr), *n.* the utterance of false reports about a person in order to defame or injure him; also, the reports themselves:—*v.t.* to injure the reputation of (a person) by spreading false reports.—*n.* **slan′der-er.**—*adj.* **slan′der-ous.**

slang (slang), *n.* **1,** those words or phrases which, though regarded as not permissible in formal or written language, are used in popular speech for the sake of picturesqueness or novelty; **2,** the language or jargon of a particular group or profession; as, thieves' *slang.* —*adj.* **slang′y.**

slant (slant), *n.* **1,** an inclined plane; a slope; as, the *slant* of a roof; **2,** *Colloq.*, a point of view; attitude; as, he has a modern *slant* on the problem:—*v.t.* to give a sloping direction to; as, *slant* your ruler a little more:—*v.i.* to slope; as, tilt the easel so that it *slants* a bit: —*adj.* sloping.—*adj.* **slant′ing.**—*adv.* **slant′ing-ly.**

slap (slap), *n.* **1,** a blow with the open hand; **2,** an insult; a repulse:—*v.t.* [slapped, slap-ping], **1,** to strike with the open hand; **2,** *Colloq.*, to lay down with, or as with, a bang.

slap-dash (slap′dash′), *adv. Colloq.* in a boldly careless manner; recklessly: —*adv.* dashing; impetuous; hasty: as, a *slapdash* style.

slap—hap-py (slap′—hap′i), *adj. Slang,* as though dazed or bewildered; **2,** foolish.

slap-stick (slap′stik′), *n.* crude comedy, as the humour depends upon horseplay, etc.:—*adj.* crudely and noisily humorous; as, *slapstick* comedy.

slash (slash), *v.t.* **1,** to cut by striking violently and aimlessly; **2,** to cut slits in (a garment) to expose the material beneath; **3,** to lash with a whip; **4,** to criticize harshly; as, the critics *slashed* the novel unmercifully:—*v.i.* to strike out violently and at random:—*n.* **1,** a long cut or gash; **2,** the stroke of a whip; **3,** a slit, as in a sleeve, showing other material beneath; **4,** a low, swampy area covered with brush.

slat (slat), *n.* a thin, narrow strip of wood or metal.

slate (slāt), *n.* **1,** a kind of fine-grained rock that splits into thin layers; **2,** the dark bluish-grey colour of this rock; **3,** a thin plate of this rock prepared for use, as for roof covering, blackboards, writing-tablets, etc.; **4,** a list of proposed candidates for nomination or election:—*v.t.* [slat-ed, slat-ing], **1,** to cover with slate; **2,** to register or suggest (a person) for an office, a rôle, or an appointment; **3,** *Colloq.*, to blame or criticize severely.—*adj.* **slat′y.**

slat-tern (slat′ẽrn), *n.* a slovenly woman.—*adj.* and *adv.* **slat′tern-ly.**

slaugh-ter (slô′tẽr), *n.* **1,** the act of killing; great and wanton destruction of life; **2,** the killing of animals for food:—*v.t.* **1,** to kill with violence; **2,** to butcher (animals) for the market.—*n.* **slaugh′ter-er.**—*n.* **slaugh′ter-house′** (an abattoir, or place where animals are killed for meat).

slave (slāv), *n.* **1,** a person owned by another; a bondsman; **2,** one who works like a slave; a drudge; **3,** a person in the power of habit or vice; as, a *slave* to drink:—*adj.* pertaining to slaves; as, *slave* labour:—*v.i.* [slaved, slav-ing], to work like a drudge; toil.—*n.* **slav′er.**—*n.* **slav′er-y.**

slav-ish (slāv′ish), *adj.* **1,** characteristic of slaves; servile; mean; base; **2,** without originality or independence.—*n.* **slav′ish-ness.**

slaw (slô), *n.* sliced cabbage mixed with a dressing, served as a relish or salad.

slay (slā), *v.t.* [*p.t.* slew (slōō), *p.p.* slain (slān), *p.pr.* slay-ing], to kill or put to death by violence.—*n.* **slay′er.**

slea-zy (slē′zi), *adj.* **1,** of *fabrics*, thin; flimsy; as *sleazy* silk, rayon, muslin, etc.; **2,** *Colloq.* slippery; unprincipled; two-faced; revolting; as, *sleazy* conduct; a *sleazy* person.—*n.* **slea′zi-ness.**

sled (sled), *n.* a vehicle on runners, used for coasting, or for carrying loads, on snow or ice:—*v.i.* and *v.t.* [sled-ded,

sled-ding], to travel or carry by sled.—*n.* **sled′ding.**

¹sledge (slej), *n.* a vehicle on runners for carrying heavy loads over snow or ice:—*v.i.* and *v.t.* [sledged, sledg-ing], to travel or carry on a sledge.

²sledge (slej), *n.* a large, heavy hammer, used by blacksmiths: also called *sledge-hammer.*

sleek (slēk), *adj.* **1,** smooth; glossy; as, the *sleek* coat of a seal; **2,** smooth or flattering in speech; as, a *sleek* betrayer:—*v.t.* to make smooth or shiny, esp. by rubbing or brushing.—*n.* **sleek′ness.**

sleep (slēp), *n.* **1,** the condition of not being conscious or awake; slumber; **2,** any condition like sleep; as, death is called eternal *sleep:*—*v.i.* [slept (slept), sleep-ing], **1,** to be asleep; slumber; **2,** to be motionless; remain inactive:—*v.t.* **1,** to rest in (sleep); as, he *slept* a sound sleep; **2,** to spend, waste, or rid oneself of, by sleeping; as, he *slept* away half the morning; he *slept* off his headache; **3,** *Colloq.*, to provide with a place to sleep; as, we *slept* three guests overnight.—*adj.* **sleep′less.**

sleep-er (slēp′ẽr), *n.* **1,** one who sleeps; hence, one who likes to sleep; a lazy person; **2,** a horizontal beam, on or near the ground level, that serves as support for some structure above, as railway ties for rails; **3,** a sleeping-car.

sleep-y (slēp′i), *adj.* [sleep-i-er, sleep-i-est], **1,** inclined to, or ready for, slumber; **2,** producing drowsiness; as, *sleepy* weather; **3,** drowsy; inactive; as, a *sleepy* town.—*adv.* **sleep′i-ly.**—*n.* **sleep′i-ness.**

sleet (slēt), *n.* driving rain that is partly frozen or that freezes as it falls:—*v.i.* to shower frozen rain.—*adj.* **sleet′y.**

sleeve (slēv), *n.* **1,** the part of a garment that covers the arm; **2,** something, as a part of a machine, that covers or protects another part.—*adj.* **sleeve′less.**

sleigh (slā), *n.* a vehicle, equipped with runners, for use on snow or ice:—*v.i.* to travel by sleigh.

sleigh-ing (slā′-ing), *n.* **1,** the act of riding in a sleigh; **2,** the condition of snow which permits such travel.

sleight of hand (slīt), *n.* skill or dexterity in using the hands to deceive or confuse onlookers, as in magic; legerdemain. Also, **sleight-of-hand.**

slen-der (slen′dẽr), *adj.* **1,** narrow in proportion to length or height; slim; **2,** scanty; slight; scarcely sufficient; as, *slender* meals; *slender* opportunities.

cat, āge, fär, câre, ásk; ten, ēve, latẽr; (i) pity, rely, senate; īce; top; nō.

sleuth (slōōth), *n.* **1,** a bloodhound; **2,** a detective. Also, **sleuth′—hound′.**

¹slew (slōō), *p.t.* of *slay.*

²slew (slōō), *n.* Same as *slough.*

³slew or **slue** (slōō), *n.* a twist; turn: —*v.t.* and *v.i.* to swing around, yaw, or pivot on a fixed point; as, the sled *slewed* (*slued*) about on the ice.

slice (slīs), *n.* a thin, broad piece cut from something; as, a *slice* of bread: —*v.t.* [sliced, slic-ing], **1,** to cut into thin pieces or layers; as, *slice* the entire cake; also, to cut into; as, *slice* open the melon; **2,** to cut (a layer) from something; as, to *slice* off a piece of meat:—**slice bar,** an iron bar with a broad, thin end, used to break up clinkers or slag in furnaces, clear out ashes, etc.—*n.* **slic′er.**

slick (slik), *adj.* **1,** smooth; sleek; as, *slick* hair; slippery, as wet roads; **2,** too smooth in speech and manners; **3,** *Slang:* **a,** tricky; sly; **b,** first-rate; as, a *slick* time:—*v.t.* to make smooth or glossy, as hair:—*n. Slang,* a magazine printed on paper of glossy finish: opposite of *pulp;* **2,** a smooth area or patch on the surface of water; as, an oil *slick.*

slick-er (slik′ẽr), *n.* a loose waterproof coat.

slide (slīd), *v.i.* [*p.t.* slid (slid), *p.p.* slid or slid-den (slid′n), *p.pr.* slid-ing], **1,** to move smoothly over a surface, as over ice; glide; **2,** to move quietly or secretly; slip; as, he *slid* into a seat; **3,** to move or pass gradually or without being noticed; as, time *slides* by: —**to let slide,** to let (something) take care of itself; as, I'll *let* my lessons *slide* until tomorrow:—*v.t.* **1,** to push along; cause to slip into place; as, they *slid* the canoe into the water; **2,** to put quietly; slip; as, he *slid* his left hand into his pocket:—*n.* **1,** the act of sliding; **2,** a surface of snow or ice for sliding; **3,** any smooth slope or incline; **4,** a mass of earth, rock, or snow that slides down a mountain; **5,** a thin glass plate upon which is a picture to be projected on a screen; also, a plate of glass upon which is mounted a specimen for examination under a microscope; **6,** that part of a device upon which anything slides; also, the part that slides.

slight (slīt), *adj.* **1,** slender; frail; not strong; as, a *slight* figure; **2,** small in amount or degree; as, a *slight* trace of gas; **3,** not important; trivial; as, a *slight* difference in colour:—*v.t.* **1,** to treat with indifference; as, she *slighted* her guests; **2,** to neglect or perform

carelessly; as, she was so engrossed in her music that she *slighted* her studies: —*n.* an act of discourtesy; a snub. —*n.* **slight′ness.**—*adv.* **slight′ly.**

slim (slim), *adj.* [slim-mer, slim-mest], **1,** slender; as, a *slim* figure; **2,** scant; slight; insufficient; as, a *slim* excuse.

slime (slīm), *n.* **1,** soft, sticky mud; any sticky, dirty substance; **2,** a sticky external secretion of certain animals, such as fishes and snails, and of certain plants.—*adj.* **slim′y.**

sling (sling), *n.* **1,** an implement for hurling a missile, as a stone; **2,** the act of hurling or flinging; a throw; **3,** any of various devices for hoisting or lowering heavy articles, or for suspending a gun, pack, etc., from the shoulder; **4,** a supporting bandage, as for a wounded arm:—*v.t.* [slung (slung), sling-ing], **1,** to hurl with, or as with, a sling; **2,** to hang (a hammock) so that it will swing; **3,** to place or suspend in a device for hoisting or lowering.

sling-shot (sling′shot′), *n.* a forked stick with a rubber band attached, for shooting small stones.

slink (slingk), *v.i.* [slunk (slungk), slink-ing], to go furtively; sneak or steal along.

slip (slip), *v.i.* [slipped, slip-ping], **1,** to glide or slide smoothly; as, the drawers *slip* in and out easily; **2,** to miss one's foothold; lose one's balance; **3,** to move or pass without being seen; as, she *slipped* into the room; **4,** to move suddenly out of place; as, the knife *slipped;* **5,** to escape; as, the address has *slipped* from my mind:—*v.t.* **1,** to put on or off with ease; as, to *slip* on a ring; *slip* off a coat; **2,** to cause to slide; as, to *slip* a rod into place; **3,** to lose or allow to escape; as, to *slip* a stitch; to cause to slide off; as, the horse *slips* his bridle; **4,** to escape from; as, his name has *slipped* my mind; **5,** to cut a small shoot from, in order to grow a new plant; as, to *slip* a rose-bush:—*n.* **1,** the act of sliding or missing one's foothold; also, an escaping or eluding; as, to give someone the *slip;* **2,** a fault; an error; as, a *slip* in grammar; **3,** a cutting from a plant; **4,** a space between wharves for vessels; a dock; **5,** something that may be put on or off with ease, as a kind of under-garment, a pillow-case, etc.; **6,** a long narrow piece of something; a strip; **7,** a slim person; as, a *slip* of a girl.

slip-knot (slip′not′), *n.* a knot which slips along the cord around which it is formed.

slip-per (slip'er), *n.* a low, comfortable shoe, usually intended for indoor wear.

slip-per-y (slip'er-i), *adj.* [slipper-i-er, slipper-i-est], **1,** having a surface so smooth or slimy as to yield no firm hold or footing; as, a *slippery* pavement; **2,** of persons, shifty; not trustworthy.—*n.* **slip′per-i-ness.**

slip-shod (slip'shod'), *adj.* **1,** wearing shoes down at the heel; **2,** hence, slovenly; careless.

slip—up (slip'-up'), *n. Colloq.* a mistake; error; as, minor *slip-ups* in grammar.

slit (slit), *v.t.* [slit (slit), slit-ting], **1,** to cut or tear lengthwise or into long strips; as, to *slit* cloth for bandages; **2,** to cut or make a lengthwise opening in; as, to *slit* a skirt for a placket:—*n.* **1,** a long cut or tear; **2,** a narrow opening.—*n.* **slit′ter.**

slith-er (slith'er), *v.i.* to slip or slide, esp. on a loose or gravelly slope, with some noise or friction.

sliv-er (sliv'er), *n.* a long, thin, sharp-pointed piece, as of wood; a splinter: —*v.t.* and *v.i.* to break off or split into long, thin pieces.

slob (slob), *n.* **1,** soft or mushy ice or snow, esp. in Newfoundland and the sealing fields of the Arctic; **2,** *Slang,* a clumsy or slovenly person.

slob-ber (slob'er), *v.i.* **1,** to let saliva dribble from the mouth; drool; **2,** to show or express feeling gushingly:—*v.t.* to wet by letting liquid run from the mouth; as, to *slobber* a dress; to spill so as to soil something; as, to *slobber* milk over a dress.

sloe (slō), *n.* a small, bitter plum of the blackthorn tree:—**sloe-eyed,** dark-eyed.

slog (slog), *v.i. Colloq.* to plod one's way heavily and with effort; toil; **2,** to hit hard; slug (a ball, opponent, etc.).

slo-gan (slō'gan), *n.* **1,** a war-cry or rallying cry; **2,** a word or phrase used as a motto by a party or group, or as a catchword to advertise a product.

sloop (slōōp), *n.* a one-masted vessel with a fore-and-aft rig, a mainsail, and a single jib.

slop (slop), *n.* **1,** water or other liquid carelessly spilled; **2,** poor or weak liquid food: used contemptuously; **3,** (often *slops*): **a,** refuse or dirty water from kitchen or bedrooms; **b,** refuse or garbage used as food for swine:—*v.t.* [slopped, slop-ping], **1,** to soil by letting liquid fall upon; as, to *slop* the floor: —*v.i.* to be spilled; also, to overflow. —*adj.* **slop′py.**

slope (slōp), *n.* **1,** a slanting line; also, a tilted surface; **2,** the degree of such a slant or tilt; as, a steep *slope;* **3,** any stretch of descending ground; esp., the land that descends toward the ocean; as, the Pacific *slope:—v.i.* and *v.t.* [sloped, slop-ing], to incline; slant; as, the ground *slopes;* to *slope* a roof.

slosh (slosh), *v.i.* to splash about or flounder in slush, mire, etc.; as, to *slosh* through a puddle:—*v.t.* to stir in a fluid; as, to *slosh* a mop through a pail.

slot (slot), *n.* **1,** a narrow groove or depression in which something fits or moves snugly; **2,** a narrow opening through which something can be slipped; as, a mail-*slot* in a door; a *slot* for a coin:—*v.t.* [slot-ted, slot-ting], to cut a slot or slots in.

sloth (slōth; slôth), *n.* **1,** laziness; indolence; **2,** a tree-dwelling animal of South and Central America which clings upside down to the branches: so called from its slow movements.— *adj.* **sloth′ful.**

slouch (slouch), *n.* **1,** a stooping or droop, as of the head or shoulders; **2,** an incompetent, lazy fellow:—*v.i.* to stand or move in a loose, ungainly manner.—*adj.* **slouch′y.**

¹slough (slou; in def. 2, slōō), *n.* **1,** a miry place; a mud hole; **2,** (slōō), a swamp: also, an inlet from a river: also spelled *slue;* **3,** a state of depression or gloom into which one sinks and from which it is difficult to free oneself; as, the *slough* of despair.

²slough (sluf), *n.* **1,** the cast-off skin of a snake or other animal; **2,** anything that has been or can be cast off, as dead tissue, a bad habit, etc.—*v.i.* **1,** to come off or be shed, as the skin of a snake; **2,** to shed or cast the skin:—*v.t.* to cast off, as the skin; hence, to discard.

slov-en (sluv'n), *n.* an untidy, slipshod, or lazy person, esp. a man: such a woman is a *slattern.*

slov-en-ly (sluv'en-li), *adj.* [sloven-li-er, sloven-li-est], untidy in appearance; careless; not neat.—*n.* **slov′en-li-ness.**

slow (slō), *adj.* **1,** not rapid in motion; as, a *slow* march; **2,** not prompt; as, *slow* in arriving; **3,** taking a long time; as, a *slow* journey; **4,** not rash or hasty; as, *slow* to anger; **5,** behind the correct time; as, the clock is *slow;* **6,** mentally dull; as, a *slow* pupil; **7,** tending to hinder rapid motion; as, a *slow* track; **8,** *Colloq.,* dull; not lively; as, a *slow* party:—*adv.* in a manner not rapid:— *v.i.* to move with less and less speed; as, the train *slowed* down:—*v.t.* **1,** to cause to move with less speed; as, to *slow down* a car; **2,** to delay; as, heavy rains *slowed* up the haying.—*adv.* **slow′ly.**

slow-down (slō′doun′), *n.* a planned slowing down of production either by workers or management.

sludge (sluj), *n.* **1,** the sediment that forms in steam boilers, water tanks, etc; **2,** mud, ooze, slush, or mire; **3,** refuse from soap-making, bleaching, oil-refining, washing of ores, etc.—*adj.* **sludg′y.**

slue (slōō), *n.* a swamp. See ¹**slough.**

¹**slug** (slug), *n.* **1,** an animal like a snail, except that it has no shell or only a very thin one; **2,** a sluglike larva or caterpillar; **3,** *Archaic,* a sluggard.

²**slug** (slug), *n.* a small, unshaped piece of metal; specifically, a kind of small, rough bullet.

³**slug** (slug), *v.t.* [slugged, slug-ging], to strike hard, esp. with the fist, as in boxing:—*n.* a hard blow, as with the fist or a club.—*n.* **slug′ger.**

slug-gard (slug′ėrd), *n.* a person who is naturally lazy and idle:—*adj.* lazy. Also, **slug′a-bed′** (one who lies in bed after others are up).

slug-gish (slug′ish), *adj.* **1,** habitually lazy and idle; dull; slothful; **2,** inactive; slow; as, a *sluggish* river.

sluice (slōōs), *n.* **1,** an artificial channel for conducting water, having a gate, called *sluice-gate,* to regulate the flow; **2,** a floodgate for controlling the flow of water; **3,** a channel through which anything flows; **4,** an inclined trough for washing gold ore, carrying down logs, etc.:—*v.t.* [sluiced, sluic-ing], **1,** to wash with water from, or as from, a sluice; as, to *sluice* gold; **2,** to draw off (water) by a channel or floodgate; **3,** to transport (logs) by such means.

slum (slum), *n.* **1,** a dirty, densely populated street or district of a town or city; **2, slums,** a neighbourhood composed of such streets:—*v.i.* [slummed, slum-ming], to visit such neighbourhoods for the purpose of study or charity, or out of curiosity.

slum-ber (slum′bėr), *v.i.* **1,** to sleep peacefully; **2,** to be in a state of rest or inactivity; as, his suspicions *slumbered:*—*n.* sleep.—*adj.* **slum′brous** or **slum′ber-ous.**

slump (slump), *v.i.* **1,** to fall or sink suddenly, as into a marsh; **2,** to sink down heavily; as, he *slumped* in his

chair; **3,** to fall or decline suddenly, as prices, stocks, business, etc.:—*n.* **1,** the act of sinking down; **2,** a sudden drop or decline; as, a *slump* in business.

slung (slung), *p.t.* and *p.p.* of *sling.*

slunk (slungk), *p.t.* and *p.p.* of *slink.*

slur (slûr), *v.t.* [slurred, slur-ring], **1,** to pass over hurriedly or briefly; as, to *slur* over an incident; **2,** to pronounce hastily or indistinctly (a sound or syllable); **3,** in *music,* to sing or sound (two or more successive tones of different pitch) without a break; also, to mark (notes that are to be so sounded) with the sign ⌢ or ⌣:—*n.* **1,** a stain or blot; **2,** a slight reproach, or a remark conveying such reproach; **3,** in *music,* a mark [⌢ or ⌣] connecting notes that are to be sung or played without a break; also, the notes to be so treated.

slush (slush), *n.* **1,** partly melted snow; **2,** silly, sentimental talk or writing:—*v.t.* **1,** to wet or splash with slush; **2,** *Colloq.,* to wash by dashing water upon.—*adj.* **slush′y.**

slut (slut), *n.* **1,** a dirty, untidy woman; slattern; also, a woman of loose character; hussy.

sly (slī), *adj.* [sly-er or sli-er, sly-est or sli-est], **1,** furtive; working or acting secretly; underhand; deceitful; as, a *sly* schemer; a *sly* scheme; **2,** playfully mischievous; roguish:—**on the sly,** in secret.—*adv.* **sly′ly** or **sli′ly.**

¹**smack** (smak), *n.* a slight taste or flavour; tinge:—*v.i.* to convey a suggestion; as, this *smacks* of treason.

²**smack** (smak), *n.* **1,** a quick, sharp noise made with the lips; **2,** a loud, hearty kiss; **3,** a quick, resounding blow or slap:—*v.t.* **1,** to make a loud noise with (the lips); **2,** to strike or slap.

³**smack** (smak), *n.* a small sailing-vessel used in fishing; a fishing sloop.

smack-ing (smak′ing), *adj.* **1,** making a sharp noise; **2,** lively; brisk; as, the wind blew up a *smacking* breeze.

small (smôl), *adj.* **1,** little in size, amount, number, degree, etc.; as, a *small* boy; a *small* school; a *small* dose; **2,** not important; insignificant; as, his opinion is of *small* value; **3,** doing business in a limited way; as, a *small* farmer; **4,** petty; not generous; narrow; as, a *small* mind. **Small fry, 1,** small or young fish; **2,** youngsters; **3,** people or things considered unimportant or petty (also called *small potatoes*).

small-pox (smôl′poks′), *n.* a contagious disease marked by fever and a characteristic skin eruption.

smart (smärt), *v.i.* **1,** to feel a sharp stinging pain; as, my hand *smarts;* **2,** to cause a stinging sensation; as, iodine *smarts;* **3,** to suffer; have one's feelings wounded:—*n.* **1,** a quick lively pain; **2,** a pang of grief:—*adj.* **1,** causing a sharp, stinging sensation; also, severe; as, a *smart* thrashing; **2,** brisk; fresh; as, a *smart* breeze; **3,** clever; shrewd; as, a *smart* business man; also, quick to learn; as, a *smart* child; **4,** amusingly witty as, a *smart* saying; **5,** up-to-date; fashionable; as, a *smart* gown; the *smart* set.—*adv.* **smart′ly.**—*n.* **smart′-ness.**—*v.t.* **smart′en** (*up*).

smart-weed (smärt′wēd′), *n.* a weed growing in wet places: it has tiny flowers and leaves that make the skin smart on contact: also called *lover's pride, redweed, pinkweed, redshank, willowweed, blackheart, spotted knot weed,* and *water pepper.*

smash (smash), *v.t.* to break (something) into pieces by dropping it, hitting it, or striking it against something else; as, to *smash* a vase, window, car:—*v.i.* **1,** to break into many pieces; as, fine glass *smashes* easily; **2,** to rush or be thrown violently against something; as, the car *smashed* into the fence; **3,** to go to pieces, as a business that fails: —*n.* **1,** an act or the sound of breaking to pieces; a crash; **2,** a violent collision; **3,** complete destruction or ruin.

smat-ter-ing (smat′ėr-ing), *n.* slight, superficial knowledge: used with *of.*

smear (smēr), *v.t.* **1,** to spread with anything greasy, oily, or sticky; daub; **2,** to spread (oil, paint, etc.) over something:—*n.* a blot or stain; a streak.

smell (smel), *v.t.* [*p.t.* and *p.p.* smelt (smelt) or smelled (smeld), *p.pr.* smelling], **1,** to perceive by means of the nose; obtain the scent of; as, to *smell* smoke; **2,** to inhale the odour of; as, to *smell* a flower; **3,** to suspect; detect; as, to smell trouble:—*v.i.* to have an odour; as, this room *smells* of lilacs:—*n.* **1,** that quality of things which is perceived by the nose; an odour; **2,** the sense by which odours are perceived; **3,** the act of smelling.—*adj.* **smell′y.**—*n.* **smell′er.**

¹**smelt** (smelt), *n.* a small, silvery food fish found in northern waters.

²**smelt** (smelt), *v.t.* to fuse or melt (ore) in order to refine the metal; also, to obtain (metal) by this process.—*n.* **smelt′er.**

smile (smīl), *n.* an expression on the face, particularly around the mouth, indicating amusement, pleasure, or affection; also, a facial expression conveying irony or contempt:—*v.i.* [smiled, smil-ing], **1,** to show a smile; look pleasant; as, the photographer told her to *smile;* **2,** to show pleasure or amusement, contempt or disdain, by smiling; **3,** to look with favour as, Fortune *smiled* upon his efforts; **4,** to present a gay or cheerful aspect; as a *smiling* landscape:—*v.t.* to express by smiling; as, to *smile* assent.

smirch smûrch, *v.t.* Same as *besmirch*

smirk (smûrk), *v.i.* to smile affectedly or conceitedly:—*n.* an affected smile

smite (smīt), *v.t.* [*p.t.* smote (smōt), *p.p.* smit-ten (smit′n), *p.pr.* smit-ing], **1,** to hit; strike with the hand, or with a weapon or implement; **2,** to strike with disaster; afflict; as, Jehovah *smote* Egypt with plagues; **3,** to cause to strike; as he *smote* his staff upon the ground; **4,** to affect with the suddenness of a blow; as, a cry *smote* the silence; **5,** to affect with any strong feeling, as love, grief, fear, etc.; **6,** to cause to feel regret or sorrow; as, his conscience *smote* him.

smith (smith), *n.* one who works or shapes metal with hammer and anvil

smith-er-eens (smi*th*′ėr-ēnz′), *n. pl* *Colloq.* tiny fragments; as, to smash into *smithereens.*

smith-y (smi*th*′i; smi*th*′i), *n.* [*pl* smithies], a forge; a blacksmith's shop

smock (smok), *n.* a long, loose blouse or garment worn to protect the clothing —*v.t.* to trim (a blouse or dress) with gathers fastened into a pattern by fancy stitches.—*n.* **smock′ing.**

smog (smog), *n.* a mixture of smoke and fog.

smoke (smōk), *n.* **1,** the visible gas that escapes from a burning substance; **2,** a column, cloud, or mass of smoke; **3,** the act of inhaling the fumes of burning tobacco, opium, etc.; **4,** anything that resembles smoke, as fumes or vapour:— *v.t.* [smoked, smok-ing], **1,** to preserve (fish or meat) by exposure to smoke; **2,** to inhale and puff out the fumes of as, to *smoke* tobacco; **3,** to force out by smoke; as, to *smoke* out snakes:—*v.i.* **1,** to give out fumes, as a chimney; **2,** to inhale and puff out the fumes of tobacco, opium, etc.; **3,** to give off anything like smoke.—*n.* **smok′er.**— *adj.* **smok′y.**—*adj.* **smoke′less.**

smoke-stack (smōk′stak′), *n.* a tall chimney, as on a factory or steamship

smolt (smōlt), *n.* a salmon in its second year, when it has acquired silver scales and descended to the sea.

smooth (smō͞o*th*), *adj.* **1,** not rough; even in surface or texture as a road; **2,** perfectly blended; free from lumps; as, *smooth* gravy; **3,** gently flowing, as a river; hence, serene; calm; pleasant; **4,** easy and polished; as, a *smooth* style in speaking or writing; **5,** flattering; fluent; as, *smooth* words; a *smooth* talker; **6,** without beard; as, a *smooth* face; **7,** steady in motion; not jerky or jarring; as, the *smooth* running of a car; **8,** of liquors, aged; free from sharpness; pleasant:—*adv.* in a smooth manner:—*v.t.* **1,** to remove roughness from; **2,** to make even, steady, or calm; **3,** to soothe; as, to *smooth* a person's feelings; **4,** to make easy; as, to *smooth* a person's way; also, to remove; as, to *smooth* away difficulties.

smor-gas-bord (smôr′gas-bōrd′), *n.* a Swedish type of meal, buffet style, in which one serves oneself hot or cold meats, fish, sausage, cheese, salads, desserts, etc.: the choice may run to 50 dishes.

smote (smōt), *p.t.* and *p.p.* of *smite*.

smoth-er (smu*th*′ẽr), *v.t.* **1,** to kill by depriving of air; stifle; also, to deaden by suffocating, as a fire; **2,** to suppress or conceal; cover up; as, to *smother* one's anger; **3,** in *cookery*, to cover, as with onions, and cook in a covered dish:—*v.i.* **1,** to be deprived of air; **2,** to be restrained:—*n.* a dense smoke or dust.

smoul-der or **smol-der** (smōl′dẽr), *v.i.* **1,** to burn slowly, giving forth smoke without flame; **2,** to burn beneath the surface; as, hate *smouldered* in his heart.

smudge (smuj), *n.* **1,** a smear or stain; **2,** a smouldering fire that produces a dense smoke for protecting fruit-trees from frost or for keeping off insects:—*v.t.* [smudged, smudg-ing], **1,** to smear or stain; **2,** to keep away by a smudge. —*adj.* smudg′y.

smug (smug), *adj.* [smug-ger, smug-gest], **1,** precise; rather too prim; **2,** self-satisfied; pleased with oneself.— *adv.* smug′ly.

smug-gle (smug′l), *v.t.* and *v.i.* [smug-gled, smug-gling], to bring or send (goods) into or out of a country secretly, without paying duties.—*n.* **smug′gler** (smug′lẽr).

smut (smut), *n.* **1,** a spot or stain made by soot or dirt; also, that which causes the spot; **2,** a disease affecting corn, wheat, etc.; **3,** foul or indecent language:—*v.t.* [smut-ted, smut-ting], to soil or blacken with, or as with, soot: —*v.i.* to become blackened by soot; also, to be affected by mildew or smut, as grain.

smut-ty (smut′i), *adj.* [smut-ti-er, smut-ti-est], **1,** soiled or stained with dirt or soot; **2,** indecent; **3,** of *grain*, diseased.

snack (snak), *n.* a slight, hurried meal.

snag (snag), *n.* **1,** the stump of a branch projecting from the trunk of a tree; **2,** some part of a tree sticking up from the bottom of a river or lake and dangerous to boats; **3,** a broken or decayed tooth; **4,** any unexpected obstacle or difficulty: —*v.t.* [snagged, snag-ging], **1,** to catch or damage on a snag; **2,** to clear of obstructions or snags.

snail (snāl), *n.* **1,** a small land or water animal with a spiral shell into which it withdraws for protection; **2,** a person slow-moving as a snail.

snake (snāk), *n.* **1,** a long, legless, slim-bodied reptile which preys on insects and small animals; **2,** a treacherous person:—*v.t.* [snaked, snak-ing], *Colloq.*, to drag, esp. at full length; jerk; as, to *snake* a log out of a swamp:—*v.i.* to crawl along like a snake.—*adj.* snak′y.

snap (snap), *v.i.* [snapped, snap-ping], **1,** to break suddenly; as, the glass *snapped* in my hand; **2,** to snatch at something suddenly, esp. with the teeth; as, a dog *snaps* at a bone; **3,** to produce a sharp, sudden sound; as, twigs *snap* underfoot; **4,** to speak crossly or angrily; **5,** to sparkle; as, her eyes *snapped*:—*v.t.* **1,** to break off short; crack; **2,** to seize suddenly; as, the fish *snapped* up the bait; **3,** to cause to make a sudden, sharp sound; **4,** to close with a sharp sound; as, to *snap* down a lid; **5,** in *football*, to put (the ball) in play by passing it back from the line of scrimmage; **6,** to take a quick photograph of:—*n.* **1,** the act of seizing suddenly; **2,** the sudden breaking of something stiff or tightly stretched; as, the *snap* of a wire; **3,** a sudden, sharp sound; **4,** a spring-lock or catch; **5,** a kind of thin, crisp biscuit; a ginger-snap; **6,** a sudden, short period of severe weather; **7,** *Colloq.*, energy or vim:—*adj.* **1,** done in haste or without much thought; as, a *snap* decision; **2,** closing with a click, or with a special closing device; as, a *snap* bracelet; **3,** *Colloq.*, easy; requiring little effort.

snap-back (snap′bak′), *n.* in *football*, the centre player who passes the ball back to put it into play; the pass-out itself.

snap-drag-on (snap′drag′un), *n.* a plant with showy white, yellow, or reddish flowers.

snap-per (snap′ėr), *n.* **1,** a fighting, edible fish inhabiting warm seas; **2,** a fresh-water turtle, valued as food.

snap-pish (snap′ish), *adj.* **1,** likely to snap or bite; as, a *snappish* dog; **2,** sharp in speech; easily irritated.—*n.* **snap′pish-ness.**

snap-py (snap′i), *adj.* [snap-pi-er, snap-pi-est], **1,** sharp and irritable in speech; **2,** *Colloq.;* **a,** lively; brisk, as conversation; **b,** stylish; smart, as clothes.

snap-shot (snap′shot′), *n.* a photograph taken quickly or instantaneously.

snare (snâr), *n.* **1,** a running noose or a loop of cord or wire, for catching an animal or a bird; **2,** hence, anything that entangles or entraps:—*v.t.* [snared, snar-ing], to catch with, or as with, a snare.—*n.* **snar′er.**

snare drum, a small drum with catgut strings, or snares, stretched across the lower head to produce a rattling sound, when the upper head is beaten.

¹**snarl** (snärl), *v.i.* **1,** to make a growling noise, as an angry dog; **2,** to speak in harsh, surly tones:—*v.t.* to utter in a growl or in a harsh, surly tone:—*n.* **1,** the act of growling; **2,** a surly tone.

²**snarl** (snärl), *n.* a tangle or knot, as of yarn or hair; hence, a state of confusion; a complicated situation:—*v.t.* and *v.i.* to make or become tangled.

snatch (snach), *v.t.* to seize suddenly or rudely:—*v.i.* to try to seize something suddenly; as, the child *snatched* at a flower:—*n.* **1,** a hasty catch; **2,** a small fragment; as, *snatches* of verse; **3,** a brief period; as, to work in *snatches.*—*n.* **snatch′er.**

snath (snath), *n.* the handle or curved shaft of a scythe.

sneak (snēk), *v.i.* **1,** to creep or move about secretly or slyly; slink; **2,** to act in a cowardly or mean way:—*n.* **1,** a mean, cowardly fellow; **2,** a petty thief; **3,** **sneakers,** canvas shoes with rubber soles.—*adj.* **sneak′y.**

sneer (snēr), *v.i.* **1,** to show contempt by an expression of the face, as by curling the lips; **2,** to speak contemptuously or with ridicule:—*n.* **1,** contempt or scorn shown in speech; **2,** a contemptuous smile.

sneeze (snēz), *n.* a sudden brief spasm of the breathing organs, causing a violent and audible rush of air out through the mouth and nostrils:—*v.i.* [sneezed, sneezing], to be seized with such a spasm.

snick (snik), *v.t.* **1,** to cut; snip; **2,** nick; notch; **3,** click.

snick-er (snik′ėr) or **snig-ger** (snig′ėr), *n.* a half-suppressed laugh; a giggle:—*v.i.* to laugh slyly; giggle.

snide (snīd), *adj.* *Slang,* sly; malicious; as, *snide* remarks.

sniff (snif), *v.i.* **1,** to draw in the breath audibly through the nose; to clear the nose; **2,** to express contempt; as, he *sniffed* at the suggestion:—*v.t.* **1,** to smell quickly and audibly; **2,** to smell out; as, to *sniff* danger:—*n.* **1,** the act of smelling; **2,** an audible, often scornful, inhaling through the nose.

snif-fle (snif′l), *v.i.* [snif-fled, snif-fling], to draw air through the nose audibly and repeatedly; to snuffle.

snip (snip), *v.t.* [snipped, snip-ping], to cut or clip, with scissors or shears, in short, quick strokes:—*n.* **1,** a single cut with scissors; a clip; **2,** a small piece; bit.—*adj.* **snip′py,** *Colloq.,* sharp; curt; esp. in an insolent or supercilious way.

snipe (snīp), *n.* [*pl.* snipe], a long-billed shore-bird akin to the woodcock:—*v.i.* [sniped, snip-ing], **1,** to hunt such birds; **2,** in *war,* to shoot enemies, one by one, from ambush:—*v.t.* to shoot (soldiers) in this way.—*n.* **snip′er.**

snitch (snich), *v.i.* *Slang,* to inform *on;* tell; blab:—*v.t.* *Slang,* to pilfer.

sniv-el (sniv′l), *v.i.* [snivelled, snivel-ling], **1,** to run at the nose; to snuffle; **2,** to cry in a complaining way.—*n.* **sniv′el-ler.**

snob (snob), *n.* one who apes and is slavishly humble to persons of wealth or position and ignores those he considers socially inferior.—*adj.* **snob′bish.** —*n.* **snob′ber-y.**

snook-er (snook′ėr), *n.* a game like pool (or billiards) played with balls numbered 1 to 15, which must be sunk in order, with this difference, that a red ball must be sunk each time before a coloured numbered one.

snoop (snoop), *v.i.* to peer or pry in a sneaking way:—*n.* one who thus pries.

snooze (snooz), *Colloq.: v.i.* [snoozed, snooz-ing], to take a nap; doze:—*n.* a nap.

snore (snōr), *v.i.* [snored, snor-ing], to breathe with a hoarse sound through the nose, or nose and mouth, in sleep: *n.* a noisy breathing in sleep.—*n.* **snor′er.**

snor-kel (snôr'kl), *n.* a device for underwater breathing consisting of two vertical tubes (or one tube with two passages) for taking in and blowing out air: it permits submersion for long periods.

snort (snôrt), *v.i.* **1,** to force the air out through the nose with a loud sound; **2,** to express feeling by such a sound; as, to *snort* with anger:—*n.* a loud, abrupt sound so made; as, a *snort* of rage.

snot (snot), *n. Vulgar*, mucus from the nose.—*adj.* **snot'ty.**

snout (snout), *n.* **1,** the projecting nose, and often jaws, of a beast, esp. of a hog; the muzzle; **2,** anything like a snout.

snow (snō), *n.* frozen water vapour in the form of white, feathery flakes, or crystals, falling through the air; also, masses of such flakes lying on the ground:—*v.i.* to fall in frozen crystals:—*v.t.* **1,** to pour out thickly like falling snow, as confetti; **2,** to obstruct or shut in with masses of snow.—*n.* **snow'ball'; snow'drift'; snow'fall'; snow'storm'.**

snow-bird (snō'bûrd'), *n.* **1,** the junco, an American blue-grey-and-white finch; **2,** the snow bunting.

snow—bound (snō'—bound'), *adj.* shut in by a heavy snowstorm.

snow bun-ting (bun'ting), a black-and-white finch nesting in the arctic regions. Its winter plumage is white overcast with brown.

snow-drop (snō'drop'), *n.* **1,** a plant with white flowers, which blooms in very early spring; **2,** its flower; also, its bulb.

snow-flake (snō'flāk'), *n.* a white feathery crystal or small mass of snow.

snow-mo-bile (snō'mō-bēl'), *n.* the first such vehicle, driven by air-pro-peller, was called *ski-peep* and *snow-plane:* today, an effective type equip-ped with powerful motors, broad caterpillar treads (with snow cleats) and aluminum cabins, is used in the Arctic by trappers, surveyors, sportsmen, doctors, hydro and telephone crews, and military and airforce personnel.

snow-plough (snō'plou') or **snow-plow** (plou), *n.* a machine used to clear roads, tracks, etc., of heavy snow.

snow-shoe (snō'shōō'), *n.* a network of rawhide stretched upon a racket-shaped wooden frame, fastened by thongs to the foot and worn for travelling over deep snow.

snow-y (snō'i), *adj.* [snow-i-er, snow-i-est], **1,** covered with, or full of, snow; **2,** white like fresh snow; as, *snowy* linen.

snub (snub), *v.t.* [snubbed, snub-bing], **1,** to check, answer, or interrupt with rude or scornful words; **2,** to treat with scorn; slight intentionally; **3,** to check the motion of; as, to *snub* a boat by means of a rope wound round a post:—*n.* **1,** an intentional slight; **2,** a check:—*adj.* short and slightly turned up; as, a *snub* nose.

¹snuff (snuf), *v.t.* **1,** to draw in through the nose; **2,** to smell; sniff at:—*n.* **1,** the act of snuffing; **2,** powdered tobacco to be inhaled through the nose.—*n.* **snuff'er.**

²snuff (snuf), *n.* the burned part of a wick:—*v.t.* **1,** to cut or pinch the charred part from; as, to *snuff* a candle; **2,** to put out (a candle); hence, to put a sudden end to; as, the accident *snuffed* out his life.

snuffers (snuf'èrz), *n.pl.* a device resembling small tongs, for snuffing a candle.

snuf-fle (snuf'l), *v.i.* [snuf-fled, snuf-fling], to speak or breathe noisily through the nose, esp. when it is stopped up:—*n.* **1,** a noisy breathing through the nose; **2, snuffles,** a cold in the head.

snug (snug), *adj.* [snug-ger, snug-gest], **1,** sheltered and warm; cosy; as, a *snug* house; *snug* in bed; **2,** fitting closely; as, a *snug* jacket; **3,** modest but sufficient; as, a *snug* fortune.—*adv.* **snug'ly.**

snug-gle (snug'l), *v.i.* [snug-gled, snug-gling], to cuddle or nestle close for warmth and comfort:—*v.t.* to hold close and make comfortable.

¹so (sō), *adv.* **1,** in like manner or degree; as, I can run fast; *so* can she; today is not *so* hot as yesterday; **2,** to such a degree; as, this fabric is *so* old that it tears; **3,** as stated, indicated, or implied; as, I told you she would come, and *so* she did; hold your needle *so;* **4,** well: expressing surprise; as, *so* here you are:—*pron.* **1,** a person or thing already indicated; as, he is a poor student and will always remain *so;* **2,** approximately that which has been indicated; a little more or less; as, it costs a dollar or so:—*adv. connective.* therefore; consequently: it is raining; *so* we must stay at home.

²so (sō) or **sol** (sol; sōl), *n.* in *music*, the fifth note of the scale.

soak (sōk), *v.t.* **1,** to wet thoroughly; as,

the rain *soaked* him; **2,** to wet so as to soften; as, to *soak* dried apricots before cooking; **3,** to absorb; as, blotting-paper *soaks* up ink:—*v.i.* **1,** to become thoroughly wet; **2,** to enter by pores or small openings; as, water *soaks* into a sponge; also, to penetrate the mind, as words or ideas:—*n.* the act or process of wetting thoroughly.

soak-ers (sōk'ẽrz), *n.pl.* absorbent knitted (wool) pants put on over a baby's diapers.

soap (sōp), *n.* a substance for cleansing, made by combining fats or oils with an alkali:—*v.t.* to cover or wash with soap. —*adj.* **soap'y.**

soap opera, *Colloq.* a daytime radio or television serial drama, usually melodramatic, emotional, etc., sponsored by a soap company.

soap-suds (sōp'sudz'), *n.* soapy water whipped into a froth or foam.

soar (sōr), *v.i.* **1,** to fly high, as a bird; mount upward with wings; **2,** to rise far above what is usual; as, prices *soared.*

sob (sob), *v.i.* [sobbed, sob-bing], to catch the breath convulsively; also, to weep with a convulsive heaving of the breast:—*v.t.* to utter while catching the breath; as, to *sob* out a confession: —*n.* **1,** a convulsive sigh; **2,** any similar sound.

so-ber (sō'bẽr), *adj.* **1,** temperate by habit, esp. in the use of intoxicating liquors; **2,** not intoxicated; **3,** calm; steady; as, *sober* judgment; **4,** solemn; grave; as, a *sober* face; **5,** plain; subdued; as, *sober* colours:—*v.t.* and *v.i.* to make or become sober.—*adv.* **so'ber-ly.**

so-bri-e-ty (sō-brī'e-ti), *n.* **1,** moderation; temperance, esp. in the use of liquor; **2,** calmness; seriousness; gravity.

so-bri-quet (sō'bri-kā') or **sou-bri-quet** (sōō'bri-kā'), *n.* a nickname; epithet.

soc-cer (sok'ẽr), *n.* a form of football in which the ball is controlled by the feet, legs, body, or head, the use of the hands and arms being prohibited.

so-cia-ble (sō'sha-bl), *adj.* **1,** friendly; companionable; **2,** giving opportunity for friendly companionship; as, a *sociable* neighbourhood; **3,** marked by friendliness; not formal:—*n.* an informal, friendly party.—*adv.* **so'cia-bly.** —*n.* **so'cia-bil'i-ty.**

so-cial (sō'shal), *adj.* **1,** pertaining to human beings living in association with one another; **2,** relating to human life

in general; as, *social* welfare; **3,** sociable; **4,** pertaining to the life of people of we⌐lth and fashion; as, the *social* whirl; **5,** of insects, living in organized communities, as ants or bees do:—*n.* an informal gathering; a sociable: —**box social,** an informal party, to which each of the ladies brings a box of eatables: the men bid for the boxes to get partners and provide money, usually for a church, or other worthy, cause.—*n. Colloq.* **so'cial-ite'** (a member of fashionable society).—*adv.* **so'cial-ly.**

so-cial-ism (sō'shal-izm), *n.* the economic, social and political doctrine which holds that, for the greatest good of the people, the resources of a country and its industries should be placed permanently under public or government ownership and operation.—*n.* and *adj.* **so'cial-ist.**—*adj.* **so'cial-is'tic.**

so-ci-e-ty (sō-sī'e-ti), *n.* [*pl.* societies], **1,** people in general, considered as living in relationship with one another; **2,** people of culture and of good standing in any community: sometimes applied only to people of wealth and fashion; **3,** an organized body of persons united by a common interest or purpose; as, a debating *society;* **4,** association; companionship.

so-ci-ol-o-gy (sō'shi-ol'o-ji; sō'si-), *n.* the science of the origin, development, organization, functions, laws, etc., of human society.—*n.* **so'ci-ol'o-gist.**—*adj.* **so'ci-o-log'i-cal.**

¹sock (sok), *n.* a short stocking not reaching the knee.

²sock (sok), *v.t. Slang,* **1,** to strike or hit hard, esp. with the fist; **2,** to stow away; as, he *socks* his money in the bank. —*n. Slang,* a blow.

sock-et (sok'it), *n.* a hollow into which something is fitted; as, the *socket* of the eye; the *socket* for the bulb of an electric light.

sock-eye (sok'ī'), *n.* and *adj.* one of five species of Pacific salmon that (unlike Atlantic salmon) spawn but once and die in their freshwater spawning grounds: genus, *Oncorrhynchus nerka,* average length 26″, weight 6 lbs.: large runs enter such rivers as the Columbia, Fraser, Skeena, and Nass.

sod (sod), *n.* **1,** the top layer of the soil, containing the roots of grass; turf, usually cut square; **3,** the surface of the ground:—*v.t.* [sod-ded, sod-ding], to cover with turf or pieces of turf.

so-da (sō'da), *n.* **1,** the name given to either of two compounds of sodium: **a,** a white powdery substance, sodium bicarbonate, or baking soda; **b,** a white crystalline substance, sodium carbonate, or washing soda; **2,** soda-water; also, a soft drink made from it.

sod-den (sod′n), *adj.* **1,** soaked; heavy with moisture; as, *sodden* shoes; **2,** badly cooked or baked; as, *sodden* piecrust; **3,** spiritless; dull; as, a *sodden* crowd.

so-di-um (sō′di-um), *n.* a silvery-white, alkaline metallic element always occurring in nature in combination, as in common salt, rock-salt, borax, etc.:—**sodium bicarbonate,** $NaHCO_3$, or *baking soda.*—**sodium carbonate,** Na_2CO_3, or *washing* soda.—**sodium chloride,** NaCl, or *common salt.*—**sodium hydroxide,** NaOH, a white *caustic* solid.—**sodium nitrate,** $NaNO_3$, a clear, odourless *salt:* also called **Chili saltpetre.**—**sodium peroxide,** Na_2O_2, a yellowish-white *powder,* used as an antiseptic.—**sodium sulphate,** Na_2SO_4, a white, crystalline *salt* (of Saskatchewan) used as a detergent.

so-fa (sō′fa), *n.* a long, upholstered seat with a back and arms.

soft (sôft), *adj.* **1,** easily yielding to pressure; lacking in hardness; as, *soft* clay; **2,** easily moulded or shaped; as, *soft* wax; **3,** smooth and yielding to the touch; as, *soft* fur; **4,** not glaring; as, a *soft* light; **5,** not loud; as, *soft* music; **6,** kind; courteous; mild or gentle; as, a *soft* answer; **7,** easily touched or moved; as, a *soft* heart; **8,** mild; as, *soft* winds; **9,** weak; unmanly; **10,** pronounced with the sound of "c" in "cell" or "g" in "gem"; not hard, like the "c" in "case" or "g" in "gate"; **11,** *Colloq.:* **a,** not in good physical condition; flabby; as, *soft* muscles; **b,** containing no alcohol; as, *soft* drinks:—*adv.* quietly.—*adv.* **soft′ly.**

soft-ball (sôft′bôl′), *n.* a game using a bigger, softer ball and smaller diamond than ordinary baseball.

sof-ten (sôf′n; sôf′en), *v.t.* and *v.i.* to make or become less hard, loud, glaring, severe, or rude.

soft-wood (sôft′wood′), *n.* any light, easily worked wood, esp. that of cone-bearing trees, such as the spruce or pine: opposite of *hardwood.* Also written **soft wood.**

sog-gy (sog′i), *adj.* [sog-gi-er, sog-gi-est], soaked; as, *soggy* clothes; also, wet and heavy; as, *soggy* cake.—*n.* **sog′gi-ness.**

¹soil (soil), *n.* **1,** the loose top layer of the earth's surface, as distinguished

from solid rock; ground; earth; **2,** land; the country; as, to go back to the *soil.*

²soil (soil), *v.t.* to make dirty; stain, as, to *soil* the hands; **2,** to mar or sully; as a reputation:—*v.i.* to become stained or dirty:—*n.* **1,** dirt; stain; **2,** manure.

so-journ (sō′jûrn; so-jûrn′), *v.i.* to dwell for a time:—*n.* a short stay; as, a *sojourn* in the mountains.—*n.* **sojourn′er.**

sol (sol; sōl), *n.* in *music,* the fifth note of the scale; so.

sol-ace (sol′is), *n.* comfort in sorrow; consolation; as, to find *solace* in music:—*v.t.* [solaced, solac-ing], to comfort in sorrow; console.

so-lar (sō′lėr), *adj.* pertaining to, measured by, or proceeding from, the sun; as, *solar* rays; *solar* time:—**solar system,** the sun together with the planets and the other bodies that circle round it:—**so-lar plex-us,** a great network of nerves lying behind the stomach: it runs to the intestines, stomach, and glands of the upper abdomen.

so-lar-i-um (sō-lâr′i-um), *n.* a sun-room, esp. for medicinal sunbathing.

sold (sōld), *p.t.* and *p.p.* of *sell.*

sol-der (sol′dėr; sod′ėr), *n.* a metal or metallic alloy used, when melted, to join metal surfaces, or to mend breaks in metal:—*v.t.* to join or patch with such an alloy.

sol-dier (sōl′jėr), *n.* **1,** a man engaged in military service; **2,** a private as distinguished from a commissioned officer; **3,** a man of military experience:—**soldier of fortune,** an adventurer; esp. a military adventurer:—*v.i.* **1,** to serve in the army; **2,** to pretend to be working; shirk.—*adj.* **sol′dier-ly.**

sol-dier-y (sōl′jėr-i), *n.* military forces; troops.

¹sole (sōl), *n.* a kind of flatfish used for food.

²sole (sōl), *n.* **1,** the under side of the foot; **2,** the bottom of a shoe or slipper:—*v.t.* [soled, sol-ing], to furnish with a sole.

³sole (sōl), *adj.* alone; only; single; as, the *sole* survivor.—*adv.* **sole′ly.**

sol-e-cism (sol′e-sizm), *n.* **1,** an error or blunder, esp. in grammar or syntax; as, *I seen it; they was;* **2,** a breach of etiquette.

sol-emn (sol′em), *adj.* **1,** attended with sacred rites or ceremonies; as, a *solemn* religious service; **2,** inspiring awe or fear; as, a *solemn* occasion; **3**, sober; serious; as, a *solemn* expression; **4**, grave; deliberate; as, a *solemn* oath.—*adv.* **sol'emn-ly.**—*v.t.* **sol'em-nize'.**

so-lem-ni-ty (so-lem'ni-ti), *n.* [*pl.* solem-nities], **1**, a sacred rite or ceremony; **2**, a formal and grave celebration; **3**, impressiveness; seriousness; gravity.

so-le-noid (sō'le-noid), *n.* a coil of wire wound in spiral form, used to produce a magnetic field or as an inductance coil.

sol—fa (sōl'—fä; sol'), *n., adj.* and *v.,* the syllables *do, re, mi, fa,* etc., used in singing the scale.

so-lic-it (so-lis'it), *v.t.* to ask for urgently; implore; entreat; seek; as, to *solicit* a favour; to *solicit* trade:—*v.i.* to seek orders, support, votes, etc.—*n.* **so-lic'i-ta'tion.**

so-lic-i-tor (so-lis'i-tėr), *n.* **1**, one who seeks trade, votes, etc.; **2**, an attorney or lawyer; **3**, the civil law officer of a city, town, department, or government.

so-lic-it-ous (so-lis'i-tus), *adj.* anxious; concerned; also, eager; as, *solicitous* to repay a debt.—*n.* **so-lic'i-tude.**

sol-id (sol'id), *adj.* **1**, keeping its shape despite pressure; not in the form of a fluid or gas; **2**, not hollow; as, a *solid* foundation; also, substantial; as, a man of *solid* means; **4**, all of a piece; the same throughout; as, *solid* silver or gold; **5**, unbroken; as, a *solid* line of defence; **6**, *Colloq.,* whole; uninterrupted; as, a *solid* hour:—*n.* **1**, a body whose shape cannot be changed by pressure; a substance not fluid or gaseous; **2**, in *geometry,* a body having length, breadth, and thickness; as, a prism is a *solid.*—*n.* **sol'id-ness.**—*n.* **so-lid'i-ty** (so-lid'i-ti).—*n.* **sol'i-dar'-i-ty.**

so-lid-i-fy (so-lid'i-fī'), *v.t.* and *v.i.* [solidi-fied, solidify-ing], to make or become hard or firm.—*n.* **so-lid'i-fi-ca'tion.**

so-lil-o-quy (so-lil'o-kwi), *n.* the act of talking to oneself:—*v.t.* and *v.i.* **so-lil'o-quize'.**

sol-i-taire (sol'i-târ'), *n.* **1**, a game of cards played by one person; **2**, a gem, esp. a diamond, mounted alone.

sol-i-tar-y (sol'i-tėr-i), *adj.* **1**, living by oneself; without companions; as, a *solitary* hermit; **2**, done, passed, or suffered alone; as, *solitary* confinement; **3**, rarely visited; remote; secluded;

as, a *solitary* house; a *solitary* inn; **4**, only; single; as, a *solitary* example.

sol-i-tude (sol'i-tūd'), *n.* **1**, the state of being by oneself; loneliness; seclusion; **2**, a remote and lonely place.

so-lo (sō'lō), *n.* [*pl.* solos (sō'lōz) or soli (sō'lē)], **1**, a musical composition, or a part of one, played or sung by a single person; **2**, any performance, as an aeroplane flight, by one person:—*adj.* done by one person; as, a *solo* flight; also, performing alone; as, a *solo* violinist.—*n.* **so'lo-ist.**

sol-stice (sol'stis), *n.* either of the two points in the sun's path at which the sun is farthest from the equator, either north of it or south of it.

sol-u-ble (sol'ū-bl), *adj.* **1**, capable of being dissolved in a fluid, as sugar in water; **2**, capable of being solved or explained.—*n.* **sol'u-bil'i-ty.**

so-lu-tion (so-lū'shun; lōō), *n.* **1**, the process of solving, or arriving at the answer to, a problem; an answer; **2**, the process by which a gas, liquid, or solid is dissolved in and mixed with a liquid; also, the resulting liquid as, an ammonia *solution.*

solve (solv), *v.t.* [solved, solv-ing], **1**, to explain; find out; esp., to find the answer to (a problem); **2**, to make clear; as, to *solve* a mystery.

sol-vent (sol'vent), *adj.* **1**, capable of dissolving another substance; as, turpentine has a *solvent* action; **2**, able to pay one's debts:—*n.* any liquid, as water, alcohol, etc., capable of dissolving other substances.—*n.* **sol'ven-cy.**

som-bre or **som-ber** (som'bėr), *adj.* **1**, dull; dark; **2**, dismal; gloomy.

som-bre-ro (som-brâ'rō), *n.* [*pl.* sombreros], a kind of broad-brimmed hat worn esp. in Latin America and southwestern U.S.

some (sum), *adj.* **1**, a certain; particular, but not named; as, *some* boy did it; *some* other time; there were *some* men here today; **2**, of an indefinite number, amount, extent, etc.; as, have *some* potatoes; I have *some* money:—*pron.* **1**, particular persons not named; as, *some* came early; **2**, an indefinite number or amount; as, I'll have *some* of these pencils; *some* of the cake:—*adv.* about; nearly; as, *some* ten men came.

some-body (sum'bud'i; sum'bod-i), *pron.* a person unknown or not named:—*n.* [*pl.* somebodies], a person of importance.

some-how (sum'hou), *adv.* in one way or another; by some means.

some-one (sum'wun'), *pron.* a person unknown or not named; somebody.

som-er-sault (sum'ẽr-sôlt), *n.* a spring or leap in which one turns heels over head.

som-er-set (sum'ẽr-set), *n.* a somersault.

some-thing (sum'thing), *pron.* 1, a thing not definitely known, named, decided, or stated; 2, a thing of unnamed amount or degree; as, one should give *something* to charity; 3, a person or thing of importance.

some-time (sum'tim'), *adv.* 1, at a time not exactly known or not definitely stated; as, *sometime* in June; 2, at a time in the future, not yet decided upon:—*adj.* former.

some-times (sum'tīmz'), *adv.* once in a while; now and then.

some-what (sum'hwot'; sum'hwôt'), *pron.* 1, an indefinite amount; 2, a person or thing to some extent like another; as, he was *somewhat* of a shirker:—*adv.* to an indefinite degree or extent; rather; as, *somewhat* tired.

some-where (sum'hwâr'), *adv.* 1, in one place or another; 2, in, at, or to, a place not named or not known.

som-nam-bu-list (som-nam'bū-list), *n.* a sleepwalker.—*n.* **som-nam'bu-lism.**

som-no-lent (som'nō-lent), *n.* sleepy, or inducing sleep; as, a *somnolent* day, air, etc.—*n.* **som'no-lence.**

son (sun), *n.* 1, a male child; a boy or man in relation to his parent or parents; 2, any male descendant; 3, a native of a particular country; 4, a person thought of as the product of an age, civilization, etc.; as, a true *son* of the Middle Ages:—**the Son,** Jesus Christ: also called *Son of God.*

so-nar (sō'när), *n.* a device used to locate submarines, schools of fish, and ocean depths, by means of sound vibrations reflected from them.

so-na-ta (sō-nä'ta), *n.* a musical composition in three or four movements, usually for the piano.

song (sông), *n.* 1, a series of rhythmic and tuneful musical sounds uttered vocally, as by a bird; 2, music produced by the human voice; 3, poetry; esp., a lyric or ballad which can be set to music; 4, a musical composition to be sung; 5, *Colloq.*, a mere trifle; as, he sold it for a *song.*

song-bird (sông'bûrd'), *n.* 1, a singing bird; 2, a woman who sings.

song-ster (sông'stẽr), *n.* 1, a person who sings; also, a singing bird; 2, one who writes songs or lyric poetry.—*n.fem.* **song'stress.**

son—in—law (sun'—in—lô'), *n.* [*pl.* sons-in-law], the husband of one's daughter.

son-net (son'it), *n.* a poem, usually of fourteen lines, arranged in any one of several rhyme schemes.

so-nor-ous (so-nôr'us), *adj.* 1, resonant; giving a full or loud sound; as, *sonorous* bells; 2, having a full, rich sound; as, *sonorous* poetry.

soon (sōōn), *adv.* 1, in a short time; in the near future; as, it will *soon* be dark; 2, shortly; quickly; as, he came *soon* afterwards; 3, gladly; willingly; as, I'd as *soon* do it as not.

soot (soot; sōōt), *n.* the very fine black powder which colours smoke, formed when anything is burned, and which is deposited in chimneys, stove-pipes, etc.—*adj.* **soot'y.**

sooth (sōōth), *n. Archaic,* truth.

soothe (sōō*th*), *v.t.* [soothed, sooth-ing], 1, to make quiet or calm; comfort or console; 2, to make less severe, as pain.

sooth-say-er (sōōth'sā'ẽr), *n.* one who claims to have the power of foretelling the future; a fortune-teller.—*n.* **sooth'-say-ing.**

sop (sop), *n.* 1, anything soaked, dipped, or softened in a liquid, as bread in broth; 2, something given to pacify; as, a *sop* to injured feelings:—*v.t.* [sopped, sop-ping], 1, to dip or soak, as biscuits in coffee; 2, to mop up, as gravy with bread.—*adj.* **sop'py.**

so-phis-ti-cat-ed (so-fis'ti-kāt'id), *adj.* wise in the ways of the world.

soph-ist-ry (sof'is-tri), *n.* reasoning which appears to be sound but is not so; a false argument; as, his ingenious *sophistry* deceived us.—*n.* **soph'ist.**

soph-o-more (sof'o-mōr'), *n.* in Canadian and American universities, colleges, and high schools, a student in the second year of a four-year course.

so-po-rif-ic (sō'po-rif'ik; sop'), *adj.* and *n.* inducing sleep: used esp. of a medicine, drug, etc.

so-pra-no (so-prä'nō; so-pran'ō), *n.* [*pl.* sopranos], 1, the highest singing voice; 2, a singer with such a voice.—*adj.* **so-pra'no.**

sor-cer-er (sôr'sẽr-ẽr), *n.* a magician; conjurer.—*n.fem.* **sor'cer-ess.**

sor-cer-y (sôr'sẽr-i), *n.* [*pl.* sorceries], witchcraft; magic; enchantment.

sor-did (sôr'did), *adj.* **1,** filthy; squalid; as, *sordid* slums; **2,** vile; base; degraded; as, a *sordid* soul.—*adv.* **sor'-did-ly.**

sore (sōr), *adj.* [sor-er, sor-est], **1,** tender or painful to the touch; inflamed; **2,** afflicted; grieved; as, her heart was *sore;* **3,** severe; intense; as, a *sore* struggle; **4,** *Colloq.*, vexed; annoyed; resentful:—*adv.* grievously; severely; deeply:—*n.* **1,** a painful or diseased spot on the body; an ulcer; **2,** a cause of trouble or distress.—*adv.* **sore'ly.** —*n.* **sore'ness.**

sor-ghum (sôr'gum), *n.* a canelike, cereal grass with sweet juicy stalk, grown for grain, fodder, syrup, etc.

so-ror-i-ty (so-rôr'i-ti), *n.* a women's or girls' club, esp. in a school or college.

¹sor-rel (sor'el), *n.* any of several flowering herbs with sour juice.

²sor-rel (sôr'el), *adj.* reddish brown: —*n.* **1,** a reddish-brown colour; **2,** a reddish-brown horse.

sor-row (sor'ō), *n.* **1,** mental pain caused by loss, regret, disappointment, etc.; grief; **2,** that which causes grief; trouble:—*v.i.* to feel sorrow; be sorrowful; grieve.—*n.* **sor'row-er.**—*adj.* **sor'-row-ful.**

sor-ry (sor'i), *adj.* [sor-ri-er, sor-ri-est], **1,** feeling regret for one's own loss, disappointment, wrongdoing, etc.; **2,** feeling pity or regret for another; **3,** wretched; shabby; as, a *sorry* fellow; also, dismal; miserable; as, a *sorry* plight.

sort (sôrt), *n.* **1,** a kind or species; as, there are many *sorts* of roses; **2,** quality; character; as, material of this *sort* wears longest:—**out of sorts,** ill; out of humour:—*v.t.* to place in different classes, according to kind; as, to *sort* beads by colour.

sor-tie (sôr'tē), *n.* a sudden sally or attack, esp. of troops from a defensive position.

SOS (es'ō'es'), *n.* the international wireless distress signal [. . . – – – . . .] used by ships, aircraft, etc.

sot (sot), *n.* a confirmed drunkard.

sou (sōō), *n. French,* a 5-centime piece, the 20th part of a franc.

souf-fle (sōō'flā), *n.* a dish of eggs, milk, cheese, salmon, etc., made light and fluffy by the adding of beaten egg whites before baking.—*adj.* puffed up.

sough (sou) *v.i.* to sigh, rustle, or murmur, as, the wind *soughing* in the trees. —*n.* such a sound.

sought (sôt), *p.t.* and *p.p.* of *seek.*

soul (sōl), *n.* **1,** that part of man which is supposed to be the centre of mental and spiritual life, believed by many to survive death; **2,** the part that gives vigour and character; as, the *soul* of art; **3,** a person who leads and inspires; as, the *soul* of the team; **4,** a person; as, not a *soul* was there; **5,** personification; as, the *soul* of honour.—*adj.* **soul'ful.**

¹sound (sound), *adj.* **1,** whole; not hurt; in good condition; as, safe and *sound;* **2,** deep; as, *sound* slumber; **3,** healthy; not decayed; as, a *sound* tooth; **4,** founded on what is believed to be true and right; free from error; as, *sound* doctrine; carefully thought out; as, a *sound* plan; **5,** conservative; dependable; as, a *sound* business man; solvent; as, a *sound* business; **6,** legal; valid; as, a *sound* title; **7,** firm; safe; as, a *sound* floor; **8,** thorough; as, a *sound* thrashing:—*adv.* deeply; thoroughly; as, *sound* asleep.—*n.* **sound'-ness.**

²sound (sound), *n.* **1,** that which is heard; the sensation perceived through the ear; as, the *sound* of a drum; a loud *sound;* **2,** meaning attached to what is heard; as, I don't like the *sound* of what you say; **3,** the distance to which a sound is audible; as, within *sound* of the bell:—*v.t.* **1,** to cause to make a sound; as, to *sound* a bell; **2,** to cause (a sound) to be heard; to utter, play, etc.; as, to *sound* a high note; **3,** to examine or test by causing to give forth sound; as, to *sound* the walls of a building; **4,** to order or announce by sound; as, to *sound* an alarm:—*v.i.* **1,** to make a noise or sound; **2,** to be played upon, as an instrument; make music; **3,** to give a certain impression when heard; as, her voice *sounds* sad.—*adj.* **sound'-less; sound'proof'.**

³sound (sound), *v.t.* **1,** to measure the depth of (water, etc.), as by lowering a weighted line from the surface; to fathom; **2,** to examine indirectly; try to find out the opinions or attitude of; as, to *sound* a person on a delicate subject:—*v.i.* **1,** to measure the depth of water; **2,** to dive deeply, as do whales.

⁴sound (sound), *n.* **1,** a long stretch of water, wider than a strait, connecting two large bodies of water, or lying between the mainland and an island; as, Long Island *Sound;* **2,** the air-bladder of a fish.

sound-er (sound'ẽr), *n.* a landline telegraph device that converts electric code impulses into sound.

sound-ly (sound′li), *adv.* **1,** thoroughly; as, *soundly* thrashed; **2,** deeply; as, he sleeps *soundly;* **3,** well and wisely; as, *soundly* reasoned.

sound track, the part of a motion picture film on which sound is recorded.

soup (sōōp), *n.* liquid food, or broth, made by simmering meat or vegetables, or both together, in a large quantity of liquid.—*adj.* **soupy′.**

sour (sour), *adj.* **1,** having a sharp, biting taste, as vinegar or green fruit; **2,** acid, esp. as a result of fermentation; as, *sour* cream; **3,** disagreeable; cross; as, a *sour* disposition:—*v.t.* **1,** to cause to become acid or fermented; **2,** to cause to become cross and disagreeable:—*v.i.* to become acid or fermented.
—*n.* **sour′ness.**—*adv.* **sour′ly.**

source (sōrs), *n.* **1,** a spring or fountain; the beginning of a stream; **2,** that from which anything rises or originates; as, books are a *source* of information.

sour-dough (sour′dō′), *n.* a Canadian or Alaskan prospector, who usually carried dough from camp to camp for use as a leaven in making bread: since 1930 the annual international Yukon Sourdough Reunion has been held on the West coast: see Service's *Songs of a Sourdough* (1907).

souse (sous), *v.t.* **1,** to dash; splash; as he *soused* water on me; **2,** to soak thoroughly by plunging into water; **3,** to steep in brine; **4,** *Slang,* to intoxicate.—*n.* the act of steeping in brine or plunging into water, etc.

south (south), *n.* **1,** one of the four points of the compass; the point opposite to the north, or to the right of a person facing the sunrise; **2,** the section of a country lying to the south; as, the *south* of France:—*adj.* having to do with, or coming from, the south; as, a *south* wind:—*adv.* to the south; as, turn *south.*
  South, in the U.S., that district lying generally south of the Ohio River and the southern boundary of Pennsylvania; **South Pole,** the southern end of the earth's axis.

south-east (south′ēst′), *n.* **1,** the point on the compass halfway between south and east; **2,** a region lying in the direction of that point:—*adj.* having to do with the southeast, or in or from the southeast; as, a *southeast* wind:—*adv.* toward the southeast.—*adj.,* *adv.* and *n.* **south′east′ward.**

south-east-er (south′ēs′tėr), *n.* a storm or gale coming from the southeast.

south-east-er-ly (south′ēs′tėr-li), *adj.* and *adv.* from or toward the southeast.

south-east-ern (south′ēst′ėrn), *adj.* of, from, or situated in, the southeast.

south-er-ly (su*th*′ėr-li), *adj.* pertaining to, situated in, or coming from, the south:—*adv.* toward the south.

south-ern (su*th*′ėrn), *adj.* in, from, or toward, the south:—Southern, pertaining to the South, or the southern United States.—*adj.* **south′ern-most.**

south-ern-er (su*th*′ėr-nėr), *n.* a person living in, or coming from, the south:—Southerner, a person living in, or coming from, the southern part of U.S.

south-paw (south′pô′), *adj. Slang,* left-handed, esp. in pitching a baseball.
—*n.* a left-handed person.

south—south-east (south′–south′- ēst′), *n.* halfway between southeast and south.

south—south-west (south′–south′- west′), *n.* halfway between southwest and south.

south-ward (south′wėrd), *adj.* and *adv.* to or toward the south; leading to the south. Also, *adv.* **south′wards** (south′wėrdz).

south-west (south′west′), *n.* **1,** the point of the compass halfway between south and west; **2,** a region lying in the direction of that point:—*adj.* having to do with the southwest, or in or from the southwest:—*adv.* toward the southwest.—*adj., adv.,* and *n.* **south′west′ward.**—*adv.* **south′west′- ward-ly.**

south-west-er (south′wes′tėr), *n.* a strong wind or storm from the southwest.

south-west-ern (south′wes′tėrn), *adj.* of, from, or situated in, the southwest.

sou-ve-nir (sōō′vė-nēr′; sōō′vė-nēr), *n.* a thing by which to remember a person or an event; a memento or keepsake.

sou′-west-er (sou′wes′tėr), *n.* **1,** a southwester; **2,** a painted canvas or oilskin hat with a brim that is wide at the back, worn in stormy weather by sailors and fishermen.

sov-er-eign (sov′rin; sov′ėr-in; suv′rin; suv′ėr-in), *adj.* **1,** chief; supreme; as, *sovereign* power; **2,** possessing absolute and independent power; as,

SOU′WESTER def. 2

a *sovereign* state; **3,** principal; greatest; also, best and most effective; as, a *sovereign* remedy:—*n.* **1,** a ruler, as a king, emperor, or queen; **2,** a British gold coin equal to twenty shillings, or about $2.80.

sov-er-eign-ty (sov′rin-ti; sov′ẽr-in-ti; suv′rin-ti; suv′ẽr-in-ti), *n,* [*pl.* sovereignties], supreme power or dominion, whether vested in a monarch or, as in a limited monarchy or a republic, in the people.

so-vi-et (sō′vi-et; sō′vi-et′), *n.* **1,** a council; **2,** (usually *Soviet*), one of the local councils or governing bodies of the Union of Soviet Socialist Republics, which are elected by the people, and send delegates to the higher congresses. —*n.* **so′vi-et′ism.**

¹sow (sou), *n.* a female hog.

²sow (sō), *v.t.* [*p.t.* sowed (sōd), *p.p.* sown (sōn) or sowed, *p.pr.* sow-ing], **1,** to strew, as seed, upon the earth; **2,** to strew seed in, on, or over; as, to *sow* a lawn; **3,** to cause to grow or spread; as, to *sow* discord:—*v.i.* to strew seed for growing.

sow-bug (sou), a water bug with shieldlike plate on abdomen, that scavenges in the oozes of stagnant ponds and pools.

sow thistle, a common coarse weed with yellow flowers, spiny leaves, and milky juice.

soy or **soy-bean** (soi′bēn′), *n.* a legume with white or purple flowers and hairy, brownish pods: the seed yields flour, oil, etc.

spa (spä), *n.* a mineral-spring resort.

space (spās), *n.* **1,** the boundless expanse in which our universe moves, and all known things exist; **2,** a definite, or limited, distance or area; room; as, the *space* between the desk and the wall; that advertisement takes up too much *space;* **3,** length of time; as, in the *space* of a few months; **4,** in *music,* one of the open places between the lines of the staff; **5,** in typewritten or printed matter, one of the open spaces separating letters or words:—*v.t.* [spaced, spac-ing], to arrange, as letters or words, by separating them with spaces.—*n.* **space′man′; space′ship′.**—*adj.* **spa′tial** or **spa′cial.**

spa-cious (spā′shus), *adj.* **1,** capacious; roomy; as, a *spacious* house; **2,** extensive; as, a *spacious* domain.—*adv.* **spa′cious-ly.**—*n.* **spa′cious-ness.**

spade (spād), *n.* **1,** a digging tool, consisting of a broad, flat blade of iron with a long handle; **2,** one of a suit,

called *spades,* of playing-cards, marked with a black figure like a pointed spade: —*v.t.* [spaded, spad-ing], to dig or work [ground] with a spade; as, to *spade* a garden.—*n.* **spade′ful′; spade′work′.**

spa-ghet-ti (spa-get′i), *n.* a flour-product like macaroni, except that it is solid, and smaller in circumference.

span (span), *n.* **1,** the distance from the end of the thumb to the tip of the little finger when the thumb and fingers are extended wide open; also, regarded as a measure of length, nine inches; **2,** a short space of time; **3,** extent having two definite bounds; as, the *span* of a river; **4,** the distance between the supports of an arch, a beam, etc.; also, the sections of an arch; a beam, etc., between two supports, **5,** a pair of horses, harnessed as a team: —*v.t.* [spanned, span-ning], **1,** to measure by the extended thumb and fingers; **2,** to extend across; as, a plank *spanned* the gully.

span-gle (spang′gl), *n.* **1,** one of the tiny, shining, metallic disks used to ornament dresses; **2,** any small, glittering ornament:—*v.t.* [span-gled, span-gling], to adorn with bits of shining material.

span-iel (span′yel), *n.* any of various small or medium-sized dogs with drooping ears and long, silky hair.

spank (spangk), *v.t.* to strike; punish by striking the buttocks with the hand, a slipper, etc.:—*n.* a slap.

spank-ing (spank′ing), *adj.* rapid; brisk; fresh; as, a *spanking* breeze.

span-ner (span′ẽr), *n.* a wrench, esp. one with a jaw or socket at both ends.

¹spar (spär), *n.* a mast, yard, boom, etc., on a vessel:—*v.t.* [sparred, spar-ring], to fit with spars.

²spar (spär), *v.i.* [sparred, spar-ring], **1,** to fight with the fists; to box; esp., to box skilfully or scientifically; **2,** to engage in a contest of words; wrangle.

spare (spâr), *v.t.* [spared, spar-ing], **1,** to use in a frugal or saving manner. use rarely; as, *spare* the rod; **2,** to do without conveniently; as, can you *spare* this book? **3,** to refrain from; omit; as, I shall *spare* no expense; **4,** to save (a person) from something; as, this will *spare* me trouble; **5,** to avoid injuring; treat carefully; as, to *spare* a person's feelings:—*adj.* [spar-er, spar-est], **1,** thin; lean; **2,** held in reserve; as, a *spare* tire; also, extra; as, *spare* cash:—*n.* **1,** a spare part; esp., a spare tire; **2,** in *bowling,* the knocking over of all the pins in two attempts; also, the score for this.

spar-ing (spâr'ing), *adj.* **1,** frugal; **2,** scanty; limited; as, a *sparing* use of salt.—*adv.* **spar'ing-ly.**

¹spark (spärk), *n.* **1,** a tiny, burning particle thrown off by a body that is on fire; **2,** any bright, small flash; **3,** hence, any sudden flash; as, a *spark* of genius; **4,** a small sign or particle; as, not a *spark* of life remained; **5,** the flash of light produced by a discharge of electricity between two conductors; **6,** the discharge of electricity in a spark-plug; also, the mechanism controlling this discharge:—*v.i.* **1,** to send out sparks; **2,** to produce an electric spark:—**spark coil,** an induction coil consisting of many turns of insulated wire on an iron core, that produces a spark, as in an internal-combustion engine.

²spark (spärk), *n.* a gay, dashing, young fellow; a beau; gallant:—*v.i.* and *v.t. Colloq.,* to play the gallant; court.

spar-kle (spär'kl), *v.i.* [spar-kled, spar-kling], **1,** to give off light in small flashes; glisten; gleam; **2,** to flash; scintillate, as wit; **3,** to bubble, as wine:—*n.* a gleam or glitter, as of gems; also, a flash, as of wit.—*n.* **spar'kler.**

spark–plug (spärk'–plug'), *n.* a device used in many engines, such as the engine of an automobile, for igniting a mixture of air and gasoline vapour by means of an electric spark.

spar-row (spar'ō), *n.* a common bird of the finch family, small, not brightly coloured, found in most parts of the world.

sparse (spärs), *adj.* [spars-er, spars-est], thinly scattered; scant and thinly distributed; as, *sparse* vegetation.

spasm (spazm), *n.* **1,** a sudden, violent, involuntary contraction, or shortening of the muscles; **2,** a sudden, violent, but brief, movement, emotion, etc.:—*adj.* **spas-mod'ic** (spaz-mod'ik).—*adv.* **spas-mod'i-cal-ly.**

spas-tic (spas'tik), *adj.* denoting a form of paralysis in which there is a sudden involuntary contraction of muscles.

¹spat (spat), *Colloq., n.* **1,** a slight blow with the open hand; a slap; **2,** a spatter, as of rain; **3,** a petty quarrel:—*v.i.* [spat-ted, spat-ting], to engage in a petty quarrel:—*v.t.* to slap.

²spat (spat), *n.* a kind of short cloth gaiter fastened under the instep.

spate (spāt), *n.* a great outpouring; a flood; as, a *spate* of words, rumours, books, etc.

spa-tial (spā'shal), *adj.* pertaining to space: also, **spa'cial.**

spat-ter (spat'ėr), *v.t.* **1,** to splash a liquid upon; soil by splashing; as, to *spatter* the tablecloth with grease; **2,** to scatter in drops or by splashing; as, to *spatter* milk over the floor; **3,** to cover, as with splashes; as, a field *spattered* with flowers:—*v.i.* to splash in drops:—*n.* **1,** a splashing or sprinkling; **2,** a spot so made; **3,** a pattering, as of rain.

spat-u-la (spat'ū-la), *n.* an implement with a broad, flat, fairly flexible blade for mixing ointments, spreading frostings, etc.: used by painters, druggists, cooks, etc.

spav-in (spav'in). *n.* a disease of horses, marked by a bony deposit in the hock joint (near knee) that causes lameness.—*adj.* **spav'ined.**

spawn (spôn), *n.* **1,** the eggs of fish, oysters, and other water animals which lay great numbers of small eggs; **2,** offspring:—*v.t.* and *v.i.* **1,** to lay or produce (eggs or spawn); **2,** to produce (offspring) in great numbers.

spay (spā), *v.t.* to sterilize (a female animal, as a bitch) by removing the ovaries.

speak (spēk), *v.i.* [*p.t.* spoke (spōk) or, *Archaic,* spake (spāk), *p.p.* spo-ken (spō'ken), *p.pr.* speak-ing], **1,** to utter words; talk; **2,** to tell; mention; as, do not *speak* of this; **3,** to make an address or speech; **4,** to sound, as a gun; **5,** to convey ideas, though not in words; as, our actions *speak* for us:—*v.t.* **1,** to utter, as a word; pronounce; **2,** to express in words; as, to *speak* the truth; **3,** to use, or be able to use, in conversation; as, he *speaks* four languages; **4,** to address or hail, as a ship.—*n.* **speak'er.**

spear (spēr), *n.* **1,** a weapon with a long shaft and sharp, pointed head, to be thrust or thrown; a lance; **2,** an instrument with barbed prongs for catching fish; **3,** a slender blade or shoot; as, a *spear* of grass:—*v.t.* to pierce or kill with a spear.—*n.* **spear'head'.**

spear-mint (spēr'mint'), *n.* a pungent, spicy herb, the common garden mint.

spe-cial (spesh'al), *adj.* **1,** characterizing a single person or thing, or a single class; as, the *special* qualities of a leader; **2,** designed for a particular purpose; as, a *special* course of study; **3,** particular; unusual; as, a *special* favour; a *special* point of interest; **4,** esteemed beyond others, intimate; as, a *special* companion.

spe-cial-ist (spesh′al-ist), *n.* a person who limits himself to one particular field of work or study; as, an eye *specialist.*

spe-ci-al-i-ty (spesh′i-al′i-ti), *n.* **1,** the distinctive mark of a person or thing; as the *speciality* of an author's style; in *pl.* [specialities] details; particulars; **2,** a specialty (definitions 1, 2).

spe-cial-ize (spesh′al-īz′), *v.i.* [specialized, specializ-ing], to pursue a particular line of action or course of study; as, to *specialize* in science:—*v.t.* to modify or adapt for a particular purpose or use.—*n.* **spe′cial-i-za′tion.**

spe-cial-ty (spesh′al-ti), *n.* **1,** a line of work or study to which one is particularly devoted; as, my *specialty* is music; **2,** an article dealt in exclusively or chiefly; as, their *specialty* is calculating machines; **3,** a speciality (definition 1).

spe-cie (spē′shi), *n.* coin or currency, like silver or gold: opposite of paper money.

spe-cies (spē′shiz; spē′shēz), *n.* [*pl.* species], **1,** a kind; variety; **2,** a group of animals or plants differing from each other in unimportant respects, and having certain common characteristics which clearly distinguish the group from other groups.

spe-cif-ic (spi-sif′ik), *adj.* **1,** pertaining to a species; as, a *specific* name; **2,** definite or particular; precise; as, *specific* information; **3,** having some particular curing or healing quality; as, a *specific* medicine:—*n.* anything that is suited to a particular use or purpose; esp., a remedy for a certain disease.—**specific duty,** a tax on goods per yard, pound, etc., not on the price (which is an *ad valorem* duty):—**specific gravity,** the ratio of the weight of a given mass or volume of substance to that of an equal volume of water (for solids and liquids) or of hydrogen (for gases):—**specific heat, 1,** the number of calories required to raise the temperature of 1 gram to 1° Centigrade; **2,** the ratio of the heat needed to raise the temperature of a substance one degree to that needed to raise the temperature of an equal volume or mass of water one degree.

spe-cif-i-cal-ly (spi-sif′i-kal-i), *adv.*

1, with respect to one particular point; **2,** definitely; in particular.

spec-i-fi-ca-tion (spes′i-fi-kā′shun), *n.* **1,** the act of stating or specifying in detail; **2, specifications,** the items of a detailed statement of requirements for carrying out some work or project; also, the statement; as, the *specifications* for a building.

spec-i-fy (spes′i-fī′), *v.t.* [specified, specify-ing], to mention or name particularly; state fully and clearly.

spec-i-men (spes′i-men), *n.* **1,** a part which represents, or shows the quality of, the whole; as, a *specimen* of ore; **2,** one of a group from which the characteristics of the entire group may be studied; as, an insect *specimen:* [*pl.* add *s*].

spe-cious (spē′shus), *adj.* seeming to be right or logical, but not really so; apparently fair or just, but not genuine; as, *specious* arguments; reasoning, etc.

speck (spek), *n.* **1,** a spot or flaw; blemish; as, a *speck* of decay in fruit; **2,** a very small thing; particle; as, a *speck* of dust:—*v.t.* to spot, or stain with small spots; speckle.

speck-le (spek′l), *n.* a small spot in or on something:—*v.t.* [speck-led, speckling], to mark with speckles:—**speckled trout,** a general term of trout, *Salmo,* embracing Atlantic salmon (*S. salar*), rainbow trout (*S. gairdner*), brown trout *S. trutta*), and cutthroat trout (*S. clarki*): found in Canada from the Atlantic to the Pacific.

spec-ta-cle (spek′ta-kl), *n.* **1,** something displayed to view, esp. something unusual or worthy of notice; a public exhibition; pageant; **2, spectacles,** a pair of lenses for assisting or correcting vision, set in a frame, with a bridge to fit over the nose and bows to pass over the ears.—*adj.* **spec-tac′u-lar.**

spec-tac-u-lar (spek-tak′ū-lér), *n.* a lavishly elaborate television programme, esp. in colour.

spec-ta-tor (spek-tā′tér; spek′tā-tér), *n.* one who looks on, as at a theatre or parade; an observer.

spec-tral (spek′tral), *adj.* **1,** pertaining to, or like, a ghost; ghostly; as, a *spectral* light; **2,** pertaining to a spectrum; as, *spectral* analysis.—*adv.* **spec′-tral-ly.**

spec-tre or **spec-ter** (spek′tér), *n.* a ghost or apparition.

spec-tro-scope (spek′trō-skōp′), *n.* an instrument used for breaking down a beam of light or radiant energy into its component parts.

spec-trum (spek′trum), *n.* [*pl.* spectra (spek′tra) or spectrums], the image formed when light is broken up into its constituent parts and these are arranged according to their different wave-lengths, as in the rainbow or when light passes through a prism.

spec-u-late (spek′ū-lāt′), *v.i.* [speculated, speculat-ing], 1, to meditate; consider a subject from every side before forming an opinion; 2, to buy or sell, with the idea of profiting by a rise or fall in prices.—*n.* spec′u-la′tion.—*adj.* spec′u-la′tive.—*n.* spec′u-la′tor.

speech (spēch), *n.* 1, the power of uttering sounds or words that are understandable; 2, the expression of thought in words; the act of speaking; 3, manner of speaking; as, his *speech* is indistinct; 4, that which is spoken; words; remarks; 5, a language or dialect; as, Italian is a musical *speech;* 6, a formal talk, delivered in public.—*adj.* speech′less.—*n.* speech′less-ness.

speed (spēd), *n.* 1, swiftness of motion; 2, rate of motion; 3, *Archaic,* good fortune; success; as, he wished her all *speed:*—*v.t.* [sped (sped) or speed-ed, speed-ing], 1, to bid farewell to; as, to *speed* the parting guest; 2, to favour; to aid; as, may God *speed you;* 3, to cause to move faster; as, to *speed* an engine; he *sped* the job to completion:—*v.i.* 1, to move quickly; as, the car *sped* toward him; 2, [speed-ed, speeding], to move at too great speed.—*n.* speed′er—*adj.* speed′y.—*adv.* speed′i-ly.—*n.* speed′way′.

speed-om-e-ter (spē-dom′e-tėr), *n.* a device on a vehicle, esp. an automobile, to show the speed in miles per hour and the distance travelled.

¹spell (spel), *n.* 1, a spoken word, or words, supposed to act as a charm; 2, hence, fascination.

²spell (spel), *v.i.* [spelled (speld) or spelt (spelt), spell-ing], to form words with letters:—*v.t.* 1, to give, in order, the proper letters of (a word); 2, to make out or decipher with difficulty; as, to *spell* out an inscription; 3, to make up or form; as, the letters d, o, g, *spell* "dog"; 4, to indicate or mean; as, war *spells* hardship.

³spell (spel), *n.* 1, a turn at work to relieve another; as, a *spell* at the oars; 2, any short period of time; as, a hot *spell;* 3, *Colloq.*, a short attack of illness; as, a dizzy *spell:*—*v.t.* [spelled, spell-ing]

to take the place of, or do a turn for; as, let me *spell* you at the oars.

spell-bound (spel′bound′), *adj.* fascinated; enchanted.

spell-er (spel′ėr), *n.* 1, one who spells, esp. one who spells in a particular way; as, a good *speller;* a poor *speller;* 2, a book with exercises for teaching pupils how to spell; a spelling-book.

spend (spend), *v.t.* [spent (spent), spending], 1, to pay out, as money; expend or use up, as strength or energy; 2, to squander; exhaust; 3, to pass (time); as, I *spent* an hour shopping.—*n.* spend′er.

spend-thrift (spend′thrift′), *adj.* wasteful; extravagant:—*n.* one who spends money foolishly or wastefully.

sperm (spûrm), *n.* the fertilizing fluid of male animals; also, one of the many living germ cells which it contains.—**sperm oil,** a lubricating oil from the head of the sperm whale:—**sperm whale** or **cach′a-lot′,** a large whale (up to 60′ long and 60 tons in weight), found in all oceans: *Moby Dick* was of this species.

spew (spū), *v.t.* to vomit; cast up or forth. Also, **spue.**

sphag-num (sfag′num), *n,* a soft moss from the surface of bogs, used in packing and potting plants, and for surgical dressing of wounds.

sphere (sfēr), *n.* 1, a round, solid body with a continuous surface, every point of which is equally distant from the point within called its centre; 2, a globe or globelike body; a ball; also, a planet; 3, extent or range of knowledge, influence, action, etc.; as, to seek a wider *sphere* for one's abilities.—*adj.* spher′i-cal (sfer′i-kal).

sphe-roid (sfē′roid), *n.* a body nearly spherical, as the earth (an oblate *spheroid,* being flattened at the poles).

sphinx (sfingks), *n.* [*pl.* sphinxes (sfingk′sez)], in *Greek mythology,* a monster with the body of a winged lion and a woman's head and breasts.

spice (spīs), *n.* 1, an aromatic vegetable substance, sometimes ground or powdered, used for seasoning, as cinnamon, nutmeg, or pepper; 2, that which gives flavour or zest; relish; as, a *spice* of humour:—*v.t.* [spiced, spic-ing], to season or flavour with spice or spices.—*adj.* spic′y.

spider (spī′dėr), *n.* 1, a small, insect-like animal, wingless, with four pairs of legs, capable of spinning silken threads of which it makes cocoons for eggs, and in some instances, webs for catching prey; **2,** anything thought to resemble or recall a spider; **3,** a cast-iron frying-pan.—*adj.* **spi'der-y.**

spiel (spēl), *n.* **1,** *Slang,* a talk or speech: —*v.i. Slang,* to talk or speak; **2,** short for **bon'spiel'** (a curling tournament).

spig-ot (spig'ut), *n.* **1,** a plug or peg used to stop a cask; **2,** a tap.

¹spike (spīk), *n.* **1,** a sharp point; **2,** any slender pointed object, as a kind of large nail; **3,** one of the metal pieces fastened to the soles of certain shoes used in sports, to prevent slipping:—*v.t.* [spiked, spik-ing], **1,** to fasten or equip with large nails or sharp points; **2,** to run through with a sharp point; **3,** to make (a gun, cannon, etc.) useless by driving a spike into an opening; **4,** hence, to make ineffective; as, to *spike* gossip.

²spike (spīk), *n.* **1,** an ear of grain; **2,** a long, often tapering, flower-cluster, in which the flowers grow along the sides of the stalk, as in the hyacinth.—*n.* **spike'let** (a secondary spike).

spile (spīl), *n.* a spout or spigot driven into a hole bored in a tree, as the sugar maple, to drain off the sap.

spill (spil), *v.t.* [spilt (spilt) or spilled (spild), spill-ing], **1,** to permit to run over, or fall out of, a vessel or other container; as, don't *spill* the water; **2,** to cause to be scattered, wasted, lost, etc.; as, to *spill* blood:—*v.i.* to flow over, fall out, be scattered, etc.:—*n.* **1,** an overflowing or downpour, as of liquid or rain; **2,** a fall or tumble; **3,** the overflow of a dam.

spill-way (spil'wā'), *n.* a channel for carrying away the overflow of a dam.

spin (spin), *v.t.* [*p.t.* spun (spun) or, *Archaic,* span (span), *p.p.* spun, *p.pr.* spinning], **1,** to draw out and twist (fibre) into threads; as, to *spin* cotton; **2,** to form (a web or cocoon) by drawing out threads of fluid from a gland; said of spiders, silkworms, etc.; **3,** to draw out to some length; as, to *spin* a long story; **4,** to cause to whirl rapidly, as a top:—*v.i.* **1,** to engage in drawing out and twisting fibre into threads, or in making a thread as a spider does; **2,** to whirl; **3,** *Colloq.,* to move swiftly; as, to *spin* along on a bicycle:—*n.* **1,** the act of spinning; esp., a rapid whirling; **2,** *Colloq.,* a short drive, as in an automobile.—*n.* **spin'ner.**

spin-ach (spin'ich; spin'ij), *n.* a common garden vegetable, the leaves of which are cooked and eaten.

spi-nal (spī'nal), *adj.* pertaining to the backbone, or spinal column; as, the *spinal* fluid; a *spinal* puncture.

spin-dle (spin'dl), *n.* **1,** in spinning, a long, thin rod, or a tapering stick, used for twisting and winding the thread; **2,** a slender rod or pin on which something turns.—*adj.* **spin'dling** (long and thin); **spin'dly.**

spin-drift (spin'drift), *n.* spray or foam blown up from the surface of a stormy sea.

spine (spīn), *n.* **1,** the backbone, or spinal column; **2,** something like the backbone in position or function; hence, that which supports or strengthens; endurance or courage; **3,** a stiff, thorn-shaped or pointed growth on a plant, as the hawthorn or barberry, or on an animal, as the hedgehog or porcupine.—*adj.* **spin'y.**—*adj.* **spi'nous; spi'nose.**—*adj.* **spine'less.**

spin-et (spin'it), *n.* an early form of piano.

spin-na-ker (spin'a-kėr), *n.* a large triangular sail used with a light boom (**spinnaker boom**) on the side opposite the mainsail when a yacht is running before the wind.

spin-ning jen-ny, a machine with several spindles so that several threads could be spun at once: invented in 1767.

spin-ning wheel, a hand- or foot-operated machine on which fibres, as cotton or wool, were twisted into thread or yarn.

spin-ster (spin'stėr), *n.* a woman who has not married.—*n.* **spin'ster-hood'.**

spi-rae-a (spī-rē'a), *n.* a shrub, cultivated or wild, bearing small white or pink flowers.

spi-ra-cle (spī'ra-kl), *n.* a small opening for taking in and expelling air or water, as in the whale or some crustaceans, insects, etc.

spi-ral (spī'ral), *adj.* **1,** winding around a fixed point or centre in increasingly larger circles, like a watch-spring; **2,** winding about a cylindrical surface, like the thread of a screw, or the stripes on a barber pole:—*n.* a spiral curve; a curve like that of a watch-spring or the thread of a screw:—*v.i.* and *v.t.* [spiralled, spiral-ling], to follow, or cause to follow, a spiral course; as, the smoke slowly *spiralled* upward; the aeroplane *spiralled* downward.—*adv.* **spi'ral-ly.**

spire (spīr), *n,* **1,** a slender leaf or blade, as of grass; **2,** a form that tapers to a point; esp., the slender, tapering top of a tower or steeple; also, a steeple.

spir-it (spir'it), *n.* **1,** the soul; the immortal, non-physical part of man; **2,** a supernatural being, as a sprite or fairy; a ghost; also, a being without a body; as, departed *spirits;* **3,** a person considered with reference to qualities of mind or character; as, the poet is a noble *spirit;* **4, spirits,** state of mind; mood; as, to be in low *spirits;* **5,** courage; energy and vim; as, the troops advanced with *spirit;* **6,** enthusiasm for an object; as, school *spirit;* **7,** real meaning; intent; as, I expect you to keep the *spirit* as well as the words of your promise; also, the chief characteristic or influence; as, the scientific *spirit* of the 20th century; **8,** (usually *spirits*): **a,** any strong distilled alcoholic liquor, as brandy, whisky, etc.; **b,** an alcoholic solution of certain drugs which evaporate easily; as, *spirits* of ammonia:—**Spirit,** the third person of the Trinity: also called *Holy Spirit, Holy Ghost:*—*v.t.* to carry off (a person) suddenly and secretly.

spir-it-ed (spir'i-tid), *adj.* full of vigour or life; animated; lively; as, a *spirited* horse.

spir-it-u-al (spir'it-ū-al), *adj.* **1,** pertaining to the mind or spirit, as distinguished from matter; **2,** pertaining to the soul or higher nature of man; pure; holy; **3,** pertaining to sacred or religious things; as, *spiritual* guidance:—*n.* a hymn or sacred song, esp. one originating among the Negroes of the southern U.S.—*n.* spir'it-u-al'i-ty.—*adv.* spir'it-u-al-ly.

spir-it-u-al-ism or **spir-it-ism** (spir'it-ū-al-izm; spir'i-tizm), *n.* the belief that departed spirits communicate with the living, esp. through a medium, as by rapping, writing, etc.—*n.* spir'it-u-al-ist.

spir-it-u-ous (spir'i-tū-us), *n.* like or containing, alcohol; as *spirituous* liquors; intoxicating; distilled (as opposed to *fermented*).

spirt (spûrt), *v.t., v.i., n.* Same as **spurt.**

¹spit (spit), *n.* **1,** a long pointed rod or bar, used to hold meat for roasting over an open fire; **2,** a point of land extending into the sea:—*v.t.* [spit-ted, spitting], to pierce with a spit; impale.

²spit (spit), *v.t.* [spat (spat) or, sometimes, spit, spit-ting], **1,** to eject (saliva or blood) from the mouth; **2,** to eject or expel; as, the cannon *spat* fire:—*v.i.* **1,** to eject saliva from the mouth; **2,** to make a hissing noise: said esp. of cats:—*n.* **1,** saliva; **2,** the act of ejecting saliva; **3,** exact likeness; as, she is the spit and image of her mother.—*n.* spit'ter.

spit-ball (spit'bôl'), *n.* **1,** a pellet of chewed paper; **2,** in *baseball*, a pitch made to curve by moistening one side of the ball with saliva: now illegal. Also called a *spitter.*

spite (spīt), *n.* ill will or hatred toward another; malice:—in spite of, in defiance of; notwithstanding:—*v.t.* [spit-ed, spiting], to show malice toward; try to injure or baffle; annoy.—*adj.* spite'ful.

spit-fire (spit'fīr'), *n.* a hot-tempered person.

spit-tle (spit'l), *n.* **1,** spit; saliva; **2,** the froth that surrounds the larvae of spittle insects (froghoppers).

spit-toon (spi-tōōn'), *n.* a vessel into which one may spit; a cuspidor.

splash (splash), *v.t.* **1,** to spatter or toss about; as, to *splash* water; **2,** to spatter or soil with water, mud, etc.:—*v.i.* **1,** to dash or spatter a liquid about in drops; as, don't *splash;* **2,** to move or proceed with a splashing noise; as, to *splash* into, or through, a puddle; **3,** to fall or fly about in drops; as, the paint *splashed* over the floor:—*n.* **1,** a spot or daub; as, I have a *splash* of mud on my dress; **2,** an irregular spot of colour; a blotch; as, the dog has a *splash* of black on his head; **3,** a noise as from sudden, violent contact with water; as, he plunged into the pool with a *splash.*—*adj.* splash'y.—*n.* splash'er.

splat-ter (splat'ẽr), *v.t. and v.i.* to spatter; splash.

splay (splā), *v.t., v.i. and adj.* **1,** to spread out; as *splay*-toed, *splay*-footed; **2,** to bevel, as the outward edge of a doorway, window, etc.

spleen (splēn), *n.* **1,** one of the ductless glands near the stomach, supposed by the ancients to be the seat of anger, melancholy, etc.: **2,** hence, melancholy, ill temper or spite.

splen-did (splen'did), *adj.* magnificent; gorgeous; inspiring; as, a *splendid* spectacle.—*adv.* splen'did-ly.

splen-dour (splen'dẽr), *n.* **1,** dazzling brightness; as, the *splendour* of diamonds; **2,** magnificence; pomp; as, the *splendour* of a king's court. In American usage, **splen'dor.**

splice (splīs), *v.t.* [spliced, splic-ing], **1,** to unite without knots, as two ropes, by interweaving the ends of the strands; **2,** to connect (pieces of wood or metal) by overlapping and making fast the ends:—*n.* the union, or place of union, of slopes, timbers, etc., by splicing.

splint (splint), *n.* **1,** one of a number of thin strips of wood interwoven to form chair seats, baskets, etc.; **2,** a device or appliance for holding in place a broken or fractured bone until it knits.

splin-ter (splin'tẽr), *n.* a thin fragment of wood, metal, etc., split or torn off lengthwise; a fragment:—*v.t.* and *v.i.* to split into long, thin pieces.—*adj.* splin'ter-y.

split (split), *v.t.* [split, split-ting], **1,** to divide or cut lengthwise; as, to *split* wood; **2,** to rend or tear apart; as, the frost *splits* rocks; **3,** to divide or break up into parts; as, to *split* a large class into several sections:—**split hairs,** to make too fine distinctions:—*v.i.* **1,** to burst; break apart; as, my sleeve *split;* **2,** to divide lengthwise, or with the grain; as, wood *splits* easily; **3,** to separate into groups; as, a political party *splits:*—*n.* **1,** a rent or crack; **2,** a division or separation, as in a group. —**split infinitive,** one with a word between the *to* and the verb; as, *to slowly change* (justifiable when used to avoid ambiguity or awkwardness).

splotch (sploch), *n.* a stain; daub; blotch:—*v.t.* to mark with stains or blotches:—*adj.* **splotch'y.**

splurge (splûrj), *n. Colloq.* a showy display or effort; a conceited personal showing off; as, we made a *splurge* and bought new blazers:—*v.i.* to show off.

splut-ter (splut'ẽr), *v.i.* **1,** to speak hastily and confusedly; as, to *splutter* with excitement; **2,** to make a hissing noise; sputter; as, the candles *spluttered* in their holders:—*v.t. Colloq.* to utter in a quick, incoherent manner: —*n.* a confused noise; stir.

spoil (spoil), *v.t.* [spoilt (spoilt) or spoiled (spoild), spoil-ing], **1,** to damage or impair the good qualities of; mar; as, the rain *spoiled* the party; **2,** to indulge (a child) with harmful effects on its character; pamper:—*v.i.* to decay; as, food sometimes *spoils* in warm weather:—*n.* **1,** pillage; plunder; booty; as, they shared the *spoil;* **2,** **spoils,** public offices and the gain derived from them, appropriated as plunder by the successful party in an election.

spoke (spōk), *n.* **1,** one of the bars of a wheel connecting the hub with the rim; **2,** a round or rung of a ladder.

spokes-man (spōks'man), *n.* [*pl.* spokesmen (-men)], a person who speaks for others; an agent or representative.

spon-dee (spon'dē), *n.* a poetic foot of two long or accented syllables [– –]; as, "Rōse frŏm theĭr/sēa-wēed/ chām-bĕrs the/mȳstĭcăl/choĭr ŏf the/sēa-maĭds" (Kingsley's *Andromeda*).

sponge (spunj), *n.* **1,** the porous elastic mass of horny fibres forming the skeleton of certain salt-water animals and capable of absorbing a large quantity of water; also, any of these animals; **2,** the act of bathing or cleaning with a sponge; **3,** any light and porous substance, as raised dough: —*v.t.* [sponged, spong-ing], **1,** to cleanse, wipe out, or dampen with a sponge; as, to *sponge* cloth; **2,** to take up or absorb, as with a sponge; **3,** *Colloq,* to obtain by imposing upon someone; as, to *sponge* a dinner:—*v.i.* **1,** *Colloq.,* to live as a parasite upon others, or to get something without paying for it, by imposing upon someone; **2,** to gather sponges.—*adj.* **spon'gy.**—*n.* **spon'gi-ness.**—*n.* **spong'er.**

spon-sor (spon'sẽr), *n.* **1,** one who endorses or lends support to a person, movement, etc.; as, the *sponsor* of a radio program; **2,** a godfather or godmother:—*v.t.* to endorse or support; as, to *sponsor* a bill in Parliament.

spon-ta-ne-ous (spon-tā'ni-us), *adj.* **1,** acting or springing from natural impulse; as, *spontaneous* applause; **2,** produced by internal forces rather than by an external cause; as, *spontaneous* combustion.—*n.* **spon'ta-ne'i-ty** (spon'-ta-nē'i-ti).

spoof (spoof), *v.t.* and *v.i. Slang,* to deceive as by a yarn or story; hoax; guy.

spook (spook), *n.* a ghost or spirit; apparition: used humorously.—*adj.* **spook'y.**

spool (spool), *n.* a hollow cylinder or reel of wood or metal, with a rim at each end, for winding thread, wire, etc.: —*v.t.* to wind on a spool; as, to *spool* thread.

spoon (spoon), *n.* **1,** a utensil with a shallow bowl at the end of a handle, used in preparing, serving, or eating food; **2,** something resembling a spoon, as an oar with a curved blade:—*v.t.* to take up with, or as with, a spoon. —*n.* **spoon'ful.**

spoon-bill (spoon'bill), *n.* a wading bird with long legs and a bill which is extremely broad and flattened at the tip.

spoon-er-ism (spoon'ẽr-izm), *n.* the

accidental interchange of two sounds; as, it is *kis*tomary to *cuss* the bride; dickens and *chucks.*

spoor (spo͝or), *n.* the track, trail, or scent of a (wild) animal; footprint.

spo-rad-ic (spō-rad′ik), *adj.* occasional; scattered; as, *sporadic strikes; sporadic* outbreaks of disease.

spore (spōr), *n.* a very small cell, occurring in flowerless plants, such as ferns, and in certain plantlike animals. It is capable of developing into a new plant or a new animal.

spor-ran (spōr′an), *n.* a large pouch or purse, often of fur or hair, worn hanging in front of a Scottish kilt.

sport (spōrt), *n.* **1,** pastime; amusement; **2,** jest or pleasantry; as, he said it in *sport;* **3,** mockery or derision; as, they made *sport* of him; **4,** outdoor play or recreation, as hunting or shooting; also, an athletic game, as baseball or hockey; **5,** a person willing to take a chance; a good loser: often called *good sport:—v.i.* **1,** to play or frolic; **2,** to make merry or jest; trifle:—*v.t. Colloq.,* to show off, or wear in public; as, to *sport* a diamond ring:—*adj.* (also *sports*), relating to, or suitable for, outdoor games or recreation; also, adapted to informal outdoor wear; as, *sports* clothes.—*adj.* **sport′ing.**—*adj.* **spor′tive.**—*adj.* **sport′y** (*Colloq.*)

sports-man (spōrts′man), *n.* [*pl.* sportsmen (-men)], **1,** one who engages in sports,esp. hunting, racing, or fishing; **2,** one who is fair and honourable in sports.—*adj.* **sports′man-like′.**— *n.* **sports′man-ship′.**

spot (spot), *n.* **1,** a blot or mark; a discoloured place or stain; as, a *spot* of ink; **2,** a blemish; as, a *spot* on his reputation; **3,** locality; place; as, the exact *spot* where he fell; **4,** a small part of a surface, differing from the background in colour; as, *spots* on a playing-card:—*v.t.* [spot-ted, spot-ting], **1,** to mark with spots; discolour; stain; **2,** to disgrace or blemish; **3,** *Colloq.,* to mark or note; recognize; as, we *spotted* the guilty man:—*v.i.* to become marked or stained; as, velvet always *spots* with water.—*adj.* **spot′ty.**—*n.* **spot′ter**—*adj.* **spot′less.**

spot-light (spot′līt), *n.* **1,** a brilliant beam of light directed at a particular object or person, as an actor on a stage; also, the lamp or apparatus which throws this light; **2,** hence, prominence; public notice; as, his fight against gangsters kept him in the *spotlight.*

spouse (spouz), *n.* either one of a married couple.

spout (spout), *v.t.* **1,** to throw out (liquid) forcibly in a jet or stream, as does a pipe; **2,** to utter pompously; as, to *spout* poetry:—*v.i.* **1,** to come forth with violence in a jet or stream, as blood from a wound; **2,** to force out fluid in a jet or stream, as does a whale; **3,** to speak in a pompous manner:—*n.* **1,** the projecting tube, nozzle, etc., through which a liquid pours; as, the *spout* of a teapot; also, a trough or pipe for carrying rain off a roof; **2,** a stream or jet of liquid.

sprain (sprān), *n.* a severe twisting or straining of the muscles or ligaments around a joint:—*v.t.* to injure by wrenching or twisting severely; as, to *sprain* a wrist.

sprang (sprang), *p.t.* of *spring.*

sprawl (sprôl), *v.i.* **1,** to lie or sit in a careless, ungraceful position; **2,** to move or crawl along awkwardly, as a very young puppy; **3,** to spread in an irregular, straggling manner, as a plant, or a person's handwriting:—*v.t.* to spread or cause to spread awkwardly or ungracefully:—*n.* an awkward spreading position or movement.

¹spray (sprā), *n.* a small branch of a tree or plant, bearing leaves or flowers; sprig; a bouquet; as, a *spray* (of flowers).

²spray (sprā), *n.* **1,** water driven in small drops or particles by the wind, the dashing of waves, etc.; **2,** medicine or other liquid applied, in the form of vapour, by an atomizer or spraying machine; **3,** an instrument for throwing fine drops of liquid or vapour; an atomizer:—*v.t.* **1,** to apply fine drops of liquid to; as, to *spray* trees; **2,** to scatter (a liquid) in fine drops.

spread (spred), *v.t.* [spread (spred), spreading], **1,** to cause to cover a surface; as, to *spread* butter on bread; also, to cover (a surface) with something; as, to *spread* bread with jam; **2,** to unfold; stretch forth; expand; as, the peacock *spreads* his tail; **3,** to publish or make widely known; as, to *spread* the good news; **4,** to place food upon; as, to *spread* the table; **5,** to communicate or carry from person to person; as, flies *spread* disease:—*v.i.* **1,** to be extended over a surface; as, smoke *spread* over the city; **2,** to be dispersed or scattered; as, rumours *spread;* **3,** to be forced apart, as rails: —*n.* **1,** extension; growth; as, the *spread* of civilization; **2,** the limit or area of expansion; as, the *spread* of an eagle's wings; **3,** a covering for a bed, table, etc.; **4,** *Colloq.*, a table set with provisions; a feast; **5,** any substance, as butter or jam, used to spread on bread.—*n.* **spread′er.**

spree (sprē), *n.* **1,** a merry frolic; **2,** a drunken debauch.

sprig (sprig), *n.* **1,** a small branch; a twig or shoot; **2,** an ornamental figure or design in the form of a spray.

spright-ly (sprīt′li), *adj.* [spright-li-er, spright-li-est], vivacious; gay.—*n.* **spright′li-ness.**

spring (spring), *v.i.* [*p.t.* sprang (sprang) *p.p.* sprung, *p.pr.* spring-ing], **1,** to leap; bound; as, to *spring* into action; **2,** to rise suddenly; dart out, as an animal from a covert; **3,** to start up or forth; appear; as, a breeze has *sprung* up; **4,** to result; have a beginning; as, superstitions *spring* from fear; **5,** to recoil; rebound; as, an elastic *springs* back; **6,** to become warped or bent, as a board:—*v.t.* **1,** to reveal or produce with unexpected suddenness; as, to *spring* a surprise; **2,** to release the catch of (a trap); also, to explode or discharge (a mine); **3,** to weaken by a crack or strain; as, I have *sprung* my tennis-racket; also, to develop (an opening) at the seams; as, the roof has *sprung* a leak:—*n.* **1,** the act of springing; a leap; also, the length of the leap; **2,** a contrivance, usually of metal that yields to pressure and returns to its original form when the force is removed; as, automobile *springs;* **3,** the quality of being elastic; as, the *spring* of a rubber band; also, the shooting back from a tense position; recoil; **4,** cause; origin; as, the *springs* of conduct; **5,** a natural fountain or supply of water rising to the surface of the earth; **6,** the season of the year between winter and summer; usually, in the Northern Hemisphere, from March 21 to June 21:—*adj.* pertaining to the spring.—*adj.* **spring′y.** —*n.* **spring′time′; spring′board′.**

spring-er (spring′ẽr). *n.* a spaniel used in rousing game from cover.

sprin-kle (spring′kl), *v.t.* [sprin-kled, spring-kling], **1,** to scatter in small drops or particles; as, to *sprinkle* salt on food; **2,** to spray with small drops or particles; as, to *sprinkle* the lawn:—*v.i.* to rain lightly:—*n.* **1,** a light shower of rain; **2,** a small quantity; as, a *sprinkle* of salt. —*n.* **sprin′kler.**

sprint (sprint), *n.* **1,** a short run at full speed; **2,** a race over a short distance:

—*v.i.* to run a rather short distance at full speed; dash.—*n.* **sprin′ter.**

sprit (sprit), *n.* **1,** a spar extending diagonally upward from a mast to the highest corner of a fore-and-aft sail; **2,** a bowsprit.

sprite (sprīt), *n.* an elf, goblin, or fairy.

sprock-et (sprok′it), *n.* **1,** a toothlike projection as on the outer rim of a wheel, shaped so as to engage with the links of a driving chain; **2,** a wheel having such teeth on its rim.

sprout (sprout) *v.i.* **1,** to begin to grow **2,** to put forth shoots, as the seed of a plant:—*v.t.* to cause to put forth shoots; as, plants may be *sprouted* indoors:—*n.* a new shoot; bud.

¹spruce (sprōōs), *adj.* [spruc-er, spruc-est], smart; trim; neat:—*v.i.* and *v.t.* [spruced, spruc-ing], *Colloq.*, to dress smartly; arrange in a neat and tidy manner.

²spruce (sprōōs), *n.* an evergreen tree bearing cones and needle-shaped leaves; also, its wood.

sprung (sprung), *p.p.* of *spring.*

spry (sprī), *adj.* [spry-er or spr-ier, spry-est or spri-est], nimble; active; agile.

spud (spud), *n.* *Colloq.* a potato.

spue (spū), *v.t.* Same as *spew.*

spume (spūm), *n.* froth, foam; scum.

spun (spun), *p.t.* and *p.p.* of spin.

spunk (spungk), *n.* *Colloq.*, courage; spirit; pluck.—*adj.* **spunk′y.**

spur (spûr), *n.* **1,** a pointed instrument worn on the heel of a horseman's boot, used to urge on a horse; **2,** anything that urges to action; an incentive; as, to offer a prize as a *spur* to good work; **3,** anything resembling a spur, as the hollow, projecting part of the flower in the larkspur and the columbine; **4,** a mountain ridge running out to the side from a range of mountains; **5,** the stiff, sharp spine on a rooster's leg; **6,** a short railway line connected with a main line at only one end; a short railway branch line over which regular service is not maintained:——*v.t.* [spurred, spur-ring], **1,** to prick with a spur; as, to *spur* a horse; **2,** to excite or drive on to action:—*v.i.* to travel with haste: press onward.

spurge (spûrj), *n.* a genus of 280 herbs, shrubs, and trees (*Euphorbia*), including those yielding rubber, tung-oil, tapioca, castor beans, etc: only 4 of the genera are found in Canada.

spu-ri-ous (spū′ri-us), *adj.* not

genuine; false; not authentic; as, *spurious* coins.

spurn (spûrn), *v.t.* **1,** to push away, as with the foot; **2,** to reject with contempt; scorn to accept; as, to *spurn* a suitor.

spurt (spûrt), *v.i.* to gush forth suddenly in a stream or jet; as, water *spurted* from the leak in the pipe:—*v.t.* to throw or force out in a stream or jet; squirt:—*n.* **1,** a sudden gushing forth of liquid; **2,** any brief and sudden outbreak, as of passion or anger; **3,** a sudden and extraordinary burst of strength or energy for a brief period, as in a race; also, a sharp and sudden increase in business.

sput-ter (sput'ẽr), *v.i.* **1,** to throw out small particles, as sparks from burning wood; **2,** to spit small, scattered drops of saliva, as in rapid or excited speech; **3,** to speak rapidly and indistinctly: —*v.t.* to utter in an excited or confused way:—*n.* **1,** the act of sputtering; also, the sound; **2,** excited and indistinct talk; **3,** fuss; bustle.

spu-tum (spū'tum), *n.* spit or saliva, often mixed with mucus from nose, throat, or lungs.

spy (spī), *n.* [*pl.* spies], **1,** a person who enters the enemy's territory secretly in time of war, to gain information; **2,** one who keeps watch on others; a secret agent:—*v.t.* [spied, spy-ing], **1,** to catch sight of, esp. at a distance; as, she *spied* a friend in the crowd; **2,** to watch closely or explore secretly; as, to *spy* out the land:—*v.i.* **1,** to make a careful examination; **2,** to act as a spy.

squab (skwob; skwôb), *n.* a young pigeon.

squab-ble (skwôb'l; skwob'l), *n.* a noisy quarrel; dispute:—*v.i.* [squabbled, squab-bling], to wrangle; dispute noisily.

squad (skwod; skwôd), *n.* **1,** a small party of soldiers assembled for drill, etc.; **2,** any small group of persons engaged in a common effort; as, a *squad* of police.

squad-ron (skwod'run; skwôd'run), *n.* **1,** any group of men in regular formation; **2,** in the British Army, a unit of a cavalry regiment containing four troops; **3,** in the Navy, a group of war vessels employed on a particular service; **4,** a unit of an airplane fleet.

squal-id (skwol'id; skwôl'id), *adj.* extremely dirty and neglected; wret-

ched; as, a *squalid* tenement. —*n.* **squal'or.**

¹squall (skwôl), *n.* **1,** a sudden and violent gust of wind, often accompanied by rain, sleet, or snow; **2,** *Colloq.,* trouble or danger of any sort.—*adj.* **squall'y.**

²squall (skwôl), *v.i.* and *v.t.* to weep, scream, or utter violently, as a child in pain:—*n.* a loud, harsh scream.

squan-der (skwon'dẽr; skwôn'dẽr), *v.t.* to spend lavishly or wastefully.

square (skwâr), *n.* **1,** a plane figure with four right angles and four equal sides; **2,** anything shaped like a square; as, silk *squares* for patchwork; **3,** a city block consisting of a four-sided space on each side of which is a street; **4,** the distance from one cross street to the next; as, the nearest store is three *squares* from our house; **5,** an open space or area, often used as a small park; **6,** an instrument, consisting usually of two straight edges at right angles to each other, used for measuring or laying out right angles; **7,** in *mathematics,* the product obtained by multiplying a number by itself; as, 4 is the *square* of 2:—*v.t.* [squared, squaring], **1,** to give (an object) the shape of a square; **2,** to cause (a line or side) to make a right angle with another; also, to bring into a position producing such an angle; **3,** to balance (accounts); **4,** in *mathematics,* to multiply (a number) by itself:—*v.i.* to accord or agree; coincide; fit; as, his story does not *square* with mine:—*adj.* **1,** having the same shape as a square; **2,** forming a right angle; rectangular; as, a *square* outline; **3,** straight and angular, rather than curved, in outline; as, a *square* jaw; **4,** true; honest; just; as, a man who is *square* in his dealings; **5,** balanced; settled, as accounts; **6,** *Colloq.,* satisfying; substantial; as, a *square* meal:—*adv.* exactly; as, he hit the nail *square* on the head.—*adv.* **square'ly**—*n.* **square'ness.**

square–rigged (skwâr'-rigd'), *adj.* having rectangular sails stretched along yards which are slung horizontally to the mast. A brig is a *square*-rigged craft.

square root, the quantity which, multiplied by itself, produces a given quantity; as, 3 is the *square root* of 9.

¹squash (skwosh; skwôsh), *n.* a green, yellow, or white gourdlike fruit used as a vegetable; also, the vine bearing it.

²squash (skwosh; skwôsh), *v.t.* **1,** to beat or mash into pulp; to crush; **2,** to put down or suppress; as, to *squash* a rumour:—*v.i.* **1**, to fall in a soft mass; be crushed to a pulp, as from a fall; **2**, *Colloq.*, to make a noise like that of a sodden mass falling:—*n.* **1**, a crushed object or mass; **2**, the sudden fall of something soft and heavy; also, the noise made when such a thing falls; **3**, a game similar to tennis, played in a walled court with rackets and a ball.

squat (skwot; skwôt), *v.i.* [squat-ted, squat-ting], **1**, to sit on the heels, or with knees drawn up; **2**, to crouch on the ground, as an animal; **3**, to settle on public land with a view to gaining title to it; also, to settle on new or unoccupied land without permission or right:—*adj.* [squatter, squat-test], **1**, crouching; **2**, short and thick; as, a *squat* vase:—*n.* a squatting position —*n.* **squat′ter.**—*adj.* **squat′ty.**

squaw (skwô), *n.* an American Indian woman.

squaw-fish (skwô′fish), *n.* a long, slender fish of the carp family found in rivers of the northern Pacific coast of Canada and U.S.

squawk (skwôk), *n.* a loud, harsh cry, as of a duck or hen:—*v.i.* to utter a loud, harsh cry: *Slang*, to complain vehemently; protest.

squeak (skwēk), *n.* a short, shrill, sharp sound; as, the *squeak* of a mouse:—*v.i.* **1**, to utter a short, shrill, sharp cry; **2**, to make a grating, disagreeable noise, as a rusty hinge. —*adj.* **squeak′y.**

squeal (skwēl), *n.* a shrill, prolonged cry, as of a pig:—*v.i.* **1**, to utter a shrill, prolonged cry; **2**, *Colloq.* to betray a plot or a companion in a crime or fault.

squeam-ish (skwēm′ish), *adj.* **1**, having a stomach easily upset or nauseated; **2**, easily shocked or disgusted; **3**, dainty; fastidious.

squee-gee (skwē′jē), *n.* **1**, a T-shaped, rubber-edged tool for removing water from windows, decks, etc.; **2**, a rubber roller used in photography to remove water from negatives or prints:—*v.t.* (skwē-jē′), to use a squeegee.

squeeze (skwēz), *v.t.* [squeezed, squeez-ing], **1**, to exert pressure on; compress; as, clothes *squeezed* into a bag; **2**, to draw forth by pressure; extract; as to *squeeze* water from a wet garment; also, to cause to yield juice; as, to *squeeze* a lemon; **3**, to thrust forcibly; crowd into too small a space; as, to *squeeze* people into a hall:—*v.i.* to press; force one's way; push; as, to *squeeze* through a crowd:—*n.* **1**, pressure; a

crowding together; **2**, the act of squeezing.—*n.* **squeez′er.**

squelch (skwelch), *v.t.* to crush; silence by a rebuke; as, to *squelch* a quarrelsome child:—*v.i.* to make a squashing sound, such as is made by walking through slush.

squib (skwib), *n.* **1**, a short, sarcastic or satirical article (or speech), often malicious or abusive in tone; **2**, a broken firecracker, whose powder burns with a fizz; **3**, any ball or roll of paper filled with powder (to be set off).

squid (skwid), *n.* a cigar-shaped, ten-armed, shell-less mollusc: the sea arrow grows to 8″ in length: famed sea-serpents are giant squids up to 50′ long: found on both coasts of Canada and U.S.

squint (skwint), *n.* **1**, the condition of being cross-eyed; **2**, a sidelong, stealthy glance:—*v.i.* **1**, to look sideways; **2**, to have the eyes half closed, as in bright sunlight; **3**, to be cross-eyed:—*v.t.* to half close (the eyes):—*adj.* **1**, looking sideways; **2**, cross-eyed.

squire (skwīr), *n.* **1**, formerly, the shield-bearer of a knight; **2**, in the U.S., a justice of the peace; **3**, in England, the chief landholder of a district; **4**, a lady's escort:—*v.t.* [squired, squir-ing], to accompany (a lady) as a squire or escort.

squirm (skwûrm), *v.i.* to twist about like an eel or a snake; wriggle; writhe.

squir-rel (skwir′el; skwur′el), *n.* a small bushy-tailed, grey, black, or reddish-brown animal that lives mostly in trees and feeds largely on grains and nuts; also, its fur.

squirt (skwûrt), *v.i.* to gush forth in a stream or jet from a small opening; to spurt:—*v.t.* to force out in a quick jet; as, a squid *squirts* an inky liquid;—*n.* **1**, a small stream or jet squirted forth; **2**, an instrument for squirting water or other liquid.

squish (skwish), *v.t.* and *v.i. Colloq.* to squash; squeeze; as, to *squish* mud between the toes.

stab (stab), *v.t.* [stabbed, stab-bing], **1**, to pierce with a pointed weapon; **2**, to wound the feelings of; as, conscience *stabbed* him with remorse:—*v.i.* **1**, to pierce something with a pointed weapon; **2**, to wound a person's feelings:—*n.* **1**, a thrust with a sharp-pointed weapon; **2**, a wound so made.—*n.* **stab′ber.**

stab-i-lize (stā′bi-līz′; stab′i-līz′), *v.t.* [stabilized, stabiliz-ing], **1**, to make firm, steady, regular, or dependable; as, to *stabilize* one's life, or one's income; **2,** to secure or maintain the balance of (a boat or aircraft) by a special device.—*n.* **stab'i-li-za'tion.**—*n.* **stab'i-liz'er.**—*n.* **sta-bil'i-ty.**

¹sta-ble (stā'bl). *adj.* **1,** firm; securely established; hence, having permanence; continuing without change; as, *stable* institutions; **2,** steadfast; unwavering; as, a man of *stable* purpose.

²sta-ble (stā'bl), *n.* a building, usually divided into stalls, in which horses, or sometimes cattle, are housed:—*v.t.* [sta-bled, sta-bling], to put into, or keep in, such a building:—*v.t.* to be so lodged.

stac-ca-to (sta-kä'tō), *adj.* and *adv.* **1,** in *music*, played, or to be played, in an abrupt, disconnected fashion, with breaks between the notes: opposite of *legato;* **2,** expressed in this way; as, a *staccato* remark.

stack (stak), *n.* **1,** a large quantity of hay, wood, etc., piled up in orderly fashion; **2,** a somewhat orderly mass or heap; as, a *stack* of letters; **3,** a chimney; often, a vent for smoke, as on a factory; **4,** rifles, bean poles, etc., arranged to form a pyramid; **5,** a rack or set of shelves for books:—*v.t.* to heap or pile up.

sta-di-um (stā'di-um), *n.* [*pl.* stadia (stā'-di-a) or stadiums], a large structure consisting of seats in tiers around a field which is used for outdoor athletic contests.

staff (stȧf), *n.* [*pl.* staffs or staves (stȧfs; stāvz)], **1,** a pole, rod, or stick used as a support in walking or climbing, as a means of defence, or as an emblem or evidence of authority; **2,** a long, slender pole serving as a support; as, a flag*staff;* **3,** [*pl.* staffs], a body of persons engaged in a single task; as, a teaching *staff;* an office *staff;* also, in the army, a body of assistant advisory officers; **4,** [*pl.* staves], in *music*, the set of five horizontal lines and four intervening spaces on which the notes are written: also called *stave.*

stag (stag), *n.* the full-grown male of the red deer and certain other large deer.

stag bee-tle, a family (of beetles), the males of which have branched, horny, toothed mandibles like a stag's horns.

stage (stāj), *n.* **1,** a raised platform, as in a theatre or concert hall; **2,** the theatre; the theatrical profession; as, she is reluctant to leave the *stage;* **3,** a place or field of action; as, the political *stage;* the scene of any celebrated event or career; as, London was the *stage* of her debut; **4,** a part, or lap, as

of a journey; **5,** degree of progress in any business, process, etc.; a point or period of development; as, an advanced *stage* of civilization; **6,** a stage coach: —*v.t.* [staged, stag-ing], to put (a play) on the stage:—*v.i.* to be adapted to the stage; as, but few poetic plays *stage* well.—*n.* **stage'coach';** **stage'craft'.** —*adj.* **stag'y** (theatrical).

stag-ger (stag'ẽr), *v.i.* to totter or reel; walk unsteadily; as, a drunkard *staggers:*—*v.t.* **1,** to cause to totter or reel; **2,** to shock; as, the truth *staggered* him; **3,** to make less sure or certain; as, the setback *staggered* his self-confidence; **4,** to arrange in shifts; as, working hours were *staggered* so that some workers came at 8, some at 8:30, some at 9; also, to arrange alternately on opposite sides of the centre, as the hub ends of the spokes of a wheel:—*n.* **1,** a reeling or tottering; **2,** staggers, *n.pl.* used as *sing.* a nerve disease of horses, sheep, and cattle, marked by staggering and falling; often called *blind staggers.*

stag-nate (stag'nāt), *v.i.* **1,** to cease to flow or run; be or become motionless; **2,** to be or become inert or dull; **3,** to be or become foul or unwholesome.—*n.* **stag-na'tion.**

stag-nant (stag'nant), *adj.* **1,** not flowing; stale or foul from standing; as, *stagnant* water; **2,** not brisk; sluggish.

staid (stād), *adj.* quiet; sedate; steady.

stain (stān), *n.* **1,** a discoloured spot or blot; **2,** a dye; as, walnut *stain;* **3,** the taint of guilt or crime; as, a reputation without *stain;*—*v.t.* **1,** to blot or spot; as, to *stain* a tie; **2,** to tinge with colouring matter; as, to *stain* walls; **3,** to tarnish or dim:—*v.i.* to take or give a dye or stain.—*adj.* **stain'less.**

stair (stâr), *n.* **1,** any one of a set of steps or treads connecting different levels; **2,** (usually *stairs*), a flight of steps.

stair-case (stâr'kās'), *n.* a flight of steps; a stairway.

stair-way (stâr'wā') *n.* a flight of steps; a staircase.

stake (stāk), *n.* **1,** a strong stick sharpened at one end and fixed into the ground as a marker or support; **2,** the post to which a person condemned to be burned is bound; hence, death by burning; **3,** (often *stakes*), money wagered or risked on an event; as, to play for high *stakes;*—**at stake,** risked or hazarded:—*v.t.* [staked, stak-ing], **1,** to fasten, support, or provide with stakes; as, to *stake* tomatoes; **2,** to mark the limits of; as, he *staked* all he had on the success of his invention.

sta-lac-tite (sta-lak′tīt), *n.* an iciclelike formation of calcium carbonate hanging from the roof of a cave: caused by the dripping of water with a high lime content.

sta-lag-mite (sta-lag′mīt), *n.* a cone of carbonate of lime, often formed under a stalactite and gradually uniting with it to form a column.

stale (stāl), *adj.* [stal-er, stal-est], **1,** not fresh or new; tasteless; dried out: used esp. of food; **2,** worn out by constant repetition or use; as, a *stale* plot; **3,** out of condition, as an athlete who is not in training or who has trained too hard or too long:—*v.t.* [staled, stal-ing], to make stale; destroy the novelty of:—*v.i.* to lose newness or freshness; wear out.

stale-mate (stāl′māt), *n.* **1,** in *chess,* a situation in which the king, not being in check, cannot move without being placed in check, and when no move can be made by any other piece; hence, a draw; **2,** a deadlock:—*v.t.* to bring to a standstill.

¹**stalk** (stôk), *n.* **1,** the stem of a plant, or of a leaf, flower, or fruit; **2,** any stemlike support, as of a goblet.

²**stalk** (stôk), *v.t.* to approach (game) cautiously and under cover:—*v.i.* to walk in a haughty manner:—*n.* **1,** the act of creeping up on game; **2,** a proud, haughty step.

stall (stôl), *n,* **1,** a stable; cattle shed; also, an enclosed space in a stable for one animal; **2,** a table on which goods are exposed for sale; as, a flower *stall;* **3,** a seat in the choir of a church; also, a church pew:—*v.t.* **1,** to place or keep in a stall; **2,** to cause to stick fast or stop; as, the snowdrifts *stalled* the train; unskilled driving *stalled* the engine:—*v.t.* **1,** to stick fast, as in mud; **2,** to come to a forced standstill; cease running.

stal-lion (stal′yun), *n.* a male horse, esp. one kept for breeding purposes.

stal-wart (stôl′wèrt; stol′wèrt), *adj.* **1,** sturdy; strong and muscular; as, a man of *stalwart* build; **2,** brave; daring; as, a *stalwart* fighter:—*n.* a firm, loyal partisan.

sta-men (stā′men), *n.* the pollen-bearing part of a flower. (See *flower,* illustration.)

stam-i-na (stam′i-na), *n.pl.* used as *sing.,* vigour; strength or staying power; power of endurance.

stam-mer (stam′ėr), *v.i.* to hesitate

or falter in speaking; stutter:—*v.t.* to utter with difficulty or hesitation; as, he *stammered* out an excuse:—*n.* **1,** hesitating or faltering speech; **2,** any difficulty in pronouncing; a stutter. —*n.* **stam′mer-er.**

stamp (stamp), *v.t.* **1,** to mark with a design by means of a die, pattern, etc.: as, to *stamp* a coin; **2,** to put a postage or other official stamp upon; as, to *stamp* a letter; **3,** to label; brand; as, our acts *stamp* our characters; **4,** to set (the foot) down heavily; **5,** to crush or grind (ore) into powder; **6,** to shape or cut out, as by pressure of a die or stamp:—**stamp out,** to destroy; end; as, to *stamp out* crime:—*v.i.* to bring down the foot forcibly or with pressure: —*n.* **1,** a mark or design impressed upon a surface; as, the *stamp* on a coin; **2,** a die; **3,** a small piece of paper, sold by the government and stuck to a letter, document, etc., to show payment of a fee or tax; as, a revenue *stamp;* **4,** a characteristic mark or imprint; as, his actions bear the *stamp* of refinement; **5,** a heavy downward blow with the foot: —**stamp-ing ground,** *Colloq.* the place to which an animal or person habitually resorts.

stam-pede (stam-pēd′), *n.* **1,** a sudden, wild running away, as of a herd of animals; **2,** any sudden, impulsive movement on the part of a crowd; a general rush; as, a *stampede* for the exits:—*v.t.* [stamped-ed, stamped-ing], to put to sudden flight; as, to *stampede* cattle:—*v.i.* **1,** to start off in a general panic; **2,** to act together from a sudden impulse.

stance (stans), *n.* **1,** posture; **2,** a position; station; **3,** in *golf,* the position of a player's feet when making a stroke.

stanch or **staunch** (stônch; stánch), *v.t.* **1,** to stop the flow of; as, to *stanch* blood; **2,** to stop a flowing from; as, to *stanch* a wound:—*adj.* (usually *staunch*), **1,** seaworthy, as a ship; **2,** loyal; firm; strong; as, a *staunch* friend.

stan-chion (stan′shun), *n.* an upright, supporting bar, post, or pillar, esp. one of two upright bars, or props, that hold an animal by the head in a stall.

stand (stand), *v.i.* [stood (stood), standing], **1,** to be stationary on the feet in an erect position; **2,** to be in a certain condition, attitude, or position; as, I *stand* ready to pay; he *stands* acquitted; **3,** to be a substitute; as, a pronoun *stands* for a noun; **4,** to remain firm or in force; as, the agreement *stands;* **5,** to maintain a certain attitude toward a question or a principle; as, he *stands* for free trade:— *v.t.* **1,** to set on the feet, or on end, in an upright position; put in place; as, *stand* the broom in the corner; **2,** to put up with; endure; as, to *stand* pain:—*n.* **1,** a stop or halt to maintain a position or to offer resistance; as, they made a *stand* at the river; **2,** position; place of standing; as, he took his *stand* behind the counter; **3,** an outdoor platform for spectators, usually with seats in tiers; **4,** a booth or station used for business; as, a cigar *stand;* **5,** a piece of furniture on which things may be placed or kept; a small table; **6,** a standing growth; as, a good *stand* of wheat.—*n.* **stand′still′.**

stand-ard (stan′dẽrd), *n.* **1,** a figure, flag, etc., used as an emblem; as, to rally around the *standard;* **2,** an established measure of weight, length, quality, etc.; **3,** any state or degree that is accepted as the desirable one; as, a high *standard* of living; **4,** an upright support; as, a lamp on a tall *standard:*—*adj.* **1,** serving as an accepted basis for comparison, reference, etc.; as, *standard* time; **2,** of a certain or recognized level of excellence; as, *standard* English.—*v.t.* **stand′ard-ize′.**

stan-dard time, official civil time. Canada has seven standard time zones, each based on a specific meridian: Newfoundland (St. John's meridian, 3½ hours slower than Greenwich time), Atlantic (60°), Eastern (75°), Central (90°), Mountain (105°), Pacific (120°), and Yukon (135°). Atlantic is 4 hrs. behind Greenwich time, and Yukon 9 hrs. behind.

stand—by (stand′-bī′), *n.* [*pl.* –bys], *Colloq.* one who, or that which, may be depended upon.

stand-off-ish (stand′ôf′ish), *adj.* aloof; reserved; unsocial.

stand-point (stand′point′), *n.* a position, principle, or standard from which things are considered or judged; as, from the *standpoint* of justice, the man should be given a fair trial.

stank (stangk), *p.t.* of *stink.*

stan-za (stan′zä), *n.* a group of lines or verses, varying in number, forming a unit or section of a poem or song.

¹sta-ple (stā′pl), *n.* **1,** the chief thing produced in a district; as, wheat is the *staple* of the Northwest; **2,** the principal part, or an important element, of something; chief item; as, bread is a *staple* of most meals; **3,** raw material for manufacture; **4,** the fibre of cotton,

flax, or wool; as, wool of long *staple:*—*adj.* **1,** important because produced regularly and in large amounts; as, *staple* goods; **2,** in commerce, fixed; as, a *staple* demand:—*v.t.* [sta-pled, sta-pling], to sort according to the quality of its fibre; as, to *staple* wool.

²sta-ple (stā′pl), *n.* a small, U-shaped piece of metal which may be driven into wood, and into which is fitted a hook or other locking device, as on a door or gate; also, a small piece of light wire bent to hold papers together—*n.* **sta′pler.**

star (stär), *n.* **1,** any heavenly body seen as a point of light; **2,** a figure whose points make it look like a star, as an asterisk; **3,** in *astrology,* a planet supposed to influence a person's life; **4,** a brilliant, outstanding person, esp. on the stage or in athletics:—*v.t.* [starred, star-ring], **1,** to deck or adorn with stars; **2,** to cast (a person) as the principal actor in a play:—*v.i.* **1,** to be illustrious or prominent; **2,** to appear as the principal actor in a play.—*adj.* **star′less.**—*adj.* **star′like′.**—*n.* **star′dom** (as, he attained *stardom* on TV).—*n.* **star′gaz′er; star′light′.**—*adj.* **star′lit.**

star-board (stär′bẽrd; stär′bōrd), *n.* the right side of the ship as one faces the bow: opposite of *port:*—*adj.* on the right side of a ship; as, a *starboard* cabin:—*v.t.* to turn to the starboard side of a ship; as, to *starboard* the helm.

starch (stärch), *n.* **1,** a white, odourless, tasteless substance obtained commercially from grain and potatoes, but found in nearly all plants; **2,** a commercial preparation of this substance used in laundering to stiffen fabrics or clothes; **3,** hence, stiffness of conduct or manner:—*v.t.* to stiffen with starch. —*adj.* **starch′y.**

stare (stâr), *v.i.* [stared, star-ing], **1,** to look with eyes wide open; gaze fixedly in one direction; **2,** to glare, as lights or bright colours:—*v.t.* to be visible to; confront; as, disaster *stared* them in the face; also, to embarrass or dismay by staring; as, she *stared* him down: —*n.* a fixed steady look with wide-open eyes.

star-fish (stär′fish′), *n.* a sea animal with a body shaped like a star. It usually has five arms, or rays.

stark (stärk), *adj.* **1,** stiff; rigid; as, *stark* with cold; **2,** utter; complete; as, *stark* nonsense:—*adv.* wholly; as, *stark* naked.—*adv.* **stark′ly.**

STARFISH (⅛)

star-light (stär′līt′), *n.* light from the stars:—*adj.* lighted by the stars.

star-ling (stär′ling), *n.* a bird, varying in plumage from brown with light speckles in winter to greenish black in summer, brought to America from Europe and now something of a pest. The starling is a sociable bird flying in flocks, and building near human habitations.

star-ry (stär′i), *adj.* [star-ri-er, star-ri-est], **1,** spangled or lighted with stars; as, a *starry* night; **2,** shining like stars; as, *starry* eyes.—*n.* **star′ri-ness.**

start (stärt), *v.i.* **1,** to spring suddenly; leap; bound; **2,** to make a sudden involuntary movement, as of surprise, pain, or shock; **3,** to begin; set out; as, to *start* on a journey; to *start* in business; **4,** to become loosened, as a nail or screw:—*v.t.* **1,** to originate action in; set going; as, to *start* a clock; **2,** to rouse suddenly, as game; **3,** to originate; begin; as, to *start* a quarrel; **4,** to loosen (a nail); **5,** to cause or help (a person) to begin; as, to *start* a man in business:—*n.* **1,** a sudden leap or bound; an involuntary movement, caused by surprise, fear, or joy; as, the prisoner gave a *start* when he heard the sentence; **2,** a brief effort; as, to work by fits and *starts;* **3,** a beginning; as, a *start* in business; **4,** a lead or advantage; as, he had a good *start.*—*n.* **start′er.**

star-tle (stär′tl), *v.t.* [star-tled, star-tling], to cause to start or move suddenly; scare; shock; as, the noise *startled* her.

starve (stärv), *v.i.* [starved, starv-ing], to suffer or die from extreme hunger:—*v.t.* to cause to suffer or die from hunger.—*n.* **star-va′tion.**—*n.* and *adj.* **starve′ling.**

stash (stash), *v.t.* and *v.i. Slang,* to hide or store away in a safe place (money or valuables) for future use.

state (stāt), *n.* **1,** the condition in which a person or thing is; as, a *state* of health; a confused *state* of affairs; **2,** great style or formal dignity; as, to receive an ambassador in *state;* **3,** a body of people united under one government; a commonwealth; **4,** the territory or the civil powers of such a commonwealth; **5,** (often *State*), one of several political units forming a federation; as, the *State* of Texas:—*adj.* **1,** pertaining to a state; as, a *state* tax; **2,** formal; ceremonious; as, *state* occasions:—*v.t.* [stat-ed, stat-ing], to set forth clearly and formally; tell; declare; as, to *state* the facts.

stat-ed (stāt′id), *adj.* fixed; regular; as, a *stated* meeting; at *stated* times.

state-craft (stāt′kråft′), *n.* the art of managing the political affairs of a commonwealth or state; statesmanship.

state-ly (stāt′li), *adj.* [state-li-er, state-li-est], having a grand or imposing appearance or manner; noble; majestic; as, a *stately* tree.—*n.* **state′li-ness.**

state-ment (stāt′ment), *n.* **1,** the act of presenting or expressing formally in words; also, that which is so expressed; **2,** a report or summary of financial condition; as, a bank *statement.*

state-room (stāt′rōōm′), *n.* a private room or compartment on a passenger vessel or in a railroad car.

states-man (stāts′man), *n.* [*pl.* statesmen (-men)], one skilled in public affairs and the art of government.—*adj.* **states′man-like′.**—*n.* **states′man-ship′.**

stat-ic (stat′ik), *n.* in *radio,* a sharp, jarring noise made by electrical disturbances, such as thunderstorms, in the air:—*adj.* **1,** pertaining to bodies at rest, or to forces in balance; **2,** standing still; inactive; **3,** in *radio,* caused by static.

stat-ics (stat′iks), *n. pl.* used as *sing.,* the branch of dynamics that treats of bodies, masses, or forces, at rest or in equilibrium.

sta-tion (stā′shun), *n.* **1,** a place where a person or thing usually remains; position; as, the guard took his *station* before the door; **2,** the place to which a person or force is appointed for duty; as, a fire *station;* **3,** a regular stopping place on a railroad; also, the buildings there; **4,** rank; standing; as, a man of high *station:*—*v.t.* to set or place in a certain position; assign; as, to *station* troops on the border.

sta-tion-ar-y (stā′shun-ėr-i), *adj.* **1,** not to be moved; fixed; as, a *stationary* tub; **2,** without change in condition, numbers, etc.; stable; as, a *stationary* population.

sta-tion-er-y (stā′shun-ėr-i), *n.* paper and other writing materials.

sta-tis-tics (sta-tis′tiks), *n. pl.* **1,** numerical facts or data relating to a community, a special industry, etc., collected and arranged for study; **2,** *pl.* used as *sing.* the science of collecting and interpreting such data.—*adj.* **sta-tis′ti-cal.**—*n.* **stat′is-ti′cian.**

sta-tor (stā′tėr; stat′ėr), *n.* in a dynamo, etc., the stationary part that influences or reacts upon a rotating part: opposite of *rotor*.

stat-u-ar-y (stat′u-ẽr-i), *n*. 1, the art of sculpture; 2, a collection of statues.

stat-ue (stat′ū), *n*. the figure of a person or an animal, sculptured, as in marble, or cast, as in bronze.—*adj*. **stat′u-esque′.**—*n*. **stat′u-ette′.**

stat-ure (stat′ūr), *n*. the height of a person or an animal; as, a man of average *stature*.

sta-tus (stā′tus), *n*. [*pl*. statuses], 1, the position, state, or condition of a person; standing; as, the *status* of an alien; 2, the position or condition of affairs; as, what is the present *status* of the negotiations?

sta-tus quo (stā′tus kwō′; stat′), *n*. the existing state of things.

stat-ute (stat′ūt), *n*. an ordinance or law passed by a law-making body.—*adj*. **stat′u-to-ry.**

staunch (stônch; stânch), *v.t*. and *adj*. Same as **stanch**.

stave (stāv), *n*. 1, a staff or heavy stick; 2, one of the curved, narrow strips of wood forming the sides of a cask or barrel; 3, a verse or stanza; 4, in *music*, the set of five horizontal lines and four intervening spaces on which the notes are written; a staff:—*v.t*. [*p.t*. and *p.p*. staved (stāvd) or stove (stōv), *p.pr*. stav-ing], 1, to knock a hole through the side of; as, to *stave* in a barrel or a boat; 2, to keep back or drive away; as, to *stave* off disease.

stay (stā), *v.t*. 1, to put off; postpone; as, to *stay* a trial; 2, to satisfy for a time; as, to *stay* the stomach:—*v.i*. 1, to remain; wait; as, you must *stay* until I return; 2, to dwell temporarily; as, to *stay* at a hotel; *stay* south for the winter:—*n*. 1, a postponement; as, the *stay* of a trial; 2, a prop or support; esp., a rope or wire used to steady or support a mast or spar on a vessel; 3, one that supports; as, he is the *stay* of the family; 4, a stop or halt; sojourn; as, a *stay* of three days; 5, **stays**, a corset.—**in stays**, heading into the wind while going about from one tack to the other.

stay-sail (stā′sl), *n*. any sail on a stay (strong rope or wire); a jib.

stead (sted), *n*. 1, the place which another had or might have; as, to go to war in another's *stead;* 2, use; service; advantage; as, it will stand you in good *stead*.

stead-fast or **sted-fast** (sted′fast),

adj. 1, fixed firmly; immovable; as, the troops stood *steadfast*; 2, steady; constant; as, *steadfast* faith.—*adv*. **stead′fast-ly.**

stead-y (sted′i), *adj*. [stead-i-er, stead-i-est], 1, firmly fixed or supported; as, a *steady* foundation; 2, constant in feeling or purpose; resolute; unwavering; as, a *steady* faith; 3, regular; uniform; even; as, a *steady* tread; 4, sober; industrious; as, a *steady* young man:—*v.t*. and *v.i*. [steadied, steadying], to make or become steady.—*adv*. **stead′i-ly.**—*n*. **stead′i-ness.**

steak (stāk), *n*. a slice of beef or other meat cut for broiling or frying.

steal (stēl), *v.t*. [*p.t*. stole (stōl), *p.p*. sto-len (stō′len), steal-ing], 1, to take by theft; take without leave or right; 2, to take or get by craft or surprise; as, to *steal* a kiss; 3, to gain gradually; as, the child *stole* its way into the man's heart:—*v.i*. 1, to take what belongs to another; 2, to move or act stealthily or secretly; as, to *steal* about on tiptoes:—*n*. a theft; also, that which is stolen.

stealth (stelth), *n*. secret means used to accomplish an object; secret action.—*adj*. **stealth′y.**

steam (stēm), *n*. 1, the invisible vapour which rises from boiling water; 2, this vapour used as a source of power; as, the engine was driven by *steam*:—*v.i*. 1, to throw off visible vapour; as, a teakettle *steams*; 2, to rise or pass off in visible vapour; as, moisture *steams* from the earth; 3, to move under the power of steam; as, the vessel *steamed* away:—*v.t*. to expose to, or treat by, steam.—*adj*. **steam′y.**—*n*. and *v*. **steam′rol′ler.**

steam-boat (stēm′bōt′), *n*. a ship driven by steam.

steam-er (stēm′ẽr), *n*. 1, a steamship; 2, an apparatus in which articles are subjected to steam.

steam-ship (stēm′ship), *n*. a vessel driven by steam power.

sted-fast (sted′fast), *adj*. Same as **stead-fast**.

steed (stēd), *n*. a horse, esp. a spirited war or parade horse.

steel (stēl), *n*. 1, an alloy of iron and carbon, treated to make a hard, tough metal; 2, any instrument or weapon of steel; 3, a piece of steel for striking fire from flint:—*adj*. made of steel; as, a *steel* blade:—*v.t*. to make hard or strong; as, to *steel* one's courage.—*adj*. **steel′y.**

steel-head (stēl′hed′), *n*. a large rainbow trout of the Pacific Coast.

¹steep (stēp), *adj.* **1,** having a sharp pitch or slope; nearly vertical; as, a *steep* cliff; **2,** *Colloq.*, very high; as, *steep* prices:—*n.* a cliff or precipice.—*adv.* **steep′ly.**

²steep (stēp), *v.t.* **1,** to soak, usually in a liquid just below the boiling-point; as, to *steep* tea; **2,** to soak or dye; hence, to saturate; fill thoroughly; as, the sun *steeped* the valley in sunshine:—*v.i.* to be soaked or steeped in a liquid.

stee-ple (stē′pl), *n.* a high tapering tower above the roof of a church.

stee-ple-chase (stē′pl-chās′), *n.* **1,** a cross-country race on horseback; **2,** any race over a course made difficult with artificial obstacles.—*n.* **stee′ ple-chas′-ing.**—*n.* **stee′ple-chas′er.**

stee-ple-jack (stē′pl-jak′), *n.* a workman who climbs steeples, smokestacks, etc., to paint or repair them.

¹steer (stēr), *n.* a bull, or male of the family of domestic cattle, that has been castrated, esp. one that is to be slaughtered for market.

²steer (stēr), *v.t.* to direct or guide (a ship, automobile, etc.) by means of a rudder, wheel, or other gear:—*v.i.* **1,** to direct a ship, vehicle, etc., in its course; **2,** to direct one's course in a given direction; as, *steer* toward shore; **3,** to obey the helm; be steered.

steer-age (stēr′ij), *n.* that part of a ship set aside for passengers paying the lowest rates.

steer-age-way (stēr′ij-wā′), *n.* the least speed needed to make a ship react to its helm.

steg-o-sau-rus (steg′o-sô′rus), *n.* a reptile (18′ to 40′ long) of the age of dinosaurs, having a small head and heavy, bony plates with sharp spines along the back.

stel-lar (stel′ẽr), *adj.* **1,** relating to the stars; as, *stellar* photography; **2,** excellent; as, a *stellar* performance.

¹stem (stem), *n.* **1,** the main stalk of a plant; also, any slender stalk that bears a leaf, flower, or fruit; **2,** any shaft, support, or handle, resembling the stalk of a plant; as, the *stem* of a wineglass; **3,** the curved wooden or metal piece to which the two sides of a ship are joined in the front; as, from *stem* to stern; **4,** the part of a word to which various endings may be attached:—*v.t.* [stemmed, stem-ming], to pluck the stem or stems from; as, to *stem* cherries.

²stem (stem), *v.t.* [stemmed, stem-ming], **1,** to stop or check; dam up; as, to

stem a flow of water; **2,** to make headway against; as, to *stem* the tide.

stench (stench), *n.* a strong, disagreeable odour; very bad smell; stink.

sten-cil (sten′sil), *n.* **1,** a thin sheet of metal, paper, etc., cut with an open pattern, so that, when it is placed on a surface and colour is brushed over it, the design appears on the surface beneath; **2,** a design or decoration so made:—*v.t.* [stencilled, stencil-ling], to mark or decorate in this manner.

ste-nog-ra-phy (ste-nog′ra-fi), *n.* a rapid, abbreviated method of writing; shorthand; also, the process of taking dictation in shorthand notes and transcribing them.—*n.* **ste-nog′ra-pher.**—*adj.* **sten′o-graph′ic.**

sten-to-ri-an (sten-tō′ri-an), *adj.* very loud; as, *stentorian* tones.

step (step), *v.i.* [stepped, step-ping], **1,** to move the feet alternately, as in walking forward, backward, or sidewise; **2,** to walk, esp. a short distance; as, to *step* across the street; **3,** to take possession without effort; as, to *step* into a fortune; **4,** to place the foot (on); as, to *step* on a tack:—*v.t.* **1,** to set or place (the foot); **2,** to measure by steps; as, to *step* off a yard; **3,** to place the heel, or foot, of (a mast) in the socket:—*n.* **1,** the complete movement made in raising and setting down the foot, as in walking or dancing; a pace; **2,** the distance gained in one such movement; hence, any short distance; **3,** a degree of progress; as, a *step* nearer to fame; **4,** a tread in a stairway; **5,** one of a series of actions or measures; as, the first *step* in an undertaking; **6,** in *music*, the interval between two successive degrees on a scale or staff.—*n.* **step′per; step′ping—stone′.**

step-broth-er (step′bruth′ẽr), *n.* the son, by a former marriage, of one's stepfather or stepmother.

step-child (step′chīld′), *n.* [*pl.* stepchildren], the child, by a former marriage, of one's husband or wife.

step-daugh-ter (step′dô′tẽr), *n.* the daughter, by a former marriage, of one's husband or wife.

step-fa-ther (step′fä′thẽr), *n.* the husband of one's mother by a later marriage.

step-lad-der (step′–lad′ẽr), *n.* a short, portable set of steps, supported at the back by a hinged prop.

step-moth-er (step′muth′ẽr), *n.* the wife of one's father by a later marriage.

steppe (step), *n.* a vast level plain without forests, as in Siberia.

step-sis-ter (step′sis′tėr), *n.* the daughter, by a former marriage, of one's stepfather or stepmother.

step-son (step′sun′), *n.* the son, by a former marriage, of one's husband or wife.

ster-e-o— (ster′i-ō–), *prefix,* meaning *three-dimensional, firm,* or *solid,* as in ster′e-o-scop′ic or ster′e-o-scope′ (an optical instrument that gives three-dimensional effect to a photograph), and ster′e-o-type′ (a one-piece printing plate cast in type metal from a mould of a printing surface, as a page of type).

ster-e-o-phon-ic (ster′i-ō-fon′ik), *adj.* pertaining to the use of several loud speakers so placed or combined as to impart greater realism or fidelity to sound recordings.

ster-e-op-ti-con (ster′i-op′ti-kon; stē′ ri-op′ti-kon), *n.* a kind of magic lantern for magnifying and projecting pictures on a screen.

ster-ile (ster′īl; ster′il), *adj.* **1,** not fertile or fruitful; barren; not producing fruit, seed, crops, or young; **2,** free from living germs or microbes; as, a *sterile* bandage.—*n.* ste-ril′i-ty.—*v.t.* ster′i-lize′.—*n.* ster′i-li-za′tion.

ster-ling (stûr′ling), *n.* English money; as, *sterling* rose when the U.S. went off the gold standard:—*adj.* **1,** of standard weight or purity; as, *sterling* silver; **2,** pure; genuine; of acknowledged worth; as, a *sterling* character.

¹stern (stûrn), *adj.* **1,** severe; rigorous; strict; as, *stern* discipline; **2,** forbidding; repelling; as, a *stern* look.—*adv.* stern′ly.

²stern (stûrn), *n.* the aft or rear part of a vessel.

steth-o-scope (steth′o-skōp′), *n.* an instrument used by doctors for listening to the sounds made by heart, lungs, etc.

ste-ve-dore (stē′vi-dôr′), *n.* one who loads and unloads ship cargoes.

stew (stū), *v.t.* and *v.i.* to boil slowly; simmer:—*n.* **1,** a dish of food, usually of meat and vegetables, prepared by simmering; **2,** *Colloq.,* nervous anxiety; worry.

stew-ard (stū′ėrd), *n.* **1,** one who manages the household affairs of a family or institution; also, the manager of a large estate or farm; **2,** a person employed at a hotel, club, or on board ship, as a waiter or an attendant in staterooms; **3,** one who controls financial affairs: as, the *steward* of a

church.—*n. fem.* stew′ard-ship′.

stew′ard-ess.—*n.*

¹stick (stik), *n.* **1,** a piece of wood, generally long and slender; a small branch from a tree or shrub; **2,** something long and slender, as a long piece of candy, a cane, the baton of a musical director, etc.; **3,** a sports implement; as, a hockey or lacrosse *stick.*

²stick (stik), *v.t.* [stuck (stuk), stick-ing], **1,** to puncture with a pointed instrument; prick; pierce; as, he *stuck* his hand with a pin; to cause (a pin or a needle) to go through fabric; **2,** to attach or hold in place by means of a point; as, to fasten in place by causing to adhere; as, to *stick* a stamp on an envelope; **3,** to push or thrust (something); as, he *stuck* the letter under the door:—*v.i.* **1,** to penetrate by means of a pointed end; as, the pin *stuck* in his arm; **2,** to adhere closely; as, dough *sticks* to the hands; **3,** to stay in one place; as, to *stick* at home; **4,** to hold fast; as, he *sticks* to his ideals; **5,** to persist; persevere; as, to *stick* to a job; **6,** to protrude; as, his handkerchief *stuck* out of his pocket; **7,** to be checked; lose the power of motion; as, to *stick* in a rut; hence, to become blocked or jammed; as, an engine *sticks;* **8,** to be checked by fear; hesitate; as, to *stick* at nothing.—*n.* stick′er.

stick-le-back (stik′l-bak′), *n.* a small pugnacious, spiny-backed, scaleless fish: there are 5 Canadian varieties: the 3-spined on both coasts, the 5-spined (or brook) in inland waters, and the 2-, 4-, and 9-spined in both sea and fresh waters.

stick-y (stik′i), *adj.* [stick-i-er, stick-i-est], **1,** tending to stick or adhere, like glue; **2,** *Colloq.,* hot and humid; as, *sticky* weather.—*n.* stick′i-ness.

stiff (stif), *adj.* **1,** not easily bent; rigid; firm; as, *stiff* cardboard; also, moved or bent with difficulty or with pain; as, a *stiff* knee; **2,** not easily operated; not working smoothly; as, a *stiff* engine; **3,** strong; fresh; as, a *stiff* breeze; **4,** unnatural; formal; as, a *stiff* manner; **5,** firm; thick; not fluid; as, *stiff* gelatin; **6,** difficult; as, a *stiff* test; **6,** *Colloq.,* high; dear; as, a *stiff* charge.—*adv.* stiff′ly.

stiff-en (stif′en), *v.t.* and *v.i.* to make or become rigid, stiff, or less flexible.

sti-fle (stī-fl), *v.t.* [sti-fled, sti-fling], **1,** to suffocate; smother; **2,** to put out (a fire); also, to stop or muffle (sounds); **3,** to suppress; choke back; as, to *stifle* a yawn.

stig-ma (stig'ma), *n.* **1,** [*pl.* stigmas], a mark of disgrace or dishonour; as, the *stigma* attached to a prison term; **2,** [*pl.* stigmata (stig'ma-ta)], a distinguishing mark; esp., the sign of some particular disorder; as, the *stigmata* of hysteria; **3, stigmata,** marks resembling the wounds on the body of Christ, said to have appeared on the bodies of certain saints; **4,** [*pl.* stigmas], the upper part of a flower pistil on which the pollen falls (see illustration under *flower*).—*v.t.* **stig'ma-tize'.**

stig-ma-tism (stig'ma-tism), *n.* the normal condition of the eye in focusing on a single point rays of light from a single point: opposite of **a-stig'ma-tism.**

stile (stīl), *n.* **1,** a set of steps leading over a fence or wall; also, a turnstile; **2,** in framing or panelling, a vertical side-piece.

sti-let-to (sti-let'ō), *n.* [*pl.* stilettos or stilettoes], **1,** a small, slender dagger; **2,** a tool for making holes in needlework.

¹**still** (stil), *adj.* **1,** motionless; also, peaceful and calm; tranquil; as, a *still* pond; **2,** quiet; silent; as, a *still* evening:—*n. Poetic,* stillness; profound silence:—*adv.* **1,** up to this time; up to any particular time; as, he is *still* sleeping; he was *still* sleeping when I saw him; **2,** nevertheless; in spite of something; as, though he failed, his friends loved him *still;* **3,** even; as, louder *still;—conj.* however; yet; as, he was in pain; *still* he uttered no sound:—*v.t.* to check motion, disturbance, or sound in; calm; put at rest; as, to *still* a baby; *still* one's fears.

²**still** (stil), *n.* an apparatus for distilling alcoholic liquors.

still-born (stil'bôrn')—*adj.* dead at birth.

still-son wrench, a wrench used esp. for turning pipes, made with a movable jaw so pivoted that its grip is tightened as turning force is applied to the handle.

stilt (stilt), *n.* one of a pair of wooden poles, each with an elevated footrest. They are used to hold one high above the ground in walking.

stilt-ed (stilt'id), *adj.* pompous; stiffly formal; as *stilted* speech.

stim-u-lant (stim'ū-lant), *n.* **1,** that which excites or spurs on; **2,** that which quickens some bodily function for a short time; as, coffee is a heart *stimulant.*

stim-u-late (stim'ū-lāt'), *v.t.* [stim-

ulat-ed, stimulat-ing], **1,** to rouse to activity; animate; as, danger *stimulated* us to action; **2,** to produce greater activity in; as, coffee *stimulates* the heart.—*n.* **stim'u-la'tion.**

stim-u-lus (stim'ū-lus), *n.* [*pl.* stimuli (stim'ū-lī)], **1,** something that rouses to action; **2,** something that excites an organ or tissue to a specific activity.

sting (sting), *n.* **1,** the sharp, often poisonous, organ with which certain animals, as the scorpion and bee, are armed; **2,** the thrust of such an organ; also, the wound made by it; **3,** keen, smarting, mental or physical pain: —*v.t.* [stung (stung), sting-ing], **1,** to prick or wound with a sharp point; cause a sharp, smarting pain to; as, cold *stings* the face; **2,** to incite to action, as by taunts:—*v.i.* **1,** to be sharply painful; as, my eyes *sting;* **2,** to be able to prick and wound; as, bees and wasps *sting.*—*n.* **sting'er.**

stin-gy (stin'ji), *adj.* [stin-gi-er, stin-gi-est], **1,** meanly saving of money; miserly; **2,** scanty; meagre; as, a *stingy* portion.—*n.* **stin'gi-ness.**

stink (stingk), *n.* an offensive odour; disgusting smell:—*v.i.* [*p.t.* stank (stangk) or stunk (stungk), *p.p.* stunk, *p.pr.* stinking], to throw off a strong, offensive odour.—*n.* **stink'er.**

stink-bug (stingk'bug'), *n,* any of various small bugs which give forth an unpleasant odour.

stink-weed (stingk'wēd'), any of the various plants, as the Jimson weed, with strong offensive scent.

stint (stint), *v.t.* to keep within narrow limits; skimp; as, to *stint* food; to limit to a scant allowance; as, to *stint* a child:—*v.i.* to be sparing or frugal: —*n.* **1,** a limit or bound; as, generosity without *stint;* **2,** a task assigned; as, his weekly *stint* was to cut the grass. —*adj.* **stint'ed.**

sti-pend (stī'pend), *n.* **1,** fixed pay for services; salary; **2,** a periodic payment, as a pension.

stip-ple (stip'l), *v.t.* to paint or draw by means of light touches or dots.—*n.* the effect so produced.—*n.* **stip'pler.**

stip-u-late (stip'ū-lāt'), *v.t.* [stipulat-ed, stipulat-ing], to arrange or settle definitely; specify; as part of an agreement; as, he *stipulated* that he be paid in advance.—*n.* **stip'u-la'tion.**

stir (stûr), *v.t.* [stirred, stir-ring], **1,** to change the position of; move; as, he *stirred* neither hand nor foot; **2,** to set in motion; as, the wind *stirred* the leaves; **3,** to shake or mix up the parts of, by moving, beating, poking, etc., with some utensil; as, *stir* the cake with a spoon; *stir* the fire with a poker; **4,** to move or rouse; as, to *stir* men to pity:—*v.i.* **1,** to move or be moved; budge; as, he would not *stir* from his chair; **2,** to be in motion; as, the leaves *stirred* in the trees; **3,** to be roused; as, pity *stirred* in his heart:—*n.* **1,** the act of stirring or mixing; as, give the soup a *stir;* **2,** hustle; excitement; as, his announcement created quite a *stir.*

stir-rup (stir′up; stûr′up), *n.* one of a pair of loop-shaped supports for the feet of a horseback rider, attached to the saddle by a strap.

stitch (stich), *n.* **1,** in *sewing,* a single passing of a threaded needle in and out of the material; also, the section of thread left in the fabric; **2,** in *knitting, crocheting,* and such work, a single complete movement of the needle or hook; also, the link or loop so formed; **3,** a particular type of stitch or arrangement of stitches, as the buttonhole stitch in needlework; **4,** a sudden, sharp pain; as, a *stitch* in the side:—*v.t.* to join by stitches; hence, to sew; also, to ornament by stitches:—*v.i.* to sew.—*n.* **stitch′er.**

stoat (stōt), *n,* the ermine, esp. when in its brown summer coat.

stock (stok), *n.* **1,** a wooden stump or block; **2,** hence, a dull or senseless person; also, the object or butt of some action or notice; as, a laughing*stock;* **3,** the main stem or trunk of a plant or tree; also, a growing plant in which a graft is placed, as a quince *stock;* **4,** the race or line of a family; ancestry; as, he comes of old *stock;* **5,** the part of an implement or machine that serves as the body or main support for other parts, as the part of a gun to which the barrel, lock, etc., are attached, the cross-piece of an anchor, etc. (see illustration under *anchor*); **6,** the capital of a corporation in the form of shares; **7,** the supply of goods which a merchant keeps on hand; as, to replenish *stock;* **8,** hence, a supply of anything; as, a *stock* of information; **9,** domestic animals kept on a farm; livestock; **10,** raw material ready for manufacture; as, paper *stock;* also, the juices of meats or vegetables from which soups, gravies, etc., are made; **11,** a close-fitting wide band or cloth for the neck; **12,** a company of actors presenting one play after another; **13,** a commonly cultivated plant with

single or double sweet-scented flowers growing along the stalk: also called *gillyflower;* **14, stocks,** an old instrument of punishment for minor offences, consisting of a wooden frame with holes in which to confine the hands, feet, and, sometimes, the head of offenders:—*v.t.* to lay in a stock or supply of.—*n.* **stock′room′.**—*adj.* **stock′still′.**

stock-ade (sto-kād′), *n.* **1,** a fence of upright posts or logs set close together in the earth, used as a defensive barrier or to form an enclosure for cattle; **2,** the space so enclosed:—*v.t.* [stockad-ed, stockad-ing], to surround with, or defend by, such a fence.

stock-brok-er (stok′brōk′ér), *n.* one who buys and sells shares of stock.—*n.* **stock′hold′er** (one who owns shares of capital stock in a corporation or joint stock company).

stock-ing (stok′ing), *n.* a woven or knit covering for the foot and leg.

stock-y (stok′i), *adj.* [stock-i-er, stock-i-est] short and stoutly built; thickset.

stock-yard (stok′yärd′), *n.* a large pen for cattle, swine, and sheep, usually for those which are to be slaughtered.

stodg-y (stoj′i), *adj.* **1,** dull; as a book; **2,** lacking in vivacity, as a person; **3,** bulky; stuffed.

sto-ic (stō′ik) or **sto-i-cal** (stō′i-kal), *adj.* self-controlled; able to suffer without complaining.—*n.* **sto′ic.**—*adv.* **sto′i-cal-ly.**

stoke (stōk), *v.t.* and *v.i.* [stoked, stok-ing], to tend (a fire or furnace).—*n.* **stok′er.**

¹stole (stōl), *p.t.* of *steal.*

²stole (stōl), *n.* **1,** a woman's long scarf, usually of fur or cloth, worn with the ends hanging in front; **2,** a long scarflike vestment worn by a bishop or priest.

stol-id (stol′id), *adj.* not easily aroused or excited.—*adv.* **stol′id-ly.**—*n.* **sto-lid′i-ty.**

stom-ach (stum′ak), *n.* **1,** a part of the digestive tract; in man, the sac at the end of the gullet to which food goes when it is swallowed; **2,** desire; inclination; as, he had no *stomach* for revenge:—*v.t.* to put up with; tolerate.

stomp (stômp), *v.i. Corruption* of *stamp:* used to indicate anger, etc.

stone (stōn), *n.* **1,** a small piece of rock; **2,** the hard, non-metallic mineral matter of which rock consists; **3,** a piece of rock cut and shaped for a special use; as, a hearth*stone;* **4,** a gem; as, a perfect ruby is a rare *stone;* **5,** in

Great Britain, a measure of weight equal to fourteen pounds; **6,** something resembling a small stone in hardness and shape; as, a hail*stone*;—*v.t.* [stoned, ston-ing], **1,** to pelt with pieces of rock; kill by hurling pieces of rock; **2,** to remove the stones, or pits, from; as, to *stone* dates:—*adj.* made of stoneware or earthenware:—**stone—blind,** entirely blind.—*adj.* **ston′y.**

stone-boat (stōn′bōt′), *n.* a few planks fastened firmly together, usually on runners, and equipped with a coupling for horses or oxen: used in pioneer days in Canada and U.S. to clear farms of stones, etc.

stood (stood), *p.t.* and *p.p.* of *stand.*

stooge (stōōj), *n. Slang,* one who acts as an underling or a foil to another, esp. in a secretive or obsequious fashion.

stook (stōōk), *n.* a pile or bundle of sheaves, esp. when stacked in a field: —*v.t.* to pile sheaves: *stook* is the preferred term in Canada, *shock* in U.S.

stool (stōōl), *n.* **1,** a seat without a back, having three or four legs; **2,** a rest for the feet; also, a rest for the knees in kneeling.—**stool pi-geon, 1,** a decoy; **2,** *Colloq.* an informer; spy.

stoop (stōōp), *v.i.* **1,** to bend the body down and, usually, forward; also, to carry the head and shoulders habitually bowed forward; **2,** to condescend; as, the king *stooped* to dine with the peasant; **3,** to submit; yield:—*n.* **1,** a bending down and forward, esp. of the head and shoulders. **2,** a small porch or platform with steps (at the door of a house).

stop (stop), *v.t.* [stopped, stop-ping], **1,** to fill up (a hole or an opening); also, to close (a container); as, to *stop* a keg; **2,** to obstruct or make impassable; as, to *stop* a road; **3,** to check the progress or motion of; cause to come to a state of rest; as, to *stop* a car; cause to cease; as, to *stop* an annoyance; **4,** to desist from; as, *stop* all that noise:—*v.i.* **1,** to cease; desist; halt; **2,** *Colloq.*, to tarry; lodge; as, to *stop* at an inn:—*n.* **1,** a pause or delay; **2,** a halt; also, a halting place; **3,** a punctuation mark; **4,** any of several devices, as a block, peg, plug, or pin, to regulate or check motion, or to keep a movable part in place; as, a window *stop;* **6,** in *music,* any means or device for regulating pitch; also, in an organ. a set of pipes producing tones of the same quality.

stope (stōp), *n.* a horizontal level excavated in a mine:—*v.t.* and *v.i.* to

mine horizontally, layer after layer; to extract ore in this way.

stop-gap (stop′gap′), *n.* a temporary substitute; a makeshift or expedient.

stop-page (stop′ij), *n.* the arresting of motion or action; also, the state of arrested motion; obstruction.

stop-per (stop′ẽr), *n.* a plug, as of glass, wood, or cork, that closes a bottle, etc.

stor-age (stōr′ij), *n.* the placing of goods in a warehouse, for safekeeping; also, the space thus occupied or the price charged for the service.

store (stōr), *n.* **1,** a great quantity or number; **2,** (often *stores*), an accumulation or supply kept in reserve or ready for use; **3,** a shop where goods are kept for sale:—**in store,** in reserve: —*v.t.* [stored, stor-ing], **1,** to furnish or stock; equip; as, a mind *stored* with knowledge; **2,** to collect; hoard; **3,** to put in a warehouse for safekeeping. —*n.* **store′house′; store′keep′er; store′room′.**

stor-ey (stōr′i), *n.* [*pl.* storeys], a floor of a building, usually divided into rooms.

sto-ried (stō′rid), *adj.* **1,** famous in story or history; **2,** of a building, as three-*storied* (*storeyed*).

stork (stôrk), *n.* a kind of wading bird with long legs and a long bill.

storm (stôrm), *n.* **1,** a violent disturbance of the atmosphere, often with a heavy fall of rain, snow, or hail; also, a thunderstorm; **2,** an outburst of passion or excitement; as, a *storm* of rage; **3,** a sudden violent attack on a fortified place:—*v.t.* to attack suddenly with violence; as, to *storm* a fort:—*v.i.* **1,** to blow violently, or to rain, hail, snow, etc.; **2,** to rage.—*adj.* **storm′y.** —*adv.* **storm′i-ly.**—*n.* **storm′i-ness.**

stor-y (stōr′i), *n.* [*pl.* stories], **1,** real or imagined events narrated in prose or verse; a tale, either written or spoken; **2,** a report or statement; rumour; **3,** *Colloq.*, a lie.

stout (stout), *adj.* **1,** brave; resolute; as, a *stout* heart; **2,** tough; strong; as, the *stout* oak; **3,** bulky; thickset; as, a *stout* figure:—*n.* strong, dark porter, ale, or beer.—*adv.* **stout′ly.**—*n.* **stout′ness.**

stove (stōv), *n.* an apparatus of iron, steel, etc., for producing heat with which to cook, warm a room, etc.

stow (stō), *v.t.* **1,** to fill by close packing; as, to *stow* a trunk with articles; **2,** to store (a cargo) compactly; **3,** to hide away; conceal.

stow-a-way (stō′a-wā′), *n.* one who hides on a ship, train, etc., to travel free.

strad-dle (strad′l), *v.t.* [strad-dled, strad-dling], **1,** to stand or sit astride of; as, to *straddle* a fence; **2,** *Colloq.*, to support, or seem to support, both sides of; as, to *straddle* an issue:—*v.i.* to sit, stand, or walk with the legs wide apart; **2,** *Colloq.*, to support, or seem to support, both sides of a question:—*n.* the act of straddling; also, the space between the legs of one who straddles.

strafe (strāf; sträf), *v.t.* to punish; subject to rapid fire, esp. from airplane machine-guns.

strag-gle (strag′l), *v.i.* [strag-gled, strag-gling], **1,** to wander away from the main group; stray; ramble; as, on the hike, certain boys *straggled* behind the rest; **2,** to spread about; occur here and there; grow unevenly; as, weeds *straggle* along a roadside.—*n.* **strag′gler.**—*adj.* **strag′gly.**

straight (strāt), *adj.* **1,** not crooked or curved; extending directly without change in direction; as, a *straight* line; **2,** honest; upright; as, *straight* living; **3,** logical; clear; as, *straight* thinking; **4,** accurate; in order, as accounts; **5,** orderly; tidy:—*adv.* directly; without swerving; as, the arrow flew *straight.*—*n.* **straight′ness.**

straight-a-way (strāt′a-wā′), *n.* and *adj.* a track or course that extends in a straight line.

straight-en (strāt′n), *v.t.* **1,** to make free of turns or curves; as, to *straighten* a road; **2,** to arrange in a desired position or condition; as, to *straighten* a necktie; to *straighten* a room; **3,** to make clear; as, to *straighten* out a mystery:—*v.i.* to become straight.

straight-for-ward (strāt′fôr′wẻrd), *adj.* proceeding in a direct course or manner; hence, honest.—*n.* **straight′-for′ward-ness.**

straight-way (strāt′wā′), *adv.* at once.

¹strain (strān), *n.* **1,** stock; race; line of descent; hence, family: ancestry; breed; **2,** inborn disposition; tendency; **3,** manner; tone; as, to speak in lofty *strain;* **4,** a vein or streak; as, a *strain* of humour; **5,** a tune or melody.

²strain (strān), *v.t.* **1,** to put to its utmost strength; exert as much as possible; as, to *strain* every muscle; stretch even beyond proper limits; as, to *strain* the law: **2,** to weaken or injure by excessive use; as, to *strain* one's voice; **3,** to put through a sieve; as, to *strain* soup; also, to remove by filtering:—*v.i.* **1,** to make violent efforts; strive; **2,** to pass through a sieve or filter; be strained; **3,** to become injured by excessive use or exertion:—*n.* **1,** extreme stretching; tension; **2,** a violent effort; **3,** injury due to violent effort or to overwork.—*adj.* **strained.**—*n.* **strain′er.**

strait (strāt), *n.* **1,** a narrow passage of water connecting two larger bodies of water; as, the *Strait* of Magellan; **2,** **straits,** perplexity; difficulties; as, financial *straits:*—*adj.* narrow; confining; strict; as, the *strait* and narrow path; a *strait* jacket.

strait-ened (strāt′nd), *adj.* contracted; narrowed:—**straitened circumstances,** poverty; want.

strait—laced (strāt′–lāst′), *adj.* very strict in conduct or morality; puritanical; prudish.

¹strand (strand), *n.* the shore, as of an ocean:—*v.t.* **1,** to drive ashore; run aground; as, the storm *stranded* the ship on a reef; **2,** to leave in a state of embarrassment or difficulty; as, he was *stranded* in a strange city without money:—*v.i.* to run aground.

²strand (strand), *n.* one of a number of flexible strings, as of wire or hemp, twisted together into a rope; also, any similar string, as of pearls, beads, or hair.

strange (strānj), *adj.* [strang-er, strang-est], **1,** belonging to some other person or place; as, to sleep in a *strange* bed; **2,** not familiar; as, a *strange* voice; **3,** odd; remarkable; unusual; as *strange* ideas; **4,** reserved; shy; timid; as, to feel *strange* in company; **5,** inexperienced; as, he is *strange* to the new work.—*adv.* **strange′ly.**

stran-ger (strān′jẻr), *n.* **1,** a person from another place; as, "a *stranger* in a strange land"; **2,** a newcomer; visitor; as, *strangers* are welcome in this church; **3,** a person not known to one; as, he was a *stranger* to me.

stran-gle (strang′gl), *v.t.* [stran-gled, stran-gling], **1,** to choke; kill by squeezing the throat; **2,** to suppress; as, to *strangle* an impulse:—*v.i.* to be choked or suffocated.—*n.* **stran′gu-la′tion.**

strap (strap), *n.* **1,** a narrow strip of leather, etc., used to fasten objects together or hold them in place; as, a book *strap;* **2,** a razor-strop:—*v.t.* [strapped, strap-ping], **1,** to fasten or bind with a strap; **2,** to flog with a strap; **3,** to sharpen (a razor) on a strop.

strap-ping (strap′ing), *adj.* tall and well built; robust; strong; as, a *strapping* youth.

strat-a-gem (strat′a-jem), *n.* 1, a trick for deceiving an enemy, esp. in war; 2, any trick for gaining some advantage.

strat-e-gy (strat′i-ji), *n.* 1, the art or science of war; the art of maneuvering troops or ships on a large scale; 2, skill in managing any affair; 3, the use of a ruse or a trick; artifice.—*adj.* stra-te′-gic.—*adj.* stra-te′gi-cal.—*adv.* stra-te′-gi-cal-ly.—*n.* strat′e-gist.

strat-i-fy (strat′i-fī′), *v.t.* and *v.i.* to form, arrange, or harden in layers; as, *stratified* rock.

stra-to—cu-mu-lus (strā′tō–kū′mū-lus), *n.* a low cloud or cloud layer made up of large dark masses that appear like mounds piled on top of one another, seen esp. in winter.

stra-to-sphere (strā′to-sfēr′; strat′-o-sfēr′), *n.* the portion of the earth's atmosphere seven miles or more above the earth.

stra-tum (strā′tum; strat′um), *n.* [*pl.* strata (strā′ta; strat′a) or stra-tums], 1, one of a series of layers of rock or earth; as, a *stratum* of rock between *strata* of clay; 2, a class in society; as, he belongs to the upper *stratum.*

straw (strô), *n.* 1, the stalk of grain; 2, such stalks when cut and threshed, used for fodder, packing, etc.; 3, anything practically worthless; as, he is not worth a *straw;* 4, a hollow stalk, or something resembling one; as, she drank her soda through a *straw:*—*adj.* 1, made of straw; as, a *straw* hat; stuffed with straw; as, a *straw* mattress; 2, of the color of straw.

straw-ber-ry (strô′ber′i), *n.* [*pl.* strawberries], a tart, fleshy, edible berry, red when fully ripe; also the low-growing plant of which it is the fruit.

stray (strā), *v.i.* to wander from one's path; hence, to wander from the path of duty; err:—*adj.* 1, wandering; lost; as, a *stray* dog; 2, occasional; incidental; as, a *stray* remark:—*n.* a lost person or domestic animal; as, the cow is a *stray.*

streak (strēk) *n.* 1, a line differing in color from its background; stripe; 2, a trait of character; as, a *streak* of meanness; 3, layer; as, *streaks* of lean in bacon:—*v.t.* mark with streaks.—*adj.* streak′y.

stream (strēm), *n.* 1, flowing water; a creek, small river, etc.; 2, anything flowing forth like a stream; as, a *stream* of people; a *stream* of light; 3, hence, a continued flow; drift; course; as, the *stream* of civilization:—*v.i.* 1, to flow or move continuously; run in a current; 2, to pour or drip; as, an umbrella *streams* with rain; 3, to float; as, banners *stream* in the air.

stream-er (strēm′ėr), *n.* 1, a long, narrow pennant or ribbon; 2, a shaft of light, as in the northern lights; 3, a newspaper headline which stretches across the page.

stream-let (strēm′lit), *n.* a little stream.

stream-line (strēm′līn′), *adj.* shaped in long smooth curves so as to offer the least resistance to air or water; as, *streamline* design:—*v.t.* to make or remodel in such a form; hence, to modernize or reorganize for efficiency.

stream-lin-er (strēm′lī′nėr), *n.* a streamlined passenger train.

street (strēt), *n.* a public way in a city or town, usually lined with buildings.

street-car (strēt′kär′), *n.* a car, usually an electric passenger car, run on tracks laid on the surface of a street.

strength (strength; strengkth), *n.* 1, the quality of being strong; muscular force; also, the ability to do or endure; 2, firmness; toughness; as, the *strength* of a rope; 3, power; vigor; intensity; as, *strength* of will; 4, force in numbers; as, the *strength* of an army.—*v.t.* and *v.i.* strength′en.

stren-u-ous (stren′ū-us), *adj.* 1, urgent; zealous; as, a *strenuous* reformer; 2, full of effort or exertion; as, a *strenuous* life.—*adv.* stren′u-ous-ly.

strep-to-coc-cus (strep′tō-kok′us), *n.* one of a group of bacteria that occur in pairs or chains, and cause diseases that affect the lungs, joints, blood, etc., as scarlet fever, pneumonia, erysipelas, blood-poisoning, etc. *Colloq.* strep.

strep-to-my-cin (strep′tō-mī′sin), *n.* an antibiotic extracted from a bacterium found in the soil, used in the treatment of tuberculosis, certain kinds of meningitis, etc.

stress (stres), *n.* 1, impelling force; pressure; as, the *stress* of work; 2, importance; emphasis; as, to lay *stress* on a particular fact; 3, in *physics*, a force, esp. one causing change of shape or volume:—*v.t.* 1, to emphasize; 2, accent; as, *stress* the first word; 3, in *physics*, subject to mechanical pressure.

stretch (strech), *v.t.* 1, to draw out in length or width; hence, to draw taut; as, to *stretch* a rubber band; 2, to extend; as, to *stretch* out an arm; to extend between two points; as, to *stretch* a tennis net; **3,** to strain; exert to the utmost; as, *stretch* every effort to get there; **4,** to exaggerate; as, to *stretch* the truth; **5,** to make the most of; as, *stretch* the pennies:—*v.i.* **1,** to spread; reach; as, the rope *stretched* across the street; **2,** to admit of being extended; as, elastic *stretches;* **3,** to extend or spread the body or limbs:— *n.* **1,** the act of straining or extending; **2,** reach; scope; extent; **3,** a continuous line, space, or time; as, a *stretch* of good road.

stretch-er (strech'ẽr), *n.* **1,** a device which draws something out to the desired shape; as, a curtain *stretcher;* **2,** a frame, usually covered with canvas, for carrying the disabled; **3,** a brace or footrest in a rowboat.

strew (strōō), *v.t.* [*p.t.* strewed (strōōd), *p.p.* strewed or strewn (strōōn), *p.pr.* strew-ing], **1,** to scatter; let fall loosely; as, to strew flowers on a path; **2,** to cover by scattering small objects; as, to *strew* a walk with pebbles.

stri-at-ed (strī'āt-id), *adj.* streaked; striped; furrowed; grooved; as *striated* rocks, shells, etc.

strick-en (strik'en), *adj.* afflicted; affected by illness, age, misfortune, etc.

strict (strikt), *adj.* **1,** exacting; severe; as, *strict* laws; **2,** rigid; unswerving; as, *strict* honesty; **3,** accurate; precise; as, the *strict* sense of a word.—*adv.* **strict'ly**.

stride (strīd), *n.* a long step; also, the space covered by a long step:—*v.i.* [*p.t.* strode (strōd), *p.p.* strid-den (strid'n), *p.pr.* strid-ing], to walk with long steps: —*v.t.* to straddle; hence, to ride (a horse).

stri-dent (strī'dent), *adj.* shrill; harsh; grating; as, *strident* tones.

strife (strīf), *n.* conflict; hostilities; rivalry.

strike (strīk), *v.t.* [*p.t.* struck (struk), *p.p.* struck or, in senses 5 and 8 in the passive, also strick-en (strik'en), *p.pr.* strik-ing], **1,** to hit; dash against; **2,** to deal (a blow); also, to deal a blow to; as, John *struck* him in the face; **3,** to collide, or cause to collide, with; as, my foot *struck* the table; I *struck* my foot on the table; **4,** to come to the mind of; occur to; as, an idea *struck* her; **5,** to afflict or affect; as, to be *struck* with horror; to be *stricken* with illness; **6,** to come upon, as gold; **7,** to conclude, as a bargain; **8,** to cancel; as, the remarks were then *struck* (or *stricken*) from the

record; **9,** to cause (a match) to ignite; **10,** to produce by printing; as, to *strike* off a new issue of stamps; **11,** to cause to sound; as, to *strike* a bell; also, to announce by sound; as, the clock *strikes* twelve; **12,** to lower (a flag or sail) as a sign of submission:—*v.i.* **1,** to deal a quick blow or thrust; make an attack; fight; **2,** to hit; collide; become stranded, as a ship; **3,** to proceed; as, they *struck* into the woods; **4,** to sound, as a bell or a clock; **5,** to cease from work in order to secure or prevent a change in working conditions or pay:— *n.* **1,** the act of striking; **2,** a stopping of work by a number of employees in order to secure or prevent a change in working conditions, rate of pay, etc.; **3,** a fortunate discovery of ore or oil; hence, any sudden success; **4,** in *baseball,* an unsuccessful attempt by the batter to hit the ball, or a ball so pitched that the batter should have struck at it; **5,** in *bowling,* the upsetting, by a player, of all the pins with the first ball bowled; also, the score so made.—*n.* **strike'-break'er** (a scab).

strik-er (strīk'ẽr), *n.* **1,** a person or thing that strikes; **2,** a workman who with others quits work in protest against existing or proposed working conditions, rates of pay, etc.

string (string), *n.* **1,** a thin cord; thick thread; twine; also, something used for tying; as, apron-*strings;* **2,** a set of things, as beads, arranged on a cord; also, a series of things in, or as in, a line; as a *string* of jokes; a *string* of cars; **3,** a vegetable fibre, as of string beans; **4,** a tightly stretched cord for musical instruments, whose vibration produces a tone; **5, strings,** stringed musical instruments:—*v.t.* [strung (strung), string-ing], **1,** to furnish (a bow, violin, etc.) with a string or strings; **2,** to thread on a cord, as beads; **3,** to form into a line or series; **4,** to fasten or hang with a cord; as, to *string* pictures on a wall; **5,** to take the strings from (beans): —*v.i.* **1,** to form strings; become stringy, as glue; **2,** to move along in a single file.

string—bean (string'-bēn'), *n.* a kind of bean, grown for its edible pods; one of the pods.

stringed (stringd), *adj.* fitted with strings, as the violin, cello, mandolin, etc.

strin-gent (strin'jent), *adj.* strict; severe; as, *stringent* rules.—*n.* **strin'-gen-cy**.

string-piece (string'pēs'), *n.* a main timber supporting the edge of a framework, as of a floor.

string-y (string'i), *adj.* [string-i-er, string-i-est], **1,** long and thin; as, a *stringy* youth; **2,** full of fibres or strings; as, *stringy* meat; **3,** capable of being drawn out into strings, as glue.

strip (strip), *v.t.* [stripped, strip-ping], **1,** to make naked; deprive of a covering; hence, to rob; bare; as, to *strip* a man of his riches; to *strip* a tree of apples; **2,** to pull off (a covering); as, to *strip* bark from a tree; **3,** to milk (a cow) dry: —*v.i.* to undress:—*n.* a long, narrow piece of anything.

stripe (strīp), *n.* **1,** a line, band, or streak; **2,** a strip of different colour or material attached to anything; as, a *stripe* on a uniform; **3,** a discoloured bruise on the skin made by the blow of a whip; also, a blow by a whip; **4,** distinctive sort or kind; as, they are persons of the same *stripe:*—*v.t.* [striped, strip-ing], to mark with lines or bands.

strip-ling (strip'ling), *n.* a youth; lad.

strive (strīv), *v.i.* [*p.t.* strove (strōv), *p.p.* striv-en (striv'en), *p.pr.* striving,] **1.** to make an effort; try hard; as, to *strive* for success; **2,** to struggle; battle; as, the swimmer *strove* against the current.

strode (strōd), *p.t.* of *stride.*

stroke (strōk), *n.* **1,** the act of dealing a blow or the blow dealt; as, the *stroke* of a hammer; **2,** a sudden action or effect suggesting the violence of a blow; as, a *stroke* of apoplexy; **3,** a single effort, or the result produced; as, a *stroke* of business; **4,** a gentle touch; as, a *stroke* of the hand; **5,** a single movement with an instrument; as, a pencil *stroke;* the result or mark made by such a movement; **6,** the sound of a bell or clock; also, the time marked; as, at the *stroke* of three; **7,** one of a series of repeated movements in air or water; as, the *stroke* of a swimmer; **8,** in *rowing,* the oarsman nearest the stern who sets the time:—*v.t.* [stroked, strok-ing], **1,** to rub gently with the hand; **2,** to set the pace for (rowers); as, he *stroked* the crew for two years.

stroll (strōl), *n.* a quiet walk or ramble: —*v.i.* to wander on foot from place to place; to ramble.—*n.* **stroll'er.**

strong (strông), *adj.* **1,** physically powerful; muscular; robust; as, a *strong* horse; a *strong* physique; **2,** upright; firm; as, a *strong* character; **3,** powerful in wealth, numbers, or other resources; as, a *strong* party; also, of a specified numerical force; as, 9,000 *strong;* **4,** violent, as a high wind; **5,** ardent or warm, as the affections; **6,** vigorous or forceful, as an argument; **7,** stable or settled, as a government; **8,** intense, as a bright light; concentrated; as, *strong* tea or coffee; also, containing alcohol; as, *strong* drink; **9,** firm in opinion; ardent; as, a *strong* partisan; **10,** deeply rooted; positive; as, *strong* beliefs; **11,** solid; not easily broken; as, a *strong* plank.

strong-hold (strông'hōld'), *n.* a fort or fortress; a place of refuge.

stron-ti-um (stron'shi-um; shum), a metallic chemical element with properties like those of calcium: a deadly radioactive isotope of it, *strontium* 90, is present in fallout from atomic explosions.

strop (strop), *n.* a strip of leather, as for sharpening a razor:—*v.t.* [stropped, strop-ping], to sharpen (a razor) on a strop.

strove (strōv), alternative *p.t.* of *strive.*

struck (struk), *p.t.* and *p.p.* of *strike.*

struc-ture (struk'tūr), *n.* **1,** that which is built, as a bridge or a house; **2,** the manner in which something is built; as, the *structure* of ships has been improved; **3,** the form or arrangement of parts or elements; as, the *structure* of a flower. —*adj.* **struc'tur-al.**—*adv.* **struc'tur-al-ly.**

strug-gle (strug'l), *v.i.* [strug-gled, strug-gling], **1,** to put forth violent effort, as in trying to escape from a grasp; **2,** to labour; strive; as, he *struggled* to get a start:—*n.* **1,** a violent effort; **2,** a contest; strife.

strum (strum), *v.t.* and *v.i.* to pluck the strings (as of a guitar, banjo, etc.) unskillfully and noisily.

strung (strung), *p.t.* and *p.p.* of *string.*

¹strut (strut), *v.i.* [strut-ted, strut-ting], to walk with a proud step or false dignity:—*n.* a proud and haughty step.

²strut (strut), *n.* a brace or bar to support or receive weight or pressure in the direction of its length.

strych-nine (strik'nin; nēn; nīn), *n.* a powerful, poisonous drug, obtained from such tropical plants as nux vomica: used as a tonic, stimulant, etc.

stub (stub), *n.* **1,** the stump of a tree; **2,** the short, blunt, remaining part of anything, as of a cigar; **3,** the part of a leaf left in a cheque-book after a cheque is torn out, used for a memorandum; **4,** a pen with a short, blunt point:—*v.t.*

[stubbed, stub-bing], to strike (one's toe) against some fixed object—*adj.* **stub′by** (as, *stubby* bristles).

stub-ble (stub′l), *n.* **1,** the stumps of grain left in the ground after cutting; **2,** a short growth of beard.—*adj.* **stub′bly.**

stub-born (stub′ern), *adj.* **1,** fixed in opinion or purpose; determined; obstinate; as, a *stubborn* child; **2,** obstinately followed or held to; as, a *stubborn* attempt; **3,** hard to treat; as, a *stubborn* cold.

stuc-co (stuk′ō), *n.* [*pl.* stuccoes or stuccos], a kind of plaster used on inside walls or on the outside of houses: —*v.t.* [stuccoed (stuk′ōd), stucco-ing (stuk′ō-ing)], to cover with stucco.

stuck (stuk), *p.t.* and *p.p.* of *stick*.

¹stud (stud), *n.* **1,** an upright timber in walls to which the laths are nailed; **2,** an ornamental boss or knob projecting from a surface; as, a belt with brass *studs;* **3,** a device like a button used as a fastener; as, shirt *studs:*—*v.t.* [studded, stud-ding], **1,** to furnish with upright props; **2,** to adorn or set with studs; as, a sky *studded* with stars:— **stud-ding sail,** a sail set (in light weather) outside the edge of a working sail by an extensible boom.

²stud (stud), *n.* a male horse, or stallion, kept for breeding; a stable of such horses.—*adj.* pertaining to a stud; as, a *stud* farm.

stu-dent (stū′dent), *n.* **1,** a person who attends school; **2,** a person devoted to books or learning; **3,** a close observer; as, a *student* of life.

stu-di-o (stū′di-ō), *n.* [*pl.* studios], **1,** the workroom of an artist; **2,** a place where motion pictures are filmed; **3,** a room equipped for the broadcasting of radio or television programmes.

stu-di-ous (stū′di-us), *adj.* **1,** given to study; fond of books; as, a *studious* youth; **2,** thoughtful; earnest; as, *studious* attention.—*n.* **stu′di-ous-ness.**

stud-y (stud′i), *n.* [*pl.* studies], **1,** the application of the mind to books, science, etc., for the gaining of knowledge; **2,** a special branch of learning; as, mathematics is a difficult *study;* **3,** careful examination of a particular question; as, a *study* of foreign trade; also, the result of such examination; as, this book is a *study* of the tariff; **4,** reverie; deep thought; as, to be in a brown *study;* **5,** in *painting,* a preliminary sketch for a picture; **6,** in *music,* a piece for a special kind of practice;

7, earnest effort; aim; as, his constant *study* is how to please; **8,** a room set apart for reading or writing:—*v.i.* [studied, study-ing], to devote oneself to the gaining of knowledge; as, he is *studying* at college:—*v.t.* **1,** to learn the details of; as, to *study* Latin; **2,** to investigate or examine closely; think over carefully; as, to *study* labour disputes.

stuff (stuf), *n.* **1,** the material of which anything is composed or may be made; **2,** the essential part of anything; as, he is of the *stuff* of heroes; **3,** woven fabrics or cloth; **4,** belongings; portable property; **5,** refuse or waste matter; hence, nonsense; as, *stuff* and nonsense:—*v.t.* **1,** to crowd, cram, or pack; as, to *stuff* clothes into a bag; also, to fill by cramming; as, to *stuff* a bag with clothes; **2,** to fill with specially prepared material; as, to *stuff* a chicken; **3,** to fill the skin of (a dead animal) so as to make it look lifelike; **4,** to put dishonest votes into (a ballot-box).—*n.* **stuf′fing.**

stuff-y (stuf′i), *adj.* [stuff-i-er, stuff-i-est], **1,** close or badly ventilated; as, a *stuffy* room; **2,** choked or stopped up, as with a cold in the head.—*n.* **stuff′i-ness.**

stul-ti-fy (stul′ti-fī′), *v.t.* to make foolish or absurd; as, don't *stultify* yourself; this decision *stultifies* the other.

stum-ble (stum′bl), *v.i.* [stum-bled, stum-bling], **1,** to trip or fall in walking; **2,** to walk in an unsteady manner; **3,** to fall into error:—**stumble on** or **upon,** to come upon by chance; as, to *stumble* on a valuable secret:—*n.* **1,** a tripping, as in walking; **2,** an error or blunder.

stump (stump), *n.* **1,** that part of a tree which remains in the ground after the trunk is cut down; **2,** the part, as of an arm, tail, etc., remaining after the main part has been removed; a stub; **3,** a platform for political speaking: from the early custom of speaking from tree stumps:—*v.i.* to walk heavily:—*v.t. Colloq.:* **1,** to canvass (a district) making political speeches; **2,** to block or hinder; as, he was *stumped* and could go no further.—*adj.* **stump′y.**

stun (stun), *v.t.* [stunned, stun-ning], **1,** to make senseless by a blow; **2,** to confuse, daze, or overpower.—*n.* **stun′ner.**

stung (stung), *p.t.* and *p.p.* of *sting*.

stunk (stungk), *p.t.* and *p.p.* of *stink*.

¹stunt (stunt), *v.t.* to check the growth or development of; dwarf.

²stunt (stunt), *n. Colloq.*, a striking feat or performance, as of strength or skill.

stu-pe-fy (stū'pe-fī'), *v.t.* [stupefied, stupefy-ing], to dull the senses of; make stupid.—*n.* **stu'pe-fac'tion.**

stu-pen-dous (stū-pen'dus), *adj.* overpowering the senses by great size, speed, etc.; amazing; remarkable.

stu-pid (stū'pid), *adj.* dull; unintelligent; as, a *stupid* person; also, foolish; as, a *stupid* error.—*n.* **stu-pid'i-ty.**

stu-por (stū'pėr), *n.* a condition of more or less complete unconsciousness; lethargy.

stur-dy (stûr'di), *adj.* [stur-di-er, stur-di-est], **1,** hardy; robust; stout; as, a *sturdy* oak; **2,** firm and unyielding; as, a man of *sturdy* principles.

stur-geon (stûr'jun), *n.* a large food fish, having rows of bony plates along the body.

stut-ter (stut'ėr), *v.i.* in speaking, to hesitate over or repeat the initial sounds of words; to stammer:—*v.t.* to utter with difficulty:—*n.* a stammer.

¹sty (stī), *n.* [*pl.* sties], **1,** a pen for swine; **2,** a filthy or vile place.

²sty (stī), *n.* [*pl.* sties], an inflamed swelling of the eyelid.

¹style (stīl), *n.* **1,** a pointed instrument used by the ancients for writing upon wax tablets; hence, any of various similar instruments, as an engraver's tool; **2,** a characteristic manner of writing or speaking; as, a polished *style;* also, literary excellence; as, the speech lacked *style;* **3,** mode of expression or execution in any art; as, the Colonial *style* in architecture; **4,** manner of conduct or action; as, a graceful *style* of dancing; also, fine or dashing appearance; as, she has *style;* **5,** fashion; as, a coat of the latest *style:*—*v.t.* [styled, styl-ing], to term, name, or call; as, Moses is *styled* the Great Lawgiver.

²style (stīl), *n.* the stemlike part of the pistil. (See illustration under *flower*.)

styl-ish (stīl'ish), *adj.* very fashionable; modern.—*adv.* **styl'ish-ly.**

styl-ist (stīl'ist), *n.* a person, esp. a writer, who is a master of style.

sty-lus (stī'lus), *n.* **1,** a style (definition 1); **2,** a sharp, needlelike device for cutting grooves in records or for reproducing their sound.

sty-mie (stī'mi), *n.* in *golf*, an opponent's ball lying directly between the player's ball and the hole of a putting green; the occurrence of this:—*v.t.* to hinder; block; obstruct; as, I was *stymied* by this move.

styp-tic (stip'tik), *adj.* tending to stop bleeding; as a *styptic* pencil (for cuts or nicks in shaving).

sua-sion (swā'zhun), *n.* urging; persuading; as in moral *suasion:* opposed to physical force.

suave (swāv; swäv), *adj.* polite; smooth; bland.—*n.* **suav'i-ty** (swä'vi-ti; swav'i-ti).

sub- (sub-), *prefix* meaning (1) *under, below, beneath,* as in *sub*marine (2) *inferior, smaller, lesser,* as in *sub*standard, *sub*division, *sub*heading (3) *secondary,* as in *sub*lease, *sub*tenant (4) *bordering,* as in *sub*tropical.

sub-al-tern (sub-ôl'tėrn; sub'l-tûrn'), *adj.* and *n.* holding an inferior position, esp. in the army one below the rank of captain.

sub-con-scious (sub-kon'shus), *adj.* pertaining to mental activity of which one is not aware.—*n.* unconscious mental functioning or processes.—*n.* **sub-con'scious-ness.**

sub-di-vide (sub'di-vīd'), *v.t.* [subdivid-ed, sub-divid-ing], to separate the parts of into other parts:—*v.i.* to divide or separate again.—*n.* **sub-di-vi'sion.**

sub-due (sub-dū'), *v.t.* [subdued, sub-du-ing], **1,** to conquer; vanquish; as, to *subdue* an enemy; **2,** to bring under control; master, as an impulse; **3,** to tone down.

sub-ject (sub'jekt), *adj.* **1,** under the power or control of another; as, a *subject* nation; **2,** exposed; liable; as, he is *subject* to malaria; **3,** dependent on; as, a plan *subject* to your approval: —*n.* **1,** a person under the control of another; esp., one who owes allegiance to a government or a sovereign; **2,** a person, animal, or thing made to undergo an operation or treatment; as, the *subject* of an experiment; **3,** the matter, theme, or topic, about which something is said or written; **4,** in a sentence, the word or group of words of which something is said or asked; as, in "our vacation begins tomorrow" the *subject* is "our vacation":—*v.t.* (sub-jekt'), **1,** to bring under control; **2,** to make liable; expose; as, to be *subjected* to insult; **3,** to cause to undergo; as, to *subject* iron to heat.

sub-jec-tion (sub-jek'shun), *n.* **1,** the act of bringing others under control; **2,** the state of being under the control of another.

sub-jec-tive (sub-jek'tiv), *n.* in *grammar,* the case of the subject:—*adj.* existing in the mind; not produced by

outside objects: opposite of *objective*.—
n. **sub′jec-tiv′i-ty.**

sub-ju-gate (sub′joo-gāt′), *v.t.* [subjugated, subjugat-ing], to conquer; subdue, as savage tribes.—*n.* **sub′-ju-ga′tion.**

sub-junc-tive (sub-jungk′tiv), *adj.* in *grammar*, pertaining to that mood of a verb which expresses state or action, not as a fact, but as something possible, desired, feared, or doubtful:—*n.* the subjunctive mood.

sub-lieu-ten-ant (sub′lef-ten′ant; lū or lōō), *n.* a subordinate or second lieutenant.

sub-li-mate (sub′li-māt′), *v.t.* in *chemistry*, to purify a solid by heating it to a gaseous state and condensing the vapour back to solid form.—*n.* **sub′li-ma′tion.**—*adj.* **sub-lim′i-nal** (below the threshold of consciousness).

sub-lime (sub-līm′), *adj.* [sublim-er, sublim-est], **1,** inspiring a feeling of awe, reverence, greatness, power, or grandeur; **2,** exalted; noble:—*n.* that which is lofty, awe-inspiring, or grand: —*v.t.* [sublimed, sublim-ing], to exalt or dignify:—*v.i.* **1,** in *chemistry*, to pass from solid to vapour form by heat, and, on cooling, back to solid form without becoming liquid: the Chinook winds sometimes do this to southern Alberta snows; **2,** sublimate (definition 2):— *v.t.* to dignify; exalt; ennoble; purify; as, his selfishness was *sublimed* to public devotion.—*adv.* **sub-lime′ly.**—*n.* **sub-lim′i-ty** (sub-lim′i-ti).

sub-lu-nar-y (sub′lū-na-ri; loo), *adj.* beneath the moon; earthly or terrestrial; as, this *sublunary* abode.

sub-ma-rine (sub′ma-rēn′), *adj.* living, situated, or used, beneath the surface of the sea; as, *submarine* plant life:—*n.* (sub′ma-rēn′), a vessel, usually a war-vessel, which can be operated under water.

sub-merge (sub-mûrj′), *v.t.* [submerged, submerg-ing], **1,** to put or sink under water; as, to *submerge* a boat; **2,** to cover with water; flood; overwhelm:—*v.i.* to sink under water or out of sight.—*n.* **sub-mer′sion** (sub-mûr′-shun; sub-mûr′zhun).—*n.* and *adj.* **sub-mers′i-ble.**

sub-mis-sion (sub-mish′un), *n.* **1,** the act of referring to the judgment, or yielding to the power or authority, of another; **2,** humility or meekness. —*adj.* **sub-mis′sive.**

sub-mit (sub-mit′), *v.t.* [submit-ted, submit-ting], **1,** to yield (oneself) to the will of another; **2,** to present for, or

refer to, the judgment of another; as, to *submit* an offer:—*v.i.* to yield or surrender.

sub-or-di-nate (su-bôr′di-nit), *adj.* **1,** lower in rank, value, power, or importance; as, a *subordinate* rank; **2,** subject to another; as, a *subordinate* official; **3,** in *grammar*, designating the dependent clause in a complex sentence, or any conjunction which introduces it:—*n.* one who is below another in rank, power, etc.—*v.t.* (su-bôr′di-nāt′), [subordinat-ed, subordinat-ing], **1,** to place in a lower order or rank; **2,** to make subject or obedient.—*n.* **sub-or′di-na′tion.**

sub-orn (su-bôrn′), *v.t.* to induce to do a wrong act, as by bribery, etc., esp. to commit perjury; as, he *suborned* the witnesses.—*n.* **sub′or-na′tion.**

sub-poe-na (sub-pē′na), *n.* a legal written order that a person appear in court (as a witness):—*v.t.* [-naed (-nid), -naing], to serve or summon with such writ.

sub-scribe (sub-skrīb′), *v.t.* [subscribed, subscrib-ing], **1,** to write or put (one's name) to a paper or document; **2,** to sign one's name at the end of (a document); **3,** to give or promise (a sum of money) to a cause; as, he *subscribed* $40 to the milk fund:—*v.i.* **1,** to sign one's name to a letter or other document; **2,** to agree; give assent; as, to *subscribe* to a protest; **3,** to promise to give a certain sum; as, to *subscribe* to a charity; also, to agree to take or buy something.—*n.* **sub-scrib′er.**

sub-scrip-tion (sub-skrip′shun), *n.* **1,** the act of signing one's name by way of agreement; **2,** a formal agreement to give or contribute a sum of money; also, the sum of money promised; **3,** an order for a certain number of issues of a periodical.

sub-se-quent (sub′si-kwent), *adj.* following; coming after; as, *subsequent* events.—*adv.* **sub′se-quent-ly.**

sub-ser-vi-ent (sub-sûr′vi-ent), *adj.* servile; cringing.—*n.* **sub-ser′vi-ence.**

sub-side (sub-sīd′), *v.i.* [subsid-ed, subsid-ing], **1,** to sink or fall to the bottom; settle, as sediment; **2,** to sink to a lower level; as, the swollen river will *subside;* **3,** to become quiet or less violent, as anger, fever, a storm, etc.

sub-sid-i-a-ry (sub-sid′i-a-ri), *adj.* and *n.* [*pl.* -aries], **1,** serving to aid or supplement; auxiliary; tributary; as, a *subsidiary* stream, valley, etc.; **2,** subordinate; as, a *subsidiary* company (one in which the controlling interest is owned by another company).—*n.* **1,** one who assists or supplies; **2,** a *subsidiary* person or organization.

sub-si-dize (sub′si-dīz′), *v.t.* **1,** to help or encourage with financial aid, esp. by a government; as, to *subsidize* a railroad, hospital, industry, etc.; **2,** to bribe.—*n.* **sub′si-dy.**

sub-sist (sub-sist′), *v.i.* **1,** to continue to be; exist; **2,** to be supported; live; as, to *subsist* on fish.—*n.* **sub-sis′tence.**

sub-soil (sub′soil′), *n.* the layer of soil below the topsoil.

sub-stance (sub′stans), *n.* **1,** the real or essential part of anything; **2,** the stuff, matter, or material of which something is made; **3,** the gist or real point of a speech or an article; **4,** wealth; property.

sub-stan-tial (sub-stan′shal), *adj.* **1,** having real existence; actual; not imaginary; **2,** made of good substance; solid; strong; as, a car *substantial* enough to stand ordinary wear and tear; **3,** of real worth; considerable; as, a *substantial* gift; also, nourishing; ample; as, *substantial* food; **4,** prosperous; responsible; as, *substantial* business men; **5,** real or true for the most part; virtual; as, the two stories were in *substantial* accord.—*adv.* **sub-stan′tial-ly.**

sub-stan-ti-ate (sub-stan′shi-āt′), *v.t.* to prove by evidence; verify; as to *substantiate* a charge, claim, etc.

sub-stan-tive (sub′stan-tiv), *adj.* **1,** real; permanent; substantial; **2,** in *grammar*: **a,** expressing existence; as, "to be" is a *substantive* verb; **b,** of the nature of a noun or used as a noun; as, a *substantive* clause:—*n.* a noun or a group of words used as a noun.—*adv.* **sub′stan-tive-ly.**

sub-sti-tute (sub′sti-tūt′), *n.* a person or thing that takes the place of another: —*v.t.* [substitut-ed, substitut-ing], to put in the place of another person or thing:—*v.i.* to take the place of another; as, to *substitute* for a teacher.—*n.* **sub′sti-tu′tion.**

sub-stra-tum (sub-strā′tum), *n.* [*pl.* -ta or -tums], **1,** an underlayer, or stratum, as of rock or soil; **2,** a basis or foundation; as, a *substratum* of truth; children are the *substratum* of society.

sub-tend (sub-tend′), *v.t.* **1,** in *geometry*, to lie opposite to; as, the chord that *subtends* an arc; **2,** in *botany*, to fold or enclose in an axil; as, a leaf *subtends* a bud.

sub-ter-fuge (sub′tẽr-fūj′), *n.* a scheme, excuse, or trick by which one seeks to escape from a difficulty.

sub-ter-ra-ne-an (sub′te-rā′ni-an), *adj.* **1,** below the surface of the earth; underground; as, a *subterranean* cave; **2,** hidden; secret; as, *subterranean* manoeuvres.

sub-tle (sut′l), *adj.* [sub-tler, sub-tlest], **1,** delicate; elusive; as, a *subtle* odour; **2,** clever; discerning; keen; as, a *subtle* mind; **3,** artful; crafty; cunning; as, a *subtle* scheme; **4,** intricate; hard to follow; as, *subtle* reasoning.—*n.* **sub′tle-ty.**—*adv.* **sub′tly** (sut′li).

sub-tract (sub-trakt′), *v.t.* to take away (a part) from the whole.—*n.* **sub-trac′tion.**

sub-tra-hend (sub′tra-hend′), *n.* the number subtracted from the *minuend*.

sub-urb (sub′ûrb), *n.* a residential district on the outskirts of a city.—*adj.* **sub-ur′ban.**—*n.* **sub-ur′ban-ite′** (**1,** one who lives in a suburb; **2,** a snow tire).

sub-vert (sub-vûrt′), *v.t.* **1,** to turn upside down; overthrow (a government); **2,** to ruin or corrupt, as a person's principles.—*n.* **sub-ver′sion.** —*adj.* **sub-ver′sive.**

sub-way (sub′wā′), *n.* **1,** an underground passage for water or gas pipes, wires, etc.; **2,** an underground electric railway.

suc-ceed (suk-sēd′), *v.t.* **1,** to take the place of; be the successor of (a ruler); **2,** to follow; as, Friday *succeeds* Thursday:—*v.i.* **1,** to become heir (to); as, he *succeeded* to the family estate; **2,** to be successful; meet with success; as, all his plans *succeed;* he *succeeded* in finding what he wanted to know.

suc-cess (suk-ses′), *n.* **1,** the favourable end or result of an undertaking; the gaining of wealth, fame, etc. **2,** a person or thing that turns out well; as, his book was a great *success.*—*adj.* **suc-cess′ful.**

suc-ces-sion (suk-sesh′un), *n.* **1,** a following of one person or thing after another; as, things happened in quick *succession;* also, a series; as, a *succession* of misfortunes; **2,** the act or right of succeeding to the place, office, property, title, or throne of another.—*adj.* **suc-ces′sive.**

suc-ces-sor (suk-ses′ẽr), *n.* one who follows, or takes the place of, another; opposite of *predecessor.*

suc-cinct (suk-singkt′), *adj.* concise; terse; expressed in few words; as, a *succinct* narrative.

---

suc-co-tash (suk′o-tash′), *n.* corn and beans stewed together.

suc-cour (suk′ẽr), *v.t.* to help or relieve (someone) in difficulty or distress:—*n.* **1,** relief; aid; help; **2,** one who or that which brings help.

suc-cu-lent (suk′ū-lent), *adj.* full of juice, as fruit.—*n.* **suc′cu-lence; suc′-cu-len-cy.**

suc-cumb (su-kum′), *v.i.* **1,** to yield or submit; **2,** hence, to die.

such (such), *adj.* **1,** of that kind; of the like kind; as, pens, pencils, and *such* things; **2,** the same; as, this flour is *such* as I have always used; **3,** a certain or particular; as, on *such* a date; **4,** so great, so good, so bad, etc.; as, he is *such* a fool; he did *such* work that he took honours:—*pron.* a certain person or thing; also, these or those; as, *such* of you as are going may start.

suck (suk), *v.t.* **1,** to draw (a liquid) into the mouth by action of the lips and tongue; as, to *suck* juice from an orange; **2,** to draw a liquid from (something) with the mouth; as, to *suck* an orange; **3,** to drink in or absorb; as, a blotter *sucks* up moisture; **4,** to draw in or engulf, as does quicksand:—*v.i.* to draw milk from the breast or udder:—*n.* the act of drawing in a liquid.

suck-er (suk′ẽr), *n.* **1,** a person or thing that sucks; a young animal; a suckling; **2,** a shoot of a plant from the roots or the lower part of the stem; **3,** a freshwater fish with thick, soft lips; **4,** in some animals, a disk-shaped organ by which they adhere to other animals; **5,** *Colloq.*, a lollipop; **6,** *Slang*, a person easily taken in.

suck-le (suk′l), *v.t.* [suck-led, suck-ling], to nurse at the breast:—*v.i.* to suck; take the breast.

suck-ling (suk′ling), *n.* a baby or young animal that nurses at the breast.

suc-tion (suk′shun), *n.* **1,** the act or condition of sucking; **2,** the drawing of liquid, dust, etc., into a container as air is withdrawn from it; as, liquid is drawn into a syringe by *suction;* **3,** the sticking together of two bodies when the air between them is removed.

sud-den (sud′n), *adj.* **1,** happening unexpectedly; as, a *sudden* turn for the worse; **2,** quickly done; hasty; as, a *sudden* job.—*adv.* **sud′den-ly.**—*n.* **sud′den-ness.**

suds (sudz), *n.pl.* soapy water; also, the froth or bubbles floating on it. —*adj.* **sud′sy** (sud′zi).

sue (sū), *v.t.* [sued (sūd), su-ing (sū′ing)], to start an action in law against (a person); prosecute; as, to *sue* a man for libel:—*v.i.* **1,** to entreat, beg, or petition; as, to *sue* for pardon; **2,** to pay court; as, to *sue* for a lady's hand; **3,** to begin ɑ lawsuit; as, to *sue* for damages.

suède (swād), *n.* soft, unglazed kid with a slight nap, used for gloves, shoes, etc.

su-et (sū′it), *n.* the hard fat around the kidneys and loins of mutton and beef. It is used in cooking and for making tallow.

suf-fer (suf′ẽr), *v.t.* **1,** to feel or endure; as, to *suffer* pain; bear up under; as, to *suffer* a wrong; **2,** to experience; as, all things *suffer* change; **3,** to permit; allow:—*v.i.* **1,** to feel pain, distress, or loss; **2,** to sustain loss or damage; as, illness made his work *suffer*.—*adj.* **suf′fer-a-ble.**—*n.* **suf′fer-er.**

suf-fer-ance (suf′ẽr-ans), *n.* **1,** implied consent or permission; as, he remained in the house on *sufferance* only; **2,** the ability to endure; endurance; as, cruelty beyond *sufferance*.

suf-fer-ing (suf′ẽr-ing), *n.* **1,** the bearing of physical or mental pain; **2,** the pain borne; the loss or injury endured.

suf-fice (su-fīs′; su-fīz′), *v.i.* [sufficed, suffic-ing], to be enough or sufficient: —*v.t.* to be sufficient for; satisfy; as, the small amount *sufficed* him.

suf-fi-cient (su-fish′ent), *adj.* equal to the need; enough; as, *sufficient* coal for the winter.—*n.* **suf-fi′cien-cy.**—*adv.* **suf-fi′cient-ly.**

suf-fix (suf′iks), *n.* a syllable or syllables, added at the end of a word or word stem, to form a new word related in meaning, as *-ant* in "assistant" or *-ion* in "erection":—*v.t.* (su-fiks′), to add (a syllable) to the end of a word in order to form a new word.

suf-fo-cate (suf′o-kāt′), *v.t.* [suffocat-ed, suffocat-ing], to kill by stopping the breath of; smother; stifle:—*v.i.* to be choked or stifled.—*n.* **suf′fo-ca′-tion.**

suf-frage (suf′rij), *n.* **1,** a vote upon a measure or candidate; **2,** the right to vote; also, the act of voting.

suf-fuse (su-fūz′), *v.t.* [suffused, suffus-ing], to spread over; as, a blush *suffused* her cheeks.—*n.* **suf-fu′sion.**

sug-ar (shoog′ẽr), *n.* **1,** a sweet substance obtained usually from the sugar-cane or sugar-beet, but also from many other plants, such as the maple; **2,** any sweet substance like sugar obtained from corn, milk, etc.:—*v.t.* **1,** to mix or sprinkle with sugar; as, to *sugar* berries; **2,** to make less disagreeable:—*v.i.* to turn into sugar; as, syrup *sugars* if boiled long.—*adj.* **sug′ar-y.**

sugar—cane (shoog′ẽr–kān′), *n.* a tall, jointed, maizelike grass from the sap of which sugar is obtained.

sugar-plum (shoog′ẽr-plum′), *n.* a bonbon; sweetmeat.

sug-gest (su-jest′), *v.t.* **1,** to propose, as a plan or method; **2,** to cause (an idea) to come to a person's mind through some natural connection or relationship; as crocuses *suggest* spring.

sug-ges-tion (su-jes′chun), *n.* **1,** the act of proposing something; also, the thing proposed; as, we accepted his *suggestion* for a ride; **2,** the process by which an idea causes another idea to come to mind through some natural connection; also, the idea thus brought to mind.

sug-ges-tive (su-jes′tiv), *adj.* **1,** tending to bring thoughts, ideas, etc., to the mind; **2,** tending to bring to the mind something improper or indecent.

su-i-cide (sū′i-sīd′), *n.* **1,** the act of intentionally taking one's own life; **2,** a person who kills himself intentionally.—*adj.* **su′i-cid′al.**

suit (sūt), *n.* **1,** the act of seeking favour; esp. in wooing or courtship; **2,** an action or process at law; **3,** a set or number of things used together; as, a *suit* of clothes; **4,** any of the four sets in a deck of cards:—*v.t.* **1,** to fit; adapt; as, *suit* your words to the occasion; **2,** to be proper or suitable to; become; befit; as, your behaviour does not *suit* your position; **3,** to please; satisfy; as, I hope this will *suit* you.

suit-a-ble (sūt′a-bl), *adj.* fitting; becoming; appropriate.—*adv.* **suit′a-bly.** —*n.* **suit′a-ble-ness.**—*n.* **suit′a-bil′i-ty.**

suit-case (sūt′kās′), *n.* a flat travelling-bag for carrying clothes, toilet articles, etc.

suite (swēt), *n.* **1,** a corps of attendants; as, a king and his *suite;* **2,** a series or set, as of rooms, furniture, etc.

suit-ing (sūt′ing), *n.* cloth, as used by a tailor, to make suits of clothes.

suit-or (sūt′ẽr), *n.* one who sues or entreats; esp., a man who courts or woos a woman.

sulk (sulk), *v.i.* to be sullen or ill-humoured:—**sulks,** *n.pl.* a sullen mood. —*adj.* **sulk′y.**

sul-len (sul′en), *adj.* **1,** gloomy; unsociable; as, a *sullen* disposition; **2,** dismal; lowering; as, *sullen* weather. —*adv.* **sul′len-ly.**

sul-ly (sul′i), *v.t.* [sullied, sully-ing], to tarnish or soil; dirty or stain.

sul-pha or **sul-fa** (sul′fa), *n., adj.* and *prefix.* Short for a group of synthetic drugs of the sulphanilamide family, that destroy certain disease-producing bacteria, as *sulpha*diazene, *sulpha*pyridine, *sulpha*thiazole, etc. Usually, *sulpha* drugs.

sul-phur (sul′fẽr), *n.* **1,** a yellow, non-metallic element, found in many places and in various forms, which burns with a blue flame and a suffocating odour, and is used in manufacturing gunpowder and matches, as a disinfectant, in medicine, etc.; **2,** a small yellow butterfly, usually spotted or streaked with black.—*adj.* **sul′phu-rous** (sul′fū-rus; sul-fū′rus).—*adj.* **sul-phu′ric** (sul-fū′rik):—**sulphur dioxide,** SO_2, a colourless, suffocating gas, easy to liquefy: used as a disinfectant, bleach, refrigerant, etc.—**sulphuric acid,** H_2SO_4, a corrosive, colourless, oily liquid made from SO_3, used in making paints, dyes, explosives, fertilizers, etc.

sul-tan (sul′tan; sool-tän′), *n.* a Mohammedan ruler:—**Sultan,** formerly, the emperor of Turkey.

sul-tan-a (sul-tan′a; sul-tä′na), *n.* the wife, daughter, mother, or sister, of a sultan.

sul-try (sul′tri), *adj.* [sul-tri-er, sul-tri-est], **1,** very hot, close, moist, and oppressive; as, a *sultry* day; **2,** marked by heat, as of passion or lust.

sum (sum), *n.* **1,** the total of two or more numbers, quantities, etc.; the whole; **2,** the amount resulting from addition; as, 5 is the *sum* of 3 + 2; **3,** a problem in arithmetic; **4,** a quantity, as of money; **5,** summary; substance; as, the *sum* of the evidence:—*v.t.* [summed, sum-ming], **1,** to add into one amount; **2,** to condense into few words:—*v.i.* to make a summary; as, and now, let me *sum* up.

su-mac or **su-mach** (shōō′mak; sū′-mak), *n.* **1,** a shrub or small tree with divided green leaves turning to a vivid red in the fall, and clusters of flowers followed by red or white berries; **2,** the dried leaves and roots of the sumac, used in tanning and dyeing.

sum-ma-rize (sum′-a-rīz′), *v.t.* [summarized, summariz-ing], to sum up; as, to *summarize* the evidence.

---

cat, āge, fär, cåre, åsk; ten, ēve, latẽr; (i) pity, rely, senate; īce; top; nō.

sum-ma-ry (sum′a-ri), *n.* [*pl.* summaries], a brief account containing the sum or substance of a fuller account; an abridgment:—*adj.* **1,** giving the general idea; brief; concise; **2,** performed instantly and without formalities; as, *summary* punishment.—*adv.* **sum′ma-ri-ly** (instantly).

sum-ma-tion (sum-ā′shun), *n.* a final adding, totaling, or summing up (of conditions, influences, qualities, etc.); as, Maugham's *summation* of Tolstoi.

sum-mer (sum′ẽr), *n.* the hottest season of the year; the season of the year when the sun shines most directly; in the Northern Hemisphere, the period from the summer solstice, about June 21st, to the autumnal equinox, about September 22d:—*adj.* of or characteristic of summer:—*v.i.* to pass the summer; as, to *summer* at the shore:—*v.t.* to care for during the summer: as, to *summer* horses in a pasture.—*n.* **sum′mer-time′.**—*adj.* **sum′mer-y.**

sum-mer-sault (sum′ẽr-sôlt′), *n.* and *v.* Same as *somersault.*

sum-mit (sum′it), *n.* the top or highest point; as, the *summit* of a hill.

sum-mon (sum′un), *v.t.* **1,** to require the presence of; order to appear in court; **2,** to send for; call; as, to *summon* a doctor; **3,** to arouse; gather up; as, to *summon* one's strength.

sum-mons (sum′unz), *n.* [*pl.* summonses (sum′un-zez)], **1,** an order to appear in court on a certain day; **2,** a document containing such a notice; **3,** a call to duty.

sump (sump), *n.* **1,** the bottom of a mine shaft or crankcase where water or oil collects; **2,** a cesspool: a *sump* pit is drained by a *sump* pump.

sump-tu-ous (sump′tū-us), *adj.* costly; lavish; as, a *sumptuous* feast.

sun (sun), *n.* **1,** the heavenly body round which the earth and other planets of our solar system revolve, and which gives us light and heat; **2,** a heavenly body which, like our sun, is the centre of a system of planets; **3,** sunshine:—*v.t.* [sunned, sun-ning], to expose to the sun's rays for warming, drying, sterilizing, or bleaching purposes.—*adj.* **sun′less.**—*n.* **sun′beam′; sun′room′; sun′shade′** (as a hat, parasol, or awning); **sun′stroke′.**

sun-burn (sun′bûrn′), *n.* an inflammation of the skin caused by exposure to the sun:—*v.t.* and *v.i.* to tan by exposure to the sun.

sun-dae (sun′di), *n.* a serving of ice cream topped with a sirup, fruit, or nuts.

Sun-day (sun′di; dā), *n.* the first day of the week.

sun-der (sun′dẽr), *v.t.* to divide or sever; separate; as, friends long *sundered.*

sun-di-al (sun′dī′al), *n.* an instrument for showing the time by the casting of a shadow from an indicator (the gnomon) on a dial: *see illustration under gnomon.*

sun-dog (sun′dog′), *n.* **1,** a mock sun, or parhelion, a bright spot of light near the sun, sometimes coloured, caused by refraction of light from ice crystals in the air; **2,** a small rainbow or halo near the horizon.

sun-down (sun′doun′), *n.* sunset.

sun-dry (sun′dri), *adj.* various; several: **—sundries,** *n.pl.* various trifles too small or too numerous to be specified.

sun-fish (sun′fish′), *n.* **1,** a very large, round, short-tailed fish, found in all warm seas, basking in the sun near the surface; **2,** a small American freshwater fish.

sun-flow-er (sun′flou′ẽr), *n.* a tall plant with large leaves and round, flattened, showy yellow flower-heads.

sung (sung), *p.p.* of *sing.*

sunk (sungk), *p.p.* of *sink.*

sunk-en (sungk′en), *adj.* **1,** below the surface, depressed; as, a *sunken* ship; *sunken* gardens; **2,** hollow; as, *sunken* eyes or cheeks.

sun-light (sun′līt′), *n.* the light of the sun.

sun-ny (sun′i), *adj.* [sun-ni-er, sun-ni-est], **1,** bright; cheerful; as, a *sunny* disposition; **2,** exposed to the warmth and light of the sun; as, a *sunny* room.

sun-rise (sun′rīz′), *n.* **1,** the daily appearance of the sun above the horizon; **2,** the time at which the sun appears; **3,** the brightening of the sky at that time; **4,** the east.

sun-set (sun′set′), *n.* **1,** the daily disappearance of the sun below the horizon; **2,** the time at which the sun disappears; **3,** the colours of the sunset sky; **4,** the west.

sun-shine (sun′shīn′), *n.* **1,** the light or rays of the sun; also, the place where they fall; **2,** brightness; cheer.

sun-spot (sun′spot′), *n.* a dark patch or spot on the sun's disk, thought to be a cyclonic sunstorm that affects the earth's magnetism, etc.

sup (sup), *v.t.* [supped, sup-ping], to

take into the mouth a little at a time; sip:—*v.i.* **1,** to take supper; **2,** to sip: —*n.* a small mouthful of liquid; a sip.

su-per- (sū′pėr-), *prefix* meaning *above, over;* as, **su′per-a-bun′dant; su′per-struc′ture.**

su-per (sū′pėr), *n.* the removable upper story of a beehive where the honey is stored:—*adj. esp.* good or fine.

su-per-an-nu-ate (sū′pėr-an′ū-āt′), *v.t.* to retire on pension, as from age or infirmity.—*adj.* **su′per-an′nu-at′ed, 1,** retired (on pension); **2,** antiquated; obsolete.—*n.* **su′per-an′nu-a′tion.**

su-perb (sū-pûrb′), *adj.* **1,** grand; proud; stately; as, a *superb* residence; **2,** rich; elegant; as, *superb* attire; **3,** exceedingly good; of finest quality; as, *superb* acting.

su-per-cil-i-ous (sū′pėr-sil′i-us), *adj.* contemptuously haughty; proud.

su-per-fi-cial (sū′pėr-fish′al), *adj.* **1,** lying on the surface only; not deep; as, *superficial* wounds; **2,** not thorough; hasty.—*adv.* **su′per-fi′cial-ly.**

su-per-flu-ous (sū-pûr′floo-us), *adj.* beyond what is necessary or desirable; excessive; as, *superfluous* remarks. —*n.* **su′per-flu′i-ty.**

su-per-high-way (sū′pėr-hī′wā′), *n.* a modern public road, esp. designed and constructed for speedy, but safe, travel.

su-per-hu-man (sū′pėr-hū′man), *adj.* **1,** beyond what is human; seeming to exceed human powers; as, *superhuman* strength; **2,** supernatural; divine; as, *superhuman* beings.

su-per-in-tend (sū′pėr-in-tend′), *v.t.* to have, or exercise, the charge or oversight of; supervise and direct.—*n.* **su′per-in-tend′ent.**—*n.* **su′per-in-tend′-ence.**

su-pe-ri-or (soo-pir′i-ėr; sū-), *adj.* **1,** higher in place, position, rank, dignity, or office; as, a *superior* officer; **2,** of higher or better quality; preferable; as, this cloth is far *superior;* **3,** not stooping (to); not yielding (to); as, *superior* to petty jealousies; **4,** pretending to greater rank or dignity than that of others; arrogant; as, a *superior* attitude:—*n.* **1,** one who is better, greater, or higher in rank; **2,** the head of a religious house; as, a Mother *Superior.*—*n.* **su-pe′ri-or′i-ty.**

su-per-la-tive (soo-pûr′la-tiv; sū-), *adj.* **1,** best, highest, or greatest in degree; as, a man of *superlative* wisdom; **2,** in *grammar,* naming that form of an adjective or adverb, as *greatest* or *best,* that expresses the highest degree of the quality indicated by the simple word in

the positive degree:—*n.* the superlative degree; also, a superlative form; as, "best" is the *superlative* of "good."

su-per-man (soo′pėr-man′; sū′), *n.* [*pl.* super-men (-men)], a man of unusual strength and ability, or with more than human powers.

su-per-mar-ket (soo′pėr-mär′kit; sū′), *n.* a large food store with most articles so arranged that customers can wait on themselves.

su-per-nal (sū-pûr′nl), *adj.* heavenly.

su-per-nat-u-ral (sū′pėr-nat′ū-ral), *adj.* outside, or exceeding, the laws of nature; miraculous:—*n.* that which is outside the usual course of nature.

su-per-nu-mer-ar-y (sū′pėr-nū′mėr-a-ri), *n.* a person or thing above the usual number or complement, esp. one not on a regular staff, as an army officer, or an actor who does bit parts (in mob scenes).—*adj.* more than needed; superfluous.

su-per-sat-u-rat-ed (sū′pėr-sat′ū-rāt′id), *adj.* saturated beyond normal; as, a *supersaturated* solution.—*n.* **su′-per-sat′u-ra′tion.**

su-per-scrip-tion (sū′pėr-skrip′-shun), *n.* the writing or engraving on the outside or top of something, esp. the address on a letter or envelope.

su-per-sede (sū′pėr-sēd′), *v.t.* [super-seded, supersed-ing], to take the place of; supplant; as, automobiles *super-seded* carriages.

su-per-son-ic (soo′pėr-son′ik; sū′), *adj.* of sound, having a frequency higher than can be heard by the human ear; of speed, faster than the speed of sound in air (about 738 miles per hour).—*n. pl.* **su′per-son′ics.**

su-per-sti-tion (soo′pėr-stish′un; sū′), *n.* **1,** belief in, fear of, or reverence for the unknown or mysterious; **2,** beliefs or practices, often of a religious character, based on fear of the unknown; also, any popular belief in the power of omens, charms, etc.—*adj.* **su′per-sti′tious.**

su-per-vise (soo′pėr-vīz′; sū′pėr-vīz′) *v.t.* [supervised, supervis-ing], to oversee; superintend.—*adj.* **su′per-vi′so-ry.** —*n.* **su′per-vi′sion.**—*n.* **su′per-vi′sor.**

su-pine (sū′pīn; sū-pīn′), *adj.* **1,** lying on the back; opposite of *prone;* **2,** careless; inefficient; listless; as, *supine* indolence; a *supine* attitude.—*n.* the Latin verbal noun, esp. ending in *-um*

sup-per (sup′ėr), *n.* the evening meal, the last meal of the day.—*adj.* **sup′per-less.**

sup-plant (su-plant′), *v.t.* **1,** to take the place of; as, electric lighting has *supplanted* gas lighting; **2,** to take the place of (another), sometimes by underhand means.

sup-ple (sup′l), *adj.* [sup-pler, sup-plest], **1,** easily bent; flexible; **2,** submissive.

sup-ple-ment (sup′li-ment), *n.* that which completes an unfinished thing or adds something to a completed thing; esp., a part at the end of a book or an article adding information or making corrections:—*v.t.* (sup′li-ment′), to make additions to; complete.—*adj.* sup′ple-men′tal.—*adj.* sup′ple-men′ta-ry.

sup-pli-ant (sup′li-ant), *n.* one who implores or entreats:—*adj.* **1,** asking earnestly and humbly; **2,** expressive of entreaty; as, bend the *suppliant* knee.

sup-pli-cate (sup′li-kāt′), *v.t.* [supplicat-ed, supplicat-ing], **1,** to ask for humbly and earnestly; as, to *supplicate* Heaven's blessing; **2,** to address or appeal to in prayer:—*v.i.* to pray or beseech humbly and earnestly.—*n.* sup′pli-ca′tion.

sup-ply (su-plī′), *v.t.* [supplied, supplying], **1,** to furnish; provide; as, to *supply* men with food; to *supply* food for men; **2,** to make up for; fill; as, to *supply* a lack:—*n.* [*pl.* supplies], **1,** the act of furnishing what is needed; **2,** that which is needed; an amount required; as, a winter's *supply* of coal; **3,** the total amount available.—*n* sup-pli′er.

sup-port (su-pōrt′), *v.t.* **1,** to bear the weight of; as, the pedestal *supports* the statue; **2,** to endure; bear; as, he *supported* his agony bravely; **3,** to encourage; sustain; **4,** to verify; prove; as, the figures *support* my claim; **5,** to aid, favour, or defend, as a political party; **6,** to provide for; as, to *support* a family:—*n.* **1,** the act of maintaining or upholding; **2,** one who or that which maintains or upholds; a prop; pillar; as, he is the chief *support* of the cause; the column is a strong *support* for the roof; **3,** maintenance; livelihood; **4,** one who furnishes means of living; as, she is the *support* of the family.—*n.* sup-port′er.—*adj.* sup-port′a-ble.

sup-pose (su-pōz′), *v.t.* [supposed, supposing], **1,** to accept as true; imagine; think; **2,** to assume as a basis of argument; as, but *suppose* you lose; **3,** to imply; require as a condition; as, creation *supposes* a creator:—

v.i. to think; imagine.—*n.* sup′po-si′-tion.—*adv.* sup-pos′ed-ly.

sup-pos-i-to-ry (su-poz′i-tėr-i), *n.* a medical preparation, in the form of a cone or cylinder that melts at body temperature, inserted into a body cavity, as the rectum (to stimulate bowel action).

sup-press (su-pres′), *v.t.* **1,** to subdue; crush; as, to *suppress* a revolt; **2,** to keep in; restrain; as, to *suppress* a cough; **3,** to conceal; also, to stop the publication of; as, to *suppress* news.— *n.* sup-pres′sion.

su-prem-a-cy (sū-prem′a-si; sōō-prem′a-si), *n.* the highest authority or power.

su-preme (sū-prēm′; sōō-prēm′), *adj.* **1,** highest in power or authority; as, a *supreme* court; **2,** highest in degree; greatest possible; as, *supreme* indifference; **3,** crucial; most important; as, the climax is the *supreme* moment in the play.

sur-charge (sûr′chärj), *n.* **1,** an excessive or extra charge; **2,** an additional or secondary printing stamped on the face of a postage stamp, giving a new valuation, date, etc.:— *v.t.* (sûr-chärj′), to levy an extra charge; overcharge; overstock.

surd (sûrd), *n.* in *algebra*, a root that cannot be obtained exactly, as $\sqrt{15}$.— *adj.* irrational: said of a quantity that cannot be expressed in ordinary numbers or quantities.

sure (shoor), *adj.* [sur-er, sur-est], **1,** knowing and believing; confident; as, I am *sure* you will succeed; **2,** destined; certain; as, you are *sure* to succeed; **3,** dependable; reliable; as, the only *sure* way; **4,** firmly fixed; as, a *sure* foundation:—*adv.* surely; as, *sure* as fate.—*n.* sure′ness.—*adv.* sure′ly.

sure-ty (shoor′ti; shoor′i-ti), *n.* [*pl.* sureties], **1,** certainty; **2,** that which makes for security; esp., a guarantee against loss or damage; **3,** one who makes himself responsible for certain acts of another, as for the payment of a debt.

surf (sûrf), *n.* the waves of the sea as they break in foam upon the shore.

sur-face (sûr′fis), *n.* **1,** the outside part of a solid body, or the upper face of a body of liquid; as, a rough *surface*; the *surface* of a lake; **2,** external or outward appearance:—*adj.* **1,** pertaining to the top or surface; **2,** insincere; as, *surface* politeness:—*v.t.* [surfaced, surfac-ing], to give an outside covering or polish to.

sur-feit (sûr′fit), *n*. **1**, indulgence to excess, esp. in eating or drinking; **2**, fullness or sickness caused by such excess:—*v.t.* to feed to excess; cloy; glut; satiate.

surf-fish (sûrf′fish′), *n*. a small, spiny-finned variety of Pacific sea perch, whose young are born alive along rocky or sandy beaches or about wharves and kelp beds: seven B.C. varieties are known, the commonest being the yellow shiner.

surge (sûrj), *n*. **1**, a large wave, swell, or billow; **2**, a great rolling motion; rush; as, the *surge* of a mob:—*v.i.* [surged, surging], to rise high and roll; swell.

sur-geon (sûr′jun), *n*. a doctor trained to perform operations.

sur-ger-y (sûr′jẽr-i), *n*. [*pl*. surgeries], the science and practice of treating injuries, deformities, or diseases by operations, esp. by the use of the knife. —*adj*. **sur′gi-cal** (sûr′ji-kl).

sur-ly (sûr′li), *adj*. [sur-li-er, sur-li-est], ill-humoured; uncivil; rudely abrupt. —*n*. **sur′li-ness.**

sur-mise (sûr-mīz′; sûr′mīz), *n*. a thought or conjecture based upon little evidence; a guess:—*v.t.* and *v.i.* (sûr-mīz′), [surmised, surmis-ing], to guess, or make a guess on insufficient evidence.

sur-mount (sûr-mount′), *v.t.* **1**, to overcome; conquer; as, to *surmount* difficulties; **2**, to be placed at the top of; as, a castle *surmounts* the hill.

sur-name (sûr′nām′), *n*. originally, a name, often descriptive, added to the Christian name, as in "Charles the Bold"; now, the last or family name, shared by all the members of one family:—*v.t.* (sûr′nām′; sûr-nām′), [surnamed, surnam-ing], to give a sur-name, or additional name, to; as, Alexander was *surnamed* the Great.

sur-pass (sẽr-pås′), *v.t.* **1**, to exceed; go beyond the limits of; as, wonders that *surpass* belief; **2**, to excel; as, he *surpasses* all others in wisdom.

sur-plice (sûr′plis), *n*. an outer white linen garment with wide sleeves, worn in some churches by the clergy and the choir.

sur-plus (sûr′plus), *n*. that which remains over and above what is used or required; excess: opposite of *deficit:* —*adj*. exceeding what is used or needed.

sur-prise (sẽr-prīz′), *n*. **1**, the act of coming upon or attacking un-expectedly; as, the enemy was taken by *surprise;* **2**, the feeling aroused by what is sudden and strange; wonder;

astonishment; **3**, a sudden or unex-pected event or fact; as, his dismissal came as a *surprise:*—*v.t.* [surprised, surpris-ing], **1**, to take unawares; come upon or attack without warning; as, they *surprised* the conspirators; **2**, to strike with wonder, as does some-thing unexpected; **3**, to hurry (a person) into doing something unin-tended; as, to *surprise* a thief into confessing.

sur-re-al-ism (su-rē′al-izm), *n*. a movement in art and literature that tries to show activities of the sub-conscious mind by images without order, as in a dream.—*adj*. **sur-re′al-is′tic.**—*n*. and *adj*. **sur-re′al-ist.**

sur-ren-der (su-ren′dẽr), *v.t.* **1**, to yield (oneself) under pressure to the power of another; **2**, to resign posses-sion of; give up; as, to *surrender* arms; *surrender* one's claim to property; **3**, to yield (oneself) to an influence or emotion:—*v.i.* to yield; give up the struggle:—*n*. the act of yielding to an outside influence; also, the giving up of a claim or privilege.

sur-rep-ti-tious (sûr′ep-tish′us), *adj*. done by stealth, or by secret or improper means; as, a *surreptitious* entry, will, etc.

sur-rey (sûr′i), *n*. a light, 4-wheeled carriage with two seats, both facing forward.

sur-ro-gate (sûr′ō-gāt′; -git), *n*. and *adj*. **1**, a court that probates wills, administers estates, etc.; **2**, a substi-tute; deputy; esp. for a judge, bishop, etc.

sur-round (su-round′), *v.t.* **1**, to enclose on all sides; as, the city is *surrounded* by suburbs; **2**, to encircle or cause to be encircled; as, to *surround* oneself with luxuries.

sur-round-ings (su-roun′dingz), *n.pl.* neighbourhood; environment.

sur-tax (sûr′taks′), *n*. a tax added to a normal tax, often graduated as that on large incomes.

sur-veil-lance (sûr-vāl′ans; sûr-vāl′-yans), *n*. a close watch; supervision.

sur-vey (sẽr-vā′), *v.t.* **1**, to look at, as from a height; take a broad, general view of; as, to *survey* a landscape; *survey* a series of events; **2**, to examine closely, with respect to condition, value, etc.; as, to *survey* a factory; **3**, to measure and determine the boundaries or other features of (a portion of land): —*n*. (sûr′vā; sẽr-vā′), **1**, the act of looking over or examining carefully; **2**, an investigation, often of official nature; as, a *survey* of unemployment; **3,** a summary or outline; **4,** the process of determining the exact measurements, outline, position, etc., of any part of the earth's surface; also, an accurate plan and description, based on these measurements.—*n.* **sur-vey'or.**

sur-vive (sêr-vīv'), *v.t.* [survived, surviv-ing], to live longer than (others); to outlive; also, to live beyond or through (an event, state, etc.); as, to *survive* a tornado:—*v.i.* to remain alive or in existence.—*n.* **sur-vi'vor.**—*n.* **sur-viv'al.**

sus-cep-ti-ble (su-sep'ti-bl), *adj.* **1,** capable of; admitting; as, a statement *susceptible* of proof; **2,** capable of being changed, influenced, or easily affected; as, a person *susceptible* to flattery; **3,** sensitive; impressionable; as, *suscept-ible* youth.—*n.* **sus-cep'ti-bil'i-ty.**

sus-pect (sus-pekt'), *v.t.* **1,** to conjec-ture; surmise; as, I *suspect* that illness kept her home; **2,** to believe in the possible guilt of, without having proof; **3,** to consider as questionable; doubt; as, to *suspect* the accuracy of a report: —*n.* (also sus'pekt), a person believed, but not proved, to be guilty of crime.

sus-pend (sus-pend'), *v.t.* **1,** to cause to hang down; as, to *suspend* a rope from a roof; **2,** to hold, as if hanging; as, particles of dust are *suspended* in the air; **3,** to delay; hold undecided; as, to *suspend* judgment; **4,** to set aside or waive temporarily; disregard for a time; as, to *suspend* a rule; **5,** to debar, or keep out, for a time, from some privilege, office, etc.; as, to *suspend* a student.—*n.* **sus-pen'sion.**

sus-pend-ers (sus-pen'dêrz), *n.pl.* **1,** a device for holding up the socks; **2,** two straps or bands worn over the shoulders to hold up the trousers.

sus-pense (sus-pens'), *n.* a state of uncertainty, doubt, or anxiety.

sus-pi-cion (sus-pish'un), *n.* **1,** the feeling or imagining that something is wrong; mistrust; doubt; **2,** a notion or inkling; as, a *suspicion* of trouble; **3,** a very small amount; hint; as, a *suspicion* of humour.

sus-pi-cious (sus-pish'us), *adj.* **1,** inclined to imagine without proof; distrustful; as, a *suspicious* parent; **2,** open to, or exciting, unbelief; as, a *suspicious* alibi; **3,** showing, or suggest-ing, doubt or suspicion; as, a *suspicious* glance.

sus-tain (sus-tān'), *v.t.* **1,** to support, as weight or pressure; **2,** to maintain or keep up, as an argument; **3,** to keep going; as, food *sustains* life; **4,** to suffer; undergo, as a loss; **5,** to bear up under; receive, as a blow; **6,** to keep up the spirit of; as, his faith *sustained* him; **7,** to confirm; bear out; as, to *sustain* an accusation with proof; **8,** to uphold, as a decision.—*n.* **sus'te-nance** (sus'ti-nans).

su-ture (sū'tūr; sōō'chêr), *n.* **1,** the act of sewing; **2,** in *surgery*, the drawing together of the edges of a wound with stitches; **3,** a joining together or junc-tion, as of the bones of the skull, valves of a mollusc, etc.

su-ze-rain (sū'zê-rān'), *n.* a feudal lord whose vassals owed allegiance in return for use of the land.—*n.* **su'ze-rain-ty.**

svelte (svelt), *n.* lithe; supple; slender: said of a woman's figure.

swab (swob), *n.* **1,** a mop for cleaning decks, floors, etc.; **2,** a bit of cotton, cloth, sponge, etc., used to clean the mouth or throat of a sick person, or to apply medicine; **3,** *Slang,* a clumsy fellow; lout:—*v.t.* to clean, wipe, or treat with a swab.—*n.* **swab'ber.**

swad-dle (swod'l), *v.t.* to wrap tightly in clothes, esp. a new-born child.

swag (swag), *n. Slang,* plundered goods; booty.

swag-ger (swag'êr), *v.i.* to strut about; also, to boast noisily; bluster:—*n.* an affected, insolent walk or strut; also, noisy boastfulness.

swain (swān), *n.* **1,** a country lad; **2,** a young suitor.

swale (swāl), *n.* a meadow, often marshy and rank with vegetation.

¹**swal-low** (swol'ō; swôl'ō), *n.* any one of several small migratory birds, with long, forked tail and pointed wings, noted for graceful, swift flight.

²**swal-low** (swol'ō; swôl'ō), *v.t.* **1,** to transfer, as food, from the mouth to the stomach through the gullet; **2,** to absorb; as, expenses *swallow* up income; engulf; as, night *swallowed* the earth; **3,** to endure quietly, as an insult; **4,** to accept as true without asking for proof; as, to *swallow* an improbable story:— *v.i.* to perform the act of taking down food or liquid; as, to *swallow* quickly: —*n.* the act of swallowing; also, the amount swallowed at one time.

swam (swam), *p.t.* of *swim.*

swa-mi (swä'mi), *n.* pundit; lord; master; a title of respect for a Hindu religious teacher.

swamp (swomp; swômp), *n.* wet, marshy land:—*v.t.* **1,** to cause to sink in a swamp or bog; **2,** to sink by filling with water; as, to *swamp* a boat; **3,** to overwhelm; submerge; as, the business was *swamped* by old debts.—*adj.* **swamp′ish.**—*adj.* **swamp′y.**

swan (swon; swôn), *n.* a large, graceful aquatic bird with a long neck.

swank (swangk), *adj. Slang,* pretentiously stylish, smart, or dashing:—*v.i. Slang,* to swagger; show off.—*adj.* **swank′y.**

swap (swop), *v.t. Colloq.* to exchange; barter; as to *swap* wives.—*n. Colloq.* an exchange. Also, **swop.**

sward (swôrd), *n.* a stretch of land covered thickly with short grass; turf.

swarm (swôrm), *n.* **1,** a large number of moving birds, animals, insects, etc.; as, a *swarm* of locusts; **2,** a large number of honey-bees, accompanied by a queen, leaving one hive to establish a new home in another; also, a colony of bees settled in a hive permanently; **3,** a great number; a crowd; as, *swarms* of people:—*v.i.* **1,** to move about in great numbers; as, people *swarmed* into the theatre; **2,** to be crowded; as, the town *swarmed* with soldiers; **3,** of bees, to leave a hive in a swarm to form a new colony:—*v.t.* to throng; as, people *swarmed* the streets.

swarth-y (swôr′thi; swôr′thi), *adj.* [swarth-i-er, swarth-i-est], of a dusky colour; dark-skinned.—*n.* **swarth′-i-ness.**

swash-buck-ler (swosh′buk′lẽr; swôsh′ buk′lẽr), *n.* a blustering bully; a swaggerer.

swas-ti-ka or **swas-ti-ca** (swos′ti-ka; swôs′ti-ka; swas′-ti-ka), *n.* a crosslike symbol, dating from ancient times, shaped like four capital L's joined together: adopted by the Nazis as the national emblem of Germany.

SWASTIKA

swat (swot), *v.t. Slang,* to strike smartly or violently:—*n.* a smart rap:—*n.* **swat′ter.** Also, **swot.**

¹**swathe** (swāth), *v.t.* [swathed, swathing], **1,** to bind with a band or bandage; **2,** to wrap; enclose; as, to *swathe* oneself in furs:—*n.* a bandage.

²**swathe** (swôth), *n.* the amount of grass cut, or the space left clear, by a single sweep of a scythe, etc. Also, **swath.**

sway (swā), *v.i.* **1,** to move or swing from side to side, or backward and forward, as tree-tops in a breeze; **2,** to lean to one side; waver; as, the tight-rope dancer *swayed* and fell:—*v.t.* **1,** to cause to bend or to move backward and

forward, or from side to side; **2,** to cause to lean to one side; bias; as, to *sway* opinion; **3,** to influence by power; direct; rule; as, to *sway* the lives of a people:—*n.* **1,** the act of swaying; **2,** a controlling force or influence; as, under the *sway* of anger; **3,** rule or control; as, the *sway* of the press over public opinion.

swear (swâr), *v.i.* [*p.t.* swore (swōr) or, *Archaic,* sware (swâr), *p.p.* sworn (swōrn), *p.pr.* swear-ing], **1,** to make a solemn declaration, with an appeal to God as witness, to the truth of what is affirmed; **2,** to make a solemn vow or promise; **3,** to give evidence on oath; **4,** to use profane language:—*v.t.* **1,** to declare solemnly, with an appeal to God or to some sacred object; **2,** to vow or promise solemnly; **3,** to cause (a person) to take an oath.

sweat (swet), *n.* **1,** the moisture which is given off through the pores of the skin; perspiration; **2,** moisture given off by any substance; **3,** the act of perspiring; also, the condition of one who is perspiring:—*v.i.* [*p.t.* and *p.p.* sweat or sweat-ed, *p.pr.* sweat-ing], **1,** to perspire; **2,** to form moisture in drops on the outside; as, a glass of water *sweats*; **3,** *Colloq.,* to labour hard; drudge:—*v.t.* **1,** to cause to perspire freely; as, to *sweat* a horse; **2,** to wet with perspiration; **3,** to employ at long hours of work for very low wages.—*adj.* **sweat′y.**—*n.* **sweat′band′**; **sweat′shop′.**

sweat-er (swet′ẽr), *n.* **1,** a person who overworks and underpays those who work for him; **2,** a knitted or crocheted jacket.

sweep (swēp), *v.t.* [swept (swept), sweep-ing], **1,** to brush or clean with a broom, brush, etc.; as, to *sweep* a rug; **2,** to remove or clean away; as, to *sweep* up bits of paper; **3,** to drive, flow over, or carry along or off, with force; as, waves *swept* the deck; **4,** to pass lightly over or across; as, to *sweep* the strings of a guitar; **5,** to scan or gaze at; move or traverse swiftly; as, to *sweep* the seas:—*v.i.* **1,** to clean or clear away dirt with a brush, broom, etc.; **2,** to pass with speed or force; as, the cavalry *swept* down the field; **3,** to move with stateliness or dignity; **4,** to extend in a continuous line or curve; as, the lawn *sweeps* down to the river:—*n.* **1,** the act of sweeping, clearing out, or getting rid of; **2,** a sweeping motion; as, a *sweep* of the arm; **3,** the range of such a motion; **4,** a bend or curve, as of a drive; **5,** one who makes a business of cleaning chimneys; **6,** a long pole, attached to a post, for drawing a bucket from a well; **7,** a long oar for moving or steering a boat.—*n.* **sweep′er.**

sweep-stake (swēp′stāk′), *n.* a winning of all the stakes or prizes by one contestant or bettor: *pl.* used as *sing.* or *pl.*, a lottery in which each buys a stake, often a ticket on a horse-race, to form a common fund, which goes as a prize to the winner or in shares to several winners; as, the Irish *sweepstakes.*

sweet (swēt), *adj.* **1,** tasting like sugar; **2,** not stale or sour; as, *sweet* milk; **3,** not salt; as, *sweet* butter; **4,** fragrant; **5,** pleasing in sound; soft; as, the *sweet* tones of a violin; **6,** charming or attractive in manner or appearance; **7,** gentle; mild; as, a *sweet* disposition: —*n.* **1,** one dearly loved; a darling; **2,** a tart, pudding, etc.; dessert; **3,** sweets, confectionery or candy.—*n.* **sweet′ness.**—*adj.* **sweet′ish.**

sweet a-lys-sum (a-lis′um), a low-growing garden plant with small fragrant white flowers.

sweet-bread (swēt′bred′), *n.* the pancreas of a calf or lamb, cooked for food.

sweet-en (swēt′n), *v.t.* to make sweet; as, to *sweeten* tea:—*v.i.* to become sweet.

sweet-heart (swēt′härt′), *n.* one who is beloved; a lover.

sweet mar-jo-ram (mär′jo-ram), a fragrant mint used as a flavouring in cooking: also called *marjoram.*

sweet-meat (swēt′mēt′), *n.* a piece of crystallized fruit, ginger, etc.; a candy.

sweet pea, a plant with slender, climbing stems and fragrant flowers of various colours; also, the flower.

sweet po-ta-to, the sweet, starchy root of a tropical American vine, used as a vegetable; also, the vine.

sweet—wil-liam (swēt′–wil′yam), *n.* a plant of the pink family with flowers of various colours in dense flat clusters.

swell (swel), *v.i.* [*p.t.* swelled (sweld), *p.p.* swol-len (swōl′en) or swelled, *p.pr.* swell-ing], **1,** to increase in size, volume, force, importance, value, etc.; as, her sprained ankle began to *swell;* it is hoped that profits will *swell* this year; the music *swelled* to a climax; **2,** to be inflated or bulge, as sails; **3,** to be puffed up; as, to *swell* with pride; **4,** to rise above the surrounding surface; as, the ground *swells:—v.t.* **1,** to cause to rise or increase; fill; puff up; **2,** to inflate with pride; **3,** in *music,* to play or sing (notes) with gradual increase and decrease of volume:—*n.* **1,** the act of swelling; an increase in volume, force, value, etc.; **2,** in *music,* gradual increase and decrease of sound; **3,** a long, continuous wave; **4,** *Colloq.,* a very fashionable person.

swel-ter (swel′tėr), *v.i.* to suffer from the heat; perspire freely.

swerve (swûrv), *v.i.* and *v.t.* [swerved, swerv-ing], to turn aside, or cause to turn aside, from a direct course:—*n.* a sudden turning aside.

swift (swift), *adj.* rapid; quick; alert: —*n.* a bird, related to the humming-bird, but resembling the swallow.

swig (swig), *n. Colloq.* a deep draught (draft), as of liquor:—*v.t.* and *v.i. Colloq.* to drink deeply; gulp; as, to *swig* from a flask or bottle.

swill (swil), *n.* **1,** liquid food for animals, esp. kitchen refuse given to pigs; **2,** a swig (of liquor); **3,** garbage; slop:—*v.t.* to drink or gulp greedily; guzzle.

swim (swim), *v.i.* [*p.t.* swam (swam), *p.p.* swum (swum), *p.pr.* swim-ming], **1,** to propel or push oneself forward in the water, with the arms and legs, as does man, or with fins and tail, as do fish, etc.; **2,** to float on a liquid; **3,** to be carried along smoothly by a current; **4,** to overflow; as, eyes *swimming* with tears; **5,** to be dizzy; as, my head *swims;* also, to reel or seem to reel; as, the room *swam* before her eyes:—*v.t.* **1,** to cause to swim or float; as, to *swim* cattle across a stream; **2,** to traverse by swimming; as, to *swim* a lake:—*n.* swimming, esp. as a sport.—*n.* **swim′-mer.**

swin-dle (swin′dl), *v.t.* and *v.i.* [swin-dled, swin-dling], to get money or something else from (someone) on false pretences; cheat:—*n.* the act of cheating; also, a fraudulent scheme.— *n.* **swin′dler.**

swine (swīn), *n.* [*pl.* swine], **1,** any animal of the hog family; **2,** a person with greedy or coarse habits.—*adj.* **swin′ish.**

swing (swing), *v.i.* [swung (swung), swing-ing], **1,** to move to and fro regularly, as the pendulum of a clock; **2,** to turn on, or as on, a hinge, or axis; as, the gate *swings* open; **3,** to move with a loose, free, swaying gait; **4,** to turn or wheel round; veer, as the wind: —*v.t.* **1,** to cause to move to and fro; as, to *swing* a child in a hammock; **2,** to move or wave to and fro; brandish, as a cane; **3,** to cause to turn or wheel about; **4,** to put up so as to hang freely; as, to *swing* a hammock; hang on hinges; as, to *swing* a gate; **5,** to manage successfully; as, to *swing* a business deal:—*n.* **1,** the act of swinging; also, the distance through which an object swings; **2,** a loose, free gait; **3,** an apparatus, usually a rope holding a seat, for swinging; **4,** strongly marked rhythm, as of poetry or music.

swipe (swīp), *n.* a vigorous blow, as with a club:—*v.t.* [swiped, swip-ing], **1,** to hit with force; **2,** *Slang*, to steal.

swirl (swûrl), *v.i.* to move with a circular or whirling motion:—*v.t.* to cause to eddy or whirl:—*n.* **1,** a whirl or eddy; **2,** a curve or twist; as, a *swirl* of hair.

swish (swish), *n.* a rustling sound, or the movement that makes it:—*v.t.* to brandish, as a cane; cause to make a rustling sound:—*v.i.* to move with a rustling sound.

switch (swich), *n.* **1,** a thin, flexible twig or rod; **2,** a blow with such a switch or whip; **3,** a movable section of rail for shifting cars from one track to another; **4,** a device for making, breaking, or shifting electric circuits; **5,** a tress of false hair, used by women in dressing the hair:—*v.t.* **1,** to whip or lash with a switch; **2,** to swing or jerk; as, the horse *switched* its tail; **3,** to shift (cars) to another track; **4,** to shift to another circuit, or on or off a circuit; as, to *switch* off the electric light:—*v.i.* **1,** to shift to another track; **2,** hence, to change course suddenly.

switch-board (swich'bōrd'), *n.* a board or panel with apparatus controlling and combining electric circuits, as in a telephone exchange.

swiv-el (swiv'l), *n.* **1,** anything that turns on a headed bolt or pin; as, the *swivel* of a watch-chain; **2,** a link in two parts connected by a bolt or pin, so that each part can turn independently:—*v.t.* and *v.i.* [swivelled, swivel-ling], to turn on a swivel.

swoll-en (swōl'en), *p.p.* of swell.

swoon (swoon), *v.i.* to faint:—*n.* a faint.

swoop (swoop), *v.i.* to sweep (down) swiftly and suddenly; pounce; as, the eagle *swoops* down upon its prey:—*n.* a sudden downward plunge, as of a bird of prey.

swop (swop), *v.t.* Same as *swap*.

sword (sōrd), *n.* **1,** a weapon consisting of a long pointed blade, with one or with two sharp edges, set in a handle or hilt, and kept, when not in actual use, in a sheath or scabbard; **2,** the symbol of military power, of justice, or of vengeance; **3,** conflict or war; as, to resort to the *sword.*—*n.* **swords'man.**

sword-fish (sōrd'fish'), *n.* a large, edible sea fish, whose upper jaw lengthens out into a swordlike projection.

sword-tail (sōrd'tāl'), *n.* an aquarium fish, *Xiphophorus helleri*, native of Central America fresh water: about 4″ long, with bright olive-brown on back and stripings of brown green, blue, and red on body and tail: to escape parents, the young need weeds.

swore (swōr), *p.t.* of *swear*.

sworn (swōrn), *p.p.* of *swear.*—*adj.* bound by oath; as, a *sworn* enemy.

swum (swum), *p.p.* and one of the past tenses of *swim*.

swung (swung), *p.t.* and *p.p.* of *swing*.

syc-a-more (sik'a-mōr'), *n.* **1,** the American buttonwood; **2,** a fig-tree of Syria and Egypt; **3,** in Europe and Asia, a kind of maple.

syc-o-phant (sik'ō-fant), *n.* a servile flatterer; parasite; toady.

syl-lab-i-fy (si-lab'i-fī'), *v.t.* [syllabified, syllabify-ing], to divide into syllables.—*n.* **syl-lab'i-fi-ca'tion.**—*v.t.* **syl-lab'i-cate'** (to divide into syllables) —*n.* **syl-lab'i-ca'tion.**

syl-la-ble (sil'a-bl), *n.* **1,** a unit of pronunciation consisting of a vowel sound or a vowel sound grouped with one or more consonant sounds, pronounced by a single impulse of the voice, and forming either a complete word or one of the units which, together, make a word; as, "dog" is the first *syllable* or "dog-mat-ic"; **2,** the written or printed letters corresponding, though not always exactly, to a syllable as pronounced.—*adj.* **syl-lab'ic** (si-lab'ik).

syl-la-bus (sil'a-bus), *n.* [*pl.* syllabi (sil'a-bī) or syllabuses], a brief statement of the main points of a lecture book, etc.

syl-lo-gism (sil'ō-jizm), *n.* a form of logic or reasoning consisting of a major premise, a minor premise and a conclusion; as, all men are mortal: AB is a man; therefore AB is mortal.

sylph (silf), *n.* **1,** an imaginary being living in the air; **2,** a slender, graceful young woman.—*adj.* **sylph'like'.**

syl-van (sil'van), *adj.* Same as **silvan**

sym-bol (sim'bl), *n.* **1,** something that stands for or represents something else; an emblem; as, the hearth is the *symbol* of home; **2,** a mark, character, combination of letters, etc.; as, the letters of the alphabet are *symbols;* the sign ÷ is the *symbol* of division; H_2O is the chemical *symbol* for water.—*adj.* **sym-bol'ic** (sim-bol'ik); **sym-bol'i-cal.**—*adv.* **sym-bol'i-cal-ly.**

sym-bol-ize (sim'bul-īz'), *v.t.* [symbolized, symboliz-ing], to stand for, or represent; as, the lily *symbolizes* purity; also, to represent by means of a symbol. —*n.* **sym'bol-ism.**

sym-me-try (sim'i-tri), *n.* [*pl.* symmetries], **1,** the balanced structure of an object, the halves of which are alike; as, the *symmetry* of a sphere; **2,** beauty of proportion.—*adj.* **sym-met'ri-cal** (si-met'ri-kal).

sym-pa-thy (sim'pa-thi), *n.* [*pl.* sympathies], **1,** the sharing of another's emotions; as, I feel *sympathy* with your indignation; **2,** compassion for another's trouble; **3,** harmony or agreement of affections or tastes; congeniality; **4,** friendly understanding and interest.—*adj.* **sym'pa-thet'ic.**—*v.i.* **sym'pa-thize.**

sym-pho-ny (sim'fo-ni), *n.* [*pl.* symphonies], **1,** harmony of sound; **2,** an agreeable blending of any kind; as, a *symphony* in blue and grey; **3,** an elaborate musical composition, consisting of three or four movements, for a full orchestra.—*adj.* **sym-phon'ic.**

sym-po-si-um (sim-pō'zi-um), *n.* **1,** a conference organized to discuss a particular subject; **2,** a meeting or social gathering for the free exchange of ideas; **3,** a collection of brief essays in which writers express their views on a given topic.

symp-tom (simp'tum), *n.* **1,** any change or special condition in the body or its functions, as an evidence of disease; **2,** a sign of the existence of something; as, a *symptom* of unrest.—*adj.* **symp'to-mat'ic.**

syn-a-gogue (sin'a-gog'), *n.* **1,** an assembly or gathering of Jews for worship; **2,** the building used for such worship.

syn-chro-nize (sing'kro-nīz'), *v.t.* **1,** to cause to agree in time, speed, or rate of vibration; **2,** to assign to the same date or period of time:—*v.i.* to coincide as to date, period of vibration, rate, etc.; to happen at the same time or rate. —*n.* **syn'chro-nism; syn'chro-ni-za'-tion.**—*adj.* **syn'chro-nous.**

syn-co-pate (sing'kō-pāt'), *v.t.* in *music,* to begin a tone on an unaccented beat and sustain it through the next accented beat, or on the last half of a beat and sustain it through the first half of the next; in *grammar,* to con-tract (a word) by omitting a letter, as in *e'er* for *ever.*—*n.* **syn'co-pa'tion.**

syn-co-pe (sing'kō-pē'), *n.* in *grammar,* the omitting of a letter or letters from a word, as in *ne'er,* or of a sound, as in *Wooster* for *Worcester;* in *medicine,* fainting (from temporary lack of blood circulation in the brain).

syn-di-cate (sin'di-kāt'; kit), *n.* a group or company of persons formed to carry out a particular enterprise, esp. one requiring much capital; as, a motion-picture *syndicate:*—*v.t.* (sin'di-kāt'), [syndicat-ed, syndicat-ing], **1,** to form into a syndicate; **2,** to manage, control, or sell through a syndicate; as, to *syndicate* a bond issue.

syne (sīn), *adv. Scottish,* since:—**auld lang syne,** days of long ago.

syn-od (sin'ud), *n.* **1,** a church council, or meeting to consult on religious matters; **2,** any deliberative assembly or council.

syn-o-nym (sin'o-nim), *n.* a word having the same or nearly the same meaning as another; as, "keen" is a *synonym* of "sharp": opposite of *antonym.*—*adj.* **syn-on'y-mous.**

syn-op-sis (si-nop'sis), *n.* [*pl.* synopses (si-nop'sēz)], a condensed statement or summary, as of a book or play.—*adj.* **syn-op'tic.**

syn-tax (sin'taks), *n.* that part of grammar which treats of the relationship of the words in a sentence to one another.—*adj.* **syn-tac'ti-cal.**

syn-the-sis (sin'thi-sis), *n.* [*pl.* syntheses (sin'thi-sēz')], the combining of separate elements, substances, or parts to make a new form or whole.—*adj.* **syn-thet'ic.**—*v.t.* **syn'the-size'.**

sy-rin-ga (si-ring'ga), *n.* a kind of orna-mental garden shrub with white or cream-coloured flowers: also called *mock orange.*

syr-inge (sir'inj), *n.* an appliance for ejecting liquid in a jet under pressure, used in gardening, surgery, and esp. for injecting a liquid into the body:—*v.t.* [syringed, syring-ing], to wash or cleanse by the use of a syringe.

syr-up (sir'up), *n.* **1,** a thick, sticky liquid made from the juice of fruits, herbs, etc., boiled with sugar; **2,** any similar liquid; as, maple *syrup.*—*adj.* **syr'up-y.** Also, **sir'up.**

sys-tem (sis'tem), *n.* **1,** a group or combination of parts or units func-tioning together as a whole according to some common law or purpose; as, the solar *system;* **2,** an orderly collection of rules and principles; as, a *system* of laws; **3,** an orderly grouping of facts and objects; as, a filing *system;*

4, regular routine; hence efficiency; **5,** the human body considered as a unit.— *adj.* sys′tem-at′ic; sys′tem-at′i-cal.— *v.* sys′tem-a-tize.—*adj.* sys-tem′ic.

T

T, t (tē), *n.* [*pl.* T's, t's], **1,** the 20th letter of the alphabet, following S; **2,** anything with the shape of a T:—*adj.* shaped like a T; as, a *T* bone.

tab (tab), *n.* **1,** a small flap or tag attached to the edge of something; as, shoulder-*tabs;* **2,** *Colloq.,* account; check; as, to keep close *tab* on his work.

tab-by (tab′i), *n.* [*pl.* tabbies], a domestic cat, esp. a female, yellowish grey and marked with black.

tab-er-nac-le (tab′ẽr-nak′l), *n.* **1,** a place of worship, esp. one erected temporarily; also, a large and imposing church; **2,** a Jewish temple; **3,** in some churches, an ornamental box resting on the altar and containing the sacred Host; **4,** a temporary dwelling; a tent:— **Tabernacle,** the movable structure used by the Israelites as a place of worship in the wilderness.

ta-ble (tā′bl), *n.* **1,** a piece of furniture consisting of a flat smooth top supported by legs; **2,** the persons sitting around a table; as, a *table* of bridge; **3,** food; fare in general; as, a hotel noted for its food *table;* **4,** an arrangement of words, facts, figures, etc., in systematic order for reference; as, statistical *tables;* **5,** a thin slab of wood, stone, metal, etc., with a flat surface, esp. one on which an inscription may be written or carved:—*v.t.* [tabled, ta-bling], **1,** to lay aside so as to postpone consideration of; as to *table* a report; **2,** to lay (cards, money, etc.) upon a table; **3,** to put in list form; tabulate.—*n.* **ta′ble-cloth′.**

tab-leau (tab′lō; tȧ′blō′), *n.* [*pl.* tableaux (tab′lōz; tȧ′blō′) or tableaus (tab′-lōz)], a representation, as of a scene from history, in which silent and motionless living models pose.

ta-ble d'hote (tȧ′bl-dōt′; tȧ′b′l-dōt′), *n.* a complete meal in a restaurant, hotel, etc., served at a set hour for a set price: opposite of *à la carte.*

ta-ble-land (tā′bl-land′), *n.* a plateau, or elevated level stretch of land.

ta-ble-spoon (tā′bl-spoon′), *n.* a large spoon used in preparing and serving

meals, and holding three times as much as a teaspoon.—*n.* ta′ble-spoon′ful.

tab-let (tab′lit), *n.* **1,** a small flat piece of some hard material, as wood or ivory, for writing upon; **2,** blank sheets of paper fastened together at one end and used for writing; a scribbler; **3,** a flat panel, often of stone, brass, or bronze, fastened in a wall and bearing an inscription; **4,** medicine in the form of a small flat disk; **5,** a small, flat cake of soap, candy, etc.

tab-loid (tab′loid), *n.* a daily newspaper, small in size, and usually containing many photographs:—*adj.* condensed; concentrated; as, medicine in *tabloid* form.

ta-boo or **ta-bu** (ta-boo′), *n.* a system or practice, among primitive races, in which certain things are held sacred, and contact with them forbidden; hence, a ban or prohibition:—*v.t.* to place under a ban; forbid; prohibit:— *adj.* **1,** set apart; made untouchable or sacred; **2,** prohibited by social custom; as, bad manners are *taboo.*

tab-u-lar (tab′ū-lẽr), *adj.* flat; having a tablelike surface; as, a *tabular* rock.

tab-u-late (tab′ū-lāt′), *v.t.* [tabulat-ed, tabulat-ing], to set up, or arrange in, a systematic outline, usually in columns; as, to *tabulate* data.—*n.* **tab′u-la′tion.**

tac-it (tas′it), *adj.* silent, not spoken; implied, but not stated outright; as, a *tacit* agreement.—*adv.* **tac′it-ly.**

tac-i-turn (tas′i-tûrn), *adj.* silent or reserved; disinclined to talk.—*adv.* **tac′i-turn-ly.**—*n.* **tac′i-tur′ni-ty.**

tack (tak), *n.* **1,** a small, sharp-pointed nail with a flat head; as, upholstery *tacks;* **2,** a rope for lashing down the lower forward corner of certain sails; also, the corner of the sail so held down; **3,** the direction of a ship as determined by the position of her sails; **4,** a change in a ship's direction to take advantage of side winds; **5,** hence, any course or policy of action:—*v.t.* **1,** to fasten with tacks; as, to *tack* down matting; **2,** to stitch lightly together; attach; as, to *tack* a bow on a dress; **3,** to change the course of (a vessel) by using the helm and shifting the sails:—*v.i.* to change the course of a vessel by shifting the position of its sails.

tack-le (tak′l), *n.* **1,** an instrument consisting of pulleys and ropes, used for raising or lowering weights; esp., on a vessel, the pulleys and ropes for managing sails and spars, taking on cargo, etc.; **2,** equipment; gear; as, fishing-*tackle;* **3** in *football,* the act of seizing and stopping an opponent who is running with the ball; also, a player in the line next to either end player, or the position next to either end position: —*v.t.* [tack-led, tack-ling], **1,** to grapple with (a person); try to solve (a problem); **2,** to fasten with ropes and pulleys; **3,** to seize and stop by a tackle, as in football.

tack-y (tak′i), *adj.* [-ier, -iest], sticky, as varnish, glue, etc., before dry.

tact (takt), *n.* natural ability to deal wisely with others; skill in saying and doing the appropriate thing.—*adj.* tact′ful.

tac-tics (tak′tiks), *n.pl.* **1,** the science or practice of handling military or naval forces in the presence of an enemy; **2,** any skilful manœuvring to gain an end. —*adj.* **tac′ti-cal.**—*n.* **tac-ti′cian.**

tac-tile (tak′til; til), *adj.* **1,** pertaining to the sense of touch; as, *tactile* organs; **2,** perceptible by touch; as, *tactile* qualities; tangible.

tact-less (takt′lis), *adj.* lacking, or not showing, readiness to say and do the most suitable thing; lacking tact, or diplomacy.—*n.* **tact′less-ness.**

tac-tu-al (tak′tū-al; tak′chōō-al), *adj.* **1,** caused by touch; as, *tactual* impressions; **2,** tactile.

d-pole (tad′pōl′), *n.* a frog or toad in an immature stage, with gills and a tail.

af-fe-ta (taf′i-ta), *n.* a shiny, fine, rustling silk or rayon, slightly stiffened, used esp. as dress material.

aff-rail (taf′rāl′), *n.* the rail around the stern of a ship.

af-fy (taf′i), *n.* **1,** candy made of brown sugar, or molasses, and butter; **2,** *Colloq.,* in the U.S., flattery.

ag (tag), *n.* **1,** an attached identifying card or label; as, a price *tag;* **2,** a children's game in which one chases the others in order to touch, or "tag" them; **3,** a reinforcement at the end of a shoestring, as to stiffen it; **4,** a loose end:— *v.t.* [tagged, tag-ging], **1,** to fix a tag to;

2, in the game of tag, to catch by touching; **3,** *Colloq.,* to follow closely and persistently:—*v.i. Colloq.,* to follow another closely.—*n.* **tag′ger.**

tail (tāl), *n.* **1,** the hindmost part of an animal, extending beyond the rest of the body; **2,** hence, something resembling a tail in position, shape, etc.; as, a comet's *tail;* **3,** the end part of anything; as, the *tail* of a parade; **4,** the side of a coin opposite the side bearing the impression of a head; **5,** a plane or planes at the rear of an aeroplane to give it balance:—*v.t.* to furnish with a tail: —*v.i.* to follow close behind; tag.

tail-ings (tāl′ingz), *n.pl.* the waste or leavings from various processes, as milling grains, washing ores, distilling, etc.; chaff; dregs.

tai-lor (tā′lẽr), *n.* one whose business it is to make and repair outer garments for men and women:—*v.i.* to follow the trade of a tailor.—*n.* **tai′lor-ing.**

tail-skid (tāl′skid′), *n.* a runner at the rear of an aeroplane to keep the tail off the ground.

tail-spin (tāl′spin′), *n.* the descent of an airplane, nose down and tail spinning in circles overhead.

taint (tānt), *n.* a spot, trace, or tinge of decay, corruption, or pollution:—*v.t.* **1,** to spoil by mixing with something unpleasant or poisonous; infect; **2,** to defile; corrupt:—*v.i.* to become spoiled, as meat.

take (tāk), *v.t.* [*p.t.* took (took), *p.p.* tak-en (tāk′en), *p.pr.* tak-ing], **1,** to lay hold of, as with the hands; grasp; as, to *take* a man by the throat; also, to seize or capture; as, the troops *took* the city; **2,** to assume possession of; as, he *took* the store on a year's lease; also, to buy regularly; subscribe to; as, I *take* this magazine every month; **3,** to eat, drink, or inhale; as, to *take* breakfast; to *take* gas; **4,** to carry; as, *take* your purse; also, to conduct or escort; as, to *take* a guest home; **5,** to remove; subtract; as, to *take* three from five; also, to steal; as, to *take* another's idea; **6,** to experience; feel; as, to *take* pride in one's work; **7,** to perform, do, make, etc.; as, to *take* exercise; to *take* a picture; **8,** to require; as, it *takes* two to make a bargain; **9,** to pick out; choose; as, *take* the largest plum; **10,** to be infected with; catch; as, to *take* cold; **11,** to attract the attention of; please; as, the hat *took* her fancy:— *v.i.* **1,** to have the intended effect; act; be successful; as, the vaccination *took;* **2,** to proceed; go; as, they *took* to the boats; **3,** to prove attractive; as, the song *took*:—*n.* the amount or quantity received or taken: said esp. of fish.—*n.* **tak′er.**

take—off (tāk′-ôf′), *n.* **1,** a parody; as, a *take-off* of an actress; **2,** a place from which one makes a start in running or jumping, in an aeroplane flight, etc.; also, the act of taking off.

tak-ing (tāk′ing), *adj.* **1,** attractive; pleasing; as, *taking* manners; **2,** contagious, as a disease:—*n.* **1,** the act of gaining possession; **2, takings,** the amount taken or received; receipts.

talc (talk), *n.* a soft mineral, greasy to the touch, used in rubber manufacture, toilet powders, etc.: also called *soapstone*.

tal-cum (tal′kum), *n.* talc:—**talcum powder,** a toilet powder of finely pulverized talc.

tale (tāl), *n.* **1,** that which is told; a story; fable; **2,** a false report or piece of gossip; **3,** a count; a summing or sum; as, the *tale* of bricks made in a day.

tal-ent (tal′ent), *n.* **1,** an ancient weight and coin; **2,** mental ability; skill; cleverness; **3,** a special gift for a particular business, art, or profession; as, the school boasts a variety of *talent;* **4,** skilled persons.—*adj.* **tal′ent-ed.**

tal-is-man (tal′is-man; tal′iz-man), *n.* [*pl.* talismans], a figure engraved on a stone or ring, supposed to possess magical powers; a charm; an amulet.

talk (tôk), *v.i.* **1,** to utter words; express and try to communicate thoughts through speech; **2,** to speak familiarly; converse; **3,** to confer; discuss; as, to *talk* with one's doctor; **4,** to chatter; gossip; **5,** to communicate ideas without speech; as, to *talk* by gestures:—*v.t.* **1,** to speak of; discuss; as, to talk business; **2,** to speak a language fluently; as, to *talk* French; **3,** to influence or affect by speech; as, they *talked* him over to their side:—*n.* **1,** speech; conversation; as, an evening of friendly *talk;* **2,** a subject of discussion; as, the *talk* of the town; **3,** rumour; as, there is *talk* of a strike; **4,** meaningless speech; as, idle *talk;* **5,** a conference; **6,** an informal address; as, a short *talk* on art.—*adj.* **talk′a-tive.**

tall (tôl), *adj.* **1,** of more than average height; as, a *tall* boy; **2,** of a certain specified height; as, a man six feet *tall.*

tal-low (tal′ō), *n.* the fat of animals, as beef or mutton suet, melted and used for making candles, soap, etc.:—*adj.* made of tallow.—*adj.* **tal′low-y.**

tal-ly (tal′i), *n.* [*pl.* tallies], **1,** originally, a stick on which scores were recorded by notches; **2,** anything on which a score or account is kept; also, the score; **3,** a duplicate; counterpart:—*v.t.* [tallied, tally-ing], to keep score of; count; reckon:—*v.i.* to match; balance; as, the two accounts *tally.*

tal-on (tal′un), *n.* the claw of a bird of prey; as, the *talon* of a hawk or eagle.

ta-lus (tā′lus), *n.* **1,** in *geology*, a sloping pile of rock fragments at the base of a cliff; **2,** the anklebone.

tam (tam), *n.* a tam-o'-shanter.

ta-ma-le (ta-mä′li), *n.* a Mexican dish of chopped meat and corn-meal, seasoned with red pepper, wrapped in cornhusks, dipped in oil, boiled or steamed, and served hot.

tam-a-rack (tam′a-rak), *n.* an American larch tree.

tam-bou-rine (tam′boo-rēn′), *n.* a small hand drum, with pairs of little metallic disks. The performer in playing shakes it or strikes it with the knuckles.

tame (tām), *adj.* [tam-er, tam-est], **1,** changed from a wild state; made useful to man; **2,** harmless; gentle; also, without fear; as, these squirrels are very *tame;* **3,** tedious; dull; as, the debate was *tame:*—*v.t.* [tamed, tam-ing], **1,** to make (an animal) useful to man; as, to *tame* an elephant; also, to make less wild or timid; as, to *tame* a bird; **2,** to crush the spirit or courage of; subdue.—*adv.* **tame′ly.** —*n.* **tam′er.**—*adj.* **tam′a-ble** or **tame′a-ble.**

tam-o'—shan-ter (tam′-o-shan′tèr), *n.* a Scotch cap with a tight band, and a loose, round top: often called *tammy.*

tamp (tamp), *v.t.* **1,** in blasting, to fill in (a hole containing the charge) with clay, earth, etc.; **2,** to drive in or down by repeated light strokes; as, the gardener has *tamped* down the sod.—*n.* **tamp′er.**

tam-per (tam′pèr), *v.i.* to meddle so as to injure or alter anything; as, to *tamper* with a lock.

tan (tan), *n.* **1,** oak bark, or other bark containing tannic acid, used in treating hides; **2,** a yellowish-brown colour, like that of such bark; **3,** a brown colour given to the skin by exposure to the sun:—*v.t.* [tanned, tan-ning], **1,** to convert (raw hide) into leather by treating with tannic acid or with mineral salts; **2,** to make brown by exposure to the sun; **3,** *Colloq.,* to thrash; beat:—*v.i.* **1,** to be made into leather; **2,** to become brown in the sun:—*adj.* yellowish brown.

tan-a-ger (tan′a-jėr), *n.* any of a family of American songbirds closely related to the finches, and usually of brilliant plumage, as the scarlet tanager.

tan-dem (tan′dem), *adv.* one behind another:—*adj.* arranged one behind the other, as horses, or seats on a bicycle:—*n.* **1,** a pair of horses harnessed one before the other; **2,** a carriage with horses tandem, or a bicycle with seats tandem.

tang (tang), *n.* **1,** a strong sharp taste or flavour; **2,** the part of a knife or similar tool that fits into the handle.—*adj.* **tang′y.**

tan-gent (tan′jent), *adj.* **1,** touching; **2,** in *geometry,* touching a line or surface at one point only, but not passing through it:—*n.* a tangent line or surface.

tan-ge-rine (tan′je-rēn′; tan′je-rēn′), *n.* a small, deep-coloured, sweet orange.

tan-gi-ble (tan′ji-bl) *adj.* **1,** touchable; capable of being felt by the touch; **2,** definite; real; as, *tangible* proof.—*adv.* **tan′gi-bly.**

tan-gle (tang′gl), *v.t.* [tan-gled, tan-gling], to knot so as to make difficult to unravel; entangle:—*v.i.* to be or become entangled; —*n.* **1,** a snarl; a confused mass; as, a *tangle* of string; **2,** hence, a confused state.

tan-go (tang′gō), *n.* [*pl.* tangos], a dance, originally from South America, in two-four time and with a great variety of steps.

tank (tangk), *n.* **1,** a large cistern, basin, or circular container for holding water or other fluid; as, an oil-*tank;* a gasoline-*tank;* **2,** a kind of armoured motorcar, built like a caterpillar tractor and equipped with guns: used in modern warfare for advancing over rough ground:—*v.t.* to put or store in a tank.—*n.* **tank′ful.**—*n.* **tank′age** (dried animal residues, used as fertilizer and coarse foodstuffs).

tank-ard (tangk′ėrd), *n.* a large drinking vessel with one handle, and a hinged cover.

tank-er (tangk′ėr), *n.* a ship esp. built with tanks for carrying oil, molasses, etc., in bulk.

tan-ner (tan′ėr), *n.* one whose business is the tanning of hides into leather.

tan-nic (tan′ik), *adj.* pertaining to, or

obtained from, any bark, as oak or hemlock, which produces tan:—**tannic acid,** a strong acid obtained from tea, sumac, etc., and used in tanning, dyeing, and medicine: also called *tannin.*

tan-ta-lize (tan′ta-līz′), *v.t.* [tantalized, tantaliz-ing], to tease by exciting hopes or fears which will not be realized.

tan-ta-mount (tan′ta-mount′), *adj.* equivalent, or equal to, in effect, value, or importance; as, silence may be *tantamount* to consent.

tan-trum (tan′trum), *n.* *Colloq.,* a sudden outburst of temper or passion.

¹tap (tap), *n.* **1,** a pipe or cock through which liquor is drawn from a cask; also, a faucet or spigot for drawing water; **2,** a place where liquor is drawn and sold; a tap-room; **3,** liquor drawn from a cask; **4,** a tool for cutting screw-threads on an inner surface, as of a nut; **5,** in *electricity,* a device for making connection with a wire:—*v.t.* [tapped, tap-ping], **1,** to furnish with a cock or spigot; pierce the side of a cask or the bark of a tree), in order to draw out liquid; **2,** to draw or let out (liquid); **3,** to make connections so as to draw from or extract from; as, to *tap* secret sources of information; **4,** to make connection with (a wire) so as to draw off current.

²tap (tap), *v.t.* [tapped, tap-ping], **1,** to strike or touch lightly; as, he *tapped* me on the shoulder; **2,** to cause to strike or touch lightly; as, he *tapped* his foot impatiently:—*v.i.* to strike light blows:—*n.* a light blow or touch; pat; rap.

tape (tāp), *n.* **1,** a narrow woven band of linen or cotton, used for tying packages, in sewing, etc.; **2,** the narrow strip of paper on which a telegraph or stock-ticker prints; **3,** the rope or line stretched across the track to mark the finish of a race; **4,** a narrow strip of cloth, paper, or steel, marked for measuring length:—*v.t.* [taped, tap-ing], **1,** to bind or cover with tape; as, he *taped* the handle of his tennis-racket; **2,** to measure off with a tape.

ta-per (tā′pėr), *n.* **1,** a long, slender candle; **2,** a gradual lessening of thickness toward a point; as, the *taper* of a cone:—*v.i.* and *v.t.* **1,** to narrow to a point; **2,** to decrease gradually; as, a boxer *tapers* off his training as the date for the fight draws near.

tape—recorder, a device that records

speech (or other sound) on electromagnetic tape.

tap-es-try (tap′es-tri), *n.* [*pl.* tapestries], an ornamental fabric in which a picture or design is woven, used as a wall hanging or furniture covering.

tape-worm (tāp′wûrm′), *n.* any of several long, parasitic flatworms that infest the intestines of man and other animals: the larvae and adult stages are often in different hosts.

tap-i-o-ca (tap′i-ō′ka), *n.* a starchy, granular substance prepared from the roots of a South American plant called the cassava, used for puddings and as a thickening.

ta-pir (tā′pèr), *n.* a heavy, brownish-black, short-legged animal with a flexible snout, found in South and Central America.

tap-pet (tap′it), *n.* in a machine, a small lever, cam, etc., that moves, or is moved by, intermittent contact with another part in order to regulate motion, as by the opening and closing of valves.

tap-root (tap′rōōt′), *n.* a main root that grows straight down, as the radish or dandelion: small lateral roots grow out from it.

taps (taps), *n.pl.* in the army and navy, the last signal of the day, on drum or bugle, ordering lights out. Taps are also sounded over the grave of a soldier or sailor.

¹tar (tär), *n.* a thick, black, oily substance obtained from wood, coal, peat, etc.:—*v.t.* [tarred, tar-ring], to cover with, or as with, tar; as, the sailors *tarred* the ropes.

²tar (tär), *n. Colloq.*, a sailor; seaman.

ta-ran-tu-la (ta-ran′tū-la), *n.* a large hairy, poisonous spider, found in many warm countries.

tar-dy (tär′di), *adj.* [tar-di-er, tar-di-est], **1,** moving or progressing slowly; as, *tardy* growth; **2,** not prompt; late. —*adv.* **tar′di-ly.**—*n.* **tar′di-ness.**

tare (târ), *n.* in the Bible, a weed.

tar-get (tär′git). *n.* **1,** formerly, a small shield or buckler; **2,** a mark set up for archery, rifle, or artillery practice; **3,** one who or that which is made the object of attack, criticism, ridicule, etc.; as, he is the *target* of abuse.

tar-iff (tar′if), *n.* **1,** a schedule of duties or taxes placed by a government on goods entering, or leaving, the country; **2,** a tax or duty levied according to such a schedule; **3,** any schedule of

rates, charges, etc.; as, he asked for a copy of the new *tariff.*

tar-mac (tär′mak′), *n.* a paved runway, flight strip, or apron at an airport or in front of a hangar.

tarn (tärn), *n.* a small mountain lake.

tar-nish (tär′nish), *v.t.* to dull the brightness of; discolour or stain:—*v.i.* to lose brightness; as, silver *tarnishes* easily:—*n.* dullness; loss of polish; *stain.*

tar-pau-lin (tär-pô′lin), *n.* **1,** heavy waterproof canvas used for covering a ship's hatches, boats, etc.; **2,** a hat or coat of waterproof canvas.

tar-pon (tär′pon), *n.* a large game-fish found in West Indian waters and along the coasts of Georgia and Florida.

¹tar-ry (tär′i), *adj.* [tar-ri-er, tar-ri-est], of, like, or covered with, tar; dirty.

²tar-ry (tar′i), *v.i.* [tarried, tarry-ing], **1,** to live in a place for a time; stay; as, he *tarried* there for a week; **2,** to be late; delay; linger.

tar-sal (tär′sal), *adj.* **1,** pertaining to the tarsus or ankle, or to any of its bones; as, a *tarsal* bone or joint; **2,** pertaining to a plate of connective tissue in the eyelid (the *tarsus*).

¹tart (tärt), *adj.* sharp to the taste; as, a *tart* jelly; hence, severe; cutting; as, a *tart* reply.—*adv.* **tart′ly.**—*n.* **tart′ness.**

²tart (tärt), *n.* a small pastry shell without a top crust, filled with fruit or jam.

tar-tan (tär′tan), *n.* a woollen cloth, woven with a plaid pattern, worn particularly in the Scottish Highlands: —*adj.* of, or in the pattern of, tartan.

tar-tar (tär′tèr), *n.* **1,** a whitish-yellow substance often found on teeth; **2,** an acid substance, present in grape juice, which is deposited on the inside of wine-casks during fermentation; also, a purified form, called *cream of tartar,* used in baking-powder.

tar-tar-ic acid (tär-tar′ik), an acid present in the juice of grapes, oranges, etc.: obtained commercially from tartar, and used in medicine, photography, dyeing, etc.

task (tȧsk). *n.* a piece of work given out to be done; as, daily *tasks:*—**take to task,** to censure:—*v.t.* to burden with work.—*n.* **task′mas′ter.**

tas-sel (tas′l), *n.* **1,** a hanging ornament made of a tuft of threads or cords of silk, wool, etc.; **2,** the hanging flower or head of certain plants; as, corn *tassels:*—*v.i.* [tasselled, tassel-ling], to put forth hanging flowery heads:—*v.t.* to trim with, or make into, tassels.

taste (tāst), *v.t.* [tast-ed, tast-ing], **1,** to perceive or know by the tongue and palate; as, I *taste* vanilla in the cocoa; **2,** to test the flavour of, by eating or drinking a little; as, to *taste* tea; **3,** to experience; as, to *taste* the joys of living:—*v.i.* **1,** to try food by the tongue or palate; **2,** to have a certain flavour; as, candy *tastes* sweet:—*n.* **1,** the flavour of a substance as perceived by the tongue and palate; as, a spicy *taste;* **2,** a little bit or piece; esp., a small portion tasted; as, take a *taste;* **3,** the sense by which the flavour of substances is perceived; **4,** liking or inclination; as, a *taste* for reading; **5,** ability to see what is beautiful; as, she has good *taste* in clothes.—*adj.* **tast/y; taste/less.**—*n.* **tast/er.**

taste-ful (tāst/fool), *adj.* marked by good taste.—*adv.* **taste/ful-ly.**—*n.* **taste/ful-ness.**

¹**tat** (tat), *v.t.* and *v.i.* [tat-ted, tat-ting], to make (trimming or lace) by looping and knotting thread wound on a shuttle.—*n.* **tat/ting.**

²**tat** (tat), *n.* See **tit for tat** (under ²*tit*).

tat-ter (tat/ẽr), *n.* **1,** a loose-hanging rag; **2, tatters,** ragged clothing.—*adj.* **tat/tered.**

tat-tle (tat/l), *v.i.* [tat-tled, tat-tling], to chatter; to tell tales:—*v.t.* to tell (tales or secrets):—*n.* trifling or idle talk; gossip.—*n.* **tat/tler.**—*n.* **tat/tling.**

¹**tat-too** (ta-tōō/), *n.* a drum or bugle signal to call soldiers to their quarters; also, a continuous beating or strumming; as, he beat a *tattoo* on the desk.

²**tat-too** (ta-tōō/), *n.* [*pl.* tattoos], a design made by puncturing the skin and rubbing indelible stain or dye into the punctures:—*v.t.* [tattooed (ta-tōōd/), tattoo-ing], to mark with tattoos.—*n.* **tat-too/ing.**

taught (tôt), *p.t.* and *p.p.* of *teach.*

taunt (tônt), *n.* a bitter or mocking gibe:—*v.t.* to ridicule with bitter, sarcastic, or insulting language; as, they *taunted* John on his failure to pass the examination.

taupe (tōp), *n.* a dark-grey colour with a slight tinge of dull yellow.

Tau-rus (tô/rus), *n.* **1,** the Bull, a northern constellation containing the Pleiades and the Hyades; **2,** the second sign of the zodiac (♉).

taut (tôt), *adj.* **1,** tight, as a stretched rope; **2,** in good condition; shipshape.

tau-tol-o-gy (tô-tol/o-ji), *n.* needless repetition of an idea in different words; as, to *descend down,* or *necessary essentials;* redundance.

tav-ern (tav/ẽrn), *n.* **1,** an inn; a hotel, esp. one in a rural section; **2,** a place where liquors are sold to be drunk on the premises.

taw (tô), *n.* **1,** a mark or line from which players shoot in playing marbles; **2,** the game of marbles; **3,** a marble, esp. one with which a player shoots.

taw-dry (tô/dri), *adj.* [taw-dri-er, taw-dri-est], showy but cheap; gaudy; as, *tawdry* jewellry.—*n.* **taw/dri-ness.**

taw-ny (tô/ni), *adj.* [taw-ni-er, taw-ni-est], tan-coloured; of a yellowish-brown colour.

tax (taks), *n.* **1,** a charge or duty on income or property, imposed by a government; as, public schools are supported by the *taxes* paid by the people; **2,** a heavy or oppressive burden; as, a *tax* on one's patience:—*v.t.* **1,** to impose a rate or duty upon, esp. for the support of a government; as, to *tax* all incomes above a certain amount; **2,** to burden; oppress; as, to *tax* the mind with too much detail; **3,** to accuse; as, to *tax* a person with bribery.—*adj.* **tax/a-ble.**—*n.* **tax/pay/er.**

tax-a-tion (taks-ā/shun), *n.* **1,** the act or system of raising money for public use by imposing a charge or duty upon persons or property; **2,** the sum, or tax, imposed.

tax-i (tak/si), *n.* [*pl.* taxis], a taxicab:—*v.i.* [taxied, taxi-ing or taxy-ing], **1,** of an aeroplane, to run along on water or land, as when preparing to rise or after landing; **2,** to ride in a taxicab.

tax-i-cab (tak/si-kab/), *n.* a motor-driven cab provided with a meter that measures and records the fare according to the distance travelled.

tax-i-der-my (tak/si-dûr/mi), *n.* the art of preparing, stuffing, and mounting the skins of animals to give them a lifelike appearance.—*n.* **tax/i-der/mist.**

tea (tē), *n.* **1,** a shrub of eastern Asia, cultivated for its leaves; **2,** the dried leaves of the tea-plant; **3,** the drink obtained by pouring boiling water on these leaves; **4,** any of various mild beverages resembling tea; as, beef *tea;* **5,** a light afternoon meal at which tea is served; **6,** hence, an evening meal, when dinner is eaten in the middle of the day; **7,** an afternoon social affair where tea is served.—*n.* **tea/room/.**

teach (tēch), *v.t.* [taught (tôt), teach-ing], **1,** to instruct; educate; as, to *teach* a pupil; **2,** to give instruction in; as, to *teach* English; **3,** to inform; help to learn; as, experience has *taught* me to work carefully:—*v.i.* to give instruction; engage in teaching.

teach-er (tēch′ėr), *n.* a person whose profession is teaching or instructing.

teach-er-age (tēch′ėr-ij), *n.* an early 20th-century residence of Western Canada, erected near a school to attract married teachers for longer tenure: analogous with *parsonage.*

teach-ing (tēch′ing), *n.* **1,** the profession of instructing or educating; as, she went into *teaching;* **2,** that which is taught; as, the *teachings* of Jesus.

tea-cup (tē′kup′), *n.* **1,** a cup, usually smaller than a coffee-cup, in which tea is served; also, any cup of this size; **2,** the amount which such a cup holds; a teacupful.

teak (tēk), *n.* **1,** a tall East Indian tree the leaves of which yield a red dye; **2,** its hard, durable timber much used in the making of ships and furniture.

tea-ket-tle (tē′ket′l), *n.* a covered kettle with a spout and handle, in which water is heated.

teal (tēl), *n.* a swift, small, freshwater wild duck (in Canada, blue-winged).

team (tēm), *n.* two or more horses, oxen, etc., harnessed together to one plough, cart, or carriage; **2,** a number of persons working or playing together; as, a basketball *team:*—*v.t.* **1,** to join together in a team; as, to *team* horses; **2,** to transport with a team; as, to *team* lumber:—*v.i.* **1,** to make one's living by driving a team; **2,** to work with a group or team; as, he *teamed* up with the other boys.

team-ster (tēm′stėr), *n.* **1,** the driver of a team of horses or other animals; **2,** one whose business is driving a truck, esp. on long hauls.

team-work (tēm′wûrk′), *n.* work done by several persons acting as a unit, as distinguished from work done by one person alone; as, superior *teamwork* won for our side.

tea-pot (tē′pot′), *n.* a vessel with a spout, handle, and cover, for making and serving tea.

¹tear (târ), *v.t.* [*p.t.* tore (tōr), *p.p.* torn (tōrn), *p.pr.* tear-ing], **1,** to pull apart; rend; as, I *tore* my dress when I fell; **2,** to cut deeply; gash; as, to *tear* the flesh; **3,** to produce or cause by the action of rending; as, to *tear* a hole in paper; **4,** to remove by force; as, he *tore* the plant up by the roots; **5,** to

cause great pain to; as, it *tore* his heart to leave his friend:—*v.i.* **1,** to part on being pulled or roughly handled; as, the cloth *tears* easily; **2,** to move or act with force or excited haste; as, to *tear* across the street:—*n.* **1,** the act of tearing; also, damage caused by tearing; **2,** a rent; a hole made by pulling apart; as, there is a large *tear* in my coat.

²tear (tēr), *n.* a small drop of salty, watery liquid secreted by a gland of the eye.—*n.* **tear′drop′.**—*adj.* **tear′less.**

tear-ful (tēr′fool), *adj.* shedding tears; weeping.—*adv.* **tear′ful-ly.**

tease (tēz), *v.t.* [teased, teas-ing], **1,** to comb or unravel (wool or flax); separate the fibres of; **2,** to roughen the surface of; as, to *tease* cloth; **3,** to annoy by petty requests or by good-natured ridicule:—*n. Colloq.,* one who teases.—*n.* **teas′er.**

tea-spoon (tē′spoon′), *n.* a small spoon, the ordinary size for table use, which holds about one third as much as a tablespoon.—*n.* **tea′spoon-ful.**

teat (tēt), *n.* the nipple on the breast or udder through which milk passes.

tech-ni-cal (tek′ni-kal), *adj.* **1,** having to do with the industrial or mechanical arts and sciences; as, a *technical* school; **2,** having to do with a certain occupation or science; as, "raceme" is a *technical* botanical word; **3,** having to do with technique; as, she has mastered the *technical* details of rhyme, but she cannot write good poetry.—*adv.* **tech′-ni-cal-ly.**

tech-ni-cal-i-ty (tek′ni-kal′i-ti), *n.* [*pl.* technicalities], **1,** the quality of belonging to, or being characteristic of, a particular occupation or science; as, the *technicality* of scientific language; **2,** a small point, formally exact but often of a quibbling nature; as, he was acquitted on a *technicality.*

tech-nique (tek-nēk′), *n.* the method of handling details in the practice of any fine art or in doing anything that requires special skill.—*n.* **tech-ni′cian** (tek-nish′an).

tech-noc-ra-cy (tek-nok′ra-si), *n.* about 1932, a proposed social and economic system that would allow capital investments and energy resources to be fully utilized under technical experts (scientists and engineers).

tech-nol-o-gy (tek-nol′o-ji), **1,** the science of industrial arts and manu-factures; **2,** the terms used in science, art, etc.—*adj.* **tech′no-log′i-cal.**

ted-der (ted'ẽr), *n.* a machine (or person) that turns or spreads (hay) for drying in the sun:—*v.t.* **ted.**

ted-dy—bear (ted'i–bâr'), *n.* a child's toy somewhat like a small stuffed bear (in plush): named after Theodore Roosevelt, U.S. President (1907).

te-di-ous (tē'di-us; tēd'yus; tē'jus), *adj.* wearisome; tiresome; as, *tedious* work.—*n.* **te'di-um** (boredom; ennui).

¹tee (tē), *n.* in *golf*, **1**, a small pointed plastic or wooden pin with cupped top on which a ball is placed for the first stroke on a hole (formerly a small cone of sand); **2**, the place or area set apart for making the first stroke on a hole:— *v.t.* and *v.i.* [teed (tēd), tee-ing], to place (a ball) on a tee; as, he *teed* off at 8 a.m.

²tee (tē), *n.* the letter T; also, something shaped like a T, as a metal beam.

teem (tēm), *v.i.* to be very productive; be full; be stocked or crowded to overflowing; as, the city *teemed* with tourists.

teen-ag-er or **teen—ag-er** (tēn'āj'ẽr), *n.* a person in his teens.—*adj.* **teen'—age'.**

teens (tēnz), *n.pl.* the years of one's age marked by numbers ending in *-teen*, from 13 to 19; as, a girl in her *teens*.

tee-ny (tē'ni), *adj. Colloq.* tiny.

tee-pee (tē'pē), *n.* Same as **tepee.**

tee-ter (tē'tẽr), *v.t.* and *v.i.* to seesaw; sway from side to side:—*n.* a seesaw; a swaying motion.

tee-ter—tot-ter (tē'tẽr–tot'ẽr), *n.* a seesaw.

teeth (tēth), *n.pl.* of *tooth.*

teethe (tē*th*), *v.i.* [teethed, teeth-ing], to cut teeth; also, to grow or develop teeth.

tee-to-tal-er (tē-tō'tal-ẽr), *n.* a total abstainer from intoxicating liquors. —*adj.* **tee-to'tal.**

tel-e- (tel'e-), *Greek prefix* meaning *at a distance*, as in **tel'e-pho'to-graph'** (a picture sent by wire or radio) and **tel'e-type'writ'er** (an instrument with a keyboard like that of a typewriter, which, when operated, sends signals that are received by a distant instrument of the same kind).

tel-e-cast (tel'e-kast'), *n.* a television program; the reproduction on a screen of distant objects, actions, or events.

tel-e-gram (tel'e-gram'), *n.* a message sent by telegraph.

tel-e-graph (tel'e-gràf'), *n.* an equipment or system for sending and receiving signals, or messages, at a distance by means of electricity:—*v.t.* to send by means of such an instrument; as, to *telegraph* news; also, to send a message to, by such means; as, to *telegraph* a friend:—*v.i.* to send a message by telegraph.—*adj.* **tel'e-graph'ic.**—*n.* **te-leg'ra-pher** (te-leg'ra-fẽr; tel'e-gràf'ẽr).

te-leg-ra-phy (te-leg'ra-fi), *n.* the science or process of sending messages by telegraph.

te-lep-a-thy (te-lep'a-thi), *n.* the apparent transferring of thought from one mind to another other than through the recognized sense organs.

tel-e-phone (tel'e-fōn'), *n.* an instrument for transmitting speech over a distance by means of electricity:—*v.t.* [telephoned, telephon-ing], to send (a message) by telephone; also, to communicate with, by telephone; as, to *telephone* a friend:—*v.i.* to send a message by telephone.—*adj.* **tel'e-phon'ic.**—*n.* **te-leph'o-ny.**

tel-e-pho-to (tel'i-fō'tō), *adj.* relating to the process of photographing distant objects, as by a *telephoto* lens.

tel-e-scope (tel'e-skōp'), *n.* an optical instrument used for viewing objects at a distance, esp. the moon, stars, etc.: —*v.t.* [telescoped, telescop-ing], to drive or force together, as colliding railway cars, so that one part slides into another, like sections of a collapsible telescope:—*v.i.* to be forced together in this manner.—*adj.* **tel'e-scop'ic** (tel'e-skop'ik).

tel-e-vise (tel'e-vīz'), *v.t.* to broadcast by television.

tel-e-vi-sion (tel'e-vizh'un), *n.* the process of sending and receiving, by means of radio waves, images of events as they are happening; as, by the use of *television* we can see, as well as hear, people singing over the radio: often written *TV.*

tell (tel), *v.t.* [told (tōld), tell-ing], **1**, to count; mention one by one; as, to *tell* the beads of a rosary; **2**, to relate in words: narrate; as, to *tell* a story; also, to say; utter; as, to *tell* a falsehood; **3**, to disclose; confess; as, to *tell* a secret; **4**, to decide; as, I cannot *tell* what is best to do; also, to recognize; as, to *tell* the difference; **5**, to order; as, he *told* her to buy meat:—*v.i.* **1**, to give an account; as, he *told* of days gone by; **2**, *Colloq.*, to play the informer; as, John *told* on Billy; **3**, to have a marked effect; as, each blow *told.*

tell-er (tel′ẽr), *n.* **1,** one who tells, discloses, narrates, etc.; as, a story writer is sometimes called a *teller* of tales; **2,** a bank clerk who receives and pays out money over the counter; **3,** one who counts the votes in a legislative body, meeting, etc.

tell-ing (tel′ing), *adj.* striking; impressive; as, his words had a *telling* effect.

tell-tale (tel′tāl′), *adj.* revealing or betraying (something intended to be secret); as, a *telltale* blush.—*n.* a tattler; informer; talebearer.

te-mer-i-ty (te-mer′i-ti), *n.* boldness; rashness; as, the clerk had the *temerity* to criticize his employer.

tem-per (tem′pẽr), *v.t.* **1,** to mix to the proper degree of softness; as, to *temper* clay; also, to soften; as to *temper* a rebuke with a smile; **2,** to bring to the proper degree of hardness or toughness; as, to *temper* steel; **3,** to reduce; moderate; as, sympathy *tempers* grief:—*n.* **1,** the degree of hardness softness, toughness, etc., of a substance, as of steel, clay, or mortar; consistency; **2,** disposition or mood; as, he is in a bad *temper* today; **3,** anger; as, to show *temper;* **4,** control of one's anger; as, to lose one's *temper.*—*adj.* **tem′pered.**

tem-per-a-ment (tem′pẽr-a-ment), *n.* disposition; the characteristic mental and emotional make-up of a person; as, an artistic *temperament.*—*adj.* **tem′per-a-men′tal.**

tem-per-ance (tem′pẽr-ans), *n.* **1,** moderation; avoidance of extremes, esp. in eating and drinking; **2,** moderation in, or abstinence from, the use of alcoholic liquors.

tem-per-ate (tem′pẽr-it), *adj.* **1,** inclined not to eat or drink to excess; moderate; also, seldom using alcoholic liquors; **2,** calm; restrained; as, a *temperate* disposition; **3,** free from extremes of heat or cold; as, a *temperate* climate.—*adv.* **tem′per-ate-ly.** —*n.* **tem′per-ate-ness.**

tem-per-a-ture (tem′pẽr-a-tūr), *n.* the degree or amount of heat or cold as measured by a thermometer; also, the degree of heat of the human body or an excess of this heat above the normal; as, a child, when ill, often has a high *temperature.*

tem-pest (tem′pest), *n.* **1,** a violent windstorm, usually accompanied by rain, hail, etc.; **2,** any violent tumult or agitation; as, a *tempest* of fury.

tem-pes-tu-ous (tem-pes′tū-us), *adj.* stormy; agitated; as, *tempestuous* seas.

tem-plate (tem′plāt) or **tem-plet** (tem′plit), *n.* **1,** a thin pattern of wood or metal serving as a gauge or guide, esp. a flat plate or strip with holes for use in riveting, drilling, etc.; **2,** in a wall, a horizontal stone, timber, etc., to take and distribute the weight of a girder, beam, etc.

¹**tem-ple** (tem′pl), *n.* **1,** a building dedicated to the worship of a deity; as, a *temple* of Jupiter; **2,** a building for Christian public worship; esp., a Protestant church in France.

²**tem-ple** (tem′pl), *n.* the flat part of the head at each side, between the eye and the upper part of the ear.

tem-po (tem′pō), *n.* **1,** characteristic speed and rhythm; as, the *tempo* of city life; **2,** in *music,* the relative pace or time, as adagio, allegro, etc.

tem-po-ral (tem′po-ral), *adj.* **1,** limited in time; not eternal or everlasting; also, worldly or earthly; **2,** pertaining to civil matters, or to affairs of political life; secular; not of the church; as, *temporal* powers.

tem-po-rar-y (tem′po-rẽr-i), *adj.* continuing for a limited time only; not permanent; as, *temporary* relief.—*adv.* **tem′po-rar-i-ly.**

tem-po-rize (tem′po-rīz′), *v.i.* [temporized, temporiz-ing], **1,** to yield temporarily to current opinion or circumstances; **2,** to adopt a policy of delay.

tempt (tempt), *v.t.* **1,** to persuade, or try to persuade, to evil ways; to entice; as, he was *tempted* to cheat; **2,** to attract; invite; as, some foods *tempt* me much more than others.—*adj.* **tempt′ing.**—*n.* **tempt′er.**

temp-ta-tion (temp-tā′shun), *n.* **1,** the act of leading, or the state of being led, into evil; an effort to lure, esp. to evil; as, the *temptation* of Christ by Satan; **2,** an enticement; that which allures; as, the chance to fly was a great *temptation.*

ten (ten), *adj.* composed of one more than nine, or twice five:—*n.* **1,** the number consisting of five and five; **2,** a sign representing ten units, as 10 or x.

ten-a-ble (ten′a-bl), *adj.* capable of being held, maintained, or defended as, a *tenable* theory.

te-na-cious (te-nā′shus), *adj.* **1,** holding fast or firmly; as, the *tenacious* grip of a bulldog; a miser is *tenacious* of his gold; also, stubborn in holding fast to one's purpose; **2,** sticky, as glue; **3,** tough, as steel; **4,** capable of holding or retaining; as, a *tenacious* mind.—*n.* **te-nac′i-ty** (te-nas′i-ti).

ten-ant (ten′ant), *n.* **1,** one who has use or possession of property for a certain length of time on the payment of rent; **2,** an occupant or dweller; as, Eskimos are the only *tenants* of this icy waste: —*v.t.* to hold as a tenant; occupy. —*adj.* **ten′ant-less.**—*n.* **ten′an-cy.**

¹tend (tend), *v.i.* **1,** to move or go in a certain direction; as, the point to which an argument *tends;* also, to exhibit a natural tendency toward something; as her talents *tend* toward music; **2,** to be likely to have a certain result; as, ill health *tends* to produce irritation.

²tend (tend), *v.t.* to attend to; watch over; protect; as, the shepherd *tends* his sheep; to have charge of; as, to *tend* a machine.

tend-en-cy (ten′den-si), *n.* [*pl.* tendencies], **1,** direction; trend or movement in some direction; as, there was a *tendency* toward anarchy in the state; **2,** natural bent or inclination; as, he had a *tendency* to get angry easily.

¹tend-er (ten′dẽr), *n.* **1,** one who attends or takes care of; as, a bar-*tender;* **2,** a small car containing coal and water, attached behind a locomotive; **3,** a small vessel attending and supplying a larger one, with fuel, provisions, etc.; **4,** a small boat used to land passengers from a ship.

²ten-der (ten′dẽr), *v.t.* **1,** to offer for acceptance; as, to *tender* one's resignation; **2,** to offer (money) in payment of a debt:—*n.* an offer, bid, or proposal for acceptance; also, the thing offered: —**legal tender,** currency that a lender must, by law, accept when it is offered in repayment of money due to him.

³ten-der (ten′dẽr), *adj.* **1,** easily broken, chewed, or cut; **2,** not hardy or tough; as, the *tender* shoots of a plant; also, easily hurt or injured; as, a *tender* skin; **3,** easily touched by pain, grief, love, or kindness; as, a *tender* heart; also, gentle; kind; loving; as, *tender* words; **4,** immature; youthful; as, a *tender* age.—*n.* **ten′der-ness.**

ten-der-foot (ten′dẽr-foot′), *n.* [*pl.* tenderfeet (-fēt′)], **1,** one who has had no experience of rough living or hardships; esp., a greenhorn or newcomer to pioneer life in the West; **2,** the beginning rank, or class, of the Boy Scouts and the Girl Guides; also, a member of this class.

ten-der-ize (ten′dẽr-īz′), *v.t.* to make tender, as meat.

ten-der-loin (ten′dẽr-loin′), *n.* the tenderest part of the loin of beef or pork.

ten-der-pad (ten′dẽr-pad′), *n. Boy Scouts,* a wolf cub who has learned the promise, salute, grand howl, and laws of the cub pack.

ten-don (ten′dun), *n.* a tough cord or band of fibrous tissue attaching a muscle to a bone, to another muscle, or to an organ of the body.

ten-dril (ten′dril), *n.* **1,** a slender, twining plant structure, which, by attaching itself to a support, enables the plant to climb or to hold itself up; **2,** any such thing, as a curl or ringlet.

ten-e-ment (ten′e-ment), *n.* **1,** in *law,* any kind of permanent property rented by one person from another; **2,** a dwelling-house; **3,** an apartment, or set of rooms, usually of inferior grade.

ten-et (ten′it), *n.* a creed, principle, or belief.

ten-fold (ten′fōld′), *adj.* and *adv.* ten times as much or as great.

ten-nis (ten′is), *n.* a game played by batting a ball with rackets back and forth over a net stretched across a specially marked surface called a court.

ten-on (ten′un), *n.* a projection at the end of a piece of wood, etc., shaped to fit a corresponding cavity or hole (mortise), so as to form a joint.

ten-or (ten′ẽr), *n.* **1,** settled tendency, direction, or course; as, the even *tenor* of the life of a nun; **2,** general character; purport; as, the *tenor* of a conversation; **3,** the highest of adult male voices; also, a part written for this voice; **4,** one who sings such a part; also, an instrument, as the viola, which plays it.

ten-pins (ten′pinz′), *n.* a bowling game played with ten pins set up at one end of a bowling alley.

¹tense (tens), *adj.* [tens-er, tens-est], stretched taut; rigid; as, *tense* muscles; also, showing or feeling mental strain; high-strung.—*adv.* **tense′ly.**

²tense (tens), *n.* in *grammar,* the form a verb takes to indicate the time of an action or state of being.

ten-sile (ten′sil), *adj.* **1,** pertaining to tension or the act of stretching; as, the *tensile* strain; **2,** capable of being stretched or strained; as, *tensile* wire.

ten-sion (ten′shun), *n.* **1,** the act of stretching or straining; **2,** the state of being stretched or strained; **3,** mental strain; intensity of feeling; **4,** strained relations; as, *tension* between relatives.

tent (tent), *n.* a portable shelter, usually of canvas, stretched over poles and fastened down by ropes attached to pegs driven into the ground:—*v.i.* to camp out in a tent.

ten-ta-cle (ten′ta-kl), *n.* **1,** a thin, flexible feeler, or organ, attached to the mouth parts or to the head of certain insects, fishes, etc., and used to aid feeling, moving, etc.; **2,** a feeler on the leaf of a plant.

ten-ta-tive (ten′ta-tiv), *adj.* done as a trial or experiment; as, a *tentative* solution (to a problem); provisional.

ten-ter-hooks (ten′tėr-hooks′), *n.* **1,** hooks that hold cloth (stretched on a framework or tenter); **2,** to **be on tenterhooks,** to be in a state of painful suspense.

tenth (tenth), *adj.* next after the ninth: the ordinal of *ten:—n.* one of the ten equal parts into which anything is or may be divided.

ten-u-ous (ten′ū-us), *adj.* **1,** thin; slender; slight; as, a *tenuous* hold (on life); **2,** flimsy; unsubstantial; meagre; as, a *tenuous* plot (to a story).

ten-ure (ten′ūr), *n.* **1,** the right, or manner, of holding real estate; **2,** the period during· which anything is held; as, do so during my *tenure* of office.

te-pee (tē′pē; tep′ē), *n.* the cone-shaped tent, or wigwam, of the North American Indians. Also spelled **tee′pee.**

tep-id (tep′id), *adj.* moderately warm; lukewarm; as, a *tepid* bath.

ter-cen-te-na-ry (tûr-sen′ti-na-ri), *adj.* comprising 300 years; as, a *tercentenary* celebration.—*n.* the 300th anniversary of an event.

ter-cet (tûr′sit), *n.* **1,** a group of three successive lines rhyming together, esp. the triplets of *terza rima;* **2,** each of the two triplets forming the last six lines of an Italian sonnet.

term (tûrm), *n.* **1,** a fixed period of time; the time during which a thing lasts; as, a *term* of office; the school's fall *term;* a prison *term;* **2,** a word or expression, esp. one belonging to a particular art, business, etc.; as, chemical *terms;* **3,** in *mathematics,* one of the parts of a proportion or ratio; **4, terms: a,** conditions or arrangements; as, *terms* of a sale; **b,** relationships; footing; as, to be on good *terms* with a person:—*v.t.* to name or call; as, the police *termed* his mysterious death murder.

ter-ma-gant (tûr′ma-gant), *n.* a noisy, violent, turbulent woman; a shrew. —*adj.* quarrelsome; scolding.

ter-mi-nal (tûr′mi-nal), *adj.* **1,** forming the end; growing at the end of a shoot or branch; as, a *terminal* bud; **2,** having to do with the end of a railroad, bus, or airline; as, a *terminal* station:—*n.* **1,** a limit or boundary; an end; **2,** the end of a railroad line, including the station, switches, etc.; **3,** one end of an electrical circuit.

ter-mi-nate (tûr′mi-nāt′), *v.t.* [terminated, terminat-ing], **1,** to limit or bound; **2,** to bring to an end; finish; as, the two countries *terminated* friendly relations:—*v.i.* **1,** to be limited or bounded; **2,** to end; as, the contract *terminates* in June.—*n.* **ter′mi-na′tion.**

ter-mi-nol-o-gy (tûr′mi-nol′o-ji), *n.* the special terms or expressions belonging to a science, art, or business; as, the *terminology* of nuclear physics; nomenclature.

ter-mi-nus (tûr′mi-nus), *n.* [*pl.* terminuses or termini (tûr′mi-nī′)], **1,** a limit or goal; **2,** an end of a railway, bus, or airline; the town and station there.

ter-mite (tûr′mīt), *n.* the white ant, which lives in large colonies, and is destructive to books, timbers, etc.

tern (tûrn), *n.* a sea-bird resembling the gull, but smaller, slenderer, and swifter in flight. It has long, deeply forked wings, and a slim, straight bill.

ter-race (ter′is), *n.* **1,** a raised level space or platform of earth with sloping sides; as, a garden *terrace;* **2,** a row of houses set along the top of a bank or slope; also, a short street lined with such a row of houses:—*v.t.* [terraced, terracing], to furnish with, a terrace or terraces; as, to *terrace* a lawn.

ter-ra—cot-ta (ter′a—kot′a), *n.* pottery of baked clay or earth; also, its reddish-brown or yellowish-brown colour.

ter-rain (te-rān′; ter′ān), *n.* ground considered with regard to its fitness for a special purpose, as for landing aircraft, camping, manoeuvring, etc.

ter-ra-pin (ter′a-pin), *n.* a North American turtle living in fresh, or tide, water; also, its flesh used as food.

ter-raz-zo (ter-rät′sō; -räz′ō), *n.* and *adj.* flooring made of small chips of marble set irregularly in cement and polished.

ter-res-tri-al (te-res′tri-al), *adj.* **1,** consisting of earth or land; as, the *terrestrial* globe; consisting of land as distinguished from water; as, *terrestrial* portions of the earth; **2,** belonging to the earth, not to the heavens; as, a *terrestrial* being; **3,** existing on land, not in the water, trees, or air; as, *terrestrial* animals.

ter-ri-ble (ter′i-bl), *adj.* **1,** exciting or causing fear or dread; dreadful; as, a *terrible* disaster; **2,** *Colloq.*, extreme; excessive; as, a *terrible* hurry.—*adv.* **ter′ri-bly.**

ter-ri-er (ter′i-ėr), *n.* an active, intelligent dog, usually of small size, and noted for its alertness and gameness, esp. in killing rats and mice, and in starting game from a burrow.

ter-rif-ic (te-rif′ik), *adj.* **1,** such as to cause fear or terror; alarming; dreadful; as, a *terrific* explosion; **2,** *Colloq.*, excessive; extreme; as, a *terrific* amount of work; **3,** *Colloq.*, extraordinary.

ter-r-ify (ter′i-fī′), *v.t.* [terrified, terrify-ing], to fill with great alarm or terror; frighten greatly; as, the storm *terrified* her.

ter-ri-tor-y (ter′i-tėr-i), *n.* [*pl.* territories], **1,** a large tract of land; region; as, Canada covers a large *territory;* also, an assigned district; as, the salesman's *territory* covers the entire state; **2,** the entire extent of land and water under the control of one ruler or government; as, British *territory:* —**Territory,** a region of the country not yet admitted as a province or state. —*adj.* and *n.* **ter′ri-tor′i-al.**

ter-ror (ter′ėr), *n.* **1,** very great fear; alarm; **2,** one who or that which causes such fear; as, the tyrant was a *terror* to his subjects.—*adj.* **ter′ror-strick′en.**

ter-ror-ize (ter′ėr-īz′), *v.t.* [terrorized, terroriz-ing], **1,** to fill with great alarm or fear; reduce to a state of terror; **2,** to govern by methods which arouse fear.—*n.* **ter′ror-ism;** **ter′ror-ist.**

terse (tûrs), *adj.* [ters-er, ters-est], concise or brief; exactly to the point; as, a *terse* literary style.—*adv.* **terse′ly.**—*n.* **terse′ness.**

ter-ti-a-ry (tûr′shi-a-ri; -sha-ri), *adj.* and *n.* **1,** third, in rank, degree, class, etc.; as, a *tertiary* defence (in football); **2,** in *geology*, the Third Period of rock formations from 60 to 12 million years ago: the great reptiles had disappeared, the mammals were beginning, and the great mountains (Alps, Andes, Himalayas, etc.) were forming.

test (test), *n.* **1,** trial; proof; as, his character was put to a *test;* examination; as, a *test* in typewriting; **2,** a criterion or standard by which a person or thing may be gauged; as, self-control is the *test* of a man's power; **3,** in *chemistry*, an experiment for discovering the presence of any particular substance in a compound:—*v.t.* **1,** to put to test; try; as, to *test* a man's ability; **2,** in *chemistry*, to try to find a particular substance in; as, to *test* alcohol for poison.—*n.* **test′er.**

tes-ta-ment (tes′ta-ment), *n.* a written document in which a person provides for the disposal of his property after his death: usually in the phrase *last will and testament:*—**Testament, 1,** either of the two main parts of the Bible; **2,** a book containing only the New Testament.—*adj.* **tes′ta-men′ta-ry** (bequeathed by will).

tes-ta-tor (tes-tā′tėr), *n.* a man who leaves a valid will at his death: *fem.* **tes-ta′trix.**—*adj.* **tes′tate** (leaving a valid will).

tes-ti-cle (tes′ti-kl) or **tes′tis** (tes′tis), *n.* [*pl.* testicles; testes (-tēz)] either of the two male sex glands that secrete the germ cells (to fertilize the ovum, or egg, of the female).

tes-ti-fy (tes′ti-fī′), *v.i.* [testified, testify-ing], **1,** to bear witness; to declare under oath before a court of law; as, the witness *testified* in the prisoner's behalf; **3,** to serve as evidence; as, his works *testify* to his industry:—*v.t.* to declare solemnly on oath; bear witness to.—*n.* **tes′ti-fi′er.**

tes-ti-mo-ni-al (tes′ti-mō′ni-al), *n.* **1,** a writing or certificate regarding the character, ability, etc., of a person, or the value of a thing; **2,** a token of respect, acknowledgement of services, etc., presented to a person.

tes-ti-mo-ny (tes′ti-mo-ni), *n.* [*pl.* testimonies], **1,** evidence; proof; as, fossil-bearing rocks give *testimony* of life in former ages; **2,** in *law*, a spoken or written declaration furnished by a witness under oath; **3,** testimonies, the Scriptures.

testy (tes′ti), *adj.* [tes-ti-er, tes-ti-est], touchy; irritable.—*adv.* **tes′ti-ly.**—*n.* **tes′ti-ness.**

tet-a-nus (tet′a-nus), *n.* an acute, infectious, often fatal, disease marked by muscular spasms or rigidity caused by a bacillus that enters through wounds: also called *lockjaw* (when in the lower jaw).

tête-à-tête (tāt′-a-tāt′; tâ′-tȧ-tât′), *n.* confidential, friendly talk between two persons:—*adj.* face to face; confidential.

teth-er (teth′ėr), *n.* **1,** a rope or chain to fasten an animal; **2,** hence, power; endurance; as, she was at the end of her *tether:*—*v.t.* to tie with a rope or chain.

tet-ra- (tet′ra-), *Greek prefix* meaning *four*, as in **tet′ra-chlo′ride** (a chemical compound with 4 chlorine atoms to the molecule), **tet′ra-eth′yl** (a poisonous lead compound added to gasoline to increase power and prevent engine knock), and **tet′ra-he′dron** (a solid figure with four triangular surfaces).

te-tram-e-ter (te-tram′e-tėr), *n.* in *poetry*, a 4-foot line; as, "Ĭ sprắng / tŏ thē sắd / dĭe and Jór / ĭs aňd hé" (anapaestic *tetrameter* of Browning's "Ride from Ghent to Aix").

Teu-ton-ic (tū-ton′ik), *adj.* pertaining to the Teutons, a group including German, Dutch, Scandinavian, British, and related peoples.

text (tekst), *n.* **1,** the main body of any piece of written or printed matter as distinguished from the illustrations, notes, etc.; **2,** a verse of Scripture forming the subject of a sermon; **3,** the subject of a discussion, speech, etc.; theme.

text-book (tekst′book′), *n.* a standard book of instruction in a branch of study.

tex-tile (teks′tĭl; teks′til), *adj.* **1,** pertaining to weaving; as, a *textile* mill; **2,** woven; suitable for weaving:—*n.* woven goods.

tex-ture (teks′tūr), *n.* **1,** the structure or arrangement of threads making up a fabric; as, damask has a smooth *texture;* **2,** composition; structure; as, the compact *texture* of clay.

thal-lus (thal′us), *n.* the simple plant body (not differentiated into true leaves, stem, and root) of the algae, fungi, lichens, and liverworts (called **thal′lo-phytes′**).

than (*th*an), *conj.* **1,** in comparison with; as, you are taller *than* James; also, in comparison with one's desire; as, I'd rather stay *than* go; **2,** besides; but; as, none other *than* my parents can help me.

thane (thān), *n.* the former title of a Scottish knight or baron; as the *thane* of Cawdor.

thank (thangk), *v.t.* to express gratitude to:—**thanks,** *n.pl.* expression of gratitude.—*adj.* **thank′ful.**

thank-less (thangk′lis), *adj.* **1,** ungrateful; not feeling or expressing gratitude; as, a *thankless* child; **2,** not gaining gratitude; unprofitable; as, a *thankless* task.—*adv.* **thank′less-ly.**

thanks-giv-ing (thangks′giv′ing;

thangks-giv′ing), *n.* the act of expressing gratitude; esp., a form of prayer expressing thanks to God.—**Thanksgiving Day,** in Canada, an annual religious and social festival celebrated on the second Monday in October, in U.S. on the last Thursday of November.

that (*th*at), *adj.* [*pl.* those (*th*ōz)], **1,** indicating someone or something at a distance in time or space; the farther; yon; as, please take *that* chair upstairs; who are *those* people? **2,** pointing out a single, particular, or known thing or person; as, ask *those* people best able to pay; **3,** the other; the second; the latter; as, on this side and *that* side: —*demonstrative pron.* **1,** a person or thing at a distance; not this; as, *that* is not fair; these must stay, *those* may go; **2,** a person or thing already indicated or to be indicated; as, so *that* is what he said; *that* is the man you mean; **3,** the other, second, or farther person or thing; as, this wood is softer than *that:*—*relative pron.* **1,** who or whom; which; as, the man *that* you saw; **2,** in, on, or at which; when; as, all those years *that* he was gone; also, for which; as, the reason *that* he came:—*conj.* **1,** used to introduce a clause which is the object or the subject of a verb; as, he said *that* he would come; *that* he lied is bad; **2,** with a purpose; as, work *that* you may succeed; **3,** with the result; as, I am so sleepy *that* I can hardly see; **4,** I wish; as, oh, *that* you were here!

thatch (thach), *n.* a roof or covering made of straw, reeds, etc.; also, the material used:—*v.t.* to cover with, or as with, a roof of straw, reeds, etc.

thaw (thô), *v.i.* **1,** to melt or become liquid, as ice or snow; **2,** to grow warm enough to melt ice and snow; **3,** to become milder or more genial; to unbend; as, his manner *thawed* perceptibly:—*v.t.* to cause to melt:—*n.* the melting of ice or snow as a result of warm weather; also, a state of weather when ice and snow melt.

the (*th*ė when unaccented before a consonant, as in *the cat; th*ē or *th*i when unaccented before a vowel, as in *the ear; th*ē when emphatic or alone), *adj.* or *definite article;* **1,** pointing out a specific or known person or thing; as, *the* boy in the back row; *the* book I gave you; **2,** a; any; every; as, *the* cow is a useful animal; **3,** that which is, or those who are; as, *the* beautiful; *the* great; **4,** being best, greatest, or most important; as, *the* event of the year:—*prep.* a; to each; as, 20 lines *the* page.

cat, āge, fär, cåre, åsk; ten, ēve, latėr; (i) pity, rely, senate; ïce; top; nō.

the-a-tre or **the-a-ter** (thē′a-tėr), *n.*
1, a building where plays, motion
pictures, etc. are given; 2, dramatic
art; the drama; 3, a place where
important action takes place; as,
Waterloo was once the *theatre* of battle.

the-at-ri-cal (thi-at′ri-kal), *adj.* 1, pertaining to the theatre, a dramatic performance, or actors; as, *theatrical* costumes; 2, suitable for, or characteristic
of, the stage; conspicuous; as, a
theatrical entrance:—**theatricals**, *n.pl.*
dramatic performances, esp. by
amateurs.

thee (thē), *pron.* objective case of *thou;*
used mainly in prayer, poetry, or in
poetic prose.

theft (theft), *n.* 1, the act of stealing;
robbery; 2, the property stolen; as,
the *theft* amounted to ten dollars.

their (thâr), *adj.* a possessive form of the
personal pronoun *they:* 1, belonging to
them; of them; as, *their* house; 2,
coming from them; as, *their* kindness.

theirs (thârz), a possessive form of *they,*
used alone: 1, as *adj.* in the predicate,
belonging to them; as, whose is that
car? it is *theirs;* 2, as *pron.*, a person or
thing that belongs to them; as, our car
is blue, *theirs* is black.

them (*th*em), *pron.* objective case of
they.

theme (thēm), *n.* 1, the subject or topic
of a speech, essay, etc.; 2, a short essay
or composition on a given subject; 3,
in *music*, a series of notes forming the
subject of a composition or movement.

them-selves (*th*em-selvz′), *pron.* the
plural form of *himself, herself,* and
itself; the emphatic form of *they* or
reflexive form of *them;* as, they *themselves* are going; they caused *themselves*
much trouble.

then (*th*en), *adv.* 1, in that case; therefore; in consequence: go *then* and buy
what we need; if you must, *then* do it;
2, next; immediately after: wash it;
then dry it; 3, at that time: *then* Rome
fell; 4, later; at another time: come
then instead:—*adj. Colloq.* existing at
the time mentioned; as, the *then* poet
laureate:—*n.* a time mentioned; as, by
then he was ready.

thence (*th*ens), *adv.* 1, from that place;
as, he departed *thence;* 2, from or after
that time; as, a week *thence;* 3, from
that cause, fact, or source.

thence-forth (*th*ens′fôrth′; *th*ens′-
fôrth′), *adv.* from then on; thereafter.

thence-for-ward (*th*ens′fôr′wėrd),
adv. forward; from that time or place·

the-ol-o-gy (thē-ol′o-ji), *n.* [*pl.* theolo-

gies], the study of the nature, powers,
and laws of God, esp. as they affect
man; divinity; the science of religion.
—*adj.* **the′o-log′i-cal** (thē′o-loj′i-kal).
—*n.* **the′o-lo′gian.**

the-o-rem (thē′o-rem), *n.* a proposition to be proved, esp. a law of geometry, algebra, or physics; as, 'the
angles at the base of an isosceles
triangle are equal'.

the-o-ret-i-cal (thē′o-ret′i-kal) or
the-o-ret-ic (thē′o-ret′ik), *adj.* 1,
pertaining to, or depending on, abstract
principles or theories; 2, based on ideas
rather than on fact or experience; not
practical; as, *theoretical* knowledge.—
adv. **the′o-ret′i-cal-ly.**

the-o-ry (thē′o-ri), *n.* [*pl.* theories], 1, a
statement of the fundamental principles
of an art or science rather than of the
method of practising it; as, the *theory*
of music; 2, an opinion, based on
observed facts, offered by a person to
explain how something has been
brought about; as, the *theory* of evolution; also, a view or opinion, not
necessarily based on facts; a guess;
conjecture; as, his *theory* of the crime.
—*n.* **the′o-rist.**

ther-a-py (ther′a-pi), *n.* in *medicine,*
the treatment, cure, or prevention of
disease; as, electro*therapy*, radio*-
therapy*, etc. Also, **ther′a-peu′tics**, *n.pl.*
the science and art of healing.—*adj.*
ther′a-peu′tic (healing; curative).

there (thâr), *adv.* 1, in or at that place;
not here; as, put the book *there;* 2, to
or toward that place; as, I will go *there*
today; 3, in that matter, respect, etc.;
as, you're wrong *there,* I think; 4, used
preceding a verb or in questions to
introduce a sentence; as, is *there* time?
there is time:—*interj.* 1, expressing
defiance, triumph, etc.; as, I won't go.
So *there!* 2, expressing sympathy; as,
there, there, don't fret.

there-a-bouts (thâr′a-bouts) or
there-a-bout (thâr′a-bout′), *adv.* near
that place, time, number, etc.; nearly.

there-aft-er (thâr-àf′tėr), *adv.* after
that; thereupon.

there-at (thâr-at′), *adv.* 1, at that place;
there; 2, on that account; therefore.

there-by (thâr-bī′), *adv.* 1, by that
means; 2, near by; 3, in that connection; as, *thereby* hangs a tale.

there-fore (thâr′fôr), *adv.* for that
reason; on that account.

there-in (thâr-in′), *adv.* 1, in or into
this or that place, time, etc.; 2, in this
or that respect; as, *therein* you err.

there-of (thâr-ov′), *adv.* **1,** of or concerning that or this; **2,** from this or that cause.

there-on (thâr-on′), *adv.* **1,** on that or this place or thing; **2,** thereafter; consequently.

there-to (thâr-tōō′), *adv.* **1,** to that or this place or thing; **2,** moreover; also.

there-up-on (thâr′u-pon′), *adv.* **1,** thereon; upon that; **2,** therefore; by reason of that; **3,** immediately; thereafter.

there-with (thâr-with′; thâr-with′), *adv.* **1,** with that or this; **2,** at the same time; immediately thereafter.

ther-mal (thûr′mal), *adj.* [*Greek, thermos*, hot] **1,** pertaining to heat; as, a *thermal* unit, *thermal* capacity; **2,** warm; hot; as, *thermal* baths or springs.

ther-mom-e-ter (thėr-mom′e-tėr), *n.* an instrument for measuring temperature and temperature changes, esp. one consisting of a sealed glass tube partly filled with mercury or coloured alcohol, whose expansion or contraction due to heat changes, is indicated on a graduated scale.

Fahrenheit thermometer, one with a scale marking the freezing-point of water at 32 degrees and the boiling-point at 212 degrees; **centigrade thermometer,** one with a scale marking the freezing-point at 0 and the boiling-point at 100 degrees.

ther-mo-nu-cle-ar (thûr′mō-nū′kli-ėr), *adj.* using heat energy released in nuclear fission.

ther-mos (thûr′mos), *adj. Greek,* hot.

ther-mo-stat (thûr′mō-stat′), *n.* an automatic apparatus for controlling temperature, by regulating dampers, the flow of fuel-oil, etc.

the-sau-rus (thi-sô′rus), *n.* a dictionary of classified synonyms and antonyms.

these (thēz), *adj.* and *pron. pl.* of *this:* opposite of *those;* as, *those* are yours, but *these* are mine.

the-sis (thē′sis), *n.* [*pl.* theses (thē′sēz)], **1,** something laid down or stated; esp., a statement by a person who undertakes to support it by argument; **2,** a long essay, based on original research, offered by a candidate for an advanced degree at a college or university.

thews (thūz), *n.pl.* muscles; brawn.

they (thā), *personal pron.* **1,** nominative plural of *he, she,* or *it;* **2,** people in general; men; as, so *they* say.

thick (thik), *adj.* **1,** large in diameter; coarse; as, a *thick* stem; **2,** of specified, or relatively great, depth between two opposite surfaces; as, a board two inches *thick;* a *thick* book; **3,** of compact or dense texture, consistency, etc.; as, *thick* glue; **4,** close together; abundant; as, *thick* foliage; also, densely set or overgrown; as, a garden *thick* with weeds; **5,** stupid; dense; **6,** not clear; muddy; foggy; as, the air was *thick* with smoke; **7,** throaty; hoarse; as, a *thick* voice; **8,** *Colloq.,* extremely friendly or intimate; as, she's too *thick* with Mary:—*adv.* close together; following closely or quickly; as, the blows came *thick* and fast:—*n.* **1,** the thickest part of anything; as, the *thick* of the thumb; **2,** the most intense moment; the place where action is liveliest; as, the *thick* of the combat.— *n.* **thick′ness.**—*adj.* (figuratively) **thick′—skinned′; thick′—wit′ted.**

thick-en (thik′en), *v.t.* to make (a liquid) less thin; as, to *thicken* gravy:— *v.i.* **1,** to become denser; as, the clouds *thicken;* **2,** to become complicated; as, the plot *thickens.*

thick-et (thik′it), *n.* a dense growth of tangled shrubs, trees, etc.

thick-set (thik′set′), *adj.* **1,** closely planted; **2,** having a short, stout body; as, a *thickset* fighter.

thief (thēf), *n.* [*pl.* thieves (thēvz)], a person who steals or robs.

thieve (thēv), *v.t.* and *v.i.* [thieved, thiev-ing], to steal; rob.—*n.* **thiev′er-y.** —*adj.* **thiev′ish.**

thigh (thī), *n.* **1,** in man, the muscular part of the leg between the knee and the trunk; **2,** the corresponding part in other animals.

thim-ble (thim′bl), *n.* a cap of metal, celluloid, etc., worn to protect the tip of the finger in sewing.

thim-ble-ber-ry (thim′bl-ber′i), *n.* any species of raspberry or blackberry having thimble-shaped fruit.

thin (thin), *adj.* [thin-ner, thin-nest], **1,** small in diameter; fine; slim; slender; **2,** having the two opposite surfaces close together; of little thickness; as, *thin* board; **3,** transparent; sheer; as, *thin* muslin; **4,** hence, easily seen through; slight; shallow; as, a *thin* excuse; **5,** lacking density; rarefied; as, *thin* air; **6,** high-pitched; shrill; faint; as, a *thin* voice; **7,** lacking roundness or plumpness of figure; gaunt; **8,** scanty; lacking substance or vigour; as, *thin* blood; **9,** lacking abundance; scanty; as, *thin* vegeta-tion:—*v.t.* [thinned, thin-ning], **1,** to

cat, āge, fär, câre, ásk; ten, ēve, latėr; (i) pity, rely, senate; ice; top; nō.

make thin or less dense; **2**, to reduce in numbers:—*v.i.* to become less dense or numerous:—*n.* in the U.S., a kind of small, dry biscuit.—*n.* **thin′ness.**—*adj.* (figuratively) **thin′—skinned′** (sensitive; easily hurt).

thine (*thīn*), *Archaic* or *Poetic*, a possessive form of *thou:* **1**, as *adj.*, belonging or relating to thee: **a**, in the predicate; as, whose is the glory? it is *thine;* **b**, used in place of *thy* before a vowel sound; as, *thine* own self; guard *thine* honour; **2**, as *pron.*, a person or thing belonging to thee; as, joy to thee and *thine.*

thing (thing), *n.* **1**, any object which may be perceived through the senses, as a stone, a book, etc.; also, anything which may be made an object of thought, or which exists in the imagination only, as courage or valour, a fairy, etc.; **2**, a particular act, course, or affair; as, this *thing* must not occur again; **3**, a person or animal: usually a term of pity, sympathy, affection, or contempt; as, poor *thing!* **4**, **things**: **a**, wraps; personal possessions, as property or baggage; **b**, circumstances; as, *things* are improving.

think (thingk), *v.i.* [thought (thôt), thinking], **1**, to develop ideas; to form a conception, opinion, or judgment; **2**, to consider; to meditate; muse; **3**, to have in mind, or call to mind, a thought idea, or image of something; as, to *think* of a picture; **4**, to have an opinion or judgment; as, he *thinks* well of you; **5**, to purpose, plan, or intend; as I had not *thought* of going until tomorrow:—*v.t.* **1**, to occupy the mind with; imagine; as, *think* no evil; **2**, to review or examine mentally; as, to *think* out a problem; **3**, to hold as an opinion; as, you may *think* what you please.—*n.* **think′er.**

third (thûrd), *adj.* next after the second: the ordinal of *three:*—*n.* one of the three equal parts of anything.

third-ly (thûrd′li), *adv.* in the third place.

thirst (thûrst), *n.* **1**, a desire for drink; also, the sensation relieved only by drinking, usually a feeling of dryness and heat in the mouth, throat, and stomach; **2**, a great craving; a yearning; as, a *thirst* for fame:—*v.i.* **1**, to desire drink; **2**, to be eager; as, to *thirst* for revenge.—*adj.* **thirst′y.**

thir-teen (thûr′tēn′), *adj.* composed of one more than twelve:—*n.* **1**, the sum of twelve plus one; **2**, a sign representing thirteen units, as 13 or xiii.

thir-teenth (thûr′tēnth′), *adj.* next after the 12th: the ordinal of *thirteen:* —*n.* one of thirteen equal parts.

thir-ti-eth (thûr′ti-eth), *adj.* next after the 29th: the ordinal of *thirty:*—*n.* one of the 30 equal parts of anything.

thir-ty (thûr′ti), *adj.* composed of one more than 29:—*n.* **1**, the sum of 29 plus one; **2**, a sign representing 30 units, as 30 or xxx.

thir-ty—one (thûr′ti–wun′), *n.* and *adj.* the numbers *thirty-one* to *thirty-nine* are hyphenated.

this (*th*is), *adj.* [*pl.* these (*th*ēz)], **1**, indicating something or someone near in time or space; as, will you mail *this* letter for me? *these* guests came; **2**, pointing out a single, particular, or known thing or person; as, *this* whole matter is a joke; *these* students best able to work; **3**, the first; the nearer; the former; as, *this* side and that:— *demonstrative pron.* **1**, a person or thing near at hand; not that; as, *this* is my house; **2**, a person or thing just indicated or to be indicated; as, I have heard *this* before; *this* is the violinist who excels them all; **3**, the first or nearer person or thing; as, *this* is a better cake than that.

this-tle (this′l), *n.* a plant of the aster family with rough, thorny stems, finely-divided, prickly leaves, and yellow, purple, or white flowers.—*adj.* **this′tly.** —*n.* **this′tle-down′** (silky fibres attached to thistle seeds, enabling them to be wind-borne).

thith-er (*th*ith′ėr), *adv. Archaic*, to that place; in that direction:—*adj.* more remote; farther.

thong (thông), *n.* **1**, a thin leather strap or string for fastening something; **2**, the lash of a whip.

Thor (thôr), *n.* the Scandinavian god of thunder, war, and strength, for whom Thursday is named.

thor-ax (thōr′aks), *n.* **1**, in the human body, the chest, containing the heart, lungs, etc.; **2**, in insects, the middle of the three main sections of the body.— *adj.* **thorac′ic** (thō-ras′ik).

tho-ri-um (thō′ri-um), *n.* a rare radio-active element (atomic number, 90) used in radio-tube filaments, gas mantles, magnesium alloys, etc.

thorn (thôrn), *n.* **1**, in plants, a stiff, sharp-pointed, slender projection, as on the locust; in animals, a similar sharp projection, usually called *spine;* **2**, any tree or shrub bearing thorns; **3**, hence, anything that annoys; a source of worry.—*adj.* **thorn′y.**—*adj.* **thorn′less.** —*n.* **thorn′i-ness.**

all (ôl), ôr; up, mūte, cûr, cōōl, book; oil, out; th, thin; *th*, the.

thor-ough (thûr'ō), *adj.* **1,** finished; complete; not superficial; as, a *thorough* cleaning; **2,** accurate; careful; as, a *thorough* worker.—*n.* **thor'ough-ness.**

thor-ough-bred (thûr'ō-bred'), *adj.* **1,** of pure and unmixed breed; as, a *thoroughbred* dog; **2,** showing the characteristics of good birth and breeding; **3,** high-spirited:—*n.* **1,** an animal of pure breed; **2,** a person of fine breeding.

thor-ough-fare (thûr'ō-fâr'), *n.* a street, road, or passage open at both ends; **2,** in the *Maritimes,* a water passage between lakes or ponds of the same level.

those (thōz), *adj.* and *pron.; pl.* of *that:* opposite of *these.*

thou (thou), *pron.* [*nominative* thou, *possessive* thy (*thī*) or thine (*thīn*), *objective* thee (*thē*); *pl. nominative* ye (yē) or you (yōō), *possessive* your (yōōr) or yours (yōōrz), *objective* you], *Archaic* or *Poetic,* the personal pronoun of the second person.

though (thō), *conj.* **1,** notwithstanding the fact that; as, I shall go, *though* it is late; **2,** even if; as, *though* he go, I'll stay:—*adv.* nevertheless; however.

thought (thôt), *n.* **1,** mental activity; meditation; reflection; **2,** that which the mind conceives, considers, remembers, or imagines; an idea; opinion; notion; **3,** the power of imagining and reasoning; intellect; as, man is endowed with *thought;* **4,** concern; care; worry; as, take *thought* for the morrow; **5,** a way of thinking, or a group of ideas or beliefs, characteristic of a period, nation, class, society, etc.; as, modern *thought,* etc.

thought-ful (thôt'fool), *adj.* **1,** thinking; full of thought; **2,** considerate of others; kind.—*adv.* **thought'ful-ly.**

thought-less (thôt'lis), *adj.* **1,** not thinking; careless; **2,** without consideration for others.—*adv.* **thought'-less-ly.**

thou-sand (thou'zand), *adj.* **1,** composed of ten times 100; **2,** indefinitely great in number:—*n.* **1,** the number consisting of ten hundreds; **2,** a sign representing this number, as 1000 or M; **3,** a large number.

thou-sandth (thou'zandth), *adj.* next after the 999th: the ordinal of *thousand:*—*n.* one of the 1000 equal parts of anything.

thrall (thrôl), *n.* **1,** a slave or serf; **2,** slavery or bondage; as, held in *thrall.*—*n.* **thral'dom.**

thrash (thrash), *v.t.* **1,** (preferably

thresh), to beat out (grain) from the hull or husk; **2,** to discuss thoroughly, or over and over; as, to *thrash* out the solution to a problem; **3,** to beat or flog:—*v.i.* **1,** (preferably *thresh*), to beat out grain; **2,** to toss or move wildly; as, the patient with a high fever *thrashed* about in bed.

thrash-er (thrash'ẽr), *n.* **1,** a person who thrashes; **2,** a North American thrushlike bird.

thread (thred), *n.* **1,** a thin, twisted strand of flax, cotton, silk, or other fibrous substance; **2,** a filament; anything threadlike; as, a *thread* of glass or metal; a fibre; **3,** something running through and connecting the parts of anything; as, the *thread* of a story; **4,** the spiral ridge of a screw or nut:—*v.t.* **1,** to provide with, or as with, a thread; as, to *thread* a screw; **2,** to put a thread through the eye of (a needle); **3,** to string (beads); **4,** to pass or pierce through; as, to *thread* a narrow street; also, to make (one's way) with difficulty.

thread-bare (thred'bâr'), *adj.* **1,** worn down to the threads; shabby; as, *threadbare* upholstery; **2,** hackneyed or worn-out; as, a *threadbare* plot to a play or story.

threat (thret), *n.* **1,** the declaration of an intention to hurt or punish; as, he never carried out his *threats;* **2,** a warning of coming evil or danger.

threat-en (thret'n), *v.i.* to give notice of coming evil or danger:—*v.t.* **1,** to warn of punishment or injury; as, the law *threatens* criminals with punishment; **2,** to portend; give evidence of (a coming event or coming calamity); as, the clouds *threaten* a storm.—*adj.* **threat'en-ing.**—*adv.* **threat'en-ing-ly.**

three (thrē), *adj.* composed of one more than two:—*n.* **1,** the number consisting of two plus one; **2,** a sign representing three units, as 3 or iii.—*n.* **three'—bag'-ger** (*Slang,* a 3-base hit).

three-fold (thrē'fōld'), *adj.* triple; in three layers, forms, etc.; consisting of three:—*adv.* (thrē'fōld'), in a threefold manner; triply.

three-score (thrē'skōr'), *adj.* three times twenty; sixty.

three-some (thrē'sum), *n.* a group of three, esp. of three persons playing a round of golf.

thresh (thresh), *v.t.* **1,** to beat out (grain) from the husk or (husks) from grain; **2,** (usually *thrash*), to discuss thoroughly; **3,** (usually *thrash*), to beat or flog:—*v.i.* **1,** to beat out grain; **2,** (usually *thrash*), to toss or move wildly.

cat, āge, fär, câre, àsk; ten, ēve, latẽr; (i) pity, rely, senate; īce; top; nō.

thresh-er (thresh′ẽr), *n.* a person or a machine that threshes.

thresh-old (thresh′ōld; thresh′hōld), *n.* **1,** the stone, plank, or piece of timber under a door; a door-sill; **2,** an entrance; the place or time of entrance; as, on the *threshold* of manhood.

threw (thrōō), *p.t.* of *throw.*

thrice (thrīs), *adv.* **1,** three times; **2,** in a threefold manner or degree.

thrift (thrift), *n.* careful management; frugality; economy.—*adv.* **thrift′i-ly.**

thrift-less (thrift′lis), *adj.* extravagant; wasteful.—*n.* **thrift′less-ness.**

thrift-y (thrif′ti), *adj.* [thrift-i-er, thrift-i-est], **1,** saving; not extravagant; **2,** prosperous; thriving; also, growing well; flourishing; as, a *thrifty* plant.—*n.* **thrift′i-ness.**

thrill (thril), *v.t.* to fill with intense emotion; stir deeply; as, the great actress *thrilled* her audience:—*v.i.* **1,** to experience a sharp tingling sensation or a wave of emotion; as, they *thrilled* with delight; **2,** to quiver; as, his voice *thrilled* with anger:—*n.* **1,** a tingling, vibrating sensation; **2,** a quiver of emotion.—*n.* **thrill′er** (*Slang,* a sensational story, play, etc.)

thrips (thrips), *n.pl.* minute insects (with long narrow wings fringed with hairs) that feed on plant juices; as onion *thrips;* tobacco *thrips.*

thrive (thrīv), *v.i.* [*p.t.* throve (thrōv) or thrived, *p.p.* thriv-en (thriv′en) or, rarely, thrived, *p.pr.* thriv-ing], **1,** to prosper by industry, economy, and good management; **2,** to increase or prosper in any way; succeed; **3,** to grow sturdily; increase; flourish.

throat (thrōt), *n.* **1,** the front part of the neck between the collar-bone and the chin; also, the passage through it; **2,** hence, a narrow entrance or passage; as, the *throat* of a cannon.

throb (throb), *v.i.* [throbbed, throbbing], **1,** to beat, as the pulse; sometimes, to beat with more than usual force; palpitate; **2,** hence, to thrill, as with joy:—*n.* **1,** a strong pulsation or beat; **2,** a thrill; as, a *throb* of joy.

throe (thrō), *n.* agony; violent pain; extreme anguish.

throm-bo-sis (throm-bō′sis), *n.* the forming of a blood-clot, or thrombus, in a blood-vessel, causing local stoppage of circulation (often fatal if in brain or heart).

throne (thrōn), *n.* **1,** the chair of state of a king, bishop, etc.; **2,** sovereign or kingly power; also, one who holds sovereign power:—*v.t.* [throned, throning], to place in a position of kingly power; raise to the throne.

throng (thrông), *n.* a multitude or great number; a crowd:—*v.t.* to crowd into; fill; as, soldiers *thronged* the streets:—*v.i.* to assemble in great numbers.

throt-tle (throt′l), *v.t.* [throt-tled, throt-tling], **1,** to strangle or choke by pressure on the windpipe; **2,** to shut off fuel from; as, to *throttle* an engine:—*n.* a valve to control the supply of fuel to an engine.

through (thrōō), *prep.* **1,** from beginning to end; as, *through* life; *through* a tunnel; *through* thick and thin; **2,** into at one place and out of at another; as, to bore *through* a plank; **3,** in the midst of; as, to walk *through* the woods; **4,** by means of; as, *through* the influence of a friend; **5,** on account of; by reason of; as, he departed *through* fear of being discovered:—*adv.* **1,** from end to end, or from side to side; as, to drive a nail *through;* **2,** from the beginning to the end; as, he played the music *through;* **3,** to the end or to a conclusion; as, we will put the job *through:*—*adj.* **1,** extending from one place or point to another; as, a *through* passage; a *through* bolt; **2,** transporting passengers or freight from one place to another without stop or change of cars; as, a *through* train.

through-out (thrōō-out′), *adv.* everywhere; in every part; as, the jewellery is gold *throughout:*—*prep.* during; in every part of; as, *throughout* the year.

throw (thrō), *v.t.* [*p.t.* threw (thrōō), *p.p.* thrown (thrōn), *p.pr.* throw-ing], **1,** to fling or hurl with the arm; pitch; toss; as, to *throw* a stone; **2,** to give forth or cast; as, the lamp *threw* a faint light; she *threw* him a quick glance; **3,** to upset; to make (someone) fall in any way; as, his horse *threw* him; the wrestler *threw* his opponent; **4,** to put or place in a particular position, state, etc.; as, the fire *threw* the people into confusion:—*n.* **1,** the act of twirling, casting, or flinging; **2,** a cast of dice.—*n.* **throw′back′,** reversion to an ancestral type.

thrush (thrush), *n.* any of a large family of songbirds, most often of plain colour, but sometimes with spotted throat and breast.

thrust (thrust), *v.t.* [thrust, thrust-ing], **1,** to push or shove forcibly; as, he *thrust* me into the car; **2,** to pierce; as, their swords *thrust* him through:—*v.i.* to attack, with a pointed weapon; as, to *thrust* with a dagger:—*n.* **1,** a violent or sudden push; **2,** a stab; as, the *thrust* of a sword.

thud (thud), *n.* a dull sound:—*v.i.* [thud-ded, thud-ding], to make, or strike so as to make, a dull sound: the apples *thudded* on the ground.

thug (thug), *n.* an assassin; a ruffian.

thumb (thum), *n.* **1,** the thickest finger of the human hand, consisting of two joints only; **2,** the part of a glove which covers the thumb:—*v.t.* **1,** to turn rapidly with the thumb; as, to *thumb* the leaves of a book; **2,** to rub or soil with the thumb or by handling; as, don't *thumb* up your new reading-book. —*n.* thumb′—tack′.

thumb-screw (thum′skrōō′), *n.* **1,** a screw with flattened head, that can be turned by thumb and forefinger; **2,** a former instrument of torture used to squeeze the thumb.

thump (thump), *n.* **1,** a hard, heavy blow; as he hit him a thump on the back; **2,** a heavy fall, or the sound of it; as, the man fell with a *thump:*—*v.t.* to pound; strike or beat with dull, heavy blows; as, he *thumped* the door:—*v.i.* to pound or throb, as the heart.—*n.* thump′er.

thun-der (thun′dẽr), *n.* **1,** the noise which is heard immediately after a flash of lightning; **2,** any similar loud noise; as, the *thunder* of the guns:— *v.i.* **1,** to send forth peals of thunder; **2,** to send forth a sound like thunder; as, the sea *thundered* against the rocks. —*adj.* thun′der-ous.—*n.* thun′der-clap′; thun′der-cloud′; thun′der-er.— *adj.* thun′der-struck′.

thun-der-bolt (thun′dẽr-bōlt′), *n* **1,** a flash of lightning accompanied by a clap of thunder; **2,** something swift, sudden, and terrible, like lightning and thunder; as, the news of the bank's failure was a *thunderbolt.*

thun-der-head (thun′dẽr-hed′), *n.* a mass of dark cloud with shining white edges, often seen before a thunderstorm.

thun-der-storm (thun′dẽr-stôrm′), *n.* a storm with thunder and lightning.

Thurs-day (thûrz′di; dā), *n.* the 5th day of the week.

thus (thus), *adv.* **1,** in this or that manner; as, write it *thus;* **2,** to this degree or extent; as, *thus* far; **3,** so; therefore; as, *thus* plants need light.

thwart (thwôrt), *adj.* situated or placed across something:—*n.* a rower's seat in a boat, extending from side to side:— *v.t.* to oppose; baffle; outwit; as, to *thwart* an enemy.

thy (thī), *Archaic* or *Poetic,* a possessive form of the personal pronoun *thou:*

belonging or relating to thee; as, honour *thy* father and *thy* mother.

thyme (tīm), *n.* an herb with small aromatic leaves, used for seasoning.

thy-roid (thī′roid), *n.* and *adj.* a gland lying on either side of the windpipe below the pharynx: it secretes a hormone, **thy-rox′ine,** used in treating *goitre* and *cretinism* (caused by its lack).

thy-self (thī-self′), *pron.* an emphatic or reflexive form of *thee* and *thou;* as, thou *thyself* must be the judge; know *thyself.*

ti (tē), *n.* in *music,* the seventh note of the scale: formerly called *si.*

ti-ar-a (ti-ä′ra; tī-âr′a; ti-âr′a), *n.* **1,** the triple crown worn by the Pope; **2,** a coronet for the head; as, a *tiara* of diamonds.

tib-i-a (tib′i-a), *n.* the inner and larger of the two bones between knee and ankle; the shinbone: the smaller one is the *fibula.*

tic (tik), *n.* the habitual, convulsive twitching of a muscle, esp. of the face.

¹tick (tik), *v.i.* to make a slight, quick, regularly repeated sound; as, a watch *ticks:*—*v.t.* **1,** to mark or check off with dots or other small marks; as, he *ticked* each item as he came to it; **2,** to mark off (time) by repeated ticking sounds, as does a clock:—*n.* **1,** a light, repeated ticking sound; **2,** time shown by the sound made by a clock; an instant; as, I'll do it in a *tick;* **3,** a tiny mark, as a dot, check, etc., used in checking off, or in marking something for attention.

²tick (tik), *n.* **1,** a tiny, blood-sucking spider which attaches itself to the skin of man and other animals; **2,** an insect which attaches itself to the skin of animals and sucks their blood; as, the bat-*tick;* sheep-*tick.*

³tick (tik), *n.* a cloth case or covering which contains feathers or other filling for a mattress.—*n.* tick′ing.

tick-er (tik′ẽr), *n.* a telegraphic device that records stock-market quotations, etc., on a narrow strip of paper called tick′er—tape′.

tick-et (tik′it), *n.* **1,** a certificate or card which entitles the holder to certain stated privileges, such as admission to an entertainment, transportation by rail or ship, etc.; **2,** a small card stating price, size, etc., of goods; a label or tag; **3,** a list of candidates to be voted for; as, the Conservative *ticket:*—*v.t.* to mark by a label.

tick-le (tik′l), *v.t.* [tick-led, tick-ling], **1,** to touch lightly so as to produce a peculiar nervous tingle; **2,** to please or

amuse; as, your speech *tickled* me:—
v.i. to feel a tingling sensation; as, my
ear *tickles:*—*n.* a peculiar thrill or
tingle, or the touch causing this
sensation.

tick-lish (tik′lish), *adj.* 1, easily tickled;
2, delicate to handle or cope with; as, a
ticklish problem; 3, risky; unstable;
unsteady; as, *ticklish* footing; 4, of
persons, over-sensitive; touchy; easily
disturbed; as, she is *ticklish* on that
point.—*n.* tick′lish-ness.

tick-tack (tik′tak′), *n.* 1, a light beating
or ticking, as of a heart or a clock; 2, a
device to make such a sound, esp. one
made to tap against a window (as a
prank).

tick-tack-toe (tik′tak-tō′), *n.* 1, a
children's game of trying,
with eyes shut, to bring down
a pencil on one set of numbers, etc.; 2, the game of
noughts and crosses. Also, TICK-TACK-
tick′tack-too′.   TOE

tid-bit (tid′bit′), *n.* Same as titbit.

tid-al (tīd′al), *adj.* pertaining to, or
affected by, the tide; as, a *tidal* river;
tidal flats.

tid-dly-winks (tid′li-winks′), *n.* a
game in which a player tries to be the
first to snap all his disks into a small
cup. Also, tid′dle-dy-winks′.

tide (tīd), *n.* 1, time; season; used very
often in combination; as, Easter*tide,*
spring-*tide;* 2, the regular rise and fall
twice every day of the oceans and the
bodies of water connected with them,
due to the unequal attraction of the sun
and the moon on the waters; 3, anything which increases and decreases,
like the tide; as, the economic *tide:*—
v.t. [tid-ed, tid-ing], 1, to carry along
with the current or tide; 2, to help (a
person) along; assist in time of need;
as, this money will *tide* him over until
he gets a job.

tide-rip (tīd′rip′), *n.* rough water
caused by the meeting of cross currents
or tides. Also called *rip* and *riptide.*

tide-wa-ter (tīd′wô′tẽr), *n.* 1, water
affected by the rise and fall of the tide;
2, land bordered by such water.

ti-dings (tī′dingz), *n.pl.* news; information; a message; as, glad *tidings.*

ti-dy (tī′di), *adj.* [ti-di-er, ti-di-est], 1,
trim; neat; orderly; 2, *Colloq.,* considerable; as, a *tidy* sum of money:—
v.t. and *v.i.* [tidied, tidy-ing], to make
neat; put things in proper order:—*n.*
ti′di-ness.

tie (tī), *v.t.* [tied, ty-ing], 1, to attach by
a cord or rope drawn together and
knotted; as, to *tie* a tag to a box; to
tie flowers in a bunch; 2, to bind
together the parts of, by a cord that is
drawn up and knotted; as, to *tie* a
shoe; 3, to make a knot or bow in; as,
to *tie* a scarf; also, to form (a knot, bow,
etc.) by looping and securing the ends
of a cord or rope; 4, to restrict or limit;
as, his business *ties* him down; 5, to
equal in score; make the same score as;
as, we *tied* the other team in football;
6, in *music,* to unite (two notes) by a
curved line:—*v.i.* 1, to form a bow or
knot; as, the sash *ties* in the back; 2,
to make the same score:—*n.* 1, something, as a band, rope, or ribbon, used
to bind, draw, or fasten together; 2, a
plank or rod to which the rails of a railroad track are attached; 3, something
tied, as a ribbon, and used as a fastening
or ornament; esp., a necktie; 4, a
relationship or connection; as, business
ties; 5, a common interest which unites;
as, a strong family *tie;* 6, equality of
numbers, as of votes; equal scores in a
contest, race, etc.; 7, in *music,* a
curved line [⌢] connecting two notes
of the same pitch, to indicate that only
the first note is to be sung or played but
that this note is to be held the length of
the two notes.—*n.* tie′beam′ (a horizontal beam connecting the lower ends
of two opposite rafters); tie′pin′;
tie′—up′.

tier (tẽr), *n.* a row or rank; esp., one of
a set of such rows arranged one above
the other; as, a *tier* of seats in a theatre.

tiff (tif), *n.* 1, a slight quarrel; spat; 2,
a fit of anger or resentment; huff; ill
humour.

ti-ger (tī′gẽr), *n.* a large, fierce Asiatic
beast of prey of the cat family, having
yellow fur with black cross stripes.—*n.*
fem. ti′gress:—**tiger beetle,** an active
species of beetle (with spots of various
colours) whose larvae burrow in the soil
and feed on other insects:—**tiger lily,** a
garden lily of orange-coloured flowers
spotted with black:—**tiger moth,** a
stout-bodied moth with brightly striped
or spotted wings: the larva has a
central band of reddish-brown hairs
between two black bands.

tight (tīt), *adj.* 1, not loose; fastened
firmly; as, a *tight* knot; compact; as,
a *tight* weave; 2, closely built, so that
water or other liquid cannot pass
through; as, a *tight* barrel; 3, fitting
close to a part of the body, usually too
close for comfort; as, a *tight* glove; 4,

---

all (ôl), ôr; up, mūte, cûr, cōōl, book; oil, out; th, thin; *th,* the.

taut or stretched; as, a *tight*rope; **5,** not easily obtained; not plentiful; as during a depression, money is *tight;* **6,** *Colloq.,* stingy:—*adv.* tightly; firmly; as, he closed the window *tight:*— **tights,** *n.pl.* close-fitting garments for the lower part of the body, worn by actors, acrobats, etc. Also called *leotards.*—*adv.* **tight′ly.**—*adj.* **tight′—fist′ed; tight′—lipped′.**

tight-en (tīt′n), *v.t.* and *v.i.* to make or become tight; as, to *tighten* a screw.

tight-rope (tīt′rōp′), *n.* a taut or stretched rope or cable on which acrobats balance themselves while performing.

tike (tīk), *n.* **1,** a dog or cur; **2,** *Colloq.* a mischievous child: used playfully of any child. Also, **tyke.**

til-de (til′dè), *n.* a pronunciation mark [~] used to denote the Spanish ñ, as in cañon, señor: also used in pronunciation keys of dictionaries.

tile (tīl), *n.* a thin slab of baked clay, stone, etc., used for roofing, floors, wall decoration, etc.; **2,** a pipe made of baked clay and used as a drain:—*v.t.* [tiled, til-ing], **1,** to cover with tiles; **2,** to protect a lodge or meeting from intrusion by posting a *tyler* (*tiler*) at the door.

¹**till** (til), *n.* a money-drawer.

²**till** (til), *prep.* to the time of; as far as; as, wait *till* one o'clock:—*conj.* **1,** until; to the time when; as, wait *till* I return; **2,** before; unless; as, he won't come *till* you call him.

³**till** (til), *v.t.* to prepare for seed, as by ploughing; cultivate; as, to *till* the soil. —*n.* **till′er.**—*adj.* **till′a-ble.**

till-age (til′ij), *n.* **1,** the act or art of tilling land; **2,** land under cultivation.

till-er (til′èr), *n.* a steering lever of wood or metal for turning the rudder of a vessel.

tilt (tilt), *v.i.* **1,** to lean or tip; keel over; **2,** to fight or make a charge on horseback, armed with a lance:—*v.t.* to raise at one end; tip; as, to *tilt* a stone:—*n.* **1,** the act of tipping; the state of being tipped; as, the *tilt* of her head; **2,** that which slopes; an incline; **3,** a combat between opponents on horseback armed with lances or spears with which each one tried to unhorse the other.

tim-ber (tim′bèr), *n.* **1,** wood suitable for carpentry, shipbuilding, etc.; **2,** a large thick piece of wood prepared for use; **3,** wooded land from which timber may be obtained:—*v.t.* to furnish or construct with timber.—*adj.* **tim′bered.**

tim-bre (tim′bèr; taṅ′br), *n.* the quality or tone identity of a sound (determined by the number and character of its overtones); as, the *timbre* of a voice, violin, etc.: also called *tone colour* and *tone quality.*

time (tīm), *n.* **1,** the moment when something happens or occurs; as, his father was away at the *time* of the fire; **2,** the period during which something is going on; as, the play continued for two hours' *time;* **3,** the regular or appointed hour when something is supposed to begin, take place, or end; as, it is *time* for lunch; **4,** the proper moment for something to happen; opportunity; as, this is the *time* to buy; **5,** a definite or precise moment as shown by a clock; as, the *time* for his departure is five o'clock; **6,** a period with more or less definite limits; an age; as, in the *time* of Julius Caesar; ancient *times;* **7,** a period marked by definite physical characteristics; as, summer-*time;* day*time;* **8,** a period characterized by special qualities, experiences, or conditions; as, to have a good *time;* hard *times;* **9,** the period required or consumed in performing an action; as, the winner's *time* was 11.5 seconds; **10,** one of a series of repeated actions; as, do this exercise five *times;* **11,** the lapse or passing of all the days, months, and years, taken as a whole; as, *time* will make him forget; **12,** a system of reckoning or measuring the passage of hours, days, etc.; as, solar *time;* standard *time;* **13,** the rate at which something is done; as, to run in double-quick *time;* **14,** in *music,* the arrangement of the rhythmic beats of a composition into equal measures included between successive bars; as, two-four *time;* also, the tempo at which a passage or composition should be, or is, played; **15,** a period long enough for something to be done; as, I have no *time* to finish this work; **16, times,** an indication that one number is to be multiplied by another: often used in place of the multiplication sign (×) as, five *times* two is ten:—*v.t.* [timed, tim-ing], **1,** to adapt to the occasion; arrange the time of; as, I will *time* my visit to suit your convenience; **2,** to regulate; as, to *time* the speed of a machine; **3,** to find out or record the speed of; as, to *time* a runner.—*adj.* **time′less; time′worn′.**—*n.* **time′keep′er.**

time-ly (tīm′li), *adj.* [time-li-er, time-li-est], suitable to the time or occasion; well-timed; as, *timely* help.—*n.* **time′-li-ness.**

time-piece (tīm′pēs′), *n.* any instrument that records the time; a clock or watch.

tim-er (tīm′ẽr), *n.* **1,** an instrument that shows or records the passage of time, as a stop-watch; **2,** a device for causing the spark in an internal-combustion engine to occur at the proper time.

time-serv-er (tīm′sûr′vẽr), *n.* one who selfishly or basely fits his conduct or principles to views that are in favour at the moment with persons in power.

time-ta-ble (tīm′tā′bl), *n.* a systematically arranged list of the dates and hours for events; esp., a list of trains, boats, etc., with their times of arrival and departure from various stations.

tim-id (tim′id), *adj.* shy; wanting in courage.—*adv.* **tim′id-ly.**—*n.* **ti-mid′-i-ty.**

tim-or-ous (tim′ẽr-us), *adj.* **1,** fearful of danger; timid; as, a *timorous* cur; **2,** expressing fear or alarm; as, a *timorous* look.

tim-o-thy (tim′o-thi), *n.* a valuable grass with long, closely packed flower spikes, used for hay: also called *timothy-grass.*

tim-pa-ni (tim′pa-nē′), *n.pl.* kettle-drums.—*n.* **tim′pa-nist** (one who plays a set of *timpani*).

tin (tin), *n.* **1,** a silvery-white, soft metal from which many useful articles are made, such as boxes, cans, and pans; **2,** thin plates of iron or steel covered with this metal; **3,** ware made of tin plate; esp., a can made of tin plate; also, the contents of such a can:—*adj.* made of tin or tin plate:—*v.t.* [tinned, tin-ning], **1,** to cover with tin, or with tinned iron; **2,** to put into tins, as food. —*adj.* **tin′ny.**—*n.* **tin′ware′.**

tinc-ture (tingk′tūr), *n.* **1,** a medicinal substance in an alcoholic solution; as, *tincture* of iodine; **2,** a small amount; touch; as, a *tincture* of hope:—*v.t.* [tinc-tured, tinctur-ing], to colour; tinge; imbue.

tin-der (tin′dẽr), *n.* any material which catches fire easily, esp. when used to kindle a fire from a spark.

tine (tīn), *n.* a tooth or spike; a prong, esp. of a fork.

tin-foil (tin′foil′), *n.* tin, or an alloy of tin and lead, rolled into thin sheets, and used as protective wrapping, etc.

ting (ting), *n.* a tinkling sound, as of a single stroke on a small bell. Also, **ting′-a—ling′.**

tinge (tinj), *v.t.* [tinged, ting-ing or tinge-ing], **1,** to stain slightly with colour; dye faintly; **2,** to give a certain characteristic flavour or quality to; as, envy *tinged* all his remarks:—*n.* **1,** a slight degree of some colour; tint; **2,** a touch; trace; as, there was a *tinge* of sarcasm in his remarks.

tin-gle (ting′gl), *v.i.* [tin-gled, tin-gling], to feel or have a stinging sensation or pricking pain; as, his fingers *tingled* with the cold:—*n.* a stinging sensation or pain, as from cold or a slap.

tink-er (tingk′ẽr), *n.* **1,** a mender of metal pots, kettles, etc.; **2,** a person able to do almost any kind of small repairing:—*v.t.* to mend, esp. in a bungling way; to patch:—*v.i.* **1,** to try in a bungling way to mend metal ware; **2,** to work at anything in a bungling or careless manner.

tin-kle (ting′kl), *n.* a small, quick, sharp, ringing sound; as, the *tinkle* of a bell:—*v.i.* and *v.t.* [tin-kled, tin-kling], to make or cause to make such a sound.

tin-sel (tin′sel), *n.* **1,** a fabric originally of silk, or silk and wool, covered or woven with gold and silver threads; **2,** strips of glittering, metallic material, used as an inexpensive trimming, as for Christmas-trees; **3,** something showy but of little value; hence, false show; pretence:—*v.t.* [tinselled, tinsel-ling], to decorate with, or as with, tinsel.

tin-smith (tin′smith′), *n.* one who works in or with tin.

tint (tint), *n.* **1,** a slight colouring; a pale tinge; as, just a *tint* of gold in the hair; **2,** a delicate or pale colour or a pale tinge of a colour; as, her dress and shoes were different *tints* of blue:—*v.t.* to give a slight colouring to.

tin-type (tin′tīp′), *n.* a photographic positive taken on a sensitized plate of iron or enameled tin.

ti-ny (tī′ni), *adj.* [ti-ni-er, ti-ni-est], very small; wee.

¹**tip** (tip), *n.* **1,** the point or end of anything; as, the *tip* of a finger; **2,** a small piece or part attached to the end of a thing; as, the *tip* of a cane:—*v.t.* [tipped, tip-ping], **1,** to form or put a point on; **2,** to cover the end of.

²**tip** (tip), *v.t.* [tipped, tip-ping], **1,** to slant or tilt; raise at one end or side; as, to *tip* a chair; **2,** to overturn; cause to lose balance; as, to *tip* a vase over; **3,** to raise (one's hat) in greeting:—*v.i.*

to lean, slant, or fall over; as, the boat *tipped* dangerously.

³tip (tip), *v.t.* [tipped, tip-ping], **1,** to strike or hit lightly; to give a slight blow to; as, his bat just *tipped* the ball; **2,** *Colloq.,* to give a private hint to; as, *tip* me off on this race; **3,** to give a small present to for service; as, to *tip* a waiter:—*v.i.* to give a fee or present, as to a servant:—*n.* **1,** a light blow or tap; **2,** a present, as to a servant; **3,** a friendly hint; secret or advance information.—*n.* **tip′—off′** (*Colloq.*)

tip-ple (tip′l), *v.i.* [tip-pled, tip-pling], to drink liquor habitually but in small amounts; also, to sip liquor:—*v.t.* to drink (liquor), esp. in small amounts:—*n.* liquor; drink.—*n.* **tip′pler.**

tip-sy (tip′si), *adj.* [tip-si-er, tip-si-est], almost drunk; unsteady or foolish from the effect of liquor.

tip-toe (tip′tō′), *n.* the end or point of a toe or the toes:—**on tiptoe,** on the tips of the toes; hence, alert; expectant:—*v.i.* [tiptoed, tiptoe-ing], to walk or stand on the toes; walk softly; as, the nurse *tiptoed* down the hall.

tip-top (tip′top′), *adj.* the highest point or degree, esp. of excellence; *Colloq.* in the best of health, spirits, etc.; as, to feel *tiptop.*

ti-rade (ti-rād′; tī′), *n.* a long, vehement speech, esp. of blame or abuse.

¹tire (tīr), *n.* a band or hoop of steel or rubber, which is placed on the rim of a wheel of an automobile, wagon, carriage; etc.:—*v.t.* [tired, tir-ing], to furnish (a wheel) with a tire.

²tire (tīr), *v.t.* [tired, tir-ing], to exhaust or wear out the strength, interest, or patience of; as, hard work *tired* him:—*v.i.* to become physically weary; as, he *tires* easily.

tired (tīrd), *adj.* weary; exhausted; fatigued; as, a *tired* mother.

tire-less (tīr′lis), *adj.* unwearying; not to be wearied; as, *tireless* hands.

tire-some (tīr′sum), *adj.* wearisome; tedious; as, a *tiresome* journey; also, annoying; boring; as, *tiresome* talk.

tis-sue (tish′ōō; tish′ū), *n.* **1,** a woven fabric or cloth, esp. thin, transparent silk material; fine cloth or gauze; **2,** the cells and connecting parts that form the structure and substance of any part of an animal or plant; as, bone *tissue;* **3,** a web or network; as, a *tissue* of lies: —**tissue—paper,** very thin, gauzelike paper used to wrap up delicate articles, protect engravings, etc.

¹tit (tit), *n.* any one of several small birds, esp. the titmouse.

²tit (tit), *n.* a blow; tap: used only in the expression *tit for tat,* blow for blow; retaliation.

ti-tan (tī′tan), *n.* a person of enormous strength (like the fabled giants of Greek mythology).—**Titan,** the largest satellite of Saturn.—*adj.* **ti-tan′ic.**

ti-ta-ni-um (tī-tā′ni-um), *n.* a metallic element, its chief ores being *rutile* and *ilmenite:* large deposits of the latter are mined at Lake Allard in Quebec and smelted at Sorel: used in metallurgy, also as a pigment for paints, and in making cosmetics, ceramics, and paper.

tit-bit (tit′bit′), *n.* **1,** a small bit or choice morsel of food; **2,** hence, a choice bit, as of gossip. Also, **tid′bit′** (tid′).

tithe (tī*th*), *n.* **1,** the tenth part of anything; esp., the tenth part of one's income or possessions given to the support of the church; **2,** loosely, any small part:—*v.t.* [tithed, tith-ing], **1,** to grant or pay a tenth of, esp. to the support of the church; **2,** to impose tithes upon.

ti-tian (tish′an; tish′i-an), *adj.* golden brown; auburn or red; as, hair of *titian* hue.

tit-il-late (tit′i-lāt′), *v.t.* [-lated, -lating], to tickle or excite pleasurably; as, to *titillate* the fancy, palate, etc.

ti-tle (tī′tl), *n.* **1,** the name of a book, poem, play, etc.; **2,** a designation of dignity, rank, or distinction, generally used in front of a person's name; **3,** a claim or right; as, a *title* to respect; **4,** the legal right to property, esp. real estate; as, a *title* to land; also, the paper giving such right:—*v.t.* [ti-tled ti-tling], to entitle; give a name to:— **titled,** having a title, esp. of nobility.— *adj.* **tit′u-lar** (tit′ū-lėr) (existing in name only).

tit-mouse (tit′mous′), *n.* [*pl.* titmice (tit′mīs)], any one of a number of small songbirds, including the chickadee, the tufted titmouse, etc.

tit-ter (tit′ėr), *v.i.* to laugh or giggle in a suppressed fashion:—*n.* a suppressed giggle.

tit-tle (tit′l), *n.* a very small part or particle; iota; jot; as the dot over an *i,* a punctuation or pronunciation mark a pip on a dice, etc.

tit-tle—tat-tle (tit′l-tat′l), *n.* and *v.i.* chatter; gossip.

tiz-zy (tiz′i), *n.* [*pl.* -zies], *Slang,* a dither.

TNT *trinitrotoluene,* a high explosive

to (tōō; when not emphatic, too), *prep.* expressing: **1,** in the direction of; towards; as, on my way *to* work; the earth turns from west *to* east; **2,** as far as; so as to arrive at or be in; as, he came *to* my office today; **3,** against; opposite; as, face *to* face; compared with; as, the score was six *to* four; **4,** into the possession of; as, give the book *to* John; **5,** in agreement or harmony with; as, words set *to* music; true *to* life; **6,** fitting; for; as, a key *to* the car; ten pounds *to* a bag; a room *to* himself; **7,** within the scope of; as, *to* my knowledge he has not come; **8,** till or until; as, I shall stay *to* midnight; before; as, ten minutes *to* five:—used to introduce an infinitive: **a,** in a noun construction; as, she began *to* sing; *to* err is human; **b,** expressing purpose; as, we work *to* succeed; **c,** completing the meaning of a preceding adjective or noun; as, fit *to* wear:—*adv.* **1,** in or into a position or contact; as, the wind blew the door *to;* **2,** to the normal position or condition; as, she came *to* slowly.

toad (tōd), *n.* a tailless, leaping, froglike animal, which breeds in water, but lives on land and eats worms, flies, etc.

toad-flax (tōd′flaks′), *n.* a common perennial weed akin to the cultivated snapdragon, with yellow flowers spotted with orange: called *butter and eggs.*

toad-stool (tōd′stōōl), *n.* any umbrella-shaped fungus which grows on decaying matter; esp., a poisonous mushroom.

toad-y (tōd′i), *n.* [*pl.* toadies], one who caters to the rich or powerful for the sake of gain or favour:—*v.t.* and *v.i.* [toadied, toady-ing], to flatter in order to gain reward.

¹toast (tōst), *n.* sliced bread browned by heat:—*v.t.* **1,** to brown or heat at a fire; as, to *toast* bread; **2,** to heat or warm thoroughly; as, *toast* your hands at the fire.—*n.* **toast′er.**

²toast (tōst), *n.* **1,** the act of drinking or proposing a drink in honour of some person or thing; as, they called for a *toast* to the winner; **2,** the person or thing toasted; as, she was the *toast* of the evening:—*v.t.* to drink or propose a toast to.

toast-mas-ter (tōst′mȧs′tẽr), *n.* a person who presides at a dinner, proposing the toasts and introducing the speakers.

to-bac-co (to-bak′ō), *n.* [*pl.* tobaccos], **1,** a large-leaved plant with pink or white trumpet-shaped flowers; **2,** the dried leaves of this plant treated in various ways and used for smoking and chewing, or as snuff.—*n.* **to-bac′co-nist.**

to-bog-gan (to-bog′an), *n.* a kind of long, flat sled without runners, curving up at the front and often carrying four or more persons: used in winter sports: —*v.i.* to ride or coast on such a sled.— *n.* **to-bog′gan-er; to-bog′gan-ist.**

to-day or **to—day** (too-dā′), *adv.* **1,** on the present day; as, you must go *today;* **2,** in these times; as, *today* many people travel by aeroplane:—*n.* **1,** the present day; as, *today* is Tuesday; **2,** this present time or age; as, the fashions of *today* change fast.

tod-dle (tod′l), *v.i.* [tod-dled, tod-dling], to walk with short, uncertain steps.—*n.* **tod′dler.**

tod-dy (tod′i), *n.* a sweetened drink of alcoholic liquor and hot water, often spiced with cloves.

to-do (too-dōō′), *n. Colloq.* a fuss; commotion; stir.

toe (tō), *n.* **1,** one of the five separate divisions or digits of the foot; **2,** the front of the foot, or of a stocking or other foot covering; as, he tore the *toe* of his sock; **3,** anything resembling a toe:—*v.t.* [toed, toe-ing], to touch, reach, or strike with the toe; as, to *toe* the mark in a race.—*n.* **toe′nail′.**

tof-fee (tof′i), *n.* a hard, chewy taffy, made with molasses or brown sugar.

to-ga (tō′ga), *n.* a loose, outer garment, once worn by Roman citizens.

to-geth-er (too-geth′ẽr), *adv.* **1,** in company or association; as, to live *together;* **2,** without interruption; at a stretch; as, we talked for hours *together;* **3,** at the same time; simultaneously; as, the firecrackers exploded *together.*

tog-ger-y (tog′ẽr-i), *n. Colloq.* **1,** togs; clothes; **2,** a haberdashery; clothing store.

tog-gle switch (tog′l), a switch in which a projecting arm or lever is moved through a small arc to open or close an electric circuit.

togs (togz), *n.pl.* clothes, esp. for a particular use; as, tennis-*togs.*

¹toil (toil), *v.i.* **1,** to work hard or long; labour; **2,** to move with difficulty; plod; trudge:—*n.* work or effort that exhausts the body or mind.—*n.* **toil′er.**—*adj.* **toil′worn′.**

²toil (toil), *n.* **1,** *Archaic,* a trap, as of net or cord, for ensnaring game; **2,** **toils,** figuratively, a snare; as, in the *toils* of crime.

toi-let (toi′lit), *n.* **1,** the act or process of washing and dressing, arranging the hair, etc.; **2,** style of dress; also, a particular costume; **3,** in Canada, a lavatory, esp. one with a water-closet; also, a water-closet. Also, **toi′lette.**

to-ken (tō′ken), *n.* **1,** something representing something else; a sign, symbol, or indication; as, the four-leaf clover is a *token* of good luck; **2,** a memento; keepsake; as, the old locket was a *token* from her sister; **3,** a piece of metal used as money, the face value of which exceeds its real value; hence, any piece of currency, as a bill or note; **4,** a coin-like piece of metal issued at a fixed price and used in payment of a streetcar or railway fare.

told (tōld), *p.t.* and *p.p.* of *tell.*

tol-er-a-ble (tol′ér-a-bl), *adj.* **1,** capable of being suffered or endured; **2,** passable; fairly good.—*adv.* **tol′-er-a-bly.**

tol-er-ant (tol′ér-ant), *adj.* willing or inclined to put up with views or opinions which are different from one's own.—*adv.* **tol′er-ant-ly.**—*n.* **tol′-er-ance.**

tol-er-ate (tol′ér-āt′), *v.t.* [tolerat-ed, tolerat-ing], **1,** to permit to exist or continue without interference; endure; as, he could not *tolerate* their dishonesty any longer; **2,** in *medicine,* to be able to take (a drug or treatment) without evil effects.—*n.* **tol′er-a′tion.**

¹toll (tōl), *n.* **1,** a tax paid for some special privilege, as for using a bridge, highway, or canal; **2,** in telephoning, the charge made for a call.

²toll (tōl), *v.t.* **1,** to cause to sound with slow strokes spaced at regular intervals; as, the sexton *tolls* the bell; **2,** to sound or strike; as, "the curfew *tolls* the knell of parting day":—*v.i.* to give forth a slow, regular, ringing sound, as a bell in announcing a death.

toll-gate (tōl′gāt′), *n.* a gate, as on a bridge or road, where toll is paid.

tom (tom), *adj.* male, as in *tom*cat or *tom* turkey.

tom-a-hawk (tom′a-hôk), *n.* a kind of hatchet or axe used by the North American Indians as a weapon in war and as a tool:—*v.t.* to strike, cut, or kill with a tomahawk.

to-ma-to (to-mā′tō; to-mä′tō), *n.* [*pl.* tomatoes], a garden plant with yellow flowers, and a red or yellow fruit which is used for food; also, the fruit.

tomb (tōōm), *n.* a grave or vault for the dead:—*v.t.* to put in a grave; bury.

tom-boy (tom′boi′), *n.* a girl who acts like a lively, noisy boy.

tomb-stone (tōōm′stōn′), *n.* a stone marking a grave.

tom-cod (tom′kod′), *n.* any of several small, edible, saltwater fishes of the cod family.

tome (tōm), *n.* a large book or volume, esp. one that is part of a larger work.

tom-fool (tom′fōōl′), *n. Colloq.* a silly or foolish person.—*n.* **tom′fool′er-y.**

tom-my-rot (tom′i-rot′), *n.* and *interj. Slang,* rubbish; nonsense!

to-mor-row or **to—mor-row** (too-mor′ō), *n.* the day after the present day; the morrow:—*adv.* on, or for, the morrow, or the day after today.

tom-tit (tom′tit), *n.* a family of small songbirds including the chickadee, wren, etc.

tom-tom (tom′tom′), *n.* a primitive drum, often beaten with the hands; used in the East Indies and among most barbaric peoples.

ton (tun), *n.* any of various relatively large measures of weight; specifically, the weight of 2,240 pounds used in Great Britain, commonly called a *long ton;* the weight of 2,000 pounds, used in Canada, the U.S., often called a *short ton;* or the weight of 2,204.6 pounds, called a *metric ton.*

ton-al (tōn′al), *adj.* pertaining to the character or quality of sound.—*n.* **to-nal′i-ty.**

tone (tōn), *n.* **1,** a sound or the quality of a sound; as, the loud *tones* of music; **2,** the voice, as expressive of feeling; as, she spoke in an imploring *tone;* **3,** one of the larger intervals in a musical scale, as that from C to D: preferably called *step;* **4,** normal or healthy condition; as, good muscular *tone;* **5,** the quality and harmony of the colours of a painting; **6,** a hue, tint, or shade of colour; as, a grey *tone;* **7,** the general character or spirit; as, I did not like the *tone* of the letter:—*v.t.* [toned, toning], **1,** to bring to a required shade or colour; as, to *tone* a photographic print, a painting, etc.; **2,** to give a particular sound, character, etc., to:—*v.i.* to harmonize in colour; as, the wallpaper *tones* with the curtains.

tongs (tôngz), *n.pl.* a device with two arms joined by a hinge, used for grasping, lifting, etc.; as, sugar-*tongs;* fire-*tongs.*

tongue (tung), *n.* **1,** the muscular organ in the mouth, used in tasting, and also, in man, for speech; **2,** a language; as, his native *tongue;* **3,** manner of speaking; as, a sharp *tongue;* **4,** anything resembling a tongue in shape, position, or use, as the clapper or hammer of a bell, the point of a flame, the vibrating reed in the mouthpiece of some musical instruments, etc. —*adj.* **tongue′less.**—*v.t.* to modify an instrument's tone, esp. to *tongue* a mouth-organ.

tongue—tied (tung′-tīd′), *adj.* **1,** unable to speak clearly because of a defect of the tongue; **2,** hence, speechless because of fear, shyness, etc.

ton-ic (ton′ik), *adj.* **1,** tending to strengthen; bracing; as, the *tonic* effect of a high altitude; **2,** pertaining to sounds; **3,** in *music*, pertaining to the keynote:—*n.* **1,** a strengthening medicine; **2,** in *music*, the keynote of a scale or composition.

ton-ic sol—fa (sōl′fä′), used for instruction in vocal music: the syllables *do, re, mi,* etc., are substituted for the staff symbols and letters of the scale.

to-night or **to—night** (too-nīt′), *n.* the present night or the night of today:—*adv.* on, or during, the present or coming night.

ton-nage (tun′ij), *n.* **1,** the weight of goods carried in a ship; **2,** the carrying capacity of a vessel, stated in tons; **3,** the duty or toll on vessels, based on the burden carried; **4,** the entire shipping of any port or country, stated in tons.

ton-sil (ton′sil), *n.* one of two almond-shaped masses of tissue on either side of the throat, near the base of the tongue.

ton-sil-lec-to-my (ton′si-lek′to-mi), *n.* surgical removal of the tonsils.

ton-sil-li-tis (ton′si-lī′tis), *n.* inflammation of the tonsils (a form of sore throat).

ton-so-ri-al (ton-sōr′i-al), *adj.* said (humorously) of a barber or his work; as, a *tonsorial* artist.—*n.* and *v.t.* **ton′sure** (shoor; shẽr).—*adj.* **ton′sured,** having the head or crown shaved, as a priest or a monk.

too (too), *adv.* **1,** also; likewise; as, he is going, *too;* **2,** more than enough; as, *too* long; **3,** so much more than enough as to be painful, intolerable, etc.; as, that is *too* annoying; **4,** *Colloq.,* exceedingly; very; as, I am *too* happy to see you.

took (took), *p.t.* of *take.*

tool (tool), *n.* **1,** an instrument used in doing work, esp. one used with the hand, as a chisel, hammer, saw, etc.; **2,** a person used as the agent of another; as, Tom was William's *tool* in the scheme; **3,** anything used as a tool, as books, money, etc.:—*v.t.* **1,** to shape with a tool; **2,** to make (leather) with a design pressed on it with a heated tool.—*n.* **tool′mak′er.**

toot (toot), *v.t.* to cause (a horn, whistle, etc.) to sound:—*v.i.* to give forth short, quick sounds:—*n.* a short blast on a horn.

tooth (tooth), *n.* [*pl.* teeth (tēth)], **1,** one of the hard, bony structures set in the jaws and used for biting and chewing, and sometimes for attacking and defending; **2,** any projection resembling a tooth, as on a gear-wheel, a comb, a rake, or a saw:—*v.t.* **1,** to indent or form into jagged points; as, to *tooth* a saw; **2,** to supply with projections or teeth.—*adj.* **toothed**; **tooth′some.**—*n.* **tooth′ache′**; **tooth′brush′**; **tooth′pick′.**

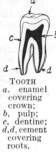

TOOTH
a, enamel covering crown; *b,* pulp; *c,* dentine; *d,d,* cement covering roots.

too-tle (too′tl), *v.i.* and *n.* to toot softly or continuously on a whistle, flute, etc.

¹top (top), *n.* **1,** the highest part; summit; as, the *top* of a hill; **2,** the upper surface, side, or part, as of a table, a carriage, a shoe, or a page; **3,** head; upper end; as, the *top* of a street; **4,** the most important person, place, or rank; as, the *top* of his profession; **5,** the crown of the head; **6,** the part of a plant above the ground: used of plants with edible roots; **7,** the very highest step or degree; as, he has reached the *top* of his ambition; **8,** a small platform at the upper end of the lower mast of a ship:—*v.i.* [topped, top-ping], **1,** to put a cover on; cap; as, to *top* a box; to *top* a bottle; **2,** to be at the head of; as, she *tops* the list of graduates; **3,** to surmount; reach or go over the top of; as, to *top* a hill; **4,** to surpass; as, he *topped* his own record; **5,** to cut off the upper part of (a plant):—*v.i.* **1,** to rise to a height; tower; **2,** to excel; surpass:—*adj.* **1,** pertaining to the highest part; highest; as, the *top* shelf; **2,** highest in degree; greatest; as, at *top* speed.—*adj.* **top′-flight′** (best); **top′—heav′y; top′—notch′.**—*n.* **top′soil′.**

²top (top), *n.* a child's cone-shaped toy with a point on which it can be made to spin rapidly by means of a spring or string.

to-paz (tō′paz), *n.* a mineral often used as a gem, varying in colour from yellow to blue or green.

top-coat (top′kōt′), *n.* a lightweight overcoat.

top—dress-ing (top′-dres′ing), *n.* fertilizer spread over the surface of land (without being ploughed in).

top-er (tōp′ėr), *n.* a chronic drunkard: —*v.t.* **tope.**

top-ic (top′ik), *n.* the subject of conversation, argument, literary composition, etc.—*adj.* **top′i-cal.**

top-knot (top′not′), *n.* a tuft of hair on the head; a crest of feathers on a bird's head.

top-mast (top′mȧst), *n.* the second mast above the deck of a ship, erected on the top of the mainmast, foremast, or mizzen-mast.

top-most (top′mōst), *adj.* highest; at the very top or summit.

to-pog-ra-phy (to-pog′ra-fi), *n.* [*pl.* topographies], **1,** the surface features of the earth of a particular region, including such physical characteristics as mountains, rivers, cities, communication routes, etc.; also, a detailed description or representation on a map of these features; **2,** the science which treats of such features; also, the science or art of making a map or other drawing on which the physical characteristics of a region are shown.—*adj.* **top′o-graph′i-cal.**

top-ple (top′l), *v.t.* [top-pled, top-pling], to overturn:—*v.i.* to fall top foremost; as, the flagstaff *toppled* in the wind.

top-sail (top′sāl′; top′sl), *n.* **1,** the second sail from the deck of a square-rigged vessel; **2,** a sail which is set above, or sometimes on, the gaff of a fore-and-aft-rigged vessel.

top-sy-tur-vy (top′si-tûr′vi), *adv.* and *adj.* **1,** upside down; **2,** in confusion: —*n.* a state of upset or confusion.

toque (tōk), *n.* a knitted stocking cap, closed at both ends, one end being tucked into the other: worn, esp. by French-Canadian *habitants*, for snowshoeing, tobogganing, etc. Also, **tuque.**

torch (tôrch), *n.* **1,** a light, made by burning wood, flax, etc., carried at the end of a pole or handle; **2,** any of various devices which give out a flare or hot flame; as, a plumber's *torch.* —*n.* **torch′light′.**

tore (tōr), *p.t.* of *tear.*

tor-e-a-dor (tôr′i-a-dôr′), *n.* a bull-fighter, esp. a mounted one: the term is not now used in bullfighting.

tor-ment (tôr′ment), *n.* **1,** extreme mental or physical suffering; **2,** that which causes pain or anguish:—*v.t.* (tôr-ment′), **1,** to put to extreme pain of mind or body; torture; as, he was *tormented* with doubt and fear; **2,** to tease; annoy; as, he *tormented* his mother with questions.—*n.* **tor-men′-tor; tor-ment′er.**

torn (tōrn), *p.p.* of *tear.*

tor-na-do (tôr-nā′dō), *n.* [*pl.* tornadoes], a violent storm of whirling, destructive wind, produced from a funnel-shaped cloud that travels rapidly along a narrow path.

tor-pe-do (tôr-pē′dō), *n.* [*pl.* torpedoes], **1,** a cigar-shaped, self-moving, underwater projectile, containing explosives which may be set off by contact with a vessel, by a timing apparatus, or by radio: usually launched from a submarine or torpedo-boat; **2,** any shell or case filled with explosives, as an undersea mine; **3,** a kind of cartridge that is placed on a railroad track and, when exploded by a locomotive wheel, warns the engineer of danger; **4,** a kind of firework which explodes when thrown against a hard surface; **5,** a fish which gives an electric shock:—*v.t.* to destroy or blow up with a torpedo; as, to *torpedo* a ship.

tor-pe-do—boat (tôr-pē′dō–bōt′), *n.* a small, fast, war vessel equipped with tubes for firing torpedoes.

tor-pid (tôr′pid), *adj.* **1,** inactive; sluggish; as, a *torpid* liver; **2,** dormant; as, a snake is *torpid* in winter; **3,** dull; stupid; as, a *torpid* intellect.—*n.* **tor′por.**—*n.* **tor-pid′i-ty.**

torque (tôrk), *n.* a force that tends to produce a rotating or twisting motion; as, the *torque* exerted on a shaft.

tor-rent (tor′ent), *n.* **1,** a violent, raging stream; **2,** hence, any similar violent flow; as, a *torrent* of words; *torrents* of rain.—*adj.* **tor-ren′tial** (to-ren′shal).

tor-rid (tor′id), *adj.* dried by the sun's heat; extremely hot; as, a *torrid* desert.

tor-sion (tôr′shun), *n.* **1,** a twisting force, applied esp. to one end of a body while the other is held fast; **2,** the force with which a twisted rod, wire, etc., tends to return to its previous position.

tor-so (tôr′sō), *n.* the trunk of (1) the human body (2) a statue, esp. one without head or limbs.

tort (tôrt), *n.* in *law*, any wrong, injury, or damage (not involving a breach of contract) for which a civil action can be brought.

tor-toise (tôr′tis), *n.* a turtle, esp. one that lives on land.

tor-tu-ous (tôr′tū-us), *adj.* **1,** crooked; winding; as, a *tortuous* channel; **2,** not straightforward; as, *tortuous* business policies.—*adv.* **tor′tu-ous-ly.**

tor-ture (tôr′tūr), *n.* **1,** agony of mind or body; extreme pain; **2,** the inflicting of extreme pain or torment; as, they used *torture* to make the man confess: —*v.t.* [tortured, tortur-ing], to inflict extreme agony upon, as a punishment or as a means of persuasion.—*adj.* **tor′tur-ous** (causing torture).—*n.* **tor′-tur-er.**

To-ry (tōr′i), a member of the Conservative party, esp. in Canada or Gt. Britain: opposed to radical parties or policies.

toss (tôs), *v.t.* **1,** to throw with the palm of the hand up; throw upward; pitch; as, to *toss* a ball; **2,** to lift or throw up quickly; as, to *toss* the head; **3,** to put into violent motion; cause to rise and fall; as, the waves *tossed* the vessel: —*v.i.* **1,** to roll or tumble; throw oneself from side to side; be restless; as, she *tossed* on the bed in pain; **2,** to be made to rise and fall; as, the ship *tossed* on the waves:—*n.* **1,** a throwing upward; pitch; as, a *toss* of the ball; **2,** a fling, as of the head.

¹tot (tot), *n.* a small child.

²tot (tot), *v.i. Colloq.* to total: with *up*, to add.

to-tal (tō′tal), *adj.* **1,** whole; not divided; as, the *total* amount; **2,** complete; utter; as, *total* silence:—*n.* the whole sum or amount:—*v.t.* [totalled, total-ling], **1,** to find the sum of; add; as, to *total* figures; **2,** to amount to; as, the costs *total* $500.—*adv.* **to′tal-ly.** —*n.* **to-tal′i-ty.**

to-tal-i-ta-ri-an (tō-tal′i-tâ′ri-an), *adj.* relating to a state in which one political group or party has complete control and allows no rival parties or loyalties.—*n.* **to-tal′i-tar′i-an-ism.**

tote (tōt), *v.t. Colloq.* **1,** to carry, esp. in person; as, to *tote* an armful of wood; **2,** to haul, as by wagon or sled.—*n.* **tote′box′** (one for carrying personal effects, etc.).

to-tem (tō′tem), *n.* **1,** an animal or object thought of by a primitive people as being closely related to their tribe or clan; **2,** a carved or painted representation of this animal or plant, as a pole or post.

tot-ter (tot′ẽr), *v.i.* **1,** to be unsteady on one's feet; stagger; **2,** to shake as if about to collapse; lose strength and firmness; as, the building *tottered.*

tou-can (tōō′kan; tōō′kän), *n.* a noisy, fruit-eating bird with a very large beak and bright plumage, found in Central and South America.

touch (tuch), *v.t.* **1,** to come into contact with; extend the hand so as to come into contact with; as, don't *touch* the wet paint; **2,** to bring into contact with; as, he *touched* his hand to his hat; **3,** to be in contact with; join; as, the two estates *touch* each other; **4,** to strike lightly; play on; as, he *touched* the keys of the piano; **5,** to add a light stroke to; also, to improve; as, he *touched* up the drawing; **6,** to mark slightly with some aspect of colour; as, the sky was *touched* with rose and gold at sunset; **7,** to take a portion of; taste; as, he has not *touched* food for three days; **8,** to affect; injure or hurt; as, the books were not *touched* by the fire; this decision does not *touch* you; **9,** to affect mentally; derange; as, he has been *touched* by sorrow; **10,** to affect the senses or feelings of; as, her sorrow *touches* us deeply; **11,** to refer to; as, to *touch* a subject in conversation; **12,** to reach; as, to *touch* one's goal; **13,** to equal; compare with; as, your books can't *touch* mine; **14,** *Slang,* to borrow from; as, he *touched* me for a dollar:—*v.i.* **1,** to be in contact, as, the two benches *touch;* **2,** to speak of a subject briefly; as, to *touch* on art; **3,** to call at a port: said of ships:—*n.* **1,** the act or state of coming into, or being in, contact; **2,** a slight tap; as, she attracted my attention by a *touch* on the arm; **3,** the sense of feeling; **4,** a distinctive manner of execution; as, the *touch* of a master in painting; **5,** the manner of action of the fingers or hand; as, she plays the piano with a light *touch;* **6,** a single delicate stroke on a painting, drawing, etc.; also, the result produced by such a stroke; **7,** communication; as, she kept in *touch* with her family while she was away; **8,** a very slight amount; as, a *touch* of pepper; a light attack; as, a *touch* of influenza:—**touch football,** an informal game (like rugby) played chiefly in schools (without defensive equipment), the ball carrier being 'downed' by a touch rather than a tackle.

touch-down (tuch′doun′), *n.* in *football,* a score (6 points), made by moving the ball, or otherwise legally possessing it, beyond the opponent's goal-line.

all (ôl), **ôr; up, mūte, cûr, cōōl, book; oil, out; th, thin;** *th,* **the.**

tou-ché (tōō′shā′; tōō-shā′), *adj.* and *interj.* **1**, being scored against in an argument, or an acknowledgment of this; **2**, in *fencing*, touched by the opponent's weapon.

touch-ing (tuch′ing), *adj.* arousing sympathy; pathetic; as, a *touching* tale of a dog's devotion.

touch-me-not (tuch′mi-not′), *n.* a plant of the balsam family having flowers with spurs, and seed pods that burst open at a touch when ripe: the *Impatiens capensis* grows from Newfoundland to Alaska.

touch-stone (tuch′stōn′), *n.* any standard for testing quality; as, time is the *touchstone* of merit.

touch-y (tuch′i), *adj.* [touch-i-er, touch-i-est], irritable; peevish; easily offended.—*n.* **touch′i-ness.**

tough (tuf), *adj.* **1**, standing great strain without breaking; not easily broken or split; as, *tough* wood; hard to cut or chew; as, *tough* meat; **2**, able to endure hardship or strain; as, a *tough* body; **3**, hard to change; stubborn; as, a *tough* will; **4**, difficult; as, a *tough* problem; **5**, rough and bad; as, a *tough* district:—*n.* a rough fellow; a rowdy.—*n.* **tough′ness.**

tough-en (tuf′en), *v.t.* and *v.i.* **1**, to make or become hard to break or divide; **2**, to make or become strong, stubborn, etc.

tou-pee (tōō-pā′; -pē′), *n.* a small wig to cover a bald spot.

tour (tōōr), *n.* a journey; an excursion or a trip; as, to make a *tour* of America: —*v.i.* to make a journey:—*v.t.* to make a trip through; as, to *tour* the country.

tour-ist (tōōr′ist), *n.* one who travels, esp. for sight-seeing or pleasure.

tour-ma-line (tōōr′ma-lin; toor′ma-lēn), *n.* a mineral that is usually black, but sometimes, red, blue, green, or, rarely, colourless: often used as a gem.

tour-na-ment (tōōr′na-ment; tûr′na-ment), *n.* **1**, in the Middle Ages, a contest with blunt lances or swords, by knights on horseback; also, a complete series of such contests occurring at one meeting; **2**, in modern times, any meeting for a trial of skill; esp., a series of meetings to determine a championship, as in tennis.

tour-ni-quet (tōōr′ni-ket′), *n.* a device for compressing a blood vessel to control the flow of blood, consisting of a bandage twisted tight by a stick, an elastic rubber bandage, a pad that can be pressed tight by a screw, etc.

tou-sle or **tou-zle** (tou′zl), *v.t.* to dishevel; put into disorder; as, *tousled* hair, clothes, etc.

¹**tow** (tō), *v.t.* to pull or drag by a rope or line; as, to *tow* a boat; *tow* an automobile:—*n.* **1**, the act of pulling or the condition of being pulled; as, a boat in *tow;* **2**, anything pulled along by, or as by, a rope; **3**, a rope or line used in pulling.—*n.* **tow′rope′.**

²**tow** (tō), *n.* the short, coarse part of flax or hemp, made ready for spinning.

¹**to-ward** (tō′ẽrd; tōrd; too-wôrd′) or **to-wards** (tō′ẽrdz; tōrdz; too-wôrdz′), *prep.* **1**, in the direction of; as, go *toward* the city; **2**, with respect to; regarding; as, his attitude *toward* free trade; **3**, near to; close upon; as, *toward* evening; **4**, with a view to; for; contributing to; as, take this money *toward* your charity drive.

²**to-ward** (tō′ẽrd; tōrd), *adj.* **1**, *Archaic*, ready to learn; promising; **2**, going on; being done; as, what's *toward?*

tow-el (tou′el), *n.* a cloth or piece of absorbent paper for drying anything wet:—*v.t.* to wipe or dry; as, he *toweled* himself after his shower.—*n.* **tow′el-ing.** Also, **tow′elled** and **tow′-ell-ing.**

tow-er (tou′ẽr), *n.* **1**, a high structure, rising above its surroundings, and either standing alone or attached to a building; as, a church *tower;* **2**, a citadel or fortress; **3**, anything resembling a tower in actual height or in being above other things or people in strength, endurance, etc.:—*v.i.* to rise to a height; overtop other objects or persons; as, the giant *towered* above everyone.

tow-er-ing (tou′ẽr-ing), *adj.* **1**, very high; lofty; as, a *towering* tree; **2**, intense; violent; as, a *towering* fury.

town (toun), *n.* **1**, a collection of houses, buildings, etc., making a place with a name, larger than a village but not organized as a city; **2**, the citizens of such a place; as, the *town* opposed the tax; **3**, the business or shopping centre; **4**, the city as opposed to the country. —*n.* **towns′folk′.**

town-ship (toun′ship), *n.* **1**, a district or unit of local government; **2**, a land unit six miles square divided into 36 sections of one square mile each; **3**, a division of a Canadian province.

tox-in (tok′sin), *n.* a poison produced by action within animal or vegetable tissue.—*adj.* **tox′ic** (poisonous).

tox-oid (toks′oid), *n.* a toxin, like that

of diphtheria, which has been chemically treated to remove the poisonous elements, but left capable of inducing the formation of antibodies upon injection.

toy (toi), *n.* **1,** a child's plaything; **2,** something of no real value; a trinket; **3,** a thing very small of its kind; as, her dog won the prize among the *toys:—v.i.* to play with something; handle or treat something idly; as, she *toyed* with her purse; to *toy* with the idea of going abroad:—*adj.* like, or made as, a plaything; as, a *toy* soldier.

trace (trās), *v.t.* [traced, trac-ing], **1,** to draw or sketch by means of lines; **2,** to copy by following the lines of, as with a pencil on transparent paper placed over the original; **3,** to form (characters in writing) laboriously or with extreme care; **4,** to follow up; study out; as, to *trace* a family record; **5,** to follow, as by tracking; as, to *trace* a fox; **6,** to decorate with ornamental lines:—*v.i.* to make one's way; follow a trail:—*n.* **1,** a mark, indication, or sign left by something that has passed by or disappeared; as, there were *traces* of carriage wheels in the snow; **2,** a small quantity or portion of something; as, a *trace* of poison was found in the food.—*adj.* **trace'a-ble.**

trac-er (trā'sẽr), *n.* a small firework which, burning slowly, shows the path of a projectile to which it is attached.

trac-er-y (trās'ẽr-i), *n.* **1,** delicately interlaced design work, as in a Gothic window; **2,** embroidery, tree-branching, etc.

tra-che-a (trā'kē-a; tra-kē'a), *n.* [*pl.* tracheae (trā'ki-ē; tra-kē'ē)], the windpipe; the air tube leading to the lungs.
—tra'che-al (trā'ki-al; tra-kē'al).

trac-ing (trā'sing), *n.* that which is copied, as a copy of a pattern or design made by marking on thin paper over the original.

track (trak), *n.* **1,** a mark or impression left by the foot, a wheel, etc.; a trace; **2,** a beaten path; road; as, a *track* has been worn through the woods; also, the path which something takes; as, the *track* of a storm; **3,** the state of maintaining contact with current events, people, etc.; as, he kept *track* of all the graduates of the school; **4,** a course laid out for a special purpose, as, for horse-racing, foot-races, etc.; also, the sports which take place on such a track; **5,** a set of metal rails supported by ties, upon which cars or trains run:—*v.t.* **1,** to seek or follow by means of traces or marks; to trail; as, to *track* a deer; **2,** to make footprints upon or with; as, to *track* a floor with dirt; to *track* dirt across a floor.—*n.* **track'er.**—*adj.* **track'less.**

¹tract (trakt), *n.* a pamphlet, usually on some moral or religious subject.

²tract (trakt), *n.* **1,** a region or area of land; as, a sandy *tract;* **2,** *Poetic,* a period of time; **3,** in the body, an entire system of related organs, performing a specific function; as, the digestive *tract.*

trac-ta-ble (trak'ta-bl), *adj.* **1,** docile; easily led or managed; as, a *tractable* child; **2,** easily handled or worked; as, gold is a *tractable* metal.

trac-tion (trak'shun), *n.* **1,** the act of drawing or pulling, as by a tractor, etc., **2,** adhesive friction, esp. of wheels; as, the car got little *traction* on the ice.

trac-tor (trak'tẽr), *n.* anything that draws or hauls; esp., a heavy motor vehicle for pulling trucks, ploughs, machinery, etc.

trade (trād), *n.* **1,** an occupation; business; **2,** a particular means of livelihood, usually manual or mechanical, which a person learns and engages in; as, he is a mason by *trade;* **3,** buying and selling for money; commerce; **4,** all the persons engaged in a particular business; as, he deals with the clothing *trade;* **5,** the total amount of business transacted at one place; **6,** a deal; bargain; also, an exchange; as, a horse *trade;* **7, trades,** the trade-winds:—*adj.* relating to business; as, a *trade* journal:—*v.i.* [trad-ed, trad-ing], **1,** to buy and sell goods; as, to *trade* in furs; **2,** to take unfair advantage; as, to *trade* on a person's sympathy: —*v.t.* to exchange.—*n.* **trad'er.**—*n.* **trade'—in'.**

trademark or **trade—mark** (trād'—märk'), *n.* a word, mark, or design, used by a merchant or manufacturer to distinguish his goods from the goods made or sold by others.

trades-man (trādz'man), *n.* [*pl.* tradesmen (-men)], a shopkeeper.

trade—wind (trād'—wind'), *n.* a wind in or near the Torrid Zone which blows steadily towards the equator from the northeast and southeast respectively.

trad-ing stamp, a stamp given as a premium to a customer, usually redeemable (in quantity) for merchandise.

tra-di-tion (tra-dish'un), *n.* **1,** the

handing down of information, opinions, doctrines, practices, etc., by word of mouth, from generation to generation; **2,** that which is so handed down; as, family *traditions;* **3,** an old custom so well established as to be almost as effective as a law.—*adj.* **tra-di′tion-al.** —*adv.* **tra-di′tion-al-ly.**

tra-duce (tra-dūs′), *v.t.* to slander, defame, or vilify; bring shame upon; as, by ignoble conduct they *traduced* (disgraced) their ancestors; to *traduce* a man.'s character.

traf-fic (traf′ik), *n.* **1,** interchange of goods; business or trade; as, the liquor *traffic;* **2,** the transportation business done by a railway, steamship line, etc., carrying persons or goods; **3,** the passing of vehicles, persons, or animals, in a street; as, city *traffic:* —*v.i.* [trafficked, traffick-ing], **1,** to barter; buy or sell goods; as, to *traffic* in hides; **2,** to do business in a mean or dishonest way.—*n.* **traf′fick-er.**

tra-ge-di-an (tra-jē′di-an), *n.* **1,** a writer of tragedies; **2,** an actor who plays tragic parts.—*n.fem.* **tra-ge′di-enne′.**

trag-e-dy (traj′ę-di), *n.* [*pl.* tragedies], **1,** a play which ends unhappily, arousing pity or terror by the misfortunes that befall the principal characters; **2,** a story, poem, etc., of similar character; **3,** a melancholy occurrence; a fatal event; calamity.

trag-ic (traj′ik) or **trag-i-cal** (traj′i-kal), *adj.* **1,** relating to tragedy; as, a *tragic* play; **2,** terrible; sad; as, a *tragic* accident.

trail (trāl), *v.t.* **1,** to draw or drag along behind; as, to *trail* oars in the water; **2,** to hunt or follow by tracking; as, the hunters *trailed* the bear:—*v.i.* **1,** to fall or hang down so as to sweep along the ground; as, her dress *trailed;* **2,** to grow to some length; as, the morning-glory *trails* along the wall; **3,** to follow; also, to move in a long and straggling line; as, they *trailed* home one by one; **4,** to lag behind; be last; as, to *trail* in a race:—*n.* **1,** a track left by a person, an animal, or a moving object; as, the hurricane left a *trail* of ruin; **2,** a footpath or track through a wilderness; **3,** the scent followed in hunting; as, the dogs lost the *trail* when they came to the river; hence, a trace or clue; **4,** anything drawn out in the wake of something; as, a *trail* of dust followed the car.

trail-er (trāl′ẽr), *n.* **1,** any vehicle drawn by a motorcar, truck, tractor, etc., **2,** in *motion pictures,* a short advertising film with scenes from a forthcoming feature picture.

trail-ing ar-bu-tus (är-bū′tus), *n.* a plant whose fragrant pink-and-white flowers bloom in early spring: floral emblem of Nova Scotia.

train (trān), *n.* **1,** a connected line of railway cars; **2,** that part of a dress or robe that trails on the ground; **3,** a retinue or body of servants; **4,** a line of men, animals, vehicles, etc., moving in procession; **5,** any series of connected things; as, a *train* of ideas; **6,** a line of gunpowder laid to fire a charge:—*v.t.* **1,** to instruct by practice; to drill; discipline; educate; **2,** to aim or point, as a gun; as, to *train* artillery on a town, **3,** to teach to perform certain motions, tricks, etc.; as, to *train* seals; *train* horses; **4,** to direct the growth of; as, to *train* a plant:—*v.i.* to prepare oneself for a contest of strength or skill; drill.—*n.* **train′er.**—*n.* **train-ee′** (one in course of training).

traipse (trāps), *v.i. Colloq.* **1,** to trudge; gad; wander idly; **2,** to trail untidily.

trait (trāt; trā), *n.* a feature or characteristic; as, a *trait* of character.

trai-tor (trā′tẽr), *n.* a person guilty of treason; one who betrays his country, cause, or friends.—*adj.* **trai′tor-ous.** —*n. fem.* **trai′tress.**

tra-jec-to-ry (tra-jek′to-ri), *n.* the curve described by a body moving through space, as the path of a bullet shot from a rifle.

tram (tram), *n.* a streetcar.

tram-mel (tram′el), *n.* **1,** (often in *pl.*) restraint; anything that checks or impedes progress, activity, or freedom; as, the *trammels* of custom; **2,** a net for catching birds, fish, etc.:—*v.t.* to hamper, catch, or entangle; as, *trammeled* (*trammelled*) by red tape.

tramp (tramp), *v.t.* **1,** to step upon forcibly and repeatedly; as, to *tramp* the grass down; **2,** to travel over on foot; **2,** to walk with a heavy step: —*n.* **1,** a foot traveller; esp., a roving, shiftless person; **2,** a walk or hike; **3,** the sound of heavy footsteps; **4,** a freight steamer that picks up a cargo wherever it can.

tram-ple (tram′pl), *v.t.* [tram-pled, tram-pling], to tread down under the feet; as, don't *trample* the grass:—*v.i.* to tread heavily; hence, to inflict hurt or grief by unkind treatment; as, to *trample* on a person's feelings.

tram-po-line (tram′po-lin), *n.* a strong canvas net tightly stretched on a frame, used by acrobats and gymnasts for feats of jumping, tumbling, etc.

trance (tråns), *n.* **1,** a condition of the body in which the mind and senses cannot be aroused; a daze; stupor; **2,** a deep sleep due to illness or hypnotism.

tran-quil (trang′kwil; tran′kwil), *adj.* tranquil-ler, tranquil-lest], calm; quiet; serene; as, a *tranquil* mind; a *tranquil* scene.—*adv.* **tran′quil-ly.**—*n.* **tran-quil′li-ty; tran-quil′i-ty.**

tran-quil-liz-er (trang′kwi-līz′ėr; tran′), *n.* a drug taken to reduce tension, anxiety, etc.:—*v.t.* **tran′quil-lize′.** Also, **tran′quil-ize′; tran′quil-iz′er.**

trans-act (tran-zakt′; trans-akt′), *v.t.* to conduct or manage, as business; also, to close; complete; as, to *transact* a deal.—*n.* **trans-ac′tion.**

trans-at-lan-tic (trans′at-lan′tik), *adj.* **1,** beyond the Atlantic; **2,** crossing the Atlantic; as, a *transatlantic* flight.

tran-scend (tran-send′), *v.t.* **1,** to rise above or go beyond; exceed; as, miracles *transcend* human knowledge; **2,** to surpass; excel; as, his ability *transcends* mine.—*adj.* **tran-scend′ent.** —*n.* **tran-scend′ence.**—*adj.* **tran′scend-en′tal.**

trans-con-ti-nen-tal (trans′kon-ti-nen′tal; tranz′), *adj.* extending across a continent; as, a *transcontinental* road.

tran-scribe (tran-skrīb′), *v.t.* [transcribed, transcrib-ing], **1,** to copy in writing; as, the mediaeval monks *transcribed* many manuscripts; **2,** to translate (shorthand notes) into longhand.—*n.* **tran-scrip′tion.**

tran-script (tran′skript), *n.* **1,** a written or typewritten copy; **2,** any copy; an imitation.

tran-sept (tran′sept), *n.* the part of a cross-shaped church at right angles to the long main section or nave; either arm of this section.

trans-fer (trans-fûr′), *v.t.* [transferred, transfer-ring], **1,** to convey or carry from one person or place to another; as, to *transfer* baggage; **2,** in *law*, to give or make over the possession or ownership of; as, to *transfer* a piece of land; **3,** to copy from one surface to another; as, to *transfer* designs by a stencil:—*v.i.* to change from one streetcar, train, bus, etc., to another at a junction point:—*n.* (trans′fûr), **1,** the making over of a right, title, property, etc., from one person to another; **3,** a removal from one place to another; **3,** a ticket permitting a person to change from one streetcar, bus, etc., to another.—*adj.* **trans-fer′a-ble** (trans-fûr′a-bl; trans′fėr-a-bl).—*n.* **trans′fer-ence** (trans′fėr-ens; trans-fûr′ens).

trans-fig-ure (trans-fig′ūr), *v.t.* [transfigured, transfigur-ing], **1,** to change the form or appearance of; **2,** to make glow or shine; illumine; as, hope *transfigured* his face.—*n.* **trans-fig′u-ra′tion.**

trans-fix (trans-fiks′), *v.t.* **1,** to pierce completely through; as, he was *transfixed* on the long point of the lance; **2,** to hold motionless; as, the sight *transfixed* me with horror.

trans-form (trans-fôrm′), *v.t.* **1,** to change the shape or appearance of; to change into something else; **2,** to change the nature of; convert; as, to *transform* a child by kindness; **3,** to change (an electric current) from higher to lower, or from lower to higher, voltage; **4,** to change (one form of energy) into another.—*n.* **trans′for-ma′tion.**—*n.* **trans-form′er.**

trans-fu-sion (trans-fū′zhun), *n.* a transference, as of blood from the blood-vessels of one person to those of another.

trans-gress (trans-gres′), *v.i.* to break a law, rule, etc.; sin:—*v.t.* **1,** to break, sin against, or violate; as, to *transgress* a law; **2,** to go beyond (any limit or bounds); as, to *transgress* the bounds of good manners.—*n.* **trans-gres′sor.** —*n.* **trans-gres′sion.**

tran-sient (tran′zi-ent; tran′shent), *adj.* **1,** fleeting; brief; passing; as, *transient* hopes; **2,** coming and going; temporary; as, *transient* lodgers:—*n.* a temporary lodger.

tran-sis-tor (tran-zis′tėr; -sis′), *n.* a tiny electronic device employing germanium embedded in plastic, that performs the functions of a vacuum tube, esp. in very small hearing aids, radios, etc.

trans-it (tran′zit; tran′sit), *n.* **1,** a passing through or over; passage; as, rapid *transit;* **2,** the act of carrying over or through; conveyance; as, goods lost in *transit;* **3,** in *surveying,* an instrument for measuring angles.

tran-si-tion (tran-zish′un; tran-sizh′-un; tran-sish′un), *n.* the passage from one place, period, state, subject, etc. to another; in *music*, an abrupt change from one key to another.—*adj.* **tran-si′tion-al.**

tran-si-tive (tran′si-tiv), *adj.* in *grammar*, requiring or taking a direct object to complete the meaning; as, "wrote" and "mailed" in the sentence "I wrote a card and mailed it" are *transitive* verbs.

tran-si-tory (tran′si-tẽr-i), *adj.* brief; lasting but a short time; quickly passing; as, this *transitory* life.

trans-late (trans-lāt′), *v.t.* [translat-ed, translat-ing], **1,** to change from one language into another; as, to *translate* a story from French into English; **2,** to remove to another place or position; specifically, to remove to heaven without death; as, Elijah did not die; he was *translated.*—*n.* **trans-la′tor.** —*n.* **trans-la′tion.**

trans-lu-cent (trans-lū′sent), *adj.* permitting light to go through, but not transparent; as, frosted glass is *translucent.*

trans-mi-gra-tion (tranz′mī-grā′-shun; trans′), *n.* the passing of the soul at death into another body or successive bodies, human or animal (called the doctrine of *transmigration* of souls).

trans-mit (tranz-mit′; trans-), *v.t.* [transmit-ted, transmit-ting], **1,** to cause or allow to pass over or through something; as, to *transmit* news by wire; **2,** to conduct; as, iron *transmits* heat; **3,** to transfer from one person to another; pass on, as a title.—*n.* **trans-mis′sion** (tranz-mish′un).

trans-mit-ter (tranz-mit′ẽr; trans-), *n.* a person by whom, or a thing through which, something is sent; esp., a device for transmitting, as the mouth-piece of a telephone, the sending instrument of a telegraph, or a radio transmitting-set.

trans-mute (tranz-mūt′; trans-), *v.t.* to change from one form, substance, or class to another; as, to *transmute* a base metal into gold; to *transmute* aimlessness into purpose.—*n.* **trans′mu-ta′tion.**

trans-o-ce-an-ic (tranz′ō-shi-an′ik; trans′), *adj.* across, or crossing, the ocean.

tran-som (tran′sum), *n.* **1,** a crossbar, as in a window or over a door; **2,** a window over a door or other window, usually hinged to the crossbar.

trans-par-ent (trans-pâr′ent; trans-

par′ent), *adj.* **1,** so clear or thin that one can see through it; as, *transparent* glass; *transparent* gauze; **2,** easy to understand; easily detected; as, a *transparent* lie.

tran-spire (tran-spīr′), *v.t.* to give off (vapour, moisture, etc.) through the skin or surface; as, in summer some plants *transpire* many times their weight of water:—*v.i. Colloq.* to leak out; become public; as, it *transpired* that he had no qualifications for the job.—*n.* **tran′spi-ra′tion.**

trans-plant (trans-plant′), *v.t.* to remove and establish in another place, as trees.

trans-port (trans-pōrt′), *v.t.* **1,** to carry from one place to another; as, to *transport* supplies or soldiers; **2,** to carry away emotionally; as, he was *transported* with delight; **3,** to banish or deport (a criminal) from a country:—*n.* (trans′pōrt), **1,** the act of conveying or being conveyed; as, the *transport* of grain; **2,** a means of conveyance; esp. a vessel for transporting troops, stores, etc.; an airplane (for freight or passengers); a van or trailer (pulled by tractor); **3,** a strong burst of emotion; as, a *transport* of rage.

trans-por-ta-tion (trans′pōr-tā′-shun), *n.* **1,** the act of carrying, or state of being carried, from one place to another; **2,** a means of conveyance; also, the charge for conveyance; **3,** the act of banishing, or sending away, a convicted criminal.

trans-pose (trans-pōz′), *v.t.* [transposed, transpos-ing], **1,** to change the place or order of; as, to *transpose* letters in a word; **2,** in *music*, to change the key of; **3,** in *algebra*, to change (a term) from one side of an equation to the other.—*n.* **trans′po-si′tion.**—*n.* **trans-pos′er.**

tran-sub-stan-ti-a-tion (tran′sub-stan′shi-ā′shun), *n.* the changing of one substance into another; specifically, the belief that in the Eucharist the bread and wine are changed into the body and blood of Christ (only the appearance of bread and wine remaining): a doctrine of the Roman Catholic Church.

trans-verse (trans-vûrs′; trans′vûrs), *adj.* lying across, or crosswise; as, *transverse* lines:—*n.* anything that lies crosswise.—*n.* and *adj.* **trans-ver′sal.**

trap (trap), *n.* **1,** a device, such as a snare or pitfall, for catching animals; **2,** an ambush; a means of tricking people; also, a hazard on a golf-course; **3,** a device, as an S-shaped or a U-shaped bend, for sealing a drain-pipe with water against the return of sewer-gas; **4,** any of various straining or separating devices; **5,** a device for throwing into the air clay disks, balls, etc., to be shot at; **6,** a trap-door; **7,** a light, two-wheeled carriage:—*v.t.* [trapped, trap-ping], **1,** to catch in, or as in, a snare or spring; as, to *trap* rabbits; **2,** to ambush (an enemy); to capture by trickery:—*v.i.* to set traps.

trap-door (trap′dōr′), *n.* a door which lifts up, as in a floor.

tra-peze (tra-pēz′), *n.* a swinging horizontal bar hung on ropes.

tra-pe-zi-um (tra-pē′zi-um), *n.* a four-sided plane figure, of which no two sides, or only two sides, are parallel.

trap-e-zoid (trap′i-zoid′), *n.* a plane figure with four sides, only two of which are parallel.

trap-per (trap′ẽr), *n.* one who snares or traps animals, esp. fur-bearing animals, for their skins. TRAPEZOID

trap-pings (trap′ingz), *n.pl.* ornaments, esp. adornments of dress; as, the *trappings* of royalty: originally used of horses.

trap-shoot-ing (trap′shoōt′ing), *n.* shooting at clay pigeons (or live ones) released from, or thrown into the air by, a *trap* (definition 5).

trash (trash), *n.* anything that is worthless or useless; refuse; rubbish.—*adj.* trash′y.

trau-ma (trô′ma), *n.* **1,** bodily injury; a wound; **2,** shock.—*adj.* trau-mat′ic.

trav-ail (trav′āl; trav′l), *n.* **1,** the suffering endured in childbirth; **2,** physical or mental agony or severe pain; as, a mind in *travail*:—*v.i.* to suffer in childbirth.

trav-el (trav′el), *v.i.* [travelled, travelling], **1,** to journey from place to place for pleasure, recreation, or adventure; **2,** to journey from place to place in the course of business; as, he *travels* for a paint firm; **3,** to move onward or proceed; as, a train *travels* faster than a horse:—*v.t.* to journey over or through; as, to *travel* a hard road; he has *travelled* the South from end to end:—*n.* **1,** a journey or journeying; as, to seek health in *travel*; a record of one's *travels*; **2,** the number of persons, vehicles, etc., on the road; traffic; as, heavy *travel*.—*n.* trav′el-ler.

trav-e-logue or **trav-e-log** (trav′e-lôg′), *n.* **1,** a lecture on travels, illustrated by motion pictures; **2,** a film of travels.

trav-erse (trav′ẽrs), *v.t.* [traversed, travers-ing], **1,** to cross in travelling; travel or pass over; as, to *traverse* a city; also, to move forward and backward over; cross and recross; as, the beams of a searchlight *traverse* the sky; **2,** to extend across; as, canals *traverse* the country:—*n.* something placed or lying across something else; a crosspiece:—*adj.* lying across.

trav-es-ty (trav′is-ti), *n.* **1,** a burlesque or parody; an absurd or fantastic imitation of an originally serious literary work; **3,** any noble subject ridiculed; as, a *travesty* of justice:—*v.t.* to burlesque, parody, or cause to appear ridiculous.

tra-vois (tra-voi′), *n.* a primitive vehicle used by the Indians of the Canadian and U.S. prairies, consisting of two trailing poles serving as shafts (for dog or horse), with a platform or net for the load.

trawl (trôl), *n.* **1,** a dragnet used in sea fishing; also called *trawlnet*; **2,** a long fishing line to which many short lines are attached; a trawl line:—*v.i.* and *v.t.* to fish with a net, trawl, or trawl line.—*n.* trawl′er (a ship for trawling).

tray (trā), *n.* a flat, shallow receptacle of wood, metal, etc., with a raised rim.

treach-er-ous (trech′ẽr-us), *adj.* **1,** betraying a trust or pledge; **2,** not to be trusted in spite of appearances; as, a *treacherous* friend; not safe; as, a *treacherous* floor.—*adv.* treach′er-ous-ly.—*n.* treach′er-y.

tread (tred), *v.i.* [*p.t.* trod (trod), *p.p.* trod-den (trod′n) or trod, *p.pr.* treading], **1,** to step or walk; as, *tread* carefully on the carpet; **2,** to press something beneath the foot; trample; as, don't *tread* on my toes:—*v.t.* **1,** to walk on; **2,** to press or crush under the feet; as, peasants *tread* grapes; **3,** to dance; as, to *tread* a minuet:—*n.* **1,** a walking or stepping; also, the manner or style of walking; as, a firm *tread*; **2,** in a flight of stairs, the horizontal surface of a step; **3,** the part of a wheel or tire that touches the road or rail; also, the mark or rut left by a wheel or tire on a road.

trea-dle (tred′l), *n.* a device, as a lever or pedal worked by foot, to operate a sewing-machine, lathe, etc.

tread-mill (tred′mil′) *n.* **1,** a mill worked by persons or animals walking on a wheel or endless belt; **2,** any tiresome routine.

trea-son (trē′zn), *n.* **1,** the betrayal of one's country; an attempt to overthrow the government of one's country; in a monarchy, an attempt to injure the sovereign; **2,** treachery; betrayal of faith.—*adj.* **trea′son-ous.**—*adj.* **trea′son-a-ble.**

treas-ure (trezh′ẽr), *n.* **1,** a hoard, as of money or jewels; abundance or wealth; **2,** anything highly valued; a person dear to one:—*v.t.* [treasured, treasur-ing], **1,** to lay up or store for future use; hoard; also, to retain in the mind; as, to *treasure* up memories; **2,** to value highly; as, to *treasure* an heirloom:—**treasure–trove, 1,** treasure found hidden, the original owner being unknown; **2,** any valuable discovery.

treas-ur-er (trezh′ẽr-ẽr), *n.* one who has charge of receiving and paying out money.

treas-ur-y (trezh′ẽr-i), *n.* [*pl.* treasuries], **1,** a place where wealth is stored; esp., a place where public funds, or the funds of an organization, are kept and paid out; also, the funds; **2,** (also *Treasury*): **a,** that department of a government which has charge of the public funds; **b,** the officials of such a department.

treat (trēt), *v.t.* **1,** to handle, deal with, or manage; as, the speaker *treated* his subject cleverly; **2,** to behave or act toward; as, to *treat* others kindly; **3,** to regard or consider; as, to *treat* a matter lightly; **4,** to cause (something) to undergo a process for a special purpose; as, to *treat* corn with lye to make hominy; **5,** to entertain; as, he *treated* his guests to music; also, to pay the cost of entertainment for (someone); **6,** to deal with, for some desired result; as, a doctor *treats* his patients; to *treat* a cold:—*v.i.* **1,** to discuss or deal with; as, the book *treats* of Russia; **2,** to negotiate; as, they were ready to *treat* with the outlaws:—*n.* **1,** the act of paying for entertainment, food, etc., for a friend; also, the entertainment or food so given; **2,** something which gives great pleasure; as, the circus is a *treat.*

trea-tise (trē′tiz), *n.* a long, written discussion or essay on a particular subject.

treat-ment (trēt′ment), *n.* **1,** manner of dealing with a person, problem, etc.; as, a firm's generous *treatment* of employees; **2,** medical or surgical care of a person.

trea-ty (trē′ti), *n.* [*pl.* treaties], an

agreement or contract between nations, as for settling differences or arranging commerical relations.

tre-ble (treb′l), *adj.* **1,** threefold or triple; **2,** in *music,* relating to the highest vocal or instrumental part; of high pitch:—*n.* **1,** in *music,* the highest part; **2,** a soprano singer or instrument; also, a high-pitched voice or sound:—*v.t.* and *v.i.* [tre-bled, tre-bling], to make or become three times as great.—*adv.* **tre′bly.**

tree (trē), *n.* **1,** a large woody plant with a high main trunk, branches, and leaves; **2,** sometimes, a bush trained to grow like a tree; **3,** a piece of timber used as part of a structure; as, an axle-*tree:*—**family tree,** an outline or diagram, sometimes shaped like a tree, showing family descent and relationships:—*v.t.* [treed, tree-ing], to drive up a tree; as, to *tree* an opossum.

tre-foil (trē′foil), *n.* any plant of the pea family (*Trifolium*), having three leaflets, as the clover.

tree–frog (trē′–frog′), *n.* **1,** any of several tree-dwelling frogs with adhesive pads on toes, or webbed feet (like the flying frog); **2,** loosely, a tree–toad.

tree–toad (trē′–tōd′), *n.* any of many small tree-dwelling amphibians with shrill, piping call and adhesive pads on toes: incorrectly called *tree-frog.*

trek (trek), *v.i.* **1,** to travel or migrate, as by ox-wagon (esp. in South Africa); **2,** to travel slowly or laboriously: as, they *trekked* across prairies, deserts, and mountains.

trel-lis (trel′is), *n.* a frame of wood or metal network to support climbing vines; a lattice-work:—*v.t.* to provide with a lattice for vines; train (vines) on a lattice.

trem-ble (trem′bl), *v.i.* [trem-bled, trem-bling], **1,** to shake or shiver, as with fear or cold; shudder; **2,** to quaver, as a sound:—*n.* an involuntary shaking; a shiver; shudder.—*n.* **trem′bler.**—*adj.* and *n.* **trem′bling.**—*adv.* **trem′bling-ly.**

tre-men-dous (tri-men′dus), *adj.* **1,** exciting fear or terror because of unusual size or violence; terrible; as, a *tremendous* crash; **2,** *Colloq.,* astonishing; extraordinary; as, a *tremendous* feat.

trem-o-lo (trem′o-lō′), *n. Music,* a tremulous or vibrating effect, as made by a rapid or fluttering repetition of a tone or chord; **2,** a device in an organ for making such a tone.

trem-or (trem'ĕr; trē'mĕr), *n.* **1**, a trembling, quivering, or shaking; as, an earthquake *tremor;* **2**, a thrill or quiver of excitement.

trem-u-lous (trem'ū-lus), *adj.* **1**, trembling; quivering; shaking; **2**, showing fear or timidity; as, a *tremulous* voice; **3**, marked by unsteadiness; as, *tremulous* writing.—*adv.* **trem'u-lous-ly.**

trench (trench), *n.* **1**, a long, narrow ditch in the earth; an open ditch for draining; **2**, a deep ditch dug in a zone of battle and held as a defensive position or as a base from which to attack:—*v.t.* **1**, to cut a ditch in; to drain by ditches; **2**, to dig trenches for (an army):—*v.i.* to encroach, as upon someone's property:—**trench coat,** a short, lined, belted raincoat.

trench-ant (tren'chant), *adj.* **1**, sharp; keen; as, a *trenchant* sword; also, cutting or biting; as, *trenchant* satire; **2**, forceful and clear; as, a *trenchant* explanation.

trench-er (tren'chĕr), *n. Archaic,* a wooden plate or platter for food.—*n.* **trench'er-man** (a hearty eater).

trend (trend), *n.* the general direction taken by something; as, the northeasterly *trend* of the Gulf Stream; general tendency or drift; as, the *trend* of public opinion:—*v.i.* **1**, to take a particular direction or course; **2**, to have a general tendency; as, prices are *trending* upward.

trep-i-da-tion (trep'i-dā'shun), *n.* **1**, a trembling or vibration; **2**, a state of nervous alarm; fear mingled with uncertainty.

tres-pass (tres'pas), *v.i.* to commit any offence; sin; as, to *trespass* against the Lord; **2**, to enter unlawfully upon the property of another; **3**, to make an inroad upon a person's time, presence, attention, etc.:—*n.* **1**, a violation of a moral law; a sin; **2**, an unlawful encroachment on the property of another.—*n.* **tres'pass-er.**

tress (tres), *n.* a long curl or lock of hair, esp. of woman's hair.

tres-tle (tres'l), *n.* **1**, a movable frame, made of a horizontal beam and spreading legs, for supporting a platform, table top, etc.; **2**, a rigid framework of timbers or steel for supporting a road or bridge across a ravine, etc.

trey (trā), *n.* a three at dice; a card or domino with three spots; as, the *trey* of clubs.

tri-ad (trī'ad), *n.* a group of three; as, a *triad* of virtues; in *music,* a common chord; in *chemistry,* an element, atom,

or radical with the power of combining with three hydrogen atoms.

tri-al (trī'al), *n.* **1**, the act of testing or putting to a test; as, the *trial* of the new aeroplane proved it unsatisfactory; **2**, the state of being tested; a chance to make good; as, give this coffee a week's *trial;* **3**, hardship; as, a time of *trial* and suffering; **4**, a person or thing that puts faith, mercy, or patience to the test; as, he was a great *trial* to his family; **5**, the hearing and deciding of a case in law court.

tri-an-gle (trī'ang'gl), *n.* **1**, a plane figure with three sides and three angles; **2**, anything shaped like a triangle; **3**, a musical instrument used in orchestras, etc., consisting of a steel rod bent in the form of a triangle open at one corner, sounded with a light metal rod.—*adj.* **tri-an'gu-lar.**

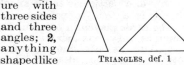

TRIANGLES, def. 1

tribe (trīb), *n.* **1**, a group of uncivilized people, usually consisting of several clans, under one chief; as, a Tartar *tribe;* loosely, any similar group; as, a gipsy *tribe;* **2**, among the ancient Israelites, one of the twelve divisions of the nation; as, the *tribe* of Judah; **3**, a group of people akin to one another because of a common occupation or trait; as, the *tribe* of moneylenders; **4**, a class or division of plants or animals.—*adj.* **trib'al.**

trib-u-la-tion (trib'ū-lā'shun), *n.* severe affliction or distress; deep sorrow; also, a cause of affliction or distress.

tri-bu-nal (trī-bū'nal; tri-bū'nal), *n.* **1**, the seat occupied by a judge or magistrate; **2**, a court of justice; any judicial assembly; **3**, any final authority; as, the *tribunal* of conscience.

¹tri-bune (trib'ūn), *n.* a champion of the people (in Roman times).

²tri-bune (trib'ūn), *n.* a raised platform for speakers.

trib-u-tar-y (trib' ū-tĕr-i), *adj.* **1**, paying tribute or taxes; hence, subordinate or subject; as, *tributary* states; **2**, flowing into another; as, a *tributary* river:—*n. [pl.* tributaries], **1**, a state or government which pays taxes to, or is under the control of, a superior government; **2**, a river flowing into a larger river or into a lake.

trib-ute (trib'ūt), *n.* **1**, an annual or stated sum of money paid by one state or ruler to another to acknowledge submission, obtain protection, or to fulfil the terms of a treaty; **2,** an acknowledgment of worth, service rendered, etc.; praise; as, *tribute* paid to a national hero.

trice (trīs), *n.* an instant; as, in a *trice.*

trick (trik), *n.* **1,** a clever, crafty, or deceitful device or action, used in order to gain an advantage; a stratagem; artifice; **2,** a foolish or stupid act; as, why did he do such a *trick?* **3,** an exhibition of skill and dexterity; as, a card *trick;* **4,** a mischievous, sometimes annoying, prank; **5,** a peculiarity of manner; habit; as, a *trick* of twitching the ears; **6,** a particular skill; knack; as, there is a *trick* to pole-vaulting; **7,** all the cards played in one round of a game; as, they took four *tricks;* **8,** a turn of duty, as on a ship:—*v.t.* **1,** to cheat; impose upon; deceive; **2,** to dress; deck; as, *tricked* out in new clothes.—*n.* **trick′ster.**

trick-ery (trik′ẽr-i), *n.* [*pl.* trickeries], deception; cheating; fraud.

trick-le (trik′l), *v.i.* [trick-led, trick-ling], to flow gently in a small stream; also, to drip; fall in drops; as, water *trickled* from the tap:—*n.* a small amount (of liquid) flowing gently or dripping; as, a *trickle* of visitors.

trick-y (trik′i), *adj.* [trick-i-er, trick-i-est], inclined to play tricks; also, deceptive; unreliable; as, a *tricky* horse.

tri-col-our (trī′kul′ẽr), *n.* a flag of three colours arranged in equal stripes; esp., the national flag of France, of blue, white, and red vertical stripes.

tri-cy-cle (trī′sik-l), *n.* **1,** a light, three-wheeled vehicle, with a single seat, and usually operated by pedals; **2,** a motor-cycle with three wheels.

tri-dent (trī′dent), *n.* a three-pronged fish-spear, as of Neptune or Britannia.

tried (trīd), *p.t.* and *p.p.* of *try.*

tri-fle (trī′fl), *n.* **1,** anything of little value or importance; **2,** a small amount, as of money; as the repairs cost only a *trifle:*—**a trifle,** rather; somewhat; as, a *trifle* disturbed:—*v.i.* [tri-fled, tri-fling], **1,** to act or talk without seriousness; **2,** to dally; toy; play; as, she *trifled* with her necklace as she talked:—*v.t.* to waste; as, to *trifle* away time.—*n.* **tri′fler.**—*adj.* and *n.* **tri′fling.**

trig-ger (trig′ẽr), *n.* a lever which, when pulled by the finger, releases the hammer of a gun; also, a catch serving a similar purpose, as for springing a trap.

trig-o-nom-e-try (trig′o-nom′e-tri), *n.* the branch of mathematics dealing with the ratios among the sides and angles of triangles, esp. the right triangle; the application of these ratios to surveying, navigating, engineering, etc.

trill (tril), *n.* **1,** a trembling or quavering on a musical tone; as, the *trill* of a bird; also, a vibration of the tongue, as in pronouncing *r,* or the sound produced by such vibration; **2,** in *music,* a quick alternation of two notes a step or a half step apart; also, the mark indicating this:—*v.t.* to utter with a vibration; as, to *trill* one's r's:—*v.i.* to make the voice vibrate.

tril-lion (tril′yun), *n.* in France and America, the unit 1 followed by 12 ciphers, in Gt. Britain by 18 ciphers. —*adj.* and *n.* **tril′lionth.**

tril-li-um (tril′i-um), *n.* a plant with three leaves surrounding a large, three-petalled flower; also, the flower:—the **white trillium** (also called *wake-robin* and *white lily*) was adopted in 1937 as Ontario's floral emblem.

TRILLIUM

tri-lo-bite (trī′lo-bīt′), *n.* any of the earliest known fossils of extinct crustaceans and spiders having the body divided into three distinct lobes (head, thorax, and abdomen), in size from 1″ to 2′ long.

tril-o-gy (tril′o-ji), *n.* a series of three plays, or three musical, literary, or artistic compositions, closely related in spirit or theme, but each complete in itself, as Shakespeare's *Henry VI.*

trim (trim), *v.t.* [trimmed, trim-ming], **1,** to make tidy and neat; set in order; as, a bird *trims* its feathers; **2,** to decorate or adorn; as, to *trim* a dress with lace; **3,** to make smooth or ready for use; as, to *trim* lumber by planing it; **4,** to make neat, as the hair by cutting, or a plant by clipping; also, to cut or clip (unnecessary parts) from a plant; **5,** to adjust or balance (a ship) by proper distribution of cargo; also, to arrange (the yards and sails) to take advantage of the wind; **6,** *Colloq.,* to defeat; as, we were *trimmed* by 40 points:—*v.i.* to maintain a middle course; try to please both sides or parties at the same time:—*n*. 1, order; adjustment; suitable condition; 2, dress; style; appearance; 3, the inside woodwork of a building around the windows, doors, etc.; 4, of a vessel, fitness for sailing; also, its position in the water:—*adj*. [trim-mer, trim-mest], neat; tidy; as, a *trim* cabin.—*adv*. **trim′ly**.—*n*. **trim′mer**.

trim-e-ter (trim′e-tėr), *n*. a verse of three feet; as, 'Now where| fore stopp' st| thou me' (iambic *trimeter*).

tri-month-ly (trī-munth′li), *adj*. occurring every three months.

Trin-i-ty (trin′i-ti), *n*. in *theology*, the mystical union in one being of the three persons of the Godhead: the Father (God's creating, preserving, and controlling power), the Son (God's human embodiment), and the Holy Ghost (the indwelling inspiration of God).

trin-ket (tring′kit), *n*. 1, a small ornament or jewel; 2, a trifle; toy.

tri-o (trē′ō), *n*. [*pl*. trios], 1, a set of three; 2, in *music*, a composition for three performers; also, a group of three musicians, either vocal or instrumental.

trip (trip), *v.i*. [tripped, trip-ping], 1, to run or step lightly or nimbly; take short, quick steps; skip; 2, to stumble; hence, to make a mistake; err:—*v.t*. 1, to perform with light, agile steps, as a dance; 2, to cause to stumble or trip; as, the rug *tripped* me; 3, to catch in a mistake or deception; as, I *tripped* you up that time; 4, to release or set free by pulling a catch, trigger, etc.—*n*. 1, a quick, short step; 2, a misstep or mistake; 3, a journey or excursion.

tripe (trīp), *n*. a part of the stomach of the ox or cow, used for food.

triph-thong (trif′thong), *n*. the combining of three vowel sounds in a single syllable, as in *wye* (oo + ä + ē); three vowels used to represent one vowel sound, as in b*eau*ty (ū).

tri-ple (trip′l), *adj*. 1, being in threes; threefold; as, a *triple* window; 2, three times as much or as many; three times the size, strength, value, etc.; also, done three times; as, a *triple* knock:— *n*. 1, a group or combination of three; 2, in baseball, a three-base hit:—*v.t*. [tri-pled, tri-pling], to increase three-fold; multiply by three; as, he *tripled* his efforts:—*v.i*. 1, to increase to three times as much; 2, in baseball, to make a three-base hit.

tri-plet (trip′lit), *n*. 1, a set of three of a

kind or three united; 2, one of three children born at one birth.

tri-plex (trī′pleks), *n*. and *adj*. threefold, or something triple, as a *triplex* measure in music, a *triplex* building with three apartments, etc.

trip-li-cate (trip′li-kit; -kāt′), *adj*. and *n*. (made in) three identical copies: —*v.t*. to produce by threes.

tri-pod (trī′pod), *n*. 1, a three-legged support, as for a surveying instrument; 2, any article, such as a stool or vase with three feet or legs.

tri-sect (trī-sekt′), *v.t*. in *geometry*, to cut into three equal parts, as a line, surface, or angle.—*n*. **tri-sec′tion**.

tri-syl-la-ble (tri-sil′a-bl; trī-), *n*. a word of three syllables, as *telephone*.

trite (trīt), *adj*. worn out; used far too much; commonplace; as, a *trite* reply.

tri-umph (trī′umf), *n*. 1, exultation over success; 2, in ancient Rome, a grand parade and celebration in honour of a victorious general; 3, a marked success or conquest; as, the new singer scored a *triumph*:—*v.i*. 1, to rejoice in success; 2, to be successful or victorious.—*adj*. **tri-um′phal** (trī-um′fal). —*adj*. **tri-um′phant**.

tri-um-vi-rate (trī-um′vi-rit; -rāt′), *n*. a government of three men ruling jointly; as, Caesar, Pompey, and Crassus (the First *Triumvirate*, B.C. 59).

tri-une (trī′ūn), *adj*. being three in one; as, the *Triune* God.

triv-i-al (triv′i-al), *adj*. trifling; insignificant; of little worth or importance.—*n*. **triv′i-al′i-ty**.

tro-chee (trō′kē), *n*. in *verse*, a foot of two syllables, the first long or accented, the second short or unaccented; as, 'Ōpen| nōw the| gātes ŏf|Āthŏl.'—*adj*. **tro-cha′ic** (trō-kā′ik).

trod (trod), *p.t*. and *p.p*. of *tread; p.p*. also **trod′den**.

¹troll (trōl), *v.t*. 1, to sing the parts of (a song) in succession, as in a round like "Scotland's Burning"; also, to carol lustily; 2, to fish for, or in, by dragging a line from a boat; as, to *troll* pike; to *troll* a stream:—*v.i*. 1, to share in a round or part song; also, to sing a song lustily; 2, to fish, as for pike, with a hook and line drawn along through the water from a moving boat:—*n*. 1, a round, or part song; 2, the rod, line, etc., used in trolling.

²troll (trōl), in Scandinavian *folklore*, a cave-dwelling dwarf.

trol-ley (trol′i), *n*. [*pl*. trolleys], 1, a

kind of truck running on an overhead track and carrying a load suspended from it; **2,** on an electric car, a grooved metal wheel at the end of a pole forming a contact with a live electric wire to convey current to the car; **3,** an electric car; a streetcar. Also spelled **trol′ly** *pl.* [trollies].

trol-lop (trol′up), *n.* **1,** a careless, slovenly woman; **2,** a prostitute.

trom-bone (trom′bōn; trom-bōn′), *n.* a long brass wind-instrument with a U-shaped sliding tube by which variations in tone are produced.

troop (trōop), *n.* **1,** a number of persons, or sometimes of animals, gathered together; a company; **2,** in the Boy Scouts and the Girl Guides, a unit consisting of from two to four patrols; **3,** a unit of cavalry, under the command of a captain; **4, troops,** armed forces:— *v.i.* to move in crowds; flock together; as, we all *trooped* into the hall:— *v.t.* to organize (persons) into a troop:—**troop the colours,** to perform a ceremony that includes carrying the colours before troops drawn up in single file.

troop-er (trōop′ẽr), *n.* **1,** a member of a troop of mounted police or soldiers; **2,** a cavalry horse.

tro-phy (trō′fi), *n.* [*pl.* trophies], **1,** anything captured in battle and kept in memory of victory, as arms, flags, cannon, etc.; **2,** any memento of deeds, achievements, etc.; as, an explorer's *trophies;* also, a prize in a contest; as, a tennis *trophy.*

trop-ic (trop′ik), *n.* **1,** either of the two imaginary circles on the earth's surface, parallel to the equator, at a distance of 23°30′ north and south of it, called *Tropic of Cancer* and *Tropic of Capricorn* respectively, marking the limits of the Torrid Zone; **2, tropics,** the region of the earth lying between these two circles; the Torrid Zone.—*adj.* **trop′i-cal; trop′ic.**

trot (trot), *n.* **1,** a jogging pace, as of a horse, faster than a walk, in which the right forefoot and left hind foot are lifted together, and then the left forefoot and right hind foot; **2,** any jogging gait:—*v.i.* [trot-ted, trot-ting], **1,** to move at a trot; **2,** to run in a jogging gait:—*v.t.* to cause (a horse) to trot.

troth (trōth; trôth), *n.* **1,** faith or fidelity; as, to plight one's *troth;* **2,** truth to one's word; as, by my *troth;* **3,** *Archaic,* betrothal.

trot-ter (trot′ẽr), *n.* **1,** a trotting-horse; **2,** the foot of an animal, esp. when used for food.

trou-ba-dour (trōo′ba-door′, trōo′-ba-dōr′), *n.* one of a class of poets and singers of love songs, who flourished in France and Italy during the 11th, 12th, and 13th centuries.

trou-ble (trub′l), *v.t.* [trou-bled, troubling], **1,** to distress, perturb, or worry; as, he was *troubled* by her silence; **2,** to cause inconvenience to; as, may I *trouble* you for a glass of water? **3,** to stir up or agitate, as water:—*v.i.* to take pains; put oneself out; as, don't *trouble* to apologize:—*n.* **1,** mental excitement, distress, or worry; **2,** the cause of such disturbance; as, a wayward child is a great *trouble* to his parents; **3,** inconvenience; effort; as, she went to much *trouble* to be present; **4,** illness; an ailment; as, heart *trouble.* —*adj.* **trou′ble-some.**—*adj.* **trou′blous.**

trough (trôf), *n.* **1,** a long, shallow, uncovered container of wood, metal, or concrete, for watering or feeding livestock; **2,** any similar container, for kneading dough, washing ore, etc.; **3,** a long, narrow uncovered gutter or drain for carrying off water; as, a pump *trough;* an eaves *trough;* **4,** any long, natural hollow; as, a *trough* between waves or hills.

trounce (trouns), *v.t.* [trounced, trouncing], to beat soundly; flog; also, to overcome or get the better of (an opponent).

troupe (trōop), *n.* a company, as of actors.—*n.* **troup′er** (an actor of long experience).

trou-sers (trou′zẽrz), *n.pl.* an outer garment covering the body from the waist to the knees, or ankles, and so divided as to cover each leg separately.

trous-seau (trōo′sō′; trōo′sō), *n.* [*pl.* trousseaux (trōo′sō′) or trousseaus (trōo′sōz′; trōo′sōz)], a bride's outfit.

trout (trout), *n.* [*pl.* trout], **1,** a medium-sized, fresh-water food fish of the salmon family, as the brook trout; **2,** any of various similar fishes.

trow (trō), *v.i.* *Archaic,* to think; believe.

trow-el (trou′el), *n.* **1,** a flat-bladed hand tool, used by bricklayers, masons, and plasterers, for spreading mortar, plaster, etc.; **2,** a scoop-shaped tool used by gardeners for moving small plants.

troy weight, a system of weights with twelve ounces to the pound, used for gold, silver, etc.

tru-ant (trōo′ant), *n.* **1,** a pupil who stays away from school without permission; **2,** a shirker or loafer:—*adj.*

cat, āge, fär, câre, åsk; ten, ēve, latẽr; (i) pity, rely, senate; ice; top; nō.

playing the truant; idle; wandering; as, a *truant* lad; *truant* fancies.—*n.* **tru′an-cy.**

truce (trōōs), *n.* **1,** a temporary peace or interruption of war by mutual agreement; an armistice; **2,** a lull in a period of stress and strain.

¹**truck** (truk), *v.t.* and *v.i.* to give in exchange; barter:—*n.* **1,** commodities for sale; articles of commerce; **2,** the system of paying wages in commodities instead of in money; **3,** fresh vegetables cultivated for sale; **4,** *Colloq.:* **a,** useless articles or rubbish; as, the old house is full of *truck;* **b,** dealings; as, have no *truck* with a cheat.

²**truck** (truk), *n.* **1,** originally, a strong, small wheel; **2,** now, a wheeled vehicle for carrying heavy or bulky loads, esp. a large motor vehicle for this purpose; **3,** a strong frame or platform on wheels used for hauling baggage in railroad stations; **4,** a set of wheels, or a frame mounted on wheels, to support one end of a locomotive, railroad car, etc.:—*v.t.* to carry by truck:—*v.i.* **1,** to carry goods by truck; **2,** to drive a truck for a livelihood.—*n.* **truck′er.**

truck-le (truk′l), *v.i.* to submit to another's will; as, to *truckle* to a superior.—*v.t.* and *adj.* to move on rollers or casters, as a *truckle*-bed.

truc-u-lent (truk′ū-lent; trōō′), *adj.* **1,** quarrelsome; savagely threatening or bullying; **2,** fierce; cruel, **3,** rude; scathing, esp. in speech or writing.—*n.* **truc′u-lence.**

trudge (truj), *v.i.* [trudged, trudg-ing], to travel on foot, usually with effort or labour:—*n.* a long or fatiguing walk; as, a long *trudge* to the station.

trudg-en stroke (truj′en), in *swimming,* a racing stroke using a double overarm motion and a scissors kick.

true (trōō), *adj.* [tru-er, tru-est], **1,** in accord with fact or reality; as, hers was the only *true* account of the robbery; **2,** faithful and loyal; reliable; as, a *true* friend; **3,** genuine; not pretended; as, *true* love; **4,** rightful; legitimate; as, the *true* heir; **5,** corresponding to a standard; as, a *true* colour; the spider is not a *true* insect; **6,** correct; exact; as, a *true* square:—*adv.* **1,** truthfully; **2,** accurately; as, the hunter aimed *true:*—*n.* the condition of being accurate; as, the wall is out of *true:*—*v.t.* [trued, tru-ing or true-ing], to make accurate; as, to *true* a window-frame. —*n.* **tru′ism** (platitude).

tru-ly (trōō′li), *adv.* **1,** in agreement with truth or fact; precisely; as, *truly* told; **2,** sincerely; honestly; as, *truly*

grateful; **3,** in fact; indeed; as, *truly,* I am sorry.

trump (trump), *n.* in *cards,* the suit which temporarily outranks the other suits; also, any card of this suit:—*v.t.* **1,** to play a trump when trump has not been led; as, to *trump* a trick; **2,** to think up or invent; as, to *trump* up an excuse:—*v.i.* **1,** to play trump when trump has not been led:—*adj.* relating to the suit named as trump.

trump-er-y (trump′ẽr-i), *n.* [*pl.* trumperies], worthless finery; rubbish:— *adj.* showy but worthless; trashy.

trum-pet (trum′pit), *n.* **1,** a metal wind-instrument formed of a single curved tube with a bell-shaped mouth, regulating keys, valves, etc.; **2,** something shaped like this instrument; as, a speaking-*trumpet;* an ear-*trumpet;* **3,** a sound like that of a trumpet; as, the elephant's *trumpet* in the jungle:—*v.t.* to noise abroad:—*v.i.* to utter a sound like that of a trumpet.—*n.* **trum′pet-er.**

trun-cat-ed (trung′kā-tid), *adj.* having the top or apex cut off; as, a *truncated* cone or pyramid.

trun-dle (trun′dl), *v.t.* [trun-dled, trun-dling], to roll, as a hoop; to cause to move on wheels; as, to *trundle* a gocart:—*v.i.* to roll along; move on, or as on, small wheels:—*n.* **1,** a small wheel; caster; **2,** a kind of low-wheeled truck; **3,** a kind of low bed on casters: also called *trundle-bed.*

trunk (trungk), *n.* **1,** the upright stem or body of a tree; **2,** in man and other animals, the body exclusive of the head and limbs; **3,** the chief part, or stem, of anything that branches; as, the *trunk* of a nerve; **4,** the elongated nose, or proboscis, of an elephant; **5,** a large box or chest to hold clothes and other personal belongings for a journey; **6, trunks,** short breeches reaching about halfway to the knee, worn by athletes, acrobats, etc.; in the 16th and 17th centuries, very full and wide dress breeches of about the same length: known also as *trunk hose:*—*adj.* pertaining to a main line; as, a *trunk*-line on a railroad; a telephone *trunk*-line.

truss (trus), *n.* **1,** a brace or framework of timbers or bars supporting a roof or bridge; **2,** a bandage or support for a rupture; **3,** a weighed measure, or a bundle, of hay or straw:—*v.t.* **1,** to bind or fasten with skewers and string; as, to *truss* a turkey; **2,** to support with a brace, framework, etc.

trust (trust), *n.* **1,** confidence; faith; belief in someone's goodness; also, the source of faith and belief; as, God is our *trust*; **2,** expectation or hope, as she put no *trust* in the future; **3,** credit granted to a buyer or borrower, because of belief in his honesty; as, to sell goods on *trust;* **4,** something involving duties and responsibilities; as, he regarded his wealth as a public *trust;* **5,** property, or an interest in property, held and managed by one party (the trustee) for the benefit of another; as, the will created *trusts* for the children; also, the state of property so held; as, the estate was held in *trust* for him; **6,** a combination of business or commercial interests into a corporation so large that it has a virtual monopoly in its field, and is able to fix prices, etc.:—*v.t.* **1,** to place confidence in; rely upon; as, to *trust* one's own judgment; **2,** to believe; as, I *trust* his word; **3,** to entrust to someone's care; **4,** to sell to on credit; **5,** to hope with confidence; as, we *trust* that you will come again:—*v.i.* to have confidence; as, *trust* in the Lord:—*adj.* held in charge for someone else; as, a *trust* fund.—*adj.* **trust′ful.**—*adj.* **trust′worth′y.**

trus-tee (trus-tē′), *n.* a person or firm to whom property, or the management of property, is entrusted.

trust-ing (trus′ting), *adj.* inclined to believe in others; unsuspicious.

trust-y (trus′ti), *adj.* [trust-i-er, trust-i-est], faithful; as, a *trusty* messenger; reliable; as, a *trusty* sword:—*n.* a person to be trusted; esp., a convict found worthy of special privileges in prison.

truth (trooth), *n.* **1,** the quality of being according to fact; agreement with facts; as, his testimony has the ring of *truth;* also, correctness; accuracy; **2,** sincerity of speech and action; as, there is no *truth* in him; **3,** a generally accepted or proved fact; as, the *truths* of science.

truth-ful (trooth′fool), *adj.* **1,** according to the facts; true; as, a *truthful* statement; **2,** naturally given to telling the truth; as, a *truthful* nature.—*adv.* **truth′ful-ly.**—*n.* **truth′ful-ness.**

try (trī), *v.t.* [tried, try-ing], **1,** to put to a trial or experiment; test; as, to *try* a new dish in cooking; **2,** to become acquainted with, by actual use; as, to *try* a new brand of tea; **3,** to subject to trouble, affliction, or annoyance; as, she *tries* her parents sorely; **4,** to test the strength or endurance of; as, she *tries* my patience; **5,** to strain; weary; as, bright light *tries* the eyes; **6,** to decide by argument or contest; as, to *try* an issue by war; **7,** to attempt;

endeavour to use; as, I have *tried* argument in vain; **8,** to melt or render; as, to *try* out fat; **9,** in *law:* **a,** to examine (the case of an accused person) before a court, as does a lawyer; **b,** to act as judge at the trial of (a person or case):—*v.i.* to make an effort; as, do *try* to come:—*n.* [*pl.* tries], an attempt; as, to succeed after several *tries.*—*n.* **try′out′** (*Colloq.*)

try-ing (trī′ing), *adj.* annoying; hard to bear; distressing.

tryst (trist; trīst), *n.* **1,** an engagement to meet at a certain time and place, esp. between lovers; **2,** a meeting, or place of meeting, called a **tryst′ing place:**—*v.t.* and *v.i.* to arrange or agree to a time or place of meeting.

tsar (tsär), *n.* Same as **czar.**

tsa-ri-na (tsä-rē′na), *n.* Same as **czarina.**

tset-se (tset′si), *n.* **1,** a small African fly which by its bite causes germs to enter the blood of domestic animals, producing a severe disease; **2,** another fly of this kind which in the same way produces in man a disease called sleeping-sickness. Also, *tsetse-fly.*

T-shirt (tē′shûrt), *n.* a collarless, pullover, cotton shirt with short sleeves.

T—square (tē′–skwâr), *n.* ruler with a crossbar at one end, used in mechanical drawing.

tub (tub), *n.* **1,** an open circular vessel of wood or metal, used for washing, etc.; **2,** a large, deep, stationary receptacle in a laundry, kitchen, or bathroom, used for washing, bathing, etc.; **3,** a small wooden cask for lard, butter, etc.; **4,** the amount contained in a tub; as, a *tub* of water; **5,** *Colloq.:* **a,** a bath; as, a hot *tub;* **b,** a slow or clumsy boat:—*v.t.* and, *Colloq.*, *v.i.* [tubbed, tub-bing], to bathe in a tub.—*adj.* **tub′by** (*Colloq.* short and fat).

tu-ba (tū′ba), *n.* a large brass wind-instrument, very low in pitch, used in bands and orchestras.

tube (tūb), *n.* **1,** a hollow cylinder, much longer than it is wide, of glass, rubber, metal, etc., for holding or conveying liquids or gases; as, a test *tube;* also, any living structure of similar shape; as, the bronchial *tubes;* **2,** a small cylinder of flexible metal, fitted with a screw cap, for holding lotions, cold cream, etc.; **3,** an underground tunnel; a subway; hence, an underground railway; **4,** a bulb or tube containing a more or less perfect vacuum; as, the vacuum-*tube*, one form of which is used to produce X-rays and another, in radio, to detect and amplify sound-waves.—*adj.* **tube'less.**

tu-ber (tū'bėr), *n.* a thick, roundish part of an underground stem, bearing small buds or eyes, as the potato.—*adj.* **tu'ber-ous** or **tu'ber-ose'** (-ōs).

tu-ber-cle (tū'bėr-kl), *n.* **1,** a natural healthy, knoblike growth, as on a bone or on the root of a plant; **2,** a small diseased lump on the skin or in the soft tissues of the body, characteristic of tuberculosis.

tu-ber-cu-lo-sis (tū-bûr'kū-lō'sis), *n.* a wasting, infectious disease characterized by the growth of tubercles in any part of the body; esp., this disease affecting the lungs: commonly called *consumption.*—*adj.* **tu-ber'cu-lous.**—*adj.* **tu-ber'cu-lar.**

tube-rose (tūb'rōz'; tū'bėr-ōs'), *n.* a Mexican plant, growing from a bulb, cultivated for its spike of fragrant white flowers.

tub-ing (tūb'ing), *n.* **1,** a piece of tube; **2,** cylindrical material for tubes; also, a set or series of tubes.

tu-bu-lar (tū'bū-lėr), *adj.* pertaining to, shaped like, or consisting of, one or more hollow cylinders, or tubes.

tuck (tuk), *v.t.* **1,** to roll or fold; as, to *tuck* up one's sleeves; also, to turn under the loose ends of; as, to *tuck* up one's hair; **2,** to cover snugly; as to *tuck* a child into bed; **3,** to stow away neatly or into a small space; as, to *tuck* bills into a purse; **4,** to make and sew folds in; as, to *tuck* a skirt:—*n.* a stitched fold.—*n.* **tuck'er.**

tuck-ered (tuk'ėrd), *adj. Colloq.* tired; exhausted: used with *out;* as, he was *tuckered out.*

Tues-day (tūz'di; dā), *n.* the 3rd day of the week.

tuft (tuft), *n.* **1,** a small, compact bunch of feathers, threads, etc., growing together or held together at the base; as, a *tuft* of grass; *tufts* in a mattress; **2,** a cluster or clump; as, a *tuft* of asters: —*v.t.* to provide with a tuft or tufts; specifically, to reinforce (mattresses, quilts, upholstery, etc.) with thread drawn through tightly at regular intervals, tied, and finished with cotton tufts or buttons.—*adj.* **tuft'ed.**

tug (tug), *v.t.* [tugged, tug-ging], **1,** to pull or haul with an effort; **2,** to tow with a tugboat:—*v.i.* to pull; as, the child *tugs* at his mother's skirt:—*n.* **1,** a strain or pull with great effort; also, a struggle; **2,** a rope or chain used for pulling; esp., a trace of a harness; **3,** a

small powerful boat for towing vessels. Also, **tug'boat'.**

tu-i-tion (tū-ish'un), *n.* **1,** instruction; teaching; **2,** the fee charged for instruction.

tu-lip (tū'lip), *n.* a plant of the lily family, bearing brilliantly coloured, cup-shaped flowers; also, its bulb or its flower.

tulip—tree (tū'lip-trē'), *n.* an American tree of the magnolia family, bearing greenish-yellow flowers resembling a double tulip.

tulle (tül; tōōl), *n.* a delicate network material, made of silk, etc., for veils, scarfs, and dresses.

tul-li-bee (tul'i-bē'), *n.* a smaller, deep-bodied cisco or whitefish of the larger Canadian prairie lakes and Great Lakes: marketed fresh, frozen, or smoked.

tum-ble (tum'bl), *v.i.* [tumbled, tum-bling], **1,** to fall suddenly and hard; **2,** to roll in play; as, the baby *tumbled* about on the floor; **3,** to perform acrobatic feats, such as springs, somersaults, etc.; **4,** to move in a careless, blundering fashion; as, he *tumbled* wearily into the chair:—*v.t.* **1,** to fling down; **2,** to cause to roll over and over like a football; **3,** to rumple; disorder; as, to *tumble* a heap of clothes:—*n.* **1,** a fall; **2,** a state of confusion or disorder; also, a disordered heap.

tum-bler (tum'blėr), *n.* **1,** a person who performs feats of leaping, somersaulting, etc.; an acrobat; **2,** a stemless drinking glass with straight sides; also, the amount it holds; as, a *tumbler* of milk; **3,** that part of a lock which must be put into a certain position, generally by a key, before the lock will open; **4,** a kind of pigeon which turns somersaults in the air: also called *tumbler pigeon.*—*n.* **tum'ble-weed'.**

tum-brel or **tum-bril** (tum'bril), *n.* a dumpcart, used esp. during the French Revolution to carry victims to the guillotine.

tu-mid (tū'mid), *adj.* bulging; swollen; enlarged; in *writing,* pompous; as, a *tumid* style.

tu-mour (tū'mėr), *n.* an abnormal swelling or growth of tissue within or upon the body.—*adj.* **tu'mor-ous.**

tump-line (tump'lin'), *n.* a strap placed across the forehead to assist in carrying a pack on the back.

tu-mult (tū'mult), *n.* **1,** such noise and confusion as proceeds from a crowd of excited people; **2,** violent agitation, as of the mind.—*adj.* **tu-mul'tu-ous.**

tun (tun), *n.* a large cask or vat, esp. for wines.

tu-na (tōō′na), *n.* [*pl.* tuna or tunas], a large game and food fish found in warm seas; the tunny: also called *tuna fish.*

tun-dra (tun′dra), *n.* flat, rolling, or treeless plains in the Arctic, with permanently frozen subsoil but mucky topsoil of mosses, lichens, dwarf herbs, and shrubs, as the tundra of the Canadian Shield and of Siberia.

tune (tūn), *n.* **1,** a series of musical tones having rhythm and melody and forming a complete theme; an air or melody; **2,** a musical setting, as for a hymn or ballad; also, any easy, simple musical composition; as, I love an old *tune;* **3,** the state of giving forth tones of the proper pitch; **4,** proper adjustment in respect to musical sounds; as, the piano and the violin are in *tune;* **5,** state of harmonious adjustment; fitting mood; as, to be in *tune* with one's surroundings:—*v.t.* [tuned, tun-ing], **1,** to cause to produce the proper sounds; adjust (a voice or an instrument) to the correct musical pitch; **2,** to put into harmony with something; as, he was *tuned* with the gaiety of the party; **3,** to put into proper working condition; as, to *tune* a motor; **4,** to adjust (a radio receiver) to a certain wave-length or frequency:—*v.i.* to be in harmony.—*adj.* tune′less.—*n.* tun′er.

tune-ful (tūn′fool), *adj.* full of music or melody; harmonious; as, a *tuneful* voice.

tung-sten (tung′sten), *n.* a metal which in its impure form is hard, brittle, and grey: used as an alloy of steel and in electric lamp filaments.

tu-nic (tū′nik), *n.* **1,** a kind of shirt worn as an undergarment by both men and women in ancient Greece and Rome; **2,** now, a woman's loose outer garment or overblouse reaching down to, or below, the hips; **3,** the close-fitting short coat of a soldier's or policeman's uniform.

tun-nel (tun′el), *n.* an underground passage cut through a hill or under a river; as, a railroad *tunnel;* also, an underground passage dug by a burrowing animal:—*v.i.* and *v.t.* [tunnelled, tunnel-ling], to make or dig a tunnel (through).

tun-ny (tun′i), *n.* [*pl.* tunnies], a food fish and game-fish found in all warm seas; the tuna fish. Largest of the mackerel family, it sometimes attains a length of ten feet and a weight of more than 1,000 pounds.

tuque (tük; tūk) *n.* a knitted stocking-cap of French-Canadian origin, worn with one end tucked into the other. Also, **toque.**

tur-ban (tûr′ban), *n.* **1,** in the Orient, a man's headdress, consisting of a cap around which a scarf is wrapped, worn esp. by Mohammedans; **2,** any similar headdress, as the bandanna worn by Negro mammies; **3,** a small close-fitting, brimless hat for women.

tur-bid (tûr′bid), *adj.* **1,** having the sediment stirred up; hence, muddy; thick; as, *turbid* waters; **2,** unsettled; confused; as, a *turbid* state of mind.

tur-bine (tûr′bīn); tûr′bin), *n.* a form of motor in which the power is derived from water, steam, or air, driven against curved vanes or cups on the rim of a wheel.

tur-bo-gen-er-a-tor (tûr′bō-jen′ėr-ā′tėr), *n.* a generator coupled with, and driven by, a turbine.

tur-bo-jet (tûr′bō-jet′), *n.* a jet engine in which air from a turbine-driven compressor supplies a chamber equipped with a discharge nozzle that directs exhaust gases rearward for thrust.

tur-bo-prop (tûr′bō-prop′), *n.* a jet engine that operates a turbine, which in turn drives the propeller.

tur-bu-lent (tûr′bū-lent), *adj.* **1,** violent; not easily controlled; as, *turbulent* emotions; **2,** agitated; wild, as a stormy sea; **3,** riotous; creating disturbance; as, a *turbulent* crowd.—*n.* tur′bu-lence.

tu-reen (tu-rēn′), *n.* a deep, covered dish, as for soup.

turf (tûrf), *n.* **1,** the top layer of ground, containing plant debris, matted grass roots, etc.; sod; also, a piece of sod; peat:—**the turf, 1,** a track for horse-racing; **2,** horse-racing:—*v.t.* to cover with sod.

tur-gid (tûr′jid), *adj.* **1,** swollen; inflated; bloated; as, *turgid* waters; **2,** bombastic; pompous; as, *turgid* prose.

tur-key (tûr′ki), *n.* [*pl.* turkeys], a large wild or domestic American fowl; also, its flesh used as food.

tur-key buz-zard, a large carrion-eating vulture of South and Central America and the southern U.S.: also called *turkey vulture.*

Turk-ish (tûr′kish) **bath,** a bath in which one is made to perspire freely in a very hot room, and then washed and rubbed down.

Turk-ish de-light, a jellylike candy dusted with powdered sugar and cut into cubes.

tur-moil (tûr′moil), *n.* confusion and disturbance; upheaval; agitation; unrest.

turn (tûrn), *v.t.* **1,** to cause to revolve or go round; as, to *turn* a wheel; hence, to revolve in the mind or ponder; as, to *turn* over a new idea; **2,** to do or perform by means of a revolving motion; as, to *turn* a handspring; **3,** to shape by revolving against a sharp edge, as in a lathe; **4,** to change the direction, attitude, or position of; as, to *turn* an automobile; **5,** to unsettle or upset (the stomach); **6,** to change (something) into something else; as, to *turn* failure into success; **7,** to cause to go; send; as, to *turn* a beggar away; to *turn* an employee off; **8,** to move to the other side of; go around; as, to *turn* a corner; **9,** to invert; reverse; as, to *turn* a blouse; **10,** to spoil; sour; as, the hot weather *turned* the cream:—*v.i.* **1,** to have a circular motion; revolve; rotate; as, the earth *turns* on its axis; **2,** to depend; hinge; as, my action *turns* on yours; **3,** to change one's direction or position; as, he *turned* away; also, to change one's attitude; as, he *turned* against his friend; **4,** to seem to whirl or spin; reel; as, my head is *turning;* **5,** to change in condition; as, the cider *turned* to vinegar:—*n.* **1,** the act of revolving; a single revolution or twisting; as, the *turn* of a wheel; **2,** a change of direction; also, a bend or curve; as, a *turn* in the road; **3,** a short walk for exercise; **4,** a deed or act; as, you did me a good *turn;* **5,** the time for some act which one does in rotation with others; as, it's your *turn* now; **6,** a change in condition; as, his fortune took a *turn* for the better; **7,** tendency; bent; particular cast of mind; as, he is of a mechanical *turn;* **8,** a short piece or act on the stage; **9,** *Colloq.,* a startling surprise or shock; as, the news gave me a *turn.—n.* **turn′er.—n.** **turn′—out′; turn′o′ver.**

turn-buck-le (tûrn′buk′l), *n.* a metal sleeve or loop with a thread at one end and a swivel at the other: used to join wires or rods; a right-and-left screw coupling.

turn-coat (tûrn′kōt′), *n.* a person who forsakes his principles; one who goes over to the opposite camp; a deserter; renegade.

tur-nip (tûr′nip), *n.* **1,** the fleshy, rounded, edible root, white or yellow, of a certain plant, the leaves of which may also, when tender, be cooked and eaten; **2,** the plant.

turn-pike (tûrn′pīk′), *n.* **1,** a gate or bar to stop wagons, carriages, etc., until toll is paid; a tollgate; **2,** a road which now has or once had tollgates; **3,** loosely, a main highway: also called *turnpike road* or *pike.*

turn-stile (tûrn′stīl′), *n.* **1,** formerly, a gate at the entrance of a road, bridge, etc., made of four arms pivoted on the top of a post and turning to let persons through, one by one; **2,** now a similar but more complicated device, as at a doorway or subway entrance, to regulate or record the number of persons passing through.

tur-pen-tine (tûr′pen-tīn′), *n.* **1,** the sap obtained from certain trees, such as the pine and fir; **2,** commonly, a light-coloured fluid distilled from this sap, used in paints and varnishes, and also in medicine.

tur-pi-tude (tûr′pi-tūd′), *n.* baseness; depravity; as, the moral *turpitude* of sin.

tur-quoise (tûr′koiz; tûr′kwoiz), *n.* **1,** an opaque, light-blue or greenish-blue stone, much used as a gem; **2,** the greenish-blue colour of this stone.

tur-ret (tur′it), *n.* **1,** a small tower, usually at the corner of a building, sometimes merely decorative; **2,** a low towerlike, rotating structure or platform, mounted on battleships, fortifications, or tanks, to house one or more guns.

tur-tle (tûr′tl), *n.* a reptile whose short, broad body is enclosed in a bony or horny shell; a tortoise.

tur-tle-dove (tur′tl-duv′), *n.* any of several Old World doves, esp. a European dove, noted for its gentleness and its soft cooing.

tush (tush), *interj.* an expression of impatience, contempt, or reproof.

tusk (tusk), *n.* **1,** one of the two outside pointed teeth which project from the mouth, when closed, of certain animals, such as the elephant and walrus; **2,** any abnormally large, projecting tooth.

tus-sle (tus′l), *n.* a scuffle, as in sport:—*v.i.* [tus-sled, tus-sling], to scuffle or struggle.

tus-sock (tus′uk), *n.* a hummock of grass or twigs; also, a tuft of hair or feathers.

tus-sock moth, any of a large group of moths whose larvae are covered with long tufts of hair.

all (ôl), ôr; up, mūte, cûr, cōōl, book; oil, out; th, thin; *th,* the.

tut (tut), *interj.* hush! be quiet! expressing rebuke, impatience, etc.

tu-te-lage (tū′ti-lij), *n.* protection; the act of guarding or teaching; as, the *tutelage* of a patron saint.—*adj.* **tu′te-la-ry** (as, a *tutelary* deity).

tu-tor (tū′tẽr), *n.* **1,** a person whose profession it is to teach or instruct; esp., a private teacher; **2,** in some American colleges, a teacher ranking below an instructor:—*v.t.* to instruct or teach privately:—*v.i.* **1,** to do the work of a tutor; **2,** *Colloq.,* to be taught privately; as, he had to *tutor* in Latin.—*adj.* **tu-tor′i-al** (tū-tōr′i-al).

tux-e-do (tuk-sē′dō), *n. Colloq.* a man's tailless dinner-jacket, less formal than a swallowtail coat: *Colloq. tux* (tuks) and *tails* (short for both kinds of formal wear).

twad-dle (twod′l), *n.* and *v.i.* silly talk.

twain (twān), *Poetic* or *Archaic: adj.* two:—*n.* a pair; two.

twang (twang), *n.* **1,** a sharp, quick, vibrating sound; **2,** a sharp nasal tone in speech; as, a Yankee *twang:*—*v.t.* to cause to sound with a twang:—*v.i.* to sound or speak with a twang.

tweak (twēk), *v.t.* to pinch or twist with a jerk:—*n.* a sudden, sharp pinch.

tweed (twēd), *n.* a twilled fabric, usually woollen, showing two or more colours generally mixed in the yarn.

tweet (twēt), *n.* and *v.i.* a thin, chirping note, as a bird's.

tweez-ers (twēz′ẽrz), *n.pl.* a small instrument for taking hold of, or pulling out, something tiny, as a hair.

twelfth (twelfth), *adj.* next after the 11th: the ordinal of *twelve:*—*n.* one of the twelve equal parts of anything.

twelve (twelv), *adj.* composed of one more than eleven:—*n.* **1,** the number consisting of eleven plus one; a dozen; **2,** a sign representing twelve units, as 12 or xii.

twen-ti-eth (twen′ti-eth), *adj.* next after the 19th: the ordinal of *twenty:*—*n.* one of the twenty equal parts of anything.

twen-ty (twen′ti), *adj.* composed of one more than nineteen:—*n.* [*pl.* twenties], **1,** the number consisting of nineteen plus one; a score; **2,** a sign representing twenty units, as 20 or xx.

twen-ty—one (twen′ti–wun′), *n.* and *adj.* the numbers twenty-one to twenty-nine are hyphenated.

twice (twīs), *adv.* **1,** two times; as, I told him *twice;* **2,** doubly; as *twice* as old.

twid-dle (twid′l), *v.t.* [twid-dled, twid-dling], to twirl; as, to *twiddle* one's thumbs.

twig (twig), *n.* a small branch or shoot.

twi-light (twī′līt′), *n.* **1,** the faint light that prevails before sunrise and after sunset; **2,** partial light; dimness:—*adj.* **1,** pertaining to the time before sunrise or after sunset; **2,** dim; obscure.

twill (twil), *n.* **1,** a weave of cloth that shows diagonal lines or ribs on the surface; **2,** a fabric woven with such ribs, as serge:—*v.t.* to weave (cloth) so as to show diagonal lines or ribs.

twin (twin), *adj.* **1,** made of two separate, but equal, parts; double; as, *twin* towers; **2,** very like each other; **3,** born at the same birth; as, *twin* brothers:—*n.* **1,** one of two born at one birth; **2,** a person or thing very like another.

twine (twīn), *n.* **1,** a kind of strong thread or string; **2,** a twist or tangle:—*v.t.* [twined, twin-ing], **1,** to make by twisting; as, to *twine* a garland; **2,** to encircle; as, to *twine* a pole with ribbons:—*v.i.* to wind; as, the vine *twines* over the porch.

twinge (twinj), *n.* a sudden, darting pain.

twin-kle (twing′kl), *v.i.* [twin-kled, twin-kling], **1,** to shine with a gleam that grows alternately dimmer and brighter; flicker; as, a star *twinkles;* hence, to sparkle, as the eyes; **2,** to flash in and out rapidly, as the feet in dancing:—*v.t.* to open and shut (the eyelids) rapidly; wink:—*n.* **1,** a flicker or quiver; **2,** a sparkle or gleam; **3,** the time occupied by a wink; a moment; twinkling.—*n.* **twin′kling.**

twirl (twûrl), *v.t.* **1,** to turn (something) around rapidly; whirl; as, to *twirl* a cane; **2,** *Slang,* in baseball, to pitch:—*v.i.* **1,** to rotate rapidly; **2,** *Slang,* to pitch:—*n.* a quick, circular motion; a twist.

twist (twist), *v.t.* **1,** to wind (strands together; also, to form (a rope or twine by this means; **2,** to twine or wind; as to *twist* a scarf around one's neck; **3,** to wrench or turn; as, to *twist* one's wrist:—*v.i.* **1,** to become joined by winding; also, to form knots; as, this silk *twists* badly; **2,** to become wrenched or turned; as, my ankle *twisted;* **3,** to take a winding course; as, the stream *twists* round the bend:—*n.* **1,** the act of manner of winding or twining; **2,** something made by winding strands together, as certain kinds of silk o cotton thread; **3,** a wrench, as of a

---

cat, āge, fär, câre, ásk; ten, ēve, latẽr; (i) pity, rely, senate; īce; top; nō

muscle; **4,** a special tendency of mind; as, a poetical *twist*.

twist-er (twis'tėr), *n.* a tornado, cyclone, waterspout, dust whirl, etc.; **2,** a ball, thrown or batted, that curves or weaves, as in baseball or cricket.

twit (twit), *v.t.* [twit-ted, twit-ting], to upbraid or tease, often good-naturedly, by reminding a person of a mistake or fault.

twitch (twich), *v.i.* **1,** to pull at something with a sudden jerk; **2,** to move jerkily; as, her fingers *twitched:*—*n.* **1,** a sudden jerk or pull; **2,** a short, jerky contraction of a muscle.

twitch grass, a coarse, weedlike grass that spreads rapidly by creeping rootstocks: also called *couch grass* and *quick grass*.

twit-ter (twit'ėr), *v.i.* **1,** to chirp; make a series of small, sharp sounds, as does a bird; **2,** to feel a slight nervous excitement:—*v.t.* to utter in short, broken sounds:—*n.* **1,** a series of short, broken sounds; **2,** a nervous trembling.

two (tōō), *adj.* composed of one more than one:—*n.* [*pl.* twos], **1,** the sum of one and one; **2,** a sign representing two units, as 2 or ii.—*adj.* **two'—piece'.**—*n.* and *adj.* **two'some** (a game for two, or two people who play it).—**two bits,** *Slang,* twenty-five cents.

two—by—four (tōō'-bī-fôr'), *n.* a length of lumber, 2″ by 4″ in size; scantling.—*adj.Colloq.* small; cramped.

two-fold (tōō'fōld'), *adj.* made of two parts; double; as, a *twofold* errand:— *adv.* (tōō'fōld'), doubly.

two-pence (tup'ens; if used as two words, tōō pens), *n.* **1,** the sum of two English pennies; **2,** formerly, a coin worth that amount of money.

two—step (tōō'-step'), *n.* a ballroom dance, or the music for it, in march or polka time (usually 2/4), done with a sliding step.

ty-coon (tī-kōōn'), *n. Colloq.* a prominent financier, industrialist, etc.

ty-ing (tī'ing), *p.pr.* of *tie.*

tyke (tīk), *n.* **1,** a dog or cur, esp. a mongrel; **2,** *Colloq.* a lively or mischievous child: used affectionately.

tym-pa-num (tim'pa-num), *n.* [*pl.* tympanums or tympana (tim'pa-na)], **1,** the eardrum, or middle ear; **2,** the thin membrane dividing the outer from the middle ear: also called *tympanic membrane.*—*adj.* **tym-pan'ic** (tim-pan'ik).

type (tīp), *n.* **1,** a person or thing possessing the characteristic qualities of a group; an example; as, many of Dickens's characters are *types* of middle-class English life; **2,** a particular class or kind; as, a high *type* of person; a juicy *type* of apple; **3,** a group of persons or things having common characteristics; as, men of an athletic *type;* also, in *biology,* a group or division of animals, plants, etc., having a common structure or form; as, an animal of the cat *type;* **4,** in *printing*: **a,** a metal or wooden block bearing on one end a raised letter, figure, or other character, an impression of which may be transferred, after inking, to paper; **b,** a series or group of such blocks; **c,** the impression from them:—*v.t.* [typed, typ-ing], to write on a typewriter.

type-script (tīp'skript'), *n.* typewritten matter.

type-set-ter (tīp'set'ėr), *n.* one who sets type.

type-writ-er (tīp'rīt'ėr), *n.* **1,** a machine, with a keyboard operated by the fingers, which produces writing similar to printing; **2,** one who writes on a typewriter.—*n.* **type'writ'ing.**— *v.t.* and *v.i.* **type'write'.**

ty-phoid (tī'foid), *n.* an infectious, often fatal, disease, traceable to germ-infected food or drinking-water: also called *typhoid fever.*

ty-phoon (tī-fōōn'), *n.* a violent tornado, usually occurring in the China Seas.

ty-phus (tī'fus), *n.* an infectious disease from the bite of lice, fleas, etc., marked by fever, mental disorder, and eruption of red spots on the skin.

typ-i-cal (tip'i-kl), *adj.* **1,** characteristic; like others of its class; as, my son is *typical* of all small boys; a *typical* country store; **2,** symbolic; representing a whole class.—*adv.* **typ'i-cal-ly.**

typ-i-fy (tip'i-fī'), *v.t.* [typified, typifying], **1,** to bear or show the striking characteristics of (a class or group); represent; **2,** to symbolize; as, the lamb *typifies* meekness.

typ-ist (tīp'ist), *n.* one whose business it is to operate a typewriting machine.

ty-po-graph-i-cal (tī'po-graf'i-kl), *adj.* dealing with printing, esp. type-setting; as, a *typographical* error.—*n.* **ty-pog'ra-phy.**

ty-ran-no-saur-us (ti-ran'ō-sôr'us), *n.* a huge, flesh-eating dinosaur that walked erect on powerful hind limbs: fossil remains found esp. in western areas as Alberta, Montana, Utah, etc.

tyr-an-ny (tir'a-ni), *n.* [*pl.* tyrannies], **1,** the government or conduct of a cruel and unjust ruler; **2,** undue severity.— *adj.* **tyran'ni-cal.**—*adj.* **tyr'an-nous.**

ty-rant (tī'rant), *n.* **1,** an absolute monarch; a despot; **2,** a ruler or

master who uses his power to oppress those under him.

ty-ro (tī'rō), *n.* a beginner, novice, or learner.

tzar (tsär), *n.* Same as **czar.** *Fem.* **tsa-ri'na.**

U

U, u (ū), *n.* [*pl.* U's, u's], **1,** the 21st letter of the alphabet, following T; **2,** anything with the shape of a U.

u-biq-ui-tous (ū-bik'wi-tus), *adj.* being, or seeming to be, everywhere at the same time.—*n.* **u-biq'ui-ty.**

ud-der (ud'ẽr), *n.* in certain animals, a baglike milk gland with teats.

ugh (ookh; oo; u; ukh), *interj.* an exclamation of aversion, disgust, or horror.

ug-ly (ug'li), *adj.* [ug-li-er, ug-li-est], **1,** displeasing to the eye; hideous; **2,** morally repulsive; evil; as, *ugly* deeds; **3,** *Colloq.*: **a,** suggesting trouble; as, an *ugly* rumour; **b,** quarrelsome; as, an *ugly* disposition.—*n.* **ug'li-ness.**

u-ku-le-le (ū/ku-lā'li), *n.* a four-stringed, guitar-shaped Hawaiian instrument of Portuguese origin.

ul-cer (ul'sẽr), *n.* **1,** an open sore which secretes pus; **2,** hence, a corrupt influence; a public evil.—*adj.* **ul'cer-ous.**

ul-na (ul'na), *n.* the inner and larger of the two bones of the forearm: the other is the *radius.*

ul-ster (ul'stẽr), *n.* a long, loose overcoat.

ul-te-ri-or (ul-tē'ri-ẽr), *adj.* **1,** lying beyond; more distant; **2,** beyond what is expressed or admitted; as, an *ulterior* purpose.

ul-ti-mate (ul'ti-mit), *adj.* **1,** last; final; as, the *ultimate* decision; **2,** fundamental; basic; as, *ultimate* facts of nature.—*adv.* **ul'ti-mate-ly.**

ul-ti-ma-tum (ul'ti-mā'tum), *n.* [*pl.* ultimatums or ultimata (ul'ti-mā'ta)], a final condition; one's last word on a matter; esp., the final terms stated by one nation to another, the rejection of which may be expected to lead to war.

ul-tra (ul'tra), *adj.* extreme; going to extremes; as, an *ultra*-conservative.

ul-tra- (ul'tra-), *prefix* meaning *beyond;* as *ultra*marine (a deep blue), *ultra*red (infrared, designating the invisible rays just beyond the red of the visible

spectrum), and *ultra*violet (designating the rays of very short wave-length that lie just beyond the violet end of the visible spectrum: used for healing and for photography). Also, *ultra*-fashionable; *ultra*-microscopic; etc.

ul-tra vi-res (ul'tra vī'rēz), *Latin,* beyond the legal power or authority of a court, corporation, etc.

u-lu (ōō'lōō), *n.* a primitive knife, like an axe-head, used by Eskimo women.

ul-u-la-tion (ūl'ū-lā'shun), *n.* howling; wailing; as, the *ululation* of wolves, jackals, etc., at night:—*v.i.* **ul'u-late'.**

um-bel (um'bel), *n.* a flower-cluster in which all the flowerstalks, of nearly equal length, grow from a common centre, and spread out to form a flat or rounded head.

um-ber (um'bẽr), *n.* **1,** a brown earth used as colouring matter; **2,** a rich, dark-brown colour:—*adj.* of or like umber; umber-coloured.

um-bil-i-cus (um-bil'i-kus; um'bi-li'kus), *n.* the navel.—*adj.* **um-bil'i-cal** (relating to the cord through which the foetus receives food and eliminates waste into the circulatory system of the mother).

um-bra (um'bra), *n.* the dark cone of shadow cast by a planet or satellite on the side opposite the sun.

um-brage (um'brij), *n.* resentful displeasure; offence; as, he took *umbrage* at my remark.

um-brel-la (um-brel'a), *n.* a device for protection against rain, sun, etc., consisting of a folding frame, covered with silk, cotton, etc., on a stick which ends in a handle.

u-mi-ak or **oo-mi-ak** (ōō'mi-ak), *n.* an Eskimo open boat, made of skins stretched over a frame.

um-laut (oom'lout), *n.* a diacritical or pronunciation mark ["] placed over a vowel, esp. in German, to show that its sound is modified because of a vowel that follows: in English called *diaeresis.*

um-pire (um'pīr), *n.* a person chosen

to decide a controversy; esp., one who oversees a game, to enforce the rules and decide disputed points:—*v.t.* and *v.i.* [umpired, umpir-ing], to supervise or decide as an umpire.

un- (un-), *prefix* meaning *not, no, lack of, opposite to,* as in un′ac-cent′ed; un′ac-count′ed—for′; un′a-dul′ter-at′ed; un-aid′ed; un′al-loyed′ (pure, as *unalloyed* bliss); un-bri′dled (uncontrolled); un′com-plain′ing; un-com′-pro-mis′ing; un′con-ven′tion-al; un′-de-terred′; un-earned′; un′es-sen′tial; un′e-quiv′o-cal; un-fath′om-a-ble; un-fath′omed; un-fet′tered; un-for-get′-ta-ble; un-friend′li-ness; un-friend′ly; un-grac′ious; un′gram-mat′i-cal; un-guard′ed; un-hurt′; un-in′ter-est-ed; un-know′a-ble; un-learn′; un-loved′; un-love′ly; un-man′age-a-ble; un-men′tion-a-ble; un′ob-tru′sive; un-or′tho-dox′; un-par′don-a-ble; un′-par-lia-men′ta-ry; un-pop′u-lar; un′-pre-med′i-tat′ed; un′pre-ten′tious; un-quench′a-ble; un-ques′tioned; un-read′; un-read′a-ble; un-read′y; un-re′al; un′re-al′i-ty; un′re-gen′er-ate; un-re-li′a-ble; un-re′pen′tant; un-right′eous; un-san′i-ta-ry; un′sat-is-fac′to-ry; un-schooled′; un-search′-a-ble; un′sci-en-tif′ic; un-serv′ice-a-ble; un-shav′en; un-slaked′; un-so′ci-a-ble; un-spar′ing; un-spo′ken; un-ster′-i-lized′; un-stressed′; un-stud′ied; un′suc-ces′ful; un-suit′a-ble; un-sul′lied; un′sur-passed′; un′-sus-pect′ing; un′sym-pa-thet′ic; un-taught′; un-ten′a-ble; un-tram′meled or un-tram′melled; un-trust′wor′thy; un-ut′tered; un-var′y-ing; un-want′-ed; un-wept′; un-whole′some; un-world′ly; un-wrap′; un-yield′ing.

un-a-ble (un-ā′bl), *adj.* incapable; not able; lacking power or ability.

un-ac-count-a-ble (un′a-koun′ta-bl), *adj.* 1, not capable of explanation; as, an *unaccountable* delay; 2, not responsible; irresponsible.—*adv.* un′ac-count′-a-bly.

un-ac-cus-tomed (un′a-kus′tumd), *adj.* 1, not usual or customary; as, *unaccustomed* speed; 2, not familiar with or used to; as, she is *unaccustomed* to the work.

un-ad-vised (un′ad-vīzd′), *adj.* 1, not discreet or prudent; rash; as, an *unadvised* person; an *unadvised* act; 2, without having received advice. —*adv.* un′ad-vis′ed-ly.

un-af-fect-ed (un′a-fek′tid), *adj.* 1, without pretence; natural in manner; 2, not influenced.—*adv.* un′af-fect′ed-ly.

u-nan-i-mous (ū-nan′i-mus), *adj.* 1, united in a single opinion; agreeing;

as, we were *unanimous* in our decision; 2, showing that all agree; as, a *unanimous* vote.—*n.* u′na-nim′i-ty (ū-na-nim′i-ti).

un-armed (un-ärmd′), *adj.* without weapons; defenceless.

un-as-sum-ing (un′a-sūm′ing), *adj.* modest; unaffected.

un-a-vail-ing (un′a-vāl′ing), *adj.* without effect; useless; as, *unavailing* efforts to rescue a person from drowning.

un-a-void-a-ble (un′a-void′a-bl), *adj.* not to be escaped; inevitable; as, an *unavoidable* accident.—*adv.* un′a-void′-a-bly.

un-a-ware (un′a-wâr′), *adj.* not knowing; ignorant of; as, he was *unaware* of my presence.

un-a-wares (un′a-wârz′), *adv.* 1, without previous planning; 2, by surprise; as, they caught the enemy *unawares*.

un-bal-anced (un-bal′anst), *adj.* 1, of unequal weight; out of equilibrium; as, *unbalanced* scales; 2, hence, mentally disordered; slightly insane.

un-bear-a-ble (un-bâr′a-bl), *adj.* that cannot be endured; intolerable.—*adv.* un-bear′a-bly.

un-be-com-ing (un′bi-kum′ing), *adj.* 1, not suitable or fit; improper; as, conduct *unbecoming* a lady; 2, not suited to one's appearance; as, an *unbecoming* hat.

un-be-lief (un′bi-lēf′), *n.* lack of positive faith or belief; esp., refusal to accept the teachings of religion.—*n.* un′be-liev′er.

un-bend (un-bend′), *v.t.* [unbent (un-bent′), unbend-ing], 1, to make straight; loosen; as, to *unbend* a bow; 2, to free from strain; relax; as, to *unbend* the mind; 3, to unfasten (a sail) from a spar:—*v.i.* 1, to become straight; 2, to become less severe or stiff; become gracious.

un-bend-ing (un-ben′ding), *adj.* 1, stiff; rigid; 2, unyielding; obstinate.

un-bi-ased or **un-bi-assed** (un-bī′ast), *adj.* impartial; without prejudice.

un-bind (un-bīnd′), *v.t.* [unbound (un-bound′), unbind-ing], 1, to make loose; untie; as, to *unbind* a bandage; 2, to release; free (a person) from bonds.

un-blem-ished (un-blem′isht), *adj.* stainless; unmarred.

un-blush-ing (un-blush′ing), *adj.* shameless.

un-bolt (un-bōlt′), *v.t.* to draw back a bolt from; unfasten; as, to *unbolt* a gate.

un-born (un-bôrn′), *adj.* not yet born; hence, yet to come; future.

un-bos-om (un-booz′um; boōz′), *v.t.* to unburden (oneself) of a secret:—*v.i.* to free one's mind by telling one's thoughts.

un-bound-ed (un-boun′did), *adj.* **1,** without limits; as, *unbounded* space; **2,** extreme; as, *unbounded* admiration.

un-bri-dled (un-brī′dld), *adj.* **1,** not fastened with a bridle; **2,** not restrained ; as, an *unbridled* tongue.

un-bro-ken (un-brō′kn), *adj.* **1,** whole; intact; **2,** untamed; **3,** continuous; **4,** not impaired, disorganized, or disordered.

un-buck-le (un-buk′l), *v.t.* [unbuckled, unbuck-ling], to undo the buckle or buckles of; as, to *unbuckle* a belt.

un-bur-den (un-bûr′dn), *v.t.* **1,** to relieve of a burden; as, to *unburden* oneself of a secret; **2,** to throw off (a burden).

un-but-ton (un-but′n), *v.t.* to unfasten the button or buttons of.

un-called—for (un-kôld′-fôr′), *adj.* not needed; out of place; as, an *uncalled-for* comment.

un-can-ny (un-kan′i), *adj.* not to be explained by reason; unearthly.

un-cer-e-mo-ni-ous (un′ser-e-mō′-ni-us), *adj.* **1,** informal; familiar, as a visit; **2,** abrupt; discourteous.—*adv.* **un-cer′e-mo′ni-ous-ly.**

un-cer-tain (un-sûr′tin), *adj.* **1,** not sure; doubtful; as, the result is *uncertain;* **2,** indefinite as to quantity or quality; as, an *uncertain* number; an *uncertain* flavour; **3,** not positive; not decided; as, we are *uncertain* about going; **4,** not steady; as, the platform gave but *uncertain* support; **5,** changing; fluctuating; as, the *uncertain* tide. —*n.* **un-cer′tain-ty.**

un-chain (un-chān′), *v.t.* to unfasten the chains of; let loose; as, to *unchain* a dog.

un-char-i-ta-ble (un-char′i-ta-bl), *adj.* **1,** not generous toward the needy; **2,** unkind; harsh in judging others.

un-chris-tian (un-kris′chan)', *adj.* **1,** heathen; **2,** unbecoming to, or unlike, a Christian; as, *unchristian* conduct.

un-civ-il (un-siv′il), *adj.* rude; discourteous.

un-civ-i-lized (un-siv′i-līzd′), *adj.* savage; barbarous.

un-clasp (un-klásp′), *v.t.* to release the clasp of; as, to *unclasp* a necklace; to unfasten; as, to *unclasp* one's fingers.

unc-le (ung′kl), *n.* **1,** the brother of one's father or mother; **2,** the husband of one's aunt; **3,** *Colloq.*, an old man.

un-clean (un-klēn′), *adj.* **1,** soiled; filthy; **2,** impure; obscene.

un-clean-ly (un-klen′li), *adj.* **1,** habitually dirty; foul; filthy; **2,** unchaste; obscene.—*n.* **un-clean′li-ness.**

un-clothe (un-klōth′), *v.t.* [unclothed, uncloth-ing], to remove the clothes or covering from; undress.

un-coil (un-koil′), *v.t.* to unwind; as, to *uncoil* a spring:—*v.i.* to become loose or unwound; as, a snake *uncoils.*

un-com-fort-a-ble (un-kum′fèrt-a-bl), *adj.* **1,** not at ease physically or mentally; **2,** causing discomfort; as, an *uncomfortable* chair.—*adv.* **un-com′-fort-a-bly.**

un-com-mon (un-kom′un), *adj.* out of the ordinary; rare; strange.

un-con-cern (un′kon-sûrn′), *n.* lack of interest or anxiety.

un-con-cerned (un′kon-sûrnd′), *adj.* **1,** not anxious; **2,** uninterested.

un-con-di-tion-al (un′kon-dish′un-al), *adj.* without any limitations; absolute; as, an *unconditional* promise. —*adv.* **un′con-di′tion-al-ly.**

un-con-scion-a-ble (un-kon′shun-a-bl), *adj.* **1,** unreasonable, immoderate, or excessive; as, an *unconscionable* delay; **2,** unscrupulous.—*adv.* **un-con′-scion-a-bly.**

un-con-scious (un-kon′shus), *adj.* **1,** without consciousness; without apparent life; **2,** without realization or understanding; as, a person *unconscious* of ridicule; **3,** not deliberate; accidental; as, an *unconscious* omission.—*n.* **un-con′scious-ness.**

un-con-sti-tu-tion-al (un′kon-sti-tū′shun-al), *adj.* not in accord with the constitution or political principles of a country.—*n.* **un′con-sti-tu′tion-al′i-ty.**

un-cork (un-kôrk′), *v.t.* to pull out the cork of; as, to *uncork* a jug.

un-cou-ple (un-kup′l), *v.t.* [uncoupled, uncou-pling], to set free; to unleash; also, to unloose from a coupling; detach; as, to *uncouple* a locomotive.

un-couth (un-koŏth′), *adj.* **1,** awkward; ungainly; **2,** crude; boorish.

un-cov-er (un-kuv′èr), *v.t.* **1,** to remove a top or cover from; **2,** to take the hat or cap from; **3,** to make known; bring to light, as a plot:—*v.i.* to take off the hat or cap; as, to *uncover* for the flag.

unc-tion (ungk′shun), *n.* **1,** the act of

anointing as a sign of consecration; **2,** an ointment; hence, anything soothing; **3,** excessive courtesy; a smooth, oily manner.

unc-tu-ous (ungk/tū-us), *adj.* **1,** oily; smooth; **2,** complacently agreeable; suave; bland; as, an *unctuous* speech. —*n.* unc/tu-ous-ness.

un-cul-ti-vat-ed (un-kul/ti-vāt/id), *adj.* **1,** untilled; as, *uncultivated* land; also, undeveloped; as, an *uncultivated* talent; **2,** uncivilized; unrefined.

un-curl (un-kûrl/), *v.t.* to cause to straighten out; as, to *uncurl* feathers: —*v.i.* to become straight.

un-de-ceived (un/di-sēvd/), *p.t.* and *p.p.* of *undeceive,* to set free from error or mistaken conception.

un-de-cid-ed (un/di-sīd/id), *adj.* **1,** doubtful; unsettled; as, an *undecided* issue; **2,** wavering; as, *undecided* what to do.

un-de-filed (un/di-fīld/), *adj.* not corrupted; pure.

un-de-ni-a-ble (un/di-nī/a-bl), *adj.* **1,** not to be contradicted; unquestionable; as, he possesses *undeniable* skill; **2,** decidedly good; as, a person of *undeniable* character.—*adv.* un/de-ni/-a-bly.

un-der (un/dėr), *prep.* **1,** below or beneath; as, *under* a ladder; *under* the skin; *under* the sea; also, lower than, in position, authority, excellence, or value; as, a captain is *under* a major; cotton sells *under* silk; **2,** less than, in height, weight, age, or number; as, *under* six feet; *under* ten years; *under* five dollars; **3,** subject to the action or effect of; as, *under* treatment; *under* a strain; *under* orders; **4,** because of; as, *under* the circumstances; **5,** in conformity with; as, *under* a rule of the firm; classified beneath; as, *under* this topic; **6,** during the rule of; as, England *under* the Tudors:—*adj.* **1,** lower in position; as, the *under* surface; **2,** lower in rank; as, an *under*-waiter:—*adv.* in or to a lower place or subordinate position.—*n.* un/der-clothes/.—*adj.* un/der-cov/er;—*v.t.* un/der-charge/; un/der-es/ti-mate/.

un-der-brush (un/dėr-brush/), *n.* bushes, shrubs, and small trees growing thickly in a forest; undergrowth.

un-der-cur-rent (un/dėr-kûr/ent), *n.* **1,** a current, as of air or water, below another current or below the surface; **2,** hence, a concealed tendency of thought or feeling.

un-der-gar-ment (un/dėr-gär/ment),

n. a garment worn under the outer clothing.

un-der-go (un/dėr-gō/), *v.t.* [*p.t.* underwent (-went/), *p.p.* undergone (-gôn/), *p.pr.* undergo-ing], to be subjected to; experience; as, to *undergo* an operation.

un-der-grad-u-ate (un/dėr-grad/ū-it), *n.* a college or university student who has not yet taken a degree.

un-der-ground (un/dėr-ground/), *adj.* **1,** below the surface of the earth; as, an *underground* railway; **2,** acting in secret; as, an *underground* system of spying:—*adv.* (un/dėr-ground/), beneath the earth's surface:—*n.* (un/dėr-ground/), something below the surface of the earth; as, in London, the subway is called the *underground.*

un-der-growth (un/dėr-grōth/), *n.* low shrubs and bushes in a forest; underbrush.

un-der-hand (un/dėr-hand/), *adj.,* **1** acting secretly or deceitfully; also, characterized by deceit; as, *underhand* methods; **2,** of a ball, thrown with an upward swing of the arm, with the palm of the hand turned up:—*adv.* (un/dėr-hand/), **1,** secretly; **2,** unfairly.

un-der-hand-ed (un/dėr-han/did), *adj.* dishonest; not aboveboard; underhand.

un-der-lay (un/dėr-lā/), *v.t.* to put something under, as paper or cardboard under (type) to raise it (for printing):—*v.i.* in *mining,* to incline, as a vein or lode, from the vertical. Also used as *n.* (un/dėr-lā/).

un-der-lie (un/dėr-lī/), *v.t.* [*p.t.* underlay (-lā/), *p.p.* underlain (-lān/), *p.pr.* underly-ing], **1,** to lie or be beneath; **2,** hence, to be at the bottom of; serve as the basis of; as, what motives *underlie* his acts?

un-der-line (un/dėr-līn/; un/dėr-līn/), *v.t.* [underlined, underlin-ing], *v.t.* to draw a line beneath; underscore; as, to *underline* a word.

un-der-ling (un/dėr-ling), *n.* a person occupying a low position; a subordinate.

un-der-mine (un/dėr-mīn/), *v.t.* [undermined, undermin-ing], **1,** to dig beneath; form a tunnel under; **2,** hence, to weaken; work against secretly; as, to *undermine* one's health; *undermine* one's influence.

un-der-most (un/dėr-mōst/), *adj.* lowest in place, position, or rank.

un-der-neath (un/dėr-nēth/), *adv.* and *prep.* beneath; below.

un-der-pin-ning (un/dėr-pin/ing), *n.*

1, a foundation, esp. beneath a wall; **2,** a support; **3,** *pl. Colloq.* the legs.

un-der-priv-i-leged (un′dẽr-priv′i-lijd), *adj.* lacking fundamental social rights or security, through poverty, discrimination, etc.

un-der-rate (un′dẽr-rāt′), *v.t.* [under-rat-ed, underrat-ing], to place too low a value or estimate upon.

un-der-score (un′dẽr-skōr′), *v.t.* [underscored, underscor-ing], to draw a line under; underline.

un-der-sell (un′dẽr-sel′), *v.t.* [under-sold (-sōld′), undersell-ing], to sell at a lower price than (another).

un-der-shirt (un′dẽr-shûrt′), *n.* a garment for the upper half of the body worn under other clothing, next to the skin.

un-der-skirt (un′dẽr-skûrt′), *n.* a skirt worn under an outer garment; a petticoat.

un-der-stand (un′dẽr-stand′), *v.t.* [understood (-stood′), understand-ing], **1,** to comprehend or grasp; as, she doesn't *understand* what you mean; **2,** to know thoroughly; as, to *understand* one's business; **3,** to see clearly; realize; as, you do not *understand* what the consequences will be; **4,** to accept as a fact without positive knowledge; believe; as, I *understand* he will come; **5,** in *grammar,* to supply mentally (a word which is not expressed); as, in the phrase, "red roses and white," "roses" may be *understood* after "white":—*v.i.* to comprehend; as, say no more; I *understand.*—*adj.* un′der-stan′da-ble.—*adv.* un′der-stan′da-bly.

un-der-stand-ing (un′dẽr-stan′ding), *adj.* intelligent; also, sympathetic:—*n.* **1,** knowledge; as, an *understanding* of algebra; **2,** ability to understand; intelligence; as, John is superior to him in *understanding;* **3,** the agreement of two minds; as, the perfect *understanding* between them.

un-der-state (un′dẽr-stāt′), *v.t.* [understat-ed, understat-ing], to tell less than the truth about; state (facts) too weakly.

un-der-stud-y (un′dẽr-stud′i), *n.* and *v.t.* **1,** one who learns the rôle of another (actor) to be ready to substitute if necessary; hence, **2,** one trained to take another's place.

un-der-take (un′dẽr-tāk′), *v.t.* [*p.t.* undertook (-took′), *p.p.* undertak-en (-tāk′en), *p.pr.* undertak-ing], **1,** to take upon oneself; attempt; as, to *under-*

take a task; **2,** to contract to do; promise; as, he *undertook* to finish the work by June.

un-der-tak-er (un′dẽr-tāk′ẽr), *n.* one who makes a business of preparing the dead for burial, and of conducting funerals.

un-der-tak-ing (un′dẽr-tāk′ing), *n.* **1,** the taking upon oneself of a task or responsibility; **2,** task or enterprise; **3,** (un′dẽr-tāk′ing), the business of preparing the dead for burial, and managing funerals.

un-der-tone (un′dẽr-tōn′), *n.* a subdued tone of voice or sound (much lower than normal); **2,** any subordinate element, as a subdued shade of colour.

un-der-tow (un′dẽr-tō′), *n.* a current below the surface of water, moving in a direction opposite to the current of the surface; esp., at the seashore, the outgoing current below the incoming breakers.

un-der-val-ue (un′dẽr-val′ū), *v.t.* to rate below actual worth; as, to *undervalue* honour.

un-der-wear (un′dẽr-wâr′), *n.* garments worn under the ordinary outer clothing.

un-der-world (un′dẽr-wûrld′), *n.* **1,** the criminal portion of humanity; **2,** the place of departed souls, as *Hades, Sheol, Hell.*

un-der-write (un′dẽr-rīt′), *v.t.* **1,** in *insurance,* to sign a policy (on behalf of a company) as a guarantee that certain liability will be met in event of loss, damage, death, etc.; **2,** to sign one's name to:—*v.i.* to carry on the business of insurance.—*n.* un′der-writ′er.

un-de-sir-a-ble (un′di-zīr′a-bl), *adj.* objectionable.

un-de-vi-at-ing (un-dē′vi-āt′ing), *adj.* not turning aside, diverging, or erring (from a proper standard, etc.)

un-dis-ci-plined (un-dis′i-plind), *adj.* not trained in self-control, character, orderliness, efficiency, etc.

un-do (un-dōō′), *v.t.* [*p.t.* undid (-did′), *p.p.* undone (-dun′), *p.pr.* undo-ing], **1,** to do away with the result of; as, going out in the rain will *undo* the effect of the medicine; **2,** to destroy; ruin; as, evil company will *undo* him; **3,** to loosen; unfasten; as, to *undo* a knot.—*n.* un-do′er.

un-do-ing (un-dōō′ing), *n.* **1,** a setting aside, or reversal, of something that has been done; **2,** ruin; downfall; as, gambling was his *undoing.*

un-doubt-ed (un-dout′id), *adj.* certain; not to be doubted; as, an *undoubted* fact.

un-dress (un-dres′), *v.i.* to take off one's clothes or covering of; strip:—*n.* (un′-dres′; un-dres′), everyday clothes:—*adj.* (un′dres′), informal; as, an *undress* uniform.

un-due (un-dū′; un′dū′), *adj.* 1, wrong or illegal; as, an *undue* course of action; 2, more than is proper or suitable; excessive; as, *undue* attention to trifles.

un-du-late (un′dū-lāt′), *v.i.* and *v.t.* [undulat-ed, undulat-ing], to move, or cause to move, with a wavy motion; as, a field of grain *undulates* in the wind. —*n.* **un′du-la′tion.**

un-du-ly (un-dū′li), *adv.* 1, improperly; 2, excessively.

un-dy-ing (un-dī′ing), *adj.* lasting; seeming to last forever; eternal.

un-earth (un-ûrth′), *v.t.* 1, to take from the earth; dig from underground; uncover; 2, hence, to bring to light; discover; as, to *unearth* a crime.

un-earth-ly (un-ûrth′li), *adj.* 1, not according to, or like, nature; supernatural; 2, weird; uncanny; as, an *unearthly* light.

un-easy (un-ēz′i), *adj.* [uneas-i-er, un-eas-i-est], 1, not at ease in mind or body; disturbed; anxious; as, John's failure in school made him *uneasy;* 2, awkward in manner; constrained. —*n.* **un-eas′i-ness.**—*adv.* **un-eas′i-ly.** —*n.* **un-eas′i-ness.**

un-em-ployed (un′em-ploid′), *adj.* 1, not being used; as, *unemployed* funds; 2, out of work:—**the unemployed,** all the people out of work.—*n.* **un′em-ploy′ment.**—*adj.* **un′em-ploy′-a-ble.**

un-e-qual (un-ē′kwal), *adj.* 1, not of the same strength, amount, size, etc.; as, *unequal* triangles; 2, not well balanced or matched; as, *unequal* teams; 3, not sufficiently large, strong, or able; as, *unequal* to the job; 4, irregular.—*adv.* **un-e′qual-ly.**

UNESCO (ū-nes′kō), *n.* the United Nations Educational, Scientific, and Cultural Organization.

un-e-ven (un-ē′ven), *adj.* 1, not level; not smooth or flat; as, an *uneven* board; 2, not uniform; as, *uneven* pressure; 3, not even; odd; as, seven is an *uneven* number.

un-ex-celled (un′ek-seld′), *adj.* best of its kind; unsurpassed.

un-ex-cep-tion-a-ble (un′ek-sep′-shun-a-bl), *adj.* blameless; faultless; irreproachable; as, *unexceptional* conduct.

un-ex-cep-tion-al (un′ek-sep′shun-al), *adj.* 1, usual; not out of the ordinary; 2, not to be deviated from; as, *unexceptional* orders.

un-ex-pect-ed (un′eks-pek′tid), *adj.* not looked for.—*n.* **un′ex-pect′ed-ness.**

un-fail-ing (un-fāl′ing), *adj.* 1, not likely to fail; as, an *unfailing* water supply; 2, reliable; as, an *unfailing* friend.

un-fair (un-fâr′), *adj.* not fair; not impartial.—*adv.* **un-fair′ly.**—*n.* **un-fair′ness.**

un-faith-ful (un-fāth′fool), *adj.* 1, false; untrue; 2, not exact; not reliable.—*adv.* **un-faith′ful-ly.**—*n.* **un-faith′ful-ness.**

un-fa-mil-iar (un′fa-mil′yėr), *adj.* 1, strange; unknown; 2, without knowledge; not acquainted; as, *unfamiliar* with law.

un-fas-ten (un-fàs′n), *v.t.* to untie; loosen:—*v.i.* to become untied.

un-fa-vour-a-ble (un-fā′vėr-a-bl), *adj.* disapproving; adverse; as, an *unfavourable* opinion.—*adv.* **un-fa′vour-a-bly.**

un-feel-ing (un-fēl′ing), *adj.* 1, cruel; brutal; 2, without feeling or sensation.

un-feigned (un-fānd′), *adj.* real; sincere; without pretense; as, *unfeigned* liking.

un-fin-ished (un-fin′isht), *adj.* 1, not complete; imperfect; 2, not perfected; lacking artistic finish.

un-fit (un-fit′), *v.t.* (unfit-ted, unfit-ting], to make unsuitable or unable: —*adj.* not suitable; not qualified.—*n.* **un-fit′ness.**

un-flag-ging (un-flag′ing), *adj.* not drooping or languishing; as, *unflagging* zeal, courage, energy, etc.

un-fledged (un-flejd′), *adj.* 1, without feathers, as a very young bird; 2, hence, undeveloped; immature.

un-flinch-ing (un-flinch′ing), *adj.* standing steadfast; resolute; firm; as, *unflinching* courage.

un-fold (un-fōld′), *v.t.* 1, to spread open, as a pocket map; 2, to reveal by degrees:—*v.i.* to open, as a flower.

un-for-tu-nate (un-fôr′tū-nit), *adj.* 1, not lucky; not prosperous; 2, badly chosen; regrettable; as, an *unfortunate* speech:—*n.* an unlucky or unsuccessful person.—*adv.* **un-for'tu-nate-ly.**

un-found-ed (un-foun'did), *adj.* **1,** without basis; not established; **2,** hence, without basis of fact; as, an *unfounded* rumor.

un-furl (un-fûrl'), *v.t.* to loose from its fastenings and spread out, as a flag or sail:—*v.i.* to be spread out or unfolded.

un-gain-ly (un-gān'li), *adj.* clumsy; uncouth; as, a tall, *ungainly* figure.

un-god-ly (un-god'li), *adj.* wicked; sinful; unholy.—*n.* **un-god'li-ness.**

un-gov-ern-a-ble (un-guv'ẽr-na-bl), *adj.* uncontrollable; unruly; rebellious; as, an *ungovernable* temper.

un-grate-ful (un-grāt'fool), *adj.* not thankful; not appreciative.—*adv.* **un-grate'ful-ly.**—*n.* **un-grate'ful-ness.**

un-ground-ed (un-groun'did), *adj.* **1,** without reason; baseless; as, *ungrounded* fear; **2,** without instruction; untaught.

un-guent (ung'gwent), an ointment or salve for burns, sores, etc.

un-gu-late (ung'gū-lit), *adj.* hoofed. —*n.* a hoofed animal.

un-hal-lowed (un-hal'ōd), *adj.* **1,** not set apart as sacred; **2,** wicked; godless.

un-hand (un-hand'), *v.t.* to let go of; release from one's grasp.

un-hand-y (un-han'di), *adj.* [unhand-i-er, unhand-i-est], clumsy; inconvenient.

un-hap-py (un-hap'i), *adj.* [unhap-pi-er, unhap-pi-est], **1,** sorrowful; wretched; **2,** unfortunate; unsuccessful; as, an *unhappy* venture; **3,** unsuitable; as, an *unhappy* choice.—*n.* **un-hap'pi-ness.**

un-health-y (un-hel'thi), *adj.* [un-health-i-er, unhealth-i-est], **1,** not well; sickly; **2,** harmful to health.

un-heard (un-hûrd'), *adj.* **1,** not heard; as, an *unheard* cry; **2,** not given a hearing:—**unheard—of,** not heard of before; strange.

un-hinged (un-hinjd'), *adj.* unsettled; disordered (of a mind, person, opinions, etc.).

un-ho-ly (un-hō'li), *adj.* [unho-li-er, unho-li-est], not sacred; godless; wicked.—*adv.* **un-ho'li-ly.**—*n.* **un-ho'li-ness.**

un-horse (un-hôrs'), *v.t.* [unhorsed, unhors-ing], to throw or drag from the back of a horse; unseat.

u-ni-corn (ū'ni-kôrn'), *n.* a fabulous animal resembling a horse, with one straight horn projecting from its forehead.

u-ni-cy-cle (ū'ni-sī'kl), *n.* a vehicle with but one wheel (used in circuses, on stages, etc.)

u-ni-form (ū'ni-fôrm'), *adj.* **1,** not changing in form, degree, or character; unvarying; as, a *uniform* climate; **2,** like one another; as, the two cities have *uniform* traffic laws:—*n.* an official or regulation dress belonging to a particular class or profession: —*v.t.* to furnish with uniforms.—*adv.* **u'ni-form'ly.**—*n.* **u'ni-form'i-ty.**

u-ni-fy (ū'ni-fī'), *v.t.* [unified, unify-ing], **1,** to form into one; unite; **2,** to make alike in form.—*n.* **u'ni-fi-ca'tion.**

u-ni-lat-er-al (ū'ni-lat'ẽr-al), *adj.* pertaining to, involving, or affecting one (side, party, nation, etc.) only; as, a *unilateral* leaf (like that of the elm); a *unilateral* contract (binding on one party; *unilateral* action (by one member of an associated group).

un-in-tel-li-gi-ble (un'in-tel'i-ji-bl), *adj.* incapable of being understood.

un-ion (ūn'yun), **1,** *n.* the act of joining two or more things into one whole; the state of being so joined; **2,** that which is made one by the joining of parts; **3,** a league; confederation; **4,** an association of workers often called *labor union* or *trade union;* **5,** a coupling for connecting pipes or rods; **6,** agreement; harmony; as, we work together in perfect *union:*—**the Union,** the United States of America.—*v.t.* **un'ion-ize'.**—*n.* **un'ion-ist; un'ion-ism.**

union jack, a jack, or small flag, emblematic of union:—**Union Jack,** the British flag; also, a U.S. naval flag which consists of 50 white stars on a blue ground.

u-nique (ū-nēk'), *adj.* **1,** unlike anything else; without an equal; **2,** extremely unusual; striking; as, a *unique* design.

u-ni-son (ū'ni-sun; ū'ni-zun), *n.* **1,** harmony; agreement; concord; **2,** a selection or passage of music in which all performers sing or play the same part together.

u-nit (ū'nit), *n.* **1,** one person or thing of a number constituting a group; as, each citizen is a *unit* in the national body; also, a single group in an association made up of groups; as, a patrol is one of the *units* of a scout troop; **2,** in *mathematics,* the smallest whole number; one; **3,** a fixed amount, quantity, distance, etc., taken as a

standard of measurement; as, the
pound is a *unit* of weight.

U-ni-tar-i-an (ū'ni-târ'i-an), *n.* one
who denies the doctrine of the Trinity
(holding that God exists in only one
person), and believes the teachings,
but rejects the divinity, of Jesus.

u-nite (ū-nīt'), *v.t.* [unit-ed, unit-ing],
1, to join together; combine so as to
make one; as, to *unite* states into a
nation; **2,** to bring into close association; ally, as to be *united* in fellowship:
—*v.i.* **1,** to be joined together; **2,** to
act together; as, let us *unite* to make
this a success.—*adj.* **u'ni-tive.**

U-nit-ed Na-tions, an international
organization for coöperation in the
preservation of peace, formed after
World War II on a charter drawn up
in San Francisco in 1945. It has three
main bodies: a Security Council,
General Assembly, and Secretariat,
along with many specialized agencies.
Its permanent headquarters are in
New York City.

u-ni-ty (ū'ni-ti), *n.* [*pl.* unities], **1,** the
state of being one; union of parts;
2, harmony; agreement; as, to act in
unity; **3,** the number one.

u-ni-va-lent (ū'ni-vā'lent; ū-niv'a-
lent), *adj.* **1,** in *chemistry,* the capacity
of an element or radical to combine
with but one atomic weight of hydrogen, chlorine, sodium, etc.; **2,** in
biology, single or unpaired: said of a
chromosome.

u-ni-ver-sal (ū'ni-vûr'sal), *adj.* **1,**
pertaining to the entire universe; as,
the *universal* law of gravitation; also,
embracing or including the whole;
prevailing everywhere; as, *universal*
peace; **2,** entire; whole.—*adv.* **u'ni-
ver'sal-ly.**—*n.* **u'ni-ver-sal'i-ty.**

u-ni-verse (ū'ni-vûrs'), *n.* the whole
system of existing material things;
all creation; loosely, the world.

u-ni-ver-si-ty (ū'ni-vûr'si-ti), *n.* [*pl.*
universities], an institution for instruction and study in the higher branches
of learning, as in the arts, medicine,
law, etc.

un-just (un-just'), *adj.* unfair; not
just.—*adv.* **un-just'ly.**—*n.* **un-just'ness.**

un-kempt (un-kempt'), *adj.* **1,** not
combed; dishevelled; **2,** slovenly.

un-kind (un-kīnd'), *adj.* not kind or
sympathetic; harsh; as, *unkind* words.
—*adv.* **un-kind'ly.**—*n.* **un-kind'ness.**

un-known (un-nōn'), *adj.* not appre-
hended; not recognized or discovered.
—*n.* an unknown person or thing, esp.

in *mathematics* the symbol for an
unknown quantity.

un-lace (un-lās'), *v.t.* [unlaced, unlac-
ing], to undo the lacing of; as, to
unlace a shoe.

un-law-ful (un-lô'fool), *adj.* contrary
to law; illegal.—*adv.* **un-law'ful-ly.**

un-less (un-les'), *conj.* if not; except
when; as, we can't be promoted *unless*
we study.

un-let-tered (un-let'ẽrd), *adj.* untaught; also, unable to read or write.

un-like (un-līk'), *adj.* having no resemblance; different.—*n.* **un-like'ness.**

un-like-ly (un-līk'li), *adj.* [unlike-li-er,
unlike-li-est], **1,** not probable; not
likely to happen; **2,** not giving promise
of success; as, an *unlikely* plan.

un-like-li-hood (un-līk'li-hood') *n.*
improbability.

un-lim-it-ed (un-lim'i-tid), *adj.* without boundaries; as, an *unlimited* area;
also, without restriction; as, *unlimited*
power.

un-load (un-lōd'), *v.t.* **1,** to remove
freight or a cargo from; as, to *unload*
a wagon; **2,** to remove from a car,
wagon, ship, etc.; as, to *unload* freight;
3, to free or relieve from care or trouble:
—*v.i.* to discharge freight.

un-lock (un-lok'), *v.t.* **1,** to unfasten;
to release the catch on (a door, trunk,
etc., that has been fastened with a
lock); **2,** to make clear; reveal; as,
to *unlock* a mystery.

un-loose (un-lōōs'), *v.t.* [unloosed,
unloos-ing], to unfasten; set at liberty.

un-luck-y (un-luk'i), *adj.* [unluck-i-er,
unluck-i-est], **1,** not lucky or fortunate;
as, an *unlucky* speculator; **2,** accompanied by, or tending to bring, bad
luck; as, an *unlucky* day.—*adv.* **un-
luck'i-ly.**

un-man (un-man'), *v.t.* [unmanned,
unman-ning], to rob of courage and
strength.

un-man-ly (un-man'li), *adj.* [unman-
li-er, unman-li-est], not manly; lacking
courage.

un-man-ner-ly (un-man'ẽr-li), *adj.*
rude; without courtesy; impolite.

un-mask (un-màsk'), *v.t.* to remove a
disguise from; show the true nature of:
—*v.i.* to lay aside a mask; also, to
reveal one's true nature.

un-mean-ing (un-mēn'ing), *adj.* senseless; without significance.

un-mer-ci-ful (un-mûr'si-fool), *adj.*
without kindness or pity; cruel.—*adv.*

un-mer′ci-ful-ly.—*n.* **un-mer′ci-ful-ness.**

un-mis-tak-a-ble (un′mis-tāk′a-bl), *adj.* incapable of being mistaken or misunderstood; clear.—*adv.* **un′mis-tak′a-bly.**

un-mit-i-gat-ed (un-mit′i-gāt′id), *adj.* **1,** not lessened or softened; as, *unmitigated* suffering; **2,** absolute; as, an *unmitigated* liar.

un-nat-u-ral (un-nat′ū-ral), *adj.* **1,** not like or representing nature; artificial; **2,** cruel; inhuman.

un-nec-es-sar-y (un-nes′e-sèr-i), *adj.* not needed.—*adv.* **un-nec′es-sar-i-ly.**

un-nerve (un-nûrv′), *v.t.* [unnerved, unnerv-ing], to deprive of control, strength, or courage; as, the accident *unnerved* him.

un-num-bered (un-num′bèrd), *adj.* **1,** not counted; **2,** countless; numerous.

un-pack (un-pak′), *v.t.* **1,** to take out; as, to *unpack* books from a box; **2,** to remove the contents of; as, to *unpack* the box.

un-par-al-leled (un-par′a-leld), *adj.* unrivalled; without an equal; having no parallel.

un-pin (un-pin′), *v.t.* [unpinned, unpin-ning], to unfasten by taking out pins.

un-pleas-ant (un-plez′ant), *adj.* disagreeable; distasteful.—*n.* **un-pleas′-ant-ness.**

un-pop-u-lar (un-pop′ū-lèr), *adj.* not generally liked or approved.

un-prec-e-dent-ed (un-pres′i-den′-tid), *adj.* without precedent; unusual; novel.

un-pre-pared (un′pri-pârd′), *adj.* not ready; not equipped; done without preparation.

un-prin-ci-pled (un-prin′si-pld), *adj.* lacking moral standards; unscrupulous.

un-qual-i-fied (un-kwol′i-fīd′; un-kwôl′i-fīd′), *adj.* **1,** lacking the proper qualifications; unfit; **2,** absolute; utter; as, *unqualified* disapproval.

un-ques-tion-a-ble (un-kwes′chun-a-bl), *adj.* not to be doubted or questioned; indisputable.—*adv.* **un-ques′-tion-a-bly.**

un-rav-el (un-rav′el), *v.t.* [unravelled, unravel-ling], **1,** to untangle; pull out, as knitting; **2,** to solve, as a mystery: —*v.i.* to become untangled or solved.

un-rea-son-a-ble (un-rē′zn-a-bl), *adj.* **1,** not influenced or controlled by reason; **2,** demanding too much; exorbitant; as, *unreasonable* prices. —*adv.* **un-rea′son-a-bly.**

un-re-served (un′ri-zûrvd′), *adj.* **1,** not held in reserve; **2,** frank; outspoken.—*adv.* **un′re-serv′ed-ly.**

un-ri-valled or **un-ri-valed** (un-rī′vald), *adj.* unequalled; without a rival; peerless.

un-roll (un-rōl′), *v.t.* **1,** to open out (something which is rolled); **2,** to display:—*v.i.* to unfold; develop.

un-ruf-fled (un-ruf′ld), *adj.* serene; calm; smooth; not agitated or disturbed: used of a person, water, etc.

un-rul-y (un-rōōl′i), *adj.* paying no attention to rules or commands; hard to manage; ungovernable.—*n.* **un-rul′i-ness.**

un-sa-vour-y (un-sā′vèr-i), *adj.* **1,** lacking taste or seasoning; **2,** disagreeable to taste or smell; **3,** morally bad.

un-say (un-sā′), *v.t.* [unsaid (un-sed′), unsay-ing], to take back (something that has been said).

un-scathed (un-skāthd′), *adj.* uninjured.

un-screw (un-skrōō′), *v.t.* to take the screws from; **2,** to take out or loosen by turning; as, to *unscrew* a nut.

un-scru-pu-lous (un-skrōō′pū-lus), *adj.* unprincipled; indifferent to right and wrong.—*n.* **un-scru′pu-lous-ness.**

un-seal (un-sēl′), *v.t.* to open by breaking or removing the seal.

un-sea-son-a-ble (un-sē′zn-a-bl), *adj.* **1,** coming at an ill-chosen time; untimely; as, an *unseasonable* request; **2,** out of season.

un-seat (un-sēt′), *v.t.* **1,** to remove from a seat; also, to unhorse; **2,** to depose; deprive of the right to sit as representative; as, to *unseat* a senator or member of Parliament.

un-seem-ly (un-sēm′li), *adj.* improper; not fitting:—*adv.* in an unsuitable manner.

un-seen (un-sēn′), *adj.* **1,** not seen; beyond the range of vision; **2,** invisible.

un-self-ish (un-sel′fish), *adj.* not selfish; generous; thoughtful of others.

un-set-tle (un-set′l), *v.t.* [unset-tled, unset-tling], to change from a firm position or state; disturb; make uncertain.

un-set-tled (un-set′ld), *adj.* **1,** not determined; undecided: an *unsettled* question; **2,** not settled; uncertain; as weather; **3,** unpaid: an *unsettled* bill; **4,** uninhabited by settlers; **5,** disturbed; disordered: *unsettled* times.

un-shake-a-ble (un-shāk′a-bl), *adj.*

firm; determined; as, an *unshakeable* belief. Also, **un-shak′a-ble.**

un-sheathe (un-sheth′), *v.t.* [unsheathed, unsheath-ing], to take from its scabbard, as a dagger or sword.

un-sight-ly (un-sīt′li), *adj.* not pleasant to see; ugly.

un-skil-ful or **un-skill-ful** (un-skil′-fool), *adj.* not expert or skilful; awkward.

un-skilled (un-skild′), *adj.* not expert; untrained; not having learned a trade.

un-so-phis-ti-cat-ed (un′so-fis′ti-kāt′id), *adj.* 1, not worldly wise; simple; artless; 2, pure; genuine.

un-sound (un-sound′), *adj.* not sound; not healthy; weak.—*n.* **un-sound′ness.**

un-speak-a-ble (un-spēk′a-bl), *adj.* 1, not to be expressed or described in words; as, *unspeakable* happiness; 2, inexpressibly bad; as, an *unspeakable* crime.—*adv.* **un-speak′a-bly.**

un-sta-ble (un-stā′bl), *adj.* not firm or stable; easily unbalanced.

un-stead-y (un-sted′i), *adj.* not steady; shaky; as, *unsteady* nerves; also, unreliable.

un-strung (un-strung′), *adj.* 1, having the strings loosened or missing, as a harp, banjo, violin, etc.; 2, nervously upset; unnerved.

un-sub-stan-tial (un′sub-stan′shal), *adj.* 1, not strong; not firmly put together; 2, imaginary; not real.

un-tan-gle (un-tang′gl), *v.t.* [untangled, untan-gling], to take out knots or snarls from; as, to *untangle* yarn.

un-ti-dy (un-tī′di), *adj.* [unti-di-er, unti-di-est], not neat; slatternly; slovenly.—*adv.* **un-ti′di-ly.**—*n.* **un-ti′di-ness.**

un-tie (un-tī′), *v.t.* [untied, unty-ing], to unfasten by loosening (a knot); to unfasten (an object) by loosening the knot that holds it; as, to *untie* a necktie; to *untie* a shoe; hence, to loose or set free; as, to *untie* a dog: —*v.i.* to become unfastened.

un-til (un-til′), *prep.* to or up to; as, he played *until* noon:—*conj.* to the degree, time, or place that; as, he talked *until* he became hoarse; he studied *until* the sun was high.

un-time-ly (un-tīm′li), *adj.* not at the right moment or on the right occasion; happening too soon:—*adv.* inopportunely; too soon.

un-to (un′tōō; un′tŏŏ), *prep. Archaic* or *Poetic*, to; as, "Suffer little children to come *unto* me."

un-told (un-tōld′), *adj.* 1, not expressed or revealed; 2, not numbered; hence, very great; as, *untold* riches.

un-true (un-trōō′), *adj.* 1, false; contrary to the truth; 2, not faithful to one's duty; disloyal; 3, varying from a standard; not straight, as lines, angles, etc.

un-truth (un-trōōth′), *n.* 1, lack of adherance to fact; incorrectness; 2, a falsehood, or lie.

un-tu-tored (un-tū′tĕrd), *adj.* not taught; having little learning.

un-used (un-ūzd′), *adj.* 1, not put to use; 2, not accustomed; as, *unused* to luxury.

un-u-su-al (un-ū′zhoo-al), *adj.* uncommon; strange; remarkable.

un-ut-ter-a-ble (un-ut′ĕr-a-ble), *adj.* unspeakable; not to be expressed in words; as, *unutterable* grief.—*adv.* **un-ut′ter-a-bly.**

un-veil (un-vāl′), *v.t.* to reveal by taking off a veil or covering; uncover, as a monument:—*v.i.* to take off one's veil.

un-war-y (un-wâr′i), *adj.* not cautious; careless; heedless.—*adv.* **un-war′i-ly.**

un-well (un-wel′), *adj.* not in good health.

un-wield-y (un-wēl′di), *adj.* difficult to move or manage because of size, shape, or weight; bulky; clumsy.—*n.* **un-wield′i-ness.**

un-will-ing (un-wil′ing), *adj.* reluctant; not willing; disinclined.—*adv.* **un-will′ing-ly.**—*n.* **un-will′ing-ness.**

up-wind (un-wīnd′), *v.t.* and *v.i.* [unwound (un-wound′), unwind-ing], to loosen or become loose by uncoiling.

un-wise (un-wīz′), *adj.* lacking good judgment; indiscreet.—*adv.* **un-wise′ly.**

un-wit-ting (un-wit′ing), *adj.* unaware; unconscious; not deliberate; as, he was the *unwitting* cause of all our trouble.—*adv.* **un-wit′ting-ly.**

un-wont-ed (un-wun′tid; un-wōn′-tid), *adj.* unusual; uncommon; as, *unwonted* kindness.

un-wor-thy (un-wûr′thi), *adj.* [unwor-thi-er, unwor-thi-est], 1, lacking merit; hence, discreditable; as, an *unworthy* suggestion; 2, not deserving; as, he is *unworthy* of our confidence; 3, not suitable or becoming; as, such conduct is *unworthy* of you.—*n.* **un-wor′thi-ness.**

un-writ-ten (un-rit′n), *adj.* 1, not expressed or recorded in writing; as, *unwritten* legends; 2, blank; without writing; as, an *unwritten* page.

up (up), *adv.* 1, from a lower to a higher

position or degree; opposite of *down;* as, to go *up* in an elevator; come *up* from a mine; **2,** into notice or consideration; as, to bring *up* a question; **3,** at or to a higher scale, price, or volume; as, the prices are going *up;* to swell *up;* **4,** even with something in time, degree, space, amount, etc.; as, to catch *up* in a race; keep *up* with the news; **5,** on one's feet; out of bed; **6,** to a person, point, or place; as, he came *up* to us to ask directions; **7,** used with many verbs to give emphasis or to indicate that the action is finished; as, to tear *up* a report; to store *up* wealth; to finish *up* a job; to nail *up* a box; to be swallowed *up* in a crowd; the stream has dried *up:—prep.* **1,** from a lower to a higher place on or along; as, to walk *up* the hill; **2,** toward the source of; as, *up* the river; also, toward the interior of (a country or region); **3,** to, at, or near the top of; as, to climb *up* a rope:—*adj.* **1,** leading, moving, or sloping toward a higher place; upward; as, on the *up* grade; **2,** in *golf*, ahead of an opponent; as, two holes *up;* **3,** well-informed; abreast of the times; as, *up* on politics; **4,** exhausted; at an end; as, my stay is *up;* **5,** above the horizon; as, the sun is *up;* **6,** out of bed; as, the patient will be *up* tomorrow.

up-braid (up-brād′), *v.t.* to chide or blame; reprove severely.

up-bring-ing (up′bring′ing), *n.* one's rearing from childhood; care and training of the young while growing up.

up-heav-al (up-hēv′al), *n.* **1,** a lifting from below; esp., an elevation of some part of the earth's crust, as in an earthquake; **2,** a violent political or social disturbance, as a revolution.

up-hill (up′hil′), *adv.* to a higher level or point on a slope; upward; as, we climbed *uphill:—adj.* (up′hil′), **1,** sloping upward; ascending; **2,** hence, tiresome; difficult; as, study is sometimes *uphill* work.

up-hold (up-hōld′), *v.t.* [upheld (-held′), uphold-ing], **1,** to support; hold up; keep erect; **2,** to encourage or aid; also, to defend; as, to *uphold* the right of free speech; **3,** to maintain or confirm; as, the umpire's decision was *upheld.*

up-hol-ster (up-hōl′stẽr), *v.t.* to provide (furniture) with cushions, springs, and coverings.—*n.* **up-hol′ster-er.**—*n.* **up-hol′ster-y.**

up-keep (up′kēp′), *n.* the maintaining of a house, automobile, etc., in good

order and repair; also, the cost of maintenance.

up-land (up′land′; up′land), *n.* an elevated region, esp. in the interior of a country:—*adj.* pertaining to an elevated region or to a hilly land.

up-lift (up-lift′), *v.t.* **1,** to raise; elevate; **2,** to better the condition of, esp. morally, socially, or intellectually:—*n.* (up′lift′), **1,** an elevation; **2,** hence, a tendency to move toward a higher standard.

up-on (u-pon′), *prep.* **1,** on; resting on the top or surface of; as, *upon* the shelf; **2,** against; as, *upon* the wall; **3,** at the moment of; as, *upon* arrival; **4,** so as to meet or find; as, to come *upon* a bargain.

up-per (up′ẽr), *adj.* **1,** higher in place, position, rank, etc.; as, the *upper* storey of a house; the *upper* classes; **2,** farther inland; as, the *upper* Nile.

up-per-most (up′ẽr-mōst′), *adj.* highest in place, rank, or authority: opposite of *lowermost.*

up-right (up′rīt′; up-rīt′), *adj.* **1,** standing erect; in a vertical position; **2,** just; honest; honourable:—*adv.* in an erect position:—*n.* (up′rīt′), something set or standing straight up, as a timber supporting a beam.—*n.* **up-right′ness.**

up-rise (up-rīz′), *v.i.* [*p.t.* uprose (-rōz′), *p.p.* upris-en (-riz′n), *p.pr.* upris-ing], **1,** to get up; rise; **2,** to ascend or rise into view; as, the sun then *uprose.*

up-ris-ing (up-rīz′ing; up′rīz′ing), *n.* a rebellion against authority; revolt.

up-roar (up′rōr′), *n.* tumult; confusion.

up-root (up-rōōt′), *v.t.* to pull up by the roots; hence, to remove; get rid of.

up-set (up-set′), *v.t.* [upset, upset-ting], **1,** to knock over; overturn; as, to *upset* a chair; also, to interfere with; as, our arrangements have been *upset;* **2,** to disturb the normal mental or physical condition of; as, the news of the accident *upset* her:—*v.i.* to overturn; as, the car *upset* at the corner:—*adj.* **1,** overturned; also, interfered with; **2,** physically or mentally disturbed:—*n.* (up′set′), **1,** the act of overturning or disturbing; **2,** the state of being overturned; **3,** mental or physical disturbance.

up-shot (up′shot′), *n.* final result; conclusion; outcome.

up-side (up′sīd′), *n.* the upper part:—**up-side—down,** with the top part at the bottom; topsyturvy.

up-stage (up'stāj'), *adv.* towards the rear of the stage.—*adj.* **1,** pertaining to the back of the stage; **2,** *Colloq.* haughtily aloof; conceited.

up-stairs (up'stârz'), *adv.* toward or on an upper floor:—*adj.* (up'stârz'), belonging to, or on, an upper floor; as, an *upstairs* room:—*n.* (up'stârz'), the part of a building above the first floor.

up-stand-ing (up-stan'ding), *adj.* **1,** of *persons,* erect and tall (with good posture); **2,** upright; honourable.

up-start (up'stärt'), *n.* a person who has suddenly risen from obscurity to wealth, power, or honour, esp. one who presumes on his success:—*v.i.* and *v.t.* (up-stärt'), to start or cause to start up.

up-stream (up'strēm'), *adv.* against the current.—*adj.* situated, directed, or taking place upstream.

up-surge (up'sûrj'), *n.* a surge upward: —*v.i.* (up-sûrj'), to surge up.

up-swing (up'swing'), *n.* a trend upward:—*v.i.* (up-swing'), to advance or improve.

up-thrust (up'thrust'), *n.* **1,** a push upward; **2,** in *geology,* an upward lift (often violent) of part of the earth's crust.

up—to—date (up'—too–dāt'), *adj.* up to the minute in style, fads, information, etc.

up-town (up'town), *adv.* towards the upper part of a town or city, esp. the part away from the main business section.

up-turn (up-tûrn'), *v.t.* to turn upward or over; as, to *upturn* sod:—*n.* (up'-tûrn'), a change for the better; as, there has been an *upturn* in business.

up-ward (up'wĕrd), *adj.* moving toward a higher place or level; as, an *upward* march.

up-ward (up'wĕrd) or **up-wards** (up'wĕrdz), *adv.* **1,** in an ascending direction; from lower to higher; **2,** toward a higher rank or position; as, to climb *upward* in a profession; **3,** toward the source; as, the explorers followed the river *upward;* **4,** indefinitely more; as, children of three years and *upward.*

u-ran-i-nite (ū-ran'i-nīt'), *n.* a black mineral containing uranium, radium, thorium, and lead: the massive variety, pitchblende, was first mined by Eldorado Mining and Refining Ltd. at Port Radium, N.W.T., later north of Lake Athabasca in Saskatchewan, and by 1957 at Elliot Lake in Northern Ontario.

u-ra-ni-um (ū-rā'ni-um), *n.* a hard, malleable, white, radioactive metallic chemical element: over 99% occurs as the isotope U-238, less than 1% as the isotope U-235, the basic ingredient in some types of atom bombs and nuclear piles. (See *uraninite.*)

ur-ban (ûr'ban), *adj.* pertaining to a city or town; as, *urban* residents.

ur-bane (ûr-bān'), *adj.* suavely courteous; polite; affable.—*adv.* **ur-bane'-ly.**—*n.* **ur-ban'i-ty.**

ur-chin (ûr'chin), *n.* a small boy, esp. a mischievous one.

u-re-thra (ū-rē'thra), *n.* the canal by which urine is discharged from the bladder.

urge (ûrj), *v.t.* [urged, urg-ing], **1,** to force onward; drive faster; as, he *urged* on his steed; **2,** to advocate strongly; as, to *urge* the necessity of help; **3,** to try to influence (a person) by arguments, entreaties, etc.; as, we *urged* him to accept the nomination.

ur-gen-cy (ûr'jen-si), *n.* the pressure of necessity; need for instant action; as, the *urgency* of the case is unquestioned.

ur-gent (ûr'jent), *adj.* **1,** calling for immediate attention; pressing; as, an *urgent* need; **2,** insistent; eager; as, an *urgent* plea.

u-rine (ū'rin), *n.* the fluid secreted by the kidneys, and cast off as waste.—*n.* **u'ri-nal** (a place for urinating):—*v.i.* **u'ri-nate'** (to pass urine).—*n.* **u'ri-nal'y-sis** (analysis of the urine).—*adj.* **u'ri-na-ry.**

urn (ûrn), *n.* **1,** a kind of vase, usually with a rounded body and a base or pedestal; **2,** a closed vessel with a tap and a heating device, used for making and keeping hot such beverages as tea and coffee.

us (us), objective case of *we.*

us-a-ble (ūz'a-bl), *adj.* fit to be employed or used.

us-age (ūz'ij; ūs'ij), *n.* **1,** the way of using; treatment; as, the furniture shows rough *usage;* **2,** settled habit or custom; established use; as, in accordance with the best *usage.*

use (ūz), *v.t.* [used, us-ing], **1,** to make use of; employ; as, to *use* the best material; **2,** to practice or make habitual use of; as, to *use* economy; **3,** to treat, act, or behave toward; as, she *uses* her servants harshly; **4,** to make accustomed; as, man is *used* to ease:—*v.i.* to be accustomed; as, they *used* to work together:—*n.* (ūs), **1,** the act of employing; the application of anything to a particular purpose; as, the *use* of steel for rails; **2,** the condition of being used; as, this room is in *use;* **3,** the method of using; treatment; **4,** familiarity; custom; continued practice; **5,** practical worth; utility; as, an ornament of no *use;* also, advantage; as, there is no *use* in apologizing; **6,** reason for employing; as, we have no *use* for the goods.—*adj.* use′ful.—*adv.* use′ful-ly.—*n.* use′ful-ness.—*n.* us′er.

use-less (ūs′lis), *adj.* **1,** having, or being of, no practical worth; as, *useless* rubbish; **2,** without results; as, *useless* efforts.

ush-er (ush′ẽr), *n.* **1,** one who escorts or directs persons to seats in a church, theatre, etc.:—*v.t.* **1,** to escort or accompany; **2,** to announce; herald; as, high winds often *usher* in the month of March.

u-su-al (ū′zhoo-al), *adj.* customary; regular; as, come at the *usual* time.—*adv.* u′su-al-ly.—*n.* u′su-al-ness.

u-su-rer (ū′zhoo-rẽr), *n.* a person who lends money and demands an unlawfully high rate of interest.

u-surp (ū-zûrp′), *v.t.* to take possession of by force or unjust means; as, to *usurp* the power of a king.—*n.* u-surp′er.—*n.* u′sur-pa′tion (ū′zûr-pā′-shun).

u-su-ry (ū′zhoo-ri), *n.* **1,** the practice of lending money at a rate higher than the lawful rate; **2,** a very high rate of interest.

u-ten-sil (ū-ten′sl), *n.* an implement or vessel for use in practical work; esp., one for use in housework.

u-ter-us (ū′tẽr-us), *n.* [*pl.* uteri (-ī)], the womb, a hollow muscular organ in which the young are conceived, developed, and nourished till birth.

u-til-i-tar-i-an (ū′til-i-târ′i-an); *adj.* characterized primarily by usefulness rather than by beauty of appearance.—*n.* u-til′i-tar′i-an-ism.

u-til-i-ty (ū-til′i-ti), *n.* [*pl.* utilities], **1,** the quality or state of being suitable for use; general usefulness; **2,** (often *public utility*), an organization, as a gas or electric company, a railroad, etc., that sells a service to a community.

u-ti-lize or **u-ti-lise** (ū′ti-līz′), *v.t.* [utilized, utiliz-ing], to make profitable; make use of; as, surgery now *utilizes* X-rays.—*n.* u′ti-li-za′tion.

ut-most (ut′mōst), *adj.* **1,** greatest; of the highest degree; as, use the *utmost* care; **2,** most removed in space or time; farthest; as, the radio reaches the *utmost* points of the globe:—*n.* **1,** the extreme limit; as, he can be trusted to the *utmost;* **2,** all that is possible; as, I will do my *utmost* to aid.

u-to-pi-an (ū-tō′pi-an), *adj.* visionary; ideal; impossibly perfect; as, *utopian* schemes, dreams, etc.—*n.* an idealist or visionary: from **U-to′pi-a**, [Greek, no place], an imaginary island with a perfect (or sinless) society flourishing on it.

¹ut-ter (ut′ẽr), *adj.* entire; absolute; complete; as, *utter* absurdity; *utter* gloom.—*adv.* ut′ter-ly.

²ut-ter (ut′ẽr), *v.t.* to speak; sound.

ut-ter-ance (ut′ẽr-ans), *n.* **1,** expression by the voice; speech; also, style of speaking; as, indistinct *utterance;* **2,** something, usually of importance, expressed in words.

ut-ter-most (ut′ẽr-mōst′), *adj.* utmost; in the farthest, greatest, or highest degree:—*n.* the furthest extent or degree; as, he worked to the *uttermost* to finish the job.

u-vu-la (ū′vū-la), *n.* the small, fleshy projection hanging from the soft palate above the back of the tongue.

ux-o-ri-ous (uk-sō′ri-us; ug-zō′), *adj.* excessively, or foolishly fond of, or submissive to, one's wife.

V

V, v (vē), *n.* [*pl.* V's, v's], **1,** the 22nd letter of the alphabet, following U; **2,** anything shaped like the letter V; **3,** the Roman numeral for five.

va-can-cy (vā′kan-si), *n.* [*pl.* vacancies], **1,** the state of being empty; emptiness; **2,** a position open to applicants; **3,** a room or rooms offered for rent; **4,** an empty space; blank.

va-cant (vā′kant), *adj.* **1,** empty, as an unoccupied room; **2,** lacking thought or expression; as, a *vacant* look.

va-cate (va-kāt′), *v.t.* [vacat-ed, vacat-ing], to make empty; give up the possession of; as, to *vacate* a house:—*v.i.* to give up a house, office, etc.; move out.

va-ca-tion (va-kā′shun), *n.* a time of

recreation or rest from regular duties:—
v.i. to pass one's vacation.—*n.* **va-ca'-tion-er**; **va-ca'tion-ist**.

vac-ci-nate (vak'si-nāt'), *v.t.* [vac-cinat-ed, vaccinat-ing], to inoculate, or give a mild form of a disease to, in order to prevent a severe attack of the disease; esp., to make immune to smallpox.—*n.* **vac'ci-na'tion**.

vac-cine (vak'sēn; vak'sin), *n.* **1,** a virus, or poison, obtained from cows affected with a disease called cow-pox, and injected into the human body to prevent smallpox; **2,** any substance used for inoculation.

vac-il-late (vas'i-lāt'), *v.i.* [vacillat-ed, vacillat-ing], to be changeable or uncertain in opinion, course of action, etc.—*n.* **vac'il-la'tion**.

va-cu-i-ty (va-kū'i-ti), *n.* [*pl.* vacuities], **1,** space not filled or occupied; **2,** mental inactivity or emptiness; **3,** lack of intelligence in facial expression.—*adj.* **vac'u-ous**.

vac-u-um (vak'ū-um), *n.* **1,** a space entirely empty of matter; **2,** a sealed space, such as the inside of an incandescent lamp bulb, emptied or nearly emptied of air by artificial means.— **vacuum tube**, a sealed glass or metal tube, as for radio or television, containing a filament (cathode), a plate (anode), and a grid for controlling the flow of electrons.

vag-a-bond (vag'a-bond), *n.* one who roams about with no permanent abode; esp., an idle fellow without honest means of support; a vagrant or tramp:—*adj.* wandering about without a fixed dwelling-place; roaming.

va-gar-y (va-gâr'i), *n.* [*pl.* vagaries], a wild or extravagant notion or act; eccentricity; freak of fancy; whim; as, *vagaries* of conduct; the *vagaries* of fortune.

va-gi-na (va-jī'na), *n.* [*Latin,* a sheath], the canal leading from the uterus to the vulva (external genital organs).—*adj.* **vag'i-nal** (as, a *vaginal* douche).

va-grant (vā'grant), *adj.* wandering from place to place without purpose and without a settled home:—*n.* a tramp.—*n.* **va'gran-cy** (as, he was held on a charge of *vagrancy*).

vague (vāg), *adj.* [va-guer, va-guest], not clearly seen, stated, or understood; hazy; as, a *vague* answer.—*adv.* **vague'ly**.

vail (vāl), *n.* Same as *veil.* (*Archaic.*)

vain (vān), *adj.* **1,** valueless; empty; idle; as, *vain* boasting; **2,** without

force or effect; useless; as, *vain* efforts; **3,** proud of small accomplishments or of personal appearance; conceited.—*adv.* **vain'ly**.

vain-glor-y (vān'glōr'i), *n.* excessive vanity or pride in oneself or one's accomplishments.—*adj.***vain'glor'i-ous**.

val-ance (val'ans) *n.* a short curtain hung across the top of a window or around a bedstead.

vale (vāl), *n.* *Poetic,* a valley.

val-e-dic-to-ry (val'e-dik'to-ri), *n.* and *adj.* a farewell speech, esp. one given at a school or college commencement.—*n.* **val'e-dic-to'ri-an** (the person who gives the farewell oration).

va-lence (vā'lens), *n.* **1,** in *chemistry,* the combining power of an element measured by the number of hydrogen atoms which one atom or one radical of the element will unite with: thus, oxygen has a *valence* of two since it combines with two atoms of hydrogen; **2,** in *biology,* the degree of power existing between chromosomes, serums, etc., to combine or produce a specific effect upon each other.

val-en-tine (val'en-tīn'), *n.* **1,** a greeting card or gift sent on Saint Valentine's Day, February 14; **2,** a sweetheart chosen on that day.

va-le-ri-an (va-lē'ri-an), *n.* **1,** an herb with small pink or white flowers and a peculiarly pungent odour; **2,** a drug obtained from the dried root of this plant.

val-et (val'it; val'ā), *n.* a manservant who personally attends a man, taking care of his apartment, clothes, etc.:—*v.t.* to serve (someone) as a valet.

val-iant (val'yant), *adj.* brave; heroic; as, *valiant* warriors; *valiant* deeds.

val-id (val'id), *adj.* **1,** based on fact; sound; as, a *valid* argument; **2,** executed with all formalities required by law; legally binding; as, a *valid* contract.—*adv.* **val'id-ly.**—*n.* **va-lid'it-y** (va-lid'i-ti).

val-i-date (val'i-dāt'), *v.t.* [validat-ed, validat-ing], to ratify; confirm; make valid.

va-lise (va-lēs'), *n.* a travelling-bag, usually of leather, for holding clothes and toilet articles.

val-ley (val'i), *n.* [*pl.* valleys], low land between hills or mountains.

val-our or **val-or** (val'ẽr), *n.* fearlessness in facing danger; bravery.—*adj.* **val'or-ous**.

val-u-a-ble (val'ū-a-bl), *adj.* **1,** costly, or worth a good price; as, a *valuable* jewel; **2,** of great importance or use; as, a *valuable* hint:—**valuables,** *n.pl.* costly possessions, esp. small personal things, as jewellery.

val-u-a-tion (val′ū-ā′shun), *n.* **1,** the act of estimating the worth of something; **2,** an estimated worth or price.

val-ue (val′ū), *n.* **1,** worth; the quality which makes a thing worth possessing; as, this ring has only a sentimental *value;* **2,** a fair or adequate return; as, to receive *value* for money spent; **3,** worth in money; as, the *value* of the property increased; **4,** estimated worth; as, he gives his ability a high *value:*—*v.t.* [valued, valu-ing], **1,** to estimate the worth of; put a price on; as, to *value* an estate; **2,** to esteem highly; hold dear; as, to *value* a friendship.

valve (valv), *n.* **1,** a mechanical device for opening and closing a pipe, and thus regulating or directing the movement through it of a gas, liquid, etc.; **2,** a device, as in a blood-vessel, consisting often of two or more folds, or flaps, that open in the direction of the flow of the blood and are closed by a reversal of the flow; **3,** either of the two pieces of the shell of a clam, oyster, etc.—*adj.* **val′vu-lar.** ·

vamp (vamp), *n.* **1,** the part of a shoe just above the sole, covering the toes and extending to the sides; **2,** anything patched up; esp., a literary work based on old material:—*v.t.* to patch with new material.

vam-pire (vam′pīr), *n.* **1,** according to superstition, a ghost, or a corpse restored to life, supposed to suck the blood of sleeping persons; **2,** one who preys on others, or makes a living at the expense of others; **3,** any of various South American bats which suck the blood of animals.

¹van (van), *n.* the front line or front part of an army or fleet; hence, a pioneering or leading position; as, in the *van* of progress.

²van (van), *n.* a large covered truck.

va-na-di-um (va-nā′di-um), *n.* a rare, silver-white, chemical element found in iron, lead, and uranium ores: used to toughen steel and make it shock-resistant.

van-dal (van′d'l), *n.* one who wilfully destroys or defaces anything beautiful or valuable, esp. a work of art.—*n.* **van′dal-ism.**

vane (vān), *n.* **1,** a movable device fastened to an elevated object to show which way the wind blows; a weather-

cock; **2,** a flat surface that is moved around an axis by wind or water; as, the *vane* that turns the wheel of a wind-mill into the wind; **3,** the flat, spreading part of a feather.

van-guard (van′gärd′), *n.* the first line or advance guard of an army; the van.

va-nil-la (va-nil′a), *n.* **1,** a tropical American climbing plant of the orchid family; **2,** the pod or bean of various species of this plant, used to make a flavouring extract; **3,** the flavouring so obtained.

van-ish (van′ish), *v.i.* **1,** to disappear; fade from sight; as, the ship *vanished* beyond the horizon; **2,** to pass out of existence; be lost; as, hopes *vanish.*

van-i-ty (van′i-ti), *n.* [*pl.* vanities], **1,** shallow pride, as in one's appearance or attainments; conceit; **2,** the quality of being worthless; futility; as, the *vanity* of human pomp; **3,** a small case, usually of metal, containing a mirror, face powder, and rouge.

van-quish (vang′kwish), *v.t.* to conquer; subdue; defeat; as, to *vanquish* an enemy.

van-tage (vàn′tij), *n.* **1,** a superior position or opportunity; advantage; as, to gain a point of *vantage* in a battle; **2,** in tennis, advantage; the first point scored following deuce.

vap-id (vap′id), *adj.* lacking life or spirit; flat; pointless; as, *vapid* talk.

va-por-ize (vā′pėr-īz′), *v.t.* and *v.i.* [vaporized, vaporiz-ing], to change, or be changed, into vapour.

va-pour or **va-por** (vā′pėr), *n.* the gaseous form of a liquid or solid; as, water *vapour,* or steam, is formed when water is boiled; **2,** moisture floating in the air, as fog or mist; also, a cloudlike substance floating in the air and robbing it of clearness, as smoke.—*adj.* **va′por-ous.**—*adj.* **va′pour-y.**

va-pour-ing (vā′pėr-ing), *adj.* foolishly boastful.—*n.* bragging; bluster; windy talk (esp. in *pl.*)

var-i-a-ble (vâr′i-a-bl), *adj.* changeable; inconstant; fitful; as, a *variable* wind:—*n.* that which is subject to change.—*n.* **var′i-a-bil′i-ty; var′i-a-ble-ness.**

var-i-ance (vâr′i-ans), *n.* **1,** the state of being changeable or different; change; difference; also, the degree of change; as, a *variance* of several dollars in price; **2,** a difference of opinion; discord; as, it is painful to be at *variance* with one's friends.

var-i-ant (vâr′i-ant), *adj.* differing from others in the same general class; showing variation; as, a *variant* form of a word:—*n.* something that differs from another thing in form, though essentially the same; as, "color" is a *variant* of "colour."

var-i-a-tion (vâr′i-ā′shun), *n.* **1,** a modification or change; diversity; as, dahlias show great *variations* in colour; **2,** amount or extent of change or difference; as, there is little *variation* in the temperature; **3,** in *music,* the repetition of a single melody with changes and elaborations.

var-i-cose (var′i-kōs′; vâr′), *adj.* swollen or dilated; as, *varicose* veins.

var-ied (vâr′id), *adj.* **1,** of different sorts; diversified; as, a *varied* collection of pictures; **2,** variegated.

var-i-e-gate (vâr′i-e-gāt′; vâr′i-gāt′), *v.t.* [variegat-ed, variegat-ing], to change the appearance of, by marking with different colours; streak; spot.—*n.* **var′i-e-ga′tion.**

va-ri-e-ty (va-rī′e-ti), *n.* [*pl.* varieties], **1,** the state of being different; diversity; change; as, we like the *variety* of city life; **2,** a collection of unlike objects; as, she received a *variety* of gifts; **3,** a plant or animal differing in some details from others of the same general class or kind; as, one *variety* of palm bears dates, another *variety* bears coconuts.

var-i-om-e-ter (vâr′i-om′e-tẽr), *n.* **1,** an instrument for determining changes in magnetism, esp. in the earth's magnetic field; **2,** a device consisting of two coils of wire connected in series and arranged so that one coil may rotate within the other: used for radio tuning by varying the inductance in the circuit.

var-i-ous (vâr′i-us), *adj.* **1,** different; diverse; of several sorts; as, the *various* colours of autumn leaves; **2,** several; as, he met the man on *various* occasions.

var-nish (vär′nish), *n.* **1,** a liquid preparation of resin used for giving gloss to the surface of wood, metal, etc.; **2,** the coating of gloss resulting from an application of varnish; **3,** superficial smoothness or polish; outside show:—*v.t.* **1,** to cover with varnish; give a gloss to; **2,** to cover up the defects of; gloss over.

var-si-ty (vär′si-ti), *n. Colloq.* the team (usually athletic) representing a college or university (as distinguished from the scrub, or second, team).

var-y (vâr′i), *v.t.* [varied, vary-ing], to alter in appearance, shape, substance,

etc.; change; as, to *vary* the order of events:—*v.i.* to undergo a change; differ; as, the price *varies* daily.

vas-cu-lar (vas′kū-lẽr), *adj.* pertaining to the vessels of an animal or vegetable body which carry or convey fluids, as blood-vessels and lymph vessels in animals, and sap ducts in plants:—**vascular bundle,** in stems, roots, and leaves of plants, the sheaf of tissues composed of the actively growing cells (cambium), the woody tissue (xylem), and the food-conducting tissue (phloëm).

vas-cu-lum (vas′kū-lum), *n.* a metal case used by botanists for carrying specimens as they are collected.

vase (vās; väz; vāz), *n.* a vessel of glass, pottery, etc., used as an ornament or for holding flowers.

vas-sal (vas′al), *n.* **1,** in the feudal system, one who placed himself under the protection of a lord or master, and in return rendered homage and service; one who held land under feudal tenure; **2,** a servant.

vast (väst), *adj.* very great in size, extent, amount, etc.; as, a *vast* plain; a *vast* fortune.—*n.* **vast′ness.**

vat (vat), *n.* a large tank, tub, or vessel, esp. one for holding liquors, dyes, etc., in process of manufacture.

vaude-ville (vōd′vil; vô′di-vil), *n.* a kind of theatrical performance consisting of a series of songs, dances, acrobatic feats, short dramatic sketches, etc.

¹vault (vôlt), *n.* a leap or jump made with the use of the hands or with the aid of a pole:—*v.i.* and *v.t.* to leap over; jump; as, to *vault* a fence.—*n.* **vault′er.**

²vault (vôlt), *n.* **1,** an arched roof or ceiling; also, any arched covering; esp., the arch of the sky; **2,** storage space, as in a cellar; **3,** a cavern; tomb; **4,** a steel room, as in a bank, in which valuables are kept:—*v.t.* to shape like a vault; provide with an arched ceiling.

vaunt (vônt; vänt), *v.i.* to brag:—*v.t.* to boast of; display boastfully; as, to *vaunt* one's courage:—*n.* a boast; brag; vain display.—*adj.* **vaunt′ing.**

veal (vēl), *n.* the meat of the calf.

vec-tor (vek′tẽr), *n.* and *adj.* **1,** in *biology,* an organism, as, an insect, that transmits a disease-producing virus; **2,** in *mathematics,* a quantity having direction as well as magnitude, denoted by a system of equal and

AX, AY, Vectors
AB, Resultant

parallel line segments; **3,** in *astronomy,* an imaginary line joining the centre of a body with gravitational pull, as the sun, to the centre of a satellite revolving around it (called *radius vector*).

veer (vēr), *v.t.* and *v.i.* to change in direction; shift; as, the ship *veered* suddenly to the south.

veer-y (vēr'i), *n.* a thrush (*Hylocichla fuscescens*), found from Newfoundland to B.C.: smaller than the wood thrush, it is noted for the rare beauty of its song, delivered on a descending scale.

Ve-ga (vē'ga), *n.* [*Arabic,* falling vulture], a blue-white star of the constellation Lyra, one of the brightest in the Northern Hemisphere.

veg-e-ta-ble (vej'e-ta-bl), *n.* **1,** a plant, esp. one cultivated for food, as potatoes, corn, beans, etc.; **2,** the edible portion of such a plant:—*adj.* **1,** pertaining to plants; **2,** derived from plants; as, *vegetable* fats.

veg-e-tar-i-an (vej'e-târ'i-an), *n.* one who avoids meat as an element of diet, and advocates vegetable food, usually with the addition of butter, milk, and eggs:—*adj.* **1,** pertaining to vegetarians; **2,** consisting· of vegetables; as, a *vegetarian* diet.

veg-e-tate (vej'e-tāt'), *v.i.* [vegetat-ed, vegetat-ing], to grow as a plant does; hence, of persons; to lead an idle, unthinking existence.—*adj.* **veg'-e-ta'tive.**

veg-e-ta-tion (vej'e-tā'shun), *n.* **1,** the act of growing or vegetating; **2,** plant life; plants in general; as, the dense *vegetation* of the jungle.

ve-he-ment (vē'e-ment), *adj.* **1,** very violent; furious; as, a *vehement* wind; **2,** passionate; earnest; as, *vehement* words.—*adv.* **ve'he-ment-ly.**—*n.* **ve'he-mence.**

ve-hi-cle (vē'i-kl;. vē'hi-kl), *n.* **1,** any kind of conveyance, esp. one used on land, as a car, wagon, bicycle, etc.; **2,** anything which may be used as a medium for communicating thought, feeling, knowledge, etc., as a newspaper, radio, etc.—*adj.* **ve-hic'u-lar** (vē-hik'ū-lėr).

veil (vāl), *n.* **1,** a thin, gauzy, ornamental covering for the face; **2,** a piece of fabric hanging from the head over the shoulders, as worn by a nun; **3,** a curtain or covering which conceals something; as, a *veil* of clouds over the mountains; **4,** anything which hides; as, a *veil* of mystery:—**to take the veil,**

to become a nun:—*v.t.* **1,** to cover with, or as with, a veil or curtain; **2,** to hide.

vein (vān), *n.* **1,** one of the tubelike vessels which carry the blood to or toward the heart; **2,** one of the branching ribs of a leaf or of the wing of an insect; **3,** a crack or seam in rock; also, ore, etc., filling a fissure in rock; as, a *vein* of coal; **4,** a long streak of a different colour, as in wood or marble; **5,** a particular strain or disposition; peculiarity of mood, speech, etc.; as, he spoke in a solemn *vein*:—*v.t.* to cover, fill, or form with veins.—*adj.* **veined** (vānd).—*adj.* **vein'y.**

veld or **veldt** (felt; velt), *n.* the open grasslands of South Africa (with very few shrubs or trees).

vel-lum (vel'um), *n.* **1,** a fine parchment, usually made of calfskin, intended for binding books, writing upon, etc.; **2,** a kind of paper or cotton cloth made in imitation of this.

ve-loc-i-pede (ve-los'i-pēd'), *n.* **1,** a light vehicle for children, with a large wheel in front and two small wheels behind, and moved by pedals; **2,** an early form of the bicycle or tricycle; **3,** a railroad hand- or gas-driven car.

ve-loc-i-ty (ve-los'i-ti), *n.* [*pl.* velocities], the rate of motion of a moving object; speed; swiftness; as, the *velocity* of a bullet.

ve-lours (ve-lōōr'), *n.* [*pl.* velours], any of various woven fabrics having a pile, or nap, like that of velvet.

vel-vet (vel'vit), *n.* a closely woven silk material with a short, thick pile, or nap, of fine upright threads:—*adj.* **1,** made of velvet; **2,** as soft as velvet.

vel-vet-een (vel've-tēn'), *n.* a cotton material resembling velvet; imitation velvet.

vel-vet-y (vel'vi-ti), *adj.* soft; like velvet, esp. to the touch.

ve-nal (vē'nl), *adj.* **1,** that can be bribed; as, a *venal* judge; **2,** that can be bought; as, *venal* services; **3,** mercenary; corrupt; as, a *venal* bargain, arrangement, etc.—*n.* **ve-nal'i-ty.**

ve-na-tion (vē-nā'shun), *n.* the vein structure or arrangement, as in a plant leaf or an insect's wing.

vend (vend), *v.t.* to sell; offer for sale.

ven-det-ta (ven-det'a), *n.* a private feud for revenge by bloodshed, usually carried on by the relatives of a murdered man.

ven-dor or **vend-er** (ven'dėr), *n.* a seller; usually, a hawker or pedlar.

Ve-ne-tian (vi-nē′shan) **blind**, a window shade of horizontal, overlapping slats on cords, (turnable so as to admit or exclude light or air).

ve-neer (ve-nēr′), *v.t.* **1**, to overlay with a thin surface of more valuable or beautiful material; as, to *veneer* a pine table with walnut; **2**, hence, to cover or conceal (something cheap or mean) with a surface polish; give a gloss to: —*n.* **1**, a thin surface of fine wood overlaying wood of a poorer quality; **2**, outside show; pretence; surface elegance; as, a *veneer* of fine manners.

ven-er-a-ble (ven′ėr-a-bl), *adj.* **1**, so old and wise as to be worthy of reverence; as, a *venerable* judge; **2**, sacred by reason of associations of a religious or historic nature; as, a *venerable* cathedral.—*adv.* **ven′er-a-bly.**

ven-er-ate (ven′ėr-āt′), *v.t.* [venerated, venerat-ing], to regard with the highest respect and honour; reverence. —*n.* **ven′er-a′tion.**

venge-ance (ven′jans), *n.* punishment inflicted for a wrong endured; repayment for an offence; as, he swore *vengeance* on his enemy.

venge-ful (venj′fool), *adj.* vindictive; desiring revenge.—*adv.* **venge′ful-ly.**

ve-ni-al (vē′ni-al), *adj.* **1**, pardonable; as, a *venial* sin (opposite of *mortal*); **2**, excusable, as a fault, error or slip.

ven-i-son (ven′zn; ven′i-zn), *n.* deer's flesh used for meat.

ven-om (ven′um), *n.* **1**, the poison secreted by certain serpents, spiders, etc., which makes their bite or sting injurious and sometimes fatal; **2**, spite; malignity.

ven-om-ous (ven′um-us), *adj.* **1**, full of poison; **2**, capable of giving a poisonous bite or sting; as, a *venomous* snake; **3**, spiteful; as, a *venomous* rumour.—*adv.* **ven′om-ous-ly.**

ve-nous (vē′nus), *adj.* pertaining to veins; as, *venous* blood (which has lost its oxygen, become charged with carbon dioxide, and is now dark red).

vent (vent), *n.* **1**, a small opening for the passage of air, smoke, etc.; **2**, an outlet; free play; utterance; as, to give *vent* to one's indignation:—*v.t.* **1**, to let out through a hole, as steam; **2**, to give an outlet to; relieve by speech or action; as, she *vented* her displeasure in words.

ven-ti-late (ven′ti-lāt′), *v.t.* [ventilated, ventilat-ing], **1**, to provide with a proper circulation of air, by letting in fresh and driving out stale air, as through open windows, shafts, etc.; **2**, to purify by exposure to fresh air; **3**, to bring out (a subject) for public examination and discussion.—*n.* **ven′ti-la′tion.**

ven-ti-la-tor (ven′ti-lā′tėr), *n.* a contrivance for admitting fresh air and letting out foul or stagnant air.

ven-tral (ven′tral), *adj.* pertaining to, or situated on or near, the belly of an animal; as, the *ventral* fins of a fish.

ven-tri-cle (ven′tri-kl), *n.* either of the two lower chambers of the heart, from which blood is forced into the arteries.

ven-tril-o-quism (ven-tril′o-kwizm), *n.* the art of speaking in such a way that the voice appears to come from another person or place.—*n.* **ven-tril′o-quist.**

ven-ture (ven′tūr), *n.* **1**, a dangerous or daring undertaking; **2**, an enterprise involving risk; as, a business *venture:* —*v.t.* [ventured, ventur-ing], **1**, to risk; expose to danger; as, he *ventured* his life in the attempt; also, to stake; as, he *ventured* all his money in the enterprise; **2**, to hazard; give; as, to *venture* a guess:—*v.i.* **1**, to dare; **2**, to take a chance; run a risk.

ven-ture-some (ven′tūr-sum), *adj.* **1**, daring; bold; as, a *venturesome* spirit; **2**, dangerous; as, a *venturesome* undertaking.

ven-tur-ous (ven′tūr-us), *adj.* **1**, fearless; venturesome; **2**, full of risks.

ve-ra-cious (ve-rā′shus), *adj.* **1**, habitually telling the truth; **2**, true; reliable; as, a *veracious* report.—*n.* **ve-rac′i-ty.**

ve-ran-da or **ve-ran-dah** (ve-ran′da), *n.* a long open porch, usually roofed.

verb (vûrb), *n.* that part of speech which expresses action, state of being, or condition; a word which states something; as, in the sentence "John studied his lesson," the *verb* is "studied."

ver-bal (vûr′b'l), *adj.* **1**, pertaining to words; also, consisting merely of words; as, his penitence was only *verbal;* **2**, spoken; not written; as, a *verbal* agreement; **3**, pertaining to a verb; as, a *verbal* prefix; **4**, literal; word for word, as a translation: —**verbal noun**, a noun formed by adding -*ing* to a verb; as, in "Seeing is believing," "seeing" and "believing" are *verbal nouns.*—*adv.* **ver′bal-ly.**

ver-ba-tim (vėr-bā′tim), *adv.* word for word; as, to report a speech *verbatim:*—*adj.* literal.

all (ôl), ôr; up, mūte, cûr, cōōl, book; oil, out; th, thin; *th,* the.

ver-be-na (vėr-bē′na), *n.* a garden plant with large heads of flowers of various colours and spicy fragrance.

ver-bi-age (vûr′bi-ij), *n.* the use of many unnecessary words in speech or writing; wordiness; verbosity.

ver-bose (vėr-bōs′), *adj.* wordy, long-winded; prolix.—*n.* **ver-bos′i-ty** (-bos′).

ver-dant (vûr′dant), *adj.* **1,** covered with fresh green grass or foliage; fresh; green; as, a *verdant* landscape; **2,** *Colloq.*, fresh and untried in knowledge or judgment; inexperienced; as, a *verdant* freshman.

ver-dict (vûr′dikt), *n.* **1,** the decision of a jury on a case in court; as, the jury's *verdict* was for acquittal; **2,** the expression of any important decision.

ver-di-gris (vûr′di-grēs′), *n.* a green-blue film of copper carbonate that forms on copper, brass, or bronze surfaces: it is used as a medicine, pigment, and dye.

ver-dure (vûr′dūr), *n.* **1,** greenness or freshness, esp. of grass and growing plants; **2,** green grass, growing plants, etc.—*adj.* **ver′dur-ous.**

¹verge (vûrj), *n.* a boundary; brink; an extreme edge; as, the country was on the *verge* of revolution.

²verge (vûrj), *v.i.* [verged, verg-ing], **1,** to approach closely; be on the border; as, his actions *verge* on treason; **2,** to tend; incline; as, a day *verging* toward its close.

ver-ger (vûr′jėr), *n.* **1,** one who carries a rod or staff (verge) before a bishop, dean, etc., in a procession; **2,** one who takes care of a church interior.

ver-i-fy (ver′i-fī′), *v.t.* [verified, verifying], to check the truth or correctness of; as, to *verify* the answer to an arithmetic problem.—*n.* **ver′i-fi′er.**—*n.* **ver′i-fi-ca′tion.**—*adj.* **ver′i-fi′a-ble.**

ver-i-ly (ver′i-li), *adv.* in truth; truly.

ver-i-ta-ble (ver′i-ta-bl), *adj.* actual; genuine; true; as, the rain was a *veritable* godsend.—*adv.* **ver′i-ta-bly.**

ver-i-ty (ver′i-ti), *n.* [*pl.* verities], the quality or state of being true; reality; also, that which is true; a truth; fact.

ver-mi-form (vûr′mi-fôrm′) **appendix,** a blind, wormlike tube, about as thick as a pencil, 3″ to 6″ long, in the lower right-hand part of the abdomen: it serves no known useful function.

ver-mil-ion (vėr-mil′yun), *n.* a brilliant red pigment; a vivid red colour like this pigment:—*adj.* of the colour of vermilion.

ver-min (vûr′min), *n.* [*pl.* vermin], usually in *pl.*, harmful and offensive insects or small animals, as flies, lice, rats, etc.—*adj.* **ver′min-ous.**—*n.* **ver′-mi-cide′** (a drug, etc., used to kill parasitic worms, esp. intestinal worms).

ver-mouth (vûr-mōōth′), *n.* a liqueur made of white wine flavoured with wormwood, etc.: used esp. in cocktails.

ver-nac-u-lar (vėr-nak′ū-lėr), *n.* and *adj.* **1,** one's native tongue; **2,** the dialect of a particular country or place: often distinguished from *literary;* **3,** the vocabulary peculiar to a business, profession, etc.; as, the *vernacular* of the stage.

ver-nal (vûr′nal), *adj.* **1,** pertaining to, or appearing in, the spring; as, *vernal* breezes; **2,** springlike; hence, youthful.

ver-sa-tile (vûr′sa-tĭl′; vûr′sa-til), *adj.* capable of dealing with many subjects, or of doing many things equally well; as, a *versatile* writer; a *versatile* workman.—*n.* **ver′sa-til′i-ty** (vûr′sa-til′i-ti).

verse (vûrs), *n.* **1,** a single metrical line in poetry; **2,** loosely, a group of metrical lines; a stanza; **3,** a form of literary composition possessing rhythm; poetry: distinguished from *prose;* **4,** any of the short divisions of a chapter in the Bible.—*v.i.* **ver′si-fy′.**—*n.* **ver′-si-fi-ca′tion.**

versed (vûrst), *adj.* thoroughly trained; skilled; learned; as, *versed* in law.

ver-sion (vûr′zhun; vûr′shun), *n.* **1,** a translation from one language into another; as, a revised *version* of the Bible; **2,** a report or description of an occurrence from an individual point of view; as, his *version* of the accident differs from mine.

vers li-bre (vâr′lēbr′′), *n.* [*French,* free verse], a verse form marked by lack of rhyme, by irregular metre, and by a length of line based on cadence (or rhythm) and thought content.

ver-sus (vûr′sus), *prep.* against; as, Toronto *versus* Montreal.

ver-te-bra (vûr′te-bra), *n.* [*pl.* vertebrae (vûr′te-brē′) or vertebras (vûr′te-braz)], one of the single bones, or segments, which are joined together to make the backbone.

ver-te-brate (vûr′te-brāt′; -brit), *adj.* having a backbone, or spinal column:—*n.* an animal with a spinal column.

ver-tex (vûr′teks), *n.* [*pl.* vertices (vûr′ti-sēz′) or vertexes (vûr′tek-sez)], the highest point; top; apex; as, the *vertex* of a pyramid.

cat, āge, fär, câre, ȧsk; ten, ēve, latėr; (i) pity, rely, senāte; ice; top; nō.

ver-ti-cal (vûr′ti-k'l), *adj.* upright; in the direction in which a tree grows: opposite of *horizontal;* as, the flagpole in our schoolyard is *vertical.—adv.* **ver′ti-cal-ly.**

ver-ti-go (vûr′ti-gō′), *n.* in *medicine,* dizziness or giddiness.

verve (vûrv), *adj.* enthusiasm, vigour, or energy, esp. in literary or artistic work; as, his sculpture has life and *verve.*

ver-y (ver′i), *adj.* [ver-i-er, ver-i-est], **1,** absolute; complete; as, the *very* truth; **2,** identical; the same; as, that is the *very* dress; **3,** mere; as, the *very* thought of an accident frightens me:—*adv.* in a high degree; extremely; as, she does *very* good work; the book was *very* dull.

ves-per (ves′pėr), *n.* and *adj.* an evening prayer, hymn, or service: usually **ves′pers.**

ves-sel (ves′l), *n.* **1,** a hollow container, usually for liquids, as a barrel, cup, etc.; **2,** a tube or canal in the body through which a fluid passes; as, a blood-*vessel;* **3,** a ship; boat, esp. a large one.

vest (vest), *n.* **1,** a waistcoat; a man's sleeveless garment, worn beneath the coat; also, a similar jacket worn by women; **2,** a woven or knitted undershirt; an undervest; **3,** an ornamental insertion in the front of a woman's dress or jacket; vestee:—*v.t.* **1,** to dress in a garment; as, they *vested* the choir in white robes; **2,** to clothe or endow with authority, power, etc.; as, the church *vests* its bishops with certain powers; **3,** to put into the care of another; as, the management of the company is *vested* in its officials:—*v.i.* to clothe oneself with vestments.

ves-tal (ves′tl), *adj.* and *n.* pertaining to a virgin or nun; pure; chaste. **—Vestal Virgins,** six virgin priestesses who tended the sacred, perpetual fire on the altar in the temple of Vesta in ancient Rome.

ves-ti-bule (ves′ti-būl′), *n.* a small, enclosed entry between the outer and inner doors of a house or other building; also, an enclosed entrance to a railway coach.

ves-tige (ves′tij), *n.* originally, a footprint or track; hence, a visible sign or trace of something that is gone or has disappeared; as, not a *vestige* of the house remained.—*adj.* **ves-tig′i-al** (imperfectly developed or rudimentary).

vest-ment (vest′ment), *n.* a robe; esp. an official or ceremonial garment, or one worn by priests, ministers, choir, etc., during services.

ves-try (ves′tri), *n.* [*pl.* vestries], **1,** a room in a church where the clergy put on their vestments, or where the sacred vessels of the service are kept; **2,** in some Protestant churches, a room or building attached to a church, and used as a chapel or Sunday-school room; **3,** in the Anglican Church, a body of men who direct the affairs of a parish.—*n.* **ves′try-man.**

ves-ture (ves′tūr; chėr), *n. Archaic,* clothing.

vetch (vech), *n.* any of several plants of the pea family (*Vicia*) grown as fodder or catch crops.

vet-er-an (vet′ėr-an), *adj.* possessing experience due to age; long trained or practised, esp. as a soldier:—*n.* **1,** a person of age and experience; one grown old in service; **2,** a soldier of any age who has seen active service in war.

vet-er-i-nar-y (vet′ėr-i-nėr-i), *adj.* pertaining to the treatment of diseases and injuries of animals; as, a *veterinary* surgeon:—*n.* [*pl.* veterinaries], one who practises veterinary medicine or surgery.—*n.* **vet′er-i-nar′i-an.**

ve-to (vē′tō), *n.* [*pl.* vetoes], the right of a president, governor, or other executive, to prevent temporarily or permanently the enactment of a measure as law; a prohibition by someone in authority:—*v.t.* to prohibit; refuse to approve; as, the teacher *vetoed* the idea of a class party; esp., to refuse assent to (a bill) so as to prevent its becoming a law, or to cause its reconsideration.—*n.* **ve′to-er.**

vex (veks), *v.t.* **1,** to irritate by small annoyances; harass; make angry; **2,** to agitate; disquiet; as, angry winds *vexed* the sea.

vex-a-tion (veks-ā′shun), *n.* annoyance; displeasure; irritation; as, he plainly showed his *vexation;* a source of annoyance; as, the sore finger was a *vexation.—adj.* **vex-a′tious.**

vi-a (vī′a), *prep.* by the way of; as, he travelled *via* the Great Lakes.

vi-a-ble (vī′a-bl), *adj.* able to live, grow, or maintain a separate existence; as a *viable* child (esp. one of premature birth); *viable* seeds.—*n.* **vi′a-bil′i-ty.**

vi-a-duct (vī′a-dukt), *n.* a bridge, usually built of arched masonry or of steel, for carrying a road or a railway over a valley or ravine.

vi-al (vī′al), *n.* a small glass bottle with a stopper, as for medicines; a phial.

vi-and (vī′and), *n.* **1,** an article of food; **2, viands,** provisions; food.

all (ôl), ôr; up, mūte, cûr, cōol, book; oil, out; th, thin; *th,* the.

vi-brant (vī′brant), *adj.* **1,** vigorous; full of life and feeling; **2,** resonant; resounding; sonorous; as, the *vibrant* tones of a violin.

vi-brate (vī-brāt′), *v.i.* [vibrat-ed, vibrat-ing], **1,** to move back and forth with a regular motion; **2,** to quiver, as the voice; make a tremulous sound: —*v.t.* **1,** to cause to move to and fro; **2,** to cause to quiver.—*n.* **vi-bra′tor.** —*n.* **vi-bra′to** (vi-brä′tō), in *music*, a tremulous effect.—*adj.* **vi′bra-to-ry.**

vi-bra-tion (vī-brā′shun), *n.* a quivering or trembling, as of the voice; also, regular motion to and fro.

vi-bur-num (vī-bûr′num), *n.* a genus of shrub or small tree, as the bush cranberry, or snowball (with large round clusters of small white flowers), cultivated for ornament.

vic-ar (vik′ẽr), *n.* **1,** in the Roman Catholic Church, a member of the clergy acting as representative of one of the higher clergy; **2,** in the Anglican Church, a minister who is the head of one chapel in a large parish; also, a bishop's representative in charge of a church.—*n.* **vic′ar-age.**

vi-ca-ri-ous (vī-kâr′i-us), *adj.* **1,** substituted; endured for another; as, Christ's *vicarious* sacrifice, punishment, or suffering (for sin) on the Cross; **2,** deputed; as, *vicarious* authority; felt by sympathetic participation in another's experience; as, *vicarious* pleasure.

vice (vīs), *n.* **1,** a debasing practice or habit, as drunkenness; **2,** wickedness; corruption; **3,** a bad trick or habit, as of a horse, dog, etc.

vice- (vīs-), *prefix* meaning *in place of, deputy;* as, *vice*-chancellor, *vice*-regal.

vice—pres-i-dent (vīs′-prez′i-dent), *n.* the officer next in rank below a president, who takes the place of the president during the latter's absence or disability. Also written **vice president.**

vice-roy (vīs′roi), *n.* a ruler of a colony or province, representing, and ruling with the authority of, a king.—*adj.* **vice′re-gal.**

vi-ce ver-sa (vī′si vûr′sa), the terms being reversed; the other way around; as, that man calls black white and, *vice versa,* white black.

vi-cin-i-ty (vi-sin′i-ti), *n.* [*pl.* vicinities], **1,** nearness; closeness; **2,** a region about or near; neighbourhood.

vi-cious (vish′us), *adj.* **1,** faulty; defective; as, *vicious* reasoning; **2,** corrupt; depraved; wicked; as, a *vicious* life; **3,** bad-tempered; malicious; as, *vicious* remarks.

vi-cis-si-tude (vi-sis′i-tūd′), *n.* a complete, unexpected change of circumstances; as, the *vicissitudes* of war.

vic-tim (vik′tim), *n.* **1,** a living being sacrificed in a religious ceremony; **2,** a person or animal injured or killed in some misfortune or calamity; **3,** a sufferer from mental or physical disease; **4,** a person who is cheated; a dupe.—*v.t.* **vic′tim-ize′.**

vic-tor (vik′tẽr), *n.* a conqueror; one who wins:—*adj.* conquering.

vic-tor-i-ous (vik-tōr′i-us), *adj.* **1,** having conquered in battle or contest; triumphant; as, a *victorious* army; **2,** marked by or ending in victory.

vic-to-ry (vik′to-ri), *n.* [*pl.* victories], **1,** the defeat of an enemy; **2,** any triumph.

vict-ual (vit′l), *v.t.* to supply or stock with food:—**victuals,** *n.pl.* food for human beings; provisions.

vi-cu-na (vi-kōōn′ya), *n.* and *adj.* a cud-chewing mammal of the high Andes, resembling the alpaca and the llama, that furnishes a very soft, fine, reddish wool, the source of *vicuna* cloth.

vi-del-i-cet (vi-del′i-sit), *adv.* full form of *viz.*; namely.

vid-e-o (vid′i-ō′), *n.* and *adj.* television, esp. the picture phase of a broadcast as distinct from the *audio,* or sound, portion; as, *video* frequency; *video* channel.

vie (vī), *v.i.* [vied, vying], to compete, as in games, school-work, etc.; contend for superiority.

view (vū), *n.* **1,** the act of seeing; inspection; as, this is worth a nearer *view;* **2,** that which is seen; scene; as, a splendid *view* of the river; **3,** a range of mental perception; as, to take a broad *view* of the matter; **4,** range of vision; as, the top of the hill is beyond our *view;* **5,** a picture of a scene, object, or person; **6,** a way of looking at anything mentally; opinion; as, he held advanced *views;* **7,** purpose or aim; as, to make your plans with a *view* to success:—*v.t.* **1,** to see; gaze at; look upon; **2,** to survey mentally; form an opinion of.

view-point (vū′point′), *n.* the position or place from which one looks at something; esp., a way of looking at or judging things; as, a person of very narrow *viewpoint.*

vig-il (vij′il), *n.* **1,** a keeping awake during a time usually devoted to sleep; watchfulness; **2,** (usually *vigils*), religious devotions in the evening or night; **3,** the eve of a feast day.

vig-i-lant (vij′i-lant), *adj.* keenly watchful; alert.—*n.* **vig′i-lance.**

vig-i-lan-te (vij′i-lan′ti) *n. U.S.* a member of a vigilance committee.

vi-gnette (vin-yet′), *n.* **1,** a short literary composition marked by grace, delicacy, or subtlety; **2,** an ornamental design (as of vine leaves, grapes, etc.) used on a title page, or as the headpiece or tailpiece of a chapter, etc.; **3,** any engraving, etc., that shades off gradually into the background or the unprinted paper.

vig-our or **vig-or** (vig′ẽr), *n.* physical or mental strength or energy; vitality. —*adj.* **vig′or-ous.**

vi-king (vī′king), *n.* one of the Scandinavian, or Norse, sea rovers, who terrorized the coasts of Europe from the eighth to the tenth century.

vile (vīl), *adj.* [vil-er, vil-est], **1,** mean; ignoble; **2,** morally base or impure; as, a *vile* person; **3,** foul or offensive; bad; as, *vile* odours.

vil-i-fy (vil′i-fī′), *v.t.* to speak evil of; slander; defame; as, he *vilified* his mother-in-law.—*n.* **vil′i-fi-ca′tion.**

vil-la (vil′a), *n.* a large surburban or country residence, usually set in extensive grounds.

vil-lage (vil′ij), *n.* a small group of houses in a country district, smaller than a town; also, the people who live in a village.—*n.* **vil′lag-er.**

vil-lain (vil′in), *n.* **1,** a wicked person; scoundrel; **2,** in a play or novel, the character who opposes the hero; **3,** (usually *villein*), a feudal serf.

vil-lain-ous (vil′in-us), *adj.* evil; base; also, *Colloq.*, very bad; abominable.

vil-lain-y (vil′in-i), *n.* [*pl.* villainies], **1,** wickedness; **2,** an act of wickedness; a crime.

vil-lein or **vil-lain** (vil′in), *n.* under the feudal system, a serf, or half-free tiller of the soil, bound to his lord but legally free in his relations with others.

vim (vim), *n.* energy; vitality.

vin-di-cate (vin′di-kāt′), *v.t.* [vindicat-ed, vindicat-ing], to defend successfully against unjust accusation; clear from suspicion of wrong or dishonour.—*n.* **vin′di-ca′tion.**

vin-dic-tive (vin-dik′tiv), *adj.* revengeful; inclined to hold a grudge.

vine (vīn), *n.* **1,** a climbing, woody-stemmed plant; esp., the grapevine; **2,** any climbing or trailing plant.

vin-e-gar (vin′i-gẽr), *n.* a sour liquid obtained by the fermentation of cider, wine, etc., and used to season or preserve food.—*adj.* **vin′e-gar-y.**

vine-yard (vin′yẽrd), *n.* a place where grapevines are cultivated.

vin-tage (vin′tij), *n.* **1,** the act of, or the season for, gathering grapes and making wine; **2,** the yearly produce of a vineyard, or of the vineyards of a country; **3,** the wine produced in a given season; as, the *vintage* of 1872.

vi-nyl (vī′nil), *n.* a radical (CH_2CH) of hard, resistant synthetic resins and plastics used in high-fidelity records, surface coatings, and moulded articles.

vi-ol (vī′ul), *n.* a mediaeval musical instrument, the forerunner of the violin.

vi-o-la (vī-ō′la; vi-ō′la), *n.* a stringed instrument of the violin class, between the violin and violoncello in size and range.

vi-o-late (vī′ō-lāt′), *v.t.* [violat-ed, violat-ing], **1,** to treat roughly or severely; ill-use; **2,** to trespass upon; **3,** to treat irreverently; as, to *violate* a tomb; **4,** to transgress; as, to *violate* the law; also, to disregard or break, as a promise.

vi-o-la-tion (vī′ō-lā′shun), *n.* **1,** interruption; disturbance; as, *violation* of a person's privacy; **2,** irreverent treatment, as of sacred or venerable things; **3,** the act of breaking a promise, law, etc.

vi-o-lence (vī′ō-lens), *n.* **1,** great strength; as, the *violence* of the wind; **2,** furious, vehement feeling or action; **3,** an outrage; attack; **4,** injury to something that should be respected; as, to do *violence* to a shrine.

vi-o-lent (vī′ō-lent), *adj.* **1,** marked by or acting with, great physical force; as, a *violent* storm; **2,** marked by, or due to, strong feeling; intense; as, a *violent* dislike; **3,** resulting from the use of force; as, a *violent* death; **4,** extreme; as, a *violent* shock.—*adv.* **vi′o-lent-ly.**

vi-o-let (vī′ō-lit), *n.* **1,** a colour made up of blue and a small amount of red; a bluish-purple colour; the colour of the common violet; **2,** a low-growing plant with violet, yellow, or white flowers; also, the flower:—*adj.* of a violet colour: the purple violet (*Viola palmata*, var. *cucullata*) was adopted in

1936 as New Brunswick's official floral emblem.

vi-o-lin (vī/ō-lin/), *n.* **1,** the smallest and highest-tuned of modern four-string musical instruments played with a bow; **2,** a violin player.—*n.* **vi/o-lin/-ist.**

vi-o-lon-cel-lo (vī/ō-lon-chel/ō; vē/ō-lon-chel/ō), *n.* [*pl.* violoncellos], a large four-string instrument of the violin class, tuned below the viola: often shortened to *'cello* or *cello* (chel/ō).—*n.* **vi/o-lon-cel/list.**

vi-per (vī/pèr), *n.* **1,** a kind of Old World poisonous snake; an adder; also, less correctly, any poisonous snake; **2,** hence, a malignant or evil person.

vi-per—fish (vī/pèr-fish/), *n.* a small, slender fish with fanglike teeth in a gaping mouth and two rows of phosphorescent points (photophores) on each side: numerous at 50 to 500 fathoms off Vancouver and Queen Charlotte islands.

vi-ra-go (vi-rā/gō), *n.* a shrew; amazon; termagant.

vir-e-o (vir/i-ō), *n.* [*pl.* vireos], any of a family of small, American, insect-eating songbirds, olive-green or grey in colour, as, the red-eyed vireo, the yellow-throated vireo, etc.

vir-gin (vûr/jin), *n.* a maid; a chaste woman:—*adj.* **1,** chaste; maidenly; **2,** spotless; undefiled; as, *virgin* white; **3,** fresh; untouched; as, *virgin* soil. —*n.* vir-gin/i-ty.

vir-gin-al (vûr/ji-nal; vûr/ji-nl), *adj.* pertaining to a maid; chaste.

Vir-gin-i-a creep-er (vèr-jin/i-a; vèr-jin/ya), a North American woody vine, with leaves divided into five or seven parts: it has bluish-black berries: also called *woodbine* or *American ivy.*

Vir-go (vûr/gō), *n.* **1,** an equatorial constellation, the Virgin, due south of the handle of the Dipper: of its 39 visible stars Spica is the brightest; **2,** the 6th sign of the zodiac (♍), which the sun enters about August 22.

vir-gule (vûr/gūl), *n.* a slanting stroke (/) between two words to show that either may be used in interpreting the sense; as, *and/or.*

vir-ile (vir/īl; vī/rīl), *adj.* **1,** characteristic of, or befitting, a man; masculine; as, *virile* strength; **2,** forceful; masterful.—*n.* vi-ril/i-ty (vi-ril/i-ti; vī-ril/i-ti).

vir-tu-al (vûr/tū-al), *adj.* existing in effect, though not in fact; as, his words

amounted to a *virtual* confession of guilt.—*adv.* **vir/tu-al-ly.**

vir-tue (vûr/tū), *n.* **1,** moral excellence; uprightness; goodness; **2,** a particular kind of goodness; as, patience is a *virtue;* **3,** excellence or merit; as, this room has the *virtue* of being cool in summer; **4,** efficacy or effectiveness; as, the *virtue* of physical exercise; **5,** chastity; purity:—**by virtue of,** because of; as, he won *by virtue* of superior strength.

vir-tu-o-so (vûr/tū-ō/sō; chōō-), *n.* **1,** a person of great technical skill in a fine art, as singing or playing a piano, violin, etc.—*n.* **vir/tu-os/i-ty.**

vir-tu-ous (vûr/tū-us), *adj.* possessing or showing moral uprightness; chaste.

vir-u-lent (vir/ū-lent; vir/oo-lent), *adj.* **1,** poisonous; deadly; as, a *virulent* disease; **2,** hostile; bitter; as, *virulent* abuse.—*n.* **vir/u-lence.**

vi-rus (vī/rus), *n.* **1,** a poison produced in the body by a disease, and capable of causing the same disease in another body; **2,** hence, a poison that affects the mind or soul.

vis-age (viz/ij), *n.* the face.

vis-count (vī/kount/), *n.* a title of nobility next below that of earl or count and next above that of baron —*n.fem.* **vis/count/ess.**

vise (vīs), *n.* a device with two jaws which may be drawn together to hold objects firmly while work is being done on them.

vi-sé (vē/zā; vi-zā/) or **vi-sa** (vē/za), *n.* an official endorsement, as by a consul, etc., on a passport or document: —*v.t.* [*p.t.* and *p.p.* **vi/séed** (vē/zād; vi-zād/) or **vi/saed** (vē/zad); *p.pr.* **vi/sa-ing**], to examine and mark as approved.

vis-ible (viz/i-bl), *adj.* **1,** in sight; as, the ocean is *visible* from here; **2,** apparent; open; as, *visible* signs of grief.—*adv.* **vis/i-bly.**—*n.* **vis/i-bil/i-ty.**

vi-sion (vizh/un), *n.* **1,** the sense of sight; also, the act or faculty of seeing; sight; as, the accident impaired his *vision;* **2,** that which is seen in a dream or trance; as, the *visions* of a prophet; also, a phantom; **3,** a mental image; a picture created by the fancy; as, a boy's *visions* of glory; **4,** imagination; foresight; as, a leader must be a man of *vision:*—*v.t.* to see in, or as in, a vision; imagine.

vi-sion-ar-y (vizh/un-ėr-i), *adj.* **1,** dreamy; inclined to accept fancies as realities; **2,** not practical; as, a *visionary* undertaking:—*n.* [*pl.* visionaries], an impractical person.

vis-it (viz′it), *v.t.* **1**, to go or come to see, as on pleasure, friendship, business, or courtesy; **2**, to come upon, either as a blessing or as an affliction; as, *visit* us with thy mercies; the city was *visited* with an epidemic:—*v.i.* to be a guest:—*n.* **1**, a brief stay as a guest; **2**, an official or professional call; **3**, the act of going to see a person, place, or thing.—*n.* **vis′i-tor.**

vis-i-tant (viz′i-tant), *n.* **1**, a visitor, esp. a temporary guest or resident from abroad; **2**, a supernatural being (as revealed to a human being), **3**, a migratory bird or other animal; as, a summer (or winter) *visitant.*

vis-it-a-tion (viz′i-tā′shun), *n.* **1**, the act of visiting, or state of being visited; **2**, reward or punishment from God; hence, any unusual event causing pleasure or pain; esp., a severe affliction.

vi-sor or **vi-zor** (vī′zėr), *n.* **1**, the movable front piece of a helmet that protects the upper part of the face, so made that it can be pushed up; **2**, the brim of a cap; **3**, a fixed or movable shade affixed to a car's windshield: called sun-*visor.*

Visor (V)

vis-ta (vis′ta), *n.* **1**, a long, narrow view, as between trees or buildings; also the trees, buildings, etc., forming such a view; **2**, a mental view of a series of events.

vis-u-al (vizh′ū-al), *adj.* **1**, concerned with, or used in, seeing; **2**, capable of being seen; visible; **3**, received through the sense of sight; as, *visual* impressions:—*v.t.* **vis′u-al-ize′** (form a mental picture).—*adv.* **vis′u-al-ly.**

vi-tal (vī′t'l), *adj.* **1**, pertaining to, or concerned with, life; as, *vital* functions; **2**, essential to life; as, air is a *vital* necessity; **3**, affecting life; ending life; as, a *vital* wound; **4**, hence, very important; as, a *vital* question:—**vitals,** *n.pl.* the parts of the body necessary to life, as the heart, lungs, etc.—*adv.* **vi′tal-ly.**

vi-tal-i-ty (vī-tal′i-ti), *n.* **1**, ability to sustain life; **2**, strength; energy.

vi-ta-min (vī′ta-min; vit′a-min) or **vi-ta-mine** (vī′ta-min; vī′ta-mēn′; vit′a-min; vit′a-mēn′), *n.* any of a class of invisible substances which are present in certain foods in their natural state and which are necessary to the health and normal growth of people and animals.

vi-ti-ate (vish′i-āt′), *v.t.* **1**, to corrupt; debase; pervert; as, these plays *vitiate* one's taste; **2**, to contaminate; pollute; as, bus fumes *vitiate* the air; **3**, to make legally ineffective; as, fraud *vitiates* a contract.

vit-re-ous (vit′ri-us), *adj.* transparent, brittle, and hard, like glass; as, *vitreous* rocks.

vit-ri-fy (vit′ri-fī′), *v.t.* to turn into glass or a glassy substance, or to give a smooth, hard surface (to) by heating and fusing.

vit-ri-ol (vit′ri-ul), *n.* **1**, sulphuric acid: also called *oil of vitriol;* **2**, any of several of the salts of this acid, as blue vitriol, or copper sulphate; **3**, anything sharp or biting.—*adj.* **vit′ri-ol′ic** (vit′ri-ol′ik).

vi-tu-per-a-tion (vi-tū′pėr-ā′shun) *n.* wordy abuse:—*v.t.* **vi-tu′per-ate′** (berate; revile).—*adj.* **vi-tu′per-a-tive** (abusive).

vi-va-cious (vī-vā′shus; vi-vā′shus), *adj.* lively; full of spirit.—*adv.* **vi-va′-cious-ly.**—*n.* **vi-vac′i-ty** (vī-vas′i-ti; vi-vas′i-ti).

vi-va-ri-um (vī-vâr′i-um), *n.* a place, as a zoo or laboratory, where animals are kept alive under their normal conditions.

viv-id (viv′id), *adj.* **1**, brilliant; intense: said of light or colours; as, *vivid* red; **2**, active; clear; realistic; as, a *vivid* description; a *vivid* imagination.

viv-i-fy (viv′i-fī′), *v.t.* to give life to; quicken; animate; as, the spring sun *vivifies* all nature.

viv-i-sec-tion (viv′i-sek′shun), *n.* dissecting, or experimenting upon, lower animals in order to gain scientific knowledge calculated to save human life:—*v.t.* **viv′i-sect′.**

vix-en (vik′sn), *n.* **1**, a female fox; **2**, a quarrelsome, ill-tempered woman.

viz (read as *namely*), *adv.* and *n.* [abbreviation of **vi-del′i-cet**], namely; that is.

vi-zier (vi-zēr′; viz′i-er; viz′yėr), *n.* in Moslem countries, a minister of state.

vi-zor (vī′zėr), *n.* Same as **visor.**

vo-cab-u-lar-y (vō-kab′ū-lėr-i), *n.* [*pl.* vocabularies], **1**, a list or collection of words arranged alphabetically and explained or translated; **2**, the stock of words employed by a language, class, or individual.

---

all (ôl), ôr; up, mūte, cûr, cōol, book; oil, out; th, thin; *th*, the.

vo-cal (vō'k'l), *adj.* **1,** pertaining to, or uttered by, the voice; as, a *vocal* protest; **2,** expressing oneself by the voice; hence, loud; vehement; as, he was *vocal* in his denial of guilt: —**vocal chords,** either of two pairs of bands of fibrous tissue, called the *false* and the *true* vocal cords, situated in the larynx, the voice being produced by the vibration of the lower pair, or true vocal cords, as the air is passed out through them.—*adv.* **vo'cal-ly.**—*n.* **vo'cal-ist.**—*v.t.* and *v.i.* **vo'cal-ize'.**

vo-ca-tion (vō-kā'shun), *n.* occupation; trade; profession; as, his *vocation* is the law.—*adj.* **vo-ca'tion-al.**

voc-a-tive (vok'a-tiv), *adj.* and *n.* the case indicating the person or thing addressed, whether *n.*, *adj.*, or *pron.*: in 'O King, live forever!' *king* is in the *vocative* case.

vo-cif-er-ous (vō-sif'ẽr-us), *adj.* making a loud outcry; clamorous; noisy.

vod-ka (vod'ka), *n.* a Russian alcoholic liquor distilled from corn, rye, and potatoes.

vogue (vōg), *n.* **1,** the fashion of the moment; as, long skirts are the *vogue;* **2,** popularity; as, his books had a great *vogue.*

voice (vois), *n.* **1,** sound proceeding from the mouth; esp., human utterance; specifically, sound produced by the vibration of the vocal cords; **2,** the power of speech; as, he lost his *voice;* **3,** anything resembling or likened to human speech or utterance; **4,** opinion, or an expression of opinion; as, the *voice* of the majority; **5,** the right to express a choice or opinion; as, she had no *voice* in the decision; **6,** in *grammar*, the form of the verb showing whether the subject acts or is acted upon; as, active or passive *voice:*—*v.t.* [voiced, voic-ing], to give expression to; put into speech; as, he *voiced* his protest. —*adj.* **voice'less.**

void (void), *adj.* **1,** empty; vacant; **2,** lacking; wanting; as, *void* of humour; **3,** without effect; useless; esp., in *law,* having no force; as, a *void* contract: —*v.t.* **1,** to cause to be empty; **2,** to annul or cancel; as, to *void* a law:—*n.* an empty space.

voile (voil), *n.* a thin, semi-transparent dress material made of silk, cotton, or wool.

vol-a-tile (vol'a-tīl; vol'a-til), *adj.* **1,** readily evaporating or changing into vapour; as, ether is a *volatile* liquid; **2,** hence, lively; gay; also, changeable; fickle.

vol-ca-no (vol-kā'nō), *n.* [*pl.* volcanoes or volcanos], an opening in the earth's surface, generally surrounded by a mass of ejected material forming a hill or mountain, from which molten rock, gases, etc., are expelled.—*adj.* **vol-can'-ic** (vol-kan'ik).

vole (vōl), *n.* any of several ratlike or mouselike rodents of heavy build and with short limbs and tails, esp. the *field mouse.* and the *meadow mouse.*

vo-li-tion (vō-lish'un), *n.* **1,** the exercise or use of the will; choice; as, he came of his own *volition;* **2,** the power of willing.

vol-ley (vol'i), *n.* [*pl.* volleys], **1,** the throwing of many missiles, as arrows, bullets, etc., at the same time; also, the missiles so thrown; **2,** a sudden burst of any sort; as, a *volley* of words: —*v.t.* and *v.i.* to discharge, or be discharged, all at the same time.

vol-plane (vol'plān'), *v.i.* to glide in an airplane with engine power cut down or off.

volt (vōlt), *n.* a unit for measuring the force needed to cause a current of electricity to flow through a conductor against resistance.

volt-age (vōl'tij), *n.* the total number of volts in a particular electrical current, measuring its electrical power.

vol-ta-ic (vol-tā'ik), *adj.* pertaining to electricity produced by chemical action; galvanic; as, a *voltaic* cell or battery.

vol-tam-e-ter (vol-tam'e-tẽr), *n.* an instrument for measuring the quantity of electricity passing through a conductor (by the amount of electrolysis it produces).

volt-me-ter (vōlt'mē'tẽr), *n.* an instrument for measuring the pressure of electricity in volts.

vol-u-ble (vol'ū-bl), *adj.* smooth or ready in speech; talkative.—*n.* **vol'u-bil'i-ty.**—*adv.* **vol'u-bly.**

vol-ume (vol'ūm), *n.* **1,** a number of printed sheets bound together; a book; **2,** one of the books within a series of books that form a complete work; as, the second *volume* of an encyclopaedia; **3,** the amount of space occupied by a body, as measured by cubic units; as, the *volume* of water in a tank; **4,** a large quantity; **5,** fullness of tone; as, a voice lacking in *volume.*

vo-lu-mi-nous (vo-lū'mi-nus), *adj.* **1,** large; bulky; **2,** filling many volumes; as, a *voluminous* history.

vol-un-tary (vol'un-tẽr-i), *adj.* **1,** done or made freely; not forced by another; as, a *voluntary* choice; **2,** acting of one' own free will; as, a *voluntary* worker; **3,** intentional; deliberate; as, *voluntary* manslaughter; **4,** controlled by the will; as, *voluntary* muscles.—*adv.* **vol′un-tar-i-ly** (vol′un-tĕr-i-li).

vol-un-teer (vol′un-tēr′), *n.* one who enters into any service of his own free will; esp., one who offers himself for military service of his own free will: —*v.i.* to offer one's services freely:—*v.t.* to offer freely of one's own accord; as, to *volunteer* information:—*adj.* pertaining to free services; voluntary.

vo-lup-tu-ous (vo-lup′tū-us), *adj.* **1,** giving delight to the senses; sensuous; **2,** devoted to luxurious pleasures; as, *voluptuous* living.—*n.* **vo-lup′tu-ous-ness.**

vom-it (vom′it), *v.i.* to throw up the contents of the stomach; spew:—*v.t.* **1,** to throw up from the stomach; **2,** to discharge with violence; belch forth; as, a locomotive *vomits* clouds of black smoke:—*n.* matter thrown up by the stomach.

voo-doo (vōō′dōō; vōō-dōō′), *n.* **1,** primitive rites based on a belief in sorcery, serpent-worship, etc.; **2,** a Negro sorcerer; **3,** a form of magic; as, to work *voodoo;* a *voodoo* charm or fetish. Also, **voo′doo-ism.**

vo-ra-cious (vō-rā′shus), *adj.* **1,** greedy in eating; as, the wolf is a *voracious* animal; **2,** marked by greediness; as, a *voracious* appetite; **3,** extremely eager in any pursuit; as, a *voracious* reader. —*adv.* **vo-ra′cious-ly.**—*n.* **vo-rac′i-ty** (vō-ras′i-ti).

vor-tex (vôr′teks), *n.* [*pl.* vortices (vôr′ti-sēz′) or vortexes (vôr′tek-sez)], air or water with a rotary motion tending to suck bodies caught in it into a depression or vacuum at the centre; an eddy or whirlpool.

vo-ta-ry (vō′ta-ri), *n.* [*pl.* votaries], a person bound by a vow or promise to some service; as, a nun is a *votary* of the church; also, one devoted to any pursuit; as, a *votary* of music.

vote (vōt), *n.* **1,** a formal expression of the choice, judgment, or wish of a person or group of persons, as in an election; as, a president is elected by the *vote* of the people; **2,** the means of expressing such choice; as, an oral *vote;* **3,** the right to express such a choice; as, women were given the *vote;* **4,** the entire number of such expressions; as, the *vote* was 55 to 30; also, such expressions of a particular class or group taken as a whole; as, the student *vote;* **5,** a resolution resulting from the formal expression of the choice or will of a majority; as, a *vote*

of thanks:—*v.t.* [vot-ed, vot-ing], **1,** to declare or authorize by a vote; as, to *vote* a reform; **2,** to grant; as, to *vote* money; **3,** *Colloq.*, to pronounce, by general consent; as, we *voted* the meeting a failure:—*v.i.* to cast a ballot. —*n.* **vot′er.**

vo-tive (vō′tiv), *adj.* given, offered, etc., in consecration or fulfilment of a vow; as, *votive* offerings.

vouch (vouch), *v.i.* to bear witness; give evidence or assurance; as, I can *vouch* for the truth of his statement.

vouch-er (vouch′ẽr), *n.* a paper, etc., which bears witness to something; specifically, a receipt for payment.

vouch-safe (vouch-sāf′), *v.t.* [vouch-safed, vouchsaf-ing], to deign to grant or give; concede; as, to *vouchsafe* an opinion.

vow (vou), *n.* **1,** a solemn promise or pledge, esp. one made to God or some deity; **2,** a pledge of love and faithfulness:—*v.t.* to promise or assert solemnly; swear:—*v.i.* to make a solemn promise; to declare with emphasis.

vow-el (vou′el), *n.* **1,** a simple vocal sound made with the mouth and lips more or less open and the vocal cords vibrating; **2,** a letter representing such a sound, as *a, e, i, o, u:*—*adj.* pertaining to a vowel.

voy-age (voi′ij), *n.* a journey by water, esp. a long one:—*v.i.* [voyaged, voyaging], to make a journey by water:—*v.t.* to sail, or travel, over; traverse.

voy-a-geur (vwȧ′yȧ′zhûr′), *n. French*, **1,** a French-Canadian or half-breed, usually an expert woodsman and boatman, hired to carry goods and men via streams and lakes to distant outposts; **2,** any such person who trapped in the Northwest.

vul-can-ize (vul′kan-īz′), *v.t.* [vulcanized, vulcaniz-ing], to harden (rubber, etc.) by treating, esp. with sulphur, at a high temperature.—*n.* **vul′can-i-za′tion.**

vul-gar (vul′gẽr), *adj.* **1,** pertaining to the common people; **2,** unrefined; in bad taste.—*adv.* **vul′gar-ly.**—*n.* **vul′gar′i-ty.**—*n.* **vul′gar-ism.**

vul-ner-a-ble (vul′nẽr-a-bl), *adj.* **1,** capable of being wounded or hurt; **2,** open to injury or criticism; as, a *vulnerable* reputation.—*n.* **vul′ner-a-bil′i-ty.**

vul-ture (vul′tūr), *n.* a large bird of prey that feeds on carrion, and is allied to the hawks and eagles.

vy-ing (vī′ing), *p.pr.* of *vie.*

W

W, w (dub′l-ū), *n.* [*pl.* W's, w's], the 23rd letter of the alphabet, following V.

wab-ble (wob′l; wôb′l), *v.i.* and *v.t.* Same as **wobble.**—*adj.* **wab′bly.**

wad (wod; wôd), *n.* **1,** a small mass or bundle of soft material; **2,** a soft bunch of cotton, wool, rope, etc., used to stop an opening, pad a garment, etc.; **3,** a plug to hold a charge of powder or shot in position in a muzzle-loading gun or in a cartridge:—*v.t.* [wad-ded, wad-ding], **1,** to form, as some soft material, into a compact mass or bunch; **2,** to insert a wad into; close, as an opening with a small compact mass; **3,** to provide with a pad.

wad-dle (wod′l; wôd′l), *v.i.* [wad-dled, wad-dling], to sway from side to side in walking; walk with short, clumsy steps, as does a short, fat person, or an animal like a duck with short legs set wide apart:—*n.* **wad′dler.**

wade (wād), *v.i.* [wad-ed, wad-ing], **1,** to walk through water, mud, snow, or other substance that hinders progress; **2,** hence, to proceed with difficulty; as, to *wade* through a tiresome lesson; **3,** to go at something with great force; as, to *wade* into one's work:—*v.t.* to cross by walking through water, mud, etc.—*n.* **wad′er.**

wa-fer (wā′fẽr), *n.* **1,** a thin cake or biscuit; **2,** a thin disk of unleavened, or unraised, bread, used in the communion service in certain churches: in the Roman Catholic Church, called the *Host;* **3,** a small, coloured disk of adhesive paper, paste, etc., for fastening letters, sealing documents, etc.

waf-fle (wof′l; wôf′l), *n.* a flat batter cake baked in a waffle-iron:—**waffle-iron,** a device for baking waffles, consisting of a pair of iron plates, hinged so as to close over batter poured upon one of them.

waft (wáft), *v.i.* and *v.t.* to float along through the air or on the water; as, the current *wafted* the leaves downstream:—*n.* **1,** a waving or beckoning movement of the hand; **2,** a gust or puff, as of wind.

¹wag (wag), *v.t.* [wagged, wag-ging], to move, or cause to swing, from side to side; as, to *wag* a finger:—*v.i.* to move from side to side:—*n.* a wagging movement.

²wag (wag), *n.* a practical joker; a wit. —*n.* **wag′ger-y.**

wage (wāj), *v.t.* [waged, wag-ing], to engage in vigorously; carry on; as, to *wage* war:—*n.* that which is paid or received for services; as, a weekly *wage.*

wa-ger (wā′jẽr), *n.* something risked on an uncertainty; a bet:—*v.t.* and *v.i.* to bet.

wag-es (wāj′iz), *n.pl.* money paid or received for labour, reckoned by the hour, day, week, etc.

wag-gish (wag′ish), *adj.* **1,** given to playing good-natured jokes on others; **2,** done in good-humoured jesting; mischievous.

wag-gle (wag′l), *v.t.* to wag with short, quick motions; as, to *waggle* a finger; to *waggle* a golf club (above a ball in line of play).

wag-on (wag′un), *n.* a four-wheeled vehicle, used for hauling freight, etc., and drawn by draught animals. Also, **wag′gon.**

waif (wāf), *n.* a homeless wanderer; a lost person or animal; esp., a lost or homeless child.

wail (wāl), *v.t.* to mourn or lament aloud:—*v.i.* to utter a cry of lament; make a mournful sound:—*n.* a mournful cry.

wain (wān), *n. Poetic,* a wagon. —**Charles's Wain,** the seven principal stars of the Great Dipper (*Ursa Major*).

wain-scot (wān′skot; wān′skut), *n.* a wooden lining, generally panelled, of a room wall or the lower portion of it: —*v.t.* [wainscot-ed, wainscot-ing], to line or face (the walls of a room) with wood.

wain-scot-ing (wān′skot-ing; wān′-skut-ing), *n.* wall lining or panelling.

waist (wāst), *n.* **1,** the narrowest part of the body, just below the ribs; **2,** a garment, or that section of a garment, which covers the body from shoulders to waist; **3,** the middle part of a vessel's deck, between the forecastle and quarter-deck.—*n.* **waist′band′; waist′line′.**

waist-coat (wāst′kōt′; wes′kut), *n.* a short, sleeveless garment for men, formerly ornamental, worn under the coat; a vest.

wait (wāt), *v.i.* **1,** to linger or tarry; remain; **2,** to continue in a state of expecting; as, to *wait* for news: —**wait upon, 1,** to attend or serve; **2,** to call on formally; as, he *waited upon* the Premier:—*v.t.* **1,** to expect or tarry for; as, to *wait* permission; **2,**

Colloq., to delay; as, to *wait* supper:
—*n*. **1**, the act of delaying or lingering; **2**, the length of time during which one lingers in expectation; delay; as, a *wait* of half an hour; **3**, ambush; hiding; as, to lie in *wait* for an enemy.

wait-er (wāt/ẽr), *n*. **1**, one who serves at table; **2**, a serving tray for dishes. —*n. fem.* **wait/ress.**

waive (wāv), *v.t.* [waived, waiv-ing], to give up a claim to; forgo; forbear to insist upon; as, to *waive* an inheritance. —*n*. **waiv/er.**

¹**wake** (wāk), *v.i.* [*p.t.* woke (wōk) or waked, *p.p.* waked, *p.pr.* wak-ing], **1**, to cease to sleep; as, to *wake* at ten o'clock; also, to be roused from sleep; **2**, to be aroused, excited, or made aware; as, let us *wake* to the danger; to *wake* to duty; the principal *woke* to the situation; **3**, to keep a watch or vigil at night:—*v.t.* **1**, to rouse from sleep; awake; as, John *woke* his father; **2**, to make active; arouse; as, music *wakes* the soul:—*n*. a vigil; esp., a keeping awake to watch over a dead body before burial.

²**wake** (wāk), *n*. the trail left behind a moving ship; hence, a track or trail; as, in the *wake* of explorers come merchants.

wake-ful (wāk/fool), *adj*. **1**, free from sleepiness; unable to sleep; **2**, watchful; vigilant; as, a *wakeful* sentinel.— *n*. **wake/ful-ness.**

wak-en (wāk/en), *v.t.* **1**, to rouse from sleep or inaction; **2**, to excite; move to action:—*v.i.* to become awake.

wake—rob-in (wāk/-rob/in), *n*. **1**, the trillium, esp. the *red* and *white* varieties: the latter was adopted in 1937 as Ontario's floral emblem; **2**, in Europe, the arums, as the cuckoopint. (See *trillium*.)

walk (wôk), *v.i.* **1**, to go by foot; proceed by steps at a moderate pace: distinguished from *run;* **2**, to take a stroll:—*v.t.* **1**, to pass over on foot; as, to *walk* a golf-course; **2**, to cause to go on foot; as, the guide *walked* us ten miles; also, to ride or drive at a slow pace; as, to *walk* a horse:—*n*. **1**, a proceeding on foot without running; also, a stroll or promenade; **2**, manner of walking; gait; **3**, a special place for walking, as a path around a lake; **4**, a distance that may be covered by walking; as, the park is a short *walk* from here; **5**, one's circle or environment; as, he was from a humble *walk* of life.—*n*. **walk/er.**

walk-ing—stick (wôk/ing–stik/), *n*. **1**,

a cane; staff; **2**, any insect of the *Phasmidae* family, with long, slender bodies resembling twigs or sticks.

walk-out (wôk/out/), *n. Colloq.* a strike (of workers).

wall (wôl), *n*. **1**, a solid structure, usually vertical, which forms any one of the sides of a building or the side of a room; **2**, a structure of stone, brick, etc., serving as an enclosure, a defence, etc.; **3**, the side or inside surface of any cavity, vessel, or receptacle; **4**, **walls**, fortifications:—*v.t.* **1**, to surround with, or as with, a structure for enclosure, security, or defence; **2**, to fill in or close up, as an opening.—*n*. **wall/board/; wall/pa/per.**

wal-la-by (wäl/a-bi), *n*. in Australia, a species of small kangaroo including the *nail-tailed, rock, hare,* and *banded* wallabies.

wal-la-roo (wäl/a-rōō/), *n*. in Australia, a species of kangaroo with long narrow hind feet and black fur (New South Wales) or grey fur (Queensland).

wal-let (wol/it; wôl/it), *n*. **1**, a bag or knapsack for the articles necessary for a journey; **2**, a folding pocketbook.

wall-eye (wôl/ī/), *n*. a term applied to the pike-perch: two varieties in Canada are the sauger or sand pickerel and the common pickerel, *Stizostedion vitreum,* also called yellow pickerel, blue pickerel, and doré. But the pickerel is not a true pike-perch.

wall-eyed (wôl/īd/), *adj*. **1**, having the iris of one eye different in hue or markings from the other, or turning outward and showing more of the white than normal; as, a *wall-eyed* horse; **2**, having large, staring eyes, as in some fishes, esp. the *wall-eyed* pike, pollock, surf-fish, and alewife: opposite of *cross-eyed.*

wal-lop (wol/up; wôl/up), *v.t.* **1**, *Colloq.*, to beat soundly; flog; **2**, *Slang*, to strike very hard; as, to *wallop* a ball:—*n. Slang*, a very hard blow.

wal-low (wol/ō; wôl/ō), *v.i.* **1**, to roll about in, or as in, mud, as a hog does; **2**, to live in and enjoy; as, to *wallow* in luxury:—*n*. **1**, the act of rolling or revelling in mud, vice, etc.; **2**, a muddy place in which an animal rolls about.

wal-nut (wôl/nut), *n*. **1**, any of several trees bearing edible nuts, esp. the black walnut-tree and the English walnut-tree; **2**, the nut of such a tree; **3**, the wood of the tree, valuable in making furniture.

wal-rus (wôl/rus; wol/rus), *n*. a large

arctic sea animal related to the seal, and valuable for its blubber, skin, and tusks.

waltz (wôlts), *n.* **1,** a smooth, graceful dance in triple time; **2,** music for such a dance:—*v.i.* to dance a waltz.—*n.* **waltz′er.**

wam-pum (wom′pum; wôm′pum), *n.* beads made of shells, strung into strands, or woven into belts, used by the North American Indians as money, ornaments, etc.

wan (won; wôn), *adj.* [wan-ner, wan-nest], pale; sickly; languid; as, a *wan* child; a *wan* smile.—*adv.* **wan′ly.**

wand (wond; wônd), *n.* a slender rod.

wan-der (won′dėr; wôn′dėr), *v.i.* **1,** to ramble; stroll about with no definite purpose or direction; **2,** to stray; as, he *wandered* from the right path; **3,** to come slowly in a long, winding course; as, the sheep *wandered* back to the fold; **4,** to be delirious:—*n.* the act of wandering.—*n.* **wan′der-er.**

wan-der-lust (wôn′dėr-lust′), *n.* eager desire or impulse to travel.

wane (wān), *v.i.* [waned, wan-ing], **1,** to grow smaller; decrease: applied esp. to the moon; **2,** to decline in power, importance, etc.:—*n.* **1,** the decrease in the visible bright part of the moon from full to new; also, the period of that decrease; **2,** decrease, as of power, importance, etc.

wan-gle (wang′gl), *v.t. Colloq.* to persuade or induce someone to procure or do something by dubious, wheedling, or indirect methods; as, he *wangled* a pass to the game; he *wangled* the records to show a profit:—*v.i.* to wriggle (out of some difficult situation).

want (wont; wônt), *n.* **1,** state of being without; lack; scarcity; as, there is a *want* of supplies in this district; **2,** state of being without necessaries; hence, poverty; as, a family in *want;* **3,** a thing needed or greatly desired; a necessity; as, my *wants* are few:—*v.t.* **1,** to be without; lack; as, the soldier does not *want* courage; **2,** to need; require; as, we *want* food when we are hungry; **3,** to desire; as, I *want* to take a trip to Europe:—*v.i.* to be in poverty.

want-ing (won′ting; wôn′ting), *adj.* **1,** short of; lacking; as, one o'clock *wanting* two minutes; **2,** falling short of what is expected; as, *wanting* in courage; **3,** missing; as, one page *wanting.*

wan-ton (won′tun; wôn′tun), *adj.* **1,** sportive; playful; mischievous; as, a *wanton* wind; **2,** unrestrained; unruly; as, *wanton* curls; **3,** loose in morals; **4,** heartless; outrageous; as, a *wanton* murder:—*n.* a person of loose morals, esp. a woman:—*v.i.* to sport and play.—*adv.* **wan′ton-ly.**—*n.* **wan′ton-ness.**

wap-i-ti (wop′i-ti; wôp′i-ti), *n.* [*pl.* wapitis or wapiti], a large American elk, reddish buff in colour, with large, heavy antlers. It is similar to the European red deer but much larger.

war (wôr), *n.* **1,** a conflict by force of arms between nations, or parts of the same nation; also, the condition created by such a conflict; as, to be at *war;* **2,** the science or art of the profession of arms; as, skilled in *war;* **3,** any contest or contention; as, a *war* of words:—*v.i.* [warred, war-ring], **1,** to engage in an armed conflict; fight; **2,** to contend.—*n.* **war′path′; war′ship′; war′time′.**

¹**war-ble** (wôr′bl), *v.i.* [war-bled, war-bling], to trill; carol, as a bird; also, to make a melodious sound, as a stream:—*v.t.* to sing with trills; also, to relate in verse:—*n.* **1,** the act of warbling; **2,** a soft, sweet flow of sounds; a carol.

²**war-ble** (wôr′bl), *n.* **1,** a tumour on the back of cattle, horses, deer, etc., caused by larvae of the warble fly, botfly, gadfly, etc.; **2,** a hard lump on a horse's back caused by galling or rubbing of the saddle.—**warble fly,** any of several botflies whose larvae live under the skin of horses and cattle.

war-bler (wôr′blėr), *n.* **1,** one who carols; a singer; **2,** any of several small, singing birds, often brightly coloured.

ward (wôrd), *v.t.* **1,** to turn aside; avert; as, to *ward* off an attack; **2,** *Archaic,* to guard:—*n.* **1,** the act of guarding; protection; **2,** a person under guard or protection; esp., a person who, because of youth, insanity, etc., is placed under protection of the court or of a person chosen as guardian; **3,** one of the sections into which a town or city is divided for election or other purposes; **4,** a section of a hospital or prison.—*n.* **ward′ship.**

ward-en (wôr′dn), *n.* **1,** one who keeps watch; a guardian; **2,** a keeper; esp., the head keeper of a prison; **3,** in England, the chief officer of government in a college or guild; **4,** an officer in a church.

ward-er (wôr′dėr), *n.* a guard or keeper.

ward-robe (wôrd′rōb′), *n.* **1,** a cupboard or cabinet for clothes; **2,** one's stock of wearing apparel.

---

cat, āge, fär, cāre, àsk; ten, ēve, latėr; (i) pity, rely, senate; īce; top; nō.

ward-room (wôrd'rōōm'), *n.* in a warship, the messroom of officers above non-commissioned rank.

ware (wâr), *n.* **1,** manufactured articles; as, glazed *ware;* silver*ware;* **2, wares,** articles for sale; as, the merchant peddled his *wares.*

ware-house (wâr'hous'), *n.* a building for storing goods.

war-fare (wôr'fâr'), *n.* open hostilities between enemies; armed conflict.

war-i-ly (wâr'i-li), *adv.* cautiously.

war-like (wôr'līk'), *adj.* **1,** fit for, or fond of, military life or fighting; as, *warlike* peoples; **2,** of or for war; as, *warlike* preparations; **3,** threatening war.

warm (wôrm), *adj.* **1,** moderately heated; not cold; as, *warm* water; *warm* weather; **2,** having little cold weather; as, a *warm* climate; **3,** giving out warmth; as, a *warm* fire; also, serving to keep heat near the body; as, *warm* fur; **4,** heated with passion, anger, excitement, etc.; as, a *warm* dispute; **5,** kindly; affectionate; as, a *warm* greeting; **6,** having tones which give a feeling of warmth, as red, yellow, or orange:—*v.t.* and *v.i.* **1,** to make or become warm; as, to *warm* milk; the milk is *warming* on the stove; **2,** to make or become eager, excited, etc.— *adv.* **warm'ly.**

war-mon-ger (wôr'mung'gẽr), *n.* one who advocates war or tries to bring it about.

warmth (wôrmth), *n.* **1,** the quality or state of having moderate heat; as, the *warmth* of the climate; **2,** earnestness; zeal; as, the *warmth* of an appeal.

warm-up (wôrm'up'), *n.* a workout or practice before a game, contest, race, etc.

warn (wôrn), *v.t.* **1,** to put on guard; make aware of possible danger; caution; as, we *warned* him not to go out in the storm; **2,** to notify; as, why didn't you *warn* us that you were coming?

warn-ing (wôr'ning), *n.* previous notice, esp. of danger; as, the black clouds gave *warning* of an approaching storm; also, that which notifies or cautions; as, this is a *warning* to you.

warp (wôrp), *n.* **1,** the lengthwise thread in weaving: distinguished from *woof;* **2,** a rope attached at one end to a fixed object, used in towing a boat; **3,** a twist, as in a board:—*v.t.* **1,** to turn or twist out of shape; as, dampness *warps*

wood; his mind is *warped* by misfortune; **2,** to tow (a vessel) with a warp: —*v.i.* to become twisted.

war-rant (wor'ant; wôr'ant), *n.* **1,** an official paper giving authority to receive money, to make an arrest, etc.; also, authorization so given; **2,** that which vouches for or guarantees anything; as, his presence is a *warrant* of his sincerity; **3,** justification; as, he acted without *warrant:*—*v.t.* **1,** to guarantee; as, this silver is *warranted* sterling; **2,** to give (a person) authority to do something; also, to authorize (a course of action); **3,** to justify; give just grounds for or to; as, this state of affairs *warrants* action; **4,** *Colloq.,* to declare as certain; as, I *warrant* this will happen.—*n.* **war'ran-ty** (guarantee; justification).

war-ren (wor'en; wôr'en), *n.* a place for breeding rabbits or other small animals; also, a place where small animals abound.

war-ri-or (wor'i-ẽr; wôr'i-ẽr; wôr'-yẽr), *n.* a soldier; a man in military life.

war-ship (wôr'ship'), *n.* a government ship equipped and used for war.

wart (wôrt), *n.* **1,** a small, usually hard, lump on the skin; **2,** a similar lump on a plant stem.—*adj.* **wart'y.**

wart—hog (wôrt'–hog'), *n.* a wild hog of Africa, with warty growths on the face, and large tusks.

war-y (wâr'i), *adj.* [war-i-er, war-i-est], **1,** constantly on guard; as, a *wary* foe; **2,** marked by caution; as, *wary* speeches.

was (woz; wuz), *p.t.* (1st and 3rd person sing.) of *be.*

wash (wosh; wôsh), *v.t.* **1,** to cleanse with a liquid, usually water; as, to *wash* the hands; **2,** to cover with water; flow against; as, the breakers *wash* the shore; **3,** to take away, or remove, by the action of water; as, the flood *washed* the bridge away; **4,** to overlay with a thin coat of metal, colour, etc:— *v.i.* **1,** to become clean by the use of water; **2,** to cleanse clothes, linen, etc., in water; as, she *washes* on Monday; **3,** to stand without injury the process of being cleaned in water; as, this material will *wash* well; **4,** to be eroded or worn away by the action of water; as, the spot will *wash* out; the bank has *washed* away; **5,** to move with a flowing, lapping sound; to splash:— *n.* **1,** the act of washing; **2,** a collection of articles which are to be, or have been, washed; as, there are six sheets in the *wash;* **3,** the dash or sound of a body of water; **4,** material deposited by water, as wreckage on a beach; **5,** disturbed water behind the propellers, oars, etc., of a boat; also, disturbed air behind a moving aeroplane; **6,** liquid with which anything is tinted or washed; as, white*wash;* eye*wash;* **1,** waste liquid; esp., kitchen waste for feeding pigs.—*adj.* **wash'a-ble.**—*n.* **wash'board'; wash'cloth'; wash'-day'; wash'rag'; wash'tub'.**

wash-er (wosh'ẽr; wôsh'ẽr), *n.* **1,** one who or that which washes; specifically, a machine for washing dishes, clothes, etc.; **2,** a flat ring of metal, leather, etc., used to secure the tightness of a joint or screw.—*n.* **wash'er-wom'an.**

wasp (wosp; wôsp), *n.* an insect with strong wings, very slender body, and powerful sting.—*adj.* **wasp'ish** (bad-tempered).

was-sail (wos'il; was'il), *n. Anglo-Saxon,* **1,** a festive occasion, marked by drinking and carousing; **2,** the wine, ale, etc., used in a drinking bout, often flavoured with spices, sugar, etc. Also used as *v.*

waste (wāst), *v.t.* [wast-ed, wast-ing], **1,** to lay in ruins; destroy; **2,** to wear away gradually the strength of; as, disease *wastes* the body; **3,** to spend recklessly, as, to *waste* money:—*v.i.* to lose vigour, substance, or strength gradually; as, she is *wasting* away with the disease:—*adj.* **1,** useless or unused, as unproductive land; **2,** desolate; dreary; **3,** discarded; no longer useful; as, *waste* products; **4,** used for carrying away or holding waste products; as, a *waste*-pipe:—*n.* **1,** the act or process of spending carelessly, of wearing gradually away, destroying, etc.; also, the state of being destroyed, used up, etc.; **2,** that which is of no value; refuse; **3,** something thrown aside in a manufacturing process; as, cotton *waste;* **4,** that which is devastated, desolate, or unproductive; a desert.—*adj.* **waste'ful.**—*n.* **wast'age; waste'-bas'ket; waste'pa'per.**

wast-rel (wās'trel) or **wast-er** (wās'-tẽr), *n.* a spendthrift.

watch (woch; wôch), *n.* **1,** wakefulness for the purpose of guarding or protecting; a vigil; **2,** the state of being alert or on the lookout; as, always on the *watch;* close observation; as, keep a good *watch* over the child; **3,** a watch-man; guard; **4,** the time a guard is on duty; also, any one of the periods into which the day is divided, during which

a given part of a ship's crew is on duty; **5,** a spring-driven wrist or pocket timepiece:—*v.i.* **1,** to be or keep awake; as, to *watch* at night by the bedside of the sick; **2,** to keep guard; **3,** to be on the lookout; **4,** to wait; as, to *watch* for an opening to speak:—*v.t.* **1,** to tend; guard; as, the shepherd *watches* his flock; **2,** to keep in sight; observe; as, to *watch* a game; **3,** to wait for; as, *watch* your turn.—*n.* **watch'er.**—*n.* **watch'dog'; watch'mak'er; watch'tow'er.**

watch-ful (woch'fool; wôch'fool), *adj.* vigilant; on the lookout; as, a *watchful* guard.

watch-man (woch'man; wôch'man), *n.* [*pl.* watchmen (-men)], a guard; as, a night *watchman.*

watch-word (woch'wûrd'; wôch'-wûrd'), *n.* **1,** a password; **2,** a rallying cry.

wa-ter (wô'tẽr), *n.* **1,** the common liquid which forms lakes, rivers, etc., and which comes from the clouds as rain; also, this liquid used for cooking, washing, drinking, etc.; **2,** any clear liquid like or containing water, as tears; **3,** a body of water, as a sea, river, lake, etc.; as, to cross the *water* in a steamer; **4,** a kind of wavy, shiny pattern, as in some silks, metals, etc.:—*v.t.* **1,** to moisten, sprinkle, or provide with water; as, to *water* the lawn; **2,** to treat (fabric) so as to produce a wavy, shiny pattern upon it; **3,** to flow through; irrigate; as, the Columbia River *waters* a large valley; **4,** to give a drink to; as, to *water* the horses; **5,** to dilute with water; as, to *water* wine:—*v.i.* **1,** to obtain or take in water; also, to drink water: said usually of animals; **2,** to secrete or fill with liquid; as, his eyes *watered:*—*adj.* **1,** used for holding or conducting water; **2,** living, feeding, etc., in, on, or near water.—*n.* **wa'ter-cress'; wa'ter-mark'; wa'ter-side'; wa'ter-works'.**

wa-ter buf-fa-lo, the East Indian buffalo, often domesticated for its milk and used as a draft animal: also called *carabao* and *water ox.*

wa-ter—col-our (wô'tẽr–kul'ẽr), *n.* **1,** a paint moistened with water; **2,** a picture made with paints of this kind, as distinguished from one painted with oil-colours; **3,** the art of painting with such colours.

wa-ter-course (wô'tẽr-kōrs'), *n.* **1,** a stream of water; **2,** a channel for water.

wa-tered (wô'tẽrd), *adj.* **1,** in *finance,* inflated above the real value; as, *watered* stock; **2,** having a wavy, lustrous pattern, as some kinds of cloth, metal surfaces, etc.

wa-ter-fall (wô′tẽr-fôl′), *n.* a steep descent or fall of water; a cataract.

wa-ter-fowl (wô′tẽr-foul′), *n.* [*pl.* waterfowl or waterfowls], a bird which lives on or close to a body of water, as a wild-duck; also, all such birds as a class.

wa-ter—lil-y (wô′tẽr–lil′i), *n.* a plant which grows in the water, bearing a fragrant, beautiful flower and broad floating leaves; also, the flower itself.

wa-ter-logged (wô′tẽr-logd′), *adj.* so soaked or filled with water as to be heavy and unmanageable.

wa-ter-mark (wô′tẽr-märk′), *n.* **1,** a mark that shows the height or limit of the rise of water; **2,** a faintly visible marking or design in some kinds of paper, seen when the paper is held to the light.

wa-ter-mel-on (wô′tẽr-mel′un), *n.* a trailing plant of the cucumber family cultivated for its large, edible fruit, which has a green rind and red, sweet, juicy pulp; also, the fruit.

wa-ter ou-zel (ōō′zl), *n.* a genus of plump, thick-plumaged bird akin to the wren: it jerks the body or ‘dips’ as it perches, walks, etc.; a dipper.

wa-ter plan-tain, a family (*Alismataceae*) of white-flowered marsh plants, with fibrous or tuberous roots, growing in shallow water and furnishing food for waterfowl and other wildlife: Canadian varieties (1 of *Lophotocarpus,* 9 of arrowhead, *Sagittarius*).

wa-ter-proof (wô′tẽr-prōōf′), *adj.* not permitting water to come through; as, *waterproof* garments:—*n.* (wô′tẽr-prōōf′), any material treated so as to shed water; esp., a raincoat made of such material:—*v.t.* (wô′tẽr-prōōf′), to make secure against water; as, to *waterproof* a fabric.

wa-ter-shed (wô′tẽr-shed′), *n.* **1,** a height or ridge of land lying between areas drained by different river systems; **2,** an area drained by a single river or lake system.

wa-ter-spout (wô′tẽr-spout′), *n.* **1,** a column of water drawn up by a whirlwind at sea to meet a descending funnel-shaped cloud; **2,** a spout for the discharge of water, esp. of rain-water.

wa-ter—star-wort (wô′tẽr-stär′-wûrt), *n.* a genus, *Callitriche,* of small aquatic herbs: 6 native Canadian species grow from coast to coast in shallow, brackish, calcareous (or lime-charged) waters.

wa-ter-tight (wô′tẽr-tīt′), *adj.* so closely made or fastened as to permit no water to leak out or to enter.

wa-ter-way (wô′tẽr-wā′), *n.* **1,** a channel for water; **2,** a body of water permitting navigation.

wa-ter-wort (wô′tẽr-wûrt), *n.* a genus, *Elatinaceae* (there are 3 Canadian species), of low, creeping, matted herbs that often root at the nodes and grow on sandy, peaty, or muddy margins of ponds and sluggish streams.

wa-ter-y (wô′tẽr-i), *adj.* **1,** pertaining to, or like, water; **2,** containing or discharging water; as, *watery* eyes; **3,** soggy; soft; as, *watery* potatoes.

watt (wot; wôt), *n.* the unit of electric power.—*adj.* **watt′less** (as, a *wattless* alternating current or electromotive force, that is, one that differs in phase by 90°).

wat-tle (wot′l; wôt′l), *n.* **1,** a twig; a rod easily bent; also, a framework of pliant rods; **2,** material made of pliant twigs twisted together and used for walls, fences, etc.; **3, wattles,** rods used in a roof to support thatch made of straw, etc.; **4,** the folds of loose red flesh under the throat of certain birds or reptiles:—*v.t.* [wattled, wat-tling], **1,** to twist or interweave (twigs or rods) into a framework, fence, etc.; **2,** to cover or fence in with rods.—*adj.* **wat′tled.**

wave(wāv), *n.* **1,** a swell on the surface of water; a billow; **2,** the wavelike motion by which sound, light, etc., are carried; **3,** anything like a wave, whether natural or artificial; as, *waves* in hair; **4,** a steady increase or sweeping advance of any feeling, condition, etc.; as, a *wave* of enthusiasm; a crime *wave;* a heat-*wave;* **5,** an up-and-down motion, as with the hand; also, a signal made by motions of the hand or some object:—*v.i.* [waved, wav-ing], **1,** to move up and down or back and forth; as, the flag *waved* in the breeze; **2,** to signal by such a motion; as, he *waved* to us to stop; **3,** to form into ripples; as, her hair *waves* beautifully:—*v.t.* **1,** to cause to move back and forth; as, to *wave* a banner; **2,** to signal by such a movement; as, to *wave* good-bye; **3,** to form into ripples; as, to *wave* the hair.

wave—length (wāv′–length′), *n.* the distance (a) between the crests or hollows of two adjacent waves of a liquid (b) between two successive points of maximum compression or rarefaction in sound-waves (c) between points in the same phase on two successive heat, light, or electromagnetic waves, esp. the latter as used in radio and television broadcasting.

waver (wā′vẽr), *v.i.* **1,** to tremble; sway; flicker, as a flame; **2,** to hesitate as in opinion; **3,** to begin to give way; as, the line of troops *wavered.—adj.* **wa′ver-ing.**

wav-y (wāv′i), *adj.* [wav-i-er, wav-i-est], moving to and fro in waves or swells; as, *wavy* grass; full of waves or curves; sinuous; wavering; as, *wavy* lines.—*n.* **wav′i-ness.**

¹**wax** (waks), *v.i.* **1,** to increase in size, power, degree, etc.; grow: used of the moon in its first and second quarters; **2,** to pass gradually into a specified condition; become; as, the party *waxed* gay.

²**wax** (waks), *n.* **1,** a sticky, yellowish substance, made by bees, from which the honeycomb is built; beeswax; **2,** any similar substance; as, ear*wax;* sealing-*wax;—v.t.* to smear, polish, or treat the surface of, with wax; as, to *wax* floors:—*adj.* made of or like wax; as, a *wax* candle.

wax-en (wak′sen), *adj.* **1,** made of, or covered with, wax; as, a *waxen* image; **2,** resembling wax; as, *waxen* paleness.

wax-wing (waks′wing′), *n.* a crested, brownish bird with waxy red tips on certain wing feathers, as the cedarbird, or cedar waxwing.

wax-y (wak′si), *adj.* [wax-i-er, wax-i-est], **1,** resembling wax; **2,** made of, or coated with, wax.—*n.* **wax′i-ness.**

way (wā), *n.* **1,** a road, street, path, or passage; as, a covered *way;* hence, room for passing; as, make *way* for the procession; **2,** the route from one place to another; the direction or best route to go; as, please tell me the *way* to the post-office; also, distance in general; as, it is a long *way* to China; **3,** progress; advance; headway; as, the ship gathers *way;* he made his *way* in business; **4,** manner; as, she has a winning *way;* also, methods or means; as, Franklin found a *way* to succeed; find a *way* to do it; **5,** a habitual or determined course of action or mode of life; as, she goes her *way* through life; he was set in his *ways;* have your own *way* about it; **6,** aspect; feature; respect; as, in some *ways* it proved a success; **7,** the line of the weave in cloth; **8, ways,** a structure of timbers on which a ship is built and down which

it slides when being launched; **9,** *Colloq.,* neighbourhood; as, out our *way;* **10,** *Colloq.,* condition; state; as, we're in a bad *way.*

way-bill (wā′bil′), *n.* a document issued with a freight shipment to show the precise nature of contents, route, charges, etc.

way-far-er (wā′fâr′ẽr), *n.* a traveller, esp. one who goes on foot.

way-lay (wā′lā′; wā′lā′), *v.t.* [way-laid (-lād′; -lād′), waylay-ing], to lie in wait for with intent to rob, kill, etc.; to seize or attack on the way.—*n.* **way′lay′er.**

way-side (wā′sīd′), *n.* the edge of a road or path:—*adj.* located or growing near the edge of the road; as, *wayside* flowers.

way-ward (wā′wẽrd), *adj.* **1,** disobedient; as, a *wayward* son; **2,** freakish; unaccountable.

we (wē), *pron.* the first person plural of the personal pronoun *I* [*nominative* we, *possessive* our, ours, *objective* us], **1,** the pronoun by which the writer or speaker denotes himself and the group of which he is a part; **2,** the pronoun sometimes used by sovereigns and writers instead of the singular "I" in official proclamations, unsigned articles, editorials, etc.

weak (wēk), *adj.* **1,** lacking in strength of body or in endurance; as, he is *weak* from illness; also, not capable of supporting a heavy weight; as, a *weak* platform; **2,** easily overcome; as, *weak* objections; **3,** wanting in mental or moral strength; easily influenced; as, a *weak* will; **4,** faulty; below standard; as, a *weak* point in the plan; *weak* in arithmetic; **5,** faint in sound; feeble; as, a *weak* cry; also, diluted; thin; watery; as, *weak* wine; **6,** not skilful, experienced, etc.; as, a *weak* swimmer.—*adj.* and *adv.* **weak′ly.** —*n.* **weak′ness.**—*adj.* **weak′—kneed′; weak′—mind′ed.**

weak-en (wēk′en), *v.t.* and *v.i.* to make or become less strong.

weak-fish (wēk′fish′), *n.* an edible sea-fish found along the Atlantic coast: so named from its tender mouth.

weak-ling (wēk′ling), *n.* a person lacking strength of body or character.

weal (wēl), *n. Archaic,* well-being; welfare; as, for *weal* or woe; the common *weal.*

wealth (welth), *n.* **1,** riches; large amounts of money or worldly possessions; **2,** abundance of anything; as,

there is a *wealth* of detail in this story.
—*adj.* **wealth'y.**

wean (wēn), *v.t.* **1,** to accustom (a child or any young animal) to substitute other food for the mother's milk; **2,** to draw away the affections or interests of (a person or animal) from any object or habit; as, they *weaned* him from smoking.

weap-on (wep'un), *n.* any instrument for fighting or for defence.

wear (wâr), *v.t.* [*p.t.* wore (wōr), *p.p.* worn (wōrn), *p.pr.* wear-ing], **1,** to carry on or about the body; as, to *wear* a coat; **2,** to bear or maintain about one; to show; as, to *wear* a careless manner; **3,** to use up or consume, wholly or in part, esp. by personal use; as, he *wears* clothes out rapidly; **4,** to diminish or lessen the quality or value of, by rubbing, scraping, etc.; as, the steps were *worn* by the children's feet; hence, to weaken; weary; fatigue; as, anxiety *wore* the woman out; **5,** to bring about by use, friction, etc.; as, to *wear* a hole in a rug:—*v.i.* **1,** to go through, or endure, the process of being used; as, these gloves *wear* like iron; **2,** to become used up; be diminished in value as a result of use; as, these shoes *wore* out too soon; **3,** to pass gradually; as, the night *wore* on:—*n.* **1,** the act of using or state of being used; use; as, suits for spring *wear;* **2,** garments; clothing; as, they deal in children's *wear;* **3,** damage caused by use; as, to show *wear;* **4,** lasting quality; service; as, these stockings give good *wear.*—*adj.* **wear'a-ble.**

wea-ri-some (wē'ri-sum), *adj.* causing fatigue; tedious; as, *wearisome* work.

wea-ry (wē'ri), *adj.* [wea-ri-er, wea-ri-est], **1,** fatigued, tired; as *weary* in body and mind; **2,** exhausted, as in patience, by continuance of something tiresome; **3,** characteristic of, or showing, fatigue; as, a *weary* sigh; **4,** causing, or accompanied by, fatigue; as, to walk many *weary* miles:—*v.t.* [wearied, weary-ing], **1,** to wear out or make tired; **2,** harass or worry by something irksome:—*v.i.* to become weary.—*adv.* **wea'ri-ly.**—*n.* **wea'ri-ness.**

wea-sel (wē'zl), *n.* a small, active animal of the same family as the mink and the skunk, mostly reddish brown in colour, with a pointed face and a long, thin body: destructive to poultry, mice, etc.:—**weasel words,** remarks that are deliberately ambiguous.

weath-er (weth'ẽr), *n.* the state of the air or atmosphere as to cold, heat, wetness, dryness, etc.; as, fair *weather:*—*v.t.* **1,** to expose to the air; season by exposure to the elements; also, to break down; as, wind and water *weather* rocks; **2,** to sail to the windward of; **3,** to endure or resist; withstand; as, to *weather* a gale at sea:—*v.i.* to undergo action of the air, sun, rain, etc.:—*adj.* windward; facing the wind.—*n.* **weath'er-man'.**—*adj.* **weath'er—beat'en.**

weath-er-cock (weth'ẽr-kok'), *n.* a figure, often shaped like a cock, fastened to a high spire, roof, pole, etc., and turning with the wind to show which way it is blowing; a weather-vane.

weath-er-vane (weth'ẽr-vān'), *n.* a movable device fastened to a spire, roof, or pole to show which way the wind blows; a weathercock: also called *vane.*

weave (wēv), *v.t.* [*p.t.* wove (wōv) or, sometimes, weaved, *p.p.* wo-ven (wō'ven) or wove, *p.pr.* weav-ing], **1,** to twist, interlace, or unite, as threads; **2,** to form by interlacing or twisting, as cloth on a loom; **3,** to spin: as, the spider *weaves* a web; **4,** to compose or fabricate; as, to *weave* a story; **5,** to direct (one's way) in a winding course, as through a crowd:—*v.i.* **1,** to make cloth on a loom; to spin a web; **2,** to become twisted together or interlaced; **3,** to wind in and out:—*n.* a particular pattern in weaving; as, cloth with a plain *weave.*—*n.* **weav'er.**

web (web), *n.* **1,** a woven fabric, esp. a whole piece of cloth; **2,** a substance or piece of material resembling woven cloth; specifically, a cobweb; **3,** anything of complicated structure or arrangement, as an intricate plot; **4,** the skin between the toes of many water birds and some water animals:—*v.t.* [webbed, web-bing], to unite or surround with, or as with, a web; entangle.—*adj.* **web'—toed'.**

webbed (webd), *adj.* **1,** having a web; **2,** having fingers or toes joined by webs; as, the *webbed* hind feet of beavers.

web-foot-ed (web'-foot'id), *adj.* having toes which are joined by webs; as, swans are *web-footed.*

wed (wed), *v.t.* [*p.t.* wed-ded, *p.p.* wed-ded or wed, *p.pr.* wed-ding], **1,** to marry; **2,** to join in marriage:—*v.i.* to marry.

wed-ding (wed'ing), *n.* **1,** a marriage; a marriage ceremony; **2,** a marriage anniversary; as, a golden *wedding.*

wedge (wej), *n.* **1,** a piece of wood or metal, thick at one end and thin at the other, used for splitting wood or rocks, raising heavy objects, etc.; **2,** anything of a similar shape; as, a *wedge* of land; **3,** any action used to create an opening or lead to further developments:—*v.t.* [wedged, wedg-ing], **1,** to split or force apart with a wedge; **2,** to fasten with a wedge, as a door or wheel; **3,** to force in (something) to serve as a wedge; to press or crowd in; as, to *wedge* packing into a crack.

wed-lock (wed′lok), *n.* the state of being married; matrimony.

Wednes-day (wenz′di; dā), *n.* the 4th day of the week.

wee (wē), *adj.* [wee-er, wee-est], very little; tiny.

¹weed (wēd), *n.* a wild plant that grows in cultivated fields, and is unsightly or useless:—*v.t.* **1,** to root out or remove, as undesirable plants; **2,** to free from wild and useless plants; as, to *weed* a garden; **3,** to remove from a group (the inferior, useless, and harmful parts); as, to *weed* out the troublemakers:—*v.i.* to take out weeds or anything obnoxious.—*adj.* **weed′y.**—*n.* **weed′er.**

²weed (wēd), *n.* **1,** a garment; **2, weeds,** mourning garments; as, widow's *weeds.*

week (wēk), *n.* **1,** a period of seven days; **2,** the six working days of the week; as, the museum is open during the *week.*—*n.* **week′end′.**

week-day (wēk′dā′), *n.* any day of the week except Sunday.

week-ly (wēk′li), *adj.* **1,** of a week; for a week; as, a *weekly* wage; **2,** happening or coming every seven days; as, a *weekly* paper:—*adv.* once a week:—*n.* [*pl.* weeklies], a paper or magazine issued once every seven days.

ween (wēn), *v.t.* and *v.i. Archaic,* to suppose; think.

weep (wēp), *v.i.* [wept (wept), weep-ing], **1,** to shed tears; cry; **2,** to give forth moisture; as, the skies *weep:—v.t.* **1,** to shed, as tears; **2,** to shed tears for; hence, to lament or mourn.—*n.* **weep′er.**

wee-vil (wē′vl; wē′vil), *n.* a small hard-shelled beetle having the head extended into a beak with the mouth parts at the end: destructive to grain, nuts, fruits, leaves, etc.

weigh (wā), *v.t.* **1,** to find the heaviness of, by use of a scale or balance or by lifting; as, I *weighed* the stone in my hand; **2,** to ponder; reflect on carefully; as, to *weigh* the evidence; **3,** to distribute in definite quantities as by the use of scales; as to *weigh* out sugar; **4,** to press heavily upon; as, care *weighs* him down; **5,** to raise: used only in to *weigh anchor:—v.i.* **1,** to have a certain weight; as, these bricks *weigh* over a ton; **2,** to bear heavily; **3,** to be considered important; as his testimony didn't *weigh* much with the jury.

weight (wāt) *n.* **1,** heaviness; the tendency of bodies to fall toward the earth; **2,** a system of units used in finding the heaviness or quantity of objects or substances; as, apothecaries' *weight;* **3,** a unit of weight, as pound, ounce, gram, ton; **4,** the amount a thing weighs; as, its *weight* is 100 pounds; **5,** degree of heaviness; as, two boys of the same *weight;* **6,** a piece of metal used as a balance in finding the heaviness of other bodies; **7,** a heavy object; as, the *weight* in a clock; **8,** something oppressive; as, care is a *weight* on the mind; **9,** power; importance; as, a man of great *weight* in the community:—*v.t.* **1,** to put weight upon; load down; as, to *weight* a sack with stones; **2,** to oppress with a load; as, he's *weighted* down with cares.

weight-y (wāt′i) *adj.* [weight-i-er, weight-i-est], **1,** heavy; as, a *weighty* body; hence, burdensome; as, *weighty* cares; **2,** important; influential; as, *weighty* considerations; **3,** serious in aspect; as, a *weighty* countenance. —*adv.* **weight′i-ly.**—*n.* **weight′i-ness.**

weir (wēr), *n. British,* a dam (as for a mill) or net, etc., across a stream (for fish).

weird (wērd), *adj.* pertaining to the supernatural; uncanny or unearthly.

welch (welch), *v.* Same as *welsh.*

wel-come (wel′kum) *adj.* **1,** received with gladness or hospitality; as a *welcome* guest; producing gladness; as, *welcome* gifts; **2,** permitted gladly; as, you're *welcome* to stay:—*n.* a kindly greeting:—*v.t.* [welcomed, welcom-ing], to greet with kindness; receive with hospitality.

weld (weld), *v.t.* **1,** to join (pieces of metal) by heating to the melting-point and pressing or hammering together or permitting to flow together; **2,** hence, to unite closely; as, he *welded* the tribes into a nation:—*v.i.* to become welded, or firmly joined together; as, iron *welds* easily:—*n.* **1,** the state of being welded; **2,** a welded joint.

wel-fare (wel′fâr′), *n.* the state or

condition of having good health, prosperity, etc.:—*adj.* pertaining tò welfare.

wel-kin (wel′kin), *n. Poetic*, the sky.

¹**well** (wel), *n.* **1,** a spring or fountain; **2,** a shaft sunk deep in the earth, for obtaining water, gas, oil, etc.; **3,** an enclosed or sunken space resembling such a shaft; **4,** a source of steady or continuous supply :—*v.i.* to flow, as from a spring; as, tears *welled* into her eyes.

²**well** (wel), *adv.* [*comp.* bet-ter, *superl.* best], **1,** in a right, just, or praiseworthy manner; as, the work was *well* done; **2,** satisfactorily or suitably; as, to dine *well;* **3,** with reason; justifiably; as, he may *well* question the verdict; **4,** fortunately; favourably; as, the store is *well* situated; **5,** to a considerable extent or degree; as, the man was *well* over 50; **6,** intimately; as, we are *well* acquainted with him; **7,** definitely; clearly; as, they knew perfectly *well* the outcome:—*adj.* **1,** in good health; **2,** in a satisfactory state; as, all is *well:*—*interj.* an exclamation of wonder, relief, resignation, etc. —*n.* well′do′ing.—*adj.* well′— groomed′; well′—in-ten′tioned; well′- made′; well′—man′nered; well′— read′.

well—be-ing (wel⌐–bē′ing), *n.* generaι health and prosperity; welfare.

well—bred (wel′—bred′), *adj.* refined in manners; cultivated; polite.

well—known (wel′—nōn′), *adj.* familiar; famed; generally recognized; as, a *well-known* nursery tale; a *well-known* author.

welsh (welsh), *v.t.* and *v.i. Slang*, to cheat, as by evading payment.

Welsh rab-bit, *n.* a dish of melted cheese, cooked with milk, ale, beer, etc., seasoned and spread on toast or crackers (erroneously called *Welsh rarebit*).

welt (welt), *n.* **1,** an edge or border fastened to something, for strengthening or ornamenting it, as the narrow strip of leather around a shoe between the upper and the sole; **2,** *Colloq.*, a red, swollen mark raised on the skin by a blow:—*v.t.* **1,** to secure or ornament with a welt, or narrow strip; **2,** *Colloq.*, to flog.

wel-ter (wel′tėr), *v.i.* **1** to roll; wallow, as a pig in mire; **2,** to rise and fall with violent tossing or rolling, as of waves; **2,** a state of confusion.

wen (wen), *n.* **1,** a harmless tumour, cyst, or sac filled with fatty secretions of the skin; **2,** any such swelling or protuberance.

wench (wench), *n.* **1,** a young girl or woman; **2,** a female servant.

wend (wend), *v.i.* to go; journey:—*v.t.* to direct or continue; as, to *wend* one's way.

Wen-di-go (wen′di-gō′), *n.* Same as *Windigo.*

went (went), *p.t.* of *go.*

wept (wept), *p.t.* and *p.p.* of *weep.*

were (wûr; wâr), **1,** past indicative *pl.* of *be;* **2,** past subjunctive, *sing.* and *pl.* of *be.*

were-wolf or **wer-wolf** (wēr′woolf′; wer′woolf′), *n.* in *folklore*, a person changed into a wolf by an evil spell or able at will to assume a wolf's shape for cannibalistic or other beastly purposes.

west (west), *n.* **1,** that part of the heavens where the sun is seen to set; one of the four points of the compass: opposite of *east;* **2,** the part of the earth lying toward the sunset:—**West, 1,** the Occident; Europe and the Americas, as distinguished from Asia, or the Orient; **2,** in Canada, the territory lying between the western boundary of Ontario and the Pacific Ocean:—*adj.* coming from the west; as, a *west* wind; in the direction of the west ; as, a *west* door:—*adv.* toward the west; as, facing *west.*

west-er-ly (wes′tėr-li), *adj.* **1,** toward the west; **2,** from the west, as a wind: —*adv.* in the direction of the west:—*n.* [*pl.* westerlies], a wind blowing from the west.

west-ern (wes′tėrn), *adj.* **1,** grown or produced in the west; as, *western* apples; **2,** situated in the west; as, a *western* city; also, going toward, or coming from, the west; as, a *western* train:—**Western,** relating to any district or region called the West.

west—north-west (west′—nôrth′—west′), *adv.*, *adj.* and *n.* two points, or 22° 30′ north of due west.

west—south-west (west′—south′—west′), *adv.*, *adj.* and *n.* two points, or 22° 30′ south of due west.

¹**west-ward** (west′wėrd), *adj.* toward the west; as, steer a *westward* course.

²**west-ward** (west′wėrd) or **west-wards** (-wėrdz), *adv.* toward the west; as, to travel *westward.*—*adv.* west′-ward-ly.

wet (wet), *v.t.* [wet or wet-ted, wet-ting], to moisten or soak with water or some other liquid:—*n.* **1,** water; moisture; also, rainy or misty weather; **2,**

Colloq., an opponent of prohibition: —*adj.* [wet-ter, wet-test], **1,** containing, consisting of, or soaked with, water or some other liquid; as, *wet* streets; also, of paint, varnish, ink, etc., not dry; **2,** rainy or misty; as, *wet* weather; **3,** *Colloq.*, favouring the manufacture and sale of alcoholic beverages.

weth-er (weth/ẽr), *n.* a castrated ram.

whack (hwak), *n. Colloq.* a sharp, resounding blow, or the sound of it; *Slang*, an attempt; trial:—*v.t.* and *v.i.* **1,** to slap or strike (a sharp, resounding blow).—*adj.* **whack/y;** *Slang*, **wack/y** (erratic, irrational, or eccentric).

whale (hwāl), *n.* a huge, warm-blooded, air-breathing sea mammal with finlike fore limbs, no external hind limbs, and a fishlike tail: valued for oil, whalebone, etc.:—*v.i.* [whaled, whal-ing], to hunt whales.—*n.* **whal/ing.**—*n.* **whal/er.**

whale-bone (hwāl/bōn/), *n.* **1,** a stiff, springy substance in the upper jaw of certain whales; **2,** something made of whalebone.

whang (hwang), *v.t.* and *n.* [Imitative], *Colloq.* to strike with a sharp, ringing, resounding blow, as on metal.

wharf (hwôrf), *n.* [*pl.* wharves (hwôrvz) or wharfs], a structure of wood, steel, or stone built at the water's edge, at which ships may be moored; a pier or quay.

what (hwot; hwôt), *pron.* **1,** in *questions*, which thing or things; as, *what* is wrong? *what* is your business? **2,** in *relative clauses*, that or those which; the thing or things that; as, *what* you have just said is wrong; also, anything that; everything that; all that; as, give him *what* he wants; I'll give *what* I can; **3,** in *exclamations*, what things; how much; as, *what* he has suffered! —*adj.* **1,** in *questions*, which; as, *what* trade do you follow? how much; as, *what* good will that do? **2,** in *relative clauses*, that or those which; which in particular; as, I want to know *what* car I should take; also, any; all; whatever; as, I'll contribute *what* flowers I have; as many as; as, take *what* pencils you please; as much as; as, take *what* ink you need; what sort of; as, I wonder *what* magazines he likes; **3,** in *exclamations*, how great, strange, unusual, etc.; as, *what* recklessness!—*adv.* **1,** partly; in part; as, *what* with the cold and *what* with the darkness we could go no farther; **2,** in *questions*, how much; in what way; as, *what* does it profit a man? **3,** in

exclamations, such; as, *what* bright colours!—*conj. Colloq.* that; as, I do not know but *what* it is true:—**what though**, even though; even granting that; as, *what though* we failed today, all is not lost:—*interj.* an exclamation expressing surprise; as, *what!* the boat stolen?

what-ev-er (hwot-ev/ẽr; hwôt-), *pron.* **1,** all that; anything that; as, give *whatever* you can; **2,** no matter what; as, we must have sugar, *whatever* its cost; **3,** used interrogatively, as an emphatic form of *what*, expressing surprise, wonder, etc.; as, *whatever* made you do it?—*adj.* of any kind; as, he owns no property *whatever*.

what-not (hwôt/not/), *n.* a stand of shelves for ornaments, bric-à-brac, books, etc.

what-so-ev-er (hwot/sō-ev/ẽr; hwôt/-), *pron.* and *adj.* the formal or emphatic form of *whatever*.

¹**wheal** (hwēl), *n.* **1,** a pimple; pustule; **2,** a whitish lump on the skin, as from the sting of an insect.

²**wheal** (hwēl), *n.* a ridge raised on the flesh, as by flogging.

wheat (hwēt), *n.* **1,** a tall, slender, cultivated grass bearing long spikes of seeds, the most important of the cereal grains; **2,** the seed of this grass, used in the making of flour and cereals.

Wheat-stone's bridge (hwēt/stōnz/), in *electricity*, a device for measuring resistances. Also, **Wheat/stone bridge.**

DIAGRAM OF WHEAT-STONE'S BRIDGE
A, B, C, D, resistances; G, galvanometer.

whee-dle (hwē/dl), *v.t.* [whee-dled, whee-dling], **1,** to persuade by flattery; cajole; coax; as, she *wheedled* her father into consenting; **2,** to get by coaxing or flattery: —*v.i.* to coax.

wheel (hwēl), *n.* **1,** a circular frame or disk designed to turn on a central axis or axle; **2,** a vehicle or machine in which a frame or disk of this kind is the characteristic or essential part, as a bicycle; **3,** something resembling a wheel, as a circular, revolving firework; **4,** a complete turning around; hence, a turn made by a line of troops or of ships moving abreast, by pivoting at one end of the line; **5, wheels,** the inner workings of anything; as, the *wheels* of state:—*v.t.* **1,** to move (something) on wheels; **2,** to cause to turn, as a line of troops:—*v.i.* **1,** to turn on, or as if on, an axis; **2,** to move on wheels, as a vehicle.—*adj.* **wheeled.**

wheel-bar-row (hwēl′bar′ō), *n.* a light vehicle with two handles and usually one wheel, used for moving small loads.

wheel-house (hwēl′hous′), *n.* the pilothouse of a ship.—*n.* **wheels′man** or **wheel′man** (helmsman).

wheeze (hwēz), *v.i.* [wheezed, wheezing], **1,** to breathe noisily and with difficulty; **2,** to make a whistling or gasping sound; as, the pump *wheezes:* —*n.* a whistling or gasping breath, as in asthma, or any similar sound.—*adj.* **wheez′y.**

whelp (hwelp), *n.* **1,** the young of a dog, lion, fox, etc.; a cub; **2,** a worthless, disagreeable child or youth:—*v.t.* and *v.i.* of animals, to give birth to (young).

when (hwen), *adv.* **1,** in *questions,* at or during what time; as, *when* are you coming? **2,** in *relative clauses,* at which time; as, he knew *when* he had to work: —*conj.* **1,** at or after the time; as, *when* he came, it was too late; on any occasion that; whenever; at whatever time; as, *when* I meet him, he does not speak; as soon as; as, *when* dinner is over, you may leave; **2,** whereas; while on the contrary; in spite of the fact that; as, he gave me ten dollars *when* he owed me only five:—*pron.* **1,** what time; as, since *when* have you been here? **2,** the time or occasion just spoken of; as, since *when,* his work has improved.

whence (hwens), *adv.* **1,** in *questions,* from what place, source, or origin; hence, for what reason; **2,** in *relative clauses,* from which; as, the place *whence* I came.

when-ev-er (hwen-ev′ér), *adv.* and *conj.* at whatever time; as often as.

where (hwâr), *adv.* **1,** in *questions,* at or in what place; as, *where* do they live? hence, in what part; in what respect; as, *where* am I wrong? to what place; whither; as, *where* are you going? from what source or place; as, *where* did you get that? **2,** in *relative clauses,* in, at, or to which; as, the house *where* I lived; in, at, or to whatever place; wherever; as, stay *where* you are:—*conj.* whereas; as, he did much, *where* we expected little:—*pron.* the place at, in, or to which; as, that is *where* I made my mistake.

where-a-bouts (hwâr′a-bouts′), *adv.* in or near what place:—*n.* (also *where-*

about) the place where a person or thing is; as, her *whereabouts* is still unknown.

where-as (hwâr-az′), *conj.* **1,** considering that; it being the case that; **2,** while on the contrary; as, he thought he was late, *whereas* he was early.

where-at (hwâr-at′), *adv.* **1,** in *relative clauses,* at or upon which; **2,** whereupon; on which account.

where-by (hwâr-bī′), *adv.* **1,** in *relative clauses,* by which; **2,** in *questions,* by what means; how.

where-fore (hwâr′fôr), *adv.* **1,** in *relative clauses,* for which reason; **2,** in *questions,* why:—*n.* a cause or reason; as, the whys and *wherefores.*

where-in (hwâr-in′), *adv.* **1,** in *relative clauses,* in which; in which time, place, respect, etc.; **2,** in *questions,* in what; as, *wherein* am I mistaken?

where-of (hwâr-ov′), *adv.* **1,** in *relative clauses,* of which; of whom; **2,** in *questions,* of what.

where-on (hwâr-on′), *adv.* **1,** in *relative clauses,* on which; **2,** in *questions,* on what; as, *whereon* do you rely?

where-so-ev-er (hwâr′sō-ev′ér), *adv.* and *conj.* in or to whatever place; wherever.

where-to (hwâr-tōō′), *adv.* **1,** in *relative clauses,* to which; **2,** in *questions,* to what; to what end or place.

where-up-on (hwâr u-pon′), *adv.* **1,** in *relative clauses,* upon which; as the result of which; after which; as, *whereupon* he rose to speak; **2,** in *questions,* upon what; upon what grounds.

wher-ev-er (hwâr-ev′ér), *adv.* at, to, or in whatever place.

where-with (hwâr-with′; hwâr-with′) *adv.* **1,** in *relative clauses,* with which; as, he had no tools *wherewith* to work; **2,** in *questions,* with what:—*pron.* that with which; as, he has *wherewith* to buy a car.

where-with-al (hwâr′with-ôl′), *adv.* with which:—*pron.* wherewith:—*n.* (hwâr′with-ôl′), that with which a thing can be bought or done; as, he has the *wherewithal* to buy a house.

whet (hwet), *v.t.* [whet-ted, whet-ting], **1,** to sharpen on or with a whetstone; as, to *whet* an axe; **2,** to make eager; stimulate; as, the rumour *whets* my curiosity.

wheth-er (hweth′ér), *conj.* **1,** in case that; no matter if; as, *whether* you go or *whether* you stay, I shall help you; *whether* he fails or not, it's worth trying; **2,** if; as, I wonder *whether* they will come today.

whet-stone (hwet′stōn′), _n._ a fine-grained stone for sharpening edged tools.

whew (hwū; hū), _interj._ an exclamation expressing surprise, disgust, or dismay.

whey (hwā), _n._ the thin, watery part of milk, which may be separated from the curds, as in making cheese.

which (hwich), _pron._ **1**, in _questions_, what one or ones (of several); as, _which_ is your book? **2** in _relative clauses:_ **a**, that; as the books _which_ we have read; _Archaic_, who or whom; as, Our Father _which_ art in heaven; **b**, the one that; as, point out _which_ is yours; also, any that; whichever; as, take _which_ of these books you please:—_adj._ **1**, in _questions_, what; as, _which_ house is yours? **2**, in _relative clauses_, what; as, after a month, during _which_ time he did nothing; point out _which_ hat is yours.

which-ev-er (hwich-ev′ẽr), _pron._ any one or ones that; as, take _whichever_ you please:—_adj._ no matter which; any; whatever; as, _whichever_ book you choose.

whiff (hwif), _n._ **1**, a sudden breath or gust, as of air or smoke; a puff; **2**, a faint odour; a trace:—_v.t._ and _v.i._ to puff or blow out or away in sudden breaths; waft.

whif-fle (hwif′l), _v.i._ to blow fitfully or in gusts, as the wind; **2**, hence, to be fickle or unsteady:—_v.t._ to disperse, emit, or expel, as by a whiff or puff.—_n._ **whif′fler**.

whif-fle-tree (hwif′l-trē′), _n._ Same as _whippletree_,

while (hwil), _n._ **1**, a period of time; as, he stayed only a little _while;_ **2**, time or pains required in doing something; as, it will be worth your _while_ to go:—_conj._ **1**, as long as; during the time that; at the same time that; as, you might read _while_ I am gone; **2**, less correctly, although; as, _while_ I like fruit, I dislike apples:—_v.t._ [whiled, whil-ing], to cause to pass; spend; as, to _while_ away the time between trains.

whilst (hwīlst), _conj._ while.

whim (hwim), _n._ a fancy; caprice; notion.

whim-per (hwim′pẽr), _v.i._ to cry in a low, whining voice:—_n._ a fretful whining.

whim-si-cal (hwim′zi-k′l), _adj._ **1**, full of odd or fanciful notions; **2**, odd; quaint.

whim-sy or **whim-sey** (hwim′zi), _n._ [_pl._ -sies or -seys], **1**, a whim, caprice, or odd fancy; a sudden freak; **2**, quaint or fanciful humour; as, a poem or play full of _whimsy_.

whine (hwīn), _v.i._ [whined, whin-ing], **1**, to utter a plaintive, long-drawn cry; esp., to show distress by such a cry; as, the dog _whined_ to be let in; **2**, to coax or complain in a plaintive or fretful tone:—_v.t._ to utter in a fretful or complaining way:—_n._ **1**, a plaintive tone or cry; **2**, a weak, fretful complaining.—_adj._ **whin′y**—_n._ **whin′er**.

whin-ny (hwin′i), _v.i._ [whinnied, whinny-ing], to neigh:—_n._ [_pl._ whinnies], a neigh.

whip (hwip), _v.t._ [whipped or whipt (hwipt), whip-ping], **1**, to strike, as with a lash or rod; beat; **2**, to beat into froth, as cream; **3**, to move or take suddenly; snatch; jerk; as, he _whipped_ off his coat; **4**, _Colloq._, to defeat in a contest; conquer:—_v.i._ **1**, to thrash about, as a loose sail; **2**, to move quickly or nimbly; as, the fox _whipped_ out of sight:—_n._ **1**, a flexible rod, often tapering to a lash, or a rod with a lash attached; **2**, anyone who uses such a rod or lash; a driver; **3**, in _cookery_, a preparation, usually a dessert, which is made up largely of cream or the whites of eggs beaten stiff.—**party whip**, in _politics_, an officer who maintains discipline, and rounds up members when a vote is to be taken.—_n._ **whip′per**.

whip-cord (hwip′kôrd′), _n._ a close-woven worsted cloth, diagonally ribbed; **2**, catgut cord; **3**, a hard-braided or twisted cord.

whip-per-snap-per (hwip′ẽr-snap′ẽr), _n. Colloq._ a petty person who feels important, esp. a brisk or impertinent young fellow.

whip-pet (hwip′it), _n._ a very fleet smooth-coated dog, resembling a greyhound, but somewhat smaller, used esp. for racing.

whip-ple-tree (hwip′l-trē′), _n._ a pivoted crossbar to the ends of which the traces of the harness are fastened; a whiffletree; swingletree (British).

whip-poor-will (hwip′poor-wil′; hwip′poor-wil′), _n._ a small American bird, mottled brown, black, and buff; so called from its frequently repeated note.

whir or **whirr** (hwûr), _v.i._ [whirred, whir-ring], to move, fly, or revolve with a buzzing noise:—_n._ a buzzing or humming noise caused by rapid motion; as, the _whir_ of an aeroplane propeller.

whirl (hwûrl), *v.t.* **1,** to turn or cause to revolve rapidly; as, to *whirl* a hat on one's finger; **2,** to carry onward or away quickly, with a revolving motion: —*v.i.* **1,** to revolve with great speed; as, the earth *whirls* on its axis; **2,** to move along swiftly; as, the carriage *whirled* away; **3,** to seem to spin around; as, my brain *whirled:*—*n.* **1,** a rapid rotation or circular motion; **2,** something revolving rapidly; as, a *whirl* of dust; **3,** confused and bustling activity; as, the *whirl* of social life.

whirl-i-gig (hwûr'li-gig'), *n.* **1,** a child's toy that spins or whirls round; **2,** a merry-go-round; **3,** anything that turns or whirls around rapidly.

whirl-pool (hwûrl'pōōl'), *n.* a swift-moving, circling eddy or current in a river or sea, with a central depression into which floating objects are drawn by suction.

whirl-wind (hwûrl'wind'), *n.* a violent windstorm marked by a whirling, spiral motion of the air.

whisk (hwisk), *v.t.* **1,** to sweep or brush lightly and rapidly; **2,** to take or carry off with a quick, sweeping motion; as, the wind *whisked* away the scrap of paper; **3,** to beat (eggs, cream, etc.) into a froth:—*v.i.* to move rapidly and nimbly; as, the squirrel *whisked* up the tree:—*n.* **1,** the act of brushing with a quick motion; **2,** a quick, nimble movement; **3,** a small broom or brush with a short handle; **4,** a kitchen utensil for whipping eggs, cream, etc.

whisk-er (hwis'kẽr), *n.* **1,** (usually *whiskers*), the hair growing on the side of a man's face, or on his upper lip or his chin; **2,** one of the long, bristly hairs growing near the mouth of a cat, rat, etc.—*adj.* **whisk'ered.**

whis-ky or **whis-key** (hwis'ki), *n.* [*pl.* whiskies or whiskeys], a strong alcoholic liquor distilled from grains, as corn or rye.

whis-per (hwis'pẽr), *v.i.* **1,** to speak in a low voice or under the breath; **2,** to rustle; as, leaves *whispered* in the breeze:—*v.t.* to say under the breath; tell privately:—*n.* **1,** a low, hushed tone of voice; **2,** a hint or suggestion; rumour; as, a *whisper* of scandal; **3,** a soft, rustling sound.

whist (hwist), *n.* a card game for four persons, from which the modern game of bridge has been developed.

whis-tle (hwis'l), *v.i.* [whis-tled, whis-tling], **1,** to make a shrill sound by forcing the breath between the teeth or puckered lips, or by forcing air, steam, etc., through a small opening, as in a valve; **2,** to make any similar shrill sound; as, the wind *whistles*; **3,** to go or pass swiftly with a sharp, shrill sound; as, arrows *whistled* past him:— *v.t.* **1,** to utter by whistling; as, to *whistle* a tune; **2,** to call or signal by whistling:—*n.* **1,** the shrill noise made by forcing air, steam, etc., through an opening; **2,** an instrument to produce such a sound.—*n.* **whis'tler.**

whit (hwit), *n.* the smallest particle; as, there is not a *whit* of truth in the rumour.

white (hwīt), *adj.* [whit-er, whit-est], **1,** of the colour of clean snow: opposite of *black;* **2,** hence, pure; innocent; **3,** silvery; grey, as hair; **4,** fair-skinned: —*n.* **1,** the colour of clean snow; **2,** a Caucasian, or white person; **3,** white clothing; as, nurses wear *white;* **4,** the albumen of an egg.—*n.* **white'ness.**— **white admiral,** a butterfly with showy white bands on its wings.

white ant, a tropical insect, the termite, most abundant in Africa: destructive to books, wooden structures, etc.

white-cap (hwīt'kap'), *n.* a wave crest whitened with foam.

white-fish (hwīt'fish'), *n.* an edible, freshwater fish of the salmon family.

whit-en (hwīt'n), *v.t.* to bleach or make white:—*v.i.* to become white; to bleach or blanch; as, linen *whitens* in the sun. —*n.* **whit'en-ing; whit'en-er.**

white-wash (hwīt'wosh'; -wôsh'), *n.* a white mixture of lime and water, for coating walls, fences, etc.:—*v.t.* **1,** to cover with whitewash; **2,** hence to gloss over the faults or misdeeds of.—*n.* **white'wash'er.**

white-wood (hwīt'wood'), *n.* light-coloured wood, esp. of the tulip (used for house finishings and boatbuilding), basswood, cottonwood, cinnamon, etc.

whith-er (hwith'ẽr), *adv.* **1,** in *questions,* to what place; as, *whither* goest thou? **2,** anywhere; wherever; as, go *whither* you will; you will go *whither* you are sent.

¹**whit-ing** (hwīt'ing), *n.* powdered chalk used in making whitewash, silver polish, putty, etc.

²**whit-ing** (hwīt'ing), *n.* **1,** a food fish of the cod family (Europe); **2,** a general term for hake, drumfish, weakfish, and menhaden.

Whit-sun-day (hwit'sun'di; hwit'-sn-dā'), *n.* the 7th Sunday after Easter commemorating the day of Pentecost, when the Holy Spirit descended upon the apostles.

whit-tle (hwit′l), *v.t.* [whit-tled, whit-tling], **1,** to cut, shape, or carve with a knife; as, to *whittle* a toy; **2,** to reduce bit by bit by, or as if by, cutting away: —*v.i.* to shape a piece of wood slowly with a knife.

whiz or **whizz** (hwiz), *v.i.* [whizzed, whiz-zing], to move rapidly with a humming or hissing sound; as, the car *whizzed* past us:—*n.* a humming or hissing noise.

who (hōō), *pron.* [*nominative* who, *possessive* whose (hōōz), *objective* whom (hōōm)], **1,** in *questions*, what person or persons; as, *who* else was there with you? *whom* did you choose? also, what sort of person or persons; as, *who* am I to be so honoured? **2,** in *relative clauses*, that; as, Mr. Smith, *who* lives near me; the one that; the person that; as, I know *who* was there; I don't know *who* you are; he that or they that; whoever; as, "*who* steals my purse, steals trash."

whoa (hwō), *interj.* Stop! (used esp. to horses).

who-ev-er (hōō-ev′ẽr), *pron.* anyone or everyone who; whatever person or persons; as, *whoever* wishes, may come along.

whole (hōl), *adj.* **1,** in good health; uninjured; **2,** not defective or broken; intact; **3,** not divided into parts; not broken, cut up, or ground; as, *whole* cloves; hence, undivided in devotion, allegiance, etc.; as, to work with one's *whole* heart and soul; **4,** complete; entire; containing all the parts or members; as, the *whole* school:—*n.* all the parts or members of something taken together; a total; as, the *whole* of a nation.—*n.* **whole′ness.**

whole-heart-ed (hōl′här′tid), *adj.* sincere; completely earnest; hearty; as, *wholehearted* co-operation.

whole-sale (hōl′sāl′), *n.* the sale or purchase of goods in large quantities: opposite of *retail:*—*adj.* buying or selling in large quantities; also, pertaining to such trade:—*v.t.* [wholesaled, wholesal-ing], to sell at wholesale.—*n.* **whole′sal′er.**

whole-some (hōl′sum), *adj.* [wholesom-er, wholesom-est], **1,** tending to promote health of body or mind; as, a *wholesome* meal; **2,** characteristic of, or suggesting, health; as, a *wholesome* appearance.

whol-ly (hōl′li; hōl′i), *adv.* completely; entirely; altogether; as, he was *wholly* satisfied with his purchase.

whom (hōōm), *pron.* the objective case of *who.* Also, *relative* or *conj. pron.*, **whom-ev′er** (objective case of *whoever*) and **whom′so-ev′er** (objective case of *whosoever*).

whoop (hōōp), *v.i.* **1,** to utter a loud and prolonged cry; shout; halloo; **2,** to make the gasping sound that follows a fit of coughing in whooping-cough:— *v.t.* to drive, call, or urge with loud cries or shouts:—*n.* **1,** a loud shout; **2,** a gasping sound following a fit of coughing.

whoop-ee (hwŏŏ′pē′; hŏŏp′ē′), *interj.* expressing hilarious enjoyment.—*n.* gay and noisy hilarity; as, to make *whoopee* (*Colloq.*)

whoop-ing—cough (hōōp′ing–kôf′), *n.* an infectious disease to which children are particularly susceptible, characterized by violent coughing.

whoop-ing crane, a graceful snow-white bird with black-tipped wings and red crown and forehead: breeding grounds, Wood Buffalo Park, northern Alberta: wintering grounds, Aransas Marsh, Texas, which is reached by flight southward across the great plains: about 35 birds are in existence (1960).

whoosh (hwŏŏsh), *interj.* and *v.i.* [Imitative], to emit a sibilant or hissing sound, as of something rushing through the air; as, the transport *whooshed* past; it passed with a *whoosh.*

whop-per (hwop′ẽr), *n. Colloq.* **1,** something unusually large; **2,** a big lie.— *adj. Colloq.* **whop′ping.**

whore (hōr), *n.* an unchaste woman; prostitute; harlot:—*v.i.* [whored, whor-ing], to have unlawful sexual intercourse for hire.—*n.* **whore′house′; whore′mon′ger.**

whorl (hwûrl; hwôrl), *n.* **1,** the circular arrangement of leaves, petals, etc., at one level on a stem; **2,** one of the turns of a spiral shell.—*adj.* **whorled.**

whose (hōōz), *pron. adj.* the possessive case of *who.*

who-so (hōō′sō), *pron.* whoever.

who-so-ev-er (hōō′-sō-ev′ẽr), *pron.* any person who; whoever.

Whorl (W) OF LEAVES

why (hwī), *adv.* **1,** in *questions*, for what reason, with what motive or for what purpose; on what account; wherefore; as, *why* did you leave? **2,** in *relative* *clauses*, on account of which; for which; as, the reason *why* he went I don't know; the reason for which; as, I do not understand *why* he is so angry:—*n.* [*pl.* whys (hwīz)], a cause or reason; motive; as, psychology explains the *why* of human conduct:—*interj.* expressing surprise; as, *why*! it's snowing!

wick (wik), *n.* the cord or tape of twisted fibres in a candle or lamp, through which the melted tallow or oil is drawn to feed the flame.

wick-ed (wik′id), *adj.* 1, evil; sinful; base; immoral; as, a *wicked* sinner; 2, mischievous; roguish; as, a *wicked* look; 3, harmful; dangerous; as, a *wicked* blow.—*n.* **wick′ed-ness.**

wick-er (wik′ėr), *n.* 1, a pliant willow rod; 2, such twigs woven into baskets, furniture, etc.:—*adj.* made of wicker; as, a *wicker* table.—*n.* **wick′er-work′.**

wick-et (wik′it), *n.* 1, a small door or gate, esp. one in a larger door or gate; 2, a windowlike opening, esp. one with a grill or grate, as in a ticket office; 3, in *cricket*, either of the two frames at which the ball is bowled, behind which stands the *wicket-keeper*; 4, in *croquet*, one of the arches through which the ball must be driven.

wide (wīd), *adj.* [wid-er, wid-est], 1, of considerable extent from side to side; broad; as, a *wide* road; also, stretching for a specified distance from side to side; as, the room is nine feet *wide*; 2, vast; spacious; as, a *wide* domain; 3, inclusive of much; comprehensive; as, a person of *wide* experience; 4, far from a point aimed at; as, *wide* of the mark; 5, opened to the fullest extent; as, eyes *wide* with wonder:—*adv.* 1, over or to a considerable distance or extent; widely; as, his fame spread far and *wide*; 2, of a door, gate, window, etc., fully open; 3, far from the point aimed at.—*adv.* **wide′ly.**—*n.* **wide′ness.**

wid-en (wīd′n), *v.t.* and *v.i.* to make or become broader or larger.

wide-spread (wīd′spred′), *adj.* 1, opened or spread to the fullest extent; as, a *widespread* fan; 2, widely distributed; as, English is a *widespread* language.

wid-ow (wid′ō), *n.* a woman whose husband is dead.

wid-ow-er (wid′ō-ėr), *n.* a man whose wife is dead.

wid-ow-hood (wid′ō-hood), *n.* the state or condition of being a widow.

width (width), *n.* the extent of a thing from side to side; breadth; as, this lot is 50 feet in *width*.

wield (wēld), *v.t.* 1, to use with the hands; as, to *wield* an axe; 2, to exercise (power, authority, etc.).—*n.* **wield′er.**

wie-ner (wē′nėr), *n.* a kind of smoked sausage made with beef and pork; a frankfurter.

wife (wīf), *n.* [*pl.* wives (wīvz)], a married woman.—*n.* **wife′hood.**—*adj.* **wife′ly.**

wig (wig), *n.* an artificial covering of hair for the head, to conceal baldness, to adorn, or to form part of official dress.—*adj.* **wigged.**

wig-gle (wig′l), *v.i.* and *v.t.* [wig-gled, wig-gling], to squirm; wriggle.—*n.* **wig′gler** (esp. the larva of a mosquito). —*adj.* **wig′gly.**

wight (wīt), *n.* *Archaic*, a person.

wig-wag (wig′wag′), *v.t.* and *v.i.* [wig-wagged, wigwag-ging], 1, to move back and forth; 2, to signal with flags or lights, moved or flashed according to a code.

wig-wam (wig′wäm; wig′wôm), *n.* a hut made of a framework of poles, covered with bark or hides, used by the North American Indians.

wild (wīld), *adj.* 1, living in the natural state; untamed; as, the lion is a *wild* animal; also, not cultivated; as *wild* flowers; 2, not civilized; savage; as, a *wild* tribe; 3, of a region, uninhabited; like a wilderness; 4, uncontrolled; as, *wild* anger; 5, fantastic; unreasonable; as, a *wild* scheme; 6, wide of the mark; 7, *Colloq.*, eager; as, I am *wild* to go:— *adv.* without control; wildly:—**wilds,** *n.pl.* a desert or wilderness.—*n.* **wild′-flow′er** or **wild flower; wild′life′.**

¹**wild-cat** (wīld′kat′), *n.* a savage cat-like animal, as the lynx and the Texas wildcat: also written *wild cat*:—*adj.* 1, risky; unreliable; as, *wildcat* banks; 2, illegal or unethical; as, a *wildcat* strike.

²**wild-cat** (wīld′kat′), *v.i.* and *v.t.* 1, to promote a risky or fraudulent adventure; 2, to prospect or drill for oil, ore, etc., in an area hitherto considered unproductive.—*n.* **wild′cat′ter.**

wil-der-ness (wil′dėr-nis), *n.* a wild uncultivated region not inhabited by man.

wild-fire (wīld′fīr′), *n.* a composition, as of certain chemicals, that catches fire readily and is hard to put out; hence, anything that spreads swiftly; as, the story spread like *wildfire*.

wild rose, any of many varieties with but one circle of petals in the flower, as the sweetbrier: the *wild prairie rose*,

(*R. arkansana*, variety *suffulta*), is the floral emblem of Alberta.

wile (wīl), *n.* a subtle, crafty trick or subtle words, meant to lure or deceive:—*v.t.* [wiled, wil-ing], **1,** to obtain by trickery; **2,** to pass (time): incorrect for *while*.

wil-ful or **will-ful** (wil′fool), *adj.* **1,** headstrong; stubborn; as, a *wilful* child; **2,** intentional; deliberate; as, *wilful* murder.—*adv.* **wil′ful-ly.**—*n.* **wil′ful-ness.**

¹**will** (wil), *n.* **1,** the power of the mind to decide upon and carry out a course of action; **2,** control exercised over impulse; self-control; as, *will* conquers habit; **3,** a deliberate choice, desire, intention, or determination directed towards a special end or purpose; as, the *will* to live helps a patient to recover; **4,** strong determination; hence, enthusiasm; energy; as, he went to work with a *will;* **5,** that which has been desired, or determined upon; as, thy *will* be done; he always had his *will;* **6,** the power to act as one wishes or sees fit; as, he comes and goes at *will;* **7,** disposition or attitude towards others; as, peace on earth and good*will* toward men; **8,** a legal paper in which a person directs how his property is to be disposed of after his death; as, his last *will* and testament:—*v.t.* [willed, will-ing], **1,** to have as a wish or determination; to have in mind as a purpose; as, to *will* success is partly to win it; **2,** to influence or compel by exercising the power of the mind; as, she *willed* him to turn around; **3,** to bequeath; as, he *willed* half his estate to his cousin:—*v.i.* to decide, choose, or determine; as, if God so *wills*, we'll win this struggle yet.

²**will** (wil), *v.t.* [*sing.* I will, thou wilt, he will, *pl.* will; *p.t.* would (wood); no other parts], *Archaic*, to wish or desire; as, what *will* you?—*v.i. and auxiliary* **1,** is or are going to; as, she *will* like this novel; they *will* be there; **2,** to wish to; want to; as, which *will* you have? come and go as you *will;* **3,** to wish; as, it shall be as you *will;* often with the subject omitted; as, *would* it were spring; **4,** to be willing to; consent to; intend to; to be inclined or disposed to; as, he *will* not work any more; also, in polite commands, to be ordered to; as, you *will* please take this report to your father; **5,** to be determined to; as, I *will* do it whether you approve or not; he *will* go in spite of the weather; **6,** to be destined to; as, children *will* grow up; accidents *will* happen; **7,** to be

accustomed to; as, she *would* sit and read for hours on end; **8,** to be able to; can; as, the bridge *will* not bear so heavy a load.

wil-lies (wil′iz), *n. Slang*, a fit of nervousness; (the) jitters; as, it gives me the *willies*.

will-ing (wil′ing), *adj.* **1.** cheerfully ready; not lazy or slow; as, a *willing* worker; **2,** given or done freely or gladly; as, a *willing* service; **3,** favourably disposed; as, he is *willing* to buy it.—*adv.* **will′ing-ly.**

will—o′—the—wisp (wil′-o-*thĕ*-wisp′), *n.* **1,** a light that is seen flitting above marshy ground at night; **2,** anything that misleads one or eludes one's grasp.

wil-low (wil′ō), *n.* a tree or shrub with slender flexible branches, usually growing near water; also, its wood, used in making baskets, furniture, etc.:—**weeping willow,** a species of willow whose drooping branches are a symbol of grief.—*adj.* **wil′low-y.**

wil-ly—nil-ly (wil′i–nil′i), *adv.* willingly or unwillingly; without choice; as he must go, *willy-nilly*.—*adj.* loosely, irresolute; uncertain; as, a *willy-nilly* customer.

wilt (wilt), *v.i.* **1,** to wither or droop, as a flower; **2,** to lose strength; become faint or weak:—*v.t.* to cause to wither.

wil-y (wīl′i), *adj.* [wil-i-er, wil-i-est], cunning; crafty; as, the *wily* fox.—*n.* **wil′i-ness.**

win (win), *v.i.* [won (wun), win-ning], to gain a victory; prevail; as, to *win* in a battle:—*v.t.* **1,** to acquire by effort or perseverance; obtain; as, to *win* promotion; earn, as a living; **2,** to gain in a contest; as, he *won* the prize; **3,** to be victorious in; as, to *win* a game; **4,** to persuade; induce; as, try to *win* him over to our side.

wince (wins), *v.i.* [winced, winc-ing], to shrink or draw back suddenly, as from a blow; flinch:—*n.* the act of flinching.

winch (winch), *n.* a hoisting-machine or windlass in which a rope or chain is wound up on a drum turned by a crank.

¹**wind** (wind; *Poetic*, wīnd), *n.* **1,** a natural current of air; breeze; **2,** breath; also, the ability to breathe without difficulty while engaged in exercise; as, a man out of training quickly loses his *wind;* **3,** scent; as, the hounds got *wind* of game; **4,** gas formed in the digestive organs; **5,** **winds,** brass and wooden wind-instruments in an orchestra:—*v.t.* (wind), **1,**

to detect or follow by scent; as, hounds failed to *wind* the deer; **2,** to put out of breath; as, fast going *winded* our horses; also, to allow to rest, as a horse, so as to permit recovery of breath.—*n.* **wind'storm'.**

²**wind** (wĭnd), *v.i.* [wound (wound), wind-ing], **1,** to turn; move with changing direction; as, the stream *winds* through the valley; **2,** to twine round and round; as, the ivy *winds* around the tree:—*v.t.* **1,** to twist or coil around on something; as, to *wind* yarn on a spool; **2,** to cover with something wrapped around; as, to *wind* a tire with tape; **3,** to tighten the springs of, by turning; as, to *wind* a watch or a music-box; **4,** to make or pursue (one's way); as, he *wound* his course across the hill.—*n.* **wind'er.**

wind-break (wind'brāk'), *n.* a shelter or protection from the wind, as a wall or a grove of trees.

wind-break-er (wind'brāk'ẽr), *n.* a short sports jacket of suede, chamois, wool, etc., with close-fitting elastic cuffs and waistband.

wind-ed (wĭn'did), *adj.* out of breath.

wind-fall (wind'fôl'), *n.* **1,** something blown down, as ripe fruit, etc.; **2,** an unexpected piece of good fortune, as a legacy.

wind-flow-er (wind'flou'ẽr), *n.* the anemone.

win-di-go (win'di-gō') or **wen-di-go** (wen'), *n.* [*Ojibway* and *Cree*], a malevolent, cannibalistic spirit of Indian folklore: an Indian afflicted with it, would, it was believed, turn into a cannibal.

wind—in-stru-ment (wind'—in'stroo-ment), *n.* a musical instrument, as the flute, oboe, or clarinet, sounded by a current of air blown into it. The organ is also a wind-instrument.

wind-lass (wind'las), *n.* a machine for hoisting or hauling; a winch.

wind-mill (wind'mil'), *n.* a mill operated by a large wheel whose oblique sails or vanes are turned as they catch the wind.

win-dow (wĭn'dō), *n.* **1,** an opening in the wall of a building, the side of an automobile or railway car, etc., to let in light and air; **2,** the framework and glass which fills such an opening.—*n.* **win'dow-pane'.**

wind-pipe (wind'pīp'), *n.* the trachea, or breathing-tube, leading from the larynx to the lungs.

wind-shield (wind'shēld'), *n.* a pane of glass attached to an automobile or aeroplane, in front of the seats, to shield the passengers from wind, rain, dust, etc.

wind-up (wind'up'), *n.* **1,** conclusion; end; close; **2,** in *baseball,* a preliminary motion of the arm before pitching the ball.

wind-ward (wind'wẽrd), *n.* the direction from which the wind is blowing: *adj.* on the side from which the wind blows:—*adv.* toward the wind.

wind-y (win'di), *adj.* [wind-i-er, wind-i-est], **1,** characterized by winds; breezy; as, March is a *windy* month; also, exposed to the wind; as, the *windy* side of the house; **2,** noisy, wordy, or boastful; as, a *windy* braggart.—*n.* **wind'i-ness.**

wine (wīn), *n.* the fermented juice of grapes, used as a drink; **2,** the fermented juice of other fruits or plants used similarly:—*v.t.* [wined, win-ing], to furnish or entertain with wine, as a guest.

wing (wing), *n.* **1,** one of the broad, flat organs or parts of birds, insects, and bats, by means of which they fly; **2,** one of the main supporting surfaces of an aeroplane; **3,** a part of a building projecting from the main structure; as, the north *wing* of the house; **4,** in a theatre, the stage platform extended at either side, or one of the pieces of scenery for these sides; **5,** in the army or navy, a force at the extreme right or left of the main force:—**on the wing,** in flight; as, to shoot a bird *on the wing:*—*v.i.* **1,** to equip for, or as for, flying; as, to *wing* an arrow; **2,** to traverse by flying; as, the bees *winged* their way to the clover; **3,** to wound in the wing:—*v.i.* to fly.—*adj.* **winged** (wingd; wing'id).

wink (wingk), *v.i.* **1,** to close and open quickly one or both eyelids; blink; **2,** to convey a hint or signal by a quick motion of one eyelid; **3,** to keep oneself from seeing something; as, to *wink* at slight errors; **4,** to twinkle; gleam at regular intervals, as the light of a lighthouse:—*v.t.* **1,** to close and open quickly, as the eyelids; **2,** to remove by winking; as, to *wink* the tears away:—*n.* **1,** the act of winking; esp. the act of closing one eye for a moment as a signal; also, a hint or command thus given; **2,** the time required for a wink; an instant; as, he came a *wink* too soon.

win-ner (win'ẽr), *n.* a person or thing that wins; a victor; hence, anything exceptionally good.

win-ning (win'ing), *adj.* **1,** successful, as in a competition; as, the *winning* horse; **2,** attractive; charming; as, a *winning* personality:—*n.* **1,** the act of gaining or conquering; **2, winnings,** that which one gains; esp., money won in gambling.

win-now (win'ō), *v.t.* **1,** to blow chaff and refuse from (grain) by a current of air; **2,** to sift; separate; as, to *winnow* truth from falsehood:—*v.i.* to separate chaff from grain by winnowing.—*n.* **win'now-er.**

win-some (win'sum), *adj.* attractive; charming.—*adv.* **win'some-ly.**

win-ter (win'tėr), *n.* **1,** the coldest season of the year; in any region, that one of the four seasons of the year when the sun shines least directly; in the Northern Hemisphere, the period from the winter solstice, about December 21, to the vernal equinox, about March 21; **2,** any time, as of gloom or sorrow, suggesting winter; also, figuratively, a year of life:—*adj.* pertaining to winter:—*v.i.* to pass the months of the cold season; as, snakes *winter* in the ground:—*v.t.* to keep during the cold season; as, to *winter* cattle.—*adj.* **win'try.**—*n.* **win'ter-time':**—*v.i.* and *v.t.* **win'ter-kill'.** —**winter solstice,** in the Northern Hemisphere, the time when the sun reaches the Tropic of Capricorn (Dec. 21); in the Southern Hemisphere, when it reaches the Tropic of Cancer (June 21).

win-ter—green (win'tėr-grēn'), *n.* **1,** a low-growing, woody, evergreen plant that bears white blossoms, pungent red berries, and leaves which yield an aromatic oil called *oil of winter-green;* **2,** this oil; also, its flavour.

win-ter-ize (win'tėr-īz'), *v.t.* to prepare for winter use, esp. an automobile or airplane, by employing antifreeze, lighter greasing, etc.

wipe (wīp), *v.t.* [wiped, wip-ing], **1,** to dry or cleanse by rubbing with something soft; as, to *wipe* dishes; to *wipe* furniture; **2,** to remove by rubbing; as, to *wipe* away tears; *wipe* off dirt: —*n.* the act of cleansing or rubbing. —*n.* **wip'er.**

wire (wīr), *n.* **1,** metal drawn out into a strand of comparatively small, often minute, diameter, usually flexible and of great length; **2,** such metal used, either singly or in cables, in telephone and telegraph systems; **3,** *Colloq.,* a telegram; as, to send a *wire:*—*v.t.* [wired, wir-ing], **1,** to bind, fit, or provide with wire; as, to *wire* a house for electricity; *wire* a broken chair together; **2,** *Colloq.,* to send (a message), or send a message to (a person), by telegraph; also, as, *wire* the results of the game; *wire* him to come.—*n.* **wir'ing.**

wire-less (wīr'lis), *adj.* without the use of wires; as, *wireless* telegraphy or telephony:—*n.* a wireless telegraph or telephone system; as, to send news by *wireless;* also, a message transmitted thus:—*v.t.* to send (a message), or send a message to (a person), by wireless; to radio; as, they *wirelessed* the news of the discovery.

wire-worm (wīr'wûrm'), *n.* the slender, hard-bodied larva of the click beetle: over 25 species from coast to coast injure the cereal, potato, root, and tobacco crops of Canada.

wiry (wīr'i), *adj.* [wir-i-er, wir-i-est], **1,** like wire; stiff; **2,** lean and slight, but sinewy; as, a *wiry* child.—*n.* **wir'i-ness.**

wis-dom (wiz'dum), *n.* **1,** the ability to form sound judgments; common sense; **2,** learning; knowledge:—**wisdom—tooth,** the third molar, or extreme back tooth, on each side in each jaw.

¹**wise** (wīz), *adj.* [wis-er, wis-est], having knowledge and the ability to use it; having good judgment; sage.—*adv.* **wise'ly.**

²**wise** (wīz), *n.* way; manner; mode; as, in such *wise* it happened.

wise-a-cre (wīz'ā/kėr), *n.* **1,** a foolish person who affects to possess wisdom; **2,** a wise or learned person (ironically or contemptuously).

wise-crack (wīz'krak'), *n.* and *v.i.* *Slang,* a flippant or facetious remark, esp. a quip, gibe, etc.

wish (wish), *v.i.* to have a strong desire; as, I *wish* to stay; we *wish* for peace:—*v.t.* **1,** to desire; as, what do you *wish?* also, to express (a desire); as, I *wish* I had a dog; **2,** to express (a hope, etc.) for, or against, someone; as, to *wish* a person good fortune; also, to express (a greeting); as, I *wish* you good morning:—*n.* **1,** a strong or eager desire; **2,** the object or thing desired; as, popularity in school was his only *wish;* **3,** a request.—*n.* **wish'er.**—*adj.* **wish'ful.**

wish-y—wash-y (wish'i-wosh'i), *adj.* *Colloq.* insipid; feeble; forceless; as, a *wishy-washy* address.

wisp (wisp), *n.* **1,** a handful or small bundle, as of straw or hay; **2,** a thin fragment or bit, as of smoke, cotton, etc.—*adj.* **wisp'y.**

wis-ta-ri-a (wis-tâ'ri-a) or **wis-te-ri-a** (wis-tē'ri-a), *n.* a climbing shrub of the pea family, with drooping clusters of lavender flowers.

wist-ful (wist′fool), *adj.* pensive; longing; wishful; as, a *wistful* expression.

wit (wit), *n.* **1,** wisdom; intelligence; as, he hasn't the *wit* to meet an emergency; **2,** wits, mental faculty or power; as, keep your *wits* about you; **3,** the ability quickly to perceive that which is odd or amusing in a situation or idea and to express it in an unexpected and amusing way; **4,** a person noted for this ability; also, the clever or brilliant things he says or writes.—*adj.* wit′less.

witch (wich), *n.* **1,** a woman supposed to have supernatural powers given her by the devil or by evil spirits; an enchantress; **2,** an old crone; a hag; **3,** *Colloq.*, a charming young woman:—*v.t.* to bewitch; enchant.—*n.* witch′-er-y.

witch-craft (wich′krȧft′), *n.* dealings with evil spirits; sorcery; magic.

witch ha-zel (hā′zl), **1,** a shrub with small yellow flowers which appear after the leaves have gone; **2,** an extract from the bark of this shrub, used as a lotion.

with (with; with), *prep.* **1,** by the side of; as, put the glove *with* its mate; in the employ, association, or company of; as, he has been *with* the firm for years; favourable to; as, we have the wind *with* us; **2,** between oneself and another; as, we trade *with* England; **3,** in the care, keeping, or possession of; as, leave the child *with* me; **4,** characterized by; as, a man *with* a sad expression; **5,** by means of; as, slain *with* a dagger; **6,** in the state, condition, or manner of; as, he performed *with* ease; **7,** as a result of; as, to perish *with* hunger; **8,** in spite of; as, *with* all his learning, he was a fool; **9,** during; as, the river rose higher *with* every minute; at the same time as; as, he was up *with* the sun; **10,** from; as, we parted *with* our friends at noon; **11,** in opposition to; against; as, I played tennis *with* my brother.

with-al (with-ôl′), *adv.* Archaic, **1,** moreover; besides; **2,** still; nevertheless.—*prep.* Archaic, with (intensive); as, a low stool *withal*.

with-draw (with-drô′; with-drô′), *v.t.* [*p.t.* withdrew (-drōō′), *p.p.* withdrawn (-drôn′), *p.pr.* withdraw-ing], **1,** to remove; take away; as, the school *withdrew* its team from the tournament; **2,** to retract; take back; as, to *withdraw* a charge in court:—*v.i.* to leave; depart.

with-draw-al (with-drô′al; with-drô′-al), *n.* a removal; also, a taking back; as, the *withdrawal* of a promise.

with-er (with′ẽr), *v.t.* to cause to shrink, fade, droop, or decay:—*v.t.* to lose sap or juice; dry up or fade; languish.

with-ers (with′ẽrz), *n.* the ridge between a horse's shoulder bones.

with-hold (with-hōld′; with-hōld′), *v.t.* [withheld (with-held′; with-held′), withhold-ing], **1,** to hold back, as from action; restrain; **2,** to keep back; refuse to give.

with-in (with-in′), *adv.* **1,** in the inner part; inside; **2,** inwardly; **3,** in the house; indoors:—*prep.* **1,** inside of; **2,** in the limits of; as, *within* an hour; *within* hail.

with-out (with-out′), *adv.* **1,** outside; **2,** outwardly; **3,** outdoors:—*prep.* **1,** outside of; **2,** beyond; as, *without* question; **3,** in the absence of; lacking in; as, *without* hope.

with-stand (with-stand′; withstand′), *v.t.* [withstood (-stood′), withstand-ing], to oppose; resist; endure; as, to *withstand* a siege.

wit-ness (wit′nis), *n.* **1,** testimony; evidence; as, his friends bore *witness* to his good character; **2,** a person or thing that gives evidence; as, a receipted bill is *witness* that the bill has been paid; **3,** a person who tells in court under oath what he knows of a fact or event; **4,** one who puts his signature to a document to show that he has seen it signed; **5,** one who from actual presence knows of an occurrence: also called *eyewitness*:—*v.t.* **1,** to give evidence of, as in court; **2,** to reveal; betray; as, her startling pallor *witnessed* her sudden fear; **3,** to sign (a document) to indicate knowledge of another's signing; **4,** to see or know personally; as, to *witness* a performance of a play:—*v.i.* to testify.

wit-ti-cism (wit′i-sizm), *n.* a witty remark; a clever saying.

wit-ting-ly (wit′ing-li), *adv.* with knowledge; intentionally; as, I would not *wittingly* hurt your feelings.

wit-ty (wit′i), *adj.* [wit-ti-er, wit-ti-est], **1,** having the faculty of arousing laughter by a clever and amusing way of expressing ideas; **2,** marked by wit.—*adv.* wit′ti-ly.

wiz-ard (wiz′ẽrd), *n.* **1,** a magician; conjurer; **2,** *Colloq.*, a very clever person; as, a financial *wizard*.—*n.* wiz′ard-ry.

wiz-ened (wiz′nd), *adj.* dried up; shrivelled:—*v.t.* and *v.i.* **wiz′en.**

wob-ble (wob′l; wôb′l), *v.i.* [wobbled, wob-bling], **1,** to move unsteadily from side to side; **2,** to be undecided in opinion or actions:—*v.t.* to cause to waver or totter:—*n.* a swaying motion. Also spelled **wab′ble.**—*adj.* **wob′bly.**

woe (wō), *n.* **1,** deep sorrow; inconsolable grief; **2,** the cause of sorrow or grief; an affliction.

woe-be-gone (wō′bi-gôn′), *adj.* overwhelmed with woe; showing great grief or misery; as, a *woebegone* appearance.

woe-ful (wō′fool), *adj.* **1,** sorrowful; miserable; **2,** mean; paltry; wretched. —*adv.* **woe′ful-ly.**

wolf (woolf), *n.* [*pl.* wolves (woolvz)], **1,** a savage, flesh-eating animal of the dog family, usually a tawny grey in colour, which hunts in packs, and preys on sheep and other animals; **2,** a fierce, greedy, or destructive person.—*adj.* **wolf′ish.**—**wolf–eel,** a preying species of Pacific coast wolf-fish (up to 8″ long). —**wolf–fish,** a preying fish with long, lithe body and grasping, grinding teeth: 3 species on Atlantic coast, esp. the 5′, 30-lb. common catfish (*Anarhichas lupus*).

wolf-hound (woolf′hound′), *n.* any of several breeds of tall, swift dogs, esp. Irish and Russian, formerly used for hunting wolves.

wol-ver-ene or **wol-ver-ine** (wool′vėr-ēn′), *n.* a ferocious, flesh-eating animal of Canada and the northern U.S., between two and three feet long, with a thick-set form and shaggy blackish fur.

wom-an (woom′an), *n.* [*pl.* women (wim′in)], **1,** an adult female of the human race; **2,** the female sex; **3,** a female servant or attendant.—*n.* **wom′-an-hood.**

wom-an-ly (woom′an-li), *adj.* like, or befitting, a woman; feminine; as, *womanly* modesty.—*n.* **wom′an-li-ness.**

womb (woom), *n.* the uterus.

wom-bat (wom′bat), *n.* an Australian mammal about 3′ long related to the kangaroo, opossum, and other marsupials: it looks like a small bear.

won (wun), *p.t.* and *p.p.* of *win.*

won-der (wun′dėr), *n.* **1,** the state of mind produced by anything new, strange, unexpected, or surprising; astonishment; **2,** a cause of surprise; marvel; miracle:—*v.i.* to feel surprise or amazement; be astonished; **2,** to feel doubt or curiosity; speculate:—*v.t.*

to be doubtful about; have a desire to know; as, I *wonder* what I ought to do. —*n.* **won′der-ment; won′der-land′.**

won-der-ful (wun′dėr-fool), *adj.* astonishing; strange; marvellous.

won-drous (wun′drus), *adj.* marvellous; remarkable.—*adv.* **won′drous-ly.**

wont (wunt; wōnt), *adj.* used or accustomed; as, she is *wont* to give much to charity:—*n.* habit or custom; as, he dined late, as was his *wont.*

wont-ed (wun′tid; wōn′tid), *adj.* habitual; customary; as, his *wonted* tasks.

woo (woo), *v.t.* **1,** to court or make love to; **2,** to coax; entreat; **3,** to seek; as, to *woo* success:—*v.i.* to go courting. —*n.* **woo′er.**

wood (wood), *n.* **1,** a large number of trees growing on an extensive tract of land; a grove or forest; **2,** the hard part of a tree under the bark; **3,** trees cut for firewood or trimmed ready for use in building; lumber; timber; **4, woods,** used as *sing.* or *pl.,* a thick growth of trees; a forest.—*adj.* **wood′-en.**—*adj.* **wood′y.**—*adj.* **wood′ed.**—*n.* **wood′shed′.**

wood-bine (wood′bīn′), *n.* any of several vines of the honeysuckle family, including the wild honeysuckle and the Virginia creeper.

wood-chuck (wood′chuk′), *n.* a coarse-furred, greyish-brown animal of the rat family, about eighteen inches long, which burrows in the ground and hibernates in winter, found in Canada and the U.S.: also called *groundhog.*

wood-cock (wood′kok′), *n.* a small brown game-bird with a long, straight bill and a short, rounded tail.

wood-craft (wood′krâft′) *n.* knowledge of the woods and woodland life, together with skill in hunting, trapping, camping, etc.

wood-cut (wood′kut′), *n.* an engraving cut on wood; a print from such an engraving: also called *wood engraving.*

wood-land (wood′land′; wood′land), *n.* land covered with trees; a forest: —*adj.* peculiar to, or dwelling in, the woods.

wood–louse (wood′–lous′), *n.* **1,** any of several small crustaceans with flattened, oval, segmented bodies, found under stones, decaying wood, etc., that roll up into a ball: also called *pill-bug* and *sow-bug;* **2,** any of several insects, as the white ant, termite, etc., that eat wood, old books, etc.

wood-peck-er (wood′pek′ėr), *n.* a

cat, āge, fär, câre, åsk; ten, ēve, latėr; (i) pity, rely, senate; īce; top; nō.

bird with feet and tail feathers adapted for climbing, and a strong beak for piercing the bark of trees for insects.

woods-man (woodz′man), *n.* [*pl.* woodsmen (-men)], one who lives or works in the woods, as a hunter, trapper, or lumberman.

wood thrush, a migratory North American thrush with a bell-like note: also called *wood robin.*

wood—winds (wood′—windz′), *n.* in an orchestra, the wooden wind-instruments collectively, including oboe, bassoon, clarinet, English horn, flute, and piccolo.

wood-work (wood′wûrk′), *n.* objects, or parts of objects, made of wood; esp., the wooden finishings of a house, as staircases, doors, etc.—*n.* **wood′-work′er.**

woof (woŏf), *n.* **1,** in *weaving,* the threads carried back and forth by the shuttle, as distinguished from *warp,* the threads fixed in the loom; **2,** the texture of a fabric.

wool (wool), *n.* **1,** the soft, curly coat of the sheep and some related animals; **2,** anything like wool; **3,** yarn or cloth made of wool.—*adj.* **wool′len.** —*adj.* **wool′ly.**

wool-gath-er-ing (wool′gath/ėr-ing), *n.* daydreaming.

wool-sack (wool′sak′), *n.* the wool-stuffed cushion on which the Lord Chancellor of the British House of Lords sits; his office.

word (wûrd), *n.* **1,** a sound or combination of sounds used in any language as a symbol of an idea, and forming a grammatical part of speech; **2,** the printed or written letters or other characters which represent the spoken word; **3,** a brief speech; saying; remark; as, a *word* of praise; **4,** information; message; report; as, he received *word* of their arrival; **5,** a password; **6,** a command; **7,** a promise; as, to keep one's *word;* **8, words,** language used in anger; as, they had *words* yesterday:—*v.t.* to express in words; as, to *word* a message. —*adj.* **word′y.**

wore (wōr), *p.t.* of *wear.*

work (wûrk), *v.i.* [worked (wûrkt) or in certain meanings, wrought (rôt), work-ing], **1,** to put forth physical or mental effort; labour; toil; **2,** to be occupied in business; be employed; as, he *works* in the steel mill; **3,** to act, operate, or run; esp., to act effectively; as, the machine *works* well; **4,** to ferment, as liquors; **5,** to progress

slowly or laboriously; as, the nail *worked* loose; the rain *worked* through the roof:—*v.t.* **1,** to operate, manage, or set in motion; as, to *work* a mine; *work* a scheme; **2,** to prepare for use; manipulate; as, to *work* the soil; **3,** to bring or move gradually or laboriously; as, he *worked* the stone into place; **4,** to perform, produce, or cause; as, he *wrought* marvellous cures; the storm *wrought* great ruin; **5,** to make or fashion; also, to embroider; as, the metal was beautifully *wrought;* she *worked* the linen with fine stitches; **6,** to exact labour from; cause to labour, as horses; **7,** to solve; as, to *work,* or *work* out, a problem; **8,** to canvass in the interest of one's trade; as, a salesman *works* a town:—*n.* **1,** physical or mental effort directed to some end or purpose; toil; labour; **2,** occupation; employment; job; **3,** a task; undertaking; **4,** a product of mental or physical effort; as, the *works* of Shakespeare; **5,** manner or style of working; as, painstaking *work;* **6, works: a,** the moving parts of any machinery; as, the *works* of a watch; **b,** structures connected with engineering projects as bridges, docks, dams, embankments, etc.; **c,** often used as *sing.,* a manufacturing plant, etc., with its contents, outbuildings, etc.; as, a dye *works.*—*n.* **work′er.**—*n.* **work′book′; work′house′; work′out′; work′shop′.**—*adj.* **work′a-ble; work′-a-day′** (prosaic; commonplace).

work-day (wûrk′dā′), *n.* a day for working, as distinguished from Sundays, holidays, etc.; also, the length of such a day.

work-man (wûrk′man), *n.* [*pl.* workmen (-men)], a man who is employed in work with his hands; esp., a skilled labourer; mechanic.—*adj.* **work′man-like′.**

work-man-ship (wûrk′man-ship′), *n.* **1,** the skill and methods of a workman; **2,** the finish or peculiar quality of anything made; as, a vase of exquisite *workmanship.*

world (wûrld), *n.* **1,** the earth with all living things and the traces of them, esp. man and his works; **2,** any one of the planets or stars imagined as similar to the earth; as, are there other *worlds* than ours? **3,** some special branch of civilization; as, the Roman *world;* **4,** any separate system, state, or sphere of existence, conceived as a whole; as the literary *world;* the *world* of dreams; **5,** the inhabitants of the earth and their affairs; esp., people in general as the bearers of public opinion; as, the *world*

---

all (ôl), ôr; up, mūte, cûr, coŏl, book; oil, out; th, thin; *th,* the.

admired him; **6,** those people who are esp. devoted to pleasure; also, material affairs as opposed to spiritual.—*n.* **world′li-ness; world′ling** (worldly person).—*adj.* **world′—wide′; world′ly-wise′.**

world-ly (wûrld′li), *adj.* [world-li-er, world-li-est], earthly; devoted to the pleasures and advantages of this life.

worm (wûrm), *n.* **1,** any small, slender, creeping or crawling, legless animal, usually having a soft, hairless body, as an earthworm; **2,** any device resembling such an animal, as a short rotating screw, made to mesh with a worm-wheel; **3,** an insignificant or contemptible person: used in scorn or disgust; **4, worms,** any illness due to worms living in the body:—**worm—wheel,** a wheel fitted with teeth which gear with a short rotating screw, or worm:—*v.t.* to bring out, put in, or move along, by methods suggesting a worm's motion; as, to *worm* his secret from him; he *wormed* himself into favour.—*adj.* **worm′y.**—*n.* **worm′hole′.**

worm-wood (wûrm′wood′), *n.* **1,** a bitter, aromatic, dark-green oil used in making absinthe; **2,** bitterness; as, remorse is *wormwood* to man.

worn (wōrn), *p.p.* of *wear.*

wor-ry (wûr′i), *v.t.* [worried, worrying], **1,** to shake, tear, or mangle with the teeth; as, the cat *worried* the mouse; **2,** to trouble; tease; harass; as, John *worried* his father:—*v.i.* to be anxious; fret; as, he *worried* about the safety of the children:—*n.* [*pl.* worries], anxiety; disturbance of mind.—*n.* **wor′ri-er.**—*adj.* **wor′ri-some.**

worse (wûrs), *adj.* [*comp.* of *bad* or *ill*], **1,** more bad, ill, or evil; more extreme in degree; as, he's a *worse* liar than his brother; **2,** less well in health; sicker; as, the sick man is *worse:*—*adv.* [*comp.* of *badly* or *ill*], **1,** in a more evil or extreme manner; less well; as, John plays the piano *worse* than Peter; **2,** less; as, even *worse* suited to one business than to another:—*n.* a thing or state even more undesirable than another; as, the patient took a turn for the *worse.*

wor-ship (wûr′ship), *n.* **1,** the act of paying reverence, adoration, or homage, esp. to God; **2,** excessive admiration; devotion; adoration; as, hero *worship:*—*v.t.* [worshipped, worship-ping], **1,** to adore or show honour to (a divinity); **2,** to admire excessively; idolize:—*v.i.* **1,** to perform religious service; **2,** feel excessive admiration.— *n.* **wor′ship-per.**

wor-ship-ful (wûr′ship-fool), *adj.* **1,** worthy of respect or honour; **2,** honourable: a title of respect used in formal address.

worst (wûrst), *adj.* [*superl.* of *bad* or *ill*], bad, evil, or ill in the highest degree:— *adv.* [*superl.* of *badly* or *ill*], in the most bad or evil way; most extreme in degree; least well:—*n.* that which is most bad or evil; as, the *worst* has happened:—*v.t.* to defeat; as, our team *worsted* theirs.

wor-sted (woos′tid), *n.* **1,** a twisted yarn spun out of wool; also, the cloth made from such yarn; **2,** a softer woollen yarn, twisted little or not at all, used in knitting and embroidery.

worth (wûrth), *n.* **1,** excellence or desirable qualities; merit; as, a person of great *worth;* a gift of much *worth;* **2,** value as expressed in money; as, the *worth* of the chair is three dollars; **3,** personal wealth; as, his total *worth* is in the millions:—*adj.* **1,** meriting; as, *worth* attention; **2,** of the actual value of; as, *worth* the price; **3,** priced at; as, *worth* ten dollars; **4,** possessed of.— *adj.* **worth′less.**—*adj.* **worth′—while′** or **worth′while′.**

wor-thy (wûr′thi), *adj.* [wor-thi-er, wor-thi-est], **1,** having value or excellence; as, a *worthy* man; **2,** deserving; as, a *worthy* charity:—*n.* [*pl.* worthies], a person of distinction: often used humorously.—*adv.* **wor′thi-ly.**—*n.* **wor′thi-ness.**

would (wood), past tense of ²*will,* used to express: **1,** intention; as, he said he *would* go; **2,** determination; as, you *would* play, although you were told not to; **3,** expectation; as, he said you *would* return soon; **4,** wish; as, I *would* spring were here; **5,** custom or habit; as, he *would* come to see us every day.

¹**wound** (wōōnd; *Archaic,* wound), *n.* **1,** a hurt or injury caused by violence; a cut; stab; as, he had a bullet *wound* in his foot; **2,** an injury to one's feelings or good name:—*v.t.* to hurt by violence; cut; slash; also, to hurt the feelings of.

²**wound** (wound), *p.t.* and *p.p.* of *wind.*

wove (wōv), *p.t.* and *p.p.* of *weave.*— **wo′ven,** *p.p.* of *weave.*

wrack (rak), *n.* **1,** wreck; ruin: now used only in the phrase *wrack and ruin;* also spelled *rack;* **2,** seaweed, etc., cast ashore by the sea.

wraith (rāth), *n.* the ghost of a person, supposed to be seen just before or just after his death; a spectre.

wran-gle (rang′gl), *v.i.* [wran-gled, wran-gling], to dispute noisily:—*n.* a noisy, angry dispute:—*v.t.* to herd or round up livestock.—*n.* **wran′gler, 1,** one who argues or bickers; **2,** a cowboy.

wrap (rap), *v.t.* [wrapped, wrap-ping], **1,** to roll or fold around something; as, *wrap* the blanket around the child; **2,** to envelop; conceal by enveloping with something; as, Mary *wrapped* her doll in a towel; **3,** to do up securely; as, *wrap* the book in paper:—*n.* **1,** an article of dress to be folded around a person; **2, wraps,** outer garments, such as coats.

wrap-per (rap′ẽr), *n.* **1,** a person or thing which enfolds or covers; as, a candy *wrapper;* **2,** a loose garment resembling a dressing-gown, worn indoors by women.

wrap-ping (rap′ing), *n.* covering, as for a package, parcel, bundle, etc.

wrath (ràth; räth), *n.* **1,** deep indignation; violent anger; fury; **2,** punishment; vengeance.—*adj.* **wrath′ful.**—*adj.* **wrath′y.**

wreak (rēk), *v.t.* to give rein to; inflict; as, he *wreaked* his fury on the dog.

wreath (rēth), *n.* [*pl.* wreaths (rēthz)], **1,** flowers or leaves wound or twined into a circular band; a garland or chaplet; **2,** something twisted into circular form.

wreathe (rēth), *v.t.* [wreathed, wreathing], **1,** to give a turned or twisted form to; as, to *wreathe* a garland; **2,** to make by twisting and intertwining; as, to *wreathe* a necklace of daisies; **3,** to encircle; adorn with something like a wreath; as, clouds *wreathed* the mountain.

wreck (rek), *n.* **1,** destruction by collision, fire, storm, etc.; esp., the destruction of a vessel afloat; shipwreck; **2,** anything that has been ruined or disabled, as a ship, automobile, house, etc.:—*v.t.* **1,** to ruin or disable by violence; as, the accident *wrecked* his health; **2,** to involve in destruction or ruin; **3,** to dismantle; as, to *wreck* a building.—*n.* **wreck′er.**

wreck-age (rek′ij), *n.* the remains of a destroyed ship, train, building, etc.

wren (ren), *n.* a small, brown, singing bird with a short, perky, erect tail.

wrench (rench), *n.* **1,** a violent turn; a sideways pull or twist; **2,** a sprain, as at a joint; **3,** a pang; a sudden distressed feeling; **4,** a tool for grasping and turning nuts, bolts, etc.:—*v.t.* **1,** to twist; wring or pull sideways with effort; wrest; as, to *wrench* the top off a box; **2,** to twist; sprain; as, she *wrenched* her ankle.

wrest (rest), *v.t.* to turn or wrench, esp. from a normal state; pull or take away by force or violence; as, he *wrested* the football from my arms.

wres-tle (res′l), *v.i.* [wres-tled, wrestling], **1,** to grapple with an opponent in an effort to force him to the ground; **2,** to struggle; strive earnestly, esp. with something difficult; as, to *wrestle* with arithmetic:—*n.* a wrestling-match; also, a hard struggle.—*n.* **wres′tler.**—*n.* **wres′tling.**

wretch (rech), *n.* **1,** an unfortunate or miserable person; **2,** a mean, contemptible person.

wretch-ed (rech′id), *adj.* **1,** miserable; unhappy; **2,** causing misery; as, *wretched* health; **3,** mean; as, a *wretched* hovel; **4,** poor; as, *wretched* work.—*n.* **wretch′ed-ness.**

wrig-gle (rig′l), *v.i.* [wrig-gled, wriggling], **1,** to move by twisting and turning; squirm; as, the pupils *wriggled* in their seats; **2,** hence, to proceed by trickery or underhand means; as, to *wriggle* out of a lie:—*n.* the act of twisting or squirming; a squirming motion.—*n.* **wrig′gler.**

wring (ring), *v.t.* [wrung (rung), wringing], **1,** to twist and squeeze; as, to *wring* wet clothes; **2,** to force out by twisting or pressure; extort; as, to *wring* water from clothes; to *wring* a confession; **3,** to give pain to, as if by twisting; to distress.—*n.* **wring′er.**

¹**wrin-kle** (ring′kl), *n.* a slight ridge or crease caused by folding, puckering, or rumpling:—*v.t.* [wrin-kled, wrin-kling], to form small ridges or creases in; pucker; as, the rain *wrinkled* his suit:—*v.i.* to become creased; as, my dress *wrinkles* easily.—*adj.* **wrin′kly.**

²**wrin-kle** (ring′kl), *n.* a clever trick, idea, or device; as, the latest *wrinkle.*

wrist (rist), *n.* the joint between the hand and forearm.—*n.* **wrist′band′.**

writ (rit), *n.* **1,** anything written: mainly applied to Scripture; as, Holy *Writ;* **2,** a written order of a court of justice.

write (rīt), *v.t.* [*p.t.* wrote (rōt) or, *Archaic,* writ (rit), *p.p.* writ-ten (rit′n) or, *Archaic,* writ, *p.pr.* writ-ing], **1,** to trace, as letters, etc., on a surface with an instrument, as a pen, pencil, etc.; **2,** to express in words or characters on paper with a pen or pencil; as, to *write* one's name; **3,** to produce as an author; compose; as, he *wrote* a book of adventure; **4,** to leave traces on; as, trouble is *written* on his face; **5,** to compose and send a letter to; as, I *wrote* my sister today:—*v.i.* **1**, to form letters, as with a pen; **2**, to compose; write books, etc.; **3**, to communicate by letter.

writ-er (rīt′er), *n.* **1**, one who writes; as, the *writer* of this letter is known to me; **2**, a person whose occupation in life is writing; as, Mark Twain was a versatile *writer*.

write—up (rīt′–up′), *n. Colloq.* **1**, a newspaper account, etc., esp. one that is laudatory (of the subject in hand); **2**, in *finance*, an illegally excessive statement of assets.

writhe (rīth), *v.i.* [writhed, writh-ing], to squirm or twist, as from acute pain or distress; also, to be shamed or bitterly annoyed; as, to *writhe* at an insult.

writ-ing (rīt′ing), *n.* **1**, the act of forming letters with a pen, pencil, etc. as on paper; **2**, that which is so set down, as an essay; **3**, the art of literary production; **4**, **writings**, things written; literary work; as, his *writings* include poetry and prose.

wrong (rông), *adj.* **1**, not morally right or just; wicked; as, it is *wrong* to cheat; **2**, not according to fact; incorrect; as, he gave me the *wrong* directions; **3**, amiss; out of order; as, the clock is *wrong;* **4**, contrary to law; illegal; as, the judge ruled that it was *wrong* of Mr. Smith to speed; **5**, of a side of a piece of cloth, garment, etc., meant to be turned away from view or wear:—*n.* that which is contrary to moral right, fact, principles, intention, or purpose, etc.; evil; injury; crime: opposite of *right;* as, you are in the *wrong:*—*adv.* **1**, in a manner not right morally; as, to go *wrong;* **2**, incorrectly; as, to guess *wrong:*—*v.t.* to treat unjustly; harm.— *adv.* **wrong′ly.**—*n.* **wrong′do′er; wrong′do′ing.**

wrong-ful (rông′fool), *adj.* evil; injurious; unjust.—*adv.* **wrong′ful-ly.**

wrote (rōt), *p.t.* of *write.*

wroth (rôth), *adj.* wrathful; indignant.

wrought (rôt), *adj.* worked; fashioned or moulded from the rough; as, a bowl of *wrought* silver.—*v.t.* and *v.i. Archaic p.t.* and *p.p.* of *work.*

wrung (rung), *p.t.* and *p.p.* of *wring.*

wry (rī), *adj.* [wri-er, wri-est], twisted out of shape; as, a *wry* mouth.—*adv.* **wry′ly.**

X

X, x (eks), *n.* [*pl.* X's, x's], **1**, the 24th letter of the alphabet, following W; **2**, the Roman numeral for ten.

xe-bec (zē′bek), *n.* an old type of three-masted sailing-ship, formerly used on the Mediterranean, as by corsairs.

xe-ni-a (zē′ni-a), *n.* in *cross-pollination*, the influence of foreign pollen upon the seed or fruit which is pollinated.

xe-no— (zen′ō–), *prefix* meaning (1) *stranger* or *foreigner* (2) *strange* or *foreign;* as in **xen′o-gen′e-sis** (production of offspring completely different from parent), **xen′o-mor′phic** (having a form other than its usual form as certain crystals of igneous rock), and **xen′o-pho′bi-a** (fear of strangers).

xe-nog-a-my (zi-nog′a-mi), *n. Botany*, cross-fertilization.

xe-non (zē′non), a heavy, inert gaseous element present in the air (about 1 part in 170 millions by volume).

xe-ro— (zēr′ō–), *prefix* meaning *dry*, as in **xe′ro-phyte′** (a plant adapted to dry conditions).

X—ray (eks′–rā′), **1**, a ray produced by an electric discharge in a vacuum-tube, now known to be similar to a light ray, but of very short wave-length, capable of penetrating many substances, as the human body, which ordinary light rays cannot penetrate: also called *Röntgen* or *Roentgen, ray;* **2**, a photograph, as of an internal diseased part of the human body, of a bone fracture, etc., made with the aid of such rays.

xy-lem (zī′lem), *n. Botany*, the woody tissue, esp. of timber trees: it conveys water and minerals, gives mechanical support, and stores food in dormant periods.

xy-lo-phone (zī′lo-fōn′; zil′o-fōn′), *n.* a musical instrument of great antiquity, XYLOPHONE made of parallel wooden bars of graduated length which are struck with two small, flexible, wooden mallets.—*n.* **xy-loph′o-nist.**

Y

Y, y (wī), *n.* [*pl.* Y's, y's], the 25th letter of the alphabet, following X.

yacht (yot), *n.* a light vessel, propelled by sails, steam, or electricity, used for pleasure or racing:—*v.i.* to sail in a yacht.—*n.* **yacht′ing.**—*n.* **yachts′man.**

yak (yak), *n.* a wild or domesticated ox of central Asia, with a hump and with long hair hanging from its shoulders, sides, and tail.

yam (yam), *n.* **1,** a tropical vine with edible, potato-like roots; also, the root; **2,** in the southern U.S., a kind of sweet potato.

yam-mer (yam′ẽr), *v.t.* and *n. Colloq.* **1,** to whimper; whine; complain; **2,** to make a loud outcry; wail.

yank (yangk), *v.t. Colloq.*, to jerk or pull quickly; as, to *yank* a coat from a hook: —*n. Colloq.*, a hard, sudden pull.

yap (yap), *v.i.* and *n.* to bark or yelp: *Slang,* to jabber; chatter.

¹yard (yärd), *n.* **1,** the standard unit of linear measure, equal to three feet, or 36 inches; **2,** a measuring-rod of 36 inches; yardstick; **3,** a slender spar slung crosswise to a mast, used to support a sail.—*n.* **yard′stick′.**

²yard (yärd), *n.* **1,** a small piece of enclosed ground beside or around a building; as, a front *yard;* **2,** a space, often enclosed, where a specific kind of work is carried on; as, a railroad *yard.*

yard-arm (yärd′ärm′), *n.* either end of a yard that supports a square sail.

yarn (yärn), *n.* **1,** a spun thread; esp., thread used for weaving, or heavy woollen thread used for knitting; **2,** *Colloq.*, an exaggerated story.

yar-row (yar′ō), *n.* a genus of plant (*Achillea millefolium*) with pungent smell and taste: it bears finely dissected leaves and small white flowers.

yaw (yô), *v.i.* of a ship or an aeroplane, to fail to hold a steady course; also, of a pilot, to steer off the straight line of a course:—*n.* a temporary change from a straight course, as of a ship or an aeroplane.

yawl (yôl), *n.* **1,** a two-masted, fore-and-aft-rigged sailing-vessel with the smaller mast aft of the rudder post; **2,** a ship's small boat.

yawn (yôn), *n.* an unintentional opening of the jaws, as from sleepiness:—*v.i.* **1,** to open the mouth wide, as from hunger, surprise, etc.; **2,** esp., to open the mouth unintentionally as wide as possible while inhaling deeply, as the result of sleepiness or boredom; **3,** to open wide; as, the mouth of a cave *yawned* before us:—*v.t.* to utter with a yawn.—*n.* **yawn′er.**

ye (yē), *pron. Archaic* and *Poetic,* a nominative plural form of *you.*

yea (yā), *adv. Archaic,* yes; indeed; truly:—*n.* (now usually *aye*), an affirmative vote.

year (yēr), *n.* **1,** the length of time it takes the earth to make one complete revolution around the sun, or 365 days, 5 hours, 48 minutes, and 46 seconds; **2,** a period of twelve months, consisting of 365 days, or, in the case of leap-year, 366 days; **3,** a period of time, usually less than a year, devoted to some particular activity; as, the college *year.* —*n.* **year′book′.**

year-ling (yēr′ling; yûr′ling), *n.* an animal between one and two years old: —*adj.* one year old; of a year's duration.

year-ly (yēr′li; yûr′li), *adj.* **1,** occurring once a year or every year; as, a *yearly* visit; **2,** by the year; as, a *yearly* rent; **3,** for a year; as, a *yearly* lease.

yearn (yûrn), *v.i.* to be filled with longing, compassion, or tenderness; as, to *yearn* for rest; to *yearn* over a child.

yeast (yēst), *n.* a growth of minute cells, causing fermentation in sugar solutions and starchy substances, used in making beer, and in causing bread-dough to rise. —*adj.* **yeast′y.**

yell (yel), *n.* **1,** a sharp, loud cry, as of pain, rage, or terror; a shriek; **2,** a characteristic shout, as used in warfare or by a group of persons; as, a college *yell:* —*v.t.* to cry out loudly; as, to *yell* defiance:—*v.i.* to cry out, as with pain.

yel-low (yel′ō), *adj.* **1,** of the colour of gold, buttercups, etc.; **2,** cowardly; mean; dishonourable; as, that boy has a *yellow* streak; **3,** melodramatic; sensational; as, a *yellow* newspaper:— *n.* **1,** a bright elementary colour, between orange and green; **2,** any dye or paint that gives this colour; **3,** the yolk of an egg.

yel-low fe-ver, a dangerous, infectious fever of the tropics, marked by a yellow skin, vomiting, etc., and carried to man by the bite of a certain species of mosquito.

yel-low-ish (yel′ō-ish), *adj.* coloured

somewhat like yellow; having a yellow tinge.

yel-low jack-et, any of several American wasps, with a black abdomen marked with yellow: often called *hornet*. Wasps live in colonies; one kind builds nests of a paperlike material; others nest in the ground.

yelp (yelp), *v.i.* to utter a sharp bark, as a dog when hurt:—*n.* a sharp, quick bark.

¹yen (yen), *n.* Japan's unit of coinage, worth 100 sen or about 20 cents.

²yen (yen), *n. Slang*, a longing; intense desire or urge.

yeo-man (yō'man), *n.* [*pl.* yeomen (-men)], **1**, in England, a soldier of the royal bodyguard; **2**, in England, a small landowner; **3**, in the U.S. Navy, a petty officer with clerical duties.

yeo-man-ry (yō'man-ri), *n.* **1**, yeomen collectively; **2**, in England, the common people, esp. the farming class.

yes (yes), *adv.* **1**, it is so: the affirmative answer to a question, opposite of *no;* **2**, furthermore; more than this; as, he is strong, *yes*, very strong.

yes-ter-day (yes'tėr-di; yes'tėr-dā'), *n.* **1**, the day before today; **2**, hence, a recent day; as, it seems only *yesterday* that we came:—*adv.* on the day before today.

yet (yet), *adv.* **1**, up until now; as, he has not come *yet;* **2**, now as previously; still; as, I have your present *yet;* **3**, even; still; besides; as, more important *yet;* **4**, sooner or later; as, the day will *yet* come; **5**, even though this is so; as, *yet* I cannot understand:—*conj.* **1**, nevertheless; however; **2**, although; though.

yew (ū), *n.* **1**, a large, cone-bearing, evergreen tree of the Old World, with darkgreen leaves; also, its fine-grained wood, used for making bows; **2**, a small evergreen tree of Pacific North America; **3**, a dwarf evergreen shrub of eastern Canada; **4, Japanese yew**, an ornamental shrub (*Taxus cuspidata*).

yield (yēld), *v.t.* **1**, to produce; as, the land *yields* wheat; **2**, to concede; as, I *yield* the point; **3**, to surrender; **4**, to afford; permit; as, to *yield* space; **5**, to give as return for labour, money invested, etc.:—*v.i.* **1**, to assent; comply; **2**, to give way; submit; **3**, to give a return; produce:—*n.* the return for labour expended or for capital invested.

yo-del (yō'dl), *v.t.* and *v.i.* [yodelled, yodel-ling], to sing or call with sudden changes in the voice from chest tones to falsetto:—*n.* a call or song so sung.

Also spelled **yo'dle**.—*n.* **yo'del-ler, yo'del-er,** or **yo'dler**.

yo-ga (yō'ga) or **yo-gi** (yō'gi), *n. Hinduism*, intense contemplation and ascetic discipline practised to establish identity of consciousness with the object of concentration, namely, God, and free the soul from further migrations; an ascetic (*yogi*).

yo-gurt (yō'goort), *n.* a thick, fermented liquor made from milk, or an artificially curdled milk product taken for the health (esp. in the East).

yoke (yōk), *n.* **1**, a wooden frame to couple together draught animals, esp. oxen, for work; **2**, two animals so coupled together; as, a *yoke* of oxen; **3**, a frame of wood fitted to a person's shoulders, for carrying buckets hung from each end; **4**, the upper part of a garment made to fit the neck and shoulders; also, the upper part of a skirt made to fit the hips; **5**, that which binds; a bond or tie; **6**, hence, bondage; as, the *yoke* of slavery:—*v.t.* [yoked, yok-ing], **1**, to put a yoke on; as, to *yoke* oxen; **2**, to couple or link.

yo-kel (yō'kl), *n.* a rustic; country bumpkin.

yolk (yōk), *n.* the yellow part of an egg, surrounded by the white.

Yom Kip-pur (yom kip'oor), the Hebrew Day of Atonement, observed on the 10th day of the first month of the Jewish civil year (usually in early October).

yon (yon), *adj.* and *adv. Poetic*, yonder.

yon-der (yon'dėr), *adj.* **1**, situated at a distance, but in sight; over there; as, *yonder* hills; **2**, more distant; as, the *yonder* side of the valley:—*adv.* at that place; there; as, situated *yonder*.

yore (yōr), *n.* time long since past; as, days of *yore*.

you (ū), *pron.* the second person of the personal pronoun (*sing.* or *pl.*, but always taking a plural verb), [*nominative* you, *possessive* your, yours, *objective* you], **1**, the person or persons spoken to; as, how are *you?* **2**, one; anyone; a person; people.

young (yung), *adj.* **1**, being in the early part of life or growth; as, a father with his *young* son; **2**, vigorous; fresh; strong; as, old in body, but *young* in heart:—*n.* **1**, those who are young; as, *young* and old came to hear him; **2**, the offspring of animals; as, a wolf with its *young*.

young-ster (yung'stėr), *n.* a person in early years; a child or youth; a lad.

your (yoor), *adj.* a possessive form of the

personal pronoun *you:* **1,** belonging to you; as, *your* coat; **2,** coming from, or relating to, you; as, *your* kindness.

yours (yoorz), a possessive form of the personal pronoun *you,* used alone: **1,** as *adj.,* in the predicate, belonging or relating to you; as, whose is this glass? it is *yours;* **2,** as *pron.,* a person or thing that belongs to you; as, which car shall we use? let's take *yours.*

your-self (yoor-self′), *pron.* [*pl.* yourselves (-selvz′)], **1,** a reflexive form of *you;* as, you fooled *yourself;* **2,** an emphatic form of *you;* as, you *yourself* must go.

youth (ūth), *n.* [*pl.* youths (ū*th*z; ūths) or, collectively, youth], **1,** the state or quality of being young; **2,** the time of life between childhood and maturity;

3, a young man; **4,** young people; as, the *youth* of a nation.

youth-ful (ūth′fool), *adj.* **1,** not old; as, a *youthful* person; **2,** pertaining or fitting to youth; as, *youthful* pleasures.

yowl (youl), *n.* and *v.i.* a howl; a long yell, esp. a mournful one.

yo—yo (yō′-yō′), *n.* a grooved, disc-shaped top spun up and down a cord attached to one's hand or finger.

yuc-ca (yuk′a), *n.* a plant of the lily family, having long, pointed leaves and white flowers; also, the flowers.

yule (ūl), *n.* Christmas or the Christmas feast:—**yule—log,** a huge log brought indoors for an open fire on Christmas Eve.

yule-tide (ūl′tīd′), *n.* Christmas-time.

Z

Z, z (zed; zē), *n.* [*pl.* Z's, z's], the 26th letter of the alphabet, following Y.

za-ny (zā′ni), *n.* and *adj.* **1,** a silly person; dolt; simpleton; **2,** a clown or apish buffoon.

zeal (zēl), *n.* ardour; great earnestness.

zeal-ot (zel′ut), *n.* an enthusiast; a person of too great zeal.

zeal-ous (zel′us), *adj.* eager; enthusiastic.—*adv.* **zeal′ous-ly.**

ze-bec (zē′bek), *n.* Same as **xe′bec.**

ze-bra (zē′bra), *n.* an African wild animal belonging to the horse family, esp. one with dark stripes on a white or tawny body.

ze-bu (zē′bū), *n.* a domestic animal of India with long ears, short horns, and a large hump on the shoulders.

ze-nith (zē′nith; zen′ith), *n.* **1,** that part of the heavens directly above the place where one stands; **2,** the greatest height.

ze-o-lite (zē′ō-līt′), *n.* any of a group of hydrated silicates of aluminum, sodium, or calcium, closely allied to the feldspars.

zeph-yr (zef′ėr), **1,** a mild, gentle breeze; **2,** *Poetic,* the west wind.

zep-pe-lin (zep′i-lin), *n.* a large, cigar-shaped dirigible balloon.

ze-ro (zē′rō), *n.* [*pl.* zeros or zeroes], **1,** a cipher; **2,** nothing; **3,** the point on a scale from which reckoning begins; **4,** the lowest point; as, her courage sank to *zero.*

zest (zest), *n.* relish; keen enjoyment.—*adj.* **zest′ful.**

Zeus (zūs), *n.* in *Greek mythology,* the son of Cronus, who overthrew his father and became the supreme god: identified with Roman *Jupiter.*

zig-zag (zig′zag′), *n.* **1,** one of a number of short, sharp angles or turns; **2,** something characterized by sharp turns, as. a path:—*adj.* having short, sharp turns; as, a *zigzag* line:—*adv.* crookedly; with sharp turns; as, the path climbs *zigzag:*—*v.t.* and *v.i.* [zig-zagged, zigzag-ging], to move or be in, or form, quick, sharp turns; as, to *zigzag* one's way; a path *zigzags* up the hill.

zinc (zingk), *n.* a bluish-white metal, which can stand exposure to air and moisture: used in making paint, in electric cells, and as a protective coating on iron sheets, wire, etc.

zing (zing), *n.* a shrill, high-pitched humming sound.

zin-ni-a (zin′i-a), *n.* a plant bearing bright-coloured, showy flowers; also, a flower of this plant.

zip (zip), *n.* and *v.i.* **1,** a sharp hissing sound as of a bullet in flight, or like the tearing of canvas, etc.; **2,** *Colloq.* energy; vim:—*v.t.* to fasten with a zipper.

zip-per (zip′ėr), *n.* a fastening device for galoshes, purses, tobacco-pouches, clothing, etc., sewed on both edges of an opening, with a locking mechanism

---

all (ôl), ôr; up, mūte, cûr, cōōl, book; oil, out; th, thin; *th,* the.

pulled by an attached tab which causes the two edges to lock together.

zir-con (zŭr′kon), *n.* a silicate of zirconium occurring in square prisms, etc., of brown, yellow, and red: when transparent used as gems (called *hyacinths*).

zir-co-ni-um (zẻr-kō′ni-um), *n.* a gray or black metallic element found in zircon, etc., used in alloys and as a heat and an acid resistant.—**zir-co′ni-a**, a white powder, ZrO₂, used in making furnace linings, crucibles, etc.

zith-er (zith′ẻr), *n.* a musical instrument with about 36 strings over a shallow sounding-box, played with a small piece of metal or ivory.

zo-di-ac (zō′di-ak), *n.* an imaginary belt encircling the heavens, extending eight degrees on each side of the path of the sun, containing the paths of the moon and the important planets, and divided into twelve equal parts, called *signs:*—**signs of the zodiac**, the twelve divisions of the zodiac, each with a specific name.—*adj.* **zo-di′a-cal** (-dī′).

zom-bie or **zom-bi** (zom′bi), *n.* [*pl.* -bies or -bis], **1,** in West Africa, Haiti, etc., the snake deity (python) of voodoo rites; **2,** a reanimated corpse; **3,** *Slang,* a dull, unattractive person; **4,** a drink of rum or brandy and fruit juices mixed.

zone (zōn), *n.* **1,** any encircling belt, band, stripe, or path; as, a *zone* of colour; **2,** any one of the five sections into which the earth's surface is divided by imaginary lines, north and south of the equator; as, the Torrid *Zone* (about the equator), the two Frigid *Zones* (about the poles), and the two Temperate *Zones* (lying between); **3,** in the Canadian parcel-post system, telephone system, etc., a specified area throughout which a certain rate is charged; **4,** an area or region distinct because of its use, its natural characteristics, etc.; as, a safety *zone;* a cotton *zone:*—*v.t.* [zoned, zon-ing], **1,** to divide into areas or zones; as, the city is *zoned* into five sections; **2,** to include within an area or zone:—*v.i.* to be divided into zones.—*adj.* **zo′nal.**

zo-o— (zō′ō–), *Greek prefix* meaning *animal,* as in **zo′o-chem′is-try** (chemistry of animal bodies), **zo′o-ge-og′-ra-phy** (geographical distribution of animals), **zo′o-phyte′** (an animal, as a sponge, coral, sea anemone, etc., with some of the characteristics of plants), **zo′o-sperm′** (the male germ cell of semen), and **zo′o-spore′** (the spore of certain fungi and algae able to move by cilia).

zoo (zo͞o), *n.* a park or other large enclosure in which living animals are kept for public exhibition; a zoological garden.

zo-o-log-i-cal (zō′ō-loj′i-kal), *adj.* pertaining to zoology, the science of animal life:—**zoological garden**, a park in which animals are kept for exhibition; a zoo.

zo-ol-o-gy (zō-ol′o-ji), *n.* [*pl.* zoologies], the branch of biology dealing with animal life.—*n.* **zo-ol′o-gist.**

zoom (zo͞om), *v.i.* **1,** to move with a humming or buzzing sound; **2,** in *aviation,* to climb for a short time at a very steep angle:—*v.t.* to cause (an aeroplane) to zoom.

zoot suit (zo͞ot), *n.* about the time of World War II, a flashy style of young man's suit having baggy trousers with narrow cuffs, and long, draped coat.

zwie-back (tswē′bäk′; tsvē′bäk′; swĭ′bak′; zwĭ′bak), *n.* a kind of bread baked in a loaf, sliced, and baked again.

zy-go- (zī′gō-), *Greek prefix* meaning *yoke* or *pair,* as in **zy′go-mor′phic** (with identical or symmetrical halves), **zy′go-phyte′** (a plant that reproduces by union of two similar cells as with some algae and fungi), and **zy′go-spore′** (a spore formed by the union of two similar sexual spores, called gametes).

zy-mo- (zī′mō-), *Greek prefix* meaning *fermentation,* as in **zy-mol′o-gy** (science of fermentation), **zy-mol′y-sis** (fermenting action of enzymes), and **zy-mo′sis** (any process similar to fermentation by which an infectious disease develops).

cat, āge, fär, câre, ȧsk; ten, ēve, latẻr; (i) pity, rely, senate; īce; top; nō.